D0152445

Encyclopedia of

THE ESSAY

Encyclopedia of

THE ESSAY

Editor

TRACY CHEVALIER

FITZROY DEARBORN PUBLISHERS
LONDON AND CHICAGO

Ypsilanti District Library
5577 Whittaker Rd.
Ypsilanti, MI 48197-9752

Copyright © 1997 by
FITZROY DEARBORN PUBLISHERS

All rights reserved including the right of reproduction in whole or
in part in any form. For information write to:

FITZROY DEARBORN PUBLISHERS
70 East Walton Street
Chicago, Illinois 60611
USA

or

11 Rathbone Place
London WIP IDE
England

British Library Cataloguing in Publication Data
Encyclopedia of the essay
   1. Essays – Encyclopedias   2. Essays – History and criticism – Encyclopedias
   I. Chevalier, Tracy, 1962–
809.4′003

ISBN 1–884964–30–3

Library of Congress Cataloging in Publication Data is available.

First published in the USA and UK 1997

Typeset by Florencetype Ltd, Stoodleigh, Devon
Printed by Braun-Brumfield, Inc., Ann Arbor, Michigan

Cover illustration: from the title page of *Essayes* by
Sir William Cornwallis, the Younger; 1632 printing

CONTENTS

EDITOR'S NOTE

The entries in this book were chosen primarily by the advisory board (listed on page ix), with advice from contributors when appropriate. Choosing what is to go in reference books is notoriously difficult. There are the subjects that must obviously have entries, and those that must obviously not. In between lies a vast block of those for which an argument can be made for or against. This is where the problems lie, and I expect our choices will inevitably raise a few quibbles.

Some gaps reflect the nature of the essay and essay scholarship rather than ignorance. There are markedly fewer entries on women, for instance, because historically women's opinions have not been encouraged, certainly not in written form. Moreover, when women did write they usually chose genres that made them money; the essay has not been known for being lucrative. In the 20th century women at last gained both leisure time and an authoritative voice; that change is reflected here in the greater number of entries on contemporary women writers. Nor does every country have a survey, even when there are several entries on individuals. Italian essay writing, for example, dates from Machiavelli, but there has never yet been any consideration of the Italian essay as a whole.

While the majority of the entries are biographical, in a handful of cases when an author's oeuvre is not sufficiently essayistic to warrant an entry and yet he has written a significant individual essay, that essay has its own entry: e.g. John Locke's *An Essay Concerning Human Understanding* or Alexander Pope's *An Essay on Criticism*.

The Essays and Related Prose lists at the end of biographical entries are selective rather than comprehensive, listing the most important essay works; the date following the title is of first publication, followed sometimes by a modern edition. Also listed are available selections and compilations. Further reading lists have as a rule been suggested by contributors.

Names and phrases in bold throughout the text indicate topics with their own entries.

Individual essays mentioned in the text are followed by the date of first publication, either in periodical or book form, though occasionally the date written and the date published are both listed if they are far enough apart to be noteworthy.

I would like to thank the advisory board for their spirited advice which helped me launch the project, and the contributors for their enthusiasm which kept me going through the endless days and nights of it. In particular, I am grateful for the help of Melba Cuddy-Keene, who wrote the first entry (on Virginia Woolf) and showed us all the way.

Thanks go to Mark Hawkins-Dady, Susan Mackervoy, Tracey Mais, and Carol Jones for their work on various parts of the book; also to Jonathan Drori for explaining the mysteries of the computer, e-mail, and the Internet, as well as for putting up with piles of manuscript in a corner of our flat for three years. Thanks too to Lesley Henderson, long-time partner in reference crime, who could be relied on for both sound editorial advice and a good line on the sometimes absurd nature of our work.

Thanks, finally, to my editor Daniel Kirkpatrick, who taught me how to make reference books in the first place; he paid me his highest compliment by leaving me alone for two years to get on with it, and then came along and quietly corrected my many and varied mistakes, making it a better book.

It has been a pleasure rather than a trial to work on this volume. Every time I go into a bookstore and see a newly appointed Essay section I am more certain that the appearance of *Encyclopedia of the Essay* reflects a growing interest. It's nice to feel relevant.

TRACY CHEVALIER

ADVISERS

Chris Anderson
Robert Atwan
Alexander J. Butrym
Richard M. Chadbourne
Anna Lisa Crone
Peter G. Earle
Graham Good

R. Lane Kauffmann
Phillip Lopate
John A. McCarthy
Janet Pérez
Elizabeth Perkins
D. E. Pollard

CONTRIBUTORS

Stephen M. Adams
Onésimo T. Almeida
Daniel Altamiranda
Nora M. Alter
Harry Amana
Adelaide P. Amore
Andrew J. Angyal
Janet Baker
Jacqueline Bardolph
Maurine H. Beasley
Gino Bedani
Michael Beddow
Ronald J. Black
Charles Blinderman
Ed Block, Jr.
Alfredo Bonadeo
Vittoria Borsò
Maura Brady
Mary Lee Bretz
Stephen W. Brown
Martine Watson Brownley
Siobhan Craft Brownson
Michael Bruce
Ralph W. Buechler

John J. Burke, Jr.
William Bush
Robert Carballo
Geoffrey Carnall
Federico A. Chachagua
Richard M. Chadbourne
Linda H. Chance
David W. Chapman
Kathryn Chittick
Albrecht Classen
Edith W. Clowes
William Connor
Thomas L. Cooksey
Kevin L. Cope
Aurelian Crăiuţu
Anna Lisa Crone
Christine Crow
Melba Cuddy-Keane
Dalia Daniel
David Darby
Sarah B. Daugherty
Pamela Davidson
David R. Davies
Duane H. Davis

Charles de Paolo
Augustinus P. Dierick
Marion Doebeling
Diane Dowdey
Joseph Duemer
Klay Dyer
Wilton Eckley
Ronald Egan
Hans Eichner
Stanisław Eile
Antonio Elorza
John Elsworth
Rainer Emig
Sandra A. Engel
Steven Epley
Colin Evans
Timothy J. Evans
Lydia Fakundiny
Jennifer Farrar
Peter Faulkner
Robert K. Faulkner
John Ferns
John Fletcher
I. P. Foote
Richard D. Fulton
Steven H. Gale
Blanca M. García Monsivais
Michael D. Garval
Daniel D. Gilfillan
Kathleen M. Glenn
Willi Goetschel
Miguel Gomes
José Luis Gómez-Martínez
Vivian Greene-Gantzberg
Benoît Grevisse
Carlos M. Gutiérrez
John H. Haddox
Garry L. Hagberg
Nicholas Hammond
William E. Harkins
Mark Harman
Thomas S. Harrington
Jane Gary Harris
Dale E. Haskell
Donald M. Hassler
Mark Hawkins-Dady
Heather Henderson
Paul Hendon
Laurie Hergenhan
Harry Heseltine
Douglas Hesse
Astrid Heyer
Peter Hinchcliffe
Darrell Hinchliffe
Petr Holman
John R. Holmes
Jiří Holý
Brian Horowitz
Bernard Howells
Alina C. Hunt

Maura Ives
Gregory S. Jackson
Zbigniew Janowski
Gloria Godfrey Jones
Jep C. Jonson
Linda A. Julian
Arpad Kadarkay
Andrzej Karcz
William H. Katra
R. Lane Kauffmann
Karen A. Keely
John Pavel Kehlen
Arnold Keller
Gary Kelly
Malcolm Kelsall
Ian Ker
Sonia I. Ketchian
Rolf Kieser
George L. Kline
Gerhard P. Knapp
Wulf Koepke
Michael S. Koppisch
Krzysztof Kozłowski
Allen J. Kuharski
James M. Kuist
Edward T. Larkin
David Lazar
Anthony Levi
Marc Lits
Donald W. Livingston
Rosemary Lloyd
Jennifer Lonergan
Luis Lorenzo-Rivero
Barbara Lounsberry
Steven Lynn
John A. McCarthy
Christopher P. McClintick
Brian McCrea
Margery Palmer McCulloch
Josephine McDonagh
Richard D. McGhee
Alan T. McKenzie
Susan Mackervoy
John McLaren
James Maharg
John L. Mahoney
Laurent Mailhot
Gilles Marcotte
Christine Masuy
Beverly J. Matiko
Sigrid Mayer
Laurence W. Mazzeno
Benoît Melançon
Thomas Mermall
David Midgley
Călin-Andrei Mihăilescu
Anthony Miller
Stephen Miller
P. M. Mitchell
Katia Mitova-Janowski

Gerald Monsman
Howard Moss
Vanna Motta
Agnes C. Müller
James Mulvihill
Pedro Maria Muñoz
Isobel Murray
Michael D. Murray
Brian Musgrove
Eunice Doman Myers
William F. Naufftus
Virgil Nemoianu
Catherine O'Neil
Charles L. O'Neill
Barbara Mary Onslow
José Miguel Oviedo
George S. Pahomov
Pamela Park
Paul Nicholas Pavich
Ann Pearson
Ted-Larry Pebworth
Janet Pérez
Elizabeth Perkins
Jill Piggott
Mary Ellen Pitts
D. E. Pollard
John H. R. Polt
Richard Polt
Valentina Polukhina
Jonathan F. S. Post
John T. Price
Suzanne R. Pucci
Michael Pursglove
Nanxiu Qian
Patricia Rae
Harold Raley
Nigel Rapport
Velma Bourgeois Richmond
Daniel E. Ritchie
William Roberts
Ian Ross Robertson
Daniel Robinson
Dan Roche
John H. Rogers
Lourdes Rojas
Judson Rosengrant
Jan Peter F. van Rosevelt
Noel Rowe
Joaquín Roy
Pilar G. Sáenz
Diego Saglia
Ciro A. Sandoval-B.
Verónica Saunero-Ward
Lilia Savova
Richard Schell
Barry P. Scherr

Karen Schiff
Eric Schwab
Richard Sheldon
Alvin F. Sherman, Jr.
James R. Simmons, Jr.
Anne Skabarnicki
David A. Sloane
Christopher Smith
Vivian Smith
Robert V. Smythe
Alvin Snider
María Soledad Carrasco
Steven P. Sondrup
Clara Speer
Barry Spurr
George J. Stack
David Staines
Robert C. Steensma
Patricia Owen Steiner
Ralph Stewart
Staci L. Stone
Richard E. Strassberg
Ned Stuckey-French
David Suchoff
Imre Szeman
Richard C. Taylor
Rodney Taylor
Carmen Chaves Tesser
Gillian Thomas
Matthew Titolo
Richard C. Tobias
Tamara Trojanowska
Brian Turner
Pierre L. Ullman
Nicasio Urbina
Antonio Urrello
Andrius Valevičius
James M. van der Laan
Camille Villafañe
Charlotte Zoë Walker
Harry Walsh
George Wasserman
Laura D. Weeks
Paul L. Wenske
Theresa Werner
Alan G. H. West
Terry Whalen
Kathleen M. Wheeler
Keith Wilson
Michael Winkler
Allen G. Wood
Servanne Woodward
Linda Mills Woolsey
Jerald Zaslove
William Zeiger
Robert Zweig

LIST OF ENTRIES

PREFACE

An encyclopedia of the essay sounds at first like a paradoxical enterprise: how can the essay's elusive multiplicity of forms and themes be contained within the systematic scope of an encyclopedia? The essay is often characterized by its spontaneity, its unpredictability, its very lack of system. Yet precisely these qualities have made it the little noticed (though much practiced) of the literary genres, and hence the most in need of some kind of comprehensive guide. Of course there can be no complete mapping of such a diverse literary form: to define all of its varieties and enumerate all its practitioners would take a much larger volume than this. Nevertheless, the *Encyclopedia of the Essay* does bring together the essential information for exploring this protean form of writing, and each entry has a section of suggestions for further reading.

The *Encyclopedia* does not apply a rigid, exclusive definition of what is or is not an essay, nor does it aim at exhaustive cataloguing of every author who has ever written an essay. Rather, it provides several types of entry as ways to access the vast and heterogeneous field of essayistic writing: 1) *generic* – considerations of different types of essay (moral essay, travel essay, autobiographical essay, for example) and different adjacent forms (aphorism, chapter, *feuilleton*, sermon, and so on); 2) *national* – entries on the major national traditions (French, British, Japanese, for example); 3) *individual* – entries on those writers who have produced a significant body of work in the genre. In addition, there is consideration of 4) the significance of *periodicals* in creating a market for essay writing, and entries on particularly important journals, along with 5) a few entries on especially significant single essays. Those interested in the theory of the essay are referred to the entries on Lukács, Adorno, and Bense – curiously, in view of the fact that the European essay first established itself in France and England, the theorists of the genre have come mainly from the Germanic cultural sphere. The four main categories of entry – formal, national, individual, and periodical – give four different routes into the territory of essayistic literature.

Despite the huge variety of its forms, there are certain features which recur often enough to give the word "essay" a specific though not rigid meaning. Generally it is used of nonfictional prose texts of between one and about 50 pages, though in some cases book-length works are also called essays. The term also frequently connotes a certain quality of approach to a topic, variously characterized as provisional and exploratory, rather than systematic and definitive. The essay can be contrasted with the academic article, which is usually a contribution to a recognized discipline and to a collaborative inquiry, previous inquiries being taken account of by means of quotations and footnotes. The essay tends to be personal rather than collaborative in its approach, and usually lacks this kind of scholarly apparatus. The essayist's authority is not based on formal credentials or academic expertise, but on his or her personality as reflected in the style of writing. Persuasiveness is based on distinctiveness of style rather than on the use of an accepted professional or technical vocabulary. The essay typically eschews specialized jargon and is addressed to the "general reader" in a friendly, informal tone. It also avoids the application of pre-established methodology to particular cases, but rather works from the particular toward the general, and even then is not concerned to produce conclusions applicable to other cases. Its concerns are personal and particular, more than professional and systematic.

Nevertheless, the essay can flourish around the margins of academic disciplines or at their origins. A topic that initially forms the subject matter of essays can later be treated within a discipline. For example, many of Freud's short texts are classics of essayistic inquiry, even though Freud considered them contributions to a systematic science of psychoanalysis, despite their literary references and style. Within the European context, the modern essay originated at the same time as modern science, in the late 16th century, and shares many characteristics with it, chiefly the stress on empirical investigation rather than on established authorities such as Aristotle. Bacon, the founder of the English essay, was also the first writer to lay out a program for what we now call science. Yet as science became collectively organized it tended to become less essayistic. The essay stayed on the margins of science, as a vehicle either for unorthodox speculations or for communicating some of science's results to a non-specialist audience, as in the writings of Stephen Jay Gould and others. Another example of an essayistic topic being institutionalized is Cultural Studies. Essayists like Robert Louis Stevenson and George Orwell wrote about "penny dreadful" comics, dirty postcards, and pulp fiction long before these topics were taken up in the academy and made into the matter of research within a new discipline.

Literary theory is another interesting case. Informal speculative essays like T. S. Eliot's "Tradition and the Individual Talent" or Walter Benjamin's "The Work of Art in the Age of Mechanical Reproduction" can acquire almost canonical status within academic theory, even though they were produced outside that context. Roland Barthes wrote highly theoretical works, but also quite personal, semi-autobiographical essays. Current literary theory seems partly in tune with the essay in the common stress on the provisional, unfixed nature of meaning, yet out of sympathy with the essayistic assumptions of a distinctive, autonomous personality and a concretely rendered reality.

The essay can provide a home for academics wanting a broader context and a wider audience for their work. Some who begin their writing within a disciplinary framework later move outside it into essayistic inquiry. Philosophy provides several examples. Heidegger moved from systematic philosophy to short poetic meditations and essays on poets like Hölderlin, Benn, and Rilke. Nietzsche forsook academia altogether and devised his own form of essayistic philosophy-writing which has paradoxically become influential in academia once again (though in literature rather than philosophy departments). Although academics can also be essayists, many essayists have been independent writers, without academic affiliations.

Besides its ambivalent relations with institutional discourses, the essay is also usually perceived as marginal to other literary genres. Just as the essay is considered to be "not quite" science or philosophy or theory, it is also "not quite" art. At least, it is not perceived "great" art, since it is a seemingly "minor" form. Many, perhaps most, essayists have made their reputations in other genres. The example of Montaigne, who founded the essay form and wrote in it almost exclusively, was not followed often. Essayists are commonly also poets, philosophers, theorists, and so on, though usually this statement is put the other way round: poets and the others are also essayists. This way of stating the matter reflects the ancillary or secondary status of the essay as the least prestigious of the literary forms. T. S. Eliot's essays have had as much influence as his poetry, yet they have had much less attention as literary works in their own right. Virginia Woolf's essays are at least as important as her fiction, yet they are still often used as a quarry for insights into the fiction. Orwell's essays are of higher literary quality than many of his novels, yet the prestige of the fictional form means that they are relatively neglected.

There are, however, signs that this critical neglect is ending, in the publication of works such as my own book *The Observing Self: Rediscovering the Essay* (London and New York: Routledge, 1988) and Claire de Obaldia's *The Essayistic Spirit: Literature, Modern Criticism, and the Essay* (Oxford: Clarendon Press, and New York: Oxford University Press, 1995), as well as a number of shorter studies listed in the bibliographical entries. This renewal of critical interest coincides with the continuing flourishing of the genre itself. The number of current or recent essayists included in this encyclopedia testifies to the vitality of the form, which has seen as rich a harvest in the 20th century as in any of the preceding ones. Many of the most famous Modernist authors, like T. S. Eliot, D. H. Lawrence, Aldous Huxley, Virginia Woolf, Thomas Mann, Paul Valéry, and W. H. Auden have left outstanding collections of essays, while among contemporaries, Susan Sontag, Joan Didion, Barry Lopez, or Stephen Jay Gould could be cited among many others as skilled practitioners of the art. Moreover, the success of recent anthologies such as John Gross' *The Oxford Book of Essays* (Oxford and New York: Oxford University Press, 1991), Phillip Lopate's *The Art of the Personal Essay* (New York: Doubleday, 1994), and Robert Atwan's *The Best American Essays* series (Boston: Houghton Mifflin, 1986–) indicates that there is an appetite among the general public for essays.

The *Encyclopedia* reflects the geographical and historical concentration of the essay form in the Euro-American world from Montaigne to the present. But the classical antecedents of the form in Greece and Rome are also noted in several entries, and the global dimension of the form is also amply represented. The Japanese and Chinese essay each receive an entry, contrasting the prose forms which predate Montaigne with the later Western-influenced types of essay. In the 20th century the list of individual authors treated includes African, Australian, Asian, as well as European and North and South American writers. The range of locations of contributors to the *Encyclopedia* also reflects the breadth of interest in the form. The essay has become truly global as the preconditions for it become more widespread: a sufficient number of suitable periodicals, a regime which tolerates criticism, an informed general readership, and writers who cultivate a distinctive, individual view of culture.

At heart, the essay is the voice of the individual. Wherever that is heard and heeded, the essay will flourish. Orwell in the 1940s pessimistically foresaw the perishing of the essay (and other forms of realistic prose, such as the novel) in the coming age of totalitarianism. The success of his own essays, particularly "Politics and the English Language," in the postwar period disproved his prediction, at least temporarily. This *Encyclopedia*, besides providing a guide to the enormous richness of the essay's past and present, is also a good augury for its continuing vitality in the future.

GRAHAM GOOD

A

Achebe, Chinua

Nigerian, 1930–

Chinua Achebe is the first major African novelist to be widely read and recognized both inside and outside Africa, and is also renowned for his role as the founding editor of the African Writers series published by Heinemann. His career as an essayist is limited to two collections of essays, *Morning Yet on Creation Day* (1975) and *Hopes and Impediments* (1988), as well as *The Trouble with Nigeria* (1983), a long essay which diagnoses the reasons for the political stagnation of post-colonial Nigeria. However, the influence and importance of his essays have far exceeded their actual number. They have been instrumental in establishing the critical and theoretical issues with which other African writers such as **Ngugi wa Thiong'o**, **Wole Soyinka**, and the *bolekaja* critics (Chinweizu and Madubuike) have had to grapple, and along with the work of the Frantz Fanon are among the earliest examples of the type of critical writing that has come to be known as "post-colonial" criticism.

Achebe's essays are mainly conversational in nature, written for lectures that he has been invited to give in response to specific questions and situations. In the essays in *Morning Yet on Creation Day* and *Hopes and Impediments* (which reproduces five essays from the earlier collection), he articulates three characteristic concerns in his self-appointed role as spokesperson for the African novel. In essays such as "Colonialist Criticism" (1974), he is critical of the failure of European critics to understand African literature on its own terms. In their demand that African fiction be concerned with issues and themes that are "universal," Achebe sees European critics as perpetuating a colonialist attitude which views "the African writer as a somewhat unfinished European who with patient guidance will grow up one day and write like every other European." For Achebe, evidence of the autonomy and uniqueness of African literature from its European counterpart can be seen, for example, in the very different role that the African writer must have toward his or her society. In "The Novelist as Teacher" (1965), he attacks the notion that the African writer should adopt the Western Modernist pose of the angst-ridden writer living on the fringes of society. The African novelist has an obligation to educate, to "help society regain belief in itself and put away the complexes of the years of denigration and self-abasement." Achebe is aware this might mean that "... perhaps what I write is applied art as distinct from pure. But who cares? Art is important, but so is education of the kind I have in mind." The Igbo ceremony of *mbari*, a festival of images in which every member of the society participates, provides him with an example of artistic production in which "there is no rigid tension between makers of culture and its consumers. Art belongs to all and is a 'function' of society" (*Morning*).

More controversially, Achebe has defended the use of English and other European languages in the production of African fiction against those critics who suggest that authentic African experience can only be represented in an African language. On the one hand, this is because for Achebe, English – being "a language spoken by Africans on African soil" (*Morning*) – is an African language. As he suggests in "The African Writer and the English Language" (1964), English (as well as French and Arabic) also makes it possible for there to be national literatures in Africa which cut across the enormous linguistic differences present within each nation. Although he feels that the English language can express his experiences as an African, it is important to recognize that "it will have to be a new English, still in full communion with its ancestral home but altered to suit its African surroundings" (*Morning*) – a point which critics of Achebe's stance have often failed to understand.

One of Achebe's most famous and important essays – an essay which he has described as his "standard-bearer" (*Hopes*) – is "An Image of Africa: Racism in Conrad's *Heart of Darkness*" (1975). While admitting that Conrad is "undoubtedly one of the great stylists of modern fiction," Achebe draws attention to the fact that he is nevertheless "a thoroughgoing racist." In Achebe's opinion, Western critics have praised Conrad's novella while never addressing the racism at its core; Conrad depicts Africa as incomprehensible, frenzied, dark, grotesque, and dangerous, and Africans as ugly, inarticulate, inhuman, and savage. Achebe criticizes this failure, and effectively deals with a range of rejoinders which might be used to "save" Conrad from being labeled a racist. For example, while it may be possible to see these attitudes as those of Conrad's character Marlow, Achebe claims that Conrad "neglects to hint, clearly and adequately, at an alternative form of reference by which we may judge the actions and opinions of his characters." While it is now common for literary critics to approach fictional works through a consideration of issues such as race, Achebe's criticism of Conrad is an early and influential example of the shift of literary criticism toward a more explicit treatment of the broader politics of fiction.

Since the publication of *Hopes*, Achebe has produced little in the way of either essays or fiction. As the founding editor of *Okike: A Nigerian Journal of New Writing* (begun 1971; subtitle later changed from *Nigerian* to *African*), he has nevertheless continued to play a prominent role in providing a forum for literary and critical writing in Africa. The main thrust of his critical writing has remained the same throughout his career: "What I am saying really boils down to a simple plea for the African novel. Don't fence me in" (*Morning*).

IMRE SZEMAN

Biography

Born Albert Chinualumogu, 16 November 1930 in Ogidi. Studied at Government College, Umuahia, 1944–47; University College, Ibadan, 1948–53, B.A. (London), 1953. Worked in various positions for the Nigerian Broadcasting Corporation in Lagos and Enugu, 1954–66. Married Christiana Chinwe Okoli, 1961: two sons and two daughters. Founding editor, Heinemann African Writers series, 1962–72, and director, Heinemann Educational Books (Nigeria), and Nwankwo-Ifejika (later Nwamife) publishers, Enugu, from 1970; chair, Citadel Books, Enugu, 1967. Senior research fellow, 1967–73, and professor of English, 1973–81, now emeritus, University of Nigeria, Nsukka; also visiting professor or lecturer at various American universities, 1972–90. Served on diplomatic missions for Biafra during the Nigerian Civil War, 1967–69. Founding editor, *Okike: An African Journal of New Writing*, from 1971; founder and publisher, *Uwa Ndi Igbo: A Bilingual Journal of Igbo Life and Arts*, from 1984. Pro-chancellor and chair of the council, Anambra State University of Technology, Enugu, 1986–88. Awards: many, including the Margaret Wrong Memorial Prize, 1959; Nigerian National Trophy, 1960; New Statesman Jock Campbell Award, 1965; Commonwealth Poetry Prize, 1973; Nigerian National Merit Award, 1979; Commonwealth Foundation Award, 1984; honorary degrees from 16 universities. Member, Order of the Federal Republic of Nigeria, 1979; Honorary Member, American Academy of Arts and Letters, 1982; Fellow, Royal Society of Literature, 1983.

Selected Writings

Essays and Related Prose
Morning Yet on Creation Day, 1975
The Trouble with Nigeria, 1983
Hopes and Impediments: Selected Essays, 1965–1987, 1988

Other writings: five novels (*Things Fall Apart*, 1958; *No Longer at Ease*, 1960; *Arrow of God*, 1964; *A Man of the People*, 1966; *Anthills of the Savannah*, 1987), two collections of short stories, a collection of poetry, and books for children.

Bibliography

Okpu, B. M., *Chinua Achebe: A Bibliography*, Lagos: Libriservice, 1984

Further Reading

Carroll, David, *Chinua Achebe: Novelist, Poet, Critic*, Basingstoke: Macmillan, 1990 (original edition, 1980)
Gikandi, Simon, *Reading Chinua Achebe: Language and Ideology in Fiction*, Portsmouth, New Hampshire: Heinemann, and London: Currey, 1991
Innes, C. L., *Chinua Achebe: A Critical Study*, Cambridge: Cambridge University Press, 1990
Innes, C. L., and Bernth Lindfors, editors, *Critical Perspectives on Chinua Achebe*, Washington, D.C.: Three Continents Press, 1978; London: Heinemann Educational, 1979
JanMohammed, Abdul R., *Manichean Aesthetics: The Politics of Literature in Colonial Africa*, Amherst: University of Massachusetts Press, 1988 (original edition, 1983)
Killam, G. D., *The Writings of Chinua Achebe*, London: Heinemann Educational, 1977 (original edition, as *The Novels of Chinua Achebe*, 1969)
Moses, Michael Valdez, *The Novel and the Globalization of Culture*, New York and Oxford: Oxford University Press, 1995
Ngugi wa Thiong'o, "Chinua Achebe: *A Man of the People*," in his *Homecoming: Essays on African and Caribbean Literature, Culture and Politics*, London: Heinemann, 1972
Ojinmah, Umelo, *Chinua Achebe: New Perspectives*, Ibadan: Spectrum, 1991
Peterson, Kirsten Holt, and Anna Rutherford, editors, *Chinua Achebe: A Celebration*, Portsmouth, New Hampshire: Heinemann International, 1991
Ugah, Ada, *In the Beginning: Chinua Achebe at Work*, Ibadan: Heinemann Educational, 1990
Wanjala, Chris L., editor, *Standpoints on African Literature: A Critical Anthology*, Nairobi: East African Literature Bureau, 1973
Wren, Robert, *Achebe's World: The Historical and Cultural Context of the Novels of Chinua Achebe*, Washington, D.C.: Three Continents Press, 1980; Harlow: Longman, 1981

Addison, Joseph

English, 1672–1719

Joseph Addison's major reputation as a moralist, stylist, and critic in the 18th and 19th centuries was based primarily on his essays for the *Spectator* (1711–12), a daily periodical he edited in conjunction with **Richard Steele**. After a short intermission the journal was revived in 1714 under Addison's control. The *Spectator* was a development from Steele's *Tatler* (1709–11) and led on to the *Guardian* (1713), both of which Addison wrote for. It was considered exemplary in both style and morality by 18th-century critics such as **Samuel Johnson** and Hugh Blair. In the 19th century **Thomas Babington Macaulay** (in "Life and Writings of Addison," 1843) was to praise Addison's cumulative essays for the journal as "perhaps the finest ... both serious and playful, in the English language." There were many imitations, notably Johnson's *Idler* (1758–60) and *Rambler* (1750–52), John Hawkesworth's *Adventurer* (1752–54), and Robert Dodsley and Edward Moore's *World* (1753–56), as well as continental *Spectators* in French, German, Italian, and other languages.

Addison was not a professional journalist and his venture into essay writing was in some respects "time out" from the more serious aspects of his career. He had begun as an academic, spending 12 years at Oxford, where he became a Fellow of Magdalen College. He had then entered the service of the Whig party, achieving high office as secretary to the Earl of Wharton, Lord Lieutenant of Ireland. It was his loss of office with the fall of the Whigs in 1710 that provided him with the leisure for sustained periodical journalism, which he quit on resuming his political career after the death of Queen Anne. His last venture into essay writing was with the *Freeholder* (1715–16), the title of which is indicative of the Whig association of political freedom with men of independent property.

It is Addison's immersion both in the world of academic learning and in the work of the politicized civil service which gives particular experiential weight to his essays. But, although written at a time of bitter partisan controversy in politics and religion, the essays endeavor to be nonpartisan in expression. Their success, in this respect, is indicative of Addison's major historical role in establishing the parameters and discourse of a generally acceptable "polite" culture in the 18th century.

That polite culture was centered upon "the club," both in the real world (where Addison was a member of a Whig literary group, the Kit-Cats) and in the fictional world of "Mr. Spectator." As the first numbers of the *Spectator* indicate, it purports to be the record of a small club of representative gentlemen, including Sir Roger de Coverley (an old-fashioned country squire), Sir Andrew Freeport (a man representative of the trading interest), Captain Sentry (the military), Will Honeycomb (a man about town and a wit), and "a clergyman, a very philosophic man, of general learning, great sanctity of life, and the most exact breeding." The Saturday *Spectators* are a form of lay sermon by Addison (earning him the sobriquet "parson in a tie-wig"), and major influences in the promulgation of Anglican rationalism. Mr. Spectator himself claimed to write the papers of the club and is a peculiarly neutral figure, being a man of learning who has traveled widely, frequents London as an observer, but keeps free from political and religious strife.

The creation of a club of characters was an important element in providing variety in the journal and establishing the modes of discourse which united a wide-ranging body of contributors. Individual columnists were invited to assume an appropriate persona, with that of the Addisonian Spectator as normative. This was a new mode of organization of the journal as miscellany, as represented by the earlier *Tatler* and the subsequent *Guardian*. It has its roots in Horace's **satires** and epistles (rather than in the formal model of the Senecan **philosophical essay**) and in the Socratic and Ciceronian symposium. Diverse points of view are put in friendly exchange. The Horatian statement *nullius addictus iurare in verba magistri* (it is not my habit to swear by the words of any master) had been recently adopted as the motto for the Royal Society, and this skeptical empiricism (rather than dogmatic enthusiasm) was the sign of polite society. To the classical examples should be added **Montaigne**'s equally skeptical essays and those of the weary, worldly-wise Epicurean, **Sir William Temple**.

These formal models carry an ideological implication. Even in summary it is apparent that this is a masculine society and the readership was being shaped from male norms. Within the club itself certain members are privileged over others. Sir Andrew Freeport represents all that is best in developing commercial society, whereas Sir Roger, although a delightful comic eccentric, signifies an out-of-date, small-world squirearchy (and thus votes Tory). In morality, the clergyman is normative, whereas Will Honeycomb carries with him certain aspects of "Restoration" society whose libertinage had been corrected or purged by societies for the reformation of manners. Likewise, in matters of taste, a correct canon of literature is representative of proper thinking. Addison was a major influence in establishing *Paradise Lost* as an English classic (Milton being purged of his republican and regicide views expressed elsewhere).

The enormous success of Addison in shaping polite society seems to have been achieved by his ability to present his substantial learning in an accessible manner and to clarify complex arguments. This is done with good-humored wit, in an easy tone, and always from a moral viewpoint. He claimed, "I have brought Philosophy out of Closets and Libraries, Schools and Colleges, to dwell in Clubs and Assemblies, at Tea-Tables, and in Coffee-Houses" (*Spectator* no. 10). He is thus a popularizer who found (and made) a public eager to learn but alienated by pedantry, obscurity, and vicious partisan controversy.

Certain groups of essays provide (in easy "sound-bites," as it were) both the most accessible, and the most advanced, treatment of current topics. In literature the series on "The Pleasures of the Imagination" (nos. 411–21) constitutes an important source for the development of Romantic theory and sensibility emerging from Lockean psychology, establishing key terms such as "fancy" and "beauty" (as well as "imagination" itself) and distinguishing between primary natural sources and those to be found in literature. Addison's social agenda is always prominent: "A Man of a Polite Imagination is let into a great many Pleasures, that the Vulgar are not capable of receiving. He can converse with a Picture, and find an agreeable Companion in a Statue. He meets with a secret Refreshment in a Description, and often feels a greater Satisfaction in the Prospect of Fields and Meadows, than another does in the Possession" (no. 411).

The religious agenda is implicit in setting the long series of essays on *Paradise Lost* on Saturdays, the lay-sermon days (nos. 267–369), but the emphasis here is on the pleasure of a great Christian poem, amply represented by quotation and easily placed within the classical tradition: "I have therefore bestowed a Paper upon each Book, and endeavoured not only to prove that the Poem is beautiful in general, but to point out its particular Beauties, and to determine wherein they consist. I have endeavoured to show how some Passages are beautiful by being Sublime, others, by being Soft, others, by being Natural; which of them are recommended by the Passion, which by the Moral, which by the Sentiment, and which by the Expression" (no. 369).

But for many readers it has been Addison's and Steele's Sir Roger de Coverley who runs away with the text. In this respect he is a median figure between Shakespeare's Falstaff (who destabilizes the ideology of the History plays) and characters in the sentimental novel like Laurence Sterne's Uncle Toby in *Tristram Shandy*. His objection to anyone sleeping in church except himself (no. 112), his remedy for love in fox hunting (no. 115), or the account of his death by his servant, Edward Biscuit (no. 517), show both how much the essay here owes to drama, and how much it is involved with the development of the heteroglossia of the novel. Thus, Biscuit: "Upon his coming home, the first Complaint he made was, that he had lost his Roast-Beef Stomach, not being able to touch a Sirloin, which was served up according to Custom: and you know how he used to take great Delight in it. From that Time forward he grew worse and worse, but still kept a good Heart to the last."

Equally important for the development of the novel is Addison's critical banter on gender relations. "The Moral World, as consisting of Males and Females, is of a Mixt Nature, and filled with several Customs, Fashion and Ceremonies, which would have no place in it were there but *One Sex*. Had our Species no Females in it, Men would be quite different Creatures from what they are at present; their Endeavours to please the Opposite Sex, polishes and refines them out of those Manners which are most Natural to them ..." (no. 433). This is a constant motif, but the account of Amazons and hermaphrodites which follows may now have acquired an unforeseen comedy. Paradoxically it is in the area in which his essays were particularly effective – the education of "the fair sex" – that Addison's writing may have acquired a provocative edge which originally it eschewed.

MALCOLM KELSALL

Biography
Born 1 May 1672 in Milston, Wiltshire. Studied at Charterhouse, London, where he met Richard Steele, 1686–87; Queen's College, Oxford, 1687–89; Magdalen College, Oxford, 1689–93, M.A., 1693. Fellow, Magdalen College, 1698–1711. Received a government pension, 1699, and traveled on the continent, 1699–1704. Moved to London, 1704; became a member of the Kit-Cat Club; served the Whig party, holding various appointed positions, 1704–10, including secretary to Lord Wharton, Lord Lieutenant of Ireland, 1709–10; Member of Parliament for Lostwithiel, 1708–10, and Malmesbury, 1710–19. Contributor to Richard Steele's *Tatler*, 1709–11, and the *Guardian*, 1713; editor of the *Whig Examiner*, 1710, the *Spectator*, with Steele, 1711–12, and alone, 1714, and the *Freeholder*, 1715–16. Secretary to the Earl of Sunderland, Lord Lieutenant of Ireland, 1714–15; appointed commissioner for trade and the colonies, 1715. Married Charlotte, Dowager Countess of Warwick, 1716: one daughter. Secretary of state in the Sunderland cabinet, 1717–18. Died in London (as a result of a degenerative heart condition and dropsy), 17 June 1719.

Selected Writings

Essays and Related Prose
The Tatler (periodical), edited by Richard Steele, nos. 1–271, 12 April 1709–2 January 1711; edited by Donald F. Bond, 3 vols., 1987
The Spectator (periodical), written and edited with Richard Steele, nos. 1–555, 1 March 1711–6 December 1712; second series (written and edited by Addison alone), nos. 556–635, 18 June–20 December 1714; edited by Gregory Smith (Everyman Edition), 4 vols., 1907, reprinted 1979, and by Donald F. Bond (Clarendon Edition), 5 vols., 1965; selection, as *Critical Essays from "The Spectator"*, edited by Bond, 1970
The Guardian (periodical), with others, nos. 1–175, 12 March–1 October 1713; edited by John Calhoun Stephens, 1982
The Free-Holder; or, Political Essays, nos. 1–55, 23 December 1715–29 June 1716; as *The Freeholder*, edited by James Leheny, 1979
Selections from the Tatler and the Spectator, edited by Angus Ross, 1982

Other writings: poetry, three plays (including the tragedy *Cato*, 1713), travel writing (*Remarks on Italy*, 1705), and correspondence (collected in *The Letters of Joseph Addison*, edited by Walter Graham, 1941).

Collected works edition: *The Works of the Right Honourable Joseph Addison*, edited by Thomas Tickell, 4 vols., 1721, revised edition, 6 vols., 1811.

Bibliography
Rogal, Samuel J., "Joseph Addison (1672–1719): A Check List of Works and Major Scholarship," *Bulletin of the New York Public Library* (Winter 1974): 236–50

Further Reading
Bloom, Edward A., and Lillian D. Bloom, *Addison's Sociable Animal: In the Market Place, on the Hustings, in the Pulpit*, Providence, Rhode Island: Brown University Press, 1971
Bloom, Edward A., and Lillian D. Bloom, editors, *Addison and Steele: The Critical Heritage*, London: Routledge, 1980
Bloom, Edward A., Lillian D. Bloom, and Edmund Leites, editors, *Educating the Audience: Addison, Steele, and Eighteenth-Century Culture*, Los Angeles: University of California William Andrews Clark Memorial Library, 1984
Elioseff, Lee A., *The Cultural Milieu of Addison's Literary Criticism*, Austin: University of Texas Press, 1963
Humphreys, A. R., *Steele, Addison, and Their Periodical Essays*, London: Longman Green, 1959
Ketcham, Michael G., *Transparent Designs: Reading, Performance, and Form in the Spectator Papers*, Athens: University of Georgia Press, 1985
Nablow, Ralph A., *The Addisonian Tradition in France: Passion and Objectivity and Social Observation*, Rutherford, New Jersey: Fairleigh Dickinson University Press, 1990
Rau, Fritz, *Zur Verbreitung und Nachahmung des Tatler und Spectator*, Heidelberg: Winter, 1980
Smithers, Peter, *The Life of Addison*, Oxford: Clarendon Press, 1968 (original edition, 1954)

Adorno, Theodor W.
German, 1903–1969

Theodor W. Adorno, the son of a Jewish merchant and an Italian singer, became famous as a philosopher and aesthetic theorist, not only for his many essays on literature and art, but chiefly for the critical theory he developed together with Max Horkheimer at the Frankfurt Institute for Social Research. His most famous work, written with Horkheimer during the years of exile in America, is the *Dialektik der Aufklärung* (1947; *Dialectic of Enlightenment*), which tackles the question of how the horror of National Socialism could have happened in a highly civilized country. In answering this question Horkheimer and Adorno provide a general critique of the modern age and capitalism, which reaches far beyond the narrow historical context of World War II to examine how Enlightenment thought made way for positivist philosophy as a "myth" of reality. With the resulting disintegration of reality into isolated facts, Western rationalism reaches its limit. This terminal state of affairs has had a destructive effect on the Western world itself.

In this work, and in his second, pessimistically tinged philosophical work, the *Negative Dialektik* (1966; *Negative Dialectics*), Adorno stands in opposition to his more optimistic colleague Ernst Bloch, whose *Das Prinzip Hoffnung* (1953; *The Principle of Hope*) he dismissed as naive. In what is known as the positivism dispute, Adorno also accused conventional philosophy (Karl Popper and **Martin Heidegger**) of positing an object independent of the subject, when the object is in fact subjectively defined and equally arbitrary. This, according to Adorno, obscures the real interrelations between individual and society, subject and object, essence and appearance. He therefore calls for a fundamental redefinition of the evaluating subject in society and art. In consequence, the posthumously published *Ästhetische Theorie* (1970; *Aesthetic Theory*) refers mainly to the concept of art in the context of the modern age, a bias that is also apparent in the subjects of his many essays on art and literature produced from 1930 onward.

Both Adorno's style of philosophy and his critique of social systems, based on the theories of Hegel, **Marx**, and **Freud**, are shaped by his predominant dialectic mode of thought. In historical reality and therefore also in philosophical thought, Adorno sees contradictions that cannot be resolved. These contradictions also give art a dual character: on the one hand art is socially determined, yet on the other the work of art is autonomous and independent of the social conditions that produced it. According to Adorno, we should not seek to resolve this contradiction but rather should accept it as it is, using the work of art as a means to achieve knowledge. He therefore criticizes the rigid, dogmatic conception of realism in art (as represented by **Georg Lukács** and Marxist aesthetics), which assumes that art's only function is to reflect social injustices. On the other hand, Adorno declares himself in favor of an art of protest, an art that refuses to endorse existing social conditions. His essays give new form to the concept of the avant-garde. Especially in the period following World War II, after his return in 1949 from exile in America, Adorno produced some of his most important writings on art and literature, written in his distinctive dialectic-artistic style; these works can themselves be considered as avant-garde works of art.

An impressive example of Adorno's artistic style of writing is provided by the manifesto-like "Der Essay als Form" ("The Essay as Form"), first published in the *Noten zur Literatur I (Notes to Literature)* in 1958. Here, following his earlier theories, according to which the increasing power of science had led to the demythologization of the world and of thought, Adorno accords particular importance to the essay form, as it avoids both absolute concepts and strict definitions. According to Adorno, the essay as a genre comes close to being a form of art, operating in the sphere of unmediated thought, where the different logical stages have not yet been separated from one another. As Adorno notes at the beginning of his essay, the essay as a form has been accorded less recognition than it deserves, precisely because of its position halfway between art and the objectivizing sciences. Although the neglect of the essay form had also been lamented by Lukács, Adorno sees this neglect as the logical consequence of an overemphasis on the scientific method of discovering truth. In this work, Adorno describes the way the perceiving subject organizes concepts within the essay form by comparing it with the behavior of a traveler who finds himself in a foreign land with no formal education and has to view concepts in their experiential context in order to understand them. Formal philosophy, by contrast, gets out a grammar book and dictionary, losing sight of the broader context which is created by the essay. The essay, with its provocative, skeptical outlook, treats science and the concepts of formal philosophy "in a systematically unsystematic way." Therefore, although the essay by definition cannot claim to achieve completeness or objective truth, it does succeed, through the very negation of these claims, in coming close to the truth of the matter. Thus the essay's "art-like quality" consists in this "awareness of the non-identity of representation and object." For Adorno this also means that the concepts used in the essay are related to theory, although the essay itself is not, as Lukács assumed, derived from theory. Adorno agrees with **Max Bense** that the essay is

"the critical form *par excellence*" and therefore also a tool for the critique of ideology. It is precisely because the essay can also incorporate untruth, and because it includes its own negation, that it does not conform to rigid, hierarchical ideological schemes. This means, finally, that the essay is an anachronistic form, caught between an omnipotent science and the last remnants of a philosophy retreating into abstract realms.

This pessimistic but aesthetically productive analysis of the state of the essay form in the late 20th century seems to have inspired Adorno to produce many of his essays in the *Notes on Literature*. The title of this work in itself (which could equally be translated as "notes for literature") indicates that Adorno accords poetic language a central significance, viewing literature in terms of musical composition. Most of the essays consider the role of language in society and in the modern age. In his essay "Zum Klassizismus von Goethes *Iphigenie*" (1974; On the classicism of Goethe's *Iphigenia*), for example, Adorno recognizes the redemptive power of language as a medium of truth and appeasement in **Goethe**'s classical work. Language helps unravel the entanglement of barbarism and civilization. "Language becomes the representative of order and at the same time produces order from freedom, from subjectivity," is Adorno's verdict on Goethe's treatment of the Iphigenia story. Here, Adorno turns against the traditional view that Goethe's work "denied the power of negativity and fabricated a spurious harmony." He quotes directly from the text to show that Orestes "by dint of his stark antithesis to the myth, threatens to fall victim to it." In this way, according to Adorno, Goethe's play prophesies the transition from Enlightenment to mythology. This farsighted and controversial critique of the Enlightenment through the interpretation of Goethe's *Iphigenia* can succeed only because Adorno presents it in the form of the essay, which can incorporate antithetical elements and in which a dialectical method of argumentation can be deployed to the full.

The contradictions which, according to Adorno, arise from the fact that language simultaneously represents and creates order, are becoming ever more acute as the modern age progresses. Just as the possibility of order seems to be increasingly elusive, so the utopia of language is disappearing in the representation of this impossibility. For this reason, as Adorno describes in his essay on Beckett ("Versuch, das *Endspiel* zu verstehen" [1961; "Attempt to Understand *Endgame*"]), the language of modern art is now no more than a differential of silence. The failure of language, which Beckett expresses in a number of ways, is interpreted by Adorno as the crisis of an existential terror which is literally lost for words. Beckett's existentialism gives expression to the catastrophe of the modern age, by reducing the drama (*Endgame*) to silent gestures. The organized meaninglessness that characterizes Beckett's work is apparent in the fact that the play has neither beginning, end, nor dramatic progression in between. Instead the whole drama is composed using techniques of reversal and negation. For Adorno this is a dramatic depiction of the final stage in the historical disintegration of subjectivity. The suffering of the figures in the play, and that of the reader who recognizes this existential finality, become for Adorno the measure of human awareness.

The foundation for Adorno's detailed and reflective analyses of many other literary texts can be found in his view that the disinterested contemplation of art is the only honest form of historical contemplation. Eichendorff, Heine, Balzac, **Valéry**, Proust, **Thomas Mann**, **Dickens**, George, Hochhuth, and Wedekind are just a few examples of the many authors and subjects Adorno considered in his essays. In refusing to give itself over to superficial beauty, art – and especially the art and literature of the modern age – was taking the guilt of the world upon itself. Thus for Adorno the modern work of art takes the empty place of Christ, a view demonstrated with particular clarity in his essay on Hölderlin's poetry ("Parataxis," 1965). In this way art fulfills the task of depicting the negative aspects of the world as it is.

Adorno's dialectic procedure in the essayistic description of his objects brings him close to the methods of some of his colleagues from the Frankfurt School, especially **Walter Benjamin**. Adorno also quotes Max Bense with approval. However, a feature that is uniquely characteristic of Adorno as a philosopher and ideological critic is the inversion of all relations that had previously been viewed as static, a product of his "negative dialectic" mode of thought. In this way he turns away from conventional, formal philosophy on the one hand, while at the same time reworking its conclusions in his own artistic-essayistic style of thinking and writing. Even Adorno's famous doctrine that after Auschwitz no more poems could be written is no rigid dogmatism, but the point of departure for a process of reflection which really does view its object from all sides. For Adorno this process is a prerequisite, not only for the essay as a literary form, but also for his entire philosophical undertaking.

AGNES C. MÜLLER
translated by Susan Mackervoy

Biography

Theodor Wiesengrund Adorno. Born 11 September 1903 in Frankfurt-on-Main. Studied at the University of Frankfurt, Ph.D., 1924; studied music composition under Alban Berg, from 1925; postgraduate studies in Frankfurt. Associated with the Institut für Sozialforschung (Institute for Social Research), Frankfurt, from 1928. Editor, *Anbruch* (Beginning) music journal, Vienna. Fled Nazi regime to Oxford, 1934, then to New York and Los Angeles, 1938. Married Gretel Karplus, 1937. Head of music study, Institute Office of Radio Research, Princeton, New Jersey, 1938–41, and in California, 1941–49; returned to Frankfurt, 1949; assistant director, 1950–55, codirector, 1955–58, and director, 1958–69, Institute for Social Research, Frankfurt; professor of philosophy and sociology, University of Frankfurt, 1958–69. Awards: Arnold Schoenberg Medal, 1954; Critics' Prize for Literature, 1959; Goethe Medal, 1963. Died (of a heart attack) in Visp, near Zermatt, Switzerland, 6 August 1969.

Selected Writings

Essays and Related Prose

Kierkegaard, Konstruktion des Ästhetischen, 1933; as *Kierkegaard: Construction of the Aesthetic*, edited and translated by Robert Hullot-Kentor, 1989
Philosophische Fragmente, with Max Horkheimer, 1944; as *Dialektik der Aufklärung: Philosophische Fragmente*, 1947; as *Dialectic of Enlightenment*, translated by John Cumming, 1972
Minima Moralia: Reflexionen aus dem beschädigten Leben (aphorisms), 1951; as *Minima Moralia: Reflections from Damaged Life*, translated by E. F. N. Jephcott, 1974

Versuch über Wagner, 1952; as *In Search of Wagner*, translated by Rodney Livingstone, 1981
Prismen: Kulturkritik und Gesellschaft, 1955; as *Prisms*, translated by Samuel and Shierry Weber, 1967
Noten zur Literatur, 4 vols., 1958–74; as *Notes to Literature*, vols. 1–2, edited by Rolf Tiedemann, translated by Shierry Weber Nicholsen, 1991–92
Klangfiguren: Musikalische Schriften I, 1959
Einleitung in die Musiksoziologie, 1962; as *Introduction to the Sociology of Music*, translated by E. B. Ashton, 1976
Quasi una fantasia: Musikalische Schriften II, 1963; as *Quasi una fantasia: Essays on Modern Music*, translated by Rodney Livingstone, 1992
Eingriffe: Neun kritische Modelle, 1963
Moments musicaux: Neu gedruckte Aufsätze 1928-1962, 1964
Negative Dialektik, 1966; as *Negative Dialectics*, translated by E. B. Ashton, 1973
Drei Studien zu Hegel, 1966; as *Hegel: Three Studies*, translated by Shierry Weber Nicholsen, 1993
Ohne Leitbild: Parva Aesthetica, 1967
Impromptus: Zweite Folge neu gedruckter musikalischer Aufsätze, 1968
Nervenpunkte der Neuen Musik, 1969
Stichworte: Kritische Modelle 2, 1969
Über Walter Benjamin, edited by Rolf Tiedemann, 1970; revised edition, 1990
Ästhetische Theorie, edited by Gretel Adorno and Rolf Tiedemann, 1970; as *Aesthetic Theory*, translated by C. Lenhardt, 1984
Aufsätze zur Gesellschaftstheorie und Methodologie, 1970
Die musikalischen Monographien, 1971
Kritik: Kleine Schriften zur Gesellschaft, edited by Rolf Tiedemann, 1971
Aufsätze zur Literatur des 20. Jahrhunderts, vol. 1: *Versuch, das Endspiel zu verstehen*; vol. 2: *Zur Dialektik des Engagements*, 1973
Vorlesung zur Einleitung in die Erkenntnistheorie, 1973
Vorlesung zur Einleitung in die Soziologie hielt, 1973
Vorlesungen zur Ästhetik, 1967–68, 1973
The Culture Industry: Selected Essays on Mass Culture, edited by J. M. Bernstein, 1991
The Stars Come Down to Earth and Other Essays on the Irrational in Culture, edited by Stephen Crook, 1994

Other writings: works on philosophy, sociology, and musicology.

Collected works edition: *Gesammelte Schriften*, edited by Rolf Tiedemann, 22 vols., 1973–80.

Bibliographies

Görtzen, R., "Theodor W. Adorno: Vorläufige Bibliographie seiner Schriften und der Sekundärliteratur," in *Adorno-Konferenz 1983*, edited by Ludwig von Friedeburg and Jürgen Habermas, Frankfurt-on-Main: Suhrkamp, 1983: 404–71
Pettazzi, Carlo, "Kommentierte Bibliographie zu Theodor W. Adorno," in *Theodor W. Adorno*, edited by Heinz Ludwig Arnold, Munich: Text + Kritik, 1977: 176–91
Schultz, Klaus, "Vorläufige Bibliographie der Schriften," in *Theodor W. Adorno zum Gedächtnis*, edited by Hermann Schweppenhäuser, Frankfurt-on-Main: Suhrkamp, 1971: 177–239

Further Reading

Alway, Joan, *Critical Theory and Political Possibilities: Conceptions of Emancipatory Politics in the Works of Horkheimer, Adorno, Marcuse, and Habermas*, Westport, Connecticut: Greenwood Press, 1995
Asiain, Martin, *Theodor W. Adorno, Dialektik des Aporetischen: Untersuchungen zur Rolle der Kunst in der Philosophie Theodor W. Adornos*, Fribourg: Alber, 1996

Bernstein, J. M., *The Fate of Art: Aesthetic Alienation from Kant to Derrida and Adorno*, University Park: Pennsylvania State University Press, and Cambridge: Polity Press, 1992

Bronner, Stephen Eric, *Of Critical Theory and Its Theorists*, Oxford and Cambridge, Massachusetts: Blackwell, 1994

Buck-Morss, Susan, *The Origin of Negative Dialectics: Theodor W. Adorno, Walter Benjamin and the Frankfurt Institute*, New York: Free Press, 1977

Cook, Deborah, *The Culture Industry Revisited: Theodor W. Adorno on Mass Culture*, Lanham, Maryland: Rowman and Littlefield, 1996

Hohendahl, Peter Uwe, *Prismatic Thought: Theodor W. Adorno*, Lincoln: University of Nebraska Press, 1995

Jameson, Frederic, *Late Marxism: Adorno, or, the Persistence of the Dialectic*, London and New York: Verso, 1990

Liessmann, Konrad Paul, *Ohne Mitleid: Zum Begriff der Distanz als ästhetische Kategorie mit ständiger Rücksicht auf Theodor W. Adorno*, Vienna: Passagen, 1991

Rose, Gillian, *The Melancholy Science: An Introduction to the Thought of Theodor W. Adorno*, London: Macmillan, and New York: Columbia University Press, 1978

Stamps, Judith, *Unthinking Modernity: Innis, McLuhan and the Frankfurt School*, Montreal: McGill-Queen's University Press, 1995

Tar, Zoltan, *The Frankfurt School: The Critical Theories of Max Horkheimer and Theodor W. Adorno*, New York: Wiley, 1977

Zimmermann, Norbert, *Der ästhetische Augenblick: Theodor W. Adornos Theorie der Zeitstruktur von Kunst und ästhetischer Erfahrung*, Frankfurt-on-Main and New York: Lang, 1989

Zuidervaart, Lambert, *Adorno's Aesthetic Theory: The Redemption of Illusion*, Cambridge, Massachusetts: MIT Press, 1991

The Adventurer

British periodical, 1752–1754

Together with **Joseph Addison**'s *Spectator* and **Samuel Johnson**'s *Rambler*, the *Adventurer* was one of the three most influential English-language periodicals of the 18th century. Published serially twice a week by London bookseller John Payne, and running to 140 numbers between 7 November 1752 and 9 March 1754, it was consciously designed to succeed the *Rambler*, which made its final appearance on 14 March 1752, but greatly outstripped the *Rambler*'s popularity, peaking at a circulation three times that of Johnson's publication. A contemporary hack journalist, Arthur Murphy, author of the competing *Gray's Inn Journal*, complained in print about the "attachment to the Adventurer" felt by so many readers and the impediment such loyalty placed in the way of his own efforts to generate a reliable circulation (no. 53, 20 October 1753). Another indication of the *Adventurer*'s success was the personal profit it brought to the publisher John Payne, who netted the then considerable sum of £422 from the sale of the 2000 sets of the second edition of the complete *Adventurer* and an additional £120 from the sale of half the copyright.

When Payne decided to follow up the *Rambler* with another serial of moral, aesthetic, and reflective essays, he turned to John Hawkesworth, then a little known but widely employed journalist and a fellow member of the Ivy Lane Club, which met at the King's Head, a tavern and beefsteak house located in Ivy Lane near St. Paul's Cathedral. Hawkesworth was a particularly astute choice on Payne's part: he was a regular contributor to Edward Cave's *Gentleman's Magazine*, where he worked closely with Samuel Johnson and developed an essayistic style so like Johnson's that contemporary and subsequent readers have struggled to distinguish among their many contributions to the *Gentleman's Magazine*. Furthermore, Johnson had used the weekly Tuesday night meeting of the Ivy Lane Club to test and develop ideas for his *Rambler* papers. Johnson was the star attraction of that literary society, whose membership included, with Payne and Hawkesworth, the dissenting clergyman Samuel Dyer, the magistrate and editor John Hawkins, and three physicians, William McGhie, Edmund Barker, and Richard Bathurst. The Ivy Lane Club became Hawkesworth's finishing school as an intellectual, and it was there that he learned to emulate so convincingly the moral and literary voice of Johnson.

The *Adventurer* followed Johnson's *Rambler* in its thematic content and varied in style only in being a little less difficult in its vocabulary and less baroque in its sentence structures. There were, however, two deliberate breaks with the editorial practice of the *Rambler*: Payne decided to solicit contributions to the *Adventurer* from several hands, rather than leave the entire burden of the writing to Hawkesworth; and it was decided from the outset that the number of issues would be finite. The number of 140 was determined with an eye to publishing the complete *Adventurer* in ready sets as soon as the final paper had been issued. seventy essays printed in folio made an ideal single volume, and Payne guessed from its conception that the *Adventurer* would sell best as a two-volume first edition in folio and a four-volume second edition in pocket-sized duodecimo. Whatever moral excellence we may now attribute to the *Adventurer*'s reflective essays, its format was entirely determined by a bookseller's understanding of what would be the most valuable way to approach the marketplace.

Along with Hawkesworth, the principal contributors to the *Adventurer* were Johnson himself, the literary critic Joseph Warton, and the journalist Bonnell Thornton, author of the periodical the *Connoisseur*. Various individual papers have also been attributed to Thomas Warton, his sister Jane Warton, the early feminist Elizabeth Carter, Hester Mulson, George Colman, and Catherine Talbot. Certainly Hawkesworth and Payne approached a wide community of possible contributors with the intention of insuring that the *Adventurer* offered a variety of style and opinions in its essays. Despite the ultimate range of hands evident in the *Adventurer*, Hawkesworth found himself solely responsible for most of the early papers. Johnson first appears with *Adventurer* no. 34; he would contribute 29 essays in all. There is some speculation that Richard Bathurst of the Ivy Lane Club was originally solicited to contribute but failed to do so, and that Hawkesworth urged Johnson to take Bathurst's place as the periodical prospered and Hawkesworth himself felt the strain of compensating for the delinquent Bathurst. At any rate, the three main authors of the papers each took up different essayistic approaches: Johnson contributed papers that continued the moral reflections which had characterized the *Rambler*; Joseph Warton wrote on aesthetic matters, producing papers on literary criticism, taste, and scholarship, including memorable pieces on Shakespeare; and Hawkesworth, who wrote the lion's share of the periodical, was particularly predisposed to contribute short fiction, especially oriental tales.

The *Adventurer* combines aspects of both the *Spectator* and the *Rambler* in defining its own place in the history of the essay. As a sort of sequel to the *Rambler*, it sustained that periodical's philosophical disposition and its determination to instruct its readers in morality and conscience. It reached back to the *Spectator* in its ambition to attain a popular readership. Where the *Rambler* is meditative and solitary in its ruminations on the human scene, the *Adventurer* tends more toward the conversational and the social. Certainly, the *Adventurer* must be credited with demonstrating the importance of collaboration in sustaining variety and debate in a periodical, especially where the essay was concerned. Looking back on its accumulated achievement in the final issue of the *Adventurer*, Hawkesworth emphasizes this collaborative effort as crucial to the paper's popular success. Essays from several hands were essential, he writes, "not because I wanted sufficient leisure, but because some degree of sameness is produced by the peculiarities of every writer; and it was thought that the conceptions and expressions of another, whose pieces should have a general coincidence with mine, would produce variety, and by increasing entertainment facilitate instruction" (*Adventurer* no. 140).

The influence of the *Adventurer* was, perhaps, strongest in the late 18th century, when Edinburgh fostered a resurgence of interest in the periodical essay. The *Mirror*, the *Lounger*, and the *Bee* would all be conceived after the collaborative model of the *Adventurer*, acknowledging the truth of Hawkesworth's simple assertion.

STEPHEN W. BROWN

Editions
The Adventurer, 140 nos., 7 November 1752–9 March 1754; in 2 vols., 1753–54; in *The Works of Samuel Johnson* (Yale Edition) vol. 2: *"The Idler" and "The Adventurer"*, edited by Walter Jackson Bate, John M. Bullitt, and L. F. Powell, 1963; selections in *Essays from the Rambler, Adventurer, and Idler*, edited by Walter Jackson Bate, 1968

Further Reading
Abbott, John Lawrence, *John Hawkesworth: Eighteenth-Century Man of Letters*, Madison: University of Wisconsin Press, 1982
Bate, W. Jackson, *Samuel Johnson*, New York: Harcourt Brace Jovanovich, 1977
Fairer, David, "Authorship Problems in *The Adventurer*," *Review of English Studies* 25 (1974): 137–51
Powell, L. F., "Introduction to *The Adventurer*," in *"The Idler" and "The Adventurer"*, *The Works of Samuel Johnson* (Yale Edition), vol. 2, New Haven, Connecticut: Yale University Press, 1963: 323–38
Sherbo, Arthur, *Samuel Johnson, Editor of Shakespeare, with an Essay on the "Adventurer"*, Urbana: University of Illinois Press, 1956

Agee, James
American, 1909–1955

Although James Agee produced journalism, **review** essays, and short nonfiction pieces throughout his career, his reputation as an essayist derives primarily from his book with Walker Evans, *Let Us Now Praise Famous Men* (1941), a long study in prose and photographs of the lives of three Southern sharecropper families. Agee both documents the lives of his human subjects – families with whom he and Evans lived during the summer of 1936 – and reflects on the problems of documenting without either inventing or concealing. Because Agee confronts the philosophical problems of truth-telling so directly in this work, because he enacts these problems stylistically, and perhaps above all because these have been critical, recurring questions for the essay throughout the genre's history, *Let Us Now Praise Famous Men* holds great interest for students of the essay, as well as a place of increasing importance in the canon of 20th-century American literature.

For Agee, as for **Montaigne**, the essay was not a form for conveying a whole and universal truth clearly perceived; on the contrary, it was useful for highlighting both the partiality of any one observer's vision and the great difficulties involved in perceiving the world and communicating one's experience of it to an audience. A form of truth is possible, says Agee, if one is as faithful as possible to one's own knowledge and experience of the world, but it will, of course, be at best a relative truth. Moreover, it is no simple thing to confront that world in an immediate way, "without either dissection into science, or digestion into art, but with the whole of consciousness, seeking to perceive it as it stands"; to do so an observer must strip his or her consciousness until it stands "weaponless" before its subject. This confrontation of two existents, observer and subject, is crucial to Agee's understanding and use of the nonfiction essay form because the meaning of his real, human subjects does not derive from the writer's work (as it does in fiction); both the subject and the writer's writing about this subject have their meaning in the fact that subject and writer both exist. Thus the essayist's responsibility is not to "art" but to that experience, the confrontation of living people. The essay is a form that Agee uses to reveal himself as a "spy," one with the specific goals of observing, recording, and exposing the lives of these families. He uses the reflective, questioning, and self-revealing aspects of the essayistic persona to give voice to the moral and ethical problems of his position – that of an anxious, indignant, and sensitive person, alive to his subjects and at times agonizingly self-conscious about what he is doing.

Agee's style is sometimes called "baroque"; critics have often found his syntax and vocabulary dense, mannered, even "tortured." Certainly his inversions of word order, the intricate syntax of some of his clauses, and his occasionally unorthodox punctuation make careful reading imperative; Agee himself cautions that the reader will have to listen carefully to his prose. But the effects of this are to draw attention to the prose as a thing composed, constructed; thus the reader is discouraged from seeing the writing merely as a transparent "screen" through which to read the world, and encouraged to see it as a reconstruction of the original experience – perhaps a problematic one at that. Although one reviewer of *Let Us Now Praise Famous Men* doubted Agee's ability to write a clear sentence, Agee had certainly developed a range of styles from which to choose. Much of his writing, here and in his journalism, displays a simple, more "transparent" style, one in which verbs do more of the work and prepositions less. In such "straightforward" passages, however, Agee often makes heavy use of figures of speech to mark the experience as distinctly his.

The critical reception of *Let Us Now Praise Famous Men* has been varied. Reviewers both praised and criticized its variety and stylistic innovations; some found Agee's *tour de force* "dazzling," brilliant in its very failure to satisfy conventional expectations, "a distinguished failure," while others thought it self-indulgent and self-important. Commercially the book was not a success, but it did attract a certain following among the literary establishment after **Lionel Trilling**'s favorable review in 1942. It was not until its reissue in 1960 that it began to gain in popularity and influence; it was embraced by young activists eager for social reform, and had a particular impact among practitioners of **New Journalism**, who, like Agee, questioned the possibility of objectivity, favored recreations of personal experiences, and pushed their craft to stylistic extremes.

Of Agee's other nonfiction, the journalistic pieces he wrote for *Fortune* reveal flashes of the style and voice of *Let Us Now Praise Famous Men*, but the articles are, for the most part, journalism rather than essays; he allows himself (or his editors allow him) no reflective excursions from the facts at hand. One exception to this is "Southeast of the Island: Travel Notes" (*Collected Short Prose*, 1968); tellingly, the piece was never published by *Fortune*, for whom he was working at the time. The film reviews he wrote for *Time* and the *Nation* are more essayistic in their occasional meditations on art, philosophy, and the American culture of the day. Much of Agee's fiction is autobiographical; the novel *A Death in the Family* (1957) drew so heavily on his childhood experiences that at least one reviewer called it a memoir, and two of the early stories anthologized in the *Collected Short Prose*, "Death in the Desert" and "They That Sow in Sorrow Shall Reap," both feature the intercutting of narrated experience and reflection characteristic of the essay, as well as being stories which, according to editor Robert Fitzgerald, were based on real occurrences. Yet for all the essayistic elements and overtones of his other work, *Let Us Now Praise Famous Men* stands as Agee's preeminent work of nonfiction prose. In no other work of nonfiction are his voice, his style, and his ideas about writing given freer rein or clearer expression. In itself, the book has made Agee's reputation as one of the great writers of nonfiction in this century.

MAURA BRADY

Biography
James Rufus Agee. Born 27 November 1909 in Knoxville, Tennessee. Studied at Phillips Exeter Academy, Exeter, New Hampshire, 1925–28; Harvard University, Cambridge, Massachusetts, where he edited the *Harvard Advocate*, 1928–32, A.B., 1932. Reporter and staff writer, *Fortune*, 1932–39. Married Olivia Saunders, 1933 (divorced, 1937). Book reviewer, from 1939, and feature writer and film reviewer, 1941–48, *Time* magazine. Married Alma Mailman, 1939 (later divorced): one son. Film columnist, *Nation*, 1942–48. Married Mia Fritsch, 1946: one daughter. Codirector of the film *In the Street*, 1948. Awards: Pulitzer Prize, for *A Death in the Family*, 1957 (posthumous). Died (of a heart attack) in New York, 16 May 1955.

Selected Writings

Essays and Related Prose
Let Us Now Praise Famous Men, photographs by Walker Evans, 1941

Agee on Film: Reviews and Comments, 1958
Collected Short Prose, edited by Robert Fitzgerald, 1968
Selected Journalism, edited by Paul Ashdown, 1985

Other writings: two novels (*The Morning Watch*, 1951; *A Death in the Family*, 1957) and several screenplays (including *The African Queen*, with John Huston, 1951; *The Night of the Hunter*, 1955).

Bibliography
Moss, Mary, "James Agee: A Bibliography of Secondary Sources," in *James Agee: Reconsiderations*, edited by Michael A. Lofaro, Knoxville: University of Tennessee Press, 1992

Further Reading
Barson, Alfred, *A Way of Seeing: A Critical Study of James Agee*, Amherst: University of Massachusetts Press, 1972
Bergreen, Laurence, *James Agee: A Life*, New York: Dutton, 1984
Hersey, John, "A Critic at Large," *New Yorker*, 18 July 1988: 72–82
Kramer, Victor A., *James Agee*, Boston: Twayne, 1975
Kramer, Victor A., *Agee and Actuality: Artistic Vision in His Work*, Troy, New York: Whitston, 1991
Larsen, Erling, *James Agee*, Minneapolis: University of Minnesota Press, 1971
Lofaro, Michael A., editor, *James Agee: Reconsiderations*, Knoxville: University of Tennessee Press, 1992
Lowe, James, *The Creative Process of James Agee*, Baton Rouge: Louisiana State University Press, 1994
Madden, David, editor, *Remembering James Agee*, Baton Rouge: Louisiana State University Press, 1974
Maharidge, Dale, and Michael Williamson, *And Their Children After Them: The Legacy of Let Us Now Praise Famous Men, James Agee, Walker Evans, and the Rise and Fall of Cotton in the South*, New York: Pantheon, 1989
Moreau, Genevieve, *The Restless Journey of James Agee*, New York: Morrow, 1977
Ohlin, Peter H., *Agee*, New York: Obolensky, 1966
Seib, Kenneth, *James Agee: Promise and Fulfillment*, Pittsburgh: University of Pittsburgh Press, 1969
Spears, Ross, and Jude Cassidy, editors, *Agee: His Life Remembered*, New York: Holt Rinehart, 1985

Die Akzente
German journal, 1954–

Die Akzente: Zeitschrift für Literatur (Accent: journal for literature) is one of Germany's most important post-World War II literary journals, both enabling the recovery of literary movements and works brutally suppressed by the National Socialists, and encouraging avant-garde poetry and drama. Founded in 1954 by Walter Höllerer and Hans Bender, with the original subtitle *Zeitschrift für Dichtung* (Journal for poetry), the journal continues to appear in bimonthly issues, and has a circulation of about 4500. *DA* has presented works by nearly every major postwar German writer, from fiction by **Günter Grass** and Gabriele Wohmann to essays concerning aesthetics and politics by **Theodor W. Adorno** and **Martin Heidegger**. It has also been an important source of literature and criticism from other European countries and North America. Recent issues of the periodical have included works by Thomas Bernhard, Tankred Dorst, and Günter Kunert.

Essays in *DA* have often provided the theoretical basis for reclaiming German Modernist literature and for encouraging postwar artistic and cultural movements. Essays in the first years of *DA* discuss dadaism and surrealism, expressionists such as the poet Georg Heym, and Bertolt Brecht's epic theater, helping to reestablish the importance of these movements and authors. Indeed, Höllerer has remarked that the recovery of these works, and of German literary tradition in general, was a primary motivation for establishing the journal. The first issue of *DA* (February 1954) included works from the literary estates of the philosopher and cultural critic **Walter Benjamin** and the Jewish poet Gertrud Kolmar, both of whom had been killed by the Nazis. The same issue included three essays concerning **Robert Musil**'s influential Modernist novel, *Der Mann ohne Eigenschaften* (1930–43; *The Man Without Qualities*). Other essays of this period concerning the radio play and the form of the novel, such as Adorno's "Form und Gehalt des zeitgenössischen Romans" (August 1954; Form and content of the contemporary novel), suggest the importance of *DA* for the development of postwar German literary aesthetics. *DA* was also an important source of works and criticism by members of Gruppe 47 (Group 47), a union of writers who demanded discussion of the Nazi period and its implications for postwar German culture. Similarly innovative works by the novelist Uwe Johnson and the documentary dramatist Peter Weiss have often appeared in the periodical.

Most characteristic of *DA*, however, has been its focus on poetry. Höllerer, who is himself a poet and playwright, encouraged other writers of experimental and avant-garde poetry and is largely responsible for the journal's early emphasis on the lyric. Bender, too, has contributed many essays on poetry to *DA* and other periodicals, and has edited several anthologies of poems. Poems have appeared by such central figures as Helmut Heissenbüttel and **Hans Magnus Enzensberger**, and poetry continues to play an important role in the journal.

It has always been an important source of works in translation, and has included essays and literature by writers from the United States, England, France, Scandinavia, and Eastern Europe. In 1956 it published essays by **Roland Barthes**, Luc Estang, and Alain Robbe-Grillet, providing an important forum in Germany for these French thinkers. Robbe-Grillet's essay concerning the contemporary novel, "Für einen Realismus des Hierseins" (August 1956; For a realism of the present), also helped fuel German literary debate and conceptions of the postwar German novel. In 1958 *DA* introduced the Beat poets to many German readers, publishing works such as Gregory Corso's essay, "Dichter und Gesellschaft in Amerika" (The poet and society in America). The February 1968 edition of *DA* featured works by Americans Richard Brautigan and **Susan Sontag**. Since the reunification of Germany in 1990, much attention has been given to writers in the East. In the February 1992 issue of *DA*, a section of the periodical was devoted to Estonian poets including Doris Kareval and Viivi Luik.

In 1968 Walter Höllerer left *DA* and Hans Bender became the sole editor of the journal. At that time, Bender changed the subtitle to *Zeitschrift für Literatur*, indicating more fully the diverse forms of writing included in the journal. Shortly after Höllerer's departure, Michael Krüger was named co-editor, becoming sole editor in 1981, a position he retains today. Krüger continues to include the combination of literature and essays that has characterized *DA* since its inception. The format of the journal has largely remained the same as well. Book-size, it includes few illustrations or advertisements. With the first issue of 1981, *DA* began to include photographs on the front cover and in various sections of the journal.

Under Krüger's editorship of *DA*, editorials have become more polemical, and more willing to discuss specific political and social issues. In 1992, for instance, the opening editorial discussed two ostensible Western "victories": the War in the Persian Gulf, and the dissolution of the East European communist governments. Subsequent issues of *DA* have brought attention to the literature and culture of Iraq and Bosnia.

While editors of *DA* have tended toward political liberalism, their understanding of *Kultur* has changed little since the journal's initial appearance. Krüger, for instance, maintains *DA*'s long tradition of distinguishing between what he calls a German "Vernunftskultur" (high culture) and a "Subkultur" (low culture). Common targets of Krüger's editorials are the media and particularly television, and the destabilizing influence of postmodernism.

CHRISTOPHER P. McCLINTICK

Further Reading

Bolz, Rüdiger, "Literatur, wie wir sie sehen, kommt nie nach Hause . . . *Akzente*: Ein publizistisches Forum der Nachkriegsjahre," *Der Deutschunterricht* 33, no. 3 (1981): 31–39
Lass, R. H., "Accent on the Sixties," *Modern Language Review* 61 (1966): 455–66
Schroedel, Folker, *"Akzente" 1954–1967* (M.A. thesis), Erlangen-Nürnberg: University of Erlangen-Nürnberg, 1987
25 Jahre Akzente (catalogue), Sulzbach-Rosenberg: Literaturarchiv Sulzbach-Rosenberg, 1979

Alain

French, 1868–1951

Alain's career was closely connected with the educational system in France, since he served as professor of rhetoric at the Lycée Henri IV from 1909 until 1933, and had a profound influence on the thinking of a generation of French intellectuals. In his essays he often adopted a professorial position, providing insights and stimulating thought in a concise, meditative prose style. As with so many French essayists, Alain was a philosopher in the style of **Montaigne** rather than of Descartes. He did not leave a systematic philosophy, nor a major opus, but a large and disparate collection of personal observations that are both penetrating and amusing. The substance of his thought, however, was profoundly influenced by rigorous Cartesian logic.

Starting in 1906 he began writing daily articles, under the pseudonym Alain (in homage to the 15th-century Norman poet Alain Chartier), for *La Dépêche de Rouen* (The Rouen dispatch), which he entitled "Propos d'un Normand" (Remarks of a Norman). These *propos* had a set length (two small pages of handwritten script) due to journalistic constraints, and focused on a specific issue in an unpretentious style. In the course of the next eight years over 3000 *propos* appeared, written on a wide variety of topics, including politics, society, and psychology. The first series of *propos* ended in 1914, but was followed by two other periods (1921–24 and 1927–36). His writings on specific topics were collected and published, from 1908 until the 1930s, and enjoyed great success. Although in later years Alain wrote more fully developed works, it is the *propos* that remain synonymous with his name.

Alain once considered becoming a novelist, but rejected both the length of the form and the fictionality of its content. Being a philosopher, a lover of wisdom, he favored the short, fleeting images of the storyteller, who is more free to blend diverse materials and examine the paradoxes of actual, everyday events. Alain preferred to give his thought and imagination the liberty to follow their own course, and develop their own associations, without the constraints of traditional generic conventions. In each *propos*, the progression is usually thematic rather than argumentative, since ideas and images spiral around a central point, providing different, unexpected perspectives on the main issue. Capable of rigorous thought, as seen in many passages of his work, Alain nonetheless presented his ideas as an interruption in the daily routine, a reexamination of common beliefs. Usually each piece ends with a memorable final statement, which may summarize the preceding ideas with a fresh insight or indicate a practical lesson or action to take. In short, his brief prose pieces are each highly crafted artifacts which are both artistically pleasing and pragmatically useful.

In the *Propos sur le bonheur* (1925, 1928; *Alain on Happiness*), Alain contended in general that passions are the major cause of unhappiness, which affects us physically as well as emotionally. Willpower plays a central role in these *propos*, as in so many others, but Alain was quick to recognize that while we are not able to control our thoughts or emotions, control of the physical body and movement can modify or alleviate causes of unhappiness. It is not through accident that we are happy or unhappy, and happiness must be cultivated, since it is only through individual efforts that we can attain our own *bonheur*. The physical and mental faculties cannot be separated. The wise and happy person should strive for a healthy mind and body, which will serve for both reflective thought and judicious action. Happiness is equated with virtue, liberty, and justice, as revealed in the wisdom of the classical writers of antiquity, of whose work Alain was a passionate and happy admirer.

A contemporary of **Freud**, Alain disagreed with the founder of psychoanalysis on the importance of sexuality in human conduct, as well as with Freud's views concerning the composition and role of the unconscious in mental activity. The basis for Alain's disagreement can be found in his belief that the soul, and by extension consciousness and thought, are not states of being, nor entities apart, but functions of an integrated self. For him, there can be no unconscious which exists separately, or which contains material hidden from the self. But rather than attempt to refute what he considered "Freud's ingenious system" with logical arguments, he chose instead to refuse it, claiming that Freud's views on psychic activity were vague and ultimately useless.

According to Alain, consciousness, thought, judgment, and reflection are all interconnected, so that critical reasoning and examination are elementary to all conscious states. By opposition, the unconscious, including sleep, is merely an absence of functionality and rationality. Alain applied his theories on states of consciousness in his observations (*Les Arts et les dieux* [1958; The arts and the gods]) on **Paul Valéry's** *La Jeune Parque* (1917; The young fate), a poem describing the transitional states of mind. Consciousness is characterized as reflection and light, which allows no partial states, but either is, or is not. Alain also commented on Proust, who "speaks of the unconscious, but doesn't need to in order to account for human actions and passions" ("Propos de littérature" [1922; Remarks on literature]). As for thought, which reveals consciousness, it is considered to be primarily a critical, negating activity. Alain's style of writing is aphoristic in nature; one of his better-known sayings is "Thought is saying no, and it is to itself that thought says no" ("Propos sur la religion" [1924; Remarks on religion]). By these negations consciousness is highly moral in its workings, frequently contrasting an ideal self with the real self. It is the morality of the human will that Alain placed in opposition to Freud's model of the unconscious.

Alain's concept of the interconnection between body and mind was primarily Cartesian, with its emphasis on the role of physical, corporeal determinants. He believed that Freud misinterpreted the symptoms and signs of human behavior, and attributed motives incorrectly to an autonomous and murky unconscious. Physiology plays a more important role in behavior than Freud allowed, and this led him to create an unruly unconscious to explain what are often, in fact, physical causes. As for dreams, they are not the messengers of a hidden spirit, but the weakened, distorted perceptions of a drowsy mind. Finally, Alain did not trust the complicated mechanisms of Freud's concepts, preferring a simpler, more practical, natural explanation of mental phenomena. He saw in psychoanalysis an overly pessimistic view of humankind, which emphasized misery and depravity rather than encouraging nobility of action and the exercise of the will.

With regard to another major influence on modern thought, **Marx**, the writings of Alain again reveal criticism and reservation. Although he can be considered a socialist, Alain espoused a dialectic which was more specific, emphasizing the individual and each person's role within the class struggle. He was also much less of a dogmatic absolutist than Marx, and his views of politics and history do not reveal the same systematic approach or the inevitability of social revolution. As for war, whose horrors he witnessed firsthand between 1914 and 1917 and which occupied his later thought, he also disagreed with Marxist ideology. He criticized the Marxists for oversimplifying historical and social causes; they blamed capitalists and their greed for causing war when in fact the causes were far more complex, and involved in addition a kind of collective madness of a people intent on war. In *Mars* (1921) the importance of passion, both individual and collective, and its relationship to war, a "crime of passion," are explored at length. Alain, a determined pacifist, believed that a Marxist state would be just as militaristic as a capitalistic one, since all governing groups have a will to power which tends to be expressed in warfare. Each individual is tempted by the moral perversions of war and violence, which are so often justified by false claims of a transcendent or ultimate justice.

Whatever the content of his writing, Alain often used concrete and innovative images to capture his reader's attention or make a point. These images are often taken from everyday life: a crying baby, a loaf of bread, or a farmer resting in his field. Besides these arresting, poetic images, he formulated his thought in striking phrases, which comprise a stockpile of **maxims**. He saw ideas as instruments which allow us to grasp reality and to conduct our life with dignity and morality. The issues he discussed were often quite complex, but stated in a simple prose, without philosophical terms or jargon. Although his writing often opposed prevailing thought, the freshness of his style and the rigor of his thought earned him a great reputation. During the first half of the 20th century, a period marked by global atrocities, his *propos* indicated a path for humankind's secular salvation through reflective thought and moral action.

ALLEN G. WOOD

Biography
Born Émile Auguste Chartier, 3 March 1868 in Mortagne-sur-Huisne (now Mortagne-au-Perche), Normandy. Studied at lycées in Alençon, 1881–86, and Vanves, 1886–89; École Normale Supérieure, Paris, 1889–92, agrégation in philosophy, 1892. Taught at lycées in Pontivy, 1892–93, Lorient, 1893–1900, Rouen, 1900–02, Lycée Condorcet, Paris, 1903–06, Lycée Michelet, Vanves, 1906–09, Lycée Henri IV (where he taught **Simone Weil**, **Henri Massis**, and Jean Prévost), Paris, 1909–33, and Collège Sévigné, Paris, 1917–33. Columnist of *propos*, occasionally, 1903–06, and daily (called "Propos d'un Normand," 1906–14), from 1906, which he signed "Alain" and which appeared in *La Dépêche de Rouen*, 1903–14, *Libres Propos*, 1921–24 and 1927–36, and *L'Émancipation*, 1924–27. Served in the French Army, 1914–17. Married Gabrielle Landormy, 1945. Awards: National Grand Prize for Literature, 1951. Died in Le Vésinet, 2 June 1951.

Selected Writings

Essays and Related Prose
Les cent un Propos, series 1–5, 1908–28
Vingt et un Propos d'Alain: Méditations pour les non-combattants, 1915
Quatre-vingt-un Chapitres sur l'esprit et les passions, 1915; revised edition, as *Éléments de philosophie*, 1941
Les Marchands de sommeil, 1919
Système des beaux-arts, 1920
Mars; ou, La Guerre jugée, 1921; as *Mars; or, The Truth About War*, translated by Doris Mudie and Elizabeth Hill, 1930
Propos sur l'esthétique, 1923
Propos sur le christianisme, 1924
Propos sur le bonheur, 1925; enlarged edition, 1928; as *Alain on Happiness*, translated by Robert D. and Jane E. Cottrell, 1973
Jeanne d'Arc, 1925
Éléments d'une doctrine radicale, 1925
Le Citoyen contre les pouvoirs, 1926
Sentiments, passions, et signes, 1926
Visite au musicien, 1927
Esquisses de l'homme, 1927; revised, enlarged edition, 1938
Les Idées et les âges, 1927
Onze Chapitres sur Platon, 1928
Étude sur Descartes, 1928
Vingt Leçons sur les beaux-arts, 1931
Préliminaires à la mythologie, 1932
Propos sur l'éducation, 1932
Propos de littérature, 1933
Les Dieux, 1934; as *The Gods*, translated by Richard Pevear, 1974
Propos de politique, 1934
Stendhal, 1935
Propos d'économie, 1935

En lisant Balzac, 1935; enlarged edition, as *Avec Balzac*, 1937
Histoire de mes pensées, 1936
Entretiens chez le sculpteur, 1937
Les Saisons de l'esprit, 1937
Propos sur la religion, 1938
Minerve; ou, De la sagesse, 1939
Préliminaires à l'esthétique, 1939
Suite à Mars, 2 vols., 1939
Vigiles de l'esprit, 1942
En lisant Dickens, 1945
Humanités, 1946; revised, enlarged edition, 1960
Politique, 1952
Propos d'un Normand, 1906–1914, 5 vols., 1952–60
Propos (Pléiade Edition), edited by Maurice Savin, 1956
Les Arts et les dieux, 1958
Propos sur des philosophes, 1961

Other writings: works on literature and writers.

Bibliographies
Dewit, Suzanne, "Alain: Essai de bibliographie," *Bibliographia Belgica* 62 (1961)
Drevit, A., "Bio-Bibliographie d'Alain," *Association des Amis d'Alain: Annuaire* (1966)

Further Reading
Assoun, P. L., and others, *Alain–Freud: Essai pour mesurer un déplacement anthropologique*, Le Vésinet: Institut Alain, 1992
Bénézé, Georges, *Généreux Alain*, Paris: Presses Universitaires de France, 1962
Bourgeois, B., "Alain, lecteur de Hegel," *Revue de Métaphysique et de Morale* 2 (April–June 1987): 238–56
Bourgne, Robert, editor, *Alain, lecteur des philosophes*, Paris: Bordas, 1987
Bulletin de l'Association des Amis d'Alain: Annuaire (1954–)
Gil, Didier, *Alain, la République ou le matérialisme*, Paris: Klincksieck, 1990
Halda, Bernard, *Alain*, Paris: Éditions Universitaires, 1965
Maurois, André, *Alain*, Paris: Domat, 1950
Miquel, Jean, *Les "Propos" d'Alain*, Paris: La Pensée Moderne, 1967
Mondor, Henri, *Alain*, Paris: Gallimard, 1953
Pascal, Georges, *Pour connaître la pensée d'Alain*, Paris: Bordas, 1946
Pascal, Georges, *Alain éducateur*, Paris: Presses Universitaires de France, 1964
Pascal, Georges, *L'Idée de philosophie chez Alain*, Paris: Bordas, 1970
Reboul, Olivier, *L'Homme et ses passions d'après Alain*, Paris: Presses Universitaires de France, 2 vols., 1968
Sernin, André, *Alain: Un Sage dans la cité, 1868–1951*, Paris: Laffont, 1985

Amar y Borbón, Josefa
Spanish, 1749–1833

During the last few years of the 18th century, Spanish letters focused almost exclusively on the essay. These writings, much maligned by 19th-century Romantics who saw little of value produced during the Spanish "enlightenment," provided a critical step in the development of the modern Spanish essay. Josefa Amar y Borbón belongs to a group of intellectuals who read prohibited books, met periodically to discuss issues of concern, and wrote extensively on topics that were bound together by a common theme – a concern for the decadent conditions of Spain and a desire to rectify the situation through education. Whether these writings were called *discursos* (speeches), *cartas* (letters), *memorias* (memoirs), or *ensayos* (essays), they are recognized today as basic elements of the Spanish essay.

Aragonese by birth, but reared and educated in Madrid, Amar y Borbón was the product, as well as an example, of the enlightened elite in Bourbon Spain. Well versed in Greek, Latin, French, English, and Italian, Amar y Borbón translated many works from these languages into Spanish. In the 1780s she began publishing essays and treatises whose subjects fall into three broad categories: those concerning science and medicine, those dealing with the study of letters and the humanities, and those combating superstition. Aside from her translations, the author's original literary production, as catalogued to date, includes eight essays published between 1783 and 1787, and a book, *Discurso sobre la educación física y moral de las mugeres* (1790; Discourse on the physical and moral education of women).

Each of Amar y Borbón's essays has three main structural components: authority, tradition, and synthesis. Authority is expressed by numerous citations of classical sources. These *autoridades*, whom the author quotes in the original language before translating, are from all epochs. Tradition refers to Spanish customs; this component not only provides a point of comparison and contrast with "authority," but is also a minute description of 18th-century society. Tradition also provides the reader with some insight concerning Amar y Borbón's point of view in many instances. The last component, synthesis, combines what "should be" (authority) with "what is" (tradition) to form what "might be" – the synthesis.

While these structural components appear in most of the author's essays, her style is far from simple, for like many of her contemporaries, she interjects numerous digressions in the form of philosophical musings: questions about the nature of religion and the religious education of children; diatribes against current practices in Spanish society such as men reserving all honors, awards, and recognition for themselves and wishing to deprive women of their intellects; or historical cataloguing of a subject such as the history of corsets from ancient times to the 18th century.

Authority, tradition, synthesis, and abundant digressions form the basic structure of the essayist's work: these elements are combined as in a mathematical formula; however, the "solution" is seldom stated. Indeed, in many cases Amar y Borbón leaves the solution of the issue to the readers, whether she does so overtly or not. As she defined her style as an essayist, she perfected the rhetorical form of argumentation that moves from the general to the specific. Most of her essays begin with a statement introducing the major theme. Then, as if in a musical variation, the same theme is presented in a series of analogous and yet distinct forms.

Within this basic structure and development, Amar y Borbón presents the reader with a healthy dose of wit and sarcasm. For example, when she describes the benefit of good health for women in her book, she states the obvious need for women to be fit for physical work and interjects that "all ladies, and those not worthy of being called so, must be physically fit for pregnancy, childbirth, and nursing." At other times her sarcasm is not as subtle. For example in her essay, "Discurso en defensa del talento de las mugeres ..." (1786; *Essay in Defense of Women's Talent*), written in response to Francisco, Conde de Cabarrús' fear that allowing women to participate in the Economic Society of Madrid would ruin the organization, she states: "It is obvious that men and women should live entirely separately, and this separation should be complete and forever ... but ... this scenario remains impossible – there being a thousand reasons for men and women to come together ... not the least of which is that the opposite would bring the destruction of the human race ..."

Like her contemporaries, Josefa Amar y Borbón wrote a form of literature characterized by multiple topics bound together by a common major theme: education, enlightenment, and progress. These writers added to the traditions established in the Spanish Golden Age and began to define the literary style later recognized as the modern essay.

CARMEN CHAVES TESSER

Biography
Born February 1749 in Saragossa. Grew up and studied privately in Madrid, tutored in Latin, French, Greek, and literature; taught herself Italian and English. Married Joaquín Fuertes Piquer (died, 1798), 1764: at least one child (a son). Returned to Saragossa, 1772. First female member, Aragonese Economic Society, 1782; member of Ladies' Group, Madrid Economic Society, 1787; member, Medical Society of Barcelona, 1790. Died in Saragossa, February 1833.

Selected Writings

Essays and Related Prose
"Discurso en defensa del talento de las mugeres y de su aptitud para el gobierno, y otros cargos en que se emplean los hombres," in *Memorial literario, instructivo y curioso de la Corte de Madrid*, 1786: 399–430; edited by Carmen Chaves McClendon, in *Dieciocho* 3 (1980): 144–61, and by Olegario Negrín Fajardo, in *Ilustración y educación: La sociedad económica matritense*, 1984: 162–76; as *Essay in Defense of Women's Talent*, translated by Carmen Chaves McClendon (dissertation), 1976
Discurso sobre la educación física y moral de las mugeres, 1790; edited by Constance A. Sullivan, 1994

Other writings: translated a six-volume work on Spanish literature by Francisco Lampillas (1782–84) and a work by Francesco Griselini (1784).

Further Reading
Franklin, Elizabeth M., "Feijóo, Josefa Amar y Borbón, and the Feminist Debate in Eighteenth-Century Spain," *Dieciocho* 12, no. 2 (1989): 188–203
McClendon, Carmen Chaves, "Josefa Amar y Borbón: A Forgotten Figure of the Spanish Enlightenment," in *Seven Studies in Medieval English History and Other Historical Essays*, edited by Richard H. Bowers, Jackson: University Press of Mississippi, 1983: 133–39
Sullivan, Constance A., "Josefa Amar y Borbón and the Royal Aragonese Economic Society," *Dieciocho* 15, no. 1 (1992): 95–148
Sullivan, Constance A., "Josefa Amar y Borbón," in *Spanish Women Writers: A Bio-Bibliographical Source Book*, edited by Linda Gould Levine, Ellen Engelson Marson, and Gloria Feiman Waldman, Westport, Connecticut: Greenwood Press, 1993: 33–43

American Essay

1. The Colonial Age

In its broadest denotation, the essay has existed in America almost from the arrival of the first English settlers in 1607. While 17th-century colonists had little or no leisure time in which to produce *belles-lettres*, there did exist what we might now call nonfictional literature, ranging from a paragraph or two of the almanac – short expositions that questioned natural phenomena – to the long chronicle histories. Growing out of the almanacs were early **science essays**, primarily on astronomical observations but also on other branches of science such as agriculture, zoology, botany, mineralogy, and meteorology. The clergy of the time, who were often the most educated of the colonists, generally adopted the belief that while God's mysteries were forever unknowable to humans, it was still their duty to ponder those mysteries. Hence, the end aim of science was contemplation. This purpose meant that their scientific writings (which appeared not only in almanacs but also in journals and **letters** to members of England's Royal Society) were not coldly scientific but tended toward moral interpretation.

The short prose works of the time, in fact, fell into definite literary types, including the "**pamphlet** of newes" (which described the new country), papers of timely interest on witchcraft and matters of immediate concern, the almanac (which contained short pieces of a moral or scientific nature), and the **sermon** – in which, apart from spiritual matters, ethics, manners, and social and national progress were also discussed – as well as its related form, the **meditation**, in which was displayed the most prolific and perhaps most creative prose of the time.

Cotton Mather (1663–1728) wrote what is considered the first verifiable book of American essays, *Bonifacius* (1710; the later edition was called *Essays to Do Good*). The book is divided into sections which are similar to 17th-century essays in being axiomatic and didactic philosophical reflections on abstract subjects, commentaries emerging from the wisdom and experience of the author. Nevertheless, the book is a departure from the writings of the early Puritans in that it contains no tedious laudatory biographies of ministers, no accusations of witchcraft, not even the display of pedantry and scriptural learning ordinarily associated with Mather. Instead it provides, in brief, simple, and forthright prose, a discussion of daily conduct, rules of behavior for ministers, doctors, and teachers, and objections to intemperance and corporal punishment. Each essay (and Mather uses the word literally, meaning "*attempts to do good*") is complete in itself, and each is suggestive rather than exhaustive; the work is unique for its time in both spirit and method.

2. The 18th Century: The Development of the Periodical and Serial Essays

The American essay began in earnest with the mushrooming of American **periodicals** in the early 18th century. It was modeled closely on the essays of the great contemporary British periodical essayists – **Steele**, **Swift**, **Goldsmith**, and especially **Addison**. Most early American essays were Addisonian in the sense that they were informal in tone, occasionally satiric, often humorous, most often brief. And like the British essays, American **periodical essays** were personal, always establishing a sociable intimacy between author and reader. The *New-England Courant*, a Boston weekly established by Benjamin Franklin's older brother James in 1721, was the first colonial newspaper to carry original essays. In his *Autobiography* (begun 1771 and published in full only in 1868), **Benjamin Franklin** (1706–90) recalled that his brother James "had some ingenious Men among his Friends who amus'd themselves by writing little Pieces for this Paper, which gained it Credit, and made it more in Demand." The group, who called themselves the "Couranteers," included Matthew Adams, John Checkley, Dr. William Douglass, and a mysterious Mr. Gardner. Initially unbeknownst to James was the fact that Benjamin himself was also a part of that group. Franklin submitted his earliest essays to his brother's newspaper with the signature "Silence Dogood" (1722). In these 14 pieces, Franklin deliberately copied the style of Addison's *Spectator*. However, he also took the Dogood papers beyond mere imitation, primarily because the *Spectator* claimed never to have "espoused any Party with Violence," while Mrs. Silence Dogood is a frugal, industrious, prosaic widow, sworn mortal enemy "to arbitrary Government and unlimited Power." Moreover, for all his English borrowings and choice of conventional subjects, Franklin succeeded in imparting to the Dogood essays a measure of originality and American coloration.

Mather Byles (1706–88), grandson of the clergyman Increase Mather, nephew of Cotton Mather, and lifelong friend of Franklin's, was also an early periodical essayist. He joined former Couranteer Matthew Adams and his grandson John Adams (1704–40) to write a serial for the *New-England Weekly Journal* (1727–41). Called *Proteus Echo*, it contained essays and poems and appeared weekly for a year. It was more didactic and less diverting than the Dogood papers, containing **moral essays** on such deadly sins as avarice, idleness, envy, and pride, **philosophical essays** on the ardor for knowledge, the way love blinds man's reason, and the love of country, and, finally, essays on manners and character. It was more nearly Addisonian than the Dogood papers, particularly because Proteus Echo is an old bachelor and widely traveled scholar like Mr. Spectator. While Franklin's Dogood papers are on balance the more successful of the two (Silence Dogood has more earthy vitality and dramatic energy, and the papers contain a sense of native idiom and environment that is almost wholly missing from *Proteus Echo*), the two serials firmly established the tradition of periodical essays in Boston, and led the way for others, which soon appeared in Philadelphia, Annapolis, Williamsburg, and Charleston.

Franklin left Boston for Philadelphia in 1723, and six years later launched a new essay serial in the *American Weekly Mercury* (1719–46) called *The Busy-Body*. He wrote the first four essays in the series and parts of two others, then withdrew; Joseph Breintnall finished the series, which when it ended in September 1729 contained 32 papers in all. The *Busy-Body* papers range through all the conventional subjects for periodical essays except criticism: manners, morality, philosophical reflection, character, humor. The liveliest entries are those by Breintnall which focus on the battle of the sexes.

Later in the 18th century – during the two decades before the Revolution – the chief outlet for essay serials became the magazine rather than the newspaper, and it was in magazines that the most notable American literary serials appeared. One of these, called *The Prattler*, appeared in the *American Magazine and Monthly Chronicle for the British Colonies* (1757–58), a magazine which promised that part of each issue would be "set aside for MONTHLY ESSAYS, in prose and verse" and that it would try to print every essay submitted "so far as they tend to promote peace and good government, industry and public spirit, a love of LIBERTY and our excellent constitution, and above all a veneration of our holy undefiled CHRISTIANITY." *The Prattler* generally appeared over the name "Timothy Timbertoe," but was probably the work of several hands. Timbertoe is a dilettante, most at home gossiping over tea tables or in coffeehouses and gathering scandal.

A more ambitious and successful serial was *The Old Bachelor*, which appeared in the *Pennsylvania Magazine; or American Monthly Museum* (1775–76). **Thomas Paine** (1737–1809) was a contributing editor to the magazine and also one of the principal authors of *The Old Bachelor*, though he seems to have contributed only to the early numbers, and left the rest to be written by Francis Hopkinson (1737–91), whose three-volume *Miscellaneous Essays and Occasional Writings* (1792) includes not only his *Old Bachelor* contributions but essays published in other periodicals. The old bachelor had been a convention in the periodical essays of England, and Hopkinson's creation – a character named George Sanby who is inconvenienced by being a bachelor but too chauvinistic to get married – is as good-natured, old-fashioned, and eccentric as any of his British predecessors or American followers (who would include Philip Freneau's Hezekiah Salem, Joseph Dennie's Lay Preacher, William Wirt's Dr. Robert Cecil, and **Washington Irving**'s Jonathan Oldstyle).

The *Maryland Gazette*, established in Annapolis in 1727, carried one literary serial, *The Plain-Dealer*, though of its ten essays only two were original. Southern periodical essays got a surer foothold seven years later when the *Virginia Gazette* (1736–66) was established in Williamsburg. The serial in that newspaper, *The Monitor* (1736–37), conformed closely in manner and matter to the English periodical essay. It managed the conventions and ranged through the traditional subjects in a lively way. As in other early American serial essays, there was heavy emphasis on manners, and the Monitor and his assistants discussed subjects such as French fashions, being in love, keeping one's temper, and good nature. Maintaining the essentially lighthearted tone of *The Monitor*, the subject of morality was seldom broached.

The *South-Carolina Gazette* was established at Charleston in 1731–32, and ran, with occasional interruptions, until 1775. Individual essays began appearing as early as the second number, and in 1735 *The Meddlers Club*, a serial whose name calls to mind Franklin and Breintnall's *Busy-Body*, ran for a short time. The only full-fledged literary serial in the *South-Carolina Gazette*, however, appeared in Winter 1753–54, and was authored by "The Humourist." This series again covered the conventional subjects, with special attention to manners and literary criticism. In fact, the relative lack of topicality in *The Humourist* and the emphasis on literary criticism reflect the influence of **Samuel Johnson**'s *Rambler* essays, which the *South-Carolina Gazette* began reprinting at the end of 1750.

With the rise of the magazine in the late 18th and early 19th centuries, the essay became perhaps the most clearly defined and popular American literary form. Essayist Nathan Fiske (1733–99) remarked near the turn of the century that any periodical without an essay series was doomed. Dozens of anonymous contributors with names like "The Censor," "The Hermit," "Gentleman at Large," and "The Lady's Friend" filled the magazines with comments on fashion, education, manners, courtship, social life, and other topics common to the tradition of Addison, Steele, and the rest. In the rush to print, few essayists distinguished themselves.

One who did was John Trumbull (1750–1831) who, while a graduate student and tutor at Yale, produced two serials, *The Meddler* (published in the *Boston Chronicle*, 1769–70) and *The Correspondent* (published in two series in the *Connecticut Journal*, 1770 and 1773). *The Meddler* had the stated purpose (from the first number) of publishing "essays, chiefly of the moral, critical and poetical kinds, upon miscellaneous and mostly unconnected subjects ... [which] carefully avoid all strokes of party spirit and personal satire, with everything that had the least tendency to immorality." Indeed, *The Meddler* was noncontroversial – as well as frequently clumsy and amateurish – choosing instead to depict the coquette and fop so popular with 18th-century readers and to castigate false wit. *The Correspondent*, while also part of Trumbull's apprenticeship as a serial essayist (he later found his literary calling more successfully in poetry), was a more ambitious serial than *The Meddler*, instructing the reader more and diverting him less than the Meddler had done. The Correspondent was a more contentious, less genial character than the Meddler, and he frequently attacked Church authority in Connecticut; there was even one essay against slavery, written at a time when almost the only anti-slavery advocates in America were Quakers.

Philip Freneau (1752–1832) was also best known as a poet, though he produced over 400 prose pieces in his career, publishing them in a variety of literary serials. *The Pilgrim* essays (1781–82) appeared in the *Freeman's Journal*; six years later, in *The Miscellaneous Works of Mr. Philip Freneau* (1788), the series was extended and renamed *The Philosopher of the Forest*. In both incarnations, the speaker resembled Addison's Mr. Spectator in being an old bachelor who wished simply to observe life, though there were partisan essays – Freneau was strongly anti-Tory – in which the angry voice of the author was clear and unmistakable. His serial *Tomo Cheeki* (1795) appeared in the *Jersey Chronicle* with a grave and melancholy title character based on an historical figure. Freneau had him visit Philadelphia, where he made observations on manners and morality and offered philosophical reflections, all tending to elevate the Native American above the white population. In general, it was a more relaxed and conversational series of essays than *The Pilgrim*. Hezekiah Salem (1797) is a wholly whimsical series of seven essays with titles such as "On the Culture of Pumpkins" and "A Few Words on Duelling." Freneau's most extensive and impressive serial was *Robert Slender* (1799–1801), published in the *Aurora* (1794–1822, 1834–35), the foremost Republican newspaper of the day. The *Slender* letters were the most steadily partisan of Freneau's literary serials, though the character of Robert Slender and his Philadelphia milieu were full bodied and alive.

It was a series in the British coffeehouse tradition – witty and filled with strong opinions.

In 1794 Joseph Dennie (1768–1812) characterized American essays as having been "hitherto unmarked except for flimsy expression & jejune ideas, they have allowed me the praise of reviving in some degree the Goldsmith vivacity in thought & the Addisonian sweetness in expression." He was at the time writing his first literary serial, *The Farrago* (1792–95), and in the first number of that series, he commented on the continuing popularity of essays: "To a lover of abstruse science, desultory essays may appear a minor species of literature. But the majority of mankind are not scholars ... They content themselves with the simplest dishes of the literary banquet. Hence the currency of Essays ..." Dennie's essays were widely popular, but his unsuccessful attempts to have them published in book form contributed to the literary eclipse into which he was to fall after his death.

Judith Sargent Murray (1751–1820) produced two concurrent serials from 1792 to 1794: *The Repository*, 27 short moralistic essays, and *The Gleaner*. Both appeared in the *Massachusetts Magazine* (1789–96). Murray was married to John Murray, the founder of universalism in America, and was eventually accused of using her essays to propagate universalism; this led to her serials for the *Massachusetts Magazine* ending in 1794. While in publication, though, her essays distinguished themselves in several ways from the great bulk of other serials of the late 18th century. *The Gleaner*, which in some of its numbers had a mildly partisan flavor, biased toward Federalism, also showed Murray's concern for the future of American drama. These essays stood out because they appeared at a time when American writers were uncertain of how to develop an American tradition (an uncertainty that would, in fact, last for at least another century). Perhaps *The Gleaner*'s most important contribution to American literature was a sentimental novel – *The Story of Margaretta* – embedded within the framework of a series of moral essays, allowing Murray not only to tell the story as if it were true (a favored method of making a sentimental novel respectable), but also to make observations on the proper role of the novel in American life.

Another essayist who made it his concern that the new nation have a literature of its own was William Wirt (1772–1834), a Virginian who published three serials, first in local newspapers, then in book form: *The Letters of the British Spy* (1803), *The Rainbow* (1804–05), and *The Old Bachelor* (1810–11). *The British Spy* provided evidence that the Addisonian essay had all but run its course in America, since Wirt employed only one Addisonian convention (the foreign visitor). Instead, the series contained elements of the **travel essay** then coming into vogue, especially in its descriptions of the Virginia landscape. *The Old Bachelor* was undeniably a literary serial, more Addisonian in its manner and matter than *The British Spy*. It was a series devoted to morals: "virtuously to instruct, or innocently to amuse," as Wirt phrased it. The Old Bachelor sought, as he said in 1811, "to awaken the taste of the body of the people for literary attainments" and to "see whether a group of statesmen, scholars, orators, and patriots, as enlightened and illustrious as their father, cannot be produced without the aid of such another bloody and fatal stimulant [as the Revolutionary War]." Publication of the series in book form in 1814 helped solidify the reputation of *The Old Bachelor*. Wirt himself confessed, "I am afraid that both the Old Bachelor and the British Spy will be considered by the world as rather too light and *bagatellish* for a mind pretending either to stability or vigor," but critics well into the 19th century highly regarded *The Old Bachelor*.

Also of note in the last part of the 18th century were the writers who adopted the essay form largely for political purposes. Its most significant practitioners included **Thomas Paine** (1737–1809), who achieved instant success and lasting fame with his pamphlet *Common Sense* (1776), and Alexander Hamilton (1757–1804), James Madison (1751–1836), and John Jay (1745–1829), who together anonymously published in 1787–88 a series of political essays called *The Federalist Papers* in support of the proposed U.S. Constitution. Later collected in book form and called *The Federalist*, they provide a classic exposition of the U.S. federal system.

3. The 19th Century: The Familiar Essay and Other Essay Types

Washington Irving (1783–1859) provided the last link in American essay writing to the periodical essay which had dominated the 18th century. Irving began his career as a serial essayist and only later moved into writing **familiar essays** along the lines of the great English Romantic essayists **Charles Lamb**, **William Hazlitt**, and **Leigh Hunt**. Irving made his first foray into essay writing with the *Oldstyle* letters he published in his brother Peter's *Morning Chronicle* (1802–03). The nine letters from Jonathan Oldstyle were highly conventional – three of the letters focusing on manners, the other six on theatrical criticism. Despite their popularity, Irving quickly distanced himself from the essay serial altogether by parodying it in *Salmagundi* (1807–08), a periodical published irregularly by Irving and a group of young New Yorkers, including the other principal writer, James Kirke Paulding (1778–1860). The work quickly became a bestseller and remained in print throughout the 19th century.

After the War of 1812, the didacticism of the "morals and manners" type of essay gave way to the kind of subjectivity more common to the familiar essay. Irving matured as a familiar essayist with *The Sketch Book of Geoffrey Crayon, Gent.* (1819–20), then all but abandoned the essay for the tale, travel romance, history, and biography. Still, through his choice of subject and the development of his own style, he gave the familiar essay a particularly American feel, and is considered by many to be the first American essayist.

If any essay form is particularly indigenous to American soil it is the **nature essay**. French-American J. Hector St. John de Crèvecoeur (1735–1813) wrote *Letters from an American Farmer* (1782), which are concerned with the plight of the colonial farmer, politics, and economics, but also closely scrutinize phenomena as disparate as snakes, hummingbirds, snowstorms, and anthills. The essays are seasoned with an antipathy toward urban life and industrialism, and give vivid, idealistic pictures of the emergent New World. William Bartram (1739–1823), a more skillful observer of plants and flowers, wrote of his travels in Georgia and Florida. John James Audubon (1785–1851) interrupted the technical descriptions of his ornithological biography to insert charming vignettes of southwestern life, which ranged in subject matter from Mississippi squatters and Kentucky deer to scenes of bird life on the Florida Keys. The American nature essay would later in the century reach a high point in the work of **John Burroughs** (1837–1921), who wrote over 100 essays devoted chiefly to the birds and flowers and forest paths of the Adirondacks. A contemporary of Burroughs, **John Muir** (1838–1914), had his own significant influence on American attitudes toward ecology by writing vigorous essays in support of forest conservation, many of them detailing his walking journeys through the northwest United States and Alaska.

Earlier, however, at the same time as the familiar essay was gaining popularity in America, the founding of the great American magazines and quarterlies – the *North American Review* (1815–1940), the *Western Review* (1819–21), the *American Quarterly Review* (1827–37), the *Southern Review* (1828–32), and others – was encouraging the production of longer, more serious, philosophical or **critical essays**. Many of the most important and influential of these essays were written by the transcendentalists – including **Ralph Waldo Emerson** (1803–82), **Henry David Thoreau** (1817–62), **Margaret Fuller** (1810–50), and Amos Bronson Alcott (1799–1888). Emerson and Thoreau exerted frequently acknowledged influence on American literature, but Fuller was also a fixture in the transcendentalist scene, as editor of the *Dial* (1840–44) and writer of both critical essays and longer personal nonfiction such as *Summer on the Lakes in 1843* (1844). Alcott left his impression on the essay with his *Concord Days* (1872) and *Table Talk* (1877).

Emerson was an agitating and fermentative force, a liberator from convention and timidity, a questioner and an instigator to valor. He did more than any other man, said John Jay Chapman, "to rescue the youth of the next generation and fit them for the fierce times to follow. It will not be denied that he sent ten thousand sons to war." The form in which he spread his original beliefs was not always the essay: his earliest compositions were sermons, and he turned from the sermon to the lecture. His essays grew out of this form of public speech, but it was only with the appearance of his second published volume, *Essays: First Series* (1841), that he placed himself before his readers explicitly in the role of essayist. Once there, his work constituted a new kind of American essay – abstract and aphoristic in a way that probably no writer since has been able to match. Emerson pieced together his essays from his **journals**, often leaving out explicit transitions from one sentence or one paragraph to the next, for he was willing to leave some of the work of thinking to his readers; he thought of continuity not as a logical but as a superlogical principle. His essays do, however, have a compositional wholeness, and a more orderly one than that in the essays of one of his true influences, **Montaigne**. As an essayist, Emerson was a masterful rhetorician, not only gifted in crafting the single sentences or phrases that can be lifted from their contexts and quoted with delight, but also blessed with a strong and delicate talent for all the rhythms of English prose.

Thoreau's fascination with nature gave rise to almost all his most important works, including *A Week on the Concord and Merrimack Rivers* (1849), *Walden; or, Life in the Woods* (1854), *The Maine Woods* (1864), *Cape Cod* (1865), and *A Yankee in Canada* (1866). An exacting sense of detail marks Thoreau's writing about nature, and he wrote in a style deliberately meant to awaken his readers – through surprising plays on language, arresting turns of speech, unusual images or metaphors. He became and remains one of the strongest influences on American nature writers. His influence also extends into politics. In 1845 he refused to pay his poll tax as a form of protest against the Mexican War and against slavery. He was jailed, an experience which led him to write "Civil Disobedience" (1849), one of his most famous essays. It became a guiding document for eminent 20th-century proponents of passive resistance such as Mohandas Gandhi and Martin Luther King, Jr.

Even with the dominance of transcendentalism among the best American essayists of the early to mid-19th century, the conversational essay practiced earlier by Washington Irving did not die. In fact, it flourished so much in the works of **Oliver Wendell Holmes** (1809–1914) that his collections became the most popular American works in England since Irving's *Sketch Book*. Holmes, a physician who wrote many controversial and ground-breaking **medical essays**, gained his greatest popularity beginning in 1857 with his Breakfast-Table essays, which were published monthly in the new *Atlantic Monthly* (1857–). They were often poetic essays filled with wise and witty observations, and threaded through with narratives. Different incarnations of the Breakfast-Table essays ran until 1890.

The greatest American poet of the second half of the 19th century, Walt Whitman (1819–92), published in 1870 a small book called *Democratic Vistas*, intended to explain the role of the poet in the success and failure of, on the one hand, American civilization and, on the other, civilization as a whole. "Above all previous lands, a great original literature is surely to become the justification and reliance (in some respects the sole reliance) of American democracy," he wrote. The essays contained the pragmatic idea that democracy is not so much a political institution as a "training school" in character formation. Whitman's other prose publication was *Specimen Days and Collect* (1882), the title essay of which is based on diary notes of Whitman's observations during the Civil War. To fill out the book, he added "Democratic Vistas" and a "Collect" of his **prefaces** and literary essays.

The **humorous essay** had many practitioners in the second half of the 19th century – including the popular Artemus Ward (1834–67) and David Ross Locke (1833–88), both of whom wrote primarily for newspapers – but few of their works hold up today anywhere near as well as do those of **Mark Twain** (1835–1910). Twain was of course a popular novelist and a lecturer, but his essays – which often combined fictional and nonfictional elements, and so are sometimes difficult to categorize – displayed his deep talent as a humorist just as well as his other work did. Never limiting himself to short pieces, Twain engaged instead in a broad range of essay forms, from travel letters to memoirs to social and political commentary. Though some of his pieces were journalistic and ephemeral, and others – especially later in his career – were polemical and pessimistic, what characterized almost all of his nonfiction work was not only humor but an interest in storytelling, whether a brief anecdote or a full-fledged account. Such a style complemented his skills as a lecturer – though they were much different skills from those of other popular American essayist-lecturers such as, for example, Emerson. For Twain, essays were about the "high and delicate art" or "how a story ought to be told."

Literary essays by lesser-known writers had also taken their place in the American essay tradition in the early to mid-19th century, many of them under the intangible influence of Washington Irving. Soon after his success, American writers began to develop a faculty for the criticism of literature as well as its creation. Henry Wadsworth Longfellow (1807–82), whose volume of essays *Outre-Mer* was published in 1835 after he had traveled for three years in Europe, was one of the most prominent critical essayists, despite the fact that his criticism was chiefly appreciative rather than analytical. He succeeded, as far as the essay is concerned, in conveying instruction at the same time as he imbued his writing with his personality, never overstepping the bounds of the familiar essay and veering into didactic formality. Edgar Allan Poe (1809–49) made his most famous contributions to the field of critical essays with "The Poetic Principle," "The Rationale of Verse," and "Philosophy of Composition" – all careful and brilliant studies in the art and aesthetics of authorship. One of the few essayists of the 19th century who made criticism his life's work to the exclusion of all other forms of literary creation was Edwin Percy Whipple (1819–86). He wrote finished, formal essays distinctively American in that they emphasized grit and determination and were filled with moral earnestness. James Russell Lowell (1819–91) wrote both critical and **personal essays**. His first prose work, *Conversations on Some of the Old Poets* (1845), revived the neglected **dialogue** essay, and among his later books of criticism was *Political Essays* (1888). Other writers of both critical and personal essays include George William Curtis (1824–92), who collected his writings for *Harper's* (1850–) in two volumes called *Essays from the Easy Chair* (1892, 1897), and Thomas Wentworth Higginson (1823–1911), who wrote reminiscences of great 19th-century writers. Higginson's tendency to look backwards was perhaps prescient, since the next stage in the life of the American essay would have as its focus the essay's impending death.

4. The "Death" of the Essay
The titles and dates tell the tale: "The Passing of the Essay" (1894), "Once and for All" (1929), "A Little Old Lady Passes Away" (1933), "A Disappearing Art" (1933), "The Lost Art of the Essay" (1935), "On Burying the Essay" (1948), "No Essays, Please!" (1951), "A Gentle Dirge for the Familiar Essay" (1955), and "The Essay Lives – in Disguise" (1984). The story of the modern American essay has been the story of its "death," a death that like Mark Twain's has been greatly exaggerated, for even as critics declared it dead, the essay thrived by taking up new subjects, reworking old forms, and accommodating new voices.

What was actually dying was not the essay, but a particular kind of essay and the age and essayist associated with it. This type of essay was variously described as the genteel, light, or Lambian essay, and for at least the first four decades of the century American essayists were preoccupied with whether the essay could be anything but light. The alternatives, it was argued, were the column or the article, both of which were largely seen as less literary and more journalistic than the essay. Their ascendancy marked the death of the essay. What at least a few astute critics and some of the practitioners of these new forms recognized was that many columns or articles were actually essays: they were personal in subject matter and familiar in style in the way that the essay has always been. What has changed during the 20th century is that the essay has become increasingly political, revealing, and weighty.

5. The Turn of the Century and the Genteel Tradition
The genteel tradition held sway in American letters at least until World War I. Promoted by an interlocking network of literary critics, magazine editors, and Ivy League English professors, this tradition argued for art that reflected upper-middle-class American values, Christian morality, the classical unity of truth and beauty, and a belief in the progress of (Anglo-American) civilization. Many, if not most, of the leading figures of the genteel tradition were essayists, and much of the tradition's cultural work was done in that genre. These "custodians of culture," as Henry May labeled them in his *The End of American Innocence* (1959), were troubled by the industrialization of America during the Gilded Age and sought to ameliorate the accompanying materialism by holding tight to Christian traditions and British literary conventions. They distrusted the new waves of immigration, the new rich, and America's new role as a leader in international affairs. These essayists produced work that was generally sentimental, idealistic, nostalgic, and sometimes pious. They often sported three names and were sometimes more "English" than their English counterparts. They adopted a tone that was decidedly conversational and sometimes even chatty, and cultivated a view of the essayist as a "friend." In order to maintain this chumminess they kept their subject matter light and noncontroversial. If politics or religion was broached, it was discussed matter-of-factly, with the assumption that the reader would agree with what "we," all right-thinking people, thought. More often, however, their essays took as their subjects gardening, reading, Christmas dinner, or the family pet. Some representative titles suggest the standard tone and subjects – *Reveries of a Bachelor* (1850) by Donald Grant Mitchell (1822–1908), *My Summer in a Garden* (1871) by Charles Dudley Warner (1829–1900), *Days Off, and Other Digressions* (1907) by Henry Van Dyke (1852–1933), *Among Friends* (1910) by Samuel McChord Crothers (1857–1927), *Days Out, and Other Papers* (1917) by Elisabeth Woodbridge Morris (1870–1964), and *Like Summer's Cloud* (1925) by Charles Brooks (1878–1934). The work of these essayists was tremendously popular and influential; *Reveries of a Bachelor*, for example, led Scribner's list for 50 years.

These writers sometimes published in other genres, usually poetry or the short story, and often worked as academics or book reviewers. Some were regular critics for outlets of "higher journalism" – Paul Elmer More (1864–1937) and Stuart Pratt Sherman (1881–1926) in the *Nation*, Hamilton Wright Mabie (1846–1916) in the *Outlook* (and later, the *Ladies Home Journal*), Bliss Perry (1860–1954) in the *Atlantic Monthly*, and Robert Underwood Johnson (1853–1937) in the *Century*. Their **review** essays were generally conservative and prescriptive, often enforcing what was called "the parlor table" or "young girl" standard, which specified what reading material was fit to appear on a family's parlor table and, more particularly, to be read aloud by a father to his daughter.

6. The 1920s and 1930s: The Rise of the Columnists and Other Developments

The relatively settled world of the late Victorians, which had allowed the whimsical dalliance with the everyday as well as the enforcement of a strict understanding of good manners, may never have been quite as ordered and sedate as it sometimes appeared, but certainly by the turn of the century it was being challenged by the revelations of the muckrakers, the flood of new immigrants, the rise of the "New Woman," and the gathering war clouds in Europe. In literature, naturalism and imagism were shaking up fiction and poetry respectively, but the essay was slower to change. Soon, however, World War I began to force essayists out of their libraries and gardens. As **Agnes Repplier** (1855–1950) put it in a 1918 piece entitled "The American Essay in Wartime," "The personal essay, the little bit of sentiment or observation, the lightly offered commentary which aims to appear the artless thing it isn't, – this exotic, of which Lamb was a rare exponent, has withered in the blasts of war."

Repplier's lament may have been a bit hyperbolic, but things were changing. In 1911, Harvard philosopher and cultural critic **George Santayana** (1863–1952) had named the genteel tradition and argued that it was an outmoded form of New England parochialism. Randolph Bourne (1886–1918), along with Van Wyck Brooks (1886–1963) and **H. L. Mencken** (1880–1956), built on Santayana's analysis in their critique of "Puritanism" and search for what Brooks called a "usable past." Bourne died early and Brooks focused on literary criticism, but Mencken, in a prodigious outpouring of personal commentary and cultural criticism, did more than anyone during the immediate prewar and postwar periods to redefine the American essay. His sarcasm and irony poked fun at the genial tone of the light essay, and his love for, knowledge of, and talent at employing a distinctly American idiom helped do for the American essay what Twain had done for fiction and Whitman for poetry – Mencken took the essay from the hands of the Anglophiles who had dominated it and showed that it could be written in American.

The work of Mencken and other new essayists during the 1920s to modernize the essay was undertaken in a rapidly changing social and cultural climate. Thousands of soldiers, including midwestern farm boys and African American sharecroppers from the South, had traveled through New York and other eastern ports on their way to and from war. After the war many of them returned to the cities and stayed on, often working in the fast-growing automobile industry. All of the cities of the North and East were growing, but it was New York that was the center of modern culture. Motion pictures, radio, and mass circulation magazines told New York's story, but so too did the many new syndicated newspaper columns.

Columns or departments had already begun to appear in American newspapers – Eugene Field's (1850–95) "Sharps and Flats" ran in the Chicago *Daily News* from 1883 to 1895, and Bert Leston Taylor's (1866–1921) "A Line o' Type or Two" appeared in the Chicago *Tribune* between 1901 and 1920 – but the 1920s and 1930s marked the heyday of the column. Not all of the new columns were strictly in the essay tradition. Some were editorials or political commentary, others were a hodgepodge of jokes and jingles sent in by readers. Sunday editions often offered a dozen or more columns on specialized topics such as gossip, sports, movies, fashion, radio, and books, as well as how-to columns on subjects as varied as cooking, bridge, and grammar.

There were also "essay" columns that were more personal, familiar, and discursive. These columns might indulge in gossip, review a book, or tender some light verse, but they consisted mainly of the author's thoughts and stories about everyday life. The popularity of these columns led to versions of them appearing as well in newly established magazines like the *New Yorker* (1925–) and the *Saturday Review of Literature* (1924–86). As such, they were more modern, somewhat less bookish versions of departments like "The Editor's Study" and "The Easy Chair" in *Harper's* or "The Contributor's Club" in the *Atlantic Monthly*.

Many major critics of the period, including Henry Seidel Canby (1878–1961) in "Out with the Dilettante" (1922), Burton Rascoe (1892–1957) in "What of Our Essayists?" (1922), Carl Van Doren (1885–1950) in "Day In and Day Out: Manhattan Wits" (1923), Stuart Sherman (1881–1926) in "Apology for Essayists of the Press" (1924), and Simeon Strunsky (1879–1948) in "The Essay of Today" (1928), argued that several of these columnists were negotiating their daily deadlines successfully enough to have begun to create a new kind of American essay, one that observed life in the American cities, especially New York, and evoked the idiom of city streets. They praised, in particular, Heywood Broun (1888–1939), Robert Cortes Holliday (1880–1947), **Christopher Morley** (1890–1957), **Robert Benchley** (1889–1945), Frank Moore Colby (1865–1925), Don Marquis (1878–1937), and Franklin P. Adams (1881–1960).

These "colyumnists," as they called themselves, took different approaches, but all were essentially essayists. Marquis parodied Modernist poetry by pretending his columns were written by a cockroach named Archy whose use of lowercase was not a choice (as it was for e. e. cummings) but a consequence of the fact that he could hop on only one key at a time and so was unable to hit the shift key at the same time. Morley, a more old-fashioned Anglophile, wrote largely about books in "The Bowling Green," which ran first in the New York *Post* and then moved to the *Saturday Review of Literature*. Broun argued for various left-liberal political positions, but, like Benchley, also adopted a kind of bumbling "little man" persona in order to tell stories about himself. Adams began with a column called "A Little of Everything" in the *Chicago Journal* in 1903, but gained greater fame when he moved to New York and created the syndicated column "The Conning Tower," which was a kind of potpourri of light verse and readers' contributions, with occasional mock diaries in the manner of Samuel Pepys in which Adams revealed the goings-on of his Algonquin Round Table pals, a group of literary types who met regularly at the Algonquin Hotel to drink and talk.

On the whole, these men were highly educated: Benchley and Broun were Harvard graduates, Colby taught at Columbia and New York Universities, Morley was a Rhodes Scholar. And yet, as **E. B. White** remarked of Marquis, they were "never quite certified by intellectuals and serious critics of *belles lettres*." Though considered hopelessly middlebrow by more academic critics, the "colyumnists" saw themselves as having sought popularity by choice, as having chosen to write for and educate a broad readership. Their pieces retained some Victorian traits, but on the whole tended to emphasize the humorous and nostalgic over the prim and proper. In his defense of the New York wits, Sherman noted that these "busy newspaper men" had "blazed their way out to the new public" that was "truly democratic," the "wide circle composed of every man and woman who reads a newspaper." Van Doren agreed and added that these essayists were not a completely new phenomenon. "They are," he said, "town wits, as Addison and Steele were in their merry London, as Irving and Paulding were in the New York of a hundred years ago."

Perhaps the most important event in the development of the American essay during this period was the founding in 1925 of the *New Yorker* by Harold Ross (1892–1951). Influenced by the columnists (Benchley was an early and frequent contributor), Ross' magazine, especially in its "Talk of the Town" department, told the rest of the nation what was going on in New York even as it claimed (perhaps somewhat disingenuously) not to be for the "little old lady in Dubuque." It was in the *New Yorker* that the most popular essayists of the 1930s and 1940s developed their styles. **James Thurber** (1894–1961) built on Benchley's little man persona in a number of comic autobiographical pieces (as well as short stories such as "The Secret Life of Walter Mitty"). **E. B. White** (1899–1985) developed his own mild-mannered, somewhat genteel, well-read man-on-the-street persona in "Notes and Comments." Alexander Woollcott (1887–1943) poked fun at his own version of the effete urban dandy in a series of celebrity profiles and his back-page column, "Shouts and Murmurs."

1925 also marked the publication of *The New Negro*, an anthology of essays and other work edited by Alain Locke (1886–1954) that launched the Harlem Renaissance and with it several African American poets and fiction writers who also wrote essays, especially Langston Hughes (1902–67), Richard Wright (1908–60), and Zora Neale Hurston (1891–1960). These younger writers worked out of a tradition of African American autobiographical nonfiction in which the writer revealed a life in order to claim selfhood, but brought to it the new rhythms of black speech and music emerging from the growing black urban communities of the North, especially Harlem. These voices ranged from the angry polemics of Wright to the affirmative comedy of Hurston, but they were all more informal, less academic, and more likely to employ dialect than the previous generations of African American essayists, which included, besides Locke, the political conscience of freed slave **Frederick Douglass** (1818–95), anti-lynching crusader Ida B. Wells Barnett (1862–1931), and the magisterial voice of **W. E. B. Du Bois** (1868–1963).

The work of the columnists offered probably the most widely read kind of essay and the most important development in the form during the period between the wars, but essays were also put to other kinds of use during this period. Many modern American novelists wrote essays, most notably Ernest Hemingway (1899–1961) in his war dispatches and F. Scott Fitzgerald (1896–1940) in a series of pieces for *Esquire* about his mental breakdown. Leftist literary critics such as **Edmund Wilson** (1895–1972), Mike Gold (1894–1967), and Meridel Le Sueur (1900–96) wrote reviews and **polemical essays** that were only occasionally more personal. Finally, high Modernists such as William Carlos Williams (1883–1963),

T. S. Eliot (1888–1965), **Ezra Pound** (1885–1972), and Gertrude Stein (1874–1946) used the essay mainly to explain and defend their experiments in other genres.

Despite the use of the essay by writers primarily known for their work in fiction or poetry, and the popularity of the essays appearing in magazines and newspaper columns, the essay, especially the personal essay, remained under attack during the 1930s. As editor of the *Saturday Review of Literature*, Henry Seidel Canby tried to temper and control the debate over the death of the essay, but found this harder to do as the 1930s grew more and more politicized. Katharine Fullerton Gerould (1879–1944), along with Agnes Repplier, had long been leading the defense of the traditional light essay. Throughout the 1920s Gerould had decried the rise of commercialism, the lowering of standards, and what she called "the plight of the genteel." In 1934, Canby let Gerould call for a "plebiscite" on the essay in the pages of his magazine. "The perfect essayist," she wrote, "could write a good essay on Hitler or on hogs, and I should be enchanted to read it – but he has not done it yet, and I am not yet enchanted." Harking back to a distinction **William Dean Howells** (1837–1920) had noted as early as 1902, Gerould asked if readers wanted mere "articles," or rather the leisure, the meditations, and the light touch of the genteel essay. Then, making her distinction into a dogmatic either/or, she asked if they wanted "news" or "truth." Her appeal backfired: she and the essay were branded as retrograde. As one reader put it, "Mrs. Gerould is complacent, slightly irritating. My plebeian vote is in favor of the present and the future against the past." The editor of Scribner's got on the bandwagon as well, writing to Gerould that "this is not an age of polite letters, and writing has ceased to be the province of the cultured." He polled his readers, proudly quantified the results, and notified Gerould that only three per cent wanted a return to her kind of essay. For the time, the debate seemed to be over. Gerould and the genteel essay had lost.

7. The 1940s: The Example of E. B. White
It was E. B. White, himself an Ivy League-educated son of the same Eastern genteel upper middle class that Gerould defended, who provided a way out of the dilemma that threatened to kill the essay. However, he had to leave the *New Yorker* and become haunted by the rise of fascism in order to do it. In 1938, tired of weekly deadlines and Ross' insistence that he use the editorial "we," White decided to leave New York for Maine and the *New Yorker* for *Harper's*. For the next five years he wrote a monthly column entitled "One Man's Meat." In these pieces (collected in a book with the same title in 1942), he found a voice that was at once personal and public. He talked about everyday life on his saltwater farm but also attacked fascism, defended democracy, supported American intervention in Europe, and anticipated the United Nations by calling for world government, or what he called "supranationalism."

White's ability to talk about such politically charged issues in the quiet voice of a Yankee farmer (or at least New York writer playing Yankee farmer) set a precedent and did much to solve a problem that had been facing the American essay since the first challenges to the genteel tradition around the turn of the century. He added weight to the light essay, allowing it to take on controversial public issues while retaining the charm of its familiar style.

In 1943 White returned full-time to the *New Yorker*, and if he never burned with quite as blue a flame as he had during the period of "One Man's Meat," a period he referred to later as "one of those rare interludes that can never be repeated, a time of enchantment," he would still write enough wonderful essays to remain the dominant voice in the field for at least another 20 years. White continued to write familiar, sometimes almost folksy, pieces, but the political commitment that had fueled "One Man's Meat" remained a part of him; his essays of the 1950s and 1960s spoke eloquently to issues such as civil rights, nuclear testing, and the environment.

8. The 1950s: Political Voices in a Quiet Time

White was hardly the only essayist to take political stands during the 1950s. On the contrary, that decade, usually seen as quiet and complacent, witnessed the appearance of many strong, committed nonfiction writers. But White was the exception in the sense that his voice was generally more personal than those of **Lionel Trilling** (1905–75), **Irving Howe** (1920–93), Alfred Kazin (1915–), **Mary McCarthy** (1912–89), Harold Rosenberg (1906–78), Elizabeth Hardwick (1916–), Stanley Edgar Hyman (1919–70), and Leslie Fiedler (1917–). Primarily literary critics (or in Rosenberg's case, art critic), these New York intellectuals had roots in 1930s radicalism, were associated with journals of cultural criticism such as *Partisan Review* (1934–) and *Dissent*, and were public intellectuals in the tradition of Edmund Wilson (himself still quite active in the 1950s) rather than personal essayists like White.

The decade also saw the emergence of three young writers who, though they saw themselves as novelists first, will perhaps be best remembered for their work in nonfiction – **James Baldwin** (1924–87), **Norman Mailer** (1923–), and **Gore Vidal** (1925–). All three brought deep political commitment (Mailer and Vidal both ran for public office) as well as their experience as fiction writers to their essay writing. Sometimes, they also seemed to live their private lives in public: Baldwin and Vidal were openly gay even before the Stonewall Rebellion of 1968, and Vidal and Mailer acquired celebrity status through their work in films and on television. They used their essays to create these well-defined, sometimes defiant public personae.

9. The 1960s and 1970s: Social Upheaval and the New Journalism

Mailer's propensity for putting himself as a character into his narrative essays (and often referring to that self in the third person) made him a pioneer of the **New Journalism**, which has had a tremendous impact on the development of the personal essay at the end of the century. Many New Journalists used techniques similar to Mailer's to challenge what they felt to be an impossible obsession with objectivity on the part of traditional journalism. Mailer, **Tom Wolfe** (1930–), Gay Talese (1932–), and others borrowed techniques from fiction such as the extensive use of dialogue, developed scenes, sensory details, experimental punctuation, colloquialisms, and neologisms, and in so doing made their magazine articles more essayistic. Many of these New Journalists focused on longer, book-length pieces,

leading to their association (particularly in the case of Truman Capote [1924–84]) with the "non-fiction novel," but even then their chapters sometimes had the feel of self-contained essays. All in all, they had a major influence on the essay by creatively blurring some of the old distinctions between journalism and *belles-lettres* that had long dogged the essay.

These and other practitioners of the New Journalism such as Pete Hamill (1935–), Dan Wakefield (1932–), Seymour Krim (1922–89), and **Joan Didion** (1934–) changed not only the form of creative nonfiction but also broadened its subject matter by reporting as participating observers from the turbulent centers of their times – Mailer marching on the Pentagon to protest the Vietnam War, Krim hobnobbing with his fellow Beats, Didion mixing with the star culture of Los Angeles and Hollywood, and Wolfe spending extended periods with everyone from acid-dropping hippies to strait-laced astronauts.

Debates over the future of the novel, intersections with European culture (especially French critical theory after May 1968), the founding of the *New York Review of Books* (1963–), accounting for the boom in Latin American literature, and other developments in and out of the academy prompted much activity among more formal, intellectual essayists during this period. As with the New Journalism, much of this work was done by practicing novelists including Didion, **William H. Gass** (1924–), John Barth (1930–), **Susan Sontag** (1933–), **Cynthia Ozick** (1928–), and Stanley Elkin (1930–95). These writers wrote a personal, richly allusive, highly stylized kind of critical essay on subjects ranging from the nature of fiction to the role writers should or should not play in the political movements of the times.

10. The 1980s to the Present: The Revival of the Essay

The political movements of the 1960s and 1970s had a tremendous effect on the development of the essay. Through the experiments of the New Journalists, not only did they make the already loose form of the essay even more open than it had been since at least the 1920s, they also led to new voices using the essay to speak to new constituencies of readers. The result has been an explosion in the number of skilled essayists publishing in America at the century's end.

The civil rights movement, for instance, forced much debate and discussion of issues of race, and the personal essay was a form particularly suited to testimony, witness, and stirring anecdote. During the 1960s leaders of the civil rights movement such as Martin Luther King, Jr. (1929–68), Eldridge Cleaver (1935–), and George Jackson (1941–71) used the essay to advance the cause. The intersection of the women's movement with the civil rights movement resulted in several new voices that focused on the interconnectedness of racism and sexism, among them **Alice Walker** (1944–), Angela Davis (1944–), Toni Morrison (1931–), and Audre Lorde (1934–92). Other struggles for democratic rights during this period have led to essays emerging from communities that had not normally been associated with the form in the past. Among these new voices are Maxine Hong Kingston (1940–), Richard Rodriguez (1944–), Judith Ortiz Cofer (1952–), Gary Soto (1952–), Leslie Marmon Silko (1948–), and Naomi Shihab Nye (1952–). The success of many of these movements has led to the establishment of new areas of specialization within the academy, the recovery of lost texts, and the insertion of new voices into the canon of Western literature. The backlash against these changes during the Reagan years led to the culture wars of the late 1980s and early 1990s, during which a number of minority academics made names for themselves while using the personal essay to argue their case; these included Henry Louis Gates, Jr. (1950–), Gerald Early (1952–), bell hooks (1955?–), and Shelby Steele (1946–).

The second wave of feminism in the 1970s also swept in a number of new writers intent on breaking down barriers between the personal and the political. Besides the minority feminists listed above, other women who have found the essay particularly conducive to this goal are **Adrienne Rich** (1929–), Gloria Steinem (1934–), Katha Pollitt (1949–), and Nancy Mairs (1943–).

A final kind of essay which has attracted a considerable number of skilled practitioners in recent years is the nature essay. Working from a strong tradition that developed in the 19th century, and energized by the environmental movement, mid-20th-century greats such as **Aldo Leopold** (1886–1948), **Loren Eiseley** (1907–77), and Rachel Carson (1907–64) have been joined by a new generation of nature writers, including practicing scientists such as **Lewis Thomas** (1913–93), Edward O. Wilson (1929–), **Stephen Jay Gould** (1941–), and popularizers of science such as **John McPhee** (1931–) and David Quammen (1948–). A host of other writers produce both fiction and nonfiction, but in their nonfiction have often focused on nature and landscape; these include Edward Abbey (1927–89), **Edward Hoagland** (1932–), **Annie Dillard** (1945–), **Barry Lopez** (1945–), Gretel Ehrlich (1946–), and **Scott Russell Sanders** (1945–).3

11. Conclusion

The view that the essay is inherently precious and irrelevant persists. In the preface to the most recent full-length study of the genre, *The Observing Self: Rediscovering the Essay* (1988), Graham Good admits that he launched his project with some trepidation because the word "essay" still "conjures up the image of a middle-aged man in a worn tweed jacket in an armchair smoking a pipe by a fire in his private library in a country house somewhere in southern England, in about 1910, maundering on about the delights of idleness, country walks, tobacco, old wine, and old books . . ."

Despite Good's concerns, the essay seems more alive than ever, even if it "lives in disguise," as Phillip Lopate (1943–), an important contemporary American essayist and anthologist, put it in a 1984 essay. Whether it is labeled New Journalism, creative nonfiction, or just nature writing, the American essay has, at least since Fitzgerald's pieces about his mental breakdown or E. B. White's essays about Hitler and hogs in *One Man's Meat*, been moving inexorably toward subjects that are at once more intimate and more public than the safe and chatty reveries of the genteel essayists of the late Victorian era. Today the most respected American essayists write uninhibitedly and skillfully about issues as personal as their own addictions and maladies and as public as women's liberation and environmental awareness, often within the same essay.

DAN ROCHE (PARTS 1–3)
NED STUCKEY-FRENCH (PARTS 4–11)

Anthologies

The Art of the Essay, edited by Leslie Fiedler, New York: Crowell, 1969 (original edition, 1958)
Best American Essays series, edited by Robert Atwan and guest editors, Boston: Houghton Mifflin, 1986–
The Bread Loaf Anthology of Contemporary American Essays, edited by Robert Pack and Jay Parini, Hanover, New Hampshire: University Press of New England, 1989
Modern Essays, edited by Russel Nye and Arra M. Garab, Glenview, Illinois: Foresman, 1969 (original edition, 1953)
The Open Form: Essays for Our Time, edited by Alfred Kazin, New York: Harcourt Brace and World, 1970 (original edition, 1961)
The Oxford Book of American Essays, edited by Brander Matthews, New York: Oxford University Press, 1914
The Penguin Book of Contemporary American Essays, edited by Maureen Howard, New York: Viking, 1984
Speech and Power: The African-American Essay and Its Cultural Content from Polemics to Pulpit, edited by Gerald Early, New York: Ecco Press, 2 vols., 1992–93

Further Reading

Anderson, Chris, editor, *Literary Nonfiction: Theory, Practice, Pedagogy*, Carbondale: Southern Illinois University Press, 1989
Atkins, G. Douglas, *Estranging the Familiar: Toward a Revitalized Critical Writing*, Athens: University of Georgia Press, 1992
Brodbeck, May, *American Non-Fiction, 1900–1950*, Chicago: Regnery, 1952
Butrym, Alexander J., editor, *Essays on the Essay: Redefining the Genre*, Athens: University of Georgia Press, 1989
Davis, Hallam Walker, *The Column*, New York: Knopf, 1926
Drew, Elizabeth, "The Lost Art of the Essay," *Saturday Review of Literature*, 16 February 1935
Eaton, W. P., "On Burying the Essay," *Virginia Quarterly Review* 24 (1948): 574–83
Edson, C. L., *The Gentle Art of Columning: A Treatise on Comic Journalism*, New York: Brentano, 1920
Emerson, Everett, editor, *Major Writers of Early American Literature*, Madison: University of Wisconsin Press, 1972
Fadiman, Clifton, "A Gentle Dirge for the Familiar Essay," in his *Party of One*, Cleveland: World, 1955: 349–53
Flanagan, John T., "A Word for the American Essay," *American Scholar* 14, no. 4 (October 1944): 459–66
Good, Graham, *The Observing Self: Rediscovering the Essay*, London and New York: Routledge, 1988
Granger, Bruce, *American Essay Serials from Franklin to Irving*, Knoxville: University of Tennessee Press, 1978
Howells, William Dean, "The Old-Fashioned Essay," *Harper's* (October 1902): 802–03
Krutch, Joseph Wood, "No Essays, Please!," *Saturday Review of Literature*, 10 March 1951: 18–19+
Lopate, Phillip, "The Essay Lives – in Disguise," *New York Times Book Review*, 18 November 1984
Loveman, Amy, "A Disappearing Art," *Saturday Review of Literature*, 23 July 1932: 1
McCord, David, "Once and for All," *Saturday Review of Literature*, 5 October 1929: 208
Piercy, Josephine K., *Studies in Literary Types in Seventeenth Century America, 1607–1710*, Hamden, Connecticut: Archon, 1969 (original edition, 1939)
Rascoe, Burton, "What of Our Essayists?," *Bookman* 55 (1922): 74–75
Repplier, Agnes, "The Passing of the Essay," in her *In the Dozy Hours*, Boston: Houghton Mifflin, 1894: 226–35
Repplier, Agnes, "The American Essay in Wartime," *Yale Review* 7, no. 2 (January 1918): 249–59
Sherman, Stuart, "An Apology for Essayists of the Press," in his *Points of View*, New York: Scribner, 1924: 173–85

Strunsky, Simeon, "The Essay of Today," *English Journal* 17, no. 1 (January 1928): 8–16

Tanner, William, General Introduction, *Essays and Essay-Writing*, edited by Tanner, Boston: Little Brown, 1935 (original edition, 1918)

Van Doren, Carl, "Day In and Day Out: Manhattan Wits," in his *Many Minds*, Port Washington, New York: Kennikat Press, 1966: 181–99 (original edition, 1924)

Waters, John P., "A Little Old Lady Passes Away," *Forum and Century* 90, no. 1 (July 1933): 27–29

The American Scholar

American journal, 1932–

Every issue of the current *American Scholar* begins with a **personal essay** by "Aristides," the *nom de plume* of editor and renowned essayist Joseph Epstein. His familiar writing on such topics as napping, name-dropping, and personal musical tastes is not at all academic in the traditional sense, but then, despite its title, the *American Scholar* is not a traditional scholarly journal. Rather it draws its name from the 1837 Phi Beta Kappa address at Harvard University by the great American essayist **Ralph Waldo Emerson**, who enlarged the definition of a scholar to "man thinking." In this speech, which James Russell Lowell called "an event without any former parallel in our literary annals" and **Oliver Wendell Holmes** hailed as "our intellectual Declaration of Independence," Emerson declared that "Man is not a farmer, or a professor, or an engineer, but he is all. Man is priest, and scholar, and statesman, and producer, and soldier." Unfortunately, Emerson concluded, in our time these functions have been divided one from another so that each person inhabits only one aspect of his or her potential. The *American Scholar* strives to mitigate this trend by helping its readers embrace all aspects of this Emersonian selfhood.

The *American Scholar* began publication in 1932 as the successor to the *Phi Beta Kappa Key*, publishing for members of PBK (the national academic honor society) as well as "for all who have general intellectual interests." In its first issue, the editorial board promised that the *American Scholar* would be "devoted to general scholarship," an assurance reiterated over 60 years later by the current editorial team, who characterized the publication as "fill[ing] the gap between learned journals and good magazines for a popular audience." In its current format, each quarterly issue leads off with general essays, followed by more specifically **topical essays** (marked by their smaller print) on the arts, sciences, social sciences, literature, politics, legal issues, and current events, as well as categories such as "memoir" and "reappraisal." Book **reviews**, some poetry, and the occasional book excerpt fill out the journal's offerings; as one reviewer noted, it is "an ideal magazine to be read leisurely." Commenting on the magazine's continuing interest in the current affairs of the world, the Winter 1939–40 editorial noted that "The table of contents of a journal of contemporary thought, such as *The American Scholar* aspires to be, may reflect, more than its editors are aware, the salient features of the modern scene."

Although the magazine's first essays were strictly formal, by the 1940s the tone was becoming increasingly familiar as the journal began including more addresses and speeches, thus easing its transition into publishing informal essays. It is this personal tone, one which recognizes that sophisticated and erudite readers not only appreciate serious discussion about wide-ranging issues but also have both a compassionate interest in their fellow humans and a sense of humor, that remains at the forefront of the *American Scholar*'s publishing sensibility. During much of its history, the magazine has included in every issue a long-running series of **familiar essays** by a single author, including philosopher Irwin Edman's "Under Whatever Sky" (1945–54), **Joseph Wood Krutch**'s "If You Don't Mind My Saying So" (1955–70), and Epstein's quarterly "Aristides" essay (1975–). While the journal has also regularly published more formal essays, including René Dubos' "The Despairing Optimist" series (1970–77), it is the magazine's personal, informal essays, following in the tradition of **Addison**, **Steele**, **Edmund Burke**, and **Montaigne**, that have contributed to the popularity of the essay form in contemporary culture. According to Epstein, "The familiar essayist lives, and takes his professional sustenance, in the everyday flow of things," and the American audience has responded well, giving the journal a circulation of 26,000 (as of 1993), large for a magazine of its type. The *American Scholar* has clearly played a leading role in claiming for the personal essay its own territory in the American literary landscape.

For a magazine so long-lived, the *American Scholar* has had a remarkable consistency of editors. The founding editor, William Allison Shimer, held that position until 1943, when he joined the armed forces to fight in World War II. Marjorie Hope Nicolson, president of the United Chapters of PBK, served as interim editor for one year before handing over the reins to Hiram Haydn, editor from Autumn 1944 until his death in 1973. During Haydn's tenure, the magazine was subtitled "A Quarterly for the Independent Thinker," reminding readers of the journal's Emersonian roots. Following Haydn's death, editorial board member Peter Gay served as acting editor for two issues until Joseph Epstein stepped into the editorial role, a position he still holds. This consistency of leadership has also been expressed in the journal's physical appearance, for the packaging of the magazine remains very similar to that of the first issue – quiet, understated, and discreet. The editorial board has seen far more diversity, having included such disparate thinkers as **Hannah Arendt**, Jacques Barzun, Saul Bellow, Ralph Ellison, Erik Erikson, John Erskine, John Kenneth Galbraith, Clifford Geertz, Lillian Hellman, Randall Jarrell, Judith Martin, Margaret Mead, Daniel P. Moynihan, and Robert Penn Warren, many of whom are themselves innovators of the essay in its various manifestations.

In Winter 1976–77, the editors paused to commemorate the Phi Beta Kappa bicentennial and reexamine the purpose of the *American Scholar*, one of the honor society's major public activities. Epstein and the editorial board noted that the journal – and by extension the essay genre itself – linked society and the intellectual world, striving to play the same role that **David Hume** (quoted in that issue's editorial) attributed to his own essay writing: "I cannot but consider myself as a kind of resident or ambassador from the dominions of learning to those of conversation, and shall think it my constant duty to promote a good correspondence betwixt these two states, which have so great a dependence on each other." In fulfilling this function, the *American Scholar* has changed its focus very little over the years. Echoing the journal's first editorial policy, Epstein recently remarked, "We hope chiefly to be interesting and entertaining to people who are interested in ideas and culture" – people, that is, who are American Scholars.

KAREN A. KEELY

The Anatomy of Melancholy
by Robert Burton, 1621; subsequent revised editions

Robert Burton (1577–1640) was one of the most prolific essayists of the 17th century. He published only one book; yet that book, *The Anatomy of Melancholy*, was his life's work. Nor did that single volume cramp the range of his style, which flowed, he wrote in his preface, "now serious, then light; now comical, then satirical; now more elaborate, then remiss, as the present subject required, or as at that time I was affected." Burton's claims for the variety of his style are not exaggerated. The title of the work suggests a twofold narrowness of focus, yet Burton somehow escapes the confines of both types of narrowness.

The first restriction is a structural one suggested by *Anatomy*: an anatomy is both analytical and synthetic, distinguishing a thing into its constituent parts, and highlighting relationships of each to each and each to the whole. Such a genre suggests a clinical, scientific style, which Burton supplies where necessary: "The upper of the hypochondries, in whose right side is the liver, the left the spleen; from which is denominated hypochondriacal melancholy." Yet within each of the compartments of the anatomy Burton feels free to indulge a more personal, subjective style, echoing his preface, wherein he urges the reader not to read his book, for "'Tis not worth the reading" and "thou canst not think worse of me than I do of myself." Further freedom comes from the nature of anatomy: interconnecting all aspects of melancholy not only allows but requires Burton to touch on a variety of subtopics.

The limitation of the major topic presents the second restriction, one of content. Yet in Burton's treatment, to write about melancholy is to write about the human condition, the subject of all great writing. To discuss melancholy is to discuss war, love, religion, imagination, sorrow, fear, or virtually any other essential element of human nature. Within the rigid structure of the anatomy Burton has imbedded essays on topics as manifold as **Montaigne**'s or **Bacon**'s.

While Burton's style may vary from scientific to personal, one element is constant: his prose is macaronic, playing Latin off against English. To some extent, this is true of almost all Jacobean prose: Latin intrudes more or less naturally in the works of educated writers of all European languages in the 17th century. Yet what is remarkable about Burton's Latinity is that it confines itself to parenthetical quotations and, sometimes, to word order: it has comparatively little effect on his diction. The Latinate "inkhorn" terms so prevalent in the writings of his contemporaries appear much less frequently in Burton's, and those that do tend to be personal favorites used habitually rather than nonce-words. For every *constringe*, *clancular*, or *calamistrate* in Burton's prose, we find half a dozen Anglo-Saxon colloquialisms such as *gubber-tushed*, *fuzzled*, or *dizzard*. The native vocabulary increases his verbal range, as English, in his century as in ours, has by far the largest vocabulary of any European language: to confine oneself to Latinate diction, even with inkhorn neologisms, is to narrow one's range severely in comparison to English. Burton's sentence structure also tends to be less Latinate than that of many contemporaries; rarely subordinating, his clauses and phrases tend to progress by apposition or accretion.

Structurally Burton's style illustrates the early 17th-century reaction to the Elizabethan imitations of **Cicero**'s Latin style. Ciceronian prose triumphed in the periodic sentence, lengthy constructions filled out by subordinate clauses and balanced antitheses. Burton and many of his contemporaries (particularly **John Donne** in his sermons, and **Sir Thomas Browne**) imitated the contrasting Silver Age style of **Seneca** and Tacitus, characterized by epigrammatic concision. The epigrammatic unit of Burton's Senecan style, however, was usually the clause, not the sentence, making his sentences as long as any Ciceronian period, but less symmetrical. The lack of balance and parallelism created the illusion of spontaneity; parallelism is obviously an artistic choice, whereas a Burtonian list or parenthesis sounds like a sudden outburst.

The impression of spontaneity and colloquialism in Burton's prose is all the more delightful for its ironic context: *The Anatomy of Melancholy* is a bookworm's distillation of a long life spent in libraries. The word "anatomy" suggests a logical order which this particular anatomy demonstrates only on the surface, in its table of contents and chapter headings. Within an individual topic, which can often be considered a separate essay, Burton's organizing principle seems to be not logical connection but rather free association. One anecdote suggests another, tangentially related, which suggests another, related more to the second than the first, so that a section might end quite a distance from its starting point. This syntactical looseness makes Burton's prose sound quite modern to many 20th-century critics.

JOHN R. HOLMES

Editions
The Anatomy of Melancholy, What It Is, 1621; revised editions, 1624, 1628, 1632, 1638, 1651; edited by Holbrook Jackson, 1932, and Thomas C. Faulkner, Nicolas K. Kiessling, and Rhonda L. Blair, 3 vols., 1989–94

Further Reading
Babb, Lawrence, *Sanity in Bedlam: A Study of Robert Burton's "Anatomy of Melancholy"*, East Lansing: Michigan State University Press, 1959
Browne, Robert M., "Robert Burton and the New Cosmology," *Modern Language Quarterly* 13 (1952): 131–48
Burgess, Anthony, "The Anatomy of Melancholy," *Horizon* 12 (Autumn 1970): 48–53
Colie, Rosalie, "Some Notes on Burton's Erasmus," *Renaissance Quarterly* 20 (1967): 335–41
Evans, Bergen, *The Psychiatry of Robert Burton*, New York: Columbia University Press, 1944
Fox, Ruth A., *The Tangled Chain: The Structure of Disorder in the "Anatomy of Melancholy"*, Berkeley: University of California Press, 1976

Gardiner, Judith Kegan, "Elizabethan Psychology and Burton's *Anatomy of Melancholy*," *Journal of the History of Ideas* 38 (1977): 373–88

Gottlieb, Hans Jordan, *Robert Burton's Knowledge of English Poetry*, Berkeley: University of California, 1937

Korkowski, Bud, "Genre and Satiric Strategy in Burton's *Anatomy of Melancholy*," *Genre* 8 (1979): 74–87

Mueller, William R., *The Anatomy of Robert Burton's England*, Berkeley: University of California Press, 1952

Osler, Sir William, "Robert Burton: The Man, His Book, His Library," *Oxford Bibliographical Society, Proceedings and Papers* 1 (1922–26): 162–90

Simon, Jean Robert, *Robert Burton (1577–1640) et "L'Anatomie de la Mélancolie"*, Paris: Didier, 1964

Traister, Barbara H., "New Evidence About Burton's Melancholy," *Renaissance Quarterly* 29 (1976): 66–70

Andersch, Alfred

German, 1914–1980

Alfred Andersch had a prolific career as an essayist: besides composing a lengthy treatise on the state of German literature after two world wars, he published four volumes of collected essays, produced and hosted numerous radio programs (among them the "radio-essay") for West Germany's leading broadcasting companies, and founded two important journals – *Der Ruf: Unabhängige Blätter der jungen Generation* (The call: independent journal of the young generation) and *Texte und Zeichen* (Texts and signs), which nurtured the essay tradition among the postwar generation of German writers. The scope and depth of his essays are as diverse as the roles he took on as author, editor, journalist, publisher, and radio man. Scattered among his many literary essays are astute social and political commentaries, art, film, and theater reviews, travel prose, author portraits (**Thomas Mann, Ernst Jünger**), aphorisms, and short philosophical glosses. The recent critical attention being given to Andersch's essays and radio work not only provides a glimpse into a brilliant career as a nonfiction writer, but also demonstrates in Andersch an important media figure and cultural talent scout. While foregrounding Andersch's interest in issues concerned with writing, cultural literacy, and aesthetics, the essays reveal a dynamic style that seeks to mediate continually between the historical, political, and socioeconomic contexts of modernity.

Andersch's capacity as editor and journalist for *Der Ruf* sparked his foray into essay writing. Along with Hans Werner Richter, Andersch sought to produce a journal that would capture the energy of the new generation of postwar writers and intellectuals. Throughout his career as an essayist, Andersch published essays in some of West Germany's principal literary and political journals, including *Frankfurter Hefte* (Frankfurt numbers), *Merkur* (Mercury), *konkret* (concrete), and *Kürbiskern* (Pumpkins). With the first meeting of the Gruppe 47 (Group 47) in 1947, which he organized, and the publication of the treatise *Deutsche Literatur in der Entscheidung* (German literature at the turning point) in 1948, Andersch established himself as a perceptive critic of German literature and advocate of Germany's younger generation of writers. When he began work in broadcasting at Radio Frankfurt (later Hessischer Rundfunk) in 1948, these

convictions became guiding forces. Andersch spent the next ten years of his life working for the leading broadcasting companies in West Germany. His creation of such programs as the *Abendstudio* and the "radio-essay" expanded the role of radio beyond reporting to include literary and artistic productions. In the *Funkkurier* (1955; Radio courier) Andersch described the "radio-essay" as a "poetic document of the reality of our world and of the life of men in that world." The unique synthesis in the "radio-essay" of artistic and political expression, musical and literary pieces, forged such critically acclaimed endeavors as the series entitled "Die Professoren" (The professors), which invited scholars like Walter Jens, **Theodor W. Adorno**, Walter Muschg, and **Max Bense** out of the classroom and into the studio to perform their ideas and put their theories into practice. The popularity of these talk-based programs stemmed from the expertise which they assumed of their audience, and made Andersch a household name. It is from his development of the "radio-essay" that his conception of the essay is brought forth. Influenced by Adorno's notion of the "constellation," Andersch's inclusion of music, literature, criticism, and politics in any one broadcast allowed for a montage of constantly shifting discourses, thereby illustrating the multifarious nature of the modern world. Andersch himself emphasized the word "trial," seeing the essay component of these radio broadcasts as providing for "the lively character of the trial or attempt, which remains continuously open to all possibilities." This intriguing definition of the "radio-essay" acts as an underlying premise for Andersch's written essays, and thus suggests some motifs common to his essays, radio broadcasts, and editorial ideals.

The essays highlight an attempt to reanimate the spirit of German Modernism, which had fallen victim to the Third Reich. The treatise *Deutsche Literatur in der Entscheidung*, the essays "Thomas Mann als Politiker" (1955; Thomas Mann as a politician) and "Achtzig und Jünger: Ein politischer Diskurs" (1975; Eighty and Jünger: a political discourse), and the review essays of work by young artists like Heinrich Böll, Arno Schmidt, Pierre Claudel, and Elio Vittorini speak to Andersch's desire to reconcile the tradition of German Modernism (Mann, Jünger) with the postwar generation's resuscitation of an avant-garde style attested to in *Europäische Avantgarde* (1949; European avant-garde), an anthology he edited. Andersch's work with the technological medium of the radio influenced the pieces he wrote and produced for his weekly features. His realization that his capacity as both radio broadcaster and author magnified the intensity of consumerist culture prompted such radio features as "Denk-Zettel für Kulturkonsumenten" (1959; Thoughts for cultural consumers) and written essays like "Die Blindheit des Kunstwerks" (1956; The blindness of art), "Notiz über die Schriftsteller und den Staat" (1966; Note concerning writers and the state), and "Literatur in den schweizerischen Massenmedien" (1977–78; Literature in the Swiss mass media).

Through Andersch's editorial ingenuity, which resulted in *Der Ruf, Europäische Avantgarde*, the brochure-series "studio frankfurt" (1951), and the literary journal *Texte und Zeichen*, young poets, artists, and essayists were given an intellectual venue where they could showcase their talents. The constellation of ideas set up by Andersch's role as essayist, radio figure, and editor sketches a trajectory between the height of German

Modernism and the birth of a postwar literary tradition, between the machinations of the Third Reich and the economic miracle of the 1950s. The importance of these essays, the care and detail with which they were written and their perceptive analyses of contemporary German culture demonstrate in Alfred Andersch an essayist of great significance in a continued and lively tradition of essay writing in Germany.

DANIEL D. GILFILLAN

Biography
Born 4 February 1914 in Munich. Studied at the Wittelsbacher Gymnasium, Munich, 1924–28. Worked for a publisher, 1928–30. Member of the youth organization of the Communist Party, 1932, and as a result spent six months in Dachau concentration camp, 1933. Office worker, Munich and Hamburg, 1933–40. Married Angelika Albert, 1935 (divorced, 1943): one daughter. Served in the German army, 1940–41, 1943–44: deserted on the Italian front and became a prisoner of war in the United States, where he worked on *Der Ruf* prisoners' publication, 1945. Editorial assistant to Erich Kästner, *Neue Zeitung* (New gazette), Munich, 1945–46; coeditor, *Der Ruf*, Munich, 1946–47. Cofounder, Gruppe 47, 1947. Founder and director of *Abendstudio*, Frankfurt Radio, 1948–50, and of "radio-essays" for South German Radio, Stuttgart, 1955–58 (assisted by **Hans Magnus Enzensberger**). Married Gisela Groneuer-Dichgans, 1950: two sons and one daughter. Founder and editor, *Texte und Zeichen*, 1955–57. Moved to Switzerland, 1958, and became a Swiss citizen, 1973. Led an expedition to the Arctic, 1965. Member, German Academy of Languages and Literature. Awards: German Critics' Prize, 1958; Nelly Sachs Prize, 1968; Charles Veillon Prize, 1968; Bavarian Academy Literature Prize. Died (of kidney failure) in Berzona, 21 February 1980.

Selected Writings

Essays and Related Prose
Deutsche Literatur in der Entscheidung, 1948
Wanderungen im Norden, 1962
Die Blindheit des Kunstwerks und andere Aufsätze, 1965
Aus einem römischen Winter: Reisebilder, 1966
Hohe Breitengrade, oder Nachrichten von der Grenze, 1969
Norden, Süden, rechts und links: Von Reisen und Büchern 1951–1971, 1972
Einige Zeichnungen, 1977
Öffentlicher Brief an einen sowjetischen Schriftsteller, das Überholte betreffend: Reportagen und Aufsätze, 1977
Ein neuer Scheiterhaufen für alte Ketzer: Kritiken und Rezensionen, 1979
Selected Writings, 1979
Es gibt kein fremdes Leid (Briefe und Essays zu Krieg und Frieden), with Konstantin Simonow, edited by Friedrich Hitzer, 1981

Other writings: four novels (*Sansibar oder der letzte Grund* [*Flight to Afar*], 1957; *Die Rote* [*The Red-Head*], 1960; *Efraim* [*Efraim's Book*], 1967; *Winterspelt*, 1974), short stories, radio plays, poetry, and an autobiography (1952).

Bibliographies
Kieser, Harro, "Alfred Andersch: Bibliographie der Sekundärliteratur, 1984–1993," in *Alfred Andersch, Perspektiven zu Leben und Werk*, edited by Irene Heidelberger-Leonard and Volker Wehdeking, Opladen: Westdeutscher Verlag, 1994: 221–25
Williams, R., "Alfred Andersch," *Kritisches Lexikon zur Deutschsprachigen Gegenwartsliteratur* 1, no. 1 (1984)

Further Reading
Haffmans, Gerd, editor, *Über Alfred Andersch*, Zurich: Diogenes, 1987 (original edition, 1974)
Jendricke, Bernhard, *Alfred Andersch in Selbstzeugnissen und Bilddokumenten*, Reinbek bei Hamburg: Rowohlt, 1988
Kunz, Eleonore, *Das publizistische und literarische Wirken Alfred Anderschs von 1945 bis zum Ende der fünfziger Jahre* (dissertation), Leipzig: University of Leipzig, 1984
Kunz, Eleonore, "Reise- und Landschaftsprosa seit 1944," in *Alfred Andersch, Perspektiven zu Leben und Werk*, edited by Irene Heidelberger-Leonard and Volker Wehdeking, Opladen: Westdeutscher Verlag, 1994: 65–74
Liebe, Matthias, *Alfred Andersch und sein "Radio-Essay"*, Frankfurt-on-Main and New York: Lang, 1990
Liebe, Matthias, "Alfred Andersch als Gründer und Leiter des 'Radio-Essays'," in *Alfred Andersch, Perspektiven zu Leben und Werk*, edited by Irene Heidelberger-Leonard and Volker Wehdeking, Opladen: Westdeutscher Verlag, 1994: 171–77
Reinhardt, Stephan, *Alfred Andersch, eine Biographie*, Zurich: Diogenes, 1990
Schmidt, Arno, *Das essayistische Werk zur deutschen Literatur in 4 Bänden, Sämtliche Nachtprogramme und Aufsätze*, Zurich: Arno-Schmidt-Stiftung in Haffmanns Verlag, 4 vols., 1988
Schütz, Erhard, "Alfred Andersch: Reiseprosa und Reportagen," in *Zu Alfred Andersch*, edited by Volker Wehdeking, Stuttgart: Klett, 1983: 132–42
Wehdeking, Volker, *Alfred Andersch*, Stuttgart: Metzler, 1983

Aphorism

"Aphorism" is a general, all-encompassing term for a condensed sentence or statement. Short and concise, it is a written or spoken expression of an observation, principle, or precept of truth or advice. (The *Oxford English Dictionary* defines the aphorism as a "short, pithy sentence expressing a truth of general import.") The etymology of the aphorism is revealing: *apo* plus *horizein* denote "away from a marked area or limited boundary." Thus it proceeds by a dual process, of initial divergence from the terms of a given discourse followed by a return to it, but importing an unusual perspective, a process often characterized by a fusion of logic and imagination, or wit. By the 18th century the aphorism had developed into an autonomous literary short form. Descending from the terse scientific-medical precepts of Hippocrates, it extended its range to include **Francis Bacon**'s *Novum organum* (1620) and the 17th-century philosophical aphorisms of the French moralists such as **La Rochefoucauld, La Bruyère**, and Chamfort.

The aphorism has included such small forms of brief discourse as the reflection, the **apothegm**, the axiom, the sentence, the *aperçu*, the proverb, the adage, the motto, and the **maxim**. These definitions are determined by a variety of criteria, such as whether the statements are oral or written, authorial or anonymous, practical or theoretical, prosaic or poetic, concrete or metaphorical, descriptive or prescriptive, etc.

The various studies of the aphorism agree in regarding it as a specific mode of inquiry or a particular intellectual response to the relationship between the individual (author, reader) and society. Further, that relationship is articulated through a distinct verbal structure, a literary representation which renders concrete the tension and conflict between individual observation and abstract reflection. Thus, the aphorism is often said to express the uncertainty of experience or a crisis of consciousness.

For many literary critics and theorists, the aphorism remains the sole form of discourse to refuse integration into any system or dominant order of thought. But in breaking up or subverting the status quo from the perspective of observation and presentation, the aphorism simultaneously implies an Other, a contrary order of the "not yet realized." The aphorism uses rhetorical verbal structures like antithesis, parallelism, proportion, oxymoron, chiasmus, metaphor, and paradox, in a concise, emphatic manner to address this matrix of oppositions.

Like all literary constructions, the aphorism mediates an insight or perception through language. However, the aphorism is highly conscious of the manner in which this mediation occurs. Indeed, it has often been called the literary form that is most aware of itself. But the resulting relationship between writer and reader is neither direct nor conversational, thus differing from that created by the essay. The aphorism's meaning is not immediately obvious; indeed often at first glance it is impenetrable. It typically works dialectically, through paradox, pun, mixed metaphor, or similarly unexpected verbal and semantic juxtaposition, forcing the reader to rethink, to complete the dialectical process of an active search for an unexpected meaning. Writer and reader require both logic and imagination: first to establish or recognize the digression, the antithesis, the paradox, the hiatus across the linear progression of discourse, and second to make the reconnection.

The essay and the aphorism share many borders, but also demonstrate key contrasts. Both forms require a high degree of learning and sociocultural sophistication by the writer and the reader; both are anti-systematic in their modes of discourse. But the essay is something much greater than an expansion and extension of an aphorism, and an aphorism is more than merely the nucleus of an essay. Whereas the essay is the discourse of experience and observation by the author, subsequently related to an idea or theme, the aphorism proceeds more independently from individual experience. It begins *in media res* with the initial idea turned inside out. With its greater self-consciousness of language and its closed, inverted form – it is read in an instant, but encourages, even requires, multiple rereadings – the aphorism provides insight but does not provide a basis for dialogue or a dialogic stance by the author toward the reader. In contrast, the essay requires a substantial period of time for its reading, and encourages, with its looser, more open form, a dialogue of thought between author and reader. The aphorism is essentially dictatorial, while the essay is suggestive.

RALPH W. BUECHLER

Anthologies
The Oxford Book of Aphorisms, edited by John Gross, Oxford and New York: Oxford University Press, 1983
The Viking Book of Aphorisms, edited by W. H. Auden and Louis Kronenberger, New York: Viking, and London: Faber, 1962

Further Reading
Blin, Jean-Pierre, "L'Aphorisme dans les romans," *Revue Littéraire Mensuelle* (November–December 1989): 93–103
Cantarruti, Giulia, and Hans Schumacher, editors, *Neuere Studien zur Aphoristik und Essayistik*, Frankfurt-on-Main: Lang, 1986
Crane, Mary Thomas, *Proverbial and Aphoristic Sayings: Sources of Authority in the English Renaissance* (dissertation), Cambridge, Massachusetts: Harvard University, 1986
Engel, William E., "Aphorism, Anecdote, and Anamnesis in Montaigne and Bacon," *Montaigne Studies* 1 (1989): 158–76
Faber, Marion, "The Metamorphosis of the French Aphorism: La Rochefoucauld and Nietzsche," *Comparative Literature Studies* 23, no. 2 (1986): 205–17
Fricke, Harald, *Aphorismus*, Stuttgart: Metzler, 1984
Grenzmann, Wilhelm, "Aphorismus," in *Reallexikon der deutschen Literaturgeschichte*, edited by Klaus Kanzog, Berlin: de Gruyter, 4 vols., 1958–88 (original edition, edited by Paul Merker and Wolfgang Stammler, 1925–31)
Jaouen, Françoise, *Discours aphoristique et pensée minimaliste: Le Classicisme en petits morceaux* (dissertation), Berkeley: University of California, 1991
Johnston, William M., "The Vienna School of Aphorists 1880–1930: Reflections on a Neglected Genre," in *The Turn of the Century: German Literature and Art 1890–1915*, edited by Gerald Chapple and Hans H. Schulte, Bonn: Bouvier, 1981
Kronenberger, Louis, *The Last Word: Portraits of Fourteen Master Aphorists*, New York: Macmillan, 1972
Lind, L. R., "The Aphorism: Wisdom in a Nutshell," *Classical and Modern Literature* 14, no. 4 (Summer 1994): 311–22
Morley, John, *Aphorisms: An Address Delivered Before the Edinburgh Philosophical Institution, November 11, 1887*, London and New York: Macmillan, 1887
Neumann, Gerhard, editor, *Aphorismus*, Darmstadt: Wissenschaftliche Buchgesellschaft, 1976
Snider, Alvin, "Francis Bacon and the Authority of Aphorism," *Prose Studies* 11, no. 2 (1988): 60–71
Wescott, Roger W., "From Proverb to Aphorism: The Evolution of a Verbal Art Form," *Forum Linguisticum* 5, no. 3 (1981): 213–25

Apothegm

Since the Renaissance, "apothegm" has been virtually synonymous with "**aphorism**" – a short, pithy statement of a general truth. Earlier, however, an aphorism was a statement of principle or scientific knowledge, while an apothegm was a statement of ethical, moral, or religious advice from a wise person.

The apothegm emerges in the tradition of "wisdom literature" that stretches back to ancient Egypt. As early as 2500 BCE, Egyptian kings and courtiers instructed their sons or protégés by means of short sayings on good and wise conduct. Jews living in Egypt adopted this practice and, after their expulsion, adapted it to augment religious teachings from the Torah and Talmud. Written records of these oral teachings form the earliest body of wisdom literature.

The early Christians inherited both traditions. In the 4th century, the apothegm appeared as a piece of profoundly considered and heartfelt advice from a holy sage to a seeker after God. At this time, in remote areas of Egypt, an ascetic movement arose: Christians, seeking pure knowledge of God, isolated themselves in the deserts, praying, fasting, and enduring lives of extreme privation, believing that discipline of the flesh brought them closer to God. Some of these anchorites gained reputations as holy men, and younger seekers came to them craving "a word," in the belief that the older men, through their experience, would be able to direct the younger men's way to God. Eventually, accounts of the advice thus given were recorded, and came to be known as *apophtheg-mata patrum* (sayings of the fathers).

The apothegm as transmitted from the sage to the seeker differs from the *bon mot*, with which it has more recently been identified. First, the apothegm was delivered to a particular person under particular circumstances: the seeker described his situation and requested guidance; the sage gave advice suited to that unique request. Moreover, the words of advice did not necessarily form the entire message. The face-to-face interaction of seeker and sage – wherein a look or a sign or simply a general sense of the other – was considered a significant element of the transmission of wisdom. Thus the apothegm was not intended to be written down for subsequent generations to apply to their own lives. Nevertheless, sayings were recorded as a way of preserving at least some part of the desert experience, and were later treated as wise sayings of general application. Second, although many hundreds of apothegms came to be collected, so that a medieval monk might read several a day, there might not have been more than a few such sayings received by any one seeker. One story tells of a man who got a word of advice from a sage, practiced it for 20 years, and then returned for another "word." A single saying, from one who distrusted words to begin with, was a rare event, worthy of much rumination.

The collections of *apophthegmata* to some extent preserved the context of the sayings by reporting the circumstances under which advice was sought. Although some apothegms are very short ("Abba Alonios said, 'If I had not destroyed myself completely, I should not have been able to rebuild and shape myself again'"), some are intricate stories of over 1000 words, reporting the condition of the seeker, his relation to the sage, and the circumstances of the question and reply. Thus a longer apothegm resembles a fable.

These sayings were passed down during the Middle Ages in the eastern part of the Christian world, and also made their way, translated and transcribed, into medieval Europe. It seems likely that the transmission process altered the character of these apothegms over time, retaining emphasis on the kernel of the sage's advice and neglecting the contextualizing story, until by the late 16th century the apothegm was understood among the literate in England as a well-said truth of any sort.

The apothegm clearly influenced the essays of **Francis Bacon**, who would have been familiar with sayings from the writings of St. Basil the Great, John Cassian, and others. Bacon preserved something like the original concept of the apothegm, in that he treated it as a bit of stored wisdom and sometimes included information about context to clarify the meaning of the saying. With Bacon's emphasis on scientific knowledge, however, the apothegm lost some of its earlier status. In his hands it was no longer the quintessential counsel of an anchorite, but a notable quotation from a famous person. Accordingly, the degree of wisdom that Bacon attributed to the apothegm also diminished. Whereas in ancient times it was the clearest possible statement of transcendent knowledge, with Bacon the apothegm became a rhetorical resource, a means of reinforcing or embellishing an idea already stated. It was the aphorism that was, for Bacon, a vehicle of clear and simple truth; the apothegm was a kind of seasoning or enhancement. Nevertheless Bacon considered this seasoning an important means of making ideas intelligible for a reader, and

recommended that apothegms be memorized and used to enliven a text. In Bacon's essay "Of Revenge" (1625) after declaring, "Revenge is a kinde of Wilde Justice . . ." he adds, among other things:

> Cosmus Duke of Florence, had a Desperate Saying, against Perfidious or Neglecting Friends, as if those wrongs were unpardonable: *You shall reade* (saith he) *that we are commanded to forgive our Enemies; But you never read, that wee are commanded, to forgive our Friends.*

The anthology *Apophthegms New and Old* (1625), edited by Bacon, contains nearly 300 examples. His essays, like those of later essayists, are sprinkled with quotations. Because the ideas of such quotations were more important to the essayist than the sources from which they came, however, the sources of quotations were often omitted, and the apothegm became simply the pithy statement of truth that we know it as today.

WILLIAM ZEIGER

Anthologies

The Sayings of the Desert Fathers: The Alphabetical Collection, translated by Sister Benedicta Ward, London: Mowbrays, 1975; revised edition, Kalamazoo, Michigan: Cistercian Publications, 1984

The Wisdom of the Desert: Sayings from the Desert Fathers of the Fourth Century, translated by Thomas Merton, New York: New Directions, 1960

The Wisdom of the Desert Fathers: The Apophthemagta Patrum (the Anonymous Series), translated by Sister Benedicta Ward, Oxford: S. L. G. Press, 1975

Further Reading

Brown, Peter, *The Body and Society: Men, Women, and Sexual Renunciation in Early Christianity*, New York: Columbia University Press, 1988

Murphy, Roland E., "Introduction to Wisdom Literature," in *The Jerome Biblical Commentary*, edited by Raymond E. Brown, Joseph A. Fitzmyer, and Murphy, Englewood Cliffs, New Jersey: Prentice Hall, 1986

Stanton, Leonard J., "Zedergol'm's *Life of Elder Leonid of Optima*: Apophthegm, Person, and the Chronotope of Encounter," *Religion and Literature* (Spring 1990): 19–38

Stephens, James, *Francis Bacon and the Style of Science*, Chicago: University of Chicago Press, 1975

Torrance, Thomas F., *Space, Time and Incarnation*, London and New York: Oxford University Press, 1969

Arciniegas, Germán

Colombian, 1900–

The two main forms of literary activity that have earned Colombia's Germán Arciniegas a prominent place in the Latin American essay are his mastery of a distinctive variation of the Spanish and Latin American newspaper column ("Arciniegas' column style," as it is known) and his talent for direct, interesting, and revealing commentary on history. "Elegant," "lucid," and "entertaining" are some of the standard descriptions bestowed by his critics. In both variations of his literary craft (Arciniegas is a writer rather than an informative journalist or bestselling popularizer of history), Latin America – and its relationship with the United States, Spain, and Europe – is the focus of his writings. In the case of the U.S., his essays reveal the uncanny perception of a Latin American observer, making Arciniegas a prominent figure on the level of such figures as **Domingo Faustino Sarmiento, José Martí,** and **Rubén Darío.**

For Arciniegas, the mystery of Latin America is a "problem," a temptation, a provocation, and an intellectual challenge. This explains why, in his view, the essay has so often been used to explore the unique features of Latin American culture and the hidden dimensions of its most prominent historical figures, its political and economic factors, and its cultural development. He writes that the essay in Latin America "is not literary entertainment, but an obligatory reflection on the problems that each epoch has imposed upon us. These problems challenge us in more definitive terms than in any other region of the world." Thus, the fitting title of one of his essays is "Nuestra América es un ensayo" (1963; Our America is an essay).

For most of this century readers of the op-ed pages in literally dozens of Latin American newspapers have rarely skipped the articles of the undisputed dean of this journalistic venture. There are crucial explanations for this addiction. When asked by a press syndicate of which he was the founding contributor to provide a clue on how he wrote his columns, Arciniegas said: "I write with the innocent intention of communicating certain personal experiences that give pleasure only to myself, and I invite others to partake in this pleasure . . . the problem is that I am interested in things lacking importance . . . I have a sort of inclination for subjects which are dead for most of the people, but they are alive for me" ("Asuntos vivos y asuntos muertos" [1979; Live topics and dead topics]). Arciniegas converts insignificant non-news events or trends into relevant features fit for columns. Circumventing the passage of time, his newspaper contributions can still be read as literature. It is not surprising that a collection of his best columns was edited and enriched with grammatical exercises as a textbook for learning Spanish in U.S. universities because of the clarity of his language, the currency of the subjects, and (most difficult) their attractiveness to young readers belonging to another cultural tradition. Anything might find itself the subject of an Arciniegas column: a black-out in New York, the multiple dimensions of U.S.-Latin American relations, Midwest towns, Christmas in New Jersey, Cuban verbosity, the problems of youth, local conferences and groups, and the lesser-known aspects of literary and political figures, as well as hidden corners of the cities he has visited. His limitless cadre of topics is a characteristic shared with other contributors to Latin American and Spanish newspapers, in contrast to the more specialized U.S. syndicated pundits.

The unique personal form of his columns combines the most outstanding features of both the traditional journalistic *crónica* and the modern *columna* in Spanish. Early on Arciniegas understood that newspaper readers do not have the time to discover the hidden message of a column cloaked in convoluted language. Readers are first hooked by a catchy title summoned from his cultural background, a technique Arciniegas uses in the titles of some of his books, such as *En el país de los rascacielos y las zanahorias* (1945; In the land

of skyscrapers and carrots) or *El continente de siete colores* (1965; The seven-colored continent). Then, instead of offering a summary of the facts as in an information story, Arciniegas complies with the aesthetics of the *crónica* and gives the reader an opening paragraph full of paradoxes, contradictions, exaggerations, and "news" in personal experiences or in history. From this intriguing beginning, the reader is obliged to follow Arciniegas' argument until he offers a convincing and usually unforgettable ending which is, in reality, a return to the main point or salient aspect of the piece. Adhering to one of the most important tenets of modern journalism, Arciniegas never overwhelms his readers with unnecessary proof of scholarship or signs of empty erudition. On the other hand, he never insults their intelligence and culture with obvious, elementary facts or interpretations. "Keep the reader in mind" is an American journalism motto which has been mastered best in Latin America by Arciniegas. It is not surprising that his best-known books consist of carefully crafted structures of short columns and essays, each paragraph revealing his distinctive, personal, and humanizing style.

Over the course of his career, Arciniegas has worn many hats – as lawyer and diplomat, minister of education and university professor, newspaper editor and novelist, and member of the Colombian academies of language and history. He has managed at all times through his writings to contribute to the open-ended search to explain Latin American culture with humility, clarity, and good humor.

JOAQUÍN ROY

Biography

Born 6 December 1900 in Bogotá. Studied at the National University, Bogotá, law degree, 1924; delegate to the first National Student Conference; founder and editor, *La Voz de la Juventud* (The voice of youth) magazine, 1919–20; helped to unionize students in Colombia. Professor of sociology, National University, Bogotá, 1925–28. Founder and editor, *Universidad*, 1925–29; founder, Ediciones Colombia publishers, 1926. Married Gabriela Vieira, 1926: two daughters. Editor, 1928–30, London correspondent, 1930–33, and editor-in-chief, 1933–39, *El Tiempo* (The times) newspaper. Vice consul, London, 1930. Member of the Colombian Parliament, 1933–34, 1939–40, and 1957–58, and minister of education, 1941–42 and 1945–46. Chargé d'affaires, Buenos Aires, 1939–41. Director, *Revista de las Indias* (Review of the Indies), 1939–44; codirector, *Revista de America* (American magazine), 1945–57. Taught at Columbia University, New York, 1947–59. Ambassador to Italy, 1959–62, Israel, 1960–62, Venezuela, 1967–70, and the Vatican City, 1976–78. Director, *Cuadernos* (Notebooks), Paris, 1963–65, and *Correo de los Andes* (Courier of the Andes), 1978–79. Dean of Faculty of Philosophy and Letters, University of the Andes, Bogotá, 1979–81. Awards: Dag Hammarsjkold Prize, 1967; honorary degrees from two academic institutions.

Selected Writings

Essays and Related Prose
La universidad colombiana, 1932
El estudiante de la mesa redonda, 1932
Diario de un peatón, 1936
América, tierra firma: Sociología, 1937
¿Qué haremos con la historia?, 1940
Los alemanes en la conquista de América, 1941
Este pueblo de América, 1945

Biografía del Caribe, 1945
En el país de los rascacielos y las zanahorias, 2 vols., 1945
En medio del camino de la vida, 1949
Entre la libertad y el miedo, 1952; as *The State of Latin America*, translated by Harriet de Onís, 1952
América mágica, 2 vols., 1959–61
El continente de siete colores, 1965; condensed version, as *Latinoamérica: El continente de siete colores*, 1967; as *Latin America: A Cultural History*, translated by Joan MacLean, 1966
Medio mundo entre un zapato: De Lumumba en el Congo a las brujas en Suecia (travel writing), 1969
Nuevo diario de Noé, 1969
Nueva imagen del Caribe, 1970
Transparencias de Colombia, 1973
América en Europa, 1975; as *America in Europe: A History of the New World in Reverse*, translated by Gabriela Arciniegas and R. Victoria Araña, 1986
El revés de la historia, 1980
Con América nace la nueva historia, edited by Juan Gustavo Cobo Borda, 1990
América es otra cosa, edited by Juan Gustavo Cobo Borda, 1992
América Ladina, edited by Juan Gustavo Cobo Borda, 1993
El mundo cambio en América, edited by Juan Gustavo Cobo Borda, 1993
Cuadernos de un estudiante americano, edited by Juan Gustavo Cobo Borda, 1994

Other writings: works on Latin American history, biographies of Jiménez de Quesada (1942), Amerigo Vespucci (1955), and Simonetta Cattaneo (1962), a travel guide to Israel, and a memoir of student days (1932). Also edited *The Green Continent* (1944), a collection of essays on Latin America.

Bibliography

Cobo Borda, Juan Gustavo, "Germán Arciniegas: 90 años escribiendo un intento de bibliografía," in *Imágenes de América en Alfonso Reyes y en Germán Arciniegas* by James Willis Robb, Bogotá: National University, 1990

Further Reading

Cobo Borda, Juan Gustavo, *Arciniegas de cuerpo entero*, Bogotá: Planeta, 1987
Cobo Borda, Juan Gustavo, editor, *Una visión de América: La obra de Germán Arciniegas desde la perspectiva de sus contemporáneos*, Bogotá: Instituto Caro y Cuervo, 1990
Córdova y Quesada, Federico, *Vida y obras de Germán Arciniegas*, Havana: Publications of the Ministry of Education, 1950
González Blanco, Pedro, *Adversus Arciniegas: Crítica violenta*, Mexico City: Rex, 1946
Robb, James Willis, *Imágenes de América en Alfonso Reyes y en Germán Arciniegas*, Bogotá: National University, 1990

Arendt, Hannah

German/American, 1906–1975

Hannah Arendt's chief mode of expression was the essay. Several of her books consist of essays she wrote and later assembled and published in book form or added to another work. She preferred the essay genre, because its dialogic form and flexible nature suited her dialectical method of argumentation. Greatly influenced by the German philosophers **Martin Heidegger** and Karl Jaspers, both of whom she studied under, Arendt was introduced to German *Existenz* philosophy combined with Søren Kierkegaard's angst and existential themes such as man's solitude and meaningless existence. Moreover, as a German Jew she was influenced by the question "Die Frage nach dem Sinn von Sein" (to question what it means to be) and by Heidegger's "being-question." Throughout her life she explored concepts such as the meaning of existence and the nature of being.

Arendt's first work, the dissertation *Der Liebesbegriff bei Augustin* (1929; *Love and St. Augustine*), consumed her for many years. Arendt was obsessed with the concepts of love and goodness, and all of her later topics – political morality, the human condition, evil and totalitarianism, Christian love, and God's love – were related to the ideas she explored in her dissertation. In *The Human Condition* (1958) she wrote: "Love, although it is one of the rarest occurrences in human lives, possesses an unequaled clarity for the disclosure of WHO, precisely because it is unconcerned to the point of total unworldliness with what the loved person may be, with his qualities and shortcomings no less than with his achievements, failings and transgressions … Love, by its very nature, is unworldly, and it is for this reason that it is not only apolitical but anti-political, perhaps the most powerful of all anti-political human forces."

For Arendt's mentor Heidegger, the question of being, the relationship between subject and object, and the problem of truth and rational language signaled the end of traditional philosophy. The pre-Socratic philosophers were already occupied with the question of being and the "unhiddenness" (*Unverborgenbeit*) of being, a question which proves impossible to understand by rational philosophy. Heidegger thought philosophy's most important task was how to bring being into the "openness" of its essence. Man must clear the "dark forest," as was claimed by Giambattista Vico, whose work provided the framework for the humanist controversy raging at the time. From this controversy emerged Heidegger's assertion that philosophy has come to an end as metaphysics. Arendt preferred to sidestep this issue, concentrating instead on human action, judgment, and affirmation of man's ontological world and the need for justification of our reality and our connectedness to the world and ourselves. Her philosophical and personal quest, both as a human and as a Jew, was to view the world we live in as more secure and less alien. For Arendt, life is fleeting and precarious, based ontologically on appearance; only judgment allows the historian or philosopher to bestow meaning on our past, our memory, our historical narratives, and our worldliness.

Originally a student of philosophy, Arendt became involved in political theory with the rise of Nazism. Only later did she find her way through political thought back to philosophy. The tension between philosophy and politics represented for her a major impasse; she claimed that the activity of thinking can make philosophers unwilling to go along with political action and inclined to favor tyranny. Historically, she explained, this discord had not always been present. In the days of the Greek *polis* (city-state), for example, speech and thought went hand in hand. Each Greek had a *doxa* (opinion), and there were many different views. All this changed with the death of Socrates. Arendt believed his death produced Plato's opposition to politics, as well as his attempt to replace pluralism with absolute truth, something Socrates never dared.

This historical schism between philosophy and politics became even more acute in Arendt's own life experience. In 1933, when she and other Jews were in danger from Nazism, Heidegger, her mentor and intimate companion of many years, proclaimed his affiliation with the Nazis. This eye-opening experience taught her that indeed there may be a link between philosophy and tyranny. In a 1946 essay on German *Existenz* philosophy, she blasted Heidegger's views and compared him to Karl Jaspers, who always opposed Nazism and behaved more responsibly politically, and in her judgment was a better philosopher; with him there was no impasse between philosophy and politics, or between thought and action. Yet, despite the high esteem she held for Jaspers, she chose to disregard his advice to pay attention to **Max Weber**, who envisaged violence as at the core of all politics. Nevertheless, Arendt came close to Weber's assertions in her work on tyranny and totalitarianism. She did not call for imitation of Christian goodness as a response to totalitarianism, but insisted on the need for and responsibility of every citizen to keep the world free of tyranny. In the paper "Collective Responsibility" (wr. 1968) she wrote: "In the center of moral considerations of human conduct stands the self; in the center of political considerations of conduct stands the world. If we strip moral imperatives of their religious connotations and origins we are left with the Socratic proposition: it is better to suffer wrong than to do wrong ... The political answer to the Socratic proposition would be: what is important in the world is that there be no wrong ... never mind who suffers it; your duty is to prevent it."

For Arendt what was unprecedented in totalitarianism was the event of totalitarian domination itself and its relation to racism and racist theories. In *The Origins of Totalitarianism* (1951), a study of Nazism and Stalinism whose publication linked her name with controversy and made her both famous and infamous, Arendt reiterated that totalitarianism is a new, unprecedented, and terrible phenomenon. It is not simply a form of tyranny, or a special form of cruelty: what is at stake, she believed, is human nature. She wrote of totalitarianism's attempt to "change human nature," not by making something new and good but, much more sinister, by trying "to rob a human being of his nature under the pretext of changing it"; in that way her characterization of totalitarianism is "absolute" and "radical evil." She cited as an example the extermination camps as "laboratories in which the fundamental belief of totalitarianism that everything is possible is verified," by a process in which men became subhuman, deprived of human freedom or moral responsibility, reduced to "ghastly marionettes with human faces who march docilely to death." Arendt claimed that what was truly sinister was the attempt to turn human beings into "specimens of human beast" by stripping men of any human action. Totalitarian regimes are absolute evil, for they destroy all forms of humanity for the sake of total tyranny and domination of members of the herd. Thus, she wrote to Karl Jaspers, men become "superfluous" as human beings. Moreover, the quest for human omnipotence dictates no human plurality. If man is to be omnipotent, human beings as individuals must disappear. The core idea of totalitarianism is the attempt to maintain total tyranny and prove that "everything is possible" by eliminating human plurality, moral decision making, and freedoms of all kinds to fit a predictable ideology. Tyranny and totalitarianism create a drive for expansion of power, "expansion for expansion's sake," as a self-propelled momentum to which everything else is sacrificed; this was manifested in Nazism, with global conquest on the one hand and "total domination" in the camps on the other.

Arendt believed the impetus for this deadly drive began with Western imperialism, particularly with the "scramble for Africa" in the 1880s. Although of economic origin, based on capitalism, the danger developed when a new kind of politics of cut-throat competition and global expansion emerged. Arendt maintained that racism was part of the ideology of imperialism, providing a comfortable excuse for the exploitation of natives removed from their dominated lands. Arendt feared, and wrote in *The Origins of Totalitarianism*, that although Nazism was finally defeated, racism would continue to be a problem.

Even more than 20 years since her death, Hannah Arendt continues to echo a contemporary voice, carrying humanistic and universal consciousness. Her work is gaining new interest and popularity possibly because of her fears, premonitions, and timely warnings.

DALIA DANIEL

Biography

Born 14 October 1906 in Hannover, Germany. Studied at Königsberg University, B.A., 1924; University of Marburg; University of Freiburg; University of Heidelberg, studying under Martin Heidegger and Karl Jaspers, from 1926, Ph.D., 1928. Married Günther Stern, 1929 (divorced, 1937). Worked for the Youth Aliyah, Paris, 1934–40. Married Heinrich Blücher, 1940. Emigrated to the United States, 1941, becoming a U.S. citizen, 1950. Research director, Conference on Jewish Relations, New York, 1944–46; chief editor, Schocken Books, New York, 1946–48; executive director, Jewish Cultural Reconstruction, New York, 1949–52. Professor at the University of Chicago, 1963–67, and the New School for Social Research, New York, 1967–75; also visiting professor at various American universities and colleges, 1955–60. Awards: many, including the National Institute of Arts and Letters Award, 1954; Lessing Prize, 1959; Freud Prize, 1967; Sonning Prize, 1975; honorary degrees from eight universities. Died in New York, 4 December 1975.

Selected Writings

Essays and Related Prose

Sechs Essays, 1948
The Origins of Totalitarianism, 1951; as *The Burden of Our Time*, 1951; enlarged edition, 1958
The Human Condition, 1958
Between Past and Future: Six Exercises in Political Thought, 1961; enlarged edition, as *Between Past and Future: Eight Exercises in Political Thought*, 1968
Eichmann in Jerusalem: A Report on the Banality of Evil, 1963; revised, enlarged edition, 1964
On Revolution, 1963
Men in Dark Times, 1968
On Violence, 1970
Die verborgene Tradition: Acht Essays, 1976
The Life of the Mind, 2 vols., 1978
Lectures on Kant's Political Philosophy, edited by Ronald Beiner, 1982
Essays in Understanding, 1930–1954, edited by Jerome Kohn, 1994

Other writings: works on political philosophy, Zionism, and other Jewish issues, and correspondence.

Further Reading

Arendt, Hannah, and Mary McCarthy, *Between Friends: The Correspondence of Hannah Arendt and Mary McCarthy, 1949–1975*, New York: Harcourt Brace Jovanovich, 1995

Bradshaw, Leah, *Acting and Thinking: The Political Thought of Hannah Arendt*, Toronto: University of Toronto Press, 1989

Canovan, Margaret, *Hannah Arendt: A Reinterpretation of Her Political Thought*, Cambridge and New York: Cambridge University Press, 1992

Disch, Lisa Jane, *Hannah Arendt and the Limits of Philosophy*, Ithaca, New York: Cornell University Press, 1994

Ettinger, Elzbieta, *Hannah Arendt/Martin Heidegger*, New Haven, Connecticut: Yale University Press, 1995

Isaac, Jeffrey C., *Arendt, Camus, and Modern Rebellion*, New Haven, Connecticut: Yale University Press, 1992

Kateb, George, *Hannah Arendt*, Totowa, New Jersey: Rowman and Allanheld, and Oxford: Robertson, 1984

May, Derwent, *Hannah Arendt*, Harmondsworth and New York: Penguin, 1986

Young-Bruehl, Elizabeth, *For Love of the World: A Biography of Hannah Arendt*, New Haven, Connecticut: Yale University Press, 1982

Areopagitica

by John Milton, 1644

Areopagitica reiterates the title of an oration delivered to the Athenian assembly by Isocrates (436–338 BCE). The Greek patriot and teacher of rhetoric, who rarely spoke publicly himself, pleaded for the reinstitution of the ancient court of the Areopagus, named for Ares, god of war, and essentially a council of nobles. But John Milton (1608–74) would also expect his readers to have in mind St. Paul's address to the Council of the Areopagus (in Acts 17.22–23). There the God of Christianity is proclaimed as the true object of the pagan altar to an unknown god.

Milton's **tract**, published rather than delivered, Ciceronian in style and redolent with the cadences of spoken English, is a plea to the English Parliament for the withdrawal of a new order for the licensing of book publication. Parliamentary reforms in the early 1640s had abolished Archbishop Laud's elaborate and repressive licensing measures and the courts of the Star Chamber and the High Commission that enforced them. Now Milton saw the new licensing measure, brought in as Presbyterian discipline and authority prevailed in Parliament over Congregational, as dangerously retrograde. Milton's target was not accountability for the printed word (in which he staunchly believed), let alone for obscene or pornographic materials, but front-end censorship of religious ideas, his own *Doctrine and Discipline of Divorce* (August 1643) being an egregious target of the new measures. (His vision was not, however, wide enough to include toleration of Catholic writing, which he regarded as radically destructive of true religion and of the state itself.)

Areopagitica follows closely much of the standard rhetorical prescription for classical oration (narration, proposition, proof, etc.). It also runs through a considerable range of tones of address, first assuming the rationality, honor, and goodwill of its parliamentary audience, and pleading for sober attention to "the voice of reason." Then it turns blisteringly polemical and, at the same time, staunchly patriotic in its mocking attack on censorship as Italianate and Catholic, reminiscent of Inquisition, inappropriate to a "nation not slow and dull, but of a quick, ingenious, and piercing spirit . . . not beneath the reach of the highest that human capacity can soar to." Pragmatism raises the problem of the censor, beleaguered by tedium and contamination. Idealistically the concept of the life of the reading intellect as a moral purifying by trial finds context in the spirit of Milton's "reforming of reformation itself." It also waxes heroic, celebrating the purifying effects of moral trial: "I cannot praise a fugitive and cloistered virtue, unexercised and unbreathed, that never sallies out and seeks her adversary, but slinks out of the race where that immortal garland is to be run for not without dust and heat." Quintessentially protestant, it privileges individual conscience, without which a man may be a "heretic in truth": "There is not any burden that some would gladlier post off to another than the charge and care of their religion."

Areopagitica, like almost everything Milton wrote, situates its concerns mythologically within the cycle of fall and recuperation, which Milton characteristically reconstructs as the vitiation and reclamation of God's creation. The writing of books thus becomes a kind of reiteration of the creative act, and censorship thus mindlessly counters creation and Creator alike: "who kills a man kills a reasonable creature, God's image; but he who destroys a good book, kills reason itself, kills the image of God, as it were, in the eye." Milton's fall of man is quintessentially a fall of reason, Adam's and Eve's fall being an act of disobedience to God that is also constructed as an act of allowing their reason to be clouded by their appetites. *Areopagitica* construes man as morally adequate in a world unprotected by "a perpetual childhood of prescription" by virtue of the continuity of man's prelapsarian freedom of choice. "For reason is but choosing," Milton proclaims, in phrasing that in the later *Paradise Lost* (1667; 3.108) becomes God's defense of Adam's sufficiency, since "Reason also is choice."

Areopagitica's power as an essay depends in large measure on its projection from more primal bodies of mythology drawn by Milton from the classics. Thus the fall is seen to reiterate an *ananagnorisis* (recognition) in which Truth, like Osiris, is torn apart, and the reclamation of man's original state comprehends the obligation "to unite those severed pieces which are yet wanting to the body of Truth." Elsewhere man's restoration becomes a mythic reawakening in which the fall vanishes into nothingness like a nightmare past: "Methinks I see a noble and puissant nation rousing herself like a strong man after sleep, and shaking her invincible locks." (Blake's conception of his audience as Albion, the giant sleeping form of the English nation, needful of a similar rousing from a state of mental and moral torpor, is obviously in Milton's debt.) Similarly, Milton's "eagle muing her mighty youth, and kindling her undazzled eyes at the full midday beam" constructs his vision on the folklore eagle that can gaze unblinkered at the sun and also on **Plato**'s account of man's emergence from the cave (*Republic*, Book 7). Also reiterated here is the primal myth of a cosmos snatched from darkness that informs the Genesis creation account, reconstructed by Milton into an analogy of man's mental state in which "those also that love the twilight" are condemned to a state of intentional self-damnation. And finally there is the appropriating of the Gospel's reiteration of a primal myth of salvation as a harvest for which "the fields are white already."

RICHARD SCHELL

See also Pamphlet

Editions
Areopagitica, 1644; many subsequent editions, including in Milton's *Complete Poems and Major Prose*, edited by Merritt Y. Hughes, 1957, *Complete Prose Works*, vol. 2, edited by Ernest Sirluck, 1959, and *Selected Prose*, edited by C. A. Patrides, 1974

Further Reading
Achinstein, Sharon, *Milton and the Revolutionary Reader*, Princeton, New Jersey: Princeton University Press, 1994

Barker, Arthur E., *Milton and the Puritan Dilemma, 1641–1660*, Toronto: University of Toronto Press, 1971 (original edition, 1942)

Corns, Thomas N., *The Development of Milton's Prose Style*, New York: Oxford University Press, 1982

Dowling, Paul M., *Polite Wisdom: Heathen Rhetoric in Milton's "Areopagitica"*, Lanham, Maryland: Rowman and Littlefield, 1995

Haller, William, *Liberty and Reformation in the Puritan Revolution*, New York: Columbia University Press, 1963 (original edition, 1955)

Hunter, G. K., "The Structure of Milton's *Areopagitica*," *English Studies* 39 (1958): 117–19

Kendrick, Christopher, *Milton: A Study in Ideology and Form*, New York: Methuen, 1986

Parker, William Riley, *Milton: A Biography*, Oxford: Clarendon Press, 2 vols., 1968; revised edition, 1996

Stavely, Keith W., *The Politics of Milton's Prose Style*, New Haven, Connecticut: Yale University Press, 1975

Wolfe, Don M., *Milton in the Puritan Revolution*, New York: Humanities Press, and London: Cohen and West, 1963 (original edition, 1941)

Arnold, Matthew
British, 1822–1888

Matthew Arnold's poetic works would be sufficient to establish him as one of the important figures of English literature. Poems such as "Dover Beach," "Thyrsis," and "The Scholar Gypsy" fuse, as Arnold himself says in a letter to his mother, some of Tennyson's "poetical sense" and "Browning's intellectual vigor." However, by the late 1850s he had written most of his poems, and for the next three decades until the end of his life devoted himself single-mindedly to the essay. In the 1860s he wrote numerous essays of literary and social criticism; in the 1870s he concentrated on religious and pedagogical writings; and in the 1880s he returned to the essay of literary criticism. Arnold's poetic decade could be considered a preparation, a period of intellectual gestation. During this time he first considered the questions he later sought to resolve in his essays, an opus of such magnitude (*The Complete Prose*

Works edited by R. H. Super comes to 11 volumes) that had Arnold not written a single poem he would still occupy an important place in the pantheon of Victorian sages. His movement between the two worlds of poetry and nonfiction prose is, nevertheless, to be understood in an organic sense: the poetry and the prose are part of the coherent growth of Arnold's mind.

Confronted with the advance of modern science, the decline of religion, the impact of industrialization and mechanization on labor and the worker, and the rise of intellectual skepticism, Arnold seeks in his essays ways to answer the age-old question of how a good life is to be lived in the rapidly changing modern world. While treating issues as diverse as literature, science, education, religion, the Bible, and culture in general, Arnold's aim remains constant: to guide and inspire modern man, both ethically and intellectually. His major essays retain a moral force that often surprises the serious reader today.

Although Arnold's intended audience was the ordinary man and woman, particularly those belonging to that middle class which his long experience as school inspector taught him to regard as narrow and lacking in authentic culture (but still educable), the essays were primarily read by the agents of cultural change, those he calls "the men of culture" and "the true apostles of equality" (*Culture and Anarchy*, 1869). Arnold hoped that the men of culture would transform the masses, bringing out in them what he calls in *Culture and Anarchy* the "best self." He therefore used the extended **philosophical essay** rather than more popular essay forms, such as the polemical pamphlet or the **familiar essay**, to reach those catalysts of social and intellectual change.

Arnold excels in the formal essay, using its impersonal, analytical approach even when engaging in polemics, as we can see in the tightly reasoned reply to **T. H. Huxley**, defending humanistic learning in "Literature and Science" (1885). But he also experiments with the humorous, **satiric essay**, as witness the dramatic letters of Baron Arminius von Thunder-ten-Tronckh, later collected as *Friendship's Garland* (1871). In any case, with Arnold we are always in the presence of the teacher and lecturer rather than the religious or political zealot or the utilitarian popularizer of ideas. Many of the individual essays, although later collected in various volumes, were first delivered as lectures or appeared in various Victorian periodicals, which served at the time as a forum for lively debate and exposition of ideas. His intellectual and academic conception of the essay – befitting a school inspector and an Oxford Professor of Poetry – influences not only the type of essay Arnold writes but also his prose style.

Arnold's style has many salient virtues, but also some flaws. His critics point to a certain syntactical stiffness, a stilted quality that deadens for some the very real vigor of his ideas. His defenders counter that what those critics are really objecting to are the requirements of austere detachment or objectivity inherent in the formal essay. Less debatable as faults in his prose are Arnold's tendency to repeat himself at times (probably a by-product of his didactic intent and professorial habit of mind) and to leave key concepts, such as the "best self" and "culture," somewhat vaguely defined. Arnold is, however, a strict logician, and his respect for the exigencies of reason results in essays which are lucid, tightly argued, and convincing. They would have pleased classical rhetoricians like Aristotle.

Just as pleasing to a rhetorician is his sense of the essay's structure. Typically, the shorter Arnold essay has an engaging *exordium* or introduction, an ample expository section (containing both a refutation of opposing views and a defense of the thesis), and a clipped, rhetorically effective *peroratio* or conclusion. A good example of this classical structure can be found in "Literature and Science." His more expansive essays retain the structural coherence of the shorter pieces even though they present what Arnold in reference to his poetry called "the main movement of mind of the last quarter of a century," indeed a great panorama of some of the most important ideas debated in England and other parts of the Western world throughout the 19th century.

In the first two volumes of *Essays in Criticism* (1865, 1888), Arnold mainly evaluates through the works of authors from different periods and nations – Homer, Spinoza, Milton, Wordsworth, and **Tolstoi**, among others – the virtues of good literature: primarily an unadorned, plain style and seriousness or elevation of ideas. In these **critical essays**, which include the well-known "The Function of Criticism at the Present Time" and "The Study of Poetry," Arnold mainly considers literature as a civilizing, ethical force. It is, therefore, not surprising that there is a connection between his literary and his social criticism. The most important of the latter is perhaps *Culture and Anarchy*, where Arnold posits that the "priests of culture" can deliver modern men and women from their idolatrous submission to the god of industrial materialism and help restore them to a condition of social and personal wholeness. In this work we encounter Arnold's famous notion of culture, derived mainly from **Johann Gottfried Herder**, which essentially entails an openness of mind that rejects the embracing of ideas because of tradition or convention.

On the Study of Celtic Literature (1867) is another example of Arnold's combination of literary, political, ethnic, and racial criticism. It remains a delightful apologia for Irish and Welsh poetry, and his argument influenced the eventual establishment of a chair of Celtic studies at Oxford. *Irish Essays and Others* (1882), which includes "The Future of Liberalism" as well as prefaces to various editions of his poetry, contains essays on both literary and social topics and is an eclectic volume much like the earlier *Mixed Essays* (1879).

The religious essays are an important part of Arnold's work and in a sense can be considered an extension of his literary and social criticism. They also provide the reader with a vivid sense of Arnold as a moderately liberal Victorian representative of that brand of modern skepticism which remains sympathetic to what it disbelieves. *Literature and Dogma* (1873) and *God and the Bible* (1875) expound his theological relativism and propose an ethical system as a substitute for traditional religion's doctrinal strictures. Still, for Arnold the Bible and the Church remain important civilizing forces. *St. Paul and Protestantism* (1870) contains incisive analyses of the Church of England; *A Bible Reading for Schools* (1871), edited by Arnold, is basically a catechetical instruction for school children based on the prophecies of the Old Testament and the parables and stories of the New. Although skeptical of the supernatural teachings of Christianity, Arnold nevertheless remained convinced that the Bible and the Church, and even ritualistic worship, are powerful sources of culture.

Arnold's vitality as a major English essayist has not diminished today. He embodies the classical traits of the great writers of expository prose: a humble but firm conviction that the humanist tradition he proposes can enrich both the individual person and society; a breadth of interests that encompasses many disciplines and intellectual traditions; a strong sense of responsibility toward the exigencies of the rational process; a respectful open-mindedness toward the past and the present; and an intellectual curiosity that best illustrates the Arnoldian concept of culture. Whether as a critic of literature, religion, the Bible, or society, in Matthew Arnold we meet that rare individual – the humanist who earnestly and honestly seeks, as does the reticent pilgrim of "Stanzas from the Grande Chartreuse," "the high, wide star of Truth" wherever it may be found. It was natural, then, that the expansive and accommodating scope of the essay should recommend it as the ideal literary vehicle for his quest, and that Arnold should have been for the greater part of his career a tireless and prolific essayist.

ROBERT CARBALLO

Biography

Born 24 December 1822 in Laleham-on-Thames, Middlesex. Studied at Winchester College, Hampshire, 1836–37; Rugby School, Warwickshire, 1837–41; Balliol College, Oxford, 1841–44, graduated, 1844. Fellow, Oriel College, Oxford, 1845–46; assistant master, Rugby School, 1846; private secretary to Lord Lansdowne (lord president of the Privy Council), 1847–51. Married Frances Lucy Wightman, 1851: four sons and two daughters. Inspector of schools, 1851–86: sent several times to the continent to study education systems. Professor of Poetry, Oxford University, 1857–67. Contributor to many journals, including the *National Review*, *Fraser's Magazine*, *Cornhill Magazine*, *Macmillan's Magazine*, *Pall Mall Gazette*, *Victoria Magazine*, *Nineteenth Century*, and the *Fortnightly Review*. Died in Liverpool, 15 April 1888.

Selected Writings

Essays and Related Prose
On Translating Homer (lectures), 1861; edited by W. H. D. Rouse, 1905
Essays in Criticism, 3 vols., 1865–1910; vol. 1 edited by Sister Thomas Marion Hoctor, 1964
On the Study of Celtic Literature, 1867
Culture and Anarchy: An Essay in Political and Social Criticism, 1869; edited by J. Dover Wilson, 1932, Ian Gregor, 1971, and Samuel Lipman, 1994
St. Paul and Protestantism, 1870
Friendship's Garland, Being the Conversations, Letters, and Opinions of the Late Arminius, Baron von Thunder-ten-Tronckh, 1871
Literature and Dogma: An Essay Towards a Better Apprehension of the Bible, 1873; edited by James C. Livingston, 1970
God and the Bible: A Review of Objections to "Literature and Dogma", 1875
Last Essays on Church and Religion, 1877
Mixed Essays, 1879
Irish Essays and Others, 1882
Discourses in America, 1885
Arnold as Dramatic Critic, 1903; as *Letters of an Old Playgoer*, 1919
Selections from the Prose Works, edited by William Savage Johnson, 1913
Selections from the Prose Writings, edited by Lewis E. Gates, 1926
Five Uncollected Essays, edited by Kenneth Allott, 1953

The Portable Matthew Arnold, edited by Lionel Trilling, 1959; as
  The Essential Matthew Arnold, 1969
Essays, Letters, and Reviews, edited by Fraser Neiman, 1960
The Complete Prose Works, edited by R. H. Super, 11 vols.,
  1960–77
Essays, Letters and Reviews, edited by Fraser Neiman, 1960
Selected Essays, edited by Noel Annan, 1964
Selected Prose, edited by P. J. Keating, 1970
Selected Poems and Prose, edited by Miriam Allott, 1978
Culture and Anarchy and Other Writings, edited by Stefan Collini,
  1993

Other writings: many collections of poetry, a play, volumes of
correspondence, and reports on elementary education, particularly
on the continent.

Collected works edition: *The Works of Matthew Arnold*, 15 vols.,
1904, reprinted 1970.

Bibliographies

Magoon, Joseph, *A Bibliography of the Editions of, and Writings
  About, Matthew Arnold's Works from 1971 to 1985*,
  Bournemouth: privately printed, 1988
Smart, Thomas B., *The Bibliography of Matthew Arnold*, London:
  Davy, 1892
Tollers, Vincent L., editor, *A Bibliography of Matthew Arnold,
  1932–1970*, University Park: Pennsylvania State University Press,
  1974

Further Reading

Anderson, Warren D., *Matthew Arnold and the Classical Tradition*,
  Ann Arbor: University of Michigan Press, 1965
Brown, E. K., *Studies in the Text of Matthew Arnold's Prose
  Works*, New York: Russell and Russell, 1969 (original edition,
  1935)
Carroll, Joseph, *The Cultural Theory of Matthew Arnold*, Berkeley:
  University of California Press, 1982
Chambers, E. K., *Matthew Arnold: A Study*, Oxford: Clarendon
  Press, 1947; New York: Russell and Russell, 1964
Dawson, William Harbutt, *Matthew Arnold and His Relation to the
  Thought of Our Time*, New York: Putnam, 1904
DeLaura, David J., *Hebrew and Hellene in Victorian England:
  Newman, Arnold, and Pater*, Austin: University of Texas Press,
  1969
Eells, John Shepard, Jr., *The Touchstones of Matthew Arnold*, New
  Haven, Connecticut: College and University Press, 1955
Faverty, Frederic E., *Matthew Arnold the Ethnologist*, New York:
  AMS Press, 1968 (original edition, 1951)
Holloway, John, *The Victorian Sage: Studies in Argument*, London:
  Macmillan, 1953; Hamden, Connecticut: Archon, 1962
Honan, Park, *Matthew Arnold: A Life*, New York: McGraw Hill,
  and London: Weidenfeld and Nicolson, 1981
Jump, John D., *Matthew Arnold*, London: Longman, 1955
Lowry, Howard F., *Matthew Arnold and the Modern Spirit*,
  Folcroft, Pennsylvania: Folcroft
1974
McCarthy, Patrick J., *Matthew Arnold and the Three Classes*, New
  York: Columbia University Press, 1964
Miyoshi, Masao, *The Divided Self: A Perspective on the Literature
  of the Victorians*, New York: New York University Press, 1969
Murray, Nicholas, *A Life of Matthew Arnold*, London: Hodder and
  Stoughton, 1996
Robbins, William, *The Arnoldian Principle of Flexibility*, Victoria,
  British Columbia: University of Victoria, 1979
apRoberts, Ruth, *Arnold and God*, Berkeley: University of
  California Press, 1983
Trilling, Lionel, *Matthew Arnold*, New York: Harcourt Brace
  Jovanovich, 1977 (original edition, 1939)

Athenäum

German periodical, 1798–1800

This biannual publication was founded by the brothers
Schlegel primarily as an outlet for their own writings, although
they also printed contributions by others, notably the poet
and novelist **Novalis** and the theologian Friedrich Daniel
Schleiermacher. August Wilhelm Schlegel is now remembered primarily as a translator of Shakespeare and for his
Vorlesungen über dramatische Kunst und Literatur (1808; *A
Course of Lectures on Dramatic Art and Literature*), which,
translated into English and French, spread the doctrine
of "Romantic poetry" throughout Europe. The essays he
contributed to the *Athenäum* can be dealt with briefly. The
first issue of the periodical begins with a long parody and criticism of a dialogue in praise of the German language by the
poet Friedrich Gottlieb Klopstock, which is now at best of
historical interest. His second contribution to the periodical,
"Die Gemälde: Gespräch" (The paintings: dialogue), cowritten
with his wife Caroline, mingles remarks on the theory of art
with descriptions of paintings in the famous art gallery in
Dresden. The speakers being a woman and two men, one of
them an artist, the dialogue form is used to juxtapose different
points of view, male and female, artist and critic. August
Wilhelm Schlegel also displays his talent as an art critic in a
long essay on John Flaxman.

The contributions to the *Athenäum* by **Friedrich Schlegel**
were much more substantial: they laid the foundations of the
German Romantic theory of literature. The bulk of the second
issue of the periodical (Fall 1798) is taken up by a collection
of **aphorism**s ("Fragmente"), mostly by him, but with substantial contributions by his friends; they quickly became famous
for their wit and incisiveness and at the same time notorious
for their extravagant terminology. The same issue of the
Athenäum also contains an essay about the most important
German novel of its time, **Goethe**'s *Wilhelm Meisters Lehrjahre*
(1795–96; *Wilhelm Meister's Apprenticeship*). According to the
neoclassical canon that prevailed throughout Europe at that
time, the novel was an inferior genre, "mere prose." Schlegel
provided a structural analysis of *Wilhelm Meister* which
showed that by an ingenious narrative technique, the use of
contrasts and parallels, foreshadowing, echoes, and similar
devices, Goethe had given his novel a kind of unity in diversity that rivaled that achievable in the classical genres and
raised his work to the status of "poetry in prose." In his own
essay, Schlegel attempted something similar. He held that critics
should not merely provide an objective account of a work of
art, but also communicate to their readers their own emotional
reaction to the work – a task that is, he thought, best performed
by poetry, i.e. by writing "a poem about a poem." In his essay
on *Wilhelm Meister*, he did the next best thing: he wrote it in
elevated, poetic prose – an unusual undertaking at that time
for a critic.

By contrast, the form of Friedrich Schlegel's major essay in
the *Athenäum*, *Gespräch über die Poesie* (1800; *Dialogue on
Poetry*), is quite traditional: it follows the form of **Plato**'s
Symposium, though it does not, like that work, privilege a
single speaker. In Schlegel's essay, six friends – four men and
two women – meet from time to time to talk about literature.

The four men give papers, which are discussed by the whole group. Together with the "Fragmente," these papers and discussions are the earliest, and arguably still the most important formulations of the German theory of Romantic poetry.

The two other essays that Friedrich Schlegel contributed to the *Athenäum*, "Über die Philosophie: An Dorothea" (1799; On philosophy: to Dorothea) and "Über die Unverständlichkeit" (1800; "On Incomprehensibility"), are less important. The first is interesting mainly because of its form: it is a fictitious letter to a real person – his mistress and later wife, the daughter of the philosopher **Moses Mendelssohn**. The second, with which Schlegel rang down the periodical when it folded in Fall 1800, is a brilliant exercise in sustained irony – a welcome reminder of the fact that Friedrich Schlegel played such a central role in the modern history of this elusive term.

It is striking how often the Schlegels used the dialogue form in the *Athenäum*. Assertive and cocksure in their aphorisms and shorter reviews, they reveal in their dialogue essays their conviction that nothing can be more damaging to creativity than holding to a system. The dialogue form as they used it precludes systematization and reminds us of an older meaning of "essay": a tentative approach to a subject. This was, however, not seen by most of their readers. Their virulent attacks on a number of established and beloved writers and poets made them anathema to most of their older contemporaries, though Goethe appreciated and befriended them. Among the younger generation, the Schlegels had an ardent following; but while the young tend to be the most enthusiastic readers, they can rarely afford to be enthusiastic buyers. The *Athenäum* did not sell well enough to be continued past the third volume. Today, it counts as a major source for the study of German Romanticism and as a milestone in the history of literary criticism.

HANS EICHNER

Editions and Selections

Athenäum, edited by August Wilhelm Schlegel and Friedrich Schlegel, 3 vols., 1798-1800, reprinted 1960
Schlegel, Friedrich, in *Kritische Ausgabe*, edited by Ernst Behler and others, 28 vols., 1958-95
Schlegel, Friedrich, *Dialogue on Poetry; Literary Aphorisms*, edited and translated by Ernst Behler and Roman Struc, 1968
Schlegel, Friedrich, *Lucinde and The Fragments* (includes the novel *Lucinde*; "Critical Fragments"; "Athenaeum Fragments"; "Ideas"; "On Incomprehensibility"), translated by Peter Firchow, 1971

Further Reading

Behler, Ernst, "Goethes *Wilhelm Meister* und die Romantheorie der Frühromantik," *Études Germaniques* 44 (1989): 409-28
Behler, Ernst, *German Romantic Literary Theory*, Cambridge: Cambridge University Press, 1993
Behler, Ernst, "Le Dialogue des 'Tableaux' d'August Wilhelm Schlegel et la conception de la peinture dans le premier romantisme," *Revue Germanique Internationale* 2 (1994): 29-37
Eichner, Hans, "Friedrich Schlegel's Theory of Romantic Poetry," *PMLA* 71 (1956): 1018-41
Eichner, Hans, *Friedrich Schlegel*, New York: Twayne, 1970
Eichner, Hans, "Friedrich Schlegel's Theory of Literary Criticism," in *Romanticism Today*, Bonn: Inter Nationes, 1973: 17-26
Hamlin, Cyrus, "Platonic Dialogue and Romantic Irony: Prolegomena of a Theory of Literary Narrative," *Canadian Review of Comparative Literature* (1976): 5-24
Stoljar, Margaret, *Athenäum: A Critical Commentary*, Berne and Frankfurt-on-Main: Lang, 1973
Wellek, René, "Friedrich Schlegel" and "August Wilhelm Schlegel," in his *A History of Modern Criticism 1750-1950*, 2. *The Romantic Age*, Cambridge and New York: Cambridge University Press, 1981: 1-73 (original edition, 1955)

The Atlantic Monthly
American magazine, 1857–

The *Atlantic Monthly* was founded in Boston in 1857 by Francis Underwood (an assistant to the publisher Moses Phillips) and a group of New England writers including **Ralph Waldo Emerson**, **Oliver Wendell Holmes**, James Russell Lowell, and Harriet Beecher Stowe. Underwood had been trying for several years to launch a uniquely American magazine that would publish primarily contributions from American writers – in contrast to other magazines in New York which relied heavily on pirating or importing English authors – and was finally able to get backing because he had the assurance of contributions not only from his founding collaborators but also from other important and popular writers of the time such as Nathaniel Hawthorne, **Henry David Thoreau**, Walt Whitman, and Thomas Wentworth Higginson.

Underwood and his cofounders, all Yankee humanists, had two additional goals. First, they intended the *Atlantic* to be an agent for propagating their own high ethical, aesthetic, and intellectual values; none of them doubted, as Higginson himself explained, that New England "was appointed to guide the nation, to humanize it," and the *Atlantic* was the focal point of this cultural mission. Second, and more specifically, the group wanted "to bring the literary influence of New England to aid the antislavery cause."

Lowell, popular as a poet and widely known for his spirited patriotism, agreed to be the first editor. Under his editorship (1857–61), essays in the *Atlantic* were characteristically literary, using brief observations of contemporary life as springboards for speculations on immutable truths of morality or human nature. During James T. Fields' tenure as editor (1861–71), the magazine tried to increase its popularity, in part by publishing essays which were more journalistic than philosophical, observing and recording the contemporary scene. Their subjects were more topical, their styles more direct and concrete. Fields also solicited travel sketches – especially the ones by Hawthorne which later became *Our Old Home* (1863) – and, knowing that half of his readers were women, he eagerly published several long series of domestic essays. These series, many of their entries written by Stowe under the masculine pseudonym Christopher Crowfield, influenced *Harper's* to initiate a domestic department – an imitation which suggested the two magazines were beginning to compete for readers.

Even with his eye toward a more general reading public, Fields did not deviate from the magazine's original goal of being a forum for the presentation of ideas. In fact, he published, among other essays of intellectual debate and inquiry, both Emerson's essay on Thoreau, Thoreau's own "Life Without Principle," Henry James, Sr.'s four-part investigation of the ethics of marriage, and Louis Agassiz's "Methods of Study of Natural History." Fields merely changed the mixture of the *Atlantic*'s nonfiction prose.

Through the rest of the 19th century and the early part of the 20th, the *Atlantic* struggled to find a balance between its traditional literary essays and more journalistic articles, between highbrow intellectualism and the mass culture which was giving rise to higher-circulation magazines such as the *Century* and *Ladies' Home Journal*. During the editorships of Thomas Bailey Aldrich (1881–90) and Horace Elisha Scudder (1890–98), the magazine clung tightly to what it saw as its intellectual integrity, frequently publishing essays that discussed the major texts and authors of the Western canon. The *Atlantic* was, in fact, one of the last general periodicals to carry extensive commentary on the Greek and Roman classics and to defend the study of these works.

Though later, more progressive editors would decide such essays on the classics explored unpromising subjects for the magazine's audience, the *Atlantic* continued into the 20th century to be widely recognized as a leading exponent of high culture in America. Most of the writers whom editor Ellery Sedgwick (1909–38) chose to voice the magazine's views on culture and literature were women: **Agnes Repplier**, a prolific writer of astringent essays on contemporary manners and morals; Margaret Sherwood and Cornelia Comer, who produced polite essays; and Katherine Gerould, an acute and reactionary Bryn Mawr professor. By 1918, however, as Repplier noted in the *Yale Review*, the **personal essay** of the type the *Atlantic* often published had "withered in the blasts of war." Gerould and other *Atlantic* essayists such as Henry Dwight Sedgwick, longing for the rapidly disappearing Victorian ethics of their childhoods, began to see themselves as futile relics of a dying culture.

Under the editorships of Ellery Sedgwick and Edward Weeks (1938–66), the *Atlantic* also renewed its interest in social and political issues, publishing essays such as Booker T. Washington's "The Case of the Negro," Bertrand Russell's "Individual Liberty and Public Control," and Woodrow Wilson's "The Road Away from Revolution." Throughout most of the 20th century, in fact, the magazine has continued to supplement its in-depth journalistic articles on public policy with long essays on related topics: for example, Albert Einstein's "Atomic War or Peace," George Kennan's "Training for Statesmanship," and Martin Luther King, Jr.'s "The Negro Is Your Brother."

As far back as the 1860s, *Atlantic* editors had been aware that the magazine could be perceived, especially by the publishing industry in New York, as too literary, and hence sought out lighter essays which would serve as relief from the "Emersonian and Whippletonian articles" – and increase circulation. The magazine has consequently long been a major outlet for **humorous essays**. **Mark Twain** was one of the first – and certainly one of the most influential – humorists to write for the *Atlantic*, and there has been a long trail of humorists behind him, especially many who are more closely associated with the *New Yorker*: **James Thurber**, **E. B. White**, Garrison Keillor. In the past 25 years, under the editorships of Robert Manning (1966–80) and William Whitworth (1981–), the magazine has been an outlet for many short, humorous essays, often domestic in nature, which hark back to the genteel tradition preceding

World War I, written by such contributors as Andrew Ward, Ian Frazier, and Roy Blount, Jr.

The *Atlantic*'s devotion to cultural criticism has also led it to be an important voice on environmental issues. Literary essays on nature, in fact, began early, with **John Burroughs'** first piece in 1865, and have continued through **John Muir** and up to recent contributions from writers such as **Annie Dillard** and Gretel Ehrlich.

DAN ROCHE

Anthologies
Jubilee: One Hundred Years of the Atlantic, edited by Edward Weeks and Emily Flint, Boston: Little Brown, 1957
119 Years of the Atlantic, edited by Louise Desaulniers, Boston: Little Brown, 1977; enlarged edition, as *Highlights from 125 Years of the Atlantic*, Boston: Atlantic Monthly Press, 1982

Further Reading
Howe, M. A. De Wolfe, *The Atlantic Monthly and Its Makers*, Boston: Atlantic Monthly Press, 1919
Sedgwick, Ellery, "The American Genteel Tradition in the Early Twentieth Century," *American Studies* 25, no. 1 (1984): 49–67
Sedgwick, Ellery, *The Atlantic Monthly, 1857–1909: Yankee Humanism at High Tide and Ebb*, Amherst: University of Massachusetts Press, 1994

Auden, W. H.

British/American, 1907–1973

W. H. Auden produced an astonishing range of prose works, and his particular and quirky intelligence painted new and challenging portraits of such "major" artists as Shakespeare and **Goethe** as well as "minor" writers such as Walter de la Mare and **G. K. Chesterton**. The distinctions between essay and **review**, criticism and history, philosophy and anthropology, melt in Auden's prose, leaving the reader bewildered by a series of erudite, yet sometimes seriously questionable arguments. The two collections *The Dyer's Hand* (1962) and *Forewords and Afterwords* (1973) contain selections of his later essays, while Edward Mendelson's *The English Auden* (1977) provides a useful cross-section of the vibrant pre-1940 pieces.

In "Psychology and Art To-Day" (1935) Auden suggested that "To a situation of danger and difficulty there are five solutions." It was after rejecting the "solutions" of the idiot, the schizophrenic, the criminal, and the invalid that he accepted the positive and healing fifth solution shared by the scientist and the artist: "To understand the mechanism of the trap." Much of the syncretism and eclecticism that underlie the easy transitions in his prose between various political and religious issues, as well as between disciplines, resulted from his search for synoptic understanding "as the hawk sees it, or the helmeted airman."

Rarely providing an orthodox interpretation of books, events, or artists, Auden thrived on experimental creative error, and the liberties he took with established knowledge – in addition to the half-serious assertion that he "needed the money"

– formed part of the price he asked for writing prose. In the early essays, for example, Auden's treatment of **Freud** and **D. H. Lawrence** demonstrated how he followed the spirit but rarely the letter of their theories, while in "The Good Life" of 1935 he observed, following **T. S. Eliot** and I. A. Richards, that "unless people have substantially the same experience, logical controversy is nothing more than systemised misunderstanding." The scientist in Auden saw through to the structures of knowledge and its transmission, hence his preference for "a critic's notebooks to his treatises."

In "Psychology and Art To-Day," Auden claimed that art consists in telling parables "from which each according to his immediate and peculiar needs may draw his own conclusions." For Auden the parable was a secular story, the "only kind of literature which has gospel authority." Politically charged in the 1930s, the later Auden sometimes used the parable as a means of speaking about Christianity at a distance, as in the 1954 essay "Balaam and his Ass": "To illustrate the use of the master-servant relationship as a parable of agape, I will take two examples . . ." In "The Guilty Vicarage" (1948) Auden found in the detective story a Christian parable of existential guilt. These analogies are typical, and Auden's acknowledgment that "Man is an analogy-drawing animal" applies particularly to himself.

Auden's remark in "The Prolific and the Devourer" (1939) that he found pornographic stories more erotic than physical sexual encounters emphasizes the importance of language and story to Auden's sense of self; this is reflected in his prose when the artist tempers the scientist. The 1938 article "In Praise of Gossip," for example, emphasized the importance of telling a story well, rather than adhering to some notion of veracity which ultimately tames and reduces a narrative to a tedious and factual account. Auden's own tendency toward the anecdote and the **aphorism** fulfilled this demand throughout his work, while his eye for the revealing quotation was often employed in an arch fashion, as when he complained about the lack of privacy in published letters and then reproduced the most personal letters himself. It is not surprising, then, that as an epigraph to *The Dyer's Hand* Auden selected **Nietzsche**'s aphorism, "We have Art in order that we may not perish from Truth."

In the autobiographical poem "Letter to Lord Byron" (1936), Auden tells us that it was his precocious desire to observe the "various types of boys" that shocked the matron at his public school; the amateur but perceptive anthropologist was another of Auden's roles. In a later essay, "Notes on the Comic" (1952), Auden described the abuse hurled between truck drivers and cab drivers on the New York streets as a form of flyting, arguing that the participants were more interested in playing with language than insulting each other.

Auden's homosexuality rarely surfaced in his prose, but he occasionally offered some thoughts on the subject (as in the essay "C. P. Cavafy," 1961). When he did discuss homosexuality it was without guilt, sensation, or prevarication; it was simply a choice of object, the important point being the quality of a relationship rather than its constitution. His obvious enjoyment in discussing the sex life of J. R. Ackerley in the essay "Papa Was a Wise Old Sly-Boots" (1969) is a fine example of Auden's double standard when considering biographical material, complaining that Ackerley never said what he "*really* preferred to do in bed."

Auden's essays combine the confessions of the innocent, the certainty of the dogmatist, the schematizing of the scientist, and the skepticism of the man in the street. These traits occur time and again from the earliest pieces, brash with "youth's intolerant certainty" to the pose of the "booming old bore" of the late prose. Hence while the tone of his later essays emulated the curmudgeonly don rather than the bright young schoolmaster, Auden remained an entertaining teacher, utilizing techniques of defamiliarization alongside a sometimes shocking familiarity. But whether written in the role of parable promoting politician or grand old man of letters bristling with *ex cathedra* statements, Auden's prose acknowledges itself as a limited and partial offering, revealing a writer intensely aware that his voice is one among thousands, and that an air of impropriety or even charlatanism hangs over his words. There remains a deceptive, studied informality in Auden's prose which allowed him to make risky and unsupported judgments through the pose of the homely amateur. His 1956 inaugural lecture as Professor of Poetry at Oxford captures this tone: "I shall now proceed to make some general statements of my own. I hope they are not nonsense, but I cannot be sure."

In the essay "Hic et Ille" (1956), using the mirror as an analogy for the ego, Auden stated that "Every man carries with him through life a mirror, as unique and impossible to get rid of as his shadow." The roles Auden played in his prose constitute a series of ingenious games played with his "mirror," and take on retrospective meaning from his remark that "We shall be judged, not by the kind of mirror found on us, but by the use we have made of it, by our *riposte* to our reflection." Auden's unique blend of storytelling and analysis, his self-conscious manipulation of knowledge, and his ability to discuss the underlying structures of power and identity constitute a *riposte* that at once disarms and disquiets.

PAUL HENDON

Biography
Wystan Hugh Auden. Born 21 February 1907 in York. Studied at Gresham's School, Holt, Norfolk, 1920–25; Christ Church, Oxford, 1925–28, B.A. in English, 1928. Lived in Berlin, 1928–29. Taught privately in London, 1930, at Larchfield Academy, Helensburgh, Scotland, 1930–32, and at Downs School, Colwall, Herefordshire, 1932–35. Married Erika Mann, daughter of the writer **Thomas Mann**, so that she could get a British passport, 1935. Staff member, GPO Film Unit, London, 1935–36. Traveled in Iceland with Louis MacNeice, 1936, and in China with Christopher Isherwood, 1938; gave radio broadcasts for the Republican forces during the Spanish Civil War, 1937. Emigrated to the United States, 1939, and became a U.S. citizen, 1946; lived primarily in New York, though from 1957 spent summers in Kirchstetten, Austria. Taught at various schools and universities in the U.S., 1939–53. Relationship with the writer Chester Kallman, from 1939. Member of the editorial board, *Decision* magazine, 1940–41, and *Delos* magazine, 1968, and editor, Yale Series of Younger Poets, 1947–62. Major with the U.S. Army Strategic Bombing Survey in Germany, 1945. Member, American Academy, 1954. Professor of Poetry, Oxford University, 1956–61. Awards: many, including King's Gold Medal for Poetry, 1937; American Academy Award of Merit Medal, 1945, and Gold Medal, 1968; Pulitzer Prize, 1948; Bollingen Prize, 1954; National Book Award, 1956; Feltrinelli Prize, 1957; Guinness Award, 1959; Poetry Society of America Droutskoy Medal, 1959; Austrian State Prize, 1966; National Medal for Literature, 1967; honorary degrees from seven colleges and universities. Died in Vienna, 29 September 1973.

Selected Writings

Essays and Related Prose
The Dyer's Hand and Other Essays, 1962
Selected Essays, 1964
Forewords and Afterwords, edited by Edward Mendelson, 1973
*The English Auden: Poems, Essays, and Dramatic Writings
1927–1939*, edited by Edward Mendelson, 1977
Essays and Reviews and Travel Books in Prose and Verse, vol. 1:
Prose 1926–1938, edited by Edward Mendelson, 1997

Other writings: many volumes of poetry (collected in *Collected Poems*, edited by Edward Mendelson, 1976), plays with Christopher Isherwood, and several libretti. Also edited many anthologies of poetry; translated works by Goethe and Scandinavian writers.

Collected works edition: *The Complete Works*, edited by Edward Mendelson, 1988– (in progress).

Bibliographies
Bloomfield, B. C., and Edward Mendelson, *W. H. Auden: A Bibliography*, Charlottesville: University of Virginia Press, 1972
Gingerich, Martin E., *W. H. Auden: A Reference Guide*, Boston: Hall, 1977

Further Reading
Bold, Alan, editor, *W. H. Auden: The Far Interior*, London: Vision Press, and Totowa, New Jersey: Barnes and Noble, 1985
Bucknell, Katherine, and Nicholas Jenkins, editors, *W. H. Auden: "The Map of All My Youth": Early Works, Friends and Influences*, Oxford: Clarendon Press, and New York: Oxford University Press, 1990
Carpenter, Humphrey, *W. H. Auden: A Biography*, London: Allen Unwin, and Boston: Houghton Mifflin, 1981
Davenport-Hines, Richard, *Auden*, London: Heinemann, and New York: Pantheon, 1995
Fuller, John, *A Reader's Guide to W. H. Auden*, London: Thames and Hudson, and New York: Farrar Straus, 1970
Haffenden, John, editor, *W. H. Auden: The Critical Heritage*, London and Boston: Routledge and Kegan Paul, 1983
Hecht, Anthony, *The Hidden Law: The Poetry of W. H. Auden*, Cambridge, Massachusetts: Harvard University Press, 1993
Hynes, Samuel, *The Auden Generation: Literature and Politics in England in the 1930s*, London: Bodley Head, 1976; New York: Viking Press, 1977
McDiarmid, Lucy, *Auden's Apologies for Poetry*, Princeton, New Jersey: Princeton University Press, 1990
Mendelson, Edward, *Early Auden*, London: Faber, and New York: Viking, 1981
Smith, Stan, *W. H. Auden*, Oxford and New York: Blackwell, 1985
Spears, Monroe K., *The Poetry of W. H. Auden: The Disenchanted Island*, New York: Oxford University Press, 1963

Australian Essay

Henry Savery (1791–1842), transported to Van Diemen's Land for forgery, is best known as the author of the novel *Quintus Servinton* (1831). It is widely accepted, however, that under the *nom de plume* of "Simon Stukeley" he also wrote a series of 30 sketches of Hobart Town and its inhabitants which, appearing in the *Colonial Times* through 1829, were published in the following year under the title *The Hermit in Van Diemen's Land*. This work makes him the first essayist in Australian literary history.

Following *The Hermit in Van Diemen's Land*, the next significant contribution to the form was *The Australian Sketch Book* (1838), written when its author, James Martin (1820–86), was only 18, and in acknowledged imitation of **Washington Irving**. Thereafter, H. M. Green asserts in his *History of Australian Literature* (1961, revised 1985) that between 1850 and 1890 "the only example of the essayist pure and simple was Richard Birnie." For 18 years from 1870 Birnie (1808–88) was retained to write a regular column for the *Australasian*, the weekly supplement of the Melbourne *Age*. Some of these were published as *Essays: Social, Moral and Political* in 1879. High minded and hortatory, they seem badly dated today.

The prose of other colonial writers, however, retains a livelier appeal. Among them were two short-term visitors from Britain, Richard Rowe (1828–79) and Frank Fowler (1833–63). Rowe's contributions to a range of Sydney newspapers and journals were collected in 1858 as *Peter Possum's Portfolio*. In the following year, and after he had returned to England, Fowler produced *Southern Lights and Shadows*. Like Rowe, he had written for a number of Sydney publications, and had indeed been the founding editor in 1857 of the *Month*.

Between the later 1860s and the early 1880s Australia's most important essayists lived in Melbourne, and wrote for its leading newspapers, the *Argus* and the *Age*. Among the earliest and probably the best was **Marcus Clarke** (1846–81), most widely remembered for his convict novel, *His Natural Life* (1874). Clarke, who had emigrated to Australia in 1863, began writing for newspapers and magazines soon after his arrival. Most notably from 1867 to 1870, and using the *nom de plume* "The Peripatetic Philosopher," he contributed a series of sketches of city life to the *Argus* and the *Australasian*.

Another shrewd and lively recorder of Melbourne's low life was John Stanley James (1843–96), who came to Australia by way of the United States in 1875. From late 1875 to late 1877 he contributed "Notes on Current Events by a Vagabond" to Melbourne *Punch*. In 1876 he began writing for the *Argus* under the same pseudonym. His columns proved so popular that they were collected in 1877 and 1878 as *The Vagabond Papers*. Michael Cannon, his modern editor, described James' normal method as "the straightforward, sympathetic, never sentimentalized description of his experiences and observations . . . a cool unemotional statement of the survival technique of a man who has almost no money and no home of his own." A third writer to chronicle the life of colonial Melbourne through the prose sketch was Edmund Finn (1819–98), who used both "An Old Colonist" and "Garryowen" as his *noms de plume*. The *Garryowen Sketches* (1880) reflect an earlier Melbourne than the observations of either Clarke or James.

By the turn of the 19th into the 20th century, more than 100 years of European experience in Australia had produced a substantial body of literature offering scope for interpretation through the **critical essay**. Individuals like Douglas Sladen (1856–1946), George Burnett Barton (1836–1901), Henry Gyles Turner (1831–1920), and Alexander Sutherland (1852–1902) had all advanced the understanding and knowledge of Australian writing both at home and abroad well before the 1890s. However, it was that decade which saw the emergence of Australia's first major literary essayist. A. G. Stephens (1865–1933) used his editorship of the Sydney *Bulletin*'s Red Page (a full-page literary section) both to encourage native talent and to create a matrix of critical discussion within which the creative writers might develop their skills. Through his own writing as well as through his editorial authority, Stephens made a major contribution to the development of an informed critical environment in Australia; *The Red Pagan* (1904), a collection of some of his *Bulletin* writings, is a landmark volume in the development of the Australian literary-critical essay.

Probably Stephens' most formidable contemporary in the domain of criticism was the poet C. J. Brennan (1870–1932). Around 1900, Brennan wrote a number of substantial critical essays which were included in the edition of his prose works by A. R. Chisholm and J. J. Quinn in 1962.

The decade of the 1890s has acquired legendary status in Australian literary history, a phenomenon partly explained by the appearance of a number of reminiscences by individuals who had participated in the events of those years. Among the most important of these are *Those Were the Days* (1918) by G. A. Taylor (1872–1928), *Knocking Round* (1930) by John le Gay Brereton (1871–1933), and *The Romantic Nineties* (1933) by A. W. Jose (1863–1934).

In the years between the two World Wars there was a steady output of recollections and nostalgia of one kind or another. Bush life in pioneering days, for instance, was a popular subject represented by Mary Fullerton's (1868–1946) *Bark House Days* (1921) and Mary Gilmore's (1865–1962) *Hound of the Road* (1922). Pen sketches of old bush ways merged readily into descriptions of the bush itself, ranging from the observations of amateur nature lovers to the more exact observations of serious natural historians. The various works of R. H. Croll (1869–1947) are toward the amateur end of this spectrum, as are the books of Donald Alister Macdonald (1857–1932), James Edmond (1859–1933), Bernard Cronin (1864–1968), and Charles Barrett (1879–1959). The apogee of the lyrical evocation of Australian nature was reached in *Images in Water* (1947) by Elyne Mitchell (1913–), largely devoted to the alpine regions in the southeastern part of the continent, while probably the most prolific and influential nature writer over many decades was A. H. Chisholm (1890–1977). An intermittent English visitor, Grant Watson (1885–1970), combined scientific inquiry and metaphysical speculation in some highly original essays, some of which were collected by **Dorothy Green** in *Descent of Spirit* (1990).

In the middle 1930s two anthologies of essays marked the success the form by that time had achieved: *Essays: Imaginative and Critical, Chosen from Australian Writers* edited by George Mackaness and J. D. Holmes (1933), and *Australian Essays* edited by George H. Cowling and Furnley Maurice [i.e. Frank Wilmot] (1935). The editors of the latter had this to say, *inter alia*, in their introduction: "The Australian essay is the product of that most potent force in the cultural development of Australia, the newspaper. The magazine and review have not flourished here ... most of our essays have seen the light of day in the columns of newspapers, especially in the Saturday journals, rather than in more ambitious periodicals. The essay began in Australia with the example of **Charles Lamb, William Hazlitt,** and **Leigh Hunt** before it, and it has flourished in their

tradition. Reminiscence, description and discussion are its modes." Their observation was, with only minor qualifications, to prove as accurate in prospect as it was true in retrospect.

One medium for comment at essay length not recognized by Cowling and Maurice was radio, which enjoyed considerable popularity and influence through the 1930s and 1940s. The book reviews of **Vance Palmer** (1885–1959), one of the leading literary figures of the day, reached a wide audience through his weekly broadcasts over the Australian Broadcasting Commission (ABC). Vance's wife **Nettie Palmer** (1885–1964) also occupied an influential position in the literary community; some of her best and most representative work in the essay form appears in *Modern Australian Literature 1900–1923* (1924) and *Talking It Over* (1932).

Undoubtedly, however, the supreme practitioner of the essay in Australia during the first half of the 20th century was **Walter Murdoch** (1874–1970). His prose pieces, which cover an astonishing array of subjects from the most trivial to the most profound, are unmistakably in the tradition of Lamb, Hazlitt, and Hunt. Appearing in the press over more than four decades, they were brought together in a number of volumes of which *Speaking Personally* (1930) and *Selected Essays* (1956) are representative. Murdoch remains a rare figure in the Australian literary landscape – an essayist first, last, and foremost.

Not all the essayists of the 1930s were content to write within purely belletristic conventions. At least three deserve mention for the intellectual weight and polemical passion they brought to their subjects: John Anderson (1893–1962), P. R. Stephensen (1901–65), and Rex Ingamells (1913–55). For many years professor of philosophy at Sydney University, Anderson used the essay form to expound his own version of the liberal tradition as well as to explain and defend the achievement of then new and challenging writers like James Joyce. Some of his essays were brought together under the title *Art and Reality: John Anderson on Literature and Aesthetics* (1982) by Janet Anderson, Graham Cullum, and Kimon Lycos. Stephensen's *The Foundations of Culture in Australia* (1936) was a strongly nationalistic tract which in turn inspired Ingamells, the founder of the Jindyworobak movement, to write (with Ian Tilbrook) *Conditional Culture* in 1938.

At the other end of the spectrum from such high seriousness, the interwar years also had their quota of essayists who looked at life from a comic point of view. Hal Eyre's *Hilarities* (1929) touched its subjects with a light brush. Later and more robust humorists included Lennie Lower (1903–47), Ross Campbell (1910–82), and Bernard Hesling (1905–88). Their tradition is continued by current writers like Barry Oakley (1931–), Morris Gleitzman (1953–), and Wendy Harmer, all of whom have contributed regularly to the metropolitan press.

World War II brought something of a hiatus to the development of the essay in Australia. While established writers like Murdoch and the Palmers maintained their positions of eminence, it was not until the late 1940s and early 1950s that any significant new names began to appear. By then there was at least a handful of serious literary and cultural journals capable of publishing sustained analytical essays on literary, cultural, social, and political matters. The career of A. A. Phillips (1900–85) was thus closely associated with *Meanjin Quarterly*, the best of his critical pieces being collected in 1958 as *The Australian Tradition*, a volume which remains admired today. *For the Uncanny Man* (1963) by Clement Semmler (1914–) has also stood up well to the passage of time.

Phillips and Semmler were both literary critics rather than creative writers. Since 1958, however, some of the most distinguished collections of literary essays have come from poets or novelists. They include *Poetry and Morality* (1959) by **Vincent Buckley** (1925–88), *Because I Was Invited* (1975) by **Judith Wright** (1915–), *The Pack of Autolycus* (1978) and *The New Cratylus* (1979) by **A. D. Hope** (1907–), *The Peasant Mandarin* (1978) and *Persistence in Folly* (1984) by Les Murray (1938–), *The Music of Love* (1984) by **Dorothy Green** (1915–91), and *The Lyre in the Pawnshop* (1986) by Fay Zwicky (1933–).

Closely allied to the critical essay is the study which fuses literary insight with comment on broader historical and cultural issues. Many examples of this genre have appeared over the past 20 to 30 years, some of the most impressive being *Ockers* (1975) and *The Unknown Great Australian* (1983) by Max Harris (1921–95), *Days of Wine and Rage* (1980) by Frank Moorhouse (1938–), *Gallipoli to Petrov* (1984) by Humphrey McQueen (1942–), *Hot Copy* (1986) by Don Anderson (1939–), and *Soundtrack for the Eighties* (1983) by Craig McGregor (1933–). In the introduction to this last collection, McGregor asks, "'Why a book of essays?" His reply to his own question indicates the essential continuity of the genre from its beginnings with Savery to the present day: "I've always liked the essay ever since reading Hazlitt at school . . . So to a certain extent this is a deliberate exercise in an honourable and enduring literary form . . . a conscious attempt to stretch and expand the traditional essay form."

Other essayists have had less lofty intentions, a number, for instance, being content to continue the tradition of reminiscences of people and places – A. R. Chisholm's (1888–1981) *Men Were My Milestones* (1958), for instance, or John Morrison's (1904–) *The Happy Warrior* (1987). Probably the most accomplished Australian essayist since World War II was Charmian Clift (1923–69). Returning to Australia in 1964 with her novelist husband, George Johnston, she was soon writing a weekly column for the Sydney *Morning Herald* which both acquired a wide popular readership and represented the most elegant writing in the belletristic mode since Walter Murdoch. Her topics ranged from the challenges of expatriation through the pangs and pleasures of family life to the changing urban experience of Australians. After her death Johnston brought together many of her best pieces as *The World of Charmian Clift* (1970).

While Clift did not fully realize her gift as an essayist until after her return home from a long period overseas, it is necessary to conclude this survey by observing that some notable Australian writers have followed the opposite path on their way to achieving a deserved reputation in the essay form. Morris Lurie (1938–), Clive James (1939–), Kate Jennings (1948–), and Meaghan Morris (1950–) have all published collections of essays of real interest and distinction – but only during or after periods of residence away from their native land. Lurie's *The English in Heat* (1972) transports the Australian capacity for deflating comedy to London of the 1960s, while Clive James in a collection like *Visions Before Midnight* (1977) focuses a sardonic eye on British television. Kate Jennings has turned her residence in New York City to

real advantage in *Save Me, Joe Louis* (1988) and *Bad Manners* (1993), while Meaghan Morris' *The Pirate's Fiancée* (1988) brings a powerful intelligence to bear on contemporary issues in feminism, cultural politics, film, and literary theory.

It is fair to say that the essay as a literary genre has never occupied a central place in the history of Australian writing. Its most important literary practitioners have, with few exceptions, reserved their principal energies for the cultivation of other forms – fiction, poetry, or drama. Literary critics, most notably in the 20th century, have used the essay to offer an interpretation of the emerging corpus of creative achievement. Starting from their own disciplinary base, leading figures in other areas of intellectual endeavor – history, philosophy, science, politics, sociology – have made important contributions. By and large, however, the essay in Australia has developed no distinctively local features of style or structure. The result is a body of work providing a valuable commentary on the changing concerns of Australians and rising at its best to an elegance of expression and force of argument which are part of the common currency of good writing anywhere.

HARRY HESELTINE

Anthologies
Australian Essays, edited by George H. Cowling and Furnley Maurice, Melbourne: Melbourne University Press, 1935
Essays: Imaginative and Critical, Chosen from Australian Writers, edited by George Mackaness and J. D. Holmes, Sydney: Angus and Robertson, 1933
Forum: Contemporary Australian Essays, edited by Bruce Elder, Sydney: Wiley and Sons, 1972

Further Reading
Green, H. M., *A History of Australian Literature: Pure and Applied*, revised by Dorothy Green, Sydney: Angus and Robertson, 1985 (original edition, 1961)
Hooton, Joy, and Harry Heseltine, *Annals of Australian Literature*, Melbourne and Oxford: Oxford University Press, 1992 (original edition, 1970)
Wilde, William H., Joy Hooton, and Barry Andrews, *The Oxford Companion to Australian Litterature*, Melbourne and Oxford: Oxford University Press, 1994 (original edition, 1985)

Autobiographical Essay

The autobiographical essay may be viewed either as a kind of essay recounting some part of the writer's own life or as short autobiography having the character of an essay. Both approaches disclose the formal tensions shaping autobiographical essays: their participation in two genres – essay and autobiography – which, although traditionally distinguished, are here so joined as to foreground the historical dynamism and instability of each.

Although autobiographical essays are found occasionally among the works of the older essayists, their proliferation is largely a 20th-century phenomenon. The term itself appears only at mid-century, despite the much earlier establishment of its components, "essay" (about 1600) and "autobiography" (about 1800). One sometimes finds "autobiographical sketch" used by earlier writers to designate essay-length texts which, from a contemporary standpoint, look like genuine autobiographical essays (e.g. Abraham Cowley's "Of Myself," 1668) as well as applied to short self-narratives that lack the ruminative texture of essays (e.g. Sir Thomas Bodley's "Life," 1609). Only in recent years has the autobiographical essay begun to assume theoretical status as a "type" which, though often incorporating features of other essay "types" (e.g. the **travel essay**, the **moral essay**, the **critical essay**), is marked by its focus on retrospection and remembrance (Graham Good, 1988).

As modern practices, both autobiography and the essay have their roots in the European Renaissance and enact that cultural epoch's reconception of the individual life. The essay's matrix is meditative and epistolary, and, despite its early anti-rhetorical cast in both French and English, its formal affinities lie with the thematizing schemata of commonplace books. Autobiography, on the other hand, may be understood as a confluence of traditions whose characteristic modes are narrative: allegory, hagiography, and history, specifically biography. If both autobiography and the essay are, broadly speaking, genres of self-representation, it is the culturally and historically variable impetus to recount the writer's own life that informs autobiography and the projection of the writer's point of view – the reflective and often reflexive gaze provisionally shaping observation and experience – that directs the essay. The autobiographical essay, then, may be viewed as a practice at the intersection of autobiography and essay, a movement between the narratively self-centered imperatives of the former and the worldly discursiveness of the latter. Alfred Kazin's much-cited delineation in *The Open Form: Essays for Our Time* (1961) of the essay's domain – "not the self, but the self thinking" – brings into sharp relief the problematical hybrid character of the autobiographical essay's simultaneous concern with both "the self" *and* "the self thinking." The essay as autobiographical space attempts to accommodate and to bring into artful relation autobiography's traditional search, by way of writing, for a significant personal past and the essay's more or less self-conscious immersion in the pleasures and aporias of writing as such. Certain well-known autobiographical essays assume their very form through the negotiative processes entailed in this accommodation. Thus **Montaigne**'s "De l'exercitation" (1588; "Of Practice") embeds a self-revising piecemeal account of an accident in an expanding self-meditation; **Walter Benjamin**'s "Berliner Chronik" (1932; "A Berlin Chronicle") configures the life of childhood as personal and cultural topography; **Virginia Woolf**'s "A Sketch of the Past" (1940) juxtaposes then and now in an ever-shifting and evolving retrospective framework; Katherine Anne Porter's "St. Augustine and the Bullfight" (1955) interweaves a continually deferred autobiographical anecdote with digressive speculation about the autobiographical act itself; Yukio Mishima's *Taiyo to tetsu* (1968; *Sun and Steel*) joins reminiscence and confession to literary and social commentary in a discourse that calls itself "confidential criticism."

More typically, it is through various foreshortenings and dispersals of narrative that the essay, with its conventions of fragmentariness and provisionality, assimilates to its relatively short span and its characteristically discursive modes the task of recounting the writer's life. Essays may scale down the amplitude of autobiography by narrowing their retrospective gaze to a single significant experience, as in **Washington Irving**'s "The Voyage" (1819), **William Hazlitt**'s "My First Acquaintance with Poets" (1823), **G. K. Chesterton**'s "A Piece of Chalk" (1905), **George Orwell**'s "Shooting an Elephant" (1936), **W. E. B. Du Bois**' "The Guilt of the Cane" (1948), or **Graham Greene**'s "The Revolver in the Corner Cupboard" (1951); or by focusing on a formative stage of the writer's life, the places and people associated with it, as in **Thomas De Quincey**'s "The English Mailcoach" (1849), **T. H. Huxley**'s "Autobiography" (1889), **W. B. Yeats**' "Reveries over Childhood and Youth" (1914), Eudora Welty's "A Sweet Devouring" (1957), **Wallace Stegner**'s "The Town Dump" (1959), **Nadine Gordimer**'s "A Bolter and the Invincible Summer" (1963), or Shiva Naipaul's "Beyond the Dragon's Mouth" (1984). Most commonly, essays limit their autobiographical scope by pondering some aspect or crux of the writer's creative, social, or spiritual existence, e.g. Jonathan Edwards' "Personal Narrative" (1739), **David Hume**'s "My Own Life" (1776), Zora Neale Hurston's "How It Feels to Be Colored Me" (1928), F. Scott Fitzgerald's "The Crack-Up" (1936), Elizabeth Bowen's "Out of a Book" (1950), Margaret Laurence's "Where the World Began" (1971), or **Alice Walker**'s "Beauty: When the Other Dancer Is the Self" (1983). This alternative has had particular appeal for distinguished writers in languages other than English, as exemplified in **Lev Tolstoi**'s *Ispoved'* (1884; *A Confession*), **Ernest Renan**'s "St. Renan" (1883), Franz Kafka's "Brief an den Vater" (1919; "Letter to His Father"), **Thomas Mann**'s "Okkulte Erlebnisse" (1924; "An Experience in the Occult"), **Albert Camus**' "La Mort dans l'âme" (1937; "Death in the Soul"), **Jerzy Stempowski**'s "Księgozbiór przemypników" (1948; "The Smugglers' Library"), **Christa Wolf**'s "Blickwechsel" (1970; "Changing Viewpoint"), and José Donoso's *Historia personal del "boom"* (1971; *The Boom in Spanish American Literature: A Personal History*). In all such instances it may be said that, even as autobiography urges its quest for self as life story upon the essay, so, in turn, the essay conducts that quest on a scale suitable to its own rhetorical habits. Nowhere is this generic transaction more intricately sustained than in the autobiographical book composed as a series of separately titled, and sometimes independently published, pieces, e.g. Vladimir Nabokov's *Speak Memory* (1966), Sara Suleri's *Meatless Days* (1989), and Tobias Wolff's *In Pharaoh's Army* (1994); a notable early example is **Jean-Jacques Rousseau**'s *Les Rêveries du promeneur solitaire* (1782; *Reveries of the Solitary Walker*). While the chapters that make up such books work as self-contained essays, their internal resonances, thematic coalescences, and cumulative effects create the amplitude, if not the continuity, of autobiography.

Beyond all such patently autobiographical essays lies the larger body of texts drawing upon autobiographical material whose narrativity is so attenuated or diffuse and so persistently subordinate to wide-ranging speculation that many students of the genre would be hard put to call them autobiographical essays. Most of Montaigne's *Essais* (1580, 1588) belong here, as do, among the works of the early writers, the "Meditations" of **John Donne**'s *Devotions upon Emergent Occasions* (1624) and, among those of later practitioners in English, William Hazlitt's miscellaneous essays, much of Washington Irving's

Sketchbook (1819), **William Makepeace Thackeray's** *Roundabout Papers* (1863), and countless 20th-century essays traditionally labeled "familiar" or "informal." Indeed, self-narrative may recede to the vanishing point in works that are, nonetheless, deeply self-revelatory and/or passionately apologetic (e.g. **Henry David Thoreau's** "Life Without Principle," 1863, **Robert Louis Stevenson's** "An Apology for Idlers," 1876, and **E. M. Forster's** "What I Believe," 1939). The strongly personal character of all such essays suggests deep affinities with autobiography as a mode of self-location; at the same time, it raises difficult, if highly productive, questions about the relationship between the autobiographical essay and what has throughout this century (at least as far back as Virginia Woolf's 1905 piece, "The Decay of Essay Writing") been termed "the **personal essay**." From one standpoint, the emergence and modern flowering of the autobiographical essay appears as a specialization of this broader "type" in which the writer's perspective and sensibility (what writers such as Woolf called "personality") move into the foreground. On this account, the autobiographical essay represents the most focused historical enactment of the anti-systematic and anti-institutional tendencies that have marked the essay since its beginnings.

But what if, like many students of the essay past and present, we regard the "personal" as characterizing not a certain range of essays but the genre as a whole? To appreciate the persistence of this view we need only observe how widespread in critical and pedagogic literature has been the sometimes deliberate, sometimes inadvertent, conflation of the terms "personal essay" and "essay," no doubt because of the normative sway of Montaigne's eminently "personal" – some would say "autobiographical" – *Essais* over the genre's multifarious practices. The theoretical implications of this terminological slippage for both traditions, essay and autobiography, are considerable. Scholars such as Hugo Friedrich (*Montaigne*, 1949) and Michel Beaujour (*The Poetics of the Literary Self-Portrait*, 1980) read Montaigne's influential work not as autobiography but as self-writing of a kind that Beaujour terms "autoportrait" (a genre which might claim such postmodern texts of the self as *Roland Barthes par Roland Barthes*, 1975). Suppose, however, that the autobiographical mark of Montaigne's essays is their recounting not of the writer's "life" as a past to be recollected but of the autobiographical act *per se* as self-inscriptive process; the autobiographical essay, in this view, opens the door to a kind of meta-story. Thus the status we assign to Montaigne's *Essais* positions our conception of both essay and autobiography as discourses of the "personal" and frames our theoretical accounts of such salient notions as "narrative" and "self." In its academically transgressive guise as "autobiographical" or "personal" or "narrative" criticism, the contemporary autobiographical essay engages these and other issues, now explicitly, now implicitly, and demonstrates yet again the protean energies of the two genres in which it participates.

LYDIA FAKUNDINY

Anthologies

American Lives, edited by Robert F. Sayre, Madison: University of Wisconsin Press, 1994
The Art of the Essay, edited by Lydia Fakundiny, Boston: Houghton Mifflin, 1991

The Intimate Critique: Autobiographical Literary Criticism, edited by Diane Freedman and others, Durham, North Carolina: Duke University Press, 1993

Further Reading

Ashley, Kathleen, Leigh Gilmore, and Gerald Peters, editors, *Autobiography and Postmodernism*, Amherst: University of Massachusetts Press, 1994
Bruss, Elizabeth W., *Autobiographical Acts: The Changing Situation of a Literary Genre*, Baltimore: Johns Hopkins University Press, 1976
Eakin, Paul John, *Fictions in Autobiography: Studies in the Art of Self-Invention*, Princeton, New Jersey: Princeton University Press, 1985
Good, Graham, *The Observing Self: Rediscovering the Essay*, London and New York: Routledge, 1988
Good, Graham, "Identity and Form in the Modern Autobiographical Essay," *Prose Studies* 15, no. 1 (April 1992): 99–117
Hart, Francis R., "Notes for an Anatomy of Modern Autobiography," *New Literary History* 1, no. 3 (Spring 1970): 485–511
Lejeune, Philippe, *Le Pacte autobiographique*, Paris: Seuil, 1975
Olney, James, *Metaphors of Self: The Meaning of Autobiography*, Princeton, New Jersey: Princeton University Press, 1972
Peterson, Linda, "Gender and the Autobiographical Essay: Research Perspectives, Pedagogical Practices," *College Composition and Communication* 42 (May 1991): 171–93
Terms of Identity: Essays on the Theoretical Terminology of Life-Writing, special issue of *Auto/Biography Studies* 10, no. 1 (1995)

Ayala, Francisco

Spanish, 1906–

Having studied political philosophy and sociology in Germany and earned his doctorate in law from the University of Madrid, Francisco Ayala published essays in numerous professional fields, as well as an abundant output of fiction. As a critic for **José Ortega y Gasset's** prestigious literary periodical, *Revista de Occidente* (Western review), his literary and cultural essays reflect that master philosopher's tutelage. He has written legal, sociological, and philosophical treatises while teaching at the University of Madrid, journalism and works on political science during his Latin American exile, and studies in linguistics, history, literary theory, and culture. In other words, there are few subjects that have not come under Ayala's scrutiny.

Ayala's essays and fiction are closely interrelated: writings in both genres explore existential alienation, ethical dilemmas, pedagogy, the abuse of power, philosophical and moral questions concerning the mass media, corruption in government, and terrorism. The basic, underlying problem he explores in his essays is the tension between individual liberty and social order, between personal dignity and equality and the common good. Ayala's essays and fiction often contemplate the power exercised by human beings over others, viewed as usurpation capable of destroying basic humanity and degrading humans to animalism. Degradation through loss of liberty (expressed in Ayala's fiction by metaphors of bestiality) appears in his essays as an ethical problem of equilibrium between personal freedom and tyranny or dictatorship.

In *Derechos de la persona individual para una sociedad de masas* (1953; Individual rights in mass society) and *El escritor en la sociedad de masas* (1956; The writer in mass society) Ayala paints a portrait of a society in crisis. Concern with juvenile gangs, gratuitous violence, and disregard for the rights of others inspires many pages in these collections and numerous fictional works. Without overt moralizing, Ayala depicts the results of pervasive abdication of moral responsibility (an attribute of the "mass man" mentality analyzed by Ortega). Dehumanization resulting from socialized conformity is a frequent motif. Ayala examines demagoguery, propaganda, censorship, and "information management" calculated to mislead public opinion, exposing (as had Ortega) artifices calculated to deprive the masses of the exercise of conscience. In *La crisis actual de la enseñanza* (1958; The current educational crisis) and *Tecnología y libertad* (1959; Technology and liberty), he critiques permissive educational policies, juvenile delinquency, antisocial activity, and gratuitous crime, analyzing discrepancies between technological and moral progress, examining material civilization and the "culture lag," contemporary political institutions' inability to cope with state invasion of individual privacy.

Razón del mundo (1944; Worldly reason) examines historiography and relationships between history and fiction, arguing that philosophy, history, and fiction all attempt to provide orientation and guidance. Without undue insistence upon history's being written by the victors, Ayala suggests its frequent fictionality, implicitly including "official versions" of the past with other forms of usurpation. Challenging readers to think autonomously, he exposes the weaknesses of historical and philosophical dogma. *Realidad y ensueño* (1963; Reality and daydreams) considers intuition sometimes superior to reason in its epistemological epiphanies. Existentially, Ayala (like Ortega) shows more concern for epistemology than ontology, but balances the psychological and sociological.

Ayala's work, whether fiction or nonfiction, constitutes a continuing linguistic probing of the human condition as a moral and aesthetic project. Seamlessly interfacing reality and literature, he explores and reexamines the implications of their relationship while elaborating his personal, intellectual perception of historical process. As Ortega's disciple, Ayala made contributions to the master's historiographic "method of generations." Profoundly preoccupied by his observations of moral mutability, Ayala offers reflections upon creativity, freedom, power, and poetry in the context of social flux, paradox, and fragmentation. The wide-ranging, polyfaceted nature of his essays overwhelms the average reader, obscuring his significant contributions to literary theory (narratology, genre theory, perspectivism), theory in the social sciences (sociology, political science, history), and more abstract philosophical theorizing (epistemological speculation, reflections on the role of memory, analysis of the psychology of everyday experience in relation to the established order and traditional culture).

Many critical works treat fields related to Ayala's teaching of Spanish literature: Cervantes, the *Lazarillo*, Quevedo, the Golden Age, Galdós, and major Spanish and Latin American writers of the 20th century. Ayala believes criticism's role is to help reconstruct circumstances at the moment of writing, but he also writes theoretical criticism, documents his readings, identifies antecedents, and traces points of coincidence.

Further critical interests include dreams, tragedy and comedy, and relationships between comedy and the grotesque, autobiography and creativity, and an author's sociohistorical reality and his or her work. Ayala's essays also facilitate understanding of his own fiction, indirectly indicating intertexts, apocryphal citations, and tricks on the unwary reader.

Writing with irony and humor, inspired by news items and current events, Ayala frequently addresses themes in his essays such as responsibility and guilt in the anonymous "mass society," existential authenticity, and the ambivalence accompanying recognition of individual responsibility. He treats radical solitude, the difficulties of authentic communication, alienation, and helplessness or desperation in both fiction and essays, believing the writer should investigate the meaning of human life and ultimate mysteries, penetrate profound questions of contemporary existence, and seek answers to questions concerning time, death, and oblivion.

JANET PÉREZ

Biography

Francisco de Paula Ayala y García-Duarte. Born 16 March 1906 in Granada. Studied at the University of Madrid, law degree, 1929, Ph.D., 1931; studied in Germany, 1929–30. Married Etelvina Silva, 1931: one daughter. Professor of law, University of Madrid, 1932–35. Diplomat for the Spanish Republic, 1937; exiled in Buenos Aires, where he taught sociology and founded *Realidad* (Reality) magazine, 1939–50, Puerto Rico, where he founded *La Torre* (The tower), 1950–58, New York, 1958–66, and Chicago, 1966–73. Professor at Rutgers University, New Brunswick, New Jersey, Bryn Mawr College, Pennsylvania, University of Chicago, and New York University. United States representative to UNESCO. Began visiting Spain, from 1960, and returned to live there, mid-1980s. Elected to the Royal Spanish Academy, 1983. Awards: National Critics' Prize, 1972; National Literature Prize, 1983; National Prize of Spanish Letters, 1988; Cervantes Prize, 1991.

Selected Writings

Essays and Related Prose

Indagación del cinema, 1929
El derecho social en la constitución de la República española (treatise), 1932
El pensamiento vivo de Saavedra Fajardo, 1941
El problema del liberalismo, 1941
Historia de la libertad, 1942
Oppenheimer, 1942
Razón del mundo (La preocupación de España), 1944
Histrionismo y representación, 1944
Los políticos, 1944
Una doble experiencia política: España e Italia, 1944
Jovellanos, 1945
Ensayo sobre la libertad, 1945
Tratado de sociología (treatise), 3 vols., 1947
La invención del "Quijote", 1950
Ensayos de sociología política, 1952
Introducción a las ciencias sociales, 1952
Derechos de la persona individual para una sociedad de masas, 1953
El escritor en la sociedad de masas, 1956
Breve teoría de la traducción, 1956; as *Problemas de la traducción*, 1965
La integración social en América, 1958
La crisis actual de la enseñanza, 1958

Tecnología y libertad, 1959
Experiencia e invención, 1960
Realidad y ensueño, 1963
La evasión de los intelectuales, with H. A. Murena, 1963
De este mundo y el otro, 1963
España, a la fecha, 1965; enlarged edition, 1977
El cine: Arte y espectáculo, 1966
España y la cultura germánica, 1968
Reflexiones sobre la estructura narrativa, 1970
El "Lazarillo": Nuevo examen de algunos aspectos, 1971
Confrontaciones, 1972
Los ensayos: Teoría y crítica literaria, 1972
La novela: Galdós y Unamuno, 1974
Cervantes y Quevedo, 1974
El escritor y su imagen: Ortega y Gasset, Azorín, Valle-Inclán, Machado, 1975
El escritor y el cine, 1975
Galdós en su tiempo, 1978
España, 1975–1980: Conflictos y logros de la democracia, 1982
Palabras y letras, 1983
La estructura narrativa, y otras experiencias literarias, 1984
La retórica del periodismo y otras retóricas, 1985
La imagen de España: Continuidad y cambio en la sociedad española, 1986
Obra periodística, 1986
Las plumas del fénix: Estudios de literatura española, 1989
Contra el poder y otros ensayos, 1992
El tiempo y yo, o, El mundo a la espalda, 1992

Other writings: many works of fiction (including *La cabeza del cordero* [*The Lamb's Head*], 1949; *Los usurpadores* [*Usurpers*], 1949; *Muertes de perro* [*Death as a Way of Life*], 1958; *El fondo del vaso*, 1962), autobiography, and books on philosophy, sociology, history, and criticism.

Bibliographies

Alvarez Calleja, José, *Bibliografía de Francisco Ayala*, Madrid: Serie Bibliografias, 1983
Amorós, Andrés, *Bibliografía de Francisco Ayala*, New York: Syracuse University, 1973

Further Reading

Anthropos issue on Ayala, 139 (December 1992)
Hiriart, Rosario, *Conversaciones con Francisco Ayala*, Madrid: Espasa-Calpe, 1982
Irizarry, Estelle, *Francisco Ayala*, Boston: Twayne, 1977
Kollatz, Elisabeth, *Krieg, Macht, Politik im essayistischen und narrativen Werk Francisco Ayalas*, Frankfurt-on-Main: Lang, 1995
Lindstrom, Naomi, "Creation in Criticism, Criticism in Creation: Four Ibero Exemplars," *Discurso Literario* 6, no. 2 (Spring 1989): 423–44
Martínez, Antonio, "The Powers That Usurped Peace: Testimony and Denunciation of Francisco Ayala," in *German and International Perspectives on the Spanish Civil War: The Aesthetics of Partisanship*, edited by Luis Costa and others, Columbia, South Carolina: Camden House, 1992: 376–85
Mermall, Thomas, *Alegorías del poder en Francisco Ayala*, Madrid: Espiral, 1983
Vásquez Medel, Manuel Angel, editor, *El universo plural de Francisco Ayala*, Seville: Alfar, 1995

Azaña, Manuel

Spanish, 1880–1940

Although Azaña the President and statesman has overshadowed Azaña the essayist and novelist, this tragic figure of Spanish liberalism never retreated from the belief that rational public action, like art, must arise from an all-embracing aesthetics which he referred to as a collective "style." But if his driving intellectual passion was to be the architect of this new order characterized by rhetorical excellence and rational cordiality, his introspective aloofness as a writer often placed him at a remove from his own grand design. Toward the end of his life in his *Memorias* (Memoirs) he drifted finally into personal detachment in ironic and self-conscious musings over his failures.

In several essays Azaña professed a special fondness for the writings of 19th-century novelist and essayist Juan Valera. Critics J. Ferrer Solà and Francisco Daudet, among others, claim to detect in his own prose a certain imitative resemblance to his predecessor in the archaic overtones, impeccable lexical purity, and classical tenor of his phrasing. Yet unlike Valera, Azaña resisted the lure of belletrism for its own sake; for him art and ideology remained inseparable, although one must add that they did so as an unresolved personal conflict. For if Azaña leaned intellectually toward ideology, his art and oratory remained grounded in vibrant aesthetic instincts. Thus in *El jardín de los frailes* (1927; The friars' garden), a partially autobiographical novel of his student days in the Escorial, the young protagonist finds consolation for his prison-like confinement in the pleasurable, almost erotic contemplation of pure beauty, a beauty suggested by the interplay of real and imaginary light reflecting a baroque and sometimes grotesque material world. His vision is at once sensuous and sensitive yet defined at more or less regular intervals by introspective rational markers tinged with occasional self-doubt and, for his opponents, frequent sarcasm. As a result of these binary swings between lyric exuberance and critical scrutiny his style exhibits a syncopated cadence that suggests both a predisposition to psychological testimonialism and an affinity for baroque syntax, qualities that seemed to serve him better as an orator than as a novelist or essayist.

The essays of Azaña veer closer in style to his oratory than to his novels. In the latter his penchant for detachment and distance seemed to prevail over the fundamental realism which, generally speaking, was predominant in the other genres he cultivated. It is particularly significant in this regard that for Azaña the creation of a style involved not only the search for a relevant ideological and literary posture before the world but also the means of escaping from it. At his dialectical best in the essay, Azaña achieves a superior level of persuasive communicativeness by the precise logical structure of his prose and by the rigorously clear exposition of arguments informed by a unique view of Spain.

Azaña has been described as "a man without a generation," but even though he publicized his disagreements with the Generation of 1898, he shared with his older compatriots much of their "landscape lyricism" and the literary temperament that informs their work. Furthermore, within his own generation he exhibited with **José Ortega y Gasset, Eugenio d'Ors, Ramón**

Pérez de Ayala, and Juan Ramón Jiménez a Modernist penchant for metaphorical precision and conceptual elegance.

In the *Memorias* and other essays an ironic note serves Azaña as a means of distancing himself from the technical incompetence, backwardness, and bad faith of certain contemporaries. As a general rule, his procedure consists of creating a spiral of contrasting images before suddenly demolishing them with a verbal *contre-coup* that reveals in unmistakable clarity not only the person's shortcomings but the author's contempt for mediocrity. Irony in the essays often introduces moments of sarcastic humor which serve to counterbalance the somber intervals of private reflections. Thus he delights in ridiculing the pompous speeches of other political figures, in caricaturing professional groups such as medical doctors, and, occasionally, in poking fun at himself.

In a general way, these moments of irony and humor serve to alleviate a style that tends toward the transcendent. Functionally, therefore, they act as humanizing components by making the text more accessible and, ultimately, more understandable. Nevertheless, the same acerbity of this irony and humor may also point to personal flaws. At times the hauteur that slips into his language seems to betray an impatient, supercilious intellectual who, though sincere and intimate with an anonymous public, scorned his less gifted peers.

Both the style and the person of Manuel Azaña raise contradictory questions. Undeniably of classical, even elitist propensities in his native literary preferences, he nevertheless sought to create a democratic ideological style for the Spanish masses. He inclined naturally to art for art's sake yet stubbornly insisted publicly that art must be subservient to ideology. And although as President of the Republic he kept watch over Spanish liberalism during its most tragic period, he also jealously guarded and cultivated an inner personal domain remote from politics and devastation, though replete with sympathies for the human condition at the nadir. It was a personal region of ideal hues and sensuous resonance articulated by the aesthetic sentiments of a literary purist. Most likely there, beyond his ideological obsessions, is where one must seek his most enduring legacy.

HAROLD RALEY

Biography

Manuel Azaña y Díaz. Born 10 January 1880 in Alcalá de Henares. Studied at the Real Colegio de Estudios Superiores, San Lorenzo de El Escorial, 1893–97; University of Saragossa, law degree, 1898; University of Madrid, Ph.D., 1900; also studied in Paris. Secretary, 1913, and president, 1930, Ateneo cultural center, Madrid. Founder, with José Ortega y Gasset, League of Political Education, 1913. Joined the Reformist Party, 1913. Cofounder, *La Pluma* (The pen), 1920–23, and *España*, 1923–24. Founder, Political Action republican group, 1925. Married Dolores Rivas Cherif, 1929. Minister of war, 1931, Prime Minister, 1931–33, and President of the Republic, 1936–39; then exiled to France. Awards: National Literature Prize, 1926. Died in Montauban, France, 3 November 1940.

Selected Writings

Essays and Related Prose
Don Juan Valera, 1926
Valera en Rusia, 1926
La novela de Pepita Jiménez, 1927
Valera en Italia, 1929
Plumas y palabras, 1930
Una política (1930–1932) (speeches), 1932
En el poder y en la Oposición (1932–1934) (speeches), 2 vols., 1934
La invencion del Quijote y otros ensayos, 1934
Discursos en campo abierto (speeches), 1936
Memorias intimas, 1938
La velada en Benicarló (dialogue), 1939; edited by Manuel Aragón, 1974; as *Vigil in Benicarló*, translated by Josephine and Paul Stewart, 1982
Ensayos sobre Valera, 1971
Memorias políticas y de guerras, 4 vols., 1976–81
Antología 1: Ensayos, edited by Federico Jiménez Losantos, 1982
Antología 1: Discursos, edited by Federico Jiménez Losantos, 1983
Apuntas de memoria (inédito), edited by Enrique de Rivas, 1990
Discursos parlamentaros, edited by Javier Paniagua Fuentes, 1992

Other writings: the autobiographical novel *El jardín de los frailes* (1927), two plays, diaries, and correspondence.

Collected works edition: *Obras completas*, edited by Juan Marichal, 4 vols., 1966–68.

Bibliography

Rivas, Enrique de, *Comentarios y notas a "Apuntes de memoria" de Manuel Azaña y a las cartas de 1938, 1939, 1940*, Valencia: Pre-Textos, 1990: 187–244

Further Reading

Alpert, Michael, *La reforma militar de Azaña (1931–1933)*, Madrid: Siglo XXI, 1982
Aragón, Manuel, "Manuel Azaña: Un intento de modernización política," *Sistema* 2 (May 1973): 101–04
Arias, Luis, *Azaña o el sueño de la razón*, Madrid: Nerea, 1990
Espín, Eduardo, *Azaña en el poder: El partido de Acción Republicana*, Madrid: Centro de Investigaciones Sociológicas, 1980
Ferrer Solà, Jesus, *Manuel Azaña: Una pasión intelectual*, Barcelona: Anthropos, 1991
Giménez Caballero, Ernesto, *Manuel Azaña (Profecías Españolas)*, Madrid: Turner, 1974 (original edition, 1932)
Jackson, Gabriel, *Costa, Azaña, el Frente Popular y otros ensayos*, Madrid: Turner, 1976
Jiménez Losantos, Federico, "El desdén con el desdén: Manuel Azaña," in his *Lo que queda de España*, Saragossa: Alcrudo, 1979
Juliá, Santos, *Manuel Azaña: Una biografía política, del Ateneo al Palacio Nacional*, Madrid: Alianza, 1990
Mainer, José-Carlos, "El retorno de Azaña," *Insula* 342 (May 1975): 4
Marco, José María, *La inteligencia republicana, Manuel Azaña, 1897–1930*, Madrid: Biblioteca Nueva, 1988
Marco, José María, *Azaña*, Madrid: Mondadori, 1990
Marichal, Juan, *La vocación de Manuel Azaña*, Madrid: Alianza, 1982
Marichal, Juan, *El intelectual y la política, 1898–1936: Unamuno, Ortega, Azaña, Negrín*, Madrid: Publicaciones de la Residencia de Estudiantes, 1990
Montero, José, *El drama de la verdad en Manuel Azaña*, Seville: University of Seville, 1979
Peña González, José, *Los ideales políticos de Manuel Azaña*, Madrid: University of Madrid, 1981
Rivas, Enrique de, *Comentarios y notas a "Apuntes de memoria" de Manuel Azaña y a las cartas de 1938, 1939, 1940*, Valencia: Pre-Textos, 1990

Rivas Cherif, Cipriano, *Retrato de un desconocido: Vida de Manuel Azaña*, Barcelona: Grijalbo, 1979

Sedwick, Frank, *The Tragedy of Manuel Azaña and the Fate of the Spanish Republic*, Columbus: Ohio State University Press, 1963

Serrano, Vicente-Alberto, and José-María San Luciano, editors, *Azaña*, Madrid: Edascal, 1980

Azorín

Spanish, 1873–1967

Early in his career, José Martínez Ruiz adopted the pen name "Azorín," under which he published novels, short stories, literary essays, plays, and countless articles in multiple turn-of-the-century magazines and newspapers and, beginning in 1905, in the leading conservative Spanish newspaper, *ABC*. Azorín was one of a group of important Spanish writers who began publishing in the 1890s and attained their greatest achievements between 1900 and 1930. With **Miguel de Unamuno**, Antonio and Manuel Machado, Pío Baroja, Jacinto Benavente, Ramón del Valle-Inclán, and others, Azorín undertook a reexamination of the Spanish nation and the modern Spanish subject. Formerly, critics divided these writers and their contemporaries into two distinct groups, the "Modernistas" and the Generation of 1898, but recently the trend has been to collapse this distinction and to classify all as "Modernistas" and to link them more broadly with the Anglo-European Modernist project while allowing for cultural variations according to local historical and social conditions. Modernism represents a break with the traditional sociosymbolic order and a search for new modes to express new experiences and perspectives.

Azorín's essayistic writing demonstrates a Modernist rejection of the rationalist and scientific discourses that prevailed in the late 19th century and introduces a subjective, impressionistic, and highly poetic style. In some respects, it forges a link with the powerful but abbreviated production of the Romantic writer **Mariano José de Larra**, but in others it cultivates new modalities of writing in response to new modes of perception. Azorín's "essays" include both literary criticism and studies of the Spanish character and landscape; frequently these two categories blend in a single text. *La ruta de don Quijote* (1905; Don Quixote's route) chronicles Azorín's retracing of the wanderings of Don Quixote and Sancho Panza in La Mancha, with a continuous melding of literary reminiscence and contemporary commentary. *Lecturas españolas* (1912; Spanish readings), *Clásicos y modernos* (1913; Classics and moderns), and *De Granada a Castelar* (1922; From Granada to Castelar), among others, offer highly personal rereadings of classical and contemporary texts. In works such as *Los pueblos* (1905; The villages), *España* (1909; Spain), and *Castilla* (1912; Castile), literary criticism also appears, but in the service of a re-creation of the Spanish and, in particular, of the Castilian landscape, peoples, and history.

Like many of his contemporaries, Azorín distrusted official history and the 19th-century belief in the objective reconstruction of facts; consequently, his texts repudiate the dispassionate tone, the emphasis on politics, and the reliance on government documents that characterize historical discourse of the period. In contrast, they foreground literary texts as a means to access the past and feature the lesser-known, sometimes anonymous figures of rural and small-town life as better guides to a reconstruction of previous periods than the biographies of notable public statesmen. In novels as well as essays, Azorín obsessively explores the theme of time and its passage, confronting the accelerated rhythm of modernity with a languorous exploration of the past as captured in the non-urban areas of Spain.

Azorín also breaks with literary and journalistic traditions in style and structure. His syntax represents a sharp departure from the heavily rhetorical style of 19th-century oratory, eschewing long sentences with multiple dependent clauses for short sentences with coordinate clauses. In keeping with a desire to bring the Spanish past into the present without sacrificing the cultural and linguistic specificity of Spain, Azorín and his contemporaries employ a rich lexicon that borrows freely from other languages while simultaneously resurrecting forgotten Spanish words drafted from specialized rural vocabularies.

Structurally, Azorín's texts often defy traditional generic boundaries. Many of the "essays" incorporate techniques borrowed from narrative and poetry, and dialogue is a frequent visitor in Azorín's essayistic writing. *Castilla*, one of his most widely-read publications, deliberately questions the established generic divisions through the careful construction of a collection of essays that move from conventional essay form through those incorporating poetic discourse, to those that take on a decidedly narrative form, and finally to the closing set of three that borrow strongly from dramatic techniques. Furthermore, the final essays introduce yet another form through the use of ekphrasis and the introduction of visual art, thus questioning the borders of literature itself.

Many critics view Azorín's experimentation with language and form as pure aestheticism, with no social or political implications. However, theorists of Modernism have refuted such a separation of content and form, and Azorín's writing can benefit from a revision along the lines that have guided other rereadings of Anglo-European Modernist writers. Notwithstanding the emphasis on Castilian texts, landscape, and culture, Azorín's publications insistently explore margins and boundaries, revising the canon, revisiting and reconstructing the past according to new visions, and denying the separation of art and life.

España, another important collection, demonstrates the insistence on multiple perspectives that cross traditional lines of separation and open up new possibilities for the perception of modern experience. The book combines the diachronic and the synchronic; the first 15 texts follow a chronological order, with each connected to a specific date, while the last 15 essays deal with contemporary issues and are devoid of historical references. Many of the essays emphasize the continuity of the past, while others foreground a disjointed historical evolution that places past and present in opposition.

Moreover, the marginalization of Spain, whether by its own choice or by foreign design, receives close scrutiny. Notwithstanding the title and the insistent examination of Spanish countryside, history, and culture, the text opens with an epigraph from Petrarch which appears in Italian and closes with an epilogue that was written in the French Pyrenees. Throughout the essays, the text speaker intrudes on the materials discussed in a constant reminder of the influence of the observer on what is observed and described, thus debunking any pretense of objectivity. Azorín's essays thus reflect the Modernist impulse to develop new modes of writing and thinking in order to represent the complexities of modern experience.

MARY LEE BRETZ

Biography

Born José Martínez Ruiz, 8 June 1873 in Monóvar, Alicante. Also used the pseudonyms Cándido and Ahrimán. Studied at the Colegio de los Padres Escolapios, Yecla, 1881–88; law at the University of Valencia, from 1888. Moved to Madrid, 1896. Journalist for various newspapers, including *ABC*, *El País* (The country), *El Progreso* (Progress), and *El Imparcial* (The impartial). Elected deputy to the Spanish Parliament, 1907. Married Julia Guinda Urzanqui, 1908. Undersecretary for the Ministry of Public Instruction, 1917, 1919. Drama critic during the 1920s. Elected to the Royal Spanish Academy, 1924. Columnist for *La Nación* (Buenos Aires), 1930–67. Lived in Paris, 1936–39. Died in Madrid, 2 March 1967.

Selected Writings

Essays and Related Prose
La crítica literaria en España, 1893
Moratín esbozo por Cándido, 1893
Buscapiés, 1894
Anarquistas literarios, 1895
Notas sociales, 1895
Literatura, 1896
Charivari, 1897
Soledades, 1898
La evolución de la crítica, 1899
La sociología criminal, 1899
Los hidalgos, 1900
El alma castellana, 1900
Los pueblos, 1905
La ruta de don Quijote, 1905
El político, 1908
España: Hombres y paisajes, 1909
La Cierva, 1910
Lecturas españolas, 1912
Castilla, 1912
Clásicos y modernos, 1913
Los valores literarios, 1913
Al margen de los clásicos, 1915
Rivas y Larra, 1916
Un pueblecito: Riofrío de Ávila, 1916
Páginas escogidas, 1917
Entre España y Francia, 1917
El paisaje de España visto por los españoles, 1917
Madrid-Guía sentimental, 1918
Paris bombardeado, 1919

Fantasías y devaneos, 1920
Los dos Luises y otros ensayos, 1921
De Granada a Castelar, 1922
El chirrión de los políticos, 1923
Una hora de España, 1924; edited by José Montero Padilla, 1993
Racine y Molière, 1924
Los Quintero y otras páginas, 1925
Andando y pensando, 1929
Lope en silueta, 1935
Trasuntos de España, 1938
Valencia, 1941
Madrid, 1941
París, 1945
Memorias inmemoriales, 1946
Con permiso de los cervantistas, 1948
La cabeza de Castilla, 1950
Con bandera de Francia, 1950
Verano en Mallorca, 1952
El oasis de los clásicos, edited by J. García Marcada, 1952
El cine y el momento, 1953
El efímero cine, 1955
El pasado, 1955
Agenda, 1959
Posdata, 1959
Ejercicios de castellano, 1960
La hora de la pluma, edited by Victor Ouimette, 1987
Artículos anarquistas, edited by José María Valverde, 1992

Other writings: many novels, short stories, and plays.

Collected works edition: *Obras completas*, edited by Ángel Cruz Rueda, 9 vols., 1947–54.

Bibliographies
Fox, E. Inman, *Azorín: Guía de la obra completa*, Madrid: Castalia, 1992
Sáinz de Bujanda, Fernando, *Clausura de un centenario: Guía bibliográfica de Azorín*, Madrid: Revista de Occidente, 1974

Further Reading
Fox, E. Inman, *Azorín as a Literary Critic*, New York: Hispanic Institute, 1962
Glenn, Kathleen M., *Azorín*, Boston: Twayne, 1981
Granell, Manuel, *Estética de Azorín*, Madrid: Biblioteca Nueva, 1949
Krause, Anna, *Azorín, the Little Philosopher: Inquiry into the Birth of a Literary Personality*, Berkeley: University of California Publications in Modern Philosophy, 1948
Pérez de Ayala, Ramón, *Ante Azorín*, Madrid: Biblioteca Nueva, 1964
Ríopérez y Milá, Santiago, *Azorín íntegro: Estudio biográfico, crítico, bibliográfico y antológico*, Madrid: Bibilioteca Nueva, 1979
Torre, Guillermo de, *Del 98 al barroco*, Madrid: Gredos, 1965
Valverde, José María, *Azorín*, Barcelona: Planeta, 1971

B

Bacon, Francis

English, 1561–1626

Francis Bacon was the first master of the essay form in English and a philosopher of this and other literary formulas for spreading enlightened thought. While he wrote in an astonishing variety of styles, as to the essay he was essentially a one-book author. But there were three versions of this book. While the *Essayes* of 1597 marked the first appearance of the term as part of an English book title, it contained only ten compositions, and these were hardly more than little collections of sharp sayings. The Baconian masterwork in the genre is clearly the third version, *The Essayes or Counsels, Civill and Morall* of 1625. Standing alone like the 1612 edition, but enlarged "both in number and weight," it is indeed the "new work" which the dedication advertises. There are 58 essays (20 more than in 1612), and those carried over are reordered and revised, and fattened by quotation, authority, and a flow of insinuating reasoning. Of this version Bacon thought well and predicted much. While in summarizing his literary motives he called the work a "recreation," he added at once that the *Essayes* had been the easy road to his fame. It was the most popular of his writings then and has been ever since. Bacon had the final version translated into Latin (with small variations) and expected that "in the universal language" it may "last as long as books last." He included the work among the "civil and moral writings" to be inserted in *The Great Instauration*, his vast collection of useful arts and sciences that could give man power over his environment. The civil and moral writings show what powers are truly useful, and they elaborate on civil powers such as the nation-state and moral powers such as the work ethic.

Bacon's *Essayes* is a variation on **Montaigne**'s *Essais*, which was published first in 1580 and then in its full three volumes in 1588. After 1600 a wave of imitative volumes appeared in English, most citing and quoting one of Bacon's versions, but others showing the influence of the *Essais*. Bacon himself refers only once to Montaigne, but it is in the first essay, "Of Truth," and as a sly guide in attacking truth, particularly religious truth. "Of Truth" develops circumspectly the universality and power of falsehood, not least in religious matters. Montaigne saw the worldly passion beneath the pretense; he "saith prettily" that he who lies fears God less and men more.

Like Montaigne, Bacon found in the essay form an informal and winning appeal, which served not least to circumvent the authority of theological works. The *Essayes* like the *Essais* are first and foremost in the vernacular, the language of the layman. Each is composed of discrete little compositions, less likely to strain the ordinary attention span. Both have a casual and even disorderly tenor; they avoid the distant formality of an oration, or even of a comedy or tragedy. Bacon no more than Montaigne imposes exhortations, or satires and laments as to virtue and vice. Also, and substantively, the *Essayes* like the *Essais* entertains men's opinions. Each adopts a tolerant stance; neither imposes a righteous way. The *Essayes* is not an application of the Bible or a eulogy of ancient morals (except in quick bows to **Seneca** and the Stoics as the reader is maneuvered past theological morals and the Peripatetics).

Yet the work directs opinion, albeit indirectly. The *Essayes* is a self-help book, but the reader is directed deep into a novel spirit of self-help. The extraordinary essay "Of Goodness and Goodness of Nature" moves past charity through humanity, then redefines goodness as self-reliance, even the self-reliance of the maliciously ambitious founder of a state. At the foundation of politics is self-making and badness, rather than goodness, of nature. The *Essayes* appeals not so much to self-expression as to self-interest, and does so by supplying enlightened ways to satisfy one's interest. The essays have been popular, the dedication explains, because "they come home to men's business and bosoms." Typical titles are "Of Death," "Of Love," "Of Great Place," "Of Riches," and "Of Ambition." Still, all this guidance is under an appearance of reticence. Bacon in his way, like Montaigne in his, seems most unauthoritative. In the only essay devoted to literary style, Bacon explains how literary diffidence can go with literary leadership; it was a lesson that followers like **Benjamin Franklin** took to heart. "The honorablest part of talk is to give the occasion; and again to moderate and pass to somewhat else; for then a man leads the dance" ("Of Discourse").

Bacon's collection is both more succinct and less charming than Montaigne's. It is more "pragmatic"; his essays are "counsels civill and morall" which concentrate on advancing one's business and state. Montaigne appears eccentric, leisurely, pleasure-seeking, and bemused; he pointedly alludes to the pleasures of freedom, food, sex, talk, and friends. Bacon by contrast writes essays that are comparatively short, intense, and businesslike. The central essay of the *Essais* is the skeptical "Apologie de Raimond Sebond" ("Apology of Raymond Sebond") and is as long as Bacon's whole volume. The greatest of Bacon's essays, "Of the True Greatness of Kingdoms and Estates," advances ten compressed counsels for building a republican empire. This is a naval and economic variation on **Machiavelli**'s plan for a warlike and imperial republic; several examples come straight from *I discorsi* (1531; *Discourses on Livy*). While Montaigne concentrated on inducing skepticism about the old other-worldly faith and learning, reminding the reader of natural pleasures, Bacon could also offer a rival object of belief, a new project of security through a this-worldly nation-state. The *Essayes* are disciplined by such a plan, and by being one building block in a whole vision of progress, scientific and technological as well as economic and political.

Given the modified Machiavellianism in the content of the *Essayes*, one must wonder whether there is also a link in form, a relation between a Baconian essay and a Machiavellian "discourse." Bacon writes of speech as "discourse," and the discussions are colored by a Machiavellian concentration on efficacy: on force and fraud in literary "transmission." Still, Bacon's essays are more compressed and less apparently wandering than Machiavelli's discourses, forego the stalking horse of ancient Rome, and thematically address civil, moral, and religious topics. In their focus they resemble Seneca's *Moral Epistles to Lucilius*, which Bacon once mentions as an "ancient" precedent. But Bacon transforms the precedent. Seneca's 124 compositions had little to do with politics and demonstrated little confidence in political reform. They meditate on the inevitable trials of life (e.g. "On the Futility of Planning Ahead") and exhort to moral restraint and a philosophic life. Bacon's essays are more devious; they follow Machiavelli's *Il principe* (wr. 1513, pub. 1532; *The Prince*) and the *Discourses* in replacing morality with modes of worldly success and meditation with comprehensive planning. Such considerations also dispose of the suggestion that a Baconian essay is like a Platonic dialogue. Bacon disdains Socrates' dialectical winnowing of opinions, as if one could get to wisdom through words rather than through managing forces. In "Of Seeming Wisdom," Bacon identifies dialectic with a wordy pretentiousness that plays with mere seemings and is "the bane of business."

What the essay is, and why Bacon favors it, is clarified in the formulations of literary theory in *Advancement of Learning* (1605) and its Latin version, *De augmentis* (1623). Both recommend sharp "fragments," rather than methodical or "magistral" texts, especially when attempting to change belief rather than confirm it. Pungent writings provoke the sharp and conceal from the dull. Being short and seminal, they encourage one's "initiative" in reconsidering "the roots of knowledge" and in progressing for oneself. But being "enigmatical," they baffle "vulgar capacities"; they reserve a teaching for "wits of such sharpness as can pierce the veil." The brief writing Bacon discusses is not the essay but the clipped sentence called the **aphorism**: "short and scattered sentences not linked together by an artificial method." A Baconian aphorism catches an observation at the core of matters. It catches especially the cause of an important effect. For example: "He that has Wife and Children, hath given Hostage to Fortune, for they are Impediments to great enterprises, either of Virtue, or Mischief" ("Of Marriage and Single Life"). The aphorism is the ammunition of the Baconian essay. The first essays of 1597 were like machine-gun fire, hardly more than staccato collections of these "dispersed directions" for pursuing one's interests.

The developed Baconian essay is typically fattened. Bland, often dense with lists, it oozes quotation and authority. This style seems both to baffle the lazy and to exhibit the politic sugar-coating recommended in *De augmentis*: introduce "knowledge which is new" with a gloss of the familiar, "with similitudes and comparisons." Govern speech by policy, and therefore with a view to obstacles in the way. This explains many of the apparently traditional doctrines in the developed essays and also the disorderly interspersing of replies to predictable objections. A typical Baconian essay starts with principles that sound like religious or moral orthodoxies and then suppresses or transforms these by degrees until they are replaced. The more closely one follows the precise terms of an argument, and its successive reformulations, qualifications, and manipulation of authorities, the more clearly a direction appears. For example, "Of Riches" begins by treating "riches" in a rather Aristotelian way, as merely "the baggage of virtue." But it jogs quickly to liberate wealth-getting from moral limit, and by the end elaborates the modes of multiplying "riches exceedingly" with only prudential limits. By adopting a disorderly receptivity to other views, one can provoke, guide, and lead – and the more effectively as one's control is hidden. One can "lead the dance" ("Of Discourse"). Dancing with the opinions dear to others, Bacon turns traditional opinions toward enlightened opinions, doing so more effectively by disguising the transformation and the direction beneath the disorder. D'Alembert, in the "Preliminary Discourse" to the *Encyclopédie*, caught this art. The great Bacon used "subdivisions fashionable in his time," even "scholastic principles," for, despite "the most rigorous precision" of style, he was "too wise to astonish anyone." Hence he and his followers could "prepare from afar the light which gradually, by imperceptible degrees, would illuminate the world."

Perhaps one could show that the *Essayes* as a whole develops like each essay, that is, from undermining the old ways of Christian Europe to establishing enlightened new ways. It moves from corrosion of the most authoritative pieties, at its beginning ("Of Truth," "Of Death," "Of Unity of Religion"), to the production of a new-model, progressive nation-state and of the priority of self-preservation, in its middle ("Of the True Greatness of Kingdoms and Estates," "Of Regiment of Health"), to intimations of a new-model progressive civilization, at its end ("Of Vicissitude of Things"). There seem to be four stages. The first essays (nos. 1–19) chiefly commit sedition on morality, religion, and the established hierarchy of estates, church, and king. Insofar as innovations are proposed, such as the priority of one's own rising to great place and the priority of economic development, they borrow a traditional surface, such as duty and the priority of repulsing sedition. The second stage (20–29) tutors those under cover but consciously rising in the new politics. Counselors who seem to advance the business of kingdoms and estates can promote their own place in an expanding and rather republican nation-state. The third stage (30–46) concentrates on what is in the new project for individuals, especially rising individuals, and becomes more open in unveiling the corresponding possibilities of a rather self-regulating civil society based on mutual utility. Moral attitudes are recast as personal incentives, channeled to attract planters of economic colonies, entrepreneurs, investors, and financiers. The final stage (47–58) shows how a superior prince provides honors and other incentives for his superior followers, such as counselors and judges who will introduce the new state of things. In turn, such enlightened public figures will help raise a founding leader to the "sovereign honor" – the dominating fame – for which he is ambitious.

The *Essayes* is a plan for civil nations and civil states, of a kind that will support the scientific civilization that Bacon also proposes. It supplements Bacon's other political works, such as his models of a state-builder (*The History of the Reign of Henry VII*, 1622) and of a humane but autonomous scientific-technological establishment (*New Atlantis*, 1626). The Baconian essay is a literary formula used to spread the new teachings to rising entrepreneurs and politicians, just as the form of political history appeals to founders and ministers of states, and that of a future-oriented scientific utopia, to visionary intellectuals.

ROBERT K. FAULKNER

Biography
Born 22 January 1561 in London. Studied at Trinity College, Cambridge, 1573–76; Gray's Inn, London, 1576, 1579–82; admitted to the bar, 1582. Attaché to Ambassador Sir Amias Paulet, British Embassy, Paris, 1576–79. Member of Parliament for Melcombe Regis, Dorset, 1584, Taunton, 1586, Liverpool, 1589, Middlesex, 1593, Southampton, 1597, Ipswich, 1604, and Cambridge University, 1614. Bencher, 1586, Lent reader, 1588, and double reader, 1600, Gray's Inn; member of a committee of lawyers appointed to review statutes, 1588. Patronized by the Earl of Essex, from 1591, but took part in treason trial against him, 1601; queen's counsel extraordinary, 1595–1603, and king's counsel, from 1604; commissioner for the union of Scotland and England, 1603. Knighted, 1603. Married Alice Barnham, 1606. Solicitor general, 1607–13; attorney general, 1613–17; member of the Privy Council, 1616; lord keeper of the great seal, 1617–18; lord chancellor, 1618. Created Baron Verulam, and admitted to the House of Lords, 1618. Accused of bribery, found guilty by the House of Lords, and stripped of offices, fined, and temporarily imprisoned, 1621; later pardoned by the king. Created Viscount St. Albans, 1621. Died in Highgate, London, 9 April 1626.

Selected Writings

Essays and Related Prose
Essayes, 1597; revised, enlarged editions, as *Essaies*, 1612, and as *The Essayes or Counsels, Civill and Morall*, 1625; many critical editions, including those edited by Michael J. Hawkins (Everyman Edition), 1973, Michael Kiernan, 1985, and John Pitcher, 1985
Francis Bacon (selections), edited by Brian Vickers, 1996

Other writings: longer works on history, law, science, religion, and politics, especially *Novum organum* (1620), which sets forth the experimental method of useful knowledge, *The Advancement of Learning* (1605), which recasts all learning, and the fable *New Atlantis* (1626).

Collected works edition: *Works* (including life and letters), edited by James Spedding, R. L. Ellis, and D. D. Heath, 14 vols., 1857–74, reprinted 1968.

Bibliography
Gibson, Reginald W., *Francis Bacon: A Bibliography of His Works and of Baconiana to the Year 1750*, Oxford: Scrivener Press, 1950; supplement privately printed, 1959

Further Reading
Adolph, Robert, *The Rise of Modern Prose Style*, Cambridge, Massachusetts: MIT Press, 1968: Chapter 2
Cochrane, Rexmond C., "Francis Bacon and the Architecture of Fortune," *Studies in the Renaissance* 5 (1958): 176–95
Crane, R. S., "The Relation of Bacon's *Essayes* to His Program for the Advancement of Learning," in *Schelling Anniversary Papers*, New York: Century, 1923
Engel, William E., "Aphorism, Anecdote, and Anamnesis in Montaigne and Bacon," *Montaigne Studies* 1 (November 1989): 158–76
Faulkner, Robert K., "The Art of Enlightenment," in his *Francis Bacon and the Project of Progress*, Lanham, Maryland: Rowman and Littlefield, 1993: Chapter 2
Fish, Stanley, "Georgics of the Mind: The Experience of Bacon's *Essayes*," in his *Self-Consuming Artifacts: The Experience of Seventeenth-Century Literature*, Berkeley: University of California Press, 1972
Fuller, Jean Overton, *Sir Francis Bacon*, Maidstone, Kent: George Mann Books, revised edition, 1994 (original edition, 1981)
Good, Graham, "Bacon: Ramifications of Counsel," in his *The Observing Self: Rediscovering the Essay*, London and New York: Routledge, 1988: 43–54
Green, A. Wigfall, *Sir Francis Bacon*, New York: Twayne, 1966
Hall, Joan Wylie, "Bacon's Triple Curative: The 1597 Essayes, Meditations, and Places," *Papers on Language and Literature* 21, no. 4 (Fall 1985): 345–58
Jardine, Lisa, *Francis Bacon: Discovery and the Art of Discourse*, Cambridge: Cambridge University Press, 1974
Kiernan, Michael, General Introduction and Textual Introduction to *The Essayes* by Bacon, Oxford: Clarendon Press, 1985
Knights, L. C., "Bacon and the Seventeenth-Century Dissociation of Sensibility," *Scrutiny* 11 (1943): 268–85
Levy, F. J., "Francis Bacon and the Style of Politics," *English Literary Renaissance* 16, no. 1 (Winter 1986): 101–22
Mazzeo, Joseph, *Renaissance and Revolution: The Remaking of European Thought*, New York: Pantheon, and London: Secker and Warburg, 1965: Chapter 4
Vickers, Brian, editor, *Essential Articles for the Study of Francis Bacon*, Hamden, Connecticut: Archon, 1968; London: Sidgwick and Jackson, 1972
Vickers, Brian, *Francis Bacon and Renaissance Prose*, Cambridge: Cambridge University Press, 1968

Baldwin, James
American, 1924–1987

For more than three decades beginning in the mid-1950s, James Baldwin was one of the most prominent and prolific writers on race and identity in the United States. Delving into almost every genre, he wrote six novels, three plays, a children's storybook, a book of short stories, a book of poetry, and more than 100 essays. Beginning with a **review** of a **Maksim Gor'kii** book in the *Nation* in 1947, his reviews, critiques, memoirs, and open **letters** were published extensively in some of the best-known publications, including *New Leader*, *Freedomways*, *Commentary*, **Harper's**, *Mademoiselle*, **Partisan Review**, **Atlantic Monthly**, *Saturday Review*, *Playboy*, *Esquire*, and the *New York Times*. Topics included his views on literature, film, history, children, and a host of prominent and not-so-prominent individuals, always infused with the issue of race. For Baldwin the essay was a weapon for change. His reports on the civil rights activities of the 1960s provided a definitive analysis of its progress and made him an enemy of the state: James Campbell writes in *Talking at the Gates* (1991) that the U.S. Federal Bureau of Investigation alone accumulated a 1750-page file on him.

Baldwin's nonfiction is often defined by the autobiographical template he seems unable to escape. In the midst of flowing, poetic prose, he is apt to digress to his life in Harlem, Paris, or elsewhere. Such asides frequently relate the story of his strict Protestant upbringing, of being told by his cruel, minister stepfather – and believing – that he is ugly. This story also includes accounts of his early sexual ambiguities; his brief career as a teenage minister; his determination against all odds to become a writer; his numerous, dangerous encounters with policemen, bar owners, and restaurateurs; and the constant rage that engulfed him – that could ultimately have led to his death – causing him to flee to Paris in 1948.

Stylistically his essays are defined by two elements. The first is a rolling, sometimes convoluted (almost stream-of-consciousness) language, whose rhythms and imagery are born of the fire-and-brimstone sermons of the African American Protestant church. This is seen in what many believe to be his greatest work, *The Fire Next Time* (1963), when he writes: "... this urgency of American Negroes is *not to be forgotten!* As they watch black men elsewhere rise, the promise held out, at last, that they may walk the earth with the authority with which white men walk, protected by the power that white men shall have no longer, is enough, and more than enough, to empty prisons and pull God down from Heaven." Many of the titles of his nonfiction also bear witness to his reliance on religious themes and symbols: *The Fire Next Time* (biblical slave song), *No Name in the Street* (Job), *The Devil Finds Work* (a religious homily), *The Evidence of Things Not Seen* (St. Paul). The second, more subtle element is his bitingly sardonic, blues-inspired commentary, as in the streetwise metaphor he gives his last collection: *The Price of the Ticket* (1985). And in *The Evidence of Things Not Seen* (1985), he deconstructs the mythology of U.S. capitalism and its relationship to the slave auction: "*Honest toil and the magic of the marketplace* sums up Black American history with a terrifying precision, and is the key to our continuing dilemma. Our first sight of America was this marketplace and our legal existence, here, begins with the signature on the bill of sale."

Early in his career, as he painfully worked on his first novel, Baldwin earned a reputation as a literary critic of some merit, publishing exclusively in the *Nation*, *Commentary*, and *New Leader* from 1947 to 1949. He was also heralded as the next Richard Wright, an African American novelist and social commentator who befriended him and whom he idolized, but from whom he would later become deeply estranged. Both he and Wright were viewed as "protest" writers because of their persistent criticism of the legacy of racism that they perceived in the United States and Europe, but Baldwin eschewed "protest" as a shallow and futile goal. The role of the artist, he said, "is to illuminate that darkness, blaze roads through that vast forest, so that we will not, in all our doing, lose sight of its purpose, which is after all, to make the world a more human dwelling place" ("The Creative Process," 1962).

Baldwin's fiction was much influenced by Wright's masterwork novel, *Native Son* (1940), which was heralded as the quintessential **treatise** on the psyche of the black American.

For Baldwin, Wright, who mentored the young writer, represented a kind of literary father figure. Yet in much the same way that Baldwin had undermined his minister stepfather's power over him by outdoing him as a teenage minister, he usurped Wright with devastatingly critical analyses of his novel. The first of these criticisms ("Everybody's Protest Novel") was published by a short-lived French publication, *Zéro* (Spring 1949), and subsequently republished in *Partisan Review* (June 1949). Two years later, as a split developed between Baldwin and Wright, Baldwin would insure the schism with a thorough, accurate, but unflattering critique of *Native Son* in "Many Thousands Gone" (*Partisan Review*, November/December 1951). *Native Son*, Baldwin says, is unquestionably "the most powerful and celebrated statement we have yet had of what it means to be a Negro in America." But, he opined, it is incomplete: "... though we follow [the anti-hero Bigger Thomas] step by step from the tenement room to the death cell, we know as little about him when his journey is ended as we did when it began; and what is even more remarkable, we know almost as little about the social dynamic which we are to believe created him." For Baldwin, therefore, Bigger Thomas "does not redeem the pains of a despised people, but reveals, on the contrary, nothing more than his own fierce bitterness at having been born one of them."

Though Baldwin's world view is frequently expressed in biting commentary, it is always tempered, paradoxically, with an urgent cry for blacks and whites to come together, in love, to liberate themselves from a history of racism. And his philosophical view of race remains constant throughout his career. Simply put, Baldwin believed that Europeans came to the New World as nationalities, but quickly became "white" as they unified in ritualistic violence, murdered the peoples they found there, and imported African slaves. In their attempt to deny the reality and horrors of the Native American and African "holocaust[s]," whites have trapped themselves in a mythological history that will not allow them to be rid of the guilt and shame of their actions. "Americans passionately believe in their avowed ideals, amorphous as they are, and are terrified of waking from a radiant dream," he writes in "Lockridge: 'The American Myth'" (*The New Leader*, 10 April 1948), a critique of Ross Lockridge's *Raintree County*. Almost four decades later, in an open letter to South African Bishop Desmond Tutu in the *Los Angeles Times* (21 January 1986), he says, "The wealth of England and my country, the wealth of the Western world, in short, is based on slave labor, and the intolerable guilt thus engendered in hearts and minds of the Civilized is the root of what we call racism."

A consequence of this falsified American history is that "[It] has allowed white people, with scarcely any pangs of conscience whatever, to *create*, in every generation, only the Negro they wished to see" ("A Fly in Buttermilk," 1958). Blacks, on the other hand, are expected to believe the lie, or, under pain of death (by vigilantes, policemen, or the state), at least to *act* as if they believe it. The price of such delusion – *The Price of the Ticket* he calls it in the title essay of his collected nonfiction – is, for blacks, self-hatred, or rebellion, or both. For the white American, the price is "to become white ... nothing less," and to continue to live with the guilt. To illustrate the paradoxical nature of this "conundrum," he repeats, in scores of essays, some form of the dialectical paradigm: "... by means of what the white man imagines the black man to be, the black man is enabled to know who the white man is" ("Stranger in the Village," 1953). Or, conversely, "... if I am not what I've been told I am, then it means that *you're* not what you thought you were either!" ("A Talk to Teachers," 1963).

The resolution of this demented game falls heavily on African Americans in a kind of distorted, redemptive process that mirrored the 1960s civil rights movement, in which Baldwin became actively involved as a writer, interpreter, and demonstrator. For example, in August 1965 he writes: "... one enters into battle with that historical creation, Oneself, and attempts to recreate oneself according to a principle more humane and more liberating; one begins the attempt to achieve a level of personal maturity and freedom which robs history of its tyrannical power, and also changes history" ("White Man's Guilt"). But, he is always careful to add, this cathartic confrontation must be accomplished with love: "And if the word *integration* means anything, this is what it means: that we, with love, shall force our brothers to see themselves as they are, to cease fleeing from reality and begin to change it" (*The Fire Next Time*).

Baldwin's timely explanation of the imperative of nonviolent struggle made him the darling of the mainstream media of the 1960s. Though he sometimes published in African American publications such as *Ebony* and *Freedomways*, he wrote almost exclusively to whites, pleading for liberals to get on board, change their ways, before it was too late. Again, in *The Fire Next Time*, he describes the profound effect of his visit with Elijah Muhammad, the Nation of Islam's black separatist leader. He notes the unerring logic that brings Mr. Muhammad to an indictment against whites as devils whose reign must end, probably in violence: "All my evidence would be thrown out of court as irrelevant to the main body of the case, for I could cite only exceptions. The South Side [of Chicago] proved the justice of the indictment; the state of the world proved the justice of the indictment." Still, Baldwin concludes, "one has no choice but to do all in one's power to change that fate, and at no matter what risk – eviction, imprisonment, torture, death. For the sake of one's children, in order to minimize the bill that *they* must pay, one must be careful not to take refuge in any delusion – and the value placed on the color of the skin is always and everywhere and forever a delusion." Finally, he warns his reader in the last words of the book: "If we do not now dare everything, the fulfillment of that prophecy, recreated from the Bible in song by a slave, is upon us: *God gave Noah the rainbow sign, No more water, the fire next time!*"

After the assassination of Martin Luther King, Jr. in 1968, when many African Americans had turned away from the civil rights movement and toward more militant strategies, Baldwin began to acknowledge the possibility of some inevitable, cataclysmic confrontation between the races. Though he still clung to his basic notion about the need for love and change, *No Name in the Street* (1972) ends with a hint that he might have come to the end of his rope: "... it is terrible to watch people cling to their captivity and insist on their own destruction. I think black people have always felt this about America, and Americans, and have always seen, spinning above the thoughtless American head, the shape of the wrath to come."

Some optimism would later return, particularly with the changes he witnessed with the appointment and election of African Americans in the political arena. But the slow progress made in South Africa against apartheid and his investigation of a series of child murders in Atlanta (*The Evidence of Things Not Seen*, 1985) kept alive the Baldwinian paradox, which he himself identifies, less than two years before his death, in his 1986 letter to Bishop Tutu: "I am sure that you believe, with me, this paradox: Black freedom will make white freedom possible. Indeed, our freedom, which we have been forced to buy at so high a price, is the only hope of freedom that they have."

HARRY AMANA

Biography

James Arthur Baldwin. Born 2 August 1924 in New York City. Studied at Public School 134, Harlem, New York, and DeWitt Clinton High School, Bronx, New York, graduated 1942. Briefly a storefront preacher in Harlem during adolescence; worked at various odd jobs in New York, and in defense work, Belle Meade, New Jersey, early 1940s. Lived primarily in Europe (mainly Paris and Istanbul), from 1948, making frequent trips to the U.S. Contributor to many journals and magazines, including the *Partisan Review*, *New Yorker*, *Atlantic Monthly*, *Freedomways*, *New Leader*, *Esquire*, *Ebony*, and the *Nation*. Awards: several, including four fellowships; American Academy Award, 1956; George Polk Award, for magazine articles, 1963; Foreign Drama Critics Award, 1964; Martin Luther King, Jr. Award, 1978; honorary degree from the University of British Columbia. Member of the American Academy, 1964; Commander, Legion of Honor (France), 1986. Died (of stomach cancer) in St. Paul de Vence, France, 30 November 1987.

Selected Writings

Essays and Related Prose
Notes of a Native Son, 1955
Nobody Knows My Name: More Notes of a Native Son, 1961
The Fire Next Time, 1963
No Name in the Street, 1972
The Devil Finds Work, 1976
The Evidence of Things Not Seen, 1985
The Price of the Ticket: Collected Nonfiction, 1948–1985, 1985

Other writings: six novels (*Go Tell It on the Mountain*, 1953; *Giovanni's Room*, 1956; *Another Country*, 1962; *Tell Me How Long the Train's Been Gone*, 1968; *If Beale Street Could Talk*, 1974; *Just Above My Head*, 1979), the collection of short stories *Going to Meet the Man* (1965), three plays, and poetry.

Bibliographies
Fischer, Russell G., "James Baldwin: A Bibliography 1947–1962," *Bulletin of Bibliography* (January–April 1965): 127–30
Kindt, Kathleen A., "James Baldwin: A Checklist 1947–1962," *Bulletin of Bibliography* (January–April 1965): 123–26
Standley, Fred L., and Nancy Standley, *James Baldwin: A Reference Guide*, Boston: Hall, 1980

Further Reading
Bloom, Harold, editor, *James Baldwin*, New York: Chelsea House, 1986
Campbell, James, *Talking at the Gates: A Life of James Baldwin*, London: Faber, and New York: Viking, 1991

Cunningham, James, "Public and Private Rhetorical Modes in the Essays of James Baldwin," in *Essays on the Essay: Redefining the Genre*, edited by Alexander J. Butrym, Athens: University of Georgia Press, 1989

Dailey, Peter, "Jimmy (The Life of Writer James Baldwin)," *American Scholar* 62, no. 1 (Winter 1994): 102–11

Early, Gerald, "James Baldwin's Neglected Essay: Prizefighting, the White Intellectual and the Racial Symbols of American Culture," *Antaeus* 62 (Spring 1989): 150–65

Eckman, Fern Marja, *The Furious Passage of James Baldwin*, New York: Evans, and London: Michael Joseph, 1966

Gates, Henry Louis, Jr., "The Fire Last Time: What James Baldwin Can and Can't Teach America," *New Republic*, 1 June 1992: 37–43

Jothiprakash, R., *Commitment as a Theme in African American Literature: A Study of James Baldwin and Ralph Ellison*, Bristol, Indiana: Wyndham Hall, 1994

Kinnamon, Keneth, editor, *James Baldwin: A Collection of Critical Essays*, Englewood Cliffs, New Jersey: Prentice Hall, 1974

Leeming, David, *James Baldwin: A Biography*, New York: Knopf, and London: Michael Joseph, 1994

Lester, Julius, "Academic Freedom and the Black Intellectual," *Black Scholar* 19, no. 6 (November–December 1988): 16–27

Macebuh, Stanley, *James Baldwin: A Critical Study*, New York: Third Press, 1973

Möller, Karin, *The Theme of Identity in the Essays of James Baldwin: An Interpretation*, Gothenburg: Acta Universitatis Gothoburgensis, 1975

Porter, Horace A., *Stealing the Fire: The Art and Protest of James Baldwin*, Middletown, Connecticut: Wesleyan University Press, 1989

Pratt, Louis H., *James Baldwin*, Boston: Twayne, 1978

Ro, Sigmund, *Rage and Celebration: Essays on Contemporary Afro-American Writing*, Atlantic Highlands, New Jersey: Humanities Press, 1984

Standley, Fred L., and Nancy V. Burt, *Critical Essays on James Baldwin*, Boston: Hall, 1988

Sylvander, Carolyn Wedin, *James Baldwin*, New York: Ungar, 1980

Troupe, Quincy, editor, *James Baldwin: The Legacy*, New York: Simon and Schuster, 1989

Waldrep, Shelton, "'Being Bridges': Cleaver/Baldwin/Lorde and African-American Sexism and Sexuality," *Journal of Homosexuality* 26, nos. 2–3 (August–September 1993): 167–80

Weatherby, W. J., *James Baldwin, Artist on Fire: A Portrait*, New York: Fine, and London: Michael Joseph, 1989

Wedin, Carolyn, "James Baldwin: Out of the Amen Corner," *Christian Century*, 16 November 1988: 1042–47

Balzac, Jean-Louis Guez de

French, 1597–1654

Jean-Louis Guez de Balzac's production as an essayist spans his literary lifetime. Reflections on politics, literature, religion, and manners are found in all of his writings: **letters**, **treatises** (e.g. *Le Prince* [1631; *The Prince*]), discourses (e.g. *La Harangue célèbre faite à la Reyne sur sa Régence* [1641; The famous harangue made to the Queen on her Regency]). It was especially in his letters that his readers found his judgments most compelling, and it is because of the correspondence that literary historians have acknowledged Balzac as a definitive master of French prose. In the first half of the 17th century, he demonstrated to members of the literary and privileged social milieux how to write eloquent, forceful, and pleasing French.

Balzac's letters launched his literary career. From the beginning, his letters circulated in aristocratic homes and salons, where they were avidly read. They provoked admiration (Richelieu early encouraged Balzac to continue in this vein) and quarrels, for Balzac ridiculed the authority of the entrenched humanists at the Sorbonne. His criticism of pedantry constituted one of the first outbreaks of the Battle of the Ancients and the Moderns, destined to rage in the 1680s. The success and notoriety of his letters prompted Balzac to publish collections of them, the most famous being the *Premières lettres* (First letters) of 1624 and 1627. Letters appeared in diverse publications throughout his lifetime, and before the end of his life, Balzac had been preparing a new collection, published posthumously as *Les Entretiens* (1657; The conversations).

Balzac spent most of his adult life in solitary retirement in the countryside of the Charente, nursing a frail body, removed from the exhausting Parisian circles, and writing letters to influential men of politics, to literary friends and foes, and to intimates. He hoped that the success of these letters would earn him a brilliant position, where he could make a life for himself. In hindsight, it seems clear that because *The Prince* (Balzac's apology for Richelieu and Louis XIII's political program for the French state) failed to clinch the Cardinal's patronage, Balzac's aspirations were not to be realized; he had been passed over. However, after the treatise's disappointing reception in 1631, Balzac continued to write, suggesting that he never really gave up hope for a brilliant appointment on the basis of his literary accomplishments.

That Balzac could attach the practical consequence of receiving a position of power to his literary endeavors is apparent from the contents and style of his letters and from the very choice of the letter as a literary medium in which to shine. As Jean Jehasse (1977) notes, the humanist Jesuits, who schooled Balzac, accorded great importance to the epistle, conceived of as a literary exercise and occasion for their pupils to prepare persuasive essays on manners, politics, or literature. The *hermite* of Charente, withdrawn from influential circles, selected this medium as the appropriate means to address topical concerns that would establish and advertise his stand on issues pertinent to his readers – both the specific addressees and their milieux – as well as reveal his commitments and loyalties. In his letters to Richelieu and to other figures of political power he promotes the value of public service and supports the authority of the State grounded in the centralized monarchy, which requires good ministers and subordinate nobles. His correspondence with other men of letters (who were more often to become his addressees as Balzac's hopes for a worthy appointment receded) situates him in the camp of the Moderns. He rejects the humanists' blind acknowledgment of the superiority of the Ancients and pedantic criticism of writing that does not strictly conform to classical models. Insisting on the superiority of judgment and of reason over unquestioning imitation, Balzac defends the educated person's power to assess reality and to act appropriately based on practiced judgment.

However, as an advocate of trained discernment, Balzac appreciates only too well the literary power of the Ancients, who indeed were capable of great writing because they exercised their judgment and aesthetic sense. Despite siding with the Moderns, he owes a debt to the Ancients, and his works testify to it throughout. Balzac sought to emulate them, especially the Roman writers – **Cicero, Seneca**, Pliny – who took upon themselves the hortatory roles of counselors to the powerful or judges of the state of human affairs. Balzac as a correspondent readily saw himself as an adviser. He set himself the task of persuading his readers about political and literary matters as effectively as possible in order to bring about appropriate thinking and behavior. In concert with the Ancients, he held this role to be a noble vocation, requiring untiring industry and continual polishing. This calling was also to serve as Balzac's ticket to immortality, as it had for the Ancients.

His letters, especially the *Premières lettres*, strike the modern reader as florid. His reasoning, though cogent, resides in an abundant display of classical rhetoric – images, antitheses, enumerations, crafted transitions – which calls attention to the artistry of the writing and implicitly, to the writer's talent. However, since these flourishes – learned from Roman oratory – are couched in letters, which naturally include direct address, compliments, and personal observations, the form relieves the weight of the pervasive Ciceronian style. The topical issues are necessarily brief, because of the conventions of the epistolary genre, but they were considered well-written because of their style. This balance of brevity and style, which satisfied the mind and aesthetic sensibility of his readers while not taxing them, made for a rewarding experience, to which the enthusiasm of Balzac's audience testifies. This correspondence became an ideal of intelligent discourse directed toward a cultivated though not necessarily learned readership (which included women). Thus, Balzac's letters contributed to the creation of *l'honnêteté*, an urbane, sophisticated, and elevated comportment, developed in aristocratic salons during Balzac's lifetime and designed to govern the intellectual, moral, and social life of the elite, giving it meaning and beauty. Balzac demonstrated, then, how to write a cultured and persuasive French.

PAMELA PARK

Biography
Born probably May 1597 (baptized 1 June 1597) in Angoulême. Studied at Jesuit colleges in Angoulême and Poitiers; Collège de la Marche, Paris, 1610; enrolled at the University of Leiden, 1615; returned to Paris, c. 1616. Secretary to the Duke of Epernon and one of his sons; aided in the rescue of Marie de Medicis from prison at Blois, 1619; agent to Cardinal de la Valette, Rome, 1620–22; appointed historiographer of France, from 1624; visited Paris, 1624–25, 1626–28. Lived mostly in Angoulême, from 1628. Elected to the French Academy, 1634. Died (after a long illness) in Angoulême, 18 February 1654.

Selected Writings

Essays and Related Prose
Lettres, 1624; revised edition, 1627; as *Les Premières Lettres (1618–1627)*, edited by H. Bibas and K. T. Butler, 2 vols., 1933–34
The Letters of Monsieur de Balzac, translated by W. Tirwhyt, vol. 1, 1634; vols. 2 and 3, as *New Epistles by Monsieur d'Balzac*, translated by Richard Baker, 1638; vol. 4, as *A Collection of Some Modern Epistles of Monsieur De Balzac*, translated anonymously, 1639; in 1 vol., 1654

Lettres, seconde partie, 2 vols., 1636
Recueil de nouvelles lettres, 1637
Œuvres diverses, 1644
Lettres choisies, 2 vols., 1647
Lettres familières à M. Chapelain, 1656; as *Lettres inédites à J. Chapelain*, edited by Tamizey de Larroque, 1873
Lettres diverses, 1657
Les Entretiens, 1657; edited by Bernard Beugnot, 2 vols., 1972
Lettres à M. Conrart, 1659

Other writings: books on political and moral philosophy (including *Le Prince* [The Prince], 1631; *Le Socrate chrétien*, 1652; *Aristippe* [Aristippus], 1658).

Collected works edition: *Les Œuvres de Monsieur de Balzac*, 2 vols., 1665.

Bibliography
Beugnot, Bernard, *Guez de Balzac: Bibliographie générale*, Montreal: Presses de l'Université de Montréal, 1967; supplement, 1969

Further Reading
Carr, Thomas M., Jr., *Descartes and the Resilience of Rhetoric: Varieties of Cartesian Rhetorical Theory*, Carbondale: Southern Illinois University Press, 1990
Guillaumie, Gaston, *Jean-Louis Guez de Balzac et la prose française*, Paris: Picard, 1927
Jehasse, Jean, *Guez de Balzac et le génie romain, 1597–1645*, Saint-Étienne: Université de Saint-Étienne, 1977
Sabrie, Jean Baptiste, *Les Idées religieuses de J.-L. Guez de Balzac*, Paris: Alcan, 1913
Sutcliffe, Frank E., *Guez de Balzac et son temps: Littérature et politique*, Paris: Nizet, 1959
Winter, John Francis, *A Seventeenth-Century Concept of the Individual and Society: Guez de Balzac* (dissertation), Princeton, New Jersey: Princeton University, 1950
Youssef, Zobeidah, *Polémique et littérature chez Guez de Balzac*, Paris: Nizet, 1972
Zuber, Roger, *Les "Belles Infidèles" et la formation du goût classique: Perrot d'Ablancourt et Guez de Balzac*, Paris: Colin, 1968

Barańczak, Stanisław
Polish, 1946–

Stanisław Barańczak belongs to the so-called "Generation of '68" (after the student protests in 1968) in Polish literature, whose main discoveries were, as he himself put it (in an interview for *Na Głos* [Aloud], 1991), that in the age of collective values imposed by communism, "the attempt to save or to defend one's individuality and one's right to be an individual is a most subversive act of public significance"; that Marxism cannot be "revised" or improved; and that censorship renders cultural authenticity impossible. When martial law was introduced in Poland in 1981, Barańczak was a visiting professor of literature at Harvard University and he remained there as a full professor, joining the group of prominent Polish writers in exile. Although living in the United States, Barańczak is very much a presence on the Polish literary market with his poetry, essays, and translations.

Barańczak is a "translator" in both the metaphoric and the literal meanings of this term – a mediator between different spheres of life and literature, between English and Polish literature, and between East European experience and the West. He has published 12 volumes of poetry in which the political and the metaphysical coexist, 12 books of essays and literary criticism, translations of 12 Shakespeare plays, and numerous collections of English, American, and Russian poetry in translation.

Barańczak's most representative collections of essays – *Etyka i poetyka* (1979; Ethics and poetics), and *Breathing Under Water and Other East European Essays* (1990) – show his mediative talent in its full lucidity. The author's reflections on the likenesses, analogies, and contrasts between ethics and poetics involve the works of **Thomas Mann**, Dietrich Bonhoeffer, **Osip Mandel'shtam**, **Joseph Brodsky**, **Czesław Miłosz**, and **Zbigniew Herbert**, but also minor works of contemporary Polish authors. In the essay "Zmieniony głos Settembriniego" (1975; The changed voice of Settembrini) Barańczak discusses the possible foundations of a new ethics that is not supported by an irrational authority: in the world without God, any authoritative ethics would be pernicious; the only possible ethical measure is "the other man," hence everyone is individually responsible for his deeds and has to make his own choice. Poetry has a special mission in this new situation: not only must it adopt some of the traditional functions of the humanistic sciences – that is, as the vehicle of socially important ideas – it must also control the consequences of vague slogans and remote goals introduced into society by ideological dogma. Barańczak believes that poetry, with its inclination toward the concrete, demonstrates how those slogans are fulfilled and by what means the goals of the ideologies are pursued. The dogma, which sets to work on the media, uses methods designed for subliminal persuasion and manipulation of the masses; poetry, on the contrary, rescues man from the automatism of his thinking and speaking – "it teaches him to think, to speak, and to act on his own and therefore responsibly." This new social mission of poetry, however, is not supposed to humble it to the level of the so-called mass audience. To be socially useful, poetry should rather try to uplift the reader ("Uwagi krótkowidza" [1972; Remarks of a short-sighted person]). Barańczak is to a great extent optimistic about the future of the new ethics without authorities. Thus, in "Notatki na marginesach Bonhoeffera" (1974; Notes on the margins of Bonhoeffer), he writes that it is not necessary for the Ten Commandments to disappear with the decline of Christianity. Pure atheism, he notes, reflecting Miłosz, is an unbearable burden; most people who simply want to "be good" feel obliged by Christian ethics even if they have no access to Revelation ("Summa Czesława Miłosza" [1978; The *summa* of Czesław Miłosz]).

In order to pursue its ethical tasks, literature must be born of doubt and creative disagreement, and awaken these in the reader. This seems to be Barańczak's main criterion as a literary critic in *Nieufni i zadufani* (1971; The diffident and the proud), *Ironia i harmonia* (1973; Irony and harmony), *Etyka i poetyka*, *Książki najgorsze* (1981, enlarged edition, 1990; The worst books), and *Przed i po* (1988; Before and after). Other indispensable qualities of good literature and especially of poetry, according to Barańczak, are the uniqueness of the individual poetic language (a theme explored in his study *Język poetycki Mirona Białoszewskiego* [1974; The poetic language of Miron Białoszewski] and summarized in the essay "Proszę pokazać język" [1974; Show your tongue, please]), and the taste for paradox and irony. Zbigniew Herbert's poetry, to which Barańczak devoted his book *Uciekinier z utopii* (1984; *A Fugitive from Utopia*), can be seen both as a source of these criteria and as their incarnation.

After years of mediating between life and literature, in the U.S. Barańczak also became a mediator between the political and cultural idioms of the East and the West. His collection of essays *Breathing Under Water* was praised by critics as "an impressive contribution to bridge-building between separate cultures" (George Gömöri, 1992). According to the author's own confession (in an interview for *Dziennik Poznański*, 1991), it follows the stylistic formula of **George Orwell**'s essays: an "impossible" alloy of richness and simplicity, complexity and transparency The relation between ethics and poetics continues to be the main object of Barańczak's reflections, but now he concentrates, on the one hand, on great creative or public figures such as the 20th century's most important Polish writers, **Witold Gombrowicz**, Bruno Schulz, Alexander Wat, Czesław Miłosz, Miron Białoszewski, and Wisława Szymborska, as well as figures like Pope John Paul II, Lech Wałęsa, **Václav Havel**, Adam Michnik, and Miklós Haraszti; and, on the other hand, on the untranslatable phenomena of the communist era in East Europe, such as censorship, *samizdat* (underground publishing), and the "state artist." Once he has delineated America "under Eastern eyes," Barańczak distances himself from the Eastern European mind-set and thus manages, if not to "translate" the Eastern reality into the language of the West, at least to explain it convincingly and to abolish the myth that communism is not necessarily antagonistic to creativity. It is clear from *Breathing Under Water* that anything of value that has been created under communism was born despite it or against it.

Katia Mitova-Janowski

Biography

Born 13 November 1946 in Poznań. Studied at Adam Mickiewicz University, Poznań, 1964–69, M.A. in Polish literature, 1969, Ph.D., 1973. Married Anna Barańczak, 1968: one son and one daughter. Assistant professor, Adam Mickiewicz University, 1970–77: expelled for political reasons, but allowed to teach again, 1980–81; invited by Harvard University as a guest lecturer, 1977, but had to wait four years for an exit visa; associate professor, 1981–84, and professor in Polish literature, from 1984, Harvard University, Cambridge, Massachusetts. Active in the Polish human rights movement in the 1980s: one of the cofounders of KOR (Committee for the defense of workers, later renamed Committee for society's self-defense); editor of the underground literary quarterly *Zapis* (Record); blacklisted from 1975 for signing letters of protest; in 1983 the Polish consulate in New York refused to renew his passport and in effect exiled him. Awards: Kościelski Foundation Prize, 1973; Jurzykowski Prize, 1981; Terrence Des Pres Prize for Poetry, for *The Weight of the Body: Selected Poems*, 1989; Polish PEN Club Award, 1990.

Selected Writings

Essays and Related Prose

Nieufni i zadufani: Romantyzm i klasycyzm w młodej poezji lat sześćdziesiątych, 1971

Ironia i harmonia: Szkice o najnowszej literaturze polskiej, 1973

Język poetycki Mirona Białoszewskiego, 1974
Etyka i poetyka: Szkice 1970–1978, 1979
Książki najgorsze (1975–1980), 1981; enlarged edition, 1990
*Czytelnik ubezwłasnowolniony: Perswazja w masowej kulturze
    literackiej PRL,* 1983
Uciekinier z utopii: O poezji Zbigniewa Herberta, 1984; as *A
    Fugitive from Utopia: The Poetry of Zbigniew Herbert,* 1987
*Przed i po: Szkice o poezji krajowej przeło mu lat siedemdziesiątych
    i osiemdziesiątych,* 1988
*Tablica z Macondo: Osiem naście prób wytłumaczenia, po co i
    dlaczego się pisze,* 1990
Breathing Under Water and Other East European Essays, 1990
*Ocalone w tłumaczeniu: Szkice o warsztacie tłumacza poezji z
    dołączeniem małej antologii przekładów,* 1992
Zaufać nieufności: Osiem rozmów o sensie poezji, 1990–1992, 1993

Other writings: 12 volumes of poetry (including *Selected Poems:
The Weight of the Body,* 1989). Also edited anthologies of English
metaphysical poetry, English and American religious lyric, English
and American love poetry, and English and American poetry;
translated into English (with Clare Cavanagh) the poetry of
Wisława Szymborska (*View with a Grain of Sand,* 1995); translated
into Polish plays by Shakespeare, as well as poems by Dylan
Thomas, Osip Mandel'shtam, Joseph Brodsky, Gerard Manley
Hopkins, e. e. cummings, **John Donne,** Emily Dickinson, James
Merrill, Philip Larkin, Robert Frost, Robert Herrick, Andrew
Marvell, Thomas Hardy, and **W. H. Auden.**

Further Reading

Czerwinski, E. J., Review of *Breathing Under Water, World
    Literature Today* 65, no. 3 (1991): 512–13
Gildner, Gary, Review of *Breathing Under Water, Georgia Review*
    45, no. 1 (1991): 191–93
Gömöri, George, Review of *Breathing Under Water, Journal of
    European Studies* 22, no. 89 (1992): 288–89
Gross, Irena G., Review of *Czytelnik ubezwłasnowolniony, Slavic
    Review* 46, no. 1 (Spring 1987): 172–73
Stamirowska, Krystyna, Review of *Breathing Under Water, English
    Studies* 74, no. 4 (1993): 404–05
Taylor, Nina, Review of *A Fugitive from Utopia, Modern
    Languages Review* 84 (1989): 815–16
Zaczek, Barbara, Review of *A Fugitive from Utopia, Comparative
    Literature* 44, no.1 (1992): 108–10

Barthes, Roland

French, 1915–1980

Roland Barthes' intellectual course did not follow the traditional university path, due, among other things, to his recurrent health problems. Numerous relapses with tuberculosis
prevented him from carrying out his doctoral research: this
explains why he published more essays than substantial scientific studies. And because he was not attached to a particular
university faculty, he was able to diversify his interests. To
begin with, Barthes wanted to be a semiologist and analyze
different systems of signification as they are revealed in
language (*Le Degré zéro de l'écriture* [1953; *Writing Degree
Zero*]), everyday life (*Mythologies,* 1957), or clothes (*Système
de la mode* [1967; *The Fashion System*]). The introduction to
Writing Degree Zero specifies that we are reading an essay, in
both meanings of the term. It consists of an attempt, "an introduction to what could be a History of Writing," but also of
a marked commitment to an ideological concept of literature

perceived as value and as institution. Writing has always functioned as a sign, so much so that the act of writing was claimed
by the bourgeoisie as early as the 17th century. The utopia of
denotation must therefore be denounced and semiology, among
other things, embraced; hence the later editions of this first
essay are completed by the *Éléments de sémiologie* (1965;
Elements of Semiology). These two volumes supply the reader
with the necessary tools to decode, with the linguistic apparatus, the different discourses that make up the social field.

All signs are full of connotations; that is, they consist of
systems of second senses that are well marked ideologically,
allowing many signs to reach mythic status. These myths must
be exposed, insofar as social objects tend to portray the cultural
for the natural, to found common opinion in absolute truth.
In *Mythologies,* then, Barthes points out the mythical dimension of "the face of Garbo," "steak and chips," "the Tour de
France," or "the new Citroën," based on the two-level conno-
tative system analyzed in "Le Mythe, aujourd'hui" ("The Myth
Today"), the closing essay of the collection. In the same way,
he studies the clothing code in a structuralist manner in *The
Fashion System* by looking for the way this particular type of
sign possesses its rhetoric and its poetry. With this semiological approach, it is not surprising that Barthes is fascinated by
Japan and that the essay he dedicates to that country is entitled *L'Empire des signes* (1970; *Empire of Signs*). He considers
Japan as another system, and discovers the symbolic in calligraphy, clothes, food, and urban geography.

But Barthes cannot be reduced simply to a systematic semiologist. On the one hand, he quickly takes issue with those
who denounce the common opinion as a new totalitarian
system ("Changer l'objet lui-même" [1971; Changing the
object itself]); on the other hand, he continues to be fascinated
by the classic literary texts of Michelet, **Chateaubriand,** or
Proust. For a time he attempted to unite semiology and literature in an article that has become a classic, "Introduction à
l'analyse structurale des récits" (1966; "Introduction to the
Structural Analysis of Narratives"), where he again talks about
the heritage of Russian formalists to try to extract the elementary functions that make up any narrative. But he quickly
perceives that literary work cannot be reduced to a system.
Already, in his first literary essay, *Michelet par lui-même* (1954;
Michelet), he is more interested in reconstituting Michelet's
"organized network of obsessions" in a "pre-critique" that
clearly illustrates Barthes' own vocation as an essayist, than in
attempting to formalize Michelet's writing style. In *Essais
critiques* (1964; *Critical Essays*) and *Nouveaux essais critiques*
(1972; *New Critical Essays*), Barthes multiplies the "plural"
readings of authors as different as Brecht, La Fontaine, Robbe-
Grillet, **Voltaire,** and Kafka.

This freedom in analysis, which is hardly as concerned with
critical machinery and philological designs as that practiced in
the Sorbonne, was strongly reproached by the university circle
when Barthes wrote *Sur Racine* (1963; *On Racine*). Raymond
Picard wrote a pamphlet about him, *Nouvelle critique ou
nouvelle imposture* (1965; *New Criticism or New Fraud?*),
which reveals the tension between those who believe in traditional biographical criticism and those who take part in a
renewed approach to literary criticism, open to the contributions of both semiology and psychoanalysis. Barthes answers
these reproaches in *Critique et vérité* (1966; *Criticism and*

Truth), denouncing the institution of a criticism which would be based on objectivity, good taste, and clarity, without grounding these self-proclaimed values scientifically. He continues his task of tearing down literary work, either by analyzing authors who prefer extremes (*Sade, Fourier, Loyola,* 1971) or by microanalyzing brief texts such as Balzac's short story "Sarrasine," dissected in 561 sequences in *S/Z* (1970).

In a way *S/Z* bids farewell to the structural utopia and to Barthes' pursuit of generalized systematization. The notion of text appears here (and this is Barthes' central point) as an opposition between "readable," i.e. classical texts that are no longer likely to be rewritten by the reader, and "writable" – texts that we can desire, write, and rewrite while reading. The text is also seen as a shattered, broken structure which allows itself to be analyzed from many angles.

This idea of the personal dimension in the relationship with the text flourishes in *Le Plaisir du texte* (1973; *The Pleasure of the Text*), where 46 entries, classified in alphabetical order, demonstrate the pleasurable relationship Barthes maintains with literary narratives, in the form of an autobiography of him as a reader. The plural form of the text, the enjoyment of reading, the game of intertextuality, the importance of reading aloud, the texture of the voice and the dialogue – all important ideas in the theoretical debates of the moment – were developed here by Barthes, not in the form of theoretical postulates, but in subjective **aphorisms**.

The subjectivity of style asserts itself with more and more power and independence in relation to the intellectual styles of the moment. The distinction between the critical part of the work and its "literary" dimension decreases to the point that the critic who talks about the writer Barthes is none other than Barthes himself. *Roland Barthes par Roland Barthes* (1975; *Roland Barthes*) thus stages this passage to a writing that is no longer separate from critical and autobiographical activity. The essay plays unceasingly on ambiguity, since it begins with his handwritten words – "It must all be considered as if spoken by a character in a novel" – but is full of the author's photographs and souvenirs. Life, literature, and criticism intermix, with enjoyment as the only rule, as confirmed in these last, also handwritten words: "One writes with one's desire, and I am not through desiring."

It is therefore not surprising that Barthes' next essay is entitled *Fragments d'un discours amoureux* (1977; *A Lover's Discourse: Fragments*). The first fragment, entitled "Comment est fait ce livre" ("How This Book Is Made"), insists on the importance of speech in the first person, "in order to portray an enunciation, not an analysis." Then Barthes evokes the listed "figures" of the feeling of love, the repertory of which is supposed to be systematic, but with variable contents. Their order is randomly set and their place in the book "absolutely insignificant" since it is based on the arbitrary nature of the alphabet. Without saying so, Barthes is setting the stage for an essay in these introductory directions.

He returns to literature in his study on *Sollers, écrivain* (1979; *Sollers, Writer*) and his *Leçon inaugurale* (1978; "Inaugural Lecture") to the Collège de France. Here he asks questions about intellectual power, language, literature, and semiology in a masterly synthesis of his great topics of reflection, but concludes by evoking the wisdom he has attained and defines as "no power, a little knowledge, a little wisdom,

and as much flavor as possible." He looks for this flavor again in a last semiological investigation of photography. But *La Chambre claire: Note sur la photographie* (1980; *Camera Lucida: Reflections on Photography*) is less a phenomenology of the image than an analysis of the emotional relationship Barthes maintains with the photographs, portraits, and landscapes he has encountered in his life. The time for remembering and admitting to intimate passions has arrived, as shown in the posthumous texts in *Incidents* (1987), which reveal the author's homosexuality and secret passions.

Since his death, Barthes' work has been constantly re-edited and commented upon. A three-volume complete edition of his works and articles has recently been published, a rarity for an essayist who appealed to the intellectual class more than to the public at large. Barthes' popularity in France and in the world, the pertinence and the originality of his analyses, their diversity and lively actuality, all explain his exceptional posthumous survival.

MARC LITS

Biography

Roland Gérard Barthes. Born 12 November 1915 in Cherbourg. Studied at the Lycée Montaigne, Paris, 1924–30; Lycée Louis-le-Grand, Paris, 1930–34, baccalauréat, 1934; the Sorbonne, Paris, from 1936, licence in classical letters, 1939, diploma in Greek tragedy, 1941, licence in grammar and philology, 1943. Contracted tuberculosis, 1934, and relapsed periodically, staying in sanatoria, 1934–35 and 1942–46. Taught at lycées in Biarritz, 1939, Bayonne, 1939–40, and Paris, 1940–41, and at the French Institute, Bucharest, 1948–49, University of Alexandria, 1949–50, and the Direction Générale des Affaires Culturelles, Paris, 1950–52; research appointments with Centre National de la Recherche Scientifique, 1952–59; chair, 1960–62, and director of studies, 1960–76, École Pratique des Hautes Études, Paris; taught at Johns Hopkins University, Baltimore, 1967–68; chair of literary semiology, Collège de France, Paris, 1976–80. Cofounder, *Théâtre Populaire* (Popular theater), 1953, and *Arguments*, 1956; contributor to various periodicals, including *Communications*, *La Quinzaine Littéraire* (The literary fortnightly), *Les Lettres Nouvelles* (New letters), and *Tel Quel* (As is). Chevalier des Palmes Académiques. Died (as the result of a street accident) in Paris, 26 March 1980.

Selected Writings

Essays and Related Prose

Le Degré zéro de l'écriture, 1953; as *Writing Degree Zero*, with *Elements of Semiology*, translated by Annette Lavers and Colin Smith, 1967
Michelet par lui-même, 1954; as *Michelet*, translated by Richard Howard, 1987
Mythologies, 1957; part as *Mythologies*, translated by Annette Lavers, 1972
Sur Racine, 1963; as *On Racine*, translated by Richard Howard, 1964
La Tour Eiffel, 1964; as *The Eiffel Tower and Other Mythologies*, translated by Richard Howard, 1979
Essais critiques, 1964; as *Critical Essays*, translated by Richard Howard, 1972
Éléments de sémiologie, 1965; as *Elements of Semiology*, with *Writing Degree Zero*, translated by Annette Lavers and Colin Smith, 1967
Critique et vérité, 1966; as *Criticism and Truth*, edited and translated by Katrine Pilcher Keuneman, 1987
Système de la mode, 1967; as *The Fashion System*, translated by Matthew Ward and Richard Howard, 1985

S/Z, 1970; as *S/Z*, translated by Richard Miller, 1974
L'Empire des signes, 1970; as *Empire of Signs*, translated by
    Richard Howard, 1983
Sade, Fourier, Loyola, 1971; as *Sade, Fourier, Loyola*, translated by
    Richard Miller, 1976
Nouveaux essais critiques, 1972; as *New Critical Essays*, translated
    by Richard Howard, 1980
Le Plaisir du texte, 1973; as *The Pleasure of the Text*, translated by
    Richard Miller, 1975
Roland Barthes par Roland Barthes, 1975; as *Roland Barthes*,
    translated by Richard Howard, 1977
Fragments d'un discours amoureux, 1977; as *A Lover's Discourse:
    Fragments*, translated by Richard Howard, 1978
Image, Music, Text (selections), edited and translated by Stephen
    Heath, 1977
Leçon inaugurale au Collège de France, 1978; as "Inaugural
    Lecture, Collège de France," translated by Richard Howard, in *A
    Barthes Reader*, 1982
Sollers, écrivain, 1979; as *Sollers, Writer*, translated by Philip
    Thody, 1987
La Chambre claire: Note sur la photographie, 1980; as *Camera
    Lucida: Reflections on Photography*, translated by Richard
    Howard, 1981
A Barthes Reader (various translators), edited by Susan Sontag,
    1982; as *Selected Writings*, 1983
L'Obvie et l'obtus, 1982; as *The Responsibility of Forms: Critical
    Essays on Music, Art, and Representation*, translated by Richard
    Howard, 1985
Le Bruissement de la langue, 1984; as *The Rustle of Language*,
    translated by Richard Howard, 1986
L'Aventure sémiologique, 1985; as *The Semiotic Challenge*,
    translated by Richard Howard, 1988
Incidents, 1987; as *Incidents*, translated by Richard Howard, 1992

Other writings: works on semiology, literary theory, and culture.

Collected works edition: *Œuvres complètes*, edited by Eric Marty, 3
vols., 1993–95.

Bibliographies
Freedman, Sanford, and Carole Anne Taylor, *Roland Barthes: A
    Bibliographical Reader's Guide*, New York and London: Garland,
    1983
Nordquist, Joan, *Roland Barthes: A Bibliography*, Santa Cruz,
    California: Reference and Research Services, 1994

Further Reading
Bensmaïa, Réda, *The Barthes Effect: The Essay as Reflective Text*,
    Minneapolis: University of Minnesota Press, 1987 (original French
    edition, 1986)
Calvet, Louis-Jean, *Roland Barthes, un regard politique sur le signe*,
    Paris: Payot, 1973
Calvet, Louis-Jean, *Roland Barthes*, Oxford: Polity Press, 1994;
    Bloomington: Indiana University Press, 1995 (original French
    edition, 1990)
Communications issue on Barthes, 36 (1982)
Culler, Jonathan, *Roland Barthes*, Oxford and New York: Oxford
    University Press, 1983
Heath, Stephen, *Vertige du déplacement: Lecture de Barthes*, Paris:
    Fayard, 1974
Jouve, Vincent, *La Littérature selon Barthes*, Paris: Minuit, 1986
Lavers, Annette, *Roland Barthes: Structuralism and After*,
    Cambridge, Massachusetts: Harvard University Press, 1982
Magazine Littéraire issue on Barthes, 314 (October 1993)
Poétique issue on Barthes, 47 (September 1981)
Sontag, Susan, *Under the Sign of Saturn*, New York: Farrar Straus
    Giroux, 1980; London: Writers and Readers, 1983

Thody, Philip, *Roland Barthes: A Conservative Estimate*, London:
    Macmillan, and Atlantic Highlands, New Jersey: Humanities
    Press, 1977
Ungar, Steven, *Roland Barthes, the Professor of Desire*, Lincoln:
    University of Nebraska Press, 1983
Wasserman, George R., *Roland Barthes*, Boston: Twayne, 1981

Bataille, Georges
French, 1897–1962

Georges Bataille was an adventurer in the world of ideas and
sensations, an explorer who, because he could not abstain from
questioning every alternative as it was offered him, intrepidly
embarked on an intellectual quest that would go beyond rationality. Endowed with a penetrating and nagging intelligence
that he nourished by wide-ranging reading, with concentration
on Hegel, **Nietzsche**, and **Heidegger**, he was never content with
others' speculations even though he never succeeded in systematizing his own, perhaps because it was in their very nature
that such a task would remain impossible.

Sharing fully in all the problems of what, at the opening of
the essay collection *La Littérature et le mal* (1957; *Literature
and Evil*) he characterized as a "tumultuous generation,"
Bataille's first endeavor to compensate for a difficult childhood
was a failure, yet it was a tell-tale one. Brought up in the
French lay tradition by his blind, paralyzed father, he first
attempted to assuage the tempests of his inner life by embracing
a religious vocation, entering the seminary of Saint-Fleur to
train for the priesthood, and spending a period with the
Benedictine congregation at Quarr, on the Isle of Wight.
Though the Abbey had a reputation for deepening spirituality,
particularly through the beauty of its liturgical observances,
Bataille's mystic phase passed rapidly. Despite his faith he
continued, as his critics have noted, to crave for deeper satisfactions than reason could offer; henceforth he would seek
them not in religion but in the arts, especially literature, which
he linked with anthropology.

Surrealism naturally attracted Bataille, though only for a
time. As he explains in "Le Surréalisme au jour le jour"
("Surrealism Day by Day"), his restless mind could not brook
André Breton's domineering ways, and, though like many other
French intellectuals he was attracted by left-wing politics, the
Communist Party could not count on his loyalty for long. He
joined with Roger Caillois and Michel Leiris to form the so-
called Collège de Sociologie and founded journals, but these
enterprises were short-lived. Bataille's preference was for the
lonely furrow, and his reputation was at its highest not during
his lifetime but posthumously, when his thought was taken up
and promoted in *Tel Quel* (As is) in the 1970s.

"A mystic without God," in Boisdeffre's phrase, Bataille
discerned the source of all literary creation in the problem of
evil, exploring the issue in *Literature and Evil*. In a wide-
ranging series of essays that were originally published separately in the journal *Critique* and that are more accessible than
some of his other writings, he discusses not only Proust and,
inevitably, Sade, **Baudelaire**, and Genet, but also Franz Kafka,
William Blake, and Emily Brontë. He marvels that *Wuthering
Heights* should have been written by a woman whose life was

apparently so circumscribed and who still achieved such awareness of what for him are the most significant issues of existence. Bataille's interest in eroticism had found early expression
in *Histoire de l'œil* (*Story of the Eye*), a novel published under
a pseudonym because the frank, if somewhat limited, pornographic first-person narrative would have clashed with his
chosen profession in librarianship. In *Literature and Evil*
Bataille presents his case in the more acceptable guise of criticism. Eroticism takes a central place, affirming existence,
releasing the individual from the isolation that is otherwise a
fundamental concomitant of consciousness, and finding its
culmination in death. Where an ancient philosopher might
have placed a premium on the equanimity that is the reward
of moderation, Bataille values anguish, the emotional turmoil
that is the product of excess. This becomes all the stronger
when excess can be experienced as transgression, with a
genuine and alarming sense of going beyond all normal bounds
in search of novel and unprecedented inner responses. The link
with sexuality is, of course, strong, but not exclusive, for the
special liberating response may equally be triggered by other
exceptional stimuli. Bataille returns repeatedly and possibly
with some retrospective elaboration to certain experiences,
such as witnessing particular horrors at a bull fight.
Paradoxically for him, cruelty has positive as well as negative
aspects. These ideas, which some might think depend to
some degree on religious and social orthodoxies that have
been rejected but never totally forgotten, are developed by
Bataille in his essay *L'Érotisme* (1957; *Eroticism*) and, with
a rather different context, in *L'Histoire de l'érotisme* (History
of eroticism).

Another approach to Bataille is through the art criticism
that constitutes a significant and characteristically multi-disci-
plinary part of his work from early on. In 1955 he published
not only an essay on Manet, dwelling in particular on the
significance of the rejection of his art by his contemporaries,
but also a study of the cave painting at Lascaux. Some of the
anthropological statements can be considered speculative, but
this study offers Bataille the opportunity for reflections on
the nature of art and its role in human existence. Arguing
that the true dawn of art dates not from ancient Greece
but from the time of Lascaux, he salutes a major advance as
humankind becomes differentiated from beasts when the self
acquires an inner life in the awareness of death and the desire
for communication. Previously humans had devoted their energies to practical ends, but now arose the possibilities for something that Bataille regards as far more important: the ludic,
which leads directly to ritual and art.

Bataille can write with all the clarity and elegance conventionally regarded as typical of French authors. But he can
also be difficult. Modern French prose has a tendency toward
ellipsis, and that suits him well. He is content to present his
thought in a way that engages his readers by leaving it to them
to make connections as best they may, and he is indeed a
master of the pregnant pause. He is also fearless in the employment of abstract nouns, the significance of which in the particular context he has created can remain puzzling. This means
that reading Bataille can itself be a challenging intellectual
adventure.

CHRISTOPHER SMITH

Biography

Born 10 September 1897 in Billom, Puy-de-Dôme. Used many
pseudonyms, including Lord Auch and Pierre Angélique. In ill health
all of his life, and suffered from periods of depression. Converted to
Catholicism, 1914: renounced, 1922. Military service, 1916–17:
discharged because of tuberculosis. Joined seminary at Saint-Fleur,
1917–18. Studied at the École des Chartes, Paris, 1918–22;
fellowship at the School of Advanced Hispanic Studies, Madrid,
1922. Librarian and deputy keeper, Bibliothèque Nationale, Paris,
1922–42: resigned because of tuberculosis. Married Silvia Maklès,
1928 (divorced, 1934): one daughter. Editor, *Documents*, 1929–31.
Liaison with "Laure" (i.e. Colette Peignot; died, 1938), 1934–38.
Cofounder, with André Breton, Contre-Attaque (Counter-Attack)
political group, 1935–36; cofounder, Collège de Sociologie,
1936–39, and a secret society, which published *Acéphale* review,
1936–39; moved to Vézelay, 1942–49. Married Diane de
Beauharnais, 1946: one daughter. Cofounder and editor, *Critique*,
1946–62; librarian in Carpentras, 1949–51, and Orléans, from
1951. Died in Paris, 8 July 1962.

Selected Writings

Essays and Related Prose

L'Expérience intérieure, 1943; revised edition, 1954; as *Inner
Experience*, translated by Leslie Anne Boldt, 1988
Sur Nietzsche: Volonté de chance, 1945; as *On Nietzsche*, translated
by Bruce Boone, 1992
La Part maudite: Essai d'économie générale, 1949; as *The Accursed
Share: An Essay on General Economy*, translated by Robert
Hurley, 2 vols., 1988–91
Somme athéologique I–II , 2 vols., 1954–61
Lascaux; or, The Birth of Art, translated by Austryn Wainhouse,
1955; as *Lascaux, ou, La Naissance de l'art*, 1980
L'Érotisme, 1957; as *Death and Sensuality*, and as *Eroticism*,
translated by Mary Dalwood, 1962
La Littérature et le mal, 1957; revised edition, 1967; as *Literature
and Evil*, translated by Alastair Hamilton, 1973
Les Larmes d'Éros, 1961; enlarged edition, 1971; as *The Tears of
Eros*, translated by Peter Connor, 1989
La Pratique de la joie avant la mort, edited by Bernard Noël, 1967
Documents (articles and reviews), edited by Bernard Noël, 1968
Le Collège de sociologie (1937–1939), with others (includes 8
lectures by Bataille), 1979; as *The College of Sociology
(1937–1939)*, edited by Denis Hollier, translated by Betsy Wing,
1988
Visions of Excess: Selected Writings, 1927–1939, edited by Allan
Stoekl, translated by Stoekl, Carl R. Lovitt, and Donald M.
Leslie, Jr., 1985
Le Dictionnaire critique, 1993
The Absence of Myth: Writings on Surrealism, 1994

Other writings: novels (including *Le Coupable* [*Guilty*], 1944;
L'Abbé C, 1950; *Le Bleu du ciel* [*Blue of Noon*], 1957), poetry,
and works on art, eroticism, and literature.

Collected works edition: *Œuvres complètes*, edited by Michel
Foucault and Francis Marmande, 12 vols., 1970–88.

Bibliography

Nordquist, Joan, *Georges Bataille: A Bibliography*, Santa Cruz,
California: Reference and Research Services, 1994

Further Reading

L'Arc issue on Bataille, 32 (May 1967)
Critique issue on Bataille (August–September 1963)
Gill, Carolyn Bailey, *Bataille: Writing the Sacred*, London and New
York: Routledge, 1995

Hollier, Denis, *Against Architecture: The Writings of Georges Bataille*, Cambridge, Massachusetts: MIT Press, 1989 (original French edition, 1974)

Land, Nick, *The Taste for Annihilation: Georges Bataille and Virulent Nihilism*, London and New York: Routledge, 1992

Richardson, Michael, *Georges Bataille*, London and New York: Routledge, 1994

Richman, Michèle, *Beyond the Gift: Reading Georges Bataille*, Baltimore: Johns Hopkins University Press, 1982

Shaviro, Steven, *Passion and Excess: Blanchot, Bataille, and Literary Theory*, Tallahassee: Florida State University Press, 1990

*Yale French Studie*s issue on Bataille, 78 (1990)

Baudelaire, Charles

French, 1821–1867

Charles Baudelaire is chiefly known as the author of *Les Fleurs du mal* (1857, 1861; *The Flowers of Evil*) and of a collection of experimental prose poems, *Le Spleen de Paris* (1869; *Paris Spleen*). But he is also important as a critic of painting and, to a much lesser extent, of literature and music. The essays on art are usually published under the collective title *Curiosités esthétiques* (Aesthetic curiosities), those on literature and music under the title *L'Art romantique* (Romantic art; a title not chosen by Baudelaire). The *Salon de 1846* (Salon of 1846) first established his reputation as a writer and aesthete, and he is now judged one of the greatest art critics of 19th-century France. Over the last 50 years his **critical essays** have come to be considered an extension of his creative work because of the insights they provide into his aesthetics as a poet. The best exhibit the qualities one might expect of a poet – imaginative and emotional investment in his subject, allusive intellectual density, sensuous evocativeness – in keeping with Baudelaire's conviction that the only aesthetics worthy of the name are *a posteriori*, the subsequent analysis of a richly sensuous lived experience, and not a matter of "principles" or abstract preconceptions about the beautiful. We can see this exemplified in "Richard Wagner et 'Tannhäuser' à Paris" (1861; Richard Wagner and *Tannhäuser* in Paris). Baudelaire's musical experience was limited, but a concert of excerpts from Wagner's music and the premiere of *Tannhäuser* in Paris in 1861 produced an overwhelming impression, evoked in the essay in terms of the poetic theory of *correspondances* (mystical correspondences) or synesthesia (in this case, sound suggesting qualities of light and color). Baudelaire referred to experience of this kind – sensation carried in the imagination to a point of almost preternatural intensity – as *le surnaturalisme* (supernaturalism). Wagner was to Baudelaire in music what Delacroix had been 15 years earlier in painting. A series of essays on drugs, published together under the title *Les Paradis artificiels* (1860; *Artificial Paradise*), explore similar states of heightened consciousness produced by alcohol, hashish, and opium, but Baudelaire's celebration of their poetic effects is counterbalanced by his condemnation of drugs in terms of irresponsibility, delusion, and moral disintegration.

The literary criticism does not have quite the same intensity, though Baudelaire's passion for Delacroix and Wagner was matched by his enthusiasm for Poe, whom he translated extensively. Poe provided not so much the revelation of a new experience as the confirmation of a theory of poetry toward which Baudelaire's own intuition was guiding him. His most important collection of essays on literature, *Réflexions sur quelques-uns de mes contemporains* (1861; Reflections on some of my contemporaries), was commissioned as a series of prefatory essays for an anthology of French poetry produced by Eugène Crépet. Many of the poets discussed would now be considered minor and do not engage Baudelaire's imagination in the same way as music or painting, the essays on Gautier and Hugo being exceptions. In these essays, Baudelaire, reflecting on the work of his contemporaries and thinking back over his own best poetry, comes closest to formulating his own ideal of a "pure poetry."

The "Salon" – a critical account of the annual exhibition of contemporary painting held in Paris – became, in the wake of Diderot, an essay subgenre in the 19th century. They were commissioned by leading Parisian papers and journals and often published separately as brochures. They were often written by established or avant-garde writers (Musset, Heine, Champfleury) and were typical of the cross-fertilization between literature and the fine arts that was a feature of the intense artistic life of Paris from the Constitutional Monarchy onward. The aim in the first place was to offer an intellectual tour of the paintings on view and to act as a guide and stimulus to bourgeois buyers. Baudelaire's first *Salon* in 1845 follows this format. A year later, electrified by his recent acquaintance with Delacroix, Baudelaire wrote the *Salon de 1846* and transformed the genre from a catalogue with commentary into an essay in high aesthetics. The *Salon de 1846* is intellectually taut in its construction and polemically committed. In it Baudelaire states his own convictions as an artist at the outset of his career and promotes the genius of Delacroix, seen as the representative of the Romantic movement in France. Much of the essay turns on the distinction and opposition of color (Delacroix) and line (Ingres). Line artificially separates objects and parts of objects from each other and creates stable conceptual identities; color blurs distinctions, including the distinction between subject (the viewer) and object (the viewed) and tends toward a poetic state of coalescence. The opposition of Delacroix and Ingres, as the two main rival representatives of contemporary French painting, is repeated in the text Baudelaire devoted to the Paris Exposition Universelle of 1855, which is perhaps more interesting in the brief glimpses it affords of the impact of non-European art (for example Chinese art) on Baudelaire's sensibility. The Exposition made Baudelaire aware of the narrowness of the controversies (e.g. Romantic versus neoclassical) that were still feeding artistic debate in France.

Two essays on caricature, "Quelques caricaturistes français" (1857; Some French caricaturists) and "Quelques caricaturistes étrangers" (1857; Some foreign caricaturists), prefaced by a short metaphysical theory of the comic, "De l'essence du rire" (1855; The essence of laughter), show a Baudelaire fascinated by the moral suggestiveness of this genre, which he refused to consider as minor. On the contrary, caricature exhibits, in quintessential form, the processes of simplification and expressive generalization (what Baudelaire calls "idealization") common to all the visual arts.

Baudelaire's last *Salon* in 1859 is tightly organized around the concept of imagination, in the name of which he rejects realism as a philosophically untenable position. As a subjective idealist, he argues that we do not know nature in any objective sense; all we have are the ways in which individual imaginations totalize experience. Baudelaire's abiding commitment to Delacroix made him hostile to Courbet and unsympathetic to the contemporary developments in French landscape painting that would lead to impressionism (he could not tolerate the erosion of compositional values). It also blinded him to the novel genius of Manet. *Le Peintre de la vie moderne* (1863; The painter of modern life) is the fullest development of a preoccupation announced as early as the *Salons* of 1845 and 1846 – the necessity for modern painters to find the material of their art in the reality and lifestyle of their own historical moment. A comparatively minor illustrator of worldly life, Constantin Guys, is hailed as the artist who has opened his eyes to the bizarre beauty of Second Empire Paris, its types, its fashions, and the whole new world of nightlife made possible by gas lighting. The essay was influential in creating the climate of thought and sensibility that made possible the work of artists like Toulouse-Lautrec, Degas, and, of course, Manet himself.

BERNARD HOWELLS

Biography

Charles Pierre Baudelaire. Born 9 April 1821 in Paris. Studied at the Collège Royal, Lyon, 1832–36; Lycée Louis-le-Grand, Paris, 1836–39: expelled; Pension Levêque et Bailly, Paris, baccalauréat, 1839; enrolled as a law student at the University of Paris, but led a bohemian life, contracted venereal disease, and fell into debt, 1839–40. Sent on a voyage to India by his parents, 1841, but left the ship at Mauritius and returned to Paris, 1842. Began a lifelong affair with Jeanne Duval, 1842. Lived on an inheritance from his father, from 1842: deprived by law of control over it by the Conseil Judiciaire, 1844. Cofounder, *Le Salut Public* (The public salute), 1848. Fought on the barricades during the Revolution of 1848; associated with Proudhon and opposed the coup d'état of Louis-Napoleon Bonaparte, December 1851, but subsequently remained aloof from politics and adopted increasingly reactionary attitudes. Involved with Marie Daubrun, 1854–55, 1859, and Apollonie Sabatier, 1857. Publication of *Les Fleurs du mal*, 1857, led to a trial for indecency, a fine, and suppression of six poems; extended stay in Brussels, 1864; returned to Paris and stayed in a sanatorium, 1866. Died aphasiac and hemiplagiac in Paris, 31 August 1867.

Selected Writings

Essays and Related Prose

Salon de 1845, 1845; edited by André Ferran, 1933
Salon de 1846, 1846; edited by David Kelley, 1975
Les Paradis artificiels, 1860; as *Artificial Paradise: On Hashish and Wine as a Means of Expanding Individuality*, translated by Ellen Fox, 1971
Réflexions sur quelques-uns de mes contemporains, 1861
Le Peintre de la vie moderne, 1863
Curiosités esthétiques, 1868
L'Art romantique, 1869
Selected Critical Studies, edited by Douglas Parmée, 1949
My Heart Laid Bare and Other Prose Writings, edited by Peter Quennell, translated by Norman Cameron, 1950
The Mirror of Art: Critical Studies, edited and translated by Jonathan Mayne, 1955
The Essence of Laughter, and Other Essays, Journals, and Letters, edited by Peter Quennell, 1956
Curiosités esthétiques, L'Art romantique, et autres œuvres critiques, edited by Henri Lemaître, 1962

Baudelaire as a Literary Critic, edited and translated by Lois Boe Hyslop and Francis E. Hyslop, Jr., 1964
The Painter of Modern Life and Other Essays, edited and translated by Jonathan Mayne, 1964
Art in Paris 1845–1862: Salons and Other Exhibitions, edited and translated by Jonathan Mayne, 1965
Selected Writings on Art and Artists, translated by P. E. Charvet, 1972
Critique d'art; Critique musicale, edited by Claude Pichois, 1992

Other writings: poetry (including the collections *Les Fleurs du mal* [*The Flowers of Evil*], 1857 and 1861, and *Petits Poèmes en prose* [or *Le Spleen de Paris*], 1869). Also translated tales by Edgar Allan Poe.

Collected works editions: *Œuvres complètes*, edited by Jacques Crépet and Claude Pichois, 19 vols., 1922–53; *Œuvres complètes* (Pléiade Edition), edited by Claude Pichois, 2 vols., 1975–76.

Bibliography

Cargo, Robert T., *Baudelaire Criticism 1950–1967*, Tuscaloosa: University of Alabama Press, 1968

Further Reading

Gilman, Margaret, *Baudelaire the Critic*, New York: Columbia University Press, 1943
Hyslop, Lois Boe, *Charles Baudelaire Revisited*, Boston: Twayne, 1992
Lloyd, Rosemary, *Baudelaire's Literary Criticism*, Cambridge and New York: Cambridge University Press, 1981
Loncke, Joycelynne, *Baudelaire et la musique*, Paris: Nizet, 1975
Pichois, Claude, and Jean Ziegler, *Baudelaire*, New York: Viking Penguin, and London: Hamilton, 1989
Raser, Timothy, *A Poetics of Art Criticism: The Case of Baudelaire*, Chapel Hill: North Carolina Studies in the Romance Languages and Literatures, 1989
Richardson, Joanna, *Baudelaire*, London: Murray, and New York: St. Martin's Press, 1994
Starkie, Enid, *Baudelaire*, London: Faber, 1957; New York: New Directions, 1958

Bayle, Pierre

French, 1647–1706

Pierre Bayle expressed his views on Protestantism and religious tolerance in brief prose forms (**letters**, thoughts, dictionary entries) which convey the style and methods of an essayist. He is often considered a forerunner to the Enlightenment because of his rigorous examination of religious dogma based on erudition and reason coupled with a perspective that respected a variety of belief systems. He relied upon Cartesian methods and tenets, as filtered through the writings of Malebranche, in the many domains covered in his writings.

Bayle grew up poor, provincial, and Protestant, which marked him an outsider in 17th-century Catholic France and had a profound effect upon his writing. He left his country, in fact, and spent most of his life in Holland to avoid religious persecution and enjoy the freedom of uncensored writing. In the *Lettre sur la comète* (1682; Letter on the comet), enlarged a year later to *Pensées diverses sur la comète* (*Miscellaneous Reflections Occasioned by the Comet*), the letter form proved an effective means for his arguments disproving any supernatural significance attributed to comets, which Bayle showed to be natural phenomena explained by Cartesian physics. Even in this early text we find the lively, entertaining digressions which characterize Bayle's later style of composition.

He applied his scientific inquiry conveyed with a derisive tone to a review of history in the *Critique générale de l'Histoire du calvinisme du P. Maimbourg* (1682, 1683; General critique of the History of Calvinism by P. Maimbourg). In this work he adapted his Cartesian principles to the study of history, and stressed the need for historical objectivity and impartiality, based on a careful examination of sources. It signaled a new style of controversy, and one of its most contested concepts was the idea that superstition is the worst of our evils, even worse than atheism. The work was burned by the hangman in Paris, and was a huge success in clandestine circulation.

Bayle's most important and influential work, the two-volume *Dictionnaire historique et critique* (1697; *An Historical and Critical Dictionary*), was the only work to bear his name. Its enormous success can be seen in the fact that it was the work most often found in private libraries in the 18th century. It consists of a series of concise biographies marked by a witty, impersonal style. His skepticism often touched on pessimism, and his critique of superstitious, dogmatic elements in all religions earned him enemies among Catholics and Protestants alike. Irony and satire were often used to strip away hypocritical notions and practices, as Bayle displayed the naked truth of human error. His ambiguous treatment of the Bible as an historical document appealing to faith but requiring scrupulous rational examination was one of the most controversial elements of the *Dictionary*. He believed the practice of supporting governments and justifying political and institutional systems by a biased interpretation of the designs of Providence to be a morally corrupt practice and subversion of the truth.

In Bayle's writing in general, as well as in the *Dictionary* in particular, the existing order of things is considered better than the chaos that change would entail. To this extent Bayle represents well the transitional period between the 17th and 18th centuries, between an acceptance, albeit critical, of contemporary political and ideological systems, and the more radical rejection of the status quo by writers of the Enlightenment. Bayle's thought reveals the fluid orthodox Calvinism prevalent during the reign of Louis XIV, which encompassed a variety of apparent contradictions (skepticism and faith, monarchy and dissent). But if he refused the role of a revolutionary, Bayle was an ardent and relentless reformer. He destroyed commonplaces, facile logic, and totems in his work, which tends toward an individualistic perspective on society, due perhaps in part to his Protestant background.

A second edition of the *Dictionary*, which was greatly augmented, appeared in 1702, and conveyed some of Bayle's more recent debates and philosophical arguments. Even in this work there is the journalistic aspect which characterizes so much of his writings, so that we can trace the evolution of his thought and of his polemical contests. His primary opponent was Pierre Jurieu, a fellow Protestant and former friend, who refused the spirit of compromise and tolerance toward the Catholics of France that can be found in Bayle's works. Since he fought dogmatism wherever he found it, all the dogmatists

of the period were naturally allied against him. His last texts focused on these ideological conflicts: a five-volume *Réponse aux questions d'un provincial* (1703–07; Response to questions of a provincial) and the *Continuation des Pensées diverses* (1705; Continuation of the Miscellaneous reflections).

Bayle was not interested in the earthly rewards of money or honor, but was driven by a tireless pursuit of discovering and expressing the truth, a philosophical goal which he sought with a religious zeal. He can be considered a moralist to the extent that his theological views often emphasize the social consequences of beliefs, and the relationships among peoples as affected by their religious attitudes. He had a great impact upon **Voltaire**, who found encouragement in his work to criticize Christian doctrine. It was as much the strength of his arguments as his style of writing, humanly imperfect in its rambling digressions yet lively in its witty understatement and sarcasm, that distinguished him as a writer. In many ways he resembled more the humanists of the 16th century than the philosophers of the 18th.

ALLEN G. WOOD

Biography

Born 18 November 1647 in Carla (now Carla-Bayle), southeast of Toulouse. Studied at home; Calvinist academy, Puylaurens, sporadically from 1666; Jesuit college, Toulouse, 1669, where he converted to Catholicism; reverted to Calvinism 17 months later and fled to Geneva to avoid exile as a lapsed Catholic; studied philosophy at the University of Geneva, 1670; tutor in Geneva and Coppet, 1672–74, and Rouen and Paris, 1674; taught philosophy at a Huguenot academy, Sedan, 1675–81, where he became friends with the Calvinist minister Pierre Jurieu; taught philosophy and history at the École Illustre, Rotterdam, 1681–93. *Critique générale* banned on first publication, 1682, and Bayle's brother Jacob was arrested in France as a result, dying in prison, 1685. Founder and coeditor, with Henry Desbordes, *Nouvelles de la République des Lettres* (News from the Republic of Letters), 1684–89. Deterioration of his friendship with Jurieu, from 1686. Died (of tuberculosis) in Rotterdam, 28 December 1706.

Selected Writings

Essays and Related Prose

Lettre sur la comète, 1682; enlarged edition, as *Pensées diverses sur la comète*, 1683; edited by A. Prat, 2 vols., 1911–12; revised edition edited by P. Rétat, 1982; as *Miscellaneous Reflections Occasioned by the Comet*, translated anonymously, 1708
Critique générale de l'Histoire du calvinisme du P. Maimbourg, 1682; revised edition, 1683
Commentaire philosophique sur ces paroles de Jésus-Christ, "Contrain-les d'entrer", 1686; as *Commentary on These Words of the Gospel Luke XIV.23 . . .*, translated anonymously, 2 vols., 1708; as *Philosophical Commentary*, translated by Amie Godman Tannenbaum, 1987
Dictionnaire historique et critique, 2 vols., 1697; revised and enlarged edition, 3 vols., 1702; edited by A. J. Q. Beuchot, 16 vols., 1820–24, and Alain Niderst, 1974; as *An Historical and Critical Dictionary*, translated anonymously, 4 vols., 1710; as *The Dictionary, Historical and Critical*, various translators, 5 vols., 1734–38, reprinted 1984; as *A General Dictionary, Historical and Critical*, various translators, 10 vols., 1734–41; selections edited and translated by Elmer A. Beller and Marguerite du Pont Lee, 1952, and Richard H. Popkin and Craig Brush, 1965
Réponse aux questions d'un provincial, 5 vols., 1703–07
Continuation des Pensées diverses, 2 vols., 1705

The Great Contest of Faith and Reason: Selections, edited and
translated by Karl C. Sandberg, 1963

Other writings: works on religion and moral philosophy, and
correspondence.

Collected works editions: *Œuvres diverses*, 5 vols., 1964–82; *Œuvres
diverses*, edited by Alain Niderst, 1971.

Further Reading

Brush, Craig B., *Montaigne and Bayle: Variations on the Theme of
  Skepticism*, The Hague: Nijhoff, 1966
Delvolvé, Jean, *Religion, critique, et philosophie positive chez Pierre
  Bayle*, Paris: Alcan, 1906
Dibon, Paul, editor, *Pierre Bayle, le philosophe de Rotterdam*
  (essays in French and English), Amsterdam: Elsevier, 1959
Kenshur, O., "Pierre Bayle and the Structures of Doubt,"
  Eighteenth-Century Studies 21, no. 3 (Spring 1988): 297–315
Labrousse, Elisabeth, *Pierre Bayle*, The Hague: Nijhoff, 2 vols.,
  1963–64
Labrousse, Elisabeth, "The Political Ideas of the Huguenot
  Diaspora: Bayle and Jurieu," in *Church, State, and Society Under
  the Bourbon Kings of France*, edited by Richard M. Golden,
  Lawrence, Kansas: Coronado Press, 1982
Labrousse, Elisabeth, *Bayle*, London and New York: Oxford
  University Press, 1983
O'Cathasaigh, S., "Skepticism and Belief in Pierre Bayle's *Nouvelles
  Lettres critiques*," *Journal of the History of Ideas* 45, no. 3
  (July–September 1984): 421–33
Rétat, Pierre, *Le Dictionnaire de Bayle et la lutte philosophique au
  XVIIIe siècle*, Paris: Les Belles-Lettres, 1971
Rex, Walter E., *Essays on Pierre Bayle and Religious Controversy*,
  The Hague: Nijhoff, 1965
Robinson, Howard, *Bayle, the Skeptic*, New York: Columbia
  University Press, 1931
Sandberg, Karl C., *At the Crossroads of Faith and Reason: An
  Essay on Pierre Bayle*, Tucson: University of Arizona Press, 1966
Smith, Horatio E., *The Literary Criticism of Pierre Bayle*
  (dissertation), Albany, New York: Brandow, 1912
Tannenbaum, Amie Godman, and D. Tannenbaum, "John Locke
  and Pierre Bayle on Religious Toleration," *Studies on Voltaire
  and the Eighteenth Century* 303 (1992): 418–21
Whelan, R., "The Anatomy of Superstition: A Study of the
  Historical Theory and Practice of Pierre Bayle," *Studies on
  Voltaire and the Eighteenth Century* 259 (1989): 1–269

Beauvoir, Simone de

French, 1908–1986

Simone de Beauvoir was a prominent French existentialist
writer who worked alongside such notables as **Jean-Paul Sartre**,
Maurice Merleau-Ponty, and **Albert Camus**. Among the hallmarks of existentialism, and hence of her thought, are an
emphasis on radical freedom and its commensurate responsibility, a rejection of the traditional idealistic assumptions about
the importance of rationality and universality in favor of an
emphasis upon the non-rational and the individual, and a sensitivity to style of expression. The existentialists wrote in a
variety of different styles: novels, plays, short stories, as well
as essays. Often their essays were more expository than analytic
in style, and were occasionally lyrical.

Yet, at her best, Beauvoir is not quite like any of her fellow
existentialists. Her unique voice emerged while she directed her

thought to the problems affecting her. Sartre, her collaborator
and intimate companion for over 50 years, said of her work
in an interview in 1965: "I don't pay compliments and I say
things simply. She seems to me a very good writer. She has
achieved something which has manifested itself particularly
since *The Mandarins*. It's apparent in the memoirs and in her
book *A Very Peaceful Death*, which I consider the best thing
she's written. What she has achieved is immediate communication with the public" (Madeleine Gobeil, "Sartre Talks of
Beauvoir: An Interview with Madeleine Gobeil," in *Marks*,
1987). Sartre went on to describe how this immediacy had
been achieved through a proper balance of intellectual and
emotional reflection: "She has the right relationship with
herself. That's what's meant by seeing oneself in perspective.
It's not only a matter of literature, it's a matter of life."

Another hallmark of existentialism is the engagement of the
author within his or her situation, referred to as "situated" or
"committed" literature, in which writing both reflects the situation the author and readers are in and addresses itself to
change and revolution rather than settling for the safe accuracy of benign description. This style of writing was meant to
emerge spontaneously from a way of living. Unfortunately, this
attempt was not always successful. The literary critic **Edmund
Wilson** once said of Sartre – this surely applies to much other
existentialist writing – that this style came off as contrived and
self-conscious rather than as effective realism: ". . . a virtuosity
of realism and a rhetoric of moral passion which make you
feel not merely that the fiction is a dramatic heightening of
life but that the literary fantasy takes place on a plane which
does not have any real connection with the actual human experience which it is intending to represent" (Edmund Wilson,
"Jean-Paul Sartre, the Novelist and the Existentialist," *New
Yorker*, 2 August 1947). However, Beauvoir's essays became
more and more effective – more situated and committed – as
she found her voice.

Beauvoir enjoyed success with her novels, such as *L'Invitée*
(1943; *She Came to Stay*), *Le Sang des autres* (1945; *The Blood
of Others*), and *Les Mandarins* (1954; *The Mandarins*). While
her initial fame as a novelist was well deserved, it has been
eclipsed by the attention resulting from her essays concerning
ethics, the social status of women, sexuality, politics, aging,
and death. Through her own style of committed literature, she
chronicled the myriad social changes of postwar Europe.

Her essay on ethics, *Pour une morale de l'ambiguïté* (1947;
The Ethics of Ambiguity), was an attempt to develop an ethics
from existentialism. Some have seen her account as the first
step in moving away from the overly individuated world view
characteristic of early existentialism toward the socially
oriented approach existentialists would later adopt.

She is often seen as a pioneer of contemporary feminist
writing. With her classic *Le Deuxième Sexe* (1949; *The Second
Sex*), a style emerged which was unique among her existentialist cohorts as she began a tradition which describes the
human predicament "in a different voice." While subscribing
to both existentialism and Marxism, neither existentialism's
theoretical emphasis on freedom and authenticity nor
Marxism's emphasis on class conflict was sufficient to account
for woman's plight as a second-class citizen in a male-domi-
nated world. Indeed, she foresaw an important threat within
the promise of both these schools of thought: they must not

be allowed to reduce the issues of woman's suffering into generic existential, social, or economic terms.

Beauvoir offers outstanding accounts of death throughout her career, describing the death of her friend Elizabeth Mabille ("Zaza"), the death of her mother, and finally the death of Sartre. In these works we see in excruciating detail how one comes to live in a world limned with death. The latter two deaths receive book-length analyses in *Une mort très douce* (1964; *A Very Easy Death*) and *La Cérémonie des adieux* (1982; *Adieux: A Farewell to Sartre*). Her account of aging and growing old in *La Vieillesse* (1970; *The Coming of Age*) provides a situated account of another topic our society has tended to avoid: aging is something which will happen to most of us, yet we tend to live as if it should not be discussed. Beauvoir effectively illustrates the social problems of relegating the elderly to the margins of society.

Beauvoir's four volumes of autobiographical reflections offer a valuable inside look into the world of a woman coming to recognize her own outstanding abilities, as well as the personal longitudinal account of aging, sexuality, her relationship with Sartre, her friendships, and the changing intellectual, political, and public scenes in France and elsewhere. These volumes offer a genuine and often courageous personal account from the perspective of a woman engaged in a lifelong struggle to speak, write, and live in a way best described as honest and free.

DUANE H. DAVIS

Biography

Simone Lucie Ernestine Marie de Beauvoir. Born 9 January 1908 in Paris. Studied at the Cours Désir, Paris, 1913–25, baccalauréat; Institut Sainte-Marie, Neuilly-sur-Seine, and Institut Catholique, Paris, 1925–26; the Sorbonne, Paris, 1926–28; École Normale Supérieure, Paris, 1928–29, agrégation in philosophy, 1929. Began a lifelong relationship with Jean-Paul Sartre, 1929. Taught at lycées in Paris, Marseilles, and Rouen, 1929–43. Founding editor, with Sartre, *Les Temps Modernes* (Modern times), from 1945. Lectured in the United States, 1947; liaison with the writer Nelson Algren, 1947–51; lived with the writer Claude Lanzmann, 1952–58. Cofounder and president, Choisir (Choose) feminist group, 1972, and president, League of Women's Rights, 1974. Awards: Goncourt Prize, 1954; Jerusalem Prize, 1975; Austrian State Prize for European Literature, 1978; honorary degree from Cambridge University. Died in Paris, 14 April 1986.

Selected Writings

Essays and Related Prose

Pyrrhus et Cinéas, 1944
Pour une morale de l'ambiguïté, 1947; as *The Ethics of Ambiguity*, translated by Bernard Frechtman, 1948
L'Existentialisme et la sagesse des nations, 1948
L'Amérique au jour le jour, 1948; as *America Day by Day*, translated by Patrick Dudley, 1952
Le Deuxième Sexe: Les Faits et les mythes and *L'Expérience vécue*, 2 vols., 1949; as *The Second Sex*, edited and translated by H. M. Parshley, 1953; vol. 1 as *A History of Sex*, 1961; vol. 2 as *Nature of the Second Sex*, 1963
Privilèges, 1955; one essay as *Must We Burn de Sade?*, translated by Annette Michelson, 1953
La Longue Marche: Essai sur la Chine, 1957; as *The Long March*, translated by Austryn Wainhouse, 1958
Mémoires d'une jeune fille rangée (autobiography), 1958; as *Memoirs of a Dutiful Daughter*, translated by James Kirkup, 1959

La Force de l'âge, 1960; as *The Prime of Life*, translated by Peter Green, 1962
Djamila Boupacha, with Gisèle Halimi, 1962; as *Djamila Boupacha*, translated by Peter Green, 1962
La Force des choses, 1963; as *Force of Circumstance*, translated by Richard Howard, 1965
Une mort très douce, 1964; as *A Very Easy Death*, translated by Patrick O'Brian, 1966
La Vieillesse, 1970; as *The Coming of Age*, and as *Old Age*, translated by Patrick O'Brian, 1972
Toute compte fait, 1972; as *All Said and Done*, translated by Patrick O'Brian, 1974
La Cérémonie des adieux, 1982; as *Adieux: A Farewell to Sartre*, translated by Patrick O'Brian, 1984

Other writings: four novels (*L'Invitée* [*She Came to Stay*], 1943; *Le Sang des autres* [*The Blood of Others*], 1945; *Tous les hommes sont mortels* [*All Men Are Mortal*], 1946; *Les Mandarins* [*The Mandarins*], 1954; *Les Belles Images*, 1966), short stories, two plays, biography, and memoirs.

Bibliographies

Bennett, Joy, and Gabriella Hochmann, *Simone de Beauvoir: An Annotated Bibliography* (criticism on Beauvoir), New York: Garland, 1988
Francis, Claude, and Fernande Gontier, *Les Écrits de Simone de Beauvoir*, Paris: Gallimard, 1979

Further Reading

Barnes, Hazel E., *The Literature of Possibility*, Lincoln: University of Nebraska Press, 1959
Marks, Elaine, editor, *Critical Essays on Simone de Beauvoir*, Boston: Hall, 1987
Oakley, Judith, *Simone de Beauvoir*, New York: Pantheon, 1986
Schwarzer, Alice, *After The Second Sex: Conversations with Simone de Beauvoir*, New York: Pantheon, 1984

Beerbohm, Max

British, 1872–1956

In 1921 Max Beerbohm urged Bohun Lynch, an early biographer, not to overanalyze his work, saying of himself that "My gifts are small. I've used them very well and discreetly, never straining them; and the result is that I've made a charming little reputation." The blend of self-mockery and self-assertion, as well as the offhand and understated accuracy of the observation, are essential elements of Beerbohm's style and approach to the essay. Beerbohm was never an especially prolific or an especially innovative writer, but within the limits he set for himself he at times achieved near-perfection in the familiar style of the **personal essay**.

Beerbohm's most interesting essays came at the beginning and the end of his literary career. In his earlier work he was, as he mockingly said of himself, "of the Beardsley period," and his essays of the 1890s reflect certain aspects of the current Aesthetic Movement. Beerbohm's first published essay, "The Pervasion of Rouge," appeared, appropriately, in the first issue of John Lane's *Yellow Book* in 1894. This essay, written while Beerbohm was still an Oxford undergraduate and with tongue very firmly in cheek, extols the arrival of the "era of rouge" and concludes that the increased use of cosmetics will be a good thing for women, because with the emphasis on cosmetics "surface will finally be severed from soul" and people will now look on women's faces as things of beauty rather than as indexes of character. "The Pervasion of Rouge" met with the incomprehension often accorded satire, and in the second issue of the *Yellow Book* Beerbohm had to explain that he was joking.

The first readers of "The Pervasion of Rouge" should not be judged too harshly, for Beerbohm was at this point far from the master satirist and parodist he would soon become, and, while the essay was intended as a parody of preciosity, the style and substance of it and several other essays are themselves somewhat precious. The subjects, style, and narrative voice of the early work were later refined but not transformed. The appreciation of artifice and display, the respect for Beau Brummell and any artist devoted completely to his art ("Dandies and Dandies," 1896), the new and sympathetic perspectives on unpopular or unknown historical figures ("King George the Fourth," 1894; Romeo Coates in "Poor Romeo," 1896) remained constant, as did the characteristic blend of historical background, iconoclastic point of view, use of mild fantasy, and the perception of the extraordinary in the seemingly commonplace, all presented with mild irony in a style of considerable polish and sophistication.

The most lasting and important achievement of Beerbohm's early essays, however, was their development of the Beerbohm persona, that of an elderly man looking wistfully back to the past. In "1880" (1895), Beerbohm's description of the birth of the Aesthetic Movement, he treats his recent youth as ancient history, noting with the truth of paradox that 1880, a mere 14 years earlier, is "now so remote from us that much in it is nearly impossible to understand." In "Diminuendo" (1896), Beerbohm perpetuates this voice of an elderly aesthete when, at the ripe old age of 24, he concludes that "Surely I could have no part in modern life" and bids farewell to literature, finding that as a writer he is already "a trifle outmoded." The self-characterization and the sense of play pervade Beerbohm's first book of essays, a slim volume published, with complete bibliography, as *The Works of Max Beerbohm* (1896).

With his characteristic blend of self-deflation and self-praise Beerbohm remarked of the Aesthetic period when he began writing that "To give an accurate and exhausting account of that period would need a far less brilliant pen than mine" and moved on to new subject matter. The narrative voice, however – so successfully employed that **Oscar Wilde** remarked that the gods had bestowed on Max the gift of perpetual old age – remained, as did the purity of style. Beerbohm's powers of observation were soon sharpened by his work as a caricaturist, his style by his experiences as a parodist and the 14 years he spent as a working journalist, primarily as the theater critic of the *Saturday Review*. Beerbohm was a diligent journalist, and his theater criticism can still be read with pleasure, but the essay remained his preferred form. Beerbohm felt that "what distinguishes literature from journalism is not vigour and sharpness of expression; it is beauty of expression." Beauty of expression marks all of Beerbohm's later essays, particularly those in his last and best collection, *And Even Now*.

By the time *And Even Now* was published in 1920 Beerbohm had become what he had always pretended to be, "an interesting link with the past" ("A Small Boy Seeing Giants"). While several of the essays in *And Even Now* treat such recurring Beerbohm themes as the difficulties of current social practices ("Hosts and Guests," "Servants") and the preference for imaginary rather than actual works of art (books by fictional characters in "Books Within Books," the "museum of incomplete masterpieces" in "Quia Imperfectum," his hilarious deflation of **Goethe**), the best of the later essays are informed by the real or imagined past. The imagined past is the background for Beerbohm's remarkable re-creation of an 18th-century conversation in "A Clergyman" (1918), a figure who, Beerbohm informs us, "forever haunts my memory and solicits my weak imagination" by becoming the unwitting victim of **Samuel Johnson**'s wrath and disdain.

Two other "reminiscial" essays of a more personal nature provide excellent examples of Beerbohm's differing approaches to the actual past of his youth. "No. 2. The Pines" (1920) is a distillation of several of Beerbohm's continual themes and techniques. The description of Swinburne's life in suburbia is a literal example of the fantastic residing in the commonplace. The past intrudes upon the present as Beerbohm enters the house inhabited by Swinburne and Theodore Watts-Dunton and has the "instant sense of having slipped away from the harsh light of the ordinary and contemporary into the dimness of an odd, august past. Here, in this dark hall, the past was the present." A young writer's awe and pleasure at meeting one of his idols is beautifully conveyed, but the solemnity of the occasion is leavened by such characteristic touches of humor as the young and old writer nearly colliding as they respectfully bow to each other and by such evocative neologisms as the "tupperrossettine" drawing room. Beerbohm's use of fantasy appears in his final vision of Swinburne, restored to youth, still being watched over and cared for by Watts-Dunton, even though the two of them are now in Elysium.

"William and Mary" (1920), Beerbohm's most personal and perhaps best essay, also plays with memory. Reflecting that as one ages "The World has ceased to be remarkable, and one tends to think more and more often of the days when it was so very remarkable indeed," Beerbohm uses a common sight, in this case a railway station, as a springboard to his past in which he was friends with William and Mary, two figures whose personalities and happy marriage are given permanence by Beerbohm's superb description of their lasting effect on him. Acting on impulse, Beerbohm returns to their deserted cottage and hesitantly rings the doorbell, producing "a whole quick sequence of notes, faint but clear, playful, yet poignantly sad, like a trill of laughter echoing out of the past," and concludes, "I must have rung again and again, tenaciously, vehemently, in my folly" – the folly of the attempt to resurrect the ghosts of his departed friends and so recapture his own past. "Playful, yet poignantly sad, like a trill of laughter echoing out of the past" aptly describes the usual tone of a Beerbohm essay, and the employment of two little-known characters both to demonstrate his belief that "the truth about anyone, however commonplace, must always be interesting" ("A Memory of a Midnight Express," 1909) and to provide a way of objectifying personal emotion, is characteristic of Beerbohm's detached approach.

Beerbohm's "charming little reputation" has never really changed. From the beginning of his career his essays have elicited a strong response from a relatively small but intensely devoted group of readers who relish their wit, their offbeat but fascinating subjects and themes, and above all their exquisite craftsmanship. In a review of *The Prisoner of Zenda* Beerbohm stated that he was "quite happy to sacrifice a story for style. I rate the essayist far higher than the romancer," the credo of a man and essayist who, as Beerbohm said of Aubrey Beardsley, "enjoyed life but . . . was never wholly of it."

JOHN H. ROGERS

See also Humorous Essay

Biography

Henry Maximilian Beerbohm. Born 24 August 1872 in London. Studied at Charterhouse, Godalming, Surrey, 1885–90; Merton College, Oxford, 1890–94. Journalist and caricaturist, contributing to various periodicals, including the *Yellow Book*, the *Strand* magazine, and the *Saturday Review*, for which he was drama critic, 1898–1910. Married Florence Kahn, 1910 (died, 1951). Lived in Rapallo, Italy, 1911–14, 1919–37, and 1948–56. Broadcaster, BBC, from 1935. Knighted, 1939. Rede Lecturer, Cambridge University, 1943. Honorary Fellow, Merton College, 1945. Married Elisabeth Jungmann, 1956. Awards: honorary degrees from three universities. Died in Rapallo, 20 May 1956.

Selected Writings

Essays and Related Prose

The Works of Max Beerbohm, with a Bibliography by John Lane, 1896
More, 1899
Yet Again, 1909
And Even Now, 1920
Around Theatres (theater reviews), 2 vols., 1924
A Variety of Things, 1928
Mainly on the Air (radio broadcasts), 1946; enlarged edition, 1957
Selected Essays, edited by N. L. Clay, 1958
The Incomparable Max: A Selection, edited by S. C. Roberts, 1962
More Theatres, 1898–1903 (theater reviews), 1969
Last Theatres, 1904–1910 (theater reviews), 1970
The Bodley Head Max Beerbohm, edited by David Cecil, 1970; as *Selected Prose*, 1971
A Peep into the Past and Other Prose Pieces, edited by Rupert Hart-Davis, 1972

Other writings: fiction (including the novel *Zuleika Dobson*, 1911), three plays, several volumes of cartoons and caricatures, a study of **Lytton Strachey** (1943), and correspondence (collected in *Letters of Max Beerbohm, 1892–1956*, edited by Rupert Hart-Davis, 1988).

Bibliography

Gallatin, Albert E., and Leslie M. Oliver, *A Bibliography of the Works of Max Beerbohm*, Cambridge, Massachusetts: Harvard University Press, 1952

Further Reading

Behrman, Samuel N., *Portrait of Max*, New York: Random House, 1960; as *Conversation with Max*, London: Hamilton, 1960
Cecil, David, *Max: A Biography*, London: Constable, 1964; Boston: Houghton Mifflin, 1965
Danson, Lawrence, *Max Beerbohm and the Act of Writing*, Oxford: Clarendon Press, 1989; New York: Oxford University Press, 1991
Grushaw, Ira, *The Imaginary Reminiscences of Sir Max Beerbohm*, Athens: Ohio University Press, 1984
Lynch, John Gilbert Bohun, *Max in Perspective*, London: Heinemann, 1921

McElderry, Bruce, *Max Beerbohm*, Boston: Twayne, revised edition, 1987
Moers, Ellen, *The Dandy: Brummell to Beerbohm*, London: Secker and Warburg, 1960
Riewald, J. G., *Sir Max Beerbohm, Man and Writer: A Critical Analysis with a Brief Life and a Biography*, The Hague: Nijhoff, 1953
Riewald, J. G., editor, *The Surprise of Excellence: Modern Essays on Max Beerbohm*, Hamden, Connecticut: Archon, 1974
Viscusi, Robert, *Max Beerbohm; or, The Dandy Dante: Rereading with Mirrors*, Baltimore: Johns Hopkins University Press, 1986

Belinskii, Vissarion

Russian, 1811–1848

"Vissarion the furious" was the founding father of Russian literary criticism. During his short life he wrote with "mercurial speed and fanatical enthusiasm." "Somehow I always run to extremes," he was to say of himself. Belinskii came from a modest background but soon symbolized the appearance of a new vocal class in Russia, the intelligentsia, those concerned about the state of Russian society and who saw in art and literature a means of improvement. He was also a *raznochinets* (someone not of the gentry), who had to survive upon his own capabilities as a writer and literary critic.

After studying for three years at Moscow University, Belinskii was expelled for writing a play entitled *Dmitrii Kalinin* which criticized serfdom (although the official reason was because of poor health). He then went on to become the chief literary critic of the most important journals of the day: *Teleskop* (The telescope), *Moskovskii Nabliudatel'* (The Moscow observer), *Otechestvennye Zapiski* (Fatherland notes), and ***Sovremennik*** (The contemporary). However, the pressures of journalism left him little time for polishing or refining his thoughts and style. In the same way, he paid almost no attention to the style or use of language of the writers he was criticizing. For him, content was the most important issue: language was meant to communicate, not be an end in itself. Belinskii's own style was erratic, ponderous, and diffuse, marked by repetition, digression, too many quotations, incessant polemic, rhetorical overemphasis aiming at immediate and startling effects, and elementary explanations for a public whose level of critical discrimination was still very low.

After an early infatuation with German idealism and his famous essay "Ideia iskysstva" (1841; "The Idea of Art"), which is saturated with Hegelianism, Belinskii came to see art and literature as primarily utilitarian. It had to go beyond the aesthetic, the romantic, the fantastic, and the grotesque; it had to transform society. He urged literature to be "natural, original and national." In this sense he accomplished much in encouraging the birth of a national Russian literature after Russian writers of the 18th century had spent most of their time imitating the French classical writers. He was in good part responsible for the fame that Nikolai Gogol', Mikhail Lermontov, **Fedor Dostoevskii**, and **Ivan Turgenev** enjoyed. However, he always rejected naturalism and would not have appreciated a writer such as Émile Zola. In his essay "Gore ot uma" (1840; Woe from wit) he wrote: "A man drinks, eats, and dresses – this is a world of phantoms . . . but as man feels, thinks and recognizes himself as an organ, a vessel of the spirit, a finite particle of the general and the infinite – this is the world of reality."

As a critic, Belinskii did not use the methodology of French or English critics, who worked close to the text. He never wrote systematic treatises. However, he made up for this lack of method by his complete belief in the power of literature. If he liked a literary work, he put his heart and soul into it, fulfilling Victor Hugo's belief that "true criticism begins with enthusiasm." As an essayist he was a powerful and passionate writer; many of his sayings were adopted by the Soviet regime. For example, after his conversion to socialism (c. 1841–42), Belinskii wrote "my God is negation" and "men are so witless that they must be led to happiness by force." In a letter to V. P. Botkin he wrote: "Socialism, socialism – or death! That is my motto. What care I for the existence of the universal when individuality is suffering? What care I if genius on earth live in heaven when the crowd is wallowing in the dirt? . . . My heart bleeds and shudders when I view the crowd and its representatives . . . And that is life: to sit in the street in rags with an idiotic expression of face collecting farthings in the daytime to be spent on booze in the evening – and men see it and no one cares about it!"

Belinskii greatly influenced Russian national tastes. His dislike of Slavic folklore and Old Russian literature affected the Russian population for an entire century. But he also refined the Russian language by introducing into it a large body of abstract, philosophical, and literary terminology. All in all, the tone and methods he used set the standard for all Russian 19th-century literary criticism. After the Revolution he became enshrined in the official Marxist-Leninist social realist school of literary criticism.

In his last piece, "Pis'mo k Gogoliu" (1847; "Letter to Gogol'"), Belinskii criticized Russian society and the role of religion in society. In it he wrote: "The basis of religion is pietism, reverence, fear of God. Whereas the Russian man utters the name of the Lord while scratching himself somewhere." Belinskii addressed Gogol', who in *Izbrannye mesta iz perepiski s druz'iami* (1847; *Selected Passages from Correspondence with Friends*) had given an odd defense of the status quo. Belinskii wrote: "One could endure an outraged sense of self-esteem, and I should have sense enough to let the matter pass in silence were that the whole gist of the matter; but one cannot endure an outraged sense of truth and human dignity; one cannot keep silent when lies and immorality are preached as truth and virtue under the guise of religion and the protection of the knout [flogging whip]." It was during a reading of this letter by the Petrashevskii circle that Dostoevskii was arrested. The article went on to become the manifesto of Russian liberals for decades to come.

ANDRIUS VALEVIČIUS

Biography

Vissarion Grigorievich Belinskii. Born 12 July 1811 in Sveaborg, Finland. Studied at a gymnasium in Penza, from 1825; Moscow University, 1829–32: expelled for writing a play seen to oppose serfdom. Wrote for *Teleskop*, 1834–36; editor, *Moskovskii Nabliudatel'*, 1838–39; moved to St. Petersburg, 1839; critic, *Otechestvennye Zapiski*, 1839. Married Mariia Vasil'evna Orlova, 1843: one son (died, 1847) and one daughter. Suffered from tuberculosis and went abroad briefly, May–November 1847. Wrote briefly for *Sovremennik*, 1847. Died (of consumption) in St. Petersburg, May 1848.

Selected Writings

Essays and Related Prose
Selected Philosophical Works, 1956
Belinsky, Chernyshevsky, and Dobrolyubov: Selected Criticism, edited by Ralph E. Matlaw, 1962

Other writings: many articles for journals (not collected during his life) and the play *Dmitrii Kalinin* (c. 1832).

Collected works edition: *Polnoe sobranie sochinenii*, 13 vols., 1953–59.

Further Reading

Annenkov, P. V., *The Extraordinary Decade: Literary Memoirs*, edited by Arthur P. Mendel, Ann Arbor: University of Michigan Press, 1968
Bowman, Herbert E., *Vissarion Belinski, 1811–1848: A Study in the Origins of Social Criticism in Russia*, Cambridge, Massachusetts: Harvard University Press, 1954
Proctor, Thelwall, *Dostoevskij and the Belinskij School of Literary Criticism*, The Hague: Mouton, 1969
Stacy, R. H., *Russian Literary Criticism: A Short History*, Syracuse, New York: Syracuse University Press, 1974: Chapter 3
Terras, Victor, *Belinskij and Russian Literary Criticism: The Heritage of Organic Aesthetics*, Cambridge, Massachusetts: Harvard University Press, 1954
Turgenev, Ivan, *Literary Reminiscences*, New York: Farrar Straus Cudahy, 1958; London: Faber, 1959 (original Russian edition, 1874)
Wellek, René, *A History of Modern Criticism: 1750–1950, 3. The Age of Transition*, Cambridge and New York: Cambridge University Press, 1982: Chapter 7 (original edition, 1965)

Belleau, André

French Canadian, 1930–1986

In a seminal essay entitled "Petite essayistique" (1983; Little essayistic piece), André Belleau claims that "At 18, one can be Rimbaud, but not an essayist" - since an essayist needs time to learn and master the languages of culture. This remark aptly describes Belleau's own career, for he came late to essay writing. During his many years as a civil servant he often wrote short stories and book or film reviews for various literary journals, most notably for the influential *Liberté* (Liberty), which he cofounded in 1959. Despite these publications, he did not begin to consider himself as a writer until the end of the 1960s. He then completely changed his professional activities: he left the government, went back to school, and subsequently (in 1969) became a literature professor at the newly born University of Quebec in Montreal. This Renaissance scholar was influenced by different theoreticians, but some of Belleau's more technical readings also changed his relationship to his own writing. Mikhail Bakhtin, for example, not only helped him grasp more firmly the nature of the Québécois novel, he also provided him with the means of creating a personal style.

What distinguishes Belleau's writing before and after the end of the 1960s is the fact that he finally came to terms with a problem he had faced for almost 15 years: how a writer is to incorporate in his work the many "voices" that inhabit him and, more importantly, that make him what he is. The title of Belleau's second collection of essays, Surprendre les voix (To catch the voices), shows the reader what the writer had discovered about both the nature of literature and the essayist's work. Belleau asserts that a writer is someone who listens to the words and phrases traded around him before turning them into something personal, and is thus engaged in what Belleau would later call the polemics of language ("polémique des langages"). From this point on, Belleau paid a tremendous amount of attention to his society's discourses, whether in literature, journalism, mass media, or everyday life. Some of his best-known essays deal with a French television broadcaster's English pronunciation ("L'Effet Derome, ou, Comment Radio-Canada colonise et aliène son public" [1980; The Derome effect; or, how Radio-Canada colonizes and alienates its public]), Montreal streets and their idioms, and his political opponents' use of language (Belleau was a fervent supporter of Quebec's independence while maintaining a skeptical distance from any form of nationalist thought). Belleau's interests went far beyond the confines of Quebec, however. He was fond of German philosophy, literature, and music; he wrote essays about Morocco and Guadeloupe; he loved French culture both high and low (Fauré as well as popular singers from his youth); he was well read in cybernetics and linguistics; he was an avid reader of European and North American mystery and gothic novels (as revealed in his reviews and his unpublished Cahiers de lecture [Reader's notebooks]). Belleau's openness and curiosity were also evident when in 1972 he cofounded the Rencontre Québécoise Internationale des Écrivains (International Québécois meeting of writers): this annual gathering continues to bring together writers from all over the world.

Belleau published only four books, but they are milestones in Quebec's literary culture, especially for those interested in sociocriticism. In Le Romancier fictif (1980; The fictional novelist) the critic uses the Quebec novel from 1940 to 1980 as a basis for contrasting the narrative techniques of novelists of the parole (for whom literature is perceived as pure interiority) with those of the code (here, the literary institution takes precedence). Notre Rabelais (1990; Our Rabelais), edited by Belleau's colleagues after his untimely death, contains radio interviews and scholarly essays on an author to whom Belleau had devoted many years of work, and who fascinated him because of the relationship between his oeuvre and contemporary popular or carnavalesque culture.

While these two books are more critical studies than essays per se, such is not the case with Y a-t-il un intellectuel dans la salle? (1984; Is there an intellectual in the house?) and Surprendre les voix (1986). These are collections of short pieces originally published between 1959 and 1985, although over half of the 51 pieces date from 1976. (Many texts appear in both the collections, for Belleau was dissatisfied with the 1984 publication, and reorganized it two years later.) Here, the voice of Belleau the essayist is heard loud and clear – in his theory of the essay as a "récit idéel" (narrative of ideas), his defense of the intellectual's role, his conception of language and politics, his ground-breaking reflections on the nature of Quebec's literary institutions, his love for his city and its culture. Particularly remarkable is Belleau's personal style of writing, which blends Quebec slang and so-called universal French, his attention to detail, and his fiery comments mixed with self-restraint (in matters of faith and spirituality, for example). Belleau's use of irony and paradox as well as his need to reach his reader are among the elements that structure his essays. At the same time, the essays are self-reflexive and consistently question the writer's own identity.

Belleau's lessons are still heard in Quebec's culture. To measure his importance, one needs only look at the magazine issues published in his honor by friends and colleagues (Liberté, 1987), and by younger scholars who wished to follow in his footsteps (Études Françaises [1988; French studies]). His passion – for knowledge, literature, and the essay as a genre – did not go unnoticed.

BENOÎT MELANÇON

Biography

Born 18 April 1930 in Montreal. Studied literature at the Collège Marie-Médiatrice; philosophy at Collège Sainte-Marie, B.A., 1952; psychology and literature at the University of Montreal, from 1953, licence, 1968, M.A., 1970, Ph.D., 1979. Federal civil servant, 1954–67, working for the Ministry of Public Health, the Public Service Commission, and the National Film Board. Cofounder, Liberté, 1959. Professor, University of Quebec, Montreal, 1969–86. Cofounder, Rencontre Québécoise Internationale des Écrivains, 1972. Married Jacqueline Belleau: two children. Awards: Prize of Excellence in Canadian Studies, 1984. Died in Montreal, 13 September 1986.

Selected Writings

Essays and Related Prose

Le Romancier fictif: Essai sur la représentation de l'écrivain dans le roman québécois, 1980
Y a-t-il un intellectuel dans la salle?, 1984
Surprendre les voix, 1986
Notre Rabelais, 1990

Other writings: short stories and numerous texts for radio programs (some were published in Notre Rabelais).

Further Reading

Cantin, Serge, "André Belleau, ou, Le Malheur d'être touriste," Liberté (December 1995): 27–69
Cousineau, Gérald, André Belleau, essayiste, Montreal: University of Montreal Department of French Studies, 1989
Dumont, François, "L'Essai littéraire québécois des années quatre-vingt: La Collection 'Papiers collés'," Recherches Sociographiques 33, no. 2 (1992): 323–35
Dumont, François, "La Littérature comme point de vue: Trois essayistes québécois contemporains: André Belleau, Jean Larose et François Ricard," Itinéraires et Contacts de Culture 18–19 (1995): 89–96
Dumont, François, "La Théorisation de l'essai au Québec," in Le Discours de l'université sur la littérature québécoise, edited by Joseph Melançon, Quebec City: Nuit Blanche, 1996: 331–56
Études Françaises issue on Belleau, 23, no. 3 (Winter 1988)
Liberté issue on Belleau, 169 (February 1987)
Melançon, Benoît, "Le Statut de la langue populaire dans l'œuvre d'André Belleau, ou, La Reine et la guidoune," Études Françaises 27, no. 1 (Spring 1991): 121–32

Montreuil, Sophie, *Le Travail du recueil*, Montreal: University of Montreal Department of French Studies, 1996

Schendel, Michel van, "Cher André (portrait intellectuel d'un chercheur)," in his *Rebonds critiques: Questions de littérature: Essais*, vol. 1, Montreal: l'Hexagone, 1992: 29–186

Schnierle, Martina, "André Belleau: Indépendance du discours et discours de l'indépendance," *Französisch Heute* 22, no. 1 (March 1991): 41–42, 51–55

Bello, Andrés

Venezuelan, 1781–1865

One of the pillars of Latin America's 19th-century intellectual thought, Andrés Bello is heir to the ideas of the Enlightenment in his rationalist struggle to reconcile national interests with universal good.

His essays on the conception of Latin America as a model society for all nations leading the way toward progress planted seeds among Latin American thinkers of the new generation. Bello was one of the first Latin American writers to articulate the ideology of a Latin American destiny, which would later find a resounding echo in the essayist **Pedro Henríquez Ureña**'s "La utopía americana" (1926; The American utopia). Yet Bello's dreams for Latin America were not mere utopian fabrications, as Adalbert Dessau explains in "Revista de crítica literaria latinoamericana" (1982): he proposed clear and specific goals to the emerging Latin American nations to achieve that objective. This shared aspiration for a common good, Bello adds, calls for an alliance or "society of nations" that will insure a strong and united Latin America.

In many of his writings, but particularly in his *Principios de derecho de gentes* (1832; Principles of the rights of people), Bello argues for the need for a progressive development of the emerging nation-states toward the formation of civilized bourgeois societies. Keenly aware of the lack of solid economic foundations in Latin American societies to propel economic development, Bello designs a model structure that would function as a catalyst for economic growth in Latin America. Both his essays on theories of culture and literature as well as his treatises on education and international law delineate Bello's proposed model for socioeconomic development that would bring Latin America to the forefront of Western civilization.

Bello's philosophical ideas lean toward what his critics have called an "objective idealism," tempered by his scientific vision of the world. In his *Filosofía del entendimiento* (posthumously pub. 1881; *Philosophy of the Understanding*), Bello develops his theory of society based on knowledge of the laws of nature. The need to use common sense in our understanding of reality is another important premise in Bello's philosophy. His contribution to Latin America's intellectual history is his synthesis of the legacies of modern European philosophy combined with his own philosophical theories. His views emerge from his desire to elaborate an ideology that addresses the needs and specific conditions of the newly independent Latin American countries, while at the same time keeping in mind universal values and principles.

In his essays on historiography, Bello discusses the need to distinguish between principles that are universally viable and those that can be applied only to particular situations. Bello's essential methodology proposes the use of experience and reason in the application, in Latin America, of laws developed in other countries. If Latin Americans were directly to copy the lessons learned by European nations, he cautions his readers, they would be unfaithful to the very spirit of those lessons, which advocate free discussion, observation, and thorough convictions. This creative application of universal ideas calls for a clear understanding of the particular needs and goals of the Latin American people.

Bello's familiarity with English philosophy – from **Francis Bacon** to **David Hume** – as well as his knowledge of Scottish thinkers such as Thomas Reid and Dugald Stewart, informs his vision of humankind and constitutes a substantive presence in his theory of knowledge, as Fernando Murillo Rubiera discusses in *Andrés Bello: Historia de una vida y de una obra* (1986). Bello also translated some of Locke's essays, and most critics indicate that Bello had knowledge of the works of Jeremy Bentham and **John Stuart Mill**. On the other hand, Bello's ties with the Latin American Enlightenment provide a clear basis for his Americanist thought, as seen in his defense of reason and virtue as essential components of the new Latin American societies.

Bello is considered the precursor of a Latin American school of thought which proposes the construction of a society that would benefit from the material progress achieved by European nations, while also avoiding the pitfalls already evident in the capitalist world.

Bello's search for "human happiness" goes hand in hand with his notion of "progressive improvement." His belief in the social need to promote progress for all is at the root of his Americanist thought. As a jurist he worked to build a society that would ensure all civil liberties and the enjoyment of progress and culture for its citizens, within a system based in the rightful administration of justice.

Bello was one of the most prolific and versatile writers of his time, and his intellectual curiosity was unbounded; his books and essays encompass such diverse topics as cosmography, philosophy, literature, education, science, politics, international law, and Spanish grammar. He is widely known as the poet who sang the beauty of the Americas and traced a social document for peace and creativity in the New World in his *Silvas americanas* (1823; Odes to America), and as the original author of *Gramática de la lengua castellana* (1847; A Spanish grammar), a pioneer work in the study of the structure of the Spanish language in Spanish America. His *Philosophy of the Understanding* has been acclaimed as the most mature expression of his philosophical ideas, and his *Principios de derecho de gentes* is considered the first work of its kind in the Americas.

LOURDES ROJAS

Biography

Andrés Bartolomé Bello. Born 29 November 1781 in Caracas. Studied at the Royal and Pontifical University, Caracas, 1797–1800, B.A., 1800. Second official of the Captaincy General of Venezuela, 1802–10. Editor of the first Caracas newspaper, *Gaceta de Caracas* (Caracas gazette), 1808. Traveled to England on diplomatic service, as aide to Simón Bolívar and Luis López Méndez, 1810, but funding withdrawn because of civil strife in Venezuela, 1812. Lived in London, 1810–30. Married Ann Boyland, 1814 (died, 1821).

Secretary, Chilean legation, 1822–24, and legation of Great Colombia, 1824–29, both London. Founding editor, *Biblioteca Americana* (American library), 1823, and *El Repertorio Americano* (The American repertoire), 1826–27, both London. Married Isabel Antonia Dunn, 1824. Elected to the Venezuelan National Academy, 1826. Moved to Santiago at the invitation of the Chilean government, 1829; named senior official, Chilean Ministry of Finance, and held post in the Foreign Ministry, from 1830. Editor, *El Araucano*, 1830–53. Senator of the Chilean Republic, 1837–55. Rector, University of Chile, Santiago, from 1843. Elected honorary member, Royal Spanish Academy, 1851. Died in Santiago, 15 October 1865.

Selected Writings

Essays and Related Prose

Principios de derecho de gentes, 1832; as *Principios de derecho internacional*, 1844
Filosofía del entendimiento, in *Obras completas*, vol. 1, 1881; as *Philosophy of the Understanding*, translated by O. Carlos Stoetzer, 1984
Antología de discursos y escritos, edited by José Vila Selma, 1976
Anthology, edited by Pedro Grases, translated by Barbara D. Huntley and Pilar Liria, 1981

Other writings: poetry, a play, a guide to Castilian grammar (1847), and works on the Spanish epic, philology, civil law, astronomy, and education.

Collected works editions: *Obras completas*, 15 vols., 1881–93; *Obras completas*, 9 vols., 1930–35; *Obras completas* (Ministerio de Educación Edition), various editors, 22 vols., 1951–69.

Bibliographies

Becco, Horacio Jorge, *Bibliografía de Andrés Bello*, Caracas: Fundación la Casa de Bello, 2 vols., 1987–89
Millares Carlo, Agustín, *Bibliografía de Andrés Bello*, Madrid: Fundación Universitaria Española, 1978

Further Reading

Alfonso, Paulino, "Don Andrés Bello: Antecedentes de influencias y rasgos íntimos," in *Estudios sobre Andrés Bello*, vol. 1, edited by Guillermo Feliú Cruz, Santiago: Fondo Andrés Bello, 1966: 163–72
Amunátegui Aldunate, Miguel Luis, "De la influéncia de don Andrés Bello en los orígenes del movimiento intelectual de Chile de 1842," in *Estudios sobre Andrés Bello*, vol. 1, edited by Guillermo Feliú Cruz, Santiago: Fondo Andrés Bello, 1966: 13–60
Ardao, Arturo, "La etapa filosófica de Bello en Londres," in *Bello y Londres*, vol. 1, Caracas: Fundación la Casa de Bello, 1981: 145–70
Ardao, Arturo, "La relación de Bello con Stuart Gill," in *Bello y Chile*, vol. 1, Caracas: Fundación la Casa de Bello, 1981: 317–38
Ardao, Arturo, "Bello y la filosofía latinoamericana," in *Bello y la América Latina*, Caracas: Fundación la Casa de Bello, 1982: 179–92
Avila Martel, Alamiro de, "The Influence of Bentham in the Teaching of Penal Law in Chile," *Revista de Estudios Historico-Juridicos* 5 (1980): 257–65
Brewer-Carías, Allan R., "La concepción del estado en la obra de Andrés Bello," in *Bello y la América Latina*, Caracas: Fundación la Casa de Bello, 1982: 99–154
Dessau, Adalbert, "La contribución de Andres Bello a la filosofía latinoamericana," in *Bello y la América Latina*, Caracas: Fundación la Casa de Bello, 1982: 165–78
Dinwiddy, John Rocoland, "Los círculos liberales y benthamistas en Londres, 1810–1829," in *Bello y Londres*, vol. 1, Caracas: Fundación la Casa de Bello, 1981: 377–98

Fernández Larraín, Sergio, *Cartas a Bello en Londres, 1810–1829*, Santiago: Editorial Andrés Bello, 1968
Galoo, Angel C., "Filosofía de Andrés Bello," in *Estudios sobre Andrés Bello*, vol. 2, Santiago: Fundación la Casa de Bello, 1971: 125–30
Gaos, José, *Filosofía del Entendimiénto: Introducción*, Mexico City: Fondo de Cultura Económica, 1948
Gazmuri, Cristián, "Algunas influencias europeas en el método historiográfico de Bello," in *Bello y Chile*, vol. 2, Caracas: Fundación la Casa de Bello, 1981: 325–38
Grases, Pedro, *Tiempo de Bello en Londres, y otros ensayos*, Caracas: Ministry of Education, 1962
Grases, Pedro, "Bello, humanista y universitario," in *Bello y la América Latina*, Caracas: Fundación la Casa de Bello, 1982: 469–78
Herrera, Felipe, "Presencia de Bello en la integración cultural latinoamericana," *Atenea* (1972): 175–92
Kilgore, W. J., "Notes on the Philosophy of Education of Andrés Bello," *Journal of the History of Ideas* 22, no. 4 (October–December 1961): 550–60
Murillo Rubiera, Fernando, "Andrés Bello en Inglaterra," *Cuadernos Hispanoamericanos* (1948): 5–44
Murillo Rubiera, Fernando, *Andrés Bello: Historia de una vida y de una obra*, Caracas: Fundación la Casa de Bello, 1986
Peers, E. Allison, "The Literary Activities of the Spanish Emigrados in England," *Modern Language Review* 19 (1924)
Rodriguez Monegal, Emir, "Bello y la inglesa en el primer tercio del siglo XIX," in *Bello y Londres*, vol. 2, Caracas: Fundación la Casa de Bello, 1980: 113–18

Belloc, Hilaire

British, 1870–1953

Hilaire Belloc was a writer of great vigor and variety, whose work included poetry, history, biographies, and travel accounts, as well as essays. He is regarded by some as the best prose stylist of his generation. He chose early to write in English rather than French, using simple, unadorned language, only occasionally employing metaphor or other rhetorical embellishment. His plain style is sometimes likened to the "piety of speech" of the 17th century, or described simply as grave and majestic, yet unmistakably Belloc.

Belloc's interests ranged widely, as did his knowledge and experience. His French and English ancestry insured him an unusual combination of insular and continental interests and sympathies as well as an acute way of analyzing everything he encountered. The essay form was particularly well chosen for his highly personal observations, which are consistently informed by his Roman Catholic sense of order as it existed in the Middle Ages, whose fragmenting with the Reformation Belloc saw as the West's greatest scandal. But an antipathy to contemporary life does not inhibit Belloc's enjoyment of the modern fools he saw everywhere. In "Fun for Clio" (1940) he noted: "The times in which we live have one great compensating advantage for their beastliness. They are vulgar and they are chaotic, they are murderous, they are dirty, they are atheist, they are intolerably wearisome, they have every vice, but they are a magnificent aid to the understanding of history." Such sentiments explain why the essays are not presently in favor; they are dismissed as too conservative because few understand the radical attitudes of Catholic faith when it decries the failings of the world yet celebrates material creation.

Some of Belloc's essays were published in the *Sunday Times*, the *Weekly Review*, and the *Tablet*. He was a close associate of **G. K. Chesterton**, with whom he published a weekly political newspaper the *Witness*. Belloc served as a Liberal Member of Parliament from 1906 to 1910, and many of his attitudes are Edwardian: a belief in arguing issues, social concern and delight in such pleasures of life as wine, but also a sense of foreboding and melancholy. The titles of volumes of essays suggest the quality of his mind: *On Nothing and Kindred Subjects* (1908), *On Everything* (1909), *On Anything* (1910), *On Something* (1910), *First and Last* (1911), *This and That and the Other* (1912), *On* (1923), *Places* (1941). Two others, *The Silence of the Sea and Other Essays* (1940) and *Hills and the Sea* (1906), reveal Belloc's lifelong enthusiasm for the sea, ships, and sailing, which coexisted with a delight in landscape that is quintessentially English.

Whatever the subject of an essay, Belloc brings to it energy, thoughtful analysis, and deep feeling. He relishes opposing current fashion and expectation, but is never facile. "On the 'Bucolics' of Virgil, a Café in Paris, the Length of Essays, Phoebus, Bacchus, a Wanton Maid, and Other Matters" (1923) more than any other title indicates Belloc's view of the essay as a free form, but he also acknowledges that there are exact expectations of length that lead to random padding. In "The Higher Criticism" he parodies the ludicrous excesses of Germanic academic analysis, concluding, "That is how the damned fools write." In "On Footnotes" (1923) Belloc identifies the practice as a form of lying in modern history that begins with Gibbon but is enforced because professional critics accuse authors who lack footnotes of "romancing." Among British writers Belloc wrote essays on Sir Walter Scott, John Bunyan, Jane Austen, James Boswell, William Tyndale, and John Milton. In "On Milton" he identifies two common qualities of English literature – adventure and mystery – and the English hunger for landscape, which he sees as proceeding from the love of adventure. Such conceptualizing from the particular is typical of how Belloc thinks. His own delight in and ruminations about landscape appear in "About Volcanoes" (1940), "On Town Walls" (1940), and most fully in *The Path to Rome* (1902). According to "On History in Travel" (1941), guidebooks should present the whole road as a piece of history, and specific descriptions in "On Old Towns" (1909) culminate in the statement that "The Old Towns are ourselves: they are mankind." For Belloc a place is "a sacramental thing," encountered on the journey, the pilgrimage of life: "We see some one thing in this world, and suddenly it becomes particular and sacramental . . . there is a resurrection, and we are refreshed and renewed."

Part of Belloc's mental quality is curiosity and skepticism, but beneath this there is a core of conviction rooted in his Catholic belief, which he identifies with European civilization. Belloc saw the decay of much European strength, culminating in World War I and repeated in World War II. He affirmed Europe's base in Christianity and attacked contemporary views of progress, capitalism, and industrial wealth. Thus in "On an Educational Reform" (1923) he urges that Fraud is the new subject needed to prepare the sons of the wealthy. In "On Truth and the Admiralty" (1923) he observes that only sea charts are trustworthy: "The war has produced propaganda. Truth took to its bed in the spring of 1915 and died unregretted, with few attendants, about a year later. Everything since then has been propaganda." An essay "On Statistics" (1940) classifies the subject as lies, since truth depends upon proportion, which can be distorted with mere figures. Writing "On Latin," from which all of the West proceeded, Belloc argues its older openness to all classes; he identifies its residual role as a liturgical language, even though "all religion has now arrived at such a stage that it may be called obsolescent." The essays become more cogent over the years, as Western society developed in ways that support Belloc, opponent of the Barbarians, as prophet of the 20th century.

The so-called progress of the 20th century that rejected Catholic experience was anathema to Belloc. He was a Liberal, but not of the classical European variety that denied life rooted in the past. His analysis of history is grounded in one tradition, and he becomes a part of its continuity. Like other Edwardians he writes of Northernness, but he avoids simple Teutonic/Nordic enthusiasm, voicing his suspicion of Prussia, made strong in the Reformation and thus not tied to European Catholic morality. Belloc warns against blond supermen. Such anticipations validate many of his essays.

VELMA BOURGEOIS RICHMOND

Biography

Joseph Hilaire Pierre Belloc. Born 27 July 1870 in La Celle, St. Cloud, near Paris. Family moved to England, 1870. Studied at the Oratory School, Edgbaston, Warwickshire; Balliol College, Oxford, 1892–95, B.A. in history, 1895. Editor, with A. H. Pollen, *Paternoster Review*, 1890–91. Served in the 8th Artillery Regiment of the French Army, 1891. Married Elodie Agnes Hogan, 1896 (died, 1914): three sons (two died) and two daughters. Became a British citizen, 1902. Freelance journalist, tutor, and prolific lecturer. Liberal Member of Parliament for South Salford, 1906–10. Editor, coeditor, or founder of the London *Morning Post*, 1906–09, *North Street Gazette*, 1910, *Eye Witness*, 1911–12, and *G. K.'s Weekly*, 1936–38; columnist of "A Wanderer's Notebook," London *Sunday Times*, 1938–53. Awards: honorary degree from the University of Glasgow; Knight Commander with Star, Order of St. Gregory the Great, 1934. Died in Guildford, Surrey, 16 July 1953.

Selected Writings

Essays and Related Prose
The Path to Rome (travel sketches), 1902
The Aftermath; or, Gleanings from a Busy Life (sketches), 1903
Varied Types, 1903
Avril, Being Essays on the Poetry of the French Renaissance, 1904
Hills and the Sea, 1906
On Nothing and Kindred Subjects, 1908
On Everything, 1909
On Anything, 1910
On Something, 1910
First and Last, 1911
This and That and the Other, 1912
At the Sign of the Lion, and Other Essays, 1916
On, 1923
Short Talks with the Dead and Others, 1926
A Conversation with an Angel, and Other Essays, 1928
Essays of a Catholic Layman in England, 1931; as *Essays of a Catholic*, 1931
A Conversation with a Cat, and Others, 1931
An Essay on the Restoration of Property, 1936; as *The Restoration of Property*, 1936

Selected Essays, edited by John Edward Dineen, 1936
An Essay on the Nature of Contemporary England, 1937
The Crisis of Civilization (lectures), 1937
The Silence of the Sea and Other Essays, 1940
Places, 1941
Selected Essays, edited by J. B. Morton, 1948
One Thing and Another: A Miscellany from His Uncollected Essays, edited by Patrick Cahill, 1955
Essays, edited by Anthony Forster, 1955
Selected Essays, edited by J. B. Morton, 1958

Other writings: light verse (including *The Bad Child's Book of Beasts*, 1896; *Cautionary Tales*, 1907), a play, fiction, and books on travel, religion, topography, and history, including biographies of Danton (1899), Robespierre (1901), Marie Antoinette (1909), Richelieu (1929), and Napoleon (1932).

Bibliography

Cahill, Patrick, *The English First Editions of Hilaire Belloc*, London: Tabard Press, 198-? (original edition, 1953)

Further Reading

Belloc Lowndes, Marie Adelaide, *The Young Hilaire Belloc*, New York: Kenedy, 1956
Corrin, Jay P., *G. K. Chesterton and Hilaire Belloc: The Battle Against Modernity*, Athens: Ohio University Press, 1981
Markel, Michael H., *Hilaire Belloc*, Boston: Twayne, 1982
Speaight, Robert, *The Life of Hilaire Belloc*, New York: Farrar Straus Cudahy, and London: Hollis and Carter, 1957
Wilhelmsen, Frederick D., *Hilaire Belloc: No Alienated Man: A Study in Christian Integration*, London: Sheed and Ward, 1953
Wilson, A. N., *Hilaire Belloc*, London: Hamilton, 1984

Belyi, Andrei

Russian, 1880–1934

Even disregarding short book reviews, Andrei Belyi's total output of articles and essays numbers close to 300. The essay is central to his oeuvre, providing a versatile form which can be used to address the reader in a wide variety of ways, and on a wide variety of topics. It is possible to classify Belyi's essays into three broad categories, but individual works frequently straddle the boundaries of different types. Some early essays are close in form to his lyrical prose fragments, while others expand to the dimensions of monographs. He wrote half his output of essays between 1902 and 1910; they are predominantly on literary and philosophical subjects. Even here the manner in which he addresses his reader varies widely between the academic and the lyrical. After 1910 he wrote many pieces about his travels; they are unified by a concern with discovering the inner impulse and identifying the spiritual essence of the cultures he observed. The death of **Aleksandr Blok** in 1921 stimulated Belyi to write memoirs and autobiography, the third category of essays which accompanied the other two, in the last decade of his life.

Belyi's first substantial essay was "Formy iskusstva" ("The Forms of Art"), published in Diaghilev's journal *Mir Iskusstva* (The world of art) in December 1902, where he outlined a theory of the hierarchy of art forms closely modeled on **Schopenhauer**, and reached the lyrical conclusion that all art

is moving inexorably toward its highest manifestation – music. Throughout the decade he published extensively in all the major symbolist and allied journals and almanacs – *Novyi Put'* (The new path), *Zolotoe Runo* (The golden fleece), *Svobodnaia Sovest'* (The free conscience) – but above all in the flagship journal of the Moscow symbolists, *Vesy* (The scales). His essays covered every aspect of symbolist theory, ranging between neo-Kantian epistemology and brash internecine polemics. In 1910 and 1911 the most important of his essays were republished, along with a number of new works, in the three volumes *Simvolizm* (1910; Symbolism), *Lug zelenyi* (1910; The green meadow), and *Arabeski* (1911; Arabesques). *Simvolizm* contains the most important of Belyi's philosophical and literary-theoretical essays, ten of which had not been published previously. These include "Smysl iskusstva" (The meaning of art), "Emblematika smysla" ("The Emblematics of Meaning"), "Magiia slov" ("The Magic of Words"), and a series of essays on the analysis of verse rhythm, in which Belyi was a pioneer. *Arabeski* and *Lug zelenyi* contain both literary-critical works and a range of essays that express the broader cultural hopes of the symbolists for a total transformation of humankind, culture, and society, such as "Simvolizm kak miroponimanie" ("Symbolism as a World-View") or "Apokalipsis v russkoi poezii" (The apocalypse in Russian poetry).

Belyi continued to write on these topics throughout his life. The teleology of culture is the subject of many works written later, such as *Tragediia tvorchestva* (1911; The tragedy of creativity), *Revoliutsiia i kul'tura* (1917; Revolution and culture), and the three long essays under the general title *Na perevale* (1918–20; At the watershed). His literary-critical studies include a series of essays on contemporary writers (Aleksandr Blok, **Viacheslav Ivanov**, V. F. Khodasevich) and culminate in his monograph, *Masterstvo Gogolia* (1934; Gogol's craftsmanship). The study of language is continued in "Zhezl Aarona" (1917; Aaron's rod) and *Glossolaliia* (1922; Glossolalia), in which he set out his ideas on the intrinsic meaning of the sounds of human speech in all languages. The rhythm of poetry formed the subject of a number of shorter pieces in the immediate post-revolutionary period, and found its fullest expression in *Ritm kak dialektika i "Mednyi vsadnik"* (1929; Rhythm as dialectics and "The Bronze Horseman"), in which he sought to interpret **Pushkin**'s poem on the basis of a dialectical tension between the surface semantics and the rhythm.

The genre of travel notes first makes its appearance in Belyi's oeuvre after his visit to Italy and North Africa in 1910–11. Short newspaper pieces were published in 1911, and two longer sections on his sojourn in Egypt appeared in the journal *Sovremennik* (The contemporary) in 1912. Book-form publication had to wait until the appearance of *Ofeira: Putevye zametki, chast' pervaia* (1921; Ofeira: travel notes, part one); some sections never did appear in his lifetime and were published only in 1984. The interest of his notes lies not merely in his detailed observation, but in his sense that every cultural monument he describes contains and still exudes the spirit of the culture that created it. There is no dividing line between his work on cultural history and his personal observations in these notes. The same is true of the newspaper articles he published in *Birzhevye Vedomosti* (The stock exchange gazette) in 1916 about his impressions of Europe at war, gained from his vantage point in Switzerland. Later works in this genre were *Odna iz obitelei tsarstva tenei* (1924; One of the mansions of the realm of shadows), a damning indictment of postwar Berlin, and *Veter s Kavkaza* (1928; A wind from the Caucasus) and "Armeniia" (1928; Armenia), in which he tried to adapt his vein of cultural criticism to the new Soviet reality.

Memoirs are one of the genres for which Belyi is best known, and the three volumes he published toward the end of his life (*Na rubezhe dvukh stoletii* [1930; On the border of two centuries]; *Nachalo veka* [1933; The turn of the century]; *Mezhdu dvukh revoliutsii* [1934; Between two revolutions]) are perhaps the most important single source for the study of the period. These grew out of the original *Vospominaniia ob A. A. Bloke* (1922–23; Recollections of Aleksandr Blok) and went through several revisions, not all of which have been published. Also related to the autobiographical novels Belyi was working on before Blok's death, the memoir genre includes sketches of the Moscow of his childhood, such as "Arbat" (1923; The Arbat).

Contemporaries often speak of Belyi as a man whose mercurial temperament resisted complete expression in any of his literary works. It is in his essays that his extraordinary range and versatility, his protean ability to vary voice and stance, come fully to the fore. A reliable picture of Belyi will never be attained without his essays. And without such a picture it is doubtful whether Russian symbolism as a whole is to be understood. Belyi embodied its spirit like no one else, and his essays are an indispensable – and almost inexhaustible – source for any student of the period.

JOHN ELSWORTH

Biography
Born Boris Nikolaevich Bugaev, 26 October 1880 in Moscow. Studied at the Polivanov gymnasium, 1891–99; science, philology, and philosophy at Moscow University, 1899–1903, degree in natural sciences. Began using the pseudonym Andrei Belyi with the publication of his first prose work, 1902; reviewer and writer for many periodicals and journals, 1902–10. Close friendship with Aleksandr Blok began through correspondence in 1903, developing later into a painful triangular relationship with Blok's wife; despite personal conflict they retained a deep and sympathetic awareness of each other's spiritual quest until Blok's death in 1921. Associate editor, *Vesy*, 1907–09; associated with Musagetes publishers, 1909–10. Traveled in Italy and North Africa, 1910–11; lived mostly in Western Europe, from 1912. Married Asia Turgeneva, 1914 (separated, 1921). Became interested in the philosophy of Rudolph Steiner, from 1912: helped with the construction of the Anthroposophical Temple in Dornach, Switzerland. Returned to Russia to join the military reserve, 1916, but was never called up. Archivist and librarian during the revolutionary period; founder and lecturer, Vol'fila (Free philosophical society). Returned to Western Europe, 1921, but was not well received by his wife or Rudolph Steiner; lecturer in Berlin, 1921–23; editor, *Epopeia*, 1922–23. Returned to Russia, 1923. Married Klavdiia Vasil'eva, 1931. Died in Moscow, 8 January 1934.

Selected Writings

Essays and Related Prose
Simvolizm, 1910
Lug zelenyi, 1910
Arabeski, 1911
Tragediia tvorchestva: Dostoevskii i Tolstoi, 1911
Rudol'f Shteiner i Gete v mirovozzrenii sovremennosti (Rudolf Steiner and Goethe in the philosophy of the present age), 1917

Revoliutsiia i kul'tura, 1917
Na perevale, 3 vols., 1918–20
Ofeira: Putevye zametki, chast' pervaia, 1921; later section published as "Afrika zhdet menia (iz Afrikanskogo dnevnika A. Belogo)," in *Vstrechi s proshlym*, 1984: 150–69
Glossolaliia, 1922
Sirin uchenogo varvarstva (The siren bird of scholastic barbarism), 1922
O smysle poznaniia (On the meaning of cognition), 1922
Poeziia slova (Poetry of the word), 1922
Vospominaniia ob A. A. Bloke, 1922–23
Odna iz obitelei tsarstva tenei (One of the mansions of the realm of shadows), 1924
Veter s Kavkaza, 1928
Ritm kak dialektika i "Mednyi vsadnik", 1929
Na rubezhe dvukh stoletii, 1930; revised edition, edited by A. V. Lavrov, 1989
Nachalo veka, 1933; revised edition, edited by A. V. Lavrov, 1990
Mezhdu dvukh revoliutsii, 1934; revised edition, edited by A. V. Lavrov, 1990
Masterstvo Gogolia, 1934
Selected Essays, edited and translated by Steven Cassedy, 1985

Other writings: six novels (*Serebryanyi golub'* [The Silver Dove], 1909–10; *Petersburg*, 1916; *Kotik Letaev*, 1922; *Moskva*, 1926; *Kreshchenyi kitaets* [The Christened Chinaman], 1927; *Maski*, 1932), and collections of poetry.

Collected works edition: *Sochineniia*, edited by V. Piskarev, 1990.

Bibliographies
Benina, M. A., "Andrei Belyi: Bibliograficheskii ukazatel', 1976–avgust 1986," in *Andrei Belyi: Problemy tvorchestva*, edited by S. Lesnevskii and A. Mikhailov, Moscow: Sovetskii Pisatel', 1988: 806–29
Bugaeva, K. N., and G. Nivat, "L'Œuvre polémique, critique et journalistique d'Andrej Belyj," *Cahiers du Monde Russe et Soviétique* 15 (1974): 21–39
Elsworth, John, "Bely Studies Since the Centenary," *Scottish Slavonic Review* 12–13 (1989): 69–98
Russkie sovetskie pisateli: Poety: Biobibliograficheskii ukazatel', vol. 3, part 1, Moscow, 1979: 114–96

Further Reading
Cioran, Samuel D., *The Apocalyptic Symbolism of Andrej Belyj*, The Hague: Mouton, 1973
Elsworth, J. D., *Andrey Bely: A Critical Study of the Novels*, Cambridge: Cambridge Unversity Press, 1983
Keys, Roger, *The Reluctant Modernist: Andrei Belyi and the Development of Russian Fiction, 1902–1914*, Oxford: Clarendon Press, and New York: Oxford University Press, 1996
Malmstad, John E., editor, *Andrey Bely: Spirit of Symbolism*, Ithaca, New York: Cornell University Press, 1987
Peterson, Ronald E., editor and translator, *The Russian Symbolists: An Anthology of Critical and Theoretical Writings*, Ann Arbor, Michigan: Ardis, 1986
Pyman, Avril, *A History of Russian Symbolism*, Cambridge and New York: Cambridge University Press, 1994

Benchley, Robert
American, 1889–1945

Most of Robert Benchley's best essays were written during a 20-year period following the end of World War I, when he was writing columns and serving in various editorial positions, first with *Vanity Fair*, then with the *Life* magazine of his day, and finally, from the late 1920s on, with the **New Yorker**. In addition to his regular columns, Benchley often wrote freelance essays for his own and other periodicals during this productive period. In the late 1930s, fearing that he was beginning to repeat himself, and often short of money, he gave up writing professionally to concentrate on his more financially rewarding alternative career as a radio and motion-picture performer. Books that appeared after 1940 are comprised mostly of pieces written earlier.

Apart from occasional parodies and skits, Benchley showed little interest in writing fiction or drama, and his books were simply compilations under catchy titles of essays published previously in magazines and newspapers. While he wrote many drama reviews and did some other more or less serious journalistic work, he was essentially a humorist and an essayist. Benchley's concentration on humor, often humor of a very playful, almost nonsensical sort, and his apparent disregard for theme, source, or time of original publication in compiling his books encourage the misconception that he took his work lightly. In fact, he wrote with a strong sense of obligation to maintain the quality and freshness of his humor and to resist relying on the stock devices and situations he attacked in his drama reviews; in addition, his diligent, almost obsessive revision made meeting deadlines a constant struggle.

Benchley's style is difficult to characterize because, within the limits of his chosen form, he was so versatile. Moreover, he frequently adopted the voices of personas, worked with parody, and employed stylistic incongruity for humorous effect. Even when writing more or less as himself, Benchley deliberately inflated his style; for the kinds of humorous effects he wanted, a degree of pomposity was essential. The seriousness with which Benchley's central persona took himself, his insecurities, and the things that annoyed him accentuated by contrast the silliness of what he had to say. In general, the further a persona was from Benchley himself, the more pronounced this incongruity between style and substance became. It should be added, however, that most of the inflation in Benchley's prose involved diction and general tone. On the whole, apart from occasional humorous interruptions, his style profited from his early work in newspapers in being syntactically straightforward and easy to read.

As well as being, in his narrow field, a creative, highly original artist, Benchley was also a craftsman, and there were few humorous devices he did not employ effectively. A few suited him particularly well, however. Benchley specialized in logical and structural confusion, usually delivered through an earnest, self-important persona who gave no indication of wanting to be funny. He particularly liked long, apologetic, or self-justifying openings, which he often followed with incongruously short, increasingly illogical essays that set readers up for anticlimactic endings. These structural games supported another of Benchley's favorite devices – satirical reduction through misinterpretation and oversimplification. As usual, working through a persona, characteristically one self-deluded about his grasp of his subject and excessively eager to appear as an authority, Benchley would expose the pretentiousness and sham he saw in some specialized field in the course of attempting to explain it. He frequently used parody to the same end. Psychoanalysis, scientific fads, overly erudite literary

criticism, the jargon of professional sports, conventions of operatic plots, stylized crime reporting, obscurity in modern art and literature – such were the typical targets of Benchley's satire. These basic techniques for deflation were hardly new in American humor, but Benchley raised the level. He wrote not for people who distrusted urban values and cultural innovations on principle, but for an audience which, while sharing his dislike of overspecialization, pseudo-sophistication, and needless obscurity, was interested in and informed about the subjects he made fun of.

But Benchley lacked the anger of a true satirist. He used his gift for discovering and revealing the ridiculous side of serious subjects more to amuse than to reform, and he was inclined by temperament to make fun of himself more than any other subject. Many of his best essays were based on humorous experiences in his own life: the challenges and aggravations of parenthood, the frustration of mastering machines and gadgets, the annoyances of traveling and dining out. Even Benchley's eccentric dislike – mutual, apparently – of birds became part of his literary act. This comic representation of himself as a bumbling, insecure, somewhat neurotic, middle-class American male challenged to comprehend and cope with the rapid social and technological changes of his time was central to his popular appeal, as both a writer and a performer. Despite his weaknesses and eccentricities, the central Benchley persona often displayed an estimable pluckiness in situations largely beyond his control. He also embodied, in exaggerated form, a skepticism about trends and fads of the period with which many readers would have identified.

Benchley played a central part in the sophistication of popular American humor that took place between the World Wars. While he maintained the vitality and adapted basic techniques of folk humor and its literary offshoots, he dramatically raised the tonal and intellectual level in order to reach a better educated, more cultured, urban audience. His craftsmanship, originality, and wit won him a following not only among readers but also among other writers, and his influence is especially noticeable in the work of such younger contemporaries as **S. J. Perelman**, **James Thurber**, and **E. B. White**.

WILLIAM CONNOR

See also Humorous Essay

Biography

Robert Charles Benchley. Born 15 September 1889 in Worcester, Massachusetts. Studied at Phillips Exeter Academy, Exeter, New Hampshire, 1907–08; Harvard University, Cambridge, Massachusetts, 1908–12, B.A., 1912; president of the editorial board, *Harvard Lampoon*. Worked for Curtis publishers, 1912–14, and in the personnel office of a paper company, Boston, 1914–15. Married Gertrude Darling, 1914: two sons. Editor and contributor, New York *Tribune* and *Tribune* magazine, 1916–17, and the *Tribune Graphic* Sunday supplement, 1918. Secretary, Aircraft Board, Washington, DC, 1917–18. Managing editor, *Vanity Fair*, 1919–20; columnist of "Books and Other Things," New York *World*, 1920–21; dramatic editor, 1921–29, and editor, 1924–29, *Life* magazine; contributor, 1925–40, and dramatic editor, 1929–40, the *New Yorker*. Founder, with Dorothy Parker and others, Algonquin Hotel Round Table, 1920. Also actor: with the Music Box Revue, 1923–24, and in many films (mostly shorts), 1923–45; radio broadcaster, from 1938. Awards: Academy Award (Oscar), for short film, 1936. Died (of a stroke) in New York, 21 November 1945.

Selected Writings

Essays and Related Prose
Of All Things, 1921
Love Conquers All, 1922
Pluck and Luck, 1925
The Early Worm, 1927
20,000 Leagues Under the Sea; or, David Copperfield, 1928
The Treasurer's Report and Other Aspects of Community Singing, 1930
No Poems; or, Around the World Backwards and Sideways, 1932
From Bed to Worse; or, Comforting Thoughts About the Bison, 1934
My Ten Years in a Quandary and How They Grew, 1936
After 1903 – What?, 1938
Inside Benchley (selection), 1942
Benchley Beside Himself, 1943
One Minute Please, 1945
Benchley – or Else!, 1947
Chips off the Old Benchley, 1949
The "Reel" Benchley, edited by George Hornby, 1950
The Bedside Manner; or, No More Nightmares, 1952
The Benchley Roundup, edited by Nathaniel Benchley, 1954
Benchley Lost and Found: 39 Prodigal Pieces, 1970
Benchley at the Theatre: Dramatic Criticism, 1920–1940, edited by Charles Getchell, 1985

Other writings: 14 screenplays.

Bibliography
Ernst, Gordon E., Jr., *Robert Benchley: An Annotated Bibliography*, Westport, Connecticut: Greenwood Press, 1995

Further Reading
Altman, Billy, *Laughter's Gentle Soul: The Life of Robert Benchley*, New York: Norton, 1997
Benchley, Nathaniel, *Robert Benchley, a Biography*, New York: McGraw Hill, 1955; London: Cassell, 1956
Gehring, Wes D., *"Mr. B."; or, Comforting Thoughts About the Bison: A Critical Biography of Robert Benchley*, Westport, Connecticut: Greenwood Press, 1992
Rosmond, Babette, *Robert Benchley: His Life and Good Times*, Garden City, New York: Doubleday, 1970
Yates, Norris W., *Robert Benchley*, New York: Twayne, 1968

Benda, Julien

French, 1867–1956

Despite the wide range of his interests, which cover such diverse fields as philosophy, aesthetics, history, sociology, literature, and politics, Benda was and remains known as a man of one idea. It was he more than anyone else in the 20th century who conceptualized the notion of the intellectual. In 1927 Benda published *La Trahison des clercs* (*The Betrayal of the Intellectuals*), in which he formulated his famous thesis of the intellectuals' betrayal of their vocation as the guardians of Truth and its absolute character. The book instantly caused a commotion, and its title, like that of **Ortega y Gasset**'s *La rebelión de las masas* (1930; *The Revolt of the Masses*), Hermann Rauschning's *Die Revolution des Nihilismus* (1938;

The Revolution of Nihilism), or Raymond Aron's *L'Opium des intellectuels* (1955; *The Opium of the Intellectuals*), became a catch-phrase among political scientists. Benda's other works are an elaboration upon the thesis advanced in *The Betrayal of the Intellectuals*, and they can be properly understood only when read against its background.

The term *clerc*, which Benda used in the title rather than *intellectuel*, was applied in the Middle Ages to all those who devoted their lives exclusively to the pursuit of Truth and who, on account of their concerns with "unworldly causes," were not subject to civil jurisdiction. Paradigmatic examples of the *clercs* whom Benda mentions are Socrates and Jesus, and several thinkers (St. Thomas, Descartes, **Pascal**, Spinoza, Malebranche, Newton, **Kant**, Husserl) who openly declared "their kingdom not to be of this world." In contrast to the *clerc* of old, the modern *clerc* abandoned his vocation, making Truth subservient to a political program or an ideology. "What a joy for them to learn that this universal is a mere phantom, that there exist only particular truths, Lorraine truths, Provençal truths, Brittany truths ... Humanity hears the same teaching about classes and learns that there is a bourgeois truth and a working-class truth; better still, that the functioning of our minds should be different according to whether we are working men or bourgeois." Again, in contrast to the *clerc* of old, for whom his homeland was a spiritual realm, the modern *clerc* asserts that he is first of all a member of a nation, a race, a class of which he claims to be the spokesman. "The modern world has made the 'clerk' into a citizen ... Humanity is national. The layman has won ... The 'clerk' is not only conquered, he is assimilated. The man of science, the artist, the philosopher are attached to their nations as much as the day-laborer and the merchant."

Benda links the process of the "nationalization" of the *clerc* with the gradual demise of Hellenistic metaphysics. He devoted three works to describing this phenomenon: *La Fin de l'éternel* (1927; The end of the eternal), *Essai d'un discours cohérent sur les rapports de Dieu et du monde* (1931; Essay on the discourse on the relationship between God and the world), and *La Crise du rationalisme* (1949; The crisis of rationalism). Although the crisis of rationalism was, as Benda called it, a triumph of "Luther over Erasmus," it was only after the appearance of German philosophy (especially the philosophies of **Schlegel, Fichte, Nietzsche**, Lotze) that "Luther's triumph" became a palpable fact which could be observed in art and literature. In *Belphégor* (1918), Benda notices that the current public no longer knows how to derive *intellectual* pleasure from art; it demands instead that art give rise to emotions and sensations. There are essentially three culprits in this situation: the Romantics, the "intuitionists," and various critics of rationalism. The Romantics declared "artistic sensibility" as the criterion of judgment. As a result a work of art is considered "great as soon it achieves a literary and artistic success," the intellectual content being of no interest; consequently, when "all arguments are equally defensible ... error is no more false than truth" (*The Betrayal of the Intellectuals*). The authors guilty of "Romanticism" are **Mallarmé**, Proust, **Gide, Valéry, Alain**, Giraudoux, Suarès, and the Surrealists (*La France byzantine* [1945; Byzantine France]). Other culprits are philosophers of a different provenance: Blondel, Lacroix, Rouyer, Gonseth, Bachelard, Le Roy, Rougier, Cuvillier, Brunschvicg, and

Lefebvre. All of them rejected "classical rationalism" either as an "inferior form of cognition" on account of its being incapable of "inventing" (*La Crise du rationalisme*) or, as in the case of the Marxist Lefebvre, as "defective."

Benda's true intellectual foe is Henri Bergson. In his three books, *Le Bergsonisme, ou, une philosophie de la mobilité* (1912; Bergsonism, or, a philosophy of mobilization), *Une philosophie pathétique* (1913; A pathetic philosophy), and *Sur le succès du Bergsonisme* (1914; On the success of Bergsonism), Benda attacked Bergson's concept of "intuition." However, what in Bergson was an intellectual error became a real threat from the American "apostle" of pragmatism, **William James**: after over 20 centuries of humankind's being taught that the morality of an action lies in its disinterestedness, James declared that the moral is that which fits the circumstances.

Benda's analysis does not stop at the theoretical level, however. The changes which the new intellectual movements brought about in the 19th century lie at the root of the political and social crises in which Europe found itself in the middle of that century. Having rejected the Hellenistic idea of the timeless Absolute, the modern *clerc* found his vocation in exalting the value of that which exists only "in time" – namely, a nation. It was not until the middle of the 19th century – called by Benda "the age of the intellectual organization of political hatred" – that nations began to see themselves as bearers of Truth in the name of which they fought wars. Benda is far from expressing a naive view of the peaceful coexistence of nations in the past. However, as he observes, in contrast to the 19th century, wars had been for the most part motivated by a desire to annex the other's territory or to extend one's own political control over another nation; they were essentially the wars of kings. In the 19th century wars became an instrument of demonstrating the "cultural superiority" of one nation over another. "This form of patriotism was so little known to preceding ages that there are countless examples of nations adopting the cultures of other nations, even of those with whom they were at war, and in addition reverencing the culture adopted" (*The Betrayal of the Intellectuals*).

As a result of the growing need for a "unified Europe" in response to the nationalistic tendencies that led to World War I, Benda published *Discours à la nation européenne* (1933; Discourse on the European nation). He scornfully rejected the European project, finding it to be nothing but an empty idea ("pure reason has never founded anything in the terrestrial order"). Those who had such a dream in the past (Emperor Justinian, Charlemagne, Charles V) were either actual or aspiring tyrants. The new dreamers, like the old, "completely ignore the fact that Europe's peoples have their respective histories, their ideas, their languages." Europe is a spiritual realm; if the European project is ever to come true, its proponents need first to repudiate the myth of **Marx** (who conceived of man as a product of economic relationships) on behalf of the myth of **Plato**, who believed man to be first and foremost a spiritual being.

Most of Benda's works did not survive much beyond their author's death, and only a handful are known today by their titles. What remains truly durable in Benda's output is his book-length essay on intellectuals. Benda had written it before the "Great Conversion" of intellectuals to fascism, Nazism, and communism. Most of the names (Mommsen, Treitschke,

Ostwald, **Brunetière**, Barrès, Lemaître, **Péguy**, Maurras, D'Annunzio, Kipling) and historical events (e.g. the Dreyfus Affair) which served Benda as the material to formulate his thesis, do not say much to a contemporary reader. Yet, if Benda's *The Betrayal of the Intellectuals* did not share the fate of his other works, it is due to the correctness of his diagnosis of the reasons which lie at the root of the Great Betrayal.

ZBIGNIEW JANOWSKI

Biography
Born 26 (some sources say 28) December 1867 in Paris. Studied at the Lycées Charlemagne, 1876–84, Condorcet, from 1884, Henri IV, 1884–87, Saint-Louis, 1887–88, and the École Centrale, 1888–91; military service, 1891–92; the Sorbonne, 1892–94, licence in history, 1894. Contributor to various periodicals, including *Revue Blanche* (White review), *Revue de Paris* (Paris review), **Nouvelle Revue Française** (New French review), *Mercure de France* (Mercury of France), *Divan*, and *Le Figaro*. Frequented the salon of Simone Casimir-Périer. Went bankrupt, 1913. Lectured at various American universities, 1936–38. Lived in Carcassonne during World War II. Married late in life. Commander, Legion of Honor, 1938. Died in Fontenay-aux-Roses, near Paris, 7 June 1956.

Selected Writings

Essays and Related Prose
Dialogues à Byzance, 1900
Mon premier Testament, 1910
Le Bergsonisme, ou, une philosophie de la mobilité, 1912
Une philosophie pathétique, 1913
Sur le succès du Bergsonisme, 1914
Les Sentiments de Critias (articles), 1917
Belphégor: Essai sur l'esthétique de la présente société française, 1918; as *Belphegor*, translated by Sarah J. I. Lawson, 1929
Billets de Sirius (articles), 1925
Lettres à Mélisande, 1925
La Fin de l'éternel, 1927
La Trahison des clercs, 1927; as *The Great Betrayal*, and as *The Treason of the Intellectuals*, translated by Richard Aldington, 1928; as *The Betrayal of the Intellectuals*, 1955
Essai d'un discours cohérent sur les rapports de Dieu et du monde, 1931
Esquisse d'une histoire des Français dans leur volonté d'être une nation, 1932
Discours à la nation européenne, 1933
Précision, 1930–1937 (articles), 1937
Le Rapport d'Uriel, 1943
La Grande Épreuve des démocraties: Essai sur les principes démocratiques, leur nature, leur histoire, leur valeur philosophique, 1945
La France byzantine; ou, Le Triomphe de la littérature pure, Mallarmé, Gide, Proust, Valéry, Alain, Giraudoux, Suarès, les surréalistes: Essai d'une psychologie originelle du littérateur, 1945
Les Cahiers d'un clerc (1936-1949), 1949
La Crise du rationalisme, 1949

Other writings: three novels (*L'Ordination* [*The Yoke of Pity*], 1911–12; *Les Amorandes*, 1922; *Songes d'Eleuthère*, 1949), a collection of short stories, autobiography, and works on politics, philosophy, and literature. Also edited the *Œuvres complètes* by **La Bruyère** and the *Dictionnaire philosophique* by **Voltaire**.

Further Reading
Aron, Raymond, *The Opium of the Intellectuals*, Lanham, Maryland: University Press of America, 1985 (original French edition, 1955)

Furet, François, *Le Passé d'une illusion: Essai sur l'idée communiste au XXe siècle*, Paris: Laffont/Lévy, 1995

Kołakowski, Leszek, *Bergson*, Oxford and New York: Oxford University Press, 1985: 88–93

Kołakowski, Leszek, "The Intellectuals," in his *Modernity on Endless Trial*, Chicago: University of Chicago Press, 1990: 32–43

Niess, Robert J., *Julien Benda*, Ann Arbor: University of Michigan Press, 1956

Read, Herbert, Introduction to *The Betrayal of the Intellectuals* by Benda, Boston: Beacon Press, 1955: xiii–xxxii

Bengtsson, Frans G.

Swedish, 1894–1954

Frans G. Bengtsson was the pre-eminent Swedish essayist of the 20th century, successful as the first practitioner of the informal essay in Sweden. Bengtsson associated with literary circles formed at the University of Lund in the early part of the 20th century, although his indifferent performance as a student camouflaged a brilliant mind later given full rein in his essays.

Bengtsson won a large reading public with his historical novel, *Röde orm* (1941–45; *The Long Ships*), a work considered by some to have contributed to a reawakening of interest in Viking civilization. He was particularly interested in history, as many of the essays demonstrate, being in some sense historical or based on historical incidents or people. In the 1920s he began publishing historical sketches in the Swedish periodical *Ord och Bild* (Word and picture), the first of which dealt with Joseph Conrad (1924). It was with his first volume of essays, *Litteratörer och militärer* (1929; Literary and military figures), that his career as an essayist blossomed. The collection contains several historical sketches, as well as pieces of literary criticism and literary history. Subjects include Sir Walter Scott, sagas, and King Charles XII of Sweden (whose biography he also wrote). He was also interested in historic figures from the American Civil War such as Abraham Lincoln, Jeb Stuart, and Nathan Bedford Forrest. Subsequent essay collections include *Silversköldarna* (1931; The silver shields), *De långhåriga merovingerna* (1933; The long-haired Merovingians), *Sällskap för en eremit* (1938; Company for a hermit), *För nöjes skull* (1947; For pleasure's sake), and the posthumous *Folk som sjöng* (1955; People who sang), as well as a volumes of selected essays in Swedish and in translation (*A Walk to an Ant Hill*, 1950).

Bengtsson was an intensely personal writer, indeed reserved to the point of being secretive. Anyone looking for biographical information will find little available. Whether this reflects his pessimistic philosophy and aestheticism is a matter of conjecture. Swedish critics have pointed out parallels with both Klara Johanson and German idealism, going back to **Schopenhauer**. Others have identified Bengtsson as both an aesthete and an entertainer.

Bengtsson's use of language, his diction, his large vocabulary, and the literary quality of his formulations are clear indications of why he has not been surpassed by his countrymen as an essayist. He characteristically quotes in foreign languages, but nonetheless carries his learning lightly, managing to combine an encyclopedic knowledge with a relaxed, informal tone and style. As Alrik Gustafson describes in *A History of Swedish Literature* (1961), Bengtsson's essays are an amalgam of "the whimsicalities of Charles Lamb, the vigor and independence of spirit of William Hazlitt, and the heroic-romantic idealism of Robert Louis Stevenson." His progress through an essay can best be described as leisurely, displaying a penchant for tangents, interjections, and personal reflections. He writes with charm and enthusiasm, particularly for historical subjects. Apart from his historical sketches, his subject matter ranges widely – from the art of lying, detective literature, and chess playing, to battles between red and black ants, ghost stories, and a childhood visit to a photographer – the more exotic and whimsical the better.

In addition to being an essayist, Bengtsson was a successful translator, translating into Swedish such works as **Henry David Thoreau**'s *Walden* and John Milton's *Paradise Lost*. In both his essays and translations, Bengtsson was a storyteller and was thus not necessarily aiming for historical accuracy. His work has been "unparalleled" – deserved praise for both the translations and the essays.

P. M. MITCHELL

Biography

Frans Gunnar Bengtsson. Born 4 October 1894 in Tossjö, near Kristianstad. Studied at the University of Lund, fil.kand., 1920, fil.lic.,1930. Married Gerda Fineman, 1939. Died in Ribbingsfors, 19 December 1954.

Selected Writings

Essays and Related Prose
Litteratörer och militärer, 1929
Silversköldarna, och andra essayer, 1931
De långhåriga merovingerna, och andra essayer, 1933
Sällskap för en eremit, 1938
För nöjes skull, 1947
A Walk to an Ant Hill and Other Essays, translated by Michael Roberts and Elspeth Schubert, 1950
Tankar i gröngräset (selected essays), 1953
Folk som sjöng, och andra essayer, 1955
Äreräddning för Campeadoren (selected articles), 1986

Other writings: novels (including *Röde orm* [*The Long Ships*], 1941–45), poetry, a two-volume biography of King Charles XII of Sweden (1935–36), and memoirs (1953). Also translated several works, including Milton's *Paradise Lost*.

Collected works edition: *Samlade skrifter*, 1950–55.

Further Reading

Ehnmark, Elof, *Frans G. Bengtsson*, Stockholm: Norstedt, 1946
Harrie, Ivar, *Legenden om Bengtsson*, Stockholm: Norstedt, 1971
Lundkvist, A., *Frans G. Bengtsson, essayisten*, Stockholm: Tiden, 1941
Thompson, L. S., "Frans G. Bengtsson, 1894–1954," *Kentucky Foreign Language Quarterly* 2 (1955)

Benjamin, Walter

German, 1892–1940

Walter Benjamin is one of the central essayists of the German-Jewish intellectual tradition. Born and raised in Berlin in a bourgeois household representing both stability and confinement, Benjamin grew into a critic of literature, Western philosophy, and contemporary European culture. His oeuvre consists of hundreds of essays on literature, culture, history, and philosophy as well as book reviews and records of his travels throughout Europe. Benjamin was not in the strict sense a philosopher, nor entirely a creative writer, but a hybrid author who fused his philosophical as well as creative talents. These in turn were often intermingled with early German Romantic ideas on language and translation, Jewish mysticism, and Marxist materialism.

His persona as cultural critic was formed in the years of childhood and youth in Berlin, where the Wilhelmian environment provided both conservatism and confinement. Benjamin's powerful sense of cultural criticism was ignited while participating in the traditional German educational system, notable for its academic rigor and excellence, but also for its suppression of originality and creativity. Benjamin's involvement in educational reform under the auspices of the Youth Movement (1912–17) was instrumental to his future role as cultural critic as well as intellectual and social outsider. His articles of 1913 in the youth journal *Der Anfang* (The beginning) consistently address issues of repression as well as the multifaceted hypocrisies of bourgeois life.

By means of cultural criticism, the early Benjamin developed a challenging methodology of cognition which earned him mostly criticism from the contemporary German academic establishment. His friends at the Institute for Social Research in Frankfurt-on-Main, including Max Horkheimer and **Theodor W. Adorno**, were often puzzled by Benjamin's opaque visions and representations. Critical and anti-systematic thinking for Benjamin was the central and almost metaphysical pillar from which he set out as essayist, and to which he returned at the end of most essays. In his well-known essays on **Charles Baudelaire**, Marcel Proust, Franz Kafka, and Karl Kraus, critical thought is directed and informed by its relation to the autonomous work of art. However, the traditional notions of this autonomy are curiously short-circuited by Benjamin's powerful reflections on the fragmentary constellation of 19th-century and contemporary European culture. For Benjamin, literary works are "irreducible as deeds"; it is to this philosophical and literary complexity that his many essays on writers from the French, German, and Russian literary tradition of Modernism speak.

1924 was a decisive year for Benjamin in his development from eclectic philosopher to more politically engaged essayist as the political force field of the Weimar Republic became more overtly established. His essays of this time were influenced by Marxist dialectical materialism – strangely wed, however, to early Romantic language theories. The collection of this period, *Einbahnstrasse* (1928; *One-Way Street*), pays homage to the surrealist avant-garde tradition of representation which would be crucial to his later and most central, yet also most controversial project, *Das Passagenwerk* (The Arcades project). As the essays of *One-Way Street* already suggest, objects or marginalia of daily life rather than Platonic ideas would from then on provide the discursive ground from which the most pressing, yet also the most decentering and fragmentary, experiences of Modernism were to be evaluated and rewritten. Moreover, by introducing collage and montage into

the essayistic structures of textual representation, Benjamin inaugurated a new way of writing history – the materialist history of modernity as seen from an essayist's perspective.

Modernism as an aesthetic, philosophical, and cultural phenomenon emerged during the 19th century. For Benjamin this historical moment, when long-cherished symbolic affinities in the material and ideistic world began to crumble, revealed layers of meaning which could then be explored and represented in more fragmentary and allegorical ways. From *One-Way Street* to the curious *Passagenwerk* Benjamin explores how meaning is primarily constructed and suspended in relation to objects of daily life which, ordained as "profane illuminations," hold their own ground as both entirely real and entirely imaginary. Thus Benjamin's essayistic work addresses in incisive prose the most challenging questions and representational concerns of the German, French, and Russian traditions of Modernism.

At the point of intersection between eclectic philosophy and cultural criticism, Benjamin creates in the almost two thousand pages of the *Passagenwerk* a materialist philosophy of history consisting of thousands of quotations, reflections, and essays on 19th-century Paris. This test ground for the emergence of Modernism on all fronts represents a collection of raw data in addition to reflective essays and aphorisms rather than a consistent and more traditional univocal narrative. Much like the essay in **Montaigne**'s tradition of skepticism, understood in the etymological sense of "seeing" and "perceiving," Benjamin's essays challenge the boundaries and limits of traditional forms of thought and representation. Readers of this work are forced into a curious paradoxical position: they must both reconstruct and create elements of a former dialogue of cultural construction which in a univocal way will never again be accessible. It is against this curious representational paradox and silence that Benjamin's work begins to resonate.

Benjamin will always be remembered for his courage to remain a visionary as well as an intellectual outsider somewhere, as he himself put it, "in the folds of time."

MARION DOEBELING

Biography

Walter Benedix Schönflies Benjamin. Born 15 July 1892 in Berlin. Studied at the Universities of Freiburg, 1912, Berlin, 1913, Munich, 1915–17, Berne, Ph.D., 1919, and Frankfurt-on-Main, thesis rejected, 1925. Married Sophie Pollak, 1917 (divorced, 1930): one son. Contributor to various journals, from the early 1920s. Visited Russia, 1926–27. Forced to leave Germany when the Nazis rose to power, 1933; lived in Paris. Associated with the Institute for Social Research, Frankfurt-on-Main, 1934–37, and wrote for its journal *Zeitschrift für Sozialforschung* (Journal for social research). Attempted to escape Nazi regime by emigrating to the United States via Spain, but committed suicide when in danger of being betrayed to the Gestapo. Died (suicide by morphine overdose) in Port Bou, 26 September 1940.

Selected Writings

Essays and Related Prose
Einbahnstrasse, 1928; as *One-Way Street*, in *One-Way Street, and Other Writings*, translated by Edmund Jephcott and Kingsley Shorter, 1979

Illuminationen: Ausgewählte Schriften, edited by Siegfried Unseld,
1961; as *Illuminations*, edited by Hannah Arendt, translated by
Harry Zohn, 1968
Goethes Wahlverwandtschaften, 1964
Zur Kritik der Gewalt und andere Aufsätze, 1965
Versuche über Brecht, edited by Rolf Tiedemann, 1966; as
Understanding Brecht, translated by Anna Bostock, 1973
Angelus novus, 1966
Über Literatur, 1969
Charles Baudelaire: Ein Lyriker im Zeitalter des Hochkapitalismus,
edited by Rolf Tiedemann, 1969; as *Charles Baudelaire: A
Poet in the Era of High Capitalism*, translated by Harry Zohn,
1973
Berliner Chronik, edited by Gershom Scholem, 1970
Drei Hörmodelle, 1971
Der Stratege im Literaturkampf: Zu Literaturwiss, edited by Hella
Tiedemann-Bartels, 1974
Aussichten: Illustrierte Aufsätze, 1977
Reflections: Essays, Aphorisms, Autobiographical Writings, edited by
Peter Demetz, translated by Edmund Jephcott, 1978
One-Way Street, and Other Writings, translated by Edmund
Jephcott and Kingsley Shorter, 1979
Moskauer Tagebuch, edited by Gary Smith, 1980; as *Moscow
Diary*, edited by Gary Smith, translated by Richard Sieburth,
1985
Benjamin über Kafka: Texte, Briefzeugnisse, Aufzeichnungen, edited
by Hermann Schweppenhäuser, 1981
Passagenwerk, vol. 5 of *Gesammelte Schriften*, edited by Rolf
Tiedemann, 1983; part as "N [Re the Theory of Knowledge,
Theory of Progress]," translated by Leigh Hafrey and Richard
Sieburth Smith, in *Walter Benjamin: Philosophy, Aesthetics,
History*, edited by Gary Smith, 1989

Other writings: works on language, and correspondence (collected
and translated in *The Correspondence of Walter Benjamin,
1910–1940*, 1994). Also translated works by Charles Baudelaire and
others.

Collected works edition: *Gesammelte Schriften*, edited by Rolf
Tiedemann and Hermann Schweppenhäuser, 7 vols., 1972–89.

Bibliographies

Nordquist, Joan, *Walter Benjamin*, Santa Cruz, California:
Reference and Research Services, 1989
Smith, Gary, "Walter Benjamin in English: A Bibliography of
Translations," in *Walter Benjamin: Philosophy, Aesthetics,
History*, edited by Smith, Chicago: University of Chicago Press,
1989

Further Reading

Adorno, Theodor W., "Benjamin the Letter Writer," in *Notes to
Literature*, vol. 2, edited by Rolf Tiedemann, New York:
Columbia University Press, 1992
Alter, Robert, *Necessary Angels: Tradition and Modernity in Kafka,
Benjamin, and Scholem*, Cambridge, Massachusetts: Harvard
University Press, and Cincinnati: Hebrew Union College Press,
1991
Arendt, Hannah, Introduction to *Illuminations* by Benjamin, edited
by Arendt, New York: Harcourt Brace and World, 1968
Buck-Morss, Susan, *The Dialectics of Seeing: Walter Benjamin and
the Arcades Project*, Cambridge, Massachusetts: MIT Press, 1991
Bullock, Marcus Paul, *Romanticism and Marxism: The
Philosophical Development of Literary Theory and Literary
History in Walter Benjamin and Friedrich Schlegel*, New York:
Lang, 1987
Cohen, Margaret, *Profane Illumination: Walter Benjamin and the
Paris of Surreal Revolution*, Berkeley: University of California
Press, 1993

Frisby, David, *Fragments of Modernity: Theories of Modernity in
the Work of Simmel, Kracauer, and Benjamin*, Cambridge: Polity
Press, 1985; Cambridge, Massachusetts: MIT Press, 1986
Gilloch, Graeme, *Myth and Metropolis: Walter Benjamin and the
City*, Cambridge: Polity Press, and Cambridge, Massachusetts:
Blackwell, 1996
Handelman, Susan A., *Fragments of Redemption: Jewish Thought
and Literary Theory in Benjamin, Scholem, and Levinas*,
Bloomington: Indiana University Press, 1991
Jennings, Michael William, *Dialectical Images: Walter Benjamin's
Theory of Literary Criticism*, Ithaca, New York: Cornell
University Press, 1987
McCole, John, *Walter Benjamin and the Antinomies of Tradition*,
Ithaca, New York: Cornell University Press, 1993
Mitchell, Stanley, Introduction to *Understanding Brecht* by
Benjamin, London: Verso, 1983
Nägele, Rainer, editor, *Benjamin's Ground: New Readings of
Walter Benjamin*, Detroit: Wayne State University Press, 1988
Nägele, Rainer, *Theater, Theory, Speculation: Walter Benjamin and
the Scenes of Modernity*, Baltimore: Johns Hopkins University
Press, 1991
New German Critique issue on Benjamin, 39 (Fall 1986)
Scholem, Gershom, *Walter Benjamin: The Story of a Friendship*,
Philadelphia: Jewish Publication Society of America, 1981;
London: Faber, 1982 (original German edition, 1975)
Smith, Gary, editor, *On Walter Benjamin: Critical Essays and
Recollections*, Cambridge, Massachusetts: MIT Press, 1988
Smith, Gary, editor, *Walter Benjamin: Philosophy, Aesthetics,
History*, Chicago: University of Chicago Press, 1989
Witte, Bernd, *Walter Benjamin: An Intellectual Biography*, Detroit:
Wayne State University Press, 1991 (original German edition,
1976)
Wolin, Richard, *Walter Benjamin, an Aesthetic of Redemption*,
Berkeley: University of California Press, 1994 (original edition,
1982)

Benn, Gottfried

German, 1886–1956

The importance of the essay form varied with each period in
Gottfried Benn's life. He particularly favored prose in situations of crisis; his use of the essay in the crucial period of the
1930s, for example, is not only a preference for the essay form,
but also for its potential readership, since the essay reaches a
much wider audience than poetry. Over half of all Benn's essays
appeared between 1930 and 1934, when he found himself
forced from the position of the outsider to that of a crucially
important participant in the conflict between Left and Right.

Benn was never a typical essayist: his greatest achievement
was to place current situations into historical, even anthropological frameworks and thus create surprising perspectives. He
was a superb stylist, even when his vocabulary at times
obscured his subject. He was a master of darkly fascinating
statements, but he was a poet rather than a thinker. His essays
cannot be compared in argumentative originality and lucidity
with those of **Robert Musil**, Hermann Broch, or **Thomas
Mann**, and many critics have in fact emphasized the stylistic
proximity of these essays to poetry, while others have charged
that they misuse an essentially philosophical form. Benn's
method, to replace logical content with lyrical images, does
give his essays a certain monotony, and occasionally betrays
intellectual and stylistic sloppiness and carelessness.

A major problem in these essays is the question of public and private, of representative and subjective viewpoints. Indeed, Benn's first essay, *Das moderne Ich* (1920; The modern self), hovers between the two spheres. On the one hand it is a "public" speech to students of the natural sciences, intended to give an overview of the post-World War I mentality. On the other hand, the shift from politics to the "inner" emotional and spiritual life already betrays Benn's preferences. Benn reveals a more political side in his next major essay, "Neben dem Schriftstellerberuf" (1927; Beside the profession of writer), when he not only affirms the asocial and nihilistic nature of art, but also presents himself as an opponent of the Weimar Republic, though it is as yet difficult to place him in either a leftist or rightist camp.

Increasingly in the late 1920s Benn's interest turned to the definition of art and the artist. In "Totenrede für Klabund" (1928; Eulogy for Klabund), he stresses the sense of mission of the artist, contending that the artist lives between social levels, despised and unknown, while himself a despiser. It was precisely because of this constellation that Benn was vulnerable to the temptation to seek a recognition which lies outside the realm of art, and can only be bestowed at the terrible price of political compromise.

A first indication of the increasing polarization of the German literary scene in fact involved Max Herrmann-Neisse's review of Benn's prose in *Die neue Bücherschau* (The new book review) in 1929. Herrmann-Neisse's enthusiastic comments included a derogatory remark against literary suppliers of political **propaganda** materials and the claim that Benn was more "revolutionary" than the propaganda writers on the Left. Two of the magazine's contributors reacted with a **letter** to the editor, in which they resigned. Benn himself was invited to respond to these letters and did so in his essay "Über die Rolle des Schriftstellers in dieser Zeit" (1929; Concerning the role of the writer in this era). In 1930 there followed "Zur Problematik des Dichterischen" (On the problem of the poetic), Benn's first full-blown poetic "theory" in which he concludes that at no time has art been able to fit into a contemporary context, nor have artists been able to influence the contemporary scene. Rather, the poet-artist is a purveyor of dreams and visions, the prophet of ecstatic existence.

Benn was able to conceive of his idea of the poet as having access to archaic visions because of his "geological" interpretation of the personality, which he presented in "Der Aufbau der Persönlichkeit" (1930; The structure of personality). Here he argues for a new image of man built on the latest developments in psychoanalysis, psychiatry, biology, and anthropology. Benn makes Jung's theory of the collective unconscious the basis for his belief that earlier stages of human development can be accessed in privileged states, such as under the influence of drugs or in a trance. Two further ideas are introduced: that of mutation and that of the phenotype and genotype. His belief in the biological and geological nature of personality allowed him to see the history of humankind in terms of "natural" history. This idea suggested to him that Germany in 1933 entered a phase of mutation, and therefore allowed him to embrace the Nazi doctrine.

Benn's next collection of essays, *Fazit der Perspektiven* (1930; The balance sheet of perspectives), met with considerable antagonism. Moreover, in 1931 there took place the incident which some critics have seen as the main reason for Benn's ultimate decision to move into the rightist camp: his speech at the banquet of the Schutzverband Deutscher Schriftsteller on the occasion of **Heinrich Mann**'s 60th birthday. Benn's attempt to pass over completely Mann's political convictions, and instead to celebrate the earlier, late Romantic and "aesthetic" Mann, met with massive rejection not only in the leftist press but elsewhere as well. In response to the attacks by primarily leftist writers, Benn inevitably found himself in the conservative camp; once there, it was difficult to extract himself from it, as the essays in *Nach dem Nihilismus* (1932; After nihilism) demonstrate.

Much has been written about the events which in 1933 led to Benn's complete accommodation with the Nazi regime. Whether his reactions were purely emotional or he placed his hope for social and cultural stability on the Nazi regime, whether opportunism or political blindness, is difficult to ascertain. More than with any other essay, perhaps, critics have had difficulty with "Dorische Welt" (1934; The Doric world), the glorification of the militaristic and eugenic values of the world of Sparta. Benn does not advance our knowledge of the Doric world beyond the positions of **Nietzsche** and **Jacob Christoph Burckhardt**; the essay's force lies in the positive interpretation of Sparta and the parallels Benn provides with the contemporary scene. It is difficult to determine whether or not the piece is blatant propaganda for the Hitler state or the first obvious break with its ideology. History itself has played a role in our assessment of what Benn advances in this essay, yet many critics remain unreconciled to the idea that Benn, as he wrote affirmatively of the virtues of Sparta, anticipated the Nazi state and its death camps.

Benn's efforts to ingratiate himself with the new regime did not prevent him from falling victim to the relentless drive for uniformity of the Nazi ideology. His clinging to a special status for the artist, his defense of certain traditions of which he felt himself part, notably the expressionist movement, caused him, in 1936, to be accused of "Artistik." The publication of his *Ausgewählte Gedichte* (1936; Selected poems) then provoked the scandal which removed him definitively from the scene he had, perhaps reluctantly in the beginning, occupied in so controversial a fashion. With the collapse of his forum and his readership, Benn almost completely abandoned the genre until after 1945.

1949 saw the publication of *Ausdruckswelt* (Expressive world), a number of essays Benn had written during the period when he was forbidden to publish. They portray him in the old situation of critic of contemporary situations, as dissector and interpreter, but recent events have changed his attitude: his tone is milder, gentler, almost elegiac. The hoped-for mutation, the new race has not been realized. But if it is true that Benn now attacks the Nazis, he also criticizes the German people as a whole, using the criterion not only of nationalism, but also of archaism and barbarism.

Most of the essays take up familiar themes from the 1920s and 1930s, dealing with the dialectic between nihilism and "Artistik." Benn sees in the rejection of the immediate European past a prerequisite for new art. In "Provoziertes Leben" (1943; A provoked life), he claims that salvation lies in a return to "das Primäre" (the primeval), to the prelogical which would do away with the schizoid split in modern man.

In the essay "Pallas" (1943), Benn makes the motherless goddess the symbol of the initial separation between form and formlessness. The goddess becomes not the symbol of nature, but of *Geist* (spirit or intellect). Both come together in the creative act, which, however, is no longer concerned with "natural" nature, but "thinking" nature, or "stylized" nature – in other words, art.

If Benn's autobiography *Doppelleben* (1950; Double life) generally found an ambivalent response, the same cannot be said of critical reactions to "Probleme der Lyrik" (1959; Problems of poetry), which originated as a lecture at the University of Marburg in 1951. Many critics have seen in this text a key to the understanding of Benn's poetic practice not only of the late phase, but of his whole career. Benn situates modern poetry squarely in the hallucinatory-constructive tradition, and reacts, consistently with his beliefs expressed both in the lyric poetry and in the essays of the 1930s and 1940s, to the mixing of sociological and poetological categories in poetry.

Benn's insistence in "Probleme der Lyrik" that modern poetry is monologic in essence reiterates a theme he had elaborated in the essays of the 1930s. In "Altern als Problem für Künstler" (1954; "Artists and Old Age") and "Über mich selbst" (1956; About myself), no further shifts of position can be discerned in his religious beliefs, nor in his poetic theory and practice. "Über mich selbst" in fact effortlessly returns to the definition of the "lyrisches Ich" (the lyric "I") of more than 30 years before.

AUGUSTINUS P. DIERICK

Biography

Born 2 May 1886 in Mansfeld. Studied philosophy and theology at the University of Marburg, 1903–04; medicine at the University of Berlin, 1904–05; medicine at the Kaiser Wilhelm Academy, Berlin, 1905–12, Ph.D., 1912. Worked at a hospital, and as a ship's physician, 1912–13. Served in the army: discharged for health problems, 1912; served in the army medical corps, 1914–18, 1935–45: awarded the Iron Cross (second class), 1914. Married Edith Brosin, 1914 (died, 1922): one daughter and one stepson. Skin and venereal diseases specialist, Berlin, after 1917. Supported National Socialism, from 1932, but renounced the National Socialist Party, 1934. Briefly appointed by Nazis acting chair of literary section, Prussian Academy of Arts, 1933. Denounced at various times throughout the 1930s and 1940s by Nazis, Communists, and Democrats. Works banned, 1938–48. Married Herta von Wedemeyer, 1938 (committed suicide, 1945). Ran a private medical practice, Berlin, from 1945. Married Ilse Kaul, 1946. Awards: Büchner Prize, 1951; Order of Merit (Federal Republic of Germany), 1952. Died (of cancer) in Bad Schlangenbad, 7 July 1956.

Selected Writings

Essays and Related Prose

Das moderne Ich, 1920
Gesammelte Prosa, 1928
Fazit der Perspektiven, 1930
Nach dem Nihilismus, 1932
Der neue Staat und die Intellektuellen, 1933
Kunst und Macht, 1934
Ausdruckswelt: Essays und Aphorismen, 1949
Frühe Prosa und Reden, 1950
Dr. Rönne: Frühe Prosa, 1950
Essays, 1951

Primal Vision: Selected Writings (includes poetry, essays, short stories, and dramatic sketches), edited by E. B. Ashton, 1960
Medizinische Schriften, edited by Werner Rübe, 1965
Weinhaus Wolf und andere Prosa, 1967
Das Gottfried-Benn-Brevier: Aphorismen, Reflexionen, Maximen aus Werken und Briefen, edited by Jürgen P. Wallmann, 1979
Prose, Essays, Poetry (various translators), edited by Volkmar Sander, 1987

Other writings: poetry, plays, correspondence, and the autobiography *Doppelleben* (1950).

Collected works editions: *Gesammelte Werke*, edited by Dieter Wellershoff, 4 vols., 1958–61; *Gesammelte Werke in der Fassung der Erstdrucke*, edited by Bruno Hillebrand, 1983–90; *Sämtliche Werke*, edited by Gerhard Schuster, 5 vols., 1986–91 (in progress).

Bibliographies

Dierick, A. P., *Gottfried Benn and His Critics: Major Interpretations, 1912–1992*, Columbia, South Carolina: Camden House, 1992: 84–106
Lohner, Edgar, "Gottfried Benn-Bibliographie, 1912–1955," *Philobiblon: Eine Vierteljahrsschrift für Buch- und Graphik-Sammler* 1 (1957): 59–70
Lohner, Edgar, and Timm Zenner, *Gottfried Benn: Bibliographie, 1910–1956*, Munich: Cicero Presse, 1985
Schönemann, Peter, and Oskar Sahlberg, "Bibliographie Gottfried Benn," *Text + Kritik* 44 (1985): 156–66
Über Gottfried Benn: Kritische Stimmen 1986, vol. 2, edited by Bruno Hillebrand, Frankfurt-on-Main: Fischer, 1987: 436–507

Further Reading

Alter, Reinhard, *Gottfried Benn: The Artist and Politics (1910–1934)*, Berne and Frankfurt-on-Main: Lang, 1976
Alter, Reinhard, "Gottfried Benn – zwischen Weimarer Republik und Bundesrepublik," in *"Die Mühen der Ebene": Kontinuität und Wandel in der deutschen Literatur und Gesellschaft 1945–1949*, edited by Bernd Hüppauf, Heidelberg: Winter, 1981
Balser, Hans-Dieter, *Das Problem des Nihilismus im Werke Gottfried Benns*, Bonn: Bouvier, 1970 (original edition, 1965)
Bense, Max, "Gottfried Benn: *Kunst und Macht*," *Europäische Revue* 11 (1935): 560–62
Dierick, A. P., *Gottfried Benn and His Critics: Major Interpretations, 1912–1992*, Columbia, South Carolina: Camden House, 1992
Erval, François, "Gottfried Benn ou la double vie des intellectuels allemands," *Les Temps Modernes* 103 (1954)
Exner, Richard, "Zum Problem einer Definition und einer Methodik des Essays als dichterischer Kunstform," *Neophilologus* 46 (1962): 169–82
Eykman, Christoph, "Der Verlust der Geschichte in der deutschen Literatur des zwanzigsten Jahrhunderts," *Neophilologus* 55 (1971): 58–72
Garnier, Pierre, *Gottfried Benn*, Paris: Silvaire, 1959
Grimm, Reinhold, "Ergriffen und dennoch unbeteiligt: Über Gottfried Benns Verhältnis zur Geschichte," *Welt und Wort* 14 (1961): 269–73
Grundlehner, Philip, *The Lyrical Bridge: Essays from Hölderlin to Benn*, Rutherford, New Jersey: Fairleigh Dickinson University Press, 1979
Hartung, Günter, "Über die deutsche faschistische Literatur," *Weimarer Beiträge* 14 (1968): 146–52
Heller, Erich, "Gottfried Benns Hordenzauber," *Die neue Weltbühne* 2 (1933): 688–91
Jens, Inge, *Dichter zwischen Rechts und Links: Die Geschichte der Sektion für Dichtkunst an der Preussischen Akademie der Künste dargestellt nach den Dokumenten*, Leipzig: Kiepenheuer, 1994 (original edition, 1971)

Kügler, Hans, "Künstler und Geschichte im Werk Gottfried Benns," in his *Weg und Weglosigkeit: Neun Essays zur Geschichte der deutschen Literatur im Zwanzigsten Jahrhundert*, Heidenheim: Heidenheimer Verlagsanstalt, 1970: 77–104

Mann, Klaus, "Gottfried Benn: Die Geschichte einer Verirrung," *Das Wort* 9 (1937): 35–42

Mannzen, Walter, "Die Stunde Gottfried Benns: Die Essays," *Frankfurter Hefte* 5 (1950): 550–53

Rohner, Ludwig, "Gottfried Benn: 'Dorische Welt'," in his *Der deutsche Essay: Materialien zur Geschichte und Ästhetik einer literarischen Gattung*, Neuwied and Berlin: Luchterhand, 1966: 259–80

Wuthenow, Ralph-Rainer, "Literaturkritik, Tradition und Politik: Zum deutschen Essay in der Zeit der Weimarer Republik," in *Die deutsche Literatur in der Weimarer Republik*, edited by Wolfgang Rothe, Stuttgart: Reclam, 1974: 434–57

Bense, Max

German, 1910–1990

"Such prose clarifies and vivifies the objects of which it is talking and which it seeks to perceive and communicate, but at the same time such prose is talking about itself, communicates itself as an authentic state of mind ..." wrote German philosopher and literary critic Max Bense, describing the essay ("Über den Essay und seine Prosa" [1947; On the essay and its prose]). Having produced numerous essays on topics ranging from the sciences to art and literary criticism, Bense viewed the essay as an expression of the experimental method of thinking and writing – similar to the role of the essay during the 18th-century Enlightenment. What distinguishes his theoretical approach from those of his predecessors, however, is the clear notion that any successful essay creates a certain atmosphere that builds a relationship between the subject matter discussed and the author as well as the reader, an atmosphere which allows the reader to draw further insights. The goal of an essay therefore should be to sum up all possible configurations in which the subject matter can be perceived. Moreover, while the essay is written in prose, it can also become poetry. In each essay there are certain basic sentences, seeds, which are concurrently prosaic and poetic. An essay can therefore never *be* a theory in itself, it can only be the beginnings, the birth of a theory, if the interaction between the atmosphere created by the essay and the author or reader is productive and thus leads to critical insights on the subject matter.

It is especially in his capacity as a critic that Bense's theoretical work has been so beneficial for literary theory and criticism as well as for philosophy. Even though he is one of the most quoted authors in German intellectual life, Bense's voluminous work has not yet become the subject of a comprehensive monograph. Perhaps this is due to the exceptionally wide range of subject matter with which he dealt, making a successful compilation difficult. Even his studies at the Universities of Bonn, Cologne, and Basle ranged from mathematics and physics to philosophy. After World War II, during which he worked as a laboratory physicist, he combined these three fields as a professor of mathematical logic and the philosophy of technology. Striving for justice and equality, he first took up his professorship in Jena, but soon became disillusioned with developments in the east and moved to Stuttgart in 1949.

Bense's major achievement for aesthetics and literary theory lies in the innovative connection of art and technology based on Hegel's aesthetics and Wittgenstein's speech-theories. He introduced scientific methods to traditional aesthetics resulting in a "technological," "material" aesthetics which could be applied to art works as well as scientific objects. This combination, formulated especially in the *Aesthetica* tetralogy (1954–60) and *Theorie der Texte* (1962; Textual theory), results in a fundamentally new approach to semiotics, which uses theories and sign systems that originate in mathematic-cybernetic contexts for language and texts. A "text" can thus be anything that consists of linguistic material, such as advertisements, scientific research, and artistic compositions. Harshly attacked by his opponents, who thought of his entire semiotic approach as being "objectivistic," "barbaric," and "anarchic," Bense nevertheless had a tremendous impact on Germany's so-called "experimental" literature and literary theories of the 1950s and early 1960s, especially on the movement called "Konkrete Poesie" (concrete poetry), including important authors such as Helmut Heissenbüttel, Eugen Gomringer, and Franz Mon.

Besides all his scientific accomplishments, and despite numerous attacks by critics that he was "too scientific" to be a humanist, Bense was deeply concerned with the question of humanitarian tasks for individuals in modern society. This concern seems particularly lucid in his essays on literature: "If the objective of knowledge lies not only in the objectivity of facts but, as in our society, rather in the external habitable condition of the world, a new type of thinker needs to be developed: a thinker who exhausts the rich possibilities of human intelligence not only as researcher or scholar, but at the same time as critic and as writer. Maybe that thinker could adapt to tasks in our society, a society based on a frightening density of outward communications, and an equally frightening lack of inner communications" (*Ein Geräusch in der Strasse: Descartes und die Folgen II* [1960; Sound in the street: Descartes and the consequences II]). Bense himself embodied this type of thinker by writing essays on such contemporaries as Gertrude Stein, Francis Ponge, **Walter Benjamin**, Helmut Heissenbüttel, **Alfred Andersch**, Ferdinand Lyon, Ludwig Harig, Ernst Jandl, Friederike Mayröcker, and many more, who were all concerned with artistically experimental art forms, and who therefore had the potential to add to the "inner communications" of society. These intimate portraits share one of Bense's most fundamental insights into literature, also advocated by members of the Frankfurt School (**Adorno**, Benjamin): "reality" is not a category that can be measured or described in scientific terms. It rather manifests itself in one singular act of reflection, while different literary realities coexist. The (literary) text for Bense becomes the object of different realities, one of which remains to be interpreted by the reader of that text – or by the writer of an essay.

AGNES C. MÜLLER

Biography

Born 7 February 1910 in Strasbourg. Studied mathematics, physics, and philosophy at the University of Bonn, diploma in physics, 1932, and geology, 1933, Ph.D., 1937; Universities of Cologne, 1935–36, and Basle. Industrial physicist for two years. Married

Elisabeth Bauer (died, 1939), 1938: one son. Served in the German Air Force, 1939. Editor of a science series, Munich, 1940. Married Maria Bauer (died, 1979), 1944: three daughters. Professor of philosophy, mathematical logic, and the theory of science, University of Jena, 1946–49; professor of the philosophy of technology and the theory of science, Technische Hochschule, Stuttgart, from 1949. Traveled extensively in North America, from 1969. Married Elisabeth Walter, 1988: one daughter. Died in Stuttgart, 29 April 1990.

Selected Writings

Essays and Related Prose

Aufstand des Geistes: Eine Verteidigung der Erkenntis, 1935
Vom Wesen deutscher Denker; oder, Zwischen Kritik und
    Imperativ, 1938
Geist der Mathematik: Abschnitte aus der Philosophie der
    Arithmetik und Geometrie, 1939
Das Leben der Mathematiker: Bilder aus der Geistesgeschichte der
    Mathematik, 1944
Umgang mit Philosophen, 1947
Technische Existenz, 1949
Ptolemäer und Mauretanier; oder, Die theologische Emigration der
    deutschen Literatur, 1950
Plakatwelt: Vier Essays, 1952
Descartes und die Folgen: Ein aktueller Traktat, 1955
Rationalismus und Sensibilität: Präsentationen, 1956
Ein Geräusch in der Strasse: Descartes und die Folgen II, 1960
Ungehorsam der Ideen: Abschliessender Traktat über Intelligenz und
    technische Welt, 1965
Artistik und Engagement: Präsentation ästhetischer Objekte,
    1970
Die Realität der Literatur: Autoren und ihre Texte, 1971
Das Universum der Zeichen: Essays über die Expansionen der
    Semiotik, 1983

Other writings: poetry, and books on philosophy, aesthetics (including the Aesthetica tetralogy, 1954–60), semiotics, mathematics, and existentialism.

Bibliography

Walter, Elisabeth, Bibliographie der veröffentlichten Schriften von Max Bense, Baden-Baden: Agis, 1994

Further Reading

Rohner, Ludwig, Deutsche Essays: Prosa aus zwei Jahrhunderten, vol. 1, Berlin and Neuwied: Luchterhand 1968: 54–69

Benson, A. C.

British, 1862–1925

For nearly 30 years, from the late 1890s to his death in the mid-1920s, A. C. Benson was one of England's most prolific, popular, and respected essayists, although the respect came more from the myriad of general readers who conferred the popularity than from his intellectual and social peers at Eton and Cambridge. A man of letters in the fullest 19th-century sense of the term, he also wrote poetry, fiction, biographies, and personal memoirs, to a total of more than 70 books. His editorial work included a three-volume selection of the correspondence of Queen Victoria (1907). Despite this prodigious output, he is today a largely forgotten figure whose tenuous

hold on posthumous reputation rests almost solely on his authorship of the words to "Land of Hope and Glory" (1902), written as an ode to welcome Edward VII to the throne and rapidly transformed, in conjunction with Edward Elgar's "Pomp and Circumstance March No. 1," into a surrogate national anthem.

Benson's essays were essentially lay **sermon**s, musings on spiritual, aesthetic, and existential matters directed always toward salutary, and often consolatory, ends. Even when the content is biographical – as in his first essay collection, entitled simply Essays (1896) and containing 13 biographical sketches, all but one of which had been previously published in **periodical**s – the eulogistic judgments on worthy lives are upliftingly homiletic. His concluding comment on Edmund Gosse's poetry ("to have made some exquisite mood your own, and to have presented it with passionate accuracy, is no light achievement") implicitly glosses the modal intensities of many of his own later essays. Their recording of the fruits of moments of quasi-epiphanic insight generates moralistic conclusions that spoke comfortingly to the emotional needs, particularly in times of despair or bereavement, of his worldwide readership. Among those who found solace in Benson's work was the poet Wilfred Owen, who recorded his admiration of Where No Fear Was: A Book About Fear (1914), read in 1917 during Owen's treatment for shellshock at Craiglockhart War Hospital (Simon Wormleighton, 1990).

Benson's distinctive tone owed much to his 18 years as a schoolmaster at Eton, the legacy of which informs one of his most influential books, The Schoolmaster: A Commentary upon the Aims and Methods of an Assistant-Master in a Public School (1902). Confident in their sense of the importance of the schoolmaster's vocation, these 16 essays are forthright in their recognition of the frequency with which the ideal and the actual part company, particularly in relation to the two great shibboleths of Victorian educational theory and practice, compulsory team sports and classics. The emphasis on both helps account in Benson's eyes for the unfortunate fact "that we send out from our public schools year after year many boys who hate knowledge and think books dreary, who are perfectly self-satisfied and entirely ignorant." The stranglehold retained on school curricula by Greek and Latin was a surprising obsession for a man who had himself achieved distinction as a Cambridge classicist. Among the 18 essays included in At Large (1908), published five years after Benson's departure from Eton for Cambridge, is "A Speech Day," in which the former schoolmaster worries again at a familiar bête noire: "to persist in regarding the classics as the high-water mark of the human intellect seems to me to argue a melancholy want of faith in the progress of the race."

When Benson addresses less pragmatic concerns, the tone becomes more precious, its tenor caught in some of the titles of his most spiritually emotive books: The Thread of Gold (1905), Along the Road (1913), and Joyous Gard (1913). The Thread of Gold, which divides into 42 sections of sentimental and vaguely theological rumination on human circumstance, has as its governing metaphor the observation "that there is a certain golden thread of hope and love interwoven with all our lives, running consistently through the coarsest and darkest fabric." Similarly, all 62 essays in Along the Road, varied as their notional subjects are ("Old England," "Mr. Gladstone," "Compulsory Greek," "Vulgarity," "Gossip," "On Being Interrupted") rarely move far from the Christian apologetics that inform Benson's advice to his readers: ". . . if the loneliest soul on earth, lying in darkness of spirit and pain of body, breathes one voiceless prayer upon the night, the world can never be the same as though that prayer had been unprayed" ("Brain Waves"). The paradoxically effete muscularity of Benson's message is caught in his explanation of the title attached to the *Joyous Gard* collection: "I have called this book ... *Joyous Gard*, because it speaks of a stronghold that we can win with our own hands, where we can abide in great content, so long as we are careful not to linger there in sloth and idleness, but are ready to ride abroad at the call for help."

But this chivalric impulse assumed an intransigently sedentary and privileged form, evidenced nowhere more palpably than in Benson's most famous and popular collection, *From a College Window* (1906), comprising 18 essays – 12 of them formerly published in *Cornhill Magazine* – written after his election to a fellowship at Magdalene College, Cambridge. Its appeal, like that of most of his work, can in part be explained by the recurrent rhetorical strategy explained in its opening essay, "The Point of View": "My desire is but to converse with my readers, to speak as in a comfortable *tête-à-tête*, of experience, and hope, and patience." For all the conversational manner, with its blend of the avuncular and the priestly, Benson's essays, even those charting his own recurrent dark nights of the soul, assume an oracular authority that owes more to class confidence than great intellectual insight. A period in which burgeoning literacy rates and the consequent demand for printed materials of a broadly "improving" kind were not yet matched by a correspondingly widespread enlargement of speculative sophistication may arguably have been the only context in which work like Benson's could enjoy such an appreciative reception.

The vogue for both Benson and the ruminative essay was passing by the end of World War I, whose cataclysm helped create an audience less deferentially accepting of paternalistic bromides about "how to enjoy life or how to endure it" ("Literature and Life," *Escape, and Other Essays*, 1915). Benson's many books are now little more than period pieces, redolent of the sentimentalized world of male companionship that he fostered and was himself cocooned by at Eton and Magdalene.

KEITH WILSON

Biography

Arthur Christopher Benson. Born 24 April 1862 at Wellington College, Crowthorne, Berkshire. Studied at Temple Grove School, Mortlake, south London, 1872–74; Eton College (King's scholar), Windsor, Berkshire, 1874–81; King's College, Cambridge, 1881–84, B.A. in classics, 1884. Taught at Eton College, 1885–1903; fellow, from 1904, president, 1912–15, and master, 1915–25, Magdalene College, Cambridge. Contributor to various journals, including *Macmillan's Magazine*, *National Review*, *Contemporary Review*, and *Cornhill Magazine*. Suffered from depression and breakdowns, 1907–09 and 1917–22. Commander, Royal Victorian Order. Died (of heart failure) at Magdalene College, Cambridge, 17 June 1925.

Selected Writings

Essays and Related Prose
Essays, 1896
The Schoolmaster: A Commentary upon the Aims and Methods of an Assistant-Master in a Public School, 1902
The Thread of Gold, 1905
From a College Window, 1906
At Large, 1908
The Leaves of the Tree: Studies in Biography, 1911
Along the Road, 1913
Joyous Gard, 1913
Escape, and Other Essays, 1915
Memories and Friends, 1924
Rambles and Reflections, edited by E. F. Benson, 1926

Other writings: poetry, short stories, two novels, a two-volume biography of his father (1899–1900), biographies of writers, works of autobiography and fictionalized meditation (including *The Upton Letters*, 1905), and a lengthy diary (selections edited by Percy Lubbock, 1926, and David Newsome, 1981). Also edited a selection of the correspondence of Queen Victoria (3 vols., 1907).

Further Reading

Benson, E. F., *Our Family Affairs, 1867–1896*, London: Cassell, 1920; New York: Doran, 1921
Benson, E. F., *As We Were: A Victorian Peep-Show*, London: Hogarth Press, 1985 (original edition, 1930)
Benson, E. F., *Final Edition: Informal Autobiography*, London: Longman, and New York: Appleton Century, 1940
Brake, Laurel, "Judas and the Widow: Thomas Wright and A. C. Benson as Biographers of Walter Pater: The Widow," *Prose Studies* 4 (1981): 39–54
Cunich, Peter, David Hoyle, Eamon Duffy, and Ronald Hyam, editors, *A History of Magdalene College Cambridge, 1428–1988*, Cambridge: Magdalene College, 1994
Howarth, T. E. B., *Cambridge Between Two Wars*, London: Collins, 1978
James, M. R., *Eton and King's: Recollections, Mostly Trivial, 1875–1925*, London: Williams and Norgate, 1926
Lubbock, Percy, editor, *The Diary of Arthur Christopher Benson*, London: Hutchinson, and New York, Longman Green, 1926
Newsome, David, *Godliness and Good Learning: Four Studies on a Victorian Ideal*, London: Murray, 1961
Newsome, David, *On the Edge of Paradise: A. C. Benson, the Diarist*, London: Murray, and Chicago: University of Chicago Press, 1980
Newsome, David, editor, *Edwardian Excursions: From the Diaries of A. C. Benson 1898–1904*, London: Murray, 1981
Ryle, E. H., editor, *Arthur Christopher Benson, as Seen by Some Friends*, London: Bell, 1925; New York: Putnam, 1926
Warren, Austin, "The Happy, Vanished World of A. C. Benson," *Sewanee Review* 75 (1967): 268–81
Wilson, Keith, "A. C. Benson," in *Modern British Essayists, First Series*, edited by Robert Beum, *The Dictionary of Literary Biography*, vol. 98, Detroit: Gale Research, 1990: 21–33
Wormleighton, Simon, "Wilfred Owen and A. C. Benson," *Notes and Queries* 37 (December 1990): 435–37

Bernanos, Georges

French, 1888–1948

Georges Bernanos' essays are far more voluminous than his better-known fiction. Six volumes appeared during his lifetime: *La Grande Peur des bien-pensants* (The great fear of conformist thinkers) in 1931; *Les Grands Cimetières sous la lune* (The great cemeteries in the moonlight; translated as *Diary of My Times*) in 1938; *Scandale de la vérité* (The scandal of truth) and *Nous autres Français* (We French) in 1939; *Lettre aux Anglais* (*Plea for Liberty: Letters to the English, the Americans, the Europeans*) in 1942; and, finally, *La France contre les robots* (*Tradition of Freedom*) in 1944. A further half-dozen compilations of Bernanos' articles and occasional texts were published posthumously. The two most substantial are *Le Chemin de la Croix-des-Ames* (1948; The way of the Cross-of-Souls), which assembled Bernanos' Brazilian wartime articles in one volume with an important **preface**-essay by the dying author, and *Français, si vous saviez* (1961; Frenchmen, if you only knew), a compilation of articles written between his return to France from Brazil in 1945 and his death in Paris in 1948.

Seven additional volumes of essays were published posthumously by Albert Béguin, Bernanos' literary executor. *Les Enfants humiliés* (The humiliated children), lost during the war and brought out only in 1949, contained Bernanos' 1939–40 poetic meditations on France's plunge into war again. *La Liberté, pour quoi faire?* (*Last Essays*) in 1953 brought together lectures from 1946–47. In 1956 Béguin assembled Bernanos' literary criticism and interviews from 1909–39 in *Le Crépuscule des vieux* (The twilight of old men). Four more recent compilations, prepared by Jean-Loup Bernanos, indiscriminately combine published and unpublished texts. *Le Lendemain, c'est vous!* (The next day it's you!), published in 1969, was followed in 1970 by a volume deceptively entitled *La France contre les robots* (France against the robots), even though the 1944 text (translated as *Tradition of Freedom*) bearing the same title comprises barely half the compilation. Further articles appeared in *La Vocation spirituelle de la France* (The spiritual vocation of France) in 1975, and *Les Prédestinés* (1983; The predestined ones) assembled texts on St. Dominic, Joan of Arc, Martin Luther, the few pages of Bernanos' *Life of Jesus*, and, from *Last Essays*, Bernanos' famous "last lecture," "Nos Amis, les saints" ("Our Friends the Saints"), in which the author gives a synthesis of his views on God, man, and creation as well as on freedom and human suffering.

As an essayist Bernanos moves effortlessly from the strident tone he learned from Édouard Drumont and Léon Bloy to the subtle, nostalgic irony of **Charles Péguy**, whom he profoundly admired. His most powerful quality as an essayist, however, is a rare gift he developed as a novelist and shared with **Dostoevskii**: the ability to pierce his reader's heart through a sorrowing tenderness he himself called the "lost language of childhood." Readers attesting to their admiration for this gift include Antonin Artaud, **Jean-Paul Sartre**, **Simone de Beauvoir**, André Malraux, Gaston Gallimard, and Charles de Gaulle.

Bernanos' desire to convince his reader of what he called "that part of the truth" given to him was rooted in his conviction that he must answer to God for all he wrote. For Bernanos, as for Bloy, writing was a divine calling, a vocation, and all true vocations, he said, must lead to Calvary. Having opted at age 18 for a writer's vocation over that of a priest, he strove to defend both Christian civilization and France – for him the foremost Christian country of Europe – with sacerdotal fervor.

As he sought in his essays to make his ideas live, Bernanos often personified them so that they might directly challenge his reader. As for his readers, Bernanos once said he liked to think that they were simply "all those men of good will" to whom the angel of Bethlehem first promised peace. In darker moments, however, he admitted that only those not totally subject to the technological seduction of the modern world remain intact enough to hear his voice.

Bernanos' audience did evolve radically from the right-wing nationalists of the *Action Française* (French action) for whom he started writing as a student. His long evolution carried him beyond any definable political position. By the end of his life communists no less than the ultra-right claimed him as one of their own. Even in his first essay volume in 1931, *La Grande Peur des bien-pensants*, Bernanos was already far more preoccupied with the future of French Christian society than with Édouard Drumont, whose biography he was supposedly writing.

His best-known essay, *Diary of My Times*, determined Gaston Gallimard to attach Bernanos to his publishing house and caused **Simone Weil** to write that Bernanos alone expressed what she herself had experienced in the Spanish Civil War. Launching "whole squads of images," as he liked to say, Bernanos denounced the Roman Catholic hierarchy for its stance on the Ethiopian conquest as well as on the "crusade" of General Franco.

When Charles Maurras, head of the *Action Française*, was elected to the French Academy in 1938, Bernanos, from Brazil, denounced the revered master of his youth in *Scandale de la vérité* for approving the Munich Pact, accurately foreseeing the fate awaiting the French Right during the war. Then, as war loomed, the essayist glorified those Christian values he particularly associated with French history and culture in *Nous autres Français*.

France's defeat was the subject for his *Plea for Liberty: Letters to the English, the Americans, the Europeans*, a work triggered by a request in 1940 from the *Dublin Review* for an article on that subject. After May 1940, and for the duration of the war, Bernanos devoted himself exclusively to essays on the meaning of the conflict, both to France and to the world.

Bernanos' seven years in Brazil (1938–45) and the devotion of the Brazilian elite to French civilization much softened the author's strident nationalism. He now attempted to define France's supernatural destiny to lead the whole postwar world in a spiritual revolution. His violent voice still surged up, however, in both *Tradition of Freedom* and *Last Essays* as he denounced technology's increasing threat to human freedom.

Bernanos' wartime essays won him a reputation as "bard of the French Resistance," but after his return to France in 1945 his inability to fuse his ideals with political realities in postwar France disappointed those who had relied on his voice for strength and moral courage during the occupation. To the end, however, Bernanos' articles in newspapers such as *La Bataille* (The battle), *Carrefour* (Crossroads), *Combat*, *Le Figaro*, and *L'Intransigeant* won him devoted readers from all social and political strata. Even half a century after his death Bernanos' passionate and thought-provoking assessment of two World Wars, the German occupation of France, and the significance of the atomic bomb remains hardly less gripping than his astonishingly fresh, pertinent, and eloquently challenging denunciation of the threats posed to the freedom of a human race increasingly enslaved by technology.

WILLIAM BUSH

Biography

Born 20 February 1888 in Paris. Studied at the Collège des Jésuits, until 1901; Collège Notre-Dame-des-Champs, Paris, 1901–03; Collège Saint-Célestin, Bourges, 1903–04; Collège Sainte-Marie, Aire-sur-la-Lys, 1904–06, baccalauréat, 1906; the Sorbonne, Paris, 1906–09, licence in law and literature, 1909. Military service, 1909–10. Editor, *L'Avant-Garde de Normandie*, 1913–14. Served in the French army, 1914–19: wounded. Married Jeanne Talbert d'Arc, 1917: three sons and three daughters. Sold insurance, 1919–27. Columnist, *Le Figaro*, 1930–32. Crippled for life in a motorcycle accident, 1933. Evicted from family home because of debts, and moved to Majorca, 1934–37, then returned to France; settled in Brazil, and involved in the resistance movement, 1938–44; returned to France, 1945. Contributor to many journals, including *Combat*, *Carrefour*, *L'Intransigeant*, and *La Bataille*. Gave lectures in Switzerland, Belgium, and North Africa. Awards: Prix Fémina, for novel, 1929; French Academy Grand Prize, for novel, 1936. Died (of liver problems) in Paris, 5 July 1948.

Selected Writings

Essays and Related Prose

La Grande Peur des bien-pensants, 1931
Jeanne, relapse et sainte, 1934; as *Sanctity Will Out: An Essay on St. Joan*, translated by Rosamond Batchelor, 1947
Les Grands Cimetières sous la lune, 1938; as *Diary of My Times*, translated by Pamela Morris, 1938
Scandale de la vérité, 1939
Nous autres Français, 1939
Lettre aux Anglais, 1942; as *Plea for Liberty: Letters to the English, the Americans, the Europeans*, translated by Harry Lorin Binsse and Ruth Bethel, 1945
Le Chemin de la Croix-des-Ames (articles), 4 vols., 1943–45; in 1 vol., 1948; revised edition, edited by Jean-Loup Bernanos and Brigitte Bernanos, 1987
La France contre les robots, 1944; as *Tradition of Freedom*, translated by Helen B. Clark, 1950
Essais et témoignages, edited by Albert Béguin, 1949
Les Enfants humiliés, 1949
La Liberté, pour quoi faire?, edited by Albert Béguin, 1953; as *Last Essays*, translated by Joan and Barry Ulanov, 1955
Le Crépuscule des vieux (articles), edited by Albert Béguin, 1956
Français, si vous saviez, 1945–1948 (articles), 1961
Le Lendemain, c'est vous!, edited by Jean-Loup Bernanos, 1969
La France contre les robots, edited by Jean-Loup Bernanos, 1970
Essais et écrits de combat (Pléiade Edition), edited by Yves Bridel, Jacques Chabot, and Joseph Jurt, 1971
La Vocation spirituelle de la France, edited by Jean-Loup Bernanos, 1975
Les Prédestinés, edited by Jean-Loup Bernanos, 1983

Other writings: eight novels (*Sous le soleil de Satan* [*The Star of Satan*], 1926; *L'Imposture*, 1927; *La Joie* [*Joy*], 1929; *Un crime* [*The Crime*], 1935; *Journal d'un curé de campagne* [*The Diary of a Country Priest*], 1936; *Nouvelle histoire de Mouchette*, 1937; *Monsieur Ouine* [*The Open Mind*], 1943; *Un mauvais rêve* [*Night Is Darkest*], 1951), the screen scenario *Dialogues des Carmélites* (1949; *The Fearless Heart*), short stories, and correspondence.

Bibliography

Jurt, Joseph, *Georges Bernanos: Essai de bibliographie des études en langue française consacrées à Georges Bernanos*, Paris: Minard, 3 vols., 1972–75

Further Reading

Béguin, Albert, *Bernanos par lui-même*, Paris: Seuil, 1982 (original edition, 1954)

Bénier, Jean, *Les Royaumes de Georges Bernanos*, Troyes: Librairie Bleu, 1994
Bernanos, Jean-Loup, *Georges Bernanos à la merci des passants*, Paris: Plon, 1986
Bush, William, *Georges Bernanos*, New York: Twayne, 1969
Bush, William, "Georges Bernanos," in *French Novelists, 1930–1960*, edited by Catharine Savage Brosman, *Dictionary of Literary Biography*, vol. 72, Detroit: Gale Research, 1988: 58–76
Chesterton Review issues on Bernanos, edited by William Bush, 15, no. 4 (November 1989) and 16, no. 1 (February 1990)
Cooke, John E., *Georges Bernanos: A Study of Christian Commitment*, Amersham, Buckinghamshire: Avebury Publishing, 1981
Estang, Luc, *Présence de Bernanos, précédé de "Dans l'amitié de Léon Bloy" de Georges Bernanos*, Paris: Plon, 1947
Estève, Michel, *Bernanos*, Paris: Gallimard, 1965
Estève, Michel, *Georges Bernanos: Un triple itinéraire*, Paris: Hachette, 1981
Gaucher, Guy, *Georges Bernanos; ou, L'Invincible espérance*, Paris: Cerf, 1994
Georges Bernanos in His Time and Ours, 1888–1948, special double issue of *Renascence: Essays on Values in Literature*, edited by William Bush, 41, nos. 1–2 (Fall 1988/Winter 1989)
Gillemin, Henri, *Regards sur Bernanos*, Paris: Gallimard, 1976
Hebblethwaite, Peter, *Bernanos: An Introduction*, London: Bowes and Bowes, 1965
Milner, Max, *Georges Bernanos*, Paris: Desclée de Brouwer, 1967
Molnar, Thomas, *Bernanos: His Political Thought and Prophecy*, New York: Sheed and Ward, 1960
Speaight, Robert, *Georges Bernanos: A Study of the Man and the Writer*, London: Collins and Harvill, 1973
Urs von Balthasar, Hans, *Le Chrétien Bernanos*, Paris: Seuil, 1956 (original German edition, 1954)

Berry, Wendell

American, 1934–

Farmer, naturalist, and conservationist Wendell Berry has published nine essay volumes and three additional nonfiction works, along with novels and poetry. His **nature essays** have called attention to the economic and environmental problems in modern American agriculture, especially the loss of traditional farm communities and rural culture. As a Jeffersonian agrarian, Berry has defended the moral, civic, and environmental values of the family farm. He first gained widespread recognition for *The Unsettling of America: Culture and Agriculture* (1977), a polemic against the excesses of corporate agribusiness.

Berry's career as an essayist coincided with the American environmental movement, beginning with the first Earth Day in 1972. His essays have appeared in publications ranging from the *Whole Earth Catalogue* to *Smithsonian* magazine. As a contributing editor with Rodale Press from 1977 to 1979, Berry promoted the organic farming movement in essays and articles in the *New Farm* and *Organic Gardening*. A self-proclaimed generalist in an age of specialists, Berry addresses his essays to a broad and diverse audience of general readers, promoting with evangelistic fervor the values of economic and cultural self-reliance.

The early **autobiographical essays**, *The Long-Legged House* (1969) and "A Native Hill" (1969), established Berry's roots as a Kentucky regionalist and agrarian. The long philosophical essay "Discipline and Hope" (1972) presents his criticism of the American consumer culture and calls for renewal through simplicity and self-reliance. As a farmer and writer, Berry writes out of his deep love for land and place. He offers an articulate defense of traditional farming ("A Defense of the Family Farm," 1986) as a viable economic and cultural alternative to corporate consumerism. In "The Making of a Marginal Farm" (1980), he explains his decision to leave a teaching career in New York and return to Kentucky to farm and write. As an agrarian regionalist, Berry is both conservative and radical. His cultural conservatism ("The Work of Local Culture," 1988) has led him to be politically radical in his opposition to the social and economic forces destroying family farms and rural communities. As a regionalist ("The Regional Motive," 1972) who has struggled to create a wholesome economic, ecological, and moral order within his family, farm, and community, he favors economic self-sufficiency ("The Tyranny of Charity," 1965) for the Cumberland region and opposes industrialism, urbanization, and technology ("Property, Patriotism, and National Defense," 1984), but he sharpens his advocacy of rural life with an informed ecological vision and a clear understanding of the complex relationships among the health of the individual, family, community, and environment ("Does Community Have a Value?," 1986). The themes of home, work, husbandry, rootedness, stewardship, responsibility, thrift, order, memory, atonement, and harmony resonate throughout his essays.

Berry's regional loyalty has led him to speak out against the ravages of strip-mining in the Cumberland region ("The Landscaping of Hell: Strip-Mine Morality in East Kentucky," 1965); to protest against the pollution of the Kentucky River by vacationers ("The Nature Consumers," 1967); and to write an eloquent plea to preserve Kentucky's Red River Gorge ("The Unforeseen Wilderness," 1971). But the major target of Berry's wrath has been the destructive farming practices of corporate agribusiness ("The Body and the Earth," 1977).

Berry's ecological essays often assume an almost religious tone. In "A Secular Pilgrimage" (1972), he traces the origins of the environmental crisis to our disdain for the earth. Berry calls for a renewal of biblical stewardship in "The Gift of Good Land" (1979); promotes the idea of usufruct in "God and Country" (1990); and outlines a nondualistic natural theology that affirms the sacredness of the world in "Christianity and the Survival of Creation" (1992). Protection of wildness and careful land use are not incompatible, he argues in "Preserving Wildness" (1985).

As a social critic, Berry examines the cultural influences of industrialism and the consumer economy. He writes about the effects of corporate greed on American culture: the vulgarization of popular culture and the debasement of language; the decline of public education; the destruction of family and community life; and the degradation of the environment. He reaffirms the dignity and value of work ("People, Land, and Community," 1983); criticizes the destructive assumptions of free market economics ("Two Economies," 1983); praises the thrift and resourcefulness of Amish culture ("Does Community Have a Value?"); defends marriage against feminist attacks ("Feminism, the Body, and the Machine," 1987); and protests against the exploitation of sex in American consumer culture ("Sex, Economy, Freedom, and Community," 1992).

In his literary essays, Berry stresses the importance of regionalism, respect for language, and traditional poetic forms. He values pastoral poetry for its ability to connect us with nature ("A Secular Pilgrimage"); laments the loss of readership for contemporary poetry ("The Specialization of Poetry," 1974); insists upon the need to protect the integrity of language to prevent cultural decline ("Standing by Words," 1983); and praises **Mark Twain**, Sarah Orne Jewett, and **Wallace Stegner** for their regional loyalty ("Writer and Region," 1987).

Berry is a polemical writer who emphasizes theme and argument over purely literary stylistics. More didactic than discursive as an essayist, he is nevertheless a clear and forceful writer who resembles Edward Abbey in his passionate defense of environmental concerns. Berry is also a moralist in the tradition of **Henry David Thoreau**, for whom simplicity and self-reliance are essential virtues. Like Thoreau, he is a writer of deep personal conviction who has articulated the social and economic principles by which he would live and write. He has striven to achieve clarity and directness in his essays by insisting upon the basic harmony among work, vocation, family, community, and nature. One finds in Berry's essays a continual effort to unify life, work, and art.

Berry is essentially a pastoral writer whose inspiration comes from his rural Kentucky heritage. In his essays, he celebrates the personal satisfactions of farming and husbandry. He cares deeply about his subjects: the dignity of work; the proper care of the land; the importance of marriage, family, and community; and the continuities of history and region. Though he regrets the loss of the discipline of thrift, care, and conservation that farming teaches, most of all it is the spiritual value and restorative power of living in harmony with nature that Berry cherishes. Perhaps best known for his agricultural and environmental essays, Berry is an important social and cultural critic whose works have helped preserve the heritage of rural American culture.

ANDREW J. ANGYAL

Biography

Wendell Erdman Berry. Born 5 August 1934 in Henry County, Kentucky. Studied at the University of Kentucky, Lexington, A.B., 1956, M.A., 1957; Wallace Stegner Writing Fellow, Stanford University, California, 1958–59. Married Tanya Amyx, 1957: one daughter and one son. Taught at Stanford University, 1959–60; traveled on a Guggenheim Fellowship to Italy and France, 1961–62; taught at New York University, 1962–64, and the University of Kentucky, 1964–77, and from 1987; staff member, Rodale Press, Emmaus, Pennsylvania, 1977–79. Awards: several grants and fellowships; *Poetry* magazine Vachel Lindsay Prize, 1962, and Bess Hokin Prize, 1967; Friends of American Writers Award, for novel, 1975.

Selected Writings

Essays and Related Prose
The Long-Legged House, 1969
The Hidden Wound, 1970
The Unforeseen Wilderness: An Essay on Kentucky's Red River Gorge, 1971
A Continuous Harmony: Essays Cultural and Agricultural, 1972
The Unsettling of America: Culture and Agriculture, 1977
Recollected Essays 1965–1980, 1981

The Gift of Good Land: Further Essays Cultural and Agricultural,
  1981
Standing by Words, 1983
Home Economics, 1987
What Are People For?, 1990
Harlan Hubbard: Life and Work (lectures), 1990
Standing on Earth: Selected Essays, 1991
Sex, Economy, Freedom & Community, 1993
Another Turn of the Crank, 1995

Other writings: many collections of poetry, four novels (*Nathan
Coulter,* 1960; *A Place on Earth,* 1967; *The Memory of Old Jack,*
1974; *Remembering,* 1988), short stories, and a play.

Bibliographies
Griffin, John B., "An Update to the Wendell Berry Checklist,
  1979–Present," *Bulletin of Bibliography* 50, no. 3 (September
  1993): 173–80
Hicks, Jack, "A Wendell Berry Checklist," *Bulletin of Bibliography*
  37 (1980): 127–31

Further Reading
Angyal, Andrew J., *Wendell Berry,* New York: Twayne, and
  London: Prentice Hall International, 1995
Merchant, Paul, editor, *Wendell Berry,* Lewiston, Idaho: Confluence,
  1991

Biography and the Essay

Biography is difficult to define succinctly or convincingly. As a genre, its boundaries are elusive, its subject slippery; it is expressive of a human need rather than the answer to that need. In its widest application, the term "biography" describes any attempt to tell the story of what it is to be human; broadly speaking, whatever artifacts, monuments, pictures, or writings people have left behind to mark the spaces they once occupied are kinds of biography. Cave paintings, petroglyphs, hieroglyphs, pyramids, and stone circles are life writings in this sense. Biography is a reflexive human gesture that points to others and says: "You are and, therefore, I am." It is the process by which individuals and cultures codify their consciousness of what it feels like to live a life of significance in time and space. That is the import of **Samuel Johnson**'s much-quoted and deeply felt explanation of how biography works upon the reader: "All joy or sorrow for the happiness or calamities of others is produced by an act of the imagination, that realises the event however fictitious, or approximates it however remote, by placing us, for a time, in the condition of him whose fortune we contemplate; so that we feel, while the deception lasts, whatever motions would be excited by the same good or evil happening to ourselves" (*Rambler* no. 60). What Johnson describes is not necessarily a literary activity but an imaginative and emotional one, predicated upon the human capacity for empathy. Perhaps this is the closest we can come to a workable definition of biography: the imagining that another life is like our own.

Perhaps the first biographer to meet Johnson's standard in life writing was **Plato**, whose exploration of the character and mind of Socrates in the **dialogues** is compellingly intimate. In a similar way the life of Christ is evoked in narrative and dramatic snatches by the Apostles who, like Socrates, achieve their biographical portraits through emphasizing the language of their subject. Recording speeches was one of the more common forms of biography before the advent of the essay in Renaissance Europe; indeed, the best biographical accounts in classical Greek are the dramatic speeches recorded by Thucydides and Herodotus in their *Histories*. Xenophon's portrayal of Socrates in his 4th-century *Memorabilia*, however, is the closest approximation to biography to be found before **Plutarch**'s *Vitae parallelae* (*Lives of the Noble Grecians and Romans*), a compilation of 44 comparative life studies in which Plutarch sets Greek against Roman, as in his comparison of Alexander and Caesar as generals or Demosthenes and **Cicero** as orators. Gaius Suetonius Tranquillus, Plutarch's contemporary, produced two important works of biography, the *Lives of the Caesars* and *Agricola*, his memoir of his father-in-law.

Medieval biographers like the Venerable Bede in *Historia ecclesiastica gentis Anglorum* (c. 732; *Ecclesiastical History of the English People*), with its life of St. Cuthbert, and the monk Eadmer who wrote *Vita Anselmi* (c. 1124; *The Life of St. Anselm*) were producing encomia that lacked the sense of personality present in the best classical biographies. Their moral perspective is typical of the pattern we see in the lives of the saints throughout the Middle Ages, but it is their emphasis upon the life to come at the expense of the life lived that diminishes their literary significance as biography. It is only with the return to secular subjects in works like Giovanni Boccaccio's *De casibus virorum illustrium* (*The Fates of Illustrious Men*) in the 14th century that life writing comes back to a focus on the shared humanity of the subject and the reader. In fact, before Boccaccio, only Einhard's *Vita Caroli Magni* (c. 829–36; *Life of Charlemagne*) offered any sustained human interest as a biography. After Boccaccio, three biographical compilations are particularly important: Giorgio Vasari's *Vite de' piu eccellenti pittori, scultori e architettori italiani* (1550; *Lives of the Most Eminent Painters, Sculptors, and Architects*), the biographies of Italian artists from Cimabue to Michelangelo; John Foxe's *The Acts and Monuments of the Church*, also known as *The Book of the Martyrs* (1563), the collected lives of the English Reformers persecuted under Mary Tudor; and the eccentric *Mirror for Magistrates* (1563 and subsequent expanded editions), edited by George Ferrers, a sort of English imitation of Boccaccio's work. These books are also among the first serious attempts to produce national biographies in the vernacular. The 16th century in England saw the greatest surge in life writing with Thomas More, William Roper, and George Cavendish establishing the return of secular and humanist biography and setting the stage for **Francis Bacon**'s *The History of the Reign of Henry VII* (1622). In France, Pierre de Bourdeille produced collections of brief lives which explored the social intimacy of court life in his *Les Vies des dames illustres, Les Vies des dames galantes, Les Vies des hommes illustres et grands capitaines français,* and *Les Vies des hommes illustres et des grands capitaines étrangers* (1665–66). However, it was Izaak Walton and Roger North who moved biography closest to its modern expression. Walton's lives of **John Donne**, George Herbert, Henry Wotton, Richard Hooker, and Robert Sanderson published between 1640 and 1678 are portraits shaded with private and domestic details, while North's narratives of the lives of his three brothers, accompanied by a prefatory essay on the art of biography and not published until 1742–44, are intimate and imaginatively engaging memoirs of the private lives of regular citizens.

Biography as Johnson described it is the creation of the European Enlightenment and finds its landmark achievements in 18th-century English literature. Notably, this great age of biographic writing was preceded by and coincident with the zenith of portrait painting in Europe. An increasingly secular emphasis in politics and art further emphasized the significance of the individual in his or her own life, but that cultural impulse required a philosophical and linguistic imperative which was provided, ultimately, by such works as Robert Burton's **The Anatomy of Melancholy** (1621 and subsequent revised editions) and John Locke's **An Essay Concerning Human Understanding** (1689). The modern notion of private psychology expressed in works like these brought a new language and way of seeing to the practice of life writing, and biographers began to examine the emotional and motivational forces behind the actions of men and women. Rather than looking to an external impetus for actions in life, whether God or the public duty demanded by the state, which had provided the focus of classical, medieval, and Renaissance biographies, the Enlightenment explored the interior terrain of emotional and private motivation. Thus, in his best biography, *An Account of the Life of Mr. Richard Savage* (1744), Samuel Johnson undertakes to tell the story of a minor writer who was a total failure and died mad, not as an example of a life to be avoided, but as a study of depression and of those ways in which every life is more an experience of disappointment than of fulfillment. He is interested in psychological understanding, not moral allegory. Johnson's own biography, arguably the greatest example of its kind, was written from a similar perspective by the Scot James Boswell. A compulsive diarist, Boswell's exhaustive *Life of Samuel Johnson* (1791) was based largely upon his extensive notes of Johnson's conversations. Boswell treats Johnson's early life with some abruptness, concentrating the bulk of his massive narration on those years he shared with Johnson. In this, the biography is also a kind of memoir evoking not one but two personalities, those of Johnson and Boswell. It is this impetus to give a psychologically compelling sense of the individual, to paint a personality in words, that is the hallmark of Enlightenment biographies and is a feature held in common with the novel which arose simultaneously with modern biography all across Europe. Biography of this sort shares with the novel an emphasis on domesticity.

Still, 18th-century biography is distinguished by its reliance on the essay for its rhetorical structure. This is especially true in the French tradition where the eulogy (*éloge*) dominated the style of life writing until Marie-Jean Caritat, Marquis de Condorcet broke entirely with that convention in the biographies of Turgot (1786) and **Voltaire** (1789). Among other important examples of life writing in Enlightenment France were Voltaire's at times satiric *Histoire de Charles XII, roi de Suède* (1731; *The History of Charles XII, King of Sweden*), **Diderot**'s *Essai sur Sénèque* (1778; Essay on Seneca), and La Beaumelle's *Mémoires pour servir à l'histoire de Madame de Maintenon* (1756; *Memoire for the History of Madame de Maintenon*). But it is the early work of **Pierre**

Bayle, the dictionary maker, that alone among French life writing has any long-reaching influence. His *Dictionnaire historique et critique* (1697; *An Historical and Critical Dictionary*) is arguably the first example of a modern biographical compilation, taking the tradition of the brief lives that originated with Suetonius and had its English expression in John Aubrey and Anthony Wood's *Athenae Oxoniensis* (1691) and developing it into an encyclopedic form. Bayle's innovation was introduced to England by Thomas Birch, a hack biographer, and eventually influenced William Oldys, the first editor of the *Biography Britannica* (1747–66), which was corrected and enlarged in a second edition by Andrew Kippis (1778–93). The biographical dictionary took a number of subsequent forms until biographical essays became a regular feature of the *Encyclopedia Britannica* in its third edition (1788–97). Among the many imitators of Bayle, William Owen and William Johnston were the first to attempt an internationally and historically inclusive compendium of biographical essays in their *New and General Biographical Dictionary . . . of the Lives and Writings of the Most Eminent People of Every Nation* (1761–67). All of these works point forward to the late 19th-century schemes for dictionaries of national biography, such as that edited by **Leslie Stephen**.

Where Locke's theories tended to shape the idea of biography during the Enlightenment, **Charles Darwin** eventually dominated 19th-century and **Sigmund Freud** 20th-century concepts of life writing. In the early 19th century, politics began to displace the domestic as the fulcrum of biographical studies, a trend especially evident in **Thomas Carlyle**'s life of Frederick the Great, some 13 years in the writing and finally published in three massive volumes over a seven-year period (1858–65). David Masson, however, best illustrates the Victorian tendency toward historical inclusiveness with his seven-volume *Life of Milton in Connection with the History of His Times*, which appeared over a 35-year span (1859–94). While English biography was becoming more historically and politically obsessed, French life writing was taking an inward turn. Introspection is the dominant feature of work like Étienne Pivert de Senancour's *Obermann* (1804) and continues to be the theme in the biographical writing of Alphonse de Lamartine and Alfred de Musset.

Lytton Strachey's *Eminent Victorians* (1918) did more than any single work since Boswell to redirect and revive the art of biography. Strachey eschewed the 19th century's respect for biographical subjects, whom he treated with irreverence and irony, writing in a highly individualistic style that harkened back to the elegance of Johnson's essays. *Eminent Victorians* shows utter disregard for historical veracity and never hesitates to embellish or invent where the events of the subject's life are absent or dull. Here was the beginning of a biographical mode that sought to reveal human weaknesses and folly while setting identification and empathy at a problematic distance. Recognition of shared humanity between the reader and the subject of the biography is more an experience of humiliation than reassurance in Strachey. Biography in the 20th century has continued and refined Strachey's methods, developing a kind of life writing that treats the subject as an opponent to be exposed. Political biography in particular is so directed, among the best examples being William Manchester's life of John F. Kennedy, *Death of a President* (1967).

Biography and the essay are closely tied for a number of reasons, but the most interesting is their shared inclination toward introspection. The essay after **Montaigne** offered a medium for intense self-examination that is autobiographical by nature. The most innovative of the early modern biographers, like Diderot, Johnson, and Boswell, were themselves outstanding essayists. But the essay is also essentially an empirical tool, designed to seek out, identify, and convey knowledge of the world as it relates to the self. This dichotomy of the introspective and the empirical that defines the essay as a genre also well describes the activity of life writing where what can be ascertained about a life and what can only be intuited are brought together uneasily into a narrative that is ultimately more an art than a science.

STEPHEN W. BROWN

Further Reading

Aaron, Daniel, editor, *Studies in Biography*, Cambridge, Massachusetts: Harvard University Press, 1978

Altick, Richard D., *Lives and Letters: A History of Literary Biography in England and America*, New York: Knopf, 1966

Clifford, James L., *Biography as Art: Selected Criticism, 1560–1960*, Oxford and New York: Oxford University Press, 1962

Garraty, John A., *The Nature of Biography*, New York: Knopf, 1957

Kendall, Paul M., *The Art of Biography*, New York: Norton, 1985 (original edition, 1965)

Meyers, Jeffrey, *The Spirit of Biography*, Ann Arbor, Michigan: UMI Research Press, 1989

Stauffer, Donald A., *English Biography Before 1700*, New York: Russell and Russell, 1964 (original edition, 1930)

Blackwood's Edinburgh Magazine

British periodical, 1817–1980

The sheer longevity of *Blackwood's Edinburgh Magazine* – 163 years – makes it noteworthy among 19th-century **periodicals**. Following its foundation by William Blackwood, successive generations of the publishing family of Blackwood owned and edited *Maga*, as it was familiarly known to its proprietors, contributors, and readers. Its founders originally saw *Blackwood's* as providing a more energetic and powerful Tory opposition to the Whig *Edinburgh Review* than the *Quarterly Review* then offered; but its monthly issue and the breadth of its scope made it from the start also a stronger vehicle for creative literature and criticism than the quarterlies.

William Blackwood's aim to produce a daring, sparkling, and successful magazine was in no way met by the editors of his first venture, the *Edinburgh Monthly Magazine*. They were replaced after a few months, and the new *Blackwood's*, produced by John Gibson Lockhart, John Wilson, and James Hogg was launched with great *élan*. In **Margaret Oliphant**'s words, the new number had to be "a sort of fiery meteor to blaze across the Edinburgh sky and call every man's attention" (*Annals* vol. 1, 1897). It succeeded. In particular its satiric "Chaldee Manuscript," lampooning the deposed editors and local notables, took Edinburgh by storm. In another piece **Coleridge**'s *Biographia Literaria* was savaged. This combative style marked the early years, notable for the virulence of the attacks on "The Cockney School," i.e. **Leigh Hunt**, **William Hazlitt**, and John Keats. The personal assaults brought actions for libel and Blackwood more than once had to pay damages. The "unholy zest and aptitude for the fray" (J. H. Lobban, 1897) shared by Lockhart, Wilson, and Hogg tested Blackwood's powers of control to the full, but the success of the magazine was established.

The popular "Noctes Ambrosianae" series of papers, humorous tavern conversations between a group of friends discussing contemporary events, books, and people, began in 1822. It featured some fictional characters, but mainly real people under sobriquets, including *Maga* writers themselves, "Christopher North" (Wilson), "The Ettrick Shepherd" (Hogg), "The Opium-Eater" (**Thomas De Quincey**), and "Ensign O'Doherty" (William Maginn). De Quincey began writing for the magazine in 1820 and continued on a sporadic, somewhat wayward basis for a decade. Maginn had been appointed Irish correspondent a few months earlier. His witty contributions were valued, though Blackwood had to restrain his propensity both to abuse and to puff.

By the mid-1830s *Maga* had established the respectable character which was to secure its position in Victorian and Edwardian cultural society, a mix of creative literature, **reviews**, essays, and serious papers on foreign and domestic issues. William Blackwood's worries about the damage caused by "the coarse and reckless" vein of writing, and his concern that "anything approaching to grossness or profane feeling" would make his magazine "a sealed book to many families" (Oliphant, *Annals* vol. 1) eventually triumphed over the rash exuberance of the early years. The magazine became much less contentious, though it developed its own personality and continued to attract writers of calibre. Many of its contributors, as *Maga* was proud to publicize, were loyal and long-standing, and held for it an affection Margaret Oliphant compared to that which a ship held for its crew. Over its long life it attracted to its ranks such writers as Oliphant herself, **George Eliot**, Anthony Trollope, Joseph Conrad, Andrew Lang, May Sinclair, Alfred Noyes, and John Buchan.

Within the parameters of decorum it set, the Blackwood dynasty was relatively restrained in its editing of such work as it accepted for publication. "One of the secrets of *Maga*'s success has been the strictly impersonal nature of her editorship," wrote J. H. Lobban, reviewing Oliphant's history. On the whole the editors preferred to discuss and persuade rather than ruthlessly hack and rewrite or bowdlerize. F. D. Tredrey (1954) regarded John Blackwood (editor 1845–79) as an editor whose "methods of conveying suggestions and criticism are models in a difficult art."

From the beginning William Blackwood had encouraged new writers, and his successors continued this policy. *Maga* maintained the tradition of anonymity long after other periodicals had introduced the signed article. A. Innes Shand (1897) claimed this enabled more "unknowns" to be given an opportunity. It also prevented an established writer from relying solely upon the power of his name, "forcing him to take more care in his work." Equally important, it gave the periodical as strong an awareness of its own identity as **Charles Dickens**, a much more intrusive editor than any of the Blackwoods, bestowed on *Household Words* and *All the Year*

Round. The magisterial "we" commonly employed in reviews and commentaries established *Maga*'s air of authority.

But already by the end of the 1860s, its lack of illustrations, in contrast to the *Cornhill Magazine*, made it appear somewhat old-fashioned, and circulation was adversely affected. The loyalty of its diminished band of readers and the commitment of its publishers, however, enabled it to survive until the final decades of this century. The magazine's early interest in foreign affairs and the ambition of "Christopher North" "that our wit shall be local all over the world" was never quite abandoned. During the two World Wars vivid dispatches from the fronts and topical fiction mingled with lighter reading. More staid, but still entertaining its middle-class readers, *Maga* traveled in the wake of colonials and expatriate communities, its bound volumes keeping them in touch with home. By the mid-20th century it was becoming something of an anachronism, in Tredrey's words "one of the very few markets left to writers of craftsmanship and integrity who are unable, or who do not wish, to write for the avant-garde journals or the popular press."

Maga always had a powerful sense of its own history. To mark its 1000th appearance in 1899 a special double number contained a celebratory revival of "Noctes," and its centenary issue of 225 pages was similarly nostalgic.

BARBARA MARY ONSLOW

See also Periodical Essay

Further Reading

Oliphant, Margaret, *Annals of a Publishing House: William Blackwood and His Sons, Their Magazine and Friends*, New York: AMS Press, 3 vols., 1974 (original edition, 1897–98)

Lobban, J. H., "Maga and Her Publishers," *Blackwood's Magazine* (1897): 860–72

Shand, A. Innes, "Contemporary Literature III: Magazine Writers," *Blackwood's Magazine* (1897): 225–47

Tredrey, Frank D., *The House of Blackwood 1804–1954: The History of a Publishing Firm*, Edinburgh: Blackwood, 1954

Blok, Aleksandr

Russian, 1880–1921

Aleksandr Blok, Russia's most celebrated and arguably most gifted symbolist poet, is known primarily for his lyrics (*Stikhi o prekrasnoi dame* [1903; Verses about the beautiful lady], "Neznakomka" [1907; "The Incognita"], the cycle "Rodina" [1912; Native land]) and for a narrative poem about the Bolshevik Revolution (*Dvenadtsat'* [1918; The Twelve]). He is also known for his drama *Balaganchik* (The Puppet Show), which was staged by the famous director Vsevolod Meyerhold in 1906. By comparison, Blok's critical, philosophical, and historical prose, which consists of over 250 separate pieces, has received rather spotty attention. For Blok's contemporaries, however, his book **reviews**, essays, and public lectures were major events on the cultural landscape. From the outset of his career, Blok himself considered expository prose an essential part of his creative legacy, very nearly on a par with his poetry. It is significant that he begins the rough draft of his first article

with the statement: "The following essay . . . emerges from the pain of my soul . . . This is a small work but an inspired one, which I want to leave posterity in addition to my songs" (1902).

An effort must be made to classify Blok's voluminous prose inventory, if only to determine which items can justifiably be called "essays" in the sense he intended ("inspired" pieces that express "the pain of my soul"). Setting aside 40–50 brief reports and notices which clearly do not qualify, we can identify about 100 articles and speeches of substantial length that bear the imprint of Blok's emotional sensibilities and definitely warrant the designation "essays." Occupying a median ground are 150 or so reviews of books and plays, ranging in length from one to five pages. Roughly half of these – especially those devoted to works which had special significance for Blok – are also miniature "essays" inasmuch as they convey not only Blok's judgment but his creative personality.

It is possible to break the inventory down further into various subgenres – articles about individual writers, literary surveys, historical **treatises**, autobiographical sketches, *feuilletons*, travel notes, and essay-narratives, to name the most common types. But there is reason to dispense with such categories and group Blok's essays according to the criterion of their relative poeticity, as Dmitrii Maksimov (1981) does. The majority of Blok's essays are written in a highly lyrical, metaphoric, and symbolic style that exploits ambiguity for aesthetic ends. Unabashedly impressionistic, they give free rein to Blok's prodigious imagination. By contrast, the nonpoetic essays, which are fewer in number and less idiosyncratic, tend to be discursive, logical, even academic in manner. They avoid metaphoric leaps and have a better-defined structure.

All of Blok's essays gravitate to one of these poles regardless of their subject matter. Hence there are lyrical book reviews ("Andrei Belyi: *Simfoniia*," 1903; "Valerii Briusov: *Urbi et Orbi*," wr. 1903), scholarly articles that tell us more about Blok's experience as a poet than about the topics they ostensibly treat ("Poeziia zagovorov i zaklinanii" [1908; The poetry of magical sayings and incantations]; "O sovremennom sostoianii russkogo simvolizma" [1910; On the contemporary state of Russian symbolism]), and personal memoirs that resemble fairytales ("Devushka rozovoi kalitki i murav'inyi tsar'" [1907; The girl at the pink fence and the ant king]; "Ni sny ni iav'" [1921; Neither dream nor reality]). On the other hand, there are also sober, almost academic essays on poetic topics ("Sud'ba Apollona Grigor'eva" [1916; The fate of Apollon Grigor'ev]; "Iskusstvo i revoliutsiia" [1919; "Art and the Revolution"]) which lack Blok's customary lyricism. His prose exists in a dynamic, complementary relationship with his poetry, and the boundary between the two is constantly fluctuating. Unlike **Pushkin**, Blok did not believe that prose and poetry were inherently different media that ought to be kept discrete.

In poeticizing the essay Blok followed the norm of his time. Rebelling against the rationalistic bias of the previous century, most essayists of the symbolist era, like Blok, replaced logical persuasion with emotive, imagistic reasoning. Nevertheless, the authorial persona of Blok's essays is unique. Less outlandish than **Andrei Belyi**, less vain than Konstantin Bal'mont, less cerebral than **Viacheslav Ivanov**, less pedantic than Valerii Briusov, and more socially committed than all of them, Blok spoke in his own distinct voice. His essays have an affinity to Innokentii Annenskii's in their brazen whimsicality, but they lack Annenskii's intellectuality. In relation to Western essayists, Blok comes closest to Wagner and **Nietzsche**, whom he knew well.

Not surprisingly, Blok acquired his reputation as an essayist in symbolist journals with an educated and aesthetically refined readership – most notably in *Zolotoe Runo* (The golden fleece), for which he edited the literary criticism section from 1907. When *Zolotoe Runo* closed in 1909, Blok was left without a suitable forum for the poetic type of essay which came most naturally to him. His ideal audience had always been an aesthetic elite who read and appreciated his poetry – his prose in fact was designed in part to explicate his own verses. Publishing in daily newspapers, he was forced to tone down his lyricism and reorient himself to a less sophisticated readership. In the years 1910 to 1916 he could hardly tolerate such constraints and contemplated abandoning the genre of the essay entirely. To reach his ideal audience, he relied increasingly on speeches, where he could freely indulge in esotericism.

One of the few symbolists who welcomed the Bolshevik Revolution, Blok experienced a new creative surge as an essayist after 1917. Some of his most inspired pieces were composed shortly after the Revolution ("Ispoved' iazychnika" [1918; A heathen's confession]; "Katalina" [1919; Cataline]; "Krushenie gumanizma" [1919; "The Collapse of Humanism"]). A handful of these found their way into the collection *Rossiia i intelligentsiia* (1918; Russia and the intelligentsia). Nevertheless, the Bolsheviks were disturbed by Blok's independent thinking and ultimately suppressed his best prose. Blok himself soured toward Bolshevism after he was arrested and nearly executed in February 1919 on the erroneous charge that he was a counter-revolutionary. The essays of his last years, therefore, reached an extremely limited public. Only two complete editions of his essays appeared in the Soviet era, the earliest of which was prefaced by a stern warning that they were "intolerable" and represented "the ideology of the bourgeoisie" (Vasilii Desnitskii, 1935). Only a small fraction of his essays have been translated into English (more are available in French and German translation).

Blok's essays treat many topics, but beneath the particulars is an abiding concern over Russia's fate during the cataclysmic changes of the early 20th century. In his first true essay, written during the Revolution of 1905 ("Tvorchestvo Viacheslava Ivanova" [Work of Viacheslav Ivanov]), Blok quoted Fedor Tiutchev's words: "Blessed is he who visited this world/In its fateful moments." Near the end of his life, when Bolshevik authority was thoroughly consolidated, he spoke about the social-political changes of his time as commensurate with those of "several centuries" ("Vladimir Solov'ev i nashi dni" [1920; Vladimir Solov'ev and our times]). Thus Blok thought of himself as a privileged witness of an historic upheaval, and in his essays he continually tried to register its spiritual significance both for himself and his generation. In "Narod i intelligentsia" (1908; "The People and the Intelligentsia"), Blok attributes Russia's trials to the fragmentation of national culture, to the split between the Westernized elite and the native peasantry. In "Stikhiia i kul'tura" (1909; The natural elements and culture), he describes the popular revolution as kind of natural cataclysm, the nation's primordial revenge against an alien and artificial culture. Blok believed that the violence of revolution was a necessary stage in the ritual of Russia's spiritual purification ("Intelligentsia i revoliutsiia" [1918; "The Intelligentsia and the Revolution"]), and in a stark indictment of his own former values, he even welcomed the demise of Western individualism and its humanistic heritage ("The Collapse of Humanism").

The perspective from which Blok passed such scathing judgments was that of a prophet or seer using poetic clairvoyance to demystify political phenomena. The role of the poet, he believed, was to discern the cosmic harmonies that resonated beyond the chaos of visible experience ("Dusha pisatelia" [1909; The writer's soul]; "O naznachenii poeta" [1921; On the calling of the poet]), and he found in the peasant's primitive aestheticism a model for such an oracular art ("Poeziia zagovorov i zaklinanii"). There was, of course, an inherent contradiction between the language of Blok's essays and this defense of primitivism. He could hardly expect an uneducated reader to follow the trajectories of metaphoric thought in his prose. Nor did he rid his essays of symbolic vagueness – a tendency that infuriated even sophisticated readers like Belyi and Zinaida Gippius. Like many Russian writers, Blok revered the common folk as a repository of truth but could not express this faith in an idiom it understood.

Because Blok's most inspired essays are written in the arcane idiom of a symbolist poet, reading them as a whole poses the question of how he understood their relation to the purely lyric form. It is interesting that in a plan for his collected works compiled in 1917, Blok referred to the essays simply as "prose," suggesting that despite their convergence, there was still an inherent difference between his essays and his verse. This difference would seem to be primarily one of focus. Blok's lyric poetry, in its aggregate, is a mesmerizingly intimate confession which draws the reader deep into the recesses of the poet's soul. It requires a phenomenal capacity for contextual reading – a knowledge not just of one poem, but of whole cycles and volumes. To the reader who embarks upon the arduous task of deciphering his lyrics, the poems reveal a complex personality, the avenues and alleyways of a vast buried labyrinth. In order not to lose the way through this labyrinth it is essential to recall the paths traversed and strive to divine those ahead – that is, to contemplate the design of the whole poetic oeuvre and the intellect which devised it.

The essays, by contrast, are directed mainly toward external phenomena. They do not have Blok's inner self as their focus, nor do they reveal (and conceal) a secret world. Whereas his verse is self-referential to an obsessive degree, the essays open onto a wider horizon and show Blok pondering a different reality: the social and political events, the cultural and aesthetic currents of his time. Blok's persona comes across no less vividly, but the environment is not claustrophobic. It is as if he is contemplating his place in the vast philosophical landscape that history has opened before him.

DAVID A. SLOANE

Biography

Aleksandr Aleksandrovich Blok. Born 28 November 1880 in St. Petersburg. Studied at Vvedenskii School, St. Petersburg, 1891–99; studied law, then philosophy at the University of St. Petersburg,

1899–1906. Married Liubov Dmitrievna Mendeleeva, 1903. Literary editor, *Zolotoe Runo*, from 1907. Traveled abroad several times, including to Italy and Warsaw, 1909. Served in the army as a record keeper with an engineering unit, stationed at the front near Pskov, 1916–17. Edited testimony of former ministers of the Tsar for the provisional government's Extraordinary Investigative Commission, 1917–18. Worked for Gor'kii publishers' Vsemirnaia Literatura (World literature) series, 1918–21, and the Vol'naia Filosofskaia Assotsiatsiia (Free philosophical association). Arrested briefly for supposed counter-revolutionary activities, 1919. Chair, Directorate of the Bolshoi Theater, 1919–21, and the Petrograd division of the All-Russian Union of Poets, 1920–21. Died (of heart failure) in Petrograd, 7 August 1921.

Selected Writings

Essays and Related Prose

Molnii iskusstva (Lightning flashes of art), 1909–20(?)
Rossiia i intelligentsiia, 1918; revised edition, 1919
Poslednie dni imperatorskoi vlasti (The last days of the Imperial
    Regime), 1921
The Spirit of Music: Selected Essays, translated by I. Freiman,
    1943

Other writings: three volumes of poetry (including *Dvenadtsat'*
[1918; *The Twelve*]) and several plays.

Collected works editions: *Sobranie sochinenii*, 12 vols., 1932–36;
edited by Vladimir N. Orlov and others, 8 vols., 1960–63, and in 6
vols., 1971.

Bibliographies

Kolpakova, E., and others, in *Vilniusskii gosudarstvennyi
    pedagogicheskii Institut* 6 (1959)
Pomirchiy, P. E., in *Blokovskii Sbornik* 2 (1972)
Pyman, Avril, in *Blokovskii Sbornik* 1 (1964)

Further Reading

Chukovskii, Kornei, *Alexander Blok as Man and Poet*, Ann Arbor,
    Michigan: Ardis, 1982
Desnitskii, Vasilii, "A. Blok kak literaturnyi kritik," in *Sobranie
    sochinenii* by Blok, vol. 10, Leningrad: Izdatel'stvo Pisatelei v
    Leningrad, 1935: 5–16
Kisch, Cecil H., *Alexander Blok: The Prophet of Revolution*,
    London: Weidenfeld and Nicolson, 1960
Kluge, Rolf-Dieter, *Westeuropa und Russland im Weltbild Aleksandr
    Bloks*, Munich: Slavistische Beiträge, 1967
Maksimov, Dmitrii E., "Kriticheskaia proza Bloka," in his
    Poeziia i proza Aleksandra Bloka, Leningrad: Sovetskii Pisatel',
    1981
Potsepnia, Dina M., *Proza A. Bloka: Stilisticheskie problemy*,
    Leningrad: Izdatel'stvo Leningradskogo Universiteta, 1976
Pyman, Avril, *The Life of Aleksandr Blok*, Oxford and New York:
    Oxford University Press, 2 vols., 1979–80
Pyman, Avril, "Blok v angliiskom i amerikanskom
    literaturovedenii," in *Literaturnoe nasledstvo*, vol. 92, book 5,
    Moscow: Nauka, 1993: 362–401
Reeve, F. D., *Aleksandr Blok: Between Image and Idea*, New York:
    Octagon, 1981 (original edition, 1962)
Vogel, Lucy, editor and translator, *Blok: An Anthology of Essays
    and Memoirs*, Ann Arbor, Michigan: Ardis, 1982

Borchardt, Rudolf

German, 1877–1945

Rudolf Borchardt once referred to his life's work as the cultivation of three adjacent fields: those of poetry, philology, and public speaking – a contiguous domain within which he allowed no confining boundaries or frivolous experimentation. He was a prodigiously talented scholar-poet, a *poeta doctus* in the classicist mold, and a polemical historian who had acquired the full compass of a traditional humanistic education. Yet his output as a writer, primarily of essays, monographs, and carefully crafted speeches, was neither prolific nor multifaceted. This is due at least in part to the fact that his work represents the eccentric position of an outsider. It purposely goes against the grain of contemporary debates or ideological controversies, and it is often freighted with the connoisseur's exquisite erudition, with the learned arcana and suggestive allusions of the expert. Stylistically, this work is animated by an unwavering sense of self-assurance, often enough by an imperious rhetorical will that, for all its politeness, does not seek to persuade so much as to grip and overpower. While it may be easy to list the many experiences and issues of his time which Borchardt haughtily refused to admit even to the periphery of his interests, it is difficult to delineate his work through a survey of its central themes.

There is recognizable, however, a pervasive tendency, sustained over many years, if not decades, to return to a small number of all-important concerns. These are then discussed from shifting vantage points and with added perspectives. This intellectual process brings forth a series of ever-expanding (and occasionally contradictory) refractions and variations. In the end it leads to the conviction that a profound and elusive problem has at last yielded its innermost truth.

Borchardt's concentration, over a lifetime, on a few fundamental verities and their inevitable consequences is rooted in the one premise and overriding experience that defined the impulse behind his entire oeuvre. He was sure to have recognized even as a student that the recently triumphant Germany (both the imperial state Bismarck had created and the ideas of its most vociferous critic, **Nietzsche**) was about to inaugurate an era of enormous barbarities. To this insight he reacted with the hauteur of the insulted aristocrat and with the sensibilities of an aesthete. The feeling that he and his nation had suffered a profound loss, his sense of chaotic ruptures with their destruction of traditions and of historically vindicated values, elicited a response of inexorable condemnation as well as an alternative program of cultural restitution. Borchardt disdained, maligned, overlooked, or misunderstood nearly every separate aspect of modern life as well as the complex interplay of its constituent forces.

But he did search for causes, and came to hold the country's rapidly expansive transformation from a richly diverse *Volk* into an industrial mass society responsible for most of its ills. He attributed the triviality of its artistic pursuits to a materialistic faith in instrumental reason – to a simplistic trust in scientific progress, in laissez-faire capitalism, in military recklessness. He despised socialism for the fervor with which it tried to destroy conventions and hierarchies; and he saw nothing but propagandistic mendacity lurking behind every emancipatory effort. This deep disorientation in the face of technological modernity traumatized many cultured individualists of the generation that had grown to adulthood around 1900. Their escape was usually the affectation of an amoral dandyism and of a dignified conservatism.

Borchardt, however, offered a more radical and thus even less pragmatic solution. He was unable to find anything worth preserving from the past hundred years, and he therefore scorned all of the proliferating programs of reform or revival as nostalgic. He considered their purposes ineffectual and a harmful illusion in an age that has replaced the guiding relevance of ideas with the dictates of doctrines. Instead of a gradual assimilation of the new to the old (and vice versa), he advocated a "creative restoration" (1927). He took his cue for this project from the work of classical philologists and archaeologists, who reassemble the surviving fragments of ancient cultures with an insightful logic that, he thought, is akin to the imaginative order of poetry. Yet he was less interested in ascertaining "what actually was" than in reclaiming "what under more propitious circumstances could have been." Thus he searched for possibilities of historical development that had been suppressed or not fully realized and then lost to posterity. And he looked to discover their continued presence in history as future potential, as a palimpsest beneath the surface of victorious reality.

It was the era of Romanticism, with its universalist and also with its specifically German university culture, from which – as from the last unified European epoch – Borchardt drew his strongest inspiration, and from which the "restitution *in integrum* of the ideal German people as a whole" would have to originate. This process he saw as a revitalization ("Rückbelebung"), if not a re-experiencing ("Rückerlebnis") that may have to retrace its historical studies and stages all the way back to "the day of creation and the life-giving spirit from God's mouth." The complementary alternative – with its "determined will to renounce our time instead of flattering it with iniquitous optimism" – demands that "we reverse ourselves and go into the underworld like Hercules in order to bring back the dead, or, like Theseus, the friend," as Borchardt wrote in 1927 in "Die geistesgeschichtliche Bedeutung des neunzehnten Jahrhunderts" (The significance of the 19th century in terms of the history of ideas). Such a reawakening of cultural vitality through a return to its sacred sources or as a descent into the realm of heroic death reveals the extremist logic of a religious fundamentalism that has erased all societal compromises in favor of metahistorical absolutes.

Even before 1900, Borchardt's poetic defiance of his age had found exemplary support in the verse and personality of Stefan George, who was unwilling, however, to admit so ambitious a rival into his inner circle. His admiring suitor then attached himself to the more tractable **Hugo von Hofmannsthal** and began to castigate George's aesthetic politics, ultimately equating it with the work of the Antichrist, who had prepared Germany for submission to Hitler. But when the Viennese poet began to develop his own ideas about a conservative revolution (1927 and earlier), Borchardt drew back again, this time from what he considered an anachronistic concept. Yet the 15 essays he wrote about Hofmannsthal reflect his most consistent critical preoccupation with one author, more specifically

with his corpus of "classicist" works. For these he could treat as if they were emanations of his own personality, and therefore he discussed them as their creator's narcissistic *Doppelgänger*.

Borchardt's readers (and audience) were mostly members of the prosperous, educated, conservative bourgeoisie, including both notables and the young academic elite. The preferred venue for his public addresses were the auditoriums of traditional ("prestigious") universities or similar halls in old merchant cities. When he published his articles in cultural journals and in a few select newspapers he made few concessions to the *modus operandi* of the medium. He neither popularized his ideas nor softened his often abstract diction, which still makes it difficult to pin him down on specific points. Consequently, the captivating momentum of his political rhetoric, for example, did not derive from a stringent analysis of empirical data or from a critical engagement with provocative opinions. It is rather the elusive openness of his key terms (and in general of the vocabulary of cultural pessimism), and the suggestive tone of his forceful pleadings, that may explain his appeal, which was strongest during the 1920s.

As early as 1902 Borchardt had inherited a substantial private fortune, which allowed him to live with his family where he felt most at home, in the villas of Tuscany. After 1933, when he was prohibited from publishing in Germany because his mother had Jewish ancestors, he returned to historical and philological studies. He wrote, for example, an excellent monograph on Pisa (1938) and unfinished interpretations of Homer (1944), the latter largely from memory because he had no access to library resources. Some 50 years later, little of his copious output – five volumes of collected nonfictional prose, a total of some 2500 pages – arouses more than historical interest. These days, respect for his stylish erudition is invariably coupled with an apologetic discomfiture, to put it mildly, over his *Ideenpolitik*, his vexatious politics of ideas.

MICHAEL WINKLER

Biography

Born 9 June 1877 in Königsberg. Grew up in Moscow, and Berlin, from 1882. Studied archaeology and classical languages at the Universities of Berlin, from 1895, Bonn, and Göttingen. Became friends with Hugo von Hofmannsthal. Traveled to Italy and England, and took special interest in the Pre-Raphaelite painters; lived in Lucca, from 1903. Married Karoline Ehrmann (divorced, 1919). Served in the German army, 1914–18. Married Marie Luise Voigt, 1919: four children. Lived in Lucca, 1921–44; arrested by the Gestapo, 1944, then released; took refuge at Trins am Brenner. Died in Trins am Brenner, 10 January 1945.

Selected Writings

Essays and Related Prose
Rede über Hofmannsthal, 1905
Villa, 1908
Der Krieg und die deutsche Selbsteinkehr, 1915
Rede am Grabe Eberhard von Bodenhausens, 1918
Prosa I, 1920
Über den Dichter und das Dichterische, 1924
Handlungen und Abhandlungen, 1928
Die Aufgaben der Zeit gegenüber der Literatur, 1929
Villa, und andere Prosa: Essays, 1952

Other writings: poetry, plays, a novel, and correspondence, especially with Hugo von Hofmannsthal. Also translated works by various English poets, and Dante; edited anthologies of German authors.

Collected works edition: *Gesammelte Werke in Einzelbänden*, edited by Marie Luise Borchardt, 14 vols., 1955–85.

Bibliographies

Beerbohm, A. W., *Rudolf Borchardt: A Biographical and Bibliographical Guide*, New York: New York University, 1952
Rizzi, Silvio, *Rudolf Borchardt als Theoretiker des Dichterischen*, Dornbirn: Mayer, 1958: 109–15

Further Reading

Barstad, Noel Kraig, *Rudolf Borchardt's Critical Assessment of Hugo von Hofmannsthal* (dissertation), Minneapolis: University of Minnesota, 1973
Beerbohm, A. W., *Rudolf Borchardt: A Biographical and Bibliographical Guide*, New York: New York University, 1952
Caffrey, George, "Rudolf Borchardt," *New Criterion* 5, no. 1 (1927): 81–87
Glaser, Horst Albert, editor, *Rudolf Borchardt 1877–1945: Referate des Pisaner Colloquiums*, Frankfurt-on-Main and New York: Lang, 1987
Sommer, Inge, "Das 'klassische Land' in Rudolf Borchardts Essay *Villa*," *Arcadia* 1 (1966): 83–96
Tgahrt, Reinhard, and others, editors, *Rudolf Borchardt, Alfred Walter Heymel, Rudolf Alexander Schröder: Eine Ausstellung des Deutschen Literaturarchivs im Schiller-Nationalmuseum, Marbach am Neckar*, Munich: Kösel, 1978
Vordtriede, Werner, "Rudolf Borchardt und die europäische Tradition," *Jahrbuch der Deutschen Schillergesellschaft* 22 (1978): 728–41
Wagner, Fred, "Restitutio in integrum: Rudolf Borchardt and the Middle Ages," *Mosaic* 10 (1976): 165–82
Wagner, Fred, *Rudolf Borchardt and the Middle Ages: Translation, Anthology and Nationalism*, Frankfurt-on-Main: Lang, 1981

Borges, Jorge Luis

Argentine, 1899–1986

Although his fame rests mainly on his production of short stories, Jorge Luis Borges began his career writing poems and essays, and continued to do so throughout his life. However, there is no separate Borges the essayist, Borges the poet, or Borges the short-story writer: he continually crossed the boundaries of genre, and could philosophize as a fiction writer or be a poet when he wrote essays. For example, a text such as "Borges y yo" ("Borges and I") is a story that is also an essay that is also a poem.

Borges' output of essays as such is not extensive. If we include prologues (a form in which he achieved a mastery of allusion and synthesis), texts from conferences, and short essays included in miscellanies, his work in this genre amounts to no more than a dozen titles. The essays in this body of work appear somewhat disparate, like the browsings of a casual reader: reflections on *gauchesco* poetry, meditations on the nature of time, the exhumation of a minor poet like Evaristo Carriego – unlikely to be remembered were it not for Borges – or a note on the artificial language invented by John Wilkins in the 17th century. The three key books from this output are

Discusión (1932; Discussion), *Historia de la eternidad* (1936; History of eternity), and *Otras inquisiciones* (1952; *Other Inquisitions*).

What strikes the reader immediately is that, in spite of the breathtaking literary knowledge he displays and the precise form in which he manages it, Borges' tone is almost always cordial and serene, his erudition tempered by self-irony and simplicity of exposition. This was not always the case: the young essayist of the first series of *Inquisiciones* (1925; Inquisitions) or *El tamaño de mi esperanza* (1926; The length of my hope) sounds surprisingly baroque, aggressive, and labored to the point of appearing somewhat pedantic. Those were Borges' avant-garde years, when he placed his revolutionary ardor at the service of a militant and iconoclastic *criollismo*, of which he was soon to recant.

Perhaps with the exception of Baldomero Sanín Cano, no one in the Americas had written essays like Borges', because few people had read certain authors in the way he had; still less had anyone written about them with such disconcerting mastery and familiarity. As an essayist, he adopted a literary culture almost entirely alien to Latin American literature and which, thanks to Borges, would become part of its tradition. It is a culture rich in oriental books, ancient philosophers and mystics, Jewish cabbalists and gnostics, forgotten French poets, but above all in English authors. He brought attention to British writers who were little known in the Hispanic world, such as **Sir Thomas Browne**, John Milton, **Samuel Taylor Coleridge, Thomas De Quincey, G. K. Chesterton**, John Keats, William Beckford, and **George Bernard Shaw**, as well as to other writers such as Franz Kafka, **Paul Valéry**, and Walt Whitman.

What is striking is not only the uniqueness of his literary subjects as an essayist, but also his ability to say something unexpected about them. Like Paul de Man, one can say that these are "imaginary essays," if we take this expression to mean essays from a personal imagination stimulated by the imagination of others. One of the surprises awaiting a reader who refers to the sources that inspired Borges is to discover that, on reading and interpreting them, the author added as much as (or more than) he took from them, and in this way gave them new meaning. His readings are a form of appropriation and reflected creation; he translates what he reads into his own literary language and his own aesthetic world. This secondhand creativity – of unforgettable suggestion and magic – is characteristic of Borges.

In this way Borges takes possession of all the literature he knows and integrates it into his own system. His books make up a library created by an imagination stimulated by another library. This can be seen especially in the way in which Borges read religious, metaphysical, and philosophical texts; he himself said that in authors such as Spinoza, George Berkeley, **Arthur Schopenhauer**, and Emanuel Swedenborg he was not interested in the truth of their theories, but rather in their aesthetic value and their ability to amaze. That is, he read them as pure exercises in thought (valid in themselves, not for their objective content) and as fictions conceived in order to explain the world.

Whatever their subject (eternity or the metaphor, Homer or the cyclic nature of time, our idea of Hell or Xeno's paradox), however modest the form they took (book **reviews**, footnotes, refutations of a thesis), Borges' essays are above all unconventional propositions, an invitation to think in a new way about something commonly accepted, a quiet intellectual dissidence. What is admirable about these proposals is that they do not impose on us a formula: everything is transformed into a hypothesis that we are free to agree with or not. The skill and seduction of the text is that, however absurd or incredible the hypothesis may appear at first, in the end the temptation to accept it is irresistible.

The major question underlying a study of Borges, essential to any investigation of literature, concerns the limits of language and how to represent the world with a succession of sounds and conventional signs (Borges, quoting Chesterton, writes of "grunts and squawks"). The very nature of language is a sober warning to the writer who wants to create something new: the most language allows us is to reiterate, with variations, what has already been said. That is, we can achieve success only by working within the tradition, not against it. In this way it is possible to understand why the theorists of modern linguistics and representatives of the French "new criticism" have found Borges' ideas so stimulating and have added him – to their own surprise – to the list of forerunners of their most sophisticated luminaries.

JOSÉ MIGUEL OVIEDO
translated by Richard Shaw

Biography

Born 24 August 1899 in Buenos Aires. Lived with his family in Europe, 1914–21. Studied at the Collège Calvin, Geneva, 1914–18. Cofounding editor, *Prisma*, 1921, *Proa*, 1922–26, and *Sur*, 1931; literary adviser, Emecé Editores, Buenos Aires; columnist, *El Hogar* (The hearth) weekly, Buenos Aires, 1936–39. Municipal librarian, Buenos Aires, 1939–46: fired by the Perón regime. Poultry inspector, 1946–54. President, Argentine Writers Society, 1950–53. Lost his sight, 1955. Director (after Perón's deposition), National Library, 1955–73. Taught at the University of Buenos Aires, 1955–70. Married Elsa Millán, 1967 (divorced, 1970); married María Kodama, 1986. Awards: many, including Argentine Writers Society Prize, 1945; National Prize for Literature, 1957; Prix Formentor, 1961; Ingram Merrill Award, 1966; Jerusalem Prize, 1971; Reyes Prize, 1973; Cervantes Prize, 1979; Yoliztli Prize, 1981; honorary degrees from seven universities. Member, Argentine National Academy; member, Legion of Honor (France); Order of Merit (Italy), 1968; Order of Merit (German Federal Republic), 1979; Honorary Knight Commander, Order of the British Empire (KBE). Died (of liver cancer) in Geneva, 14 June 1986.

Selected Writings

Essays and Related Prose
Inquisiciones, 1925
El tamaño de mi esperanza, 1926
El idioma de los argentinos, 1928; enlarged edition, as *El lenguaje de Buenos Aires*, with José Edmundo Clemente, 1963
Discusión, 1932; revised edition, 1976
Historia de la eternidad, 1936; revised, enlarged edition, 1953
Otras inquisiciones, 1937–1952, 1952; as *Other Inquisitions, 1937–1952*, translated by Ruth L. C. Simms, 1964
Prólogos con un prólogo de prólogos, 1975
Siete noches, 1980; as *Seven Nights*, translated by Eliot Weinberger, 1984
Nueve ensayos dantescos, 1982
Textos Cautivos: Ensayos y reseñas en El Hogar (1936–1939), edited by Enrique Sacerio-Gari and Emir Rodríguez Monegal, 1986

El aleph borgiano (book reviews), edited by Juan Gustavo Cobo Borda and Martha Kovasics de Cubides, 1987
Borges, el judaismo e Israel (selected essays on Judaism), 1988
Biblioteca personal: Prólogos, 1988

Other writings: many short stories, poetry, a screenplay, and works on literature. Also edited anthologies of stories (including *Antología de la literatura fantástica* [*The Book of Fantasy*], with Silvana Ocampo and Adolfo Bioy Casares, 1940; *Cuentos breves y extraordinarios* [*Extraordinary Tales*], with Bioy Casares, 1955); translated works by Franz Kafka, Herman Melville, **Thomas Carlyle**, **Virginia Woolf**, William Faulkner, and **Ralph Waldo Emerson**.

Collected works editions: *Obras completas*, 9 vols., 1953–60, revised edition in 1 vol., edited by Carlos V. Frías, 1974; *Obras completas*, 2 vols., 1989.

Bibliographies
Becco, Horacio Jorge, *Jorge Luis Borges: Bibliografía total, 1923–1973*, Buenos Aires: Casa Pardo, 1973
Foster, David William, *Jorge Luis Borges: An Annotated Primary and Secondary Bibliography*, New York and London: Garland, 1984

Further Reading
Alazraki, Jaime, "Borges: Una nueva técnica ensayística," in *El ensayo y la crítica literaria en Iberoamérica*, Toronto: University of Toronto, 1970: 137–43
Alazraki, Jaime, "Oxymoronic Structure in Borges' Essays," *Books Abroad* 45 (1971): 421–27
Hahn, Oscar, "Borges y el arte de la dedicatoria," *Revista Iberoamericana* 43 (1977): 691–96
Omil de Piérola, Alba, "Jorge Luis Borges: Del ensayo a la ficción narrativa," in *El ensayo y la crítica literaria en Iberoamérica*, Toronto: University of Toronto, 1970: 155–60
Phillips, Katharine Kaiper, "Borges as Concomitant Critic," *Latin American Literary Review* 3 (1973): 7–17
Piérola, Raúl Alberto, "Temas de Jorge Luis Borges, ensayista," in *El ensayo y la crítica literaria en Iberoamérica*, Toronto: University of Toronto, 1970: 109–15
Rodríguez Monegal, Emir, "Borges essayiste," *L'Herne* (1964): 343–51
Stabb, Martin S., "Utopia and Antiutopia: The Theme in Selected Essayistic Writings of Spanish America," *Revista de Estudios Hispánicos* 15 (1981): 377–93
Xirau, Ramón, "Borges refuta el tiempo," in his *Antología personal*, Mexico City: Fondo de Cultura Económica, 1976: 36–42
Zalazar, Daniel E., "Los conceptos de 'instante' y 'eternidad' en la obra de Borges," in his *Ensayos de interpretación*, Buenos Aires: Crisol, 1976

Bourget, Paul
French, 1852–1935

Though best known for the novels of psychological analysis that gained him a wide reputation in his lifetime, Paul Bourget also made frequent use of the opportunities provided by the French periodical press of his day to present in essays his thoughts about pressing contemporary issues.

His travel writings reveal a good deal about his approach. Crossing over to the United Kingdom for a succession of short visits in the 1880s and 1890s, he came not only well prepared by his wide reading of English classics and what were then the most modern authors, but also with his intellectual agenda already drawn up. Whether on the Isle of Wight in the holiday season, in an Ireland simmering with political discontent, or at Oxford in high summer, the same questions concern him: in what ways does Britain differ from France? And what can discontented Frenchmen learn from the island on the other side of the Channel? In this he is not unlike **Voltaire**, author of the 18th-century *Letters Concerning the English Nation* (1733; *Lettres philosophiques*), with his urge to observe and his restless intellectual curiosity; like Voltaire, Bourget uses to good effect the dodge of sometimes posing as the innocent abroad while in fact pursuing his own theories and analysis. Though he offers alert and entertaining descriptions of the manners of Victorian England and presents Ireland as a country with a different set of acute problems of its own, he is not primarily concerned with evoking the places he visits. By the same token, despite a few personal details to give an initial narrative impetus to his accounts, lend them an air of authenticity, or else provide variety in authorial stance, his travel writings are not really concerned with what he did and felt, where he went and what he saw. Instead, he uses his experience of Britain for an analysis of a country which he realizes is different from his own yet which, despite the problems, prejudices, and incongruities of the Victorian age, he feels is also in many respects more successful than France. To some degree the difference is material; influenced by **Hippolyte Taine**, Bourget is not predisposed to underestimate economic factors, but in them he sees the consequences of decades of peace under stable monarchical government, especially for a middle class that establishes and maintains its ever more crucial position between an aristocracy whose importance is fading and a proletariat that threatens established values. The implication throughout Bourget's travel writing is that France is in a comparatively parlous state and would be well advised to consider carefully, if not to follow closely, the example of Britain.

A similar spirit informs Bourget's literary essays. In 1883 he set out his program in the **preface** to his first set of *Essais de psychologie contemporaine* (Essays in contemporary psychology). His concern, he declares, is not to analyze the literary means by which authors have sought to express themselves, and he also abjures the Sainte-Beuvean temptation to present or explain this or that trait in a writer by reference to a supposedly revealing anecdote. He has, he says, no desire to assess the talents of authors or to depict their personalities. Instead, his ambition is to provide observations that will be of value when historians turn to writing an intellectual history of France in the second half of the 19th century. While conceding that many factors contribute to the intellectual climate of any age, Bourget argues for granting a more significant part to literature in the 19th century for two reasons in particular: other, traditional formative influences are steadily forfeiting their importance, and the reading of printed material is playing an ever greater role in contemporary culture. In the preface to the second volume (1885) of *Essais de psychologie contemporaine*, Bourget is more explicit. What he seeks to portray in his studies of 19th-century authors are, he explains, the social tendencies in French literature during the Second Empire. In an aside ostensibly providing a clarification that none of his original readers can in fact have needed, he adds the ominous reminder that the period stretched from Louis-Napoleon's *coup d'état* to the disastrous Franco-Prussian War and the 1871 Commune. One could perhaps have supposed that the imperial debacle itself was explanation enough for the malaise endemic among young people in France during the Third Republic. For Bourget, however, it is the literature of the preceding generation that has left them imbued with deep-rooted pessimism, fatal mental lassitude, and the gloomy conviction that all effort is futile. His answer to the problem, when critics asked him, is that he has none. It seems, however, that his diagnosis points at least to a change of literary role models, just as his travel writing and his novels suggest that the Third Republic was not the ideal response to ills inherited from the discredited Third Empire.

Though Bourget avers that other French authors might well have been considered, those on whom he concentrates make an impressive list: **Baudelaire, Renan**, Flaubert, Taine, Stendhal, Alexandre Dumas *fils*, Leconte de Lisle, the Goncourt brothers, the Russian novelist **Turgenev**, and the Genevan diarist Amiel. Notwithstanding his intention of putting forward his thesis, Bourget discusses these writers sympathetically and in measured tones. He does justice to Dumas as a successful and serious-minded dramatist before drawing our attention to the vein of pessimism about human nature that he sees as fundamental to the plays. He is at pains to be fair to Amiel too, before going on to argue that the diarist stands at the convergence of two traditions, which he calls Germanic and Latin respectively, using the former term to designate a pattern of negative attitudes and response that might be summed up in the convenient shorthand of the adjective "Hamletic." Before turning to an analysis of Flaubert's nihilism, Bourget pauses for a penetrating account of the role Romanticism played in the development of the novelist's outlook.

Well informed and informative, couched in lucid French with crisp formulations, Bourget's literary essays offer insights that retain their validity even for readers who may prefer not to adhere to the general thesis that he draws from his serious study of the writers of his day.

CHRISTOPHER SMITH

Biography

Paul Charles Joseph Bourget. Born 2 September 1852 in Amiens. Abandoned Catholicism, 1867. Studied at the Lycée Louis-le-Grand, Paris, 1867–71, baccalauréat, 1871, licence in philosophy, 1872. Contributor to various periodicals, including the **Revue des Deux Mondes** (Review of two worlds), from 1873, and **Journal des Débats** (Journal of debates); drama critic, *Le Globe*, 1879, and *Le Parlement*, 1880–82. Married Minnie David (died, 1932), 1890. Visited Palestine, 1893; lived in New York, 1893–94, writing for the New York *Herald* and *Le Figaro*. Elected to the French Academy, 1895. Reverted to Catholicism, 1901. Died (of pneumonia) in Paris, 25 December 1935.

Selected Writings

Essays and Related Prose
Essais de psychologie contemporaine, 2 vols., 1883–85; revised and enlarged edition, 2 vols., 1901
Études et portraits, 2 vols., 1888; revised edition, 3 vols., 1906; part as *Some Impressions of Oxford*, translated by M. C. Warrilow, 1901
Pastels: Dix portraits de femmes, 1889

Nouveaux pastels: Dix portraits d'hommes, 1891; as *Pastels of Men*, translated by Katharine Wormeley, 2 vols., 1891–92
Pages de critique et de doctrine, 2 vols., 1912
Nouvelles pages de critique et de doctrine, 2 vols., 1922
Quelques témoignages, 2 vols., 1928–33
Sur la Toscane, 1929
Au service de l'ordre, 2 vols., 1929–33

Other writings: 28 novels (including *Le Disciple* [*The Disciple*], 1889), many collections of short stories, seven plays, travel writing, and poetry.

Collected works edition: *Œuvres complètes*, 9 vols., 1899–1911 (incomplete).

Further Reading

Austin, Lloyd J., *Paul Bourget: Sa vie et son œuvre jusqu'en 1889*, Paris: Droz, 1940
Crouzet, Michel, "La Mode, le moderne, le contemporain chez Paul Bourget: Une lecture des *Essais de psychologie contemporaine*," *Saggi e Ricerce di Letteratura Francese* 26 (1987): 27–63
Feuillerat, Albert, *Paul Bourget: Histoire d'un esprit sous la Troisième République*, Paris: Plon, 1937
Garrett, Crister, *Paul Bourget and the Politics of Traditionalism* (dissertation), Los Angeles: University of California, 1993
Giraud, Victor, *Paul Bourget*, Paris: Bloud et Gay, 1934
Klerkx, Henri, *Paul Bourget et ses idées littéraires*, Nimègue-Utrecht: Dekker en van de Vegt, 1946
Mansuy, Michel, *Un moderne: Paul Bourget: De l'enfance au disciple*, Paris: Les Belles-Lettres, 1960
Singer, Armand E., *Paul Bourget*, Boston: Twayne, 1976

Boy-Żeleński

Polish, 1874–1941

Tadeusz Żeleński, called Boy, is one of the most unusual and colorful personalities in the cultural life of 20th-century Poland. He was a practicing doctor, poet, theater critic, columnist, sometime literary director of the Polish Theater, professor of French literature, but above all the most ingenious translator of French literature Poland has had. The role Boy-Żeleński played in the literary world in Poland can be compared to that of **Sainte-Beuve** in France or of George Saintsbury in England. In old-fashioned cultural terms, one might call him a libertine; in political terms he was a liberal. For all his vast interests, erudition, and tremendous output, he was not, however, an original mind; rather, he was a perceptive, talented, and provocative essayist.

Although Boy-Żeleński is chiefly known as an expert on French literature, his most significant essays are those devoted to his native literature. Most of them are, so to speak, "correctives" to established interpretations. With his characteristic wit and irony and his beautiful style, Boy-Żeleński attacked and ridiculed the recognized scholars – called by him the "gilders" (*brązownicy*) – for purposely glossing over the "uncomfortable" details from the lives of great writers and for treating literature as national mythology rather than as a source of human self-knowledge. A model of literary culture for Boy-Żeleński was France, where "one walks around the great genius, one describes him, as if he were a lion or a tiger. One assumes a disinterested scientific approach . . . One buries him

in the Pantheon – but one never overlooks any of his weaknesses. Profanation? I do not think so; rather, the conviction that the mystery of genius lies elsewhere than in ordinary perfection. This 'mundane, archmundane,' from which it is born, is the most touching mystery . . . to catch the moment when genius gels is the most fantastic task of literary criticism" ("Mickiewicz a my" [1928; Mickiewicz and us]). Unlike in France, in Poland, Boy-Żeleński claims, the poets are treated like "gilded gods." In his provocative essay "Mickiewicz a my" – devoted to the greatest of the Polish Romantics – he launches an unprecedented attack on Mickiewicz's messianism and his critics. Messianism, according to Boy-Żeleński, is the reaction of an emigrant poet from a country erased from the political map of Europe to the newborn bourgeoisie indifferent to everything that cannot be translated into the values of a commercial society. "Destroy all the monuments of Mickiewicz," Boy-Żeleński states in his conclusion, "melt them down and cast from them a cannon, and load it with a number of critics of Mickiewicz's works." His essay, in which he concentrates on pointing out what was truly original in Mickiewicz, is a novelty in the traditional approach. The Mickiewicz who emerges from Boy-Żeleński's pen is not a national hero but a great Romantic, perhaps the greatest of all the European Romantics; but as a man, however ingenious, he is not free from weaknesses and errors. Messianism was an "illness" – the illness which afflicted Mickiewicz and then was thoughtlessly glorified by his critics.

Many of Boy-Żeleński's objections are fully justified and insightful. He is at his worst, however, when his reading is informed by his anticlericalism and his liberal attitude to social life. For example, in "Tajemnica Pascala" (1931; Pascal's secret), he draws a comparison between the "canonization" of Mickiewicz by his critics in Poland and the attempt on the part of the members of Port-Royal to hide certain details of Pascal's life in order to attain for him the status of a saint, without noticing, however, that Pascal's case weakens his own claim about the objectivity of the French approach to literature.

Boy-Żeleński's work as a translator – quite apart from his intention of filling in the gaps of Polish literary culture – was not merely a matter of rendering in his native tongue the best of French literary achievements. He considered his translations to be a means of counteracting "the didactic tone, temerity, and narrow moral considerations" characteristic of Polish literature. In "O literaturze niemoralnej" (1924; On immoral literature), Boy-Żeleński invokes as examples Octave from Alfred de Musset's *La Confession d'un enfant du siècle* (1836; *The Confession of a Child of the Century*) and **Montaigne**'s "sober analysis of drunkenness" in order to illustrate the salutary character of "immorality" for "self-knowledge": "This exhibitionism of one's self, to its most hidden throbs of thought, the analysis of the motivation standing behind man's every deed, the attempts to show the shortcomings of human nature in man's fraudulence – this is the content of almost the whole of French literature. The Pole does all that, perhaps, only at the confessional."

This search for self-knowledge went hand-in-hand with the development of the French language. In his essay (1925) on **La Rochefoucauld**'s *Maxims* (1664), Boy-Żeleński emphasizes the beneficial character of the word games played in

17th-century salons for the precision of the French language. For instance, the **maxim** questioning whether "one forgives infidelity, but one does not forget it," or whether "one forgets infidelity, but one does not forgive it," was originally half a page long; only after the process of "purification" in the course of heated salon discussions did it take on its present form. Such apparent idle considerations contributed to making French as precise as possible.

The soundness and brilliance of many of his observations notwithstanding, a closer look at Boy-Żeleński's methodology reveals weaknesses. For one thing, French literature is really the only literature with which he makes comparisons; many of his criticisms of Polish literature could with equal force be applied to English and German literature. It seems that the differences between Polish and French literatures – which Boy-Żeleński sometimes claimed had their roots in the Poles' being "genetically" deprived of the sense of curiosity so characteristic in the French – stem simply from the different historical circumstances which shaped the literary, political, and social lives of the two nations. Probably Boy-Żeleński's greatest merit was to stir up the Polish literary world, making later critics analyze Polish literature in a broader context.

ZBIGNIEW JANOWSKI

Biography

Born 21 December 1874 in Warsaw. Studied medicine at Jagiellonian University, Cracow, 1892–99. Medical doctor, Cracow, 1901–18. Script writer for Zielony Balonik (Green balloon), the celebrated cabaret in Cracow, from 1906; theater critic, from 1919; literary director, Polish Theater, Warsaw, 1922–23. Contributor to various journals, including *Kurier Poranny* (Morning messenger), *IKC*, and the London émigré weekly *Wiadomości Literackie* (Literary news). Worked on behalf of the organization of "conscious motherhood," 1930s; fought for the reform of marital law and against the supremacy of clericalism in culture and social life. Moved to Lvov after the outbreak of World War II. Chair of the Department of the French Literature, University of Lvov, after 1939. Member, Polish Academy of Literature. Awards: French Academy Award for Translation, 1914; Knight, Legion of Honor, 1922; Polish Society of Publishers Award, 1928; Warsaw Literary Prize, 1933. Arrested by Nazis after the seizure of Lvov: executed, along with other members of the Polish intelligentsia, 3 July 1941.

Selected Writings

Essays and Related Prose

Słówka, 1913
Flirt z Melpomeną (theater reviews), 10 vols., 1920–32
Studia i szkice z literatury francuskiej, 1920
Nowe studia z literatury francuskiej, 1922
Ludzie żywi, 1929
Brązownicy, 1930
Zmysły-zmysły, 1932
Nieco mitologii, 1935
Szkice o literaturze francuskiej (includes *Studia i szkice z literatury francuskiej* and *Nowe studia z literatury francuskiej*), edited by Wanda Balicka, 2 vols., 1956
Romanse cieniów: Wybór recenzji teatralnych (theater reviews), edited by Józef Hen, 1987
O literaturze niemoralnej: Szkice literackie, edited by Henryk Markiewicz, 1990

Other writings: poetry, works on literature, books defending birth control (*Piekło kobiet*, 1930) and advocating the reform of marriage laws (*Dziewice Konsystorskie*), a biography of King John III Sobieski's French wife, and memoirs (*Znasz li ten kraj?*, 1931). Also translated many authors from the French, including Montaigne, Balzac, Molière, Beaumarchais, **Marivaux**, Musset, Villon, Brantôme, La Rochefoucauld, Descartes, **Pascal**, Rabelais, **Diderot**, **Voltaire**, Constant, **Chateaubriand**, **Rousseau**, Stendhal, Proust, **Gide**, and Jarry, as well as *Tristan et Iseut* and *La Chanson de Roland*.

Collected works edition: *Pisma*, edited by Henryk Markiewicz, 28 vols. 1956–75.

Further Reading

Bouteron, Marcel, *Études balzaciennes*, Paris: Jouve, 1954
Makowiecki, Andrzej, *Tadeusz Żeleński Boy*, Warsaw: Wiedza Powszechna, 1974
Miłosz, Czesław, *The History of Polish Literature*, Berkeley: University of California Press, 2nd edition, 1983 (original edition, 1969)
Natanson, Wojciech, *Boy-Żeleński: Opowieść biograficzna*, Warsaw: Ludowa Spółdzielnia Wydawnicza, 1977

Brault, Jacques

French Canadian, 1933–

If one were to choose a single essay as most representative of Jacques Brault's work, "Petite suite émilienne" (1986; A suite of Emilys) would probably come to mind. After meandering about Emily Dickinson's poetry, the author goes on to discover "other Emilys" all over the world, in England (Emily Brontë), in Germany (Annette von Droste-Hülshoff), in France (Danielle Collobert), in Scotland (Margaret Tait), and finally in his native Quebec, for his last Emily – or more precisely Émilienne – is the essayist's own mother. His "rêverie textuelle" (textual reverie) has led him from literature to autobiography, thus stressing the fact that reading is a double gesture: reaching out is always reaching in.

A medievalist by trade, Brault is a professor, poet, novelist, dramatist, editor, translator, critic, publisher, and essayist – a complete *homme de lettres*. His works of criticism concern mostly Quebec poets (Émile Nelligan, Alain Grandbois, Saint-Denys Garneau, Gaston Miron, Juan Garcia), but, whatever the nature of his writing, it is nurtured by texts from all countries and periods, be it Japanese haiku or **Diderot**'s *Neveu de Rameau*, E. M. Cioran's **aphorism**s, or modern French poetry (**Baudelaire**, Laforgue, Verlaine, Apollinaire, Char, Michaux). Among the many topics he addresses, melancholy, friendship, solidarity, time, and silence are especially frequent. In the visual arts (painting, engraving, collage, drawing), he describes himself as an amateur and apprentice, eager to master yet another language (he illustrates his own books as well as those of others).

It is tempting to explain this hunger for learning new modes of expression by referring to one of Brault's most frequent metaphors, that of the road. His first book of essays was called *Chemin faisant* (1975; On the way), and his second, *La Poussière du chemin* (1989; The dirt of the road). Many of his books of poetry convey similar images: *Migration* (1979), *Trois fois passera* (1981; It will come around three times), *Il n'y a plus de chemin* (1990; On the Road No More). The street and the neighborhood are the poet's favorite loci. For the essayist, everything is always evolving: people, works of art, knowledge and the ways to achieve it. A writer worthy of the name never ceases to learn how to read and to follow new paths.

Humility and humor are needed if one is to be a good student and a good reader. The first quality is most visible in Brault's attention to the texts or works of art he comments on; far from submitting them to any preconceived method of analysis, he instead reveals where he believes their meaning lies by means of comparisons and parallels. He makes no apologies for his subjectivity or for using the present time and his own person as the basis for his analysis. There is a humility in this method that is underlined by the recurrent use of the adjective "petit" (small), as if Brault's investigations must be limited in scope to be effective. As for Brault's humor, often overlooked by critics, this is evidenced by his many tongue-in-cheek remarks, as in *Ô saisons, ô châteaux* (1991; Oh seasons, oh castles; the title is borrowed from Rimbaud), as well as by the word games he plays and his propensity for mocking intellectual fashions.

Brault's style is striking, as a close reading of "Petite Suite émilienne" reveals. His background in philosophy and medieval literature is often visible in his choice of vocabulary. Since he refuses to see the world dualistically, he needs words that will deal with its complexity – hence the many neologisms created with negative prefixes: "désenferme," "inévidence," "non-savoir," and the importance of oxymora, as in "éternité d'un instant" (eternity of an instant). Paradoxes abound in his texts: "She is young and old. Provider and sterile." Brault also likes words seldom used in modern French – "inconnaissance," "trembleuse" – and is fond of Québécois colloquialisms. He likes to quote at length, for he refuses to lose sight of the object of his divagations. This is not to say that his essays read like affected prose; his language adapts well to the contours of his subject matter.

Brault's humility leads him to provide his readers, whom he often addresses directly, as in a **dialogue** or a **letter**, with his personal recollections of his contacts with the world of art. He depicts himself as a reader ("I have only one craft: reading"), as an amateur, and as an apprentice constantly refining his tools – words and images. Central to his work is the "I" who proceeds cautiously to approach the world from his particular point of view. That is the "I" perceived in the marginalia of *Chemin faisant*, and heard in the last lines of "Petite Suite émilienne": "Émilienne loved me so much – in spite of herself, in spite of me." These closing lines are not a conclusion; they do not summarize a literary analysis. They leave open the essayist's relation to his subject matter, as well as his personal history. This openness, this surrender to the power of the literary and artistic journey, characterizes Jacques Brault as an essayist.

BENOÎT MELANÇON

Biography
Born 29 March 1933 in Montreal. Studied at the Collège Sainte-Marie, Montreal, graduated 1954; philosophy at the University of Montreal, M.A., 1958; the Sorbonne, Paris, and at Poitiers, 1958–60. Married Madeleine Breton, 1955: one daughter. Professor of medieval studies (and later of French literature), University of Montreal, 1960–96. Contributor to various magazines and journals, including *Parti Pris* (We affirm) and *Liberté* (Liberty); literary critic and producer of literary radio programming for Radio-Canada. Awards: France-Canada Prize, for poetry, 1969; Duvernay Prize, 1978; Governor-General's Award, for drama, 1970, and for fiction, 1984; David Prize, 1986.

Selected Writings

Essays and Related Prose
Chemin faisant, 1975
La Poussière du chemin, 1989
Ô saisons, ô châteaux, 1991

Other writings: poetry, short plays, work for television and radio, short stories, a novel (*Agonie* [*Death-Watch*], 1984), and a study on Alain Grandbois (1968). Also coedited the work of Saint-Denys Garneau (1971).

Further Reading
Dumont, François, "L'Essai littéraire québécois des années quatre-vingt: La Collection 'Papiers collés'," *Recherches Sociographiques* 33, no. 2 (1992): 323–35
Lemaire, Michel, "Jacques Brault essayiste," *Voix et Images* 35 (Winter 1987): 222–38
Lévesque, Claude, *Le Proche et le lointain*, Montreal: VLB, 1994
Paquin, Jacques, "Écriture et interlocution chez Jacques Brault," *Voix et Images* 57 (Spring 1994): 568–84

Březina, Otokar
Czech, 1868–1929

Between 1895 and 1901 Otokar Březina, the leading representative of Czech literary symbolism, published five collections of poetry. These received the attention of the foremost critics of the day and have surpassed all other literature of that period in their importance. It is no coincidence that, in addition to his poetry, Březina also wrote essays. He soon realized – probably stimulated by his reading of Maurice Maeterlinck and Ernest Hello – that great versatility was possible in the essay form. The 1890s, when Březina's essays began appearing in magazines, is now considered the period of some of the best Czech essayistic works. The authors of that time, particularly František Xaver Šalda, the founder of the Czech **critical essay**, and Březina, the most prominent personality of the poetic essay, laid the foundations of Czech essay writing.

Březina's first book of essays, *Hudba pramenů* (1903; The music of the springs), and the second, *Skryté dějiny* (*Hidden History*) – not published until 1970, long after his death – are artistic expressions of the positive qualities of life, as well as a rich source of Březina's artistic and aesthetic views. In both books the poet deals with fundamental questions of life and art. The essays of *Hudba pramenů*, written at the same time as his books of poems, make the spiritual and imaginative process of these books in a certain sense more complete, bringing them closer to the reader. *Hudba pramenů* is a transitional book in the sense that it represents an intermediate stage linking Březina's artistic, aesthetic, and philosophical attitudes with those he had arrived at when he was still writing verse. In *Hidden History*, written mostly during World War I, the center of interest shifts from art to life. Březina's extraordinary inner strength and certainty in such an uncertain period are clear from the fact that he did not lose his belief in humankind and his creative abilities even in the most difficult years of the war.

In his essays Březina tries, in his often overly rich metaphorical language, to express all the infinite changes of the "hidden history" of the human soul, earth, and cosmos, which – although they take place in a latent, invisible manner, as if under the surface – nonetheless remain the moving force, and therefore the real reason, of all life. It was especially in his essays that the poet was able to find enough space to contemplate freely all the disturbing problems whose solutions became partial contributions to his efforts to achieve a synthesis; he never gave up the search for life's inner core or its unifying meaning, its coherence with truth, beauty, and action. Březina never abandoned his attempt to penetrate – "burn through" – to the essence of things. His will for truth and consequently his will for action did not diminish in spite of his literary silence. The poet's "eternal longing" for a harmonization of all contradictions of life and art, his longing to embrace the world in the totality of its changes and to arrive at the original unity of all cosmic beings, the compelling inner necessity to satisfy fully and truthfully the need for the essence of things, became a fully concrete expression of man trying to achieve unity with himself and the world.

Březina's essays frequently return to the themes of social inequality, poverty, and misery. During the war the poet experienced the oppression of nations and the suffering of the masses. In his essays, from a deep conviction about the importance of a spiritual reality for humankind, grows the permanent necessity for a love which can overcome pain and suffering. There is a great longing for collectivity as well as for peace. In particular, the essay "Mír" ("Peace") which concludes *Hidden History* represents the highest values in Czech literature. According to the Czech literary critic Miloš Dvořák, this is one of the most profound works to emerge from Czech literature and should be read and analyzed by all nations.

In the history of Czech literature Březina's essays occupy an exceptional position, even though until now their importance has not been fully understood or appreciated. They are considered to be the most mature form of poetic prose of the 1890s, a time characterized by contradictions in both society and culture as well as in literature, philosophy, politics, and aesthetics. In this sense, his works also represent a search for a way to overcome and harmonize all contradictions; they are one of the solutions which, by their greatness, originality, and courage of conception, won the admiration and respect of those who were not otherwise among the admirers of the poet's work. The mere existence of essays of this caliber is an "utter novelty" in Czech literature, according to Józef Zarek (1979), who describes them as "a work so unique that we may have difficulty in finding analogies with them in present-day literature." Miroslav Červenka (1969) explains that these essays are meant to "present the reader with the drama of ideas themselves, the drama of human collectives, cosmic processes, and even earthly matters." While they undoubtedly contribute to an understanding of his poetry, they are also Březina's most systematic aesthetic confession, from which later Czech artistic and literary criticism was derived.

While the essays make understanding Březina's poetic work easier, they are not a mere accompaniment, appendix, or explanatory commentary on the verses; they represent an autonomous work of art. From them and Březina's correspondence we can clearly see that the poet never gave himself up to uncritical admiration of the works of the Indian poets and philosophers or Christian mystics and intellectuals of the Middle Ages. Even when he is fully occupied with the study of Maeterlinck, Hello, **Schopenhauer**, **Nietzsche**, **Novalis**, Poe, **Emerson**, or Solov'ev, Březina is fully conscious of his own art, preserving his independence and critical distance from the start.

The list of synonyms by which Březina's essays were designated in the past (prose, poetic prose, philosophical prose, **meditation**, essayistic meditation, philosophical meditation, rhapsody, essay, **philosophical essay**), indicates how difficult it was to classify them appropriately and how unusual their position was in the literary world. Whatever name we may give them, clearly Březina gave concrete support to Šalda's principle of synthesism, trying to realize in his essays his theoretical idea of the integration of art and life, in a completely new kind of essay writing.

PETR HOLMAN

Biography

Born Václav Ignác Jebavy, 13 September 1868 in Počátky, South Bohemia. Used the pseudonyms Václav Danšovský, 1886–92, and Otokar Březina, from 1892. Studied at primary and lower secondary schools in Počátky and at higher secondary school in Telč. Taught at schools in Jinošov, 1887–88, Nová Říše, 1888–1901, and Jaroměřice nad Rokytnou, from 1901. Published his first lyric and epic compositions, sketches, and short stories in the journals *Vesna* (Spring) and *Orel* (Eagle), from 1886; worked on the never published and ultimately destroyed *Román Eduarda Brunnera* (Novel of Eduard Brunner), from 1888; his poems began to appear regularly in journals such as *Vesna*, *Moderní revue* (The modern review), *Rozhledy* (Outlook), *Almanach secese* (The almanac of secession), and *Nový život* (The new life), from 1892; his essays began to appear in various journals, from 1897. Corresponding member, 1913, and full member, 1923, Czech Academy of Arts and Sciences. Awards: Czech State Prize, 1928; honorary degree from Charles University, Prague. Died in Jaroměřice nad Rokytnou, 25 March 1929.

Selected Writings

Essays and Related Prose
Hudba pramenů, 1903
Prvotiny, edited by Miloslav Hýsek, 1933
Prosa, edited by Miloslav Hýsek, 1933
Nové eseje, edited by Otakar Fiala, Matěj Lukšů, and Emanuel Chalupný, 1934
Eseje z pozůstalosti, edited by Otakar Fiala, 1967
Skryté dějiny, edited by Josef Zika, 1970; as *Hidden History*, translated by Carleton Myles Bulkin, forthcoming
Esej, edited by Josef Glivický, 1988
Hudba pramenů a jiné eseje, edited by Petr Holman, 1989; revised, enlarged edition, as *Eseje*, 1996
Fragmenty, edited by Petr Holman, 1989 (unofficial publication)
Dokumenty, edited by Petr Holman, 1991 (unofficial publication)

Other writings: five volumes of poetry (*Tajemné dálky*, 1895; *Svítání na západě*, 1896; *Větry od pólu*, 1897; *Stavitelé chrámu*, 1899; *Ruce*, 1901), short stories, and correspondence.

Collected works editions: *Spisy*, edited by Miloslav Hýsek, 3 vols., 1933–39; *Básnické spisy*, edited by Miroslav Červenka, 1975.

Bibliographies
Holman, Petr, and Jana Sedláková, *Otokar Březina, Bibliografie 3*, Brno: Státní Vědecká Knihovna, 1988
Kubíček, Jaromír, *Otokar Březina: Soupis literatury o jeho životě a díle*, Brno: Universitní Knihovna v Brně, 1971
Papírník, Miloš, and Anna Zykmundová, *Knižní dílo Otokara Březiny*, Brno: Universitní Knihovna v Brně, 1969
Riess, Jiří, "Bibliografie," in *Stavitel chrámu*, edited by Emanuel Chalupný and others, Prague: (in, 1941: 255–74

Further Reading
Červenka, Miroslav, "Tematické posloupnosti v Březinově próze," *Česká Literatura* 17 (1969): 141–58
Deml, Jakub, *Mé svědectví o Otokaru Březinovi*, Olomouc: VOTOBIA, 1994 (original edition, 1931)
Fraenkl, Pavel, *Otokar Březina*, Prague: Melantrich, 1937
Heftrich, Urs, *Otokar Březina, zur Rezeption Schopenhauers und Nietzsches im tschechischen Symbolismus*, Heidelberg: Winter, 1993
Holman, Petr, *K historii vzniku a vydávání Březinových esejů*, Prague: Literární Archiv, Sborník Památníku Národního Písemnictví, 1989: 135–85
Holman, Petr, *Frequenzwörterbuch zum lyrischen Werk von Otokar Březina*, Cologne, Weimar, and Vienna: Böhlau, 2 vols., 1993
Hyde, Lawrence, "Otokar Březina – A Czech Mystic," *Slavonic Review* 2, no. 6 (March 1924): 547–57
Jelínek, Hanuš, "Un poète de la fraternité des âmes: Otokar Březina," *Revue de Genève* 2 (1929): 223–36
Králík, Oldřich, *Otokar Březina 1892–1907: Logika jeho díla*, Prague: Melantrich, 1948
Lakomá, Emilie, *Úlomky hovorů Otokara Březiny*, edited by Petr Holman, Brno: Jota & Arca Jimfa, 1992
Lakomá, Emilie, "Dodatky k Úlomkům hovorů Otokara Březiny," *BOX* 1, no. 1 (1994): 40–47
Marten, Miloš, *Otokar Březina*, Prague: Symposion, 1903
Marten, Miloš, *Akkord: Mácha, Zeyer, Březina*, Prague: Kočí, 1916
Novák, Arne, "Otokar Březina, Obituary," *Slavonic Review* 8, no. 22 (June 1929): 206–09
Selver, Percy Paul, *Otokar Březina: A Study in Czech Literature*, Oxford: Blackwell, 1921
Slavík, Bedřich, "Březinův essay," *Archa* 18, no. 4 (1930): 257–78
Slavík, Bedřich, "Essay Březinův a Unamunův," *Akord* 3, no. 9 (1930): 374–80; 3, no. 10 (1930): 403–07
Vesely, Antonín, *Otokar Březina*, Brno: Moravské kolo Spisovatelů, 1928
Zarek, Józef, *Eseistyka Otokara Březiny*, Wrocław: Ossolineum, 1979
Zika, Josef, *Otokar Březina*, Prague: Melantrich, 1970

British Essay

The history of the British essay traces a complex, entwined rise and fall of various emphases. At certain moments, as in the early 19th century, essays celebrate the experiences and personalities of their authors, while at others, as during the Victorian period, the exploration of ideas predominates. At times the essayist's goal is to entertain or render an aesthetic effect, while at others it is to argue a point, and in still others, as in the case of **George Orwell**, it is to do both. Essayists take their subject matter variously from minor casual events, from literary performances, from political situations, or from the exploration of timeless truths. The genre shifts in relation to neighboring genres – the **treatise**, the article, the **letter**, the **character sketch**, the short story – and even breaks out occasionally in verse. Nonetheless, the steady trajectory of the genre in the 400 years since its British inception is toward short prose pieces that represent ideas as being formed and shaped not through a formal method, but through the consciousness and experience of writers as they interact with the world.

1. Origins and the 17th Century

Perhaps no other genre in British literature appears to have had so clear a beginning. When **Francis Bacon** (1561–1626) published the first edition of his *Essayes or Counsels, Civill and Morall* in 1597, he introduced the genre to the English-speaking world, some 17 years after **Montaigne** had done the same for the French. (As early as 1584 James VI of Scotland, later James I of England, had characterized some writings as essays, though these do not match the genre as presently recognized.) Fittingly, the definitional issues that have marked the essay throughout its history were present at its very birth. A few 20th-century critics, including the essayist **J. B. Priestley**, have gone so far as to argue that Bacon's works are not essays in the core sense of the genre.

Montaigne's essays are characterized by an insistent first-person voice. Whether he discusses his reading, his thoughts, or his experiences, the consciousness that shapes his writing is transparently his own. His essays meander and digress, though always more purposefully than might first appear, and their effect is of a man exploring his world and regularly being surprised at what he discovers in the process. In contrast, Bacon's essays almost entirely lack personal references. Propositional rather than experiential, they strike modern readers as having a sermonic, rhetorical quality that contrasts sharply with Montaigne's more casual works, a quality reflected even in their titles: "Of Truth," "Of Studies," "Of Death," and so on. Contributing to this aphoristic effect is the brevity of Bacon's essays, most of them only a page or so long. Bacon published three editions, in 1597, 1612, and 1625, and each was marked by the addition of more essays and the revision, usually by expansion, of works from earlier editions. However, even the pieces in the 1625 edition remain shorter and less obviously personal than those by Montaigne.

Still, Bacon's essays enact qualities beyond relative brevity that would, over the centuries, define the genre. Most importantly, they present multiple perspectives on a given topic. The successions of **aphorisms** that constitute the essays generally take one position, then its almost opposite, before eventually landing somewhere in the middle. The effect is to represent thought as it occurs rather than to report its results. Later essayists would join Bacon's exploratory method of thinking-in-progress with more explicit narratives of experience and self.

Two factors promoted the rise of the essay during the early 17th century. As demonstrated by Bacon's other works, such as *The Advancement of Learning* (1605), the bases of knowledge were shifting at this time. Previously, knowledge was still founded on the authority of earlier writers and on principles of deduction. Around 1600, however, observation and experiment began to emerge as plausible and desirable. Since observations were a function of observers, the nature, circumstances, and experiences of the writer became an element for consideration, not just disdain.

Second, during the 17th century several new prose forms proliferated. Three types of writings approached the essayistic: aphoristic writings, such as Ben Jonson's (1572–1637) *Timber, or Discoveries* (1641), character sketches, such as those by Sir Thomas Overbury (1581–1613) and Nicholas Breton (c. 1545/55–c. 1626), and meditative prose, such as Robert Burton's (1577–1640) *Anatomy of Melancholy* (1621) and **Sir Thomas Browne**'s (1605–82) *Religio Medici* (1642, revised 1643), many **chapters** of which are frequently anthologized as essays and were criticized by some on publication for narrating personal concerns. **John Donne**'s (1572–1631) *Meditations* (wr. 1612–15, pub. 1651), by virtue of their brevity, occasional nature, and reflective quality are directly in the essay tradition.

Though perhaps less grounded in presentations of self than these three, the argumentative philosophical treatises of writers like Thomas Hobbes (1588–1679) influenced the genre. John Locke's (1632–1704) *An Essay Concerning Human Understanding* (1689) is the most obvious such work, but it is also problematic because its sheer length distinguishes it from essays as usually understood. Locke's decision to call his work an essay reflects, ultimately, his sense of the method and conditional nature of the work, and it prefigures a later common tendency to speak of "essayistic" qualities of works that themselves are not strictly essays. Finally, and perhaps most significantly, the 17th century also witnessed an expansion of various other types of what might be called "utilitarian" prose writing: travels, biographies, diaries and **journals**, **pamphlets**, journalism, and letters. The close affinities during this period between the essay and the letter, both characterized by informality, spontaneity, and a measure of egotism on the part of the author, can be noted in the publishing practice of mixing the genres, as in Charles Gildon's (1665–1724) *Miscellaneous Letters and Essays* (1694).

Shortly following the publication of Bacon's essays, **Sir William Cornwallis the Younger** (1579–1614) published two volumes of *Essayes* (1600, 1601), in them characterizing the genre in ways that would be repeated through its history: the essay as tentative practice work, "like a Scrivenor trying his pen," the result being prose that at best is "undigested motions." Cornwallis' writings inhabited a territory between Bacon and Montaigne, demonstrating more of the latter's presentation of self. Even further in this direction were Abraham Cowley's (1618–67) *Several Discourses by Way of Essays, in Verse and Prose* (1668), terse pieces each concluding in verse that further challenged the formal definitions of the new genre.

2. The 18th Century: The Essay Transformed by Periodicals

A significant development in the evolution of the essay was the rise of periodical journalism near the beginning of the 18th century. News had been published as early as the 1620s to 1650s; however, by the end of the century **periodicals** were actively publishing more than accounts of events. The advent of popular periodicals had two important consequences for essays and essayists. First, the regular access to a consistent readership invited essayists to adopt a more familiar, as opposed to formal, style, as if they were corresponding with known readers. Second, the periodical format enhanced the occasional and topical nature of the essay. Not only could writers use current events as points of departure, but the range of appropriate occasions expanded to include personal experiences in the lives of the authors (as in **Addison**'s "A Visit to Westminster Abbey") and even fictional ones, as in the *Spectator*'s Sir Roger de Coverley papers.

Daniel Defoe's (1660–1731) copious journalistic efforts helped create a space for **periodical essays**. His works appeared in such short-lived magazines as *Mist's Journal* and *Applebee's Journal*. In *A Review of the Affairs of France* (1704–13), most of which he wrote as well as edited, Defoe published opinions on current political topics as well as lighter articles on topics like marriage and gambling. One section of the *Review*, "Mercure Scandale, or Advice from the Scandalous Club," provided the germ of the *Tatler* and *Spectator*, without a doubt the most important periodicals in the early history of the genre.

Richard Steele (1672–1729) began publishing the *Tatler* in April 1709 and was quickly joined by **Joseph Addison** (1672–1719). The *Tatler* appeared three times a week, and its newspaper-like format invited casual reading in spare moments. As a result its essays were compact and graceful, balancing a need to entertain with its authors' desires to comment on contemporary life and suggest attitudes and behaviors to a middle-class audience. The original design was to have individual essays emanating from various London coffeehouses and chocolate houses, thereby borrowing from news reportage the veneer of the dispatch but with a lighter spirit, facilitated by the ostensible narrator of the periodical, Sir Isaac Bickerstaff. Bickerstaff's name was borrowed from **Jonathan Swift** (1667–1745), who himself wrote occasional pieces for the *Tatler*, including a famous one on style (no. 230).

The *Tatler* closed in January 1711 but was succeeded in March of that year by the *Spectator*, this periodical chiefly Addison's effort, though both men contributed numerous essays. The *Spectator* introduced a cast of fictional characters who figured in a number of the pieces and represented different segments of society, for example Sir Roger de Coverley, representative of the gentry, and Will Honeycomb, representative of the town. With this device the essay genre mingled with the tale and short story. By the time the *Spectator* ceased publication in December 1712, it and the *Tatler* had published hundreds of essays of various types, ranging from character sketches like "Tom Folio" and "Ned Softly" to more philosophical pieces like "Meditation on Animal Life" (*Spectator* no. 519) and the frequently jocular narratives of the Spectator Club. The periodicals had also established criticism as an aim of the essay, a tradition that flowered in 19th century periodicals and continued into the 20th century, as is most thoroughly demonstrated by **Virginia Woolf**'s collection *The Common Reader* (1925). At the broadest level, the aim of these papers was to explore the individual's proper relationship to and behavior in a changing public life, one of whose many facets included not only politics but also social gatherings and the arts.

Addison, Steele, and Jonathan Swift wrote for papers that followed the *Spectator*, most notably the *Guardian*, the *Intelligencer*, and the *Examiner* (1710–16), a forthright political paper that Swift briefly edited. Swift brought to the genre a stance that was frequently polemical, though polemic is often couched in **satire**, as in his famous "A Modest Proposal" (1729).

Many of Swift's works appeared as pamphlets or **tracts**, and others at this time were, of course, publishing essays in venues other than periodicals. Anthony Ashley Cooper, Third **Earl of Shaftesbury** (1671–1713) published *Characteristicks of Men, Manners, Opinions, Times* in 1711, a volume accompanied by a collection of "Miscellaneous Reflections," which had more of the light character of Addison's and Steele's works. The letters that Philip Dormer Stanhope, Fourth **Earl of Chesterfield** (1694–1773), wrote to his son in the 1740s are frequently anthologized as essays and have something of the flavor of Bacon's aphoristic style. However, Chesterfield did not intend them for publication and, in fact, wrote frequently for mid-century periodicals like the *World*. **Henry Fielding's** (1707–54) eminence as a novelist all but occludes his own essay writings, although the introductory chapters to the books of *Tom Jones* (1749) function as essays, and Fielding additionally wrote for periodicals like the *Champion* (1739–41) and the *Covent-Garden Journal* (1752).

The greatest periodical essayist of the mid-century was **Samuel Johnson** (1709–84). He wrote the *Rambler* from 1750 to 1752, a twice-weekly magazine that appeared on Tuesdays and Saturdays. The *Rambler* obviously owed a great deal to the *Tatler* and *Spectator* in terms of conception and even variety of essay forms: letters, characters, tales, and so on. But in other respects, Johnson's essays were of quite a different quality. In seeking to avoid "mere topicality" for what he perceived as more general moral truths, Johnson reached back to the traditions of both Bacon and Montaigne and "serious" 17th-century writers like Browne and Jeremy Taylor (1613–67), a tradition perpetuated in the 18th century by essayists like **David Hume** (1711–76) in works such as *Essays Moral and Political* (1741–42). Johnson's *Rambler* essays are generally more serious than those of his immediate periodical predecessors. Occasionally they contain autobiographical elements, as in no. 134, "Idleness an Anxious and Miserable State," but these elements tend to introduce more abstract subject matter rather than to serve as the ongoing basis of the essay. Johnson's sense of the proper position of the essayist *vis-à-vis* the work is suggested by his initial decision to conceal the authorship of the *Rambler* papers, although not long after publication his hand was revealed.

Johnson's apparent self-distancing is reflected by the fact that some 60 of the approximately 200 essays that he wrote for the *Rambler* are in the form of letters attributed to correspondents to the magazine. There are letters, for example, in the persona of girls "less than sixteen," of young bachelors, and of women of "antiquated virginity." About half of the *Rambler* papers are straightforward essays dealing with philosophical or moral topics such as religion and superstition, the vanity of stoicism, the sources of disagreement in marriage, and the value of fame. Approximately 15 are short tales or sketches, including a dream allegory set in "the garden of hope." Some narrative works are "Orientals," fictions set in the exotic locations of the Middle and Far East, a tradition that had preceded Johnson and was later extended by Oliver Goldsmith. Of the remaining works, some 30 are pieces of literary criticism.

The *Rambler* was hardly a financial triumph, with most issues selling fewer than 500 copies. But later collections of the essays sold well, broadening their readership and thus establishing their place in the genre's history. Johnson went on to contribute a series of essays, known collectively as **The Idler**, to the *Universal Chronicle* from 1758 to 1760; these pieces were generally lighter in tone, more like works in the *Tatler* and *Spectator*. He also contributed frequently to John Hawkesworth's (1715–73) *Adventurer* (1752–54), a periodical notable for its frequent narratives and sketches.

Oliver Goldsmith's (1730–74) success with the essay as a periodical genre parallels Johnson's. The *Bee* (1759) survived for only eight numbers; however, each issue contained several essays, and collectively they demonstrate how far the genre had come. Most striking is how they mingle the aesthetic with the political and moralistic. Essays like "A City Night Piece" and "A Reverie at the Boar's Head Tavern in East Cheap" seem to exist as much to create an atmosphere and to entertain as to instruct or deliver a point. Characters like "The Man in Black" and "Beau Tibbs" are marked by a subtlety not found in earlier works, and even ostensibly instructive and persuasive pieces like "National Prejudices" are carefully given a narrative occasion, so that their topics seem to emerge out of naturally occurring events rather than stock commonplaces. Following the demise of the *Bee*, Goldsmith published a series of essays in the *Public Ledger* (1760–61). Collected as *The Citizen of the World* in 1762, these essays were unified by the conceit of their having been written by a Chinese visitor to England.

Goldsmith's career as essayist encapsulates a number of essay trends during the 18th century. Beyond the influence of periodicals and periodical publication on the readership, style, and subject matter of the genre, two additional qualities are noteworthy. First, a surprising number of essays, from Swift to Addison and Steele to Johnson to Goldsmith, were attributed to a persona other than the author. Despite Montaigne's declaration nearly two centuries earlier that he was the subject of his book and despite the earlier publication of essays like Cowley's "Of Myself" (1668), there remained uncertainty about the propriety and desirability of having one's own experience explicitly serve as the source and object of presentation and exploration. Second, most of the essays appearing in the prominent periodicals were written by the editors of those periodicals. In a sense, then, the periodicals functioned in much the same way that present-day single-author volumes of essays do. While each essay could – and did – stand on its own, it also benefited from its readers' associating it with a larger sense of the author and his work. In some cases, as with the Spectator Club, the essays even cross-refer to one another, thus forming a whole larger than the individual works. Later writers, like **Charles Lamb** in his Elia essays, would meld and transform the issues of the essayist's persona and of the essay in relation to other essays.

3. The Romantic Movement

If ever a literary and intellectual movement were suited to the essay, it was Romanticism. By emphasizing qualities of emotion, of direct apprehension and interpretation of the natural world beyond social institutions, and, especially, of the centrality of the individual interpreting his or her experience, Romanticism revived and transformed the essay tradition growing out of Montaigne. One hundred seventy-five years later, the American essayist **Edward Hoagland** would characterize the genre as "existing on a line between 'what I think' and 'what I am'." The second pole of Hoagland's formulation is present only by indirection in most essays written before 1800. That would change in the first third of the 19th century.

The Romantic movement is defined through its poetry, and some poets did, in fact, make a substantial contribution as essayists. The works that come most easily to mind are the **prefaces** of William Wordsworth (1770–1850) and **Percy Bysshe Shelley** (1792–1822). Robert Southey (1774–1843), who became Poet Laureate in 1813, wrote **reviews** for magazines like the **Quarterly Review**, published aphoristic commonplaces and essayistic observations in *Omniana* (1812), and wrote more conventional essays of ideas which were collected in the 1832 volume *Essays, Moral and Political*. **Samuel Taylor Coleridge**'s (1772–1834) reviews, interpretations, and aphorisms were collected in volumes like *Aids to Reflection* (1825); his weekly periodical the *Friend* (1809–10) contained essays more general in their occasion, especially those he designated "Landing Places." Most interesting and problematic as an essayistic work is his *Biographia Literaria* (1817). Too long to be easily considered a single essay, some of its individual chapters able to stand alone but most of them integrated into the larger whole, the *Biographia Literaria* nonetheless has a strong essayistic quality, intermixing criticism with philosophy and autobiography. Coleridge's critique of empiricism and his privileging of the individual mind's creative powers carved a philosophical pretext for the genre.

But the best and most influential essayists of the period were those writers who worked almost exclusively in prose and almost exclusively in the genre, writers like Lamb, **Hunt**, **Hazlitt**, and **De Quincey**. Leigh Hunt's (1784–1859) career exemplifies the broad belletristic role performed by many of his contemporary essayists, who published a mixture of criticism and reviews, **familiar essays**, and political and occasional writings. Hunt began as a theater critic before starting, with his brother John in 1808, the *Examiner*, a weekly political periodical. However, his familiar essays, published in such magazines as the *Reflector* (1811–12), are most significant in terms of the genre. Works like "Getting up on Cold Mornings" and "A Few Thoughts on Sleep" (both 1820) deal with subjects notable for their plainness and apparent triviality, serving as occasions for Hunt's sometimes whimsical analysis, as if the game of the essay were to see what could be made of such an apparently unpromising topic. Lamb's "A Dissertation on Roast Pig" (1822) also stems from this vein, and the conceit is evident in later essays like **G. K. Chesterton**'s "A Piece of Chalk" (1909). Critics have sometimes pointed to extreme tendencies to inflate minor subjects as evidence of shallowness or the pursuit of style for style's sake.

A more important essayist was **William Hazlitt** (1778–1830), whose extensive prose output can also be divided into the two broad classes of literary criticism and familiar essays on miscellaneous topics ranging from politics to prize-fighting, sometimes with an autobiographical element. In her essay on Hazlitt (1930), Virginia Woolf comments that by both the estimations of his contemporaries and the evidence of his published work, Hazlitt was frequently a hard man and writer to endure. That Woolf was ultimately able to commend his writing, especially in light of such works as "Education of Women" (1815), in which Hazlitt claims that "the writer of this article confesses that he never met with any woman who could reason," suggests his achievement almost despite himself. In "On Prejudice," he declares that individuals must "attend to the 'still, small voice of our own hearts and feelings' instead of being browbeat by . . . pedants and sophists," a Romantic pronouncement that claims not only the right but also the obligation for the essayist's stance. This viewpoint infused his literary essays, such as those published in *Characters of Shakespeare's Plays* (1817) and *Lectures on the English Comic Writers* (1819), the latter of which contains "On the Periodical Essayists," an important discussion of the genre in the 18th century. "On Familiar Style" (1821–22) presents a credo for what many have before and since taken to be a defining characteristic of the essay: a precise conversational style free from pomp and flourish but also free from cant and low language.

Hazlitt's interpretation of this quality is clearest in his two volumes of *Table-Talk; or, Original Essays* (1821–22). In these essays he most clearly represents his ideas as products ultimately of his own experience and views. "On the Feelings of Immortality in Youth" (1821) begins with observations of how a general universal "we" only gradually come to perceive our own deaths, but by the middle of the essay Hazlitt reveals his personal stake in the issue, musing that "For my part, I started in life with the French Revolution, and I have lived, alas! to see the end of it." "On Going a Journey" (1822) articulates a now prominent essay convention, the narrative of a journey or even merely a walk. The writer's progress through a physical space provides the sufficient occasion to organize the mental space of apparently disparate ideas and topics. When Hazlitt writes, "With change of place we change our ideas; nay our opinions and feelings," he means in a figurative sense as well as a literal one. Just as the decision to travel sets up a range of possible encounters but does not determine precisely what those encounters will be or any logical connection between them, so the decision to essay does not determine the contents or shape of the ensuing text.

Perhaps the most original essayist of the Romantic period was **Charles Lamb** (1775–1834). In some ways, Lamb's position as a Romantic writer is contradictory since, like Samuel Johnson, he was more a writer of urban life than of nature, and he affected an older style and voice contrasting with the familiar style that Hazlitt favored; Hazlitt admitted that Lamb was the only practitioner of that style he could tolerate. Lamb's essays are marked by their pervading sense of nostalgia, their nearly excessive self-deprecation, and most importantly, their central focus on Lamb's relationship to the world, a relationship usually slightly out of step.

As did many of his essayist contemporaries, Lamb wrote in genres other than the familiar essay, including reviews, poems, plays, and with his sister Mary the successful *Tales from Shakespeare* (1807). Unlike many of his contemporaries, Lamb never pursued a solely belletristic career. From 1790 until 1825 he worked as a clerk and accountant, which gave him some artistic distance from the literary world. In 1820, he began publishing essays in *London Magazine*, which also printed Hazlitt's *Table-Talk* and De Quincey's *Opium Eater* essays. Collected in 1823 as *The Essays of Elia* and again in 1833 as *The Last Essays of Elia*, these pieces quietly long for a vaguely distant past. Elia, a persona Lamb named after a clerk at the South Sea House, portrays a genteel sense of life and business at the Inns of Court in "The Old Benchers of the Inner Temple" (1821). In "Old China" (1823), Lamb writes of the nostalgic beauty evoked by old plates, cups, and saucers. In "New Year's Eve" (1821), he bravely (and unconvincingly) embraces the New Year as an optimistic antidote for an almost paralytic longing for times past; Lamb represents his mind as almost painfully introspective, and confesses: "That I am fond of indulging, beyond a hope of sympathy, in such retrospection, may be the symptom of some sickly idiosyncrasy." The essayist's gaze is turned unabashedly inward, topics merely serving as occasions for reflection. Lamb himself recognized the preciousness and self-indulgence this conceit risked. In "A Character of the Late Elia" (1823), a mock literary obituary, he jokes that, "To say truth, it is time he were gone. The humour of the thing, if there was ever much in it, was pretty well exhausted." *The Essays of Elia* bring to the genre the quality that Goethe's *Die Leiden des jungen Werthers* (1774; *Sufferings of Young Werther*) brought to the novel. The degree of introspection in essays since then has varied, but its existence in the genre today can be traced from Montaigne through Lamb.

One of his contemporaries, **Mary Russell Mitford** (1787–1855), shared Lamb's intimate style and tone, though the focus of her works was ostensibly less that of portraying a sensibility than a way of life. In *Our Village*, five volumes written between 1824 and 1832, Mitford presented a series of essays, sketches, and stories of life in a fictionalized and romanticized rural village. Rendering country life has become a stock trope for the essay genre, showing up for example in **Richard Jefferies'** works and Alexander Smith's *Dreamthorp* (1863), and crossing the Atlantic to manifest itself in works like those of the American essayist **E. B. White**.

Contrasting sharply with Lamb's rather staid and self-deprecating style are the essays of **Thomas De Quincey** (1785–1859). De Quincey himself named his style "impassioned prose," an apt description for the writing in "The English Mail Coach" (1849), especially a section narrating an accident entitled "Dream-Fugue." His dramatic flair can be seen in the **critical essay** "On the Knocking at the Gate in *Macbeth*" (1823), and in his series "On Murder Considered as One of the Fine Arts" (1827, 1839, 1854) published in *Blackwood's*, both of which use sensational killings to ground contemplations that are nearly decadent in their lack of clear moral pronouncement. Such a quality is hardly surprising from the author of the autobiographical *Confessions of an English Opium Eater*, published first in *London Magazine* (1821–22). In "Suspiria de Profundis" (wr. 1845, pub. 1871) De Quincey presents **meditations** and autobiographical reminiscences from his childhood, many exploring dreams and the subconscious, in a lyric style that Virginia Woolf would later explore in essays like "Old Mrs. Grey" (1942) or "The Moment" (1947). His brief theoretical distinction between "The Literature of Knowledge and the Literature of Power" (the former having as its goal

"teaching," the latter "moving") has been embraced by later critics and theorists to distinguish essays, as a literature of power, from other nonfiction prose.

Qualities important to the essay in the previous century continued to be manifested during the Romantic period. **Maria Edgeworth's** (1768–1849) essays in *Practical Education* (1798) and elsewhere provided the conceptual underpinnings of her didactic novels and continued the tradition of the essay as a genre for transmitting cultural values. Periodicals continued to instruct too, though in a manner different from that of the early 18th century. Magazines and journals published creative and topical works. But a shift in emphasis can be seen with the rise of the **review**. In reviews the occasions of essays and articles were not events, real or imagined, ideas, or issues but rather published works; reviews approached events or ideas through the gateway of others' writings. The liberal *Edinburgh Review* (1802–1929), published several of Hazlitt's essays between 1814 and 1830, as well as works by **Carlyle and Macaulay**, by the middle of the century introducing essays on topical as well as literary matters. The *Quarterly Review* (1809–1967) condemned Hunt, Hazlitt, and Lamb and provided conservative views through the middle of the century on issues of science, religion, and culture. *Blackwood's Edinburgh Magazine* (1817–1980) published creative works as well as reviews, essays, and treatises on political matters. De Quincey wrote occasionally for the magazine during the 1820s, the "Noctes Ambrosianae" series of conversations among a cast of individuals echoing the Spectator Club of more than a century earlier.

4. The Essay of Ideas in the Victorian Age
The character of the essay changed significantly by the middle of the 19th century, as 18th-century and Romantic concerns with developing polite sensibility (and correcting its lack), presenting individual reflection, and celebrating (and critiquing) *belles-lettres* were eclipsed by advances in science and technology, and their impact on religion, the economy, and education, which commanded essayists' attention in new ways. Previous writers had dealt with abstract issues, as Bacon's essays demonstrate and Johnson's essays frequently suggest. However, by the Victorian age, philosophical ideas and their implications directly occasioned essays rather than emerging obliquely from the exploration of a specific incident or reading. One sign of this development was the relative disappearance of the familiar essay during the middle third of the century, as the genre bent more toward the treatise, history, or article. (More precisely, one might say that familiar essays were still being written, but they have not endured as the canonical works from this period.) Illustrating this shift was the emergence of periodicals like the *Spectator* in 1828, which featured political articles and "interesting topics of a general nature" (5 July 1828) along with reviews.

Of course, the essayistic self did not disappear completely during this period. **Harriet Martineau's** (1802–76) essays frequently employ narrative and anecdotes, her own life circumstances furnishing the impetus for many of them. Her "Letter to the Deaf" (1834) was informed by her own deafness, as was the collection *Life in the Sick-Room* (1844) by her illness and *Letters on Mesmerism* (1844) by her treatments. Still, the bulk of Martineau's work, as with the 14 years of articles written for the *Daily News*, dealt with current events and issues, including many on women's rights.

Thomas Babington Macaulay's (1800–59) numerous essays in the *Edinburgh Review* (collected as *Critical and Historical Essays* in 1843) are similarly infused with political concepts, though this was less the cause of their popularity than Macaulay's manner of expression. Many of the essays existed to explain historical events and ideas, and Macaulay frequently created dramatic scenes to do so. Socrates and Phaedrus, for example, talk on "a fine summer day under the plane-tree, while the fountains warbled at their feet, and the cicadas chirped overhead." Although the impulse is historical, the mood is essayistic to the extent that Macaulay colors factual material with an aesthestic sensibility, as well as using history to serve the argument, as in the essay "Lord Bacon" (1837), in which the writer is revealed through thought and style, not autobiography.

Thomas Carlyle's (1795–1881) essays share some of these features with Macaulay's, particularly his lectures *On Heroes, Hero-Worship, and the Heroic in History* (1841) and *Past and Present* (1843). However, Carlyle is much more the social critic and philosopher. While he began as a literary reviewer and critic for the *Edinburgh Review*, continuing this work in places like *Fraser's Magazine*, essays such as "Signs of the Times" (1829) and "Characteristics" (1831) more clearly signal Carlyle's turn – and the genre's. In "Signs of the Times," Carlyle says that the 19th century should be called "not an Heroical, Devotional, Philosophical, or Moral Age, but, above all others, the Mechanical Age." Most of his subsequent essays critique the times and call for the spiritualism and strength of individual character and leadership that Carlyle perceived in the past. His tone is often polemical and always assured, and while he writes characteristically in the essayistic first person, as in the late essay *Shooting Niagara: And After?* (1867), his stance is much less that of "friend" than "lecturer." The possible exception is *Sartor Resartus* (1836), part novel, part autobiography (through the persona of Diogenes Teufelsdroech), part philosophy, the mixture of exposition, narrative, and reflection placing the work in the essayistic mode.

John Ruskin (1819–1900) shared Carlyle's vision of modern times, critiquing them in a spirit that was, if anything, ultimately more fierce. Late in life, in the apocalyptic essay "The Storm Cloud of the Nineteenth Century" (1884), Ruskin used the occasion of a walk from Abingdon to Oxford to locate his perception, literally and metaphorically, that a "dark" and "malignant" "plague wind" was destroying the age. Whereas Carlyle grounded his ideas in literary criticism and philosophy, Ruskin grounded his in art criticism and theory. Essays in his five-volume *Modern Painters* (1843–60) comment as much on the social contexts of art as on the works themselves, as for example in "The Two Boyhoods" (vol. 5, 1860). *The Stones of Venice* (1851–53) is simultaneously history, descriptive travel writing, and cultural theory. Many of Ruskin's other works, some published in journals like *Cornhill Magazine*, are more overtly political, such as those collected in *The Two Paths* (1859) and *Unto This Last* (1862). Autobiographical moments or scenes appear in several of these essays, unlike those written by most of his contemporary "sages," though he did write a separate autobiography, *Praeterita* (1886–89). Ruskin wrote

several of his essays (as letters) for *Fors Clavigera*, a journal he wrote for the Guild of St. George, thus working in a politicized variant of the single-author periodical tradition last practiced by Johnson and Goldsmith.

John Stuart Mill's (1806–73) writings were more conventional. He reserved the personal narratives and explicitly self-reflexive materials of his own personal crises for his *Autobiography*, published posthumously in 1873. Beginning in the 1820s, he wrote review essays in periodicals like the *Westminster Review* and continued in that mode of publication throughout his life, also publishing pamphlets and monographs. Mill's essays (in contrast to the *Autobiography*) argue specific positions, on topics ranging from political economy to women's issues. Their method is to establish a thoughtful dialectic, in which opposing ideas serve to complicate one another, in an essayistic move that is, however, more purposeful than digressive. The effect on readers is to perceive the essay as driven by inquiry rather than dogma, though Mill's positions are assuredly evident. The clearest examples of his method (and most influential works) are *Principles of Political Economy* (1848) and *On Liberty* (1859); the five chapters of the latter each constitute an essay exploring the relationship of the individual to the group.

John Henry Newman's (1801–90) essayistic work bears interesting parallels to Mill's. He too saved personal narratives for an autobiography (*Apologia Pro Vita Sua*, 1865), and his essays focus squarely on philosophical, educational, religious, and social issues. Logically, owing to Newman's status as a clergyman who eventually was made Cardinal, many of his essays had their origins as **sermons** or lectures, as for example, the *Oxford University Sermons* (1843) and *The Idea of a University* (published in various forms in 1852 and 1859 and in standard form in 1873). As a result, the essays have a conversational tone, familiar not in the sense of the author telling intimate details of his life but in the sense of a speaker addressing a present and known audience. Yet their purpose is didactic and persuasive, and they demonstrate the blurred boundaries between the essay and various oratorical genres. Two book-length works, *An Essay on the Development of Christian Doctrine* (1845) and *An Essay in Aid of a Grammar of Assent* (1870) might better be considered treatises or, rather, be viewed as essays in the same sense as Locke's *An Essay Concerning Human Understanding*.

What Newman was to religious culture **Matthew Arnold** (1822–88) was to more secular culture, though both writers shared moral, ethical, intellectual, and even spiritual concerns, and even when Arnold took exception to historical religion, as in *Literature and Dogma* (1873), he did so with respect. Arnold's essays are philosophical, even academic in character, and can be divided into two broad but interpenetrating categories. *Essays in Criticism* (1865, 1888) discusses specific authors but, more importantly for literary studies, articulates theoretical and literary principles, most famously in "The Function of Criticism at the Present Time" (1864), "The Study of Poetry" (1880), and "The Literary Influence of Academies" (1864). Of broader purview are his social essays, many published originally in *Cornhill Magazine* and collected in *Culture and Anarchy* (1869). These works, later given their now familiar chapter titles such as "Sweetness and Light" and "Hebraism and Hellenism," seek directly to influence contemporary culture through carefully reasoned analyses of broad issues. His sustained defense of humanistic learning is exemplified by his later essay "Literature and Science" (1885).

Arnold felt compelled to write such substantial defenses because it was not only poets, artists, and clergy who wrote essays during the period. T. H. Huxley's (1825–95) hundreds of professional and popular essays articulated basic tenets of the new science, most prominently the work of Charles Darwin (1809–82), who himself wrote popular essays as well as the ground-breaking *On the Origin of Species* (1859). In the *Fortnightly* and *Westminster Reviews* (serving as science columnist for the second), Huxley explored the range from specific topics, as in "On the Physical Basis of Life" (1869), to broader implications of science, as in "Science and Culture" (1881); a corpus of essays was later collected in nine volumes. Huxley is important for establishing the subgenre of essays popularizing and commenting on scientific ideas, practiced in the 20th century by the American writers Loren Eiseley, Lewis Thomas, and Stephen Jay Gould.

Walter Pater's (1839–94) essays looked back rather than forward, both for subject matter, as in his most celebrated work *The Renaissance* (1873, 1877), and for style, as he privileged imagination, sensation, and private visions, qualities more characteristic of Romantic prose than Victorian utilitarianism. Pater wrote appreciations of Montaigne, Browne, and Lamb, as well as a volume of *Imaginary Portraits* (1887). Leslie Stephen's (1832–1904) career included numerous studies of earlier writers, as can be seen in *Hours in a Library* (1874–79) and *Studies of a Biographer* (1898–1902). However, his first essays are narratives of hiking and mountain climbing (*The Playground of Europe*, 1871), befitting someone who edited the *Alpine Journal*. Other essays deal with issues of modern life and proper conduct in an age "after" religion, for instance in *An Agnostic's Apology* (1893).

Although the genre from the 1830s to the 1880s is most characteristically defined by the essay of ideas, not all its practitioners were political or moral philosophers or scholars. William Makepeace Thackeray (1811–63), for example, represented that venerable tradition of novelists who include the essay among their palette of genres. Thackeray began as a journalist, writing characters, satires, sketches, and articles, many with a satiric and burlesque quality, which were collected in *Comic Tales and Sketches* (1841). He reinvigorated the tradition of the character in *The Book of Snobs* (1848), which first appeared in *Punch*, where he published extensively. His primary contributions to the genre, though, are the *Roundabout Papers* (1863), originally published in *Cornhill Magazine*, of which he was the first editor.

Other prominent Victorian writers also wrote essays. Charles Dickens (1812–70) began his career writing descriptive sketches and essays of places and characters, primarily in London, collected as *Sketches by Boz Illustrative of Every-Day Life and Every-Day People* (1836). The scenic quality and narrative sense of these essays convey the social criticism that Dickens featured in his novels and that more explicitly formed the subject of later essays like "Wapping Workhouse" (1860). As founder of *Household Words*, he published dozens of short pieces on various subjects, including rather plain aspects of contemporary life. George Eliot (1819–80) published numerous reviews in *Westminster Review*, the *Leader*, and elsewhere,

works that, though occasioned as literary criticism, enabled her essayistically to expand to broader topics, as in "Margaret Fuller and Mary Wollstonecraft" (1855). Late in life she published a relatively experimental work, a series of fictional/essayistic sketches, *The Impressions of Theophrastus Such* (1879).

In addition to her novels, Margaret Oliphant (1828–97) published essays in a number of periodicals, especially *Blackwood's*, where she was a prolific literary reviewer for nearly the last half of the century, often focusing on groups of authors or works rather than single works. Poet and novelist William Morris' (1834–96) essays, written between 1877 and 1896, articulated the relationship he saw between politics, art, and society, echoing Ruskin's sentiments and, to some extent, style. Oscar Wilde (1854–1900) wrote literary criticism, reviews, and more political works, including "The Soul of Man Under Socialism" (1891), in the tradition of Arnold. Most famous are his clever essays in the form of dialogues, "The Decay of Lying" (1889) and "The Critic as Artist" (1890), which invert typical relationships, putting art over life, and criticism over creation.

5. Century's End and Beyond and the Return of the Familiar Essay

In 1863, Alexander Smith (1830?–67) published *Dreamthorp: A Book of Essays Written in the Country*, which marks the return and evolution of a familiar essay spirit that had waned during the middle third of the century. The essays in this slim book celebrate life on a rural estate and, more importantly, the perspective of Smith himself. Overtly narrative and autobiographical in their content, they demonstrate the qualities Smith describes in "On the Writing of Essays," in which he distinguishes between the "serious and stately" tradition out of Bacon and the "garrulous and communicative" tradition out of Montaigne. Smith notes that "The essayist plays with his subject, now in whimsical, now in grave, now in melancholy mood . . . His main gift is an eye to discover the suggestiveness of common things; to find a sermon in the most unpromising texts." Plain country life is one such text, but Smith's essays are hardly trivial. "A Lark's Flight," for example, deals with issues of capital punishment, but his method is primarily narrative. He recounts watching the hanging of two prisoners and how, at a pivotal moment, a lark flies off singing, the poignancy of the event indicating to him the horror of such occasions. (George Orwell's "A Hanging" [1931] would later use a happy dog to similar effect.) These essays are grounded not in abstract ideas or books but in direct experience.

Richard Jefferies (1848–87) shared both Smith's topical matter and his stance, representing the countryside to a largely urban audience. Like Smith, he centers much of his work in place (as in *Round About a Great Estate*, 1880) and relishes close descriptions of scenes from nature.

More famous than either Smith or Jefferies is Robert Louis Stevenson (1850–94), whose essays in *Virginibus Puerisque* (1881), *Familiar Studies of Men and Books* (1882), and *Memories and Portraits* (1887) recall the style of Lamb and Hazlitt. In several of his essays, such as "An Apology for Idlers" (1877), Stevenson writes successions of aphoristic pronouncements in a vein growing out of Bacon; in others, such as "A College Magazine" (1887), he narrates his own experiences. The interaction of these poles in the bulk of his work distinguishes the familiar essay at the end of the century from the critical and philosophical works of writers like Arnold and Mill. Ruskin's essays have some of this quality but with the dramatic difference that Ruskin had a sharp political edge and little of the drawing room sentimentality that some have found in Stevenson.

The end and turn of the century thus saw the rise of an essay genre which contrasted strongly with the intellectual essay: the familiar essay as leisure reading and entertainment, an essay less serious in either form or intention. **Max Beerbohm's** (1872–1956) essays are perhaps the highest achievement in this manner, and though he published essays well into the 1920s, he is most often associated with the turn of the century. Partly this is because of Beerbohm's own themes and persona as a man out of step with his times, as much older than his years. In "Diminuendo" (1896), written when he was 24, he describes himself (Elia-like) as already outmoded, and this gentle self-deprecating presentation characterizes most of his essays. Beginning as a writer for the *Yellow Book* and the *Strand*, Beerbohm published numerous collections, including the satirically titled *Works of Max Beerbohm, with a Bibliography* (1896), *More* (1899), *Yet Again* (1909), and *And Even Now* (1920), the very titles suggesting the playful enterprise that he and his readers enjoyed. The quality can be seen in a piece like "Going out for a Walk," which begins with "It is a fact that not once in all my life have I gone out for a walk. I have been taken out for walks; but that is another matter," signaling in tone, topic, and stance the easy personal tone and relationship his readers had come to expect.

Beerbohm's contemporary, **Hilaire Belloc** (1870–1953), shares elements of both his ethos and his sense of the essay as entertainment, as can be seen through the titles of his own volumes, including *On Nothing and Kindred Subjects* (1908), *On Everything* (1909), *On Anything* (1910), *On Something* (1910), and four others in a similar vein. Belloc writes on places and landscapes and on past authors (thus appreciations rather than reviews), as well as on "minor" occasional topics, such as "The Crooked Streets" (1912), in which a whole quality of life is invoked by the way a town deploys its roads. In "An Essay upon Essays upon Essays" (1951), he spoofs the already common subgenre.

A third contemporary and a friend of Belloc, **G. K. Chesterton** (1874–1936), similarly used a casual, even light tone in his diverse essays on familiar topics. A voluminous writer, of novels and detective stories as well as nonfiction, recalling in many respects Hazlitt in his critical as well as familiar essays and in his journalistic interests (including cofounding and editing the periodical *Eye Witness* in 1911), Chesterton filled a belletristic role common since Addison, Johnson, and the Romantics. Virginia Woolf would fill this role, too, but in a manner more distinctly modern. Chesterton's many essay volumes, including *The Defendant* (1901), *All Things Considered* (1908), *Alarms and Discursions* (1910), *A Defence of Nonsense and Other Essays* (1911), and *All I Survey* (1933) demonstrate through their diversity of subject matter and confidence of narrative voice a quality essential to the essay: the claim of a right to explore and explain a position on any topic, simply by virtue of being a careful and sensitive observer.

The revitalization of the familiar essay hardly came at the expense of critical works. **Henry James'** (1843–1916) discussions of various writers in *Partial Portraits* (1888) exemplify his extensive critical writings, which include those essays he wrote as critical prefaces to his own novels. However, James also wrote numerous **travel essays**, primarily for American magazines like the *Atlantic Monthly*, the *Nation*, and the *North American Review*. Collected in such volumes as *Transatlantic Sketches* (1875) and *Portraits of Places* (1883), these essays reveal subtle changes in periodicals as distant travel becomes more possible (or at least imaginable), and magazines extend their editorial borders to new places.

James, of course, belongs to that growing tradition throughout the 19th century of writers best known in one literary genre but who wrote essays "on the side." Not only novelists like James or poets like Arnold but also dramatists like **George Bernard Shaw** (1856–1950) are customarily acknowledged secondarily (if at all) as essayists. This common idea of the essay as a genre supplemental to one's "real work" perhaps originates with Montaigne's modesty, and it may have resulted in essays being excluded from serious study throughout much of their history. That writers like Beerbohm, Belloc, and Chesterton could be known primarily as essayists is a new development in many ways and, in others, a rebirth of the early 18th century.

6. The 20th Century
The essay during the 20th century continues along many of the trajectories traced during the previous period, though the contributions of Virginia Woolf and George Orwell, the genre's leading figures, challenge the boundaries of the personal, the political, and the aesthetic. The tradition of the **critical essay** and biographical essay was prominently extended by **Lytton Strachey** (1880–1932), who began publishing in the *Spectator* and continued in places like the *Athenaeum* and the *Edinburgh Review*; he most notably published *Eminent Victorians* (1918) and *Portraits in Miniature and Other Essays* (1931). **T. S. Eliot** (1888–1965), like Arnold and other prominent poet-essayists before him, published numerous literary critical works, many of them, like "The Function of Criticism" (1923) and "Essay on Style and Order" (1928), articulating broad perspectives about literary matters rather than reviews or appreciations of individual authors. Most famous among these works is "Tradition and the Individual Talent" (1919). Eliot published essays about social and educational issues too, but his literary essays best define him. They are noteworthy today for the utter confidence of his voice and an authoritative stance that contrasts with the more carefully couched and qualified views of most critics and essayists since then. Fellow poet **W. H. Auden** (1907–73) also published numerous essays from the 1930s to the 1960s, many of them also works of criticism. However, his pieces demonstrated a somewhat broader range of topics, including analyses of art tempered by views of science.

John Eglinton's (1868–1961) critical essays (especially those collected in *Two Essays on the Remnant* [1894] and *Pebbles from a Brook* [1901]) use criticism to the additional ends of nationalistic advocacy. As a theorist of the Irish Literary Renaissance, Eglinton wrote about **Yeats**, Joyce, George Moore, and others, for a mostly intellectual as opposed to popular audience. In his later *Irish Literary Portraits* (1935), he tempers the critical essay of ideas with elements of memoir. **W. B. Yeats** (1865–1939) himself wrote numerous critical essays and prefaces, including some, like "Magic" (1901), that intricately weave autobiographical, critical, and reflective elements.

D. H. Lawrence (1885–1930) continued the tradition of the novelist-essayist. Like James (but reversing him in part by writing from America rather than England), Lawrence published many travel essays collected in four books, including *Twilight in Italy* (1916) and *Mornings in Mexico* (1927). His travel writings are a mix of narrative and reflection, intended to render for a general readership a sense of the primitive or strange. Lawrence's literary criticism similarly tours foreign writers, as in *Studies in Classic American Literature* (1923), but the critical work frequently expands beyond the boundaries of "the literary" *per se* into broader areas of social criticism. Similarly, his novels, like those of his Austrian contemporary **Robert Musil**, contain occasional essayistic passages.

However, by far the most important novelist-essayist – in fact, the most important English essayist of the first half of the century – was **Virginia Woolf** (1882–1941). Like her predecessors, Woolf published in overtly literary forums such as the **Times Literary Supplement** and the *Criterion*, but she also published in more popular magazines like *Vogue*, the **Atlantic Monthly**, and even *Time and Tide*. In doing so, she followed a path blazed by **Alice Meynell** (1847–1922), who wrote for the *Pall Mall Gazette* as well as the *Spectator*. Like Woolf after her, Meynell wrote extensively about literary and language subjects (as for example in the collection *The Second Person Singular and Other Essays*, 1921), but she also wrote about place (*London Impressions*, 1898) and domestic and other issues, most notably the lives of children (*The Children*, 1897; *Childhood*, 1913).

Woolf's publishing outlets demonstrate a quality to which she aspired in even her *TLS* pieces, namely the suitability of her writings for a "common reader" – as, in fact, two of her volumes were titled (*The Common Reader*, 1925; *The Second Common Reader*, 1932). At a time when the world of literary criticism was increasingly shrinking to the province of professionals, Woolf represents the reassertion of the essay's position as a more democratic genre in which the distance between writer and reader is minimized rather than exaggerated. Obviously, Woolf's common reader is not Everyman or Everywoman. Especially her writings about literature assume a fairly high level of reading, background knowledge, and literary interest. But her style is anything but that of the pedant or sage, enacting her own belief that "the principle which controls it [the essay] is simply that it should give pleasure; the desire which impels us when we take it from the shelf is simply to receive pleasure" ("The Modern Essay," 1922). In so privileging the aesthetic over the didactic, Woolf reverses the assumptions of the Victorian sage essayists. Writers like Beerbohm aspired to this, too, but Woolf is striking because she employs the principle in her criticism as well as her experiential essays.

Among her critical works are several about essayists, including Montaigne, Addison, Goldsmith, Hazlitt, Ruskin, and her own father Leslie Stephen, this last in a curiously distanced tone that scarcely calls attention to his being her father. But more important are her occasional and autobiographical works, especially those collected in *The Death of the Moth* (1942), *The Moment* (1947), and *The Captain's Death Bed* (1950), all published after her death. "The Death of the Moth" (1942) and "Thoughts on Peace in an Air Raid" (1940) demonstrates Woolf's ability to use the narrative of events ranging from the trivial to the dramatic as the occasion for meditation and speculation. "Street Haunting" (1927), "Flying over London" (1950), and "To Spain" (1923) evoke places and times in a lyric mode that reaches its zenith in essays like "The Moment: Summer's Night" (1947) and "Old Mrs. Grey" (1942), in which the essay verges on the prose poem, a static yet dynamic object rich in metaphor, simultaneously drawing a picture of the world and of the author's consciousness. However, Woolf's essays were impelled by political as well as belletristic concerns. "Thoughts on Peace in an Air Raid" calls for an end to war. "Professions for Women" (1931) and "Women and Fiction" (1929) are now classic articulations of problems that women have faced in trying to move beyond a narrow domestic sphere.

Woolf's novelist contemporary **E. M. Forster** (1879–1970) inhabited much of the essayist space that she helped to establish. Forster turned to essays in the 1920s after he had tired of novels, and his works meld autobiography, literary criticism, and contemporary social issues. Those collected in *Abinger Harvest* (1936) and *Two Cheers for Democracy* (1951) are particularly noteworthy in the way they balance the political issues of the day, especially the rise of European fascism, with personal perspectives; in an essay like "My Wood" (1926), for example, Forster's owning a piece of land gives rise to broader considerations about the effect of possession. During the 1940s, **Cyril Connolly** (1903–74) published essays that more overtly merged politics and literary/cultural criticism in his left-wing periodical *Horizon*. Connolly's earlier volume *Enemies of Promise* (1938) blended personal memories with views of earlier writers, and four books of essays published between 1945 and 1973 feature literary and art criticism.

The most artful political essayist of the 20th century is **George Orwell** (1903–50), whose "Why I Write" (1946) provides a key to his aesthetic. Orwell claims that circumstances of a given age direct writers, and the circumstances of his age – colonialism, fascism, poverty, and war – compel his writing to a political purpose, against totalitarianism and for democratic socialism. Orwell pursues this purpose sometimes in essays that are explicitly argumentative, such as "Politics and the English Language" (1946) or "Antisemitism in Britain" (1945). But his real contribution to the genre are those essays that embed political arguments in personal narratives with fictional qualities. For example, "A Hanging" (1931) consists entirely of an objective account of a prisoner's execution, the narrator commenting only briefly on events that otherwise are left to speak for themselves. "Shooting an Elephant" (1936) contains realizations about imperialism in a dramatic story of Orwell's having to kill a rogue elephant. "Marrakech" (1939) relies on the juxtaposition of several closely described themes to convey an argument about how colonialists treat those they colonize – and the consequences. "How the Poor Die" (wr. 1946, pub. 1950) is a close narrative of Orwell's stay in a

Paris hospital for the impoverished. Orwell's essays combine journalism, fictional techniques (if not fiction itself, as some critics have speculated certain events never happened), and autobiography to develop a new form that, nonetheless, is still essayistic in articulating ideas and the mind of its author.

Rebecca West (1892–1983) followed her early political essays on the women's movement, in *Freewoman* and the *Clarion*, with journalistic and essayistic analyses of World War II and its political and social implications. West published widely in American magazines like *Harper's* and the *New Yorker*, and her essays are collected in a few volumes, including *The Strange Necessity* (1928) and *The Meaning of Treason* (1947).

As one might assume, the political events of the first half of the 20th century directly and indirectly affected essay writing, topically, tonally, and formally. However, not every essayist was overtly political. **Herbert Read** (1893–1968) critiqued modern industrial culture and World War II, even publishing collections like *The Politics of the Unpolitical* (1943); however, he complemented this work with a vast amount of literary criticism in a neo-Romantic vein, as with *In Defence of Shelley and Other Essays* (1936), and he additionally published autobiographical pieces. **Aldous Huxley** (1894–1963) wrote numerous travel essays (as, for example, in *Along the Road: Notes and Essays of a Tourist* [1925] and *Essays New and Old* [1926]), but his most important works are those in which he explores the conditions of modern culture by considering developments in science and technology, philosophy, and art, as in *Proper Studies* (1927) and *Ends and Means* (1937). A good example of Huxley's stance is "Tragedy and the Whole Truth" (1931), which explores the nature of truth in science versus the nature of truth in literature. The grandson of T. H. Huxley, he wrote for a similarly broad, popular audience in a voice that is simultaneously familiar and didactic. **C. S. Lewis** (1898–1963) employs – to quite different intellectual ends – the same voice. As a Christian apologist whose autobiography *Surprised by Joy* (1955) recalls in purpose, at least, those of Mill and Newman, Lewis seeks to defend theological principles in an age of skepticism; important collections are *The Case for Christianity* (1943), *Mere Christianity* (1952), and *The Four Loves* (1960).

Other essayists throughout the century have embraced the familiar voice minus the overt didacticism. Prominent among them is **J. B. Priestley** (1894–1984), whose numerous essays cover a wide range of topics and are frequently occasioned by his own experience, as in "On Doing Nothing" and "Money for Nothing." His collections include *Papers from Lilliput* (1922), *I for One* (1923), *Open House: A Book of Essays* (1927), *Thoughts in the Wilderness* (1957), and *Outcries and Asides* (1974). In the introduction to his edited collection *Essayists Past and Present* (1925), Priestley rejects "all the philosophers and historians and scientists masquerading as essayists," using De Quincey's distinction to label such works as belonging merely to the "literature of knowledge." Thus Macaulay and most of the Victorian essayists are denied the status of true essayists; the debate over the definition of the genre as critical versus creative work continues.

The works of more contemporary writers continue to raise these issues. **V. S. Pritchett**'s (1900–97) literary criticism over the past 60 years imagines Woolf's common reader, and other

writings enact the travel tradition. **Kenneth Tynan** (1927–80) accompanied criticism with longer essays on theater and film and the people, places, and events associated with them, most notably in profile essays that appeared originally in the *New Yorker* and are collected in *Show People* (1980). **Graham Greene** (1901–91) similarly published numerous movie reviews in the 1930s but also memoirs, characters, criticism, and even travel pieces, several of them gathered in *Collected Essays* (1969). The Irish writer **Hubert Butler** (1900–91) wove together strands of the personal, the political, and the literary in a familiar voice recalling Orwell's, in essays collected in volumes such as *Escape from the Anthill* (1985) and *Grandmother and Wolfe Tone* (1990).

7. Conclusion

It would be reductive to assert that in the 400 years of its history, the British and Irish essay has developed along simple, unidirectional lines. The essay in every age has wandered between various apparently polar qualities: the formal versus the informal, the critical versus the creative, the argumentative versus the meditative, the aesthetic versus the didactic, expert knowledge versus lay knowledge. Every period has generated both essays whose central occasion is the presentation of ideas or arguments and essays whose central occasion is the presentation of writers' experiences or perspectives.

Probably the truest general point that can be made about the development of the essay is that it has emerged as a lasting genre, significant in its own right. Periodical publication played a complex role in this transition. At the dawn of the genre, published in collections as books by writers like Montaigne, Bacon, and Cowley, the essay had at least the trappings of permanence and significance enjoyed by other genres. On the one hand, periodical publication in the 18th century as well as today constructs essays as transitory, occasional works, often supplemental to other literary and philosophical texts. Yet, on the other hand, periodical publication both expands a reading audience and has given many writers the constant forum needed to establish their reputations as essayists. The circle is completed when periodically published essays are collected into book volumes, a practice occurring with Samuel Johnson and even before – and certainly since. Most such collections are unified not by subject matter but by their authors' experiences, personalities, and particular ways of seeing the world. While many British and Irish authors have been known as essayists only secondarily in relation to their work as novelists, poets, or dramatists, it is also true that many authors are known primarily as essayists. The sense of the genre has evolved to accommodate such a status. As knowledge has become more specialized and culture more fragmented (or, rather, as the fragments that have always existed become more apparent), the essayist increasingly figures the consoling ability – and right – of individuals to make sense of things, in a genre that consistently acts out the limits and conditional nature of that sense.

DOUGLAS HESSE

Anthologies

A Century of English Essays, edited by Ernest Rhys and Lloyd Vaughan, London: Dent, and New York: Dutton, 1929 (original edition, 1913)

A Century of the Essay, British and American, edited by David
Daiches, New York: Harcourt Brace, 1951
The Hutchinson Book of Essays, edited by Frank Delaney, London:
Hutchinson, 1990
The Oxford Book of Essays, edited by John Gross, Oxford and
New York: Oxford University Press, 1991

Further Reading

Dobrée, Bonamy, English Essayists, London: Collins, 1946
Good, Graham, The Observing Self: Rediscovering the Essay,
London and New York: Routledge, 1988
Pebworth, Ted-Larry, "'Real English Evidence': Stoicism and the
English Essay Tradition," PMLA 87 (1972): 101–02
Pebworth, Ted-Larry, "Not Being, but Passing: Defining the Early
English Essay," Studies in the Literary Imagination 10, no. 2
(1977): 17–27
Stapleton, Laurence, The Elected Circle: Studies in the Art of Prose,
Princeton, New Jersey: Princeton University Press, 1973
Thompson, Elbert N. S., The Seventeenth-Century English Essay,
New York: Haskell House, 1967 (original edition, 1926)
Walker, Hugh, The English Essay and Essayist, London: Dent, and
New York: Dutton, 1915

Brodsky, Joseph

Russian/American, 1940–1996

As an essayist Joseph Brodsky (best known to the West by this
anglicized form of his Russian name, Iosif Brodskii) was versatile and prolific: in addition to two large, impressive collections of essays and Watermark (1992), an extended essay on
Venice, he published more than 100 **reviews**, introductions,
lectures, occasional critical pieces, contributions to conferences,
appeals, and **letters**, in Russian, English, and American periodicals and magazines. Some of his best essays are based on
his lectures and seminars, like the painstakingly detailed
analyses of the poetry of **W. H. Auden**, Robert Frost, and
Thomas Hardy; others are extensions of introductions. His
literary essays, especially on Russian authors, particularly
impressed his Western critics. Brodsky brought with him to
the West "the most valuable thing Russia can give us – a reaf-
firmation of the belief that 'art is an alternative form of existence'" (Henry Gifford, 1986). While in Russia Brodsky's
reputation is based primarily on his achievement as a poet, in
the West his essays have played a major part in creating his
ultimate stature as a writer, while also bringing an immense
benefit to Russian literature as a whole.

Brodsky made his first excursions into the essay genre soon
after his forced emigration in 1972. He wrote his first essays
in Russian, but soon switched to English and became a regular
contributor to the New York Review of Books, **Partisan
Review**, and the **Times Literary Supplement.** He wrote mainly
about poets whose verses influenced his work or who shared
his aesthetic values. His own aesthetic standards were high,
demanding much of the people he wrote about, but he was
also extremely generous in his evaluation of them. He called
Auden "the greatest mind of the twentieth century" and **Osip
Mandel'shtam** "a poet of and for civilization." His essays are
marked by quality of perception and supersensitivity toward
other writers' use of language. He praised Andrei Platonov for
inventing a language which compromises not only the Soviet

ideology but also "time, space, life itself and death," while the
novels of such writers as Aleksandr Solzhenitsyn and Vasilii
Grossman he saw as socialist realism in reverse because they
adopted the language strategies of their opponents.

Apart from literature, Brodsky discussed a wide range of
topics: civilization, history, political forces, ethical choices,
time, faith, memory, and other major themes. He also assimilated and processed material from his ceaseless travels. He
viewed Venice as a gigantic orchestra, with a restless chorus
of waves and "the falsetto of a star in the winter sky." His
ethical and philosophical interpretations of historical events
were as ambivalent and polemical as his scattered comments
on political affairs reflecting the intensely political nature of
his experience, although his political views were never openly
expressed. He captured a feeling about tyranny; the Empire,
as one of his principal themes, also figured in his essays and
was interpreted as a conceptual metaphor for what Yakov
Gordin called "forced harmonization in the face of deep
internal troubles" (Valentina Polukhina, 1992). We are offered
some of his liveliest controversies on time and space when he
meditates upon man's relationship with time: "What can we
learn about ourselves from time? – What does it mean to be
insignificant?" According to Brodsky, man in all his vulnerability to time and history should structure himself around reliable ethical and aesthetic principles.

"The Guide to a Renamed City" (1979) is a beautiful evocation of St. Petersburg, a city "where it's somehow easier to
endure loneliness than anywhere else: because the city itself is
so lonely." He also wrote about his childhood and his parents
("In a Room and a Half," 1985) and the terror inflicted by
the state. Perhaps in order to avoid granting himself the status
of a victim, he said very little about his life in prison or in
exile. In his essays, as in his poems, Brodsky remains an impersonal author, a man of intellectual sobriety with a sense of
perspective. He did not believe that a writer's ego, even a
wounded ego, was the best material for literature.

Brodsky's message can be reduced to one main idea: what
a great poet leaves behind is his language. Language, for him,
is the vessel and vehicle of civilization. In "On Cavafy's Side"
(1977) he demonstrates how language can triumph when
empire fails. Language is older than any state, and superior
to history: "language is a millenarian device, history isn't."
Language operates through and within time but outside
history, enlarging writers' appreciation of life in ethical terms.
The writer's only duty is to his language, to keep it alive
"in the light of conscience and culture." The effect of the
Revolution on the Russian language, according to Brodsky,
has been "an unprecedented anthropological tragedy . . . whose
net result is a drastic reduction in human potential."

Exquisite style, poetic energy, sharp intelligence, wit, and
paradox are the natural ingredients of his prose. Brodsky's
voice is authoritative, his approach to a subject stripped of
sentimentality. In his use of syntax, word order, and lexical
nuances he works on extreme levels. Writing at the edge of
speech, he increases the depth of the ethical drama played out
within his work. "We never forget or are allowed to forget
that the critic is a poet" (Gifford). The tension of his essays
is created by the rational, skeptical attitude toward what
cannot be rationally explained (faith, time, creativity). Believing
that "aesthetics is the mother of ethics," he never fails to make

an intrinsic connection between them. He openly declares the unpardonable subjectivity of his views, saying that "extreme subjectivity, prejudice and idiosyncrasy are what helps art to avoid cliché."

A subtle relationship exists between the style of his essays and his poetry. In his essays Brodsky employs free association, internal rhyme, convoluted syntax, and poetic composition. His first collection of essays, *Less than One* (1986), forms a cycle, beginning and ending with personal memoirs, with two magnificent pieces on **Marina Tsvetaeva** at the center, surrounded by essays on Anna Akhmatova, Mandel'shtam, Auden (his "ideal double"), Derek Walcott, appreciations of C. P. Cavafy and Eugenio Montale, homage to Osip's wife Nadezhda Mandel'shtam, and a criticism of modern Russian prose. Each of his essays, like each of his poems, is a part of the whole. Although they stand as independent, self-sufficient pieces, they benefit enormously from being read in context: their essence becomes more visible.

In 1995, just before Brodsky's untimely death, his second collection of essays, *On Grief and Reason*, was published in New York. Like the first collection, it also includes **travel essays** ("After a Journey"), historical pieces ("Collector's Item" and "Homage to Marcus Aurelius"), essays on political displacement ("The Condition We Call Exile"), tributes to his favorite poets (Frost, Hardy, Rainer Maria Rilke), and **meditations** on the past ("Spoils of War"). Inspired by Mozart and Haydn, Brodsky cultivated his own technique of developing "themes and variations": ideas circulate and reverberate from one essay to the next throughout the book. His Christian attitude toward art is openly stated: every poem is an act of love, a flash of memory and faith.

Two particular qualities characterize his essays. First, Brodsky used the full force of his intellectual power to offer new answers to old questions, thus providing an unforgettable intellectual education. Second, he possessed a remarkable power of observation and a sharp eye for detail. Like Mandel'shtam and Tsvetaeva before him, Brodsky played a pivotal role in re-creating and redefining the essay genre. Like the latter, he allowed the agonies of spirit to flower, taking ideas to their most extreme conclusions; like the former, he tried to control his arguments with the discipline of logic. Like both, he responded to a large diversity of world literature by assimilating not so much Greek, French, or German literary traditions, but those of the Latin, American, and English. His essays are characterized by a dynamic interaction between dazzling language, conceptual thought, and poetic narrative process. They are as brilliant as his poetry, in both their philosophical complexity and their verbal inventiveness. His studies of the poets are models of close reading, a valid demonstration of how poetry works: "how to get to the marrow of every image and phrase" (D. Rayfield, 1986). These essays "should be required reading for students of modern Russian literature and history. They imply a canon" (G. S. Smith, 1988). They are the best introduction to his poetry, for as Brodsky himself put it, poets' prose is "nothing but a continuation of poetry by other means": the same precision, speed and intensity of thought, the same syntactic ambiguity, the same density of tropes. They offer an intellectual feast prepared by the master.

VALENTINA POLUKHINA

Biography

Iosif Aleksandrovich Brodskii. Born 24 May 1940 in Leningrad. Studied at schools in Leningrad to the age of 15. Convicted as a "social parasite," 1964, and served 20 months of a five-years' hard labor sentence; later exiled by the Soviet government: emigrated to the United States, 1972, and became a U.S. citizen, 1977. Taught at the University of Michigan, Ann Arbor, Queen's College, City University of New York, Columbia University, New York, New York University, Smith College, Northampton, Massachusetts, Amherst College, Massachusetts, Hampshire College, and Mount Holyoke College, South Hadley, Massachusetts, 1972–96. U.S. Poet Laureate, 1991–92. Married Maria Sozzani: one daughter; also had a son with Marina Basmanova. Awards: Mondello Prize (Italy), 1979; National Book Critics' Circle Award, 1987; Nobel Prize for Literature, 1987; Guggenheim Fellowship; MacArthur Fellowship; honorary degrees from ten universities. Member, American Academy of Arts and Letters (resigned in protest over the honorary membership of the Russian poet Evgenii Evtushenko, 1987); corresponding member, Bavarian Academy of Sciences; Legion of Honor (France), 1991. Died (of a heart attack) in New York, 28 January 1996.

Selected Writings

Essays and Related Prose
Less than One: Selected Essays, 1986
Watermark, 1992
On Grief and Reason, 1995

Other writings: many collections of poetry and two plays.

Collected works edition: *Sochineniia*, 4 vols., 1992–95.

Bibliographies

Bigelow, Thomas, *Joseph Brodsky: A Descriptive Bibliography 1962–1996*, forthcoming
Kline, George L., in *10 Bibliographies of 20th Century Russian Literature*, edited by Fred Moody, Ann Arbor, Michigan: Ardis, 1977: 159–75

Further Reading

Bayley, John, "Mastering Speech," *New York Review of Books*, 12 June 1986: 3–4
Bethea, David M., "Conjurer in Exile," *New York Times Book Review*, 13 July 1986: 3, 38
Bethea, David M., *Joseph Brodsky and the Creation of Exile*, Princeton, New Jersey: Princeton University Press, 1994
Coetzee, J. M., "Speaking for Language," *New York Review of Books*, 1 February 1996: 28–31
Dunn, Douglas, "In Whom the Language Lives," *Poetry Review* 76, no. 3 (1986): 4–6
Gifford, Henry, "Of Petersburg, Poetry and Human Ties," *Times Literary Supplement*, 19 October 1986: 1019
Philips, William, "Brodsky's *Less than One*," *Partisan Review* 1 (1987): 139–45
Polukhina, Valentina, *Joseph Brodsky: A Poet for Our Time*, Cambridge: Cambridge University Press, 1989
Polukhina, Valentina, *Brodsky Through the Eyes of His Contemporaries*, Basingstoke: Macmillan, and New York: St. Martin's Press, 1992
Rayfield, D., "Grist to the Mill," *Times Higher Education Supplement*, 10 October 1986: 18
Russian Literature issue on "Brodsky's Genres," edited by Valentina Polukhina, 37, nos. 2–3 (April 1995)
Smith, G. S., "Brodsky's *Less than One*," *Slavonic and East European Review* 66, no. 2 (1988)

Venclova, Tomas, "A Journey from Petersburg to Istanbul," in *Joseph Brodsky's Poetics and Aesthetics*, edited by Lev Loseff and Valentina Polukhina, Basingstoke: Macmillan, 1990: 134–49

Brown, E. K.
Canadian, 1905–1951

In his brief career, E. K. Brown produced – besides six critical books, four edited works, and two translations from the French of full-length works – over 80 articles and 135 reviews. Since he held academic positions in the Departments of English at four universities between 1929 and 1951, his essays and reviews were often scholarly and critical in nature. They appeared in such North American academic journals as *American Literature*, *College English*, *Modern Philology*, *Sewanee Review*, *University of Toronto Quarterly*, *Queen's Quarterly*, and *Yale Review*. He wrote literary-critical articles and reviews chiefly on 19th- and 20th-century American, Canadian, and English literature; however, he also wrote for encyclopedias, newspapers and popular reviews such as *Chambers*, the *Winnipeg Free Press*, *Canadian Forum*, and *Saturday Night*.

In the late 1920s, Brown wrote two doctoral dissertations at the Sorbonne, one of which concerned **Matthew Arnold**. One of the principal motives for his essays and reviews was an Arnoldian impulse to disseminate culture. More particularly he sought to improve Canadian culture, and to broaden and deepen awareness of the tradition of Canadian poetry in English. This he attempted not only in his ground-breaking book *On Canadian Poetry* (1943), which he calls in the preface "less an historical enquiry than a **critical essay**," and in his preface to the second edition "this essay," but also in a series of annual review articles on the year's books of Canadian poetry in English which he contributed to the *University of Toronto Quarterly* from 1935 to 1949. He wrote an introductory essay to a selection of Victorian poetry as well as introductions to selections of poems by Archibald Lampman and Duncan Campbell Scott whom, together with E. J. Pratt, he considered English Canada's foremost poets. Brown introduced a selection he had made of Canadian poetry for a special issue of *Poetry* (Chicago) in 1941. He also wrote essays on English and French Canadian politicians and historians for *Harper's* and *Canadian Forum*, and 46 essays on literary topics, several of which were Canadian, for the "Causeries" column of the *Winnipeg Free Press* between 1947 and his death in 1951.

Brown's friends and colleagues Leon Edel and A. S. P. Woodhouse gathered, but failed to publish a collection of his essays shortly after his death. However, David Staines in 1977 (at a high point of renewed interest in Canadian literature) was able to publish a collection of Brown's essays in the New Canadian Library series, entitled *Responses and Evaluations: Essays on Canada*. Brown is more highly regarded as a pioneer critic in the study of Canadian literature, a position he achieved in part through the writing of essays and reviews, than he is as an Arnold scholar, though his Alexander lectures, *Rhythm in the Novel* (1950), and his biography of Willa Cather are still kindly remembered.

Brown's biographer, Laura Smyth Groening (1993), argues convincingly that "He wrote articles carefully adapted in tone, style, and content for the general reading public." Of his "Causeries," she remarks that they "allowed him to indulge a less formal voice (for which he had a distinct and perhaps surprising ear) than he needed for his academic prose." However, Brown's two voices are modulated rather than being sharply distinct. Brown always writes clearly and directly; he never patronizes or condescends to his general reader, nor is his style pedantic. A representative example of Brown's essay style can be found in an early essay on Abbé **Lionel Groulx** for the *Canadian Forum* published in 1929:

> The vials of his wrath are, it will be seen, copious; but in their flow, the British lion has the lion's share. The Abbé Groulx's references to Britain are mostly in the strains of the popular song which long ago ran like wild-fire through Quebec: "*Les Français aiment l'équité,/Les Anglais la duplicité,/Voilà la différence.*"
>
> This, if a little distressing, is explicable. The Abbé Groulx exhorts, he does not expound; history is to him a mine not for science, but for art, and in particular for the art of preaching.

The elegant repetition of "the British lion has the lion's share" is characteristic, as is the delicate irony of the ending. Imagine the effect of omitting the words "and in particular for"; Brown eschews such brutal directness.

In "The Immediate Present in Canadian Literature" (1933), Brown implies the importance of the essay in literary culture when he connects what he calls "the poverty of our criticism" with the lack of Canadian literary periodicals as venues for critical discussion in essay form:

> As Mr. Norris Hodgkins remarks in the excellent introduction to his recent collection *Some Canadian Essays*: "Essays are rarely written in bookfuls." Essays flourish where literary periodicals flourish; and literary periodicals do not flourish in Canada. How many of Mr. Paul Elmer More's essays would have remained unwritten had he not edited the New York *Nation*? or of Mr. Middleton Murry's had he not edited *The Adelphi*, or even of Mr. T. S. Eliot's without his *Criterion* as a platform? We have no periodicals of importance in which literature is the sole concern, or even the admittedly chief concern. The periodical which seems to me to have done most for the erection and diffusion of critical standards in Canada is *The Canadian Forum*.

Though Brown's essays are not well known internationally, they are not likely to be forgotten in his "home and native land," where he entreated and cajoled his countrymen to take literature (particularly their own literature) more seriously. In one of the last "Causeries" pieces written before his death, Brown noted that "Canadians do not care what other Canadians think." Brown cared passionately about what his fellow Canadians thought. In his essays for a wide variety of American and Canadian journals, he sought to leaven the lump of Canadian culture.

JOHN FERNS

Biography

Edward Killoran Brown. Born 15 August 1905 in Toronto. Studied at the University of Toronto, B.A., 1926; the Sorbonne, Paris, Docteur-ès-Lettres, 1935. Taught English at the University of Toronto, 1929–41, University of Manitoba, 1935–37, Cornell University, Ithaca, New York, 1941–44, and the University of Chicago, 1944–51. Contributor to many journals and newspapers; coeditor, *Canadian Forum*, 1930–33, and the *University of Toronto Quarterly*, 1932–41. Married Margaret Deaver, 1936: two sons. Died in Chicago, 24 April 1951.

Selected Writings

Essays and Related Prose
On Canadian Poetry, 1943
Rhythm in the Novel (Alexander lectures), 1950
Responses and Evaluations: Essays on Canada, edited by David
   Staines, 1977

Other writings: a biography of Willa Cather (1953) and books on literature. Also translated Balzac and Louis Cazamian; edited works by English and Canadian writers.

Bibliography

Staines, David, "E. K. Brown (1905–1951): The Critic and His
   Writings," *Canadian Literature* 83 (Winter 1979): 176–89

Further Reading

Breen, Melwyn, "Man of Letters: A Talk with Professor E. K.
   Brown and Some Facts About the State of the Nation's Fiction,"
   Saturday Night, 27 December 1949: 12
Bush, Douglas, "E. K. Brown and the Evolution of Canadian
   Poetry," *Sewanee Review* 87 (January–March 1979): 186–90
Fee, Margery, "On E. K. Brown," *Canadian Literature* 86 (Autumn
   1980): 142–43
Fee, Margery, *English-Canadian Literary Criticism, 1890–1950:
   Defining and Establishing a National Literature* (dissertation),
   Toronto: University of Toronto, 1981
McDougall, Robert L., Introduction and Notes to *The Poet and the
   Critic: A Literary Correspondence Between D. C. Scott and E. K.
   Brown*, Ottawa: Carleton University Press, 1983
Smyth Groening, Laura, *Art, Vision, and Process: The Literary
   Criticism of E. K. Brown* (dissertation), Ottawa: Carleton
   University, 1985
Smyth Groening, Laura, "Critic and Publisher: Another Chapter in
   E. K. Brown's Correspondence," *Canadian Literature* 110 (Fall
   1986): 46–58
Smyth Groening, Laura, *E. K. Brown: A Study in Conflict*, Toronto:
   University of Toronto Press, 1993
Staines, David, Introduction to *Responses and Evaluations: Essays
   on Canada* by Brown, Toronto: McClelland and Stewart, 1977:
   i–xviii
Steele, Apollonia, "On E. K. Brown," *Canadian Literature* 89
   (Summer 1981): 186–87

Browne, Sir Thomas

English, 1605–1682

Sir Thomas Browne, the Norwich physician, is one of the early masters of the English essay. In addition to writing one of the century's most celebrated autobiographies in *Religio Medici* (1642), he produced a huge inquiry into popular errors of the times in his *Pseudodoxia Epidemica* (1646), a pair of elegant treatises on the contrasting subjects of urns and gardens in *Hydriotaphia* (popularly known as *Urn Burial*) and *The Garden of Cyrus* (1658), and a number of shorter works, the best known being the formal **letter** of consolation entitled *A Letter to a Friend*, the explicitly didactic *Christian Morals*, and the brief fragment on dreams – none of which can be dated precisely. Without possessing either the foundational or canonical status of a **Montaigne** or a **Bacon**, Browne has nonetheless woven himself deeply into the fabric of the essay tradition. **Samuel Johnson** wrote a "Life of Browne" (1756), which remains the best introduction to his works. Browne has also been a favorite with later writers on both sides of the Atlantic: most notably Herman Melville and **Henry David Thoreau** on the one, and **Walter Pater**, **Leslie Stephen**, and **Lytton Strachey** on the other.

As an essayist, Browne's interests reflect those of the educated elite in the mid-17th century, a period when scientific curiosity and antiquarianism were both on the rise, the one not always distinguishable from the other, and both only in the process of becoming organized as distinct branches of knowledge in England at this time. (Browne's eldest son, Edward, also a physician, was made a member of the Royal Society five years after its official inception in 1662; the first museum in England was established at Oxford in 1677, with the help of the noted collector, Elias Ashmole, with whom Browne occasionally corresponded.) To Browne these overlapping fields of inquiry at times blurred with, or were subordinated to, a third: religious belief of a broad Protestant order. An avowed purpose of *Religio Medici* was to counter the popular saying "ubi tres medici, duo Athei" (of every three physicians, two are atheists), and *Urn Burial* intones at the outset that the "ancient of dayes" – God – ought to be the antiquarian's "truest object."

To these many kinds of inquiry, Browne brought his enormous erudition, his fascination for paradox, his passion for mystery, and his seeming desire for endless questions. Almost no topic was too arcane to be investigated: "What Song the *Syrens* Sang, or what name *Achilles* assumed when he hid himself among women, though puzling Questions are not beyond all conjecture" (*Urn Burial*). Indeed, the more arcane the better since the challenge to ingenuity would then be the greater, regardless of whether the topic involved querying the particular species of fruit used by the serpent to tempt Eve, the origins of blackness in Negroes, the meaning of burial urns discovered in a field near Walsingham, the possibility that the quincunx was the basic ordering design of the universe, or simply whether elephants had knees – though "simply" turns out to be just the wrong word since Browne also goes on to consider a whole host of other possibilities, including whether elephants were capable of talking. About the only topic this lay philosopher, scientist, physician, antiquarian, and amateur theologian did not puzzle over in print was contemporary politics. On the great events of the day – civil war, the execution of Charles I, the emergence of Cromwell – the irenic Browne is conspicuously silent.

Given Browne's projected, and sometimes explicitly identified, audience of like-minded inquirers, and his dispassionate temperament, the essay was the ideal vehicle for purposeful expression. Its conceptual and discursive flexibility allowed Browne to set forth, in undogmatic fashion, the principal tenets of his religious beliefs in the manner of a **personal essay** in *Religio Medici*. Here Browne describes, for example, his youthful heresies, the delight he takes in exploring the "wingy mysteries in Divinity and the ayery subtleties in Religion," himself as a microcosm of the world. In the many individual sections or brief essays that make up the two parts of *Religio*, the often familiar topics of faith serve as the substance out of which Browne fashions his silk-like subjectivity. At the same time, but in a different context, the essay also encourages an equally undogmatic, scrupulous, open-ended inquiry into the many popular beliefs recorded in *Pseudodoxia Epidemica*. Here Browne speaks in a more scholarly and "scientific" voice, seeking to test the truth of an opinion by invoking the three-fold criteria of past authorities, reason, and experience.

Nonetheless, the distance between the rhetorically inflected prose of Browne and, say, the descriptively exact writings of a Newton seems greater than can be accounted for by chronology alone, even by a sea change as large as the emergence of science. Although Browne often wrote about what he observed, his prose is most memorable for its succinct phrasing and rich patterning of sounds, conspicuous in the frequent use of formal devices that we more normally associate with poetry, such as assonance, alliteration, internal rhyme, and parallel and antithetical phrases often of nearly equal syllabic count. These rhetorical effects could be intensified to match the gravity of subject matter, as in a sentence like the following from the famous last chapter of *Urn Burial*: "Time which antiquates Antiquities,/and hath an art to make dust of all things,/hath yet spared these *minor* Monuments." This is prose informed by the cadences of near-perfect blank verse. Or they could be invoked to suggest the proliferating exuberance of nature in *The Garden of Cyrus*: "The calicular leaves inclose the tender flowers,/and the flowers themselves lye wrapt about the seeds,/in their rudiment and first formations." "Rudiment" is there to give amplitude to the cadence, to help fill out the line.

The American poet Elizabeth Bishop, having just purchased the elegant six-volume Keynes Edition of Browne's *Works* (1928–31), jubilantly remarked: "I should like to do nothing but sit all evening and copy off such sentences as 'That wee call a bee bird is a small dark gray bird,' or 'What word you give our knotts or gnatts, a small marsh bird, very fatte and a daintye dish.' But Cotton Mather still awaits me with his prayers and groans" (*One Art*, 1994). Although the choice of sentences to copy might differ from one reader to another, Bishop's response, right down to the felt contrast with the Puritan Mather, seems otherwise typical of the intoxicating effect Browne has on his readers.

JONATHAN F. S. POST

Biography

Born 19 October (or 19 November) 1605 in London. Studied at Winchester College, Hampshire, 1616–23; Broadgates Hall (now Pembroke College), Oxford, 1623–26, B.A., 1626, M.A., 1629; studied medicine in Montpellier and Padua and at the University of Leiden, M.D., 1633; medical apprenticeship in Oxfordshire and possibly Yorkshire, 1634–37; granted Oxford M.D., 1637. Moved to Norwich and practiced as a physician, 1637–82. Married Dorothy Mileham, 1641: 12 children (five died in youth, two as young adults). Died in Norwich, 19 October 1682.

Selected Writings

Essays and Related Prose
Religio Medici, 1642; revised edition, 1643; edited by W. A. Greenhill, 1881, reprinted 1990, W. Murison, 1922, Jean-Jacques Denonain, 1953, Vittoria Sanna, 2 vols., 1959, and Robin H. A. Robbins, with *Urn Burial*, 1972
Pseudodoxia Epidemica; or, Enquiries into Very Many Received Tenents and Commonly Presumed Truths, 1646; edited by Robin H. A. Robbins, 2 vols., 1981
Hydriotaphia, Urn-Burial; or, A Discourse of the Sepulchral Urns Lately Found in Norfolk, Together with the Garden of Cyrus; or, The Quincuncial Lozenge, or Network Plantations of the Ancients, Artificially, Naturally, Mystically Considered, 1658; edited by W. A. Greenhill, 1896, John Carter, 1958, and Robin H. A. Robbins, with *Religio Medici*, 1972
Religio Medici and Other Works, edited by L. C. Martin, 1964
The Prose of Sir Thomas Browne, edited by Norman Endicott, 1968
Selected Writings, edited by Geoffrey Keynes, 1968
The Major Works, edited by C. A. Patrides, 1977
Selected Writings, edited by Claire Preston, 1995

Other writings: tracts and notes on natural history.

Collected works editions: *Works*, edited by Simon Wilkin, 4 vols., 1835–36; *Works*, edited by Geoffrey Keynes, 6 vols., 1928–31, revised edition, 4 vols., 1964.

Bibliographies
Donovan, Dennis G., *Sir Thomas Browne and Robert Burton: A Reference Guide*, Boston: Hall, 1981
Keynes, Geoffrey, *A Bibliography of Sir Thomas Browne*, Oxford: Clarendon Press, revised edition, 1968 (original edition, 1924)
Sununu, Andrea, "Recent Studies in Sir Thomas Browne (1970–1986)," *English Literary Renaissance* 19 (1989): 118–29

Further Reading
Bennett, Joan, *Sir Thomas Browne: A Man of Achievement in Literature*, Cambridge: Cambridge University Press, 1962
Croll, Morris W., *Style, Rhetoric, and Rhythm: Essays*, edited by J. Max Patrick and others, Princeton: Princeton University Press, 1966
Davis, Walter R., "*Urne Buriall*: A Descent into the Underworld," *Studies in the Literary Imagination* 10 (1977): 73–87
Finch, Jeremiah S., Introduction and Notes to *A Catalogue of the Libraries of Sir Thomas Browne and Dr. Edward Browne, His Son*, Leiden: Brill (facsimile reprint), 1986
Fish, Stanley E., *Self-Consuming Artifacts: The Experience of Seventeenth-Century Literature*, Berkeley: University of California Press, 1972
Gosse, Edmund, *Sir Thomas Browne*, Westport, Connecticut: Greenwood Press, 1970 (original edition, 1905)
Grey, Robin, *The Complicity of Imagination: The American Renaissance, Contests of Authority, and Seventeenth-Century English Culture*, Cambridge: Cambridge University Press, 1996
Guibbory, Achsah, "'A Rationall of Old Rites': Sir Thomas Browne's *Urn Buriall* and the Conflict over Ceremony," *Yearbook of English Studies* 21 (1991): 229–41
Hall, Anne Drury, "Epistle, Meditation, and Sir Thomas Browne's *Religio Medici*," *PMLA* 94 (1979): 234–46
Huntley, Frank L., *Sir Thomas Browne: A Biographical and Critical Study*, Ann Arbor: University of Michigan Press, 1962
Johnson, Samuel, "Life of Browne," in his *Christian Morals*, edited by S. C. Roberts, Cambridge: Cambridge University Press, 1927; New York: Kraus, 1960 (original edition, 1756)
Leroy, Olivier, *Le Chevalier Thomas Browne, 1605–1682: Médecin, styliste et métaphysicien*, Paris: Gamber, 1931

Loffler, Arno, *Sir Thomas Browne als Virtuoso*, Nuremberg: Carl, 1972

Nathanson, Leonard, *The Strategy of Truth: A Study of Sir Thomas Browne*, Chicago: University of Chicago Press, 1967

Pater, Walter, "Sir Thomas Browne," in his *Appreciations*, edited by William E. Buckler, in *Walter Pater: Three Major Texts*, New York: New York University Press, 1986 (original edition, 1889, 1890)

Post, Jonathan F. S., *Sir Thomas Browne*, Boston: Twayne, 1987

Silver, Victoria, "Liberal Theology and Sir Thomas Browne's 'Soft and Flexible' Discourse," *English Literary Renaissance* 20 (1990): 69–105

Stapleton, Laurence, *The Elected Circle: Studies in the Art of Prose*, Princeton, New Jersey: Princeton University Press, 1973

Warren, Austin, "The Style of Sir Thomas Browne," *Kenyon Review* 13 (Autumn 1951): 674–87

Webber, Joan, *The Eloquent "I": Style and Self in Seventeenth-Century Prose*, Madison: University of Wisconsin Press, 1968

Brunetière, Ferdinand

French, 1849–1906

Ferdinand Brunetière, literary historian and Catholic apologist, achieved fame for his teaching as a professor at the École Normale Supérieure and, above all, as editor from 1893 to 1906 of the influential **Revue des Deux Mondes** (Review of two worlds). Brunetière was introduced to the review in 1875 by **Paul Bourget**, when an essay on contemporary literature was required. Like the editors François and Charles Buloz before him, Brunetière contrived to be slightly ahead of the public opinion he led. A pessimist of the school of **Schopenhauer**, hostile to Zola and his "naturalist" school, Brunetière also moved toward Catholicism slightly ahead of the general revival of interest in religion in early 20th-century France. He was opposed to Anatole France, whose work he nevertheless published, in his desire to limit the permissible bounds of philosophical speculation in matters of morality, and was favorable to the "Parnassian" poets, particularly Leconte de Lisle and Heredia.

Brunetière's contribution to the essay form in France was concerned with the elevation of pieces of literary criticism above **Sainte-Beuve**'s affectations of intimacy and social analyses into a critical genre based on a strong moral vision. His collected volumes are typically entitled *Études critiques* (1880–1925; Critical studies), *Questions de critique* (1889; Questions of criticism), *Essais sur la littérature contemporaine* (1892; Essays on contemporary literature), *Discours académiques* (1901; Academic discourses), and *Variétés littéraires* (1904; Literary varieties). It was the need to find support for his moral vision which led Brunetière to his conversion to Catholicism, writing, "I hope that symbolism will bring poetry toward the realization of its highest definition, which is to be a metaphysic manifested in images and enabled to touch the heart . . . a conception of the world, or a theory of the relations between individuals." This view was also behind Brunetière's hostility to naturalism, which he felt deliberately restricted our vision to the external aspects of life. The whole corpus of his critical writing was essentially directed at detecting in the past the true sources of the national spirit which had been extinguished by defeat in the Franco-Prussian war. He found it, no doubt too exclusively, expressed in the literature of the 17th century.

Brunetière's name is also too exclusively linked to a new critical method, more forcefully expressed than consistently realized by him at the apogee of **Darwin**'s intellectual influence. It is not surprising that the idea of linking methods of literary criticism to those of scientific inquiry should be conceived and prove attractive in the last decade of the 19th century in France, but Brunetière's expressions, derived from **Hippolyte Taine**, go beyond an interest in "the evolution of genres" to assume some process of natural selection. He believed he could achieve a balance between understanding the variety of literary genres and the individual personal contribution of each great author. The famous course given at the École Normale in 1889–90 was published in essay form in 1890 as *L'Évolution des genres* (The evolution of genres), with the 55 lectures divided into four groups. They were devoted to the history of criticism in France, the theory of the evolution of genres, a detailed study of three applications of the theory, and a protracted consideration of the conclusions to which the whole course had led. The three examples chosen for detailed consideration illustrated the history of tragedy, the development of sacred eloquence into lyric poetry, and the genesis of the novel.

The combination of criticism, of editing France's foremost literary review, and of giving important professorial lectures naturally led Brunetière to the essay form. Arguably a stricter form than the large academic study, it obliged Brunetière to make his points succinctly and thus sharpen his ideas for presentation to a potential readership of educated nonspecialists and students. In fact, despite the considerable impact of his essays, Brunetière was not a master of the essay form. Indeed, the celebrated article "Après une visite au Vatican" (1895; After a visit to the Vatican) scarcely hangs together in any formal way. It consists of three badly connected parts: the first attacks the scientism of **Ernest Renan**'s 1890 *L'Avenir de la science* (*The Future of Science*), while the other two deal with the development of social Christianity and with the prospect of eventual agreement between the Church and the social moralists. The arguments are intelligent and powerful, and in 1895 capable of stirring considerable passion, but their formal presentation does not suggest a natural essayist, however much Brunetière was accustomed to thinking in terms suitable for articles or lectures.

The essay, or such of its analogues as the **letter**, were, however, the forms to which Brunetière, by trade more a journalist than a professor, most naturally turned. When, in September 1903, the government wanted officially to inaugurate a statue of Renan, who had died in 1892, Brunetière was invited to attack Renan's lingering influence. The form he chose was the letter, of which he wrote five, the *Cinq lettres sur Ernest Renan* (1904; Five letters on Ernest Renan).

Brunetière has never passed for a great writer, though he was, in his day and for some time thereafter, an influential thinker. It is not specifically as an essayist that he is best remembered, but as a contributor to the necessary re-evaluation of France's literary culture after the era of positivism which nourished him had passed away. His work emphasizes above all the social and moral value of religion in a way which helped to restore the balance between secular and religious spheres at a time, during the last decade of the 19th century, when French academic life was permeated with hostility to the church and its institutions.

ANTHONY LEVI

Biography

Born 19 July 1849 in Toulon. Studied at a lycée in Marseilles; Lycée Louis-le-Grand, Paris, until 1869; studied law briefly at Rennes, 1871. Tutor for five years. Book reviewer, *Revue Bleue*, from 1874; contributor, from 1875, editorial secretary, 1877–93, and director, 1893–1906, *Revue des Deux Mondes*. Professor of French literature, École Normale Supérieure, Paris, 1883–1904. Director, *Revue de Paris*, from 1894. Elected to the French Academy, 1894. Died in Paris, 6 December 1906.

Selected Writings

Essays and Related Prose

Études critiques sur l'histoire de la littérature française, 9 vols., 1880–1925
Questions de critique, 1889
L'Évolution des genres dans l'histoire de la littérature, 1890
Nouvelles questions de critique, 1890
Essais sur la littérature contemporaine, 1892
Nouveaux essais sur la littérature contemporaine, 1895
Conférence de l'Odéon: Les Époques du théâtre français (1636–1850), 1896
Essays in French Literature (selection), translated by D. Nichol Smith, 1898
Discours de combat, 3 vols., 1900–07
Discours académiques, 1901
Variétés littéraires, 1904
Cinq Lettres sur Ernest Renan, 1904

Other writings: many works on French literature, including a four-volume history of classical French literature (1904–17) and a study of Balzac (1905).

Further Reading

Bondy, Louis J., *Le Classicisme de Ferdinand Brunetière*, Paris: Flor Burton, 1930
Clark, John, *La Pensée de Ferdinand Brunetière*, Paris: Nizet, 1954
Giraud, Victor, *Brunetière*, Paris: Flammarion, 1932
Gullace, Giovanni, *Taine and Brunetière on Criticism*, Lawrence, Kansas: Coronado Press, 1982
Hocking, Elton, *Ferdinand Brunetière: The Evolution of a Critic*, Madison: University of Wisconsin Studies in Language and Literature, 1936
Jequier, Walter, *Ferdinand Brunetière et la critique littéraire*, Tübingen: Laupp, 1923
Nanteuil, Jacques, *Ferdinand Brunetière*, Paris: Bloud et Gay, 1933

Brzozowski, Stanisław

Polish, 1878–1911

Despite his premature death at 33, Stanisław Brzozowski left behind an impressive number of books and articles, which exerted great influence on his contemporaries and successors, contributing much to the intellectual climate of 20th-century Poland. His range of interests is equally phenomenal. Known chiefly as a leading literary critic of early Modernism, familiar with Polish and European authors of the 19th century, he was also interested in philosophy, religion, and social problems. Essays on Polish Romantic philosophy and poetry, contemporary fiction, and criticism accompanied portrayals of **Dostoevskii** and Chekhov, articles about **Kant, Taine, Nietzsche,** Spencerean ethics, the educational values of English literature, and the syndicalism of Georges Sorel. Brzozowski's memoir (*Pamiętnik* [Diary; wr. 1910–11, pub. 1913]) leaves aside the mundane course of his life and is dedicated to a personal contemplation of the books and events that shaped his spiritual development or stimulated further reflection or vehement opposition. Moreover, he accumulates a variety of intellectual inspirations into a single *Weltanschauung*, which he expects will transform Poland and the world.

Brzozowski's ideas underwent various modifications and were related to different philosophers such as **Marx**, Nietzsche, and Bergson. Finally, he became fascinated by the teaching of Cardinal **Newman**, whose *Grammar of Assent* (1870) he translated into Polish (*Przeświadczenie wiary*, 1915). However, once espoused, those ideas became a creed, which Brzozowski promoted with fervor and a characteristic lack of tolerance for any opposing view. As a result, he played the role of national preacher, who considered the future of Poland and of all humanity, and believed in his ability to postulate their tasks and moral obligations.

If the essay is normally regarded as more relaxed and less complete than other forms of discourse, Brzozowski's works only partly comply with that pattern. He never indulges in detached contemplation or witty paradoxes, and overburdens his writings with many references to contemporary thinkers. Yet his effusive rhetoric creates emotional tension, where the reader feels overwhelmed by the ardor of the dedicated author even more than by the undoubted authority of his arguments. In these national "sermons," Brzozowski's digressive style transgresses the logical sequence of arguments, its free progress approaching essayistic models. He is also capable of encompassing complex thoughts within well-chosen metaphors, which would later become part of Polish critical language – for example, his often quoted description of Romanticism as "a flower rebelled against its roots."

Brzozowski's career is linked with notoriety, as he made himself known by fierce attacks against two recognized luminaries of Polish contemporary literature, Henryk Sienkiewicz and Zenon Przesmycki. The aggressive tone and denigrating assessment of these writers founded his reputation as the Zoilus of Polish criticism. The same uncompromising attitude became the hallmark of his later works as well. Some contained articles printed earlier in literary journals, such as *Głos* (Voice), *Przegląd Społeczny* (Social review), and *Krytyka* (Criticism), but some appeared only as books that immediately galvanized their readers and fomented vigorous disputes, as did his most influential publication, *Legenda Młodej Polski* (1910; The legend of Young Poland). Brzozowski's most important critical and philosophical works also include *Współczesna powieść polska* (1906; The contemporary Polish novel), *Kultura i życie* (1907; Culture and life), *Współczesna krytyka literacka w Polsce* (1907; Contemporary literary criticism in Poland), *Idee* (1910; Ideas), and *Głosy wśród nocy* (1912; Voices in the night).

Best known as a literary critic, Brzozowski developed his own idea of professional responsibility. He treated his task seriously, believing it should surpass personal impressions and establish a deeper order of understanding life than literary works themselves: "Literary criticism constitutes a higher form of contemplating art, it is a further stage of evolution toward the ultimate comprehension of those human activities that produce art" (*Współczesna krytyka literacka w Polsce*). In accordance with his moralist stance, Brzozowski believed in the practical value of critical appraisals, as they were expected to help writers in solving their dilemmas and benefit readers by advancing their knowledge of modern human life. Since he related literature and the arts to ethics, the problem of aesthetic form eventually became linked with moral judgment and regarded as its unwitting or subconscious expression: "Our art always constitutes our judgment on life, a verdict of condemnation or of elevated rapture" (*Współczesna krytyka literacka w Polsce*). In the course of time, Brzozowski developed his own philosophy of culture, which then served as a point of reference for his re-evaluation of various forms of human activity. Starting from a "philosophy of action," he eventually developed his acclaimed "philosophy of labor," which also found admirers long after his death. What he had in mind was a major physical effort, capable of reshaping reality in accordance with human will. Consequently, intellectual exertion might have turned into genuine labor only by its links with and influence upon manual toil. Since Brzozowski loftily extolled the gigantic endeavor to conquer nature and struggle with "suprahuman forces," his grand theory, regarded by only a few as utopian, attracted many Polish intellectuals. As a kind of national messianism, revitalized long after the Romantic movement, it proclaimed the emergence of a new Polish mission, whose major message would "reveal ideas undiscovered so far by the rest of the world" (*Legenda Młodej Polski*).

Brzozowski holds a unique position as an astute critic of Polish contemporary culture, known as Young Poland or Neo-Romanticism. His *Legenda Młodej Polski* represents the most comprehensive denunciation of those forms of the Polish mind, which, in Brzozowski's words, represent "the delusion of cultural consciousness." (Was he, however, free of those delusions himself?) Inspired partly by Marxism, he was convinced that all humans reflected their economic and social conditions. Therefore Romantic attempts at controlling life from above – that is, from high "prophetic" posts of national bards – are regarded as misconceived and deceptive. Similar criteria motivate Brzozowski's condemnation of the shortcomings of leading Young Poland writers such as Stefan Żeromski and Stanisław Wyspiański. Still, he shared the views of his peers that intuition is superior to rational thinking, and that inner life is much more interesting than outer reality, reflected in the novels of conventional realists like Sienkiewicz or Władysław Reymont. His lasting impact and popularity has been confirmed by the critical works of **Czesław Miłosz**, Kazimierz Wyka, and many others.

STANISŁAW EILE

Biography

Leopold Stanisław Brzozowski. Born 28 June 1878 in Maziarnia, near Lublin. Studied at the Russian Imperial University, Warsaw, 1896–97: suspended for demonstrating against a Russian nationalist professor. Arrested for his activities in the illegal group, Society for Popular Education, and imprisoned for a month, where he contracted tuberculosis, 1898; treated at a sanatorium at Otwock, near Warsaw, 1899, and worked there as a librarian, 1900. Married Antonina Kolberg, 1901: one daughter. Contributor to various journals, including *Głos*, from 1902, and *Naprzód* (Forward), 1906. Moved to Zakopane in the Tatra Mountains for treatment of TB, 1905; lectured at Lvov Technical University, from 1905. Went for treatment to Nervi, Italy, 1906, and moved to Florence, 1907. Accused of being an agent of the tsarist police, 1908: he denied charges, the case went to trial, and no verdict was reached. Died (of tuberculosis) in Florence, 30 April 1911.

Selected Writings

Essays and Related Prose

Kultura i życie, 1907; enlarged edition, edited by Andrzej Walicki, 1973

Legenda Młodej Polski: Studia o strukturze duszy kulturalnej, 1910

Głosy wśród nocy: Studia nad przesileniem romantycznym kultury europejskiej, 1912

Aforyzmy, edited by Andrzej Mencwel, 1979

Humor i prawo: Wybrane studia krytyczne, edited by Tomasz Burek, 1988

Eseje i studia o literaturze, edited by Henryk Markiewicz, 2 vols., 1990

Other writings: several novels (including *Pod ciężarem Bogo*, 1901; *Wiry*, 1904–05; *Płomienie*, 1908; *Sam wśród ludzi*, 1911; *Książka o starej Kobiecie* [unfinished], 1914), a treatise on Henryk Sienkiewicz (1903), plays, books on literature (including *Współczesna powieść polska*, 1906) literary criticism (including *Współczesna krytyka literacka w Polsce*, 1907), and writers (including on Hippolyte Taine, Jan Śniadecki, Stefan Żeromski, Friedrich Nietzsche, and Fedor Dostoevskii), philosophy, letters (collected in *Listy*, edited by M. Sroka, 2 vols., 1970), and a diary (*Pamiętnik*, 1913). Also translated *Grammar of Assent* by John Henry Newman (1915).

Collected works edition: *Dzieła wszystkie*, edited by A. Górski and S. Kołaczkowski, 4 vols., 1936–38 (never completed).

Further Reading

Kołakowski, Leszek, *Main Currents of Marxism*, vol. 2, Oxford: Oxford University Press, 1978: 215–39

Mackiewicz, Witold, *Brzozowski*, Warsaw: Wiedza Powszechna, 1979

Mencwel, Andrzej, *Stanisław Brzozowski: Kształtowanie myśli krytycznej*, Warsaw: Czytelnik, 1976

Miłosz, Czesław, "A Controversial Polish Writer: Stanisław Brzozowski," in *California Slavic Studies*, vol. 2, Berkeley: University of California Press, 1963: 53–95

Miłosz, Czesław, *Człowiek wśród skorpionów: Studium o Stanisławie Brzozowskim*, Warsaw: Młoda Polska, 1982

Miłosz, Czesław, *The History of Polish Literature*, Berkeley: University of California Press, 2nd edition, 1983: 373–79

Syska-Lamparska, Rena A., *Stanisław Brzozowski: A Polish Vision*, Florence: Le Lettere Firenze, 1987

Walicki, Andrzej, *Stanisław Brzozowski – drogi myśli*, Warsaw: Pánstwowe Wydawnictwo Naukowe, 1977

Walicki, Andrzej, *Stanisław Brzozowski and the Polish Beginnings of "Western Marxism"*, Oxford: Clarendon Press, and New York: Oxford University Press, 1989

Walicki, Andrzej, and Roman Zimand, editors, *Wokół myśli Stanisława Brzozowskiego*, Cracow: Wydawnictwo Literackie, 1974

Buckley, Vincent
Australian, 1925–1988

In the essays collected as *Essays in Poetry, Mainly Australian* (1957), the poet Vincent Buckley made a unique contribution to discussions about cultural identity and Australian poetry. Writing in an independent and definitive style, he challenged popular critical opinion, judging the realist-nationalist "Australian Tradition" too descriptive and nostalgic, naming vitalism and nationalism as the main retarding forces on Australian poetry, and favoring writing which demonstrated "a deepening of sensibility to the point where the land is conceived and imagined in terms which are at once spiritual, moral, sensory and directed to the drama of human existence." The most influential of these essays, "The Image of Man in Australian Poetry," established what was to become a characteristic interplay of social and metaphysical, spiritual and sensual, inward and outward perspectives. This incarnational poetics informs particular essays on Kenneth Slessor, **A. D. Hope**, **Judith Wright**, and James McAuley, as well as critiques of contemporary leftwing poets and Stephen Spender's "a-social aesthetic" ("Helicon as Jordan"). Although contested (and often simplified as "metaphysical"), *Essays in Poetry, Mainly Australian*, as well as "Patrick White and His Epic" (1958) and "Capricornia" (1960), were very important to the development of Australian literature as a subject worthy of detailed and extensive criticism.

Questions surrounding national identity are pursued in later essays. "Utopianism and Vitalism" (1958) rejects literary nationalism as the main "line of influence" in Australian writing, nominating instead "two chief lines of influence . . . a kind of utopian humanism or insistence on the soul's radical innocence, and a kind of vitalism, or insistence on releasing the basic powers of life." "National and International" (1978) recalls the nationalist debates of the 1950s as locked into an either/or structure, which Buckley still disputes, preferring to uncover depths of history and myth in immediate social fact. "A Later Note on 'Identity'" (1980) remembers how, in the 1950s, it was necessary to avoid both imperialism and nationalism, finding Australian culture now "more in danger from imperialism than from nationalism." "Ease of American Language" (1982) outlines some of Buckley's own American influences, but his recognition of the "special naturalness" of American literary speech (especially Gary Snyder's) serves a notion of "the idiom of sensation" which recapitulates and extends an earlier use of "holy place" into a poetics of interconnected rhythms (of place, sensation, perception, and language). At the time Buckley was trying to make his own poetry "locally mimetic," so that it discovered and developed the intimate relation between the world outside the self and the language that the self had learned. This did not, however, degenerate into nationalism: "Imagination's Home" (1979) identifies "Ireland as a source-country . . . in the sense that the psyche grows from and in it, and remains profoundly attuned to it." Ireland becomes an active symbol for mythic imagination (not a surrogate mythology) and occupies a central place in Buckley's late poetry and prose.

Buckley's attention to "the spiritual and social fact of Australia" derived in part from his Christology, which saw the Incarnation as the prototype of "the union of the sacred and the secular." Influenced by Cardinal Emmanuel Suhard and Yves Congar as well as by the Apostolate movement at the University of Melbourne, Buckley argued, in "The World Awaiting Redemption" (1957), for a Christian humanism that reconciles freedom and grace, immanence and transcendence, declaring that the Church manifests itself fully in a society when it lives at the center of the problems and values of that society. This theology was to be modified and muted as Buckley became more interested in mythic imagination and less identified with institutionalized Catholicism, but the mediatory act coded into the Incarnation metaphor remained integral to his writing. Buckley's theopoetics is best represented by *Poetry and the Sacred* (1968), where individual essays on Wyatt, **Donne**, Blake, **Yeats**, and **Eliot** play out the suggestive opening essay, "Specifying the Sacred." Buckley's approach, influenced by Mircea Eliade, was as much anthropological as theological, and his central distinction, between "religion in poetry" and "poetry as a religious act," provided new ways of discussing the relationship between religion and poetry where religion was not reduced to doctrine, nor religious poetry to piety. Another influential **religious essay** was "The Strange Personality of Christ" (1970), a provocative piece that took issue with two images of Christ then prevalent in popular theology – "man for others" and political agitator – and reasserted his essential mystery by applying Eliade's concept of "hierophany." This essay is characteristic of Buckley's mature religious writing, standing within and against the Christian tradition, defining a shift from dogma to myth and exploring an imagination which is sacramental because deeply sensate.

Buckley also wrote a number of reminiscences and portraits, writing in such a way that descriptive and speculative memories merged. "Remembering What You Have To" (1968) outlines the origins of his gradualist politics (Irish-Catholic working-class background, Labour sympathies, and distrust of power) and discusses his own relationship to Catholicism, communism, and the Labour Party in the 1940s and 1950s. Such essays in memory dominated his late career. The autobiographical *Cutting Green Hay* (1983) might be approached as an extended sequence of essays, speculating on such topics as the Irish in Australia, Catholic social action of the 1950s, the Labour Split, and university controversies over Vietnam, and providing memorable portraits of figures such as Archbishop Mannix and James McAuley. *Memory Ireland* (1985) might be similarly read: the chapter "Election and Death of Bobby Sands," discovering Sands "at the centre of the mythopoeic universe" and in a deeply realized social context, releasing a voice inflected with Ireland, is a particularly fine example of how Buckley used the essay to mediate mythic and social, deliberative and evocative, subject and style. He often employed the term "rhythm" to indicate the interpenetration of style and insight. This idea receives a final and characteristically supple treatment in "Self Portrait" (1986) in which Buckley tells a "self": "You affirmed a rhythm in all things: the rhythm *in* the eye as well as the rhythm *of* the eye . . ."

NOEL ROWE

Biography
Born 8 July 1925 in Romsey, Victoria. Studied at the Jesuit college in Melbourne; University of Melbourne, B.A., 1950, M.A., 1954;

Cambridge University, 1955–57. Married twice: four children. Lockie Fellow, 1958–60, reader, 1960–67, and Personal Chair in Poetry, from 1967, University of Melbourne. Editor, *Prospect*, 1958–64; poetry editor, *Bulletin*, 1961–63. Founder, Committee for Civil Rights in Ireland, 1969. Awards: Australian Literature Society Gold Medal, 1959; Myer Award, for poetry, 1967. Vincent Buckley Prize established, 1993. Died in Melbourne, 12 November 1988.

Selected Writings

Essays and Related Prose
Essays in Poetry, Mainly Australian, 1957
Poetry and Morality: Studies in the Criticism of Matthew Arnold, T. S. Eliot, and F. R. Leavis, 1959
Poetry and the Sacred, 1968
Cutting Green Hay: Friendships, Movements and Cultural Conflicts in Australia's Great Decades, 1983
Memory Ireland: Insights into the Contemporary Irish Condition, 1985

Other writings: several collections of poetry.

Further Reading
Booth, Elizabeth, "Vincent Buckley, an Interview," *Quadrant* (August 1976): 27–32
Brady, Veronica, "Return to the Centre: Vincent Buckley's *Golden Builders*," *Westerly* 2 (1973): 68–76
Buckley, Brian, "Vincent Buckley's Melbourne," *Quadrant* (August 1983): 35–58
Colmer, John, "The Quest for Roots: Vincent Buckley and Sally Morgan," in his *Australian Autobiography: A Personal Quest*, Melbourne: Oxford University Press, 1989: 98–116
Davidson, Jim, "Vincent Buckley," *Meanjin* 4 (1979): 443–58
Kavanagh, Paul, and Peter Kuch, "Scored for the Voice: An Interview with Vincent Buckley," *Southerly* 3 (1987): 249–66
O'Sullivan, Vincent, "Singing Mastery: The Poetics of Vincent Buckley," *Westerly* 2 (1989): 50–57
Rosenbloom, Henry, "An Interview with Vincent Buckley," *Meanjin* 3 (1969): 317–25
Rowe, Noel, "Believing More and Less: The Later Poetry of Vincent Buckley," *Meridian* (May 1991): 4–18
Steele, Peter, "Vincent Buckley as Critic," *Meanjin* 3 (1969): 309–16
Thomson, A. K., "The Poetry of Vincent Buckley: An Essay in Interpretation," *Meanjin* 3 (1969): 293–308
Wallace-Crabbe, Chris, "Vincent Buckley: The Poetry of Presence," *Overland* 114 (1989) 31–34

Buies, Arthur

French Canadian, 1840–1901

Arthur Buies is without a doubt the *enfant terrible* of French Canadian literature. He has been accused of having no philosophical culture or direction, of being an eternal adolescent, a greedy seducer, a bored bourgeois, a cheater, narcissistic, maniacal, and inconsistent; yet he is one of the few French Canadian writers of the 19th century whose legacy still continues. It is said that he was the only writer capable of earning his living from his work at the time. During his lifetime and for many years afterwards, he was both loved and hated, either admired as a writer or totally defamed by his critics.

Buies began his writing career after returning from France where he studied at the Lycée Saint-Louis and the Sorbonne. His first major contribution to French Canadian literature came with his return to Canada in 1862 when he began to publish in the journal *Pays* (Country), which the then Archbishop of Montreal described as "anti-christian, anti-catholic, anti-social, immoral and dangerous to the young." Buies made himself defender of the liberal ideas he had absorbed while living in France and which were far from making their way to French Canada, still very much under the dominance of the Catholic Church. In 1864 he published the first and second of his *Lettres sur le Canada* (Letters on Canada); here the diversity and style of Buies is made manifest. The first **letter** is a description of the port of Quebec City, where Buies exercises his talent as a descriptive and geographical writer (he went on to write several other geographical monographs later in life). Here he expresses his infatuation with the beauty of the landscape surrounding Quebec City. The letter is dreamy, tender, full of enchantment, but at the same the cold, irresistible force of nature is present. Nature is savage and ferocious, majestically monotonous, stormy and aggressive. Buies, who emerges in the second letter (written in the same year) as a vehement enemy of the clergy and the Catholic Church, reveals in this first letter a strong sense of religiosity, bordering on the mystical: "In the silence of the Infinite, we were alone. The Unknowable appeared to encompass us in his mystical sphere, a Universal enveloped heaven and earth. I thought I saw the hills rise slowly, garlanded by long vapors bathing in the sun."

The second letter contains none of this enchantment. It is an attack against the obscurantist dominance of the Catholic Church and the occult power of the clergy, who, together with the British colonialists, held the French Canadian people under their oppression and in a state of almost total ignorance. "A clerical education is the poisoning of the people," he claims. Referring to candidates for the priesthood, he writes: ". . . are they not certain of the truth that great men of history have sought for a very long time, but which has cost them only five or six mea culpas a day and many genuflections?"

As **polemical essay**ist, **pamphlet**eer, and descriptive writer, Buies retains similar characteristics: his style in all contexts is colorful and artistic, romantic, poetical, and allegorical. His descriptive works are full of small portraits of everyday life, tender, fleeting moments which his observing eye catches and relays in language readers can identify with. Today he would be described as a cinematographic writer. This was undoubtedly the reason for his popularity, even though many were shocked by his libertine and anticlerical positions. However, while his style can be rather basic and common, he never misses the sublime. He also disliked the conventional. His descriptions are exotic, and he enjoys playing on opposites: clear and obscure, classical and romantic, realistic and artistic. His work is full of antitheses: laughter and tears, cradle and tomb. He also uses hyperbole, especially when describing moments of emotional intensity.

Buies' first notion of the essay consisted in not harboring any notions. He "wrote to write," as he himself said. "I wrote by imagination, by inclination, according to taste so that I would not become rusty and to fill, here and there, a few hours of existence . . ." However, writing essays was also a practical and utilitarian activity with which he encouraged change in French Canadian society. He wanted to raise the cultural level of his society, believing this could come about only through a solid knowledge of the French language and of French literature. He wrote several works against the use of angli-cisms and barbarisms in French Canada, and he dreamed of seeing the birth of a national, French Canadian literature. As well as denouncing the ecclesiastically-run educational system, he also wrote to bring about a separation of Church and State according to the American model, to denounce intolerance against other forms of thinking and belief, and to sound a cry of alarm to all French Canadians contemplating emigration to the United States. He was one of the first ideologists of a sepa-rate and independent French Canadian nation in North America. He spent the last 20 years of his life writing geograph-ical surveys, attempting to convince French Canadians to popu-late the vast, rich, uninhabited, and unexplored expanses of the Province of Quebec.

ANDRIUS VALEVIČIUS

Biography

Born 24 January 1840 in Montreal. Studied at the Collèges de Nicolet and Sainte Anne de la Pocatière, Quebec, expelled 1855; joined his father in British Guiana, 1856; studied at Trinity College, Dublin, 1856; moved to Paris, and studied at the Lycée Saint-Louis, 1857–59; joined Garibaldi's army in Italy, 1860; returned to Paris, where he studied at the Sorbonne and failed the baccalauréat examination three times; returned to Canada, 1862; studied at the Institut Canadien; called to the bar, 1866. Editor, *La Lanterne*, 1868–69, *L'Indépendant*, 1870, and *Le Réveil* (The awakening), 1876. Married Maria Mila Catellier, 1887: five children. Died in Quebec City, 26 January 1901.

Selected Writings

Essays and Related Prose

Lettres sur le Canada, 3 vols., 1864–67; reprinted 1968
Chroniques, 2 vols., 1873–75; edited by Francis Parmentier, 2 vols., 1986–91
Petites chroniques pour 1877, 1878
Chroniques canadiennes: Humeurs et caprices, 1884; reprinted 1978
La Lanterne (periodical), 1884; as *La Lanterne d'Arthur Buies: Propos révolutionnaires et chroniques scandaleuses, confessions publiques*, edited by Marcel A. Gagnon, 1964
Anglicismes et canadianismes, 1888; reprinted 1979
Arthur Buies, 1840–1901, edited by Léopold Lamontagne, 1959
Anthologie d'Arthur Buies, edited by Laurent Mailhot, 1978

Other writings: books about the Saguenay and Outaouais Rivers, Canadian flora and fauna, and other travel writing.

Bibliography

Tessier, Rachel, *Bio-Bibliographie d'Arthur Buies*, Montreal: University of Montreal, 1943

Further Reading

Bender, Prosper, "Arthur Buies," in *Literary Sheaves, or, La Littérature au Canada français*, Montreal: Dawson, 1881: 129–34
Douville, Raymond, *La Vie aventureuse d'Arthur Buies*, Montreal: Lévesque, 1933
Falardeau, Jean-Charles, "Arthur Buies, l'antizouave," *Canadian Literature* 11, no. 27 (May 1960): 25–32
Gagnon, Marcel A., *Le Ciel et l'enfer d'Arthur Buies*, Quebec City: Presses de l'Université Laval, 1965
Genest, Jean-Guy, "*La Lanterne*, 1868–1869," *Recherches Sociographiques* 10, nos. 2–3 (1969): 389–407
Hare, John, "Arthur Buies, essayiste: Une Introduction à la lecture de son œuvre," in *L'Essai et la prose d'idées au Québec*, Montreal: Fides, 1985: 295–310
Lamontagne, Léopold, *Arthur Buies, homme de lettres*, Quebec City: Presses de l'Université Laval, 1957
Marion, Séraphin, "La Citadelle classique," in *Les Lettres canadiennes d'autrefois*, vol. 7, Ottawa: L'Éclair, 1952
Roy, Pierre-Georges, "Les Ouvrages d'Arthur Buies," *Bulletin des Recherches Historiques* 7, no. 5 (1901): 150–53
Tusseau, J.-P., "La Fin édifiante d'Arthur Buies," *Études Françaises* 9, no. 1 (February 1973): 45–54
Vachon, G.-André, "Arthur Buies, écrivain," *Études Françaises* 6, no. 3 (1970): 283–95

Bulgarian Essay

The essay is one of the typical genres of 20th-century Bulgarian literature, the fruit of both the native prose tradition and inte-riorized foreign influence (particularly German, French, and Russian). The native origins of the Bulgarian essay can be traced back to *Istoriia sloveno-Bulgarskaia* (1762; The Slavic-Bulgarian history), written by Father Paisii Khilendarski (1722–73), the biographical and **historical essays** of Zakhari Stoianov (1850–89), and Aleko Konstantinov's (1863–97) **travel essay** *Do Chikago i nazad* (1894; To Chicago and back). These works are representative of the leading themes in the Bulgarian essay: national identity (initially seen as the institu-tional unity of the State, the independent Orthodox Church, and common past, but from the beginning of the 20th century understood primarily as cultural identity) and Bulgaria's rela-tionship to the rest of Europe. In general, the Bulgarian essay reflects the peculiarity of the nation's political and social history: from the second half of the 19th century, when Bulgaria was liberated from the Ottoman yoke, the essay was considered to be a means of public discussion of the major problems of the nation.

In Bulgarian literature and fine art at the beginning of the 20th century, the traditional society and the "national soul" were aestheticized. The genre of the essay in its turn was thematically dominated by the idea of "Bulgarian-ness," systematically introduced by the pioneer of the modern Bulgarian essay, **Pencho Slaveikov** (1866–1912), whose essen-tial contribution to Bulgarian culture was to reject utilitarian tendencies and reconcile the "traditional" and the "modern," for instance in his works on Bulgarian folksongs and on **Nietzsche**'s *Also sprach Zarathustra* (1883–85; Thus Spoke Zarathustra).

Krustyu Krustev (1866–1912), Boian Penev (1882–1927), Spiridon Kazandzhiev (1882–1951), Petar Mutafchiev (1883–1943), Vladimir Vasilev (1883–1963), **Chavdar Mutafov** (1889–1954), Nikolai Rainov (1889–1954), Konstantin Petkanov (1891–1952), Konstantin Gulabov (1892–1980), Atanas Iliev (1893–1985), Geo Milev (1895–1925), Atanas Dalchev (1904–77), and Ivan Khadzhiiski (1907–44), each in his own fashion, reflected on a few particular issues that stemmed from the theme of cultural identity: the national psy-chology of Bulgarians in contrast to Western European or other Balkan nations; changes in the emotional world of Bulgarians in modern times; the spiritual and social state of the Bulgarian intelligentsia; Bulgarian literature and fine art in the context of

European culture; cultural kinship of Bulgarians and other Slavic nations. German influence can be detected in the idea of Bulgarian "spirit," "soul," or "fate" (the equivalent of *Geist*) which preoccupied students of national psychology and culture. By the time of World War II, a whole mythology of national psychology ("narodopsikhologiia") had developed, ranging from the most positive to the most negative features: the former were seen as the heritage of the idyllic past, while the latter were explained as the result of the lost innocence of peasant life and the lack of national self-consciousness, spiritual and social unity, and stability in the present day. In this period the Bulgarian essay revolved around the questions "Who are we? Where do we come from? Where are we going?," as Ivan Elenkov formulates them in his **preface** to the most representative anthology of Bulgarian essays, *Zashto sme takiva?* (1994; Why are we thus?).

Along with and through the elaboration of the theme of cultural identity, the main characteristics of the Bulgarian essay were constituted: a tendency toward formal objectiveness (the narrative point of view is not "I," the author, but "we," which can be denoted as Bulgarians, the Bulgarian intelligentsia, or a group gathered around a particular cultural magazine); a tendency toward generalization and a prophetic tone in some essays which followed naturally from the ambition to answer the most important questions about national existence and the future, even when discussing fleeting subjects; and a succinct style, especially characteristic of followers of the German school of the essay.

After World War II, communists seized political power in Bulgaria. The idea of a gradual Europeanization of Bulgaria, dominant in the interwar period, was replaced by the ideology of the "internationalization" of Bulgarian culture. Literary and art criticism was proclaimed to have a "leading function" in cultural life; critics were supposed to "transmit" the ideological directives of the Communist Party into art, to propagate the "most recent course of the Party" and the "most advanced" literary method – that of "socialist realism" (see *The Cultural Policy of Socialism* [1986], the selected speeches of Todor Zhivkov, the first secretary of the Communist Party). Because the genre of the essay was treated as an effective literary means of communist control over cultural life, and because, unlike other communist countries, in Bulgaria *samizdat* (underground) publishing hardly existed, the essay was more deeply harmed than other literary genres.

The 1970s brought the first significant breakthrough to this stagnation. **Georgi Markov** (1920–78) began broadcasting his political essays about Bulgaria from Radio Free Europe (collected in *The Truth That Killed*, 1983). Blaga Dimitrova (1922–) and Iordan Vasilev (1928–) published a two-volume essay in 1975 devoted to the Bulgarian poet Elisaveta Bagriana (*Mladostta na Bagriana* [Bagriana's youth] and *Dni cherni i beli* [Days black and white]) and Toncho Zhechev (1929–) brought out a series of essays under the title *Mitut za Odisei* (1979; The myth of Odysseus). Both publications evoked storms of negative criticism incited by the Communist Party. The 1980s, however, began with the official acceptance of Zhechev's essay *Bulgarskiiat Velikden ili strastite Bulgarski* (1980; Bulgarian Easter, or the passion of Bulgarians), which restored the interwar interest in the riddles of national mentality and posed anew the question: Why are we thus?

In the 1980s the essay genre became more popular and obtained greater liberty. Several publishing houses (e.g. Narodna Kultura [National culture], Izdatelstvo na Otechestveniia Front [Publishing house of the Fatherland Front], Knigoizdatelstvo "Georgi Bakalov" [Georgi Bakalov publishing house]) issued series of essay collections by Bulgarian and foreign authors. The philosopher Isak Pasi (1929–), himself author of essays on German, French, and Spanish thinkers, began promoting European classical essays in Bulgarian translation. In the 1980s two essayists who cherished their spiritual link with the interwar period attracted readers' attention: Mikhail Nedelchev (1942–) with his *Sotsialni stilove, kriticheski siuzheti* (1987; Social styles, critical subjects), and Svetlozar Igov (1945–) with his **critical essays** (*Groznite pateta* [1984, 1989; Ugly ducklings]) and essayistic fragments *Prizori* (1988; Before dawn). Thematic variety and relative liberty of expression notwithstanding, the Bulgarian essay still had to keep its most important messages "between the lines" in order to avoid censorship or to react playfully to the "deficiencies" and "simulations" of the totalitarian epoch, as did Alexander Kiossev (1953–), Ivailo Dichev (1955–), Vladislav Todorov (1956–), and Ivan Kristev (1965–) in their essays collected in *Post-Theory, Games, and Discursive Resistance: The Bulgarian Case* (1995).

After the collapse of communism at the end of 1989, Bulgaria found itself "in the hall of democracy," to use the title of one of the typical collections of essays from the first two years of the political changes (Georgi Velichkov [1938–], *V antreto na demokratsiyata*, 1990). Liberated from the restraints of censorship, Bulgarian publishers hastened to issue books by émigré writers: Georgi Markov's political essays *Zadochni reportazhi za Bulgaria* (1990; Broadcasts about Bulgaria) and *Novi zadochni reportazhi za Bulgaria* (1991; New broadcasts about Bulgaria); Stefan Popov's (1906–89) *Bezsunitsi* (1992; Insomnia), which combines memoir and travel essay features and belongs to the national identity trend in the Bulgarian essay; Atanas Slavov's (1925–) **autobiographical essay** *S tochnostta na prilepi* (1992; *With the Precision of Bats*) and *Bulgarskata literatura na "razmraziavaneto"* (1994; *The "Thaw" in Bulgarian Literature*), as well as a selection of his political essays, *Politika: Belezhki po dilemite na promianata* (1992; Politics: notes on the dilemmas of the change), in which Slavov reflects on the specifics of the national political tradition which allowed communism to root itself deeper in Bulgaria than in some other East European countries and points out the importance of the well-functioning state institutions for the transition from totalitarianism to parliamentary democracy. Konstantin Katsarov's (1898–1980) two-volume travel essay *Svetut otblizo* (1947; The world from close up), once on the censorship index, was reprinted in 1995. Step by step, the higher standards of the interwar Bulgarian essay are returning. The liberation of thought was accompanied by the liberation of language and style; awareness of personal responsibility for the written word along with the immense variety of political opinions brought a new subjectivity to the Bulgarian essay. At the same time, interest in "hot topics," as well as the fact that during the period of transition to a market economy most of the literary and cultural magazines collapsed and were replaced by newspapers, made a journalistic style prevail in most writings. Typical examples of the contemporary Bulgarian essay can be found in Blaga Dimitrova's *Raznoglasitsy* (1996; Discords), in *Beliia svyat* (1994; The wide world), travel essays by Vera Mutafchieva (1929–), or in the essays of Dimitar Koroudzhiev (1941–), whose main concern is the deformation inflicted by totalitarianism on the human soul (e.g. *Hristiianskata svoboda* [1996; Christian freedom]).

At the end of the 20th century the Bulgarian essay is returning to the question "Why are we thus?," burdened – or perhaps enriched – with reflections on the consequences of more than four decades of communist stagnation. Once again the audience expects the essay to address the pivotal problems of the future of Bulgaria, to be a genre with a social mission.

KATIA MITOVA-JANOWSKI

Anthologies

Izbrani Bulgarski eseta: Bulgarski eseisti mezhdu dvete voini (Select Bulgarian essays: Bulgarian essayists between the wars), edited by Zdravko Petrov, Varna: Knigoizdatelswo "Georgi Bakalov," 1981

Post-Theory, Games, and Discursive Resistance: The Bulgarian Case, edited by Alexander Kiossev, Albany: State University of New York Press, 1995

We własnych oczach: XX-wieczny esej zachodnio- i południowosłowiański (In [their] own eyes: the 20th-century West and South Slavic essay), edited by Halina Janaszek-Ivaničzkova, Warsaw: Panstwowy Instytut Wydawniczy, 1977

Zashto sme takiva? V tursene na Bulgarskata kulturna identichnost (Why are we thus? In search of Bulgarian cultural identity) edited by Ivan Elenkovn and Rumen Daskalov, Sofia: Izdatelstvo Prosveta, 1994

Further Reading

Elenkov, Ivan, and Rumen Daskalov, Prefaces to *Zashto sme takiva? V tursene na Bulgarskata kulturna identichnost* (Why are we such? In search of Bulgarian cultural identity), edited by Elenkov and Daskalov, Sofia: Izdatelstvo Prosveta, 1994

Burckhardt, Jacob Christoph

Swiss, 1818–1897

Although Jacob Christoph Burckhardt gained the greatest respect for his seminal study *Die Kultur der Renaissance in Italien* (1860; *The Civilization of the Renaissance in Italy*), his contribution as an essayist is equally remarkable, though much less known today and relatively difficult to fathom. Born in Basle, he spent most of his life there teaching and writing, reaching out to the public through lectures and essays and through editorial work with the *Baseler Zeitung* (Basle news) and other publications. Whereas his books are primarily concerned with historical and art historical subjects, such as *Die Zeit Constantins des Grossen* (1853; *The Age of Constantine the Great*), *Der Cicerone* (1855), *The Civilization of the Renaissance in Italy*, and, finally, *Geschichte der Renaissance in Italien* (1867; *The History of the Renaissance in Italy*), all his other publications, many posthumous, are based on philosophical reflections, lecture notes, and drafts. Burckhardt did not compose essays in the narrow sense of the word, but dealt with history in an essayistic manner. In particular he expressed his view of history in *Weltgeschichtliche Betrachtungen* (1905; *Reflections on History*), in *Historische Fragmente* (1929; *Judgements on History and Historians*), and in many letters, which were revised and edited by Werner Kägi, Burckhardt's successor in the chair of history at the University of Basle.

Burckhardt was reticent about his lecture notes, refusing to let them be published during his lifetime. Only on his deathbed did he give permission for the printing of his insightful historical-philosophical studies. These lectures focus on the historical process itself, on humans' dependency on time, and on the interaction of state, religion, and culture; others analyze what makes some people famous and what constitutes their fortune. But the majority are purely historical, emphasizing individual periods or personalities.

Friedrich Nietzsche, who came to Basle in 1869 as professor of classics, was one of the few who seemed to have fully understood Burckhardt's complex and not always clearly structured presentations. He praised him for being an individual thinker and an enemy of fashions and modern trends in scholarship. In 1910 Carl Neumann lauded Burckhardt's works as masterpieces of the "cultural-historical" style. Johann Huizinga admired him as the "wisest spirit of the 19th century," and he is now considered to have been one of the finest essayists of the 19th century in the field of world history and art history.

Whereas traditional historians have pursued an interest in the process of times and events, Burckhardt investigated the constitutive elements of specific epochs such as the Italian Renaissance and attempted to grasp its universal characteristics. Moreover, he deliberately distanced himself from structural, social-historical, and economic approaches. Instead he emphasized the individual person, both an active and passive being in history, as the only worthwhile object of study. For that reason he dismissed any questions about the prehistorical origin of peoples and countries because the data about those early periods are too fragmented and do not inform us about actual people from that time. "Primitive" people and religions were of no interest to Burckhardt because he only examined "sophisticated" or "high" European cultures, which excelled through their intellectual productivity and corresponding art forms. The entity of culture as a holistic phenomenon dominated his thinking, but he ignored, deliberately and entirely, Asian and any other non-European cultures, concentrating instead on the history of ancient and modern Europe.

At the same time Burckhardt was neither an idealist nor an elitist, and did not believe in the absolute goodness of humankind. According to his view, in his later years strongly colored by **Arthur Schopenhauer**'s teachings, historical investigations always reveal the good and the evil in humans, and the dream of reform to establish an ideal society is in vain. Even happiness is no guaranteed goal; the best that can be hoped for is the absence of misfortune. In his essayistic writing Burckhardt increasingly expressed a distrust of historical progress and lamented the decline of modern culture in terms of the loss of communication, individualism, leisure, and cultural education.

His essays are cultural-historical studies that examine the totality of a period, a people, or a genre (e.g. arch forms in architecture, madonna paintings in art). Burckhardt studied the difference between barbarism and culture, the contrast between antiquity and the modern world. Characteristic features in his lectures are the reliance on anthropomorphic images (e.g. the youth of the Middle Ages), the preference for organic concepts (e.g. "life of humankind"), emphasis on idealistic concepts, and naive but possibly brilliant generalizations (e.g. "Christianity," "the Church," "the Jews," "Heathendom," and "the forces of a time period").

Burckhardt's basic concept of past cultures was not limited by the approaches and methods traditionally pursued by historians. His essays addressed a more nonacademic audience, being written from a philosopher's rather than an academic scholar's point of view. His understanding of history as an academic discipline was based on the concept of a universal spirit expressed in culture, and the spirit of individual epochs of history, captured in their art. Nevertheless Burckhardt did not believe in the religious *telos* of history, and considered Christianity, like any other religion, as an historical phenomenon in the cultural process from the past to the present.

Art history represented an important aspect of Burckhardt's research and teaching, and in many of his critical writings he examined the art works from the past as reflections of the human dimension. For many years Burckhardt lectured on both history and art history at the University of Basle; later he even abandoned the purely historical discipline. His highly acclaimed study on *The Civilization of the Renaissance in Italy* is based not only on many art historical observations, but also includes extensive and detailed examinations of Renaissance art. In this sense Burckhardt developed into a perceptive cultural historian who incorporated the various elements of past cultures in his essays and analyses of those times. The purpose of art was, according to Burckhardt, to serve religion, even during the Italian Renaissance. Yet art appeared to him as an expression of the ineffable, a reflection of the mystical realm, a phenomenon which can be appreciated but not intellectually penetrated. Art is autonomous and can only be approached through feeling and intuition. Art objects are therefore representations of the "true" world and contain the key to absolute truth. Burckhardt did not consider art history from a chronological point of view, but in terms of genres, aesthetics, and styles. He believed art enjoys a form of autonomy and cannot be interpreted using social, economic, and political criteria.

Burckhardt pursued history through the eyes of an art historian, art history through the eyes of a theologian, and the history of religion through the eyes of an historian. For him, cultural history is intellectual history, or the history of the spirit of a culture. Not surprisingly, the individual, as it emerged in the age of the Italian Renaissance, appears as the major factor in the development of culture. The historian must therefore examine all aspects of daily life, in particular literature, arts, religion, the state, the educational system, festivities, and morality. The individual, Burckhardt's prime object of study, reflects the totality of society. The historian's purpose, then, is to trace the development of humanity as it is expressed through both the visible and the invisible, i.e. the factual and the spiritual world. Although this contradicts the search for the individual, Burckhardt was convinced that great men and women determine the course of history and lead to humankind's *telos*.

Burckhardt writes succinct and carefully crafted sentences, and successfully conveys his opinions and conclusions to his readers. His writings and lectures were especially aimed for the enlightenment of the public, without losing the quality of academic scholarship. With his publications he targeted the thinking reader, those among his audience who could enjoy true beauty and the teachings of the past.

ALBRECHT CLASSEN

Biography

Born 25 May 1818 in Basle. Studied theology at the University of Basle, 1836–39; history and the history of art under **Leopold von Ranke**, University of Berlin, 1841–43. Editor, *Baseler Zeitung*, 1844–45. Visited Italy, 1846. Revised and edited the *Geschichte der Malerei* (History of painting) and the *Handbuch der Kunstgeschichte* (Handbook of art history) by his teacher Franz Kugler, 1847. Taught at the Pädagogium, Basle, 1848, and at the Polytechnic Institute, Zurich, 1855; chair of history and art history, University of Basle, 1858–93. Rejected offer to succeed von Ranke as chair of history, University of Berlin. Died in Basle, 8 August 1897.

Selected Writings

Essays and Related Prose

Die Kunstwerke der belgischen Städte, 1842; in *Frühe Schriften*, edited by Hans Trog and Emil Dürr, 1930
Griechische Kulturgeschichte (lecture course), edited by Jacob Oeri, 4 vols., 1898–1902, and Rudolf Marx, 3 vols., 1952; abridged version as *History of Greek Culture*, translated by Palmer Hilty, 1963
Weltgeschichtliche Betrachtungen, edited by Jacob Oeri, 1905, Rudolf Stadelmann, 1949, Rudolf Marx, 1955, and (with *Über das Studium der Geschichte*), Peter Ganz, 1982; as *Force and Freedom: Reflections on History*, edited and translated by James Hastings Nichols, 1943; as *Reflections on History*, translated by M. D. H., 1943
Vorträge, 1844–1887, edited by Emil Dürr, 1918
Unbekannte Aufsätze . . . aus Paris, Rom und Mailand, edited by Josef Oswald, 1922
Historische Fragmente (vol. 7 of his *Gesamtausgabe*), 1929; as *Judgements on History and Historians*, translated by Harry Zohn, 1958
Weisheit aus der Geschichte, edited by Otto Heuschele, 1968
Die Kunst der Betrachtung: Aufsätze und Vorträge zur bildenden Kunst, edited by Henning Ritter, 1984

Other writings: works on the history of art (including *Die Zeit Constantins des Grossen* [*The Age of Constantine the Great*], 1853; *Der Cicerone* [*The Cicerone; or, Art Guide to Painting in Italy*], 1855; *Die Kultur der Renaissance in Italien* [*The Civilization of the Renaissance in Italy*], 1860), poetry, and correspondence.

Collected works editions: *Gesamtausgabe*, edited by Hans Trog, Emil Dürr, and others, 14 vols., 1929–34; *Gesammelte Werke*, 10 vols., 1955–59.

Further Reading

Flaig, Egon, *Angeschaute Geschichte, zu Jacob Burckhardts "Griechische Kulturgeschichte"*, Rheinfelden: Schäuble, 1987
Gitermann, Valentin, *Jacob Burckhardt als politischer Denker*, Wiesbaden: Steiner, 1957
Hardtwig, Wolfgang, *Geschichtsschreibung zwischen Alteuropa und moderner Welt: Jacob Burckhardt in seiner Zeit*, Göttingen: Vandenhoeck & Ruprecht, 1974
Heftrich, Eckhard, *Hegel und Jacob Burckhardt: Zur Krisis der geschichtlichen Bewusstseins*, Frankfurt-on-Main: Klostermann, 1967

Jaeger, Friedrich, *Bürgerliche Modernisierungskrise und historische Sinnbildung: Kulturgeschichte bei Droysen, Burckhardt, und Max Weber*, Göttingen: Vandenhoeck & Ruprecht, 1994

Kaegi, Werner, *Jacob Burckhardt: Eine Biographie*, Basle: Schwabe, 8 vols., 1947–82

Maikuma, Yoshihiko, *Der Begriff der Kultur bei Warburg, Nietzsche und Burckhardt*, Königstein/Ts.: Hain, 1985

Siebert, Irmgard, Introduction to *Aesthetik der bildenden Kunst* by Burckhardt, Darmstadt: Wissenschaftliche Buchgesellschaft, 1992: 1–34

Winners, Richard, *Weltanschauung und Geschichtsauffassung Jakob Burckhardts*, Hildesheim: Gerstenberg, 1971 (original edition, 1929)

Burke, Edmund

Irish, 1729–1797

Edmund Burke's first published writings were **periodical essays** for the *Reformer*, a miscellany largely produced by Burke himself at the close of his undergraduate career at Trinity College, Dublin. In the very first paragraph of this paper, which ran to 13 numbers from January to April 1748, Burke asserts the link between taste and morals that underlies his writings for nearly 50 years: "the morals of a Nation have so great Dependance on their taste and Writings, that the fixing the latter, seems the first and surest Method of establishing the former."

In 1758 a more significant opportunity opened for him in London as editor of the *Annual Register*. Burke wrote the *Register*'s original articles singlehandedly until at least 1764. This job had three main consequences for his later writings and speeches. The *Annual Register* reprinted a broad variety of historical, scientific, antiquarian, and literary research, whose scope is later revealed in Burke's wide-ranging imagery, diction, and general knowledge. Second, the ideas he expressed in his book reviews developed into longstanding principles which guided his entire life. In 1759 he criticized **Rousseau**'s "satire on civilized society," for instance, because it would "unsettle our notions of right and wrong." He returns to this theme in the *Letter to a Member of the National Assembly* (1791), where he charges that Rousseau's "paradoxical morality ... led directly" to the cultural revolution that preceded the French Revolution.

Most important, the *Annual Register*'s long historical articles, broken up into essay-length **chapters**, gave Burke practice in making historical exposition interesting to his audience. In these early articles, he experiments with combining extensive knowledge of the events of the year – from the military operations of the Seven Years' War to the conquests of the East India Company – with the strategic significance of any given event and an estimate of the characters of the persons involved. Burke refines and expands this combination of data, character, and underlying historical significance into the powerful rhetoric of his later political writings. It is a logical development from Burke's ironic description of English "astonishment and indignation at finding that an Asiatic prince of their own creation had dared to be a sovereign" (1764) to his bitter sarcasm at the end of Warren Hastings' trial, where he casts Hastings as Macbeth: "'Thou has it now, King, Cawdor, Glamis, all'" (1794).

In Burke's writings, definitions and principles arise out of example and experience, rather than vice versa. Even in the very theoretical "Introduction on Taste" (1759) to his *A Philosophical Enquiry into ... the Sublime and Beautiful*, Burke argues that the definition of taste "seems rather to follow than to precede our enquiry ..." While he does define taste, he contrasts his inquiry with one based on "naked reason." The one work where Burke proceeds strictly from propositions to conclusions (*A Vindication of Natural Society*, 1756) is a **satire** – undetected by some – on the Enlightenment notion that unaided human reason can establish secure foundations for society, apart from custom and historical precedent.

While the "Introduction on Taste" is sometimes called an "essay," Burke himself used that term in only one title, "An Essay Toward an Abridgement of English History" (wr. 1756–57, pub. 1812). Only a few sheets of this work, which runs to over 200 pages, were published in Burke's lifetime. The work is an "essay" in the literal sense of an attempt to account for the growth of the British Constitution, as Burke describes **David Hume**'s *History of Great Britain*. Many of his later themes – such as the significance of manners and the historical context for the growth of practical liberty – are found here. Burke probably abandoned it in 1757 because he could not produce a history that would both surpass Hume's work and satisfy his high expectations of what he should do for his audience and for his own integrity. That balance, between Burke's self-imposed task and his relation to his audience, is present in all of his writings, from the speeches he prepared for publication as an M.P., to the open **letters** he wrote after his exile from the Whig Party, through the memos he penned for the eyes of William Pitt.

For Burke, it was not enough to introduce his audience to the proper principles of politics: like many essayists of the 18th century, he felt he was educating his readers' taste. While he could admit the brilliance of Rousseau, therefore, he simultaneously dismisses him as "totally destitute of taste in any sense of the word." Burke's theatrical, highly charged rhetoric reflects his union of an educated taste with an educated moral and political intelligence. For instance, his *Reflections on the Revolution in France* (1790) describes the fall of Marie Antoinette in the terms of Aristotle on tragedy ("what a heart must I have to contemplate without emotion that elevation and that fall"), then employs Horace's **Poetic Art** in a critique of the French revolutionaries' political system: "The precept given by a wise man as well as a great critic, for the construction of poems, is equally true as to states: *Non satis est pulchra esse poemata, dulcia sunto ...* To make us love our country, our country ought to be lovely."

The **aphorism** at the end of this quotation brings up another striking element of Burke's style. Like English essayists from **Francis Bacon** through **Samuel Johnson**, Burke often distills his analysis of history and character into single moments of jewel-like precision, balance, and beauty. For instance, his response to the exponents of natural rights – "art is man's nature" – arises from a historical and biographical exposition of the controversies surrounding the Revolution of 1688 (*An Appeal from the New, to the Old Whigs*, 1791). Similarly, his description of the French political situation in 1791 concludes thus: "It is ordained in the eternal constitution of things, that men of intemperate minds cannot be free. Their passions forge their fetters" (*Letter to a Member of the National Assembly*). Here, as often, Burke's prose is simultaneously aphoristic, alliterative, and self-consciously rhythmic.

Like many **science** and **philosophical essay**ists of his century, Burke frequently appeals to experience. Yet he is often self-consciously opposed to the Enlightenment. He sees habit, custom, tradition, and even prejudice as more reliable guides than "the naked reason." For writers, politicians, philosophers, and historians who have sought an alternative to the purely rationalistic and anti-traditionalist strands of the Enlightenment, Burke's writings have proven useful for over 200 years.

DANIEL E. RITCHIE

Biography
Born 12 January 1729 in Dublin. Studied at Abraham Shackleton's Quaker school, Ballitore, County Kildare, 1741–43; Trinity College, Dublin, 1744–48, A.B., 1748; editor, the *Reformer*, 1748; entered the Middle Temple, London, 1750; left law for literary work, 1755. Married Jane Nugent, 1757: two sons (one died in youth). Editor, 1758–66, and contributor, until 1788, *Annual Register*, London. Private secretary to William Gerard Hamilton, 1759–64, accompanying him to Ireland, 1763–64, and receiving a pension on Hamilton's retirement, 1764. Whig Member of Parliament for Wendover, 1765–74, Bristol, 1774–80, and Malton, Yorkshire, 1781–94: active, contentious M.P., opposing Tory government, advocating economic reform, peace with the American colonies, and the limitation of slave trade. Private secretary to the Marquis of Rockingham, 1765; paymaster-general of the Forces in the new Whig government, under Rockingham, 1782, and Portland, 1783, but never given a cabinet post; quarreled with Fox and the Whigs, 1791, and advised support for Pitt and the Tories, 1792; retired from Parliament, and granted government pension, 1794. Member of Samuel Johnson's literary Club, from 1764. Rector, University of Glasgow, 1784, 1785. Awards: honorary degree from Dublin University, 1791. Died (of stomach cancer) at his Beaconsfield estate, Buckinghamshire, 9 July 1797.

Selected Writings

Essays and Related Prose
The Reformer (periodical), 13 nos., 28 January–21 April 1748
A Vindication of Natural Society, 1756; edited by Frank N. Pagano, 1982
A Philosophical Enquiry into the Origin of Our Ideas of the Sublime and Beautiful, 1757; revised edition, 1759; edited by James T. Boulton, 1958, revised 1987, and Adam Phillips, 1990
Reflections on the Revolution in France, 1790; edited by Conor Cruise O'Brien, 1969, J. G. A. Pocock, 1987, and L. G. Mitchell, 1993
Letter to a Member of the National Assembly, in Answer to Some Objections to His Book on French Affairs, 1791; facsimile reprint, 1990
An Appeal from the New, to the Old Whigs, in Consequence of Some Late Discussions in Parliament, Relative to the Reflections on the French Revolution, 1791
Thoughts on the Prospect of a Regicide Peace, 1796
Three Memorials on French Affairs, 1797
Select Works, edited by E. J. Payne, 5 vols., 1874–78
A Note-Book of Edmund Burke: Poems, Characters, Essays and Other Sketches, edited by Henry V. F. Somerset, 1957
Selected Writings and Speeches, edited by Peter J. Stanlis, 1963
On Government, Politics and Society, edited by B. W. Hill, 1975
The Political Philosophy, edited by Iain Hampsher-Monk, 1987
Pre-Revolutionary Writings, edited by Ian Harris, 1993

Other writings: works on history and politics, reports, speeches, and correspondence (collected in *The Correspondence*, edited by Thomas W. Copeland and others, 10 vols., 1958–78).

Collected works editions: *Works*, edited by French Laurence and Walker King, 8 vols., 1792–1827; *The Works of the Right Honourable Edmund Burke*, 9 vols., 1854–62; *The Writings and Speeches* (Clarendon Edition), general editor Paul Langford, 1981– (in progress; 12 vols. projected).

Bibliographies
Cowie, Leonard W., *Edmund Burke, 1729–1797: A Bibliography*, Westport, Connecticut: Greenwood Press, 1994
Gandy, Clara I., and Peter J. Stanlis, *Edmund Burke: A Bibliography of Secondary Studies to 1982*, New York: Garland, 1983
Todd, William B., *A Bibliography of Edmund Burke*, Godalming, Surrey: St. Paul's Bibliographies, 1982 (original edition, 1964)

Further Reading
Blakemore, Steven, *Burke and the Fall of Language: The French Revolution as Linguistic Event*, Hanover, New Hampshire: University Press of New England, 1988
Boulton, James T., *The Language of Politics in the Age of Wilkes and Burke*, London: Routledge and Kegan Paul, 1963
Canavan, Francis, *The Political Reason of Edmund Burke*, Durham, North Carolina: Duke University Press, 1960
Chapman, Gerald W., *Edmund Burke: The Practical Imagination*, Cambridge, Massachusetts: Harvard University Press, 1967
Cone, Carl B., *Burke and the Nature of Politics*, Lexington: University of Kentucky Press, 2 vols., 1957–64
Copeland, Thomas W., *Our Eminent Friend: Edmund Burke*, Westport, Connecticut: Greenwood Press, 1970 (original edition, 1949)
Gengembre, Gérard, "Burke," in *A Critical Dictionary of the French Revolution*, edited by François Furet and Mona Ozouf, Cambridge, Massachusetts: Harvard University Press, 1989 (original French edition, 1988)
Janes, Regina, "Edmund Burke's Flying Leap from India to France," *History of European Ideas* 7 (1986): 509–27
Kirk, Russell, "Burke and the Politics of Prescription," in his *The Conservative Mind*, Washington, D.C.: Regnery, 1986 (original edition, 1953)
Mansfield, Harvey, *Statesmanship and Party Government: A Study of Burke and Bolingbroke*, Chicago: University of Chicago Press, 1965
O'Brien, Conor Cruise, *The Great Melody: A Thematic Biography and Commented Anthology of Edmund Burke*, Chicago: University of Chicago Press, and London: Sinclair Stevenson, 1992
Parkin, Charles, *The Moral Basis of Burke's Political Thought*, Cambridge: Cambridge University Press, 1956
Paulson, Ronald, "Burke's Sublime and the Representation of Revolution," in *Culture and Politics from Puritanism to the Enlightenment*, edited by Perez Zagorin, Berkeley: University of California Press, 1980
Pocock, J. G. A., "Burke and the Ancient Constitution," in his *Politics, Language, and Time: Essays on Political Thought and History*, New York: Atheneum, 1971; London: Methuen, 1972
Reid, Christopher, *Edmund Burke and the Practice of Political Writing*, Dublin: Gill and Macmillan, 1985
Stanlis, Peter, *Edmund Burke and the Natural Law*, Ann Arbor: University of Michigan Press, 1958
Weinsheimer, Joel, "Burke's Reflections: On Imitation as Prejudice," *Southern Humanities Review* 16 (1982): 223–32
Weston, John C., "Edmund Burke's View of History," *Review of Politics* 23 (1961): 203–29

White, James Boyd, "Making a Public World," in his *When Words Lose Their Meaning: Constitutions and Reconstitutions of Language, Character and Community*, Chicago: University of Chicago Press, 1984

Wilkins, Burleigh Taylor, *The Problem of Burke's Political Philosophy*, Oxford: Clarendon Press, 1967

Burke, Kenneth

American, 1897–1993

A poet, novelist, and short story writer, Kenneth Burke is best known as one of the most important literary critics and rhetoricians of the 20th century. His essays and **reviews** encompass a range of subjects from aesthetics and music to anthropology and sociology, and have been influential in areas such as linguistics, communication theory, semiotics, and composition studies. In recent years, Burke's reputation has grown exponentially as his insights and ideas have been rediscovered and applied in a variety of fields.

Burke was first published in the avant-garde magazines of the 1920s, such as *Broom* and the *Dial*. In the 1930s, the major outlets for his essays, book and music reviews were the *Nation* and the *New Republic*, magazines that reached a larger general audience. By the 1940s, he had found an academic audience in the critical quarterlies and specialized publications. He began collecting his work in book form in 1931; many important essays, however, remain uncollected.

Stanley Edgar Hyman (1948), an early admirer of Burke, claimed that "Like Bacon, Burke has set out to do no less than to integrate all man's knowledge into one workable critical frame." Returning to the Baconian roots of the essay as a vehicle for investigation, Burke devoted his critical efforts to analyzing the effects that symbols, when elaborated into rhetorical systems – whether literary, philosophical, or social – have on human beings. He defined man as "the symbol-using animal" and literature as a variety of "symbolic action" ("Definition of Man," 1966). The use of language, moreover, is never disinterested, but always motivated; works of art, he stressed, are strategies for encompassing situations ("Literature as Equipment for Living," 1941). A poet, for example, might write a poem as a way of working out an oppressive sense of guilt (see "The Philosophy of Literary Form," 1941, on **Coleridge**). All texts, for Burke, are potential subjects for probing rhetorical analysis.

Burke's first collection of essays, *Counter-Statement* (1931), treated artists known for their aestheticism: **André Gide, Walter Pater**, Gustave Flaubert, **Remy de Gourmont**. Throughout these essays, Burke considers not only what each artist's work did for them, but also what it did for the audience they addressed – what "situations" the "strategies" encompassed. Many of Burke's most memorable **aphorisms** are found here: "Beauty is the term we apply to the poet's success in evoking our emotions" ("The Poetic Process") or "An art may be of value purely through preventing a society from becoming too assertively, too hopelessly, itself" ("Thomas Mann and André Gide").

In the shadow of the Depression, Burke began to stress "Literature as Equipment for Living." That essay, and others collected in *The Philosophy of Literary Form* (1941), treat "a *sociological* criticism of literature." In "The Rhetoric of Hitler's Battle," for example, Burke analyzes how *Mein Kampf* helped "unify" the German people by offering Hitler's "strategy for encompassing a situation" – finding a scapegoat for his own persecution mania – as a "world-view" they might adopt.

Books such as *Permanence and Change* (1935) and *Attitudes Toward History* (1937) explore symbolic action in such areas as magic, ritual, history, and religion, while *A Grammar of Motives* (1945) and *A Rhetoric of Motives* (1950) work out what Burke calls the "dramatistic" basis of all symbolic action. He argues that "any complete statement about motives will offer *some kind* of answers to these five questions: what was done (act), when or where it was done (scene), who did it (agent), how he did it (agency), and why (purpose)" (*A Grammar of Motives*).

Burke's last major collection, *Language as Symbolic Action* (1966), contains "Five Summarizing Essays," including his "Definition of Man." In elaborate "dramatistic" analyses of several plays by Shakespeare, **Goethe**'s *Faust*, Coleridge's "Kubla Khan," and **Emerson**'s *Nature*, Burke displays the strengths and weaknesses of his style and methods. The essays are, as usual, provocative and surprising, but the style could be seen as abstract, often obscure, repetitive, and too much in debt to Burke's own terminology. Critics have seized on such phrases as "Where, then, are we?" as evidence of the author's Byzantine elaboration. Burke's prose, like Bacon's, is at its most resonant when it is most aphoristic, e.g. "The poet, in his pious or tragic role, would immunize us by stylistically infecting us with his disease" ("The Philosophy of Literary Form").

Burke once wrote, "The main ideal of criticism, as I conceive it, is to use all that there is to use" ("The Philosophy of Literary Form"). As modern criticism moves away from an exclusively text-centered study to engage all forms of human behavior – "symbolic actions" – Burke has come increasingly to be seen as a central figure. His essays provoke, inspire, even infuriate. Burke has become, according to the critic Denis Donoghue (in the *New York Review of Books*, 26 September 1985), an American "sage."

CHARLES L. O'NEILL

Biography

Kenneth Duva Burke. Born 5 May 1897 in Pittsburgh, Pennsylvania. Studied at Ohio State University, Columbus, 1916–17; Columbia University, New York, 1917–18. Married Lillian Mary Batterham, 1919 (divorced, early 1930s): three daughters. Coeditor, *Secession*, 1923; member of the research staff, Laura Spelman Rockefeller Memorial, New York, 1926–27; music critic, *Dial*, 1927–29, and the *Nation*, 1934–36; editor, Bureau of Social Hygiene, New York, 1928–29. Married Elizabeth Batterham, 1933: two sons. Lectured and taught at various American colleges and universities, 1937–76. Awards: many, including several grants and fellowships; National Endowment for the Arts Award, 1968; Ingram Merrill Foundation Award, 1970; American Academy Gold Medal, 1975; American Academy of Arts and Sciences Award, 1977; National Medal for Literature, 1981; Bobst Award, 1983; honorary degrees from eight universities. Member, American Academy of Arts and Letters, and American Academy of Arts and Sciences. Died in Andover, New Jersey, 19 November 1993.

Selected Writings

Essays and Related Prose
Counter-Statement, 1931
Permanence and Change: An Anatomy of Purpose, 1935
Attitudes Toward History, 1937
The Philosophy of Literary Form: Studies in Symbolic Action, 1941; revised edition, 1957
A Grammar of Motives, 1945
A Rhetoric of Motives, 1950
The Rhetoric of Religion: Studies in Logology, 1961
Perspectives by Incongruity; Terms for Order, edited by Stanley Edgar Hyman and Barbara Karmiller, 1964
Language as Symbolic Action: Essays on Life, Literature and Method, 1966

Other writings: the novel *Towards a Better Life* (1932), poetry, short stories, and literary criticism. Also translated works from the German, including *Death in Venice* by **Thomas Mann** (1925).

Further Reading

Bewley, Marius, "Kenneth Burke as Literary Critic," in *The Complex Fate: Hawthorne, Henry James and Some Other American Writers*, London: Chatto and Windus, 1952; New York: Grove Press, 1954

Brown, Merle E., *Kenneth Burke*, Minneapolis: University of Minnesota Press, 1969

Crusius, Timothy, "A Case for Kenneth Burke's Dialectic and Rhetoric," *Philosophy and Rhetoric* 19, no. 1 (1986): 23–37

Duncan, Hugh Dalziel, *Language and Literature in Society: A Sociological Essay*, Chicago: University of Chicago Press, 1953

Duncan, Hugh Dalziel, *Communication and Social Order*, New York: Bedminster Press, 1962; London: Oxford University Press, 1968

Frank, Armin Paul, *Kenneth Burke*, New York: Twayne, 1969

Heath, Robert L., *Realism and Relativism: A Perspective on Kenneth Burke*, Macon, Georgia: Mercer University Press, 1986

Henderson, Greig E., *Kenneth Burke: Literature and Language as Symbolic Action*, Athens: University of Georgia Press, 1988

Holland, L. Virginia, *Counterpoint: Kenneth Burke and Aristotle's Theories of Rhetoric*, New York: Philosophical Library, 1959

Hyman, Stanley Edgar, "Kenneth Burke and the Criticism of Symbolic Action," in his *The Armed Vision*, New York: Knopf, 1948; revised edition, 1955

Knox, George, *Critical Moments: Kenneth Burke's Categories and Critiques*, Seattle: University of Washington Press, 1957

Lentricchia, Frank, *Criticism and Social Change*, Chicago: University of Chicago Press, 1983

Nemerov, Howard, "Everything, Preferably All at Once: Coming to Terms with Kenneth Burke," *Sewanee Review* 79 (April–June 1971): 189–205

Ransom, John Crowe, "An Address to Kenneth Burke," *Kenyon Review* 4 (Spring 1942): 219–37

Rueckert, William H., *Kenneth Burke and the Drama of Human Relations*, Berkeley and Los Angeles: University of California Press, 1982 (original edition, 1963)

Rueckert, William H., editor, *Critical Responses to Kenneth Burke, 1924–1966*, Minneapolis: University of Minnesota Press, 1969

Rueckert, William H., *Encounters with Kenneth Burke*, Urbana: University of Illinois Press, 1994

Southwell, Samuel B., *Kenneth Burke and Martin Heidegger – with a Note Against Deconstructionism*, Gainesville: University Presses of Florida, 1987

Wellek, René, "Kenneth Burke," in *A History of Modern Criticism, Volume 6: American Criticism, 1900–1950*, New Haven, Connecticut: Yale University Press, 1986

White, Hayden, and Margaret Brose, *Representing Kenneth Burke*, Baltimore: Johns Hopkins University Press, 1982

Burroughs, John

American, 1837–1921

During his lifetime the American nature writer John Burroughs achieved a fame which seemed somehow incongruent with the simplicity of his life and the quiet nature of his work. Growing up in the Catskill Mountains of New York State, "the son of a farmer who was the son of a farmer who was the son of a farmer," as he put it in his autobiography *My Boyhood* (1922), he lived simply all his life, and in his middle years returned to making part of his living from fruit and vegetable crops. He walked in nature with unceasing pleasure and perceptiveness, and wrote about it in informal, inviting, yet scientifically responsible essays. His work struck a chord with the public, and his lifetime work of some two dozen books went through many printings. He became the sought-out friend of famous men of the world, such as Henry Ford, Thomas Edison, and Theodore Roosevelt. More significantly, his writings on nature were placed in schools throughout the United States, and became the model through which children learned to observe and appreciate nature; some schools were even named after him.

Because of the tremendous popularity of Burroughs in his own time, and especially his friendships with leading figures of his day, his work was later either forgotten in the shadow of his celebrity, or its literary value underestimated. Either way, Burroughs the public figure seemed to shoulder aside Burroughs the writer. This is not what Burroughs himself would have wanted; his lifelong commitment to his writing for its own sake, and to the active engagement with nature which his writing urges, far outweighed his honest but sometimes ambivalent enjoyment of his fame. For Burroughs, his life was indeed inextricably mingled with his writing: "My books are, in a way, a record of my life – that part of it that came to flower and fruit in my mind. You could reconstruct my days pretty well from these volumes. A writer who gleans his literary harvest in the fields and woods reaps mainly where he has sown himself. He is a husbandman whose crop springs from the seed of his own heart" (*My Boyhood*).

The accomplishment of his writing, and its great contribution to American nature writing, is in the sunlit work itself, and in the wooded, bird-attended path it helped create for other writers. (Burroughs, sometimes known as "John-O'Birds," was more likely to lavish his sentences and paragraphs on a bird's song or its nest than on a "scenic view.") Fortunately, recent reassessments of Burroughs have accompanied a general revival of interest in nature writing, and his work is receiving new attention and appreciation. As a writer Burroughs was greatly influenced by the American transcendentalists, **Emerson** in particular. As Burroughs wrote of his first reading of Emerson: "I read him in a sort of ecstasy. I got him in my blood, and he colored my whole intellectual outlook. He appealed to my spiritual side; his boldness and unconventionality took a deep hold upon me." Throughout his writing, Burroughs continually returns to the "gospel of nature," finding spirituality there rather than in conventional religion. In his late work, *Accepting the Universe* (1920), Burroughs explores epistemological questions in a way that reflects both his transcendentalist roots and his interest in

Darwin and science. He writes, "I have never tried to clothe myself in the delusive garments of a superstitious age. I have ever pinned my faith to a man-made God, however venerable. I have opened my mind to the open air of the universe, to things as they are ..."

Burroughs' work also reveals strong ties to the American Romanticism of Walt Whitman, the close friend of his years in Washington, D.C. Burroughs wrote his first book about Whitman's work, and it was Whitman who helped him decide on the title of his first book of essays, *Wake-Robin* (1871). It is likely that the many hours and days spent with Whitman helped to nourish the generous, openhearted, and often lyrical spirit of Burroughs' own writing style.

Burroughs' approach to the **nature essay** was uniquely his own, and yet far more influential than is commonly realized. The writers who extolled the great vistas of the American West and the drama of wilderness explorations and adventures became the more celebrated examples of American nature writing as the 20th century developed. Yet Burroughs' more quiet and close-to-home approach to experiencing, enjoying, and writing about nature has gained renewed appreciation toward the end of the century. His essays are always close to human life, as well as to nature. They are artfully composed, though casual in style. The sensibility in his essays is a reliable one, which the reader can trust for the "science" of its observations, and for the friendliness of its invitations to participate, appreciate, respect, and enjoy. True essayist that he is, Burroughs builds his observations and interpretations at a comfortable pace, as if taking the reader on one of his countless walks. An observation is followed by interpretation, by further illustration and observation, until a new light of understanding seems to come over writer and reader at the same time. Burroughs trusts the reader to have reached that enlarged understanding with him, and typically does not belabor it in his conclusion. The essay will simply end – often with a graceful echo of the main topic, rather than a methodical reiteration. In "The Spring Bird Procession" (1919), for instance, Burroughs expresses his pleasure at the spring migration of birds, but dwells particularly on the lost pleasure of the great migrations of the now extinct passenger pigeon: "In my boyhood the vast armies of the passenger pigeons were one of the most notable spring tokens. Often late in March, or early in April, the naked beechwoods would suddenly become blue with them, and vocal with their soft, childlike calls." He describes the last great migration of pigeons he witnessed, concluding, "The pigeons never came back. Death and destruction, in the shape of the greed and cupidity of man, were on their trail." With typical forthrightness, he confesses to having killed the last passenger pigeon that he himself ever saw, "little dreaming that, so far as I was concerned, I was killing the last pigeon." He follows this with the rueful statement, "What man now in his old age who witnessed in youth that spring or fall festival and migration of the passenger pigeons would not hail it as one of the gladdest hours of his life if he could be permitted to witness it once more? It was such a spectacle of bounty, of joyous, copious animal life, of fertility in the air and in the wilderness, as to make the heart glad."

The essay might have ended here, but instead it goes on to describe the migrations of other bird species, and to speculate about their lives, closing many pages later with the description of purple finches stealing cherry blossoms from his orchard. After his alarm that they might ruin his crop, he discovered that "they had only done a little of the much-needed thinning. Out of a cluster of six or eight blossoms they seldom took more than two or three, as if they knew precisely what they were about, and were intent on rendering me a service." He does not spell out the contrast between the finches' considerate thinning of his cherry blossoms and the human "greed and cupidity" that drove the passenger pigeon to extinction, but leaves it to the reader to make the connection.

Burroughs is probably best known for his close observation of particular birds, plants, or animals. Yet, as his biographer Edward Renehan (1992) notes, "As an artist interpreting nature, Burroughs was never to become what he called 'a strict man of science.' He evolved not into a naturalist, *per se*, but into a new hybrid: a literary naturalist with a duty to record his own unique perceptions of the natural world. While remaining loyal to the truth of natural facts, he also remained true to his personal vision of these facts." His clearsightedness and free use of his own voice, expressing his delight in nature, are the elements of Burroughs' writing that have been most influential on later nature writers. In his essay "Sharp Eyes" (1879), Burroughs speculates:

> Noting how one eye seconds and reinforces the other, I have often amused myself by wondering what the effect would be if one could go on opening eye after eye to the number say of a dozen or more. What would he see? Perhaps not the invisible – not the odor of flowers or the fever germs in the air – not the infinitely small of the microscope nor the infinitely distant of the telescope ... We open another eye whenever we see beyond the first general features or outlines of things – whenever we grasp the special details and characteristic markings that this mask covers. Whenever you have learned to discriminate the birds, or the plants, or the geological features of a country, it is as if new and keener eyes were added.

CHARLOTTE ZOË WALKER

Biography

Born 3 April 1837 near Roxbury, New York. Grew up on a farm in the Catskill Mountains, New York. Taught in schools in New York, New Jersey, and Illinois, 1854–63; studied briefly at Hedding Literary Institute, Ashland, New York, and Cooperstown Seminary, 1856. Married Ursula North (died, 1917), 1857: one son. Contributor to various journals and newspapers, from 1860, including the *Atlantic Monthly*. Studied medicine privately, Tongore, New York, 1862. Moved to Washington, D.C., 1863, where he met and became lifelong friends with Walt Whitman. Clerk, 1864–72; special bank examiner, from 1873, Currency Bureau, Treasury Department. Traveled to England, 1871 and 1882. Bought a fruit farm on the Hudson River, West Park, New York, 1873, and built on it the house Riverby, living there from 1874, where he soon gave up office work to make his living through writing and farming; later built the cabin Slabsides, near Riverby, 1894, and renovated the farmhouse Woodchuck Lodge, near Roxbury, 1920. Became good friends with Theodore Roosevelt, Henry Ford, and fellow naturalist John Muir; accompanied Muir on a trip to Yosemite, and Roosevelt to Yellowstone National Park. Awards: American Institute of Arts and Letters Gold Medal, 1916; honorary degrees from three universities. Died on a train in Ohio (returning from California to New York State), 29 March 1921.

Selected Writings

Essays and Related Prose

Wake-Robin, 1871
Winter Sunshine, 1875; revised, enlarged edition, 1877
Birds and Poets, with Other Papers, 1877
Locusts and Wild Honey, 1879
Pepacton, 1881
Fresh Fields, 1884
Signs and Seasons, 1886
Sharp Eyes, and Other Papers, 1886
Birds and Bees, 1887
Indoor Studies, 1889
Riverby: Essays on Birds, Trees, and Prairies, 1894
A Bunch of Herbs, and Other Papers, 1896
The Light of Day, 1900
Literary Values, and Other Papers, 1902
Far and Near, 1904
The Complete Nature Writings, 9 vols., 1904–21
Ways of Nature, 1905
Leaf and Tendril, 1908
Time and Change, 1912
The Summit of the Years, 1913
The Wit of a Duck, and Other Papers, 1913
The Breath of Life, 1915
Under the Apple-Trees, 1916
Field and Study, 1919
Nature near Home and Other Papers, 1919
Accepting the Universe, 1920
Under the Maples, 1921
The Last Harvest, 1922
The Heart of John Burroughs's Journals, edited by Clara Barrus, 1928
John Burroughs's America (selections), edited by Julian Burroughs, 1951
The Birds of John Burroughs, edited by Jack Kligerman, 1976
A River View and Other Hudson Valley Essays, edited by Edward Renehan, 1981
A Sharp Lookout: Selected Nature Essays, edited by Frank Bergon, 1987
Birch Browsings: A John Burroughs Reader, edited by Bill McKibben, 1992

Other writings: the collection of poetry *Bird and Bough* (1906), a book about mammals (*Squirrels and Other Fur-Bearers*, 1900), *Camping with President Roosevelt* (1906; enlarged edition, as *Camping and Tramping with Roosevelt*, 1907), studies of Whitman (*Walt Whitman as Poet and Person*, 1867; *Walt Whitman*, 1896) and John James Audubon (1902), the autobiography *My Boyhood* (1922), and correspondence. Also edited *Songs of Nature* (1901), an anthology of nature poetry.

Collected works editions: *The Writings* (Riverside Edition), 23 vols., 1895–1922; Riverby Edition, 23 vols., 1904–23, reissued as the Wake-Robin Edition, 1924, 1968.

Bibliographies

Blanck, Jacob, "John Burroughs," in *Bibliography of American Literature*, vol. 1, New Haven, Connecticut: Yale University Press, 1955: 433–48
Garrison, Joseph M., Jr., "John Burroughs," *Bulletin of Bibliography* 24 (May–August 1964): 95–96

Further Reading

Kanze, Edward, *The World of John Burroughs*, New York: Abrams, 1993
Kelly, Elizabeth Burroughs, *John Burroughs, Naturalist: The Story of His Work and Family by His Granddaughter*, West Park, New York: Riverby Books, 1959
Renehan, Edward J., Jr., *John Burroughs, an American Naturalist*, Post Mills, Vermont: Chelsea Green, 1992
Walker, Charlotte Zoë, editor, *Sharp Eyes: John Burroughs and American Nature Writing: A Collection of Essays*, New York: Lang, 1997
Westbrook, Perry D., *John Burroughs*, New York: Twayne, 1974

Butler, Hubert

Irish, 1900–1991

Hubert Butler began publishing essays in the 1930s in Irish newspapers and literary magazines such as the *Bell*, the *Twentieth Century*, the *Irish Times*, and the *Dublin Magazine*. It seems extraordinary that, for whatever combination of personal, political, and literary reasons, his essays did not appear in book form until the Lilliput Press in Dublin published *Escape from the Anthill* (1985), *The Children of Drancy* (1988), and *Grandmother and Wolfe Tone* (1990). Penguin drew from these three for *The Sub-Prefect Should Have Held His Tongue and Other Essays* (1990). Butler's recent place as a major 20th-century essayist adds to the essay form the sort of late-emergence story that has occasionally marked undiscovered poets or fiction writers, except that Butler wrote and published essays for almost 60 years. His mature vitality (although many of the collected essays are decades old, they are frequently subject to revisions, additions, and epilogues) might be compared to Henry Roth and **M. F. K. Fisher** (who also had a vibrant autumnal output) in the United States.

Butler's essays have some of the epigrammatic force, allusive erudition, and philosophical range of **Montaigne**'s. As for his 20th-century generic compatriots, Butler moves into the personal and political in ways similar at times to **Virginia Woolf**, at others to **George Orwell**. Butler, Woolf, and Orwell also attend to moral conundrums and outrages on large and small scales, from the international, to the intranational, to the small but telling personal decisions that are symptomatic of cultural dis-ease and decline. All three share a balance of jeremiadical pessimism and small sparks of hope.

In "A Fragment of Autobiography" (1987), Butler strikes Orwellian notes, speaking respectively of his school days and his days at Oxford: "I remember all the shrubs between the pavvy and the swimming bath. Hundreds of episodes present themselves in heavy type. Everything else is in italics"; "Religion had become a subject, like Philosophy or Physics. You either took it or you didn't." Butler's attention to detail, image, and metaphor, and his demystifying sardonic nature has some of the flavor of Orwell's "Such, Such Were the Joys" (1953) or "England, Your England" (1953), as well as the tonal complexity that hedges bets against absolute pronouncement. Butler's voice, though, has a kind of lyrical crankiness distinctly his own in essays such as "Beside the Nore" (1984): "Various economic causes can be alleged for their [local industry's] failure but often there is nothing to be said except that men grow old and have bored or stupid sons and that today there are many prosperous industries which would be more admirable as ruins covered with valerian and wild wall flowers." In "Aunt Harriet" (1987), Butler curves back around toward his topic, following a typical digression, with a mixture of sentiment, self-effacement, and harsh but muted statement:

"I have left Aunt Harriet in her coffin a long way behind, but am thinking of the memories she took with her; they were all unimportant but the past is a mosaic of tiny pieces, a fragment of a larger picture, Ireland in the twenties and the last days of the Anglo Irish, and I will continue with more minutiae ... It is only because my elder relations are all dead and I am an old man now, soon to go into a box myself, that I can write like this. Perhaps I should for I have nothing interesting to relate, only what happened in my mind, and that is discreditable but not exciting."

Butler's range is wide, but certain subjects and themes dominate his essays: his experience in the Balkans and Russia in the 1930s, and in Vienna working to arrange exit visas for Jews in 1938–39, and the war's incomplete moral reckoning; his ancestral environs above the River Nore in the village of Bennettsbridge, County Kilkenny; telling moments in Irish history; the "troubles," along with his perspective on both his own Anglo-Irish and the Catholic cultures of Ireland; the impoverished role of religion in late modern life and values, from the failure of sectarian theology in Ireland to the capitulations of religious institutions to nationalist governments and human atrocity during the war; literary essays on writers from **Maria Edgeworth** (a relation) to **Graham Greene** (he writes memorably in "Graham Greene and Stephen Spender: The Sense of Evil and the Sense of Guilt," 1951: "They are inseparable in their dissent, like two sisters quarrelling in the family home. The one wants the front door locked in case there's a burglar, the other wants it ajar, in case there's a fire. Or so they say"); and more general "speculative" essays, as Butler called them.

Echoing **Auden**'s dark imperative at the end of "September, 1939," Butler frequently calls for realistic or pragmatic peace as a first step toward reconstructing human relations. In "Divided Loyalties" (1984) he writes, "Opposites often attract each other but the attraction seldom lasts if the full extent of the opposition is ignored. It is as neighbours, full of ineradicable prejudices, that we must love each other, not as fortuitously 'separated brethren.'" Butler often strikes the kind of Montaignean note of "Des cannibales" (1580; "Of Cannibals"), signaling as classical **personal essay**ists always have an ability to step outside of his own culture and find it not only flawed, but ridiculous, ludicrous even in the perpetuation of stagnant modes of thought and inscribed prejudices. In "The Auction" (1957), Butler tells us that "Living in social harmony is a most difficult art; the most absolute concentration is required, and perfect equilibrium. Our island is dangerously tilted towards England and towards Rome, good places in themselves but best seen on the level. Everybody is rolling off it and those that remain, struggling hard for a foothold, drag each other down. But it is not necessary to argue, it is only necessary to look."

In "Grandmother and Wolfe Tone" (1962) Butler displays his ability to shine the beacon of aphoristic humanism on the murky and intractable conflicts between Irish Catholic and Protestant: "No educated man now dares take up a cause till he has mastered 90 per cent of the facts and all the background ... There is only one way out, the way of Jefferson and Tone. In the North the Protestant Parliament for the Protestant people must go and in the South the separation of Church and State must be introduced and adhered to

absolutely." In "The Sub-Prefect Should Have Held His Tongue" (1956), perhaps Butler's most trenchant analysis of human iniquity married to historical revisionism and ignorance, he speaks specifically of the Catholic responsibility for the forced conversion of thousands of the Serbian Orthodox, including the following indictment of moral compromise and delusion: "In countries where the old beliefs are dying it is the custom for educated people to handle them with nostalgic reverence ... If you suppress a fact because it is awkward, you will next be asked to contradict it."

Two other essays from Butler's body of work must be singled out: "The Eggman and the Fairies" (1960) and "Little K" (1967). "The Eggman and the Fairies" is a riveting novelistic account of the barbaric attempt in 1895 to exorcise Bridget Cleary, committed by her husband and abetted by the active participation of friends and the indifference of almost all, in a town in the shadow of Slevenaman mountain, host to ancient natural beauty and persistent superstition. Butler's reconstruction and commentary are masterly, distinguished by a kind of shocked horror at the past mixed with restraint and a balance of sympathy. Butler ends the essay with another kind of mystery: the mystery of the missing eggman, the (fellow?) traveler Bridget Cleary claimed to have met on her not-so-mysterious excursion, and whom no one seemed to remember to inquire about.

"Little K" is one of Butler's longest and most complex essays, a personal lament for a retarded granddaughter (Little K), an ethical history of euthanasia, an accusation of the way an indifferent legal system has appropriated the prerogatives of family and community, and a somber judgment of Christianity. Speaking of Spartan eugenic practices, Butler writes, "All this is very shocking to Christians, if Christians have not forfeited their right to be shocked at such things by their connivance at Auschwitz and Hiroshima ... The gospels say that a darkness fell upon the earth when Christ was crucified and when a new era began. Surely the Silence of Pius [concerning the Nazis and their exterminations] has the same symbolic quality. It was mysterious and ominous, like the silence of woods and fields that precedes a total eclipse of the sun." The end of the essay, a stoical coda, typically combines the qualities of resignation and hope that make one wish Butler's voice in the wilderness had been more widely available earlier: "Maybe in ten or twenty years, as little K climbing very slowly has reached the highest rung she will ever reach, she will meet me there descending much more rapidly. If that were so, she would be the companion that I would choose above all others to travel back with me into nothingness."

DAVID LAZAR

Biography

Hubert Marshal Butler. Born 2 October 1900 in Kilkenny. Studied at Charterhouse, Godalming, Surrey; St. John's College, Oxford. Worked for county libraries movement in Ireland, 1922–23; lived and taught abroad, in Alexandria, Egypt, 1927, Latvia, 1930, Leningrad, 1931, and Zagreb, 1934–37; also traveled in Russia, China, America, and the Balkans. Married Peggy Guthrie, 1930: one daughter. Worked for a Quaker organization helping to obtain exit visas for Jews, Vienna, 1938–39. Returned to Ireland, 1941, when he inherited Maiden Hall country house in Bennettsbridge, near Kilkenny. Journalist, contributing to various newspapers and journals; review editor, the *Bell*, 1950. Revived the Kilkenny Archaeological Society, 1945. Awards: several literary prizes for his essay collections in the 1980s. Died near Kilkenny, 5 January 1991.

Selected Writings

Essays and Related Prose
Escape from the Anthill, 1985
The Children of Drancy, 1988
Grandmother and Wolfe Tone, 1990
The Sub-Prefect Should Have Held His Tongue and Other Essays, 1990

Other writings: a study of saints (1972). Also translated Leonov's *The Thief* (1931) and Chekhov's *The Cherry Orchard* (1934).

Further Reading

Longley, Edna, "'Defending Ireland's Soul': Protestant Writers and Irish Nationalism After Independence," in *Literature and Nationalism*, edited by Newey Vincent and Ann Thompson, Liverpool: Liverpool University Press, and Savage, Maryland: Barnes and Noble, 1991: 198–224

Butor, Michel

French, 1926–

The objective of Michel Butor's essays corresponds to the title *Répertoire* (5 vols., 1960–82), which refers to what is performed during a theater season (repertoire), as well as to the place of a discovery (repertory). Butor's essays are, in fact, the place of an intertextual discovery, not only because they offer a new interpretation of the canonic literary heritage, but also because they reveal the importance of literary and nonliterary traditions, including tales, popular novels, science fiction, travel sketches, and radio plays, all of which have been considered peripheral genres. His essays also explore the intertextual relationship between other artistic systems like music, painting, and literary discourse.

In the first two volumes of *Répertoire*, Butor expounds the program of the *nouveau roman* (new novel) in reviewing his own two novels, *Passage de Milan* (1954; Passage from Milan) and *L'Emploi du temps* (1956; *Passing Time*). It is not just explicit statements, but also the open structure of the essays that establish the character of the *nouveau roman*, a style of novel which Butor founded together with Nathalie Sarraute, Alain Robbe-Grillet, and Claude Simon. In accordance with the experimental conception of literature that emerged in France after World War II within the existentialist movement, Butor also rejects historical and biographical factors as determinants for the novel. His polyphonic writing prefigures the theory of intertextuality developed by Julia Kristeva and the group Tel Quel (As is), which conceives the subject of writing as the point of interconnection of other voices. The subject gets lost in the intricate net of memory and becomes incapable of dominating the outer world. As a result, the concept of author is abandoned. Not surprisingly, then, Butor emphasizes the temporality of the subject of writing. The decline of subject implies denying the mimetic power of narrative. Descriptions work independently from the observer, who is incapable of organizing them into a coherent representation of the world. Things thus appear "deanthropomorphized" and alien. Although descriptions are an invention of heterogeneous realms of the world, Butor nevertheless does not renounce reality. Literature becomes a phenomenological laboratory where the reflection of reality implies the self-reflection of writing. It is an intentional, metafictional (metadiscursive) elucidation of reality and at the same time a mystification of the narrator's ability to grasp it.

The heterogeneity of topics considered in the *Répertoire* volumes defines the status of literature itself, including all kinds of texts and re-creating the literary discourse as a dialogue between texts and media. In this way Butor transforms the concept of modern literature inherited from **Baudelaire** and **Mallarmé**. On the one hand, his essays intertwine narrative and essayistic discourses; on the other, his novels include metafictional considerations. With *Répertoire*, Butor dissolves the epistemological difference between fiction and nonfiction. Both are a global project theatricalizing the relationship between world and language. Butor's writings are a polyphonic network without center, whose purpose is the renovation of narrative through the destruction of the author as a subject dominating his own discourse. This implies refusing the mimetic status of narrative as well as the epistemological superiority of the narrator. Storytelling is a self-referential process ("mise en abîme") and a series of ruptures of the mimetic illusion. The narrator searches for past events through different stratifications of memory, temporality, and historicity, a labyrinthine confusion between the time of narration and the narrated time; this confusion effaces the narrator. In his commentary on his third novel (*La Modification* [1957; *A Change of Heart*]), Butor claims the necessity of an inner monologue in a sphere between the first and the third person beyond the dimension of human beings. Accordingly, in his novel *Degrés* (1960; *Degrees*), after the destruction of linearity and the integrity of the narrator, the latter becomes part of the narrated material, to whom a second narrator speaks in the second person.

In his *Essais sur "Les Essais"* (1968), a study on **Montaigne** and at the same time the definition of his own theory on essays, Butor underscores the reference to visual arts as the principle organizing the syntactic composition of the essays. As he points out, the architecture of Montaigne's essays corresponds to the composition of mannerist or baroque painting stressing grotesque heterogeneity. The centrifugal "montage" and the hybrid entourage around the central concern of the painting force the viewer to "travel" within the picture. This (cinematographic) "traveling" is the path toward building meaning as a result of the reading process. Butor illustrated this affinity between literature and visual arts (including film), which is a common concern of authors of the *nouveau roman*. The most important and original "invention" of Butor is the discovery of polyphony as a consequence of the death of the individual. Butor considers the individual an outdated historical narrative category from the 18th and 19th centuries, when individuals were established as heroes coping with the social world. Today, individuals must surrender themselves to the discursive network of the general memory of society.

VITTORIA BORSÒ

Biography

Michel Marie François Butor. Born 14 September 1926 in Mons-en-Barœul. Studied at the Collège Saint-François-de-Sales, Evreux, and Lycée Louis-le-Grand, Paris, 1936–44; the Sorbonne, Paris, 1945–49, licence in philosophy, 1946, diploma in philosophy, 1947. Taught at lycées in Sens, 1950, and El Minya, Egypt, 1950–51, University of Manchester, England, 1951–53, in Salonika, 1954–55, École Internationale, Geneva, 1956–57, Centre Universitaire, Vincennes, 1969, University of Nice, 1970–75, and the University of Geneva, from 1975; also visiting professor of French at several American universities and colleges, 1959–74. Advisory editor, Gallimard publishers, Paris, from 1958. Married Marie-Josèphe Mas, 1958: four daughters. Awards: Fénéon Prize, for novel, 1956; Renaudot Prize, for novel, 1957; Grand Prize for Literary Criticism, 1960. Chevalier, National Order of Merit.

Selected Writings

Essays and Related Prose

Répertoire, 5 vols., 1960–82
Une histoire extraordinaire: Essai sur un rêve de Baudelaire, 1961; as Histoire Extraordinaire: Essay on a Dream of Baudelaire's, translated anonymously, 1969
Mobile: Étude pour une représentation des États-Unis, 1962
Essais sur les modernes, 1964
Illustrations (includes poetry), 4 vols., 1964–76
Essais sur "Les Essais" (on Montaigne), 1968
Inventory: Essays (various translators), edited by Richard Howard, 1968
Essais sur le roman, 1969
Improvisations sur Flaubert, 1984
Improvisations sur Henri Michaux, 1985
Improvisations sur Rimbaud, 1989
Improvisations sur Michel Butor, l'écriture en transformation, 1993

Other writings: several novels (including Passage de Milan, 1954; L'Emploi du temps [Passing Time], 1956; La Modification [A Change of Heart], 1957; Degrés [Degrees], 1960), the opera Notre Faust (1962), five books about dreams, several collections of poetry, and works on art, culture, and many other topics.

Bibliography

Mason, Barbara, Michel Butor: A Checklist, London: Grant and Cutler, 1979

Further Reading

Godin, Georges, Michel Butor: Pédagogie, littérature, La Salle, Quebec: Hurtubise, 1987
Lancry, Yehuda, Michel Butor, ou, La Résistance, Paris: Lattès, 1994
Lydon, Mary, Perpetuum Mobile: A Study of the Novels and Aesthetics of Michel Butor, Edmonton: University of Alberta Press, 1980
Mason, Barbara, "Criticism and Invention in Michel Butor's Répertoire Series," New Zealand Journal of French Studies 1 (1986): 23–43
Roudiez, Leon S., Michel Butor, New York: Columbia University Press, 1965
Spencer, Michael, Michel Butor, New York: Twayne, 1974
Waelti-Walters, Jennifer, Michel Butor, Victoria, British Columbia: Sono Nis, 1977
Waelti-Walters, Jennifer, "Œuvres et critique: Les Répertoires," Œuvres et critiques: Michel Butor 2 (1985): 145–61
Waelti-Walters, Jennifer, Michel Butor (in French), Amsterdam and Atlanta: Rodopi, 1992
World Literature Today issue on Butor (Spring 1982)

C

Cadalso, José

Spanish, 1741–1782

The texts of José Cadalso exemplify the ambiguity in style, mood, and tension experienced in the second half of 18th-century Spain. Under the pseudonym "Dalmiro," Cadalso dedicated many verses to his Filis – was he the first Romantic writer in Spain? Was he one of the first politically charged writers of his time? Was he one of the first to demonstrate psychological development in his characters? All of these questions have concerned Cadalso's critics throughout the years. This troubled figure of the Spanish Enlightenment is an example of rational aesthetics combined with romantic desperation. During his relatively short life, he wrote drama, poetry, short fiction, and essays. As with many of his contemporaries, the strict lines of genre division do not apply to his texts. Thus, his *Cartas marruecas* (wr. 1789, pub. 1793; Moroccan letters), a work of fiction by his admission, can be classified as an essay, and *Los eruditos a la violeta* (1772; The pseudo-intellectuals), an essay satirizing the intellectual climate of the country, can also be classified as fiction.

In his texts Cadalso is able to create tension through differing points of view – what today we would call different voices – through internal dialogue as well as dialogue with contemporary 18th-century characters. In *Cartas marruecas*, a work that follows the 18th-century utopian tradition, three voices mirror ideological positions in society. Nuño Nuñez, a true Christian beloved by his contemporaries, lives incarcerated within himself. His tone is humorous and accepting of a society that cannot be changed. Gazel, the optimistic young African diplomat, becomes more pessimistic as the text develops. Ben-Beley, an old wise man, provides a philosophical view of the circumstances. The three complement one another in the portrayal of a bitter satire that questions the ideological foundation of Bourbon Spain. Using three different voices, Cadalso presents the reader of this text, as well as of his other essays, with the dilemma faced by the virtuous man – "el hombre de bien" – who is confronted with social evils. This triangular debate highlights one of the most controversial 18th-century polemics: that juxtaposing stoicism and Christianity.

In the tradition of **Seneca** and **Cicero**, as well as the Spanish classics, Cadalso reflects on several themes in his essays, debating issues such as virtue, moderation, human misery, and truth. Throughout the *Cartas*, Cadalso aspires to an impartiality in keeping with the scientific spirit of the Enlightenment. In line with other 18th-century essayists, his texts reveal a concern for Spain's industrial progress, economic stability, educational system, social and political reform, and human welfare.

If in *Cartas marruecas* Cadalso presents the reader with philosophical debates in his satire, in *Eruditos a la violeta* his satire is more caustic toward the frivolity of appearances as opposed to well-educated "cultured" people. The stoic, ascetic criticism found in *Cartas* is replaced by a lighthearted, humorous parody of social conditions and daily customs. More in the tradition of Padre Isla's *Fray Gerundio* (1787), Cadalso presents a method for educating Spain's idle elite so that they will succeed within the superficiality of manners imposed by society.

When considering the context in which Cadalso lived and wrote, his essays become more cohesive. In all of his texts, whether philosophical, humorous, satirical, or political, Cadalso questions the ability of mortals to survive in a world governed by rational laws. The rules of the Enlightenment that permeated Spanish society in his time also presented a great opportunity for hypocrisy in a society concerned with appearances. Critics have pointed to the fragmentation exhibited by 18th-century essayists in facing, debating, and theorizing about issues of "heart" and "mind." In Spain, Cadalso's essays best exemplify this fragmentation and basic skepticism toward rationality while at the same time creating a world that rejects sentimentalism.

Current Cadalso criticism has focused on the epistemology of madness (Paul Ilie, 1986), which can be seen in the fragmentation of discourse more than in thematic development. This more recent reading of the 18th-century essayist may provide more insights into the discursive fragmentation that mirrors philosophical and thematic issues in Bourbon Spain. The complexity of Cadalso's essays, in terms of both rhetoric and theme, indicates a talented observer of society. His constant struggle between optimism and pessimism, reason and emotion, reform and restoration serves to highlight his genius. Through his essays, the 20th-century reader may glimpse the complexity of Spain's French century and the psychological implications of reform and enlightenment. Cadalso's essays present us with one of the best examples of the beginning of modernity: the idea of moving toward a more positive future – the idea of progress.

CARMEN CHAVES TESSER

Biography

José Juan Antonio Ignacio Francisco de Borja de Cadalso. Born 8 October 1741 in Cádiz. Studied at Jesuit schools in Cádiz, Paris, 1750–54, and the Royal Seminary for Nobles, Madrid, 1758–60. Traveled in Europe, 1755–58 and 1760–62. Military career: enlisted for the Portuguese campaign, 1762; made knight of Santiago, 1766. Banished from Madrid under suspicion of writing *Calendario manual*, which was critical of Madrid customs, 1768, and lived in Aragón, 1768–70. Liaison with the actress María Ignacia Ibáñez (died, 1771). Attended *tertulias* (literary gatherings) at San Sebastián Inn, Madrid, 1772. Lived in Salamanca, 1773–74. Made colonel shortly before his death. Killed at the siege of Gibraltar, 26 February 1782.

Selected Writings

Essays and Related Prose

Los eruditos a la violeta, 1772; edited by Nigel Glendinning, 1967, and José Luis Aguirre, 1967
Suplemento al Los eruditos a la violeta, 1772
El buen militar a la violeta, 1790
Cartas marruecas, 1793; edited by Juan Tamayo y Rubio, 1935 (revised 1953), Lucien Dupuis and Nigel Glendinning, 1966, José Sánchez Reboredo, 1978, Aurora Cruzado Díaz, 1984, Manuel Camarero, 1984, Francisco Alonso, 1985, Salvador Sole Camps and José Palomar Ros, 1986, Mariano Baquero Goyanes, 1988, José Miguel Caso González, 1989, Rogelio Reyes Cano, 1989, and Joaquín Arce, 1993

Other writings: the fiction *Noches lúgubres* (1792), plays, poetry, and autobiography.

Collected works edition: *Obras*, 3 vols., 1818.

Further Reading

Barnette, Linda-Jane, "Male-Female Relationships in Cadalso's Prose: Distancing Techniques," in *Selected Proceedings of the Thirty-Eighth Annual Mountain Interstate Foreign Language Conference*, edited by Sixto E. Torres and Carl S. King, Clemson, South Carolina: Clemson University Press, 1991
Coloquio internacional sobre José Cadalso, Abano Terme, Italy: Piovan, 1985
Cuadernos Hispanoamericanos issue on Cadalso, 389 (1982)
Edwards, June K., *Tres imágenes de José Cadalso: El crítico, el moralista, el creador*, Seville: University of Seville, 1976
Glendinning, Nigel, *Vida y obra de Cadalso*, Madrid: Gredos, 1962
Goldman, Peter B., "What's in a Word? 'Class' and Its Evolution in the Eighteenth Century," *Romance Quarterly* 39, no. 1 (February 1992): 7–16
Ilie, Paul, "Cadalso and the Epistemology of Madness," *Dieciocho* 9, nos. 1–2 (1986): 174–87
Moreno Hernandez, Carlos, "Cadalso y Larra: El fracaso del hombre de bien," *Cuadernos de Investigación Filológica* 12–13 (May–December 1987): 45–68
Sebold, Russell P., *Colonel Don José Cadalso*, New York: Twayne, 1971

Călinescu, George

Romanian, 1899–1965

The impressive variety of George Călinescu's essayistic output has a distinct place in 20th-century Romanian literature. The essay is protean, impressionistic, and artificial in the oeuvre of this most famous and controversial literary critic, also a noted novelist and a well-known playwright, poet, and translator. His essays elude classical definitions of the genre, but neither do they impose a new definition. These "impure" essays often extend over the borders into the literary **review**, the **treatise**, and the monograph. Often contradicting himself, Călinescu ranges from extreme congeniality and playfulness (e.g. "Domina bona" [1946], on I. L. Cararagiale's plays), to pedantic, outright misunderstanding (e.g. his interpretation of Ion Barbu's "Mallarméan" poetry). Pedantry brands many of Călinescu's essays during his later years (after Romania came within the zone of Soviet influence), when he shifted his attention to opportunistic issues, writing admiring essays on socialist-realist authors and using lukewarm **satire** against the weaknesses of the petty bourgeoisie. Throughout his career, however, Călinescu's writing is always agile, exploiting the powers of **aphorism** and metaphor. If, at times, the attitude of the critic is unreasonable, the style is always recognizable, with passages of imposing beauty.

After translating into Romanian many Italian writers, as well as Horace, Laurence Sterne, and Hans Jacob Christoffel von Grimmelshausen, and having determined his priorities ("I never read a book: I translated it . . . When I judge, I create . . . I had to be a bad poet in order to become a just critic," *Ulysse*, 1967), Călinescu set out to analyze the life and works of Mihai Eminescu, the "national poet" whose legacy was to become intertwined with Călinescu. The mythological aura of this last European Romantic touched Călinescu, who came to be called, in the Romania of the 1970s and 1980s, "the divine critic."

Călinescu's vocation was that of a builder (expressed especially in his 1953 novel *Bietul Ioanide* [Poor Ioanide]), who dreams of transforming the Balkanic city of Bucharest into a majestic metropolis with imposing monuments and vast plazas. The grandiose – Călinescu's mode of choice – is advocated by his essays in ways unprecedented in Romanian culture. The inspiration from both the urban utopias of the Italian Renaissance and his own whim accounts for his fetish of the monumental. Some of Călinescu's most influential essays follow in the same grandiose vein. His 1941 *Istoria literaturii române de la origini pînă în prezent* (History of Romanian Literature) is conceived as collection of historical essays on authors and periods written with verve, little objectivity, and in the highly personal style characteristic of Călinescu's criticism. The monumental *History* (over 1000 pages in folio) concludes with a powerful and controversial *mise en abîme* of the entire history of Romanian literature, an essay entitled "Specificul național" ("The National Specificity"), in which Călinescu articulates a geo-national and racial theory of his personal reading of this history.

A sense of classicism pervades much of Călinescu's late output. *Impresii asupra literaturii spaniole* (1946; On Spanish literature: impressions), a collection of essays on Spanish and comparative literature, begins with his influential "Clasicism, romantism, baroc" (Classicism, Romanticism, Baroque), in which the essayist analyzes the opposition between classicism and Romanticism viewed as ideal types: the classical is healthy and well balanced, while the Romantic is abnormal, exceptional, unbalanced, and "sick."

Călinescu finds that friendship, proper to French neoclassicism and to such 19th-century Romanian writers as Vasile Alecsandri, Mihail Kogălniceanu, Costache Negruzzi, Ion

Ghica, Titu Maiorescu, and Ioan Slavici, fades rapidly in the first decades of the 20th century (*Ulysse*). The classical mind is indifferent to events, rather than being absorbed by them. According to Călinescu, modern Romanian culture presents a monochromatic interest in the event, which is sanctioned as the non-negotiable truth of the past and dealt with in the form of the novel. The typically novelistic character is driven by primary instincts, accompanied by a twisted consciousness and complex overinterpretive techniques. The classical is to be seen in the abolition of the genius, reduction of the biographical, of the inner diary. Accompanying his taste for nationally oriented traditionalism is Călinescu's view on the the classicism of the *Volk* (people), whose imposing anonymity and objectivity destroy personal invention and discard claims to creative subjectivity.

Any great writer is, ultimately, a classic, a dispassionate "peripathetician" in dialogue with his friends. The classic writer attains universality, gives **apothegm**atic, "architectural" formulations, and "builds solid bodies." Călinescu's self-assured attack on the French aphoristic writings of the exiled Romanian writer **E. M. Cioran**, at the time a *persona non grata* in Romania, depends heavily on metaphor to demonstrate "the banality of Cioran's aphorisms" in a heavy-handed dismissal of the "failed architectonic function of Cioran's aphorisms."

Călinescu's fidgety essayistic production reveals an author unable to abstain from writing or tame his desire for glory. It is hard to find a week, between 1930 and his death 35 years later, in which Călinescu's name did not appear in print. His ridiculing satires against the Orthodox poets obsessed with the angels of the late 1920s and 1930s, and his dislike of quiet understatement, made him into a champion of the overblown. In a crucial reversal of the Montaignean legacy of the genre, Călinescu's essays resist both radical self-questioning and the appetite for silence.

CĂLIN-ANDREI MIHĂILESCU

Biography

Born 19 June 1899 in Bucharest. Studied philosophy at the University of Bucharest, from 1918; University of Jassy, Ph.D., 1936. Taught at the Romanian School, Rome, 1923–26, and French and Italian in Bucharest, 1926–35. Contributor to various journals, from 1926; coeditor, *Viaţa Românească* (Romanian life), 1927–36. Married Alice Vera Trifu, 1929. Member of the Faculty of Letters, University of Jassy, 1937–45. Founder, *Jurnalul Literar* (Literary journal), 1939. Chair of Romanian literature, University of Bucharest, from 1945. Editor, *Lumea* (The world), 1945–46, and *Naţiunea* (The nation), 1946–49. Elected to the Romanian Academy, 1948. Director, Institute of the History of Literature and Folklore, from 1948. Awards: Romanian National Prize, 1964. Died in Bucharest, 12 March 1965.

Selected Writings

Essays and Related Prose

Opera lui Mihaai Eminescu, 5 vols., 1934–36
Principii de estetică, 1939; edited by Alexandru Piru, 1974
Istoria literaturii române de la origini pînă în prezent, 1941; revised edition, edited by Alexandru Piru, 1982; as *History of Romanian Literature*, translated by Leon Levitchi, 1989
Impresii asupra literaturii spaniole, 1946; part in *Studies in Poetics*, translated by Andrei Bantaş and Anda Teodorescu, 1972

Studii şi conferinte Horaţiu, Tasso, Cervantes, Tolstoi, Cehov, 1956
Cronicile optimistului, Cu un cuvînt înainte al autorului, 1964
Studii şi cercetări de istorie literară, 1966
Studii şi comunicări, edited by Alexandru Piru, 1966
Ulysse, 1967
Scriitori străini, edited by Vasile Nicolescu and Adrian Marino, 1967
Scrieri despre artă, edited by George Muntean, 2 vols., 1968
Universul poeziei, edited by Alexandru Piru, 1971; part in *Studies in Poetics*, translated by Andrei Bantaş and Anda Teodorescu, 1972
Texte social-politice, 1944–1965, edited by Gheorghe Tuţui and Gheorghe Matei, 1971
Literatura nouă, edited by Alexandru Piru, 1972
Gîlceava înţeleptului cu lumea: Pseudojurnal de moralist, edited by G. Şerban, 2 vols., 1973–74
Mihai Eminescu: Studii şi articole, edited by Maria and Constantin Teodorovici, 1978
Aforisme şi reflecţii, edited by I. Pîrvănescu and Al. Stănciulescu-Birda, 1984
Însemnări şi polemice (selected essays), edited by Andrei Rusu, 1988
Cronici literare şi recenzii, edited by Andrei Rusu, 1991

Other writings: four novels (*Cartea nunţii*, 1933; *Enigma Otiliei*, 1938; *Bietul Ioanide*, 1953; *Scrinul negru*, 1960), plays (*Teatru*, 1956), poetry, and works on Romanian literature and writers (including a biography of Mihai Eminescu, 1932). Also translated many writers from the Italian.

Collected works edition: *Opere*, 14 vols., 1965–83 (in progress).

Bibliography

Bălu, Ion, *G. Călinescu, 1899–1965: Biobibliografie*, Bucharest: Editura Ştiinţifică şi Enciclopedică, 1975

Further Reading

Bălu, Ion, *G. Călinescu: Eseu despre etapele creaţiei*, Bucharest: Cartea Românească, 1981
Călin, Vera, "Romanian Contributions to the European Avant-Garde," *Cross-Currents* 4 (1985): 337–50
Livadă, Melania, *G. Călinescu, poet şi teoretician al poeziei*, Bucharest: Cartea Românească, 1982
Martin, Mircea, *G. Călinescu şi "complexele" literaturii române*, Bucharest: Albatros, 1981
Micu, Dumitru, *G. Călinescu: Între Apollo şi Dionysos*, Bucharest: Minerva, 1979
Negoiţescu, Ion, *Istoria literaturii române*, Bucharest: Minerva, 1991: 184–88
Niţescu, Marin, "G. Călinescu," in his *Sub zodia proletcultismului: Dialectic puterii*, Bucharest: Humanitas, 1995: 188–208

Calvino, Italo
Italian, 1923–1985

"I will begin by saying that I was born under the sign of Libra," notes Italo Calvino in the brief autobiography offered in the guise of an appendix to *Una pietra sopra: Discorsi di letteratura e società* (1980; *The Uses of Literature*). The astrological detail may seem innocuous, but it is perhaps revealing of the ambivalence running through the Italian writer's work. Calvino does, in fact, use humor to express his concern over what the modern world is becoming, and the place that man may yet take in it. Bearing at one and the same time the imprint of realism and the fantastic, his fiction writing – novels and extended short stories – has shown him to be one of the most original authors of postwar Italian literature. But it is also through his work as an editor, journalist, and essayist that Calvino has commanded attention as one of the outstanding figures of the cultural life of his country.

At the close of World War II, during which he had joined the Resistance, Calvino made his debut as a writer and journalist in the columns of *Politecnico*, a Marxist-inspired weekly. The experience did not last long, but from it Calvino acquired the certainty that "only a critical attention to everyday reality could underwrite the validity of his [literary and intellectual] commitment" (Germana Pescio Bottino, 1967). More prosaically, the *Politecnico* venture introduced Calvino to Elio Vittorini – at that time editor of the magazine – who, along with Cesar Pavese, noticed his first novel, *Il sentiero dei nido di ragno* (1947; *The Path to the Nest of Spiders*), and introduced him to Einaudi, the Turin publishing house where Calvino was to work for many years. It was with Vittorini, too, that he was subsequently to start *Il Menabò di Letteratura* (1959–67), a militant cultural magazine which was to introduce many young writers. Calvino himself published a variety of essays in it, most memorably "Il mare dell'oggettività" (1960; "The Sea of Objectivity"), in which he denounced the belief in objectivity which spared the intellectual the need to subject real events to his critical judgment, and "La sfida al labirinto" (1962; "The Challenge to the Labyrinth"), in which he examined the consequences of industrial development on the human condition and contemporary culture.

In the post-1956 period, marked by the events in Hungary which were to cause him to leave the Italian Communist Party, Calvino devoted himself more to his work as an editor than to his literary work. But the novels of this period are also clearly influenced by the uncertainty of the times. The trilogy *I nostri antenati* (*Our Ancestors*) – *Il visconte dimezzato* (1952; *The Cloven Viscount*), *Il barone rampante* (1957; *The Baron in the Trees*), and *Il cavaliere inesistente* (1959; *The Non-Existent Knight*) – which was to win Calvino a permanent place in the history of Italian literature, stands out from the ambient neorealistic vein to give precedence to fantasy which came close to fairytale, and which had already been glimpsed in his first novel. Behind the fantastic digressions, the irreverent tone, and the linguistic inventions characterizing these three improbable stories can be seen all of Calvino's questioning about the precise relationship between the individual conscience and the course of history. Exactly like his Baron (who lives in the trees in order to withdraw from the world, but does so without misanthropy, concerned first and foremost with his neighbor), Calvino was never to stop his anxious reflections on the gradual progress of a dehumanized world. Although, over the course of the years, the fantastic assumed an increasingly important place in his literary work, his factual writing and approach, influenced particularly by the group OULIPO (Ouvroir de Littérature Potentielle [Workroom of potential literature]), was often to come close to sheer virtuosity.

At the same time, various texts and essays he published (collected in 1980 under the title *Una pietra sopra*) were concerned with the execution of literature, the way a literary text works, the combinative processes which give it shape, and the levels of reality it presupposes. Calvino subsequently put his ideas to the test in a series of lectures (collected in 1991 under the title *Perché leggere i classici* [Why read the classics]) ranging from the Odyssey to Pavese, taking in Ariosto and **Voltaire** on the way. Another collection of essays and non-literary texts appeared in 1984 under the title *Collezione di sabbia* (Collection of sand). In the first section of the collection, Calvino brings together a series of articles written for the newspapers he worked on (among them *Il Corriere della Sera* [The evening courier], *La Repubblica*, *L'Espresso*, and *Le Monde* [The world]). These articles, devoted to the most unusual subjects, enabled him to comment on the world via an exploration of various unexpected objects. A second section was devoted to the visible, and the very act of seeing, including vision born from the imagination. The last part of the book is dedicated to various incidental reflections during three journeys (to Japan, Mexico, and Iran), which raise questions about other dimensions of the mind.

Six Memos for the Next Millennium (1988) brings together in one place five lectures (he had not yet written the sixth when he died), which Calvino was to have given at Harvard University. Working around five themes which he anchored within a literary discussion – lightness, quickness, exactitude, visibility, and multiplicity – Calvino attempted to draw up a memorandum for the forthcoming millennium, so that the aging world, with the weight of its problems and anxieties, should not find itself unprepared to face the future. In this posthumous book, we once again find the literary and existentialist questionings which guided Calvino throughout his work.

Christine Masuy

Biography

Born 15 October 1923 in Santiago de las Vegas, Cuba; moved to San Remo, Italy, 1925. Studied at the University of Turin, 1941–47; Royal University, Florence, 1943. Drafted into the Young Fascists, 1940, but left and sought refuge in the Alps, and joined the Communist Resistance, 1943–45. Wrote for various periodicals throughout his life, including *L'Unità* (Unity), *La Nostra Lotta* (Our struggle), *Il Garibaldino*, *Voce della Democrazia* (Voice of democracy), *Contemporaneo*, *Città Aperta* (Open city), and *La Repubblica*, from 1945. Staff member, Einaudi publishers, Turin, 1948–84. Coeditor, with Elio Vittorini, *Il Menabò di Letteratura*, 1959–67. Traveled to the Soviet Union, 1952, and the United States, 1959–60. Married Esther Judith Singer, 1964: one daughter. Moved to Paris, 1967, and to Rome, 1979. Member of the editorial board, Garzanti publishers, 1984. Awards: several, including *L'Unità* Prize, 1945; Viareggio Prize, 1957; Bagutta Prize, 1959; Veillon Prize, 1963; Feltrinelli Prize, 1972. Honorary Member, American Academy, 1975. Died (of a cerebral hemorrhage) in Siena, 19 September 1985.

Selected Writings

Essays and Related Prose

Una pietra sopra: Discorsi di letteratura e società, 1980; part as *The Uses of Literature*, 1986, and as *The Literature Machine*, 1987, translated by Patrick Creagh
Collezione di sabbia, 1984
Six Memos for the Next Millennium (texts for Charles Eliot Norton lectures), translated by Patrick Creagh, 1988; as *Lezioni americane: Sei proposte per il prossimo millennio*, 1988
Perché leggere i classici, 1991

Other writings: several novels (including *Il sentiero dei nidi di ragno* [The Path to the Nest of Spiders], 1947; *I nostri antenati* [Our Ancestors] trilogy, 1952–59; *Le città invisibili* [Invisible Cities], 1972; *Il castello dei destini incrociati* [The Castle of Crossed Destinies], 1973; *Se una notte d'inverno un viaggiatore* [If on a Winter's Night a Traveller], 1979; *Palomar*, 1983), short stories, and three libretti.

Further Reading

Baroni, Giorgio, *Italo Calvino: Introduzione e guida allo studio dell'opera Calviniana, storia e antologia della critica*, Florence: Le Monnier, 1988

Bertoni, Roberto, *Int'abrigu int'ubagu: Discorsi su alcuni aspetti dell'opera di Italo Calvino*, Turin: Tirrenia, 1993

Bonura, Giuseppe, *Invito alla lettura di Italo Calvino*, Milan: Mursia, 1972

Bresciani Califano, Mimma, *Uno spazio senza miti: Scienza e letteratura: Quattro saggi su Italo Calvino*, Florence: Le Lettere, 1993

Calligaris, Contardo, *Italo Calvino*, Milan: Mursia, 1973

Cannon, JoAnn, *Italo Calvino: Writer and Critic*, Ravenna: Longo, 1981

Carter, Albert Howard, *Italo Calvino: Metamorphoses of Fantasy*, Ann Arbor, Michigan: UMI Research Press, 1987

Ferretti, Gian Carlo, *Le capre di Bikini: Calvino giornalista e saggista, 1945–1985*, Rome: Riuniti, 1989

Gabriele, Tommasina, *Italo Calvino: Eros and Language*, Rutherford, New Jersey: Fairleigh Dickinson University Press, and London: Associated University Press, 1994

Hume, Kathryn, *Calvino's Fictions: Cogito and Cosmos*, Oxford: Clarendon Press, 1992

Milanini, Claudio, *L'utopia discontinua: Saggio su Italo Calvino*, Milan: Garzanti, 1990

Pescio Bottino, Germana, *Calvino*, Florence: Nuova Italia, 1967

Puletti, Ruggero, *Un millenarismo improbabile: Le "Lezioni americane" di Italo Calvino*, Rome: Lucarini, 1991

Ricci, Franco, editor, *Calvino Revisited*, Ottawa: Dovehouse Press, 1989

Camus, Albert

French, 1913–1960

In his monumental biography of Albert Camus, Olivier Todd (1996) makes the point that Camus and **George Orwell** had much in common; the one big difference, however, was that Orwell's essays were much better than his novels, whereas with Camus it was the other way around: he was a greater novelist than essayist. And yet – like Orwell's fiction – Camus' essays contain some of his finest prose, and have been enormously influential. Like Orwell, too, Camus was remarkably consistent throughout his relatively short life as a writer. His art develops with astonishing internal coherence; there are no abrupt changes of direction.

In 1937, shortly after Camus had at the age of 24 completed his university studies in philosophy with a diploma essay on Plotinus and St. Augustine, his first collection of essays, *L'Envers et l'endroit* (The wrong side and the right side), was published in Algiers. This short book, some 50 pages long, consists of five essays; unlike *Le Mythe de Sisyphe* (The Myth of Sisyphus) and *L'Homme révolté* (The Rebel) it presents no sustained argument, but offers instead a blend of lyrical reflection with self-portrayal, even self-scrutiny, that will come to be seen as characteristically Camusian. Sometimes, when relating his 1936 visit to Prague, for instance, he speaks in the first person, but at other times, for example when speaking of more intimate family matters, he uses the third person: "There were five of them living in the flat: the grandmother, her younger son, her elder daughter and the latter's two sons." The stark poverty of Camus' childhood as described here is contrasted with the superabundant generosity of nature in a country where the sun and the sea cost nothing and are freely available to all. This play of opposites is a constant theme of the collection and helps explain its title. The day of the grandmother's funeral, for instance, is a fine, cold, clear winter's day: ". . . from the cemetery high above the town the bright transparent sun could be seen shining on the sea which was quivering with light like a moist lip." One person's existence may have come to an end, but life in all its glory flaunts its sensuous splendors unabashed.

This theme recurs in *Noces* (1939; Nuptials), a collection of four essays published in Algiers two years later. They describe different places in North Africa and Italy, and the title is taken from a passage of characteristically sensual lyricism which concludes the third essay, "L'Été à Alger" (Summer in Algiers): "In the evening or after rain the whole earth, her belly moistened with a seed that gives off an odor of bitter almonds, takes her rest after giving herself all summer to the sun. And so once again this smell hallows the nuptials between man and the earth, and fills our hearts with the only truly virile love available in this world: a love that is generous but cannot last." In tune with the note sounded here – of impermanence and perishability experienced in the midst of the most intense manifestations of ecstasy and joy – Camus' two youthful collections foreshadow the major essays to come, particularly in a revealing remark in *Noces*, which has rightly been called Camus' manual of happiness, to the effect that whatever exalts life increases its absurdity at the same time.

The absurd is, famously, the theme of Camus' greatest essay, *The Myth of Sisyphus* (1942). In what Olivier Todd aptly describes as "a philosophical prose poem," Camus explores the implications of the fact that humanity has to learn to live with a historically unprecedented situation, namely a world in which God does not exist. Camus' atheism is no modish affectation, but absolutely fundamental to his thinking; such efforts as are occasionally made to portray him as a kind of covert Christian are doomed to failure, because the texts will simply not bear out such a reading. On the contrary: Camus takes the nonexistence of God for granted, as something needing neither detailed demonstration nor further explanation. If there is no God – if in other words there is no permanent, transcendent being governing the universe – then there can be no such thing as life after death. Indeed, positing the existence of a soul which goes on functioning after our earthly body wears out makes sense only in a universe where a God of sorts presides over some kind of empyrean to which the soul is dispatched pending (according to which faith is involved) reincarnation or resurrection. But if there is no life after death, if death is indeed final, it is death's very finality that raises questions which Camus tackles head-on in *The Myth of Sisyphus*. He goes straight to the point in the essay's famous opening sentences: "There is only one really serious philosophical question, and that is suicide. Deciding whether or not life is worth living is to answer the fundamental question in philosophy.

All other questions follow from that." Humankind finds the finality of death hard to take: hence the existence of religions which claim to abolish it. Once human beings face up to the fact of their mortality they experience the absurd, which is the feeling that since death is the end of everything so far as the individual is concerned, nothing makes sense any more; and if life is not worth living, it is only reasonable to commit suicide.

Camus wrote *The Myth of Sisyphus* to rebut this argument. He fully accepts the fact of the absurd, but not the conclusions drawn from it. Humankind, he says, can (indeed must) renounce all hope of immortality and accept the transitoriness of life, but it should never assume that this denies the possibility of finding happiness and a sense of purpose in the here-and-now. Suicide is, in fact, a totally unwarranted act of irrational despair; there are instead, he argues, three valid, rational, nonreligious ways of responding to the absurd. The first is to acknowledge that the acceptance of the absurd sets a person free: free to act and function as a genuinely independent being, no longer trammeled by the givens of an illusory transcendent reality. The second is passion, the enthusiasm to make the utmost of the present moment; or as the epigraph, taken from Pindar, eloquently puts it: "Aspire not, oh my soul, to immortal life, but exhaust the realm of the possible."

The last is revolt, the refusal to be cowed by the absurd: such an act of rebellion gives value and dignity to life, and is epitomized by the figure at the center of this philosophical meditation, the Greek hero Sisyphus. For daring to flout the wishes of the gods, Sisyphus, according to legend, was condemned through all eternity to push a boulder to the top of a hill and watch helplessly as it rolled down again. But the most unpleasant truths lose their power of discouragement once we recognize and accept them. That explains why, in the magnificently defiant words on which this essay closes, "the struggle toward the summit is itself enough to fill a man's heart: Sisyphus should be seen as someone who has found happiness."

Camus' next, much longer essay, *The Rebel* (1951), develops the idea of revolt as humanity's only recourse in a world without religious faith, and further defines this kind of metaphysical rebellion as "the urge that impels individuals to defend a dignity common to all humankind." This time Camus misjudges the nature and scope of the essay as a genre; *The Rebel* lacks the punch of *The Myth of Sisyphus*, being too ambitious and too liable to get bogged down in historical and political detail to function effectively as an essay. Whereas in the earlier work the end convincingly answers the question raised at the beginning, in the course of *The Rebel* the definition of the central concept – revolt – shifts unnervingly from a philosophical to a political one. The essay is therefore unsatisfying, even broken-backed. It reads more like the doctoral dissertation Camus (because of ill health) was never allowed to submit than an essay in the usual sense of the term.

His last work in this genre was *L'Été* (1954; Summer), a collection of eight lyrical essays written between 1939, the year of *Noces*, and 1951, the year of *The Rebel*. It therefore harks back to an earlier and better form of the essay as practiced by Camus and to what as a writer of lyrical prose he was best at – celebrating the harsh light and untamed beauty of his native land:

There is an Italian softness about Algiers. The cruel brilliance of Oran has something Spanish about it. Perched on a rock above the Rummel gorges, Constantine reminds one of Toledo. But Spain and Italy are steeped in history, whereas the [three Algerian] towns I'm speaking of have no past at all. During the tedium of the siesta, sadness is both implacable and free from melancholy, while joy lacks softness in the morning light or in the natural luxury of our nights.

JOHN FLETCHER

Biography
Born 7 November 1913 in Mondovi, Algeria. Studied at the Grand Lycée, Algiers, 1924–32, baccalauréat; University of Algiers, 1933–36, licence in philosophy and graduate studies diploma, 1936. Contracted tuberculosis, 1930, with recurrences, 1942–43, and 1949–50. Married Simone Hié, 1934 (divorced, 1940). Held various jobs in Algiers, 1935–39; member of the Communist Party, 1935–39; worked for the *Alger-Républicain* (Algiers republican; later the *Soir-Républicain* [Evening republican]), 1938–40, Algiers, and *Paris-Soir* (Paris-evening), 1940. Married Francine Faure, 1940: twin son and daughter. Taught in Oran, Algeria, 1942; reader and editor of Espoir series, Gallimard publishers, Paris, from 1943; journalist, Paris, 1943–45; cofounding editor, *Combat*, 1944–47; journalist for *L'Express*, 1955–56. Awards: Critics Prize (France), 1947; Nobel Prize for Literature, 1957. Died (in a car accident) at Villeblevin, near Montereau, 4 January 1960.

Selected Writings

Essays and Related Prose
L'Envers et l'endroit, 1937
Noces, 1939
Le Mythe de Sisyphe, 1942; as *The Myth of Sisyphus and Other Essays*, translated by Justin O'Brien, 1955
Actuelles 1–3: Chroniques, 1944–1948, Chroniques, 1948–1953, and *Chroniques algériennes, 1939–1958*, 3 vols., 1950–58
L'Homme révolté, 1951; as *The Rebel: An Essay on Man in Revolt*, translated by Anthony Bower, 1953
L'Été, 1954
Resistance, Rebellion, and Death (selection), translated by Justin O'Brien, 1961
Essais (Pléiade Edition), edited by Roger Quilliot and Louis Faucon, 1965
Lyrical and Critical (selection), edited by Philip Thody, translated by Ellen Conroy Kennedy, 1967; as *Lyrical and Critical Essays*, 1968
Selected Essays and Notebooks, edited and translated by Philip Thody, 1970

Other writings: five novels (*L'Étranger* [*The Stranger*], 1942; *La Peste* [*The Plague*], 1947; *La Chute* [*The Fall*], 1956; *La Mort heureuse* [*A Happy Death*], 1971; *Le Premier Homme* [*The First Man*] (incomplete), 1994), short stories, several plays, and notebooks.

Collected works edition: *Œuvres complètes*, edited by Roger Grenier, 9 vols., 1983.

Bibliographies
Crepin, Simone, "Albert Camus: Essai de bibliographie," *Bibliographia Belgica* 55 (1960)
Roeming, Robert F., *Albert Camus: A Bibliography*, Madison: University of Wisconsin Press, 1968

Further Reading

Brée, Germaine, *Camus*, New Brunswick, New Jersey: Rutgers University Press, revised edition, 1961

Cruickshank, John, *Albert Camus and the Literature of Revolt*, Oxford: Oxford University Press, 1959; New York: Oxford University Press, 1960

Grenier, Roger, *Albert Camus, soleil et ombre: Une Biographie intellectuelle*, Paris: Gallimard, 1987

Lottman, Herbert R., *Albert Camus*, Garden City, New York: Doubleday, and London: Weidenfeld and Nicolson, 1979

McCarthy, Patrick, *Camus: A Critical Study of His Life and Work*, London: Hamilton, 1982

Rhein, Phillip H., *Albert Camus*, Boston: Twayne, revised edition, 1989

Thody, Philip, *Albert Camus: A Study of His Work*, London: Hamilton, 1957

Thody, Philip, *Albert Camus, 1913–1960: A Biographical Study*, London: Hamilton, 1961

Todd, Olivier, *Albert Camus: Une Vie*, Paris: Gallimard, 1996

Canadian Essay (English)

The great majority of English Canadian essayists of literary quality have preferred the informal, personal approach of the **familiar essay**, and a discussion of the essay in Canada is therefore essentially a discussion of the familiar essay. The familiar essay became a serious literary art form in Canada only around the turn of the present century. There were of course a great many essays published in Canadian periodicals during the 1800s, and a even few undistinguished collections, but these early essays were written by individuals for whom writing, let alone writing essays, was very much a sideline. Making a living by writing alone was out of the question in 19th-century Canada, and those few who managed to derive significant supplementary income from their pens found themselves better served by other forms than the essay. This general lack of commitment to the genre inhibited its development and often had a detrimental effect on individual essays.

Albeit more distinguished than those of his contemporaries who dabbled with the essay, the career of **Joseph Howe** (1804–73), who is commonly credited with being the first Canadian essayist of note, serves well to represent the diversity of interests typical of essay writers of his day. In addition to editing and managing newspapers, Howe was a politician and a locally celebrated orator. He served both as premier of Nova Scotia and, after Confederation, briefly as lieutenant-governor. What Howe wrote served practical concerns – promoting his political views and career, encouraging cultural improvement in his province, and, not least, selling newspapers. While the purposes for which other writers adapted the essay varied considerably, all had to be mindful of the demands of life in what amounted to a frontier, encouraging a focus on practical, immediate concerns; rarely, then, were their ambitions purely literary. Howe's flexible understanding of the genre is also typical. If his style often seems heavily rhetorical by comparison with that of British and American essayists of the same period, this is to some extent a result of his practice of recycling his speeches as essays. Though less rhetorically pretentious and generally more interesting than his essays, the anecdotes and observations that Howe published in his newspaper the *Novascotian* as "Rambles" are less essays than travel sketches.

The success of Howe's sketches suggests a characteristic of popular taste in his time. Particularly in 19th-century Canada, the popularity of sketches both limited and influenced the development of the familiar essay, leading writers away from abstract reflection toward detailed recording of local color. Tending more toward narration and description than most essays, the sketch proved more attractive than conventional essays in a new land in which most readers were inclined to accept the authority of writers in established cultural centers where general ideas were concerned, and in which the diversity and novelty of experience invested observations on local life and the local setting with special interest. As was the case with Howe's rambles, there was often a good deal of overlap between familiar essays and sketches, and an extended discussion of the essay in Canada might well consider the elements of the essay present in (to suggest only a few of the most notable) the autobiographical sketches of Susanna Moodie (1803–85) and Catharine Parr Traill (1802–99), and Anna Jameson's (1794–1860) *Winter Studies and Summer Rambles in Canada* (1838). In this century, the sketch has often been blended with the essay for humorous purposes, notably by **Stephen Leacock, Robertson Davies** in many of his Samuel Marchbanks columns, and in personal recollections, such as those of Emily Carr (1871–1945), most notably in *Klee Wyck* (1941), Ernest Buckler (1908–84) in *Ox Bells and Fireflies* (1968), and Kildare Dobbs (1923–) in *Running to Paradise* (1962).

Individual essayists being unremarkable, a useful source of insight into 19th-century Canadian essays is provided by the periodicals for which they were written. While dozens of **periodicals** willing to publish original Canadian essays followed the first, the *Nova-Scotia Magazine* (1789–92), most were short-lived, tenuous operations capable of paying little if anything for the material they published. Particularly in the first half of the century, most relied heavily on reprinted material from British and American publications, where the interest of most readers was still focused, and even as locally written material gradually became more common, it consisted more of journalistic reporting, political commentary and polemics, sketches, tales, and poetry, depending on the focus of individual periodicals, than of familiar essays. Colonial Canada lacked anything like the large, intellectually sophisticated audience that encouraged the British familiar essay tradition, and the scattering of the population further limited the potential circulation of early periodicals.

Notwithstanding the obstacles facing them as business ventures, newspapers and periodicals kept springing up, and, in reaching the political and social leaders of the time, they exerted more influence than their numerical readership or the brevity of their individual periods of publication would suggest. Interestingly, more periodicals mainly concerned with literature were initiated between 1820 and 1840 than between 1840 and 1860. The reason was less a decreasing interest in literature than an increase in political excitement. Toward the middle of the century political debates, particularly those related to Confederation, were beginning to overshadow *belles-lettres* in periodicals, and the topicality of most mid-century essays gives them more historical than literary interest. Among the more literary periodicals, Montreal's *Literary Garland* (1838–51) stands out as a singular success story. The *Garland* was distinguished by its comparatively long survival and its willingness to encourage local writers to the almost unheard-of extent of paying them for their contributions. Patterned on the successful *Godey's Lady's Book* in the United States, the *Garland* assumed as its primary mission the improvement of literary culture. The essay played a relatively small part in this scheme, however, and while the *Garland* did publish essays on cultural and literary subjects, those on literature were generally no more than reviews, mainly of foreign fiction. Locally written fiction, sometimes long enough to run in serial form, and sketches were far more common than familiar essays.

Following Confederation in 1867, increasing readership and a growing understanding that nationhood depended on cultural as well as political maturity encouraged the founding of several periodicals intended to promote Canadian writing. Although the *Canadian Monthly and National Review* (1872–78) (which became *Rose-Belford's Canadian Monthly and National Review* [1878–82]), deserves honorable mention, the best and most influential of the post-Confederation periodicals was the *Week* (1883–96). Both were published in Toronto, a reflection of a general movement of the publishing industry to the center where it remains focused today. In addition to publishing most of the good young poets of the time, the *Week* published essays by many of the most interesting Canadian thinkers. Few of these could be thought of as being primarily essayists, however. Sir Charles G. D. Roberts (1860–1943), the *Week*'s first editor, became much better known later for his poetry and animal stories, as did Sara Jeannette Duncan (1861–1922) for her fiction and travel writing. More of an essayist was Goldwin Smith (1823–1910), one of the founders of the magazine, who stated his opinions on a wide range of social issues. Less topical and combative in his stance than Smith was his associate Theodore Arnold Haultain (1857–1941), who later moved on from his social and cultural comment in the *Week* to write pieces concerned with humans' relationship with nature in *Two Country Walks in Canada* (1903) and other collections. Of recurrent contributors to the *Week*, the one most consciously writing in the familiar essay tradition was **Archibald MacMechan** (1862–1933).

MacMechan is one of three writers, the others being **Andrew Macphail** and **Bliss Carman**, whose collections of often estimable essays, published in the first decade of this century, signal the maturing of the essay in Canada as literature. Writing with a confident sense that he was well suited to his assumed purpose of improving society, MacMechan's thinking was guided by Christian ethics, Victorian morality, and a response to the natural world influenced by Romanticism. In addition to literary criticism, including *Headwaters of Canadian Literature* (1924), verse, and various books concerned with the history and geography of his adopted province, Nova Scotia, MacMechan collected many of his best familiar essays in *The Porter of Bagdad and Other Fantasies* (1901) and *The Life of a Little College* (1914).

A medical doctor and eventually a professor of the history of medicine at McGill University, **Andrew Macphail** (1864–1938) took writing as seriously as he did his profession. After editing medical journals and trying his hand at fiction and drama, he took on the editorship of McGill's *University Magazine* (1907–20) (formerly *McGill University Magazine* [1901–06]), during its final 13 years of publication. Many of his collected essays were first published here. *Essays in Puritanism* (1905), perhaps the best of Macphail's collections, works from biography to celebrate his conception of puritan ideals of independent moral thinking and his belief in social progress based on puritan self-reliance. *Essays in Politics* (1909) and *Essays in Fallacy* (1910) demonstrate Macphail's ability to write with authority on a wide range of subjects.

Better known for his poetry, **Bliss Carman** (1861–1929) was also a prolific writer of essays. Carman contributed essays to a wide range of periodicals, mainly American, throughout the 1890s and brought out his first collection, *The Kinship of Nature*, in 1903. *The Friendship of Art* (1904), *The Poetry of Life* (1905), *The Making of Personality* (1908), and *Talks on Poetry and Life* (1926) tend to be similar in their strengths and weaknesses. Carman was too fond of making vaguely Emersonian pronouncements and overly zealous in his advocacy of a variety of self-development activities, but he could also express complex ideas clearly and forcefully, and his prose, like his poetry, benefited from his creative imagery and sensitivity to the rhythms of language.

Although their collections appeared in the 20th century, these three writers tended to echo 19th-century values and ideas. Other Canadian essayists writing only slightly later were much less influenced by the Victorian past. The primary factor contributing to this change in perspective was the growth of journalism – in ever larger daily newspapers and in magazines reaching a much wider audience than was the case with even the most successful 19th-century periodicals. The audience for these publications was growing not only in size; it was also becoming less genteel and more down-to-earth in its interests. A second important factor leading Canadian essayists away from Victorian gentility and Romantic ideas of nature was the inadequacy of the Romantic-Victorian perspective to accommodate genuine responses to Canadian nature and the realities of rural Canadian living. It is significant that these were the focal subjects of several of Canada's more modern essayists early in the century.

Though born in the same year as Bliss Carman, William Hume Blake (1861–1924) took a much more prosaic approach to Canadian nature. A lawyer by profession, Blake was also an avid outdoorsman whose essays express his sensible appreciation of nature and rural life, particularly as he found it in his fishing trips in the Quebec woods, and the satisfactions of outdoor recreation. Blake's essays are collected in *Brown Waters and Other Sketches* (1915) and *In a Fishing Country* (1922). Like Blake, **Peter McArthur** (1866–1924) took a realistic approach to his primary subject – humans' relationship with nature. McArthur's nature, however, was that of farm life rather than the wilderness, and his approach was often humorous. After working for two decades as a journalist, mainly in New York, McArthur retired in 1909 to his family farm in the village of Ekfrid, Ontario, from which he wrote a popular column on rural life for the Toronto *Globe* (1909–24) and contributed regularly to the *Farmer's Advocate*. His columns were revised for *In Pastures Green* (1915), *The Red Cow and Her Friends* (1919), *The Affable Stranger* (1920), and various posthumously published collections. Although McArthur also had a good deal to say about political and economic subjects, his primary strengths were his ability to convey the satisfactions of farming and his own deep appreciation of the vitality of nature. McArthur retained the journalist's habit of writing quickly and tended to be careless about structure and style, but his prose is readable and appropriate for his chosen role of farmer-philosopher.

Rural living has provided the subject matter and the inspiration for a number of minor Canadian essayists who to some extent resemble McArthur in approach. Showing most clearly the influence of McArthur's writing, Kenneth McNeill Wells (1905–) concentrated on the lighter side of rural life, but his essays and sketches about farm life, animals, and country people are nonetheless believable. Wells' contributions to the Toronto *Evening Telegram* were collected in *The Owl Pen* (1947), *By Moonstone Creek* (1949), *Up Medonte Way* (1951), and *By Jumping Cat Bridge* (1956). His essays benefit from keenly observed descriptive details as well as common sense. Carrying on this rural theme in a mood which by the 1960s had become nostalgic, H. Gordon Greene (1912–) and Harry Boyle (1915–) each produced several collections recalling their youths in small places and simpler times, and Ernest Buckler's *Ox Bells and Fireflies* stands out for both its subtle perceptions and Buckler's deft handling of language.

Foremost among those essayists who take a more naturalistic approach to Canadian nature are Frederick Philip Grove (1879–1948) and **Roderick Haig-Brown** (1908–76). Though better known for his novels, Grove was also an accomplished essayist who, notwithstanding his strongly held opinions on social issues, wrote his most memorable essays about nature and pioneer life. *Over Prairie Trails* (1922), based on weekend journeys he made while teaching in rural Manitoba, and *The Turn of the Year* (1923), which follows the changing seasons on the prairie, are grounded in keen, almost scientific observation. In powerful prose, they capture both the beauty and the harshness of the prairie environment and pioneer life. While the individual pieces in these collections resemble sketches in consisting largely of description and narration, Grove's continuing search for meaning in what he relates brings them closer to the essay. Grove also wrote more conventional essays for periodical publication, and one collection, *It Needs to Be Said* (1929), mainly concerned with writing. Haig-Brown is arguably the most accomplished Canadian essayist primarily concerned with nature. After concentrating on fiction, often for young readers, for more than a decade, Haig-Brown discovered his natural medium in the familiar essay. Although he wrote well on a wide range of subjects, his best essays are about nature and fishing. Most were written for such integrated collections as *A River Never Sleeps* (1946), *Fisherman's Spring* (1951), which explores the essential meaning fishing holds for him, and *Fisherman's Summer* (1959), which shows a growing concern with conservation. Haig-Brown's success rests not only on his descriptive power but on his extensive firsthand knowledge of game fish, Canadian waters, and the techniques of fishing, as well as an ability to convey his enthusiasm about nature and fishing that remained undiminished throughout his long career.

Like Grove and Haig-Brown, many of the best Canadian essayists of this century have been novelists as well. **Hugh MacLennan** (1907–90) concentrated on novels for several years before taking up the essay. MacLennan began by writing comparatively formal essays on topics of public concern in order to support himself between novels, but he gradually developed a deep affection for the familiar essay. His first two collections, *Cross Country* (1949) and *Thirty and Three* (1954) won him Governor-General's Awards for nonfiction, and *Seven Rivers of Canada* (1961), which, in revised form, was the basis of *The Rivers of Canada* (1974), includes some of the best familiar essays on Canadian regions yet written. MacLennan excelled at explaining complex subjects lucidly and memorably, and his essays reflect the wide range of his enthusiasms. His central concern, however, is personal and national identity, and his explorations of what it meant to be a Canadian in his time played a central role in shaping national self-perception.

Unlike MacLennan and Haig-Brown, who took up the essay only after writing several novels, **Robertson Davies** (1913–95) began by writing essays and developed his talent for fiction later. Initially, Davies worked through the irascible but perceptive persona of Samuel Marchbanks. As often as not his Marchbanks columns amounted to little more than humorous sketches, but this eccentric, intolerant persona provided Davies with an excellent medium for criticizing Canadian society. Davies published selections from his Marchbanks columns in *The Diary of Samuel Marchbanks* (1947) and *The Table Talk of Samuel Marchbanks* (1949), and revived the character in *Marchbanks' Almanack* (1967) and *The Papers of Samuel Marchbanks* (1985). Writing in his own voice (which was not unlike that of Marchbanks) Davies wrote numerous periodical essays on a remarkable variety of subjects. These appeared in several collections, such as *A Voice from the Attic* (1960), *The Enthusiasms of Robertson Davies* (1979), and *The Well-Tempered Critic* (1981), which is devoted mainly to literature and Canadian theater. Davies' essays reflect his wide-ranging literary interests, his distaste for intellectual narrowness, and his impressive knowledge of arcane subjects.

Perhaps because Davies drew heavily on his sense of humor in building a following, he took a special interest in the work of another essayist whose intelligence and extensive learning were often overshadowed by his success as a humorist. While **Stephen Leacock** (1869–1944) is best known for many amusing sketches and essays, he also wrote more serious essays in such general areas as history, politics, education, popular entertainment, and the media, as well as economics, his primary academic interest. Leacock was without rival the foremost Canadian humorist of his day, but his success encouraged others. Canadian journalists especially have relied on humor to build readership for their columns. In addition to Davies, McArthur, and Wells, Greg Clark (1892–1977) and later Eric Nicol (1919–) stand out among the many capable newspaper columnists who owed their popularity largely to their ability to amuse readers. In addition to winning awards for straight reportage, Clark reached a wide audience in the Toronto *Star Weekly* and later in *Weekend Magazine* with humorous sketches and essays in which hunting and fishing figure prominently. Before turning to drama in the mid-1970s, Nicol wrote a popular column for the Vancouver *Province*, in which he specialized in making fun of himself and the trials of middle-class family living, and saw his essays and sketches collected in numerous books. The work of these two writers is typical of humorous columns in Canada through mid-century in that it is amusing rather than pointedly satirical. These columnists often make fun of themselves, partly because establishing themselves as personalities whose foibles, failings, and insights readers can understand easily and quickly saves space in individual essays, and partly because the approach allows them to poke fun at weaknesses often shared by their readers without giving offense. Written under deadline pressure for an audience more concerned with being entertained than enlightened, humorous columns tend to be somewhat repetitive and to rely on formulaic humor.

Journalism has, of course, affected more serious essay writing as well as humor, and there can be no doubt that the continuing growth of newspapers and general interest magazines in this century has made journalism, along with the related focus on a mass audience of average readers, the primary factor shaping the development of the familiar essay in Canada. There is, however, another secondary but still important outlet for publication that has run counter to the leveling effects of popular journalism. University-based journals, which began to appear around the turn of the century, have encouraged a more intellectual, somewhat more formal approach to the familiar essay than that of newspapers and large magazines. While the circulation of journals such as the *Queen's Quarterly* (1893–), the *Dalhousie Review* (1921–), and the *University of Toronto Quarterly* (1895–) has remained relatively small, the essays they publish have reached a more thoughtful and better informed audience; in so doing, they have – as was the case with the early 19th-century periodicals – exerted influence out of proportion to their numerical readership. With the expansion of the university system starting in the mid-1960s came a related increase in the number of more specialized academic journals and little magazines dedicated mainly to poetry and short fiction. A few journals in both these categories publish informal essays along with their usual fare, but the established university journals continue to offer the main outlet for academic essayists seeking to reach an intellectual audience with essays on general topics.

While most essays published in the university-based journals differ in tone and focus from those in the popular press, the distinction between academic and journalistic writers is less clear in that many Canadian academics have also written for popular magazines. Goldwin Smith was a professor at Oxford and Cornell before becoming a driving force behind Canadian periodical publishing in the 1870s and 1880s. Macphail, MacMechan, and Leacock – all professors – were able to appeal to both academic and general audiences. Although primarily creative writers, MacLennan and Davies worked as both journalists and academics. Moreover, Canada has produced a good number of academic writers who, while keeping mainly within their areas of expertise, have managed to capture the interest of a wider, nonspecialist audience. Outstanding in this group were **E. K. Brown** (1905–51) and **Northrop Frye** (1912–91). Brown was an accomplished stylist and a prolific writer on literary topics. He edited the *University of Toronto Quarterly* from 1932 to 1941 and, in addition to his many well-written articles in academic journals, published numerous essays on literature accessible to nonspecialists in better magazines such as **Harper's** and *Canadian Forum*. Frye's reputation as one of the foremost literary theorists of the 20th century rests mainly on his highly original and persuasive books, such as *Anatomy of Criticism: Four Essays* (1957) and

The Bush Garden: Essays on the Canadian Imagination (1971), but Frye's books are generally made up of sections constructed with the tradition of the familiar essay in mind. In addition to practical and theoretical criticism, Frye also wrote essays on more general cultural and historical topics for nonspecialized periodicals such as the *University of Toronto Quarterly* and *Canadian Forum*, which he edited from 1948 to 1952.

Canadian Forum (1920–) is an interesting instance of a Canadian magazine that bridges the gap between the university-based journals and the popular press. Though eventually expanded, the *Forum* was started by faculty and students at the University of Toronto. Reaching a wider audience than the university periodicals, the *Forum* provided a more searching, intellectual alternative to mass-circulation magazines like *Maclean's* (1896–) and *Chatelaine* (1928–). More journalistic than the *Forum* yet still intended for a readership more culturally and socially aware than average, *Saturday Night* (1887–) stands out, particularly in the 30 or so years after World War I, as the leading outlet for thoughtful Canadian essays. Under the editorial guidance of such accomplished essayists as William Arthur Deacon (1890–1977) and B. K. Sandwell (1876–1954), *Saturday Night* set the standard for serious essays on Canadian political, cultural, and literary topics. Deacon collected his own essays in *Pens and Pirates* (1923) and *Poteen* (1926), Sandwell his in *The Privacity Agent and Other Modest Proposals* (1928) and *The Diversions of Duchesstown and Other Essays* (1955). Robertson Davies worked as literary editor for *Saturday Night* during World War II and continued to contribute later on. Though certainly not without humor, these magazines were devoted to promoting serious consideration of Canada's cultural and literary achievements and failings.

After mid-century the critical temper characteristic of *Canadian Forum* and *Saturday Night* intensified and gradually became the norm. Out of the social ferment of the 1960s came a loss of confidence in the traditional values that underlay the writing of most earlier Canadian essayists, even those critical of many aspects of Canadian life. Many writers moved from social criticism toward social activism, and this impatience with things as they are is reflected in stylistic experimentation. The questioning mood of the times has done nothing to slow the production of good essays, however, and the number of essayists writing well on a wide variety of subjects – sports, Canadian politics, world affairs, business, lifestyles, entertainment, literature, to mention a few – has grown with the population and an increasing tendency among educated readers to become involved in social and political movements. Many recent essays are so closely tied to the news of the day that they tend to become dated quickly; this, along with the volume of good writing, makes it difficult to estimate which writers will achieve continuing recognition. A few of the older generation of contemporary essayists – those born before World War II – who transcend topicality and who have seen their work collected in book form seem likely to continue to be read.

Robert Fulford (1932–) began his career in journalism in the early 1950s when still a teenager and worked his way up to become editor of *Saturday Night* in 1968. In the same year, he published *Crisis at the Victory Burlesk*, a collection of previously published essays on a variety of mainly cultural topics.

Fulford continues to write prolifically on an impressive range of subjects, both cultural and, more recently, political. Poet-novelist Alden Nowlan (1933–83) brought shrewd wisdom and a characteristically old-fashioned East Coast perspective to contemporary Canadian subjects in *Double Exposure* (1978). Another accomplished essayist with roots in the Atlantic provinces is Harry Bruce (1934–). Writing through the persona of Max MacPherson for the Toronto *Daily Star*, Bruce produced a readable column using the Toronto scene as a starting point. The best of these essays are available in *The Short Happy Walks of Max MacPherson* (1968). Continuing his practice of using places as a starting point for his reflections, Bruce later moved to his family home in Nova Scotia and based several books of essays, including the exceptionally perceptive collection *Down Home* (1988), on his explorations of his East Coast cultural roots.

Nature writing since the 1960s reflects the concern with promoting social action common in many recent essays. After a distinguished career as an academic and journalist, David Suzuki (1936–) has turned increasingly to the familiar essay to educate Canadians about nature and promote conservation. In *Inventing the Future: Reflections on Science, Technology, and Nature* (1989) and *Time to Change* (1994) Suzuki expresses his personal views on a range of cultural, political, and economic topics, always with a sense of our relationships with the natural environment in the background.

Many prominent Canadian novelists have taken up the informal essay and published excellent collections in recent decades – Hugh Hood (1928–) in *The Governor's Bridge Is Closed* (1973), Margaret Laurence (1926–87) in *Heart of a Stranger* (1976), Margaret Atwood (1939–) in *Second Words: Selected Critical Prose* (1982), a collection of informal essays on literature – but by far the most dedicated and prolific familiar essayist among these has been **Mordecai Richler** (1931–). Richler has published widely in magazines in Canada and abroad and has collected only a fraction of his periodical publications in such books as *Hunting Tigers Under Glass* (1968), *Shovelling Trouble* (1972), *Notes on an Endangered Species and Others* (1974), and *The Great Comic Book Heroes and Other Essays* (1978). Richler's essays are more personal than those of most of his contemporaries in that he is characteristically outspoken about his likes and dislikes and writes in a colloquial style that creates a strong impression of his speaking voice. Although Richler owes much of his wide appeal to his well-developed sense of the ridiculous and the satirical cast of his mind, he is a serious critic of society, culture, and, increasingly, in *Home Sweet Home: My Canadian Album* (1984) and *Oh Canada! Oh Quebec!* (1992), of political trends, particularly in his native province of Quebec.

Dozens of promising younger essayists are writing in Canada today, many as full-time journalists and many more freelancing, often supported through connection in some capacity with colleges or universities. The latter group are more typically experimental, but both groups are tending to take the familiar essay toward persuasion rather than detached observation and reflection. It might be argued that personal journalism and essays clearly aimed at changing the attitudes of readers stand somewhat apart from the traditional model of the familiar essay, but the essay has at many points in its history been an agent for social change, and the frankness of Canadian writers today about where they stand in relation to controversial subjects reflects the openness of the time. Whatever developments the new century may bring in the familiar essay, the current interest in this flexible but distinctive genre suggests that it will become more central in Canadian literature.

WILLIAM CONNOR

Anthologies
The Canadian Essay, edited by Gerald Lynch and David Rampton, Toronto: Copp Clark Pitman, 1991
Modern Canadian Essays, edited by W. H. New, Toronto: Macmillan, 1976

Further Reading
Cameron, Elspeth, "Essays in English," in *The Oxford Companion to Canadian Literature*, edited by William Toye, Toronto: Oxford University Press, 1983: 231–35
Conron, Brandon, "Essays 1880–1920," "Essays 1920–1960," and "Essays," in *Literary History of Canada: Canadian Literature in English*, 2nd edition, edited by Carl F. Klinck and others, Toronto: University of Toronto Press, 3 vols., 1976: vol. 1: 354–60; vol. 2: 119–25; vol. 3: 176–79 (original edition, 1965)
Gerson, Carole, and Kathy Mezei, Introduction to *The Prose of Life: Sketches from Victorian Canada*, edited by Gerson and Mezei, Downsview, Ontario: ECW Press, 1981
Hjartarson, Paul, "Essays (Canada)," in *Encyclopedia of Post-Colonial Literature in English*, vol. 1, edited by Eugene Benson and L. W. Connolly, London and New York: Routledge, 1994: 450–54
McDougall, Robert L., *A Study of Canadian Periodical Literature of the Nineteenth Century* (dissertation), Toronto: University of Toronto, 1950
Sutherland, Fraser, *The Monthly Epic: A History of Canadian Magazines 1789–1989*, Markham, Ontario: Fitzhenry and Whiteside, 1989

Canadian Essay (French)

Until the 1930s, when genuine novels and poems began to be published in Quebec, the largest and most interesting part of French literature in Canada was to be found in all kinds of essays, from "relations de voyages" (travel narratives) to public-speaking and journalism.

Discoverers, pioneers, missionaries, and administrators of New France (1534–1760) left rich narratives describing their explorations, as well as private and public letters, annals, and reports. *Jesuit Relations* (1632–73) is the best known and most varied collection of journals, documents, moral reflections, and mystical meditations on day-to-day and major events. *Mémoires* and *Dialogues* (1703) with a "bon sauvage" (noble savage), by the secular, liberal, republican – perhaps even anarchist – Baron de Lahontan (1666–1716), are the first steps on the road to the Enlightenment and the French Revolution. Father Joseph François Lafitau (1681–1746), comparing Amerindian customs with primitive Christian culture (1724), provides systematic methods which are seen as forerunners to modern ethnology and anthropology. Another Jesuit humanist, Pierre François Xavier de Charlevoix (1682–1761), is a precursor of modern history. In the 19th century, he was read by François-Xavier Garneau (1809–66), author of the first extensive *Histoire du Canada* (1845–52; *History of Canada*). This romantic, nationalist, yet sober and realistic *History* is considered the keystone of French Canadian literature, thought, and ideology.

With the British regime and the importation of printing presses (1764), newspapermen and journalists came to be the most active thinkers, writers, and publishers. *La Gazette de Montréal* (1778–; The Montreal gazette) – first French, later bilingual, and today an English newspaper – was founded by two French immigrants, both disciples of **Voltaire** and friends of **Benjamin Franklin**. *Le Canadien* (1806–93; The Canadian), run by liberal professionals and members of the new Parliament in Quebec City, was not a neutral observer of events, but rather a fighter for the nationalist cause. Its writers were the forebears of the 1837–38 Patriots; it was they who gave the French Canadian essay its main themes for decades to come. They were the first to give form and utterance to resistance, survival, and hopes of autonomy.

Étienne Parent (1802–74), editor of *Le Canadien*, was a moderate who became a respected high official in the civil service and the best lecturer of the 19th century on subjects like industry, economy, education, labor, priesthood, and society. He was a political philosopher, a kind of sociologist, but at the same time a writer. His papers are true *texts*, serious, free, and open.

The letters that the poet Octave Crémazie (1827–79) wrote to the Abbé Henri Raymond Casgrain (1831–1904), leader of the folklorist Mouvement Littéraire et Patriotique de Québec (Literary and patriotic movement of Quebec), are interpreted by today's readers as essays of a sort. Crémazie, a good prose writer, critic, and theoretician, dealt in his letters with literature and translation, languages and peoples, cultural institutions and the writer – whom he defined as a desperate prophet in a society of philistine "grocers."

Arthur Buies (1840–1901) returned to Montreal from his formative years in France with revolutionary ideas and a literary style to match. His *Lettres sur le Canada* (1864–67; Letters on Canada) are pamphlets in the form of letters against what he termed the contemporary dark ages, characterized by sluggishness, cowardice, and intellectual lethargy. His collected newspaper articles are more tense and passionate than Hector Fabre's (1834–1910) *Chroniques* (1877; Columns). The latter are descriptions of promenades and streets, pieces of diplomatic irony, glances and twinklings of a sympathetic eyewitness. Edmond de Nevers (i.e. Edmond Boisvert, 1862–1906), a cultivated polyglot, lived and worked in Berlin, Vienna, and Paris, where he published *L'Avenir du peuple canadien-français* (1896; The future of the French Canadian people). The utopia he defines in this essay is, in reality, the European past interpreted as a museum of progress in the arts and sciences.

Since almost all schools, colleges, and universities were under the complete control of the clergy until World War II, French Canadian lay intellectuals turned to politics, civil service, newspapers, radio, and later television to express themselves. Among the best journalists and essayists of the first years of the 20th century were two friends: Olivar Asselin (1874–1937) (*Pensée française* [1937; French thought]) and Jules Fournier (1884–1918) (*Mon encrier* [1922; My inkpot]), both francophile purists and polemicists. Another bright young nationalist was André Laurendeau (1912–68), editor of *Le Devoir* (The duty) and disciple of **Lionel Groulx** (1878–1967): he used his daily to oppose Quebec's conservative Premier Maurice Duplessis. He was later named royal commissioner on bilinguism and biculturalism.

Fournier and Laurendeau were occasional literary critics, whereas professor Victor Barbeau (1896–1994) and novelist Claude-Henri Grignon (1894–1976) were lonely pamphleteers. The first professional critics in newspapers, magazines, journals, or reviews were a diplomat (René Garneau [1907–83]), a notary (Albert Pelletier [1895–1971]), a neorealist poet enamored of the United States (Alfred DesRochers [1901–78]), and a printer (Louis Dantin [i.e. Eugène Seers, 1865–1945], at Harvard University Press). Dantin's *Gloses critiques* (1931; Critical glosses) are often about theories, ideologies, or general questions such as regionalism, subjectivity, art, and morals.

A moralist in the French classical tradition, Pierre Baillargeon (1916–67) is concise, confidential, pessimistic, and rightist. His classmates Jacques Ferron (1921–85) and **Pierre Vadeboncoeur** (1920–) are more artful in mixing wisdom and freedom, French wit and political insight, ethics and aesthetics. So is **Jacques Brault** (1933–), who, like Ferron and Vadeboncoeur, contributed regularly to the left-wing, secessionist *Parti pris* (1965–68; We affirm) as well as to the more moderate *Liberté* (1959–). More than philosophers or historians, sociologists were the kings and the king-makers of the 1960s and 1970s in universities, mass media, and sometimes in literature. Marcel Rioux's (1919–92) *Les Québécois* (1974) is a colorful portrait of Quebec society. Fernand Dumont (1927–) goes from a theoretical *Lieu de l'homme* (1968; Man's locus) to a more timely *La Vigile du Québec* (1971; Quebec's vigil), about terrorism during the October Crisis of 1970.

What came to be known as the Quiet Revolution – the period of intense social rupture and radical reforms in politics, economy, and lifestyles that started in 1960 – was preceded by many cultural movements: manifestos (*Refus global* [1948; Global refusal] by Paul-Émile Borduas [1905–60]), journals (*Cité Libre* [1950–66; Free city]), cooperatives of poets (L'Hexagone [1953–]), collections of essays like *La Grève de l'amiante* (1956; The Asbestos Strike) edited by future Prime Minister Pierre Elliott Trudeau (1919–). Another forerunner of this revolution is the **personal essay**, for example *L'Homme d'ici* (1952; The man from here) by the Jesuit Ernest Gagnon (1905–78), in which modern Catholicism meets psychoanalysis, existentialism, and African and Oriental myths.

The Quiet Revolution was accelerated by a bestselling essay, *Les Insolences du Frère Untel* (1960; The Impertinences of Brother Anonymous) by Jean-Paul Desbiens (1927–). The author of this anonymously published book, who was a friar and a teacher, attacked bishops and popularized the word *joual* to designate the sloppy French spoken mostly in Montreal's East End. Another angry young man of the period was Gilles Leclerc (1928–), whose *Journal d'un inquisiteur* (1960; An inquisitor's diary) is a dense pamphlet directed at all establishments. **Jean Le Moyne**'s (1913–96) *Convergences* (1961) concentrated its fire not only on the traditional family, as well as the Jansenism or puritanism of Quebec's society, but also attacked nationalism and separatism – Le Moyne being one of the few essayists to do so.

Jean-Paul Sartre, Albert Memmi, and Frantz Fanon were read by the young founders of *Parti pris*, Paul Chamberland (1939–) and Pierre Maheu (1939–79). Their collaborators included former terrorist Pierre Vallières (1938–) – his *Nègres blancs d'Amérique* (1968; *White Niggers of America*) is an explosive mix of autobiography and ideology – and the journalist Jean Bouthillette (1929–), author of *Le Canadien français et son double* (1972; The French Canadian and his double), an attempt at political psychoanalysis. For the latter, "French Canadian" – neither French from France nor Canadian in Canada – is a word and concept to be replaced by "Québécois." This is also the point of view of Hubert Aquin (1929–77), a novelist, political scientist, and philosopher, who wrote about "cultural fatigue," or Prime Minister Trudeau's constitutional obsessions. His collection *Blocs erratiques* (1977; Erratic blocks) was published after his suicide.

Less tragic and impatient than the revolutionary Aquin is the novelist and filmmaker Jacques Godbout (1933–), who has a nose for fads, slogans, and day-to-day images in Montreal, Paris, New York, or California. Before *Le Murmure marchand* (1984; The rumor of merchandise), on media, commerce, and publicity, he published *Le Réformiste: Textes tranquilles* (1975; The reformist: quiet texts). Playwright and novelist Jacques Ferron mixed political and literary essays with many genres: open letters, autobiography, portraits, **satire**, history (as in *Historiettes* [1969; Anecdotes]), and book **reviews** (as in *Escarmouches* [1975; Skirmishes]).

A few other novelists, journalists, and poets – for example, **Fernand Ouellette** (1930–) – are also occasional essayists. Naïm Kattan (1928–), born in Baghdad, educated in Paris, and now living in Montreal, plays on his "triple existence" and on twofold titles to contrast and blend the East and the West, Judaism and Christianity, *Le Désir et le pouvoir* (1983; The desire and the power). Diplomat **Pierre Trottier** (1925–) explores similar themes, but expresses them in other ways.

From the 1960s to the 1980s, the so-called "national question" – the vexed issue of the identity of the Québécois people as a nation, as well as the debate on the status of the Province of Quebec within the Canadian Confederation – was one of the principal obsessions of essayists. This issue permeated many domains of thought; it flowed over into discussions of language, individualism and collectivity, fear, action, and freedom. But other subjects – literature and silence, for example – were not neglected. Links between reading, thinking, and writing are the main issues in *Le Jeu en étoile* (1978; The star-shaped game) and *Entre l'écriture et la parole* (1984; Between writing and speech) by Jean-Louis Major (1937–). The most influential French Canadian literary critic since the 1950s is Gilles Marcotte (1925–), who wrote *Une littérature qui se fait* (1962; A literature that builds itself), *Littérature et circonstances* (1989; Literature and circumstances), and *La Littérature et le reste* (1980; Literature and what remains), which contains correspondence and dialogue with Marcotte's colleague André Brochu (1942–), himself a scholar, critic, and essayist. Jean Éthier-Blais (1925–95) was more conservative and subjective than Marcotte in his reviews (*Signets* [1967; Bookmarks]) and in his clever *Dictionnaire de moi-même* (1976; Dictionary of myself). Georges-André Vachon's (1926–94) *Esthétique pour Patricia* (1980; Aesthetics for Patricia) subverted all distinctions between reality and fiction, reading and writing, science and art.

The rise of the essay in Quebec since the Quiet Revolution has depended greatly on two publishers. HMH – later Hurtubise HMH – created the longest lasting series of essays in 1961 with the publication of Le Moyne's *Convergences*. The "Constantes" series includes texts by Pierre Baillargeon, Maurice Blain (1925–96) (*Approximations*, 1967), Fernand Dumont, Ernest Gagnon, Naïm Kattan, Jean-Louis Major, Gilles Marcotte, Fernand Ouellette, Jean Simard (1916–) (*Nouveau répertoire* [1965; New repository]), Pierre Trottier, and Pierre Vadeboncoeur. Many series were created in the wake of "Constantes" – most notably "Prose exacte" by the Éditions Quinze, and "Essais littéraires" by L'Hexagone – but the most important editor of essays after Hurtubise HMH is clearly Boréal. Created in 1984, the "Papiers collés" series publishes collections of essays, "books of scattered texts, whose assemblage underlines their eclecticism as well as the continuity of thought and style of their authors." *Surprendre les voix* (1986; To catch the voices) by **André Belleau** (1930–86), *La Poussière du chemin* (1989; The dirt of the road) by Jacques Brault, and *La Petite Noirceur* (1987; The small darkness) by **Jean Larose** (1948–), the most important collections of the 1980s, were published in this series, alongside books by Gilles Archambault (1933–), André Brochu, Jacques Godbout, Yvon Rivard (1945–), and François Ricard (1947–), who is the director of the series. It is also in this series that Bernard Arcand (1945–) and Serge Bouchard (1947–) like to pin down the "lieux communs" (commonplaces) of modern life. With the journal *Liberté*, these two series have been crucial in the field of the Québécois essay. It is still too early to assess the importance of the most recent series of essays in Quebec. "Pour en finir avec" (To be done with, also published by Boréal) attempts to maintain the polemical tradition that dates back to Louis-Antoine Dessaulles (1819–95) or Louis Fréchette (1839–1908) in the 19th century.

Few women writers have seen their books included in series such as "Constantes" or "Papiers collés," a fact that may partially explain why critics and anthologists seem to be so ill at ease with these books and their place within the genre of the essay in Quebec. Besides journalists whose articles are frequently collected – Rolande Allard-Lacerte, Lise Bissonnette, Ariane Émond, Lysiane Gagnon, Judith Jasmin (1916–72), Catherine Lord, Hélène Pedneault (1952–), Nathalie Petrowski (1954–) – many women writers use genres that are difficult to categorize, for they often refuse the boundaries imposed upon them by the genres themselves. Nicole Brossard (1943–), Madeleine Gagnon (1938–), and France Théoret (1942–) write about their private lives as well as their theories and ideas in their texts. Michèle Lalonde (1937–) is concerned with matters of language and politics. Louky Bersianik (i.e. Lucile Durand [1930–]) is a novelist and a utopian. Marcelle Brisson (1929–) and Madeleine Ouellette-Michalska (1935–) mix philosophy, anthropology, and feminist theory. Fernande Saint-Martin (1927–) is a historian of both art and literature, and also a semiotician. Simonne Monet-Chartrand (1919–93) used all forms of autobiographical expression in her series of books. Suzanne Lamy (1929–87) wrote literary criticism that was well-informed, firmly rooted theoretically, ideologically oriented, and personal in the strongest possible sense of the word: she constantly stressed the intimate pleasures of reading and writing. One has to wonder if women writers' choices of publishing houses, coupled with their fondness for personal narratives and political prose, as well as with the literary institution's tendency to treat them as a separate corpus, have not led critics to overlook their role in the Québécois essay.

With the exception of Janusz Przychodzen (1962–) and Lise Gauvin (1940–), who herself published a book of essays in 1984, critics of the genre have not advanced coherent ideas on the matter of essays written by women, a curious oversight given how eagerly Quebec's essayists theorize their own writing. Fernand Ouellette, André Belleau, Jean-Louis Major, Jean-Marcel Paquette (1941–), and François Ricard, all essayists themselves, have written at length on the nature of the essay, its relationship with other genres, its stylistic devices (including the use of paradox), and its peculiar efficiency: "Anybody who has used the essay," Belleau wrote, "knows that it allows him to discover." Critics such as Laurent Mailhot (1931–), Robert Vigneault (1927–), Marc Angenot (1941–), François Dumont (1956–), Janusz Przychodzen, and Jean Terrasse (1940–) have also been concerned with the genre's characteristics and history – in Quebec as elsewhere.

Studies written by these critics are similar to the thoughts of contemporary essayists who deal with the powers of literature. Be it Modernism (Philippe Haeck [1946–]), great literary figures of the past (Victor-Lévy Beaulieu [1945–]), the teaching of literature (Jean Larose), or every author's fight with language (Thomas Pavel [1941–]), Quebec essayists are constantly reassessing questions that confront today's literary theorists and readers alike. What are the "ends" of literature (*Chutes: La Littérature et ses fins* [1990] by Pierre Ouellet [1950–])? What can it do "against itself" (*La Littérature contre elle-même* [1985] by François Ricard)? Does it promote a particular "ecology" (*L'Écologie du réel* [1988] by Pierre Nepveu [1946–])? The spatial metaphors that abound in the texts of the 1990s – the road (*Le Bout cassé de tous les chemins* [1993] by Yvon Rivard), narrowness (*Les Littératures de l'exiguïté* [1992] by François Paré), distance (*Le Proche et le lointain* [1994] by Claude Lévesque [1927–]) – remind its reader that the genre of the essay is especially helpful for those who wish to travel along the road of literature.

LAURENT MAILHOT
BENOÎT MELANÇON

Anthologies
Écrivains contemporains du Québec depuis 1950, edited by Lise Gauvin and Gaston Miron, Paris: Seghers, 1989
Essais québécois, 1837–1983: Anthologie littéraire, edited by Laurent Mailhot and Benoît Melançon, Montreal: Hurtubise HMH, 1984

Further Reading
Andrès, Bernard, "Essai de typologie du discours pamphlétaire québécois," *Voix et Images* 1, no. 3 (April 1976): 417–31
Angenot, Marc, *La Parole pamphlétaire: Contribution à la typologie des discours modernes*, Paris: Payot, 1982
Belleau, André, "Approches et situation de l'essai québécois," in his *Y a-t-il un intellectuel dans la salle?*, Montreal: Primeur, 1984: 148–53
Bonenfant, Joseph, "Divergences de l'essai québécois," in *Culture populaire et littératures au Québec*, edited by René Bouchard, Saratoga, California: Anma Libri, 1980: 243–56

Brisson, Marcelle, "L'Écriture réflexive au Québec," *La Nouvelle Barre du Jour* 60 (November 1977): 53–63
Dorais, Fernand, *L'Essai au Canada français de 1930 à 1970: Lieu d'appropriation d'une conscience ethnique*, Sudbury: Prise de Parole, 1984
Dumont, François, "L'Essai littéraire québécois des années quatre-vingt: La Collection 'Papiers collés,'" *Recherches Sociographiques* 33, no. 2 (1992): 323–35
Dumont, François, "La Théorisation de l'essai au Québec," in *Le Discours de l'université sur la littérature québécoise*, edited by Joseph Melançon, Quebec City: Nuit Blanche, 1996: 331–56
L'Essai et la prose d'idées au Québec, Montreal: Fides, 1985
Études Littéraires issue on the essay, 5, no. 1 (April 1972)
Études Littéraires issue on the pamphlet, 11, no. 2 (August 1978)
Gauvin, Lise, "Petit Essai sur l'essai au féminin," in *L'Autre Lecture: La Critique au féminin et les textes québécois*, vol. 2, edited by Lori Saint-Martin, Montreal: XYZ, 1992: 117–27
Mailhot, Laurent, *Ouvrir le livre*, Montreal: L'Hexagone, 1992
Marcel, Jean, *Pensées, passions et proses*, Montreal: L'Hexagone, 1992
Przychodzen, Janusz, *Un projet de liberté: L'Essai littéraire au Québec (1970–1990)*, Quebec City: Institut Québécois de Recherche sur la Culture, 1993
Québec Français issue on the essay, 53 (March 1984)
Ricard, François, "La Littérature québécoise contemporaine 1960–1977; IV. L'Essai," *Études Françaises* 13, no. 3–4 (October 1977): 365–81
Simard, Sylvain, "L'Essai québécois au XIXe siècle," *Voix et Images* 6, no. 2 (Winter 1981): 365–81
Terrasse, Jean, *Rhétorique de l'essai littéraire*, Montreal: University of Quebec Press, 1977
Vachon, Stéphane, "Problématique d'une nouvelle forme: L'Essai-pamphlet au Québec," *Itinéraires et Contacts de Culture* 6 (1985): 47–57
Vidricaire, André, "Pour une politique de l'essai en littérature," *Livres et Auteurs Québécois 1979* (1980): 275–82
Vidricaire, André, "Les Genres en littérature, en histoire, en art, etc.: Un Conflit de disciplines," *Livres et Auteurs Québécois 1980* (1981): 241–46
Vigneault, Robert, *L'Écriture de l'essai*, Montreal: L'Hexagone, 1994
Vincenthier, Georges, *Une idéologie québécoise de Louis-Joseph Papineau à Pierre Vallières*, Montreal: Hurtubise HMH, 1979
Voix et Images issue on the age of criticism, 1920–1940, 17, no. 2 (Winter 1992)

Cândido, Antônio

Brazilian, 1918–

After completing a degree in social sciences and beginning a career as a sociologist, Antonio Cândido embarked on a brilliant career as a literary critic. His essays have helped to define the writings of a generation of young Brazilian critics. His objective, as his students and followers have indicated, is not simply to define the parameters of the discipline of literary criticism, but rather to articulate the question of aesthetics through psychology, sociology, economics, philosophy, and art. One could say that he has inaugurated the field of Cultural Studies in Brazil. To this end, Cândido integrates the practice and experience of the critic with the objective data obtained through his investigations. As a trained social scientist, Cândido is just as likely to pursue empirical research – usually considered anathema to literary criticism – as critical textual analysis.

Cândido's essays mobilize information from structuralism, psychological criticism, and sociopolitical empiricism. His genius lies in his ability to combine the disciplines without producing impressionistic texts and, more importantly, without falling into the reductionist trap of a mechanical approximation to a text. Indeed, he has labeled some critics imperialistic for their use of the scientific method alone in the analysis of texts.

Well ahead of the now fashionable New Historicism, Cândido proposed a revisionist reading of Brazilian literature. His project involves a recontextualization of Brazilian letters from the point of view of literary tradition juxtaposed to a critical perspective that he finds missing in most textual analyses. His method, or as some have called it, his theory, involves analyzing the formalistic aspects of a text as merely a step toward comprehending the diversity that encompasses a work of literary art. Once analyzed, the text then becomes organic and dialogic.

To reach his own maximum critical creativity, Cândido attempts "to focus simultaneously on the work as its own reality and on its context as a system of texts" (*Formação da literatura brasîleira* [1959; The formation of Brazilian literature]). For Cândido, the contextualization of a work of literary art involves bringing it into dialogue with all other texts surrounding it, be they literary or not. In this process, he proposes placing the literary text on an equal level with all other texts present when the literary text was written, and more importantly, when it is being read. In the introduction to *Formação da literatura brasîleira* Cândido writes that "it is necessary to see simplicity where there is complexity, trying to point to the harmony in contradiction. The spirit of the system intervenes as form to translate the multiplicity of the real: be this an art form applied to life, or scientific form applied to data." Cândido proposes that literature and its analysis make up a system of intrinsically linked texts. To understand this system, one must analyze in chronological, sociopolitical, and economic contexts not only the critical terms that are used to define it, but also the very discourse that is present in the text. Rather than discarding some literary works as unworthy of analysis, Cândido proposes a different kind of reading – the deconstruction of these texts' position in the "literary system." Not to do so, according to Cândido, is to fall into the trap of "colonizing" the literary text, much as the indigenous ideologies were colonized by the ideal of "civilization."

Perhaps more so than his contemporaries, Cândido has been able to maintain a balance between ideology and culture. Ideology as he defines it presents all of the political underpinnings suggested by or projected onto the text. Culture, on the other hand, is a mirror of a period's aesthetic judgment. Within these definitions lies the system that will guide the rereading of all past literary texts.

Cândido's essays are both products and examples of his system, for he enters into dialogue not only with the literary texts, but also with his own context and ideology. As Celia Pedrosa (1990) has indicated, the essayist "may articulate intelligence and sensibility, information and evaluation, mobilizing at the same time the theoretical-methodological recourses of several disciplines."

Antonio Cândido continues to develop his essays within an organic system. He has helped to define the field of literary analysis in a culture where imitation is often valued over originality, and the adaptation of foreign models over the development of national ones. Cândido breaks with this tradition in his essays, in doing so pointing an entire generation of young Brazilian critics toward a new vision of Brazilian literature.

CARMEN CHAVES TESSER

Biography
Antônio Cândido Mello e Souza. Born 1918. Studied at home; moved to Paris at age 11, where he was tutored in French culture and language; returned to Brazil as a teenager; studied anthropology at the University of São Paulo. Taught sociology for 15 years at the Universidade Estadual Paulista; coordinator of language studies, Universidade Estadual de Campinas; currently professor of literary theory, University of São Paulo. Founding member, Partido dos Trabalhadores (Workers' party).

Selected Writings

Essays and Related Prose
Brigada ligeira, 1945
Ficção e confissão: Ensaio sôbre a obra de Graciliano Ramos, 1956
O observador literário, 1959
Tese e antítese, 1964; revised edition, 1971
Literatura e sociedade: Estudos de teoria e história literária, 1965; as *On Literature and Society*, edited and translated by Howard S. Becker, 1995
Vários escritos, 1970
Teresina, etc., 1980
A educação pela noite e outros ensaios, 1987
Brigada ligeira e outros escritos, 1992
O discurso e a cidade, 1993
Recortes, 1993

Other writings: *Formação da literatura brasîleira: Momentos decisivos* (2 vols., 1959) and a book on Sylvio Romero (1963). Also edited several collections by other writers.

Further Reading
Gomes, Renato Cordeiro, "Um olhar para além das fronteiras: 'Literatura e subdesenvolvimento' de Antonio Cândido," in *Toward Socio-Criticism: Selected Proceedings of the Conference "Luso-Brazilian Literatures, a Socio-Critical Approach"*, edited by Roberto Reis, Tempe: Arizona State University Center for Latin American Studies, 1991: 87–94
Leite, Ligia Chiappini Moraes, *Formación de la literatura brasileña o la historia de un deseo*, Miami: Casa de las Américas, 1990
Pedrosa, Celia, "Antonio Cândido e a crítica como experiência," *Chasqui* 19, no. 1 (1990): 64–76
Schwarz, Roberto, "Presupuestos, salvo engano, de 'Dialectica del malandrinaje'," *Revista de Teoria y Crítica Literarias* 4, no. 8 (1979): 191–211

Canetti, Elias
Bulgarian-born, 1905–1994

Elias Canetti's reputation as an essayist was established on the basis of 15 essays collected in the volume *Das Gewissen der Worte* (enlarged edition, 1976; *The Conscience of Words*). With one exception, these essays date from the 1960s and 1970s and so postdate his major study of social collectivities and their rulers, *Masse und Macht* (1960; *Crowds and Power*). Most first appeared either in smaller collections of Canetti's essays or in literary periodicals.

The collected essays, while predominantly preoccupied with literary topics, at first glance suggest some thematic diversity. Several take writers as their nominal topic: Büchner, **Tolstoi**, Kafka, Broch, and Kraus. Others consider different aspects of Canetti's own writing, one treating the autobiographical background of his novel *Die Blendung* (1936; *Auto-da-Fé*), another considering what constitutes realistic writing in the new reality of the 20th century, and a third discussing his own unpublished diaries, partly in relation to his extensive production as an aphorist. Others discuss the problems of language and exile and the profession of the writer in the 20th century. Not all the texts on which Canetti writes are purely literary: he also writes on Confucius, on Albert Speer's memoirs, and on a Japanese diary recording the aftermath of the bombing of Hiroshima. Only one essay, "Macht und Überleben" (1972; "Power and Survival"), has no obvious textual or literary referent, but rather elaborates two of the central categories developed in *Crowds and Power*.

Canetti's **preface** to the collection argues that any apparent thematic disunity is the result only of a distinction between the public and the private spheres that is no longer tenable in the face of humankind's potential to destroy the earth. What the essays present, according to Canetti, is a series of positive and negative models of behavior – and particularly of writing – *vis-à-vis* the forms of power explored at length in *Crowds and Power* and represented here explicitly in one essay. These essays' posteriority to that study is therefore significant since, in their reliance on predominantly modern material, they offer a response to the early criticism of *Crowds and Power*, which questioned the contemporary usefulness of analytic categories derived almost exclusively from remote historical or anthropological data.

These models cluster around the four main, interrelated themes of his work: crowds, power, death, and metamorphosis. Hitler, for example, is presented as the paranoiac ruler of crowds, obsessed with and fascinated by the size of the crowds of living and dead which he commands ("Hitler, nach Speer" [1972; "Hitler, According to Speer"]); while Kafka, whose whole consciousness as a writer is revealed as negotiating between power and powerlessness, emerges "among all writers as the greatest expert on power" (*Der andere Prozess* [1969; *Kafka's Other Trial*]). Similarly, models for Canetti's dogmatic refusal to make peace with the power of death are found in Confucius, who refuses even to discuss death ("Konfuzius in seinen Gesprächen" [1972; "Confucius in His Conversations"]), and in Kraus' lonely and resolute defiance of authority in protesting against World War I ("Der neue Karl Kraus" [1972; "The New Karl Kraus"]). Tolstoi, however, though a clear and uncompromising critic of power in all its forms for most of his life, is rejected as a model for having "struck a kind of pact with death" in his late turn to religion ("Tolstoi, der letzte Ahne" [1972; "Tolstoy: The Final Ancestor"]).

This accumulation of strategic variations on his central themes is typical of Canetti's reflective writings. Indeed it defines the form of *Crowds and Power* which, though itself subtitled "Essay," is more satisfactorily described as an intricate, kaleidoscopic structure of essayistic fragments whose whole is finally greater than the sum of its parts. (With the difference of its chronological axis, Canetti's autobiography can be seen in similar terms, inviting the suggestion that essayistic forms become Canetti's principal mode of writing following his one early novel.) While some of the collected essays thematize the problems of representing the fractured reality of modernity, the experiments conducted in others are concerned with the essaying of interconnected, passionately subjective approaches to a world which can only be glimpsed, according to Canetti, in small "splinters of astonishment" ("Hermann Broch," 1936).

Canetti's approach to the contemporary topics of these essays echoes his approach to the more esoteric material of *Crowds and Power*. Thus, for example, he accords Kafka's and Kraus' letters, the Hiroshima diary, and Büchner's play *Woyzeck* the same degree of reverence which he elsewhere reserves for the most ancient and sacred of myths. In the final essay in the collection, Canetti describes the immense responsibility of the writer – the *Dichter* – as the "keeper of metamorphosis" ("Der Beruf des Dichters" [1976; "The Writer's Profession"]), a term which implies a quasi-religious responsibility for the preservation, revivification, and invention of life-sustaining myths and their meanings. The texts he discusses contain for him the fragmentary truths of our age, the myths which recent history has produced. In his essays he effects their perpetuation through what Dagmar Barnouw (1975) has termed a technique of "concentrated retelling." Like many sections of *Crowds and Power*, then, these essays have an especially strong narrative component.

The truths which these narratives aim to reveal stand, by virtue of their mythic status, essentially independent of any prior scholarship. Canetti's essays neither acknowledge other discourses on his topic nor invite discussion. Functioning outside any received terminology, they propagate their truths with a remarkable clarity of expression and argument, the rhythm of their revelations attesting to their author's expertise as a storyteller. Canetti's own terminology is provocatively original, often saturated with strikingly evocative metaphors, such as those cited above or his characterization of the writer's role as "the thrall of his time, its serf and bondman, its lowest slave . . . the dog of his time" ("Hermann Broch"). These essays aim less to persuade than to initiate their reader into the mystery, and the general tone of the critical discussion they have provoked – outside the supporting role they have played in the study of *Crowds and Power* – suggests the broad success of their project.

DAVID DARBY

Biography

Born 25 July 1905 in Ruse (Ruschuk), Bulgaria. Studied at schools in England, Austria, Switzerland, and Germany; University of Vienna, 1924–29, Ph.D. in chemistry, 1929. Married Veza Taubner-Calderón, 1934 (died, 1963). Left Vienna, 1938; lived in England, from 1938 or 1939; also maintained a home in Zurich, from the 1970s. Married Hera Buschor (died, 1988), 1971: one daughter. Awards: many, including the Foreign Book Prize (France), 1949; Vienna Prize, 1966; Critics Prize (Germany), 1967; Great Austrian State Prize, 1967; Bavarian Academy of Fine Arts Prize, 1969; Büchner Prize, 1972; Nelly Sachs Prize, 1975; Order of Merit (Germany), 1979; Europa Prato Prize (Italy), 1980; Hebbel Prize,

1980; Nobel Prize for Literature, 1981; Kafka Prize, 1981; Great Service Cross (Germany), 1983; honorary degrees from two universities. Died in Zurich, 14 August 1994.

Selected Writings

Essays and Related Prose

Masse und Macht, 1960; as *Crowds and Power*, translated by Carol Stewart, 1962
Aufzeichnungen, 1942–1948, 1965
Die Stimmen von Marrakesch: Aufzeichnungen nach einer Reise, 1967; as *The Voices of Marrakesh: A Record of a Visit*, translated by J. A. Underwood, 1978
Der andere Prozess: Kafkas Briefe an Felice, 1969; as *Kafka's Other Trial: The Letters to Felice*, translated by Christopher Middleton, 1974
Alle vergeudete Verehrung: Aufzeichnungen, 1949–1960, 1970
Macht und Überleben: Drei Essays, 1972
Die gespaltene Zukunft: Aufsätze und Gespräche, 1972
Die Provinz des Menschen: Aufzeichnungen, 1942–1972, 1973; as *The Human Province*, translated by Joachim Neugroschel, 1978
Das Gewissen der Worte: Essays, 1975; enlarged edition, 1976; as *The Conscience of Words*, translated by Joachim Neugroschel, 1979
Die gerettete Zunge: Geschichte einer Jugend (autobiography), 1977; as *The Tongue Set Free: Remembrance of a European Childhood*, translated by Joachim Neugroschel, 1979
Die Fackel im Ohr: Lebensgeschichte, 1921–1931 (autobiography), 1980; as *The Torch in My Ear*, translated by Joachim Neugroschel, 1982
Das Augenspiel: Lebensgeschichte, 1931–1937 (autobiography), 1985; as *The Play of the Eyes*, translated by Ralph Manheim, 1986
Das Geheimherz der Uhr: Aufzeichnungen, 1973–1985, 1987; as *The Secret Heart of the Clock: Notes, Aphorisms, Fragments, 1973–1985*, translated by Joel Agee, 1989
Die Fliegenpein: Aufzeichnungen, 1992; as *The Agony of Flies: Notes and Notations*, translated by H. F. Broch de Rothermann, 1994
Aufzeichnungen, 1942–1985, 1993
Nachträge aus Hampstead: Aus den Aufzeichnungen, 1954–1971, 1994
Wortmasken: Texte zu Leben und Werk von Elias Canetti (includes seven essays by Canetti), edited by Ortrun Huber, 1995: 105–44

Other writings: the novel *Die Blendung* (1936; *Auto-da-Fé*) and three plays.

Bibliography
Bensel, Walter, editor, *Elias Canetti: Eine Personalbibliographie*, Giessen: DUX, 1989

Further Reading
Barnouw, Dagmar, "Elias Canettis poetische Anthropologie," in *Canetti lesen: Erfahrungen mit seinen Büchern*, edited by Herbert G. Göpfert, Munich: Hanser, 1975: 11–31
Barnouw, Dagmar, *Elias Canetti*, Stuttgart: Metzler, 1979: especially 1–16 and 87–100
Barnouw, Dagmar, "Elias Canetti: Poet and Intellectual," in *Major Figures of Contemporary Austrian Literature*, edited by Donald G. Daviau, New York: Lang, 1987: 117–41
Bayley, John, "Canetti and Power," in his *Selected Essays*, Cambridge and New York: Cambridge University Press, 1984: 176–91
Düssel, Reinhard, "Aspects of Confucianism in Elias Canetti's Notes and Essays," *Tamkang Review* 18 (1987): 333–41
Falk, Thomas H., *Elias Canetti*, New York: Twayne, 1993: especially 119–45
Hartung, Rudolf, "Ein neues Kafka-Bild: Anmerkung zu Canettis Essay *Der andere Prozess*," *Text und Kritik* 28 (1970): 44–49
Lawson, Richard H., *Understanding Elias Canetti*, Columbia: University of South Carolina Press, 1991: especially 79–89
Parry, Idris, "Attitudes to Power: Canetti, Kafka, Crowds, and Paranoia," *Times Literary Supplement*, 15 January 1971: 67–68
Piel, Edgar, *Elias Canetti*, Munich: Beck, 1984: especially 7–14 and 147–59
Sontag, Susan, "Mind as Passion," *New York Review of Books*, 25 September 1980: 47–52
Stern, J. P., "Canetti's Later Work," in his *The Heart of Europe: Essays on Literature and Ideology*, Oxford and Cambridge, Massachusetts: Blackwell, 1992: 331–40
Zagari, Luciano, "'Die Splitter des Staunens': Canetti über Kafka und Broch," *Annali: Studi Tedeschi* 25 (1982): 189–212

Čapek, Karel

Czech, 1890–1938

Karel Čapek was almost certainly the Czech nation's greatest writer, as well as a noted philosopher, political thinker, and teacher. He sought to make his people worthy of the independence they had achieved as a nation, almost without cost (as the gift of the Versailles Treaty). He sought to educate them – in spite of the condescension this implied. He even dared to try to amuse them.

For most of his life Čapek combined a dual role as journalist and creative writer. His numerous essays are the product of both impulses. He was hired to furnish *Lidové Noviny* (The people's news), the paper to which he contributed, with one **feuilleton** or column nearly every day. Not all of these columns were essays, of course. Indeed, most were not: they were daily columns that might present book reviews or articles on Prague and its sights, or on mundane national habits. In them Čapek followed the inspiration of Jan Neruda, the leading Czech feuilletonist, most often employing the point of view of an author chatting familiarly with his reader. Yet a substantial number are essays – enough to make their author the greatest Czech essayist. These are deeply reflective and introspective, frequently centered on nature, and dominated by a profoundly aesthetic view of life. They tend to fuse with the philosophical and lyric reflections we find in Čapek's fiction, except that introspection – the rule of a lyrical "I" – dominates the essays.

From his literary beginnings – in writings done jointly with his elder brother Josef – Čapek took up the essay. The pieces contained in their early collection, *Krakonošova zahrada* (1918; The garden of Krakonoš), are customarily referred to as *causeries*, but at least two are superb essays: one concerned with metaphysical time ("... solitary confinement is the torment of time. And time is suffering and endurance"), the other with artificial flowers ("In the widest sense, artificial flowers are made only from paper and the restless movements of fine hands which feel themselves deserted"). Later Čapek was to employ the predominantly aesthetic point of view implicit in these short pieces, but to forego their effeteness.

Čapek's greatest essays were written for newspapers in the early 1920s; a collection of them was published in book form under the title of *O nejbližších věcech* (1925; *Intimate Things*). They deal with a variety of matters, but all are small and intimate, and the Čapekovian pan-aesthetic principle applies to almost all of them. We read of frost flowers forming on a windowpane, of maps and the landscapes they symbolize, of the smell of home, of dreams, of being laid up by a cold. Only rarely does Čapek work on a grand scale, such as the essay on Ibsen's heroes as melancholics condemned to live rather than die. One piece voices the playful conceit that the contours and colors of farmland should be copied on a map; another the notion that humankind would move far more efficiently if Nature had supplied us with wheels rather than legs.

Earlier Čapek, inspired by Henri Bergson, the American pragmatists, and the Viennese journalist Karl Kraus, had written a specialized cycle on words and language, the separate essays of which were collected as *Kritika slov* (1920; A critique of language). Later cycles of essays on particular topics, also published both individually in newspapers as well as in collections, include *Zahradníkův rok* (1929; *The Gardener's Year*), *Marsyas; čili, Na okraj literatury* (1931; *In Praise of Newspapers*), *O věcech obecných; čili, Zoon politikon* (1932; On political affairs; or, *Zoon Politikon*), and *Měl jsem psa a kočku* (1939; *I Had a Dog and a Cat*). There are also five volumes of travel sketches of trips Čapek made to Italy, England, Spain, Holland, and Scandinavia, but these are closer to humorously tinged reportage than to essays as such.

A majority of these essays are playful or humorous, although those on domestic pets are interwoven with original and valid observations. The political essays are quite serious and two, "Betlém" (1924; "Bethlehem") and "O malých poměrech (1925; "On a Small Scale"), preach the Čapkovian gospel of smallness as a model for his homeland: Czechoslovakia, like Holland, can become great. The most famous is without doubt "Proč nejsem komunistou" (1924; "Why I Am Not a Communist"), which was suppressed during the whole period of communist rule in Czechoslovakia. Finally, *In Praise of Newspapers* is actually in praise of all the minor literary arts, including folklore and the romance novels popular with maid-servants; there is even a lighthearted essay on pornography.

Later in life Čapek, perhaps with age and under the pressure of his quasi-official position (he was the close friend as well as biographer of the president, T. G. Masaryk), moved away from humor; his columns are devoted more to other writers and outstanding personalities, and often have a decidedly official quality to them. As essays they rank below the earlier pieces.

More perhaps than in his other work, in his essays Karel Čapek created a broad panorama of life and the world as he himself viewed it. The diversity of his essays can in part be explained by his need to educate his people in many things, as well as to reconcile them to the small size of their nation's world.

WILLIAM E. HARKINS

Biography

Born 9 January 1890 in Malé Svatoňovice, Bohemia. Studied at Charles University, Prague, 1909–15, Ph.D. in philosophy, 1915; Universities of Paris and Berlin, 1909–10. Wrote for *Lidové Noviny* (Literary journal). Cofounder, with his brother Josef Čapek, František Langer, and Edmond Konrad, Pátnici (Friday circle) avant-garde group. Associated with the Vinohrady Theater, Prague,

1921–23. Married Olga Scheinpflugová, 1935. Died in Prague, 25 December 1938.

Selected Writings

Essays and Related Prose
Krakonošova zahrada, with Josef Čapek, 1918
Kritika slov, 1920
Italské listy, 1923; as *Letters from Italy*, translated by Francis P. Marchant, 1929
Anglické listy, 1924; as *Letters from England*, translated by Paul Selver, 1925
O nejbližších věcech, 1925; as *Intimate Things*, translated by Dora Round, 1935
Zahradníkův rok, 1929; as *The Gardener's Year*, translated by M. and R. Weatherall, 1931
Vylet do Španěl, 1930; as *Letters from Spain*, translated by Paul Selver, 1932
Marsyas; čili, Na okraj literatury (1919–1931), 1931; as *In Praise of Newspapers and Other Essays on the Margin of Literature*, translated by M. and R. Weatherall, 1951
Obrázky z Holandska, 1932; as *Letters from Holland*, translated by Paul Selver, 1933
O věcech obecných; čili, Zoon politikon, 1932
Cesta na sever, 1936; as *Travels in the North*, translated by M. and R. Weatherall, 1939
Měl jsem psa a kočku, with Josef Čapek, 1939; as *I Had a Dog and a Cat*, translated by M. and R. Weatherall, 1940
Kalendář, 1940
O lidech, 1940
Neuskutečněný dialog (selected essays), edited by Gustav Földi, 1978

Other writings: several novels (including *Hordubal*, 1933; *Povětroň* [*Meteor*], 1934; *Obyčejny život* [*An Ordinary Life*], 1934), plays with his brother Josef Čapek (including *R.U.R.* [*Rossum's Universal Robots*], 1920; *Ze života hmyzu* [*The Insect Play*], 1921), short stories, a biography of T. G. Masaryk (3 vols., 1928–35), and correspondence.

Collected works edition: *Spisky bratří*, 51 vols., 1928–47.

Bibliography
Křepinská, Margita, *Karel Čapek, bibliografie díla a literatury o životě a díle*, Prague: Národní Knihovna, 4 vols., 1991

Further Reading
Černy, Václav, *Karel Čapek*, Prague: Borový, 1936
Doležel, Lubomír, "Karel Čapek and Vladislav Vančura: An Essay in Comparative Stylistics," in *Narrative Modes in Czech Literature*, Toronto: University of Toronto Press, 1973: 91–111
Harkins, William E., *Karel Čapek*, New York: Columbia University Press, 1962
Harkins, William E., "Karel Čapek and the Ordinary Life," *Books Abroad* 36 (1962): 273–76
Harkins, William E., "Karel Čapek," in *European Writers*, vol. 10, edited by George Stade, New York: Scribner, 1990: 1565–89
Klíma, Ivan, *Karel Čapek*, Prague: Československý Spisovatel, 1962
Králik, Oldřich, *První řada v díle Karla Čapka*, Ostrava: Profil, 1972
Makin, Michael, and Jindřich Toman, editors, *Karel Čapek*, Ann Arbor: Michigan Slavic Publications, 1992
Matuška, Alexander, *Karel Čapek, an Essay*, London: Allen and Unwin, 1964 (original Czech edition, 1963)
Mukařovský, Jan, "Karel Čapek," in *Kapitoly z české poetiky*, Prague: Svoboda, 1948: 325–400
Wellek, René, "Karel Čapek," in *Essays on Czech Literature*, The Hague: Mouton, 1963: 46–61

Cardoza y Aragón, Luis

Guatemalan, 1904–1992

Better known in international literary circles for his poetry and his seminal works on Mexican mural painting, Luis Cardoza y Aragón left behind an important body of essays. A constant search for innovation and a surrealist perspective characterize his extensive literary production. This experimentation with literary forms led him to conceptualize the essay as a "genre that has much of poetry and the most rigorous thought." In his essays, Cardoza y Aragón blends poetic prose, chronicles, memoirs, and other literary forms to provide texture and depth to his analysis. He explores complex issues from several perspectives, allowing tension and doubt to emerge.

A lifetime radical, committed to the cause of socialism, freedom, and democracy, Cardoza y Aragón struggled against all forms of "isms" in the cultural and political arena. In his essays on art production he staunchly defends artistic freedom and rejects any attempt to value the work of art on political or ideological merits. Throughout the years, Cardoza y Aragón openly debated with leftist intellectuals and artists on this question, while proclaiming the need to develop a Marxist aesthetics.

His best-known essay, *Guatemala, las líneas de su mano* (1955; Guatemala, the lines in her hand), exemplifies both Cardoza y Aragón's political thought and his hybrid approach to the genre. The book is a mixture of memoirs, short stories, literary and cultural criticism, and political and historical analysis. Exiled in Mexico from 1932, Cardoza y Aragón returned to Guatemala in 1944 to participate in the revolutionary process that took place under the administrations of Juan José Arevalo (1944–51) and Jacobo Arbenz (1951–54). During those years Cardoza y Aragón began to write the essay, but had to finish it in Mexico shortly after the 1954 military coup that ended the Guatemalan democratic experiment. Regarded as a literary classic, *Guatemala, las líneas de su mano* is a detailed and vivid portrayal of the land and its people. The book is divided into three thematic sections: a nostalgic and poetic evocation of his childhood and the geography of his native land, an overview of Guatemala's history from the Popol Vuh to the present, and, finally, a sociopolitical essay which portrays Guatemala as the "land of the eternal tyranny." Using Marxist analysis, Cardoza y Aragón discusses those issues he considers key to understanding the crossroads facing Guatemala at that historical moment. He questions the idea of a Guatemalan national unity, while bringing the Indian question to the forefront. He also proposes the need for a sweeping revolution to bring about the consolidation of Guatemalan nationality as well as equality and freedom to all its people. Although decidedly anti-imperialist in tone, the essay also emphasizes the internal structure of class and racial oppression, thus breaking away from the nationalist interpretation of Guatemala's socioeconomic plight that dominated the political discourse of the period.

Cardoza y Aragón further develops his thesis regarding the national question and the revolution in *La revolución guatemalteca* (1955; The Guatemalan revolution). Written during the last days of the Arbenz administration, this controversial essay discusses the external and internal conditions that brought about the 1954 military takeover. Although a rigorous analytical piece, the essay lacks the polished style displayed by Cardoza y Aragón in his previous work.

One of the most important themes of *Guatemala, las líneas de su mano*, which is further developed in Cardoza y Aragón's subsequent essays, is the role of the indigenous element in the forging of Guatemala's past, present, and future. Cardoza y Aragón sets the liberation and incorporation of this sector into the social, economic, political, and cultural life as a precondition for establishing Guatemalan nationality. While emphasizing the prevalence of the pre-Hispanic culture in contemporary Guatemala, Cardoza y Aragón, however, sharply criticizes the *indigenista* literary movement for its romantic and simplistic representation of the Indian experience. On the other hand, critics have found Cardoza y Aragón guilty of promoting a static view of the Indian population and culture. Still, *Guatemala, las líneas de su mano* remains one of the most penetrating and profound analyses of Guatemalan society, having laid the foundations for further discussion concerning the Guatemalan national question, specifically on the role of the indigenous population in the nation-building process.

Cardoza y Aragón's essays on Mexican art are recognized as some of the most thought-provoking works on Mexican artistic trends and their main exponents. *La nube y el reloj* (1940; The cloud and the clock) is widely regarded as an indispensable work on Mexican painting. In this seminal essay, Cardoza y Aragón traces the historical evolution of Mexican painting, discusses the work of contemporary Mexican painters, and offers his thoughts concerning artistic creation. While recognizing Mexican mural painting as one of the highest expressions of the Mexican Revolution, he also stresses its universal character. In *Orozco* (1959) and *México: Pintura de hoy* (1964; *Mexican Art Today*), as well as in other full-length studies, Cardoza y Aragón offers illuminating insights into the work and personality of the major Mexican artists of this century. Guatemalan artists and writers such as Rafael Landivar and Miguel Ángel Asturias were also the object of Cardoza y Aragón's inquisitive mind. His last major work, *Miguel Angel Asturias: Casi novela* (1991; Miguel Angel Asturias: almost a novel), is another fine example of his hybrid essay and poetic prose.

Cardoza y Aragón also wrote an array of essays in journals and newspapers. Some of his most important essays, published in the influential journal **Cuadernos Americanos** (American notebooks), were later included in *Guatemala con una piedra adentro* (1983; Guatemala with a stone inside). Contrary to what the title seems to imply, the book is not exclusively dedicated to Guatemalan political and cultural themes; it also contains important essays on Mexican artistic life, including sketches of several major Mexican artists and writers, such as David Alfaro Siqueiros and **Alfonso Reyes**.

CAMILLE VILLAFAÑE

Biography

Born 21 June 1904 in Antigua, Guatemala. Self-taught. Lived in Paris and studied first medicine, then arts and politics, 1921–29. Lived in Mexico, 1932–44, 1954–92. Returned to Guatemala during the rebellion against Ubizo, 1944, and collaborated with the new president, Juan José Arevalo. Cofounder, *Revista de Guatemala*

(Guatemala review), 1945–51. Founder, Casa de la Cultura y el Movimiento Guatemalteco por la Paz (House of culture and Guatemalan movement for peace). Diplomat in Sweden, Norway, and the Soviet Union; Guatemalan ambassador to Colombia and Chile. Married Lya Kostakowsky. Contributor to *El Nacional Dominical* and *Los Suplementos de El Nacional* (Supplements to The national). José Clemente Orozco professor, National Autonomous University of Mexico, Mexico City, from 1980. Awards: Quetzal de Jade Award, 1979; Rubén Darío Prize, 1986. Order of Aguila Azteca, 1979. Died in Mexico City in 1992.

Selected Writings

Essays and Related Prose
Carlos Mérida, 1927
Torre de Babel, 1930
Rufino Tamayo, 1934
La nube y el reloj, 1940
Apolo y Coatlicue: Ensayos mexicanos de espina y flor, 1944
El pueblo de Guatemala, la United Fruit y la protesta de Washington, 1954
Guatemala, las líneas de su mano, 1955
La revolución guatemalteca, 1955
Orozco, 1959
Nuevo Mundo, 1960
José Guadalupe Posada, 1964
México: Pintura de hoy, 1964; as *Mexican Art Today*, 1966
Perfiles, 1964
Círculos concéntricos, 1967
Guatemala con una piedra adentro, 1983
Malevich: Apuntes sobre su aventura icárica, 1983
Antología (selections), 1987
Ojo/Voz, 1988
Tierra de belleza convulsiva, edited by Alberto Enríquez Perea, 1991
Miguel Angel Asturias: Casi novela, 1991

Other writings: poetry, memoirs, exhibition catalogues, and books about travels in Russia (1946) and Mexican art and culture.

Further Reading

Albizúres Palma, Francisco, "Cardoza y Aragón," in *Diccionario de autores guatemaltecos*, Guatemala City: Tipografía Nacional, Colección Guatemala, vol. 13, 1984
Arias, Arturo, "Consideraciones en torno al género y la génesis de *Guatemala, las líneas de su mano*," *Tragaluz* 2, no. 15 (May 1987): 24–28
Figueroa Ibarra, Carlos, "Luis Cardoza y Aragón: La redención del desterrado," *Plural* 14, no. 160 (January 1985): 26–31
Flores, Angel, "Luis Cardoza y Aragón," in *Spanish American Authors: The Twentieth Century*, New York: Wilson, 1992
Mandujano Jacobo, Pilar, "Luis Cardoza y Aragón," in *Diccionario de escritores mexicanos, siglo XX*, Mexico City: National Autonomous University of Mexico, 1988
Paz, Octavio, "Luis Cardoza y Aragón (1904–1992)," *Vuelta* 16, no. 191 (October 1992): 50–51
Rodríguez, Francisco, "Luis Cardoza y Aragón: Las paradojas de la escritura," *Plural* 22, no. 264 (September 1993): 52–55
Salgado, María A., "Guatemala," in *Handbook of Latin American Literature*, edited by David William Foster, New York: Garland, 1992: 317–32
Talavera, Laura, "Luis Cardoza y Aragón: La última entrevista," *Nexos* 15, no. 178 (October 92): 5–7
Xirau, Ramón, "Review of *Poesías completas y algunas prosas* by Luis Cardoza y Aragón," *Vuelta* 1, no. 6 (May 1977): 32–33
Zimmerman, Marc, and Raúl Rojas, *Guatemala: Voces desde el silencio: Un collage épico*, Guatemala City: Oscar de León Palacios y Palo de Hormigo, 1993

Carlyle, Thomas

British, 1795–1881

Thomas Carlyle's essay writing career began with two pieces in the **Edinburgh Review** in 1827: "John Paul Friedrich Richter" and "The State of German Literature." Reviews of books on Richter and German literature, these first essays were a hybrid of literary criticism and cultural critique. The same can be said – despite their lesser scope – of a number of essays on German literature published in the *Foreign Review* in 1828 and 1829. Here, and later in *Fraser's Magazine*, Carlyle earned a reputation as the interpreter of German literature to England.

In "Burns" (1828), Carlyle took the publication of Lockhart's life of Burns as an opportunity to articulate a view of Burns and biography which anticipated his own later work in that vein. Combining aphoristic style with Augustan periods, Carlyle emphasized his points with alliteration and antithesis.

Among subsequent essays which identify Carlyle's unique tone and style are "Signs of the Times" (1829), "Thoughts on History" (1830), "Characteristics" (1831), and "Biography" (1832). "Signs of the Times" articulates an anti-utilitarian philosophy in a style both idiosyncratic and broadly allusive. Neologisms, compounds, and wordplay abound, which critics attribute in part to Carlyle's familiarity with and love of German language and literature. "Thoughts on History," a **familiar essay** manifesting the cadences of Augustan prose, classifies the sources and kinds of history but is also sprinkled with neologisms, references to "the Unknown, the Infinite in man's life," and social-critical asides. The essay defends the uses of the past and articulates assumptions which guide Carlyle in such later works as *The French Revolution* (1837).

If any single essay by Carlyle earns him the honorific, "Sage of Chelsea," it is the aphoristic and allusive "Characteristics." Critical of the philosophical and moral state of the modern world, Carlyle stresses the "dynamical" and the "vital," arguing for "a spiritual principle" in society. Contrasting the health of past societies with the "maladies" and "diseases" that afflict the thought and behavior of the present, Carlyle strikes the first notes of a theme he elaborates on in *Past and Present* (1843). Highly figured, "Characteristics" trades heavily in images of light and darkness and oppositions of the natural and the artificial, employing metaphors of chaos and the whirlwind.

Like the essay on history, "Biography" manifests the more analytical qualities of Carlyle's style. Subordinating as he classifies various fictional forms of the biographical, Carlyle praises "the smallest historical *fact*" because "it is not a dream, but a reality." Even more than "Thoughts on History," "Biography" anticipates the biographies Carlyle was to write on John Sterling, Robert Burns, and Frederick the Great.

Modern critics usually class *Sartor Resartus* (1836) as a hybrid autobiographical novel, philosophical **treatise**, and cultural critique, but seen in a certain light, it also manifests its affinity with the essay form. Structurally, tonally, and specifically, it focuses on the essayist/editor/reviewer relation. The "editor," who gathers and presents the papers of one Diogenes Teufelsdröch, is a parody of the journal editor. Teufelsdröch and his pedantic style are a caricature of the more pompous reviewer/essayist – and of Carlyle himself. The subjects *Sartor Resartus* treats – fashion, philosophy, and mores – are also as varied as the subjects considered in any of the early 19th-century **reviews**.

Originally written for **John Stuart Mill**'s utilitarian *Westminster Review*, the long essay *Chartism* was rejected by Mill and J. G. Lockhart, editor of the Tory **Quarterly Review**. Published by itself in 1839, it expresses sympathy for the conditions of the working class but is generally agreed to be an uneven work.

With his reputation assured by the publication of *The French Revolution*, Carlyle capitalized on that book's popularity by developing a series of six lectures which became *On Heroes, Hero-Worship, and the Heroic in History* (1841). Combining his interest in history and a focus on individuals, the six lectures expand the conception of the essay as they reflect on different ideas of the hero: as divinity, prophet, poet, priest, man of letters, and king. Structurally, *On Heroes* is more narrative and descriptive than Carlyle's earlier review essays. Stylistically, the book owes a debt to the lecture hall, its emphatic and oratorical redundancies diluting some of the more Germanic features of the earlier essays. The conservative, authoritarian tone evident in *Chartism* takes on a new form in *On Heroes*.

Somewhat in the manner of *Sartor Resartus* and *On Heroes*, *Past and Present* expands the notion of the essay form inasmuch as Carlyle combines historical re-creation, social analysis, and cultural criticism to descry the paradoxical prosperity amid poverty and waste that characterized England as it approached the end of the first half of the 19th century.

The latter 1840s found Carlyle contributing occasional pieces primarily to newspapers. "Occasional Discourse on the Negro-Question" (the more offensive "Nigger" became part of the title when it was published separately in 1853) appeared anonymously in *Fraser's Magazine* in 1849. It was followed by *Latter-Day Pamphlets* in 1850, eight essays published separately – possibly because no periodical would print them. In "The Negro Question" Carlyle addresses the subject of West Indian slavery in intemperate and (for the 20th century) doubly repugnant terms. In this essay and the *Latter-Day Pamphlets* Carlyle's frustration and cynicism with English society become prominent. Strident, satirical, and offensive to former friends like John Stuart Mill, these essays nevertheless raise serious questions about democracy, mass persuasion, and politics in modern society.

Longer biographical essays on Sterling, **Samuel Johnson**, and Burns followed in the 1850s, along with the monumental *History of Friedrich the Second called Frederick the Great* (1858–65). *Shooting Niagara: and After?* appeared first in *Macmillan's Magazine* in 1867 before being published separately. Critical of England's move toward democracy and its wallowing in hypocrisy, Carlyle in this long essay nevertheless holds out some hope, should the natural aristocrats of the nation "develop themselves into something of heroic Well-doing by act and by word."

One of Carlyle's ablest critics, G. B. Tennyson (1966), has said that Carlyle "created the taste for serious works of non-fiction prose," adding that he was a "pioneer" for the essay as "a form for carrying ideas to a mass audience." Carlyle's passionate, often irreverent tone, and what increasingly reads like oratory, nevertheless elaborates a vision and a critique of England in the middle four decades of the 19th century which remains a landmark not only of social criticism but of the powerful and persuasive force of the essay.

ED BLOCK, JR.

Biography

Born 4 December 1795 in Ecclefechan, Dumfriesshire. Studied at the Annan Academy, 1805–09; University of Edinburgh, 1809–14, B.A., 1813; studied for the ministry of the Church of Scotland, 1813–18; studied Scottish law, 1819. Taught at Annan Academy, 1814–16, Kirkcaldy Grammar School, 1816–18, and privately in Edinburgh, 1818–22. Wrote for the *Edinburgh Encyclopaedia*; full-time writer, from 1824, contributing to journals such as the *Edinburgh Review* and *Fraser's Magazine*. Married Jane Welsh, 1826 (died, 1866). Lived in Craigenputtock, Dumfriesshire, 1828–34, and Chelsea, London, 1834–81. Rector, University of Edinburgh, 1866. Awards: Prussian Order of Merit, 1874; declined a baronetcy from Disraeli. Died in London, 5 February 1881.

Selected Writings

Essays and Related Prose
Critical and Miscellaneous Essays, 4 vols., 1838
Chartism, 1839
On Heroes, Hero-Worship, and the Heroic in History (lectures), 1841; edited by Michael K. Goldberg, 1993
Past and Present, 1843
Latter-Day Pamphlets (*The Present Time*; *Model Prisons*; *Downing Street*; *The New Downing Street*; *Stump-Orator*; *Parliaments*; *Hudson's Statue*; *Jesuitism*), 8 vols. bound into 1 vol., 1850
Occasional Discourse on the Nigger Question, 1853
Shooting Niagara: and After?, 1867
Rescued Essays, edited by Percy Newberry, 1892
Unpublished Lectures: Lectures on the History of Literature or the Successive Periods of European Culture, edited by R. P. Karkaria, 1892
Montaigne and Other Essays, Chiefly Biographical, 1897
Historical Sketches of Notable Persons and Events in the Reigns of James I and Charles I, edited by Alexander Carlyle, 1898
A Carlyle Reader (selections), edited by G. B. Tennyson, 1969

Other writings: the fiction work *Sartor Resartus* (1836), a three-volume history *The French Revolution* (1837), a six-volume history of Frederick the Great of Prussia (1858–65), other works on history and biography, and several volumes of correspondence to members of his family and figures such as **Goethe**, John Stuart Mill, **John Ruskin**, and **Ralph Waldo Emerson**. Translated Goethe's *Wilhelm Meister's Apprenticeship* (1824) and works by other German writers.

Collected works edition: *Works* (Centenary Edition), edited by H. D. Traill, 30 vols., 1896–99.

Bibliographies
Dillon, R. W., "A Centenary Bibliography of Carlylean Studies, 1928–1974," *Bulletin of Bibliography* (October–December 1975); supplements, 1975–1980, 1983
Dyer, I. W., *A Bibliography of Thomas Carlyle's Writings and Ana*, New York: Octagon, 1968 (original edition, 1928)
Tarr, Rodger L., *Thomas Carlyle: A Bibliography of English-Language Criticism, 1824–1974*, Charlottesville: University Press of Virginia, 1976
Tarr, Rodger L., *Thomas Carlyle: A Descriptive Bibliography*, Pittsburgh: University of Pittsburgh Press, and Oxford: Clarendon Press, 1989

Further Reading

Harrold, Charles Frederick, *Carlyle and German Thought, 1819–1834*, New Haven, Connecticut: Yale University Press, and London: Oxford University Press, 1934

Heffer, Simon, *Moral Desperado: A Life of Thomas Carlyle*, London: Weidenfeld and Nicolson, 1995

Holloway, John, *The Victorian Sage: Studies in Argument*, London: Macmillan, 1953; New York: Norton, 1965

LaValley, Albert J., *Carlyle and the Idea of the Modern: Studies in Carlyle's Prophetic Literature and Its Relation to Blake, Nietzsche, Marx and Others*, New Haven, Connecticut: Yale University Press, 1968

Leopold, Werner F., *Die religiöse Wurzel von Carlyles literarischer Wirksamkeit dargestellt an seinem Aufsatz "State of German Literature" (1827)*, Halle: Niemeyer, 1922

Levine, George, *The Boundaries of Fiction: Carlyle, Macaulay, Newman*, Princeton, New Jersey: Princeton University Press, 1968

Roellinger, F. X., "The Early Development of Carlyle's Style," *PMLA* (1957)

Shine, Hill, *Carlyle's Early Reading, to 1834, with an Introductory Essay on His Intellectual Development*, Lexington: University of Kentucky Libraries, 1953

Sussman, Herbert L., *Fact into Figure: Typology in Carlyle, Ruskin, and the Pre-Raphaelite Brotherhood*, Columbus: Ohio State University Press, 1979

Taylor, Alan Carey, *Carlyle, sa première fortune littéraire en France (1825–1865)*, Paris: Champion, 1929

Tennyson, G. B., *Sartor Called Resartus: The Genesis, Structure and Style of Thomas Carlyle's First Major Work*, Princeton, New Jersey: Princeton University Press, 1966

Carman, Bliss

Canadian, 1861–1929

While known primarily as a poet, Bliss Carman also developed a considerable reputation in his day as cultural commentator in the American magazine world and as a Canadian and American literary critic, in the period from 1888 to 1922. His essays on everything from canoeing and hiking through to the philosophy of poetry were published mainly from 1890 to about 1905 and appeared in such publications as the *Book News Monthly*, *Bookman*, *Boston Evening Transcript*, *Chap-Book*, *Commercial Advertiser*, *Criterion*, *Critic*, *Forum*, *Independent*, *Literary World*, *Literary Miscellany*, *New York Times*, *Progress*, *Saturday Night*, and the *World*.

Carman had a solid reputation as a readable columnist and critic, and many of his efforts were assembled in his lifetime in four collections. *The Poetry of Life* (1905) is the most representative collection, as it displays the variety of his work and contains some of his best writing. These collections do not contain all of Carman's prose, and a large number of his best pieces (especially his reviews) are today uncollected newspaper clippings in Canadian archives. Work is under way to collect and republish a larger selection from all of Carman's prose.

Carman was a professional, journalistic writer who well understood that his popular audience would not stand for long-windedness, tonal dullness, obscurity of reference, or elaborate theoretical postures. He was an entertaining, cheerful writer, an excellent popular philosopher, and a good scholar who included his scholarly interests in an entertaining, or at least agile, way. He could write about the most potentially banal of topics (the history of the human foot, for example) with a

natural intelligence, charm, and wit. He was highly conscious of the limitations of magazine journalism, and once said in a column that "The beauty of style is like the beauty of nature, achieved through infinite care of results, with infinite carelessness of time. The successes of journalism are achieved through infinite care of time, with infinite carelessness of the manner in which results are expressed" ("The Modern Athenian: A Note on Style," 1896). He challenged and provoked his audience as much as possible, within the constraints of popular taste.

As a social critic his efforts ranged from essays advocating socialism and commenting on the moral shame of American imperialism through to his sometimes missionary-like advocacy of mind cure and self-development. He was a vigorous apologist for all sorts of improving spiritual activities (e.g. meditation, nature observation, dance, art and poetry appreciation), and some of his essays had their origin as lectures he gave when on cross-country tours in both Canada and the United States. His audience was more American than Canadian, so his comments on modern society are focused primarily on the American scene. He saw modern American culture as essentially mechanical, soulless, and mentally unhealthy. His readings of Romantic, transcendentalist, and Victorian authors, of advocates of Unitarianism like François Delsarte, and of philosophers such as Josiah Royce and **George Santayana** (the latter both professors of his when he attended Harvard University), inspired him to write innumerable popular essays in moral philosophy in which he spoke against the distractions of materialism and on behalf of the antidote value of spiritual cultivation. Just as much of his poetry has a proto-hippie ring to it, most of his prose falls within the broadly mystical, curative, and countercultural aims of current New Age writing. His progressive ideas and attitudes give to his prose a very contemporary quality.

Carman always wrote from a solid core of common sense, and this prevented his mind-cure writing from the worst excesses of avuncularity, while it stabilized his literary criticism with a likable tone and a convincing, durable set of aesthetic standards. He could be tough-minded in his reviews of his contemporaries, but most of his works of literary criticism were idealistic, appreciative essays advocating the poets and literary movements he saw as most fit to answer the soullessness of Victorian and impending modern times. He wrote general essays on literary criticism itself, on the artist's role in society, and on the relationships between religion and art. In such pieces he often showed a generous and nicely explorative temperament as an advocate of "the masters and sustainers of the spiritual life, the seers and prophets, but the loving skeptics as well" ("Marginal Notes: Scribes and Pharisees," 1899). As a theorist he commonly reminded himself and others to hold all literary "doctrines lovingly but lightly" ("The Artist and His Critic," 1897). He was a dialogic rather than an authoritarian critic.

Most of Carman's literary criticism advocates the work of the Romantics and the transcendentalist writers, but as editor, with Richard Hovey, of *Chap-Book* during the 1890s, he became aware of various manifestations of symbolist art and loudly advocated that tradition of writing as he saw it manifested in writers as otherwise diverse as Stephen Crane, Emily Dickinson, Maurice Maeterlinck, and **William Butler Yeats**.

Carman is commonly seen as a straightbackwardly moving writer because of his scorn for the ironic mode, and he was to write that in his view, "Evil is the irony of the universe, the giant sarcasm of existence, the titanic gibe in the teeth of good" ("The Modern Athenian"). Consequently, he appears anti-Modernist in his literary tastes, but his vigorous and very expressive advocacy of the symbolist tradition inspires some of his best critical essays and demonstrates that he understood an affinity between the symbolist writers' aim to "create a sacred book" ("Marginal Notes," 1898) and the more mystical compulsions of emerging Modernism.

Carman's literary criticism was aimed at a popular audience and was clearly and thoughtfully written. It remains highly readable today because of its social progressiveness, its centrality in the literary-critical milieu of North America at the turn of the century, and as prose written by a sage who as a popular writer did not permit himself to become a hack.

TERRY WHALEN

Biography
William Bliss Carman. Cousin of the poet and fiction writer Charles G. D. Roberts and distant relative of **Ralph Waldo Emerson**. Born 15 April 1861 in Fredericton, New Brunswick. Studied at the University of New Brunswick, Fredericton, B.A. in Latin and Greek, 1881, M.A. in English literature, 1884; Oxford University and Edinburgh University, 1882–83; Harvard University, Cambridge, Massachusetts, 1886–88. Remained a "genteel vagabond" and bachelor all his life. Lived mostly in the United States, working as a literary journalist for journals and magazines in New York and Boston; traveled extensively in both North America and Europe. Cofounding editor, *Chap-Book*, from 1894. Met Mary Perry King, who became his patron and lifelong friend, 1896. Awards: Lorne Pierce Medal, 1928; many honorary degrees. Died (of a heart seizure) in New Canaan, Connecticut, 8 June 1929.

Selected Writings

Essays and Related Prose
The Kinship of Nature, 1903
The Friendship of Art, 1904
The Poetry of Life, 1905
The Making of Personality, 1908

Other writings: many volumes of poetry (including *Low Tide on Grand Pré: A Book of Lyrics*, 1893; *Vagabondia* series, with Richard Hovey, 1894–1900; *Ballads and Lyrics*, 1902, revised edition, 1923; *Sappho: One Hundred Lyrics*, 1903; *Sanctuary: Sunshine House Sonnets*, 1929), broadsheets, lyrical pageants, and correspondence (including in *Letters*, edited by H. Pearson Gundy, 1981, and *Bliss Carman's Letters to Margaret Lawrence 1927–1929*, edited by D. M. R. Bentley, 1995).

Bibliography
Sorfleet, John R., "A Primary and Secondary Bibliography of Bliss Carman's Work," in *Bliss Carman: A Reappraisal*, edited by Gerald Lynch, Ottawa: University of Ottawa Press, 1990

Further Reading
Bentley, D. M. R., "Carman and Mind Cure: Theory and Technique," in *Bliss Carman: A Reappraisal*, edited by Gerald Lynch, Ottawa: University of Ottawa Press, 1990
Sorfleet, John R., Introduction to *The Poems of Bliss Carman*, Toronto: McClelland and Stewart, 1976
Whalen, Terry, *Bliss Carman and His Works*, Downsview, Ontario: ECW Press, 1983
Whalen, Terry, "Carman as Critic," in *Bliss Carman: A Reappraisal*, edited by Gerald Lynch, Ottawa: University of Ottawa Press, 1990

Castellanos, Rosario
Mexican, 1925–1974

Despite meeting an untimely death in 1974, Rosario Castellanos left her readers a sizeable legacy: 12 books of poetry, three novels (one unpublished), three volumes of short stories, several plays, and four collections of essays. Lifelong friend Oscar Bonifaz explains in *Remembering Rosario* (1990) that Castellanos, best known initially for her poetry, was encouraged by her colleagues to explore additional outlets for her creative and socially conscious talent. Under these auspices, Castellanos' most productive period of prose writing occurred while she was working on her prize-winning second novel, *Oficio de tinieblas* (1962; *The Book of Lamentations*), which is considered by many to be her masterpiece. In fact, the years following the writing of *The Book of Lamentations* reflect a marked change in her writing: where alienation, loneliness, and melancholy were key elements in her early poetry, later literary works are characterized by irony, humor, and wit, as if she had arrived at some point of inner peace.

It is through her craft as an essayist that this development is especially evident. Like many fellow writers, Castellanos was a journalist as well as an author, contributing articles regularly to Mexican newspapers (*Novedades* [News], *¡Siempre!* [Always], and *Excélsior*) and periodicals (*Revista de la Universidad de México* [University of Mexico review] and *La Palabra y el Hombre* [The word and the man]). Many of these are included in Castellanos' collections: *Juicios sumarios* (1966; Summary judgments), *Mujer que sabe latín ...* (1973; A woman who knows Latin ...), *El uso de la palabra* (1974; The use of the word), and *El mar y sus pescaditos* (1975; The sea and its little fish). There are also more than 100 uncollected essays.

In this particular genre Castillos cultivates an intimate space in which to discuss a variety of topics, characterized by frequent interior dialogues with her readers in which she shares particular insights or confidences. According to colleague and confidant Emilio Carbadillo, Castellanos' stylistic evolution was due to the relative anonymity of the reading public, which provided her with a "safe" venue in which to reveal perspectives previously stifled by her characteristic reserve. To this assertion Myralyn F. Allgood (1990) adds that Castellanos' reading public was highly receptive, as she was already a household name, synonymous with prize-winning novels, short stories, and poetry. Both Carbadillo and Allgood echo what the author herself describes in "El escritor como periodista" (1972; The writer as journalist), in which she muses about what would have happened had she remained in the "limbo" of her own private world of poetry. She likens her essay style to a spontaneous conversation with friends, finding herself comfortable with the notion of chatting with her reading public as an anonymous and multiple "you."

This is not to say her topics are necessarily informal. With humor and often biting irony, Castellanos' essays address what she considered transcendent truths across personal, social, political, and feminist lines. Her first collection, *Juicios sumarios*, reveals the strong intellectual influence of existentialist **Simone de Beauvoir**, social and religious thinker **Simone Weil**, and literary figures Sor Juana Inés de la Cruz, Gabriela Mistral, Emily Dickinson, and **Virginia Woolf**. In this volume, Castellanos problematizes specific philosophical positions with regard to social issues.

If *Juicios sumarios* indicates an interest in "cultural ideology and gender" (Allgood), her next collection, *Mujer que sabe latín . . .*, "argues an overtly feminist viewpoint" (Naomi Lindstrom, 1980). Lindstrom posits that this collection reflects thoughts on the status of women and indicates a future for feminist criticism by superseding the simple denunciation and specific grievances so popular in her time, most notably by contextualizing woman's experience in order to re-examine specific gender roles, as in "Las amistades peligrosas" (1973; Dangerous liaisons). Bonifaz states that her focus is primarily the condition of woman in Mexican culture. This may be the case in "La mujer mexicana del siglo 19" (1973; "19th-Century Mexican Woman"), in which Castellanos describes how myth keeps women marginalized within the culture and history of Mexico (Maureen Ahern, 1988). However, her discussion of the symbiotic relationship between the oppressed and the oppressor in "La participación de la mujer mexicana en la educación formal" (1973; The participation of the Mexican woman in formal education) could well describe a more universal social condition. According to Ahern, this is especially apparent in "La mujer y su imagen" (1973; "Woman and Her Image"), in which Castellanos refutes the idea of biological determinism by way of a parody of scientific language.

The generalizability of Castellanos' themes seem to increase in *El uso de la palabra*, a collection compiled posthumously by José Emilio Pacheco, and including essays from the period 1963 to 1974. The topics span commentaries on local and current events as well as personal and professional issues. In all cases, Castellanos illuminates that transcendent kernel of truth for her readers with humor and irony. In "Una propiedad privada" (1969; Private property), she analyzes the social and psychological constructs behind a father's murder of his sons. In later essays, Castellanos reveals a deeply personal facet, for example in "Anticipación a la nostalgia" (1971; Anticipating nostalgia), in which she confronts the sense of loss with regard to good friends and Mexico. Her experiences as a mother surface as well, for instance in "Mundo de cambios" (1973; World of changes), where a single incident with her son leads her to extrapolate on the experience of motherhood as a whole. On a lighter note, her irascible humor with regard to her role as a diplomat is revealed in "La diplomacia al desnudo" (1974; "Sheer Diplomacy"), where diplomatic subtleties are reduced to one simple recommendation: weather as the suggested topic of conversation.

The last collection Castellanos submitted was received two days before her death. *El mar y sus pescaditos* was oriented toward literature, including critiques and reviews of Latin American writers and their works.

A review of the material written about Castellanos and her literary work reveals that the bulk of research deals with her novels and poetry as well as feminist thematics. However, her essays, short stories and theater, as well as the social and political themes interwoven in her texts, remain to be fully examined and contextualized. Rosario Castellanos was much more than a talented writer with a specific social agenda: she was diplomat, philosopher, mother, wife, social activist, intellectual, educator, and perhaps most importantly, an artist endowed with the unique ability to connect with her readership through her insightful writing.

JENNIFER FARRAR

Biography
Born 25 May 1925 in Mexico City. Studied at the College of Philosophy and Letters, National Autonomous University of Mexico, Mexico City, 1944–50, M.A. in philosophy, 1950; University of Madrid, 1950–51. Director of cultural programs, 1951–53, and staff member, Institute of Arts and Sciences, both in Tuxtla Gutiérrez, Chiapas. Director, El Teatro Guiñol/Petul (puppet theater) for the National Indigenist Institute, San Cristóbal, 1956–59, and toured Chiapas, 1956–58. Married Ricardo Guerra, 1958 (later divorced): one son. Journalist for various newspapers and periodicals, including *Novedades*, *¡Siempre!*, and *Excélsior*, 1960–74. Press and information director, 1960–66, and chair of comparative literature, 1967–71, National Autonomous University of Mexico, Mexico City; visiting professor of Latin American literature at various American universities, 1967. Ambassador to Israel, Tel Aviv, and lecturer in Latin American literature, Hebrew University, Jerusalem, 1971–74. Awards: Mexican Critics' Award, for novel, 1957; Chiapas Prize, 1958; Xavier Villaurrutia Prize, 1961; Woman of the Year Award, Mexico, 1967. Died (by accidental electrocution) in Tel Aviv, 7 August 1974.

Selected Writings

Essays and Related Prose
Juicios sumarios, 1966; revised edition, as *Juicios sumarios: Ensayos sobre literatura*, 2 vols., 1984
Mujer que sabe latín . . ., 1973
El uso de la palabra, edited by José Emilio Pacheco and Danubio Torres Fierro, 1974
El mar y sus pescaditos, 1975
A Rosario Castellanos Reader (includes short stories, poetry, and essays), edited by Maureen Ahern, translated by Ahern and others, 1988
Another Way to Be: Selected Works (includes poetry, essays, and stories), edited and translated by Myralyn F. Allgood, 1990

Other writings: two novels (*Balún-Canán* [*The Nine Guardians*], 1957; *Oficio de tinieblas* [*The Book of Lamentations*], 1962), short stories, poetry, and plays.

Collected works edition: *Obras*, edited by Eduardo Mejía, 1989– (in progress).

Bibliographies
Ahern, Maureen, in *Spanish American Women Writers: A Bio-Bibliographical Source Book*, edited by Diane E. Marting, Westport, Connecticut: Greenwood Press, 1990
Foster, David William, in *Mexican Literature: A Bibliography of Secondary Sources*, Metuchen, New Jersey: Scarecrow Press, 1992

Further Reading
Ahern, Maureen, Introduction to *A Rosario Castellanos Reader*, Austin: University of Texas Press, 1988

Allgood, Myralyn F., Introduction to *Another Way to Be* by Castellanos, Athens: University of Georgia Press, 1990

Anderson, Helene, "Rosario Castellanos and the Structures of Power," in *Contemporary Women Authors of Latin America*, edited by Doris Meyer and Margarite Fernández Olmos, New York: Brooklyn College Press, 2 vols., 1983

Bonifaz, Oscar, *Rosario*, Mexico City: Presencia Latinoamericana, 1984

Bonifaz, Oscar, *Remembering Rosario: A Personal Glimpse into the Life and Works of Rosario Castellanos*, Potomac, Maryland: Scripta Humanística, 1990

Cordero, Dolores, "Rosario Castellanos: 'La mujer mexicana, cómplice de su verdugo'," *Revista de Revistas*, supplement to *Excélsior* (10 November 1971): 24–27

Cresta de Leguizamón, Maria Luisa, "En recuerdo de Rosario Castellanos," *La Palabra y el Hombre* 19 (July–September 1976): 3–18

Dybvig, Rhoda, *Rosario Castellanos, biografía y novelística*, Mexico City: Andrea, 1965

Franco, Jean, *The Modern Culture of Latin America: Society and the Artist*, London: Pall Mall Press, 1967

Franco, Jean, *Spanish American Literature Since Independence*, London: Benn, and New York: Barnes and Noble, 1973

Gómez Parham, Mary, "Intellectual Influences on the Works of Rosario Castellanos," *Foro Literario: Revista de Literatura y Lenguaje* 7, no. 12 (1984): 34–40

González Peña, Carlos, *History of Mexican Literature*, Dallas: Southern Methodist University Press, 1969 (original Mexican edition, 1940)

Lindstrom, Naomi, *Rosario Castellanos: Pioneer of Feminist Criticism*, edited by Maureen Ahern and Mary S. Vásquez, Valencia: Albatros Hispanófila, 1980

Miller, Beth, "Women and Feminism in the Works of Rosario Castellanos," in *Feminist Criticism: Essays on Theory, Poetry and Prose*, edited by Cheryl L. Brown and Karen Olson, Metuchen, New Jersey: Scarecrow Press, 1978

Miller, Beth, editor, *Women in Hispanic Literature, Icons and Fallen Idols*, Berkeley: University of California Press, 1983

Poniatowska, Elena, "¡Te hicieron parque, Rosario!," *Revista de Bellas Artes* 18 (November–December 1971): 2

Poniatowska, Elena, "Rosario Castellanos, las letras que quedan de tu nombre," *La Cultura en México*, supplement to *¡Siempre!*, 4 September 1974: 6–8

Ruta, Suzanne, "Adiós, Machismo: Rosario Castellanos Goes Her Own Way," *Latin American Literary Review* 6, no. 11 (Fall–Winter 1977): 68–80

Urbano, Victoria E., "La justicia femenina de Rosario Castellanos," *Letras Femeninas* 1, no. 2 (1975): 9–20

Vásquez, Mary S., "Rosario Castellanos, Image and Idea," in *Homenaje a Rosario Castellanos*, edited by Maureen Ahern and Mary S. Vásquez, Valencia: Albatros Hispanófila, 1980

Castro, Américo

Spanish, 1885–1972

Américo Castro continued the intellectual tradition of Francisco Giner de los Ríos and the Krausists – followers of the philosophy of Karl Friedrich Christian Krause, a movement begun in Madrid by Sanz del Río in 1868 – as well as that of **Miguel de Unamuno**, example *par excellence* of the Generation of 1898. The recurrent self-reflections on the Spanish character are characteristic of the period that begins with the Generation of '98. A renewed concept of what Spain is – its reinvention, as we would say today – becomes part of the themes treated not only in the essay (by **Ángel Ganivet**,

Miguel de Unamuno, **José Ortega y Gasset**, Pedro Laín Entralgo) but in poetry as well (Antonio Machado). The Spanish reality, present or historic, becomes part of the Spanish essay of the time, be it erudite, scientific, polemic, or political in nature.

Américo Castro wrote essays exclusively, with two clearly distinguishable periods in his work, the first phase encompassing essays of literary criticism with a rigorous philological base, the second stage containing his contributions to historiography. The well-defined periods of his work correlate with circumstances, Castro writing the former before the Spanish Civil War and the latter while already in exile and teaching at Princeton University. It is there, and in the subsequent period until his death, that his work reaches full fruition. Nevertheless, in spite of this chronological division, there is a unity in his work.

Before 1936 Castro's work centered on literary figures of the Spanish Golden Age (Lope de Vega, Tirso de Molina, Quevedo, St. Teresa), a study of Cervantes that he later partially repudiated, **Erasmus**, and theme studies on the concept of honor and the Don Juan figure in Spanish literature. From 1940, and without abandoning essays on literary criticism, Castro began concentrating more and more on themes dealing with historiography: the meaning of Spanish civilization, Ibero-America, Erasmus in Spain, Castile, the concept of historiography, St. James of Galicia, the nature and existence of being Spanish. All these issues culminate in his monumental book *España en su historia: Cristianos, moros y judíos* (1948; Spain in its history: Christians, Moors and Jews), a revised version entitled *La realidad histórica de España* (1954; The Structure of Spanish History), and *The Spaniards: An Introduction to Their History* (1971), fundamental contributions to a new approach to the study of Spanish historiography which in his day provoked heated debate and controversy. To this day Castro's theory has both followers and opponents, but no serious study of Spanish historiography can ignore it.

The first stage of Castro's work is an attempt to place Spanish Erasmists, Cervantes, Lope de Vega, St. Teresa, Quevedo, and Golden Age drama as well as the picaresque novel within the universal European literary movements. The historiographical essays of the second phase deal with the historic meaning of culture through interpretations of Spanish culture on aesthetic and philosophical bases. While using the philological-scientific methods learned with his master Ramón Menéndez Pidal, Castro is influenced by the ideology of Ortega y Gasset and his vitalist philosophy, by new currents of German thought (the philologist Karl Vossler, the philosopher Wilhelm Dilthey), and by other European thinkers (Oswald Spengler, A. J. Toynbee).

Castro acknowledges his work to be a continuation of the Generation of '98 and states first in *España en su historia* and then in *The Structure of Spanish History* his intention to be the rendition of "an intellection of what Spain is at present and has been in the past," thus enabling him "to penetrate the entrails of Spanish life." The point of departure is human history, human actions within the life where they happen and where they exist. His postulates originate with concrete and specific facts of life, and then are considered in the generic and universal background of humanity. To that effect he coins his own terminology to express his ideological position: the "vividura" (living or functional context), the "morada vital" (historical dwelling place), the "vivir desviviéndose" (living by denying the reality of one's existence).

Castro proposes not to study the Spanish past but first to establish the peculiarities that are distinctive of the Spanish way of life, that differentiate Spaniards from other peoples, and then to explain the causes of such differences. He believes that the essence of that peculiarity and distinctiveness rests in the medieval cohabitation in the Iberian Peninsula of Christians, Moors, and Jews, called the three castes by Castro. The manner of living was formed in the 8th century when Islam became a presence in the peninsula, while the consciousness of being a Spaniard originated in the 10th and 11th centuries. Hence Viriato, **Seneca**, and St. Isidore, reputed by many to be Spaniards, for Castro are merely inhabitants of what we call Spain.

The term "morada vital," an original metaphor of Castro's and the center of his theory, is not unrelated to Unamuno's concept of "intrahistoria" (a spiritual history underlying the conventional body of historical data). Ortega y Gasset refers to "the innermost abode of Spaniards" but it is Castro who gives to his term the meaning of a "horizon of possibilities and obstacles – internal and external – that confront our lives." In Castro the "historical dwelling place" is related to *el estar* (to be in a given place) and not to *el ser* (the essence of being).

As expected, his theories became the center of controversy with supporters (Marcel Bataillon, Laín Entralgo) as well as opponents, the most prominent being Claudio Sánchez Albornoz, who wrote *España, un enigma histórico* (1956; Spain, an historic enigma) as a rebuttal to Castro's *The Structure of Spanish History*. There is no doubt that the polemic generated from Castro's work is one of the most significant in the history of Spanish thought.

Castro's essays are exploratory in nature but scholarly in form, solidly based in the methodologies of a philologist, conveying both information and the author's thought and experience. His literary interpretation follows the lines of the Spanish Krausists, with an emphasis on order and progress and a questioning based on reason and documented in science. The structure of the essay is expository as well as argumentative since Castro, in addressing his reader, aims to inform and convince. To that effect he resorts to textual verification in his quest to get the reader to accept his viewpoint.

Castro subjects himself to continual self-examination, constantly going back to previous work in order to submit it to rigorous self-criticism, and at times the reflection serves as a point of departure for a new interpretation. Aware that language is an important tool, he searches to improve his work with more vigorous and exact use of such a critical vehicle.

PILAR G. SÁENZ

Biography

Américo Castro Quesada. Born 4 May 1885 in Cantagalo, Brazil. Family moved to Granada, Spain, 1889. Studied at the University of Granada, arts degree, 1904; the Sorbonne, Paris, 1905–08; Center for Historical Studies, University of Madrid, Ph.D. in history, 1911; Institución Libre de Enseñanza. Married Carmen Medinabeitia. Contributor, *Revista de Filología* (Philological review), from 1914,

and *El Sol* (The sun), from 1923. Chair of the history of Spanish language, University of Madrid, 1915–36. Toured and lectured in South America and the United States, 1923–24; visiting professor, University of Berlin, 1930–31. Cofounder, International University of Santander, 1933. Left Spain during the Civil War: lived briefly in Argentina, then in United States, where he taught at the Universities of Wisconsin and Texas, then as Emory L. Ford Chair of Spanish, Princeton University, New Jersey, 1940–53; visiting professor at various American universities; post-retirement appointment at University of California San Diego, La Jolla, 1964–68. Returned to live in Madrid, 1969. Awards: honorary degrees from five universities. Officer, Legion of Honor (France); Member, Argentine Academy of Letters. Died (of a seizure while swimming) in Lloret de Mar, Gerona, 25 July 1972.

Selected Writings

Essays and Related Prose
Lengua, enseñanza y literatura, 1924
Santa Teresa y otros ensayos, 1929; as *Teresa la Santa; Gracián y los separatismos; con otros ensayos*, 1972
España en su historia: Cristianos, moros y judíos, 1948; revised edition as *La realidad histórica de España*, 1954; as *The Structure of Spanish History*, translated by Edmund L. King, 1954
Ensayo de historiología: Analogías y diferencias entre hispanos y musulmanes, 1950
Dos ensayos: Descripción, narración, historiografía; Discrepancias y mal entender, 1956
The Spaniards: An Introduction to Their History, translated by Willard F. King and Selma Margaretten, 1971
An Idea of History: Selected Essays, edited and translated by Stephen Gilman and Edmund L. King, 1977

Other writings: works about Spanish history and literature.

Bibliography

Brent, Albert, and Robert Kirsner, "A Bibliography of the Writings of Américo Castro," in *Américo Castro: The Impact of His Thought: Essays to Mark the Centenary of His Birth*, edited by Ronald E. Surtz, Jaime Ferrán, and Daniel P. Testa, Madison, Wisconsin: Hispanic Seminary of Medieval Studies, 1988

Further Reading

Araya, Guillermo, *El pensamiento de Américo Castro*, Madrid: Alianza, 1983
Brancaforte, Benito, "Américo Castro and Michel Foucault's 'Filosofia del sospetto'," in *Hispanic Studies in Honor of Joseph H. Silverman*, edited by Joseph V. Ricapito, Newark, Delaware: Juan de la Cuesta, 1988: 371–79
Garagorri, Paulino, "Un mitoclasta nacional: En torno a la tarea desmitificadora de Américo Castro," *Revista de Occidente* 41, no. 4 (1966): 234–44
García Gabaldón, Jesús, "Makbara, espacio de encuentros," *La Torre* 15, no. 4 (1990): 353–60
Gómez Martínez, José Luis, *Américo Castro y el origen de los españoles: Historia de una polémica*, Madrid: Gredos, 1975
Hornik, M. P., editor, *Collected Studies in Honour of Américo Castro's Eightieth Year*, Oxford: Lincombe Lodge Research Library, 1965
Insula issue in honor of Castro (1973)
King, Willard, "Américo Castro y Lope de Vega," *Boletín Real Academia Española* 68, no. 243 (1988): 169–75
Laín Entralgo, Pedro, editor, *Estudios sobre la obra de Américo Castro*, Madrid: Taurus, 1971
Marichal, Juan, *Teoría e historia del ensayismo hispánico*, Madrid: Alianza, 1984

Martín, Marina, "Juan Goytisolo en deuda con Américo Castro: *Reivindicación del Conde don Julián*," *Letras Peninsulares* 2, no. 2 (1989): 211–23

Peña, Aniano, *Américo Castro y su visión de España y de Cervantes*, Madrid: Gredos, 1975

Pi-Sunyer, Oriol, "The Historiography of Américo Castro: An Anthropological Interpretation," *Bulletin of Hispanic Studies* 49 (1972): 40–50

Rubia Barcia, José, editor, *Américo Castro and the Meaning of Spanish Civilization*, Berkeley: University of California Press, 1976

Sánchez-Albornoz y Menduiña, Claudio, *España, un enigma histórico*, Buenos Aires: Sudamericana, 2 vols., 1956

Sotomayor, Carmen, *Una lectura orientalista de Juan Goytisolo*, Madrid: Fundamentos, 1990

Surtz, Ronald E., Jaime Ferrán, and Daniel P. Testa, editors, *Américo Castro: The Impact of His Thought: Essays to Mark the Centenary of His Birth*, Madison, Wisconsin: Hispanic Seminary of Medieval Studies, 1988

Varela, Javier, "La tragedia de los intelectuales y la historiografía de Américo Castro," *Insula* 48, no. 563 (1993): 20–22

Cattaneo, Carlo

Italian, 1801–1869

Carlo Cattaneo, principally known for the active role he played as leader of the War Council during the revolutionary "Five Days" of Milan in 1848, which he related in his highly personal account *Dell'insurrezione di Milano nel 1848* (1848; Of the insurrection in Milan in 1848), has recently been rediscovered as one of the most original thinkers of his day and a precursor of positivist philosophy in Italy. He was one of the most dynamic figures in the cultural life of Lombardy, and Milan in particular, during the period of the Risorgimento.

His first articles were published in the *Annali di Statistica* (Statistical annals) and the *Bollettino di Notizie Statistiche* (Bulletin of statistical notices), two journals founded by the philosopher and jurist Giandomenico Romagnosi, who taught Cattaneo, and whose influence was considerable in shaping Lombard culture at the turn of the 18th and 19th centuries. Already in these early works, which explore topics in the field of social sciences, it is possible to detect the influence on Cattaneo of Milanese Enlightenment thinking, which, in the previous century, had permeated the social and administrative fabric of the Lombard-Venetian kingdom.

In 1839, after years of effort, he obtained permission from the Austrian rulers to edit his own journal, called *Il Politecnico*. The first series ran until 1844. In the **preface** to the first number, Cattaneo clearly stated that the aim of his journal was to further the study of all sciences, in particular applied sciences, in order to promote social progress. His **"reviews,"** a genre which aimed to inform and educate the public by expounding the most up-to-date ideas, covered a variety of subjects, even though his main interests were economics, history, and literature. His aim was to make Milanese culture less provincial by opening it up to all streams of contemporary debate, and more particularly to the new thinking on economics. This renewal of intellectual life in the capital was intended to modernize the Lombard state, "to free it from many of the anti-scientific opinions in agriculture, public economy, religion and everyday life" (preface to *Il Politecnico*).

The *Politecnico* cultivated a vigorous dialogue with the mainstream of European thinking in a deliberate attempt to break away from the narrowly academic and humanistic tradition of Italian culture in favor of a more positive engagement with studies of a scientific and technical nature.

The journal was directed at a middle-class public with a sound literary and scientific background. Occasionally, Cattaneo also wrote on *arti belle* – the theater, opera, painting, architecture, and literature. In these pieces, which were often several pages long and possessed the style and authority of literary essays, Cattaneo sought to demonstrate the interdependence between artistic form and social reality, between literature and life. While recognizing that the creative process was distinct from the rational and practical, he asserted that art, as the expression of beauty, ennobled the human spirit and constituted the most sublime ingredient of social existence. Although his ideas on art and literature were influenced by the Romantics, whose major exponents had lived and worked in Milan a few years earlier, Cattaneo's philosophy was closer to the Enlightenment, and also to Giambattista Vico, whose work, *La scienza nuova* (1725; *The New Science*), he had studied in depth. Utilizing Vico's ideas, Cattaneo developed his theory that the study of history does not produce merely passive knowledge of the past. Through the investigation of the complex relationship between the individual, his culture, and civilization, and an examination of the "istoria delle idee dei popoli" (history of ideas of the people), it deepens our understanding of human nature. Thus his philosophy is "una filosofia della istoria" (philosophy of history) aimed at discovering the laws of human progress and, through them, enhancing our capacity to shape events; philosophy is a "scola pratica" (school of practice) and has a primarily social role ("La scienza nuova," *Il Politecnico*, 1839).

The last reviews in the *Politecnico* dealt with the problem of the Italian language, a live issue which Cattaneo shared with all the intellectuals of his day. Against the classicists, who proposed a national language derived from popular Florentine dialect, Cattaneo, while recognizing the immense contribution of Dante's works to Italian literature, puts forward the case for a language which, far from being archaic and academic, should be clear and comprehensible to the majority of the population, but also suitable for expressing elevated concepts.

After winding up the first series of the *Politecnico*, Cattaneo found more time to dedicate to his geographical articles, which he wrote for *Il Crepuscolo* (Twilight), a Milanese journal published by Carlo Tenca. He also completed his historical work, *Introduzione alle notizie culturali e civili su la Lombardia* (1844; Introduction to cultural and civic events in Lombardy), a book which, in the words of Mario Fubini in *Romanticismo italiano* (1965), celebrates the social, economic, and cultural history of Milan and which, together with his *La città considerata come il principio ideale delle istorie italiane* (1858; The town considered as the ideal principle of Italian history), provides a clear outline of his vision of a unified and federal Italy.

The main objective of the second series of the *Politecnico*, which was published immediately on the departure of the Austrians from Lombardy in 1859 and continued until 1864, was to influence the new ruling classes in Italy in supporting scientific progress throughout the newly formed nation. The new *Politecnico* published mainly economic and technical material, with a few exceptions, for example the now famous literary essay on "Ugo Foscolo e l'Italia" (1860; Ugo Foscolo and Italy), an impassioned defense of the Romantic poet, and a grateful acknowledgment of his undisputed influence on the whole generation that participated in the Risorgimento.

Through his writings, Cattaneo played a crucial role in the development of nationalist ideas throughout Northern Italy. His style, compared by M. Balestrieri in his *Antologia della letteratura italiana* (1967) to that of the Latin historian Tacitus for his concise paragraphs and the clarity of his "istoriche e esperimentali" (historical and scientific) descriptions, is closely associated with a need for intelligibility and rationality. In this respect, it reflects the position he holds as a transitional figure between the humanistic orientation of the early protagonists of the Risorgimento and the later development of a more technical approach rooted in the social sciences.

VANNA MOTTA

Biography

Born 15 June 1801 in Milan. Studied at a seminary near Milan; Liceo Sant'Alessandro, Milan, from 1817; law courses taught privately by Giandomenico Romagnosi, 1820–21; law degree granted from the University of Pavia, 1824. Taught in public schools, Milan, 1820–35. Contributor to various journals, including *Annali di Statistica*, from 1828; legal adviser for Società degli Editori (Society of publishers), early 1830s. Married Anna Woodcock, 1835. Legal advisor, then secretary, Società della Strada Ferrata Venezia a Milano (Society for the Venice-Milan railroad), from 1837. Cofounder and editor, *Il Politecnico*, 1839–44 and 1859–64. Leader in the Five Days of Milan march during the revolutionary uprising of 1848. Fled to Switzerland, August 1848, then Paris, then back to Switzerland, living permanently in Castagnola, near Lugano; became a Swiss citizen, 1859. Died in Castagnola, 5 February 1869.

Selected Writings

Essays and Related Prose

Scritti politici ed epistolario, edited by Gabriele Rosa and Jessie White Mario, 3 vols., 1892–1901
Saggi di economia rurale, edited by Luigi Einaudi, 1939
Scritti letterari, artistici, linguistici e vari, edited by Agostino Bertani, 2 vols., 1948
Scritti critici, edited by Mario Fubini, 1954
Scritti economici, edited by Alberto Bertolino, 3 vols., 1956
Scritti storici e geografici, edited by Gaetano Salvemini and Ernesto Sestan, 4 vols., 1957
Scritti filosofici, letterari e vari, edited by Franco Alessio, 1957
Scritti filosofici, edited by Norberto Bobbio, 3 vols., 1960
Scritti politici, edited by Mario Boneschi, 4 vols., 1964–65
Scritti filosofici, edited by Alfredo Saloni, 1965
Scritti sulla Lombarda, edited by Giuseppe Anceschi and Giuseppe Armani, 2 vols., 1971
Antologia degli scritti politici, edited by Giuseppe Galasso, 1978
Scritti letterari, edited by Piero Treves, 2 vols., 1981
Scritti su Milano e la Lombardia, edited by Ettore Mazzali, 1990

Other writings: *La città considerata come il principio ideale delle istorie italiane* (1858), a history of Lombardy (1844), and a book on the 1848 uprising.

Collected works edition: *Opere inedite*, edited by Agostino Bertani, 7 vols., 1881–92.

Bibliography

Brignoli, Marziano, and Danilo L. Massagrande, *Bibliografia degli scritti su Carlo Cattaneo (1836–1987)*, Florence: Le Monnier, 1988

Further Reading

Ambrosoli, L., "Giuseppe Mazzini e Carlo Cattaneo dal Risorgimento all'unità," *Belfagor* 24 (1969)
Angelini, Cesare, *Nostro Ottocento: Foscolo, Monti, Leopardi, Cattaneo, Carducci, Lettere di Domenico Gnoli*, Bologna: Boni, 1970
Della Peruta, Franco, *Conservatori, liberali e democratici nel Risorgimento*, Milan: Angeli, 1989
Della Peruta, Franco, *Milano nel Risorgimento*, Milan: La Storia, 1992
Fubini, Mario, "Introduzione alla lettura del Cattaneo" and "Gli scritti letterari di Carlo Cattaneo," in his *Romanticismo italiano*, Bari: Laterza, 1965
Galante Garrone, Alessandro, and Franco Della Peruta, *La stampa italiana del Risorgimento*, Rome/Bari: Laterza, 1978
Gobetti, Piero, "Cattaneo" (1922), in his *Scritti storici, letterari e filosofici*, edited by P. Spriano, Turin: Einaudi, 1960
Maturi, Walter, "La scuola democratica: Carlo Cattaneo," in his *Interpretazioni del Risorgimento*, Turin: Einaudi, 1962
Salvemini, Gaetano, Preface to *Scritti storici e geografici* by Cattaneo, Florence: Le Monnier, 1957
Sestan, Ernesto, editor, *Romagnosi, Cattaneo, Ferrari*, Milan and Naples: Classici Ricciardi, 1957
Voza, Pasquale, *Letteratura e rivoluzione passiva: Mazzini, Cattaneo, Tenca*, Bari: Dedalo, 1978
Woolf, Stuart, *The Italian Risorgimento*, London: Longman, and New York: Barnes and Noble, 1969

Chacel, Rosa

Spanish, 1898–1994

Rosa Chacel's works, essays and fiction, share a common discursive tone: logical, measured, dispassionate, abstract, and clear. Chacel studied painting and sculpture before turning to literature, and artistic preoccupations characterize her writing as a whole. This widely traveled, cosmopolitan Modernist was influenced by James Joyce (fiction) and **José Ortega y Gasset** (essays and thought); other significant writers included **Goethe**, Jaspers, Rilke, **Nietzsche**, **Kierkegaard**, and **Freud**.

Chacel began writing essays on literature, art, and culture in the 1920s, in the heady atmosphere of vanguardism, and continued during the Spanish Civil War, when she contributed several articles to the wartime republican periodical *Hora de España* (Spain's hour). Notwithstanding her republican sympathies, she was convinced of the superiority of things of the spirit and that aesthetics and ideology should remain separate; hence her writings have an ahistorical, detached quality seldom reflecting the circumstances of composition.

Chacel's first book of essays was a miscellaneous volume, *Poesía de la circunstancia: Cómo y por qué de la novela* (1958; Circumstantial poetry: how and why of the novel), followed by *La confesión* (1970; Confessions), in which Chacel examines the genre and attempts to respond to Ortega's query as to reasons for the scarcity of memoirs and confessional writing in Spanish. Seeking the fundamental condition of all confessions, she examines those she considers most important – St. Augustine (cf. **Confessions**), **Rousseau**, Kierkegaard –

determining that the most dramatic ones are inspired by guilt, and are thus most truthful. Chacel applies "confessional" principles to a *sui generis* meditation on Cervantes, Galdós, and **Unamuno**, concluding that all of the latter's work is a huge, personified confession, while *Don Quixote* springs from the conclusion that to believe and love, one must be crazy. Special attention is given these writers' pronouncements on love, a major subtheme, as are reflections on contemporary life.

Chacel's longest and most significant work of nonfiction, *Saturnal* (1972; Saturnalia), was some four decades in the writing. Love constitutes the primary preoccupation, not as passion, charity, *agape*, or sexual attraction, but as unique poetic truth. Parting from the basic, unstated premise of sexual equality, *Saturnal*'s more than 400 pages elaborate and extend an article first published in **Revista de Occidente** (Western review) in 1931, "Esquema de los actuales problemas prácticos del amor" (Outline of current practical problems of love). Chacel situates herself between the extremes represented by Denis de Rougemont's *L'Amour et l'Occident* (1939; *Love in the Western World*) – passionate love, mystic Christian overtones, and love-death – and Herbert Marcuse's *Eros and Civilization* (1955) – Freudian implications, Eros as vital impulse, economic factors as discouraging eroticism, death as fatigue. Chacel views love as a blend of the ideal, erotic, and sexual, adding existentialist tones and references to clearly existentialist sources (Kierkegaard, **Camus**, Unamuno).

Her discussion of relations between the sexes centers around attempts to isolate the essence of feminine psychology, resulting in the conclusion that its distinguishing characteristic is a deep, ancestral fear of rape on the level of the collective unconscious. Chacel discusses various feminists, noting specific divergences: **Virginia Woolf, Simone de Beauvoir**, the Spanish Countess of Campo Alange. She touches upon homosexuality, maternity, and prostitution, citing readings from Jung to Rosa Luxemburg and Madame Curie. Loosely following Ortega's theory of generations and his method of defining the sensibility of the times, she elucidates characteristics of her own generation, differentiating it from those before and after. For Chacel, one distinguishing "sign of the times" is the "unisex" phenomenon.

Deeply preoccupied with ethical dilemmas, she contemplates good and evil, tolerance, war, the "right to kill," and responsibility (which she believes all share equally). Chacel rejects the cliché blaming wars on men and viewing women as war's enemies, contending that tolerance allows wars to exist and women are to blame for passivity. *Saturnal* treats many marginal topics, related only most tangentially to the male-female axis, such as the cinema, to which she accords special significance as a force shaping the modern mentality. She makes excursions into the plastic arts, contemporary painting – areas in which Chacel was very knowledgeable, as was her mentor, Ortega – and fashion. Her theories on love repeatedly parallel those of Ortega, and her readings frequently coincide with his, as she consults sources from Socrates, **Plato**, Ovid, and Quevedo to Bergson, Kierkegaard, **Heidegger**, and Freud. Chacel considers platonic love, the nature of beauty, immortality and eternity, good and evil, and several other dense, universal themes in the course of what amounts to an unfinished intellectual journey, expressed with clarity and precision. While the relationship between the sexes forms the axis around which everything else revolves, and sexual relationships are

viewed as paradigmatic or symbolic of all others, *Saturnal* weaves a complex tapestry of topics. Only two acts are recognized as being the same for all: birth and death.

Chacel's writing, whether narrative, essay, or poetry, constitutes in its entirety a vehicle of self-discovery, an aesthetic quest centering around time as genesis of the word (*logos*), of life and memory and hence of autobiography, history, intimate dialogue, and all creative material. The writer – a pilgrim of illumination – travels toward light, form, truth, will-to-being, creating an aesthetics of rich expressiveness, seeking self-revelation in data extracted from the preconsciousness of time, before truth.

Los títulos (1981; Titles) contains selected articles by Chacel, but was not composed as a volume; nor was *Rebañaduras* (1986; Slices), a collection of 18 articles written between 1937 and the 1980s and divided into five thematic categories: 1) the feminine condition, love, and genesis; 2) Ortega y Gasset's significance in the 1920s, especially for Chacel's beginnings; 3) Spanish writers Quevedo, Sor Juana, Corpus Barga, and Justo Alejo (two baroque greats, two little-known contemporaries); 4) wartime articles from *Hora de España*; 5) Chacel's lecture presenting her book on her late husband, their meeting, and his art, *Timoteo Pérez Rubio y sus retratos del jardín* (1980; Timoteo Pérez Rubio and his portraits of the garden) – part tale, part dream, a strangely beautiful essay reflecting on the mechanisms of memory.

Chacel's novels are very essayistic, especially *La sinrazón* (1960; Unreason), whose protagonist is meditative, philosophical, preoccupied with truth, beauty, essence and form, time and eternity, pleasure and the forbidden, good and evil, the divine and the transitory, body and soul, faith and doubt, reason and passion, love and death. This most dense and complex of Chacel's novels presents multiple changes of genre – story, confession, essay, diary, autobiography – and treats the aesthetics of peril, will, life as a struggle between loves, love as dialogue, the problems of duplicity, doubt and suicide, and the metaphor of life as a road, with the necessity of choosing a destination.

Other books, of difficult classification, are both autobiographical and essayistic, dealing with the gestation of early works, Chacel's own intellectual formation and that of her generation: *Desde el amanecer* (1972; From dawn) and *La lectura es secreto* (1989; Reading is secret). Obsession with her point of origin, repetitive themes, autobiographical character, and constant stylistic rigor endow Chacel's works with unity despite diversity.

JANET PÉREZ

Biography

Rosa Arimón Chacel. Born 3 June 1898 in Valladolid. Studied at the Escuela de Artes y Oficios and Escuela Superior de Bellas Artes de San Fernando, Madrid, 1908–18. Married Timoteo Pérez Rubio, 1921 (died, 1977): one son. Lived in Italy, 1921–27, in France during the Spanish Civil War, 1936–39 and after, in Greece, and in Rio de Janeiro and Buenos Aires, 1940–77. Contributor, *Revista de Occidente, Ultra, Caballo Verde para la Poesía* (The green horse for poetry), *El Mono Azul* (The blue monkey), and *Hora de España*, 1927–36, and *Sur, La Nación*, and *Realidad*, 1939–60. Awards: two fellowships; National Critics' Prize, 1970, 1976; National Literature Prize, 1987; honorary degree from the University of Valladolid. Died in Madrid, 27 July 1994.

Selected Writings

Essays and Related Prose
Poesía de la circunstancia: Cómo y por qué de la novela, 1958
La confesión, 1970
Saturnal, 1972
Desde el amanecer, 1972
Los títulos, edited by Clara Janés, 1981
Rebañaduras: Colección de artículos, edited by Moisés Mori, 1986
Memoria, narrativa y poetica de las presencias: Poesias, relatos, novelas y ensayos, 1988
La lectura es secreto, 1989

Other writings: seven novels (*Estación, ida y vuelta*, 1930; *Teresa*, 1941; *Memorias de Leticia Valle* [*Memoirs of Leticia Valle*], 1945; *La sinrazón*, 1960; *Barrio de maravillas* [*The Maravillas District*], 1976; *Acrópolis*, 1984; *Ciencias naturales*, 1988), two collections of short stories, poetry, diaries, autobiography, two volumes of memoirs (*Alcancía: Ida* and *Alcancía: Vuelta*, 1982), and a study of her husband's painting. Also translated works by Albert Camus and Jean Racine.

Collected works edition: *Obras completas*, 4 vols., 1989– (in progress).

Further Reading

Beneyto, Antonio, "Rosa Chacel: Esencialmente un ser libre," in his *Censura y política en los escritores españoles*, Barcelona: Euros, 1975

Bergés, Consuelo, "Rosa Chacel y la literatura responsable," *Insula* 183 (February 1962)

Conte, Rafael, "La realidad de una escritora intelectual," *El País*, 30 January 1983

Crispin, John, "Rosa Chacel y las 'Ideas sobre la novela'," *Insula* 262 (September 1968)

Gimferrer, Pedro, "Una conciencia puesta en pie hasta el fin," *ABC*, 3 June 1988

Herrero, F., "Ciencias naturales: La subversión de la palabra escrita," *El Norte de Castilla*, 4 June 1988

Janés, Clara, "Rosa Chacel y la luz," *El País*, 5 January 1977

Janés, Clara, Prologue to *Los títulos* by Chacel, Barcelona: EDHASA, 1981

Janés, Clara, "Diario de una escritora," *Nueva Estafeta* 53 (1983): 90–92

Janés, Clara, "El reclamo de la razón," *Diario 16*, 20 July 1989

Mangini, Shirley, "Women and Spanish Modernism: The Case of Rosa Chacel," *Anales de la Literatura Española Contemporánea* 12 (1987): 17–28

Marra-López, José R., "Rosa Chacel: La búsqueda intelectual del mundo," in his *Narrativa española fuera de España, 1939–1961*, Madrid: Guadarrama, 1963

Moix, Ana María, "Rosa Chacel, un clásico: El amor, fuente de creación y armonía," *Destino*, 10–16 December 1979

Moix, Ana María, "La agonía de la razón," *Camp de l'Arpa* 74 (April 1980): 74–76

Moix, Ana María, "El fuego sagrado del diálogo," *Diario 16*, 28 May 1988

Pardo, F., "La serena meditación de una filosofía," *El Norte de Castilla*, 4 July 1988

Pardo, F., "Estudio preliminar," in *Obra completa, 2: Ensayos y poesía* by Chacel, Valladolid: Centro Jorge Guillén, 1989: 7–43

Piedra, Antonio, "*Saturnal*, el laberinto lúcido," *Anthropos* 85 (1988): 54–58

Rodríguez Fischer, A., "Los diarios de Rosa Chacel," *Cuadernos Hispanoamericanos* 399 (September 1983): 135–47

Rodríguez Fischer, A., "Cronología intelectual de Rosa Chacel," *Anthropos* 85 (June 1988): 28–34

Rosa Chacel, premio nacional de las letras españolas 1987, Barcelona: Anthropos, and Madrid: Ministry of Culture, 1990

Chapter

The word "chapter" is derived from the Latin *capitulum*, which is also the source of the word "capital." An enlarged capital letter was used to signal a division of thought in early manuscripts. When paper began to replace parchment as the principal writing material, it became economically feasible to start each new chapter on a separate page. Some ancient manuscripts, such as the Bible, were divided into chapters by printers for the convenience of the reader. By the 18th century most long prose works were created with chapter divisions, and the conventions were well enough established by 1760 to enable Laurence Sterne's infamous experiments with chapters (blank chapters, chapters out of order) in *Tristram Shandy*. In the 19th century, chapter divisions were an important feature of serial publication, and both novels and essays were frequently published by installment. *Cornhill Magazine*, for instance, published serialized novels by authors such as **George Eliot**, Hardy, and **Thackeray** in this manner, along with essays by **Arnold, Ruskin**, and others.

Chapter divisions are usually indicated by numbers, but practice is quite varied. In Christine de Pizan's *Le Livre de la Cité des Dames* (wr. 1405; *The Book of the City of Ladies*), the chapters are marked off with numbers and with running heads that describe the contents and orient the reader to the text. For instance, the opening chapter is headed: "HERE BEGINS THE BOOK OF THE CITY OF LADIES, WHOSE FIRST CHAPTER TELLS WHY AND FOR WHAT PURPOSE THE BOOK WAS WRITTEN." Such practice was also followed by Cervantes in *Don Quixote* (1605–15); however, Cervantes' chapter headings also contribute to the mockery of his hero. When he titles I: 20, "Of the unparalleled Adventure achieved by the valorous Don Quixote de la Mancha with less peril than any ever achieved by any famous knight in the whole world," the hyperbole and ironic stance are unmistakable. Although the practice of numbering the text suggests narrative progression, it may also be used to show the logical progression of an argument from premise to deduction, as it does in **Bacon**'s *Novum organum* (1620). In contrast to Bacon's plain style, novelists of the 18th and 19th centuries revived the tradition of elaborate and self-conscious titles, such as **Henry Fielding**'s Chapter 1 of Book 8 of *Tom Jones*: "A wonderful long chapter concerning the marvellous; being much the longest of all our introductory chapters." Victorian essayists tended both to number and to title the chapters of long works – a practice followed by **Carlyle**, Ruskin, **Mill**, Arnold, and others. Modern writers have tended to minimize editorial apparatus, omitting titles and using white space to indicate textual divisions. Contemporary essayists are much less likely to follow the practice of numbering the chapters of book-length works.

Traditional definitions of the essay have emphasized that the individual essay is a complete and self-contained unit. The chapter, on the other hand, is generally considered to be part of a larger work, one division within a sequence. In reality, the concepts of chapter and essay are much more fluid than these definitions suggest. When **Montaigne** applied the title *Essais* to his writing, he was referring not to the structural divisions of his work, but to the general enterprise he had undertaken. In his books, he was "essaying," that is, attempting to come to some understanding on a matter of personal concern. The individual units of each book were identified as *chapitres* and numbered consecutively. Although the chapters do not represent a linear progression of thought, the individual chapters cannot be completely understood without reference to the entire work that Montaigne undertook.

Since the rise of popular journalism in the 18th and 19th centuries, the concept of the essay has also been linked to its means of publication. Essays are generally associated with periodical publication, while chapters are divisions of books. However, many essays appear first in book form, and some chapters of books are published first as essays in periodicals. The distinction, then, between a collection of essays and a nonfiction book may be more slippery than is generally imagined. **Thoreau**'s *Walden* (1854), for instance, appears to be a collection of essays loosely related to a general theme. A closer inspection, however, reveals a conscious ordering of the essays as part of a larger design.

The distinction between essay and chapter is probably best understood as a tendency rather than as a clear demarcation. The term "essay" stresses the author's approach to the subject – tentative, reflective, individual. A chapter, conversely, emphasizes a convenient division for purposes of publication. Indeed, long essays may be subdivided into chapters. Although the chapter may signify a continuation of the narrative in fictional works, there may be little distinction at all between an essay and a chapter in a work of nonfiction.

DAVID W. CHAPMAN

Further Reading

Avrin, Leila, *Scribes, Script and Books: The Book Arts from Antiquity to the Renaissance*, Chicago: American Library Association, and London: British Library, 1991

Febvre, Lucien, and Henri-Jean Martin, *Coming of the Book: The Impact of Printing, 1450–1800*, edited by Geoffrey Nowell Smith and David Wootton, London: NLB, 1976; New York: Verso, 1990 (original French edition, 1958)

Marr, George S., *The Periodical Essayists of the Eighteenth Century*, London: Clarke, 1923; New York: Appleton, 1924

Stevick, Philip, *The Chapter in Fiction: Theories of Narrative Division*, Syracuse, New York: Syracuse University Press, 1970

Sultana, Niloufar, "The Principle of Chapter and Volume Division in *Tristram Shandy*," *Language and Style* 20 (1981): 185–202

Walker, Hugh, *The English Essay and Essayist*, London: Dent, and New York: Dutton, 1915

Character Sketch

The character sketch is a brief prose description of a person or type. The form originated in second-century Greece with Theophrastus (c. 371–c. 287 BCE), a student and friend of Aristotle, whose lasting fame rests on one of his minor works, the **Characters**. Warren Anderson points out in his translation of Theophrastus (*The Character Sketches*, 1970) that although modern critics view the philosopher as a proto-scientist collecting observations of character as data, earlier writers saw him as a moralist, with the *Characters* as illustrations of Aristotle's doctrine of the golden mean.

There are two main kinds: 1) the type character, known as the Theophrastan character, which generalizes individuals; and 2) the historical character, which depicts a particular individual. Although their purposes are different, both kinds of character sketch have classical roots, the type character in Theophrastus and the historical character in **Plutarch**, Tacitus, and Suetonius. Rhetoric is another important influence on the character sketch. A number of rhetorical terms were connected with character descriptions (*descriptio, ethologia, prosopopoeia, characterismos*, etc.), and for centuries the writing of characters was a common rhetorical exercise.

The primary characteristic of the character sketch is its brevity and concision. Very much a set piece and a static form, the character tends toward artificiality, primarily due to the self-consciously literary style in which it is usually written. Wit and irony as well as **aphorism**s abound in the character sketch. A moral bias is generally prominent, probably derived from Theophrastan connections with morality as well as from the wide use of the character in religious and spiritual writings. All character sketches show considerable abstraction and reductiveness; even the historical characters tend to make their subjects become models of their kind, rather than realistic human beings. Indeed, despite the traditional critical distinction between the two types of character sketches, in practice they often tended to merge, and tracing a specific strain in later manifestations can be difficult.

Aside from Theophrastus himself, the type character is found in Roman comedy, medieval hagiography, homiletic writings, humor characters in drama (particularly Ben Jonson's plays), and literature based on concepts such as the "ruling passion" (as in certain of Alexander Pope's poems). After the classical historians' characters, the form reappeared prominently in the work of 17th-century English historians.

After its original Greek appearance with Theophrastus, the great flowering of the character sketch occurred in 17th-century England, continuing well into the 18th century, and, to a lesser extent, in France. The type character experienced a rapid rise and development in the early part of the 17th century in England. Joseph Hall's *Characters of Vertues and Vices*, the first English collection of characters, was published in 1608, and by 1632 the English Theophrastan character was, according to Benjamin Boyce (1947), "perfectly developed." Major English writers of the Theophrastan character were Hall and Thomas Overbury. John Earle is generally considered the best; his *Micro-Cosmographie* (1628) went through ten editions by 1665. During the Restoration Samuel "Hudibras" Butler wrote type characters, but they remained unpublished until 1759. The 18th-century Theophrastan character is best represented by William Law in *A Serious Call to a Devout and Holy Life* (1728).

During the middle and later years of the 17th century, and well into the 18th, the historical character flourished in England. Civil War and Restoration polemicists drew on it constantly. In historical writings, character sketches had appeared as early as the 16th century in Polydore Vergil, and early 17th-century historians such as William Camden, Edward Hall, and John Speed also employed them. But the greatest historical characters of the period were written at mid-century and during the Restoration by Edward Hyde, the first Earl of Clarendon, and Bishop Gilbert Burnet, both of whom wrote memoirs as well as histories. The most famous character sketch by Clarendon, who is generally acknowledged as the master of the form, is the portrait of his close friend Lord Falkland. Later 18th-century historians such as **David Hume** and, particularly, Edward Gibbon in his monumental *Decline and Fall of the Roman Empire* (1776–88) also deployed character sketches effectively.

In France the historical character appeared early in Phillippe de Commines' *Mémoires* (wr. 1489–90 and 1497–98; pub. 1524–28). More famous were the character sketches of mid-17th-century French memoirs and romances. The master of the French character sketch is **Jean de La Bruyère**, who translated Theophrastus' *Characters* and added other portraits to them in his own *Caractères* (1688; *Characters*). Among the portraits La Bruyère added were some of his contemporaries, whom he depicted under pseudonyms.

By the early 19th century, the English character sketch had by and large disappeared as an independent genre, although Richard Phillips published his *Public Characters* each year from 1798 to 1810. Historians obviously continued to describe characters in their works, and journalistic prose and the emerging novel, over the course of the 18th century, incorporated character sketches in different ways. But the character sketch was inherently a genre with limited possibilities for development. In addition to its brevity, it lacked both flexibility and realism. Thus the character was difficult to integrate into narratives; self-contained and too often abstract, it tended to remain an autonomous element, a set piece lacking natural connections to other prose.

The character sketch and the essay emerged at roughly the same time in England, and they are closely related genres. Indeed, the character is in essence a very brief essay. Early 18th-century essayists such as **Joseph Addison** and **Richard Steele**, along with **Samuel Johnson** and others later in the century, produced a number of essays that are basically expanded character sketches. But the character did not typically incorporate either the overtly personal elements or the serious moral and political ideas that have traditionally marked the essay; nor did its brevity, abstraction, and resistance to narrative integration make it particularly suitable for essayists to use. Ultimately, the major contribution of the character sketch was to hasten the development of other genres, particularly biography and autobiography; the essay was a subsidiary beneficiary in this generic process.

MARTINE WATSON BROWNLEY

Anthologies and Collections

A Book of "Characters", edited by Richard Aldington, London: Routledge, and New York: Dutton, 1924

A Cabinet of Characters, edited by Gwendolen Murphy, London: Oxford University Press, 1925

The Character Sketches by Theophrastus, translated by Warren Anderson, Kent, Ohio: Kent State University Press, 1970

The Characters by Jean de La Bruyère, translated by Henri Van Laun, London and New York: Oxford University Press, 1963 (original French edition, 1688)

Characters from the Histories and Memoirs of the Seventeenth Century, edited by David Smith, Oxford: Clarendon Press, 1918

Bibliographies

Greenough, Chester Noyes, *Bibliography of the Theophrastan Character in English*, Westport, Connecticut: Greenwood Press, 1970 (original edition, 1947)

Murphy, Gwendolen, *A Bibliography of English Character-Books, 1608–1700*, London: Oxford University Press, 1925

Further Reading

Boyce, Benjamin, *The Theophrastan Character in England to 1642*, Cambridge, Massachusetts: Harvard University Press, 1947

Boyce, Benjamin, *The Polemic Character, 1640–1661: A Chapter in English Literary History*, Lincoln: University of Nebraska Press, 1955

Brownley, Martine Watson, "Johnson's *Lives of the English Poets* and Earlier Traditions of the Character Sketch in England," in *Johnson and His Age*, edited by James Engell, Cambridge, Massachusetts: Harvard University Press, 1984

Clausen, Wendell, "The Beginnings of English Character-Writing in the Early Seventeenth Century," *Philological Quarterly* 25 (1946): 32–45

Ernst, Charles A. S., *Contextualizing the Character: Generic Studies of Text and Canon, Rhetoric, Style, and Quantitative Analysis in the Seventeenth-Century English Prose Character* (dissertation), Philadelphia: University of Pennsylvania, 1988

Smeed, J. W., *The Theophrastan Character: The History of a Literary Genre*, Oxford: Clarendon Press, and New York: Oxford University Press, 1985

Characters

by Theophrastus, c. 319 BCE

Characteres (*Characters*) is a collection of 30 short prose descriptions of human vices written c. 319 BCE by the Greek polymath Theophrastus (c. 371–c. 287 BCE), a student of Aristotle and, after the latter's retirement, his successor as head of the Peripatetic School; it is also the name given to the 17th- and 18th-century examples of this literary genre produced by English and French writers. The form of the Character by Theophrastus consists of a title naming a vice, an opening sentence that defines this vice first in abstract terms and then in terms of a man who represents it, followed by a collection of human actions or speeches that further illustrates it. As the word "character" originally meant an engraved mark or brand and, by extension, the instrument that makes such a mark, the Theophrastan Character conflates these two meanings, presenting both the distinctive marks or traits that define a particular moral quality and the human type whose behavior habitually enacts them. In this respect, a Character is like a riddle, the answer to which is given at the beginning rather than guessed at the end.

The form of the Theophrastan Character is unique in other respects. Its affinities with Aristotle's system of ethics and with Theophrastus' own (now lost) rhetorical treatises are suggestive, but inconclusive. If virtue, for Aristotle, is the mean between the extremes of excess and deficiency, Theophrastus supplies images only of the extremes (the reference to "good" men in the dedication of his book, suggesting a lost second part, may be spurious); furthermore, only a few of his vices (e.g. "Flattery" and "Surliness") fit Aristotle's "too much/too little" pairing, and even these are too widely separated in the collection to function as contrasting extremes. Moreover, Theophrastus' vices are not, for the most part, truly vicious qualities. The norms from which his subjects diverge are social or cultural rather than moral, representing forms of overdoing

("Talkativeness," "Officiousness") or underdoing ("Absent-mindedness," "Stinginess") that would be ignored in existing categories of moral admonition and that are as much a testimony to the observer's perceptiveness as criticism of the observed. The Theophrastan voice is objective, neutral; its effect depends solely upon the recognition value of the details it cites, as these call forth a representative type of human nature.

In England, the Character emerged as a distinct literary form at about the same time as the essay (**Bacon**'s *Essayes* appeared in 1597, 1612, and 1625), and there is a tendency to blur the distinctions between the two genres. Both make use of the curt, pointed, Senecan "Attic" prose that (at least in Bacon's essays) lends itself to discontinuous **aphorism**; in their later manifestations, moreover, essays may include illustrative Characters, and Characters become more methodical and discursive. Yet while native traditions of character representation played a part in the development of Character writing in England, writers in the first half of the 17th century found the basic elements of the Character in Isaac Casaubon's edition and Latin translation of 23 (later 28) of Theophrastus' *Characters*, published on the continent in 1592 and 1599. Of the countless imitations and adaptations of this basic model, three collections stand out. The earliest of these, Joseph Hall's *Characters of Vertues and Vices* (1608), bears the closest resemblance to the Theophrastan model, notwithstanding its nine innovative virtue-types. But Hall, a churchman and Juvenalian satirist, introduced an element of sincere moral concern to the Character, an exhortative voice that tends to comment and interpret and that undercuts the dramatic objectivity of his model. In a collection of (finally) 83 Characters attached to succeeding editions of Sir Thomas Overbury's long poem, *A Wife* (1614), drama and moral earnestness are alike abandoned for the sake of wit and epigram, qualities that would remain standard features of the English Character. The writers of the "Overburian" Characters (John Webster, Thomas Dekker, **John Donne**, and others) also replaced the ethical subjects of Theophrastus and Hall with the occupational and social types of their own times, often selected as ideological targets for satiric ridicule. Wit and an English repertoire of social and occupational types are also marks of the Characters included in John Earle's *Micro-Cosmographie* (1628), the most admired of the English collections. But Earle's wit is more often sympathetic than satirical, and his subjects do not exclude the ethical dimensions of Theophrastus' Characters. His commitment to humanist ideals is implicit in the title of the collection, "a discovery of the little world," i.e. Man.

In France, Casaubon's Latin version of Theophrastus' Characters was translated by **Jean de La Bruyère**, although this seems little more than a pretext for the translator's own *Les Caractères ou mœurs de ce siècle* (1688; *The Characters, or the Manners of the Age*). If the Overburian writers made the **character sketch** the vehicle of satirical wit and epigram, La Bruyère made satirical portraiture only one element in a larger and expandable medley of **maxim** and moral reflection on a general topic (e.g. Women, Courtiers, Freethinkers). Framed in this moral discourse, his portraits seem less like specimens of an abstract anatomy and more like the characters of fiction – La Bruyère gives them classical names rather than taxonomic labels. **Addison** and **Steele** later adopted this successful pattern in the *Tatler* and *Spectator*.

In the 1640s and 1650s, the fragmenting of English society into political and religious factions provided a new field of subject matter for Character writers, self-identified types (the Puritan, the Non-Conformist, the Cavalier, etc.) that afforded writers the luxury of indulging their talent for inventing witty variations on the recognized characteristics of the subject. As a consequence, Characters grew longer, at times reaching **pamphlet** or essay length, and were often published singly rather than in collections. In the late 1660s, Samuel Butler, the author of the Puritan satire *Hudibras* (1662–77), produced (but did not publish) 198 Characters, several of them ("A Modern Politician," "A Small Poet," "An Hermetic Philosopher") running to a dozen pages or more. By this time the "Character" label was also attached to the verbal portrait of an historical personage who epitomized a social or political class (e.g. Butler's "A Duke of Bucks," i.e. George Villiers), and even to the biographical sketch of an individual (e.g. Edward Hyde's "Character of Charles II"). As Benjamin Boyce remarked in *The Polemic Character* (1955), however, "when literary terminology becomes so blurred that the tradition of Plutarch can no longer be distinguished from that of Theophrastus it is time to stop."

GEORGE WASSERMAN

See also Classical Influences

Editions
Characteres (Greek and Latin text), edited by Isaac Casaubon, 1592, 1599, Hermann Diels, 1909, O. Navarre, 1920, O. Immisch, 1923, and R. G. Ussher (with commentary), 1960, revised edition, 1993; as *The Characters*, edited and translated by J. M. Edmonds (Loeb Edition), 1929, and Jeffrey Ruslen, I. C. Cunningham, and A. D. Knox, 1929; translated by John Healey, 1616 (reprinted 1899), R. C. Jebb, 1870 (revised by J. E. Sandys, 1909), Jean Stewart, 1970, and Warren Anderson, 1970

Bibliography
Greenough, Chester Noyes, *A Bibliography of the Theophrastan Character*, Westport, Connecticut: Greenwood Press, 1970 (original edition, 1947)

Further Reading
Baldwin, Edward C., "La Bruyère's Influence upon Addison," *PMLA* 29 (1904): 479–95
Boyce, Benjamin, *The Theophrastan Character in England to 1642*, Cambridge, Massachusetts: Harvard University Press, 1947
Boyce, Benjamin, *The Polemic Character, 1640–1661: A Chapter in English Literary History*, Lincoln: University of Nebraska Press, 1955
Boyce, Benjamin, *The Character-Sketches in Pope's Poems*, Durham, North Carolina: Duke University Press, 1962
Bush, Douglas, *English Literature in the Earlier Seventeenth Century, 1600–1660*, Oxford: Oxford University Press, revised edition, 1973 (original edition, 1945)
Fortenbaugh, William W., and others, editors and translators, *Theophrastus of Eresus: Sources for His Life, Writings, Thought and Influence*, Leiden and New York: Brill, 1991
Smeed, J. W., *The Theophrastan "Character": The History of a Literary Genre*, Oxford: Clarendon Press, and New York: Oxford University Press, 1985
Turner, Margaret, "The Influence of La Bruyère on the 'Tatler' and the 'Spectator,'" *Modern Language Review* 48 (1953): 10–16

Chateaubriand

French, 1768–1848

Despite his grandiose overarching projects, titles, and suggestions, Chateaubriand's writing is expressed, as often as not, as familiar conversation and concrete fragmentariness. Having spent several years of his youth in England, and gained an acquaintance with the traditions of English literature (he wrote a sketchy, subjective history of English literature and culture), Chateaubriand was also influenced by a mode of writing much better established north than south of the English Channel.

Some of Chateaubriand's writings, particularly in the second half of his life, have the length and manner usually expected from the journalistic essay and *feuilleton*. These appeared largely between 1815 and 1830 when the author was deeply involved in French political life. He fiercely defended the freedom of the press, argued in favor of a constitutional monarchy based on legitimacy and continuity, and philosophized on the accelerated modernization of society and the resulting implicit dangers. Although the purposes of these essays (many of them in periodicals he himself initiated, such as *Le Conservateur* [The conservative]) are ideological and political, they are always founded on a tone of unabashed subjectivity and appeal to personal preferences and choices.

More significantly and typically, Chateaubriand's two chief works, *Les Mémoires d'outre-tombe* (wr. c. 1811–41, pub. 1849–50; Memoirs from beyond the grave, translated simply as *Memoirs*) and *Le Génie du christianisme* (1802; *The Genius of Christianity*), consist of short pieces that are not always connected, unless in a somewhat general and abstract way. Thus the latter, which made the young author famous, contains pieces of literary criticism (e.g. the famous comparison between biblical Hebrew poetics and Homeric writings, claiming the superiority of the former), as well as passages of whimsical erudition such as the detailed parallels between the tables of laws and commandments of different cultures, or between the cosmogony of Moses and various philosophies of classical antiquity. Even more typically recognizable as autonomous essays within *The Genius of Christianity* are "chapters" such as those on the aesthetic appeal of ruins, the vindication of reptiles and amphibians within natural economy, the human relevance of bird song, the evocative power of church bells, and the typology and meaning of cemeteries.

The memoirs of Chateaubriand, perhaps his most durable literary work, are formed from disjointed fragments of varying lengths arranged in approximately chronological order; the great majority can be read separately without any significant loss of sense. Among these are memorable portraits, often devastatingly sarcastic, of major historical figures of the French Revolution and Restoration, or of different imperial and royal courts.

Some of the units or modules into which the text of the memoirs is divided are meditations on issues of political and historical interest, such as the future of the United States, a global society in which mass democracy prevails, or, even more important, the long essay on the life of Napoleon placed at the center of the book. Others are straightforward essays on, for instance, the description of Venice and of Silvio Pellico's prison, an anti-mountain diatribe during his 1832 journey from Paris to Lugano and back via Switzerland, or the parallels between Washington and Bonaparte.

More generally it must be said that Chateaubriand lived and worked under the sign of the essay to the extent to which he rejected the definitive and the complete. He decided he was not in a position to write a history of English literature, but simply a connected series of separate vignettes on some of its highlights, and thus called his work an "essay." Similarly he could not convince himself that his comments on the patterns of revolutions in different historical ages added up to a **treatise** or manual on the philosophy of history and so, again, he gave it the title of "essay." An exquisite mixture of erudition, subjectivity, moral gravity, and dreamy delight in the face of the world's spectacle characterizes all of these works.

Chateaubriand's style was flamboyant and passionate, expressing his proud, bold, and egocentric temperament. His daring ideological intiatives proved to be of lasting influence: the whole of Christian apologetics of the 19th century was deeply marked by his argument that beauty and the emotional and subjective resources of humankind are the proper environment for spiritual and religious concerns, rather than logic, science, or even the realm of ethical action. Chateaubriand differs from other essayists of the day (particularly from the English tradition) in that he lacks their lightly humorous and playful manner, choosing a discourse of melancholy and pathos. (There are a few exceptions, for instance in parts of the memoirs.) Nevertheless, he shares in the general project of Romantic essayism: finding a place where a trust in completeness and universality meets a firm commitment to the fragmentary and the symptomatic. In this respect, Chateaubriand can be classed with both **Lamb** and the **Schlegel** brothers.

VIRGIL NEMOIANU

Biography

François-René August, Vicomte de Chateaubriand. Born 4 September 1768 in Saint-Malo. Studied at the Collège de Rennes, 1781–83; Collège de Dinan, 1783–84. Entered the army, 1786; visited America, 1791; served briefly in the Prussian army, 1792. Married Céleste Buisson de la Vigne (died, 1847), 1792. Exiled to Jersey, 1792, and England, 1793–1800, then returned to France; diplomat, 1803–04. Traveled to the Middle East and Spain, 1806–07. Elected to the French Academy, 1811; exiled by Napoleon to Ghent, 1815; appointed Minister of Interior of the Government in exile, 1815; created peer of France, 1815, and President of the Electoral College of Orléans, 1815. Founder, *Le Conservateur*, 1818–20. Ambassador to Berlin, 1820–21, London, 1822, and Rome, 1828; Minister of Foreign Affairs, 1822–24. Arrested briefly on suspicion of a conspiracy to overthrow the monarchy, 1832. Liaisons with many women throughout his life. Died in Paris, 4 July 1848.

Selected Writings

Essays and Related Prose

Essai historique, politique, et moral sur les révolutions anciennes et modernes, 1797; edited by Maurice Regard, 1978

Le Génie du christianisme; ou, Beautés de la religion chrétienne, 5 vols., 1802; edited by Maurice Regard, 1978; as *The Genius of Christianity*, translated by Charles I. White, 1802, and Rev. E. O'Donnell, 1854; as *The Beauties of Christianity*, 3 vols., translated by Frederic Shoberl, 1813

Réflexions politiques, 1814; as *Political Reflections*, translated anonymously, 1814

Mélanges de politique, 2 vols., 1816
Études ou discours historiques sur la chute de l'empire romain, la naissance et les progrès du christianisme, et l'invasion des barbares, 4 vols., 1831
Essai sur la littérature anglaise, 2 vols., 1836
Les Mémoires d'outre-tombe, 12 vols., 1849–50; edited by Maurice Levaillant and Georges Moulinier, 2 vols., 1951, and Jean-Claude Berchet, 1989; as *Memoirs*, translated anonymously, 3 vols., 1848, and by Alexander Teixeira de Mattos, 6 vols., 1902; selections edited and translated by Robert Baldick, 1961
Réflexions et aphorismes, edited by Jean-Paul Clément, 1993
Grands Écrits politiques, edited by Jean-Paul Clément, 2 vols., 1993

Other writings: two short stories (*Atala*, 1801; *René*, 1802), a novel (*Les Martyrs* [*The Martyrs*], 1809), a play (*Moïse*, 1831), travel writing (including *Itinéraire de Paris à Jérusalem* [*Travels in Greece, Palestine, Egypt, and Barbary*], 1811), studies of literary history, a biography (*La Vie de Rancé*, 1844), and numerous political and ideological pamphlets and articles.

Collected works editions: *Œuvres complètes*, 31 vols., 1826–31, 36 vols., 1836–39, and 12 vols., 1859–61; *Œuvres romanesques et voyages* (Pléiade Edition), edited by Maurice Regard, 2 vols., 1969.

Bibliography
Dubé, Pierre H., and Ann Dubé, *Bibliographie de la critique sur François-René de Chateaubriand: 1801–1986*, Paris: Nizet, 1988

Further Reading
Barberis, Pierre, *À la recherche d'une écriture: Chateaubriand*, Tours: Mame, 1974
Barberis, Pierre, *Chateaubriand: Une Réaction au monde moderne*, Paris: Larousse, 1976
Clarac, Pierre, *À la recherche de Chateaubriand*, Paris: Nizet, 1975
Lelièvre, Michel, *Chateaubriand polémiste*, Paris: Presses Universitaires de France, 1983
Moreau, Pierre, *Chateaubriand, l'homme et l'œuvre*, Paris: Hatier, 1956
Painter, George D., *Chateaubriand: A Biography*, vol. 1, London: Chatto and Windus, 1977
Porter, Charles A., *Chateaubriand: Composition, Imagination, and Poetry*, Saratoga, California: Anma Libri, 1978
Richard, Jean-Pierre, *Paysage de Chateaubriand*, Paris: Seuil, 1967
Sainte-Beuve, *Chateaubriand et son groupe littéraire sous l'Empire*, Paris: Garnier, 2 vols., 1948 (original edition, 1861)
Switzer, Richard, *Chateaubriand*, New York: Twayne, 1971
Vial, André, *Chateaubriand et le temps perdu*, Paris: Julliard, 1963

Chernyshevskii, Nikolai
Russian, 1828–1889

Born the son of a priest, Nikolai Chernyshevskii was himself intended for the priesthood. His seminary education, however, was cut short in 1845, but his publicistic writings, characterized by dogmatism, moral fervor, zeal, and dedication, bear its stamp. In 1846, Chernyshevskii entered the University of St. Petersburg. During his years in the capital, acquaintance with members of the Petrashevskii circle and with the works of many Western thinkers, especially **Ludwig Feuerbach**, Louis Blanc, P.-J. Proudhon, and Charles Fourier, as well as his witnessing the failed revolutions of 1848, persuaded him of the futility of liberalism and helped him to mold a radical world

view. After graduation, he taught in Saratov for several years, but returned to St. Petersburg in 1853 to write his Master's thesis. His views also found a new outlet: that year, he began his journalistic career, publishing a few articles for the liberal journal *Otechestvennye Zapiski* (Fatherland notes) before moving to *Sovremennik* (The contemporary) early in 1854.

Initially he published mainly literary criticism. Like his predecessor **Vissarion Belinskii**, who deeply influenced him and whose post as leading critic of Russian literature he would later fill, Chernyshevskii demanded civic responsibility in art, believing that literature was one of the key forces of progress. In his work he maintained that the role of art was to portray real life, to make it understandable to the reader, and to pass judgment on it. However, the extreme materialist aesthetics ("beauty is life") that he formulated in his Master's thesis, *Esteticheskie otnosheniia iskusstva k deistvital'nosti* ("The Aesthetic Relation of Art to Reality"), which he defended unsuccessfully in 1855, proved to be as offensive to many of his coworkers as they had been to his thesis supervisor, Aleksandr Nikitenko. He succeeded in alienating many of *Sovremennik*'s important writers, including **Lev Tolstoi, Ivan Turgenev**, and Aleksandr Druzhinin, who eventually left the journal. He continued to express and elaborate his views on the role of the writer and literature in a number of critical **reviews**, most importantly in "Ocherki gogolevskogo perioda russkoi literatury" (1855–56; "Essays on the Gogol Period of Russian Literature"), in which he hailed Gogol', long revered for what was considered his faithful depiction of the corrupt aspects of Russia, as Russia's greatest writer. Supported by the editor, Nikolai Nekrasov, Chernyshevskii was the leading critic of *Sovremennik* and, by 1856, exerted considerable influence on all editorial questions.

In 1857, Chernyshevskii left *Sovremennik*'s literary criticism section in the hands of his protégé, Nikolai Dobroliubov. Hopeful about the possibility of reform under the new tsar, Alexander II, Chernyshevskii was pleased to deal more explicitly with socioeconomic questions, although his literary criticism had always served as a forum for critique of the existing order. In 1858 and 1859, he wrote numerous essays about serfdom and the potential value of the peasant commune, as well as proposals for land reform, which have since caused him to be referred to as a "utopian" socialist. For several years he wrote monthly reviews of political and historical events relevant to Russia's development. In addition to his many articles of a political nature, Chernyshevskii wrote the ethical **treatise** "Antropologicheskii printsip v filosofii" (1860; "The Anthropological Principle in Philosophy"), which was strongly influenced by the utilitarian principles of **John Stuart Mill**. In it he maintained that all human behavior is motivated exclusively by self-interest, and that the interests of the individual are inextricably linked to the interests of society; hence man can be taught to serve the common good if he is made to understand that it will ultimately benefit his own interests.

By the close of the decade, however, Chernyshevskii had become doubtful about the prospect of reform from above and began to be recognized as the leader of a section of the intelligentsia which was becoming increasingly radical. Provoked by an alarming rash of peasant disturbances and student unrest, the authorities thought it prudent to remove the apparent leader of the radicals, who had been under surveillance by the

Third Section for almost a year. Though they were not able to prove that Chernyshevskii was connected with the events, a **letter** from **Aleksandr Herzen** to Nikolai Serno-Solov'evich, in which Herzen offered to print the prohibited *Sovremennik* in London, gave the authorities a sufficient pretext for his arrest. On 7 July 1862, Chernyshevskii was arrested and imprisoned in the Peter and Paul Fortress. While in prison, he wrote the novel *Chto delat'?* (1863; *What Is to Be Done?*), which the censors mistakenly permitted to be serially published in *Sovremennik*. It was Chernyshevskii's first and last noteworthy work of fiction. Though widely considered didactic and poorly written, the novel was wildly popular and went on to influence a number of later revolutionaries, including Vera Zasulich and Lenin.

Despite an obvious lack of evidence, Chernyshevskii was found guilty of attempting to overthrow the regime, and was sentenced to seven years' hard labor and exile for life. His unreasonably hard sentence helped further to alienate many from the regime, and assured Chernyshevskii's status as a martyr. He was finally permitted to return to his birthplace in 1889, where he died later that year.

JENNIFER LONERGAN

Biography

Nikolai Gavrilovich Chernyshevskii. Born 12 July 1828 in Saratov. Studied at a seminary in Saratov, 1842–45; history and philology at the University of St. Petersburg, 1846–50, graduated 1850. Taught at a gymnasium in Saratov, 1851–53. Married Olga Sokratovna Vasil'eva, 1853: two sons. Returned to St. Petersburg, 1853; contributor, *Otechestvennye Zapiski*, 1853; contributor, from 1854, and co-editor, 1856–62, *Sovremennik*. Arrested and imprisoned for criticizing as insufficient the terms of Tsar Alexander II's emancipation of the serfs, 1862: went through a mock execution, then exiled to Siberia, 1864; worked in silver mines in Irkutsk region for seven years; lived in the Arctic village Vilyuisk for 12 years; suffered from malaria; allowed to return to Astrakhan, 1883, and Saratov, 1889. Died in Saratov, 17 October 1889.

Selected Writings

Essays and Related Prose

Esteticheskie otnosheniia iskusstva k deistvitel'nosti, 1855; as "The Aesthetic Relation of Art to Reality," in *Selected Philosophical Essays*, 1953

Ocherki gogolevskogo perioda russkoi literatury, in *Sovremennik*, 1855–56; as "Essays on the Gogol Period of Russian Literature," in *Selected Philosophical Essays*, 1953

"Antropologicheskii printsip v filosofii," in *Sovremennik*, 1860; as "The Anthropological Principle in Philosophy," in *Selected Philosophical Essays* 1953

Selected Philosophical Essays, 1953

Belinsky, Chernyshevsky, Dobrolyubov: Selected Criticism, edited by Ralph E. Matlaw, 1962

Other writings: the novels *Chto delat'?* (1863; *What Is to Be Done?*) and *Prolog* (1918; *Prologue*), and some short stories.

Collected works edition: *Polnoe sobranie sochinenii*, 16 vols., 1939–53.

Further Reading

Frank, Joseph, "Nikolay Chernyshevsky: A Russian Utopia," in his *Through the Russian Prism: Essays on Literature and Culture*, Princeton, New Jersey: Princeton University Press, 1990

Paperno, Irina, *Chernyshevsky and the Age of Realism: A Study in the Semiotics of Behavior*, Stanford, California: Stanford University Press, 1988
Pereira, N. G. O., *The Thought and Teachings of N. G. Cernyshevskij*, The Hague: Mouton, 1975
Randall, Francis B., *N. G. Chernyshevski*, New York: Twayne, 1967
Woehrlin, William F., *Chernyshevskii: The Man and the Journalist*, Cambridge, Massachusetts: Harvard University Press, 1971

Chesterfield, Earl of

English, 1694–1773

The essays of Philip Dormer Stanhope, fourth Earl of Chesterfield, comment on the politics and manners of his contemporaries from the lofty social, political, and intellectual positions available only to someone with Chesterfield's lineage, connections, and talents. The essays draw strength from a long and successful career in diplomacy and a lifetime of reading and writing. They exhibit wit, thought, style, integrity, and contempt – commodities of character and thought too rare to be ignored or forgotten, wherever they may be found. Like his notorious **letters** to his illegitimate son on how to succeed in the courts of Europe, his essays, several of which metamorphosed into separate political **pamphlets**, combine long experience in high places with thoughtful reading of classical texts, and great powers of observation and discernment. They exercise a judgment sharpened, but not embittered, by an unsentimental assessment of human nature and its capacities. They also, it must be admitted, reflect, or rather magnify, the prejudices of party and class held by this eloquent earl.

Well-born, well-bred, well-educated, well-read, well-traveled, well-connected, and exceedingly well-spoken, Chesterfield turned his polished hand to social and political essays at several points in his career. He had prepared himself as a writer by translating, memorizing, and emulating **Cicero**, Horace, Martial, and Ovid, and by reading and meeting all the best writers, French and English, of his own time. The contents of his elegant library resonate in his essays, his letters, and his speeches, proving again and again that this library was for use rather than ostentation.

None of Chesterfield's essays was published under his name. Some 45 essays have been attributed to Chesterfield on the good authority of his first biographer and editor, Matthew Maty, who reprinted them in his *Miscellaneous Works* edition of 1777. The attributions are discussed by Roger Coxon (1925), who reprints 11 essays. The earliest essays (17, 24 January and 10 April 1736) appeared in *Fog's Journal*, a weekly paper emanating from, and amplifying, the opposition to Sir Robert Walpole. In the first of them a self-congratulatory "projector" suggests that, based on a German (i.e. Hanoverian) model, the English army should be replaced with wax figures driven by clockwork. This contrivance would provide soldiers of a more uniform appearance and a fiercer demeanor, at great savings to the country, which had not, in any case, sent its army to battle for 25 years, "notwithstanding the almost uninterrupted disturbances that have been in Europe, in which our interests have been as nearly concerned as ever they are likely to be for these five and twenty years to come." Being made of wax, these new soldiers will be more pliable to the demands of the politicians and less of a threat to English liberty than a "standing army." This witty invention attacks the two military policies to which the Opposition most objected – that of maintaining a standing army and the failure to use any army to develop and maintain trade. The second essay deplores flattery as the tickling of the ear. Chesterfield had seen far too much, and practiced far too little, of this commodity in the course of his long diplomatic and short political career. The third essay draws on the same experience to ridicule the distortions of curiosity, vanity, and partiality in the guise of a survey of various optical instruments.

The 17 essays Chesterfield wrote for *Common Sense* from February 1737 through January 1739 discuss the rare and not very fashionable commodity named in its title and then apply it to such perennial topics of the essay as the balance of power, fashionable attire, misconceptions of honor, corrupt ministers (i.e. advisers such as Walpole), ill-advised efforts to regulate plays, party zeal, country living, coxcombs, the witlessness and ignorance of his competitors, taste, a foolish preference for all things French (few Englishmen understood the French and their language better than Chesterfield), and foreign and military policy. Two of them compete with the *Spectator* on its own ground, but without notable success. One argues that it is in January, not May, that the virtue and state of mind of women is most threatened, while the other considers, without real regret, the decline of opera.

In two numbers of *Old England, or the Constitutional Journal* of February 1743 attributed to Chesterfield by Maty, "Jeffrey Broadbottom" defends constitutional opposition and deplores faction and foreign entanglements. These two essays fail noticeably – whether using wit or wisdom – to enlarge upon the issues they consider.

The 23 numbers Chesterfield wrote for the *World* from retirement between 1753 and 1756 discuss, sometimes at too much leisure, such concerns of the time as family expeditions to the continent in search of fashion and diversion, elegant handwriting, honor, foreign operas, make-up, duels, decorum, and restraint. Two numbers make a halfhearted effort to construct a club of caricatures like that which Sir Roger de Coverley made famous in the *Spectator*. Given the lineage and nature of their author, three essays on exaggerated notions of noble birth, mistaken ideas of rank and fortune, and good breeding are among the most interesting and surprising. The two most important papers are those of 28 November and 5 December 1754, commending **Samuel Johnson**'s forthcoming *Dictionary*. Johnson vigorously repudiated Chesterfield's support as belated and condescending in one of the most famous letters of rejection ever written (7 February 1755). Nevertheless, Chesterfield's essays show an admirable understanding of the nature and state of the English language and the power of the English state, as well as a strong sense of Johnson's abilities and the difficulties facing him. The second essay is bold enough to comment on "the incontinency of female eloquence" and orthography.

The elegance, wit, and experience evident in these social and political essays blend nicely with malice and admiration in a series of 20 **character sketch**es cum memoirs published posthumously as *Characters of Eminent Personages of His Own Time* (1777). The portraits of George I and II, Queen Caroline, Walpole, and Newcastle are especially vivid, intimate, and severe. Those of Pope, Bolingbroke, and Scarborough are admiring and eloquent. Chesterfield's life and temperament seem to have qualified him almost uniquely to contribute to this subgenre of the essay.

Many of the 400 surviving letters to his son for which Chesterfield is best known, indeed infamous, are, in effect, essays on the politics of politeness, written with a more specific audience and, sometimes, a more particularized occasion in mind than most essays. Like his political essays, they draw on his long career and studious habits, while exhibiting wit, judgment, discernment, and prejudices of class and culture – in short, the character of their author. Few writers were in a better position to comment on civility than this polite and practiced earl. These letters also exhibit a gift for **maxim** that would have looked good in the essays (e.g. "Whoever is in a hurry, shows that the thing he is about is too big for him" – 10 August 1749).

Writing to educate his illegitimate and, evidently, unpromising and ungainly son for a diplomatic career and to instruct him in ways to prosper in the courts of Europe, Chesterfield provides devastating insights into the courts and the careerism of his era. Many of the manners, morals, and political and economic devices that he exposes seem still to be practiced in courtly and other venues. Whole pages are given over to the discussion of such perennial essay topics as frivolity, dissimulation, handwriting, Italian literature, pedantry, domestic politics, Roman history, treaties, mercenary armies, French politics and manners (a letter of 25 December 1753 seems to predict the French Revolution), sexual liaisons (the eight letters that treat or mention this topic are what made the correspondence notorious), and paternal authority. To the extent that an essay is thoughtful prose by someone who knows what he or she is writing about, and why, most of these letters are essays.

ALAN T. McKENZIE

Biography

Philip Dormer Stanhope, fourth Earl of Chesterfield. Born 22 September 1694 in London. Studied privately; Trinity Hall, Cambridge, 1712–14. Traveled on the continent, 1714–15. Whig Member of Parliament for St. Germans, Cornwall, from 1715, and Lostwithiel, from 1722; gentleman of the bedchamber, from 1715, and lord of the bedchamber, from 1727, to George, Prince of Wales (George II from 1727); appointed captain of the gentlemen-pensioners, 1723. Upon father's death in 1726 became the fourth Earl of Chesterfield and a member of the House of Lords; appointed privy councillor, 1728, and lord steward of the king's household, 1730. British Ambassador in The Hague, 1728–32, where he negotiated the marriage between William, prince of Orange, and Ann, princess royal of England, 1730. Made knight of the garter, 1730. Had one son, Philip Stanhope (died, 1768) by Elizabeth du Bouchet, 1732. Married Melusina de Schulemburg, Countess of Walsingham and Baroness of Aldeburgh, 1733. Began writing to his son, 1736 (over 400 letters extant), and to his godson, from 1761 (236 letters extant). Lord lieutenant of Ireland, 1745–46; secretary of state, 1746–48, then retired from politics. Contributor to various journals, including *Common Sense* and the *World*. Died in London, 24 March 1773.

Selected Writings

Essays and Related Prose

Letters to His Son Philip Stanhope, 2 vols., 1774; several revised, enlarged editions, 1776–1800; edited by Lord Mahon, 5 vols., 1845–53, John Bradshaw (with *Characters*), 3 vols., 1892, Charles Strachey and Annette Calthrop, 2 vols., 1901, and Bonamy Dobrée, 6 vols., 1932; selections, as *The Art of Pleasing; or, Instructions for Youth in the First Stage of Life*, 1783, *Letters to His Son*, edited by James Harding, 1973, *Dear Boy: Lord Chesterfield's Letters to His Son*, edited by Piers Dudgeon and Jonathan Jones, 1989, and *Letters*, edited by David Roberts, 1992

Miscellaneous Works, vols. 1–2 edited by Matthew Maty, 1777; vol. 3 edited by Benjamin Way, 1778

Characters of Eminent Personages of His Own Time, 1777; enlarged edition, 1778, reprinted 1990; edited by John Bradshaw (with *Letters to His Son*), 3 vols., 1892, and Colin Franklin, 1993

Letters to His Godson and Successor, edited by the Earl of Carnarvon, 1890

Some Unpublished Letters, edited by Sidney L. Gulick, Jr., 1937

Other writings: poetry, and letters to colleagues and friends (especially his friend Solomon Dayrolles).

Bibliographies

Gulick, Sidney L., *A Chesterfield Bibliography to 1800*, Charlottesville: University Press of Virginia, revised edition, 1979 (original edition, 1935)

Todd, W. B., "The Number, Order and Authorship of the Hanover Pamphlets Attributed to Chesterfield," *Papers of the Bibliographical Society of America* 44 (1950)

Further Reading

Connely, Willard, *The True Chesterfield: Manners – Women – Education*, London: Cassell, 1939

Coxon, Roger, *Chesterfield and His Critics*, London: Routledge, 1925

Dobrée, Bonamy, "The Life of Philip Dormer Stanhope, Fourth Earl of Chesterfield," in *The Letters of Philip Dormer Stanhope, Fourth Earl of Chesterfield*, vol. 1, edited by Dobrée, London: Eyre and Spottiswoode, and New York: Viking Press, 1932

Franklin, Colin, *Lord Chesterfield: His Character and Characters*, Aldershot, Hampshire: Scolar Press, 1993

Fullen, Charles, "Lord Chesterfield and Eighteenth-Century Appearance and Reality," *SEL: Studies in English Literature, 1500–1900* 8 (1968): 501–15

Korshin, Paul J., "The Johnson-Chesterfield Relationship: A New Hypothesis," *PMLA* 85 (1970): 247–59

Lucas, F. L., "Lord Chesterfield," in his *The Search for Good Sense: Four Eighteenth-Century Characters: Johnson, Chesterfield, Boswell and Goldsmith*, London: Cassell, and New York: Macmillan, 1958

McKenzie, Alan T., Introduction to *Characters* by Chesterfield, Los Angeles: Clark Memorial Library, 1990: iii–xii

McKenzie, Alan T., "History, Genre and Insight in the Characters of Lord Chesterfield," in *Studies in Eighteenth-Century Culture*, vol. 21, edited by Patricia B. Craddock and Carla H. Hay, East Lansing, Michigan: Colleagues Press, 1991: 159–76

McKenzie, Alan T., "Philip Dormer Stanhope, Lord Chesterfield," in *British Prose Writers, 1660–1800, Second Series*, edited by Donald T. Siebert, *Dictionary of Literary Biography*, vol. 104, Detroit: Gale Research, 1991: 61–77

Maty, Matthew, "Memoirs of Lord Chesterfield," in *Miscellaneous Works of the Late Philip Dormer Stanhope, Earl of Chesterfield*, vol. 1, edited by Maty, London: Edward and Charles Dilly, 1777

Neumann, J. H., "Chesterfield and the Standard of Usage in English," *Modern Language Quarterly* 7 (1946): 463–75

Shellabarger, Samuel, *Lord Chesterfield and His World*, 1935; Boston: Little Brown, 1951 (original edition, 1935)

Weinbrot, Howard, "Johnson's 'Dictionary' and 'The World': The Papers of Lord Chesterfield and Richard Owen Cambridge," *Philological Quarterly* 50 (1971): 663–69

Willey, Basil, "Lord Chesterfield (1694–1773)," in his *The English Moralists*, New York: Norton, and London: Chatto and Windus, 1964: 269–82

Chesterton, G. K.

British, 1874–1936

G. K. Chesterton was one of the 20th century's most prolific writers, his range including poetry, dramas, biographies, and novels. As an essayist, however, he was no less productive, and his collected efforts in this category fill dozens of volumes. Considered by some critics to be one of the last of the great "men of letters," Chesterton wrote essays on a wide variety of topics over a span of more than 40 years. As with any author producing such an enormous yield of literature, the quality often varied, but as T. S. Eliot noted in Chesterton's obituary in the *Tablet* (20 June 1936), "it is not, I think, for any piece of writing in particular that Chesterton is of importance, but for the place that he occupied, the position that he represented, during the better part of a generation."

When his first collection of essays, *The Defendant*, appeared in 1901, Chesterton had already gained something of a reputation as an essayist for his contributions to a number of English periodicals such as the *Speaker*, the *Bookman*, and the *Daily News*. Thus, as most reviewers were already familiar with Chesterton's style and his sometimes paradoxical approach to his subject matter, few were disappointed in this collection of largely humorous essays on topics ranging from nonsense to ugly things. As an anonymous reviewer for the *Whitehall Review* (27 February 1902) wrote, "The whole book, in short, is one of the most delightful companions possible for a man to have with him, and if it does not run through two or three editions rapidly then there is no humor left in these decadent days."

This critical observation made so early in his career notes perhaps one of the defining characteristics of many of Chesterton's essays: his humor. While not given to writing overtly funny, rollicking essays, Chesterton was always cognizant of the fact that a little humor in an otherwise serious work could strengthen its argument and draw attention to the essay's salient points. However, these touches of humor were to be consistently observed by critics as evidence of Chesterton's flippancy, charges that he failed to appreciate. In the preface to *Orthodoxy* (1908), Chesterton – by this time the author of a number of works – refuted his critics' assertions of his often cavalier attitude by claiming that even if the work were dull, "dullness will, however, free me from the charge which I most lament; the charge of being flippant. Mere light sophistry is the thing that I happen to despise most of all things, and it is perhaps a wholesome fact that this is the thing of which I am generally accused."

However, even today it is difficult to read Chesterton's literature without feeling that he is purposely making light of certain situations, leaving the reader uncertain as to whether he is actually attempting to be humorous or not. For example, in one of his most famous works, *Charles Dickens* (1906), Chesterton makes a typically paradoxical comment concerning **Dickens'** marriage to Catherine Hogarth. Noting Dickens' often obsessive devotion to her sisters Mary and Georgina, Chesterton claims that Dickens was overwhelmed by the attentions of all of the sisters, and "as sometimes happens in undeveloped youth, an abstract femininity simply intoxicated him. And again, I think we shall not be accused of harshness if we put the point this way: that by a kind of accident he got hold of the wrong sister." While Dickensian purists might begrudgingly admit that there is perhaps a modicum of truth in the assertion, no doubt the statement ultimately appears to be a humorous attempt to define the reason Dickens chose what appeared to be an incompatible mate. In this and other cases, Chesterton was simply a victim of his own success: he often came across as being funny whether he intended to or not. As for *Charles Dickens* as a work, critics pointed out that although it purported to be a biography, it was in itself a collection of related essays, much of it literary criticism, relating to the famous author.

In addition to his humor, perhaps the other characteristic Chesterton's work was noted for was his occasional laudatory stance on Orthodox Christianity. Then, as now, alluding to one's religious beliefs could be literary suicide, but Chesterton never appeared to worry about offending his readers; in fact he seemed aware that his place as a man of letters provided him a unique opportunity to share his views and religious opinions. Generally, Chesterton was able to avoid being heavy-handed, even in works that were intrinsically religious, such as *Orthodoxy*, *St. Thomas Aquinas* (1933), *The Everlasting Man* (1925), and *St. Francis of Assisi* (1923). Like many of his volume-length works, these were essentially collections of interrelated essays, and most critics recognized them as such.

Today Chesterton's reputation as an essayist has been somewhat eclipsed by the continuing popularity of his fictional works, and he is now probably best known for his Father Brown detective stories. Yet there is still much that can be gained by reading Chesterton's essays. Perhaps his friend **Hilaire Belloc** best defined how we should evaluate Chesterton's place as an essayist when he wrote in the *Observer* (21 June 1936), at Chesterton's death, that his "was a voice from which I learnt continually, from the first day I heard it until the last; acquiring its discoveries, explanations, definitions which continue to increase my possessions. Nor does it cease. Nor will it cease."

JAMES R. SIMMONS, JR.

Biography

Gilbert Keith Chesterton. Born in London, 29 May 1874. Studied at St. Paul's School, London, 1887–92, where he edited the *Debater*; Slade School of Art, London, 1893–96. Worked for Redway publishers, London, 1896, and T. Fisher Unwin publishers, London, 1896–1902. Married Frances Alice Blogg, 1901. Columnist for the London *Daily News*, 1901–13, and the *Illustrated London News*, 1905–36. Moved to Beaconsfield, Buckinghamshire, 1909. Founder, with his brother Cecil Chesterton and Hilaire Belloc, and editor, with others, *Eye Witness*, 1911–12; contributor, London *Daily Herald*, 1913–14; editor, *New Witness*, 1916–23, and *G. K.'s Weekly*, 1925–36. Leader of the Distributist movement, from 1919, and president of the Distributist League. Joined the Roman Catholic Church, 1922. Radio broadcaster, BBC, 1930s. Illustrated some of his own works and books by others. Awards: honorary degrees from three universities. Fellow, Royal Society of Literature; Knight Commander with Star, Order of St. Gregory the Great, 1934. Died in Beaconsfield, 14 June 1936.

Selected Writings

Essays and Related Prose

The Defendant, 1901; revised edition, 1903
Twelve Types, 1902; enlarged edition, as *Varied Types*, 1903
Charles Dickens, 1906
Orthodoxy, 1908
All Things Considered, 1908
Tremendous Trifles, 1909
Alarms and Discursions, 1910
A Defence of Nonsense and Other Essays, 1911
A Miscellany of Men, 1912
The Victorian Age of Literature, 1913
The Barbarism of Berlin, 1914
Utopia of Usurers and Other Essays, 1917
The Uses of Diversity: A Book of Essays, 1920
St. Francis of Assisi, 1923
The Everlasting Man, 1925
Generally Speaking: A Book of Essays, 1928
(Essays), 1928
The Thing, 1929
Come to Think of It: A Book of Essays, 1930
All Is Grist: A Book of Essays, 1931
Sidelights on New London and Newer York and Other Essays, 1932
All I Survey: A Book of Essays, 1933
St. Thomas Aquinas, 1933
Avowals and Denials: A Book of Essays, 1934
The Well and the Shallows, 1935
As I Was Saying: A Book of Essays, 1936
Essays, edited by John Guest, 1939
Selected Essays, edited by Dorothy Collins, 1949
The Common Man, 1950
Essays, edited by K. E. Whitehorn, 1953
A Handful of Authors: Essays on Books and Writers, edited by Dorothy Collins, 1953
The Glass Walking-Stick and Other Essays from the Illustrated London News, 1905–1936, edited by Dorothy Collins, 1955
Lunacy and Letters, edited by Dorothy Collins, 1958
The Spice of Life and Other Essays, edited by Dorothy Collins, 1964
G. K. Chesterton: A Selection from His Non-Fictional Prose, edited by W. H. Auden, 1970
The Apostle and the Wild Ducks, and Other Essays, edited by Dorothy Collins, 1975
As I Was Saying: A Chesterton Reader, edited by Robert Knille, 1985
The Bodley Head Chesterton, edited by P. J. Kavanagh, 1985; as *The Essential Chesterton*, 1987
G. K.'s Weekly: A Sampler, edited by Lyle W. Dorsett, 1986

Other writings: several novels, Father Brown detective stories, collections of poetry, plays, and an autobiography.

Collected works edition: *Collected Works*, edited by D. J. Conlon, 1986– (in progress).

Bibliography

Sullivan, John, *G. K. Chesterton: A Bibliography*, London: University of London, 1958; supplement, 1968; and *G. K. Chesterton 3: A Bibliographical Postscript*, 1980

Further Reading

Auden, W. H., Introduction to *G. K. Chesterton: A Selection from His Non-Fictional Prose*, edited by Auden, London: Faber, 1970

Boyd, Ian, *The Novels of G. K. Chesterton: A Study in Art and Propaganda*, New York: Barnes and Noble, and London: Elek, 1975

Cammaerts, Emile, *The Laughing Prophet: The Seven Virtues and G. K. Chesterton*, Folcroft, Pennsylvania: Folcroft, 1979 (original edition, 1937)

Conlon, D. J., *G. K. Chesterton: The Critical Judgments, Part 1: 1900–1937*, Antwerp: Antwerp Studies in English Literature, 1976

Conlon, D. J., editor, *G. K. Chesterton: A Half Century of Views*, Oxford and New York: Oxford University Press, 1987

Evans, Maurice, *G. K. Chesterton*, New York: Haskell House, 1972 (original edition, 1939)

Kenner, Hugh, *Paradox in Chesterton*, New York: Sheed and Ward, 1947; London: Sheed and Ward, 1948

Ward, Maisie, *Return to Chesterton*, London and New York: Sheed and Ward, 1952

Wills, Gary, *Chesterton: Man and Mask*, New York: Sheed and Ward, 1961

Chinese Essay

In his book *My Country and My People* (1936), Lin Yutang (1895–1976), a 40-year-old intellectual educated in China, the United States, and Europe, described traditional Chinese prose literature in terms which if accepted would make the present survey rather short. His opening sentence was "There was very little good prose in the classical Chinese literature." By "good," he meant good by modern standards: that is, having a broad sweep and wide canvas, substantial intellectual content, the rhythms of speech, and a familiar, personal tone. Classical Chinese prose, in contrast, was typically euphuistic and poetic, impersonal and stereotyped, economical with words, and cast in a dead language. As an example of its limitations, Lin cited Hou Fangyu's (1618–54) biography of Li Xiangjun. The liaison between the red-blooded young scholar Hou and the patriotic courtesan Li was the stuff that plays are made of (and, indeed, famously were), yet, as Lin put it, "Hou did his 'Biography of Miss Li' in exactly 375 words [characters], written in a manner as if he was describing the virtues of his neighbour's grandmother." Another swipe is aimed at the venerated poet Tao Yuanming (365–427 CE), whose portrait of himself, "Mr. Five Willows," is even shorter (125 characters); this composition, though regarded as a model in the past, Lin found completely devoid of intellectual content. Both criticisms are correct: Hou's "biography" is insipid, and Tao's self-portrait vacuous. It is also true that both disappointments can be laid at the door of weaknesses endemic in Chinese prose literature. However, that is the start, not the end, of the story.

It will occasion no surprise to record that Chinese prose goes back a long way. In a divided empire of warring states for several centuries prior to reunification at the end of the third century BCE, many clever men found employment as political advisers. They spoke and wrote voluminously. More permanently employed court historians quite properly also had a great deal to say. If we unpick their works we find a multitude of finely composed "essays" on history and contemporary life and conduct. With the spread of literacy in succeeding ages, the number and output of occasional pieces expressing their author's views or giving vent to his feelings grew exponentially. However, the channels and compartments for views and feelings differed from those that evolved in Europe; chronologically speaking they were all in place, indeed solidified, before the European "essay" that served as Lin Yutang's yardstick for prose was ever thought of, and very little tinkering with them was done until the 20th century.

In ancient China those with a high degree of literacy served the state as civil servants. Their best thoughts on social and ethical matters were addressed to the court in the first instance, with all the formality that entailed. Furthermore, as is the way with bureaucracies, forms were codified and rapidly acquired their conventions. Of the many vehicles for prose contained in Chinese anthologies of literature from the sixth to the 19th centuries, few allowed much freedom for maneuver. Personal letters (*shu*), widely circulated, were sometimes used for informal discussion of general topics, but the very fact that they had to be pressed into service is a token of the rigidity of established forms. Another constraint, before paper and print became common, was the costliness of writing materials and the laboriousness of copying, which naturally encouraged pithiness; those early days set the models and standards for later literature. The search for a personalized essay with a wide canvas as Lin Yutang did was therefore bound to end in disappointment.

The characteristic of euphuism that Lin Yutang objected to was a natural concomitant of brevity: if words were to be few, a premium was placed on craftsmanship. (Conversely, where space is limitless and cost negligible, the opposite holds true – craftsmanship is taboo.) Hence in the first historical period which enjoyed freedom of thought after Confucianism was set up as state orthodoxy, that advantage was offset by the bondage of formalism. The Six Dynasties (third to sixth centuries CE) saw the emergence of some of the most flamboyant individuals in Chinese history, but also the apogee of *pianwen* (parallel prose, composed in syntactically matching couplets). Even very long treatises and personal letters adopted this form, despite the impediment to the natural flow of thought it constituted. In the same period there developed a sophisticated aesthetic for literature, which reinforced the tendency to strive for artistic effect. The emphasis of this criticism was on performance rather than content, as with a concert where the score is taken as given and the interest is in the virtuosity of the soloist. Within the general directive that *belles-lettres* should "give pleasure to the ear, delight to the eye," different genres were assigned their tone-coloring. For instance, the *lun* (disquisition) was said to be "rarefied and subtle, bright and smooth," the *shuo* (plea) "dazzlingly bright and extravagantly bizarre" (*Wenfu* [3rd century CE; Description of literature]) – these formulas themselves being expressed in parallel prose.

While performance criteria were being laid down on a generic level, ideas were formulated on how to assess and describe individual style. The seminal notion was that of *qi*, a kind of energy or life force, immanent in the author and perceptible in his work, that determined the pace and vigor of a composition. More superficially, works were described in terms of flavors and colors. What the great majority of critical statements had in common was their attention to the aesthetic or sensual experience of reader reception; thought content or mental power was rarely mentioned. The interest was less on what was said than on how it was said. Though this criticism could be extremely perceptive, it could also be looked upon as overrefined, and contributing to the kinship between classical prose and poetry that Lin Yutang deplored.

All was not lost, though: there was an alternative. Even in the heyday of parallel prose, plain prose continued to be written. In time this plain kind of prose came to be known as *guwen* (ancient prose), as it looked back to the "attic" simplicity of the classics and early histories. *Guwen* did not become a popular notion until the Tang dynasty (618–907), when the pendulum swing against the mellifluity – associated with decadence – of the preceding age occurred. The *guwen* school's view of prose style was close to that taken in the West: a good style consisted of no more and no less than putting in the best order the words that could best express one's thoughts. Along with disdain for ornament naturally went esteem for substantial content. On the other hand, the emphasis on restoring ancient virtues was not conducive to the independence of thought we associate with the prose essay. Forceful argument, skillful reasoning, vehemence, and subtlety of expression are to be found in quantity in Tang prose, as they should be, considering that the *Quan Tang wen* (Complete Tang prose) includes 18,000 pieces by 3042 authors. What was lacking was an "I" and a "you"; discourse on serious subjects tended to be delivered from an imaginary pulpit and addressed to the whole of the civilized world, when not to the emperor.

As all scholars were perforce students of Chinese history, **historical essays** featured prominently among their occasional pieces, highlighting things they admired or censured or found a reinterpretation for. In the works of the two acknowledged *guwen* masters of the Tang dynasty, Han Yu (768–824) and **Liu Zongyuan** (773–819), many examples can be found. As the intention was to prove a point, their focus was on clear and cogent reasoning, with no frills attached. Relaxed discussion of familiar matters had to find a home in letters (as mentioned), and of cultural matters in **prefaces**, neither of which allowed for much expansiveness. In three respects, however, they pushed forward the frontiers of prose composition. First, they used the *zhuan* (biography) to write of humble tradesmen (masons, nurserymen, snake catchers), not so much for the people themselves but as spokesmen for ways of life or healthy, common-sense attitudes that they, the authors, endorsed; in other words, the subjects were hardly more than borrowed voices. Second, they developed the parable, Han Yu with his "Maoying zhuan" (Mr. Brush Tip) and Liu Zongyuan with his animal parables, which were very like Aesop's fables. Third, Liu Zongyuan established the landscape essay as an art form. His "Yongzhou ba ji" (809; Eight descriptions of Yongzhou), each taking up on average no more than half a page in a modern edition, are like panels of a painting which put together form a broad vista. Yongzhou was on the remote southwest fringe of Hunan province, a wild region to which Liu had been demoted. There for the first time he apprehended Nature as an overwhelming presence that made his mind "congeal" and his body "dissolve." From this

communion derived the sketches that would inform the consciousness of nearly all subsequent practitioners of this genre.

The next high point in the history of Chinese prose came in the 11th century with the revival of *guwen*, which had in the interim been overshadowed again by *pianwen*. Compositions on matters of historical, philosophical, and general interest, previously the province of the disembodied intellect, were personalized in the hands of **Ouyang Xiu** (1007–72), **Su Shi** (1037–1101), and their like, and the taut and compact, heavily freighted language of Tang prose loosened and lightened. The sophistication and civility of the Song dynasty (960–1279) brought relatively ordinary and routine aspects of life into the ambit of prose composition, there to be celebrated precisely because they represented sophistication and civility. Ouyang Xiu's best-remembered pieces are those about pavilions constructed in beauty spots – civilization brought to the wilderness. They gave occasion to talk about the surroundings, local history, and local personages, the author included. "Zuiwen ting ji" (1046; "The Old Drunkard's Pavilion"), the most famous of all, pictures a scene of perfect rural harmony under the benevolent rule of the prefect – himself. Despite relaxing some tensions, though, Ouyang was still constrained by his literary vehicles: his thoughts on retirement had to be framed as *zizhuan* (autobiography), and his thoughts on autumn framed as a dialogue and called a *fu* (description).

His protégé Su Shi went further than Ouyang in shaping what one might call the occasional essay, combining the elements of narrative, description, and reflection. Persuaded of his own genius, justifiably it must be admitted, Su was the first writer in the pantheon of Chinese prose whom modern essayists were willing to recognize as a precursor, on account of his free thinking and uninhibitedness. Though Han Yu could be very witty, Su Shi's writing was unprecedented in its liberal display of humor, not to say jokiness. His sense of superiority, in being attuned to the true harmonies of creation, led him to put forward his own view of everything, so he is almost always entertaining. On the other hand, his perspective is too elevated for modern tastes: as author he places himself far above what he writes about. This characteristic is general among classical scholar-essayists, but is particularly salient in Su's case. His occasional essays typically set a scene, introduce someone else's response to it, then cap that response with his own wiser view, leading to a serene resolution. They are faultlessly written, but they leave the impression that with Su Shi the magic of words takes precedence over truthfulness to experience.

The mainstream of classical prose after Su Shi flowed along a smooth bed for several hundred years. Lin Yutang discovered in it only a purely linguistic craftsmanship, "laid over a paucity of characterization, a vacuity of facts, and a baldness of sentiment." That criticism was made specially to deflate the reputation of Gui Youguang's (1506–71) finest piece, "Xianbi shilüe," in memory of his mother. But there Lin erred. Granted the brevity (this and similar pieces are only about a page long) and baldness of statement; yet more sympathetic readers have found this piece extremely vivid and unbearably moving. Facts may be few, but they are tellingly chosen; as for sentiment, Lin does not seem to have realized that things half-said or unsaid may be more powerfully affective than things said at length. Classical Chinese prose in fact made as much use of empty spaces as Chinese painting.

The next highwater came with a surge toward individualism at the end of the 16th century, which threw up the Gongan school, headed by **Yuan Hongdao** (1568–1610), and its successors. Like Su Shi they believed in genius, but unlike him they did not think of genius as a superior accomplishment but rather as innate in all individuals. Hence they rejoiced in popular entertainments and all interests pursued with gusto. Consistent with this attitude, the language they used, while still basically classical – for who would wish to relinquish such a rich inheritance? – straddled the boundary between the refined and vulgar, making raids in both directions, and frequently echoed the rhythms of speech. **Zhang Dai** (1597–1679) was the last and best exponent of this style and persuasion. The new authoritarian Manchu dynasty closed down their business.

The grip of the classical language was loosened toward the end of the 19th century with the founding of journals and magazines in the principal cities, the heaviest concentration being in Shanghai. At last the time was ripe for the type of essay that the West had been familiar with since the same conditions pertained there: generous space to expatiate in, a readership no longer exclusively of the elite, but increasingly of middle-class citizens eager to expand their horizons, and financial rewards adequate to make writing for journals a valuable source of income. A new kind of written language, popularized by the leading journalist-intellectual of the day, Liang Qichao (1873–1929), became the standard medium for practical purposes. This still employed classical syntax, but its range was limited; more positively, it opened its doors wide to the vocabulary of the social sciences which had been introduced by translations of Western works. Within one generation there was a revolution in the way thoughts were formulated.

History decreed, however, that this simplified literary language would only be transitional. The flower of Chinese youth came back from being educated abroad to support the argument that survival in the 20th century required the unification of written and spoken languages, and the New Literature that took off around 1920 was all written in the vernacular (*baihua*). To sustain its newness the New Literature looked to foreign models, which included the foreign – principally English – essay. For the first few years when the New Literature was fighting its factional wars the **polemical essay** reigned supreme: that was when **Lu Xun** (1881–1936) won his spurs. Thereafter the civil essay shared the living space of prose: in the 1930s the "gentlemanly" essays of **Zhou Zuoren** (1885–1967) and the **humorous essay**s of Lin Yutang gained a large following; by then the notion that the purpose of the essay was to enrich life, rather than pursue controversy, had taken firm hold.

In this Republican period (1912–49) the Chinese vernacular essay resembled the English essay in the manner of taking its readers into its confidence, and being frank and open; the author placed himself on a level with the reader, in fact often inferior to him, confessing weakness and failings. It also likewise took its subject matter from daily life and personal experience. Nevertheless, comparatively few followed the English model in taking a topic and discussing it intelligently and entertainingly from a variety of angles. Only two writers stand out in this respect: **Liang Yuchun** (1906–32), who earned the

sobriquet of "the Chinese Elia," and Liang Shiqiu (1902–87), whose wartime essays reached a peak of urbanity. Adopting a droll and quizzical tone, these essays dealt with universal, everyday topics such as haircuts, illness, and anonymous letters. They included only enough personal matter to create familiarity; otherwise they drew upon observed behavior and the wit and wisdom of others. Liang Shiqiu's great strength, apart from his way with words, was his knowledge of his native culture and way of life, of course, but also his extensive education in Western literature (he had studied at Harvard). Chinese and foreign old saws and modern instances therefore came easily to him, and put the stamp of a genuine man of the world on his work.

The great majority of modern essayists were, understandably, more native in their values and inclinations. They did not appreciate the rambling sentences and involved reasoning of the foreign essay. Argument, whether or not alleviated with wit or energized by histrionics, they preferred to assign to a separate category known as *zawen*, or contentious essays. Pure prose, in their book, should exemplify such virtues as sparkling freshness, intricate description, and "truthfulness" (*zhen*), by which in practice they meant something like soulfulness. In sum, the bent of their essays was toward lyricism – hence the popularity of "sketches" and reminiscences.

In the second half of the 20th century, essay writing did not go into the decline suffered in the West; on the other hand, it is difficult to name any really outstanding exponents of the art. In communist China it was impossible for three decades to write honestly: laudatory "reportage" was the order of the day. Since the relaxation of controls in the 1980s new reputations have yet to be made. In Taiwan the trend in prose has been toward narrative and dramatization, employing a large amount of dialogue. Those who have published most have been academics, but that has not guaranteed freedom from slackness and shallowness. An honorable mention should, however, be made of Yu Guangzhong (1928–), who can be relied upon to write wittily.

To return to where we began, euphuism has not disappeared from Chinese prose: encomia of people and places that bear little relation to reality are still tolerated, especially in mainland China. Nor is wisdom at a premium in the present age; perhaps it is out of fashion everywhere. Wisdom tends to do its work covertly, as in what may be called the "existential" essays of Hong Kong writer Xiao Si (1938–), which hint at the lessons that may be drawn from cameos of commonplace experience, and in the bizarre perceptions of the Taiwanese prose-poet Shang Qin (1920–). Of more lengthy compositions, the most interesting, particularly to the foreign reader, are those that capture the character of life in the community in which the author grew up, cherished mostly as memories now that impersonal urbanization has spread or is spreading everywhere.

D. E. POLLARD

Anthologies

Chinese Classical Prose: The Eight Masters of the T'ang-Sung Period, edited by Liu Shih-shun, Hong Kong: Chinese University of Hong Kong Research Centre for Translation, 1979

The Columbia Anthology of Modern Chinese Literature, edited by Joseph S. M. Lau and Howard Goldblatt, New York: Columbia University Press, 1995: 585–716

The Columbia Anthology of Traditional Chinese Literature, edited by Victor Mair, New York: Columbia University Press, 1994: 507–756

Gems of Chinese Literature, edited by Herbert A. Giles, Shanghai and London: Kelly and Walsh, revised edition, 1922 (original edition, 1884)

Renditions issue on classical Chinese prose, 33–34 (1990)

Renditions issue on classical Chinese letters, 41–42 (1994)

Further Reading

Lin Yutang, *My Country and My People*, London: Heinemann, 1936

Liu Yan, editor, *Zhongguo sanwen shigang* (An outline history of Chinese prose), Hunan: Hunan jiaoyu chubanshe, 1994

Pollard, D. E., *A Chinese Look at Literature: The Literary Values of Chou Tso-jen in Relation to the Tradition*, London: Hurst, 1973

Pollard, D. E., "Ch'i in Chinese Literary Theory," in *Chinese Approaches to Literature from Confucius to Liang Ch'i-ch'ao*, edited by Adele Austin Rickett, Princeton, New Jersey: Princeton University Press, 1978: 43–66

Cicero

Roman, 106–43 BCE

Few writers succeed in becoming an eponym for writing itself. There is no doubt that Cicero is one of those few. To be called a "Cicero" is to be dubbed a master of the periodic sentence and the *clausula*. Quintilian declared Cicero the name "not of a man, but of eloquence itself." Throughout Europe, from his own century (or at least from Quintilian's) until ours, Cicero's **letters** and orations became the premier model for prose style, not only in Latin, but in modern European languages as well.

Cicero's prose composition is actually oratorical composition: it is written to be declaimed, to imitate the cadences of formal speech before a public body. Perhaps this is not as much of a distinction as it first appears, for to some extent all prose style imitates speech. Yet the speech patterns Cicero's prose records are those of his speeches in the Roman Senate. It would be another generation, the generation of Tacitus and **Seneca**, before Roman writers would turn to the rhythms of conversational speech for models.

Though the essay as we know it is largely a product of the Renaissance, Cicero's prose works imitating orations on various subjects certainly qualify as essays in the widest sense, even those which were actually declaimed in the Senate or cast in the form of **dialogue**s. Certainly many of our modern essays were first delivered as lectures or speeches. Cicero's **treatise**s, whatever form, touch on as many subjects, general and specific, as **Montaigne**'s essays: oratory itself (*De oratore, Brutus, De inventione*), old age (*De senectute*), prophecy (*De divinatione*), political science (*De re publica*), law (*De legibus*), duty (*De officiis*), friendship (*De amicitia*).

The hallmarks of Cicero's prose style are the period and the rhythmic *clausula*. The period is a long, stately sentence which suspends the verb until the end (a natural tendency in Latin style) with chains of subordinate clauses and balanced antitheses. Because the clauses and phrases between subject and predicate can vary in length, the periodic sentence is capable of a variety of rhythmic effects. The *clausula* or *cursus*,

the rhetorical term for the closing words of a sentence, is another rhythmic device for Cicero. Whether the sentence is short or long, Cicero's control of its final cadence almost invariably follows a specific metrical pattern. Thus the cadence at the end of the period gives to the ear the same sense of closure as the grammatical resolution of the sentence gives to the understanding.

As famous as the more stately effects of period and *clausula* are in Ciceronian style, Cicero was just as capable of short, swift, staccato rhythms which set his longer sentences into relief. As Cicero himself put it, he could use the dagger (*pugiunculus*) as well as the broadsword. His most quoted phrase is not only itself a simple vocative phrase, but is also followed by equally simple two- and three-word clauses: "o tempora, o mores! Senatus haec intelligit, consul videt: hic tamen vivit" ("O the times, o the mores! The Senate knows these things, the consul sees them; yet this man lives") (first oration, *In Catalinam*).

Furthermore, what makes Cicero's use of rhythmic techniques so effective is that they appear to be unstudied, though of course they must be consciously crafted. Though his treatises on rhetoric make clear that he distinguished the composition of oratory from that of the written word, all writing for Cicero should appeal to the ear. Petrarch reported that he fell in love with Cicero's prose by hearing it declaimed, charmed by the sound, long before he could understand what the words meant. Yet euphony at the expense of meaning was anathema to Cicero. He criticized precisely that as a fault of the "Asianist" style of some of his contemporaries. Cicero's choice of a word may depend on its sound value, but it is always found to be precisely the right word in meaning as well.

The direct influence that Cicero has had on modern European prose style is tremendous. Yet indirectly he also influenced virtually every Christian writer of the Middle Ages, for having been St. Jerome's stylistic guide in translating the Bible. In fact, in a fevered nightmare Jerome saw himself at the gates of heaven, begging entrance as a devout Christian, only to be told he was not a Christian but rather a Ciceronian. Though Jerome felt guilty for the association with the pagan writer, few stylists after his day gave it a second thought. Cardinal **Newman** called Cicero "the only master of style I have ever had." That is what he has represented for many essayists over the centuries: a master of style – a Cicero.

JOHN R. HOLMES

See also Classical Influences

Biography

Marcus Tullius Cicero. Born 3 January 106 BCE in Arpinum (now Arpino, central Italy). Served in the army of Pompeius Strabo, 89. Appeared in courts as a lawyer, from 81. Married Terentia, 80 (divorced, 47): one daughter and one son. *Quaestor* (financial administrator) in western Sicily, 75; *praetor* (judicial officer), 66; consul, 63: exposed Catiline's conspiracy to carry out uprisings in Italy and arson in Rome; declared an exile by Clodius, 58, and lived in Thessalonica and Illyricum, but recalled with the help of Pompey, 57; reluctantly allied himself with triumvirate of Pompey, Caesar, and Crassus, 56, and retired from public life until 51; elected augur of the college of diviners, 53; governor of Cilicia, Asia Minor, 51–50; allied with Pompey in civil war, 49–48: after Pompey's defeat Cicero's safety was guaranteed by Caesar. Married

Publilia (divorced, 45). After Caesar's assassination, 44, supported general amnesty (delivered 14 Philippic orations against Antony, 44–43); the triumvirate of Octavian, Antony, and Lepidus put Cicero on the execution list, 43: he was captured and killed in Formiae (now Formia), 7 December 43 BCE.

Selected Writings

Related Prose

Brutus, edited by H. Malcovati, 1963, and A. E. Douglas, 1966; translated by H. M. Poteat, 1950

De amicitia, edited by H. E. Gould, 1983; as *On Friendship*, translated by Benjamin E. Smith, 1897, and edited and translated by J. G. F. Powell, 1990

De divinatione, edited by Arthur S. Pease, 4 vols., 1920–23; translated by William Arthur Falconer, 1922; as *On Divination*, translated by H. M. Poteat, 1950

De domo sua, edited by R. G. Nisbet, 1939

De finibus, edited by J. N. Madvid, 1876; part edited by J. S. Reid, 1925

De inventione, edited and translated by H. M. Hubbell (Loeb Edition), 1949

De legibus, with *De re publica*, translated by Clinton Walker Keyes (Loeb Edition), 1928; Book I edited by Niall Rudd and Thomas Wiedemann, 1987

De natura deorum, edited by A. S. Pease, 2 vols., 1955–58; as *On the Nature of the Gods*, translated by H. M. Poteat, 1950, and H. C. P. McGregor, 1972

De officiis, edited by P. Fedeli, 1965; as *On Duties*, translated by H. M. Poteat, 1950, John Higginbotham, 1967, Harry G. Edinger, 1974, M. T. Griffin and E. M. Atkins, 1991, and M. Winterbottom, 1994

De oratore, edited by H. Rackham, translated by E. W. Sutton (Loeb Edition), 2 vols., 1959–60

De re publica, with *De legibus*, translated by Clinton Walker Keyes (Loeb Edition), 1928; as *On the Commonwealth*, translated by G. H. Sabine and S. B. Smith, 1929; selections as *Res Publica*, translated by W. K. Lacey and Harry G. Edinger, 1974; selections edited by James E. G. Zetzel, 1995

De senectute, edited by Leonard Huxley, revised edition, 1923, Ioannes Salanitro, 1987, and J. G. F. Powell, 1988; translated by William Armistead Falconer, 1922; as *On Old Age*, translated by Frank Copley, 1967

Epistulae ad Atticum: Letters to Atticus, edited by W. S. Watt, 2 vols., 1961–65; edited and translated by D. R. Shackleton Bailey, 7 vols., 1965–70

Epistulae ad familiares, edited by D. R. Shackleton Bailey, 2 vols., 1977, and W. S. Watt, 1982; translated by D. R. Shackleton Bailey, 1978

Epistulae ad Quintum fratrem et M. Brutum, edited by W. S. Watt, 1958, and D. R. Shackleton Bailey, 1980; translated by D. R. Shackleton Bailey, 1978

In Catalinam, edited by H. Bornecque, 1963

In Pisonem, edited by R. G. Nisbet, 1961

In Vatinium, edited by L. F. Pocock, 1926

Kerrines II, translated by T. N. Mitchell, 1986

Laelius, edited by Frank Stock, revised edition, 1930; as *On Friendship*, translated by Frank Copley, 1967, and J. G. F. Powell, 1990

[Letters], edited by R. Y. Tyrrell and L. C. Purser, 7 vols., 1899–1918; selections as *Letters*, translated by L. P. Wilkinson, 1949; *Selected Letters*, translated by D. R. Shackleton Bailey, 1980

Philippics I–II, edited by J. D. Denniston, 1939, and D. R. Shackleton Bailey, 1986

Pro M. Caelio, edited by R. G. Austin, 1960

Somnium Scipionis, as *The Dream of Scipio*, with *Nine Orations*, translated by Smith P. Bovie, 1967, Percy Bullock, 1983, and J. G. F. Powell, 1990

Tusculanae disputationes, edited by Thomas W. Dougan and Robert M. Henry, 2 vols., 1905; as *Tusculan Disputations* (Loeb Edition), translated by J. E. King, 1927; part translated by A. E. Douglas, 1990

Selected Works, translated by Michael Grant, 1960

The Caesarian Orations, translated by G. J. Acheson, 1965

Nine Orations and the Dream of Scipio, translated by Smith P. Bovie, 1967

Selected Political Speeches, translated by Michael Grant, 1969; revised edition, 1973

On the Good Life (selections), translated by Michael Grant, 1971

Murder Trials (selected orations), translated by Michael Grant, 1975

Back from Exile: Six Speeches upon His Return, edited and translated by D. R. Shackleton Bailey, 1991

Caesarian Speeches, edited by Harold C. Gotoff, 1993

On Government, translated by Michael Grant, 1993

The Fragmentary Speeches, edited by Jane W. Crawford, 1994

Collected works edition: *Works* (Loeb Edition; bilingual), translated by C. Macdonald, 28 vols., 1977.

Further Reading

Douglas, Alan Edward, "The Intellectual Background of Cicero's *Rhetorica*," in *Aufstieg und Niedergang der römischen Welt*, vol. 2, edited by Hildegard Temporini, Berlin: de Gruyter, 1973

Gotoff, Harold C., *Cicero's Elegant Style: An Analysis of the "Pro Archia"*, Urbana: University of Illinois Press, 1979

Haskell, H. J., *This Was Cicero: Modern Politics in a Roman Toga*, Greenwich, Connecticut: Fawcett, 1964 (original edition, 1942)

Hunt, H. A. K., *The Humanism of Cicero*, Melbourne: Melbourne University Press, 1954

Johnson, Walter R., *Luxuriance and Economy: Cicero and the Alien Style*, Berkeley: University of California Press, 1971

Laurand, Louis, *Études sur le style des discours de Cicéron*, Paris: Hachette, 1928 (original edition, 1907)

Mitchell, Thomas N., *Cicero: The Ascending Years*, New Haven, Connecticut: Yale University Press, 1979

Petersson, Torsten, *Cicero: A Biography*, Berkeley: University of California Press, 1920

Rawson, Elizabeth, *Cicero: A Portrait*, Ithaca, New York: Cornell University Press, and Bristol: Bristol Classical Press, revised edition, 1983 (original edition, 1975)

Shackleton Bailey, D. R., *Cicero*, London: Duckworth, 1971; New York: Scribner, 1972

Stockton, David L., *Cicero: A Political Biography*, London: Oxford University Press, 1971

Cioran, E. M.

Romanian/French, 1911–1995

E. M. Cioran's work bears the stamp of despair, expressed from the outset in finely honed **aphorisms**. At the age of 23, after finishing his studies in philosophy, he published a first collection in Romanian, *Pe culmile disperării* (1934; *On the Heights of Despair*), in which he was already broaching questions about the meaning of existence, the relationship between man and God, and the problem of death. Here he comes across as a thinker who is convinced of the futility of philosophy and is immersed in tedium, in an agonizing emptiness, even, all of which consumes him to the point of insomnia and brings him close to madness. The titles of the opening sections, "Unable to live any longer" and "The passion for the absurd," give an indication of the work to come, which is an apologia for skepticism, but one that still measures itself against the divine, as does *Lacrimi si sfinţi* (1937; Tears and saints). He wishes then to be the equal of **Schopenhauer**, or be nothing.

After several other collections written in Romanian, Cioran settled in France in 1937 and made a permanent choice to use the French language, "the ideal idiom for delicately translating elusive feelings," in order to express an increasingly dark pessimism, as is voiced in uncompromising titles: from the *Précis de décomposition* (1949; *A Short History of Decay*), *De l'inconvénient d'être né* (1973; *The Trouble with Being Born*), or *La Tentation d'exister* (1956; *Temptation to Exist*), to the recent *Aveux et anathèmes* (1987; *Anathemas and Admirations*). The brief form here is closely implicated with paradox and irony, making it possible for Cioran to escape the overweening presumption of philosophy while still writing rigorously. He resembles Heraclitus in his sense of conciseness, and **Mallarmé** in the attention he gives to language. This lover of aphorisms has henceforth chosen the humility of the essayist: "How is it possible to be a philosopher? To have the audacity to attack time, beauty, God and the rest? The mind puffs up and struts shamelessly. Metaphysics, poetry – the impertinences of a louse . . ." (*Syllogismes de l'amertume* [1952; *Syllogisms of bitterness*]).

In fact, the philosopher speaks of ideas, constructs a system of abstracts, while the essayist speaks of his own existence: "The aphorism is cultivated only by those who have known fear *amidst* words, that fear of collapsing *with all the words*." This existential quest always goes hand in hand with the work of writing, Cioran's tone being particularly easy to locate, in the succinctness of his pessimistic sentences and his taste for paradoxical statements, sarcasm, and derision. Such derision led him, in his early beginnings in Romania, to reactionary statements, and to virulent anti-Semitic positions, which he was to repudiate after World War II in a new awareness of the suffering inflicted upon European Judaism.

Side by side with these aphorisms, a few books are made up of longer pieces, such as *Histoire et utopie* (1960; *History and Utopia*), in which he attempts to denounce all ideologies, since no political undertaking could make good the loss of the vanished paradise of one's origins. He therefore followed a course which ran parallel to that of his compatriot Eugène Ionesco, choosing the French language, the better to tell of the absurdity of life. But, being more radical than Ionesco in his options, Cioran also modeled himself on Joseph de Maistre, whom he admired, on another foreigner who chose to write in French, the Irishman Samuel Beckett, and also on Maurice Blanchot and Henri Michaux, other literary figures who were haunted by suicide. Since the irreparable had been committed from birth ("Not to have been born, just to think of it – what happiness, what freedom, what space!"), Cioran was left to live like Job on his dung heap, torn between lamentation and fatalism, but with an increasing mistrust of God, or any other form of the absolute, and a cynicism which held at a distance any new idols we might be tempted to set up. Only lucidity had any importance: according to Cioran we must be mistrustful of ourselves, and resist the desire to organize philosophy like "a coherent vision of chaos." There is no outcome to be hoped for, since "the tragedy of detachment is that we cannot measure its progress. We move forward in a wilderness, and never know where we are." Man, for Cioran, emerged from the Apocalypse to end in disaster. Only music finds favor with him, principally that of Bach – "to whom God owes everything" – and a few writers such as Beckett, **Paul Valéry**, his compatriot Mircea Eliade, and Michaux, to whom he dedicated his "exercises in admiration."

It is Cioran's lucidity which explains the constant success of an author who never wished to be modern, long after existentialism and the writers of the absurd ceased to occupy center stage. The man who dreamed of writing "a light and unhealthy book, which would be at the edge of everything, and would be addressed to no one," who declared, "a book, which, after demolishing everything, did not demolish itself, will have infuriated us in vain," keeps a large audience of admirers, as much for his uncompromising ethics as for his incisive style. Although the last words of his late book, *Anathemas and Admirations*, put forward an ultimate paradox – "After all, I have not wasted my time, I, too, have been flung up and down, just like anybody else, in this aberrant universe" – readers are not wasting their time, either, in facing up to the question of the meaning of existence, in a body of work which is the heir to the French moralists of the 18th century.

MARC LITS

Biography
Émile Michel Cioran. Born 8 April 1911 in Rasinari, Romania. Studied at the lycée in Sibiu, 1920–27; philosophy at the University of Bucharest, 1928–31; fellowship to study in Germany, 1934–35; teaching certificate in philosophy, 1936. Won a fellowship from the French Institute, Bucharest, and moved permanently to Paris, 1937. Studied English at the Sorbonne. Part-time translator and manuscript reader, from 1949. Awards: King Carol II Foundation for Art and Literature Award (Romania), 1934; French Language Prize, 1949. Died in Paris, 20 June 1995.

Selected Writings

Essays and Related Prose
Pe culmile disperării, 1934; as *Sur les cimes du désespoir*, 1990; as *On the Heights of Despair*, translated by Ilinca Zarifopol-Johnston, 1992
Cartea amăgirilor, 1936; as *Le Livre des leurres*, 1992
Schimbarea la faţă a României, 1936
Lacrimi si sfinţi, 1937; as *Des Larmes et des saints*, 1986
Amurgal Gândurilor, 1940; as *Le Crépuscule des pensées*, 1991
Précis de décomposition, 1949; as *A Short History of Decay*, translated by Richard Howard, 1975
Syllogismes de l'amertume, 1952
La Tentation d'exister, 1956; as *Temptation to Exist*, translated by Richard Howard, 1968
Histoire et utopie, 1960; as *History and Utopia*, translated by Richard Howard, 1987
La Chute dans le temps, 1964; as *The Fall into Time*, translated by Richard Howard, 1970
Le Mauvais Démiurge, 1969; as *The New Gods*, translated by Richard Howard, 1974
Valéry face à ses idoles, 1970
De l'inconvénient d'être né, 1973; as *The Trouble with Being Born*, translated by Richard Howard, 1976
Écartèlement, 1979; as *Drawn and Quartered*, translated by Richard Howard, 1983
Exercices d'admiration, 1986
Aveux et anathèmes, 1987; as *Anathemas and Admirations*, translated by Richard Howard, 1991

Revelatiile durerii, edited by Mariana Vartic and Aurel Sasu, 1991
Bréviaire des vaincus, 1993

Collected works edition: *Œuvres*, 1995.

Further Reading
Cioran, E. M., *Entretiens avec Sylvie Jaudeau*, Paris: Corti, 1990
Gruzinska, Aleksandra, "Émile Michel Cioran," *Miorita: A Journal of Romanian Studies* 10 (1986): 27–53
Gruzinska, Aleksandra, "E. M. Cioran and the Idea of Admiration," *Journal of the American Romanian Academy of Arts and Sciences* 13–14 (1990): 145–61
Jaudeau, Sylvie, *Cioran, ou le dernier homme*, Paris: Corti, 1990
Kimball, Roger, "The Anguishes of E. M. Cioran," *New Criterion* 6, no.7 (March 1988): 37–44
Liiceanu, Gabriel, *Itinéraire d'une vie: E. M. Cioran*, Paris: Michalon, 1995
Massmer, Michael W., "In Complicity with Words: The Asymptotic Consciousness of E. M. Cioran," in *The Secular Mind: Transformations of Faith in Modern Europe*, edited by W. Warren Wagar, New York: Holmes and Meier, 1982: 220–38
Savater, Fernando, *Ensayo sobre Cioran*, Madrid: Taurus, 1974
Sora, Mariana, *Cioran jadis et naguère*, Paris: L'Herne, 1988
Tiffrea, Philippe, *Cioran, ou la dissection du gouffre*, Paris: Veyrier, 1991

Clarke, Marcus

Australian, 1846–1881

Marcus Clarke is today acknowledged as the most notable prose writer of colonial Australia. Like many postcolonial writers, particularly those of the 19th century, his reputation did not begin to emerge until the 1950s. Even then he was critically reclaimed mainly as the author of the widely read novel, *His Natural Life* (1874), which dramatizes and explores in depth the horrors of the system of convict transportation. As a consequence, his considerable body of essays, written as a necessary part of the output of most authors of his time, was neglected. In addition, his essays were not collected in substantial (if still incomplete) form until the 1970s because journalism, of which they form a part, was for a long time regarded as an inferior and ephemeral branch of literature. This is ironic because in everything he wrote Clarke was the most literary of writers.

Clarke was an unwilling English emigrant to Australia, uprooted from a comfortable position in upper-middle-class English life and the prospects that went with it at an early age and under the shadow of family tragedy: his widower father collapsed physically and mentally and died shortly after Clarke arrived in Australia when he was 17, having emigrated on the advice of relations. But if he retained traces of exile, he also drew upon the resources of his fertile if mercurial temperament to meet, indeed to enjoy the challenges of post-goldrush Melbourne, which mushroomed into one of the world's considerable and progressive cities.

One of his fellow students at Highgate School in London, Gerard Manley Hopkins, described him as "a kaleidoscopic, particoloured, harlequinesque, thaumatropic being." Clarke's subject matter and styles grew out of his cross-cultural experiences and the nature of his audience. He had the background

to stand apart from the pretensions and rawness of colonial society, yet he could also appreciate its vitality, nascent spirit of difference, and unconventionality. Correspondingly, as a stylist he was able to draw on the intertextuality of British, French, German, and classical literature, not simply to call up tradition but to show how writing is open to rejuvenating change when subjected to the pressures of registering the difference of a new culture.

Hence in writing of Melbourne low life in a series of essays called "Lower Bohemia" (1869), he could remind readers that the misery he was depicting "exists here," not in Europe but in Europe transposed or translated, and that the low-life genre drew on literary models ranging from popular writers such as Paul de Kock, Eugène Sue, Beranger, Mayhew, Wilkie Collins, back to **Defoe**, Dante, and beyond. Clarke could call these up, not to echo them, but to appropriate them. Similarly, in "In Outer Darkness" (1869), he alluded to "the wild and fascinating life of the prairies – history told by Cooper, Aimard, Reid and a hundred minor chatterers," for Clarke was sensitive to emerging American literature and aware of its parallels with Australian literature.

If Clarke could cast a sympathetic yet observant eye on Melbourne low life, he turned his writerly hand to a variety of subgenres and appropriate styles: satirical sketches of the rising professional classes of doctors, lawyers, and nouveaux riches in a series called "The Wicked World" (1874); an out-and-about weekly column, "The Peripatetic Philosopher" (1867–70), using the persona of a literary cynic and fringe dweller who commented on personalities, events (such as the visit of the Duke of Edinburgh), topics of the day, and set pieces, such as colonial holiday-making; write-ups of the theater, to which he was himself a contributor; sketches for a short-lived comic journal he edited, *Humbug* (1869–70), a rival of the *Melbourne Punch*; controversy in *Civilisation Without Delusion* (1880; later as *What Is Religion?*, 1895), a public debate with the Anglican bishop; and literary criticism or *belles-lettres*, including **reviews** and perceptive essays on his two main fictional models, **Dickens** and Balzac. He also wrote a pioneering piece on the connections between contemporary graphic art and literature, "Modern Art and Gustave Doré" (1867). An essay of art criticism, reprinted as a **preface** to a volume of Adam Lindsay Gordon's poetry (1876), was influential in setting the "keynote" of Australian scenery as "weird melancholy," with reminiscences of E. T. A. Hoffmann and Edgar Allan Poe, for Clarke's landscapes were typically literary.

In his preface to selections from *The Peripatetic Philosopher* (1869), Clarke named his models as "Thackeray, Dickens, Balzac, George Sala and Douglas Jerrold" – in other words, the popular novelists and journalists of the day noted for their vivid and satirical social sketches. Clarke hoped to "equal Thackeray in satire and Dickens in description." He also aimed to capture what he saw in Defoe and Dickens as "the romance of reality," the extrarealistic.

Clarke's audience was a local one, the Melbourne metropolis, though he achieved some interstate fame in Australia and sent several dispatches to the London *Daily Telegraph*. Local magazines were precariously short-lived and Clarke's main contributions were to the weekend magazines of the leading papers, the *Australasian* (published by the *Argus*) and the *Leader* (the *Age*). These were the counterparts of British literary weeklies and often had to compete with them and British magazines available at comparative prices. Some of the Australian outlets looked nostalgically back to England, others to the local, developing society, and some swung between the two. Clarke catered for both tastes. His allusiveness appealed to the one, his gusto, tinged with satire, to the other. He was criticized by some contemporaries for his "fluency," a superficial wit and cleverness, but his stylistic flair, together with his observant eye and his manipulation of the market, made him popular and a target for envy if not an easy model to follow. These qualities insure that many of his essays repay reading today.

LAURIE HERGENHAN

Biography
Marcus Andrew Hislop Clarke. Born 24 April 1846 in London. Studied at Highgate School, London, with fellow students Cyril and Gerard Manley Hopkins. Father committed to an insane asylum, and Clarke emigrated to Australia, 1863. Worked for the Bank of Australia, Melbourne, 1864; worked on sheep stations in Western Victoria, 1865–67, then returned to Melbourne. Began contributing to journals and magazines, from 1865, including the *Argus*, *Australian Monthly Magazine*, the *Age*, the *Leader*, *Melbourne Review*, *Victorian Review*, and the London *Daily Telegraph*; columnist, as "The Peripatetic Philosopher," the *Australasian*, 1867–70; editor, *Colonial Monthly*, 1868–69, *Humbug*, 1869–70, and the *Australian Journal*, 1870–71. Cofounder, Yorick Club, Melbourne, 1868. Married Marian Dunn, 1869: six children. Worked for the Melbourne Public Library, from 1870. Went bankrupt, 1874, 1881. Died (of pleurisy and liver problems) in St. Kilda, 2 August 1881.

Selected Writings

Essays and Related Prose
The Peripatetic Philosopher (under the name "Q"), 1869
The Future Australian Race, 1877
Civilisation Without Delusion, 1880; revised edition, as *What Is Religion?*, 1895
The Marcus Clarke Memorial Volume, edited by Hamilton Mackinnon, 1884
Selected Works (Austral Edition), edited by Hamilton Mackinnon, 1890
A Marcus Clarke Reader, edited by Bill Wannan, 1963
A Colonial City: High and Low Life: Selected Journalism, edited by L. T. Hergenhan, 1972
Marcus Clarke: Portable Australian Authors (also contains the novel *His Natural Life*), edited by Michael Wilding, 1976

Other writings: three novels (*Long Odds*, 1869; *His Natural Life*, 1874 [as *For the Term of His Natural Life*, 1884]; *Chidiock Tichbourne*, 1893) tales (including *Old Tales of a Young Country*, 1871; *Stories*, edited by Michael Wilding, 1983), plays, and an operetta.

Bibliography
McLaren, Ian F., *Marcus Clarke: An Annotated Bibliography*, Melbourne: Library Council of Victoria, 1982

Further Reading
Elliott, Brian, *Marcus Clarke*, Oxford: Clarendon Press, 1958
Hergenhan, L. T., Introduction to *A Colonial City: High and Low Life: Selected Journalism by Clarke*, St. Lucia: University of Queensland Press, 1972

McCann, Andrew, "Marcus Clarke and the Society of the Spectacle: Reflections on Writing and Commodity Capitalism in Nineteenth-Century Melbourne," *Australian Literary Studies* 17, no. 2 (October 1995): 222–34
Wilding, Michael, *Marcus Clarke*, Melbourne: Oxford University Press, 1977 (includes a select bibliography)

Classical Influences

The essay genre as pioneered by **Michel de Montaigne**, **Erasmus**, **Francis Bacon**, and their Renaissance contemporaries rose out of the attempt by the first modern theorists of language to negotiate a settlement with the inheritance of classical rhetorical theories. Writers in the 16th and 17th centuries explored the possibilities of exploiting the achievements of classical rhetoric to provide a foundation for the new vernacular humanist culture. As Morris Croll argues in *Style, Rhetoric, and Rhythm* (1966), his definitive study of 17th-century Attic prose, the conflict between "the oratorical style and the essay style" characterized the debate over the inheritance of classical rhetoric in the Renaissance. The first style, the Gorgian and Isocratean *genus grande*, was meant to signify the powerful voice of the virtuous public advocate and statesman. This style originated as the rhetorical basis of sophistic education, survived in the dominant Roman tradition of Ciceronianism, and continued to exert a powerful influence on medieval Latin culture. It is characterized by symmetrical phrasing, ornate sentences, and flamboyant periods, and is first and foremost the rhetoric of oral presentation. The style that grew in opposition to the "sophistic" rhetoric of this first school came to be called the *genus humile*. Finding its ultimate authority in Socratic dialectic, the flexible, formless, "humble" species of discourse is well suited to conversation and philosophical speculation. While we should recognize in this latter tradition the practice of writing that ultimately became the early modern essay, we must also remember that the essay as a literary genre developed out of the various attempts to reconcile and interweave these conflicting traditions.

The most frequently cited classical precursors to the modern essay form are Horace (65–8 BCE), **Seneca** (c. 4 BCE–65 CE), Tacitus (c. 56–116 CE), **Plato** (c. 429/27–347 BCE), and Demosthenes (c. 384–322 BCE), among many others. The "curt" and "loose" styles of what became known as the modern essay sought to imitate the pointed language of the mature, self-reflective, and humble mode of the great **letter** writers and dialecticians of the classical era. Montaigne, inventor of the modern *essai*, admired the self-critical and autobiographical spirit of skeptical inquiry that he found in this tradition, and sought a vernacular prose form for exploring its possibilities. In the moral **treatises** of **Plutarch** (c. 46–c. 120/25 CE) and Seneca, Montaigne found inspiration for his own varied speculations. The titles of Montaigne's essays, such as "Toutes Choses ont leur saison" ("All Things Have Their Season") and "Que philosopher c'est apprendre à mourir" ("To Philosophize Is to Learn How to Die"), reflect the influences of classical moralism. A reader of Montaigne's essays overhears the author's musings and wanderings across a variety of topics, a "realistic" method that, according to Montaigne's own admission, harkens back to the Roman **satires** of Horace and Lucilius

(c. 180–c. 102 BCE). "Sur des vers de Virgile" ("On Some Verses of Virgil") provides an occasion for Montaigne to reflect on his mind's capacity to produce capricious and fleeting impressions: "But I am displeased with my mind for ordinarily producing its most profound and maddest fancies, and those I like the best, unexpectedly and when I am least looking for them; which suddenly vanish, having nothing to attach themselves to on the spot . . . So of these chance thoughts that drop into my mind there remains in my memory only a vain notion, only as much as I need to make me rack my brains and fret in quest of them to no particular purpose. Now then, leaving books aside and speaking more materially and simply . . ." The gesture implied by the final sentence is the signature of the new *genus humile* characteristic of the essay, which transports the reader out of the monastery and into the worldly experiences and pragmatic wisdom of the new cosmopolitan genre.

When Erasmus published his textbook on producing copious Latin prose, *De duplici copia verborum ac rerum* (1512; *On Copia* [the abundance] *of Words and Ideas*), arguably the first modern book on the subject, the opening gambit had been made in the move from the study of rhetoric as technical achievement to the modern study of the experience of writing itself. His *Encomium moriae* (1511; *The Praise of Folly*) had already shifted the ground of traditional imitation theory by adding the self-conscious sense of a rapidly developing modern subjectivity to the pursuit of truth through a fallen, linguistic medium; and the *Adagia* (1500; *Adages*), generically speaking, laid the foundation for the construction of the first properly named *Essais* (1580, 1588) by Montaigne. The chief intertext for *On Copia*, as it was for much of the Renaissance, was the tenth book of Quintilian's (c. 35–c. 100 CE) *Institutionis oratoriae* (*Institutes of Oratory*). In that section, Quintilian writes, "We must return to what we have read and reconsider it with care, while, just as we do not swallow our food till we have chewed it and reduced it almost to a state of liquefaction to assist the process of digestion, so what we read must not be committed to the memory for subsequent imitation while it is still in a crude state, but must be softened and, if I may use the phrase, reduced to a pulp through frequent perusal." This passage summarizes a central problem of modern interpretation theory: how should the *sensus germanus* of an *Ur*-text be rendered adequately by later generations? If texts were to be digested and synthesized, what exegetical principles would ensure that a remnant of the original text would remain? In *The Cornucopian Text: Problems of Writing in the French Renaissance* (1979), Terrence Cave demonstrates the movement from classical mimesis as technique to exploratory writing as the modern obsession *par excellence*, arguing that "the Erasmian text, by its very movement from *verba* towards *res*, uncovers the essential duplicity of *copia*."

Another major break with the Ciceronianism of classical rhetorical education came in the last quarter of the 16th century. If the confident rhetoric of Ciceronian education had flourished in a time of relative political and social stability, further cracks began to appear in the classical façade when Marc-Antoine Muret delivered his lectures of 1582, appended to the *Episotalae ad Atticum*. Muret argues that the training offered by the old *genus grande* failed adequately to prepare young gentlemen for modern statecraft, a vocation that required the cultivation of conversation, wit, and dialectic.

Public oratory rapidly began to be suspected as providing undue might to a mob scarcely ready to assume the mantle of power. As Montaigne suggests in his essay "De la vanité des paroles" ("The Vanity of Words"), public oratory became suspect as the material sign of a dangerously unstable republic. Modern societies needed the "good institution and sound counsel" fostered by the cultivation of dialectic, best instituted by a flexible essayistic rhetoric of self-criticism. This line of thought would be adopted by Milton, Hartlib, Bacon, and English educational reform.

Another force contributing to the decline of the grand style in the late Renaissance is the rapid displacement of classical authority by empirical methodology. The new plain prose style developed by Erasmus, Muret, Justus Lipsius, Francis Bacon, **Blaise Pascal**, **Sir Thomas Browne**, Robert Burton, Montaigne, and John Milton in the 16th and 17th centuries sought an appropriate forum for representing "man thinking," a process necessitated by the new experimental priorities in political and scientific culture.

Rhetorical style – whether oral or written – illustrated the complex interrelationship of political, moral, and ethical positions available to Renaissance culture. Well aware of this connection, political and religious reformers in Britain, taking their cue from continental intellectuals such as Erasmus and Comenius, argued that in order for England to thrive as a rapidly expanding commercial nation, it must produce a confident, outward-looking national leadership, educated in the practical arts of navigation, cartography, and commerce. Not least among these reformers, John Milton added his voice to a national movement that sought radically to shift the foundation of education, a reformation that looked primarily to language and rhetorical training – deeply informed by classical theories – as the key to nation building. From the perspective of the language reformers and new essay writers, the standard academic curriculum in classical scholarship encouraged the development of a psychologically and socially stunted individual. In *De augmentis scientiarum* (1623), Bacon includes a supplementary comment not included in the English version (*The Advancement of Learning*) of 1605, which compares the new, plain style favorably to the old expansive rhetoric. He writes ". . . somewhat sounder is another form of style . . . [which] consists wholly in this: that the words be sharp and pointed; sentences concise; a style in short that may be called 'turned' rather than fused. Whence it happens that everything dealt with by this kind of art seems rather ingenious than lofty. Such a style is found in Seneca very freely used, in Tacitus and the younger Pliny more moderately; and is beginning to suit the ears of our age as never before."

The practical advantages of this new style for constructing a national identity were explored most extensively by John Milton. As Milton writes in the seventh of the *Prolusiones oratoriae*, his series of Latin addresses to Oxford – quite plausibly conceived as self-reflexive and playful essays in the Erasmian and Montaignean style – "I confess that the man who shuts himself up and is almost entirely immured in study, is readier to talk with the gods than with men, either because he is habitually at home among celestial affairs . . . or because a mind which has been enlarged by the steady pursuit of divine interests is irked by physical constraints and disqualified from the more formal social amenities." The social amenities that would be required in modern political culture would be best cultivated through a plain style of speaking and writing that in turn would be best nourished by the self-reflexive practice of writing.

The new continental essayism of Erasmus had as its goal, as Milton suggests, the production of a fully socialized individual, unburdened of the worst aspects of classical rhetoric that Erasmus and later Bacon and the continental reformers were busily revising. The old rhetorical and logical training – specifically, Milton argues, the oversubtle scholasticism comprising the traditional university curriculum in classical humanism – taught young men to be querulous self-doubters, unfit for public life, for which, presumably, the study of classical Greek and Roman rhetoric ought to prepare them. Citing Erasmus' reformation of classical style as a precursor, Milton writes of the old, unreformed rhetoricians: ". . . like an evil spirit, they have filled men's breasts with thorns and briars and have brought endless discord into the schools" – and thus into the nation at large. In his Latin orations, Milton describes this scholarly disputation over the fine points in classical rhetoric, against which Erasmus and other reforming humanists would rail, as an "impudent battle of words [which] does nothing for the good of society or for the honor or profit of our fatherland, the first priority, by common consent, in the sciences."

For the new rhetorical reformers the Aristotelian notion that empirical learning produces useful and instructive mental pleasure, contrary to Platonic interdictions against mere *mimesis* and sensory knowledge, provides another classical authority to replace the now discredited mechanical dryness of classical education. The intellectual pleasure taken in reinventing the correspondent universe that had been celebrated in the essays of Montaigne, Bacon, and Erasmus would be recuperable by a generation of reformers searching for solid rhetorical principles to insure the responsible administration of the nation. As Milton writes in *Prolusion VII*, "how great an additional pleasure of mind it is to take our flight over all the history and regions of the world, to view the conditions and changes of kingdoms, nations, cities, and people . . . This is the way to live in all the epochs of history . . . and to become a contemporary of time itself. And while we are looking forward to the future glory of our name, this will also be the way to extend life backward from the womb and to extort from unwilling Fate a kind of immortality in the past." Figures of spatial and temporal mastery, strongly linking the success of education to the pleasurable experience of acquiring and mastering knowledge, abound in Milton's work. Recalling Adam's panoramic survey of the future from atop a hill in Books XI and XII of *Paradise Lost* (1667), this new, pleasurable mastery must be achieved by a properly aerial perspective that encompasses the known world. Thus, references to maps, globes, charts, and compasses proliferate in the early modern essay.

A clear precursor to the Enlightenment rationalists, then, Milton's essays, **tracts**, and **pamphlets** turn back to Aristotle (384–322 BCE), advocating a detailed knowledge of the sensory experience of every living creature. This reliance on the cultivation of the senses in the early modern essay anticipated the 18th-century medicalization of the body in terms of a fully "disciplined" national individual, a vision which Milton articulates in *Prolusion VI*: "But if by living a modest and temperate life we . . . keep the heavenly powers of the mind clean and unstained from all filth and pollution . . . we would look back after a few years, to see how much distance we had covered, and what a mighty sea of learning we had quietly navigated." But the modest and temperate life advocated here must be enriched by the cultivation of wit and speculation. The connection between the pleasure of learning and the early French essays is clear from Milton's subtitle, "That sportive exercises are occasionally not adverse to philosophic studies," and he later cites Erasmus' *The Praise of Folly* as an exemplary bridge between duty and necessity provided by the early modern essay.

In Milton's *Of Education* (1644), even the study of grammar and rhetoric are concretely figured as images of exploration and commerce: "So that they having but newly left those grammatic flats and shallows where they stuck unreasonably to learn a few words of lamentable construction and now on the sudden transported under another climate to be tossed and turmoiled with their unballasted wits in fathomless and unquiet deeps of controversy, do for the most part grow into hatred and contempt of learning." Milton's sailing metaphor – so common in the early modern essay – recalls Quintilian's image of the proper domain of Roman rhetoric in *Institutes of Oratory*: "Greek keels, even the little ones, know well their ports; let ours usually travel under fuller sails, with a stronger breeze swelling our canvas . . . They have the art of threading their way through the shallows; I would seek somewhat deeper waters, where my bark may be in no danger of foundering." If the 17th-century rhetorical reforms had begun by deploring the unfortunate "psychological" consequences of hasty learning, perhaps a grounded flotilla represents the most frightening image of collective failure for the republican imagination in the habit of linking the metaphorical explorations of knowledge with the literal explorations of global expansion. The young student trained in the habit of rote memorization encouraged by the uncritical imitation of the old rhetoricians, hastily entered a public career for which the old rhetoric ill prepared him, and "ground[ed] [his] purposes not on the prudent and heavenly contemplation of justice and equity which was never taught them, but on the promising and pleasing thoughts of litigious terms, fat contentions, and flowing fees . . ." The metaphor of rhetorical education as grounding, getting solid footing on the moral soil of a Christian commonwealth, seems almost irrelevant here, in light of the massive emphasis placed throughout the reformist essays of the 17th century on secular travel and practical mastery.

The 17th-century essays of Bacon and Milton, in boldly advocating education's socializing function – as strongly influenced by classical republicanism as by modern *Realpolitik* – laid the foundation for notions of sentimental education and *Bildung* that would begin to circulate throughout Europe by the end of the 18th century. It was this new scholarly and public-political rhetoric that would eventually yield the empiricist tradition of Hobbes and Locke, and further the dissemination of Enlightenment ideas in the 18th-century essay. A century after the prose revolution inspired by Milton, Bacon, and their French precursors, however, for many intellectuals, the practical rhetorical education – the plain style – that Erasmus' generation had identified with republican reform, began to look like a force for repression. **Friedrich von Schiller**'s *Briefe über die ästhetische Erziehung des Menschen*

(1795; *Letters on the Aesthetic Education of Man*) is an example of the Romantic tenor of this critique: "But today Necessity is master, and bends a degraded humanity beneath its tyrannous yoke. *Utility* is the great idol of the age, to which all powers must do service and all talents swear allegiance." For a whole generation of Romantic essayists, the sublime wonders of the work of art would prepare the skeptical individual for the often unpleasant tasks mandated by the public duties and responsibilities at the moral core of the classical Roman essay and its early modern inheritors.

MATTHEW TITOLO

Further Reading

Cave, Terrence, *The Cornucopian Text: Problems of Writing in the French Renaissance*, Oxford: Clarendon Press, and New York: Oxford University Press, 1979

Croll, Morris W., *Style, Rhetoric, and Rhythm*, edited by J. Max Patrick and others, Woodbridge, Connecticut: Ox Bow Press, 1989 (original edition, 1966)

Curtius, Ernst Robert, *European Literature and the Latin Middle Ages*, Princeton, New Jersey: Princeton University Press, 1990 (original German edition, 1948)

Fallon, Stephen M., *Milton Among the Philosophers: Poetry and Materialism in Seventeenth Century England*, Ithaca, New York: Cornell University Press, 1991

Greengrass, Mark, Michael Leslie, and Timothy Raylor, editors, *Samuel Hartlib and Universal Reformation: Studies in Intellectual Communication*, Cambridge and New York: Cambridge University Press, 1994

Highet, Gilbert, *The Classical Tradition: Greek and Roman Influences on Western Literature*, Oxford and New York: Oxford University Press, 1985 (original edition, 1949)

Hill, Christopher, *Milton and the English Revolution*, London: Faber, and New York: Viking Press, 1977

Lopate, Phillip, Introduction to *The Art of the Personal Essay*, edited by Lopate, New York: Anchor Doubleday, 1994

Patrides, C. A., and Raymond B. Waddington, editors, *The Age of Milton: Backgrounds to Seventeenth Century Literature*, Manchester: Manchester University Press, and Totowa, New Jersey: Barnes and Noble, 1980

Raab, Felix, *The English Face of Machiavelli: A Changing Interpretation, 1500–1700*, London: Routledge and Kegan Paul, 1964

Schoeck, R. J., *Erasmus Grandescens: The Growth of a Humanist's Mind and Spirituality*, Nieuwkoop: De Graaf, 1988

Schoeck, R. J., *Erasmus of Europe: The Making of a Humanist, 1467–1500*, Edinburgh: Edinburgh University Press, and Savage, Maryland: Barnes and Noble, 1990

Smith, Henry Goodwin, "The Triumph of Erasmus in Modern Protestantism," *Hibbert Journal* 3 (1905): 64–82

Coleridge, Samuel Taylor

British, 1772–1834

Of the 16 volumes comprising Samuel Taylor Coleridge's collected works, 15 consist of prose discourse. If we add to this corpus eight volumes of **letters**, four volumes of notes (published thus far), not to mention a considerable amount of manuscript material in collections at the British Museum and at the University of Toronto, we find that Coleridge was a prolific, interdisciplinary prose writer. This brings us to the difficult question: aside from better-known pieces (e.g. "On the Prometheus of Aeschylus," 1825; "On the Principles of Genial Criticism," 1814), what parts of this enormous bulk of material qualify as discrete essays?

The *OED* defines an essay as "A composition of moderate length on any particular subject, or branch of a subject originally implying want of finish ... but now said of a composition more or less elaborate in style, though limited in range." We need only consult **Samuel Johnson**'s *Dictionary of the English Language* (1755) to see that, by the middle of the 18th century, the essay was an endeavor considered lacking in "finish." The authorities Johnson cites agree that the essay is little more than an early draft: "(Smith). A Loose sally of the mind; an irregular indigested piece. (Bacon). A trial; an experiment. (Glanville). First taste of anything." By the turn of the century, however, the essay had become a more serious, formal, and purposeful effort. As Vicesimus Knox wrote in 1819: "Essays ... may now convey the idea of regular treatises." It is important to recognize that the Coleridgean essay is closer to the 20th than to the 18th century, for, in most instances, it exhibits self-conscious craft and persuasive intent.

If an essay is any prose work of limited range having a clearly articulated purpose, as well as formal style and rhetoric, then many more of Coleridge's writings qualify for inclusion in the genre. Reasoning along these lines, it is possible, therefore, to identify six sets of Coleridgean prose as kinds of "essays": the topical (periodic, nonperiodic, lectural, homiletic); the aphoristic; the **review**; the notational (annotative, marginal); the epistolary (confessional, correspondent); and the conversational.

The **topical essay**, with its four subsets, is the largest category of the Coleridgean essay. Coleridge composed periodical essays intermittently for over 20 years. He contributed an essay to almost every issue of the *Watchman* (1 March–13 May 1796), most notably "On the Slave Trade," a reworking of a 1795 Bristol lecture. He was a primary contributor to the *Morning Post* (1799–1802), submitting over 90 pieces, ranging from paraphrases of parliamentary proceedings to original historical and political analyses. He submitted 140 articles to the *Courier* (24 February 1804–31 March 1818). Add to these totals nearly 100 conjectural and collaborative pieces, and we have what for many would be the work of a lifetime. Demonstrating an extraordinary understanding of contemporary issues, especially of the French Wars, Coleridge's journalism is qualitatively impressive as well. Noteworthy are essays on Pitt, Napoleon, ancient Rome, contemporary France, and Wellington's Peninsular campaign. A third journalistic venue, consisting of 26 numbers (1 June 1809–15 March 1810), is the *Friend*. In this privately financed journal, Coleridge outlined his political philosophy, expanding upon ideas broached in the public journalism.

Each of Coleridge's nonperiodic essays has its own history. Some of his best pieces, such as "Essay on Scrofula," were undelivered and recently published from manuscript. His eclectic and interdisciplinary essays – e.g. "On Free Will" (1800), "On Miracles" (1807), or "On Language and Thought" (1815) – are among the most widely known. The revised "Treatise on Method," appearing in the 1818 *Friend*, would introduce the *Encyclopedia Metropolitana* (1818–45).

One of his most intricate, theoretical works on natural philosophy, "Theory of Life," was published posthumously in 1848.

Coleridge's lectural essays have great interdisciplinary appeal. His earliest, delivered at Bristol in 1795, were both political and theological in emphasis; "A Moral and Political Lecture," six "Lectures on Revealed Religion," and "Lecture on the Two Bills" are the most famous. The sequence of lectures on literature and on philosophy (1808–19) demonstrates Coleridge's erudition as an historian of ideas. He lectured on many subjects, including poetry, Shakespeare, Milton, Cervantes, Dante, Spenser, Ariosto, European drama, and *belles-lettres*, as well as delivering philosophical lectures. The coverage in these lectures is encyclopedic: in literature, from Achilles to Ywain; in philosophy, from Abelard to Zoroaster.

As "a discourse, usually delivered from a pulpit and based upon a text of Scripture, for the purpose of giving religious instruction or exhortation" (*OED*), the **sermon**, like the essay, is a text that is limited in scope, persuasive in intent, and elaborate in style. Probably the earliest examples of Coleridge's homiletic essay are "A Sermon Written When the Author Was But 17 Years Old" (1789–90) and the "College Commemorative Sermon" (1799). Better known are the three lay sermons Coleridge planned to publish in a single volume; however, he only wrote two of the three, under the titles *The Statesman's Manual; or, The Bible the Best Guide to Political Skill and Foresight* (1816) and *A Lay Sermon* (1817).

Since an **aphorism** is an incisive statement conveying a general truth, the notion of an "aphoristic essay" sounds oxymoronic. Occasionally Coleridge begins a piece aphoristically – that is, with a terse, general truth – and then expands upon this idea. He uses this modality in the *Omniana* (1812), a collection of collaborative essays with **Robert Southey**; for example, item no. 297 begins aphoristically ("It is the mark of a noble nature to be more shocked with the unjust condemnation of a bad man than of a virtuous one . . .") and is developed into a cohesive essay. *Aids to Reflection* (1825), on the writings of Archbishop Robert Leighton (1611–84), contains "aphorisms" (those of Leighton), upon which Coleridge meditates. In one frequently anthologized example, Aphorism 8, Coleridge ruminates on Leighton's statement: "Faith elevates the soul not only above Sense and sensible things, but above Reason itself . . ." Contained in Coleridge's response is the important section "On the Differences in Kind of the Reason and the Understanding."

The review constitutes a third category of the Coleridgean essay. The reviews in the *Watchman* – e.g. of Thomas Lovell Beddoes' "Essay on the Public Merit of Mr. Pitt" and "A Letter to . . . Pitt, on . . . Scarcity"; of **Edmund Burke**'s "A Letter . . . to a Noble Lord"; and of Count Rumford's "Essays" – vary in critical depth, the Rumford review, for example, consisting mainly of historical paraphrase and of direct quotation. On the other hand, there is the **Edinburgh Review** essay on Thomas Clarkson's *History of the Abolition of the Slave Trade*. An encomium to his friend, this review provides a synopsis, a sketch of the abolition movement, references to parliamentary proceedings, and Coleridge's original ideas on the issue.

Embedded in over 6000 notes (published and unpublished), in thousands of marginalia, and in innumerable extended footnotes to his own texts, is a surprising resource: clearly discernible essays, some embryonic, some fragmentary, some mature. Amidst the published notes, for instance, is a coherent exposition on the atrocities of the French Revolution (1810; no. 3845); amidst the unpublished manuscripts, an essay on "the true system of philosophy"; and amidst the marginalia, his reaction to Joseph Hughes' theories on soul and body.

The epistolary essay takes "confessional" and correspondent forms. *Confessions of an Inquiring Spirit* (1840) comprises six letters, each one beginning with the formulaic salutation, "My dear Friend." Frequently, in the over 2000 letters, Coleridge wrote small essays, the corpus of which cannot be adequately described in this context. His letters, touching on innumerable topics, exhibit the workings of an inquisitive and encyclopedic intelligence; particularly erudite examples, worth independent study, are letters to Lord Liverpool and to Hyman Hurwitz, a scholar of Jewish studies.

Coleridge was known to be a great talker who could expostulate intelligently on many subjects. Many of the recorded conversations in the *Table Talk* (posthumously pub. 1835) are cohesive essays. Those on parliamentary reform and on the threat of civil discord (20 March 1831–9 April 1833) are, in part and parcel, a perfect example of Coleridge's oral discourse. Consisting of small and medium-sized essays, the series presents the intricacies of this national crisis vividly and comprehensively.

Coleridge's use of discrete essays to build larger works (e.g. for the 1818 *Friend*) sheds some light on the genre and unity of such works as *Biographia Literaria; or, Biographical Sketches of My Literary Life and Opinions* (1817), the *Logic* (wr. c. 1823), and *On the Constitution of the Church and State* (1830). In the *Biographia*, for example, he states that, under autobiography, he has unified "miscellaneous reflections" on literary criticism, philosophy, and politics, and the narrative provides "continuity to the work." Scholars have devoted much attention to the unity, structure, and compositional process involved in the *Biographia* (Max F. Schulz, 1985). Specifically, with regard to the essay genre, the organization of these sketches or essays provides the *Biographia* with relative coherence. Two interwoven strands of essays unify the work to a degree: the first, concerned with Coleridge's literary life and opinions (chapters 1–4, 10–11, 14–23); and the second, with his philosophical, psychological, and theological speculations (chapters 5–9, 12–13, 24). Unifying these two themes is an emphasis on "the Scheme of Christianity" and on the idea that the pursuit of knowledge should be directed toward communion with God. The *Biographia* is also important for how it adumbrates – stylistically, organizationally, and methodologically – the 1818–19 commentaries on literature and philosophy, as well as the 1818 revision of the *Friend*, the culmination of his work in the genre.

CHARLES DE PAOLO

Biography
Born 21 October 1772 in Ottery St. Mary, Devon. Studied at Christ's Hospital, London, 1782–90; Jesus College, Cambridge, 1791–94; University of Göttingen, 1798. Married Sara Fricker, 1794 (separated, 1807): three sons (one died in infancy) and one daughter. Lived in Bristol, 1794–96, Clevedon, Somerset, 1796, and Nether Stowey, Somerset, near William and Dorothy Wordsworth at Alfoxden, 1797. Editor, the *Watchman*, 1796, the *Friend*, 1809–10,

and assistant editor, the *Courier*, 1810–11; contributor to various other journals and newspapers. Given an annuity by the Wedgwood family, 1798; moved to Greta Hall, Keswick, near Robert Southey and the Wordsworths, 1800. Became addicted to opium, by 1800, and lived in Malta in an effort to restore his health, 1804–06, where he was secretary to the governor, Sir Alexander Bell, 1804–05. Lectured extensively in London, 1808–19. Lived in London, Calne, Wiltshire, and Bath, 1811–15, and in Highgate, London, under the care of Dr. James Gillman, 1816–34. Associate, Royal Society of Literature (with pension), 1824. Died in Highgate, London, 25 July 1834.

Selected Writings

Essays and Related Prose

The Watchman (periodical), nos. 1–10, 1 March–13 May 1796
The Friend (periodical), nos. 1–27 (and one supernumerary), 1 June 1809–15 March 1810; in 1 vol., as *The Friend: A Series of Essays*, 1812; revised edition, 3 vols., 1818
Omniana, or Horae Otiosiores, with Robert Southey, 2 vols., 1812; edited by Robert Gittings, 1969
The Statesman's Manual; or, The Bible the Best Guide to Political Skill and Foresight (sermon), 1816
A Lay Sermon, 1817
Biographia Literaria; or, Biographical Sketches of My Literary Life and Opinions, 1817; edited by George Watson, 1956
Aids to Reflection in the Formation of a Manly Character on the Several Grounds of Prudence, Morality, and Religion (aphorisms), 1825
On the Constitution of the Church and State, According to the Idea of Each, 1830
Specimens of the Table Talk of the Late Samuel Taylor Coleridge, edited by Henry Helson Coleridge, 2 vols., 1835, and Carl Woodring, 2 vols., 1990
Confessions of an Inquiring Spirit, 1840; edited by H. St. J. Hart, 1956
Notes and Lectures upon Shakespeare and Some of the Old Poets and Dramatists; with Other Literary Remains, edited by Sara Coleridge, 2 vols., 1849
Essays on His Own Times (2nd series of *The Friend*), edited by Sara Coleridge, 3 vols., 1850; edited by David V. Erdman, with additional material, in *Collected Works*, 3 vols., 1978
The Philosophical Lectures, edited by Kathleen Coburn, 1949
The Notebooks, edited by Kathleen Coburn, 4 vols., 1957–90
Writings on Shakespeare, edited by Terence Hawkes, 1959; as *Coleridge on Shakespeare*, 1969
Shakespearean Criticism, edited by T. M. Raysor, 1960
Coleridge on Shakespeare, edited by R. A. Foakes, 1971; as *Coleridge's Criticism of Shakespeare*, 1989
Lectures 1808–1819 on Literature, edited by R. A. Foakes, 2 vols., 1987

Other writings: the poems "Kubla Khan" (wr. 1797, pub. 1816), "The Rime of the Ancient Mariner" (1798), and "Christabel" (1816), as well as many others, four plays, and several volumes of correspondence (collected in *The Collected Letters*, edited by Earl Leslie Griggs, 6 vols., 1956–71).

Collected works editions: *Complete Works*, edited by William Greenough Thayer Shedd, 7 vols., 1853; *Collected Works*, edited by Kathleen Coburn, 16 vols., 1969– (in progress); *Coleridge's Writings*, general editor John Beer, 1991– (in progress).

Bibliographies

Crawford, Walter B., Edward S. Lauterbach, and Ann M. Crawford, *Samuel Taylor Coleridge: An Annotated Bibliography of Criticism and Scholarship 2: 1900–1939 (with Additional Entries for 1795–1899)*, Boston: Hall, 1983
Haven, Josephine, Richard Haven, and Maurianne Adams, *Samuel Taylor Coleridge: An Annotated Bibliography of Criticism and Scholarship 1: 1793–1899*, Boston: Hall, 1976
Wise, Thomas J., *A Bibliography of the Writings in Prose and Verse of Samuel Taylor Coleridge*, London: Bibliographical Society, 2 vols., 1913–19

Further Reading

Chambers, E. K., *Samuel Taylor Coleridge: A Biographical Study*, Oxford: Clarendon Press, 1938
Coleman, Dierdre, *Coleridge and The Friend (1809–1810)*, Oxford: Clarendon Press, 1988
Fogle, Richard H., *The Idea of Coleridge's Criticism*, Westport, Connecticut: Greenwood Press, 1978 (original edition, 1962)
Goodson, A. C., *Verbal Imagination: Coleridge and the Language of Modern Criticism*, New York and Oxford: Oxford University Press, 1988
Holmes, Richard, *Coleridge*, Oxford: Oxford University Press, 1982
Holmes, Richard, *Samuel Taylor Coleridge: Early Visions*, London: Hodder and Stoughton, and New York: Viking, 1989
Jackson, James Robert de Jager, *Method and Imagination in Coleridge's Criticism*, London: Routledge, 1969
Jenkins, Patricia Mavis, *Coleridge's Literary Theory: The Chronology of Its Development, 1790–1818*, Fairfield, Connecticut: Fairfield University Department of English, 1984
Leask, Nigel, *The Politics of Imagination in Coleridge's Critical Thought*, Basingstoke: Macmillan, 1988
Schulz, Max F., "Coleridge: Prose Writings," in *The English Romantic Poets: A Review of Research and Criticism*, edited by Frank Jordan and others, New York: Modern Language Association of America, 1985: 410–63
Wellek, René, "Coleridge's Philosophy and Criticism," in *The English Romantic Poets: A Review of Research*, edited by T. M. Raysor, New York: Modern Language Association of America, revised edition, 1956: 110–37

The Compleat Angler

by Izaak Walton, 1653; revised editions 1655 and later

The Compleat Angler by Izaak Walton (1593–1683) is one of the most widely published books in the English language, having appeared in several hundred editions since the author's death. It was first published in 1653 after Walton had already published biographies of **John Donne** (1640) and Sir Henry Wotton (1651) and before he wrote his lives of Richard Hooker (1665), George Herbert (1670), and Robert Sanderson (1678). Later, he invited his friend, Charles Cotton, to write a continuation, which appeared in 1676.

Ostensibly a book on the sport of fishing, *The Compleat Angler, or, The Contemplative Man's Recreation, Being a Discourse of Fish and Fishing Not Unworthy the Perusal of Most Anglers* is also a long essay which relates angling to literature and philosophy. Its polished artistry, achieved through numerous revisions, pays high tribute to the ideal of the English literary pastoral tradition in its evocation of personality and landscape. Written and published during one of the most socially, religiously, and politically traumatic periods in British history, the book reflects an ideal world from which all the evils attendant to the human condition have been purged. As Jonquil Bevan (1988) has suggested, the book is in part a royalist's "reaction to the exile and imprisonment of his friends," many of whom had been ravaged by the violent political and religious sectarianism of the times.

The Compleat Angler is a long **dialogue** involving Piscator (an angler), Venator (a hunter), and Auceps (a falconer) in an area a few miles north of London. Much of the text deals with angling: the kinds of fish available (he lists about 20, ranging from minnow and carp to trout and salmon), their locations, their habits, and the best methods and baits for catching them. The evidence of Walton's extensive reading is everywhere apparent in the text as he cites over 60 writers and works from classical times to the Renaissance. Much of the essay's charm derives from the simple, straightforward way he describes the mechanics of angling and the innocent pleasures derived from it. Angling is an art much like poetry, Piscator tells Venator. People inclined to either must be born with inclinations to it: "He that hopes to be a good Angler must not only bring an inquiring, searching, observing wit; but he must bring a large measure of hope and patience, and a love and propensity to the Art itself; but having once got and practis'd it, then doubt not but what Angling will prove to be so pleasant, that it will prove to be like Virtue, a reward to itself."

Typical of Walton's method is the section on the trout in Chapter 4: "The trout is a fish highly valued both in this and foreign nations; he may be justly said (as the old poet said of wine, and we English say of venison) to be a generous fish: a fish that is so like the buck that he also has his seasons, for it is observed that he goes in and out of season with the stag and buck ... and he may justly contend with all fresh-water fish, as the mullet may with all sea-fish for precedency and daintiness of taste, and that being in right season, the most dainty palates have allowed presidency to him." He goes on to describe the kinds and habitats of the trout. In Chapter 5 he gives further directions for fishing for trout and how to make artificial minnows and flies for lures.

But The Compleat Angler is more than just a fishing manual. It is a book that celebrates the wholesomeness of creation and the rural life in which a simple pleasure such as angling can heal the body, cleanse the mind, and refresh the spirit. As Venator says at the end of the book: "So when I would beget content, and increase confidence in the Power, and Wisdom, and Providence of Almighty God, I will walk the Meadows by some gliding Stream, and there contemplate the Lillies [sic] that take no care, and those very many other various little living creatures that are not only created but fed (man knows not how) by the goodness of the God of Nature, and therefore trust in him." Walton's book thus takes its place in the tradition of the literature of retirement so prominent in the 17th century.

Walton's delightful treatment of fishing as sport, recreation, and spiritual refreshment and its smooth, flowing, and engaging style make the book a classic. Overarching The Compleat Angler is his belief that the traditional in state, church, society, and culture, as symbolized in the art of angling, are being overthrown by the religious fanatics who have taken control of England.

ROBERT C. STEENSMA

Editions

The Compleat Angler, or, The Contemplative Man's Recreation, Being a Discourse of Fish and Fishing Not Unworthy the Perusal of Most Anglers, 1653; revised editions, 1655, 1661; in The Universal Angler, with Charles Cotton, 1676; many subsequent editions, including those edited by Richard Le Gallienne, 1897, John Buxton, 1982, and Jonquil Bevan, 1983

Further Reading

Bevan, Jonquil, Izaak Walton's The Compleat Angler: The Art of Recreation, New York: St. Martin's Press, 1988

Bottrall, Margaret Smith, Izaak Walton, London and New York: Longman Green, 1955

Coon, A. M., The Life of Izaak Walton (dissertation), Ithaca, New York: Cornell University, 1938

Cooper, John, The Art of the Compleat Angler, Durham, North Carolina: Duke University Press, 1968

The Confessions

by St. Augustine, 397–398 CE

St. Augustine of Hippo (354–430 CE) is a major figure in the history and development of Western experience. Many biographical details come from the Confessions. Augustine was born in Tageste, in Numidia, the son of Patricius, a small landowner and local official who became a Christian late in life, and of Monica, a devout Christian from girlhood who was a major influence on Augustine. He was educated in the grammar school at Madura, where he became skilled in late Latin literature, if imperfect in Greek. Then came a year at home, while his father saved enough to send him to Carthage, where he trained in rhetoric. As was customary, Augustine took a concubine and fathered a son, called Adeodatus, before he was 20. After teaching a year in Tagaste, Augustine taught in Carthage from 376 to 383, and was drawn to the Manichaeans. In 384 he went to Milan to be a professor of rhetoric. There he met Ambrose, a major influence because of his learned eloquence and fervent belief. Several events in 386 – the persecution of Justina, the reading of Plotinus that made Augustine a Platonist, the recognition that a Christian soldier like Ponticianus was capable of greater discipline and renunciation than the thoughtful Augustine, the moment of conversion through the episode in the garden, followed by a summer of intellectual dialogues with non-Christian friends near Como – led to his return to Milan and baptism on Holy Saturday, 24 April 387, when he was 32. Augustine decided to return to Africa, with Monica, who died on the journey at Ostia. Here the autobiographical account in the Confessions ends. Subsequent details of his life include three years of study and devotion at Tagaste, during which time Adeodatus died. While on a visit to Hippo Regius, Augustine was selected by the aged bishop's flock and ordained to be a priest in 391. He was consecrated bishop in 395, a fixed appointment from the age of 40, and continued to live and work in this rather remote seaport.

Augustine wrote prodigiously – **letters**, **sermons**, and great **treatises**, notably De trinitate (The Trinity) and De civitate dei (The City of God) – in a style of contemporary Latin with greater flexibility than the classics and a mastery for memorable phrases. Augustine was not so much a systematic thinker as a responder to current opponents and heretics (Donatists, Manichaeans, Pelagians). Obscurely situated during his lifetime, a period of imperial decline, Augustine became the most accessible author in early Christendom, one of the four Latin fathers and a Doctor of the Church. His works were widely circulated, in manuscript and early printings, though first collected in 11 volumes in a Benedictine edition (1679), which became part of *Patrologiae latina*, edited by J. P. Migne (1845). Comparable to Augustine's place in the Catholic tradition was his impact upon the Reformation, since his thinking was also fundamental to Lutheranism, Calvinism, and Jansenism in the 16th and 17th centuries. Trained as a rhetorician, not as a philosopher, Augustine had a powerful appeal; he wrote always of the journey of the Christian soul to God, concerned with understanding the Scripture and living the Christian life, and vividly asserting the self-knowledge of the individual.

Augustine is not usually thought of as a writer of essays; he lived centuries before **Montaigne**, whom many identify as the progenitor of the essay form, although there were distinguished classical precedents in Latin writers like **Cicero**, Marcus Aurelius (*Meditations*), and **Plutarch**. The essay is typically defined as "a moderately brief prose discussion of a restricted topic." The length of the *Confessions* argues against consideration, but his discursive writing and highlighting of episodes create sections of the book in which can be seen many characteristics of content and style that anticipate the modern essay. Augustine's topic is restricted; he writes always of the Christian soul's relation to God. Seriousness of purpose, an intent to persuade, and dignity of style give the *Confessions* the quality of a formal essay; but the personal and confidential manner, the use of "I" and indeed the formulation of a "self," as well as exposition of tentative understanding (albeit leading to truth) suggest the informal essay.

Three selections from the text illustrate how portions of the *Confessions* can be identified as essays, or attempts at understanding coming from personal analysis. The story of the pear theft (Book II. 4–10) is among the most famous passages, in which Augustine describes his action as a 16 year old and analyzes the meaning of his behavior. With his fellows he steals quantities of pears, not because of hunger but to throw them to the pigs. The real reason for the theft is to do something that is forbidden; the flavor tasted is not pear but sin, and the pleasure is in doing something that is wrong, for the act would have held no appeal but for the companions who shared it. Thus Augustine questions logically and finds answers that culminate in a recognition of a most unfriendly friendship. The conclusion is to compare his wandering away from God into a barren waste with the joy of being with God. Augustine exposes his youthful failings with the skill of a psychologist and an immediacy that vividly evokes the difficulties of adolescence. His style is personal and confessional, with an openness and directness that the best essayists seek.

A slightly shorter passage (Book VII. 9–10) might be called "Of Books," to use the title of an essay by **Francis Bacon**. Here Augustine describes how God has mercifully kept him from pride by putting before him many books of the Platonists that helped him to think of God as a Spiritual Being. The classical philosophers give the framework, but the quotations are from Scripture – the Gospels, St. Paul, and the Psalms. The purpose is sober, and the method is an intellectual argument through close reading of texts. In the last section Augustine departs from his narrative recounting and textual presentation to a praise of God as eternal Truth, known through His creation.

A much longer section (Book X. 8–28), analogous to 19th-century longer and more **personal essays**, may be called "On Memory," which is again devoted to Augustine's seeking God. Here his Platonist account, the rising through stages, goes beyond the experiences of the senses to consider the nature of memory, a storehouse of images. Very systematically Augustine explores the nature of memory, how things are preserved – sense experiences, knowledge from study, the process of thought that assembles. He posits that at some time in the past we were happy, and thus all long for happiness, more specifically for God, always in his memory from when Augustine first learned of Him. The style is questioning, with frequent qualifications, and an answer of personal struggle and self-affirmation, memorably expressed through illustrative descriptive details and exclamations.

VELMA BOURGEOIS RICHMOND

See also Autobiographical Essay; Religious Essay

Editions

Confessiones, edited by P. Knöll, 1909, M. Kutella, revised by H. Juergens and W. Schaub, 1969, revised by James J. O'Donnell, 3 vols., 1992, and Gillian Clark, 1995; as *The Confessions*, many translations, including by F. J. Sheed, 1943, J. M. Lelen, 1952, R. S. Pine-Coffin, 1961, Rex Warner, 1963, E. M. Blaiklock, 1983, Hal M. Helms, 1986, and Henry Chadwick, 1991

Further Reading

Brown, Peter, *Augustine of Hippo*, Berkeley: University of California Press, and London: Faber, 1967
McWilliam, Joanne, editor, *Augustine: From Rhetor to Theologian*, Waterloo, Ontario: Wilfrid Laurier University Press, 1992
Mallard, William, *Language and Love: Introducing Augustine's Religious Thought Through the Confessions Story*, University Park: Pennsylvania State University Press, 1994
Pope, Hugh, *Saint Augustine of Hippo: Essays Dealing with His Life and Times and Some Features of His Work*, London: Sand and Co., 1937; Westminster, Maryland: Newman Press, 1949

Connolly, Cyril

British, 1903–1974

Although he wrote and published from the late 1920s until the mid-1970s, Cyril Connolly is commonly associated with the 1930s and 1940s. This is due to the lasting impact of his assessment of the period in *Enemies of Promise* (1938). The book merges Connolly's personal memories, their historical backdrop, and his views on selected authors, mostly Modernists, but also from his favorite period, the 18th century. *Enemies of Promise* sets the tone for Connolly's career as an essayist, but it also hints at his restricted outlook and the contradictory impulses which shape his essayistic work.

As the editor of *Horizon* Connolly went on to produce one of the most stimulating periodicals of World War II and the immediate postwar years. First published in 1939, it survived financial and organizational difficulties until 1950. In *Ideas and Places* (1953) Connolly assembled essays from *Horizon* (but also from *Art News*, *World Review*, *Go*, the *Geographical Magazine*, **Partisan Review**, the *New Statesman*, the **Times Literary Supplement**, and the *Listener*) and prefaced them with a summary of *Horizon*'s intention and problems. Born from the idealistic idea of a "renewal of the world and of letters," the journal maneuvered through left-wing politics, a disenchantment with Russia, and an equally thorough disappointment by the "philistine attitude of the Labour government to culture." Already in 1947 it showed signs of turning away from politics and drifting into an increasingly monotonous condemnation of postwar society. Halfway between initial enthusiasm and eventual decline, *Horizon* produced some of the most inspired antiwar essays of World War II. The fictional "Letter from a Civilian" of September 1944, which placed the suffering of the so-called "homefront" against the shallow heroism of the fighting troops, especially caused a stir. The wartime issues embraced an eclectic mix of Georgian writers, 1930s authors around **W. H. Auden**, and new names, such as Alun Lewis, William Sansom, Julian Maclaren Ross, and Laurie Lee. Toward the end of the war *Horizon* began to feature the literature of the French Resistance.

The problems of Connolly's cultural politics and the internal rift of many of his writings derive from a deeply ambivalent attitude toward the relationship of art and society. His claim to be working for "a new humanism which considers human life vulgar but sacred" encapsulates the impasse. Marxist critics such as Julian Symons were as little pleased with "the quite frankly belles-lettrist *Horizon*" and its "fagends of the Twenties . . . bound together by no organized view of Life or Society" as the conservative media who resented *Horizon*'s struggle against puritanism, identity cards, and the death penalty. On the positive side, Connolly used *Horizon* to fight, among other things, for prison reform and – interestingly enough – a culturally united Europe. Like many authors who grew up in the 1920s, Connolly was torn between a traditional privileged education (he went to Eton and Balliol College, Oxford) and the attempt to transcend it in the direction of a socially responsible, if not socialist perspective. His essentially elitist outlook and its source, his nostalgic and anachronistic orientation toward classical Greece and Rome, the French and English Enlightenment, and the *fin de siècle*, eventually pushed him toward nostalgia and cultural pessimism.

In a 1946 survey called "The Cost of Letters," for instance, *Horizon* had still sought to demonstrate in a very materialistic vein the link between art and real life. The questionnaire on authors' incomes was answered by John Betjeman, Elizabeth Bowen, C. Day Lewis, Robert Graves, Laurie Lee, Rose Macaulay, **George Orwell**, Stephen Spender, and Dylan Thomas, among others. In the "Centenary" essay of 1948, on the other hand, Connolly complains about the "continuous decline in all the arts." After lamenting the deaths of Joyce, **Yeats, Woolf, Valéry, Freud**, H. G. Wells, and J. G. Frazer, he goes on to state that "their places are not being filled. This is not because there is a decline in talent, but on account of the gradual dissolution of the environment in which it ripens. There is a decay in communication owing to the collapse of that highly cultivated well-to-do world bourgeoisie who provided the avant-garde artists – writer, painter, musician, architect – with the perfect audience."

A traditionalist liberal humanism which often collapses into an art for art's sake position is perhaps the best characterization of Connolly's essays. Yet even his critics applauded the grace and wit of his style. As a confirmed francophile Connolly also introduced a large number of French authors to the British audience. He translated Alfred Jarry's *Ubu* plays and promoted Louis Aragon, Paul Éluard, **Jean-Paul Sartre**, **Albert Camus**, Francis Ponge, Raymond Queneau, and Maurice Blanchot. His continued praise for Paul Valéry showed Connolly once more establishing his idiosyncratic connection between modern writing, the 19th-century aestheticism of **Baudelaire**, Rimbaud, **Mallarmé**, and Huysmans, and his beloved 18th century. Connolly's old fascination with Modernism (incidentally, he seems to have been the first to write about Joyce's *Finnegans Wake* in an essay entitled "The Position of Joyce" of 1929) found an outlet in his book *The Modern Movement* (1965).

After the demise of *Horizon*, Connolly continued to contribute to the intellectual debates of the postwar years, though his voice sounded more and more outmoded. Despite his unflinching attachment to his favorite subjects (which culminated in a book on 18th-century French pavilions), he also wrote approvingly about Francis Bacon's rather antihumanist paintings. The contradictory nature of his politics is evident from the fact that he had no problems working as literary editor for the *Observer* and writing for the *New Statesman*, but also for the conservative *Sunday Times*.

Four volumes of essays arranged by Connolly himself give an overview of his career: *The Condemned Playground* (1945), *Ideas and Places* (1953), *Previous Convictions* (1963), and the rather somber *The Evening Colonnade* (1973). There, Connolly's perceptive literary studies are united with his art criticism, but also with often surprisingly superficial travel writings. All this adds up to the curious impression of a Modernist traditionalist, a profoundly English snob with an interest in social reform, in short (and in the words of Peter Quennell): a "jet-propelled armchair."

RAINER EMIG

Biography

Cyril Vernon Connolly. Born 10 September 1903 in Whitley, near Coventry, Warwickshire. Lived in South Africa as a child, 1906–10, and Ireland, 1910–14. Studied at St. Cyprian's school, Eastbourne, where he met Eric Blair (i.e. George Orwell), 1914–18; Eton College, Berkshire, 1918–22; Balliol College, Oxford, 1922–25, B.A. in history, 1925. Tutor in Jamaica, 1925–26; secretary to Logan Pearsall Smith, 1926–27. Reviewer for the *New Statesman*, London, 1927–29. Married Frances Jean Bakewell, 1930 (divorced, 1947). Founder, with Stephen Spender, and editor, 1939–50, *Horizon*; literary editor, the *Observer*, London, 1942–43. Married Barbara Skelton, 1950 (marriage dissolved, 1954). Columnist and book reviewer, London *Sunday Times*, 1951–74. Married Deirdre Craig, 1959: one daughter and one son. Fellow, and Companion of Literature, 1972, Royal Society of Literature; Commander, Order of the British Empire (CBE), 1972; Chevalier, Legion of Honor (France). Died in London, 26 November 1974.

Selected Writings

Essays and Related Prose

Enemies of Promise, 1938; revised edition, 1948
The Condemned Playground: Essays, 1927–1944, 1945

Ideas and Places, 1953
Enemies of Promise and Other Essays: An Autobiography of Ideas, 1960
Previous Convictions, 1963
The Evening Colonnade, 1973
Selected Essays, edited by Peter Quennell, 1984

Other writings: the "word cycle" *The Unquiet Grave* (1944), two novels (one unfinished), letters, journals (included in *Journal and Memoirs*, edited by David Pryce-Jones, 1983), and *The Modern Movement* (1965), a study of Modernism.

Further Reading
Fisher, Clive, *Cyril Connolly: A Nostalgic Life*, London: Macmillan, 1995
Kramer, Hilton, "Cyril Connolly's *Horizon*," *New Criterion* 8, no. 1 (September 1989): 5–11
Lewis, Jeremy, *Cyril Connolly: A Life*, London: Cape, 1997
Ozick, Cynthia, "Cyril Connolly and the Groans of Success," *New Criterion* 2, no. 7 (March 1984): 21–27
Sheldon, Michael, *Friends of Promise: Cyril Connolly and the World of "Horizon"*, London: Hamilton, 1989
Spender, Stephen, *Cyril Connolly: A Memoir*, Edinburgh: Tragara Press, 1978

Cornwallis, Sir William, the Younger
English, c. 1579–1614

Sir William Cornwallis the Younger has some claim to the title of England's first essayist; certainly, he was the first to write a substantial book of **"familiar"** essays with the critical consciousness of working within a new vernacular prose genre. His *Essayes* were initially published in two parts: 25 essays in 1600 (reprinted with stylistic changes in 1606) and 24 essays in 1601. In 1610 there appeared a "newly enlarged" volume comprising the 1606 edition and a somewhat revised version of the 1601 edition, along with three new essays, bringing the total to 52. A posthumous edition (1632) testifies to the continuing appeal of the *Essayes*, reflected in Richard Whitlock's tribute to them as an authority for his own "manner of writing" (*Zootomia*, 1654). Although **Francis Bacon**'s brief aphoristic *Essayes* were available three years before Cornwallis' first publication, the mature Baconian essay did not reach the public until his revised editions of 1612 and 1625, and there is no evidence to suggest that the two essayists had any direct influence on each other. (Despite their appearance under the title *Essayes* . . ., Cornwallis' six posthumously issued pieces of 1616 belong to another genre popular in the Renaissance: the paradox.)

The Cornwallian essay, ranging in length from barely a page to ten or more pages, grafts an informal engagement with humanist learning to the moral typologies of "character" writing. It reads somewhat like the exercise of a youthful **Montaigne** coming of age in the social and political milieu of a late Elizabethan courtier, poor and debt-ridden but resolved upon taking his own measure through explorations of the world's virtues and vices. The essay titles – e.g. "Of Resolution," "Of Suspition," "Of Love," "Of Feare," "Of Vanitie," "Of Alehouses," "Of Knowledge," "Of Discourse" – give some notion of their author's topical range, the associative movement

of his thought testing its vernacular muscle among the neo-Stoic moral commonplaces that guide him like his own personal courtesy book. Cornwallis read the ancients, including the Greeks, in Latin, and he knew Italian (as well as some Spanish), especially the writings of **Guicciardini**, Sannazaro, **Machiavelli**, Petrarch, and Tasso; the ideal of humanist learning is affirmed in his own vision of courts of "gentlemen" enacting the virtues, each according to his capacity and station. In his writing, he appears intent upon preparing himself for a post in such a court by essaying moral commonplaces that have the power to make or break him. Thus, for instance, the discourses of professional men such as surgeons and attorneys are, in Cornwallis' eyes, "places to grow fat in, not wise," and those of scholars "too finicall," prone to fall apart unless they are made to "goe Methodically to worke"; "a Gentleman," he insists, "should talke like a Gentleman," whose knowledge is "generall." A specialized knowledge is "but one part of the house, a baywindow or a gable-ende," and he is brought to ask: "Who builds his house so maimed, much lesse himselfe?" Characteristically, Cornwallis searches out his own moral location in the space of discourse: "It shal be my course . . . not to loose my self in my tale, to speak words that may be understood, and, to my power, to meane wisely rather than to speake eloquently" ("Of Discourse").

Viewing his essays as conversations with himself, Cornwallis counterposes a "talking style" ("Of Ambition") to the Ciceronian model, corrupted, to his way of thinking, by rhetorical verbosity. Avowing allegiance to **Seneca** and Tacitus, he writes in the "loose" style combined with "curt" elements, but with little of either Ben Jonson's pointed verve or **John Donne**'s mannered wit – he counted both among his friends. He leans toward Montaigne's discursiveness, but with little capacity to sustain the great French essayist's ruminative and narrative range. "Plainnesse" ("Of Essaies and Bookes") functions for him as a textual mirror to reflect his mind's movement; it serves to mediate between thought and action and to bring the particulars of his individuality into accord with the universal "minde." Thus, says Cornwallis, "I would be as I talke" ("Of Fortune and her Children"). Having read a partial translation of Montaigne's essays ("divers of his pieces" ["Of Censuring"]) before their appearance in English, he declares that neither they nor those of the ancients are "rightly tearmed Essayes; for . . . they are strong and able to endure the sharpest tryall." "But mine," he claims, "are Essayes, who am but newly bound Prentise to the inquisition of knowledge and use these papers as a Painter's boy a board, that is trying to bring his hand and his fancie acquainted" ("Of Essaies and Bookes"). At times immediate and self-referential ("I Write this in an Alehouse, into which I am driven by night" ["Of Alehouses"]), or vaguely confessional ("About nothing doe I suffer greater conflicts in my selfe then about induring wrongs" ["Of Patience"]), or casually conversational ("It is a pretty soft thing this same Love, an excellent company keeper" ["Of Love"]), or gnomically brooding ("We are all in darkenesse" ["Of Ambition"]), the openings of the *Essayes* not infrequently strike a strong personal and experiential note. A crotchety, even harsh sensibility colors many of these pieces, suggesting a spirited youth whose early disillusionment with the world and himself drives him into reclusion, where he earnestly searches his books for understanding. Unlike Bacon, bringing counsel to others on the path to power, Cornwallis writes as physician to his own soul: "without any company but Inke & Paper, & them I use in stead of talking to my selfe" ("Of Alehouses"). Essay writing furnishes him with the "Marchandise of the mind" ("Of Keeping State") that will, he writes, "cure my bodie in his innate diseases" ("Of Life, and the Fashions of Life").

England's first essayist in the spirit of Montaigne, scarcely past adolescence when he embarked on his opus, contemplates himself as a creature of time ("the stuffe that life is made of" ["Of Vanitie"]): the self of his past destined by birth for an "active course" ("Of Life") but already lost to folly; the self of his present uncertainly taking shape in writing; the self of his anticipated future resolutely adjusting to a neo-Stoic regimen, an increasingly shared nostalgia of the Jacobean age. Thus the temporality of the self unfolds in the Cornwallian essay as a discourse for moral measurement. "Shall it not bee lawful then for us to build our Tombes in our Papers?" asks Cornwallis in "Of Trappes for Fame."

Although interest in the *Essayes* waned after the middle of the 17th century, their colloquial candor infuses a tincture of Montaigne into the English practice of the genre, even as the Baconian alternative is still discovering its own form. For the modern reader, the dogged moralizing of Cornwallis' book somewhat dulls its often engaging immediacy but leaves, at the same time, the emblematic stamp of a rugged, rough-and-ready self-portraiture.

LYDIA FAKUNDINY

Biography
Born probably 1579 in Suffolk. Nephew of Sir William Cornwallis, the Elder. Probably educated privately; knew Spanish and Italian but no French. Married Katherine Parker, 1595: 11 children (three died). Member of Parliament for Lostwithiel, 1597, and Orford, Suffolk, 1604, 1614. Accompanied Robert Devereux, second Earl of Essex on his Irish campaign, 1599: knighted as a result. Involved in court life, 1601–05: member of King James' privy chamber, 1603, and carried dispatches between Spain and England for his ambassador father, 1605; renounced court when he failed to win the king's preferment. Friend of Ben Jonson, commissioning him to write *Penates, or a Private Entertainment for the King and Queen*, 1604. Also associated with John Donne and Thomas Overbury. Apparently lived extravagantly until he lost the inheritance of his uncle's estate; at his death left his wife and children in poverty. Died 1 July 1614.

Selected Writings

Essays and Related Prose
Essayes, 2 vols., 1600–01; enlarged edition, 1610; edited by Don Cameron Allen, 1946

Other writings: *Discourses upon Seneca the Tragedian* (1601); *The Miraculous and Happie Union of England and Scotland* (1604); *Essayes; or Rather Encomions, Prayses of Sadnesse* (1616); and *Essayes of Certain Paradoxes* (1616).

Further Reading
Bennett, Roger E., *The Life and Works of Sir William Cornwallis* (dissertation), Cambridge, Massachusetts: Harvard University, 1931
Bennett, Roger E., "Sir William Cornwallis' Use of Montaigne," *PMLA* 48 (December 1933): 1080–89
Bush, Douglas, "Essays and Characters," in his *English Literature in the Earlier Seventeenth Century, 1600–1660*, Oxford: Clarendon Press, revised edition, 1962 (original edition, 1945)
MacDonald, W. L., "The Earliest English Essayists," *Englische Studien* 64 (September 1929): 20–52
Price, Michael W., "Sir William Cornwallis," in *British Prose Writers of the Early Seventeenth Century*, edited by Clayton D. Lein, *Dictionary of Literary Biography*, vol. 151, Detroit: Gale Research, 1995: 82–87
Salmon, J. H. M., "Seneca and Tacitus in Jacobean England," in *The Mental World of the Jacobean Court*, edited by Linda Levy Peck, Cambridge and New York: Cambridge University Press, 1991: 169–88
Sandbank, S., "On the Structure of Some Seventeenth-Century Metaphors," *English Studies* 52 (August 1971): 323–30
Thompson, Elbert N. S., *The Seventeenth-Century English Essay*, Iowa City: University of Iowa Press, 1926
Upham, A. H., "Montaigne," in his *The French Influence in English Literature, from the Accession of Elizabeth to the Restoration*, New York: Octagon, 1965 (original edition, 1908)
Wedgwood, C. V., "The Later Evolution of Prose," in her *Seventeenth-Century English Literature*, Oxford and New York: Oxford University Press, 1970 (original edition, 1950)
Whitt, P. B., "New Light on Cornwallis the Essayist," *Review of English Studies* 8 (1932): 155–69
Williamson, George, "Aculeate Style and the Cult of Form," in his *The Senecan Amble: A Study in Prose Form from Bacon to Collier*, London: Faber, and Chicago: University of Chicago Press, 1951

Critical Essay

The critical essay has its distant origins in Aristotle's *Poetics*, especially in his analysis of the work of Sophocles, and in the work *Peri hypsous* (**On the Sublime**), attributed to the first-century Greek critic Longinus. But true critical prose in the modern sense – cultural criticism that takes full advantage of the rhetorical possibilities of the **familiar essay** – only began during the late 17th century in Europe, coming fully into its own as a genre with the rise of literary periodical journalism in the 18th century. One might reach back in time to include a few earlier seminal expressions of criticism, including such Renaissance works as the *Poetice* (1562; *On Poetry*) by the Italian scholar Julius Caesar Scaliger, which gave classicism its first voice, or Sir Philip Sidney's **The Defence of Poesy** (wr. 1580–82, pub. 1595), perhaps the earliest example of modern literary criticism. But it was the appearance of John Dryden's **An Essay of Dramatic Poesy** in 1667–68 that firmly established the critical essay in prose as a distinct and culturally influential genre. Dryden's essay took ownership of the literary space between the older form of the **treatise**, with its theoretical preoccupation, and the soon-to-evolve **review**, with its emphasis on the evaluation of texts. The critical essay after Dryden has continued to mix a general appreciation of literary history with the analysis of specific works and authors, and has always set its discussion within the contexts of contemporary cultural and political discourse. Whether or not it employs a theoretical framework, the critical essay is always textually grounded and very much preoccupied with the sociological and psychological process of reading.

The 18th century saw a proliferation in production of the critical essay across Europe. John Dennis, the first professional critic, found a popular readership in England and France for criticism in which he stressed the primacy of passion in the literary arts; he published controversial essays on *The Usefulness of the Stage* (1698), *The Advancement and Reformation of Modern Poetry* (1701), *The Grounds of Criticism in Poetry* (1704), and *An Essay upon the Genius and Writings of Shakespeare* (1712). Dennis' generation of writers included **Richard Steele** and **Joseph Addison**, whose *Spectator* (1711–12, 1714) was the first periodical to adapt literary criticism to serious journalism. In this periodical Addison published serialized essays on Milton, the ballad, and the theory of the imagination, and did much to make literature a conversational topic in the coffee houses. But it was **Samuel Johnson** who made of the critical essay in English something definitive: his *Lives of the English Poets* (1779–81), a series of critical **prefaces** written for a ten-volume historical collection of English poetry, developed an essay style that mingled moral and aesthetic criticism of literature while showing equal appreciation for classical and contemporary works. Among Johnson's earliest attempts at criticism, his *Life of Mr. Richard Savage* (1744) emphasized the humanist values that would continue to underpin most critical essays for the next three centuries, even in writers otherwise as diverse as **Denis Diderot**, **Matthew Arnold**, and **Edmund Wilson**.

The French encyclopedists, especially Montesquieu, **Voltaire**, **Rousseau**, and of course, Diderot, did much to advance the critical essay on the continent, having themselves been influenced by the style of Addison in particular. They added to the sophisticated classicism of their English models a radicalism that in turn affected much late 18th- and early 19th-century critical writing. The Scottish encyclopedist, essayist, and editor William Smellie and his colleague, the historian Dr. Gilbert Stuart, launched the *Edinburgh Magazine and Review* (1773–76), which took the radical combination of literature, politics, and opinion to its ultimate expression. They wrote and published regular critical essays which undertook to review current publications against an erudite and idiosyncratic background of selective literary traditions. Their aggressive and very personal critical postures were often inflammatory, and even libelous, but always intelligently original. Their approach to criticism was somewhat before its time, but they defined the anarchic end of the spectrum of critical essay writing, in opposition to Samuel Johnson's position of consolation: where Johnson, even when derogatory, sought to instruct his reader with informed wit, Stuart and Smellie undertook to outrage and alarm. This Scottish style made its real mark in the 19th century in the essays of John Gibson Lockhart, a chief contributor to *Blackwood's Edinburgh Magazine* and editor of the *Quarterly Review*, both important trend setters in their day. The criticism of most English-language essays down to the 20th century can be grouped around one or other of the two poles defined by Johnson and the Scottish reviewers: there are the antagonists like **Thomas Carlyle**, **Oscar Wilde**, and F. R. Leavis, and the consolers like Matthew Arnold, **Henry James**, and **Lionel Trilling**.

While the English-language critical essay became more polemical as the 18th century closed, criticism in German tended toward the philosophic and speculative. Following the publications of the classicist **Gotthold Ephraim Lessing** (*Laokoon* [1766; *Laocoon*] and *Hamburgische Dramaturgie* [1767–69; *Hamburg Dramaturgy*]), German Romanticism produced lasting contributions to critical-essay writing in the nationalistic work of **Johann Gottfried Herder** and **Friedrich von Schiller**, especially Herder's *Über die neuere Deutsche Litteratur: Fragmente* (1767; Fragments on modern German literature) and Schiller's *Über naive und sentimentalische Dichtung* (1795–96; *On the Naive and Sentimental in Literature*). The German critical essay became obsessed with the intricacies of language, in particular etymology, and developed an almost exclusive concern for philology as it proceeded through the 19th century. **Friedrich Schlegel**'s essays in the *Athenäum* (1798–1800) laid the groundwork for the German critical focus on irony and the inadequacy of literary language. Meanwhile, French criticism in the 19th century continued to reflect the more sociological concerns of the earlier form of the critical essay. **Charles-Augustin Sainte-Beuve**, in such works as his *Critiques et portraits littéraires* (1832–39; Literary critiques and portraits) and the collected volumes of his essays in criticism, *Causeries du lundi* (1851–62; *Monday Chats*) and *Nouveaux Lundis* (1863–70; New Mondays), carefully positioned his studies of an author's work against an understanding of the life and times. **Hippolyte Taine** extended Sainte-Beuve's portraiture into a fully racial and historical account of literary culture in his *Histoire de la littérature anglaise* (1863–64; *History of English Literature*). But it was Émile Zola who epitomized the French style in criticism, centering his approach on an exhaustive consideration of literature and the arts as a reflection of the human social condition.

The critical essay became a literary institution in 19th-century Europe when periodicals and magazines as well as daily newspapers established review criticism as the public forum for a nation's examination of its artistic identity. The Scottish reviewers of the early 1800s, so devastatingly satirized by Lord Byron after an *Edinburgh Review* essay attacked his poetry (*English Bards and Scotch Reviewers*, 1809), can in fact be credited with making the critical essay an important political and sociological exercise. *Blackwood's* (established 1817) and the *Edinburgh Review* (established 1802) greatly influenced both the form of the critical essay and the development of publications in which it was to appear. *Scrutiny* (1932–53), the *Paris Review* (1953–), the *Times Literary Supplement* (1902–), and the *New Yorker* (1925–) all trace their genealogy back to these sources by one route or another.

If all critical essays can be said, despite their otherwise apparently diverse thematic concerns, to have one common defining feature, it is this: the critical essay is chiefly concerned with engaging its audience in a reflective analysis of the politics of the act of reading. The best essayists of this kind value the texts they critique not for what is said but for how it is said, struggling with the ambiguity of literary language to describe a rhetoric of reading.

STEPHEN W. BROWN

Anthologies

The English Critical Tradition: An Anthology of English Literary Criticism, edited by S. Ramaswami and V. S. Seturaman, Bombay: Macmillan, 2 vols., 1977–78

The Great Criticism: An Anthology of Literary Criticism, edited by James Harry Smith and Edd Winfield Parks, 3rd edition, New York: Norton, 1951 (original edition, edited by Smith only, 1932)

Literature in America: An Anthology of Literary Criticism, edited by Philip Rahv, Cleveland: World, 1957

Further Reading

The Cambridge History of Literary Criticism, Cambridge: Cambridge University Press, 1989– (in progress)

Hall, Vernon, Jr., *A Short History of Literary Criticism*, New York: New York University Press, 1963

Saintsbury, George, *A History of Criticism and Literary Taste in Europe, from the Earliest Texts to the Present Day*, New York: Humanities Press, 3 vols., 1961 (original edition, 1902–04)

Wellek, René, *A History of Modern Criticism*, 8 vols., New Haven, Connecticut and (vols. 7–8) London: Yale University Press, 1955–92; vols. 1–2 and 5–6, London: Cape, 1955, 1986; vols. 1–4, Cambridge: Cambridge University Press, 1981–83

Wimsatt, W. K., and Cleanth Brooks, *Literary Criticism: A Short History*, New York: Knopf, and London: Routledge, 1957

Croce, Benedetto

Italian, 1866–1952

Benedetto Croce was the dominant figure in Italian culture for the first 50 years of the 20th century. His formidable output covers well over a hundred volumes, over half of which consist of collections of essays in philosophy, aesthetics, literary criticism, philosophy of history, narrative history, and politics. Although the essay form was the dominant mode of Croce's writing – even the chapters of his monographs can often be read as self-contained pieces – it was for him an instrument in a literary life dominated by cultural battles rather than a genre chosen for its own sake. Ironically, Croce, one of the most prodigious and effective users of the essay in the 20th century, produced an aesthetic theory which allowed no space for critical consideration of the genre as such.

Croce burst onto the cultural scene in 1896 with the publication in essay form of two lectures given in 1893 and 1894 under the title *Il concetto della storia nelle sue relazioni col concetto dell'arte* (The concept of history in its relationship to the concept of art). One of the immediate effects of these essays was to bring cultural debate in Italy into the mainstream of European thought. In these writings Croce engaged with the German neo-Kantians in a common enterprise to establish the theoretical foundations of humanistic studies *vis-à-vis* the natural sciences and to clarify the distinction between *Naturwissenschaften* (natural sciences) and *Geisteswissenschaften/Kulturwissenschaften* (sciences of the humanities). In these early writings Croce was not as antipositivist as he later claimed. He attempted to establish the autonomy of art (and historiography as an art form) on the philosophical terrain of naive or uncritical realism. But this was the terrain *par excellence* of the natural sciences, firmly based on the epistemological assumption that human understanding has an unmediated access to reality. The natural sciences thus had the unassailable advantage of being able to analyze reality with greater explanatory power than the arts, by implication relegating the latter to a second-order, divertive, cognitive activity. Croce's observation in *Il concetto della storia nelle sue relazioni col concetto dell'arte* that the philosophical foundations of aesthetics did not yet exist was made in recognition of this temporary defeat.

From this point onward, the direction of his thinking took a decisive anti-positivist turn, and began to shift in emphasis away from the desire of the German neo-Kantians to establish the *autonomy* of the arts; Croce's objective became to demonstrate their cognitive *superiority* over the natural sciences. His discovery of Hegel (and a strongly idealist **Kant**), revealed in his **letters** of the period to Giovanni Gentile, led him to abandon uncritical realism, and with a complete *volte face* to construct an epistemology in which the human mind or spirit does not so much perceive reality as actually construct it. His monumental *Estetica come scienza dell'espressione e linguistica generale* (1902; *Aesthetic as Science of Expression and General Linguistic*), which also contains a collection of discrete essays and studies on the history of aesthetics, and the *Logica come scienza del concetto puro* (1905; *Logic as the Science of the Pure Concept*), laid the foundations of Croce's solution to the problem. In these works he establishes a hierarchy in which philosophy, dealing with "pure concepts," is epistemologically superior to the more mundane "pseudo-concepts" of the natural sciences. Art, based on intuition, and philosophy, based on reasoning, are given equal status as the two "cognitive" activities of the human spirit, while science is consigned to the sphere of the multifarious moral and economic "practical" activities of the human spirit. Historiography is transferred from art to become a branch of philosophy. Karl Vossler observed that no previous thinker had put aesthetic theory on the map so effectively, and Croce's influence spread well beyond Italy to inspire critics abroad. These writings, along with his *Filosofia della pratica: Economica ed etica* (1909; *Philosophy of the Practical: Economic and Ethic*), laid the foundations of Croce's subsequent theoretical labors. Later, when the positivist threat receded, Croce's antipathy toward the incursions of the scientific mentality into the arts took the form of opposition to methodological developments, whether in literary analysis, historiography, or the study of language.

A deep-rooted conservatism lay at the heart of Croce's thinking: not a sterile conservatism, but a tortured, creative, and challenging questioning of all that was new. Thus while he had an inhibiting effect in many fields of inquiry (e.g. historical and literary methodologies, linguistics, psychology), his passionate commitment to debating all the issues of the day nevertheless broadened the horizons of Italian intellectuals, and his journal *La Critica* (Criticism), founded in 1903 in collaboration with Giovanni Gentile, remained a critical point of reference for the next 40 years.

As a literary critic Croce developed the theory that the "poetic" core of all art was independent of genre, structure, and intellectual and ethical content. This theory, underlying the *Aesthetic*, discussed in his collection *Problemi di estetica* (1910; Problems in aesthetics), clearly enunciated in the *Breviario di estetica* (1913; *The Breviary of Aesthetic*), and further elaborated in the essays *Nuovi saggi di estetica* (1920; New essays on aesthetics), was finalized in *La poesia* (1936; *Benedetto Croce's Poetry and Literature*). Croce's inability to define the ineffable "poetic" essence of art, which escaped all specificities, made the critic's task impossible to formulate. The critic with true perception simply knows "poetry" when he sees it. The purpose of this "purist" theory (art was simply "art," or in essence "poetry") was twofold: to keep criticism free of "particular" theories (art as pleasure, feeling, moral purpose, etc.), which would transform art into a different order of activity of the spirit, and to protect art from the methodological "technicians" who would collapse genius or inspiration into *tecnica*. Croce's own literary criticism followed the practice of dichotomizing the work of art into a "poetic" core on the one hand and "extraneous" intellectual, moral, and structural elements on the other.

Some of Croce's most notable collections of **critical essays** appear in his six-volume *La letteratura della nuova Italia* (1914–40; Literature of the new Italy), *La poesia di Dante* (1921; The Poetry of Dante), *Ariosto, Shakespeare e Corneille* (1920; Ariosto, Shakespeare, and Corneille), *Poesia e non poesia* (1923; European Literature in the Nineteenth Century), *Poesia "popolare" e poesia d'arte* (1933; "Popular" poetry and true poetry), the two volumes of *Saggi sulla letteratura italiana del Seicento* (1911, 1931; Essays on Italian literature of the 17th century), *Conversazioni critiche* (1918–39; Critical conversations), *Poesia antica e moderna* (1941; Ancient and modern poetry), and *Letture di poeti* (1950; Poetic readings). His classical taste led him to view the experimental movements of the day as decadent. In his Dante essays he contrasted the positive lyrical elements in the *Divine Comedy* with its "non-poetic" rational and structural dimensions, while his opponents saw the interpenetration of these elements as the very reason for the work's poetic power. His similar treatment of Manzoni, **Leopardi**, and other writers produced vigorous opposition to what increasingly came to be seen as an overschematic system of analysis, resulting in the eventual discrediting of the aesthetic theory on which Croce's style of criticism was based.

His evolving idealist historicism eventually reduced philosophy to historiography according to the formula that the defining cognitive constituent of reality, the spirit, is quintessentially historical. Croce initially defined the historical process as an inscrutable impersonal force that progressively enriches our understanding of the "truth" content of reality. Attempts to steer the course of history violate this process. In his World War I essays *Pagine sulla guerra* (Notes on the war) – eventually published in 1928 – he exhorts Italians to stop debating whether or not Italy should enter the conflict, and to follow their political leaders since "such compliance, such obedience to the word of command issued by the few in number, by the ruling classes, is not blindness but a profound instinct for survival . . . a profound sense of necessity, of obedience to the laws of history." This deeply conservative view of history was modified when Croce turned against fascism, from which point he perceived the force of history as promoting the emergence of "liberty" rather than "truth." His subsequent historical writings reflect this injection of a greater moral purpose into the activities of individuals (but not collective forces) and into the historical process, a position theorized in the collection *La storia come pensiero e come azione* (1938; *History as the Story of Liberty*). Yet this new orientation never resolved the tensions between the moral purpose inherent in human activity and Croce's insistence on ultimate surrender to history's lofty design. Thus, despite his championing of liberty, his political writings in such collections as *Elementi di politica* (1925; *Politics and Morals*), *Etica e politica* (1931; Ethics and politics), *Pensiero politico e politica attuale* (1945; Political thought and current politics), and *Scritti e discorsi politici* (1943–1947)

(1963; Political writings and speeches) greatly disappointed the more radical anti-fascist elements of the Liberal party, the postwar reconstitution of which he presided over until 1947. His attachment to the theory of history as an impersonal force led Croce to see political programs for systematic reform as futile attempts to interfere with history's mysterious purpose. His leadership divided Liberal intellectuals and left the party as a right-wing rump on the margins of postwar Italian politics.

GINO BEDANI

Biography

Born 25 February 1866 in Pescassèroli. Lost his parents and sister in an earthquake on the island of Ischia, 1883. Studied law at the University of Rome, 1883–86. Returned to Naples, and administered family estate, 1886–90. Founder, with Giovanni Gentile, and editor, *La Critica*, 1903–44, later the *Quaderni della "Critica"*, 1945–51; adviser, Laterza and Sons publishers, Bari, from 1904. Appointed senator for life, 1910. Married Adele Rossi, 1914: four daughters. Minister of education, 1920–21; denounced the fascist dictatorship, 1925; president of the Liberal party, 1943–47, minister without portfolio of the new democratic government, 1944, and member of the Constituent Assembly, 1946–47. Founder, Istituto Italiano per gli Studi Storici (Italian institute of historical studies), Naples, 1947. Awards: honorary degrees from three universities. Died in Naples, 20 November 1952.

Selected Writings

Essays and Related Prose

Il concetto della storia nelle sue relazioni col concetto dell'arte, 1896
Materialismo storico ed economia marxistica, 1900; as *Historical Materialism and the Economics of Karl Marx*, translated by C. M. Meredith, 1914
Estetica come scienza dell'espressione e linguistica generale, 1902; as *Aesthetic as Science of Expression and General Linguistic*, translated by Douglas Ainslie, 1909, revised edition, 1953; as *The Aesthetic as the Science of Expression and of the Linguistic in General*, translated by Colin Lyas, 1992
Logica come scienza del concetto puro, 1905; as *Logic as the Science of the Pure Concept*, translated by Douglas Ainslie, 1917
Letteratura e critica della letteratura contemporanea in Italia, 1908
Filosofia della pratica: Economica ed etica, 1909; as *Philosophy of the Practical: Economic and Ethic*, translated by Douglas Ainslie, 1913
Problemi di estetica e contributi alla storia dell'estetica italiana, 1910
La filosofia di Giambattista Vico, 1911; as *The Philosophy of Giambattista Vico*, translated by R. G. Collingwood, 1964
Saggi sulla letteratura italiana del Seicento, 1911
Breviario di estetica, 1913; as *The Breviary of Aesthetic*, translated by Douglas Ainslie, 1915, and as *The Essence of Aesthetic*, 1921; as *Guide to Aesthetics*, translated by Patrick Romanell, 1965
Saggio sullo Hegel, seguito da altri scritti di storia della filosofia, 1913; part as *What Is Living and What Is Dead of the Philosophy of Hegel*, translated by Douglas Ainslie, 1915
La letteratura della nuova Italia, 6 vols., 1914–40
Aneddoti e profili sette centeschi, 1914
Cultura e vita morale, 1914
Teoria e storia della storiografia, 1917; as *History: Its Theory and Practice*, translated by Douglas Ainslie, 1921, and as *Theory and History of Historiography*, 1921
Conversazioni critiche, 5 vols., 1918–39
Primi saggi, 1919
Curiosità storiche, 1919
Storie e leggende napoletane, 1919

Una famiglia di patrioti, ed altri saggi storici e critici, 1919
Pagine sparse, edited by G. Castellano, 3 vols., 1919–26
Goethe, 1919; revised edition, 1939; as *Goethe*, translated by Emily Anderson, 1923
Nuovi saggi di estetica, 1920
Giosuè Carducci, 1920
Giovanni Pascoli, 1920
Ariosto, Shakespeare e Corneille, 1920; as *Ariosto, Shakespeare, and Corneille*, translated by Douglas Ainslie, 1920
Storia della storiografia italiana nel secolo decimonono, 2 vols., 1921
La poesia di Dante, 1921; as *The Poetry of Dante*, translated by Douglas Ainslie, 1922
Nuove curiosità storiche, 1922
Frammenti di etica, 1922; as *The Conduct of Life*, translated by Arthur Livingston, 1924
Poesia e non poesia, 1923; as *European Literature in the Nineteenth Century*, translated by Douglas Ainslie, 1924
Elementi di politica, 1925; as *Politics and Morals*, translated by Salvatore J. Castiglione, 1945
Storia del Regno di Napoli, 1925; as *History of the Kingdom of Naples*, translated by F. Frenaje, 1970
Pagine sparse, edited by G. Castellano, 1927
Uomini e cose della vecchia Italia, 1927
Pagine sulla guerra, 1928
Storia d'Italia dal 1871 al 1915, 1928; as *A History of Italy, 1871–1915*, translated by C. M. Ady, 1929
Storia dell'età barocca in Italia: Pensiero – Poesia e letteratura – Vita morale, 1929
Alessandro Manzoni, 1930
Eternità e storicità della filosofia, 1930
Nuovi saggi sulla letteratura italiana del seicento, 1931; revised edition, 1949
Etica e politica, 1931
Storia d'Europa nel secolo decimonono, 1932; as *History of Europe in the Nineteenth Century*, translated by H. Furst, 1933
Poesia "popolare" e poesia d'arte, 1933
Nuovi saggi sul Goethe, 1934
Orientamenti: Piccoli saggi di filosofia politica, 1934
La critica e la storia della arti figurative, 1934
Ultimi saggi, 1935
La poesia: Introduzione alla critica storia della poesia e della letteratura, 1936; as *Benedetto Croce's Poetry and Literature: An Introduction to Its Criticism and History*, translated by Giovanni Gullace, 1981
Vite di avventure, di fede e di passione, 1936
La storia come pensiero e come azione, 1938; as *History as the Story of Liberty*, translated by Sylvia Sprigge, 1941
Poesia antica e moderna, 1941
Il carattere della filosofia moderna, 1941
Storia dell'estetica per saggi, 1942
Aneddoti di varia letteratura, 3 vols., 1942; enlarged edition, 4 vols., 1953–54
Pagine sparse, 3 vols., 1943
Considerazioni sul problema morale del tempo nostro, 1945
Pensiero politico e politica attuale, scritti e discorsi, 1945
Il carattere della filosofia moderna, 1945
Discorsi di varia filosofia, 2 vols., 1945; selection in *My Philosophy and Other Essays on the Moral and Political Problems of Our Time*, 1949
Poeti e scrittori del pieno e del tardo Rinascimento, 3 vols., 1945–52
Nuove pagine sparse, 2 vols., 1948–49
Filosofia e storiografia, 1949; selection in *My Philosophy and Other Essays on the Moral and Political Problems of Our Time*, 1949
My Philosophy and Other Essays on the Moral and Political Problems of Our Time, edited by R. Klibansky, translated by E. F. Carritt, 1949
La letteratura italiana del Settecento – Note critiche, 1949

Letture di poeti e riflessioni sulla teoria e la critica della poesia, 1950
Filosofia, poesia, storia: Pagine tratte da tutte le opere, 1951; as *Philosophy, Poetry, History: An Anthology of Essays*, translated by Cecil Sprigge, 1966
Indagini su Hegel, 1952
Terze pagine sparse, 2 vols., 1955
Scritti e discorsi politici (1943–1947), 1963; edited by Angela Carella, 1993
Essays on Marx and Russia, edited and translated by Angelo A. De Gennaro, 1966
Essays on Literature and Literary Criticism, translated by M. E. Moss, 1990

Other writings: works on aesthetics, logic, economics, ethics, literary criticism, historiography, and Marxism.

Collected works edition: *Edizione nazionale delle opere*, 1991– (in progress).

Bibliographies

Borsari, Silvano, *L'opera di Benedetto Croce*, Naples: Istituto Italiano per gli Studi Storici, 1964
Cione, Edmondo, *Bibliografia crociana*, Turin: Fratelli Bocca, 1956
Nicolini, Fausto, *L'"editio ne varietur" delle opere di B. Croce: Saggio bibliografico con taluni riassunti o passi testuali e ventinove fuori testo*, Naples: Biblioteca del "Bollettino" dell'Archivio Storico del Banco di Napoli, 1960
Palmer, L. M., and H. S. Harris, editors, *Thought, Action and Intuition: A Symposium on the Philosophy of Benedetto Croce*, Hildesheim and New York: Olms, 1975

Further Reading

Adamson, Walter L., "Benedetto Croce and the Death of Ideology," *Journal of Modern History* 55 (June 1983): 208–36
Allan, George, "Croce's Theory of Historical Judgement: A Reassessment," *Modern Schoolman* (January 1975): 169–87
Bedani, Gino, "Art as 'Poesia': The Strategic Dimension of Croce's Aesthetic," in *The Italian Lyric Tradition*, edited by Gino Bedani, Remo Catani, and Monica Slowikowska, Cardiff: University of Wales Press, 1993: 7–22
Bedani, Gino, "Art, Poetry and Science: Theory and Rhetoric in Croce's Early Anti-Positivist Epistemology," *Italian Studies* 49 (1994): 91–110
Bobbio, Norberto, *Profilo ideologico del Novecento italiano*, Turin: Einaudi, 1986
Bonetti, Paolo, *Introduzione a Croce*, Rome: Laterza, 1984
Brown, Merle E., *Neo-Idealistic Aesthetics: Croce–Gentile–Collingwood*, Detroit: Wayne State University Press, 1966
Carr, Herbert Wildon, *The Philosophy of Benedetto Croce*, New York: Russell and Russell, 1969 (original edition 1917)
Corsi, Mario, *Le origini del pensiero di Benedetto Croce*, Naples: Giannini, 1974
Garin, Eugenio, *Intellettuali italiani del XX secolo*, Rome: Riuniti, 1974
Montale, Eugenio, "Lesson on Croce: Esthetics and Criticism," *Italian Quarterly* 7 (1963): 48–65
Moss, M. E., *Benedetto Croce Reconsidered*, Hanover, New Hampshire: University Press of New England, 1987
Orsini, Gian N. G., *Benedetto Croce: Philosopher of Art and Literary Critic*, Carbondale: Southern Illinois University Press, 1961
Palmer, L. M., and H. S. Harris, editors, *Thought, Action and Intuition: A Symposium on the Philosophy of Benedetto Croce*, Hildesheim and New York: Olms, 1975
Parente, Alfredo, "Estetica e gusto nell'opera critica di Croce," *Rivista di Studi Crociani* 3 (1966): 293–94

Roberts, David D., "Benedetto Croce and the Dilemmas of Liberal Restoration," *Review of Politics* 44 (April 1982): 214–41

Roberts, David D., *Benedetto Croce and the Uses of Historicism*, Berkeley: University of California Press, 1987

Sprigge, Cecil J. S., *Benedetto Croce: Man and Thinker*, New Haven, Connecticut: Yale University Press, and Cambridge: Bowes and Bowes, 1952

Wellek, René, *Four Critics: Croce, Valéry, Lukács, and Ingarden*, Seattle: University of Washington Press, 1981

White, Hayden V., "The Abiding Relevance of Croce's Idea of History," *Journal of Modern History* 37 (June 1963): 109–24

Cuadernos Americanos

Mexican journal, 1942–

The launch of the first volume of *Cuadernos Americanos* (American notebooks) was celebrated on 30 December 1941 in Mexico City. Since that time, the six annual issues of *CA* have appeared without interruption. The original objectives of *CA*, on both the international and the national levels, have remained constant. Yet in its evolution it has followed the transformation of Latin American countries; we can distinguish two clearly delineated stages which correspond to the periods under the direction of Jesús Silva Herzog (1942–86) and **Leopoldo Zea** (since 1987, under the auspices of the National Autonomous University of Mexico).

CA emerged in 1942 in the middle of what was still an indecisive discourse, which was beginning to be recognized as Mexican but which was also inspired by several mentors who saw the Mexicanness in function with the human and sensed the possibility of formulating a discourse with universal repercussions. From its beginning, *CA* projected an essayistic perspective with interdisciplinary focus. The original Executive Board had 11 members, six Mexicans (Alfonso Caso, Daniel Cosío Villegas, Mario de la Cueva, Manuel Martínez Báez, **Alfonso Reyes**, and Jesús Silva Herzog) and five Spanish exiles (Pedro Bosch Gimpera, Eugenio Imaz, Juan Larrea, Manuel Márquez, and Agustín Millares). All were established intellectuals with significant humanist cultural experience and were not only recognized internationally for their essays, but also associated with various fields of specialization, ranging from literature to anthropology, economics, medicine, history, and sociology. For them, *CA* was responding to a sense of mission which Alfonso Reyes expressed in these words during the launch of the periodical: "The task that presents itself today is not just another literary venture, but rather has been defined by a sense of continental and human service ... We understand our work as a moral imperative, as one of the many efforts for the salvation of culture, that is to say, the salvation of man." From its first issues, *CA* was the most prestigious Latin American magazine, and had an appeal to the whole continent.

Within the context of World War II, this select group of intellectuals, as Reyes indicates in his statement of purpose, feels destiny's calling: "[There] has been placed upon us the grave duty of preserving and promoting religion, philosophy, science, ethics, politics, urbanity, courtesy, poetry, music, the arts, industries and professions: as much as it is language that preserves and transmits the conquests of the species, in short, all that is culture." *CA* proposed to be a forum reflecting the present, communicating with the world from a Latin American context. For the first time, the Latin American nations felt included in the international community; Reyes reaffirmed what motivated the magazine: "We are an integral and necessary part in the representation of man by man. Whoever does not recognize us is not a whole man." The prestige of the essayists who collaborated from the beginning (**Mariano Picón-Salas**, Alfonso Reyes, Raúl Haya de la Torre, Francisco Romero, Waldo Frank, Joaquín Xirau, José Gaos, Edmundo O'Gorman, and Samuel Ramos, among many others) and the quality of the essays that were published served as a model for the Latin American essay during the formative years of the 1940s and 1950s.

During this first stage, the magazine was precisely structured. It consisted of four parts: 1. "Nuestro tiempo" (Our time), 2. "Aventura del pensamiento" (The adventure of thinking), 3. "Presencia del pasado" (Presence of the past), and 4. "Dimensión imaginaria" (The imaginary dimension). Each part was divided into two sections; the first section of each part included essays of variable length (generally between five and 25 pages); the second section, which was much shorter, included critical notes (generally two to ten pages) on the most notable European and American books of the moment.

In 1987, the second stage of *CA* began, as a "Nueva época" (new period), even though its director, Leopoldo Zea, was among the most frequent contributors to the magazine from the first issues in 1942. In this context, the title "Nueva época" has the double meaning of both "a return" to some of the initial objectives and a formulation of new ideal objectives that serve as a model for the new period. Today, the "aventura del pensamiento" has reached "nuestro tiempo": the explicit division into four sections has been eliminated. All the fields these sections covered are currently represented by national and international associations promoting their study. They continue to be the center of *CA*'s concerns, but it is no longer considered necessary to categorize so rigidly the journal's contents. What was once used to define its objectives would today limit its freedom.

Much more significant than these changes to the structure of the magazine are the new ideals that accompany the "Nueva época." As the objectives formulated in 1942 by Herzog and Reyes have been realized, Zea now extends his vision: "To know how to recognize oneself in others and upon that recognition, to respect them in order to be respected. Such is the spirit that will have to be maintained in this new stage of *Cuadernos Americanos*, open to the times that rapidly pass by in our America and in the world of which it is a part. One will have to review and actualize the problems of the region and of the world of which it is now expression" ("Palabras del Director" [1987; Words of the editor]). In order to achieve such goals, *CA* now relies on the collaboration, as editor, of the essayist and literary critic Liliana Weinberg; in addition to an Editorial Board, it possesses an International Board of recognized essayists (Roberto Fernández Retamar, Domingo Miliani, Francisco Miró Quesada, Gregorio Weinberg, Fernando Ainsa, Tzvi Medin, and Amy Oliver, among others) who encourage the global dimension of contemporary Latin American thought.

JOSÉ LUIS GÓMEZ-MARTÍNEZ

Further Reading

Gómez-Martínez, José Luis, "La nueva época de *Cuadernos Americanos* en el desarrollo del pensamiento mexicano," *Cuadernos Americanos* 31 (1992): 72–81

Larrea, Juan, "Gestación de *Cuadernos Americanos*," *Cuadernos Americanos* 31 (1992): 16–40

Morales Benítez, Otto, "*Cuadernos Americanos*: Una tribuna para la verdad y la libertad," *Cuadernos Americanos* 31 (1992): 41–71

Muñoz, Humberto, Leopoldo Zea, Marcos Kaplan, and Juan Ortega y Medina, "Crónica de la presentación de la nueva época de *Cuadernos Americanos*," *Cuadernos Americanos* 4 (1987): 225–36

Reyes, Alfonso, "América y los *Cuadernos Americanos*," *Cuadernos Americanos* 2 (1942): 7–10

Weinberg, Gregorio, "Por mis palabras testimonios," *Cuadernos Americanos* 31 (1992): 82–86

Weinberg, Liliana Irene, "*Cuadernos Americanos* como empresa de cultura," *Cuadernos Americanos* 31 (1992): 89–93

Zea, Leopoldo, "Palabras del Director," *Cuadernos Americanos* 1 (1987): 9–11

Zea, Leopoldo, "*Cuadernos Americanos* cincuenta años después," *Cuadernos Americanos* 31 (1992): 11–15

Cunha, Euclides da

Brazilian, 1866–1909

When Samuel Putman translated Euclides da Cunha's *Os sertões* (1902; *Rebellion in the Backlands*), he called it "Brazil's greatest book." Cunha's masterpiece, as it was labeled, was one of the first prose pieces effectively to combine two genres: essay and fiction. The text is too scientific to be called an historical novel, although it was based on an historical event, and too fictitious to be called a scientific treatise. The essays that make up this "novel" can be classified as geographical, geological, ethnographic, philosophical, sociological, and historical.

All but forgotten, except by students of Brazilian letters, Cunha was once again discovered and analyzed when Mário Vargas Llosa published his *La guerra del fin del mundo* (1981; *The War of the End of the World*), a novel based on Cunha's *Rebellion*. In *A Writer's Reality* (1990), Vargas Llosa describes his reaction to Cunha's text: "For me all of this was like seeing in a small laboratory the pattern of something that had been happening all over Latin America since the beginning of our independence." Thus, Vargas Llosa recognizes in the turn-of-the-century text the beginning of the current debate on "barbarism and civilization" that still fuels the passions of Latin American essayists.

The three sections of *Rebellion* – "Land," "Man," "Struggle" – reflect Cunha's scientific knowledge, which is greatly influenced by European positivism. Cunha "proves" that the *jagunço* (ruffian) is not guilty of rebellion, but is the product of racial, geographical, and historical factors that create a kind of semi-barbaric existence. To be sure, Cunha represented the view of the elite of the time: the struggle between the "primitive" citizens of the interior and the "civilized" citizenry of the coastal areas. Cunha's essay becomes, then, a description of turn-of-the-century Brazilian ideology.

Although one cannot deny the racist implications in Cunha's text, such as the "degeneration" of the races in America due to miscegenation, the author also saw that not all barbarism

lay on the side of the rebels, and that civilization meant more than the political and military establishment of Brazil. Cunha's primary purpose was to re-create the peasant revolt against the republic, but what he achieved has been recognized as the first attempt within Brazilian letters to probe beneath the surface of Brazilian reality and to expose forbidden topics of discussion. For the student of turn-of-the-century Brazilian literature, Cunha provides a backdrop against which to measure current trends in the attempt to describe and define Brazilian identity in terms of what is European or North American (i.e. foreign); what is "native" – meaning authentically Brazilian and a problematic term in itself; and what is African. Many critics continue to live under the positivism that gave Brazil its motto "Order and Progress," while unwilling to discuss openly issues of miscegenation, racism, discrimination, and classism. In many cases in the contemporary debate, critics fall into the same trap experienced by Cunha. Raymond Williams, in his book *Mário Vargas Llosa* (1986), concludes that "Da Cunha was ultimately seduced by the beleaguered inhabitants of Canudos. Consequently, everything that supposedly stood for the opposite of civilization appealed to him most strongly." It is in this very attraction to the "Brazilian race" – the mixed races that comprise the majority of the population – that Cunha's essays need re-evaluation. He opened the way for a "scientific" view of culture that today has become fashionable once again.

Cunha's style is excessively baroque, characterized by antithesis, hyperbole, paradox, and an inordinate use of adjectives and repetition. Critics have noted these flaws in his style, but most have also acknowledged his extraordinary facility with and manipulation of the language. A journalist by training, Cunha was able to combine journalistic prose with a poetic artistry of discourse that made most of his essays masterpieces of discursive development.

CARMEN CHAVES TESSER

Biography

Euclides Rodrigues Pimenta da Cunha. Born 20 January 1866 in Santa Rita do Rio Negro. Studied at the Colégio Aquino, Rio de Janeiro, 1883–84: cofounder, with fellow students, *O Democrata* (Democracy); Polytechnic School, Rio, 1884–86; Praia Vermelha military school, Rio, 1886–88: expelled for openly insulting minister of war, and briefly imprisoned; traveled briefly to São Paulo, 1888, and began writing for *A Província de São Paulo* (Province of São Paulo); resumed military education at Praia Vermelha, 1889–92, degree in military engineering. Married, 1890. Worked as a government engineer, from 1892, traveling often on government commissions. Journalist for various newspapers, and covered the War of Canudos for *O Estado de São Paulo* (The state of São Paulo), 1897. Lived in São José do Rio Pardo, 1898–1901, where he wrote *Os Sertões* (*Rebellion in the Backlands*). Member, Brazilian Academy of Letters, 1903. Died (shot by his wife's lover) 15 August 1909.

Selected Writings

Essays and Related Prose

Os sertões, 1902; edited by Walnice Nogueira Galvão, 1985; as *Rebellion in the Backlands*, 1944, and as *Revolt in the Backlands*, 1947, translated by Samuel Putnam

Contrastes e confrontos, 1907; edited by Dermal de Camargo Montrê, 1967, and Araripe Júnior, 1975

À margem da história, 1909; edited by Dermal de Camargo Montrê, 1967
Canudos e inéditos, edited by Olímpio de Souza Andrade, 1967; revised, enlarged edition, as *Canudos e outros temas*, edited by Cyl Gallindo, 1994
Uma paraíso perdido: Reunião dos ensaios amazônicos, edited by Leandro Tocantins, 1976

Other writings: notebooks and letters.

Collected works edition: *Obra completa*, edited by Afrânio Coutinho, 2 vols., 1966.

Bibliographies

Reis, Irene Monteiro, *Bibliografia de Euclides da Cunha*, Rio de Janeiro: Ministry of Education and Culture, 1971
Sousa, J. Galante de, "Algumas fontes para o estudo de Euclides da Cunha," *Revista do Livro* 15, no. 4 (1959): 183–219
Venâncio Filho, Francisco, *Euclides da Cunha: Ensaio bio-bibliográphico*, Rio de Janeiro: Officina Industrial Graphica, 1931

Further Reading

Bernucci, Leopoldo M., *Historia de un malentendido: Un estudio transtextual de "La guerra del fin del mundo" de Mário Vargas Llosa*, New York: Lang, 1989
Booker, M. Keith, *Vargas Llosa Among the Postmodernists*, Gainesville: University Press of Florida, 1994
Levine, Robert M., *Vale of Tears: Revisiting the Canudos Massacre in Northeastern Brazil*, Berkeley: University of California Press, 1992
Reale, Miguel, *Face oculta de Euclides da Cunha*, Rio de Janeiro: Topbooks, 1993
Vargas Llosa, Mário, *A Writer's Reality*, Syracuse, New York: Syracuse University Press, 1990; London: Faber, 1991
Wasserman, Renata R. Mautner, "Mário Vargas Llosa, Euclides da Cunha, and the Strategy of Intertextuality," *PMLA* 108, no. 3 (1993): 460–73
Williams, Raymond Leslie, *Mário Vargas Llosa*, New York: Ungar, 1986

Curtius, Ernst Robert

German, 1886–1956

In his magisterial study *Europäische Literatur und lateinisches Mittelalter* (1948; *European Literature and the Latin Middle Ages*), Curtius collected many of his important essays and articles written during nearly 30 years of philological research. This book made him famous among both medievalists and early modern literary scholars. In it he discussed the cultural world of the Latin Middle Ages, the role of literature and education from the early through the late Middle Ages, rhetoric, *topoi* or topics, the function of the poetic figure of goddess Natura, the relationship of poetry and rhetoric, the *topos* of the ideal landscape, the concept of classicism, mannerism, the book as a symbol, the relevance of Dante for medieval literature, and the interplay between theology and poetry among Italian writers of the 14th and 15th centuries. In a voluminous appendix Curtius added a collection of other essays dedicated to themes such as devotional formulae and humility, jest and earnest in the Middle Ages, divine frenzy among poets, numerical composition, the relationship between

poetry and scholasticism, self-references of medieval poets, the cultural development of Spain in the 16th and 17th centuries, and, finally, essays on Calderón, Montesquieu, **Diderot**, and Horace.

Curtius was deeply influenced by classical schooling, and was an ardent defender of the cultural values representative of the European traditions rooted in classical antiquity. He was brought up as a Catholic, but later espoused Anglicanism. His religious orientation connected him with such philosophers and writers as Max Scheler, **T. S. Eliot**, Romain Rolland, **José Ortega y Gasset**, and **André Gide**. The same traditional outlook led Curtius to despise current political events and the trivialization of public culture during the 1930s. In his polemical **pamphlet** and essay *Deutscher Geist in Gefahr* (1932; German ideals in danger), he argued against the futile squabbles of the various political parties, seeing grave dangers for German culture resulting from the rise of the mass movement. Individualism and elitism, as represented by his role models Stefan George and Friedrich Gundolf, were much more to Curtius' liking. He also stayed away from narrow nationalism and defended the view of a European political unity with a broadly conceived culture shared by all European nations.

To reach a comprehensive understanding of this culture, the critic himself has to realize the highest educational goals possible and turn into a high priest for the rest of society. As Curtius argued, the essayist best represents this high priest, as demonstrated by the Romanticist **Friedrich Schlegel**, whom Curtius deeply admired. In Schlegel he also discovered a fighter for "culture," not simply for "civilization," the former supported by the national *Geist* (spirit), the latter by the masses. Nevertheless, Curtius strove for a cosmopolitan approach to culture, as he outlined in his study on T. S. Eliot (1927). From this perspective the writing of James Joyce, particularly *Ulysses*, was a true experiment in exploring the essence of human existence, similar to Homer's *Odyssey*. In this and other essays from this time Curtius hailed the idea of a cult of elite leaders steeped in European traditions. At the same time he rejected the positivistic and scientific method of analysis, instead favoring a form of intuition and the quality of affinities between great spirits as the only meaningful avenue toward true learning.

In a 1950 article on Balzac, Curtius discussed the mystical harmony of spiritual unity and the creative act of writing poetry – aspects academic critics cannot comprehend because of their lack of adequate methodologies with which to grasp a "seer's unity of vision." He expressed similar ideas in his important essay on Proust, which was first published in his book *Französischer Geist im neuen Europa* (1925; French spirit in the new Europe) and reprinted in *Französischer Geist im zwanzigsten Jahrhundert* (1952; French spirit in the 20th century). Following Proust in his concept of the "unique spiritual life," Curtius argued that receptivity and musical sensibility are the crucial vehicles for a profound perception of art and the truths of life.

At a time of great political, military, and economic pressure on Germany after World War I, Curtius struggled hard to overcome the cultural differences between France and Germany and to reveal in his many essays and articles the common historical roots connecting both countries. Latinity and the world of classical antiquity were for him the foundation of the entire European culture, a shared heritage that, properly understood, should overcome modern conflicts and nationalistic tensions.

Despite Curtius' efforts to awaken his contemporaries to the values of humanism based on classical learning, the trends of his time were against him. In *Deutscher Geist in Gefahr* he attacked the new barbarism of the National Socialists and the general decline of cultural values. In particular, he challenged the suddenly fashionable view of Charlemagne as the first perpetrator who alienated the Germanic world from its indigenous values and allowed Christianity and Roman culture to enter the minds of his people. Curtius desperately stressed the European orientation of the emperor and the absolute importance of classical antiquity for the emergence of medieval and Renaissance civilization on North European soil.

On the other hand, Curtius attacked the rise of new schools of thinking and new academic disciplines such as sociology because, as he saw it, they engendered nothing but useless knowledge, whereas traditional humanism would be the only trustworthy guarantor for the survival of culture. The study of the past, in particular of the Middle Ages, would provide modern students with an instrument to grasp both their origins and their present. But Curtius differentiated here, since the study of Greek culture was in such a decline that there was no possibility of its revival in the schools. Instead, the world of Rome and the Middle Ages based on the Latin language promised hope for the future.

Ernst Troeltsch's criticism of historicism, A. J. Toynbee's historical studies, and **Jacob Christoph Burckhardt**'s concept of universal truths and ideals all deeply influenced Curtius' essays. Nevertheless, he carved his own approach to history in his many articles and essays published during the 1930s and 1940s in which he explored the relevance of medieval Latin literature, comparing it with texts from classical antiquity and the postmedieval world. Curtius firmly believed in the importance of medieval Latin writings from which the modern reader could gain profound insights into the basic aspects of life. The study of the Latin Middle Ages, which for him lasted from the 8th through the 18th century, became a struggle for the preservation of Western culture on a large scale.

Curtius repeatedly voiced his conviction that only a solid familiarity with medieval Latin and a great concern for the detailed facts of medieval culture could provide a firm foundation for any philological study of that past. With these two tools Curtius fought against the speculative nature of the so-called "Geistesgeschichte" (history of ideas), a methodology aiming for a broad picture of past cultures, taking into account the various forms of cultural expression. Yet Curtius himself followed the school of Carl Jung in many respects, rejecting art history as an elusive academic subject.

Many of Curtius' essays became the basis for chapters in his famous monograph *European Literature and the Latin Middle Ages*, which stirred up academic disciplines for many years to come. In particular his perception of *topoi* as deciding elements in medieval literature was heavily attacked, as was his exclusive focus on Roman heritage, omitting the important Jewish, Arabic, Celtic, and Slavic influences on medieval Europe. Moreover, as critics pointed out, Curtius paid little attention to lyric poetry and the drama.

Nevertheless, Curtius' essays continue to be seminal interpretations despite their denial of the historical individuality of particular periods. His belief in a *Zeitgeist* was highly provocative, while also demonstrating the superior quality of his essayistic writing. Many of his views may no longer be fully accepted today, but as essays they preserve their historical value, not to speak of their importance as scholarly landmarks.

ALBRECHT CLASSEN

Biography

Born 14 April 1886 in Thann. Traveled widely throughout Europe during his formative years. Studied Sanskrit and comparative literature at the University of Berlin, 1904–11, Ph.D. Traveled to Rome, 1912, where he met Romain Rolland. Privatdozent, 1913, and associate professor, 1914–20, University of Bonn; chair of philology, University of Marburg, 1920–24, and University of Heidelberg, from 1924; chair of Romance philology, University of Bonn, from 1929. Died in Rome, 19 April 1956.

Selected Writings

Essays and Related Prose

Französischer Geist im neuen Europa, 1925
Die französische Kultur, eine Einführung, 1930; as *The Civilization of France*, translated by Olive Wyon, 1932
Deutscher Geist in Gefahr, 1932
Europäische Literatur und lateinisches Mittelalter, 1948; as *European Literature and the Latin Middle Ages*, translated by Willard R. Trask, 1953
Kritische Essays zur europäischen Literatur, 1950; enlarged edition, 1954; as *Essays on European Literature*, translated by Michael Kowal, 1973
Französischer Geist im zwanzigsten Jahrhundert, 1952
Gesammelte Aufsätze zur romanischen Philologie, 1960
Büchertagebuch, 1960
Kosmopolis der Wissenschaft: Ernst Robert Curtius und das Warburg Institut: Briefe, 1928–1953 und andere Dokumente, edited by Dieter Wuttke, 1989

Other writings: books on French literature, and correspondence (including with André Gide, **Charles Du Bos**, and Valery Larbaud). Also translated works by Gide, Jorge Guillén, William Goyen, and *The Wasteland* by T. S. Eliot.

Bibliography

Richards, Earl Jeffrey, *Modernism, Medievalism and Humanism: A Research Bibliography on the Reception of the Works of Ernst Robert Curtius*, Tübingen: Niemeyer, 1983

Further Reading

Berschin, Walter, and Arnold Rothe, editors, *Ernst Robert Curtius: Werk, Wirkung, Zukunftsperspektiven*, Heidelberg: Winter, 1989
Christmann, Hans Helmut, *Ernst Robert Curtius und die deutschen Romanisten*, Mainz: Akademie der Wissenschaften und der Literatur, and Stuttgart: Steiner, 1987
Evans, Arthur R., in *On Four Modern Humanists: Hofmannsthal, Gundolf, Curtius, Kantorowicz*, edited by Evans, Princeton, New Jersey: Princeton University Press, 1970: 85–145
Forster, L., "Ernst Robert Curtius Commemorated," *New Comparisons* 4 (1987): 164–72
Freundesgabe für Ernst Robert Curtius zum 14. April 1956, Berne: Francke, 1956

Godman, Peter, "The Ideas of Ernst Robert Curtius and the Genesis of ELLMA," in *European Literature and the Latin Middle Ages* by Curtius, Princeton, New Jersey: Princeton University Press, 1990: 599–653

Hoege, Dirk, *Kontroverse am Abgrund: Ernst Robert Curtius und Karl Mannheim*, Frankfurt-on-Main: Fischer, 1994

Lange, Wolf-Dieter, editor, *In Ihnen begegnet sich das Abendland: Bonner Vorträge zur Erinnerung an ERC*, Bonn: Bouvier, 1990

Theis, Raimund, *Auf der Suche nach dem besten Frankreich: Zum Briefwechsel von Ernst Robert Curtius mit André Gide und Charles Du Bos*, Frankfurt-on-Main: Klostermann, 1984

D

Dalin, Olof von

Swedish, 1708–1763

Olof von Dalin's name is preserved in Swedish history with something of a halo above it. He was not only the first author of weekly and monthly periodicals in Sweden, but was the founder of the important moral weekly in Sweden, *Then Swänska Argus* (The Swedish Argus), which enjoyed an overwhelming success and great popularity during the two years it appeared. Credit for issuing the first moral weekly goes to the brothers Carl and Edvard Carleson with their important journal *Sedolärande Mercurius* (Didactic Mercury), which appeared between June 1730 and October 1731. Begun anonymously in December 1732, *Argus* may have been founded to fill the gap left when the widely-read Carleson brothers' journal ceased publishing. The public may have been surprised by the change, but they took to the *Argus* enthusiastically.

The *Argus* was actually an offspring – even an imitation – of the British weeklies the *Tatler* and *Spectator* of **Addison** and **Steele**, and sometimes published translated material from the British periodicals. The original material appears to have been written by one person, though many found it hard to believe that an unknown young man like Dalin could be the author of such a sophisticated and enlightened periodical. According to Greek mythology, the name Argus signifies a vigilant observer. Dalin not only proved to have a sharp eye, he also wielded his pen with flair and wrote on many subjects satirically – yet cautiously too, as befitted the times. He did not allow himself seriously to satirize the church or the monarchy; nonetheless, his writings about the character of Swedish clergymen managed to be both negatively critical and positively descriptive.

Like the British periodicals, the Swedish *Argus* was a champion of the Enlightenment and aimed to raise the level of culture in Sweden. Several subjects of concern to Addison and Steele – such as literary standards and social behavior – were also considered in the *Argus*. While Dalin's essays were hardly original or unusual in style, nonetheless, as Ingemar Algulin explains in *A History of Swedish Literature* (1989), "their significance lies in Dalin's ability to transfer the ideas to Swedish conditions and to fit the Swedish language to the demands of the genre: a realistic depiction of society, a nimble and satirical analysis of customs and societal conditions, an enlightening, effective discussion of ideas. *Then Swänska Argus* marks the beginning of a new period in the development of the Swedish language through its realism, its clear form and its effective means of expression."

After its demise in December 1734, the *Argus* was sorely missed. Although the journal was of lasting importance and influence in Sweden, it did not evoke imitations. Nor did Dalin attempt to resurrect it or replace it with other journals; instead he turned to poetry and drama, and later produced the allegorical tale *Sagan om hästen* (1740; The tale of the horse), in which he relates the history of Sweden through the eyes of a horse. His popularity, begun with the *Argus*, accelerated; he was a favorite at court and in 1751 he was ennobled. However, his position *vis-à-vis* the Swedish court was not secure and he eventually lost his favored status.

Although Dalin was a champion of modern Swedish, he was not without connections to classical literature. He often cited classical sources: Plautus, Hesiod, Horace, Boileau, and numerous others. Thoroughly grounded in the classics, he was of the old school of the 18th century, which made use of antiquity's literary models. **La Bruyère** had the greatest influence of any foreign writer besides the British on Dalin. Dalin said of La Bruyère that despite occasionally "losing himself," his lively **character sketch**es were invaluable.

While Dalin did occasionally write **satiric essays** on historical subjects, none was as sophisticated and widely read as his *Argus*.

P. M. MITCHELL

Biography

Born 29 August 1708 in Vinberg. Studied at the University of Lund, 1721. Visited Stockholm, 1723, and moved there, 1727, where he was a tutor to various families. Founder and principal contributor, *Then Swänska Argus*, 1732–34. Tutor to the crown prince (later Gustaf III), 1750. Ennobled, 1751. Associated with the salon of Queen Lovisa Ulrika. Tried for political intrigue: acquitted, but banned from the court, 1756–59. Died in Stockholm, 12 August 1763.

Selected Writings

Essays and Related Prose

Then Swänska Argus, 104 nos., December 1732–December 1734; edited by Bengt Hesselman and M. Lamm, 3 vols., 1910–19; selections translated by W. H. Carpenter, in *Warner's Library of the World's Best Literature*, vol. 10, 1917: 4278–84

Other writings: two plays, the historical allegory *Sagan om hästen* (1740), the epic poem *Svenska Friherten* (1742), and a four-volume history of Sweden.

Further Reading
Hillman, Rolf, *Svensk prosastil under 1700-talet: Dalin, Linné, gustaviansk talekonst*, Stockholm: Läromedelsförlaget (Svenska Bokförlaget), 1970

Warburg, Karl Johan, *Olof Dalin: Hans life och gerning: Litterturhistorisk Avhandling*, Stockholm: Norstedt, 1884

Wikander, Ruth, *Studier över stil och språk i Dalins Argus*, Uppsala: Appelberg, 1924

Darío, Rubén
Nicaraguan, 1867–1916

Critics and editors of the Latin American essay usually include Nicaraguan Rubén Darío in their survey of this genre in Spanish America. Darío is best remembered, however, as a poet who knitted his craft into standard, well-defined structures in verse, applying and enriching rhyme rules available in Spanish as no one had done before. *Cantos de vida y esperanza* (1905; Songs of life and hope) is among his most famous collections of verse. He is also recognized for his short stories, some of which are examples of the fantastic, a subgenre dominated by the masters of the Americas such as the U.S. writer Edgar Allan Poe and Argentines **Jorge Luis Borges** and Julio Cortázar.

However, Darío's creativity challenged the rules by skillfully mixing subgenres in what critics have called prose poems, which he published along with versified compositions in *Azul* (1888; Blue), the collection that propelled him to literary stardom. As a consequence, his prose has been the subject of conflicting interpretations. For the novice reader, the titles of his collections are deceptive; for example, *Prosas profanas* (1896; Profane prose) is composed of standard poetic composition using orthodox metrics.

Darío's essayistic production can be divided into at least three distinct categories. The best known takes the form of standard literary criticism as well as highly personalized literary portraits of outstanding figures and the subjects of his artistic admiration. The second category can be considered journalism and is composed of distinctively personal and impressionistic columns resulting from his travels in the United States, Latin America, and Europe. The third is unique pieces in the form of an autobiography and a long essay in which he narrates his return to his native country.

Most of Darío's literary comments meet the canonical expectations of the genre and reveal his innate skills. They are dispersed in numerous literary journals, as **prefaces** to several of his best-known books of poetry, and collected in anthologies such as *Los raros* (1896; The rare ones). In these pieces Darío is semantically and lexically precise in his use of language, displays strong cultural sensitivity, and is extremely opinionated. Most of the linguistic characteristics of his best-known poems in the tradition of *modernismo* are also revealed in his literary comments. Musical tones, baroque variations, and an overwhelming richness of vocabulary and syntactic structures often appear in his literary articles.

It is ironic that Darío himself had little respect for what has become his best-known writing besides his poetry. His articles published in newspapers, especially those commissioned by *La Nación* (The nation) of Buenos Aires, are among the most impressive generated in Spanish American literature. Darío labeled this task "el trabajo diario y preciso y fatal" (daily, precise, and fatal work), a characterization frequently made by others who have had to earn a living as journalists; however, in Darío's case his journalism had no discernible negative impact on his poetic craft (for which he was paid nothing). The journalistic genre that best applies to Darío is the freestyle *crónica*, a hybrid of reportage and informative column pieces. In his case, as well as in the journalistic ventures of other established Spanish and Latin American writers, the presence of his voice is paramount, constituting the trademark of the pieces. Still relevant are his lively turn-of-the-century commentaries on post-'98 Spain in *España contemporánea* (1901; Contemporary Spain), in which he shows increasing awareness of that country's regional and social differences, its rich multilingual cultural heritage, and its search for a new identity as it would be expressed by the Generation of 1898. Several Latin American settings (especially Argentina and Chile, where he resided) became the center of his attention, as did different aspects of the United States, inter-American relations, Italy, and France. In most cases, these articles still reveal a freshness in their analysis and point of view.

A third variation came in the form of personal "artistic prose," timeless essays loaded with commentaries on local customs and less anchored in sentimental diversions; this approach is mostly reserved for his autobiographical pieces. *La vida de Rubén Darío escrita por él mismo* (1915; The life of Rubén Darío as written by himself) is a short, meticulous document, a fine example of autobiography as a variation of the essay. The use of journalistic leads at the beginning of each chapter captures the attention of readers just as it does in his best poems. *El viaje a Nicaragua* (1909; Travel to Nicaragua), mixed with poems under the subheading *Intermezzo tropical*, is a narrative essay, a hybrid of memoirs and journalism, full of personal impressions as well as information and commentary on local mores.

Apart from his standard prose writing, some of Darío's best poems have essayistic qualities. Because of the intimacy between political ideas and the evolution of the essay in Latin America, these poems, as "essays in verse," a common subgenre in Latin American literature, were milestones in the changing attitudes concerning Latin America's search for cultural and political identity, and the use of the United States as a model. Historians of diplomatic and inter-American relations admire these works not so much for their lyricism as for the ideas expressed in them. Three of these poems are classics: "Oda a Roosevelt" (1904; Ode to Roosevelt), "A Colón" (1892; To Columbus), and "Salutación al Aguila" (1906; Salutation to the eagle). They are among the most used and abused documents by politicians, historians, and other essayists in discussing the Latin American perception of and relationship with the U.S. With these poems Darío, along with other *modernista* masters such as Cuba's **José Martí** and Uruguay's **José Enrique Rodó**, ushered in a new era in Spanish American literature and intellectual history.

JOAQUÍN ROY

Biography
Born Félix Rubén García Sarmiento, 18 January 1867 in Metapa (now Ciudad Darío), Nicaragua. Worked for newspapers in Santiago, Valparaíso, and Buenos Aires, from age 14; correspondent

for Latin American papers in various parts of Latin America, including *La Nación*, Buenos Aires, from 1889, and in Paris and Madrid. Served Guatemala in various diplomatic and representative functions. Married Rafaela Contreras, 1890 (died, 1892): one son. Married (under duress) Rosario Murillo, 1893. Colombian consul to Argentina, 1893–94. Cofounder, *Revista de América* (American review), Buenos Aires, 1896. Long liaison with Francisca Sánchez, from 1899: one son (two other children died in infancy). Traveled in Europe, from 1900; Nicaraguan consul to France, 1903–07. Died (of cirrhosis of the liver) in León, Nicaragua, 6 February 1916.

Selected Writings

Essays and Related Prose
Los raros, 1896
España contemporánea, 1901
Peregrinaciones, 1901
La caravana pasa, 1902
Tierras solares, 1904; edited by Noel Rivas, 1991
Parisiana, 1907
El viaje a Nicaragua: Intermezzo tropical (travel writing), 1909
Letras, 1911
Todo al vuelo, 1912
La vida de Rubén Darío escrita por él mismo, 1915
El mundo de los sueños: Prosas póstumas, 1917
Alfonso XIII, y Sus primeras notas, 1921
Rubén Darío periodista (selection), 1964
Escritos dispersos de Rubén Darío (recogidos de periódicos de Buenos Aires), edited by Pedro Luis Barca, 1968
El mundo de los sueños (selected essays), edited by Ángel Rama, 1973
El modernismo y otros ensayos, edited by Iris M. Zavala, 1989

Other writings: poetry (including the collections *Azul*, 1888; *Prosas profanas y otros poemas*, 1896; *Cantos de vida y esperanza*, 1905), three novels, short stories, and two works of autobiography.

Collected works editions: *Obras completas*, edited by Rubén Darío Sánchez, 22 vols., 1917–19, Alberto Ghiraldo and Andrés González-Blanco, 21 vols., 1923–29, and M. Sanmiguel Raimúndez, 5 vols., 1950–55.

Bibliographies

Greco, Arnold Armand del, *Repertorio bibliográfico del mundo de Rubén Darío*, New York: Las Américas, 1969
Jirón Terán, José, *Bibliografía activa de Rubén Darío*, Managua: Ministry of Culture, 1981
Woodbridge, Hensley C., *Rubén Darío: A Selective Classified and Annotated Bibliography*, Metuchen, New Jersey: Scarecrow Press, 1975

Further Reading

Ellis, Keith, *Critical Approaches to Rubén Darío*, Toronto: University of Toronto Press, 1974
Ingwersen, Sonya A., *Light and Longing: Silva and Darío: Modernism and Religious Heterodoxy*, New York: Lang, 1986
Jrade, Cathy Login, *Rubén Darío and the Romantic Search for Unity: The Modernist Recourse to Esoteric Tradition*, Austin: University of Texas Press, 1983
Reyes Huete, Alejandro, *Darío en su prosa*, Granada, Nicaragua: Editorial Hospicio, 1960
Rodríguez-Hernández, Raúl, "*Los raros*: La otra estética modernista de Rubén Darío," *Texto-Crítico* 14, no. 38 (January–June 1988): 51–58
Schick Gutiérrez, René, *Rubén Darío y la política*, Managua: Editorial Nicaraguense, 1966
Schräder, Ludwig, "Rubén Darío, crítico literario en *Los raros*," in *El ensayo y la crítica literaria en Latinoamérica*, Toronto: University of Toronto Press, 1970: 95–99
Watland, Charles Dutton, *Poet-Errant: A Biography of Rubén Darío*, New York: Philosophical Library, 1965

Darwin, Charles
British, 1809–1882

Charles Darwin's *Journal of Researches* (1839), written during the five-year global voyage of the HMS *Beagle*, and his larger studies, primarily *On the Origin of Species* (1859) and *The Descent of Man* (1871), belong to an era in which travel writing, autobiography, literary allusions, scientific observation, and natural philosophy could still be combined in the same work. In this light, Darwin's fusing of discursive genres as a means of observing and classifying places him firmly in the Baconian empiricist tradition, a tradition codified by the great 18th-century skeptics. Darwin's ingenious use of the hypothetical-deductive method, with its presuppositions and mediated introspection, received energy from the essay form, which had since **Bacon** been pressed into the service of natural philosophy. **Montaigne**'s depiction of the essay as a kind of blueprint of cognition – or as **Theodor W. Adorno**'s later description of the form as the mimetic representation of "man thinking" – helps to explain why much of Darwin's work seems essayistic even when it fails to conform fully to the conventions of the genre. As a record of cognition, the essay is conducive to science's deductive analysis, even as the essay's open form and resistance to closure dovetail nicely with the Enlightenment ideal (embodied in both **Diderot** and William Smellie's encyclopedia projects) that each empirical study become a stepping stone to further reflection, observation, and finally greater knowledge. In this tradition, then, taken together, Darwin's monographs and essays represent a single persuasive argument for the mutability of plant and animal species throughout history, a unity of thought that represents a major turning point in the history and philosophy of natural science. Thus, through deductive reasoning and associative analysis, Darwin looked beyond specific historical events and particular species in an attempt to formulate a larger world picture of organic history.

Darwin was the heir to Enlightenment naturalism, and his works register the continued evolution of a new form of personal and historical narration, a narration generated after the Western intellectual tradition broke free in the early modern period from the fetters of the Platonic/Aristotelian theories of knowledge. In essence, the essay is the form this new narration takes when the intellectual tradition makes a major shift in perception from a theory of *ontic logos*, a belief that the external world announces its own truths to the revolutionary understanding of knowledge as a representational construct that becomes dominant with Descartes and Locke. That is, ideas (*ontic*) for Plato (in an immaterial realm) or forms for Aristotle (in the material realm) are not just objects waiting to be perceived and valuated, but rather are self-manifesting sources of light (*logos*). In contrast, the Cartesian/Lockean theory of knowledge places the valuation of the object solely with the subject. Thus, before we can begin to understand the reason for the compelling form Darwin's great **treatises** take, much less understand natural philosophy's (or science's) collusion with the essay form, we need to understand how profoundly the New Science, with its empirical basis, influenced Western intellectual tradition.

The essay had colluded with science since Bacon (following Galileo's precedent) made the account of scientific knowledge representational. According to this modern model, to understand reality is to have a correct representation of ideas and fundamental principles. In the well-known phrase from a letter to Gibieuf (19 January 1642), Descartes writes that he is "certain that I can have no knowledge of what is outside me except by means of the ideas I have within me." Implicit here is the demise of a Platonic self-revealing reality, or realm of ideas; now reality is constructed, not received. Knowledge is not only personalized in the sense that it is the product of self-examination, but it is also personalized by the language of the subject, recorded, as it is, in the first person. But for Descartes and his 18th- and 19th-century scientific heirs, representations have to be ordered through a chain of deductively connected perceptions. Descartes perhaps theorizes this causal order most effectively in the *Discours de la méthode* (1637; *Discourse on Method*), where he tells us to break down our perceptions into parts and then to connect those disparate parts, "assuming an order, even if a fictitious one, among those which do not follow a natural sequence relative to one another." Darwin articulated precisely this methodological model in his **journals** of the late 1830s. Facts, he argued, are meaningless unless ordered by a coherent theory; a theory is useless unless it unites several significant facts; and a new theory is pointless if it does not advance the work of its predecessors. Thus, the essay as the discursive vehicle for the process of cognition is as tenable for the theoretical work of Darwin as it was for Descartes.

The Cartesian model with its narrative component helps to explain why Darwin's scientific journals join empirical observation with classical and contemporary literary tropes and historical allusions, and mix critical analysis with personal anecdotes and autobiographical references. But Darwin's more literary style also owed something to the intervening rise of the essay in popular culture. On the discursive level, his conversational style of writing reflects the didactic essay tradition of **Joseph Addison** and **Richard Steele**. Such textual heteroglossia and stylistic hybridization between the social and **science essay** aside, however, Darwin's intellectual activity was, in and of itself, never a purely endogenous process. His *Beagle* journals, later synthesized into *Journal of Researches* and expanded and developed into the *Voyage of the Beagle*, refer to numerous conversations, scientific books, and articles, all adding to Darwin's explanatory theory of evolution and species dissemination. On the theoretical level, his work depended upon the larger scientific community, an innovation of the "new science," which later reached it apogee with the philosophical and scientific communities of Aufklärer in Germany, the Philosophes in France, and the Enlightenment thinkers in Britain and America. After all, Diderot, La Mettrie, **Kant**, **Goethe**, and Hegel, among others, were all moving toward an evolutionary world conception.

Darwin's study, then, drew upon the work of predecessors and contemporaries alike, a fact which helps to explain Alfred Russel Wallace's independent formulation of the theory of evolution in 1858. For example, in his journal for 7 September 1838, Darwin credits his scientific debt: "Seeing what Von Buch [Humboldt], G. St. Hilaire, and [Jean-Baptiste] Lamarck have written I pretend to no originality of ideas." Yet less than three weeks after this entry, Darwin's synthesis and extension of these earlier ideas led him to a recognition of the evolutionary significance of natural selection. This realization compelled him to revise his first monad theory, which had proposed that all species created from the monad die to make room for the progeny of new monads. The new theory accounted for the explanatory mechanism undergirding his later theory of evolution: a species lives on only if it gives rise to new species – that is, if it produces variations.

Among Darwin's and Wallace's other important predecessors in biology, Darwin also named Georges Buffon, his own grandfather, Erasmus Darwin, and later Gregor Mendel for his developments in genetics. In geology his thought built upon the work of Charles Lyell, James Hutton, and John Playfair. On the other end of the epistemological and temporal spectrum, there is no evidence that Darwin had read the presocratic natural philosopher Empedocles, who had introduced the ideas of species variation and adaptation, survival and extinction, a strong prelude to Darwin's and Wallace's explanatory mechanism for natural selection, or that Darwin was familiar with Lucretius, whose narrative poem *On the Nature of Things* accorded to humans a socio-cultural evolution that began in a cave. Nonetheless, given Darwin's repeated emphasis on his scientific debt, it is easy to underestimate the originality of his work and its impact on Western thought. Ultimately, what Newton had accomplished for the physical cosmos, Darwin accomplished for organic nature. While Newtonian theory set new parameters for the spatial dimensions of the universe, Darwinian theory established new parameters for the temporal dimension of nature, both the scale of its existence and the conceptual immensity of its qualitative organic transformations.

Because of Darwin's work with fossils and his association with the geological work of Charles Lyell, he not only added empirical evidence to organic evolution's (and thus speciation's) encroachment upon the Aristotelian and Thomist belief in the immutability of all animal types, but his work as a whole also reflected the 18th- and 19th-century change in imagination and in the sense of man's place in nature. Such a conceptual revolution in the sweeping geological framework of space, time, and transformation had a dramatic impact upon science and human subjectivity, all of which was imagined and explored through the discursive and elastic dimensions of the essay. To fully appreciate why *On the Origin of Species* proved explosively controversial, earning it the label "the book that shook the world," we need to consider the intellectual foundations of the world in which Darwin was born and his part in the overthrow of more than 2000 years of philosophical stasis.

By recovering Aristotelian natural philosophy for theological ends (in much the same way Augustine had appropriated the Platonic paradigm of the material and immaterial realm for Christian metaphysics), Thomas Aquinas extended the Aristotelian hold over natural philosophy for another millennium. Despite his study of reproductive methods as well as the growth and development of organisms, Aristotle (and later

Thomas Aquinas) grounded his view of life in the concept of the immutability of biological types, arguing that each organic kind has its own eternally fixed natural place in this hierarchical order of the living world depending on its degree of complexity and intelligence. Imbricated in religious dogma and a model of static metaphysics, natural philosophy sought, with few exceptions even during the Enlightenment, to support only literal interpretations of biblical narrative and causality. Even in the early modern period when science began to break free from the logic of Aristotelian syllogism, the Christian concept of the "Great Chain of Being," adapted from Aristotle's terrestrial continuum, dominated, legislating organic evolution as heretical even to science. Moreover, the rise of Deism in the 18th century had cooperated with the concept of Platonic/Aristotelian stasis to derail material and mechanistic science from inquiry that might have otherwise developed into earlier theories of organic evolution.

In primarily Protestant countries in the two centuries preceding Darwin, the design of nature – or on a grander scale, the universe – supported the existence of the supreme Deity. Alexander Pope's *Essay on Man* (1733–34) is the quintessential exemplar of just this: that in God's universe "All are but parts of one stupendous whole,/Whose body Nature is, and God the soul." But Deism means that Pope's harmonious natural order is not ontic like the Aristotelian/Thomist universal order. Rather it is interconnected in a kind of ecological economy that will presage Adam Smith's political and social theories: although each being has its own internal purpose, by serving itself, it serves the entire order. This is precisely why organic evolution was eventually to have such dramatic consequences for religious belief. The intellectual structures of Christianity had become inextricably tied to the design of nature. Thus by demonstrating that there could be a design without a Designer – not to mention a design with a dynamic, mutable, and organic pattern – Darwin undermined a theological superstructure that had grounded religious faith in a theory of moral sentiment derived (through the **Earl of Shaftesbury** and Francis Hutcheson) from a hybrid of Lockean rationalism and the humanism of the Cambridge Platonists.

Darwin's essayistic journals reflect the age's dawning of a real sense of geological time. Not since Copernicus' cosmological revolution had such new expanses been opened to the mind and imagination of philosophers. Certainly not since the demise of the geocentric universe in the 16th century did Judeo-Christian mysticism receive such a blow from scientific materialism. Significantly, in both historic instances the rent in the ecclesiastic fabric allowed for further secular inquiry. Temporal order played an important part in encouraging literal interpretations of biblical narrative since the Reformation, a trend marked by the gradual displacement of the archetype and allegory for the particular in 17th- and 18th-century narratives. Thus, it is not by chance that the essay and modern novel are products of modernity: the novel for its specificity of time, place, and character; the essay because nothing could be more particular than an infusion of the first person. Not only did the eons required for Darwin's mechanisms of natural selection and adaptation punch a hole in biblical time, but his study proved that these were eons altogether unnarrated, requiring a new kind of imaginative framework for what **Walter Benjamin** has called "homogenous, empty time."

Darwin's work also turned the scientific lens inward upon the unexplored dimensions of the human mind. His early theories about "primitive" man led to his chapter on "Instinct" in *Origin*, and a more sophisticated development of that thesis in *Descent of Man*, opening the way for the 20th century's abiding preoccuption with man's psychological motivations and social unconsciousness. Both **Marx** and **Freud** brought Darwin's study to its logical conclusion in the increasing perception of the human as a product of unconscious political, economic, and instinctual impulses of a naturalistic order.

GREGORY S. JACKSON

Biography

Charles Robert Darwin. Born 12 February 1809 in Shrewsbury, Shropshire. Studied at Dr. Butler's boarding school, 1818–25; medical studies at Edinburgh University, 1825–27; theology at Christ's College, Cambridge, 1828–31, B.A., 1831. Investigated biological, zoological, and geological phenomena throughout his life. Sailed to South America as a naturalist on board HMS *Beagle*, 1831–36; in ill health after return, and for the rest of his life could work only a few hours a day. Lived in London, 1837–42, and in Down, Kent, from 1842. Married Emma Wedgwood, 1839: six sons and four daughters (two children died young). Elected to the Royal Society, 1839. Awards: Royal Society Medal, 1853; Copley Medal, 1864; Royal College of Physicians Daly Medal, 1879; honorary degrees from four universities. Died in Down, Kent, 19 April 1882.

Selected Writings

Essays and Related Prose
Letters on Geology, 1835
Journal and Remarks, 1832–1836 (on his voyage on the *Beagle*), 1839; as *Journal of Researches into the Geology and Natural History of the Various Countries Visited by HMS Beagle*, 1839; edited by Gavin de Beer, 1959; as *Diary of the Voyage of the Beagle*, edited by Nora Barlow, 1933, Millicent E. Selsam, 1959, Leonard Engel, 1962, Richard Darwin Keynes, 1988, and Janet Browne and Michael Neve, 1989
On the Origin of Species by Natural Selection, 1859; edited by J. W. Burrow, 1968
The Descent of Man, and Selection in Relation to Sex, 2 vols., 1871; several subsequent revised editions
The Foundations of the Origin of Species: Two Essays Written in 1842 and 1844, edited by Francis Darwin, 1909
The Darwin Reader, edited by Marston Bates and Philip S. Humphrey, 1957
Evolution and Natural Selection, edited by Bert James Loewenberg, 1959
Darwin for Today: The Essence of His Works, edited by Stanley Edgar Hyman, 1963
The Essential Darwin, edited by Mark Ridley, 1987; as *The Darwin Reader*, 1987
The Portable Darwin, edited by Duncan M. Porter and Peter W. Graham, 1993

Other writings: many scientific works (on coral reefs, mold, earthworms, barnacles, plants, and other subjects), journals, an autobiography, and correspondence (collected in *The Correspondence*, 9 vols., 1985–94 [incomplete]).

Collected works editions: *Works*, 15 vols., 1910; *Works* (Appleton Edition), 18 vols., reprinted 1972; *The Works*, edited by Paul H. Barrett and R. B. Freeman, 29 vols., 1986–89; *The Darwin CD-Rom*, 1992.

Bibliography

Freeman, Richard B., *The Works of Charles Darwin: An Annotated Bibliographical Handlist*, London: Dawson, 1965; revised edition, 1977

Further Reading

Culler, A. Dwight, "The Darwinian Revolution and Literary Form," in *The Art of Victorian Prose*, edited by George Levine and William Madden, New York: Oxford University Press, 1968

Descartes, René, *Philosophical Letters*, Oxford: Clarendon Press, 1970; Minneapolis: University of Minnesota Press, 1981

Descartes, René, *Discourse on Method*, Notre Dame, Indiana: University of Notre Dame Press, 1994 (original French edition, 1637)

Friedrich, Hugo, *Montaigne*, Berkeley: University of California Press, 1991 (original German edition, 1949)

Gibson, Walker, "Behind the Veil: A Distinction Between Poetic and Scientific Language in Tennyson, Lyell, and Darwin," *Victorian Studies* 2 (1958–59): 60–68

Levine, George, "Darwin Among the Critics," *Victorian Studies* 30 (Winter 1987): 253–60

Morton, Peter, *The Vital Science: Biology and the Literary Imagination*, London and Boston: Allen and Unwin, 1984

Young, Robert, *Darwin's Metaphor: Nature's Place in Victorian Culture*, Cambridge and New York: Cambridge University Press, 1985

Davies, Robertson

Canadian, 1913–1995

Robertson Davies' accomplishments as a dramatist and novelist tend to overshadow his achievements with the essay, but he wrote a great many essays and was a master of the form. Davies' essays profit from their author's rare but happy combination of, on the one hand, extensive learning coupled with formidable intelligence and, on the other, a fine sense of humor. Opinionated, sometimes defiantly nonconformist, Davies was never dull, and, in addition to the intrinsic interest of their subjects, his essays hold the added attraction of revealing one of the most fascinating and memorable literary personalities of our time.

Although he never abandoned the form completely, Davies wrote most of his essays between 1940 and the mid-1960s, when he turned from journalism to academic life as Master of Massey College at the University of Toronto and began devoting his creative energy increasingly to writing novels. The 1940s and 1950s were extremely busy years for Davies. He was extensively involved in Canadian theater and was widely acknowledged as his country's leading dramatist, and he also turned out three very entertaining novels. His main work, however, was in journalism. In addition to freelancing vigorously, Davies edited and later managed the Peterborough *Examiner* and wrote columns for his own paper, *Saturday Night*, and, from 1959 to 1963, the Toronto *Star*. Most of the material in Davies' columns belongs in one of two general classes: essays on the arts, often reviews or essays growing out of reviews of books or theatrical performances, and the discursive, more oblique cultural criticism he delivered through the humorous persona of Samuel Marchbanks.

The Marchbanks columns appeared between 1943 and 1953, first in Davies' Peterborough *Examiner*, and gradually, as the character caught on with the reading public, in other Canadian newspapers. Somewhat revised, the Marchbanks writings reached a wider audience in *The Diary of Samuel Marchbanks* (1947), *The Table Talk of Samuel Marchbanks* (1949), and *Samuel Marchbanks' Almanack* (1967). *The Papers of Samuel Marchbanks* (1985) brought together material from the earlier books with previously uncollected writings. While Marchbanks was initially conceived of as a vehicle for humor, he shared Davies' love of reading, his delight in arcane subjects, and his impatience with cultural narrowness; in time he came to express many of Davies' personal views. The Marchbanks persona also provided Davies with a means of perfecting a writing style that would have seemed more at home in an 18th-century periodical than in a contemporary newspaper. Although the Marchbanks columns consist more of material related to the essay – short humorous sketches, diary entries, observations about human nature and society – than of essays proper, *Table Talk* at least can be thought of as a collection of genuine essays. While its individual pieces are rarely more than 300 words long, and many are written primarily for humorous effect, more than a few develop ideas that Davies himself takes very seriously. For example, "The man who writes only for the eye generally writes badly; the man who writes to be heard will write with some eloquence, some regard for the music of words, and will reach nearer to his reader's heart and mind" ("The Inner Voice"). In passages like this, we see the rhetorical balance, the emphatic, carefully placed repetition, and the sensitivity to the cadence of speech characteristic of Davies' own mature style.

Davies' essays on theater and books, particularly those that appeared in *Saturday Night* during his two terms as literary editor (first for a year and a half beginning in November 1940 and later from 1953 to 1959), played an important part in promoting discerning taste and cosmopolitan thinking in Canadian readers. Few were collected, however, until the success of his novels in the 1970s generated widespread interest in his ideas. Containing essays on characters, books, and other subjects he finds stimulating, *The Enthusiasms of Robertson Davies* (1979) demonstrates Davies' extensive, eclectic erudition. *The Well-Tempered Critic: One Man's View of Theatre and Letters in Canada* (1981) is aptly described by its title. Both collections were edited by Davies' biographer, Judith Skelton Grant. Davies himself gathered the pieces *One Half of Robertson Davies: Provocative Pronouncements on a Wide Range of Topics* (1977), a collection of speeches that were for the most part essays written to be read aloud. But the best and most personally revealing of Davies' essay collections came earlier. *A Voice from the Attic* (1960; published in Britain a year later as *The Personal Art: Reading to Good Purpose*) is directed to an audience of serious but nonspecialist readers which Davies terms "the clerisy." To Davies, "Curiosity, the free mind, belief in good taste, and belief in the human race are the marks of the clerisy, allied with a genuine love of literature, not as a manifestation of fashion, not as a substitute for life, but as one of the greatest of the arts, existing for the delight of mankind" ("The Shame of Brains"). It is in the "informed, rational, and intellectually adventurous individuality" ("Epilogue") of the clerisy that Davies sees the best hope for Western civilization.

Davies' own essays exemplify splendidly the qualities he values in his projected readers. His wisdom, clarity of thought, and wide learning are always much in evidence, but perhaps the most memorable characteristic of Davies' serious writing is its enthusiasm – the intense intellectual excitement with which he explores the diverse subjects that capture his imagination.

WILLIAM CONNOR

Biography
William Robertson Davies. Born 28 August 1913 in Thamesville, Ontario. Studied at Queen's University, Kingston, Ontario; Balliol College, Oxford, 1936–38, B.Litt., 1938. Teacher and actor, Old Vic Theatre School and Repertory Company, London, 1938–40. Married Brenda Mathews, 1940: three daughters. Literary editor, *Saturday Night*, Toronto, 1940–42 and 1953–59; editor, and columnist under the pseudonym Samuel Marchbanks, Peterborough *Examiner*, Ontario, 1942–63. Governor, Stratford Shakespeare Festival, Ontario, 1953–71. Professor, 1960–81, and Master of Massey College, 1963–81, University of Toronto. Elected to the Royal Society of Canada, 1967. Awards: many, including the Leacock Medal, 1955; Lorne Pierce Medal, 1961; Governor-General's Award, for fiction, 1973; World Fantasy Convention Award, for fiction, 1984; City of Toronto Book Award, 1986; Canadian Authors' Association Award, for fiction, 1986; Toronto Arts Lifetime Achievement Award, 1986; U.S. National Arts Club Medal of Honor, 1987 (first Canadian recipient); Molson Prize, 1988; Foundation for the Advancement of Canadian Letters Award, 1990; honorary degrees from 23 colleges and universities. Fellow, Balliol College, Oxford, 1986, and Trinity College, Toronto, 1987. Companion, Order of Canada, 1972; Fellow, Royal Society of Literature, 1984; Honorary Member, American Academy, 1981 (first Canadian elected). Died in Orangeville, Ontario, 4 December 1995.

Selected Writings

Essays and Related Prose
The Diary of Samuel Marchbanks, 1947
The Table Talk of Samuel Marchbanks, 1949
A Voice from the Attic: Essays on the Art of Reading, 1960; as *The Personal Art: Reading to Good Purpose*, 1961; revised edition, 1990
Samuel Marchbanks' Almanack, 1967
One Half of Robertson Davies: Provocative Pronouncements on a Wide Range of Topics, 1977
The Enthusiasms of Robertson Davies, edited by Judith Skelton Grant, 1979
The Well-Tempered Critic: One Man's View of Theatre and Letters in Canada, edited by Judith Skelton Grant, 1981
The Mirror of Nature (lectures), 1983
The Papers of Samuel Marchbanks (selections from earlier Marchbanks collections), 1985
Reading and Writing (lectures), 1993
The Merry Heart: Reflections on Reading, Writing, and the World of Books, 1997

Other writings: 11 novels (*The Salterton Trilogy*, 1951–58; *The Deptford Trilogy*, 1970–75; *The Cornish Trilogy*, 1981–88; *Murther and Walking Spirits*, 1991; *The Cunning Man*, 1994), a collection of ghost stories, 16 plays, a critical study of **Stephen Leacock**, and several books on the Stratford Shakespeare Festival.

Bibliography
Ryrie, John, *The Annotated Bibliography of Canada's Major Authors*, vol. 3, edited by Robert Lecker and Jack David, Downsview, Ontario: ECW Press, 1981: 57–280

Further Reading
Buitenhuis, Elspeth, *Robertson Davies*, Toronto: Forum House, 1972
Cluett, Robert, "Robertson Davies: The Tory Mode," *Journal of Canadian Studies* 12, no. 1 (February 1977): 41–46
Cockburn, Robert H., Introduction to *A Voice from the Attic* by Davies, Toronto: McClelland and Stewart, 1972: viii–xii
Grant, Judith Skelton, *Robertson Davies*, Toronto: McClelland and Stewart, 1978
Grant, Judith Skelton, *Robertson Davies: Man of Myth*, Toronto and New York: Viking, 1994
Peterman, Michael, *Robertson Davies*, Boston: Twayne, 1986

The Defence of Poesy
by Sir Philip Sidney, written c. 1580–82; published 1595

Member of a family that had risen to prominence under the Tudor monarchy, Sir Philip Sidney (1554–86) won admiration at an early age for his courtly skills and intellectual curiosity. His wide travel in continental Europe included diplomatic missions on behalf of Elizabeth I. He advocated support for the Protestant Netherlands in their military resistance to the rule of Catholic Spain. When an English force was sent to the Netherlands in 1585, Sidney was given command of a garrison, and died from wounds sustained in a military engagement.

Sidney's major writings probably belong to the period 1578–84, though none can be dated with certainty. *Arcadia*, a prose narrative interspersed with verse, combines chivalric romance, pastoral, comedy, and debate on ethics and politics. It survives in a complete earlier version and an unfinished expanded version. *Astrophil and Stella*, a cycle of 108 sonnets and 11 songs, is one of the first English adaptations of Petrarchan love poetry. By turns witty and tormented, it is a lightly disguised and no doubt fictionally embellished treatment of Sidney's thwarted love for Penelope Devereux, sister of the Earl of Essex.

The most likely date for the composition of the *Defence* is 1580–82. Like Sidney's other writings, it circulated only in manuscript during his lifetime, and was published by two separate printers in 1595 under the titles *Defence of Poesy* and *Apology for Poetry*. It is one of several English defenses against moralistic or philosophical attacks on poetry, drama, and music. One of these attacks, Stephen Gosson's *School of Abuse* (1579), was dedicated to Sidney and possibly prompted the writing of the *Defence*.

The *Defence* has the structure of a classical oration, a literary form much utilized in Renaissance education and later adopted in Milton's **Areopagitica** (1644). Rejecting the methodical order of a **treatise** and the fantastic elaboration of euphuism, the fashionable literary style of his day, Sidney adopts the varying voice of a public speaker. The *Defence* expounds ideas with clarity and concision; it wins over the reader through politeness and humor; it assails poetry's enemies with satirical caricature and impassioned rhetorical questions; it rises to a rhapsodic enthusiasm in praising poetry. The persona created by Sidney's style exhibits the *sprezzatura* of the Renaissance gentleman, in which seriousness and effort were masked by the appearance of ease and casualness.

In the theoretical part of Sidney's *Defence*, "poetry" means imaginative literature. His purpose is to defend creative writing, whether in verse or prose, against the ethical charges of falsehood and frivolity. Sidney's basic argument is that poetry feigns "notable images of virtues, vices, or what else" and thus provides "delightful teaching." In developing this argument he makes well-informed and quite sophisticated use of the ancient writers **Plato**, Aristotle, and Horace. He also draws on medieval doctrines and Italian Renaissance criticism.

From Aristotle comes Sidney's definition of poetry as "mimesis" or imitation. Imitation is not the copying of particulars but a generalized rendering, in which a particular action and characters are universally representative. For the means by which this imitation is achieved, Sidney adopts the language of Renaissance neoplatonism, which drew a parallel between the activity of God in creating nature and the activity of the human mind, able to "grow in effect another nature." Possibly on religious grounds, Sidney is reluctant to press the high claim that the poet has intuitive apprehension of an ideal world.

Sidney quotes from Horace's *Ars poetica* (**Poetic Art**) the view that the aim of poetry is "to teach and delight." The way these purposes work together is the central theme of the essay. The delightfulness of the poet's fiction and the vividness of his "speaking picture" are the source of his ability to move hearers or readers to virtue. In this ability the poet is superior to his main rivals in the enterprise of Renaissance humanism, the philosopher and the historian. The philosopher's teaching is too "abstract and general," while the historian's is too narrow, tied "to the particular truth of things and not to the general reason of things." The poet uniquely combines the strengths of the two: "he coupleth the general notion with the particular example."

Sidney's emphasis on the power of poetry to move readers to virtuous conduct, and in particular to military valor, is characteristic of the practically oriented Christian humanism of the northern European Renaissance. His lament over the shortcomings of contemporary English poetry shows a cultural nationalism that is also characteristic of the Renaissance. In his review of English poetry, as well as in his earlier discussion of the traditional poetic genres, Sidney drops his broad definition of poetry as fiction and adopts the more conventional definition of poetry as writing in verse. His criticisms of English poetry and drama are based on a more rigid neoclassical ideal of formal "correctness" than is found in the early part of the essay.

The prescriptions about style in the *Defence* are well applied in Sidney's other writings. The *Defence* criticizes English love poets "as men that had rather read lovers' writings . . . than that in truth they feel those passions, which easily (as I think) may be bewrayed [revealed] by that same forcibleness or *energia* (as the Greeks call it) of the writer." *Astrophil and Stella* is a brilliant exercise in *energia*, giving dramatic verisimilitude to Astrophil's passion. Sidney's application of the "teaching" power of poetry is more problematic. The *Defence* makes a sharp division between the representation of vicious characters who show "nothing that is not to be shunned" and virtuous characters who show "each thing to be followed." Such clearcut characters are rarely exhibited in Sidney's fictions, or in any fictions. This is a fact that the reader of the *Defence* can forget under the impact of Sidney's powerful advocacy.

Like most Renaissance writers on poetry, Sidney restates and reinterprets classical doctrines. Later Renaissance writings that seem to derive from the *Defence* may simply share the same sources. **Shelley**'s "A Defence of Poetry" (1821), an answer to Thomas Love Peacock's satirical *The Four Ages of Poetry* (1820), borrows Sidney's title, adopts many of his arguments, and develops his neoplatonic suggestions into a Romantic claim for the transcendent status of the imagination.

ANTHONY MILLER

See also Critical Essay

Editions

The Defence of Poesy, 1595; as *Apology for Poetry*, 1595; edited by Geoffrey Shepherd, 1965, Jan van Dorsten, 1966, and in *Selected Writings*, edited by Richard Dutton, 1987

Further Reading

Atkins, J. W. H., *English Literary Criticism: The Renascence*, London: Methuen, 1947

Barnes, Catherine, "The Hidden Persuader: The Complex Speaking Voice of Sidney's *Defence of Poetry*," *PMLA* 86 (1971): 422–27

Craig, D. H., "A Hybrid Growth: Sidney's Theory of Poetry in *An Apology for Poetry*," *English Literary Renaissance* 10 (1980): 183–201

DeNeef, A. Leigh, "Rereading Sidney's *Apology*," *Journal of Medieval and Renaissance Studies* 10 (1980): 155–91

Ferguson, Margaret W., *Trials of Desire: Renaissance Defenses of Poetry*, New Haven, Connecticut: Yale University Press, 1983

Hamilton, A. C., *Sir Philip Sidney: A Study of His Life and Works*, Cambridge and New York: Cambridge University Press, 1977

Hardison, O. B., Jr., "The Two Voices of Sidney's *Apology for Poetry*," *English Literary Renaissance* 2 (1972): 83–99

Heninger, S. K., Jr., *Sidney and Spenser: The Poet as Maker*, University Park: Pennsylvania State University Press, 1989

Kinney, Arthur F., "Parody and Its Implications in Sidney's *Defence of Poetry*," *Studies in English Literature 1500–1900* 12 (1972): 1–19

Miller, Anthony, "Sidney's *Apology for Poetry* and Plutarch's *Moralia*," *English Literary Renaissance* 17 (1987): 259–76

Myrick, Kenneth, *Sir Philip Sidney as a Literary Craftsman*, Cambridge, Massachusetts: Harvard University Press, 1965 (original edition, 1935)

Robinson, Forrest G., *The Shape of Things Known: Sidney's "Apology" in Its Philosophical Tradition*, Cambridge, Massachusetts: Harvard University Press, 1972

Rudenstine, Neil L., *Sidney's Poetic Development*, Cambridge, Massachusetts: Harvard University Press, 1967

Sinfield, Alan, "The Cultural Politics of the *Defence of Poetry*," in *Sir Philip Sidney and the Interpretation of Renaissance Culture*, edited by Gary F. Waller and Michael D. Moore, London: Croom Helm, and Totowa, New Jersey: Barnes and Noble, 1984

Defoe, Daniel

English, c. 1660–1731

The most prolific essayist of early 18th-century England, Daniel Defoe produced some 200 works of nonfiction prose in addition to close to 2000 short essays in periodical publications, several of which he also edited, such as *A Review of the Affairs of France*. Such profuse output earned for Defoe a contemptuous mention as "Restless Daniel" in Alexander Pope's

Dunciad (1728), but the energy and intelligence of the writing gained for Defoe an influential voice in public affairs from the end of the previous century until his death in 1731, spanning the reigns of William, Anne, and George I.

Defoe's first success as an essayist came in 1697–98, at the age of 37, with the publication of two **pamphlets** on the standing army controversy and a longer work, *An Essay upon Projects*, a collection of proposals for public ventures such as an academy for women, an institution for those born with mental defects, and an expanded national system of roads. Until this time he had published mainly verse pamphlets and concentrated on his business concerns; but after the success of these prose works – and the failure of his mercantile enterprises – he worked almost solely in nonfiction prose for the next two decades, and even after turning to fiction with *Robinson Crusoe* in 1719, remained prolific in nonfiction, producing in his last five years several of his most substantial and interesting volumes: *The Complete English Tradesman* (1725–27), *A Plan of the English Commerce* (1728), the economic geography *Atlas Maritimus* (1728), and two works involving the supernatural, *The Political History of the Devil* (1726) and *An Essay on the History and Reality of Apparitions* (1727). Much more than the novels, the nonfiction works provided Defoe his comfortable income.

Despite (or perhaps because of) this prodigious output, Defoe has until recently not held a secure place in the history of the essay, existing instead in the borderlands between the belletristic essay writing of **Addison**, **Swift**, and **Johnson**, on one side, and the anonymous ephemera of Grub Street, on the other. Certainly his work does not exhibit the self-exploration of **Montaigne**'s *Essais* (1580, 1588) or the timelessness of the commonplace topics of **Bacon**'s *Essayes* (1597, 1612, 1625); only Defoe's *A Tour Thro' the Whole Island of Great Britain* (1724–27) is widely recognized as having the aesthetic qualities of the *belles-lettres*. However, recent interest in the rhetorical nature of a wider range of nonfiction has prompted a new exploration of Defoe as a writer who used the flexibility and openness of the essay to investigate and shape the social life around him.

Defoe does share with Montaigne a notion of the essay as an informal and experimental kind of writing. When he uses the word "essay" in a title of a text (as he does a dozen times, e.g. *An Essay upon Publick Credit*, 1710, or *An Essay on the Late Storm*, 1704), its primary meaning is an experimental or initial attempt to treat a subject, only secondarily referring to the resulting text. There are several instances of this use of the word, as in Defoe's remark in the introduction to *An Essay upon Projects* that "If I have given an Essay towards any thing New, or made Discovery to advantage of any Contrivance now on foot, all Men are at liberty to make use of the Improvement." In the conclusion to the same work he refers to the essay as a kind of text but one defined only by a "Free and Familiar" language unconcerned with "Exactness of Style."

The informality and freedom of Defoe's essays, however, are in their style and tone, not in their structure. Despite the self-effacing tone of the introduction to *Upon Projects*, the individual essays proceed carefully, if casually, from an exposition of a public problem to a "Proposal" section that lays out the solution methodically, often in enumerated steps.

Likewise, the *Tour* combines an often casual description of landscapes and cityscapes with a meaningful narrative pattern, each essay following a trip out from London and back. The relaxed but consistent repetition of this pattern helps Defoe depict Britain as a regionally diverse but economically unified whole, with London as its heart. When he pauses to reflect on a vista of fine country houses or a once bustling town now desolate, it becomes not a Montaignean digression but simply another illustration of the theme of national growth and decay.

But in tone and style the essays seem thoroughly "Free and Familiar," and it is this aspect that readers have always found noteworthy. Most of Defoe's pronouncements on writing urge the use of "Language plain, artless, and true" for the aim of broad comprehension: "A man speaking to five hundred people, of all common and various capacities . . . should be understood by them all, in the same manner with one another, and in the same sense which the speaker intended to be understood" (*Tradesman*). Recent studies have discovered in Defoe's "plain style" an intriguing variety of figures of speech (especially irony and allegory) and levels of formality. But his essays are almost without exception conversational and accessible, and he is credited with being influential in the increasing use of the lower range of styles in 18th-century prose. Defoe's own style was inspired by a variety of sources: the plain style of Dryden and the Royal Society, the popular preaching style of Defoe's Presbyterian upbringing, and the premium upon familiar, unadorned prose among merchants.

The broader significance of Defoe's essays, however, lies in the remarkable range of his work. From his formative commercial beginnings he took a lasting admiration of the merchant, who through his trade "converses with all parts of the world" and builds his enterprises from what is at first "all project, contrivance, and invention" (*Upon Projects*). That Defoe used the essay as a form whose openness would allow both wide converse and the projector's focus on the present makes him a pivotal figure in the explosion of nonfiction, in both kind and quantity, for which the 18th century is still known.

STEPHEN M. ADAMS

Biography
Born Daniel Foe c. 1660 in London; used the name Defoe from c. 1703. Studied at Charles Morton's Academy, London. Hosiery manufacturer and commission merchant, early 1680s: went bankrupt, 1691. Married Mary Tuffley, 1684: two sons and five daughters. Involved in Duke of Monmouth's rebellion against James II, 1685. Associated with a brick and tile works in Tilbury: business failed, 1703; accountant to the commissioners of the glass duty, 1695–99. Convicted and jailed for seditious libel with *The Shortest Way with the Dissenters*, 1703. Political writer for Robert Harley, later Earl of Oxford, 1704–11; editor, *A Review of the Affairs of France, and of All Europe*, 1704–13, *Mercurius Politicus*, 1716–20, the *Manufacturer*, 1720, and the *Director*, 1720–21; contributor to periodicals published by Nathaniel Mist, from 1715. Died in London, 26 April 1731.

Selected Writings

Essays and Related Prose
An Essay upon Projects, 1697; facsimile reprint, 1969; as *Several Essays Relating to Academies*, 1700, and as *Essays upon Several Projects*, 1702

An Essay on the Late Storm, 1704
An Essay at Removing National Prejudices Against a Union with Scotland, 6 vols., 1706–07
An Essay upon Publick Credit, 1710
An Essay on the South Sea Trade, 1712
An Essay on the Treaty of Commerce with France, 1713
A Tour Thro' the Whole Island of Great Britain, 3 vols., 1724–27; edited by G. D. H. Cole, 2 vols., 1927, and Pat Rogers, 1971; abridged edition, 1989
The Complete English Tradesman, 2 vols., 1725–27; reprinted 1969
An Essay on the History and Reality of Apparitions, 1727; as *The Secrets of the Invisible World Disclosed; or, An Universal History of Apparitions*, 1728
The Shortest Way with the Dissenters and Other Pamphlets, 1927
A Review of the Affairs of France, and of All Europe, edited by Arthur Wellesley Secord, 22 vols., 1938; reprinted 1965; *Index* by William L. Payne, 1948; selection as *The Best of Defoe's Review*, edited by Payne, 1951
Selected Poetry and Prose, edited by Michael F. Shugrue, 1968
Selected Writings, edited by James T. Boulton, 1975
"The Manufacturer" (1719–1721); Together with Related Issues of "The British Merchant" and "The Weaver", facsimile reprint, 1978
The Versatile Defoe: An Anthology of Uncollected Writings, edited by Laura Ann Curtis, 1979

Other writings: novels (including *Robinson Crusoe*, 1719; *Moll Flanders*, 1722; *A Journal of the Plague Year*, 1722; *Roxana*, 1724), poetry, and many **tracts**, **pamphlets**, broadsides, and other journalism.

Bibliographies

Moore, John R., *A Checklist of the Writings of Daniel Defoe*, Hamden, Connecticut: Archon, 1971 (original edition, 1960, revised edition, 1961)
Peterson, Spiro, *Daniel Defoe: A Reference Guide, 1731–1924*, Boston: Hall, 1987
Stoler, John A., *Daniel Defoe: An Annotated Bibliography of Modern Criticism, 1900–1980*, New York: Garland, 1984

Further Reading

Backscheider, Paula R., *Daniel Defoe: Ambition and Innovation*, Lexington: University of Kentucky Press, 1986
Backscheider, Paula R., *Daniel Defoe: His Life*, Baltimore: Johns Hopkins University Press, 1989
Curtis, Laura, "A Rhetorical Approach to the Prose of Daniel Defoe," *Rhetorica* 11 (1993): 293–319
Furbank, P. N., and W. R. Owens, *The Canonisation of Daniel Defoe*, New Haven, Connecticut and London: Yale University Press, 1988
Novak, Maximillian E., *Economics and the Fiction of Daniel Defoe*, Berkeley: University of California Press, 1962
Novak, Maximillian E., *Defoe and the Nature of Man*, London: Oxford University Press, 1963
Richetti, John J., *Daniel Defoe*, Boston: Twayne, 1987
Rogers, Pat, "Literary Art in Defoe's *Tour*: The Rhetoric of Growth and Decay," *Eighteenth-Century Studies* 6 (1972–73): 153–85
Schellenberg, Betty A., "Imagining the Nation in Defoe's *A Tour Thro' the Whole Island of Great Britain*," *English Literary History* 62 (1995): 295–311
Schonhorn, Manuel, *Defoe's Politics: Parliament, Power, Kingship, and Robinson Crusoe*, Cambridge: Cambridge University Press, 1991

De Quincey, Thomas

British, 1785–1859

With **William Hazlitt** and **Charles Lamb**, Thomas De Quincey takes his place as one of the most influential and prolific essayists in Britain in the first half of the 19th century. His *Collected Writings* (1889–90) edited by David Masson comprises 14 volumes, and includes his autobiography, *Confessions of an English Opium Eater* (1822), a small number of short stories, the novel *Klosterheim* (1832), and a dissertation on David Ricardo's economic theory, *The Logic of Political Economy* (1844). By far his largest output, however, are his essays on topics ranging from philology to astronomy, from ancient history to political affairs, from literary reviews to works of political economy.

De Quincey's literary reputation, as the master of a lyrical and digressive prose style, was established through the *Confessions*, his first work, published initially in four parts in *London Magazine*. In it he told the story of his peripatetic, bohemian youth, alongside breathtaking accounts of his opium dream visions. In his lifetime his name came to be synonymous with a lavish and poetic prose style, named by himself as "impassioned prose," but also with an eccentricity and disorderliness held to be characteristic of an opium addict. Less well known is the fact that after the success of the *Confessions* he became a major contributor to the periodical press, notably for the Edinburgh magazines **Blackwood's** and *Tait's*, writing essays on a strikingly broad range of subjects. Although his astute but eccentric intelligence gave an unusual slant to many of the topics he dealt with, he nevertheless played a significant role in the dissemination of contemporary ideas to a more general reading public. He was an enthusiast for German idealist philosophy, and an early translator of **Kant** and of German Romantic fiction; he had an interest in contemporary linguistic scholarship, in Ricardian economic theory, in new developments in astronomy, and in the new historiography of Barthold Georg Niebuhr. De Quincey was an eccentric polymath and hack journalist, and his works amount to an uneven but unusually broad corpus.

Much of his best prose is to be found in his autobiographical writings: *Confessions*, and its sequel, *Suspiria de Profundis* (1845). The latter is a series of reminiscences from his infancy, interspersed with passages of a lyrical and mythic character, such as his short piece on the palimpsest, which for De Quincey acts as a metaphor for the human memory. It is significant that in his autobiographical works he lingers on his childhood and adolescence, playing into the Romantic fascination for the state of childhood as a period of enhanced sensitivity and creativity. His own recurrent documentation of his childhood years has been in part responsible for the somewhat anachronistic estimation of De Quincey as an English Romantic writer, rather than the Victorian he properly is: he published from the 1820s to the 1850s and, moreover, was based in Scotland rather than England. This misplacing of his work has been exacerbated by his early association with the Wordsworths. From 1809 for a period of about 11 years, De Quincey was part of the Wordsworth coterie, a close companion of Dorothy Wordsworth, and intensely involved with the Wordsworth children. Through Wordsworth he was made editor of the provincial newspaper, the *Westmorland Gazette* – an appointment which, although short-lived, launched his journalistic career. As relations with the Wordsworths soured, he accepted an invitation from John Wilson, editor of *Blackwood's*, to write for that journal, and eventually moved with his family permanently to Edinburgh in 1830. Notoriously impecunious, spending long periods in a debtors' sanctuary, De Quincey was nevertheless a well-respected figure among Scottish intellectuals and academics, including among his friends Robert Chambers, the philosophers Sir William Hamilton and J. F. Ferrier, the classicist E. L. Lushington, and the astronomer John Pringle Nichol. These contacts account for many of the interests revealed in his journalism. Recent historicist criticism of De Quincey has paid attention to the Scottish context of his work, which for earlier critics had been eclipsed by his Wordsworthian connections.

Noteworthy among his contributions to *Blackwood's* are the three essays "On Murder Considered as One of the Fine Arts" (1827, 1839, 1854). The first two essays explore the ambiguities of Kantian philosophy, and expose the absurdities of contemporary interest in the lurid and the grotesque. While the jokes are often obscure, these essays nevertheless provide good examples of De Quincey's wit, presenting absurd situations matter-of-factly, and literalizing metaphors to comic effect. The moral ambiguities of the essays give a sense of decadence characteristic of De Quincey's work, and anticipate later Victorian writers such as **Oscar Wilde**. The final essay in the series provides a chilling and suspenseful account of two recent murder cases, and was influential in the developing trend of crime writing. Also published in *Blackwood's* was "The English Mail Coach" (1849), a fine example of De Quincey's "impassioned prose."

Less critical attention has been paid to his political commentaries. The essays on the collapse of the Wellington government and on the 1830 revolution in France give clear demonstration of his high Tory affiliations. Seemingly at odds with his political sympathies are his essays on political economy, "The Dialogues of the Three Templars" (1824) in *London Magazine* and "Ricardo Made Easy" (1842) in *Blackwood's*, designed to popularize the works of the Whig economist David Ricardo.

In 1833 De Quincey began a series of anecdotal essays for *Tait's*, which would include his "Autobiographical Sketches" (1834–41), "Lake Reminiscences" (1839), and three essays on **Samuel Taylor Coleridge** (1834–35). The essays on Wordsworth and his circle were particularly popular, as they incorporated frank discussion of the personal lives of these well-known figures, including the revelations of Coleridge's drug addiction and his plagiarisms. Although they widened the rift between the Wordsworths and De Quincey, they nevertheless enhanced his literary reputation, and have been frequently republished as important documents of English Romanticism.

JOSEPHINE MCDONAGH

Biography

Born 15 August 1785 in Manchester. Studied at Worcester College, Oxford, 1803–08; entered Middle Temple, London, 1812. First took opium, 1804, and later became addicted for life. Met William Wordsworth, 1807, and became associated with him, Dorothy Wordsworth, Coleridge, and **Robert Southey**. Settled in Grasmere, Westmorland, 1809. Married Margaret Simpson, 1817 (died, 1837): five sons (three died) and three daughters. Editor, *Westmorland Gazette*, 1818–19. Moved to Edinburgh, 1830. Contributor to various journals, including *London Magazine*, Edinburgh *Saturday Post* and *Evening Post*, *Edinburgh Literary Gazette*, *Blackwood's*, and *Tait's*. Contributor to the *Encyclopaedia Britannica* of entries on German and British writers, from 1837. Died in Edinburgh, 8 December 1859.

Selected Writings

Essays and Related Prose

Confessions of an English Opium Eater, 1822; facsimile reprint, 1989; revised edition, 1856; edited by Malcolm Elwin, 1956, and Alethea Hayter, 1971
China: A Revised Imprint of Articles from "Titan", 1857
Recollections of the Lakes and the Lake Poets, 1862; edited by Edward Sackville-West, 1948, and David Wright, 1970
Suspiria de Profundis, with *Confessions of an English Opium Eater*, 1871; edited by Malcolm Elwin, 1956
The Uncollected Writings, edited by James Hogg, 2 vols., 1890
Posthumous Works, edited by Alexander Japp, 2 vols., 1891–93
New Essays by De Quincey: His Contributions to the Edinburgh Saturday Post and the Edinburgh Evening Post, 1827–1828, edited by Stuart M. Tave, 1966
Confessions of an English Opium Eater, and Other Writings, edited by Aileen Ward, 1966
Thomas De Quincey as Critic, edited by J. E. Jordan, 1973
Confessions of an English Opium Eater, and Other Writings, edited by Grevel Lindop, 1985

Other writings: the novel *Klosterheim* (1832), short stories, and works on political economy.

Collected works edition: *Collected Writings*, edited by David Masson, 14 vols., 1889–90.

Bibliographies

Dendurent, H. O., *Thomas De Quincey: A Reference Guide*, Boston: Hall, and London: Prior, 1978
Green, John A., *Thomas De Quincey: A Bibliography*, New York: Franklin, 1968 (original edition, 1908)

Further Reading

Abrams, M. H., *The Milk of Paradise: The Effect of Opium Visions on the Works of De Quincey, Crabbe, Francis Thompson and Coleridge*, New York: Harper and Row, 1970 (original edition, 1934)
Barrell, John, *The Infection of Thomas De Quincey: A Psychopathology of Imperialism*, New Haven, Connecticut and London: Yale University Press, 1991
Baxter, Edmund, *De Quincey's Art of Autobiography*, Edinburgh: Edinburgh University Press, and Savage, Maryland: Barnes and Noble, 1990
Hayter, Alethea, *Opium and the Romantic Imagination*, London: Faber, and Berkeley: University of California Press, 1968
Leighton, Angela, "De Quincey and Women," in *Beyond Romanticism: New Approaches to Texts and Contexts 1780–1832*, edited by Stephen Copley and John C. Whale, London and New York: Routledge, 1992: 160–77
Lindop, Grevel, *The Opium-Eater: A Life of Thomas De Quincey*, London: Dent, and New York: Taplinger, 1981
McDonagh, Josephine, *De Quincey's Disciplines*, Oxford: Clarendon Press, and New York: Oxford University Press, 1994

Maniquis, Robert M., "Lonely Empires: Personal and Public Visions of Thomas De Quincey," in *Mid-Nineteenth Century Writers: Eliot, De Quincey, Emerson*, edited by Eric Rothstein and Joseph Anthony Wittreich, Jr., Madison: University of Wisconsin Press, 1976

Russett, Margaret, "De Quincey's Gothic Interpreter: De Quincey Personifies 'We Are Seven'," *Studies in Romanticism* 30 (1991): 345–65

Rzepka, Charles J., *Sacramental Commodities: Gift, Text, and the Sublime in De Quincey*, Amherst: University of Massachusetts Press, 1995

Snyder, Robert Lance, editor, *Thomas De Quincey: Bicentenary Studies*, Norman: University of Oklahoma Press, 1985

Whale, John C., *Thomas De Quincey's Reluctant Autobiography*, London: Croom Helm, and Totowa, New Jersey: Barnes and Noble, 1984

De Voto, Bernard

American, 1897–1955

Bernard De Voto was a novelist and distinguished historian, critic, and journalist, whose *Mark Twain's America* (1932), *Mark Twain in Eruption* (1940), *Mark Twain at Work* (1942), *The Year of Decision: 1846* (1943), *The Course of Empire* (1952), and *The Journals of Lewis and Clark* (1953) are still standard works in American literature and historiography. But a major part of De Voto's long career involved writing essays for a wide variety of **periodicals**, beginning with a little essay on world peace in the Ogden, Utah *Standard* in May 1913 and continuing until his death in 1955, after which about a dozen appeared posthumously.

Over these four decades, De Voto's essays appeared in, among others, *American Heritage*, *American Mercury*, **Atlantic Monthly**, *Fortune*, **Harper's**, *Holiday*, *Reader's Digest*, *Redbook*, *Saturday Evening Post*, *Saturday Review of Literature*, *Woman's Day*, the *Writer*, and other magazines. The best known of these are the 243 "Easy Chair" essays which appeared in *Harper's* from November 1935 to January 1956 and made him perhaps the most widely recognized magazine columnist of his time. De Voto's most important and distinguished essays are to be found in three collections: *Forays and Rebuttals* (1936), *Minority Report* (1940), and *The Easy Chair* (1955), the latter a selection of essays written for *Harper's*.

In his essays De Voto focused on many of the same topics that engaged his attention in his nonfiction books: literary criticism, Western American history, and conservation. Much of his writing, in whatever form it took, was concerned with the American West, and his essays on the West reflect his fearlessness in attacking that region's mistaken notions and also defending it against its Eastern exploiters.

The quality of De Voto's essays might well be described in terms that he himself used in explaining the purpose of "The Easy Chair" as it had been carried on by his predecessors (including **William Dean Howells**): "to have a connotation of urbane informality, of a graceful interplay of thought and personality that used to be more highly regarded as literature than it is now ... It has always had a quality it could not get in the study but only down the street, at the square, and in the city hall. If study and reflection have gone into it, so have

legwork, sweat, and the opinion that is based not on research but on experience and participation."

Forays and Rebuttals brings together 23 essays, most of them from *Harper's* and the *Saturday Review of Literature*. They deal with a wide variety of topics: the American West as a "plundered province" of the East, Mormonism, the education of women, college faculties, New England, historiography, and works by prominent American writers – Mari Sandoz's *Old Jules*, Sinclair Lewis' *Ann Vickers*, Malcolm Cowley's *Exile's Return*, Ernest Hemingway's *Green Hills of Africa*, and Lloyd Douglas' *Green Light*. The volume concludes with two addresses: "Mark Twain: The Ink of History" (delivered at the University of Missouri in December 1935) and "Mark Twain and the Limits of Criticism" (given at the annual meeting of the Modern Language Association of America at Cincinnati on 1 January 1936).

Minority Report contains 36 essays reprinted from *Harper's* and the *Saturday Review of Literature*. As with his other two volumes of essays, this book demonstrates the range of De Voto's interests. "Passage to India" deals with the Lewis and Clark expedition, "Gettysburg" the fascination that the battlefield has held for generations of Americans. In other essays he discusses the election of 1860, the significance of Christmas in America, life in New York City, the failures of journalism, scholarly conferences, liberalism, literary criticism, semantics, Havelock Ellis, William Faulkner, Ernest Hemingway, Eugene O'Neill, the economics of writing, grammar, the cowboy story, and literary scholarship.

The final book of essays, *The Easy Chair*, brings together 31 pieces, all but one from *Harper's*. Again, De Voto's omnivorous mind ranges across many areas: 20th-century American life, communism and ex-communists, Don Marquis and his poetry, doctors and medicine, smoke-jumpers (fire-fighting parachutists), motels, radio and television, the television series "Victory at Sea," the Civil War, the FBI, censorship and pornography, the American West, federal land policy, the U.S. Forest Service, and conservation.

The guiding principle behind all of De Voto's essays is perhaps contained in a passage from Easy Chair 241: "I have assumed that there was no public demand for me to write about anything at all but that if I was interested in something, some readers would be interested in it too. But also I have written about a good many subjects not primarily because I wanted to write about them but because it seemed likely that no one else would."

De Voto's essays, early and late, reflect the mind of a writer who did not hesitate to take an unpopular stand on contemporary issues, to support the underdog, and to deflate hypocrisy wherever it might be found – in politics, business, education, religion, or literary criticism.

ROBERT C. STEENSMA

Biography

Bernard Augustine De Voto. Born 11 January 1897 in Ogden, Utah. Studied at the Sacred Heart Academy and Ogden High School; University of Utah, one year; Harvard University, Cambridge, Massachusetts, 1915–20, B.A., 1920. Served in the U.S. Army for two years. Taught English at Northwestern University, Evanston, Illinois, 1922–27, and Harvard University, 1929–36. Married Helen Avis MacVicar, 1923: two sons. Editor, *Harvard Graduates'*

Magazine, 1929–32, and *Saturday Review of Literature,* 1936–38; columnist of "The Easy Chair," *Harper's,* 1935–55. Regular staff member, Bread Loaf Writers' Conference, Middlebury College, Vermont, Summers 1939–49. Literary editor of the **Mark Twain** estate. Awards: Pulitzer Prize, for *Across the Wide Missouri,* 1948. Died (of a heart attack) in New York City, 13 November 1955.

Selected Writings

Essays and Related Prose
Forays and Rebuttals, 1936
Minority Report, 1940
The Literary Fallacy (lectures), 1944
The Easy Chair, 1955

Other writings: five serious novels (*The Crooked Mile,* 1924; *The Chariot of Fire,* 1926; *The House of Sun-Goes-Down,* 1928; *We Accept with Pleasure,* 1934; *Mountain Time,* 1947), four novels under the pseudonym John August, books about Mark Twain, and a trilogy on American history (*The Year of Decision: 1846,* 1943; *Across the Wide Missouri,* 1947; *The Course of Empire,* 1952 [also as *Westward the Course of Empire*], 1953).

Bibliography
Barclay, Julius P., in *Four Portraits and One Subject: Bernard De Voto,* edited by Wallace Stegner, Boston: Houghton Mifflin, 1963

Further Reading
Sawey, Orlan, *Bernard De Voto,* New York: Twayne, 1969
Stegner, Wallace, editor, *Four Portraits and One Subject: Bernard De Voto,* Boston: Houghton Mifflin, 1963
Stegner, Wallace, *The Uneasy Chair: A Biography of Bernard De Voto,* Garden City, New York: Doubleday, 1974

Dialogue

Throughout its half-millennium history, the essay has proved inseparable from dialogue. Defined as "trials" or "tests" or "attempts," "essays" keep their distance from the information they would discover. Were the truth about their topics close at hand, the explorations that they undertake would seem superfluous. In dialogue, similarly, diverse interlocutors probe opposing opinions while keeping consensus at bay. To divide essays from dialogue would be then to separate the genre from the dramatic foundations of its defining qualities. Without dialogue, the open rhetorical space of the essay would contract into solid **treatises** and preacherly monologues. Our contemporary stereotype of the essay as a brash, confident, opinionated, and didactic form should be moderated by an understanding of the fact that almost all essayists, at one time or another, have cast works in dialogic form, made ample use of dialogic elements, or presented themselves as conversationalists.

Buoyed by the renewal of learning during the Renaissance, but befuddled by the resulting wealth of information, the early essayists reconciled ancient authority with modern skepticism by *conversing with* rather than simply citing the sages of old. **Montaigne,** a founder of the modern essay genre, creates the illusion of a conversation among the ancients by juxtaposing disparate extracts from their unrelated works and deeds:

Plutarch goes further, asserting that to appear to excel in such unnecessary accomplishments is to bear witness against yourself of time ill-spent on leisure and study which ought to be better spent on things more necessary and more useful. So Philip, King of Macedonia, when he heard his son Alexander the Great singing of a feast and rivaling the best musicians, remarked: "Are you not ashamed of singing so well?" ... A king should be able to reply like Iphicrates did to the ambassador who was haranguing him with invectives: "[I am] None of these," he replied. "But I am the one who can lead them all."

In classical antiquity, dialogue was a trademark of skepticism, especially of that of the Platonic and Pyrrhic schools. Such mock conversations permitted moderns like Montaigne to tighten this longstanding link between doubt and discussion. Moderns could confirm their skepticism by crediting ancient authorities even while counterpointing differences in ancient opinion.

Britain's **Francis Bacon** emulated Montaigne's method. Although Bacon's *Essayes* (1597, 1612, 1625) seldom take an overtly dialogic form, they proceed from, and work within, a conversable environment. The famous prelude to Bacon's "Of Truth" – "*What is Truth,* said jesting Pilate, and would not stay for an answer" – is a conclusion to a prior conversation. Pilate has just finished elaborating on the topic of truth with some unknown Judaean colleague, closing his discussion with dialogic inconclusivity. Bacon, indeed, could be described as an unacknowledged master of aborted conversations, for many of his essays begin with tacit conversational referents. Interrupted offstage discussions lead into dislocated mock conversations comprised of decontextualized quotations. Bacon's simulated discussions replicate the mixed uncertainty and optimism of early empiricism. As an essayist and empirical scientist, Bacon faced an abundance of new experimental and philological evidence, but had at his disposal only the most provisional, "inductive" methods with which to organize it. Vigorous use of dialogue about diverse discoveries was one robust way of raising a temporary canopy over a circus of seeming contradictions.

Many early essayists applied the dialogic method to religious controversies, of which the later Renaissance never ran short. Essayists on religious topics affected the confidence that comes from zeal, yet the dialogic character of their discourses discloses all the uncertainties and instabilities that riddled the secular lucubrations of Bacon and Montaigne. Doubt-wracked **John Donne** bolstered his essays on theology with authoritative Scriptural quotations, yet he showed a marked preference for excerpts of a dialogic rather than definitive tone:

> *In the Morning ye shall see the glory of God,* (sayes Moses to them) *for, he hath heard your grudging against him.* And again, *At evening shall the Lord give you flesh; for the Lord hath heard your murmuring. They murmur'd for water, saying, What shall we drink? ... When they saw it* [Manna] *they said to one another, it is Man, for they wist not what it was ...* (*Essayes in Divinity,* 1651)

People talk, God listens, Israelites *say* things to one another. Conversations pack and pile together in close quarters. God himself drops in on conversations.

The density and compactness that distinguish the early essay interact in later eras with the openendedness of conversation. Bacon's *brevia* cannot compare quantitatively with John Locke's colossal *Essay Concerning Human Understanding* (1690), yet Locke's encyclopedia of Restoration epistemology is less a unified work than a baroque array of essayistic conversations. The famous (and comical) case of Prince Maurice's rational (and dialogical) Brazilian parrot, who bantered with the best of wits, is one of hundreds of miniature discussions. As scrupulous Locke explained, "I set down the words of this worthy dialogue [with the parrot] in French, just as prince Maurice said them to me." Locke was not the only Restoration researcher to construct agglutinative essays from multiple recorded conversations. John Dryden, the author of *Essay of Dramatic Poesy* (1668), Lady Margaret Cavendish, and Henry More were only a few of the more notable practitioners of this art.

The inflationary tendencies of the Lockean essay joined with the didactical powers of the Baconian anecdote to propel the doubt-driven essay of the Renaissance toward the comical-instructive essays of the Addisonian era. Early 18th-century periodical essayists used extended dialogues to teach the proper application of abstractions rather than merely to undercut scholastic generalities. Dialogue in early periodical essays advanced Lockean empiricism, for it showed not only the content of an idea or theory, but also the character and motivations of its advocates. Such dialogue compressed a range of invisible psychological and moral factors into palpable form. The result was a jolly, optimistic skepticism that balanced hard facts and clear ideas against peculiar personalities and private agendas. **Joseph Addison** relied on dialogue to popularize neoclassical critical ideas while also satirizing their overzealous advocates, and proposing milder manifestos:

> In short, sir, (says he), the author [of the comedy under discussion] has not observed a single unity in his whole play; the scene shifts in every dialogue; the villain has hurried me up and down at such a rate, that I am tired off my legs ... For my part, (says she), I never knew a play that was written up to your rules ... I must confess ... I laughed very heartily at the last new comedy which you found so much fault with ... Madam (says he), there are such people in the world as Rapin, Dacier, and others that ought to have spoiled your mirth ... I must confess, (continued she), I would not be troubled with so fine a judgment as yours is; for I find you feel more vexation in a bad comedy, than I do in a deep tragedy ... (*Tatler* no. 165, 1710)

Extended essay sequences like those in the *Tatler* or the *Spectator* expanded this comical, empirical, and above all dialogical enterprise. Sequenced essays permit the examination of numerous related phenomena from countless viewpoints in an infinity of settings. The serial technique was taken to the outer limits by the buoyant **Lord Shaftesbury**, whose gargantuan essay collection *Characteristicks of Men, Manners, Opinions, Times* (1711, revised 1714) overflows with nonstop dialogues written from every conceivable viewpoint, from St. Paul's to the dung heap's. Later in the 18th century, letter-writing essayists like Philip Dormer Stanhope, the **Earl of Chesterfield**, interspersed reams of instructive epistles with

comic re-creations of cocktail conversations. Repeated satiric dialogues tested the social and psychological limits of essayistic advice. Even the dour objectivist **Samuel Johnson** capitulated to the delights of serialized dialogic essays, with many of the essays in the *Rambler*, the *Idler*, and the *Adventurer* being comprised completely of dialogue, juxtaposed letters, or simulated conversation. And the trajectory that leads from the melancholy to the comic essay bisects the career of **Samuel Taylor Coleridge**. Coleridge is most often remembered for such sober (albeit Shaftesburian) projects as his *Biographia Literaria* (1817); but his most voluminous contributions came in the genre of the tart political essay, sometimes sounding like a highly serious version of coffee house Addison.

From our post-Hegelian perspective, we want to see Romantic essayists as capacious, organic, monumental, and full of grandeur. In fact, they relied on the same sort of conversational snippets as did their Augustan predecessors. **William Hazlitt**, the unremitting author of 21 immense volumes, could conjure up sublimities concerning just four lines of conversation from Shakespeare:

> The character of Cleopatra is a masterpiece ... The luxurious pomp and gorgeous extravagance of the Egyptian queen are displayed in all their force and lustre, as well as the irregular grandeur of the soul of Mark Antony. Take only the first four lines that they speak as an example of the regal style of love-making.
> *Cleopatra.* If it be love indeed, tell me how much?
> *Antony.* There's beggary in the love that can be reckon'd.
> *Cleopatra.* I'll set a bourn how far to be belov'd.
> *Antony.* Then must thou needs find out new heav'n, new earth.

As a mode of contrast, dialogue compares characters and views. In Hazlitt's consideration, it compares fragmentary utterances with immense conceptions. Hazlitt's metaphysical extrapolation of essayistic patter received a personal touch from **Charles Lamb**, who entered into simulated conversations with earlier authors hoping that he himself could give voice to a kind of transcendental shock at the inadequacy of their conceptions:

> "We read the Paradise Lost as a task," says Dr. Johnson. Nay, rather as a celestial recreation, of which the dullard mind is not at all hours alike recipient. "Nobody ever wished it longer," nor the moon rounder, he might have added. Why, 'tis the perfectness and completeness of it which makes us imagine that not a line could be added to it, or diminished from it, with advantage. Would we have a cubit added to the stature of the Medicean Venus? Do we wish her taller?

Later in the 19th century, the satiric superman **Thomas Carlyle** continued this practice of turning intended meanings inside-out in order to evoke shattered images of sublimity. Carlyle even suggested that Sir Walter Scott's physical maladies constituted a kind of corporeal conversation with Nature. "A vigorous health seems to have been given by Nature; yet, as if Nature had said withal, 'Let it be a health to express itself by mind, not body,' a lameness is added in childhood." In Carlyle's twisted world, bad health is dialogically if not dialectically essential to writing good essays.

Wandering wits like Carlyle travel in and around the interstices between individual speakers and impersonal ideas – between quoted speakers, unscrolling essays, and immense conceptions. In earlier times, the confrontation with these rhetorical and epistemological instabilities drove Coleridge to drugs and Montaigne to his tower. In the 20th century, it has produced a darkly erudite, amusingly insufficient climax to the essay tradition: morosely entertaining fragments on the complexities and directionlessness of postmodernity. The collapse of essayistic openness is exemplified by the urbanely essayistic chit-chat of **T. S. Eliot** (e.g. in "A Dialogue on Dramatic Poetry," 1928):

B. . . . But the questions which he [Dryden] discussed are not out of date.

E. The Unities of Place and Time, for instance. Dryden gives what is the soundest and most commonsense view for his time and place. But the Unities have for me, at least, a perpetual fascination. I believe they will be found highly desirable for the drama of the future. For one thing, we want more concentration. All plays are now much too long. I never go to the theatre, because I hate to hurry over my dinner, and I dislike to dine early. A continuous hour and a half of *intense* interest is what we need. No intervals, no chocolate-sellers or ignoble trays. The Unities do make for intensity, as does verse rhythm.

A. You think we need stronger stimulants, in a shorter space of time, to get the same exaltation out of the theatre that a sensitive contemporary may be supposed to have got out of a tragedy by Shakespeare or even out of one by Dryden.

E. And meanwhile let us drink another glass of port to the memory of John Dryden.

Deeply if unwillingly immersed in the contradictions and self-consciousness that characterize the modern and contemporary eras, essayists like Eliot have looped themselves into a dialogue about former dialogues, into wryly repetitive essays about past essays about the future of dramatic poesy. Eliot and his successors have anticipated the dislocation of essay-dialogues into serialized television debates about future views of what happened in the past or about past anticipations of future retrospectives. They have captured that strange combination of optimism and despair, certainty and turbulence, that makes essays dialogues rather than declamations.

KEVIN L. COPE

Further Reading

Adams, D. J., *Diderot, Dialogue and Debate*, Liverpool: Cairns, 1986
Brewer, Daniel, "The Philosophical Dialogue and the Forcing of Truth," *Modern Language Notes* 98, no. 5 (1983): 1234–47
Carron, Jean-Claude, "The Persuasive Seduction: Dialogue in Sixteenth-Century France," in *Contending Kingdoms: Historical, Psychological and Feminist Approaches to the Literature of Sixteenth-Century England and France*, edited by Marie-Rose Logan and Peter L. Rudnytsky, Detroit: Wayne State University Press, 1991
Cope, Kevin L., editor, *Compendious Conversations: The Method of Dialogue in the Early Enlightenment*, Frankfurt-on-Main and New York: Lang, 1992
Gilman, Donald, "The Reconstruction of a Genre: Carolus Sigonius and the Theorization of Renaissance Dialogue," in *Acta Conventus Neo-Latini Torontonensis*, edited by Alexander Dalzell, Charles Fantazzi, and Richard J. Schoeck, Binghamton, New York: Medieval and Renaissance Texts and Studies, 1981
Haynes, Robert William, *The Dramaturgy of the Early Tudor Dialogue* (dissertation; on More, Thomas Starkey, Thomas Elyot, and Thomas Lupset), Athens: University of Georgia, 1991
Himmelfarb, Anne, *A Mirror of Conversation: Studies in Late Seventeenth and Eighteenth Century English Dialogue* (dissertation), New York: Columbia University, 1990
Himmelfarb, Anne, "Argument as Imitation: The Prose Dialogue," *Age of Johnson: A Scholarly Annual* 3 (1990): 281–99
Keener, Frederick M., *English Dialogues of the Dead: A Critical History, an Anthology, and a Checklist*, New York: Columbia University Press, 1973
McCutcheon, R. R., *Thomas More and the Limits of Dialogue* (dissertation), Stanford, California: Stanford University, 1991
McCutcheon, R. R., "Heresy and Dialogue: The Humanist Approaches of Erasmus and More," *Viator: Medieval and Renaissance Studies* 24 (1993): 357–84
Mortier, Roland, "Variations on the Dialogue in the French Enlightenment," *Studies in Eighteenth-Century Culture* 16 (1986): 225–40
Prince, Michael Benjamin, *Strains of Enlightenment: Philosophical and Religious Dialogue in England, 1700–1780* (dissertation), Charlottesville: University of Virginia, 1990
Snyder, Jon R., *Writing the Scene of Speaking: Theories of Dialogue in the Late Italian Renaissance*, Stanford, California: Stanford University Press, 1989
Trueblood, Alan S., "The Art of Dialogue in the Early Seventeenth Century: Two Examples," in *Studies in Honor of Bruce W. Wardropper*, edited by Dian Fox, Harry Sieber, and Robert TerHorst, Newark, Delaware: Juan de la Cuesta, 1989
Wilson, Kenneth J., "The Continuity of Post-Classical Dialogue," *Cithara: Essays in the Judaeo-Christian Tradition* 21, no. 1 (1981): 23–44
Wilson, Kenneth J., *Incomplete Fictions: The Formations of English Renaissance Dialogue*, Washington, D.C.: Catholic University of America Press, 1985

Diary *see* Journal

Dickens, Charles

British, 1812–1870

The sketches, polemical pieces, and **familiar essays** written by Charles Dickens from 1833 to 1869 form a body of remarkable work that doubtless would have assured him fame as a writer had his novels, numerous tales, several plays, and annual Christmas stories never been written. Dickens' career as a novelist has greatly eclipsed his career as an essayist. Although his essays have received much scholarly attention, critics have generally focused on their revelation of Dickens' social views, his relationship to the periodicals publishing them, the autobiographical information embedded in them, and, most often, the connections between the essays and the novels. In addition to these legitimate critical interests, examination of Dickens' style has begun to enrich appreciation for the complexities of his essays. He wrote hundreds of essays and rewrote and edited hundreds of others submitted to the various periodicals he edited.

Although Dickens wrote some sketches as early as 1833, he began to distinguish himself as an essayist in 1834 when he started writing under the pseudonym Boz for publication in the *Morning Chronicle*. Other essays by Boz and under the pseudonym Tibbs appeared in the *Evening Chronicle* and *Bell's Life in London*. Many of these essays, particularly those describing London, are reminiscent of descriptive essays by **Oliver Goldsmith**, **Charles Lamb**, **Leigh Hunt**, and **Washington Irving**. The social concerns that figure significantly in all genres of Dickens' work appear in such early sketches as "Gin Shops," "The Pawnbroker's Shop," and "The Prisoner's Van," all published in 1835. The comic satire that was to blossom in later essays appears in many of the early essays and is especially notable in the six published in 1835 under the heading "Our Parish." In these, Dickens reveals the techniques – the dramatic scene, detailed and often detached observation, parallelism, and comic exaggeration – that he would refine in later pieces. In the "Our Parish" group, he satirizes the office and process of electing the beadle, the fickle regard of the parish for the curate, and the lofty but fruitless busy-ness of the ladies' societies of the parish, whose members held their meetings "with great order and regularity: not more than four members being allowed to speak at one time on any pretense whatever" ("The Ladies Societies," 1835).

On a more somber note, other essays by Boz reveal Dickens' skills as a journalist whose detachment from the subject creates irony or who frames the essay with detachment but allows his opinions about social issues to erupt at the core. For instance, in "A Visit to Newgate" (1836), Dickens begins with a matter-of-fact description of the prison and prisoners but breaks this tone by passionately reiterating one of his recurrent themes: the loss of childhood innocence. Observing a young girl visiting her inmate mother, Dickens writes: ". . . she was one of those children, born and bred in neglect and vice, who have never known what childhood is . . . Tell them of hunger and the streets, beggary and stripes, the gin shops, the station house, and the pawnbroker's, and they will understand you." This eruption of emotion about child visiting parent in prison likely reflects Dickens' painful memory of visiting his own family in the Marshalsea Prison, where his father was imprisoned for debt in 1824. After this emotional outpouring, the detached observer leads the reader through the rest of the prison, the prison yards, the chapel, the press yard, to the cells of condemned prisoners. At this point, detachment dissolves into a fervent expression of sympathy for the condemned prisoner contemplating his impending execution. Here, as he often does, Dickens requires the reader to participate imaginatively, creating not simply a picture of the condemned man but also a series of the prisoner's dreams of his loving wife, the scenes in the courtroom, and his desperate escape.

From 1836 to 1839 Dickens edited *Bentley's Miscellany*, where some essays and the serialized *Oliver Twist* appeared (1836–39), but problems with the owner provoked him to begin in 1840 the periodical *Master Humphrey's Clock*, a weekly he said owed much to the *Tatler*, the *Spectator*, and the *Bee*. Public pressure for serialized novels forced him to reduce the number of essays he was publishing in it and to make it more modern than its 18th-century counterparts had been. In 1850 he founded *Household Words*, where he published about 200 essays of his own and collaborated on or

substantially rewrote many others. Essays in *Household Words* were aimed at a wide audience, including less well-educated middle-class readers; as such, these pieces include a broad range of subjects and techniques. As Harry Stone points out in his detailed introduction to *Uncollected Writings from Household Words 1850–1859* (1968), a new kind of essay, the "process essay," explained to readers what it was like to be in a certain place or to follow a particular process of experiencing or making something – for example, "Valentine's Day at the Post-Office" (wr. with W. H. Wills, 1850), "A Paper Mill" (with Mark Lemon, 1850), and "Post-Office Money Orders" (with W. H. Wills, 1852).

In the weekly *All the Year Round*, which Dickens edited from 1859 until his death, his mastery of the essay is clear. In many pieces (such as those published in a volume entitled *The Uncommercial Traveller*, 1860), the connections between childhood and adulthood are explored through a skillfully created complex of tone and sensory detail. As Gordon Spence (1977) points out, the self-revelation of the narrator is at the core of a familiar essay. Identifying himself as one who travels for "the great house of Human Interest Brothers" ("His General Line of Business," 1860), the narrator sets up the framework for his observations in England and on the continent, in the city and in the country. One of the best known of these essays is "Mr. Barlow" (1869), where the narrator reveals his detestation of a former tutor who had no sense of humor or fun and who delighted in destroying all imaginative pleasure his young pupils could have in reading such works as *The Arabian Nights*. In "Travelling Abroad" (1860) the narrator tells the story of seeing a great house near Chatham when he was a boy and being told by his father that if he worked hard, he could some day buy it. The reference is to Dickens' conversation with his father when he first saw Gadshill, the house which indeed he did buy.

Dickens' social conscience appears in such essays as "Wapping Workhouse" (1860), where he argues that "those Foul wards . . . ought not to exist; no person of common decency and humanity can see them and doubt it"; "The Great Tasmania's Cargo" (1860), where he urges the country to do its duty by its soldiers; and "The Short-Timers" (1863), which states that the way children, cripples, and paupers are treated is "a disgrace to civilisation, and an outrage on Christianity." The most poignant of the essays urging social reform is "A Small Star in the East" (1868), which juxtaposes scenes of despair and hope. In the first scene, the narrator visits a woman nearly dead from lead poisoning as a result of her work in the lead mills, and interviews a much younger woman who wants to work in the mills because, she says, "Better be ulcerated and paralyzed for eighteen-pence a day, while it lasted, than see the children starve." In the second scene, he visits the East London Children's Hospital, where honest and selfless concern for the malnourished and abused children have reclaimed them from miserable and premature deaths.

Many essays in *The Uncommercial Traveller*, like those collected in *Reprinted Pieces* (1861) and other works, explore such topics as church architecture, theater buildings and plays, social customs such as eating in restaurants, morbid settings like the Paris Morgue or a Welsh seacoast where 500 men had been lost in a shipwreck, "shy" neighborhoods where birds, dogs, and cats are personified, travel customs and difficulties, and places and people in London and abroad who are invisible to the masses of people passing them daily. With such a range of topics, Dickens attracted a broad spectrum of readers and engaged them through techniques and tones extending from whimsicality to somberness and zeal.

LINDA A. JULIAN

Biography

Charles John Huffam Dickens. Born 7 February 1812 in Portsmouth, Hampshire. Lived with his family in London, 1814–16, Chatham, Kent, 1817–21, where he attended a school, and London, 1822; worked in a blacking factory, Hungerford Market, London, while his family was in Marshalsea debtor's prison, 1824; studied at Wellington House Academy, London, 1824–27; Mr. Dawson's school, London, 1827. Married Catherine Hogarth, 1836 (separated, 1858): seven sons and three daughters. Long liaison with the actress Ellen Ternan. Law office clerk, London, 1827–28; shorthand reporter, Doctors' Commons, 1828–30, and in Parliament for *True Son*, 1830–32, *Mirror of Parliament*, 1832–34, and the *Morning Chronicle*, 1834–36. Contributor, *Monthly Magazine*, 1833–34 (as Boz, 1834), and the *Evening Chronicle*, 1835–36; editor, *Bentley's Miscellany*, 1836–39, and the London *Daily News*, 1846; founding editor, *Master Humphrey's Clock*, 1840. Lived in Italy, 1844–45, and Switzerland and Paris, 1846. Founding editor, *Household Words*, 1850–59, and its successor, *All the Year Round*, 1859–70. Gave reading tours in Britain and the United States, 1858–68. Lived at Gadshill Place, near Rochester, Kent, from 1860. Died at Gadshill, 9 June 1870.

Selected Writings

Essays and Related Prose

Sketches by Boz Illustrative of Every-Day Life and Every-Day People, 1836; second series, 1836
American Notes for General Circulation, 1842; edited by John S. Whitley and Arnold Goldman, 1972
Pictures from Italy, 1846; edited by David Paroissien, 1973
The Uncommercial Traveller, 1860
Reprinted Pieces, vol. 2 of *Works* (Library Edition), 1861
Speeches Literary and Social, edited by R. H. Shepherd, 1870; revised edition, as *The Speeches 1841–1870*, 1884; edited by K. J. Fielding, 1960
Speeches, Letters, and Sayings, 1870
To Be Read at Dusk and Other Stories, Sketches, and Essays, edited by F. G. Kitton, 1898
Miscellaneous Papers, edited by B. W. Matz, 2 vols., 1908
Uncollected Writings from Household Words 1850–1859, edited by Harry Stone, 2 vols., 1968
Household Words: A Weekly Journal 1850–1859, edited by Anne Lohrli, 1974
A December Vision: Social Journalism, edited by Neil Philip and Victor Neuburg, 1986
Dickens's Journalism, Volume I: Sketches by Boz and Other Early Papers, 1833–39, edited by Michael Slater, 1993
Dickens's Journalism, Volume II: The Amusements of the People and Other Papers: Reports, Essays and Reviews, 1834–51, edited by Michael Slater, 1997

Other writings: 15 novels (*The Pickwick Papers*, 1837; *Oliver Twist*, 1838; *Nicholas Nickleby*, 1839; *The Old Curiosity Shop*, 1840; *Barnaby Rudge*, 1841; *A Christmas Carol*, 1843; *Martin Chuzzlewit*, 1844; *Dombey and Son*, 1848; *David Copperfield*, 1850; *Bleak House*, 1853; *Hard Times*, 1854; *Little Dorrit*, 1857; *A Tale of Two Cities*, 1859; *Great Expectations*, 1861; *Our Mutual Friend*, 1865), the unfinished novel *The Mystery of Edwin Drood* (1870), and several plays, including three with Wilkie Collins.

Collected works editions: The Charles Dickens Edition, 21 vols., 1867–75; Nonesuch Edition, edited by Arthur Waugh and others, 23 vols., 1937–38; *The New Oxford Illustrated Dickens*, 21 vols., 1947–58; *The Clarendon Dickens*, edited by Kathleen Tillotson and others, 1966– (in progress).

Bibliographies

Chittick, Kathryn, *The Critical Reception of Charles Dickens 1833–1841*, New York: Garland, 1989
Churchill, R. C., *A Bibliography of Dickensian Criticism 1836–1975*, New York: Garland, and London: Macmillan, 1975
Cohn, Alan M., and K. K. Collins, *The Cumulated Dickens Checklist 1970–1979*, Troy, New York: Whitston, 1982
Eckel, John C., *The First Editions of the Writings of Charles Dickens*, New York: Inman, and London: Maggs Bros., revised edition, 1932 (original edition, 1913)
Hatton, Thomas, and Arthur H. Cleaver, *A Bibliography of the Periodical Works of Charles Dickens*, London: Chapman and Hall, 1933

Further Reading

Ackroyd, Peter, *Dickens*, London: Sinclair Stevenson, and New York: Harper Collins, 1990
Butt, John, and Kathleen Tillotson, *Dickens at Work*, London: Methuen, 1957
Easson, Angus, "Who Is Boz? Dickens and His Sketches," *Dickensian* 81 (1985): 13–22
Slater, Michael, Introduction to *Dickens' Journalism: Sketches by Boz and Other Early Papers 1833–39*, edited by Slater, London: Dent, 1993; Columbus: Ohio State University Press, 1994
Spence, Gordon, *Charles Dickens as a Familiar Essayist*, Salzburg: University of Salzburg Institute for English Language and Literature, 1977
Stone, Harry, Introduction to *Uncollected Writings from Household Words 1850–1859* by Dickens, edited by Stone, Bloomington: Indiana University Press, 1968; London: Allen Lane, 1969

Diderot, Denis

French, 1713–1784

Although Denis Diderot wrote only a small number of texts bearing the title "essay," his writing owes much to the essay's conceptual and formal design. Those very essay traits have in fact contributed to a renewed interest in this *philosophe*'s texts and to a transformation of his legacy. Until the 1960s, and from as early as 18th- and 19th-century criticism and commentary, intellectual historians and literary critics – Sainte-Beuve, the Goncourt brothers, and others – often judged Diderot's thinking to be unfocused, digressive, even derivative. As compared with other 18th-century French Enlightenment *philosophes* – for example, Montesquieu (*De l'esprit des lois* [1749; *The Spirit of the Laws*]), Buffon (*Histoire naturelle* [1749–1804; *Natural history*]), Rousseau (*Du contrat social* [1762; *Of the Social Contract*]) – and the 19th-century discipline of philosophy itself, it was thought that Diderot's texts failed to produce either a new system of thought or of knowledge. Nor were his texts esteemed for any rigorous systematic method. In the last 30 years, however, those very properties of the essay which are characteristic of Diderot's texts and of the judgment levied against him have taken on a different significance. Diderot has been projected into a new critical spotlight provided by contemporary criticism in semiotics and poststructuralist analysis.

Indeed, the same characteristics of Diderot's writing which once served as the basis for negative critique now function in an opposite capacity as his indisputable intellectual and literary attributes, and in effect echo some of the basic literary and philosophical traits of the "essay." According to **Theodor W. Adorno** ("Der Essay als Form" [1958; "The Essay as Form"]), the essay "does not let its domain be prescribed for it. Instead of accomplishing something scientifically or creating something artistically," the essay thus can seem derivative, taking its inspiration from multiple sources, from "what others have done before him. The essay reflects what is loved and hated instead of presenting the mind as creation *ex nihilo* . . ." The essay proclaims a different kind of interdisciplinary, unsystematic allegiance, faithful neither to absolutes nor to preconceived models of truth or knowledge; this defines the salient aspects of Diderot's writing. But Diderot also influenced the direction of the essay by bringing new elements to this paradoxical writing.

Using "essay" in the actual title, Diderot wrote *Essai sur le mérite et la vertu* (1745; Essay on merit and virtue); *Essai sur Sénèque* (1778; Essay on Seneca); *Essai sur les règnes de Claude et de Néron* (1782; Essay on the reigns of Claudius and Nero); *Essais sur la peinture* (1795; Essays on painting). Despite this small corpus, essay writing constitutes a paradigm for Diderot's thinking in texts carrying such diverse titles as *Pensées* (Thoughts), *Discours* (Discourse), *Entretiens* (Discussions), and *Lettre* (Letter). In each text, in each title, the fragment dominates: in thought, in direction, in the proliferation of different narrative voices, disclaiming exhaustive study of any one particular field, often disavowing any discovery of first or final principles and yet consistently seeking out new directions and territory. Says Adorno, "The essay thinks in fragments."

Diderot's equivalent of **Francis Bacon**'s *Novum organum* (1622), his *Pensées sur l'interprétation de la nature* (1753; Thoughts on the interpretation of nature), introduce an 18th-century emphasis on experimental science ("physique expérimentale") based on a notion implicit in the semantics and form of the essay, that of a trial, an experiment, experience. Empiricism is based here on a renunciation of prescribed principles imposed on nature. Indeed, as Adorno says, the "essay alone has successfully raised doubts about the absolute privilege of method . . ."

Thus, just as Adorno names Descartes' perspective as the antithesis to the spirit of the essay, which is "a protest against the four rules established by Descartes' *Discours de la méthode*" (**Discourse on Method**), Diderot also challenges the Cartesian system, distinguishing between "two sorts of philosophy, the experimental and the rational. One has its eyes blindfolded, always goes along groping, seizes everything that comes to it and encounters in the end precious things. The other collects these precious materials and tries to form a torch; but this so-called torch has until now served less than the groping of its rival." This "groping" is also textually manifest as isolated *pensées* in the form of fragments: "Experimental philosophy which does not propose anything is always content with what comes to it; rational philosophy is always learned, even when what it proposes does not come to it."

Emphasis on observation and experience reverses a thinking based on *a priori* truths established in advance of any direct experience of nature. Both in the *Pensées sur l'interprétation de la nature* as well as in other writings Diderot places great value on the observer's experience of discovery and reception. This crucial reversal also finds expression in the text's narrative voice and direction. In the first fragment of *L'Interprétation*, Diderot the narrator models his writing on the lack of directed inquiry inherent in the experimental method: "It is of nature that I am going to write. I will let thoughts succeed themselves under my pen, in the same order according to which objects offered themselves to my reflection." The text's division into fragments is modeled on the often disconnected trials in nature unearthed by the experimenter and observer. In other words, the attributes of the essay are consonant with the tenets of experimental science in Diderot's writing; the *philosophe* always makes an explicit link to the unprogrammatic fragmentary development and uncharted direction of his thought and expression. Adorno says that the "essay allows for the consciousness of nonidentity, without expressing it directly; it is radical in its nonradicalism, in refraining from any reduction to a principle, in its accentuation of the partial against the total in its fragmentary character."

This seemingly modest concept of hypothesis based in experience delegates new power to the observer. Whether in epistemological, philosophical, aesthetic, or even fictional terms, Diderot's texts testify to a new concern with the experience of an observer/spectator who is writing in the first person. The letter novel (*La Religieuse* [1796; *The Nun*]), and the philosophical novel (*Le Neveu de Rameau* [1821; *Rameau's Nephew*]) derive from fragments which are written **letters**, or **dialogue** broken into multiple voices. A new kind of partial agency endows such a spectator with the ability to judge and to experience.

The still dominant norms of 17th-century French classicism were thus also challenged by Diderot's testimony to a new kind of aesthetic judgment. His texts (*Les Salons*, 1759–72) on the painting and sculpture exhibited biannually in the Salon Carré of the Louvre form many short essays on artists and their exhibited art work. Such commentaries have long been viewed as digressive and verbose, but also as having inaugurated modern art criticism (see Michael Fried, *Absorption and Theatricality*, 1980). In fact, Diderot's art criticism comes into existence precisely through a progressive union of the observer, the spectator, of painting and sculpture with first-person narrators who react to the experience, to the art work on exhibit. Thus, the individual observer's perspective is embodied in a figure of discourse as a sentient narrative "I/you."

Each essay in Diderot's *Essais sur la peinture* (posthumously pub. 1795), written to accompany his *Salon* of 1765, treats another aspect of painting: design, color, *chiaroscuro*, expression, composition, even architecture. Throughout these essays, the reader becomes both listener and spectator. The narrator addresses Grimm, editor of the journal *Correspondance Littéraire* (Literary correspondence), for whom Diderot wrote both the *Salons* and his accompanying essays. But it is not solely to address Grimm that Diderot employs forms of direct address: he uses first-person discourse throughout the *Essais*, creating an atmosphere of informal conversation that contributes to the unfettered free flow of thought and experience. Direct discourse, in which the narrator communicates ostensibly to Grimm, also structures his address to various painters and spectators, adopting alternately formal and informal modes of address: *vous/tu*; "Look at that woman who lost her eyesight in her youth"; or "Turn your gaze on that man whose back and chest have assumed a convex shape." The narrator urges the painter to provide new experience: "Touch me, astonish me, rend my heart, make me shudder, cry, tremble, rouse me first; you will remake my eyes afterward, if you can." The spectators/readers, like the narrator, respond to experience that touches and transfixes them. Other figures also appropriate the "I" of the spectator, including characters from the canvas of painting, or spectators from the exhibit hall who are endowed in Diderot's *Salons* with spoken language and who begin to speak in their own person.

The classical, generally accepted academic criteria of good painting and sculpture are challenged through this structure of discourse. And the same characteristics of direct discourse mark both Diderot's *Salons* and his *Essais sur la peinture*. As one critic remarked already in 1796 in the journal *La Décade Philosophique* (The philosophical decade): "... those who have already heard him [Diderot] converse have only to open the pages of the *Essais* at random and will think they hear him speaking." Centuries later, in an introduction to the 1957 edition of Diderot's *Salons*, Jean Seznec uses almost identical words in describing Diderot's commentary on diverse tableaux and sculpture. Whether labeled "essay," "salon," or "lettre," and whether his essays treat historical, fictional, or pictorial personnages, the (dis)order and immediacy of dialogue stage the voices of active controversy. This familiar, idiomatic language coincides with new criteria for painting itself: new appreciation of domestic genre scenes rather than exclusively of the grand canvases of history and mythology. Scenes from everyday life portray experience recognizable by all. Instead of the perfectly formed model, posed within the academy classroom, the narrator encourages painters to dwell outside in the experience of individual subjects whose particular, rare traits, even deformities, should be traced in their influence on all aspects of the body and character ("a system of deformities necessarily interrelated"). The essay is itself a deformity, a heterodoxy. Multiple speakers interrupt the univocal voice of third-person narrative and the unitary coherence of any set of philosophical, epistemological, historical, and aesthetic prescriptions to introduce the immediacy of both thought and experience.

As editor of the *Encyclopédie* (1746–72), Diderot composed another text of many voices, fragments offering further testimony to the uneven and unresolved experiences and experiments of an entire culture. Like the essay, all Diderot's texts consistently challenge the reigning method and accepted system of knowledge. "Heresy," Adorno says, "is the innermost formal law of the essay." Thus does this *philosophe* radicalize the notion of essay itself, his hybrid texts remaining unconfined to any single rubric or genre. Diderot reinvents the essay precisely through a new dialogue of proliferating voices which constitute the variegated weave of his diverse experiments.

SUZANNE R. PUCCI

See also Encyclopedias and the Essay

Biography

Born 5 October 1713 in Langres. Studied at a Jesuit school in Langres, 1723–28; Collège d'Harcourt or Lycée Louis-le-Grand, Paris, from 1728; University of Paris, master of arts, 1732. Worked for the attorney Clément de Ris, 1732–34; tutor, freelance writer, and translator, 1734–46. Married Antoinette Champion, 1743: two daughters and two sons (all but one daughter died young). Liaison with Madeleine d'Arsant de Puisieux, 1745–51. General editor and main contributor, Le Breton's *Encyclopédie*, 1746–72 (first volume published 1751). Imprisoned for three months because of writings, 1749. Intimate friendship with Sophie Volland, from 1755. Contributor, F. M. Grimm's private periodical *Correspondance Littéraire*, from 1759. Patronized by Catherine the Great, from 1765, and visited Russia, 1773–74. Member, Prussian Royal Academy, 1751; Foreign Member, Russian Academy of Sciences, 1773. Died (of emphysema and dropsy) in Paris, 31 July 1784.

Selected Writings

Essays and Related Prose
Essai sur le mérite et la vertu, 1745
Pensées philosophiques, 1746; as *Early Philosophical Works*, translated by Margaret Jourdain, 1916
Lettre sur les aveugles, 1749; edited by Robert Niklaus, 1951; as *An Essay on Blindness*, translated anonymously, 1750; as *A Letter upon the Blind*, translated by S. C. Howe, 1857
Lettre sur les sourds et muets, 1751; edited by Paul H. Meyer, 1965
Pensées sur l'interprétation de la nature, 1753
Select Essays from the Encyclopedy (includes essays by others), translated anonymously, 1772
Essai sur Sénèque, 1778
Essai sur les règnes de Claude et de Néron, 1782; edited by Hisayasu Nakagawa, 2 vols., 1966
Essais sur la peinture, 1795
Mémoires, correspondance et ouvrages inédites, 4 vols., 1830–31
Thoughts on Art and Style, with Some of His Shorter Essays, edited and translated by Beatrix L. Tollemache, 1893
Dialogues, translated by Francis Birrell, 1927
Interpreter of Nature: Selected Writings, edited by Jonathan Kemp, translated by Kemp and Jean Stewart, 1937
Selected Philosophical Writings, edited by John Lough, 1953
Les Salons, edited by Jean Seznec and Jean Adhémar, 4 vols., 1957–67
Selections from the Encyclopedia, edited and translated by Stephen Gendzier, 1959
Œuvres philosophiques, edited by Paul Vernière, 1964
Selected Writings, edited by Lester G. Crocker, translated by Derek Coltman, 1966
Political Writings, edited and translated by Robert Wokler and John H. Mason, 1992
Diderot on Art, translated by John Goodman, 2 vols., 1995

Other writings: two novels (*Les Bijoux indiscrets* [*The Indiscreet Toys*], 2 vols., 1748; *La Religieuse* [*The Nun*], 1796), two dialogues (*Jacques le fataliste et son maître* [*James the Fatalist and His Master*], 1796; *Le Neveu de Rameau* [*Rameau's Nephew*], 1821), and several plays.

Collected works editions: *Œuvres complètes*, edited by Jules Asségat and Maurice Tourneux, 20 vols., 1875–77, and Herbert Dieckmann, Robert Mauzi, Jean Varloot, and Jacques Proust, 20 vols., 1975–90 (in progress; 36 vols. projected); *Œuvres*, edited by Laurent Versini, 3 vols., 1994–95 (in progress; 5 vols. projected).

Bibliography
Spear, Frederick A., *Bibliographie de Diderot*, Geneva: Droz, 2 vols., 1980–88

Further Reading
Adorno, Theodor W., "The Essay as Form," in his *Notes to Literature*, vol. 1, edited by Rolf Tiedemann, New York: Columbia University Press, 1991: 3–23 (original edition, 1958)

Bukdahl, Else Marie, *Diderot, critique d'art*, Copenhagen: Rosenkilde & Bagger, 1980

Cassirer, Ernst, *The Philosophy of the Enlightenment*, Princeton, New Jersey: Princeton University Press, 1968 (original edition, 1951)

Chouillet, Jacques, *La Formation des idées esthétiques de Diderot, 1745–1763*, Paris: Colin, 1973

Creech, James, *Diderot: Thresholds of Representation*, Columbus: Ohio State University Press, 1986

Fellows, Otis, *Diderot*, Boston: Twayne, 1977

France, Peter, *Diderot*, Oxford: Oxford University Press, 1983

Fried, Michael, *Absorption and Theatricality: Painting and the Beholder in the Age of Diderot*, Berkeley: University of California Press, 1980

Furbank, P. N., *Diderot: A Critical Biography*, London: Secker and Warburg, 1992

Goncourt, Jules, and Edmond Goncourt, *The Goncourt Journals*, vol. 7, edited by Lewis Galantière, New York: Greenwood Press, 1968 (original edition, 1891)

Lacoue-Labarthe, Philippe, "Le Paradoxe et la mimésis," in his *L'Imitation des modernes*, Paris: Galilée, 1986: 15–36

Pucci, Suzanne, "The Art, Nature and Fiction of Diderot's Beholder," *Stanford French Review* 8 (Fall 1984): 273–94

Pucci, Suzanne, *Diderot and a Poetics of Science*, New York: Lang, 1986

Pucci, Suzanne, editor, *Diderot in the Wake of Modern Critical Thought*, special issue of *L'Esprit Créateur* 24, no. 1 (Spring 1984)

Didion, Joan
American, 1934–

An angelic rattlesnake in our blighted Eden is an apt description of Joan Didion, the penetrating American prose stylist who is likely to be remembered more for her striking essays than for the five novels she has written to date. Her output as a magazine travel writer, book and film reviewer, feature writer, and columnist outweighs her work in fiction. Indeed, certain Didion essays have become classics: "Slouching Towards Bethlehem" (1967) is widely considered the definitive portrait of the "flower children" of the 1960s who flocked to San Francisco in search of peace and love; "The White Album" (1979) is a quintessential evocation of the entire 1960s era. Didion, in fact, is often grouped with the 1960s "new journalists."

As a sixth-generation Californian, Didion writes with authority on a range of Western American subjects. She has made the Californian and Hawaiian landscapes her own, and has interpreted the Hollywood film industry to a world bedazzled by its glamour. Didion's greatest gift, in fact, is for exposing the romantic fantasies which propel individual citizens, communities, and the American government as well. Her most recent essays invariably focus on the "narratives" we tell ourselves, and their often damaging consequences.

Didion's career can be tracked through her magazine associations. The first half of the 1960s mark her apprenticeship as a New York magazine writer. She wrote travel articles for *Mademoiselle* and *Holiday*, film reviews for *Vogue*, and book reviews for William Buckley's conservative *National Review*. Then she said "Farewell to the Enchanted City" (1967) and fled to California. The late 1960s and 1970s saw Didion's emergence as a columnist for the *Saturday Evening Post*, *Life*, and *Esquire* magazines; the 1980s, her book-length travel and political reportage written for the *New York Review of Books*, collected as *Salvador* (1983) and *Miami* (1987); and the 1990s, writing on Washington, D.C., New York City, and California for the *New York Review of Books*, the **New Yorker** ("Letters from Los Angeles"), and *New West* (collected as *After Henry*, 1992).

Didion writes for the cultural intelligentsia, for style-conscious upscale readers interested in politics and cultural analysis. These readers can (or aspire to) buy the clothes modeled in *Vogue* and the holidays heralded in *Holiday*. Nuances of fashion or upper-class life, therefore, often go untranslated in a Didion essay, which will note the Charles Jourdan suede pumps worn by Colombian women (*Miami*), or the "access to corporate G-3s" possessed by publishers and editors, though not by writers ("After Henry"). Didion's upscale readers need no gloss of these items. At the same time, such detailed rendering of status life lends an aura of insider authority to Didion's essays, providing readers with a sense of being both "in the know" with Didion and aware of the barriers to entry illuminated by these codes.

Although the cultural intelligentsia remain Didion's primary audience, she has secured a larger, popular audience as well through her interest in American icons and in news stories which illuminate the times. Readers of the *Saturday Evening Post*, *Life*, and *Esquire* have been drawn to her telling portraits of John Wayne, Howard Hughes, and Joan Baez – all figures who have engaged the popular imagination. In her later work she dissects the Patti Hearst kidnap and trial and the web of events following the attack on New York's Central Park jogger in April 1989. What may seem tabloid topics to some become narratives of complex misperceptions in Didion's enriching hands. Readers seeking the sensational come away with sobering new perspectives on the individual and cultural histories which inform the event, but are misunderstood by most of the story's major players. Like **Virginia Woolf**, Didion allows readers to inhabit differing points of view in her essays. Also like Woolf, she employs her outsider's perspective to critique dominant ideologies, particularly those of the government and press.

Didion's essays offer an illustration of how a writer's style and artistic vision may be inescapable embodiments, not only of her personal history, geography, and literary assimilation, but of her very corporeal being. In her "Points West" and "The Coast" columns and her "Letters from Los Angeles," Didion repeatedly insists that California's history and geography instill a specific perspective in Californians widely misunderstood by those not native to the terrain. Much of Didion's mission as a writer seems to be to correct these misconceptions. Didion's Western perspective explains her defense of Patti Hearst and appreciation of Howard Hughes' grand antisocial privacy. It explains her suspicion of "civic

virtue," in its myriad forms, and her California-bred awareness of America's "golden dreamers" who erect their homes
on sand.

Didion's work reflects the strong influence of fellow
American writer F. Scott Fitzgerald, who also toiled in the
vineyards of fiction and nonfiction. Her early writings contain
at least 20 references to Fitzgerald or his work, and the bond
is more than parallel histories – of "Westerners" drawn and
repelled by the East, of writers of Hollywood movies living in
Malibu. It is more than their shared interests in wealth and
illusion, the beautiful and the damned, the lost Eden of the
American Dream and the dark night of the American soul. It
is even more than Didion's willingness to follow Fitzgerald's
advice of "tearing your . . . tragic love story out of your heart
and putting it on pages for people to see," which she did
in her inaugural *Life* column ("A Problem of Making
Connections," 1969), as well as when she reprinted the psychiatric report of her own nervous breakdown in "The White
Album." Even more important than these parallels is Didion's
special affinity for Fitzgerald's "golden moments." In a lecture
at Berkeley in 1976 Didion described an illustration of a cat
drawn by a patient suffering from schizophrenia. The cat had
a shimmer around it. "Writing is the attempt to understand
what's going on in the shimmer," Didion explained. "To find
the cat in the shimmer, if the cat is the important thing, or to
find what the shimmer is." Here, symbolically presented, is
Didion's ideological project. She employs the perceptions of
her (often afflicted) nervous system as a metaphor for illusion
and reality in the American experience.

This ideological project explains many of the traits of
Didion's remarkable style. She often begins an essay with
description of a place; however, place soon becomes a "landscape of the mind" – with the shimmers of mind sets carefully
limned. Didion's essays are often cautionary tales, parables of
illusion, of betrayed or lost promise. She employs anaphora
to foreground the dissonant elements of her narratives –
even narratives of her own illusions. She writes, for example,
in "The White Album": "It was a time of my life when I
was frequently named. I was named godmother to children.
I was named lecturer and panelist, colloquist and conferee. I
was even named, in 1968, a *Los Angeles Times* 'Woman of
the Year,' along with Mrs. Ronald Reagan, the Olympic
swimmer Debbie Meyer, and ten other California women
who seemed to keep in touch and do good works." Ironic
humor is part of this style. "I did no good works but I tried
to keep in touch," Didion continues. After reprinting her
psychiatric report in this same essay, she adds, "By way of
comment I offer only that an attack of vertigo and nausea does
not now seem to me an inappropriate response to the summer
of 1968."

Didion's wry and sympathetic persona, in fact, is one of her
most successful creations. She uses herself as a probe and as
a model of American society. Her confessions of personal illusions both invite reader identification and sympathy with her
views, and demonstrate how prone Americans are to illusion.
Her effort to discipline her illusions likewise becomes a model
for reader behavior. Most cleverly, her assertion in many essays
that she can find no meaning to the narrative has the effect of
spurring readers to moral understandings she herself refuses
overtly to claim.

Those who have read Didion's descriptions of her migraine
attacks and possible multiple sclerosis cannot help but wonder
if her mythos of shimmering light may be an exquisitely
rendered translation of her physical condition. Didion wears
oversized sunglasses even indoors to protect her light-sensitive
eyes. An "aura" (or shimmer) is a documented early stage in
most migraine attacks, preceding the actual headache. Didion
has written that "When I am in a migraine aura . . . I . . . lose
the ability to focus my eyes or frame coherent sentences" ("In
Bed," 1968). Dehydration is thought beneficial for migraine
sufferers and excessive water harmful. Didion's obsession with
water and tropical climates may, therefore, have physical as
well as spiritual nuance. Additionally, weariness with life and
a wish to die are oft-reported experiences of migraine sufferers.

Certainly Didion's struggle with and acceptance of her physical afflictions have influenced her adamant stance against
human improvability. The snakes in our gardens – the wormy
truths of error, corruption, and death – are the reality which
Didion's essays perpetually sound. We await, almost with
dread, her continued rarefied perceptions.

BARBARA LOUNSBERRY

See also New Journalism

Biography

Born 5 December 1934 in Sacramento, California. Studied at the
University of California, Berkeley, 1952–56, B.A. in English, 1956.
Associate feature editor, *Vogue*, New York, 1956–63; moved to Los
Angeles, 1964. Married the writer John Gregory Dunne, 1964: one
adopted daughter. Columnist of "Points West," with Dunne,
Saturday Evening Post, 1967–69, and "The Coast," *Esquire*
magazine, 1976–77; contributor to several other magazines,
including *Harper's Bazaar*, *New Yorker*, *Ms.*, *New York Review of
Books*, and the *New York Times Book Review*; contributing editor,
National Review; Visiting Regents' Lecturer, University of
California, Berkeley, 1975. Awards: *Vogue* Paris Prize, 1956;
National Institute of Arts and Letters Morton Dauwen Zabel
Award, 1979.

Selected Writings

Essays and Related Prose
Slouching Towards Bethlehem, 1968
The White Album, 1979
Salvador, 1983
Miami, 1987
After Henry: Sentimental Journeys, 1992

Other writings: five novels (*Run River*, 1963; *Play It as It Lays*,
1970; *A Book of Common Prayer*, 1977; *Democracy*, 1984; *The
Last Thing He Wanted*, 1996), short stories, four screenplays with
John Gregory Dunne (*Panic in Needle Park*, 1971; *Play It as It
Lays*, 1972; *True Confessions*, 1981; *Up Close and Personal*, 1996).

Bibliography
Oldendorf, Donna, "Joan Didion: A Checklist, 1955–1980,"
   Bulletin of Bibliography (January–March 1981): 33–44

Further Reading
Anderson, Chris, "Joan Didion: The Cat in the Shimmer," in his
   Style as Argument: Contemporary American Nonfiction,
   Carbondale: Southern Illinois University Press, 1987: 133–73
Braman, Sandra, "The 'Facts' of El Salvador According to Objective
   and New Journalism," *Journal of Communication Inquiry* 9
   (1985): 75–96

Braman, Sandra, "Joan Didion," in *A Sourcebook of American Literary Journalism: Representative Writers in an Emerging Genre*, edited by Thomas B. Connery, New York: Greenwood Press, 1992: 353–58

Braudy, Susan, "A Day in the Life of Joan Didion," *Ms.*, February 1977: 65–68

Diamonstein, Barbaralee, *Open Secrets: Ninety-Four Women in Touch with Our Time*, New York: Viking Press, 1972

Friedman, Ellen G., editor, *Joan Didion: Essays and Conversations*, Princeton, New Jersey: Ontario Review Press, 1984

Johnson, Michael L., *The New Journalism: The Underground Press, the Artists of Nonfiction, and Changes in the Established Media*, Lawrence: University Press of Kansas, 1971

Lounsberry, Barbara, "Joan Didion's Lambent Light," in her *The Art of Fact: Contemporary Artists of Nonfiction*, Westport, Connecticut: Greenwood Press, 1990: 107–37

Martin, Stoddard, *California Writers*, London: Macmillan, and New York: St. Martin's Press, 1983

Weber, Ronald, editor, *The Reporter as Artist: A Look at the New Journalism Controversy*, New York: Hastings House, 1974

Winchell, Mark Royden, *Joan Didion*, Boston: Twayne, revised edition, 1989

Dillard, Annie

American, 1945–

In an author's note to her collection of 14 essays, *Teaching a Stone to Talk: Expeditions and Encounters* (1982), Annie Dillard asserts that "this is not a collection of occasional pieces, such as a writer brings out to supplement his real work; instead this is my real work, such as it is." This statement attests to Dillard's passionate conviction about the validity and artistic merit of the essay; it also acknowledges the speculation, confusion, and misreading that can arise when a writer refuses to confine herself to one genre. In addition to a wide variety of books of nonfiction prose, including a foray into the natural world, a memoir of childhood, reflections on the writer's craft, an account of her experiences as a member of a literary delegation, an exploration of human suffering, and a book of literary criticism, Dillard has published a novel and two collections of poetry. *The Annie Dillard Reader*, which draws from a number of these works, was published in 1994.

Though Dillard is quick to assert that *Teaching a Stone to Talk* is her only essay collection, to her displeasure many continue to use that label to describe *Pilgrim at Tinker Creek* (1974), which won a Pulitzer prize for general nonfiction. In a 1989 interview, Dillard describes *Pilgrim at Tinker Creek* as "a single sustained nonfiction narrative." She acknowledges that her decision to give each chapter a separate title has led readers and critics to call *Pilgrim at Tinker Creek* a book of essays. Selected chapters of the book have appeared in magazines and anthologies of essays, also contributing to what Dillard regards as genre mislabeling.

While the most fitting classification for any piece of Dillard's prose can be debated, certainly not in dispute is Dillard's contribution to modern nonfictional prose. She is often compared with **Thoreau** and Melville and to her own contemporaries such as **Loren Eiseley**. Her essays can be found in numerous magazines including *Antaeus*, the

Atlantic Monthly, *Christian Science Monitor*, *Esquire*, *Harper's*, *Harvard Magazine*, *Living Wilderness*, *New York Times Review of Books*, *North American Review*, *Parnassus*, *Ploughshares*, *Yale Literary Magazine*, and the *Yale Review*.

In her introduction to the 1988 volume of *The Best American Essays*, which she edited with Robert Atwan, Dillard observes, "The essayist does what we do with our lives; the essayist thinks about actual things. He can make sense of them analytically or artistically. In either case he renders the real world coherent and meaningful, even if only bits of it, and even if that coherence and meaning reside only inside small texts." She restates this assessment of her writerly lot and the company she keeps a year later in an interview recorded for the American Audio Prose Library: "One great advantage of the essay is that it mimics on paper what it is we do with our own minds at their best which is try to make sense of experience – actual experience. Fiction makes sense of imagined experience; nonfiction makes sense of actual experience." Nowhere does Dillard recast this more eloquently than in "Total Eclipse," the essay from her collection that is most often anthologized: "The mind – the culture – has two little tools, grammar and lexicon: a decorated sand bucket and a matching shovel. With these we bluster about the continents and do all the world's work. With these we try to save our very lives."

In this same interview Dillard admits that she dislikes opinion essays. It is narrative essays that interest her, and these constitute her offerings in *Teaching a Stone to Talk*. The essays in this collection recall many of the images and themes developed earlier in *Pilgrim at Tinker Creek*. But unlike *Pilgrim at Tinker Creek*, which focuses primarily on one geographical location and the reading experiences that Dillard brings to bear on her time spent there, *Teaching a Stone to Talk* covers much more distance geographically and topically. The essay collection includes "Life on the Rocks: The Galápagos," "An Expedition to the Pole," "In the Jungle," "The Deer at Providencia," and "Total Eclipse," an account of that natural phenomenon as viewed near Yakima, Washington in 1979.

In *Teaching a Stone to Talk*, Dillard continues to probe the act of seeing which she began in *Pilgrim at Tinker Creek*. In "An Expedition to the Pole," she says, "I stood on the island's ocean shore and saw what there was to see . . ." This sounds very much like a passage early in *Pilgrim at Tinker Creek*, "Like the bear who went over the mountain, I went out to see what I could see." She returns to this idea in "In the Jungle": "The point of going somewhere like the Wapo River in Ecuador is not to see the most spectacular anything. It is simply to see what is there." This passage is followed by an observation that sounds as if it could easily have come from *Pilgrim at Tinker Creek*: "We are here on the planet only once, and might as well get a feel for the place." Dillard entitles one of the chapters in *Pilgrim at Tinker Creek* "Seeing." Titles of two essays in *Teaching a Stone to Talk*, "Lenses" and "Mirages," also make seeing the subject.

Dillard moves beyond a discussion of seeing in both *Pilgrim at Tinker Creek* and *Teaching a Stone to Talk* to an exploration of perception and consciousness. The main focus of *Pilgrim at Tinker Creek*'s chapter "The Present," the quest for "experiencing the present purely," is also of primary concern in "Total Eclipse." Here Dillard says, "We teach our children one thing only, as we were taught: to wake up. We teach our children to look alive there, to join by words and activities the life of human culture on the planet's crust." She laments that "We live half our waking lives and all of our sleeping lives in some private, useless, and insensible waters we never mention or recall." Much of Dillard's exuberant prose serves as a wake-up call to her reader. Here she keeps company with the young man in "Total Eclipse" whom she labels affectionately "a walking alarm clock."

Readers of Dillard's prose are struck as much by her sense of mystery as they are by her sense of humor. At times she can be a prankster and even mislead her readers. She admits in her interview with Kay Bonetti (1989), for example, that when she found out that it was virtually impossible to determine when the next solar eclipse in Yakima would occur, she simply invented a date. While Dillard's tone can be flippant and whimsical, it can also be celebratory and awestruck. She returns often to an acknowledgment and exploration of the transcendent in her prose. Her Christianity is most evident in *Teaching a Stone to Talk*'s shortest essay, "God in the Doorway," and in the *Yale Review* essay, "Singing with the Fundamentalists." To her credit, Dillard zealously privileges art over ideology in her writing. When asked if she has a theology, she quips, "I have a prose style."

BEVERLY J. MATIKO

See also Nature Essay

Biography
Born Annie Doak, 30 April 1945 in Pittsburgh. Studied at Hollins College, Roanoke, Virginia, B.A., 1967, M.A., 1968. Married Richard Dillard, 1964 (divorced, 1974). Columnist, *Living Wilderness*, 1974–76; contributing editor, *Harper's*, 1974–81 and 1983–85; contributor to many other journals and magazines. Scholar-in-residence, Western Washington University, Bellingham, 1975–78. Married Gary Clevidence, 1980 (later divorced): one child and two stepchildren. Visiting professor, 1979–83, full adjunct professor, from 1983, and writer-in-residence, from 1987, Wesleyan University, Middletown, Connecticut. Married Robert D. Richardson, Jr., c. 1988. Awards: several, including the Pulitzer Prize, for *Pilgrim at Tinker Creek*, 1975; New York Presswomen's Award for Excellence, 1975; Washington Governor's Award, 1978; Appalachian Gold Medallion, 1989; honorary degrees from three universities.

Selected Writings

Essays and Related Prose
Pilgrim at Tinker Creek, 1974
Teaching a Stone to Talk: Expeditions and Encounters, 1982
The Annie Dillard Reader, 1994

Other writings: the novel *The Living* (1992), two collections of poetry (*Tickets for a Prayer Wheel*, 1974; *Mornings Like This*, 1995), *Holy the Firm* (1977), on religious and metaphysical questions, books on literature and writing, and the autobiography *An American Childhood* (1987).

Further Reading
Bonetti, Kay, "Interview with Annie Dillard," Audio Prose Library, June 1989
Chénetier, Marc, "Tinkering, Extravagance: Thoreau, Melville, and Annie Dillard," *Critique* 31, no. 3 (1990): 157–72
Clark, Suzanne, "The Woman in Nature and the Subject of Nonfiction," in *Literary Nonfiction: Theory, Criticism, Pedagogy*, edited by Chris Anderson, Carbondale: Southern Illinois University Press, 1989
Dunn, Robert Paul, "The Artist as Nun: Theme, Tone and Vision in the Writings of Annie Dillard," *Studia Mystica* 1, no. 4 (1978): 17–31
Felch, Susan M., "Annie Dillard: Modern Physics in a Contemporary Mystic," *Mosaic* 22, no. 2 (1989): 1–14
Hammond, Karla M., "Drawing the Curtains: An Interview with Annie Dillard," *Bennington Review* 10 (1981): 30–38
Johnson, Sandra Humble, *The Space Between: Literary Epiphany in the Work of Annie Dillard*, Kent, Ohio: Kent State University Press, 1992
Keller, Joseph, "The Function of Paradox in Mystical Discourse," *Studia Mystica* 6, no. 3 (1983): 3–19
Lavery, David, "Noticer: The Visionary Art of Annie Dillard," *Massachusetts Review* 21 (1980): 255–70
McClintock, James, *Nature's Kindred Spirits: Aldo Leopold, Joseph Wood Krutch, Edward Abbey, Annie Dillard, Gary Snyder*, Madison: University of Wisconsin Press, 1994
McConahay, Mary Davidson, "'Into the Bladelike Arms of God': The Quest for Meaning Through Symbolic Language in Thoreau and Annie Dillard," *Denver Quarterly* 20 (Fall 1985): 103–16
McFadden-Gerber, Margaret, "The I in Nature," *American Notes and Queries* 16 (1977): 3–5
McIlroy, Gary, "*Pilgrim at Tinker Creek* and the Social Legacy of Walden," *South Atlantic Quarterly* 85, no. 2 (Spring 1986): 111–22
McIlroy, Gary, "*Pilgrim at Tinker Creek* and the Burden of Science," *American Literature* 59, no. 1 (1987): 71–84
Reimer, Margaret Loewen, "The Dialectical Vision of Annie Dillard's *Pilgrim at Tinker Creek*," *Critique: Studies in Modern Fiction* 24, no. 3 (1983): 182–91
Scheick, William J., "Annie Dillard: Narrative Fringe," in *Contemporary American Women Writers: Narrative Strategies*, edited by Catherine Rainwater and William J. Scheick, Lexington: University Press of Kentucky, 1985
Yancey, Philip, "A Face Aflame: An Interview with Annie Dillard," *Christianity Today* 22 (1978): 14–19

Discourse on Method
by René Descartes, 1637

Published in 1637, the *Discours de la méthode* (*Discourse on Method*) stands at a crucial point of transition in the philosophical and scientific thinking of René Descartes (1596–1650). On the one hand it looks back at early works such as the *Regulae ad directionem ingenii* (wr. 1628, pub. 1701; *Rules for the Direction of the Mind*), and the aborted *Le Monde* (begun 1629; The world), Descartes' vision of the cosmos in response to Galileo's *Dialogo dove si discorre sopra il due massimi sistemi del mondo* (1632; *Dialogue Concerning the Two Chief World Systems*). On the other, it anticipates the famous *Meditationes de prima philosophia* (1641; *Meditations on First Philosophy*) and the influential *Les Passions de l'âme* (1649; *Passions of the Soul*). Presented as an introduction or prologue to his works on optics, meteorology, and geometry, it is concerned with the problem of legitimizing natural philosophy after the condemnation of Galileo by the Church.

Writing in French rather than the more conventional Latin, Descartes addresses himself ostensibly to the general reader in search of truth. At the same time, while he hopes that others will find some value in his intellectual journey, he emphasizes the highly personal nature of the quest. If the *Meditations* are patterned after the spiritual exercises of Loyola, the *Discourse* finds its prototype in St. Augustine's **Confessions** (397–98 CE) and **Montaigne**'s *Essais* (1580, 1588). He characterizes the *Discourse* as an autobiographical "story" or "fable," divided into six parts for easy contemplation. Implicitly portraying himself as a sort of Socrates in search of truth and wisdom through skepticism and doubt, he traces his intellectual journey from his early classical education through the breakdown of his certainty and subsequent spiritual and intellectual revelation, to the current state of his thinking. Descartes builds this fable around a series of architectural and travel metaphors, evoking images of foundations and construction, dark forests and roads.

The first two parts of the *Discourse* present his early philosophical doubts, culminating in the discovery of his "method," while enjoying the solitude of the famous stove-heated room. Echoing the *Regulae*, he describes four rules for reforming his own ways of thinking: first, accept nothing that is not clear and distinct; second, divide difficult subjects into many small parts; third, start with the simplest problems; and fourth, be comprehensive. By means of the "method" Descartes rehearses his ontological arguments for the existence of God, and enunciates the famous "cogito ergo sum" ("I think therefore I am"), all of which he develops more fully, systematically, and in a different order in the *Meditations*. In the third part, he suggests a series of moral **maxim**s, positing tolerance and restraint in the face of uncertainty, an ethical stance that looks back to both Socrates and Montaigne.

After explaining his system of morality in Part 3, and his metaphysics in Part 4, Descartes turns in Part 5 to a summary of the doctrines found in the suppressed *Le Monde*, and in *L'Homme* (wr. 1629–33, pub. 1664; *Treatise on Man*). Of particular importance to Descartes was the theory of automata and the workings of the circulatory system, both developed more fully later in the *Passions of the Soul*. Playing on the theme of the fable, he describes his model of the cosmos and the mechanics of the human body in terms of an elaborate fantasy rather than an actuality, a speculative portrait of how the world would be if his assumptions on the nature of God were true. In this way, he can present his theories, suggest their reasonableness, yet not commit himself to their ultimate validity. He cuts off any lengthy scholastic disputation, short-circuiting the traditional philosophical doctrines that he feels stand in the way of scientific discovery. Part 6 provides an introduction to the essays on meteorology and optics, indicating the present state of his scientific investigations. Having thus explained the method and his state of progress as a result of the method, a movement from the past to the present, Descartes offers a veiled invitation to any patron who would help him continue his search, a turn toward the future.

First published in Leiden by Elzevier, the *Discourse* had an initial run of 3000 copies. Having already circulated in proof to a number of noted figures, the book attracted a wide and immediate reaction, and Descartes spent the next two years responding to questions and objections. If the *Discourse* did not provide Descartes with the economic independence he desired, at least until the fateful patronage of Queen Christina of Sweden, it contributed to the composition of the *Meditations* and his subsequent philosophical works. Perhaps

more importantly, however, by introducing the doctrine of the *cogito*, and the exploration of the limits of human knowledge, Descartes' philosophical fable influenced all subsequent Western philosophy, from the various empirical schools that accept the role of consciousness in the constitution of reality even while rejecting the proofs of God and the theory of innate knowledge, to the phenomenologists and their followers among the existentialists and poststructuralists who purport to radicalize the Cartesian self. His most personal work, the *Discourse* stands as the starting point for all modern philosophy.

While Descartes was not the first to use the **personal essay**, he is one of the first to use it for the development of a full system. **Erasmus**' *Adagia* (1500; *The Adages*) and *Colloquia familiaria* (1516; *The Colloquies*), More's *Utopia* (1516), or even Montaigne's *Essais* are more modest and random in their treatments; when Erasmus or More wished to explicate a topic systematically, they fell back on the conventions of the scholastic **treatise**. Informality, flexibility, and narrative qualities were well suited to Descartes' philosophical and scientific purposes, allowing him to discuss a wide variety of matter with conciseness and clarity without having to address the given body of scholarship. In turn, the essay form allowed him to present his ideas without committing himself to them or having to engage in lengthy scholastic debate. The effect was to take philosophical and scientific discussion out of the university and bring it to the general public, marking the beginning of modern philosophy, and establishing the personal essay as a popular vehicle of discourse.

THOMAS L. COOKSEY

See also Philosophical Essay

Editions
Discours de la méthode pour bien conduire sa raison et chercher la verité dans les sciences, 1637; edited by Étienne Gilson, 1925 (reprinted 1989), M. Robert Derathe, 1937, Gilbert Gadoffre, 1961, L. Meynard, 2 vols., 1966–68, Jean Costilhes, 1966, François Misrachi, 1977, and Simone Mazauric, 1983; as *Discourse of a Method for the Well Guiding of Reason, and the Discovery of Truth in the Sciences*, translated anonymously, 1649; as *Discourse on Method*, translated by John Veitch, 1870, Laurence J. Lafleur, 1950, Arthur Wollaston, 1960, F. E. Sutcliffe, 1968, Donald A. Cress, 1980, and George Heffernan, 1994

Further Reading
Beck, Leslie, *The Metaphysics of Descartes*, Oxford: Oxford University Press, 1965
Cottingham, John, *Descartes*, Oxford and New York: Blackwell, 1986
Cottingham, John, editor, *The Cambridge Companion to Descartes*, Cambridge and New York: Cambridge University Press, 1992
Dicker, Georges, *Descartes: An Analytical and Historical Introduction*, Oxford and New York: Oxford University Press, 1993
Frankfurt, Harry G., *Demons, Dreamers, and Madmen: The Defense of Reason in Descartes's Meditations*, New York: Garland, 1987 (original edition, 1970)
Garber, Daniel, *Descartes' Metaphysical Physics*, Chicago: University of Chicago Press, 1992
Gaukroger, Stephen, *Descartes: An Intellectual Biography*, Oxford: Clarendon Press, and New York: Oxford University Press, 1995
Gueroult, Martial, *Descartes' Philosophy Interpreted According to the Order of Reasons*, Minneapolis: University of Minnesota Press, 2 vols., 1984–85

Kenny, Anthony, *Descartes: A Study of His Philosophy*, New York: Random House, 1968

Schouls, Peter A., *Descartes and the Enlightenment*, Edinburgh: University of Edinburgh Press, 1989

Sorell, Tom, *Descartes*, Oxford and New York: Oxford University Press, 1987

Williams, Bernard, *Descartes: The Project of Pure Enquiry*, Atlantic Highlands, New Jersey: Humanities Press, and Hassocks: Harvester, 1978

Wilson, Margaret, *Descartes*, London and Boston: Routlege and Kegan Paul, 1978

Donne, John

English, 1572–1631

Although he is best known for the poetry composed during the first half of his adult life and the **sermons** written in the latter half, John Donne also produced four collections of brief prose works in the essay and related genres as well as an essay and two characters intended to stand alone. These works are all marked with his characteristic cleverness of thought and expression, and the best reflect an attractive generosity of spirit.

The three uncollected pieces all date from the early part of his career. "An Essay of Valour," probably written in the late 1590s, may reflect Donne's service in two of the Earl of Essex's expeditions. Written in the manner of **Montaigne**, it consists of a series of arguments proving "that nothinge is so potent eyther to procure, or merrit Love, As Valour." It was first published in the 11th edition of Sir Thomas Overbury's *A Wife* (1622). His "Character of a Dunce," also first published in the same volume, is in the Theophrastan tradition characterizing vices. It lists unflattering attributes possessed by one who "Is a Soule drownd in a lump of flesh, Or a peece of earth that *Prometheus* put not halfe his proportion of fire into." The equally derogatory "Description of a Scot at First Sight" probably dates from the early years of the reign of James I, when many poor Scots came to London to seek their fortunes. No doubt for political reasons it was left unpublished during Donne's lifetime. Some modern editors have questioned Donne's authorship of these works, but all three are included in authoritative manuscripts of his poetry and prose compiled during his lifetime.

The two earliest collections of Donne's short prose pieces were first printed posthumously in an unauthorized edition as *Juvenilia, or Certaine Paradoxes, and Problems* (1633), which included eleven of the former and ten of the latter. An "authorized" edition of 1652, prepared by Donne's son and namesake, added a twelfth paradox and seven additional problems. The younger Donne is not accurate in calling these collections "the entertainment of the Author's Youth." While the paradoxes were begun during Donne's years at the Inns of Court in the 1590s and probably completed by 1600, the problems date from the first decade of the 17th century, when Donne was in his thirties.

Two kinds of literary paradoxes were written in the Renaissance, both tracing their roots to classical models: the mock encomium and the argument against received opinion.

Donne's paradoxes are in the latter tradition, and they rejoice in their own cleverness, proving "That Nature is our worst Guide," "That the guifts of the body are better then those of the Mind or of Fortune," "That good is more common then evill," and "That by Discord things increase." Their wit resides in the framing of each premise in such a way as to disguise its outrageousness so that the conclusions drawn seem to follow logically. For example, Donne begins the paradox "That a wise man is knowne by much Laughinge" with this premise: ". . . since the powers of discourse, and reason, and laughter, be equally proper to only man, why shall not he be most wise which hath most use of laughing, as well as he which hath most of reasoning and discoursing."

The problem as a genre also had classical roots, in the problems posed by Aristotle as a method of education. In the Renaissance, the form found expression as a social diversion designed to entertain and to exercise wit. By Donne's time, problems could be either brief, consisting of a few statements suggesting possible answers to the question posed, or lengthy, consisting of carefully wrought arguments with appeals to authority. Donne wrote both kinds. "Why doth Sir Walter Ralegh write the Historie of these times?" has three suggested answers; "Why doth not Gold soyle the fingers?" has four, all in question form. At the other extreme, "Why hath the common opinion affoorded woemen Soules?" is argued in approximately 270 words; "Why have Bastards best Fortune?" and "Why doth the Poxe so much affect to undermine the nose?" both extend to 380 words. Donne's problems, apparently the earliest literary problems written in English, are as witty as his paradoxes, but they are much darker in tone, doubtless reflecting his straitened circumstances at the time of their composition.

The *Essayes in Divinity*, first published in 1651, were probably written in 1614, when Donne was preparing himself to enter Holy Orders in the Church of England. Described by his son as "Disquisitions, Interwoven with Meditations and Prayers," the book contains true essays, in the sense of "attempts" to set down scattered thoughts provoked by the first verse each of Genesis and Exodus. Drawing on Donne's extensive reading in theology and on his own experience, they explore such topics as "Of Genesis," "Of the Name of God," "Diversity in Names," and "Of Number." While they are not as polished as his *Devotions upon Emergent Occasions*, the *Essayes in Divinity* present Donne in a most attractive light as he deplores the narrow sectarianism of his day and declares, "so Synagogue and Church is the same thing, and of the Church, *Roman* and *Reformed*, and all other distinctions of place, Discipline, or Person, but one Church, journying to one *Hierusalem*, and directed by one guide, Christ Jesus."

Certainly the best known of Donne's short prose works are the 23 "Meditations *vpon our Humane Condition*" included in *Devotions upon Emergent Occasions*, written over the Winter of 1623, when Donne was gravely ill, and published in 1624. These meditations react to the stages of his illness, beginning with its onset, progressing to a state near death, and ending in recovery, though with a warning of relapse. The most famous of these meditations (no. 17) is a soaring declaration of the interdependence of humankind: "No Man is an *Iland*, intire of it selfe; every man is a peece of the *Continent*, a part of the *maine*; if a *Clod* bee washed away by the *Sea*, *Europe* is the lesse, as well as if a *Promontorie* were, as well as if a *Mannor* of thy *friends*, or of *thine owne* were; Any Mans *death* diminishes *me*, because I am involved in *Mankinde*; And therefore never send to know for whom the *bell* tolls; It tolls for *thee*." The first clause of this passage, which has become as much identified with Donne as any of his poetry, is the most quoted nonbiblical prose passage in English.

TED-LARRY PEBWORTH

See also Religious Essay

Biography

Born between January and June 1572 in London. Studied privately with Catholic tutors, and at Hart Hall (now Hertford College), Oxford, 1584–87; possibly studied at Cambridge University; Thavies Inn, London, 1591; Lincoln's Inn, London (master of the revels, 1593–95), from 1592. Renounced his Catholicism, c. 1593. Volunteer on the Earl of Essex's expeditions to Cadiz, 1596, and to the Azores, 1597. Private secretary to Sir Thomas Egerton, lord keeper, London, 1598–1601; member of Parliament for Brackley, 1601. Secretly married Egerton's niece Ann More, 1601 (died, 1617): 12 children (six died before his death); discovery of his marriage caused him to be dismissed from his post and briefly imprisoned, destroying his hopes for a political career. Lived in Pyrford, Surrey, 1602–06, and Mitcham, Surrey, 1606–11; traveled in Europe with Sir Walter Chute, 1605–06, and Sir Robert Drury, 1611–12. Ordained in the Church of England, 1615; chaplain-in-ordinary to James I at Cambridge; rector, Keyton, Hampshire, 1616–21, and Sevenoaks, Kent, 1616; reader in divinity, Lincoln's Inn, 1616–21; held various church positions, 1619–26, including dean of St. Paul's, London, 1621. Justice of the peace, Kent and Bedfordshire, 1622, and Bedfordshire, 1626; served on the Court of Delegates, 1622–31. Awards: honorary degrees from Oxford and Cambridge Universities. Died in London, 31 March 1631.

Selected Writings

Essays and Related Prose

Devotions upon Emergent Occasions, 1624; edited by J. Sparrow, 1923, Anthony Raspa, 1975, and Elizabeth Savage, 2 vols., 1975
Juvenilia, or Certaine Paradoxes, and Problems, 1633; revised, enlarged edition, as *Paradoxes, Problems, Essayes*, edited by John Donne (the son), 1652; as *Paradoxes and Problems*, edited by Helen Peters, 1980
Essayes in Divinity, Interwoven with Meditations and Prayers, 1651; edited by Evelyn M. Simpson, 1952
Selected Prose, edited by Evelyn M. Simpson, 1967
Selected Prose, edited by Neil Rhodes, 1987

Other writings: poetry, satires, a book about suicide (*Biathanatos*, wr. 1607–08, pub. 1647), and sermons (collected in *Sermons*, edited by G. R. Potter and Evelyn M. Simpson, 10 vols., 1953–62).

Bibliographies

Keynes, Geoffrey, *A Bibliography of Dr. John Donne*, Oxford: Clarendon Press, revised edition, 1973 (original edition, 1914)
Roberts, John R., *John Donne: An Annotated Bibliography of Modern Criticism, 1912–1967 and 1968–1978*, Columbia: University of Missouri Press, 2 vols., 1973–82

Further Reading

Bald, R. C., *John Donne: A Life*, Oxford: Clarendon Press, and New York: Oxford University Press, 1970
Simpson, Evelyn M., *A Study of the Prose Works of John Donne*, Oxford: Clarendon Press, 1962 (original edition, 1924)

Dostoevskii, Fedor

Russian, 1821–1881

In the course of a literary career spanning about 35 years Fedor Dostoevskii produced over 50 separate essays in addition to a large number of unsigned editorial notes and longer essayistic works – particularly the travelogue *Zimnie zametki o letnikh vpechatleniiakh* (1863; *Winter Notes on Summer Impressions*) and the periodical miscellany *Dnevnik Pisatelia* (1873–81; *A Writer's Diary*), which itself consists of over 200 essay entries. The genre of these essays has its roots in the newspaper *feuilleton* but builds in other directions to include review essays, editorial notes, testimony, travel account, diary, and aesthetic, social, and political polemic. Dostoevskii's essays range over a large number of topics relating to public life: cultural events of current interest, contemporary social and political issues, current aesthetic debates in which the author himself participates, and questions of national identity, as well as questions of historical interest such as Dostoevskii's participation in the "radical" Petrashevskii reading circle.

The topics and genres of Dostoevskii's essay writing emerge from two different traditions. In spirit they are particularly Russian, belonging to and helping to shape the tone of Russian social polemics of the 1860s. In form they are strongly influenced by the French popular news *feuilleton*. The polyphonic quality of Dostoevskii's journalism reveals it to be the direct heir to the polemics between the Westernizers and the Slavophiles of the generation of the 1840s concerning the fate and national character of Russia. The Westernizers believed that the secularization and modernization of Russia by Peter the Great had been for the best, bringing Russia from a condition of ahistorical stagnation into the family of nations, while the Slavophiles argued that Peter had badly fragmented Russian society and had buried age-old Russian social and cultural values. Dostoevskii was strongly influenced by such leading Westernizing writers as the political thinker **Aleksandr Herzen** and the literary critic **Vissarion Belinskii**. Dostoevskii's longer works, especially *Winter Notes on Summer Impressions* and *A Writer's Diary*, respond to Herzen's *S togo berega* (pub. in German, 1850, in Russian, 1855; *From the Other Shore*), a brilliant philosophical dialogue about the meaning of history and historical change. This influence is felt both in the author's tendency to carry on an imagined argument with his readers and in his ongoing meditations about the possible paths of change in Russia and Europe. Belinskii's presence is felt in Dostoevskii's focus on arousing and shaping the social conscience of his readers.

In the 1840s Dostoevskii was one of four or five promising young writers (among them, Ivan Goncharov, Nikolai Nekrasov, and **Ivan Turgenev**) who were practitioners of the new French fashion of the *feuilleton*. Assuming the point of view of the *flâneur* – or the dreamy young wanderer strolling through St. Petersburg's streets – Dostoevskii in his earliest work, "Peterburgskaia letopis'" (1847; "A Petersburg Chronicle"), plays with the lighthearted reportage of current cultural events, typical of the *feuilleton*. He uses parody of this form as a way to introduce more serious ethical and aesthetic issues, at times dealing with questions about censorship or the suffering of the poor or, in other instances, arguing about the true social function of art.

After a hiatus of 13 years spent in prison, labor camp, and in exile in the army, all for his participation in the radical Petrashevskii reading group, Dostoevskii developed longer genres building partly from the *feuilleton*. More weighty essays of the early 1860s, for example, "G. -bov i vopros ob iskusstve" (1861; "Mr. -bov and the Question of Art"), form an important part of the debate between moderates and radical utilitarians (**Nikolai Chernyshevskii**, Nikolai Dobroliubov, Dmitrii Pisarev). Dostoevskii defends a middle ground between pure aestheticism and a social utilitarian aesthetic, arguing that great art must have liberty to develop its own forms, themes, and techniques, but that great art is always of contemporary interest and always addresses central social concerns.

Dostoevskii once characterized himself as a writer "possessed of a nostalgia for the current moment." Indeed, his essay writing always focuses attention on two things: the voices of the writer and his interlocutors and the events of the present moment. Selfhood, which is the thematic core of Dostoevskii's essays, takes shape through discussion and polemic, through forming a position, and through keeping one's thinking oriented toward the ever-evolving present. Thus, his essay writing is essential to understanding the person and the writer. There is a creative symbiosis between his essays and the great novels written after his incarceration; the essays provide the polemical material for the fictional work. What Mikhail Bakhtin calls the "polyphonic" quality of Dostoevskii's art, the counterpoint of a number of ideologically distinct voices within one work, is directly related to his experience as an essayist and polemicist. Thus, the travel notes *Winter Notes on Summer Impressions* have been shown to interact substantially with the later *Zapiski iz podpol'ia* (1864; *Notes from the Underground*). *A Writer's Diary* was an important laboratory for the generic experiments and polemical complexities of *Brat'ia Karamazovy* (1880; *The Brothers Karamazov*).

Dostoevskii's impact on later essay writing, both philosophical and literary-critical, is overwhelming. "Rech' o Pushkine" (1880; Pushkin speech) announced a Russian national culture which had the power to redeem a moribund Western European spirit. The Russian symbolists, particularly Dmitrii Merezhkovskii, responded in force. Dostoevskii's writing inspired a generation of major religious thinkers, including Nikolai Berdiaev, **Lev Shestov**, and Semion Frank. Probably the clearest example of the influence of his essay writing can be seen in the writings of one of Russia's most brilliant if problematic essayists, **Vasilii Rozanov**, whose greatest works emerge directly from *A Writer's Diary*.

EDITH W. CLOWES

Biography

Born 30 October 1821 in Moscow. Studied at schools in Moscow; Army Chief Engineering Academy, St. Petersburg, 1838–43, then brief military service, until 1844. Translated Balzac's *Eugénie Grandet*, 1844; began writing fiction. Joined the Petrashevskii circle, 1847–49: group arrested in 1849 for reading a banned letter by Vissarion Belinskii; mock execution arranged by Tsar Nicholas I: after reprieve, sentenced to four years' hard labor, 1850–54, then exiled as a soldier, 1854–59; suffered worsening epilepsy while in prison and in exile. Married Maria Dmitrievna Isaeva, 1857 (died, 1864): one stepson. Cofounder, with his brother, *Vremia* (Time), 1861–63, and *Epokha* (Epoch), 1864–65; took on the debts of his brother's and wife's families when they died, 1864. Had a difficult

affair with Apollinaria Suslova, and began gambling, 1865–66. Married Anna Grigorievna Snitkina, 1867: two daughters (one died) and two sons (one died). Lived in Western Europe, partly to escape debts, 1867–71. Editor, *Grazhdanin* (The citizen), 1873–78, and *Dnevnik Pisatelia*, 1876–77 (also major contributor, 1873–81). Visited Germany, usually Ems, for treatment of emphysema. Died (of emphysema) in St. Petersburg, 28 January 1881.

Selected Writings

Essays and Related Prose

Zimnie zametki o letnikh vpechatleniiakh, 1863; as *Winter Notes on Summer Impressions*, translated by R. Renfield, 1954, Kyril FitzLyon, 1954, and D. Patterson, 1988

Dnevnik Pisatelia, 1873–81; as *The Diary of a Writer* and as *A Writer's Diary 1873–1876*, translated by Boris Leo Brasol, 2 vols., 1949, and by Kenneth Lantz, 2 vols., 1993–94

Fel'etony sorokovykh godov: Zhurnal'naia i gazetnaia proza I. A. Goncharova, F. M. Dostoevskogo, i drugikh (Feuilletons of the 1840s: the journal and newspaper prose of I. A. Goncharov, F. M. Dostoevskii, and others), edited by Iu. G. Oksman, 1930

Occasional Writings, edited and translated by David Magarshack, 1963

Ob iskusstve (Of art), 1973

Iskaniia i razmyshleniia (Quests and thoughts), 1983

O russkoi literature (On Russian literature), 1987

Other writings: four novels (*Prestuplenie i nakazanie* [*Crime and Punishment*], 1867; *Idiot* [*The Idiot*], 1869; *Besy* [*The Possessed*], 1872; *Brat'ia Karamazovy* [*The Brothers Karamazov*], 1880), four novellas, short stories, the prose work *Zapiski iz podpol'ia* (1864; *Notes from the Underground*), and memoirs.

Collected works editions: *Polnoe sobranie sochinenii*, edited by G. M. Fridlender and others, 30 vols., 1972–90; *Sobranie sochinenii*, 15 vols., 1988.

Bibliographies

Belkin, A. A., A. S. Dolinin, and V. V. Kozhinov, editors, *Dostoevskii: Bibliografiia proizvedenii Dostoevskogo i literatury o nem 1917–65*, Moscow: Kniga, 1968

Dostoevskii: Materialy i issledovaniia, Leningrad: Nauka, 1974– (in progress)

Grossman, Leonid Petrovich, *Seminarii po Dostoevskomu: Materialy, bibliografiia i kommentarii*, Moscow: Gosizdat, 1922

Leatherbarrow, W. J., *Fedor Dostoevsky: A Reference Guide*, Boston: Hall, 1990

Further Reading

Chances, Ellen, *The Ideology of Pochvennichestvo in Dostoevsky's Thick Journals "Vremja" and "Epoxa"* (dissertation), Princeton, New Jersey: Princeton University, 1972

Jackson, Robert Louis, *Dostoevsky's Quest for Form*, New Haven, Connecticut: Yale University Press, 1966

Kelly, Aileen, "Irony and Utopia in Herzen and Dostoevsky: *From the Other Shore* and *Diary of a Writer*," *Russian Review* 50, no. 4 (October 1991): 397–416

Kjetsaa, Geir, "Written by Dostoevsky?" *Scando-Slavica* 26 (1980): 19–31

Lvovski, Zinovy, "Dostoievsky feuilletoniste," *Revue Politique et Littéraire* 69, no. 4 (1931): 527–31

Morson, Gary Saul, *The Boundaries of Genre: Dostoevsky's "Diary of a Writer" and the Traditions of Literary Utopia*, Austin: University of Texas Press, 1981

Morson, Gary Saul, "Introductory Study: Dostoevsky's Great Experiment," in *A Writer's Diary* by Dostoevskii, Evanston, Illinois: Northwestern University Press, 1993: 1–117

Moser, Charles A. "Dostoevsky and the Aesthetics of Journalism," *Dostoevsky Studies* 3 (1982): 27–41

Nechaeva, V. S., *Zhurnal M. M. i F. M. Dostoevskikh "Vremia", 1861–1863*, Moscow, 1972

Perlina, Nina, "Vozdeistvie gertsenovskogo zhurnalizma na arkhitektoniku i polifonicheskoe stroenie 'Dnevnika pisatelia' Dostoevskogo," *Dostoevsky Studies* 5 (1984): 141–55

Zakharov, V. N., *Sistema zhanrov Dostoevskogo: Tipologiia i poetika*, Leningrad: Izdatel'stvo Leningradskogo Universiteta, 1985

Zhurbina, Evgeniya Isaakovna, *Teoriia i praktika khudozhestvenno-publitsisticheskikh zhanrov: Ocherk, fel'eton*, Moscow: Mysl', 1969

Douglass, Frederick

American, 1818–1895

Frederick Douglass, a self-taught escaped slave, published *Narrative of the Life of Frederick Douglass, an American Slave* in 1845 to launch an activist writing career that would make him the dominant African American for the next half century. He wrote two subsequent autobiographies (1855 and 1881) and excelled as statesman, orator, and journalist. He left more than 500 speeches and published abolitionist newspapers for nearly 16 years, and a postwar weekly for nearly four. His commentaries were published in **Atlantic Monthly**, the London *Times*, and the New York *Herald*.

Douglass' fluency with rhythm and imagery is in evidence in his *Narrative*. Critics note, however, that the narrative owes less to the autobiography genre than to the slave narrative tradition. It is a chronological testimony delivered in understated language, whose shape was determined by abolitionist printers and editors. Its purpose was to document for whites the horrors of slavery and to persuade them to abolish slavery. But the restrained approach of the slave narrative, juxtaposed with Douglass' rhythmic portrayals of anguish, fear, and pathos, creates a tension generally associated with literature. The narrative is hailed as an artistic masterpiece. Its 11 **chapters** – essays of sorts – chronicle Douglass' birth in Maryland to a mother he would see only a few times and a father rumored to be a white slave owner. It follows his bestial existence across plantations, his abuse by seven different owners or overseers, his introduction to reading and writing by a kind mistress, and his clever schemes as a shipyard worker to get others to help with his education.

The *Narrative* was an immediate success, with editions published in England, Ireland, and France, but its publication in the U.S. in May 1845, replete with specific names and places (excluding details of his means of escape) put Douglass in danger of being returned to slavery. He left for Europe in August 1845 to lecture in England, Scotland, and Ireland. After British friends purchased his freedom for 150 pounds (750 dollars) in 1846, he returned to the U.S. in 1847 and settled in Rochester, New York, where he published his first newspaper, the *North Star*.

Douglass' decision to publish, against the wishes of his abolitionist mentor William Lloyd Garrison, marked the beginning of his re-creation – as a writer, as an independent person of color, as an intellectual. African American newspapers had been published since 1827, but none for more than a few years. Douglass was determined that the *North Star* would survive, and prove that a man of color could sustain a quality newspaper over a long period of time. "Our race must be vindicated from the embarrassing imputations resulting from former non-success," he wrote in the inaugural issue. Most of its readers were white. The *North Star* also provided Douglass the forum he needed for an independent exploration of questions regarding slavery. By early 1848, a *North Star* article ("The Constitution and Slavery") confirmed that his break with the Garrisonians was complete. Now he rejected Garrison's notion that the U.S. Constitution was by nature a pro-slavery document that should not be honored, and that, consequently, abolitionists, through the sheer weight of logic and persuasion, would convince good men to effect radical change.

For nearly 13 years the newspaper – changed in name in 1851 to *Frederick Douglass's Paper* – was the vehicle for hundreds of articles, editorials, and reprinted speeches by Douglass. His best writing is infused with elements of his oratorical delivery: long, sermonesque sentences, filled with anguish, anger, or ridicule, sometimes drawing wry analogies from Old Testament imagery. He railed against colonization, supported women's suffrage, and recorded the resolutions of African American conventions. When the weekly failed in 1860, Douglass relied on *Frederick Douglass's Monthly* – founded in 1858 as a monthly compendium primarily for foreign distribution – to carry his views. After Abraham Lincoln's election as president, Douglass held him to be "the most dangerous advocate of slave-hunting and slave-catching in the land" ("The Inaugural Address," April 1861). After the outbreak of the Civil War, Douglass remained critical, lambasting Lincoln and Congress for not outlawing slavery ("The Slave Power Still Omnipotent at Washington," January 1862) and agitating for the enlistment of African American volunteers in the Union Army ("Services of Colored Men," July 1862). Not until Lincoln signed the Emancipation Proclamation did Douglass relent, somewhat. Even then he was not completely satisfied: there was still work to be done ("The Work of the Future," November 1862) and there were still profound questions to be answered ("What Shall Be Done with the Freed Slaves?," November 1862). In the last issue of the monthly, marking the end of almost 16 years of continuous publication in some form or another, Douglass took one last broadside at Lincoln for not speaking out against Confederate abuse of captured African American troops ("Black Soldiers," August 1863).

Douglass returned to writing full-time in 1870 when he took control of the *New Era*, renaming it the *New National Era*. Here he examined the problems of the newly freed slave, the need for federal commitment to Reconstruction, the evils of Chinese worker exploitation, and the urgency of women's suffrage. The *Era* folded in 1874, and Douglass wrote for mainstream publications.

In 1892, Douglass, journalist Ida B. Wells, newspaper historian I. Garland Penn, and attorney Ferdinand L. Barnett published *The Reason Why the Colored American Is Not in the World's Columbian Exposition, 1892*; Douglass' introduction to the **pamphlet** devoted a few pages to lynchings. He returned to this topic in the *North American Review* ("Lynch Law in the South," June 1894), and later in 1894, less than a year before his death, he published a pamphlet addressing the issue fully (*Why Is the Negro Lynched? The Lesson of the Hour*). In the pamphlet, he notes that at the root of lynchings is the accusation that black men have assaulted white women and, in some cases, white children. Douglass defends, as if before a court of law, the integrity of the Negro "as a class" against this accusation. "Throughout the war," Douglass writes, "while the slave-masters of the South were absent ... in the field of rebellion, with bullets in their pockets, treason in their hearts, broad blades in their bloody hands, seeking the life of the nation ... their wives, their daughters, their sisters and their mothers were left in the absolute custody of these same Negroes ... and there was never a single instance of such crime reported." Douglass also notes that slavery "was a system of unmitigated, legalized outrage upon black women of the South, and no white man was ever shot, burned or hanged for availing himself of all the power that slavery gave him."

When he died in 1895, Douglass left behind an enormous collection of writing, which has yet to be fully evaluated. Clearly his legacy as an intellectual, politically motivated African American has had a marked effect on African American politics and on American political writing in general. His use of the essay form is a good example of the effectiveness of the genre as a tool for political discussion and change, underpinning Douglass' stature as a man of conscience.

HARRY AMANA

Biography

Born Frederick Augustus Washington Bailey, probably 1818 in Tuckahoe, Talbot County, Maryland; changed his name to Douglass when he escaped slavery. Worked on a plantation, until 1825; house servant, Baltimore, 1825–33; field hand, St. Michael's, Maryland, 1833–36; ship's caulker, 1837–38; escaped from slavery to New York, 1838. Married Anna Murray, 1838: one daughter and three sons. Worked in shipyards in Massachusetts, 1838–42. Worked on various anti-slavery campaigns, from 1841, and later on women's rights campaigns. Published the first of three autobiographical volumes, 1845; lectured in Britain and Ireland, 1845–47. Friends bought his freedom and he returned to the U.S., 1847. Founder, editor, and main contributor, *North Star* abolitionist paper, 1847–60 (name changed to *Frederick Douglass's Paper*, 1851), and *Frederick Douglass's Monthly*, 1858–63; owner, *New National Era* newspaper, 1870–74. President, Freedman's Savings and Trust Company, 1873–74; U.S. marshal, 1877–81; recorder of deeds, after 1881. Married Helen Pitts, 1884. U.S. minister to Haiti, 1889–91. Died in Washington, D.C., 20 February 1895.

Selected Writings

Essays and Related Prose
Narrative of the Life of Frederick Douglass, an American Slave, 1845; edited by Benjamin Quarles, 1960, Houston A. Baker, Jr., 1982, and David W. Blight, 1993
My Bondage and My Freedom, 1855; edited by William L. Andrews, 1987
Life and Times of Frederick Douglass, 1881; revised edition, 1892
On Women's Rights, edited by Philip S. Foner, 1976
The Narrative and Selected Writings, edited by Michael Meyer, 1984
The Oxford Frederick Douglass Reader, edited by William L. Andrews, 1996

Collected works editions: *Life and Writings*, edited by Philip S. Foner, 4 vols., 1950–55; *The Frederick Douglass Papers*, edited by John W. Blassingame and John R. McKivigan, 5 vols., 1979–92 (in progress).

Further Reading

Andrews, William L., *Critical Essays on Frederick Douglass*, Boston: Hall, 1991
Baker, Houston A., Jr., "Autobiographical Acts and the Voice of the Southern Slave," in his *The Journey Back: Issues in Black Literature and Criticism*, Chicago: University of Chicago Press, 1980
Castronovo, Russ, "'As to nation, I belong to none:' Ambivalence, Diaspora, and Frederick Douglass," *American Transcendental Quarterly* 9, no. 3 (September 1995)
Foner, Philip S., Introduction to *Frederick Douglass on Women's Rights*, edited by Foner, Westport, Connecticut: Greenwood Press, 1976
Garvey, Gregory T., "Frederick Douglass's Change of Opinion on the U.S. Constitution: Abolitionism and the 'elements of moral power'," *American Transcendental Quarterly* 9, no. 3 (September 1995)
Gates, Henry Louis, Jr.,"Binary Oppositions in Chapter One of the *Narrative*," in *Afro-American Literature: The Reconstruction of Instruction*, edited by Dexter Fisher and Robert B. Stepto, New York: Modern Language Association of America, 1979
Gates, Henry Louis, Jr., "A Dangerous Literacy: The Legacy of Frederick Douglass," *New York Times Book Review*, 28 May 1995: 3
McFeely, William S., *Frederick Douglass*, New York: Norton, 1991
Royer, Daniel J., "The Process of Literacy as Communal Involvement in the Narratives of Frederick Douglass," *African American Review* 28, no. 3 (Fall 1994)
Sekora, John, "Comprehending Slavery: Language and Personal History in the *Narrative*," *CLA Journal* 29, no. 2 (December 1985)
Sekora, John, "'Mr. Editor, if you please': Frederick Douglass, *My Bondage and My Freedom*, and the End of the Abolitionist Imprint," *Callaloo* 17, no. 2 (Spring 1994)
Stone, Albert E., "Identity and Art in Frederick Douglass's *Narrative*," *CLA Journal* 17, no. 2 (December 1973)
Sundquist, Eric J., editor, *Frederick Douglass: New Literary and Historical Essays*, Cambridge and New York: Cambridge University Press, 1990

Du Bois, W. E. B.
American, 1868–1963

W. E. B. Du Bois was the preeminent African American writer, scholar, editor, and activist of the first 50 years of the 20th century. He published scores of essays, which range in style from the lyrical to the polemical and in subject matter from the personal to the historical. His influence as an essayist, especially inspiring to African American writers, has been immense. Du Bois showed that the essay could be used to do battle in the struggle for justice and equality as well as to explore the self. In his autobiography, *Along This Way* (1933), James Weldon Johnson refers to Du Bois' collection of essays *The Souls of Black Folk* (1903) as "a work, which, I think, has had greater effect upon and within the Negro race in America than any single book published in this country since *Uncle Tom's Cabin*."

The range of Du Bois' voice as an essayist originates in his awareness that as an African American he could not write a strictly "personal" essay. He believed that the black writer must always speak publicly and politically as well as personally. The Negro, he wrote in "Of Our Spiritual Strivings" (1903), has "no true self-consciousness," but only a "double-consciousness," for he must always "see himself through the revelation of the other world." For Du Bois this meant that he must address the issue of racism even in his most **personal essays**.

In "Criteria of Negro Art" (1926), Du Bois wrote that he could "conceive" that "somehow, somewhere eternal and perfect beauty sits above truth and right, but here and now in the world in which I work they are for me unseparated and inseparable." For him, "all art is propaganda and ever must be" and "whatever art I have for writing has been used always for propaganda for gaining the right of black folk to love and enjoy."

But, if art was a weapon, it was also art and all the more effective if beautiful. Du Bois' conception of beauty was classical. Raised in the Congregational Church of New England and educated at Harvard and in Berlin, Du Bois was torn at an early age between the elitism and gentility of his education and the militance and outrage forced on him by white racism. A white artist might be able to aspire to beauty in and of itself; a black artist could not. For Du Bois, beauty had to serve truth and justice, and to such ends the plasticity of the essay was well suited. Du Bois was a committed student of the essay, especially the 19th-century English and American essayists. He admired the specific rendering of personality in **Hazlitt** and **Lamb**, and the abstract theorizing and magisterial pronouncements of **Emerson** and **Carlyle**. He saw the essay as a form that could accommodate scholarship and objectivity as well as opinion and lyricism.

From 1910 until 1934 Du Bois was editor of *Crisis*, the journal of the National Association for the Advancement of Colored People. Though he published many of the writers of the emerging Harlem Renaissance, his support of the New Negro movement was qualified. His own classicism and his belief in the leadership of the "talented tenth" of the Negro population led him to want to put the "best foot forward," and he had difficulty with the blues rhythms, street argot, and sometimes seamy material of the younger writers. Nevertheless, he recognized the difficulties renaissance writers faced as they tried to steer between "the Scylla of prudery and Charybdis of unbounded license" ("Harlem," 1927) and, in fact, his own writing, especially his essays, presented the example of one who was willing to take political and stylistic risks. In a 1903 essay, "Of Mr. Booker T. Washington and Others" (1903), he had challenged Washington's accommodationist views on education and the hegemony the older man maintained among black intellectuals. The break with Washington marked a move by Du Bois toward more and more radical positions. First exposed to Marxism during graduate work in Berlin (1892–94), Du Bois maintained an uneasy relationship with socialist thought for the next several decades. Though he did not join the Communist Party until 1961, he used the opinion page of the *Crisis* from the beginning to support socialist causes, and even, after a 1926 visit, the young Union of Soviet Socialist Republics. Du Bois continued to write political essays throughout his life, promoting pan-Africanism, women's rights, and the civil rights movement while attacking lynching, segregation, the Ku Klux Klan, fascism, and McCarthyism.

In his attempts to get black readers to adopt a sense of racial pride and white readers to take the issue of race seriously, Du Bois employed a variety of stylistic approaches in his essays. In essays in the *Crisis*, he turned the style of the gossip column and the celebrity profile to political ends. He even offered a send-up of **Swift**'s *A Modest Proposal* (1729) entitled "A Mild Suggestion" (1912), sarcastically proposing to whites that they pick a night on which they might each lure a few blacks into their homes and massacre them: "The next morning there would be ten million funerals, and therefore no Negro problem. Think how quietly the thing would be settled!"

Du Bois employed satire elsewhere (for instance in "The Black Man Brings His Gifts," 1925), but it was not his favored tone. More often he chose to take seriously that which was too often ignored, such as black spirituals ("Of the Sorrow Songs," 1903), everyday racial slights ("On Being Black," 1920), and the lives of poor Negroes in the rural South ("Of the Black Belt," 1903).

Du Bois exploited a wide range of what the essay offers. He wrote lyrically and allegorically, used classical allusions and rigorous research, and revealed a most personal and even nostalgic voice at times, but almost invariably his subject was too serious for the whimsy and wit of the light essay of the late Victorian period. Even an essay occasioned by his daughter's wedding makes clear at the outset that it will be about racism: "The problem of marriage among our present American Negroes is a difficult one" ("So the Girl Marries," 1928). When the subject is a much sadder one – for example, the death of his son – Du Bois knows that the real subject remains racism. In "Of the Passing of the First-Born" (1903), he adds anger to the grand and somber tones of the classical elegy, apostrophizing Death and confronting his own despair before deciding he must return to his work so that some "young souls," if not his own son, might know a "morning" when the "veil" of racism is lifted.

NED STUCKEY-FRENCH

Biography

William Edward Burghardt Du Bois. Born 23 February 1868 in Great Barrington, Massachusetts. Studied at public schools in Great Barrington; Fisk University, Nashville, Tennessee, 1885–88, A.B., 1888; Harvard University, Cambridge, Massachusetts, 1888–90, A.M., 1891, Ph.D., 1895; University of Berlin, 1892–94. Taught at Wilberforce University, Ohio, 1894–96, the University of Pennsylvania, Philadelphia, 1896–97, and Atlanta University, 1897–1910. Married Nina Gomer, 1896 (died, 1950): one son (died in youth) and one daughter. Founder, Pan-African Congress, 1900, and the Niagara Movement, 1904. Editor, *Moon Illustrated Weekly*, Memphis, Tennessee, 1906–07, and *Horizon*, Washington, D.C., 1907–10. Cofounder, National Association for the Advancement of Colored People, 1910: director of publicity and research, editor of its magazine the *Crisis*, 1910–34, and director of Special Research, 1944–48. Editor, with A. G. Dill, *Brownies' Book*, 1920–21; columnist for the Pittsburgh *Courier*, 1936–38, *Amsterdam News*, New York, 1938–44, Chicago *Defender*, 1945–48, and *People's Voice*, 1947–48; also wrote for *Current History*, the *Journal of Negro Education*, *Foreign Affairs*, and **American Scholar**, editor, *Phylon*, Atlanta, 1940–44. Vice chair, Council on African Affairs, 1949–54; candidate for U.S. Senate for New York, 1950. Married Shirley Graham, 1951. Emigrated to Ghana, 1961, and became citizen, 1963. Awards: Spingarn Medal, 1920; International Peace Prize, 1952; Lenin Peace Prize, 1959. Knight Commander, Liberian

Order of African Redemption; Fellow, American Association for the Advancement of Science; Member, American Academy. Died in Accra, Ghana, 27 August 1963.

Selected Writings

Essays and Related Prose

The Souls of Black Folk: Essays and Sketches, 1903; revised edition, 1953
Darkwater: Voices from Within the Veil, 1920
The Gift of Black Folk: The Negroes in the Making of America, 1924
Black Reconstruction in America: An Essay Toward a History of the Part Which Black Folk Played in the Attempt to Reconstruct Democracy in America, 1860–1880, 1935
Black Folk, Then and Now: An Essay in the History and Sociology of the Negro Race, 1939
Dusk of Dawn: An Essay Toward an Autobiography of a Race Concept, 1940
An ABC of Color: Selections from over Half a Century of the Writings, 1964
W. E. B. Du Bois Speaks: Speeches and Addresses 1890–1963, edited by Philip Foner, 2 vols., 1970
Selected Writings, edited by Walter Wilson, 1970
W. E. B. Du Bois: A Reader, edited by Meyer Weinberg, 1970
The Seventh Son: The Thought and Writings of W. E. B. Du Bois, edited by Julius Lester, 2 vols., 1971
A W. E. B. Du Bois Reader, edited by Andrew D. Paschal, 1971
The Crisis Writings, edited by Daniel Walden, 1972
The Emerging Thought of W. E. B. Du Bois: Essays and Editorials from The Crisis, edited by Henry Lee Moon, 1972
The Education of Black People: Ten Critiques 1906–1960, edited by Herbert Aptheker, 1973
The Writings of W. E. B. Du Bois (selection), edited by Virginia Hamilton, 1975
Against Racism: Unpublished Essays, Papers, Addresses 1887–1961, edited by Herbert Aptheker, 1985
W. E. B. Du Bois: A Reader, edited by David Levering Lewis, 1995
The Oxford W. E. B. Dubois Reader, edited by Eric J. Sundquist, 1996

Other writings: five novels (*The Quest of the Silver Fleece*, 1911; *Dark Princess*, 1928; *The Black Flame* trilogy, 1957–61), poetry, many works on African American politics and social conditions, an autobiography (published posthumously, 1968), and correspondence.

Collected works edition: *The Complete Published Works* (Kraus-Thomson Organization Edition), edited by Herbert Aptheker, 20 vols., 1973–86.

Bibliographies
Aptheker, Herbert, *Annotated Bibliography of the Published Writings of W. E. B. Du Bois* (part of *The Complete Published Works*), Millwood, New York: Kraus-Thomson Organization, 1973
Partington, Paul G., *W. E. B. Du Bois: A Bibliography of His Published Writings*, Whittier, California: privately printed, 1979; supplement, 1984

Further Reading
Andrews, William, editor, *Critical Essays on W. E. B. Du Bois*, Boston: Hall, 1985
Byerman, Keith E., "Hearts of Darkness: Narrative Voices in *The Souls of Black Folk*," *American Literary Realism* 14 (1981): 43–51
Byerman, Keith E., *Seizing the Word: History, Art, and Self in the Work of W. E. B. Du Bois*, Athens: University of Georgia Press, 1994
Ikonné, Chidi, *From Du Bois to Van Vechten: The Early New Negro Literature, 1903–1926*, Westport, Connecticut: Greenwood Press, 1981
Rampersad, Arnold, *The Art and Imagination of W. E. B. Du Bois*, Cambridge, Massachusetts: Harvard University Press, 1976

Du Bos, Charles

French, 1882–1939

Educated in France, England, and Germany in the most select schools, Charles Du Bos was an avid reader, who considered that encountering an author was meant to transform one's life. A man who valued spiritual life above all else, he points out that he was born in 1889, the year Henri Bergson published the *Essai sur les données immédiates de la conscience* (Essay on the immediate givens of the conscience; translated as *Time and Free Will*). He wrote that he owed to Bergson "what in me is myself," according to the type of spiritual expression also found in Paul Claudel. This spiritual bent led Du Bos to convert from theism to Catholicism in 1927.

At the time of his death, Du Bos had published only a small part of his writings; most readers knew him for his *Approximations* (1922–37), a seven-volume collection of critical essays and lectures. In 1929 he also published a collection of extracts from his **journal**, as well as passages in various scholarly magazines. Today readers know him because of his **dialogue**s with **André Gide**.

Most of Du Bos' publication is posthumous. Nevertheless, in 1939 he was well received in England, where he represented a new kind of French criticism, less attached to reason and lucidity, and more sincerely emotional, according to Charles Morgan. On the continent he had a limited following: Albert Béguin, Georges Poulet, and the brilliant Jean Starobinski may be cited as inheritors of his critical tradition. Du Bos met numerous authors, including Marcel Proust, Bernard Berenson, **Ernst Robert Curtius**, Rainer Maria Rilke, **Georg Simmel**, André Maurois, Herbert Dieckmann, **Stéphane Mallarmé**, **Paul Valéry**, Edith Wharton, Percy Lubbock, and Marguerite Yourcenar; he became close friends with Gide. Du Bos admired Gide as an author, and shared his spiritual concerns, though he eventually rejected his evangelical leanings. Their friendship is somewhat reminiscent of that of **Montaigne** and La Boétie: Du Bos felt that he was engaged in a dialogue with Gide "in the margins" of his writings. In 1931, when their friendship declined, Du Bos' assessment was that Gide's "rigorous" and sober literary style displayed a lack of imagination, and an "intricacy" devoid of "complexity."

Du Bos' written production is threefold: literary and aesthetic analysis (*Approximations*); his autobiographical *Journal* (composed 1902–39, published in complete form 1946–61); and literary theory with *What Is Literature?* (1940), a piece composed in English and made up of four lectures on Keats and **Shelley**, delivered in 1938 at the University of Notre Dame, where he briefly taught. There is much debate as to which of his works is most important, but in 1918 Gide told Du Bos not to abandon his *Journal*, for this would be his completed oeuvre. As did many of his friends, Gide considered Du Bos essentially a man of dialogue.

Marie-Anne Gouhier (1951) notes Du Bos' frequent use of parentheses and inserted propositions in *Approximations*. The same could be observed in his *Journal*. She finds that he needed to integrate ideas complementary or external to the main thrust of his thought without compromising the linearity of his expression. She believes this facet corresponds to a necessity for temporal simultaneity, when a new explanation, a pause for reflection, traverses the text without interrupting it. This method of writing parallels Bergson's conversational style with Du Bos. The philosopher said to him that "Genius consists in . . . keeping in contact with an internal current," and Du Bos observed that "Bergson thinks aloud in front of you, approves your answer, and continues his thought, without ever an exchange, properly speaking" (*Journal*, 1922). Du Bos' friends described him as a great conversationalist, who always penetrated his interlocutor's thoughts and showed great receptiveness; but his parenthetical style in *Approximations* and the *Journal* resembles an internal Bergsonian-Dubosian dialogue which the readers are invited to witness. A common point between his oral and written expression may have been that he used both to think, explore, and weigh, as in Montaigne's "balance pérenne" (eternal movement of the scales). Yet passages from his journal explain why Du Bos preferred **Pascal** to Montaigne: Pascal proceeded by a series of provisory certainties, proving to be a resolute, decisive genius inherently necessitating the "parti pris" (*Journal*, 1923). It is in this spirit that one may understand Du Bos' certainties.

One of the major themes of Dubosian criticism stems from a reaction against the 1913–14 popular conviction that literature is divorced from life. Du Bos repeats that literature and life are one: in *Approximations*, he declares that "life owes more to literature than literature to life," for literature survives life. He lives through the authors he selects, gathering his essays and critical reflections in *Approximations* and his *Journal*. His manner of composing agreed with his method of literary perception, exploring the musical "tempo" of an author and the harmonies (or Baudelairean "correspondences") resulting from it. François Mauriac pointed out that Du Bos was criticized for being so biographical that "one would forget the authors he studied ever wrote." The method of "approximation" relates to an exploration of the author's essential identity, defined not so much by what is said, but rather by what the author cannot refrain from repeating – the monotony inherent to individual genius. The *Approximations* have been compared to an encyclopedia of Du Bos' favorite European authors, such as Browning, **Carlyle**, and Keats, from whom he borrowed: "I have relapsed into those abstractions which are my only life."

Compared to the volumes of *Approximations*, the *Journal* is at once more intimate and more fragmentary. The contingencies of daily life are often points of departure for literary essays – for instance, bright insights into the creative psychology of Flaubert and Degas. Sometimes a sentence begun in French ends in English. An occasional day will be recorded entirely in English. The fragmentary aspect allowed by the diary form suits Du Bos. He thus avoids the unified coherence of the thesis essay and the task of forcibly organizing materials within a given frame (in 1922 he had already refused to give cohesion to his collection of *Approximations*).

According to his wife's testimony, in 1921 Du Bos began dictating the *Journal* to save time. But in 1928 he was taking as much care with it as with any of his writings. During the last ten years of his life, he apparently dictated (and occasionally wrote) his *Journal* in a masterful delivery exempt from hesitations. In his effort to pinpoint the essential qualities of the authors he studied, Du Bos focused on the "soul" his intuition pursued.

This idea was developed fully in "Literature and the Spirit," the first part of *What Is Literature?*. In it, the conversation tends to become a catechism. Questions about literature must be answered by the scriptures, which clearly state the meaning of life. The text proceeds by a series of metaphysical equations: "Intellects are God"; they are souls which become themselves by means of the heart; life reaches self-consciousness in creating; literary creation is God's Creation; creation is emotion; the Creator gives himself and receives the artist's joy. Thus, Marcelin Pleynet and Michèle Leleu (in *Charles Du Bos*, edited by Dominique Bourel and Hubert Join, 1985) find that Du Bos was somewhat foreign to skepticism. It is difficult to pinpoint the cause of this change of tone. Ian D. McFarlane (1981) notes a "puzzling lack of reference to Montaigne," whom Du Bos had saluted for his "heroism of non-heroism" in 1933. Du Bos seems to have shied away from Montaigne's "prudence and moderation" for the sake of "warmth and audacity," preferring the "pathetic spirituality" of Pascal, **Baudelaire**, and **Péguy**.

In *What Is Literature?* Du Bos advocates a "creative reading" equal to writing, whereby literature becomes consubstantial to its readers. "Literature and Light" shows that culture is a study in perfection, with each literary piece the meeting point of two souls, initiated in wordless communication in the spiritual world. "Literature and Beauty" demonstrates that beauty is order, mathematical and moral, and humans' *raison d'être*. "Literature and the Word" criticizes Hamlet's "words, words, words" to describe books, and Faust's transformation of "In the beginning was the word" into "was the action" – Du Bos would have preferred "was the act" because the word is active. It is the Word made flesh. In his conclusion to *What Is Literature?* Du Bos called for the advent of a true Catholic literature to the world.

Du Bos intended to reach a plenitude that the journal form could not reach, because, as he observed during a 1914 discussion with Gide, **Goethe** once wrote to Lavater that a journal was composed predominantly during moments of emptiness and depression, thus underrepresenting the moments of possession and joy. Perhaps, then, the four lectures from Notre Dame form the complementary counterpart to Du Bos' *Journal*.

SERVANNE WOODWARD

Biography
Born 27 October 1882 in Paris. Studied at Lycée Janson de Sailly, from 1895; Balliol College, Oxford, 1901–02. Military service at Évreux, 1902–03. Traveled in Italy, Germany, and England, 1903–05. Contributor to various periodicals, including the *Nouvelle Revue Française* (New French Review) and the *Gazette des Beaux-Arts*. Married Juliette Siry: one daughter. Became friends with André Gide during World War I, founding the Foyer Franco-Belge to host people fleeing the German invasion. Suffered from a spiritual crisis, 1918–27, then converted to Catholicism. Organizer, with Paul

Desjardin, "The Decades of Pontigny" intellectual debates, 1922–34. Founder, with François Mauriac, *Vigile* (Vigil), 1930. Taught at Saint Mary's College, University of Notre Dame, Indiana, 1937–38 and 1938–39. Died in La Celle-Saint-Cloud, 5 August 1939.

Selected Writings

Essays and Related Prose
Notes sur Mérimée, 1920
Approximations, 7 vols., 1922–37; in 1 vol., 1965
Extrait d'un journal, 1908–1928, 1929; enlarged edition, 1931
Le Dialogue avec André Gide, 1929
Byron et le besoin de la fatalité, 1929; as *Byron and the Need of Fatality*, translated by Ethel Colburn Mayne, 1932
François Mauriac et le problème du romancier catholique, 1933
What Is Literature?, 1940
Commentaires, 1946
Grandeur et misère de Benjamin Constant, 1946
Journal, 9 vols., 1946–61; the years 1902–20 published in *Cahiers Charles Du Bos* 10–25 (1966–81)
Goethe, 1949
La Comtesse de Noailles et le climat du génie, 1949
Du spirituel dans l'ordre littéraire, 1967
Robert et Elizabeth Browning, ou, La Plénitude de l'amour humain, 1982

Other writings: letters to and dialogues with André Gide.

Bibliographies
Bourel, Dominique, and Hubert Juin, editors, *Charles Du Bos, inédits de Charles Du Bos et d'André Gide*, Paris: FAC, 1985: 16–18
Resurrection: Cahiers de Culture Chrétienne issue on Du Bos, 4, no. 13 (1946)

Further Reading
Angles, Auguste, "Charles Du Bos ou l'esthétique d'une belle âme," *Bulletin des Amis d'André Gide* 12, no. 17 (January 1984): 7–10, 61
Bertocci, Angelo, *Charles Du Bos and English Literature*, New York: King's Crown Press, 1949
Bodart, Roger, *À la rencontre de Charles Du Bos*, n.p.: La Sixaine, 1946
Bossière, Jacques, *Perception critique et sentiment de vivre chez Charles Du Bos*, Paris: Nizet, 1969
Bourel, Dominique, and Hubert Juin, editors, *Charles Du Bos, inédits de Charles Du Bos et d'André Gide*, Paris: FAC, 1985
Crépu, Michel, *Charles Du Bos ou la tentation de l'irréprochable*, Paris: Félin, 1990
Dédéyan, Charles, *Le Cosmopolitisme littéraire de Charles Du Bos*, 6 vols., Paris: Société d'Enseignement Supérieur, 1965–71
Devaux, André A., "Charles Du Bos, Jacques Maritain et Gabriel Marcel, ou, Peut-on aller de Bergson à Saint Thomas d'Aquin," *Cahiers Charles Du Bos* 18 (May 1974): 87–103
Didier, Béatrice, *Un dialogue à distance: Gide et Du Bos*, Paris: Desclée de Brouwer, 1976
Gouhier, Marie-Anne, *Charles Du Bos*, Paris: Vrin, 1951
Halda, Bernard, *Charles Du Bos*, Paris: Wesmael-Charlier, 1966
Jodogne, Pierre, "Charles Du Bos à Florence: Le Dossier de Carlo Placci," *Studi Francesi* 25, no. 3 (September–December 1981): 472–78
Leleu, Michèle, *Charles Du Bos, Approximations et certitude*, Paris: Desclée de Brouwer, 1976
McFarlane, Ian D., "Charles Du Bos and Montaigne," in *Columbia Montaigne Conference Papers*, edited by Donald M. Frame and Mary B. McKinley, Lexington, Kentucky: French Forum, 1981: 70–83

Mertens, Cornelis Joseph, *Émotion et critique chez Charles Du Bos*, Nijmegen: Janssen, 1967
Mouton, Jean, *Charles Du Bos: Sa relation avec la vie et avec la mort*, Paris: Desclée de Brouwer, 1954
O'Rourke, Maire, *L'Article de Charles Du Bos sur Proust: L'Idée de l'exaltation*, Berne: Lang, 1979
Poulet, Georges, and others, editors, *Permanence de Charles Du Bos: Colloque de Cerisy*, Paris: Desclée de Brouwer, 1976

Dürrenmatt, Friedrich
Swiss, 1921–1990

Friedrich Dürrenmatt's international acclaim as a playwright has long overshadowed his accomplishments as an author of fiction and essays. During the last two decades of his life, when he became gradually disenchanted with the stage, Dürrenmatt increased his production of narrative and essayistic texts. This, in turn, generated renewed critical interest in his work within these genres and a reappraisal – especially of his essays – which is far from complete. From 1947 until 1990, literally a few days before his death, he produced more than 150 essays, speeches, reviews, and critiques. These include six book-length essays, which are outgrowths of public lectures or, in one case, a sequel to his dramatic writings.

Dürrenmatt never saw a clear demarcation between genres: his speeches proliferated into essays, which often display a "dramaturgic" structure interspersed with narration. Some of his essays seamlessly incorporate fictional material. His playful disregard for traditional literary forms and his impromptu creation of strikingly unconventional, often meandering prose lend these essays their unique textuality. Most are concerned with literary/aesthetic or social/political matters. Already in the mid-1950s, these issues became so inextricably entwined that his dramaturgical statements are invariably political, and vice versa. His novel amalgam of the aesthetic and the sociopolitical contributes to Dürrenmatt's original essayistic voice.

The early essays may be divided into two distinct groups: theater critiques and occasional pieces on political topics. Dürrenmatt's growth as an essayist parallels his struggle for his own idiom as a playwright. Between 1947 and 1952, he wrote critiques of current stage performances and short essays on theater for the Berne *Nation* and the Zurich *Weltwoche* (The weekly world). Their common thrust lies in their anti-classicist stance and in their plea for a new, "objective" form of comedy: the only kind of theater fit to visualize contemporary reality on stage. At the same time, he sharpened his pen as a political essayist in brief, aphoristic pieces like "Sätze für Zeitgenossen" (1947–48; Sentences for contemporaries) and "Hingeschriebenes" (1947–48; Jottings). In the latter, the effortless transition from literary to political matters typical in all his later essays is already evident: "One must never cease to imagine the world in its most reasonable configuration."

A summation of the early essays and a reflection of Dürrenmatt's experience with the stage (he had in the meantime produced five plays) is the lecture *Theaterprobleme* (1955; *Problems of the Theatre*). Here he presents his own, full-fledged theory of (tragi)comedy and of the grotesque as its premier revelatory device. The aesthetic and the political are now intricately linked, as only tragicomedy can conceptualize the amorphous, chaotic, and regimented world of the mid-20th century: a world of nuclear threats, oppression, economic exploitation, and total warfare. Ultimate responsibility for humanity's future rests not with collectives but with the "courageous individual," as portrayed on stage. The dramatist aims to present viable alternatives to a destructive reality. *Problems of the Theatre*, Dürrenmatt's most cogent and polished dramaturgical essay, remains one of the truly innovative and influential statements on theater in the 20th century. Like all his writings, it addresses (and is widely read by) an educated, predominantly bourgeois audience.

By the late 1950s, Dürrenmatt had found his own literary voice. The essays of this period reflect his growing international fame as a playwright; they often provide programmatic commentaries on his plays and on the role of the writer in a capitalist society. Among the more remarkable texts in this group are "Vom Sinn der Dichtung in unserer Zeit" (1958; On the purpose of literature today) and "Friedrich Schiller" (1959). In the former, Dürrenmatt emphasizes the importance of the sciences for modern life – a recurring theme in his works. The latter differentiates his own dramaturgy from that of both **Schiller** and Bertolt Brecht, as he lays claim to a middle ground between idealistic and materialist ideologies.

In the late 1960s and 1970s, Dürrenmatt's writings became more overtly political. A second book-length essay, *Monstervortrag über Gerechtigkeit und Recht nebst einem helvetischen Zwischenspiel: Eine kleine Dramaturgie der Politik* (1969; "A Monster Lecture on Justice and Law Together with a Helvetian Interlude: A Small Dramaturgy of Politics"), which had once again originated as a speech, dramaturgically thematizes the dialectical relationship of individual justice versus organized law – another central aspect in the political essays to come. Many of these essays react polemically to world events, for instance, "Israels Lebensrecht" (1967; Israel's right to live), a response to the Six-Day War, or "Tschechoslowakei 1968" (1968; Czechoslovakia in 1968), an eloquent protest against Soviet suppression of the Prague Spring. Others are written as the result of Dürrenmatt's extensive travels: *Sätze aus Amerika* (1970; Sentences from America) or the most voluminous of all, *Zusammenhänge: Essay über Israel* (1976; Connections: essay on Israel), with its 1980 addendum "Nachgedanken" (Afterthoughts). All propound Dürrenmatt's critical position between the ideological camps, and his bellicose, often strained neutrality.

Zusammenhänge marks the apex of his production of large-scale political essays. Originally conceived as a speech he delivered in Beersheba, its subject matter grew into a substantial book upon first publication. The essay's structure – typical of the nonfictional prose from *Monstervortrag* until the end of the 1970s – is sprawling and loose-jointed, interspersed with authorial comments and long narrative passages. Dürrenmatt develops his argument in a rambling, peripatetic fashion. The lack of an authoritative, linear structure makes for a persuasive, almost private voice and a work-in-progress appearance. *Zusammenhänge* is his best and most personal political essay. The much less coherent "Nachgedanken" – with their strident anticommunism and their barrage of familiar clichés from the militant pseudo-liberal discourse of their time – pale in comparison.

Equally sprawling but not as convincing as *Zusammenhänge* is its dramaturgic counterpart, *Der Mitmacher: Ein Komplex* (1976; The collaborator: a complex). Here Dürrenmatt delivers a huge, convoluted essayistic-fictional-rhetorical sequel to his weak drama *Der Mitmacher*. The text ostensibly deals with the play's political underpinnings in contemporary totalitarianism, but it is hardly more than a rambling, random sequence of stories, polemic, and tedious gripes of a frustrated playwright. Dürrenmatt must have realized that he overextended the essay form into a monstrous parody. From here on, his political prose returns to more manageable proportions. Less freewheeling and somewhat more disciplined in their discourse, the later essays still retain their personal, nonauthoritative tone. Once more they mostly derive from public speeches. In his last major essay, "Über Toleranz" (1977; On tolerance), Dürrenmatt makes a plea for political tolerance and lambasts Marxism as an oppressive concept. For the sake of humanity, he hopes that reason – as a beacon in the search for humane solutions to global problems – may prevail. This quasi-utopian faith in human reason – in the arrival of a new, sober enlightenment – provides the leitmotif for Dürrenmatt's essays after "Albert Einstein" (1979). Among the many shorter political texts from the last decade of his life, those on **Václav Havel** ("Die Schweiz – ein Gefängnis" [1990; Switzerland – a prison]) and Mikhail Gorbachev ("Die Hoffnung, uns am eigenen Schopfe aus dem Untergang zu ziehen" [1990; Hoping to pull ourselves out of doom by our own bootstraps]) stand out as final assertions of his hope that humanity, after all, may yet conquer the future and avert catastrophe through reason without fear.

Highly improvisational discourse, an innovative textuality, and unflagging humanism are the hallmarks of Dürrenmatt's essayistic oeuvre. Seen as a whole, it appears clearly a cut above much of contemporary nonfiction prose, though uneven and closely bound to the given sociopolitical context at the time of writing. Individual pieces weather the test of time fairly well as the century draws to a close. But even these ultimately fail to attain greatness. A disturbing lack of stringency and intellectual discipline – the trade-off for their spontaneity and work-in-progress openness – mars even the best of the lot.

GERHARD P. KNAPP

Biography

Born 5 January 1921 in Konolfingen, near Berne, Switzerland. Studied at the University of Berne, 1941–42 and 1943–45; University of Zurich, 1942–43. Married Lotti Geissler, 1946 (died, 1983): one son and two daughters. First play, *Es steht geschrieben*, premiered in Zurich, April 1947. Drama critic, *Die Weltwoche*, Zurich, 1951–53. Codirector, Basle Theatre, 1968–69. Coeditor, *Züricher Sonntags-Journal* (Zurich Sunday journal), 1969–71. Traveled to the United States, 1959, 1969, 1981, the U.S.S.R., 1964, 1967, Israel, 1974, Greece and South America, 1983–84, and Egypt, 1985. Married Charlotte Kerr, 1984. Awards: many, including the Schiller Prize (Mannheim), 1959, (Switzerland), 1960; Grillparzer Prize, 1968; Buber-Rosenzweig Medal, 1977; Zuckmayer Medal, 1984; Austrian State Prize, 1984; Bavarian Literature Prize, 1985; Büchner Prize, 1986; Schiller Prize (Stuttgart), 1986; Ernst Robert Curtius Prize, for essays, 1989; honorary degrees from five universities. Died (of heart failure) in Neuchâtel, Switzerland, 14 December 1990.

Selected Writings

Essays and Related Prose

Theaterprobleme, 1955; as *Problems of the Theatre*, translated by Gerhard Nellhaus, in *Four Plays*, 1964, and with *The Marriage of Mr. Mississippi*, 1966

Friedrich Schiller: Eine Rede, 1960

Theater-Schriften und Reden, edited by Elisabeth Brock-Sulzer, 2 vols., 1966–72; part as *Writings on Theatre and Drama*, edited and translated by H. M. Waidson, 1976

Monstervortrag über Gerechtigkeit und Recht nebst einem helvetischen Zwischenspiel: Eine kleine Dramaturgie der Politik, 1969; as "A Monster Lecture on Justice and Law Together with a Helvetian Interlude: A Small Dramaturgy of Politics," in *Plays and Essays*, edited by Volkmar Sander, 1982

Sätze aus Amerika, 1970

Zusammenhänge: Essay über Israel, 1976; enlarged edition, 1980

Der Mitmacher: Ein Komplex (includes a play), 1976

Stoffe I–III, 3 vols., 1981; revised edition, as *Labyrinth: Stoffe I–III*, 1 vol., 1990

Plays and Essays (various translators), edited by Volkmar Sander, 1982

Rollenspiele, with Charlotte Kerr, 1986

Versuche, 1988

Turmbau: Stoffe IV–IX, 1990

Gedankenfuge, 1992

Other writings: many plays (including *Der Besuch der alten Dame* [*The Visit*], 1956; *Die Physiker* [*The Physicists*], 1962), screenplays, radio plays, and several novels (including *Der Richter und sein Henker* [*The Judge and His Hangman*], 1952; *Die Panne* [*A Dangerous Game*], 1956; *Justiz* [*The Execution of Justice*], 1985; *Der Auftrag* [*The Assignment*], 1986).

Collected works editions: *Werkausgabe*, 30 vols., 1980–90; *Gesammelte Werke*, edited by Franz Josef Görtz, 7 vols., 1988.

Bibliographies

Knapp, Gerhard P., in *Friedrich Dürrenmatt*, Stuttgart: Metzler, 1993

Whitton, Kenneth S., in *Dürrenmatt: Reinterpretation in Retrospect*, New York and Oxford: Berg, 1990

Further Reading

Arnold, Armin, editor, *Zu Friedrich Dürrenmatt*, Stuttgart: Klett, 1982

Bänziger, Hans, *Frisch und Dürrenmatt*, Berne: Francke, 1976 (original edition, 1960)

Federico, Joseph A., "The Political Philosophy of Friedrich Dürrenmatt," *German Studies Review* 12 (1989): 91–109

Keel, Daniel, editor, *Über Friedrich Dürrenmatt*, Zürich: Diogenes, 1980

Keel, Daniel, editor, *Herkules und Atlas: Lobreden und andere Versuche über Friedrich Dürrenmatt*, Zürich: Diogenes, 1990

Knapp, Gerhard P., and Gerd Labroisse, editors, *Facetten: Studien zum 60. Geburtstag Friedrich Dürrenmatts*, Berne: Lang, 1981

Knapp, Gerhard P., *Friedrich Dürrenmatt*, Stuttgart: Metzler, 1993

Knapp, Mona, and Gerhard P. Knapp, "Recht – Gerechtigkeit – Politik: Zur Genese der Begriffe im Werk Friedrich Dürrenmatts," *Text+Kritik* 56 (1977): 23–40

Knopf, Jan, *Friedrich Dürrenmatt*, Munich: Beck, 1988 (original edition, 1976)

Lazar, Moshe, editor, *Play Dürrenmatt*, Malibu: Undena, 1983

Sheppard, Vera, "Friedrich Dürrenmatt as a Dramatic Theorist," *Drama Survey* 4 (1965): 244–63

Whitton, Kenneth S., *Dürrenmatt: Reinterpretation in Retrospect*, New York and Oxford: Berg, 1990, particularly "The Essays": 158–209

E

Eco, Umberto

Italian, 1932–

Umberto Eco has pursued scientific research to the limits of philosophy and semiology; he has also published many articles and reports destined for a wider public, in newspapers such as the *Times Literary Supplement* and *L'Espresso* and in collections. More recently, he has also been tempted by novels and has found worldwide success with *Il nome della rosa* (1980; *The Name of the Rose*), *Il pendolo di Foucault* (1988; *Foucault's Pendulum*), and *L'isola del giorno prima* (1994; *The Island of the Day Before*).

He first became known with *Opera aperta* (1962; *The Open Work*), a work in which he develops thoughts on the plural character of artistic productions in an intuitive semiological approach he would later expand thanks to his discovery of structuralist thinkers. From this point on, Eco's work as an essayist oscillates between two issues: on the one hand, the founding of a general semiology sensitive to the questions of interpretation and reception, and on the other, shorter, more personal reflections on the little details of life that he feels illustrate signs of cultural phenomena.

The semiological subjects he focuses on belong to literature as well as to diverse manifestations of popular culture, particularly to the mass media. Thus, in *Apocalittici e integrati* (1964; Apocalyptic and integrated), Eco opposes both the believers of a superior elitist culture, nostalgic for the past, who keep their distance from the media (which they consider to be akin to bearers of the apocalypse), and the "integrated," who are not only open to this mass culture but so fascinated by it that they submit to its power. Eco advises the consumer to adopt a critical standpoint, to confront actively this media explosion in which modern kitsch takes refuge. Here he develops his first thoughts on Superman and, later, James Bond and other heroes he will discuss in *Il superuomo di massa* (1976; The mass superman). He also analyzes the social importance of television and the beginning of its evolution, propositions he had already developed in *The Open Work*, where he questions the aesthetic possibilities of direct televiewing, and which he takes up again in *Faith in Fakes* (1986; also published as *Travels in Hyperreality*) and *Il secondo diario minimo* (1992; *How to Travel with a Salmon and Other Essays*).

In the preface to *Faith in Fakes*, Eco describes the methods of composition for his articles, which are not semiological exercises but appeal to what Barthes called "semiological flair."

He clearly distinguishes between what is particular to scientific work and what is specific to essays: "At white heat, in the rush of an emotion, stimulated by an event, you write your reflections, hoping that someone will read them and then forget them. I don't believe there is any gap between what I write in my 'academic' books and what I write in the papers." Eco continues that "It is true there is a difference in tone, because in reading about daily events day after day . . . you don't start with theoretical hypotheses to underscore concrete examples, you start with events to make them 'talk' without having to conclude in definite theoretical terms." Eco then shows that this "mind wandering," when faced with particular facts, may be the first necessary step in the elaboration of a scientific project. Thus *Diario minimo* (1963; *Misreadings*), published just after *The Open Work*, uses imitations, parodies, and anachronisms abundantly, and develops ideas on the war games children love or on the passion for football in Italy, but always based on Eco's knowledge of rhetoric, Aristotelian philosophy, or Charles S. Peirce's semiology.

The interpenetration between Eco's journalistic entertainment and his fundamental theoretical reflection becomes clear when comparing these articles with his more rigorous full-length works such as *La struttura assente* (1968; The absent structure), *Lector in fabula* (1979; *Role of the Reader*), or *I limiti dell'interpretazione* (1990; *The Limits of Interpretation*). He begins by reinserting structures in the written codes of a story, and thus strongly denies the structuralist negation of the story, with the aim of founding a social semiology that also rehabilitates the reader's role. Eco works on the assumption that "the text is a lazy machine demanding strenuous cooperation from the reader to fill in the unspoken or already spoken blanks." The interpretative adventure builds up, essentially with the help of three notions: the encyclopedia, the topic, and the possible world. The activity of the reader is especially "inferential," which means that "reading signifies deducing, conjecturing, inferring from a text a possible context that the rest of the book must either confirm or correct." Thus, while remaining loyal to the notion of sign, which is the basis of his treatise *Il segno* (1971; The sign) or *Trattato di semiotica generale* (1975; *A Theory of Semiotics*), he also gives an important place to what he calls the "Model Reader" and to the procedures of interpretation, in a constant dialectic between the injunctions of the textual sign and their acknowledgment. Even in essays on literary theory, Eco's choice of works he writes about is significant: serial novels by Dumas or Eugène Sue, spy novels, and comic books, all of which are objects of the popular culture ignored by traditional criticism and which appear as significant witnesses of an era, outside all ideological value judgments.

More recently, Eco's role as denouncer of all the pretenses invented by mass culture seems to be softened by his fiction writing. But even then he feels the need to put his novels in perspective, for example in *Postille a "Il nome della rosa"* (1984; *Reflections on "The Name of the Rose"*), where he reveals his methods as an author by discussing again his conception of intertextuality and the reader's role, all the while speaking of suspense novels or postmodernism, which he magnificently defines as the triumph of irony in an era of lost innocence. Thus, the creator cannot hide the fact that he is above all a lover of language – of all languages – and of comic books, television series, medieval philosophy, and science fiction. All these beckon to those who can interpret them. This is Eco's quest.

MARC LITS

Biography

Born 5 January 1932 in Alessandria. Also uses the pseudonym Dedalus. Studied at the University of Turin, Ph.D., 1954. Editor of cultural programs, RAI Italian Radio-Television, Milan, 1954–59; taught at the Universities of Turin, 1956–64, Milan, 1964–65, Florence, 1965–69, and Bologna, from 1971 (chair of semiotics, from 1975), and at Milan Polytechnic, 1969–71. Served in the Italian Army, 1958–59. Senior editor of nonfiction, Bompiani publishers, Milan, 1959–75. Columnist of "Diario minimo" for *Il Verri*, 1959–61. Married Renate Ramge, 1962: one son and one daughter. Visiting professor at various American universities, 1969–84. Cofounder, *Marcatré*, 1961, and *Quindici* (Fifteen), 1967; editor, *Versus*, from 1971; member of editorial board, *Semiotica, Poetics Today, Degrés, Structuralist Review, Text, Communication, Problemi dell'Informazione* (Problems of information), and *Alfabeta*. Secretary-general, 1972–79, and vice president, from 1979, International Association for Semiotic Studies. Awards: Strega Prize, 1981; Viareggio Prize, 1981; Anghiari Prize, 1981; Medicis Prize, 1982; McLuhan Teleglobe Prize, 1985; honorary degrees from four universities.

Selected Writings

Essays and Related Prose

Opera aperta, 1962; revised edition, 1967; as *The Open Work*, translated by Anna Cancogni, 1989

Diario minimo, 1963; as *Misreadings*, translated by William Weaver, 1993

Le forme del contenuto, 1971

Il costume di casa: Evidenze e misteri dell'ideologia italiano (articles), 1973

Dalla periferia dell'Impero (articles), 1976

Lector in fabula: La cooperazione interpretativa nei testi narrativi, 1979; as *Role of the Reader: Explorations in the Semiotics of Texts*, 1979

Semiotics and the Philosophy of Language, 1984

Sugli specchi e altri saggi, 1985

Faith in Fakes, and as *Travels in Hyperreality*, translated by William Weaver, 1986

Il secondo diario minimo, 1992; as *How to Travel with a Salmon and Other Essays*, 1994

Interpretation and Overinterpretation, with others, edited by Stefan Collini, 1992

Six Walks in the Fictional Woods (Charles Eliot Norton lectures), 1994

Apocalypse Postponed (various translators), edited by Robert Lumley, 1994

Other writings: three novels (*Il nome della rosa* [*The Name of the Rose*], 1980; *Il pendolo di Foucault* [*Foucault's Pendulum*], 1988; *L'isola del giorno prima* [*The Island of the Day Before*], 1994), poetry, and many books on semiotics, art, and culture.

Bibliography
Ganeri, Margherita, in *Il "caso" Eco*, Palermo: Palumbo, 1991: 159–216

Further Reading
Coletti, Theresa, *Naming the Rose: Eco, Medieval Signs and Modern Theory*, Ithaca, New York: Cornell University Press, 1988

De Lauretis, Teresa, *Umberto Eco*, Florence: La Nuova Italia, 1981

Ganeri, Margherita, *Il "caso" Eco*, Palermo: Palumbo, 1991

Gritti, Jules, *Umberto Eco*, Paris: Éditions Universitaires, 1991

Magazine Littéraire issue on Eco, 262 (1989)

Pansa, Francesca, and Anna Vinci, *Effetto Eco*, Rome: Gallo, 1990

Robey, David, "Umberto Eco," in *Writers and Society in Contemporary Italy*, edited by Michael Caesar and Peter Hainsworth, Leamington Spa: Berg, 1984

Edgeworth, Maria

Irish, 1768–1849

Maria Edgeworth was one of the most popular and widely read authors of her time, as the numerous editions of her works reveal. She is recognized as an early innovator of the regional novel and an important writer of instructional tales for children. Current critical interest in Edgeworth focuses mainly on these novels and tales, which established her reputation as a writer. The critical attention given to her best-known works – *Castle Rackrent* (1800), *Belinda* (1801), and *The Absentee* (1812) – dominates Edgeworth scholarship, so that her essays, which launched her literary career, have been ignored by most critics. This dismissal is unwarranted, for, in addition to being valuable in themselves, the essays explain the moral instruction that is the basis for her novels and stories. As her father Richard Lovell Edgeworth states in the preface to *Moral Tales for Young People* (1801), the tales were intended to serve as illustrations of the opinions delivered in *Practical Education* (1798). Maria Edgeworth followed this creative process throughout her literary career: she repeatedly used her essays as foundations for her longer works, either expanding an essay into a tale or writing didactic stories to exemplify the concepts presented in the essays.

Although Edgeworth dabbled in several genres, such as translation, drama, tale, and novel, her first published work, *Letters for Literary Ladies* (1795), is a collection of three pieces: two written in epistolary form and the third in essay form. "An Essay on the Noble Science of Self-Justification" humorously explores the feminine argumentative method. As Marilyn Butler points out in *Maria Edgeworth* (1972), Edgeworth later expanded this essay into *The Modern Griselda: A Tale* (1805), a didactic novel that contrasts two wives: Griselda, the silly wife, and Emma Granby, the sensible wife. The tale comically exemplifies the arguments set forth in the essay, as Griselda insists on having the last word in every argument with her husband.

Edgeworth and her father worked collaboratively on *Practical Education*; however, she wrote the majority of the essays. *Practical Education* explains the theories underlying the educational techniques utilized in the Edgeworth family. These theories also served as guidance for Edgeworth in her literary endeavors. In the chapter entitled "Books," she warns that fiction can give false ideas to children and recommends that writing fiction "should be attended to with care in all books for young people; nor should we sacrifice the understanding to the enthusiasm of eloquence, or the affectation of sensibility." Edgeworth practiced this cautious approach in writing *The Parent's Assistant* (1800) and *Moral Tales*: the stories in these collections popularized the themes expounded in *Practical Education*.

Another essay that profoundly affected Edgeworth's literary career is *Essays on Professional Education* (1809). In 1807 Edgeworth decided, at her father's suggestion, to write an essay examining male education, and thus was forced to investigate an unfamiliar, masculine topic. In order to write *Professional Education* she spent two years researching, reading, and writing about the selection of vocations and the proper education for sons. This rigorous scholarship greatly influenced the topics in her fiction. According to Butler, the later tales in *Tales of Fashionable Life* (1809–12) illustrate the principles set out in the essay, while *Ormond* (1817) qualifies them.

In addition to the essays that served as sources for her tales and novels, Edgeworth published *Essay on Irish Bulls* (1802), a work closely connected to her best-known novel, *Castle Rackrent*. In the essay she humorously relates numerous verbal blunders, called "bulls," many of which were personally observed by either herself or her father. The essay demonstrates that blunders are made by people of all nationalities, not just the Irish. While Butler calls *Essay on Irish Bulls* an apology for *Castle Rackrent*, in *Family Chronicles* (1987) Coilin Owens insists on a closer connection between the essay and the novel: "that the Irish Bull – a general term for a variety of rhetorical tropes in which sense is cunningly encased in apparent nonsense – is a paradigm for the entire novel." The humor found in *Essay on Irish Bulls* also exists in Edgeworth's "Thoughts on Bores" (1826), published anonymously in the almanac *Janus*. This essay gives a comical overview of the different types of bores, ranging from the parliamentary bore, who is "Fond of high places; but not always found in them," to bluestocking bores. These humorous essays exhibit Edgeworth's ability simultaneously to entertain and to instruct the reader.

Because of their important connections to her popular novels and tales, Edgeworth's essays deserve more critical attention. Although she is remembered as an author of children's fiction and as an Irish regional novelist, the foundations of her works of fiction exist in her essays. "Essayist" is an appropriate label for Edgeworth, and one she probably would have approved of: she despised being called a "novelist" because of the emphasis on fiction the term implied. Throughout her life, Edgeworth insisted on the truthfulness of the representations in her fictional works, which were intended to illustrate the principles explained in her many essays. Thus, the essays are a major part of the Edgeworth canon, and require further examination.

STACI L. STONE

Biography

Born 1 January 1768 in Black Bourton, Oxfordshire; daughter of the educationist Richard Lovell Edgeworth (died, 1817). Studied at Mrs. Lattuffiere's school, Derby, 1775–80; Mrs. Devis' school, London, 1781–82. Moved with her family to Ireland, living in Edgeworthstown, Longford, from 1782, and helped run the family estates. Lived in England, 1791–93; collaborated with her father on educational works, 1798–1802. First novel published anonymously, 1800. Traveled in England, France, and Scotland, 1802–03, and in France and Switzerland, 1820–21; frequently visited London and made occasional tours of Britain. Died in Edgeworthstown, 22 May 1849.

Selected Writings

Essays and Related Prose

Letters for Literary Ladies, 1795; Everyman Edition, 1993
Practical Education, with Richard Lovell Edgeworth, 1798; revised edition, 3 vols., 1801; as *Essays on Practical Education*, 2 vols., 1811
Essay on Irish Bulls, 1802
Essays on Professional Education, 1809

Other writings: moral tales, regional novels (including *Castle Rackrent*, 1800), plays, and correspondence.

Collected works edition: *Tales and Novels* (Longford Edition), 10 vols., 1893, reprinted 1969.

Bibliographies

Finneran, Richard J., editor, *Anglo-Irish Literature: A Review of Research*, New York: Modern Language Association of America, 1976
Slade, Bertha Coolidge, *Maria Edgeworth, 1767–1849: A Bibliographical Tribute*, London: Constable, 1937

Further Reading

Butler, Marilyn, *Maria Edgeworth: A Literary Biography*, Oxford: Clarendon Press, 1972
Harden, Elizabeth, *Maria Edgeworth*, Boston: Twayne, 1984
Kelly, Gary, "Amelia Opie, Lady Caroline Lamb, and Maria Edgeworth: Official and Unofficial Ideology," *ARIEL* 12, no. 4 (1981): 3–24
Kestner, Joseph, "Defamiliarization in the Romantic Regional Novel: Maria Edgeworth, Walter Scott, John Gibson Lockhart, Susan Ferrier, and John Galt," *Wordsworth Circle* 10, no. 4 (1979): 326–30
Kowaleski-Wallace, Elizabeth, *Their Fathers' Daughters: Hannah More, Maria Edgeworth, and Patriarchal Complicity*, New York: Oxford University Press, 1991
Myers, Mitzi, "De-Romanticizing the Subject: Maria Edgeworth's 'The Bracelets,' Mythologies of Origin, and the Daughter's Coming to Writing," in *Romantic Women Writers: Voices and Countervoices*, edited by Paula R. Feldman and Theresa M. Kelley, Hanover, New Hampshire: University Press of New England, 1995: 88–110
Myers, Mitzi, "The Dilemmas of Gender as Double-Voiced Narrative; or, Maria Edgeworth Mothers the Bildungsroman," in *The Idea of the Novel in the Eighteenth Century*, edited by Robert W. Uphaus, East Lansing, Michigan: Colleagues Press, 1988: 67–96
Owens, Coilin, editor, *Family Chronicles: Maria Edgeworth's Castle Rackrent*, Dublin: Wolfhound Press, and Totowa, New Jersey: Barnes and Noble, 1987
Tracy, Robert, "Maria Edgeworth and Lady Morgan: Legality Versus Legitimacy," *Nineteenth-Century Fiction* 48, no. 1 (1985): 1–22

Wilson, Carol Shiner, "Lost Needles, Tangled Threads: Stitchery, Domesticity, and the Artistic Enterprise in Barbauld, Edgeworth, Taylor, and Lamb," in *Re-Visioning Romanticism: British Women Writers, 1776–1837*, edited by Carol Shiner Wilson and Joel Haefner, Philadelphia: University of Pennsylvania Press, 1994: 167–90

The Edinburgh Review
British periodical, 1802–1929

In 18th-century Britain, with the number of publications increasing enormously, there was a corresponding increase in the demand for **periodicals** that would enable readers to select from the mass, and to be offered judgments that they could repeat or contradict. Earlier reviews, like the *Monthly*, attempted something like comprehensive coverage, with readers in mind like Lady Russell in Jane Austen's *Persuasion*, who was said to "get all the new publications." The foundation in 1802 of the *Edinburgh Review* marked the point at which any such attempt was abandoned; instead, a few items were given relatively elaborate consideration. As time went on, the books selected became fewer, the **reviews** discussing them longer – a development that underlined the salience of the reviewer in comparison to the books reviewed.

The earlier decades of the 19th century saw the emergence of the weightily anonymous reviewer. With the *Edinburgh* it was well known that the review was in the hands of a group of liberal-minded members of the Scottish capital's establishment, and readers were usually able to recognize the mercurial eloquence of Francis Jeffrey, the editor after the first number, or the animated humor of Sydney Smith, who after editing the first number remained one of the most entertaining contributors, or the slashing vigor of Henry Brougham. But the review itself counted for more than the individuals who composed it, and there is a distinctive *Edinburgh* house style, supremely confident, determinedly enlightened and humane, avoiding bigotry and exalting good sense, but colored by a severity summed up in the motto that graced the title page of every number: *Judex damnatur cum nocens absolvitur* – "The judge is condemned when the guilty is acquitted." A presiding judge is a fitting emblem of the editor's role as seen by Jeffrey and his colleagues and imitators. Many years later, Walter Bagehot was to give him the credit for inventing the trade of editorship – no longer a bookseller's drudge, but "a distinguished functionary." But more than that, to be an *Edinburgh* reviewer was to be a high priest of the Spirit of the Age, an implicit claim that annoyed the many authors whose work was treated unfavorably, and the even greater number of conservative-minded readers who found reformist views objectionable. Of the many rejoinders to the *Edinburgh*'s pretensions, at least one, Edward Copleston's *Advice to a Young Reviewer* (1807), with its specimen review of Milton's "L'Allegro," is very telling. But nothing could undermine the *Edinburgh*'s commercial success, and this inevitably generated imitators, notably, in 1809, the **Quarterly Review**. Still, for many years the *Edinburgh* remained required reading even for those who found its views very disagreeable.

Of the early contributors, Jeffrey and Smith retained the most enduring reputation, and their collected *Edinburgh* essays were widely read. Jeffrey has earned some notoriety for his dismissive reviews of Wordsworth, and he is probably best remembered for his opening words on *The Excursion* – "This will never do!" But while his ridicule of Wordsworth's infelicities may now seem obtuse, it is not difficult to appreciate the pleasure a sympathetic reader might have felt at his flamboyant obliteration of a political opponent, e.g. "Though the learned author has not always the gift of writing intelligibly, it is impossible for a diligent reader not to see what he would be at" (in this instance a high Tory trying to discredit libertarian institutions). Sydney Smith shared in this destructive *joie de vivre*: when he and Brougham had drafted one such review, "we sat trying to find one more chink, one more crevice, through which we might drop one more drop of verjuice, to eat into his bones." But Smith's drollery is usually more humane than this would suggest, and much of it is in the service of a generous indignation against injustice, its perpetrators exposed by their absurdity. His imagination warms to a persecuting bishop or a suppressor of vice; landowners who set spring-guns and mantraps to protect their game do not, he allows, positively *want* to kill poachers, but if there is a choice between game and poacher, the less worthy must suffer – "the rustic without a soul, – not the Christian partridge – not the immortal pheasant – not the rational woodcock, or the accountable hare" (March 1821).

A startlingly high proportion of the first 20 years of the *Edinburgh* was written by the founding group, but as time went on new and even more talented writers joined them. **William Hazlitt** contributed some 16 reviews between 1814 and 1830, and although they are recognizably his work, he is not there quite the fierce radical of the **Examiner** or the *Yellow Dwarf*. **Thomas Carlyle** contrived to gain admission for his idiosyncratic style, perhaps because he was an acknowledged authority on German literature; this was part of the process of introducing readers to an unfamiliar but crucially important agency of enlightenment. As for **Thomas Babington Macaulay**'s disquisitions upon a wide range of literary and historical subjects, these were probably the most widely admired productions of the *Edinburgh Review*, with a reputation extending far beyond readers of the periodical for which they were written.

Although Macaulay was very much a partisan of the liberalism with which the *Edinburgh* was associated from the outset, his frequently reprinted essays became part of the broad intellectual culture of the Victorian period to which the periodicals of the time contributed so weightily. In mid-century and afterwards, particularly during the long editorship of Henry Reeve (1855–95), the *Edinburgh* became just one of a number of serious journals devoted to keeping readers abreast of current information and discussion. Sir Alfred Lyall's articles on India are a fair example, including in 1884 an astonishingly far-sighted analysis of the contradictions between a bureaucratic ruling apparatus and the libertarian ideas cultivated by English education.

The *Edinburgh Review* continued until 1929, but perhaps was never quite the same after 1912, when its contributors began to be named, as in other journals. While anonymity continued, even though it was an anonymity designed to be penetrated, the immense pretensions of the original publication still left an afterglow. But those pretensions belonged to the world of the early 19th century, and could not be sustained indefinitely.

GEOFFREY CARNALL

See also Periodical Essay

Further Reading
Clive, John Leonard, *Scotch Reviewers: The Edinburgh Review, 1802–1815*, London: Faber, 1957
Fontana, Biancamaria, *Rethinking the Politics of Commercial Society: The Edinburgh Review, 1802–1832*, Cambridge: Cambridge University Press, 1985
Greig, James Alexander, *Francis Jeffrey of the Edinburgh Review*, Edinburgh: Oliver and Boyd, 1948
Koss, Stephen, *The Rise and Fall of the Political Press in Britain*, vol. 1: *The Nineteenth Century*, London: Hamilton, 1981
Newton, Judith, "Engendering History for the Middle Class: Sex and Political Economy in the *Edinburgh Review*," in *Rewriting the Victorians: Theory, History, and the Politics of Gender*, London and New York: Routledge, 1992: 1–17
Pottinger, George, *Heirs of the Enlightenment: Edinburgh Reviewers and Writers, 1800–1830*, Edinburgh: Scottish Academic Press, 1992
Shattock, Joanne, *Politics and Reviewers: "The Edinburgh" and "The Quarterly" in the Early Victorian Age*, Leicester: Leicester University Press, 1989

Eglinton, John

Irish, 1868–1961

Although remembered now as a caricature in James Joyce's *Ulysses*, during the early 20th century "John Eglinton" (the pseudonym for William Kirkpatrick Magee) was one of the most influential critics in Irish literature and one of the leading theorists of the Irish Literary Renaissance. The early members of this movement, now associated primarily with Joyce and **William Butler Yeats**, sought to establish an independent, Irish publishing industry as an element of a distinct national literary culture, and the essay was accordingly central to the movement's development. As an essayist, Eglinton helped formulate the defining issues of Irish cultural independence, centering on whether Ireland's literary aspirations lay more in a cosmopolitan, English-speaking, European future or in a concentration on a Celtic, Gaelic-speaking, legendary past. Eglinton's stance on these issues was consistently Anglo-Irish, cosmopolitan, and European; but, however little the modern Irish political map conforms to his ideals, the Modernism of the novels of Joyce and the late poetry of Yeats demonstrates the literary importance of Eglinton's influence.

 Eglinton's essays appeared predominantly in the Irish literary magazines and newspapers that sprung up in Dublin around the turn of the century, most of which proved short-lived. Among the more influential to which he contributed were the *Shanachie*, the *Irish Review*, the Dublin *Daily Express*, and *Dana: An Irish Magazine of Independent Thought*, which he edited (1904–05). He broadened his audience beyond ephemeral publications by collecting many of his essays in

books: *Two Essays on the Remnant* (1894), *Pebbles from a Brook* (1901), *Bards and Saints* (1906), and *Anglo-Irish Essays* (1917). Additionally, Yeats published *Some Essays and Passages by John Eglinton* (1905). Eglinton also edited an influential series of letters that he, Yeats, and other members of the Irish Renaissance had written to the *Daily Express* and published them as *Literary Ideals in Ireland* (1899). Because it helped to frame the issues of the Renaissance, *Literary Ideals* is one of the most important Irish books of the 1890s. After 1921, responding to the establishment of a Republican government in Ireland, Eglinton lived in voluntary exile in England. There he wrote several reminiscences of key figures in the Irish Renaissance – Yeats, George Russell (Æ), Edward Dowden, George Moore, and James Joyce – published as *Irish Literary Portraits* (1935).

 As an essayist, Eglinton saw himself as a "philosopher-priest," following an essentially scientific, materialist mysticism developed from early exposure to theosophy. His essays can seem esoteric and abstract, but the abstraction masks a concrete reality, creating parables of the material world, almost always with a counterpart in the practical debates surrounding Irish nationalism. Always concerned with the relation between art and society, Eglinton saw more clearly than most the trajectory that led from old legends of a heroic Ireland to the Irish Revolution and Civil War. Even in his early *Two Essays on the Remnant* Eglinton warns of what Yeats realized only after the fact: the power of art to unloose the "blood-dimmed tide" of war.

 Eglinton's essays fall into three stylistic periods. The tone of *Two Essays on the Remnant* is prophetic and oracular, drawing heavily on images from the Bible and comparing Ireland with Old Testament Israel (a common trope of the Irish Renaissance). *Pebbles from a Brook* marks Eglinton's second stylistic period, in which he discontinues the oracular style and develops the detached, ironic tone usually associated with him, and the one parodied in *Ulysses*. Allusive and dryly witty, he clearly writes for fellow intellectuals, including a wide range of reference to classical literature, oriental religions, and German Romantic philosophy, as well as the English literary tradition. His tone is conversational, but it is the conversation of the literary salon, often as condescending as it is recondite. The third stylistic phase of his *Irish Literary Portraits* occurs after his voluntary exile in England. These essays are personal reminiscences – often as much memoir as portrait. The erudition remains but is less ostentatiously presented.

 Although Eglinton's style changed over his career, the themes of his essays reflected a remarkably consistent world view, based on the idea that old cultures die and are superseded in a process combining aspects of a natural life cycle with a Hegelian historic synthesis. Claiming Anglo-Irish culture as a new synthesis of decadent Celtic and Anglo-Saxon cultures, Eglinton uses this view to argue for an Anglo-Irish rather than a Celtic Ireland. Although no longer plausible as a theory of history, it did lead him to some trenchant criticism of the romantic nostalgia at the heart of Yeats' "Celtic Twilight" movement. Arguing for a "natural" succession of national cultures, he warned that arousing nationalist feelings for purely aesthetic purposes, as Yeats was doing, would lead only to chaos and unrest. His warnings came true in the Easter Rising of 1916 and the subsequent Irish Revolution.

Although Eglinton's early essays retain an historical interest, their late Victorian style limits their interest for modern readers. They are important to an understanding of the Irish Renaissance Movement, and in many ways Eglinton was a perceptive and far-sighted critic of the divorce of aesthetics from social and political concerns. But for all their attempts to generalize and make universal, Eglinton's **philosophical essays** are, ironically, the most strictly local and time-constrained essays he wrote.

The later *Irish Literary Portraits* is Eglinton's best work, not merely because it has lost the Victorian hypotaxis of his earlier style but because it is his most human, more concerned with people than ideas. He also has the advantages not only of fascinating subjects, but of an intimate acquaintance with them. The portraits of Yeats and Joyce are particularly worthwhile. He writes of Yeats with a mixture of admiration and near bitterness: admiration for Yeats' accomplishments in poetry, bitterness for Yeats' role in dividing Ireland from the Union. There is a poignancy in his description of his literary pretensions being eclipsed by James Joyce, the callow literary poseur to whom Eglinton once could condescend, but who has since become his unquestioned literary master. Joyce's brother Stanislaus accused Eglinton of envious sniping, but his portrait of Eglinton seems more petty than Eglinton's of his brother; and Eglinton, for all his obvious jealousy, is much more willing to give James Joyce his due. Eglinton's humanity – manifest in his pettiness as well as his generosity – gives these essays an interest that his earlier essays lack. They are important because of the portraits they give of writers far more significant than Eglinton himself; but they are also rewarding in their own right as the record of an intelligent, idiosyncratic writer coming to grips with a literary tradition that has passed him by.

JEP C. JONSON

Biography

Born William Kirkpatrick Magee, 1868 in Dublin. Studied at the High School, Dublin, where he met William Butler Yeats; Trinity College, Dublin: won the Vice-Chancellor's Prize four times. Worked at the National Library, Dublin, 1895–1921. Member of the theosophical movement in Dublin, associating with Æ, Stephen McKenna, and George Moore; secretary to Moore for a time. Cofounder, *Dana: An Irish Magazine of Independent Thought*, 1904–05; contributor to various other Irish journals. Married M. L. O'Leary, 1920. Moved to England after the formation of the Free State, 1921. Died in Bournemouth, 9 May 1961.

Selected Writings

Essays and Related Prose
Two Essays on the Remnant, 1894
Pebbles from a Brook, 1901
Some Essays and Passages by John Eglinton, edited by W. B. Yeats, 1905
Bards and Saints, 1906
Anglo-Irish Essays, 1917
Irish Literary Portraits, 1935

Other writings: poems (including *Confidential; or, Take It or Leave It*, 1951), and a memoir of Æ (1937). Also edited and contributed to *Literary Ideals in Ireland* (1899); edited the *Letters* of Edward Dowden (1914); translated letters written by George Moore to Édouard Dujardin (1929).

Further Reading
Boyd, Ernest A., *Ireland's Literary Renaissance*, Dublin: Figgis, 1968 (original edition, 1916)
Boyd, Ernest A., *Appreciations and Depreciations: Irish Literary Studies*, Dublin: Talbot Press, and London: Fisher Unwin, 1917; New York: Lane, 1918
Hall, Wayne E., *Shadowy Heroes: Irish Literature of the 1890s*, Syracuse, New York: Syracuse University Press, 1980
Joyce, Stanislaus, *My Brother's Keeper: James Joyce's Early Years*, edited by Richard Ellmann, London: Faber, and New York: Viking, 1958
Morris, Lloyd R., *The Celtic Dawn: A Survey of the Renascence in Ireland, 1889–1916*, New York: Cooper Square, 1970 (original edition, 1917)

Eiseley, Loren
American, 1907–1977

Best known as the poet-scientist who wrote hauntingly of time and evolution, Loren Eiseley turned to the popular essay in mid-career, gaining widespread recognition with *The Immense Journey* (1957). He wrote over 75 essays, along with scientific articles, reviews, and science-fiction sketches, many of which were later incorporated into his books and his autobiography, *All the Strange Hours: The Excavation of a Life* (1975). A respected anthropologist and expert on evolutionary history, he preferred to write for the general audience, blending scientific insights with moments of wonder and delight. His persona of the compassionate scientist appealed to many readers. A master stylist, Eiseley was a writer of grace and eloquence whose finest essays extend the tradition of American meditative natural history writing.

Eiseley's career as a popular essayist began with a series of science articles he wrote for **Harper's** and *Scientific American* during the 1940s. These articles came to the attention of editor John Fisher, who invited Eiseley to rework them in book form. Eiseley spent over eight years preparing the manuscript, which became *The Immense Journey*. His subsequent books were generally assembled from previously published essays, often revised and adapted for their new context.

Eiseley's mastery of the **personal essay** developed gradually. His "concealed essay" blends personal anecdotes with thoughts of a more scientific nature. He structured his essays with a kind of "reenactment through memory," in which a dramatically intensified account of past experiences leads the reader to unexpected insights. Memory, landscape, and metaphor combine to shape many of Eiseley's most powerful passages. The "concealed essay" often begins with a vivid reminiscence ("The Slit," 1957) and gradually expands it in a scientific or contemplative direction. The subject matter of the essay is framed or "concealed" by the personal approach ("The Judgment of the Birds," 1957). The "concealed essay" became for Eiseley an elaborate form, combining personal anecdotes, literary allusions, quotations, multiple themes, and a contemplative perspective ("How Natural Is 'Natural'," 1960). Eiseley's later essays evolved toward a more impressionistic, almost surrealistic style ("The Star Thrower," 1969), which depicts the limitations of a strictly scientific world view.

Eiseley's **familiar essays** often blend the ordinary and the exotic, or point to the miraculous in the commonplace.

Beginning with a specific setting or thematic description, sometimes in a remote time or place, his essays create a series of dramatic incidents to illustrate a theme ("The Brown Wasps," 1969). Often there is a touch of the gothic sensibility in Eiseley's use of nocturnal imagery ("Instruments of Darkness," 1971), insomnia ("One Night's Dying," 1971), painful childhood memories ("The Gold Wheel," 1971), bizarre or grotesque events ("The Relic Men," 1971), physical deformities ("The Last Neanderthal," 1969), or grotesque fantasy ("The Dance of the Frogs," 1978).

Through the personal essay, Eiseley was able to connect ideas that seemed quite disparate. Beginning with a specific setting or thematic description, such as the bleak uplands of western Nebraska ("The Slit"), he takes the reader on a metaphoric journey backwards in time, accentuated by his vivid descriptions of a primitive mammal's skull embedded in a sandstone wall. His essays create a dramatic situation, such as a chance encounter on a beach in Costabel ("The Star Thrower"), or take readers on an intellectual journey ("The Ghost Continent," 1969) and bring them back with new insights. Along the way, Eiseley maintains the voice of informed conversation on a common theme, sharing a range of intellectual interests in literature, science, religion, philosophy, and biography.

Eiseley conveys his musings with vivid, arresting images rather than abstract theories. His essays feature a variety of fossilized and living mammals, birds and plants set in past and present dramatic landscapes. They range through topics as diverse as the miracle of water ("The Flow of the River," 1957), the appearance of flowering plants ("How Flowers Changed the World," 1957), the mechanisms of evolutionary adaptation ("The Snout," 1957), and the mystery of the rapid emergence of the human brain ("The Dream Animal," 1957). Several themes unify these speculations: an antimaterialistic bias, an opposition to scientism, and a desire to recover the past by using imagination to transcend temporal restraints.

Central to Eiseley's personal essays is a distinctive voice that appeals to public misgivings about the ideology of science. Eiseley's persona combines the insights of a disillusioned scientist with a distinctly romantic, often pessimistic sensibility. Skeptical of the claims of science and technology, he insists on the uniqueness of the individual and the need for compassion ("The Chresmologue," 1971). We are mysteries to ourselves, he observes ("Strangeness in the Proportion," 1971), part of the unaccountable strangeness and novelty of the universe. Evolution holds no favorites, he warns, and there are no guarantees for our future ("The Spore Bearers," 1970).

Dissatisfied with the restrictive, value-free orientation of modern science, Eiseley turned to the personal essay as a form through which he could articulate his sense of the mystery and wonder of life. For some time he had been disillusioned with the "religion of science," with its rigid assumption that every natural event in the universe could be measured, analyzed, and explained by prior events. He disliked the scientific detachment that would not permit imaginative or aesthetic response to his study of nature.

With this change of orientation, Eiseley placed himself in a long, distinguished tradition of English and American natural history writing – including Gilbert White, **Richard Jefferies**, W. H. Hudson, **Ralph Waldo Emerson, Henry David Thoreau,**

John Muir, John Burroughs, Ernest Thompson Seton, and **Aldo Leopold**. Like these earlier writers, Eiseley recorded his impressions of nature in a precise, distinctive, personal style. Eiseley's natural history essays gain vividness and accuracy from the influence of empirical science. His style is both personal and factual, blending objectivity with delight. Eiseley recognized that the study of nature could be both factual *and* contemplative. He believed that description and analysis alone could not provide a full understanding of the natural world; there is also a need for contemplative natural history, an approach that "contains overtones of thought which is not science, nor intended to be, and yet without which science itself would be poorer" ("The Enchanted Glass," 1957). Contemplative natural history offers what Eiseley calls "a natural history of the soul" ("The Enchanted Glass"). This human response to the world is especially important, he notes, in an age that does not lend itself to contemplation. Eiseley's familiar essays personalize science by balancing fact and knowledge with affection and emotional insight.

Eiseley's models were the great Victorian scientists – **Charles Darwin**, Alfred Russel Wallace, T. H. Huxley – who could express complex ideas to a general audience. In many ways, Eiseley resembles these gifted Victorians, naturalists with a literary bent, who forever changed human understanding of our place in the natural world. Eiseley had the poetic vision to perceive the natural history of life's emergence as an epic event, a grand unfolding of living forms, capable of being cast in imaginative terms. It took a special kind of talent to accomplish this, one more akin to the Victorian naturalist than the modern specialist, someone not intimidated by the "two cultures" division or the challenge of bridging disciplines. Eiseley had long been pursuing separate careers as a poet and a scientist, with the hope of eventually combining them in some literary form, and the personal essay seemed best to fulfill that promise for him.

Despite these affinities with Victorian men of science, Eiseley's work is neither derivative nor anachronistic. His visionary power, his animistic descriptions, and the range of his philosophical speculations distinguish him from his Victorian predecessors. Eiseley is less optimistic about the prospects of science than either Darwin or Huxley. A strong romantic tendency reinforces his pessimistic tone, particularly in his various self-dramatizations: as the neglected child, the impoverished student, the wandering bone hunter, the midnight scholar, the weary insomniac. While this attitude is largely temperamental, it may also reflect, especially in his most melancholic or somber moods, the influence of his diverse antiquarian reading. Throughout his life, Eiseley's favorite authors remained **Coleridge, Hazlitt, De Quincey, Lamb,** Poe, **Francis Bacon,** Robert Burton, and **Sir Thomas Browne** – all masters of the essay who loved obscure and arcane references, elegant practitioners of an ornate style who emphasized tone and mood in their writing. Eiseley may have learned from Bacon the habit of balancing scientific or scholarly ideas with vivid metaphors, although he is far more candid than Bacon, especially in regard to the painful memories of his childhood. Retaining Bacon's philosophical sweep and scientific vision, Eiseley tempers it with a baroque, introspective style more reminiscent of Robert Burton, Thomas Browne, Abraham Cowley, and the later Thoreau. Like each of these writers, Eiseley cultivated the personal essay in its purest form, as a mode of personal expression.

What Eiseley accomplished through his popular essays was to create an imaginative synthesis of literature and science – one that enlarged the power and range of the personal essay. Eiseley's "literary essay turned to scientific purposes" (*All the Strange Hours*) became the ideal medium for such self-discoveries as he wished to offer, modest and unassuming, tentative and speculative without appearing dogmatic. Despite changes in literary taste, Eiseley will continue to be read as one of the great modern masters of the personal essay.

ANDREW J. ANGYAL

See also Nature Essay; Science Essay

Biography

Loren Corey Eiseley. Born 3 September 1907 in Lincoln, Nebraska. Studied at the University of Nebraska, Lincoln, B.A., 1933; University of Pennsylvania, Philadelphia, A.M., 1935, Ph.D., 1937. Taught sociology and anthropology at the University of Kansas, Lawrence, 1937–44, and Oberlin College, Ohio, 1944–47; professor of anthropology, 1947–61, and Benjamin Franklin of Professor of Anthropology and the History of Science, 1961–77, University of Pennsylvania; curator of early man, University of Pennsylvania Museum, 1948–77; visiting professor at various universities during summers. Married Mabel Langdon, 1938. Contributor to various journals (especially science), newspapers, and magazines, including the *Saturday Evening Post*, *Harper's*, *Scientific American*, *Horizon*, the New York *Herald Tribune*, and the *New York Times*. Television host of Animal Secrets program, 1966–68. Awards: many, including the Athenaeum of Philadelphia Award, for *Darwin's Century*, 1958; John Burroughs Medal, and Pierre Lecomte du Nouy Foundation Award, for *Firmament of Time*, both 1961; Joseph Wood Krutch Medal, 1976; honorary degrees from dozens of universities. Died (of cancer) in Philadelphia, 9 July 1977.

Selected Writings

Essays and Related Prose
The Immense Journey, 1957
The Firmament of Time, 1960
Francis Bacon and the Modern Dilemma, 1962; revised, enlarged edition, as *The Man Who Saw Through Time*, 1973
Man, Time, and Prophecy, 1966
Science and the Unexpected Universe, 1966
The Invisible Pyramid, 1970
The Night Country: Reflections of a Bone-Hunting Man, 1971
The Star Thrower, 1978
Darwin and the Mysterious Mr. X: New Light on the Evolutionists, 1979
The Lost Notebooks, edited by Kenneth Heuer, 1987

Other writings: poetry, books on evolution (including *Darwin's Century: Evolution and the Men Who Discovered It*, 1958) and other natural history subjects, and an autobiography (*All the Strange Hours: The Excavation of a Life*, 1975).

Further Reading

Angyal, Andrew J., *Loren Eiseley*, Boston: Twayne, 1983
Carlisle, E. Fred, *Loren Eiseley: The Development of a Writer*, Urbana: University of Illinois Press, 1983
Carlisle, E. Fred, "The Literary Achievement of Loren Eiseley," in *Essays on the Essay: Redefining the Genre*, edited by Alexander Butrym, Athens: University of Georgia Press, 1989
Carrithers, Gale H., Jr., *Mumford, Tate, Eiseley: Watchers in the Night*, Baton Rouge: Louisiana State University Press, 1991

Gerber, Leslie E., and Margaret McFadden, *Loren Eiseley*, New York: Ungar, 1983
McCrae, Murdo William, editor, *The Literature of Science: Perspectives on Popular Scientific Writings*, Athens: University of Georgia Press, 1993
Pitts, Mary Ellen, "Undermining the Authority of Science: Epistemological Symbiosis in Loren Eiseley and Lewis Thomas," *Rendezvous* 25, no. 1 (Fall 1989): 83–90

Ekelund, Vilhelm

Swedish, 1880–1949

Vilhelm Ekelund's career as an essayist began only after he had already established himself as one of Sweden's foremost poets of the early 20th century. Between 1900 and 1906 he published seven volumes of poetry which were highly original yet also full of resonances of Paul Verlaine, **Stéphane Mallarmé**, Stefan George, and **Hugo von Hofmannsthal**, thereby becoming Sweden's most important contributor to the international symbolist movement. In 1909 he published his first collection of **meditation**s, *Antik ideal* (The classical ideal), not only launching his career as an essayist but at the same time completely taking his leave of poetry. During his lifetime he published some 20 volumes of prose, consisting overwhelmingly of essays and **aphorism**s, supplemented by several posthumous volumes.

Ekelund's abandonment of poetry and cultivation of the essay was motivated on one level by a desire to maintain his mental health. His poetry, animated by shifting moods and subtle nuances, seemed to threaten the spiritual health of his overly sensitive soul. In pragmatic terms, he needed a mode of expression that at least seemed to him more objective and univocal. His desire to maintain his mental balance not only required a change in genre but also suggested the theme of mental and spiritual well-being that in some way or other informs everything else he wrote. In more specific terms, Ekelund's essays explore how anxiety, melancholy, and solipsistic introversion can be avoided, and balance, stability, and peace maintained. Although he had great admiration for Friedrich Hölderlin, he saw in him the poet who, unable to withstand the demands of his own poetry, ended in madness; a poet like Walt Whitman, however, was of a more rugged nature and could endure.

On the whole, Ekelund's essays are anti-Romantic and anti-lyrical. They both reflect and exemplify a commitment often articulated in almost moralistic terms to precision, clarity, and aesthetic rigor. Among ancient authors, they celebrate Heraclitus, Sophocles, and Pindar, while the moderation and deferential if not obsequious attitudes of Socrates are scorned. Fortitude and the search for harmony stand out as the most salient characteristics of antiquity in Ekelund's mind, and are contrasted with the servile and accommodating in contemporary life. In their disparagement of the tepid, impassive, or halfhearted, the essays reveal their kinship with the thought of **Friedrich Nietzsche**, which is also reflected in their ecstatic exultation. Like Nietzsche, Ekelund despised erudition for its own sake, believing it to be stultifying and lifeless pedantry. "Bagage" is the derisive term Ekelund uses for useless knowledge that fails to engage life. Formally, Ekelund's essays gradually discarded more and more of what was considered inessential and became more narrowly focused. Essays in the usual sense became briefer and more concentrated and were eventually completely supplanted by aphorisms.

In addition to the heroic spirit he shared with Nietzsche, Ekelund also valued the search for balance and harmony as exemplified in more moderate and humane models like **Goethe** and **Ralph Waldo Emerson**. Although in general terms Nietzsche loomed larger in Ekelund's earlier essays and Goethe predominated in the later, the two coexisted and exercised influence throughout his career. The essay "Doric Apollo" (1908) compares the two and, with striking insights, delineates the complementary relationship Ekelund saw linking them. Indeed, many of his most significant essays are a form of biographical literary criticism in which Ekelund seeks to unveil the hidden recesses of writers' psyches and reveal what makes their spirits great and of enduring interest. To be counted among such essays are "Carlyle och Emerson" (1915), "James Russell Lowell" (1914), and "Leopardi – Nietzsche" (1918).

Ekelund was an aristocratic and exclusive spirit who could never appeal to a broad audience. After an absence from Sweden of several years, he returned hoping to lead a new generation of writers, but was frustrated and disappointed to find himself isolated and alienated to a degree from the public. Nonetheless, a small group of appreciative readers loyally supported him and saw his works into print (though in relatively small editions) even after his death.

Ekelund was a master of the Swedish prose style, using the language with great flexibility and inventiveness. His fluidity and eloquence reveal frequent traces of his mastery of Greek and Latin but without being labored or heavy-handed. Although capable of great clarity and lucidity, his prose became more cryptic and at times almost opaque as he found himself more and more marginalized. He used common words in personal and unusual ways that all but precluded comprehension except by those acquainted with his specialized vocabulary. He also derived crucial terms from Greek but assigned to each his own personal semantic meaning.

One of the many ironies central to Ekelund's career as an essayist is that the enduring and most obvious influence of his essays is not so much on the genre as such but rather on the poetry of the Finland-Swedish Modernist poets, Elmer Diktonius, Olof Enckell, and Edith Södergran. Not even those who most admired his prose have tried to imitate it. Thus his essays stand as magnificent achievements – though often dense and cryptic – but singular and relatively remote.

STEVEN P. SONDRUP

Biography

Otto Vilhelm Ekelund. Born 14 October 1880 in Stehag. Studied at the University of Lund, from 1898, degree, 1937. Left Sweden to avoid a prison sentence for a minor offence, 1908, living in Berlin for four years, then Denmark until 1921, when he returned to Sweden. Married. Awards: Bellman Prize, 1944; Tegnér Prize, 1947. Died in Saltsjöbaden, 3 September 1949.

Selected Writings

Essays and Related Prose

Antik ideal, 1909
Böcker och vandrigar, 1910
Båge och lyra, 1912
Tyska utsikter, 1913
Nordiskt och klassiskt aforismer, 1914
Veri similia, 2 vols., 1915–16
Metron, 1918
Attiskt i fågelperspektiv, 1919
På hafsstranden, 1922
Sak och sken, 1922
Lefnadsstämning, 1925
Väst-östligt: Tankar till en minnesdag, 1925
Passioner emellan, 1927
Lyra och Hades, 1930
Spår och tecken, 1930
Valda sidor och essays, 1908–1930, 1933
Det andra ljuset, 1935; as The Second Light, translated by Lennart Bruce, 1986
Elpidi, 1939
Concordia animi, 1942
Atticism, humanism, 1943; enlarged edition, 1946
Plus salis-, 1945
Prosa, edited by K. A. Svensson, 2 vols., 1952
Nya vakten, 1953
Saltet och Helichrysus: Atticism, humanism II, 1956
In silvis cum libro, 1957
Skoltal, ett urval aforismer, 1961
Campus et dies, 1963
Essayer och meditationer, 1901–1943, edited by Nils Gösta Valdén, 1978
Aforismer och sentenser, 1907–1949 (selections), 1980
Den ensammes stämningar: Artikler och dikter, 1898–1910 (includes poems), edited by Jonas Ellerström, 1984

Other writings: seven volumes of poetry, and **journals**. Also translated Ralph Waldo Emerson's journal.

Further Reading

Ekman, Rolf, Vilhelm Ekelunds Estetik, Lund: Gleerup, 1953
Johannesson, Eric O., "Vilhelm Ekelund: Modernism and the Aesthetics of the Aphorism," Scandinavian Studies 56, no. 3 (Summer 1984): 213–34
Naert, Pierre, Stilen i Vilhelm Ekelunds essayer och aforismer, Lund: Gleerup, 1949
Sjoberg, Leif, and Niels Lyhne Jensen, "Early Scandinavian Symbolism," in The Symbolist Movement in the Literature of European Languages, edited by Anna Balakian, Budapest: Akademiai Kiado, 1982: 575–85
Valdén, Nils Gösta, Inledning till Vilhelm Ekelund, Lund: Gleerup, 1965
Werin, Algot, Vilhelm Ekelund, Lund: Gleerup, 2 vols., 1960–61

Eliot, George

British, 1819–1880

George Eliot produced over 60 essays and **reviews**, the majority of which were published in the period 1854–56, immediately preceding her novel-writing career. During this time she published regularly in two radical journals: the quarterly *Westminster Review* and the weekly *Leader*. She also contributed a smaller number of essays to the *Saturday Review* and *Fraser's Magazine*. The essays largely took the form of literary reviews, but the freedom of this genre allowed her to tackle issues beyond those of the literary as it is narrowly defined: for instance, she wrote a number of important essays on evangelism and religion ("Evangelical Teaching: Dr. Cumming," 1855), women's rights ("Woman in France," 1854; "Margaret Fuller and Mary Wollstonecraft," 1855), and philosophy ("R. W. Mackay's *Progress of the Intellect*," 1851; "The Future of German Philosophy," 1855).

Eliot returned to the essay form in 1865 when she was invited to contribute some pieces to the *Pall Mall Gazette* and the *Fortnightly Review*. These include a short piece on the importance of German philosophical culture, "A Word for the Germans," and an essay on "The Logic of Servants," an explanation of why the franchise should not be extended to the servant class, exposing her socially conservative political views. In 1868, **Blackwood's Edinburgh Magazine**, the journal which had published most of her fiction, invited her to write an essay on the 1867 Reform Bill in the persona of Felix Holt, the hero of her hugely successful novel of the previous year. An essay steeped in organic metaphors, the "Address to Working Men, by Felix Holt" advises the newly enfranchised class of the gravity of their responsibility, and is a clear statement of the conservatism of her beliefs.

Eliot's relationship with the *Westminster Review* began when she moved to London to seek an independent living after the death of her father. At this stage she had already published her translation of D. F. Strauss' *Das Leben Jesu* (*The Life of Jesus*) and Spinoza's *Tractatus theologicopoliticus* (*Ethics*). Later she translated **Ludwig Feuerbach**'s *Das Wesen des Christenthums* (*The Essence of Christianity*). Her translation work is significant for its introduction of German historical criticism, or Higher Criticism, into British intellectual culture. Through her friends in the Midlands she was introduced to the publisher John Chapman, who bought the *Westminster Review* in 1851. Eliot lodged with the Chapmans for a number of years, writing for the *Review*, and between 1852 and 1854 took over as managing editor, a position that gave her full editorial control.

Eliot's essays from the 1854–56 period are noteworthy for their freshness and energy, the breadth of learning they display, their judiciousness, and also their wit and sometimes savage irony. The essay "Silly Novels by Lady Novelists" (1856) is characteristic of Eliot, the essayist, at her best and funniest. However, in critical opinion her achievement as an essayist is generally considered to pale beside that of her subsequent achievements as a novelist. When critical attention is focused on the essays, it is usually to consider them as precursors to her novels. Critics find in the essays the treatment of themes that dominate the novels (e.g. a critique of religious orthodoxies, the development of humanist notions of sympathy, and so on), and the development of stylistic qualities that come to characterize her mature novelistic techniques.

In the context of a literary history of the essay, however, Eliot is significant as one of the most intelligent and elegant practitioners of the genre in the mid-Victorian period. Moreover, the authoritative and sympathetic voice that she was able to assume within the essay form contributed to the development of her distinctive narrative style in the novels. Recent historicist and feminist critics have instigated a reassessment of the essays as works in their own right. In particular her essays on women have been analyzed as an expression of a formation of a distinctive feminist position – a conservative feminism that accepted women's social inferiority but argued that women should share an equal moral and intellectual culture with men.

A number of essays from Eliot's notebooks have also been published (e.g. "Notes on Form in Art," wr. 1868; "How I Came to Write Fiction," wr. 1857). These pieces deal with technical and aesthetic issues of writing fiction and, together with pieces from her published essays (such as "The Natural History of German Life," 1856), have provided the basis for constructing Eliot's literary theory. The emphasis is largely on realism within fiction.

Also noteworthy is Eliot's last published work, *The Impressions of Theophrastus Such* (1879). This is a work that has received very little critical attention, possibly on account of its unusual generic status, on the borders of fiction and the essay: it is a series of short sketches written in the persona of bachelor clergyman Theophrastus Such. The essays deal with a variety of issues of topical interest from science, philosophy, and economics. Frequently obscure in their frames of reference and with little by way of a narrative to support them, they are a far cry from Eliot's two late masterpieces, *Middlemarch* (1872) and *Daniel Deronda* (1876); critics have tended to dismiss them as a collection of unconnected essays. Nevertheless they share the intellectual preoccupations of the late works – broadly, a desire to write about the future – and it is significant that in the end it is the essay that provides Eliot with the formal flexibility she requires to consider this in some ways unwritable project.

JOSEPHINE McDONAGH

Biography

Born Mary Ann (later Marian) Evans, 22 November 1819 in Arbury, Warwickshire. Studied at Miss Lathom's school, Attleborough; Miss Wallington's school, Nuneaton, 1828–32; Misses Franklins' school, Coventry, 1832–35. Responsible for the family household after her mother's death, 1836; lived with her father in Foleshill, near Coventry, 1841–49; lived in Geneva, 1849–50; moved to London, 1851. Contributor, from 1851, and managing editor, 1852–54, the *Westminster Review*. Lived in Germany, 1854–55, Richmond, Surrey, 1855–60, and London, 1861–80. Lived with George Henry Lewes, from 1854 (died, 1878). Married John Walter Cross, 1880. Died (of pneumonia) in London, 22 December 1880.

Selected Writings

Essays and Related Prose

The Impressions of Theophrastus Such, 1879; edited by Nancy Henry, 1994, and D. J. Enright, 1995
Essays and Leaves from a Note-Book, edited by Charles Lee Lewes, 1884
Early Essays, 1919
Essays, edited by Thomas Pinney, 1963
A Writer's Notebook, 1854–1879, and Uncollected Writings (includes 16 essays and reviews), edited by Joseph Wiesenfarth, 1981
Selected Essays, Poems, and Other Writings, edited by A. S. Byatt and Nicholas Warren, 1990
Selected Critical Writings, edited by Rosemary Ashton, 1992

Other writings: seven novels (*Adam Bede*, 1859; *The Mill on the Floss*, 1860; *Silas Marner*, 1861; *Romola*, 1863; *Felix Holt*, 1866; *Middlemarch*, 1872; *Daniel Deronda*, 1876), the collection of stories *Scenes of Clerical Life* (1858), short stories, some poetry, and correspondence (collected in *The George Eliot Letters*, edited by Gordon S. Haight, 9 vols., 1954–78). Also translated works from the German.

Collected works edition: *The Works*, 21 vols., 1878–85(?).

Bibliographies

Fulmer, Constance M., *George Eliot: A Reference Guide*, Boston: Hall, 1977
Pangallo, Karen L., *George Eliot: A Reference Guide, 1972–1987*, Boston: Hall, 1990

Further Reading

Ashton, Rosemary, *The German Idea: Four English Writers and the Reception of German Thought, 1800–1860*, Cambridge and New York: Cambridge University Press, 1980
Beer, Gillian, *George Eliot*, Brighton: Harvester, and Bloomington: Indiana University Press, 1986
Carroll, David, editor, *George Eliot: The Critical Heritage*, London: Routledge and Kegan Paul, and New York: Barnes and Noble, 1971
Ermarth, Elizabeth Deeds, *George Eliot*, Boston: Twayne, 1985
Haight, Gordon S., *George Eliot: A Biography*, Oxford: Clarendon Press, and New York: Oxford University Press, 1968
Knoepflmacher, U. C., "George Eliot, Feuerbach and the Question of Criticism," *Victorian Studies* 7, no. 3 (1964): 306–09
Myers, William, "George Eliot's Essays and Reviews," *Prose Studies* 1, no. 2 (1978): 5–20
Myers, William, *The Teaching of George Eliot*, Leicester: Leicester University Press, and Totowa, New Jersey: Barnes and Noble, 1984
Robbins, Bruce, *The Servant's Hand: English Fiction from Below*, New York: Columbia University Press, 1986
Semmel, Bernard, *George Eliot and the Politics of National Inheritance*, Oxford and New York: Oxford University Press, 1994
Shuttleworth, Sally, *George Eliot and Nineteenth-Century Science: The Make-Believe of a Beginning*, Cambridge and New York: Cambridge University Press, 1984
Stang, G. Robert, "The Voices of the Essayist," *Nineteenth Century Fiction* 35 (1980): 312–30
Uglow, Jennifer, *George Eliot*, London: Virago, and New York: Pantheon, 1987
Vogeler, Martha S., "George Eliot and the Positivists," *Nineteenth Century Fiction* 35 (1980): 406–31
Welsh, Alexander, *George Eliot and Blackmail*, Cambridge, Massachusetts: Harvard University Press, 1985
Witemeyer, Hugh, *George Eliot and the Visual Arts*, New Haven, Connecticut: Yale University Press, 1979
Wright, T. R., "George Eliot and Positivism: A Reassessment," *Modern Language Review* 76 (1981): 257–72

Eliot, T. S.

American/British, 1888–1965

The most influential and, arguably, the most important poet writing in English in the 20th century, T. S. Eliot was also a master essayist. As significant, for contemporary readers, writers, scholars, and teachers of literature in English as his thematic and stylistic innovations in Modernist poetry were his critical analyses and gnomic pronouncements in numerous essays, several of which have become classics of the genre: "Tradition and the Individual Talent" (1919), "Hamlet" (1919), "The Metaphysical Poets" (1921), "The Function of Criticism" (1923), "Dante" (1929), "Milton I" (1936), "What Is a Classic?" (1945), "To Criticize the Critic" (1961), and many more. Beyond literary criticism, there are also Eliot's essays on sociological, educational, and theological subjects: "Thoughts After Lambeth" (1931) and "Modern Education and the Classics" (1932), for example. Two longer works of this kind, *The Idea of a Christian Society* (1939) and *Notes Towards the Definition of Culture* (1948) are properly classified as extended essays. Furthermore, in the way of articles and **reviews**, in the 60 years from 1905 to his death, Eliot contributed some 600 pieces to periodicals such as the *Little Review* and the *Times Literary Supplement*. As editor of the *Criterion*, Eliot was able to nurture the careers of other essayists, just as he promoted the works of younger poets at Faber and Faber.

In his literary-critical essays, especially those gathered in his most important collection, *Selected Essays* (1932; revised and enlarged, 1934, 1951), Eliot's principal purpose is "the elucidation of works of art and the correction of taste" ("The Function of Criticism"). Most of the "works of art" to which he refers are from the English Renaissance and the "correction of taste" which he would accomplish is that to which he aspired in his own poetry: the eradication of the prevailing hegemony of Romantic priorities and practices (in their Edwardian and Georgian forms) in literary criticism and creativity. However, Eliot wanted to revive not only the appreciation of the artistry of the 17th-century poets, dramatists, and prose writers, but something, too, of the spirit of their cohesive civilization (as he envisaged it) in the fragmented modern world of *The Waste Land*.

So when Eliot defined "the general point of view" of his "Essays on Style and Order," *For Lancelot Andrewes* (1928), as "classicist in literature, royalist in politics, and anglo-catholic in religion," his inspiration for these convictions came from Jacobean and Caroline England, in the lives and works of such as Andrewes himself, a translator of the Authorised Version of the Bible (1611), and Bishop of Winchester, whose **sermons** Eliot celebrates for their harmony of "intellect and sensibility" ("Lancelot Andrewes"). Later in the 17th century, however, in the discord of the Civil War, Eliot identified "a dissociation of sensibility . . . from which we have never recovered" ("The Metaphysical Poets"). This was not merely literary, but cultural and spiritual as well.

The association of "ordonnance, or arrangement and structure, precision in the use of words, and relevant intensity" that Eliot admired in Andrewes' sermons is to be found in his own essays. They exhibit the combination of carefully evolved frameworks of argument (Eliot had begun as a philosopher), intellectual acuteness (seasoned with provocative *aperçus*), and impassioned assessment. Eliot's is a prose decidedly not written, as Milton claimed his to be, with the poet's "left hand." His intended readership was those with a measure of his own literary culture. Many examples are occasional pieces, such as reviews. Yet as Eliot emerged as the premier poet of the modern age, his prose writings were also disseminated to a wider audience. The brilliant insights and sweeping generalizations achieved the status of canon law, and toward the end of his life Eliot confessed to having been dogged by his quotable pronouncements long after they had ceased to be adequate statements of his convictions ("To Criticize the Critic").

The famous essay of 1919, "Tradition and the Individual Talent," is a case in point, its very title being a credal statement about the combination and tension between received and innovative elements in literature. It first appeared in the *Egoist* and contains an untranslated quotation from Aristotle and references to Homer and Dante, in combination with Modernist convictions about objectivity in creativity and criticism – revolutionary by the literary standards of the time. Eliot's procedure enacts his thesis, culminating in the declaration: "Poetry is not a turning loose of emotion, but an escape from emotion; it is not the expression of personality, but an escape from personality. But, of course, only those who have personality and emotions know what it means to want to escape from these things."

Such dicta transformed literary criticism in the 20th century, as Eliot enunciated the precepts by which his own poetry – with its wry, ironic, and fastidious detachment – could be enjoyed: "the more perfect the artist, the more completely separate in him will be the man who suffers and the mind which creates." The confrontation of the classical ideal and Romantic experience which Eliot constructs in his essays, and the refinement of the latter by the former, is the *leitmotif* of his theory: "Tennyson and Browning are poets, and they think; but they do not feel their thought as immediately as the odour of a rose. A thought to Donne was an experience; it modified his sensibility" ("The Metaphysical Poets").

Eliot's individualistic essays, that is to say, in their iconoclastically legislative character, belong to "the tradition," as represented in the 19th century by **Matthew Arnold**'s *Essays in Criticism* (1865–88) and, in the 18th, by **Samuel Johnson**'s *Lives of the English Poets* (1779–81). In "Hamlet," for example, Eliot employs the quasi-Arnoldian touchstone of the "objective correlative" to pronounce, with a Johnsonian absoluteness, Shakespeare's tragedy a failure. This judgment, as startling as Johnson's repudiation of Milton's "Lycidas," derives from Eliot's conviction that there is not "a set of objects, a situation, a chain of events" (that is, an "objective correlative") to justify the emotion of the central character. Hamlet is "dominated by an emotion which . . . is in *excess* of the facts as they appear."

With Milton, Eliot dealt even more rudely. F. R. Leavis, the Cambridge critic who was a principal purveyor of Eliot's poetry and literary criticism, summarized (approvingly) the devastating effect of Eliot's assessment, culminating in the essay of 1936, "Milton I": "Milton's dislodgment, in the past decade, after his two centuries of predominance, was effected with remarkably little fuss. The irresistible argument was, of course, Mr. Eliot's creative achievement; it gave his few critical asides – potent, it is true, by context – their finality" ("Milton's Verse," 1936). The matter was not finalized, however. In "Milton II" (1947), Eliot substantially repudiated his earlier indictments. Here and elsewhere, we can trace the evolution of his thought in the sequence of his essays.

Leavis took a phrase from Eliot – his definition of the collaborative process of literary criticism as "the common pursuit of true judgement" ("The Function of Criticism") – for the title of his critical collection, *The Common Pursuit* (1952), which was one of several studies by scholars and, perhaps more importantly, teachers of international stature and influence who propagated Eliot's precepts in the universities in the

mid-20th century. Their graduates took these ideas into the secondary schools to the point where, for two or three generations, Eliot's literary-**critical essays** were formative and formidable across the gamut of English studies. The origin of the so-called "New Criticism" of the 1940s, for example, may be traced to the Cambridge of Leavis, I. A. Richards, and William Empson of the 1920s, and they had taken their cue from Eliot.

The breadth of Eliot's subject matter in his essays, beyond literary criticism, must be emphasized. In "Second Thoughts About Humanism" (1929), for example, the philosopher is to the fore; in "The Aims of Education" (1950), the cultural critic and theologian; while in "Marie Lloyd" (1923), an essay on "the greatest music-hall artist of her time," we are struck by Eliot's humanity.

His two long essays remain to be mentioned. *The Idea of a Christian Society* began as a series of lectures at Corpus Christi College, Cambridge, in March 1939, which were published later that year. Eliot reflects, in the months leading up to World War II, on the future of Western civilization bereft of Christian spirituality. *The Idea of a Christian Society* is a valuable aid to the understanding of some of the themes in Eliot's last important poetic work, *Four Quartets* (1936–42).

Eliot introduces *Notes Towards the Definition of Culture* (1948) as an "essay" which he began in the closing stages of the war, after completing the *Quartets*. It is, as he says, a piece of "social criticism." Again, it is the centrality of religion in the development and sustenance of culture which is his theme: "no culture has appeared or developed except together with a religion." Although by this period in his life Eliot had attained the status of a sage, having acquired the Nobel Prize and been admitted to the Order of Merit (both in 1948), his conservative views in these essays did not achieve popular acceptance.

The influence of Eliot's essays today, especially in what remains of the discipline of English Literature, is negligible. In the 21st century – like Arnold's *Essays* and Johnson's *Lives* now – they will probably be regarded only as historical curiosities. Yet, like the essays of those earlier masters, Eliot's will remain exemplary for their style – erudite, stimulating, and, above all, readable. To paraphrase the closing observation of his essay on "John Dryden" (1921), Eliot is one of those who have set standards for English prose which it is desperate to ignore.

BARRY SPURR

Biography

Thomas Stearns Eliot. Born 26 September 1888 in St. Louis, Missouri. Studied at Harvard University, Cambridge, Massachusetts, 1906–10, 1911–14, A.B., 1909, A.M. in English, 1910; the Sorbonne, Paris, 1910–11; Merton College, Oxford, 1914–15. Married Vivienne Haigh-Wood, 1915 (separated, 1933; died, 1947). Taught at English schools, 1915–17; worked for Lloyd's Bank, London, 1917–25. Assistant editor, the *Egoist*, London, 1917–19; contributor, the *Times Literary Supplement*, London, from 1919, and the *Athenaeum*; founding editor, the *Criterion*, London, 1922–39. Editor, later director, Faber and Gwyer, 1925–28, and Faber and Faber publishers, London, 1929–65. Became a British citizen, 1927. Editorial board member, *New English Weekly*, London, 1934–44, and *Christian News Letter*, Oxford, 1939–46. Charles Eliot Norton Professor of Poetry, 1932–33, and Theodore Spencer Memorial Lecturer, 1950, Harvard University. Married Valerie Fletcher, 1957. Awards: Nobel Prize for Literature, 1948; Order of Merit, 1948; New York Drama Critics Circle Award,

1950; Hanseatic-Goethe Prize (Hamburg), 1954; Dante Gold Medal (Florence), 1959; Order of Merit (Bonn), 1959; Emerson-Thoreau Medal, 1960; U.S. Medal of Freedom, 1964; honorary degrees from 19 universities; Honorary Fellow, Magdalene College, Cambridge, 1948, and Merton College, Oxford, 1949; Officer, Legion of Honor, and Commander, Order of Arts and Letters (France), 1950. Died in London, 4 January 1965.

Selected Writings

Essays and Related Prose
The Sacred Wood: Essays on Poetry and Criticism, 1920
Homage to John Dryden: Three Essays on Poetry of the Seventeenth Century, 1924
For Lancelot Andrewes: Essays on Style and Order, 1928
John Dryden: The Poet, the Dramatist, the Critic, 1932
Selected Essays, 1917-32, 1932; revised, enlarged editions, 1934, 1951
The Use of Poetry and the Use of Criticism (lectures), 1933
After Strange Gods: A Primer of Modern Heresy (lectures), 1934
Elizabethan Essays, 1934; revised edition, as *Essays on Elizabethan Drama*, 1956; as *Elizabethan Dramatists*, 1963
Essays Ancient and Modern, 1936
The Idea of a Christian Society (lectures), 1939
Notes Towards the Definition of Culture, 1948
Selected Prose, edited by John Hayward, 1953
On Poetry and Poets, 1957
To Criticize the Critic and Other Writings, 1965
Selected Prose, edited by Frank Kermode, 1975

Other writings: several collections of poetry (including *Prufrock and Other Observations*, 1917; *The Waste Land*, 1922; *Four Quartets*, 1936-42; collected in *Complete Poems and Plays*, 1969), seven plays (including *Murder in the Cathedral*, 1935; *The Family Reunion*, 1939; *The Cocktail Party*, 1950), and works on literature and writers.

Bibliographies

Gallup, Donald, *T. S. Eliot: A Bibliography*, London: Faber, 1952; revised edition, Faber, and New York: Harcourt Brace, 1969
Gunter, Bradley, *The Merrill Checklist of T. S. Eliot*, Columbus, Ohio: Merrill, 1970
Martin, Mildred, *A Half-Century of Eliot Criticism: An Annotated Bibliography of Books and Articles in English, 1916-1965*, Lewisburg, Pennsylvania: Bucknell University Press, and London: Kaye and Ward, 1972
Ricks, Beatrice, *T. S. Eliot: A Bibliography of Secondary Works*, Metuchen, New Jersey: Scarecrow Press, 1980

Further Reading

Asher, Kenneth, *T. S. Eliot and Ideology*, Cambridge and New York: Cambridge University Press, 1995
Bergonzi, Bernard, *T. S. Eliot*, London: Macmillan, 1978 (original edition, 1972)
Freed, Lewis, *T. S. Eliot: The Critic as Philosopher*, West Lafayette, Indiana: Purdue University Press, 1979
Good, Graham, "T. S. Eliot: The Process of Refinement," in his *The Observing Self: Rediscovering the Essay*, London and New York: Routledge, 1988: 135-51
Gray, Piers, *T. S. Eliot's Intellectual and Poetic Development, 1909-1922*, Brighton: Harvester, and Atlantic Highlands, New Jersey: Humanities Press, 1982
Jain, Manju, *T. S. Eliot and American Philosophy: The Harvard Years*, Cambridge and New York: Cambridge University Press, 1992
Kojecky, Roger, *T. S. Eliot's Social Criticism*, London: Faber, and New York: Farrar Straus, 1971
Margolis, John, *T. S. Eliot's Intellectual Development, 1922-1939*, Chicago: University of Chicago Press, 1972
Newton-de Molina, David, editor, *The Literary Criticism of T. S. Eliot: New Essays*, London: Athlone Press, 1977
Rajan, Balachandra, editor, *T. S. Eliot: A Study of His Writings by Several Hands*, London: Dobson, 1947; New York: Haskell House, 1964
Ricks, Christopher, *T. S. Eliot and Prejudice*, London: Faber, and Berkeley: University of California Press, 1988
Schwartz, Sanford, *The Matrix of Modernism: Pound, Eliot, and Early Twentieth-Century Thought*, Princeton, New Jersey: Princeton University Press, 1985

Emerson, Ralph Waldo
American, 1803-1882

Ralph Waldo Emerson is undoubtedly the premier essayist in American literary history. Over a period of 34 years he produced a remarkable series of essays which expressed a unique literary philosophy characterized by the critic Harold Bloom (in *Agon*, 1982) as a "literary religion" that did nothing less than express the mythology of America itself. The buoyant spirit, the philosophical light touch, and the pithy diction Emerson injected into his numerous and diverse essays signified what **Oliver Wendell Holmes** described (particularly in regard to "Man Thinking, or the American Scholar," but applicable to all the essays of "the Yankee Sage") as "America's Declaration of Independence," its liberation from the long shadow of the dominance of European literary styles and modes of expression. His influence on subsequent American writers – Walt Whitman, William Carlos Williams, Wallace Stevens, Robert Frost, F. Scott Fitzgerald, Willa Cather, Gertrude Stein, and others – is virtually immeasurable. Emerson provided the foundation for the emphasis on immediate experience in the thought of the philosophers John Dewey and **William James** and for the spirit of the pragmatic movement in philosophy in general. Emerson was at the heart of the then new focus on individuality, on what he called "the sovereign individual." This influence even extended to the radical German philosopher **Friedrich Nietzsche**, who referred to him as "the author richest in ideas of this century." Walt Whitman was stimulated by Emerson's stress on the promise of the future, his respect for the "common man," and the transformative power of the poetic spirit. He endeavored to emulate the ideal poet depicted in Emerson's edifying essay, "The Poet" (1844).

By the time the first edition of his complete works was published in 1903-04, Emerson's international reputation was already established. Moreover, his essays have had an unusual appeal to a large and diverse audience of general readers. This is no doubt due to the nontechnical and accessible nature of his essays. One of the leading figures in the transcendentalist movement in American literature, Emerson received recognition and serious treatment from literary critics in his own time and well into the 20th century. And, over the last 15 years or so, he has undergone a significant, positive, and sophisticated reappraisal at the hands of a host of critics as a thinker, essayist, and poet. He is generally considered the quintessential American writer.

Emerson's earliest essay, *Nature*, was published in book form in 1836 and soon after was christened "the Bible of New England Transcendentalism." Despite its sometimes murky metaphysical idealism, *Nature* clearly announced the emergence of a new voice in American literature. In addition to a celebration of the salutary value of communing with nature and the elevation of the affirmative spiritual dimension of life (through the persona of the Orphic poet), Emerson presented a condensed theory of signs that anticipated some aspects of recent semiotics. As if foreshadowing his own rich use of metaphorical imagery in his later essays, Emerson called attention to our natural reliance on analogy in ordinary language, literature, poetry, and philosophical thinking. Language is construed in *Nature* as pervaded by anthropomorphic metaphors and the natural world itself is described as "a metaphor of the human mind." There is a "correspondence" between spirit and nature that is reflected in the metaphorical language by which we describe the one in images derived from the other. This general orientation colors many of his later essays insofar as moods are metaphorically expressed and invariably suggest a metaphysics or world view.

Already in *Nature* Emerson's ability to create pithy sentences, coin ingenious tropes, and produce compressed insights is apparent. Entire theories are compacted into quotable sentences: "Nature's dice are always loaded." "Nature is so pervaded with human life that there is something of humanity in all and every particular." "The corruption of man is followed by the corruption of language." Thinking of humankind's capacity to transform the world by means of its power of spiritual transcendence, Emerson proclaims that "The kingdom of man over nature" is "a dominion such as now is beyond his dream of God." Edifying prose, bracing optimism, and the centrality of subjective experience, which characterize so many of Emerson's essays, are already discernible features of his writing. *Nature* is so passionately devoted to the potentialities of humankind which have not yet been realized that, as Harold Bloom has said, it might as well be entitled "Man."

In his *Essays, First Series* (1841) and *Essays, Second Series* (1844) Emerson's thought and expression are clear and incisive. He is the master of the *aperçu*, the arresting trope. His essays have a speech-like character – several are slightly revised or polished lectures or orations, a characteristic often linked to his earlier practice, as a former Unitarian minister, of carefully preparing **sermon**s. Emerson's prose has a distinctive poetic quality, a prophetic tone. He displays in his essays an unusual talent for epigrammatic statement. Many of his taut sentences are eminently quotable and some of his phrases have long since passed into common English parlance: "the shot heard around the world," "the devil's attorney" (as "the devil's advocate"), "a minority of one," "a foolish consistency is the hobgoblin of little minds." The richness of his language and the thematic content of his essays disclose his ability to compress thoughts, to attain an accessible condensation of ideas derived from a variety of disparate domains. The American critic Malcolm Cowley, in his introduction to *The Portable Emerson* (1981), said that Emerson created "sentences" in the Latin sense of the term: "ideas briefly and pungently expressed as axioms." Some of his chiseled sentences are both profound and immediately persuasive, as this, from "Self-Reliance": "In every work of genius we recognize our own rejected thoughts; they come back to us with a certain alienated majesty." Or this, from "Fate": "Life is an ecstasy."

Emerson typically expresses in his essays, with striking rhetorical force and verve, a complexity of ideas that is not so much (as critics have often charged) a catena of contradictions as it is lucid perceptions and expressions of dialectical oppositions, a multiplicity of perspectives. With regard to the shifting standpoints typically found in virtually all of his essays, what Emerson said in "Montaigne" (1850) about the French prototype of the modern prose essay, the *Essais*, applies to his own writings as well: "An angular dogmatic house would be rent to chip and splinter in this storm of many elements." He was quite aware of being perceived as never having constructed a conceptual foundation for the flurry of ideas he spun out in his essays; he once remarked that it was his "love of truth" which led him to abstain from propounding dogmatic absolutes. Emerson's essays reveal a habit of provisional, experimental thinking, a flexibility of mind, an impressionistic mode of reflection clothed in metaphorical expression. He was cognizant of the limits of language and sensitive to the "unspeakable" encountered in experience which eludes precise linguistic determination or articulation. Although he was by no means an uncritical mystic, Emerson evoked the mystery of existence, comparing it to a more perplexing version of the riddle of the sphinx. His writings often point to the wonder of the protean metamorphoses in nature. In "Circles" he celebrates, rather than bemoans, the impermanence of things, ideas, arts, of what is prized, of people, of life itself, affirming the fluidity, volatility, and circular patterns in the world. In "The American Scholar" (1837) he embraces a nature in which "there is never a beginning, never an end, to the inexplicable continuity of this web of God, but always circular power returning into itself."

Perhaps because of his experience in delivering hundreds of lectures as a participant in the 19th-century Lyceum movement for cultural enrichment, in his essays Emerson seems to "speak" directly to the reader, to be seeking existential communication, to try to stimulate, in a Socratic manner, reflective self-consciousness. His aim is not merely to entertain or charm his readers; rather he encourages them to cultivate "self-trust," to become what they ought to be, to be open to the internal, private, intuitive, and reflective world of experience. His oracular, "uplifting" rhetoric seems to serve, in an indirect way, a psychagogic purpose. Many of his essays are motivational exhortations to seek the good, the better, the best. Over a hundred years later they still have the power, when read in a receptive mood, to stir in the reader a powerful sense of the possible.

Aside from *Nature*, it is generally held that the essays of the first series show Emerson at the peak of his form, fully in control of his aphoristic powers. The works in this collection reveal a mastery of style and a confident execution of intention not readily apparent in his last collection of essays, *Society and Solitude* (1870). There is no doubt that style and intellectual content are synergistically combined in "Self-Reliance," "Compensation," "History," and "Circles" (all 1841). However, some of the essays in the second series – in particular the striking characterization of the nature of the poetic impulse and the invocation of the liberating artist in "The Poet," as well as the trenchant discourse on the relativity of perspective and subjectivity in "Experience" – are sprightly and convincing. In "Politics" Emerson shows himself to be the opposite of naive by hurling barbs at what is deceptive, fraudulent, and corrupt in the political atmosphere of his day.

In his portraits of various types of men in *Representative Men* (1850), Emerson alters his style and approach to his material somewhat and, with the exception of a surprisingly weak depiction of Shakespeare, displays a talent for literary portraiture. "Montaigne; or, the Skeptic" is a sympathetic and perceptive depiction of the man and his writings. Of the *Essais* Emerson tersely but aptly observes that in them we find "the language of conversation transferred to a book." "Napoleon; or, the Man of the World" is an insightful summary of the positive and negative traits of this "thoroughly modern man" whose virtues, Emerson suggests, are almost deleted by his faults, "who proposed to himself simply a brilliant career, without any stipulation or scruple concerning the means."

In the book-length series of essays comprising *English Traits* (1856), Emerson tries to do for the collective character of the English in the mid-19th century what he had done for **Plato**, **Montaigne**, Napoleon, and others in *Representative Men*. *English Traits* is a departure from his usual essay form and indicates an unsuspected versatility of style and tone. The essays comprising this collection are almost reportorial, casual, friendly toward their subject, but occasionally gently ironic, even witty.

Although the essays comprising *The Conduct of Life* (1860) have often been minimized in relation to the first and second series of *Essays*, they can be powerful, surprisingly sharp and biting pieces. Essays such as "Fate," "Culture," "Power," and the barbed "Considerations by the Way" serve to dispel the traditional, projected image of Emerson as sentimental, "genteel," "naive," "starry-eyed," and excessively idealistic. In these essays he concentrates more on content than on form, more on the negative aspects of existence than on the positive, more on a hard-headed realism than edifying discourses. We see in them another aspect of "the Sage of Concord," one that emphasizes the limitation of our powers, the force of circumstances, the dangers inherent in an emerging mass society. In "Power," we find the man called "the philosopher of the common man" praising uncommon creative artists (such as Michelangelo and Leonardo) for their energy, surplus power, and boldness. The prose hymn to "The Over-Soul" in the first series of *Essays* is replaced in *The Conduct of Life* by a decidedly this-worldly emphasis. Transcendentalism seems to be replaced by an immanent cultural idealism which nonetheless advocates a "sacred courage" in face of the terrible aspects of existence. Nature, humanity, and life are seen from a darker, but not yet pessimistic, point of view.

It is generally believed that the death of his first wife Ellen Tucker at the age of 19, the loss of his six-year-old son, Waldo, and of his two brothers – over a period of a decade – made him painfully aware of the negative aspects of existence. Nonetheless, he continued to produce incisive, carefully crafted essays. Whether his later essays were informed by painful personal experiences or not, Emerson was always prone to extend the range of his interests and adopt multiple perspectives on nature, humankind, society, and life. Invariably he disclosed the oppositions, paradoxes, polarities, and stupendous "antagonisms" in reality.

The pungency, rhetorical power, and insightfulness of Emerson's essays, as well as his affirmation of "the constant fact of Life" in the face of limitations, imperfections, and the vicissitudes of fate, show him to have been a sensitive, perceptive, and persuasive literary philosopher. In terms of his supreme mastery of the essay genre, the immediacy of his communication with his readers, and his ability to express profound insights in accessible language, Emerson could, with only slight exaggeration, be characterized as the Montaigne of America.

GEORGE J. STACK

Biography
Born 25 May 1803 in Boston. Studied at Harvard University, Cambridge, Massachusetts, A.B., 1821; Harvard Divinity School, 1825, 1827. Schoolmaster during the 1820s. Married Ellen Tucker, 1829 (died, 1831). Assistant pastor, then pastor, Old Second Church, Boston, 1829–32. Traveled to Europe, 1832–33, meeting and becoming lifelong friends with **Thomas Carlyle**. Lyceum lecturer, after 1833. Moved to Concord, Massachusetts, 1834. Married Lydia Jackson, 1835: two sons (one died as a child) and two daughters. Leader of the transcendentalists, from 1836; contributor, 1849–44, and editor, 1842–44, the *Dial* transcendentalist periodical. Active abolitionist during the 1850s. Awards: honorary degree from Harvard University. Died (of pneumonia) in Concord, 27 April 1882.

Selected Writings

Essays and Related Prose
Nature, 1836; facsimile reprint, 1985; edited by Kenneth Walter Cameron, 1940, and Warner Berthoff, 1968
Essays, 1841; revised, enlarged edition, as *Essays: First Series*, 1847
Essays, Second Series, 1844; revised edition, 1850
Orations, Lectures, and Addresses, 1844
Nature: Addresses and Lectures, 1849; as *Miscellanies: Embracing Nature, Addresses, and Lectures*, 1856; as *Miscellanies*, 1884
Representative Men: Seven Lectures, 1850; edited by Pamela Schirmeister, 1995
English Traits, 1856; edited by Howard Mumford Jones, 1966
The Conduct of Life, 1860
May-Day and Other Pieces, 1867
Prose Works, 3 vols., 1868–78(?)
Society and Solitude, 1870
Letters and Social Aims, 1876
The Senses and the Soul, and Moral Sentiment in Religion: Two Essays, 1884
Two Unpublished Essays: The Character of Socrates, The Present State of Ethical Philosophy, 1896
Uncollected Writings: Essays, Addresses, Poems, Reviews and Letters, edited by Charles C. Bigelow, 1912
Uncollected Lectures, edited by Clarence Gohdes, 1932
Young Emerson Speaks: Unpublished Discourses on Many Subjects, edited by Arthur Cushman McGiffert, Jr., 1938
The Portable Emerson, edited by Mark Van Doren, 1946; revised edition, edited by Carl Bode and Malcolm Cowley, 1981
Selections, edited by Stephen E. Whicher, 1957
Early Lectures, edited by Stephen E. Whicher, Robert E. Spiller, and Wallace E. Williams, 3 vols., 1959–72
Literary Criticism, edited by Eric W. Carlson, 1979
Selected Essays, edited by Larzer Ziff, 1982
Essays and Lectures, edited by Joel Porte, 1983
Complete Sermons, 4 vols., 1989–91
Selected Writings, edited by Brooks Atkinson, 1992
Self-Reliance, and Other Essays, 1993
Nature and Other Writings, edited by Peter Turner, 1994
Antislavery Writings, edited by Len Gougeon and Joel Myerson, 1995

Other writings: poetry, letters, and journals (collected in *Journals and Miscellaneous Notebooks*, edited by William H. Gilman and others, 16 vols., 1960–83).

Collected works editions: *Complete Works* (Centenary Edition), edited by Edward Waldo Emerson, 12 vols., 1903–04; *Collected Works* (Harvard Edition), edited by Alfred R. Ferguson, 5 vols., 1971–94 (in progress).

Bibliographies

Boswell, Jeanetta, *Emerson and the Critics: A Checklist of Criticism, 1900–1977*, Metuchen, New Jersey: Scarecrow Press, 1979

Burkholder, Robert E., *Emerson: An Annotated Bibliography of Criticism, 1980–1991*, Westport, Connecticut: Greenwood Press, 1994

Burkholder, Robert E., and Joel Myerson, *Emerson: An Annotated Secondary Bibliography*, Pittsburgh: University of Pittsburgh Press, 1985

Myerson, Joel, *Emerson: A Descriptive Bibliography*, Pittsburgh: University of Pittsburgh Press, 1982

Putz, Manfred, *Ralph Waldo Emerson: A Bibliography of Twentieth-Century Criticism*, New York: Lang, 1986

Further Reading

Allen, Gay Wilson, *Waldo Emerson: A Biography*, New York: Viking Press, 1981

Atwan, Robert, "'Ecstasy & Eloquence': The Method of Emerson's Essays," in *Essays on the Essay: Redefining the Genre*, edited by Alexander Butrym, Athens: University of Georgia Press, 1989

Bishop, Jonathan, *Emerson on the Soul*, Cambridge, Massachusetts: Harvard University Press, 1964

Buell, Lawrence, *Literary Transcendentalism: Style and Vision in the American Renaissance*, Ithaca, New York: Cornell University Press, 1973

Cavell, Stanley, *Conditions Handsome and Unhandsome: The Constitution of Emersonian Perfectionism*, La Salle, Illinois: Open Court, 1990

Cheyfitz, Eric, *The Trans-Parent: Sexual Politics in the Language of Emerson*, Baltimore: Johns Hopkins University Press, 1981

Ellison, Julie, *Emerson's Romantic Style*, Princeton, New Jersey: Princeton University Press, 1984

Hughes, Gertrude Reif, *Emerson's Demanding Optimism*, Baton Rouge: Louisiana State University Press, 1984

Konvitz, Milton R., editor, *The Recognition of Ralph Waldo Emerson: Selected Criticism Since 1837*, Ann Arbor: University of Michigan Press, 1972

Michael, John, *Emerson and Skepticism: The Cipher of the World*, Baltimore: Johns Hopkins University Press, 1988

Packer, B. L., *Emerson's Fall: A New Interpretation of the Major Essays*, New York: Continuum, 1982

Paul, Sherman, *Emerson's Angle of Vision: Man and Nature in American Experience*, Cambridge, Massachusetts: Harvard University Press, 1952

Porte, Joel, *Representative Man: Ralph Waldo Emerson in His Time*, New York: Oxford University Press, 1979

Richardson, Robert D., Jr., *Emerson: The Mind on Fire: A Biography*, Berkeley: University of California Press, 1995

Robinson, David, *Apostle of Culture: Emerson as Preacher and Lecturer*, Philadelphia: University of Pennsylvania Press, 1982

Stack, George J., *Nietzsche and Emerson: An Elective Affinity*, Athens: Ohio University Press, 1992

Thurin, Erik Ingvar, *Emerson as Priest of Pan: A Study in the Metaphysics of Sex*, Lawrence: Regents Press of Kansas, 1981

Van Veer, David, *Emerson's Epistemology: The Argument of the Essays*, Cambridge: Cambridge University Press, 1986

Whicher, Stephen E., *Freedom and Fate: An Inner Life of Ralph Waldo Emerson*, Philadelphia: University of Pennsylvania Press, 1953

Yoder, R. A., *Emerson and the Orphic Poet in America*, Berkeley: University of California Press, 1978

Encyclopedias and the Essay

Encyclopedias, or comprehensive systems of learning, developed independently of one another in three distinct cultural traditions in Europe, the Near East, and the Orient. The earliest Chinese encyclopedia is recorded in 220 CE but has been completely lost; part of the text of its successor, the *Bian zhu* (String of pearls of literature), survives and was followed by at least eight other attempts before the appearance in the late 13th century of the *Wen xian tong kao* (General study of literary remains). The first Arabic encyclopedia is the 9th-century work of Ibn Qutayba, arranged in ten books, each with a defining topic: power, war, nobility, character, eloquence, asceticism, friendship, prayer, food, and women. European encyclopedia-making has its generally accepted origins in Pliny's *Historia naturalis* (Natural history) in 77 CE.

The word "encyclopedia" was first used by Paul Scalich in 1559, the term "cyclopedia" having been employed initially by Joachim Sterck van Ringelbergh in 1541. Both are derived from the Greek and translate as a "cycle of learning." There are easily hundreds of examples of compilations which could be loosely described as encylopedias, deriving from all literary traditions from as early as 350 BCE. They share the common purpose of bringing together in one source their culture's accumulated learning, but few if any of these efforts provide a unifying philosophical context for the knowledge they catalogue. Encyclopedias continued to be no more than "strings of pearls" until well into the 18th century, when in the West, the phenomenon of the **periodical essay** had a great impact on the format and especially on the ideology of encyclopedia-making. At that point the seminal European examples of the encylopedia appeared under the editorship of **Denis Diderot** in France and of William Smellie in Scotland, relying on the essay to anchor and give to the encyclopedia the integrity of a true literary construct. Such works continued to be ambitiously comprehensive in content and elaborately schematic in structure, but the whole was made to give place to the part; these encyclopedias are distinguished not for their general attempt to embrace *all* learning but for the particular achievement of individual contributions on discrete topics. This essayistic approach to compiling encyclopedias, working as it does from part to whole, characterizes all the national encyclopedias which appeared throughout the 19th and early 20th centuries.

Increasingly in the 17th century, beginning with **Francis Bacon**'s plan for the *Instauratio magna* (1620), which sets out new principles for schematizing learning, and culminating in **Pierre Bayle**'s *Dictionnaire historique et critique* (1697; *An Historical and Critical Dictionary*), the first truly "modern" work of this kind, encyclopedias in Europe incorporated the sensibility of the rationalists and became more scientific in their structure and content. But even the influential work of Ephraim Chambers, whose *Cyclopaedia* (1728) would inspire both Diderot and Smellie, lacked a strong editorial direction; Bayle and Chambers still relied on the traditional illusion of inclusiveness, the impression that their work was exhaustive in its scholarship, to assert their credentials. It was the weight of their learning rather than any professional expertise and opinions that distinguished their efforts. Theirs remained notably the achievements of individuals, encyclopedias produced by the prodigious labors of one man, not the cooperative discourse of a society of scholars and practitioners.

By the mid-18th century, quite a different sort of approach to compiling encyclopedias began to emerge. Innovations appeared in three areas: a new emphasis on the trades and professions with their technical and applied learning; a collaborative approach that enlisted some 160 contributors to Diderot's *Encyclopédie* (1751–72); and the editorial choice of the essay to embrace the more important and controversial entries with an individualistic and even polemical tone that challenges the reader to reflection rather than simply providing information. Diderot recruited an international body of experts to write essays that argued theoretical positions often at the expense of facts and particulars, as was the case with **Rousseau**'s notorious entry on Music, a discussion which continues to matter not for what it tells us about music but for what it reveals about Rousseau. Many of the articles Diderot solicited assumed socially and politically critical stances, employing the style of the **polemical essay** to attack the notion of privilege in European society. The essay as it developed after **Montaigne** and Bacon, with its emphasis upon the values of the written word and upon subjectively contextualizing its topics, makes possible during the Enlightenment a style of encyclopedia-making that is more critical, more aggressive, and more literary.

The *Encyclopaedia Britannica* made its first appearance in 1768 in Edinburgh, issued in parts. The editor, William Smellie, compiled much of the material himself, although he seems to have been aided in the original articles by fellow Scot and historian Gilbert Stuart. Smellie's approach to the encyclopedia was novel in one very important respect: as a practicing journalist, distinguished essayist, and recent editor of the *Scots Magazine*, he compiled the *Britannica* using the methods of periodical journalism. Smellie mixed in brief factual entries and definitions with long specialized essays written in the periodical style. The article on Medicine is over 100 pages long and closely reflects the essayistic method prevalent in magazine writing in the mid-18th century. In fact, Smellie conceived the *Britannica* in a periodical format; his first prospectus suggested an ongoing publication, the total number of parts not predetermined. He argued with his partners about this and the paper size; he wanted octavo, the printing size of magazines, but his partners prevailed and the *Encyclopaedia* was issued in three volumes, quarto. Still Smellie compiled and composed as if he were publishing a periodical paper, and each of the first *Britannica*'s 100 issues has the feel of a magazine.

The *Encyclopaedia Britannica* owes as much to the influence of the periodical press in the early 18th century as it does to the example of the French encyclopedists. Beginning with John Dunton's innovation, a question-and-answer periodical called the *Athenian Gazette* (1690–97), English popular journalism displayed a recurrent interest in collecting and disseminating technical and cultural knowledge through periodical essays. Most magazines carried regular columns on medicine, science, and literature, through which the editors provided serialized compilation on various topics which, taken together, comprised crucial popular reference works. William Smellie's own essays on medical and scientific topics written, extracted, and compiled for the *Scots Magazine* between 1760 and 1765 were a rudimentary version of what he would do for the first

edition of the *Encyclopaedia Britannica*, and Dunton's stunning popular success with the *Athenian Gazette* did much to influence Ephraim Chambers in his undertaking of the *Encyclopaedia* in the 1720s.

As the encyclopedia became a European phenomenon through the later 18th, 19th, and 20th centuries, the essay remained its dominant literary feature, and national encyclopedias whose knowledge and learning are now out of date continue to be important historical and cultural documents, because they contain seminal examples of the writing of important figures in the genre of the essay.

STEPHEN W. BROWN

Further Reading

Collison, Robert, *Encyclopaedias: Their History Throughout the Ages*, New York: Hafner, 1964
Darnton, Robert, *The Business of Enlightenment: A Publishing History of the Encylopédie (1775–1800)*, Cambridge, Massachusetts: Harvard University Press, 1979
Kafker, Frank A., "Notable Encylopedias of the Seventeenth and Eighteenth Centuries: Nine Predecessors of the Encyclopédie," *Studies on Voltaire* 194 (1981)
Kafker, Frank A., "Encyclopédie," in *The Blackwell Companion to the Enlightenment*, edited by John W. Yolton and others, Oxford: Blackwell, 1991: 145–50

Enzensberger, Hans Magnus

German, 1929–

Called "Germany's most important literary catalyst" by the *New York Times Book Review* in 1968, the contemporary poet, essayist, and political moralist Hans Magnus Enzensberger made his literary debut in 1955, when he was first invited to join the Gruppe 47, and with the publication of the poetry collections *Verteidigung der Wölfe* (In defense of wolves) in 1957 and *Landessprache* (Language of a country) in 1960. Since then, his eclectic production has centered around short literary forms such as the documentary, interview, book and film **review**, biography, story, and *feuilleton*. It has found the greatest resonance through mass publication in newspapers and magazines as well as in video and radio.

Widely traveled and multilingual, Enzensberger was influenced foremost by the thought of Germans Brecht, Benn, and **Adorno**, but also by such foreign writers as Poe, **Baudelaire**, **Valéry**, Maiakovskii, and William Carlos Williams. He was editor, lecturer, literary consultant, and professor of painting, as well as a fellow at the Center for Advanced Studies at Wesleyan University in the United States. In 1968 he resigned from Wesleyan in protest against U.S. foreign policy and subsequently moved to Cuba, where he resided until the mid-1970s, in order to demonstrate his personal engagement with the ideas of radical enlightenment and revolutionary change.

Ever intent on being a step ahead of the times while refusing to fall into ideological traps, Enzensberger recognized from the start of his writing career the close and crucial connection between "the medium and the message." In his enlightening communication on society and culture, he has steadfastly ignored the boundary between fiction and nonfiction and has utilized a wide spectrum of alienation strategies in his literary work of critical enlightenment of the present as well as utopian visions of the future.

Throughout his literary work, Enzensberger has explored the role of the individual in history and the dialectics of adaptation and subversion, of ideology and coercion. Such an exploration consists predominantly of questions and contradictions rather than of answers and generally accepted knowledge. By both examining the construction of the individual within the process of history and questioning the social functions of bourgeois literature itself, Enzensberger has encouraged German society to analyze itself.

Specifically and most importantly, he has posed the question of how the "consciousness industry," a phrase he coined, maintains and preserves the existing structures of power through the ideologies of capitalism, nationalism, and German history. It is not the means of production or capital nor the goods and services produced, but rather the production of consciousness for purposes of "manufacturing consent" that represents for Enzensberger the central paradigm of postindustrial society. But the consciousness industry is itself trapped in an obvious contradiction, the dialectic of the enlightenment, where it must first give what it later takes away. That is, before consciousness can be appropriated and changed, it must first exist at all. The production of ideology and consent must first raise consciousness before it can be lowered to ideological levels.

Before the enlightenment of power can be instrumentalized and utilized, it exists as the enlightenment of freedom, and, Enzensberger argues, it is within this arena that the future debates on consciousness and information will occur. It is no longer just a political arena, but a ubiquitous sphere ranging from public relations to sports, tourism, marketing, and the media. According to Enzensberger, the consciousness industry will be the key industry of the next century. This implies a change in the role of the intellectual who, voluntarily or by force, knowingly or naively becomes an accomplice to the consciousness industry.

Such a discussion – often provocative and consciously directed against the grain of common assumptions about the form, content, and functions of literature – is perhaps best characterized by the literary-cultural journal *Kursbuch* (Timetable), which Enzensberger founded in 1965 and edited until 1975, and which has been widely recognized as Germany's most vital cultural medium of critical communication. *Kursbuch* represents both a politicization of literature and the end of its traditional role. But ironically, subsequent to the 1965 declaration in *Kursbuch* of the "death of literature," Enzensberger continued to write essays and poetry with a new power and lyricism, including his epic poem *Titanic* (1978).

From the Germany of the 1950s, when, as a heretic in the land of status quo, Enzensberger thematized the issues of the Adenauer Era, to the student movement and the anti-Vietnam protests of the 1960s, to the restoration of the private and subjective in the 1970s, to the debate over nuclear power, the environment, and ecology of Germany in the 1980s, and up to the present, Enzensberger has not only instrumentalized literature, but at the same time has questioned the traditional roles of writing, publishing, and reading in the postmodern information age.

RALPH W. BUECHLER

Biography

Born 11 November 1929 in Kaufbeuren. Served in the Volkssturm, 1944–45. Studied at the Universities of Freiburg, Hamburg, and Erlangen, Ph.D., 1955; the Sorbonne, Paris, 1952–54. Assistant to **Alfred Andersch** on "radio-essays" for South German Radio, Stuttgart, 1955–57; member of Gruppe 47, from 1955; guest lecturer, Academy of Design, Ulm, 1956–57; worked for Suhrkamp publishers, Frankfurt-on-Main, 1960–75. Lived in Norway, 1961–65. Professor of poetry, University of Frankfurt, 1965. Founder, 1965, and editor, until 1975, *Kursbuch*. Fellow at Wesleyan University, Middletown, Connecticut, 1967–68 (resigned). Lived in Cuba, 1968–mid-1970s. Founding editor, *TransAtlantik*, 1980–82. Publisher, Die andere Bibliothek book series, from 1985. Married 1) Dagrun Christensen; 2) Maria Makarova (divorced); 3) Katharine Bonitz, 1986; two daughters. Awards: several, including Critics Prize (Germany), 1962, 1979; Büchner Prize, 1963; Etna-Taormina Prize, 1967; Pasolini Prize, 1982; Heinrich Böll Prize, 1985; Bavarian Academy of Fine Arts Award, 1987.

Selected Writings

Essays and Related Prose
Einzelheiten, 1962
Politik und Verbrechen, 1964
Deutschland, Deutschland unter anderm, 1967
Palaver: Politische Überlegungen (1967–1973), 1974
Raids and Reconstructions: Essays on Politics, Crime, and Culture, translated by Michael Roloff and others, 1976
Politische Brosamen, 1982; as *Political Crumbs*, translated by Martin Chalmers, 1990
Critical Essays, edited by Reinhold Grimm and Bruce Armstrong, 1982
Ach Europa!, 1987; as *Europe, Europe: Forays into a Continent*, translated by Martin Chalmers, 1989
Mittelmass und Wahn, 1988; as *Mediocrity and Delusion: Collected Diversions*, translated by Martin Chalmers, 1992
Dreamers of the Absolute: Essays on Politics, Crime, and Culture, translated by Michael Roloff, Stuart Hood, and Richard Woolley, 1988
Der fliegende Robert: Gedichte, Szenen, Essays, 1989
Aussichten auf den Bürgerkrieg, 1993; part in *Civil War*, 1994
Civil War, translated by Piers Spence and Martin Chalmers, 1994
Diderots Schatten: Unterhaltungen, Szenen, Essays, 1994

Other writings: poetry, a novel, and a play.

Further Reading

Dietschreit, Frank, and Barbara Heinze-Dietschreit, *Hans Magnus Enzensberger*, Stuttgart: Metzler, 1986
Grimm, Reinhold, *Texturen: Essays und anderes zu Hans Magnus Enzensberger*, New York: Lang, 1984
Grimm, Reinhold, editor, *Hans Magnus Enzensberger*, Frankfurt-on-Main: Suhrkamp, 1984
Schickel, J., editor, *Über Hans Magnus Enzensberger*, Frankfurt-on-Main: Suhrkamp, 1970

Erasmus
Dutch, 1467–1536

Although Erasmus had been dead nearly half a century when **Montaigne** coined the term *essai* in 1580 to refer to his new prose composition, he would undoubtedly have shared **Francis Bacon**'s observation that although Montaigne's term was new, the form itself was ancient. Certainly the essay of Montaigne owes a large debt to the *Adagia* (1500; *Adages*) and the *Colloquia familiaria* (1516; *The Colloquies*) of Erasmus. In the 1870s, at a time when academic divisions of genre did not include a category for the essay, French literary critic Baston Feugère attempted unsuccessfully to sort Erasmus' canon according to standard genres. What is noteworthy about Feugère's failure, however, is how closely his description of Erasmus' eclectic style approximates contemporary definitions of the essay: for Feugère, Erasmus' prose was a conflation of theology, ethics, pedagogy, **satire**, erudition, and even personal reminiscence; his style was easy, lightly mocking, often personal, and predominantly aphoristic. Feugère, in fact, was merely echoing a complaint that was itself as old as the works of Erasmus. In his own day, Erasmus suffered the harsh slings of the French Ciceronian Étienne Dolet (*L'Erasmianus sive Ciceronianus*, 1535), who criticized in his rhetorical style what in Montaigne's work would be praised. Dolet resented the base subject matter, the aphoristic style, the familiar and deriding tone, and the rootless and wandering prose.

Attempting to form and define a genre for the essay three decades after Feugère, Pierre Villey (*Les Sources et l'évolution des "Essais" de Montaigne*, 1908), first suggested a generic link between the literary style of Erasmus and the *essai* of Montaigne. He argued that Montaigne's *Essais* were derivative of several genres and subgenres that arose out of the cultural and philosophical milieu of the Renaissance, naming Erasmus' *Adages* and *Apophthegmes* (1531) as the *Essais'* most influential precursors. While Erasmus' works are not, then, essays *per se*, we can in retrospect recognize elements of the essay in them. Although as a corpus his works chart the development and ascendancy of his rhetorical theory, a theory that by breaking from the Ciceronian model would culminate in Montaigne's *Essais*, it is his lesser-known, more condensed theoretical works that provide a greater understanding of the Erasmian influence on the formation of the essay.

During the 16th and 17th centuries, Erasmus' rhetorical experiments (and to a lesser extent those of his younger contemporary, François Rabelais) were pivotal in the transmission of essayistic attributes from the works of such classical writers as Lucian, Quintilian, **Seneca**, and even **Plato** to the early modern works of Montaigne, Bacon, and their European and British contemporaries, in whose writings the essay began to take form. In his popular (for some heretical) handbook *De duplici copia verborum ac rerum* (1512; *On Copia* [the abundance] *of Words and Ideas*), Erasmus synthesizes the tenets of his rhetorical style into a theory of writing as an open-ended and spontaneous exercise that escapes the prescriptive parameters and artificial symmetry imposed by classical models of rhetoric and dialectic. In *De inventione* (*On Invention*), his first **treatise** on rhetoric, **Cicero** delineated five steps in his rhetorical model, placing emphasis on the first three: invention, the discovery of valid arguments; arrangement, the distribution of arguments in appropriate order; and style (*elocutio*), the expression of the arguments in proper language and syntax. Reacting against the emphasis his Ciceronian contemporaries continued to place on imitation and style over content, Erasmus reverses Cicero's paradigm, subjugating style and the symmetry of syntax to the primacy of the subject matter. Like all subgenres of the modern essay, then, the writings of Erasmus broke with traditional notions of form.

His writing burst the seams of the classical – primarily Ciceronian – model, spilling over with a plenitude of language that, although compressed in the eloquence of each individual theme, was expansive in its collective narrative. Thus, the revolution in prose style mounted against the rhetorical conventions of Ciceronianism was initiated by the pen of Erasmus and not at the hands of the earliest essayists, Montaigne and Bacon, as is so often argued.

By the inclusion in his handbook of a section on "imitation," the standard practice in rhetorical theories since classical antiquity, Erasmus would appear to embrace certain elements of standard rhetorical and pedagogic practice. But here, too, he moves counter to convention. For Erasmus, the writer asserts his independence by both replicating and fragmenting the revered classical models to create a new model of intertextuality. The process of naturalizing fragments of alien texts would later be perfected in the writings of Montaigne in terms of what he called *topoi*; and Bacon would advance the use of *topoi* by juxtaposing contradictory axioms or precepts of received wisdom, a practice he recommends in *The Advancement of Learning* (1605). But such conventions were not without their dangers. Borrowing from and alluding to older works implied that meaning was inherent in a fragment or allusion and thus transferable from one context to another. The difficulties of such a notion would be addressed repeatedly by Erasmus, most explicitly in his *Convivium religiosum* (*Religious Fellowship*), and by Montaigne and Bacon, both of whom, not incidentally, freely borrowed from Erasmus' literary corpus.

Erasmus' appropriation and integration of alien texts predicts yet another intriguing metamorphosis found in the essay. We might see such a practice as having anticipated Montaigne and later essayists' projection of the self into their writing as a way of militating against the influence and prestige of an *Ur*-text.

Finally, because Erasmus' theory of rhetoric came at a time when the high and rigid rhetorical style of Cicero was perceived as antithetical to the precepts of 16th-century humanism, his work dovetailed neatly with contemporary projects on both sides of the English Channel to explore and vigorously defend the use of the vernacular. After all, crucial to the emergence of the essay and its subsequent popularity is the simultaneous rise in literacy, the vernacular, and the bourgeois class.

In *De ratione studii* (1512; *A Method of Study*), Erasmus would complete his turn from Ciceronian style. In this text, he argues that although the choice of words is important to the writing process, the subject matter has primacy. That is, Erasmus reconfigures the ancient rhetorical and pedagogic paradigm of *natura-doctrina-exercitatio*. He elevates performance (*experientia*) above the exactness of *doctrina*, a sensibility that would be perfected in the *Essais* of Montaigne. In effect, Erasmus was guarding against what he perceived as the empty loquacity produced by imitation, a subject touched on by **Plutarch** and Petrarch, and one which Erasmus expanded upon in his proto-essay, *Lingua* (1525; *Speech*). That the motivation to write and the act of writing itself are valued above the mediation of technique helps to explain Erasmus' lifelong custom of elaborating his already printed texts. The gradual evolution of his work on the New Testament, the perennial revisions of *Paraclesis* (1519; *An Exhortation to the Diligent*

Study of Scripture), and the manifold versions of the *Ratio verae theologiae* (1518; *The Reason of True Religion*) all testify to Erasmus' view of the text as a work-in-progress. His practice of continual revision, taken together with his theory of deconstructing and incorporating alien material, reinforces his idea of the text as an object that could continue to be expanded and embedded with additional meaning. Thus, his writing already heralds a theory of textual heterogeneity, the fundamental characteristic of the essay genre that makes the essayist of every age Erasmus' literary descendant. Moreover, the gradual sedimentation of Erasmus' works clearly anticipates Montaigne and Bacon's view of the essay as an open-ended and antisyllogistic narrative, one which advances not logically but obliquely. Each "draft" simply becomes one more brick toward the foundation of reason that leads to a greater truth. This is precisely why the essay, in the empiricist tradition of Bacon, Hobbes, and Locke, flourished as a tool for the collaborative production, accumulation, and dissemination of Enlightenment ideas in the 18th century. In short, what for Erasmus was practice for the essayists would be form.

When weighing Erasmus' influence on the essay, it is essential not only to consider the texts he authored, but also the subsequent interpretations of the ideology those texts were perceived to deploy, especially their influence during the 18th century, a time when the **periodical essay** – and its division into sociological and scientific subgenres – was codified and commodified in the growing market economy as an agent of an imperial and bourgeois moralism. (Here, we have only to think of Pope's accolades for Erasmus in *Essay on Criticism* [1711], or the Erasmus invoked in the "practical moralism" of **Addison** and **Steele**.) It is Erasmus, more than any of his contemporaries, to whom the 17th- and 18th-century writers and thinkers revert, by both explicit reference and implicit allusion. Erasmus was so popular among Enlightenment thinkers, in fact, that the 18th century saw the publication of no fewer than three complete biographies of him. He is mentioned in many of the great documents of the Enlightenment, including **Diderot**'s *Encyclopédie* (1746–72) and **Voltaire**'s *Essai sur les mœurs et l'esprit des nations* (1756, 1761–63; *Essay on the Manner and Spirit of Nations*). His progressive thought resonates in still more of the period's most influential humanist essays, such as Locke's treatise, *The Reasonableness of Christianity* (1695). The 17th-century French Cartesian **Pierre Bayle** proclaimed Erasmus the church father of the Enlightenment, a title that places Erasmus at the head of a long tradition of modern skepticism, for which Bayle himself is a distinguished forerunner. In a stunning recapitulation of his role in Luther's 16th-century struggle with the papal court, Erasmus is once again cast as mediator between Catholic and Protestant, in debates that would escalate into Britain's Glorious Revolution of 1688. As in Luther's day, both sides would lay claim to Erasmus, finding in the ambiguities of his free and associative rhetorical style support for their respective partisanships.

Given the 18th century's renewed interest in the classical period, its philosophical rediscovery of neoplatonism, it is not surprising that it is Erasmus to whom pundits returned for a rehearsed argument between the classical and the nascent vernacular models of rhetoric. He was used as a symbol in the conflict between classical restraint and Romantic fervor in late 18th-century Germany. Ultimately the late 18th and early 19th centuries would consider him part of the tradition of "free-thinking" education that through Locke would give rise to the essays of **Rousseau** and Voltaire, to culminate in the work of Jeremy Bentham. Finally, in the grand scheme of the 18th century, Erasmus was summoned forth as the great humanist whose intellect and idea of progress paved the way for the likes of Descartes, Locke, and several other great architects of the Age of Reason. Yet, if it is writers in this period whose praise for Erasmus codified his position as an innovator of language and free thinking, then it is also detractors like Edward Gibbon, historians in and of this period, whose criticism has resulted in modern scholarship's having glossed too narrowly, or slighted altogether, Erasmus' manifold contribution to the emergence of the essay as a genre.

GREGORY S. JACKSON

Biography

Desiderius Erasmus. Born in Rotterdam, probably 27/28 October 1467. Studied at schools in Gouda and Deventer, until 1493; a seminary at 's Hertogenbosch; entered the monastery of Canons Regular of St. Augustine, Steyn, 1487: ordained priest, 1492; secretary to the Bishop of Cambrai, 1493–95; studied at the College of Montaigue, Paris, 1495–99 and 1500–01; University of Turin, Doctor of Divinity, 1506. Lived or traveled in England, 1499, 1505–06, 1509–14, 1515, 1516, 1517; lived in Italy, 1506–09, and Louvain, 1517–21. General editor of John Froben's press, Basle, 1521–29. Lived in Freiburg, 1529–35, and again in Basle, 1535–36. Declined the offer of becoming a Cardinal. Died 12 July 1536.

Selected Writings

Essays and Related Prose

Adagia, 1500, and later augmented editions; as *Proverbs or Adages*, translated by Richard Taverner, 1539, and Margaret Mann Phillips, 1964

Enchiridion militis Christiani, 1503; as *The Manual of the Christian Knight*, translated by William Tyndale, 1533 (reprinted 1905), and Anne M. O'Donnell, 1981; as *The Christian Manual*, translated by John Spier, 1752; as *The Handbook of the Militant Christian*, translated by John P. Dolan, 1962; as *The Enchiridion*, translated by Raymond Himelick, 1963

Encomium moriae, 1511; revised edition, 1514; edited and translated by Hoyt H. Hudson, 1941; several translations, as *The Praise of Folly*, including by Thomas Chaloner, 1549, John Wilson, 1668 (reprinted 1961), Leonard F. Dean, 1946, A. H. T. Levi and Betty Radice, 1971, and Clarence H. Miller, 1979

De ratione studii, 1512; revised edition, 1514; as *On the Aim and Method of Education*, edited by W. H. Woodward, 1904; as *A Method of Study*, translated by Brian McGregor, in *Collected Works*, 1978

De duplici copia verborum ac rerum, 1512; revised edition, 1514; as *On Copia of Words and Ideas*, translated by Donald B. King and H. David Rix, 1963; as *On Copia*, translated by Betty I. Knott, in *Collected Works*, 1978

Colloquia familiaria, 1516, and later augmented editions; edited by L.-E. Halkin, F. Bierlaire, and R. Hoven, in *Opera omnia*, 1972; as *The Colloquies*, translated by H. M. London, 1671, Roger L'Estrange, in *Twenty Select Colloquies*, 1680, revised edition, 1923, Nathan Bailey, 1725, and Craig R. Thompson, 1965; in part as *Ten Colloquies*, translated by Craig R. Thompson, 1957

Institutio principis Christiani, 1516; as *The Education of a Christian Prince*, translated by Lester K. Born, 1936

Julius Exclusus, 1517; as *The Dialogue Between Julius the Second Genius and Saint Peter*, translated anonymously, 1534; as *The Pope Shut out of Heaven Gates*, 1673; also translated by J. A. Froude, 1894

De libero arbitro, 1524; edited by J. Walter, 1910; as *Discourse on the Freedom of the Will*, edited and translated by Ernest F. Winter, 1961

Lingua, 1525

Dialogus Ciceronianus, 1528; edited by Pierre Mesnard, in *Opera omnia*, 1971; as *Ciceronianus; or, A Dialogue on the Best Style of Speaking*, edited and translated by Izora Scott, 1900

Apophthegmes, 1531; translated by Nicholas Udall, 1542, reprinted 1877

The Complaint of Peace, translated by Thomas Paynell, 1559, revised edition, 1946

Opus epistolarum (in Latin and English), edited by P. S. Allen and others, 12 vols., 1906–58; as *The Epistles*, edited and translated by Francis M. Nichols, 3 vols., 1901–18; as *Correspondence*, translated by R. A. B. Mynors and D. F. S. Thomson, annotated by Wallace K. Ferguson, James K. McConica, and Peter G. Bietenholz, in *Collected Works*, 1974

Opuscula, edited by W. K. Ferguson, 1933

The Essential Erasmus, edited by John P. Dolan, 1964

Christian Humanism and the Reformation: Selected Writings, edited by John C. Olin, 1965

Essential Works, edited by W. T. H. Jackson, 1965

The Praise of Folly, and Other Writings, edited by Robert M. Adams, 1989

The Erasmus Reader, edited by Erika Rummel, 1990

Other writings: edited works by Ambrose, Aristotle, Augustine, Basil, Cato, Chrysostom, Cicero, Cyprian, Hilary, Irenaeus, Jerome, Lactantius, Origen, Plutarch, Pseudo-Arnobius, Seneca, and others.

Collected works editions: *Opera omnia*, 6 vols., 1969–95 (in progress); *Collected Works*, 33 vols., 1974–95 (in progress).

Bibliography

Devereux, E. J., *Renaissance Translations of Erasmus: A Bibliography to 1700*, Toronto: University of Toronto Press, 1983

Further Reading

Mansfield, Bruce, *Phoenix of His Age: Interpretations of Erasmus, c. 1550–1750*, Toronto: University of Toronto Press, 1979

Mansfield, Bruce, *Man on His Own: Interpretations of Erasmus, c. 1750–1920*, Toronto: University of Toronto Press, 1992

Pavlovskis, Zoja, *The Praise of Folly: Structure and Irony*, Leiden: Brill, 1983

Schoeck, R. J., *Erasmus Grandescens: The Growth of a Humanist's Mind and Spirituality*, Nieuwkoop: De Graaf, 1988

Schoeck, R. J., *Erasmus of Europe: The Making of a Humanist, 1467–1500*, Edinburgh: Edinburgh University Press, 1990

Screech, M. A., *Ecstasy and "The Praise of Folly"*, Harmondsworth: Penguin, 1988 (original edition, 1980)

Smith, Henry Goodwin, "The Triumph of Erasmus in Modern Protestantism," *Hibbert Journal* 3 (1905): 64–82

Thompson, Geraldine, *Under Pretext of Praise: Satiric Mode in Erasmus' Fiction*, Toronto: University of Toronto Press, 1974

El Espectador

Spanish journal, 1916–1934

El Espectador (The spectator) was a one-man journal written and published by the Spanish philosopher and public intellectual **José Ortega y Gasset** between 1916 and 1934. The magazine, whose name appears to have been derived from the title of Addison's and Steele's famous 18th-century publication, was originally conceived as a vehicle which would allow Ortega to share, on a bimonthly basis, his more intimate and transcendent reflections (as opposed to the political ones for which he was already well known) with what he hoped would be a select and discriminating group of paid subscribers. As he said in the initial essay of the magazine's first issue, his goal was "to raise a fortress against politics for both myself and those that share my affection for pure vision and theory."

In founding *El Espectador* in the spring of 1916, Ortega sought, in a sense, to liberate himself from his largely self-created role as one of Spain's best-known political commentators. Ortega's rise to this status began with his much publicized polemics in 1908 and 1909 with the well-known politician Gabriel Maura and two celebrated members of the so-called Generation of '98, **Ramiro de Maeztu** and **Miguel de Unamuno**. As a result of these widely reported conflicts, his tireless journalistic activity, as well as key speeches such as "Los problemas nacionales y la juventud" (1909; National problems and youth) and "La pedagogía social como programa político" (1910; Social pedagogy as political program), Ortega came to be recognized in the years immediately preceding World War I as the leading spokesman for a European-inspired reform of Spain's political culture. In late 1913 he began organizing the Liga de Educación Política (League for political education), which he hoped would enable his generation of young intellectuals to make a clean break with what he saw as the corrupt and antiquated political practices propagated by the "Official Spain" in the years since the restoration of the Bourbon monarchy in 1875. After the publication of his influential *Meditaciones del Quijote* (1914; *Meditations on Quixote*), in which he ponders the question of Spain's historical destiny, Ortega, the son and grandson of prominent journalists as well as a veteran of two short-lived publishing ventures, founded *España* (Spain), a journal aimed at supporting and furthering the goals of the Liga de Educación Política. Within weeks of its appearance in early 1915, *España* established itself as one of the country's leading journals of social and political thought. However, in January 1916 Ortega, sensing that the Liga would never be able to effect social change on the scale he had envisioned, abruptly resigned his position as *España*'s editor and announced soon thereafter his plans to begin publishing *El Espectador*.

In the long run, Ortega's adherence to his original concept for *El Espectador* would prove to be rather inconsistent. The first installment of the series (May 1916) was, as promised, largely free of political commentary. However, as early as the magazine's second volume, published in May 1917, Ortega returned, as he would do intermittently throughout the life of the journal, to the discussion of contemporary political culture. Similarly, Ortega quickly dispensed with his proposed bimonthly schedule of publication. In 18 years, he managed to write and distribute only eight full issues of the magazine, a number of which are little more than compilations of previously written articles.

While *El Espectador* ultimately failed to engender a sustained and intimate dialogue between Ortega and what he would come to term, in *España invertebrada* (1921; *Invertebrate Spain*) and *La rebelión de las masas* (1930; *The Revolt of the Masses*), the "select minorities" of society, it nonetheless remains an important showcase of his broad interests and expressive talents. Included in its pages are in-depth analyses of the work of the Spanish novelists Pío Baroja ("Ideas sobre Baroja" [1916; Ideas on Baroja]) and José Martínez Ruiz "**Azorín**" ("Azorín o primores de lo vulgar" [1917; Azorín or the delicacy of the commonplace]), as well as articles which touch upon the key Orteguian concepts of "perspectivism" ("Verdad y perspectiva" [1916; Truth and perspective]) and "biologism" ("El Quijote en la escuela" [1921; Don Quixote in the schools]). These essentially scholarly articles are joined together with the aforementioned sprinkling of political essays – "La democracia morbosa" (1917; Ailing democracy), a review of Scheler's "El genio de la guerra y la guerra alemana" (1917; The genius of war and the German war), and "Sobre el fascismo" (1927; On fascism) – numerous travel pieces, and erudite musings on subjects ranging from wine to Egyptian culture.

El Espectador can also be seen as a significant point of departure in Ortega's longitudinal development as a thinker. The year 1923, in which he founded **Revista de Occidente** (Western review), is sometimes identified as the point at which Ortega moved from being a Spanish writer largely concerned with national issues to being a "European" philosopher more interested in commenting upon universal themes. If this is indeed the case, then *El Espectador*, especially its first three, more conscientiously crafted volumes (published in 1916, 1917, and 1921) should be seen as a precursor to the author's later, universalist production, for it was there that he first openly sought to transcend his devotion to political thought which is, in contrast to theoretical speculation, "located in the realm of man's secondary spiritual activities."

THOMAS S. HARRINGTON

Editions

El Espectador: Colección de ensayos filosóficos y literarios, 8 vols., 1916–34; in 1 vol., 1943; vols. 2–3 of Ortega y Gasset's *Obras completas*, 1957; selections edited by Gaspar Gómez de la Serna, 1969, and Paulino Garragorri, 1980

Further Reading

Gaos, José, *Sobre Ortega y Gasset y otros trabajos de historia de las ideas en España y la América Española*, Mexico City: Universidad Nacional Autónoma de México, 1957

Niedermayer, Franz, *José Ortega y Gasset*, New York: Ungar, 1973 (original German edition, 1959)

Ouimette, Victor, *José Ortega y Gasset*, Boston: Twayne, 1982

Romano García, Vicente, *José Ortega y Gasset, publicista*, Madrid: Akal, 1976

Saiz Barberá, Juan, *Ortega y Gasset ante la crítica: El idealismo en "El Espectador"*, Madrid: Iberoamericanas, 1950

An Essay Concerning Human Understanding

by John Locke, 1689; revised editions, 1694, 1700

John Locke (1632–1704) – the founding figure of the school of philosophy developed primarily in 18th-century England known as empiricism – wrote *An Essay Concerning Human Understanding* in addition to other influential books and a voluminous correspondence. The *Essay* is a vastly larger work than one might expect from its classification as an essay; in fact it constitutes one of the indisputably great works in the history of philosophy, and ranks among the most influential.

The beginnings of the *Essay* date back to 1671, at a time when Locke was participating in sustained philosophical discussions; during this period he realized that genuine philosophical progress could not be made until a thorough overview of the mind's faculties, capacities, and contents was achieved. Although this initial overarching purpose motivated the *Essay*, the book was not written during a single uninterrupted period of Locke's life. It is true that he wrote a paper on the capacities of the mind in connection with the discussions of 1671, and this formed the core of two early drafts of the *Essay* composed during the ensuing years. But in fact the *Essay* was assembled from many independent parts over many years, and grew vastly beyond its initial proportions: in his "Epistle to the Reader" Locke informs us that the *Essay* was "written by incoherent parcels; and after long intervals of neglect, resumed again, as my humour or occasions permitted."

There are a number of intersecting reasons for this great philosophical study to have been called an "essay." First, it began in conversation, and was in its earliest manifestation conceived as supplement both to philosophical **dialogue**s and to further philosophical work of a different order. Second, it was composed and augmented over a number of years, with each new section essaying, or initially and in some cases provisionally, mapping out new conceptual territory for inclusion in the large work. Third, the *Essay* comprised ultimately a very large number of individual essays on multifarious philosophical topics with considerable thematic independence.

There remains a further reason for the aptness of the title, even with the great size of the volume, and this concerns Locke's authorial voice. On Locke's arrival as a student of philosophy in Oxford in 1652 he was taught what the distinguished historian of philosophy Frederick Copleston has called in *A History of Philosophy* (1946) "a debased and rather petrified form of Scholasticism"; Copleston reports that Locke then and there "conceived a great distaste [for this philosophy], regarding it as 'perplexed' with obscure terms, and useless questions." At that time he was also philosophically stimulated by his private reading of Descartes' philosophical writings, in which the virtues of clarity and distinctness of thought are both exemplified and elevated to a position of epistemological indispensability. Locke was thus in pursuit of a style which would emphasize clarity, avoid obscure terms, facilitate the discussion of useful philosophical questions, and, as mentioned above, arise out of and contribute to philosophical dialogue. The voice at which he arrived, at an early stage in his work, is thus clear, commonsensical, rhetorically undecorated, and perfectly suited to the central philosophical tenets of empiricism. In short, Locke's voice is essayistic; indeed, it became foundational to all of the developments in British empiricism to follow, and we can plausibly argue that it has been foundational to almost all major developments in British philosophy up to the present day (including utilitarianism, positivism, and "ordinary language philosophy"). It will be clear to any reader of the *Essay* that Locke's authorial voice is integral to the philosophical method being developed and deployed in the book; this grand compendious undertaking is unthinkable in any other voice.

Locke's fundamental philosophical aspirations in the *Essay* are to delineate the boundary between opinion and knowledge, to inquire into the origins of our ideas, to determine the degree of certainty we are able to achieve with those ideas, and to investigate the nature of faith or opinion (where we give our assent to propositions as true but where we do not possess certain knowledge). These lead him to compose a broad and encompassing typology of the contents of the human mind, providing classifications that are at once psychological and epistemological; indeed, Locke's theory of human knowledge is – like Descartes' philosophy before him and to which his work is in part indebted and in part polemically opposed – inextricably intertwined with a theory of the mind.

Locke begins by observing that we have in our minds numerous ideas (he provides the examples whiteness, hardness, sweetness, thinking, motion, man, elephant, army, drunkenness, and others), and asks: How do we come by them? He answers by describing the mind as a "white paper, void of all characters, without any ideas" in its pre-experiential pure state (which he famously characterizes elsewhere in the *Essay* as a "*tabula rasa*"). All the multifarious inscriptions made on this paper, he states, are reducible to one word: experience. "In that," he writes, "all our knowledge is founded." With this one-word answer, he lays the cornerstone of British empiricism.

Locke quickly divides experience into two categories, noting that our observation is employed either with "external sensible objects" or with "internal operations of our minds perceived and reflected on by ourselves"; these two categories, ideas of *sensation* and ideas of *reflection*, are for him the "fountains of knowledge from whence all the ideas we have, or can naturally have, do spring." (With this latter remark he is initiating a theme much discussed throughout philosophy's history from his *Essay* onward: the attempt to demarcate the scope and limits of possible experience.) Examples of ideas of sensation are "yellow, white, heat, cold, soft, hard, bitter, and sweet"; examples of ideas of reflection are "perception, thinking, doubting, believing, reasoning, knowing, and willing." Locke has thus elucidated the significance of his one-word answer; at the close of this part of the *Essay* he concludes that "All of our ideas are of the one or other of these. The understanding seems to me not to have the least glimmering of any ideas which it doth not receive from one of these two. *External objects* furnish the mind with the ideas of sensible qualities, which are all those different perceptions they produce in us; and *the mind* furnishes the understanding with ideas of its own operations." Indeed, taking a polemical stand against the theory of innate ideas adumbrated by Descartes and his successors in 17th-century continental rationalism, Locke adds that we "begin to have ideas when [we] first have sensation."

Locke advances his psychological and epistemological typology by distinguishing between simple and complex ideas, as this distinction manifests itself in our experience of both sensation and reflection. Light and colors, with their many shades and combinations, or all kinds of sounds and noises, or all kinds of tastes and olfactory experience, or all sensations of touch, taken together constitute a vast range of sensory experience. Introducing another centrally significant philosophical theme that has been discussed through to the present day, Locke observes that "Few simple ideas have names." In observing that we have far more simple ideas of sensation than we have names for them, Locke gives rise to a newly focused question, inquiring into the very relation between language and perception. (He returns to this at the beginning of Book III of the *Essay*, articulating a theory of language that, consistent with everything thus far put forward, posits mental entities – ideas – as inner meanings that are contingently externalized through association or linkage to external signs, i.e. spoken or written words. The foundations and central tenets of this theory have been much discussed, and much criticized, in 20th-century analytical philosophy, notably by Ludwig Wittgenstein and his successors.) Locke's fundamental point here is that ideas such as solidity, which we obtain by the experience of, for instance, feeling resistance to the pressure of our hands on an unyielding object, are simple ideas of sensation. Simple ideas of reflection, by contrast, are given to us by direct inspection – or introspection – of the mental activities of perception or thinking, or volition or willing. There are simple ideas of both sensation and reflection: the ideas of pleasure or delight, or their opposites, pain or uneasiness; these ideas, like those of existence, unity, power, and succession, are "suggested to the understanding by every object without and every idea within."

Before moving to his examination of complex ideas of sense and of reflection, Locke renders a fundamental distinction that has also been developed and discussed ever since. He distinguishes "primary" from "secondary" qualities in objects. The power to produce an idea in us, he explains, is a quality: thus a snowball has the power to produce in us the ideas of white, cold, and round. Primary qualities are those that, for Locke, are "utterly inseparable" from the object in question, in "what state soever it be." Thus a candle, melted down, may display many changed qualities, but those that do not – that *cannot* – change are primary. Similarly, a grain of wheat divided into many parts still possesses the qualities of solidity, extension, figure, and mobility in each part. "Divide again," Locke writes, "and it retains the same qualities." By contrast, secondary qualities "in truth are nothing in the objects themselves but powers to produce various sensations in us by their primary qualities, i.e., the bulk, figure, texture and motion of their insensible parts"; colors, sounds, and tastes are in this category. Fundamental to Locke's empirical ontology is the related claim that primary qualities *resemble* the objects really out there in the world; they alone provide true reports of the nature of reality beyond the reach of subjectivity. It is thus an ontological mistake to believe that warmth is actually *in* the fire, that coldness is *in* the snow.

Indeed, Locke asserts that if we could directly perceive the primary qualities, the secondary ones would disappear. It was Locke's empiricist follower George Berkeley (1688–1753) who argued that, on these grounds, the idea of the material world must be dismissed as a crude myth, since *any* knowledge or ideas we have of primary qualities are derived in the first instance from our sensation, and thus are in fact secondary qualities – and hence not true or reliable reports of extra-subjective ontology, but rather only further secondary ideas that thus fail to resemble external reality. In Berkeley's Lockean-inspired idealist ontology, the very idea of "external reality" is highly suspect.

Locke's second great successor in the tradition of British empiricism, **David Hume** (1711–76), argued that on strict Lockean grounds causation is necessarily illusory; in fact, we only experience the constant conjunction of events in the world, not their causal relations. Causal relations, in that they are projected onto the world subjectively rather than perceived from it objectively, are similar in ontological status to secondary qualities. In short, Locke's most fundamental distinction within his larger epistemic typology, the distinction between primary and secondary qualities in objects, led to two different extreme ends of empiricism, the first being Berkeleyan idealism and the second Humean skepticism.

Locke's discussion of complex ideas of sensation and of reflection greatly extends his explanation of the origin of our ideas; complex ideas are those that are "made up of several simple ones put together," such as "beauty, gratitude, a man, an army, or the very universe." Here too integrating his concern with linguistic meaning and the philosophy of language, Locke says that while the mind may consider each simple element of these complex ideas independently, in combinations, or as one entire thing, they are still "signified by one name."

There is a vast amount of philosophy in Locke's *Essay*, including psychological and epistemological subdivisions and distinctions not mentioned here, as well as philosophical examinations of perennial conceptual quandaries such as free will versus determinism, the problem of personal identity (added in the second edition), and fundamental issues in the philosophy of religion. But throughout the *Essay* Locke remains true to his central empiricist cornerstone: "All those sublime thoughts which tower above the clouds, and reach as high as heaven itself, take their rise and footing here; in all that great extent wherein the mind wanders, in those remote speculations it may seem to be elevated with, it stirs not one jot beyond those ideas which *sense* or *reflection* have offered for its contemplation."

GARRY L. HAGBERG

See also Philosophical Essay

Editions
An Essay Concerning Human Understanding, 1689; revised editions, 1694, 1700; edited by Peter Nidditch, 1975; *Essay* draft A edited by R. I. Aaron and Jocelyn Gibb, 1936; *Essay* draft B as *An Essay Concerning the Understanding, Knowledge, Opinion, and Assent*, edited by Benjamin Rand, 1931; drafts A and B edited by Nidditch, 2 vols., 1980–82

Bibliography
Hall, Roland, and Roger Woolhouse, *Eighty Years of Locke Scholarship: A Bibliographical Guide*, Edinburgh: Edinburgh University Press, 1983

Further Reading
Aaron, R. I., *John Locke*, Oxford: Clarendon Press, 1971 (original edition, 1938)
Aarsleff, Hans, *From Locke to Saussure: Essays on the Study of Language and Intellectual History*, London: Athlone Press, 1982
Ayers, Michael, *Locke*, London: Routledge, 2 vols., 1991
Bennett, Jonathan, *Locke, Berkeley, Hume: Central Themes*, Oxford: Clarendon Press, 1971
Brandt, Reinhard, editor, *John Locke*, Berlin: de Gruyter, 1981
Colman, John, *John Locke's Moral Philosophy*, Edinburgh: Edinburgh University Press, 1983
Cranston, Maurice, *John Locke: A Biography*, London: Longman Green, and New York: Macmillan, 1957
Dunn, John, *Locke*, Oxford: Oxford University Press, 1984
Gibson, James, *Locke's Theory of Knowledge and Its Historical Relations*, Cambridge: Cambridge University Press, 1917
Mackie, J. L., *Problems from Locke*, Oxford: Clarendon Press, 1976
Tipton, I. C., editor, *Locke on Human Understanding: Selected Essays*, Oxford: Oxford University Press, 1977
Woolhouse, R. S., *Locke's Philosophy of Science and Knowledge*, Oxford: Blackwell, and New York: Barnes and Noble, 1971
Woolhouse, R. S., *Locke*, Aldershot: Gregg Revivals, 1994 (original edition, 1983)
Woolhouse, R. S., *The Empiricists*, Oxford: Oxford University Press, 1988
Yolton, John W., *John Locke and the Way of Ideas*, Oxford: Clarendon Press, 1956
Yolton, John W., editor, *John Locke: Problems and Perspectives*, Cambridge: Cambridge University Press, 1969
Yolton, John W., *Locke and the Compass of Human Understanding*, Cambridge: Cambridge University Press, 1970

Essay Film

Essay film is a relatively recent concept used to define a cinematographic (and video) genre that has been gaining growing recognition as a distinct branch of international film production. In its broadest meaning, it is a hybrid medium which falls between, and to an extent combines, the two dominant film categories: feature film and documentary. Like its literary and philosophical ancestor, the written essay, it ignores generic borders or chooses to transgress their norms conceptually and formally. It is generally shorter than standard feature films; its length may vary from one to 90 minutes and over, with an average perhaps of about an hour. The international scope of the essay film results in a great diversity among its many forms of inspiration, but its manifestations tend to have in common a sustained self-reflective questioning both of the subject position of individual filmmakers and of the global imaging technologies themselves, not only of film and video but also, increasingly, of digital electronics. Coming after a long history of film, the essay film readdresses, from a new audiovisual perspective, several basic questions raised by earlier forms of cinema about the tension between verisimilitude (documented reality) and artifice (free imagination). In that process, the essay film problematizes various traditional concepts such as narrative fiction and historical record, truth and fantasy, blurring the boundaries between the stable genres and calling into question all simplifying binary categories of representation.

Conceptually, the essay film can be traced back to a 1948 plea for its autonomous status as the most contemporary of media by the French film theorist Alexandre Astruc. Astruc claimed that if Descartes were alive today his *Discours de la méthode* (1637; **Discourse on Method**) would take the form of a 16mm film: that is, it would be "written" as an essay film. However, the essay film has become not merely a filmic rendering of a philosophical text; rather it has developed as a new form of cinema which, with its dual audio and visual dimensions, is progressively transforming the nature of the traditional philosophical discourse just as that discourse, were it filmed, would be transforming the nature of traditional films. The essay film is, moreover, not only a particular genre of film production, albeit one resisting generic norms, but also a hermeneutic procedure, that is, a way of viewing all films.

Astruc promoted the notion of a *camera-stylo* (camera-stylus) that would, in the essay film, "break free from the tyranny of what is visual, from the image for its own sake, from the immediate and concrete demands of the narrative, to become a means of writing, just as flexible and subtle as written language … more or less literal 'inscriptions' on images as 'essays'." Some essay films have included actual writing or graphic inscription on the celluloid. The result is a multi-layered product: an image track, a soundtrack, and a written track often accompanied by a voiceover reading of the written text. The properly textual track or layer is sometimes in direct contradiction with the image track, creating within the total filmic text a jarring collision of opposites and complex levels of meaning which the audience must coproduce.

In response to its literary and philosophical origins, the essay film can also borrow and translate into audiovisual dimensions various classical rhetorical devices. For example, the rhetorical figure of chiasmus (the oscillatory crossing between categories), an integral feature in the work of the German philosopher and promoter of the essay, **Theodor W. Adorno**, has been adapted to the cinematographic medium in several German essay films. Similarly, the painterly technique of anamorphosis (whereby a change of perspective alters manifest meaning) has been adapted as a methodological tool by film essayists everywhere, insofar as they use various techniques of layering images and sounds.

The earliest examples of the essay film can be found in cinema produced many years before Astruc coined the term and formulated its theory. Most of these early film essays – such as Walter Ruttmann's *Berlin: Symphonie einer Grossstadt* (1927; *Berlin: Symphony of a Great City*) or the Soviet Dziga Vertov's *Chelovek s kino-apparatom* (1929; *Man with a Movie Camera*), both of which articulated images and music tracks with considerable self-reflective artistry – were still mainly filmed in the spirit of documentary. Conversely, the surprising *Tabu* (1931) by F. W. Murnau and Robert Flaherty remains essentially a fictional feature film despite its documentary orientation, cultural displacement, and essay-like aspects. More importantly, perhaps, unlike the literary essays, few of these early movies presented an ideological argument, an explicit justification of their production as essays rather than as exclusively audiovisual works of art. It is arguably with *Les Statues meurent aussi* (Statues also die), by French directors Chris. Marker and Alain Resnais in 1953, that the combination of formal and thematic innovations with a clearly subversive (and in fact censored) ideological agenda (anticolonialism) was conceived and received as a major illustration of what an essay film could and ought to be. This medium-length film offered remarkable photography of African art, a dislocated narrative, a mixture of fact and imaginative speculation, and a sharp critique of the colonial project and its cultural legacy on location in Africa and in contemporary European museums. The model – always slightly subversive, most typically from a left-wing perspective – was set for future essay films.

In 1979, the Hamburg Declaration of New German Filmmakers officially called for an end to the artificial separation between "the feature film form [and] the documentary" and between "films that reflect on the medium (in a practical way as experiments) [and] the narrative and commercial films." The resulting hybrid was to uphold the transgressive spirit of that declaration: for instance, joining all manner of avant-gardes, promoting all sorts of artistic and political causes (particularly on the left), and maintaining a certain sympathy for gender struggles and for cultural cross-fertilization.

Internationalization of the new genre followed rapidly. Soon it became impossible to categorize the essay film on the basis of the nationality of filmmakers working alone or together in several countries at the same time – in filmic versions of a postmodernist mode of production. Most question or reject the notion of a fixed identity as filmmaker, be it national, sexual, or cultural. Many, like Chilean-born but Paris-based Raul Ruiz, or Vietnamese-born, French-educated, and U.S.-based Trinh T. Minh-ha, have been working in exile. It may even be argued that it is this state of "in-between-ness" which leads these filmmakers to adopt the essay film as a medium of expression in the first place. Falling themselves between categories, more or less finding a home in multicultural lands, they have been inspired, if not forced, to look for their inspiration to a similarly multilayered practice of filmmaking.

There are other ways to order the seeming proliferation of essay films. Some categories – with considerable overlap between them – are basically thematic, corresponding to an inferred intention on the part of the director. For instance, many essay films adopt a "travelogue" or "ethnographic" format as a means of mapping psychological space and time onto geophysical space and time. Issues of tourism and travel in foreign countries emerge on the surface of epistolary films such as Chris. Marker's *Lettre de Sibérie* (1958; *Letter from Siberia*) or frank "filmed diaries" such as the German Wim Wenders' *Tokyo-Ga* (1985). Markers' early film contains a famous sequence, seminal for the essay film, in which one image track is replayed three times, each time with a radically different, ideologically coded, voice-over. Wenders' film, although filmed on location in Japan, problematizes national identity in part by confronting national cinemas with video and television as transnational forces. In short, these films explore problems of cultural displacement, ideological conviction, and cinematographic technique formally as well as thematically. Following the theory of Claude Lévi-Strauss, this mode of essay film tends to become a form of "anthropological bricolage" – offering escape from some of the conceptual limitations of "national identity," but encountering new limits at home and abroad. In some instances, when travel is impossible, the subgenre is parodied, as in the French omnibus production *Loin du Vietnam* (1967; *Far from Vietnam*), Jill Godmillow's *Far from Poland* (1984), and Trinh T. Minh-ha's *Surname Viet, Given Name Nam* (1989). In the latter two films, manipulated and/or fabricated documentary footage and interviews are successfully presented as being "authentic," duping the audience until the end, when the artifice is revealed.

A related strategy motivates "journalistic" essay films, which offer an alternative view to the representation of current events by traditional journalism and television. This is the case for the depiction of the Romanian Revolution in German Harun Farocki's *Videograms einer Revolution* (1991; *Videograms of a Revolution*), of German reunification in French Marcel Ophüls' *November Days* (1991), and of the AIDS pandemic in the German Rosa von Praunheim's *Silence=Death* (1991). These reportage films counteract the spectacular nature of such world events as covered by other, more powerful media, seeking to communicate greater depth and ambivalence. Together with other types of essay films, they create a half-factual, half-imaginary public sphere that competes with, and undermines, both the ostensible objectivity of documentaries and the commercial subjectivity of fictional features.

Contributing to that subversive – or corrective – effect are various "historical" essay films that focus on both history in general and film history in particular. Like other subgenres, they entail the use and manipulation of documentary footage, but particularly focus on old film clips and soundtracks. This category has expanded tremendously in recent years, as the cinema celebrates its centennial, drawing attention to its own past. The most notable explicit examples are French: Jean-Luc Godard's *Histoire(s) du cinéma* (1988; *History of Cinema*) and Chris. Marker's *Silent Movie* (1995). But many essay films reflect on historical figures and problems in a manner that might be called "auto/biographical." Marker's *Le Tombeau d'Alexandre* (1993; *The Last Bolshevik*) explores the problem of representing a filmmaker who is also a party member. Some films take a clearly solipsistic autobiographical turn, as does Godard's *JLG/JLG* (1994; *JLG by JLG*).

An equally complex development is offered by the "philosophical" essay film, which claims to contribute to (Western) philosophy, to cinema aesthetics, and to their interaction. The films of Farocki (*Wie man sieht* [1986; *As You See*]; *Bilder der Welt und Inschrift des Krieges* [1988; *Images of the World and the Inscription of War*]), Wim Wenders (*Notebooks on Cities and Clothes*, 1989), Hartmut Bitmoski (*Reichsautobahn*, 1984; *VW Komplex*, 1989), Godard (*Photo et Cie.* [1976; *Photo and Co.*]), and Valie Export (*Unsichtbare Gegner* [1976; *Invisible Adversaries*]) tend to question, in diverse ways, not only differences between film and rival imaging technologies but also, in the field of public visual representations, differences between visual representation and the modern man-made environment. The essay film is thus poised to trace the history of "mechanical reproduction" since the Enlightenment, contrasting "vision" with "visuality" on the one hand, and with the "reconfigured eye" of digital manipulation and synthesis on the other.

Another important topic of essay films is centered on problems of sexual identity and gender roles. As has been noted by critics, the more traditional written essay itself can be viewed as a "feminine" form because of its rejection of categories fixed by patriarchy. Applying their general policy of cultural transgression, some essay films deconstruct the *a priori* binary opposition of male versus female, heterosexual versus homosexual. They question the conventional imagery of patriarchal structures, relativize the image of women, sometimes promote feminist theses, and offer probing views of lesbian, gay, or transvestite milieus. Among the best known of these filmmakers are Chantal Akerman (*News from Home*, 1976), Derek Jarman (*Blue*, 1992–93), Isaac Julien (*Looking for Langston*, 1989), Rosa von Praunheim (*Anita, Tanze des Lasters* [1987; *Anita, Dances of Vice*]), Yvonne Rainer (*Journeys from Berlin*, 1971, 1980), Helke Sanders (*Redupers* [1977; *All Around Reduced Personality*]), Monika Treut (*Female Misbehavior*, 1993), and Valie Export (*Menschenfrauen* [1979; *Humanwoman*]).

These essay film contributions to modern cinema are paralleled by its equally significant influence on general film production. Many documentary and feature filmmakers follow developments in the essay film, and are increasingly adapting its new themes and forms into works that reach a mass audience. For example, Marker's *La Jetée* (1962) has clearly inspired Terry Gilliam's commercial *Twelve Monkeys* (1996). Furthermore, many prestigious feature film directors (e.g. Godard, Wenders, Werner Herzog, Orson Welles) have interspersed their commercial productions with low-budget, nonprofit essays in which they carry out experiments on their more innovative theories of representation. Many avant-garde "investigations" eventually find their way into feature films, such as Oliver Stone's *Natural Born Killers* (1994). In that sense, the essay film participates in the contemporary form of what Russian and Czech formalists used to call the "canonization of the junior branch": the perpetual circulation between "high" and "low" cultural production and consumption. In this sense, the comparatively unknown essay film irrigates, fertilizes, and stimulates the cinematographic field in an increasingly post-literate technoculture, keeping the critical impulsion of the literary and **philosophical essay** alive under hostile conditions.

The future of the essay film is linked to the evolution of the major factors that generated it, such as the dispersion of national units into tribes, fragmentation of belief structures, skeptical questioning of values, breaking of traditional boundaries and genres of all types, appeal of irrational ideas and movements, multiplication of political, social, technological, and cultural debates, and the erosion of the public sphere by the mass media. There is no reason to expect a moderating change in the impact of these factors. Nor is it likely that any form of cinema will escape the process that leads aging art forms, tired of creating, to a self-reflective cannibalization of their own past, and to a more or less discrete and obsessive poaching from other disciplines. The essay film or video will likely share for some time the current successes and failures of the literary and philosophical essay, fueled by similar cultural and political disturbances around the globe.

NORA M. ALTER

Further Reading

Alter, Nora M., "The Political Im/perceptible in the Essay Film: Farocki's *Images of the World and the Inscription of War*," *New German Critique* 68 (Spring–Summer 1996): 165–92

Astruc, Alexandre, *Du stylo à la caméra – et de la caméra au stylo*, Paris: L'Archipel, 1992

Barsam, Richard M., *Non-Fiction Film: A Critical History*, Bloomington: Indiana University Press, 1992 (original edition, 1973)

Bellour, Raymond, editor, *L'Entre-image: Photo, cinéma, video*, Paris: La Différence, 1990

Bensmaïa, Réda, *The Barthes Effect: The Essay as Reflective Text*, Minneapolis: University of Minnesota Press, 1987 (original French edition, 1986)

Blümlinger, Christa, editor, *Sprung im Spiegel: Filmisches Wahrnehmen zwischen Fiktion und Wirklichkeit*, Vienna: Sonderzahl, 1990

Blümlinger, Christa, and Constantin Wulff, editors, *Schreiben Bilder Sprechen: Texte zum essayistischen Film*, Vienna: Sonderzahl, 1992

Boetcher Joeres, Ruth-Ellen, and Elizabeth Mittman, editors, *The Politics of the Essay: Feminist Perspectives*, Bloomington: Indiana University Press, 1993

Chion, Michel, *Audio-Vision: Sound on Screen*, New York: Columbia University Press, 1994 (original French edition, 1990)

Conley, Tom, *Film Hieroglyphs: Ruptures in Classical Cinema*, Minneapolis: University of Minnesota Press, 1991

Deleuze, Gilles, *Cinema 1–2*, Minneapolis: University of Minnesota Press, 2 vols., 1986–89 (original French editions, 1983–85)

Godard, Jean-Luc, *Son+Image*, New York: Museum of Modern Art, 1993

Guynn, William, *A Cinema of Nonfiction*, Rutherford, New Jersey: Fairleigh Dickinson University Press, and London: Associated University Presses, 1990

Halbreich, Kathy, and Bruce Jenkins, editors, *Bordering on Fiction: Chantal Akerman's D'Est* (exhibition catalogue), Minneapolis: Walker Art Center, 1995

Images Documentaires issue on Chris. Marker, 15 (1993)

Marker, Chris., *Commentaires I–II*, Paris: Seuil, 2 vols., 1961–67

Marker, Chris., *La Jetée: Ciné Roman*, New York: Zone, 1992

Marker, Chris., *Silent Movie* (video installation catalogue), Columbus: Ohio State University Wexner Center for the Arts, 1995

Mueller, Roswitha, *Valie Export: Fragments of the Imagination*, Bloomington: Indiana University Press, 1994

Nichols, Bill, *Representing Reality: Issues and Concepts in Documentary*, Bloomington: Indiana University Press, 1991

Nichols, Bill, *Blurred Boundaries: Questions of Meaning in Contemporary Culture*, Bloomington: Indiana University Press, 1994

Non-Fiction: Über Dokumentarfilme, Cinema special issue, 39 (1993)

Renov, Michael, "History and/as Autobiography: The Essayistic in Film and Video," *Frame/Work* 2/3 (1989): 6–13

Renov, Michael, editor, *Theorizing Documentary*, New York and London: Routledge, 1993

Rosenthal, Alan, editor, *New Challenges for Documentary*, Berkeley: University of California Press, 1988

Trinh T. Minh-ha, *When the Moon Waxes Red: Representation, Gender, and Cultural Politics*, New York and London: Routledge, 1991

Versuch über den Essayfilm, Augenblick special issue, 10 (1991)

An Essay of Dramatic Poesy
by John Dryden, 1667–68

When John Dryden (1631–1700) published the *Essay of Dramatic Poesy* late in 1667 or early in 1668, he was already actively engaged in writing for the London stage. He had written, collaborated on, or adapted some seven plays in various genres, including comedy, tragicomedy, and heroic. Inevitably, he had become embroiled in the controversies that arose after the Restoration. Playwrights and critics were beginning to assess their theatrical inheritance and to evaluate precisely what sort of drama gave best expression to the new age's sense of its own modernity.

The *Essay* was written while Dryden was out of London in flight from the plague. Between June 1665 and December 1666, he was staying at Charlton in Wiltshire, the country estate of his father-in-law, the Earl of Berkshire; this period also saw the composition of the heroically patriotic *Annus Mirabilis*, the most substantial of Dryden's early attempts to mythologize the Stuart monarchy. Both works have in common the contemporary drama of the sea battles against the Dutch, providing an epic canvas and subject for the poem, and a backdrop and extended metaphor of international conflict for the essay.

Precedent for such a confrontational setting had already been established by some unflattering remarks made upon the English stage by the French commentator Samuel Sorbière in his *Relation d'un voyage en Angleterre* (1664; Account of a voyage in England). Foreign slanders provoke indignant counterblasts, and, in the following year, Thomas Sprat, the historian of the Royal Society, published his *Observations on M. de Sorbière's Voyage into England*. At about the same time, Dryden was involved in a debate on the question of rhyme with his brother-in-law and collaborator, Sir Robert Howard (soon to become the Crites of the *Essay*). In the dedication to *The Rival Ladies* (1664), Dryden had argued in favor of rhymed drama, to which Howard replied in the preface of his *Four New Plays* (1665), rejecting the device on the grounds of its "unnaturalness." Here were all the ingredients for civil and international "war," and, in part at least, the writing of the *Essay* can be seen as an episode in a landscape of critical skirmishes.

Unlike the greater part of Dryden's criticism, which is found in **preface**s, prologues, and dedications, the *Essay* is distinguished by its formally articulated speeches, and by the poise with which conflicting critical positions are offered for the reader's consideration. We are witness to a sophisticated *débat* between four Restoration gentlemen as they float down the Thames on a barge, the better to catch the sound of "distant Thunder" as the English and Dutch navies "disputed the command of the greater half of the Globe." As *his* combatants dispute the relative merits of Ancient and Modern drama, of English and French theatrical practice, Dryden conjures up echoes of the Platonic **dialogue**, although his dramatic reconstructions lack **Plato**'s purposeful drive toward a conclusion. He is at pains to avoid the dogmatism which bedeviled much previous 17th-century criticism. If Dryden has an agenda, it is perhaps no more specific than, as **T. S. Eliot** suggested in *The Use of Poetry and the Use of Criticism* (1933), "the necessity of affirming the native element in literature." As a working dramatist, Dryden has his preferences, but resists that submission to the Rules most often identified with French theorists. Thus, his advocacy of rhyme, echoed in the *Essay* by Neander, would, in his later career, be revised. In fact, the *Essay* remains speculative in its presentation of antithetical ideas, and is best characterized by Dryden's own explanation in his *Defence of An Essay of Dramatic Poesy* (1688), "My whole discourse was sceptical . . . You see it is a dialogue sustained by persons of several opinions, all of them left doubtful, to be determined by the readers in general."

The four occupants of Dryden's Platonic barge are usually identified with contemporary figures. The three "persons [of] Wit and Quality" are Sir Robert Howard (Crites), Charles

Sackville, Lord Buckhurst (Eugenius), and Sir Charles Sedley (Lisideius), and it seems reasonable to assume that the fourth character, Neander, is Dryden himself, the names being almost anagrammatic. Their opening exchanges display the currency of ironic repartee familiar from Restoration comedy, as fears are voiced that an English victory will be heralded by a plethora of outlandish celebrations from those ever-eager "leveller[s] in poetry." These tart remarks, carrying more than a hint of cultural elitism, lead into a serious discussion of drama.

Lisideius proposes a definition for a play which all accept, although the precise meaning of "A just and lively Image of Human Nature" will be differently interpreted according to each speaker's idea of how it is that Art should imitate Nature. The *Essay* is then given over to a series of set speeches in which the companions put forward what they consider to be the best examples of dramatic representation. Crites launches the debate with his advocacy of the Ancients: the radically classical viewpoint. It is true that he states a preference for the plays of "the last age" (Elizabethan and Jacobean) over the present; his central contention, however, is that in classical drama we find the eternal verities, which have never received more powerful expression. The current age has discovered its own genius in scientific progress, but in the theater its best hope is to conform to the rules provided by its predecessors. He cites the application of the pseudo-Aristotelian "Unities" as an example of how far short of the classical model the Moderns have fallen.

Eugenius, in response, attempts to turn Crites' points against him. Progress in science has been matched by progress in the arts. The Moderns have improved upon the older dramatists' hackneyed exploitation of myth; furthermore, they are more precise observers of the "Unities," which, as he accurately observes, are mostly the product of continental criticism. Perhaps most importantly of all, the modern theater has corrected the moral laxity of the Ancients, whose plays too often condoned a "Prosperous Wickedness, and an Unhappy Piety."

The second topic of debate is introduced by Lisideius. He accepts the success of the earlier English stage, but relocates modern classicism in France. The French are strict observers of the "Unities"; they have rejected that peculiar English hybrid, the tragicomedy; they have modernized and simplified their plots to give them a familiar credibility; and they have engaged in a more searching exploration of human passion. Narration has, to an extent, replaced action, so that the performances are no longer embarrassed by inept death scenes and acts of violence. Out of such classical spareness, claims Lisideius, emerges a new verisimilitude.

It is left to Neander to reply, and to summarize, one suspects, on Dryden's behalf. He acknowledges the superior "decorum" of French drama, but then qualifies his approval by allowing French plays only the lifeless beauty of a statue. And, with a sly glance at the Unity of Place, he describes the scenery moving around two motionless characters as they endlessly declaim. Conversely, the English stage is more vital, more exciting. Subplots and tragicomedy lend variety and contrast, dramatic dialogue is better suited to passion, and even violent action is justified by deference to popular appeal. Neander is realigning the original definition of a play by shifting the focus from "just" to "lively," from an exact versimilitude to a more dynamic likeness to life.

The *Essay* has apparently sustained Dryden's claim that it is a skeptical discourse. Three versions of classicism have held the stage, but Neander's deferential conclusions have persuasively illuminated Dryden's true ambition: a vindication of English drama. It is one which will pay sufficient respect to the rules, but which will be generous enough to accommodate the wilder genius of a Shakespeare who "when he describes any thing, you more than see it, you feel it too."

MICHAEL BRUCE

Editions

Of Dramatic Poesy: An Essay, 1667 or 1668; revised edition, 1684; as *An Essay of Dramatic Poesy*, edited by Thomas Arnold, 1889, P. D. Arundell, 1929, George Watson, 1962, and John L. Mahoney, 1965

Further Reading

Aden, John M., "Dryden, Corneille, and the *Essay of Dramatic Poesy*," *Review of English Studies* 6 (1955): 147–56

Aden, John M., *The Critical Opinions of John Dryden: A Dictionary*, Nashville, Tennessee: Vanderbilt University Press, 1963

Archer, S., "The Persons in *An Essay of Dramatic Poesy*," *Papers on Language and Literature* 2 (1966): 305–14

Atkins, J. W. H., *English Literary Criticism: 17th and 18th Centuries*, London: Methuen, 1951

Davie, D., "Dramatic Poetry: Dryden's Conversation Piece," *Cambridge Journal* 5 (1952): 553–61

Hume, R. D., *Dryden's Criticism*, Ithaca, New York: Cornell University Press, 1970

Huntley, Frank L., "On the Persons of Dryden's *Essay of Dramatic Poesy*," *Modern Language Notes* 63 (1948): 88–95

Huntley, Frank L., *On Dryden's "Essay of Dramatic Poesy"*, Ann Arbor: University of Michigan Press, 1951

Jensen, H. James, *A Glossary of John Dryden's Critical Terms*, Minneapolis: University of Minnesota Press, 1969

LeClercq, R. V., "Corneille and *An Essay of Dramatic Poesy*," *Comparative Literature* 22 (1970): 319–27

LeClercq, R. V., "The Academic Nature of the Whole Discourse of *An Essay of Dramatic Poesy*," *Papers on Language and Literature* 8 (1972): 27–38

Mace, D. T., "Dryden's Dialogue on Drama," *Journal of the Warburg and Courtauld Institute* 25 (1962): 87–112

Reverand, C. D., "Dryden's 'Essay of Dramatic Poesie': The Poet and the World of Affairs," *Studies in English Literature* 22 (1982): 375–93

Thale, Mary, "Dryden's Dramatic Criticism: Polestar of the Ancients," *Comparative Literature* 18 (1966): 36–54

Williamson, G., "The Occasion of *An Essay of Dramatic Poesy*," *Modern Philology* 44 (1946): 1–9

Wimsatt, W. K., and Cleanth Brooks, *Literary Criticism: A Short History*, Chicago: University of Chicago Press, 1978 (original edition, 1957)

An Essay on Comedy

by George Meredith, given as a lecture, 1877; published separately, 1897

George Meredith (1828–1909) first presented what was to be known as the "Essay on Comedy" as a lecture to the London Institution on 1 February 1877. It was his first and only public lecture. In April of that year, the essay was published under the title "On the Idea of Comedy, and of the Uses of the Comic Spirit" in the *New Quarterly Magazine*. Its first separate publication took place in 1897, in a book titled *An Essay on Comedy, and the Uses of the Comic Spirit*.

Although Meredith was primarily known as a novelist and poet, he also worked as a journalist, especially in the early years of his career, contributing to the *Westminster Review*, the *Pall Mall Gazette*, the *Graphic*, and the *Fortnightly Review*, which he also edited for a brief period (November 1867–January 1868). Meredith served as a war correspondent for the *Morning Post* during the conflict between Italy and Austria in 1866, and, despite his liberal views, he also wrote for the conservative *Ipswich Journal* from 1858 to 1868. Within this wide range of journalistic prose, the *Essay* stands out as Meredith's most significant periodical contribution and his best-known nonfiction prose work. However, the *Essay* is more closely linked, both stylistically and thematically, to Meredith's fiction and poetry. Many of the ideas about comedy that he develops in the *Essay* are put into practice in his short fiction, also published in the *New Quarterly Magazine* ("The House on the Beach," 1877; "The Case of General Ople and Lady Camper," 1877; "The Tale of Chloe," 1879), and in his most famous novel, *The Egoist* (1879).

In the *Essay*, Meredith defines "comedy" primarily by its rarity in British and continental literature, accounting for this absence in part by explaining that comedy demands a particular sociocultural setting. Meredith's ideal comedy is intellectual; it is "the humour of the mind," and therefore requires a society "wherein ideas are current and the perceptions quick." For him, the "thoughtful laughter" of comedy was to serve as a corrective to the "Unreason and Sentimentalism" that permeated British society; its goal was to create a more rational, balanced, and progressive culture while avoiding the emotionally loaded extremes of satire (which Meredith views as mean-spirited) and of conciliatory humor. His emphasis on cultural reform provides a link between the *Essay* and the similarly inspired writings of **Matthew Arnold** (whose *Culture and Anarchy* appeared in 1869) and **Walter Pater**.

If English society, "possessed of wealth and leisure, with many whims, many strange ailments and strange doctors," was greatly in need of comedy, Meredith believed that the British were likely to be receptive to it, both because Britain's large middle class provided an appropriate audience, and because, in his view, British women enjoyed a relatively high degree of social freedom. Early in the *Essay* Meredith stipulates that comedy cannot exist in cultures where one finds a "state of marked social inequality of the sexes." Much critical attention has been paid to his attempt to link comedy with the status of women, and to promote comedy as a tool for women's advancement. Meredith's concern for women manifests itself in the *Essay*'s frequent references to the condition of women in various cultures throughout history, in its insistence that women should "recognise that the Comic Muse is one of their best friends," and in various rhetorical strategies, such as his tendency to refer to female comic characters and personifications. His favorite heroines, Molière's Célimène and Congreve's Millamant, are praised for their wit, intelligence, and verbal agility, traits that also characterize Meredith's own heroines, most notably Diana Warwick of *Diana of the Crossways* (1885).

Meredith's prose writing is notoriously idiosyncratic, and the *Essay*, while more readable than many of his novels, is no exception. The difficulty of his sometimes confusing syntax and opaque diction is compounded by the essay's loose overall structure and his wide-ranging references to ancient dramatists as well as to contemporary British and continental writers. The didactic tone of the *Essay* bears witness to its origin as a lecture, as well as to his primary stylistic influence, **Thomas Carlyle**, with whom Meredith shared a belief in the value of work and in the healing power of laughter.

Although Meredith's literary influence has lessened considerably in the 20th century, the impact of the *Essay* can be traced in writers as diverse as **Oscar Wilde** and **Virginia Woolf**. As the most extensive discussion of the comic genre produced in the 19th century, the *Essay* remains frequently cited in studies of British comedy and in discussions of the role of women in comedy.

MAURA IVES

Editions

An Essay on Comedy, and the Uses of the Comic Spirit, 1897; edited by Lane Cooper, 1918, reprinted 1972, and Maura Ives, 1997

Further Reading

Beer, Gillian, *Meredith: A Change of Masks: A Study of the Novels*, London: Athlone Press, 1970

Carlson, Susan, *Women and Comedy: Rewriting the British Theatrical Tradition*, Ann Arbor: University of Michigan Press, 1991

Henkle, Roger B., *Comedy and Culture: England, 1820–1900*, Princeton, New Jersey: Princeton University Press, 1980

McWhirter, David, "Feminism/Gender/Comedy: Meredith, Woolf, and the Reconfiguration of Comic Distance," in *Look Who's Laughing: Gender and Comedy*, edited by Gail Finney, Langhorne, Pennsylvania: Gordon and Breach, 1994: 189–204

Martin, Robert Bernard, *The Triumph of Wit: A Study of Victorian Comic Theory*, Oxford: Clarendon Press, 1974

Moses, Joseph, *The Novelist as Comedian: George Meredith and the Ironic Sensibility*, New York: Schocken, 1983

Polhemus, Robert, *Comic Faith: The Great Tradition from Austen to Joyce*, Chicago: University of Chicago Press, 1980

Stevenson, Lionel, *The Ordeal of George Meredith*, New York: Scribner, 1953; London: Owen, 1954

Stevenson, Lionel, "Carlyle and Meredith," in *Carlyle and His Contemporaries*, edited by John Clubbe, Durham, North Carolina: Duke University Press, 1976: 257–79

Wilt, Judith, *The Readable People of George Meredith*, Princeton, New Jersey: Princeton University Press, 1975

An Essay on Criticism

by Alexander Pope, 1711

Alexander Pope (1688–1744) was 23 when *An Essay on Criticism* was published anonymously in May 1711. It appeared while he was engaged in some fairly orthodox prentice work in the pastoral mode, and is flanked by the publication of the *Pastorals* (1709) and *Windsor-Forest* (1713). There is an implied context of sophisticated, metropolitan literary life very different from the landscapes of classical eclogue and georgic, although arguably both these worlds coexist in another work of that time, the first version of *The Rape of the Lock* in 1712. It has been notoriously difficult to identify a precise date of composition for the *Essay*, but it seems likely that many of the preoccupations were the direct product of what Pope described to Joseph Spence as his "great reading period" of 1701–09. These were years when Pope "went through all the best critics," and a time also when he fell under the intellectual patronage of William Walsh, who gave wise advice against the tyranny of the "mechanical rules" of neoclassicism. The poem's appearance immediately provoked a hostile response from John Dennis, who had located an ironic portrait of himself. By the end of the year, however, **Joseph Addison** had come to Pope's defense in the *Spectator* (no. 253), and a month later there was a second "issue," although a "Second Edition" was not published until November 1712.

There is a long history, extending into the Twentieth-century, of selling the *Essay* short as a meretricious compendium of critical commonplaces. In his *Spectator* paper, Addison had drawn attention to the unmethodical structure of the work, reminiscent of Horace's *Ars poetica* (**The Poetic Art**), and had noted the names that stood behind Pope's verses: in particular, Aristotle and Longinus (**On the Sublime**). He had also endorsed Pope as an example of his own **maxim**, "What oft was thought, but ne'er so well express'd." But those features that had met with the essayist's approval, and Pope's refreshing attempt to reconcile various strands of classical and 17th-century theory, were unlikely to survive the scrutiny of Romantic criticism. **De Quincey**'s reaction is predictably extreme: for him, the *Essay* was "substantially a mere versification, like a metrical multiplication-table of commonplaces the most mouldy with which criticism has baited its rat-traps." Closer attention to the text might have revealed that Pope's unwillingness to be hampered by any sort of prescriptive formalism made allowance even for the sublime ambitions of Romanticism; but it was inevitable that the debates concerning neoclassical "rules" would find little sympathy by the end of the 18th century. Twentieth-century scholarship has made efforts to rehabilitate the *Essay*; yet, as recently as 1976, James Reeves concluded that "Pope's virtuosity has succeeded in blinding [us] to the emptiness and derivative quality of most of what he says" (*The Reputation and Writings of Alexander Pope*).

Addison's citation of Horace, and his mention of the Latin poet's dependency upon Aristotle, highlight the Augustan ethos of tradition and allusion, pointing up its distance from the Romantic preoccupation with "originality." The *Spectator* essay was a reminder that Pope's poem was very much an exercise in consolidation which naturally involved a backward-looking reflex. Here was an attempt at a judicial review of various modern opinions, all of which claimed the sanction of classical authority. There was an insistence upon the positive and fostering role of the critic whose relationship with the text given into his care was figured in images of friendship rather than competition. And there was a warning against those forms of ungoverned individualism and vested interest that persistently distort critical judgment: snobbery, faction, arrogance, modishness, all encourage us in the belief that only our own watches tell the correct time. The critic had a social responsibility which took precedence over the eccentric satisfactions of ego. Taste and morality were not divisible.

By 1711, there was already a minor "tradition" of versified poetic theory. In 1674 Boileau had published his *Art poétique* (*The Art of Poetry*), one of many of its type, and soon the French inclination to codify literary "laws" had become a matter for debate among Restoration men of letters. The Earls of Mulgrave and Roscommon, both mentioned approvingly by Pope, respectively brought out an *Essay upon Poetry* (1682) and an *Essay on Translated Verse* (1684). Immediately distinctive is Pope's choice of subject, but it is quickly apparent that he is as much concerned with the business of poetry as he is with criticism. Behind all this activity stands the *Ars poetica*. The relaxed urbanity of Horace's verse **letter** provided Pope with the ideal model: "Horace still charms with graceful negligence,/And without method talks us into sense." The easy transitions of the "epistle" could perhaps have conflicted with the conventions of the "essay," but, in fact, there is both fluidity and orderliness in Pope's poem.

The risk lay in giving birth to an unacceptable hybrid. Certainly the satirical vein in Pope's verse, with its pyrotechnical wit and substratum of sexual innuendo, might be predicted to undermine the dignity associated with the traditional prose "essay." However, it is not a form which claims any structured conclusiveness; it is, after all, a "trying out," and hence possesses a resistance to formalism which was entirely appropriate to Pope's poem. In this sense, his piece had much in common with the early 18th-century journalistic essay. Both are marked by a conversational "easiness" and the balanced, periodic sentences of the prose essayists find their equivalent in Pope's deployment of the heroic couplet, and in the antithetical and epigrammatic quality of the verse. Again, there are larger structures to be discovered, but, in keeping with the tradition of the "essay," symmetry is not an ambition. It is possible to map out a tripartite division, but the sections are unequal in length and loosely coupled. Part I establishes the notion of an ideal Nature, "one clear, unchanged, and universal light," and directs us to discover it in the "Ancients." Part II catalogues the moral and psychological causes of bad criticism. Part III makes suggestions for its rehabilitation, and concludes with a roll call of exemplary critics, both ancient and modern.

In ways reminiscent of Dryden's **Essay of Dramatic Poesy** (1667–68), Pope set out to navigate between contentious positions. Opposed to neoclassicism's insistence on regulations, Pope's advice was to seek out the "useful Laws" of Greece and Rome, and his characteristically Augustan injunction was to "Avoid extremes." Thus the French were too servile in their deference to the "Rules," while the English, "fierce for the Liberties of Wit," could be too stubbornly individualistic. The crisis Pope attempts to resolve concerns the nature of authority. At times, when dealing with the "bookful blockheads," the essayist gives way to the satirist, yet above all the poem is penetrated by a conciliatory intelligence. Pope is the liberal neoclassicist who respects Horace's recommended "decorum," but never at the expense of that inspired moment of poetic passion which "gloriously offend[s]" to "snatch a grace beyond the reach of art." Pope's commitment to tradition encouraged him to normalize the idiosyncratic; he had no intention, however, of circumscribing genius by "dull receipts."

MICHAEL BRUCE

Editions

An Essay on Criticism, 1711; edited by E. Audra Williams and Aubrey Williams, 1961, Robert M. Schmitz, 1962, Raymond Southall, 1973, and S. L. Paul, 1988

Further Reading

Aden, John M., "'*First* follow nature': Strategy and Stratification in *An Essay on Criticism*," *Journal of English and Germanic Philology* 55 (1956): 604–17

Adler, Jacob H., "Balance in Pope's *Essays*," *English Studies* 43 (1962): 457–67

Atkins, G. Douglas, "Fair Art's 'Treach'rous Colours'," in his *Quests of Difference: Reading Pope's Poems*, Lexington: University Press of Kentucky, 1986

Atkins, J. W. H., *English Literary Criticism: 17th and 18th Centuries*, New York: Barnes and Noble, 1950; London: Methuen, 1951

Brown, Laura, "The 'New World' of Augustan Humanism," in her *Alexander Pope*, Oxford and New York: Blackwell, 1985

Empson, William, "Wit in the *Essay on Criticism*," in his *The Structure of Complex Words*, London: Hogarth Press, 1985; Cambridge, Massachusetts: Harvard University Press, 1989 (original edition, 1951)

Fenner, Arthur, "The Unity of Pope's *Essay on Criticism*," *Philological Quarterly* 39 (1960): 435–46

Fogle, R. H., "Metaphors of Organic Unity in Pope's *Essay on Criticism*," *Tulane Studies in English* 13 (1963): 51–58

Hooker, E. N., "Pope on Wit: The *Essay on Criticism*," in *The Seventeenth Century: Studies in the History of English Thought and Literature from Bacon to Pope* by R. F. Jones and others writing in his honor, Stanford, California: Stanford University Press, 1951

Isles, D., "Pope and Criticism," in *Alexander Pope*, edited by Peter Dixon, London: Bell and Hyman, and Athens: Ohio University Press, 1972

Morris, D. B., "Civilized Reading: The Act of Judgment in *An Essay on Criticism*," in *The Art of Alexander Pope*, edited by H. Erskine-Hill and A. Smith, London: Vision Press, and New York: Barnes and Noble, 1979

Ramsay, P., "The Watch of Judgement: Relativism in *An Essay on Criticism*," in *Criticism and Aesthetics, 1660–1800*, edited by Howard Anderson and John S. Shea, Minneapolis: University of Minnesota Press, 1967

Spacks, P. M., "Imagery and Method in *An Essay on Criticism*," in *Pope: Recent Essays by Several Hands*, edited by Maynard Mack and James A. Winn, Brighton: Harvester Press, and Hamden, Connecticut: Archon, 1980

Wimsatt, W. K., and Cleanth Brooks, *Literary Criticism: A Short History*, Chicago: University of Chicago Press, 1978 (original edition, 1957)

An Essay on Man

by Alexander Pope, 1733–34

An Essay on Man is a series of four verse epistles by Alexander Pope (1688–1744) addressed to the politician and man of letters Henry St. John, Lord Bolingbroke (1678–1751). It was intended to form Book I of a comprehensive series of essays, to be called *Ethic Epistles*, which was also to include Pope's *Epistles to Several Persons* on the characters of men and of women and on the use of riches. This plan was never finally settled or put into effect, but the *Essay on Man* stands as his most ambitious attempt at setting out his philosophical beliefs, or his "general Map of Man."

Pope began the *Essay* in 1729. By 1731 he had completed Epistles I–III and had begun Epistle IV. He may then have set the work aside for a period, before publishing Epistles I–III in 1733 and Epistle IV in 1734. Pope had made enemies in the vigorous and often scurrilous literary politics of his time; hence in order to gain the *Essay* an unprejudiced reception, its first publication was anonymous. It was reprinted with minor revisions in the nine authorized editions of Pope's works published in his lifetime as well as appearing in pirated editions.

Each of the four Epistles is in effect a separate essay, discussing man's place in the universe (I), psychology (II), society (III), and the sources of happiness (IV). These discussions touch on major controversies or developments in 18th-century thought. Epistle I employs the arguments of natural religion, the attempt to show that the existence of God and other orthodox religious doctrines could be inferred by reason. In confining himself to these arguments, Pope excludes biblical revelation. This need not mean that he rejected the authority of the Bible, though this conclusion has been drawn by some readers from the time the *Essay* was first published. It may mean rather that Pope wrote for an audience not responsive to traditional religious discourse and that he wished to demonstrate to this audience the compatibility between reason and at least some aspects of Christian orthodoxy. Epistle II expounds the doctrine that each person is governed by a particular "ruling passion," which reason cannot overcome but may guide. Throughout the poem Pope gives surprising prominence and importance to the passions and to instinct, arguing in Epistle III that human reason is less reliable than animal instinct. In its frequent allusions to the discoveries of Isaac Newton, the *Essay* reveals skepticism about the usefulness of the new empirical science. Against this science Pope asserts the humanist idea that "The proper study of Mankind is Man," and that this study is even more demanding than the physical sciences. The prevailing theme of the *Essay* is a characteristic 18th-century optimism that all aspects of creation, including apparent evils, work together to produce an inclusive good, which may however be beyond the grasp of human understanding.

The *Essay* also incorporates traditional teachings of classical and Christian philosophers and moralists. It envisages Creation as a "great chain of being," a hierarchical gradation in which each species has its allotted place. Its history of human society begins with the mythic "golden age," a state of nature in which all creatures lived in peace. The discussion of happiness in Epistle IV teaches that true happiness consists not in accidents of fortune, like wealth or social rank, nor in military or political achievements, nor even in wisdom, but in virtue. This is a teaching familiar in Roman moralists and poets such as **Seneca** and Horace. The *Essay* takes on its most sternly Christian coloration when it attacks human pride and emphasizes the limits of human knowledge and capacities.

This emphasis relates the poem to the questioning and tentative character of the essay as practiced by **Montaigne**. Pope's mistrust of systematic science also leads him to adopt the aim of **Bacon**'s essays, to treat not abstruse but everyday subjects, which "come home to men's business and bosoms." One model for Pope's style are the epistles of Horace, with their good-humored urbanity. Nevertheless there is a tension between, on the one hand, Pope's protestations of modesty and his insistence on human ignorance, and, on the other, the ambitious scope of his poem and his air of unruffled confidence in his own knowledge and understanding.

The *Essay* exhibits Pope's characteristic uses of his verse form, the rhyming couplet. It abounds in parallelism and antithesis and in epigrams and **aphorisms**. Occasionally the demands of argumentation produce excessively elliptical language, but in general the poem has an easy, conversational quality. This is created by Pope's use of question and answer and of direct address to an imagined interlocutor. Sometimes the interlocutor's understanding or opinion is presented only to be disproved or ridiculed; sometimes the interlocutor is imagined to be the poem's addressee Bolingbroke and is treated respectfully. Vigor and a sense of debate are injected by the poem's rhetorical questions, its exclamations of wonder or outrage, and its occasional ecstatic visions. An effect of comprehensiveness and variety, appropriate to the poem's large subject, is produced by its lists and catalogues. These may detail the wonders of the universe or the varieties of human nature produced under the direction of wisdom, or they may detail the follies of humanity in doubting or resisting that wisdom. Pope draws on historical examples, such as Alexander the Great or Oliver Cromwell, though the *Essay on Man* generally lacks the vivid narrative episodes and character sketches that mark his *Epistles to Several Persons*. Pope's own summary of his style is "happily to steer/From grave to gay, from lively to severe;/Correct with spirit, eloquent with ease,/Intent to reason, or polite to please."

The *Essay* was widely admired in the 18th century. Besides its English editions, about 100 translations were published. It is frequently quoted by the philosopher **Immanuel Kant** and was imitated by **Voltaire** (*Discours en vers sur l'homme* [1736; Discourse in verse on man]). However, since the 19th century the didacticism, rationalism, and optimism of the *Essay* have caused it to fall from critical favor.

ANTHONY MILLER

Editions
An Essay on Man, 4 vols., 1733–34; edited by Maynard Mack, 1950

Further Reading
Brower, Reuben A., *Alexander Pope: The Poetry of Allusion*, Oxford: Clarendon Press, 1959

Brown, Laura, *Alexander Pope*, Oxford and New York: Blackwell, 1985

Ferguson, Rebecca, *The Unbalanced Mind: Pope and the Rule of Passion*, Philadelphia: University of Pennsylvania Press, and Brighton: Harvester, 1986

Nuttall, A. D., *Pope's "Essay on Man"*, London and Boston: Allen and Unwin, 1984

Sutherland, John, "Wit, Reason, Vision and 'An Essay on Man'," *Modern Language Quarterly* 30 (1969): 356–69

White, Douglas, *Pope and the Context of Controversy: The Manipulation of Ideas in "An Essay on Man"*, Chicago: University of Chicago Press, 1970

An Essay on the Principle of Population

by Thomas Malthus, 1798; revised edition, 1803

In 1797, Thomas Malthus (1766–1834) read "Of Avarice and Profusion," an essay by **William Godwin**, author of the famous and influential *An Enquiry Concerning Political Justice* (1793). Godwin believed there could be justice and happiness for all in a society regulated by reason. To Malthus, Godwin's utopianism marked its proponent as a person blind to the biological facts of human nature. For social progress to continue, solutions would have to be found to the problem of an increasing disproportion between population growth and food supplies. This was Malthus' observation in *An Essay on the Principle of Population as It Affects the Future Improvement of Society, with Remarks on the Speculations of Mr. Godwin, M. Condorcet, and Other Writers*, which he published anonymously in 1798.

His book caused an enormous outcry, with charges that he was barbarous and inhumane, given his underlying belief that if natural disasters did not check the increase of population, then little could be done by humankind itself, short of cruelty to children: a baby is, he pointed out, "comparatively speaking, of little value to the society, as others will immediately supply its place." Malthus felt the force of his critics' charges that he lacked feeling in his pessimism. In 1803, he published a revision in which he sought to ameliorate the severity of earlier conclusions by arguing that people should exercise "moral restraint," and delay marriage, and so children, until they could afford to support them. The revised *Essay* went through six editions in Malthus' lifetime, with a seventh shortly after his death in 1834.

Malthus began with the empirical fact that nature wastes a great deal of life. Everything alive has the potential for enormous proliferation; why, then, doesn't a single species fill the earth up to its capacity for reproduction? Malthus' answer included the facts of history and experience, that death and destruction were checks to runaway population growth.

Adam Smith had demonstrated, in his *Wealth of Nations* (1776), that workers are a commodity which, when increased in production, will suffer a decline in value. In other words, when there are too many people competing for jobs, there will be a consequent decline in the number of people. The economics of wealth production and distribution were functions of population growth and food supplies. Malthus had read Smith's book, as he had read others on these subjects, and so he began with the widely understood proposition that no species of life can multiply beyond the capacity of nature to provide food. Malthus, appointed as a professor of political economy in 1805, developed the implications of his essay on population for various problems of macroeconomics.

There are two postulates from experience from which Malthus argues: "First, that food is necessary to the existence of man. Secondly, that the passion between the sexes is necessary and will remain nearly in its present state." The burden of the *Essay on Population* is to show how these postulates lead to painful conclusions that "the power of population is indefinitely greater than the power in the earth to produce subsistence for man," and "population, when unchecked, increases in a geometrical ratio. Subsistence increases only in an arithmetical ratio." This Malthusian thesis has been debated ever since.

Since Malthus was responding to the rationalist utopias of Godwin and Condorcet, his *Essay on Population* takes on the tone of polemic and often satirizes the objects of his criticism. He ridicules the argument of Condorcet for indefinite prolongation of human life, saying that "we may shut our eyes to the book of nature, as it will no longer be of any use to read it." He dismisses Godwin's abstract reasoning, asserting that "his conjectures certainly far outstrip the modesty of nature." Of Godwin's prediction that sexual passion will diminish with the progress of society, Malthus ironically observes that "no observable progress whatever has hitherto been made."

When **Charles Darwin** read Malthus' *Essay*, he found there a clue to solve the mystery of the origin of species, since Malthus wrote that "the prodigious waste of human life occasioned by this perpetual struggle for room and food was more than supplied by the mighty power of population, acting in some degree, unshackled from the constant habit of emigration." In his *Origin of Species* (1859), Darwin refers to "the doctrine of Malthus applied with manifold force to the whole animal and vegetable kingdoms." **Karl Marx**, on the other hand, in *Das Kapital* (1867–95; *Capital*) attacks Malthus' *Essay* as a "schoolboyish, superficial plagiary," and proceeds to make an *ad hominem* attack on Malthus as a parson of the English State Church.

Malthus published his *Investigation of the Cause of the Present High Price of Provisions* in 1800, explaining how increased demand, with population growth, will drive up prices, and higher prices will lead to the necessary "checks" of misery. In 1820 he published *Principles of Political Economy Considered with a View to Their Practical Application*, in which he makes the radical suggestion of public works for the unemployed, to increase means to meet increased demand. As in the *Essay on Population*, these later essays wrestled with the challenges of balancing production with consumption, though they posed the problems in less graphic and brutal terms.

Anyone who writes of economics or demographics after the publication of Malthus' *Essay on Population* must take into account the issues, problems, and solutions which were raised in that classic statement. From Darwin and Marx to John Maynard Keynes and Barry Commoner, there has continued to be a fierce debate on prospects for social progress and individual happiness in a world of burgeoning population, environmental degradation, and improved technologies for food production. It is a measure of his mark on subsequent history that Malthus has lent his name to opponents in the debate between "Anti-Malthusians" and "Neo-Malthusians."

RICHARD D. MCGHEE

Editions

An Essay on the Principle of Population as It Affects the Future Improvement of Society, with Remarks on the Speculations of Mr. Godwin, M. Condorcet, and Other Writers, 1798; revised edition, 1803; many subsequent editions, including those edited by Antony Flew, 1970, Philip Appleman, 1976, E. A. Wrigley and David Souden, 1986, and Geoffrey Gilbert, 1993

Further Reading

Commoner, Barry, *The Closing Circle: Nature, Man, and Technology*, New York: Knopf, 1971

Godwin, William, *An Enquiry Concerning Political Justice*, Harmondsworth and New York: Penguin, 1985 (original edition, 1793)

Godwin, William, *Of Population*, New York: Augustus M. Kelley, 1964 (original edition, 1820)

Heilbroner, Robert L., *An Inquiry into the Human Prospect: Updated and Reconsidered for the 1980s*, New York: Norton, 1980; revised edition, as *An Inquiry into the Human Prospect: Looked at Again for the 1990s*, Norton, 1991

James, Patricia, *Population Malthus: His Life and Times*, London and Boston: Routledge and Kegan Paul, 1979

Parsons, Jack, *Population Versus Liberty*, London: Pemberton, 1971; Buffalo, New York: Prometheus, 1973

Perrot, Michelle, "Malthusianism and Socialism," in *Malthus Past and Present*, edited by Jacques Dupaguier, Antoinette Fauve-Chamoux, and E. Grebenik, London and New York: Academic Press, 1983

Smith, Kenneth, *The Malthusian Controversy*, London: Routledge and Kegan Paul, 1951; New York: Octagon, 1978

Turner, Michael, editor, *Malthus and His Time*, Basingstoke: Macmillan, and New York: St. Martin's Press, 1986

The Examiner

British periodical, 1710–1711, 1712–14

In November 1710 **Jonathan Swift** assumed the writing of a weekly paper consisting of a single political essay, in support of the policies of Robert Harley, the moderate Tory minister. The 13 numbers already produced (by several of the foremost Tory writers, most notably Henry St. John, Francis Atterbury, and Matthew Prior) had leaned too hard to the right to suit Harley's bipartisan method. After Swift left off the project in June 1711, a few more numbers were written by Mary Delarivière Manley before the paper lapsed, to be revived in 1712 to run for two more years, with less distinction, under William Oldisworth; but the significance of the *Examiner* lies almost wholly in Swift's 33 essays.

The signal distinction of Swift's essays is their marriage of topical politics with a classical equanimity that sets a tone high above the raw-knuckled brawling of much Queen Anne period journalism. Writing from behind the veil of anonymity, Swift could lament the "mad, ridiculous Extreams" of both parties and profess a desire to lend a disinterested "impartial Hand" in the cause of national sanity (no. 16). Of course, Swift's readers have always known that under this purportedly impartial treatment, the Whigs consistently come out the worse for wear. The justly famous no. 15, "Upon the Art of *Political Lying*," for instance, decries a general decline in truth in favor of expediency but illustrates this general corruption by alluding only to Whig leaders, who, we are told, have overshadowed the "Father of lies" by their "continual Improvements" upon his art. Compared to the frontal attacks of most contemporary political essayists, however, the allusiveness of this satire gives an impression of judiciousness and restraint.

Swift maintained this elevated tone, at least in the early numbers, by ignoring with cool contempt the attacks of opposing writers – "hedge-writers," he calls them, or, in a delightfully disdainful phrase that is perhaps prescient of the

Lilliputians, his "little Antagonists" (no. 18). The most persistent antagonist, Arthur Mainwaring, whose *Medley* was published each Monday to counter the *Examiner* of the preceding Thursday, ably criticized the the Examiner's representations of the Whig leaders; but Swift kept to his satiric objects instead of being baited into defending his previous issues. As a result of this strategy – and of his obvious care with the composition – Swift's best essays seem independent and self-contained in contrast to the skirmishing of other political **periodicals** of the day.

Even more essential to the impression of equanimity was the playfully indirect manner of Swift's **satire**. In the essay commonly called the "Impeachment of Verres" (no. 18), for example, not until the midpoint does the real topic surface: the gluttonous exploitation of Ireland by Thomas Wharton during his recent term as Lord-Lieutenant. The opening paragraphs entertain the question of how one is to write on current politics without reflecting scandalously on specific politicians. Noting that some writers have mined ancient texts for parallel histories, the Examiner complains that his own search of Livy and Tacitus for a model of the corrupt senator or proconsul has failed to produce any that he could use "without doing Injury to a *Roman* memory." The expectations aroused by these tantalizing preliminaries are not disappointed when Swift's persona finally announces that he has found a workable parallel in **Cicero**'s orations impeaching Verres (whose name means "hog"), Roman Governor of Sicily, and presents a selective abstract of the speeches. Swift identifies his target only by highlighting precisely those abuses for which Wharton was criticized – selling public offices to the highest bidder, rendering the law arbitrary, defiling the churches (Verres stole statuary; Wharton smashed furniture and urinated on the altar). Although the reflections on Wharton made by this typology seem damning enough, the Examiner concludes the essay by noting his disappointment that "modern Corruptions are not to be parallel'd by ancient Examples, without having recourse to Poetry and Fable." In this final move the Examiner evinces the detachment that rankled his opponents, as he treats the demolition of a prominent politician as though merely a thorny artistic exercise.

Arguably the most powerful *Examiner* essay, the "Bill of Ingratitude" (no. 17) makes a more open attack on its object, the abuses of office by Marlborough; yet the manner again demonstrates a detached irony. It was Swift's task to deflate the charge by Whig writers that stripping Marlborough of command of the military was to reward heroic service with base ingratitude. The Examiner warms to the task by suggesting that with the enormous wealth he has accumulated from state gifts and privileges, the former Captain-General can hardly be pitied as neglected.

The master-stroke comes deep into the essay, when the Examiner inverts the charge that the British do not reward their heroes as honorably as did the Romans by tallying the gains of a Roman general, under the heading "Roman Gratitude," against the gains of Marlborough in a second column, ironically headed "British Ingratitude." Although the inclusion of a balance sheet in a political essay was not entirely new (**Defoe** had used the device in *A Review of the Affairs of France* [1704–13]), Swift recognized and took advantage of its potential for satire. The list of Roman gifts is lengthy, miscellaneous, and more honorific than substantial (a bull, a statue, a costly garment, and so on); by contrast, the British column seems meagre in number of gifts, but the items listed (estates, offices, grants, pensions) are followed by valuations in five and six digits. The last item in the British list, "Employments" valued at 100,000 pounds, is set across from "A Crown of Lawrel," at two pence, dramatizing the magnitude of Marlborough's gains and deftly implying that his aims were more pecuniary than heroic all along. Moreover, this one line of the account serves as an emblem for the disjuncture between the classical heritage of English (Tory) culture and the grasping commercial ambition of the Whigs.

The Tory readership of the *Examiner* – mostly rural gentry and parish priests – needed little persuading to believe the worst of the Whig leaders. What Swift provided them was an image of their own political orientation that communicated an unflappable confidence. More than argument or style, it is this austere tone which distinguishes the *Examiner* from all of its contemporaries.

STEPHEN M. ADAMS

See also Periodical Essay

Editions
The Prose Works of Jonathan Swift, vol. 3, edited by Herbert Davis, 1957
Swift vs. Mainwaring: "The Examiner" and "The Medley", edited by Frank H. Ellis, 1985

Further Reading
Cook, Richard I., "'Mr. *Examiner*' and 'Mr. *Review*': The Tory Apologetics of Swift and Defoe," *Huntington Library Quarterly* 29 (1966): 127–46
Ellis, Frank H., "'A Quill Worn to the Pith in the Service of the State': Swift's *Examiner*," in *Proceedings of the First Munster Symposium of Jonathan Swift*, edited by Hermann J. Real and Heinz J. Vienken, Munich: Fink, 1985
Rembert, James A. W., *Swift and the Dialectical Tradition*, Basingstoke: Macmillan, and New York: St. Martin's Press, 1988
Speck, W. A., "*The Examiner* Examined: Swift's Tory Pamphleteering," in *Swift*, edited by C. J. Rawson, London: Sphere, 1971
Speck, W. A., "*The Examiner* Re-Examined," *Prose Studies* 16 (1993): 36–43

F

Die Fackel

Austrian journal, 1899–1936

Die Fackel (The torch) was an extremely influential literary and cultural journal edited and published by Karl Kraus primarily in Vienna. Even more than contemporaneous literary and cultural journals such as Herwarth Walden's *Der Sturm* (The storm) and Franz Pfemfert's *Die Aktion* (The action), *DF* is indistinguishable from its extraordinary editor. While these other journals published numerous authors, *DF* always featured Kraus' writings and, from 1911, published only his works. Book-length collections such as Kraus' *Sittlichkeit und Kriminalität* (1923; Morality and criminality), and his apocalyptic play, *Die letzten Tage der Menschheit* (1918; *The Last Days of Mankind*), were first serialized in *DF*. Kraus expressed his often caustic **satire** in essays, **aphorism**s, and even poems, generating a large following as well as a great number of detractors who often became the subjects of Kraus' remarks.

DF appeared three times a month through 1904; after that time the journal was published quarterly, though it often appeared irregularly as the result of frequent double and multiple issues. It had a circulation of approximately 9000 copies from 1910 to 1936 (Harry Zohn, 1971). The polemical tone of *DF* was clear in the inaugural issue (April 1899) in which Kraus, playing on a Viennese daily newspaper's practice of telling readers "Was wir bringen" (What we will publish), announced in an essay "Was wir umbringen" (What we will destroy). Frequent targets of *DF* were the daily press and the Viennese justice system, both of which Kraus faulted for double standards and superficiality. Throughout the tenure of *DF*, Kraus' indignation was directed especially at the popular Viennese paper, *Die Neue Freie Presse* (The new free press). Attempting to distance himself from the dailies, Kraus refused advertising after the June 1901 issue and even purported not to take the desires of readers into account, stating that the content of each issue was determined solely by his own priorities. Kraus' satires reflected his belief that language, culture, and politics were connected; thus he linked what he perceived as a misuse of language with the immorality and injustice of Austrian cultural and political institutions.

Kraus' harsh assessments extended beyond the press and the justice system, however, and included psychoanalysis, Zionism, and educational institutions. In essays as well as sections entitled "Glossen" (glosses) and "Universitätsbummel" (A stroll around the university), Kraus criticized the educational structures of the day, implicating them in Austria's (and Europe's) decline. He attacked nepotism, rote learning, and the inculcation of bourgeois notions of morality and decorum. In a June 1899 entry Kraus suggested the extent to which nepotism affected the hiring practices of Viennese universities and provided a table listing such instances. Essays such as Adolf Loos' "Der moderne Schulmeister" (April 1904; The modern schoolmaster) identified the schoolmaster as someone who cripples students through "rules, formulas, and numbers." Other writers advancing similar critiques in *DF* before 1911 included Peter Altenberg, Else Lasker-Schüler, Franz Werfel, and Albert Ehrenstein.

Kraus was a pacifist and an incessant critic of the militarism that was leading Germany and Austria to war. He focused with great zeal on the hypocritical statements and manipulation of language that he believed characterized the actions of many of Vienna and Berlin's most educated and powerful citizens. Few people were spared Kraus' satire, and many writers and artists who were once his friends found themselves accused of commercialism and pandering to popular taste. During the war Kraus often noted the actions of politicians and professors without comment, allowing what he saw as their brutality and irrationality to speak for themselves. In "Glossen" (1916), for instance, he quoted a group of professors who said Germany should not "sheath its sword." In the same issue Kraus reprinted a popular postcard of the time that featured a model-scale church altar made out of shrapnel from grenades, a juxtaposition of war and religion that Kraus found self-evidently ludicrous.

Like **Nietzsche**, Kraus was a master stylist and often used epigrams and aphorisms to criticize cultural institutions. Kraus' aphorisms addressed nearly every aspect of Austrian culture, and were so prolific that several collections were created from *DF*. In one aphorism, he aptly described himself: "Many share my intentions, but I do not share theirs." Kraus often played upon the ambiguity of words and exploited their multiple meanings as if to counterbalance the pedestrian uses to which language had been subjected.

DF led to a number of imitative journals and **pamphlet**s within Austria, some of which, like *Der Fackel-Reiter* (The torch rider), even used the term "Fackel" in their titles. Kraus also influenced German editors and publishers including Herwarth Walden, editor of *Der Sturm*, and Kurt Wolff, who founded the Kurt Wolff publishing company. Walden helped Kraus establish a short-lived Berlin edition of *DF*, and his journal, *Der Sturm*, adopted Kraus' aesthetic and cultural criticism. Wolff was so impressed with Kraus that he established a publishing company – Verlag der Schriften von Karl Kraus – devoted solely to works by Kraus.

The end of World War I did not make Kraus any more sanguine about Austrian cultural institutions or the ethics of his fellow citizens. Poems were frequent in postwar editions of *DF* and Kraus' interest in the intricacies of language and culture was more pronounced. His prose poems were another means of exploiting the richness of language, but it was his familiar criticisms rather than his lyricism which distinguished them. In "Optimismus" (1925; Optimism) he detailed the ills of Austrian culture, wishing for a day in which the printed word is no longer analogous to lying. Because of Kraus' earlier vociferous criticism of the conditions leading to war, his silence concerning Hitler's rise to power was conspicuous; he published only one issue of *DF* in 1933. In explaining this hiatus to critics who accused him of cowardice, Kraus wrote that with regard to Hitler he had "nothing to say," a statement typical in its ambiguity and in the controversy it evoked. *DF* was published fitfully from 1934 to Kraus' death on 12 June 1936.

CHRISTOPHER P. MCCLINTICK

Further Reading

Bilke, Martina, *Zeitgenossen der "Fackel"*, Vienna: Locker, 1981

Halliday, John D., *Karl Kraus, Franz Pfemfert and the First World War: A Comparative Study of "Die Fackel" and "Die Aktion" Between 1911 and 1928*, Passau: Haller, 1986

Jenaczek, Friedrich, *Zeittafeln zur "Fackel": Themen, Ziele, Probleme*, Gräfelfing bei München: Kosel, 1965

Timms, Edward, *Karl Kraus: Apocalyptic Satirist: Culture and Catastrophe in Habsburg Vienna*, New Haven, Connecticut: Yale University Press, 1986

Zohn, Harry, *Karl Kraus*, New York: Twayne, 1971

Familiar Essay

The familiar essayist has commonly been characterized as curious – in constant search for the significance of the mundane. His or her subjects "spring naturally from the affairs of everyday life." Familiar essays themselves have traditionally been highly informal in tone, often humorous, valuing lightness of touch above all else. They have been filled with intimate personal observations and reflections, and have emphasized the concrete and tangible, the sensual enjoyment of everyday pleasures. Usually brief, familiar essays have long affected a feeling of careless spontaneity so strong that perhaps no other type of essay is as dependent for its success and popularity on its ability to "present a personality."

Montaigne, who wrote "I confess myself in public," produced essays considered familiar. The first popular familiar essayists, however, appeared in the 18th century, especially in **Joseph Addison**'s and **Richard Steele**'s *Spectator* (1711–12; 1714) and **Samuel Johnson**'s *Rambler* (1750–52) and *Idler* (1758–60). Besides their casual tone, these essays were "familiar" because they induced the reader to join the author at a double level. Addison's essays in the *Spectator*, as well as

most Eighteenth-century essays, are concerned, explicitly and implicitly, with belonging, with membership; the reader is constantly encouraged to recognize kinship, to distinguish himself from one group and ally himself with another. Eighteenth-century familiarity inevitably drew readers into the rhetoric of the essay and induced them to participate in an alliance with the author in a way that essays before that century almost never did.

However, it was in the 19th century – a period of material well-being in England, when there was a leisure class who enjoyed literature, when an education was received by many among the masses – that the familiar essay fully came into its own. The familiar essayist, as Sister Mary Eleanore wrote (1923), "is a veritable Jaques upon a mossy bank, who, while he watches the world go jostling its way down the river of life, extracts from its seemingly confused and meaningless tumbling bits of loving wisdom and quaint chuckles of fun . . ." He soothes the pains of the world's tired travel, and does so through his ability to be whimsical, grave, melancholy, through his love of living and sense of humor over "those ridiculous and pathetic incongruities which are such a necessary part of life."

The familiar essay reached its zenith with **Charles Lamb**. Though living a melancholy and often tragic life, Lamb created in his essays a narrator "in love with this green earth," one who hid wisdom under playfulness. His *Essays of Elia* (1823, 1828) includes autobiographical pieces such as "A Chapter on Ears" and "Imperfect Sympathies" (in which he is quick to admit to his prejudices), and humorous or farcical ones such as "A Dissertation upon Roast Pig" and "Mrs. Battle's Opinions on Whist."

William Hazlitt stands as the other major familiar essayist of early 19th-century England, though his persona was much harsher and crankier than Lamb's Elia. Hazlitt looked to the exotic, in such essays as "The Indian Jugglers" (1821) and to the contradictory, in such essays as "On the Ignorance of the Learned" (1821) and "On the Pleasure of Hating" (1826). His "On Familiar Style" (1821) is an argument for how precisely and purely a familiar essayist must write.

Contemporary with Lamb and Hazlitt was **Leigh Hunt**, who chose such common subjects as "Getting Up on Cold Mornings" (1820) and "A Few Thoughts on Sleep" (1820). The second half of the 19th century saw English essayists continue in this vein, such as **Robert Louis Stevenson** ("A Plea for Gas Lamps," 1878; "An Apology for Idlers," 1877), **G. K. Chesterton** ("A Defence of Nonsense," 1911; "A Piece of Chalk," 1909), and E. V. Lucas ("Concerning Clothes," 1897). In the United States, the tradition was less strong but was still practiced by writers such as Samuel McChord Crothers.

Toward the end of the 19th century, familiar essays often came to be written for their own sake, rather than for the sake of the subject; there was a shift from matter to manner. Augustine Birrell wrote good-humored and whimsical musings which were popular enough to give rise to a new literary term, "birrelling." So many essayists "birrelled" their way through that era – and were held up as models in the schoolroom – that their work helped to give the essay a bad name. **Hilaire Belloc**, a prolific familiar essayist, poked fun at these tendencies in the titles to his collections: *On Nothing, On Everything, On Anything, On Something* (1908–11), and *On* (1923).

Still, as late as 1922, the familiar essay had its host of practitioners, most notably the immensely popular **Max Beerbohm** and the prolific **J. B. Priestley**. It had, too, its fierce defenders, such as the critic F. R. Schelling, who wrote in "The Familiar Essay" (in *Appraisements and Asperities*, 1922) "He who loves the essay – especially the familiar essay, as it is called – and letters, is the aristocrat, the Brahmin among readers, because he, among all others, has the taste of the connoisseur for delicate flavor, for fragrance, for aroma . . ." But World War I brought out another view. As **Agnes Repplier** – one of the most important familiar essayists of the late 19th and early 20th centuries – wrote in "The American Essay in War Time" (1918), "To write essays in these flaming years, one must have a greater power of detachment than had Montaigne or Lamb."

The familiar essay, to review 20th-century commentary on it, was dying a slow death from World War I up through at least 1955, when Clifton Fadiman declared its "digressive and noncommitting" method nearly impossible to practice in "an age of anxiety." He noted exceptions – **E. B. White**, **Bernard De Voto**, John Mason Brown – but said they were simply "exerting their delaying action [on] the eclipse of the familiar essay." The completely "light" familiar essay has been severely marginalized in the last few decades of the 20th century – reserved for newspaper columnists like Erma Bombeck and Dave Barry, as well as for many pieces in the *New Yorker*'s "Talk of the Town" section.

The traditional lightness of the familiar essay, however, has been complemented by a new sense of political awareness. E. B. White helped bring about this evolution, by writing not only primarily **autobiographical essays** such as "Death of a Pig" (1947), but others in which he intertwined his personal stories with calls for one-world government or arguments against racial segregation. The feminist movement of the 1970s produced writers such as Nora Ephron, a humorist who, in essays such as "A Few Words About Breasts" (1972) and "Vaginal Politics" (1972), took the very personal and commonplace and presented them in the contexts of public issues. Other recent essayists who have imbued this formerly "dainty" form with commitment and thereby helped regenerate its popularity include **Scott Russell Sanders**, Martin Amis, and Fran Lebowitz. Nowadays the familiar essay is often seen as a form particularly well suited to modern rhetorical purposes, able to reach an otherwise suspicious or uninterested audience through personal discourse, which reunites the appeals of ethos (the force and charm of the writer's character) and pathos (the emotional engagement of the reader) with the intellectual appeal of *logos*.

DAN ROCHE

See also Personal Essay

Anthologies
A Book of English Essays, edited by W. E. Williams, Harmondsworth: Penguin, 1948
The English Familiar Essay: Representative Texts, edited by William Frank Bryan and R. S. Crane, Boston: Ginn, 1916
Familiar Essays, edited by Stuart Robertson, New York: Prentice Hall, 1930
Familiar Essays of Today, edited by Benjamin A. Heydrick, New York: Scribner, 1930
Modern Familiar Essays, edited by William M. Tanner, Boston: Little Brown, 1927

The Oxford Book of Essays, edited by John Gross, Oxford and New York: Oxford University Press, 1991
Thought and Form in the Essay: Expository – Familiar – Argumentative, edited by De Calvus W. Simonson and Edwin R. Coulson, New York: Harper, 1933

Further Reading
Broadhead, Glenn J., *The Rhetoric of Conversation: Essays on Eighteenth-Century English Criticism of "Familiar Discourse"* (dissertation), Davis: University of California, 1973
Drew, Elizabeth, "The Lost Art of the Essay," *Saturday Review of Literature*, 16 February 1935
Eleanore, Sister Mary, *The Literary Essay in English*, Boston: Ginn, 1923
Enright, Nancy, "William Hazlitt and His 'Familiar Style'," in *Essays on the Essay: Redefining the Genre*, edited by Alexander J. Butrym, Athens: University of Georgia Press, 1989
Fadiman, Clifton, "A Gentle Dirge for the Familiar Essay," in his *Party of One*, Cleveland: World, 1955
Gross, John, Introduction to *The Oxford Book of Essays*, edited by Gross, Oxford and New York: Oxford University Press, 1991
Hansche, Maude Bingham, *The Formative Period of English Familiar Letter-Writers and Their Contribution to the English Essay* (dissertation), Philadelphia: University of Pennsylvania, 1902
Haskell, Dale E., *The Rhetoric of the Familiar Essay: E. B. White and Personal Discourse* (dissertation), Fort Worth: Texas Christian University, 1983
Law, Marie Hamilton, *The English Familiar Essay in the Early Nineteenth Century*, New York: Russell and Russell, 1965
Repplier, Agnes, "The American Essay in War Time," *Yale Review* 7, no. 2 (1918): 249–59
Watson, Melvin R., *Magazine Serials and the Essay Tradition, 1746–1820*, Baton Rouge: Louisiana State University Press, 1956

Feijóo y Montenegro, Benito Jerónimo
Spanish, 1676–1764

One of Spain's most important 18th-century scholars, Benito Jerónimo Feijóo y Montenegro represents the burgeoning intelligentsia of the Enlightenment casting off the burdens of traditionalism, conformity, and ignorance. Unlike many of his contemporaries, Feijóo preferred the isolation of his native Galicia where he could enjoy an independence of thought not always allowed in the more confining and politically charged environment of the capital Madrid. From this unique vantage point, Feijóo could observe and synthesize the culture, politics, and social conditions of his homeland. Ivy McClelland in her study of the author (1969) notes that ". . . as an intelligent man of the perimeter, Feijóo saw things that could not be seen in such clear perspective from the center . . . when he was urged to transfer permanently to Madrid to live at the heart of Spain's activity, he resolutely refused, showing, by word or implication, that he could think better in less crowded places." Aside from the freedom that his isolation afforded him, Feijóo also had more access to books, pamphlets, and other intellectual material than he could have had in the capital, where strict censorship was enforced. The combination of these two factors created a rich interplay of intellect and practical observation in his discourses.

Feijóo's stance within the milieu of 18th-century Spanish Enlightenment thought manifests itself clearly in a multitude of essays which address a broad range of topics, including the role of women, politics, morality, literature, and medicine. The primary forum for his opinions is a multi-volume series entitled *Teatro crítico universal* (1725–40; Universal theater of criticism). Essential to Feijóo's philosophical outlook is his perception of what he considered to be the pervasive errors held by the general populace in contrast to his own truth. Feijóo explains in the prologue to *Teatro crítico universal* that these errors are comprised of "all the opinions" that contradict his perception of truth. Thus, the general tenor of Feijóo's discourses reflects the perspective of a man sitting on a mountain looking down at the clamoring masses. He is an observer whose physical isolation causes him to consider objectively, and somewhat narrowly, the world that surrounds him. This is not to say that Feijóo lacks passion, only that the author's zeal toward his topic appeals to a more restricted class of people, namely other intellectuals like himself. One might consider Feijóo's own words from "Voz del pueblo" (1726; Voice of the people) where he asserts that the masses suffer from the illusion that their numbers alone vindicate their opinions. To this premise, Feijóo warns, "The value of an opinion should be calculated by its profundity, not by the number of souls who believe it. The ignorant, even though they are numerous, do not cease to be ignorant." He later affirms that those who adhere to a single truth should not be surprised that in a time of limited understanding and learning there should be so many false ideas.

Feijóo applies the same measure of truth to all his topics. Whether he addresses politics, patriotism, the role of women, or medicine, the recurring theme is the centrality of truth versus error. Despite his Christian stance, Feijóo often experienced derision because he condemned not only the fallibility of the people, or *vulgo*, but also the fallibility of the "pueblo de Dios" (people of God). In "El no sé qué" (1733; I don't know), Feijóo reiterates his perception that there rests an air of indecision and apathy on the masses that influences the way they act or are acted upon. Feijóo explains, "This *I do not know what* is the hex over their willpower and the quagmire of their understanding."

In addition to *Teatro crítico universal*, Feijóo published his memoirs, *Cartas eruditas y curiosas* (1742–60; Intellectual letters), in five volumes. These documents provide important biographical information regarding the author and his social, political, and intellectual environment. Commenting on the content of Feijóo's autobiography, McClelland notes, "He exposes the whole structure of his personality so completely that we often see parts of it that he cannot see himself. If he is aware of his own makeup he becomes, in his complexity, an even more absorbing study. To know him is to be admitted into the engine room of universal character, to observe a mind in motion, to examine the total product of innumerable trivialities; it is to treat him as someone no less alive than we are."

The context and content of *Teatro crítico universal* and *Cartas eruditas* suggest a rich and vigorous intellect. His susceptibility to Enlightenment thought in combination with his religious training combine in a unique vision of right and wrong, truth and error. For Feijóo, as for so many of his contemporaries, Spain was on the cusp of a new age of understanding and learning. Future writers such as **Mariano José de Larra** would look to Feijóo for inspiration and number him

among the great writers of all time: "How would one write today, in our country, without the prior existence of Feijóo, Iriartes, Forner and Moratín?" Herein we see the true genius of the man, the ability to sound the trumpet of discontent and to ignite the intellectual flame not only in those who knew him, but in those who followed.

ALVIN F. SHERMAN, JR.

Biography
Born 8 October 1676 in Casdemiro, Orense. Studied at the monastery of San Julián de Samos, where he was ordained a Benedictine monk, 1690; University of Oviedo, degree in theology, 1709. Lived and taught at the monastery of San Vicente, Oviedo, from 1709; professor of theology, University of Oviedo, 1710–39. Honorary member, Royal Society of Medicine, Seville, 1727. Died in Oviedo, 26 September 1764.

Selected Writings

Essays and Related Prose
Teatro crítico universal, 9 vols., 1725–40; edited by Carmen Martín Gaite, with *Cartas eruditas*, 1970, Ángel-Raimundo González Fernández, 1980, and Giovanni Stiffoni, 1986; selection as *Essays or Discourses Selected from the Works of Feijóo*, translated by John Brett, 1779; several essays also translated anonymously and published separately, including *The Honour and Advantage of Agriculture*, 1764, *An Essay on Woman*, 1770, *An Essay on the Learning, Genius, and Abilities, of the Fair-Sex*, 1774, and *Rules for Preserving Health, Particularly with Regard to Studious Persons*, 1800(?)
Cartas eruditas y curiosas, 5 vols., 1742–60; edited by Carmen Martín Gaite, with *Teatro crítico universal*, 1970

Other writings: poetry.

Collected works edition: *Obras completas*, edited by José Miguel Caso González, 1981.

Further Reading
Aldridge, A. Owen, "Feijóo, Voltaire, and the Mathematics of Procreation," in *Studies in Eighteenth-Century Culture*, vol. 4, edited by Harold E. Pagliaro, Richard Morton, and Roy McKeen Wiles, Madison: University of Wisconsin Press, 1975: 131–38

Alvarez de Miranda, Pedro, "Aproximación al estudio del vocabulario ideológico de Feijóo," *Cuadernos Hispanoamericanos* 347 (1979): 367–93

Browning, John, "Fray Benito Jerónimo Feijóo and the Sciences in 18th-Century Spain," in *The Varied Pattern: Studies in the 18th Century*, edited by Peter Hughes and David Williams, Toronto: Hakkert, 1971: 353–71

Camarero, Manuel, "Una lectura de 'El no sé qué' de Feijóo," in *Pen and Peruke: Spanish Literature of the Eighteenth Century*, edited by Monroe Z. Hafter, Ann Arbor: University of Michigan Department of Romance Languages, 1992: 203–13

Coughlin, Edward V., "The Polemic of Feijóo's 'Defensa de las mujeres'," *Dieciocho* 9, nos. 1–2 (1986): 74–85

Crusafont y Pairo, M., "El enciclopedismo ortodoxo del Padre Feijóo y las ciencias naturales," *Boletín de la Biblioteca de Menéndez Pelayo* 40 (1964): 65–97

Domergue, Lucienne, "Feijóo y Blanco White: Homenaje de un 'hereje' al Padre Maestro," in *II simposio sobre el Padre Feijóo y su siglo*, Oviedo: Center for Eighteenth-Century Studies, 1981: 333–48

Dowling, John, "Life, Death, and Immortality in Eighteenth- and Nineteenth-Century Spain," in *Selected Proceedings of the Thirty-Fifth Annual Mountain Interstate Foreign Language Conference*, edited by Ramón Fernández Rubio, Greenville, South Carolina: Furman University, 1987: 121–34

Elizalde, Ignacio, "La influencia de Bayle y Fontenelle en Feijóo," in *Actas del VIII Congreso de la Asociación Internacional de Hispanistas*, edited by A. David Kossoff and others, Madrid: Istmo, 2 vols., 1986: 497–509

Fallows, Noel, "'True Wit,' and Feijóo's 'Chistes de N'," *Bulletin of Hispanic Studies* 70, no. 2 (April 1993): 249–53

Franklin, Elizabeth M., "Feijóo, Josefa Amar y Borbón, and the Feminist Debate in Eighteenth-Century Spain," *Dieciocho* 12, no. 2 (1989): 188–203

Livermore, A. L., "Goya y Feijóo," *Cuadernos Hispanoamericanos* 253–54 (1971): 17–45

McClelland, I. L., *Benito Jerónimo Feijóo*, New York: Twayne, 1969

Maravall, José A., "Feijóo, el europeo, desde América," *Revista de Occidente* 7 (1964): 313–34

Maravall, José A., "El espíritu de crítica y el pensamiento social de Feijóo," *Cuadernos Hispanoamericanos* 318 (1979): 736–65

Mestre, Antonio, "Reflexiones sobre el marco político-cultural de la obra del P. Feijóo," *Bulletin Hispanique* 91, no. 2 (July–December 1989): 295–312

Sebold, Russell P., "Colón, Bacon y la metáfora heroíca de Feijóo," in *Homenaje a Don Agapito Rey*, edited by Josep Roca Pons, Bloomington: Indiana University Department of Spanish and Portuguese, 1979: 333–54

Ferreira, Vergílio

Portuguese, 1916–1996

Vergílio Ferreira, one of the most acclaimed Portuguese novelists of this century, was also a first-class essayist. Early in his career he joined ranks with the neo-realists, who focused on social themes, but he soon parted company from them over their increasing links with socialist realism, as well as his own discovery of existentialism. Under the influence of **Dostoevskii**, Malraux, **Sartre**, and **Camus**, Ferreira made his own way, weaving his personal reflections upon the modern themes of absence of meaning and value in a post-Nietzschean world without foundations, with a fine yet powerful sense of the aesthetic dimension of life. The language he inherited from the prose of the 19th-century Portuguese master novelist Eça de Queiroz was a guiding inspiration for Ferreira, who envisioned the ideal writer as someone who could combine the best of Dostoevskii, Eça de Queiroz, and Malraux. The latter was one of the authors he most admired, not so much as a novelist, but as an essayist. As Ferreira said in an interview, "the Malraux of the novels aged quite a bit; the essayist I find very stimulating, almost as stimulating as listening to Bach" (*Um escritor apresenta-se* [1981; A writer presents himself]).

There is, indeed, a strong philosophical bent in the writings of this compulsive author, who throughout his life maintained a steady flow of volumes (40 in total) of fiction, essays, and, from 1980, five volumes of a **journal**, *Conta-corrente* (1980–87; Running a tab), which are filled with entries easily classifiable as essays. His novels are often philosophical, full of metaphysical obsessions (in that sense, they too are essays), but there are also several volumes of essays in which Ferreira's thoughts are expanded in an analytical yet poetic style. Of

these, perhaps *Do mundo original* (1957; Of the original world) is one key to understanding the mind of this thinker, "a kind of manifesto of his essayism," as **Eduardo Lourenço** puts it, even though Ferreira would probably have chosen *Invocação ao meu corpo* (1969; Invocation to my body) as his most representative work.

Lourenço has written extensively about Ferreira; Ferreira himself considered Lourenço to be his best interpreter "because of his exceptional capacities as well as our solid affinity of ideas." Lourenço has pointed out the reactive nature of Ferreira's essayistic discourse, written always in response to someone else's writing. Considering the issue of the originality of Ferreira's thought, Lourenço writes: "Vergílio Ferreira's essayism does not really proceed either from inner demands that are philosophical demands – in the generic or the metaphysical sense – or, even less so, from the sociological or political. The only vital object of meditation, the one in which while questioning he questions himself, in which by inventing justifications he justifies himself, is the one of Art. It is the living experience of Art – as an incomprehensible creative impulse, an incandescence of being and not as a finished product – that constitutes the matrix of all of Vergílio Ferreira's thought" (*O canto do signo*, 1994).

Reading any of Ferreira's journal volumes can be a pleasant introduction to the world of this artist and thinker, who writes fiction but who still prefers to blend it with essayism in his journal. In his later years he decided to subdivide his journal into two genres: one intellectual, addressing ideas and philosophical themes, the other more mundane, in which he writes of daily life. *Pensar* (1992; Thinking) was a concretization of the former. Its title and format reveal an affiliation with **Pascal**'s *Pensées*, which Ferreira explicitly mentions after describing his volume as "a sort of journal of the haphazard of thinking" ("*ir pensando*" in Portuguese expresses better the idea of continuity and openness). The fragmented nature of Pascal's work is compared favorably to the completeness Pascal intended for it.

The other, more quotidian segment of the journal has already resulted in four volumes – *Conta-corrente, nova série* (1993–94; Running a tab, new series). Whether he writes about the ordeal of Lisbon traffic or about a television program he happened to watch, Ferreira never abandons his penchant for the reflective. For him, the "pure" essay is creative and problematizing (*problematizante*). He establishes a difference between the purely informative or analytical essay on someone else's work and the "problematizing" essay, which should itself be an aesthetic creation, something in which "ideas detain themselves and stay where the work of art dwells"; thus "the essay comes close to the artistic work." However, the closer the essay is to being a work of art the less questionable it becomes, "because one does not argue about emotions" (*Conta-corrente, nova série*, 1993).

About the essay as a genre he has written: "The essay (in Portugal) basically informs; but what is important is that the essay may *discuss*, that it may *problematize* . . . Infinitely more useful is the *fertile error* than the *sterile truth*. But there is an element which is to be incorporated in the essay and that particularly approximates it to literary art – one that particularly makes it a candidate to succeed the novel: *emotiveness*" (*Um escritor apresenta-se*).

In another interview he explained: "For me, the novel and the essay were always parallel activities. On the one hand, I do not see the essay as a process, a means, with a merely pedagogic objective. I cultivate the essay, seeking, through it, to explicate problems. I must make clear that the problematics which preoccupy me in my essays are more or less the same as in the novels. The ideal essayistic activity is one that extends the work of the fictionalist, and not one which is subsidiary or which happens in the intervals . . . if I prefer the novel to the essay, it is because, among other reasons, the novel places me immediately in life and in myself – one exists before, and only afterwards does one speak about what one is" (*Um escritor apresenta-se*).

Ferreira continued to write both essays and novels until the very end of his life, remaining obsessed with the same themes. In 1987 he published another volume of his collection of essays under the general title of *Espaço do invisível* (Invisible space), dealing once again, as in the previous volumes of the series, with figures such as Malraux, Queiroz, Sartre, Kafka, and Foucault, and with topics such as art, the critic, death, the novel, disquietude, and the nude. Ferreira was a novelist who never ceased being a philosopher and an essayist who never stopped being a writer of narratives.

ONÉSIMO T. ALMEIDA

Biography

Born 28 January 1916 in Melo. Entered a Catholic seminary in Fundão at age ten, remaining for six years, which had a lasting impact on his religious thought: he wrote a novel about this traumatic experience, *Manhã submersa* (1954; Submerged morning). Studied classical philology at the University of Coimbra, graduated 1940. High school teacher in Évora, 1945–58, and Lisbon, 1959–81. Married: two adopted children. Awards: many Portuguese prizes; Camões Prize; International Association of Literary Critics Award; Femina Prize; Europalia Award. Died in Lisbon, 1 March 1996.

Selected Writings

Essays and Related Prose
Sobre o humorismo de Eça de Queirós, 1943
Do mundo original, 1957
Carta ao futuro, 1958
Da fenomenologia a Sartre, 1962
André Malraux: Interrogação ao destino, 1963
Espaço do invisível, 4 vols., 1965–91
Invocação ao meu corpo, 1969
Conta-corrente, 5 vols., 1980–87
Um escritor apresenta-se, edited by Maria de Glória Padrão, 1981
Arte tempo, 1988
Pensar, 1992
Conta-corrente, nova série, 4 vols., 1993–94

Other writings: many novels (including *O caminho fica longe*, 1943; *Vagão "J"*, 1946; *Mudança*, 1949; *Manhã submersa*, 1954; *Aparição*, 1959; *Estrela polar*, 1962; *Alegria breve*, 1965; *Nítido nulo*, 1972; *Para sempre*, 1983; *Em nome de terra*, 1990; *Na tua face*, 1993).

Further Reading

Anthropos issue on Ferreira (October 1989)
Arenas, Fernando, "Beauty at the Surface of Love's Nest: Myth and Narratives in Vergílio Ferreira's Contemporary Writing," *Santa Barbara Portuguese Studies* 3 (1997)
Décio, João, *Vergílio Ferreira, a ficção e o ensaio*, São Paulo: Século XXI, 1977
Godinho, Helder, editor, *Estudos sobre Vergílio Ferreira*, Lisbon: Imprensa Nacional-Casa da Moeda, 1982
Goulart, Rosa Maria, *Romance lírico: O percurso de Vergílio Ferreira*, Lisbon: Bertrand, 1990
Lourenço, Eduardo, *O canto do signo*, Lisbon: Presença, 1994

Feuerbach, Ludwig
German, 1804–1872

It was *Das Wesen des Christenthums* (1841; *The Essence of Christianity*) that gave Feuerbach an intense though brief prestige in the 1840s, and this book, together with the fact of his influence on the young **Marx**, is the main source of contemporary interest in Feuerbach's work. However, his numerous essays are forceful, entertaining, and often philosophically interesting. Some achieved a certain fame or notoriety of their own, and many are effective expressions of his main philosophical position – his critique of religion, authoritarianism, and dualistic philosophy in the name of concrete, corporeal human life.

Feuerbach's preferred form of essay was the book **review**, allowing him to engage in the polemics he clearly relished. In the years 1835–45, particularly, he wrote a flurry of reviews which take advantage of contemporary intellectual controversies or minor publications to stake out his own philosophical position. The books under review are works not only of pure philosophy and the history of philosophy, but also of medicine, theology, and devotional literature. Feuerbach's reviews do not shy away from blasphemy, as when he compares the beauty of the Virgin Mary to the charms of a Bavarian barmaid – "Über den Marienkultus" (1842; On the cult of Mary). Nor does he hesitate to use the harshest insults, as in "Kritik des 'Antihegel'" (1835; Critique of "Anti-Hegel"), an early **pamphlet** in which he defends Hegel against C. F. Bachmann: "Herr Bachmann's views on thinking display his thoughtless-empirical standpoint in all its crassness and barbarity. With a real enthusiasm for dunderheads and cretins, he writes . . ."

Notably, within a few years of writing "Kritik des 'Antihegel'," Feuerbach himself was to become a virulent anti-Hegelian and espouse a materialism quite close to the position expressed by Bachmann. Thus, while the flamboyant tone of Feuerbach's writing is a constant, the content of his opinions undergoes significant change. Yet he himself might argue that the contradictions to be found in his thought are evidence of depth rather than of carelessness. In his 1836 review of Johann Eduard Erdmann's *Geschichte der neueren Philosophie* (*History of Modern Philosophy*), Feuerbach cites paradoxical lines from **Goethe**, Petrarch, and Corneille, and asks: "Doesn't pain, the tragic moment, consist in the presence of two opposed predicates *together* in *one and the same* subject? Isn't the principle of the concurrence of opposites the characteristic principle of living modern philosophy, as against the dead, formal Scholasticism of the Middle Ages . . .?"

While Feuerbach writes for intellectuals, his fight against "dead, formal" thought and prose leads him to use vivid, colloquial language sprinkled with emphatic typography, exclamation points, and question marks. Above all, he has a flair for direct and catchy phrases. This aphoristic trait is often combined with a sense of humor, as when he writes in the long essay "Zur Kritik der Hegelschen Philosophie" (1839; Contribution to the critique of Hegelian philosophy), "Hegel's mind is a *logical* – or more precisely, I would say, an *entomological* mind."

Feuerbach puts his gift for **aphorisms** to good use in "Vorläufige Thesen zur Reform der Philosophie" (1842; Preliminary theses on the reform of philosophy). This text distills Feuerbach's thought in a series of aphorisms ranging from a sentence to a paragraph. The style recalls Luther's 95 theses, invites Marx's famous "Theses on Feuerbach" (wr. 1845), and anticipates **Nietzsche** in its economical style, its prophetic tone, and its subject matter. Feuerbach's briefer aphorisms here are thought-provoking and memorable. For example: "What there is, as it is – truth expressed truly – appears superficial; what there is, as it is not – truth expressed untruly, backwards – appears deep." This thesis illustrates and expresses Feuerbach's love of the plain statement that cuts to the core of things. In 1843 Feuerbach was to write an entire short book in this genre, *Grundsätze der Philosophie der Zukunft* (*Principles of the Philosophy of the Future*).

Feuerbach's aphoristic gift does not always protect him against effusive passages which string together long lists of adjectives. His talent is also a liability, as it can lead him into sloganeering. A case in point is his most famous (or infamous) one-liner, from "Die Naturwissenschaft und die Revolution" (1850; Natural science and the revolution), a review of a book by the physiologist Moleschott: "Man is what he eats." (In German, this is an irresistible pun: *Der Mensch ist was er isst*.) This essay verges on self-parody when it concludes that the 1848 revolution failed in Germany because of the nutritional deficiencies of the German staple, potatoes – the country can find its true salvation in a diet of beans. Such statements drew scornful satire from Feuerbach's contemporaries. But Feuerbach relished the notoriety of his phrase, and even incorporated it into the title of his piece of 1862, "Das Geheimnis des Opfers, oder der Mensch ist was er isst" (The mystery of sacrifice, or man is what he eats). The phrase in question exemplifies a pattern of hyperbole in Feuerbach's writings: he is given to identifying now one feature, now another as the sole "essence" of some phenomenon.

In general, while Feuerbach's essays should never be taken too literally, their exuberance and their flashes of wit give them real rhetorical impact.

RICHARD POLT

Biography

Ludwig Andreas Feuerbach. Born 28 July 1804 in Landshut, Bavaria. Studied at the Ansbach Gymnasium, Munich, 1817–22; theology under Theodor Lehmus at the University of Heidelberg, from 1823; theology and philosophy under Hegel and the theologian Friedrich Schleiermacher at the University of Berlin, 1824; natural sciences at the University of Erlangen, from 1826. Lecturer in the history of modern philosophy, University of Erlangen, 1829–35. Married Berta Löw, 1837. Lived in wife's family's castle near Bruckberg, 1837–60, then moved to Rechenberg, near Munich, 1860–72. Lectured in Heidelberg, 1848–49. Died in Nuremberg, 13 September 1872.

Selected Writings

Essays and Related Prose

Gedanken über Tod und Unsterblichkeit, aus den Papieren eines Denkers, edited by Johann Adam Stein, 1830; revised edition, 1847; as *Thoughts on Death and Immortality, from the Papers of a Thinker*, translated by James A. Massey, 1980

Abälard und Heloise, oder, Der Schriftsteller und der Mensch: Eine Reihe humoristisch-philosophischer Aphorismen (aphorisms), 1834

Grundsätze der Philosophie der Zukunft, 1843; as *Principles of the Philosophy of the Future*, translated by Manfred H. Vogel, 1966

Das Wesen des Glaubens im Sinne Luthers, 1844; as *The Essence of Faith According to Luther*, translated by Melvin Cherno, 1967

Vorlesungen über des Wesen der Religion: Nebst Zusätzen und Anmerkungen (*Sämtliche Werke*, vol. 8), 1851; as *Lectures on the Essence of Religion*, translated by Ralph Manheim, 1967

The Fiery Brook: Selected Writings, translated by Zawar Hanfi, 1972

Other writings: *Das Wesen des Christenthums* (1841, revised 1843, 1849; *The Essence of Christianity*), *Das Wesen der Religion* (1846; *The Essence of Religion*), histories of modern philosophy (1833, 1837), a book on **Pierre Bayle** (1838), and other works on philosophy, religion, and Greek mythology.

Collected works editions: *Sämtliche Werke*, edited by Wilhelm Bolin and Friedrich Jodl, 10 vols., 1903–11; *Gesammelte Werke* (East German Academy of Sciences Edition), edited by Werner Schuffenhauer, 1967– (in progress).

Further Reading

Cherno, Melvin, "Feuerbach's 'Man Is What He Eats': A Rectification," *Journal of the History of Ideas* 24, no. 3 (1963): 397–406

Duquette, David A., "From Disciple to Antagonist: Feuerbach's 'Critique of Hegel'," *Philosophy and Theology* 3 (Winter 1988): 183–99

Kamenka, Eugene, *The Philosophy of Ludwig Feuerbach*, London: Routledge and Kegan Paul, 1970

Wartofsky, Marx W., *Feuerbach*, Cambridge and New York: Cambridge University Press, 1977

Feuilleton

During the 19th century a famous satirical quatrain was published, mockingly wondering whether the word *feuilleton* came from the verb *feuilleter*, to flick through, or vice versa. The genre had already changed by that date, and *feuilleton* had come to mean any sort of **pamphlet**, although it usually denoted an adventure novel, and was an abbreviation of *roman-feuilleton*, which was in turn an expanded form of the original *feuilleton*. The term's meaning changed again in the 20th century in continental Europe, as it became appropriated to define episodic forms in film and television.

In France, the genre was invented by the *Journal de l'Empire* (Journal of the empire), which in 1814 became the **Journal des Débats** (Journal of debates). The early newspapers were simply folded single sheets, printed on both sides, so offering readers four printed pages. The front page was reserved for such matters of public importance as discussions in the Chamber; but on the frequent occasions when there was neither news of sufficient interest to hand, nor anything much to report from current political rhetoric, the editor of the *Journal des Débats* took to tucking the Abbé Geoffrey's pieces of theater criticism under a horizontal rule at the bottom of the front page. This slot was thereafter known, throughout the 19th century, as the "ground floor."

The first *feuilletons* were, therefore, columns of drama criticism, a subject of riveting interest in a Paris of some 630,000 people in 1815: although almost half this number were literate, in the early part of the century it was the stage that was the principal public forum for the imaginative exploration of social and political attitudes – hence the prominence given to commentary about the stage, even if it appeared only on the "ground floor." It was an important time for developments in dramatic form: by 1830 neoclassical declamatory drama was being challenged and replaced in the legitimate theater by the Romantic movement's downmarket tragedies in verse; and the boulevard theaters performed the (even) less literate cultural functions that were more than simple entertainment.

The *feuilleton* evolved as the "ground floor" enlarged its scope beyond drama criticism to include a gazette of events in the worlds of society, the arts, and politics. **Sainte-Beuve's** *Lundis* (Mondays) first appeared as *feuilletons* in a series of newspapers, as he changed his affiliations from the liberal *Le Constitutionnel* (The constitutional) to the official government organ, *Le Moniteur Universel* (The universal monitor), and then to the opposition newspaper, *Le Temps* (The times). Balzac had already used the term *feuilleton* for the 1830 newspaper *Feuilleton des Journaux Politiques* (Feuilleton of political journals), which he coedited with Victor Varaigne and Émile de Guardin. And, on 1 July 1836, Armand Dutacq issued *Le Siècle* (The century) and Girardin brought out *La Presse* at a subscription price of 40 francs, exactly half of what the established newspapers were charging, thereby launching the French popular press.

Novelists had never before written novels as *feuilletons*, for serialization; when they did, they were led inevitably to introduce cliff-hanging breaks in increasingly episodic narratives, full of incredible adventures, and empty of all but the shallowest psychology. Eventually the adventure novels began to appear on their own in weekly or monthly fascicles; these too were known as *feuilletons*. In the meantime, and until the law curbed the new development by putting a tax on advertising, competition for the best authors of *feuilletons* became fierce, and the prices they commanded were huge. In response there was an outcry led by Sainte-Beuve against the "industrial" output of literature (and Girardin, fighting what was in effect a battle for the new press, killed Armand Carrel, defending the old style, in a duel).

Balzac was the first French author to publish a novel in a newspaper: *La Vieille Fille* (The old maid) appeared in 12 installments of *La Presse* during October and November 1836, and *Le Père Goriot* (Old Man Goriot), although it originally had six parts, was written to appear in four installments. Even Flaubert's *Madame Bovary* first appeared serialized in the *Revue de Paris*. The great masters of the genre, after Balzac himself, were Frédéric Soulié, Alexandre Dumas *père*, George Sand, and above all Eugène Sue, whose *Mystères de Paris* (The mysteries of Paris), tracing the relationship between moral values and the social realities of urban life in the capital, was serialized by the *Journal des Débats* from June 1842 to October

1843. Its success was phenomenal: the newspaper's circulation doubled from 5000 to 10,000, a much greater percentage increase than Balzac had achieved in other journals. Véron saved *Le Constitutionnel* by outbidding Girardin's *La Presse* and paying a famously large 100,000-franc fee for Sue's *Le Juif errant* (The wandering Jew) serialization, from June 1844 to July 1845, which raised the newspaper's circulation from 3600 to 25,000 by 1846.

After this heyday of the *roman-feuilleton*, its decline was relatively slow; but the "ground floor" lost all importance after the Franco-Prussian War (1870–71), which few of the large-circulation French newspapers survived.

The *feuilleton* also flourished in Germany. It is sometimes associated with **Christoph Martin Wieland**, cofounder of *Der Teutsche Merkur* (The German Mercury) in 1773, and who edited the newspaper until 1800, after which it declined under K. A. Böttiger. The newspaper ceased publication in 1810. However, the definitive work of Wilmont Haacke, the three-volume *Handbuch des Feuilletons* (1950–53), regards the *feuilleton* as simply that aspect of the early newspapers dealing with cultural issues and events, and traces the form proper back to 1740 in France. Its precursor, though, he sees in the German liberal journal known as the *Vossische Zeitung* (Voss' newspaper), published from 1683 (formally titled the *Berliner Priviligierte Zeitung* [The privileged Berliner newspaper] from 1721), which itself had a forerunner in an untitled news sheet of the early 17th century. The German phrase "unterm Strich," corresponding to the "ground floor" of the French newspapers, has been traced back to the *Nürnberger Correspondenten* (Nuremberg correspondent) of 1831. Of modern German writers of *feuilletons*, the best known is Karl Kraus (1874–1936), founding editor of the Viennese satirical journal *Die Fackel* (1899–1936; The torch).

ANTHONY LEVI

Anthologies

Klassiker des Feuilletons, edited by Hans Bender, Stuttgart: Reclam, 1965
Wiener Meister-Feuilletons: Von Kürnberger bis Hofmannsthal, edited by Jörg Mauthe, Vienna: Wiener Verlag, 1946

Further Reading

Angenot, Marc, "La Littérature populaire française au dix-neuvième siècle," *Canadian Review of Comparative Literature* 9, no. 3 (1982): 307–33
Atkinson, Nora, *Eugène Sue et le roman-feuilleton* (dissertation), Paris: University of Paris, 1929
Bianchi, Angela, *La luce a gas e il feuilleton: Due invenzioni dell' Ottocento*, Naples: Liguori, 1988
Chollet, Roland, "Balzac et le 'feuilleton littéraire'," *L'Année Balzacienne* 5 (1985): 71–106
Eckstein, Ernst, *Beiträge zur Geschichte des Feuilletons*, Leipzig: Hartknoch, 2 vols., 1876
Gislason, Donald Garth, *Castil Blaze, "De l'opéra en France" and the Feuilletons of the "Journal des Débats"* (dissertation), Vancouver: University of British Columbia, 1992
Haacke, Wilmont, *Feuilletonkunde: Das Feuilleton als literarische und journalistische Gattung*, Leipzig: Hiersmann, 1943
Haacke, Wilmont, *Julius Rodenburg und die Deutsche Rundschau: Eine Studie zur Publizistik des deutschen Liberalismus (1870–1918)*, Heidelberg: Vowinckel, 1950

Haacke, Wilmont, *Handbuch des Feuilletons*, Emsdetten: Lechte, 3 vols., 1950–53

Hallig, Christian, *Das Feuilleton der Dresdener Tagespresse von 1864 bis 1880*, Borna-Leipzig: Noske, 1933

Jakoby, Ruth, *Das Feuilleton des Journal des Débats von 1814 bis 1830*, Tübingen: Narr, 1988

Meunier, Ernst, *Die Entwicklung des Feuilletons der grossen Presse*, Nuremberg: Hilz, 1914

Newby, David Ralph, *The Ideology of the Roman-Feuilleton in the French Petite Presse, 1875–1885* (dissertation), Madison: University of Wisconsin, 1993

Oscarsson, Ingemar, "Le Feuilleton dans la presse française dans les années 1790 et au début du 19e siècle," *Dix-Huitième Siècle* 25 (1993): 433–56

Peterson, Gunther, *Feuilleton und öffentliche Meinung: Zur Theorie einer Literaturgattung im Kontext mit ihrem Resonanzfeld*, Wiesbaden: Flieger, 1992

Picard, Michel, "Pouvoirs du feuilleton, ou D'Artagnan anonyme," *Littérature* (May 1983): 55–76

Queffelec, Lise, *Le Roman-Feuilleton français au XIXe siècle*, Paris: Presses Universitaires de France, 1989

Stanitzek, Georg, "Talkshow – Essay – Feuilleton – Philologie," *Weimarer Beiträge* 38, no. 4 (1992): 506–28

Wildhagen, Andreas, *Das politische Feuilleton Ferdinand Kürnbergers: Themen und Technik einer literarischen Kleinform im Zeitalter des deutschen Liberalismus in Österreich*, Frankfurt-on-Main: Lang, 1985

Fichte, Johann Gottlieb

German, 1762–1814

The *Wissenschaftslehre*, hailed by **Friedrich Schlegel** in 1798 as one of the three major accomplishments of its age, was doubtless Fichte's greatest intellectual achievement. In its attempt to reconcile the palpable epistemological dualism in Kantian philosophy between freedom and necessity, subject and object, through the concept of a practically striving, nonderivative "I," this "science of knowledge" serves as the firm starting point for many of Fichte's conceptual essays, e.g. *Das System der Sittenlehre nach den Principien der Wissenschaftslehren* (1798; *The Science of Ethics as Based on the Science of Knowledge*). Even the less technically philosophical and more practical essays, e.g. *Der geschlossne Handelstaat* (1800; The closed commercial state), are indebted to this theory of knowledge. Understandably, scholarship, encouraged by the publication since 1964 of the critical edition of Fichte's works, has tended to view his essays in the light of his philosophy of practical activity. In Fichte's hand the essay is a demonstration of a rational argument or an exhortation to act on the basis of knowledge. Employing both vehicles of formal, scholarly communication and of informal, social communication, Fichte wrote on an impressive range of topics: the desirability of revolution, the mission of the scholar, the state's economic system, the function of religion and aesthetics, patriotic nationalism and the concept of world history, and the organization of the university. His essays were published as books or in the intellectual journals *Allgemeine Literatur-Zeitung* (General literary gazette), *Die Horen* (The muses), and *Philosophisches Journal einer Gesellschaft Teutscher Gelehrtern* (Philosophical journal of the Society of German Scholars).

The essays of this prolific writer, many of which have been translated into English, are directed toward the academic philosopher and, especially after 1800, toward the educated public. To the professional philosopher, the intended reader of his first essay, the generally well-received, book-length essay *Versuch einer Kritik aller Offenbarung* (1792; *Attempt at a Critique of All Revelation*) argued that the basis of revealed religion lies in the sovereignty of a nonempirical law whose acknowledgment strengthens the moral law in humanity. Considered to be **Kant**'s long-awaited **treatise** on religion because it was published by Kant's publisher and even praised by the Königsberg sage, this essay propelled Fichte to fame and ultimately to his appointment to the philosophy faculty at the University of Jena. As successor to the Kantian Karl Reinhold, Fichte gave many successful public lectures in Jena; his *Einige Vorlesungen über die Bestimmung des Gelehrten* (1794; "Some Lectures Concerning the Scholar's Vocation") endeavors through cajoling, analysis, and exhortation to convince his largely student audience that they, as scholars, bear responsibility for supervising the advancement of mankind. Hölderlin, **Novalis**, and Friedrich Schlegel were among the listeners who applauded Fichte's impassioned closing plea for practical engagement: "Act! Act! That is what we are here for!" Following Fichte's relocation to Berlin in 1799, his essays took on a decidedly popular style. *Die Bestimmung des Menschen* (1800; *The Vocation of Man*) consciously attempts to overcome the obscurity of his earlier philosophical essays and speaks in a more conversational tone to the average reader: "And it is to be hoped that the reader . . . will actually hold converse with himself during the act of reading; that he will deliberate, draw conclusions, and form resolutions . . . and thus, by his own labor and reflection, develop and build up purely out of himself that mode of thought the mere picture of which is presented to him in the book." This polyperspective essay weighs in an even-measured, dialogical manner the alternatives of doubt, knowledge, and faith as life orientations before depicting faith's triumph over skeptical, deterministic thinking.

The tone of a Fichtean essay varies immensely. While the technical writings associated with the *Wissenschaftslehre* tend to be demonstrative and sober, the anonymously published lectures of 1794 call passionately, even defiantly, for freedom of the press and represent a rebellious affirmation of nontraditional societal reorganization in terms of Rousseauvian contractualism and Kantian autonomous ethics. The important review of C. G. Schulze's *Aenesidemus* in 1794 in the *Allgemeine Literatur-Zeitung* is remarkable as much as for its defense of Kantian epistemology against Schulze's Hume-like skepticism as it is for its sarcastic and polemical barbs. Similarly, Fichte's acridity toward his censors is revealed in the subtitle "A writing one should read before it is confiscated" of *Appellation an das Publikum . . .* (1799; Call to the public . . .). On the other hand, Fichte could speak in a more moderate voice, as for example in "Über den Grund unsers Glaubens an eine göttliche Weltregierung" (1798; "On the Foundation of Our Belief in a Divine Government of the Universe"), in which he attempted to mediate F. K. Forsberg's radical denial of Christian divinity, but apparently too closely identified God with a self-willed moral world order himself, thus precipitating the famous "Atheismusstreit." This "atheism controversy" was initially a departure of the minds between Fichte and Forsberg, but Fichte's many enemies made sure that he was accused of atheism by the Saxon authorities. The case gained wide popularity as both opponents and defenders of Fichte joined the battle. At stake was essentially Fichte's contention that the existence of God could not be inferred from the moral world order. Ultimately, the debate was a factor in Fichte's dismissal/resignation from his academic post.

If Fichte was considered an effective public orator, his writing was not always accorded equal praise. The conceptual confusion and the abstract, occasionally opaque technical language of his various tracts of the *Wissenschaftslehre*, which included the coining of new words, e.g. "Tathandlung" ("act"), frequently perplexed his contemporaries. Even Fichte himself abandoned hope that he could articulate his concepts effectively. His philosophical **letter**s *Über den Geist und Buchstab in der Philosophie: In einer Reihe von Briefen* (1794; "On the Spirit and Letter in Philosophy, in a Series of Letters") were rejected for publication in **Schiller**'s journal *Die Horen* largely because Fichte, according to Schiller, "thrust[s] the reader directly from the most abstruse abstractions right into harangues." On the other hand, **Goethe** praised *Reden an die deutsche Nation* (1808; *Addresses to the German Nation*), Fichte's most widely known and most accessible essays, for their wonderful style. Based on lectures given in the amphitheater of the Berlin Academy during the Napoleonic occupation (December 1807), these inspirational public talks delineate in a confident, nationalistic tone Fichte's plan for the education of the Germans to their true identity.

Fichte's essays reflect his forceful, occasionally alienating personality. Uncompromising, authoritative, and intense, they vibrate with his contention that "The kind of philosophy one adopts depends upon the sort of man one is . . ." (*Erste Einleitung in die Wissenschaftslehre* [1797; *First Introduction to the Science of Knowledge*]). Fichte's was a moralistic essayism, which sought through linear argument and effective strategies the purposeful if not always aesthetically successful expansion of freedom. Standing in the service of his *Strebungsphilosophie* (philosophy of activity), his essays demand that the reader act in a manner such that the noumenal idea of freedom can be realized in the practical, social world.

EDWARD T. LARKIN

Biography
Born 19 May 1762 in Rammenau, Lausitz. Studied theology at the Universities of Jena, 1780–81, and Leipzig, 1781–84. Private tutor near Leipzig, 1784–88, and in Warsaw and Danzig. Married Johanna Maria Rahn (Klopstock's niece), 1793: one son. Chair of philosophy, University of Jena, 1793–99; dean of the philosophical faculty, 1810, and rector, 1811, University of Berlin. Died (of typhoid contracted from his wife) in Berlin, 29 January 1814.

Selected Writings

Essays and Related Prose
Versuch einer Kritik aller Offenbarung, 1792; as *Attempt at a Critique of All Revelation*, translated by Garrett Green, 1978
Zurückforderung der Denkfreiheit von den Fürsten Europens, die sie bisher unterdrückten (lecture), 1793
Beitrag zur Berichtigung der Urtheile des Publikums über die französische Revolution; Zur Beurteilung ihrer Rechtmässigkeit, 2 vols., 1793; first essay edited by D. Bergner, 1957

Über den Geist und Buchstab in der Philosophie: In einer Reihe von Briefen, 1794; as "On the Spirit and Letter in Philosophy, in a Series of Letters," translated by Elizabeth Rubenstein, in *German Aesthetic and Literary Criticism: Kant, Fichte, Schelling, Schopenhauer, Hegel*, edited by David Simpson, 1984: 74–93
Einige Vorlesungen über die Bestimmung des Gelehrten, 1794; as *The Vocation of the Scholar*, translated by William Smith, 1847; as "Some Lectures Concerning the Scholar's Vocation," translated by Daniel Breazeale, in *Philosophy of German Idealism*, edited by Ernst Behler, 1987: 1–38
Über den Begriff der Wissenschaftslehre, 1794; revised edition, 1798; edited by Hans Michael Baumgartner and Wilhelm G. Jacobs, 1969; as "Concerning the Concept of *Wissenschaftslehre* or, of So-Called 'Philosophy'," translated by Daniel Breazeale, in *Early Philosophical Writings*, 1988
Grundlage der gesammten Wissenschaftslehre, 1794; edited by Hans Michael Baumgartner and Wilhelm G. Jacobs, 1969; as *The Science of Knowledge*, translated by A. E. Kroeger, 1868; as *Foundations of the Entire Science of Knowledge (Wissenschaftslehre)*, with the First and Second Introductions, edited and translated by Peter Heath and John Lachs, 1970
Grundriss des Eigentümlichen der Wissenschaftslehre, 1795; edited by Wilhelm G. Jacobs, 1975; as "Outline of the Distinctive Character of the *Wissenschaftslehre* with Respect to the Theoretical Faculty," translated by Daniel Breazeale, in *Early Philosophical Writings*, 1988
Grundlage des Naturrechts nach Prinzipien der Wissenschaftslehre, 2 vols., 1796–97; edited by Manfred Zahn, 1967; as *The Science of Rights*, translated by A. E. Kroeger, 1869; part as "The Foundations of Natural Law According to the Principles of the Theory of Science," translated by H. S. Reiss and P. Brown, in *The Political Thought of the German Romantics, 1793-1815*, edited by Reiss, 1955: 44–86
Erste und zweite Einleitung in die Wissenschaftslehre, 1797; edited by Fritz Medicus, 1920; as *The First and Second Introductions to The Science of Knowledge*, edited and translated by Peter Heath and John Lachs, 1970
Das System der Sittenlehre nach den Principien der Wissenschaftslehren, 1798; as *The Science of Ethics as Based on the Science of Knowledge*, edited by W. T. Harris, translated by A. E. Kroeger, 1897
Appellation an das Publikum über die durch ein Kurf. sächs: Confiscationsrescript ihm beigemessenen atheistischen Äusserungen: Ein Schrift, die man erst zu lesen bittet, ehe man sie confiscirt, 1799
Die Bestimmung des Menschen, 1800; edited by Theodor Ballauf and Ignaz Klein, 1966; as *The Vocation of Man*, translated by William Smith, 1848, translation revised by R. M. Chisholm, 1956, and Peter Preuss, 1987; as *The Destination of Man*, translated by Mrs. Percy Sinnett, 1846
Der geschlossne Handelstaat: Ein philosophischer Entwurf als Probe einer künftig zu liefernden Politik, 1800
Sonnenklarer Bericht an das grössere Publikum, über das eigentliche Wesen der neuesten Philosophie: Ein Versuch, die Leser zum Verstehen zu zwingen, 1801; as "A Crystal Clear Report to the General Public Concerning the Actual Essence of the Newest Philosophy: An Attempt to Force the Reader to Understand," translated by John Botterman and William Rasch, in *Philosophy of German Idealism*, edited by Ernst Behler, 1987: 39–115
Die Grundzüge des gegenwärtigen Zeitalters, 1806; as *The Characteristics of the Present Age*, translated by William Smith, 1847
Die Anweisung zum seeligen Leben, oder auch die Religionslehre, 1806; edited by Fritz Medicus, 1921; as *The Way Towards the Blessed Life; or, The Doctrine of Religion*, translated by William Smith, 1849
Über das Wesen des Gelehrten, und seine Erscheinung im Gebiete der Freiheit, 1806; as *On the Nature of the Scholar, and Its Manifestations*, translated by William Smith, 1845

Reden an die deutsche Nation, 1808; as *Addresses to the German Nation*, translated by Louis H. Gray, in *The German Classics*, vol. 5, edited by K. Francke and W. G. Howard, 1914: 69–105; edited by George Armstrong Kelly, translated by R. F. Jones and G. H. Turnbull, 1923

Die Thatsachen des Bewusstseyns (lectures), 1817; as "The Facts of Consciousness," translated by A. E. Kroeger, *Journal of Speculative Philosophy* (1871)

The Popular Works, translated by William Smith, 2 vols., 1848–49

Über patriotische Erziehung: Pädagogische Schriften und Reden, edited by Heinz Schuffenhauer, 1960

Early Philosophical Writings, edited and translated by Daniel Breazeale, 1988

Introductions to the Wissenschaftslehre and Other Writings (1797–1800), edited and translated by Daniel Breazeale, 1994

Other writings: philosophical works, and correspondence.

Collected works editions: *Sämmtliche Werke*, edited by Immanuel Hermann Fichte, 8 vols., 1845–46, reprinted 1971; *Werke*, edited by Fritz Medicus, 6 vols., 1908–12; *Gesamtausgabe* (Bavarian Academy Edition), edited by Reinhard Lauth, Hans Jacob, and Hans Gliwitzky, 1964– (in progress).

Bibliographies

Baumgartner, Hans Michael, and Wilhelm G. Jacobs, *Johann Gottlieb Fichte – Bibliographie*, Stuttgart and Bad Cannstatt: Frommann-Holzboog, 1968

Breazeale, Daniel, "Bibliography of English Translations of Fichte's Works and of Works in English About Fichte," in *Fichte: Historical Contexts/Contemporary Controversies*, edited by Breazeale and Tom Rockmore, Atlantic Highlands, New Jersey: Humanities Press, 1994: 235–63

Doyé, Sabine, *J. G. Fichte – Bibliographie (1968–1992/93)*, Amsterdam and Atlanta: Rodopi, 1993

Further Reading

Beiser, Frederick C., *The Fate of Reason: German Philosophy from Kant to Fichte*, Cambridge, Massachusetts: Harvard University Press, 1987

Beiser, Frederick C., "Philosophy and Politics in J. G. Fichte's 1794 *Wissenschaftslehre*," in his *Enlightenment, Revolution, and Romanticism: The Genesis of Modern German Political Thought, 1790–1800*, Cambridge, Massachusetts: Harvard University Press, 1992

Breazeale, Daniel, "Fichte's *Aenesidemus* Review and the Transformation of German Idealism," *Review of Metaphysics* 34 (1981): 545–68

Breazeale, Daniel, "Fichte and Schelling: The Jena Period," in *The Age of German Idealism*, edited by Robert C. Solomon and Kathleen M. Higgins, London and New York: Routledge, 1993

Ebbinghaus, Julius, "Fichtes ursprüngliche Philosophie," in his *Gesammelte Aufsätze, Vorträge und Reden*, Hildesheim: Olms, 1968: 211–25

Fichte and Contemporary Philosophy, *Philosophical Forum* special issue, 19 (1988)

Gardiner, Patrick, "Fichte and German Idealism," in *Idealism, Past and Present*, edited by Godfrey Vesey, Cambridge: Cambridge University Press, 1982: 111–26

Henrich, Dieter, "Fichte's Original Insight," in *Contemporary German Philosophy*, University Park: Pennsylvania State University Press, 1982: 15–53 (original German edition, 1967)

Idealistic Studies issue on Fichte, 62 (1979)

Jacobs, Wilhelm G., *Johann Gottlieb Fichte*, Hamburg: Rowohlt, 1984

Lachs, John, "Fichte's Idealism," *American Philosophical Quarterly* 9 (1972): 311–18

Lauth, Reinhard, "Der letzte Grund von Fichtes *Reden an die deutsche Nation*," *Fichte Studies* 4 (1992): 197–231

Lauth, Reinhard, *Vernünftige Durchdringung der Wirklichkeit: Fichte und sein Umkreis*, Neuried: Ars Una, 1994

Mandt, A. J., "Fichte's Idealism in Theory and Practice," *Idealistic Studies* 14 (1984): 127–47

Rockmore, Tom, *Fichte, Marx, and the German Philosophical Tradition*, Carbondale: Southern Illinois University Press, 1980

Seidel, George, *Activity and Ground: Fichte, Schelling, and Hegel*, Hildesheim and New York: Olms, 1976

Fielding, Henry

British, 1707–1754

Henry Fielding is justly famous for his three great novels – *Joseph Andrews* (1742), *Tom Jones* (1749), and *Amelia* (1751) – and was praised by **George Bernard Shaw** as "the greatest dramatist, with the single exception of Shakespeare, produced by England between the Middle Ages and the nineteenth century." His work as an essayist, stretching from the mid-1730s until the last years of his life, is substantial although less well known. He produced four major **periodicals** – the *Champion* (1739–40), the *True Patriot* (1745–46), the *Jacobite's Journal* (1747–48), and the *Covent-Garden Journal* (1752). In addition, it now appears that from 1734 to 1738 Fielding contributed essays to the *Craftsman*, although his ties to that journal were clandestine. In his essays, Fielding addresses major political and social issues of his day: the prime ministry of Sir Robert Walpole; the Jacobite Rebellion of 1745; problems of crime and poverty in the growing metropolis of London. He comments on literary matters less frequently than he does on political. But the periodicals do include important evaluations of major figures in 18th-century British literature – Pope, **Swift**, **Addison**, and **Steele** – as well as of Fielding's own work. Parson Abraham Adams from *Joseph Andrews* reappears in the *True Patriot*; Fielding defends *Amelia* from criticism in the *Covent-Garden Journal*.

Fielding had a complicated family background, which profoundly influenced his political and literary loyalties. Cousin to the Earls of Denbigh, Fielding's father, Edmund, achieved success and some fame as a soldier, but his splendid social connections paid no bills for him; he was improvident and chronically in debt. Fielding's mother's family was wealthy and landed, but its wealth was not Henry's to inherit. When Henry's mother died in 1718, a custody battle ensued over her children (Henry had five sisters and one brother) between Edmund Fielding and the children's maternal grandmother, who eventually won custody of them and control of their inherited property. Fielding's connections with the social elite, then, were tenuous, even traumatic. He attended Eton with classmates who included William Pitt the Elder and George Lyttelton, but while they went on to Oxford, Fielding attended the University of Leiden for a year until his funds ran out. He then returned to London, a gentleman with no fortune.

Having grown up in Dorset, Fielding tended to idealize rural life, but he chose to earn his living in London. Educated in the classics at Eton, in his career as a playwright he appealed to popular taste, struggling to win the favor of theater managers like Colley Cibber, the prince of Alexander Pope's

Dunces. While he admired the work of Swift and Pope, Fielding was loyal to the memory of his father's commander, the Duke of Marlborough, and remained throughout his life a Whig in politics. In the absence of a viable Tory opposition, however, Fielding could remain loyal to Marlborough's memory, even as he sniped at Walpole. Particularly when his essays treat of matters political, Fielding works between the models of Addison and Steele and of Swift and Pope. In their mediation between the Whig sentiment of the former and the Tory satire of the latter, Fielding's essays achieve their distinctive tone.

The format of the *Champion* – and of all Fielding's subsequent periodicals – followed that of Addison and Steele's **Tatler** and **Spectator**. Sections include a lead essay, home and foreign news (with Fielding frequently commenting wryly upon those news items), and advertisements. Appearing three times a week, the paper, like those of Addison and Steele, relies upon a persona, one Captain Hercules Vinegar. Vinegar, whose namesake was a famous cudgel fighter and prize fight promoter, sets down his club and takes up his pen as a weapon. He appoints himself head of a Court of Censorial Inquiry and brings both literary and political figures to the bar. Vinegar has an extended family, which loosely resembles the Spectator Club in that its members can comment upon all parts of British life. One relative is an expert on foreign affairs, one has studied law, another the classics, another medicine. Vinegar's sons visit theaters and other popular entertainments; his wife has connections with polite families and can report on the activities of the great.

The breadth of the *Champion* diminished over the course of its run. Fielding's coadjutor, James Ralph, who took the pseudonym "Dr. Lilbourne," is described by Fielding in his farewell to the reader (12 June 1740), as ready to "dose" them with political "Physic . . . as often as it is requisite." As the paper continued under Ralph's supervision, it became an anti-Walpole voice. After 12 June, however, Fielding did contribute a series of essays on the "Voyages of Mr. Job Vinegar." Vinegar, in this imitation of *Gulliver's Travels*, visits the Ptfghsiumgski – or "the Inconstants" – who are guilty of all manner of political tergiversation. In a paper for 6 September 1740, Fielding attacks Walpole for patronizing scribblers while the true literary giants – he mentions Pope, Swift, Gay, and Thomson – oppose him.

If Fielding's politics in the *Champion* are uncertain, his literary opinions can also be surprising. While at times he offers fairly sharp criticism of Pope, he also describes him as a poet "whose works will be coeval with the Language in which they are writ." No. 80 puts Colley Cibber on trial for "assaulting" the English language, while no. 75 attacks his *Apology* but praises his early plays. Fielding, who in some of his early satires refers to himself as "H. Scriblerus Secundus," writes essays on the model of Steele, the great rival of the Scriblerians, and uses the letters by which Addison, Pope's Atticus, identified his contributions to the *Spectator* to distinguish his contributions from Ralph's.

In his response to the crisis of 1745 and his subsequent confidence in the "Broad-Bottom" ministry of Henry Pelham, Fielding moved beyond his political uncertainty of the 1730s. The *True Patriot* gave Fielding a chance to define his political loyalties and also to put his conflicting literary loyalties behind him. In its first number, Fielding not only reports the advance of Bonnie Prince Charlie, he also offers news of the death of

Jonathan Swift and a fine eulogy upon him: "He possessed the Talents of a Lucian, a Rabelais, and a Cervantes, and in his Works exceeded them all." Throughout the *True Patriot*, Fielding's treatment of public credit parallels Addison's in *Spectator* no. 3 – a dream vision in which the Stuarts threaten a female personification of credit, and the Hanoverians rescue her. In no. 2 Fielding explicitly avows Addison's *Freeholder* no. 4 as his model for comment upon the stock exchange, particularly those companies like the East India and South Sea, which assumed part of the national debt in exchange for trade monopolies. Fielding celebrates the economic system that Addison and Steele helped to invent and that Swift detested. Defending both the Protestant Succession and the Bank of England, Fielding's loyalties to both Addison and Swift are no longer troubled by the "curse of party."

In the *Jacobite's Journal*, Fielding maintains the course he took in the *True Patriot*, placing himself within a recognizably Whiggish political and literary tradition, turning to the models of Addison and Steele, dropping the persona in which he begins the paper (John Trott-Plaid, a bibulous, bellicose Jacobite) to speak directly in support of Pelham. In no. 36, he transcribes Addison's lead essay from *Freeholder* no. 28; in no. 37, he cites Addison's analysis of the dangers of Jacobitism in 1715 and applies it to 1748. He reopens the "Office of Censor" that Steele's Isaac Bickerstaff established and publishes a letter in no. 30 that refers to "your great Patterns, *Addison* and *Steel* [sic]." But Fielding also suggests that Addison and Steele, like Swift and Pope, must now give way to others.

Fielding's *Covent-Garden Journal* was his last attempt at an ongoing periodical. He opens the paper announcing, "I disclaim any dealings in Politics," and returns to literary criticism and religious and moral instruction. Taking the persona of "Sir Alexander Drawcansir, Knight Censor of Great Britain," he puts himself one last time in the camp of the Tory satirists. Like Hercules Vinegar, Drawcansir concerns himself with "Taste." Pervasive in the journal is the sense that the taste of the social elite – the old English "Genius" – is in decline. Casting himself as an agent of reform, Fielding compares his task to Hercules' cleansing the stables of Augeus (no. 5). If Hercules Vinegar in the *Champion* occasionally brings together political and literary attitudes that reveal Fielding's uncertainty, here Drawcansir reveals an attitude closer to despair.

Throughout this final journal, however, Fielding generally manages to keep his tone light. He proceeds ironically, returning to the model of Swift. He offers mock etymologies and learned discourses that turn upon his readers. Drawcansir, like Vinegar, is a "Censor," and Fielding uses the proceedings of his court to comment upon manners. The *Covent-Garden Journal* also includes a column which reports on cases that Fielding had heard in his magistrate's court. This column, compiled by Fielding's clerk Joshua Brogden but frequently revealing Fielding's hand in it, gives great topicality to the *Journal*; so too do the news columns in which Fielding reprints items from other journals and then reflects upon or satirizes them.

Fielding's essays reveal him working between his great predecessors. As he integrates the genial and tolerant modernity of Addison and Steele with the conservative and satiric classicism of Swift and Pope, Fielding, in the course of his essays, defines a transitional moment in 18th-century British life, even as he limns the combination of sentiment and satire that enriches his novels.

BRIAN MCCREA

Biography
Born 22 April 1707 at Sharpham Park, near Glastonbury. Studied at Eton College, Berkshire, 1719–24; University of Leiden, 1728–29; Middle Temple, London, 1737–40, admitted to the bar, 1740. Playwright, 1728–37: writer and manager, Little Theatre, Haymarket, London, 1736–37. Married Charlotte Cradock, 1734 (died, 1744): one son and four daughters (all but one daughter died). Contributor, the *Craftsman*, 1734–38; editor, the *Champion* (with James Ralph), 1739–40, the *True Patriot*, 1745–46, the *Jacobite's Journal*, 1747–48, and the *Covent-Garden Journal*, 1752. Appointed high steward of the New Forest, Hampshire, 1746. Married Mary Daniel, 1747: one daughter and two sons (another child died). Principal magistrate, City of Westminster, 1748, and County of Middlesex, 1749; chair, Westminster Quarter Sessions, 1749–52. Traveled to Lisbon for health reasons, 1754. Died in Lisbon, 8 October 1754.

Selected Writings

Essays and Related Prose
The Champion; or, British Mercury, with James Ralph, nos. 1–158, 15 November 1739–December(?) 1740; in 2 vols., 1741
Miscellanies, vol. 1, 1743; vol.1 edited by Henry Knight Miller, in *The Wesleyan Edition of the Works*, 1972
The True Patriot; and The History of Our Own Times, nos. 1–33, 5 November 1745–17 June 1746; in *The True Patriot and Related Writings*, edited by W. B. Coley (part of the Wesleyan Edition), 1987
The Jacobite's Journal, nos. 1–49, 5 December 1747–5 November 1748; in *The Jacobite's Journal and Related Writings*, edited by W. B. Coley (part of the Wesleyan Edition), 1974
The Covent-Garden Journal, nos. 1–72, 4 January–25 November 1752; edited by Gerard Edward Jensen, 2 vols., 1915, and Bertrand A. Goldgar (part of the Wesleyan Edition), 1988
Criticism, edited by Ioan Williams, 1970
An Enquiry into the Causes of the Late Increase of Robbers and Related Writings, edited by Malvin R. Zirker, Jr. (part of the Wesleyan Edition), 1988
New Essays by Henry Fielding: His Contributions to the Craftsman (1734–1739) and Other Early Journalism, edited by Martin C. Battestin, 1989

Other writings: five novels (the parody *Shamela*, 1741; *Joseph Andrews*, 1742; *Jonathan Wild*, 1743; *Tom Jones*, 1749; *Amelia*, 1751), 26 plays, poetry, and works of nonfiction.

Collected works editions: *The Complete Works*, edited by William E. Henley, 16 vols., 1902; *The Wesleyan Edition of the Works*, edited by W. B. Coley and others, 1967– (in progress).

Bibliographies
Hahn, H. George, *Henry Fielding: An Annotated Bibliography*, Metuchen, New Jersey: Scarecrow Press, 1979
Morrissey, L. J., *Henry Fielding: A Reference Guide*, Boston: Hall, 1980
Stoler, John A., and Richard Fulton, *Henry Fielding: An Annotated Bibliography of Twentieth-Century Criticism, 1900–1977*, New York: Garland, 1980

Further Reading
Battestin, Martin C., and Ruthe R. Battestin, *Henry Fielding: A Life*, London and New York: Routledge, 1989
Goldgar, Bertrand A., *Walpole and the Wits: The Relation of Politics to Literature, 1722–1742*, Lincoln: University of Nebraska Press, 1976
McCrea, Brian, *Henry Fielding and the Politics of Mid-Eighteenth-Century England*, Athens: University of Georgia Press, 1981
Paulson, Ronald, *Satire and the Novel in Eighteenth-Century England*, New Haven, Connecticut: Yale University Press, 1967
Paulson, Ronald, and Thomas Lockwood, *Henry Fielding: The Critical Heritage*, London: Routledge and Kegan Paul, and New York: Barnes and Noble, 1969
Rawson, C. J., *Henry Fielding and the Augustan Ideal Under Stress*, London and Boston: Routledge and Kegan Paul, 1972
Shaw, George Bernard, Preface to *Plays Pleasant and Unpleasant*, London: Grant Richards, and Chicago: Stone, 1898
Zirker, Malvin R., Jr., *Henry Fielding's Social Pamphlets*, Berkeley: University of California Press, 1966

Fisher, M. F. K.
American, 1908–1992

While the reputation of M. F. K. Fisher as 20th-century America's finest food writer is clearly established, this prolific author and prose stylist rejected the "food writer" label. For Fisher, the writing was never devoted to food or drink itself; her fascination was with the hunger of the human race. Fisher's keen, appreciative eye and elegant, seductive voice earned a wide readership in nonfiction books and in essays, articles, and short stories published in magazines such as the *Saturday Review*, the *New Yorker*, *Gourmet*, and *Vanity Fair* over a career that spanned almost 50 years. The poet W. H. Auden, among others, noted the excellence of her prose.

Fisher, the daughter of a California newspaper editor and educated at three American colleges and the University of Dijon, began her writing career as a freelance magazine writer. She spent her early adult years in southern France, Switzerland, and Mexico before returning to California, where she worked briefly as a screenwriter at Paramount Studios.

Her first book, *Serve It Forth* (1937), established Fisher as a charming and nontraditional food writer who combined scholarship with humorous anecdotes and clever social commentary, writing about the world of food and drink as a devoted amateur who combined ambitious research with good grace. Like her subsequent books on food (*Consider the Oyster*, 1941; *How to Cook a Wolf*, 1942; *The Gastronomical Me*, 1943; and *An Alphabet for Gourmets*, 1949 – all five reprinted as the collection *The Art of Eating*, 1954), this work revealed Fisher as an intellectually ambitious and perceptive writer for whom food preparation was only a small part of a compelling human story. In *How to Cook a Wolf*, a deft and humorous treatment of wartime rationing, the resourceful Fisher offers advice on what to do when the wolf is at your door: invite him in, seduce him, and cook him for supper. In her foreword to *The Gastronomical Me*, she stakes out for herself the territory of hunger: "It seems to me that our three basic needs, for food and security and love, are so mixed and mingled and entwined that we cannot straightly think of one without the other . . . There is a communion of more than our bodies when bread is broken and wine drunk."

The decade of the 1960s marked her greatest contribution to scholarly gastronomic writing. She produced a highly entertaining study of folk remedies, elixirs, and nostrums (*A Cordiall Water*, 1961) and a comprehensive survey of the history of European and American wine-making (*The Story of Wine*, 1962). In 1968 she collaborated with fellow gourmets Julia Child and Michael Field on *The Cooking of Provincial France*. But the scholarly work for which she was most praised was her 1949 translation of Brillat-Savin's *Physiologie du goût* (1825; *Physiology of Taste*).

Fisher also enjoyed a strong reputation as a writer of memoirs whose autobiographical pieces preserve the fragile, disappearing spirit of times and places. Whether the focus of her remembrances is a Quaker community in the southern California of her childhood (*Among Friends*, 1971), the South of France where she spent some 20 years (*A Map of Another Town*, 1964; *Two Towns in Provence*, 1983; *The Boss Dog*, 1991; *Long Ago in France: The Years in Dijon*, 1991), or the northern California wine country in which she spent her final 22 years as an elegant Grande Dame of Sonoma Valley gourmet society (*As They Were*, 1982, and various essays and magazine articles 1970–92), Fisher captures and celebrates precarious 20th-century local cultures whose worlds are being impinged upon by fast food franchises and shopping malls.

Only one volume of her collected essays has been published to date (*As They Were*). Among the attributes cited by its reviewers is Fisher's capacity for drawing vignettes in powerfully sensuous language. She brings to the description of everyday activities a cultural anthropologist's sense of ritual and symbology. Clifton Fadiman has spoken of her as a philosopher of food. Taken as a whole, the body of Fisher's work celebrates the complexities of satisfying our appetites; it explores the culture of sensual and intelligent living.

Her prose style is warm yet precise, in the fashion of **E. B. White** (admired for his control of American language and closely observed life), the one essayist Fisher identified as influencing her own writing. Fisher's readers encounter a passionate and charming voice. In a 1991 interview, the 82-year-old Fisher identified her composed and seductive approach to the reader: "I have to write toward somebody I love. Express myself as that person I love would want me to be." Fisher's essaying voice conveys a rich sense of appreciating the moment, of taking joy in the world she sees around her.

After reaching her 75th year, Fisher entered an impressively productive decade in which she published seven new books and saw several of her earlier works reprinted. After developing rheumatoid arthritis and, later, Parkinson's disease in the 1980s, she wrote by dictating to an assistant. Her book of essays and meditations on aging, *Sister Age* (1984), expresses the sentiments of a woman who accumulates experience with frank, unsentimental good humor and grace. Near the end of her career, she received considerable recognition for her literary accomplishments, being elected to both the American Academy and the National Institute of Arts and Letters.

DALE E. HASKELL

Biography

Mary Frances Kennedy Fisher. Born Mary Frances Kennedy Brenton, 3 July 1908 in Albion, Missouri. Studied at Illinois College, Occidental College, the University of California, Los Angeles, and the University of Dijon, France, 1929–32. Married Alfred Young Fisher, 1929 (divorced, 1938). Lived in Dijon, from 1929, and Vevey, Switzerland, from 1938. Married Dillwyn Parrish, 1940 (died, 1942). Screenwriter in Hollywood, briefly after 1942. Married Donald Friede, 1945 (divorced, 1951): one daughter and one son. Lived in northern California for the last two decades of her life. Awards: California Literature Silver Medal, for *With Bold Knife and Fork*, 1970; Los Angeles Times Robert Kirsch Award, 1984. Member, American Academy, and the National Institute of Arts and Letters. Died in Glen Ellen, California, 22 June 1992.

Selected Writings

Essays and Related Prose
Serve It Forth, 1937
Consider the Oyster, 1941
How to Cook a Wolf, 1942
The Gastronomical Me, 1943
An Alphabet for Gourmets, 1949
The Art of Eating: The Collected Gastronomical Works, 1954
With Bold Knife and Fork, 1969
As They Were, 1982
Sister Age (includes fiction), 1984
Last House: Reflections, Dreams, and Observations, 1943–1991, 1995

Other writings: the novel *Not Now But Now* (1947) (also coauthored a novel with her second husband, 1939), short stories, books about cooking, food, and wine, and memoirs. Also translated *The Physiology of Taste* by Brillat-Savarin (1949).

Further Reading

Angelou, Maya, "M. F. K. Fisher," *People Magazine*, 24 January 1983: 63+
Eames, David, "How to Cook a Life," *Quest* 81 (June 1981): 38–42
Ferrary, Jeanette, *Between Friends: M. F. K. Fisher and Me*, New York: Atlantic Monthly Press, 1991
Fussell, Betty, "The Prime of M. F. K. Fisher," *Lear's*, July–August 1989: 67–71
Greene, Bert, "America's Finest Food Writer – M. F. K. Fisher: An Intimate Portrait," *Food and Wine*, December 1986: 28+
Hawes, Elizabeth, "M. F. K. Fisher: A Profile," *Gourmet*, November 1983: 50+
Lazar, David, *Conversations with M. F. K. Fisher*, Jackson: University Press of Mississippi, 1992
Reardon, Joan, *M. F. K. Fisher, Julia Child, and Alice Waters: Celebrating the Pleasures of the Table*, New York: Harmony, 1991
Reed, Julia, "Eating Well Is the Best Revenge," *U.S. News and World Report*, 8 September 1986: 62+
Reichel, Ruth, "M. F. K. Fisher," Los Angeles *Times*, 6 June 1991: Food Section, 1+
Shapiro, L., "The Fine Art of Remembering," *Newsweek*, 24 September 1990: 71+

Fontenelle, Bernard de

French, 1657–1757

Bernard de Fontenelle had ceased to write works of literary or philosophical importance by the date of his admission to the French Academy on 5 May 1691. He remained an important literary figure, taking part in the defense of the superiority of modern literature over the antique, and he wrote 69 panegyrics on members of the Académie Royale des Sciences who died during his tenure as permanent secretary from 1697. Those of his works which can be called essays were mostly written by 1688, when Fontenelle was 31. The principal exception, the **treatise** on religion known as *De l'origine des fables* (Of the origin of fables) and first published in 1724, a reworking of an earlier *Sur l'histoire* (On history), used to be thought of as an early work. It seems in fact to have been composed between 1691 and 1699, which actually changes its meaning, making its insinuations much more daring.

Fontenelle came from Rouen in Normandy, and **Voltaire** said of him that "he knew how to speak Norman," which means that he knew how to insinuate what he meant without even ironically stating it. Perhaps Voltaire was being unfair, but Fontenelle's early works reverberate with compromising innuendos, suggestions, implications, and questions, without actually stating very much. His cultivated literary technique makes straight-faced and perfectly defensible statements bristle with implied skepticism about conservative religious orthodoxy, and leaves the reader's mind teeming with questions which Fontenelle never presumed directly to ask. It was a technique Fontenelle might have found constraining, but which he adopted with relish, and it constitutes his chief contribution to the essay form.

Fontenelle's first work was the two-volume *Dialogues des morts* and *Nouveaux dialogues des morts* (*Dialogues from the Dead*), two sets of 18 **dialogue**s published anonymously in 1683. Loosely based on Lucian as translated by Nicolas Perrot d'Ablancourt, the *Dialogues* bring together the most unlikely of conversational partners, but permit pointed exchanges. Then appeared the *Entretiens sur la pluralité des mondes* (1686; *Conversations on the Plurality of Worlds*), which, though dialogue in form, comes quite near to being a series of conversational essays. It is an astonishing work of astronomical vulgarization, based on the 1656 translation of *Discoveries of a New World* (1638–40) by John Wilkins. Its tone is provocative. Addressed to a woman, it grossly and amusingly simplifies large concepts: "The whole of philosophy is founded on only two things: we have inquiring minds and poor eyesight."

In 1684 **Pierre Bayle** put his newly founded *Nouvelles de la République des Lettres* (News from the Republic of Letters) virtually at Fontenelle's disposal, although he may well never have met him. In January 1685 he printed Fontenelle's obituary essay on one of Fontenelle's famous uncles, the "Éloge de Pierre Corneille" (Elegy of Pierre Corneille), critical, biographical, knowledgeable, and important for the historical background. From September to November 1685 Bayle published Fontenelle's treatise on the number nine, then other pieces designed to flatter him, before anonymously publishing Fontenelle's own daring "Relation de l'île de Bornéo" (Report on the island of Borneo), a strongly satirical account of religious disputes presenting a conflict between three queens representing respectively Calvinism, Judaism, and Catholicism. Voltaire, who mostly disliked Fontenelle's oblique style, thought that he had risked imprisonment in the Bastille by allowing the "Relation" to appear.

It was possibly to avoid trouble that Fontenelle then immediately published two highly orthodox essays, "Le Triomphe de la religion sous Louis le Grand" (The triumph of religion under Louis the Great) and the "Discours sur la patience" (Discourse on patience). However, he also published his best-known essay, *Histoire des oracles* (1687; *The History of Oracles*), adapted from Antonius van Dale's 1683 *De oraculis ethnicorum*, whose purpose was to destroy a commonly used proof of Christ's divinity, that the pagan oracles which had been thought to foretell his coming fell silent after his birth. Fontenelle removed van Dale's identification of Catholicism with superstition, showing that the oracles were not the work of demons, and that they did not stop with the coming of Christ. On the other hand, Fontenelle also opened up a whole array of further questions about the changing forms historically taken by the search for the meaning of human experience.

In 1686 Fontenelle, who had kept away from metaphysics in the *Conversations*, also published a criticism of Malebranche. His "Doutes sur le système physique des causes occasionnelles" (Doubts about the physical system of occasional causes) criticized the way Malebranche had preserved the credibility of the immortality of the soul by making human knowledge independent of perception by bodily organs.

Fontenelle's literary registers had appeared insubstantial and inconsequential, but he raised by insinuation and innuendo a range of questions covering everything from the nature of the cosmos to the evolution of human belief, and from the triviality of religious disputes to the metaphysics of knowledge. His intervention in major disputes was to be rounded off with the *Digression sur les anciens et les modernes* (1688; Digression on the Ancients and the Moderns), in which another serious, complex issue is simplified to appear trivial. The whole question is "whether the trees which used to be in our countryside were taller than today's." If they were not, then nature has not exhausted itself, and modern authors can equal those of antiquity. In fact, Fontenelle maintains that the race has grown toward its maturity from former childhood, and at their best modern works are superior to those of classical Greece and Rome. Fontenelle, as usual, has protected a radical imaginative power with a flippancy of style and apparent subject.

If *De l'origine des fables* really was an early work, it is perfectly possible to take it at face value and understand it as an essay in intellectual archaeology. Before 1680 Fontenelle's development as a writer makes it unlikely that he was deliberately raising the question of whether fables were early attempts at a scientific explanation of the universe, replaced by the Christian revelation, but with the implication that Genesis, rather than revealed truth, might also have been adapted to a particular stage in our understanding of the origins of the cosmos. After about 1690, it is more likely that Fontenelle would have been raising that question, for "The more ignorant we are, and the less experience we have, the more miracles we see." The chances are that the text was relatively late, and intended to be subversive.

Fontenelle's contribution to the essay form was therefore principally to use the structured format to write at the same time in a multiplicity of registers. He liked to affect a lighthearted salon style, but had penetrating observations to make about the ultimately important subjects. He wrote half a dozen plays and operas, and some lightweight verse, but not even the dialogues gave him the form he really needed. That was the essay, but the essay of tongue-in-cheek pretense, which he brought to a balanced perfection it has scarcely known before or since.

ANTHONY LEVI

Biography

Bernard le Bovier, sieur de Fontenelle. Nephew of the dramatist Pierre Corneille and the poet and dramatist Thomas Corneille. Born 11 February 1657 in Rouen. Studied at a Jesuit college, Rouen, from 1664; studied law, 1672–77. Moved to Paris; involved in literary circles and frequented many salons, especially those of Mesdames de Lambert, de Tencin, Geoffrin, and du Deffand. Contributor, *Le Mercure Galant* (The gallant Mercury), 1677–81. Elected to the French Academy, 1691. Permanent secretary, Académie Royale des Sciences, from 1697, and edited its *Histoire de l'Académie Royale des Sciences* (History of the Royal Academy of Science), 1699–1740, which published *éloges* on many eminent scientists. Patronized by the Regent, receiving a pension and a lodging in the Palais-Royal, early 1700s–31. Elected to the Académie des Inscriptions et des Belles-Lettres, 1701; Member, Arcadian Academy of Rome, Royal Society of London, and the Academies of Berlin, Nancy, and Rouen. Died in Paris, 9 January 1757.

Selected Writings

Essays and Related Prose

Dialogues des morts and *Nouveaux dialogues des morts*, 2 vols., 1683; edited by Donald Schier, 1965, and Jean Dagen, 1971; as *Dialogues from the Dead*, translated by John Hughes, 1708; as *Dialogues of Fontenelle*, translated by Ezra Pound, 1917

Entretiens sur la pluralité des mondes, 1686; enlarged edition, 1687; edited by Robert Shackleton, 1955, and A. Calame, 1967; as *A Discourse of the Plurality of Worlds*, translated by W. D. Knight, 1687; as *A Discovery of New Worlds*, translated by Aphra Behn, 1688; as *A Plurality of Worlds*, translated by John Glanvill, 1695; as *Conversations on the Plurality of Worlds*, translated by William Gardiner, 1715, Elizabeth Gunnig, 1803, and H. A. Hargreaves, 1990

Histoire des oracles, 1687; edited by Louis Maigron, 1908; as *The History of Oracles*, translated by Aphra Behn, 1699

Lettres galantes du Chevalier d'Her***, 1687; edited by Daniel Delafarge, 1961; as *Letters of Gallantry*, translated by John Ozell, 1715

Digression sur les anciens et les modernes, 1688; edited by Robert Shackleton, 1955

Éloges historiques de tous les académiciens morts depuis ce renouvellement, 2 vols., 1709–20; revised edition, as *Éloges des Académiciens de l'Académie Royale des Sciences*, 2 vols., 1731; selections as *Choix d'éloges des savants*, edited by D. Bourel and others, 2 vols., 1981; selections as *The Lives of the French, Italian and German Philosophers*, translated by John Chamberlayne, 1717

De l'origine des fables (treatise), 1724; edited by Jean-Raoul Carré, 1932

Textes choisis, edited by M. Roelens, 1966

Rêveries diverses: Opuscules littéraires et philosophiques, edited by Alain Niderst, 1994

Other writings: poetry, plays, operas, and works on literature, the French theater, and science.

Collected works edition: *Œuvres complètes*, edited by Alain Niderst, 5 vols., 1990–93 (in progress; 6 vols. projected).

Bibliography

Delorme, Suzanne, "Contribution à la bibliographie de Fontenelle," *Revue d'Histoire des Sciences* 10, no. 4 (October–December 1957): 300–09

Further Reading

Bott, François, *L'Entremetteur: Esquisses pour un portrait de M. de Fontenelle*, Paris: Presses Universitaires de France, 1991

Cosentini, John W., *Fontenelle's Art of Dialogue*, New York: King's Crown, 1952

Maigron, Louis, *Fontenelle: L'Homme, l'œuvre, l'influence*, Paris: Plon, 1906

Marsak, Leonard, *Bernard de Fontenelle: The Idea of Science in the French Enlightenment*, Philadelphia: Transactions of the American Philosophical Society, 1959

Niderst, Alain, *Fontenelle à la recherche de lui-même*, Paris: Nizet, 1972

Niderst, Alain, editor, *Fontenelle: Actes du colloque de Rouen, 1987*, Paris: Presses Universitaires de France, 1989

Niderst, Alain, *Fontenelle*, Paris: Plon, 1991

Rendall, Steven F., "Fontenelle and His Public," *MLN* 86, pt. 2 (1971): 496–508

Williams, Charles G. S., editor, *Racine, Fontenelle: Actes du XXIe colloque de la North American Society for Seventeenth-Century French Literature, Ohio State University, Columbus, 6–8 April 1989*, Paris and Seattle: Papers on French Seventeenth-Century Literature, 1990

Forster, E. M.

British, 1879–1970

E. M. Forster's fifth novel, *A Passage to India*, was published in 1924. From then, aged 45, until his death at 91, Forster's publications took the form of essays, biographies, **reviews**, petitions, short stories, lectures, and libretti. After *Passage*, Forster once explained, his desire to write novels simply "dried up." Notwithstanding, his later writings were to sustain the wisdom of the earlier fiction and also help explain it; Forster's essays in large measure reproduce the insights of his novels, making them explicit and political.

Published originally in periodicals such as the **Atlantic Monthly**, the *Listener*, the *New Statesman*, *Oxford and Cambridge Review*, the **Spectator**, and the **Times Literary Supplement**, Forster's essays are collected in three main volumes: *Pharos and Pharillon* (1923), *Abinger Harvest* (1936), and *Two Cheers for Democracy* (1951). While the first centers on Forster's experiences as a World War I Red Cross volunteer in Egypt, the second and third range widely over literary, social, cultural, and biographical themes: from Proust to Marco Polo, music, liberty, Nazism, tolerance, censorship, chauvinism, anti-Semitism, the countryside, Cambridge, the English character, and America.

The epithet "Forsterian" (liberal, unconventional, skeptical, moral) had been in circulation since the critical success of his 1910 novel, *Howards End*. It is important in comprehending Forster's influence as an essay writer to appreciate his achievement in maintaining, through some of the most turbulent years of the 20th century, a personal philosophy of liberal humanism. By the mid-1930s, indeed, he had become a principal moralist of his age. He was a sage (with remarkably few open detractors) who brought liberalism to suburbia; who countered the excesses of the world by demonstrating the powers of self-redemption; who garnered the respect of a whole generation of writers (including **Auden**, Isherwood, Spender, MacNeice, **Cyril Connolly**, and Iris Murdoch) for prescribing in his writings and exhibiting in his life an outspoken personal integrity. As Isherwood concluded (1962), Forster's work stood for "all that is truly worth saving from Hitler."

The most famously Forsterian of the essays is perhaps *What I Believe* (1939). "I do not believe in Belief," Forster begins. "But this is an Age of Faith, and there are so many militant creeds that, in self-defence, one has to formulate a creed of one's own . . . Tolerance, good temper, and sympathy – they are what matter really, and if the human race is not to collapse they must come to the front before long. But for the moment they are not enough, their action is no stronger than a flower, battered beneath a military jack-boot. They want stiffening, even if the process coarsens them. Faith, to my mind, is a stiffening process, a sort of mental starch, which ought to be applied as sparingly as possible. I dislike the stuff. I do not believe in it, for its own sake, at all." What he does believe in, Forster then proceeds to enunciate: individualism – even though individual wholeness may be a myth, since an awareness of individual lives and deaths fosters decent personal relations with others; loyalty, trust, and love between friends – even though in theory human beings do not know themselves and cannot know others; human beings who are sensitive, imaginative, and conscientious, who endure through cruelty and chaos and do not see life in terms of power – even while all live in power's shadow; civilization – those intervals when force and violence are not to the fore, when social organization is based on the distribution of native human goodness rather than a dependence on the God of Christianity or of Government; and democracy, because it grants creative people the opportunity and liberty to make and express themselves, and shuns the hero-worship of Great Men. And he concludes: "So Two cheers for Democracy: one because it admits variety and two because it permits criticism. Two cheers are quite enough: there is not occasion to give three. Only Love the Beloved Republic deserves that."

Particularly characteristic is Forster's combination of affirmation and skepticism. He assumes a liberal humanism, for the purpose of living and as a purpose for living, not blindly, sanctimoniously, or dogmatically, but ironically, in spite of the absurdities of the world, despite the limitations of any human philosophy. Semi-cynical, Forster yet remains semi-idealistic.

Forster's technique of writing was memorably described by Isherwood (1938) as "based on the tea-table." It involves a toning down rather than a heightening of drama and import, accentuating through underemphasis. Unceremonious sentences bear a weight of meaning seemingly disproportionate to their spare scaffolding; the particular is offered as stimulus to generalities, the vivid image standing for the implicit wider idea. Hence, across a diversity of essay topics, there is a familiarity of treatment: personal and personable. Presenting particular ideas in a personal way, Forster eschews simple categorizations and conclusions and evinces instead the complexity of things: the disorder of the world, the paradoxical character of human nature. Thus he abnormalizes the everyday and brings it to consciousness. As **Virginia Woolf** noted, Forster was able to gain perspective on "the simple things which clever people overlooked." He also addresses the reader on equal terms and without trivialization, with an "unforbiddingness" which encourages intimacy and rapport. Finally, while refraining from detailing a political program, and with ready admission of personal inadequacy and provisionality, Forster makes humorous, gentle stabs at pomposity and hypocrisy; by having domestic detail impinge on political sensibility, he makes his politics experiential, of a human size and intelligibility.

Speaking with simultaneous attachment and detachment, as participant, observer, and critic, Forster's essay narration switches between a number of different voices. There is a voice of social realism; there is also a voice of social radicalism and prophecy. There is an ironic voice, veering between the comedic and the satiric, and also a voice of transcendentalism, of Forster proclaiming the inauthenticity of all manner of social exchange, through which (in art) reality only periodically erupts. There is a voice of allegory and romance, as Forster explores elemental human problems in flat characterizations. Finally, there is a voice of mysticism, of Forster seeking insinuations of the infinite in human contact with the earth. There is, in sum, a multiplicity to Forster, of many voices becoming and returning.

When these different voices are critically discussed, their relationship is often found to be perplexing. Woolf claimed an ambiguity and elusiveness at the heart of Forster's writing deriving from the problem of harmonizing the voices so that a coherent vision could emerge. But in not resolving such ambiguity, Forster heightens his writing's effectiveness; reality, he intimates, cannot be described in just one voice. Thus he demonstrates, in **Lionel Trilling**'s phrase (1943), his "whim of iron," insisting that human life must always elude essential definition.

Nonetheless, Trilling (like others) declined to rank Forster as a great critic or theorizer. His critical essays ("T. S. Eliot," 1928; "George Orwell," 1950) are seen as excessively informal, privileging neither distinctions nor judgments. His nonfiction in general is elegant, cultivated, and accomplished, but not unique; contemporary *littérateurs* – **Strachey**, Nicholson – might have written similarly. Even his more theoretical essays ("Jew-Consciousness," 1939; "Does Culture Matter?" 1940) are found to be impressionistic, not architectonic, stimulated by a personal need to validate his individual responses. But then Forster never held criticism in particularly high esteem: criticism could not approach the mystery of the creative arts. Meanwhile, his overriding liberal impulse is to extend the range of his audience's moral imagination, connecting all things, seeing all equally: good-with-evil, not good versus evil.

Since his death, a modish antihumanism has caused Forster's liberal reputation to be queried. But then, as Stephen Spender put it, if Forster appears no longer to speak to us directly, it is likely because we have listened and followed his advice: his writing (fiction and nonfiction alike) has passed into our heritage.

NIGEL RAPPORT

Biography

Edward Morgan Forster. Born 1 January 1879 in London. Studied at Kent House, Eastbourne, Sussex, 1890–93; Tonbridge School, Kent, 1893–97; King's College, Cambridge, 1897–1901, B.A., 1901, M.A., 1910. Contributor to various journals and newspapers, beginning at Cambridge and continuing later, including the *Nation*, the *Daily News*, the *Daily Herald*, the *Athenaeum*, the *Listener*, *London Mercury*, *New Criterion*, *Time and Tide*, and the *New Statesman*. Traveled in Italy, 1901–02, and in Greece and Italy, 1903. Lecturer, Working Men's College, London, 1902–07. Cofounder, *Independent Review*, 1903. Lived in India, 1912–13, and private secretary to the Maharajah of Dewas, India, 1921. Worked for the National Gallery, London, 1914–15. Red Cross volunteer worker, Alexandria, Egypt, 1915–18. Literary editor,

London *Daily Herald*, 1920. Fellow of King's College, Cambridge, and Clark Lecturer, Trinity College, Cambridge, 1927; Honorary Fellow of King's College, 1946–70. Awards: James Tait Black Memorial Prize, 1925; Femina Vie Heureuse Prize, 1925; Royal Society of Literature Benson Medal, 1937, and Companion of Literature, 1961; honorary degrees from eight universities; Honorary Member, American Academy and Bavarian Academy of Fine Arts; Companion of Honour, 1953; Order of Merit, 1969. Died in Coventry, 7 June 1970.

Selected Writings

Essays and Related Prose
Pharos and Pharillon, 1923
Anonymity: An Enquiry (pamphlet), 1925
Aspects of the Novel, 1927
A Letter to Madan Blanchard (pamphlet), 1931
Abinger Harvest, 1936
What I Believe, 1939
Two Cheers for Democracy, 1951
Albergo Empedocle and Other Writings, edited by George Thomson, 1971
Aspects of the Novel and Related Writings, edited by Oliver Stallybrass, 1974
The Uncollected Egyptian Essays, edited by Hilda D. Spear and Abdel-Moneim Aly, 1988

Other writings: six novels (*Where Angels Fear to Tread*, 1905; *The Longest Journey*, 1907; *A Room with a View*, 1908; *Howards End*, 1910; *A Passage to India*, 1924; *Maurice*, 1971 [published posthumously]), short stories, travel writing, and three plays.

Collected works edition: *Works* (Abinger Edition), edited by Oliver Stallybrass and Elizabeth Heine, 1972– (in progress).

Bibliographies

Borrello, Albert, *E. M. Forster: An Annotated Bibliography of Secondary Materials*, Metuchen, New Jersey: Scarecrow Press, 1973
Kirkpatrick, B. J., *A Bibliography of E. M. Forster*, Oxford: Clarendon Press, revised edition, 1985 (original edition, 1965)
McDowell, Frederick P. W., editor, *E. M. Forster: An Annotated Bibliography of Writing About Him*, De Kalb: Northern Illinois University Press, 1976

Further Reading

Beauman, Nicola, *Morgan: A Biography of E. M. Forster*, London: Hodder and Stoughton, 1993
Bloom, Harold, editor, *E. M. Forster*, New York: Chelsea House, 1987
Borrello, Alfredo, *An E. M. Forster Dictionary*, Metuchen, New Jersey: Scarecrow Press, 1971
Borrello, Alfredo, *An E. M. Forster Glossary*, Metuchen, New Jersey: Scarecrow Press, 1972
Bradbury, Malcolm, editor, *Forster: A Collection of Critical Essays*, Englewood Cliffs, New Jersey: Prentice Hall, 1966
Crews, Frederick, *E. M. Forster: The Perils of Humanism*, Princeton, New Jersey: Princeton University Press, 1962
Dowling, David, *Bloomsbury Aesthetics and the Novels of Forster and Woolf*, London: Macmillan, and New York: St. Martin's Press, 1985
Furbank, P. N., *E. M. Forster: A Life*, London: Secker and Warburg, 2 vols., 1977–78; New York: Harcourt Brace, 1978
Gillie, Christopher, *A Preface to Forster*, Harlow: Longman, 1983
Gransden, K. W., *E. M. Forster*, Edinburgh: Oliver and Boyd, revised edition, 1970 (original edition, 1962)
Herz, Judith Scherer, and Robert K. Martin, editors, *E. M. Forster: Centenary Revaluations*, London: Macmillan, and Toronto: University of Toronto Press, 1982
Isherwood, Christopher, *Lions and Shadows: An Education in the Twenties*, London, Hogarth Press, 1938; Norfolk, Connecticut: New Directions, 1947
Isherwood, Christopher, *Down There on a Visit*, New York: Simon and Schuster, and London: Methuen, 1962
Jones, D., "An Interview with E. M. Forster on His Life and His Books," *The Listener*, 1 January 1959
Page, Norman, *E. M. Forster*, Basingstoke: Macmillan, 1987; New York: St. Martin's Press, 1988
Stallybrass, Oliver, editor, *Aspects of E. M. Forster: Essays and Recollections Written for His Ninetieth Birthday, 1st January 1969*, London: Arnold, and New York: Harcourt Brace, 1969
Stone, Wilfred, *The Cave and the Mountain: A Study of E. M. Forster*, Stanford, California: Stanford University Press, 1966
Summers, Claude J., *E. M. Forster*, New York: Ungar, 1983
Trilling, Lionel, *E. M. Forster*, Norfolk, Connecticut: New Directions, revised edition, 1965; London: Hogarth Press, 1967 (original edition, 1943)
Warren, Austin, *Rage for Order: Essays in Criticism*, Ann Arbor: University of Michigan Press, 1948
Wilson, A., "A Conversation with E. M. Forster," *Encounter* 9 (1957)
Woolf, Virginia, "The Novels of E. M. Forster," in her *The Death of the Moth and Other Essays*, London: Hogarth Press, and New York: Harcourt Brace, 1942

Forster, Georg

German, 1754–1794

Georg Forster was born near Danzig and was the oldest of seven children. His father, Johann Reinhold Forster, was a village pastor and played a pivotal role in the younger Forster's life. In 1765 Forster's father received from the St. Petersburg Academy of Science the coveted assignment to travel 4000 kilometers to the German colony along the Volga River, where he was to study the geography, geology, and natural conditions of the region. For the young Forster, who accompanied his father, this experience represented an incomparable early opportunity to observe the relations existing among science, nature, and history. Unfortunately, rightful recognition and compensation for this journey remained mired in the feudal bureaucracy of St. Petersburg. Forster Sr. moved his family to London in 1766, where in the following 12 years the young Forster helped his father with translation work amid economic misery and squalor.

It was at this stage in Forster's development that a momentous adventure once again presented itself in the form of the famous second circumnavigation of the globe by Captain James Cook. England's burgeoning capitalism required new sources of raw materials and production and new markets, along with the knowledge to find and develop them. Such a voyage of discovery was undertaken once again in 1772 by Cook in his ship *Resolution* and Forster's father received a commission as ship's scientist. He was also granted permission to bring along his son Georg.

The three-year voyage, the longest in history, included visits to Antarctica, the Pacific, and Tahiti. Upon his return to England, the 23-year-old Forster immediately combined the experiences of the voyage with personal interpretations. The resulting essay *A Voyage Round the World* (1777) proved to be an intellectual deepening of the literary form of the **travel essay**, taking on board the philosophy of the 18th century.

As a travel essay, *Voyage* continues the search for new human existence beyond the scientific findings it reports. Rather than a series of conclusive findings, it functions as an open-ended search for and understanding of these conclusions. While facts make up the surface, human questions underlie the text. Moreover, Forster does not fall victim to sentimental Romanticism or Rousseauism; rather he seeks to explain individual qualities and traits and to integrate them into an historical framework.

Upon returning to Germany in 1778, Forster found that his long absence had rendered him a virtual foreigner in his native land. Yet it was precisely his lengthy stays in Russia and England and his sea voyage that gave him a broad perspective and an open mind.

Forster continued to expand his circle of friends and acquaintants. Perhaps most productive of these was his friendship and collaboration with Georg Christoph Lichtenberg, with whom he coedited the literary magazine *Göttingisches Magazin* (1780–85), where Forster published a dozen or so essays. Essays such as "O-Tahiti" (1783) and "Cook, der Entdecker" (1787; Cook, the discoverer) demonstrate the continuing influence of the Cook voyage. These travel and **science essay**s again emphasize the meaning of science, the search for truth, and the philosophy of life in a synthesizing treatment of nature, science, and history. It was the human face of science and the possibility of social perfectibility in an historical process that characterized Forster's contribution to the *Göttingisches Magazin*.

After a disappointing teaching stint in Vilnius, Lithuania, Forster returned to Germany in 1787 and in 1788 accepted a position as bibliographer in Mainz. It was here that he wrote the famous "Über Leckereyen" (1788; On sweets) in which he explored issues of nature and culture from the perspective of taste, both palatal and aesthetic. Eschewing both the moral-idealist and the physical-materialist traditions, this essay postulates the central theme of human perfectibility through culture, as well as an enlightened-progressive organization of society. At this time Forster also penned his "History of English Literature" (1789), an inquiry written in English into the relationship between a nation's literature and its politics and economics.

In 1789, on the eve of the momentous events in France, Forster, accompanied by the 21-year-old Alexander von Humboldt, undertook another epic journey, producing his best-known travel essay, *Ansichten vom Niederrhein, von Brabant, Flandern, Holland, England und Frankreich* (1791–94; Views of the Lower Rhine, of Brabant, Flanders, Holland, England, and France). The title *Ansichten* (Views) is deliberately ambiguous, referring both to objects and to reflection or opinion. By traveling outside of Germany – particularly through Holland, site of the first successful bourgeois revolution – Forster began to understand the connections between the rise of the bourgeoisie and the rise of industry and trade. As a travel essay, the *Ansichten* remains sketchy, open, associative, and digressive, combining literary forms such as **letter**, report, **treatise**, polemic, and **meditation**, all in a personal, conversational tone.

The final phase of Forster's life was engulfed by the French Revolution and marked his abandonment of bourgeois-humanistic enlightenment in favor of revolutionary-bourgeois democracy. Following the events of 1789 with interest and, later, the rise of the Jacobins with sympathy, Forster was drawn into the midst of the revolutionary debate, not least because he resided in Mainz, which was conquered in 1792 by the French forces. Demonstrating ever more strongly his willingness and enthusiasm for moving from theoretical enlightenment to revolutionary practice, Forster joined the "Society of Friends for Freedom and Equality" and called for political allegiance to France and the Revolution.

After the Parisian National Commune declared Mainz an independent republic in 1793, Forster felt that its survival was possible only if Mainz joined France. He was accordingly one of three representatives who traveled to Paris to petition for admittance to the French state. The petition was successful but irrelevant, for the very day Forster delivered his speech before the National Commune, the counterrevolutionary army of Prussia reconquered the Rhineland. After four months the Republic of Mainz ceased to be.

As a traitor, Forster had a price of 100 ducats placed on his head. His actions were radically unique for German history, in that he completed the transition from revolutionary writing to revolutionary action.

RALPH W. BUECHLER

Biography

Johann Georg Adam Forster. Born 27 November 1754 in Nassenhuben, near Danzig (now Gdańsk). As a child traveled to Russia, 1765, and later lived in London. Accompanied his father on Captain Cook's second voyage to the South Seas, 1772–75. Professor of natural history, Collegium Carolinum, Kassel, 1778–84, and University of Vilnius, 1784–86. Coeditor, *Göttingisches Magazin der Wissenschaften und Literatur*, 1780–85; contributor to *Göttingische Anzeigen von gelehrten Sachen*, **Der Teutsche Merkur** (The German Mercury), and other periodicals. Married Therese Heyne, 1785 (she deserted him, 1792): two daughters (two others died in infancy). Librarian at the University of Mainz, 1788. Supported the French Revolution; representative of the Mainz Republicans, Paris, 1793, and outlawed in Germany. Died (of complications arising from scurvy; possibly of a stroke) in Paris, 10 January 1794.

Selected Writings

Essays and Related Prose

A Voyage Round the World in His Britannic Majesty's Sloop, Resolution, Commanded by Capt. James Cook, During the Years 1772, 3, 4, and 5, 2 vols., 1777
Ansichten vom Niederrhein, von Brabant, Flandern, Holland, England und Frankreich im April, Mai und Junius, 3 vols., 1791–94
Ausgewählte kleine Schriften, edited by Albert Leitzmann, 1894
Tagebücher, edited by Paul Zincke and Albert Leitzmann, 1914
Ausgewählte Schriften, edited by Rudolf Leonhard, 1928
Kleine Schriften und Briefe, edited by Claus Träger, 1964
Über die Beziehung der Staatskunst auf das Glück der Menschheit und andere Schriften, edited by Wolfgang Rödel, 1966
Schriften zu Natur, Kunst, Politik, edited by Karl Otto Conrady, 1971

Other writings: books on botany, and correspondence. Also translated Kalidasa's *Sakontala* from Sanskrit.

Collected works editions: *Sämtliche Schriften*, edited by G. G. Gervinus, 9 vols., 1843; *Werke* (Germany Academy of Science Edition), 18 vols., 1958–82; *Werke*, edited by Gerhard Steiner, 4 vols., 1967–70.

Bibliography
Fiedler, Horst, *Georg-Forster-Bibliographie, 1767–1970*, Berlin: Akademischer-Verlag, 1971

Further Reading
Bodi, Leslie, "Georg Forster: The 'Pacific Expert' of Eighteenth-Century Germany," *Historical Studies of Australia and New Zealand* 32 (1959): 345–63
Döppe, Friedrich, *Forster in Mainz*, Berlin: Aufbau, 1987 (original edition, 1956)
Gordon, Joseph Stuart, *Reinhold and Georg Forster in England* (dissertation), Durham, North Carolina: Duke University, 1975
Kersten, Kurt, *Der Weltumsegler: Johann Georg Adam Forster, 1754–1794*, Frankfurt-on-Main: Europäische, 1957
Rödel, Wolfgang, *Forster und Lichtenberg*, Berlin: Rütten & Loenig, 1960
Steiner, Gerhard, *Georg Forster*, Stuttgart: Metzler, 1977
Thoma, Friedrich M., *Georg Forster: Weltreisender, Forscher, Revolutionär*, Berlin: Neues Leben, 1954

Franklin, Benjamin

American, 1706–1790

Benjamin Franklin was undoubtedly a living symbol of the Age of Reason; his essays, among the great of that genre, reflect a practical rationalism that goes far beyond a simple record of his life. If **Henry David Thoreau** was born, as he said, in "the nick of time," so too was Franklin; if Thoreau revolted against materialism, so too did Franklin revolt against the speculative and introspective reasoning of the Puritans. A materialist and pragmatist, he wanted to be directly involved in the world.

To understand Franklin and his idea of involvement, one must start with his *Autobiography* (1791). Arguably the first great work in American literature, it presents a guide for living in a world that was vastly different from that of England or Europe. While some have criticized Franklin for a faulty style and a lack of imagination, not to mention a soulless philosophy of life, the *Autobiography* is clearly a rags-to-riches success story of considerable proportion; moreover, any examination of Franklin's career will reveal him as a man who could get things done, from starting a lending library in Philadelphia to achieving a treaty with France.

Addressed to his son, the *Autobiography* has as its central theme Franklin's rise from poverty and obscurity, as he puts it, "to a state of affluence and some degree of celebrity in the world." Utilizing a personal, almost folksy, style, he works his way from his infancy to his 51st year in an attempt to create a guide to the achievement of what has come to be called the American Dream. He was mapping new ground, for the New World demanded adaptation to new conditions and a new reality. For Franklin the key was experience and reason. By applying the latter to the former, one could win in the game of life. In a very real sense life was a game to Franklin, one he enjoyed playing, just as he enjoyed the knowledge that he was a symbol of an age. It is the fact of this knowledge that gave Franklin an ironic way of seeing and presenting himself in the *Autobiography*.

At first the *Autobiography* appears to be a loosely structured reminiscence expressed in a conversational style. However, there is a method and order to the work, just as there was to Franklin's everyday life. More important, however, is the tone of the *Autobiography*, which might best be described as refreshing, not only for the times in which it was written, but also for today. Combining humor with self-exaggeration, Franklin exhibits himself to the reader as a cross between a naive bumpkin and an insightful man of the world. Ever ready to admit to errors in his career, he never lets the reader lose sight of the basis of his success: a pragmatic activism marked by optimism and the desire to make both himself and the world around him better. It may take some stretch of the imagination to agree with Franklin that virtue may be achieved by a specific set of steps or rules, yet in his view becoming virtuous was like the learning of any art. As he wrote to Lord Kanes in 1760, to acquire those virtues that are wanting "is the subject of an art." As the *Autobiography* and Franklin's other writings show, for him there was no such thing as abstract reality.

What the *Autobiography* lays out in a discursive prose style, *Poor Richard's Almanack* (begun in 1732) presents in the staccato style of axioms. The fact that Franklin's work sold out in one month attests to the popularity of almanacs at the time. For Franklin, it was the ideal medium in which to present his rules for living the successful life. Along with the sayings of Poor Richard, Franklin's **personal essays**, the *Silence Dogood Papers* (1721–23), the *Busy-Body Papers* (1728), and the *Bagatelles* (1776–85) illustrate the versatility of his creative talents. These essays cover a wide range of topics, reflecting his seemingly endless interests in the world around him. He is at his best in the *Bagatelles*, most of which were **letters** written to Mmes. Brillon and Helvetius while he was in Paris from 1776 to 1785. The bagatelle, as Franklin conceived of it, was a lighthearted essay or letter in which he could make good use of his charm and wit, as well as his broad knowledge and his consummate skill in the essay form.

As he did in so many areas, Franklin left an indelible mark on the essay in America. Perhaps he sums himself up best:

If you wou'd not be forgotten
As soon as you are dead and rotten,
Either write things worth reading
Or do things worth the writing.

WILTON ECKLEY

Biography
Born 17 January 1706 in Boston. Studied at Boston Grammar School, 1714; George Brownell's School, Boston. Apprenticed to half-brother James' printer business, from 1718; contributor of the "Silence Dogood" articles, *New-England Courant*, 1721–23; worked for printers in Philadelphia, 1723–24, 1728, and London, 1724–25; clerk for Denham merchant, Philadelphia, 1726–27; established his own printing business, publishing the *Pennsylvania Gazette*, 1728, 1729–66 (copublisher, from 1748), *Philadelphische Zeitung* (Philadelphia news), 1732, and *Poor Richard's Almanack*, 1732–57. Married Deborah Read, 1730 (died, 1774): one son and one daughter; also had a son and daughter with another woman. Served in the Pennsylvania Assembly, 1736–64: London agent for the Assembly, 1757–62, 1764–75; also colonial agent for Georgia, 1768, New Jersey, 1769, and Massachusetts, 1770; deputy

postmaster, Philadelphia, 1737–53, and joint deputy postmaster of the colonies, 1753–74; publisher and editor, *General Magazine and Historical Chronicle*, 1741; delegate to the Second Continental Congress, 1775–76; member of the drafting committee and signatory of the Declaration of Independence, 1776; sent to France as commissioner to negotiate with the French, 1776; lived at Passy, near Paris, establishing a press, 1776–85; member of commission to negotiate peace with Britain, from 1781 (treaty signed, 1783); returned to Philadelphia, 1785. Also inventor of the Franklin Stove, 1739; studied electricity and performed the famous kite, key, and lightning experiment, 1752. Awards: Royal Society Copley Medal, 1753; honorary degrees from five colleges and universities. Fellow, Royal Society (London), 1756; Member, French Academy of Sciences, 1772. Died in Philadelphia, 17 April 1790.

Selected Writings

Essays and Related Prose
The Silence Dogood Papers, in *New-England Courant*, 1721–23
The Busy-Body Papers, in *American Weekly Mercury*, 1728
Political, Miscellaneous, and Philosophical Pieces, edited by Benjamin Vaughan, 1779
Philosophical and Miscellaneous Papers, edited by Edward Bancroft, 1787
Autobiography, 1791; first complete edition edited by John Bigelow, 1868; edited by J. A. Leo Lemay and P. M. Zall, 1986, and Louis P. Masur, 1993
Satires and Bagatelles, edited by Paul McPharlin, 1937
Autobiographical Writings, edited by Carl Van Doren, 1945
Franklin's Wit and Folly: The Bagatelles, edited by Richard E. Amacher, 1953
The Political Thought, edited by Ralph L. Ketcham, 1965
The Autobiography and Other Writings, edited by Peter Shaw, 1982, Kenneth Silverman, 1986, and Ormond Seavey, 1993

Other writings: works on science, history, and politics.

Collected works editions: *Writings*, edited by Albert Henry Smyth, 10 vols., 1905–07; *The Papers of Benjamin Franklin* (Yale Edition), edited by Leonard W. Labree, Whitfield J. Bell, Jr., and others, 31 vols., 1959–95 (in progress); *Writings* (Library of America Edition), edited by J. A. Leo Lemay, 1987.

Bibliographies
Buxbaum, Melvin H., *Benjamin Franklin, 1721–1906: A Reference Guide*, Boston: Hall, 1983
Ford, Paul Leicester, *Benjamin Franklin Bibliography: A List of Books Written by, or Relating to, Benjamin Franklin*, Brooklyn: Historical Printing Club, 1889

Further Reading
Aldridge, A. O., *Benjamin Franklin and Nature's God*, Durham, North Carolina: Duke University Press, 1967
Amacher, Richard, *Benjamin Franklin*, New York: Twayne, 1962
Conner, Paul W., *Poor Richard's Politicks: Benjamin Franklin and His New American Order*, New York: Oxford University Press, 1965
Crane, Verner, *Benjamin Franklin and a Rising People*, Boston: Little Brown, 1954
Fay, Bernard, *Bernard Fay's Franklin, the Apostle of Modern Times*, Boston: Little Brown, 1929
Lingelbach, William, "Studies on Benjamin Franklin," *Proceedings of the American Philosophical Society* 99, no. 6 (December 1955): 359–73
Nolan, J. Bennett, *Benjamin Franklin in Scotland and Ireland, 1759 and 1771*, Philadelphia: University of Pennsylvania Press, 1956

Parton, James, *The Life and Times of Benjamin Franklin*, New York: De Capo, 1971 (original edition, 1864)
Sanford, Charles L., editor, *Benjamin Franklin and the American Character*, Boston: Heath, 1955
Sellers, Charles Coleman, editor, *Benjamin Franklin in Portraiture*, New Haven, Connecticut: Yale University Press, 1962
Tourtellot, Arthur Bernon, *Benjamin Franklin: The Shaping of Genius: The Boston Years*, Garden City, New York: Doubleday, 1977
Van Doren, Carl, *Benjamin Franklin*, New York: Viking Press, 1938; London: Putnam, 1939
Wright, Esmond, *Franklin of Philadelphia*, Cambridge, Massachusetts: Harvard University Press, 1986

Freire, Paulo
Brazilian, 1921–1997

Philosopher, educator, attorney, revolutionary, and later secretary of education in São Paulo, Paulo Freire is best known for his work on the themes of oppression and liberation. Literally hundreds of essays stemmed from Freire's philosophical theories of education, democratization, and "conscientization." Between 1947 and 1959, Freire was involved with literacy education in the northeast of Brazil, a center of poverty and illiteracy. In the early 1960s, he became more and more involved in literacy projects, usually centered among the student-dominated Popular Culture Movement. Among the Movement's many goals was that of consciousness-raising among the poor. Freire and his followers had to suspend their efforts abruptly with the Brazilian military coup of 1964, at which time he was arrested; he later left Brazil for Chile, where he worked as a UNESCO consultant and with the Agrarian Reform Training and Research Institute. During these tumultuous years, Freire traveled throughout the "Third World" and began refining his philosophy of education, first published in English as *Pedagogy of the Oppressed* (1970). The book was then published in Spanish because it was prohibited in Freire's own country, Brazil.

In *Pedagogy of the Oppressed*, Freire evolved his theory for the education of illiterate adults based on the conviction that every human being, no matter how "ignorant" or how far submerged in the "culture of silence," is capable of looking critically at the world in a dialectical encounter with others. This dialogue can only be achieved if each person is conscious of his or her own position in society. Education, Freire argues, cannot be of the "banking" kind. "Banking" education – in which an authoritarian figure "deposits" bits of knowledge into a learner and the latter "receives" this deposit without question – is seen as an instrument of oppression. For Freire, educational systems in the Third World are the chief tools used by oppressive elites to dominate the masses. It is only through "conscientization" that individuals may become aware of true reality.

Freire did not deny the need for factual education – perhaps even some "banking" knowledge may be required; however, this type of learning is to be a step toward the democratization and equalization of the dialectical system. Freire insisted, in both thought and action, that words and themes used in literacy programs must be relevant and common among the people being educated. The content of education is to be determined jointly with the people who are to pursue the learning. Freire's idea of "learning to question" reaches not only the learner but also the educator. It is only through the "conscientization of the educator that the learner will become more conscious of his or her oppression." Educators, he maintained, must question their own philosophical stance.

Peter L. McLaren (1994) deconstructs Freire's essays in a mirror-like opposition to "the discursive trail from consciousness to language, from the denotative to the performative, and from the hypothesis to the speech-act." What Freire attempted in his own essays was to build from speech-act to performative to denotative to language to consciousness. Is this utopian paradox possible? In *The Politics of Education* (1985), Freire establishes once again that "it is necessary to have faith in the people, solidarity with them. It is necessary to be utopian." If educators take this stance, he believes they will be able to carry out the project of "transforming and recreating the world."

From the publication of the *Pedagogy of the Oppressed* through the publication of *Pedagogy of Hope: Reliving "Pedagogy of the Oppressed"* (1994), Freire thought and rethought his position as the consciousness-raising advocate of the early 1960s. He claimed that he "writes what he does"; his essays were merely "reports" of his activities. Freire's critics claimed that his utopian society is pointless in Brazil, a country dominated by a small elite. His followers expanded his theories to industrialized nations where the "banking" model of education has failed.

In the last 30 years, Freire's work has been studied throughout the world. His philosophy has been one of the major influences to emerge from Latin America. In his own words, in an interview with Carlos Alberto Torres, Freire concludes, "the limits of education would bring a naive man or woman to desperation. A dialectical man or woman discovers in the limits of education the *raison d'être* for his or her efficiency. It is in this way that I feel that today I am an efficient Secretary of Education because I am limited." Thus, Freire returned to his main thesis that it is only through the conscientization of the educator – the understanding of limitations – that dialogue begins.

CARMEN CHAVES TESSER

Biography
Born 19 September 1921 in Recife, Pernambuco. Studied at the University of Recife, Ph.D., 1959. Married Elza Maia Costa Oliveira, 1944 (died, 1986): three daughters and two sons. General coordinator of National Plan for Adult Literacy, northeastern Brazil, 1947–59. Professor of history and the philosophy of education, University of Recife. Imprisoned briefly after military coup, 1964; moved to Chile, where he worked for UNESCO and the Chilean Institute for Agrarian Reform, for five years. Visiting professor, Harvard University School of Education, Cambridge, Massachusetts, from 1969. Consultant to the Office of Education, World Council of Churches, Geneva, 1974–81. Professor of education, Pontifical Catholic University of São Paulo, from 1981. Secretary of education, São Paulo, 1988–91. Married Ana Maria Araújo, 1988. Awards: honorary degrees from 29 universities. Died 2 May 1997.

Selected Writings

Essays and Related Prose
Educação como prática da liberdade, 1967; as *Education for Critical Consciousness*, 1973; as *Education, the Practice of Freedom*, 1976

Sobre la accion cultural: Ensayos escogidos, 1969
Pedagogy of the Oppressed, translated by Myra Bergman Ramos, 1970; revised edition, 1996
La demitificación de la concientización y otros escritos, 1975
Ação cultural para a liberdade e outros escritos, 1976
Cartas a Guine-Bissau: Registros de uma experiencia em processo, 1977; as *Pedagogy in Process: The Letters to Guinea-Bissau*, translated by Carmen St. John Hunter, 1978
The Politics of Education: Culture, Power, and Liberation, translated by Donaldo Macedo, 1985
Pedagogy of Hope: Reliving "Pedagogy of the Oppressed", translated by Robert R. Barr, 1994
Letters to Cristina, translated by Donald Macedo, 1996

Further Reading
Bullough, Robert V., Jr., and Andrew D. Gitlin, "Challenging Teacher Education as Training: Four Propositions," *Journal of Education for Teaching* 20 (1994): 67–81
Elias, John L., *Paulo Freire: Pedagogue of Liberation*, Melbourne, Florida: Krieger, 1994
Elias, John L., and Sharan B. Marriam, *Philosophical Foundations of Adult Education*, Melbourne, Florida: Krieger, 1995
Kanpol, Barry, and Peter McLaren, editors, *Critical Multiculturalism: Uncommon Voices in a Common Struggle*, Westport, Connecticut: Bergin and Garvey, 1995
McLaren, Peter L., and Colin Lankshear, *Politics of Liberation: Paths from Freire*, London and New York: Routledge, 1994
Mayo, Peter, "Synthesizing Gramsci and Freire: Possibilities for a Theory of Radical Adult Education," *International Journal of Lifelong Education* 13 (1994): 125–48
Shor, Ira, and Paulo Freire, *A Pedagogy for Liberation: Dialogues on Transforming Education*, South Hadley, Massachusetts: Bergin and Garvey, and Basingstoke: Macmillan, 1987
Wong, Pia Lindquist, "Constructing a Public Popular Education in São Paulo, Brazil," *Comparative Education Review* 39 (1995): 120–41

French Essay

1. Montaigne, The 16th and 17th Centuries
It is in 16th-century France, with the *Essais* (1580, 1588; *Essays*) of **Michel de Montaigne** (1533–92), that the essay had its origins. One of his basic tenets was to write extensively about himself. Autobiography had already been established as an acceptable form in Renaissance Italy and the acceptance of the individual self as subject matter was already affirmed when his *Essais* appeared on the scene (Peter Burke, 1981). Yet the *Essais* are not exactly autobiographical in nature, and Montaigne may not have known these autobiographical works when he began writing. As for the existence of short prose pieces on a variety of topics, Burke has this to say: "The idea of publishing a discursive treatment of different subjects within the covers of a single volume was not new in Montaigne's day." These collections were called "miscellanies" or "discourses," the latter being a "revival of the Greek *diatribe*, which may be defined as the short treatment of a moral theme, written in a vivid, immediate, and humorous way so that the reader has the sense of listening to the author." Montaigne knew, and was inspired by, **Plutarch**'s *Moralia*, a collection of such diatribes; he also knew the French translation of the Spanish author Pedro Mexía's *Silva de varia lección* (1544; *The Forest; or, Collection of Histories*), discourses which deal

with many of his own subjects; and the *Adagia* (1500) and *Apophthegmes* (1531) of **Erasmus**, an important precursor as an adversary of Ciceronian discourse. Other proto-essay forms that influenced him, especially from classical antiquity (in addition to Plutarch), were **Seneca**'s *Letters to Lucilius*, Horace's verse epistles, and **Plato**'s *Dialogues*. But in the end Montaigne's originality is unassailable. No one, as he rightly acknowledged, had ever written a work exactly like his *Essais*.

For Montaigne, his *essais* were less a literary form created by a self-conscious artist than "attempts" (the original meaning of the word) at "trying himself" in writing against a great number of challenges, with the practical goal of living more wisely. The complete title of his work is in fact *Essais de Michel de Montaigne*, or "Self-testings of Michel de Montaigne." Donald Frame (1969) points out that Montaigne's title was used "to designate not a genre but a procedure for exploring and revealing the self." Some of the features of the *Essais* were unique to their author and scarcely imitable by future essayists: the central role of his friend Étienne de La Boétie (1530–63) in their inspiration; the extensive and highly original use of quotations, especially from classical authors; the disguising of his heterodox opinions by means of misleading titles given to individual essays; the abundant additions he made from one edition to the next, rendering the definitive text a palimpsest of meanings; the profound skepticism (that of a Catholic fideist) concerning the possibility of attaining certain truth outside of Christian revelation, a skepticism embodied in the very form of his essays. On the other hand, many features of the *Essais* were to remain genetically imprinted, so to speak, in the future essay of many lands: the highlighting of the "self" as both subject and point of view, more precisely the "observing self" (Graham Good, 1988), open to reflection on an endless variety of subjects; the tendency to reflect on the essay itself as subject matter ("Others write about various subjects; Montaigne writes about writing itself," observed Marie de Gournay in her preface to the 1595 edition of the *Essais*); the fortuitous association of ideas and apparent randomness of form, resulting in a kind of artful disorder; and finally, the foregoing of the definitive expression of thought in favor of the expression of thought, so to speak, "in process."

Montaigne is a rare example in literary history: the inventor of a literary type whose mastery of the type has remained unexcelled. The Greek tragedians met their match in Shakespeare; Aristophanes and Plautus met theirs in Molière; Cervantes met his in later novelists. "The perfection of any artistic form is rarely achieved by its first inventor. To this rule Montaigne is the great and marvelous exception" (**Aldous Huxley**, preface to *Collected Essays*, 1960). Having said this, however, one must also recognize that he left the field open for many types of essays that he could hardly have envisioned, such as the **periodical essay**, and for essayistic features that would be absorbed into what we might call "disguised essays" in all their various forms.

The development of the essay in France in the late 16th and 17th centuries largely coincides with the story of how the *Essais* were received and the extent of their influence, a story that has been told by such Montaigne scholars as Frame, Pierre Villey, Alan Boase, and Ian Winter. In the 1580s his example encouraged the vogue of *discours* and even a few direct

imitations of his essay form. His influence reached abroad to Italy, Spain, and England. English followers, unlike their French counterparts, who were shy about adopting a title that seemed to be Montaigne's private property, eagerly borrowed the title. The most famous of these was **Francis Bacon**, who in his *Essayes* (1597, 1612, 1625) brilliantly reinvented the form along lines quite different from Montaigne's. In France, with changes in taste and the advent of the literary movement known as "classicism," a sharp dichotomy occurred in Montaigne's reception: on the one hand, his *thought* as moralist, skeptic, and promoter of the ideal of gentlemanly cultivation (*l'honnêteté*) was highly respected; on the other, his literary *form* (or what appeared to be formlessness) as well as his archaic, often coarse language and his abundance of personal detail were frowned upon. (This duality in the reception of his work would continue well into the 18th century.) Few were the writers who admired his whole project and imitated his form. One such was Pierre de L'Estoile (1546–1611) in his *Registre-Journal* (1606), whose title echoes the master's view of his essays as being the "register" of his experiences. The well-intentioned Pierre Charron (1541–1603) showed how little he understood Montaigne's originality as an essayist by publishing *De la sagesse* (1601; *Of Wisdom*), the first of what would be a long line of reductions of the *Essais* to a compendium of systematic thought. The jurist Étienne Pasquier (1529–1615) thought the *Essais* could be improved upon by eliminating a quarter of the text, cutting out all the self-descriptions!

If 17th-century authors tended to avoid the use of the title *essai* for their short prose pieces, preferring to call them *discours, dissertations, réflexions, considérations, traités*, etc., the usage did catch hold of calling long prose explorations of a given subject *essais*. A precedent existed for this in the 16th century, in the political work of Montaigne's friend, La Boétie, his *Discours de la servitude volontaire* (1548; *A Discourse of Voluntary Servitude*), which Montaigne himself describes as having been written "by way of *essay*" "par manière d'essai." Great momentum was given to this use of the title by the philosopher René Descartes (1596–1650), who describes his *Discours de la méthode* (1637; **Discourse on Method**) as being "essais de cette méthode." "Trials *of*" evolved into "Essays *on*," in such later works as the *Essai sur les mœurs et l'esprit des nations* (1756–63; *Essay on the Manner and Spirit of Nations*) by **Voltaire**.

Before surveying the leading 17th-century essayists the essay should be considered in its relation to classical literary doctrine and to a form of resistance to this doctrine, namely, the defense of the literary rights of fragmentary and discontinuous prose. The ideal of French classicism had as its basic principles: imitation (more exactly, emulation) of the Greco-Roman "ancients"; the assignment of the forms (mostly verse) inherited from them to a hierarchy of genres; selectivity in choice of matter; impersonality; and highly polished, well-structured form. Obviously the essay had no place in this canon: its creator was less than a century old; it was all-inclusive in subject matter, defiantly personal, embedded in personal circumstances, loosely structured, open-ended, and closer to the process of thinking itself than to any finished product of thought. But the essay's exclusion, like the novel's, from the realm of consecrated literary forms meant that, like the novel, it had no need to conform to the strictures governing such "higher" forms as epic, tragic, comic, or satirical verse and could develop with perfect freedom. Perhaps even more significantly – as has been shown in the pioneer study by Jean Lafond and others, *Les Formes brèves de la prose et le discours discontinu (XVIe–XVIIe siècles)* (1984; Brief prose forms and discontinuous discourse in the 16th and 17th centuries) – Montaigne's essays figure prominently in the assault against classical doctrine by partisans of prose forms marked by brevity, fragmentariness, and discontinuity. Traditional rhetoric, deriving in great part from oratory, favored well-rounded, self-contained discourse of a certain amplitude with a beginning, a middle, and an end; it dismissed short prose forms such as **maxim**s as being *materials* for a literary work rather than a *true literary work*. Montaigne, an enemy of rhetoric, especially of the Ciceronian style, based his writing not on an oratorical but on a conversational model and defended both discontinuity and the relative autonomy of each fragmentary member ("chaque lopin" was his term) of his discourse. He was thus a pioneer in what Lafond, apropos of **La Rochefoucauld** (1613–80), calls strikingly "the aesthetics of the unfinished" ("l'esthétique de l'inachèvement"), a concept that was to have important repercussions in the Romantic and post-Romantic eras. The *Réflexions; ou, Sentences et maximes morales* (1665; popularly known as *Maximes*) of La Rochefoucauld are too brief to qualify as true essays; but both he and **Jean de La Bruyère** (1645–96), with his *Les Caractères ou mœurs de ce siècle* (1688; *Characters, or the Manners of the Age*), made literary history by boldly defying classical doctrine and claiming for their fragmentary discourse true literary stature.

Among 17th-century essayists who have been relegated by posterity to minor status are François de La Mothe le Vayer (1588–1672), whose loosely constructed self-examination and confession, *Prose chagrine* (1661; Distressed prose), is directly imitative of the *Essais*; **Jean-Louis Guez de Balzac** (1597–1654), an important figure in the evolution of classical French prose whose *Dissertations critiques* (1657) are ambiguous in their attitude toward Montaigne, deploring the *Essais*'s "lack of construction" but admitting, in a famous phrase, the charm of their digressions: "Montaigne does not always know where he is going [but] when he casts aside something good it is usually to find something better"; and Antoine Gombaud de Méré (1607–84), friend of Balzac and of Pascal (he exerted a marked influence on Pascal's concept of the *esprit de finesse*), whose essays and letters, published posthumously (*Œuvres posthumes*, 1700), reveal imitations of Montaigne's essay form (Alan Boase, 1935).

One of the few 17th-century writers to use the title "Essays" was the Jansenist theologian, Pierre Nicole (1625–95), in his *Essais de morale* (1671; *Moral Essays*). Little attempt to imitate Montaigne here, either in form or (even less) in self-portraiture (Nicole would have agreed with Pascal that "the 'I' is detestable" – "le moi est haïssable"); the Montaignean tradition he is appealing to is that of the modest attempt to deal with a subject, in this instance Christian ethics, that is too vast to handle otherwise. In any case Nicole is a pale, minor essayist compared to the incomparably greater "essayists in disguise" (that is, who used other titles): **Blaise Pascal** (1623–62), **Madame de Sévigné**, La Bruyère, and, the most self-conscious essayist as well as the closest in inspiration to Montaigne, **Saint-Évremond**.

The unfinished apology for the Christian religion that is Pascal's *Pensées*, first published in 1670, for obvious reasons figures prominently in the 17th-century debate about the literary fragment, but it also contains Pascal's famous ridicule of Montaigne's "silly project of depicting himself." Pascal's real claim as an essayist is found in his letters to a friend in the provinces and to Jesuit Fathers concerning matters of morality and politics, published under the pseudonym of "Louis de Montalte" and familiarly known as the *Lettres provinciales* (1656–57; *The Provincial Letters*). Here he gladly acknowledged his debt to Montaigne's "insinuating" conversational style, the *style coupé* ("abrupt style") inherited by way of Montaigne from Seneca. The essay as a public **letter** also harks back to Seneca, and we recall that Montaigne viewed his essays as letters to an ideal friend. The brilliant, highly original polemical masterpiece of *The Provincial Letters* foreshadows such 18th-century polemicists as Voltaire as well as the modern journalistic essay.

Madame de Sévigné (1626–96) also used the letter form: in her case, letters primarily to her daughter which were circulated privately before being first published posthumously in 1725 and then subsequently in much enlarged editions. The 19th-century critic **Sainte-Beuve** wrote perceptively (in an essay from 1829) of what we would now call her "essayistic" qualities. He compared her humor to that of the English. "As a rule," he added, "she set down whatever sprang to her mind, and as many things as possible," letting her pen "trot along" and "glide over" (a phrase reminiscent of Montaigne) an abundance of ideas. Of the two types of style he found predominant in the 17th century, the one "austere, polished, worked-over, learned" (he cites Guez de Balzac's prose) and the other "broad, loose, abundant . . . far freer, capricious and varied, without traditional method," stemming from Montaigne, there is no doubt to which current Madame de Sévigné belonged, nor is it surprising to learn that Montaigne was among the authors she read daily.

La Bruyère's *Characters* are in some ways strongly indebted to the *Essais* and in other ways very unlike them. At first glance the looseness of the overall structure governing the 16 chapters, the apparent absence of a premeditated plan, and the individual chapter titles ("Des ouvrages de l'esprit" ["On Works of the Mind"], "Du mérite personnel" ["On Personal Merit"], etc.) suggest Montaigne, whom La Bruyère admired, from whom he borrowed many thoughts, and of whose style he even wrote a pastiche. But since he belonged to a generation formed by classical doctrine and by the conventions of the polite *salon* society of his time (the *littérature mondaine* or worldly literature), he departs in significant ways from Montaigne and thus, like Pascal and Madame de Sévigné, "reinvents" the essay. He expressly "imitates" the ancients, by basing his *Characters* on those of the Greek philosopher and moralist Theophrastus, whose **Characters** he also translated and published together with his own. His respect for "impersonality" meant that direct self-portraiture in his essays is rare: when he speaks of himself it is under fictional names or as "le philosophe." His highly polished and finely chiseled prose bears little resemblance to Montaigne's. His **chapters**, unlike Montaigne's, are broken up into numbered subdivisions, varying in length from a single sentence (often a maxim) or paragraph to two or three pages. His originality is to have renewed the essay as a collection of fragments, intermediary in form between the essays of Montaigne and the maxims of La Rochefoucauld. His originality also lies in his content. A perceptive, sometimes profound, sharply satirical commentator on the society of his time, his "world" – often surprisingly like our own – is a mini-"human comedy," limited in scope compared to the vast canvas of a Montaigne or a Sainte-Beuve but nevertheless the product of one of France's greatest moralists, a sociologist *avant la lettre*. His influence was strong on 18th-century writers, especially on **Marivaux** the essayist, another "modern Theophrastus." His relevance to 20th-century criticism, thanks to his genius as an "essayist of customs" ("essayiste d'usages"), has been recognized by the major 20th-century critic and essayist, **Roland Barthes**, in his *Essais critiques* (1964; *Critical Essays*).

Saint-Évremond (1614–1703), the descendant of an aristocratic Norman family, a career soldier and courtier, was forced by his involvement in the disgrace of Fouquet to spend roughly the latter half of his very long life as a political exile, first in Holland and then, until his death, in England. Thus, as a "spectator of the Versailles era" (Jean Prévost, *Tableau de la littérature française de Corneille à Chénier*, 1939) rather than a participant, he enjoyed something of the literary freedom that Montaigne had benefited from during his self-imposed exile in his provincial château. He wrote abundantly but published little during his lifetime. As with Montaigne, his aristocratic code prevented his acknowledging himself as an "author"; he was "the author in spite of himself" (Eugène Joliat, "L'Auteur malgré lui," *University of Toronto Quarterly*, 1955). To such writers the essay was perfectly suited as a genre, and so it comes as no surprise that apart from some verse and a few plays he wrote mostly essays, which he preferred to call "dissertations," "little treatises," "discourses," "reflections," "considerations," "eulogies," "characters" (following Theophrastus), "letters," or "portraits." His longest and most ambitious essay was his "Réflexions sur les divers génies du peuple romain dans les divers temps de la République" (1662; Reflections on diverse characteristics of the Romans during various phases of the Republic), a pioneer historical work highly esteemed by Montesquieu and other 18th-century writers. But for the most part he wrote "little works" which he considered (at least this was his playful pose, a stance found in many essayists) "trifles," "bagatelles," even, in his most self-deprecating mood, "pieces of foolishness" ("sottises"), an attitude straight out of his fellow aristocrat, Montaigne.

Saint-Évremond, traditionally esteemed as a link in the history of ideas between the 17th-century free thought of the *libertins* and the 18th-century Enlightenment, or as a moralist and literary critic, deserves to be better known as an essayist. His affinities with Montaigne, the reading of whom gave him lifelong pleasure, are many, including: writing essentially in order to know himself better and to live more wisely; the concept of writing as "conversation prolonged in written form" (Maurice Wilmotte, *Saint-Évremond critique littéraire*, 1921), which he derived also from the "long instances of table talk" in Plutarch; and the habit of presenting his thoughts "without order as they come to my mind." Morris Croll (1966) places him, with La Bruyère, among the enemies of Ciceronian rhetoric who followed Montaigne's example in the practice of Senecan or "Attic" prose (the "style coupé" or "loose style").

On the other hand, his vocabulary is severely pruned of what the grammarians of his day considered the overabundance or excrescences of Montaigne's, appearing austere beside the latter's marvelous wealth of words. His style, concise, laconic, deceptively simple, much admired by Voltaire and Stendhal for its compressed allusiveness, innuendos, and ironic overtones, lacks Montaigne's expansiveness and poetic quality. He is the least poetic of the great French essayists. Unlike Montaigne, he rarely writes directly of himself: to speak of oneself intimately and too long was deemed in bad taste by the polite *salons* he frequented. His breadth of subject matter, while impressive – history, politics, literature, language, music, psychology, morality, religion – seems restricted when placed beside Montaigne's or Sainte-Beuve's. Yet this "subdued Montaigne" ("un Montaigne adouci," in Sainte-Beuve's happy phrase) must be credited with revitalizing the essay as a form of studied or artful conversation on the part of the *honnête homme*. With Saint-Évremond, writes Quentin Hope (1962), "a new intimacy and informality [begin] to appear in literary criticism. Like letter writing, it becomes an extension and outgrowth of the art of conversation." As an essayist Saint-Évremond is important not only in himself but as a link between Montaigne and **Addison** (George Saintsbury, *Collected Papers*, 1924), and consequently, as we shall see, between Montaigne and the greatest 18th-century French essayist Marivaux, whose point of departure was the *Spectator* of Addison and **Steele**.

2. The 18th Century

The 18th century is marked by a profusion of essay types, some renewed from those already in existence and others relatively new. However, except as a title for longer works, essayists continue to be reluctant to call their short prose works *essais*, perhaps out of deference to Montaigne. As for the reception given to Montaigne himself, Maturin Dréano has shown in his exhaustive study, *La Renommée de Montaigne en France au XVIIIe siècle, 1677–1802* (1952; Montaigne's fame in the 18th century), how mixed this continued to be: defenses and imitations of his *Essais* were juxtaposed with bowdlerized versions, compilations, extracts, "breviaries" for the *honnête homme*, and other variations. Purely as a thinker, he exerted more influence than ever on the Age of Enlightenment, since "the *philosophes* carried out against classical thought a campaign very similar to that of Renaissance and Reformation writers against the Middle Ages." "As it emerged from the classical period," observes Theodore Fraser (1986), "the essay form became in turn for the *philosophes* the favored literary genre by which they could forward their assault on the traditional citadels of power and prestige." Furthermore, as the century progressed readers and critics became more appreciative of Montaigne's so-called "disorder," recognizing it as perfectly suited to the context of a "conversation."

The main development in the essay of this time is the emergence of the **periodical** (*la grande presse*) as a new vehicle for short works of philosophical, historical, literary, and artistic criticism, as well as a polemical weapon. Older journals, such as *Le Journal des Savants* (1665; The journal of the sages) and *Le Mercure Galant* (1672–1724; The gallant Mercury; then *Le Mercure de France*, 1724–1965), continued to function. The first daily paper, *Le Journal de Paris*, was founded in 1777.

The philosopher **Pierre Bayle** had established his *Nouvelles de la République des Lettres* (News from the Republic of Letters), an early example of "literary reportage," in 1684. These were followed by *Le Pour et le Contre* (1733–40; The pros and cons) of the Abbé Antoine-François Prévost (1697–1763) and by two distinguished journals produced by opponents of the *philosophes*: the *Journal* (originally *Mémoires*) *de Trévoux* (1701–62) and *L'Année Littéraire* (1754–90; The literary year) of Voltaire's worthy adversary, Elie-Catherine Fréron (1718–76). Much admired by Sainte-Beuve (in *Causeries du lundi*, 1853) as a precursor of the modern critical essay was the *Correspondance Littéraire* (1718–96; Literary correspondence) of the German-born Frédéric de Grimm (1723–1807) who, in his role as Paris correspondent of various German sovereigns for literary and artistic "news" became "the literary chronicler of the century." He also enjoyed the luck to have as his collaborator one of the century's greatest essayists, **Denis Diderot**. Many of the new journalists, or *nouvellistes* as they were also called, prepared their published ideas in the conversational atmosphere of drawing-rooms and cafés such as the Procope, the Régence, and the Rotonde. The "age of criticism," as it has been called, thus greatly favored the expansion of the essay. A vast new public for the genre appeared in the form of the *bourgeoisie libérale*, whose power was growing. The 18th was also above all the century of great prose, a fact which added to the essay's popularity. Between La Fontaine and the Romantic poets, verse went into decline, along with the classical hierarchy of genres favoring verse. As the strict separation of genres promoted by classical doctrine broke down, new forms of prose, such as the prose poem and poetic prose, absorbed lyrical elements once found in verse.

Examples from among the great number of essays in the longer form are: the aforementioned *Essay on the Manner and Spirit of Nations* by Voltaire; *De l'esprit des lois* (1748; *The Spirit of Laws*) and *Essai sur le goût* (1756; *An Essay on Taste*) of Charles de Montesquieu (1689–1755); and *De l'esprit* (1758; *Essays on the Mind*) of Charles-Adrien Helvétius (1715–71). Short essay forms may be grouped roughly under four types: the *éloge* (eulogy); the dictionary or encyclopedia article; the letter; and the *rêverie*.

The most brilliant exponent of the *éloge*, a forerunner of the biographical essay, was the witty **Bernard de Fontenelle** (1657–1757), lion of the *salons* as well as learned "perpetual secretary" of the Royal Academy of Sciences, better known for his longer works (**dialogues**, satires) popularizing scientific discoveries and boldly undermining religious dogmas. His *éloges* of Academy members, published in the *Histoire de l'Académie Royale des Sciences* (History of the Royal Academy of Sciences), a journal he edited from 1699 to 1740, were based on factual accounts and free of the panegyrical, declamatory style customary in such tributes; they were much admired by Sainte-Beuve, who recognized in them one of the sources of his own essay-portraits. Another admirer was the English biographical essayist **Lytton Strachey**; lamenting in 1918 that the art of biography "seems to have fallen on evil times in England," he added, "We have never had, like the French, a great biographical tradition; we have had no Fontenelles and Condorcets [Jean-Antoine-Nicolas de Condorcet (1749–94)], with their incomparable *éloges*, compressing into a few shining pages the manifold existences

of men" (preface to *Eminent Victorians*). Fontenelle the essayist is also important for having carried forward from Saint-Évremond, who had in turn learned it from Montaigne, the art – one of the marks of the true essayist – of treating serious subjects in a light, ironical vein.

Masterful examples of the essay as dictionary or encyclopedia article are found in the *Dictionnaire historique et critique* (1697; *An Historical and Critical Dictionary*,) of **Pierre Bayle** (1647–1706), who emulated Montaigne's digressive form; Voltaire's *Dictionnaire philosophique portatif* (1764; *Philosophical Dictionary*); and the great *Encyclopédie* (1751–72), whose chief organizer was Diderot and for which Bayle's *Dictionary* had prepared the way. Bayle, though hardly a great stylist, had brought immense learning as well as polemical wit to the essay, providing a model for later writers, including Sainte-Beuve, who named him as one of his "three masters" (the other two were Horace and Montaigne).

The epistolary essay, a firm thread running from Seneca through Montaigne to Pascal and Madame de Sévigné, continues strong into the 18th century. Its three greatest exemplars are Montesquieu's *Lettres persanes* (1721; *Persian Letters*), Voltaire's *Lettres philosophiques*, also known as *Lettres sur les Anglais* (1734; *Letters on England*), and Diderot's *Correspondance* (1830–31). Montesquieu admired his fellow Gascon, Montaigne, whom he called, with great acumen, "man thinking" as opposed to "man writing" and ranked, with Plato, as one of the great poets in prose. His own style was stronger in precision and clarity than in poetic qualities; but he learned from Montaigne how to combine "lightness of tone with basic seriousness" and, unlike Voltaire, was in no way shocked by Montaigne's "disorder." Closer in time as models for Montesquieu were La Bruyère's *Characters* and *Les Amusements sérieux et comiques d'un Siamois* (1699) of Charles Rivière Dufresny (1648–1724), the impressions of a Siamese visitor to Paris, the prototype of this kind of semifictional observation ("sociological" in import) of one's own society as seen through foreign eyes. (Montaigne's great essay "Des cannibales" ["Of Cannibals"], which criticizes his own society by comparing it with the merits of so-called "savages," may have originally sparked this type of writing.) The essay-story of Montesquieu's Persians in Paris serves as the pretext for social satire; it is also one of the earliest examples of the breakdown in the classical distinction between literary forms, leading to the fusion of genres, since it is as much a short novel in letter form as an essay work. Montesquieu was probably justified in claiming that the *Lettres persanes* "taught others how to write epistolary novels." The *Letters on England* by **Voltaire** (pseudonym of François-Marie Arouet, 1694–1778) gives a new twist to this type of satire by adopting the stance of *himself* as a foreigner (a Frenchman in exile in England) comparing the failings of the *ancien régime* with what he considered the superior merits of English society. His letters are cast in a more recognizable essay form than those of Montesquieu: in the first person, without narrative continuity, and with such essayistic chapter headings as "Sur les quakers," "Sur M. Locke," etc. He had less enthusiasm for Montaigne than did Montesquieu or Diderot, defending his self-portrayal against Pascal's attack upon it but complaining that Montaigne the writer lacked "eloquence"; he also denied him a place in his ideal "Temple of Taste" ("temple du goût"). There is, furthermore, a strong polemical strain in Voltaire (**pamphlet**s, diatribes) that is alien to the relative detachment of the *Essais*.

Denis Diderot's (1713–84) *Correspondance* belongs to the tradition of the essay as private letter later made public. Many critics consider his correspondence on a wealth of subjects, carried on over a period of 40 years with friends, family, and especially his mistress, Sophie Volland (a name he immortalized), to be his true masterpiece. Diderot also "created modern French art criticism as a literary genre" (Otis Fellows and Norman Torrey, 1942) thanks to his articles (the *Salons*, 1759–72) for his friend Grimm's *Correspondance Littéraire*. He provided a model for both Sainte-Beuve's critical essays in literature and **Charles Baudelaire**'s *Salons* on art and music. Nor should we forget the essayistic features found in his many other works (*pensées, dialogues, entretiens*), in his contributions as chief editor to the *Encyclopédie*, and even in his novels. He brought to the essay one of the greatest French prose styles, characterized by what Jean Thomas (*Histoire des littératures*, vol. 3, 1958) calls a unique kind of "lyrisme cérébral." Only Marivaux, his rival and perhaps superior as an essayist, owed more than Diderot to Montaigne's example. For Diderot the *Essais* were "superior to the work of any moralist who has appeared since his [Montaigne's] time." He admired their form as much as their content, emulating their imaginative style and their loose, wandering structure ("vagabondage"), arguing that the latter, far from being an idiosyncrasy, conformed to the very nature of the human mind itself. His own mind, like Montaigne's, "worked through digression and association rather than through logical pattern" (Fellows and Torrey).

The final 18th-century variation on the essay form to be mentioned is the *rêverie*, a new literary genre created by **Jean-Jacques Rousseau** (1712–78) in his *Rêveries du promeneur solitaire* (*The Reveries of a Solitary Walker*), published posthumously in 1782. In his much more famous *Confessions* (also posthumously published, 1782 and 1789), to which the *Reveries* are a kind of epilogue, he also invented another new genre, the modern autobiography, breaking the powerful taboo against intimate self-portraiture which had prevailed in France since Montaigne's first attempt to challenge it. Unlike Montaigne's only partly autobiographical *Essais*, the *Confessions* are a continuous, integrated narrative of their author's past; they were meant, furthermore, to surpass in frankness a Montaigne he judged to be only pseudo-sincere. Yet he called Montaigne "the master of us all" ("notre maître à tous"), worthy of emulation for his stylistic "naturalness, grace, and energy" and for his "spontaneous mind" ("esprit primesautier"). It is in the *Reveries* that Rousseau's true indebtedness to Montaigne as well as his re-creation of the essay may be found. He achieved the latter, according to Henri Roddier (in his 1960 edition of the *Reveries*), in two distinct ways: by inventing the "essai-confidence," confiding intimate feelings and sensations to the reader; and by preparing the way for the related modern genre of the intimate **journal** ("journal intime"). Having learned from Montaigne's example, he brought to the essay: 1) an association of ideas based more on sensations than on logical thought; 2) a poetic prose alien to Montesquieu's or Voltaire's but akin to that of Diderot; and 3) the concept of what may be called the "peripatetic" essay, reflections arising from his walks in the countryside around Paris, thoughts and feelings stimulated by no precise

object, often by pure chance as (so he describes it in the "Seconde Promenade") "I let my mind be completely free, and my ideas follow their inclination unopposed and unconstrained." One can hardly imagine a source of inspiration further removed from the polite conversation of the *salon* or the witty exchanges of the cafés, both of which animated other types of 18th-century essays mentioned earlier.

That it was possible to harmonize both kinds of inspiration had already been proved by the last (but the earliest in date of birth) and in many ways the greatest of the 18th-century essayists to be mentioned: **Marivaux** (1688–1763). He stands apart from the others in several ways: as the creator of the one-man *feuille périodique* (periodical folio) or *essai journalistique* (journalistic essay); as the most self-conscious heir of Montaigne; as a rare student and emulator of the English essay and author of reflections on the nature of the essay itself; and for the unique manner in which his essays are integrated into an organic whole consisting also of his novels and plays. Few French writers of any age have been more original, more daring in their experimentation, and in so many literary genres, than this avant-garde partisan of the Moderns, in the Quarrel of Ancients and Moderns, this subverter of classical doctrine and classical rhetoric, whose reputation has been unjustly overshadowed by those of Montesquieu, Voltaire, Rousseau, and Diderot. To reduce his writing to *marivaudage*, or the excessively refined, even affected or *précieux* discourse about love, is to deny its true breadth and depth: his subject was nothing less than what the anti-hero of his novel, *Le Paysan parvenu* (1734–35; *The Upstart Peasant*), calls "the art of reading people's minds and figuring out their secret feelings" – the art, in other words, of discovering not what they say but what they mean (Freud would certainly have understood his approach). An astute contemporary of Marivaux called his field of inquiry, in a memorable phrase, "the metaphysics of the human heart."

Marivaux began his essay work with a series of articles in the *Nouveau Mercure de France* (New Mercury of France) entitled *Lettres sur les habitants de Paris* (1717–18; Letters on the inhabitants of Paris), inspired by La Bruyère's *Characters* (like La Bruyère he too fancied himself as a "modern Theophrastus") and by Dufresny's *Amusements sérieux et comiques d'un Siamois*. These essays are less interesting for their satirical content than for their foreshadowing of an aesthetics of the essay which Marivaux would put into practice in his mature essay masterpieces, *Le Spectateur Français* (1721–24; The French spectator) and *L'Indigent Philosophe* (1727; The pauper philosopher). Montaigne's influence is obvious in the essential features of the essay as Marivaux conceived the genre: 1) an infinite number and variety of subjects; 2) a mixture of the serious and the lighthearted (cf. Dufresny's *sérieux et comique*), a direct contradiction of the classical doctrine's proprieties that forbad the mixture of tones and styles; 3) an ordering of subject matter depending largely on chance (cf. Montaigne: "I take the first subject that chance offers. They are all equally good to me") and on immediate circumstances; 4) a complete freedom of thought (*libertinage d'idées*) that follows fancy and natural bent (*le naturel*) rather than logic; and finally 5) the freedom to write primarily to please oneself while at the same time (a paradox here) engaging in a dialogue with one's reader. On this last point, Marivaux's self-portrayal, characteristic of the relative reticence of French essayists as compared with their English counterparts, is rarely as intimate as Montaigne's and much less so than Rousseau's. This in fact adds to his appeal, since it obliges the reader, as Jean Fabre (*Histoire des littératures*, vol. 3, 1958) has observed, to "search out the true self of Marivaux beneath the first person of *Le Spectateur français* and *L'Indigent philosophe*." These two works – the first, using Addison and Steele's *Spectator* as a springboard for innovation, and the second, an even bolder experiment, described by its author as "an essay of what could be done by writing haphazardly whatever might strike the imagination" – establish Marivaux as one of the greatest French essayists.

3. The 19th Century

The essay as a long continuous discourse prolongs its life into the 19th as well as the 20th centuries. Examples from among many include the *Essai historique, politique, et moral sur les révolutions anciennes et modernes* (1797; *An Historical, Political and Moral Essay on Revolutions, Ancient and Modern*) of the great Romantic prose writer, **Chateaubriand** (1768–1848); *De la littérature considérée dans ses rapports avec les institutions sociales* (1800; *The Influence of Literature upon Society*) and *De l'Allemagne* (1810; On Germany) of **Madame de Staël** (1766–1817); and the *Essai sur les Fables de La Fontaine* (1853) of **Hippolyte Taine**. These longer works cover the broadest range of subjects and vary in approach from the impersonal, even the erudite, to the more personal ones such as *De l'amour* (1822; *On Love*) of Stendhal (pseudonym of Henri Beyle, 1783–1842). Among recurrent types of the short essay inherited from earlier centuries are the essay as public letter and the essay as polemical – usually political – pamphlet. The Romantic poet Alfred de Musset (1810–57) exemplifies the first type in his delightful satire on certain foibles of Romanticism, published in 1836–37 in the form of four letters to the editor of the **Revue des Deux Mondes** (Review of two worlds), as the *Lettres de Dupuis et de Cotonet* (the double pseudonym assumed by their author). The *Mémoires* in letter form (1828) by Paul-Louis Courier (1772–1825), inspired by those of Pliny the Younger, contain many reminiscences of Madame de Sévigné's letters. But it is primarily as one of the last of the great pamphleteers, according to **Albert Thibaudet** (1936), that Courier deserves to be remembered. His chief model was Pascal's *Provincial Letters*. Courier defended the pamphlet as a literary genre in his *Pamphlet des pamphlets* (1824). His younger rival as political essayist was the liberal anti-Second Empire journalist Lucien-Anatole Prévost-Paradol (1829–70), especially in his *Essais de politique et de littérature* (1859; Essays on politics and literature) and their sequel, the *Nouveaux Essais . . .* (1862). Prévost-Paradol ranks high among what the French call *écrivains de combat*, the best of whom knew how to reveal permanent, universal meaning in the ephemeral issues they addressed. In his ambition for the political essay to win (as he put it) "right of entry into the highest literary regions," he anticipated **George Orwell**'s aspiration "to make political writing into an art." Among his English models were the pamphleteers Junius and **Jonathan Swift** (he wrote a doctoral dissertation on Swift).

However, overshadowing in importance these revivals of earlier forms of the essay are several major developments. The most significant is the emergence of the modern periodical; others include the renewal of the aesthetic defense of fragmentary or discontinuous prose works, the shifting relationship of the essay to other genres, and the growing number of writers whose essay work is part of their production as poets, novelists, or dramatists.

Writes Fraser: "The essay's rise in the nineteenth century to the status of an authentic, widely used, but [n.b.] still undeclared literary genre, is intimately bound up with the rapid growth of journalism in France," a phenomenon closely paralleled in England. In this great flowering, a new type of essay emerges: first published in one of the new journals or reviews – the *Revue des Deux Mondes*, the *Revue de Paris* (The Paris review), the **Journal des Débats** (Journal of debates), *Le Constitutionnel* (The constitutional), *Le Temps* (The times), to name only a few – such essays then reappeared in collections, a new vehicle for diffusion of the genre. The great pioneer in France of this revitalized essay form, its "Montaigne," is **Charles-Augustin Sainte-Beuve** (1804–69). His *Portraits* (1844–46) and *Causeries* and *Nouveaux Causeries du Lundi* (1849–69; Monday and New Monday Chats), spanning almost 30 years of production, deal with literary criticism, often (but not always) biographically oriented, and conceived in the broadest sense (he was primarily a moralist), so as to constitute a veritable "human comedy" peopled with hundreds of writers and other figures. Sainte-Beuve aimed, as **Virginia Woolf** was later to do in her role as critic for the **Times Literary Supplement**, at something much better than what she called "journalism embalmed in a book." Another writer who met the challenge – an aesthetic as much as an intellectual one – of the periodical essay was the historian and philosopher **Ernest Renan** (1823–92) who, from the 1850s until his death, produced several outstanding essay collections, including his *Études d'histoire religieuse* (1857; *Studies of Religious History*), *Essais de morale et de critique* (1859; Moral and critical essays), *Questions contemporaines* (1868; Contemporary issues), and, the year of his death, the semi-autobiographical *Feuilles détachées* (1892; Detached leaves). Sainte-Beuve modestly credited his younger contemporary Renan with being "the master of a new genre," the "article de revue." It would be more accurate to say that Renan broadened the scope of this kind of essay still further than his predecessor, to embrace religious history, philosophy, politics, and contemporary affairs, bringing to it, in addition, a depth of thought and refinement of poetic style rarely found in Sainte-Beuve. He also added new luster to the essay-as-dialogue in his *Dialogues et fragments philosophiques* (1876; *Philosophical Dialogues and Fragments*), inspired by Plato and by Nicolas de Malebranche (1638–1715), and launched the essay as speech or lecture.

Both Sainte-Beuve and Renan stimulated by example a whole succession of younger, less gifted critics and authors of *essais*, *études*, and the like, ranging from the (pseudo-) scientific (several were bent on finding physiological or psychological "explanations" for artistic creation) to the frankly subjective and "impressionistic." Among the most notable were **Hippolyte Taine** (1828–93), who proposed to make a "science" of literary criticism (*Essais de critique et d'histoire* [1858; Critical and historical essays]); Anatole France (pseudonym of Jacques Thibault, 1844–1924), for whom, on the contrary, the critic is "one who relates the adventures of his soul among masterpieces" as illustrated in his *La Vie littéraire* (1888–92; The literary life, translated as *On Life and Letters*); **Ferdinand Brunetière** (1849–1906), editor of the *Revue des Deux Mondes*, best known for his attempt to assimilate **Charles Darwin**'s theory of evolution to the history of literary genres, *L'Évolution des genres dans l'histoire de la littérature* (1890; The evolution of genres in the history of literature); **Paul Bourget** (1852–1935), whose *Essais de psychologie contemporaine* (1883–85; Essays in contemporary psychology) has outlasted in value his novels; Jules Lemaître (1853–1914), a short-story writer, drama critic for the *Journal des Débats*, and essayist in his *Les Contemporains* (1885–1918; Contemporaries), *Impressions de théâtre* (1888–1920; *Theatrical Impressions*), and *Politiques et moralistes du XIXe siècle* (1903; 19th-century political and moralist writers); and finally, in some ways the most original essayist of this later generation, admired by **T. S. Eliot, Ezra Pound**, and other exponents of Modernism, **Remy de Gourmont** (1858–1915), who invented in his *La Culture des idées* (1900; *The Culture of Ideas*) and *Promenades littéraires* (1904–27) an early form of "deconstructionism" which he called "dissociation of ideas," and whose *Promenades philosophiques* (1905–09) are **personal essays** directly inspired by Montaigne.

The great poet **Charles Baudelaire** (1821–67) stands apart as an essayist for his unique approach to criticism, and is superior in his gift to any of the aforementioned periodical essayists except Sainte-Beuve and Renan. His view that criticism should be creative and poetic in nature owed much to Sainte-Beuve; he went even further in claiming paradoxically that the ideal critic inevitably works within the horizon limited by his own passions and prejudices, while always seeking to broaden that horizon. His voluminous critical writing includes remarkable assessments of contemporary artists and penetrating reflections on the nature of the imagination, Romanticism, and modernity in art. His essays on painting and music, especially his *Salons* (1845–59), link him to the tradition launched by Diderot. The elements of surprise, digression, and paradox, as well as the shifting, multiple perspectives found in his essays, are highly reminiscent of Montaigne (Martha Evans, *The French Essay*, 1982).

The periodical essay was far from being limited to literary and other kinds of criticism. One of the liveliest guises it assumed, especially with the Romantics, was that of the **travel essay**, whose improvised, meandering form tended to mimic the unstructured nature of the voyages it described. Its most gifted practitioners were the Romantic poets Gérard de Nerval (pseudonym of Gérard Labrunie, 1808–55) and Théophile Gautier (1811–72), and the lesser-known, unjustly neglected Émile Montégut (1825–95), literary critic for the *Revue des Deux Mondes*. Although Nerval never uses the term *essai*, he does call himself an "essayiste," a word introduced from English in 1821, and refers to his "essayisme." In his essay masterpiece, *Les Nuits d'octobre* (1852; October nights), the account of his meanderings in the Île de France, he describes his *essayisme* as the tendency to wander ("vagabondage"). The spirit of Montaigne's artful disorder permeates this work and also his *Promenades et souvenirs* (1854; Walks and reminiscences), but the models he actually acknowledged were Rousseau's *The Reveries of a Solitary Walker* and *Les Nuits de Paris, ou Le Spectateur nocturne* (1788–94; Parisian nights,

or the nocturnal spectator) of Nicolas-Edme Restif de la Bretonne (1734–1806). Gautier correctly placed Nerval in their tradition of "peripatetic literature" ("la littérature ambulante"). Gautier himself was no stranger to this same type of essay or to "essayism." In addition to memorable critical articles such as *Les Grotesques* (1844), literary portraits of François Villon, Paul Scarron, and others, he published delightful travel sketches: *Un voyage en Espagne* (1843; A voyage to Spain), *Caprices et zig-zags* (1852), whose title alone invites us to place him in the essay tradition, and others. The majority of Montégut's almost 300 published articles, of which only a third have been collected in book form, deal with literary criticism, supplemented by **moral essays**, political essays, and travel essays centered on his native region of south-central France. This "encyclopedic and cosmopolitan essayist" (Pierre Alexis Muenier, *Émile Montégut*, 1925) whose breadth of knowledge and interests rivaled those of Sainte-Beuve, Taine, or Renan and included pioneer studies in comparative literature (especially English and American literatures) was also a self-conscious essayist and student of the genre, who derived much of his inspiration from **Ralph Waldo Emerson** (whom he translated) and **Thomas Carlyle**. His objective, a highly unusual one for a journalist, was to replace the "artificial linking of thoughts" endemic in the journalistic article with a freer, more "indefinite and indeterminate" order, allowing for the play of the subconscious ("l'inconscience"). His motto might have been a sentence from his *Types littéraires et fantaisies esthétiques* (1882; Literary types and aesthetic fantasies): "We never go so far as when we know not where we are going." Montaigne would have smiled on this idea across the centuries, and also on the fact that a 19th-century journalist-critic would be attacking Ciceronian rhetoric as he had attacked it in his own time.

To the flowering of the periodical essay as the most important development of the genre in the 19th century should be added the three other major developments mentioned above. The Romantic defense of fragmentary and discontinuous prose began in the late 18th century when the German critic **Friedrich Schlegel** discovered the beauty of the maxim. A whole "literature of the fragment" with an influence on the history of the essay emerged, whose vogue was akin to the Romantic taste for paintings of ruined (in other words, fragmentary) edifices. Its later exponents would include the philosopher **Friedrich Nietzsche**, the poet-essayist **Paul Valéry**, and the poet René Char (1907–88). Fragments were described by the early German Romantic philosopher and poet **Novalis** as "literary seeds" capable of germinating larger structures (Lafond, 1984). Both the fragment and the discontinuous discourse found a 19th-century apologist in France in the moralist and *pensée* writer Joseph Joubert (1754–1824), whose selected thoughts taken from his notebooks were first published by his literary protégé Chateaubriand in 1838 and, in more complete form, by Pierre de Raynal, as *Pensées, maximes, essais, et correspondance* (1842). Joubert's debt to Montaigne's *discontinu* is clear from his statement, "I am just as unsuited to continuous discourse as Montaigne."

A still further major development affecting the 19th-century essay was the decline of the classical tradition of the hierarchy and strict separation of genres, whose political implications Antoine de Rivarol (1753–1801) had shrewdly noted by comparing "the classes of styles in our language" to the "classes of subjects in our monarchy." The 18th century had already prepared the way for this transformation in such writers as Diderot, who made sport of the "rules" and advocated resorting to new literary forms whenever the traditional genres failed to meet new aspirations. The absorption of poetry into prose made possible the mastery of the *poème en prose* in such 19th-century poets as Baudelaire and **Stéphane Mallarmé** (1842–98). The latter wrote not only **critical essays** on literature, music, theater, and ballet but also prose poems such as *Divagations* (1897; Ramblings), comparable to very short essays, pondering the mystery of poetry in a difficult, challenging prose unlike that of any essayist before him. Gradually the distinction between genres became blurred (in the 20th century the very concept of genre would be radically questioned); many features of the essay were absorbed into the novel, the autobiography, the intimate journal, or intimate notebooks (*cahiers, carnets,* etc.). The novel, like the essay, having developed outside classical doctrine, was free to say "almost everything about almost anything" (Huxley). Montégut went on record as deploring the novel's tendency to "take on the most varied forms [and] to replace other genres." In a more positive vein, Patrick Henry (1987), commenting on the influence of Montaigne's concept of "continuous becoming" on such modern novelists as Proust, Joyce, and Woolf, observes: "Like the novel, the essay, which is also a narrative form of continuous becoming, can [quoting the Russian literary theorist Mikhail Bakhtin] 'include, ingest, devour other genres and still retain its status,' for once again, like the novel, it has no canon of its own." As for confessional literature, which had been growing in attraction for writers since Rousseau, it obviously usurped some of the traditional territory of the essay, especially in France, where the essay as a vehicle for intimate self-portrayal was less acceptable than in England. From the intimate journals and notebooks of Sainte-Beuve, Renan, and Baudelaire through those of **André Gide**, Valéry, and **Albert Camus** and beyond, this more direct form of self-disclosure would parallel the indirect form found in the essay.

In the 19th century, finally, the distinction between "pure" essayists and those whose essays constitute a more or less integral part of their total work as poets, novelists, or playwrights becomes firmly established. Renan, Montégut, Taine, Brunetière, and Gourmont belong to the first "family." In the preceding century, Marivaux offers the initial example of a writer whose essays are part of a total vision also involving imaginative works (in his case, novels and plays). Voltaire *conteur* and dramatist, Rousseau novelist, Diderot novelist and dramatist, also follow this pattern. Nineteenth-century examples abound: Nerval, Gautier, Baudelaire, Mallarmé, Anatole France. Sainte-Beuve's limited success as poet and novelist should not blind us to the fact that his essays are intimately related to his poems and novel. His special significance from this point of view lies in his theory and practice of criticism as a *creative* art (Richard Chadbourne, 1977), which gave new prestige to the essay by breaking down the artificial distinction between "critical" and "creative" or "imaginative" literature. "With the example of Sainte-Beuve," observes Wallace Fowlie (1957), "the critic became a writer, and literary criticism became an art of writing."

4. The 20th Century

The 20th century witnesses no decline in the fortunes of the essay. On the contrary, it has become an "eclectic kind of literary genre – and one supple enough to be adapted to the many individual styles and varied purposes" of leading 20th-century writers (Fraser). At times the essay not only rivals but surpasses in interest the so-called "creative" genres. New journals and reviews take root as vehicles for essays in their initial form, including the *Nouvelle* (and later *Nouvelle Nouvelle*) *Revue Française* (1908–43, 1953–; New French review), the *Cahiers du Sud* (1914–; Notebooks of the south), the *Nouvelles Littéraires* (1920–; Literary news), *Les Temps Modernes* (1945–; Modern times), *Critique* (1946), and *Tel Quel* (1960–82; As is; then *L'Infini*, 1982–; The infinite). French writers continue to be more reluctant than their English counterparts to use the essay for self-portraiture, preferring autobiography, journal, notebooks, and other forms. New impetus is given to the travel essay and the lyrical essay, and critical awareness grows of the essay, both as a genre unlike any other and as an "anti-genre" undermining all the others.

As in the preceding century, essayists may still be divided roughly into two groups: those who wrote primarily or only essays; and "creative" writers (for want of a better term) who have left an important body of essayistic work. To begin with the lesser lights among the former type: **Julien Benda** (1867–1956), in his *La Trahison des clercs* (1927; *The Treason of the Intellectuals*); André Suarès (1868–1948), literary, musical, and art critic, travel essayist, and moralist (*Voici l'homme* [1905; Here is man]); **Albert Thibaudet** (1874–1936), literary critic, historian of modern French literature, author of a series of *Réflexions* (1938–40) on literature, the novel, and criticism itself; **Charles Du Bos** (1882–1939), explorer of English literature and of spirituality in literature, in his *Approximations* (1922–37); **Henri Massis** (1886–1970), Catholic apologist and critic of the educational system (*Agathon, ou, L'Esprit de la nouvelle Sorbonne* [1911; Agathon, or, the spirit of the new Sorbonne]); Jean Rostand (1894–1977), who used biology as a springboard for meditations on human nature (*Pensées d'un biologiste* [1939; Thoughts of a biologist]); **Simone Weil** (1909–43), spiritual writer, searching and prophetic critic of modern society (*Oppression et liberté* [1955; *Oppression and Liberty*], edited by none other than Camus himself; the Romanian-French author **E. M. Cioran** (1911–95), a relentlessly pessimistic writer whose laconic, fragmentary texts such as *Précis de décomposition* (1949; *A Short History of Decay*), *Syllogismes de l'amertume* (1952; Syllogisms of bitterness), and *De l'inconvénient d'être né* (1973; *The Trouble with Being Born*) often read like a self-parodying intimate journal, "without chronology or intimate detail, reflecting the disorder inherent in the intellectual life itself " (Bruno Vercier and Jacques Lecarme, 1982); and **Michel Serres** (1930–), whose five-volume series of essays, from *Hermès: La Communication* (1968) to *Le Passage du Nord-Ouest* (1980; The northwest passage), propose a critique of science from the viewpoint of a new humanism.

The most original and gifted of the "pure" essayists are **Alain** (pseudonym of Emile-Auguste Chartier, 1868–1951) and **Roland Barthes** (1915–80). Journalist and lycée philosophy professor, Alain produced, over a period of some 30 years (1903–36), more than 5000 uniformly brief prose pieces which he called "propos," meaning "propositions" presented for our reflection; "proposals," plans, or designs for living more wisely; and simply, "words." As Jean Miquel puts it (*Les Propos d'Alain*, 1967), Alain "tried his hand at everything" (a Montaignean trait); hence the contents are amazing in their variety. The impulse for a given *propos* was usually less an idea than, as in the essays of Montaigne or Marivaux, a chance circumstance or occurrence, often an observed concrete phenomenon of the humblest everyday kind, out of which an idea would grow. Some *propos* are veiled or stylized self-portraits, while others (again one thinks of Montaigne's reflections on the writing of essays) are thoughts on the art of the *propos*, or, more broadly, on the creative process itself. Each *propos* can be read independently of the others, yet one leads to another, and certain themes recur: Alain recognized this last feature by grouping and publishing some of them that possessed a common theme (e.g. *Propos sur le bonheur* [1925–28; *Alain on Happiness*]). Form and style depended greatly on improvisation and the author's desire to espouse what he called "thought in action" or the process of thought (another affinity with Montaigne and Marivaux). Yet the constraints within which he worked, those cruel deadlines and severe limitations of length, worked miraculously to bring out the craftsman in him, for he is one of the most impeccable and artistic of French prose stylists. Not always the clearest, however: his elliptical style, with its unexpected juxtapositions of thought and absence of transitions, is often deliberately "obscure," so as to challenge the reader's alertness and intelligence. "Many of the *propos*," observes Sterling Madsen (in an unpublished dissertation, Duke University, 1975), "are so structured as to defy immediate interpretation." The *propos* have been variously compared to the act of breathing, mental gymnastics, choreography ("the dance of thoughts," is Alain's phrase), the fugue, and a proposition, but not a proof, in geometry (Madsen). Many *propos* are small prose poems or poetic *rêveries*.

Although he owed much to Montaigne, La Bruyère, Montesquieu, and Bayle, Alain was also very conscious of his originality as an essayist. As much as he detested Sainte-Beuve, his own journalistic feat of producing essays at frequent, regular intervals, on command, without serious sacrifice of quality, is equaled only by the author of the *Lundis*. His conviction that the essay was a creative art also links him with Sainte-Beuve. Much of his writing remains timelessly relevant, since he succeeded in uncovering general principles beneath the particulars of contemporary issues he treated; or, as he put it, "My destiny was to become a journalist raising the newspaper column to the level of metaphysics."

Like Alain, Barthes was a journalist-critic writing for the most part *sur commande* and an academic, though at a higher level than Alain's in the educational system, at the Collège de France, where he held the chair in semiology (the science of signs) created especially for him. This broad field took him well beyond the study of language and literature into writing about the language of fashion, film, theater, photography, painting, music, and other subjects. His questioning of the "establishment" was more radical than Alain's, since it challenged the very assumptions about reality embodied in the ideologies of today's power structures, the very claims of language and literature to have some privileged access to truth

undistorted by ideology. A unique feature of his essays was his ability to absorb in succession the values of various "schools" of thought – Marxism, semiology, anthropology, psychoanalysis – abandoning each in turn, not because of any "dilettantism" but because of his belief that none offered a definitive guide and out of his horror of becoming an "authority," "expert," or "true believer" (Montaigne underwent similar changes of position and for similar reasons). Giving unity to this amazing diversity of subjects, as Susan Sontag (1982) has observed, there is a central subject: writing itself and its relation to "the theory of his own mind." A hedonistic quest for pleasure in what he reads, a spirit of playfulness (reminiscent of Renan), sometimes of joy, are attractively balanced by a sense of responsibility that links his work with the kind of ethical inquiry associated with the long line of French *moralistes*.

Barthes published a number of book-length essays, such as his first book, *Le Degré zéro de l'écriture* (1953; *Writing Degree Zero*), challenging the theory of **Jean-Paul Sartre** of literature as social commitment, in the name of a purer kind of writing (*l'écriture*) freed from the dictates of the "institution of literature." Other long essays are his book on the semiology of fashion, *Système de la mode* (1967; *The Fashion System*), and the controversial essay on Japanese culture as a system of "pure signs," *L'Empire des signes* (1970; *Empire of Signs*). But Barthes had the natural-born essayist's "resistance to long forms" (Sontag); he is more at home in his short essays, which Sontag divides into two main types: the "straight essay" conceived in more or less linear, logical fashion (reviews, articles, etc.) and the later, more personal and original essays in which a "splintering of form" occurred, leading him to the essay as discontinuous fragment. Examples of the first type are his *Essais critiques* (1964; *Critical Essays*) and their sequels amounting to five volumes in all (1964–73) and *Mythologies* (1957; Mythologies), brief pieces resembling Alain's *propos* in form and, in content, both La Bruyère's *Characters* (he admired this author and emulated him as an "essayist of customs" – "un essayiste d'usages") and Marivaux's *Spectateur Français*. Although Barthes claimed in an interview not to have read Montaigne, Réda Bensmaïa (1986) has pursued a number of parallels in their use of the essay as "reflective text." In the brilliant and highly amusing *Mythologies*, originally published as monthly feature articles for the *Lettres Nouvelles* (New letters), Barthes the "mythographer" demythifies stereotypes of popular culture and everyday life, from ads for detergents to "people in the news." His boldest experimentation in the essay form, shading off into the essay "deconstructing" itself, or the "anti-essay," is found in *Roland Barthes par Roland Barthes* (1975; *Roland Barthes*) and *Fragments d'un discours amoureux* (1977; *A Lover's Discourse: Fragments*). The first, commissioned for the series *Écrivains de toujours*, in which a critic usually writes about a "classic" author or prestigious contemporary one, set the remarkable precedent of having a living author write about himself. Barthes' little volume uses the quasi-fictional pronoun *il* (he) as much as the personal *je* (I) and breaks the mold of rhetorical structure by chopping up the subject matter into small paragraphs (called "biographemes" and compared to family snapshots), arranged, in a further bold stroke, in the deliberately arbitrary alphabetical order. Barthes returns to this device of the fragmentary, discontinuous, alphabetically arranged "order" in *A Lover's Discourse*.

Among poets and novelists whose essays are more or less integrated into their total work, several deserve brief mention, while five should be highlighted for their greater originality or the way in which they recast the essay in a radically new role: **Paul Valéry, Henry de Montherlant, Albert Camus**, Maurice Blanchot (1907–), and **Michel Butor**.

For the first group, the essay tends to be an appendage to their poetry or fiction rather than an essential part of their total work. **André Gide** (1869–1951), cited by Thibaudet as an example of the pervasive presence of "essayism" in 20th-century literature, left fine critical essays such as *Prétextes* (1903–13; *Pretexts: Reflections on Literature and Morality*), but they have been overshadowed by his famous *Journal*. Valery Larbaud (1881–1957), explorer of American, English, and Spanish literatures and translator of Samuel Butler and James Joyce, best known for his creation of the fictional poet "Barnabooth," deserves remembering also for his delightful travel sketches, such as *Aux couleurs de Rome* (1938; The colors of Rome), which blend essay and short story. Primarily novelists, François Mauriac (1885–1970) and **Georges Bernanos** (1888–1948) gave new life to the journalistic (often **polemical**) essay: the first in his *Bloc-Notes* (1958–71; Writing pads), the second in such works as his *La Grande Peur des bien-pensants* (1931; The great fear of conformist thinkers). The versatile Jean Cocteau (1889–1963), who excelled in almost every genre (including film), left a delightful book of essays whose format evokes Montaigne and the English essayists, although the title, *La Difficulté d'être* (1947; *The Difficulty of Being*), was inspired by Fontenelle. The "philosopher of eroticism," **Georges Bataille** (1897–1962), in his novels and essays, ponders the meaning of sex, self-violation, societal transgression, and death with such violence of both content and style that **Jean-Paul Sartre** (1905–80) coined a new term to describe this form of the essay, in his critique of Bataille's *L'Expérience intérieure* (1943; *Inner Experience*): the "martyred essay" ("essai martyre"). The essays in Sartre's own 10-volume collection, *Situations* (1947–76), are less interesting for their form than for his literary criticism and reflections on the nature and function of literature. *Le Deuxième Sexe* (1949; *The Second Sex*), in the tradition of the long essay form, is an important contribution of **Simone de Beauvoir** (1908–86), who Toril Moi informs us (*Simone de Beauvoir: The Making of an Intellectual Woman*, 1994) preferred autobiography and fiction to essay writing.

Paul Valéry's (1871–1945) prolific essay output consists of two basic types of essay: those of the "official writer," written on commission – **prefaces**, speeches, lectures – and published under the collective title of *Variété* (1924–44; *Variety*), and those, culminating in his massive, largely posthumously published *Cahiers* (1957–61; *Notebooks*), in which the essay is splintered into fragmentary form. Although he considered the first type to be a kind of "forced labor," he was not unhappy to find that chance circumstances, confronting him with a totally strange and unexpected subject, stimulated his mind. Out of necessity he simply made a virtue. The essays in *Variety* cover literary, philosophical, and "quasi-political" subjects, as well as poetic and aesthetic theory, education, and brief "memoirs of a poet." A central theme underlies all

Valéry's writings: his lifelong inquiry (cf. Montaigne before him and Barthes after him) into the nature of his own mind, in order better to understand the human mind itself and to formulate what he called "the theory of oneself." He anticipated Barthes and the "deconstructionists" by questioning the claim to truth and authenticity of the "literary work," making exception only for poetry. His *Cahiers*, unprecedented in their deliberate apology for and practice of discontinuous, fragmentary form (only Nietzsche in philosophy had gone so far), are conceived as "anti-works, anti-finished products" (*des contre-œuvres, des contre-fini*), rejecting all claim to systematizing or totalization of knowledge, all claim to meaningful closure. Although few of these fragments resemble Montaigne's essays, it was Montaigne's term "essai" in its original meaning that he used in order to describe his lifelong habit of rising each day before daybreak to record "for myself only" these "attempts" ("essais") at defining his thought. In style, his self-described "methodical breaking up of language's ready-made forms and word-associations" echoes Montaigne's attack on Ciceronian rhetoric.

The essay collections of **Albert Camus** (1913–60) and **Henry de Montherlant** (1896–1972) share many common elements: they both bring a lyrical quality to their finest essays, which possess a beauty of their own as well as serving to throw light on their fictional and dramatic works; both practice a blending of genres which lends essayistic features to their fiction and narrative elements to their essays; both sought to preserve a sense of dignity, nobility, even heroism in a world fast losing such a sense; compared with the boldly experimental, subversive Blanchot, Barthes, and Butor, their essays appear traditional in form and even somewhat archaic. In other ways they diverge sharply from each other. Montherlant was a minor aristocrat, aloof, self-absorbed, anarchical in outlook, reveling (like Gide) in his contradictions, which he called "alternances" and rarely sought to resolve. Steeped like Montaigne in the Roman classics, especially Seneca, as well as in the classical idea of the essay as a search for the art of living wisely, and happy to emulate the sensuous, amply developed Romantic prose of Chateaubriand, he prided himself on his irrelevance to contemporary values and concerns. The theme of the self, in fact the *cult* of the self which he had learned from Maurice Barrès (1862–1923), permeates his essays, which constitute a long dialogue with himself whose ultimate aim is to construct a poetic, mythic self-image, often with little correspondence to the actual facts of his life. An unrelenting nihilist, he wrote, in his essay collection *Service inutile* (1935; Useless service), "Only the idea of myself keeps me afloat on the seas of nothingness." This tragic perspective, enriched by a wealth of reflections on many subjects, gives to *Service inutile* and to other fine collections of essays such as *Aux fontaines du désir* (1921–27; At the fountains of desire) and *Le Solstice de juin* (1941; June solstice) a unique beauty and power.

Camus, by contrast, clung to the ideal of social commitment in the name of humanism and justice. Much of his essay work consists of polemical articles first written for the significantly named newspaper, *Combat* (1944–47) and subsequently published in book form as *Actuelles* (1950–58; Current issues). As a political essayist he is a worthy successor of Renan and Prévost-Paradol. However, these "essays in rational form" couched in "the language of action" (his own description) he did not consider true "essays." He reserved this purer designation for the three collections of semi-autobiographical, lyrico-narrative pieces entitled *L'Envers et l'endroit* (1937; The wrong side and the right side), *Noces* (1939; Nuptials), and *L'Été* (1954; Summer), inspired by his revered philosophy professor, Jean Grenier (1898–1971), and by the example of Grenier's fine essay work, *Les Îles* (1933; The islands). (Camus named Grenier along with Montherlant and André Malraux as the modern writers who had most influenced him.) Unlike Montherlant, Camus had serious scruples about dwelling on himself as essay subject matter: for one thing, he expressed doubt that "any man has ever dared depict himself as he really is"; for another, he preferred what he called "objective" subjects. Finally, unlike Montherlant, he also excelled in the long form of the essay, his best work in this field probably being *Le Mythe de Sisyphe* (1942; *The Myth of Sisyphus*).

The novelist-essayists Blanchot and Butor are best understood in the context of the essay's evolution in its relationship to the "postmodern" radical questioning of the whole concept of literary genres and of the privileged status accorded to the language of "literature." Lafond has shown the venerable precedents of this movement in the 16th- and 17th-century defense of fragmentary and discontinuous literary forms (maxim, aphorism, essay). "The fragment," noted Cioran, "is doubtless a disappointing genre, but the only honest one." The philosopher Jacques Derrida (1930–) argued that "all writing is aphoristic" and that "the fragment is not a failed literary form but the very form of everything that is written." He based this view on his claim as a semiotician that the meaning of a given unit in discourse is impossible to determine without indefinite deferral (what he called *différance*). Similarly, Barthes, in his essay on Butor, wrote: "The discontinuous is the fundamental status of all communication: there are no communicative signs that are not discrete [i.e. separate from all other units]." Derrida also questioned the concept of "genre" as a "principle imposing order," that is, arbitrary order, and allowing "transgressions" only within its prescribed limits. The philosopher Édouard Morot-Sir (in an article in *The French Essay*, 1982) considers the essay as the ultimate "anti-genre," perfectly expressive of contemporary "agnosticism, subjectivism, and nominalism [i.e. the belief that the names of things correspond to no metaphysical reality beyond themselves]." The essay as "anti-essay," subversive of its own traditional forms, is but one variation among several in the 20th-century revolt against genres: the "anti-novel," the "anti-theater," the "anti-painting," etc.

Blanchot's early essays in literary criticism, such as the collection *Faux pas* (1943; False steps), were relatively "straight" in manner, before he moved to the essay as "l'écriture fragmentaire" ("fragmentary writing"), a term he invented, and to the "anti-book" or "livre écartelé" (literally "drawn and quartered") or "éclaté" ("shattered," "exploded"). His work, then, whether in fiction or criticism, became a "défense et illustration," an apology for and practice of fragmentary and discontinuous forms. His sources were many: the "negative theology" of the great medieval theologian, Meister Eckhart (language can meaningfully make only negative statements about the nature of God); Mallarmé's goal of "giving a purer meaning to the words of the tribe" and his reflections on the nature of language and of the "Book"; Nietzsche's

defense of the fragment; and Valéry's concept of the "anti-book." Drawing on these precursors, together with his contemporaries, the philosophers Michel Foucault (1926–84) and Derrida, he probed the nature of language as the essential clue to the nature of being itself. Faced with the act of writing, he asked such questions as: "Who is speaking?" and "In what sense is there truly an author?" His striving to find a "language beyond language," a "language outside itself," and his resistance to the book as completion, closure, totality are reflected in such essay collections as *L'Entretien infini* (1969; The endless dialogue), *L'Attente, l'oubli* (1962; Waiting, forgetfulness), and *Le Pas au-delà* (1973; The step/not beyond). In these texts he practices what he called "plural speech," using multiple typefaces (narrative fragments in italics juxtaposed with bold-face type for essay fragments), creating the effect of a dialogue between the different voices, creating also the illusion of an author who is "absent" (or, as he preferred to call it, "neuter"). The distinction between genres, in fact any claim that the concept of genre has meaning at all, has practically disappeared in such works.

Some of these essayistic features are also found in the work of Blanchot's younger contemporary, **Michel Butor** (1926–). A natural-born experimenter and versatile (perhaps too versatile) polygraph, moving from one artistic experiment to another in a kind of frenzy, he was a pioneer in the *nouveau roman* (new novel) before abandoning the novel for what he calls "post-novelistic texts," assimilating what he had learned of the novel into the writing of essays. In reality he was indifferent to the traditional distinction between genres and, even more significantly, to the longstanding assumption that works of "criticism" (i.e. essays) were somehow inferior to works of "invention" (novels, poems, plays). His model here was Baudelaire, on whom he wrote a critical study, *Histoire extraordinaire: Essai sur un rêve de Baudelaire* (1961; *Histoire Extraordinaire: Essay on a Dream of Baudelaire's*). His massive five-volume series of essays on literature, *Répertoires* (1960–82; Repertories) and, in four volumes, his essays on art, *Illustrations* (1964–76), are less original in form than such texts as *Mobile* (1962), described as a "kaleidoscopic presentation of travel notes, lyrical outcries, dialogues, work timetables, and quotations" (Vercier and Lecarme). For Butor himself it was akin to a musical score, calling upon the reader's collaboration to turn it into a composition; others compare it to "serialist music." Central to Butor's essays as well as his novels are his reflections on space, both "literary" and geographical space, and on reading, or, more exactly, on what it means to be a reader. This latter theme suggests a close affinity with Montaigne, which he in fact demonstrated in his *Essais sur "Les Essais"* (1968; Essays on the *Essays*), on the subject of La Boétie's role in the *Essais*. He called himself, in a phrase that Montaigne would have enjoyed, a "monstrous reader." In his reading of works of the past, again not unlike Montaigne, he sought to uncover in them their "power of subversion" (Georges Raillard, *Butor*, 1968).

5. Conclusion

Germaine Brée (1978) has written: "The French essay made such a brilliant stage entrance with Montaigne that it seems at one stroke to have reached a level of perfection designed to discourage successors." She adds: "It was in England rather than in France that the essay won a rightful place among accepted literary genres." As a title in the singular for a longish, tentative, and modest inquiry into a large subject, the *essai* took hold in France; but as a short form, for two centuries it assumed other names and guises, as though to distance itself from Montaigne. It became the invisible or nonexistent genre, unrecognized by critics and historians of letters. It was categorized – and often dismissed – as an English literary type. Rare were the French essayists such as Marivaux or Montégut willing to emulate their English counterparts. In one of his letters Flaubert hints at something deep in the French psyche that both admired the "superb parts" of English writing and distrusted its "defective composition" and "lack of plan." Sainte-Beuve, introducing his famous article, "What Is a Classic?" (*Causeries du lundi*, 1850), indulges for once in a more informal manner of writing, "of the sort that our neighbors, the English, modestly call an 'essay' and have developed into a genre." Brunetière makes no mention of the essay in his *L'Évolution des genres*, except, in the volume on criticism, to dismiss the English critics as "mere essayists." A German anthologist of French moralist writings, G. R. Hocke, affirmed in 1938: "There is no French essay." Fraser documents further evidence of this strange situation, citing French dictionaries and encyclopedias.

Gradually in our own century, however, thanks to the efforts of Chadbourne, Brée, Fraser, and others, awareness has increased that *l'essai* is much more than a vague amorphous term for "nonfiction" or "the prose of ideas" and that it deserves attention for its specific nature as a distinct literary genre, however elusive its nature may be. Among long-established, prestigious genres such as fiction, poetry, and drama, its very marginality and its freedom from the constraints of literary conventions have given it the advantage of being a uniquely flexible and adaptable instrument; so adaptable, in fact, that it is "protéiforme" (Brée), able like the Greek god Proteus to change its form at will; capable of assimilating features of the poem, the short story, or the dialogue; capable even, in the hands of a Blanchot, a Barthes, or a Butor, of subverting itself, dissolving into fragments and becoming the "anti-essay."

The paradox is that the long absence in France of critical awareness of the essay as genre has coexisted with an extraordinarily rich production of essays and "essay-relatives," almost without hiatus, from Michel de Montaigne to Michel Butor and beyond. Amidst the changing guises, certain more or less constant features of the essayist's art recur: the invitation to the reader to enter into the author's confidence and share in his or her dialogue with the self; the freedom of form sometimes called "artful disorder"; the effect of "thought-in-process" as distinct from the finished product of thought leading to conclusion and closure; reflections that are less premeditated than stimulated by chance, rooted in circumstance, using any subject as pretext. These features, which obviously derive from Montaigne, are hardly exclusive to the French essay. What may be its specific *cachet* is at least fourfold: a restrained, indirect manner of self-portraiture; a strong link with the *moraliste* literary tradition (not all *moralistes* are essayists but most essayists are *moralistes*); a greater willingness (certainly than the English essayists), especially since postmodernism, to use the essay as a tool for theoretical, often

highly abstract speculations on the profoundest philosophical questions. As for the fourth feature, it has been beautifully summed up by Sontag apropos of Barthes' essays. The French essay, she writes, provides merely one great "variation on the project of self-examination – the noblest project of French literature," a project "inaugurated by Montaigne: the self as vocation, life as a reading of the self [with] the self as the locus of all possibilities."

RICHARD M. CHADBOURNE

Anthologies

The Age of Enlightenment: An Anthology of Eighteenth Century French Literature, edited by Otis Fellows and Norman Torrey, New York: Appleton Century Crofts, 1971 (original edition, 1942)

Anthologie des essayistes français contemporains, Paris: Kra, 1929

Choix d'essais du vingtième siècle, edited by Germaine Brée and Philip Solomon, Waltham, Toronto, and London: Blaisdell, 1969

The Continental Model: Selected French Critical Essays of the Seventeenth Century, edited by Scott Elledge and Donald Schier, Ithaca, New York: Cornell University Press, revised edition, 1970 (original edition, 1960)

Découverte de l'essai, edited by Susan Lawall, Christian Garaud, and Mireille Azibert, New York: Harcourt Brace Jovanovich, 1975

Essays of French, German and Italian Essayists, New York: Colonial Press, and London: Co-operative Publication Society, 1900

Further Reading

Bensmaïa, Réda, *The Barthes Effect: The Essay as Reflective Text*, Minneapolis: University of Minnesota Press, 1987 (original French edition, 1986)

Boase, Alan, *The Fortunes of Montaigne: A History of the Essays in France, 1580–1669*, New York: Octagon, 1970 (original edition, 1935)

Brée, Germaine, *Twentieth-Century French Literature*, Chicago: University of Chicago Press, 1983 (original French edition, 1978)

Burke, Peter, *Montaigne*, Oxford: Oxford University Press, 1981; New York: Hill and Wang, 1982

Chadbourne, Richard, *Ernest Renan as an Essayist*, Ithaca, New York: Cornell University Press, 1957

Chadbourne, Richard, "Prévost-Paradol, Political Essayist," *French Review* 30 (1957): 350–57

Chadbourne, Richard, "The Essay World of Emile Montégut," *PMLA* 76 (1961): 98–120

Chadbourne, Richard, "Criticism as Creation in Sainte-Beuve," *L'Esprit Créateur* 14 (1974): 44–54

Chadbourne, Richard, *Charles-Augustin Sainte-Beuve*, Boston: Twayne, 1977

Chadbourne, Richard, "A Puzzling Literary Genre: Comparative Views of the Essay," *Comparative Literature Studies* 20 (1983): 133–53

Champigny, Robert, *Pour une esthétique de l'essai*, Paris: Minard, 1967

Croll, Morris, "Attic Prose: Lipsius, Montaigne, Bacon," in his *Style, Rhetoric, and Rhythm: Essays*, edited by J. Max Patrick and others, Princeton, New Jersey: Princeton University Press, 1966

Dréano, Maturin, *La Renommée de Montaigne en France au XVIIIe siècle, 1677–1802*, Angers: l'Ouest, 1952

Fowlie, Wallace, "The Essay," in his *A Guide to Contemporary French Literature: From Valéry to Sartre*, New York: Meridian, 1957

Frame, Donald, *Montaigne's Essais: A Study*, Englewood Cliffs, New Jersey: Prentice Hall, 1969

Fraser, Theodore, *The French Essay*, Boston: Twayne, 1986

The French Essay, Columbia: University of South Carolina Department of Foreign Languages and Literatures, 1982

Good, Graham, "Montaigne, the Growth of Experience," in his *The Observing Self: Rediscovering the Essay*, London and New York: Routledge, 1988: 26–42

Henry, Patrick, *Montaigne in Dialogue*, Saratoga, California: Anma Libri, 1987

Hope, Quentin, *Saint-Évremond, the Honnête Homme as Critic*, Bloomington: Indiana University Press, 1962

Lafond, Jean, editor, *Les Formes brèves de la prose et le discours discontinu (XVIe–XVIIe siècles)*, Paris: Vrin, 1984

Queneau, Raymond, editor, *Histoire des littératures*, vol. 3, Paris: La Pléiade, 1958

Routh, H. V., "The Origins of the Essay Compared in English and French Literatures," *Modern Language Review* 15 (1920): 28–40, 143–51

Sontag, Susan, "Writing Itself: On Roland Barthes," *The New Yorker*, 26 April 1982: 122–41

Terrasse, Jean, *Rhétorique de l'essai littéraire*, Montreal: University of Quebec Press, 1977

Thibaudet, Albert, *Histoire de la littérature française de 1789 à nos jours*, Paris: Stock, 1936; as *French Literature from 1795 to Our Era*, translated by Charles Lam Markmann, New York: Funk and Wagnall, 1968

Vercier, Bruno, and Jacques Lecarme, *La Littérature française depuis 1968*, Paris: Bordas, 1982

Freud, Sigmund

Austrian, 1856–1939

Psychoanalytic theory, whether in Sigmund Freud's original version or in the reconstruction of it by French thinkers since the 1950s, has become an inescapable feature of Western intellectual culture in the 20th century. Controversy has undeniably helped to keep it at the focus of public attention, but there are also two factors inherent in Freud's writings which have contributed to maintaining that interest. One is the intellectual appeal (in a scientific age) of an integrative theory of mind and human creativity; the other is Freud's skill as a presenter of his own insights. For, as his supporters and critics alike have acknowledged, he could write very attractive German prose.

It is not clear that Freud ever followed a particular literary model in his writing, although he did admit to a special affinity with **Lessing** (the "father of modern German literature"). However, his works abound with quotations from literary authors – from **Goethe** and Heine, E. T. A. Hoffmann and Georg Christoph Lichtenberg, and the Austrian dramatists Franz Grillparzer and Johann Nestroy, as well as Shakespeare, Sophocles, and Virgil – and it is likely that such reading helped him to develop his ease of expression as well as providing him with corroboration for some of his key psychological insights. In his technical papers, as in his public lectures and his well-known brochures (on jokes, on religion, on the psychopathology of everyday life), he used an idiom which was readily intelligible to any educated German speaker. That lucidity largely survives in the English *Standard Edition* of his works, even if some of the central concepts which Freud expressed in simple and familiar German terms have been rendered into an artificial medicalese ("ego," "id," "parapraxis"). Freud's own *Vorlesungen zur Einführung in die Psychoanalyse* (1916; *Introductory Lectures on Psycho-Analysis*) remain the most readable introduction to his system of thought.

Freud seems to have avoided the term "essay" when describing his own works, and in the early stages of his career, at least, this may have been in order to avoid the impression that his argument was in any way imprecise. In the *Standard Edition* there are just two works that are so described – the *Drei Abhandlungen zur Sexualtheorie* (1905; *Three Essays on the Theory of Sexuality*) and *Der Mann Moses und die monotheistische Religion* (1939; *Moses and Monotheism*) – and even here the German word that Freud preferred was *Abhandlung*, which is suggestive rather of "**treatise**" or "**discourse**." The distinguishing features of his writing are nevertheless recognizably the techniques of a skilled essayist, regardless of whether as readers we accept them as convincing or reject them as fanciful and beguiling. His case studies, for example, invariably provide an exposition of the patient's personal situation which is at once vivid and painstakingly constructed, as well as containing moments of calculated surprise when particularly revealing information is disclosed. (Freud himself likened these studies to novellas.) *Die Traumdeutung* (1900; *The Interpretation of Dreams*), notwithstanding its character as a scholarly dissertation, makes for lively reading because of the way that empirical experience, whether clinical or personal, is extensively described in illustration of its central propositions. And precisely when he is developing his most speculative arguments, in his cultural and metapsychological writings of the 1920s and 1930s, Freud is usually careful to anticipate likely objections on the part of the reader, and to be frank about the incomplete or insecure nature of the supporting evidence for his views.

The intellectual basis for Freud's mature writings can be found in the works he published between 1900 and 1905. That basis is the notion of an "economy" of libidinal energies at work in the unconscious mind, energies with which each of us is born and which require to be "discharged," but which become disposed in particular ways under the influence of external conditioning factors as we grow from infancy to adulthood. His central thesis in *The Interpretation of Dreams*, for example, is that every dream is an expression of wish-fulfillment, but that the wish is made manifest only in disguised forms because the original impulse from which it derived is being prevented from entering consciousness. It is a model of the mind which enabled Freud to suggest that there is a universal system of psychic mechanisms at work in the production of neuroses, dreams, and creative acts, as well as the commonplace aberrations of everyday life. It allowed him to develop a taxonomy of personality types related to the phases of physiological and psychological development in early childhood. And it permitted him to argue in the *Three Essays on the Theory of Sexuality* that all forms of sexual behavior, including bestiality, fetishism, and homosexuality, share a common source – a bold and liberalizing argument in the circumstances of 1905, when "deviant" sexuality tended to be automatically attributed to genetic disorders or "degeneracy." The mechanism which confines the determining impulse to the unconscious Freud calls "repression." His explanation for it centers on the "Oedipus complex," the notion that the growing male child, on his progress to adulthood, must pass through a phase in which he perceives his father as a threatening rival for the affections of his mother. Freud sees the internalization of the father's authority (as a power which is simultaneously terrible and admirable) as the means by which the individual acquires a sense of social restraint, a conscience; he later gives it the name "superego."

Freud's gift for imaginative intellectual constructions is most clearly apparent in *Totem und Tabu* (1913; *Totem and Taboo*), where he draws on the writings of **Darwin** and of contemporary anthropologists in order to make connections between the characteristic mental patterns of neuroses and those of "primitive" cultures. That same internalization of paternal authority which determines compulsive behavior, he now argues, also governs the incest taboo and the worship of totem animals in animistic societies. On the basis of this parallel he develops his famous scenario for the origin of social morality and monotheistic religion in the killing of the "primal father" by a band of young males previously excluded from sexual enjoyment of the females of the tribe: their act of parricide eliminates the physical presence of the dominant male, but his authority lives on in their subsequent codification of sexual behavior and in the notion of a "father in heaven." It is a scenario which Freud expressly characterizes as an intellectual scandal and a "just-so story," but it provides the foundation for his discussion of the seemingly ineradicable antipathy of human beings toward their own cultural institutions in *Das Unbehagen in der Kultur* (1930; *Civilization and Its Discontents*) as well as for his later essays on the psychological origins of religion in general and of Judaism in particular, *Die Zukunft einer Illusion* (1927; *The Future of an Illusion*) and *Moses and Monotheism*.

Freud is at his least persuasive in *Jenseits des Lustprinzips* (1920; *Beyond the Pleasure Principle*), the text in which he sought to adjust his conception of the unconscious mind to clinical evidence arising from World War I. The recurrent nightmares of shell-shocked soldiers could not be accommodated within his earlier theory of wish-fulfillment, and in order to account for them Freud suggests that alongside the "erotic" drives of the libido there is a set of conservative drives in the mind which aims at the reduction of displeasure. He calls the second set the "death instinct" because he claims that, left to itself, it would ultimately aim to restore the organism to an inanimate state; and he attributes the phenomena of sexual violence and sadism to the "death instinct" because, he says, it defies reason to attribute them to "Eros." It may be possible to see in these arguments an expression of Freud's temperamental pessimism, which is similarly apparent both in his later comments on society and culture and in his public exchange of letters with Albert Einstein in 1932 on the question of why societies go to war. But they can equally be seen as an illogical attempt to conserve the integrity of his psychological theory in the face of an empirical challenge.

Freud's theories have come under attack for a variety of reasons. He has been accused of selecting, and even suppressing, evidence in order to maintain the plausibility of the arguments he favors. He has been criticized as manifestly one-sided in his concentration on sexual energy as a determinant of human activity, and in the way he bases his account of culture exclusively on the psychology of the male. The very conception of his therapeutic regime has been attacked as oversystematized and authoritarian, entailing as it does the notion that a patient's "resistance" may be interpreted as confirmation of the accuracy of the diagnosis. Most damaging of all for Freud's psychological views, the principle of energy discharge on which he initially based his thinking has been shown since his time to be neither adequate nor accurate for a proper understanding of the nervous system.

What Freud's writings do offer is (in Wittgenstein's phrase) a "powerful mythology," a body of arguments which uses the analytical language of scientific rationalism to express a conception of human identity determined by irrational impulses, by desires and anxieties. His works have retained their provocative vigor because of the skepticism they bring to bear on the comfortable notion that thinking is a wholly rational activity.

DAVID MIDGLEY

Biography

Sigismund Solomon Freud. Born 6 May 1856 in Freiburg, Moravia. Brought up in Vienna. Studied medicine at the University of Vienna, 1873–79, M.D., 1881; neurology with J. M. Charcot in Paris, and H. Bernstein in Nancy, 1885–86. Worked at the Physiological Institute of Vienna, 1876–82, Brücke Institute, Vienna, 1881–82, and the General Hospital, Vienna, 1882–85; lectured at the University of Vienna, 1885. Private practice in Vienna, 1886–1938. Married Martha Bernays, 1886: six children. Cofounder, *Zeitschrift für Psychoanalyse und Imago*, and the *Jahrbuch der Psychoanalyse* (Yearbook of psychoanalysis); editor, *Imago* journal, from 1912. Left Vienna to escape the Nazi regime, 1938, and lived in London, setting up a private practice. Awards: Goethe Prize, 1930; honorary degree from Clark University. Corresponding member, Royal Society, London, 1936; also member of many psychiatric and psychoanalytical societies and associations. Died (of cancer) in London, 23 September 1939.

Selected Writings

Essays and Related Prose

Die Traumdeutung, 1900; as *The Interpretation of Dreams*, translated by Abraham A. Brill, 1913, and James Strachey, 1955

Drei Abhandlungen zur Sexualtheorie, 1905; as *Three Contributions to the Sexual Theory*, translated by Abraham A. Brill, 1910; as *Three Essays on the Theory of Sexuality*, translated by James Strachey, 1949

Über Psychoanalyse: Fünf Vorlesungen, 1910; as *Five Lectures on Psycho-Analysis*, edited and translated by James Strachey, 1957

Totem und Tabu: Über einige Übereinstimmungen im Seelenleben der Wilden und der Neurotiker, 1913; as *Totem and Taboo: Resemblances Between the Psychic Lives of Savages and Neurotics*, translated by Abraham A. Brill, 1918; as *Totem and Taboo: Some Points of Agreement Between the Mental Lives of Savages and Neurotics*, translated by James Strachey, 1950

Vorlesungen zur Einführung in die Psychoanalyse, 3 vols., 1916; as *A General Introduction to Psychoanalysis*, translated by Joan Riviere, 1920; as *Introductory Lectures on Psycho-Analysis*, translated by James Strachey, 1963

Das Unheimliche, 1919

Jenseits des Lustprinzips, 1920; as *Beyond the Pleasure Principle*, translated by C. J. M. Hubback, 1922, and James Strachey, 1950

Die Zukunft einer Illusion, 1927; as *The Future of an Illusion*, translated by W. D. Robson-Scott, 1928, and James Strachey, 1962

Das Unbehagen in der Kultur, 1930; as *Civilization and Its Discontents*, translated by Joan Riviere, 1930, and James Strachey, 1967

Neue Folge der Vorlesungen zur Einführung in die Psychoanalyse, 1933; as *New Introductory Lectures on Psycho-Analysis*, translated by W. J. H. Sprott, 1933, and James Strachey, 1964

Der Mann Moses und die monotheistische Religion, 1939; as *Moses and Monotheism*, translated by Katherine Jones, 1939, and James Strachey, 1974

The Freud Reader, edited by Peter Gay, 1989

Psychological Writings and Letters, edited by Sander L. Gilman, 1995

Other writings: many works on psychology and psychoanalysis, case studies of patients, diaries, and correspondence.

Collected works editions: *Gesammelte Werke*, 17 vols., 1940–52; *The Standard Edition of the Complete Psychological Works of Sigmund Freud*, general editor James Strachey, 24 vols., 1953–74; *Studienausgabe*, edited by Alexander Mitscherlich, Angela Richards, and James Strachey, 10 vols., 1969–89.

Bibliography

Grinstein, Alexander, *Sigmund Freud's Writings: A Comprehensive Bibliography*, New York: International Universities Press, 1977

Further Reading

Borch-Jacobsen, Mikkel, *The Freudian Subject*, Stanford, California: Stanford University Press, 1988; Basingstoke: Macmillan, 1989 (original French edition, 1982)

Bouveresse, Jacques, *Wittgenstein Reads Freud: The Myth of the Unconscious*, Princeton, New Jersey: Princeton University Press, 1995 (original French edition, 1991)

Clark, Ronald W., *Freud: The Man and the Cause*, London: Cape, and New York: Random House, 1980

Forrester, John, *Language and the Origin of Psychoanalysis*, London: Macmillan, 1980

Fromm, Erich, "Freud's Theory of Aggressiveness and Destructiveness," in his *The Anatomy of Human Destructiveness*, New York: Holt Rinehart and Winston, 1973; London: Cape, 1974

Gay, Peter, *Freud: A Life for Our Time*, New York: Norton, and London: Dent, 1988

Jones, Ernest, *Sigmund Freud: Life and Work*, London: Hogarth Press, and New York: Basic Books, 3 vols., 1953–57

Kitcher, Patricia, *Freud's Dream: A Complete Interdisciplinary Science of Mind*, Cambridge, Massachusetts: MIT Press, 1992

Kline, Paul, *Fact and Fantasy in Freudian Theory*, 2nd (expanded) edition, London and New York: Methuen, 1981 (original edition, 1972)

Mahony, Patrick, *Freud as a Writer*, 2nd (expanded) edition, New Haven, Connecticut and London: Yale University Press, 1987

Marcus, Steven, *Freud and the Culture of Psychoanalysis*, London and Boston: Allen and Unwin, 1984

Masson, Jeffrey Moussaieff, *Freud: The Assault on Truth: Freud's Suppression of the Seduction Theory*, New York: Farrar Straus Giroux, and London: Faber, 1984

Meisel, Perry, editor, *Freud: A Collection of Critical Essays*, Englewood Cliffs, New Jersey: Prentice Hall, 1981

Ricoeur, Paul, *Freud and Philosophy: An Essay on Interpretation*, New Haven, Connecticut and London: Yale University Press, 1970 (original French edition, 1965)

Rieff, Philip, *Freud: The Mind of the Moralist*, New York: Viking Press, 1959; London: Gollancz, 1960

Schönau, Walter, *Sigmund Freuds Prosa: Literarische Elemente seines Stils*, Stuttgart: Metzler, 1968

Storr, Anthony, *Freud*, Oxford and New York: Oxford University Press, 1989

Sulloway, Frank, *Freud: Biologist of the Mind*, New York: Basic Books, and London: Deutsch, 1979

Wallace, Edwin R. IV, *Freud and Anthropology: A History and Reappraisal*, New York: International Universities Press, 1983

Webster, Richard, *Why Freud Was Wrong: Sin, Science and Psychoanalysis*, London: HarperCollins, and New York: Basic Books, 1995

Wollheim, Richard, *Freud*, Cambridge and New York: Cambridge University Press, 1990 (original edition, 1971)

Wollheim, Richard, and James Hopkins, editors, *Philosophical Essays on Freud*, Cambridge and New York: Cambridge University Press, 1982

Freyre, Gilberto

Brazilian, 1900–1987

Gilberto Freyre is considered one of the major figures in Brazilian thought. His essays exemplify rigorous scientific training combined with a keen artistic sensitivity to provide the reader with a glimpse of Brazilian society, particularly that of the northeast region. Freyre's life and work spanned most of the 20th century; he witnessed at first-hand many of the changes that took place in his native country – revolution, dictatorship (benevolent and repressive), Modernism, political apathy, political diversification, and democracy. Throughout this turbulent century, Freyre was a methodical observer of society, and most of his insights were new and controversial, although many have come to be seen as part of the "national lore."

In 1926 he wrote the *Manifesto regionalista de 1926* (pub. 1952; Regionalist manifesto), in direct opposition to the ideals proposed during the Week of Modern Art (1922) that marked the beginning of Brazilian Modernism. The *Manifesto* develops two interrelated themes: the defense of the region as a unit of national organization and the conservation of regional and traditional values in Brazil in general and in the northeast region in particular.

As a scientist, Freyre followed the path established by **Euclides da Cunha** concerning miscegenation in the formation of the "Brazilian race." Freyre, however, was more methodical and scientific in his writings. His greatest work, *Casa-grande e senzala* (1933; *Masters and Slaves*), earned him international acclaim as the most solid interpretation of interracial relations to that date. The publication of *Masters and Slaves* marked the beginning of rigorous **science essay** production in Brazil. Critics have named this book as the first to separate scientific essays from purely academic and **critical essays**. Although other writers had already begun to study and write essays with sociocultural content, Freyre has rightfully earned recognition as the "Father of Brazilian Sociology."

The relationship between "masters" and "slaves" is the basic premise of all of Freyre's theories. Indeed, he paved the way for many of the current ideas concerning modern cultural studies and postcolonial observations. Only through understanding the nature of oppression – whatever its source – can one comprehend one's culture. Similarly, only through "reading" the oppressor's text – the text of the master – can one begin to understand one's own text. Freyre applied his own thesis in his interpretation of Brazilian society. Unlike many essayists who describe Brazil in terms of what happens in the main population centers – São Paulo and Rio de Janeiro

– Freyre studies the "periphery" of Brazilian society, including his native northeast and the northern region of Brazil. Both regions represent the "slaves" within a society, with many internal and external "masters." Indeed, he criticizes the Brazilian elite, who habitually adopted customs they judged to be modern, emphasizing the "foreign" (French) over the "national" (Brazilian).

Freyre's discourse is sober and precise. He uses a limited vocabulary characterized by only the most necessary scientific terminology. Like Graciliano Ramos, he limits the use of adjectives, providing the reader with a discourse that mirrors the dry conditions of the society and culture he describes. While not subscribing to the racist views founded on European positivism, Freyre is conservative in his views, particularly those that deal with women's roles. His much-studied "masters and slaves" thesis falls short of including women as oppressed beings within a patriarchal society. Women's roles, according to Freyre, are limited to those of wives and mothers. Indeed, his most emphatic (and, one should add, least scientific) view is that the best and only books women ought to read are cookbooks, particularly those that have been in the family for a long time; this, Freyre believes, will preserve the moral fiber of the family.

Freyre's essays influenced not only scientific writing in Brazil, but also the development of the northeastern regionalist novel. Such writers as José Lins do Rego, Rachel de Queiroz, and Jorge Amado have all mirrored in their novels the social context and the language found in Gilberto Freyre.

CARMEN CHAVES TESSER

Biography
Gilberto de Mello Freyre. Born 15 March 1900 in Recife, Pernambuco. Studied at the American Colégio Gilreath, Recife, until 1917; Baylor University, Waco, Texas, 1918–21, B.A., 1921; Columbia University, New York, 1921–22, M.A. in anthropology, 1922. Traveled in Europe, 1922–23. Private secretary to the Governor of Pernambuco, Recife, 1927–30. Editor, *A Província*, Recife, 1928–30. Taught sociology at the Escola Normal, Recife, 1928–30. Exiled to Portugal, then traveled to Africa, 1930. Professor of sociology, University of São Paulo, 1935–38; visiting professor at various universities in Brazil, Europe, and the United States. Married Maria Magdalena Guedes Pereira, 1941: one daughter and one son. Representative of Pernambuco, National Assembly, 1946, and in the House of Deputies, 1947–50. Brazilian Ambassador to the United Nations General Assembly, 1949, 1964. Supervisor, Northeast Brazil Social and Educational Research Center, Recife, 1957–87. Director, *Diogene* and *Cahiers Internationaux de Sociologie* (International notebooks of sociology). Awards: several, including the Felippe d'Oliveira Award, 1934; Machado de Assis Prize, 1963; José Vasconcelos Gold Medal (Mexico), 1974; Moinho Santista Prize, 1974; honorary degrees from five universities. Member, São Paulo Academy of Letters, 1961, Brazilian Academy of Letters, 1962, and American Academy of Arts and Sciences. Knight Commander, Order of the British Empire (KBE), 1971. Commander, Legion of Honor (France), 1986. Died in Recife, 18 July 1987.

Selected Writings

Essays and Related Prose
Casa-grande e senzala: Formação de família brasileira sob o regimen de economia patriarchal, 1933; as *Masters and Slaves*, translated by Samuel Putnam, 1946

Artigos de jornal, 1935; revised, enlarged edition, as *Retalhos de jornais velhos*, 1964
Sobrados e mucambos, 1936; as *The Mansions and the Shanties*, translated by Harriet de Onís, 1963
Região e tradição, 1941
Na Bahia em 1943, 1944
Perfil de Euclydes e outros perfis, 1944
Brazil: An Interpretation (lectures), 1945; revised, enlarged edition, as *New World in the Tropics: The Culture of Modern Brazil*, 1959
Manifesto regionalista de 1926, 1952
Um brasileiro em terras portuguesas, 1952
Problemas brasileiros de antropologia, 1959
Ordem e progresso, 1959; as *Order and Progress: Brazil from Monarchy to Republic*, edited and translated by Rod W. Horton, 1970
O Luso e o trópico, 1961
Vida, forma e côr, 1962
6 conferências em busca de um leitor, 1965
Seleta para jovens, edited by Maria Elisa Dias Collier, 1971
A condição humana e outras temas, 1972
Além do apenas moderno: Sugestões em torno de possíveis futuros do homen, em geral, e do homen brasileiro, em particular, 1973
The Gilberto Freyre Reader, translated by Barbara Shelby, 1974
O brasileiro entre os outros hispanos: Afinidades, contrastes, e possíveis futuros nas suas inter-relações, 1975
A presença do açúcar na formação brasileira, 1975
Alhos e bugalhos: Ensaios sobre temas contraditórios, 1978
Préfacios desgarrados, edited by Edson Nery de Fonseca, 2 vols., 1978
Tempo de aprendiz (articles 1918–26), edited by José Antônio Gonsalves de Mello, 2 vols., 1979
Pessoas, coisas e animais: Ensaios, edited by Edson Nery de Fonseca, 1981

Other writings: two novels, poetry, a cookbook, and many books on Brazilian history and culture.

Bibliography
Foster, David William, and Walter Rela, in *Brazilian Literature: A Research Bibliography*, New York: Garland, 1990

Further Reading
Arroyo, Jossianna, "El cuerpo del esclavo y la narrativa de la nación en *Casa-Grande e senzala* de Gilberto Freyre," *Lucero* 4 (1993): 31–42
Gilberto Freyre: Sua ciência, sua filosofia, sua arte, Rio de Janeiro: Olympio, 1962
Oliven, Ruben, *Tradition Matters: Gaúcho Diversity in Brazil*, New York: Columbia University Press, 1996
Sanchez-Eppler, Benigo, "Telling Anthropology: Zora Neale Hurston and Gilberto Freyre Disciplined in Their Field-Home-Work," *American Literary History* 4 (1992): 464–88

Frisch, Max
Swiss, 1911–1991

Max Frisch's reputation as one of this century's foremost authors of German literature is based mainly on a number of formidable novels, plays, and literary diaries. His importance as a prodigious essayist is known only in the German-speaking world since the vast majority of his essays have never been translated. Indeed, it could be stated that the essay as a literary genre is at the core of Frisch's work. Beginning in the early 1930s, when he wrote book **reviews** and short stories as a young student at the University of Zurich, a splendid array of essays extends over a period of some 60 years, ending with Frisch's last publication, "Schweiz ohne Armee?" (1989; Switzerland without an army?), an essay in dialogue form which was dedicated "with gratitude to Denis Diderot and Ulrich Bräker," two essayists of the Enlightenment tradition, which he considered the last great utopia of humankind. The subject of this last essay may explain at least partially why Frisch's essays have remained mostly unappreciated outside Switzerland: they deal to a great extent with Swiss matters, be they political or cultural. In fact, to understand the weight of Frisch's essays within his literary oeuvre, one has to recognize the central role the essay as a genre has always played in Switzerland's literary tradition, from **Rousseau**, Johann Heinrich Pestalozzi, Jeremias Gotthelf, and Gottfried Keller in the past to Carl Spitteler, Carl Burckhardt, C.-F. Ramuz, Max Rychner, Paul Nizon, and Adolf Muschg and Peter von Matt in more recent times. The literary essay is a typical art form in that country of four major cultures whose common denominator rests on political rather than cultural similarities and which is thus dependent on short and well-formulated essays as a means of intercultural and intertextual communication.

Yet to call Frisch simply an essayist on Swiss matters would do injustice to his oeuvre, whose quality, range, and depth make him one of the few world-class authors Switzerland has produced. From a biographical point of view, Frisch's literary works coincide with some of the major events of the 20th century. As a writer, he was in personal contact with some of the most significant cultural and political personalities of his age. Frisch's essays on contemporaries include those on his fellow writers, colleagues and friends Albin Zollinger, **Thomas Mann**, Bertolt Brecht, **Friedrich Dürrenmatt**, Peter Suhrkamp, Teo Otto, Kurt Hirschfeld, **Günter Grass**, Andrei D. Sakharov, Ludwig Hohl, Varlin (i.e. Willi Guggenheim), and Gottfried Honegger. Many experiences and encounters that are of interest to a greater public have entered his essays or appear in essay form in Frisch's literary diaries. (His friendship with Brecht comes to mind, or his lunch in the White House with Henry Kissinger, or a trip to China as a companion of Helmut Schmidt.)

Essays play a central role in Frisch's life as a literary diary by reflecting the writer's love for the open-ended sketch and his distrust of timeless perfection. As with the literary diary, Frisch's numerous essays provide the reader with structure and guidance through his own prolific literary work. Frisch is not an easy guide, no Baedecker for superficial readers. He makes demands that are perhaps too difficult for many who want to ignore his haunting, inescapable questions. Frisch set standards for literary thought and linguistic elegance. Since Franz Kafka, **Robert Musil**, and Thomas Mann, German literature has known no writer who handled the German language with equal precision. "Everything that is completed ceases to be the home of our spirit," he states at the end of his essay "Das erste Haus" (1942; The first house), reminding the reader of Frisch's early training as an architect.

Frisch's reflections, his intellectual analyses, his remarkable insights into the spiritual development of his epoch are nowhere more apparent than in the over 200 known essays that appear listed in his *Gesammelte Werke in zeitlicher Folge* (1976–86; Collected works in chronological order). His didactic intentions are quite obvious. He considered himself to belong to the tradition of the age of reason, which he eventually came to judge as a failed endeavor.

His lifelong battle against premature reconciliation, against any kind of ideology or compromise, made him a formidable opponent of all establishments, whether conservative, socialist, or postmodern. He taught the daring adventure of ongoing utopian thought. Frisch had many opponents among those compatriots who, as he said in his speech on the occasion of the awarding of the Schiller Prize, "have only an Establishment, complete with flag, posing as Heimat – and owned by the military to boot" ("Die Schweiz als Heimat" [1974; "Switzerland as *Heimat*"]).

Of Frisch's essays, those about politics were the most heated and passionate, those about literature the most memorable. Over the years he gradually gave up the somewhat apodictic style of his earlier writings and developed a new form of essayistic prose, the so-called "Fragebogen" (questionnaire), consisting of a list of mostly unanswerable questions regarding the human condition. With his precise questions he challenged the reader into recognizing the frailty of the world he lived in and the false assumptions on which the human condition has been built, as in his caustic but humane query at the beginning of his last "Fragebogen 1987": "Are you sure you are really interested in the preservation of the human race, once you and all the people you know are no longer living?"

ROLF KIESER

Biography
Max Rudolf Frisch. Born 15 May 1911 in Zurich. Studied at the Kantonale Realgymnasium, Zurich, 1924–30; University of Zurich, 1930–33; Zurich Technische Hochschule, 1936–41, diploma in architecture, 1941. Freelance journalist, from 1933. Served in the Swiss army, 1939–45. Married Gertrud Anna Constance von Meyenburg, 1942 (divorced, 1959): two daughters and one son. Practicing architect in Zurich, 1942–55. Traveled in Europe throughout the late 1940s; visited the United States and Mexico, 1951–52; lived in Rome, 1960–65, then moved back to Switzerland. Married Marianne Öllers, 1968 (later divorced). Awards: several, including Raabe Prize, 1954; Büchner Prize, 1958; Zurich Prize, 1958; Veillon Prize, 1958; Jerusalem Prize, 1965; Schiller Prize (Baden-Württemberg), 1965; Schiller Prize (Switzerland), 1974; Neustadt International Prize, 1986; Heine Prize, 1989; honorary degrees from five universities and colleges. Died in Zurich, 4 April 1991.

Selected Writings

Essays and Related Prose
Tagebuch mit Marion, 1947
Tagebuch 1946–1949, 1950; as *Sketchbook 1946–1949*, translated by Geoffrey Skelton, 1977
Ausgewählte Prosa, 1961; enlarged edition, 1965
Tagebuch 1966–1971, 1972; as *Sketchbook 1966–1971*, translated by Geoffrey Skelton, 1974
Forderungen des Tages: Porträts, Skizzen, Reden 1943–1982, 1983
Novels, Plays, Essays, edited by Rolf Kieser, 1989

Other writings: several novels (including *Stiller* [*I'm Not Stiller*], 1954; *Homo Faber*, 1957) and 11 plays (including *Biedermann und die Brandstifter* [*The Fire Raisers*], 1958; *Andorra*, 1961).

Collected works edition: *Gesammelte Werke in zeitlicher Folge*, edited by Hans Mayer, 7 vols., 1976–86.

Bibliographies

Gerlach, Rainer, "Bibliographie," *Text + Kritik* issue on Frisch, 47–48 (1983): 114–49

Wilbert-Collins, Elly, in *A Bibliography of Four Contemporary German-Swiss Authors: Friedrich Dürrenmatt, Max Frisch, Robert Walser, Albin Zollinger*, Berne: Francke, 1967: 33–52

Further Reading

Bodine, Jay F., "Frisch's Little White Lies: Self-Discovery and Engagement Through Skepsis of Language and Perspective," in *Perspectives on Max Frisch*, edited by Gerhard F. Probst and Jay F. Bodine, Lexington: University Press of Kentucky, 1982

Cook, Mary E., "'Countries of the mind': Max Frisch's Narrative Technique," *Modern Language Review* 65 (1970): 820–28

Pender, Malcolm, *Max Frisch: His Work and Its Swiss Background*, Stuttgart: Heinz, 1979

Petersen, Jürgen H., *Max Frisch*, Stuttgart: Metzler, 1978

Schmitz, Walter, *Max Frisch: Das Werk (1931–1961)*, Berne: Lang, 1985

Schmitz, Walter, *Max Frisch: Das Spätwerk (1962-1982)*, Tübingen: Francke, 1985

Schuchmann, Manfred E., *Der Autor als Zeitgenosse: Gesellschaftliche Aspekte in Max Frischs Werk*, Berne: Lang, 1979

Stephan, Alexander, *Max Frisch*, Munich: Beck, 1983

Weisstein, Ulrich, *Max Frisch*, New York: Twayne, 1967

Werner, Markus, *Bilder des Endgültigen, Entwürfe des Möglichen: Zum Werk von Max Frisch*, Berne: Lang, 1975

Frye, Northrop

Canadian, 1912–1991

Almost all of Northrop Frye's writings are essays in the broad sense of the word. He termed his first book, *Fearful Symmetry* (1947), an "extended critical essay in the Swinburne tradition." *Anatomy of Criticism* (1957) is subtitled "Four Essays." Most of his earlier short pieces are **reviews**, and most of his mature writings began as public lectures; but in all of these the essential features of the essay prevail. His recurrent concern is the relation of his immediate subject to the conception of literature collectively as a meaningful whole, unified by an organizing mythology and by recurrent patterns of imagery and narrative. Roughly half of his books are groupings of essays on a common author or theme; most of the others are collected reprints from his 350-odd journal articles.

Frye's essays return repeatedly to several favored topics: critical studies of Blake, Shakespeare, Milton, **Yeats, T. S. Eliot,** and Stevens; educational themes, such as examination of the purpose of studying literature, a theory of education based on the conception of the primacy of the Bible and of Greek mythology in the teaching of Western literature, and the nature and function of the university; social themes, especially the function of the study of literature as educating the imagination and thus as the quintessential tool for understanding and survival in society.

Frye's audience is almost invariably a university audience, but a relatively unspecialized one. Frye was an instinctive teacher, and even his studies of Shakespeare or Milton are designed to appeal to the not entirely converted. The blind spots and the mental blocks of the specialist and the reluctant freshman assume equal importance. Prefiguring new historicism in a sense, his assumption is constantly that the cultural highbrow, the common reader, and the barely literate unwittingly have more in common than divides them; and central to his conception of literature is the assumption that the texts of imaginative literature, from the classics to pulp romance and soap opera, are similarly informed by a common body of mythological structures. This logically required his reaction, strongly polemical in its context of the trends of the time, against the prevailing conception of criticism as evaluation.

For Frye the intellectually honest may change their opinions but not their principles or their informing mythological constructs, hence the possibility of treating the structure of their thought and imagery as a consistent unit. His studies of literary figures thus tend to deal primarily with the relation of the part to the whole, on an assumption, like Milton's, that the life of the poet is itself a poem.

Seminal to Frye's thought is the poetry of William Blake, the subject of *Fearful Symmetry*. A deep instinctive revulsion to the mechanistic elements of British empirical thought, and to the industrialized tyranny it spawned, led Blake to focus on the relevance and importance of the arts and on the centrality of human creativity, themes that Frye made his own. Human essence and existence are those of an imagination that constructs a world in its own image, a world of gardens and cities and communities and domesticated animals. The artist is thus the quintessential human, in possession of a creativity that transcends the individual; for Blake this larger personality, in which the human and the divine are the same thing, is that of Jesus. Frye's nonconformist (and sometimes destructively conservative) childhood Protestantism, to which he seems to have felt both commitment and revulsion, made Blake's exuberant optimism of spirit, and his triumphant transcendence over some of the deadlier elements of the same traditions, the breath of fresh air that enabled Frye to resolve the tensions of his own background and to find his characteristic stance and voice.

Frye claims that the genesis of his thought moved from Blake, who worked out the principles of literary symbolism and biblical typology for himself, and on to Renaissance figures like Spenser, who took them from the critical theories of his age. (Frye's first graduate teaching was on Spenser, and the Spenser essay in *Fables of Identity* [1963] is apparently the epitome of an unwritten second book.) *Anatomy of Criticism* takes from this nexus the conviction that the Western world possesses a consistent and unified mythology, encyclopedic in range, from which its literature and thought are descended or "displaced." The *Anatomy*'s project is a trial grammar or taxonomy of this integrated conception of literature. A polarization, conceived of as embedded in the structure of the imagination, and derived largely through Blake from the Bible, conceives the projection of a world of desire in comedy and romance and of anxiety in tragedy and irony or satire. Widely admired, but frequently seen as overly schematic, the *Anatomy*'s premises *per se* have not gained general acceptance. It nevertheless stands as one of the most quoted books of the postwar period.

In contrast, Frye's work on Shakespearean comedy, culminating in *A Natural Perspective* (1965), is now widely accepted. Its central themes are: first, comedy's highly conventionalized nature as a function of its descent from oral culture, folklore, and myth; second, its movement from an initial "blocking" world of rigid law and parental and social repression, through a phase of complications and release in the context of a natural world that is variously exotic, innocent, green, magic, and dream-related, to a renewed and reconfigured social world characterized by self-knowledge, marriage, and the passage of authority between the generations; finally, its vision, grounded in desire, of a union of the human imagination with a benevolent natural order, with the result that a deeper human identity is found and society is renewed on a higher level of existence.

A student and admirer of Canadian poet E. J. Pratt, Frye took an early and enduring interest in Canadian writing. This manifested itself in numerous early reviews, especially in *Canadian Forum*, which he edited for some years, and, through the 1950s, in a survey of the year's poetry, written annually for the *University of Toronto Quarterly*'s "Letters in Canada" issues. His view of Canadian literature, which he conceived of as being at a stage somewhat analogous to that of Old English, features some similarities of bleakness in what he calls a "garrison complex" and in its sense of nature as powerfully alien.

The Great Code (1982) and *Words with Power* (1990), based on the conception of the unity of the Bible's imagery and narrative, are both a late climax to Frye's career and a working out of themes he was already at work on in his Blake book. In the former, recuperating typological reading, which was much out of fashion when he first turned to it, Frye sees the Bible as a series of seven phases of revelation, all re-creations of one another. A structuring of metaphor, polarized between desire and anxiety, projects recurrent bodies of apocalyptic and demonic imagery respectively. Recurrent mythology constitutes narrative as a series of deliverances, from the escape out of Egypt to the inheritance of the Kingdom. The language of the Bible, a language of love, is seen to transcend all that divides, and to find a final antitype in the reader's mind. *Words with Power* considers the determinative and authorizing relation of the Bible to Western literature and argues the principle that its language of myth and metaphor provide the context and pattern for all literary creation and for all thought.

RICHARD SCHELL

Biography
Herman Northrop Frye. Born in Sherbrooke, Quebec, 14 July 1912. Studied at Aberdeen High School, Moncton, graduated, 1928; Victoria College, University of Toronto, 1929–33, B.A. in philosophy and English, 1933; theology at Emmanuel College, Toronto, 1933–36 (spent Summer 1934 as a student preacher near Shaunavon, Saskatchewan), ordained into the ministry of the United Church of Canada, 1936; Merton College, Oxford, 1936–39, B.A. in English, 1939, M.A., 1943. Married Helen Kemp, 1937 (died, 1986). Lecturer, from 1937, professor of English, from 1948, chair of department, from 1952, and principal, 1959, Victoria College; University Professor of English, University of Toronto, from 1967; chancellor, Victoria University, Toronto, from 1978. Editor, *Canadian Forum*, 1948–52; supervisory editor, Uses of Imagination textbook series, Harcourt Brace Jovanovich, New York. Elected to the Royal Society of Canada, 1951. Married Elizabeth Brown, 1988. Awards: Lorne Pierce Medal, 1958; Pierre Chauveau Medal, 1970; Molson Prize, 1971; Royal Bank of Canada Award, 1978; Canada Council Medal, 1978; Governor-General's Award, 1987; dozens of honorary degrees from universities worldwide, particularly Canadian. Companion, Order of Canada, 1972. Died (of a heart attack) in Toronto, 22 January 1991.

Selected Writings

Essays and Related Prose
Fearful Symmetry: A Study of William Blake, 1947
Anatomy of Criticism: Four Essays, 1957
The Educated Imagination, 1963
Fables of Identity: Studies in Poetic Mythology, 1963
T. S. Eliot, 1963
The Well-Tempered Critic, 1963
A Natural Perspective: The Development of Shakespearean Comedy and Romance, 1965
The Return of Eden: Five Essays on Milton's Epics, 1965; as *Five Essays on Milton's Epics*, 1966
Fools of Time: Studies in Shakespearean Tragedy, 1967
The Modern Century, 1967
A Study of English Romanticism, 1968
The Stubborn Structure: Essays on Criticism and Society, 1970
The Bush Garden: Essays on the Canadian Imagination, 1971
The Critical Path: An Essay on the Social Context of Literary Criticism, 1971
The Secular Scripture: A Study of the Structure of Romance, 1976
Spiritus Mundi: Essays on Literature, Myth, and Society, 1976
Northrop Frye on Culture and Literature: A Collection of Review Essays, edited by Robert D. Denham, 1978
Creation and Recreation, 1980
Divisions on a Ground: Essays on Canadian Culture, edited by James Polk, 1982
The Great Code: The Bible and Literature, 1982
The Myth of Deliverance: Reflections on Shakespeare's Problem Comedies, 1983
Northrop Frye on Shakespeare, edited by Robert Sandler, 1986
On Education, 1988
Myth and Metaphor: Selected Essays, 1974–1988, edited by Robert D. Denham, 1990
Reading the World: Selected Writings, 1935–1976, edited by Robert D. Denham, 1990
Words with Power: Being a Second Study of the Bible and Literature, 1990
The Double Vision: Language and Meaning in Religion, 1991
The Eternal Act of Creation: Essays, 1979–1990, edited by Robert D. Denham, 1993

Collected works edition: *Collected Works*, edited by Robert D. Denham, 1996– (in progress).

Bibliography
Denham, Robert D., *Northrop Frye: An Annotated Bibliography of Primary and Secondary Sources*, Toronto: University of Toronto Press, 1987

Further Reading
Ayre, John, *Northrop Frye: A Biography*, Toronto: Random House, 1989
Hamilton, A. C., *Northrop Frye: Anatomy of His Criticism*, Toronto: University of Toronto Press, 1990
Hart, Jonathan, *Northrop Frye: The Theoretical Imagination*, London and New York: Routledge, 1994
Lee, Alvin A., and Robert D. Denham, editors, *The Legacy of Northrop Frye*, Toronto: University of Toronto Press, 1994

Fuentes, Carlos

Mexican, 1928–

Carlos Fuentes is one of Latin America's greatest writers, remarkable as both a fiction writer and an intellectual. An enthusiastic participant in conferences and international forums, he has given countless interviews in which he talks about his life, literary ideas, world view, books, obsessions, and desires. He is cosmopolitan, sophisticated, and vigorous, as well as an assiduous inquirer and intense creator. Author of numerous essays, he also writes novels and stories, chronicles, articles, reviews, literary criticism, translations, plays, and movie scripts. Although he has published a dozen books of essays, many others are scattered in publications throughout the world. Of his writings his nonfiction prose is the least studied, but it is of enormous influence in political, literary, and cultural discussions.

Fuentes began his career as a critic when, along with Emmanuel Carballo and **Octavio Paz**, he founded the review *Revista Mexicana de Literatura* (Mexican review of literature) in 1954. He undertook this endeavor, he explains in an interview with Jonathan Tittler in 1980, "with the express purpose of combatting the narrowness of literary chauvinism, of opening our windows to the world, and particularly to the rest of Latin America." *París: La revolución de mayo* (1968; Paris: the May revolution), his first nonfiction published as a brief book, best defined as a political chronicle, became famous and widely read among students and leftwing intellectuals. His first book of essays, *La nueva novela hispanoamericana* (1969; The new Hispanic American novel), in which he reflects on the new Latin American narrative, is one of his best-known works, and frequently considered the theoretical exposition of his own fiction. Fuentes writes about literature, especially the novel, constantly and extensively, but he also writes on political, social, and economic subjects, as well as history, culture, and life in Latin America. His essays are not limited to explicating his own writings: they are also part of the vast project that characterizes his creative effort. As in the novel, in the essay he seeks to formulate the many complex and interacting sides of history and culture, in which writing is conceived as a boundless verbal exploration arriving at knowledge only through the imagination.

Two books center on his own country: *Tiempo mexicano* (1971; Mexican time), and *Nuevo tiempo mexicano* (1994; New Mexican time). However, although Mexico is his main concern, Fuentes characteristically extends his perspective to all of Latin America, elaborating an intricate and expansive understanding of its many manifestations, often counterpointing its past and present and conjoining its Indian and Spanish inheritance. A good example of this is the long essay, *El espejo enterrado* (1992; The Buried Mirror), where Fuentes explores the 500 years of what he considers the life of the American continent torn between dream and reality, between the precious cultural inheritance ranging from the stones of Chichén Itzá and Machu Picchu to modern Indian influences, from the baroque of colonial times to contemporary literature, and the failure and crisis of its political and economic systems.

The variegation in Fuentes' fictional prose also appears in his essays. He constantly rereads and rewrites his own tradition, dismantling old schemes in literary, historical, political, and ethnic fields. For Fuentes, there is a silence hidden behind the sterile rhetoric in Latin American literature that overshadows the vitality of language and creation, and of the history and identity of Latin America. In his work, this becomes an assertion of the American universalism expressed in an intense confluence of speeches and cultures, incessantly revolving in multiple shadings. His essay prose is not only lucid, dense, and subjugating, but also precise, erudite, and polemical. It follows a linearity in the development of thought, drawing together disparate elements and unfolding a multiple perspective with which he rejects the pretense of totality and sufficiency of closed systems.

Much of the innovation of his essays lies in their aesthetic texture. Fuentes writes in a characteristically autobiographical and anecdotal voice, but unlike the **familiar essay**, his themes are of an elevated nature. There is a constant essaying self, with attenuated variations (it almost disappears in *La nueva novela hispanoamericana*), which becomes an axis from which the tensions of his discourse are displaced and unfolded. Fuentes' essays exhibit a breadth and depth of knowledge and assume an intelligent readership not willing to be guided by formulas. Fuentes does not accept the restrictions of genre; rather he favors their intermixture. He flouts univocal views and Cartesian continuity, claiming instead the plurality and convergence of language as a cognitive process which is able to grasp a reality that is multiform and plural. In this sense, language becomes one of his main themes (José Carlos González Boixo, 1988).

In his essays, Fuentes accumulates cultural information, displaying a vigorous process of comparisons, interactions, pronouncements, remarks, convergences, and divergences. Counterpoints abound: "Desire in the western world decreases in inverse proportion to the increasing number of objects capable of satisfying it" (*Tiempo mexicano*); evocations: "Whoever has been in the city of Buenos Aires knows that the most fantastic flight of Borges was born in a backyard . . ." (*La nueva novela hispanoamericana*); counterpositions: "History is not an uninterrupted development, but a winding, spiral movement . . ." (*Valiente mundo nuevo* [1990; Brave new world]).

Fuentes often freely combines serious, highly sophisticated language with humor and slang, as well as familiar and colloquial language. He sometimes mixes tragic and comic modes or interweaves high and popular culture. His tone may be refined but can quickly become visceral and ardent. Stylistically, Fuentes leads the reader along many tangents, resulting not in aimless thought but in an intensification of the vision he offers. For him this enriching use of language compensates for the many centuries of silence in Spanish American literature.

Polemical, courageous, and outspoken (politically he defines himself as center-left), Fuentes has become a controversial writer. Nevertheless, he is admired and highly respected, for he has given expression to deep Latin American feelings, defending their justice and freedom, and maintaining a characteristically critical attitude against oppressive political schemes throughout Latin America and the rest of the world.

In his essays he is essentially critical, but also maintains what he calls the horizon of literature – that is, memory and desire as imagination in our own time, so that we can witness both the past and the future.

BLANCA M. GARCÍA MONSIVAIS

Biography

Born 11 November 1928 in Panama City. Parents were Mexican; he later became a Mexican citizen. Lived in the United States, Chile, and Argentina, then returned to Mexico at age 16. Studied at the Colegio Frances Morelos; National Autonomous University of Mexico, Mexico City, LL.B., 1948; Institut des Hautes Études Internationales, Geneva. Member, then secretary of the Mexican delegation, International Labor Organization, Geneva, 1950–52; assistant chief of press section, Ministry of Foreign Affairs, Mexico City, 1954; press secretary, United Nations Information Center, Mexico City, 1954. Editor, *Revista Mexicana de Literatura*, 1954–58, *El Espectador* (The spectator), 1959–61, *Siempre* (Always), from 1960, and *Política*, from 1960. Secretary, then assistant director of the Cultural Department, National Autonomous University of Mexico, 1955–56. Head of Department of Cultural Relations, Ministry of Foreign Affairs, 1957–59. Married Rita Macedo, 1959 (divorced, 1966): one daughter; married Sylvia Lemus, 1973: one son and one daughter. Mexican ambassador to France, 1974–77. Fellow or visiting lecturer/professor at various American and British universities, 1974–87; taught at the University of Pennsylvania, Philadelphia, 1978–83, and Harvard University, Cambridge, Massachusetts, from 1984. Awards: many, including Villaurrutia Prize, 1975; Gallegos Prize (Venezuela), 1977; Reyes Prize, 1979; Mexican National Award for Literature, 1984; Cervantes Prize, 1987; Darío Prize, 1988; New Order of Cultural Independence (Nicaragua), 1988; Prince of Asturias Prize (Spain), 1994; Grinzane Cavouch International Prize (Italy), 1994; National Order of Merit (France), 1997; honorary degrees from eight universities.

Selected Writings

Essays and Related Prose

París: La revolución de mayo, 1968
El mundo de José Luis Cuevas, 1969
La nueva novela hispanoamericana, 1969
Casa con dos puertas, 1970
Tiempo mexicano, 1971
Cervantes, o, La crítica de la lectura, 1976; as *Don Quixote; or, The Critique of Reading*, translated anonymously, 1976
Myself with Others: Selected Essays, 1988
Valiente mundo nuevo, 1990
El espejo enterrado, 1992; as *The Buried Mirror: Reflections on Spain and the New World*, 1992
Geografía de la novela, 1993
Tres discursos para dos aldeas, 1993
Nuevo tiempo mexicano, 1994
Por un progreso incluyente, 1997

Other writings: 14 novels (including *La región más transparente* [*Where the Air Is Clear*], 1958; *Las buenas conciencias* [*The Good Conscience*], 1959; *La muerte de Artemio Cruz* [*The Death of Artemio Cruz*], 1962; *Aura*, 1962; *Cambio de piel* [*A Change of Skin*], 1967; *Terra nostra*, 1975; *La cabeza de la hidra* [*The Hydra Head*], 1978; *Una familia lejana* [*Distant Relations*], 1980; *Gringo viejo* [*The Old Gringo*], 1985; *Cristóbal nonato* [*Christopher Unborn*], 1987; *La campaña* [*The Campaign*], 1990), eight collections of short stories, three plays, and books on Latin America.

Collected works edition: *Obras completas*, 3 vols., 1974– (in progress).

Bibliographies

Dunn, Sandra L., "Carlos Fuentes: A Bibliography," *Review of Contemporary Fiction* 8 (1988)
Foster, David William, in *Mexican Literature: A Bibliography of Secondary Sources*, Metuchen, New Jersey: Scarecrow Press, 1992
Jackson, Richard L., "Hacia una bibliografía de y sobre Carlos Fuentes," *Revista Iberoamericana* 31, no. 60 (July–December 1965): 297–301
Reeve, Richard, "An Annotated Bibliography on Carlos Fuentes, 1949–1969," *Hispania* 53, no. 4 (1970): 595–652

Further Reading

Anthropos issue on Fuentes, 91 (December 1988)
Benítez, Fernando, Prologue to *Obras completas* by Fuentes, vol. 1, Mexico City: Aguilar, 1974: 9–76
Blanco Aguinaga, Carlos, "Sobre la idea de la novela en Carlos Fuentes," *Cuadernos Políticos* 23 (1974): 73–108
Boschi, Liliana Befumo, and Elisa Calabrese, *Nostalgia del futuro en la obra de Carlos Fuentes*, Buenos Aires: García Cambeiro, 1974
Brody, Robert, and Charles Rossman, editors, *Carlos Fuentes: A Critical View*, Austin: University of Texas Press, 1982
Brushwood, John S., *The Spanish American Novel: A Twentieth-Century Survey*, Austin: University of Texas Press, 1975
Durán, Gloria, *The Archetypes of Carlos Fuentes: From Witch to Androgyne*, Hamden, Connecticut: Archon, 1980 (original Spanish edition, 1976)
Durán, Manuel, "Carlos Fuentes," *Tríptico Mexicano* (September 1973): 51–133
Faris, Wendy D., *Carlos Fuentes*, New York: Ungar, 1983
García Gutiérrez, Georgina, *Los disfraces: La obra mestiza de Carlos Fuentes*, Mexico City: El Colegio de México, 1981
Giacoman, Helmy F., editor, *Homenaje a Carlos Fuentes: Variaciones interpretativas en torno a su obra*, New York: Las Américas, 1974
González, Alfonso, *Carlos Fuentes: Life, Work, and Criticism*, Fredericton, New Brunswick: York, 1987
González Boixo, José Carlos, "La obra ensayística de Carlos Fuentes," *Anthropos* 91 (December 1988): 7–10
Guzman, Daniel de, *Carlos Fuentes*, New York: Twayne, 1972
Harss, Luis, and Bárbara Dohmann, "Carlos Fuentes o la nueva herejía," in Harss' *Into the Mainstream*, New York: Harper and Row, 1967
Hernández, Ana María de López, editor, *Interpretaciones a la obra de Carlos Fuentes: Un gigante de las letras hispanoamericanas*, Madrid: Beramar, 1990
Levy, Isaac Jack, and Juan Loveluck, editors, *Actas: Simposio Carlos Fuentes*, Columbia: University of South Carolina, 1980
Monsiváis, Carlos, "Notas sobre la cultura mexicana en el siglo XX," in *Historia general de México*, vol. 2, Mexico City: Colegio de México, 1977: 303–476
Paz, Octavio, "La máscara y la transparencia," Prologue to *Cuerpos y ofrendas: Antología* by Fuentes, Madrid: Alianza, 1972
Poniatowska, Elena, *¡Ay vida, no me mereces! Carlos Fuentes, Rosario Castellanos, Juan Rulfo, la literatura de la onda*, Mexico City: Mortiz, 1985
Tittler, Jonathan, interview with Fuentes in *Diacritics* (September 1980)
Vernier, Martha Elena, "Escritura lateral: Ensayos de Carlos Fuentes," in *La obra de Carlos Fuentes: Una visión multiple*, edited by Ana María Lopez de Hernandez, Madrid: Pliegos, 1988
World Literature Today issue on Fuentes, 57, no. 4 (1983)
Zúñiga, Dulce Ma., *Intertextos: Calvino, Borges, Fuentes*, Guadalajara: University of Guadalajara, 1989

Fuller, Margaret

American, 1810–1850

Margaret Fuller's short-lived career as an essayist did not prevent her from making a clear literary mark in several important areas. She wrote major works in areas including (but not limited to) feminist thought, **travel essays**, literary criticism, social activism, and Italian politics. Her essays began with reflective, literary pieces directed to an elite audience of contemporaries, including transcendentalists such as **Ralph Waldo Emerson** and Nathaniel Hawthorne, when she was editor and writer for the *Dial*. Later she became a reporter for the New York *Tribune*. As firsthand witness to the social ills of her day, she sought to move her public audience to action on social issues. *Woman in the Nineteenth Century*, developed from an earlier essay written and published in the *Dial*, is the work for which she is best remembered today. Her reputation among feminist scholars is well known, but her essays on literary, social, and political issues are enjoying renewed interest. They illustrate Fuller's prophetic insight into issues that still challenge citizens today.

Fuller's initial literary publications resulted in her editing the transcendentalist journal the *Dial*. With Emerson's encouragement she assumed the task, believing she would be free of major financial responsibilities. She saw the editorship as an opportunity: "I will try to say what I mean in print one day," she wrote in 1840. However, when writers who had promised works failed to deliver them in a timely fashion, Fuller pressed herself into essay writing. In the first issue, she set forth "Essay on Critics" (1840); she followed with "Lives of Great Composers" (1841), "Goethe" (1841; one of her favorite philosophers), and "The Great Lawsuit: Man versus Men: Woman versus Women" (1843). The latter work became the catalyst of her larger, better-known essay, *Woman in the Nineteenth Century* (1845). In "Lawsuit," Fuller formed her argumentative format using the Muse and Minerva to represent the two sides of the radical duality that exists in each man and woman. With the support of Horace Greeley, who began the New York *Tribune* (1841) in order to elevate the masses, Fuller expanded her initial essay into a book-length manuscript that Bell Gale Chevigny (1994) says gave "psychological integrity and a new attention to the claims of society and politics."

When *Woman* was published, Fuller was on a journey to the Great Lakes, where she gained valuable experiences beyond those of transcendental New England. She wrote about these experiences in a book of essays outlining the natural beauty of the area. *Summer on the Lakes in 1843* (1844) initially gave evidence of Fuller's romantic view of the plight of Native Americans. Later, however, she spent time with the Indians at Mackinaw Island and began to feel differently, writing that she understood the "soul" of their race. She further expressed this sensitivity in her subsequent social essays for the *Tribune* by addressing the plight of immigrants who faced ethnic, religious, racial, and economic discrimination. Among her most famous essays are those such as "The Irish Character" (1845), in which she exposes the common expression, "No Irish need apply." She gained her knowledge firsthand as she visited homes, workplaces, schools, prisons, and insane asylums. She

provided eloquent defenses for equality of women's education and fought the evils of capital punishment. She became a champion of the poor, the blind, the insane, and social outcasts, including prostitutes who were often viewed as social inferiors or ruined women. She tackled the issue of slavery in seven pieces, most notably her "Narrative of Frederick Douglass" (1845); she argued that everyone should read **Douglass** to understand how the human mind is "stifled in bondage."

Social issues did not prevent Fuller from maintaining her interest in literary criticism. *Papers on Literature and Art* (1846) provided her with new popularity in America and abroad. Here Fuller combined a number of her *Tribune* reviews on writers such as Nathaniel Hawthorne, Charles Brockden Brown, and Henry Wadsworth Longfellow with an original essay on the state of American literature. She also wrote "Modern British Poets" (1846), in which she assessed writers such as Byron, Keats, **Coleridge**, and Wordsworth. She completed a favorable review of Elizabeth Barrett's poems (1845), expressing her "cordial admiration" of the work.

In August 1846, Fuller became one of the first American correspondents to cover the European scene. Accompanied by philanthropist Marcus Spring and his family, Fuller visited England, France, and Italy. While she was encouraged by the roles of English women in theater and publishing, she was appalled by their general poverty and poor education. She outlined her views in "On Travel in England and Scotland" (1846–47). In France, she met and became a defender of the writer George Sand.

Because of her earlier meeting with the Italian patriot **Giuseppe Mazzini** in London, Fuller, captivated by the cause of Italian liberty, left the Springs in Venice. Remaining in Italy, she took up the patriots' cause by visiting the wounded soldiers and forming alliances with patriots such as the Marchesa Costanza Arconati, a noblewoman who introduced Fuller to important literary and political figures. Fuller's disillusionment with Pius IX resulted in an anti-Catholic turn in her *Tribune* writings (1849); this proved to be personally costly. She led with essays such as "On Austrian Rule and the Need for Revolution" (1847) and followed with "On the Pope's Flight and the Condition of Women" (1848).

Unable to have her *History of Italy* published in England, Fuller determined to return home to regain her reputation, which had been sullied by rumors of her romance with an Italian nobleman and the birth of their son. Unfortunately, Fuller, the Italian nobleman, and their son died in a shipwreck off the coast of Fire Island, New York. Her manuscript of *History of Italy* was never recovered.

ADELAIDE P. AMORE

Biography

Sarah Margaret Fuller, Marchesa d'Ossoli. Born 23 May 1810 in Cambridge, Massachusetts. Studied privately, tutored by her father. Taught at Bronson Alcott's Temple School, 1836, and Hiram Fuller's Greene Street School, two years. Involved with transcendentalism, 1836–44: editor and major contributor, the *Dial*, 1840–44. Organized the Boston Conversationalists, which ran weekly "Conversations" for women, 1839–44. Traveled in the Midwest, 1843–44. Moved to New York, 1844: journalist for the New York *Tribune*, 1844–46, and sent articles from abroad, from

1846. Traveled to Europe, 1846, and settled in Italy. Liaison with Giovanni Angelo Ossoli (possibly married, 1848): one son. Forced to leave Rome, then Italy, after the fall of Rome to the French. Died (in a shipwreck off Fire Island, New York), 19 July 1850.

Selected Writings

Essays and Related Prose

Summer on the Lakes in 1843, 1844; facsimile reprint, 1972

Woman in the Nineteenth Century, 1845; in *Woman in the 19th Century, and Kindred Papers Relating to the Sphere, Condition, and Duties of Woman*, edited by Arthur B. Fuller, 1855

Papers on Literature and Art, 1846; as *Literature and Art*, 1852; enlarged edition, as *Art, Literature, and Drama*, edited by Arthur B. Fuller, 1860

At Home and Abroad; or, Things and Thought in America and Europe, edited by Arthur B. Fuller, 1856

Life Without and Life Within; or, Reviews, Narratives, Essays, and Poems, edited by Arthur B. Fuller, 1859

Writings (selection), edited by Mason Wade, 1941

Margaret Fuller, American Romantic: A Selection from Her Writings and Correspondence, edited by Perry Miller, 1963

The Educated Woman in America: Selected Writings of Catherine Beecher, Margaret Fuller, and M. Carey Thomas, edited by Barbara M. Cross, 1965

Essays on American Life and Letters, edited by Joel Myerson, 1978

"These Sad But Glorious Days": Dispatches from Europe, 1846–1850, edited by Larry J. Reynolds and Susan Belasco Smith, 1991

The Essential Margaret Fuller, edited by Jeffrey Steele, 1992

The Portable Margaret Fuller, edited by Mary Kelley, 1994

Woman in the Nineteenth Century and Other Writings, edited by Donna Dickenson, 1994

Margaret Fuller's New York Journalism: A Biographical Essay and Key Writings, edited by Catherine C. Mitchell, 1995

Bibliographies

Myerson, Joel, *Margaret Fuller: An Annotated Secondary Bibliography*, New York: Burt Franklin, 1977

Myerson, Joel, *Margaret Fuller: A Descriptive Bibliography*, Pittsburgh: University of Pittsburgh Press, 1978

Further Reading

Allen, Margaret Vanderhaar, *The Achievement of Margaret Fuller*, University Park: Pennsylvania State University Press, 1979

Brown, Arthur W., *Margaret Fuller*, New York: Twayne, 1964

Chevigny, Bell Gale, editor, *The Woman and the Myth: Margaret Fuller's Life and Writings*, Boston: Northeastern University Press, revised edition, 1994

Myerson, Joel, editor, *Critical Essays on Margaret Fuller*, Boston: Hall, 1980

Watson, David, *Margaret Fuller, an American Romantic*, Oxford: Berg, 1988

G

Ganivet, Ángel

Spanish, 1865–1898

Ángel Ganivet's suicide at the age of 32 brought to an abrupt close the development of an innovative writer and thinker. Although necessarily limited in number, his publications had a significant impact on his contemporaries and on the development of the essay in Spain. His writings challenge the established generic borders in keeping with turn-of-the-century experimentation with limits and traditional definitions. He combines the essay and the epistolary form in *Cartas finlandesas* (1898; Letters from Finland) and in the posthumous *El porvenir de España* (1912; The future of Spain), and takes the hybrid form of **travel essay** and social commentary in a second posthumous work, *Hombres del norte* (1905; Men from the north). Ganivet writes from the stance of an outsider, analyzing Spain from his diplomatic residences in Finland and Belgium and critiquing European culture from his vantage point as a Spaniard with ties to Africa and Latin America. In his best-known essay, *Idearium español* (1897; *Spain: An Interpretation*), Ganivet breaks with the prevailing rationalist, scientific perspective to analyze the history and future of Spain by means of a new multivoiced, contradictory, and subjective discourse.

Spain: An Interpretation and Ganivet's other essays incorporate a multitude of competing voices and discourses that represent the tensions marking Spain and the rest of the world in the transition from traditional to modern society. His texts introduce terms and arguments drawn from 19th-century debates over Catholicism, positivism, imperialism, and rationalism and interweave them in a complex discursive play that undermines and redefines tradition while suggesting new forms of thinking and writing. The text speaker in *Spain: An Interpretation* appropriates a positivist, determinist characterization of nations according to their geographic identification as island, peninsula, or continent, but then deconstructs the stability of these classifications by pointing out that Spain, a peninsula, has erroneously adopted behaviors appropriate to an island nation. In a similar vein, the speaker continuously invokes history and the 19th-century notion of historical determinism, only to subvert it by suggesting that Spain's past was an error, a deviation from its true nature. The present does not mirror the past or develop naturally from it, but rather confronts it as an alien other.

Ganivet's texts display a disjunctive vision of history, as a process marked by violent shifts and discontinuity. This view coincides with a repudiation of rationalism and the adoption of a style that eschews a logical development of ideas and a clear exposition of thought. Ganivet's essays privilege a nonlinear exposition, with no clear declaration of purpose and constant changes in topic without prior explanation. The various sections of *Idearium español* have no titles and no clear section or subsection divisions. The narrator repeatedly verbalizes a lack of concern with consistency and logic and expresses a preference for "ideas redondas" (round ideas) over "ideas picudas" (sharp, pointed ideas). The latter are defined as categorical, with no contradictions and no shading, and consequently lead to conflict and disagreement, while round ideas allow for the fusion of opposites and welcome paradoxical overlappings and irregularities, creating possibilities for love and union. The acceptance and even cultivation of contradiction produces texts that defy definition and force the reader to suspend judgment and adopt an open and flexible position.

Attempts to define a clearly delineated ideological posture in Ganivet's essays fail in the face of a purposeful irrationalism and consistent shifts in position. For some readers, the repudiation of positivism, capitalism, and Kantian pure reason reflects the failure of the Enlightenment to take root in Spain and leads to an antirational stance bordering on fascism. However, Ganivet's redefinitions of history and his insistent rejection of a logic that justifies injustice and of a capitalism that promotes war can also be read as an answer to the crisis of modernity that continues to find voice in contemporary thought. Furthermore, his unrelenting attack on imperialism and respect for different cultures and values anticipate late 20th-century views. During the height of the Cuban struggle to win independence from Spain and during the years when European imperialist dominance over Africa and Asia were viewed as proof of Western superiority over the rest of the world, Ganivet's writings proposed new, nonimperialist forms of leadership. *Idearium español* argues that the greatness of a nation does not depend on territorial extension, and calls on Spain to initiate a new postcolonial order that is without precedent in world history. The text speaker makes use of nationalistic discourse in order to combat it, calling on national pride but toward a new end.

The essays of Ángel Ganivet offer new modalities of thinking and writing. His texts evade clear categorization in keeping with his rejection of 19th-century rationalist and scientific discourse and thought. The organization of ideas follows a circular pattern, with the reintroduction of previously mentioned ideas, but with significant (albeit subtle) variations.

Through a complex interweaving of inherited discourse and modern variations, Ganivet's essays seek to rewrite the past and create new forms of cultural coexistence.

MARY LEE BRETZ

Biography

Born 13 December 1865 in Granada. Studied at the Institute of Granada, 1880–85; University of Granada, degrees in the arts, 1888, and law, 1890; University of Madrid, Ph.D. in philosophy, 1890. Liaison with Amelia Roldán Llanos, from 1892: one daughter (died in infancy) and one son. Vice consul in Antwerp, 1892–96; consul in Helsinki, 1896–98, and Riga, Latvia, 1898. Died (suicide by drowning) near Riga, 29 November 1898.

Selected Writings

Essays and Related Prose

Granada la bella, 1896; edited by Antonio Gallego y Burín, 1954
Idearium español, 1897; edited by E. Inman Fox, 1990; as *Spain: An Interpretation*, translated by J. R. Carey, 1946
Cartas finlandesas, edited by Nicolás M. López, 1898
Libro de Granada (includes poetry), 1899
Hombres del norte, 1905
El porvenir de España (open newspaper letters), with Miguel de Unamuno, 1912

Other writings: two novels, a verse play, and correspondence.

Collected works editions: *Obras completas*, 10 vols., 1923–30; edited by Melchor Fernández Almagro, 2 vols., 1943.

Bibliography

Gallego Morell, Antonio, *Estudios y textos ganivetianos*, Madrid: Consejo Superior de Investigaciones Científicas, 1971: 183–214

Further Reading

Baquero Goyanes, Mariano, *Temas, formas y tonos literarios*, Madrid: Prensa Española, 1972
Fernández Almagro, Melchor, *Vida y obra de Ángel Ganivet*, Valencia: Sempere, 1925
Gallego Morell, Antonio, *Ángel Ganivet, el excéntrico del 98*, Granada: Albaicín, 1965
Ginsberg, Judith, *Ángel Ganivet*, London: Tamesis, 1985
Herrero, Javier, *Ángel Ganivet, un iluminado*, Madrid: Gredos, 1966
Olmedo Moreno, Miguel, *El pensamiento de Ganivet*, Madrid: Revista de Occidente, 1965
Ramsden, Herbert, *Ángel Ganivet's "Idearium español": A Critical Study*, Manchester: University of Manchester Press, 1967
Ramsden, Herbert, *The 1898 Movement in Spain: Towards a Reinterpretation, with Special Reference to "En torno al casticismo" and "Idearium español"*, Manchester: University of Manchester Press, and Totowa, New Jersey: Rowman and Littlefield, 1974

Gass, William H.

American, 1924–

William H. Gass is a philosopher and fiction writer as well as an essayist. In the preface to his first collection of essays, *Fiction and the Figures of Life* (1970), he acknowledged that

in his essays "we observe an author trying to be both philosopher and critic by striving to be neither," but that "in another sense" his essays are "the work of a novelist insufficiently off duty." These several roles affect Gass' essays, which always display both the rigorous abstract thinking of a philosopher and the richly figurative language of a novelist. They also determine his subject matter. Even his most **personal essays** – "Memory of a Master" (1970), "On Talking to Oneself" (1979), "On Reading to Oneself" (1984), for example – eventually come around to discussions of his theories of fiction and his philosophy of language.

Gass' dual career as both fiction writer and essayist was launched when the editors of *Accent* devoted an issue to his work in 1958 in which they published examples of his fiction ("The Triumph of Israbestis Tott," "Mrs. Mean") as well as an essay on **Henry James** ("The High Brutality of Good Intentions"). In the 40 years since, his essays have appeared regularly in literary quarterlies such as *Salmagundi* and *New American Review* and reviews such as the *New York Review of Books* and the *New York Times Book Review*. The audience he finds in these **periodicals** is both well read and highly educated, learning that undoubtedly helps them as they encounter Gass' sometimes dense, and always metaphoric and allusive prose.

Gass has long been labeled a "writers' writer." This is in part because he is a generous writer of blurbs for younger writers, a teacher of literature and writing as well as philosophy (since 1969, as David May Distinguished University Professor at Washington University in St. Louis), a performer of his own work on the reading circuit, and a writer of introductions to new editions or collections of fiction by friends such as Stanley Elkin and John Hawkes. Principally, however, he has earned the title because other writers admire his work and his uncompromising devotion to literary language, especially rhetorical persuasiveness and individual style. His essays are, as Robert Kiely put it in the *New York Times Book Review* (1971), "in the best tradition of eloquence, wit and passion … a defense of 'poesy' in a time of need."

Literature, Gass argues, finds itself in this time of need because it has allowed itself to be reduced to a commodity, to look for the quick sell and the bestseller. The threat to literary accomplishment, he says, comes mainly from those books that "trade in slogan and clichés, fads and whims, the slippery and easy, the smart and latest" ("A Letter to the Editor," 1969). His countermove has been to argue for and practice a most uncompromising aestheticism. Surrounding every work of art, he says, is only "empty space and silence" ("The Concept of Character in Fiction," 1970). His first novel, *Omensetter's Luck* (1966), "was written," he said, "to *not* have readers, while still deserving them" ("A Letter to the Editor"). His second, *The Tunnel* (1995), took him 30 years to complete.

This kind of deliberate and hermetic perfectionism would seem to be at odds with the contingencies of the essay, which, if not always engaged, is usually solicitous of its audience, occasioned by an event or issue, and, at least apparently, a kind of rendering of the mind's rambles. Gass is not unaware of this contradiction nor of how it has worked itself out in his own career, which has seen him published perhaps more widely as an essayist than as a fiction writer. On the occasional nature of the essayist's work, he has remarked that "it is embarrassing to recall that most of **Paul Valéry**'s prose pieces were replies to invitations and requests" (preface to *Fiction and the Figures of Life*); in addition to his many **review** essays, Gass' own prose pieces have been prompted by centennials ("Proust at 100," 1971), retirements ("The Ontology of the Sentence, or How to Make a World of Words," 1977), conference and symposium invitations ("Tropes of the Text," 1983; "'And'," 1984), new editions ("Gertrude Stein and the Geography of the Sentence," 1973), and university commencement exercises ("On Reading to Oneself," 1979; "On Talking to Oneself," 1984).

Gass' most extended examination of the tension inherent in the essay, the pull the essayist and the essay feel between occasion and permanence, journalism and literature, subject and self, and audience and author, appears in a long essay he wrote on **Ralph Waldo Emerson** ("Emerson and the Essay," 1982). "Emerson is himself a man of occasions," says Gass, and proceeds to examine the lecture tours from which Emerson's essays emerged, "the talks" that he "gathers up in books." As he writes of Emerson "essaying to be," of Emerson's "sacred fear of the superfluous," of the essay sparring with its "opposite," that "awful object, 'the article'," we hear Gass rehearsing again his own familiar concerns. The essay rises above the article, becomes literature and ceases to be journalism because it manifests the mind at work, tells the story of the imagination imagining, "an activity – the process, the working, the wondering." An article "represents itself as the latest cleverness." It is "footnoted and useful and certain," but it is doubtful that it "has ever contained anything of lasting value." The essay, on the other hand, is "unhurried," born of digression, allusion, and "the narrative disclosure of a thought." The essay is the site where Emerson "is giving definition to his Being."

Finally, ironically, the recognition comes for Gass that the essay's energy and its unity exist within, not apart from, the relationship between author and audience as they examine together the central concern that occasioned both the writing and the reading of the essay. He is, like Emerson, always a Platonist in search of a lasting form in a cheap and ephemeral world, and in the end he admits that "the unity of each essay is a unity achieved by the speaker for his audience as well as for himself, a kind of reassociation of his sensibility and theirs; so from its initiating center the mind moves out in widening rings the way it does in Emerson's first great essay, 'Circles,' where the sentences surround their subject, and metaphors of form control the flow of feeling." He described this mutuality more concretely and with a bit more irony early on in the essay on Emerson: "And what is the occasion for my writing, or your reading, other than some suggestion from a friend, a few fine books sent in the mail, an invitation to speak, an idle riffle through a few sheets of a stale review, the name Emerson, an essay, an open hour."

NED STUCKEY-FRENCH

Biography

William Howard Gass. Born 30 July 1924 in Fargo, North Dakota. Studied at Kenyon College, Gambier, Ohio, 1942–43, 1946–47, A.B., 1947; Ohio Wesleyan University, Delaware, Ohio, 1943;

ensign in the U.S. Navy, 1943–46; studied at Cornell University, Ithaca, New York, 1947–50, Ph.D., 1954. Married Mary Pat O'Kelly, 1952 (later divorced): two sons and one daughter. Taught philosophy at the College of Wooster, Ohio, 1950–54, Purdue University, West Lafayette, Indiana, 1954–69, and the University of Illinois, Urbana, 1958–59 (visiting); David May Distinguished University Professor in the Humanities, Washington University, St. Louis, from 1969. Married Mary Alice Henderson, 1969: two daughters. Contributor to various journals and magazines, including *Salmagundi*, the *New Republic*, *TriQuarterly*, and the *New York Review of Books*. Awards: Longview Foundation Award, 1969; American Academy Award, 1975, and Award of Merit Medal, 1979; National Book Critics Circle Award, for criticism, 1986; honorary degrees from three universities and colleges. Member, American Academy, 1983.

Selected Writings

Essays and Related Prose
Fiction and the Figures of Life, 1970
On Being Blue: A Philosophical Inquiry, 1976
The World Within the Word, 1978
Habitations of the Word, 1985
Finding a Form, 1996

Other writings: two novels (*Omensetter's Luck*, 1966; *The Tunnel*, 1995), short stories, and criticism.

Bibliography
Saltzman, Arthur M., "A William H. Gass Checklist," *Review of Contemporary Fiction* 11, no. 3 (Fall 1991): 150–58

Further Reading
Boyers, Robert, "Real Readers and Theoretical Critics," in his *After the Avant-Garde: Essays on Art and Culture*, University Park: Pennsylvania State University Press, 1988: 81–90

Bruss, Elizabeth W., *Beautiful Theories: The Spectacle of Discourse in Contemporary Criticism*, Baltimore: Johns Hopkins University Press, 1982: 135–202

Dyck, Reginald, "William Gass: A 'Purified Modernist' in a Postmodern World," *Review of Contemporary Fiction* 11, no. 3 (Fall 1991): 124–30

Eckford-Prossor, M., "Shattering Genre/Creating Self: William H. Gass's *On Being Blue*," *Style* 23 (Summer 1989): 280–99

French, Ned, "Against the Grain: Theory and Practice in the Work of William H. Gass," *Iowa Review* 7 (Winter 1976): 96–106

Gilman, Richard, "William H. Gass," in his *The Confusion of Realms*, New York: Random House, 1969: 69–81

Guttenplan, Donald, "The Wor(l)ds of William Gass," *Granta* 1 (1979): 147–60

Hassan, Ihab, "Wars of Desire, Politics of the Word," *Salmagundi* 55 (Winter 1982): 110–18

Hix, Harvey, "Morte d'Author: An Autopsy," *Iowa Review* 17 (Winter 1987): 131–50

Holloway, Watson L., *William Gass*, Boston: Twayne, 1990

Rosenfeld, Alvin H., "The Virtuoso and the Gravity of History," *Salmagundi* 55 (Winter 1982): 103–09

Saltzman, Arthur M., *The Fiction of William H. Gass: The Consolation of Language*, Carbondale: Southern Illinois University Press, 1986

Schneider, Richard J., "Rejecting the Stone: William Gass and Emerson Transcendence," *Review of Contemporary Fiction* 11, no. 3 (Fall 1991): 115–23

Stevick, Philip, "William Gass and the Real World," *Review of Contemporary Fiction* 11, no. 3 (Fall 1991): 71–77

The Georgia Review

American journal, 1947–

The *Georgia Review* has been concerned with the essay and the essayistic since its foundation in 1947. The magazine was conceived primarily as a regional journal – Georgian in subject, author, or implication – by its originating editor, John D. Wade, a contributor to the distinctly Southern, 1930 Agrarian manifesto *I'll Take My Stand*. In his introductory editorial in Spring 1947, Wade explained that the *Georgia Review*'s brand of regionalism would be fairly conservative, "avoid[ing] the obscene and blasphemous, the trivial, the Tobacco Road sort of thing, and an undue emphasis upon race matters." Either despite or because of his definition of regionalism, some readers and potential contributors protested at this emphasis, and by his second editorial in the Summer issue of the same year, Wade had to clarify that "any composition that arises from sullen earth and speaks with catholicity would be precisely what the *Review* is looking for," assuming that in such an essay there would be some, no matter how remote, connection to Georgia. Although many of the subsequent articles were distinctly academic, they were often affected by the **personal essay**istic tone associated with regional writing.

In the *Review*'s 20th-anniversary issue (Winter 1966), editor William Wallace Davidson (1957–68) and former editor John Olin Eidson (1951–57) looked back proudly on the magazine's history as a distinctly regional voice. This voice would continue under editor James Colvert (1968–72) and acting editor Edward Krickel (1972–74), although the journal abandoned its traditional "Confederate gray" cover in 1969 and the regionalism of the journal was becoming more difficult to define.

The tenor of the magazine changed in 1974 when John T. Irwin became editor. Irwin's emphasis on contemporary theory reunited the academic essay with its Baconian roots, showcasing the "open-ended" works of such renowned literary and philosophical theorists as Jacques Derrida, J. Hillis Miller, Harold Bloom, Geoffrey Hartman, Edward W. Said, Wolfgang Iser, Paul de Man, and Michael Riffaterre. In 1982, Eugene K. Garber of the *Literary Magazine Review* noted that, while the *Georgia Review* had formerly been respected but staid, its incarnation under Irwin's editorship was an altogether different journal: "Out of the improbable larva of conservative southern regionalism developed the sometimes gorgeous chrysalis of structuralist/deconstructionist criticism and avant garde fiction."

The *Review* underwent yet another dramatic transformation in 1978, when Stanley Lindberg assumed the editorship, a position he still holds. Lindberg created for the magazine "a new format – one intended to make our contents as inviting visually as they are intellectually." His first cover featured French painter André Derain's previously unreproduced 1938 *Landscape with Huntsman and Bathers* in a glossy, colorful packaging, an aesthetic change that has now become one of the journal's trademarks. The graphic portfolios begun under Irwin have grown to include beautifully reproduced paintings and photographs, thus enveloping the pictorial within the margins of the essayistic. In 1986–87, Fred Chappell surveyed the journal for *Literary Magazine Review* and concluded that

"The *Georgia Review* is physically the most attractive and intellectually the most adventurous of [current Southern literary quarterlies]; at the present time it outshines every comparable periodical in the United States."

The Georgia Review also publishes poetry, fiction (for which it is frequently a finalist in the National Magazine Award in Fiction, winning the prize in 1986), and book reviews, but remains most noted for its essays, which range topically from philosophy, music, and art to history, psychology, film and literary criticism, frequently transgressing traditional disciplinary lines. Lindberg has emphasized the familiar, thesis-driven essay over more narrowly focused scholarly articles and in doing so has greatly expanded the magazine's reading public, which has grown from fewer than 2000 subscribers in the late 1970s to more than 6000.

In recent years, contributors have included Malcolm Cowley, **N. Scott Momaday**, O. B. Hardison, Jr., Eudora Welty, Sally Fitzgerald, Rita Dove, Richard Howard, Henry Louis Gates, Jr., **Scott Russell Sanders**, Joyce Carol Oates, Ernest J. Gaines, Michael Dorris, and 1995 Nobel Laureate Seamus Heaney. The *Review* has also maintained its commitment to publishing new and sometimes nonprofessional writers, "willing to take the risk," as Davidson commented in Fall 1957, "remember[ing] that Chaucer and Rabelais were not professional writers, that Matthew Arnold was an inspector of schools, that A. E. Housman was a professor of Latin, that Virgil was a farmer, that **William Morris** was a manufacturer and decorator, that Anthony Trollope was a post office official, that Wallace Stevens was an insurance executive."

Recent special issues have included "Women and the Arts" (Spring/Summer 1990), a double issue of over 300 pages; "Focus on Nature Writing" (Spring 1993); "The Nobel Laureates of Literature" (Spring 1995), a collection of Nobel Laureate Acceptance Speeches and Lectures; and "Contemporary Literature of the American South" (Spring 1996), this last representing in some ways the best of both the new *Georgia Review* and the old.

KAREN A. KEELY

German Essay

1. Status of Research

Scholars are not in agreement on when the art of the essay in German actually began. Most argue that the genre – which generally runs in length anywhere from one page to about 50, although ideally it is easily read at one sitting – is relatively new and has a spotty tradition. Literary scholarship neglected the essay as a genre until the mid-20th century. The first edition of the *Reallexikon der deutschen Literaturgeschichte* (1925; Lexicon of German literary history) devoted a scant 40 lines to the essay. Despite efforts by Emil Dovifat in Berlin, who encouraged work on the genre and penned a brief entry on it for the *Handbuch der Zeitungswissenschaft* (1940; Handbook for the study of newspapers), and **Max Bense**'s seminal essay, "Über den Essay und seine Prosa" (1947; On the essay and its prose), scholarly interest in the essay did not intensify until after 1950.

When the second edition of the *Reallexikon* appeared in 1958, Fritz Martini replaced the original entry on the essay with a more substantial, first attempt at sketching its history. Important studies by Peter M. Schon, Klaus Günter Just, Bruno Berger, Dieter Bachmann, Ludwig Rohner, Gerhard Haas, and Heinrich Küntzel all appeared between 1954 and 1969. Furthermore, under the direction of Richard Samuel, the *Jahrbuch für internationale Germanistik* (Yearbook for international Germanics) sponsored a critical series on the German essay in the late 1970s and early 1980s. Nevertheless, in scholarly circles the essay continues to exist in the shadows of the canonical genres. This critical disinterest in the history and practice of essay writing in Germany seems to be singular within the national literatures. Even leading practitioners of the art during its classical era from **Gotthold Ephraim Lessing** to Wilhelm Dilthey did not use the designation "essay" for their essayistic writings or see themselves as essayists.

Most historical treatments of the genre date its origins from c. 1750 as the result of importations from France and England. However, some trace its beginnings to sermons, broadsides, and **treatises** dating from the time of Martin Luther (1483–1546). Regardless of where one stands on the issue, all agree that essayistic writing in Austria, Germany, and Switzerland is part and parcel of a European tradition with roots in **Michel de Montaigne** (1533–92) and **Francis Bacon** (1561–1626), but also in Nicholas Breton's *Characters upon Essays, Moral and Divine* (1615), Izaak Walton's *The Compleat Angler* (1653), **Blaise Pascal**'s *Pensées* (1670), **Jean de La Bruyère**'s *Caractères* (1688; *Characters*), and **Pierre Bayle**'s *Pensées diverses* (1683; *Miscellaneous Reflections*) and *Dictionnaire historique et critique* (1697; *An Historical and Critical Dictionary*). Most also agree that the devastating effects of the Thirty Years' War (1618–48) and the religious dogmatism of the era greatly inhibited the development of the inquisitive literary form for most of the 17th century in the German territories. Religious conservatism in Catholic Austria delayed its practice and flowering there until the second half of the 18th century in the wake of the Enlightenment. After approximately 1750 there were so many border crossings regarding essay writing in Austria, Germany, and Switzerland that it is not very feasible to differentiate strictly among three traditions of the German essay. (The German Democratic Republic [1949–89] could be seen as a fourth.) Thus they will be considered as one tradition concerning the essay.

In general, the essay has experienced intermittent periods of flowering in the German-speaking countries. These periods coincide with significant paradigmatic shifts such as the onset of humanism and the Reformation in the 15th and 16th centuries, the rise of Enlightenment ideals beginning around 1700, the radical rethinking of social intercourse in the wake of the French Revolution at the end of the 18th century, and the philosophic and scientific convulsions around 1900 prompted by **Friedrich Nietzsche**'s radical break with systemic philosophy, **Sigmund Freud**'s psychoanalytical method, Max Planck's theory of quantum physics, and Albert Einstein's relativity theory. Sweeping reassessments after 1945 pursuant to the shattering of long-held traditions and values and the advent of the atomic age continued the sense of displacement. Particularly conducive to essay writing are thus those periods marked by shifts in epistemic attitudes, scientific breakthroughs, and a general sense of decline, captured in such works as Oswald Spengler's *Der Untergang des Abendlandes* (1911; *The Decline of the West*) – which **Thomas Mann**, in reference to its essayistic nature, characterized as an "intellectual novel," "a border crossing between science and art."

The specific function of the essay mode is to insure continuing, independent debate on the value of cultural and intellectual heritage. It forces us to come to terms with a given, contemporary situation by placing it in a broader context. It seeks to articulate conceptual transformations by marking out essential tensions as well as past influences on current forces of change, and to project possible trajectories into the future. The essay is a refined means of coming to terms intellectually with the conflict inherent in the alternation between expansion and contraction. That is why the essay flourishes in times of crisis and change.

The most striking leitmotif in the history of the essay is Montaigne's famous inscription "Que sçais-je?," which has been variously interpreted by emphasizing each word independently: "*What* [can] I know?," "What do *I* know?," and "What do I *know*?" The playful ambiguity is entirely appropriate for the literary form whose *Spielcharakter* is often cited as a distinguishing trait. It might explain why a telltale sign of the essay is its sparkle and magic at the intersection of science and poetry, and clarify why essayism is frequently identified with the dialectics of the Enlightenment. That dialectic is further marked by what one critic has called the "principle of holistic rhythm" (Klaus Weissenberger, 1985): it is a constituent part of the essay's tendency to involve the reader in an interactive process of reading in the search for shared truth. The designation "essayism" in the German tradition refers to this dialectic and does not necessarily connote flaccid journalism as some have argued (Gerhard Haas, 1969).

The following survey traces the main contours of the genre within the productive tensions between scientific precision and free-spirited association. Of course, the term essay was not always applied consistently, so that other designations for the mode of writing gathered under the rubric of the "essay" must be borne in mind, especially prior to the second half of the 19th century. The actual term, "essay," did not enter common usage until **Herman Grimm** introduced it in 1859. To be sure, the term was cited in titles and texts from 1750, but remained indistinct as a concept and genre until **Friedrich Schlegel** began to muse upon it around 1800. Before Grimm succeeded in promulgating the loan word in the 19th century, essay writing appeared most commonly under the guise of the *Abhandlung* (treatise), *Bemühung* (endeavor), *Brief* (**letter**), *Denkwürdigkeiten* (memoirs), *Einfälle* (inspirations), *Fragment*, *Gespräch* (conversation), *Gedanken* (thoughts), *Meinungen* (opinions), *Predigt* (**sermon**), *Probe* (sample), *Rede* (oration), *Versuch* (attempt), *Vorrede* (**preface**), *Vortrag* (lecture), and *Wäldchen* (literally copse of trees = fragment). In contrast to the early English and French traditions which emanated from the coffeehouse, the salon, and the art of private conversation, the early German tradition of the essay emanated from the halls of academe, the pulpit, and the scholar's study.

2. The 16th and 17th Centuries: From Humanism to Baroque

Humanists, Reformists, and Counter-Reformists alike from Johannes von Saaz (i.e. Tepl, c. 1350–c. 1411), Johannes

Reuchlin (1455–1522), Martin Luther (1483–1546), Ulrich Zwingli (1484–1531), Ulrich von Hutten (1488–1523), Hans Sachs (1494–1576), and Thomas Murner (c. 1475–1537) created distant cousins of later essays with their epistles, **dialogue**s, broadsides, and political **pamphlet**s. Examples of these writings are the dialogic *Ackermann aus Böhmen* (c. 1400; The plowman of Bohemia), Reuchlin's satiric and witty *Epistolae obscurorum virorum* (1515; *Letters of Obscure Men*; penned together with Crotus Rubeanus and von Hutten), von Hutten's politically charged dialogues, *Gesprächbüchlein* (1521; Little book of conversations), and Sachs' propagandistic set of disputations, *Dialoge* (1524; Dialogues). While not essays in the narrower sense, they deserve mention here because of their success in spreading the art of ancient and medieval rhetoric to increasingly nonacademic audiences, encouraging them to weigh new possibilities in times of change.

Luther's popular *Tischreden* (table talks), sermons, letters, and pamphlets come closer to the essayistic mode with their personal appeals to the reader, engaging tone, and middle style (i.e. neither overly erudite nor crassly popular). Taken together they constitute "fragments of a major confession" (as **Goethe** described his own literary oeuvre) but are simultaneously commentaries on his age. The goal of his German writings (and translation of the Bible into contemporary German) was to establish his mother tongue as an equal alongside Greek, Hebrew, and Latin. Of special note are his call to the German nobility to break with Rome, "An den christlichen Adel deutscher Nation" (1520; An epistle to the Christian nobility of the German nation), his discourse on the nature of free will, "Von der Freiheit eines Christenmenschen" (1520; On the freedom of Christians), and his thoughts on the art of translation, "Sendbrief vom Dolmetschen" (1530; Epistle on translation). While polemicizing is foreign to the essay mode, Luther's masterful use of the vernacular had a lasting impact on all subsequent writers. For that reason alone he deserves a place in the history of the essay.

Topics such as fashion, friendship, marriage, the education of children, the relationship between faith and reason, practical philosophy, and social responsibilities, so favored by humanists and church reformers alike, were also often treated by later clerics and academics in pamphlets and sermons. Here one thinks of Georg Philipp Harsdörffer's (1607–58) conversation lexicon for women, *Frauenzimmer-Gesprächspiele* (1641–49; Garrulous games for women), the immensely popular albeit repetitive **satire**s of Abraham à Sancta Clara (1644–1709) such as *Judas, der Ertz-Schelm* (1686–95; Judas, chief rogue), the cultural critiques of Gottfried Wilhelm Leibniz, and the university lectures of Christian Thomasius.

While it must be borne in mind that the particular aesthetic of the essay cannot be derived merely from the criteria of earlier prose forms, we should be careful not to underestimate the influence of the practiced orator from Luther to Gellert on the making of the genre. Nor need we denigrate the genre because it is not pure-bred, as is the wont in German scholarship. To be sure, it can be descriptive like the narrative, intense like the drama, and magical like the lyric poem, but the essay nonetheless has its own special aesthetic derived from the "narrative" stance of the author. The key traits are conciseness of form, personal tone, active reader involvement, a dramatic inner movement, and richly nuanced perspectives.

Above all, the literary essay exists on the frontier between poetry and prose (Bense, 1947) and occupies a small, significant space between pure literature and strict science (K. G. Just, 1954). It is the marketplace of intellectual exchange, cloaked in pathos and rhetoric, but also embellished with playful irony. **Georg Lukács** revives Friedrich Schlegel's term "intellektuelles Gedicht" (intellectual poem) to describe its ambivalent nature. Yet the varying types of bond between author and reader result in different kinds of essays which can be more or less conceptual, more or less culturally critical, biographical, literary, graphic, or ironic (John A. McCarthy, 1989).

These characteristics are evident, at least in part, in essay writing in the late 17th century. Examples are Christian Thomasius' (1655–1728) book **review**s on the art of the novel in his journal, *Monats-Gespräche* (1687–88; Monthly conversations), his inaugural lecture at the University of Leipzig on the proper imitation of the French, "Discours Welcher Gestalt man denen Frantzosen in gemeinem Leben und Wandel nachahmen solle?" (1687; Discourse on the manner for imitating the French in everyday life), and his lectures on practical philosophy, "Kurtzer Entwurff der politischen Klugheit" (1710; A brief sketch of political wisdom). Each represents a step toward involving ever broader segments of the educated public in matters of practical philosophy. They have earned Thomasius acclaim as the inaugurator of the Enlightenment and of a new, enlightened reading public in the first half of the 18th century. Those efforts came to full fruition with his successors at the University of Leipzig, Christian Wolff (1679–1754), Johann Christoph Gottsched (1700–66), and Christian Fürchtegott Gellert (1715–69), but are also readily evident in the journalistic writing of Christian Garve (1742–98) and Johann Jakob Engel (1741–1802).

The length, moderate tone, and gallant style of Thomasius' 1687 lecture on the proper cultural imitation of the French clearly mark it as being in the camp of the chatty Montaigne rather than that of the sober and pithy Bacon. Its topic – the art of living – is a distinctive feature of the essay regardless of the tone adopted. With a surprisingly light, lively, and ironic touch, Thomasius addresses important cultural questions of the day by detailing the areas of life affected by the mania of imitating anything French: fashion, cuisine, household goods, language, customs, even sodomy and syphilis. The shift in focus from the usual cultural phenomena to questions of morality and personal health is brilliant in its surprise effect on the audience. The importance of rhetorical strategies is everywhere manifest. Thomasius makes liberal use of rhetorical questions, personal appeals, graphic language, allusions to historical events, evocation of authority figures, metaphors, similes, tropes, prolepses, and litotes, thus establishing a pattern for all later essayists.

In arguing for equal opportunities for women in higher education, he uses the metaphor of the writing tablet to illustrate the resilience of the human mind. The more a writing tablet has been used, the less distinct are the new letters because the old ones leave residual traces. New tablets absorb the chalk more readily because their pores are not cluttered with the dust of past scribblings. In other words, Thomasius argues persuasively that women can learn more easily because they have not been corrupted by the old academic ways he wishes to replace with a stress on critical reflection, clarity of organization, sound judgment, and lively presentation. Style and content are a harbinger of essayistic production in the 18th century (e.g. Gellert, Pitschel, Lessing, **Wieland**, Garve, **Forster**). Perhaps not coincidentally, Isaac Newton published his momentous *Principia*, which shaped our view of the cosmos until the late 19th century, in the same year Thomasius proposed his new way of thinking.

Even though Thomasius draws upon the humanistic traditions of the 16th and 17th centuries, it would nonetheless be inaccurate to claim solely endemic roots for the essay. Thomasius openly admits his indebtedness to the Spanish gallant and skeptic **Baltasar Gracián**, the French moralists (Bouhours, Malebranche, Scudéry, Bayle), and ancient thinkers (Lucian, Epictetus). The rhetorical and gallant traditions were obviously influential for both him and the subsequent development of the essay right into the late 20th century.

Leibniz's (1646–1716) importance for the European Enlightenment is well documented. Less well known is his contribution to the early art of the essay, as with his epistle "Ermahnung an die Teutschen, ihren Verstand und Sprache besser zu üben" (wr. 1683, pub. 1846; A call to the Germans to make better use of their reason and mother tongue) and its companion piece, "Unvorgreifliche Gedanken" (wr. c. 1709, pub. 1727; Provisional conjectures). They have been identified as representing a clear break with the stylistic concepts of the ornate baroque era. The first is a culturally critical essay in which Leibniz calls upon his countrymen to make refined use of German in order to compete better with the French, English, and Italians. Leibniz appeals to the patriotism of his readers by painting a positive picture of the Holy Roman Empire with its wealth distributed throughout the social classes. Nowhere are natural resources more abundant, the nobility more competent, the city republics more prosperous, or personal freedom more prevalent. Everything points to a rosy future and the realization of a perfect utopian state. All that is lacking is the individual will to be happy and content.

In the second part of the article, Leibniz shifts perspective to reveal the negative side of those same conditions and accomplishments. In the forefront of his examination is the German language, which provides the basis for cultural and national identity. Like Thomasius, Leibniz criticizes the cultural backwardness of his countrymen, the stilted and obtuse quality of German writing, the lack of decent translations, the thoughtless imitation of foreign models, and the lack of genuine understanding. The world of German writing is depicted as uninspired and lifeless, having been neglected by scholars who slavishly follow the Latin model and government officials who prefer French for diplomacy. The German vernacular must be cultivated, he argues, in order for Germany to realize its full potential.

Leibniz's progressive piece can perhaps be aligned with the more formal tone of the Baconian essay. His place among early essayists is, however, not surprising given his general role in promulgating a dramatic shift from mere geometry to a dynamic philosophy of nature, from mere mechanism to vitalistic organism. Such an intellectual stance clearly favors an essayistic mode of writing. In any event, Leibniz's treatise partakes of the provocative, avant-garde tendencies of the essay and clearly reveals the characteristic hybrid nature of scientific

tract and artistic *tour de force*. His writing is gauged to lead the reader on a dynamic journey of encirclements of an appealingly elusive solution.

The views expressed by Leibniz (and Thomasius) around 1700 resonate throughout the history of the essay. Christoph Martin Wieland's critique of the German scholar in the essay collection *Sympathien* (1756; Sympathies), which is heavily indebted to the **Earl of Shaftesbury**, picks up the theme, as do **Kant**'s lectures of the 1760s, **Schiller**'s inaugural lecture at Jena on "Was heist und zu welchem Ende studiert man Universalgeschichte?" (1789; "What Is Universal History and to What End Does One Study It?"), a veritable rhetorical masterpiece worthy of **Cicero**, Adam Müller's masterful "Vom Gespräch" (1816; On conversation), and **Arthur Schopenhauer**'s wittily incisive caricature "Über die Universitätsphilosophie" (1851; On the practice of philosophy at the university). The new mode of writing introduced by Leibniz and Thomasius bore much fruit even beyond Schopenhauer. The topic of their essays is echoed in such 20th-century classics as Josef Hofmiller's "Was ist deutsch?" (1927; What is German?), Werner Weber's musings on what it means to be Swiss in "Mut zum Erziehen" (1965; Courage to educate), **Theodor W. Adorno**'s radio essay on intellectual maturity, "Erziehung zur Mündigkeit" (1969; Education for maturity), Walter Jens' reflections on the personal and cultural locus of identity in "Nachdenken über Heimat" (1984; Reflections on the meanings of homeland), and Hans Mayer's "Rede über das eigene Land: Deutschland" (1985; Speech on our nation: Germany) or "Der Rede wert: Bemerkungen über die Beredsamkeit und die Deutschen" (1987; Worthy of mention: comments on rhetoric and the Germans). Obviously, Thomasius and Leibniz cast long shadows in the annals of the essay.

3. The 18th Century: Enlightenment; Storm and Stress; Classicism (1730–1805)

Noteworthy from the early development of the essay onward is the confluence of the essayistic mode with the desire to secularize knowledge and broaden the reading public through appeals to rhetoric and the gallant mode. The 18th century saw such a sharp rise in the number of **periodicals** and published titles that contemporary observers spoke of a "print revolution," "reader revolution," an "age of critique," an "age of journalism," and the "age of pedagogy." All this activity had a marked impact on essayistic writing, whether this took the form of individual essays, parts of a collection, or interludes in novels. While there are important differences in the various schools of literary thought which came to the fore in the course of the 18th century, those differences were later downplayed; the emphasis in essay writing centered on epistemological issues and sought to transcend schools of thought.

Johann Christoph Gottsched (1700–66), Johann Jakob Bodmer (1698–1783), and Johann Jakob Breitinger (1701–76) were very influential in communicating the ideas of Leibniz and Thomasius, as filtered through the writings of Leipzig philosopher Christian Wolff, to a large, nonacademic audience in the first decades of the century. They did this through their moral weeklies modeled on **Addison**'s and **Steele**'s *Tatler* (1709–11), *Spectator* (1711–12; 1714), and *Guardian* (1713). Other important models for the critical stance of these writings were Bayle's *Dictionnaire historique et critique* (1697; *An Historical and Critical Dictionary*) and **Bernard de Fontenelle**'s popular *Dialogues des Morts* (1683; *Dialogues from the Dead*). Gottsched translated and edited the latter, while his wife and collaborator, Luise Adelgunde Victoria Kulmus (1713–62), contributed influential translations from the moral weeklies and of French plays.

Bodmer and Breitinger published their progressive *Die Discourse der Mahlern* (1721–23; Discourses of painters) in Zurich, while Gottsched produced *Die vernünftigen Tadlerinnen* (1725–27; The reasonable critics, a misunderstanding of "tatler") and *Der Biedermann* (1727–29; The man of honor) in Leipzig. The patrician Barthold Hinrich Brockes also published a moral weekly in Hamburg under the title *Der Patriot* (1724–26). These weeklies, aimed at improving human nature, were frequently reprinted and contained many articles important to the genesis of the essay as well as for disseminating practical philosophy and aesthetics. Representative is, for example, the "19th Discourse" (1721) penned by Bodmer on the role of the imagination in poetic works. The influential topic was later treated in greater detail by both Bodmer and Breitinger in "Von dem Einfluss und Gebrauche der Einbildungs-Krafft" (1727; On the influence and use of the imagination). Gottsched also contributed essay-like articles to his weeklies such as "Furcht und Hoffnung" (1728; Fear and hope), a characteristically enlightened examination of virtue as the art of countering the paralysis of anxiety with liberating hope.

The longevity of the moral weekly format in Germany is attested by such later endeavors as *Der Gesellige* (1748–50; Sociable man), *Der Mensch* (1751–56; Humankind), *Der Redliche* (1751; The sincere person), and *Der nordische Aufseher* (1757; The Nordic guardian). They give witness to the extraordinary increase in publishing activity in the Age of Enlightenment. These moral weeklies were instrumental in spreading practical philosophy, moral values, and a fondness for instructive yet entertaining reading. Friedrich Gottlieb Klopstock (1724–1803) published pieces on literary practice and theory in *Der nordische Aufseher* such as "Von der Sprache der Poesie" (1757; On the language of poetry) and "Gedanken über die Natur der Poesie" (1757; Thoughts on the nature of poetry).

Shortly before mid-century, the moral weeklies began to give way to a new breed of journal, one more centrally interested in literary, cultural, and aesthetic matters. Gottsched led the way with his *Beyträge zur critischen Historie der deutschen Sprache, Poesie und Beredsamkeit* (1732–44; Contributions to a critical history of the German language, literature, and rhetoric) and *Der Büchersaal der schönen Wissenschaften und freyen Künste* (1742–50; Library of the humanities and fine arts). While the former emphasized questions of literary history and taste, the latter covered all areas of scholarly interest with an emphasis on philosophy and the natural sciences. Gottsched's student, Johann Joachim Schwabe (1714–84), edited *Die Belustigungen des Verstandes und Witzes* (1741–45; Entertainments of mind and wit) and other former disciples published the *Neue Beiträge zum Vergnügen des Verstandes und Witzes* (1744–57; New contributions . . .). The central significance of *Die Belustigungen* for the development of belletristic prose in the early century is still not fully appreciated. The list of contributors to the periodical reads like a Who's Who of the literary world in Northern Germany in the 1740s. Johann Elias Schlegel's (1719–49) seminal critique of dramatic technique in Shakespeare and Andreas Gryphius ("Vergleichung Shakespeares und Andreas Gryphs," 1741) appeared here, as did the accomplished essays of Theodor Lebrecht Pitschel (1716–43).

It was the 18th century that discovered Montaigne directly again. Johann Daniel Titius (i.e. Tietz) published the first German translation of the *Essais* as *Michaels Herrn von Montaigne Versuche* in 1753, and Lessing's friend Johann Joachim Christoph Bode provided a second translation of the complete opus in seven volumes (1793–97). Although Bode's translation appeared at century's end, he was already hard at work on it during the years of close contact with Lessing in Hamburg (1767–70). Moreover, Gottsched had cited Montaigne as a model for his journalistic writings around 1720 and Christian Ludwig Liscow acknowledges the impact of Montaigne's style and attitude on his satirical *Vortrefflichkeit und Notwendigkeit der elenden Scribenten* (1734; The excellence and necessity of miserable scribblers).

To be sure, Montaigne's broad, direct influence was not really felt until late in the 19th century. By contrast, the work of the Scottish Enlighteners Adam Ferguson and Francis Hutcheson and the Third Earl of Shaftesbury (especially his *Characteristics*, 1711) did have a broad and lasting impact throughout the 18th century. In any event, the period from the third quarter of the 18th century to the early 20th century (i.e. 1770–1930; from Lessing, Herder, and Wieland to Wilhelm Dilthey, **Georg Simmel**, and Josef Hofmiller) is customarily referred to as the classical period of the German essay.

A hallmark of Enlightenment anthropology, already evident in the moral weeklies, is the focus on the individual as either man reflecting or man acting. Reflective man was prone to examine his relationship to society and the universe in a new light. When the emphasis is cosmological or cultural, the tone of essayism is more detached and philosophical. When the social or personal context is foregrounded, the tone becomes more immediate and vibrant. This attitude is reflected in new literary journals which sprang up everywhere from Berlin to Vienna in the second half of the century. The most important for chronicling the history of the journalistic essay are the *Briefe die neueste Literatur betreffend* (1758–61; Letters on contemporary literature); Friedrich Nicolai's *Bibliothek der schönen Wissenschaften und schönen Künste* (1757–65; Library of the humanities and fine arts) and the *Allgemeine deutsche Bibliothek* (1765–1806; Universal German library); the Austrian statesman Josef von Sonnenfels' *Der Mann ohne Vorurteil* (1765–75; Man without prejudice); Herder's *Über die neuere deutsche Literatur* (1767; On contemporary German literature) and *Kritische Wälder* (1769; Critical forests); Johann Heinrich Merck and Johann Georg Schlosser's *Frankfurter Gelehrte Anzeigen* (1772–90; Frankfurt scholarly announcements); Wieland's **Der (neue) Teutsche Merkur** (1773–1810; The [new] German Mercury); Heinrich Christian Boie and Christian Conrad Wilhelm von Dohm's *(Neues) Deutsches Museum* (1776–91; The [new] German museum); Christian Friedrich Daniel Schubart's *Teutsche Chronik* (1774–77; German chronicle); Schiller's *Thalia* (1785–87, 1792–95) and *Die Horen* (1795–97; The muses); Johann Jakob Engel's

Philosoph für die Welt (1775–77; A philosopher for the world); Sophie La Roche's *Pomona* (1783–84); Marianne Ehrmann's progressive monthly *Amaliens Erholungsstunden* (1790–92; Amalien's leisure hours); Goethe's *Die Propyläen* (1798–1800); Leopold Friedrich Günter von Goeckingk's *Journal von und für Deutschland* (1795–1805; Journal of and for Germany); and Friedrich Justin Bertuch's *Journal des Luxus und der Moden* (1786–1827; Journal of luxury and fashion). Additionally, "Musenalmanache" (poetic almanacs) of all sorts sprang up in the 1770s and remained popular into the 19th century. They were edited by quality writers like Goeckingk, Schiller, Wieland, and Johann Heinrich Voss. The list of periodicals is merely representative of the great diversity.

The editors were themselves frequent contributors of letters, memoirs, travel descriptions, critiques, and reviews to their own journals. Most, as Schiller said of himself, wrote as "Weltbürger" (citizens of the world) and not as citizens of a particular state. Their preferred topics were historical, philosophical, and aesthetic. The publicistic work of Sophie La Roche (1731–1807) and Marianne Ehrmann (1735–95), two of the first women writers to make money from their writing careers, has yet to be examined from the point of view of the essay.

Gotthold Ephraim Lessing (1729–81), a chief representative of the Enlightenment, began his journalistic career by writing for *Die Berlinische privilegierte Zeitung* (1749–55; The privileged Berliner newspaper), coedited the *Briefe die neueste Literatur betreffend* with Friedrich Nicolai and **Moses Mendelssohn**, and published his own *Hamburgische Dramaturgie* (1767–69; Hamburg dramaturgy) as well as a series of essays and treatises on primarily theological topics, *Wolfenbütteler Beiträge zur Geschichte und Literatur* (1773–77; Wolfenbüttel contributions to literature and history). The essays contributed to these journals are the more formal kind like his philological study, *Wie die Alten den Tod gebildet* (1769; *How the Ancients Represented Death*) or "Von der Duldung der Deisten" (1774; On tolerance of deists), although the distinction is not always strict, as we know from his famous invective against Gottsched in the "17th Literary Letter." While Lessing cannot be said to have penned consciously self-contained essays in the manner of Wieland, Sturz, Goethe, or Georg Forster, nevertheless his prose is praised as exemplary for its combination of intellectual substance and stylistically light touch.

His series of five dialogues on political liberalism, *Ernst und Falk* (1778–79; *Ernst and Falk*), is a case in point. Because of its pristine clarity and deft engagement of the reader, this work can be considered a literary jewel. While emphasizing what is essential, each of the dialogues seeks to expose the falseness of a commercialized and politicized Freemasonry movement. The true aim of the Freemasons according to Lessing is the refinement of humanity itself, not personal or public gain. The presentation of the argument is a prime example of the essay as the act of thinking aloud. A later classic example of this attitude is **Heinrich von Kleist's** (1771–1811) seminal essay, "Über die allmähliche Verfertigung der Gedanken beim Reden" (1807–08; "On the Gradual Fabrication of Thoughts While Speaking"). This movement is brought out by the topos of the leisurely walk, which has been identified as a major mark of the essayistic attitude.

Lessing guides the reader through the maze of his meandering thoughts by posting metaphoric signs. At the crucial point of Falk's argument regarding the genuine deeds of the Freemasons, he interrupts his thought to chase after a butterfly. This gives Ernst time to ponder the paradox of good deeds whose purpose is to make good deeds superfluous. He goes off to a nearby tree to observe an ant colony busily pursuing its individual and collective tasks. With these two images the first discourse comes to an end. The attentive reader suspects that the butterfly is a symbol of truth which flutters about, now distant, now near, but always just out of reach. The anthill, on the other hand, symbolizes organized activity for the collective good. In the second dialogue the beehive is used further to elucidate this thought: when each member of society is capable of self-regulation, then government will not be superfluous; each individual will do what is necessary for the whole to function, for each will recognize the personal good in the commonweal. This truly democratic revolution of the spirit is dependent, however, upon genuine communication among individuals. It must be grounded on trust and attentiveness to others. Ethnic, religious, and social distances between individuals must be minimized. While humankind has not yet reached the goal, Ernst and Falk conclude, the path is clear. These dialogues are exemplary of literature's role as intellectual stimulus.

The mastery of the rhetorical arsenal and the genuine openness to truth-seeking evident in *Ernst and Falk* and Lessing's numerous other essays explain the lavish praise heaped on him by Friedrich Schlegel, Johann Gottfried Herder, and Moses Mendelssohn, who admired his combinatory wit and intellectual gymnastics. While the distinction of being the father of the German essay, as Karl Hillebrand has contended, is not necessarily true, Lessing's articles and fragments are unmistakably sparkling "fermenta cognitionis" (fermentations of his thinking), the term Lessing himself used to characterize his manner of writing and a mode which has become synonymous with essayistic writing in German because of its ability to prompt reflection and counteract rigor mortis of the spirit.

Johann Gottfried Herder, an essayist in his own right, remarked of Lessing's style that it is that "of a writer who does not simply present a finished product but rather displays the writing and thought processes themselves as they occur. Each twist and turn provides a stimulus for further reflection; each thought is presented, analyzed, dissected and then reconstructed." Herder's summary judgment describes Lessing's style in classical pithiness as "a progressive poem with interludes and episodes, always on the move, always chipping away, caught in forward progress, wrapped up in the process of becoming." What Herder espies here is recognized by Lessing himself in his own commentaries on the nexus of writing style and epistemological underpinnings. Commonly cited passages are drawn from Lessing's masterpiece, *Eine Duplik* (1778; A response) and from his *Sogenannte Briefe an verschiedene Gottesgelehrte* (So-called letters to various theologians) published posthumously. They make clear the significance of his philosophical probing for the tentativeness of the essayistic attitude. His statement that his letters are really "one-sided dialogues" is striking because it claims they are aimed at an absent interlocutor, that is, the reader, who is enjoined to participate in the exploration of ideas. Moreover, Lessing points out the absence of a logical order which allows for the lightness of touch in the treatment of issues. That open, searching manner is manifest in the late piece, *Die Erziehung des Menschengeschlechts* (1780; *The Education of the Human Race*).

The essayistic writing of **Christoph Martin Wieland** (1733–1810) during the course of the second half of the century is a mirror of the evolution and varied textures of the genre itself. Most of his essays first appeared in the pages of his journal, *Der Teutsche Merkur*. One of the chief features of his early prose is the carefully orchestrated pattern of argumentation which is clearly indebted to rhetorical technique. The "principle of holistic rhythm" is readily evident even in the early work, such as *Sympathien* (1756; Sympathies), a collection of loosely joined and frequently rhapsodic letters on the necessity of self-knowledge for proper education. With surprising adroitness the novice writer alternates long retarding cadences with abrupt, almost staccato-like phrasing, regulating the rhythm by means of questions, curt factual statements, and effective repetition of words and formulations.

Beginning in the 1760s Wieland's essays already reveal a mature style. They range from interpolations in his novels such as "Der Anti-Platonismus in Nuce" in *Agathon* (1766; Anti-Platonism in a nutshell) to journalistic pieces in the *Teutscher Merkur* such as "Was ist Wahrheit?" (1776; "What Is Truth?"), "Über die ältesten Zeitkürzungsspiele" (1781; On the oldest pastimes), "Für und Wider" (1793; Pro and contra), and "Euthanasia" (1805). They cover the full range of essayistic topics: the nature of truth, the dangers of self-deception, leisure activities, human conflict, and death. Wieland is fittingly celebrated as an early classic essayist.

Immanuel Kant (1724–1804) contributed essays as well, especially in his precritical years. Here one thinks of *Versuch über den Optimismus* (1759; Essay on optimism) and *Träume eines Geistersehers* (1766; *Dreams of a Spirit-Seer*), which have been described as lively, fresh, and witty in their use of language. The impetus for this style might well lie in the English model, for Kant was an avid reader of English literature during the 1750s and 1760s. In *Der Essay: Form und Geschichte* (1964) Bruno Berger clearly accords Kant the status of essayist. Still, the essay with the greatest impact is his famous examination of the nature of Enlightenment in "Beantwortung der Frage: Was ist Aufklärung" (1784; "What Is Enlightenment?"), which, as well as his "Idee zu einer allgemeinen Geschichte in weltbürgerlicher Sicht" (1784; "Idea for a Universal History with Cosmopolitan Intent"), reverberated well into the 20th century, inviting reactions from writers such as Theodor W. Adorno, Max Horkheimer, Jean Amery, Michel Foucault, and Jürgen Habermas. Via an arsenal of rhetorical techniques Kant leads us deep into the labyrinth of his thinking without our having suspected how demanding the reasoning really is. The impression of ease in moving from one idea to the next is conveyed largely by the judicious use of images, all related to the need to walk and to move about freely. But we are not dealing here with the topos of the leisurely walk which is the mark of the Montaignean essay; on the contrary, this is a guided tour exploring the possible routes to self-direction in all things. Kant expresses his complicated ideas in an admixture of philosophical rigor and poetic imagination.

Moses Mendelssohn (1729–86), a friend of Lessing and the Berlin publisher Friedrich Nicolai, collaborated with them in writing the important critique of contemporary 18th-century literature and aesthetics, *Briefe die neueste Literatur betreffend*. In his *Briefe über die Empfindungen* (1755; Letters on sentiment) and the dialogues *Phädon, oder über die Unsterblichkeit der Seele* (1767; *Phædon; or, The Death of Socrates*), the influence of Shaftesbury and the neo-Platonists is obvious. The preferred epistolary form frequently reveals the essentially essayistic quality of these contributions. His response to the burning question of his day on the nature of Enlightenment, "Über die Frage: Was heisst aufklären?" (1784; "On the Question: What Is Enlightenment?"), is, like most of his essayistic endeavors, a good example of the conceptual essay.

Johann Gottfried Herder (1744–1803) was a central figure in the literary life of the second half of the 18th century. He wore many hats well, as preacher, innovative cultural historian, and early semiotician. His *Über die neuere deutsche Literatur* (1767; On contemporary German literature) immediately established him as an innovative and critical thinker with the spark and sparkle of an accomplished orator. In fact, he saw himself in those years as an interpreter and rhapsodist whose sole intent was to instigate a revolution of the national spirit by adopting an anti-intellectual stance.

Perhaps the single most important collection of essays, not just as a manifesto of the *Sturm und Drang* (Storm and Stress) movement (1767–84), but for German literature in general and the essay in particular, is *Von deutscher Art und Kunst: Einige fliegende Blätter* (1773; On German art: some hastily scribbled notes), edited by Herder. In addition to seminal essays by Goethe and Paolo Frisi on Gothic architecture and Justus Möser on German history, it also contains two energetic essays by Herder, one on Ossian and another on Shakespeare. Not just Herder's but all five essays are significant documents on the German search for national and cultural identity. The volume exemplifies the culturally critical essay. After his move to Weimar in 1776, Herder contributed essays on von Hutten, Reuchlin, Johann Joachim Winckelmann, and Lessing to the *Teutscher Merkur*. Later writings such as the influential *Ideen zur Philosophie der Geschichte der Menschheit* (1784–91; *Reflections on the Philosophy of the History of Humankind*) and *Briefe zu Beförderung der Menschheit* (1793–97; Letters for the advancement of humankind) contain any number of essayistic subsections of high quality.

Johann Wolfgang von Goethe (1749–1832) was a prolific essay writer from his youth through his last years. Drawing upon the advances through the evolution of German as a literary language in the wake of Thomasius and Gellert, Goethe's essays mirror the full spectrum from conceptual essay to biographical treatise, graphic description, and cultural critique. In addition to the piece on the Strasbourg cathedral (1773) mentioned earlier, there are the tributes to Shakespeare ("Zum Shakespeares-Tag" [1771; "Shakespeare's Day"]; "Shakespeare und kein Ende" [1813–16; "Shakespeare Without End"]), the geological study, "Über den Granit" (1784; "On Granite"), his critiques of contemporary German literature, "Literarischer Sanculottismus" (1795; The literary left), and the introduction to his journal *Die Propyläen* (1798), his assessment of Winckelmann's significance for the 18th century (1805). A key feature of Goethe's essayistic style is his tendency to draw close to his central idea and then pull back again. By using telling metaphors and changing perspectives, he succeeds in drawing the reader into a process of gradual discovery. Just as drama comes to life only when performed on stage, the written text lives only through the active participation of the reader's power of imagination. Goethe's stylistic *modus operandi* corresponds to the highest goal to which human beings can aspire according to the anthropological views of the 18th century: the enhanced awareness of our own sentiments and thoughts. Goethe discerns this consciousness-raising in "natural" phenomena from Shakespeare's art to rock formations and classical aesthetic theory. The title of his later essay, "Shakespeare Without End," alludes to this never-ending process of consciousness-raising through the encounter with the texts of man and nature.

Friedrich von Schiller (1759–1805) contributed numerous compositions to the essay genre, starting with his school oration of 1779 on the nature of virtue and continuing through his discussion of the use of the Greek chorus in tragedy which prefaces his drama *Die Braut von Messina* (1803; *The Bride of Messina*). Interspersed are seminal essays with far-reaching influence such as his Mannheim lecture on the value of a national theater, "Was kann eine gute stehende Bühne eigentlich wirken?" (1785; "What Can a Good Standing Theater Actually Accomplish?"), the rhapsodic philosophical letters "Philosophische Briefe" (1786), the critical review of Gottfried August Bürger's poetry ("Bürgers Gedichte," 1791) in which Schiller begins to sketch his classical aesthetics, the programmatic and exemplary "Über Anmut und Würde" (1793; "On Grace and Dignity"), and the pace-setting *Über naive und sentimentalische Dichtung* (1795–96; *On Simple and Sentimental Poetry*). In these works we find to varying degrees the influence of Klopstock (rhapsodic tone), Goethe (intellectual energy), Leibniz (theodicy, monads), Ferguson (moral sentiment), Lessing (tolerance, perfectibility), and Kant (philosophical rigor). Although Schiller sees himself as a preceptor, he operates like the classical essayist on the belief that no single individual has sole claim to truth. Truth lies neither here nor there, but rather *both* here and there. The reader is led both to *understand* the point and to *feel* it. Schiller never theorized about the essay like Friedrich Schlegel, but he did share a common understanding with Schlegel about the need to galvanize author and reader.

Other important essays from this period include "Vom Tode fürs Vaterland" (1761; On dying for one's country) and "Vom Verdienste" (1765; On merit) by Thomas Abbt (1738–66) and "Anmerkungen über das Theater" (1774; Notes on the theater) by Jakob Michael Reinhold Lenz (1751–92), for they were frequently cited by contemporaries and others to reflect upon the meaning of patriotism and the role of theater in national life. Helferich Peter Sturz's (1736–79) epistles, fragments, dialogues, and anecdotes were penned between 1768 and 1779 on topics ranging from Klopstock to hypochondria, umbrellas, lawyers, and Duke von Bernstorf, and give evidence of Sturz's stature as a classical essayist. Other essays include Adolf von Knigge's (1752–96) "Meine eigene Apologie" (1784; My own apology), Georg Christoph Lichtenberg's (1742–99) publications in the *Göttinger Musenalmanach* (Göttinger poetic almanac) and in his *Sudelbücher*, Emilie von Berlepsch's

(1749–1818) essay on marriage and the rights of women published in the *Teutscher Merkur* in 1791, "Über einige zum Glück der Ehe nothwendige Eigenschaften und Grundsätze" (On some character traits and principles indispensable to a happy marriage) and Christian Garve's (1742–98) timely compositions on style, "Über die Popularität des Stils" (1793; On popular discourse) and "Über die prosaische Schreibart" (1798; On prose style). Sophie La Roche's Swiss diary (1787) and *Schreibetisch* (1799; Writing desk) contain essay-like commentaries which round out the picture. They give ample evidence of the popularity of essay writing by century's end.

4. The 19th Century: From Romanticism to *Fin de siècle* and a New Awakening (1798–1905)

Endings and beginnings in literary and cultural history are rarely tidy. The opening of a "modern" world view often clashes with a sense of closure at the end of a century. Thus the history of the essay around 1800 – as it was around 1700 and was again to be around 1900 – is marked by feelings of both *fin de siècle* and "Aufbruch" (new awakening). It is the oft-cited phenomenon of the "Gleichzeitigkeit des Ungleichzeitigen" (synchronism of the nonsimultaneous). The current chronological cutoffs are set by two eventful occurrences: the appearance of the *Athenäum* (1798) and Einstein's theory of relativity (1905). The classical age of the essay (from Herder to Wilhelm Dilthey, i.e. 1770–1930) coincides at the front end with the emergence of "modern" Romantic criticism with its emphasis on discovery, exploration, and rediscovery of the origins of language and of the relationship between nature and mind, and at the back end with the rise of Modernism (1880–1930). The final decade of the 19th century with its own explorations and rediscovery was clearly marked by a Modernist thrust. The essay form thrives in such a climate.

4.1. Romanticism (1798–1835)

The arch-Romanticist **Friedrich Schlegel** (1772–1829) is considered the first genuine theoretician of essayism and the true founder of hermeneutics. Drawing upon the hybrid and dialogic quality of essayistic writing evident since Lessing and Garve, he theorizes the central relationship between author and reader as a "mutual galvanism." Moreover, he argues that the essay is "a kind of experimental philosophy" which must be "rhetorical," "ironic," and "tactical" in method; "the essay is to be written the way we think, write." The mode of writing, Schlegel concludes, "should bring about movement, it should combat intellectual arthritis and promote nimbleness." In general, Schlegel sees the dominant intellectual tendency of the new era to be one of deconstructing rigid systems, what he calls the "essayification" of all disciplines. This stands in contrast to the critical age of Kant and his successors **Johann Gottlieb Fichte** (1762–1814) and Georg Wilhelm Friedrich Hegel (1770–1831), who came to dominate the 19th century. Yet, by radicalizing Kant's questioning attitude, Schlegel acts as a bridge from the Enlightenment to Romanticism and from Romanticism to the turn of the century.

This "new" *modus operandi* is everywhere evident in the ground-breaking journal *Athenäum* (1798–1800) published by Friedrich and his brother, August Wilhelm (1767–1845). Kleist's *Die Berliner Abendblätter* (1810–11; The Berlin evening news) and the early years of Johann Friedrich Cotta's

Morgenblatt für gebildete Stände (1807–65; Morning news for the educated classes) were the most important periodicals for the Romantic movement. Important for the continuing conflation of political life (as prefigured in *Berliner Abendblätter*) and literary quality (as emphasized in the *Athenäum*) were such periodicals as *Isis* (1817–48), *Zeitung für die elegante Welt* (1801–59; Newspaper for the elegant world), Theodor Mundt's *Wissenschaft und Kunst* (1835; Science and art), and Karl Gutkow's *Telegraph für Deutschland* (1835–42; Telegraph for Germany). Wolfgang Menzel edited *Das literarische Blatt* (1825–49; Literary news) as a supplement to Cotta's *Morgenblatt*. Also noteworthy is *Europa* edited by August Lewald from 1835 to 1846.

The Schlegel brothers, Dorothea Veit (1763–1839), Karoline Michaelis, and Friedrich von Hardenberg (i.e. **Novalis**, 1772–1801) published numerous pieces in the Romantic journals. Notable among them are Novalis' aphoristic "Blütenstaub" (1798; "Pollen") and the essay "Die Christenheit oder Europa" (wr. 1799, partially pub. 1826; "Christianity or Europe"). Friedrich Schlegel's essays "Über die Philosophie" (1800; "On Philosophy"), "Das Gespräch über die Poesie" (1800; "Dialogue on Poetry"), and the genial lectures *Geschichte der alten und neuen Literatur* (1812; *Lectures on the History of Literature, Ancient and Modern*) elucidate ideas on the role of myth, irony, and philosophy in prose, establishing him as a world-class essayist and theorist. His brother August Wilhelm gave form and substance to the lightning-quick ideas of his younger brother, popularizing them in his lectures such as *Über dramatische Kunst und Literatur* (1808; *Dramatic Art and Literature*).

Essayism as an ironic attitude is exemplified especially well in Friedrich Schlegel's "Über die Unverständlichkeit" (1800; "On Unintelligibility"), which appeared in response to criticism of an unintelligible style in the *Athenäum*. Schlegel makes a virtue out of a vice by arguing that irony is at the heart of the journal, for it points to the never-ending conflict between the infinite and the finite and underscores the impossibility of complete understanding. The essay, then, operates on the principle of hermeneutic indeterminacy. Essayistic compositions are written as if they were casual letters or private conversations on a moral topic in neither a strict philosophical nor a purely refined poetic style.

In this context we can also recall Schlegel's praise of **Georg Forster**'s (1754–94) style in his famous essay on the nature scientist, writer, and revolutionary. That style throbs with life because of the simultaneous appeal to the mind, the imagination, and the emotions. The effect of this broad appeal to the lower as well as higher human faculties is what has become known as genuine popularity. Schlegel's characterization of Forster's prose is valid about his own writing as well: it stimulates reflection by refining our sensitivity and broadening our perspectives.

Heinrich von Kleist (1777–1811) and Adam Müller (1779–1829) are two other superb essayists associated with the Romantic school. The former experienced an epistemological crisis which left deep marks on his literary production; the latter is especially noted for his political role. Kleist created enduring essays with his theoretically important *Über das Marionettentheater* (1810; *On Puppet Shows*) and the epistemologically seminal "Über die allmähliche Verfertigung der

Gedanken beim Reden" (wr. c. 1805–06; "On the Gradual Fabrication of Thoughts While Speaking"). In the first he argues for "a more natural coordination of the center of gravity" of each being or thing, for he values "balance, agility, and ease" above all else. In the second essay Kleist speaks of the need to think one's way through a problem and find the solution via the process. Reflection occurs only after the act; thus the act must be foregrounded in any theoretical consideration. The call for "agitation of the mind" in order to reactivate the ideas that we have already had clearly marks the essayistic mode as "intellectual midwifery" and echoes Schlegel's views on the essay.

Müller's "Vom Gespräch" (1816; On conversation) is actually a commentary on the theory and practice of essayistic writing as its own mode of writing. His topic is the trust between interlocutors prerequisite to understanding. Without mutual respect genuine communication cannot occur. The "galvanism of author and reader" cited by Schlegel is here presented as the synergy of discussants. Moreover, Müller echoes the call for *bon goût* sounded around 1700 by praising the natural light touch and sense of good taste evident in French discourse as being the "pulse beat of the nation." He exhorts his compatriots to emulate the model.

Others who must be included in the history of the essay are the women writers Karoline von Günderrode (1780–1806), Bettina von Arnim (1785–1859), Elisa von der Recke (1756–1831), and Karoline Pichler (1769–1843), as well as such canonical writers as Jean Paul Friedrich Richter (1763–1825), Ludwig Tieck (1773–1853), Friedrich Hölderlin (1770–1843), and Joseph Görres (1776–1848). Finally, we should recall Wilhelm von Humboldt (1767–1835), the Prussian Minister of Culture and Education and founder of the University of Berlin, his brother and natural scientist Alexander von Humboldt (1769–1859), and the philosophers Friedrich Schleiermacher (1768–1834), **Johann Gottlieb Fichte** (1762–1814); Friedrich Wilhelm Schelling (1775–1854), and Gotthilf Heinrich Schubert (1780–1860), who all deserve mention as well in the history of the essay during the Romantic period.

4.2. From Realism to *Fin de siècle* and a New Awakening

Arthur Schopenhauer (1788–1860) shares with the Romantics a rebellious spirit. He too is widely acclaimed as a consummate practitioner of the essay, earning the title of the "German Montaigne" (endowed by Karl Hillebrand) and serving as the expressed inspiration of Thomas Mann's own essay style. In fact, Schopenhauer appears to be a writer's writer, for in addition to the comments by Hillebrand and Mann, Franz Kafka judged Schopenhauer to be a veritable "Sprachkünstler" (language artist) who should be read for that talent alone. **Jorge Luis Borges** claimed he learned German just so that he could read Schopenhauer in the original, even apologizing for putting the philosopher ahead of Goethe and Heine. The main portion of Schopenhauer's *Parerga und Paralipomena* (1851; *Parerga and Paralipomena*) is comprised of **aphorisms** on the art of living. They have proved to be the most popular of his publications, for his manner of philosophizing was coincident with his ironic and lively style of writing. Philosophy is presented here in an accessible fashion and in stark contrast to the German idealism so widespread at the universities in the 19th century (Schelling, Fichte, Hegel). Above all

Schopenhauer sought to stimulate with his thoughts on diverse subjects further reflection on the part of his readers so that they might draw their own conclusions based on their own critical faculties. That is the main reason why he referred to professors of philosophy in the wake of Schelling, Fichte, and Hegel as "corrupters of the mind" ("Kopfverderber"). No wonder that Nietzsche found in him a kindred spirit.

Herman Grimm (1828–1901) published his first set of 11 essays in Hannover in 1859; the book bore the simple title *Essays*, was dedicated to **Ralph Waldo Emerson**, and was an immediate success. In 1865 a second set of ten essays followed under the title *Neue Essays über Kunst und Literatur* (New essays on art and literature). It opened with a homage to Emerson, and the entire collection pays tribute to the impact the American had on Grimm. Indeed the 1830s and 1840s proved to be a fertile period of incubation for the genre: **Lamb, Hunt, Hazlitt,** Landor, **De Quincey, Carlyle, Macaulay, Thackeray, Thoreau,** and **Margaret Fuller** as well as Emerson penned many of their classical essays then. Grimm refers to that impact in such pieces as "Emerson" (1865), "Friedrich der Grosse und Macaulay" (1874; Frederick the Great and Macaulay), and "Goethe und Carlyle" (1865). The 1850s and 1860s subsequently saw the birth of the genuine, self-consciously conceived and practiced essay mode.

In another essay collection from the year 1890, Grimm included a lengthy preface in which he detailed the history and distinguishing characteristics of the literary genre of the essay. In his introductory comments to his *Fragmente* (1900–02) he concedes that he perhaps has created a legacy of some import for subsequent generations of writers by cultivating the essay form. To be sure, his latter essays include reviews and articles with a more polemical tone such as "Deutscher Unterricht auf deutschen Gymnasien" (1890; German instruction in the German schools), "Wert und Wirkung der Kunstkritik" (1890; Value and impact of art criticism), and "Goethe im Dienste unserer Zeit" (1890; Goethe for our times) (Ludwig Rohner, 1966). But Emerson is given due credit for having introduced into the mainstream the loan word "essay," using it interchangeably with the native German *Aufsatz*. Nevertheless, the *Preussische Jahrbücher* found it necessary in 1857 to encourage the use of the term "essay" to designate what was already common practice.

If Herman Grimm captures the spirit of the positivistic 19th century, **Friedrich Nietzsche** (1844–1900) points to a thorough revamping of conceptions. His influence on generations of writers has been profound. As the first radically (post)modern thinker in Germany, Nietzsche found aphoristic and essayistic writing to be the most appropriate vehicle of expression for his philosophy of the future. Many of the entries in the aphoristically styled works of the 1870s and 1880s, *Menschliches, Allzumenschliches* (1878–80; *Human, All Too Human*), *Also sprach Zarathustra* (1883–85; *Thus Spoke Zarathustra*), *Jenseits von Gut und Böse* (1886; *Beyond Good and Evil*), and *Die fröhliche Wissenschaft* (1882; *The Gay Science*), contain fine examples of the essay. Earlier pieces on the birth of tragedy, the advantages and disadvantages of the use of history, David Strauss as writer, Schopenhauer as educator, and Wagner in Bayreuth, which appeared in his culturally critical *Unzeitgemässe Betrachtungen* (1873–76; *Untimely Meditations*), are veritable masterpieces of the genre whose

trademark is experimental playfulness. His thought experiments are most aptly expressed in aphoristic form, which Just considered to contain the essence of the essayist's attitude and thus labeled them "essay extracts."

Many other 19th-century essayists are worthy of note, but only a small selection can be mentioned here. At the beginning of Book III of his *Die romantische Schule* (1836; *The Romantic School*), Heinrich Heine (1797–1856) remarked that "The history of literature is as difficult to describe as natural history. In both cases one sticks to particularly dominant phenomena. Yet just as a small glass of water can contain an entire world of wondrous creatures which demonstrate the greatness of God just no less than the largest beasts, so too can the smallest poetic almanac contain innumerable miniature poets who appear just as interesting to the researcher as the largest elephants of literature." Any number of the many collections and journals mentioned here are like the *Musenalmanach* cited by Heine. The following partial list is designed to communicate a sense of that richness: Heine's *Die Harzreise* (1826; *The Harz Journey*) and *Die romantische Schule*; *Ästhetische Feldzüge* (1834; Aesthetic campaigns) by Ludolf Wienbarg (1802–72); "Das politische Gespräch" (1836; "A Dialogue on Politics") and *Über die Epochen der neueren Geschichte* (wr. 1854, pub. 1888; On the epochs of modern history) by **Leopold von Ranke** (1795–1886); *Wanderungen durch den Mark Brandenburg* (1862–82; Excursions through Mark Brandenburg) by Theodor Fontane (1819–98); *Weltgeschichtliche Betrachtungen* (1905; *Reflections on History*) by **Jacob Christoph Burckhardt** (1818–97); "Die deutsche Ideologie" (wr. 1845–46; *The German Ideology*) by **Karl Marx** (1818–83) and Friedrich Engels (1820–95); and *Zeiten, Völker und Menschen* (1874–85; Time, people, and men) by Karl Hillebrand (1829–84).

Then there are the Austrians Ferdinand Kürnberger (1821–79), Otto Gildemeister (1823–1902), Ludwig Bamberger (1823–99), **Sigmund Freud** (1856–1939), and Franz Xavier Kraus (1840–1901). These writers published their works in journals as well as in individual collections. Few of them, however, are known first and foremost as essayists.

5. The 20th Century (1900–94): From Modernism to Postwall

Given the essay's function as a means of exploring conflict in times of change, it is no surprise that the 20th century, with its repeated psychological, scientific, and political crises, has experienced a burgeoning of the essayistic style. The Austrian critic Hans Hahnle noted in 1956 that literary production is no longer centered on the epic, the lyric, or the drama as it was earlier, not even on the novel as in the 19th century; today, he averred, it is centered on the essay (Rohner). Writers of diverse backgrounds mirror these essential tensions, which re-emerged around 1900 with the Modernist movement and have continued throughout the entire century. After having long stood in the shadow of the essay as practiced in America, England, France, and Spain, the German essay moved to the forefront with a flurry of activity in the early decades of the 20th century and again immediately after World War II. Its strength has continued since then. The constellation of events and talent evident in the axis Lessing–Herder–Wieland–Goethe–Schlegel repeats itself in the constellation of

Hofmannsthal–Borchardt–Kassner–**Heinrich Mann**–**Benn** and again in the configuration Jens–Mayer–Werner Weber–Weizsäcker–**Wolf**.

5.1. *Fin de Siècle* and Modernism (1890–1930)

Together with his friend Rudolf Borchardt, **Hugo von Hofmannsthal** (1874–1929) represents the beginning of another high point in the unity of the lyric, dramatic, epic, and the essayistic. Hofmannsthal led the way with his sensitive treatments of Swinburne (1893), D'Annunzio (1894), and the poems of Stefan George (1896) as cosmopolitan phenomena. The aestheticizing thrust of these essays underscores the dallying pleasure of nuance while simultaneously prompting sublimation of the momentary pleasure. The result is a conflation of poetry and life, as Hofmannsthal entitles one of his essays ("Poesie und Leben," 1896). Nevertheless, the most influential of his essays was surely his fictive epistle, "Brief des Lord Chandos" (1901; Letter to Lord Chandos), directed to the father of the English essay, Francis Bacon, in which Hofmannsthal expresses his crisis of creative inspiration. The introductions to collected works frequently assume the shape and feel of the essay, as for example the prefaces to *1001 Nacht* (1908) and *Balzac* (1908). *Die Briefe des Zurückgekehrten* (1908; Letters of those who have returned), "Maria Theresia" (1917), "Rede auf Grillparzer" (1922; Speech on Grillparzer), and finally "Das Schrifttum als geistiger Raum der Nation" (1927; The written word as the spiritual space of nationhood) document respectively his eye for sharp cultural criticism, an appreciation of Austrian heritage, and his personal commitment to a "conservative revolution" (as he called it). Taken as a whole, Hofmannsthal's opus is a fine example of the reworking of a cosmopolitan cultural legacy to respond to the personal and intellectual crises of the day.

Rudolf Borchardt's (1877–1945) style is the counterpart to that of his friend: it is loud, sometimes irritating, even militant. An opportunity to compare and contrast offers itself readily since Borchardt also penned essays on Swinburne (1909) and George (1909). His own attitude toward and deep sense of affinity with Hofmannsthal can be gleaned from his "Rede über Hofmannsthal" (1902), "Die neue Poesie und die alte Menschheit" (1912; New poetry and traditional humanity), and "Schöpferische Restauration" (1927; Creative restoration). In his posthumously published essay on Edna St. Vincent Millay, "Die Entdeckung Amerikas" (c. 1925; The discovery of America), Borchardt was one of the first great German essayists to point out the importance of American lyrical poetry.

Rudolf Kassner (1873–1959), a great essayist of the day, is little remembered today. That is due perhaps to the fact that he wrote exclusively essays and, as noted, the essay form has stirred little interest among German scholars. Nevertheless, Kassner's essayistic production can be considered the counterpart to the early lyrics of George and Rilke. What fascinated Kassner was the relationship between the Platonic idea and the physical body. Favorite topics, therefore, are compelling beauty and transparency of the inner essence. In his first publication, "Die Mystik, die Künstler und das Leben" (1900; The mystic, the artist, and life), Kassner renders the master prose writer as the necessary counterpart to the creative poet. **Shelley**, Keats, Blake, Rossetti, and Swinburne are his models. This nuance-rich aestheticism of the turn of the century ultimately gives way to a growing concentration on the external form. The tension between antique and Christian views of man is rendered in "Von den Elementen menschlicher Grösse" (1911; On the elements of human grandeur), while physiognomy begins to dominate in the 1920s as in "Grundlagen der Physiognomik" (1921; Fundamentals of physiognomy) and "Das physiognomische Weltbild" (1930; Physiognomical world view). During the fascist years Kassner turned his attention to travel, reminiscences, and the role of the imagination. Following the war, he returned to politically sensitive issues in his interpretation of the age of the atom bomb in "Transfiguration" (1946) and the role of Christ in mediating the tensions between the age of **Plato** and the age of the Iron Curtain in "Die Geburt Jesu" (1951; The birth of Christ). Kassner was active to the end, and his intellectual agility is manifest in his "Das inwendige Reich" (1953; The inner empire), "Der Zauberer" (1955; The magician), and "Der goldene Drachen" (1957; The golden dragon). In all of these works the intellectual anxiety and aesthetic sensibilities of the first half of the 20th century from *fin de siècle* to the atom bomb are captured, mirrored, and transfigured.

The many influential essays of **Walter Benjamin** (1892–1940), penned between 1925 and 1935, capture this sense of diversity as well: "Die Aufgabe des Übersetzers" (1923; The translator's task), "Goethes Wahlverwandtschaften" (1924–25; Goethe's *Elective Affinities*), "Karl Kraus" (1931), "Der Autor als Produzent" (wr. 1934; The author as producer), and "Das Kunstwerk im Zeitalter seiner technischen Reproduzierbarkeit" (1936; "The Work of Art in the Age of Reproduction"). While each has a different thematic focus and there is a clear shift from his early idealism to his later Marxist stance, the growing emphasis on the political and ethical responsibilities of the writer goes hand in hand with the calling of the classical essayist to be responsive to the human condition. To be sure, "Karl Kraus" is considered to be the closest in form and style to the classical form of the essay, but then thematic and excursive qualities of the genre always resonate with one another as if in pre-established harmony. Benjamin summed up this tendency of the age in his *Einbahnstrasse* (1928; One-way street), where he remarks that refined prose has three dimensions: a musical one which structures the piece rhythmically, an architectonic one which provides the external structure, and a "textile" one which provides the verbal fabric and particular texture of the text (Dieter Bachmann, 1969). His "artwork essay" is one of the most important contributions to the sociology of art in the 20th century and is worthy of detailed analysis.

5.2. From Exile to Postwall (1945–94)

The essayistic style was not favored by the National Socialists, who came to power in 1933. They rejected the essay precisely because of its open, critical stance, something German exile writers of course valued all the more. The editorial reactions of *Die neue Rundschau* (1890–; The new review) and *Die Deutsche Rundschau* (1874–45, 1950–; The German review) reveal the two major forms of resistance during the Fascist regime. While the former employed cloaking devices in order to conceal its criticism of the Nazis, the latter under the direction of Rudolf Pechel was unmistakenly critical of the regime.

Two collections of essays from the pages of these journals underscore the point. In his collection, *Der goldene Schnitt: Grosse Essayisten der Neuen Rundschau 1890–1960* (1960; The golden harvest), Christoph Schwerin includes not a single essay from the period 1933–44, explaining that the journal became a secret center of anti-National Socialist thought, but that National Socialist terminology had to be adopted in order to conceal its real purpose. By contrast, Pechel penned an introduction, "Schicksale und politische Aufgabe einer deutschen Zeitschrift" (Fate and political mission of a German journal) to his collection, *Deutsche Rundschau: Acht Jahrzehnte deutschen Geisteslebens* (1961; German review: eight decades of German intellectual life) in which he explains how he used the journal as a weapon against the Ministry of Propaganda and the Gestapo. He consciously sought to unmask the Nazi regime by employing the techniques of Montesquieu, **Swift**, and Confucius (Rohner). But following World War II the essay again came into its own, rising to prominence in such publications as *Merkur* (1947–; Mercury), *Sinn und Form* (1949–; Meaning and form), *Frankfurter Hefte* (Frankfurt journal), *Der Monat* (The month), and *Kursbuch* (Timetable), as well as again in the *Deutsche Rundschau* and *Neue Rundschau*. Newspapers such as the *Frankfurter Allgemeine Zeitung* (Frankfurt general newspaper) and the *Süddeutsche Zeitung* (South German newspaper) are frequent sites of essayistic rather than merely feuilletonistic writing.

The positivism and specialization already evident in the Baconian branch of the European essay and in the 19th-century German one have come to mark the scientific attitudes of the 20th. In order to communicate the particular knowledge of a narrow specialty to the public at large, recourse was taken to essay writing. Examples of this move are provided by Sigmund Freud, Carl Jung (1875–1961), Werner Heisenberg (1901–76), Hans Blumenberg (1920–96), Carl Friedrich von Weizsäcker, and Max Planck (1858–1947). A by-product of this movement has been the importation of the mentality of precise measurements essential to science into the quintessentially ambiguous realm of art. Consequently, some critics fear the progressive disintegration of the essay (Karl August Horst, 1962) and note a significant shift from the classical essay of the 18th and 19th centuries with its goal of instigating a critical dialogue to a desire simply to win the reader over to the author's point of view. The positing of a specific ideological or dogmatic truth threatens to displace the characteristic encirclements of possible, probable truths. Thus it is imperative that the reader pay close attention to the *modus operandi*. More important than a particular style is the essential attitude reflected in the use of language.

Other critics sense a decline in the appropriateness of the classical essay of the 18th and 19th centuries as a model for writing in the 20th century because it seemed little more than a form of masquerade and prevarication (Hermann Kähler, 1982). Hugo von Hofmannsthal's Chandos letter and Hermann Hesse's "Die Brüder Karamasoff oder der Untergang Europas" (1919; The brothers Karamasov and the decline of Europe) or "Zarathustras Wiederkehr" (1919; Zarathustra's return), and **Ricarda Huch**'s "Entpersönlichung" (1921; Depersonalization) capture this feeling – paradoxically – in essay form. While the sense of decenteredness recurs after 1945, it does not stem the flow of essays. Weizsäcker, Walter

Jens (1923–), and Christa Wolf demonstrate that such fears of dissolution are exaggerated.

Gerhard Haas identifies three general categories of essayists in the 20th century which, however, are not free of overlap. The first group includes those whose point of departure is *belles-lettres* itself: **Alfred Andersch** (1914–80), Ingeborg Bachmann (1926–73), Hermann Bahr, Gottfried Benn, Ernst Bertram, Heinrich Böll (1917–85), Rudolf Borchardt, Bertholt Brecht (1898–1956), Hermann Broch, Elias Canetti, Alfred Döblin (1878–1937), **Friedrich Dürrenmatt** (1921–90), Hans Magnus Enzensberger, Max Frisch, **Günter Grass** (1927–), Hermann Hesse (1877–1962), Hugo von Hofmannsthal, **Ernst Jünger** (1895–), Oskar Loerke (1884–1941), Heinrich and Thomas Mann, Robert Musil, **Rudolf Alexander Schröder** (1878–1962), Peter Turrini (1944–), Robert Walser, Christa Wolf, and Stefan Zweig (1881–1942), among many others. The second group comprises essayists who come from the other disciplines, for example: Theodor W. Adorno, **Max Bense** (1910–90), Ernst Bloch (1885–1977), Jacob Christoph Burckhardt, **Ernst Robert Curtius** (1886–1956), Sigmund Freud, Romano Guardini (1885–1968), Friedrich Heer (1916–83), Eric Heller (1911–), Ricarda Huch, Walter Jens, Rudolf Kassner, Max Kommerell (1902–44), **Georg Lukács** (1885–1971), Hans Mayer, Alexander Mitscherlich (1908–82), Rudolf Pannwitz (1881–1969), Georg Simmel, Karl Vossler, and Carl Friedrich von Weizsäcker. Finally, a third group draws its members largely from the press and media: Peter Bamm (1897–1975), Walter Benjamin, Hans Hennecke (1897–1977), Theodor Heuss (1884–1963), Josef Hofmiller, Curt Hohoff (1913–), Hans Egon Holthusen, Siegfried Kracauer, Karl Kraus (1874–1936), Marcel Reich-Ranicki (1920–), Max Rychner, Arno Schmidt (1914–79), Dolf Sternberger (1907–), Günter Wallraff (1942–), and Werner Weber. As extensive as this list is, it is still woefully incomplete.

The 20th century has seen a veritable flood of essayistic writing which makes it prohibitive to go into any detail here. Yet it is useful to cite certain influential editions and even individual essays worthy of closer consideration. Among the telling collections are *Bildung* (1900; Education) and *Inventur* (1912; Inventory) by Hermann Bahr (1863–1934), whose titles represent essential attitudes toward stock-taking at the turn of the century. Robert Walser (1878–1956) followed with *Aufsätze* (1913; Essays), **Georg Simmel** (1858–1918) with *Fragmente und Aufsätze* (1923; Fragments and essays), Rudolf Kassner with *Essays* (1923), and Josef Hofmiller (1872–1933) with his *Über den Umgang mit Büchern* (1927; On intimacy with books). **Heinrich Mann** (1871–1950), even more noteworthy than his brother Thomas as an essayist, produced a whole series of essay collections over a 20-year span: e.g. *Macht und Mensch* (1919; Power and people), *Geist und Tat* (1931; Spirit and deed), and *Mut* (1939; Courage). **Thomas Mann** (1875–1955) had a broad impact with his literary critiques, "Goethe und Tolstoi" (1925; "Goethe and Tolstoy"), "Goethe als Repräsentant des bürgerlichen Zeitalters" (1932; "Goethe as Representative of the Bourgeois Age"), and "Leiden und Grösse Richard Wagners" (1933; "Sufferings and Greatness of Richard Wagner") as well as numerous other essays. Siegfried Kracauer's (1889–1966) Weimar essays *Das Ornament der Masse* (1936; *The Mass Ornament*) captures the mood of those years, while the autobiographical "Doppelleben" (1950;

Double life) of **Gottfried Benn** (1886–1956) reflects the tension between the individual as self-directive and the self as an insignificant test case in a large laboratory experiment.

Blätter aus dem Brotsack (1940; Pages from the food pouch) by **Max Frisch** (1911–91) and *Welt im Wort* (1949; World in the word) by Max Rychner (1897–1965) are commentaries on the war years. "Der unbehauste Mensch" (1951; Homeless man), *Ja and Nein* (1954; Yes and no), and *Das Schöne und das Wahre* (1958; The beautiful and the true) by Hans Egon Holthusen (1913–) capture the sense of marginalization and ambivalence toward the past and one's own disenfranchisement caused by the war. Rychner picked up on these themes in *Zwischen Mitte und Rand* (1964; Between center and margin). The socially and culturally critical essays in **Theodor W. Adorno**'s (1903–69) *Prismen* (1955; Prisms) proved to be highly influential, as was his edition of Benjamin's critical writings, *Schriften I und II* (1955). The same is true of *Holzwege* (1950; Woodpaths) by **Martin Heidegger** (1889–1976), although Bruno Berger (1964) is reluctant to label them essays. **Elias Canetti**'s (1905–94) *Masse und Macht* (1960; Crowds and Power) and *Die Welt im Kopf* (1962; The world in your head), Werner Weber's well-received *Tagebuch eines Lesers* (1965; Diary of a reader), and Christa Wolf's *Lesen und Schreiben* (1972; Reading and writing) evince the continuing appeal of the essay in the in the second half of the century.

Individual essays of note are *Das hilflose Europa* (1922; Helpless Europe) by **Robert Musil** (1880–1942), "Der Zerfall der Werte" (1932; "The Disintegration of Values") and "Das System der Welt-Bewältigung" (System of world control) by Hermann Broch (1886–1951), "Bildung als Konsumgut" (1962; Culture as consumer ware) by **Hans Magnus Enzensberger** (1929–), Adorno's "Zeitlose Mode" (Timeless fashion), Kracauer's "Über Erfolgsbücher und ihr Publikum" (On bestsellers and their public), **Max Weber**'s (1864–1920) "Wissenschaft als Beruf" (1919; Science as profession), "Stein" (Stone) by **Ricarda Huch** (1864–1947), and Holthusen's "Der unbehauste Mensch." Each is exemplary in style and form. Many of those written before the war were rediscovered as a way of dealing indirectly with the dark era of fascism. Huch's piece is a rare example of political essay in German. Kracauer's topology of filmic motifs and his sociological critique in "Die kleinen Ladenmädchen gehen ins Kino" (1927; The little shop girls go to the movies) are still fresh and incisive today because of their emphasis on the impact of the entertainment industry. Films reinforce bourgeois values through their choice of characterization. Film imitates life, but life also imitates film, for the young women model their own actions on the film characters.

The above-named essays also reveal a tendency in the 20th-century essay toward the more formal treatise with clear external signposts of the internal structure. This is also true of Walter Benjamin, whose influence on postwar writing has been considerable in the wake of the posthumous publication of his works in the 1950s. His "Der Autor als Produzent" (1934; The author as producer) and artwork-essay have been frequently consulted by writers and scholars alike. Completely different but equally significant for the history of the essay are his treatments of **Baudelaire** (1939) with its emphasis on the urban life of the *flâneur* and the celebration of Franz Kafka (1934) as the quintessential "homeless" intellectual adrift in the flow of time.

"Brecht und die Humanität" (1964; Brecht and humanity) by Hans Mayer (1907–) is a rhetorical *tour de force* with a strong essayistic slant toward the favored method of the combinatory principle. Mayer begins his oration significantly with the statement: "Brecht and humanitas: a questionable combination." Yet it can serve to underscore the continuous fascination with politics (Brecht) and humanistic values (humanitas) which lies at the center of the essay. Mayer is known for his mesmerizing ability to speak freely on writers and their literature, their forms and traditions, and their realized or unrealized political responsibilities. In a secular age of reason, he plays the kind of role that Luther, Zwingli, and Abraham à Sancta Clara played in the age of faith when the preacher was teacher, entertainer, and pastor all rolled into one. The rhetorical tradition continues despite obvious transformations in world view.

K. G. Just pointed out in "Der Essay" (1954), his pioneering article on the essay, that future inquiries into the history and practice of the essay would need to look explicitly at the influence on the genre emanating from scientific circles and not focus merely on the literary practice. While it is evident from the essayistic output of the Göttinger physicist Georg Christoph Lichtenberg (1742–99), the geological studies of Goethe, and the objective essays of Alexander von Humboldt that the natural sciences have always been part and parcel of the essayistic tradition, developments since 1945 have dissolved the distinction between scientific prose and the literary essay even further. Aesthetic production in all the genres has displayed a strong tendency to experiment, thus drawing closer to the stance of science and technology. Two essayists – Wolf and Weizsäcker – exemplify these border crossings between science and poetry which are at the core of essayistic writing.

Few natural scientists have shown themselves to be more accomplished essayists than the physicist, philosopher, and statesman, Carl Friedrich von Weizsäcker (1912–). A veritable *uomo universale* like Francis Bacon, Weizsäcker has contributed frequently and substantially to the genre. Of special interest in this context is the work pursuant to the transformation of his world view during the 1950s, when he began to formulate his philosophy of nature in search of a unity of nature, science, religion, and human existence. His studies of Kant, Descartes, the scholastics, Aristotle and Plato, and frequent talks with Heidegger convinced him of the dominant role that a skeptical attitude plays in gaining knowledge. Philosophy is, in fact, learning how to ask ever more questions. Of course the methodology was not unknown to him as an atomic physicist interested in spin theory and the splitting of the atom. He has held a chair in physics (Berlin) and in philosophy (Hamburg). These experiences found expression on the lecture circuit. The chief thematic foci of his essays and speeches are human consciousness, social structures, economic conditions, ecology, the concept of nation, political responsibility, and personal morality.

Christa Wolf (1929–) is an essayist in the manner of Montaigne as well as a noted novelist. Her light touch is deceiving in that her prose sentences consistently pierce the external shell of convention to stir inner movement. Her essays fly easily, breathe naturally, and animate relentlessly. This is especially true of such pieces as "Tabula Rasa" (1968) in which she invokes a universe of self-knowledge and experience resultant of her reading since childhood and concludes that without books, she could not be what she has become. "One of the greatest adventures we can have in life," she contends, is "to compare, examine, define our limits and gradually learn to see ourselves, to measure ourselves against the most well-defined figures of all time." Without books all that is impossible.

Extraordinary as an essay crossing disciplinary boundaries is the speech Wolf delivered in Bremen in 1977 entitled "Ein Satz" (1978; "A Sentence"). An intent look at the simple relationships subject-verb-object quickly reveals cracks and fissures running throughout the apparently monolithic façade. Sentences rarely match the human behavior, the internal conditions of the reader or listener. We hear and understand what we already know and accept. Prejudgment interferes, therefore, with the ability to judge what another is saying. This stance harks back to Thomasius and to Lessing and Wieland's exhortations to hear clearly, read closely, and think critically for oneself in order to escape the controlling mechanisms of tradition and customs.

In "Gedächtnis und Gedenken: Über Fred Wander" (1972; "Commemorative Medallions") Wolf deals with memory, identifying the essential tension between systole and diastole which defines human existence. Here the principle of expansion is translated into the language of imagination with its freedom to play with the open possibilities while the principle of contraction is rendered in the language of trite tradition and hardening habit. Her comment on the function of epic prose in the battle against intellectual arthritis applies equally to essayistic writing with its insistence on resistance: "Epic prose should be a genre which aims to penetrate [the] individual, the prose reader, along trails which have not yet been blazed. It must get through to his innermost core, the nucleus where the personality is formed and made solid . . . This region is accessible to the voice of another human being; prose can reach it; language can touch it and open it up – not to take control of it, but to free psychic energies whose power is comparable to those locked in the atom." As is true for essayists of any era, we must have the courage to investigate, to explore, to experiment. This Wolf does in "Abschied von Phantomen – Zur Sache: Deutschland" (1994; "Parting from Phantoms: The Business of Germany") in which she reviews – not all too kindly – the first five years after the fall of the wall and the reunification of East and West Germany. It is a far-ranging and incisive exposé which draws upon history, literature, travels to America, ethnic and cultural diversity in easy and tantalizing ways. As is the wont with classical essayists, she keeps the reader guessing where she is headed as she moves toward her goal in a seemingly associative manner. Her real topic is forgetfulness, oblivion, "the loss of reality." That aligns her with writers of the 1950s troubled by memories of the recent past. Wolf's refrain-like question "Where am I headed?" keeps the reader focused until she concludes with an image of a commonly prepared and shared meal by all Germans whether from the West or from the East.

The kind of prose Weizsäcker and Wolf offer in these pieces is truly essayistic; it is hazardous to writer and reader alike, for it is capable of altering and moving. It is supposed to alter and move. Wolf strikes a chord resonant with one sounded by the American essayist, Harold Brodkey, who deemed reading (not just consuming) to be a most dangerous game. Unfortunately, Wolf suspected that prose writers in the 1970s and 1980s had not yet arrived at the stage of science which, of course, is wholly dependent on curiosity and experimentation and without which there could be no further movement.

6. Conclusion: Maps

The German essay is like a map of middle Europe: it reveals geographical diversity and fecundity. The essays are like so many signposts; the essayists are the guides. Individual essays, essay collections, essayistic interludes in novels, even the personalities of the essayists themselves are like the hills and valleys, pastures and meadows, lakes, rivers, and streams, the towns and urban centers. All contribute a particular flavor to the terrain and give it its special character. A traveler therein can become acquainted with many different towns and landscapes. The essayist functions as a collector and transmitter of the spirit of an age – not in the sense of an objective mirror which merely reflects images but in the sense of an amplifier and filter of human thoughts and emotions. Distinguishing fine nuances, rearranging them in creative and productive ways, the essayist captures the invigorating essence of the all-too-mundane in the cultural, sociological, and philosophical matrix of the human community and sends it back out into the relational system to energize the whole with new life. Such is the function of the essay as mediator between spirit and deed, between science and poetry, from Thomasius to Christa Wolf. It dazzles with its sparkle and animates with its delicate balancing act.

JOHN A. McCARTHY

Further Reading

Bachmann, Dieter, *Essay und Essayismus: Benjamin – Broch – Kassner – H. Mann – Musil – Rychner*, Stuttgart: Kohlhammer, 1969

Bohm, Arnd, "Artful Reproduction: Benjamin's Appropriation of Adolf Behne's 'Das reproduktive Zeitalter' in the *Kunstwerk-Essay*," *Germanic Review* 68, no. 4 (1994): 146–55

Burgard, Peter J., *Idioms of Uncertainty: Goethe and the Essay*, University Park: Pennsylvania State University Press, 1992

Ginsberg, Robert, editor, *The Philosopher as Writer: The Eighteenth Century*, Selinsgrove, Pennsylvania: Susquehanna University Press, 1987

Haas, Gerhard, *Studien zur Form des Essays und zu seinen Vorformen im Roman*, Tübingen: Niemeyer, 1966

Haas, Gerhard, *Essay*, Stuttgart: Metzler, 1969

Horst, Karl August, *Kritischer Führer durch die deutsche Literatur der Gegenwart: Roman, Lyrik, Essay*, Munich: Nymphenburger, 1962

Just, K. G., "Der Essay," in *Deutsche Philologie im Aufriss*, vol. 2, edited by Wolfgang Stammler, Berlin: Schmidt, 1954: cols. 1897–1948

Kähler, Hermann, *Von Hofmannsthal bis Benjamin: Ein Streifzug durch die Essayistik der zwanziger Jahre*, Berlin and Weimar: Aufbau, 1982

Küntzel, Heinrich, *Essay und Aufklärung: Zum Ursprung einer originellen deutschen Prosa im 18. Jahrhundert*, Munich: Fink, 1969

McCarthy, John A., *Crossing Boundaries: A Theory and History of Essay Writing in German, 1680–1815*, Philadelphia: University of Pennsylvania Press, 1989

Midgley, David R., "'Das hilflose Europa': Eine Aufforderung, die politischen Essays von Robert Musil neu zu lesen," *German Quarterly* 67, no. 1 (1994): 16–26

Mittmann, Elizabeth, "Christa Wolf's Signature in and on the Essay: Woman, Science, and Authority," in *The Politics of the Essay: Feminist Perspectives*, edited by Ruth Ellen Boetcher Joeres and Elizabeth Mittmann, Bloomington: Indiana University Press, 1993: 95–112

Morchen, Helmut, "Nebensachen: Zu den Essays westdeutscher Autoren," in *Deutsche Gegenwartsliteratur: Ausgangspositionen und aktuelle Entwicklungen*, edited by Manfred Durzak, Stuttgart: Reclam, 1981: 359–73

Nordmann, Ingeborg, "Nachdenken an der Schwelle von Literatur und Theorie: Essayistinnen im 20. Jahrhundert," in *Deutsche Literatur von Frauen: 19. und 20. Jahrhundert*, edited by Gisela Brinker-Gabler, Munich: Beck, 1988: 364–79

Rohner, Ludwig, *Der deutsche Essay: Materialien zur Geschichte und Ästhetik einer literarischen Gattung*, Neuwied and Berlin: Luchterhand, 1966

Schmidt, James, editor, *What Is Enlightenment? Eighteenth-Century Answers and Twentieth-Century Questions*, Berkeley: University of California Press, 1996

van der Laan, James, *The German Essay of the Eighteenth Century: An Ecology* (dissertation), Ann Arbor: University of Michigan, 1984

Weissenberger, Klaus, "Essay," in *Prosakunst ohne Erzählen: Die Gattungen der nichtfiktionalen Kunstprosa*, edited by Weissenberger, Tübingen: Niemeyer, 1985: 105–24

Wohlleben, Joachim, *Goethe als Journalist und Essayist*, Frankfurt-on-Main and Berne: Lang, 1981

Gershenzon, Mikhail

Russian, 1869–1925

While for many writers the essay was a sideline interest, for Mikhail Gershenzon it was his first, enduring, and primary love. Although he wrote over ten books and hundreds of articles, reviews, and essays in his 30-year career as a Russian historian, critic, and philosopher, the essay served as the fundamental form from which all his work germinated. His most important contributions to Russian literature are in themselves exemplary treatments of the essay genre. For example, in the domain of political thought, Gershenzon contributed a key essay to *Vekhi* (1909; *Landmarks*), that "scandalous," anti-revolutionary volume which transformed the Russian political landscape. As a literary scholar, he wrote the famous essay, "Mudrost' Pushkina" (1917; Pushkin's wisdom), which clearly stated the Modernist attitudes toward Russia's greatest poet. As a philosopher, Gershenzon published a group of philosophical essays in the 1920s in which he described his vision of a "natural" life that should replace the hateful, unfree "world of culture."

Gershenzon's most innovative use of the essay, however, belongs to his work as an historian. His major historical books and biographies – *Istoriia molodoi Rossii* (1908; The history of young Russia), *Istoricheskie zapiski* (1910; Historical sketches), and *Obrazy prosh logo* (1912; Images of the past) – are actually simply collections of essays which were first published in journals. With the essay form, he portrayed the Russian thinkers of the 19th century, whom he depicted as seekers of a better world. To make his inimitable portraits, he needed to develop an original view of history. Criticizing historians who saw the past as a debate over ideas, systems, and ideologies, Gershenzon held that living individuals are the

subject of history. The task of historical investigation, therefore, must be to understand people. Since the human psyche is composed of far more than ideas, he claimed, the historian must be concerned with the unconscious aspects of the individual: feeling, instinct, and the drive for spiritual perfection. Among all three, Gershenzon believed the last – the religious need of the individual for unity with all other things – was the most important. This view helped him conceive of an original model for the depiction of the individual in culture. Instead of lauding the external accomplishments of individuals, Gershenzon trumpeted "internal," spiritual achievements. By internal achievement, he meant the capacity of some individuals for joining personal will to the spiritual, "divine will" of the cosmos.

Concretely, Gershenzon transformed into heroes those individuals who lived life organically, without reflection. He selected those Russian thinkers who, he felt, embodied the desire to escape logical reason and wished to embrace a religious world view. In his biographical essay on the philosopher Petr Chaadaev, he shows the thinker eagerly imbibing the ecumenical ideal of Catholicism as an alternative to the sectarian division of the Christian churches. In his essays on the Stankevich Circle, Russian intellectuals of the 1830s, he concentrates on their expressed desire for spiritual unity through revealing the hidden beauty in the world of ideas. Similarly, he admires Russia's first revolutionaries, the Decembrists, since they lived an "organic" life based on European ideas of service, pride, friendship, and loyalty.

Gershenzon's use of the essay form came from his education as a student in the Department of History and Philology at Moscow University. Loaded down with classes covering enormous bodies of knowledge, the students were periodically required to produce essay-length papers on specialized themes. From these habitual assignments, the students developed an ability succinctly to organize, analyze, and relate voluminous amounts of material. Gershenzon's earliest published works in the 1890s, on ancient Greek history, were in fact term papers. His first articles on Russian literature and history closely resemble those university projects in form and style, and it would not be an exaggeration to say that the essay form he mastered at university was the same one he employed throughout his life.

He chose to continue using the essay form for several reasons. As a Jew, he was unable to get an academic appointment in tsarist Russia, and earned his livelihood from publications in the monthly "thick" journals, which contained several sections, including one for literary studies. The essay's size was perfect for such a venue. Additionally, the essay form was elastic, permitting him to employ a lively, conversational prose style with which he could portray heroes' psychological and emotional dimensions. He also included "novelistic" techniques, such as the drawing out of the plot to create suspense, transmission of fictionalized conversations, and the insertion of epilogues.

There were other reasons for his choice of genre as well. Gershenzon used the essay form because it offered narrative possibilities lacking in academic prose and objective biography. He exploited the essay's potential as a source for moral exhortation. Gershenzon often aimed to educate or edify the reader with a direct address. In *Istoriia molodoi Rossii*, for example, he writes, "And why are the advanced individuals of our time doomed to spiritual solitude and each one, while involved in the same activity, nevertheless stands alone?" The point of these asides, quite unusual in conventional historical writing, is to force readers to evaluate their own lives in comparison with the supposedly morally superior and heroic lives of the intellectuals of an earlier time.

Gershenzon's **historical essays** enjoyed great popularity in the first two decades of the 20th century. In recognition of his refined style he was lauded as a master of the historical portrait. For his approach to biography he was called the "Russian Carlyle." His books won him national awards and were best-sellers, appearing in second and even third editions. These portraits of national heroes depicted by an engaged and sympathetic author found favor among a readership which was gradually becoming more and more interested in the religious achievements of the Russian national tradition.

In his other activities as a literary scholar, journalist, and philosopher, Gershenzon also used the essay effectively. As the author of over a hundred book reviews, he played an important role in chronicling Russian literary life between 1900 and 1920. In his journalistic writing between 1910 and 1916, he employed a critical narrative in which he judged the cumulative effect on society of phenomena as diverse in content as literature, poetry, religious life, law, military affairs, foreign policy, and anti-Semitism. As a philosopher, Gershenzon especially employed the essay, since he was not interested in a systematic, logical analysis of his ideas, preferring instead to describe his idyllic vision of a future world in unconventional ways, through allegory, epigrams, and **dialogue**. Gershenzon was not, however, an innovator in these genres. He merely applied the narrative devices and ideological perspectives worked out in his far more original historical writings.

BRIAN HOROWITZ

Biography

Mikhail Osipovich Gershenzon. Born 13 July 1869 in Kishinev. Studied in Germany for two years; studied history, philosophy, and political science at Moscow University, 1889–94, graduated 1894. Scholar, author, and lecturer, Moscow, 1894–1925: unable to obtain an official academic position because he was Jewish. Literary reviewer, *Nauchnoe Slovoe* (Scientific word), 1903–05, and *Vestnik Evropy* (Herald of Europe), 1907–08; literary editor, *Kriticheskoe Obozrenie* (Critical review), 1907–09. Common-law relationship with Mariia Gol'denveizer, from 1904 (Jews and Orthodox Christians were unable to marry legally): one daughter and one son. During the Civil War worked in various sections of the People's Commissariat of Education. First chair, Moscow Writers' Union, 1918, and the All-Russian Writers' Union, 1920–21; head of the literary section, Moscow Academy of Artistic Sciences, 1922–25. Died (of heart failure) in Moscow, 19 February 1925.

Selected Writings

Essays and Related Prose
Istoriia molodoi Rossii, 1908
Istoricheskie zapiski, 1910
Obrazy prosh logo, 1912
Troistvennyi obraz sovershenstva (The triple image of perfection) (treatise), 1918

Mechta i mysl' I. S. Turgeneva (I. S. Turgenev's dream and idea), 1919
Videnie poeta (The poet's vision), 1920
Mudrost' Pushkina (The wisdom of Pushkin) (collection), 1921
Perepiska iz dvukh uglov, with **Viacheslav Ivanov**, 1921; as "Corner-to-Corner Correspondence," translated by Gertrude Vakar, in *Russian Intellectual History: An Anthology*, edited by Marc Raeff, 1966: 372–401; as *Correspondence Across a Room*, translated by Lisa Sergio 1984
Stat'i o Pushkine (Articles about Pushkin), 1926

Other writings: books on the 19th-century Moscow intelligentsia, philosophy, and religion, and correspondence. Also organized and edited *Vekhi* essay anthology (1909; *Landmarks*).

Bibliography
Berman, Iakov Z., *M. O. Gershenzon: Bibliografiia*, Odessa: Odespoligraf, 1928

Further Reading
Florovsky, George, "Michael Gerschensohn," *Slavonic Review* 14 (1926): 315–31
Grossman, Leonid, "Gershenzon-pisatel'," in *Stat'i o Pushkine* by Gershenzon, Chicago: Russian Language Specialties, 1968: iii–xiv (original edition, 1926)
Horowitz, Brian, "M. O. Gershenzon and the Perception of a Leader in Russia's Silver-Age Culture," *Wiener Slavistischer Almanach* 29 (1992): 45–73
Horowitz, Brian, "Ot Vekh' k russkoi revoliutsii: Dva filosofa N. A. Berdiaev i M. O. Gershenzon," *Vestnik Russkogo Studencheskogo Khristianskogo Dvizheniia* 166 (1992): 89–132
Horowitz, Brian, "A Jewish-Christian Rift in Twentieth-Century Russian Philosophy: N. A. Berdiaev and M. O. Gershenzon," *Russian Review* 53, no. 4 (October 1994): 497–514
Horowitz, Brian, "From the Annals of the Literary Life of Russia's Silver Age: The Tempestuous Relationship of S. A. Vengerov and M. O. Gershenzon," *Wiener Slavistischer Almanach* 35 (1995): 77–95
Horowitz, Brian, *The Myth of A. S. Pushkin in Russia's Silver Age: M. O. Gershenzon, Pushkinist*, Evanston, Illinois: Northwestern University Press, 1996
Kotrelev, N. V., and E. B. Rashkovskii, "M. O. Gershenzon," in *Russkie pisateli: Biobibliograficheskii slovar'*, vol. 1, edited by P. A. Nikolaeva, Moscow: Prosveshchenie, 1990: 555–57
Levin, Arthur, *The Life and Work of Mikhail Osipovich Gershenzon (1869–1925): A Study in the History of the Russian Silver Age* (dissertation), Berkeley: University of California, 1968
Levin, Arthur, "M. O. Gershenzon's 'Revolutionary' Poem," *Études Slaves et Est-Européenes* 15 (1970): 69–75
Levin, Arthur, "The Making of a Russian Scholar: The Apprenticeship of M. O. Gershenzon," *California Slavic Studies* 7 (1973): 99–120
Levin, Arthur, "Andrey Bely, M. O. Gershenzon, and Vekhi: A Rejoinder to N. Valentinov," in *Andrey Bely: A Critical Review*, edited by Gerald Janaček, Lexington: University Press of Kentucky, 1978: 169–80
Poggioli, Renato, "A Correspondence from Opposite Corners," in his *The Phoenix and the Spider: A Book of Essays About Some Russian Writers and Their View of the Self*, Cambridge, Massachusetts: Harvard University Press, 1957: 208–28
Praskurina, Vera, "M. O. Gershenzon – Istorik kul'tury," in *Griboedovskaia Moskva* by Gershenzon, Moscow: Moskovskii Rabochii, 1989: 3–26
Praskurina, Vera, "Viacheslav Ivanov i Mikhail Gershenzon: Na puti k *Perepiske iz dvukh uglov*," *Cahiers du Monde Russe* 35, nos. 1–2 (1994): 377–92
Shestov, Lev, "O vechnoi knige: Pamiati o Gershenzone," *Sovremennye Zapiski* 24 (1925): 237–45

Gide, André

French, 1869–1951

If we ignore the early satirical parables and symbolist fiction, the lyrical pieces, **pamphlet**s, travel diaries, political and social **tract**s, and the major works of fiction, we are left chiefly with the lengthy major insertions in the diaries as André Gide's personal contribution to the essay genre. The distinction between what can be accounted a true essay and what cannot is blurred, but it seems reasonable to regard *Voyage au Congo*, *Le Retour du Tchad*, and *Carnets de route* (1927–28; all translated in *Travels in the Congo*) as belonging to Gide's *Journal* proper, leaving *Si le grain ne meurt* (1920–21; *If It Die . . .*), *Souvenirs de la cour d'assises* (1914; *Recollections of the Assize Court*), *Feuillets d'automne* (1949; *Autumn Leaves*), *Et nunc manet in te* (1947; *The Secret Drama of My Life*), and *Ainsi soit-il; ou, Les Jeux sont faits* (1952; *So Be It; or, The Chips Are Down*), as extended personal reflections which belong to the essay genre rather than forming part of the diary itself. There are other less **personal essays**, like those devoted to individuals – **Wilde, Dostoevskii**, Conrad, **Montaigne**, Émile Verhaeren, Jacques Rivière, Henri Michaux, and **Paul Valéry** – and those contained in *Prétextes* (1903; *Pretexts*), *Nouveaux prétextes* (1911; *New pretexts*), *Incidences* (1924), *Préfaces* (1948), and *Rencontres* (1948; *Encounters*), but their literary interest, although great, does not consist chiefly in the contribution they make to Gide's development of the essay form. At times, they slide off into polished pieces of journalism.

Gide was an uneven writer, intensely self-conscious and obsessed by a need for self-analysis, but he never wrote without a cultivated sophistication drawing on an unusually wide culture and, at least after about 1900, a generally fastidious taste. He was not only well read, but might easily have become a professional musician. His high level of mental awareness made it difficult for him to resist the temptation to write multilayered prose with disparate but distinct levels of meaning, bristling with allusions to people and events not all of which any single reader was expected to understand, and exhibiting masterly control of innuendo. The *Journal* itself (kept between 1889 and 1949) contains exquisitely subtle insights, although the cleverness is sometimes too forced for the genre and the literary judgments are not always assured. The *Journal* may not as a whole be Gide's final masterpiece, a status sometimes claimed for it.

That accolade should probably be reserved for the fastidiously precise work of self-analysis, *If It Die . . .*, written as the result of a spiritual crisis. Gide had published his imaginative exploration of homosexual and hedonist values in *L'Immoraliste* (1902; *The Immoralist*) and of rigid spiritual asceticism in *La Porte étroite* (1909; *Strait Is the Gate*), implicitly rejecting both sets of values, and completing the triptych with the multiple-ironied and vastly amusing send-up of almost everything, but especially devout Catholicism and militant atheism, in *Les Caves du Vatican* (1914; *The Vatican Cellars*). When World War I broke out in 1914, Gide, already in his mid-forties, worked for the Red Cross, from which he retired in 1916 to garden at his small estate at Cuverville. It was there that he underwent his spiritual crisis, which he writes about specifically in *Numquid et tu . . .?* (1922), kept in diary form between 1916

and 1919. It is a reflective meditation born of remorse and despair, and contains a further rejection of the confident Catholicism to which Claudel had been trying to convert him for almost a score of years. It includes an interpretation of the Christian ideal subsuming Gide's individualism into an ethic of abnegation, itself seen as the supreme happiness.

The Cuverville crisis was partly caused by the discovery by Gide's wife of a letter to him from Henri Ghéon, recently converted to Catholicism, alluding to the interest in adolescent Arab males which Gide and Ghéon had once shared. It was at this time also that Gide began the spiritual autobiography, *If It Die . . .*, also partly the product of the serious attraction felt for him by Elisabeth Van Rysselberghe, who was to bear him a daughter in 1923. The essay is much longer than the earlier works of fiction, but its form is not immediately clear. Most of the details Gide gives about his early childhood, and the places and events it involved, must have been discoverable from family sources, but not the exact verbal exchanges that Gide records. The difficulty lies in assessing the degree of fictionalization in what appears to be, but cannot be, straightforward recall. Such recall must involve some re-creation of the past, with conscious or unconscious falsification. Gide himself writes at the beginning of the work, "I know the injustice I am doing myself in recounting this [early recollection] and what is going to follow, I foresee the use that will be made of it against me. But my account has no *raison d'être* other than truthfulness. Let us suppose that I am writing in penitence." The French admits of two renderings, depending on whether *raison d'être* is used as a single phrase. Gide might be saying that there is no reason to be other than truthful (which might not itself be the case), or, if *raison d'être* is taken as a phrase, that telling the truth was his whole motive. Again "let us suppose" is only an invitation to the reader to share an assumption, while "penitence" can be taken as indicating anything from a desire to make amends for a social impropriety to performing formally ecclesiastical penance for sin. Gide is extremely skillful at creating his ambiguities.

It is left to the reader to guess whether Gide has revealed, or even knows, his true motive in writing, and how far his account may have been colored by his motive. The hedonist principles adopted by Michel in *The Immoralist* are taken to the point at which they are clearly unacceptable, as is the self-deluding asceticism of Alissa in *Strait Is the Gate*. To what degree is *If It Die . . .*, which ends with the death of Gide's mother and his own engagement to his cousin Madeleine, affected by a desire to shock, or by exaggerated or even insincere depths of self-abasement? From time to time, to reinforce the impression that he is striving after absolute, and therefore impartial accuracy, Gide reminds the reader how his memory must have been playing tricks, for instance in a passage recounting a dance, marked off from the surrounding narrative by its sudden switch into the present tense, which cannot have taken place as he remembered it, when his grandmother was still alive, because he was not yet four when she died. Occasionally Gide breaks off to address the reader directly, or as if musing to himself. He learned his art from Flaubert, and was always the supreme stylist, in perfect control of every nuance of irony.

It is easy to become lost in admiration at Gide's sheer virtuosity, the subtlety and power of the self-analysis, and the meticulous selectivity exercised in the choice of telling detail. The narrative of *If It Die . . .* is held together principally by its meticulous and penetrating implied comment. Gide once turned down the earliest section of Proust's *À la recherche du temps perdu* (1913–27; *Remembrance of Things Past*) for the **Nouvelle Revue Française** (New French review); he seems here to be mimicking Proust's style.

The most important of the nonpersonal essays are probably those contained in *Pretexts* of 1903 and *Nouveaux Prétextes* of 1911, although both these works contain pieces that are primarily *conférences*, that is, delivered before an audience, often on a topic dictated by the occasion, and of interest as essays chiefly for the way Gide deals with the intractable problem of writing at the same time for oral delivery and for subsequent publication, a feat which, however continually attempted, is seldom successfully brought off. Gide simply published what was designed to be given as an address, with short sentences, pithy paragraphs, and no obvious logical connection between paragraphs, dealing wholesale with imaginary objections to his argument. There are strong indications that the published text served only as a written basis for the partly extemporized address based on it.

The literary form of the *conférences* is really the *causerie*, and in *Pretexts* they merge into the dozen *Lettres à Angèle* (Letters to Angela), written as letters in a conversational tone – short digressive pieces on books which Gide published in the symbolist *Revue Blanche* (White review) in 1901, not really formal enough to be called essays. *Pretexts* ends with three obituary pieces of personal reminiscence, full of anecdotes, snatches of conversation, and Gide's whole repertoire of semi-colons, dashes, question marks, exclamation points, and dots to indicate incomplete thoughts and conversational style. *Nouveaux Prétextes* contains further *conférences*, diary snatches, letters, book reviews, and reminiscences. These are essentially civilized conversation pieces, bedside books rather than formal essays.

It is perhaps again stretching the meaning of the term essay too far in a different direction to include as part of Gide's contribution to the form *Souvenirs de la cour d'assises* (1914; *Recollections of the Assize Court*), a powerful social comment in the form of an account of Gide's experience as a member of an assize jury, drawing on notes he took and rendering word for word snatches of exchange between the judge and the accused. "I believed," he writes, "that a simple account of the cases that we had been called on to judge would be more eloquent than any criticism." The real importance of this brief work lies in the deftness with which the social comment is made to emerge the more powerfully for being totally implicit in the narration of what happened and what was said.

ANTHONY LEVI

Biography

André Paul Guillaume Gide. Born 22 November 1869 in Paris. Studied at the École Alsacienne, 1887; École Henri IV, baccalauréat, 1889. Traveled at various times to North Africa, Italy, Germany, and Switzerland. Married his cousin Madeleine Rondeaux, 1895 (died, 1938). Mayor of La Roque-Baignard, Normandy, 1896–1900. Cofounder, *Nouvelle Revue Française*, 1908. Liaison with Marc Allégret, from 1916. Had one daughter with Elisabeth Van Rysselberghe, 1923. Traveled to Congo and Chad, 1925–26, and Egypt and Greece, 1939; lived in North Africa, 1942–45. Awards:

Nobel Prize for Literature, 1947; honorary degree from Oxford University. Honorary Member, American Academy, 1950. Died (of pulmonary congestion) in Paris, 19 February 1951.

Selected Writings

Essays and Related Prose
Prétextes, 1903; enlarged edition, 1913; selection in *Pretexts: Reflections on Literature and Morality*, edited by Justin O'Brien, translated by O'Brien, Angelo P. Berbocci, Jeffrey J. Carre, and Blanche A. Price, 1959
Nouveaux prétextes, 1911; selection in *Pretexts: Reflections on Literature and Morality*, edited by Justin O'Brien, translated by O'Brien, Angelo P. Berbocci, Jeffrey J. Carre, and Blanche A. Price, 1959
Souvenirs de la cour d'assises, 1914; as *Recollections of the Assize Court*, translated by Philip A. Wilkins, 1941
Si le grain ne meurt, 2 vols., 1920–21; as *If It Die . . .*, translated by Dorothy Bussy, 1935
Incidences, 1924; selection in *Pretexts: Reflections on Literature and Morality*, edited by Justin O'Brien, translated by O'Brien, Angelo P. Berbocci, Jeffrey J. Carre, and Blanche A. Price, 1959
Essai sur Montaigne, 1929; as *Montaigne: An Essay in Two Parts*, translated by Stephen H. Guest and Trevor E. Blewitt, 1929; translated by Dorothy Bussy, in *The Living Thoughts of Montaigne*, 1939
Et nunc manet in te, 1947; as *The Secret Drama of My Life*, translated by Keen Wallis, 1951; as *Madeleine*, translated by Justin O'Brien, 1952
Préfaces, 1948
Rencontres, 1948
Feuillets d'automne, 1949; as *Autumn Leaves*, translated by Elsie Pell, 1950
Ainsi soit-il; ou, Les Jeux sont faits, 1952; as *So Be It; or, The Chips Are Down*, translated by Justin O'Brien, 1960

Other writings: many novels (including *L'Immoraliste* [*The Immoralist*], 1902; *La Porte étroite* [*Strait Is the Gate*], 1909; *Les Caves du Vatican* [*The Vatican Cellars*], 1914; *La Symphonie pastorale* [*The Pastoral Symphony*], 1919; *Les Faux-Monnayeurs* [*The Counterfeiters*], 1926), several plays, autobiography, travel writing, journals, and many volumes of correspondence.

Collected works editions: *Œuvres complètes*, edited by Louis Martin-Chauffier, 15 vols., 1932–39; also separate Pléiade editions, 1951–58.

Bibliographies
Brosman, Catharine Savage, *An Annotated Bibliography of Criticism on André Gide 1973–1988*, New York: Garland, 1990
Martin, Claude, *Bibliographie chronologique des livres consacrés à André Gide (1918–1986)*, Lyon: Centre d'Études Gidiennes, 1987
Naville, Arnold, *Bibliographie des écrits de Gide*, Paris: Guy Le Prat, 1949; supplement, 1953

Further Reading
Brée, Germaine, *André Gide*, New Brunswick, New Jersey: Rutgers University Press, 1963
Martin, Claude, *Gide*, Paris: Seuil, 1995
Schnyder, Peter, *Pré-textes: André Gide et la tentation de la critique*, Paris: Intertextes, 1988

Giliarovskii, Vladimir

Russian, 1853–1935

Although Vladimir Giliarovskii wrote one of the most famous books in the Russian language, *Moskva i moskvichi* (1926;

Moscow and the Muscovites), he is conspicuous by his absence from most standard histories of Russian literature published in the West. This may well be because most of his prose work falls on the boundary between the short story and the journalistic sketch (*ocherk*), a genre much used in 19th-century Russia, notably by Giliarovskii's friend the populist writer Gleb Uspenskii. Giliarovskii himself made a clear distinction between the two: "Reporting trained me to give only the filtered truth, to discern the essence of the matter immediately and to write about it briefly. The pictorial and psychological material which remained within me I used for *belles-lettres* and poetry." However, the distinction is not so clearcut. Common to both his fiction and his sketches is a strong autobiographical element. As he says in his **preface** to *Liudi teatra* (1941; Theater people): "I simply take people, events, pictures, as I remember them, and serve them up in wholly inviolable form, without any sauces or garnishments." Whether he is describing a dramatic event – the fire at the Morozov factory in Orekhovo-Zuevo, the disastrous crush on Khodynka field during the coronation of Nicholas II in 1896, or a catastrophic train crash at Kukuevka – or whether he is describing a personality, famous or humble, it is always from direct personal experience. He was known as the "king of reporters" and went to extraordinary lengths to get his story firsthand.

The enduring popularity of *Moskva i moskvichi* can be ascribed at least partly to nostalgia. Though the book appeared in Soviet times, it recorded the Moscow of the turn of the century. When that Moscow began to disappear as Stalin ruthlessly reshaped the topography of the city, the popularity of both the aged Giliarovskii and his book increased. It is a book about places rather than people: 22 of the 31 sketches have topographical names, some specific ("Sukharevka," "Lubianka"), others more general, such as "Bani" (Bathhouses) or "Traktiry" (Taverns). The colorful characters who inhabit Giliarovskii's landscape, ranging from a man who gave his wife a crocodile as a wedding present to a man who sold pastries filled with cockroaches, are all viewed externally with no attempt at psychological investigation. The places described by Giliarovskii are those which the respectable middle-class readership of the journals for which he wrote would never have visited: low taverns, brothels, doss houses, disreputable markets, and thieves' dens. In one sketch, "Tainy Neglinki" (Secrets of the Neglinka) the author even explores the Neglinka River, which flows under the city and was its main sewer.

The sketches have something in common with **Maksim Gor'kii**'s stories *Po Rusi* (1928; *Through Russia*), but Giliarovskii's descriptions are never those of a dispassionate observer. Rather they are marked by a zest, a sense of involvement, a sense of compassion for the myriad of Muscovites who passed their lives in drudgery and humiliation, a sense of enjoyment, and above all, a fearless directness, stemming from his famously intrepid approach to life, which other writers do not match. His prose reads as if meant to be read out loud. Indeed in the preface to *Liudi teatra*, he refers to his readers as "listeners" with whom he conducts "intimate chats." This gives his work a theatrical quality, no doubt derived from Giliarovskii's own experiences as a provincial actor, his friendship with, among others, Anton Chekhov and the actress Maria Ermolova, and his lifelong fascination with the theater. His theatricality includes a strong whiff of the melodramatic, with sketches bearing such lurid titles as "Iama" (The pit), and references to places known as "Dom uzhasov" (The house of horrors) and "Ad" (Hell).

Giliarovskii is quite capable of what would now probably be described as "tabloid journalism." When, for example, in "Dva kruzhka" (Two clubs) he concentrates on the more picturesque aspects of Moscow club life, he admits that he did not "describe in detail their useful social and educational activity ... because our readers find more interesting that side of life which, even while the clubs existed, was shrouded in secrecy, which concealed the true source of the wealth on which the 'social activity' of these clubs was based." Yet, for all their lurid and sometimes barely credible detail – a centenarian actor who drank 20 glasses of vodka a day, a waiter whose ability to pocket tips destined for a common pool made his name a byword for the practice – Giliarovskii's eyewitness testimony establishes the veracity of these stories.

Giliarovskii repeated the formula so successful in *Moskva i moskvichi* in two of the three books he wrote during the last decade of his life (both of which were published posthumously), *Liudi teatra* and *Gazetnaia Moskva* (1960; Newspaper Moscow). In a preface to *Moskva i moskvichi*, written in 1956 and much reprinted, Konstantin Paustovskii, with great perception, discerns Giliarovskii's position on the boundary between journalism and the great Russian tradition of *belles-lettres*, describing "Uncle Giliai" as "one of those people without whom literature cannot exist." Unfortunately, while Russian literature has found a worldwide audience through translations, Giliarovskii has been wrongly considered so archetypally Russian that no English translation of his work has been attempted.

MICHAEL PURSGLOVE

Biography

Vladimir Alekseevich Giliarovskii. Born 8 December 1853 in Vologda province. Studied at Vologda gymnasium; Junkers' School, Moscow. Traveled around Russia, 1871–81, working variously in factories, as a firefighter, barge hauler, and actor: published occasional articles on his experiences, from 1873; volunteer in the Russo-Turkish War, 1877–78. Moved to Moscow, 1881; journalist, contributing to various newspapers and journals, including *Russkaia Gazeta* (Russian gazette), *Sovremennye Izvestiia* (Contemporary news), *Budil'nik* (Alarm clock), *Moskovskii Listok* (Moscow broadsheet), *Oskolki* (Splinters), *Russkie Vedomosti* (Russian news), and *Kur'er* (The courier). Married M. I. Murzina, 1884. Died in Moscow, 1 October 1935.

Selected Writings

Essays and Related Prose
Trushchobnye liudi (People of the slums), 1887 (censored); reprinted 1927
Moskva i moskvichi, 1926; edited by N. V. Giliarovskii, 1955; edition with introduction by Konstantin Paustovskii, 1968
Moi skitaniia (My wanderings), 1928
Zapiski moskvicha (Muscovite sketches), 1931
Druz'ia i vstrechi (Friends and encounters), 1934
Liudi teatra, 1941
Gazetnaia Moskva, 1960
Rasskazy i ocherki (Essays and sketches), 1988

Other writings: poetry and short stories.

Collected works editions: *Sochineniia*, 4 vols., 1967, and 2 vols., 1994.

Further Reading
Esin, B. I., *Reportazhi V. A. Giliarovskogo*, Moscow: Izd-vo Moskovskogo Universiteta, 1985

Ginzburg, Lidiia

Russian, 1902–1990

Though largely unknown in the West and for the time being somewhat neglected in her disordered homeland, Lidiia Ginzburg is regarded by those familiar with her many writings as a brilliant student of modern European literature and as one of its leading 20th-century Russian practitioners. Her efforts as a historian, critic, and theorist are a masterful investigation of the still vital energies of the past and a penetrating analysis of the nature of verbal art. In compelling and original ways they address such diverse yet connected topics as the evolution of poetic diction and the shaping of the lyric hero in Russian poetry of the early 19th and early 20th centuries (the so-called Golden and Silver Ages); the epochal redefinition of the self in Russian epistolary prose in the third and fourth decades of the 19th century; changing conceptions of individual personality and the rendering of literary character in the 18th- and 19th-century European memoir and autobiography; the larger theoretical issue of the reciprocal relation between literary images of identity and the dominant personality types of an age; and the complex assumptions, methods, and cognitive insights of the 19th-century psychological novel and its predecessors and heirs.

In this wide-ranging discussion and in her handling of a variety of related topics, Ginzburg gives always incisive and sometimes classic treatment to an impressive array of major Russian and European literary figures, including the memoirist Saint-Simon and the autobiographers **Jean-Jacques Rousseau** and **Aleksandr Herzen**, the critic, polemicist, and **letter** writer **Vissarion Belinskii**, the novelists Gustave Flaubert, **Lev Tolstoi**, and Marcel Proust, and the poets **Aleksandr Pushkin**, Mikhail Lermontov, Fedor Tiutchev, **Aleksandr Blok**, Innokentii Annenskii, and **Osip Mandel'shtam**, as well as to a host of lesser, but historically still significant memoirists, novelists, and poets of the 18th, 19th, and 20th centuries – an achievement of extraordinary learning and broad conceptual reach.

Comparable to Ginzburg's learned legacy in importance if not in scale, and originating from the same impulse to engage evolving historical reality within the structures of literary language and form, are her *zapisi* (notebooks), memoirs, and quasi-autobiographical narratives – what she called her "documentary" prose. This work is an aesthetic achievement of very high order and an indispensable contemplation of the changing moral and intellectual climate of virtually the entire Soviet period, inasmuch as Ginzburg came of age shortly after the 1917 Revolution and died roughly a year before the Soviet Union's ultimate collapse. The sheer longevity of her career, culminating in her ninth and arguably most productive decade, is itself notable: it means she was able to witness and then at some remove address the full span of Soviet life from its tumultuous beginnings through its years of repression, war, and fitful

relaxation to its oddly feeble end. Her experience of the Russian 20th century with its terrible suffering as well as its enormous courage is deeply representative. But her transformation of that experience in her scholarly and creative writing stands forth as an individual accomplishment of surpassing integrity, stamina, and will.

Of the documentary genres practiced by Ginzburg, perhaps the most arresting is the *esse*, a form somewhat belied in her case by the usual cognate translation of "essay," since the English term suggests something rather more discursive than is appropriate. As may be seen from her principal literary publication, the compendium *Chelovek za pis'mennym stolom* (1989; A person at the writing table), with its decade-by-decade arrangement of memoiristic, philosophical, and literary-critical material taken from the notebooks she began in 1925 while a student in Leningrad and kept on a regular basis till the very end of her life, her *esse* is closer to the **pensée** or **meditation** than it is to the more relaxed, digressive form that emerged with **Montaigne** and that typifies the essay not only in English-speaking countries but also in Russia – Herzen's *S togo berega* (1847–50; *From the Other Shore*), for example, or the literary-philosophical studies of **Konstantin Leont'ev** and **Vasilii Rozanov**. Ginzburg's *esse* is highly compact, even laconic, but like the more leisurely essays of her compatriots, it is often frankly theoretical in the kinds of themes it is willing to entertain. It also reveals, in its more personal moments, an interesting affinity to the biographical sketch, the sharp delineation of individual personality stemming from the French neoclassical *portrait* and *caractère*, genres that she had taken up in *O psikhologicheskoi proze* (1971, revised 1977; *On Psychological Prose*) and that had in their day influenced those of her Russian predecessors to whom she not coincidentally gave much of her scholarly attention – the poet Petr Viazemskii, an edition of whose *Staraia zapisnaia knizhka* (1813–78; Old notebook) she had published in 1929, and Herzen, on whose vast *Byloe i dumy* (1852–68; *My Past and Thoughts*) she had written a monograph in 1957. Thus, the Ginzburg *esse* is sometimes devoted to portraits of Russian literary luminaries, of such people as the Formalist critics Iurii Tynianov, Boris Eikhenbaum, and **Viktor Shklovskii** and the poets Anna Akhmatova and Vladimir Maiakovskii, to name but a few from the earlier period of Ginzburg's long life.

Ginzburg's style in her *esse* and in the longer pieces she wrote on social and political themes – in particular her influential examinations of the intelligentsia's ambiguous role in Russian revolutionary culture and of the all-pervading moral temper of Stalinism, "Eshche raz o starom i novom (Pokolenie na povorote)" (1986; Once more on the old and the new [a generation at the turning point]) and "'I zaodno s pravoporiadkom . . .'" (1988; At one with the prevailing order . . .) – as well as in her fictional and memoiristic writing, is pithy, even aphoristic, with a rich, sometimes scholarly lexicon deployed with great precision, and a powerful analytical bent tempered by a dry sense of humor happily disinclined to leave any shibboleth unturned.

JUDSON ROSENGRANT

Biography

Lidiia Iakovlevna Ginzburg. Born 5 March 1902 in Odessa. Studied at a secondary school in Odessa, graduated 1920; State Institute for the History of the Arts (GIII), Leningrad, studying under Iurii Tynianov, Boris Eikhenbaum, Viktor Zhirmunskii, Boris Tomashevskii, and Viktor Vinogradov, 1922–26; Leningrad State University, candidate degree, 1940; Institute of Russian Literature, doctoral degree, 1959. Taught history of Russian literature at GIII, 1926–30, and in the *rabfaky* (workers' faculties) at the Civil Aeronautics Academy and the Post-Secondary School of the Labor Movement, 1931–34; lectured on Russian literature for the Leningrad Municipal and Regional Public Lecture Service and the Section for Artistic Propaganda of the Leningrad branch of the Soviet Writers' Union, 1930–40; taught history of Russian literature and Russian aesthetic doctrine at the All-Russian Academy of Arts, Leningrad, 1944–46, and at the Karelo-Finnish University, Petrozavodsk, 1947–50; taught monograph courses as a part-time instructor at Leningrad State University, 1948–50. Editor in the literature and drama section of Leningrad Radio during World War II and the Leningrad blockade, receiving two awards for valor; freelance editor responsible for numerous scholarly and academic editions of Russian classical authors, 1929–90. Awards: State Prize for Literature, 1988. Died in Leningrad, 15 July 1990.

Selected Writings

Essays and Related Prose

O starom i novom: Stat'i i ocherki (On the old and the new: articles and essays), 1982

Literatura v poiskakh real'nosti: Stat'i, esse, zametki (Literature in search of reality: articles, essays, notes), 1987

Chelovek za pis'mennym stolom: Esse, iz vospominanii, chetyre povestvovaniia, 1989

Pretvorenie opyta (The transubstantiation of experience), edited by Nikolai Kononov, 1991

Other writings: *Tvorcheskii put' Lermontova* (Lermontov's creative path), 1940; *'Byloe i dumy' Gertsena* (Herzen's *My Past and Thoughts*), 1957; *O lirike* (On Lyric Poetry, edited and translated by Judson Rosengrant, forthcoming), 1964, revised 1974; *O psikhologicheskoi proze* (On Psychological Prose, edited and translated by Judson Rosengrant, 1991), 1971, revised 1977; *O literaturnom geroe* (On the literary hero), 1979; *Blockade Diary*, translated by Alan Myers, 1995.

Bibliography

Rosengrant, Judson, "L. Ia. Ginzburg: An International Chronological Bibliography of Primary and Secondary Works," *Russian Review* 54, no. 4 (October 1995): 587–600

Further Reading

Bibler, V. S., "Lidiia Iakovlevna Ginzburg i sud'by russkoi intelligentsii," *ARKhE: Kul'turo-Logicheskii Ezhegodnik* 1 (1993): 422–27

Bitov, Andrei, "Prorvat' krug," *Novyi Mir* 12 (December 1986): 245–51

Frank, Joseph, "Subversive Activities," *New York Review of Books*, 1 December 1994: 44–48

Grekova, I., "Proza uchenogo," *Oktiabr'* 2 (February 1985): 203–05

Grekova, I., "Samoosuzhdenie i samoopravdanie," *Oktiabr'* 4 (April 1989): 200–02

Harris, Jane Gary, editor, "Lidiia Iakovlevna Ginzburg: In Memoriam," *Canadian-American Slavic Studies* 28, nos. 2–3 (Summer–Fall 1994): 125–285

Mikhailov, E., editor, "Tsel'nost': O tvorchestve L. Ia. Ginzburg," *Literaturnoe Obozrenie* 10 (October 1989): 78–86

Pratt, Sarah, editor, "Lidiia Ginzburg's Contribution to Literary Criticism," *Canadian-American Slavic Studies* 19, no. 2 (Summer 1985): 119–99

Ginzburg, Natalia

Italian, 1916–1991

Natalia Ginzburg is known primarily as a novelist but was also a significant essayist, publishing three collections: *Le piccole virtù* (1962; *The Little Virtues*), *Mai devi domandarmi* (1970; *Never Must You Ask Me*), and *Vita immaginaria* (1974; Imaginary life). She was the fifth of five children of Giuseppe Levi, a Jewish professor of anatomy who was idiosyncratic and domineering at home, and Lidia Tanzi, a non-practicing Catholic and protective figure for Natalia well into maturity. In her autobiography, *Lessico famigliare* (1963; *Family Sayings*), Ginzburg writes of the early years of her family through the war, ending with the death of Cesar Pavese, a close friend of both Natalia and Leone Ginzburg, her first husband, an anti-fascist activist who himself was tortured and executed in 1944. The autobiography is strangely unemotional at times, focusing on portraits of friends and families, many of whom are quirky, distracted, literary, and politically committed.

In 1950 Natalia Ginzburg married Gabriele Baldini, a professor of English first at the University of Trieste, then the University of Rome. Ginzburg's relationship with Baldini is the subject of one of her most anthologized essays, "Lui e io" (1962; "He and I"), a deceptively complex treatment of two people who seem to have little in common. Ginzburg begins "He and I" with a statement of utter polarity: "He always feels hot, I always feel cold." Her self-imposed challenge is to move beyond simple opposition to a complex and textured relational polarity. The essay works through subtle shifts of tone and point of view, and through the invocation of both the generic, clear in the title, and the more personal details: "I know the price of that dinner service – it was £16, but he says £12. And it is the same with the picture of King Lear that is in our dining room, and which he also bought in the Portobello Road (and then cleaned with onions and potatoes); now he says he paid a certain sum for it, but I remember that it was much more than that." One feels, at times, that Baldini is a charming brute, narcissistic, and the writer is long-suffering. There is an unmistakable edge of bitterness at times, balanced by a self-knowledge that is far from self-flattering: "And so – more than ever – I feel I do everything inadequately or mistakenly. But if I once find out that he has made a mistake I tell him so over and over again until he is exasperated. I can be very annoying at times."

As with all of Ginzburg's essays, a kind of lyrical stoicism dominates – expressed both tonally and formally through flattened tone, repetition, and the use of theme and variation to taxonomic ends – and ends up emphasizing the effort of the writer to see the world clearly and to envision the past unsentimentally: "It is not given to us to choose whether we are happy or unhappy. But we *must* choose not to be *demonically* unhappy" ("Silenzio" [1951; "Silence"]), or: "There is no peace for the son of man. The foxes and the wolves have their holes, but the son of man hath not where to lay his head. Our generation is a generation of men. It is not a generation of foxes and wolves. Each of us would dearly like to rest his head somewhere, to have a little warm, dry nest. But there is no peace for the son of man" ("Il figlio dell'uomo" [1946; "The

Son of Man"]). An early essay, "Inverno in Abruzzo" (1944; "Winter in the Abruzzi"), clarifies the effect of the war, specifically the loss of Leone Ginzburg, on Natalia Ginzburg's essay voice: "Our dreams are never realized and as soon as we see them betrayed we realize that the intensest joys of our life have nothing to do with reality. No sooner do we see them betrayed than we are consumed with regret for the time when they glowed within us ... My husband died in Rome, in the prison of Regina Coeli, a few months after we left the Abruzzi."

Many of Ginzburg's essays are melancholic; there is a constant reiteration of diminished possibilities, and a profound, but frequently implicit, sense of loss. Her spare style, however, with its bursts of the lyrical or the cantankerous, still attempts to penetrate the mysteries of love, work, friendship, and place. Ginzburg's "Il mio mestiere" (1949; "My Vocation") is one of the most unsentimental and successful essays on the writing life written in the 20th century: "It is a vocation which also feeds on terrible things, it swallows the best and worst in our lives and our evil feelings flow in its blood just as much as our benevolent feelings. It feeds itself, and grows within us." This essay also contains Ginzburg's well-known self-estimation: "I prefer to think that no one has ever been like me, however small, however much a mosquito or a flea of a writer I might be."

Ginzburg's essay "I rapporti umani" (1953; "Human Relationships") is reminiscent of **Virginia Woolf** in its imaginative re-creation of the development of relational psychology from girlhood to maturity. It contains one of her most heartfelt pleas for compassionate intersubjectivity: "All our life we have only known how to be masters and servants: but in that secret moment of perfect equilibrium, we have realized that there is no real authority or servitude on the earth. And so it is that now as we turn to that secret moment we look at others to see whether they have lived through an identical moment ... It is the highest moment in the life of a human being, and it is necessary that we stand with others whose eyes are fixed on the highest moment of their destiny."

"Le piccole virtù" (1960; "The Little Virtues") is Ginzburg's best-known essay in English. It is similar to **Montaigne's** "De l'institution des enfants" (1580; "Of the Education of Children") both in subject and classical style (formal rhetoric, antitheses, parallel structures), as the opening sentence makes abundantly clear: "As far as the education of children is concerned I think they should be taught not the little virtues but the great ones. Not thrift but generosity and an indifference to money; not caution but courage and a contempt for danger ..." The possibility of instruction and harmony between parent and child is precarious, but also more authentically possible in the postwar generation: "And so we have no authority; we have no weapons. Authority in us would be a hypocrisy and a sham. We are too aware of our own weakness, too melancholy and insecure ..." There are important feminist implications in Ginzburg's passionate plea for the necessity of vocation for the whole person, and thus the whole parent. As sharply as in any of her works, Ginzburg shows in "The Little Virtues" both her formality and reserve and the quietly radical ability to challenge convention that places her squarely and importantly in the 20th-century essay tradition, drawing on the essay's old fathers and new mothers: "And what is a human being's vocation but the highest expression

of his love of life? And so we must wait, next to him, while his vocation awakens and takes shape. His behavior can be like that of a mole, or of a lizard that holds itself still and pretends to be dead but in reality it has detected the insect that is its prey and is watching its movements, and then suddenly springs forward."

DAVID LAZAR

Biography

Born Natalia Levi, 14 July 1916 in Palermo, Sicily. Family moved to Turin, 1919. Studied at the University of Turin, 1935. Married Leone Ginzburg, 1938 (killed by Nazis, 1944): three children. Exiled to Pizzoli, Abruzzo region, 1940–43, then returned to Rome after the fall of Mussolini, 1943; went into hiding in Rome and Florence, 1944, then returned to Rome after Allied Liberation. Worked for Einaudi publishers, Rome, 1944, and Turin, 1945–49. Married Gabriele Baldini, 1950 (died, 1969). Moved to Rome, 1952. Lived in London, 1959–61. Elected to parliament as independent left-wing deputy, 1983. Awards: Tempo Prize, 1947; Veillon Prize, 1952; Viareggio Prize, 1957; Chianciano Prize, 1961; Strega Prize, 1963; Marzotto Prize, for play, 1965; Bargutta Prize, 1983. Died (of cancer) in Rome, 8 October 1991.

Selected Writings

Essays and Related Prose

Le piccole virtù, 1962; as The Little Virtues, translated by Dick Davis, 1985
Mai devi domandarmi, 1970; as Never Must You Ask Me, translated by Isabel Quigly, 1973
Vita immaginaria, 1974

Other writings: many novels and novellas (including La strada che va in città [The Road to the City], 1942; È stato così [The Dry Heart], 1947; Tutti i nostri ieri [All Our Yesterdays], 1952; La madre [The Mother], 1957; Valentino, 1957; Le voci della sera [Voices in the Evening], 1961; Caro Michele [Dear Michael], 1973; Borghesia, 1977; Famiglia [Family], 1977; La famiglia Manzoni [The Manzoni Family], 1983; La città e la casa [The City and the House], 1984), several plays, and the autobiography Lessico famigliare (Family Sayings), 1963.

Collected works edition: Opere (Mondadori Edition), edited by Cesare Garboli, 2 vols., 1986–87.

Bibliography

Giffuni, Cathe, "A Bibliography of the Writings of Natalia Ginzburg," Bulletin of Bibliography 50, no. 2 (June 1993): 139–44

Further Reading

Bullock, Allan, Natalia Ginzburg: Human Relationships in a Changing World, New York and Oxford: Berg, 1991
Cappetti, Carla, "Natalia Ginzburg," in European Writers, New York: Scribner, 1991
Janmart, Anne, "Lettres féminines en Italie: Natalia Ginzburg," Revue Générale 8–9 (August–September 1982): 53–63

Godwin, William

British, 1756–1836

William Godwin's essays form a cohesive, if small, body of work. By his own admission, their author "scarcely in any instance contributed a page to any periodical miscellany"

(*Thoughts on Man*), most of the essays appearing in three separate volumes: *The Enquirer* (1797), *Thoughts on Man* (1831), and a posthumous, rather cranky collection of **religious essays** usually designated as *Essays* (1873). The rest serve as **prefaces** to the novels, the most notable being that to *Caleb Williams* (1794), in which the organic process of creation, as distinct from *a priori* rules of composition, is carefully traced by the novelist from a psychological perspective that anticipates the organicist critiques written by Romantic poets and essayists in the following decades. Even so, like so much else he wrote, Godwin's essays are largely footnotes – of amplification and qualification, and eventually of contradiction – to the work for which he was best known, the classic **tract** of philosophic anarchism, *An Enquiry Concerning Political Justice* (1793).

It is no coincidence that Godwin's first and most notable collection, *The Enquirer: Reflections on Education, Manners, and Literature*, should allude in its title to that earlier politico-philosophical tract. Each work treats human nature and the constitution of society – both as they are and as they might be. The difference is that the later enquiry foregrounds the enquirer – or at least holds out the promise of a more humane, personalized mode of enquiring. In his preface, Godwin pointedly distinguishes the method of *Political Justice*, which proceeds synthetically from fundamental principles, from *The Enquirer*'s method, which involves "an incessant recurrence to experiment and actual observation" – for "the intellectual eye of man, perhaps, is formed rather for the inspection of minute and near, than of immense and distant objects." In addition to an empirical bent, moreover, the essayist exhibits an immediacy of address arising from "a passion for colloquial discussion." Even the rational systematizer of *Political Justice* observes that "there is a vivacity, and, if he may be permitted to say it, a richness, in the hints struck out in conversation, that are with difficulty attained in any other method."

That said, the reader of *The Enquirer* must contend with an authorial diffidence that suggests that "colloquial discussion" did not come easily to Godwin. A glance at the table of contents reveals the topics named in the book's subtitle (*Education, Manners, and Literature*) arranged in a systematic schema not unlike that of a volume of moral philosophy. The form taken by most of the essays – "Of Choice in Reading," "Of Riches and Poverty" – suggests a Baconian provenance that the essays themselves have preserved virtually intact. Like **Francis Bacon**, Godwin treats conventional topics from the perspective of a rather neutral persona. Indeed, the Enquirer behind these essays, to the extent that he has any tangible presence, is a very generalized figure with none of the idiosyncrasies or genial egoism of a **Montaigne**. More often than not, Godwin favors the editorial "we" ("We are accustomed to suppose something mysterious and supernatural in the case of men of genius" ["Of the Sources of Genius"]) or the proverbial "he" ("He that has not been accustomed to refine upon words, and discriminate their shades of meaning, will think and reason after a very inaccurate and slovenly manner" ["Of the Study of the Classics"]). The "I" of these essays, where it appears, is the hypothetical "I" of philosophical demonstration ("Again; I desire to excite a given individual to the acquisition of knowledge. The only possible method in which I can excite a sensitive being to the performance of a voluntary

action, is by the exhibition of motive" ["Of the Communication of Knowledge"]). Like Bacon, too, Godwin favors an expository style that generally resolves itself aphoristically – "The true object of education, like that of every other moral process, is the generation of happiness" ("Of Awakening the Mind") – though it lacks Bacon's witty astringency.

Godwin treats his subjects in general terms, favoring the hypothetical example over the personal anecdote. When he considers the inevitable gains and losses attendant on aging in his *Enquirer* essay, "Of the Happiness of Youth," there is no hint of the elegiac regret we would expect from **Charles Lamb**'s Elia. On the other hand, Godwin's psychological nominalism, his preoccupation with the minute particulars of character, allows for idiosyncrasy and infirmity in the human constitution – finally exhibiting Elia's tolerance, if not his poignancy. In the same way, a pedestrian style does not imply pedestrian observations in essays like "Of Choice in Reading," which addresses simplistic moral attacks on literature. In this essay Godwin distinguishes between the "moral" of a work, which is explicitly formulated, and its actual "tendency," which is not. Moreover, "the selection of the one, and the character of the other, will in great degree depend upon the previous state of mind of the reader." His conclusion, that the influence of literature is a joint product of complexity in text and reader alike, indicates a critical sophistication lacking in his conventional observations on literature in the *Enquirer*'s final section.

Separated from *The Enquirer* by more than 30 years, *Thoughts on Man* registers, if only nominally, the Romantic transformation of the essay effected by writers like Charles Lamb, **William Hazlitt**, and **Thomas De Quincey**. While it would be absurd to speak of a confessional impulse anywhere in this volume, some of the essays do betray a tendency toward autobiography – the emergence of an authentic "I." Essays like "Of Youth and Age" are premised on the subjective grounds of knowledge: "The philosophy of the wisest man that ever existed, is mainly derived from the act of introspection. We look into our own bosoms, observe attentively every thing that passes there, anatomise our motives, trace step by step the operations of thought, and diligently remark the effects of external impulses upon our feelings and conduct" ("Of Youth and Age"). This is the route followed by Romantic introspectivists in the essays and poetry of earlier decades. If the author of *Political Justice* had proceeded from the assumption that humanity could change itself and society by a rational act of will, the sadder but wiser essayist in *Thoughts on Man* yields questions of intellectual doctrine to the vagaries of character and circumstance.

JAMES MULVIHILL

Biography

Born 3 March 1756 in Wisbech, Cambridgeshire. Studied at Robert Akers' school, Hindolveston, 1764–67, 1771–72; Rev. Samuel Newton's school, Norwich, 1767–71; Hoxton Academy, near London, 1773–78. Minister at Ware, Hertfordshire, Stowmarket, Suffolk, and Beaconsfield, Buckinghamshire, 1778–83. Moved to London, 1783. Contributor, *English Review*, from 1783, and *New Annual Register*, 1784–91. Married **Mary Wollstonecraft**, 1797 (died, 1797): one daughter (the writer Mary Shelley) and one stepdaughter. Married Mary Jane Clairmont, 1801: one son (died, 1832), one stepson, and one stepdaughter. Publisher and writer of the Juvenile Library, 1805–25, when it went bankrupt. Yeoman usher of the Exchequer, 1833–36. Died in London, 7 April 1836.

Selected Writings

Essays and Related Prose
Sketches of History in Six Sermons, 1784
The Enquirer: Reflections on Education, Manners, and Literature, 1797
Essay on Sepulchres, 1809
Thoughts on Man, His Nature, Productions, and Discoveries, 1831
Essays Never Before Published, edited by C. Kegan Paul, 1873
Uncollected Writings, 1785–1822, 1968
The Anarchist Writings, edited by Peter Marshall, 1986

Other writings: the philosophical study *An Enquiry Concerning Political Justice* (1793), nine novels (*Italian Letters*, 1783; *Imogen*, 1784; *Damon and Delia*, 1784; *Caleb Williams*, 1794; *St. Leon*, 1799; *Fleetwood*, 1805; *Mandeville*, 1817; *Cloudesley*, 1830; *Deloraine*, 1833), two plays, many books on history, and a biography of Chaucer.

Collected works edition: *Collected Novels and Memoirs*, 8 vols., 1992, and *Political and Philosophical Writings*, 7 vols., 1993, general editor Mark Philp.

Bibliography
Pollin, Burton R., *Godwin Criticism: A Synoptic Bibliography*, Toronto: University of Toronto Press, 1967

Further Reading
Locke, Don, *A Fantasy of Reason: The Life and Thought of William Godwin*, London: Routledge and Kegan Paul, 1980
Marshall, Peter H., *William Godwin*, New Haven, Connecticut and London: Yale University Press, 1984
Woodcock, George, *William Godwin: A Biographical Study*, Montreal: Black Rose, 1989

Goethe, Johann Wolfgang von

German, 1749–1832

Poet, playwright, novelist, aphorist, government official, and natural scientist: all apply to the polymath and essayist Johann Wolfgang von Goethe. Goethe's essayistic production spans his long and prolific life as a writer. A reflection of a multifaceted career, his essays display an astounding range, versatility, and interdisciplinarity. Like many of his other achievements, his work as essayist is preeminent, masterful, and exemplary. He was, moreover, a leading proponent of the form, albeit *avant la lettre*, as the German language and literature of the time did not yet have a single or specific label for the genre. Even so, his essays can be readily identified or classified as such according to subsequent definitions of the term.

While it is difficult to characterize something as protean and undefinable as the essay and equally difficult to distinguish among different types of essay, Goethe's might be said to fall loosely into biographical, historical, critical, personal, general expository, and scientific categories. The subjects of his essays vary immensely and mirror his wide-ranging talents and activities. He accordingly penned essays on such topics as architecture, sculpture, painting, literature, aesthetics, the scientific (or experimental) method, botany, osteology, geology, and morphology. Though some of his prose expositions on literary and aesthetic themes have received considerable scholarly attention, his **science essays** remain mostly unappreciated and unfamiliar to many readers.

Goethe's essays provide a showcase for his mastery of prose style. Many have long been prized as models of German prose writing, among them "Zum Shakespeares Tag" (1771; "For Shakespeare: A Tribute"), "Von deutscher Baukunst" (1772; "On German Architecture"), "Über den Granit" (1781, 1784; "On Granite"), and "Winckelmann" (1805), to name only a few. His essayistic writing flows with a seeming effortlessness, natural grace, and elegance. The metaphor **Friedrich Schlegel** chose to describe Goethe's *Wilhelm Meister* (1795–96) likewise typifies Goethe's essayistic prose; it is a metaphor Goethe himself borrowed from Solomon's Proverbs (25:11): "a word aptly spoken is like apples of gold in settings of silver." In other words, his essays reflect a concern for the well-wrought phrase, for excellence in manner of expression. Characterized by clarity and facility as well as economy, they exemplify a form of simple eloquence. Neither too casual nor too erudite, they typically occupy a space somewhere between the so-called formal and **familiar essays**. **Samuel Johnson**'s description of **Addison**'s essayistic style in *The Lives of the English Poets* (1781) – "familiar but not coarse, and elegant but not ostentatious" – could easily apply to Goethe's as well.

Goethe's essayistic writing is a rich, eclectic, and expert blend of styles, voices, modes, and forms. Mood and tone vary greatly depending on topic, authorial intent, even Goethe's stage of life, and so convey in one instance the exuberance of youth and in another the equanimity of greater maturity. "On German Architecture," for example, has a decidedly rhapsodic tenor, while "Myrons Kuh" (1818; "Myron's Cow") shows more detachment. Similarly, the contentious and polemical "Literarischer Sansculottismus" (1795; "Literary Sansculottism") differs markedly from the amiable and genial "Sankt-Rochus-Fest zu Bingen" (1814; "The St. Rochus Festival in Bingen"). In addition (and such variations notwithstanding), Goethe's essays characteristically manifest a didactic tendency which is defined by the complementary action of *prodesse et delectare*, by the reciprocation of instruction and entertainment, or as the 18th century would express it, of *nützen und ergötzen*.

Associative, combinative, and collective as well as asystematic, inexhaustive, and undogmatic, Goethe's essays display the same plasticity and state of flux he admired and described in his essayistic tribute to **Christoph Martin Wieland**, "Zu brüderlichem Andenken Wielands. 1813" ("In Brotherly Remembrance of Wieland, 1813"). As employed by Goethe, the essay investigates the relation of balance to imbalance, the interplay of similarity and dissimilarity, even the possibility of harmony in disharmony. Moreover, his essays embody the tension between the static and dynamic (*Dauer im Wechsel*) and between *levitas* and *gravitas* (*Scherz und Ernst*), those concepts so fundamental to Goethe's way of thinking and writing.

Goethe takes full advantage of the essayistic potential for metalinguistic collage. In his service, the essay fulfills its promise as a generic hybrid, as a genre of genres, as an amalgam of lyric, dramatic, epic, and whatever other kinds of writing one could imagine or care to include. If one word could describe Goethe's essayistic prose, it might well be experimental – and in every sense of the word. As their various structures and contours illustrate, Goethe's essays explore the vast possibilities of short expository prose. "Ruysdael als Dichter" (1816; "Ruysdael as Poet"), for example, has no internal division to speak of, while "Das römische Karneval" (1789; "The Roman Carnival") consists of numerous subsections, each with its own heading. By turns monologic and dialogic, assertive and tentative, analytic and synthetic, Goethe's essays represent a literary space where not only style and content, but also form and function converge.

Essayistic may well describe Goethe's prose writing in general. Indeed, an essayistic style informs much if not all of his literary production. Consider, for example, the essayistic properties of his epistolary novel *Die Leiden des jungen Werthers* (1774; *The Sufferings of Young Werther*), his autobiography *Dichtung und Wahrheit* (1811–13; Poetry and truth, translated as *Memoirs of Goethe*), his travel narrative *Italienische Reise* (wr. 1817; *Travels in Italy*), the stylistically complex and varied *Wilhelm Meisters Wanderjahre* (1821; *Wilhelm Meister's Travels*), or his study in optics *Zur Farbenlehre* (1810; *Theory of Colours*). The essay is in a sense epitomic of Goethe, as it embraces and displays his literary style, scientific method, and way of thinking all at once.

Although never explicitly formulated, Goethe's notion of the essay coincides with his concept of the scientific method, and both mirror his general way of thinking and working *per se*. This correspondence is most clearly expressed in his essay on the experiment (or assay) – "Der Versuch als Vermittler von Objekt und Subjekt" (1792; "The Experiment/Essay as Mediator Between Object and Subject"). There he gives an account of his scientific *modus operandi*, which implicitly and concurrently describes his essayistic *modus scribendi*. Like his concept of experimentation, Goethe's essayistic prose attempts to take into account the many and varied particularities of a given topic, issue, or phenomenon. In the essay, he collects several different perspectives and perceptions which when taken together offer a generalized impression of the subject under consideration. His essayistic compositions in effect extrapolate wholeness from particularity, completeness from fragmentariness, generality from speciality (and perhaps vice versa as well). At the same time, such extrapolation always remains a mere approximation, since the essay never fully comprehends every aspect of the topic in question.

As plied by Goethe, the essay encircles its subject by collecting a number of various impressions, perspectives, perceptions, experiences, and observations, for example in "Der Sammler und die Seinigen" (1799; "The Collector and His Circle"). In doing so, the essay constructs and yields a composite, approximating a unified whole or, to borrow a concept from **Max Weber**, an ideal type. Goethe's essays reflect the same fundamentally morphological, typological, or synthetic thinking as that which distinguishes his science. His essayistic writing illustrates an attempt to obtain a synthesis of multiple, isolated, and disconnected experiences. With the essay, Goethe generates a unified construct in approximation of an otherwise elusive and inaccessible whole. As such a construct, one which comprises a number of fragmentary and limited points of view, the essay in a sense performs the same

function as Goethe's concept of the *Urphänomen*, the proto- or pure phenomenon he posits, but which is actually nowhere present or attainable in empirical reality (e.g. "Erfahrung und Wissenschaft" [1798; "Experience and Science"]). While Goethe's essays admit to the fragmented and fragmentary nature of his knowledge and perceptions, they simultaneously attempt to overcome such limitations with what might be called a holistic response to the all but insurmountable discrepancies and often unrelated singularities of which our experience of reality consists. A comment in his autobiography *Dichtung und Wahrheit* illustrates the holistic propensity that also informs his essayism: "only humankind taken all together is the true human being." Like his science of morphology, Goethe's essayistic method of thinking and writing bridges the gaps between objective and subjective realities as well as between incomprehensible, inconceivable totalities and multiple, even irreconcilable particularities.

Along with **Montaigne**, whom he had read extensively, Goethe could also have declared "je suis moy-mesmes la matière de mon livre," for like the great French essayist, he too was himself the subject or substance of his essays. Goethe's famous reference in his autobiography to his literary creations as fragments of a great confession ("Bruchstücke einer grossen Konfession") bears witness as well to such an understanding of writing as self-study and self-disclosure, an activity to which the essay particularly lends itself.

Even though Goethe always wrote both about and for himself, he certainly had another audience in mind. The conversational and dialogic quality of his essays in effect implies and requires a reader. Goethe thus enlists and enables the active participation of his reader; he engages and includes the reader as interlocutor. His essays invite cooperation and the opportunity to share in his deliberations, to think along with him, to enter into the process of thought itself, and to be a partner in both reflection and invention. Goethe "the creative writer" desired and posited a "creative reader," one who as **Emerson** wrote "must be an inventor to read well" ("American Scholar," 1837). In this way, Goethe's reader becomes not only a re-but also a co-producer of the essayistic text.

Besides the implied individual reader, Goethe's essays assume and address the cosmopolitan, intellectual community at large. Whether about Laocoön or the intermaxillary bone, his essays are not written for a few scholarly specialists, but for any educated, informed, knowledgable reader, all peers in the republic of letters, citizens of literary society in general. As practiced by Goethe, the essay created and afforded a "virtual" literary salon, a communal space for a meeting of the minds. Goethe's essays represent a place where author and reader come together not only to explore the coincidence of art and science, but also to experience the intersection and interaction of thinking, reading, and writing.

JAMES M. VAN DER LAAN

Biography

Born 28 August 1749 in Frankfurt-on-Main. Studied law at the University of Leipzig, 1765–68, and drawing with Adam Öser; became ill, 1768, and convalesced in Frankfurt-on-Main; studied at the University of Strasbourg, 1770–71, law degree, 1771. Practiced law in Frankfurt-on-Main, 1771–72, and Wetzlar, 1772. Invited to court of Weimar by Duke Karl August of Saxony-Weimar, 1775:

entered civil service at ducal court, 1776, appointed Privy Counsel, 1779, and held various governmental posts and carried out diverse administrative duties, directing economic, political, social, and cultural affairs of state; ennobled, 1782. Visited Italy, 1786–88. Liaison with Christiane Vulpius, from 1788, marrying her, 1806 (died, 1816): one son. First met **Friedrich von Schiller**, 1788. Director of the court theaters, 1791–1817. Accompanied Duke Karl August on a military campaign in France, 1792. Editor of various yearbooks and magazines, including *Xenien* (with Schiller), 1796–97, *Die Propyläen* (with J. H. Meyer), 1798–1800, *Kunst und Altertum*, 1816–32, and *Zur Naturwissenschaft*, 1817–24. Chancellor of the University of Jena. Died in Weimar, 22 March 1832.

Selected Writings

Essays and Related Prose

Essays on Art, translated by Samuel Gray Ward, 1845
Briefe und Aufsätze von Goethe, aus den Jahren 1766 bis 1786, edited by A. Schöll, 1846
Italienische Reise, Aufsätze und Aussprüche über bildende Kunst, edited by C. Schuchardt, 2 vols., 1862–63
Aufsätze zur Kultur-, Theater- und Literatur-Geschichte: Maximen, Reflexionen, 2 vols., 1913–14
Literary Essays, edited by J. E. Spingarn, 1921
Botanical Writings, translated by Bertha Mueller, 1952
Schriften zur Literatur, 7 vols., 1970–82
Goethe on Art, edited and translated by John Gage, 1980
Essays on Art and Literature (vol. 3 of the Suhrkamp *Collected Works*), edited by John Gearey, translated by Ellen von Nardroff and Ernest H. von Nardroff, 1986
Maximen und Reflexionen (in English), edited and translated by R. H. Stephenson, 1986
Scientific Studies (vol. 12 of the Suhrkamp *Collected Works*), edited and translated by Douglas Miller, 1988

Other writings: four novels (*Die Leiden des jungen Werthers* [*The Sufferings of Young Werther*], 1774; *Wilhelm Meisters Lehrjahre* [*Wilhelm Meister's Apprenticeship*], 1795–96; *Die Wahlverwandtschaften* [*Elective Affinities*], 1809; *Wilhelm Meisters Wanderjahre* [*Wilhelm Meister's Travels*], 1821), many plays (including *Götz von Berlichingen mit der eisernen Hand* [*Goetz of Berlichingen with the Iron Hand*], 1773; *Faust I and II*, 1808, 1832), poetry, travel sketches, scientific works, and autobiographical accounts.

Collected works editions: *Werke* (Weimar Edition), 143 vols., 1887–1919; *Werke* (Hamburg Edition), edited by Erich Trunz and others, 14 vols., 1948–64; *Gedenkausgabe der Werke, Briefe und Gespräche*, edited by Ernst Beutler, 27 vols., 1948–71; *Collected Works* (Suhrkamp Edition), edited by Victor Lange and others, translated by Michael Hamburger and others, 12 vols., 1983–89; *Sämtliche Werke* (Munich Edition), edited by Karl Richter and others, 1986– (in progress).

Bibliographies
"Goethe-Bibliographie," *Goethe: Jahrbuch der Goethe Gesellschaft*, beginning with 14/15 (1952/53); as *Goethe-Jahrbuch*, since 1972
Hermann, Helmut G., *Goethe-Bibliographie*, Stuttgart: Reclam, 1991
Pyritz, Hans, *Goethe-Bibliographie*, Heidelberg: Winter, 2 vols., 1965

Further Reading
Bennett, Benjamin, "Werther and Montaigne," *Goethe Yearbook* 3 (1986): 1–20
Blackall, Eric A., *The Emergence of German as a Literary Language*, Ithaca, New York: Cornell University Press, 1978

Bouillier, Victor, "Montaigne et Goethe," *Revue de Littérature Comparée* 5 (1925): 572–93
Burgard, Peter J., "Adorno, Goethe, and the Politics of the Essay," *Deutsche Vierteljahrsschrift für Literaturwissenschaft und Geistesgeschichte* 66 (1992): 160–91
Burgard, Peter J., *Idioms of Uncertainty: Goethe and the Essay*, University Park: Pennsylvania State University Press, 1992
Damann, Günter, "Goethes 'Unterhaltungen deutscher Ausgewanderten' als Essay über die Gattung der Prosaerzählung im 18. Jahrhundert," in *Der deutsche Roman der Spätaufklärung: Fiktion und Wirklichkeit*, edited by Harro Zimmermann, Heidelberg: Winter, 1990: 1–24
Dell' Orto, Vincent, "Audience and the Tradition of the German Essay in the Eighteenth Century," *Germanic Review* 50 (1975): 111–25
Eibl, Karl, "'. . . mehr als Prometheus . . .': Anmerkung zu Goethes 'Baukunst'-Aufsatz," *Jahrbuch der Deutschen Schillergesellschaft* 25 (1981): 238–48
Fink, Karl J., and Max L. Baeumer, editors, *Goethe as a Critic of Literature*, Lanham, Maryland: University Press of America, 1984
Haenelt, Karin, *Studien zu Goethes literarischer Kritik: Ihre Voraussetzungen und Möglichkeiten*, Frankfurt-on-Main: Lang, 1985
Krebs, Franz Joseph, "Goethes Aufsatz 'Von deutscher Baukunst' und Valerys Leonardo-Essay: Zwei Begegnungen mit dem Genius," *Französisch-Heute* (September 1983): 151–61
Küntzel, Heinrich, *Essay und Aufklärung: Zum Ursprung einer originellen deutschen Prosa im 18. Jahrhundert*, Munich: Fink, 1969
McCarthy, John A., *Crossing Boundaries: A Theory and History of Essay Writing in German, 1680–1815*, Philadelphia: University of Pennsylvania Press, 1989
van der Laan, James M., "The German Essay of the Eighteenth Century: Mirror of Its Age," *Lessing Yearbook* 18 (1986): 179–96
van der Laan, James M., "Of Goethe, Essays, and Experiments," *Deutsche Vierteljahrsschrift für Literaturwissenschaft und Geistesgeschichte* 64 (1990): 45–53
Wohlleben, Joachim, *Goethe als Journalist und Essayist*, Frankfurt-on-Main and Berne: Lang, 1981

Goldsmith, Oliver

Irish, 1730–1774

Oliver Goldsmith is best known for his comedy *She Stoops to Conquer* (1773), which is still regularly staged, for the novel *The Vicar of Wakefield* (1766), and for his poem *The Deserted Village* (1770). However, for a period roughly coinciding with the Seven Years' War – Goldsmith began reviewing books in 1757 and largely withdrew from essay writing after 1763 – he distinguished himself as a Tory critic, a guardian of English paternal authority; as a social satirist, assuming an outsider's stance; and, for better or worse, as one of the most commented-upon figures in the Johnson circle.

Goldsmith's "apprenticeship" to **Samuel Johnson** began after "Doctor Minor" published two influential books of essays, *An Enquiry into the Present State of Polite Learning in Europe* (1759) and *The Citizen of the World* (1762). Goldsmith reviewed books for Ralph Griffiths' *Monthly Review* and for its rival the *Critical Review*, edited by Tobias Smollett. He published his own single-author periodical, the *Bee* (1759), and was among the most prolific "daily historians" for the newspapers and magazines of the High Georgian era.

Goldsmith entered the field of professional authorship as a sort of intern for Griffiths. In this capacity, he reviewed some of the principal publications of the late 1750s, including works by Smollett, **Edmund Burke**, **David Hume**, and Thomas Gray. The opportunity further afforded him the chance to develop several of the authorial personae that would serve him as an essayist in the years to come: the scourge of the romance writer, the British patriot, the English gentleman, the upholder of taste and morality. Decrying the exploding popular fascination with the novel, he followed the Tory line in declaring the genre morally bankrupt and aesthetically offensive. In 1759, jumping to the rival *Critical Review*, he continued his reviewing work while beginning a productive association with Smollett, with whom he also collaborated on the *British Magazine* a year later.

At a time when single-author **periodicals** were becoming outmoded, Goldsmith attempted the *Bee* (1759), which he saw as carrying on the tradition of **Addison** and Johnson. In one of its most celebrated essays, "A Resverie," more commonly called the "Fame Machine," the author imagines himself riding in a coach toward literary immortality. The procession he joins includes Addison, **Swift**, Pope, **Steele**, Congreve, and Colley Cibber. In the later edition of his essays that the author himself compiled, *Essays by Mr. Goldsmith* (1765, revised 1766), Goldsmith appears fairly convinced of his own eventual fame, though the anonymity of his early work makes identifying his entire canon nearly impossible. Although the *Bee* demonstrated his remarkable range and stylistic panache, it suffered a meager reception and quick demise.

In 1760 Goldsmith began another productive assocation: with the bookseller John Newbery who, with Smollett, founded the *British Magazine*. In addition to essays on manners and morals, Goldsmith used the magazine to experiment with short fiction, moral tales that anticipated in tone and theme his *Vicar of Wakefield*. But it was in another Newbery periodical, the *Public Ledger*, that Goldsmith would reach the pinnacle of his achievement as an essayist. His "Chinese Letters," published on average ten times per month, appeared first as lead columns in Newbery's newspaper, and later were collected as *The Citizen of the World*. His fictional persona Lien Chi Altangi comments on the vulgarity of the British press, the hypocrisy of English society, and the peculiarity of English fashion. The work gives form to the authorial voice for which he has become best known: the genial and wise humorist, aloof from the ubiquitous foibles of his era.

Hester Thrale-Piozzi and James Boswell depict Goldsmith as a social misfit, or as an errant pupil corrected by his master, Johnson. No doubt he suffered for his being Irish, and so a target for stereotypical characterization. His being an "outsider" in London may have also contributed to the failure of his medical practice and led him to construct the fictionalized "English gentleman" and "Chinese visitor," aghast at England's literary, social, and political customs.

Throughout his essays Goldsmith carefully crafts a reputation for being apolitical, above the partisan fray. Yet he provides important political commentary on the coronation of George III in his Chinese Letter of 5 November 1760 and offers support for the new king's political housecleaning. He frequently voiced his opposition to the Pitt ministry in its execution of the Seven Years' War, and he remained suspicious of the sort of "liberty" advanced by John Wilkes and his allies in the early 1760s. Goldsmith's importance as an advocate of political, religious, and social orthodoxy has long been underestimated.

For six years, Goldsmith was among the most prolific contributors to London's newspapers and magazines, appealing to a coffeehouse readership and engaging in what was arguably the most prominent form of public discourse of that period. His adaptability to his readership and to the changing modes of essay writing, as well as his remarkable stamina and productivity, assure his position as one of the most prominent essayists of the period.

RICHARD C. TAYLOR

Biography
Born 10 November 1730 (possibly 1728 or 1731) in Pallas, near Ballymahon, County Longford. Studied at schools in Athlone, 1739–41, and Edgeworthstown, Longford, 1741–44; Trinity College, Dublin, 1745–49, B.A., 1750; medicine at the University of Edinburgh, 1752–53, and University of Leiden, 1754; failed the examination at the College of Surgeons, 1758. Traveled on the continent, 1755–56. Moved to London; briefly a physician in Southwark; usher, Dr. Milner's classical academy, Peckham, 1756, 1758. Contributor to various journals, including the *Monthly Review*, *Critical Review*, and *British Magazine*, 1757–60; editor, the *Bee*, 1759, and the *Lady's Magazine*, 1761; contributor of the "Chinese Letters" to the *Public Ledger*, 1760–61; editor, *Compendium of Biography*, 7 vols., 1762; founder member of Samuel Johnson's literary Club, 1764. Died (possibly of a kidney infection) in London, 4 April 1774.

Selected Writings

Essays and Related Prose
An Enquiry into the Present State of Polite Learning in Europe, 1759
The Bee, nos. 1–8, 6 October–24 November 1759; in 1 vol., as *The Bee: Being Essays on the Most Interesting Subjects*, 1759
The Citizen of the World; or, Letters from a Chinese Philosopher Residing in London to His Friends in the East, 2 vols., 1762
Essays by Mr. Goldsmith, 1765; revised edition, 1766
Selected Writings, edited by John Lucas, 1988

Other writings: four plays (including *She Stoops to Conquer*, 1773), the novel *The Vicar of Wakefield* (1766), poetry, and books on history.

Collected works edition: *Collected Works* (Clarendon Edition), edited by Arthur Friedman, 5 vols., 1966.

Bibliographies
Scott, Temple, *Oliver Goldsmith Bibliographically and Biographically Considered*, New York: Bowling Green Press, 1928
Woods, Samuel H., *Oliver Goldsmith: A Reference Guide*, Boston: Hall, 1982

Further Reading
Hopkins, Robert H., *The True Genius of Oliver Goldsmith*, Baltimore: Johns Hopkins Press, 1969
Quintana, Ricardo, *Oliver Goldsmith: A Georgian Study*, New York: Macmillan, 1967; London: Weidenfeld and Nicolson, 1969
Spector, Robert D., *English Literary Periodicals and the Climate of Opinion During the Seven Years' War*, The Hague: Mouton, 1966

Taylor, Richard C., *Goldsmith as Journalist*, Rutherford, New Jersey: Fairleigh Dickinson University Press, 1993

Wardle, Ralph M., *Oliver Goldsmith*, Lawrence: University of Kansas Press, and London: Constable, 1957

Gombrowicz, Witold

Polish, 1904–1969

Witold Gombrowicz – a man of contradictions, a writer-provocateur, and an eccentric intellectual – was as idiosyncratic an essayist as he was a novelist and a playwright. His formally and stylistically diversified essays range from a mock interview ("Byłem pierwszym strukturalistà" [1967; I was the first structuralist]), through a series of autobiographical radio talks, initially prepared for Radio Free Europe and published posthumously in 1977 as *Wspomnienia polskie* (Memories of Poland) and *Wędrowki po Argentynie* (Wandering in Argentina), to a highly original "Przewodnik po filozofii w sześć godzin i kwadrans" (1971; Guide through philosophy in six hours and a quarter), a collection of thoughts on **Schopenhauer**, Hegel, Husserl, **Sartre**, Heidegger, and **Marx**. To fight sickness and boredom, the bedridden Gombrowicz delivered them as lectures to his wife and a friend.

A four-volume *Dziennik* (1957–69; *Diary*) is probably Gombrowicz's most important achievement. Carefully structured for publication in the Parisian monthly *Kultura*, and later polished for book form, the *Diary* is no less a work of fiction than Gombrowicz's novels. It combines autobiographical entries with pure fiction, essays ("Przeciwko poetom" ["Against Poets"] and "Sienkiewicz" crown its first volume) and essayistic fragments with commentaries on his own works, literary criticism with personal and intellectual polemics.

The *Diary* opens with symptomatic words: "Monday/Me. /Tuesday/Me. /Wednesday/Me. /Thursday/Me." This unmistakable provocation reveals the core of Gombrowicz's artistic and philosophical position. The writer scrutinizes himself as both a human being and an artist. Consequently, Gombrowicz's most original work concerns man and art. His interests are anthropocentric and existential; his focus is on an individual life – his own; his attitude is to transcend every position he takes; his purpose is to decipher the mechanisms governing one's relation to others (the main concern is authenticity), to reality and how we communicate with it.

The writer views man as both a producer and a product of form, which he defines as "all modes of our self-expression such as language, ideas, gestures, decisions, deeds . . ." Being born in human interaction, form makes every manifestation of individuality, including artistic expression of uniqueness, irreversibly artificial. Form also dominates human perception and understanding of reality, and creates important oppositions: between our sense of self and the roles we play, between our thinking and being, between our form and the form of others, and finally between our consciousness and the world. Gombrowicz believes that the essence of culture is a dialectical relationship between man and form; the purpose of artistic creation is to enter reality by penetrating and manipulating the realm of form.

Since art is a social phenomenon, its perception is governed by social rituals and conventions, and in the case of literature by the authority of critics. Therefore it is never authentic and rarely accurate. No one reads the works everyone claims to admire, Gombrowicz alleges in "Against Poets." Poets write for other poets, remain isolated in their hierarchical milieu, and are oblivious to the important tensions in the world. He disapproves of cultural institutions and claims that museums, literary conventions and awards, academic conferences, and the coteries of critics are deadly for art and boring for their participants. Institutionalized, ritualized, and abundant, with no clear criteria for the evaluation of its merits, art exists for its own sake and loses touch with reality. This is its gravest sin, Gombrowicz maintains, for whom writing was a form of living and the most important way of saying something meaningful about the reality in which he lived.

That is not to say that art should be subjected to ideological, intellectual, or literary tenets. Despite his respect for and partial affiliation with existentialism, Gombrowicz attacks writers who use literature to propagate the doctrine. His own polemic with existentialism (as well as with Marxism and Catholicism) is part of the most captivating fragments in his writings. Gombrowicz criticizes the *nouveau roman* and the apocalyptic cries of his contemporaries with equal intensity. As a Polish writer, he also recognizes the restrictions of the national mission of literature. In "Sienkiewicz" he reproaches Polish literature and culture for being invariably immersed in virtuous mythologies and naive self-adoration, for isolating itself and for ignoring the most important contemporary philosophical and aesthetic problems. On the other hand, Gombrowicz uses his stylized identity of "a simple country bumpkin, just a Pole," to confront the West and win his artistic sovereignty from and superiority over its manifested avant-garde sophistication. Gombrowicz does not spare Paris, this mecca of modern thought, literature, and philosophy, sneering at it as ruthlessly as he does at provincial Poland.

For a writer who declares himself to be "a form in motion," Gombrowicz's most important task is to execute a strategically designed attitude to himself and his readers. "Writing is nothing more than a battle that the artist wages with others for his own prominence," Gombrowicz declares in his *Diary*. Through laughter, jokes, and outright buffoonery, through parodies of genres and styles, and through serious intellectual contemplation, he creates a dynamic artistic personality for himself, a personality based on permanent ambivalence and transformation. If a struggle with form is the main theme of Gombrowicz's works, then the main strategy in this struggle, as Jerzy Jarzębski has superbly shown in his book, *Gra w Gombrowicza* (1982; Playing Gombrowicz), is the game – a well-planned series of maneuvers that enables the writer to find a necessary distance from form and to impose the desired image of himself on his readers.

Sometimes Gombrowicz is aggressive, often unfair and petty in his artistic and intellectual battles "for his own prominence," but so long as he manages to escape final classification, he is always ready to pay the highest price for his choices – the price of dismissal, ridicule, and hostility. His contradictions, oppositions, and paralogisms, his style of direct but rarely didactic persuasion, his provocations and maneuvers, his seriousness and unmatched understanding of pain make him one of the most original Polish writers and thinkers.

TAMARA TROJANOWSKA

Biography

Born 4 August 1904 in Maloszyce. Studied at Warsaw University, 1922–27, law degree, 1927; studied philosophy and economics at the Institut des Hautes Études Internationales, Paris, 1927. Law clerk briefly, Warsaw. Wrote for Warsaw newspapers, from 1933. Visited Argentina, 1939, and stayed there once war had broken out. Wrote for Buenos Aires newspapers, from 1940; secretary, Polish Bank, Buenos Aires, 1947–53. Left Argentina, 1963, living in Berlin, 1963–64, and Vence, France, 1964–69. Married Marie-Rita Labrosse, 1969. Awards: Kultura Prize, 1961; International Literary Prize, 1967. Died in Vence, 25 July 1969.

Selected Writings

Essays and Related Prose

Dziennik, 3 vols., 1957–66; vol. 4 of fragments, in *Dzieła*, 1969; as *Diary*, edited by Jan Kott, translated by Lillian Vallee, 3 vols., 1988–93
Przewodnik po filozofii w sześć godzin i kwadrans, 1971
Wspomnienia polskie; Wędrowki po Argentynie, 1977
Gombrowicz filozof, edited by Francesco M. Cataluccio and Jerzy Illg, 1991
Aforyzmy, refleksje, myśli i sentencje, edited by Joachim Glensk, 1994

Other writings: five novels (*Ferdydurke*, 1937; *Trans-Atlantyk*, 1953; *Pornografia*, 1960; *Kosmos*, 1965; *Opętani* [*Possessed*], 1973), short stories, and four plays (*Ślub* [*The Marriage*], 1953; *Iwona, księżniczka Burgunda* [*Princess Ivona*], 1957; *Operetka* [*Operetta*], 1966; *Historia* [unfinished], 1975).

Collected works editions: *Dzieła zebrane*, 11 vols., 1969–77; *Dzieła*, 15 vols., 1986– (in progress).

Further Reading

Barilli, R., "Sartre et Camus, juges dans le journal," in *Gombrowicz*, edited by Constantin Jeleński and Dominique de Roux, Paris: L'Herne, 1971
Błoński, Jan, *Forma, śmiech i rzeczy ostateczne*, Cracow: Znák, 1994: 141–79, 215–51, 259–77
Bujnowski, Józef, *Esej, szkic literacki i krytyka artystyczna w literaturze polskiej na obczyźnie 1940–1960*, London: Związek Pisarzy Polskich, 1964
Dedieu, Jean-Claude, *Witold Gombrowicz*, Paris: Marval, 1993
Jarzębski, Jerzy, *Gra w Gombrowicza*, Warsaw: Państwowy Instytut Wydawniczy, 1982: 59–139
Karpiński, Wojciech, "Gombrowiczowska przestrzeń," *Współczesność* 20 (1969)
Kott, Jan, Introduction to *Four Decades of Polish Essays*, edited by Kott, Evanston, Illinois: Northwestern University Press, 1990
Łapiński, Zdzisław, editor, *Gombrowicz i krytycy*, Cracow: Wydawnictwo Literackie, 1984
Łapiński, Zdzisław, *Ja Ferdydurke: Gombrowicza świat interakcji*, Lublin: Katolickiego Uniwersytetu Lubelskiego, 1985
Lęgierski, Michał, *Modernizm Witolda Gombrowicza: Wybrane zagadnienia*, Stockholm: Almqvist & Wiksell, 1996
Malic, Zdravko, "Felietony literackie Witolda Gombrowicza," *Pamiętnik Literacki* 4 (1973): 251–61
Proguidis, Lakis, *Un écrivain malgré la critique: Essai sur l'œuvre de Witold Gombrowicz*, Paris: Gallimard, 1989
Thompson, Ewa M., *Witold Gombrowicz*, Boston: Twayne, 1979
Volle, Jacques, *Gombrowicz, bourreau, martyr*, Paris: Bourgois, 1972

González, José Luis

Dominican/Mexican, 1926–

José Luis González's cultural, sociological, and **historical essays** of national interpretation are some of the most provocative and ambitious works written in and on a Latin American country. They can be understood only within the context of Puerto Rico's concerns about national identity, being an ELA (Spanish acronym for Free Associated State), with but not within the United States.

González's first essay, *Literatura y sociedad en Puerto Rico* (1976; Literature and society in Puerto Rico), set up, under the aegis of socioliterary methods and using Marxist thought, the history of Puerto Rican literature from the age of Spanish conquerors until the first decades of the 20th century. His *El país de cuatro pisos y otros ensayos* (1980; The Four-Storeyed Country and Other Essays) can be considered a continuation, in a broad sense, of *Literatura*. The book, and the well-known title essay in particular, is an outstanding attempt to interpret the reality of contemporary Puerto Rico. González suggests that the role of the Creole bourgeoisie, as reflected clearly in texts, was suddenly and hopelessly frustrated because of the American intervention in 1898, and therefore disabled as a driving force of national identity. The polemical condition of the essay, as assumed by the author, is centered in literary sociology and points to the colonial condition of the island, economically attached to the United States.

The fundamental role played by the exile is a key theme in González's essays. As he points out in "El escritor en el exilio" (The writer in exile), "in certain circumstances exile can prove a very effective form of service to one's country." That is, it seems, what he means to say in in "The Four-Storeyed Country," which answers, in a Socratic manner, the question of how Puerto Rican culture has been affected by American colonial presence. González looks for a response using Marxist theories on national identities, whose roots can be found in Engels' assertion that "nation is a cultural fact," or in Italian Marxist theorist **Antonio Gramsci**'s concept of "national popular culture," as well as in dialectic dialogues with former intellectuals and activists of the national conciousness such as **Eugenio María de Hostos** or Pedro Albizu Campos.

National consciousness, according to González, has never been possible because of the "four storeys" that make up the Puerto Rican national edifice: 1) native "taínos," African slaves and Spanish conquerors; 2) immigrants of the first decades of the 19th century (Spanish American political refugees, Corsicans, Majorcans, Catalonians, Irish, English, Dutch, and French); 3) the American intervention in 1898; and 4) late American capitalism and Puerto Rican populism of the 1940s. González concludes that, generally speaking, the impact of the American presence can only be negative for the ruling class, whereas for the remaining social classes it has implied modernization.

The criticism Gonzalez's theories have received is centered, mostly, on three points: 1) the treatment given to Pedro Albizu, a former Puerto Rican independence leader, as a simplistic personification of pro-Spanish conservatism; 2) the misuse of Marxist methodology, such as the use of culture in terms of social classes, making a distinction between "culture of the masses" and "culture of the elite"; and 3) the biased racial division of two Puerto Rican nations, in economic as well as cultural terms, influenced by the surrounding Latin American examples of two-nation theories, based on the gap between native population and white conquerors or immigrants.

Nueva visita al cuatro piso (1987; New visit to the fourth storey) is not only a kind of continuation of "The Four-Storeyed Country," but also an explanation of the lack of class consciousness of Puerto Rican proletarians.

CARLOS M. GUTIÉRREZ

Biography
Born 8 March 1926 in Santo Domingo, Dominican Republic. Raised and educated in Puerto Rico. Writer, from 1943. Exiled to Mexico, 1950s: became a Mexican citizen. Professor of literature, National Autonomous University of Mexico, Coyoacán, and University of Guanajuato. Cofounder, Puerto Rican Communist Party. Awards: Villaurrutia Prize, 1978.

Selected Writings

Essays and Related Prose
Literatura y sociedad en Puerto Rico, 1976
El país de cuatro pisos y otros ensayos, 1980; as *The Four-Storeyed Country and Other Essays*, translated by Gerald Guinness, 1990
Nueva visita al cuatro piso, 1987
Historia de vecinos y otras historias, 1993

Other writings: several collections of short stories, the novel *Balada de otro tiempo* (1978; *Ballad of Another Time*), and memoirs.

Bibliographies
Foster, David William, editor, *Puerto Rican Literature: A Bibliography of Secondary Sources*, Westport, Connecticut: Greenwood Press, 1982: 118–20
Ruscadella Bercedóniz, Isabel, "Bibliografía de José Luis González," *Texto Crítico* 12 (1979): 115–27

Further Reading
Díaz Quiñones, Arcadio, *Conversación con José Luis González*, Río Piedras: Huracán, 1976
Flores, Juan, "The Puerto Rico That José Luis González Built: Comments on Cultural History," *Latin American Perspectives* 3 (Summer 1984): 173–84
Flores-Caraballo, Eliut D., "Class-Bound Reductionism vs. the Multidetermination of National Cultures: An Essay on Puerto Rican National Consciousness," *Studies in Latin American Popular Culture* 10 (1991): 25–58
Méndez, José Luis, *Para una sociología de la literatura puertorriqueña*, Havana: Casa de las Américas, 1982
Rodríguez de Laguna, Asela, *Notes on Puerto Rican Literature: Images and Identities: An Introduction*, New Brunswick, New Jersey: Rutgers University Press, 1987
Rodríguez de Laguna, Asela, editor, *Images and Identities: The Puerto Rican in Two World Contexts*, New Brunswick, New Jersey: Transaction Books, 1987

Gordimer, Nadine
South African, 1923–

A native of South Africa, Nadine Gordimer began her writing career as the white Nationalist Party assumed power in Pretoria, and she has taken as her primary subject the personal lives of those who have lived under the weight or off the fat of racist politics. Each of Gordimer's 11 novels, several collections of short fiction, and four volumes of essays deals with relations between the races, but she did not begin writing in order to express her abhorrence of apartheid. In an early **autobiographical essay**, "A Bolter and the Invincible Summer" (1963), Gordimer remembers her simple delight at producing rhythm and rhyme for a patriotic school assignment. She began to publish in newspapers as an adolescent and, though young and essentially self-taught, found that writing required her to "chip" away at "ready-made concepts" and make her "own sense of the world." Consequently, as she explains, ". . . the 'problems' of my country did not set me writing; on the contrary, it was learning to write that sent me falling, falling through the surface of 'the South African way of life'."

The importance of Gordimer's essays lies not in innovations of form (as in her novels *The Conservationist*, 1974; *Burger's Daughter*, 1979; *July's People*, 1981), nor in prose so precise, details so telling that the narrative itself gives off a poetic intensity (as in her finest short fiction, particularly stories in *A Soldier's Embrace*, 1980), for Gordimer is not among the great essayists of her day. What commands our attention in her nonfiction is her continued effort to fulfill Chekhov's demand "to describe a situation so truthfully . . . that the reader can no longer evade it" ("The Essential Gesture," 1985). No reader of Gordimer's essays can avoid seeing what it has meant to this white, middle-class woman to go "home to quiet streets . . . and secure shelter" while in the black township just eight miles from her home "children no longer go to school, fathers and sons disappear into police vans or lie shot in the dark streets, social gatherings are around coffins and social intercourse is confined to mourning" ("Letter from Johannesburg, 1985").

A central subject of the essays is writing as the means of discovering and recovering what is concealed by political force and the unconscious extension of such force into everyday habit: "The expression in art of *what really exists* beneath the surface is part of the transformation of a society. What is written, painted, sung, cannot remain ignored" ("That Other World That Was the World," 1995). Grown more radical with age and increased exposure to lives crushed under and set against racist rule, Gordimer allies herself with writers who know, with Proust, that they must "not be afraid to go too far, for the truth lies beyond" (*Writing and Being*, 1995). Like Naguib Mahfouz, **Chinua Achebe**, and Amos Oz (to whom she devotes a trilogy of essays, originally delivered in 1994 as Harvard lectures), Gordimer goes too far: "Too far for the accepted norms of loyalty to the regimes, the societies, the mores, the politics of the countries whose earth, nevertheless, they feel between bare toes, flesh of the flesh" ("Zaabalawi: The Concealed Side," 1995).

From the start, Gordimer's audience has been largely overseas, in Britain and America; not only has her work been banned several times in her own country (at one point occasioning a book she wrote with others, *What Happened to Burger's Daughter; or, How South African Censorship Works*, 1980), but she writes as a "minority within a minority ... A white; a dissident white; a white writer," as she puts it in her most important essay, "Living in the Interregnum" (1983). To that audience, far from Africa, an audience mostly white with tastes toward "literature" rather than "popular fiction," she has seemed its best interpreter of the machinations of apartheid's white minority rule. Many of her essays were written expressly for overseas publications, and hers is the voice of the teacher explaining – with wonder as well as repugnance – events as they unfold in her homeland.

The publication of *The Black Interpreters: Notes on African Writing* (1973) allowed Gordimer to use her significant status as an interpreter of South African affairs to introduce her overseas audience to little-known works by black writers. She has continued to write about African authors, and though her criticism lacks the rare genius of her fiction, it creates a community-in-print of gifted writers buried beneath – or confined to the edges of – the canon.

The subtitle of Gordimer's 1988 essay collection, *The Essential Gesture*, summarizes her interests: "writing, politics, and places," foregrounding the work of putting words down, the effort of "getting it all straight" (as a character describes storytelling in *Jump and Other Stories*, 1991). Several essays analyze the "tension" that "makes a writer": the "tension between standing apart and being fully involved" ("Selecting My Stories," 1975), or, as it is framed in a later essay, the strain between commitment to one's art and responsibility to one's society ("The Essential Gesture").

For Gordimer, politics is never abstract theory, but always an account of the force of power in people's lives, including, in her essays, both profiles of the powerful (Albert Luthuli, Nelson Mandela, white communist Bram Fischer) and guarded glimpses into the writer's own well-protected privacy. In Gordimer's essays about places, she explores Africa itself, at times in prose as beautiful as any she has written. Seen through her eyes, Abidjan in the Ivory Coast "verges knee-deep in delicate lilies like just-struck match flames" ("Merci Dieu, It Changes," 1971); out of the night noise of the Congo's banks she hears the cry of the tree hyrax, "Greek and immortal in its desperate passion, gathering up echoes from all the private wailing walls of the human soul" ("The Congo River," 1961).

Introducing her 1975 *Selected Stories*, Gordimer argues "that in a certain sense a writer is 'selected' by his subject – his subject being *the consciousness* of his own era." Nadine Gordimer's essays stand alongside her novels and stories as keen, clear testimony to her willingness to bring "the writer's questioning concentration" (from "That Other World That Was the World") to bear on the passions and politics that have defined her time and place.

JILL PIGGOTT

Biography

Born in Springs, Transvaal, 20 November 1923. Educated at home between ages 11–16; studied at the University of the Witwatersrand, Johannesburg. Married G. Gavron, 1949; married Reinhold Cassirer, 1954: one son, one daughter, and one stepdaughter. Visiting lecturer at various American institutes and universities, 1961–71; presenter, *Frontiers* television series, 1990. Awards: many, including the James Tait Black Memorial Prize, 1972; Booker Prize, 1974; Grand Aigle d'Or Prize (France), 1975; Commonwealth Award, 1981; Malaparte Prize (Italy), 1985; Nelly Sachs Prize (Germany), 1985; Royal Society of Literature Benson Medal, 1990; Nobel Prize for Literature, 1991; honorary degrees from ten universities and institutes.

Selected Writings

Essays and Related Prose
African Literature (lectures), 1972
The Black Interpreters: Notes on African Writing, 1973
The Essential Gesture: Writing, Politics, and Places, edited by Stephen Clingman, 1988
Writing and Being (Charles Eliot Norton lectures), 1995

Other writings: 11 novels (*The Lying Days*, 1953; *A World of Strangers*, 1958; *Occasion for Loving*, 1963; *The Late Bourgeois World*, 1966; *A Guest of Honour*, 1970; *The Conservationist*, 1974; *Burger's Daughter*, 1979; *July's People*, 1981; *A Sport of Nature*, 1987; *My Son's Story*, 1990; *None to Accompany Me*, 1994) and eight collections of short stories.

Bibliography

Driver, Dorothy, and others, *Nadine Gordimer: A Bibliography of Primary and Secondary Sources*, Grahamstown, South Africa: National English Literary Museum, 1993; London: Zell, 1994

Further Reading

Berthoud, Jacques, "Writing Under Apartheid," *Current Writing: Text and Reception in South Africa* 1, no. 1 (October 1989): 77–87
Ettin, Andrew V., *Betrayals of the Body Politic: The Literary Commitments of Nadine Gordimer*, Charlottesville: University Press of Virginia, 1993
Head, Dominic, *Nadine Gordimer*, Cambridge and New York: Cambridge University Press, 1994
Smith, Rowland, editor, *Critical Essays on Nadine Gordimer*, Boston: Hall, 1990
Subbarao, C., "The Writer's Conscience: A Reading of Nadine Gordimer's *The Essential Gesture*," in *Indian Response to African Writing*, New Delhi: Prestige, 1993: 113–18
Wagner, Kathrin, *Rereading Nadine Gordimer*, Bloomington: Indiana University Press, 1994

Gor'kii, Maksim

Russian, 1868–1936

Maksim Gor'kii's essays reveal a range and variety at least as great as that of his fictional writing; indeed, at times it is not easy to keep the two apart. In a letter of 1930 he remarked that many of his own works combined the *ocherk* (sketch or essay) form with that of the story. Thus some of his most notable collections of the 1910s and early 1920s hover between the two genres: his *Russkie skazki* (1911–17; Russian tales) are satirical pieces on Russia's political and cultural life in the years following the uprisings of 1905; the quasi-fictional form often provides only the thinnest of disguises for the individuals and occurrences on which they are based. Similarly, his *Zametki iz dnevnika* (1924; *Fragments from My Diary*) deals with actual events and at least ostensibly with actual people, though some of the depictions are sufficiently bizarre that Gor'kii would seem to have invented certain details. These highly fragmentary pieces in turn are closely related to his autobiographical writings, most notably his famous trilogy: *Detstvo* (1913; *My Childhood*), *V liudiakh* (1914–16; *My Apprenticeship*), and *Moi universitety* (1923; *My Universities*). Here, too, while the writing seems increasingly factual as

Gor'kii moves from his childhood years into early adulthood, he appears to have included some fictional elements to enhance his narrative. As with *Fragments from My Diary*, it is Gor'kii's eye for the striking detail that makes particular scenes or individuals memorable; the trilogy, though, is also distinguished by his ability to take portions of his life's experiences and from them create a powerful effect by focusing on a handful of key themes.

Some of Gor'kii's outstanding memoirs, while clearly works of nonfiction, reveal a literary flair that has led critics to discuss them alongside his belletristic productions. Perhaps his greatest accomplishment in this mode is "Leo Tolstoi" (1919). Typically, the work is something of a miscellany, in this case combining a series of brief notes written nearly two decades earlier, when the two writers were both spending time in the Crimea due to ill health, and a long letter originally composed after **Tolstoi**'s death in 1910. The initial impression is that Gor'kii pulled together random jottings and then filled out his essay with an old letter; only upon a careful reading (or rereading) does it become clear that the choice and ordering of the often startling observations and quotations create one of the most revealing biographical sketches of Tolstoi ever written. Gor'kii occasionally wrote about political figures (most notably, Lenin) and various individuals from his past, but the most remarkable of his memoirs tend to be devoted to writers, such as "Leonid Andreev" (1919) and "Anton Chekhov" (1904, 1923). Typically, at least part of the essay is composed under the immediate influence of the subject's death, and rather than attempt a full biography, Gor'kii relies heavily on a series of anecdotes, many based on his own contacts with the individual, to provide illuminating insights that finally coalesce into a coherent and effective portrayal.

Thus the satirical writings, the autobiographical sketches, and the memoirs devoted to prominent individuals are all distinguished by a purposefully fragmentary method of writing that tends to highlight the individual description or anecdote, often to the detriment of conventional notions as to what would constitute a well-made work. The autobiographical trilogy and a few of the memoirs maintain at least a chronological coherence and a sense of structure; however, in, for instance, the Tolstoi memoir and especially *Fragments from My Diary* Gor'kii challenges the reader to create meaning from the natural disjointedness of real life.

Not all of Gor'kii's essays contain so strong a literary flair, not even those pieces devoted specifically to questions of writing. "Besedy o remesle" (1930–31; "Chats on Craftsmanship") uses autobiographical examples in a relatively straightforward manner to show other writers how actual experience can be translated into literature. A similar manner pervades his purely political writing. An example is his "Zametki o meshchanstve" (1905; "Notes on the Bourgeois Mentality"), one of his earliest major articles, where he accuses the bourgeoisie of, among many other things, a limited outlook, total self-absorption, a determination to maintain the status quo, and a concern only with its own comfort and well-being. He is if anything even harsher in his judgment of the peasant class; "O russkom krest'ianstve" (1922; "On the Russian Peasantry") expresses virulent dislike toward a class that he sees as resistant to the new revolutionary order. His strong political commitment to bolshevism appears as well in "Gorod Zheltogo

d'iavola" (1906; "City of the Yellow Devil"), written under the influence of his hostile reception in New York and containing a scathing denunciation of American capitalism (in a manner far more one-sided than the actual personal opinions he expressed in his correspondence at the time). After the revolution the capitalist world represents for him an amalgam of social ills and anti-Soviet hostility. For instance, in his "S kem vy, 'mastera kul'tury'" (1932; "Whose Side Are You On, 'Masters of Culture'"), Gor'kii remains opposed to capitalist bourgeois culture but has much nicer things to say about Russian peasants, or at least about those who have come to accept the Communist Party's edicts encouraging collectivization and outlawing private ownership of the land.

However, around the time of the revolution itself Gor'kii expressed many doubts about the direction it was taking. These were eloquently expressed in his columns appearing in the newspaper *Novaia Zhizn'* (New life) from Spring 1917 until Summer 1918 and subsequently published under the title of their rubric, *Nesvoevremennye mysli* (*Untimely Thoughts*). He mistrusts the Bolsheviks' desire (and rush) for power, their shrill propaganda, and most of all the violence they are committing in their efforts to consolidate their rule.

Underlying most of Gor'kii's essays is a strong humanistic thrust. He opposes those who, no matter how loyal they may be to an abstract ideal, are too harsh in their judgment of people. His disagreement with **Dostoevskii**'s attitude toward individuals led to the bitter attack in "O Karamazovshchine" (1913; "On Karamazovism"), on the staging of a play based on Dostoevskii's great novel. His early opposition to the Bolsheviks, like that to the bourgeoisie in general, is based on a sense that they commit too much violence against their fellow men and also that they are in some way inimical to culture, which Gor'kii sees as the main path by which humanity can progress. That Gor'kii himself, in other essays, ended up supporting those who committed the very sins he attacked elsewhere, remains one of the paradoxes, and tragedies, of his career.

BARRY P. SCHERR

Biography

Born Aleksei Maksimovich Peshkov, 28 March 1868 in Nizhnii Novgorod. Lost his parents early and worked in various odd jobs, from age 11; self-taught. Attempted suicide, 1887; wandered through southern Russia, 1888–89, 1891–92. Published his first story in *Kavkaz* newspaper, Tbilisi, 1892; wrote for various periodicals in the Volga region, from 1892. Married Ekaterina Pavlovna Volzhina, 1896 (later separated): one son and one daughter. Arrested and briefly imprisoned for revolutionary activities, 1898, 1901. Literary editor, *Zhizn'* (Life), from 1899; editor, Znanie publishing house, St. Petersburg, from 1900; became involved in a secret printing press, and temporarily exiled to Arzamas, central Russia, 1902. Elected to the Russian Academy, 1902, but election declared invalid by the government: several members of the Academy resigned in protest. Joined the Bolshevik Party, 1905, and supported the 1905 Revolution. Traveled to the United States, 1906; lived on the island of Capri, 1906–13, then returned to Russia. Founding editor, *Letopis'* (Chronicles), 1915–17, and *Novaia Zhizn'*, 1917–18; helped to launch a series of world classics by Vsemirnaia literatura (World literature) publishing house. Left Russia, 1921, and spent three years at various German and Czech spas; editor, *Dialogue*, Berlin, 1923–25, and in Sorrento, 1924–33. Visited Russia, from 1928, and settled there, 1933;

assumed various editorial posts in Russia, from 1930. Participated in the All-Union Congress of Soviet Writers, 1934. Awards: Order of Lenin, 1932. Died (in suspicious circumstances) near Moscow, 18 June 1936.

Selected Writings

Essays and Related Prose

Nesvoevremennye mysli, 1917–18; edited by Herman Ermolaev, 1971; as *Untimely Thoughts*, translated by Herman Ermolaev, 1968

Revoliutsiia i kultura (Revolution and culture), 1918

O russkom krest'ianstve, 1922; as *On the Russian Peasantry*, translated anonymously, 1976

Zametki iz dnevnika, 1924; as *Fragments from My Diary*, translated anonymously, 1924, and by Moura Budberg, 1972, revised edition, 1975

O literature, 1933; revised edition, 1935, 1955; as *On Literature: Selected Articles*, translated by Julius Katzer and Ivy Litvinova, 1960

Reminiscences of Tolstoy, Chekhov and Andreyev, translated by Katherine Mansfield, S. S. Kotelianski, Virginia Woolf, and Leonard Woolf, 1934

Articles and Pamphlets, 1951

The City of the Yellow Devil: Pamphlets, Articles and Letters About America, translated anonymously, 1972

Literary Portraits (vol. 9 of Collected Works), 1982

On Literature (vol. 10 of Collected Works), 1982

Other writings: many novels (including *Foma Gordeev*, 1899; *Mat'* [Mother], 1906; *Zhizn' Matveia Kozhemiakina* [The Life of Matvei Kozhemyakin], 1910–11; *Delo Artamonovykh* [The Artamonov Business], 1925; *Zhizn' Klima Samgina*, 1925–36), short stories (including *Russkie skazki*, 1911–17), plays, three volumes of autobiography (1913–23), and letters.

Collected works editions: *Sobranie sochinenii*, 25 vols., 2nd edition, 1933–34; *Sobranie sochinenii*, 30 vols., 1949–56; *Polnoe sobranie sochinenii* (includes *Khudozhestvennaia literatura*, 25 vols., 1968–76, and *Varianty k khudozhestvennym proizvedeniiam*, 10 vols., 1974–82), 1968– (in progress); *Collected Works*, 10 vols., 1978–82.

Bibliographies

Clowes, Edith, *Maxim Gorky: A Reference Guide*, Boston: Hall, 1987

Terry, Garth M., *Maxim Gorky in English: A Bibliography, 1868–1986*, Nottingham: Astra Press, 1986

Further Reading

Barratt, Andrew, "Maksim Gorky's Autobiographical Trilogy: The Lure of Myth and the Power of Fact," *AUMLA* 80 (November 1993): 57–79

Bialik, Boris, *Gor'kii – Literaturnyi kritik*, Moscow: GIKhL, 1960

Borras, F. M., *Maxim Gorky the Writer: An Interpretation*, Oxford: Clarendon Press, 1967

Clowes, Edith W., "Gorky, Nietzsche and God-Building," in *Fifty Years On: Gorky and His Time*, edited by Nicholas Luker, Nottingham: Astra Press, 1987

Hare, Richard, *Maxim Gorky: Romantic Realist and Conservative Revolutionary*, London: Oxford University Press, 1962

Jackson, Robert L., "Gor'kij's Polemic with Dostoevskij," *Russian Literature* 24 (1988): 503–16

Muchnic, Helen, "Gorky from Chaliapin to Lenin," in her *Russian Writers: Notes and Essays*, New York: Random House, 1971

Ovcharenko, A. I., *Publitsistika M. Gor'kogo*, Moscow: Sovetskii pisatel', 2nd edition, 1965

Pel't, Vladimir Danilovich, *M. Gor'kii – zhurnalist (1928–1936)*, Moscow: Moskovskii universitet, 1968

Pritchett, V. S., "The Young Gorky," in his *The Living Novel*, New York: Random House, revised edition, 1964 (original edition, 1946)

Rougle, Charles, *Three Russians Consider America: America in the Works of Maksim Gor'kij, Aleksandr Blok, and Vladimir Majakovskij*, Stockholm: Almqvist & Wiksell, 1976

Scherr, Barry P., *Maxim Gorky*, Boston: Twayne, 1988

Scherr, Barry P., "Gorky's Skazki: Structure and Genre," in *The Short Story in Russia, 1900–1917*, edited by Nicholas Luker, Nottingham: Astra Press, 1991

Spiridonova, L., *M. Gor'kii: Dialog s istoriei*, Moscow: Nasledie, 1994

Steinberg, Mark D., Introduction to *Untimely Thoughts* by Gor'kii, New Haven, Connecticut: Yale University Press, 1995

Todd, William Mills, III, "Gor'kij's Essay on the Peasantry: Framing the Mirror," *Russian Literature* 24 (1988): 555–68

Weil, Irwin, *Gorky: His Literary Development and Influence on Soviet Intellectual Life*, New York: Random House, 1966

Wolfe, Bertram D., *The Bridge and the Abyss: The Troubled Friendship of Maxim Gorky and V. I. Lenin*, New York: Praeger, and London: Pall Mall Press, 1967

Yedlin, Tova, "The Political Career of Maxim Gorky, 1884–1921," in *Russian and Eastern European History*, edited by R. C. Elwood, Berkeley, California: Berkeley Slavic Specialties, 1984

Zhak, L. P., *Ot zamysla k voploshcheniiu: V tvorcheskoi masterskoi M. Gor'kogo*, Moscow: Sovetskii Pisatel', 2nd edition, 1983

Gould, Stephen Jay

American, 1941–

One of the most significant contemporary **science essay**ists is Stephen Jay Gould, recognized for his mastery of prose and for the importance of his primary topic, evolutionary biology, in an era when it is under increasing attack from those outside the scientific community. Gould, a professor of zoology, geology, and the history of science at Harvard University, has won many awards for both his scientific and his writing accomplishments. His column, "This View of Life," which has appeared in *Natural History* since 1973, was honored by winning the National Magazine Award for essays and criticism in 1980. His books have also won the American Book Award for science, the National Book Award, and the National Book Critics Circle Award. His essays have been widely anthologized.

Gould is a prolific writer, appealing to a wide variety of audiences. In addition to professional scientists and people with an avowed interest in science, he has also regularly contributed essays to the *New York Review of Books*. In all of these venues, Gould attempts to explain and address the intellectual concerns of evolutionary biology. In an interview he asserts that "there is no reason to dilute the intellectual content at all" to accommodate his audience. His essays continue and expand the tradition of popular science exemplified by 19th-century scientists such as Asa Gray and T. H. Huxley. In fact, Gould has asserted that the tradition he is working in goes back to St. Francis of Assisi's works on animal and bird life. His essays make frequent use of literary allusions, quoting from such diverse sources as Dr. Seuss, the Bible, Gilbert and Sullivan, Shakespeare, and Alexander Pope. He frequently begins his essays with literary and cultural comparisons to draw the reader into the important scientific information he wants to impart. Some of his essays are distinctly personal, revealing the immediate circumstances of their development. Similar to **Montaigne**'s *Essais*, Gould's writings try out ideas and thoughts, revealing a human voice speaking of human concerns.

The overarching theme of all his writing is evolution. Many of his essays are explicitly persuasive in explaining and defending the theory of evolution as one founded on factual evidence of variation which "must be random, or at least not preferentially inclined toward adaptation" as he writes in the prologue to his first collection, *Ever Since Darwin* (1977). Gould's belief in, and his arguing for, this view of evolution influences other themes and rhetorical strategies in his essays. One of his principal themes, supporting his view of evolution, is his definition of science, which he sees as a part of human culture; according to Gould scientists are as influenced by their personalities, personal histories, and cultural biases as they are by the objective truth of the scientific method. As he wrote in *The Mismeasure of Man* (1981):

> Science, since people must do it, is a socially embedded activity. It progresses by hunch, vision, and intuition. Much of its change through time does not record a closer approach to absolute truth, but the alteration of cultural contexts that influence it so strongly. Facts are not pure and unsullied bits of information; culture also influences what we see and how we see it. Theories, moreover, are not inexorable inductions from facts. The most creative theories are often imaginative visions imposed upon facts; the source of imagination is also strongly cultural.

This definition of science summarizes the important characteristics of Gould's view of science, which is rooted both in the traditional scientific method with its idea of factual reality, testable hypotheses, and enduring truths, and in the evidence of historical and cultural influences on science as presented by historians and sociologists of science. Gould's definition of science structures the choice of topics of most of his essays.

Many of his essays focusing on individual scientists allow him to accentuate the human activity of science and its idiosyncratic nature. Essays on scientific figures – such as **Charles Darwin**, from "Darwin's Delay" (1973) to "Spin Doctoring Darwin" (1995); **Sigmund Freud**, "Freudian Slips" (1987); "The Passion of Antoine Lavoisier" (1989); and Pierre-Simon Laplace and Georges Buffon, "The Celestial Mechanic and the Earthly Naturalist" (1994) – show how scientists arrive at their conclusions and are influenced by the culture in which they live. He also introduces readers to obscure scientists, such as William Whiston, Isaac Newton's successor as Lucasian Professor of Mathematics at Cambridge, in "The Godfather of Disaster" (1987), or Emmanuel Mendes da Costa, "the only Jewish naturalist of note in eighteenth century Britain" in "The Anatomy Lesson" (1995). He also argues that theories which have been dismissed as unscientific were often based on the best science available at the time, as in "Crazy Old Randolph Kirkpatrick" (1979) or "Kropotkin Was No Crackpot" (1988).

By using these scientists to show that the development of science, often seen as linearly progressing toward perfection, is influenced by random events, dependent on historical development, Gould implicitly asserts the correctness of evolutionary theory. Science, as in life, is constrained by its history, tied to the general cultural progression, quirks of fate, individual peculiarities, and historical biases. Gould also reveals in his essays their own origins, thus linking his definition of science with his production of essays, both of which reveal the same traits of evolutionary and historical change.

Diane Dowdey

Biography

Born 10 September 1941 in New York City. Studied at Antioch College, Yellow Springs, Ohio, A.B. in geology, 1963; Columbia University, New York, Ph.D., 1967. Married Deborah Lee, 1965: two sons. Geology instructor, Antioch College, 1966; taught geology and zoology at Harvard University, Cambridge, Massachusetts, from 1967: currently Alexander Agassiz Professor of Zoology, from 1982; also assistant curator, 1967–71, associate curator, 1971–73, and curator of invertebrate paleontology, from 1973, Harvard Museum of Comparative Zoology. Lecturer at various universities and institutions around the world. Associate editor, *Evolution*, 1970–72; member of the editorial board, *Systematic Zoology*, 1970–72, *Paleobiology*, 1974–76, *American Naturalist*, 1977–80, and *Science*, from 1986; columnist of "This View of Life," *Natural History*, from 1973; contributor to many other journals. President, American Society of Naturalists, 1979–80, and the Paleontological Society, 1985–86; vice president, 1975, and president, 1990, Society for the Study of Evolution. Member of the advisory board, *Nova* television series, from 1980. Member, American Association for the Advancement of Science, and the American Academy of Arts and Sciences. Awards: many, including National Magazine Award, for essays, 1980; American Book award, for *The Panda's Thumb*, 1981; National Book Critics Circle Award, 1981, and American Book Award, 1982, both for *The Mismeasure of Man*; MacArthur Foundation Fellowship, 1981–86; Phi Beta Kappa Book Award, for *Hen's Teeth and Horse's Toes*, 1984, and for *Wonderful Life*, 1990; Sarah Josepha Hale Medal, 1986; Vursell Award, 1987; Rhône-Poulenc Prize, for *Wonderful Life*, 1991; honorary degrees from over 30 universities and colleges.

Selected Writings

Essays and Related Prose
Ever Since Darwin: Reflections in Natural History, 1977
The Panda's Thumb: More Reflections in Natural History, 1980
Hen's Teeth and Horse's Toes: Further Reflections in Natural History, 1983
The Flamingo's Smile: Reflections in Natural History, 1985
An Urchin in the Storm: Essays About Books and Ideas, 1987
Time's Arrow, Time's Cycle: Myth and Metaphor in the Discovery of Geological Time (lectures), 1987
Bully for Brontosaurus: Reflections in Natural History, 1991
Eight Little Piggies: Reflections in Natural History, 1993
Dinosaur in a Haystack: Reflections in Natural History, 1995

Other writings: *The Mismeasure of Man* (1981), concerning the development of IQ testing, and *Wonderful Life: The Burgess Shale and the Nature of History* (1989).

Further Reading

Asante, Molefi Kete, "Locating a Text: Implications of Afrocentric Theory," in *Language and Literature in the African American Imagination*, edited by Carol Aisha Blackshire-Belay, Westport, Connecticut: Greenwood Press, 1992
Becker, John E., "A Concealed Totality: Science and Poetry in the Essays of Stephen Jay Gould," *Soundings: An Interdisciplinary Journal* 74, nos. 3-4 (Fall–Winter 1991): 559-79

Kaufer, David S., and Cheryl Geisler, "A Scheme for Representing Written Argument," *Journal of Advanced Composition* 11, no. 1 (Winter 1991): 107–22

McRae, Murdo William, "Stephen Jay Gould and the Contingent Nature of History," *CLIO: A Journal of Literature, History, and the Philosophy of History* 22, no. 3 (Spring 1993): 239–50

Masur, Louis P., "Stephen Jay Gould's Vision of History," in *The Literature of Science: Perspectives on Popular Scientific Writings*, edited by Murdo William McCrae, Athens: University of Georgia Press, 1993

Morrell, Roy, "What Happened to the Dinosaurs?," *Thomas Hardy Journal* 8, no. 1 (February 1992): 37–40

Selzer, Jack, editor, *Understanding Scientific Prose*, Madison: University of Wisconsin Press, 1993

Winterowd, W. Ross, "Rediscovering the Essay," *Journal of Advanced Composition* 8, nos. 1–2 (1988): 146–57

Gourmont, Remy de

French, 1858–1915

Aptly described by Richard Aldington as "one of France's most able and industrious journeymen of letters," Remy de Gourmont enjoyed considerable popularity and esteem both in France and in English-speaking countries during his lifetime. Today he is no doubt best remembered for his crucial role in founding the highly influential *Mercure de France* in January 1890, and for his influence on such writers as **T. S. Eliot, Ezra Pound**, and John Middleton Murry. A prolific writer who worked in many genres, he made his greatest contribution in the area of the essay, writing on a broad range of topics, from literature and art to science and philosophy.

For Gourmont, the subject matter was far from being the most important aspect either of creative or of critical writing: like **Charles Baudelaire** before him, he believed that criticism should be impassioned and personal, and unlike such contemporaries as **Hippolyte Taine**, he was convinced that critical writing was valuable for itself, as a means of expression comparable to more traditional vehicles. As he remarks in *La Culture des idées* (1900; "The Culture of Ideas"), "the craft of writing is a craft, but style is not a science." All human expression, for him, from literature and art to philosophy and science, depends, like intelligence itself, on the senses. A man for whom the external world clearly existed and whose physical drives were all the stronger for being frequently suppressed, Gourmont used his wide-ranging interests and his polymath curiosity and knowledge to create a vision of culture where the high value placed on the aesthetic, far from being effete, is always at least on the verge of being erotic. As a literary critic he was eager not to offer judgments, but rather to note his impressions as he read. Above all he focused on style, convinced, as he maintains in the fifth series of *Promenades littéraires* (1913; Literary promenades), that "the criticism of style would suffice as literary criticism; it contains all the others."

His *Le Livre des masques* (1896–98; *The Book of Masks*), which is one of the first studies to define and delimit symbolism as a school, enters into the imagination of the writers he discusses, reveals the physical and intellectual pleasures of reading and writing, and encapsulates them in heightened visual images. The Belgian poet Émile Verhaeren, for instance, is presented in the following, highly characteristic, terms: "This poet lives in an old Italian palace, on whose walls emblems and words are inscribed. He dreams, passing from room to room, and toward evening he goes down the marble staircase and wanders into the gardens, which are paved like courtyards, and there he dreams his life amidst the pools and fountains, while black swans nervously protect their nests and a peacock, as solitary as a king, seems beautifully to imbibe the dying pride of a golden dusk."

If Gourmont possessed the art of the complex and appropriate image, he also knew how to turn a pungent **aphorism**: "You have to kill many loves to arrive at love," "Hope is a great hindrance," "One never goes to bed with anyone but oneself," "University degrees were invented in order to people France with persons looking as if they had studied." Such aphorisms are frequently imbued with skepticism, especially in his *Physique de l'amour* (1903; *The Natural Philosophy of Love*), which presents a purely materialistic and Darwinian view of existence, but he also reveals a healthy refusal to take himself (or anyone else) too seriously. Thus, in *Promenades littéraires* he asserts: "Genius is almost always accompanied by a strong propensity to play."

Among his finest essays are those included in the *Lettres à l'Amazone* (1914; *Letters to the Amazon*), written for Natalie Clifford Barney. The easy intimacy between writer and reader, the polished but informal style, and the culturally sophisticated frame of reference suggest the extent to which **Montaigne** has inspired Gourmont's concept of the essay, and evoke the image of a somewhat avuncular conversationalist taking delight in forging a smoothly articulate response to whatever topic his listener suggests to him. It is this openness to the best in human thought and creation, this conviction that "the intellectual domain is a limitless landscape and not a series of little gardens enclosed in walls of suspicion and disdain" (*Esthétique de la langue française* [1899; The aesthetics of the French language]) that is most appealing in Gourmont's writing, but it is also fraught with a certain danger, the temptation of multiple possibilities rather than the determination to focus on and deepen specific areas. Crippled, like many of his time, by the prevalent misogyny, Gourmont's writing has aged most in the area of human relationships. On literature, style, and culture he is better for the broad view than the particular.

One last aphorism can serve both to sum up Gourmont's gifts and to account for his fall from favor: "Posterity is like a schoolchild condemned to learn by heart a hundred lines of verse. He remembers ten, and stammers a few syllables of the rest. The ten lines are fame; the rest is literary history."

ROSEMARY LLOYD

Biography

Remy Marie Charles de Gourmont. Born 4 April 1858 in Bazoches-au-Houlme. Studied at a lycée in Coutances, 1868–76; law at the University of Caen, 1876–79. Assistant librarian, Bibliothèque Nationale, Paris, 1881–91: dismissed for article critical of government policy toward Germany. Contributor to many periodicals, from early 1880s. Liaison with Berthe de Courrière, 1887–90. Cofounder, coeditor, and major contributor, *Mercure de France* (Mercury of France), from 1890. Facially disfigured by skin disease, 1891, resulting in seclusion and an identity crisis. Cofounder, *L'Ymagier*, 1894–96, and *La Revue des Idées* (The review of ideas), 1904. Died (of a stroke) in Paris, 27 September 1915.

Selected Writings

Essays and Related Prose

Le Latin mystique, 1892; reprinted 1981
L'Idéalisme, 1893
La Poésie populaire, 1896
Le Livre des masques: Portraits symbolistes, 2 vols., 1896–98; as
    The Book of Masks, translated by Jack Lewis, 1921
Esthétique de la langue française, 1899
La Culture des idées, 1900; as "The Culture of Ideas," translated
    by William A. Bradley, in *Decadence, and Other Essays on the
    Culture of Ideas*, 1921
Le Problème du style, 1902
Le Chemin de velours, 1902
Physique de l'amour: Essai sur l'instinct sexuel, 1903; as *The
    Natural Philosophy of Love*, translated by Ezra Pound, 1922
Épilogues: Réflexions sur la vie, 6 vols., 1903–13
Promenades littéraires, 7 vols., 1904–27
Promenades philosophiques, 3 vols., 1905–09; selection as
    Philosophic Nights in Paris, translated by Isaac Goldberg,
    1920
Dante, Béatrice, et la poésie amoureuse, 1908
Le Chat de misère: Idées et images, 1912
Lettres d'un satyre, 1913
Lettres à l'Amazone, 1914; as *Letters to the Amazon*, translated
    by Richard Aldington, 1931
La Belgique littéraire, 1915
Pendant l'orage, 1915
La Petite Ville; Paysages, 1916
Dans la tourmente, 1916
Pendant la guerre: Lettres pour l'Argentine, 1917
Les Idées du jour, 2 vols., 1917–18
Monsieur Croquant, 1918
Trois Légendes du Moyen Âge, 1919
Les Pas sur le sable, 1919
Huit aphorismes, 1920
Le Livret de l'imagier, 1920
Pensées inédites, 1920
La Patience de Griseledis, 1920
Petits crayons, 1921
Decadence, and Other Essays on the Culture of Ideas, translated
    by William A. Bradley, 1921
Le Puits de la vérité, 1922
Le Vase magique, 1923
Dernières pensées inédites, 1924
Dissociations, 1925
Nouvelles dissociations, 1925
Les Femmes et le langage, 1925
La Fin de l'art, 1925
Deux poètes de la nature: Bryant et Emerson, 1925
Le Joujou, et trois autres essais, 1926
Lettres intimes à l'Amazone, 1927
Selections, edited and translated by Richard Aldington, 2 vols.,
    1928
Selected Writings, edited and translated by Glenn S. Burne,
    1966
Le Joujou patriotisme; La Fête nationale, edited by Jean-Pierre
    Rioux, 1967

Other writings: six novels (including *Sixtine* [*Very Woman*], 1890;
Un cœur virginal [*A Virgin Heart*], 1907), tales, poetry, five plays,
and correspondence.

Collected works edition: *Œuvres*, 6 vols., 1925–32.

Bibliography

Gourmont, Jean de, and Robert D. Donne, *Bibliographie des œuvres
    de Remy de Gourmont*, Paris: Leclerc, 1922

Further Reading

Aldington, Richard, *Remy de Gourmont: A Modern Man of Letters*,
    Seattle: University of Washington Chapbook, 1928
Burne, Glenn S., *Remy de Gourmont, Literary Critic* (dissertation),
    Seattle: University of Washington, 1956
Burne, Glenn S., *Remy de Gourmont: His Ideas and Influence in
    England and America*, Carbondale: Southern Illinois University
    Press, 1963
Gosse, Edmund, *Aspects and Impressions*, London and New York:
    Cassell, 1922: 203–23
Powys, John Cowper, *Essays on De Gourmont and Byron*, Girard,
    Kansas: Haldeman-Julius, 1923; reprinted in *Suspended
    Judgments: Essays on Books and Sensations*, Norwood,
    Pennsylvania: Norwood, 1977
Sieburth, Richard, *Instigations: Ezra Pound and Remy de
    Gourmont*, Cambridge, Massachusetts: Harvard University Press,
    1978

Gracián, Baltasar

Spanish, 1601–1658

The work of this Spanish baroque moralist exemplifies the unresolvable tension between Christian values, on the one hand, and the practical philosophy geared at earthly success, on the other. A Jesuit theologian, Baltasar Gracián's unquestioned Catholicism contrasts with his elitist attitude of one who professes that most human beings are condemned to stupidity and intellectual mediocrity. The purity of his religious faith is not directly questionable; he even published a beautiful manual of preparatory prayers for Holy Communion (*El comulgatorio*, 1655); however, it is significant that almost all of Gracián's work was published under pseudonyms outside the official circles of the Jesuits. His superiors noted certain excessively "mundane" elements in his **maxim**s, which caused him continual problems in his religious career and led to repeated disciplinary measures.

Gracián influenced **La Rochefoucauld** and, especially, **Schopenhauer**, who considered *El criticón* one of the best books ever written. The Spanish Academy has always considered Góngora, Calderón, and Quevedo to be literary figures superior to Gracián; the latter, however, has remained, alongside Cervantes, the most frequently translated author of the Spanish Golden Age.

Apart from the above-mentioned brief collection of prayers, Gracián wrote six books, of which the first three – *El héroe* (1637; *The Hero*), *El político D. Fernando el Católico* (1640; The politician Ferdinand the Catholic), and *El discreto* (1646; The discreet man, translated as *The Complet Gentleman*) – continue the Renaissance tradition of Castiglione, and to a lesser degree, of **Machiavelli**. In these, he charts a characterological map of the ideal man. The fundamental difference between these heroes and Castiglione's in *Il cortegiano* lies in the distinction we find between the Renaissance and the world of the baroque era. The themes and ethos of the baroque are the same as those of the Renaissance, displaying similar references to classical heroes and authors and to the same Arcadian ideals, but the pathos has radically changed: although Reason and Nature remain as inspiring entelechies, the human condition is no longer perceived in the same way. In this period of religious crises, wars, and economic decadence the world had become a battlefield of ambitions and moral misery where one had to survive amid constant attacks of envy and general vulgarity. More than ever, the discreet man must be judicious, individualistic, astute, and outstanding in letters, arms, and politics. For Gracián, this ideal image of the politician is incarnate in King Ferdinand the Catholic, who demonstrates characteristics of valor and prudence, all the while surrounding himself with the best company.

In *The Complet Gentleman*, the profile of the perfect man is drawn with greater precision. The book's structure demonstrates a varied discourse based on allegories, maxims, **dialogue**s, and commentaries; it is comprised of 25 **chapters**, each one dedicated to a different quality. Gracián's pessimism is intensified here and the importance of astuteness is underscored, which gradually becomes the most significant element of his later work. The discreet man is one who at any moment can read the minds of others and remain in control, all the while covering those errors which are inevitable in the human condition. Gracián also values the wise man who knows to retreat in time.

Agudeza y arte de ingenio (1642, 1648; *The Mind's Wit and Art*) is Gracián's most stylistically difficult work. In it he attempts to take the cultivated reader by surprise and force him to navigate through plays on words, apparent antitheses, and twisted metaphors. Basically, the text is a system of principles in the form of **aphorism**s and allegories, whose fundamental premises are repeated in his following book, which is much easier to read. The *Oráculo manual y arte de prudencia* (1648; *The Oracle, a Manual of the Art of Discretion*), Gracián's most successful book outside of Spain, consists of 300 philosophical maxims which comprise a practical message on worldly triumph, followed by an explanatory commentary.

But Gracián's most ambitious and extensive book is *El criticón* (1651–57; *The Critick*). The title of the book does not refer to he who criticizes a great deal (which would be the accepted use of the word in modern Spanish), but rather to he who knows how to analyze or critique society. Here the ideal man, Critilo, with whom the author clearly identifies, teaches his spiritual son and disciple, Andrenio (an archetype of the common man), the secrets of life by means of a series of novelistic episodes. The world, as Calderón had already perceived it, is depicted as a great theater in which most of the actors are motivated exclusively by egoistic impulses. Once again, the value of this work lies in the philosophical digressions made by Critilo, who repeatedly advises Andrenio not to allow himself to be swayed by appearances, since great value is to be found in virtue and in the ability to survive the moral misery of one's contemporaries without being contaminated by it. *The Critick* demonstrates, like none of Gracián's other works, the contradiction inherent in the coexistence of the virtues of honesty and authenticity with astuteness and worldly wisdom.

In Gracián, the long European nonreligious moralist tradition (**Cicero**, **Seneca**, Guevara, Castiglione) converges with the baroque preference for the laconic and the stylistically hermetic. But the most interesting aspect of this work, from the point of view of intellectual history, is that it represents a milestone in the textual construction of the modern "I." Pessimism combines with emphasis on individual success and points to an intensification of the secularization process in which the individual self becomes independent of the social and religious constraints of the Old Regime. This process will be dramatically accelerated with the Enlightenment and later with Romanticism. This may be a slightly exaggerated claim, but it is significant that in the early 20th century Gracián was deemed the "Spanish Nietzsche."

PEDRO MARIA MUÑOZ

Biography

Baltasar Gracián y Morales. Born 8 January 1601 in Belmonte, near Calatayud. Lived with and taught by his priest uncle in Toledo during childhood; studied at a Jesuit school in Saragossa, 1616–19; novice with the Jesuits, Tarragona, at age 18; studied philosophy at the College of Calatayud, 1621–23; studied theology in Saragossa, 1623–27. Ordained as a priest, 1627, and took solemn vows, 1635. Taught philosophy and theology at several Jesuit schools in Aragon, the University of Gandía, 1633–36, and the Colegio de Huesca, from 1636, where he befriended the rich patron of letters, Vincencio Juan de Lastanosa, who financed the publication of his most important books. Had problems with censorship for most of his publications (disciplined twice), which embittered him and left him with enemies. Attempted unsuccessfully to leave the Jesuits and become a monk. Died in Tarragona, 6 December 1658.

Selected Writings

Essays and Related Prose

El héroe, 1637; corrected edition, 1639; edited by Adolphe Coster, 1911; as *The Heroe*, translated by John Skeffington, 1652; as *The Hero*, translated anonymously, 1726

El político D. Fernando el Católico, 1640; edited by E. Correa Calderón, 1961

Arte de ingenio, 1642; revised edition, as *Agudeza y arte de ingenio*, 1648; edited by E. Correa Calderón, 2 vols., 1969; as *The Mind's Wit and Art*, translated by Leonard H. Chambers, 1962

El discreto, 1646; edited by Miguel Romera-Navarro and Jorge M. Furt, 1960, and Arturo del Hoyo, 1963; as *The Complet Gentleman, or a Description of the Several Qualifications, Both Natural and Acquired, That Are Necessary to Form a Great Man*, translated by T. Saldkeld, 1730

Oráculo manual y arte de prudencia, 1648; edited by Miguel Romera-Navarro, 1954, E. Correa Calderón, 1968, Benito Pelegrín, 1983, and Emilio Blanco, 1995; as *The Art of Worldly Wisdom*, translated by Joseph Jacobs, 1892, Martin Fischer, 1934, Otto Eisenschmil, 1947, and Christopher Maurer, 1993; as *The Oracle, a Manual of the Art of Discretion*, translated by L. B. Walton, 1953; also translated under other titles by John Savage, 1702, and Lawrence C. Lockley, 1967; selection as *Practical Wisdom for Perilous Times: Selected Maxims*, edited and adapted by J. Leonard Kaye, 1992

El criticón (allegorical novel with essayistic qualities), 3 vols., 1651–57; edited by Miguel Romera-Navarro, 1938, Antonio Prieto, 2 vols., 1970, and E. Correa Calderón, 1971; as *The Critick*, translated by Paul Rycaut, 1681

Tratados políticos, edited by Gabriel Juliá Andreu, 1941

The Best of Gracián, translated by Thomas C. Corvan, 1964

Other writings: the collection of prayers *El comulgatorio* (1655).

Collected works editions: *Obras completas*, edited by E. Correa Calderón, 1944, Arturo del Hoyo, 1960, Miguel Batllori and Ceferino Peralta, 1969– (in progress), and Emilio Blanco, 2 vols., 1993.

Further Reading

Anceschi, Luciano, *La poética di Gracián in Europa*, Naples: Istituto Suor Orsola Bernincasa, 1989

Ayala, Jorge M., *Gracián: Vida, estilo, y reflexión*, Madrid: Cincel, 1987

Batllori, Miguel, *Gracián y el barroco*, Rome: Storia e Letteratura, 1958

Bell, Aubrey FitzGerald, *Baltasar Gracián*, London: Oxford University Press, 1921

Bouillier, Victor, *Baltasar Gracián et Nietzsche*, Paris: Champion, 1926

Chiappini, Julio O., *Borges y Baltasar Gracián*, Rosario, Argentina: Zeus, 1994

Correa Calderón, Evaristo, *Baltasar Gracián: Su vida y su obra*, Madrid: Biblioteca Románica Hispánia, 1961

Ferrari, Angel, *Fernando el Católico en Baltasar Gracián*, Madrid: Espasa-Calpe, 1945

Foster, Virginia R., *Baltasar Gracián*, Boston: Twayne, 1975

Hafter, Monroe Z., *Gracian and Perfection: Spanish Moralists of the Seventeenth Century*, Cambridge, Massachusetts: Harvard University Press, 1966

Hidalgo-Serna, Emilio, *Das ingeniöse Denken bei Baltasar Gracián: Der "concepto" und seine logische Funktion*, Munich: Fink, 1985

Kassier, Theodore L., *The Truth Disguised: Allegorical Structure and Technique in Gracián's "Criticón"*, London: Tamesis, 1976

Krabbenhoft, Kenneth, *El precio de la cortesía: Retórica e innovación en Quevedo y Gracián*, Salamanca: University of Salamanca, 1994

Krauss, Werner, *Gracians Lebenslehre*, Frankfurt-on-Main: Klostermann, 1947

Patella, Giuseppe, *Gracián o della perfezione*, Rome: Studium, 1993

Pelegrín, Benito, *Le Fil perdu du "Criticón" de Baltasar Gracián, objectif Port Royal: Allégorie et composition "conceptiste"*, Aix-en-Provence: University of Provence, 1984

Pelegrín, Benito, *Éthique et esthétique du Baroque: L'Espace jésuitique de Baltasar Gracián*, Arles: Actes Sud, 1985

Werle, Peter, *"El héroe": Zur Ethik des Baltasar Gracián*, Tübingen: Narr, 1992

Gramsci, Antonio

Italian, 1891–1937

For their range, perceptiveness, and originality Gramsci's writings on politics and society have had a considerable influence on 20th-century thought. His early production, mainly articles of both a theoretical and an unashamedly propagandistic nature for the socialist daily *Avanti!* (Forward!) (1916–20) and for *L'Ordine Nuovo* (1919–24; The new order), were written in the heat of intense political involvement and were largely concerned with supporting workers' rights and advocating revolutionary action on the Soviet model. Later collected in five volumes, they constitute a stirring record of political activism at a time of turmoil and precariousness in Italy as well as a fascinating sociohistorical document of the period.

When Gramsci's activity as a political leader (he was cofounder of the Italian Communist Party in 1921) led to his confinement in fascist prisons for the last ten years of his life (1926–37), he continued to write, committing to paper, mainly in the form of notes and short essays, his reflections on and analyses of an extraordinarily broad spread of topics: from literature through ethics to history and practical politics. The 32 *Quaderni del carcere* (Prison Notebooks), smuggled out of Italy after Gramsci's death and organized for publication in six volumes after World War II, reflect among much else the thinker's concern to reevaluate 19th- and early 20th-century

literary, moral, and political thought, especially that found in the Italian tradition of Francesco De Sanctis, Antonio Labriola, and **Benedetto Croce** but also in influential foreign figures such as Hegel, **Marx**, and Georges Sorel. Even if, by the very nature of these writings, their vision is fragmentary and incomplete, they are nevertheless marked by a vastness of design and, for the most part, by a style of exemplary clarity and vigor.

His move away from Crocean "idealism" had begun early and, despite the continued admiration for and echoes of Croce to be found in the *Prison Notebooks*, the latter are seen by most commentators, whether favorable or otherwise to Gramsci's ideas, as offering an essentially materialist analysis of history and socioeconomic structures and constituting a Marxist sociology of a new and original kind, interpretations of which have informed left-wing discussion in the cultural and political fields up to this day, both in Italy and abroad. The outstanding features of this new sociology are twofold: the positing of the lack of a "national-popular" tradition in Italy compared to other nations as the key to the kind of aulic, court-based cultural (especially literary) development that has characterized the country over the centuries; and the reassessment of the concept of and opportunity for political revolution in the West. In particular, following the failure of the Left in Italy, Gramsci comes to see revolution as essentially a long-term prospect depending on the particular traditions and conditions that exist in each individual country and needing above all as its prerequisite the gradual building of hegemony (his name for ideological domination or penetration) in all the institutions of society by those intellectuals with revolutionary ideas. Only when this task is complete, and ideological unity between intellectuals and masses ("historic bloc" is the term Gramsci uses for this) has been achieved, does the time become ripe for successful revolutionary political action. For Gramsci this is the process that has informed history; new ruling classes have succeeded in establishing a new social order only when they have had effective ideologists to make their ideas permeate the institutions of civil society.

Close analysis of Gramsci's discussion of hegemony, however, and in particular of his concept of the nature of revolution and future society, suggests that his thought continues to be marked both by much of the coercive element of his Leninist political background and by the idealism of his early intellectual formation. While now finding the Soviet model inapplicable to the more advanced societies of the West, whose histories have led them along different and varying paths, he still seems to conceive of revolution as the coercive taking of power by one minority class from another even if in different circumstances from those experienced by Lenin in Russia. This is far from a universally agreed view, however, and many find enough in Gramscian hegemony to see it as an essentially democratic concept based on mass consciousness and understanding and, as in Gino Bedani's (1979) words, "a sophisticated and flexible account of social causation."

Today, despite the collapse of Leninism and Soviet power in the East and the apparent inability of radical intellectuals to spread revolutionary hegemony in the West, Gramsci's ideas, through their depth and richness, continue to exercise considerable fascination among cultural and political commentators and to generate as much debate and controversy as they have since his writings first became widely known and circulated.

One senses that they will continue, at the hands of critics from a wide variety of disciplines, to be the object of exaggerated praise, unfair vilification, and everything in between.

HOWARD MOSS

Biography

Born 22 January 1891 in Ales, Sardinia. Suffered from rickets and spinal injury as a child, leaving him physically deformed. Studied at the University of Turin, 1911–15. Married Julka Schucht, 1922: two sons. Founder, editor, or contributor to several journals and newspapers, including *Il Grido del Popolo* (The shout of the people), from 1915, *Avanti!*, 1916–20, *La Città Futura* (The future city), 1917, *Il Club di Vita Morale* (The club of moral life), 1917, *L'Ordine Nuovo*, 1919–24, and *L'Unità* (Unity), 1922. Active with the Socialist Party, from 1917; founder member, 1921, and party secretary, 1924, Italian Communist Party; elected deputy in Veneto constituency and participated in parliamentary secession to Aventine, 1924. Arrested because of political opposition and imprisoned, 1926–37: suffered from arteriosclerosis, Potts disease, and pulmonary tuberculosis, and transferred from prison to a private clinic in Formia, 1933, and to Quisisana Clinic, Rome, 1935; mass of observations, essays, and studies written while in prison later collected as *Quaderni del carcere*. Awards: Viareggio Prize for Literature, 1947. Died (of a cerebral hemorrhage) in Rome, 27 April 1937.

Selected Writings

Essays and Related Prose

Lettere dal carcere, 1947; revised edition, edited by Sergio Caprioglio and Elsa Fubini, 1965; as *Letters from Prison*, edited by Frank Rosengarten, translated by Ray Rosenthal, 2 vols., 1994; selections as *Letters from Prison*, edited and translated by Lynne Lawner, 1973, and *Prison Letters*, translated by Hamish Henderson, 1988

Quaderni del carcere, 6 vols., 1948–51; Istituto Gramsci Edition edited by Valentino Gerratana, 4 vols., 1975; part as *Prison Notebooks*, vol. 1 (1929–33), edited by Joseph A. Buttigieg, translated by Buttigieg and Antonio Callari, 1992; various selections as *The Open Marxism of Antonio Gramsci*, translated by Carl Marzani, 1957, *The Modern Prince and Other Writings*, translated by Louis Marks, 1957, *Selections from the Prison Notebooks*, translated by Quintin Hoare and Geoffrey Nowell Smith, 1971, and *Further Selections from the Prison Notebooks*, edited and translated by Derek Boothman, 1995

History, Philosophy and Culture in the Young Gramsci, edited by Peter Cavalcanti and Paul Piccone, 1975

Selections from Political Writings, edited by Quintin Hoare, translated by Hoare and John Mathews, 2 vols., 1977–78

Cronache Torinesi (1913–17) (articles), edited by Sergio Caprioglio, 1980

La Città Futura (1917–18) (articles), edited by Sergio Caprioglio, 1982

Il Nostro Marx (1918–19) (articles), edited by Sergio Caprioglio, 1984

Selections from Cultural Writings, edited by David Forgacs and Geoffrey Nowell Smith, translated by William Boelhower, 1985

L'Ordine Nuovo (1919–20), edited by Valentino Gerratana and Antonio A. Santucci, 1987

A Gramsci Reader: Selected Writings, 1916–1935 (various translators), edited by David Forgacs, 1988

Lettere, 1908–1926, edited by Antonio A. Santucci, 1992

Pre-Prison Writings, edited by Richard Bellamy, translated by Virginia Cox, 1994

Collected works edition: *Opere*, 12 vols., 1947–71.

Bibliographies

Cammett, John M., *Bibliografia gramsciana, 1922–1988*, Rome: Riuniti, 1991

Nordquist, Joan, *Antonio Gramsci*, Santa Cruz, California: Reference and Research Services, 1987

Further Reading

Bates, Thomas Richard, "Gramsci and the Theory of Hegemony," *Journal of the History of Ideas* 36 (1975): 351–66

Bedani, Gino, "The Long-Term Strategy in Gramsci's Prison Notebooks," *Quinquereme* 2 (1979): 204–22

Bellamy, Richard, and Darrow Schechter, *Gramsci and the Italian State*, Manchester: Manchester University Press, and New York: St. Martin's Press, 1993

Bobbio, Norberto, "Gramsci and the Concept of Civil Society," in *Gramsci and Marxist Theory*, edited by Chantal Mouffe, London and Boston: Routledge and Kegan Paul, 1979

Cammett, John M., *Antonio Gramsci and the Origins of Italian Communism*, Stanford, California: Stanford University Press, 1967

Davidson, Alastair, *Antonio Gramsci: Towards an Intellectual Biography*, London: Merlin, and Atlantic Highlands, New Jersey: Humanities Press, 1977

Dombroski, Robert S., *Antonio Gramsci*, Boston: Twayne, 1989

Faenza, Liliana, *Tra Croce e Gramsci: Una concordia discors*, Rimini: Guaraldi, 1992

Gruppi, Luciano, *Il concetto di egemonia in Gramsci*, Rome: Riuniti-Istituto Gramsci, 1972

Harman, Chris, *Gramsci Versus Reformism*, London: Bookmarks, 1983

Hoffman, John, *The Gramscian Challenge: Coercion and Consent in Marxist Political Theory*, Oxford and New York: Blackwell, 1984

Holub, Renate, *Antonio Gramsci: Beyond Marxism and Postmodernism*, London and New York: Routledge, 1992

Jocteau, Gian Carlo, *Leggere Gramsci: Una guida alle interpretazioni*, Milan: Feltrinelli, 1975

Joll, James, *Gramsci*, New York: Viking Press, 1977; London: Penguin, 1978

Maier, Bruno, and Paolo Semama, *Antonio Gramsci*, Florence: Le Monnier, 1975

Moss, Howard K., "Gramsci and the Idea of Human Nature," *Italian Quarterly* 31, nos. 119–20 (1990): 7–19

Paladini Musitelli, Marina, *Introduzione a Gramsci*, Bari: Laterza, 1996

Ransome, Paul, *Antonio Gramsci: A New Introduction*, Hemel Hempstead and New York: Harvester Wheatsheaf, 1992

Scruton, Roger, "Thinkers of the Left: Antonio Gramsci," *Salisbury Review* 6 (1984): 19–22; also in his *Thinkers of the New Left*, Harlow, Essex: Longman, 1985

Simon, Roger, *Gramsci's Political Thought: An Introduction*, London: Lawrence and Wishart, 1982

Williams, Gwyn A., "Gramsci's Concept of Egemonia," *Journal of the History of Ideas* 21 (1960): 586–99

Grass, Günter

German, 1927–

The essayistic work of Günter Grass has so far received less critical attention than his novels, early plays, poetry, or graphic art. Yet the 1987 edition of his collected works includes a volume of 138 selected essays, speeches, and commentaries written over 30 years. A decade later, about 50 more essays and speeches can be added to this number.

In marked contrast to his early novelistic style, often described as baroque as it winds its way through lists of objects and grotesque juxtapositions into the surreal, Grass' voice as essayist exhibits restraint, lucidity, and sober rationality. Rather than indulging in baroque playfulness or rhetoric, Grass develops balanced arguments based on facts embedded in historical context, and on values of openness, honesty, equality, and democracy.

Most of Grass' essays written after 1963 were first conceived and delivered as speeches or published as "open **letters**," addressing political and cultural occasions and including tributes and eulogies. During the election years 1965, 1969, and 1972 Grass delivered hundreds of speeches for Willy Brandt's Social Democrat party. His political speeches clearly address a broad public, speaking to the concerns of both the older and younger generations, working people, trade unions, pensioners, students, and teachers. Indeed, with his campaign speeches of the 1960s and beyond, Grass sets a unique example for German writers. Emphasizing his political work as that of a citizen shouldering his public responsibility, Grass enters into dialogue with his audiences with the purpose of raising reasonable doubt. Exemplary campaign speeches appear in four collections from 1968 to 1984. The English collection *Speak Out!* (1969) comprises examples up to 1968; *On Writing and Politics* (1985) selects speeches up to 1983.

Grass has also written essays on writers and writing, examples appearing in *Aufsätze zur Literatur* (1980; Essays on literature) and in the recent *Die Deutschen und ihre Dichter* (1995; The Germans and their writers), which attempts to collect his essays focusing on literary figures from the historical and the contemporary scene, including writers from world literature. One name recurring in Grass' essays but missing from this collection is **Montaigne**, whom Grass designates as "Frühaufklärer" (forerunner of the age of reason).

The grouping of Grass' essays into the categories of "Writing" and "Politics" seems obvious enough, but finer thematic distinctions apply. For example, essays written in connection with the author's travels on four continents could, if collected, shed more light on his concerns with third-world and international affairs. Another persistent topic of Grass' speeches at German and international meetings is the writer's role in society and politics.

Grass' essays referring to the mutual elucidation of the arts deserve separate attention. Having trained in sculpture and graphic arts, he frequently draws inspiration from graphic sources in art history. Three essays in particular illustrate the author's affinity with some of his models in the arts. His first essay, "Die Ballerina" (1956; "The Ballerina"), is a discourse on an old print in the style of the *commedia dell'arte*, which portrays the confrontation between a poet and a ballerina who appears late at night poised on the writer's table. (Grass had married the Swiss ballet student Anna Schwarz in 1954.) By dwelling on the strict regime and discipline of the classical ballet dancer and on the asceticism her art requires, Grass presents her as inspiration and muse to the writer. Just as all ballet expressions require intense control of natural movement, the art of the poet cannot be "natural." An allusion to **Heinrich von Kleist**'s essay *Über das Marionettentheater* (1810; *On Puppet Shows*) places Grass' first essay in a demanding

aesthetic context. Suggesting that the ballerina and (Kleist's) marionette might enter into a marriage, this essay aspires to a perfection for art and the artisan which transcends the human condition.

Grass' address on the Dürer anniversary of 1971, "Vom Stillstand im Fortschritt" (On stasis in progress), draws inspiration from Dürer's engraving *Melancolia I*. He pictures the mysterious allegorical figure in a variety of roles in contemporary society: placed at a conveyor belt, she "sits wingless and as though sexless" for eight hours a day. Her utopian side is "Touristica," as the same ancient deity presides over both Melancholia and Utopia. Melancholy is also embodied in the lonesome suburban wife, and as socialist woman she holds hammer and sickle instead of the compass. Expressing Western overabundance, supply without demand, she sits on a deep freezer, a can opener in her hand. In a corresponding attitude she may refuse food, aspiring to a utopia of stern discipline. Grass attempts to demonstrate that Dürer's melancholy is a social reality rather than a suspicious eccentricity.

In the essay "Der Traum der Vernunft" (The dream of reason), addressing a 1984 conference at the Berlin Academy of Art, Grass refers to Goya's etching in aquatint with the inscription *El sueño de la razón produce monstruos* (The sleep of reason brings forth monsters). Identifying *sueño* as both sleep and dream, he points out that all ideologies are dreams of reason or terrifying utopian visions. Does this mean, he asks, that reason must never sleep, permit us no mystery, no flights of the imagination including the bat, owl, and lynx of Goya's etching? In this and other essays of the 1980s, Grass questions humankind's future: "Die Vernichtung der Menschheit hat begonnen" (The destruction of humankind has begun) he claimed at the reception of the Feltrinelli Prize in 1982. Grass was so demoralized by this vision that he stopped writing fiction for four years.

During and after the changes of 1989–91 in Germany, Grass opposed in 13 essays and speeches the hasty German reunification without appropriate changes in the constitution. Pleading for a more carefully reasoned procedure, Grass suggested a federation of the two states rather than an emotional unification, which would amount in effect to a takeover by the West of a formerly independent state. In November 1992 he dedicated a public address about the decline of political culture in the united Germany to the Turkish victims of Mölln. In a 1994 speech accepting a prize from the Bavarian Academy of Art, Grass seemed to anticipate the critical uproar that would follow the 1995 publication of his novel *Ein weites Feld* (A wide field). "Über das Sekundäre aus primärer Sicht" (On the secondary from a primary perspective) presents a skeptical evaluation of the emphasis on secondary concerns in contemporary culture and politics.

As the selected examples show, Grass the essayist tends to be underrated in relation to Grass the popular novelist, who continues to be the main focus of critical attention. More than mere political or theoretical footnotes to his main oeuvre, Grass' essays constitute a complex genre in their own right. With their formal qualities and varied content, these essays still await critical discovery.

SIGRID MAYER

Biography

Günter Wilhelm Grass. Born 16 October 1927 in Danzig (now
Gdańsk, Poland). Studied at the Volksschule and Gymnasium,
Danzig; Academy of Art, Düsseldorf, 1948–52; State Academy of
Fine Arts, Berlin, 1953–55; also trained as a stone mason and
sculptor. Prisoner of war during World War II. Married Anna
Margareta Schwarz, 1954 (divorced, 1978): one daughter and three
sons. Held various jobs; speechwriter for Willy Brandt when he was
Mayor of West Berlin. Coeditor, L, from 1976, and Verlag L '80
publishers, from 1980. Married Ute Grunert, 1979. Awards: many,
including Gruppe 47 Prize, 1958; Critics' Prize (Germany), 1960;
Foreign Book Prize (France), 1962; Büchner Prize, 1965; Fontane
Prize, 1968; Heuss Prize, 1969; Mondello Prize (Palermo), 1977;
Carl von Ossiersky Medal, 1977; Viareggio-Versilia Prize, 1978;
Majakowski Medal, 1978; Feltrinelli Prize, 1982; Leonhard Frank
Ring, 1988; honorary degrees from three colleges and universities.
Member, 1963, and President, 1983–86 (resigned), Berlin Academy
of Art.

Selected Writings

Essays and Related Prose

Über das Selbstverständliche: Reden, Aufsätze, Offene Briefe,
    Kommentare, 1968; revised and enlarged edition, as Über das
    Selbstverständliche: Politische Schriften, 1969; as Speak Out!
    Speeches, Open Letters, Commentaries, translated by Ralph
    Manheim and others, 1969
Dokumente zur politischen Wirkung, edited by Heinz Ludwig
    Arnold and Franz Josef Görtz, 1971
Der Bürger und seine Stimme: Reden-Aufsätze-Kommentare, 1974
Denkzettel: Politische Reden und Aufsätze, 1965–76, 1978
Aufsätze zur Literatur, 1980
Widerstand lernen: Politische Gegenreden, 1980–1983, 1984
On Writing and Politics, 1967–1983, translated by Ralph Manheim,
    1985
Deutscher Lastenausgleich: Wider das dumpfe Einheitsgebot: Reden
    und Gespräche, 1990
Ein Schnäppchen namens DDR, letzte Reden vorm Glockengeläut,
    1990
Gegen die verstreichende Zeit: Reden, Aufsätze und Gespräche,
    1989–1991, 1991
Cat and Mouse and Other Writings, edited by A. Leslie Willson
    (includes "The Ballerina," translated by Willson, and speeches),
    1994
Die Deutschen und ihre Dichter, edited by Daniela Hermes, 1995

Other writings: many novels (including Die Blechtrommel [The Tin
Drum], 1959; Katz und Maus [Cat and Mouse], 1961; Hundejahre
[Dog Years], 1963; Aus dem Tagebuch einer Schnecke [From the
Diary of a Snail], 1972; Der Butt [The Flounder], 1977; Das
Treffen in Telgte [The Meeting at Telgte], 1979; Kopfgeburten; oder
die Deutschen sterben aus [Headbirths; or, The Germans Are Dying
Out], 1980; Die Rättin [The Rat], 1986; Unkenrufe [The Call of
the Toad], 1992; Ein weites Feld, 1995), eight plays, poetry, books
on politics, and many collections of drawings and graphics.

Collected works edition: Werkausgabe, edited by Volker Neuhaus,
10 vols., 1987.

Bibliographies

Everett, George A., A Select Bibliography of Günter Grass (From
    1956 to 1973), New York: Franklin, 1974
Görtz, Franz Josef, "Kommentierte Auswahl-Bibliographie," Text +
    Kritik 1/1a (1978): 175–99
Görtz, Franz Josef, "Bibliographie," in Günter Grass: Auskunft für
    Leser, edited by Görtz, Darmstadt and Neuwied: Luchterhand,
    1984: 297–310
O'Neill, Patrick, Günter Grass: A Bibliography, 1955–1975,
    Toronto: University of Toronto Press, 1976

Further Reading

Arnold, Heinz Ludwig, editor, Text + Kritik issue on Grass, 1/1a
    (1978)
Ascherson, Neal, "Raw Nerves" (review of Speak Out! by Grass),
    New York Review of Books, 20 November 1969: 16–21
Brady, Philip, Timothy McFarland, and John L. White, editors,
    Günter Grass' "Der Butt": Sexual Politics and the Male Myth of
    History, Oxford: Clarendon Press, 1990
Casanova, Nicole, Günter Grass: Atelier des métamorphoses, Paris:
    Belfond, 1979
Görtz, Franz Josef, editor, Günter Grass: Auskunft für Leser,
    Darmstadt and Neuwied: Luchterhand, 1984
Hayman, Ronald, Günter Grass, London and New York: Methuen,
    1985
Hollington, Michael, Günter Grass: The Writer in a Pluralist
    Society, London and New York: Marion Boyars, 1980
Labroisse, Gerd, and Dick Van Stekelenburg, editors, Günter Grass:
    Ein Europäischer Autor?, Amsterdam and Atlanta: Rodopi, 1992
Lawson, Richard H., Günter Grass, New York: Ungar, 1985
Leonhard, Irene, Günter Grass, New York: Barnes and Noble, 1974
Mason, Ann L., The Skeptical Muse: A Study of Günter Grass'
    Conception of the Artist, Berne: Lang, 1974
Mews, Siegfried, editor, "The Fisherman and His Wife": Günter
    Grass' "The Flounder" in Critical Perspective, New York: AMS
    Press, 1983
Miles, Keith, Günter Grass, London: Vision Press, and New York:
    Barnes and Noble, 1975
O'Neill, Patrick, editor, Critical Essays on Günter Grass, Boston:
    Hall, 1987
Osterle, Heinz D., "An Orwellian Decade? Günter Grass Between
    Despair and Hope (with a Campaign Speech of 1983)," German
    Studies Review 8, no. 3 (October 1985): 481–507
Reddick, John, The "Danzig Trilogy" of Günter Grass, London:
    Secker and Warburg, and New York: Harcourt Brace Jovanovich,
    1975
Tank, Kurt Lothar, Günter Grass, New York: Ungar, 1969 (original
    German edition, 1965)
Updike, John, "Snail on the Stump," New Yorker, 15 October
    1973: 182–85
Vormweg, Heinrich, Günter Grass mit Selbstzeugnissen und
    Bilddokumenten, Reinbek: Rowohlt, 1986
Willson, Leslie A., editor, A Günter Grass Symposium, Austin:
    University of Texas Press, 1971

Green, Dorothy

Australian, 1915–1991

Dorothy Green was an intense speaker and writer. This quality
arose from a strong Christian faith which assured her that
human life has meaning and that all human beings deserve a
justice their rulers deny them. Her insistent belief that ordinary people "are still better than their culture" supported her
optimism that they will eventually realize the minimum demand
of justice – that none should go hungry in a world with technology already supplying commodities beyond any demand –
and her anger at the system that devotes this technology to
greed and aggression and at the individuals who choose to use
their intellect to serve this system.

Green, who in her earlier years was better known by
her birth name as the poet Dorothy Auchterlonie, began her
writing career while a student at the University of Sydney
where, as editor of the journal Hermes, she published an
editorial essay, "People, Politics, and 'Poetry'" (1938). The

separate words in the title identify the issues that were to remain central to her concerns throughout her life, and their juxtaposition explains her moral passion. Poetry, and literature in general, were, for Green, a means of identifying and clarifying human relationships, and her criticism is merciless in its condemnation of pretension in content and falsity in form. Hence in 1944, writing about the "Ern Malley" hoax (in which editor Max Harris mistook as real some spoof poetry written by two well-known Australian poets and published it in the avant-garde journal *Angry Penguins*) Green recognized the intellectual arrogance – which prevented Harris attending to either the opinions of others or the rhythms of the words presented to him – that led to his humiliation. More than a quarter of a century later, she was equally perspicacious in her identification of the flight from reason of many of the counterrevolutionary poets collected in Thomas Shapcott's 1969 anthology *Australian Poetry Now*, and later of the way the commodification of literature in Colleen McCullough's *The Thorn Birds* (1977) degrades the capacity for human feeling. Yet her feeling for the positive forces of life, which gave impetus to her condemnations of the shoddy, also enabled her to find virtue in works that she knew were deeply flawed. So, her review of Germaine Greer's book on women painters, *The Obstacle Race* (1979), condemns the polemic that separates women as victims from men as oppressors, yet finds in the book reason to hope that women may lead the way toward **William Morris**' ideal of a world where art is "a necessity of human life, common to the whole people."

The greater number of Green's essays were **reviews**, which take the form, when she is dealing with writers she admired, of a penetrating scrutiny of the work in question and a passionate engagement with readers to convince them of the importance of recognizing its truth. She shared with **Judith Wright** the belief that the core of morality was to be found in the wholeness of humans and nature, and that evil was what defaced or deformed either. She shared with Martin Boyd, to whose writing she brought discriminating praise, the belief that the custodians of this value were artists and aristocrats, for whom the world was to be enjoyed and praised, not exploited for material gain or delivered to the dealers of death. The religion that supported these beliefs, although formally orthodox, was in no way narrowly sectarian. She accepted the many paths to God, including the Buddhism of Robert Gray's poetry as much as the secular humanism of Christina Stead. Yet she was intolerant of the easy acceptance of any universal ideal that denied difference and division, particularly the notions that all is permitted in a fallen world, or that humans do not have to wrestle with the divisions brought about by this fall.

The search for a wholeness that would transcend division without denying it accounts for Green's interest in the biologist, anthropologist, and novelist Grant Watson, whose letters she edited and whose work she discussed in an important essay, "The Daimon and the Fringe-Dweller" (1971). In analyzing Watson's work, Green reveals her own understanding of the mysteries of existence. The English-born Watson spent only two years in Australia, but the relations between its people and its landscape provided the theme for six of his ten novels. The fringe-dwellers of the essay's title are those who move out from civilization to pursue their demons to the true center, the land where nature communicates through the senses an understanding of life that moves beyond the merely human. This understanding, which Green likens to Hindu and Chinese thought and to the way of being of the Aborigines, brings the spiritual, the biological, and the cultural into harmony. Green contrasts it with the exploitative modes of Western rationalism, which subjugate both women and the land to the masculine drive to dominate and possess. In this desire Green locates the divisions between individuals and nations alike.

Green's distrust of isolated intellectualism did not, however, mean any elevation of feeling over thought, or any romantic illusions about the innate wisdom of untutored sensibility. As she says in her essay (originally a lecture) "The Place of Literature in Society" (1986), the illiterate could exist happily only in societies where there was no pressure of population on resources. In the contemporary world, bondage to nature means misery, and the absence of public discourse means bondage to those who control the economic forces. Literature, "humanity thinking aloud," is the "great continuous discussion throughout the ages and across the world" that provides the insights into the human condition which alone can offer us the hope of freedom.

In her essay on A. G. Stephens, Green remarks that he fails the final test of a critic – the ability to develop his particular insights into a continuous argument. Green herself passes this test triumphantly. Her moral concerns are consistent from her earliest work, but develop as her understanding of the complexity of the human predicament develops to take account of the social origins of individualism, of the divisions of the self, and of the persistent and pernicious effects of power and greed. At the same time, the content of her essays provides an analysis of the developing responses of Australian writers to their environment. Her essays on A. H. Davis and Louis Stone identify the precise nature of their Australian experience, while those on Patrick White demonstrate how he uses this experience to contribute to world literature. All of this is accomplished with wit and a breadth of knowledge that places the immediate in the context of the universal, represented by the touchstones of Shakespeare, Milton, **George Eliot**, and **Tolstoi**.

Green will probably be remembered mainly as a poet and critic, but her essays are integral to her work, and contain the craftsmanship, the sharp-eyed insight into human nature and human folly, and the passionate concern for our relation to ourselves and to nature, that marks all of her writing.

JOHN MCLAREN

Biography
Born Dorothy Auchterlonie, 28 May 1915 in Sunderland, County Durham, England. Studied at the University of Sydney, B.A., 1938, M.A., 1940. Worked as a broadcaster, journalist, and news editor, Australian Broadcasting Corporation, 1942–49. Married H. M. Green, 1944 (died, 1962): one daughter and one son. Teacher and coprincipal at a girls' school, Warwick, Queensland, 1955–60; lecturer in English, Monash University, Melbourne, 1960–63, Australian National University, Canberra, 1964–72, and the Royal Military College, Duntroon, 1976–80. Awards: James Cook University Literary Award, 1973; Barbara Ramsden Award, for *Ulysses Bound*, 1973; honorary degree from the University of New South Wales. Medal, Order of Australia, 1984, and Officer, Order of Australia, 1988. Died in Canberra, 21 February 1991.

Selected Writings

Essays and Related Prose
The Music of Love: Critical Essays on Literature and Life, 1984
The Writer, the Reader and the Critic in a Monoculture (lectures),
     1986; enlarged edition, as *Writer, Reader, Critic*, 1990

Other writings: poetry (as Dorothy Auchterlonie) and the critical
study *Ulysses Bound* (1973). Also revised her husband H. M.
Green's *History of Australian Literature* (1985).

Further Reading
Dowse, Sara, "In the Nature of a Prophet: Sara Dowse Profiles
     Dorothy Green," *Australian Society* 9, no. 2 (1990): 18–21
Southerly issue on Green, 50, no. 3 (1990), particularly "The Work
     of Dorothy Green" by Elizabeth Perkins: 279–93

Greene, Graham

British, 1904–1991

Although he failed to win the Nobel Prize for Literature despite
his great achievement with over two dozen novels, four collections of short stories, four volumes of travel writing, and eight
plays, Graham Greene nevertheless also made his mark in the
essay genre with several volumes: *British Dramatists* (1942),
The Lost Childhood and Other Essays (1951), *Collected
Essays* (1969), *The Pleasure-Dome* (1972), and *Reflections*
(1990). His essays were published in a wide variety of British
periodicals, including the *New Statesman*, the *Spectator*, *Night
and Day*, the *Listener*, the *Observer*, and the *Sunday Times*.

     Greene's serious work as an essayist (he had written some
film criticism as an undergraduate at Oxford) began in 1935
with movie reviews for the *Spectator*, to which he contributed
over 400 reviews in the next four and a half years. In these
reviews (over 300 of them published in *The Pleasure-Dome*,
and a selection more recently in *Mornings in the Dark*, 1993)
Greene analyzed most of the major films of the time – *Anthony
Adverse*, *Beau Geste*, *Crime and Punishment*, *Goodbye Mr.
Chips*, *Intermezzo*, *Trail of the Lonesome Pine*, for example
– and the work of major actors, actresses, and directors from
Frank Capra, Katharine Hepburn, and Laurence Olivier to
Laurel and Hardy, the Marx Brothers, and W. C. Fields. In
one instance, his review (in *Night and Day*, October 1937)
gave him a great deal of legal trouble when he libeled Shirley
Temple and her performance in *Wee Willie Winkle*; the subse-
quent suit forced him to flee to Mexico for a time.

     As Norman Sherry (1989), his biographer, has written,
"Greene's long fascination with the cinema aroused in him
extremes of emotional response and a deeply critical attitude
toward films, their makers, and those who appeared in them."
He found a good deal wrong with the films of the 1930s
because of their sensationalism in publicity and their falseness
to life. All too often, he felt, film failed because it did not
fulfill that which should be its object: "the translation of
thought back into images."

     British Dramatists is an essay of 48 pages written at sea in
December 1941, while Greene was on his way to Africa to
serve as a spy for the British Secret Service. In the essay he
finds the genesis of British drama in the ritual of the Roman

Catholic Church, surveys the theater from the mystery plays
down to Noël Coward and Somerset Maugham, and suggests
that the theater casts its spell because "the ritual is there – the
magic." His comments on Shakespeare are particularly striking
for their insights into the playwright's verbal power.

     Greene's best work as an essayist is found in *Collected
Essays*, which contains 75 essays written and published over
a period of three decades, 39 of them having previously been
published in *The Lost Childhood and Other Essays*. Greene
wrote in his note to *Collected Essays* that in making his selections for the volume, "I have made it a principle to include
nothing of which I can say that, if I were writing today, I
would write in a different sense. The principle applies as much
to my hatreds as to my loves ... A man should be judged by
his enemies as well as by his friendships."

     The collected essays cover a wide range of topics from the
influence of childhood reading to his wartime experiences in
Sierra Leone to literature and writers. Among the many writers
he deals with are **Fielding**, Sterne, **Dickens**, **Henry James**, Ford
Madox Ford, **G. K. Chesterton**, François Mauriac, Edgar
Wallace, Beatrix Potter, Anthony à Wood, John Evelyn,
Charles Churchill, Francis Parkman, **Simone Weil**, and George
Moore.

     Reflections, a final collection of essays selected by Judith
Adamson, ranges in time from 1923 ("Impressions of Dublin")
to 1988 ("Out of the Dustbin") and covers a wide range of
topics: criticism, the Russian-Finnish War, the papacy, Indo-
China, Catholicism, Adlai Stevenson, secondhand bookstores,
Chile, **Jorge Luis Borges**, Cuba, and Papa Doc Duvalier. Like
his other essays, these pieces are lively, highly personal, often
controversial, and stylistically polished. Many had their genesis
in Greene's travels as a journalist and later served as quarries
for his novels. As Adamson says in her introduction, they let
us "see what reality looked like before it was transformed into
a unique vision of the world."

     Perhaps Greene's most enduring essays are those concerning
literature. In his brilliant essays on Henry James, for example,
Greene's admiration of James and the influence of James
on Greene's fiction are obvious. In "Henry James: The Private
Universe" (1936), "Henry James: The Religious Aspect"
(1933), "The Plays of Henry James" (1950), and "The Lesson
of the Master" (1951), he praises the writer for his treatment
of the struggle between good and evil, his deft handling of
point of view and style, and his poetic imagination. His essays
on Dickens, Fielding, Sterne, Mauriac, Chesterton, Ford, and
Moore are also significant contributions to the history of the
criticism of fiction.

     Greene's essays will never overshadow the distinguished
achievement of his fiction, but they will continue to reveal a
great deal about the workings of the mind of one of the most
important British novelists of the 20th century.

                                        ROBERT C. STEENSMA

Biography
Born 2 October 1904 in Berkhamsted, Hertfordshire. Studied at
Balliol College, Oxford, B.A., 1925. Joined the Roman Catholic
Church, 1926. Subeditor, the *Times*, London, 1926–30. Married
Vivien Dayrell-Browning (later separated), 1927: one son and one
daughter. Fiction editor, 1932–35, film critic, 1937–40, and literary
editor, 1940–41, the *Spectator*, London. Worked as a spy for the

British Secret Service during World War II. Director, Eyre and Spottiswoode publishers, London, 1944–48, and Bodley Head publishers, London, 1958–68. Contributor to many journals and magazines, including *Life*, *New Republic*, *Saturday Evening Post*, *Esquire*, **Atlantic Monthly**, and the *London Mercury*. Traveled widely. Lived in Antibes, on the French Riviera, from 1966. Awards: many, including the Hawthornden prize, 1941; James Tait Black Memorial Prize, 1949; Thomas More Medal, 1973; Dos Passos Prize, 1980; Jerusalem Prize, 1981; honorary degrees from four universities. Honorary Fellow, Balliol College, 1963; Honorary Citizen, Anacapri, 1978; Companion of Honor, 1966; Chevalier, Legion of Honor (France), 1967; Grand Cross, Order of Balboa (Panama), 1983; Commandant, Order of Arts and Letters (France), 1984; Companion of Literature, Royal Society of Literature, 1984; Order of Merit, 1986. Died in Geneva, 3 April 1991.

Selected Writings

Essays and Related Prose

British Dramatists, 1942
The Lost Childhood and Other Essays, 1951
Essais catholiques, part translated into French by Marcelle Sibon, 1953
Collected Essays, 1969
The Pleasure-Dome: The Collected Film Criticism, 1935–1940, edited by John Russell Taylor, 1972; as *Greene on Film: Collected Film Criticism, 1935–1940*, 1972
Reflections, 1923–1988, edited by Judith Adamson, 1990
Mornings in the Dark: The Graham Greene Film Reader, edited by David Parkinson, 1993; as *The Graham Greene Film Reader: Reviews, Essays, Interviews, and Film Stories*, 1994

Other writings: 28 novels (including *Brighton Rock*, 1938; *The Power and the Glory*, 1940; *The Heart of the Matter*, 1948; *The Third Man*, 1950; *The End of the Affair*, 1951; *The Quiet American*, 1955; *Our Man in Havana*, 1958; *The Comedians*, 1966; *Travels with My Aunt*, 1969; *The Honorary Consul*, 1973; *Monsignor Quixote*, 1982), four volumes of short stories, eight plays, travel books, autobiography, and books for children.

Collected works edition: *Graham Greene: The Collected Edition*, 1970– (in progress).

Bibliographies

Cassis, A. F., *Graham Greene: An Annotated Bibliography of Criticism*, Metuchen, New Jersey: Scarecrow Press, 1981
Vann, J. D., *Graham Greene: A Checklist of Criticism*, Kent, Ohio: Kent State University Press, 1970
Wobbe, R. A., *Graham Greene: A Bibliography and Guide to Research*, New York: Garland, 1979

Further Reading

Davis, Elizabeth, *Graham Greene: The Artist as Critic*, Fredericton, New Brunswick: York Press, 1984
De Vitis, A. A., *Graham Greene*, Boston: Twayne, revised edition, 1986
Shelden, Michael, *Graham Greene: The Enemy Within*, New York: Random House, and London: Heinemann, 1994
Sherry, Norman, *The Life of Graham Greene*, New York: Viking, and London: Cape, 2 vols., 1989–94 (in progress)
Stratford, Philip, *Faith and Fiction: Creative Process in Greene and Mauriac*, Notre Dame, Indiana: University of Notre Dame Press, 1964: Chapter 5

Die Grenzboten

German journal, 1841–1922

The weekly journal *Die Grenzboten* (Dispatches from the border) was published between 1841 and 1922. During the period between 1848 and 1857 it was edited primarily by Julian Schmidt and Gustav Freytag. Little has been written about this period of *GB*, though it deserves attention since the journal figured prominently in formulating the aesthetic and cultural characteristics of German literature and art. Although the post-1857 period of the journal was increasingly aligned with the right, during Schmidt and Freytag's tenure *GB* reflects its editors' moderate liberalism. Further, *GB* addressed the formative political events of the time – from the failed Frankfurt Revolution of 1848 to the end of the reign of Prussian King Friedrich Wilhelm IV in 1857. Discussions of literature and culture in the Leipzig periodical were characterized by the editors' desire to forge a common German cultural heritage, a necessity, they believed, if a politically united German state was to be formed.

GB was directed toward educated, middle-class citizens, a group whose numbers steadily increased in the 19th century. Circulation during this period was about 1000 (Joachim Kirchner, 1962). As the subtitle of the journal – "Zeitschrift für Politik und Literatur" – suggests, politics and literature were central concerns. Essays and articles on political and historical issues were the primary forms of writing in *GB*. Discussions of aesthetics and **reviews** of specific literary works accounted for the journal's literary component, although occasionally original literature appeared. Particularly in the first two years of Schmidt and Freytag's joint editorship, each approximately 40-page issue was devoted to essays concerning Prussia's and Austria's relationship to the eastern border states, the hegemony of Prussia, and the stirrings of the southern German states. Articles condemned both the more radical German parties which led the Revolution in March 1848 and the threat to individual liberties posed by the right.

Forces of the Prussian government ended the Frankfurt Assembly's attempts to demilitarize Prussia and limit the power of the nobility; supporters of the Assembly throughout the country were suppressed and even executed. Nonetheless, the re-establishment of the pre-1848 order was generally welcomed by *GB*. On the first page of the January 1849 issue of *GB* the editors condemned the "chaos" of the revolution and welcomed the imposition of order and the hope it offered of a unified Germany. Schmidt and Freytag supported a loosely (politically) unified Germany under the leadership of Prussia.

Beginning in 1849 and 1850, the editors devoted a significant portion of each issue to literature, and, to a lesser extent, the plastic arts and music. Freytag, who was himself a novelist, is best known for his contributions to conceptions of German drama. Essays in *GB* concerning dramatic form reflect his rule-based aesthetic and desire for sharply drawn unities, heroism, strong characters, and emphasis on plot development. However, it was Schmidt, the writer of the five-volume *Geschichte der deutschen Literatur von Leibniz bis auf unsere Zeit* (1886–96; History of German literature from Leibniz to the present), who was most responsible for the periodical's attempt to delineate and create a national German culture in order to reinforce the development of political unity.

The editors' political and aesthetic emphases led to the focus on works of historical literature; discussions of the role of museums, dictionaries, and fairytale collections; and increasing interest in "Volkskunde" or folklore. Romanticism and the works of writers such as E. T. A. Hoffmann and Ludwig Tieck were criticized as dangerously subjective and fantastic. Even **Heinrich von Kleist**, Georg Büchner, and Friedrich Hölderlin were censured for their attempts to portray madness, a state, Schmidt wrote in a review of Büchner's oeuvre in 1851, that cannot and should not be portrayed through literature. Writers viewed favorably in *GB* include Jeremias Gotthelf and Adalbert Stifter, authors of novellas concerned with village life and local customs, and Otto Ludwig, whose dramas exemplified the editors' desire for an aesthetic of "poetic realism."

The editors of *GB* viewed themselves as supporting the democratic ideals and rationalism of the Enlightenment. Frequent articles on the press and censorship reflected the editors' belief in the need for a free press, and liberal conception of the rights of the individual. Featured essays represent an extraordinarily wide field, from articles on the role of the press in Austria to slavery and politics in the United States. In 1854 *GB* included essays on Prussia's relationship to the Netherlands, Richard Wagner's opera *Lohengrin*, and the construction of Das Neue Museum in Berlin. Frequent essays under the heading "Zur orientalischen Frage" (On the question of the East) focused on Austria's clash with many of the states within its empire. Articles concerning Austria, Czechoslovakia, Hungary, Poland, and Turkey were written by various, often unidentified, correspondents. Ignaz Kuranda, the founder of *GB* in 1841, was responsible for *GB*'s focus on Belgium in the first years of the journal; Schmidt and Freytag shifted the emphasis to Prussia and the eastern border states.

Formulation of cultural and national identities becomes more pronounced in the later years of Schmidt and Freytag's tenure. **Goethe** and **Schiller** were especially lionized and sections entitled "Kulturbilder" (cultural images) and "Bilder aus der deutschen Vergangenheit" (images from the German past) were inaugurated, addressing everything from the book trade in Leipzig to the piety of 16th-century German mercenaries. Literature of ancient Greece and Rome as well as essays concerning the politics and culture of both were advanced as exemplary models from which Germans could learn.

CHRISTOPHER P. MCCLINTICK

Further Reading

Elster, Hanns Martin, "*Die Grenzboten*: Zeitschrift für Politik, Literatur und Kunst," in *Hundert Jahre Verlag F. W. Grunow, 1818–1919*, Leipzig, 1919: 59–74

Grunow, Johannes, "Fünfzig Jahre!," *Grenzboten* 40, no. 4 (1891)

Kirchner, Joachim, *Das deutsche Zeitschriftenwesen, seine Geschichte und seine Probleme*, vol. 2, Wiesbaden: Harrassowitz, 1962: 137–38

Leppla, Rupprecht, "Julian Schmidt (1818–1886)," *Gustav-Freytag-Blätter* 13, no. 27 (1968): 11–14

Grimm, Herman

German, 1828–1901

Herman Friedrich Grimm was the second son of Wilhelm, the younger of the famous Grimm Brothers. He grew up in a world of profuse learning, which comprised both the traditional "philological" disciplines and the sciences of the naturalist, and which valued exacting rigor as much as the inventiveness of the poetic imagination. He was introduced early in life to prominent public figures whose patriotism expressed itself in a commitment to civic welfare and to the ideals of constitutional liberalism. Grimm's education under the guidance of a private tutor, **Leopold von Ranke**, was free of coercion. Subsequent studies at the reform Universities of Berlin and Bonn seem to have destined him for a career in law and diplomacy. He chose literature instead, but became increasingly frustrated when his poems and plays (conventional historical dramas and social comedies) and a three-volume "conversational novel" *Unüberwindliche Mächte* (1867; Unvanquishable powers) proved to be less than successful. His solution to this dilemma was an extended trip in 1857 to the venues of Italian classical and Renaissance culture, from which he returned with an abiding interest in art history. He also brought back enough material for a biography of Michelangelo, the factual and intuitive description of how a great genius lived as a dominating force "in the history and culture of his time, the efflorescence of art in Florence and Rome." It both exemplified a new vision of the artist as a heroic creator of his age, and developed a new style of making that artist comprehensible to an appreciative posterity – that of the artistic essay.

It is not quite accurate historically to credit Grimm with introducing the term "essay" into the German literary vocabulary and to single him out as the first major practitioner of this new "short" form of nonfictional prose. In this respect **Novalis** and **Friedrich Schlegel** had preceded him by some 60 years. But he created a new style of essay writing, and he was the person most instrumental in gaining popular acceptance for a genre that, in contrast to the erudite study, the academic disquisition, or the empirical analysis, could capture a different spirit of inquiry and incorporate a changing attitude toward learning, insight, and information. Acknowledging his debt to the inspirational example of **Ralph Waldo Emerson**, to whom he had dedicated his first collection of 11 *Essays* (1859) "with cordial admiration," he states retrospectively in 1890 that "the real essay nowadays has to deal with something generally understandable and do so quickly, fluently, and as a sequence of individually focused insights," which have emerged from many-sided investigations "as suggestive samplings rather than in their all-inclusive completeness." Each particular essay, as one **chapter** in the accumulating variety of the ideal book, is also like "a summarizing preface to an unwritten book."

Grimm's style of controlled improvisation – open, associative, digressing, and without firm conclusions – made him an influential mediator in the cultural sphere of his generation. It is a way of writing that is altogether consonant with the aestheticism that dominated the world view of Germany's upper bourgeoisie in the era of Bismarck. This philosophy of culture, and indeed this perception of life as culture, cherished the great art of the past as representative of a higher realm of timeless values – separate from everyday existence, grandiosely independent of sociopolitical pressures, immune from forces outside their own compass. The freedom this art exemplifies is freedom from pragmatic obligations, especially from those of party politics. Against the partiality of arguments advanced in favor of special interests, the retreat into art led to an almost abstract idealism. An aesthetic orientation of this kind complemented an optimistic faith in progress with stability, in the preservation of privileges and hierarchies, in the benevolent but firm execution of power. It did not encourage the development of a modern political will or create opportunities for the exercise of civil rights. Instead, it reserved the realm of liberating enterprise to the free play of artistic creativity and its congenial contemplation. Thus the masterworks of the visual arts and literature incorporate the eternal verities that a secularized consciousness no longer found in religious truth. Such works are valuable in their own right and exist for no other but their own sake, devoid of alien purpose and ultimately inexplicable. The "new" essay is their perfect messenger: as literary art it is there for the sake of literature and art. It is a product of the empathic inspiration.

For Grimm all of this meant an obligation to preserve the cultural heritage of classicist humanism that he found personified, so far as the German people's "national creative imagination" is concerned, in **Goethe**. More even than his three other "ideal figures" – Homer, Raphael, and Michelangelo – he used the Weimar Olympian to illustrate how genius works as a historical force. He returned to Goethe at all stages of his life, in a large variety of essays and most notably in the 25 lectures he gave in 1874–75 (published as *Goethe* in 1876–77) as the first professor of aesthetics and modern art history at a German university, that of Berlin. It is both the rich life of the exceptional individual and his widely productive impact on his age and on posterity that inspired Grimm's admiring, even worshipful, and indeed mythicizing attitude. His style of presentation, committed though it is to making complicated vital processes understandable, does not sacrifice subtlety. On the contrary, his lectures are crafted so carefully as to be spoken essays. Grimm assimilated the characteristic features of Goethe's own language as an expression of continuity through legitimate stewardship. His emphatic concern is with an ever-developing life and with the time upon which it has left its imprint; therefore he pays scant attention to the analysis of specific works or characters or to the creative transformation by which life is changed into art.

Rather, Grimm seeks to re-create the ambience of open-minded sociability and cosmopolitan liberality that he knows to be an ideal construct, even as he imbues it with a discreet personal flavor. In other words, it is his own experiences and insights that bridge historical distances and societal differences. They also stimulate an interchange between the things to be apprehended and the reader's own subjectivity through which they are being refracted. This approach runs counter to the spirit of the *Critical and Historical Essays* (1843) of **Thomas Babington Macaulay**. Grimm expressed admiration for them, to be sure, but he criticized their author for letting his material (rather than his opinions of it) direct and dominate the discussion. Thus Grimm's affinity is more with **Matthew Arnold** and Emerson. The latter especially he praised as a contemplative observer who "sees in every thing the direct line that connects it with the center of life" (1861, in the essay on Emerson that is included in *Neue Essays* of 1865).

Grimm published his essays discriminately in the leading conservative periodicals – Menzel's *Literaturblatt* (Literary page), *Vossische Zeitung* (Voss' newspaper), Haym's *Preussische Jahrbücher* (Prussian yearbooks), Julius Rodenberg's *Deutsche Rundschau* (German review) – or as introductions to books he liked. He then collected his work with almost predictable regularity and, from 1874, in an unchanging format. That year his *Neue Essays über Kunst und Literatur* (1865; New essays on art and literature) appeared in an augmented edition of some 500 pages under the title of *Fünfzehn Essays* (Fifteen essays). Three more collections (1875, 1882, 1890) of 15 essays followed, and finally three volumes of *Fragmente* (1900 and 1902). Each single book is so arranged as to form a variegated entity of complementary segments and is in turn expanded in the manner of concentric circles by its subsequent companion pieces. When taken all together, they form what Klaus Günther Just (in *Von der Gründerzeit biz zur Gegenwart*, 1973) has called an "essayistic cosmos in miniature."

The collection of 1874 can serve as a typical example of how one part of this harmonious order was put together. Its table of contents lists essays on **Voltaire**, Frederick the Great and Macaulay, Goethe in Italy, **Schiller** and Goethe, Goethe and his *Elective Affinities*, Goethe and Suleika (i.e. his beloved Marianne von Willemer, who had befriended Grimm late in life), Goethe and Luise Seidler, Heinrich von Kleist's burial place, Lord Byron and **Leigh Hunt**, Alexander von Humboldt, Schleiermacher (a review of Dilthey's unfinished book), Herr von Varnhagen's diaries, (the literary historian) Georg Gervinus, Dante and the latest struggles in Italy, Ralph Waldo Emerson. Grimm presents these personages as topics in the manner of a Socratic conversation in which he himself slips into many roles and tries out any number of perspectives feigning objections, comparing, introducing private recollections, quoting with approval and reserve, embellishing his thoughts with metaphorical flourishes and imagined confessions, shifting from sensual immediacy to theoretical reasoning and interpretive summary. Always, however, he comes back to his personal opinions, sometimes casually, later on more sententiously and with the phrases of conventional wisdom.

Grimm abhorred the pedantry of historicist positivism which defined the professional ethic of his academic colleagues. But his own epigonic conservatism and his lack of interest in the living arts of his time had become a serious liability by the 1880s. More and more he wrote necrologies and commemorative appreciations (including reflections on statues and tombs), conceding that he had run out of worthy subjects and finding it difficult to enter into any current debate with his earlier enthusiastic devotion. Time had overtaken him – but not forever. During the 1940s he was rediscovered by those educated burghers who sought refuge from barbarism once again in the refined consolations of their classicist heritage.

MICHAEL WINKLER

Biography
Born 6 January 1828 in Kassel. Tutored privately by Leopold von Ranke; studied law and philology at the Universities of Berlin and Bonn. Married Gisela von Arnim, 1870. Professor of the history of modern art, University of Berlin, from 1873. Awards: honorary degree from Harvard University. Died in Berlin, 16 June 1901.

Selected Writings

Essays and Related Prose
Essays, 1859
Die Venus von Milo; Rafael und Michel Angelo, 1864; first essay as
    The Venus of Milo, translated by Alice M. Hawes, 1868
Neue Essays über Kunst und Literatur, 1865; enlarged edition, as
    Fünfzehn Essays: Erste Folge, 1874
*Zehn ausgewählte Essays zur Einführung in das Studium der
    neueren Kunst*, 1871; revised edition, 1883
Fünfzehn Essays: Neue Folge, 1875
Goethe, 2 vols., 1876–77; edited by Wilhelm Hansen, 1948; as *Das
    Leben Goethes*, edited by Reinhard Buchwald, 1939; as *The Life
    and Times of Goethe*, translated by Sarah Holland Adams, 1880
Fünfzehn Essays: Dritte Folge, 1882
Essays on Literature, translated by Sarah Holland Adams, 1885; as
    Literature, 1886
Fünfzehn Essays: Vierte Folge: Aus den letzten fünf Jahren, 1890
Beiträge zur deutschen Culturgeschichte, 1897
Fragmente, 3 vols., 1900–02
Aufsätze zur Kunst, edited by Reinhold Steig, 1915
Aufsätze zur Literatur, edited by Reinhold Steig, 1915
Deutsche Künstler: Sieben Essais, edited by Reinhard Buchwald,
    1942
Essays, edited by Rolf Welz, 1964

Other writings: plays, poetry, a novel, biographies of Michelangelo
(1860–63) and Raphael (1886), and correspondence (including with
Ralph Waldo Emerson).

Further Reading

Berger, Bruno, *Der Essay: Form und Geschichte*, Berne: Francke,
    1964
Haas, Gerhard, *Essay*, Stuttgart: Metzler, 1969
Hiebel, Friedrich, "Ralph Waldo Emerson und Herman Grimm," in
    his *Biographik und Essayistik: Zur Geschichte der schönen
    Wissenschaften*, Berne and Munich: Francke, 1970: 97–120
Jenkel, Gertrud, *Herman Grimm als Essayist* (dissertation),
    Hamburg: University of Hamburg, 1948
Rohner, Ludwig, *Der deutsche Essay: Materialien zur Geschichte
    und Ästhetik einer literarischen Gattung*, Neuwied and Berlin:
    Luchterhand, 1966
Strasser, René, *Herman Grimm: Zum Problem des Klassizismus*,
    Zurich: Atlantis, 1972

Groulx, Lionel

French Canadian, 1878–1967

A pioneer in many fields – historian, professor, lecturer, orator,
preacher, storyteller, novelist, journalist, polemicist, essayist –
Father (l'Abbé), later Canon, Lionel Groulx was the most
influential, controversial French Canadian intellectual in the
first half, if not two-thirds, of the 20th century. As Susan
Trofimenkoff explains (1973), "He developed François-Xavier
Garneau's view of the Conquest as a disaster and his idea of
history as a struggle by examining the post-Conquest period."
Thirty years after his death, books and articles are still
published about his conception of State, Church, history,
language and culture, and politics. Was he a racist because
he wrote the novel *L'Appel de la race* (1922; *The Iron Wedge*)?
Was he a Quebec separatist or a French Canadian nationalist?
A democrat, monarchist, or fascist? Everyone knows his or
her own particular Groulx, whose name has been given to a
mountain, a subway station, streets, colleges, and other institutions. He had a large audience (of both friends and opponents); his folk sketches and souvenirs of "old days, old ways,"
Les Rapaillages (1916; Haycocks), was a bestseller.

There is no doubt that he was a conservative, traditional,
right-wing citizen and historian. But he was also a dynamic,
youthful, imaginative man and writer, and above all, a freelance scholar, a free-spoken lecturer, an independent priest,
and a committed man of action. Groulx was never a pure
theoretician or researcher, but a well-documented erudite and
popularizer of knowledge. Beginning with his first book, *Une
croisade d'adolescents* (1912; A crusade of adolescents), he
launched generations of young people on moral, spiritual,
political, and patriotic crusades. Among his best-known disciples are Jean Drapeau, Montreal's longtime mayor, and André
Laurendeau, Bloc Populaire's leader, *Le Devoir* (The duty)
editor, and royal commissioner (on bilinguism and biculturalism in Canada, 1962).

A few of Groulx's students or readers became respected
scholars. Michel Brunet, Guy Frégault, and Maurice Séguin
built with and without their master a modern and complete
history department at the University of Montreal. They were
laymen, more scientific, methodical, and critical than Groulx.
His devotion to religion, language, and culture is balanced by
their interest in economics and social classes. This so-called
Montreal School (in opposition to quiet Quebec City as well
as to Ottawa or Toronto) was more radical and systematic
than Groulx in political and national matters. If Groulx is the
ancestor, this trio is the triple grandfather of the new nationalism that aims at Quebec sovereignty in or out of Canadian
Federation.

Contrary to his reluctant followers, Groulx is more a generalist than a specialist (of modern French Canadian history). If
not a true novelist – *L'Appel de la race* and *Au Cap Blomidon*
(1932; At Cape Blomidon) are more propaganda than fiction
– he is a vivid *raconteur*, a picturesque sketcher when he
evokes old-timers, draws children, grandmothers, farmers,
and craftsmen as well as explorers, missionaries, pioneers, and
heroes. For him, time is closely knit to both individual
and collective memory. The past is neither driver nor owner
(men are not slaves); the past is not God, but one of His
prophets. It is from this perspective that one should read *Chez
nos ancêtres* (1920; Among our ancestors) and other ethnological essays, *Notre maître, le passé* (1924–44; Our master,
the past) and other collections of portraits and edifying examples, *La Découverte du Canada* (1934; The discovery of
Canada) and other epic poems in prose. Lionel Groulx himself
is now *passé*, a part of history rather than an historian, but
he is still living (in a kind of purgatory) as an essayist.

LAURENT MAILHOT

Biography

Lionel Adolphe Groulx. Born 13 January 1878 in Vaudreuil,
Quebec. Studied classics at the seminary of Sainte-Thérèse-de-
Blainville; theology in Montreal and Rome, D.Th., 1908;
philosophy, literature, and history at the University of Fribourg,
Switzerland, 1908–09. Ordained priest, 1903. Taught humanities at
the Collège de Valleyfield, 1901–06, 1909–15; first chair in
Canadian history, University of Montreal, 1915–49. Elected to the
Royal Society of Canada, 1918. Lecturer or visiting professor at the

Sorbonne and the Institut Catholique, Paris, and at schools in Lyons and Lille, 1931. Founding editor, *L'Action Française*, 1920–28; founder, the Institute of the History of French America, 1946, and editor of its journal *Revue d'Histoire de l'Amérique Française*, 1948–67; contributor to *Le Devoir* and *L'Action Nationale*. Awards: French Academy Prize, 1931; Tyrrell Medal, 1948; Duvernay Prize, 1952, Léo-Parizeau Medal, 1963; honorary degrees from four universities. Died in Montreal, 23 May 1967.

Selected Writings

Essays and Related Prose
Une croisade d'adolescents, 1912
Les Rapaillages (vieilles choses, vieilles gens), 1916
La Naissance d'une race, 1919
Chez nos ancêtres, 1920
Notre maître, le passé, 3 vols., 1924–44
Le Français au Canada, 1932
La Découverte du Canada: Jacques Cartier, 1934
Orientations, 1935
Directives, 1937
Pourquoi nous sommes divisés: Une réponse du chanoine Lionel Groulx, 1943; as *Why We Are Divided: A Reply from Canon Lionel Groulx*, translated by Gordon O. Rothney, 1943
L'Indépendance du Canada, 1949
Constantes de vie, 1967
Lionel Groulx (selections), edited by Benoît Lacroix, 1967
Abbé Groulx: Variations on a Nationalist Theme, edited by Susan Trofimenkoff, translated by Joanne L'Heureux, 1973

Other writings: two novels (*L'Appel de la race* [*The Iron Wedge*], 1922; *Au Cap Blomidon*, 1932), four volumes of *Mémoires*, several volumes of diaries, speeches, lectures, portraits, biographies, and letters, and important historical studies (including *Nos luttes constitutionnelles*, 1915–16; *La Confédération canadienne*, 1918; *La Naissance d'une race*, 1919; *Lendemains de conquête*, 1920; *Vers l'émancipation*, 1921; *Histoire du Canada français depuis la découverte*, 4 vols., 1950–52; *Notre grande aventure: L'Empire français en Amérique du Nord, (1535–1760)*, 1958).

Bibliographies
Hamel, Réginald, John Hare, and Paul Wyczynski, *Dictionnaire des auteurs de langue française en Amérique du Nord*, Montreal: Fides, 1989
Lemire, Maurice, editor, *Dictionnaire des œuvres littéraires du Québec*, Montreal: Fides, 6 vols., 1978–94

Further Reading
L'Action Nationale issue on Groulx, 57, no. 10 (June 1968): 929–1115
Asselin, Olivar, *L'Œuvre de l'abbé Groulx*, Montreal: Bibliothèque de l'Action Française, 1923
Delisle, Esther, *Le Traître et le Juif*, Montreal: l'Étincelle, 1992
Éthier-Blais, Jean, *Le Siècle de l'abbé Groulx*, Montreal: Leméac, 1993
Filion, Maurice, editor, *Hommage à Lionel Groulx*, Montreal: Leméac, 1978
Frégault, Guy, *Lionel Groulx tel qu'en lui-même*, Montreal: Leméac, 1978
Gaboury, Jean-Pierre, *Le Nationalisme de Lionel Groulx: Aspects idéologiques*, Ottawa: Éditions de l'Université d'Ottawa, 1970
Ricard, François, "Lionel Groulx/Action française/État français," *Voix et Images* 9 (1975): 11–33
Trofimenkoff, Susan, Introduction to *Abbé Groulx: Variations on a Nationalist Theme* by Groulx, edited and translated by Joanne L'Heureux and Trofimenkoff, Vancouver, Calgary, Toronto, and Montreal: Copp Clark, 1973
Voix et Images issue on Groulx, 19 (Autumn 1993)

Guicciardini, Francesco
Italian, 1483–1540

Francesco Guicciardini's fame rests on his statesmanship and his historical-political writings, namely the *Storia fiorentina* (*The History of Florence*), *Dialogo del reggimento di Firenze* (*Dialogue on the Government of Florence*), *Ricordi politici e civili* (Political and civil memoirs; translated as *Maxims and Reflections*), *Considerazioni intorno ai Discorsi del Machiavelli* (Considerations on Machiavelli's *Discourses*), and his masterpiece, *Storia d'Italia* (*The History of Italy*). His works also include many orations, discourses, memoirs, reports, and letters dealing with those problems of internal and foreign policy that he faced as an ambassador, political adviser, military leader, and governor in the service of the Florentine Republic, the Medici, and Popes Leo X, Adrian VI, and Clement VII. But the publication of Guicciardini's personal and political correspondence, of which 13 volumes have so far appeared, is still to be completed. The importance of Guicciardini's works lies in the fact that their author was the protagonist or observer of the events represented in their pages, and that he was personally acquainted with many figures peopling his narrative. His opinions are today still the most valuable commentary on a crucial period of Italian political history.

None of Guicciardini's works was published in his lifetime. Not until 1561, 21 years after his death, was *The History of Italy* published in Florence by one of his nephews. The first edition comprised only the first 16 books of the work; the next four were published separately in Venice in 1564. However, three centuries passed before the remainder of Guicciardini's works were published by Giuseppe Canestrini in ten volumes under the title of *Opere inedite* (1857–67; Unpublished works). After this edition, other minor works were discovered, the most important of which is the *Cose fiorentine* (Florentine affairs), published in 1945. *The History of Italy* met with success abroad shortly after the first Italian edition. In 1579 in London there appeared the first English translation by G. Fenton dedicated to Queen Elizabeth; two more editions were printed in 1599 and 1618; the last, and most remarkable, was by Sidney Alexander in 1969. By the end of the 16th century the *History* was also translated into French, Latin, Spanish, German, and Flemish.

Guicciardini was an aristocrat by birth and a lawyer by training, and his ambition was aided by a cold, lucid intelligence. He entered public life in 1512 when he was appointed ambassador to the court of Ferdinand the Catholic of Spain, where he resided for two years. When he organized the anti-imperial League of Cognac and the military operations of the pontifical forces in 1526, Guicciardini became one of the important players in a crucial stage of Renaissance Italian history.

His writing was informed by the ideals of Florentine independence, freedom of Italy from foreign domination, opposition to both democratic extremism and tyrannical danger, and self-interest, the famous "particulare," which made Guicciardini a man hard to like and drove forward his career at the expense of his principles. *The History of Florence* (wr. 1508–09) covers his city's history from 1378 to 1509 and is distinguished by characteristics rare in a youthful work: a careful search for both facts and causation, mature and objective judgment, and a sharp depiction of historical characters. From the *Dialogue on the Government of Florence* (wr. 1525) emerges Guicciardini's vision of the government of Florence based on the rule by the "ottimati," the wise and reputable men, dictated by the author's experience.

Maxims and Reflections is recognized as one of the outstanding documents of a time in crisis and transition and, like *The History of Italy*, has been translated into many languages. It is made up of two series of **maxims** and **aphorisms**, written between 1512 and 1528 and collected by Guicciardini in 1530, after the authorities of the last Florentine Republican had banished him from Florence. They distill the essence of his experience as a statesman in a realistic and disenchanted spirit, and offer an exceptional insight into the working of the minds and hearts of men in private life, politics, and society.

The *Considerazioni intorno ai Discorsi del Machiavelli*, also written during his banishment from Florence, reveals the author's distinctive intellectual traits. Unlike his fellow citizen and sometime friend **Niccolò Machiavelli**, Guicciardini had no patience for theory. Machiavelli liked to move from general theory to the particular, Guicciardini from the particular to the general. He adhered to an empiricism that clipped the flight of the speculation that marks out Machiavelli's writings, and refused to take examples from antiquity as models for contemporary behavior and action. Guicciardini taught that the living experience is everything and warned against using models of ancient historiography, especially Roman history, as standards of judgment and guides for making decisions and taking actions.

The pragmatism and the lesson of experience that pervade the *Considerazioni* are worked into the maze of events and figures that people *The History of Italy*, which covers the period from the death of Lorenzo il Magnifico in 1492 to that of Pope Clement VII in 1534. Discarding the method used by the humanists, Guicciardini achieved a breakthrough in the writing of history. The humanists' method neglected or used only a few primary sources, aiming instead at literary eloquence and elegance and at inspiring readers with the "correct" standards of thought and action. Guicciardini, an anti-rhetorician if ever there was one, wrote the history of a whole geographical unit, following the thread of many events, using all available histories and archival documents (including those of the Florentine Republic, which he brought home). Unlike humanistic history, which dealt with only one city or region of Italy, Guicciardini's *History* brings to life the entire world of the peninsula in its complexity and, through the repercussions of its politics abroad, also that of other countries. He dictated excerpts from documents to his scribe in chronological order, then fused and reshaped the material, placing in the margins his agreement or disagreement and adding information of his own and of others. His narration shows that moral virtues have nothing to do with political success or failure, but rather with the protagonists' response to the events that touch them and with the interactions of their passions. Individuals who act out of passion, prejudice, blindness, and insight are the sole agents of historical change. Guicciardini's method has produced the classic portrait of a country in decline, illustrating how the rulers of the Italian states had gradually been deprived of all control over their own destinies.

Over-elaborate, dense, bulging with facts and details, here and there weighed down by long winding sentences and paragraphs often presenting an historical and conceptual horizon too wide to maintain comfortably, *The History of Italy* has lost the appeal it exerted on earlier generations of readers and critics. But it is only in this work that one is able to contemplate the complex structure of the Italian Renaissance and to find both the abundance of blood that coursed through the veins of its public life and the heart that regulated it: for the past four centuries the *History* has been ransacked as the chief source of Renaissance history and politics. The work offers unparalleled interpretations of events and figures; placed in ample perspectives and drawn with the broad and precise brushstrokes of a masterly hand, they have become historiographical icons: portraits of sickly but warlike Charles VIII, ambitious but bungling Emperor Maximilian, Pope Clement VII and his tortured personality; the state of Italy at the death of Lorenzo the Magnificent; the discovery of America, the invention and use of guns and gunpowder, the appearance of syphilis, the threat posed by the Turks and Luther to Christendom; the picture of gory battles and the role of bravery and cowardice; the stunning corruption of Pope Borgia, the source of the Christian church's temporal power, the sack of Rome, and the siege of Florence. The breadth and depth of representation and interpretation explains why, immediately after the *History* appeared in print, it was elevated to the rank of a masterpiece equal to the great works of ancient historiography.

ALFREDO BONADEO

Biography

Born 6 March 1483 in Florence. Studied civil law in Florence, Ferrara, and Padua, from 1498, doctorate, 1505. Married Maria Salviati secretly, 1507, publicly, 1508. Ambassador to Spain, 1512–14; replaced his father as one of the Seventeen Reformers, 1514; appointed one of the Eight of Ward, and of the Signoria, 1514; appointed consistorial advocate by Pope Leo X, 1515; named governor of Modena by Leo X, 1516, and of Reggio, 1517; became close friends with Machiavelli, 1521; appointed commissary general of the papal army against the French, 1521; named president of Romagna by Pope Clement VII, 1524; appointed lieutenant general of the papal army in the League of Cognac, 1526; banished from Florence, 1530; appointed governor of Bologna by Clement VII, 1531; returned to Florence, 1534; political advisor to Duke Alessandro de' Medici, 1534–37; retired after Alessandro's assassination and the rise of Cosimo de' Medici, 1537. Died in Florence, 22 May 1540.

Selected Writings

Essays and Related Prose
Storia d'Italia, 20 vols., 1561–64; edited by Silvana Seidel Menchi, 3 vols., 1971, Emanuella Scarano, 1981, and Ettore Mazzoli, 1988; as *The History of Italy*, translated by G. Fenton, 1579, Austin Parke Goddard, 10 vols., 1753–56, edited by John R. Hale, translated by Cecil Grayson, 1966, and edited and translated by Sidney Alexander, 1969
Considerazioni intorno ai Discorsi del Machiavelli, in *Opere inedite*, vol. 1, edited by Giuseppe Canestrini, 1857
Ricordi politici e civili, in *Opere inedite*, vol. 1, edited by Giuseppe Canestrini, 1857, Roberto Palmarocchi, 1931, Raffaele Spongano, 1951, Ettore Barelli, 1977, Sergio Marconi, 1983, Tommaso Bavaro, 1990, Tommaso Albarini, 1991, and Emanuella Scarano, 1991; as *Counsels and Reflections*, translated by Ninian Hill

Thomson, 1890; as *Maxims and Reflections*, translated by Mario Domandi, 1965; selection as *The Maxims*, translated by Emma Martin, 1845

Dialogo del reggimento di Firenze, in *Opere inedite*, vol. 2, edited by Giuseppe Canestrini, 1858, Roberto Palmarocchi, 1932, and Emanuella Scarano, 1970; as *Dialogue on the Government of Florence*, edited and translated by Alison Brown, 1994

Storia fiorentina, in *Opere inedite*, vol. 2, edited by Giuseppe Canestrini, 1858, Roberto Palmarocchi, 1931, and Emanuella Scarano, 1991; as *The History of Florence*, translated by Cecil Grayson, 1965, and Mario Domandi, 1970

Cose fiorentine, edited by Roberto Ridolfi, 1945

Selected Writings, edited by Cecil Grayson, translated by Margaret Grayson, 1965

Other writings: family memoirs and correspondence.

Collected works editions: *Opere inedite*, edited by Giuseppe Canestrini, 10 vols., 1857–67; *Opere*, edited by Vittorio de Caprariis, 1953, and Emanuella Scarano, 1970.

Bibliography

Guicciardini, Paolo, *Contributo alla bibliografia di Francesco Guicciardini*, Florence: Giuntina, 1946; supplements, 1948, 1950

Further Reading

Annali d'Italianistica issue on Guicciardini, 2 (1984)

Bonadeo, Alfredo, "Guicciardini on War and Conquest," *Il Pensiero Politico* 14 (1981): 214–42

Bondanella, Peter E., *Francesco Guicciardini*, Boston: Twayne, 1976

Cochrane, Eric, *Historians and Historiography in the Italian Renaissance*, Chicago: University of Chicago Press, 1981: 295–305

De Sanctis, Francesco, "L'uomo del Guicciardini," in his *Saggi critici*, vol. 3, edited by Luigi Russo, Bari: Laterza, 1963

Francesco Guicciardini 1483–1983: Nel V centenario della nascista, Florence: Olschki, 1984

Gilbert, Felix, *Machiavelli and Guicciardini: Politics and History in Sixteenth-Century Florence*, Princeton, New Jersey: Princeton University Press, 1965

Luciani, Vincent, *Francesco Guicciardini and His European Reputation*, New York: Otto, 1936

Palmarocchi, Roberto, *Studi guicciardiniani*, Florence: Macrì, 1947

Phillips, Mark, *Francesco Guicciardini: The Historian's Craft*, Toronto: University of Toronto Press, 1977

Ridolfi, Roberto, *The Life of Francesco Guicciardini*, London: Routledge and Kegan Paul, 1967; New York: Knopf, 1968

Treves, Paolo, *Il realismo di Francesco Guicciardini*, Florence: La Nuova Italia, 1931

H

Haig-Brown, Roderick

Canadian, 1908–1976

Roderick Haig-Brown approached writing from two perspectives – as a professional and as a literary artist. The former often took precedence, and much of his writing was motivated, in part at least, by the necessity of making a living. He turned out government-sponsored reports, instructional guides, and popular histories for young readers as circumstances and the market demanded, and the greater part of what he wrote, though interesting and entertaining, is of little literary interest. Coupled with the fact that he did his most serious writing in the neglected genre of the informal essay, the amount and variety of his commercial writing has tended to obscure Haig-Brown's literary achievement, and he has received far less attention from critics of Canadian literature than the quality of his essays and his international reputation warrant.

Another barrier to recognition is a common misconception of Haig-Brown as a local, special-interest writer, narrowly concerned with sport fishing in British Columbia. While he lived most of his adult life in the small Vancouver Island community of Campbell River, where he settled after emigrating from England as a young man, Haig-Brown was anything but provincial in his outlook. He served as a judge for over 30 years, was an officer in the Canadian Army during World War II, and later, in addition to becoming Chancellor of the University of Victoria, played leading roles in various private and governmental organizations concerned with sports, parks, and the environment. He was also an avid reader and book collector and knowledgeable about many subjects beyond fishing. Particularly in the 1960s and 1970s, these commitments limited his literary output, but they also allowed him to write with authority on a wide variety of topics and added greatly to the intellectual scope of the essays on fishing and nature, which often digress into discussions of literature, history, sociology, and the human qualities fishing develops.

Notwithstanding his professional nonfiction writing, Haig-Brown discovered his talent as an informal essayist relatively late. Early in his career he concentrated his creative energy mainly on fiction, but partly because of the instructional bent that would later serve him well in his essays, he achieved better results with his animal stories and outdoor adventure fiction for young readers than with his novels for adults. *A River Never Sleeps* (1946), his first collection of informal essays, did not appear until 15 years after his first book, and although it can be seen in retrospect to represent a breakthrough in approach and style, he continued to concentrate on fiction throughout the 1940s. Partly, it may be supposed, because he believed publishers considered the form "dead as hieroglyphics" ("Writer's Notebook: Influences," 1953), it was not until the early 1950s that Haig-Brown devoted himself mainly to writing essays. A writer's "real importance," he observed at this time, "is in the sum of experience that he can share through his writing and in the quality of what he shares . . . provided always that he has the art and skill to transmute them into new meaning" ("Writer's Notebook: Influences"). The experiences that he knew best were, of course, his own; the form that allowed him to express the deeper meaning he considered essential to quality in writing was the informal, **personal essay**.

The best of Haig-Brown's informal essays appear in six collections: *A River Never Sleeps*, *Measure of the Year* (1950), which is more concerned with his family life, his hobbies, and his experience as a local magistrate than with fishing, and the fishing tetralogy for which he is best known. In *Fisherman's Spring* (1951), Haig-Brown explores the deep significance fishing holds for him personally. *Fisherman's Winter* (1954) grows out of a fishing trip to Argentina and Chile and is on the whole a more factual book than *Spring*. *Fisherman's Summer* (1959) shows Haig-Brown's growing concern with conservation, while *Fisherman's Fall* (1964), in its fascination with game fish themselves, particularly salmon, and their underwater environment, extends this concern. All six collections demonstrate his ability to combine complex, original imagery, which is particularly effective in capturing action, with accurate, minutely observed details. They also benefit from a style so clear and fluent that it makes underestimating the complexity of the ideas being expressed all too easy. These books are not simply collections of previously published essays, but carefully structured, thematically unified works in themselves. In the essays of these six books at least, Haig-Brown was able to put aside sales expectations to write as a conscious artist, aware of his position as an inheritor of the British tradition of reflective rural writing, especially the fishing strain begun by Izaak Walton (with **The Compleat Angler**, 1653) and Charles Cotton.

Although he savored its challenge, excitement, and fun as much as anyone, Haig-Brown regarded fishing as a thinking person's sport, and in writing his fishing essays he made thinking people his primary audience. Though fishermen made up a sizable portion of his actual audience, those fishermen who were content to pursue their sport without reflecting on what it had to offer beyond pleasant recreation remained secondary. Technique, tackle, and the size of the catch were far less important to Haig-Brown than the insight to be had from a sport that was "more than a sport," a sport that offered an "intimate exploration of a part of the world hidden from the eyes and minds of ordinary people . . . a way of thinking and doing, a way of reviving the mind and body . . ." ("The Art of Fishing," 1951). Through the process of writing his essays, Haig-Brown's exploration of fishing and the world of fish became an exploration of self as well, and as central to his achievement as the narrative and descriptive excellence, for which he is more often praised, is his success in articulating the psychological, philosophical, and spiritual significance fishing and nature held for him.

WILLIAM CONNOR

See also Nature Essay

Biography

Roderick Langmere Haig-Brown. Born 21 February 1908 in Lancing, Sussex, England. Studied at Charterhouse, Godalming, Surrey. Emigrated to the United States, 1926, then to Canada, 1927. Worked as a logger, trapper, fisherman, and guide in Washington state and British Columbia, 1926–29. Married Ann Elmore, 1934: one son and three daughters. Major in the Canadian Army, 1939–45. Provincial magistrate and judge, Campbell River Children's and Family Court, British Columbia, 1942–75. Chancellor, University of Victoria, British Columbia, 1970–73. Also a frequent television broadcaster. Awards: Canadian Library Association Book of the Year Medal, 1947, 1964; Governor-General's Citation, 1948; Crandell Conservation Trophy, 1955; Vicky Metcalf Award, for children's book, 1966; honorary degree from the University of British Columbia. Died in Campbell River, British Columbia, 9 October 1976.

Selected Writings

Essays and Related Prose
A River Never Sleeps, 1946
Measure of the Year, 1950
Fisherman's Spring, 1951
Fisherman's Winter, 1954
Fisherman's Summer, 1959
Fisherman's Fall, 1964
The Master and His Fish: From the World of Roderick Haig-Brown, edited by Valerie Haig-Brown, 1981
Writings and Reflections: From the World of Roderick Haig-Brown, edited by Valerie Haig-Brown, 1982

Other writings: three novels (*Pool and Rapid*, 1932; *Timber*, 1942; *On the Highest Hill*, 1949), a collection of short stories, ten books for children, and books about fishing.

Further Reading

Keith, W. J., "Roderick Haig-Brown," *Canadian Literature* 71 (Winter 1976): 7–20
Robertson, Anthony, *Above Tide: Reflections on Roderick Haig-Brown*, Madeira Park, British Columbia: Harbour, 1984

Hamm, Peter

German, 1937–

German poet Peter Hamm plays a major role as an essayist in Germany's literary life today. However, he is neither as recognized, nor as prolific, as his older colleague **Hans Magnus Enzensberger**. Though Hamm's essayistic writings are rare, they are nevertheless unique in the way they treat their subjects. Using an intimate, plain, yet lucid style, Hamm conveys the sense that he knows personally all the authors he is writing about, even if they are removed in time (like **Goethe**) or in place (like the Portuguese poet Fernando Pessoa). Of course, Hamm does know many contemporary writers personally, and his portraits of them are intriguing accounts of their lives and works. But even if he has not met an author face to face, he takes his readers on a haunting trip into the intellectual and emotional worlds of those he is portraying. Since it is always the lives of his subjects that most interest Hamm – he once wrote that he does not have faith in people who claim to be interested only in an author's work – his approach is decidedly nonacademic and as such never claims objectivity or bothers itself with the latest theories. Instead, Hamm leaves enough space for readers to draw their own conclusions from the careful, almost caressing way in which he presents biographical details intertwined with the writings of both well-known and lesser-known writers.

Hamm's personalized yet critical method is best described by looking at one of his essays, a speech on Ingeborg Bachmann. Besides meeting her several times throughout his life, he also directed a film portrait on her. In "Rede zum 60. Geburtstag von Ingeborg Bachmann" (1986; Speech on the 60th anniversary of Ingeborg Bachmann's birth), Hamm asks himself and his audience: "What is it that I needed from Ingeborg Bachmann?" By confronting the audience with such a simple, seemingly naive, and egocentric question, Hamm invites us to ask that same question about the woman who had then already been dead for 13 years. This invitation to communal self-reflection creates an immediate bond between the listener/reader and Bachmann, the subject. At the same time, however, Hamm warns us that when we think we are close to really understanding an author, it is usually the reflection of our own self that we are projecting onto the perceived Other. Thus, ultimately, Hamm never answers his opening question. Instead, he takes his audience on a journey to Søren Kierkegaard, Franz Kafka, **E. M. Cioran**, and **T. S. Eliot**, comparing their responses to literature with his own feelings as a 16-year-old boy when reading the first lines of the celebrated poet. He goes on to describe some of his personal encounters with Bachmann, which he illuminates by references to lines of her poetry. The outcome is a description of her life and writings as the journey of a holy martyr, finally raising the question: What is it that *I* need from Ingeborg Bachmann?

René Wellek's insight, that the combination of poet and critic in one person is not always successful, is certainly justified in many cases. For Peter Hamm, the opposite is true. His essays never lack a critical perspective. This can perhaps be explained by his participation in Gruppe 47, the major literary movement of postwar Germany. The experience of being exposed to the critique of friends and colleagues – as a poet – at the meetings of the Gruppe, while at the same time developing his own critical method further, sharpened his literary instinct at a young age. Writing for the two major periodicals in German intellectual life, *Die Zeit* (The age) and *Der Spiegel* (The mirror), Hamm has often been among the first to respond in public to new and upcoming contemporaries, such as Peter Handke, Thomas Bernhard, or Martin Walser. Because of his role as a poet-critic, he is also concerned with the aims and purposes of literary criticism. He wrote about the self-image of the critic in the late 1960s and mediated a selection of different critics' reflections on their profession by editing the volume *Kritik – von wem/für wen/wie: Eine Selbstdarstellung deutscher Kritiker* (1968; Criticism – by whom/for whom/how: a self-representation of German critics).

In his essayistic writings, Hamm is mainly influenced by French philosophical thought, more specifically by **Blaise Pascal**, **Paul Valéry**, and above all **Simone Weil**. Her exploration of the loss of religion and faith in modern times is a recurring theme for Hamm, inspiring many of his essays. Because of a difficult childhood during World War II and its aftermath, Hamm turned even as a teenager to non-German cultures and avant-garde movements. He soon developed a fundamental knowledge of other European cultures, editing and translating collections of Swedish and Czechoslovakian poetry, as well as poems by Artur Lundkvist and Jesse Thoor. Hamm's ambivalent feelings toward the German tradition are best characterized by the title of his collected essays: *Der Wille zur Ohnmacht* (1992; The will to powerlessness), a play on **Nietzsche**'s *Der Wille zur Macht* (1901; *The Will to Power*), reflecting his critical, yet modest and personalized reexamination of traditionally accepted authorities.

AGNES C. MÜLLER

Biography

Born 27 February 1937 in Munich. Studied at Catholic boarding schools in Baden-Württemberg: left school at age 14. Worked for a time at a small publishing house; music, cultural, and literary critic, Bayerischer Rundfunk radio station, Munich, from 1960. Film director and producer: subjects included Ingeborg Bachmann, Heinrich Böll, Hanns Eisler, Hans Werner Henze, Alfred Brendel. Has one daughter.

Selected Writings

Essays and Related Prose
Der Wille zur Ohnmacht, 1992
Deutschland – du mein Traum: Ein Familienleben in einer menschenverachtenden Diktatur, 1994

Other writings: poetry. Also edited and translated anthologies of German, Swedish, and Czech poetry.

Harper's

American magazine, 1850–

Harper's New Monthly Magazine appeared on the American scene in June 1850, the creation of four Harper brothers – James, John, Joseph Wesley, and Fletcher – who had been in the book publishing business since 1817. The magazine was, at first, largely an advertising vehicle for the firm's book publication, though the Harper brothers declared in the first issue their intention to bring "within the reach of the great mass of the American people, an immense amount of useful and entertaining reading matter," most of which was otherwise inaccessible to these potential readers. The magazine was designed to be eclectic, a compendium of materials found in other periodicals. And because the Harper brothers – especially Fletcher, who was the real animating force behind the magazine – believed that Americans were not completely ready for a purely nationalistic fare, it was also an early goal of the magazine to present English fiction (especially serialized novels) and articles to an American audience for whom writers such as **Ralph Waldo Emerson**, James Russell Lowell, **Oliver Wendell Holmes**, and John Whittier were too highbrow. (In 1857, this group of Yankee humanists would help found the *Atlantic Monthly*.) Such presentations were easy to accomplish, since international copyright laws had not yet been created and American publishers could pirate all the writings they wanted from English books and periodicals. Within six months of its birth, *Harper's*, under the editorship of Henry J. Raymond, had a circulation of 50,000.

While Fletcher Harper and the early editors (Raymond and Alfred H. Guernsey) relied heavily on English writings, they were also quick to recognize, at a time when most American magazines focused on localism, the possibilities of a national publication. It took only a few years for *Harper's* not only to find for itself a greater purpose than advertising, but also to transform itself into a magazine with something approaching a national audience. Neither as highbrow as the *Atlantic*, nor as newsy and up-to-the-minute as *Harper's Weekly*, which Fletcher Harper added in 1857, it was a general family magazine aimed at a large common denominator of American readership. Among its nonfiction, it carried battle sketches from the Civil War, as well as **travel essays** about trips to the Western frontier by prominent writers such as Horace Greeley and **John Muir**.

Henry Mills Alden assumed the editorship in 1869, and after Fletcher Harper died a few years later Alden was chiefly responsible for the growing dignity, distinction, maturity, and range of the magazine during the later years of the 19th century. Alden would remain editor for 50 years, until 1919. Under his guidance and within the growing genteel tradition of middle- and upper-class American culture, *Harper's* steered away from mass popularity and became a select magazine for respectable and well-to-do gentlefolk of nice tastes. It was, in fact, preeminent in the golden age of the old-fashioned family magazine, rivaled only by the younger *Century* and the still younger *Scribner's* – with the *Atlantic Monthly* as a somewhat more austere competitor.

In the 1890s and the early 1900s, new magazines began to appear which pinpointed the middle class, or the average 20th-century Americans – unintellectual and half-educated, but wide awake, confident, and ready to spend their money freely. Many of the new magazines of that time were sensational, vulgar, and venal. But they were such financial successes that they were eventually able to buy the best authors away from *Harper's*, *Scribner's*, and *Century*.

In 1925, *Harper's* was saved by a daring move by the editor Thomas Bucklin Wells (1919–31). Wells realized it was no longer practical to appeal to a class or group that was supposed to combine wealth, discrimination, and literary taste. Too many people now had enough money to buy nationally advertised products, and they were mostly satisfied with the journalistic fare provided by the mass-circulation magazines. So he aimed at a somewhat different though overlapping public – thoughtful and discriminating people, of whatever income bracket, who appreciated fine quality, felt a deep sense of responsibility for the national well-being, and possessed genuine intellectual curiosity. He pulled the illustrations out of *Harper's*, put it in a plain brick-orange cover, and went in for a new program focused upon human, energetic, and often controversial articles on the burning issues of the day.

Wells was pointing the magazine not so much toward well-to-do gentlefolk as toward readers who combined brains and taste with a more-than-superficial concern with public affairs. Such was also the direction followed by editors Lee Foster Hartman (1931–41) and Frederick L. Allen (1941–60). In 1955, Allen said that *Harper's* deliberately edited for a minority of educated (though not necessarily formally educated), responsible, intelligent people. In defense of the magazine's relatively small circulation compared to slicker publications, Allen said, "The ignition system is a very small part of an automobile."

Harper's has been an important outlet for essays since its inception. From 1870 to 1920 its important essayists included **Henry James** (many of his travel pieces appeared in the magazine), **Mark Twain**, **William Dean Howells**, and Brander Matthews. **E. B. White**, one of the most influential **personal essayists** of the 20th century, contributed a monthly column called "One Man's Meat" from 1938 to 1943. He was living on a farm in Maine and, from that quiet, rural vantage point, turned a discerning and often humorous eye on a world plunging into war.

Harper's editors from Alden to John Fischer (1960–67) to Lewis Lapham (1976–81, and 1983–) have long insisted that the magazine is "a journal which traffics in ideas," a description borne out in many of its essays about art, politics, and science: Faulkner on segregation in 1956; **E. M. Forster's** "Art for Art's Sake" in 1949; Russell Lynes' famous "Highbrow, Lowbrow, Middlebrow" in 1949; Secretary of War Henry L. Stimson's important 1947 piece, "The Decision to Use the Atomic Bomb"; Vicki Hearne's 1991 "What's Wrong with Animal Rights?"; Gerald Early's 1992 "Their Malcolm, My Problem." At the same time, *Harper's* – especially under the influence of Lapham – has long insisted on a novelistic approach to journalism, in which the writer's function "is to describe and tell a story, not shove an idea down people's throats." The late 1960s and early 1970s saw *Harper's*, under the editorship of Willie Morris (1967–71), become a primary outlet for the **New Journalism**, including writers such as Truman Capote, **Norman Mailer**, **Joan Didion**, and **Tom Wolfe**.

Columns have long been an outlet for essayists, and *Harper's* "The Easy Chair" (now called, for Lewis Lapham's essays, "Notebook") is the oldest column in American journalism. Produced over the years by barely more than half a dozen writers, it has served, in the words of "Easy Chair" contributor John Fischer, "as a lens with a reasonably fixed focus on American life." Though originally intended to be "an agreeable and entertaining collection of literary miscellany," it soon became, and has remained, a place for political and cultural critique, often argumentative in tone and provoking significant controversy.

Like the **New Yorker**, though without the extensive influence on the tone of casual American writing, *Harper's* has a long tradition of publishing **humorous essays**. Besides Twain and White, humorists such as **James Thurber**, **Stephen Leacock**, Roald Dahl, Leo Rosten, and Jean Kerr have appeared in the magazine.

A major overhaul of the magazine in 1983, the fifth of its existence, refined its treatment of essays. Led by Lapham, *Harper's* set out to become, in Lapham's words, "an interpretive rather than an investigative instrument." In contrast to the mass media which Lapham saw as necessarily superficial and lacking in any individual voice or story, *Harper's* strengthened its traditional bias in favor of the essay and short story. Wanting to build even further on *Harper's*' place as the oldest of America's monthly magazines, Lapham said that "if the American experience is about people embarked on the trials of discovery, then both the essay and the short story present themselves as the most useful of the available literary forms – brief and experimental, convenient to the arts of improvisation, easily adapted to different tones of voice or modes of feeling, quickly changed into a confession, a treatise, or a traveler's tale." *Harper's* grasped more firmly onto the essay to counterbalance the less speculative forms of expository prose which it continued to publish. In the mid-1990s, perhaps its most typical essayists are those who range widely over intellectual terrain, incorporating personal stories with incisive ruminations on the defining issues of the times – essayists such as **Barry Lopez**, **Cynthia Ozick**, Joyce Carol Oates, and Stanley Elkin.

Because of financial straits, before 1992 *Harper's* limited itself to printing essays (as well as stories) of no more than seven or eight pages. In 1992, however, with the 1983 overhaul deemed a success (circulation was up to 202,000, from 140,000 in 1983), the magazine instituted a four-times-a-year section called "Folio," in which it began to publish essays and stories of substantial length. As an objective sign of its recent high stature in American literary nonfiction writing, *Harper's* has had more of its essays chosen for inclusion in the annual *Best American Essays* series (begun in 1986) than any other magazine.

DAN ROCHE

Anthologies

Gentlemen, Scholars and Scoundrels: A Treasury of the Best of Harper's Magazine from 1850 to the Present, edited by Horace Knowles, New York: Harper, 1959

Harper Essays, edited by Henry Seidel Canby, New York: Harper, 1927

Humor from Harper's, edited by John Fischer and Lucy Donaldson, New York: Harper, 1961

Six in the Easy Chair, edited by John Fischer, Urbana: University of Illinois Press, 1973

Further Reading

Baldwin, Neil, "Lewis Lapham," *Publishers Weekly*, 5 February 1988: 75–76

Dowgray, John Gray Laird, Jr., *A History of Harper's Literary Magazines, 1850–1900* (dissertation), Madison: University of Wisconsin, 1956
Lapham, Lewis, "Notes on a Newer Journalism," *Harper's*, January 1984: 10–12
Lapham, Lewis, "In the American Grain," *Harper's*, February 1984: 6–10
Lapham, Lewis, "Happy Anniversary," *Harper's*, March 1987: 10–11
Lapham, Lewis, "New Directions," *Harper's*, October 1992: 6–9
Morris, Willie, *New York Days*, Boston: Little Brown, 1993

Havel, Václav

Czech, 1936–

Václav Havel is best known as a playwright and politician, but his essays have always been an important part of his oeuvre. His essayistic work can be divided into three periods. During the 1950s and 1960s, he dwelt primarily on problems of theater and literature. During the 1970s and 1980s, he turned increasingly to problems of cultural policy, politics, and human existence. The latest period, during his presidency of his country since 1989, reflects an obvious turn toward public affairs.

From the end of the 1950s Havel concentrated on theater, including commentaries on his own plays. These essays and reflections were published in journals such as *Divadlo* (Theater), *Host do Domu* (Guest at home), and *Literární Noviny* (Literary news), and collected in *Josef Čapek* (1963). Other essays from this period were devoted to critical analysis of culture and thought. He dealt with politics only sporadically, e.g. in "Na téma opozice" (1968; "On the Theme of an Opposition"), directed against the monopoly on government enjoyed by the Communist Party. Unlike Milan Kundera and other Czech writers, Havel had no illusions concerning the humane nature of communism or the possibility of democratization.

In these early articles the typical features of Havel's style and perspective on the world are already evident. He carried on the tradition of democratic and liberal thought, as established and represented in Czech culture by Karel Havlíček, Tomáš G. Masaryk, the **Čapek** brothers, and Ferdinand Peroutka. As in his plays, Havel's style is factual, accurate, and ironic.

A new period began in the 1970s, not only in Havel's work, but in Czechoslovakian culture as a whole. After the defeat of the "revival" in 1968, many outstanding writers were forbidden to publish their works or to take part in public life. At this time Havel became a leading figure in the organization of underground culture, establishing movements such as *samizdat* publishing, in which works were privately produced and secretly circulated. (Because of such activity Havel was hounded by the police and imprisoned several times.) He began to take more interest in political, cultural, and existential questions. In the open "Dopis Dr. Gustávu Husákovi" (1975; "Letter to Dr. Gustáv Husák"), the Czech president at the time, Havel disclosed the deep moral and spiritual crisis present in Czechoslovakian society, the "order without life" he considered an inseparable part of the more general crisis of human

identity. In the famous, much quoted *Moc bezmocných* (1978; "The Power of the Powerless"), written after the foundation of the Charter 77 human rights group, he analyzed the phenomenon of dissent. Opposed to "living a lie" by colluding with totalitarian ideology, dissidents stress "living in truth." At the same time, Havel denounced the egotism of the current technical and consumer civilization of Western society. He developed these ideas in other essays such as *Politika a svědomí* (1984; "Politics and Conscience"), "Anatomie jedné zdrženlivosti" (1985; "Anatomy of a Reticence"), and "Příběh a totalita" (1987; "Stories and Totalitarianism"), revealing himself to be a modern intellectual whose skepticism is counterbalanced by his belief in transcendental spiritual values. Belief for Havel means "hope as the state of the spirit, not as the state of the world." He considered the moral revival of the individual more important than change in the social order.

Havel formulated many ideas in the **letters** he wrote from prison to his wife Olga between 1979 to 1982, and published in *Dopisy Olze* (1983; *Letters to Olga*). Often taking the form of essays on philosophy, theater, and other subjects, they differ from Havel's other work from the 1970s and 1980s in not being able to deal directly with politics (the letters had to pass through censorship) and hence being more general and oblique considerations of issues.

As the leader of his country since November 1989, Havel has not surprisingly shifted the focus of his writing to problems of public life and politics. His recent essays are less comprehensive than those of the 1970s and 1980s; more and more take the form of speeches. Even in those, however, he preserves his ability to analyze things precisely, his irony and self-irony, and the ideas he has developed in earlier works. In a speech delivered to the United States Congress in February 1990, Havel said: ". . . we are greatly influenced by a malignant and entirely selfish impression that man is the top of all creatures and hence can do anything he wants." The salvation of the contemporary world he sees in the turn toward "human heart, human consideration, human humility, and human responsibility." His essays – whether in *samizdat* publications, as letters from prison, or as presidential speeches – have consistently reflected this humanitarian perspective.

JIŘÍ HOLÝ

Biography

Born 5 October 1936 in Prague. Laboratory technician, 1951–55. Studied at a technical college, 1955–57, and the Academy of Arts, Prague, 1962–66. Military service in the Czechoslovak Army, 1957–59. Worked at the ABC Theater, Prague, 1959–60, and the Divadlo na Zábradlí (Theater on the bannister), Prague, 1960–68. Married Olga Šplíchalová (died, 1996), 1964. Passport confiscated because writings considered subversive, 1969; imprisoned for various charges of subversion or behavior opposed to the government, 1977, 1978–79, 1979–83, 1989. Cofounder, Charter 77 human rights group, 1977, and the Committee for the Defense of the Unjustly Prosecuted (VONS), 1978; member of the editorial board, and regular contributor, *Lidové Noviny* (The people's news) *samizdat* newspaper, 1987–89. Cofounder and leader, Občanské Fórum (Civic forum) political party, 1989. President of the Czech and Slovak Federal Republic, 1989–92, and of the Czech Republic, since 1993. Married Dagmar Veskrnova, 1997. Awards: many, including Obie Award, 1968, 1970; Austrian State Prize, 1969; Prix Plaisir du Théâtre, 1981; Palach Prize, 1981; Erasmus Prize, 1986; Olof Palme

Prize, 1989; UNESCO Bolívar Prize, 1990; Friedrich-Ebert Foundation Political Book of the Year Award, 1990; Malaparte Prize, 1990; Legion of Honor Grand Cross, 1990; Charlemagne Prize, 1991; Averell Harriman Democracy Award, 1991; B'nai B'rith Prize, 1991; Freedom Award, 1991; Raoul Wallenberg Human Rights Award, 1991; Leonhard-Frank-Ring, 1992; Indira Gandhi Prize, 1993; European Cultural Society Award, 1993; Order of the White Eagle (Poland), 1993; Golden Honorary Order of Freedom (Slovenia), 1993; honorary degrees from over a dozen universities.

Selected Writings

Essays and Related Prose
Josef Čapek: Dramatik a jevištní výtvarník, with Věra Ptáčková, 1963
Protokoly, 1966
Moc bezmocných, 1978; as "The Power of the Powerless," in *The Power of the Powerless: Citizens Against the State in Central-Eastern Europe*, edited by John Keane, 1985
Dopisy Olze (letters to his wife from prison), 1983; as *Letters to Olga, June 1979 to September 1982*, translated by Paul Wilson, 1988
Výzva k transcendenci, 1984
O lidskou identitu: Úvahy, fejetony, protesty, polemiky, prohlášení a rozhovory z let, 1969–1979, edited by Vilem Prečan and Alexander Tomsky, 1984
Politika a svědomí, 1984; as "Politics and Conscience," translated by Erazim Kohák and Roger Scruton, in *Living in Truth*, edited by Jan Vladislav, 1986
Living in Truth (also includes essays by other writers addressed to Havel), edited by Jan Vladislav, 1986
Do různých stran: Eseje a články z let 1983–1989, edited by Vilem Prečan, 1989
Projevy: Leden-červen 1990 (speeches), edited by Vilem Prečan, 1990
Open Letters: Selected Prose 1965–1990, edited by Paul Wilson, 1991
Letní přemítání, 1991; as *Summer Meditations: On Politics, Morality and Civility in a Time of Transition*, translated by Paul Wilson, 1992
Vážení občane (speeches), 1992
Čtyři eseje, 1993

Other writings: many plays (including *Zahradní slavnost* [*The Garden Party*], 1963; *Vyrozumění* [*The Memorandum*], 1965; *Ztížená možnost soustředění* [*The Increased Difficulty of Concentration*], 1968; *Audience*, 1975; *Vernisáž* [*A Private View*], 1975; *Žebrácká opera* [*The Beggar's Opera*], 1976; *Protest*, 1978; *Chyba* [*The Mistake*], 1983; *Largo desolato*, 1985; *Pokoušení* [*Temptation*], 1986; *Asanace* [*Redevelopment*], 1987), and correspondence.

Bibliography
Hoznauer, Miloslav, *Václav Havel: Bibliografická příručka*, Prague: Comenium, 1991

Further Reading
Candole, James de, "Václav Havel as a Conservative Thinker," *Salisbury Review* (December 1988)
Cobb, Kelton, "Ernst Troeltsch and Václav Havel on the Ethical Promise of Historical Failure," *Journal of Religious Ethics* 22 (Spring 1994): 53–74
Farrell, Thomas B., "Practicing the Arts of Rhetoric: Tradition and Invention," *Philosophy and Rhetoric* 24, no. 3 (1991): 183–212
Gibian, George, "Havel's Letters from Prison," *Cross Currents* 3 (1984): 87–119

Goetz-Stankiewicz, Marketa, "Variations of Temptation: Václav Havel's Politics of Language," *Modern Drama* 33 (March 1990): 92–105
Hejdánek, Ladislav, "Variace a reflexe na téma vězeňských dopisů Václava Havla," *Listy* 20, no. 6 (1990): 6–19
Königsmark, Václav, "Havlovy dramatické eseje," *Přítomnost* 1, no. 6 (1990): 26–27
Kriseová, Eda, *Václav Havel*, New York: St. Martin's Press, 1993 (original Czech edition, 1991)
Matustik, Martin J., *Postnational Identity: Critical Theory and Existential Philosophy in Habermas, Kierkegaard, and Havel*, New York: Guilford Press, 1993
Pithart, Peter, "Intellectuals in Politics: Double Dissent in the Past, Double Disappointment Today," *Social Research* 60 (Winter 1993): 751–61
Prochazka, Martin, "Prisoner's Predicament: Public Privacy in Havel's Letters to Olga," *Representations* 43 (Summer 1993): 126–54
Rezek, Petr, *Filosofie a politika kýče*, Prague: Institut pro Středoevropskou Kulturu a Politiku, 1991
Satterwhite, James, "Marxist Critique and Czechoslovak Reform," in *The Road to Disillusion: From Critical Marxism to Post-Communism in Eastern Europe*, edited by Raymond Taras, Armonk, New York: Sharpe, 1992: 115–34
Tucker, Aviezer, "Václav Havel's Heideggerianism," *Telos* (Fall 1990): 63–78

Hazlitt, William
British, 1778–1830

The history of essays on the essay – with **Bacon**, **Addison** and **Steele**, and **Montaigne** among those cited as Founding Fathers – reveals the genre's amazing diversity and the consequent difficulty of formulating any kind of completely satisfactory definition. In *A Glossary of Literary Terms* (1981), M. H. Abrams sets down interesting guidelines to facilitate discussion. He defines it generally as "any brief composition in prose that undertakes to discuss a matter, express a point of view, or persuade us to accept a thesis on any subject whatever." He is quick to distinguish the **personal** or **familiar** essay in which the author assumes "a tone of intimacy with his audience" and is "concerned with everyday things," writing in "a relaxed, self-revelatory, and often whimsical fashion," from the formal essay in which the writer takes on the role of "authority, or at least as highly knowledgeable, and expounds the subject in an orderly way." Whether writing informally or formally, William Hazlitt is a master in both.

Walter Jackson Bate (1970), an important critic in the 20th-century revival of Hazlitt studies, catches a key dimension of the essayist's attractiveness in his engaging comment that "There is an appearance of hastiness in almost everything Hazlitt wrote, as though the printer's boy were at the door awaiting the sheets as they came from his pen." Yet this "appearance," while the clear result of the sheer busy-ness of Hazlitt's life and career as essayist, critic, reviewer, biographer, and social and political commentator, can as easily and justly be associated with his own favorite quality, gusto: the lively, immediate mode of his expression, the quickness of his mind, the range of his ideas, the forceful commitment to the cause of freedom in almost every area of human activity.

Jacob Zeitlin (1913), one of the earliest of the modern commentators on Hazlitt, finds a "triple ancestry" for the essayist: Montaigne's "original observation of humanity," **Rousseau**'s "high-strung susceptibility to emotions, sentiments, and ideas," and **La Rochefoucauld**'s "cynicism." Hazlitt is consistently cited in histories of the essay as part of a great tradition, and indeed he does conform to certain general norms associated with the genre wherever it is discussed, but he also pushes the boundaries beyond what many would regard as its defining limits, standing back to play the role of psychologist, lecturer, and teacher of both canonical and noncanonical classics.

Hazlitt's career as reviewer began as early as 1813 when he was appointed drama critic for the *Morning Chronicle*. In 1814 he began writing art and drama criticism for the *Champion* as well as for the **Edinburgh Review** and **Leigh Hunt**'s *Examiner*. His career continued with his celebrated "Round Table" essays and theatrical criticism for the *Examiner*, which he published as *The Round Table* (1817), and in 1817 he became drama critic for the *Times*. The 1820s saw more "Table Talks" for *London Magazine* and the publication of two volumes of *Table-Talk* (1821–22). He contributed to Hunt's radical journal the *Liberal* in 1823, and from 1828 to 1830 he was associated with the weekly *Atlas* and again as drama critic with the *Examiner*. So prodigious was his essay writing of all kinds – there are thousands of items in his oeuvre – that any elaborate system of classification fails.

Hazlitt's lengthy but influential *An Essay on the Principles of Human Action* (1805) advances his favorite subject, "the natural disinterestedness of the human mind," a subject that greatly influenced Keats' ideas on Negative Capability. Essays such as "On Genius and Originality" (1814), "On Reason and Imagination" (1826), "On Poetry in General" (1818), "On Imitation" (1816), "On the Character of Rousseau" (1816), and "On Shakespeare and Milton" (1818) represent the barest sample of his work as critic/essayist; there are also hundreds of **reviews** of almost every kind of artistic performance as well as a large number of biographical sketches.

But he may be best remembered for the short familiar essays on a remarkable variety of topics: "On Consistency of Opinion" (1821), "The Character of Country People" (1819), "On the Feeling of Immortality in Youth" (1827), "On Reading New Books" (1827), "On Going a Journey" (1822), "On the Pleasure of Painting" (1820). There is also his *tour de force* account of "The Fight" (1822) of 10 December 1821 between Tom Hickman the Gas-man and Bill Neate.

It is his own term "gusto" that best captures the approach in Hazlitt's essays. The way he musters language and imagery to catch the difficult-to-describe subject, the verve and energy of the speaking voice, the power of entering into a subject, and the range of artistic allusion even now gives the essays the ring of truth. Stanley Chase (1924) describes the overall approach as classic impressionism, "the interpretation of works of art by reference to the emotions which they excite in the individual breast." Herschel Baker (1962) sees the essays as seldom following a "linear pattern," tracing "not the sharp contour of points in ordered exposition but the undulating sequence of his moods." His range of literary allusion or quotation is remarkable – from the Bible to the Book of Common Prayer, from Chaucer, Spenser, and Milton to Shakespeare,

from Sterne's *Tristram Shandy* to Scott's *Waverley*, from Dryden's *The Hind and the Panther* to Gray's *Ode on a Distant Prospect of Eton College*, to Young's *Night-Thoughts*, to Cowper's *The Task*, to Wordsworth's *Tintern Abbey*.

The personal is almost always his strongest suit. As John Nabholtz says in his introduction to Hazlitt's *Selected Essays* (1970), "his style transmits the voice of a man passionately involved with his experience and communicating that involvement through all the devices of sound and structure." "One of the pleasantest things in the world," Hazlitt writes in "On Going a Journey," "is going a journey; but I like to go by myself. I can enjoy society in a room; but out of doors, nature is company enough for me . . . The soul of a journey is liberty; perfect liberty to think, feel, do just as one pleases." Or, with his lifelong trust in feeling as guide to action, he describes himself as "one of those who do not think that mankind are exactly governed by reason or a cool calculation of consequences" ("The Main Chance," 1828).

In "The Fight" Hazlitt draws his audience into the ring with his vivid sportswriter-like journalism. "Reader," he writes at the beginning, "have you ever seen a fight? If not, you have a pleasure to come, at least if it is a fight like that between the Gas-Man and Bill Neate . . . In the first round every one thought it was all over. After making play a short time, the Gas-man flew at his adversary like a tiger, struck five blows in as many seconds, three first, and then following him as he staggered back, two more, right and left, and down he fell, a mighty ruin."

Hazlitt's keen interest in the psychological reveals itself not only in *An Essay on the Principles of Human Action*, but throughout his more formal essays and essay-reviews of literature, painting, and other arts. For him "Poetry is the language of the imagination and the passions" ("On Poetry in General"). He expects the same gusto from the work of art that he brings to his own experience: "power or passion defining any object." The color in Titian's painting has this power: "Not only do his heads seem to think – his bodies seem to feel." So do Michelangelo's forms, which "everywhere obtrude the sense of power upon the eye" ("On Gusto," 1816). The power of Milton's mind can be found almost everywhere in his work: "The fervour of his imagination melts down and renders malleable, as in a furnace, the most contradictory materials" ("On Shakespeare and Milton"). The pleasure of tragic poetry is not an anomaly of the imagination, "but has its source in the common love of strong excitement" ("On Poetry in General"). It is the sympathetic quality of the imagination – its power to enter into the reality beyond the self – which attracts Hazlitt most. Imagination "is an associating principle, and has an instinctive perception when a thing belongs to a system, or is only an exception to it" ("On Reason and Imagination"). And genius, far from self-centeredness or display, "is, for the most part, *some strong quality in the mind answering to and bringing out some new and striking quality in nature*" ("On Genius and Common Sense," 1821).

Chaucer, Spenser, Milton, as well as Wordsworth, **Coleridge**, and his Romantic contemporaries, loom large in Hazlitt's lecture-essays. But Shakespeare conquers all; he is "the least of an egotist it was possible to be." "The striking peculiarity" of his mind and genius "was its generic quality, its power of communication with all other minds . . . and had no peculiar bias, or exclusive excellence more than another. He was just like any other man, but that he was like all other men" ("On Shakespeare and Milton").

Hazlitt's splendid "A Farewell to Essay Writing" (1828) combines all the elements of the successful essay, and specifically his own special qualities. The intensely personal tone, the engaging style, the keen sensitivity to persons and places, the wide range of literary reference – these and indeed more mark his farewell. "Food, warmth, sleep, and a book; these are all at present I ask – the *ultima thule* of my wandering desires." A walk in nature is a vital necessity in his life. Sipping his morning tea, he loves to watch "the clouds sailing from the west." Metaphor quickly becomes his mode: "We walk through life, as through a narrow path, with a thin curtain drawn around it; behind it are ranged rich portraits, airy harps are strung." But we must "lift aside the veil" to see the beauty and play the music. Memory recalls another time and place 18 years earlier, which in turn evokes a memory of the Theodore-Honora story in Boccaccio's *Decameron* when the lovers return from Hell. Hazlitt resolves to return home, take up Dryden's translation, and "drawing my chair to the fire, and holding a small print close to my eyes, launch into the full tide of Dryden's couplets (a stream of sound)."

At his best – and as a somewhat overburdened journalist and reviewer he often falls short – William Hazlitt is the master essayist of the English Romantic period, a writer who inherits one tradition and sets a high standard for a new one. He is an essayist with the rare gift of capturing the vitality of his own experience of life and art and of making his readers richer for sharing that experience.

JOHN L. MAHONEY

Biography

Born 10 April 1778 in Maidstone, Kent. Family moved to Ireland, 1780, the United States, 1783–87, then to Wem, Shropshire, from 1787. Studied privately; Hackney Theological College, London, 1793–94; studied painting with his brother in Paris, 1802–03. Associated with Coleridge, **Lamb**, **Godwin**, and Wordsworth. Lived in Wem and London, 1805–08, Winterslow, near Salisbury, 1808–11, returning to London, 1812. Married Sarah Stoddart, 1808 (divorced, 1822): one son (two others died in infancy). Parliamentary reporter, 1812–13, and dramatic critic, 1813–14, *Morning Chronicle*, and for the *Times*, 1817, and the *Examiner*, 1828–30; contributor to various other journals and newspapers, including the *Edinburgh Review*, the *Champion*, the *Liberal*, *London Magazine*, *Atlas*, and the *New Monthly*. Arrested for debt, 1823. Married Isabella Bridgewater, 1824 (separated, 1827). Traveled in France and Italy, 1824–25. Died (of stomach cancer) in London, 18 September 1830.

Selected Writings

Essays and Related Prose
An Essay on the Principles of Human Action, Being an Argument in Favour of the Natural Disinterestedness of the Human Mind, 1805
Free Thoughts on Public Affairs; or, Advice to a Patriot, 1806
A Reply to the Essay on Population by Malthus, in a Series of Letters, 1807
The Round Table: A Collection of Essays on Literature, Men, and Manners, with Leigh Hunt, 2 vols., 1817; facsimile reprint, 1991
Characters of Shakespeare's Plays, 1817

A View of the English Stage; or, A Series of Dramatic Criticisms, 1818
Lectures on the English Poets, 1818
Lectures on the English Comic Writers, 1819; edited by A. Johnson, 1965
Political Essays, with Sketches of Public Characters, 1819
Lectures, Chiefly on the Dramatic Literature of the Age of Elizabeth, 1820
Table-Talk; or, Original Essays, 2 vols., 1821–22
Characteristics, in the Manner of Rochefoucault's Maxims, 1823
Sketches of the Principal Picture Galleries in England with a Criticism on "Marriage a la Mode", 1824
The Spirit of the Age; or, Contemporary Portraits, 1825; edited by E. D. Mackerness, 1969
Notes of a Journey Through France and Italy, 1826
The Plain Speaker: Opinions on Books, Men, and Things, 2 vols., 1826
Literary Remains, 2 vols., 1836
Sketches and Essays, edited by William Hazlitt, Jr., 1839; as *Men and Manners,* 1852
Criticisms on Art and Sketches of the Picture Galleries of England, edited by William Hazlitt, Jr., 2 vols., 1843–44; as *Essays on the Fine Arts,* 1873
Winterslow: Essays and Characters Written There, edited by William Hazlitt, Jr., 1850
New Writings, edited by P. P. Howe, 2 vols., 1925–27
Selected Essays, edited by Geoffrey Keynes, 1930
Hazlitt on Theatre, edited by William Archer and Robert Lowe, 1957
Selected Writings, edited by Ronald Blythe, 1970
Selected Essays, edited by John R. Nabholtz, 1970
Selected Writings, edited by Jon Cook, 1991

Other writings: a four-volume life of Napoleon (1828–30), an autobiographical account of a doomed love affair, *Liber Amoris* (1823), an English grammar book, and correspondence (collected in *The Letters,* edited by Herschel Moreland Sikes, 1978).

Collected works edition: *Complete Works* (Centenary Edition) edited by P. P. Howe, 21 vols., 1930–34.

Bibliographies
Houck, James A., *William Hazlitt: A Reference Guide,* Boston: Hall, 1977
Keynes, Geoffrey, *Bibliography of William Hazlitt,* Godalming, Surrey: St. Paul's Bibliographies, revised edition, 1981 (original edition, 1931)

Further Reading
Albrecht, W. P., *Hazlitt and the Creative Imagination,* Lawrence: University of Kansas Press, 1965 (original edition, 1953)
Baker, Herschel, *William Hazlitt,* Cambridge, Massachusetts: Harvard University Press, 1962
Bate, Walter Jackson, "William Hazlitt," in *Criticism: The Major Texts,* New York: Harcourt Brace, 1970
Bromwich, David, *Hazlitt: The Mind of a Critic,* New York and Oxford: Oxford University Press, 1983
Bullitt, John M., "Hazlitt and the Romantic Conception of the Imagination," *Philological Quarterly* 24 (1945): 343–61
Chase, Stanley P., "Hazlitt as a Critic of Art," *PMLA* 39 (1924): 179–202
Good, Graham, "Hazlitt: Ventures of the Self," in his *The Observing Self: Rediscovering the Essay,* London and New York: Routledge, 1988: 71–89
Ireland, Alexander, *William Hazlitt, Essayist and Critic: Selections from His Writings with a Memoir, Biographical and Critical,* London and New York: Warne, 1889

Kinnaird, John, *William Hazlitt: Critic of Power*, New York: Columbia University Press, 1978

Mahoney, John L., *The Logic of Passion: The Literary Criticism of William Hazlitt*, New York: Fordham University Press, revised edition, 1981

Nabholtz, John R., editor, *"My Reader My Fellow-Labourer": A Study of English Romantic Prose*, Columbia: University of Missouri Press, 1986

O'Hara, J. D., "Hazlitt and the Function of Imagination," *PMLA* 81 (1956): 552–62

Park, Roy, *Hazlitt and the Spirit of the Age: Abstraction and Critical Theory*, Oxford: Clarendon Press, 1971

Schneider, Elisabeth, *The Aesthetics of William Hazlitt: A Study of the Philosophical Basis of His Criticism*, Philadelphia: University of Pennsylvania Press, 1933

Zeitlin, Jacob, *Hazlitt on English Literature: An Introduction to the Appreciation of Literature*, New York: Oxford University Press, 1913

Heiberg, Gunnar

Norwegian, 1857–1929

Although recognized primarily as Norway's greatest dramatist of his generation – best known for his satires and his two plays with erotic themes, *Balkonen* (1894; *The Balcony*) and *Kjærlighetens tragedie* (1904; *The Tragedy of Love*) – Gunnar Heiberg also enjoyed a reputation as one of his country's established essayists. Beginning in 1879, at around the time he wrote his first play, *Tante Ulrikke* (*Aunt Ulrikke*), Heiberg worked for various newspapers in Norway and elsewhere in Europe. Living outside of Norway for some of his life and hence commanding a European perspective, he wrote frequently on topics involving theater – e.g. in *Ibsen og Bjørnson på scenen* (1918; Ibsen and Bjørnson on stage) and in *Norsk teater* (1920; Norwegian theater) – but also on Norwegian politics and the current debate on art. He wrote with a sense of urgency and clarity.

Heiberg's primary essay collection, *Pariserbreve* (1900; Letters from Paris), includes portraits of authors, travel descriptions, and political journalism surrounding the Dreyfus affair. Another volume resulting from his residence in France, *Franske visitter* (1919; Flying visits), contains portraits of that country's literary personalities. Examples of his essays on aesthetics can be found in the collections *Set og hørt* (1917; Seen and heard) and *Salt og sukker* (1924; Salt and sugar).

Heiberg contributed to the development of the impressionistic essay, which portrayed the personalities of national writers. This subgenre of the essay made possible the interpretation of works based on the temperaments of their authors. Heiberg's portrait of the patriotic Norwegian critic and poet Henrik Wergeland (1808–45), for example, is among the most inspiring Norwegian portraits.

In his essays, Heiberg speaks to man's inner strength. His descriptions are detailed studies in which he often suggests his personal engagement or observation. It has been said that Heiberg's "artikler," as they are called, afford a veritable view of his life and character. He abhorred the lack of personal conviction and personality he sometimes observed in individuals, addressing this condition with skepticism on the one hand and wit on the other. In the public sphere, he raised humanistic concerns above politics.

Along with **Nils Kjær**, Heiberg is noted for his stylistic mastery of the essay. The many nuances and associations of language in his work reflect the attitude with which he approached the multifarious sides of human experience. As James McFarlane (1993) describes Heiberg's tone and content: "Acerbic, bitingly satirical, wickedly sarcastic when his indignation took command, he was at the same time possessed of a vision of love and passion and a faith in the potential for good in the individual which inform all that he wrote."

VIVIAN GREENE-GANTZBERG

Biography
Gunnar Edvard Rode Heiberg. Born 18 November 1857 in Christiania (now Oslo). Studied law at the University of Christiania, 1874–75. Traveled to Italy, where he met Ibsen, 1878–79. Wrote his first play, *Tante Ulrikke* (*Aunt Ulrikke*), 1879: published 1883, produced 1901. Worked as a journalist in Norway and abroad, from 1879, including for the *Verdens Gang* (World progress) newspaper, Oslo. Artistic director, National Theater, Bergen, 1884–88. Married Didi Tollefson, 1885 (divorced, 1896); also married a second time. Lived abroad, especially in Paris: returned to Oslo, 1902. Died in Oslo, 22 February 1929.

Selected Writings

Essays and Related Prose
Pariserbreve, 1900
Set og hørt, 1917
Ibsen og Bjørnson på scenen, 1918
Franske visitter, 1919
Norsk teater, 1920
1905, 1923
Salt og sukker, 1924
Hugg og stikk: Artikler i utvalg, edited by Einar Skavlan, 1951
Artikler om mange ting, 1972
Artikler om teater og dramatikk, edited by Hans Heiberg, 1972

Other writings: several plays (including *Tante Ulrikke* [1883; *Aunt Ulrikke*]; *Kong Midas*, 1890; *Balkonen* [1894; *The Balcony*]; *Kjærlighetens tragedie* [1904; *The Tragedy of Love*]; *Jeg vil væ mit land*, 1912; *Paradesengen*, 1913) and poetry.

Further Reading
Beyer, Edvard, *Norsk Litteratur Historie*, Oslo: Aschehoug, 1952: 349–53

McFarlane, James, "Norwegian Literature, 1860–1910," in *A History of Norwegian Literature*, edited by Harald S. Naess, Lincoln: University of Nebraska Press, 1993: 167–71

Skavlan, Einar, *Gunnar Heiberg*, Oslo: Aschehoug, 1950: 299–336

Heidegger, Martin

German, 1889–1976

The greater part of Martin Heidegger's writings consists of lecture courses delivered during his years of teaching, but he also employed a number of other genres: **treatise, dialogue,** essay. Many of his essays were first delivered orally before reaching a broad audience through publication. These pieces include some of the most dramatic and provocative of his works. While they cannot serve as complete guides to his thought, they are highly successful as stimulants which serve to indicate that a certain topic is, as the Heideggerian expression has it, "worthy of questioning."

Heidegger's first influential essay was his inaugural lecture, "Was ist Metaphysik?" (1929; "What Is Metaphysics?") – a piece that is cited by almost all existentialists thereafter – but it was in the postwar period that the essay became his primary form of expression. His essays treat a broad range of topics: truth, art, theology, the poetry of Hölderlin, the nature of language, critiques of traditional philosophy. They also explore several subgenres. Many are exegetical essays, focused on the elucidation of a brief philosophical or poetic text. Others, such as "Brief über den Humanismus" (1947; "Letter on Humanism") and "Zur Seinsfrage" (1956; "The Question of Being") are epistolary essays, open **letters** to Jean Beaufret (and indirectly to **Jean-Paul Sartre**) and to **Ernst Jünger**, respectively.

Heidegger often begins, ends, or titles his essays with questions. An initial question is soon transformed into a surprising or enigmatic position, such as the assertion that "the essence of technology is by no means anything technological," in "Die Frage nach der Technik" (1954; "The Question Concerning Technology"). This process of transformation continues in carefully crafted but bold steps, leading to a conclusion that frequently faces the audience with a riddle. The classic example here is the final line of "What Is Metaphysics?": "Why are there beings at all, and why not rather nothing?"

Heidegger's purpose is not to answer these questions, but to raise them – to make the problems they express come alive for his audience. An essay by Heidegger is not a linear argument directed toward proving a thesis; it is a path, sometimes a circuitous one, on which we are meant to learn the art of thinking. Heidegger titles one of his collections of essays *Holzwege*, or "woodpaths." In German, to be on a *Holzweg* means to be lost, or on a wild goose chase; but for Heidegger, striking out on woodpaths, even if they are dead ends, is the only way to get to know the woods. The statements we encounter on these paths must always be read in the context of the movement of the essay as a whole; readers must develop an ear for the provisional and even ironic tone in which Heidegger writes many of his sentences, for he is likely to challenge the assumptions on which these assertions rest when he takes the next step in his thought.

Heidegger shows a gift for **apothegms**: "language is the house of being" ("Letter on Humanism"), "questioning is the piety of thought" ("The Question Concerning Technology"). He prefers a spare, concentrated style that loads each crucial word with many meanings by drawing on its phonetic and etymological resonances with other words in the essay. These resonances often prove quite difficult or impossible to translate, as when Heidegger writes in "Der Weg zur Sprache" (1959; "The Way to Language"), "Das Ereignis ereignet in seinem Er-äugen . . ." (roughly, "the event appropriates in its envisaging . . ."). This is poetic prose that depends on a gradual accumulation of sounds and senses. Heidegger both respects the history of language and is willing to experiment boldly with words and typography in order to allow this history to point us toward being itself, or the overall significance of things. He also makes demands of a different sort on his readers: he assumes that they are thoroughly familiar with the history of philosophy, so that they will understand a quotation in Greek from Aristotle or a passing reference to Hegel.

Political questions are often in the background of Heidegger's postwar essays, and many contemporary critics focus on this dimension of the texts. Heidegger is given to the trope of claiming that what ultimately matters is not some concrete fact of pressing urgency (the atom bomb, the housing crisis, poverty) but its basis or analogue in the "history of being" – which he himself is in the best position to interpret. The most notorious example is found in "Die Gefahr" (wr. 1949; Danger), where Heidegger claims that mechanized agriculture is "essentially the same" as death camps, for both are rooted in a technological understanding of being. One may surmise that these claims served as a reassurance for postwar German audiences seeking to transcend the all-too-troubling facts of their recent past, and as an apologia for Heidegger's own choices during the Nazi period.

Heidegger's style lends itself to imitation, as is proved by the work of many commentators and followers. Jacques Derrida's essays take many Heideggerian mannerisms to an extreme (for example, Derrida has often adopted the practice of crossing out words in a text – a technique used by Heidegger in "The Question of Being"). Others, such as Anglo-American analytic philosophers, have denounced Heideggerian phrases such as "the nothing nothings" (*das Nichts selbst nichtet*) as absurdities. The latter phrase, in particular, which stems from "What Is Metaphysics?," was asserted by Rudolf Carnap to be strictly meaningless in his influential essay "Überwindung der Metaphysik durch logische Analyse der Sprache" (1932; "The Elimination of Metaphysics Through Logical Analysis of Language"). Today, however, when Carnap's own "logical positivism" has long fallen out of fashion, and in a period which is more tolerant of linguistic experimentation, Heidegger's essays find a wide audience in the English-speaking world.

RICHARD POLT

Biography

Born 26 April 1889 in Messkirch. Studied at gymnasia in Konstanz and Freiburg, 1903–09; the University of Freiburg, 1909–13, Ph.D., 1913. Military service, 1915–18. Lecturer, 1915–23, and assistant to Edmund Husserl, 1920–23, University of Freiburg. Married Elfride Petri, 1917: two sons and one daughter. Associate professor of philosophy, University of Marburg, 1923–28; professor of philosophy, 1928–51, chancellor, 1933–34 (resigned), and professor emeritus, 1951–57, University of Freiburg. Banned from teaching by occupation forces, 1945–50. Member, Academy of Fine Arts, Berlin; Bavarian Academy of Fine Arts. Died in Freiburg, 26 May 1976.

Selected Writings

Essays and Related Prose

Existence and Being, edited by Werner Brock, translated by Douglas Scott, R. F. C. Hull, and Alan Crick, 1949

Holzwege, 1950

Vorträge und Aufsätze, 3 vols., 1954

Was heisst Denken? (lectures), 1954; as *What Is Called Thinking?*, translated by Fred D. Wieck and J. Glenn Gray, 1968

Was ist das – die Philosophie, 1956; as *What Is Philosophy?*, translated by Jean T. Wilde and William Kluback, 1958

Zur Seinsfrage, 1956; as *The Question of Being*, translated by Jean T. Wilde and William Kluback, 1958

Identität und Differenz, 1957; as *Identity and Difference*, translated by Kurt F. Leidecker, 1960, and Joan Stambaugh, 1969

Unterwegs zur Sprache, 1959; as *On the Way to Language*, translated by Joan Stambaugh and Peter D. Hertz, 1971
Gelassenheit, 1959; as *Discourse on Thinking*, translated by John M. Anderson and E. Hans Freund, 1966
Wegmarken, 1967
Zur Sache des Denkens, 1969; as *On Time and Being*, translated by Joan Stambaugh, 1972
Poetry, Language, Thought, translated by Albert Hofstadter, 1971
Early Greek Thinking, translated by David Farrell Krell and Frank Capuzzi, 1975
The Piety of Thinking, translated by James G. Hart and John C. Maraldo, 1976
The Question Concerning Technology and Other Essays, translated by William Lovitt, 1977
Basic Writings (various translators), edited by David Farrell Krell, 1977; revised, enlarged edition, 1993

Other writings: many philosophical works.

Collected works edition: *Gesamtausgabe*, 48 vols., 1975–94 (in progress; 100 vols. projected).

Bibliographies
Guignon, Charles B., editor, *The Cambridge Companion to Heidegger*, Cambridge and New York: Cambridge University Press, 1993: 358–80
Nordquist, Joan, *Martin Heidegger: A Bibliography*, Santa Cruz, California: Reference and Research Service, 1990
Sass, Hans-Martin, *Heidegger-Bibliographie*, Meisenheim-on-Glan: Hain, 1968
Sass, Hans-Martin, and others, *Materialien zu einer Heidegger-Bibliographie*, Meisenheim-on-Glan: Hain, 1975
Sass, Hans-Martin, *Martin Heidegger: Bibliography and Glossary*, Bowling Green, Ohio: Bowling Green State University Philosophy Documentation Center, 1982

Further Reading
Anderson, John M., Introduction to *Discourse on Thinking* by Heidegger, New York: Harper and Row, 1966
Bailiff, John, "Truth and Power: Martin Heidegger, 'The Essence of Truth,' and 'The Self-Assertion of the German University'," *Man and World* 20 (August 1987): 327–36
Biemel, Walter, "On the Composition and Unity of *Holzwege*," in *Continental Philosophy in America*, edited by Hugh J. Silverman, John Sallis, and Thomas M. Seebohm, Pittsburgh: Duquesne University Press, 1983
Caputo, John D., *Demythologizing Heidegger*, Bloomington: Indiana University Press, 1993
Dauenhauer, Bernard P., "Heidegger, the Spokesman for the Dweller," *Southern Journal of Philosophy* 15 (Summer 1977): 189–99
Fritsche, Johannes, "On Brinks and Bridges in Heidegger," *Graduate Faculty Philosophy Journal* 18, no. 1 (1995): 111–86
Hofstadter, Albert, Introduction to *Poetry, Language, Thought* by Heidegger, New York: Harper and Row, 1971
Kockelmans, Joseph J., "Heidegger on Theology," *Southwestern Journal of Philosophy* 4 (Fall 1973): 85–108
Krell, David Farrell, "*Schlag der Liebe, Schlag des Todes*: On a Theme in Heidegger and Trakl," *Research in Phenomenology* 7 (1977): 238–58
Lovitt, William, Introduction to *The Question Concerning Technology and Other Essays* by Heidegger, New York and London: Harper and Row, 1977
Maly, Kenneth, "Toward 'Ereignis'," *Research in Phenomenology* 3 (1973): 63–93

Sheehan, Thomas J., "Getting to the Topic: The New Edition of *Wegmarken*," in *Radical Phenomenology: Essays in Honor of Martin Heidegger*, edited by John Sallis, Atlantic Highlands, New Jersey: Humanities Press, 1978
Singh, R. Raj, "Heidegger and the World-Yielding Role of Language," *Journal of Value Inquiry* 27 (April 1993): 203–14
Spanos, William V., editor, *Martin Heidegger and the Question of Literature: Towards a Postmodern Literary Hermeneutics*, Bloomington: Indiana University Press, 1979

Henríquez Ureña, Pedro
Dominican, 1884–1946

The versatile work of the philosopher, humanist, and literary critic Pedro Henríquez Ureña placed him at the center of Latin American intellectual life at the turn of the century. His production offers a wide range of interests, from books and articles on literature and linguistics – the latter usually published in magazines and newspapers – to essays on Latin American culture, history, and philosophy.

His essays focus mostly on a central theme: the idea of searching for what he calls "Our America." Henríquez Ureña is heir to the literary tradition of thinkers such as Simón Bolívar, **José Martí**, **Andrés Bello**, **Eugenio María de Hostos**, and **José Enrique Rodó**, and his writings explore Spanish America's past intellectual history in an attempt to understand its present. His work's unifying thread is his insistence on defining what he calls the spirit of "Our America," which he considers indispensable if Latin Americans are to articulate their own identity and forge their own future. Although the search for identity is not a new theme in 20th-century Latin American thought, Henríquez Ureña's vision of creating an identity that projects itself onto the future, and that aims to reconcile Spanish America's various cultural traditions, is a new preoccupation among Latin American essayists of his time.

From his *Ensayos críticos* (1905; Critical essays), and his *Literary Currents in Spanish America* (1945) to his *Seis ensayos en busca de nuestra expresión* (1928; Six essays in search of our expression), Henríquez Ureña is concerned with the fundamental theme of defining a culture and an identity that are unique to Spanish America while at the same time granting each nation a solid platform from which to engage with and contribute to the universal dialogue.

Rather than advocating a return to Spain or relying only on autochthonous traditions to explain Latin American reality, as most of his 19th-century predecessors and some of his contemporaries had done, Henríquez Ureña's essays look for a genuine expression by digging into Latin America's recent past. In order to be authentic, that expression needed to incorporate the European intellectual legacy with Indian and black contributions. His essays denounce as reductionist the tendencies of some Latin American elites to identify themselves only with their European background; at the same time the author criticizes the romanticized vision of those who would like to see themselves exclusively as descendants of Indian and black cultures. For Henríquez Ureña, the true expression of Spanish America's identity must necessarily emerge from the amalgam of all cultural elements, native and imported, that Latin Americans live with in their societies and express in their literature. He searches in the past for the roots of problems that are responsible for the lack of social integration in Latin American societies. The crisis of modern civilization has left Spanish America without a solid spiritual foundation from which to nourish itself. Neither the European nor the indigenous traditions alone can offer the answer to "Our America"'s future, according to Henríquez Ureña.

In many of his lectures and essays, Henríquez Ureña proposes a vision of his America as a world that embraces difference as the welcome diversity of humankind, and combines those nuances to form a rich and harmonious unity with a plurality of voices. This vision of "Our America" – a term that he borrows from José Martí – is to be developed with the participation of all members of society: young and old, rich and poor, working together for the goal of a better world based on unity and social justice. This utopian world, which he discusses in "La utopía de América" (1925; The utopia of America), is built on the premise that the cultural history of Latin America is rooted in a bed of crisis from which nations need to design the unity of a "Magna patria" – their own motherland. The ideals of sustained cooperation, faith, justice, and hope are imbedded in the construction of this utopia, where the work of all will guarantee a prosperous future for Our America.

The need for Spanish America to find a place among the nations of the world is a corollary to this effort of self-definition. For Henríquez Ureña, Spanish America's search for itself will justify its own history in the future, and will create a model society from which the rest of the world will be able to learn a true sense of justice and liberty.

Most critics agree that Henríquez Ureña's essays share a series of stylistics traits – such as a clear sense of measure, a comfortable sobriety, and a powerful directness – that stand in sharp contrast to the luscious verbosity of some of his 19th-century predecessors. Henríquez Ureña was a philologist by training, and his command of language exhibits the elegant rigor of the academic blended with the freshness of approach of the creative writer. Cintio Vitier praises Henríquez Ureña's "intellectual prose," and Alberto Zum Felde calls him "one of the greatest Latin American literary essayists," while Juan Jacobo Lara alludes to the "dispassionate objectivity in his essays," which have served as a great source of inspiration to generations of Latin Americans.

In his quest for a genuine American expression, Henríquez Ureña unearths the ideas of his Latin American forefathers, and like them he becomes an apostle and model for later generations of thinkers such as **Leopoldo Zea**, Edmundo O'Gorman, **Octavio Paz, Mariano Picón-Salas**, and **Carlos Fuentes**.

LOURDES ROJAS

Biography
Born 29 June 1884 in Santo Domingo, Dominican Republic. Studied at a high school in Santo Domingo, graduated 1901; Columbia University, New York, 1902; moved to Cuba, 1904, and Mexico, 1906; studied law in Mexico, law degree, 1914; University of Minnesota, Minneapolis, M.A., 1917, Ph.D., 1918. Taught at the University of Minnesota, until 1921, and the National Autonomous University of Mexico, from 1921. Married, 1923. Moved to Argentina, 1924. Professor, Colegio Nacional, La Plata, until 1930; taught at the University of Buenos Aires, Instituto del Profesorado, the Colegio Libre de Estudios Superieres, and other institutions in Buenos Aires and La Plata, from 1930. General superintendent of education, Dominican Republic, 1931–33. Charles Eliot Norton Professor, Harvard University, Cambridge, Massachusetts, 1940–41. Contributor to many newspapers and journals, including the *Revista de Filología Hispánica* (Review of Hispanic philology). Director of One Hundred Master Works series for Editorial Losada publishers, Buenos Aires. Died in La Plata, Argentina, 11 May 1946.

Selected Writings

Essays and Related Prose
Ensayos críticos, 1905
Horas de estudio, 1910
El nacimiento de Dioniso: Ensayo de tragedia antigua, 1916
En la orilla: Mi España, 1922
Seis ensayos en busca de nuestra expresión, 1928
Plenitud de España: Estudios de historia de la cultura, 1940; enlarged edition, 1945
Literary Currents in Spanish America (Charles Eliot Norton lectures), 1945
Plenitud de América: Ensayos escogidos, edited by Javier Fernández, 1952
Obra crítica, edited by Emma Susana Sperati Piñero, 1960
Selección de ensayos, edited by José Rodriguez Feo, 1965; as *Ensayos*, 1973
Universidad y educación, 1969
Desde Washington, edited by Minerva Salado, 1975
Observaciones sobre el español en América y otros estudios filológicos, edited by Juan Carlos Ghiano, 1976
La utopía de América (selected essays), edited by Ángel Rama and Rafael Gutiérrez Giradot, 1978
Pedro Henríquez Ureña, del ensayo crítico a la historia literaria (selection), edited by Javier Lasarte Valcárcel, 1991

Other writings: short stories for adults and children, and a book on Spanish American culture (1947). Also edited collections of Argentine literature and Spanish poetry.

Collected works edition: *Obras completas*, edited by Juan Jacobo de Lara, 10 vols., 1976–80.

Bibliographies
Carilla, Emilio, "Pedro Henríquez Ureña: Bibliografía comentada," *Inter-American Review of Bibliography* 27, no. 3 (1977): 227–39
Speralti Piñero, Emma Susana, "Cronobibliografía de don Pedro Henríquez Ureña," in *Obra crítica* by Henríquez Ureña, Mexico City: Fondo de Cultura Económica, 1960: 751–96

Further Reading
Alvarez, Soledad, "Sobre el americanismo de Pedro Henríquez Ureña," *Casa de las Américas* 21, no. 126 (1981): 63–77
De Lara, Juan Jacobo, *Pedro Henríquez Ureña: Su vida y su obra*, Santo Domingo: UNPHU, 1975
Gutiérrez Giradot, Rafael, "La historiografía literaria de Pedro Henríquez Ureña: Promesa y desafío," *Casa de las Américas* 24, no. 144 (1984): 3–14
Henríquez Ureña, Max, "Hermano y maestro (recuerdo de infancia y juventud)," in *Pedro Henríquez Urena: Antología*, Ciudad Trujillo: Dominicana, 1950: xxi–xxii
Jiménes-Grullón, J. I., *Pedro Henríquez Ureña: Realidad y mito, y otros ensayos*, Santo Domingo: Dominicana, 1969
Leal, Luis, "Pedro Henríquez Ureña en México," *Revista Iberoamericana* 21, nos. 41–42 (1956): 19–133
Lizaso, Félix, "Pedro Henríquez Ureña y sus precencias en Cuba," *Revista Iberoamericana* 21, nos. 41–42 (1956)

Piña Conteras, Guillermo, "El universo familiar en la formación intelectual de Pedro Henríquez Ureña," *Cuadernos de Poética* 8, no. 2 (September–December 1994): 51–91

Reyes, Alfonso, "Evocación de Pedro Henríquez Ureña," in his *Obras completas*, vol. 12, México: Fondo de Cultura Económica, 1960: 163–64

Rodríguez Demorizi, Emilio, *Dominicanidad de Pedro Henríquez Ureña*, Ciudad Trujillo: University of Santo Domingo, 1947

Roggrano, Alfredo A., *Pedro Henríquez Ureña en los Estados Unidos*, Mexico City: National Autonomous University of Mexico, 1961

Sábato, Ernesto, "Significado de Pedro Henríquez Ureña," *La Torre* 14, no. 54 (September–December 1966): 75–91

Zum Felde, Alberto, *Indice crítico de la literatura hispanoamericana: El ensayo y la crítica*, Mexico City: Guarenia, 1954

Herbert, Zbigniew

Polish, 1924–

Zbigniew Herbert is an author not particularly well known for his essays; his poetry is what has earned him a reputation as one of the best contemporary writers now living in Poland. Yet his two modest collections of essays, inspired by his travels to France, Italy, and Holland – *Barbarzyńca w ogrodzie* (1962; *Barbarian in the Garden*) and *Martwa natura z wędzidłem* (1991; *Still Life with a Bridle: Essays and Apocryphas*) – secure Herbert a place among the world's most distinguished essayists. His modest output as an essayist is supplemented by his early and lesser-known attempts at prose writing. Herbert started his career in the late 1940s and early 1950s by publishing articles, *feuilletons*, and **reviews** of books, theater, painting, and photography. He wrote for such periodicals as *Dziś i Jutro* (Today and tomorrow), *Słowo Powszechne* (Universal word), *Przegląd Powszechny* (Universal review), *Tygodnik Powszechny* (Universal weekly), and *Twórczość* (Creation). Herbert's contributions to these periodicals – along with his publications in the Paris-based Polish journals *Kultura* (Culture) and *Zeszyty Literackie* (Literary notebooks) – may indicate the kind of audience to which he addresses his essays: his readers are highly select and belong to the intellectual and literary elite. During the communist period in Poland, they also represented the unyielding and politically independent circles who confronted the authorities.

What truly defines Herbert's select and intellectual audience is the very nature of his essays, which are sophisticated and witty, thoughtful and artistic. For the most part they represent the type of essay known as the **travel essay**, but not in its "pure" form: they also contain elements of the philosophical and **historical essay** as well as those of the critical article aiming to explain an historical event or interpret a work of art. Critics have noticed that these essays, like Herbert's other writings, are permeated with the spirit of humanism.

One of the main traits of Herbert's essays is their polemical character – myths, widespread beliefs, and commonly accepted opinions are often questioned, scrutinized, and revised. Herbert reveals the falsity of conventional assumptions and the fragility of established truths. His deliberations on an issue from the history of art – one of his favorite topics – almost always constitute a dispute against the "learned" judgments of savants, the immovable "wisdom" of tradition, and widely shared popular knowledge. Thus, in an essay on Gothic cathedrals, after the blunt statement, "One should finally dispose of the myth of the cathedral builders' anonymity" ("Kamień z katedry" [1962; "A Stone from the Cathedral"]), Herbert proceeds to revise the idea. Similarly, after realizing the boldness of his questioning on other occasions, he decides, "One must blaspheme against the authors of handbooks – the Orvieto frescoes are much more impressive than Michelangelo's frescoes in the Sistine Chapel" ("Il Duomo" [1962; "Orvieto's Duomo"]), or, "I realize I am allowing myself to write blasphemies, because 'Swearing of the Peace Treaty in Muenster,' according to general opinion, is a masterpiece . . . I think only that this is not Terborch's best painting . . ." ("Gerard Terborch: Dyskretny urok mieszczaństwa" [1991; "Gerard Terborch: The Discreet Charm of the Bourgeoisie"]). However, in his revisionary approach to a subject, Herbert does not pretend to be omniscient. He himself hesitates, asks questions, weighs his own words, and declares that sometimes his statements may also be simply speculations. By such deliberation Herbert not only demonstrates the limitations of human knowledge about the past and the present; he also attempts, through questioning and examining, to indicate that some understanding of historical and current events is possible. Revision of myths, beliefs, and opinions helps remove mendacities gathered like patina on works of history and art. Karl Dedecius (1975), who detects the same feature in Herbert's poetry, rightly notices that Herbert, with the same purpose in mind, travels like a "barbarian" through the "garden" of European culture and tradition. He sets out to the mythical places he has always heard of and explores them himself to uncover hidden truths and to gain authentic knowledge.

The polemical character of Herbert's essays is also revealed in the selection of his subjects. His travel essays are indeed, as the author says, a confrontation of "monuments, books, and paintings with the real sky, the real sea, and the real land" ("Delta," 1989). But when he writes about Dutch art and landscape, about French or Italian Gothic cathedrals and the shape of the terrain, and about Doric temples and the sunlight, or even when he relates the course of a 16th-century battle as recorded in a Dutch chronicle, Herbert's interest does not lie in what is obvious, typical, and expected from the choice of such a subject. Instead he searches for and describes things which are either unknown or unnoticed, as well as things traditionally considered insignificant and not worth mentioning. A famous painting as the theme of an essay serves as an inspiration for a commentary on the material conditions of painters of a given epoch ("Cena sztuki" [1991; "The Price of Art"]); the subject of a Gothic cathedral brings about a detailed account of a church construction technique in the Middle Ages ("A Stone from the Cathedral"). Critics have noticed that Herbert is interested in defeated civilizations and defeated individuals, in nations that failed and in peoples whose "tribulations and defeats left no trace and had no career in history." Herbert's selection of the subject allows him to make good use of irony, his favorite literary device. He comments frequently on history in a familiar tone of voice, and from the convenient distance of a contemporary observer.

The polemic, as one of the main traits of Herbert's essays, obviously determines his style. But this polemic is discreet; questioning, arguing, and proposing new answers are not dominant characteristics of Herbert's style. Other stylistic elements are more conspicuous. Herbert's vocabulary is simple but representative of poetic prose. Polished, subtle, and ingenious metaphors are common; especially captivating are the metaphors used in descriptions of works of art: in the Greek column "under the weight of the architrave a branchy capital is swollen from an effort" ("U Dorów" [1962; "Among the Dorians"]).

The specific artistic qualities of the two collections of essays may point to Herbert's affinities with such masters of the essay as **Paul Valéry** and **T. S. Eliot**, and place him among the best of the 20th-century Polish essayists, such as **Jerzy Stempowski**, Mieczysław Jastrun, and **Czesław Miłosz**. It is surprising that Herbert's fine essays have so far attracted little attention from critics; the fact that he is famous for his outstanding poetry cannot explain this neglect.

ANDRZEJ KARCZ

Biography
Born 29 October 1924 in Lvov. Studied at the Academy of Economics, Cracow, M.A. in economics, 1947; Nicholas Copernicus University of Toruń, M.A. in law, 1949; University of Warsaw, M.A. in philosophy, 1950; also studied briefly at Jagiellonian University and the Academy of Fine Arts, Cracow. Worked for *Twórczość* literary monthly, 1955–65; coeditor, *Poezja* (Poetry), 1965–68. Married Katarzyna Dzieduszycka, 1968. Taught at California State College, Los Angeles, 1970–71, and University of Gdańsk, 1972. Awards: several, including the Nikolaus Lenau Prize (Austria), 1965; Herder Prize, 1973; Knight's Cross, Order of Polonia Restituta, 1974; Petrarch Prize, 1979; Jerusalem Prize, 1991; Ingersoll Prize, 1995.

Selected Writings

Essays and Related Prose
Barbarzyńca w ogrodzie, 1962; as *Barbarian in the Garden*, translated by Michael March and Jarosław Anders, 1985
Still Life with a Bridle: Essays and Apocryphas, translated by John and Bogdana Carpenter, 1991; as *Martwa natura z wędzidłem*, 1993

Other writings: many collections of poetry (including *Pan Cogito* [*Mr. Cogito*], 1974; *Raport z oblężonego miasta* [*Report from the Besieged City and Other Poems*], 1983, and several *Selected Poems*), and several plays.

Further Reading
Dedecius, Karl, "Anbau der Philosophie: Zbigniew Herbert auf der Suche nach Selbstgewissheit," in his *Polnische Prophile*, Frankfurt-on-Main: Suhrkamp, 1975
Dybciak, Krzysztof, "W poszukiwaniu istoty i utraconych wartości," in his *Gry i katastrofy*, Warsaw: Biblioteka Więzi, 1980
Kijowski, Andrzej, "Pielgrzym," *Twórczość* 5 (1963): 57–60
Kijowski, Andrzej, "Outcast of Obvious Forms," *Polish Perspectives* 2 (1966): 34–41
Kott, Jan, Introduction to *Four Decades of Polish Essays*, edited by Kott, Evanston, Illinois: Northwestern University Press, 1990
Kwiatkowski, Jerzy, "Symbol trwałości," *Życie Literackie* 9 (1963)

Herder, Johann Gottfried
German, 1744–1803

Johann Gottfried Herder lived in an age of momentous change and enormous creativity in German culture. He was a student of **Immanuel Kant**, a dialogue partner of **Gotthold Ephraim Lessing**, and a mentor and friend of **Johann Wolfgang von Goethe**. Therefore, Herder is often mentioned in conjunction with others rather than for his own sake. His image is still distorted, as he is labeled a "pre-Romantic" and anti-Enlightenment thinker, whereas he tried to combine both trends. He is not remembered for one towering achievement, but for the many seeds he sowed in different disciplines such as aesthetics, literary criticism and history, philosophy of history, language theory, anthropology, psychology, and education. He was a theologian by profession, and worked as a high official in the Lutheran church. He was a renowned preacher, and contributed new ideas to Bible studies and the education of Lutheran ministers. Herder was also a singularly gifted translator and adapter of poetry from many languages and cultures. He is best remembered for his seminal anthology of folksongs from many cultures and ages, originally called *Volkslieder* (1778–79) but later renamed *Stimmen der Völker in Liedern* (Voices of the peoples in songs). This anthology and Herder's concept of folk poetry had a tremendous impact on the Romantic search for national identity, above all in Eastern and Southeastern Europe.

Herder believed in the power of the spoken word, as he practiced it in his sermons. He considered the written text a poor substitute for direct speech and enriched it with features from oral language. He considered poetry the original and most powerful form of human communication, and interspersed his prose with poems or poetic quotations. He preferred informal and communicative genres, such as dialogues, letters, and speeches. The style of his early works is effusive and intense, but even his more measured later prose remains emotional and personal, full of dashes, exclamation points, and rhetorical questions.

Herder was a universalist and had grand and ambitious projects. He considered his texts mere preliminaries for the real work, and liked to use titles such as "ideas," "fragments," "contributions," and "thoughts on . . ." Recent scholarship has defined his style and approach as "essayistic" (e.g. John A. McCarthy, 1989; James van der Laan, 1990). Even Herder's magnum opus, *Ideen zur Philosophie der Geschichte der Menschheit* (1785–91; *Ideas for a Philosophy of the History of Man*), is unfinished and fragmentary in many of its sections.

In Herder's Germany, the word "essay" had not yet entered the vocabulary; instead, other words were used, such as *Versuch*, *Aufsatz*, and *Abhandlung*, the latter dangerously close to academic writing. However, the short form of prose for an educated general audience, neither too academic and ponderous nor too flippantly superficial, and also not tied to religious observances, was in demand, especially for the emerging periodical press. It was meant for a public with no patience for complex language and deep thoughts. Such pieces could be read aloud and discussed in social circles, and applied to real-life situations. Herder was a popular author for these circles and contributed biographical essays, book **reviews**, essays on literature and the arts, and essays about philosophical and religious questions. Such essays, first published in journals, were usually republished in collections of poetry and prose, notably six installments of *Zerstreute Blätter* (1785–97; Scattered leaves). In the last decade of his life, Herder wrote short prose texts for collections, such as *Briefe zur Beförderung der Humanität* (1793–97; Letters for the advancement of humanity) and *Adrastea* (1801–04).

Herder was and is still faulted for his "unacademic" style, yet he showed perseverance in one academic genre of his age, the so-called prize essays for Academies of Science. He won prizes from the Prussian and Bavarian Academies, first with his *Abhandlung über den Ursprung der Sprache* (1772; *Essay on the Origin of Language*), but he did not win a prize with the important psychological **treatise** *Vom Erkennen und Empfinden der menschlichen Seele* (1778; On the cognition and sensation of the human soul), although he wrote three versions and submitted the essay twice. Most of Herder's prize essays held controversial positions, but the judges' major objection was their nonacademic style.

Herder is not known for really outstanding individual essays, except the treatise on the origin of language, but some deserve special mention, not least because of their impact – for instance, his two essays in *Von deutscher Art und Kunst* (1773; On German art), a volume edited by Herder that also contains texts by Goethe, Justus Möser, and Paoli Frisi. "Shakespear" is an enthusiastic defense of Shakespeare's form of the drama against classical norms, comparing Shakespeare to Sophocles. Despite its title, "Auszug aus einem Briefwechsel über Ossian und die Lieder alter Völker" (Extract from a correspondence about Ossian and the songs of ancient peoples) deals primarily with folksongs, and only secondarily with the problem of whether MacPherson's *Ossian* was genuine Gaelic folk poetry, and how his texts should be translated.

Zerstreute Blätter reprinted major pieces from previous years, and included numerous noteworthy essays. To mention two theme essays: "Nemesis: Ein lehrendes Sinnbild" (Nemesis: a didactic symbol) traces the Greek goddess and concept of Nemesis as the balance of justice in history and human affairs and reintroduces it as a key concept. "Tithon und Aurora" (1792) discusses aging and rejuvenation as well as radical changes such as revolutions, introducing the idea of evolution. The volumes also include biographical essays, such as the eulogy on Gotthold Ephraim Lessing, written after his unexpected death. "Über ein morgenländisches Drama" (1792; On an Oriental play) is a book review of the German translation of the Indian play *Sakontala* by Kalidasa, a translation by **Georg Forster** from the English. *Sakontala* is seen as a valid example of a non-Aristotelian drama, and as a demonstration of the significance of non-Western art. Herder wrote many book review essays, the most influential being the review of Heinrich Wilhelm von Gerstenberg's tragedy *Ugolino* in the *Allgemeine Deutsche Bibliothek* (General German library) of 1770, considered a model of sympathetic understanding.

The *Briefe zur Beförderung der Humanität* offer significant texts on key concepts, such as "Humanität" and "Geist der Zeit" (spirit of the age). Other collections contain Herder's influential reflections on ideas such as the immortality of the soul, palingenesis, and reincarnation. Both *Adrastea* and the *Briefe* end in sections condemning colonialism and the European domination and exploitation of the globe.

Since Herder's shorter texts were much more popular than his larger works, they were often anthologized, together with extracts from his major books. His impact was considerable though not always acknowledged, since he had committed the grave sin in his last years of opposing the critical philosophy of Kant and the classical poetics of Goethe and **Schiller**. Still, his call for an openness to all cultures and his validation of national identity and folk poetry made him a revered figure for many movements of national liberation. Postmodernism is discovering the essayistic and forward-looking features of his texts, and has a new sensibility for his idiom fusing prose and poetry.

Wulf Koepke

Biography

Born 25 August 1744 in Mohrungen (now Morag), East Prussia. Studied theology, literature, and philosophy under Immanuel Kant at the University of Kˆnigsberg, 1762–64. Teacher at the Cathedral School, Riga, 1764–69; preached in several churches in Riga. Traveled in France, and traveling companion to Prince Wilhelm of Holstein, 1769–70; stayed in Strasbourg for eye operation and met and became friends with Goethe, 1770. Pastor, consistorial councillor, and superintendent to the petty court of Schaumburg-Lippe, Bückeburg, 1771–76. Married Caroline Flachsland, 1773: six children. Consistorial councillor, general superintendent, and court preacher, Weimar, 1776–1803. Elected external member, Prussian Academy of Science, 1787. Traveled to Italy, 1788–89. Awards: Prussian Academy of Sciences Prize, for essay, 1772, 1775, and 1780 (Berlin), 1778 and 1779 (Munich). Died in Weimar, 18 December 1803.

Selected Writings

Essays and Related Prose

Haben wir noch jetzt das Publikum und Vaterland der Alten?, 1765
Über die neuere Deutsche Litteratur: Fragmente, 3 vols., 1767; parts in *Selected Early Works 1764–1767*, translated by Ernest A. Menze and Karl Menges, 1992
Abhandlung über den Ursprung der Sprache, 1772; edited by Wolfgang Pross, 1978; as *Treatise upon the Origin of Language*, translated anonymously, 1827; as *Essay on the Origin of Language*, translated by John H. Moran and Alexander Gode, 1966
Von deutscher Art und Kunst: Einige fliegende Blätter, with Goethe, Justus Möser, and Paoli Frisi, 1773; edited by Hans Dietrich Irmscher, 1968
Auch eine Philosophie der Geschichte zur Bildung der Menschheit, 1774; edited by Hans Georg Gadamer, 1967; as *Yet Another Philosophy of History for the Education of Humanity*, translated by Eva Herzfeld, 1968
Älteste Urkunde des Menschengeschlechts, 2 vols., 1774–76
Ursachen des gesunknen Geschmacks bei den verschiedenen Völkern, da er geblühet, 1775
Vom Erkennen und Empfinden der menschlichen Seele, 1778
Briefe, das Studium der Theologie betreffend, 2 vols., 1780–81
Vom Geist der ebräischen Poesie, 2 vols., 1782–83; as *The Spirit of Hebrew Poetry*, translated by James D. Marsh, 1833, reprinted 1971
Ideen zur Philosophie der Geschichte der Menschheit, 4 vols., 1785–91; as *Outlines of a Philosophy of the History of Man*, translated by T. Churchill, 1800, reprinted 1966; abridged edition, as *Ideas for a Philosophy of the History of Man*, edited by Frank E. Manuel, 1968
Zerstreute Blätter, 6 vols., 1785–97
Gott: Einige Gespräche, 1787; revised edition, 1800; as *God: Some Conversations*, translated by Frederick H. Burkhardt, 1940

Briefe zur Beförderung der Humanität, 10 collections, 1793–97
Adrastea, 6 vols., 1801–04
Johann Gottfried Herder on Social and Political Culture, edited and translated by F. M. Barnard, 1969
Selected Early Works, 1764–1767: Addresses, Essays, and Drafts; Fragments on Recent German Literature, edited and translated by Ernest A. Menze and Karl Menges, 1992
Against Pure Reason: Writings on Religion, Language, and History, edited and translated by Marcia Bunge, 1993
Vom Geist des Christentums: Aus den "Christlichen Schriften" (1793–1798), edited by Herbert von Hintzenstern, 1994
On World History: Johann Gottfried Herder: An Anthology, edited by Hans Adler and Ernest A. Menze, translated by Menze and Michael Palma, 1997

Other writings: works on philosophy (including *Metakritik* against Kant's critical philosophy, 1799), aesthetics (*Kritische Wälder*, 3 vols., 1769), theology, and history, and correspondence. Also compiled a collection of European-language folksongs (1778–79).

Collected works editions: *Sämtliche Werke*, edited by Bernhard Suphan and others, 33 vols., 1877–1913, reprinted 1994; *Werke*, edited by Wolfgang Pross, 3 vols., 1984–88; *Werke*, 10 vols., 1985– (in progress); *Ausgewählte Werke in Einzelausgaben*, edited by Regine Otto and others, 1985– (in progress).

Bibliographies

Günther, Gottfried, Albina A. Volgina, and Siegfried Seifert, *Herder-Bibliographie*, Berlin and Weimar: Aufbau, 1978
Irmscher, Hans Dietrich, and Emil Adler, *Der handschriftliche Nachlass Johann Gottfried Herders*, Wiesbaden: Harrassowitz, 1979
Kuhles, Doris, *Herder-Bibliographie 1977–1992*, Stuttgart: Metzler, 1994

Further Reading

Barnard, F. M., *Herder's Social and Political Thought: From Enlightenment to Nationalism*, Oxford: Clarendon Press, 1965
Barnard, F. M., *Self-Direction and Political Legitimacy: Rousseau and Herder*, Oxford: Clarendon Press, 1988
Berlin, Isaiah, *Vico and Herder: Two Studies on the History of Ideas*, London: Hogarth Press, and New York: Viking Press, 1976
Clark, Robert T., *Herder: His Life and Thought*, Berkeley: University of California Press, 1955
Fink, Karl J., "Tithonism: Herder's Concept of Literary Revival," in *Johann Gottfried Herder: Language, History, and the Enlightenment*, edited by Wulf Koepke, Columbia, South Carolina: Camden House, 1990: 196–208
Haym, Rudolf, *Herder nach seinem Leben und seinen Werken dargestellt*, Berlin: Weidmann, 2 vols., 1877–85
Irmscher, Hans Dietrich, "Grundzüge der Hermeneutik Herders," in *Bückeburger Gespräche über Johann Gottfried Herder 1971*, edited by Johann Gottfried Maltusch, Bückeburg: Grimme, 1973: 17–57
Irmscher, Hans Dietrich, "Herder über das Verhältnis des Autors zum Publikum," in *Bückeburger Gespräche über Johann Gottfried Herder 1975*, edited by Johann Gottfried Maltusch, Rinteln: Bösendahl, 1976: 17–57
Irmscher, Hans Dietrich, "Beobachtungen zur Funktion der Analogie im Denken Herders," *Deutsche Vierteljahrsschrift für Literaturwissenschaft und Geistesgeschichte* 55 (1981): 64–97
Koepke, Wulf, "Herders Totengespräch mit Lessing," in *Aufnahme – Weitergabe: Literarische Impulse um Lessing und Goethe*, edited by John A. McCarthy and Albert A. Kipa, Hamburg: Buske, 1982: 125–42
Koepke, Wulf, "Herder's Craft of Communication," in *The Philosopher as Writer: The Eighteenth Century*, edited by Robert Ginsberg, Selinsgrove, Pennsylvania: Susquehanna University Press, and London: Associated University Presses, 1987: 94–121
Koepke, Wulf, *Johann Gottfried Herder*, Boston: Twayne, 1987
Koepke, Wulf, "Herders *Zerstreute Blätter* und die Struktur der Sammlung," *Herder Yearbook* 1 (1992): 98–117
La Vopa, Anthony J., "Herder's *Publikum*: Language, Print, and Sociability in Eighteenth-Century Germany," *Eighteenth-Century Studies* 29 (1995): 5–24
Liebel-Weckowicz, Helen, "Herder's Place in the Development of Ideas on Human Genesis and Evolution," *Eighteenth-Century Life* 9 (1984): 62–82
McCarthy, John A., *Crossing Boundaries: A Theory and History of Essay Writing in German, 1680–1815*, Philadelphia: University of Pennsylvania Press, 1989
Moser, Walter, "Herder's System of Metaphors in the *Ideen*," in *Johann Gottfried Herder: Innovator Through the Ages*, edited by Wulf Koepke, Bonn: Bouvier, 1982: 102–24
Nisbet, H. B., *Herder and the Philosophy and History of Science*, Cambridge: Modern Humanities Research Association, 1970
Norton, Robert E., *Herder's Aesthetics and the European Enlightenment*, Ithaca, New York: Cornell University Press, 1991
van der Laan, James M., "Herder's Essayistic Style," in *Johann Gottfried Herder: Language, History, and the Enlightenment*, edited by Wulf Koepke, Columbia, South Carolina: Camden House, 1990: 108–23

Herling-Grudziński, Gustaw

Polish, 1919–

Gustaw Herling-Grudziński writes about fundamental things that determine the human condition: good and evil, love and hate, the yearnings and limitations of existence. The material for his reflections are significant examples from literature, history, art, and contemporary social and political life. The essay, with its formal flexibility, seems the best genre for both his unrestrained thinking and his eloquent style. The voice of Herling-Grudziński the essayist can be heard even in some of his short stories and in his famous novel *A World Apart* (1951; *Inny świat*), a retelling of his own experiences and observations in the Soviet labor camp Ertsevo, where he spent almost two years (1940–42). Conversely, Herling-Grudziński's eminent talent for storytelling is the moving force behind some of his essays. His affinity for mixed literary forms led to the unique *Dziennik pisany nocą* (*Journal Written at Night*), composed of essays, short stories, book reviews, and comments on political and cultural events and published in the Polish émigré monthly *Kultura* in Paris from the 1971 onward, and in six separate volumes so far.

After World War II Herling-Grudziński lived and published in Rome and London. From 1948 to 1952 he was a contributor to the London-based Polish weekly *Wiadomości Literackie* (Literary news). In 1955 he settled in Naples, and has since been a regular contributor to *Kultura* and the Italian monthly *Tempo Presente*. Although a polyglot, Herling-Grudziński writes mainly in Polish and addresses himself to Polish-speaking readers. During the 1980s Herling-Grudziński was one of the most popular émigré authors in Poland, a moral authority in the Polish effort to abolish the communist system. Beginning in 1988 his books were officially published in his native country, and he has gained the reputation of being a brilliant and original Polish essayist.

Herling-Grudziński is a real "devourer and masticator of books," as Jerzy Paszek (1992) describes him. He has published insightful essays on the works of Kafka, **Camus**, **Dostoevskii**, Pasternak, Bulgakov, Solzhenitsyn, Isaac Babel', **Simone Weil**, Joseph Conrad, **Graham Greene**, and Giuseppe Tomasi di Lampedusa. To highlight the uniqueness of each author, Herling-Grudziński often compares the approaches of two or more authors to the same question. In "Dwie świętości" (1949; Two sanctities), which is devoted to everyday human heroism (a favorite theme), he contrasts Graham Greene's appreciation for Catholic sanctity with Camus' recognition of laic sanctity: "Between the theological abstraction, which commands us to suffer in silence for reward in heaven, and the humanist abstraction, which commands us to die and kill in the name of utopia's mirage, there is and will always be room for the laic sanctity, which commands us to fight against despair for one reason only: to relieve human suffering." In "Sąd ostateczny" (1957; Last judgment), an essay on "the adventures of the soul in its quest for grace," the kinship and the polemics between Kafka's and Camus' novels – seen as ethical and metaphysical **treatises** – are traced. Through a comparison between Joseph Conrad's *Under Western Eyes* and Dostoevskii's *Crime and Punishment* ("W oczach Conrada" [1957; In Conrad's eyes]), Herling-Grudziński elaborates on the secrets of the persuasive power of fiction. He is a profound reader and interpreter of Solzhenitsyn's "polyphonic" novels ("Jegor i Iwan Denisowicz" [1963; Egor and Ivan Denisovich]; "Realizm rosyjski" [1968; Russian realism]; "Godzina prawdy" [1968; The hour of truth]) and Boris Pasternak's poems and *Doctor Zhivago* ("Zwyciestwo Borysa Pasternaka" [1957; Boris Pasternak's victory]; "Wielka Książka" [1958; A great book]). Herling-Grudziński's critical commentaries on contemporary Polish literature have been highly influential in creating the modern Polish literary sensibility.

Herling-Grudziński's essays on painting display a similar humanistic interpretive approach. His reflections on the famous works of Correggio, Caravaggio, Rembrandt, Vermeer, and Ribera reveal his intuitive perception of particular pictures as well as his expertise in this field. Animated by Herling-Grudziński's imagination, the artists' personalities loom large behind the paintings discussed.

A characteristic of Herling-Grudziński's essays is the depiction of the individual at a dramatic moment of history as a way of particularizing the human condition. The author's own experience of the turning points of 20th-century history has given his observations worldly wisdom and understanding. Whether he writes on the plague in Naples in 1656 ("Dżuma w Neapolu" [1990; The plague in Naples]) or on the martial law in Poland, whether on the idea of revolution ("Wiek rewolucji" [1952; The age of revolution]) or on the Holocaust ("Demon naszych czasów" [1963; The demon of our time, a brilliant essay on **Hannah Arendt**'s *Eichmann in Jerusalem*]), Herling-Grudziński is always concerned with the eternal problem of good and evil and the individual's responsibility in choosing between them.

Riddles of the past fascinate Herling-Grudziński. A few of his masterpieces are accounts of his own investigations into an object, a story, or a figure from the past ("Srebrna szkatułka"

[1994; The silver casket]; "Monolog o martwej mniszce" [1991; A monologue about the dead nun]; "Dżuma w Neapolu"). The essay "Siedem śmierci Maksyma Gorkiego" (1954; The seven deaths of Maksim Gor'kii) is exemplary of Herling-Grudziński's special interest in the history of communist Russia and in the totalitarian mechanisms of falsifying reality, a phenomenon he closely analyzes in *A World Apart*.

Suspicious of generalizations, Herling-Grudziński has developed a sharp sense of the importance of the concrete. By exploring the fate of the individual he unearths truths about human hope and despair, about the moral dimension of human life. In his ethical judgments, however, Herling-Grudziński is not a moralist; the hierarchy of moral values that he has adopted from the "laic saint," along with his civil courage, have earned him devoted readers, who belong to different social and professional groups but share the belief that literature, art, and culture as a whole unavoidably reflect the human condition and are, therefore, a source of knowledge about humankind.

KATIA MITOVA-JANOWSKI

Biography

Born 20 May 1919 in Kielce. Studied Polish literature at the University of Warsaw, 1937–39; editor, *Orka na Ugorze* (Plowing the fallow field) weekly. Following the 1939 September campaign at the beginning of World War II, he organized the anti-Nazi underground group PLAN and the newspaper *Biuletyn Polski* (Polish bulletin), 1939–40; deported to a Soviet labor camp near Archangelsk, 1940: released, 1942, and joined the Polish forces fighting on the side of the Allies against the Germans in Italy. Literary editor, *Orzeł Biały* (White eagle), 1945–47; frequent contributor to the Paris-based Polish émigré monthly *Kultura*, from 1947, and associated with the group of Polish émigré writers based around it, including **Czesław Miłosz**, **Witold Gombrowicz**, Józef Czapski, **Jerzy Stempowski**, Konstanty A. Jeleński, and Marek Hłasko. Lived in London and worked for the émigré weekly *Wiadomości Literackie*, 1948–52. Moved to Naples, 1955; contributor to the Italian monthly *Tempo Presente*. Visited Poland, 1991. Awards: honorary degree from the University of Poznań.

Selected Writings

Essays and Related Prose
Żywi i umarli, 1945
Drugie przyjście oraz inne opowiadania, 1963; as "The Second Coming," translated by Ronald Strom, in *The Island: Three Tales*, 1967
Upiory rewolucji, 1969
Dziennik pisany nocą, 6 vols., 1973–93; part as *Volcano and Miracle: A Selection of Fiction and Nonfiction from the Journal Written at Night*, translated by Ronald Strom, 1996
Godzina Cieni, Eseje, edited by Zdzisław Kudelski, 1991
Wyjścia z milczenia, 1993
Sześć medalionów i srebrna szkatułka, 1994

Other writings: the autobiographical novel *A World Apart* (1951; pub. in Polish as *Inny świat*, 1955), short stories (some translated in *The Island*, 1990), and literary criticism.

Collected works edition: *Pisma zebrane*, 1994– (in progress).

Further Reading
Kandulski, Henryk, "O Herlingu-Grudzińskim," *Arka* 18 (1987): 30–37

Kudelski, Zdzisław, *Pielgrzym Świętokrzyski: Szkice o Herlingu-Grudzińskim*, Lublin: Fis, 1991

Nycz, Ryszard, "Zamknięty odprysk świata," *Teksty Drugie* 1–2 (1991): 35–46

Paszek, Jerzy, *Gustaw Herling-Grudziński*, Katowice: Slask, 1992

Pomian, Krzysztof, "Herling-Grudziński: Emigracja heroiczna," *Kultura* 12 (1981): 82–86

Przybylski, Ryszard Kazimierz, *Być i pisać: O prozie Gustava Herlinga-Grudzińskiego*, Poznań: Wydawnictwo A5, 1991

Wysłouch, Seweryna, and Ryszard Przybylski, editors, *Etos i artyzm: Rzecz o Herlingu-Grudzińskim*, Poznań: Wydawnictwo A5, 1991

Herzen, Aleksandr

Russian, 1812–1870

Aleksandr Herzen was to the modern Russian essay what **Aleksandr Pushkin** was to verbal art: he created standards of language and genre that later essayists could not ignore and would use as points of departure. Claimed as their direct forebear by radical leftists and Westernizers, Herzen also exerted a considerable influence upon intellectuals of all stripes. Beginning in the mid-1830s, Herzen wrote a large number of articles, editorials, **reviews**, and open **letters**. His most famous essays were written in cycles. His first major works, the cycles *Diletantizm v nauke* (1842–43; Dilettantism in science) and *Pis'ma ob izuchenii prirody* (1845–46; Letters on the study of nature), were published in Russia in the journal *Otechestvennye Zapiski* (Fatherland notes). Herzen took his family into exile in Europe in January 1847, deciding to remain abroad as long as Russia was oppressed with censorship and serfdom. Real social change, he argued, was happening in France, far away from the stagnant regime of Tsar Nicholas I. In his first two years in Europe during and after the turmoil of 1848, Herzen wrote perhaps his greatest single essayistic cycle, *S togo berega* (first pub. in German, 1850, in Russian, 1855; *From the Other Shore*).

Disillusioned with the results of the revolution, Herzen turned his essayistic efforts to acquainting European intellectuals with the political and social conditions of Russian life. His writing no longer took the form of essay cycles, but rather of separate articles. The essay *Le Peuple russe et le socialisme* (1851; *The Russian People and Socialism*), an open letter to the French historian Jules Michelet, is among the best examples of this writing. Most importantly, Herzen saw his chief purpose in acting as a free, uncensored voice speaking to educated Russians about taboo political and social issues. In 1853 Herzen opened his Free Russian Press in London. Separate numbers of his almanac, *Poliarnaia Zvezda* (1855–69; The polar star), and his newspaper, *Kolokol* (1857–67; The bell), were smuggled across the border, where they were read avidly and in tight secrecy, so that by 1862, when the ban on Herzen's name was officially lifted, thousands of readers were at least acquainted with his ideas.

Herzen's "moral education" was strongly founded on a youthful love for the German *Sturm und Drang* movement and its most prominent writers, **Schiller** and **Goethe**, and a later affinity for German idealist philosophy, particularly that of F. W. J. von Schelling. In Schiller's writings he found a high valuation of friendship that went beyond the individuals involved to a devotion to the betterment of society, nation, indeed, all humanity. From both Schiller and Schelling he adopted a belief in the power of the conscious, knowing self to form the surrounding environment. In these early responses to literature and philosophy can be found that generosity of spirit that would distinguish his greatest essays. The concept of socialism first became known to Herzen in 1834 when he read the French utopian socialist, Henri Saint-Simon. It was in Hegel that, in the 1840s, Herzen found what he called "the algebra of revolution." Although he developed political beliefs considerably more radical than those of most of his generation, he always held onto a faith in the private and public responsibility of the individual self and was always skeptical of social utopias, philosophical systems, and political theories abstracted from life experience.

Herzen's essay style combines breadth of spirit and passion with a sharp satirical wit normally associated with Gogol'. The goal of his essays was, as he put it, "to convince by making a strong impression." Thus, the force of his argument rested frequently on a few striking points rather than on pedantic adumbration of facts. In Herzen's time most major **philosophical essays** were written in French or German. If they were written in Russian, they tended to be so narrowly scholastic as to be unreadable by all but a narrow clique of academics. Herzen had the following to say about the generation of students of the late 1830s who were devoted to the study of German philosophy: "Our young philosophers ruined not only their native language but their understanding. Their attitude toward reality became scholastic and literary ... Everything really direct, every simple feeling was reduced to an abstract category, and as a result became emptied of life – a pale, algebraic shadow." The great contribution of Herzen's early career was to make philosophical inquiry accessible to educated Russian readers and to use it to build a new practice of public discourse in the Russian language. His greatest works, *From the Other Shore* and his autobiography, *Byloe i dumy* (wr. 1852–68, pub. 1855–69; *My Past and Thoughts*), are both brilliant performances of this new discourse.

The discussion of philosophy in Russian is directly linked in all Herzen's writings to the creation of a new kind of public self. Herzen grew up in the 1820s when the chief model of social selfhood was the *honnête homme*, a kind of social chameleon who could adapt harmoniously to any circle in high society. Modeled in part on Goethe, Herzen's public self was broadly educated and conversant in a variety of contemporary scientific, literary, and, by inference, social-political developments. Aesthetically and scientifically educated people, Herzen suggested, are in a position to be socially responsible, not just to adapt to but to exert an influence upon their social environment. In his first major cycle, *Diletantizm v nauke*, Herzen made the point as clearly as the oppressive times allowed: ". . . from the temple of science [read also: philosophy] humanity will issue forth with proud uplifted brow inspired by consciousness toward the creation of the kingdom of heaven." Herzen's interest in philosophy and science was always directed away from the thin air of pure theory and toward engagement with "reality," experience, and action.

The targets of Herzen's early invective (for example, in "Moskvitianin'o kopernike" [1843; "The Muscovite" on Copernicus]) were conservative circles in educated Russian society based around such journals as *Moskvitianin* (The Muscovite) and their sycophantic concept of "nationalism" which aped that proclaimed by the court. He also made fun of their incompetence in matters of science and thought. In *Diletantizm v nauke* he wittily undermined a prevalent attitude of political quietism and argued for an outlet for scientific knowledge in the real world. *Pis'ma ob izuchenii prirody* argued against scholastic scientific inquiry and created a positive image of the well-rounded thinker, naturalist, and artist. *From the Other Shore* was addressed to issues of broad European interest. Here Herzen stood against the abstract ideals and systems of the radical elite – this time, Hegelian historical teleology. He argued instead that human history is really an outgrowth of natural chaos. Disillusioned with the French revolutionary experience, in his post-1848 writings Herzen found a new model for the realization of socialism, the Russian peasant and the peasant *mir* or commune. This new populism was expressed in the open letter to Michelet.

The motto of *Kolokol* was a quotation from Schiller: "I call to the living." Herzen announced the strongly political program of exposing every injustice and corrupt act to the light of the media: "*The Bell* [*Kolokol*] will resound with whatever touches it – the absurd decree, or the senseless persecution of Old Believers, grandees' thievery or the ignorance of the Senate. The comic and the criminal, the malicious and the crude – all will play to the sound of *The Bell*." Here for the first time in Russian history was a consistent, long-term assault on the internal politics of the tsarist regime. It is not by chance that Herzen became known as a "second government."

Herzen acted as a bridge between the 1840s generation of idealistically minded "superfluous men," and the radical utilitarians – **Nikolai Chernyshevskii** and others – of the 1860s; his achievements were strongly admired by Russia's Marxists. Nonetheless, it is essential to remember his considerable impact on writers and thinkers of other orientations, for example, Dostoevskii, whose dramatic, philosophical dialogues owe much to the thinker, **Tolstoi** and Pasternak, whose views of history were strongly influenced by Herzen, and the Marxist-turned-Idealist philosopher, Semion Frank.

EDITH W. CLOWES

Biography

Aleksandr Ivanovich Herzen. Born 25 March 1812 in Moscow. Studied physics and mathematics at Moscow University, 1829–33, degree, 1833. Joined a group of students to debate progressive ideas: arrested with other members and charged with "dangerous free-thinking," 1834: exiled as a government clerk in Perm', 1835, Viatka, 1835–37, and Vladimir, 1837–39. Married Natal'ia Zakhar'ina (died, 1852), 1838: eight children (only one son and two daughters survived infancy). Clerk, Ministry of Internal Affairs, Moscow, 1839, and St. Petersburg, 1840. Exiled again to Novgorod on the grounds of spreading baseless rumors, 1841, but permitted to return to live in Moscow, 1842. Wrote a series of essays on philosophy and the natural sciences using the name Iskander, 1842–47. Moved to Europe, 1847, living in Paris, 1847–49, then Switzerland and Nice, 1849–52. His mother and son killed in shipwreck, 1851, and his wife died after an affair with the German poet Georg Herwegh, 1852. Lived in London, 1852–64, where he was joined by Nikolai Ogar'ev, with whose wife he had an affair; coeditor, with Ogar'ev, of émigré publications throughout the 1850s and 1860s; founder, Free Russian Press, 1853, *Poliarnaia Zvezda*, 1855–69, and *Kolokol*, 1857–67. Lived mainly in Switzerland, 1865–69. Died in Paris, 11 January 1870.

Selected Writings

Essays and Related Prose

Diletantizm v nauke, 1842–43
Pis'ma ob izuchenii prirody, 1845–46
Vom anderen Ufer, 1850; as *S togo berega*, 1855; as *From the Other Shore*, translated by Moura Budberg, 1956
Le Peuple russe et le socialisme: Lettre à Monsieur J. Michelet, 1855; as *Russkii narod i sotsializm*, 1858; as *The Russian People and Their Socialism: A Letter to M. J. Michelet*, translated by V. Linton, 1855; as *The Russian People and Socialism: An Open Letter to Jules Michelet*, translated by Richard Wollheim, 1956
Byloe i dumy, in *Poliarnaia zvezda*, 1855–69; as *My Exile in Siberia*, translated by M. Meizenburg, 2 vols., 1855; as *The Memoirs of Alexander Herzen*, translated by J. D. Duff, 1923; as *My Past and Thoughts*, translated by Constance Garnett, 6 vols., 1924–27, and abridged in 1 vol., 1968, revised by Humphrey Higgins, 1982; part as *Ends and Beginnings*, edited by Alice Kelly, 1985; part as *Childhood, Youth and Exile*, translated by J. D. Duff, 1979
"*Kontsy i nachala*" (Ends and beginnings), in *Kolokol* (The bell), 1862–63; also in *Esche raz: Sbornik statei Iskandera* (Once again), 1866
Pis'ma k staromu tovarischchu: Sbornik posmertnykh statei Aleksandra Ivanovicha Gertsena (Letters to the old comrade), 1867–69
Eshche raz Bazarov (Bazarov once more), 1869
Sbornik posmertnykh statei (Posthumous essays), 1870
"*Kolokol*": *Izbrannye stat'i A. I. Gertsena, 1857–1869* (The bell: selected articles 1857–1869), 1887
Izbrannye filosofskie proizvedeniia (Selected philosophical prose works), 1946
Selected Philosophical Works, translated by Leo Navrozov, 1956
Za piat' let (1855–1860) (In the course of five years), 1960
A. I. Gertsen o literature (Herzen on literature), 1962
Estetika, kritika, problemy kul'tury (Aesthetics, criticism, cultural problems), 1987
Pis'ma iz Frantsii i Italii, as *Letters from France and Italy, 1847–1851*, edited and translated by Judith E. Zimmerman, 1995

Other writings: several novels (including *Kto vinovat?* [*Who Is to Blame*], 1845–46) and short stories.

Complete works edition: *Sobranie sochinenii*, 30 vols., 1954–66.

Bibliographies

A. I. Herzen: Materialy k bibliografii, Leningrad, 2 vols., 1970
Gillel'son, M. I., E. N. Dryzhakova, and M. K. Perkal', *A. I. Herzen seminarii*, Moscow, 1965

Further Reading

Acton, Edward, *Alexander Herzen and the Role of the Intellectual Revolutionary*, Cambridge: Cambridge University Press, 1979
Babaev, E. G., "A. I. Gertsen i 'metafizicheskii iazyk'," *Russkaia Rech'* 2 (1987): 30–35
Berlin, Isaiah, "Herzen and Bakunin on Individual Liberty," in his *Russian Thinkers*, edited by Henry Hardy, London: Hogarth Press, and New York: Viking Press, 1978: 82–113
Berlin, Isaiah, "A Remarkable Decade: IV. Alexander Herzen," in his *Russian Thinkers*, edited by Henry Hardy, London: Hogarth Press, and New York: Viking Press, 1978: 186–209
Carr, Edward Hallett, *The Romantic Exiles: A Nineteenth-Century Portrait Gallery*, Boston: Beacon Press, 1961; Harmondsworth: Penguin, 1968 (original edition, 1933)
Dryzhakova, E. N., "Dostoevskii i Gertsen: U istokov romana 'Besy'," in *Dostoevskii: Stat'i i materialy*, vol. 1, Leningrad: Nauka, 1974: 219–38

Elizavetina, G. G., "A. I. Gertsen i spory slavianofilov s zapadnikami," *Izvestiia Akademii Nauk (Seriia literatury i iazyka)* 33 (1974): 75–79

Elsberg, Iakov E., *Gertsen: zhizhn' i tvorchestvo*, Moscow: Goslitizdat, 1956 (original edition, 1948)

Gromova, L. P. "A. I. Gertsen o russkoi zhurnalistike 1940-kh godov," *Vestnik leningradskogo universiteta: Filologiia* 1 (January 1988): 33–40

Iaroslavtsev, Ia. A., "A. I. Gertsen v legal'noi pechati perioda pervoi revoliutsionnoi situatsii," *Russkaia Literatura* 2 (1989): 200–07

Kelly, Aileen, "Irony and Utopia in Herzen and Dostoevsky: *From the Other Shore and Diary of a Writer*," *Russian Review* 50, no. 4 (1991): 397–416

Koslovskii, L. S., *Gertsen – publitsist*, St. Petersburg: Energiia, 1914

Lanskii, L. P., "'Prototip' gertsenovskogo stilia," *Russkaia Rech'* 3 (1978): 33–35

Letopis' zhizni i tvorchestva A. I. Gertsena: 1812–1870, edited by B. F. Egorov and others, Moscow, 1974

Lishchiner, S. D., "Gertsen i russkaia 'intellektual'naia proza'," *Voprosy Literatury* 20, no. 4 (1976): 172–95

Malia, Martin, *Alexander Herzen and the Birth of Russian Socialism, 1812–1855*, Cambridge, Massachusetts: Harvard University Press, and London: Oxford University Press, 1961

Partridge, Monica, "Alexander Herzen and the English Philosophers, Francis Bacon and Thomas Hobbes," *Zeitschrift für Slawistik* 35, no. 1 (1990): 35–47

Perlina, Nina, "Vozdeistvie gertsenovskogo zhurnalizma na arkhitektoniku i polifonicheskoe stroenie 'Dnevnika pisatelia' Dostoevskogo," *Dostoevsky Studies* 5 (1984): 141–55

Polianina, T. V. "Poetika zaglavii v publitsistike A. I. Gertsena: Kolokol," *Voprosy Russkoi Literatury* 1 (1981): 73–80

Putinsev, V. A., *Gertsen; pisatel'*, Moscow: Iszdatel'stvo Akademii Nauk, 1963

Shostak, M. I., "Vpechatliaia – ubezhdat' Zametki o stile Gertsena-publitsista," *Russkaia Rech'* 5 (1975): 43–49

Skliarevskii, G. I., "A. I. Gertsen o russkom literaturnom iazyke," *Russkaia Rech'* 1 (1970): 17–20

Sukhomlin, E. G., "Zhanrovoe svoeobrazie pamfletov A. I. Gertsena," *Voprosy Russkoi Literatury* 2 (1973): 68–73

Sukhomlin, E. G., "U istokov russkogo fel'etona: O fel'etonakh A. I. Gertsen 1840-kh godov," *Voprosy Russkoi Literatury* 1 (1975): 57–63

Vomperskii, V. P., "K 125-letiiu so dnia vykhoda Kolokola: 'Zovu zhivykh'," *Russkaia Rech'* 4 (1982): 3–8

Historical Essay

Historiography in some form exists in the annals of the earliest civilizations; more than 20,000 clay tablets survive recording names and events from the Assyrian dynasty of Ashurbanipal, for example, and accounts from Egyptian, Babylonian, and Chinese dynastic archives are equally ancient. The modern reader, however, would find such early work difficult to identify as historical writing because of its lack of critical perspective and the absence of any genuine narrative. Indeed, until the philosophical and stylistic innovations of the essay had established literary dominance in Enlightenment Europe, few works of history were anything but eulogies, monuments, medals, or chronicles – representations of the past lacking analytical self-consciousness. Empiricism and its medium, the essay, are the true inventors of what we would recognize as historiography.

Among ancient writers, however, are two prominent exceptions to this generalization: the Greeks Herodotus and Thucydides, both of whom undertook their histories with "theses" in mind. Herodotus endeavored to show how the Greeks had withstood the Persian invasions, while Thucydides examined the causes of the Peloponnesian Wars which eventually involved all of the Greek states in internecine conflicts. It is Herodotus who first uses the word "historia," meaning inquiry, and who demands of the historian a position of skepticism toward his sources. Thucydides goes further in his acknowledgment of the essentially political nature of history and in his statement that he "always tested the accuracy of a report by the strictest standards." Both Herodotus and Thucydides are remarkable for their sense of what Virginia Hunter (1982) calls "historical space," a recognition that history required a methodology to shape it and that it was a rhetorical mode subject to techniques of analysis and persuasion. Oratory is both a model and a component of historiography for both Greeks, but especially for Thucydides. What survives of Roman history continues this tradition. Varro was remarkable for distinguishing history from antiquarianism and wrote an influential work of each kind, respectively his study of the first Triumvirate, the *Trikaranos*, and his exploration of the ancient origins of Rome, the *Antiquitates rerum humanarum et divinarum* (Human and divine antiquities). Livy and Tacitus are the two other most influential of the Roman historians: the former for his monumental history of Rome from its beginnings, *Ab urbe condita* (*History of Rome*), published in installments and running to 142 books; the latter for his *Historiae*, covering the period from the reign of Galba to that of Domitian, and his *Annales* concerning the Julian emperors from the time of Augustus.

Subsequent European historiography until the 18th century is much inferior to these classical examples and more like the recording of history in other world cultures. Such works are more accurately described as chronicles than histories and lack the element of synthesis and the critical perspective that distinguished classical history. In China, the first historical records of this sort were the *Shi chi*, dating from 85 BCE, which established a tradition that is mostly unbroken into the 20th century and is best described as bureaucratic and archival. Arabic historical writing originated with the legal records of Muslim theologians, had its zenith during the 14th century in the work of Ibn Khaldun, and was very like the Christian tradition of that time in its obsession with recording the growth of the faith and the lives of exemplary holy men. Bede's *Historia ecclesiastica gentis Anglorum* (c. 732; *Ecclesiastical History of the English People*), with its narratives of miracles and saints, is typical of medieval work of this kind in Europe, the first instance of which were the chronicles of Eusebius, called the *Historia ecclesiastica* (312–24 CE; *Ecclesiastical History*). None of these traditions is critical of its sources and all are chauvinistic in their biases toward their own cultural imperatives. There is no concept of anachronism in such writing, best witnessed in the inconsistencies of the monumental *Anglo-Saxon Chronicles* written between the 9th and 12th centuries. Only the work of the Bavarian Otto, Bishop of Freising in his *Chronica* (1146) and his *Gesta Friderici I imperatoris* (1158; *The Deeds of Frederick Barbarossa*) shows any sense of a philosophy of history that is analytical and attempts to examine events within their chronological and political contexts.

However, with the rise of secular city states during the Renaissance, historians saw themselves as more than chroniclers, a trend that began with Italian humanists like Leonardo Bruni, who wrote the *Historiae Florentini populi* (History of the Florentine people). Flavio Biondo was the most important of the humanist historians, and two of his works established new standards for accuracy in source and concern with rhetorical purpose: *Historiarum ab inclinatione Romanorum imperii decades* (1483; *The Decades*) and *Roma instaurata* (1444–46; Rome restored). Still, the true invention of history as a modern discipline belongs to the European Enlightenment.

The 18th century saw the development of two kinds of historical writing, the work of the "érudits" and the "philosophes," the former more or less antiquarians who emphasized documentation and research and the latter, theorists and interpreters who came to prevail during the century. **Voltaire** in his entry on "Histoire" in the *Encyclopédie* would emphasize the philosophical utility of history as a means of enlightening humanity by exposing the barbarity of the past. He eschewed detail in favor of opinion. On the opposite side as regards methodology were the English and Scottish historians for whom detail was crucial if opinion and theory were to be validated. Of these, Edward Gibbon and William Robertson are the most influential. **David Hume** in his essay "Of the Study of History" (1741) describes it as the narrative of human progress whose primary objective is moral by implication because it undertakes to delineate the rise and fall of civilizations by recounting "the virtues which contributed to their greatness and the vices which drew on their ruin." Indeed, the Enlightenment notion of progress, that improvement defined the historic curve of all civilizations, combined with the cultural domination of the scientific method after the 17th century, shaped the best historical writing in the period. The essay became the vehicle for historiography in the early 18th-century work of such writers as the Italian Ludovico Muratori, the French Maurist scholars, and especially **Pierre Bayle** in his *Dictionnaire historique et critique* (1697; *An Historical and Critical Dictionary*).

The mid- to late 18th-century publications of accomplished essayists like Montesquieu (*L'Esprit des lois* [1748; *The Spirit of Laws*]), Voltaire (*Le Siècle de Louis XIV* [1751; *The Age of Louis XIV*]), d'Alembert ("Discours préliminaire," *Encyclopédie*, 1751), David Hume (*History of England*, 1756–62), William Robertson (*History of Charles V*, 1769), Adam Smith (*The Wealth of Nations*, 1776), Gilbert Stuart (*The History of Scotland*, 1782), and Edward Gibbon (*Decline and Fall of the Roman Empire*, 1776–88) focused the writing of history both upon the perception of the individual as interpreter of his own history and upon the struggle of the individual within historic time as the primary subject of such writing. But it was the idea of history as much as the practice that obsessed 18th-century historians. Here the influence of the scientific method and the Enlightenment concern for applied learning were especially apparent in work like Giambattista Vico's *Scienza nuova* (1725; *The New Science*) and Voltaire's *Essai sur l'histoire générale et sur les mœurs et l'esprit des nations* (1756, 1761–63; *Essay on the Manner and Spirit of Nations, and on the Principal Occurrences in History*). Both men saw history as a mature discipline of learning which drew on all aspects of human culture from the arts through the sciences to provide theories of civilization. **Immanuel Kant** took this concept further in his "Idee zu einer allgemeinen Geschichte in weltbürgerlicher Absicht" (1784; "Idea for a Universal History with a Cosmopolitan Purpose"), where he argued that the knowledge of history would provide the basis for a just and universal society. This universalism had its opponents in Johann Winckelmann, who emphasized the unique unity of historic epochs, and **Johann Gottfried von Herder**, who presented a pluralistic model of world history in *Ideen zur Philosophie der Geschichte der Menschheit* (1785–91; *Ideas for a Philosophy of the History of Man*).

The Enlightenment development with the most impact on the 19th century was the professionalization of the study of history, especially in its establishment as an academic discipline at the University of Göttingen, with the first seminars and learned journal (1734–37). As the academic practice of history grew, so too did specialization, and after **Darwin**'s *On the Origin of Species* (1859), the scientific bias in historiography became nearly absolute. At the same time, national archives became crucial to serious historians; Jules Michelet wrote his work on medieval France entirely from archival sources, while the British Public Record Office opened government archives to the public in 1838. The Napoleonic Wars created a public appetite for contemporary history, at first satisfied by newspapers and magazines which proliferated at this time and eventually resulting in popular histories like **Macaulay**'s *History of England* (1848–61). Still, professional history became the preserve of the academic by the 20th century, as we see in the appearance of journals like the *Revue Historique* (Historical review) in France in 1876 and the founding of modern historiography by Henry Baxter Adams at Johns Hopkins University in Baltimore (1876), from where he also established the American Historical Association (1884) and launched the *American Historical Review* in 1895.

Historiography has continued to reflect the two primary traits it derived from the influence of the Enlightenment essayists: a scientific bias and an emphasis on critical scrutiny. Biases peculiar to the 20th century have made their mark, from economics in the work of Charles A. Beard (*Economic Interpretation of the American Constitution*, 1913) to the anthropological perspectives of Walter Burkert (*Homo Necans*, 1983). But it is the growth of journalism and the international press that may have had the most significant impact on how European culture looks at history. Certainly, the essay as a format for exploring and critiquing the historic moment dominates the newspaper and magazine; and popular periodical publications like *Time* magazine and more specialist magazines like *The Economist* present an experiential view of history through their presentation and analysis of the news in a culturally definitive way. Journalism in the late 20th century has helped to define history as a living encounter that changes almost daily and reflects the dynamism and uncertainty of modern society. In many ways, journalism is the ultimate expression of Voltaire's sense of historiography as an interpretive **dialogue**, not a compendium of factual detail. Its emphasis is upon history as an experience in the organic, unstable present. Thus the journalist becomes both an "eye witness" to history and its adjudicator, the document and the interpreter at once.

STEPHEN W. BROWN

Further Reading

Braudel, Fernand, *On History*, Chicago: University of Chicago Press, 1980 (original French edition, 1969)

Burke, Peter, *Sociology and History*, London and Boston: Allen and Unwin, 1980

Carey, John, editor, *Eyewitness to History*, Cambridge, Massachusetts: Harvard University Press, 1987

Froude, J. A., *Historical Essays*, New York: Alden, 1886

Gooch, G. P., *Historical Surveys and Portraits*, New York: Barnes and Noble, and London: Longman, 1966

Halévy, Daniel, *Essai sur l'accélération de l'histoire*, Paris: Îles d'Or, 1943

Hunter, Virginia, *Past and Process in Herodotus and Thucydides*, Princeton, New Jersey: Princeton University Press, 1982

Robinson, James Harvey, *The New History: Essays Illustrating the Modern Historical Outlook*, New York: Free Press, 1965 (original edition, 1912)

Hoagland, Edward

American, 1932–

Edward Hoagland sees the writer's job as "to swim upstream," to "unearth ideas that have been laid aside, reaffirm the unfashionable" ("Bicentennial Palaver," 1982). It is *his* job, certainly: he writes about subjects ranging from turtles ("The Courage of Turtles," 1985) to tiger-trainer Gunther Gebel-Williams ("Tiger Bright," 1970), from a county fair ("Americana, Etc.," 1985), to New York City ("The Problem of the Golden Rule," 1985). Hoagland writes about the disappearing wilderness, of trains and of tugboats. He writes of bear tracks, boxers, and carousels – and of his own marital infidelities and peccadilloes.

Regardless of his subject, for Hoagland the essay is a performance, something of a celebration, yet also "like the human voice talking" ("What I Think, What I Am," 1982). In his essays Hoagland notes that he stutters and characterizes himself as being in "vocal handcuffs" ("The Threshold and the Jolt of Pain," 1985); "I strangle," he notes in "The Problem of the Golden Rule" (1985). The man speaks only with difficulty.

In the tradition of **Montaigne**, Hoagland's essays are replete with multiplicity and variation; they proceed associatively. Often they are arranged around two contrasting subjects: men and women, the city and the country, lions and tigers, solitude and company. These seemingly opposing but complementary points of departure provide him with a framework within which he can digress – tacking contrapuntally, moving laterally and tangentially. His essays end with varying degrees of closure, often via metaphor and story, sometimes with the effect of Hoagland ending the essay *ex machina*. He has accurately declared himself "a rhapsodist" ("Walking the Dead Diamond River," 1970), and his essays evince a certain enthusiasm, an inclusive spirit, and a sheer joy in language.

A significant manifestation of this joy are his metaphors: "Turtles are birds with the governor turned low" ("The Courage of Turtles"), or Hoagland's analogy noting that tigers "smell like rye bread smeared with Roquefort cheese" ("Tiger Bright"). He speaks in multiples, as in "wolf pups make a frothy ribbon of sound like fat bubbling, a shiny, witchy, fluttering yapping" ("Howling Back at the Wolves," 1983). The metaphors suggest the variety within his subject: "Turtles cough, burp, whistle, grunt and hiss, and pronounce social

judgments" ("The Courage of Turtles"). Often he includes a paragraph-long list as a means to suggest multiplicity. He improvises with language, noting that when the temperature drops, mud is "architectured into shape" ("Walking the Dead Diamond River"); mountain lions play a "game of noses-and-paws" ("Hailing the Elusory Mountain Lion," 1970).

Hoagland has characterized the essayist as being "like an infielder in baseball. He performs a lot, making the pretty throw to first" ("On Being Between Books," 1982). This essayist is not the writer who hits home runs, who scores points, but one who essays on occasion. The performer, the "artful 'I'" of the essay can be a "chameleon" ("What I Think, What I Am"). In an interview Hoagland has noted that essays are "more the province of middle-aged writers" who are "cannier, less truthful" (Robert Smith, 1982). Trust the essay, not the essayist. It may well be that Hoagland would like the essayist to be kin to what he sees as the ideal politician, who "should not be many things to different people but many things within himself" ("Bicentennial Palaver," 1976).

Hoagland's abundance does not reduce well or easily; nor is it intended to. In "What I Think, What I Am" he notes that essays "don't usually boil down to a summary" and contrasts the essay with the story, which plays upon the reader's empathy. An essay is a matter of "mind speaking to mind" and while lurking in the essay is "a point which is its real center," that point "couldn't be uttered in fewer words than the essayist has used" ("What I Think, What I Am"). Hoagland locates the essay "hang[ing] somewhere on a line between two sturdy poles: this is what I think and this is what I am." His observations on the style of the essay apply to his own: it "has a 'nap' to it, a combination of personality and originality and energetic loose ends that stand up like the nap on a piece of wool and can't be brushed flat." Hoagland describes the essay in metaphors: "Essays belong to the animal kingdom, with a surface that generates sparks, like a coat of fur" ("What I Think, What I Am"). It is a live and lively genre.

For Hoagland the essay is an armchair genre but one that makes demands upon the reader. He assumes a literate reader, his essays being addressed "to an educated, perhaps middle-class reader, with certain presuppositions, a frame of reference, even a civility that is shared" ("What I Think, What I Am"). Following the movement of the essayist's mind does not make for easy reading; Hoagland says reading "is like swimming described in the Greek epics" ("Books, Movies, the News," 1985) in which Odysseus had to contend with a variety of oceanic conditions. So too does the reader with Hoagland's essays, contending with his range of subjects, metaphors, lists, stories, wordplay, and celebration of his private quirks and foibles. Although he cannot otherwise speak with ease, Edward Hoagland's essays manifest a celebration of the possibilities of language.

Sandra A. Engel

See also Nature Essay

Biography

Edward Morley Hoagland. Born 21 December 1932 in New York City. Studied at Harvard University, Cambridge, Massachusetts, 1950–54, A.B., 1954. Served in the U.S. Army, 1955–57. Married Amy Ferrara, 1960 (divorced, 1964). Taught at various American colleges and universities, including the New School for Social

Research, New York, Rutgers University, New Brunswick, New Jersey, City University of New York, Columbia University, New York, Bennington College, Vermont, Brown University, Providence, Rhode Island, and the University of California, Davis, 1963–91. Married Marion Magid, 1968 (died, 1993): one daughter. Editorial writer, the *New York Times*, 1979–89; contributor to various other newspapers, journals, and magazines, including the **Atlantic Monthly**, *Village Voice*, *New England Review*, *Sports Illustrated*, **New Yorker**, *Esquire*, and *Transatlantic Review*. General editor, Penguin Nature Library, from 1985. Awards: many, including several fellowships; Longview Foundation Award, 1961; O. Henry Award, 1971; National Book Critics Circle Award, 1979; Vursell Award, 1981; New York Public Library Literary Lion Award, 1988; National Magazine Award, 1989. Member, American Academy and Institute of Arts and Letters, 1982.

Selected Writings

Essays and Related Prose

The Courage of Turtles: Fifteen Essays About Compassion, Pain, and Love, 1971
Walking the Dead Diamond River, 1973
The Moose on the Wall: Field Notes from the Vermont Wilderness, 1974
Red Wolves and Black Bears, 1976
The Edward Hoagland Reader, edited by Geoffrey Wolff, 1979
The Tugman's Passage, 1982
The Courage of Turtles, 1985
Heart's Desire: The Best of Edward Hoagland, 1988
Balancing Acts, 1992

Other writings: four novels (*Cat Man*, 1956; *The Circle Home*, 1960; *The Peacock's Tail*, 1965; *Seven Rivers West*, 1987), a collection of short stories (*The Final Fate of the Alligators*, 1992), and two travel books (*African Calliope*, 1979; *Notes from the Century Before: A Journal from British Columbia*, 1982).

Further Reading

Engel, Sandra, *Yourself a Little Change: Reading Edward Hoagland* (dissertation), Iowa City: University of Iowa, 1992
Smith, Robert, "From Harvard to the Big Top and Beyond," *Book World*, 28 February 1982: 6–7
Strenski, Ellen, "Foreign Correspondent in the Wild Kingdom: The Essays of Edward Hoagland," *Commonweal* 4 (August 1978): 500–03
Tropp, Sandra Fehl, "Edward Hoagland," in her *Shaping Tradition: Art and Diversity in the Essay*, Fort Worth, Texas: Harcourt Brace Jovanovich College Publishers, 1992: 548–51
Wolff, Geoffrey, Introduction to *The Edward Hoagland Reader*, New York: Vintage, 1979: ix–xxx

Hofmannsthal, Hugo von

Austrian, 1874–1929

Although Hugo von Hofmannsthal showed a distinct preference for particular genres during various parts of his career, his commitment to the essay began early in his life and lasted until his death. His earliest essays, published in 1891 when he was just 17, appeared in periodicals under the pen name "Loris," the title chosen for the first publication in book form of his early essays. When he died in July 1929, he had not only already published several essays that year but was also considering plans for a collection of his late essays, which, however, never came to fruition. These nearly 40 years witnessed considerable change, growth, and development as well as an extremely varied and flexible use of the genre.

His earliest essays emerged from the tradition of cultural journalism that flourished during the late 19th and early 20th centuries throughout Europe. Hofmannsthal certainly never thought of himself as a journalist in a narrow sense of the word, and went to great lengths to distinguish himself from those who practiced that profession. He argued that a certain vulgarity had been introduced into German journalism by Heinrich Heine and subsequent authors who had fallen under his influence. Although Hofmannsthal's essays on literature, theater, music, art, travel, and general cultural developments were published for the most part in Viennese periodicals, he saw them as having an enduring quality that derived from his ability to use a contemporary cultural event as a point of departure for formulating a general principle or gaining a universal insight. If his essays are to be associated with journalism in any way, Hofmannsthal would certainly have argued that they were the basis for a new journalistic style rising above the abysmal level then current. Among the contemporaries discussed are D'Annunzio, Ibsen, Swinburne, and **Pater**. He also records his impressions during a tour through the south of France and comments frequently on contemporary painting. The style of these essays is relatively informal and has something of a conversational tone. They are never chatty or casual but seem addressed to a congenial conversation partner who is widely read and has a cultivated sensitivity to aesthetic nuance.

The mode in which Hofmannsthal's essays address their audience is extremely varied. While most are straightforward discursive presentations, others, following a long tradition extending back to **Plato**, speak out of imaginary situations such as conversations or **letters**. Perhaps the most important conversation is "Gespräch zu Gedichten" (1903; "Conversation on Poetry"), which discusses several poems by Stefan George, a contemporary poet with whom Hofmannsthal had a highly ambiguous relationship. Through the comments the two characters make about the poems, Hofmannsthal reveals his concept of the nature and challenge of poetry. Even more important than the conversations, however, are the imaginary letters; in fact the essay simply entitled "Ein Brief" (1902; "A Letter") is one of Hofmannsthal's most widely discussed and broadly influential works. It claims to be a letter written by the young Philipp Lord Chandos to **Francis Bacon**. In the most general of terms, the letter deals with the nature of language and of symbolic representation. Many have seen this letter as an expression of Hofmannsthal's deeply skeptical attitude toward the expressive power of language and his response to the uniquely Viennese crisis of confidence in language as seen particularly in the works of his contemporaries Fritz Mauthner and Ludwig Wittgenstein. Most informed recent criticism, however, has not been so willing to read the essay in such narrowly biographical terms but stresses rather its fictionality. Editors of Hofmannsthal's works have been far from consistent in their generic understanding of these conversations and letters: some have been published along with more conventional examples of the essay, while others have been classified as a genre in their own right, though collected in the same volume as indisputably fictional narratives.

World War I had a profound effect on Hofmannsthal's essays. During and immediately following the war, he often turned to broadly patriotic themes and strove to differentiate what was distinctly Austrian from what was German or, more precisely, Prussian. He wrote eloquently and with a deep sense of personal conviction on themes taken from Austrian history and on Austria's literary and cultural heritage. These essays – "Die Bejahung Österreichs" (1914; The affirmation of Austria), "Grillparzers politisches Vermächtnis" (1915; Grillparzer's political legacy), "Österreich im Spiegel seiner Dichtung" (1916; Austria in the mirror of her literature), and "Die Österreichische Idee" (1917; The Austrian idea), for example – are neither shrill nor aggressively polemical but rather nostalgic and, perhaps, somewhat conservative.

Just as Hofmannsthal saw his collaboration with the composer Richard Strauss and the director Max Reinhardt as the fusion of drama, theater, and music, he saw Austria as the place where the Germanic, Romance, and Slavic worlds met and experienced, if not a fusion, at least a richly productive interpenetration. During the last decade of his life, the idea of an inclusive Europe that extends across political as well as temporal boundaries became a motif of much of his thinking and manifested itself in his essays in a variety of ways. Some deal specifically with a common European spiritual and intellectual heritage: "Blick auf den geistigen Zustand Europas" (1922; A look at the intellectual condition of Europe), for example; others, when addressing specific figures, events, or ideas, draw on them in terms of their most broadly encompassing significance and their value for Western culture generally.

Hofmannsthal's influence on the essay as a genre is not to be found so much by seeking subsequent writers who drew on his example but rather in his extremely supple and pliant use of the genre. Situating it at the juncture of cultural reportage, fictional narration, visionary meditation, cultural critique, synthesizing analysis, congenial conversation, and edifying homily, he extended the horizon of the genre within the specific context of German literary history in ways that invite exploration.

STEVEN P. SONDRUP

Biography
Born 1 February 1874 in Vienna. Studied at Akademisches Gymnasium, Vienna, 1884–92; studied law, 1892–94, and Romantic philology, 1895–97, University of Vienna. Served with the 6th Dragoon Regiment in Göding, 1894–95. Married Gertrud Schlesinger, 1901: one daughter and two sons. Collaborated with Richard Strauss on operas, from 1909; editor, Österreichische Bibliothek, 1915–17; cofounder, with Max Reinhardt, Salzburg Festival, 1919. Died (of a stroke) in Rodaun, Austria, 15 July 1929.

Selected Writings

Essays and Related Prose
Studie über die Entwicklung des Dichters Victor Hugo (dissertation), 1901; as Victor Hugo, 1904; as Versuch über Victor Hugo, 1925
Unterhaltungen über literarische Gegenstände, 1904
Die prosaischen Schriften gesammelt, 5 vols., 1907; revised edition, 3 vols., 1917
Reden und Aufsätze, 1921

Buch der Freunde (aphorisms), 2 vols., 1922–29; part translated in Selected Prose, 1952
Früheste Prosastücke, 1926
Loris: Die Prosa des jungen Hofmannsthals, 1931
Die Berührung der Sphären, 1931
Festspiele in Salzburg, 1938
Selected Writings, vol. 1: Selected Prose (includes fiction), translated by Mary Hottinger and Tania and James Stern, 1952
Reitergeschichte: Erzählungen und Aufsätze, 1953
Selected Essays (in German), edited by Mary E. Gilbert, 1955
Österreichische Aufsätze und Reden, edited by Ludwig F. Jedlicka, 1956
Natur und Erkenntnis, 1957

Other writings: many plays (including Der Schwierige [The Difficult Man], 1921; Der Turm [The Tower], 1925), libretti (including Der Rosenkavalier, 1911), poetry, fiction, and many volumes of correspondence.

Collected works editions: Sämtliche Werke, edited by Heinz Otto Burger, Rudolf Hirsch, and others, 31 vols., 1975–94 (in progress); Gesammelte Werke, edited by Bernd Schoeller, 10 vols., 1979–80.

Bibliographies
Koch, Hans-Albrecht, and Uta Koch, Hugo von Hofmannsthal Bibliographie, 1964–1976, Freiburg: Hugo von Hofmannsthal-Gesellschaft, 1976
Köttelwesch, Clemens, "Hofmannsthal Bibliographie," Hofmannsthal Blätter 23–24 (1980), and 39 (1989)
Weber, Horst, Hugo von Hofmannsthal: Bibliographie des Schrifttums, 1892–1963, Berlin: de Gruyter, 1966
Weber, Horst, Hugo von Hofmannsthal: Bibliographie: Werke, Briefe, Gespräche, Übersetzungen, Vertonungen, Berlin and New York: de Gruyter, 1972

Further Reading
Exner, Richard, "Probleme der Methodik und der Komposition in den Essays von Thomas Mann und Hugo von Hofmannsthal," German Quarterly (1957): 145–57
Exner, Richard, "Zur Essayistik Hugo von Hofmannsthals," Schweizer Monatshefte 42, no. 2 (1962): 239–313
Gerke, Ernst-Otto, Der Essay als Kunstform bei Hugo von Hofmannsthal, Lübeck: Matthiesen, 1970
Gilbert, Mary E., "Hofmannsthal's Essays 1900–1908: A Poet in Transition," in Hofmannsthal: Studies in Commemoration, edited by F. Norman, London: University of London Institute of Germanic Studies, 1963: 29–52
Kähler, Hermann, Von Hofmannsthal bis Benjamin: Ein Streifzug durch die Essayistik der zwanziger Jahre, Berlin: Aufbau, 1982
Lengauer, Hubert, "Hofmannsthals journalistische Anfänge und das Feuilleton des späten 19. Jahrhundert," in Hofmannsthal und das Theater: Die Vorträge des Hofmannsthal Symposium Wien 1979, edited by Wolfram Mauser, Vienna: Halosar, 1981:125–40

Holberg, Ludvig
Danish, 1684–1754

Ludvig Holberg is the father of modern Scandinavian literature. Best known abroad as a writer of comedies, he was also a master in various other fields. He served, for example, as professor of history at the University of Copenhagen and wrote several historical works. Some of his works – including his autobiography – he wrote in Latin; most, however, were written in Danish, the language of Denmark and Norway. Holberg himself had been born in Bergen, Norway, and can be claimed as both a Danish and a Norwegian writer, a figure of whom both countries today are proud. Holberg was also an essayist, although his essays were written relatively late in life. The volume entitled *Moralske Tanker* (*Moral Reflections*) dates from 1744; the five volumes of *Epistler* (*Epistles*), containing 540 items in all, began appearing in 1748, with the final volume posthumously published in 1754.

Holberg traveled widely as a young man, spending two years in England (mainly in Oxford), and visiting the Netherlands and France twice, as well as Germany and Italy. Curiously, Holberg's stay in England at the beginning of the 18th century, the very time when periodicals were blossoming there, did not lead to a discernible interest on his part in English authors of the day. On the other hand, he found a major source of inspiration in French writers, particularly Jean de Clerc, whose work appeared in the Netherlands, where he lived in exile and where Holberg once called upon him.

The *Moral Reflections*, Holberg's volume of 63 essays, is more philosophical and serious than most of the essays making up the "epistles" of his second, five-volume collection. Indeed, because of the *Moral Reflections* Holberg has been called a modern **Cicero**. The earlier essays also have a clear connection with those of **Montaigne** and **Bacon**. A champion of moderation and reason, Holberg was the chief Scandinavian moralist and rationalist of his time. The *Moral Reflections* present no cohesive system of thought, however, though they are in many ways both theological and philosophical, suggesting the work of Gottfried Wilhelm von Leibniz and Leibniz's foremost disciple Christian Wolff. Many of the essays recall those by English writers of the moral weeklies, treating subjects such as virtue, decorum, reform, the best way to take criticism, and why similar deeds may be judged differently. Holberg's humor is present in these earlier essays, but subdued when compared with the humor in some of his other works, for example his *Nicolai Klimii iter subterraneum* (1741; *A Journey by Nicholas Klimius to the World Under Ground*), which strongly resembles **Jonathan Swift**'s *Gulliver's Travels*. Even the style of the *Moral Reflections* suggests British essays of the same or an earlier era. For example, the essay on studies begins, "Studies can be divided into the necessary, the useful, and the harmful" – an echo of Bacon's essay on books.

Holberg was writing the *Moral Reflections* for a learned and fairly limited audience in Denmark and Norway; he often quoted in Latin and Greek, and prefaced each essay with a Latin quotation. (In contrast, the later *Epistles* appealed to a much broader audience and, by virtue of their number, necessarily dealt with many more and different subjects.) An example of Holberg's style, wit, and attitude can be found in the following quotation from the end of the essay dealing with the arrogance of the ignorant: "I for my part would not wish to live in a country where there are no fools; a fool has the same effect in a republic as fermentation in the human stomach. The fool is like a sal volatile, which causes movement of the blood and juices; indeed, he can be compared with a hurricane which, although it may from time to time destroy houses and trees, at the same time purifies the air and prevents sicknesses which are born of too much quietude."

While the *Moral Reflections* express Holberg's personal philosophy and beliefs, the later *Epistles* deal with subjects of a non-philosophical nature. In them Holberg is as ever a spokesman for moderation and tolerance, championing what he calls the middle path. The individual epistles are, on the whole, much shorter than the **philosophical** essays in *Moral Reflections*. Nominally they are in the form of **letters** to an unknown person, a device which allowed Holberg to range considerably from the topic at hand and to insert quotations whenever it suited him. F. J. Billeskov Jansen (1938–39) demonstrates that Holberg wrote his essays using **Pierre Bayle**'s *Dictionnaire historique et critique* (1697; *An Historical and Critical Dictionary*) as a source of continuing inspiration: the sequence of essays in the *Epistles* corresponds to some extent to the sequence of articles in Bayle's dictionary, and Holberg invokes Bayle frequently in the text of the essays. In Epistle 34, for example, he states that one can profit much from Bayle's works and in particular escape the taste for the trivial with which most academics are infected. He goes on to say that no author known to him, old or new, "has written with greater pithiness and penetration and no publication has appeared which in regard to zeal, accuracy, variety of material, thorough criticism and gallant style can be compared with his critical dictionary." There are also many references to classical writers, French writers of an earlier era, and contemporary phenomena, as for example the discussion dealing with Julien Offray de La Mettrie's *L'Homme-machine*, a book of materialistic philosophy which had been published anonymously in Leiden in 1748. Works by La Mettrie had been publicly burned in The Hague in 1745, but he had the protection of King Frederick the Great of Prussia. Holberg's attitude is evidence of his liberal thought and openness to new and different ideas, without, however, raising his voice against Protestantism or the Establishment in general.

Several of the epistles are concerned with drama, specifically with Holberg's own comedies, the foreign criticism of them, and the unwillingness of the French to accept Holberg on a plane with Molière. As a dramatist Holberg identifies with Plautus and Molière but has little positive to say of contemporary writers of comedy.

Holberg's essays clearly demonstrate that he wrote as a result of studying other writers, and how dependent he was on them for his thoughts. The *Epistles* may be designated as essays evolved from his reading, his reflections, and his efforts at synthesis. On the whole they do not develop a single argument; rather they are reactive, responding to other works and to the issues of the day. Like essays in the moral weeklies of England and elsewhere, Holberg's essays are easy, pleasant reading, and it is as easy to disagree as to agree with what he writes.

P. M. MITCHELL

Biography

Born 3 December 1684 in Bergen, Norway. Studied theology at the University of Copenhagen, 1702–04. Visited the Netherlands, 1704–05, 1714–16, and 1725–26, Germany, 1705–06 and 1708–09, and England (mostly Oxford), 1706–08. Fellow, Borch's College, Copenhagen, 1709–14; professor of metaphysics, 1718–20, of Latin literature (and secretary of the university), 1720–30, of history, from 1730, and rector, 1735–36, and university bursar, 1737–51,

University of Copenhagen. Wrote for Montaigu's troupe at the Lille Grønnegade Theatre, Copenhagen, 1722–28; stopped writing plays during the ban on theatrical activity by Christian VI, 1730–46; made a baron, 1747; unoffical adviser and writer, Kongelige Teater, Copenhagen, 1748. Died in Copenhagen, 28 January 1754.

Selected Writings

Essays and Related Prose

Moralske Tanker, 1744; edited by F. J. Billeskov Jansen, 1943; as *Moral Reflections*, with *Epistles*, edited and translated by P. M. Mitchell, 1991

Epistler, 5 vols., 1748–54; edited by F. J. Billeskov Jansen, 5 vols., 1944–54; in part as *Selected Essays*, edited and translated by P. M. Mitchell, 1955, and as *Epistles*, with *Moral Reflections*, edited and translated by Mitchell, 1991

Essays, edited by Kjell Heggelund, 1977

Other writings: 32 plays (including *Den politiske kandestøber* [*The Political Tinker*], 1722; *Jeppe på Bjerget* [*Jeppe of the Hill*], 1722; *Jean de France*, 1722; *Den vægelsindede* [*The Weathercock*], 1722; *Erasmus Montanus*, 1723; *Henrik og Pernille* [*Henry and Pernilla*], 1724; *Maskarade* [*Masquerade*], 1724; *Jacob von Thyboe*, 1725; *Den Stundesløse* [*The Fussy Man*], 1726; *De usynlige* [*The Masked Ladies*], 1731), the novel *Nicolai Klimii iter subterraneum* (1741; *A Journey by Nicholas Klimius to the World Under Ground*), the mock epic poem *Peder Paars* (1719–20), many books on history, and an autobiography.

Bibliography

Ehrencron-Müller, Holger, *Bibliografi over Holbergs skrifter*, Copenhagen: Aschehoug, 3 vols., 1933–35

Further Reading

Billeskov Jansen, F. J., *Holberg som epigrammatiker og essayist*, Copenhagen: Munksgaard, 2 vols., 1938–39
Billeskov Jansen, F. J., *Ludvig Holberg*, New York: Twayne, 1974
Billeskov Jansen, F. J., *A Guide to the Writings of Ludvig Holberg and to His Manor-House Tersløsegaard*, Dianalund: Holbergske Stiftelse Tersløsegaard, 1979
Bredsdorff, Thomas, "Holberg: A Scandinavian Slant on the European Enlightenment," *Scandinavian Canadian Studies/Études Scandinaves au Canada* 4 (1991): 115–22
Greene-Gantzberg, Vivian, "Holberg and German-Speaking Europe," in *Holberg, a European Writer: A Study in Influence and Reception*, edited by Sven Rossel, Amsterdam: Rodopi, 1994: 67–103
Haarberg, Jon, "Essayet: Holberg, Montaigne og 'de gamle'," *Edda* 1 (1987): 73–83
Naess, Harald, "Holberg and the Age of Enlightenment," in *A History of Norwegian Literature*, edited by Naess, Lincoln: University of Nebraska Press, 1993: 53–81

Holmes, Oliver Wendell

American, 1809–1894

"Montaigne and Bacon under one hat" was how the American poet John Greenleaf Whittier described Oliver Wendell Holmes, the Boston physician-poet who created a new form for the essay with his popular *Autocrat of the Breakfast-Table* essays. Holmes' literary achievement is especially noteworthy in that literature was a sideline, a diversion from his full-time work as a Harvard University medical professor. Holmes defined the term Boston "Brahmin" and, in 1857, gave the

name the *Atlantic* (now known as the **Atlantic Monthly**) to the new monthly American magazine which would showcase his work. His impressive body of essays – which includes groundbreaking, highly readable **medical essays**, Civil War essays, and tributes to his famous contemporaries, as well as the Breakfast-Table essays – coincides with and expresses the golden age of Boston and provides a window on 19th-century American thought. In addition, Holmes' artful incorporation of poetry and narrative into the **familiar essay** marks him as an important figure in the development of literary nonfiction.

Holmes' first fame as an essayist came through the medical essays written on his return from Paris, where he studied medicine from 1833 to 1835. There he had breakfasted regularly at the café once frequented by **Voltaire, Rousseau,** and **Fontenelle.** In 1836 and 1837, Holmes won three of the four 50-dollar Boylston Prizes for his essays "Facts and Traditions Respecting the Existence of Indigenous Intermittent Fever in New England," "The Nature and Treatment of Neuralgia," and "The Utility and Importance of Direct Exploration in Medical Practice."

One hundred years after the publication of his controversial 1842 essay "The Contagiousness of Puerperal Fever," in which he presented overwhelming evidence that doctors often infected pregnant women with the fatal disease, an article in the *Bulletin of the Medical Library Association* called this essay "the most important contribution made in America to the advancement of medicine." Such essays, as well as "Currents and Counter-Currents in Medical Science" (1860), the most popular and quoted of all Holmes' medical writings, exhibit thorough research, lively language and thought, and even occasional humor.

Holmes devoted himself to medical rather than to political and social reform. One national issue which aroused him, however, was the secession of the Southern states, which he decried in such essays as "Bread and the Newspaper" (1861), "The Inevitable Trial" (1863), and "My Hunt After 'The Captain'" (1862), which described his search for his son and namesake, Captain Oliver Wendell Holmes, Jr., who was wounded three times during the Civil War.

Holmes knew all the leading men and women of his time. His "tributes" to **Emerson** (1882, 1885, 1889), Longfellow (1882), and Richard Henry Dana (1882) reveal his friendship and admiration. His "Remarks on the Death of Washington Irving" (1859) and *Atlantic* article on Nathaniel Hawthorne (1864) have greater interest as they recount Holmes' medical observations of the last days of **Irving** and Hawthorne's lives.

In 1857, the poet and essayist James Russell Lowell was invited to edit a new monthly literary magazine. He made a condition of his editorship that Holmes be the first contributor engaged – a surprising insistence given that the 48-year-old Holmes was known then only as a lyceum speaker and as the author of controversial medical essays and the popular poem "Old Ironsides" (1830). Holmes repaid Lowell's confidence by naming the magazine the *Atlantic* and beginning *The Autocrat of the Breakfast-Table* in its first number. *The Autocrat* was an immediate triumph. Indeed, in England its success surpassed any American work since Washington Irving's *Sketch Book* (1819–20).

The popularity of his Breakfast-Table essays caused Holmes to begin a publishing pattern he would follow to the end of his days: publishing monthly installments of his work in the *Atlantic*, which were then collected and published as a book in November in time for Christmas sales. Succeeding the "Autocrat" in January 1859 was *The Professor at the Breakfast-Table*, to be followed by *The Poet at the Breakfast-Table* in January 1872, and *Over the Teacups* in 1888. In the Breakfast-Table series Holmes created a form of the essay perfectly suited to his personality and vision. Holmes was a brilliant conversationalist, and the boarding house breakfast-table "setting" provided him a homey forum for his sharp observations and engaging "talk." In a masterful stroke he embodied the three facets of his identity (professor, poet, and "autocrat") as three separate characters in the essays. Thus in *The Autocrat* he could allow his "friend, the Professor" to express his most radical ideas, or could present the latest offerings of his "friend, the Poet." "How briskly his writing moves along," **Virginia Woolf** exclaimed in a 1909 centenary tribute to Holmes, and indeed Holmes employed his poetry (including his most famous poem, "The Chambered Nautilus") for both emphasis and variety in his essays. He created other breakfast-table companions as foils for his pronouncements: the Divinity School Student for discussions of dogma, the "young man named John" as the voice of dissent, the School Mistress for expressions of sentiment.

Holmes recognized that his readers liked stories as well as poems and wise and witty observations; he therefore also wove narrative threads into the essays. *The Autocrat of the Breakfast-Table* ends with the marriage of the Autocrat and School Mistress; *The Professor at the Breakfast-Table* with the illness and death of Little Boston, the isolated cripple. At the close of *The Poet at the Breakfast-Table* the Landlady gives up the boarding house, bringing the breakfast-table meetings to an end.

The Breakfast-Table essays display Holmes' gifts as an essayist. He writes in *The Autocrat* of "the infinite ocean of similitudes and analogies that rolls through the universe," and readers even today find Holmes' similes and metaphors engaging. His famous assertion that human beings possess one-, two-, or three-story intellects still stimulates thought. His lifelong faith in science and contempt for Calvinism's stress on human depravity is revealed in this characteristically vivid simile: "If for the Fall of man science comes to substitute the RISE of man, sir, it means the utter disintegration of all the spiritual pessimisms which have been like a spasm in the heart and a cramp in the intellect of men for so many centuries" (*The Poet at the Breakfast-Table*).

Holmes drew his figures from every imaginable source – the natural, social, commercial, historical, anatomical, nautical, pugilistical, and even "newspaporial" worlds. His use of simple, concrete figures helped him wed the classical universality and 18th-century rationalism of his idol **Samuel Johnson** with 19th-century Romantic subjectivity. Since Holmes believed his own subjective thoughts and feelings (as a well-balanced, rational individual) were shared by all people, the more subjective he was, the more universal he became. "And so I am not afraid to talk very freely with you, my precious reader or listener. You too, Beloved, were born somewhere ... Your hand is upon mine, then, as I guide my pen. Your heart frames the responses to the litany of my remembrance" (*The Poet at the Breakfast-Table*).

Dr. Johnson ranked highest in Holmes' pantheon, but he admired and saw his own strengths in fellow physician-writer Sir Thomas Browne ("With a Prelude on Nightcaps, and Comments on an Old Writer," 1883). Of his own countrymen, Holmes admired Washington Irving; certainly kinship can be found between Holmes' Autocrat and Irving's earlier Diedrich Knickerbocker and Geoffrey Crayon. Irving's essays may have shown Holmes that the public warmed to a personal tone, a winning persona, genial humor, and a rich but easy prose style.

In turn, Holmes influenced essayists who followed him, most notably **Lewis Thomas**, the Holmes of the 20th century. Thomas paid regular tribute to Holmes in his popular medical essays. Like Holmes, he created a genial persona who expressed optimistic humanism in his essays – and even many of Holmes' specific views.

Holmes was not without his limitations, however. Focused as he was on science and believing in evolutionary progress, he was not a champion of abolition, Brook Farm, transcendentalism, or other political, social, and philosophical movements of his time. More surprising, he failed to note the profound ethnic and religious changes that were transforming his own Boston during his lifetime. Holmes was concerned instead with the simple, universal emotions related to home and family affections, romantic love, friendship, aging, and the expansion of the human mind. He is unsurpassed at expressing ordinary ideas in ways that stimulate thought. Wherever the conversational essayist is evoked, Holmes' name must be mentioned, and he demonstrates that the essay can be highly congenial to poetry and fiction.

BARBARA LOUNSBERRY

Biography

Born 29 August 1809 in Cambridge, Massachusetts. Studied at Phillips Academy, Andover, Massachusetts, 1824–25; Harvard University, Cambridge, Massachusetts, B.A., 1829; Dane Law School, Cambridge, 1829–30; studied medicine at Tremont Medical School, Boston, 1830–33, in Paris, 1833–35, and at Harvard Medical School, M.D., 1836. Practiced medicine in Boston, from 1838. Professor of anatomy, Darmouth Medical College, Hanover, New Hampshire, 1838–40. Married Amelia Lee Jackson (died, 1888), 1840: two sons (one the judge Oliver Wendell Holmes, Jr.) and one daughter. Lyceum lecturer, 1841–57; Parkman Professor of Anatomy, Harvard Medical School, 1847–82, then emeritus. Contributor of the "Breakfast-Table" essay series, the *Atlantic*, from 1857. Awards: Boylston Prize, for medical essays, 1836, 1837; honorary degrees from three universities. Died in Boston, 7 October 1894.

Selected Writings

Essays and Related Prose
Boylston Prize Dissertations for 1836 and 1837, 1838
Homoeopathy and Its Kindred Delusions (lectures), 1842
The Autocrat of the Breakfast-Table, 1858
The Professor at the Breakfast-Table, 1860
Currents and Counter-Currents in Medical Science, with Other Addresses and Essays, 1861
Soundings from the Atlantic, 1864
The Poet at the Breakfast-Table, 1872
Medical Essays 1842–1882, 1883
Pages from an Old Volume of Life: A Collection of Essays, 1857–1881, 1883
Our Hundred Days in Europe, 1887

Over the Teacups, 1890
Oliver Wendell Holmes (selection), edited by S. I. Hayakawa and Howard Mumford Jones, 1939
The Autocrat's Miscellanies, edited by Albert Mordell, 1959

Other writings: three novels (*Elsie Venner*, 1861; *The Guardian Angel*, 1867; *A Moral Antipathy*, 1885), five volumes of poetry, and biographies of John Lothrop Motley (1879) and Ralph Waldo Emerson (1885).

Collected works edition: *Works* (Standard Library Edition), 15 vols., 1892–96.

Bibliographies

Currier, Thomas Franklin, and Eleanor M. Tilton, *A Bibliography of Oliver Wendell Holmes*, New York: New York University Press, 1953
Menikoff, Barry, "Oliver Wendell Holmes," in *Fifteen American Authors Before 1900: Bibliographical Essays on Research and Criticism*, edited by Earl N. Harbert and Robert A. Rees, Madison: University of Wisconsin Press, 1984
Tilton, Eleanor M., and Sidney Ives, *A Descriptive Catalogue of the Oliver Wendell Holmes Collection*, Gainesville: University Press of Florida, 1993

Further Reading

"Centenary Study of Holmes," *Edinburgh Review* 211 (April 1910): 414–34
The Critic issue on Holmes, 30 August 1884
Crothers, Samuel McChord, *Oliver Wendell Holmes: The Autocrat and His Fellow-Boarders*, Folcroft, Pennsylvania: Folcroft, 1973 (original edition, 1909)
Cullingworth, C. J., "Oliver Wendell Holmes and the Contagiousness of Puerperal Fever," *British Medical Journal* 2 (1905): 1161–67
Eccles, F. R., "Oliver Wendell Holmes, Physician and Man of Letters," *Canadian Lancet* 37 (1906): 1002–11
Ferguson, J. DeLancey, "The Unfamiliar Autocrat," *Colophon* 1 (February 1936): 388–96
Gougeon, Len, "Holmes's Emerson and the Conservative Critique of Realism," *South Atlantic Review* 59 (January 1994): 107–25
Green, R. F., "Oliver Wendell Holmes: His Writings and Philosophy," *Proceedings of the Literary and Philosophical Society* 35 (1880–81): 215–47
Grenander, M. E., "Doctors and Humanists: Transactional Analysis and Two Views of Man," *Journal of American Culture* 3 (Fall 1980): 470–79
Howe, M. A. De Wolfe, *Holmes of the Breakfast-Table*, London and New York: Oxford University Press, 1939
Hughes, J. L., "Oliver Wendell Holmes," *Canadian Magazine* 60 (February 1923): 334–40
Jennings, W. B., "Oliver Wendell Holmes: A Centenary Memoir of the Physician," *Medical Review of Reviews* 15 (1909): 107–14
Linn, H. W., "Holmes as Humorist," *University of Chicago Magazine* 2 (November 1909): 16–23
Merrill, W. S., "The Centenary of the Autocrat," *Catholic World* 134 (February 1932): 581–86
Morse, John Torrey, Jr., *Life and Letters of Oliver Wendell Holmes*, Boston: Houghton Mifflin, and London: Sampson Low, 2 vols., 1896
Pritchard, J. P., "The Autocrat and Horace," *Classical Weekly*, 16 May 1932: 217–23
Selbie, R. H., "Holmes," *Manchester Quarterly* 20 (1901): 232–58
Small, Miriam Rossiter, *Oliver Wendell Holmes*, New York: Twayne, 1962
Stephen, Leslie, *Studies of a Biographer*, vol. 2, London: Duckworth, 1931; New York: B. Franklin, 1973 (original edition, 1902)
Tilton, Eleanor M., *Amiable Autocrat: A Biography of Dr. Oliver Wendell Holmes*, New York: Henry Schuman, 1947
Woolf, Virginia, "Oliver Wendell Holmes," in her *Granite and Rainbow*, London: Hogarth Press, and New York: Harcourt Brace, 1958: 232–40

Hope, A. D.

Australian, 1907–

A. D. Hope is best known as an internationally recognized poet whose poetry has a strong, almost neoclassical sense of form and precision of language. However, some critics find his prose style more flexible, persuasive, and charming, and although his prose collections are all on literary topics, he has a well-earned reputation as a **critical essay**ist. Hope centers his prose writing on a traditional defense of poetry in a contemporary context. As a reviewer, his uncompromising, often caustic criticism has given rise to more than one literary *contretemps*, the most famous being his criticism of Patrick White's *The Tree of Man* as self-consciously provincial and the prose style as "pretentious and illiterate verbal sludge," although in general the review had some praise for the novel. Published under the title "The Bunyip Stages a Comeback" in the *Sydney Morning Herald* (16 June 1956), the review is said to have initiated White's lasting contempt of most Australian academics, and his satiric portrait (with allusions to Hope) of the academic Professor Sword in the play *Night on Bald Mountain* (1962). Hope republished the review in *Native Companions* (1974), repeating a belief unshaken by the realities of the modern novel that "The novelist needs a plain style, a clear easy stride, a good open texture of language to carry him to the end of his path."

Hope's essays take a generally prescriptive but well-reasoned stance on literary issues, including subject matter, genre, and the motives for writing; the influence of T. S. Eliot is often apparent. A typical essay from *The Cave and the Spring* (1965), a collection of essays on poetry, is "The Discursive Mode: Reflections on the Ecology of Poetry" (revised for *The New Cratylus* [1979] as "Ecology"), in which Hope draws analogies between natural and human ecology and finds that "The evil and incoherence and folly in society are also connected." This essay advocates the "middle form of poetry," the discursive mode, which does not depend, like most of the admired poetry of today, on a profusion of startling images, but on the plain resources of ordinary English used with inimitable aptness and animated by meter and rhythm. In "The Activists" (1965) Hope deplores what he calls "activism in literature" which "requires the writer to write in such a way that he promotes something" and tells him that "he has a duty to society beyond the duty of merely being a good writer." He defends the great satirists in prose and poetry, whose work is great "precisely because they are great as *satires*. And to say that they are satires is to say that they have a social purpose." Nevertheless, Hope's criticism also reveals a strong sympathy with the ideals of Romanticism, especially those implicit in the work of Keats, for example, and he frequently expounds the vatic and celebratory roles of poetry.

The most notable contributions to Australian letters made by Hope's essays are their style and their persistent advocacy of balance and control in literature and criticism, including the poetic use of rhythm, rhyme, and traditional forms. Graceful, fluent, authoritative, clear, and balanced, his essays use the minimum of critical jargon. Even when Hope's ideas seem insupportable, the prose makes them worth reading. Several essays remain a record of a good critic's errors, as in the attack on T. S. Eliot's prosody and poetic style in "Free Verse: A Post-Mortem" (1965). In the mid-century, when Australian literature found its place in university curricula, Hope maintained a vigilance against critical tendencies to approach Australian writing with less than rigorous standards, and he deplored motives of patriotism in the encouragement of local writers. He also warned against constructing canons of Australian literature that "prize those elements in Australian writing which were distinctively Australian and . . . underestimate anything which was not."

Hope had no patience with the self-consciously Australian school of Jindyworobak poets in the 1930s and 1940s, whose attempts to find primal ties with the country and its indigenous people seemed to him too strained or fictitious; he described them as "the Boy Scout School of Poetry," with "the same boyish enthusiasm for playing at being primitive." Later he acknowledged that he always had "an uneasy feeling that I had missed something important in what they were trying to say."

In the 1950s Hope was well known on ABC radio as Anthony Inkwell, giving advice to aspiring young writers in the long-running children's series The Argonauts. He also appeared as a regular reviewer and participant on many other series, on television as well as radio. *Chance Encounters* (1992), published in Hope's 85th year, is a comfortable collection of personal reminiscence and anecdotes which demonstrate his prose style at its most relaxed and graceful, the essays forming a brief account of his life, work, travels, and meetings in Australia and abroad with literary and other famous figures.

ELIZABETH PERKINS

Biography

Alec Derwent Hope. Born 21 July 1907 in Cooma, New South Wales. Studied at the University of Sydney, 1925–28, B.A., 1928; University College, Oxford University, 1928–30, B.A., 1931; Sydney Teachers' College, 1932. Teacher and vocational psychologist, Commonwealth Public Service, New South Wales, 1932–36. Married Penelope Robinson (died, 1988), 1937: one daughter (died) and two sons. Taught English at Sydney Teachers' College, 1937–44, University of Melbourne, 1945–50, Canberra University College (now Australian National University), 1951–68 (then emeritus), and Sweet Briar College, Virginia, 1970–71 (visiting). Founding member, Australian Academy of the Humanities; president, Australian Society of Authors, 1966–67; deputy chair, Australia Council for the Arts Literary Board, 1973–74. Awards: several, including the Grace Leven Prize, 1956; Britannica-Australia Award, 1965; Volkswagen Award, 1965; Myer Award, 1967; Australian Literature Society Award, 1968; *Poetry* magazine Levinson Prize, 1968; Ingram Merrill Foundation Award, 1969; Robert Frost Award, 1976; honorary degrees from four universities; Officer, Order of the British Empire (OBE), 1972; Companion, Order of Australia, 1981.

Selected Writings

Essays and Related Prose
The Structure of Verse and Prose, 1943
Australian Literature, 1950–1962, 1963
The Cave and the Spring: Essays on Poetry, 1965
The Literary Influence of Academies, 1970
Henry Kendall: A Dialogue with the Past, 1971
Native Companions: Essays and Comments on Australian Literature, 1936–1966, 1974
The Pack of Autolycus, 1978
The New Cratylus: Notes on the Craft of Poetry, 1979
Poetry and the Art of Archery, 1980
Directions in Australian Poetry, 1984
Chance Encounters, 1992

Other writings: 12 collections of poetry, a study of Dunbar's *The Tua Mariit Wemen and the Wedo* (*A Midsummer Eve's Dream*, 1970), a study of the poet Judith Wright (1975), and the play *Ladies from the Sea* (1987).

Bibliographies

Hergenhan, Laurie, and Martin Duwell, editors, *The ALS Guide to Australian Writers: A Bibliography 1963–1990*, St. Lucia: University of Queensland Press, 1992
Hooton, Joy, *A. D. Hope*, Melbourne: Oxford University Press, 1979
O'Brien, Patricia, *A. D. Hope: A Bibliography*, Adelaide: Libraries Board of Southern Australia, 1968
Phoenix Review issue on Hope includes bibliography (Winter 1987)

Further Reading

Hart, Kevin, *A. D. Hope*, Melbourne: Oxford University Press, 1992
Kramer, Leonie, *A. D. Hope*, Melbourne: Oxford University Press, 1979
Phoenix Review issue on Hope (Winter 1987)

Hostos, Eugenio María de

Puerto Rican, 1839–1903

Although Eugenio María de Hostos began his literary career as a novelist and also wrote short stories and poetry, his prestige as a philosopher and writer is primarily due to his extensive work as an essayist. His essays are a form of combat and action. For Hostos, the essayist is the "guardian of civilization" (*Moral social* [1888; Social morality]). As an artist, he pursues in his essays the expression of beauty, but also understands that "beauty is only that which is good." His essays are written in nimble prose, often with the intimate tone of an autobiographical text, but his style is always refined, even in the most private passages of his diary. His essays more closely approximate the Modernist renewal than the rhetorical prose of his age. He is direct and clear in the development of his ideas; however, he expresses them in a reflective manner and, in doing so, seeks to incite thought, to raise consciousness in order to free the human being, and in turn to advance the progress of humankind. Hostos is above all a moralist.

Influenced by the Krausist movement (Spanish followers of the German philosopher Karl Christian Friedrich Krause) and positivism, his writings are impregnated with faith in the progress of humanity. His inductive-rationalist method, radical in a period in which the scholastic system dominated the Hispanic world, made Hostos both an intellectual and a man of action. Puerto Rican by birth and educated in Spain, Hostos is a citizen of the Americas: he resided and taught in the United States, Colombia, Peru, Chile, Argentina, Brazil, Venezuela, and Santo Domingo. In his complete works, the collection of essays comes from 113 different magazines in various countries, which span the Americas and Spain, and among which seven were founded by Hostos. Two of the magazines that he founded in Santo Domingo, *Las Tres Antillas* (The three Antilles) and *Los Antillanos* (The Antillean people), had such notorious repercussions with their philosophy of independence that the Spanish government pressured the Dominican Republic into prohibiting them.

His political and social concern is part of his vision of an integral humanism that likewise demands a personal commitment: "No man is stronger than the man who fulfills his duty" ("En que se fundan los deberes sociales" [1888; On what social duties are founded]). Therefore, when his efforts failed before the revolutionary Spain of 1869, Hostos writes in his diary: "I cannot continue here . . . without renouncing my conscience and my dignity and my principles" (30 May 1869). In America, his fight for the political independence of the Antilles (Cuba and Puerto Rico) formulates itself as an imperative for human progress. He presents America as a symbol of the future where "three mother races, the native, the conquistador and the African," are in the process of achieving "the fusion of races into one civilization"; in this way, he speaks to us about an Antillean federation, a federation of Latin American nations as a preliminary step toward "the union of all nations" ("El día de América" [1883; America's day]). Politically speaking, he sees independence in the federation, and fights for the abolition of slavery as an initial step to the recovery of human dignity: "For me, the cholo [the mestizo – person of mixed blood] is not a man, he is not a type nor the example of the race; he is all of this and, in addition, a social question of future." With the cultural perspective by which this term is enriched, Hostos affirms that "America will owe its future to the fusion of races . . . the mestizo is the hope of progress" ("El cholo," 1870).

As Hostos had to confront in Spain the "liberal" intellectuals, who were denying the colonies the rights for which they were fighting, in America, particularly in the Dominican Republic, his teaching methods and ideas regarding the liberation of the individual led him to a confrontation with the hierarchy of the Catholic Church. Hostos, influenced by Krausist ideology in Spain, was promoting an interior religion in which the principles of the conscience would dominate and prepare "the transition from the traditional religions to the religions of Reason" (*Moral social*). In New York he also had to confront the greed of personal interests dividing Cuban and Puerto Rican patriots and degrading the ideals for which he was fighting.

But Hostos' place in history does not arise from his political activities or controversies. He was above all an educator who fought for cultural awareness, for an education dedicated to recuperating human dignity – a quality disregarded at that time in Latin America. In this concern he was multifarious; but there are two aspects, which, because of their present importance at the end of the 20th century, exemplify the significance of his thought: his struggle against racial discrimination and the relegation of women. In both cases, he believes that transcendence can be attained through educational reform directed toward the integral liberation of the human being. With regard to women, his position is equally strong. Hostos believes that prejudice and the abandonment of women's education impede the progress of humanity: "Vegetation, not life; fatal development, not free development; instinct, not reason; a bundle of irritable nerves, not directed faculties; woman has been made into this by the errors that burden her, social traditions, both intellectual and moral, that crush her" ("La educación científica de la mujer" [1873; The scientific education of woman]).

Hostos, indeed, belongs to a generation of 19th-century essayists (**José Martí**, Manuel González Prada, and Justo Sierra, among others) who charted the vision of Latin American thought and initiated the formulation of its discourse.

JOSÉ LUIS GÓMEZ-MARTÍNEZ

Biography

Born 11 January 1839 in Río Cañas, Mayagüez, Puerto Rico. Educated in Spain, from 1852; Central University of Madrid, law degree, c. 1860; admitted to the Spanish bar. Became active in Spanish politics, 1850s and 1860s. Immigrated to the United States, 1869; joined the Cuban Revolutionary Junta of pro-independence Cuban exiles in New York, and edited their magazine, *La Revolución*, c. 1869–70. Traveled to South America to promote Cuban and Puerto Rican independence and educational modernization, 1870–74; taught at various schools and universities throughout Latin America. Returned to New York, 1874–77. Founder of several magazines, including *Las Tres Antillas* and *Los Antillanos*, 1875. Promoted education in Venezuela, 1877–80. Founder and dean, Santo Domingo Normal School, and inspector general of public instruction, Santo Domingo, Dominican Republic, 1880–88; headmaster, Miguel Luis Amunátegui secondary school, Santiago, c. 1888–90; worked in education, Santo Domingo, 1900–03. Had one son. Died in Santo Domingo, 11 August 1903.

Selected Writings

Essays and Related Prose

Hamlet, 1873; as "An Essay on *Hamlet*," translated anonymously, in *Eugenio María de Hostos, Promoter of Pan Americanism*, 1953
Lecciones de derecho constitucional (lectures), 1887
Moral social, 1888; edited by Manuel Maldonado-Denis, with *Tratado de sociología*, 1982
Tratado de sociología (treatise), 1904; edited by Manuel Maldonado-Denis, with *Moral social*, 1982
Meditando, 1909
Romeo y Julieta, edited by Manuel Negrón Nogueras, 1939
Hostos, hispanoamericanista (includes essays by Hostos and critical essays on him), edited by Eugenio Carlos de Hostos, 1952; as *Eugenio María de Hostos, Promoter of Pan Americanism*, 1953
Ensayos inéditos, edited by Emilio Godínez Sosa, 1987
Obra literaria selecta, edited by Julio César López, 1988

Other writings: novels, plays, poetry, and children's stories.

Collected works editions: *Obras completas*, 20 vols., 1939, and 8 vols., 1988–92 (in progress).

Bibliographies

Foster, David William, editor, *Puerto Rican Literature: A Bibliography of Secondary Sources*, Westport, Connecticut: Greenwood Press, 1982: 124–43

Hostos, Adolfo de, *Indice hemero-bibliográfico de Eugenio María de Hostos, 1863–1940*, San Juan: Comisión pro Celebración del Centenario del i de Hostos, 1940

Further Reading

Álvarez, Ernesto, *La invasión pacífica: Estudios sobre Manuel Zeno Gandía y Eugenio María de Hostos*, San Juan: Asomante, 1988

Araya, Juan Gabriel, "Hostos en Chile: 1872–1873," *Hostos Para Hoy: Anuario Hostosiano* 1, no. 1 (1988): 53–65

Babín, María Teresa, "El pensamiento de Hostos (1839–1903)," *Revista del Instituto de Cultura Puertorriqueña* 59 (1973): 17–22

Bosch, Juan, *Hostos, el sembrador*, Río Piedras: Huracán, 1976

Carreras, Carlos N., *Hostos: Apóstol de la libertad*, San Juan: Cordillera, 1971

Cores Trasmonte, Baldomero, "La teoría y la acción en la obra de Hostos," *Atenea* 4, nos. 1–2 (1984): 133–66

Ferrer Canales, José, *Martí y Hostos*, Río Piedras: University of Puerto Rico, Instituto de Estudios Hostosianos, 1990

Freire de Matos, Isabel, *Eugenio María de Hostos para la juventud*, Mayagüez: Comité del Sesquicentenario de Eugenio María de Hostos, 1990

Gutiérrez Laboy, Roberto, *Hostos y su filosofía moral: Acercamiento a Moral Social*, Lajas, Puerto Rico: Sociedad Histórica de Lajas, 1992

Lugo Guernelli, Adelaida, *Eugenio María de Hostos: Ensayista y crítico literario*, San Juan: Instituto de Cultura Puertorriqueña, 1970

Maldonado-Denis, Manuel, *Hostos, América la lucha por la libertad*, Mexico City: Siglo Veintiuno, 1980

Maldonado-Denis, Manuel, *Eugenio María de Hostos, sociólogo y maestro*, Río Piedras: Antillana, 1981

Maldonado-Denis, Manuel, *Eugenio María de Hostos y el pensamiento social iberoamericano*, Mexico City: Fondo de Cultura Económica, 1992

Mora, Gabriela, *Hostos intimista: Introducción a su diario*, San Juan: Instituto de Cultura Puertorriqueña, 1976

Mora, Gabriela, "Hostos feminista: Ensayos sobre la educación de la mujer," *Revista de Estudios Hispánicos* 24, no. 2 (1990): 143–60

Pascual Morán, Anaida, *Hostos: Precursor de la educación por la paz*, Guaynabo, Puerto Rico: Soñador, 1989

Pedreira, Antonio S., *Hostos, ciudadano de América*, Río Piedras: Edil, 1976 (original edition, 1931)

Pimentel, Miguel A., *Hostos y el positivismo en Santo Domingo (filosofía y política)*, Santo Domingo: Autonomous University of Santo Domingo, 1981

Rivera Nieves, Irma N., *El tema de la mujer en el pensamiento social de Eugenio María de Hostos*, Río Piedras: University of Puerto Rico, Instituto de Estudios Hostosianos, 1992

Rojas Osorio, Carlos, *Hostos, apreciación filosófica*, Humacao, Puerto Rico: Colegio Universitario de Humacao, 1988

Howe, Irving

American, 1920–1993

Irving Howe's essays made him one of America's foremost radical cultural and literary critics in the post–World War II and Cold War generations. Though a member of the group that his essay of 1969 helped define as "The New York Intellectuals," the anti-Stalinist writers and critics who emerged around the *Partisan Review* in the late 1940s, Howe used the essay to criticize their larger move toward neoconservatism. His landmark essay of 1954, "This Age of Conformity," which attacked the Cold War complacency and complicity of American intellectuals, and **Lionel Trilling** in particular, with American power, stands today as one of the defining essays of the 1950s; it also marked Howe's conflicted refusal to give up his socialist Jewish background, and appeared simultaneously with his cofounding of the democratic socialist journal *Dissent* in that year. Howe's political pieces were often fiercely polemical, directed against perceived authoritarianism on the left almost as often as against the right, whom he was capable of joining on issues such as preserving the literary canon, and critically eviscerating, as in his 1986 essay, "Reaganism: The Spirit of the Times." Howe's essays on Yiddish literature and his substantial translations were also cultural landmarks. The historical essays of *World of Our Fathers* (1976), which evoked and bid farewell to the Yiddish culture of New York's lower East Side, produced his only best-seller. But the double-edged and even conservative nostalgia of his essays on Jewish culture never led him into the ranks of Jewish neoconservatives; instead, he joined Michael Harrington's Democratic Socialist Organizing Committee in the 1980s. Howe's essays appeared in *Dissent*, *Partisan Review*, *Commentary*, the *New York Times*, the *Nation*, and other venues, defining the terrain on which battles over high and mass culture, postmodernism, McCarthyism, relations between blacks and Jews, Israel, American Jewish identity, the New Left, and many other issues would be fought. His essays were often major cultural interventions, identifying the fault lines that would shape American cultural criticism in the postwar period.

Born Irving Horenstein, Howe began writing essays in the late 1930s for journals of the Trotskyist movement such as *Labor Action*, under pseudonyms which included R. Fahan, R. F. Fangston, and Theodore Dryden. He achieved a larger audience when his essays helped to define the particular genre of essay for which the New York Intellectuals became famous. Described by Howe himself as a kind of essayistic attempt at "brilliance," the essay Howe pioneered often yoked high and low culture together, while defending a Modernist aesthetic critical of mass society against the political reduction of literary autonomy that had occurred during the leftist period of the 1930s. The New York Intellectuals' essayistic style Howe helped create was erudite, but decidedly nonacademic, even when Howe became a faculty member at Brandeis University in the 1950s. The brash intelligence displayed, sometimes seen as "rudeness" by Howe's contemporaries with their genteel ethos, highlighted the critic's personality at times as much as did the subject. As Howe himself suggested in his autobiography, *A Margin of Hope* (1982), this style was influenced by the immigrant Jewish milieu in which he and many of the New York Intellectuals were formed. This assimilationist form of the essay allowed a new group of writers, faced with their status as cultural outsiders to the American scene, eventually to lay claim to being the United States' first "Europeanized," cosmopolitan group of urban intellectuals.

To achieve such a cosmopolitan style, while retaining his socialist and Jewish commitments, Howe's essays and their choice of subjects often walked a fine line. "The essay," Howe wrote, "required a margin of impersonality, or a showing forth of personality through indirection." This tension between polemical display and aesthetic reserve, and even ethnic withdrawal, often produced essays which defined and sometimes exemplified problems dividing American culture as a whole. One of Howe's last essays, in his posthumously published collection *A Critic's Notebook* (1994), lamented the postmodern proliferation of reading publics as the loss of the concept of the "common reader." The talent Howe credited to **T. S. Eliot** was one he himself possessed: "he had an enviable capacity for raising the shapeless concerns of his readers to the level of explicit issues." At times, Howe's commitment to such public purpose produced results which were indistinguishable from the Cold War liberalism and neoconservatism he decried. In his denunciations of the New Left, his writing-off of Kate Millett's *Sexual Politics*, his attack on Philip Roth's novel *Portnoy's Complaint*, or his siding with cultural conservatives on "The Value of the Canon" (1991), the pressures of sustaining the socialist identity of Jewish leftists through the Cold War and beyond led Howe to excoriate positions his political and cultural sympathies otherwise might have embraced. On the other hand, the critical debate Howe engaged in with Ralph Ellison over Howe's attempt to define the African American novel, "Black Boys and Native Sons" (1963) stands as a crucial document of American literature, and as a powerful articulation of tensions surrounding the expression of cultural difference in postwar America. On such contentious subjects, Howe often wrote more measured essays, such as "Universities and Intellectuals" (1964), which predicted the contesting of politics in the university during the culture wars of the early 1990s.

Howe's essayistic achievement ranged from "Mass Society and Postmodern Fiction" (1963), which provided one of the first, if hostile, definitions of postmodernism, to "The Culture of Modernism," a kind of manifesto for his generation, to belletristic appreciations of writers as diverse as **W. E. B. Du Bois**, Isaak Babel', **George Orwell**, Ignazio Silone, Theodore Dreiser, **Lev Tolstoi**, Laurence Sterne, and **Virginia Woolf**, to critiques of the behavior of intellectuals during the Red Scare, to the fate of socialism in America. Howe's importance as an essayist is represented by the scope of this work, almost all of which displayed an uncanny, eloquent ability to lay bare the tensions subtending the postwar American "consensus." Like the writing of **Julien Benda**, Howe's essays raise fundamental questions about the responsibility of intellectuals in modern and postmodern society. They remain crucial documents, and often the unconscious subtexts, for postmodern discussions of liberalism, radical politics, ethnic identity, and cultural criticism in the United States.

DAVID SUCHOFF

Biography
Born Irving Horenstein, 11 June 1920 in the East Bronx, New York. Socialist from the age of 14. Studied at the City College of New York, B.Sc., 1940; Brooklyn College, 1940–41. Served in the U.S. Army, 1942–45. Married Arien Hausknecht: one daughter and one son; later married Ilana Wiener. Contributor to various journals, including the *Nation*, *Partisan Review*, and *Commentary*. Cofounder and editor, *Dissent*, 1954–93. Taught English at Brandeis University, Waltham, Massachusetts, 1953–61, Stanford University, California, 1961–63, and Hunter College, City University of New York, 1963–86. Awards: several, including the Bollingen Award, 1959–60; National Institute of Arts and Letters Award, 1960; Jewish Heritage Award, 1975; Brandeis University Creative Arts Award, 1975–76; National Book Award, for *World of Our Fathers*, 1977. Died (of cardiovascular disease following a stroke) in New York, 5 May 1993.

Selected Writings

Essays and Related Prose
Politics and the Novel, 1957
A World More Attractive: A View of Modern Literature and Politics, 1963
Steady Work: Essays in the Politics of Democratic Radicalism, 1953–1966, 1966
Decline of the New, 1970
The Critical Point: On Literature and Culture, 1973
World of Our Fathers, 1976; as *The Immigrant Jews of New York, 1881 to the Present*, 1976
Celebrations and Attacks: Thirty Years of Literary and Cultural Commentary, 1979
The American Newness: Culture and Politics in the Age of Emerson (lectures), 1986
Selected Writings, 1950 to 1990, 1990
A Critic's Notebook, edited by Nicholas Howe, 1994

Other writings: the autobiography *A Margin of Hope* (1982), and books on American literature, literary criticism, and politics. Also edited many editions of works by major American writers, and works on socialism.

Further Reading
Bloom, Alexander, *Prodigal Sons: The New York Intellectuals and Their World*, New York and Oxford: Oxford University Press, 1986
Cain, William, "An Interview with Irving Howe," *American Literary History* 1 (Fall 1989): 554–64
Cooney, Terry A., *The Rise of the New York Intellectuals: Partisan Review and Its Circle*, Madison: University of Wisconsin Press, 1986
Isserman, Maurice, *"If I had a hammer": The Death of the Old Left and the Birth of the New Left*, New York: Basic Books, 1987: 79–118
Jumonville, Neil, *Critical Crossings: The New York Intellectuals in Postwar America*, Berkeley: University of California Press, 1991
Krupnick, Mark, "Irving Howe," in *Modern American Critics Since 1955*, edited by Gregory S. Jay, Dictionary of American Literary Biography, vol. 67, Detroit: Gale Research, 1988: 167–75
Pinsker, Sanford, "Lost Causes/Marginal Hopes: The Cultural Elegies of Irving Howe," *Virginia Quarterly Review* 65 (Spring 1989): 215–30
"Remembering Irving Howe," *Dissent* (Fall 1993): 515–49
Wald, Alan M., "Portrait: Irving Howe," in *The New York Intellectuals: The Rise of the Anti-Stalinist Left from the 1930s to the 1980s*, Chapel Hill: University of North Carolina Press, 1987: 311–21

Howe, Joseph
Canadian, 1804–1873

Journalist, politician, civil servant, and noted public speaker, Joseph Howe is sometimes considered the first Canadian essayist of note, with his speeches and formal orations designated and collected as essays during and since his own time.

Although his work appeared in a variety of forms, including **pamphlets** and collections, his reputation was established primarily through his prodigious output of editorials, public **letters**, and transcribed speeches which appeared regularly in a number of prominent contemporary newspapers, including the Halifax *Morning Chronicle* and the New York *Albion*. The most important of these journalistic associations, though, was with the *Novascotian*, which Howe edited for many years and which was quickly established as the most influential newspaper in the province.

Writing in a self-assured tone that critics past and present have suggested borders on egotism, Howe appears to the modern reader as a grandiloquent stylist. Prone, at times, to moments of excessive decoration, flights of rhetorical exuberance, and forced literary allusion, he also apparently had a strong sense of his audience, for his essays were often "looked to as stylistic models" by his contemporaries (Brandon Conron, 1965). It is not as a prose stylist that modern critics commonly remember Howe, however, but rather as a writer whose essays remain centered firmly on the social and political issues that kept him in the public's eye throughout his life: the drive for universal access to nonsectarian public education; wariness of direct taxation and excessive governmental intervention in private lives; battles for freedom of speech and of the press; advocacy of railway construction; and arguments for reciprocity with the United States. Two issues in particular define both Howe's public life and his essays: his ongoing fight for responsible government, and later in his life his passionate opposition to Canadian Confederation.

On the first count, Howe was a proponent of open, liberal politics. In essence a conservative reformer who respected the values of the emerging middle class, he saw partisan politics as the bane of Nova Scotia's future, a static system that bound people to party loyalties which could put them in opposition to their conscience. To Howe, governing was never a singularly partisan activity. As he reflected in a personal letter: "Parties form and reform, fuse and divide in all free Countries as opinions change, and new issues and exigencies arise" (1869). More important, the party-dominated system was rife with what Howe saw as systemic neglect, misconduct, and corruption on the part of the province's political elite.

During his two tenures as editor of the *Novascotian* (1827–40; 1844–46), Howe saw his editorial "chair," as he called it, become the rallying point for Nova Scotia's Reform party. It was a position he accepted gladly. As he announced in his "Opening Editorial" upon return to the paper following a stint in public office: "When one sits in it, however hard the work, they are answerable for nobody's sins or follies or shortcomings but their own; in dignity it may be somewhat less elevated, but it is second to none in . . . real substantial power . . . to influence the daily thought, to touch the hearts, to enter the dwellings of tens of thousands like an old familiar friend, and inform, excite, and guide them; power, not without its legitimate checks – for, when abused, it ceases to be power" (1844).

To his readers Howe was an old familiar "friend," and one who always wrote, first and foremost, as a native son. A dedicated promoter of the intellectual and cultural progress of the province, he developed a popular and well-known series of travel sketches known in the aggregate as his "Rambles." There

are, in fact, two distinct sets of essays comprising these travels: a series of "Western Rambles," which appeared in the *Novascotian* between 23 July and 9 October 1828, and the "Eastern Rambles," which appeared in the paper between 17 December 1829 and 19 October 1831. Both sets are organized as the descriptions and meditations of an inquiring traveler who sets out from the provincial capital to explore and study the natural and social history of the regions and towns of Nova Scotia. These are **familiar essays**, full of direct appeals to the "gentle reader," passages of sentimental meditation upon rural life and the "philosophy of nature," and moral instruction. Often, Howe tries to invoke a sense of the history that had shaped the "youthful" Nova Scotia: "Had I the happy faculty of Scott, and could evoke from the green sward the forms which once, in bravery and pride, trod where they now are lying, I could paint for the gentle traveller's eye many a singular and striking scene, and carry him away from the present, to behold the deeds and partake of the spirit of the past" (October 1828).

Although modern critics generally see Howe's "rambles" as the least political of his writings, politics and social issues are never far below the surface. Especially prominent are examples of the ubiquitous "hobgoblins" of "disaffection and bad government" (25 February 1830), the distinctions of religion which continue to divide local communities, and reflections on the sorry state of transitional economies. One of Howe's favored strategies in these essays is to reflect on how social policies and practices have shaped the lives of various "characters" he meets on the road, including the exemplary "Ploughman" (28 August 1828) and "a Village Doctor" (11 September 1828).

This dedication to the well-being of Nova Scotia also informed Howe's well-documented stance against Confederation during the 1860s. The more interesting of these anti-Confederation tracts include an insightful series of anonymous "Botheration letters" (*The Morning Chronicle*, 1865) detailing his view of the constitutional structure of post-Confederation Canada, and two pamphlets from 1866: "Confederation Considered in Relation to the Empire" and "The Organization of the Empire." Serious in tone, intricately detailed, and articulating a controlled defense of Nova Scotia's interests, these essays stand apart from those Howe produced in the months and years that followed royal assent of the British North America (BNA) Act, which are the most deeply personal of Howe's writings. A lifelong anglophile who openly celebrated Nova Scotia's links to Britain, "that great country from which we have all sprung, to which we owe allegiance" ("Speech on Elective Councils," 1837), Howe was bitterly disappointed and disillusioned with both the British public and the British political process following Confederation. As he admits publicly in the first of a series of five letters "To the Editor of *The Morning Chronicle*" following the British government's rejection of a brief anti-confederate agitation for repeal of the BNA Act, the experiences of the 1860s left their mark: "with deep sorrow, and a sense of humiliation not easily described, I [am] compelled to acknowledge that I had cherished a delusion" (1868).

An especially succinct summary of Howe's lifelong commitment to his ideals and native province comes in a widely printed public letter "To the People of Canada" (1867): "The page of my public life of which I shall ever be most justly proud is that whereon is unfolded the earnestness and sincerity with which, against fearful odds, I defended the independence of my native Province, and endeavored to protect her people from insult and spoliation."

KLAY DYER

Biography

Born 13 December 1804 in Halifax, Nova Scotia. Little formal schooling. Apprenticed to family printing and newspaper business, from age 13. Cofounding editor, the *Acadian*, 1827; editor and major contributor, the *Novascotian*, 1827–40, 1844–46. Married Catherine McNab, 1828: ten children. Elected to the Nova Scotia legislative assembly, 1836; premier, 1860–63; led opposition forces in the Confederation debate of the mid-1860s; elected as an Opposition candidate, 1867, but accepted that opposition to Confederation was futile, 1869; appointed secretary of state for the provinces, 1869–73; appointed lieutenant-governor of Nova Scotia, April 1873. Died in Halifax, 1 June 1873.

Selected Writings

Essays and Related Prose

The Speeches and Public Letters of the Hon. Joseph Howe, edited by William Annand, 2 vols., 1858; revised edition, edited by Joseph Andrew Chisholm, 2 vols., 1909
Poems and Essays, 1874; edited by M. G. Parks, 1973
The Heart of Howe: Selections from the Letters and Speeches, edited by D. C. Harvey, 1939
Joseph Howe: Voice of Nova Scotia, edited by J. Murray Beck, 1964
Western and Eastern Rambles: Travel Sketches of Nova Scotia, edited by M. G. Parks, 1973

Other writings: poetry, addresses, pamphlets, and correspondence.

Further Reading

Beck, J. Murray, *Joseph Howe*, Kingston and Montreal: McGill-Queen's University Press, 2 vols., 1982–83
Conron, Brandon, "Essays 1880–1920," in *Literary History of Canada: Canadian Literature in English*, edited by Carl F. Klinck and others, Toronto: University of Toronto Press, 1976: 354–60 (original edition, 1965)
Grant, George M., "The Late Hon. Joseph Howe," *Canadian Monthly and National Review* 7, no. 5 (May 1875): 377–87; 7, no. 6 (June 1875): 497–508; 8, no. 1 (July 1875): 20–25; 8, no. 2 (August 1875): 115–22
Hunt, Wayne A., editor, *The Proceedings of the Joseph Howe Symposium*, Sackville, New Brunswick: Mount Allison University Centre for Canadian Studies, 1984
Parks, M. G., Introduction to *Poems and Essays* by Howe, Toronto: University of Toronto Press, 1973: vii–xxxi
Parks, M. G., Introduction to *Western and Eastern Rambles: Travel Sketches of Nova Scotia* by Howe, Toronto: University of Toronto Press, 1973: 3–44
Roy, James A., *Joseph Howe: A Study in Achievement and Frustration*, Toronto: Macmillan, 1935

Howells, William Dean

American, 1837–1920

As a realist, William Dean Howells is more easily caricatured than accurately portrayed. Detractors since **H. L. Mencken** have misrepresented him as a defender of respectability and the "smiling aspects of life" ("The Editor's Study," September 1886), while scholarly critics (notably Michael Bell and Daniel Borus) have commented on his lack of theoretical rigor. But the publication of his *Selected Literary Criticism* (1993) in the *Selected Edition* of his works may prompt a better understanding of Howells as an essayist in the literal sense of the word: a writer who tested competing values without pretending to reconcile them. Though he promoted a distinctively American literature, he was an early champion of internationalism and multiculturalism; and though he fought the "realism war," he acknowledged the actual heterogeneity of modern fiction, welcoming writers who defied categorization. "True criticism," he wrote, ". . . is the function and the natural habit of every intelligent and candid mind" ("Literary Criticism," 1866) – yet honest readers should be troubled by "the inadequacy of criticism" every time they examine a new book (review of *Literature and Its Professors*, 1867). While such modesty prevented Howells from developing a consistent theory, it enabled him to appreciate the texts we still regard as canonical. This virtue was crucial in an age when writers were misunderstood by one another as well as by an increasingly diverse public.

Venetian Life (1866), a collection of essays written by Howells during his service as American consul, was his first major literary success. Reviewed favorably by James Russell Lowell, it gained the young Ohioan admission to the charmed circle of the New England Brahmins, and later the prestigious editorship of the *Atlantic Monthly*. But these sketches convey the democratic outlook that distinguished Howells from his privileged elders. "Thank God that the good old times are gone and going!" he exclaims after visiting the Jewish ghetto.

His reviews of literature were also progressive – ethically serious but devoid of Arnoldian snobbishness. He applauded such regionalist writers as Sarah Orne Jewett, Edward Eggleston, Bret Harte, and E. W. Howe, and he was equally friendly to Europeans who supplied an antidote to American provincialism. Two companion essays, both published in 1882, demonstrate Howells' gift for accepting rival geniuses on their own terms. "Mark Twain" praises **Twain** for his humor and directness, while "Henry James, Jr." defends **James**' "analytic tendency" and his subtle appeal to a more elite audience. Unfortunately for Howells, the latter piece offended British reviewers because of its casual disparagement of **Dickens** and **Thackeray** ("We could not suffer the confidential attitude of the latter now, nor the mannerism of the former"). Yet Howells was far less dogmatic than the critics who accused him of trying to establish a "new school."

In 1885 Howells was invited by Henry Alden, the editor of *Harper's Monthly*, to replace the usual book **reviews** with a column treating "any subject of current literary interest." These "Editor's Study" essays, some of which were excerpted in *Criticism and Fiction* (1891), were his strongest attempt to promote a realist aesthetic. Using a genial tone and witty metaphors, he needled the sentimentalists – those who preferred a painted model of an ideal grasshopper, "made up of wire and cardboard," to the actual commonplace thing. As for his positive standards – "the simple, the natural, and the honest" – they were sufficiently flexible to accommodate a literature still in its nascence ("The Editor's Study," December

1887). But he could not personally effect all the developments he sought. The radical views of his favorite author, **Tolstoi**, undermined his own attempts to locate self-evident values; and he was forced to admit the disparity between Russian fiction and the modest efforts of his American compatriots. His final essay (March 1892) portrays the Editor leaving his Study while his successors puzzle over his "collection of moral bric-à-brac."

Despite this valediction, Howells remained an active commentator on literature and culture. Such essays as "Are We a Plutocracy?" (1894) record his growing concern for social and economic equality, while his literary reviews (which welcome Stephen Crane, Charlotte Perkins Gilman, Frank Norris, and Thomas Hardy, among others) testify to his refusal to succumb to "Sclerosis of the Tastes" (*Imaginary Interviews*, 1910). But the pieces of most enduring interest are the reminiscences in *Literary Friends and Acquaintance* (1900) and *My Mark Twain* (1910). Here we find the details that enrich our understanding of American literary history: Lowell's habit of saying "Remember the dinner-bell" whenever the conversation turned unduly transcendental; **Emerson**'s condescending dismissal of Poe as *"the jingle-man"*; Mark Twain's disastrous speech at the Whittier birthday dinner. Howells may once have regarded Boston as the "holy land," but he had a keen sense of the Brahmins' jealousies and foibles.

On Howells' 75th birthday, Henry James conceded that "the critical intelligence" had not done justice to his friend. And yet, James added, "the more it shall be moved by the analytic and historic spirit, the more indispensable, the more a vessel of light, will you be found" ("A Letter to Mr. Howells," 1912). Howells' essays are of lasting value to students of his era – not simply an "age of realism," but one whose complexities and contradictions foreshadow those of our own culture.

SARAH B. DAUGHERTY

Biography

Born 1 March 1837 in Martin's Ferry, Ohio. Studied at schools in Hamilton and Dayton, Ohio; educated mostly at home. Compositor, *Ohio State Journal*, Columbus, 1851–60; wrote for the Jefferson *Gazette*, Ohio, from 1852, Cincinnati *Gazette*, 1857–58, 1866, Cleveland *Herald*, 1858, Boston *Advertiser*, 1863–65, the *Nation*, New York, 1865–66, and *Literature*, 1898–99. U.S. Consul, Venice, 1861–65. Married Elinor Gertrude Mead, 1862 (died, 1910): two daughters (one died) and one son. Assistant editor, 1866–71, and editor-in-chief, 1871–81, *Atlantic Monthly*, Boston. Lectured at Harvard University, Cambridge, Massachusetts, 1869–71. Columnist of "Editor's Study," 1885–92, and 1900–20, and "The Editor's Easy Chair," 1895–98, *Harper's Monthly*; coeditor, *Cosmopolitan*, New York, 1892. Lifelong friend of Mark Twain (i.e. Samuel Clemens) and Henry James. Awards: National Institute of Arts and Letters Gold Medal, 1915; honorary degrees from five universities. Honorary Fellow, Royal Society of Literature, 1901; president, American Academy, 1908–20. Died in New York, 11 May 1920.

Selected Writings

Essays and Related Prose

Venetian Life, 1866; enlarged edition, 1872
Modern Italian Poets: Essays and Versions, 1887; as *The Three Greatest Italian Poets of the Nineteenth Century*, 1983; as *Contemporary Italian Poets*, 2 vols., 1987
Criticism and Fiction, 1891
My Literary Passions, 1895

Impressions and Experiences, 1896
Literary Friends and Acquaintance: A Personal Retrospect of American Authorship, 1900
Literature and Life: Studies, 1902
London Films, 1905
Certain Delightful English Towns (travel sketches), 1906
Roman Holidays and Others (travel sketches), 1908
Seven English Cities (travel sketches), 1909
Imaginary Interviews, 1910
My Mark Twain: Reminiscences and Criticisms, 1910; edited by Marilyn Austin Baldwin, 1967, and David F. Hiatt and Edwin H. Cady, 1968
Prefaces to Contemporaries (1882–1920), edited by George Arms, William M. Gibson, and Frederic C. Marston, Jr., 1957
Criticism and Fiction, and Other Essays, edited by Clara Marburg Kirk and Rudolf Kirk, 1959
Discovery of a Genius: William Dean Howells and Henry James (articles about James), edited by Albert Mordell, 1961
Tuscan Cities, 1967
W. D. Howells as Critic, edited by Edwin H. Cady, 1973
Editor's Study: A Comprehensive Edition of W. D. Howells' Column [in *Harper's*], edited by James W. Simpson, 1983
The Early Prose Writings, edited by Thomas Wortham, 1990
A Realist in the American Theatre: Selected Drama Criticism, edited by Brenda Murphy, 1992

Other writings: many novels (including *The Undiscovered Country*, 1880; *A Modern Instance*, 1882; *The Rise of Silas Lapham*, 1885; *Indian Summer*, 1886; *A Hazard of New Fortunes*, 1889), plays, poetry, travel writing, a biography of Abraham Lincoln, and literary criticism.

Collected works edition: *A Selected Edition*, edited by Edwin H. Cady, Ronald Gottesman, Don L. Cook, and David Nordloh, 25 vols., 1968–93 (in progress).

Bibliographies

Brenni, Vito J., *William Dean Howells: A Bibliography*, Metuchen, New Jersey: Scarecrow Press, 1973
Eichelberger, Clayton L., *Published Comment on William Dean Howells Through 1920: A Research Bibliography*, Boston: Hall, 1976
Gibson, William M., and George Arms, *A Bibliography of William Dean Howells*, New York: New York Public Library, 1948

Further Reading

Arms, George, "Howells' English Travel Books: Problems in Technique," *PMLA* 82 (March 1967): 104–16
Bassett, John E., "'A heart of ideality in my realism': Howells's Early Criticism," *Papers on Language and Literature* 25 (Winter 1989): 67–82
Bell, Michael Davitt, *The Problem of American Realism: Studies in the Cultural History of a Literary Idea*, Chicago: University of Chicago Press, 1993
Borus, Daniel H., *Writing Realism: Howells, James, and Norris in the Mass Market*, Chapel Hill: University of North Carolina Press, 1989
Cady, Edwin H., editor, *W. D. Howells as Critic*, London and Boston: Routledge and Kegan Paul, 1982
Carrington, George C., "Howells and the Dramatic Essay," *American Literary Realism* 17 (Spring 1984): 44–66
Daugherty, Sarah B., "Howells Reviews James: The Transcendence of Realism," *American Literary Realism* 18 (Spring–Autumn 1985): 147–67
Dean, James L., *Howells' Travels Toward Art*, Albuquerque: University of New Mexico Press, 1970

Demoor, Marysa, "Andrew Lang Versus W. D. Howells: A Late-Victorian Literary Duel," *Journal of American Studies* 21 (December 1987): 416–22

Hough, Robert L., *The Quiet Rebel: William Dean Howells as Social Commentator*, Lincoln: University of Nebraska Press, 1959

Jacobson, Marcia, "The Mask of Fiction: William Dean Howells's Experiments in Autobiography," *Biography* 10 (Winter 1987): 55–67

Jacobson, Marcia, "Howells' *Literary Friends and Acquaintance*: An Autobiography Through Others," *American Literary Realism* 27 (Fall 1994): 59–73

James, Henry, "A Letter to Mr. Howells," *North American Review* 195 (April 1912): 558–62

Kirk, Clara Marburg, *W. D. Howells and Art in His Time*, New Brunswick: Rutgers University Press, 1965

Matthews, Brander, "Mr. Howells as a Critic," *Forum* 32 (January 1902): 629–38

Miller, Elise, "The Feminization of American Realist Theory," *American Literary Realism* 23 (Fall 1990): 20–41

Stull, William L., "The Battle of the *Century*: W. D. Howells, 'Henry James, Jr.' and the English," *American Literary Realism* 11 (Autumn 1979): 249–64

Tuttleton, James W., "William Dean Howells and the Practice of Criticism," *New Criterion* 10 (June 1992): 28–37

Woodress, James L., *Howells and Italy*, Durham, North Carolina: Duke University Press, 1952

Woodress, James L., "Howells in the Nineties: Social Critic for All Seasons," *American Literary Realism* 23 (Spring 1993): 18–26

Huch, Ricarda

German, 1864–1947

Ricarda Huch is a paradox in the history of the essay. Few of her individual works can be called "essays." Moreover, she was opposed to the prevailing attitude of "essayism" or "feuilletonism," and tried to write in a manner and form that could not be confused with the dominant modes of essay writing. Her distaste for the essay genre derives mainly from the German/Austrian understanding of that term around the turn of the century rather than from an opposition against the essay as such. Yet her texts exhibit a significant number of characteristics of the essay. She wrote for a general educated audience, and cultivated a combination of narrative and reflexive elements, with a mixture of general and personal ideas, and an appeal to both reason and emotion. Above all, the individual **chapters** of her larger works tend to be independent, self-contained units.

Huch belonged to the first generation of educated and professionally independent women in German society. She fought hard for her independence: in order to qualify for university studies, she had to leave Germany for Switzerland, where she graduated with a Ph.D. in modern history from the University of Zurich in 1892. She declined careers as teacher and researcher and became a freelance writer, producing poetry, novels (historical novels among them), historical works, literary criticism, and books on religion and philosophy. She was a person of rare integrity and courage, following her own path despite the obstacles; in 1933, for example, she resigned from the prestigious membership of the Prussian Academy of the Arts rather than collaborate with the Nazis. A pillar of the oppositional "Bekennende Kirche" (Confessional Church) within the Lutheran Church, she was treated in 1945 with reverence by the Soviet administration, the Allied military, and the German public.

There are four types of essay to be found within the context of her works: the biographical essay, the **historical essay**, the geographical essay, and the essay of ideas. Whereas her earlier works consist mainly of poetry and very personal, if not autobiographical novels, later texts combine personal empathy with objective fact. Huch's foremost preoccupation was with people and their relationships. All her works contain numerous biographical sketches; she also wrote major factual or fictional biographies. Her intense interest in the Italian Risorgimento of the 19th century led to novels on Garibaldi (1906–07) and Federigo Confalioneri (1910). She wrote a biography of the Freiherr vom und zum Stein (1925). Rather surprising, given her conservative views, is her positive biography *Michael Bakunin und die Anarchie* (1923; Mikhail Bakunin and anarchy). What attracted her to Bakunin's anarchism was his concept of a self-reliant "organic" community as opposed to artificial modern society. These works can be regarded as expansions of biographical essays.

Huch's personalism is apparent in her extensive historical work. She diagnosed "Entpersönlichung" (depersonalization) as a major illness of the age, publishing a book with that title (1921). She was fascinated by creative personalities, as shown in her writings on literary figures, and especially in her early, successful book on Romanticism, *Die Romantik* (1899, 1902). Its individual chapters can be read as essays on the leading personalities, ideas, and developments of German Romanticism. Huch's personalized view of history is also evident in *Alte und neue Götter* (1930; Old and new gods), her account of the 1848 Revolution in Germany.

The most essay-like writing can be seen in Huch's geographical tableau of old German cities, *Im alten Reich: Lebensbilder deutscher Städte* (1927–34; In the old empire: images of the life of German cities). Her descriptions of the structure of these old cities, important buildings, and conspicuous events and personalities stress the individuality of urban organisms as well as the communal spirit they generated. Huch's social ideal of the self-governing community based on personal involvement and solidarity is portrayed in living pictures of many different individual entities. In the entry on her native city of Brunswick, understandably one of the most thorough articles, there is an easy transition from such portraits combining history and geography to Huch's autobiographical sketches describing the people and the places most important to her. She had to feel part of the land, the history, and its people wherever she lived.

Huch combined a fervent Lutheran faith with a Goethean organic view of history and community. For all her belief in tradition, the importance of the home country, and family values, she accepted change as inevitable and valued individuality above all else. Her religious and philosophical books try to convey this holistic view of the human being and of human life and history. The most essay-like sections can be found in her book on Martin Luther's faith (*Luthers Glaube*, 1916), written during World War I. The book is presented in the form of **letters** to a skeptical friend, and step by step she tries to counter the arguments of modern skepticism, unfolding Luther's stature as a great man of faith rather than his skills as a founder of a new church.

The last statement of her beliefs bears the Goethean title *Urphänomene* (1946; Archetypal phenomena), archetypes of the visible forms in nature. This refers to the belief in the organic order of the world, the benign dynamics of life, and the ultimate victory of living forces over annihilation. While nature can be grasped only in individual phenomena, the gaze should always be directed to the essence and the whole. Thus, each of Huch's statements and writings is meant to convey one aspect of a larger world view. She never tired of narrating and describing, always with an eye toward the meaning of life.

It may be this very integrity of her world view and her personal life that makes Huch a stranger in our world. Today she elicits polite and distant respect, and does not seem relevant to our problems. But it could be her essay-like features that will make some of her writings accessible again.

WULF KOEPKE

Biography
Ricarda Octavia Huch. Born 18 July 1864 in Brunswick. Studied at the University of Zurich, Ph.D. in history, 1892. Archivist, Zentralbibliothek, Zurich, 1891–94; teacher in Zurich, 1894–96. Married Ermanno Ceconi, 1898 (divorced, 1906): one daughter. Married her cousin Richard Huch, 1907 (divorced, 1911). Lived at various times in Bremen, Vienna, Trieste, Munich, Berlin, Berne, Heidelberg, Freiburg, and Jena. Member, Prussian Academy of the Arts, 1927, resigned in protest at the Nazi regime's expulsion of various writers, 1933. Awards: Goethe Prize, 1931. Died in Kronberg, 17 November 1947.

Selected Writings

Essays and Related Prose
Die Romantik: Blütezeit der Romantik; Ausbreitung und Verfall der Romantik, 2 vols., 1899–1902
Das Risorgimento (treatise), 1908; as *Menschen und Schicksale aus dem Risorgimento*, 1925
Luthers Glaube: Briefe an einen Freund, 1916
Entpersönlichung, 1921
Im alten Reich: Lebensbilder deutscher Städte, 3 vols., 1927–34
Urphänomene, 1946
Gesammelte Schriften: Essays, Reden, autobiographische Aufzeichnungen (includes essays, speeches, and autobiography), 1964

Other writings: several novels (including *Erinnerungen von Ludolf Ursleu dem Jüngeren* [*Eros Invincible*], 1893; *Aus der Triumphgasse*, 1902; *Vita somnium breve*, 1903; *Das Leben des Grafen Federigo Confalonieri*, 1910; *Der Fall Deruga* [*The Deruga Trial*], 1917), short stories, poetry, plays, works on history and religion, and correspondence.

Collected works edition: *Gesammelte Werke*, edited by Wilhelm Emrich, 11 vols., 1966–74.

Further Reading
Baum, Marie, *Leuchtende Spur: Das Leben Ricarda Huchs*, Tübingen: Wunderlich, 1950
Baumgarten, Helene, *Ricarda Huch: Von ihrem Leben und Schaffen*, Weimar: Böhlau, 1964
Flandreau, Audrey, *Ricarda Huch's Weltanschauung as Expressed in Her Philosophical Works and in Her Novels* (dissertation), Chicago: University of Chicago, 1948
Gottlieb, Elfriede, *Ricarda Huch: Ein Beitrag zur Geschichte der deutschen Epik*, Leipzig and Berlin: Teubner, 1914

Hertling, Gunter H., *Wandlung der Werte im dichterischen Werk der Ricarda Huch*, Bonn: Bouvier, 1966
Hoppe, Else, *Ricarda Huch*, Stuttgart: Riederer, 1951 (original edition, 1936)
Mutzner, Paula, *Die Schweiz im Werke Ricarda Huchs*, Berne: Haupt, 1935
Walzel, Oskar, *Ricarda Huch: Ein Wort über Kunst des Erzählens*, Leipzig: Insel, 1916

Hume, David
British, 1711–1776

To appreciate David Hume as an essayist, he must be understood as a philosopher, for it was to better communicate his reconstruction of philosophy that he turned to the essay. Philosophy, as traditionally conceived, has its source in pure reason independent of pre-reflective custom and tradition. But Hume argued that the notion of pure reason is incoherent and that the true source of belief and conduct is custom. Reason, properly conceived, is a matter of methodizing and correcting the prejudices and customs of common life. The "true philosopher" is not a spectator of common life but a loyal and critical participant in it. This radical reform of philosophy was presented in Hume's first published work, *A Treatise of Human Nature* (1739–40), written in his twenties. This was a systematic and abstruse work designed for a philosophical audience, which, in Hume's time, it failed to impress. But even during its preparation, Hume was writing essays. *Essays, Moral and Political* appeared in 1741, with a second volume in 1742. Hume worked on essays throughout his career until his death in 1776, when he arranged for the posthumous publication of *Essays, Moral, Political, and Literary* (1777). Overall he published 49 essays. Of these, 27 appeared in the first two volumes. Over the years Hume dropped eight and added others, publishing 11 editions of essays. They were warmly received in Britain, America, and on the continent, where they went through numerous translations in French, German, and Italian.

It was through the essay that Hume's philosophy was made known to his contemporaries. And it was as a writer of essays that he first signed his name, the *Treatise of Human Nature* having been published anonymously and later publicly rejected by Hume as a "juvenile" work, embarrassing not because of its matter but for its form. Even the other main sources of Hume's philosophy, *An Enquiry Concerning Human Understanding* (1758) and *An Enquiry Concerning the Principles of Morals* (1751) should be viewed as eclectic extended essays or as collections of essays. In fact the former, in its first version, was published as *Philosophical Essays Concerning Human Understanding* (1748). No other philosopher of Hume's range, depth, and stature has endeavored to philosophize through the essay form. It is also remarkable that Hume is the only great philosopher who is also a great historian. His monumental *History of Great Britain* went through over 100 posthumous editions. That Hume was both essayist and historian is explained by his reconstruction of philosophy.

The "true philosopher" is a rooted participant in common life. To think critically about this order one must develop a connoisseur's knowledge of the habits, prejudices, and traditions of common life. The connoisseur is a master of the particular, which requires a knowledge of history. The philosopher seeks the universal meaning of the particular, but the true philosopher knows that the universal is revealed through a metaphor made by the imagination and not merely by a concept. The universal, so conceived, is best exhibited in the form of conversation in common life. In "Of Essay-Writing" (1742), Hume explains why the essay is the proper medium of "true philosophy." He distinguishes between two worlds: that of conversation and that of learning. The essayist is an "Ambassador from the Dominion of Learning to those of Conversation." In the past, learning was "shut up in Colleges and Cells," and "Philosophy went to Wrack by this moaping recluse Method of Study, and became as Chimerical in her Conclusions as she was unintelligible in her Stile and Manner of Delivery." Philosophy is a maker of universals, but these are rooted in metaphorical identities framed in pre-reflective common life. "The Materials of this Commerce must chiefly be furnish'd by Conversation and common Life: The manufacturing of them alone belongs to Learning." For Hume, the essay was an extension of the philosophical societies that had flourished in Edinburgh from the late 17th century and had a more serious purpose in "learning" than the French salons. He hoped to extend the conversation of these societies, through the essay form, to a more general audience that included women, whom he identified as "the Sovereigns of the Empire of Conversation."

Few philosophers have experimented with so many different literary forms in order to find the proper voice for philosophy. Hume wrote systematic **treatise**s, essays, **dialogue**s, narratives, and eclectic combinations of these forms. The essays also exhibit considerable experimentation. Some of the early ones from *Essays, Moral and Political* address serious themes to the ladies in a gallant and playful idiom, e.g. "Of the Study of History," "Of Love and Marriage," "Of Essay-Writing." Allegory appears in "Of Avarice," "Of Impudence and Modesty," and "Of the Middle Station of Life." Parable is to be found in "Of Moral Prejudices."

Some essays are to be read as a set. "The Epicurean," "The Stoic," "The Platonist," and "The Sceptic" (from *Essays, Moral and Political*, vol. 2) together explore the question of what constitutes human happiness. The first three are speeches of wisdom and employ the familiar "Thee" and "Thou." The "Sceptic" is not itself a speech about happiness so much as a reflection of the meaning of the question and speaks in the voice of "I" and "We." But this voice is not necessarily Hume's, for the author appears in footnotes to query the skeptic. In this way, the essays become orations on the good life addressed to the author and reader. In most of the essays, Hume speaks as the maker of universals, giving the complete speech on the topic at hand. All the essays are rich in references to classical authors as sources of wisdom and as evidence for historical theses in a debate between the Ancients and the Moderns that runs throughout the essays. Though Hume held that classical moral philosophy is superior to the modern, he insisted that modern moral, political, and economic practice is superior to the ancient. In "Of Eloquence" (1742), he argued that eloquence is the only art in which the Moderns have not surpassed the Ancients, and he urges revival of the art.

Over half the essays are attempts to gain a connoisseur's understanding of the vices and virtues of modern political institutions and practices. Hume explores with great subtlety the often strange and contingent origin of the modern practices of liberty, how good is interwoven with evil, and how some good drives out other good. "Of Some Remarkable Customs" (1752) demonstrates how political traditions are ingenious, reconciling opposites that political theory had declared to be impossible. But political theorizing, though limited, can provide insight into the dialectical ferment of practice. In "Idea of a Perfect Commonwealth" (1752), Hume finds intimated in modern politics a new and superior form of political association, namely, an extensive republic, thereby subverting the traditional wisdom that republics can exist only in a small territory. This essay, entering the political conversation of common life in America, influenced, among others, James Madison, who argued in the "Tenth Federalist" that, despite the vast territory of America, the states could and should unify into a republic. This is one of many episodes in which Hume's **philosophical essays** effected a fruitful commerce between the world of conversation and the world of learning.

DONALD W. LIVINGSTON

Biography

Born 26 April 1711 in Edinburgh. Studied at the University of Edinburgh, 1723–25(?); studied law and philosophy privately; worked briefly for a merchant in Bristol, then studied in France, 1734–37. Lived in London, 1737–39, 1740–44, and on Ninewells family estate, eastern Scotland, 1739–40, 1744–45. Tutor to George, Marquess of Annandale, 1745–46; secretary to General James St. Clair, 1746–47, and accompanied him to Port l'Orient, 1747, and to Vienna and Turin, 1748. Lived in Edinburgh, 1751–63 (except for a year in London, 1758–59); librarian to the Faculty of Advocates, Edinburgh, 1752–57. Personal secretary to the Ambassador of the British Embassy in Paris, 1763–66; undersecretary of state for the Northern Department, 1767–68. Returned to live in Edinburgh, 1769–76. Died in Edinburgh, 25 August 1776.

Selected Writings

Essays and Related Prose

Essays, Moral and Political, 2 vols., 1741–42; enlarged edition, 1748; in *Essays and Treatises on Several Subjects*, vol. 1, 1753; as *Essays, Moral, Political, and Literary*, in revised edition of *Essays and Treatises on Several Subjects*, vol. 1, 1758, and in its definitive edition, 1777; edited by Thomas Hill Green and Thomas Hodge Grose, 2 vols., 1875, and Eugene F. Miller, 1987

Philosophical Essays Concerning Human Understanding, 1748, reprinted 1986; revised edition, 1750; in *Essays and Treatises on Several Subjects*, vol. 2, 1756; as *An Enquiry Concerning Human Understanding*, in revised edition of *Essays and Treatises on Several Subjects*, vol. 2, 1758, and in its definitive edition, 1777; edited by L. A. Selby-Bigge, 1902 (revised by P. H. Nidditch, 1975), Charles W. Hendel, 1955, Antony Flew, 1962, Ernest Campbell Mossner, 1963, and Eric Steinberg, 1993

An Enquiry Concerning the Principles of Morals, 1751; in *Essays and Treatises on Several Subjects*, vol. 3, 1753, and in its definitive edition, 1777; edited by Charles W. Hendel, 1957

Political Discourses, 1752; in *Essays and Treatises on Several Subjects*, vol. 4, 1754, and in its definitive edition, 1777

Essays and Treatises on Several Subjects, 4 vols., 1753–56; several
   subsequent revised editions, 1758–70; definitive edition, 1777;
   edited by L. A. Selby-Bigge, 1894; as *The Philosophical Works*,
   edited by Thomas Hill Green and Thomas Hodge Grose, 4 vols.,
   1886, reprinted 1992
Four Dissertations, 1757
Two Essays, 1777; as *Essays on Suicide, and the Immortality of the
   Soul*, 1783
Dialogues Concerning Natural Religion, 1779; edited by Norman
   Kemp Smith, 1935, Henry D. Aiken, 1948, Stanley Tweyman,
   1991, and in *Principal Writings on Religion*, edited by J. C. A.
   Gaskin, 1993
Political Essays, edited by Charles W. Hendel, 1953
Of the Standard of Taste, and Other Essays, edited by John W.
   Lenz, 1965
Writings on Religion, edited by Antony Flew, 1992
Selected Essays, edited by Stephen Copley and Andrew Edgar,
   1993
Political Writings, edited by Stuart D. Warner and Donald W.
   Livingston, 1994
Political Essays, edited by Knud Haakonssen, 1994

Other writings: the philosophical work *A Treatise of Human Nature*
(1739–40), the multi-volume *History of Great Britain*, other works
on politics and history, and correspondence.

Bibliographies

Hall, Roland, *Fifty Years of Hume Scholarship: A Bibliographical
   Guide*, Edinburgh: Edinburgh University Press, 1978;
   supplements in the November issues of *Hume Studies*, 1977–
Jessop, T. E., *A Bibliography of David Hume and of Scottish
   Philosophy from Francis Hutcheson to Lord Balfour*, New York:
   Garland, 1983 (original edition, 1938)
Todd, William B., "David Hume, a Preliminary Bibliography," in
   *Hume and the Enlightenment: Essays Presented to Ernest
   Campbell Mossner*, edited by Todd, Edinburgh: Edinburgh
   University Press, and Austin: University of Texas Humanities
   Research Center, 1974

Further Reading

Bongie, Laurence L., *David Hume, Prophet of the Counter-
   Revolution*, Oxford: Clarendon Press, 1965
Box, M. A., *The Suasive Art of David Hume*, Princeton, New
   Jersey: Princeton University Press, 1990
Capaldi, Nicholas, *Hume's Place in Moral Philosophy*, New York:
   Lang, 1989
Forbes, Duncan, *Hume's Philosophical Politics*, Cambridge and New
   York: Cambridge University Press, 1975
Gaskin, J. C. A., *Hume's Philosophy of Religion*, London:
   Macmillan, and Atlantic Highlands, New Jersey: Humanities
   Press, 1988 (original edition, 1978)
Jones, Peter, *Hume's Sentiments, Their Ciceronian and French
   Context*, Edinburgh: Edinburgh University Press, 1982
Livingston, Donald W., *Hume's Philosophy of Common Life*,
   Chicago: University of Chicago Press, 1984
Miller, David, *Philosophy and Ideology in Hume's Political
   Thought*, Oxford: Clarendon Press, and New York: Oxford
   University Press, 1981
Norton, David Fate, *David Hume, Common-Sense Moralist,
   Sceptical Metaphysician*, Princeton, New Jersey: Princeton
   University Press, 1982
Penelhum, Terence, *Hume*, London: Macmillan, and New York: St.
   Martin's Press, 1975
Siebert, Donald T., *The Moral Animus of David Hume*, Newark:
   University of Delaware Press, 1990

Humorous Essay

Before the early 18th century the term "humor" referred to
any one of four chief liquids in the human body, the proportion of which was thought to determine an individual's character. Only in the 18th century did the term come to refer to
a type of writing meant to evoke laughter. The older meaning
of the word persisted in the sense that this type of writing
focused on human characteristics, personalities, foibles, and
eccentricities, as opposed to witty writing, which relied on
mental quickness, keen intellectual perceptions, and wordplay.

As a genre the essay has tended more toward the humorous
than the witty. Even before there was a such a term, the
humorous essay existed. For instance, in "Des cannibales"
(1580; "Of Cannibals"), **Montaigne** shows cannibals from the
New World to be more "civilized" than Europeans. The cannibals are shocked by the cruelty of the Portuguese invaders and
amazed that young Charles IX's hefty Swiss guardsmen
"should submit to obey a child." Tongue in cheek, Montaigne
admits grudging respect for these noble savages, but then
concludes, "All of this is not too bad – but what's the use?
They don't wear breeches."

Within the essay tradition Montaigne's anecdotal humor was
offset from the start by **Bacon**'s more serious, instructive, and
epigrammatic approach. If humor is broader, slower, and more
open, while wit is more incisive, rapid, and neat, then the
tradition of the humorous essay can be traced to Montaigne
and the witty essay to Bacon. During the 17th century, **La
Rochefoucauld** explored a sort of middle ground. His **maxims**
were aphoristic and instructive in the manner of Bacon, but
retained Montaigne's skepticism and ironic self-deprecation.

The 17th century was also marked by the rise of the **character sketch** as a kind of humorous essay. This development
grew out of the 1592 publication of a Latin translation of
Theophrastus (c. 371–c. 287 BCE), whose *Characters* offered
a model for exploring the eccentricities of the individual. These
essays sometimes pretended to be a **letter** from a neighboring
place bringing news about those who lived there. Bishop Joseph
Hall, Sir Thomas Overbury, Thomas Dekker, Thomas
Harman, John Earle, Thomas Fuller, and Laura Spencer Portor
all published collections in which they characterized such types
as the bumpkin, the glutton, the busybody, and the hypocritical nonconformist. Ben Jonson's epigrams also presented types
as social or moral models. The character was also popular in
France where **La Bruyère** created more individualized subjects
in his essays.

During the 18th century, the character evolved into the **periodical essay**, which was brief, gossipy, and topical. **Richard
Steele** developed this type of humorous essay in his *Tatler*
(1709–11) and joined with **Joseph Addison** to refine it in
the *Spectator* (1711–12, 1714). **Samuel Johnson**'s *Rambler*
(1750–52) and *Idler* (1758–60) followed, as did variations by
Jonathan Swift, Alexander Pope, the **Earl of Chesterfield** (Philip
Dormer Stanhope), Horace Walpole, **Oliver Goldsmith**, and
George Colman and Bonnell Thornton. **Henry Fielding** folded
similar kinds of essays into his novel *Tom Jones* (1749). The
periodical essayists were also popular in America, spawning
imitators such as John Trumbull, Joseph Dennie, Charles
Brockden Brown, and William Wirt.

The humor of the periodical essayists appealed to a new, urban, middle-class readership. By satirizing fashions, marriage, coffeehouse conversation, and pastimes such as duelling and card-playing, the periodical essayists sought to reform the manners, morals, and tastes of their readers. The border between fiction and nonfiction was permeable for the periodical essayists, who regularly invented characters, "correspondents," and clubs in their essays. Addison and Steele targeted women's fashions and their alleged flightiness and duplicity, charges that **Maria Edgeworth** answered in her sly *Letters for Literary Ladies* (1795).

The turn into the 19th century saw the emergence of the Romantic movement with its emphasis on individualism, sensibility, and radical politics. These concerns, along with the more leisurely deadlines and extra space provided in new literary magazines such as *Blackwood's Edinburgh Magazine* and the *London Magazine*, led to the development of a more sentimental, autobiographical, and urbane kind of humorous essay. **Charles Lamb**'s persona in his Elia essays (1823, 1828) was apparently not unlike the genial self that he showed his friends and that helped him through his melancholy life. Lamb's light, whimsical, intimate, somewhat antique style was aspired to by English essayists for a century after his death. **William Hazlitt**, the other great master of the period, had a bit more edge, writing humorously about such topics as "On the Pleasure of Hating" (1826) and "On the Disadvantages of Intellectual Superiority" (1821).

In America, **Washington Irving** added length and sentiment to the Addisonian essay in his *Sketch Book* (1819–20). Sara Payson Willis Parton, who published under the name Fanny Fern, was a professional journalist for more than 20 years. Best known for her sentimental *Fern Leaves from Fanny's Portfolio* (1853), she also had a wicked wit with which she punctured masculine pomposity. But it was Irving's lighter brand of irony and nostalgic musing that most influenced genteel American essayists such as Charles Dudley Warner and Donald Grant Mitchell, who dominated the second half of the 19th century. **Agnes Repplier** and Katherine Fuller Gerould kept the genteel or "light" essay alive well into the 1930s with their apt allusions and dry wits.

In England, the essay grew increasingly formal, decorous, and critical until the very end of the 19th century. **Oscar Wilde**, the sharpest *fin-de-siècle* wit, only occasionally wrote essays, but **Max Beerbohm**'s perfect parodies, **G. K. Chesterton**'s puns and conversational style, **Robert Louis Stevenson**'s whimsical imagination, and E. V. Lucas' single-handed resurrection of Lambian geniality brought humor back to the English essay. The problem was that these writers were sometimes so discreet in their choice of subject matter and so light in their treatment of it that their essays became almost parodies of the form. The titles of **Hilaire Belloc**'s collections demonstrate an awareness of this problem: *On Nothing, On Everything, On Anything, On Something* (1908–11), and, finally, just *On* (1923).

It was during this period that the humorous essay moved from the literary quarterlies back to the newspapers and magazines. Oswald Barron, writing as "The Londoner" in the *Evening News*, produced a light essay – at once sensible, readable, and witty – every day for two decades. Robert Lynd accomplished a similar feat, writing weekly about everything from football to eggs as "Y. Y." of the *New Statesman* until his death in 1949.

It was not until the 20th century that the United States developed its own type of the humorous essay. The rustics and cracker-barrel philosophers of 19th-century America, from Sut Lovingood to Artemus Ward to Mr. Dooley, were fictional characters whose humor was mainly dialect humor. Even real-life figures such as Davy Crockett, Mike Fink, and Jim Bridger were turned into tall tales. **Mark Twain** used the essay form to pillory James Fenimore Cooper, but was himself primarily a fiction writer, as the title of perhaps his best-known essay, "How to Tell a Story" (1895), indicates.

The first few decades of the 20th century in the United States have been called by some "the age of Mencken." From the *Baltimore Evening Sun* **H. L. Mencken**'s iconoclastic, often cynical, always American voice sounded daily. Mencken skewered puritanism, sentimentality, boosterism, pedantry, and other traits of the "*booboisie.*"

The explosion in the number of newspapers and a desire on the part of readers to be "in the know" also led to the rise of a group who called themselves "colyumnists." Several of these urban humorists frequented the famous Round Table at the Algonquin Hotel in New York. Competition forced each to pursue his own angle. Franklin Pierce Adams collected one-liners and humorous verse from readers, and wrote mock Pepysian diaries about New York goings-on; R. C. Holliday, Alexander Woollcott, and Christopher Morley displayed bookish and acerbic wits; and Don Marquis used a fictional cockroach to poke fun at the times. But it was **Robert Benchley** and Heywood Broun who most successfully re-created themselves as characters in their columns. Their version of the "little man" – a kind of bewildered, middle-class American guy doing his best in a fast-paced modern world – was developed and refined by **James Thurber** and **E. B. White** in the *New Yorker*. The beset "little man" has survived as Garrison Keillor's sentimental Midwesterner and Dave Barry's suburban father.

The "little man" has bumbled through the 20th century, but his female counterpart has not. The decline of gentility meant that women essayists no longer needed to worry quite so much about being decorous. As Victorian proprieties eroded, female essayists could be more unabashed. **Virginia Woolf** and Dorothy Parker wrote wickedly funny essays – though this activity did not allow them to escape all the restrictions on their gender in their societies. Parker, in particular, should be regarded as a 20th-century woman, not a 19th-century lady. Woolf was cleverer than most men, Parker was quicker, and both were funnier. Among contemporary female practitioners of the humorous essay, some, such as Nora Ephron, Molly Ivins, and Fran Lebowitz, find their subjects in the (still) masculine public sphere, while others, such as Jean Kerr, Shirley Jackson, Peg Bracken, and Erma Bombeck, focus on domestic life; but all feel free to be both clever and incisive.

In the United States, black and Jewish writers of humorous essays have, like women, long recognized that in a society of inequalities and prejudices, people laugh at different things. Thus, their essays tend to revolve around issues of sameness and difference. As Langston Hughes put it in the preface to his *Book of Negro Humor* (1966), "Humor is laughing at what you haven't got when you ought to have it. Of course, you laugh by proxy. You're really laughing at the other guy's lacks, not your own." He then adds that the joke may be "on you but hits the other fellow first – before it boomerangs." This doubleness in ethnic humor has meant that the African American or Jewish humorous essay often relies on dialect – be it Yiddish or the "signifyin'" codes of black speech. The best of these essays are not strictly in-jokes, however, and can be appreciated by many outside the particular ethnic group. Such doubleness has also meant that black and Jewish essayists often turn their humor back on the pretensions of their own group. Thus there is no *real* self-hatred in, for instance, Hughes' uncompromising look at the black middle class in "The Negro Artist and the Racial Mountain" (1926), Zora Neale Hurston's "How It Feels to Be Colored Me" (1928) (which opens with the line "I am colored but I offer nothing in the way of extenuating circumstances except the fact that I am the only Negro in the United States whose grandfather on the mother's side was *not* an Indian chief"), or even Woody Allen's exposure of his own neuroses and insecurities.

On the basis of a long view of the history of the humorous essay, one could, if reducing the form to its essentials, say that while it can be aphoristic, quick, and witty, it more often harks back to the 17th-century character's slower, fuller descriptions of eccentricities and foibles – sometimes another's, sometimes the essayist's, but usually both.

NED STUCKEY-FRENCH

Anthologies

Humour in English Literature: A Chronological Anthology, edited by Reginald Horace Blyth, Folcroft, Pennsylvania: Folcroft, 1970
A Subtreasury of American Humor, edited by E. B. White and Katharine S. White, New York: Coward McCann, 1941

Further Reading

Blair, Walter, and Hamlin Hill, *America's Humor: From Poor Richard to Doonesbury*, New York: Oxford University Press, 1978
Bruère, Martha Bensley, and Mary Ritter Beard, *Laughing Their Way: Women's Humor in America*, New York: Macmillan, 1934
Clark, William Bradford, and W. Craig Turner, editors, *Critical Essays on American Humor*, Boston: Hall, 1984
Eleanore, Sister Mary, *The Literary Essay in English*, Boston: Ginn, 1923
Gale, Stephen H., editor, *Encyclopedia of American Humorists*, New York: Garland, 1988
Inge, Thomas M., editor, *The Frontier Humorists: Critical Views*, Hamden, Connecticut: Archon, 1975
Little, Judy, *Comedy and the Woman Writer: Woolf, Spark and Feminism*, Lincoln: University of Nebraska Press, 1983
Morris, Linda A., *Women Vernacular Humorists in Nineteenth-Century America: Ann Stephens, Francis Whitcher, and Marietta Holley*, New York: Garland, 1988
Morris, Linda A., editor, *American Women Humorists: Critical Essays*, New York: Garland, 1994
Rourke, Constance, *American Humor: A Study of the National Character*, New York: Harcourt Brace, 1931
Tave, Stuart M., *The Amiable Humorist: A Study in the Comic Theory and Criticism of the Eighteenth and Early Nineteenth Centuries*, Chicago: University of Chicago Press, 1960
Thackeray, William Makepeace, *The English Humourists of the Eighteenth Century: A Series of Lectures*, London: Smith Elder, 1853
Trachtenberg, Stanley, editor, *Dictionary of Literary Biography: American Humorists, 1800–1950*, Detroit: Gale Research, 2 vols., 1982

Walker, Nancy A., *A Very Serious Thing: Women's Humor and American Culture*, Minneapolis: University of Minnesota Press, 1988
Ward, A. C., *Twentieth-Century Literature: 1901–1950*, London: Methuen, 1956
White, E. B., Preface to *A Subtreasury of American Humor*, edited by E. B. White and Katharine S. White, New York: Coward McCann, 1941
Yates, Norris Wilson, *The American Humorist: Conscience of the Twentieth Century*, Ames: Iowa State University Press, 1964

Hunt, Leigh

British, 1784–1859

Leigh Hunt wrote essays on a wide variety of subjects and in a number of styles. This eclecticism and versatility have established his reputation as an important figure in the Romantic period.

Beginning in 1801, Hunt wrote essays and theatrical criticism for a number of journals, one of which was his brother John's *News*. In collaboration with his brother, Leigh began the weekly political journal, the *Examiner*, in 1808. Concurrent with the *Examiner* was the short-lived *Reflector* (1810–11), a quarterly magazine devoted to literary topics, noteworthy for the **familiar essays** "A Day by the Fire" and "The Feast of the Poets." Legal trouble befell Hunt in 1813, when his unrestrained criticism of government corruption, ineptitude, and foreign policy provoked the charge of seditious libel, for which he was found guilty, fined, and incarcerated for two years.

Despite this experience, the best of Hunt's work was yet to come. Familiar essays such as "Getting up on Cold Mornings" and "A 'Now': Descriptive of a Hot Day" appeared in the weekly *Indicator* (1819–21). While in Italy in 1822, Hunt planned a joint periodical venture with Byron and **Shelley**. After Shelley's death, however, the *Liberal* produced only four numbers (1822–23), ceasing once an embittered Byron left Hunt, who remained in Genoa, destitute. By 1828, Hunt was, once again, writing high-quality essays for the *Companion*, these contributions consisting largely of theatrical criticism and occasional essays in the manner of the *Indicator*. Among his later outlets were the *Tatler* (1830–32), *Leigh Hunt's London Journal* (1834–35), and *Leigh Hunt's Journal: A Miscellany for the Cultivation of the Memorable, the Progressive, and the Beautiful* (1850–51).

One of Hunt's greatest innovations in the genre was his version of the Theophrastan character, a sketch in which the definition of a human weakness introduces a list of actions typical of such a person. An example of this motif can be found in "On Washerwomen" (1816). Hunt, whose knowledge of the fine arts was impressive, begins by describing "direct picture-making" as a means of sketching both men and things. Like a great painter who captures the intensity of a scene through color, position, and shade, or like a great composer whose overture conveys the substance of a symphony, the essayist must approach his task with incisiveness, perspicuity, and power. The "detached portrait," the form of which Chaucer and **Steele** had done much to develop, was, for Hunt, precisely such an intense scene or overture. From this theoretical preamble, he turns, not without tongue in cheek, to washerwomen. In a Wordsworthian spirit, Hunt makes his purpose clear: to celebrate the pleasures derived from contemplating "any set of one's fellow creatures and their humours, when our knowledge has acquired humility enough to look at them steadily." This topical versatility – the ability to treat theoretical material in an imaginative context – is a distinguishing feature of Hunt's talent.

A further example of Hunt's proclivity for literary innovation in the essay is "A 'Now': Descriptive of a Hot Day" (1820). In this piece, the speaker focuses on a sequence of detached scenes of rural and urban persons, things, and familiar activities. Here, mundane or commonplace subject matter is used in a highly imaginative way: the sequencing of portraits is unified spatially through the mind of the ubiquitous speaker; and the simultaneity of experience is linguistically evoked by the repetition of the adverb "Now" at the head of each sentence. "A 'Now'" demonstrates Hunt's intention of using the essay as a testing ground for his theory of detached portraiture.

Hunt underscores his idea of the amplitude of great poetry in "What Is Poetry?," the introductory essay to his larger work, *Imagination and Fancy* (1844). Defining poetry synoptically as an utterance of a passion for truth, beauty, and power, he signals his departure from neoclassical norms, stating that any subject can be legitimately considered for poetry. Thus, the means of poetry can be "whatever the universe contains"; rather than striving for a didactic or moral message, poetry should seek to convey "pleasure and exaltation." Hunt's conjectures on the creative faculties – on imagination and fancy – clearly owe much to Wordsworth, **Coleridge**, **Hazlitt**, and Keats; in fact, Hunt seems to have had Coleridge's *Biographia Literaria* in mind in his enumeration of the kinds and degrees of imagination. His sevenfold paradigm treats figurative language (the dynamics of metaphor) and emphasizes the great importance of the imagination, in all its phases, "as a constituent part of the highest poetic faculty." "What Is Poetry?" epitomizes Hunt's theoretical interests and incisive style.

Perhaps nowhere else are Hunt's critical intelligence and virtuosity with the genre exhibited more impressively than in his famous **review** of John Keats' first volume of poetry (1816). As a preamble to his evaluation of Keats' work, Hunt describes neoclassical poetry as being bereft of imagination, of intense feeling, and of sentiment and variety. Even the greatest of the 18th-century poets – Gray, Thomson, Akenside, and Collins – allegedly practiced an imitative and artificial style. Whereas the 18th-century poets were reputedly alienated from feeling and concrete reality, the Lake poets, though not above criticism themselves, were the first to revive true taste for nature, with Wordsworth epitomizing this tendency. Keats, too, is emphatically a poet of the new age, for he pursues new poetry for its own sake. Hunt's review is typically balanced, precise, and even-tempered. He begins by enumerating two faults of Keats' poetry (one of which is to overdo rhymes intentionally), but then turns to the obvious "Beauties" of his work. Three prominent aspects of Keats' verse are his "fine ear," the felicitous workings of his imagination and fancy, and "an intense feeling of external beauty in its most natural and least expressible simplicity." Besides evidencing Hunt's support of Romantic

literature, the review reflects his tactical ability, within a relatively finite space, to focus on and to interrelate a variety of topics (literary theory and history), as well to employ effectively several rhetorical strategies (comparison and exemplification).

Among his numerous essays on the theater, that on the reopening of the Covent Garden Theatre (1809) evidences Hunt's concern for his fellow man and for social equity. No dilettante, he could not detach the arts either from the living reality they imitated or from the society which they were supposed to entertain. Specifically, he castigates the hypocritical management of Covent Garden for raising ticket prices to cater to the aristocracy and probably to defray the costs of the opulent furnishings and decor. Calculating to serve only "the higher orders," the management, whom Hunt calls "tradesmen," have, in a sense, subverted the nobility of the theater, not to mention having precipitated riots. This piece, like many others, depicts Hunt as a humane, penetrating, and conscientious critic.

CHARLES DE PAOLO

Biography

James Henry Leigh Hunt. Born 19 October 1784 in Southgate, Middlesex. Studied at Christ's Hospital school, London, 1791–99. Served with the St. James regiment, 1803. Legal clerk, 1803–05; worked for the War Office, 1805–08. Married Marianne Kent, 1809 (died, 1857): seven children (one son died). Contributor throughout his career to many journals and periodicals, including the *Traveller*, 1804, the *News*, 1805–07, the *Statesman*, 1806, the *Times*, 1807, *New Monthly Magazine*, 1825–26 and occasionally until 1850, *Atlas*, 1828–30, *True Sun* and *Weekly True Sun*, 1833–34, the *Spectator*, 1858–59, and the *Morning Chronicle*; editor of many journals, including the *Examiner: A Sunday Paper*, 1808–21 (also contributor until 1825), the *Reflector*, 1810–11, the *Indicator*, 1819–21, *Literary Pocket-Book; or, Companion for the Lover of Nature and Art*, 1819–23, the *Companion*, 1828, *Chat of the Week*, 1830, the *Tatler: A Daily Journal of Literature and the Stage*, 1830–32, *Leigh Hunt's London Journal*, 1834–35, the *Monthly Repository*, 1837–38, and *Leigh Hunt's Journal*, 1850–51. Convicted and jailed for libeling the prince regent, 1813–15 (continued to edit the *Examiner* while in prison). Lived in Italy (arrived a week before Percy Bysshe Shelley's drowning), 1822–25: established the *Liberal* with Shelley, editing it with Byron after Shelley's death, 1822–23. Granted Civil List pension, 1847. Died in Putney, south London, 28 August 1859.

Selected Writings

Essays and Related Prose

Critical Essays on the Performers of the London Theatres, 1807
The Examiner (periodical), 3 January 1808–26 February 1821
The Reflector (periodical), nos. 1–4, 1 January 1811–23 March 1812; in 2 vols., 1812
The Round Table: A Collection of Essays on Literature, Men, and Manners, with William Hazlitt, 2 vols., 1817; facsimile reprint, 1991
The Indicator (periodical), nos. 1–76, 13 October 1819–21 March 1821; in 2 vols., 1820–21
The Chat of the Week (periodical), nos. 1–13, 5 June–28 August 1830
The Seer; or, Commonplaces Refreshed, 2 vols., 1840
Essays: The Indicator, The Seer, 1841
Imagination and Fancy, with an Essay in Answer to the Question What Is Poetry?, 1844

Men, Women, and Books: A Selection of Sketches, Essays and Critical Memoirs, 2 vols., 1847
A Jar of Honey from Mount Hybla, 1848
The Town: Its Memorable Characters and Events, 2 vols., 1848
Table-Talk, 1851
Essays and Miscellanies (from the *Indicator* and the *Companion*), 1851
The Old Court Suburb; or, Memorials of Kensington, Regal, Critical, and Anecdotical, 2 vols., 1855; enlarged edition, 1855
A Tale for a Chimney Corner and Other Essays, edited by Edmund Ollier, 1869
A Day by the Fire; and Other Papers Hitherto Uncollected, edited by Joseph Edward Babson, 1870
Essays and Poems, edited by R. Bromley Johnson, 2 vols., 1891
Dramatic Essays, edited by William Archer and R. W. Lowe, 1894
Prefaces by Leigh Hunt, Mainly to His Periodicals, edited by R. Brimley Johnson, 1927
Dramatic Criticism, Literary Criticism, and *Political and Occasional Essays*, edited by Lawrence H. Houtchens and Carolyn W. Houtchens, 3 vols., 1949–62
Selected Writings, edited by David Jesson-Dibley, 1990

Other writings: poetry, a novel, two plays, a book on Byron (1828), books on London, a three-volume autobiography (1850), and correspondence.

Collected works edition: *Works*, 7 vols., 1870–89.

Bibliographies

Lulofs, Timothy J., and Hans Ostrom, *Leigh Hunt: A Reference Guide*, Boston: Hall, 1985
Waltman, John L., and Gerald G. McDavid, *Leigh Hunt: A Comprehensive Bibliography*, New York: Garland, 1985

Further Reading

Blainey, Ann, *Immortal Boy: A Portrait of Leigh Hunt*, New York: St. Martin's Press, and London: Croom Helm, 1985
Blunden, Edmund, *Leigh Hunt: A Biography*, Hamden, Connecticut: Archon, 1970 (original edition, 1930)
Cheney, David R., "Leigh Hunt, Essayist," *Books at Iowa* 40 (April 1984): 31–40
Grigely, Joseph C., "Leigh Hunt and the *Examiner* Review of Keats's Poems, 1817," *Keats-Shelley Journal* 33 (1984): 30–37
Kendall, Kenneth E., *Leigh Hunt's Reflector*, The Hague: Mouton, 1971
Marshall, William H., *Byron, Shelley, Hunt, and the Liberal*, Philadelphia: University of Pennsylvania Press, 1960
Smith, David Q., "Genius and Common Sense: The Romantics and Leigh Hunt," *Books at Iowa* 40 (April 1984): 41–57
Thompson, James R., *Leigh Hunt*, Boston: Twayne, 1977

Huxley, Aldous

British, 1894–1963

Aldous Huxley was born into a well-to-do upper-middle-class family, which brought him a rich scientific and humanistic intellectual heritage. He was the grandson of **T. H. Huxley**, one of the best-known British scientists, and on his mother's side was related to **Matthew Arnold**, the great British humanist. His father was a biographer, editor, and poet, and his elder brother, Julian, was a challenging writer and well-known biologist. These facts, plus several irreversible events that marked his early life, placed him in an ambiguous relationship to both

science and literature; they also set his remarkably inquisitive mind on an unflagging search for ultimate truth, both objective and metaphysical, wherever it could be found. Given this background, and despite his success as both novelist and essayist at a very early age (in his late twenties and early thirties), Huxley at first experienced enormous frustration at not being a scientist. He later acknowledged, however, that at this time in history, especially in the aftermath of ill-fated events including World War II, being a Michael Faraday would have been more difficult than being a Shakespeare.

Huxley chose the essay as the definitive and preferred vehicle for expressing his ideas, especially after 1936 (a crucial turning point in his life when he decided to abandon pure fictional writing), for several reasons. First, the novel, despite the freedom of viewpoints it could allow the writer, was not the genre that best portrayed reality as intellectuals saw it, but only as they thought and believed it to be. Thus, for Huxley, intellectuals who wrote novels could not reflect real human attitudes. Second, Huxley saw in the essay a means to liberate himself from the restraints of form and style of an established canon, and a door through which he could pass freely among literary, technical, and scientific worlds. He openly stated that his most cherished endeavor as a writer was the achievement of the perfect fusion of the novel and the essay. This statement echoes the general perception that Huxley was an essayist who happened to write novels. It also affirms that this genre, which the Mexican humanist and essayist **Alfonso Reyes** classified as a form of "ancillary literature" as opposed to "pure literature," and which he also called "the centaur of genres" (half literature and half science), fits Huxley's pretext for bringing together his objective and subjective views about both the natural and human worlds. The essay allowed him to uncover this fusion of worlds, as well as to display his enormous knowledge and natural wit.

This hybrid form serves as a means for exploring what he called *Proper Studies* (1927), namely those dealing with the human being. This series of essays addresses some of his most puzzling themes, ideas that constantly resurfaced in his early attempts at writing poetry, short histories, and drama, through his travelogues, novels, and social and **critical essays** on painting, art, architecture, ecology, and mysticism. As a 20th-century writer, he was especially concerned with the education of the human being as an "amphibian" (one capable of living in different environments), an epithet he applied to himself.

Huxley's concerns about the power of science and technology mainly reflect on the damage they could eventually inflict on humans and nature. This view would lead him to swing repeatedly between dystopian and utopian conceptions for the society of his day, especially following World War II, conceptions that motivated his will to synthesize both philosophical and cultural views around the well-being of humanity. This can be gathered, for instance, from his collection of essays in *Ends and Means* (1937), his philosophical work *The Perennial Philosophy* (1944), his last and only utopian novel *Island* (1962), and his posthumous essayistic piece *Literature and Science* (1963). From reading these works, it is understandable that he should consider himself a Pyrrhonist (skeptical philosopher) and why his entire production can be equally considered biographical, a natural feature of the essay, and one that accounts for the confessional tone of the author.

Huxley's skepticism may also explain why he caused so much controversy as poet, novelist, and essayist among a wide audience that came to perceive him as an extremely intelligent satirist, ironist, and cold-minded thinker. Surprisingly, these latter features were especially pleasing to his younger admirers, who came to see him as an enlightened leader. These same characteristics, however, would disappoint those same fans when they realized Huxley had abandoned his fictional writing in favor of essayistic didacticism rather than break ground in literary and critical circles.

As a writer, Huxley emphasized both the spirituality and the intellectuality of human life through his rationalistic amalgamation of science, philosophy, and art. The concept of "perennial philosophy" (as an ethical, universal system) appealed to him, especially as a system underlying all the goodness of the world in its natural manifestation (*The Doors of Perception*, 1954).

As a seeker of ultimate reality, he realized that problems arise when abstract language is used to intellectualize about the modern super-specialized and industrialized world. Father Joseph of *Gray Eminence* (1941), principal adviser to Cardinal Richelieu, is for Huxley the example that best illustrates the effects of such intellectualization and abstract language. Huxley's disillusionment with abstract progress led him finally to seek after mysticism, as he gradually abandoned the belief that one can find salvation by blindly accepting the norms of a highly complex, technological society.

CIRO A. SANDOVAL-B.

Biography

Born 26 July 1894 in Godalming, Surrey. Grandson of the scientist T. H. Huxley. Studied at Eton College, Berkshire, 1908–13; Balliol College, Oxford, 1913–15, B.A. in English, 1916. Worked for the War Office, London, 1917; taught at Eton College, 1918. Married Maria Nys, 1919 (died, 1955): one son. Member of the editorial staff, the *Athenaeum*, London, 1919–20; drama critic, *Westminster Gazette*, 1920–21; assistant at the Chelsea Book Club; worked for Condé Nast Publications, 1922. Lived in Italy, 1923–30, France, 1931–36, and California, from 1937; wrote screenplays for film studios. Experimented with hallucinogenic drugs, 1950s. Married Laura Archera, 1956. Awards: American Academy Award, 1959; Companion of Literature, Royal Society of Literature, 1962. Died in Los Angeles, 22 November 1963.

Selected Writings

Essays and Related Prose

On the Margin: Notes and Essays, 1923
Along the Road: Notes and Essays of a Tourist, 1925
Essays New and Old, 1926
Proper Studies, 1927
Do What You Will: Essays, 1929
Holy Face, and Other Essays, 1929
Music at Night, and Other Essays, 1931
The Olive Tree and Other Essays, 1936
Stories, Essays, and Poems, 1937
Ends and Means: An Enquiry into the Nature of Ideals and into the Methods Employed for Their Realization, 1937
Themes and Variations, 1950
Adonis and the Alphabet, and Other Essays, 1956; as *Tomorrow and Tomorrow and Tomorrow, and Other Essays*, 1956
Collected Essays, 1959

On Art and Artists, edited by Morris Philipson, 1960
Selected Essays, edited by Harold Raymond, 1961
Literature and Science, 1963
Huxley and God, edited by Jacqueline Hazard Bridgeman, 1992
Hearst Essays, edited by James Sexton, 1994
Between the Wars: Essays and Letters, edited by David Bradshaw, 1994
The Hidden Huxley: Contempt and Compassion for the Masses, edited by David Bradshaw, 1994

Other writings: 11 novels (*Crome Yellow*, 1921; *Antic Hay*, 1923; *Those Barren Leaves*, 1925; *Point Counter Point*, 1928; *Brave New World*, 1932; *Eyeless in Gaza*, 1936; *After Many a Summer Dies the Swan*, 1939; *Time Must Have a Stop*, 1944; *Ape and Essence*, 1948; *The Genius and the Goddess*, 1955; *Island*, 1962) short story collections, several plays and screenplays, travel writing, poetry, works on philosophy, and *The Doors of Perception* (1954), a book about his drug experiences.

Collected works edition: *Collected Works*, 1948– (in progress).

Bibliographies
Bass, Eben E., *Aldous Huxley: An Annotated Bibliography of Criticism*, New York: Garland, 1981
Eschelbach, Claire John, and Joyce Lee Shober, *Aldous Huxley: A Bibliography 1916–1959*, Berkeley: University of California Press, and Cambridge: Cambridge University Press, 1961; supplements by Thomas D. Clareson and Carolyn S. Andrews, in *Extrapolation 6* (December 1964): 2–21, and by Dennis D. Davis, in *Bulletin of Bibliography* 31 (April–June 1974): 67–70

Further Reading
Atkins, John, *Aldous Huxley: A Literary Study*, New York: Orion Press, and London: Calder and Boyars, revised edition, 1967
Firchow, Peter, *Aldous Huxley: Satirist and Novelist*, Minneapolis: University of Minnesota Press, 1972
Holmes, Charles M., *Aldous Huxley and the Way to Reality*, Bloomington: Indiana University Press, 1970
Thody, Philip, *Huxley: A Biographical Introduction*, New York: Scribner, 1973
Watt, Donald, *Aldous Huxley: The Critical Heritage*, London and Boston: Routledge and Kegan Paul, 1975
Watts, Harold H., *Aldous Huxley*, New York: Twayne, 1969

Huxley, T. H.

British, 1825–1895

T. H. Huxley wrote 220 **science essays** and over 100 "fugitive pieces," popular essays devoted to promoting science as the instrument for revealing truths biological and geological, educational and political, ethical and ethical. His audience ranged from working men to Royal Institution amateurs to professional peers in the Royal Society, of which he was president between 1883 and 1885. Huxley's scientific essays exhibit his meticulous prose style, achieved by both a keen understanding of the physiological or physiographic process being analyzed and the employment of specialized terms.

In the preface to *Discourses Biological and Geological* (1894), Huxley extols prose for "lay sermons" that replaces "scholastic pedantry" with clear expression. He alludes to John Wesley's cunning in popularizing the sacred: "he did not see why the Devil should be left in possession of the best tunes."

These tunes are sometimes played in his scientific memoirs, for example in his savage **review** of a new edition of a bad book, the appearance of which "has much the effect that the inconvenient pertinacity of *Banquo* had upon *Macbeth*. 'Time was, that when the brains were out, the man would die.' So time was, that when a book had been shown to be a mass of pretentious nonsense, it, too, quietly sunk into its proper limbo" ("Vestiges of the Natural History of Creation, Tenth Edition," 1854).

The fundamental feature of Huxley's prose style is his philosophical perspective: "unity in diversity," aligning stork and the snake it swallows; beetle and bee; monkey and man; the hut and the pantheon; and agnosticism ("agnostic" is his invention), reason, science, and decent behavior. In "On Science and Art in Relation to Education" (1882), he aligned the pleasure derived from Bach's fugues with the pleasure of unifying diverse data in morphology. In his laboratory, he would select a common animal as an item stimulating generalization, moving from the specific to the general: from the entrance hall crayfish to the mansion Invertebrata. He would also shift deliberately from the known to the unknown, from a piece of chalk held in his hand to strata held by the earth below. "On a Piece of Chalk," delivered to Norwich working men in 1868, exemplifies his technique as popular lecturer, beginning with the concrete here and now and cruising strange seas of thought to transport his audience to the ancient sea bottom. The conclusion envisages burning chalk that shines like the sun, its luminous rays metamorphosing into a "fervent" and often-reprinted essay.

Huxley's "On the Physical Basis of Life" (1869) tracks down vital activities to the collaboration of carbon, hydrogen, nitrogen, and oxygen. This reduction of people to protoplasm was sufficiently subversive to send the *Fortnightly Review*, the journal in which it appeared, into seven editions, a record last accomplished by **Jonathan Swift**. It also excited a dozen jeremiads. The essay provides fine strata for investigation of Huxley's prose style: specificity of reference to biological, chemical, and geological data; imaginative and informative analogy and metaphor; an aesthetic precision of diction; allusions, e.g. to Schoolmen, Dante, Balzac, Jacob's ladder; a tone often tinged with humor if not tainted with sarcasm; and references to himself, a voice that over the decades presented him to his auditors and readers as a friendly guide.

Opening with a revelation of protoplasm as the cohering substance of all life, Huxley directs us to picture to ourselves "the great Finner whale, hugest of beasts that live, or have lived, disporting his eighty or ninety feet of bone, muscle and blubber, with easy roll, among waves in which the stoutest ship that ever left dockyard would flounder hopelessly, and contrast him with the invisible animalcules – mere gelatinous specks, multitudes of which could, in fact, dance upon the point of a needle with the same ease as the angels of the Schoolmen could, in imagination." If he, Huxley, were to sup upon lobster, the crustacean would metamorphose into humanity; and were Huxley to drown, the crustacean would "return the compliment" and convert the lecturer into lobster. A noteworthy product of the human molecular machine is the physiological event called thought. Automatism dooms people to nightmares: the eclipse of tradition "threatens to drown their souls; the tightening grasp of law impedes their freedom;

they are alarmed lest man's moral nature be debased by the increase of his wisdom."

Another feature of Huxley's prose style is the architectonic. His essays are usually so well organized, with such comforting guiding transitions, that they have been taken as models for undergraduate (as well as scholarly) writing – for example, in his "A Liberal Education" (1868), with its famous personification of Nature as a grand master playing a lethal chess game with us pawns. He did not always find his compatriots skillful at architectonics; he felt the *Origin of Species* was "An intellectual pemmican – a mass of facts crushed and pounded into shape, rather than held together by the ordinary medium of an obvious logical bond." German scientists are "magnificently laborious and accurate. But most of them have no notion of style, and seem to compose their books with a pitchfork."

Huxley was famous, or infamous, as a polemicist. Scores of his essays display his pugilistic talent, for example, *Lectures on Evolution* (pub. 1882), delivered in New York City in 1876, which earned him extensive reports in the *New York Times* and the ignoble label "Huxley Eikonoklastes" elsewhere. His most impressive polemical bouts (1885–95) were his description of Genesis as an inaccurate account of global and vital dynamics, and his attack on Messianic exorcism (the Gadarene swine episode) as an accurate account of demonology at work.

For good literary creation, Huxley focused on the importance of being earnestly stirred by the subject, of being clear and avoiding "that pestilent cosmetic, rhetoric" (which sometimes adorns his prose), and of meticulous revising. The work of good writers is characterized by "clear and vivid conceptions" embodied in "language exactly adapted to convey them to other minds"; they possess "that purely artistic sense of rhythm and proportion which [enable] them to add grace to force, and, while loyal to truth, make exactness subservient to beauty" ("Good Writing: A Gift or an Art?," 1890). Other essayists influenced by him as naturalistic writer and agnostic mentor were Thomas Hardy, H. G. Wells, **H. L. Mencken**, Clarence Darrow, and his grandsons Julian and **Aldous Huxley**.

CHARLES BLINDERMAN

Biography

Thomas Henry Huxley. Born 4 May 1825 in Ealing, west London. Studied at Ealing School, 1833–35; Charing Cross Hospital, London, 1842–45; University of London, medical degree, 1845. Assistant surgeon on HMS *Rattlesnake*, which surveyed the passage between the Great Barrier Reef and the Australian coast, 1846–50. Lecturer in natural history, Royal School of Mines (later the Royal College of Science), from 1854. Married Henrietta Heathorn, 1855: seven children (two others died), including Leonard Huxley, father of Julian and Aldous Huxley. Naturalist to the geological survey of the English coast, from 1855. Science columnist, *Westminster Review* and *Saturday Review*. President, Ethnological Society, 1868–70, Geological Society, 1869–70, and the Royal Society, 1883–85. Held many other positions, including: Croonian Lecturer, Royal Society; Fullerian Lecturer, Royal Institution; Hunterian Professor, Royal College of Surgeons; Governor of Eton College, of University College, London, and of Owen College, Manchester; and Rector, University of Aberdeen. Retired from all official appointments, 1885. Privy Councillor, 1892. Awards: Copley Medal; Darwin Medal; honorary degrees from nine universities. Died (of influenza and bronchitis) in Eastbourne, 29 June 1895.

Selected Writings

Essays and Related Prose

On Our Knowledge of the Causes of the Phenomena of Organic Nature (lectures), 1862
Evidence as to Man's Place in Nature, 1863
On the Origin of Species; or, The Causes of the Phenomena of Organic Nature (lectures), 1863
Lectures on the Elements of Comparative Anatomy, 1864
Lay Sermons, Addresses and Reviews, 1870
Essays Selected from Lay Sermons, 1871
Critiques and Addresses, 1873
American Addresses, with a Lecture in the Study of Biology, 1877
Science and Culture, and Other Essays, 1881
Lectures on Evolution, 1882
Animal Automatism, and Other Essays, 1884
Technical Education, and Other Essays, 1885
Essays upon Some Controverted Questions, 1892
Evolution and Ethics, 1893; edited by James Paradis and George C. Williams, 1989
Collected Essays, 9 vols., 1893–94; reprinted 1968
  1. *Method and Results*, 1893
  2. *Darwiniana*, 1893
  3. *Science and Education*, 1893
  4. *Science and Hebrew Tradition*, 1893
  5. *Science and Christian Tradition*, 1893
  6. *Hume, with Helps to the Study of Berkeley*, 1894
  7. *Man's Place in Nature, and Other Anthropological Essays*, 1894
  8. *Discourses Biological and Geological*, 1894
  9. *Evolution and Ethics, and Other Essays*, 1894
The Scientific Memoirs, edited by Michael Foster and E. Ray Lankester, 5 vols., 1898–1903
Autobiography and Selected Essays, edited by Ada L. F. Snell, 1903, Sarah E. Simons, 1910, E. H. Kemper McComb, 1910, and Brander Matthews, 1919
Essays on Science and Education, edited by Ada L. F. Snell, 1909
Selected Essays and Addresses, edited by Philo Melvyn Buck, Jr., 1910
Selections from the Essays, edited by Alburey Castell, 1948
The Essence of T. H. Huxley: Selections from His Writings, edited by Cyril Bibby, 1967
T. H. Huxley on Education, edited by Cyril Bibby, 1971

Other writings: a book about the *Rattlesnake* voyage (1859), and textbooks and manuals on biology, zoology, anatomy, and other natural sciences.

Bibliographies

Dawson, Warren R., *The Huxley Papers: A Descriptive Catalogue of the Correspondence, Manuscripts, and Miscellaneous Papers of the Rt. Hon. T. H. Huxley*, London: Macmillan, for the Imperial College of Science and Technology, 1946

Pingree, Jeanne, *T. H. Huxley: A List of His Scientific Notebooks, Drawings and Other Papers, Preserved in the College Library*, London: Imperial College of Science and Technology, 1968

Further Reading

Bibby, Cyril, "Huxley: Prince of Controversialists," *Twentieth Century* 161 (1957): 268–77
Blinderman, Charles, "Semantic Aspects of T. H. Huxley's Literary Style," *Journal of Communication* 12 (1962): 171–78
Blinderman, Charles, "T. H. Huxley's Theory of Aesthetics: Unity in Diversity," *Journal of Aesthetics and Art Criticism* 21 (1962): 49–55
Blinderman, Charles, "Huxley, Pater, and Protoplasm," *Journal of the History of Ideas* 3 (1982): 477–86
Block, Ed., Jr., "T. H. Huxley's Rhetoric and the Popularization of Victorian Scientific Ideas, 1854–1874," *Victorian Studies* 29 (Spring 1986): 363–86
Desmond, Adrian, *Huxley: The Devil's Disciple*, London: Michael Joseph, and New York: Viking, 1994
Gardner, Joseph H., "A Huxley Essay as 'Poem'," *Victorian Studies* 14 (1970): 177–91
Houghton Walter E., "The Rhetoric of T. H. Huxley," *University of Toronto Quarterly* 18 (1949): 159–75
Hutton, Richard, "Professor Huxley's Hidden Chess Player," *Spectator* 41 (11 January 1868): 41–42
Huxley, Aldous, "T. H. Huxley as a Literary Man," in his *The Olive Tree and Other Essays*, London: Chatto and Windus, 1936; New York: Harper and Row, 1937
Jensen, J. Vernon, *Thomas Henry Huxley: Communicating for Science*, Newark: University of Delaware Press, 1991
Lightman, Bernard, *The Origins of Agnosticism: Victorian Unbelief and the Limits of Knowledge*, Baltimore: Johns Hopkins University Press, 1987
McCartney, Jesse F., "The Pedagogical Style of T. H. Huxley in 'On the Physiological Basis of Life'," *Southern Quarterly* 14 (1976): 97–107
Paradis, James G., *T. H. Huxley: Man's Place in Nature*, Lincoln: University of Nebraska Press, 1978
Routh, James, "Huxley as a Literary Man," *The Century Magazine* 63 (1902): 392–98
Watt, Donald, "Soul-Facts: Humour and Figure in T. H. Huxley," *Prose Studies* 1 (1978): 30–40
Zappen, James P., "Scientific Rhetoric in the Nineteenth and Early Twentieth Centuries: Herbert Spencer, Thomas H. Huxley and John Dewey," in *Textual Dynamics of the Professions: Historical and Contemporary Studies of Writing in Professional Communities*, edited by Charles Bazerman and James Paradis, Madison: University of Wisconsin Press, 1991

I

The Idler

by Samuel Johnson; British periodical series, 1758–1760

Samuel Johnson's *Idler* papers appeared originally as the leading articles in the newspaper the *Universal Chronicle* on consecutive Saturdays from 15 April 1758 to 5 April 1760. The series began in the second number of the newspaper, Johnson having provided anonymously a general essay in the first number to introduce the new serial (in which he was a shareholder). Though he wrote the **periodical essay**s as Mr. Idler, this body of writing was easily recognized and widely enjoyed as his work, and it was the single feature of the newspaper in which it appeared that kept that enterprise alive. When Johnson ended the periodical essays with the 104th number, the newspaper itself stopped publication.

The *Idler* was Johnson's third substantial periodical-essay project in the decade of the 1750s. He was a major contributor to Hawkesworth's **Adventurer** in the middle of the decade, and he produced the highly successful **Rambler** essays from 1750 to 1752. It is thought that he undertook the *Idler* project as a diversion from the editorial work on Shakespeare's plays which began to preoccupy him at the end of the decade, much as he had devised the *Rambler* project to provide himself some relief from his labor on the *Dictionary* earlier. Mr. Idler's essays were not, however, simply a continuation, after some years, of Mr. Rambler's. Less deeply analytical, less learned in reference than most of Johnson's previous work in the essay form, the *Idler* papers are as a whole the most accessible pieces of Johnsonian discourse for "the common reader" – a part of his audience of which Johnson was characteristically solicitous.

For Mr. Idler, Johnson adopted a prose style far less complex and latinate than had been his practice in previous periodical writing. Consider, for instance, the opening sentence of the *Rambler* essays: "The difficulty of the first address on any new occasion, is felt by every man in his transactions with the world, and confessed by the settled and regular forms of salutation which necessity has introduced into all languages." Compare this with the sentence inaugurating the *Idler*: "Those who attempt periodical essays seem to be often stopped in the beginning, by the difficulty of finding a proper title." Almost at random throughout the *Idler*, one finds a Johnson who is charmingly straightforward and matter-of-fact: "But such is the constitution of the world, that much of life must be spent in the same manner by the wise and the ignorant, the exalted and the low ... We are all naked till we are dressed, and

hungry till we are fed; and the general's triumph, and sage's disputation, end, like the humble labors of the smith or plowman, in a dinner or in sleep" (*Idler* no. 51).

Compared with the *Rambler* essays, those in the *Idler* series may seem to cover a less diverse range. This is in part a function of sheer numbers, since there are twice as many papers in the earlier series. Some readers may also feel that there are fewer brilliant moments among the *Idlers* – no critical papers, for instance, which can match Johnson's earlier essays on the pastoral mode or on Miltonic versification. Still, the two-part **character sketch** of the absurd fashionable critic Dick Minim (nos. 60 and 61) is a brilliant critical sally, and in the character mode Minim is joined in the *Idler* by a host of other sharply etched persons: Jack Whirler (no. 19), Will Marvel (nos. 49 and 50), Ned Drugget (nos. 16 and 18), and Dick Shifter (no. 71), to name only four. These characters sketched by Mr. Idler or his correspondents are joined by some equally well-conceived fictitious **letter** writers on subjects no one else could write about so appropriately: Betty Broom (nos. 26 and 29), Sukey Savecharges (no. 54), Robin Spritely (nos. 78 and 83), Sophia Heedfull (no. 98), Tom Toy (no. 39), and a number of other worthies. Mr. Idler certainly did not lack his brilliant moments.

Although a dozen *Idlers* were, according to the standard modern edition, written by Johnson's acquaintances (including Sir Joshua Reynolds and Thomas Warton), Johnson himself wrote all the rest, allowing us to explore the breadth and perceptiveness of his interesting mind. We expect, perhaps, to find him writing about biography (no. 84) or the English language (no. 63). His commentary on practices in the serial press – on advertising (no. 40) or the corruption of news reportage (nos. 7 and 30) – is interesting in view of its original context. Although his handling of certain issues, such as charitable giving (no. 4) or imprisonment for debt (nos. 22 and 38), is rather serious, he was obviously amusing himself quite often: in the essay (no. 5), for instance, in which he suggests the creation of a female army to accompany male regiments which deplete the social world when wars must be fought. Mr. Idler moved easily from contemplating why weather is so often a topic of conversation among the English (no. 11), to discussing the custom of publishing notices of marriage (nos. 12 and 28), then on to essays on the critical reception of new actors and writers (no. 25), on punch and its effects (no. 34), on the wearing of bracelets as fashion statements by various types of people (no. 39). Reading his essay on the loss of loved ones (no. 41) and realizing that his mother had just died brings us unusually close to this eminent man. In general, of course, we are quite content to pretend, with Dr. Johnson, that he is Mr. Idler and to let him talk in this style. Such talk is pleasant, and unlike the Boswellian version of his utterances (brilliant and dramatic as that version is), his own discourse in the *Idler* essays seems to come quite naturally from the streets and shops and public places he inhabited in busy 18th-century London.

JAMES M. KUIST

Editions

The Idler, in the *Universal Chronicle, or Weekly Gazette*, 15 April 1758–5 April 1760; in 2 vols., 1761; in *The Works of Samuel Johnson* (Yale Edition) vol. 2: *"The Idler" and "The Adventurer"*, edited by Walter Jackson Bate, John M. Bullitt, and L. F. Powell, 1963; selections in *Essays from the Rambler, Adventurer, and Idler*, edited by Walter Jackson Bate, 1968

Further Reading

Bate, Walter Jackson, *Samuel Johnson*, New York: Harcourt Brace Jovanovich, 1977; London: Chatto and Windus, 1978

Kenney, W., "Addison, Johnson and the 'Energetic Style'," *Studia Neophilologica* 33 (1961): 103–14

Krutch, Joseph Wood, *Samuel Johnson*, New York: Holt, 1944; London: Cassell, 1948

McCrea, Brian, "Style or Styles: The Problem of Johnson's Prose," *Style* 14 (Summer 1980): 201–15

Wain, John, *Samuel Johnson*, London: Macmillan, 1974; New York: Viking, 1975

Wimsatt, W. K., *The Prose Style of Samuel Johnson*, New Haven, Connecticut: Yale University Press, and London: Oxford University Press, 1941

Woodruff, J. F., "Johnson's 'Idler' and the Anatomy of Idleness," *English Studies in Canada* 6 (1980): 22–38

Irving, Washington

American, 1783–1859

Washington Irving is best known as the creator of "Rip van Winkle," a fact that may say as much about the relative status of stories and essays in the hierarchy of genres as it does about Irving's formative contribution to American literature's preoccupation with fables of identity. Irving was, indeed, one of the creators of the modern short story and, beyond that, of a distinctly American literary imagination; but in his time, both in the New World and the Old, he was widely celebrated not only as an engaging purveyor of fictitious and historical tales (often transplanted and adapted from other national traditions) but also as America's answer to the stylish periodical essayists of 18th-century England.

The book in which Irving's most famous story appears is predominantly a collection of essays, or – in the metaphor of its title, *The Sketch Book of Geoffrey Crayon, Gent.* – sketches. These range from personal report ("The Voyage") and sentimental narrative ("The Broken Heart") to imaginative literary excursion ("A Royal Poet"), fanciful dream vision ("The Art of Bookmaking"), conciliatory polemic ("English Writers on America"), impassioned historical revisionism ("Philip of Pokanoket"), and warmly engaged social portraiture (the

Christmas sketches). When the *Sketch Book* was issued (1819–20), to a transatlantic acclaim never quite matched by his later works, Irving was best known as the writer behind "Diedrich Knickerbocker's" *History of New York* (1809), a masterpiece of Rabelaisian humor some chapters of which stand as self-contained ironic, even **satiric**, essays. At age 19, following essayists such as **Benjamin Franklin**, Joseph Dennie, and Philip Freneau in their use of fictional masks shaping **Addison**'s *Spectator* to an American mold, Irving had penned epistolary essays under the name "Jonathan Oldstyle" (1802–03), a theater-haunting bachelor much exercised about the "degeneracy of the present times." Soon thereafter, under a whole array of whimsical bachelor masks, Irving collaborated on the rambunctiously parodic essay periodical *Salmagundi* (1807–08). With the *Sketch Book* appeared his most durable and prolific persona, "Geoffrey Crayon," the professional writer as traveling sketch artist and perpetual "stranger in the land" ("The Voyage") also associated with several later medleys of short prose. These works contain (among various fictions, framing pieces, and narrative links) the greater part of Irving's essays and include, besides the *Sketch Book*: *Bracebridge Hall* (1822); *The Alhambra* (1832); *The Crayon Miscellany* (1835), incorporating *A Tour on the Prairies* and *Abbotsford and Newstead Abbey*; and *Chronicles of Wolfert's Roost* (1855), which, although it dropped the name, was composed of "Crayon" pieces from the late 1830s and early 1840s.

Like his earlier authorial personae, the fiction of "Geoffrey Crayon, Gent." functions as an announcement that these works are not occasions for the fullness and complexity of Washington Irving's own thoughts and feelings as a person. But the English resonance of the name is more than a pseudonymous screen for an American writer (the first to support himself by his pen) who, all of his life, despite unprecedented popular and critical success, doubted the value of his work and especially his capacity for sustained production (although he wrote, among other work, a five-volume biography of George Washington). The itinerant Crayon is both the controlling metaphor of an often interrupted literary enterprise and a shifting locus of accommodation with the project of authorship as such. As the man of "vagrant imagination" "sketching" whatever his "sauntering gaze" takes to its fancy, he is the New World's early 19th-century version of the continental traveler making drawings and notes for the entertainment of his friends back home. No cultural program, however, directs this sightseer's idiosyncratic eye, only the whimsy impelling him to "bye places," to "cottages . . . and obscure ruins" rather than to the standard tourist attractions. This earliest literary figure of the American abroad – a man of taste and sensibility, a voracious reader of wide sympathies, a worldly voyager limited only by the innocence of one who has not grown up in an old culture – Geoffrey Crayon is the keen-eyed Addisonian looker-on without his moral agenda, the Citizen of the World *sans* philosophic portfolio, the rambler as creature of "roving passion" and "idle humor" ("The Author's Account of Himself"). A self-described loiterer in sundry locales of reverie and romance, he specializes in evoking vanished and vanishing pasts of old Europe – the urban and rural landscapes of England (*Sketch Book* and *Bracebridge*), the fabled haunts of Moorish Spain (*Alhambra*), the erstwhile

Parisian hotel and the paradisiacal Dutch village (*Wolfert's Roost*). Seventeen years later, back on his own continent but still a "stranger," he rides the frontier in *A Tour on the Prairies*, discovering a literary Wild West that becomes the fount of picturesque enterprises, characters, and settings for the emergence of a national literature.

Washington Irving as Geoffrey Crayon is, most characteristically, the highly responsive observer fascinated by the great range of human life, from Granada, London, Paris, and the Scottish border country to the riverside Creole villages of Louisiana and the old Pawnee hunting grounds of Oklahoma. At times vibrantly present in his work, he more habitually recedes to the point of self-erasure, not a locus of introspection but a fluid sensibility – bemused, melancholy, shrewd, sentimental, ironical, romantic – embodied in a supplely adapted style. In the hands of this sojourning artist persona the Irvingesque essay as sketch – by definition preliminary and contingent – flows easily from scene painting and character study to fanciful elaboration; achieves unity not so much by way of thematic shaping as by focus on persons, places, or moods; prefers forays into the evocative domains of narration and description rather than reflection and analysis (except as irony or burlesque); enacts a potpourri of self-conscious techniques for rendering the immediate effects of experience rather than its profundities. Something resembling it may be found in parts of the *Spectator*, and much later, among the short nonfiction works of writers such as **Dickens**, Hawthorne, or **Mark Twain**, or, in modern times, **Joan Didion**.

Generically volatile, by turns eclectic and experimental, as varied and variable as the mundane, culturally inflected textures of life itself, Washington Irving's artfully staged essay of immediate response is to be sharply distinguished from its near contemporary Emersonian counterpart, in which nature becomes the deep of meaning to be plumbed. As far removed from the Montaignean *essai* of ruminative self-portraiture as from the elegant moral and political counsels of **Bacon**, Irving's essay as sketch adumbrates a journalistic practice to come, where the surface of experience is taken to be what is most natural, most worth portraying, and most appealing to a broadly literate audience. What may engage the postmodern reader as generic transgression is, in its historical context, an exploration of short prose forms by a literary pioneer whose work itself outlined their possibilities and thereby contributed materially to a new literature in the making.

LYDIA FAKUNDINY

Biography

Born 3 April 1783 in New York City. Studied law in the offices of Henry Masterton, 1798, Brockholst Livingston, 1801, and Josiah Ogden Hoffman, 1802; admitted to New York bar, 1806, and practiced occasionally. Contributor, including "The Letters of Jonathan Oldstyle, Gentleman," *Morning Chronicle*, 1802–03. Traveled in Europe, 1804–06. Coeditor, *Salmagundi*, 1807–08. Engaged to Martha Hoffman (died, 1809). Partner with his brothers in the family hardware business, New York and Liverpool, England, 1810, and representative of the business in England until it collapsed, 1815–18. Military aide to New York Governor Tompkins in U.S. Army during the War of 1812. Editor, *Analectic* magazine, Philadelphia and New York, 1812–14. Lived in Dresden, 1822–23, London, 1824, and Paris, 1825; worked for the U.S. Embassy,

Madrid, 1826–29, and secretary to the U.S. Embassy, London, 1829–32; returned to New York, then toured the southern and western United States, 1832. Lived at Sunnyside manor house, Tarrytown-on-Hudson, New York, 1836–42. U.S. Ambassador to Spain, 1842–45, then returned to Tarrytown. President, Astor Library (later New York Public Library), 1848–59. Awards: Royal Society of Literature Medal, 1830; honorary degrees from three universities. Corresponding member, Royal Academy of History (Spain), 1829. Died in Tarrytown, 28 November 1859.

Selected Writings

Essays and Related Prose
Salmagundi; or, The Whim-Whams and Opinions of Launcelot Longstaff, Esq. & Others, 2 vols., 1807–08; revised editions, 1814, 1824
A History of New York from the Beginning of the World to the End of the Dutch Dynasty, 2 vols., 1809; revised editions, 1812, 1848
The Sketch Book of Geoffrey Crayon, Gent., 7 vols., 1819–20
Bracebridge Hall; or, The Humorists, a Medley by Geoffrey Crayon, Gent., 2 vols., 1822
Letters of Jonathan Oldstyle, Gent., 1824
The Alhambra, 2 vols., 1832
A Tour on the Prairies, 1835
Abbotsford and Newstead Abbey, 1835
The Crayon Miscellany (includes *A Tour on the Prairies* and *Abbotsford and Newstead Abbey*), 3 vols., 1835
Essays and Sketches, 1837
Chronicles of Wolfert's Roost and Other Papers, 1855

Other writings: tales, histories, and biographies (*Tales of a Traveller by Geoffrey Crayon*, 1824; *The Life and Voyages of Christopher Columbus*, 1828; *A Chronicle of the Conquest of Granada*, 1829; *Voyages and Discoveries of the Companions of Columbus*, 1831; *Astoria, or Anecdotes of an Enterprise Beyond the Rocky Mountains*, 1836; *The Adventures of Captain Bonneville*, 1837; *Oliver Goldsmith: A Biography*, 1840, revised 1849; *Biography and Poetical Remains of the Late Margaret Miller Davidson*, 1841; *Mahomet and His Successors*, 1850; *Life of George Washington*, 1855–59), five volumes of journals and notebooks, four volumes of correspondence, and miscellaneous writings.

Collected works editions: *Works* (Author's Revised Edition), 15 vols., 1848–51; *Complete Works* (Twayne Edition), general editors Henry A. Pochmann, Herbert L. Kleinfeld, and Richard Dilworth Rust, 30 vols., 1969–89.

Bibliographies
Bowden, Edwin T., *Washington Irving: Bibliography* (vol. 30 of the *Complete Works*), Boston: Twayne, 1989
Springer, Haskell, *Washington Irving: A Reference Guide*, Boston: Hall, 1976

Further Reading
Aderman, Ralph M., *Critical Essays on Washington Irving*, Boston: Hall, 1990
Antelyes, Peter, *Tales of Adventurous Enterprises: Washington Irving and the Poetics of the Western Experience*, New York: Columbia University Press, 1990
Hedges, William L., *Washington Irving: An American Study, 1802–1832*, Baltimore: Johns Hopkins University Press, 1965
Irving, Pierre M., *The Life and Letters of Washington Irving*, Detroit: Gale Research, 4 vols., 1967 (original edition, 1862–64)
Kasson, Joy S., *Artistic Voyagers: Europe and the American Imagination in the Works of Irving, Allston, Cole, Cooper, and Hawthorne*, Westport, Connecticut: Greenwood Press, 1982

McFarland, Philip, *Sojourners*, New York: Atheneum, 1979

Roth, Martin, *Comedy and America: The Lost World of Washington Irving*, Port Washington, New York: Kennikat, 1976

Rubin-Dorsky, Jeffrey, *Adrift in the Old World: The Psychological Pilgrimage of Washington Irving*, Chicago: University of Chicago Press, 1988

Seed, D., "The Art of Literary Tourism: An Approach to Washington Irving's *Sketch Book*," *Ariel* 14, no. 2 (1977): 67–82

Tuttleton, James W., editor, *Washington Irving: The Critical Reaction*, New York: AMS Press, 1993

Wagenknecht, Edward, *Washington Irving: Moderation Displayed*, New York: Oxford University Press, 1962

Williams, Stanley T., *The Life of Washington Irving*, New York and London: Oxford University Press, 2 vols., 1935

Ivanov, Viacheslav

Russian, 1866–1949

Viacheslav Ivanov was a major poet, philosopher of culture, critic, and translator, who played an important role in literary history as the leading theoretician of the Russian symbolist movement. Using dense, highly suggestive polyphonic prose, Ivanov in his **critical essays** and **philosophical essays** expanded the metaphysical school of criticism begun by **Vladimir Solov'ev**. Although he always regarded his essays as an elaboration or elucidation of intuitions first communicated in his poetry, his prose works were in fact the primary channel through which his ideas about art and religion made their impact on European as well as Russian culture. The frequently cited description of Ivanov as a true "European Russian" reflects the wide erudition displayed in his essays, resting on a deep scholarly knowledge of ancient Greek and Latin, and on a close familiarity with the languages and cultures of Russia, Germany, Italy, France, and England.

Before emigration Ivanov published numerous essays and **reviews** in leading Russian journals; many of these were collected in the three volumes of his essays which appeared in Russia (1909, 1916, 1917). His essays on **Dostoevskii** dating from the same period were later published in book form in a German translation in 1932 and in English in 1952. From 1926 he was a less frequent but nevertheless substantial contributor to European journals (German, Swiss, French, and Italian), and to Russian émigré journals from 1936; most of these later essays were reprinted in his *Sobranie sochinenii* (Collected works).

In terms of subject matter, his essays can be divided into five main groups, reflecting the gradual development of his interests and preoccupations over the years. Although Ivanov's essays on the religion of Dionysus (1904, 1905) originated in his years of research as a scholar of classical antiquity, the philosophical, religious, and cultural issues they raise go far beyond the boundaries of academic discourse, preparing the ground for his later work by setting out his views on the relationship between pagan antiquity and Christianity, and more generally between mystical experience, religion, and myth.

The early essays on aesthetics, poetry, and drama, first published in symbolist journals and later collected in *Po zvezdam* (1909; By the stars) and *Borozdy i mezhi* (1916; Furrows and boundaries), are concerned with establishing an aesthetic platform for the movement of religious symbolism, either by drawing up a tradition of literary precedents (ranging from Dante and **Goethe** to Tiutchev and Solov'ev), or by elaborating a theory of symbolist art, based on the difference between "great art" and "intimate art," between "realist" and "idealist" symbolism. This distinction depends on whether the artist's vision is regarded as mirroring the macrocosm of the universal order, and therefore as having particular ontological significance, or as a purely private and solipsistic illusion.

Ivanov's critical essays on individual writers contribute to the same endeavor. They usually provide a highly original, stimulating reading of a classical, European, or Russian author in the light of symbolist aesthetics. Russian writers are frequently related to the classical tradition (Dostoevskii's novels are shown to be structured according to the principles of Greek tragedy, Gogol's *The Government Inspector* is linked to the drama of Aristophanes and the choral principle in Greek tragedy), **Pushkin** and Lermontov are discussed in relation to their intuition of spiritual truths, and Petrarch, **Schiller**, Goethe, **Novalis**, and Byron are interpreted through the prism of the symbolist world view.

A more limited number of essays deal with aspects of Russian national identity. An early essay of this type, "O russkoi idee" (1908; On the Russian idea), later became well known in Europe through its translation into German in 1930. Ivanov's interest in this theme reached a peak at the time of World War I and the Russian Revolution, resulting in a number of articles on Russia's historical destiny, relation to Europe, and religious mission in the light of current events. Several of these essays were collected in *Rodnoe i vselenskoe* (1917; Matters native and universal).

After the Revolution Ivanov's essays display an increasing concern with the fate of culture in the modern world and with its relation to the Christian tradition of humanism. He cultivated the genre of the **letter** as a form of essay in *Perepiska iz dvukh uglov* (1921; Correspondence Across a Room) with **Mikhail Gershenzon**, in his letter to **Charles Du Bos** with its detailed exposition of the reasons for his conversion to Catholicism (1930), and in his letter to Alessandro Pellegrini on his view of culture as a form of "docta pietas" (1934).

One of the most salient paradoxes of the symbolist movement was the gulf between its obscure, esoteric content and its professed ideal, the revival of a universal art form which would express the national soul and convey a vital message to the people. Despite these claims, the contemporary audience of Ivanov and his fellow symbolists **Aleksandr Blok** and **Andrei Belyi** remained confined to a small group of like-minded poets, critics, and disciples. Outside this circle, responses to their work mostly emanated from socially oriented critics and were largely negative.

Although Ivanov's output as an essayist was not enormous, it was nevertheless extremely influential. The breadth and depth of his essays, as well as his role as the major theoretician of religious symbolism, had a great impact on the beliefs and poetics of the next generation of post-symbolist poets, particularly on the Acmeists and Futurists. Writers (such as **Osip Mandel'shtam**) who did not accept all the philosophical and religious premises of Ivanov's world view nevertheless often retained in their prose works some of its stylistic characteristics (a multi-strand argument developed through a highly allusive use of image, metaphor, and myth, woven together into a polyphonic chorus), or returned to engage in debate with it in their later lyrics (Nikolai Gumilev, Anna Akhmatova, **Marina Tsvetaeva**).

While poets were flexible in their ability to absorb elements of Ivanov's system selectively, philosophers of a religious orientation (such as Nikolai Berdiaev and **Lev Shestov**) became increasingly impatient with his all-encompassing syncretism and attempted combination of religious and cultural values. According to one critic, Ivanov tried to reconcile too many different roles; to poets he appeared a prophet, to philosophers an artist, and to orthodox believers, a priest without God and without a church.

Ivanov's reputation as an essayist has undergone many fluctuations in the course of the 20th century. In Europe, his fame has rested almost exclusively on his essays, which have attracted the attention of prominent intellectuals such as Martin Buber, **Ernst Robert Curtius**, Gabriel Marcel, Du Bos, and Pellegrini. In Soviet Russia, he was marginalized for many decades, in part because of political circumstances, but also because his critics could not or would not recognize his view of culture as memory as the foundation of his distinctive voice. His legacy, transmitted through thinkers as varied as Mikhail Bakhtin, Lev Loseff, and Sergei Averintsev, has attracted a marked resurgence of critical interest since the mid-1980s.

PAMELA DAVIDSON

Biography

Born 16 February 1866 in Moscow. Studied at the First Moscow Gymnasium, graduated 1884; history and classical philology, Moscow University, 1884–86; University of Berlin, 1886–91. Married Dar'ia Mikhailovna Dmitrievskaia, 1886 (divorced, 1896): one daughter. Lived in Europe, including Berlin, Paris, Rome, and Geneva, from 1886. Married Lidiia Dmitrievna Zinov'eva (pseudonym: Zinov'eva-Annibal), 1899 (died, 1907): two daughters and three stepchildren. Returned to Russia, 1905: lived in St. Petersburg, hosting the literary salon at Bashnia (Tower); founder, Ory publishing house, and the Poetic Academy. Lived in Switzerland, France, and Italy, 1912–13, and Moscow, 1913–20. Married his stepdaughter Vera Shvarsalon (died, 1920), 1913: one son. Professor of classical philology, University of Baku, 1920–24. Emigrated to Italy, 1924, converting to Catholicism, 1926; lived in Rome, 1924–26, 1934–49, and in Pavia, 1926–34, lecturing and teaching in both cities. Died in Rome, 16 July 1949.

Selected Writings

Essays and Related Prose
Po zvezdam: Stat'i i aforizmy, 1909
Borozdy i mezhi: Opyty esteticheskie i kriticheskie, 1916
Rodnoe i vselenskoe: Stat'i (1914–1916), 1917
Perepiska iz dvukh uglov, with Mikhail Gershenzon, 1921; as "A Corner-to-Corner Correspondence," translated by Gertrude Vakar, in *Russian Intellectual History: An Anthology*, edited by Marc Raeff, 1966: 372–401; as *Correspondence Across a Room*, translated by Lisa Sergio, 1984
Dostojewskij: Tragödie – Mythos – Mystik, 1932; as *Freedom and the Tragic Life: A Study in Dostoevsky*, edited by S. Konovalov, translated by Norman Cameron, 1952
Esse, stat'i, perevody (Essays, articles, translations), 1985

Predchuvstviia i predvestiia: Sbornik (Premonitions and portents: a collection), edited by S. V. Stakhorskii, 1991
Lik i lichiny Rossii: Estetika i literaturnaia teoriia (The face and masks of Russia: aesthetics and literary theory), edited by S. Averintsev, 1995

Other writings: eight books of poetry (*Kormchie zvezdy: Kniga liriki*, 1903; *Prozrachnost': Vtoraia kniga liriki*, 1904; *Eros*, 1907; *Cor Ardens*, 2 vols., 1911–12; *Nezhnaia taina: Lepta*, 1912; *Mladenchestvo*, 1918; *Chelovek*, 1939; *Svet vechernii*, 1962), two plays ("Tantal," 1905; *Prometei: Tragediia*, 1919), and two books on classical antiquity (*De societatibus vectigalium publicorum populi romani*, 1910; *Dionis i pradionisiistvo*, 1923). Also translated Aeschylus, Alcaeus, Sappho, Bacchylides, Pindar, Dante, Petrarch, Michelangelo Buonarroti, **Leopardi**, Byron, **Baudelaire**, and Novalis.

Collected works edition: *Sobranie sochinenii*, edited by D. V. Ivanov and O. Deschartes, 4 vols., 1971–87 (in progress; 6 vols. projected).

Bibliography
Davidson, Pamela, *Viacheslav Ivanov: A Reference Guide*, New York: Simon and Schuster Macmillan–Hall, 1996

Further Reading
Belyi, Andrei, *Sirin uchenogo varvarstva: Po povodu knigi V. Ivanova "Rodnoe i vselenskoe"*, Berlin: Skify, 1922
Il Convegno issue on Ivanov, 8–12 (1933–34)
Davidson, Pamela, *The Poetic Imagination of Vyacheslav Ivanov: A Russian Symbolist's Perception of Dante*, Cambridge: Cambridge University Press, 1989
Egorov, B. F., "Viach. Ivanov i russkie slavianofily," *Russkii tekst* 1 (1993): 43–57
Jackson, Robert Louis, and Lowry Nelson, Jr., editors, *Vyacheslav Ivanov: Poet, Critic, and Philosopher*, New Haven, Connecticut: Yale Center for International and Area Studies, 1986
Un maître de sagesse au XXe siècle: Vjačeslav Ivanov et son temps, Cahiers du Monde Russe 35, nos. 1–2 (1994)
Malcovati, Fausto, *Vjačeslav Ivanov: Estetica i filosofia*, Florence: La Nuova Italia, 1983
Malcovati, Fausto, editor, *Cultura e memoria: Atti del terzo Simposio Internazionale dedicato a Vjačeslav Ivanov*, Florence: La Nuova Italia, 2 vols., 1988
Potthoff, Wilfried, editor, *Vjačeslav Ivanov: Russischer Dichter – Europäischer Kulturphilosoph*, Heidelberg: Winter, 1993
Pyman, Avril, *A History of Russian Symbolism*, Cambridge and New York: Cambridge University Press, 1994
Shestov, Lev, "Viacheslav Velikolepnyi: K kharakteristike russkogo upadochnichestva," *Russkaia mysl'* 10 (1916): 80–110
Stammler, Heinrich A., "Belyj's Conflict with Vjačeslav Ivanov over War and Revolution," *Slavic and East European Journal* 18, no. 3 (1974): 259–70
Tschöpl, Carin, *Vjačeslav Ivanov: Dichtung und Dichtungstheorie*, Munich: Sagner, 1968
Venclova, Tomas, "Viacheslav Ivanov and the Crisis of Russian Symbolism," in *Issues in Russian Literature Before 1917*, edited by J. Douglas Clayton, Columbus, Ohio: Slavica, 1989
Viacheslav Ivanov: Materialy i publikatsii, edited by N. V. Kotrelev, *Novoe literaturnoe obozrenie* 10 (1994)
Wachtel, Michael, *Russian Symbolism and Literary Tradition: Goethe, Novalis, and the Poetics of Vyacheslav Ivanov*, Madison: University of Wisconsin Press, 1995
Wachtel, Michael, editor, *Dichtung und Briefwechsel aus dem deutschsprachigen Nachlass*, Mainz: Liber Verlag Mainz, 1995
West, James, *Russian Symbolism: A Study of Vyacheslav Ivanov and the Russian Symbolist Aesthetic*, London: Methuen, 1970

J

James, Henry

American/British, 1843–1916

For several decades Henry James' essays have been collected and studied by scholarly connoisseurs, and are now attracting the wider audience for which they were intended. The Library of America Editions of his literary criticism (1984) and his travel writings (1993) have rescued many pieces from the obscurity of earlier anthologies and periodicals. Further, the recent attention paid to his works of cultural criticism – notably *The American Scene* (1907) and *Italian Hours* (1909) – has enhanced his status as an observer of national types and the play of differences. Cognizant of the power of richly textured language, James was equally aware of the limits of his own mastery. Even his most polemical efforts (e.g. "The Question of Our Speech," 1905) are characterized by their self-conscious use of the first person. And his **prefaces** to his fiction, once read as a formalist manifesto, are best appreciated as **personal essays** tinged with uncertainty as well as fond reminiscence.

Ironically, the young critic was far more dogmatic than the seasoned writer known to his disciples as "cher maître." British and American novels, he complained in his early reviews, were dull and formless; French fiction was "intolerably unclean" (review of Goncourt's *La Fille Elisa*, 1877); the mass public consisted of "jolly barbarians of taste who read . . . only for what they call the 'story'" ("Marian Rooke," 1865). His occasional **reviews** of drama and art exhibitions likewise reflect the brashness of an aspiring elitist whose model was **Matthew Arnold**, and whose sense of cultural mission was fostered by the journals to which he contributed: the *Atlantic Monthly*, the *Galaxy*, the *Nation*, and the *North American Review*.

However, James' critical judgments became more flexible, especially following his expatriation from the United States in 1875. Writing to Thomas S. Perry, he had expressed his hope for "a vast intellectual fusion and synthesis of the various National tendencies of the world" (20 September 1867); yet, as he admitted in "Paris Revisited" (1878), an "uncomfortable consequence" of being a cosmopolitan was "seeing many lands and feeling at home in none." Reviewers of his *French Poets and Novelists* (1878) were struck by the inconclusiveness of such pieces as the essay on Balzac, criticized for being "morally and intellectually so superficial" but lauded for his "incomparable power."

Eventually James focused on the subjects he found personally compelling. In a letter he told his British publisher, Frederick Macmillan, that the title of *Partial Portraits* (1888) – his most important collection of essays on other writers – contains a pun, suggesting "both that the picture is not down to the feet, as it were, and that the appreciation is favourable" (21 March 1888). Balancing sympathy with judgment, he paid tribute to his elders (**Emerson, George Eliot, Turgenev**) while also considering younger contemporaries (Alphonse Daudet, Guy de Maupassant) whose "cases" he found instructive. Appropriately, the volume concludes with "The Art of Fiction" (1884), which is less a defense of realism than a paean to the artist's mind: "Experience is never limited, and it is never complete; it is an immense sensibility, a kind of huge spider-web of the finest silken threads suspended in the chamber of consciousness, and catching every air-borne particle in its tissue." As Mark Spilka (1973) has noted, James was aware of his growing distance from his audience, but he opened the way for himself and other writers to create a new audience of "uncommon readers." And as William Veeder (1985) has observed, James became more generous – especially to such "unclean" authors as Zola – when he replaced "the rigidity of *a priori* propositions with the suppleness of metaphor."

This style is the hallmark of James' prefaces to the New York edition of his novels and tales (1907–09). Whereas detractors were bemused by his late manner, admirers sought to abstract theories from his richly metaphorical prose. A disciple, Percy Lubbock, expounded the principle of "showing, not telling" in *The Craft of Fiction* (1921); and R. P. Blackmur, who collected the prefaces in *The Art of the Novel* (1934), presented them as "an essay in general criticism." But contemporary readers have noticed James' disclaimers of formalist mastery: his confessions to lapses of memory as he tells "the story of [his] story," his statement that the novel appears "more true to its character as it strains or tends to burst, with a latent extravagance, its mould," and his admission that there were "more of the shining silver fish afloat in the deep sea of [his] endeavour than the net of widest casting could pretend to gather in." Here as in his later travel writings, the "restless analyst" creates a first-person narrative which undermines definitive interpretation.

"Is There a Life After Death?" (1910), James' most **philosophical essay**, affirms his desire for ongoing process rather than closure. Despite the apparent finality of death, he refuses to regard the question as settled because – "speaking for myself only and keeping to the facts of my experience – it is above all as an artist that I appreciate this beautiful and enjoyable independence of thought" which "refers me to realizations I am condemned as yet but to dream of . . . I reach beyond the laboratory-brain." For James and his many followers, uncertainty itself becomes the basis of a humanistic tradition. And his advice to aspiring authors – "Oh, do something from your point of view" ("Letter to the Deerfield Summer School," 1889) – echoes through today's classrooms and writing workshops.

SARAH B. DAUGHERTY

Biography

Born 15 April 1843 in New York City. Brother of the philosopher **William James**. Studied at the Richard Pulling Jenks School, New York; traveled in Europe with his family during youth, studying with tutors in Geneva, London, Paris, Boulogne, and Bonn, 1855–60; lived with family in Newport, Rhode Island, 1860–62. Studied at Harvard Law School, Cambridge, Massachusetts, 1862–63. Contributor to the *Nation* and the *Atlantic Monthly*, 1866–69 (art critic, 1871–72). Traveled in Europe, 1869–70, then returned to Cambridge. Lived in Europe, 1872–74, and Cambridge, 1875. Moved to Paris, 1875; contributor to New York *Tribune*, Paris, 1875–76; lived in England for the rest of his life, first in London, from 1876, then in Rye, Sussex, from 1896; traveled in the United States, 1904–05. Became a British citizen, 1915. Awards: honorary degrees from Harvard and Oxford Universities; Order of Merit, 1916. Died in Rye, 28 February 1916.

Selected Writings

Essays and Related Prose

Transatlantic Sketches, 1875; revised edition, as *Foreign Parts*, 1883
French Poets and Novelists, 1878; revised edition, 1883; edited by Leon Edel, 1964
Portraits of Places, 1883
A Little Tour in France, 1884; revised edition, 1900
Partial Portraits, 1888
Essays in London and Elsewhere, 1893
English Hours, 1905; edited by Alma Louise Lowe, 1960
The American Scene, 1907; edited by Leon Edel, 1968, and John F. Sears, 1994
Views and Reviews, 1908
Italian Hours, 1909; edited by John Auchard, 1992
Notes on Novelists with Some Other Notes, 1914
Within the Rim and Other Essays 1914–1915, 1919
The Art of the Novel: Critical Prefaces, edited by R. P. Blackmur, 1934
The Scenic Art: Notes on Acting and the Drama, 1872–1901, edited by Allan Wade, 1948
The Art of Fiction and Other Essays, edited by Morris Roberts, 1948
The Painter's Eye: Notes and Essays on the Pictorial Arts, edited by John L. Sweeney, 1956
The American Essays, edited by Leon Edel, 1956
The Future of the Novel: Essays on the Art of the Novel, edited by Leon Edel, 1956; as *The House of Fiction: Essays on the Novel*, 1957
Parisian Sketches: Letters to the New York Tribune, edited by Leon Edel and Ilse Dusoir Lind, 1957
Literary Reviews and Essays on American, English, and French Literature, edited by Albert Mordell, 1957
The Art of Travel: Scenes and Journeys in America, England, France and Italy, edited by Morton Dauwen Zabel, 1958
French Writers and American Women: Essays, edited by Peter Buitenhuis, 1960
Selected Literary Criticism, edited by Morris Schapira, 1963

Literary Criticism (Library of America Edition), edited by Leon Edel and Mark Wilson, 2 vols., 1984
The Art of Criticism: Henry James on the Theory and Practice of Fiction, edited by William Veeder and Susan M. Griffin, 1986
The Critical Muse: Selected Literary Criticism, edited by Roger Gard, 1987
Collected Travel Writing (Library of America Edition), 2 vols., 1993
Traveling in Italy with Henry James, edited by Fred Kaplan, 1994

Other writings: many novels (including *The Europeans*, 1878; *Washington Square*, 1881; *The Portrait of a Lady*, 1881; *The Bostonians*, 1886; *What Maisie Knew*, 1897; *The Sacred Fount*, 1901; *The Wings of the Dove*, 1902; *The Ambassadors*, 1903; *The Golden Bowl*, 1904), novellas (including *Daisy Miller*, 1878; *The Aspern Papers*, 1888; *The Spoils of Poynton*, 1897; *The Turn of the Screw*, 1898), short stories, several plays, correspondence, and works on travel, literature, and art.

Collected works edition: *The Novels and Tales* (New York Edition; includes the prefaces), 24 vols., 1907–09.

Bibliographies

Bradbury, Nicola, *An Annotated Critical Bibliography of Henry James*, Brighton: Harvester, 1987
Budd, John, *Henry James: A Bibliography of Criticism, 1975–1981*, Westport, Connecticut: Greenwood Press, 1983
Edel, Leon, Dan H. Laurence, and James Rambeau, *A Bibliography of Henry James*, Oxford: Clarendon Press, 1982
McColgan, Kristin Pruitt, *Henry James, 1917–1959: A Reference Guide*, Boston: Hall, and London: Prior, 1979
Ricks, Beatrice, *Henry James: A Bibliography of Secondary Works*, Metuchen, New Jersey: Scarecrow Press, 1975
Scura, Dorothy McInnis, *Henry James, 1960–1974: A Reference Guide*, Boston: Hall, and London: Prior, 1979
Taylor, Linda J., *Henry James, 1866–1916: A Reference Guide*, Boston: Hall, 1982

Further Reading

Auchard, John, Introduction to *Italian Hours* by James, edited by Auchard, University Park: Pennsylvania State University Press, 1992; London: Penguin, 1995
Blackmur, R. P., Introduction to *The Art of the Novel: Critical Prefaces* by James, New York: Scribner, 1934
Daugherty, Sarah B., *The Literary Criticism of Henry James*, Athens: Ohio University Press, 1981
Fogel, Daniel Mark, editor, *A Companion to Henry James Studies*, Westport, Connecticut: Greenwood Press, 1993
Gervais, David, "Deciphering America: The American Scene," *Cambridge Quarterly* 18 (1989): 349–62
Good, Graham, "Henry James: Patterns of Art and Life," in his *The Observing Self: Rediscovering the Essay*, London and New York: Routledge, 1988: 90–111
Griffin, Susan M., *The Historical Eye: The Texture of the Visual in Late James*, Boston: Northeastern University Press, 1991
Jones, Vivien, *James the Critic*, London: Macmillan, 1984; New York: St. Martin's Press, 1985
Leitch, Thomas M., "The Editor as Hero: Henry James and the New York Edition," *Henry James Review* 3 (1981–82): 24–32
Lubbock, Percy, *The Craft of Fiction*, London: Cape, and New York: Scribner, 1921
MacDonald, Bonney, *Henry James' Italian Hours: Revelatory and Resistant Impressions*, Ann Arbor, Michigan: UMI Research Press, 1990
Maini, Darshan Singh, "Henry James: The Writer as Critic," *Henry James Review* 8 (Spring 1987): 189–99
Miller, James E., Jr., editor, *Theory of Fiction: Henry James*, Lincoln: University of Nebraska Press, 1972

Roberts, Morris, *Henry James's Criticism*, Cambridge, Massachusetts: Harvard University Press, 1929

Rowe, John Carlos, *The Theoretical Dimensions of Henry James*, Madison: University of Wisconsin Press, 1984; London: Methuen, 1985

Schwarz, Daniel R., *The Humanistic Heritage: Critical Theories of the English Novel from James to Hillis Miller*, Philadelphia: University of Pennsylvania Press, and London: Macmillan, 1986

Spilka, Mark, "Henry James and Walter Besant: 'The Art of Fiction' Controversy," *Novel* 6 (Winter 1973): 100–19

Veeder, William, "Image as Argument: Henry James and the Style of Criticism," *Henry James Review* 6 (Spring 1985): 172–81

Wellek, René, "Henry James's Literary Theory and Criticism," *American Literature* 30 (November 1958): 293–321

James, William

American, 1842–1910

William James' most significant contributions to the literature of the essay were examples of "public philosophy" in the tradition of **Emerson**: informal exercises bringing academic insights to bear on public problems. While his major book-length studies – *The Principles of Psychology* (1890), *The Varieties of Religious Experience* (1902), and *Pragmatism* (1907) – outlined his understanding of the fundamentals of empirical psychology, the phenomenology of religion, and the philosophical method of "pragmatism," the essays (with the notable exception of those collected in *The Meaning of Truth* [1907] and the posthumously published *Essays in Radical Empiricism* [1912]) were more concerned with popularizing his ideas than with perfecting them. James himself wondered late in his life whether the energy he had devoted to public education had been at the expense of a fully developed system of thought, complaining that it had been a "tragedy" that he, having had a "bridge" begun, had "stopped in the middle of an arch" (*Letters of William James*). His sense of his legacy was remarkably prescient: while his thought has had a lasting influence on American literary culture and public discourse, it has proven vulnerable to attack by professional psychologists and analytic philosophers.

The most influential of James' popular essays translate his central psychological and philosophical tenets into practical advice for day-to-day living. Inspirational pieces like "The Will to Believe" (1896), "Is Life Worth Living?" (1895), "The Gospel of Relaxation" (1899), and "On a Certain Blindness in Human Beings" (1899) offer advice for coping with personal problems like depression and enervation, advice consistently mindful of a general public where religious faith and temperamental optimism have gone out of fashion. "The Will to Believe" is a précis of the central argument of *The Varieties of Religious Experience*: "a defense of our right to adopt a believing attitude in religious matters, in spite of the fact that our merely logical intellect may not have been coerced." Its Pascalian argument turns on the example of a man lost in a snowstorm, his very survival depending on a leap of faith, a dilemma that (along with James' solution) echoes throughout modern literature (most famously in Robert Frost's poem "The Road Not Taken"). The essay "Is Life Worth Living?" presents a series of arguments against suicide, judiciously organized to appeal first to the religious believer and then to the

atheist. Its evenhandedness reflects a policy central to Jamesian pragmatism: a commitment to respecting "tender-minded" and "tough-minded" temperaments equally.

James offers more practical advice for overcoming depression in "The Gospel of Relaxation," drawing from a theory of emotion developed with the Danish thinker Carl G. Lange and fully explicated in *The Principles of Psychology*. Since emotions have a physiological basis, it argues, the cure for depression rests in cultivating the physical signs of good cheer: the "sovereign voluntary path to cheerfulness" is "to sit up cheerfully, to look round cheerfully, and to act as if cheerfulness were already there." In its persuasive arguments about the spiritual benefits of relaxation and "muscular vigor" – arguments repeated by motivational figures from John Dewey and Malcolm X to Norman Vincent Peale – the essay is a milestone in the history of self-help literature.

The essay "On a Certain Blindness in Human Beings," finally, is vitally important for offsetting an impression the other essays give: that James encourages the fulfillment of *self*-interest, regardless of its consequences for others. In language stripped of specific political reference, but designed to challenge the imperialistic policies of the McKinley administration (1897–1901), it emphasizes the importance of checking optimistic hypotheses and self-fulfilling prophecies through consultation with the other people whose lives they will affect. Whatever our own hopes for self-improvement, it counsels, we must "tolerate, respect, and indulge those whom we see harmless, interested and happy in their own ways, however unintelligible these may be to us."

James' style as an essayist reflects both his commitment to popular education and the essentials of the "pragmatic" approach to truth-making. In "Remarks on the Occasion of the Centenary of William James" (1942), James' son, Henry James III, recalled his father's contempt for "style that makes an affectation of learning and therewith desiccates and often obscures the thought": a contempt whose positive side was an educator's love of blunt statements, homely examples, and familiar forms of address. Other aspects of James' style directly reflect *Pragmatism*'s correlation of "truths" with "hypotheses," provisional theories whose capacity to "satisfy" is subject to an ongoing empirical test. One is his frequent use of qualifying words and phrases: "if," "as if," "suppose." Another is his habit of recounting testimonies and anecdotes: the best data available, from a pragmatist's point of view, for verifying, or testing the efficacy of, propositions. Still another is his frequent use of prolepsis, or the anticipation of counterarguments: not for its usual rhetorical purpose of defeating such arguments, but for the pragmatist's purpose of incorporating them into his developing "truth." Finally, his open-minded and practically oriented philosophy is reflected in his tendency to rely upon analogy and metaphor in place of more logical forms of argumentation. As James summarizes pragmatism's sense of things in "The Will to Believe," its only criteria for admitting a proposition into consideration are that it not be "impossible," and that it be possible to "bring analogies to bear in its behalf."

Despite the survival of James' incitements to positive thinking in American popular culture, recent critical work has raised questions about the applicability of his advice across race, class, and gender lines. His suggestions, in particular, that happiness and success can be attained through the cultivation of "relaxation" and "muscular vigor," have inspired the claim that his solutions were better suited to resolving the *tedium vitae* of the privileged young men of Harvard than the tougher problems faced by women, minorities, or the poor. Jarring claims like the one that "sufferings and hardships do not, as a rule, abate the love of life" ("Is Life Worth Living?"), or that "the strength of the British Empire lies in the strength of character of the individual Englishman, taken all alone by himself" ("The Gospel of Relaxation"), suggest that James was not immune to the kind of "blindness" he warned against. But if his faith in the transformative power of optimism underestimated certain social problems, his openmindedness toward religious faith and his conception of truth-making as a consultative process have been formative examples for some social activists. In contemporary America, Cornel West, the self-described Christian-Marxist champion of African American rights, and "public philosopher" in his own right, has cited James' work both as inspiration and as example.

PATRICIA RAE

See also Philosophical Essay

Biography

Born 11 January 1842 in New York City. Brother of the writer **Henry James**. Traveled with his family in Europe, studying there, 1857–60; studied art with William Morris Hunt, Newport, Rhode Island, 1860–61; Lawrence Scientific School, Harvard University, Cambridge, Massachusetts, 1861–63, and Harvard Medical School, M.D., 1869. Accompanied the Thayer Expedition to Brazil, 1865–66; traveled and studied in Germany, 1867–68. Taught physiology, philosophy, and psychology at Harvard University, 1872–1907, then emeritus. Married Alice Howe Gibbens, 1878: four sons and one daughter. Gifford Lecturer, University of Edinburgh, 1899–1901, lecturer, Lowell Institute, Boston, 1906, and Hibbert Lecturer, Manchester College, Oxford, 1908. Awards: honorary degrees from seven universities. Died in Chocorua, New Hampshire, 26 August 1910.

Selected Writings

Essays and Related Prose

The Will to Believe, and Other Essays in Popular Philosophy, 1897
Talks to Teachers on Psychology, and to Students on Some of Life's Ideals, 1899
The Varieties of Religious Experience (Gifford lectures), 1902
Pragmatism, a New Name for Some Old Ways of Thinking: Popular Lectures on Philosophy, 1907
The Meaning of Truth: A Sequel to "Pragmatism", 1907
A Pluralistic Universe (Hibbert lectures), 1909
Memories and Studies, 1911
Essays in Radical Empiricism, edited by Ralph Barton Perry, 1912
Selected Papers on Philosophy, edited by C. M. Bakewell, 1917
Collected Essays and Reviews, edited by Ralph Barton Perry, 1920
Essays on Faith and Morals, edited by Ralph Barton Perry, 1943
Essays in Pragmatism, edited by Alburey Castell, 1948
The Moral Equivalent of War, and Other Essays, and Selections from Some Problems of Philosophy, edited by John K. Roth, 1971
The Essential Writings, edited by Bruce W. Wilshire, 1971
A William James Reader, edited by Gay Wilson Allen, 1972
Selected Writings, edited by G. H. Bird, 1995

Other writings: philosophical works and much correspondence.

Collected works edition: *Works* (Harvard Edition), edited by Frederick H. Burkhardt, Fredson Bowers, and Ignas K. Skrupskelis, 1975– (in progress).

Bibliography
Skrupskelis, Ignas K., *William James: A Reference Guide*, Boston: Hall, 1977

Further Reading
Cotkin, George, *William James, Public Philosopher*, Baltimore: Johns Hopkins University Press, 1990
Heddendorf, David, "Filling Out the What: William James, Josiah Royce and Metaphor," *American Transcendental Quarterly* 2 (1988): 125–38
Lentricchia, Frank, *Ariel and the Police: Michel Foucault, William James, Wallace Stevens*, Madison: University of Wisconsin Press, 1988
Myers, Gerald E., *William James: His Life and Thought*, New Haven, Connecticut: Yale University Press, 1986
Perry, Ralph Barton, *The Thought and Character of William James*, Boston: Little Brown, 2 vols., 1935
Posnock, Ross, *The Trial of Curiosity: Henry James, William James, and the Challenge of Modernity*, New York and Oxford: Oxford University Press, 1991
Seigfried, Charlene Haddock, *William James' Radical Reconstruction of Philosophy*, Albany: State University of New York Press, 1990
Wernham, James C. S., *James' Will-to-Believe Doctrine: A Heretical View*, Kingston, Ontario: McGill-Queen's University Press, 1987
West, Cornel, *The American Evasion of Philosophy: A Genealogy of Pragmatism*, Madison: University of Wisconsin Press, 1989

Japanese Essay

The type of prose held by many to be most characteristically Japanese is called (among other things) *zuihitsu* or *essei*. That the first term is a transliteration of a Chinese designation and the second derives from the West is a telling paradox, for Japan owes the existence of its literary tradition to China, and many of the assumptions that govern its modern genre framework to Europe. Accounts of this mode – or modes, necessarily – often dwell on whether and how the Japanese achievement may be successful or unique. It is a debate that constitutes much of the writing itself, second only to the question of what *zuihitsu*, which literally means "following the brush," is as a genre.

Just as they imported Chinese graphs to facilitate writing, so the Japanese accepted China's distinctions between formal genres, such as poetry, history, or argument, and informal modes, including fiction and personal reflections. Literate Japanese men were expected to write in Chinese, and the work of one of them, Yoshishige no Yasutane's (c. 931–1002) *Chiteiki* (982; Record of the pond pavilion), a record of his pavilion and reclusive life, is recognized as an early landscape essay. It is more common, however, to list as the first essay in Japan *Makura no sōshi* (*The Pillow Book*) of **Sei Shōnagon** (c. 965–?), one of the brilliant literary women who wrote narrative fiction and memoirs of a psychological subtlety not rivaled in Europe until the development of the novel. However, *The Pillow Book*'s heyday was not the height of the essay: that came with the maturation of hybrid Sino-Japanese language in medieval times. Hybridization is seen in syntactic parallelism and translation-equivalent phrases, as well as the high proportion of Chinese compound words. This blend of Chinese terseness with Japanese agglutination animates the famous opening meditation on the constantly metamorphosing nature of all things in **Kamo no Chōmei's** (1155?–1216) *Hōjōki* (c. 1212; *An Account of My Hut*). Today literary historians do not always treat *An Account of My Hut* as a *zuihitsu*, preferring his *Shiki monogatari* (Tales of the four seasons); *An Account of My Hut* is stylistically quite different from both *The Pillow Book* and *Tsurezuregusa* (wr. c. 1319 to as late as 1350; *Essays in Idleness*) by **Kenkō** (c. 1283–c. 1352), the third member of what became established at the end of the last century as a triumvirate. *Essays in Idleness* uses the hybrid style, and also harks back to *The Pillow Book*, often imitating its vernacular, whose purity was identified with the feminine. Although important essays centered on single themes exist, the definition canonized from the 18th century de-emphasized them in favor of the fragmentary, seemingly random work that claims to have no purpose.

The first piece actually to use the word *zuihitsu* in its title, the *Tōsai zuihitsu* (Tōsai's miscellany) of Ichijō Kaneyoshi (also known as Kanera) (1402–81), was not of this random type, being instead a collection of topically arranged anecdotes. Such compendia are usual for the Chinese *suibi*, which gave the name to the Japanese genre (although in China the designation *biji* or "records of the brush" is more common). In Korea, where they were also written in classical Chinese, the term *chapki* (miscellaneous record) is preferred to indicate literary miscellanies that may combine auotobiographical narration with other jottings. Throughout East Asia, "idleness" was held to be the key characteristic from which these writings emerged.

In a more Japanese vein is an admonitory work by Kanera, *Sayo no nezame* (1477; Awake in the night), which explains political leadership and literary studies to a woman who was virtually a *shōgun* (generalissimo) during the civil wars that tore apart the capital. It is an opinionated but elliptical work of criticism; only its audience is atypical. Other medieval writers whose works are treasured include Shinkei (1406–75), a linked verse poet. Notes on his flight from the wars and contemplation of aesthetics are interwoven in *Hitorigoto* (1468; Solitary ramblings) and *Oinokurigoto* (1471–75; Old man's prattle). Both internal commentary and the titles of Japanese essays are frequently self-denigrating and inward-looking, claiming to be mere distractions or comforts to the author, yet the reader is also consoled by the unexpected intimacy.

Still other works, particularly much Buddhist writing, broadly qualify as representative Japanese essays. *Shōbōgenzō zuimonki* (1235–38; *Record of Things Heard from the Treasury of the Eye of the True Teaching*), the collected teachings of Zen master Dōgen (1200–53), *Ichigon hōdan* (*Plain Words on the Pure Land Way*), aphoristic statements by monks and recluses, and even Zeami's (1363?–1443?) celebrated **treatises** on the Nō theater share similarities in organization and thought with more strictly lyric endeavors. Oral teaching was a central practice of the literati, and when written, records of talks on poetry and similar subjects took on the form of discursive essays.

Medieval essays can be quite short. Both brevity and the tendency toward a fragmented, incomplete treatment of topics have been linked to the literate elite's difficulty in absorbing new and and confusing trends as their world dissolved. The later emergence of the 17-syllable haiku poem reminds us that brevity is considered a virtue in Japan; indeed, many essays are divided into passages of haiku-like length. Skepticism toward the verbal permeates some religious thinking, as in the Zen sects. Nonetheless, extensive volumes of criticism, transcripted interviews, for example the Zen priest Musō Soseki's (1275–1351) *Muchū mondōshū* (1344; Dialogues in dream) and rambling discourses satisfy an equally fierce desire for verbosity.

The passion for words and knowledge yielded thousands of essays in the early modern period, many of them still unpublished. In the 1600s, *Essays in Idleness* and *The Pillow Book* enjoyed revivals, accustoming Japanese readers to desultory vignettes – often with a touch of didacticism – as a mode of essay, typified by Sano Shōeki's (1610–91) *Nigiwaigusa* (1682; Musings on prosperity), a dilettante merchant's musings. The youthful Yanagisawa Kien (1704–58) lovingly recalled life in the pleasure district of Yoshiwara in his celebrated *Hitorine* (1725; Sleeping alone). Lyrical essays may also be found in the genre known as *haibun*, light prose sketches combined with haiku poetry, such as Yokoi Yayū's (1702–83) *Uzuragoromo* (1727–79; Patchwork cloak). Matsuo Bashō's (1644–94) *Genjūan no ki* (1690; *Prose Poem on the Unreal Dwelling*), a meditation along the lines of *An Account of My Hut*, demonstrates the profundity attainable in a brief, allusive space.

At the same time, interest in Chinese models reached a new pitch. Lengthy productions like Muro Kyūsō's (1658–1734) *Sundai zatsuwa* (1732; Miscellaneous talks by Sundai, selections translated as *A Japanese Philosopher, and Other Papers upon the Chinese Philosophy in Japan*), arranged under the Five Confucian Virtues, and Amano Sadakage's (1663–1733) *Shiojiri* (1697–1733; Salt mounds) remain fascinating troves. Partly from interest in the past, partly from thirst for novelty – strange tales were common – the intelligentsia was responsible for circulating such works. Ogyū Sorai's (1666–1728) *Narubeshi* (1736; It should be), consisting of over 400 segments on language use, spurred a flurry of rebuttals. With the emergence of *kokugaku*, or national learning scholars, who unearthed texts of the Japanese past as an antidote to what they held were the crippling effects of China, Japanese *zuihitsu* were compared favorably to the Chinese. Motoori Norinaga's (1730–1801) *Tamakatsuma* (1793–1812; The beautiful basket) contains 1005 segments reflecting his research and controversial ideas. His disciple Ishihara Masaakira (1760–1821) – whose *Nennen zuihitsu* (1801–05; Jottings year by year) defines the genre as a gathering of all that is seen and heard, of varying quality but honest intent, and defends Motoori's use of it – was self-conscious about the native legacy and the virtues of its casualness. Matsudaira Sadanobu's (1758–1829) *Kagetsu sōshi* (1818; Book of moon and flowers) is a late example of the impact of *The Pillow Book* even on a conservative interested in promoting Confucian principles.

In the late 18th and early 19th centuries, *zuihitsu* publication hit its first peak, in which authors of all stripes compiled useful information. Santō Kyōden's (1761–1816) *Kottōshō* (1813; Collection of curios) is one encyclopedic example. Many works described the sights and sounds of ordinary life, as in *Miyako no teburi* (1808; Customs of the capital), the innkeeper Ishikawa Masamochi's (1753–1830) elegant chronicle of Edo, the old name for Tokyo. Suzuki Bokushi (1770–1842) detailed the seasons of the countryside in *Hokuetsu seppu* (1837; *Snow Country Tales*). A major work that bridges Japan's encounter with the West is *Ryūkyō shinshi* (1860, 1874; The new record of Yanagibashi), Narushima Ryūhoku's (1837–84) document of the Yanagibashi pleasure quarter, written in a playful, ironical, Japanized Chinese.

Along with the momentous impact of Western fiction, forms of the essay flourished from the last quarter of the 19th century. A plethora of journalists arose to write for the many newly founded magazines and newspapers. Accounts of his travels to the West by Fukuzawa Yukichi (1834–1901) were bestsellers, while his *Gakumon no susume* (1872; *An Encouragement of Learning*) was indispensable to the modernization of Japan. Essays were the vehicle for introducing such unprecedented concepts as romantic love, the theme of Kitamura Tōkoku's (1868–94) "Ensei shika to josei" (1892; The world-weary poet and woman). Hiratsuka Raichō's (1886–1971) manifesto *Genshi josei wa taiyō de atta* (In the beginning woman was the sun) – printed in the inaugural 1911 issue of *Seitō* (Bluestockings), a journal to promote women's creativity – rocked society. The poet and critic Yosano Akiko (1878–1942) published collections of essays on social questions as often as twice a year, and debated with Raichō over the protection of motherhood. Arguments and debates about the nature of argumentation evolved, with the allowance for following one's brush acting as a kind of reassurance.

Writers known for forging new forms of literature appropriate to the modern experience continued to extend the *zuihitsu* inheritance. Masaoka Shiki (1867–1902), notorious for proposing that traditional verse forms were doomed, linked *zuihitsu* to the possibilities for improving Japanese literature and creating a new colloquial written language closer to speech. His *Fudemakase* (1884–92; Leaving it to the brush) and *Gyōga manroku* (wr. 1901–02; Stray notes while lying on my back), the latter published posthumously after his death from tuberculosis, were widely read. Shiki introduced the concept of *shasei* (copying from life) into the modern literary scene. Shimazaki Tōson (1872–1943), identified with the so-called "I-novel" form that draws part of its inspiration from **personal essay** conventions, practiced this mode of creative literary observation in his *Chikumagawa no suketchi* (1911–12; *Chikuma River Sketches*). Natsume Sōseki (1867–1916), a renowned and versatile novelist, wrote both literary criticism drawn from his two-year stay in London and the highly regarded occasional piece *Garasudo no uchi* (1915; *Within My Glass Doors*). *Dōba mango* (1919), critical remarks by Saitō Mokichi (1882–1953), the chief modern *tanka* poet, drew the acclaim of Akutagawa Ryūnosuke (1892–1927), whose own *Shuju no kotoba* (1923–25; Fool's words) is a masterpiece of the **aphorism**.

The Taishō period (1912–26), when Japan experimented with democracy and cosmopolitanism, heralded a boom in *zuihitsu*. In 1923, Kikuchi Kan (1888–1948) founded *Bungei shunjū* (Literary spring and autumn), which to this day publishes numerous essays, while a journal entitled *Zuihitsu* began after the Tokyo earthquake. Terada Torahiko (1878–1935), a

physicist who wrote under the sobriquet Fuyuhiko, is credited with formulating the first original style – frank, expansive, and "scientific" – for the modern essay. Established themes mold the work of Nagai Kafū (1879–1959), chronicler of old Tokyo and its commodified women. His *Ame shōshō* (1918; *Quiet Rain*) is reminiscent of hermitage accounts (altered by time in America, France, and the gay quarters), and his miscellanies from "Dyspepsia House" (*Danchōtei*) were as copious as any earlier author's scribblings. Irony and style mark the accomplishments of career essayists such as Uchida Roan (1868–1929). *Taikutsu tokuhon* (1915–26; Boredom reader) is Satō Haruo's (1892–1964) splendid contribution to the heritage of desultory writings, in which humor is rarely far from the surface.

The mid-1930s brought another wave of *zuihitsu* popularity, in the midst of which many questioned the randomness and superficiality of Japanese essayism, including those such as Nakano Shigeharu (1902–79), poet and Marxist revolutionary, whom literary history lauds for his trenchant critique of the culture. The desire to guard the "real Japan" defined literature in some of its best and worst moments, but ultimately did not impede the writing of significant works or the delineation of the crisis of modernity. In 1933, Tanizaki Jun'ichirō's (1886–1965) *In'ei raisan* (*In Praise of Shadows*) exulted in a fading past of dark beauty. That same year, Yanagita Kunio's (1875–1962) *Tōno monogatari* (1910; *The Legends of Tōno*), the first of many ethnographic accounts modeled on *zuihitsu*, was "discovered" and Japanese folklore studies blossomed. Hagiwara Sakutarō (1886–1942), poet and essayist, found in Yasuda Yojūrō's (1910–81) *Nihon no hashi* (1936; Japanese bridges) a transcendent aestheticization of bridges read by many as a call to battle, the first work of Japanese literature with the requisite intellection to be called an essay. Yasuda's name has been expunged from lists of important essayists, perhaps due to his sympathy with the Japanese war effort.

One essayist who drew acclaim in the 1930s, Kobayashi Hideo (1902–83), remains a pillar of Japanese literature. Kawabata Yasunari (1899–1972), himself a perceptive judge, praised Kobayashi in 1931 as the first modern literary critic. "Influential" hardly describes the path of his career up to the classics *Mujō to iu koto* (1946; On impermanence) or *Kangaeru hinto* (1964; Hints for thinking). After him, the value of Japanese criticism was no longer in doubt.

A chief problem posed by "*zuihitsu* booms" was whether any distinct essay form existed in Japan. As Hagiwara lamented, all novelists write *zuihitsu* as well. Since there is often little formal difference between the novel as practiced by many Japanese and the essay, commentators raise the question whether the short pieces by Shiga Naoya (1883–1971), "deity of the novel," would not be better termed *zuihitsu*. Even the decadent author Dazai Osamu (1909–48), who considered *zuihitsu* – his **travel essay** *Tsugaru* (1944), for example – to be different from fiction may, in the judgment of others, have written his masterpieces in the genre. Japanese critics confound the issue further by applying this caveat which seems appropriate to confessional fiction – *zuihitsu* tell the naked truth about an author. This points to a fundamental and perhaps counter-intuitive contrast. Where the I-novel is based on presumptions of necessary sincerity, *zuihitsu* are more distanced, more opinion than experience. Rather than creating an interiorized portrait that frequently drives the reader away with its blunt crudity, or flaunts marks of intimacy that imply the reader is being made privy to a vast private world (the I-novel mode), *zuihitsu* build an image of a personality one would like to sit down with for a long chat. In fact, the *zuihitsu* is that long chat – by the brazier in winter, in a cotton robe sipping astringent tea in summer, according to practitioner and theorist Kuriyagawa Hakuson (1880–1923) – artlessly orchestrated for the maximum comfort of the guest, but with the host all the while complaining that he or she is unprepared and failing miserably as a companion. The author, in other words, claims not to be exposing anything, and waves the reader away with social gambits that make the audience all the more willing to listen. Thus, paradoxically the I-novel author's strategies of self-exposure lead to a fundamental posturing that hides as much as it reveals, while the *zuihitsu* author's postures of nonchalance and disinterest leave the reader feeling he or she has uncovered the author's core.

Zuihitsu today retain overwhelming popularity, and are often hailed as congenial to the Japanese world view. Women maintain their presence, with Kōda Aya (1904–90), daughter of Kōda Rohan (1867–1947), whose own essays were much loved, observing her father's death (*Shūen* [1947; Last moments]) and the domestic world. Epoch-defining works continue to be written. Sakaguchi Ango (1906–55) shocked postwar Japan out of its nostalgia by undercutting the received meanings of culture and authority with his *Darakuron* (1946; On decadence). *Taiyō to tetsu* (1965; Sun and Steel), Yukio Mishima's (1925–70) statement of literary and political ideals, would later be understood in the context of his ritual suicide. The most significant essays of the postwar period, Nobel prize winner Ōe Kenzaburō's (1935–) *Hiroshima nōto* (1965; *Hiroshima Notes*), mark his transition from spokesman for the young generation to the atomic bomb-aware and ill-appreciated conscience of a contemporary Japan he faults as irresponsible. At the end of the millennium, the essay endures as the form through which writers seek consolation and identification of what is irreducibly Japanese in their world.

LINDA H. CHANCE

Anthologies

Anthology of Japanese Literature: From the Earliest Era to the Mid-Nineteenth Century, edited by Donald Keene, New York: Grove Press, and London: Allen and Unwin, 1955; revised edition, Harmondsworth: Penguin, 1968
Classical Japanese Prose: An Anthology, edited by Helen Craig McCullough, Stanford, California: Stanford University Press, 1990

Further Reading

Ariga, Chieko, "Dephallicizing Women in *Ryukyo Shinshi*: A Critique of Gender Ideology in Japanese Literature," *Journal of Asian Studies* 51 (August 1992): 565–86
Beichman, Janine, *Masaoka Shiki*, Boston: Twayne, 1982
Fowler, Edward, *The Rhetoric of Confession: Shishōsetsu in Early Twentieth-Century Japanese Fiction*, Berkeley: University of California Press, 1988
Hare, Thomas Blenman, "Reading Kamo no Chōmei," *Harvard Journal of Asiatic Studies* 49 (June 1989): 173–228
Ivy, Marilyn, "Ghastly Insufficiencies: *Tōno monogatari* and the Origins of Nativist Ethnology," in her *Discourses of the Vanishing: Modernity, Phantasm, Japan*, Chicago: University of Chicago Press, 1995: 66–97

Karatani, Kōjin, *Origins of Modern Japanese Literature*, Durham, North Carolina: Duke University Press, 1993
Keene, Donald, *World Within Walls: Japanese Literature of the Pre-Modern Era, 1600–1867*, New York: Grove Press, and London: Secker and Warburg, 1976
Keene, Donald, *Dawn to the West: Japanese Literature of the Modern Era*, vol. 2: *Poetry, Drama, Criticism*, New York: Holt Rinehart Winston, 1984
Keene, Donald, *Seeds in the Heart: Japanese Literature from Earliest Times to the Late Sixteenth Century*, New York: Holt, 1993
Koschmann, J. Victor, Ōiwa Keibō, and Yamashita Shinji, editors, *International Perspectives on Yanagita Kunio and Japanese Folklore Studies*, Ithaca, New York: Cornell University China-Japan Program, 1985
LaFleur, William R., "Inns and Hermitages: The Structure of Impermanence," in his *The Karma of Words: Buddhism and the Literary Arts in Medieval Japan*, Princeton, New Jersey: Princeton University Press, 1983: 60–79
Ninomiya, Masayuki, *La Pensée de Kobayashi Hideo: Un intellectuel japonais au tournant de l'histoire*, Geneva: Droz, 1995
Rodd, Laurel Rasplica, "Yosano Akiko and the Taishō Debate over the 'New Woman'," in *Recreating Japanese Women, 1600–1945*, edited by Gail Lee Bernstein, Berkeley: University of California Press, 1991: 175–98
Silverberg, Miriam, *Changing Song: The Marxist Manifestos of Nakano Shigeharu*, Princeton, New Jersey: Princeton University Press, 1990
Tansman, Alan, "Bridges to Nowhere: Yasuda Yojūrō's Language of Violence and Desire," *Harvard Journal of Asiatic Studies* 56, no. 1 (June 1996): 35–75
Treat, John Whittier, "Ōe Kenzaburō: Humanism and Hiroshima," in his *Writing Ground Zero: Japanese Literature and the Atomic Bomb*, Chicago: University of Chicago Press, 1995: 229–58
Wolfe, Alan, *Suicidal Narrative in Modern Japan: The Case of Dazai Osamu*, Princeton, New Jersey: Princeton University Press, 1990

Jefferies, Richard

British, 1848–1887

Richard Jefferies, in the almost 500 published essays and articles he is known to have written, discusses topics as various as sculpture, powered flight, the intelligence of fish, the etymology of dialect, shipping on the Thames, bathing at Brighton, and the dehumanizing effect of London streets. Nevertheless, it is the rural world, in all its aspects, with which Jefferies is mainly concerned.

Jefferies targeted more than one audience in a career which began in journalism. The articles he wrote for the *Live Stock Journal* in the late 1870s, such as "America and the Meat Market" (1877) and "Haymaking by Artificial Heat" (1878), were obviously intended for agriculturalists, and have largely been forgotten. The essays he wrote for publications such as the *Globe*, the *Pall Mall Gazette*, and the *Graphic*, however, were suited to a more general urban or suburban audience to whom the countryside offered an actual or imaginative escape. These essays, ranging from descriptive accounts of rural rambles to excursions into natural mysticism, from reactionary dismissals of farm workers' appeals for improvements in their lot, have been an influence on writers such as Kenneth Grahame, Edward Thomas, W. H. Hudson, and Henry Williamson.

His formal education over by his 15th year, Jefferies makes few demands on his reader in terms of historical or cultural knowledge. Although he might mention the sculptor/engraver Benvenuto Cellini's *Autobiography* ("A Defence of Sport," 1883), his allusions are usually to culturally familiar places such as the Louvre ("The Bathing Season," 1884) or to well-known figures like **Ruskin** ("Outside London," 1885).

Nature permeates Jefferies' writing, and even, in a sense, influences the structure and style of his work. Often using, in his descriptive pieces, a narrator who situates himself in, or adjacent to, the landscape he is describing, Jefferies steers the essay on what seems to be a perfectly natural progress as the narrator relates what he sees to the reader, and then muses upon it. Although an essay may therefore seem to be somewhat rambling, the effect is deliberate; John Fowles has said in his 1987 introduction to Jefferies' *Round About a Great Estate* (1880) that his "prose is like nature itself." In pieces such as "January in the Sussex Woods" (1884), this device enables Jefferies to achieve a natural closure; the last paragraph, beginning with "the gloom of the short January evening . . . settling down fast," ends with "the wood is silent, and it is suddenly night." As the day closes, so does the essay.

Jefferies was aware of the limitations of language; in "Wild Flowers" (1885), he compares the difficulty he found in rendering visual impressions in words to that encountered by early photographers in their efforts to "fix the scene upon the plate." He wrote "I can see [the images], but how shall I fix them for you? By no process can that be accomplished." Nevertheless, it is a limitation he overcame better than most. To Jefferies ". . . the beauty of English woodland and country is in its detail" ("An English Deer-Park," 1888), and it is through a careful and intricate layering of detail that Jefferies attempts to convey his perceptions, be they of beauty or otherwise. This detail could be applied to the broad expanse of a rural scene, or to the particularity of a flower. In "Notes on Landscape-Painting" (1882), a beam of sunshine briefly penetrates a cloudy sky and sweeps across an autumnal scene of men and women threshing wheat. In the almost epiphanic "second of its presence" the shaft of light renders the ordinary extraordinary, brilliantly illuminating farmworkers, threshing machine, horse and straw. Then ". . . it is gone, and lights up the backs of the sheep yonder as it runs up the hill swifter than a hare." Elsewhere in the essay his attention turns from panoramic scenes to a single buttercup; describing the effect of scraping off the outer "enamel" of a petal, he compares the pollen on his fingers to "dust . . . from the wing of a butterfly."

His observations of the intricacies within the spatial immensity of Nature, the sense of collapsed time he felt when contemplating the Iron Age earthworks visible in the Wiltshire landscape, and his awe at the temporal infinity of the universe, led him toward a natural mysticism, expressed at length in his spiritual autobiography, *The Story of My Heart* (1883), but apparent in much of his later writing. In his essay "The Pageant of Summer" (1883) he wrote that the "exceeding beauty of the earth, in her splendour of life, yields a new thought with every petal," and he expressed his hope that eventually Nature itself would "become, as it were, interwoven into man's existence."

Jefferies' mysticism did not blind him to the more pragmatic aspects of rural life, however. In "Notes on Landscape Painting" he states his belief that the countryside absorbs innovation, so that what once seemed dramatically new soon becomes "a part of the life of the country." Eventually "the old and the new . . . shade and blend together." Elsewhere, in *Round About a Great Estate* he states "my sympathies are with the light of the future." This acceptance of, and belief in, gradual change as natural to rural life is evident also in much of his social commentary. While Jefferies' philosophy was always somewhat class-biased, distrustful of organized labor, and opposed to rapid change, he was able to view the disadvantaged with some compassion, often documenting the hardship and drudgery of laboring life in the form of vignettes; the eponymous and dull-witted protagonist of "John Smith's Shanty" (1874) is imprisoned for domestic assault, but the narrator comments on the need for an improvement in education and *gradual* change of the "whole social system." In "One of the New Voters" (1885), characteristically emphasizing that he is "describing the realities of rural life," Jefferies notes that behind "the beautiful aspects" of a golden wheat field is "the reality of human labour – hours upon hours of heat and strain."

This social analysis in Jefferies' essays, as opposed to some of his more philosophical work, has assured him, if not a place in history, then at least some space in history texts. Historians of Victorian rural England, such as Howard Newby and Pamela Horn, have often used Jefferies as a source. He remains relegated to the margins of the canon, however, and a literary reappraisal of Jefferies awaits "the light of the future."

ALAN G. H. WEST

See also Nature Essay

Biography

John Richard Jefferies. Born 6 November 1848 at Coate Farm, near Swindon, Wiltshire. Studied until age 15 at schools in Sydenham, Kent, and Swindon. Lived in Swindon, 1866–77, Surbiton, Surrey, 1877–81, and Sussex, 1882–87. Reporter, *North Wilts Herald* and *Wilts and Gloucestershire Standard*, 1866–70; contributor to various journals, from 1873, including *Fraser's Magazine, Fortnightly Review, New Quarterly Magazine, New Monthly Magazine*, the *World, Live Stock Journal*, the *Pall Mall Gazette*, and the *Standard*. Married Jessie Badon, 1874: three children. Had four operations for tubercular fistula, 1882. Died (of chronic fibroid phthisis) in Goring, Sussex, 14 August 1887.

Selected Writings

Essays and Related Prose

The Gamekeeper at Home: Sketches of Natural History and Rural Life, 1878
The Amateur Poacher, 1879
Wild Life in a Southern County, 1879; as *An English Village*, 1903
Round About a Great Estate, 1880
Hodge and His Masters, 2 vols., 1880
Nature near London, 1883
The Life of the Fields, 1884
Red Deer, 1884
The Open Air, 1885
Field and Hedgerow, Being the Last Essays, edited by Jessie Jefferies, 1889
The Toilers of the Field, 1892
Nature and Eternity, with Other Uncollected Papers, 1902

The Hills and the Vale, 1909

Beauty Is Immortal ("Felise of the Dewy Morn") with Some Hitherto Uncollected Essays and Manuscripts, edited by Samuel J. Looker, 1948

The Essential Richard Jefferies, edited by Malcolm Elwin, 1948

The Old House at Coate, and Other Hitherto Unprinted Essays, edited by Samuel J. Looker, 1948

Chronicles of the Hedges, and Other Essays, edited by Samuel J. Looker, 1948

Field and Farm: Essays Now First Collected, edited by Samuel J. Looker, 1957

Landscape and Labour: Essays and Letters, edited by John Pearson, 1979

Landscape with Figures: An Anthology of Richard Jefferies' Prose, edited by Richard Mabey, 1983

Other writings: nine novels, the autobiography The Story of My Heart (1883), and nature diaries.

Collected works edition: Works, edited by C. Henry Warren, 6 vols., 1948–49.

Bibliography

Miller, George, and Hugoe Matthews, Richard Jefferies: A Bibliographical Study, Aldershot, Hampshire: Scolar Press, and Brookfield, Vermont: Ashgate, 1993

Further Reading

Blench, J. W., "The Influence of Richard Jefferies upon Henry Williamson," Durham University Journal 69 (1986): 79–89; (1987): 327–47

Ebbatson, Roger, "Richard Jefferies," in Lawrence and the Nature Tradition: A Theme in English Fiction 1859–1914, Brighton: Harvester, 1980: 127–64

Fowles, John, Introduction to Round About a Great Estate by Jefferies, Bradford-on-Avon: Ex Libris, 1987: 9–14

Keith, W. J., Richard Jefferies: A Critical Study, Toronto: University of Toronto Press, 1965

Keith, W. J., The Rural Tradition: A Study of the Non-Fiction Prose Writers of the English Countryside, Toronto: University of Toronto Press, 1974

Leavis, Q. D., "Lives and Works of Richard Jefferies," Scrutiny 6 (1938): 435–46

Looker, Samuel J., and Crichton Porteous, Richard Jefferies, Man of the Fields: A Biography and Letters, London: Baker, 1965

Mabey, Richard, Introduction to Landscape with Figures by Jefferies, edited by Mabey, Harmondsworth: Penguin, 1983: 7–24

Manning, Edna, Richard Jefferies: A Modern Appraisal, Windsor: Goldscheider, 1984

Matthews, Hugoe, and Phyllis Treitel, The Forward Life of Richard Jefferies: A Chronological Study, Oxford: Petton Books, 1994

Pearson, John, Introduction to Landscape and Labour by Jefferies, edited by Pearson, Bradford-on-Avon: Moonraker, 1979: 7–18

Richard Jefferies Society Journal, 1992–

Rossabi, Andrew, Introduction to Hodge and His Masters by Jefferies, London: Quartet, 1979: vi–xxiii

Taylor, Brian, Richard Jefferies, Boston: Twayne, 1982

Thomas, Edward, Richard Jefferies: His Life and Work, London: Hutchinson, and Boston: Little Brown, 1909

Williams, Merryn, Thomas Hardy and Rural England, London: Macmillan, and New York: Columbia University Press, 1972

Williams, Raymond, The Country and the City, New York: Oxford University Press, 1973; London: Hogarth Press, 1985: 191–96

Wilson, Keith, "Richard Jefferies," in Modern British Essayists: First Series, edited by Robert Beum, Dictionary of Literary Biography, vol. 98, Detroit: Gale Research, 1990: 192–204

Johnson, Samuel

British, 1709–1784

What did Samuel Johnson think of the essay? His great Dictionary of 1755, a landmark in human achievement, has this to say regarding "essay" as a noun:

1. Attempt; endeavour.
Fruitless our hopes, though pious our essays;
Your's to preserve a friend, and mine to praise. Smith.
2. A loose sally of the mind; an irregular indigested piece; not a regular and orderly composition.
My essays, of all my other works, have been most current. Bac.
Yet modestly he does his work survey,
And calls his finish'd poem an essay. Poem to Roscommon.
3. A trial; an experiment.
He wrote this but as an essay, or taste of my virtue. Shak.
Repetitions wear us into a liking of what possibly, in the first essay, displeased us. Locke.
4. First taste of any thing; first experiment.
Translating the first of Homer's Iliads, I intended as an essay to the whole work. Dryden's Fables, Preface.

Within a culture that values success (over endeavor), regularity and method (over loose sallies), accomplishment (over trials), and the final (over the initial), the essay would appear always to be an inferior genre, at least as it is depicted in these definitions. The second definition in particular distinguishes the essay from more finished kinds of writing, and the illustration indicates how a writer might depreciate another kind of work by calling it an essay.

At the same time, however, Johnson's definitions and illustrations also suggest the elusive nature of what an essay is: almost any piece of writing would fit the parameters of the first and third definitions, as an "attempt" or "experiment." The second definition, to be sure, does seem to be the most restrictive, and its first illustration alludes to a tradition of "irregular indigested" pieces by citing **Bacon**, who followed the generally acknowledged inventor of the essay, **Montaigne**. But Bacon's comment points to the particular power of his essays, their currency; and the second illustration undermines any confident focusing of the term by employing a quotation in which the essay referred to is actually a poem, which may remind us of the disparate works Johnson would have known as "essays": Dryden's **Essay of Dramatic Poesy** (1668; a **dialogue**), Locke's **Essay Concerning Human Understanding** (1694; an extended philosophical speculation), Pope's poetic **Essay on Man** (1733–34) or **Essay on Criticism** (1711).

Johnson's own career also undermines any sense that the essay is a lowly or indeterminate genre. Prior to the **Rambler**, which ran from 1750 to 1752, Johnson was a promising but rather minor figure. Among his publications could be counted two long poems, London (1738) and The Vanity of Human Wishes (1749); some **reviews** and brief biographies; the "Plan" (1747) for the Dictionary; and a mediocre (at best) play, Irene (1749). After the Rambler's 208 biweekly essays had appeared (almost entirely by Johnson), he was a major figure.

In 1752 Charlotte Lennox was not alone in determining that "the Author of the Rambler" was "the greatest Genius in the present Age," as she puts it in the penultimate chapter of *The Female Quixote*. Johnson was, for the rest of his life, "the Rambler" (sometimes even "Ramblin' Sam"). The famous Nollekens bust of Johnson has written on its base, "RAMBLER."

In the 1750s, in addition to his *Dictionary* and the philosophical tale of *Rasselas* (1759), Johnson published in two other essay series, the **Idler** (1758–60) and the **Adventurer** (1752–54). By 1764, the *Biographia Dramatica*, reflecting a widespread sentiment, could refer to Johnson as "no less the glory of the present age and nation, than he will be the admiration of all succeeding ones." Johnson garnered this praise, repeated again and again by his contemporaries, before his great edition of Shakespeare's plays (1765), *Journey to the Western Islands* (1775), or *The Lives of the Poets* (1779–81). Johnson's massive reputation, in other words, was substantially the result of his work as an essayist. And the *Rambler*, as Arthur Murphy, Johnson's early biographer puts it, was his "great work" (Boulton, 1971).

Johnson's celebrity when he died, late in 1784, was indeed phenomenal. He reportedly had remarked to Boswell a few years earlier, "I believe there is hardly a day in which there is not something about me in the newspapers," and Helen McGuffie's patient search of the London and Edinburgh newspapers (1749–84) revealed (in *Samuel Johnson in the British Press, 1749–1784*, 1976) that Johnson "was closer to the truth than he may have realized." The press apparently tracked his every move and scrutinized his health; when there were no sightings or symptoms to report, they made things up, recycled anecdotes, quoted excerpts from his works, or focused on someone somehow related to Johnson (Richard Russell for instance, who was the subject of some 20 newspaper articles from 4 October to 13 November 1784: he had left money in his will to Johnson and then changed his mind [McGuffie]).

This sort of interest in Johnson as super-celebrity can only partly be explained by reference to his works. One must look as well to their reception; as Johnson put it: "It is advantageous to an author, that his book should be attacked as well as praised. Fame is a shuttlecock. If it be struck only at one end of the room, it will soon fall to the ground. To keep it up, it must be struck at both ends" (*Journey to the Western Islands*). Johnson's works certainly were struck passionately at both ends, during his lifetime and afterwards. As Vicesimus Knox put it in 1788: "Few men could stand so fiery a trial as he has done. His gold has been put into the furnace, and really, considering the violence of the fire, and the frequent repetition of the process, the quantity of dross and alloy is inconsiderable" (Boulton).

The critical purification of Johnson's essays focused primarily on the *Rambler*'s style and tone (its pious intentions could hardly be questioned). Johnson's readers naturally compared this series, and every other essay series, to **Addison**'s and **Steele**'s *Spectator* (1711–12, 1714). Arthur Murphy's assessment is fairly representative of late 18th-century views: "Addison lends grace and ornament to truth; Johnson gives it force and energy. Addison makes virtue amiable; Johnson represents it as an awful duty. Addison insinuates himself with an air of modesty; Johnson commands like a dictator" (Boulton, 1971). While the *Spectator* was spectacularly popular, the *Rambler* "increased in fame as in age," as Boswell put it. Some readers, however, never came to terms with Johnson's distinctive style: Horace Walpole, for instance, thought Johnson's manner "so encumbered, so void of ear & harmony, & consequently so harsh and unpliable that I know no modern Writer whose works could be read aloud with so little satisfaction" (Boulton).

Such a view of Johnson as a pedantic and pompous writer came to dominate the 19th century, so much so that **Macaulay** – writing in his famous 1831 review of Croker's edition of Boswell's *Life of Johnson* (1791) – could say that the "characteristic faults of his style are so familiar to all our readers, and have been so often burlesqued, that it is almost superfluous to point them out" (Boulton). But at the same time that Johnson's writings were being dismissed, his conversation and his character (some Johnsonians would prefer to say "caricature"), particularly as presented by Boswell, were being affectionately embraced: "When he talked," Macaulay asserted, "he clothed his wit and his sense in forcible and natural expressions."

The modern appreciation of Johnson the writer has been developed by many people. George Birkbeck Hill specifically set out in the 1880s to eradicate Macaulay's Johnson, which had influenced generations of readers in schoolbook anthologies. Hill's editions of Boswell, Johnson's letters, *The Lives of the Poets*, and other works helped spark a return to the texts themselves. Walter Raleigh's *Six Essays on Johnson* in 1910, and **T. S. Eliot**'s essay on Johnson as critic and poet in 1930, are particularly influential examples of early efforts to take Johnson seriously as a writer. In 1924 in *Johnson the Essayist*, O. F. Christie asserted what was becoming a commonplace – that Johnson's essays, which contain his real opinions, are being neglected, while his conversations are being read. Christie attempted to see Johnson's essays "as a consistent and coherent whole," and praised their imagery and "spiritual insight." In 1929 D. N. Smith poked a hole in Boswell's notion that Johnson's essays were not revised, and Curtis Bradford in 1939 established that the fourth edition was Johnson's final revision.

In the 1940s and 1950s interest in Johnson the essayist heightened. In 1941, for instance, W. K. Wimsatt examined the carefully crafted *Prose Style of Samuel Johnson*, looking closely at the use of parallelism, antithesis, diction, and other qualities; and in 1948, Wimsatt studied Johnson's distinctive use of scientific imagery and diction in *Philosophic Words*. In 1944 **Joseph Wood Krutch** produced the first modern biography of Johnson, which is notable for the careful analysis it provides of Johnson's own works, including his essays. Arthur Sherbo, Edward Bloom, A. T. Elder, and others deepened appreciation for Johnson's accomplishment as an essayist, as well as his influence on the essay tradition. With a simple yet important bit of basic research, R. M. Wiles showed in 1968 that the circulation of the *Rambler* essays, in reprints and excerpts, was much greater than Johnson knew.

In the 1970s and 1980s, a series of studies examined Johnson's rhetoric. In a particularly important essay, Leopold Damrosch in 1973 saw Johnson "dismantling" commonplaces in an effort "to make us stop parroting the precepts of moralists and start thinking for ourselves." Damrosch thus suggested that the experience of Johnson's essays is at least as important as the content, and subsequent scholarship tends to focus on defining the nature of that experience. James Boyd White, in *When Words Lose Their Meaning* (1984), offered a particularly revealing description of the typical Johnsonian essay's unfolding: the beginnings of Johnson's essays typically start "where the reader actually is, surrounded by truisms and clichés, in a condition of uncertainty or doubt, perhaps of essential thoughtlessness, from which he may be moved to a new position of clarity and truth"; yet White also noted that Johnson's conclusions are "open-ended" and "structurally tentative," conclusive only within the context of the particular essay. Johnson is thus engaged in teaching his reader how to think.

The insights of Damrosch and White seem to apply primarily to those essays Johnson called "professedly serious," and it is worth noting the wide variety of writing actually contained in the *Rambler*, *Idler*, and *Adventurer*: literary criticism and theory (the essays on Milton are especially interesting), Oriental tales, epistolary short fiction, allegories, and dream visions. Steven Lynn in *Samuel Johnson After Deconstruction* (1992) describes the reader's experience of the *Rambler* as a sequential series, noting (among other things) how Johnson reshapes the reader's sense of the *Spectator*'s priority, how the movement of various essays anticipates and surpasses deconstruction, and how the careful patterning of the various essays brings the reader again and again to the brink of religious faith – thus carrying out the pious intention Johnson declared at the series' outset.

For the modern reader, Johnson's essays are likely to seem rigorous, intense, and strikingly eloquent. They generally demand the reader's active attention, but even the most rigorous essays are not without a subtle humor. And the stories of Dick Minim (a lousy critic), Dick Linger (a sluggish soul), Tom Tempest and Jack Sneaker (political fanatics), and many other characters are both amusing and instructive. Johnson deals generally with "known truths," moral insights that the reader is already quite familiar with, but has perhaps stopped acting upon, or applying, or questioning. The movement of his essays as well as the style serve to enliven the reader's attention.

As Donald Greene (1989) has pointed out, the idea of "Johnson's prose style," as if he had only one, is mistaken. In his published essays, however, Johnson does tend toward quite poetic effects of balance, parallelism, alliteration, and imagery. The notion that Johnson's prose is verbose or padded, a widespread idea in the 19th century, is easily negated by anyone who reads him without prejudice. Here for instance are the first two sentences of the *Rambler*:

> The difficulty of the first address on any new occasion, is felt by every man in his transactions with the world, and confessed by the settled and regular forms of salutation which necessity has introduced into all languages. Judgment was wearied with the perplexity of being forced upon choice, where there was no motive to preference; and it was found convenient that some easy method of introduction should be established, which, if it wanted the allurement of novelty, might enjoy the security of prescription.

The first sentence efficiently sets up the problem – how does one open a channel of communication? – and looks at two aspects of it: on the one hand, the discomfort every individual experiences with first meetings, and on the other hand, the cultural consequences of this perception, namely the institution of various conventions to smooth over this difficulty. This sentence may appear, at first glance, wordy: it does have eight prepositional phrases. The reader who attempts to shorten it without loss or alteration of meaning will quickly discover, however, the efficiency of Johnson's prose. The second sentence suggests a miniature allegory in which the figure of "Judgment" deliberates (like Rasselas and many other Johnsonian characters) over the choice of introduction, and finally decides arbitrarily. The sentence's final construction reflects this balance, as "the allurement of novelty" is traded for "the security of prescription."

This kind of rich texture is easy to parody but very difficult to imitate. Although Johnson's essays have been very influential (even Macaulay's prose strategies often derive from Johnson), his voice remains quite distinctive.

STEVEN LYNN

Biography

Born 18 September 1709 in Lichfield, Staffordshire. Studied at Lichfield Grammar School and Stourbridge School, to age 16; Pembroke College, Oxford, 1728–29. Contributor to *Gentleman's Magazine*, 1734–44. Married Elizabeth (Tettie) Porter, 1735 (died, 1752). Ran a school in Edial, Staffordshire, 1735–37; moved to London, 1737. Reported on debates in Parliament, 1740–44; worked on his *Dictionary*, 1746–55; formed the Ivy Lane Club, 1749; writer and editor of the *Rambler*, 1750–52; major contributor, the *Adventurer*, 1753–54; arrested for debt, 1756: released after Samuel Richardson loaned him the money; contributor, the *Literary Magazine*, 1756–58, and the "Idler" papers for the *Universal Chronicle*, 1758–60. Granted crown pension, 1762. Cofounder of the Literary Club, 1764. Traveled with James Boswell to Scotland, 1773, and with Hester and Henry Thrale to Wales, 1774, and Paris, 1775. Formed the Essex Head Club, 1783. Awards: honorary degrees from Oxford University and Trinity College, Dublin. Died in London, 13 December 1784.

Selected Writings

Essays and Related Prose

The Rambler, 208 nos., 20 March 1750–14 March 1752; in 6 vols., 1752; selections in *Essays from the Rambler, Adventurer, and Idler*, edited by Walter Jackson Bate, 1968

The Adventurer, with others, 140 nos., 7 November 1752–9 March 1754; in 2 vols., 1753–54; selections in *Essays from the Rambler, Adventurer, and Idler*, edited by Walter Jackson Bate, 1968

The Idler papers, in the *Universal Chronicle, or Weekly Gazette*, 15 April 1758–5 April 1760; in 2 vols., 1761; selections in *Essays from the Rambler, Adventurer, and Idler*, edited by Walter Jackson Bate, 1968

Prefaces, Biographical and Critical, to the Works of the English Poets, 10 vols., 1779–81; as *The Lives of the English Poets*, 1781; revised edition, 1783; edited by George Birkbeck Hill, 3 vols., 1905; selection edited by J. P. Hardy, 1972

Essays from the Rambler, Adventurer, and Idler, edited by Walter Jackson Bate, 1968

Literary Criticism, edited by R. D. Stock, 1974

Selected Poetry and Prose, edited by Frank Brady and W. K. Wimsatt, 1977

Samuel Johnson on Literature, edited by Marlies K. Danziger, 1979

Samuel Johnson on Shakespeare, edited by H. R. Woudhuysen, 1989

Other writings: the two-volume *Dictionary of the English Language* (1755), poetry, the moral tale *Rasselas* (1759), the verse-tragedy *Irene* (1749), the travelogue *Journey to the Western Islands* (1775), letters (collected in *The Letters*, edited by Bruce Redford, 5 vols., 1992–94), biographies, and autobiography. Also edited an edition of Shakespeare's plays (1765).

Collected works edition: *Works* (Yale Edition), edited by Allen T. Hazen and others, 13 vols., 1958–90 (in progress).

Bibliographies

Clifford, James L., and Donald Greene, *Samuel Johnson: A Survey and Bibliography of Critical Studies*, Minneapolis: University of Minnesota Press, 1970

Courtney, William Prideaux, and David Nichol Smith, *A Bibliography of Samuel Johnson*, with a supplement by R. W. Chapman and Allen T. Hazen, New Castle, Delaware: Oak Knoll Books and M. Goldberg, 1984 (original edition, 1915; supplement, 1938)

Greene, Donald, and John A. Vance, *A Bibliography of Johnsonian Studies 1970–1985*, Victoria, British Columbia: University of Victoria English Literary Studies, 1987

Further Reading

Bate, Walter Jackson, *Samuel Johnson*, New York: Harcourt Brace Jovanovich, and London: Chatto and Windus, 1977

Boulton, James T., editor, *Johnson: The Critical Heritage*, London: Routledge and Kegan Paul, and New York: Barnes and Noble, 1971

Bullough, Geoffrey, "Johnson the Essayist," *New Rambler* 16 (1968): 16–33

Damrosch, Leopold, "Johnson's Manner of Proceeding in the *Rambler*," *ELH* 40 (1973): 70–89

Fussell, Paul, *Samuel Johnson and the Life of Writing*, New York: Harcourt Brace Jovanovich, 1971

Good, Graham, "Johnson: The Correction of Error," in his *The Observing Self: Rediscovering the Essay*, London and New York: Routledge, 1988: 55–71

Greene, Donald, *Samuel Johnson*, Boston: Twayne, revised edition, 1989

Koper, Peter, "Samuel Johnson's Rhetorical Stance in *The Rambler*," *Style* 12 (1978): 23–34

Lynn, Steven, *Samuel Johnson After Deconstruction: Rhetoric and "The Rambler"*, Carbondale: Southern Illinois University Press, 1992

O'Flaherty, Patrick, "Towards an Understanding of Johnson's *Rambler*," *SEL* 18 (1978): 523–36

Rewa, Michael, "Aspects of Rhetoric in Johnson's 'Professedly Serious' *Rambler* Essays," *Quarterly Journal of Speech* 56 (1970): 75–84

Schwartz, Richard, "Johnson's 'Mr. Rambler' and the Periodical Tradition," *Genre* 7 (1974): 196–204

Trowbridge, Hoyt, "The Language of Reasoned Rhetoric in *The Rambler*," in *Greene Centennial Essays: Essays Presented to Donald Greene*, edited by Paul Korshin and Robert Allen, Charlottesville: University Press of Virginia, 1984

White, James Boyd, *When Words Lose Their Meaning: Constitutions and Reconstructions of Language, Character, and Community*, Chicago: University of Chicago Press, 1984

Wimsatt, W. K., *The Prose Style of Samuel Johnson*, Hamden, Connecticut: Archon, 1972 (original edition, 1941)

Journal

The terms "journal" and "diary" are often used interchangeably to describe an account of an individual's experience written at regular intervals. Sometimes the term "diary" suggests a daily record. The term "journal" may be used to describe an ongoing record that is less regular or more elaborate than a diary, or that covers a limited period of time, but which still retains a chronological arrangement. Both the diary and the journal employ a personal perspective, even when recording historical events or scenes of travel, as the journal writer sets down what he or she is able to observe. The journal is a highly flexible form, with few rules about subject matter or narrative style, or even, for that matter, about the frequency or length of entries.

The entry, which is the basic unit of the journal, is often, but not always, given a date. Entries may follow a range of patterns, but the most common is a simple sequential recounting of the events of a particular day. Another common pattern is more like a meditative essay in miniature, which reveals the writer's inner response to what is happening at the time. While a central convention of the journal is that entries are made daily in the midst of, or shortly after, the experience, many well-known diarists, including Samuel Pepys and Dorothy Wordsworth, often wrote retrospectively, sometimes using notes made close to the time of the experience. Even when they did so, they used the dated-entry form to create the impression of regularity and immediacy.

This convention of appearing to record immediate experience makes the journal form appear casual and linear. Coupled with the ostensibly private purposes of most journals, this leads to a common notion of the journal as a naive, frank, and sincere form, although some journals are actually complex in design, developing dialectic or symbolic patterns through entries that question or echo what has gone before. Novelists have sometimes capitalized on the journal's appearance of sincerity and immediacy by giving their stories the shape of a journal. Two notable instances are **Daniel Defoe's** *A Journal of the Plague Year* (1722) and **André Gide's** *La Symphonie pastorale* (1919; *The Pastoral Symphony*).

Like an essay, a journal may enact a sort of imagined conversation in the form of a **dialogue** with one's later or earlier self, an extended epistle to a real or imagined friend, or a confession addressed to God. In *The Observing Self: Rediscovering the Essay* (1988), Graham Good suggests that the essay, as the "book of the self," bears a likeness to the journal because both forms continue **Montaigne's** practice of paying attention to one's individual experience and recording it in ways that mirror its fluidity and contradictions. But, Good points out, the essayist focuses on a series of topics even when dealing with them over time, while the journal writer concentrates on the chronological unfolding of experience.

In *Private Chronicles: A Study of English Diaries* (1974), Robert A. Fothergill lists four types of journals: the journal of travel, the public journal or eye-witness record of historic events, the journal of conscience, and the journal of personal memoranda, noting that the great journals often combine elements of several categories. Within these broad categories more specialized forms arise, such as the religious diary or prayer journal as a variety of the journal of conscience, and the journal of erotic adventures as a specialized form of personal memoranda.

Although there have probably been journals as long as there have been literate people with an interest in recording the facts of experience, the words "diary" and "journal" first began to be used in their modern senses in the 16th century. In addition to offering accounts of travel and military experience, during the 17th and 18th centuries journals focused on self-improvement, as the journal-keeper scrutinized his or her life in light of a personal, religious, or cultural ideal. Most of these journals were not made public during the lives of their writers; some were not published until the 19th and 20th centuries. By the middle of the 18th century, however, increasing interest in reading about private lives paved the way for the wider appearance of the journal as a published form. From that time on, journal writing has been characterized by a tension between reticence and the need to please readers. Isaac D'Israeli's "Some Observations on Diaries, Self-Biography and Self-Characters" (1796) presents a common justification for publishing private journals – that their truthfulness makes them useful to readers. But **Samuel Johnson**, writing in the *Idler* (no. 84), argued that private accounts must be kept private to preserve the writer's integrity. Some 19th-century reviewers of published journals feared that the popularity of such works would create a plague of self-absorption and idle curiosity. Still, the rise of the Romantic sensibility focused on the development of the individual, and the publication of important diaries, such as those by 17th-century diarists John Evelyn (1818) and Samuel Pepys (1825), added to a growing consciousness of the journal as a literary form. In some ways, Samuel Pepys is to the diary what Montaigne is to the essay, for his balance of interior and public comment, variety of subject matter, and the apparent simplicity of accounting become models for the journal. For Enlightenment rationalists, keeping a journal was an element of an ordered life, while for dissenting Christians in England and on the continent, the journal was a means of assessing one's progress in sanctity. The *Journal of John Wesley* (wr. 1725–91) set the stage for increasing interest in using the journal as a spiritual discipline. Toward the end of the 18th century the pleasure of recollection and the treasuring of memories became an important part of journal writing, and the quest to understand the unfolding self tended to replace moral self-scrutiny. The 19th century also saw the rise of the journal that recorded the life and creative processes of the artist and, in the wake of psychoanalysis, 20th-century journals often frame their accounts of self-discovery in psychological, symbolic, and therapeutic terms.

In the 20th century, the publication of complete or nearly complete unexpurgated editions of journals from the past has spurred much critical thinking about literary genres, the canon, and the complexities of self-representation. James Boswell's *Journals* (wr. 1763–78) reveal the conflicts of the private man behind the biographer. Dorothy Wordsworth's *Alfoxden Journals* (wr. 1798) and *Grasmere Journals* (wr. 1800–03), with their self-effacing but engaging pictures of ordinary life, have raised questions about the literary status of private writing and the manner in which journals, **letters**, and private memoirs can shed light on women as writers. Benjamin Robert Haydon's *Diary* (wr. 1808–46; pub. originally as *The Life of Benjamin Robert Haydon: Autobiography and Journals*, 1853) transforms the rhetoric of emotion, removing it from a religious context. Instead of writing about emotions, he writes emotionally, making it fashionable to dramatize the self as a creature of sensibility. The collaborative *Journal* kept by the brothers Edmond and Jules Goncourt from 1851 to 1870, and continued by Edmond until 1895, exemplifies the journal as a chronicle of an intellectual and artistic milieu. By the 20th century Anaïs Nin could make the keeping of a journal central to her life's work; her *Journals*, which began to appear in 1966, raises the journal of self-exploration to new levels of aesthetic and psychological awareness.

LINDA MILLS WOOLSEY

Anthologies

The Book of American Diaries, edited by Randall M. Miller and Linda Patterson Miller, New York: Avon, 1995
A Day at a Time: The Diary Literature of American Women from 1764 to the Present, edited by Margo Culley, New York: Feminist Press of the City University of New York, 1985
English Diaries of the XVIth, XVIIth, and XVIIIth Centuries, edited by James Aitken, Harmondsworth: Penguin, 1941
English Family Life: An Anthology from Diaries, edited by Ralph Houlbrooke, Oxford and New York: Blackwell, 1988
The Faber Book of Diaries, edited by Simon Brett, London and Boston: Faber, 1987
Leaves in the Storm: A Book of Diaries, edited by Stefan Schimanski and Henry Tree, London: Drummond, 1947
Private Pages: Diaries of American Women, 1830s–1970s, edited by Penelope Franklin, New York: Ballantine, 1986

Bibliographies

Arksey, Laura, Nancy Pries, and Marcia Reed, editors, *American Diaries: An Annotated Bibliography of Published American Diaries and Journals*, Detroit: Gale Research, 2 vols., 1983–87
Cline, Cheryl, *Women's Diaries, Journals, and Letters: An Annotated Bibliography*, New York: Garland, 1989
Goodfriend, Joyce D., *Published Diaries and Letters of American Women: An Annotated Bibliography*, Boston: Hall, 1987
Guide and Index to Women's Diaries: A Readex Microfilm Collection, New Canaan, Connecticut: Readex, 1984– (in progress)
Havlice, Patricia Pate, *And So to Bed: A Bibliography of Diaries Published in English*, Metuchen, New Jersey: Scarecrow Press, 1987
Matthews, William, editor, *British Diaries: An Annotated Bibliography of British Diaries Written Between 1442 and 1942*, Berkeley: University of California Press, 1950

Further Reading

Blodgett, Harriet, *Centuries of Female Days: English Women's Private Diaries*, New Brunswick, New Jersey: Rutgers University Press, 1988
Fothergill, Robert A., *Private Chronicles: A Study of English Diaries*, London and New York: Oxford University Press, 1974
Girard, Alain, *Le Journal intime*, Paris: Presses Universitaires de France, 1963
Good, Graham, *The Observing Self: Rediscovering the Essay*, London and New York: Routledge, 1988
Hocke, Gustav René, *Das Europäische Tagebuch*, Wiesbaden: Limes, 1963
Hoffman, William J., *Life Writing: A Guide to Family Journals and Personal Memoirs*, New York: St. Martin's Press, 1982
Kagle, Steven E., *American Diary Literature, 1620–1799*, Boston: Twayne, 1979
Kagle, Steven E., *Early Nineteenth-Century American Diary Literature*, Boston: Twayne, 1986
Kagle, Steven E., *Late Nineteenth-Century American Diary Literature*, Boston: Twayne, 1988
Mallon, Thomas, *A Book of One's Own: People and Their Diaries*, New York: Ticknor and Fields, 1984
Matthews, William, "The Diary as Literature," in *The Diary of Samuel Pepys: Volume 1*, edited by Robert Latham and Matthews, Berkeley: University of California Press, and London: Bell, 1970

Nin, Anaïs, *The Novel of the Future*, New York: Macmillan, 1968

Nussbaum, Felicity, *The Autobiographical Subject: Gender and Ideology in Eighteenth-Century England*, Baltimore: Johns Hopkins University Press, revised edition, 1995 (original edition, 1989)

O'Brien, Kate, *English Diaries and Journals* (Britain in Pictures series), London: Collins, 1943

Ponsonby, Arthur, *English Diaries: A Review of English Diaries from the Sixteenth to the Twentieth Century*, London: Methuen, 1923

Ponsonby, Arthur, *More English Diaries: Further Reviews of Diaries from the Sixteenth to the Nineteenth Centuries*, London: Methuen, 1927

Ponsonby, Arthur, *Scottish and Irish Diaries from the Sixteenth to the Nineteenth Centuries*, London: Methuen, 1927

Ponsonby, Arthur, *Samuel Pepys*, London: Macmillan, 1928; New York: League of America, 1929

Ponsonby, Arthur, *British Diarists*, London: Benn, 1930

Spalding, Philip Anthony, *Self Harvest: A Study of Diaries and the Diarist*, London: Independent Press, 1949

Willy, Margaret, *English Diarists: Evelyn and Pepys*, London: Longman, 1963

Willy, Margaret, *Three Women Diarists: Celia Fiennes, Dorothy Wordsworth, Katherine Mansfield*, London: Longman, 1964

Journal des Débats

French journal, 1789–1939

The *Journal des Débats, Politiques et Littéraires* (Journal of political and literary debates) was founded in 1789 to cover the proceedings of the National Assembly. Its name was changed to the *Journal de l'Empire* by Napoleon, appearing under that title through 31 March 1814, the date of the capitulation of Paris. Five days later, on 6 April, Napoleon abdicated, the Bourbon monarchy was restored in France, and the "first empire" was over. The new newspaper, using its original name and authorized by an official decree, was owned by a small group of individuals. Success was phenomenal, as the paper quickly achieved 23,000 subscribers, against 6300 for its nearest rival, *La Gazette de France*.

The paper's immediate demand for complete freedom of the press led speedily to the appointment of a police commissar for each newspaper. The *Débats*, as it soon came to be known popularly, was itself liberal-conservative, adopting the political views of Benjamin Constant, anti-Romantic in the arts, and conservative economically. Constant bravely published an outright and now famous attack on Napoleon in the *Débats* on 19 March 1815 during the welcoming phase of the hundred days. The paper consistently attacked the abuse of power and, on the collapse of the group surrounding the philosopher and economist Saint-Simon, welcomed refugees from his followers, successors to the old "ideologist" camp of materialistic social reformers with broad international interests. From 1833 to 1835 it published Michel Chevalier's "Lettres de l'Amérique du Nord" (Letters from North America), and on 10 May 1852 published a famous article by him against protectionism and in favor of free trade. The *Débats* was friendly to the English in 1857 and hostile to the Jesuits. Later on, its views were to become clearly anti-clerical.

After the sea change in French newspaper history brought about in 1836 by the simultaneous launch of Armand Dutacq's *Le Siècle* (The century) and Émile de Girardin's *La Presse* at half the ordinary subscription price, the conservatively presented *Débats*, with its conventional four pages of double columns, had to make concessions. Alongside the political speeches, reports of court occasions, and book and theater reviews, some column inches began to be devoted to *faits divers* like accidents and particularly important crimes. It also began to publish the immensely popular serial fiction which newspapers were carrying at the bottom of their front pages. The *Débats* was lucky enough to contract Eugène Sue, whose unbelievably successful, but at the time largely unwritten, *Les Mystères de Paris* (The mysteries of Paris) ran from June 1842 to October 1843, doubling the circulation from 5000 to 10,000. The office staff at the *Débats* had to help devise incidents to keep the plot going, as well as cliffhangers at the end of each episode, when Sue's inspiration flagged. The paper went on to publish George Sand, notably *François le Champi* (1848). The upmarket style and solidly bourgeois readership, of which about two-thirds came from outside Paris, enabled it to achieve an advertising revenue as high as that of *Le Constitutionnel* (The constitutional), which had more than double the circulation.

While the *Débats* was never primarily a forum for the publication of essays, **Hippolyte Taine** published in its pages many pieces which we would now call essays. The ex-prime minister and educational reformer François-Pierre-Guillaume Guizot also published complimentary pieces about Taine in the paper in 1857. The intellectual and cultural orientation of the paper was epitomized in its long association with both Taine and **Ernest Renan**, who published a collection of his essays which had first appeared in the *Débats*, and who once wrote in its pages, "What is needed at the moment is an intellectual and spiritual elite."

While the newspaper was eventually a champion of fiction – contracting Balzac to write two novels for it, serializing Alexandre Dumas and Joseph-Arthur de Gobineau – it contributed above all to the steady development of the essay as a vehicle for reviewing and discussing cultural pursuits, particularly those touching on literature and the performing arts, reflecting the way in which during the 19th century the development of literacy diminished cultural dependency on drama.

The influence of the *Débats* remained higher than is suggested by the bare circulation figures, down to 7000 by 1880. In 1884 it took over *Le Parlement* (The parliament) and in 1894 began publishing morning and evening editions, retaining a staid, conservative style until World War II, when it was closed permanently.

ANTHONY LEVI

Further Reading

Jakoby, Ruth, *Das Feuilleton des "Journal des Débats" von 1814 bis 1830, ein Beitrag zur Literaturdiskussion der Restauration*, Tübingen: Narr, 1988

Mège, Francisque, *Les Fondateurs du "Journal des Débats" en 1789*, Paris: Faure, 1865

Nettement, Alfred, *Histoire politique, anecdotique et littéraire, du "Journal des Débats"*, Paris: Echo de France, 2 vols., 1838

Pereire, Alfred, *Le "Journal des Débats" politiques et littéraires, 1814–1914*, Paris: Champion, 1914

Journalism and the Essay

The relationship between the history of journalism and the evolution of the essay has intrigued theorists who venture into interdisciplinary research. For some writers, to work as journalist has been characterized either as beneficial or as a detrimental violation of literary purity. Whatever the theorists' opinions, the list of authors who practiced journalism as a profession or as a major outlet for their literary production is lengthy and includes British writers such as **Defoe, Swift, Darwin, Dickens,** and **Thackeray**; the Americans **Twain,** Hemingway, and Steinbeck; the French **Voltaire,** Zola, Gide, Malraux, and **Camus**; the Spaniards **Larra, Ortega y Gasset,** Baroja, **Unamuno,** and **Azorín**; and the Latin Americans **Sarmiento, Montalvo, Martí, Martínez Estrada, Arciniegas,** García Márquez, and Vargas Llosa.

Two facts are important for textual and sociological analyses of these two genres. First, newspapers and magazines have been frequent vehicles for what history and the theory of literature consider to be essays. Rarely published in book form, many have been reprinted only in anthologies published solely for educational purposes, to give examples of the literary genre called essay. In other words, from an historical point of view, the history of the contemporary essay cannot be studied separately from the history of journalism. Second, the textual nature of journalism in general, especially of some of its variations, reveals numerous parallels with the features outlined by critics either for the essay in general or for some of its modern transfigurations.

Ironically, both writing trades have transgressed from their declared faithful origins and goals in order to survive. In doing so, they have taken on distinctive features that had apparently belonged exclusively to the other: the essay has incorporated clarity and economy of means, while journalism has absorbed subjective literary views and techniques. In journalism, the faculties of notation, sensation, and memory take precedence over imagination and reason. In the case where the literary energy of the essay is latent, the reverse occurs. Never appearing in pure forms, these modes combine according to the personal style and inclinations of writers, columnists, investigative reporters, and editorial writers.

Whether recognized as a separate literary genre or not, the essay has benefited from its comparative treatment with canonical counterparts. The most crucial marker for differentiating the essay from the novel, short story, drama, or poetry is that only the author is to blame for the message. The essay is without the mask of narrator, characters, actors, or even the protected introspective aspect of poetry. More than the facts, argument, or thesis of the essay, it is the manner in which essayists present their materials that makes the difference in getting the reader's attention. By persuasion and, at the same time, the revelation of a human, personal side, the author aims at sharing a point of view.

In contrast, journalism developed from an initial period dominated by ideological leanings into another obsessed with objectivity. The questions "who, what, where, when" took precedence over the "how" and the "why." The golden, heroic era of informative journalism culminated in the crafting of the perfect lead-in, the initial concept, couched in a sentence or two, that would grab readers' attention and make them read on. In this antiseptic environment writers became correspondents and were glorified by the stardom supplied by the by-line. However, they were subjected to deadlines and style directives prescribed by wire services and desk editors, necessitating the discipline of polishing their prose, a surgical operation necessary to attract the attention of readers who were increasingly distracted by other media developments in film, radio, and television.

Journalism then entered a more sophisticated stage. While still imbued with the clarity of language, it was further enriched by what was called in-depth reporting, which later developed into an investigative style, with an attitude toward the subject that crossed the line into the realm of interpretative journalism. While as old as literature itself, this **New Journalism** shattered the myth of the separation between essay and journalism.

These freestyle ruptures with the past were accompanied in the American tradition and its imitators in Europe and Latin America by two other branches of journalism. The first was made up of editorials and commentaries in the form of columns, which were fully recognized as members of the family. The second played the role of fillers, different forms of features and entertainment pieces, comics, and games, which were relegated to the supplement pages or Sunday magazines. While the editorial kept alive the flame of authoritarian, ideological journalism, the columns experienced the slow surge of a more sober, economical, specialized style practiced by pundits who stuck to the norms and limitations of their expected topics.

However, in other cultural traditions, especially in Southern Europe and Latin America, the more anarchical writers, encouraged by a freer style and anchored to the literary and political essay, enriched journalism with subgenres such as **reportage** and the Spanish *crónica*. In both cases, the pressures of limited space and the competition resulting from other media forms began to erode the freedom previously enjoyed.

Finally, this experimentation in journalism exercised an influence on the textual revolution that took place all over the world. In the past, the insertion of poetic language and dialogue had an impact on other forms of literature, such as the novel and the essay. In more recent times, techniques such as the lead-in, the economy of words, and the experience of the New Journalism have had an impact not only on the essays produced by writers, but also on their own narrative fiction.

JOAQUÍN ROY

Anthologies

The Best of the Rest: Non-Syndicated Newspaper Columnists Select Their Best Work, edited by Sam G. Riley, Westport, Connecticut: Greenwood Press, 1993

The Literary Journalists, edited by Norman Sims, New York: Ballantine, 1984

Further Reading

Botts, Jack, *The Language of News: A Journalist's Pocket Reference*, Ames: Iowa State University Press, 1994

Cray, Ed, *American Datelines*, New York: Facts on File, 1990

Roy, Joaquín, "Periodismo y ensayo," *El Ensayo Hispánico* (1984): 63–80

Sims, Norman, editor, *Literary Journalism in the Twentieth Century*, New York: Oxford University Press, 1990

Warren, Carl Nelson, *Modern News Reporting*, New York: Harper, 1951

Weber, Ronald, *Hemingway's Art of Non-Fiction*, New York: St. Martin's Press, 1990

Jovellanos, Gaspar Melchor de

Spanish, 1744–1811

In Gaspar Melchor de Jovellanos' time, the word *ensayo* did not yet denote a literary genre; but among Jovellanos' extant works are dozens, on a great range of subjects, in essayistic genres, primarily reports, addresses, **treatises**, and **letters**, frequently products of the author's activities as magistrate or as member of one of the quasi-public learned societies. Some occupy a few pages, while a handful are of book length.

Many of these essays concern economic problems, including trade, transportation, industry, labor, and, more generally, economic development. Jovellanos' most famous work (and his only essay available in English), is the book-length *Informe ... en el expediente de ley agraria* (1795; *Memoir on the Advancement of Agriculture and on Agrarian Laws*), which analyzes obstacles to agricultural development: the physical (inadequate roads, canals, etc.), the intellectual (ignorance of science and technology), and the legal, the most serious and most interesting – laws restricting the free play of self-interest and concentrating land ownership in a few great families and the Church. In describing and attacking these laws, Jovellanos makes a forceful argument for economic liberty.

Another major work, the *Memoria en defensa de la Junta Central* (1811; Defense of the Central Committee), deals with the constitutional crisis brought about by the Spanish insurrection against the Bonapartes. In it Jovellanos attempts to balance his monarchical sentiments with his love of political liberty.

Several essays, including the unfinished book-length *Memoria sobre educación pública* (wr. 1802; Treatise on public education), express Jovellanos' belief that education is the source of individual and national prosperity and must be universal and modern, stressing natural sciences and modern languages, including the students' native language – in other words, something quite different from the traditional, classically-oriented education Jovellanos had himself received.

Also of book length are the complex of descriptive and **historical essays** on the major buildings of Palma de Mallorca and the surrounding countryside (wr. c. 1805–08), and the *Memoria para el arreglo de la policía de los espectáculos y diversiones públicas, y sobre su origen en España* (wr. 1790, pub. 1812; Essay on reform of the policy on spectacles and public entertainments, and on their origin in Spain), interesting for Spanish social history and for its enlightened policy proposals.

Jovellanos' letters to Antonio Ponz (wr. 1789), intended for publication, study the geography, agriculture, arts, and customs of his native Asturias. His *Elogio de Carlos III* (1789; Eulogy of Charles III) reveals how a leading partisan of the Enlightenment viewed Spanish history.

Many of Jovellanos' essays were published posthumously by admirers and scholars; but others were printed in his lifetime by the organization that received them, and Jovellanos himself published the *Memoria en defensa de la Junta Central*, his self-defense before public opinion. The essays often aim at two publics: the immediate addressee (government, an academy or economic society, those attending a ceremony), and, for the principal writings, a potential further readership which, limited by illiteracy and poverty, consisted chiefly of men of the middle and upper classes and of the clergy, and, within these groups, of the enlightened elite that exercised political power. Many of Jovellanos' essays are thus attempts to influence the thinking and, ultimately, the policies of the leaders of state and society. In some works Jovellanos speaks for himself; in others the formal speaking subject is the body in whose name he addresses a superior entity.

Jovellanos writes a pure and elegant prose, managing to treat even specialized and technical subjects in clear and precise language accessible to an educated public, without archaisms, neologisms, or technical jargon. His skilled effort produces an appearance of effortlessness, and the attentive reader easily discerns the neat and sometimes explicit order of development. This generally rational expository style does not exclude irony, pathos, outbursts of indignation at injustice, and animated, sometimes lyrical evocations of a heroic past or an idyllic future; but whatever his tone, Jovellanos' language is a means to the end of communication, never an end in itself.

Jovellanos' essays frequently reflect the breadth of his interests and information and his ability to view problems in several dimensions: historical, political, legal, ethical, aesthetic, and simply human. Thus the *Memoir on the Advancement of Agriculture*, the *Espectáculos y diversiones públicas*, and a report on a proposed welfare fund for the nobility (wr. 1784) explain historical background and consider the social, political, and moral consequences of reform; the descriptions of the architecture of Palma lead to imaginative re-creations of medieval scenes.

Although Jovellanos often touches on theoretical questions, he generally does so tangentially: as a rule, his essays are not disinterested theoretical speculations, but responses to specific problems or circumstances. Sharing a practical purpose in the service of the ideals of the Enlightenment, they reflect their author's faith in the possibility of progress – material, intellectual, and moral – through freedom and reason.

Though Jovellanos was a poet and dramatist, his literary reputation and his broader significance for his contemporaries and posterity rest largely on the high quality of his prose and the clarity of his thought on topics hotly debated in modern Spain: the birth of constitutional government, of economic liberalism, and of modern capitalism; the status of the Catholic Church; the nature and control of education. For nearly two centuries, Spaniards of widely divergent political persuasions have attempted to use Jovellanos' essays to support their causes. These efforts have sometimes led to anachronistic interpretations of a writer best understood as embodying the complex movement of the Enlightenment.

JOHN H. R. POLT

Biography

Baltasar Gaspar Melchor María de Jovellanos. Born 5 January 1744 in Gijón. Studied canon law at the University of Ávila, licence, 1763, and the College of San Ildefonso, University of Alcalá, degree, 1764. Appointed criminal magistrate, Seville, 1768, to the Seville magistrature, 1774, to the magistrature of Madrid, 1778–80, and to the Council of Military Orders, from 1780. Elected to the Royal Spanish Academy, 1783. Banished to Asturias for defending a friend accused of corruption, 1790–97, and commissioned to study roads and mines. Founder, Royal Asturian Institute, 1794. Minister of justice, 1797–98. Exiled again to Asturias and imprisoned on Majorca, 1801–08. Joined the Central Committee, the ruling council of the Spanish provisional government, traveling with it to Seville and Cádiz, 1808–10. Died (of pneumonia) in Puerto de Vega, Asturias, 27 November 1811.

Selected Writings

Essays and Related Prose
Elogio de Carlos III, 1789
Informe . . . en el expediente de ley agraria, 1795; as *Memoir on the Advancement of Agriculture and on Agrarian Laws*, translated anonymously, in *A View of Spain*, vol. 4, by Alexandre de Laborde, 1809: 111–315
Memoria en defensa de la Junta Central, 1811; edited by José Miguel Caso González, 1992
Memoria para el arreglo de la policía de los espectáculos y diversiones públicas, y sobre su origen en España, 1812
Carta histórico-artística sobre el edificio de la Lonja de Mallorca, 1812
Memorias históricas sobre el Castillo de Bellver en la isla de Mallorca, 1813
Cartas del viaje de Asturias (Cartas a Ponz), edited by José Miguel Caso González, 1981

Other writings: poetry, plays, diaries, and correspondence.

Collected works editions: *Colección de varias obras en prosa y verso*, edited by Ramón María Cañedo, 7 vols., 1830–32; *Obras publicadas e inéditas*, edited by Cándido Nocedal and Miguel Artola, 5 vols., 1858–1956; *Obras completas*, edited by José Miguel Caso González, 6 vols., 1984–94 (in progress).

Bibliographies
Rick, Lilian L., *Bibliografía crítica de Jovellanos (1901–1976)*, Oviedo: University of Oviedo, 1977
Somoza de Montsoriú, Julio, *Inventario de un jovellanista*, Madrid: Sucesores de Rivadeneyra, 1901

Further Reading
Caso González, José Miguel, *Vida y obra de Jovellanos*, Gijón: Caja de Asturias and El Comercio, 2 vols., 1993
Ceán Bermúdez, Juan Agustín, *Memorias para la vida del Excmo. Señor D. Gaspar Melchor de Jovellanos, y noticias analíticas de sus obras*, Madrid: Fuentenebro, 1814
Del Río, Ángel, "Jovellanos," in *Historia general de las literaturas hispánicas*, vol. 4, pt. 1, edited by Guillermo Díaz-Plaja, Barcelona: Barna, 1956
Galino Carrillo, María Ángeles, *Tres hombres y un problema: Feijóo, Sarmiento y Jovellanos ante la educación moderna*, Madrid: CSIC, 1953
Helman, Edith, *Trasmundo de Goya*, Madrid: Revista de Occidente, 1963
Ilie, Paul, "Picturesque Beauty in Spain and England: Aesthetic Rapports Between Jovellanos and Gilpin," *Journal of Aesthetics and Art Criticism* 19 (1960): 167–74
Polt, John H. R., *Jovellanos and His English Sources: Economic, Philosophical, and Political Writings*, Philadelphia: Transactions of the American Philosophical Society, 1964
Polt, John H. R., "Jovellanos y la educación," in *El P. Feijoo y su siglo*, Oviedo: Cuadernos de la Cátedra Feijoo, 1966: 315–38
Polt, John H. R., *Gaspar Melchor de Jovellanos*, New York: Twayne, 1971
Varela, Javier, *Jovellanos*, Madrid: Alianza, 1988

Jünger, Ernst

German, 1895–

Severe rigidity and anti-Modernism are characteristics often attributed to Ernst Jünger's writing (by friends and foes alike, indeed sometimes by the author himself). However, the opposite is true: few writers of our century have shown an equal passion for understanding modernity and exploring its inner workings. At the same time, Jünger's writing is permeated by the spirit of the essay, with its continuous revisions and open options. Little of his enormous body of work (written over no less than 80 years) can escape the label of essay, even though much of it appeared under the form of the novel, short story, or diary.

Throughout his career Jünger's favorite vehicle has remained the collection of fragments in which short narrative episodes, **aphorisms** (or longer reflexions), reproductions of dreams, philosophical comments, presentations of readings, natural descriptions, and other forms elbow one another and constitute a kind of subtle counterpoint. Jünger's preferred position has most often been that of the cool and dispassionate outsider, always capable of describing objectively things small and large, as well as placing the ideal values of the spirit above the incidents of sociohistorical process.

To maintain this stance Jünger resorted to two main strategies. The first was to place in his hierarchy of values attention, precision, and the relentless gaze above other values such as compassion or outrage. The second was to give preferential treatment to the *symptom* as a central part of existence; several times in his works Jünger argues that it is only through a thorough and accurate grasp of the surface that we can reach the core of any phenomenon. He also sometimes describes this attention to surface and symptoms as the "stereoscopic gaze." To some extent this brings Jünger close to his contemporaries **Theodor W. Adorno**, and particularly **Walter Benjamin**, despite vast ideological differences.

Jünger liked to make himself the object of observation. He did so in war diaries when he tried to gain self-detachment and note human reactions under circumstances of extreme violence and danger, as well as during his extensive experiments with a variety of hallucinogenic drugs, chemical as well as natural. Even more frequent was his habit of jotting down and describing in great detail his oneiric experiences. In this sense Jünger's passion for entomological (and sometimes botanical) pursuits is easy to understand. The orderly and well-structured world of insects and other small beings can be grasped in both its individuality and its wholeness, and treated with benevolent neutrality.

Jünger ran into intense hostility when he tried to apply the same kind of noncommittal attention to the historical and social world: he was accused of coldness and inhuman indifference, if not of encouraging violence and suffering. This is vastly exaggerated. It is more apposite to say that Jünger was trying to place human history inside the framework of natural and cosmic history – a tradition that goes back to the 17th and 18th centuries. He described himself not as an anarchist, but as an "anarch," one who strives to preserve by all means his autonomy of thought and his independence in the face of historical trends and the consensus of majorities.

Jünger's essay style was schooled on Lichtenberg, **Schopenhauer**, and **Nietzsche**, but even more on the tradition of the French 17th- and 18th-century "moralistes." He prefers cutting, oracular statements, surprising metaphorical associations, and indulging in breviloquence: his essays seem to progress by successively stepping from stone to stone in a stream, avoiding explanation and continuity. Readers are expected to ponder and unravel the meanings and connotations of an enigmatic or metaphorical laconic statement, encouraged by Jünger's limpid and exact use of language, glittering in carefully devised multiple facets.

Jünger uses the essay in a highly personal way. For him it is the best vehicle for making judgments on the ways of the world, as well as a means of preserving the dignity of personal human independence in the face of sweeping and all-encompassing statistical tides. The essay is seen as a way of circling around a timeless pattern of reality, and is thus also a channel of communication with transcendence. In an environment that appears post-religious or uncertain about the divine, the essay can play with the mythical at the interface of immanence and transcendence without committing itself to any specific religious structure. Similarly, the orders of tradition and the centrifugal impulses of the individual seem to find a chance for cohabitation primarily in the essay. It is owing to these thoughtful propositions, rather than by any ideological inclination, that Jünger came to appeal to his diverse readership.

VIRGIL NEMOIANU

Biography

Born 29 March 1895 in Heidelberg. Grew up in Hannover, where he studied at school, 1901–13. Joined the French Foreign Legion briefly, 1913. Volunteer with the German army during World War I, serving on the Western Front, 1914–18: granted the Pour le Mérite order for bravery, September 1918. Officer in the Reichswehr, 1919–23. Studied biology in Leipzig and Naples, 1923–26, and eventually became a well-known entomologist: a number of inspect species bear his name. Married Gretha von Jeinsen, 1925 (died, 1960): two sons (one died). Contributor to radical right-wing journals, including *Standarte* (Standard), *Arminius*, *Widerstand* (Resistance), *Die Kommenden* (Future generations), and *Der Vormarsch* (The advance), 1925–31; freelance writer, from 1927. Lived in Berlin, from 1927, Goslar, 1933–36, Überlingen, 1936–39, Kirchhorst, 1939–48, Ravensburg, 1948–50, and Wiflingen, from 1950. Turned down offer to head the Nazi Writers' Union, 1933. Captain during World War II: dishonorably discharged for participation in anti-Nazi activities, 1944. Banned from publishing his work, 1945–49. Traveled extensively in the 1950s and 1960s. Coeditor, *Antaios* journal, 1959–71. Married Liselotte Lohrer, 1962. Awards: several, including the Immermann Prize, 1964; Humboldt Society Gold Medal, 1981; Goethe Prize, 1982; honorary degree from the University of Bilbao. Great Order of Merit (Federal Republic of Germany), 1959.

Selected Writings

Essays and Related Prose

Der Kampf als inneres Erlebnis, 1922; revised edition, 1926
Das abenteuerliche Herz: Aufzeichnungen bei Tag und Nacht, 1929; revised edition, 1938
Der Arbeiter: Herrschaft und Gestalt, 1932
Blätter und Steine, 1934
Geheimnisse der Sprache: Zwei Essays, 1934
Der Friede, 1945; as *The Peace*, translated by Stuart O. Hood, 1948
Über die Linie, 1950
Der Waldgang, 1951
Der gordische Knoten, 1953
Das Sanduhrbuch, 1954
An der Zeitmauer, 1959
Der Weltstaat: Organismus und Organisation, 1960
Sgraffiti, 1960
Typus; Name; Gestalt, 1963
Grenzgänge, 1966
Subtile Jagden, 1967
Ad Hoc, 1970
Annäherungen: Drogen und Rausch, 1970
Sinn und Bedeutung: Ein Figurenspiel, 1971
Zahlen und Götter; Philemon und Baucis: Zwei Essays, 1974
Flugträume (selections), 1983
Autor und Autorschaft, 1984
Die Schere, 1990

Other writings: several novels and long short stories (including *Das Wäldchen 125* [*Copse 125*], 1925; *Afrikanische Spiele*, 1936; *Auf den Marmorklippen* [*On the Marble Cliffs*], 1939 (published unofficially); *Heliopolis*, 1949; *Gläserne Bienen* [*The Glass Bees*], 1957; *Die Zwille*, 1973; *Eumeswil*, 1977; *Aladins Problem* [*Aladdin's Problem*], 1983; *Eine gefährliche Begegnung*, 1985), diaries, and works on politics, travel, and scientific inquiries.

Collected works editions: *Werke*, 10 vols., 1960–65; *Sämtliche Werke*, 18 vols., 1978–83.

Bibliographies

Coudres, Hans Peter des, and Horst Mühleisen, *Bibliographie der Werke Ernst Jüngers*, Stuttgart: Klett, 1970; revised edition, 1985
Paetel, Karl O., *Ernst Jünger: Eine Bibliographie*, Stuttgart: Klett, 1953

Further Reading

Bohrer, Karl-Heinz, *Die Ästhetik des Schreckens*, Munich and Vienna: Hanser, 1978
Bullock, Marcus Paul, *The Violent Eye: Ernst Jünger's Visions and Revisions on the European Right*, Detroit: Wayne State University Press, 1992
Kaempfer, Wolfgang, *Ernst Jünger*, Stuttgart: Metzler, 1981
Koslowski, Peter, *Der Mythos der Moderne: Die dichterische Philosophie Ernst Jüngers*, Munich: Fink, 1991
Loose, Gerhard, *Ernst Jünger*, New York: Twayne, 1974
Meyer, Martin, *Ernst Jünger*, Munich: Hanser, 1990
Schwarz, Hans Peter, *Der konservative Anarchist: Politik und Zeitkritik Ernst Jüngers*, Freiburg: Herder, 1962

K

Kamo no Chōmei

Japanese, 1155?–1216

As one of the three great essayists in the tradition of classical Japanese literature, Kamo no Chōmei occupies a median in style, sensibility, and time between the other two exemplars of the *zuihitsu* genre – the *Makura no sōshi* (*Pillow Book*) of **Sei Shōnagon** and the *Tsurezuregusa* (*Essays in Idleness*) of **Kenkō**. In sentiment lying somewhere between the aristocratic delicacy of the former and the rapid delight in life found in the latter, the *Hōjōki* (1212; *An Account of My Hut*) is both simple and complex, a unique mingling of style and wit in the tradition of Japanese prose. Yet during his lifetime Chōmei held greater renown for two other works that reflect not only his wide literary skill and interest, but the two primary influences on his prose – classical poetry and a deep Buddhist piety – which permeate the whole of his principal and most prized work.

Mumyōshō (1210?; A treatise with no name) is a subtle and joyous work, representing the culmination of Chōmei's many years spent among the poetic circles of the Imperial Court. Both a study of late Heian poetics and a personal – even chatty – recollection of personalities, places, and poem-banquets, this earlier work is in many respects a look backwards to the bright, elegant world of Shōnagon and the classical era of Japanese prose. Chōmei's skill as a poet is quite obvious – although clearly not the equal of his contemporaries Teika and Shunzei; his love of old diction and fresh images is evident in his surviving poems, and it is this mingling of old and new that becomes most manifest in the prose of *An Account of My Hut*. Another work written in parallel with *An Account of My Hut*, the *Hosshinshū* (1214?; Collected tales of awakened faith), an unorthodox collection of Buddhist tales of religious enlightenment, is pervaded with Chōmei's own reflections of his faith. While the work should not be considered a standard Japanese essay as such, nor even typical of the compilations of his day, the masterful touches of the author are unmistakable: quick, almost fluid phrasing, a keen eye for details interior and exterior, and a passionate resignation lurking behind every sentence.

Chōmei's reputation as an essayist, however, is due to the high substance and style of *An Account of My Hut*, a collocation best expressed in the single word *mujō* (impermanence). Just as the famous opening line bursts into syntactic flow – "The river's flow never ends, its waters never stay the same; bubbles appear and vanish, floating among the pools, never resting: just so our world of men and their dwellings" – the supple strength of his words serves as a wellspring for the entire work, a prolonged **meditation** on the ceaseless flux between the human and natural worlds. Writing in seclusion, in a hermit's small grass hut far from the political and aristocratic intrigues of the capital, Chōmei strives for a distinct degree of separation from the "floating world" of the court; his wariness at the uncertainty of human affairs is echoed in the loose, almost unconnected structure of the work and the pessimistic tone of his observations. In the miniature world of his hermitage, true pleasure emerges only from observation of the transience of nature or from the joys of aesthetic creation: playing at his harp or pondering over a line of verse. This disdain for the practical aspects of life – and the essay – is central to Chōmei's world; neither art, word, nor nature is for the sake of instruction or the transmission of absolute truth. The phrased rapids of *An Account of My Hut* wander through relative mountains and valleys of human experience, only to vanish into an endless, all-encompassing ocean of silence and shadow. His view of human fate is not mere pessimism: he seeks the tranquil promise of the contemplative life and the slow pursuit of artistic and spiritual perfection. At the essay's end, Chōmei sets aside his brush – but only for a moment, for his verbal peregrinations, fixed in ink, have made him into an immortal member of the Japanese canon.

Apart from the poetic currents of his day, there are two distinct influences on Chōmei's work: the prose of his Japanese predecessor Sei Shōnagon, and the semi-versified essays of the Chinese *fu* genre. The former, writing more than 200 years before Chōmei, endows him in no small part with her gift for wry observation and short, elegant phrases; his debt becomes particularly clear in his austere, uncluttered language, especially when compared with his contemporaries. From the Chinese literati such as **Su Shi** he absorbs both the loose structures and the poetic fancies of the *fu*, a literary form prone to limpid language and evanescent sensations. With these two disparate traditions of the essay before him, Chōmei fuses them to create a new style for the Japanese essayist: personal yet detached, intimate in emotion yet oblique in thought. His legacy to the essayists that follow is immense; Kenkō, among many others, is unimaginable without the lasting force of Chōmei's observations of the transient world made permanent in a liquid tangle of tears and ink.

JOHN PAVEL KEHLEN

443

Biography

Born in 1155? Brought up in Kyoto; had a classical education.
Played the lute and wrote poetry for the court; involved with poetry
circles connected to the Emperor Go-Toba (who held the throne,
1183–98); invited to be a Fellow of the Bureau of Poetry, 1201.
Took Buddhist orders and retired from court to a hermitage on Mt.
Ohara, near Kyoto; later moved to Mt. Hino, where he lived in his
"ten-foot square hut." Died in 1216.

Selected Writings

Essays and Related Prose

Hōjōki, edited by Miki Sumito, 1976, and Satake Akihiro and
  Kubota Jun, 1989; as *Notes from a Ten Feet Square Hut*,
  translated by F. Victor Dickins, 1907; as *The Ten Foot Square
  Hut*, translated by A. L. Sadler, 1928; as *The Hō-jō-ki: Private
  Papers of Kamo-no-Chōmei, of the Ten Foot Square Hut*,
  translated by Itakura Junji, 1935; as *An Account of My Hut*,
  translated by Donald Keene, in *Anthology of Japanese Literature:
  From the Earliest Era to the Mid-Nineteenth Century*, 1955; as
  Notebook of a Ten Square Rush-Mat Sized World, translated by
  Thomas Rowe and Anthony Kerrigan, 1979; as *Hōjōki, Visions
  of a Torn World*, translated by Moriguchi Yasuhiko and David
  Jenkins, 1996
Hosshinshū, edited by Miki Sumito, 1976; as *The Hosshinshū*,
  partially translated by Marian Ury (dissertation), 1965
Mumyōshō, edited by Yanase Kazuo, 1980, and Takahashi
  Kazuhiko, 1987

Other writings: poetry.

Collected works edition: *Kamo no Chōmei zenshu*, edited by Yanase
Kazuo, 2 vols., 1940.

Further Reading

Hare, Thomas Blenman, "Reading Kamo no Chōmei," *Harvard
  Journal of Asiatic Studies* 49 (June 1989): 173–228
Katō, H., "The Mumyōshō of Kamo no Chōmei and Its Significance
  in Japanese Literature," *Monumenta Nipponica* 23, nos. 3–4
  (1968): 321–430
LaFleur, William R., "Inns and Hermitages: The Structure of
  Impermanence," in his *The Karma of Words: Buddhism and the
  Literary Arts in Medieval Japan*, Princeton, New Jersey: Princeton
  University Press, 1983: 60–79

Kant, Immanuel

German, 1724–1804

Immanuel Kant's essays played a decisive role in defining the
philosophical and political meaning of "enlightenment." Indeed
Kant developed the **critical-philosophical essay** as the very site
where the process of "enlightenment" occurs. Prior to the
Kritik der reinen Vernunft (1781; *Critique of Pure Reason*) –
i.e. in his "pre-critical" period – Kant was known in Germany
primarily for his writings on natural science, metaphysics,
and psychology. His early essays – which he frequently titled
Versuch ("essay," "attempt," "experiment") – examine questions of both physics and metaphysics with one purpose: the
attempt to redefine the method and presumptions of theoretical science. Kant strove to revolutionize philosophy the way
Newton had revolutionized natural science. In the brevity and
openness of the essay form he found a literary means to challenge the dogmatic method and stale language of scholasticism.

Whether discussing proofs of God, mathematical negation,
or mental derangement, Kant's early essays aim less at exhaustive demonstration than at providing "just small beginnings,
which is how it goes if one wants to open up new perspectives
– that may, however, bring about important consequences."
Although their scholarly nature limits his audience primarily
to his peers, Kant's essays address themselves to readers
who have "a universal perspective," and he never hesitates to
deride "scholarly nonsense" when it impedes free philosophical inquiry (*Versuch, den Begriff der negativen Grössen in die
Weltweisheit einzuführen* [1763; "Attempt to Introduce the
Concept of Negative Magnitudes into Philosophy"]). Kant's
popular literary aspirations are also evident when he hopes his
results will prove "just as charming as they are instructive"
(*Beobachtungen über das Gefühl des Schönen und Erhabenen*
[1764; *Observations on the Feeling of the Beautiful and the
Sublime*]).

Stylistically the pre-critical essays take their cue not only
from the scholastic precision of Leibniz and Wolff but also
from **Montaigne**'s erudite versatility and **Rousseau**'s incisive
moral fervor. Kant cautions against the seductive style of
French authors but admires the "Swiss" Rousseau. Likewise
he draws upon the ironic wit of English writers – **Swift**, Sterne,
and Samuel Butler – not as an end in itself but as a means of
provoking understanding. Irony thus takes on an epistemological function. In the stylistically most accomplished and
theoretically most daring essay of this period, *Träume eines
Geistersehers, erläutert durch Träume der Metaphysik* (1766;
*Dreams of a Spirit-Seer, Elucidated Through Dreams of
Metaphysics*), Kant explores the related subjects of spiritualism
and metaphysics with an irony so pervasive that it turns on
the essay itself, and he predicts of his reader: "the bulk of it
he will not understand, parts of it he will not believe, and as
for the rest – he will dismiss it with scornful laughter." Yet
this ironic laughter, for Kant, is the beginning of critical
thinking.

Kant uses the essay form to experiment with literary-philosophical modes of reflection that question the theoretical
presuppositions of knowledge itself. This method comes to
fruition in the revolutionary achievement of the first *Critique*
(1781). Despite its seemingly monolithic, "architectonic" structure, the work can be read in terms of essayistic style: but now
it is the process of thinking itself that must be understood –
in other words "criticized" – as a series of "attempts" to transcend its own limitations. When knowledge can be grounded
only through such a self-critical articulation of its possibility,
the medium of thinking essentially becomes this form of
"critique." As the site where the transcendental turn is first
inscribed as such, the essay is thus transformed into the
privileged vehicle for Kant's "transcendental style" (Willi
Goetschel, 1994).

The essays of Kant's "critical" period – published in the
1780s and 1790s – combine the self-conscious irony of his
early writing with the tools of rational self-criticism developed
in the *Critiques*. In their application of a critical method
grounded in "pure" reason these essays achieve a tone of
profound self-assurance and even idealistic conviction. At times
this also leads to a presumptive sort of rigor that can be
extremely demanding to the reader unfamiliar with the
Critiques. Thus while **Schopenhauer** praises Kant's "brilliant

dryness," **Nietzsche** is unforgiving of his "bulky pedantry" – an opinion that has endured, perhaps unfairly, into the present.

Even after developing the critical method Kant continues to exploit the formal possibilities of the essay as a means of examining implications that lead beyond scientific truth. His titles indicate genre experiments: a useful but unprovable "idea" of universal history whose goal is a "cosmopolitan" republic; a "conjectural" interpretation of Genesis as an allegory of rational freedom; and a "sketch" of the "articles" of right that could lead to "perpetual peace." His unflagging concern in these essays is the rationality of moral judgment and the teleological necessity of human freedom in history. The inherently provisional, inventive quality of essayistic expression for Kant mirrors the dialectical potential of the "idea" itself: as a mode of thinking – and writing – that only posits knowledge theoretically insofar as it enacts it practically.

Kant's mature essays seek to establish and delimit a public sphere of free discourse, an intellectual "culture" that will contribute inevitably to the progress of enlightenment. The concept of public dialogue becomes the intrinsic principle in his understanding of the essay form. Thus in pieces like "Was ist Aufklärung?" (1784; "What Is Enlightenment?") and "Was heisst: Sich im Denken orientieren?" (1786; "What Does It Mean: To Orient One's Self in Thinking?"), Kant does not simply provide answers. Rather, these essays are interventions that seek to formulate the very possibility of a discourse in which such questions can occur: "But how much and how accurately would we *think* if we did not think, so to speak, in community with others to whom we *communicate* our thoughts and who communicate their thoughts to us!" For Kant, the essay is not merely a privileged forum for philosophical reflection on questions of political and moral progress; it is, in fact, the objective form of that progress.

ERIC SCHWAB

Biography

Born 22 April 1724 in Königsberg. Studied at the Collegium Fredericianum for eight years; physics and mathematics at the University of Königsberg, 1740–47. Private tutor; adjunct assistant professor, from 1755, and chair of logic and philosophy, from 1770, University of Königsberg. Also worked as assistant librarian in the royal castle. Lived alone and kept to a strict routine, which included an hour-long daily walk after lunch. Awards: Royal Academy of Science (Berlin) Award, 1754. Died in Königsberg, 12 February 1804.

Selected Writings

Essays and Related Prose
Gedanken von der wahren Schätzung der lebendigen Kräfte und Beurtheilung der Beweise, deren sich Leibnitz und andere Mechaniker in dieser Streitsache bedient haben, nebst einigen vorhergehenden Betrachtungen, welche die Kraft der Körper überhaupt betreffen, 1747
Allgemeine Naturgeschichte und Theorie des Himmels, oder Versuch von der Verfassung und dem mechanischen Ursprunge des ganzen Weltgebäudes, nach Newton'schen Grundsätzen abgehandelt, 1755; as *Universal Natural History and Theory of the Heavens*, translated by William Hastie, 1969, and Stanley L. Jaki, 1981
Principiorum primorum cognitionis metaphysicae nova delucidatio, 1755; as "A New Exposition of the First Principles of Metaphysical Knowledge," translated by John A. Reuscher, in *Latin Writings*, edited by Lewis White Beck, 1986

Versuch einiger Betrachtungen über den Optimismus, 1759
Gedanken bei dem frühzeitigen Ableben des Herrn Johann Friedrich von Funck, in einem Sendschreiben an seine Mutter, 1760
Die falsche Spitzfindigkeit der vier syllogistischen Figuren erwiesen, 1762; as "On the Mistaken Subtlety of the Four Syllogistic Figures," translated by Thomas K. Abbott, in his *Kant's Introduction to Logic*, 1885
Der einzig mögliche Beweisgrund zu einer Demonstration des Daseins Gottes, 1762; as *The Only Possible Ground for a Demonstration of the Existence of God*, translated by G. B. Kerferd and D. W. Walford, 1968
Versuch, den Begriff der negativen Grössen in die Weltweisheit einzuführen, 1763
Beobachtungen über das Gefühl des Schönen und Erhabenen, 1764; as *Observations on the Feeling of the Beautiful and the Sublime*, translated by John T. Goldthwait, 1960
Träume eines Geistersehers, erläutert durch Träume der Metaphysik, 1766; as *Dreams of a Spirit-Seer, Elucidated Through Dreams of Metaphysics*, translated by Emanuel P. Goerwitz, 1900
De mundi sensibilis atque intelligibilis forma et principiis, 1770; as "On the Form and Principles of the Sensible and the Intelligible World," translated by John Handyside, revised by Lewis White Beck, in *Latin Writings*, 1986
Kritik der reinen Vernunft, 1781; revised edition, 1787; as *Critique of Pure Reason*, translated by J. M. D. Meiklejohn, 1855, and Norman Kemp Smith, 1929
Prolegomena zu einer jeden künftigen Metaphysik, die als Wissenschaft wird auftreten können, 1783; as *Prolegomena to Every Future Metaphysic*, translated by John Richardson, 1819; as *Prolegomena to Any Future Metaphysic*, translated by Lewis White Beck, 1950; as *Prolegomena to Any Future Metaphysics That Will Be Able to Present Itself as a Science*, translated by P. G. Lucas, 1953
Grundlegung zur Metaphysik der Sitten, 1785; revised edition, 1786; as *The Moral Law*, and as *Groundwork of the Metaphysic of Morals*, translated by H. J. Paton, 1948
Metaphysische Anfangsgründe der Naturwissenschaft, 1786; as *Metaphysical Foundations of Natural Science*, translated by James Ellington, 1970
Kritik der praktischen Vernunft, 1788; as *Critique of Practical Reason*, translated by Lewis White Beck, in *Critique of Practical Reason and Other Writings in Moral Philosophy*, 1949
Kritik der Urteilskraft, 1790; as *Critique of Judgement*, translated by John Henry Bernard, 1892; revised edition, 1914; as *Critique of Aesthetic Judgement*, translated by James C. Meredith, 1911, and *Critique of Teleological Judgement*, 1928, and together as *Critique of Judgement*, 1957; as *Critique of Judgment*, translated by Werner S. Pluhar, 1987
Die Religion innerhalb der Grenzen der blossen Vernunft, 1793; as *Religion Within the Limits of Reason Alone*, translated by Theodore M. Greene and Hoyt H. Hudson, 1934; revised edition by John R. Silber, 1960
Zum ewigen Frieden: Ein philosophischer Entwurf, 1795; enlarged edition, 1796; as *Perpetual Peace*, translated by Lewis White Beck, 1957
Die Metaphysik der Sitten, 2 vols., 1797; part of vol. 1 as *The Metaphysical Elements of Justice*, translated by J. Ladd, 1965; vol. 2 as *The Doctrine of Virtue*, translated by M. J. Gregor, 1964, and as *The Metaphysical Principles of Virtue*, translated by J. Ellington, 1964
Der Streit der Fakultäten in drey Abschnitten, 1798; part as "The Contest of the Faculties," translated by H. B. Nisbet, in *Political Writings*, 1970
Anthropologie in pragmatischer Hinsicht, 1798; as *Anthropology from a Pragmatic Point of View*, translated by M. J. Gregor, 1974
Essays and Treatises on Moral, Political, and Various Philosophical Subjects, translated by John Richardson, 2 vols., 1798; reprinted, 1993

Logik: Ein Handbuch zu Vorlesungen, edited by G. B. Jäsche, 1800; as *Kant's Logic*, translated by R. S. Hartman and W. Schwartz, 1974

Critique of Practical Reason and Other Writings in Moral Philosophy, translated by Lewis White Beck, 1949

Kant on History, translated by Lewis White Beck, 1963

Political Writings, edited by Hans Reiss, translated by H. B. Nisbet, 1970

Was ist Aufklärung? Aufsätze zur Geschichte und Philosophie, edited by Jürgen Zehbe, 1975

Perpetual Peace, and Other Essays on Politics, History, and Morals, translated by Ted Humphrey, 1983

Latin Writings (various translators), edited by Lewis White Beck, 1986

Raising the Tone in Philosophy: Late Essays by Immanuel Kant, Transformative Critique by Jacques Derrida, edited and translated by Peter Fenves, 1993

Collected works editions: *Gesammelte Schriften* (Prussian Academy of Sciences Edition), 23 vols., 1902–55; *The Cambridge Edition of the Works*, general editors Paul Guyer and Allen W. Wood, 1992– (in progress; 14 vols. projected).

Bibliographies

Adickes, Erich, *German Kantian Bibliography*, Würzburg: Liebing, 1967 (original edition, 1896)

Gabel, Gernot U., *Immanuel Kant: Eine Bibliographie der Dissertationen aus den deutschsprachigen Ländern, 1900–1975*, Hamburg: Gemini, 1980

Walker, Ralph C. S., *A Selective Bibliography on Kant*, Oxford: Oxford University Sub-Faculty of Philosophy, 2nd edition, 1978 (original edition, 1975)

Further Reading

Cassirer, Ernst, *Rousseau, Kant, Goethe*, Princeton, New Jersey: Princeton University Press, 1970 (original edition, 1945)

Galay, Jean-Louis, *Philosophie et invention textuelle: Essai sur la poétique d'un texte kantien*, Paris: Klincksieck, 1977

Goetschel, Willi, *Constituting Critique: Kant's Writing as Critical Praxis*, Durham, North Carolina: Duke University Press, 1994

McCarthy, John A., "The Philosopher as Essayist: Leibniz and Kant," in *The Philosopher as Writer: The Eighteenth Century*, edited by Robert Ginsberg, Selinsgrove, Pennsylvania: Susquehanna University Press, 1987: 48–74

Reiss, Hans, Introduction and Postscript to *Political Writings* by Kant, edited by Reiss, Cambridge: Cambridge University Press, 1991 (original edition, 1970)

Kenkō

Japanese, c. 1283–c. 1352

Asked to identify the foremost essay in the Japanese tradition, most educated Japanese are likely to recite the opening line of *Tsurezuregusa* (wr. c. 1319 to as late as 1350; *Essays in Idleness*). This work by Kenkō, a recluse and poet, has been exploited by pedagogues since the late 16th century. The subject of diverse commentaries thereafter, it was, in the 17th century, first punctuated and divided into a **preface** and 243 sections, some as short as one sentence, the longest no more than a half dozen pages in modern editions. *Essays in Idleness* was evidently not circulated during its author's lifetime. This and the anomalous organization of the text were accounted for by the apocryphal story that the servant of a warrior-poet found the segments pasted to the walls of Kenkō's hermitage after his death. The putative location at Yoshida also gave rise to the misnomer "Yoshida Kenkō."

The work's popularity has perhaps been enhanced less by the stern tone in passages exhorting us to practice the Buddhist Way and more by such figures as the volatile high priest, sketched in his rapid progress from being nicknamed after his nettle tree, then after the stump left when he cut down the tree in anger, and finally by the hole left when he dug up the stump. As literacy and printing spread in the 1600s, Kenkō became one of the best-known authors, portrayed as a sage by some, accepted in spite of his inconsistencies by the more practical, and converted into a wag in stage plays and **satires**, while his work spawned numerous imitations with similar titles.

Like **Sei Shōnagon**, whose *Makura no sōshi* (*The Pillow Book*) he read and imitated in part, Kenkō was a low-ranking member of the aristocracy. His early readership, chiefly poet-priests like himself, appreciated most his fusion of the Buddhist understanding of impermanence with aesthetic appreciation. Kenkō responded to unstable times as no lyric writer before him had, not simply lamenting but acknowledging changes in the world. He shared the classical prejudice that the court at Kyoto was the sum of what was desirable in life, but was curious about the ways of the less cultured East, which he had visited. In *Essays in Idleness*, Kenkō deplores the insinuation of soldiers into a ritual at the imperial palace, yet approves of a ferocious warrior for declaring that people who do not have children cannot understand human pathos.

Kenkō's essay style incorporates subtle reframings of multiple genres, including narrative (*monogatari*), memoir, **journal**, poetic criticism, **aphorism**, Buddhist homily, admonition, court manual, and oral anecdote (*setsuwa*). Examples of the last include the crowd which pursues a woman reputed to be a demon and collapses into fistfights when the search proves fruitless; a father who will not give his daughter in marriage because she eats only chestnuts; a priest who is so single-minded that he cannot distinguish the word "horse's leg" from a Buddhist spell. Yet such anecdotes do not furnish platitudinous morals, for Kenkō's interpretative comments are often oblique or nonexistent. Moving freely from topic to topic, Kenkō dares us to accept his words (he is skeptical of much worldly talk), and defies us to form stable conclusions.

The opening line or preface tells of sitting in front of an inkstone all day long, giving in to tedium (*tsurezure*, the source of much vernacular prose), and scribbling trifles that occur to him until he senses absurdity. Such an apology is typical of medieval writers, who deny their overt authority in order to pull readers into closer engagement with the text. A reader of *Essays in Idleness* must supply logical links and otherwise enter into active dialogue with a reticent yet highly rhetorical Kenkō, who both plays upon and disappoints ordinary reactions. Even his most dogmatic passages advising swift renunciation of the world anticipate the reader's responses, while ignoring their incompatibility with his intermittent bursts of celebration of everyday life.

Kenkō is often compared to Castiglione or **Montaigne**. Kenkō's "good person" is one who "glances sidelong" at things, avoiding directness, a courtly but also contemplative stance. Unlike Montaigne, self-exposure is not his aim (however much it is achieved); he prefers to serve as an ironic foil to tales of self-mastery. Repeatedly hailing the role of experts, and deriding the human tendency toward waste, he relates how he once impressed a crowd at a racetrack by pointing out their similarity to a priest precariously dozing in a tree above them. Surely everyone needs to awaken to the futility of such things as equestrian entertainment, he exclaims. The chastened crowd ushers Kenkō to the front row.

The unsettling effect of his juxtapositions and incompleteness is the purpose of the essays. It is in his capturing of the aesthetic virtues of impermanence, next to karma the most influential Buddhist concept for the Japanese, that Kenkō made his prime contribution. The moon is gorgeous, but most valuable when clouds intervene to remind us how short our time is, or when we are shut inside and can only imagine its perfection. He leans heavily on the tradition of viewing the aesthetic object as he leads us through the gardens of beautiful young men and sensitive ladies, but never with full disclosure of anything except the fact that these paragons are now just memories.

Kenkō was a significant poet in his day, but historically he is remembered as a prose master. Each section is written in an appropriate style, whether an agglutinative, lyric Japanese in imitation of women's classics, a terse rendition of Taoist mysteries, crisp notes redolent of Chinese Confucian attitudes, or a hybrid Sino-Japanese for Buddhist thoughts. A professional in court ceremony, he frequently includes matters of custom or untangles teachings on culturally momentous points. His strong desire to preserve aristocratic culture in the face of a belief that change is inevitable is one of many contradictions animating the text.

Although many picture Kenkō as the worldly bonze (poet-priest) dispensing advice in a unified "guidebook of life," *Essays in Idleness* is on another level a guide to the instability and insubstantiality of life, a plea not to form and impose the self on the world (or the text) but to contemplate the fact that all forms are nugatory phantoms. As he quotes a man the world laughed at, "If you love life, you should love death." The essay lives by dying one word at a time.

LINDA H. CHANCE

Biography

Cognomen Yoshida; also known as Yoshida Kaneyoshi. Born Urabe Kaneyoshi, c. 1283 in Kyoto. Served in the Kyoto court as a youth. Entered the lay Buddhist priesthood as early as 1313, and thereafter attempted to live a life of refined detachment. Traveled widely, eventually settling in the Narabigaoka suburb of Kyoto. Died possibly in Iga province, c. 1352.

Selected Writings

Essays and Related Prose
Tsurezuregusa, edited by Yasuraoka Koosaku, 2 vols., 1967–68, and Kubota Jun, in *Hōjōki, Tsurezuregusa*, 1989; as *Meditations of a Recluse*, translated by G. B. Sansom, 1911, and C. E. Eby (bilingual edition), 1934; as *Idle Thoughts of a Recluse*, translated by T. Wakameda, 1914; as *The Miscellany of a Japanese Priest*, translated by William N. Porter, 1914; as *The Harvest of Leisure*, translated by Ryukichi Kurata, 1931; as *Essays in Idleness*, translated by Donald Keene, 1967, and Steven D. Carter, in *Classical Japanese Prose: An Anthology*, edited by Helen Craig McCullough, 1990

Other writings: poetry.

Further Reading

Carter, Steven D., Introduction to *Waiting for the Wind: Thirty-Six Poets of Japan's Late Medieval Age*, edited by Carter, New York: Columbia University Press, 1989
Chance, Linda H., *Formless in Form: Kenkō, Tsurezuregusa, and the Rhetoric of Japanese Fragmentary Prose*, Stanford, California: Stanford University Press, 1997
Chance, Linda H., "Constructing the Classic: *Tsurezuregusa* in Tokugawa Readings," *Journal of the American Oriental Society* 117, no. 1 (1997)
Ishigami Iagolnitzer, Mitchiko, "L'Homme devant la vie et la mort selon Kenkō et Montaigne: Essai de philosophie comparée," *Bulletin de la Société des Amis de Montaigne* 21–22 (1985): 43–53
Keene, Donald, "Japanese Aesthetics," *Philosophy East and West* 19, no. 3 (July 1969): 293–306
Keene, Donald, "Kenkō: Essays in Idleness (*Tsurezuregusa*)," in *Approaches to the Asian Classics*, edited by William Theodore de Bary and Irene Bloom, New York: Columbia University Press, 1990: 310–19
Marra, Michele, "Semi-Recluses (*tonseisha*) and Impermanence (*mujō*): Kamo no Chōmei and Urabe Kenkō," *Japanese Journal of Religious Studies* 11, no. 4 (December 1984): 313–50
Marra, Michele, "The Ideal Court: Kenkō's Search for Meaning," in his *The Aesthetics of Discontent: Politics and Reclusion in Medieval Japanese Literature*, Honolulu: University of Hawaii Press, 1991: 127–52
Thornton, Naoko Fuwa, *The Birth of the Essay: A Comparative Study of Michel de Montaigne and Yoshida Kenkō* (dissertation), Bloomington: Indiana University, 1973

Kjær, Nils

Norwegian, 1870–1924

Popularly known as "the golden pen," Nils Kjær referred to the essays of **Ludvig Holberg** to describe the character of his favorite genre, and used the same word, "epistler" (epistles), as Holberg had some 150 years earlier. He began his writing career as an essayist and developed into one of Norway's leading social critics. His writing includes travel sketches, literary portraits, and criticism, as well as descriptions of nature, especially along the south coast of Norway. As an essayist, Kjær demonstrated fluidity in style and content. While on the one hand he cultivated an elegant literary style, on the other he developed a polemical and controversial mode of expression. Despite his European bent, he intimated ongoing national concerns in his essays.

Kjær's lasting impression as an essayist is his contribution "Den litterære kritik" (Literary criticism) to the Norwegian journal *Tidssignaler* (Signs of the time) in 1895, in which he convincingly argued that the **critical essay** was on the verge of superseding the novel as an art form. The paucity of ideas in modern literature could, he felt, now be corrected. Kjær attributed part of the emerging importance of the critical essay to its role as an expression of popular philosophy and its encouragement of reflection on the part of the sensitive reader.

Another reason Kjær gave for the essay's new position in Norwegian cultural history was the increasing sophistication of the reading public. He pointed out that the need for entertainment was being replaced by the desire for intellectual stimulation. At the same time, Kjær observed how criticism assumed the responsibility of elucidating literary works as objects of art rather than of science. As a result, the new essayists of Norway should concern themselves more with the intensity of personalities than with scientific accuracy.

Intuitively European in spirit, Kjær was preoccupied with French authors. His first collection of essays was, in fact, entitled *Essays: Fremmede Forfatteren* (1895; Essays: foreign authors). In the collection, Kjær sketched the lives of the Swedish humanist Viktor Rydberg, **Blaise Pascal**, Dante, and Edgar Allan Poe. While some of the pieces recall literary **reviews**, others present broad studies of literary lives. In the case of Poe, in particular, Kjær evinced his ability to transform literary criticism from mere descriptive accounts to portraits of personality and character, doing so by allying himself with the reader and at the same time by employing equal amounts of irony and passion.

A Norwegian reader would be attuned to Kjær's emphasis on the correspondence of nature and national character in his essays. His depictions of the Norwegian people sketch the conditions under which they live and the spirit of the times. A critic of his age as well as a stylist, Kjær evolved into an essayist with high cultural values, but with a sometimes overpowering sense of pessimism and, later, increasingly reactionary views. Alongside his warm descriptions of the Norwegian landscape emerged polemics concerning modern culture. His conviction that technological progress signified the regression of humanity colored his deep concern for the humanitarian ideal and cultural values.

VIVIAN GREENE-GANTZBERG

Biography
Born 11 November 1870 in Holmestrand. Traveled a great deal in France and Italy. Died in Oslo, 9 February 1924.

Selected Writings

Essay and Related Prose
Essays: Fremmede forfatteren, 1895
Bøger og Billeder, 1898
I forbigaaende, 1903
Smaa epistler, 1908
Nye epistler, 1912
Svundne somre, 1920
Siste epistler, 1924
Brekkestø breve og andre epistler, 1955

Other writings: four plays (*Regnskabets dag*, 1902; *Mimosas hjemkomst*, 1907; *Det lykkelige valg*, 1913; *For træ er der haab*, 1917) and short stories.

Collected works edition: *Samlede skrifter*, 5 vols., 1921–22.

Further Reading
Beyer, Edvard, *Norsk Litteratur Historie*, Oslo: Aschehoug, 1952: 367–69
Madsen, Mads, *En stilkritisk studie af Nils Kjærs naturepistler* (dissertation), Oslo: University of Oslo, 1967
Noreng, Harald, *Nils Kjær: Fra radikal til reaksjonær*, Oslo: Gyldendal Norsk, 1949

Kleist, Heinrich von

German, 1777–1811

Although better known as a playwright and author of novellas, Kleist wrote a small number of essays that reveal his unique cast of mind. These essays, which are often ransacked by critics mistakenly seeking keys to Kleist's other works, are seldom explored as contributions to the art of the essay. Kleist also penned terse anecdotes, admired by Kafka, which make the reader ponder issues similar to those raised by his essays. What gives Kleist's essays their characteristic texture is the tension between his rationalistic quest for order and his intuitive grasp of the uncertainties of the human psyche. They disclose a mind caught uneasily between a hand-me-down faith in reason derived from 18th-century philosophy, Romantic notions about the importance of inner life, and a very modern sense of the inherently paradoxical nature of man's lot.

Kleist's first essay, "Aufsatz, den sichern Weg des Glücks zu finden" (Essay on the sure way of finding happiness), a juvenile piece of writing full of clichés culled from second-rate 18th-century thinkers, was probably written in 1799. His mature essays, anecdotes, theatrical reviews, and articles were written primarily for the *Berliner Abendblätter* (Berlin evening news), one of the first German dailies, which Kleist set up with the political economist Adam Müller in October 1810. Although the newspaper owed its short-lived success to the crime reports supplied by the Berlin chief of police, the occasional contributions by Kleist captivated discerning contemporaries such as the Brothers Grimm. However, after Kleist was obliged to close the newspaper in March 1811, these writings fell into oblivion until the surge of interest in his life and work in the early decades of this century.

The most famous – and most misunderstood – of Kleist's essays is *Über das Marionettentheater* (1810; *On Puppet Shows*). A number of critics have concocted systems of thought on the basis of the philosophical, aesthetic, and theological allusions scattered throughout this seminal essay. Some commentators construe the essay as a **treatise** on Romantic aesthetics, others as an exposition of a triadic philosophical scheme said to underlie all of Kleist's plays and novellas. Such attempts, however, ignore the tentative quality of the essay, which is modeled after a Platonic **dialogue**.

The essay features a dialogue between the first person narrator and a puppet master about the elegance of puppets, who have only one "center of gravity," and the clumsiness of humans, whose capacity for reflection destroys their ability to move and act naturally. What concerns Kleist about the Fall of Man is not so much sin as the loss of the primeval grace still possessed by unthinking animals. Unlike the Romantics, however, with whom he is sometimes wrongly conflated, Kleist is not tempted by past idylls. What he envisages instead is an open-ended quest for the harmony lost when man was expelled from Eden: "But Paradise is locked and bolted and the Cherub is behind us. We must make a journey around the world to see if a back door has perhaps been left open." Kleist's doubts about the possibility of ever attaining that goal, suggested by that characteristic word "perhaps," links him to later, more radical skeptics such as Kafka and **Camus**.

In other ways, too, Kleist points forwards rather than backwards. In a mere handful of essays he anticipates the insights of modern psychologists, philosophers, and linguists. In "Über die allmähliche Verfertigung der Gedanken beim Reden" (wr. c. 1805–06; "On the Gradual Fabrication of Thoughts While Speaking"), he reverses traditional notions about language by arguing that speech often creates thought rather than vice versa. He emphasizes the largely unconscious process by which we arrive at insights: "it is not *we* who 'know'; it is rather a certain condition of ourselves that 'knows'." Here he anticipates **Freud**'s exploration of different levels of consciousness. Moreover, Kleist, who covertly alludes to the political and cultural objectives of the *Berliner Abendblätter* in a piece called "Gebet des Zoroaster" (1810; "Prayer of Zarathustra"), no doubt influenced **Nietzsche**'s choice of a mouthpiece in *Also sprach Zarathustra* (1883–85; *Thus Spoke Zarathustra*).

The distinctiveness of Kleist's essays stems from his ability to write with the rigor of a scientist and the imagination of a poet. In one of his **aphorisms** Kleist states that most people think either in terms of metaphors or in terms of formulas. He himself was capable of both modes of thought. His style reflects the tension in himself between rationalism and intuition. In the essay on fabricating thought, and elsewhere, he shows a particular fondness for metaphors and analogies drawn from mechanics and physics: "Speech is not a fetter, then, like a drag chain on the wheel of the mind, but a second wheel running parallel to it on the same axle." Yet he also has a poet's flair for apt detail: "Perhaps, after all, it was only the twitch of an upper lip, or the ambiguous fingering of a wrist frill, that precipitated the overthrow of the old order in France." Kleist's sense of humor is evident in the whimsical essay, "Nützliche Erfindungen: Entwurf einer Bombenpost" (1810; "Useful Inventions: Project for a Cannonball Postal System") and in "Allerneuester Erziehungsplan" (1810; "The Very Latest Educational Scheme"), in which he advocates the establishment of a School for Vice.

Although Kleist's own writing is noted for its formal rigor, in his essays on aesthetic themes he advocates unrestrained subjectivity. Two essays in epistolary guise, "Brief eines jungen Dichters an einen Maler" (1810; "Letter from a Young Writer to a Young Painter") and "Brief eines Malers an seinen Sohn" (1810; "A Painter's Letter to His Son"), suggest that the arts are merely a vehicle for self-expression: "The objective, after all, is not to become someone else, but to be yourself: through color and design to render your very self, that most personal and inner part of you, visible." In "Brief eines Dichters an einen anderen" (1811; "Letter from One Poet to Another"), written in the year of his suicide, Kleist is even more extreme in his rejection of literary form : ". . . if I could reach into my heart, take hold of my thoughts, and with my bare hands lay them without further embellishment in your own, then, I confess, the innermost desire of my soul would be fulfilled." Although this **letter**-writing poet is not necessarily Kleist himself, it is difficult not to read such passages in existential terms as the final testament of a writer who, like Arthur Rimbaud and Robert Walser, turned away from literature and chose what Kafka, in a letter to his fiancée Felice Bauer in September 1913, described as the "right way out."

MARK HARMAN

Biography
Bernd Heinrich Wilhelm von Kleist. Born 18 October 1777 in Frankfurt-on-Oder, Brandenburg. Suffered many nervous breakdowns throughout his life. Served in the Prussian army, 1792–99, taking part in the siege of Mainz, 1793. Studied law at the University of Frankfurt, 1799–1800. Traveled in Germany, Switzerland, and France, 1800–04; civil servant, Königsberg, 1805–06; cofounder, with Adam Müller, and editor, *Phöbus*, Dresden, 1808–09, and *Berliner Abendblätter*, 1810–11; attempted unsuccessfully to publish the newspaper *Germania*, Prague, 1809. Died (suicide by gunshot) at Lake Wannsee, near Potsdam, 21 November 1811.

Selected Writings

Essays and Related Prose
Über das Marionettentheater: Aufsätze und Anekdoten, edited by Helmut Sembdner, 1935; revised edition, 1980; title essay edited by Wilhelm Neufeld, 1962, and Helmut Sembdner (including essays on the text), 1967; title essay as *On a Theatre of Marionettes*, translated by G. Wilford, 1989; as *On Puppet Shows*, translated by David Paisley, 1991
An Abyss Deep Enough: Letters of Heinrich von Kleist with a Selection of Essays and Anecdotes, edited and translated by Philip B. Miller, 1982

Other writings: seven plays (*Die Familie Schroffenstein* [*The Feud of the Schroffensteins*], 1803; *Amphitryon*, 1807; *Der zerbrochene Krug* [*The Broken Pitcher*], 1808; *Penthesilea*, 1808; *Das Käthchen von Heilbronn* [*Kate of Heilbronn*], 1810; *Prinz Friedrich von Homburg* [*The Prince of Homburg*], 1821; *Die Hermannsschlacht*, 1839), short stories (including "The Marquise of O." and *Michael Kohlhaas* [1810]), and correspondence.

Collected works editions: *Werke*, edited by Erich Schmidt and others, 5 vols., 1904–05, revised edition, 7 vols., 1936–38; *Sämtliche Werke und Briefe*, edited by Helmut Sembdner, 2 vols., 1961, revised edition, 1984; *Sämtliche Werke*, edited by Roland Reuss and Peter Staengle, 2 vols., 1988–92 (in progress).

Bibliography
Sembdner, Helmut, *Kleist-Bibliographie, 1803–1862*, Stuttgart: Eggert, 1966

Further Reading
Blöcker, Günter, *Heinrich von Kleist oder Das absolute Ich*, Frankfurt-on-Main: Fischer, 1977
Dyer, Denys, *The Stories of Kleist: A Critical Study*, London: Duckworth, 1977
Ellis, John M., *Heinrich von Kleist: Studies in the Character and Meaning of His Writings*, Chapel Hill: University of North Carolina Press, 1979
Gearey, John, *Heinrich von Kleist: A Study in Tragedy and Anxiety*, Philadelphia: University of Pennsylvania Press, 1968
Hamburger, Michael, "Heinrich von Kleist," in his *Reason and Energy: Studies in German Literature*, London: Routledge and Kegan Paul, and New York: Grove Press, 1957: 107–44; as *Contraries: Studies in German Literature*, New York: Dutton, 1971: 101–39
Harman, Mark, "An Echo of Kafka in Kleist," in *Heinrich von Kleist Studies*, edited by Alexej Ugrinsky, New York: AMS Press, and Berlin: Schmidt, 1980: 169–75
Helbling, Robert E., *The Major Works of Heinrich von Kleist*, New York: New Directions, 1975
Hohoff, Curt, *Heinrich von Kleist* (in English), Bonn and Bad Godesberg: Inter Nationes, 1977 (original German edition, 1958)
Ide, Heinz, *Der junge Kleist*, Würzburg: Holzner, 1961

Kurock, Wolfgang, "Heinrich von Kleist und die Marionette," in *Heinrich von Kleist Studies*, edited by Alexej Ugrinsky, New York: AMS Press, and Berlin: Schmidt, 1980: 103–08

Nicolai, Ralf, "Schwerpunkt Kleist: Motive des Marionettentheaters im 20. Jahrhundert," in *Heinrich von Kleist Studies*, edited by Alexej Ugrinsky, New York: AMS Press, and Berlin: Schmidt, 1980: 127–35

Reed, T. J., "The 'Goethezeit' and Its Aftermath," in *Germany: A Companion to German Studies*, edited by Malcolm Pasley, London: Methuen, 1972: 493–553

Sembdner, Helmut, editor, *Kleists Aufsatz "Über das Marionettentheater": Studien und Interpretationen*, Berlin: Jahresgabe der Heinrich-von-Kleist-Gesellschaft, 1967

Silz, Walter, *Heinrich von Kleist: Studies in His Works and Literary Character*, Philadelphia: University of Pennsylvania Press, 1961

Kołakowski, Leszek

Polish, 1927–

Leszek Kołakowski is as well known for his essays (for which he received the European Prize for the Essay in 1980) as he is for his strictly philosophical works. He launched his spectacular career as an essayist with the publication in 1959 of the influential essay "Kapłan i błazen" ("The Priest and the Jester"), which gained him the reputation as the most brilliant Marxist philosopher in Poland. In this essay Kołakowski formulates a dichotomy between the Priest, the guardian of tradition and accepted absolutes, and the skeptical Jester who "doubts all that appears self-evident." The philosophy of the Priest, Kołakowski argues, represented incurable and "unbearable traits of senility." Despite the attractiveness and force with which Kołakowski presents the Jester, the metaphor, as one of his critics observed (Ryszard Legutko, "Podzwonne dla błazna" [Requiem for the jester], in his *Bez gniewu i uprzedzenia* [1989; Without anger and prejudice]), is based on the confusion of individual temperament – such as intellectual vitality, irony, and paradox – with an intellectual world view. The inadequacy of the metaphor can be seen when it is applied to **Pascal**, the thinker to whom Kołakowski devoted an essay and made frequent allusions in that period. The irony and humor harnessed by Pascal in his *Lettres provinciales* (1656–57; *The Provincial Letters*) to mock the lax morality of the Jesuit Fathers would seem to place Pascal with the Jesters; yet in fact Pascal's humor serves to defend an austere Jansenist morality and Catholicism, which, according to Kołakowski's categorization, puts Pascal in the camp of the defenders of absolutes.

Although the dichotomy between the Priest and the Jester could, with the greatest of difficulties, become a key to the interpretation of the history of philosophy, the Jester's philosophy of the mistrust for absolutes turned out to have considerable practical consequences. The Jester's philosophy served the former Marxists, including Kołakowski himself – who was called in the 1960s "the most intelligent man in the world" – as a form of immunization against ideological traps into which they had fallen, when, in the early 1950s, they committed themselves to Marxism.

From today's perspective the "The Priest and the Jester" bears strong traces of the sociopolitical situation in which it was written; yet it is pivotal for Kołakowski's philosophical methodology. A considerable part of the essay concerns the theological underpinnings of contemporary philosophy. "Philosophy has never freed itself from its theological heritage," Kołakowski writes at the outset of the essay, "which means that theological questions were merely clumsy formulations of essential enigmas that still hold us in thrall ... theology has never been more than a projection of anthropology onto non-human reality." Thus:

> ... the problem of theodicy in its modern version is that of the "wisdom" of history ... Theodicy is, therefore, a method of transforming facts into values ... eschatology is an attempt to find absolute justification for our life outside its limits, to establish a reality that makes all other reality meaningful and comprehensible ... The most important of these questions is the problem of nature and grace ... this question concerns determinism and responsibility ... All these questions involve the relationship between man and the absolute ... Revelation is simply the absolute in the order of cognition, a collection of positive and unquestionable data, our means of communicating with the absolute ... secular revelation was the Cartesian *cogito* ... nostalgia for revelation lives on in the heart of philosophy.

All these points have been elaborated by Kołakowski in his books, many of which are written in an essayistic form: *Obecność mitu* (1972; *The Presence of Myth*), *Husserl and the Search for Certitude* (1975), *Religion: If There Is No God* (1982), and *Metaphysical Horror* (1988).

After his expulsion from Warsaw University and his arrival in the West in 1968, Kołakowski became a frequent contributor to the English *Encounter* and other European and American journals such as *Survey*, *Commentary*, **Partisan Review**, *Commentaire*, and *Merkur*. In 1982 ANEKS, the London-based Polish émigré publishing house, published the collection of his essays, *Czy diabeł może być zbawiony i 27 innych kazań* (Can the devil be saved and 27 other sermons), written mostly in English, French, and German. Similar collections appeared in French and English.

In 1990 Kołakowski published *Modernity on Endless Trial*, for which he received the Laing Award from the University of Chicago Press for the best book of the year. Unlike Kołakowski's essays written during his Marxist period – *Kultura i fetysze* (1967; Culture and fetishes, translated as *Toward a Marxist Humanism* and as *Marxism and Beyond*) and *A Leszek Kołakowski Reader* (1971) – these essays are, as Kołakowski aptly called them, "semi-philosophical sermons." The early mistrust of the Jester against the absolutes is no longer present in his later works, and the dichotomy between the Jester and the Priest is replaced by the opposition between the philosophers who seek a cognitive Absolute and those who apply "skeptical medicine" to the ever-present attempt in European thought to find the absolute "foundation of all foundations." As Kołakowski persuasively argues, "The search for the ultimate foundation is as much an unremovable part of European culture as is the denial of the legitimacy of this search" (*Metaphysical Horror*). For the most part, Kołakowski's attention is focused on the state of Christianity and Catholicism (frequent themes in his writings), the relationship between religious thought and philosophy, modernity, and ideologies. Whether the object of our analysis is philosophy, Christianity, Marxism, or liberalism, we unfailingly come across the same utopian tendency in human thinking: the belief of philosophers in attaining absolute certitude, man's search for a perfect social order, and the theocratic tendencies within Christianity. All of these express the same belief that there is a perfect solution to all human problems. Yet there are no perfect solutions; the solution to one problem always gives rise to others. There are only dilemmas with which we need to learn how to live. Kołakowski believes that "moderation in consistency" is the best way to counter this utopian thinking, which always leads to the perversion of the ideal and in the social realm finds but one solution: totalitarian temptation, exemplified in the 20th century by the rise of Marxist and Nazi states. While the specter of Marxism, the greatest utopia of the 20th century, as Kołakowski called it in his monumental work *Główne nurty marksizmu* (1976; *Main Currents of Marxism*), is behind us, cultural relativism, characteristic of the life of contemporary Western democratic liberal societies, undermines the very belief in the existence of moral and epistemological "absolutes" on which European culture has always been based.

ZBIGNIEW JANOWSKI

Biography
Born 23 October 1927 in Radom. Studied at the University of Łódź, 1945–50, Ph.D., 1953. Member of the Polish Workers' Party, 1945. Staff member, *Po Prostu* (In plain words), 1955. After the so-called "October thaw," 1956, became one of the leading voices for the democratization of life in Poland. Professor of modern philosophy, University of Warsaw: 1959–68: expelled after giving a speech at the Warsaw Chapter of the Union of Polish Writers. Delivered a famous speech at at the 10th anniversary of the "Polish October," 1966: expelled from the Polish United Workers' Party. Left Poland, November 1968; no references to his works could be made in Poland, 1968–89. Professor of philosophy, McGill University, Montreal, 1968, and University of California, Berkeley, 1969; senior research fellow, All Souls College, Oxford, 1970–95; visiting professor, Yale University, New Haven, Connecticut, 1975; professor, Committee on Social Thought and the Department of Philosophy, University of Chicago, 1980–95. Awards: several, including the German Booksellers Peace Prize, 1977; Erasmus Prize, 1980; Veillon Foundation European Prize for the Essay, 1980; Jefferson Award, 1986; MacArthur Award, 1982; University of Chicago Laing Award, 1990; Tocqueville Prize, 1994.

Selected Writings

Essays and Related Prose
Der Mensch ohne Alternative, 1960
Kultura i fetysze, 1967; as *Toward a Marxist Humanism: Essays on the Left Today*, and as *Marxism and Beyond*, translated by Jane Zielonko Peel, 1968
Traktat über die Sterblichkeit der Vernunft: Philosophische Essays, 1967
A Leszek Kołakowski Reader, TriQuarterly 22 (1971)
Obecność mitu, 1972; as *The Presence of Myth*, 1989
Husserl and the Search for Certitude, 1975
Czy diabeł może być zbawiony i 27 innych kazań, 1982
Religion: If There Is No God, 1982
Le Village introuvable, 1986
Metaphysical Horror, 1988
Pochwała niekonsekwencji: Pisma rozproszone z lat, 1955–1968, 3 vols., edited by Zbigniew Menzel, 1989

Cywilizacja na ławie oskarżonych, edited by Paweł Kłoczowski, 1990
Modernity on Endless Trial, 1990
God Owes Us Nothing: A Brief Remark on Pascal's Religion and on the Spirit of Jansenism, 1995

Other writings: one-act plays, short stories, and works on Marxism (including *Główne nurty marksizmu* [1976; *Main Currents of Marxism*]), philosophy, and religion.

Bibliography
Kline, George L., "Selective Bibliography," *TriQuarterly* 22 (1971): 239–50

Further Reading
Davis, Charles, and John C. Robertson, Jr., "Religion: If There Is No God," *Religious Studies Review* 2 (1985): 145–51
Karpiński, Wojciech, "Leszek Kołakowski: A Portrait," in *European Liberty: Four Essays on the Occasion of the 25th Anniversary of the Erasmus Prize Foundation*, The Hague: Nijhoff, 1983
Kline, George L., "Beyond Revisionism: Leszek Kołakowski's Recent Philosophical Development," *TriQuarterly* 22 (1971): 13–47
Król, Marcin, "Leszek Kołakowski: Le Philosophe et la religion," *Esprit* (October 1985): 63–81
Lenz, Siegfried, *Gespräche mit Manes Sperber und Leszek Kołakowski*, Munich: Deutscher Taschenbuch, 1982
Schwan, Gesine, *Leszek Kołakowski: Eine marxistische Philosophie der Freiheit nach Marx*, Stuttgart: Kohlhammer, 1971
Schwan, Gesine, "The Philosophical Resistance of Leszek Kołakowski," *Humanities: National Endowment for the Humanities: Leszek Kołakowski, the 1986 Jefferson Lecturer* 7, no. 2 (1986): 10–16

Kott, Jan
Polish, 1914–

Jan Kott's writing has encompassed a variety of genres – poetry, a series of translations of French literature into Polish, and the 1990 autobiography *Przyczynek do biografii* (*Still Alive*) – but his reputation is primarily based on essays related to the theater. Kott's theatrical essays have in turn embraced various forms and perspectives over the course of his career, ranging from performance reviews, to critical investigations into theater history, to visionary or speculative essays on the contemporary performance of classical drama. It is for the last of these that Kott is most renowned, particularly for the essays contained in *Szkice o Szekspirze* (1961, revised and enlarged, 1965; *Shakespeare Our Contemporary*) and *The Eating of the Gods* (1973).

The impact of Kott's essays on 20th-century theater practice was unprecedented and remains unique. Rather than merely research or critically respond to the performances of the plays he considered, Kott instead tacitly wrote from the perspective of a contemporary theatrical director or production dramaturge preparing a staging of the text. While his style of writing in early works such as *Shakespeare Our Contemporary* was energetic and designed to be accessible to a general audience, it had its most profound impact in professional theater circles in the 1960s and 1970s – particularly among those involved with experimental or alternative theater. On this score, the influence of Kott's writing could be compared to that of the earlier theoretical writings of Bertolt Brecht and Antonin Artaud. Among the directors most deeply influenced by Kott's essays in *Shakespeare Our Contemporary* were Peter Brook and Peter Hall in England, Ariane Mnouchkine in France, Giorgio Strehler in Italy, and Andrzej Wajda and Konrad Swinarski in Poland.

The popular style of *Shakespeare Our Contemporary* made it one of the most widely read and translated books by any contemporary Polish writer; the book has long been required reading in England's secondary schools as well as in American college and university theater programs. Kott's essays on Shakespeare were published and translated into various languages before he had any direct experience with theatrical production or even a reading knowledge of English. As a result of the success of *Shakespeare Our Contemporary*, Kott received his first opportunities to study and teach in the English-speaking world as well as his first invitations to work as director or dramaturge on various productions in Western Europe and the United States. In 1969, he was granted political asylum in the U.S. after being denounced by the Polish Communist Party as a result of the turmoil in Poland following the so-called "events of March 1968" – which included an anti-Semitic campaign instigated by Stalinist elements in the Party.

Kott's personal and political biography are inseparably linked to the content of his essays. He was a child of the secularized urban Jewish bourgeoisie in interwar Poland and was fully assimilated into Polish language and culture. In the wake of the fall of Poland following the combined Nazi and Soviet invasions of the country in 1939, Kott joined the tiny and embattled Polish communist underground movement, a choice that initially secured his position in the postwar Polish communist cultural establishment. He won the Polish State Prize in Literature and Literary Studies twice (in 1951 and 1955), only to resign from the Communist Party in 1957 in protest against the excesses of its Stalinist elements. In 1964, he cosigned "The Letter of the Thirty-Four" protesting against censorship in Poland, and left the country the next year to write and teach abroad.

Shakespeare Our Contemporary was a landmark in the Marxist humanist school of cultural criticism that emerged in the wake of Stalinism in Poland, Czechoslovakia, and elsewhere, with its emphasis on the dramatic play of historical forces and *realpolitik*. The book presented Shakespeare's history plays, for example, as a variety of Brechtian *Lehrstücke*, or "learning plays," on the dialectics of political history. In other regards, however, the book went beyond Marxism, with one of Kott's most famous essays connecting *King Lear* with Samuel Beckett's *Endgame*. Kott's anti-sentimental reading of Shakespeare's comedies in the book emphasized their brutality and eroticism, particularly in *A Midsummer Night's Dream*, in a manner that owed little to **Marx** but proved immensely popular with young British and Western European directors at the time. Peter Brook's landmark production of the play at the Royal Shakespeare Company in 1970 was one of several productions that acknowledged the influence of Kott's essay "Titania and the Ass's Head," and is now regarded as a turning point in the production history of the play in Great Britain.

Kott's writing changed markedly after his emigration from Poland. Marx receded as an influence; in his stead emerged a complex hybrid of archetypal mythology and the carnivalesque theories of Mikhail Bakhtin. The essay "Orestes, Electra, Hamlet," found in *The Eating of the Gods*, displays Kott's archetypal approach at its best, using the characters and scenarios of *The Oresteia* and *Hamlet* to highlight each other. The essays in *The Bottom Translation* (1987) marked the height of Kott's work under Bakhtin's influence. The book's title essay (devoted to *A Midsummer Night's Dream*) is primarily a study in the aesthetic and transcendent reconciliation of opposites, a quite different principle indeed from Marx's dialectical materialism.

Kott's influence on the "director's theater" that emerged in Europe and America in the 1960s and 1970s came full circle in several late essays devoted to the work of experimental directors such as Jerzy Grotowski, Tadeusz Kantor, and Peter Brook. His late writings in the collections *The Memory of the Body* (1992) and *Nowy Jonasz i inne szkice* (1994; The new Jonas and other sketches) and his autobiographical book *Still Alive* leave the Marxist and Bakhtinian theoretical armatures of his early and middle periods behind. Instead they freely move between autobiography, reflections on the theater, and philosophical meditations on literature, nature, and Kott's growing sense of his own mortality as a result of a series of strokes, heart attacks, and related medical crises. In spite of his declining health, Kott has taken an avid interest in Poland's cultural and political life since the fall of the Berlin Wall, after many years of being denied access to the country as a result of his public protests against the declaration of Martial Law in 1981. He remains a vital and vocal presence in Polish émigré circles in the U.S. and Western Europe.

ALLEN J. KUHARSKI

Biography

Born 27 October 1914 in Warsaw. Studied at the University of Warsaw, law degree, 1936; the Sorbonne, Paris, 1938–39; University of Łódź, Ph.D., 1947. Married Lidia Steinhaus, 1939: one daughter and one son. Served in the Polish Army, defending Warsaw, September 1939; member of the Polish resistance movement, 1942–45. Member of the Polish Communist Party, 1943–57: resigned. Professor of romance languages, University of Wrocław, 1949–52; professor of Polish literature, University of Warsaw, 1952–69: dismissed. Cosigned a public letter protesting against Polish censorship, 1964. Visiting professor of Polish literature and drama, Yale University, New Haven, Connecticut, 1966–67 and 1978–79, and of drama, Catholic University of Louvain, 1968. Sought political asylum in the United States, 1969. Professor of drama and Germanic and Slavic languages and literatures, 1969–73, and of comparative literature and English, 1973–83, State University of New York, Stony Brook; visiting professor of drama, Hebrew University. Became an American citizen, 1979. Awards: Polish State Prize in Literature, 1951, 1955; Herder Award, 1964; Guggenheim Fellowship, 1972–73; Alfred Jurzykowski Award, 1976.

Selected Writings

Essays and Related Prose
Mitologia i realizm, 1946
Po prostu, 1946
O społecznym awansie, 1947
O "Lalce" Bolesława Prusa, 1948
Szkoła klasyków, 1949; revised, enlarged edition, 1955
Trwałe wartości literatury polskiego Oświecenia, 1951
Wiktor Hugo: Pisarz walczący, 1952

Jak wam się podoba: Spotkanie pierwsze (theater reviews), 2 vols.,
1955–57
Postęp i głupstwo, 2 vols., 1956
Szkice o Szekspirze, 1961; revised, enlarged edition, as *Szekspir
współczesny*, 1965; as *Shakespeare Our Contemporary*, translated
by Bolesław Taborski, 1964
Aloes, dzienniki i małe szkice, 1966
Theatre Notebook, 1947–1967, translated by Bolesław Taborski,
1968
The Eating of the Gods: An Interpretation of Greek Tragedy,
translated by Bolesław Taborski and Edward J. Czerwiński, 1973
The Theater of Essence and Other Essays, 1984
Kamienny potok, 1986; enlarged edition, 1991
*The Bottom Translation: Marlowe and Shakespeare and the
Carnival Tradition*, translated by Daniela Międzyrzecka and
Lillian Vallee, 1987
Przyczynek do biografii, 1990; as *Still Alive: An Autobiographical
Essay*, translated by Jadwiga Kosicka, 1994
The Memory of the Body: Essays on Theater and Death, translated
by Jadwiga Kosicka, 1992
The Gender of Rosalind, translated by Jadwiga Kosicka and Mark
Rosenzweig, 1992; as *Płeć Rozolindy: Interpretacje Marlowe,
Szekspir, Webster, Büchner, Gautier*, 1992
Nowe Jonasz i inne szkice, 1994

Other writings: poetry. Also translated many writers from the
French, including Molière, **Jean-Paul Sartre**, and Eugène Ionesco.

Bibliography
Vasco, Gerhard, and Hélène Volat-Shapiro, *The Publications of Jan
Kott*, Stony Brook: State University of New York, 1979

Further Reading
Barker, Clive, and Simon Trussler, editors, "Jan Kott: An Eightieth
Birthday Celebration," *New Theater Quarterly* 10, no. 40 (1994)
Brockett, Oscar G., and Robert Findlay, *Century of Innovation: A
History of European and American Theater and Drama Since the
Late Nineteenth Century*, Englewood Cliffs, New Jersey: Prentice
Hall, 1973
Brustein, Robert, "Jan Kott, Super Dramaturge," in his *Who Needs
Theater: Dramatic Opinions*, New York: Atlantic Monthly Press,
1987; London: Faber, 1989
Elsom, John, "Is Shakespeare Still Our Contemporary?,"
Contemporary Review 249, no. 1451 (1986): 315–19
Guczalska, Beata, "Jan Kott: Pisarz i krytyk," *Dialog* 33, no. 5
(1988): 123–35
Guczalska, Beata, "Shakespeare Jana Kotta," *Dialog* 33, no. 6
(1988): 125–37
Houliston, Victor, "Shakespeare Not Our Contemporary,"
Shakespeare in South Africa 3 (1989): 67–77
Kennedy, Dennis, editor, *Foreign Shakespeare: Contemporary
Performance*, Cambridge: Cambridge University Press, 1993
Krajewska-Wieczorek, Anna, "Still Contemporary: A Conversation
with Jan Kott," *Yale/Theater* 25, no. 3 (1995): 85–89
Krzemiński, Adam, "Opowieści Jana Kotta," *Dialog* 36, no. 1
(1991): 86–91
Kuharski, Allen, "Beyond Criticism: The Theatrical Poetics of Jan
Kott," *San Francisco Review of Books* 13, no. 1 (1988): 29–30
Kuharski, Allen, "Identity and Improvisation: Backstage in the
Theater of Jan Kott," *Yale/Theater* 25, no. 3 (1995): 80–84
Lichtenstein, Leonie, "Is Shakespeare Still Our Contemporary?,"
Shakespeare in South Africa 3 (1989): 78–86
Miłosz, Czesław, *The History of Polish Literature*, Berkeley:
University of California Press, 1983 (original edition, 1969)
Pieczara, Marek, "Kott współczesny," *Dialog* 36, no. 1 (1991):
100–05
Selbourne, David, *The Making of "A Midsummer Night's Dream"*,
London: Methuen, 1982

Krutch, Joseph Wood

American, 1893–1970

Joseph Wood Krutch was a consummate practitioner of both the formal and informal essay. He published over 750 essays in both scholarly and popular journals between 1920 and 1970. The theater reviews and occasional columns which he wrote during that 50-year period bring the total number of his publications to well over 1000. Most of the 28 books he authored are collections of essays on a wide variety of topics ranging from 17th-century comedy to the geography of Baja California. While the main focus of his writing during the 1920s and 1930s was on literature and society, during the 1950s and 1960s he also became one of America's foremost nature essayists.

Krutch's life as a professional writer commenced in 1920 when he began to publish his essays in several important journals and reviews including *Smart Set*, the *Saturday Review of Literature*, and the *Nation*. Krutch's tone was skeptical, often cynical, but also always refined and cultivated, much like that of **Montaigne** and **Addison** and **Steele**. His sophisticated readers appreciated his clarity, reasonableness, and eloquence, as well as his courage in boldly addressing some of the most controversial issues of his day: the banality of modern art, the attack on the individual by various psychological and Marxist schools of thought, the joyless existence of many Americans. Krutch's scholarly, carefully crafted essays in cultural studies brought him to the attention of America's intelligentsia. At the same time he was quickly recognized as one of the most erudite and perceptive drama critics in New York. He was applauded for both his intellectual acumen and his ability to see beyond the latest theatrical fad. Krutch's opinion was so respected that even Eugene O'Neill, one of America's leading playwrights, requested his advice.

One of his most important early critical works, *The Modern Temper*, was completed in 1929. The essays making up this volume focus on the collapse of the belief in traditional humanistic values, especially free will, caused by social engineering, the influence of the mass media, and technocracy. Krutch characterizes the mood of the 20th century as pessimistic and alienated. His concluding statement seems to sum up the general mood of Western civilization: "Ours is a lost cause and there is no place for us in the natural universe, but we are not, for all that, sorry to be human. We should rather die as men than live as animals." While hailed as one of America's foremost intellectuals, Krutch was nevertheless uneasy with his own negativity and began to search for answers outside the Modernist paradigm.

Over the next four decades Krutch's writing style evolved with his new interests and an appeal to a more diverse audience. In the 1940s he published biographies of both **Samuel Johnson** and **Henry David Thoreau**, two writers who symbolized a spectrum of stylistic virtues to him: Johnson's polish, wit, and urbane insights on English life; Thoreau's humor, enthusiasm, and rhapsodic commentary on the American wilderness. During this same period Krutch had begun to enjoy writing the **familiar essay** so much that in an article entitled "No Essays, Please!" (1951) he even bemoaned the fact that the audience for this literary form was dwindling. He attributed this loss of interest to the upsurge in writing which was supposed to be spare, succinct, and objective – the language of the reporter. Such writing was meant to negate the individual's voice, to "exist in an impersonal realm." In marked contrast to this tendency toward the depersonalization of writing, many of Krutch's essays took on an intimate tone and began to focus not just on society and art but also on his increasing fascination with the world of nature.

The publication of his first collection of nature essays, *The Twelve Seasons* (1949), marked a turning point for him. Near the end of his life Krutch reflected on his mood when he began this phase of his writing career: "All of my books had been both serious and rather more solemn than I would have liked them to be. I wanted something lighter and more definitely in the manner of the now generally despised 'familiar essay'." *The Twelve Seasons* was successful enough that Krutch followed up with the publication of his reflections on a year spent in the arid environment of southern Arizona, *The Desert Year* (1952). This work was lauded as a perceptive analysis of life in the Southwest, a 20th-century version of Thoreau's *Walden*. Krutch's reputation as a disciple of Thoreau grew as he continued to expand his areas of expertise. He began to submit articles to popular journals such as *Audubon Magazine*, *House and Garden*, and *Desert Magazine* as well as continuing to contribute to the more academic journals such as the **American Scholar**, the **Atlantic Monthly**, *Commentary*, *Harper's*, and *Theater Arts*.

The range of Krutch's interests was astonishing. While he wrote formal essays about such literary luminaries as Shakespeare, Congreve, Eugene O'Neill, **Tolstoi**, **Twain**, **Shaw**, **Oscar Wilde**, and **André Gide**, he felt equally comfortable writing familiar essays about the Grand Canyon, coyotes, bats, desert frogs, and cacti. In his autobiography, *More Lives Than One* (1962), Krutch mused: "I probably know more about plants than any other drama critic and more about the theater than any botanist."

During the first half of the 20th century Krutch's academic essays on selfhood, freedom, and individuality were central to the theoretical debates about the humanistic tradition and the nature of civilization itself. Today much of this writing is seen as having value primarily to those interested in the evolution of Modernism. On the other hand, the growth of the environmental movement in America has fostered a renewed interest in Krutch's informal but discerning writing about the relationship of humanity to the larger community of nature. Krutch believed that the best nature essays were based on "the question of the moral consequences" of our actions (*The Best of Two Worlds*, 1953). Ethical concern and stylistic grace made Joseph Wood Krutch one of the most important critical voices of the 20th century.

PAUL NICHOLAS PAVICH

Biography

Born 25 November 1893 in Knoxville, Tennessee. Studied at the University of Tennessee, Knoxville, 1911–15, B.A., 1915; Columbia University, New York, M.A. in English, 1916, Ph.D., 1923. Served in the U.S. Army medical corps, 1917–18. Associate professor, Brooklyn Polytechnic Institute, 1920–23. Married Marcelle Leguia, 1923. Drama critic, 1924–32 and 1937–52, regular contributor, until the 1930s, associate editor, 1924–32, and member of the editorial board, 1932–37, the *Nation*. Taught part-time at Vassar College, Poughkeepsie, New York, 1924–25, Columbia University, 1925–31, and the New School for Social Research, New York, 1932–35; professor of English, Columbia University, 1937–52. Moved to Tucson, Arizona, 1952. Awards: several, including the Burroughs Medal, for nature writing, 1954; National Book Award, for *The Measure of Man*, 1955; Rockefeller Institute Ettinger Award, for science writing, 1964; Emerson-Thoreau Medal, 1967; honorary degrees from four universities; member, American Academy of Arts and Letters, and American Academy of Arts and Sciences. Died in Tucson, 22 May 1970.

Selected Writings

Essays and Related Prose
The Modern Temper: A Study and a Confession, 1929
Five Masters, 1930
Experience and Art, 1932
Was Europe a Success?, 1934
The Twelve Seasons, 1949
The Desert Year, 1952
The Best of Two Worlds, 1953
"Modernism" in Modern Drama: A Definition and an Estimate (lectures), 1953
The Measure of Man, 1954
The Voice of the Desert: A Naturalist's Interpretation, 1955
The Great Chain of Life, 1956
Grand Canyon: Today and All Its Yesterdays, 1958
Human Nature and Human Condition, 1959
The Forgotten Peninsula: A Naturalist in Baja California, 1961
If You Don't Mind My Saying So . . . Essays on Man and Nature, 1964
And Even if You Do: Essays on Man, Manners, and Machines, 1967
The Best Nature Writing, 1969
A Krutch Omnibus: Forty Years of Social and Literary Criticism, 1970

Other writings: the autobiography *More Lives Than One* (1962), studies of Edgar Allan Poe (1926), Samuel Johnson (1944), and Thoreau (1948), and works on literature, social criticism, and nature.

Bibliography
Lehman, Anthony L., "Joseph Wood Krutch: A Selected Annotated Bibliography of Primary Sources," *Bulletin of Bibliography* 41 (June 1984): 74–80

Further Reading
Abbey, Edward, "On Nature, the Modern Temper and the Southwest: An Interview with Joseph Wood Krutch," *Sage* 2 (1968): 13–21
Dubos, Rene, "The Despairing Optimist," *American Scholar* 40 (1971): 16–20
Gorman, John, "Joseph Wood Krutch: A Cactus *Walden*," *Journal of the Society for the Study of Multi-Ethnic Literature of the United States* 7 (Winter 1984): 93–101
Kilgo, James, "Krutch's Sonoran Pastoral: The Aesthetic Integrity of *The Desert Year*," *Southwestern American Literature* 7 (1981): 9–21
Limerick, Patricia Nelson, *Desert Passages*, Albuquerque: University of New Mexico Press, 1985: 127–48
McClintock, James, *Nature's Kindred Spirits: Aldo Leopold, Joseph Wood Krutch, Edward Abbey, Annie Dillard, Gary Snyder*, Madison: University of Wisconsin Press, 1994
Margolis, John D., *Joseph Wood Krutch: A Writer's Life*, Knoxville: University of Tennessee Press, 1980
Pavich, Paul N., *Joseph Wood Krutch*, Boise, Idaho: Boise State University, 1989

Powell, Lawrence Clark, "Southwest Classics Reread: Joseph Wood Krutch's *The Desert Year*," *Westways* (June 1971): 14–16, 66–67

Rowley, Robert, "Joseph Wood Krutch: The Forgotten Voice of the Desert," *American Scholar* 64 (1995): 438–43

Slater, Peter Gregg, "The Negative Secularism of the Modern Temper," *American Quarterly* 33 (1981): 185–205

Van Lann, Thomas F., "The Death-of-Tragedy Myth," *Journal of Dramatic Theory and Criticism* 5 (1991): 5–31

Wild, Peter, *Pioneer Conservationists of Western America*, Missoula, Montana: Mountain Press, 1979: 131–39

Wild, Peter, "Ash Heap for Bright Ruderals: Joseph Wood Krutch's *The Modern Temper*," *North Dakota Quarterly* (Fall 1989): 14–22

L

La Bruyère, Jean de

French, 1645–1696

The story is told about La Bruyère that he often visited Étienne Michallet, who would eventually become his publisher, and enjoyed playing with the book dealer's young daughter. On the day he offered Michallet the manuscript of *Les Caractères ou mœurs de ce siècle* (*The Characters, or the Manners of the Age*), La Bruyère, uncertain of the book's chances for success, proposed that any profits from the work become the dowry of Michallet's daughter. Since her dowry was substantial, the story may well be true. The author who emerges from the pages of the *Characters*, however, is anything but a carefree, resilient man given to spontaneous gestures of liberality. On the contrary, La Bruyère is a sharp, at times bitter observer of the foibles of humankind. His trenchant prose cuts to the core – often unpleasant – of issues and personalities. In its acuity of perception, attention to detail, and insistence on stylistic perfection, La Bruyère's work reflects, above all, the author's devotion to writing.

La Bruyère is best known for his *Characters*, first published in 1688 together with his translation of the **Characters** of Theophrastus (wr. c. 319 BCE). The translation of Theophrastus is based primarily upon the Latin translation by Isaac Casaubon (1592 and 1599), although La Bruyère clearly knew Greek and consulted the original text. In 1693, La Bruyère was elected to membership of the French Academy. The *Discours* (Discourse) he delivered on the day of his reception was immediately attacked, and he had it reprinted in the eighth edition of his *Characters*, this time with a **preface** in which he defends himself. Aside from some **letters**, most of them to Louis II de Bourbon, Prince de Condé about his grandson, for whom La Bruyère had been appointed tutor, the author's only other published work is the *Dialogues sur le quiétisme* (Dialogues on Quietism). Here La Bruyère sides with his friend and supporter the Bishop of Meaux, Jacques-Bénigne Bossuet, against the Quietists, a small sect of religious mystics who believed in the total abandonment of the human will in the contemplation of God's presence. The nine **dialogues** were published posthumously in 1698, but carry a 1699 publication date. Ellies du Pin, their editor, appears to have written the last two dialogues and undoubtedly altered the others. This work is not an important literary achievement. La Bruyère is, finally, a writer whose greatness rests on one text – the *Characters*.

That work was far more popular than either its author or its publisher had foreseen. During La Bruyère's lifetime, eight successive editions appeared, and in the course of their publication, the work more than doubled in size. Taking his society and its inhabitants as raw material, La Bruyère set out, as he says in the preface of the *Characters*, to "paint mankind in general." He was simply giving back to the public what it had given him. This he did in a series of **aphorisms**, remarks, descriptive passages, and portraits, organized into 16 **chapters** whose titles cover a wide diversity of subjects, among them the works of the mind, women, the heart, the court, the town, the sovereign, humankind, the pulpit, and freethinkers. La Bruyère claimed that the individual fragments of each chapter had "a certain gradual connection," but this seems to be more self-justification than the enunciation of a principle to which he consciously adhered as he wrote.

The most memorable and controversial passages in the *Characters* are the portraits of imaginary individuals. These are drawn with brilliant stylistic finesse and are recognized as models of literary portraiture. Some of the best known of these character studies are those of Ménippe, who has no thoughts of his own but merely repeats the sentiments of others; the hopelessly absent-minded Ménalque; the hyper-hypocritical Onuphre, based on Molière's Tartuffe; and the couple Giton and Phédon, whose physical beings correspond exactly to their financial circumstances of extraordinary wealth in the one case and abject penury in the other.

From shortly after the first appearance of the *Characters*, *clefs* (keys) claiming to identify the imaginary characters began to be published. However, La Bruyère maintained that he did not, in creating each portrait, take specific people as his subjects. The real interest of the *Characters* has little to do with whom La Bruyère may have had in mind in any particular passage. In the preface to his speech before the French Academy, he asserts that "every writer is a painter, and every excellent writer an excellent painter." He later defends his *Characters* as being precisely what he had said they would be: a portrayal of "mankind in general."

La Bruyère's portrait of humankind as it develops through the editions of the *Characters* has a paradoxical quality. As one of the major *moralistes* of 17th-century French literature, La Bruyère, like his counterparts **La Rochefoucauld** and **Pascal**, is a keen observer of human beings. What he observes, however, does not always correspond perfectly with what this orthodox Catholic monarchist believes; and therein lies something of the fascination that his work holds for readers today.

On the one hand, La Bruyère thinks it possible to penetrate beyond the surface of human existence to uncover a fixed reality, the essence of a human being. On the other, he wonders, "... how shall I fix this restless, giddy, and irascible man ... I depict him as devout ... and he is already a free-thinker." Whence La Bruyère's definition of a devout person as "one who under an atheistical king, would be an atheist." In the end, La Bruyère admits, "Such a man's inmost feelings can really not be described ... he is not exactly what he thinks he is himself or what he appears to be."

La Bruyère is one of the few major writers of 17th-century France to evince compassion for those on the lowest rungs of the social ladder. A committed monarchist convinced of the necessity of a social hierarchy, he believed, nonetheless, that the king should behave as a shepherd concerned for the well-being of his flock. A famous passage in the *Characters* evokes the plight of France's peasants, reduced to the state of animals and unable to reap the benefits of the crops they have sown. Given the choice between belonging to the society of a nobility that does little good and is capable of great evil and that of the common people, La Bruyère declares firmly that "I should select, without hesitation, being a plebeian."

What the *Characters* portray is not always an attractive sight, but each of the work's perfectly crafted passages reveals an author who attempts to lay bare the truth. The drama of the text lies in the disparity at times apparent between what it reveals and what its author had imagined he would discover.

MICHAEL S. KOPPISCH

See also Character Sketch

Biography
Born probably August 1645 (baptized 17 August 1645) in Paris. Studied law in Orléans, licence in law, 1665; admitted to the bar, Paris, 1665. Bought office as king's counsellor and financial treasurer, Caen, 1673 (sold, 1686); tutor to his sister's daughters, from 1674; tutor, 1684–87, then secretary and librarian to Duke Louis II de Bourbon. Elected to the French Academy, 1693. Died (of apoplexy) in Versailles, 10–11 May 1696.

Selected Writings

Essays and Related Prose
Les Caractères de Théophraste traduits du grec, avec Les Caractères ou mœurs de ce siècle, 1688; several substantially revised and enlarged editions, 1689–96; edited by R. Garapon, 1962, and J. P. Kaminker, 2 vols., 1966; as *The Characters, or the Manners of the Age* (various translators), 1699; translated by Henri van Laun, 1885 (reprinted 1992), Helen Stott, 1890, and Jean Stewart, 1970; selections translated by Elizabeth Lee, 1903

Other writings: dialogues, a discourse, and correspondence.

Collected works editions: *Œuvres complètes*, edited by Gustave Servois, 4 vols., 1865–82, revised edition, 1922; *Œuvres complètes* (Pléiade Edition), edited by Julien Benda, 1951.

Further Reading
Brody, Jules, *Du style à la pensée: Trois études sur Les Caractères de La Bruyère*, Lexington, Kentucky: French Forum, 1980
Delft, Louis van, *La Bruyère moraliste*, Geneva: Droz, 1971
Garapon, Robert, *Les Caractères de La Bruyère, La Bruyère au travail*, Paris: Société d'Édition d'Enseignement Supérieur, 1978
Gray, Floyd, *La Bruyère, amateur de Caractères*, Paris: Nizet, 1986
Jasinski, René, *Deux accès à La Bruyère*, Paris: Minard, 1971
Kirsch, Doris, *La Bruyère ou le style cruel*, Montreal: Presses de l'Université de Montréal, 1977
Knox, Edward C., *Jean de La Bruyère*, New York: Twayne, 1973
Koppisch, Michael S., *The Dissolution of Character: Changing Perspectives in La Bruyère's Caractères*, Lexington, Kentucky: French Forum, 1981
Michaut, Gustave, *La Bruyère*, Paris: Boivin, 1936
Mourgues, Odette de, *Two French Moralists: La Rochefoucauld and La Bruyère*, Cambridge: Cambridge University Press, 1978
Richard, Pierre, *La Bruyère et ses Caractères*, Paris: Nizet, 1965
Soler, Patrice, *Jean de La Bruyère, Les Caractères*, Paris: Presses Universitaires de France, 1994
Stegmann, André, *Les Caractères de La Bruyère*, Paris: Larousse, 1972

Lamb, Charles
British, 1775–1834

Charles Lamb worked as a clerk for a mercantile firm from the age of 17 until he retired at 50. A writer by avocation, he published poetry, a novel, two plays, **critical essays**, stories for children (with his sister Mary), and **familiar essays**. His critical essays earned respect, and *Tales from Shakespeare* (1807), a collection of plot sketches for children, remains popular. The familiar essays, however, are the works on which his literary reputation rests. These essays began to appear in 1820, most of them in the *London Magazine*. Lamb later collected them in three volumes: two series of *Elia* (1823, 1828) and *The Last Essays of Elia* (1833). Selections were regularly anthologized for more than a century after Lamb's death, and the collection continues to receive critical attention.

Lamb helped shape the English essay. Before the Romantic period, the essay was defined by the work of **Addison** and **Steele** – familiar in tone, social and didactic in purpose. In the hands of Lamb and his contemporaries, the essay became familiar not only in tone but also in purpose. Rather than posing as models of a social class, Lamb and writers like **William Hazlitt** and **Thomas De Quincey** appeared personally in their own texts and declared their personal opinions. The personality of the writer merged with the substance of the essay. Lamb stands apart even from his contemporaries, however, in foregrounding the writer's personality, for two reasons. First, in Lamb's essays, the personality of the writer nudges the thesis off stage. Writing in the persona of Elia, a charming, curious, and talkative London bachelor, Lamb reminisces, describes a scene or a character, proposes one opinion only to replace it with another – often all of these in a single essay – never seriously advancing a thesis. One effect is that the reader, after "conversing" with Elia, is so well entertained as not to notice, or mind, the absence of a point. Elia's personal charm is the whole essay. Another effect of the essays' taking no strong stands, however, is that Elia's personality is elusive. A feeling of intimacy combines with a sense of never knowing where the essays rest intellectually. For these reasons, in Lamb's hands the English essay becomes not a vehicle for ideas, but a plaything, a divertissement.

The familiar tone of his essays comes partly from a conversational flow of words – Lamb took great pains revising his texts in order to achieve the effect of conversational ease – and partly from a choice of the most commonplace subjects. The subjects of the essays suit the tone. Lamb – or Elia – does not try to figure out life, any more than he tries to explain himself personally. Delighting in the diversion of the moment, he chats ardently on ordinary topics. He recalls the adventure of a walk in town, portrays an odd character, or describes a familiar place. The most typical essays, and the most beloved, take up an array of homely, familiar themes, evident in a sampling of titles: "Mrs. Battle's Opinions on Whist" (1821), "The South-Sea House" (1820), "A Chapter on Ears" (1821), "Grace Before Meat" (1821), "Witches, and Other Night Fears" (1821), "The Praise of Chimney-Sweepers" (1822), "A Dissertation upon Roast Pig" (1822), "The Tombs in the Abbey" (1823), and so on.

Lamb's familiar tone was directed to a familiar audience – educated Londoners whom he knew personally. Although a stammer kept Lamb from pursuing a university education (which prepared one for the pulpit), he was gifted and well read enough to mingle with the intellectual elite. His stammer did not prevent him from attaining a reputation as a stimulating conversationalist. A sociable, kindly person, fond of jokes and puns, Lamb liked company. His eclectic social gatherings included well-known Romantics, and literature and art were frequent topics of conversation. Close to **Coleridge**, Hazlitt, **Southey**, and Wordsworth, Lamb also socialized with De Quincey, **Hunt**, and Keats, among others. In 1820 the founding of the *London Magazine* provided a public showcase for the wit of such social gatherings, and coincidentally guided Lamb to the medium best suited for his literary talents. Old friends and new literary comrades met in the *London*'s pages – and at monthly dinners – creating a milieu of fellow writers and readers who labored to impress and surpass each other, who stimulated and informed each other, and whose habitual acquaintance gave support and encouragement. It is this circle – and, by extension, the educated people of London in the 1820s – for whom Lamb primarily wrote.

Besides Elia's playfulness and familiar tone, several other features distinguish Lamb's style. His puckish humor moved him often to mix fact with fiction, historical accuracy with imagination. His love for the literature of previous centuries seasoned his essays with old-fashioned expressions and allusions to Shakespeare, Milton, and the prose writers **Sir Thomas Browne**, Robert Burton, and Thomas Fuller; even at the moment they were published, Lamb's essays had an archaic flavor because of his taste for literature over a century old. He also possessed what he called an "antithetical manner," which led him to entertain contrary viewpoints with equanimity. Finally, he was sentimental, sometimes to the point of sentimentality. Each of these idiosyncrasies contributes in its own way to the elusiveness of the essays, and together they have caused some critics to call them "quaint"; yet Lamb's ability to make his own idiosyncrasies the subject of artful reflection helped create the familiar or **personal essay**.

No single passage can illustrate all of Lamb's qualities, but perhaps a few citations can give a sense of his style. In Lamb's most anthologized essay, "A Dissertation upon Roast Pig," Elia professes to have found an ancient Chinese manuscript that describes the discovery of this delicacy. The alleged document tells how a father and son are tried for arson after they repeatedly burn down their house – the only way they know of roasting pigs, which are trapped inside. The two are acquitted, however, when the jury discover how delicious the evidence is:

> The judge, who was a shrewd fellow, winked at the manifest iniquity of the decision; and when the court was dismissed, went privily and bought up all the pigs that could be had for love or money. In a few days his lordship's town-house was observed to be on fire. The thing took wing, and now there was nothing to be seen but fires in every direction. Fuel and pigs grew enormously dear all over the district. The insurance-offices one and all shut up shop. People built slighter and slighter every day, until it was feared that the very science of architecture would in no long time be lost to the world. Thus this custom of firing houses continued, till in process of time, says my manuscript, a sage arose, like our Locke, who made a discovery that the flesh of swine, or indeed of any other animal, might be cooked . . . without the necessity of consuming a whole house to dress it.

Here broad burlesque extends beyond its initial success and transforms itself gradually into finer humor. The series of quips, each topping the one before, recalls the playfulness of the talk that Lamb so enjoyed at social gatherings. This passage also presents fanciful material as if it were true, mocking Lamb's own antiquarian bent by treating the "manuscript" with scholarly respect.

Lamb's more sentimental, less detached nature appears and reappears alongside his humor. While these two qualities often complement and mitigate each other, occasionally sentiment waxes into reverie. In "Old China" (1823), for example, Elia's cousin and living companion Bridget (modeled on Lamb's sister Mary) reminisces longingly on earlier days. Life was better when they were poor, she says, because they appreciated so much more the purchases for which they had to scrimp and save:

> Do you remember the brown suit, which you made to hang upon you, till all your friends cried shame upon you, it grew so threadbare – and all because of that folio Beaumont and Fletcher, which you dragged home late at night from Barker's in Covent Garden? Do you remember how we eyed it for weeks before we could make up our minds to the purchase, and had not come to a determination till it was near ten o'clock of the Saturday night, when you set off from Islington, fearing you should be too late – and when the old bookseller with some grumbling opened his shop, and by the twinkling taper (for he was setting bedwards) lighted out the relic from his dusty treasures – and when you lugged it home, wishing it were twice as cumbersome – and when you presented it to me – and when we were exploring the perfectness of it . . . and while I was repairing some of the loose leaves with paste, which your impatience would not suffer to be left till day-break – was there no pleasure in being a poor man?

Even in this sentimental passage, however, Lamb the craftsman does not let the essay rest on nostalgia alone. After Elia hears

Bridget out, he returns a gentle rebuttal, "It is true we were happier when we were poorer, but we were also younger, my cousin . . ." Neither Elia nor Bridget can be said to "win" their hearthside debate – Elia gets the last word, but Bridget holds the floor longer. The essay concludes in a sort of suspension or synthesis, embracing the best of both arguments. Several of Lamb's essays exhibit this "antithetical manner." "Dissertation upon Roast Pig," for example, mentioned above, emphasizes the tenderness of the suckling to the point of making it an object of pity and even a symbol of Christ-like suffering. Yet the lightness of Lamb's touch avoids a collision between sympathy and appetite.

The elusiveness created by this and other devices of Lamb's style is a focus of much criticism of the essays, both negative and positive. Critics question whether Elia is Lamb, and what the essays reveal of the author's real thoughts. Many similarities between Elia and Lamb invite further comparison; and remarkable circumstances of Lamb's life make scrutiny of his essays more intense. As a young man Lamb lived with his sister Mary (ten years older than Lamb), their father and invalid mother and an aunt. When he was 21, Lamb returned home from work to find that Mary, in a fit of madness, had killed their mother with a knife. Lamb mastered the situation at that moment, kept his poise throughout the aftermath, and from then on devoted his life to his sister, caring for her personally rather than allowing her to be confined to an asylum. Lamb himself had spent six weeks in an asylum at the age of 20. He was known in adulthood as a bit of an eccentric, incurably informal in social situations, and possessed of high tolerance for unpopular opinions.

These circumstances of Lamb's life affect critics differently. One extreme of opinion regards him as a saint, not only for the essays' constant good spirits, but also for the image of Lamb smiling in the face of disaster, sacrificing himself for Mary. The other extreme regrets that the essays lack any direct reference to his mother, his sister, or his love life, and sees Lamb as a coward for refusing to grapple intellectually with life's difficulties.

Most contemporary criticism praised the prose as the work of a person whose benignity shines through it. The essays were loved for the sake of the author, and their literary merits were described in general terms. This brand of criticism continued for about a hundred years. New Criticism tended to see Lamb's essays in a negative light. In the 1960s, however, close readings of Elia began to appear which recognized artistic achievement in the essays and attempted to account for it.

This recent criticism has interpreted Lamb's elusiveness as subtlety. Perhaps the most comprehensive view sees the essays as foils for the overly serious mind. Robert Frank (1976) suggests that Lamb felt one could not write seriously to his contemporaries because they were already too serious – stuck in moral positions and incapable of suspending judgment. Lamb took as his task, then, to teach the reader to give up judging; to open the reader's mind by calling all ideas into question. Given a reader who is opinionated, a writer seeks to deflect, to dissolve, to disqualify serious debate in an attempt to achieve level ground. This may be the sober strategy behind Elia's elusiveness. Or Lamb may simply be expressing his own inclination to dwell (Zen-like?) in the moment.

WILLIAM ZEIGER

Biography

Born 10 February 1775 in London. Studied at Christ's Hospital, London, 1782–89, where he met Samuel Taylor Coleridge. Clerk for the merchant Joseph Paice, 1790–91, in the examiner's office of the South Sea Company, 1791–92, and in the accountant's office of the East India Company, 1792–1825: retired with pension. Had a nervous breakdown and spent six weeks in an asylum, 1795–96; suffered from melancholia throughout the rest of his life; guardian from 1796 of his sister Mary, who suffered from mental illness and periodically had to be confined. Associated with Coleridge, Robert Southey, and William Hazlitt, and William and Dorothy Wordsworth. Wrote Elia essays for the London Magazine, 1820–25; also contributed to other journals. Lived in Enfield, Middlesex, 1827–32, and Edmonton, Middlesex, 1833–34. Died (of erysipelas) in Edmonton, 27 December 1834.

Selected Writings

Essays and Related Prose

Elia: Essays Which Have Appeared Under That Signature in the London Magazine, 1823; Second Series, 1828; both series, 2 vols., 1835; edited by W. Macdonald, 2 vols., 1929, Malcolm Elwin, with The Last Essays of Elia, 1952, and Jonathan Bate, with The Last Essays of Elia, 1987
The Last Essays of Elia, 1833; edited by Malcolm Elwin, with Elia, 1952, and Jonathan Bate, with Elia, 1987
Charles Lamb and Elia, edited by J. E. Morpurgo, 1948
The Portable Lamb, edited by John Masson Brown, 1949
A Lamb Selection: Letters and Essays, edited by F. B. Pinion, 1965
Lamb as Critic, edited by Roy Park, 1980
Selected Prose, edited by Adam Philips, 1985

Other writings: the Tales from Shakespeare with his sister Mary (2 vols., 1807), the novel Rosamund Gray (1798), two plays, poetry, tales and poetry for children, and several volumes of correspondence.

Collected works editions: The Works of Charles Lamb and Mary Lamb, edited by E. V. Lucas, 7 vols., 1903–05; Works (Oxford Edition), edited by Thomas Hutchinson, 2 vols., 1908.

Bibliographies

Barnett, George L., and Stuart M. Tave, "Charles Lamb," in The English Romantic Poets and Essayists: A Review of Research and Criticism, edited by Carolyn Washburn Houtchens and Lawrence Huston Houtchens, New York: New York University Press, and London: University of London Press, revised edition, 1966: 37–74
Livingston, Luther S., A Bibliography of the First Editions in Book Form of the Writings of Charles and Mary Lamb, New York: De Vinne Press, 1903
Thomson, J. C., Bibliography of the Writings of Charles and Mary Lamb, Hull: Tutin, 1908

Further Reading

Barnett, George L., Charles Lamb: The Evolution of Elia, Bloomington: Indiana University Press, 1964
Barnett, George L., Charles Lamb, Boston: Twayne, 1976
Brier, Peter A., "Dramatic Characterization in the Essays of Charles Lamb," Coronto 8 (1973): 3–24
Cecil, David, A Portrait of Charles Lamb, London: Constable, and New York: Scribner, 1983
Flesch, William, "'Friendly and Judicious' Reading: Affect and Irony in the Works of Charles Lamb," Studies in Romanticism 23 (Summer 1984): 163–81
Frank, Robert, Don't Call Me Gentle Charles! An Essay on Lamb's Essays of Elia, Corvallis: Oregon State University Press, 1976
Greene, Graham, "Lamb's Testimonials," Spectator no. 5518 (30 March 1935): 512–13

Haven, Richard, "The Romantic Art of Charles Lamb," *English Literary History* 30 (June 1963): 137–46
Jessup, Bernard, "The Mind of Elia," *Journal of the History of Ideas* 25 (1954): 246–59
Monsman, Gerald, "Charles Lamb's Art of Autobiography," *English Literary History* 50 (Fall 1983): 541–57
More, Paul Elmer, *Shelburne Essays*, 2nd series, New York: Putnam, 1905
Morley, F. V., *Lamb Before Elia*, Folcroft, Pennsylvania: Folcroft, 1973 (original edition, 1932)
Mulcahey, Daniel J., "Charles Lamb: The Antithetical Manner and the Two Planes," *Studies in English Literature, 1500–1900* 3 (Autumn 1963): 517–74
Nabholtz, John R., "Elia and the Transformed Reader," in *"My Reader My Fellow-Labourer": A Study of English Romantic Prose*, edited by Nabholtz, Columbia: University of Missouri Press, 1986
Parker, Mark, "Ideology and Editing: The Political Context of the Elia Essays," *Studies in Romanticism* 30 (Fall 1991): 473–94
Pater, Walter, *Appreciations*, Evanston, Illinois: Northwestern University Press, 1987 (original edition, 1889)
Randel, Fred V., *The World of Elia: Charles Lamb's Essayistic Romanticism*, Port Washington, New York: Kennikat, 1975
Reiman, Donald H., "The Thematic Unity in Charles Lamb's Familiar Essays," *Journal of English and Germanic Philology* 64 (July 1965): 470–78
Schoenfield, Mark, "Voices Together: Lamb, Hazlitt, and the London," *Studies in Romanticism* 29 (Summer 1990): 257–72
Thompson, Denys, "Our Debt to Lamb," in *Determinations*, edited by F. R. Leavis, New York: Haskell House, 1970 (original edition, 1934)

Lange, Per

Danish, 1901–1991

The dualistic tenor of Per Lange's essays emerged from philosophical views already crystallized at the time of his debut in 1926. His collection of lyrics entitled *Kaos og stjærnen* (Chaos and the star) alluded to the Nietzschean sentence expressed in *Also sprach Zarathustra* (1883–85; *Thus Spoke Zarathustra*): "Man must still have chaos, to give birth to a dancing star." In both his poetry and his essays, the failure to overcome the chaos coincides with the image of the insatiable, lonesome wanderer. Particularly as an essayist, Lange assumed the voice of the traveler and the skeptic. As a philosophical aesthete and intellectual aristocrat, he gave expression to man's unrest and the division between the realizations of life and art. His aesthetic program recognized the duality of Apollonian and Dionysian styles of life.

Between Lange's career as a poet, in which he produced only three collections of lyrics, and his career as an essayist lie more than 20 years. His essay collections span the years from 1953 (*Spejlinger* [Reflections]) to 1982 (*Udvalgte essays* [Selected essays]). Some have recognized him as Denmark's most accomplished essayist. Part of that recognition can be ascribed to his defining the essay for modern Danish readers. With "Om essayets kunst" (1964; On the art of the essay), he reaffirmed the foundation of the essay and placed its home outside academia. The essay, he wrote, requires a "natural tête-à-tête" between author and reader. Essentially, the essay is nothing more than an expression of a personal whim disguised in artistic form. The essayist allows his public to enjoy the same expression.

Lange insisted that the essay is short; via Polonius, he reminded his reader that "brevity is the soul of wit." The shortness of the essay not only allows the reader a sense of freedom (he does not feel bound to the opinions of the author), but also encourages trust between the essayist and the reader. The essay should appear learned, but, as Lange explained, if there are holes in one's thinking, the essayist should view the world through those holes. His insistence that the essayist should not appear better versed than his readers was central to his writing. The essayist, according to Lange, "must make his reader his equal and create a sense of trust and he must never raise his voice to the extent that he might be perceived as wanting to convince."

The distinguishing feature of the modern essay is its ability to let the reader feel that he is alone with the author. In this regard, Lange recalled the English essayist **Charles Lamb**'s notion of a "conversation with the reader." The sense of intimacy which emerges through such "conversations" gives way to the **personal essay**, for which Lange again looked to Lamb for inspiration.

In his essays Lange was not driven by the dictates of tendentious literature. He was, rather, an impressionable but discreet wanderer. The spectrum of his themes was broad; he wrote, on the one hand, on the lives of authors, composers, and artists, and, on the other, on God and death. Stylistically, Lange was indebted to **Montaigne**'s essays and to **La Rochefoucauld**'s moral **maxim**s and reflective epigrams. He also drew inspiration from the English models **Addison** and **Steele**. In both his **personal essay**s and his portraits Lange was a master of humor and irony.

VIVIAN GREENE-GANTZBERG

Biography
Son of the literary critic Sven Lange. Born 30 August 1901 in Hørsholm, near Copenhagen. Studied at Copenhagen University, from 1919. Lived in Austria, 1923, and Italy, 1926–27; visited Italy and Greece, 1958. Worked as a reader for Gyldendal publishers for many years. Contributor to *Tilskueren* (The spectator). Died in 1991.

Selected Writings

Essays and Related Prose
Spejlinger: Essays, 1953
Ved musikkens tærskel og andre essays, 1957
Samtale med et æsel, 1961
Om krig og krigsmænd, og andre essays, 1966
Dyrenes maskerade og andre essayer, 1969
Udvalgte essays, 1982

Other writings: three volumes of poetry. Also translated from the French, English, and Swedish.

Bibliography
Dansk Skønlitterært Forfatterlexikon: 1900–1950, vol. 2, Copenhagen: Grønholt Pedersen, 1960: 174–75

Further Reading
Andersen, Harry, "Per Lange og hans essays," *Nordisk Ttidskrift för Vetenskap, Konst och Industri* 51 (1975): 23–41

Frederiksen, Emil, in *Danske digtere i det 20. aarhundrede*, vol. 1, edited by Ernst Frandsen and Niels Kaas Johansen, Copenhagen: Gyldendal, 1951

Nielsen, Hans-Jørgen, "Formernes fastholdelse: Otto Gelsted, Tom Kristensen, Paul al Cour og Per Lange," in *Tilbageblik på 30'erne*, vol. 2, edited by Hans Hertel, Copenhagen: Vendelkær, 1967: 889–97

Sandersen, Vibeke, *Essayet – oprøret og tradition*, Copenhagen: Gyldendal, 1975: 33–47

Thomsen, Ejnar, *Digteren og Kaldet*, Copenhagen: Gyldendal, 1957

La Rochefoucauld

French, 1613–1680

François VI, Duc de La Rochefoucauld, is best known for the *Maximes*, a work whose last title during the author's lifetime was *Réflexions; ou, Sentences et maximes morales*. The manuscripts of these mostly brief **aphorism**s were circulated in 1663 among a select group of guests of his friend, the Marquise de Sablé. The manuscript was leaked, and published first in a pirate edition dated 1664, almost certainly without La Rochefoucauld's complicity, in the interest of advancing the rigorous spirituality associated with the Augustinian theology of Jansenism and the monastery of Port-Royal. La Rochefoucauld immediately published an authentic edition late in 1664 (but dated 1665) and then, chiefly by dropping the prefatory discourse and the long initial **maxim** on "amour-propre," distanced himself from the Augustinian interpretation of his moral vision in a second edition of 1666.

La Rochefoucauld was also the author of other related works. They included an *Apologie* of 1649, disdainful of the chief minister, Mazarin; *Mémoires*, possibly begun before 1656 and again intended for circulation only among a select group of friends, but published without La Rochefoucauld's connivance in Belgium in 1662; and a series of 19 *Réflexions diverses*, of the greatest interest in the present context on account of the light they shed on the development of the essay genre in France.

Montaigne's *Essais*, first published in 1580, had been a series of often intimate disquisitions containing much moral and historical speculation. The **chapters** of his book, although not intended to be essays in the modern sense, are regarded as early examples of the essay. Between Montaigne and La Rochefoucauld the genre had developed in France, emerging from formal **letters**, often intended for publication, on subjects of interest to the cultivated classes, and from short **treatises**, sometimes written as polemic, often speculative, and occasionally appearing as **prefaces** to books. In La Rochefoucauld's *Réflexions*, the **moral essay** and **historical essay** can be seen for the first time to have clear links with another important genre emerging in mid-17th-century France: the portrait.

The portrait as a literary genre had begun in France in the mid-1650s, largely with the immensely popular novels of Madeleine de Scudéry, whose *Clélie* (1660–62) had included often idealized but recognizable portraits of members of the new salon society emerging after the mid-century civil wars known as the Fronde. Fifty-seven of the newly fashionable portraits were collected by two well-known literary figures, Jean-Regnauld de Segrais and Pierre-Daniel Huet, for a sumptuously bound collection published as *Divers Portraits* in 1659 by Mme. de Montpensier, "la grande Mademoiselle," niece of Louis XIII, who wrote 16 of them herself. The enterprising bookseller-publishers Claude Barbin and Charles Sercy then published as many portraits as they could lay their hands on, printing over 500 in the 1659 *Recueil de portraits et éloges en vers et en prose* (Collection of portraits and eulogies in verse and in prose), including some taken from the *Divers Portraits*.

La Rochefoucauld's first "essay" was probably the subtle self-portrait of 1658 included in Mme. de Montpensier's volume. He was to write other portraits, notably of the Cardinal de Retz, as well as of Mme. de Montespan, Richelieu, and the Comte d'Harcourt, but these were published only as an appendix to the *Réflexions diverses*, some at least of which were true essays, however closely related in subject matter and viewpoint to the briefer *Maximes*. Seven of the *Réflexions diverses* were first published in 1731, the other 12 not until 1863. La Rochefoucauld is known to have revised them toward the end of his life, but the dates of earlier drafts remain uncertain. They are much longer than the *Maximes* and some are nearer to the *Mémoires* in style, but it is not impossible that the famous maxim on "amour-propre," already an essay in all but name, was first conceived as a portrait of a moral state or motive personalized by La Rochefoucauld. It was certainly first published in the third part of Sercy's *Recueil de pièces en prose* very late in 1659, and was preceded by a letter addressed to a lady and signed by "L'Amour-propre," as by a male whom the addressee had rejected. It was suppressed as too open to a Jansenist interpretation after the first authentic edition of the *Maximes*, which began with it, but may well provide an early and striking example of the way in which the portrait evolved into the essay in France in the 1650s.

The 19 *Réflexions diverses* differ too widely from one another to form a coherent whole. Three, including the long 19th with its attached portraits, are devoted rather in the manner of Montaigne to the consideration of the peculiarities of history. Another four are virtuoso exercises on common themes, "the sea and love," "the relationship between human beings and animals," "the origin of sicknesses," and "coquettes and old men." Half a dozen concern social behavior and taste, while only four – "the uncertainty of jealousy," "the difference of minds," "inconstancy," and "retirement" – are clearly related to the maxims in focus and penetration by their psychological analyses.

La Rochefoucauld's essays are nonetheless marked by the same perceptiveness, wit, and restrained cynicism as are apparent in the *Maximes*. Sometimes the *Réflexions* are harsher, emphasizing pride rather than self-interest as a principal human motive, and invariably uncovering beneath a surface of social lustre reasons for the inevitability of inconstancy, insincerity, and hypocrisy. Underlying them is always an ideal of moral attitudes, social behavior, and a hierarchical division of personal qualities which reflect the instincts of a cultivated French social elite on the whole opposed to the increasing power wielded by the non-aristocratic but wealthy and educated bourgeois classes. La Rochefoucauld's cultivated tastes, his fastidiousness, and his psychological acumen keep him above anything so vulgar as snobbery. The foundation of his lasting power as a writer lies not in any implied defense of outdated moral qualities and social attitudes, but in the penetration and analytical skill for which he found the ideal vehicle in the short forms of essay and maxim. By developing the game of intelligent and sensitive society portraiture into a new literary genre, he also brought new life to the essay form in France.

ANTHONY LEVI

Biography

François VI, le Prince de Marcillac, Duc de La Rochefoucauld. Born 15 September 1613 in Paris. Married Andrée de Vivonne, 1628 (died, 1670): eight children. Maître de camp, 1629; served in Italy, the Netherlands, 1635–36, Rocroi, 1643, and Gravelines, 1644, and severely wounded at the Battle of Mardick, 1646. Imprisoned briefly by Richelieu for conspiracy against the court, 1637, then banished to Verteuil for two years. Liaison with the Duchesse de Longueville, from 1646. Participated in the Fronde (rebellions against the ministry of Cardinal Mazarin in the reign of Louis XIV), 1648–52: almost blinded in fighting in Paris, 1652; fled to Luxembourg, then allowed back to France and lived in Verteuil, 1653; allowed to live in Paris, 1656. Lived in retirement among a small intellectual circle, including Mmes. de Sablé, de Sévigné, and de Lafayette. Took part in Louis XIV's Dutch campaign, 1667–68. Suffered from gout, from 1669. Died in Paris, 17 March 1680.

Selected Writings

Essays and Related Prose
Apologie de M. le Prince de Marcillac, 1649
Mémoires, 1662; edited by Gabriel de La Rochefoucauld, 1925; as *The Memoirs*, translated anonymously, 1684
Sentences et maximes de morale, 1664 (Dutch pirated edition); as *Réflexions; ou, Sentences et maximes morales*, 1665 (actually 1664); revised and enlarged editions, 1666, 1671, 1675, 1676, 1678 (definitive edition), and 1693; as *Maximes*, edited by Robert L. Cru, 1927, Henry A. Grubbs, 1929, Frederick C. Green, 1945, Roland Barthes, 1961, Jean Starobinski, 1964, Dominique Secretan, 1967, and Jacques Truchet (Classiques Garnier), 1967; as *Maxims*, translated by Aphra Behn, 1685, A. S. Bolton, 1884, F. C. Stevens, 1939, Constantine FitzGibbon, 1957, Louis Kronenberger, 1959, and Leonard W. Tancock, 1959
Réflexions diverses, in *Œuvres*, vol. 1, edited by D. L. Gilbert and others, 1868; edited (with *Maximes*) by Henry A. Grubbs, 1929, S. de Sacy, 1965, Jacques Truchet (Classiques Garnier), 1967, and Dominique Secretan, 1967

Other writings: the autobiography *Portrait de La Rochefoucauld par lui-même* (1659) and journals.

Collected works editions: *Œuvres*, edited by D. L. Gilbert and others, 4 vols., 1868–93; *Œuvres complètes* (Pléiade Edition), edited by Louis Martin-Chauffier, revised by Jean Marchand, 1964.

Bibliography
Marchand, Jean, *Bibliographie générale raisonnée de La Rochefoucauld*, Paris: Giraud-Badin, 1948

Further Reading
Baker, Susan Read, *Collaboration et originalité chez La Rochefoucauld*, Gainesville: University Presses of Florida, 1980
Bishop, Morris, *The Life and Adventures of La Rochefoucauld*, Ithaca, New York: Cornell University Press, 1951
Clark, Henry C., *La Rochefoucauld and the Language of Unmasking in Seventeenth-Century France*, Geneva: Droz, 1994

Hippeau, Louis, *Essai sur la morale de La Rochefoucauld*, Paris: Nizet, 1978
Hodgson, Richard G., *Falsehood Disguised: Unmasking the Truth in La Rochefoucauld*, West Lafayette, Indiana: Purdue University Press, 1995
Lafond, Jean, *La Rochefoucauld, Augustinisme et littérature*, Paris: Klincksieck, 1977
Lewis, Philip E., *La Rochefoucauld: The Art of Abstraction*, Ithaca, New York: Cornell University Press, 1977
Magne, Emile, *Le Vrai Visage de La Rochefoucauld*, Paris: Ollendorff, 1923
Moore, W. G., *La Rochefoucauld: His Mind and Art*, Oxford: Clarendon Press, 1969
Mourgues, Odette de, *Two French Moralists: La Rochefoucauld and La Bruyère*, Cambridge: Cambridge University Press, 1978
Rosso, Corrado, *Procès à La Rochefoucauld et à la maxime*, Pisa: Goliardica, 1986
Thweat, Vivien, *La Rochefoucauld and the Seventeenth-Century Concept of the Self*, Geneva: Droz, 1980
Watts, Derek, *La Rochefoucauld, Maximes et réflexions diverses*, Glasgow: University of Glasgow French and German Publications, 1993
Zeller, Mary F., *New Aspects of Style in the Maxims of La Rochefoucauld*, Washington, D.C.: Catholic University of America Press, 1954

Larose, Jean
French Canadian, 1948–

Jean Larose is many things to many people. For some, his statements about Quebec's political status within the Canadian Federation amount to sheer provocation. Others accuse him of elitism, because he has pointed out the shortcomings of the contemporary educational system, and is said to disdain mass media culture. A few nationalists reprove him for his use of European philosophy and literature. Still others think of him as one of the most important voices in the field of the Québécois essay. Despite these controversies, all would agree that, with four books in print, Larose has shown himself to be someone to be reckoned with in today's intellectual debate in French Canada.

Le Mythe de Nelligan (1981; The myth of Nelligan), Larose's first book, is closer to traditional literary criticism than the other three. The poems of Émile Nelligan serve as a starting point for the author's investigation of the origins – both of the poet and, by extension, of the nation. Born to a French Canadian mother and an Irish father, and confined to an asylum for most of his adult life, Nelligan was the sort of literary figure that lends itself easily to myth, and Larose uses that myth to scrutinize Quebec family ties from an anthropological and psychoanalytical point of view. In using a pastiche of the Marquis de Sade's epigraph to *La Philosophie dans le boudoir* (1795; *Philosophy in the Bedroom*) as the epigraph to his own book, Larose underscores the link between generations and between Europe and North America: "The son will prescribe the reading of this book to his father." Just as the complexity of family symbolic structures lies at the core of Larose's thought, so does the intricate web linking Quebec to France.

If *Le Mythe de Nelligan* was praised within literary circles, it did not get the media attention *La Petite Noirceur* (1987) was to receive six years later. Soon after it appeared, this collection of essays was nominated for the 1987 Governor-General's Award (which it subsequently won) – a prize given under the aegis of a federal government agency – and polemics raged. "Anti-Canada book up for national prize," read one headline. Most of the uproar came from a literal reading of the book's final chapter, "'Si tu reviens au Canada . . .': Lettre à une amie" ('If you come back to Canada . . .': letter to a friend). Here, in a letter to a fictional friend living in New York, Larose advises against coming back to the native country. His statements about Canada as a whole were designed to be provocative: "Leaving is the writer's last recourse against Canada."

The debate surrounding that essay diverted attention from the main issues in *La Petite Noirceur*, namely the relationship between culture and nationalism in Quebec. Larose's position was already clear from the title he gave his book: his *petite noirceur* (small darkness) refers to Quebec's *grande noirceur* (big darkness), the period that preceded the so-called *Révolution Tranquille* (Quiet Revolution) of the early 1960s. It is commonly accepted that the Quiet Revolution brought French Canada from being a closed and culturally retarded society into an open, modern nation. Not so, says Larose, who shows that the attitudes and misconceptions that precluded Quebec from producing any sustained culture for such a long time have remained the same up to this day. The author uses Lacanian theory – in a broad sense – to demonstrate how Quebec has not managed to move from imaginary modes of conscience to symbolic ones, how images matter more than the ways in which they are organized into symbols. Cultural mimesis is not culture, according to Larose.

L'Amour du pauvre (1991; Love of the poor) did not stir the same emotion throughout Canada as Larose's previous collection, although it raised many of the same issues from a slightly different perspective. What he had first called *petite noirceur* had transformed itself into *pauvreté* (poverty). Larose traces that poverty in a number of works of art, from movies to poems, as well as in the realm of teaching (the essays on that subject are the most controversial of the book). His general diagnosis remains that which he exposed in *La Petite Noirceur*: Quebec's intellectual poverty derives from its refusal to admit the distance between object and subject. The familiarity that prevails in Quebec's culture prevents its intellectuals from becoming part of "humanist modernity" in its fullest sense. This situation will not change until Quebec's intellectuals realize that, in order to liberate oneself, one has to fight against a "maître" (master).

La Souveraineté rampante (1994; Cringing sovereignty) is more explicitly political than Larose's previous works. This short **pamphlet** groups four texts that deal with the sovereignist movement's pusillanimity, and the cultural prejudices of a few of Larose's opponents. These essays are united by one theme, the resentment of Quebec nationalists toward their perceived colonizers. As a counterpoint to this resentment, Larose promotes a view of independence that is not based on traditional nationalist values, but on "vraie souveraineté" (true sovereignty) or "souveraineté souveraine" (sovereign sovereignty) – on a sovereignty that imposes itself shamelessly but in a positive rather than negative sense. For Larose, one has to be at the same time "québécois, américain et universel" (Québécois, American, and universal). Literature, argues the author here as in his other essays, should be at the forefront of that new political stance.

The essayist's description of his own writing posture in that book is worth quoting, for it characterizes his style in all of his books: "Thus I could not keep my reflections to myself. Some will find them arrogant or rash, especially as they are not without my usual dose of exaggeration, but this gives me the opportunity to find a more universal truth than that which is limited to reasonable and profitable discourse . . ." In a nutshell Larose gives his concept of the essay. Reason is important to prose writing, but it cannot bring full light to any given subject all by itself. It needs be mixed with exaggeration, as long as this is intentional. When Larose states that his motto is "juger raide" (judge tough) or that he wishes to "se dresser contre" (rise against), he never loses sight of his writing persona, that of a free intellectual promoting the radical use of language.

BENOÎT MELANÇON

Biography
Born in 1948 in Valleyfield, Quebec. Studied at the University of Paris VIII-Vincennes, Ph.D., 1979. Professor of French studies, University of Montreal, since 1979. Contributor to various journals, including *Liberté*, *Québec Studies*, *La Revue Belge de Cinéma* (The Belgian review of cinema), *La Deriva delle Francofonie*, *Québec Français*, and *Le Devoir*. For many years created radio programs for the French network of Société Radio-Canada. Awards: Governor-General's Award, for nonfiction, 1987; Victor-Barbeau Prize, for nonfiction, 1992.

Selected Writings

Essays and Related Prose
Le Mythe de Nelligan, 1981
La Petite Noirceur, 1987
L'Amour du pauvre, 1991
La Souveraineté rampante, 1994

Further Reading
Dumont, François, "La Littérature comme point de vue: Trois essayistes québécois contemporains: André Belleau, Jean Larose et François Ricard," *Itinéraires et Contacts de Culture* 18–19 (1995): 89–96
Lévesque, Claude, *Le Proche et le lointain*, Montreal: VLB, 1994
Melançon, Benoît, "La Fiction de l'Amérique dans l'essai contemporain: Pierre Vadeboncoeur et Jean Larose," *Études Françaises* 26, no. 2 (Autumn 1990): 31–39
Milot, Pierre, "La Division institutionnelle du travail intellectuel," in *Pourquoi je n'écris pas d'essais postmodernes*, Montreal: Liber, 1994: 11–28
Montreuil, Sophie, *Le Travail du recueil*, Montreal: University of Montreal Department of French Studies, 1996
Pelletier, Jacques, *Les Habits neufs de la droite culturelle: Les Néo-Conservateurs et la nostalgie de la culture d'ancien régime*, Montreal: VLB, 1994

Larra, Mariano José de
Spanish, 1809–1837

Mariano José de Larra's output as an essayist was prodigious, and he gained from his essays a reputation as the first great modern Spanish writer. In addition to a novel, three original dramas, seven play translations, and several poems, he produced over 270 articles in only nine years. The depth and variety of his essays are likewise impressive, encompassing political, social, cultural, literary, and other issues, and provoking diverse and even antagonistic opinions. During the past 35 years his essays have received tremendous attention, which is evidence of their prominence in Hispanic and global literatures.

Larra's career as an essayist began when he founded *El Duende Satírico del Día* (The satiric spirit of the day) in February 1828. It was closed by the government for its social and political **satires** on 31 December 1828, after publishing only eight articles. He wrote no more articles until August 1832, when he founded *El Pobrecito Hablador* (The poor little tattler), where he established himself as a satirist. He solidified his career in *La Revista Española* (The Spanish review) from November 1832 to 1835. He also wrote simultaneously for other periodicals and weeklies such as *El Correo de las Damas* (The ladies' post), *El Observador* (The observer), and others, until he committed suicide in 1837. He never published his essays under his real name, using several pen names until he settled on Fígaro in 1833.

The articles published in *El Duende Satírico del Día* are insignificant – Larra even excluded them from his first collection published in 1835. These first articles suffered from many of the deficiencies characteristic of Spanish literature of that time, inherited from the previous century, such as excessive use of Latin words and gross abuse of gallicisms, quotations, and epigraphs, as well as the rigid neoclassical norms. Later essays, however, better illustrate the degree of development and civilization of contemporary Spanish society. Larra had the most lucid Spanish mind of his time, leading his contemporaries by several decades. This gave his articles a modern feel, and for that reason he still is in many ways a relevant author as well as perhaps the most outstanding figure of Spanish Romanticism.

Larra's life coincided with a monumental national crisis. During this period Spain suffered the atrocities and devastation of Napoleon's war. Then, upon King Ferdinand VII's return from exile in France, he rejected the newly drafted Constitution, ruled with an iron fist, had hundreds of liberals executed, and forced thousands into exile in France and England. He even had universities closed and opened instead a bullfighting school. At his death in September 1833, the Carlist Civil War engulfed the country. During Larra's life Spain never enjoyed a truly constitutional government such as various European countries had at that time. His desire, then, was to change Spain into a modern progressive nation, as he wrote in "Dos liberales, o lo que es entenderse: Segundo artículo" (1834; Two liberals, or understanding each other: second article): "This [Spain] does not go forward, and only a continuous opposition may save us. Target them, therefore, Mr. Fígaro, and reform them with your satires."

For Larra, Spain was a grotesque deformation of Europe in which the Spanish people were subject to the will of a parasitic aristocracy and an avaricious clergy. His goal was to achieve social justice, and as late as August 1835 he believed that Spain soon would liberate itself from such horrible oppression. He wrote in "Conventos españoles: Tesoros artísticos" (Spanish convents: artistic treasures) that Spain "is at the critical moment of the transition, transition which could be more abrupt the more it has been desired and delayed." Thus Larra became perhaps the most authentic revolutionary of the entire Spanish 19th century, as some critics have stated. Less than a year later, however, he had lost all hope of reform in Spain. Although in Larra's opinion Europe had achieved a greater degree of political liberty than Spain, it still was not fully democratic either. He wrote in "Cuasi: Pesadilla política" (1835; Almost: political nightmare): "[there is] an almost eternal struggle in Europe between two principles: kings and people" – a struggle between the monarchies' desire to preserve their absolute power and the people's wish to establish democracy.

Larra's readers had an important bearing on his style, since he believed that writer and reader were bound together in a collective effort. This explains the dialogic nature of most of his essays, at times addressing his reader directly in a conversational tone. Although he addressed a large and diverse patronage, he assumed a high intellectual level in his readership. He left untranslated his quotations in Latin, French, English, and other languages, but the meanings are contextually lucid. Critics consider that he was the writer of his time who contributed most to the modernization of Spanish literary language and style. He was a precursor to the 20th-century Spanish essayists and philosophers **Miguel de Unamuno** and **José Ortega y Gasset**, although Larra's essays are less philosophical.

Larra's vocabulary, while extensive, is never obscure. It contains many neologisms and his ideas develop frequently through images and metaphors. His handling of viewpoints is complex and challenging, resorting to skillful ironies, distortion, and mirror techniques to outwit the strict censorship. His essays demand that today's reader be well-versed in Spanish culture and history of that time fully to comprehend his subtleties; they also require knowledge of Spanish, for the ironies and hidden meanings in his writings make translation difficult. Critics connect Larra's essays with the clandestine press of the end of the Spanish 18th century, especially with the writings of León de Arroyal, José Marchena, and Juan Bautista Picornell, as well as with Francisco de Quevedo and Francisco de Goya. He also had affinities to such British writers as **Addison, Steele,** and **Swift,** or the French Étienne de Jouy, Louis Sébastien Mercier, Restif de la Bretonne, and others. But Larra's essays, particularly after the death of Ferdinand VII in September 1833, capture the nature of the changes taking place in Spanish society.

As a critic Larra censured all that was an obstacle for the reform of Spain according to his progressive ideology. As a refined satirist, however, his attacks were never directed at a named person, but rather at deplorable acts. Since he takes issue with certain women's shortcomings, some shortsighted critics have accused him of misogyny, but on the contrary, he was a strong supporter of women's liberation, directly opposing the misogyny of others, for example in the review of "*Todo por mi padre,* escándalo en tres actos" (1837; Everything for my father, scandal in three acts): "It is commonly said that women are vulnerable 15 minutes a day. It would be useful to know when this occurs ... we respect them too much to pay attention to such vulgarities." He blamed men's control of Spanish society and the lack of women's education for the denial of their rights and the abuses they suffered.

Larra's essays, despite their thematic diversity, constitute a work of great unity of objectives and techniques. Spain and the problems of the Spanish people are the common thread in his essays. Sadly, seeing such a depressing situation in his country, Larra lost his hope and the will to fight any longer for his ideals, as he wrote in "El día de difuntos de 1836: Fígaro en el cementerio" (1836; All-Souls' Day 1836: Fígaro in the cemetery): "My heart is but another sepulcher . . . Here lies hope!" Three months and 11 days later he committed suicide, an act he had already committed in his mind.

LUIS LORENZO-RIVERO

Biography

Mariano José de Larra y Sánchez de Castro. Used the pseudonyms Fígaro, El Duende, El Pobrecito Hablador, and others. Born 24 March 1809 in Madrid. Father collaborated with Napoleon, and family forced to flee to France, 1813; lived six months in Bordeaux; studied in Paris; family returned to Spain, 1818. Studied at the Escuelas Pías de San Antón; Colegio Imperial de la Compañía de Jesús, Madrid, 1823–24; studied philosophy in Valladolid, 1824–25, and in Madrid, 1825–26. Founder, *El Duende Satírico del Día*, 1828, and *El Pobrecito Hablador*, 1832–33; drama critic, *La Revista Española*, 1832–35; columnist, *El Observador, Revista Mensajero* (Messenger review), and *El Correo de las Damas*, 1833–35, and *El Español, El Mundo* (The world), and *El Redactor General* (The general editor), all 1836. Married Josefina Wetoret y Martínez [Pepita Martínez], 1829 (separated, 1834): one son and two daughters. Intimate liaison with Dolores Armijo, which ended when she decided to return to her husband; he shot himself that night. Died (suicide by gunshot) in Madrid, 13 February 1837.

Selected Writings

Essays and Related Prose

Fígaro: Colección de artículos dramáticos, literarios, políticos y de costumbres, 5 vols., 1835–37; edited by Alejandro Pérez Vidal, 1989

Colección de artículos: Artículos dramáticos, literarios, políticos y de costumbres, publicados en varios periódicos de España (as Fígaro), 1844

Artículos de costumbres, 2 vols., 1874–75; edited by José R. Lomba y Pedraja, 3 vols., 1923–27; selections edited by Rubén Benítez, 1987, and Luis F. Díaz Larios, 1989

Postfígaro: Artículos no coleccionados, 2 vols., 1918

Artículos de crítica literaria y artística, edited by José R. Lomba y Pedraja, 1923

Artículos políticos y sociales, edited by José R. Lomba y Pedraja, 1927

Los mejores artículos, edited by Alberto de Segovia, 1930

Selected Essays, edited by Caroline B. Bourland, 1932

Artículos completos, edited by Melchor de Almagro San Martín, 1944

Artículos varios, edited by E. Correa Calderón, 1976

Escritos sobre teatro, edited by José Monleón, 1976

Antología, edited by Armando L. Salinas, 1977

Artículos sociales, políticos y de crítica literaria, edited by Juan Cano Ballesta, 1982

Las palabras: Artículos y ensayos, edited by José Luis Varela, 1982

Artículos, edited by Enrique Rubio, 1984

Other writings: three plays, a historical novel, and poetry.

Collected works edition: *Obras*, edited by Carlos Seco Serrano, in *Biblioteca de autores españoles*, 127–30, 4 vols., 1960.

Further Reading

Aymes, Jean-René, "Las interpretaciones de la obra de Mariano José de Larra (1837–1978)," in *Evocaciones del romanticismo hispánico*, edited by John R. Rosenberg, Madrid: Porrúa, 1988

Azorín, *Rivas y Larra*, in his *Obras completas*, vol. 3, Madrid: Aguilar, 1961

Escobar, José, "'El Pobrecito Hablador,' de Larra, y su intención satírica," *Papeles de Son Armadans* 64 (1972): 5–44

Escobar, José, *Los orígenes de la obra de Larra*, Madrid: Prensa Española, 1973

Fabra Barreiro, Gustavo, "El pensamiento vivo de Larra," *Revista de Occidente* 50 (1967): 129–52

Hendrix, William, "An Early Nineteenth Century Essayist," *Texas Review* 4 (1918–19): 238–44

Ile, Paul, "Larra's Nightmare," *Revista Hispánica Moderna* 38 (1974–75): 153–61

Kirkpatrick, Susan, *Larra: El laberinto inextricable de un romántico liberal*, Madrid: Gredos, 1977

Kirkpatrick, Susan, "Spanish Romanticism and the Liberal Project: The Crisis of M. J. de Larra," *Studies in Romanticism* 16 (1977): 451–71

Kirkpatrick, Susan, "Larra and the Spanish 'mal du siècle'," in *Evocaciones del romanticismo hispánico*, edited by John R. Rosenberg, Madrid: Porrúa, 1988

Lorenzo-Rivero, Luis, *Larra y Sarmiento: Paralelismos históricos y literarios*, Madrid: Guadarrama, 1968

Lorenzo-Rivero, Luis, *Estudios literarios sobre Mariano José de Larra*, Madrid: Porrúa, 1986

Lorenzo-Rivero, Luis, *Larra: Técnicas y perspectivas*, Madrid: Porrúa, 1988

McGuire, Elizabeth, *A Study of the Writings of D. Mariano José de Larra*, Berkeley: University of California Press, 1918

Martín, Gregorio C., "Larra: Los artículos del miedo," in *Evocaciones del romanticismo hispánico*, edited by John R. Rosenberg, Madrid: Porrúa, 1988

Ruiz Otín, Doris, *Política y sociedad en el vocabulario de Larra*, Madrid: Centro de Estudios Constitucionales, 1983

Rumeau, A., "Une copie manuscrite d'œuvres inédites de Larra: 1836," *Hispanic Review* 4 (1936): 111–23

Tarr, F. Courtney, "More Light on Larra," *Hispanic Review* 4 (1936): 89–110

Tarr, F. Courtney, "Larra's 'El duende satírico del día,'" in *Mariano José de Larra*, edited by Rubén Benítez, Madrid: Taurus, 1979

Ullman, Pierre L., *Mariano José de Larra and Spanish Political Rhetoric*, Madison: University of Wisconsin Press, 1971

Varela, José Luis, *Larra y España*, Madrid: Espasa-Calpe, 1983

Latin American Essay *see* Spanish American Essay

Lawrence, D. H.

British, 1885–1930

D. H. Lawrence is one of the most important and prolific Modernist essayists. Lawrence wrote on an eclectic range of topics: aesthetics, botany, culture, education, literature, pornography, psychoanalysis, religion, sexuality, travel, and trousers. He even wrote an unconventional school textbook for Oxford University Press: *Movements in European History* (1921) was commissioned as a series of informal short essays, "vivid sketches of movements and people." His numerous **prefaces**, introductions, and book **reviews** clearly demonstrate his critical and commercial versatility.

In England, Lawrence's essay work appeared principally in the *English Review* and, later, the *Adelphi* magazine; in America, the *Dial* was his chief publishing outlet. The *Dial*'s editorial interest in primitive art and culture was particularly germane to Lawrence's preoccupations. From 1912 Lawrence lived by his pen, and his feel for the popular journalistic market found expression in his essays for mass-circulation newspapers such as the *Evening News* and *Sunday Dispatch*. In these articles, the neglected side of Lawrence as an adaptable, professional wordsmith is evident.

In many ways, Lawrence's career starts and finishes with the essay. His earliest completed prose work, "Art and the Individual" (1908), originally delivered as a discussion paper, and his last full-scale text *Apocalypse* (1931), a death-bed commentary on the symbology of the Book of Revelations, are indicative of Lawrence's notorious tendency to preach. He adopted argumentative tactics as a distinctive stylistic means of redefining complacent literary forms. No area of Lawrence's writing is without the stamp of essayism. His novels habitually halt in mid-narrative, delivering polemics on marriage, politics, or cultural malaise; his **letters** are frequently self-contained essays or fragmentary drafts for essay projects; his later poetry is often direct commentary rather than traditional verse, indebted both to **Pascal**'s *Pensées* and **Nietzsche**'s use of the **aphorism** as guerrilla mini-essay.

As social critic, Lawrence dwells on the impact of technological change and the ways in which that change restructures "organic community," affecting consciousness and altering the sense of the physical human self. He observes how the crises of modernity reverberate in the most intimate corners of personal relationships, especially the sexual. Anticipating Michel Foucault, Lawrence regarded sex and power as vital codependants. He also believed that Western Christian culture was in decline, making way for the reemergence of ancient, esoteric knowledges which would put the human body and spirit back into a "true relation" with the cosmos.

That "true relation" was formulated and developed in a number of key essays, beginning with "Study of Thomas Hardy" (1914), a "philosophicalish" work of literary criticism combined with reflections on sexual morality and the universal principle of conflicting dualities, adopted from Heraclitus. Reacting to the outbreak of World War I Lawrence wrote: "What colossal idiocy, this war. Out of sheer rage I've begun my book about Thomas Hardy. It will be about anything but Thomas Hardy I am afraid." Lawrence's comments on his Hardy study establish two important features of his essay work. First, Lawrence always regarded the essay as historically engaged with momentous events; immediacy and combativeness color his style. He sometimes writes with the urgency of a Victorian sage – **Carlyle, Ruskin,** or **Arnold** – and his rhetoric is inflected by the prophetic language of a jeremiad. Second, Lawrence delineates his proclivity to argue laterally and vertically at the same time. A Lawrentian essay on any subject can suddenly become decentered; different knowledges multiply in the margins, unexpected propositions begin to circulate beneath the surface of the text. A good deal of Lawrence's essay work is characterized by the dissolution of discursive boundaries.

"The Crown" (1915, revised 1925) continued the Hardy investigation, and in related essays like "The Reality of Peace" (1917), "Democracy" (1919), and "Education of the People" (1920) Lawrence reconceived the essay as a form of intervention, a directive for the social implementation of his ideas. Many of his essays in the period between 1915 and 1925 are handicapped by inconsistent terminology and abstraction, as well as a tonal shift to condescension and authoritarianism. Lawrence may have written them as a trigger for political action, literally, but their didactic overdetermination makes them somewhat remote from readerly sympathies.

After 1919, Lawrence lived more or less permanently outside England, distanced geographically and ideologically from the centers of literary production and uncertain of his audience. His two psychoanalytic **pamphlets**, for example, are important lay responses to **Freud**; but *Psychoanalysis and the Unconscious* (1921) and *Fantasia of the Unconscious* (1922) also suggest Lawrence's embittered abdication of a public speaking position. The foreword to *Fantasia* unmasks Lawrence the coterie-essayist, assuming the role of explorer in difficult intellectual terrain, dismissive of the common reader who cannot follow: "I don't intend my books for the generality of readers. I count it a mistake of our mistaken democracy that every man who can read print is allowed to believe that he can read all that is printed." The foreword further avers that his speculative essays, "pollyanalytics," are "inferences made afterwards" from the "pure passionate experience" of his holistic creative moments. This is misleading, obscuring the extent to which Lawrence used the essay form to gloss his own oeuvre, to deploy the mythology of late Romanticism in imposing a false coherence upon the diversity of his writing. Lawrence needed the essay to explain himself and, indeed, to map his future moves.

In his literary criticism, Lawrence is consistently concerned with deconstructing the authority of the Logos. The essays collected as *Studies in Classic American Literature* (1923) were pioneering readings of mainstream American authors, critically observing the unstable, dialogic nature of the literary text that forever slips away from an author's conscious intentions. The *Studies* is prefaced with Lawrence's famous injunction: "Never trust the artist. Trust the tale. The proper function of a critic is to save the tale from the artist who created it." Lawrence's **critical essays** unseal subtexts which themselves are provisional to other proliferating knowledges. The reading process is complicated by the unstable subjectivity of the critic: for Lawrence, critical engagement with a text is always interactive, involving the simultaneous unraveling of the Word and a performance of the critic's deferred, divided self.

Lawrence wrote four book-length travel studies – *Twilight in Italy* (1916), *Sea and Sardinia* (1921), *Mornings in Mexico* (1927), and *Etruscan Places* (1932) – and several occasional sketches; they are major contributions to an essay form which had a special significance between the wars. The **travel essays** were aimed at a general reader, encouraging Lawrence to give material, experiential form to his beliefs within an established genre that was historically conditioned by the notion of "pleasurable instruction" and a demand for "the real." Travel writing allowed Lawrence to resolve the formal problems of essayism. Thematically, his fetishizations of the primitive, the organic, the agrarian, and "the spirit of place" are plausibly contextualized in narratives of crosscultural encounter. Structurally, the journey narrative, with defined points of departure and terminus, modulated Lawrence's lateral and vertical intellectual tendencies with a degree of accessible linearity. Tonally, Lawrence's oscillation between language registers – from the prophetic to the conversational, the waspish to the confessional – appears as a mobile response to changing psychic geographies. Lawrence could alternately represent himself as a popular interlocutor or a deracinated Arnoldian cultural remnant; as traveling, tale-telling essayist he indulged in both at once.

BRIAN MUSGROVE

Biography

David Herbert Lawrence. Born 11 September 1885 in Eastwood, Nottinghamshire. Studied at Nottingham High School, 1898–1901; University College, Nottingham (now University of Nottingham), 1906–08, teacher's certificate, 1908. Taught at Davidson Road School, Croydon, Surrey, 1908–12. Eloped with Frieda von Richthofen Weekley, 1912, and married, 1914. Lived in Germany, Italy, and Switzerland, 1912–14, then in England, 1914–19. Prosecuted for obscenity for the novel *The Rainbow*, 1915. Contributor to various journals and newspapers, including *Adelphi*, the *Dial*, the *English Review*, the *Evening News*, and the *Sunday Dispatch*; founder, with Katherine Mansfield and John Middleton Murry, *Signature* magazine, 1916. Lived in Italy, 1919–22, the United States and Mexico, 1922–23, England, France, and Germany, 1924, New Mexico and Mexico, 1924–25, Italy, 1925–28, and France, 1928–30. Died (of tuberculosis) in Vence, southern France, 2 March 1930.

Selected Writings

Essays and Related Prose
Twilight in Italy, 1916
Sea and Sardinia, 1921
Movements in European History (as Lawrence H. Davidson), 1921
Psychoanalysis and the Unconscious (pamphlet), 1921
Fantasia of the Unconscious (pamphlet), 1922
Studies in Classic American Literature, 1923
Reflections on the Death of a Porcupine and Other Essays, 1925
Mornings in Mexico, 1927
Pornography and Obscenity (pamphlet), 1929
My Skirmish with Jolly Roger, 1929; revised version as *A Propos of Lady Chatterley's Lover*, 1930
Assorted Articles, 1930
Etruscan Places, 1932
Phoenix: The Posthumous Papers, edited by Edward D. McDonald, 1936
Selected Essays, 1950
Phoenix II: Uncollected, Unpublished, and Other Prose Works, edited by Warren Roberts and Harry T. Moore, 1968
Selected Poetry and Non-Fictional Prose, edited by John Lucas, 1990

Other writings: several novels (including *Sons and Lovers*, 1913; *The Rainbow*, 1915; *Women in Love*, 1920; *Lady Chatterley's Lover*, 1928), short stories, a novella, poetry, plays, letters, and travel writing.

Collected works edition: *Works* (Cambridge Edition), general editors James T. Boulton and Warren Roberts, 1980– (in progress).

Bibliographies
Cowan, James C., *D. H. Lawrence: An Annotated Bibliography of Writings About Him*, De Kalb: Northern Illinois University Press, 2 vols., 1982–85
Phillips, Jill M., *D. H. Lawrence: A Review of the Biographies and Literary Criticism*, New York: Gordon Press, 1978
Roberts, Warren, *A Bibliography of D. H. Lawrence*, Cambridge: Cambridge University Press, revised edition, 1982 (original edition, 1963)
Stoll, John E., *D. H. Lawrence: A Bibliography*, Troy, New York: Whitston, 1977

Further Reading
Andrews, W. T., "D. H. Lawrence's Favourite Jargon," *Notes and Queries* 13 (1966): 97–98
Balbert, Peter, *D. H. Lawrence and the Phallic Imagination: Essays on Sexual Identity and Feminist Misreading*, Basingstoke: Macmillan, and New York: St. Martin's Press, 1989
Black, Michael, *D. H. Lawrence: The Early Philosophical Works*, Basingstoke: Macmillan, 1991; New York: Cambridge University Press, 1992
Edwards, Duane, "'Inferences made afterwards': Lawrence and the Essay," in *Essays on the Essay: Redefining the Genre*, edited by Alexander J. Butrym, Athens: University of Georgia Press, 1989
Eggert, Paul, "Lawrence and the Futurists: The Breakthrough in His Art," *Meridian* 1 (1983): 21–32
Ellis, David, "Reading Lawrence: The Case of Sea and Sardinia," *D. H. Lawrence Review* 10 (1977): 52–63
Ellis, David, "Lawrence and the Biological Psyche," in *D. H. Lawrence: Centenary Essays*, edited by Mara Kalnins, Bristol: Bristol Classical Press, 1986
Ellis, David, and Howard Mills, *D. H. Lawrence's Non-Fiction: Art, Thought and Genre*, Cambridge and New York: Cambridge University Press, 1988
Foster, Richard, "Criticism as Rage: D. H. Lawrence," in *A D. H. Lawrence Miscellany*, edited by Harry T. Moore, Carbondale: Southern Illinois University Press, 1959
Gutierrez, Donald, "D. H. Lawrence's Golden Age," *D. H. Lawrence Review* 9 (1976): 377–408
Herzinger, Kim A., *D. H. Lawrence in His Time, 1908–1915*, Lewisburg, Pennsylvania: Bucknell University Press, 1982
Holderness, Graham, *D. H. Lawrence: History, Ideology, and Fiction*, Dublin: Gill and Macmillan, and Atlantic Highlands, New Jersey: Humanities Press, 1982
Joost, Nicholas, and Alvin Sullivan, *D. H. Lawrence and the Dial*, Carbondale: Southern Illinois University Press, 1970
Meyers, Jeffrey, editor, *D. H. Lawrence and Tradition*, London: Athlone Press, and Amherst: University of Massachusetts Press, 1985
Musgrove, B. M., *D. H. Lawrence's Travel Books* (dissertation), Cambridge: University of Cambridge, 1988
Schneider, Daniel J., *D. H. Lawrence: The Artist as Psychologist*, Lawrence: University Press of Kansas, 1984
Schneider, Daniel J., *The Consciousness of D. H. Lawrence: An Intellectual Biography*, Lawrence: University Press of Kansas, 1986
Simpson, Hilary, *D. H. Lawrence and Feminism*, De Kalb: Northern Illinois University Press, and London: Croom Helm, 1982
Williams, Raymond, "D. H. Lawrence," in his *Culture and Society, 1780–1950*, London: Chatto and Windus, and New York: Columbia University Press, 1958
Worthen, John, *D. H. Lawrence: A Literary Life*, London: Macmillan, and New York: St. Martin's Press, 1989

Leacock, Stephen
Canadian, 1869–1944

A prolific and popular writer whose essays and books continue to garner readers both at home and abroad, Stephen Leacock was a man comfortable in many worlds. An economist who studied under Thorstein Veblen at the University of Chicago, a dedicated university professor, and an internationally renowned public speaker, he wrote virtually uncountable essays on a wide range of eclectic topics from educational theory to contemporary politics. As **Peter McArthur** suggested as early as 1923 when Leacock had more than two decades of writing still ahead of him, any attempt to summarize this immense body of work "is an exhilarating, but somewhat bewildering task." It is a mission that sweeps a reader from discussions of Western culture's shortsighted enthusiasm for the false gods of technology ("Radio: A New Form of Trouble," 1923), to explanations of "practical political economy," to lighthearted looks at current trends in film and literature.

Leacock is best remembered, though, as a humorist, a writer for whom the study and practice of humor was "in the grain of [his] intelligence" (**Robertson Davies**, 1970); this was a man, after all, who proclaimed in the autobiographical **preface** to his *Sunshine Sketches of a Little Town* (1912) that he "would sooner have written *Alice in Wonderland* than the whole *Encyclopaedia Britannica*." The essence of humor, which Leacock believed was captured most eloquently in such a work as **Dickens'** *Pickwick Papers*, is "that it must be without harm or malice, nor should it convey even incidentally any real picture of sorrow or suffering or death." The basis of humor lies, he maintained, "in the deeper contrasts offered by life itself," most notably "the strange incongruity between our aspirations and our achievement" ("Humour as I See It," 1916). Humor was a kind of consolation for the world, helping to reconcile us individually and collectively to things as they are in contrast to things as they might be. Indeed, both these definitions figure prominently in the Leacock oeuvre, proof not only of his willingness to accord humor status as "the highest product of our civilization" ("Humour as I See It") but also of his propensity for self-plagiarism.

It is important to note that Leacock rarely locates the source of this comfort in the contemporary world. His essays, both humorous and serious, are often backward-looking, engaging various strategies in order to illuminate what he considered the positive aspects of vanished or vanishing sensibilities: "It is perhaps conceivable that literature has arisen in the past mainly on the basis of the inequalities, the sufferings and the misery of the common lot that has led humanity to seek in the concepts of the imagination the happiness that seemed denied by the stern environment of reality. Thus perhaps American civilisation with its public school and the dead level of its elementary instruction, with its simple code of republicanism and its ignorance of the glamour and mystery of monarchy, with its bread and work for all and its universal hope of the betterment of personal fortune, contains in itself an atmosphere in which the flower of literature cannot live" ("Literature and Education in America," 1909).

Despite this proclivity to find solace in remembered times, Leacock was not a nostalgist. He understood progress as inevitable, and he proved an astute social historian and critic whose sense of where Canada was headed during a period of rapid social change and sudden economic development is frequently understated in critical writing about him. For him, the past represented a kind of vantage point from which he could peruse the modern world while remaining firmly grounded in what critics have called his Tory humanist belief in "the middle way," in the benefits of reconciliation over confrontation, and in the values of the golden mean. His views

on many subjects, as Gerald Lynch (1988) observes, "represent an attempt to balance the rights of the individual and the needs of the social organism, to temper the extremes of liberalism and socialism." Emerging from this dialectic was a respect for the stability of an ordered community and traditional institutions, a belief in the benefits of human and political diversity, and a deep concern for human rights and social justice. At times, his writing in these areas hints at an essential uncertainty and unwillingness to commit to a single line of thought; more often, though, Leacock writes with assurance and optimism, comfortable with the knowledge "that no opinion is altogether right, no purpose altogether laudable, and no calamity altogether deplorable" ("A Rehabilitation of Charles II," 1906).

One issue to which Leacock returned regularly in his legion of articles on history, economics, and political science was the question of "the Empire." To him, Anglo-American imperialism was never irreconcilable with his own sense of nationalism but was a complementary "recognition of a wider citizenship" (*The Unsolved Riddle*, 1920). It was the nurturing of this broader sense of cosmopolitan responsibility that Leacock believed would effectively counterbalance the growing preoccupation with self-interest and the regressive "creed and cult of self-development" ("The Devil and the Deep Sea," 1910) that he saw as threatening the stability of the modern world.

Although today's reader may find Leacock leaning at times toward the politically conservative, most obviously in his dismissive attitudes toward early feminist concerns and socialism (the latter of which he often equates with utopianism), it is his irony, wit, and optimism that endure and continue to endear him to readers.

DAVID STAINES

Biography

Stephen Butler Leacock. Born 30 December 1869 in Swanmore, Hampshire, England. Family moved to Canada, 1876. Studied at Upper Canada College, Toronto, 1882–87; University of Toronto, 1887–91, B.A. in modern languages, 1891; University of Chicago, 1899–1903, Ph.D. in political economy, 1903. Taught at Upper Canada College, 1889–99, and the University of Chicago, 1899–1903. Married Beatrix Hamilton, 1900 (died, 1925): one son. Lecturer, 1903–06, associate professor, 1906–08, William Dow Professor of Political Science and Economics, 1908–36, then emeritus, McGill University, Montreal. Elected to the Royal Society of Canada, 1919. Charter member, Canadian Authors Association, 1921. Awards: Lorne Pierce Medal, 1937; Governor-General's Award, for nonfiction, 1937; honorary degrees from three colleges and universities. Died in Toronto, 28 March 1944.

Selected Writings

Essays and Sketches (partly fictional)
Literary Lapses: A Book of Sketches, 1910
Sunshine Sketches of a Little Town, 1912
Behind the Beyond, and Other Contributions to Human Knowledge, 1913
Arcadian Adventures with the Idle Rich, 1914
Moonbeams from the Larger Lunacy, 1915
Further Foolishness: Sketches and Satires on the Follies of the Day, 1916
Essays and Literary Studies, 1916

The Hohenzollerns in America, with the Bolsheviks in Berlin and Other Impossibilities, 1919
The Unsolved Riddle, 1920
My Discovery of England, 1922
Over the Footlights, 1923
College Days, 1923
The Garden of Folly, 1924
Winnowed Wisdom, a New Book of Humour, 1926
Short Circuits, 1928
The Iron Man and the Tin Woman, with Other Such Futurities, 1929
Laugh with Leacock (selection), 1930
The Leacock Book, edited by Ben Travers, 1930
Wet Wit and Dry Humour, 1931
Afternoons in Utopia: Tales of the New Time, 1932
The Dry Pickwick and Other Incongruities, 1932
The Perfect Salesman, edited by E. V. Knox, 1934
Funny Pieces: A Book of Random Sketches, 1936
Here Are My Lectures and Stories, 1937
Model Memoirs and Other Sketches from Simple to Serious, 1938
Too Much College; or, Education Eating Up Life, with Kindred Essays in Education and Humour, 1939
Laugh Parade, 1940
My Remarkable Uncle and Other Sketches, 1942
Last Leaves, 1945
The Leacock Roundabout (selection), 1945
The Bodley Head Leacock, edited by J. B. Priestley, 1957; as *The Best of Leacock*, 1958
Feast of Stephen, edited by Robertson Davies, 1970; revised edition, 1990
The Social Criticism, edited by Alan Bowker, 1973
The Penguin Stephen Leacock, edited by Robertson Davies, 1981
My Financial Career and Other Follies, edited by David Staines, 1993

Other writings: satirical novels and parodies, a college textbook on political science, books on humor and politics, biographies of Charles Dickens and **Mark Twain**, history books, and an unfinished autobiography (*The Boy I Left Behind Me*, 1946).

Bibliography

Lomer, G. R., *Stephen Leacock: A Check-List and Index of His Writings*, Ottawa: National Library, 1954

Further Reading

Bowker, Alan, Introduction to *The Social Criticism* by Leacock, edited by Bowker, Toronto: University of Toronto Press, 1996 (original edition, 1973)
Bush, Douglas, "Stephen Leacock," in *The Canadian Imagination: Dimensions of a Literary Culture*, edited by David Staines, Cambridge, Massachusetts: Harvard University Press, 1977
Cameron, Donald, *Faces of Leacock: An Appreciation*, Toronto: Ryerson Press, 1967
Cook, Ramsay, "Stephen Leacock and the Age of Plutocracy, 1903–1921," in *Character and Circumstance*, edited by John S. Moir, Toronto: Macmillan, 1970
Curry, Ralph L., *Stephen Leacock: Humorist and Humanist*, Garden City, New York: Doubleday, 1959
Davies, Robertson, *Stephen Leacock*, Toronto: McClelland and Stewart, 1970
Legate, David M., *Stephen Leacock: A Biography*, Toronto and Garden City, New York: Doubleday, 1970
Lynch, Gerald, *Stephen Leacock: Humour and Humanity*, Kingston and Montreal: McGill-Queen's University Press, 1988
McArthur, Peter, *Stephen Leacock*, Norwood, Pennsylvania: Norwood, 1976 (original edition, 1923)
Moritz, Albert, and Theresa Moritz, *Leacock: A Biography*, Toronto: Stoddart, 1985
Pacey, Desmond, "Leacock as Satirist," *Queen's Quarterly* 58 (1951): 208–19
Staines, David, editor, *Stephen Leacock: A Reappraisal*, Ottawa: University of Ottawa Press, 1986
Taylor, Charles, *Radical Tories: The Conservative Tradition in Canada*, Toronto: Anansi, 1982

Le Moyne, Jean

French Canadian, 1913–1996

Jean Le Moyne published only one book in his lifetime, but this book is a milestone in the history of the essay in Quebec. Since it appeared in 1961, *Convergences* has won numerous prizes, and was reprinted regularly as well as translated into English in 1966. The essays and articles Le Moyne collected and organized thematically were written between 1941 and 1961, and their subject matter ranges from the author's father to friendship, from science to dreams, from the oppressive clericalist climate in Quebec to the place of women in its culture. A few of these texts – especially the biblical exegeses of the book's fourth section – have lost most of their appeal, but *Convergences* remains to this day an object of intense interest and some dispute among critics (Jean-Marcel Paquette, Jacques Pelletier, Pierre Nepveu) and fellow essayists (Jacques Ferron, **André Belleau**, Jean Bouthillette, **Jean Larose**).

Le Moyne's most widely discussed essay deals with the work of his friend, the poet Saint-Denys Garneau (1912–43). Le Moyne was part of Garneau's inner circle of friends – which included Robert Charbonneau, Claude Hurtubise, Robert Élie, and Paul Beaulieu – and participated in the publication of Garneau's *Poésies complètes* (1949; Complete poetical works), his *Journal* (1954), and a selection of his *Lettres à ses amis* (1967; Letters to his friends). The opening lines of Le Moyne's essay entitled "Saint-Denys Garneau, témoin de son temps" (1960; Saint-Denys Garneau, witness to his time) set the tone for what follows: "I cannot speak of Saint-Denys Garneau without anger. For he has been killed." In reality, no one murdered Garneau, but, for Le Moyne, French Canada was guilty of causing the poet's premature death. If Garneau did not produce the oeuvre that was expected from him, it was, according to Le Moyne, because French Canada forced upon the poet an unbearable sense of guilt in an atmosphere of spiritual poverty. The essay appeared during what was to be known as Quebec's Quiet Revolution, where it struck a responsive chord in the intellectual upheaval taking place.

Other texts in *Convergences* are of equal importance. In response to a traditional obsession on the part of Quebec's clergy and elite with their province's "spiritual" mission in an essentially "materialistic" North America, Le Moyne tackled what he called "notre différenciation nord-américaine" (our North American differentiation), most notably in "Henry James et *Les Ambassadeurs*" (1951; Henry James and *The Ambassadors*). Challenging the fear of everything American that characterized Quebec's high culture for years, Le Moyne compares **Henry James** to F. Scott Fitzgerald, and chooses the former as the model of a universal writer who, while being ever conscious of an emerging North American civilization, never forgets his European roots. For Le Moyne, the process of the adaptation of European populations to North American places and cultures is the American "devenir" (coming of age); it is an ever-changing duality, an "American ambivalence" which only James managed to master. In the perception of this cultural process lies true grandeur.

Of the 28 texts collected in *Convergences*, seven deal with music, mostly classical; most of these bear the same title: "Rencontre de . . ." (Encounter with . . .). Le Moyne "encounters" Schubert, Wagner, Beethoven, Mozart, and Bach (whose *Art of the Fugue* he ranks first among all forms of human creation), and Negro spirituals. Le Moyne was not a musicologist, but he loved music and wanted to locate it within the larger context of spirituality; his encounters are testimonies to a revelation. The "theological perspective" which Le Moyne says is at the core of *Convergences* is linked to the physical pleasure of music: "If Christ does indeed include everything, how are we to pray outside of our physical bodies and cut off from the rest of the universe?" Paradoxically, humor is not absent from such serious reflections: "No instrument has given me as much pleasure as the organ. Except the steam locomotive."

Le Moyne's book gave him a distinct reputation in Quebec letters. Unlike many of his contemporaries, he (along with Gilles Leclerc, Jean Bouthillette, and **Pierre Vadeboncoeur**) wrote nothing but essays. His robust prose is heavily tainted with a metaphysical vocabulary rarely found in the essays of those who followed him. But it is above all his iconoclastic views that made him so compelling at the time his essays were published, and that make him the subject of continued dispute. At a time when most intellectuals lined up on the side of the Quebec sovereignist movement, Le Moyne staunchly opposed nationalism. At a time of intense attacks on every form of institutionalized religion, he was a profoundly religious man, and wrote at length on spiritual matters (his frequent attacks on the dualism of the flesh and spirit were particularly vituperous). Fond as he was of French literature (Bloy, **Bernanos**, Teilhard de Chardin, Jouhandeau, Jarry), Le Moyne did not circumscribe his artistic interests to the French-speaking world. Not only did he comment on books by James and Fitzgerald, music by African Americans, and movies by the Marx Brothers (he praises their "radical anarchy"), but he went so far as to claim, in 1956, that he never felt at home within the culture of his native French province. At a time when many felt proud of their Americanness – their so-called "américanité" – he reminded them of their European cultural past and wondered if it was possible to express the reality of North America in the French language. For these reasons, Jean Le Moyne remains widely discussed and controversial among the essayists of contemporary Quebec.

BENOÎT MELANÇON

Biography
Born 17 February 1913 in Montreal. Studied at the Collège Sainte-Marie, Montreal, B.A., 1933; began to go deaf; self-educated thereafter. Cofounder, *La Relève* (The relief), from 1934 (*La Nouvelle Relève*, from 1941); journalist, *La Presse*, 1941–42; city editor and literary critic, *Le Canada*, 1942–44; managing editor, *La Revue Moderne* (The modern review), 1953–59; also contributor to other journals, including *Cité Libre* (Free city) and *Écrits du Canada Français* (Writings from French Canada). Writer and researcher for the National Film Board, 1959–69. Special assistant

and senior adviser to Prime Minister Pierre Trudeau, 1969–78. Married Suzanne Rivard, 1970. Named to the Canadian Senate, 1982–88. Awards: Governor-General's Award, 1961; France-Canada Prize, 1961; Province of Quebec Concours Littéraires, 1967; Molson Prize, 1968. Officer, Order of Canada, 1982. Died in Ottawa, 1 April 1996.

Selected Writings

Essays and Related Prose
Convergences, 1961; slightly different version, as *Convergence: Essays from Quebec*, translated by Philip Stratford, 1966

Other writings: edited works by the poet Saint-Denys Garneau.

Further Reading
La Bossière, Camille R., "Of Unity and Equivocation: Jean Le Moyne's *Convergences*," *Essays on Canadian Writing* 15 (Summer 1979): 51–68
Nepveu, Pierre, "Le Poème québécois de l'Amérique," *Études Françaises* 26, no. 2 (Autumn 1990): 9–19
Pelletier, Jacques, "Jean Le Moyne: Les Pièges de l'idéalisme," in *L'Essai et la prose d'idées au Québec*, Montreal: Fides, 1985: 697–710
Pelletier, Jacques, "Jean Le Moyne, témoin essentiel: Une relecture des *Convergences*," *Voix et Images* 54 (Spring 1993): 563–78
Pelletier, Mario, "*Convergences* trente ans après," *Écrits du Canada Français* 78 (1993): 163–73
Simon, Sherry, "Le Discours du Juif au Québec en 1948: Jean Le Moyne, Gabrielle Roy," *Québec Studies* 15 (Fall 1992–Winter 1993): 77–86

Leont'ev, Konstantin
Russian, 1831–1891

In his first two decades of literary activity (1854–76) Konstantin Leont'ev wrote mostly short stories and novels. His talent was recognized by **Turgenev**, who helped him with money, advice, and constructive criticism. Over the next two decades (roughly 1872–91) he produced a torrent of brilliant, provocative, and disturbing essays. In his final years he expressed some of his deepest insights in personal **letters**.

Two of Leont'ev's central ideas – the priority of aesthetic over moral values and the benign effect of social conflict on cultural creativity – were expressed by the character Mil'keev in the novel *V svoem kraiu* (1864; Back home): "*A single century-old magnificent tree is worth more than twenty faceless men*; and I will not cut it down in order to be able to buy medicine [to treat] the peasants' cholera!" It was doubtless the French Romantics who taught Leont'ev to view social violence as culturally creative. "Which is better," Mil'keev asks rhetorically, "the bloody, but spiritually and culturally luxuriant Renaissance or the tame, prosperous, moderate existence of contemporary . . . Switzerland?"

Leont'ev was quite prepared to replace moral criteria by aesthetic criteria for judging societies, cultures, and religions. "What is *useful to all of them*," he wrote, "we do not know and shall never know. What is beautiful, elegant, and lofty in them – it is high time we found out!" ("Srednii Evropeets kak ideal i orudie vsemirnogo razrusheniia" [1872–84; The average European as an ideal and instrument of universal destruction]).

Like **Nietzsche**, with whom he has often been compared, Leont'ev celebrated the "poetry of war," regarding security, comfort, and tranquillity as destructive of cultural vitality and creativity. But his characteristic stress was on the "aesthetics" or "poetry" of social and historical life, in contrast to Nietzsche's stress on the aesthetics of high culture. Leont'ev died before Nietzsche became known in Russia; but he would doubtless have consigned him to the despised "bookish, paper world" (*knizhnyi i bumazhnyi mir*) of universities and editorial offices.

In ancient Greece and Rome, as in medieval Europe and the present Ottoman Empire – in which he served for a decade as a Russian diplomat – Leont'ev saw vibrant diversity, held within cultural and sociopolitical bounds by the "despotism of an inner idea." But in Western Europe's present, and especially in its projected future, he saw only a dreary, prosaic conformity. He was outraged by the thought "that Moses went up to Sinai, the Greeks built their elegant acropolises, the Romans waged their Punic Wars, the handsome genius Alexander, in a plumed helmet, crossed the Granicus and fought at Arbela; that the apostles preached, martyrs suffered, poets sang, painters painted, and knights shone in the tourneys, *only in order that the French, German, or Russian bourgeois, in his ugly and comical clothing*, should sit complacently . . . on the ruins of all this past greatness" ("Pis'ma o vostochnykh delakh" [1882–83; Letters on Eastern affairs]).

Leont'ev's theoretical explanation of the decline of 19th-century European culture was based on a triadic schema of historical development borrowed from Nikolai Danilevskii. Historical cultures, like living beings, develop from a stage of "initial simplicity" to one of "flourishing complexity" and then sink, through a process of "leveling interfusion," to decay and death. Europe, which had achieved its flourishing complexity in the high Middle Ages, was already far advanced in the terminal process of leveling interfusion. It is not clear how seriously Leont'ev took this schema. But it is quite clear that it fed his "philosophical hatred" (as he himself called it) of the egalitarian, secularizing, democratizing, and standardizing tendencies of his time.

The "poetry of life," as Leont'ev saw it, could not be maintained, "without the mysticism and shaping beauty of religion, without the magnificence and threatening power of the state, without a resplendent and firmly established aristocracy" ("Plody natsional'nykh dvizhenii na Pravsolavnom vostoke" [1888–89; The fruits of national movements in the Orthodox East]). Despite Leont'ev's significant points of contact with Nietzsche, there are two key theoretical differences. The first is Leont'ev's attachment to religion and the churches (chiefly Russian Orthodoxy, but also Islam and Roman Catholicism). The second is Nietzsche's repudiation of Good Samaritanism in the name of "instrumental cruelty" toward the weak and uncreative. Leont'ev, in contrast, defended Good Samaritanism, urging compassion "for the nearest . . .the person encountered . . . – charity toward the living and real human being whose tears we can see, whose sighs and groans we hear, whose hand we can actually clasp, like a brother's, *in this present hour*" ("Nashi novye khristiane, II" [1880; Our new Christians, II]). This stands in sharpest contrast to what in 1883 Nietzsche celebrated as *Fernsten-Liebe*, "love of the high culture of the remote historical future," as he rejected *Nächstenliebe* ("love

of neighbor") and urged *Nächsten-Flucht* ("flight from one's neighbor"). Leont'ev was explicit in condemning the "feverish preoccupation" with the earthly welfare of future generations on the part of both socialists and utilitarians. Although Nietzsche was indeed feverishly preoccupied with the remote historical future, he joined Leont'ev in scorning the socialist and utilitarian concern for the "earthly welfare" of future generations. What he preached was concern for the cultural creativity of a handful of future *Übermenschen* (supermen) – quite a different matter.

Leont'ev introduced what might be called a Nietzschean corrective or corollary into his Good Samaritanism, insisting that Christian *agape* should not be one-sidedly "democratic"; it should be directed not only toward suffering workers or wounded soldiers (of whom he had direct experience during the Crimean War), but also toward the "high and mighty"– such as defeated generals or noblemen abused by the mob.

In his own time and after, Leont'ev's ideas were "heard but not heeded, read but not understood." It is only in our century, and especially in the past half-dozen years (and mostly in Russia) that this deep and original, if sometimes idiosyncratic thinker has been treated with full and deserved seriousness.

GEORGE L. KLINE

Biography

Konstantin Nikolaevich Leont'ev. Born 25 January 1831 in Kudinovo. Studied medicine at Moscow University. Served as a military surgeon in the Crimean War, 1853–56. Began publishing fiction, 1854. Married Elizaveta Pavlovna Politova, 1861. Served as a diplomat at the Russian consulate on Crete and in the Balkans, 1863–73; suffered from dysentery or cholera, 1871, then made a religious vow and lived for a year on Mt. Athos, Greece. Returned to Russia, 1874; spent much time at the Optina Pustyn monastery; censor in Moscow, 1880–87; took monastic vows and entered the Trinity Monastery, near Moscow, 1891. Died at the Trinity Monastery, 24 November 1891.

Selected Writings

Essays and Related Prose
Vostok, Rossiia i Slavianstvo (The East, Russia, and Slavdom), 2 vols., 1885–86
Essays in Russian Literature: The Conservative View: Leontiev, Rozanov, Shestov, translated by Spencer E. Roberts, 1968: 225–356
Against the Current: Selections from the Novels, Essays, Notes, and Letters of Konstantin Leontiev, edited by George Ivask, translated by George Reavey, 1969
Zapiski otshel'nika (Notes of a recluse), edited by V. Kochetkov, 1992
Tsvetushchaia slozhnost': Izbrannye stat'i (Flourishing complexity: selected articles), edited by I. Simonova, 1992
Izbrannoe (Selected writings), edited by I. N. Smirnov, 1993
Izbrannye pis'ma, 1854–1891 (Selected letters, 1854–1891), edited by D. V. Solov'ev, 1993

Other writings: several novels (including *Podlipki*, 1861; *V svoem kraiu*, 1864; *Iz zhizni khristian v Turtsii* [From the life of Christians in Turkey], 3 vols., 1876; *Egipetskii golub'* [The Egyptian Dove], 1881), short stories, and works on literary criticism, including studies of **Lev Tolstoi** and Ivan Turgenev.

Collected works edition: *Sobranie sochinenii*, 9 vols., 1912–14.

Further Reading

Auden, W. H., "A Russian Aesthete," in his *Forewords and Afterwords*, edited by Edward Mendelson, New York: Viking Press and London: Faber, 1973: 274–82 (article originally published 1970)

Berdiaev, Nikolai, *Konstantin Leont'ev*, Orono, Maine: Academic International, 1968 (original Russian edition, 1926; first English translation, 1940)

Dolgov, K. M., *Voskhozhdenie na Afon: Zhizn' ii mirosozertsanie Konstantina Leont'eva* (The ascent of Mt. Athos: Konstantin Leont'ev's life and world view), Moscow: Luch, 1995

Ivask, Iuri, *Konstantin Leont'ev: Zhizn' i tvorchestvo* (Konstantin Leont'ev: life and work), Berne: Lang, 1974

K. N. Leont'ev: Pro et contra: Lichnost' i tvorchestvo Konstantina Leont'eva v otsenke russkikh myslitelei i issledovatelei, 1891–1917 (K. N. Leont'ev: pro et contra: Konstantin Leont'ev's personality and work as appraised by Russian thinkers and scholars, 1891–1917), edited by Aleksei Kozyrev and Aleksandr Korol'kov, St. Petersburg: Izd-vo Russkogo Khristianskogo Gumanitarnogo In-ta, 1995

Kline, George L., *Religious and Anti-Religious Thought in Russia*, Chicago: University of Chicago Press, 1968: 35–54

Kologriwof, Iwan von, *Von Hellas zum Mönchtum: Leben und Denken Konstantin Leontiews, 1831–1891*, Regensburg: Gregorius Verlag, 1948

Korol'kov, Aleksandr, *Prorochestva Konstantina Leont'eva* (The prophecies of Konstantin Leont'ev), St. Petersburg: Izd-vo S.-Peterburgskogo Universiteta, 1991

Lukashevich, Stephen, *Konstantin Leontev* [sic] *(1831–1891): A Study in Russian "Heroic Vitalism"*, New York: Pageant Press, 1967

Masaryk, Thomas G., *The Spirit of Russia: Studies in History, Literature, and Philosophy*, vol. 2, London: Allen and Unwin, and New York: Macmillan, 1955: 207–20 (original German edition, 1913; first English translation, 1919)

Poliakov, Leonid, "The Conservatism of Konstantin Leontiev in Present-Day Russia: An Example of 'Encouraging Pessimism'," *Russian Studies in Philosophy* 35, no. 2 (Fall 1996): 51–60

Yanov, Aleksandr, "Tragediia velikogo myslitelia" (The tragedy of a great thinker), *Voprosy filosofii* 1 (1992): 61–88

Zenkovsky, V. V., *A History of Russian Philosophy*, vol. 1, London: Routledge and Kegan Paul, and New York: Columbia University Press, 1953: 434–53 (original Russian edition, 1948)

Leopardi, Giacomo

Italian, 1798–1837

Giacomo Leopardi forms with Ugo Foscolo and Alessandro Manzoni the great triumvirate of Italian Romanticism. His poetry, as well as his prose, shares with them a concern for Italian nationalism, the formative role of history, the problem of belief, and the tensions between past and present, humankind and nature. But where Foscolo and Manzoni played an active public role, Leopardi lived an interior life, recording and creating himself in the act of writing. This is most evident in his contributions to the essay. Aside from some early journeyman pieces, including a learned compendium on astronomy, a huge body of letters, and the essays *Saggio sopra gli errori popolari degli antichi* (wr. 1815, pub. 1846; Essay on the popular mistakes of the Ancients) and *Discorso di un italiano intorno alla poesia romantica* (wr. 1818, pub. 1906; Address by an Italian on Romantic poetry), Leopardi's most important prose writing falls into three groups: the *Zibaldone*, the *Pensieri*, and *Operette morali*.

The *Zibaldone*, literally "hodge-podge" or "commonplace book," was a sort of running diary in which Leopardi made notes and recorded his thoughts on philosophy, language, religion, science, art, politics, and history while he read and thought in his father's library. The idea came from a mentor who suggested that everyone with literary pretensions should keep a "written chaos" out of which orderly work might emerge. In a deeper sense, it became for Leopardi a dialogue with himself, what his biographer Iris Origo terms "a record of human solitude." Kept between July 1817 and December 1832, the manuscript of the *Zibaldone* fills 4526 pages with entries ranging from brief fragments and notes to fully developed essays. In these he brings together a vast learning with profound meditation to develop theories of art and poetry that are comparable to and even superior to those of **Goethe**, Wordsworth, and **Coleridge** in their appreciation of literature. The *Zibaldone* was not published until 1898–1900, and so exercised no direct influence on Leopardi's contemporaries. In retrospect, however, it offers a rich intellectual gloss on his poems and the *Operette morali*, as well as an important body of thought in and of itself.

During the last years of his life in Naples, Leopardi began to work on his *Pensieri* (Thoughts), preparing 111 entries. About two-thirds of these were derived from the *Zibaldone*. While the latter ranges over a wide variety of topics, the *Pensieri*, patterned after the *Maximes* (1665–78) of the French moralist **La Rochefoucauld**, is a melancholy examination of human character and behavior. But like **Pascal**'s *Pensées* (1670), also a prototype in theme and form, the *Pensieri* remained the fragments of a book that he could never finally bring together. They appeared only posthumously, in the 1845 edition of his collected works.

The *Operette morali* (*Moral Tales*) was the only major work of prose that Leopardi published in his lifetime. The 20 essays and dialogues that comprise the first edition (1827) were composed in a period of intense creativity from January to December 1824, running from "Storia del genere umano" ("The History of the Human Race") to "Dialogo di Timandro e di Eleandro" ("Dialogue Between Timander and Eleander"). The second edition (1834) included two more; the final, complete edition, with 24 essays, did not appear until 1845, eight years after Leopardi's death.

While ostensibly an imitation of the dialogues of the Greek satirist Lucian, *Moral Tales* represents a deeply personal exploration of human destiny and disillusion. The underlying spirit is that of Ecclesiastes as the **dialogues** weigh the various sides of human aspiration, only to find illusion and vanity. Aside from a favorable notice by Alessandro Manzoni, whose *I promessi sposi* (*The Betrothed*) was published in the same year, *Moral Tales* was largely ignored by a reading public uncomfortable with Leopardi's materialism, pessimism, and skepticism. Nominated for the prestigious prize of the Accademia della Crusca, it was rejected in favor of a mediocre history of Italy. Only later would it receive admirers as varied as the German philosopher **Arthur Schopenhauer** and the Spanish writer **Miguel de Unamuno**.

Leopardi conceived *Moral Tales* as a single unified work, rejecting offers to have individual essays published separately in periodicals. Despite that, it brings together a diverse range of styles, subject matter, and forms, playing with various combinations of narrative and dialogue. "Dialogo della Terra e della Luna" ("Dialogue Between the Earth and the Moon"), for instance, a comic dialogue looking at the indifference of nature, follows the conventions of a literary dialogue akin to those of Lucian. "Dialogo della Natura e di un Islandese" ("Dialogue Between Nature and an Icelander") treats the same theme, but with greater pathos and irony. "The History of the Human Race" and "Proposta di premi fatta dall'Accademia dei Sillografi" ("Announcement of Prizes by the Academy of Syllographs") take the form of conventional essays, even if their subject matter is not conventional. On the other hand, "Il Parini, ovvero della gloria" ("Parini's Discourse on Glory") and "Detti memorabili di Filippo Ottonieri" ("Memorable Sayings of Filippo Ottonieri") develop the frame of an essay in which lengthy passages are quoted. In fact, all of the voices appearing in *Moral Tales* are deeply personal and often auto-biographical. In this, Leopardi anticipates the pseudonymous technique used by the Danish philosopher Søren Kierkegaard. The use of the dialogue, as well as the pseudonyms and multiple perspectives, allowed Leopardi to explore his own complex and conflicted views on the tension between aesthetic enthusiasm and philosophical pessimism, and between a desire to believe and an inability to do so. *Moral Tales*, like all of Leopardi's prose, is marked by a blend of Romantic passion and classical clarity that makes him one of the masters of the 19th-century essay.

THOMAS L. COOKSEY

Biography

Born 29 June 1798 in Recanati. Suffered scoliosis as a child, and ophthalmia as an adult. Studied privately with tutors. Lived in Rome, 1822–23, Milan, 1825, Bologna, 1825–26, Florence, 1826, 1830–33, and Naples, 1833–36. Wrote for Fortunato Stella publishers, Milan, 1825–28. Became a count on the death of his father. Died in Naples, 14 June 1837.

Selected Writings

Essays and Related Prose

Operette morali, 1827; revised editions, 1834, 1845; edited by Saverio Orlando, 1976, Cesare Galimberti, 1978, Ottavio Besomi, 1979, Paolo Ruffilli, 1982, Edoardo Sanguineti, 1982, Giorgio Ficara, 1988, and Pietro Pelosi, 1990; as *Essays and Dialogues*, translated by Charles Edwards, 1882; as *Essays, Dialogues and Thoughts*, translated by Patrick Maxwell, 1893, and James Thomson, 1905; as *Operette Morali, Essays and Dialogues*, edited and translated by Giovanni Cecchetti, 1982; as *Moral Tales*, translated by Patrick Creagh, 1983
Pensieri, in *Opere*, vol. 1, edited by Antonio Ranieri, 1845, Cesare Galimberti, 1982, and Mario Fubini, 1988; edited and translated by W. S. Di Piero (bilingual edition), 1981
Saggio sopra gli errori popolari degli antichi, in *Opere*, vol. 4, edited by Prospero Viani, 1846
Zibaldone, 7 vols., 1898–1900; edited by Anna Maria Moroni, 2 vols., 1972, Emilio Peruzzi (facsimile edition), 10 vols., 1989–94, and Giuseppe Pacella, 3 vols., 1991; selection as *Zibaldone*, translated by Martha King and Daniela Bini, 1992
Discorso di un italiano intorno alla poesia romantica, 1906; edited by Ettore Mazzali, 1957, and Ottavio Besomi, 1988
Selected Prose and Poetry, edited and translated by Iris Origo and John Heath-Stubbs, 1966
Poems and Prose, edited by Angel Flores (bilingual edition), 1966

Other writings: poetry (collected and published in the *Canti*, 1831), a history of astronomy (wr. 1813, pub. 1878–80), and correspondence.

Collected works editions: *Opere*, general editor Antonio Ranieri, 6 vols., 1845–49; *Tutte le opere* (Mondadori Edition), edited by Francesco Flora, 5 vols., 1968–73; *Poesie e prose* (Mondadori Edition), edited by Rolando Damiani and Mario Andrea Rigoni, 2 vols., 1987–88.

Bibliographies

Bibliografia analitica leopardiana, Florence: Olschki, 2 vols., 1963–73
Carini, Ermanno, *Bibliografia analitica leopardiana (1971–1980)*, Florence: Olschki, 1986
Giordano, Emilio, *Il labirinto leopardiano: Bibliografia, 1976–1983, con una breve appendice, 1984–1985*, Naples: Edizioni Scientifiche Italiane, 1986
Mazzatinti, G., and M. Menghini, *Bibliografia leopardiana*, Florence: Olschki, 3 vols., 1931–53

Further Reading

Barricelli, Gian Piero, *Giacomo Leopardi*, Boston: Twayne, 1986
Bini, Daniela, *A Fragrance from the Desert: Poetry and Philosophy in Giacomo Leopardi*, Saratoga, California: Anma Libri, 1983
Caesar, Michael, "Leopardi's *Operette morali* and the Resources of Dialogue," *Italian Studies* 43 (1988): 21–40
Dotti, Ugo, "La missione dell'ironia in Giacomo Leopardi," *Belfagor* 39 (July 1984): 377–96
Getto, Giovanni, *Saggi leopardiani*, Florence: Vallecchi, 1966
Koffler, Richard, "Kant, Leopardi, and Gorgon Truth," *Journal of Aesthetics and Art Criticism* 30 (Fall 1971): 27–33
Negri, Antonio, "Between Infinity and Community: Notes on Materialism in Spinoza and Leopardi," *Studia Spinozana* 5 (1989): 151–76
Origo, Iris, *Leopardi: A Study in Solitude*, London: Hamilton, 1953
Perella, Nicholas James, *Night and the Sublime in Giacomo Leopardi*, Berkeley: University of California Press, 1970
Ragione, Regini, "Ragione architettonica delle *Operette morali*," *Rassegna della Literatura Italiana* 85 (September–December 1981): 501–10
Singh, G., *Leopardi and the Theory of Poetry*, Lexington: University of Kentucky Press, 1964

Leopold, Aldo

American, 1886–1948

A major figure in the environmentalist movement, Aldo Leopold anticipated by a generation the need to recognize the interdependence of humankind and its natural environment. Leopold studied at Yale but felt limited by the laboratory; for him, research was best carried out in the environment, where both flora and fauna worked together. For many years, he worked for the U.S. Forest Service, studying erosion and preservation of the environment. He published more than 350 articles, but his quest was for an understanding that would bring together the natural world and the human being. He is remembered as the originator of the term "land ethic," a naturalist, a hunter, and a member of the Ecological Society of America, the American Forestry Association, and the Audubon Society.

Leopold's best-known books were both published posthumously. *A Sand County Almanac* was written as observations throughout the year at his sand farm in Wisconsin and prepared for publication by his son after Leopold died in 1948; *Round River*, a second collection of essays, was published by his son in 1953. The gentle, musing quality of Leopold's essays and verbal sketches, as well as his carefully detailed observations of the unusual, the beautiful, or the wonderful in ordinary birds, fish, deer, flowers, trees, and sunrises appealed to a wide audience. Leopold has been widely read as a natural historian and for his concept of the "land ethic," which treats the land as a "community" and emphasizes the symbiosis of all things, animate and inanimate. In the foreword to *A Sand County Almanac*, Leopold explains his attempt to bring together the ecological notion of community, the need to love and respect land, and the cultural insights that land can give. In blending these three concepts, he goes beyond ecology into the ethical principle of love and respect for land and into the land as a repository for human history. Indeed, his cultural insights are among the most memorable in his work; he writes, for example, on the impact on human culture of diverting streams or eliminating the fires essential to the prairie as an ecosystem. Leopold calls for a reexamination of "unnatural" things with an eye to "things natural, wild, and free."

Leopold's major themes include not only the interdependence of all nature, but his own and, potentially, humankind's joy in participating in the ecosystem: working on the land (making a well-filed shovel "sing"), arising at 3:30 a.m. to catalogue the territorial chants of assorted birds, following the flight of migrating geese. He contextualizes his essays by noting that in the century since **Darwin** published *Origin of Species*, we should have had time to develop a sense of kinship with other life forms and an awareness that we are merely partners in the voyage of evolution.

Leopold's style is simple, laced with poetic images such as that of a tiny spring flower that is "only a postscript to hope." He is sometimes whimsically ironic, as when he writes of the "alphabetical conservationists" who work for the U.S. government but often lack a holistic view of nature and humankind, or of an educated woman, "banded [like the birds he banded to track] by Phi Beta Kappa," who had never heard the geese overhead. Leopold speculates that education seems to suggest "awareness" of material objects that are worth far less. He is poetic when he traces an atom through a cycle – outside time – from breaking off a rock to passing into the bodies of animals, into a river, and finally into the sea, where it remains trapped for thousands of years.

The essay most representative of Leopold's style and his ethic is "The Round River," the title essay of the second collection. Drawing on the legend of Paul Bunyan, who was said to have discovered a circular river that flowed into itself, Leopold takes the notion and applies it to what he calls the "biota," the circle of ongoing and constantly modifying life in which each species plays a role. Understanding this circuit, he argues, requires thinking that runs "perpendicular" to Darwin's stream of evolution, looking at the whole rather than the individual species. Continuing the metaphor, he defines conservation in terms of learning to navigate the biotic stream. Declaring that the acknowledgment of land as organism is the major discovery of 20th-century science, he argues that we must learn to keep every part rather than to be profligate in destroying streams, prairies, creatures, species. By tracing the history of a German mountain and its greater fertility on one slope, he exemplifies

the human lack of awareness of the effects of farming, cutting, trenching, diverting waterways, and otherwise tinkering with the earth as organism. Stability and diversity are interlocked, he contends, and we have neglected the small "cogs and wheels" in the larger whole. But not only do we need greater public awareness of the interweaving of individual and whole; we need to "refine" our "taste in natural objects." Whereas fertility and diversity should be the keys to conservation, public debates link economics and biology and omit other considerations.

The essay ends with a whimsical analogy based on a bird dog that, in the absence of pheasants, hunted meadowlarks. Conservationists, Leopold writes, are like the bird dog: after failing to convince landowners to practice forest conservation, wildlife management, and fire control, they decided that a bureau could take care of the problem. Bureaucracy, he concludes, is the meadowlark that helps us forget that we really wanted a pheasant. For Leopold, ethics must be added to economic and biological considerations. If we try to understand the cycle of the round river and to develop a land ethic, we may eventually achieve conservation.

Long before such awareness became fashionable, Aldo Leopold encouraged development of an ethic of environmental management, an awareness of the interrelationship of all things. To accomplish his ends, he used whimsical humor and irony, imaginary journeys of atoms, tales of animals on his sand farm, and hunting lore. He has been compared with **Henry David Thoreau** and **John Muir**, but Leopold's writings are unique: they speak of the need of one species for another, of animate life valuing the inanimate in landscape, of going beyond Darwin to a holistic view that incorporates human respect for the environment that produced us.

MARY ELLEN PITTS

See also Nature Essay

Biography

Rand Aldo Leopold. Born 11 January 1886 in Burlington, Iowa. Studied at the Sheffield Scientific School, Yale University, New Haven, Connecticut, B.S., 1908; Yale School of Forestry, Master of Forestry, 1909. U.S. Forest Service assistant, Apache National Forest, Arizona Territory, 1909–11; worked in various capacities as a forester at Carson National Forest, New Mexico, 1911–24. Married Estella Bergeve, 1914: three sons and two daughters. Secretary, Albuquerque Chamber of Commerce, 1918–19; associate director, Forest Products Laboratory, Madison, Wisconsin, 1924–28; game consultant, Sporting Arms and Ammunition Manufacturers Institute, 1928–31; professor of wildlife management, University of Wisconsin, 1933–48. Contributor to various journals, including the *Journal of Forestry* and the *Wisconsin Agriculturalist and Farmer*. President, American Wildlife Society, 1939, and Ecological Society of America, 1947; founding member, and vice president, 1945–48, Wilderness Society. Awards: Permanent Wild Life Protection Fund Medal, 1917; *Outdoor Life* Medal; John Burroughs Medal, 1977. Died (of a heart attack while fighting a grass fire) in Wisconsin, 21 April 1948.

Selected Writings

Essays and Related Prose

A Sand County Almanac, and Sketches from Here and There, 1949
Round River: From the Journals of Aldo Leopold, edited by Luna B. Leopold, 1953

Aldo Leopold's Wilderness: Selected Early Writings, edited by David
   E. Brown and Neil B. Carmony, 1990; as *Aldo Leopold's
   Southwest*, 1995
The River of the Mother of God and Other Essays, edited by Susan
   L. Flader and J. Baird Callicott, 1991

Other writings: a book on game management (1933), and game
surveys of various regions.

Further Reading
Callicott, J. Baird, editor, *A Companion to A Sand County
   Almanac: Interpretive and Critical Essays*, Madison: University of
   Wisconsin Press, 1987
Flader, Susan L., *Thinking like a Mountain: Aldo Leopold and the
   Evolution of an Ecological Attitude Toward Deer, Wolves, and
   Forests*, Madison: University of Wisconsin Press, 1994 (original
   edition, 1974)
Lobiecki, Marybeth, *Of Things Natural, Wild, and Free: A Story
   About Aldo Leopold*, Minneapolis: Carolrhoda Books, 1993
McClintock, James, *Nature's Kindred Spirits: Aldo Leopold, Joseph
   Wood Krutch, Edward Abbey, Annie Dillard, Gary Snyder*,
   Madison: University of Wisconsin Press, 1994
Meine, Curt, *Aldo Leopold: His Life and Work*, Madison:
   University of Wisconsin Press, 1988
Paul, Sherman, "The Husbandry of the Wild," in *Essays on the
   Essay: Redefining the Genre*, edited by Alexander J. Butrym,
   Athens: University of Georgia Press, 1989
Potter, Van Rensselaer, *Global Bioethics: Building on the Leopold
   Legacy*, East Lansing: Michigan State University Press, 1988
Sayre, Robert F., "Aldo Leopold's Sentimentalism: 'A Refined Taste
   in Natural Objects'," *North Dakota Quarterly* 58, no. 1 (1991):
   112–25
Scheese, Don, "'Something more than wood': Aldo Leopold and the
   Language of Landscape," *North Dakota Quarterly* 58, no. 1
   (1990): 72–89

Lessing, Gotthold Ephraim

German, 1729–1781

With Lessing German prose reached a new level of point and
power. **Nietzsche** praised Lessing's unique gusto and precision
that gave his prose new verve; Karl Jaspers described it as
"philosophy in action." While his writings contain few pieces
that fit the definition of the essay in the strict sense, the search
for an essayistic, experimental, and tentative truth informs
virtually all of Lessing's productions. The exposure and ridiculing of prejudices is already the task of the first plays like
Der Freigeist (1753; *The Freethinker*), *Die Juden* (1749; *The
Jews*), and *Der Misogyn* (1767; *The Woman-Hater*). Lessing's
insistent critical alertness produces a new, striking, razor-
sharp style. Brief, pointed, uncompromising, yet flexible in his
attacks, Lessing combines elegance, transparency, acuity, and
logical stringency. His polemical tone reflects not simply a
sublimated form of aggression but also the self-imposed imperative of honesty and veracity. The unrelenting rigor Lessing
conjures in his writings not only means to challenge and often
ridicule his opponents but, more importantly, aims to stake a
claim for a public sphere which, in mid-18th-century Germany,
was only just emerging.

Inspired by **Pierre Bayle**'s *Dictionnaire historique et critique*
(1697; *An Historical and Critical Dictionary*), Lessing wrote
a series of *Rettungen* (rescues), a particular type of essay that
attempts to redeem falsely accused or misrepresented authors
fallen from grace because of their unpopular or supposedly
dangerous opinions. There he reissues the warning against
siding too precociously with what seems to be the truth without
careful examination first. He stresses that even when the
truth seems to be found, error still plays a crucial role in its
discovery: "There is no use for the simile that one need not
care about the wrong ways once the right one is known. For
one does not get to know the former through the latter but
the latter through the former" ("Rettung des Cardanus" [1754;
Rescue of Cardanus]). When truth wins, he insists, no individual side has prevailed; rather it is a victory for all, for truth
is never won just for oneself: "The losing party does not lose
anything but its errors, and can thus partake at any moment
in the victory of the other."

The concern with developing an open, liberal, and free-
spirited public space runs through all of Lessing's dramatic,
literary, and philosophical works. A prolific journalist, critic,
playwright, **pamphlet**eer, **review**er, and editor, Lessing envisaged a free republic of letters. The ambition to become
Germany's first economically successful freelance writer
inspired him early on to emerge as a distinct critical voice. In
addition to a steady stream of reviews and critiques, he experimented with new forms in which critics could express their
concerns. In journals like *Critische Nachrichten aus dem Reiche
der Gelehrsamkeit* (Critical news from the realm of scholarship), *Berlinische privilegierte Zeitung* (Berlin privileged newspaper), *Das Neueste aus dem Reiche des Witzes* (News from
the realm of wit) – for which he also often served as editor –
Lessing advocates the acknowledgment of the public as an independent, self-regulatory power. His friendship with Friedrich
Nicolai, an energetic publisher and promoter of the Berlin
Enlightenment, and the philosopher **Moses Mendelssohn**, led
to a close and intensive collaboration resulting in the creation
of the first impartial and independent review of modern
German letters, *Briefe die neueste Literatur betreffend* (Letters
on contemporary literature). Provocative and witty, the *Briefe*
initiate a dialogue between its authors and the public as a way
of establishing a shared aesthetic and critical understanding of
the nature of drama, poetry, and literature at large.

Against the "ut pictora poesis" (painting is like poetry)
convention, the collection of essays *Laokoon; oder, Über die
Grenzen der Malerei und Poesie* (1766; *Laocoon; or, The
Limits of Poetry and Painting*) develops in a systematic fashion,
marked by digressions and excursions into philology and
conjecture, the intrinsic difference between painting and poetry.
While painting is limited to representations of spatial ideas,
poetry's limits and strengths consist in staging temporal representations, i.e. actions and processes. Unable to depict temporal
difference, representations of an event like that which the
Laocoon statue presents do not depict a process, but its "most
pregnant moment." On the other hand, spatial representations
in literature are subject to transformation into the consecutive
order of a progressing narrative.

In a series of fictitious letters, conversations, and in the
running commentary Lessing fashioned for the Hamburg
theater in his *Hamburgische Dramaturgie* (1767–68; *Hamburg*

Dramaturgy), he critiques plays and their productions, poetry, translations, and other publications. Lessing's critiques play a crucial role in preparing the stage for the essay as the proper medium in which to argue for and eventually establish standards of taste and judgment. Indeed, such standards emerge, if not via the public exchange, then at least by way of the ongoing dialogue between Lessing and his friends, especially Mendelssohn. The consequence of this dialogue is nothing less than the transformation of the conditions of the truth-finding process. The criteria for truth now appear as something that can be conceived only as an ongoing exchange, which itself can be delimited solely in and through the public.

As a persistent philosopher of the Enlightenment, Lessing breaks ground for the freedom of investigation that formulates its own rules. Repealing the traditional restrictions of competence, he insists that every truth without exception must be exposed to discussion and dispute in the public sphere: "It may very well be the case that no dispute has ever settled the truth; but in every dispute truth has gained. Dispute has nourished the spirit of examination . . ." (*Wie die Alten den Tod gebildet* [1769; How the Ancients represented death]). Truth, therefore, is no longer an entity that can securely be arrived at once and for all. Rather it becomes an ideal toward which we can only strive, which we can approach more or less but never possess. In his pitiless exchange with the reform theologian Reverend Goeze, Lessing sums this up in an image: "It is not the truth that a human being possesses but the sincere effort in getting to truth that makes a human being . . . Possession makes one at rest, inert, proud – If God were to hold in his right hand all the truth and in his left the unique ever-active spur for truth, although with the corollary to err forever, asking me to choose, I would humbly take his left and say: 'Father give! for the pure truth is for you alone!'" (*Eine Duplik* [1778; Counter-response]).

If the truth-finding process is to remain open-ended, a result only of a dialogical procedure, then this must also be reflected in the method in which the truth-finding process is enacted. As a consequence, many of Lessing's writings are presented as thought experiments. They do not arrive at definitive results but rather open up more questions. They cause the reader to address the problems anew. They emphasize the paradoxical and unresolvable features of historical truths, and the difficulties posed by a thorough application of logic.

Conceived as exercises and experiments, Lessing's essays aim at revising conventional history. In contrast to a Voltairean mode, Lessing's interventions do not pretend to reflect the truth; rather they call for a reevaluation of the entire epistemological situation. By turning answers into questions, and assumptions into problems, Lessing exposes prejudices and assertions as unproven conjectures devoid of reasonable grounds.

The work-in-progress quality of Lessing's prose, its unfinished, open-ended, investigative character makes it difficult to answer the question of which literary genre, precisely, these writings belong to. At times scholarly, historical, theological, and polemical, they form a new kind of essay. As much as they derive their force from polemical dispute, they also aim to be more than just a victorious attack against the enemy. For these essays redefine the framework wherein arguments are supposed to take place in such a way that the truth-finding process itself is transformed into a critical enterprise. Thus it is precisely the "polemical" character in Lessing's essays that frees them from the implicit, yet harmful polemics inherent in the dogmatic practice of scholastic philosophy. What presents itself as erudite and scholarly is unmasked by Lessing as the petty politics of lazy pretensions.

Some of the theological writings do take the form of theses, as was common in both Reformation and scholastic disputations. But it is not just Luther and his contemporaries whom Lessing may have followed in this: **Bacon**'s scientific **aphorisms** may have been another literary model. In Lessing the strands of vigorous Reformation and logically rigorous scientific thought combine to form a new way of reasoning. His thesis-length paragraphs sketch out the skeleton of an argument that remains strictly objective and yet also projects essayistic qualities. Exemplary of this kind of essay is *Die Erziehung des Menschengeschlechts* (1780; *The Education of the Human Race*). Conceived as a thought experiment, this piece does not advance theses for disputation; rather it suggests a rethinking of the fundamental assumptions of religion and of the course of history.

Hermäa (wr. 1763), a project abandoned by the young Lessing, shows the author as a *flâneur avant la lettre*, one who undertakes excursions and digressions that depart from the deductive reasoning of a limited rationalism. Favoring the accidental, Lessing makes chance the legitimate guide for traveling the road to knowledge. By validating chance, he emancipates curiosity from the grip of dogmatic rationalism. Freed from conventions and customs, method is replaced by spontaneity and the sense for contingency is cultivated. "Hermäa" – that which belongs to Hermes as the god of the roads, of traveling, mediation, but also of interpretation – were stone piles placed along highways dedicated to Hermes, the patron of travelers. Noting that Hermes is the god of both the roads and chance, Lessing's *Hermäa* are an implicit commentary on the contingent character of methods, literally the "meta-ways." His **preface** to *Hermäa* recalls **Montaigne**'s programmatic opening pronouncement in his *Essais*, transposing it to a German Enlightenment setting. Montaigne's preoccupation with himself – or his "self" as the central and only meaningful concern – is now displaced by the author's wandering mind, which promises rich returns from its intellectual adventures: "Imagine a human being with infinite curiosity and without the inclination for a certain discipline. Unable to give his mind a firm direction, he will wander through all fields of knowledge, admire everything, desire to recognize everything, and become disgusted with everything. If he is not without genius, he will notice a great deal, but get to the bottom of little."

Lessing's practice of writing presents a paradoxical project of controversy, dispute, and dialogical experimentation. How intimately Lessing experiences the connection of the thought-process to his writing is expressed in a paradox in "Über eine zeitige Aufgabe" (1776; On a timely task): "What a pity I cannot think without the pen in my hand! What a pity I only think for my own instruction. If my thoughts satisfy me, I tear the paper apart. If they don't, I have it printed."

WILLI GOETSCHEL

Biography

Born 23 January 1729 in Kamenz, Saxony (then part of the Holy Roman Empire). Studied theology and medicine at the University of

Leipzig, 1746–48; University of Wittenberg, 1748 and 1751–52, masters degree in theology, 1752. Editor, with Christlob Mylius, *Beiträge zur Historie und Aufnahme des Theaters*, 1750; review editor, *Berlinische privilegierte Zeitung*; editor, *Theatralische Bibliothek*, 1754–58, *Briefe die neueste Literatur betreffend*, 1759–65, and *Das Neueste aus dem Reiche des Witzes*. Secretary to General Bogislaw von Tauentzien, Breslau, 1760–65. Theater critic for the National Theater in Hamburg, 1767–68. Librarian for the Duke of Brunswick, Wolfenbüttel, 1770–81. Member, Academy of Mannheim, 1776. Married Eva König, 1776 (died, 1778): one son (died in infancy). Died in Brunswick, 15 February 1781.

Selected Writings

Essays and Related Prose
Laokoon; oder, Über die Grenzen der Malerei und Poesie, 1766; edited by Dorothy Reich, 1965; as *Laocoon; or, The Limits of Poetry and Painting*, translated by William Ross, 1836, E. C. Beasley, 1853, Robert Phillimore, 1874, Ellen Frothingham, 1874, W. B. Rönnfeldt, 1895, and Edward Allen McCormick, 1962
Hamburgische Dramaturgie, 2 vols., 1767–68; edited by Georg Zimmerman, 1879(?), Charles Harris, 1901, Julius Petersen, 1916, Hans Kaufmann, 1953(?), and Otto Mann, 1958; as *Hamburg Dramaturgy*, translated anonymously, 1962
Briefe, antiquarischen Inhalts, 2 vols., 1768
Eine Duplik, 1778
Die Erziehung des Menschengeschlechts, 1780; edited by Louis Ferdinand Helbig, 1980; as *The Education of the Human Race*, translated by F. W. Robertson, 1858, and Henry Chadwick, in *Theological Writings*, 1956
Theological Writings, translated by Henry Chadwick, 1956
Unvergängliche Prosa: Die philosophischen, theologischen und esoterischen Schriften, edited by Konrad Dietzfelbinger, 1981

Other writings: several plays (including *Minna von Barnhelm*, 1767; *Emilia Galotti*, 1772; *Nathan der Weise* [*Nathan the Wise*], 1779), fables, and correspondence.

Collected works editions: *Werke*, edited by Julius Petersen and Waldemar von Olshausen, 25 vols., 1925, supplement, 5 vols., 1929–35; *Werke*, edited by H. G. Göpfert and others, 8 vols., 1970–79; *Werke und Briefe*, edited by Wilfried Barner and others, 1985– (in progress).

Bibliographies
Bauer, Gerhard, and Sibylle Bauer, *Gotthold Ephraim Lessing*, Darmstadt: Wissenschaftliche Buchgesellschaft, 1968; revised edition, 1986
Kuhles, Doris, *Lessing-Bibliographie, 1971–1985*, Berlin: Aufbau, 1988
Seifert, Siegfried, *Lessing-Bibliographie*, Berlin and Weimar: Aufbau, 1973

Further Reading
Blackall, Eric A., *The Emergence of German as a Literary Language, 1700–1775*, Ithaca, New York: Cornell University Press, 1978 (original edition, 1959)
Dilthey, Wilhelm, "Lessing," in *Poetry and Experience*, edited by Rudolf A. Makkreel and Frithjof Rodi, Princeton, New Jersey: Princeton University Press, 1985
Goetschel, Willi, "Negotiating Truth: On Nathan's Business," *Lessing Yearbook* 28 (1997)
Heftrich, Eckhard, *Lessings Aufklärung*, Frankfurt-on-Main: Klostermann, 1978
Jaspers, Karl, "Lessing," in his *Die grossen Philosophen: Nachlass*, vol.1, edited by Hans Saner, Munich: Piper, 1981: 346–415, and vol. 2: 726–63
McCarthy, John A., *Crossing Boundaries: A Theory and History of Essay Writing in German, 1680–1815*, Philadelphia: University of Pennsylvania Press, 1989
Pikulik, Lothar, "Lessing als Vorläufer des frühromantischen Fragmentarismus," in *Wolfram Mausser und Günter Sasse*, Tübingen: Niemeyer, 1993: 428–35

Letter

Although evidence for the existence of epistles can be found from earliest antiquity, the letter, as a rhetorical vehicle used for essay writing, developed from the Athenian oratory of Isocrates, from whom we have nine surviving letters as discourses, and flourished during the Hellenistic age. Epicurus embedded much of his philosophy in letter form. Thus by the time of St. Paul the elegant Hellenistic figures were firmly a part of the epistolary tradition, though some church historians such as Adolf Deissmann (*Paulus* [1911; *St. Paul: A Study in Social and Religious History*]) have argued strongly that the Pauline epistles are unliterary "conversations" intended only for a limited community. Among the Romans, however, the epistolary essay clearly became a literary type of the highest order. **Cicero** used the letter for some of the prose on political and ethical topics that most clearly exemplifies his periodic style. Many of the stoic treatises of **Seneca**, such as the *Ad Marciam de consolatione* (wr. c. 43 CE; To Marcia on consolation), were cast in epistolary form, while the letter in verse form also became popular with the elegant Romans. The *Ars poetica* (wr. c. 12–8 BCE; **The Poetic Art**) of Horace was actually his epistle to the Pisos, and the work of Ovid also included verse epistles.

Long letters on serious topics saw their next great flowering near the end of the Middle Ages. In fact, late Victorian and modern scholars have rediscovered and delighted in the epistolary form and in the way it took on increased importance as a vehicle for political, literary, and even scientific ideas. In the preface to his late lectures on the *Life and Letters of Erasmus* (1895), the great Victorian scholar J. A. Froude wrote, "The best description of the state of Europe in the age immediately preceding the Reformation will be found in the correspondence of Erasmus." In England, Sir Thomas More was using the letter for similar purposes. Following the founding of the Royal Society, a century and a half later, the standard method for expressing new and elaborate ideas was in "letters" for publication in the transactions of the Society, a practice that continues to this day. (A typical example is the communication on "a case of squinting," dated 10 March 1777, sent to the Royal Society by Erasmus Darwin, the grandfather of **Charles Darwin**, and clearly named after the great Erasmus.)

The letter as an elaborate literary form itself, and not just as a vehicle for ideas, enjoyed a major resurgence with the neoclassicism of the late Renaissance and Enlightenment. Alexander Pope rejuvenated the verse epistle of Horace, so that his **An Essay on Man** (1733–34) is set as an epistle to Henry St. John, Lord Bolingbroke. At the same time **Voltaire** published his *Letters Concerning the English Nation*, which are also known as "philosophic" letters because of their highly essayistic quality. Similarly, Charles de Montesquieu and **Oliver Goldsmith** made use of the long letter in prose to convey their ideas on culture, and in the course of so doing produced literature of a high quality. The form was widespread throughout the 18th and early 19th centuries, ranging from the **Earl of Chesterfield**'s *Letters to His Son* (wr. 1737 onward; pub. 1774) through a number of letter-essays by **Edmund Burke**, to Thomas Malthus on the "poor laws," to de Crèvecœur's *Letters from an American Farmer* (1782), to Sydney Smith's *Peter Plymley Letters* (1807) on religion and the Church.

The complex interface between the personal letter and that crafted as literature, which troubled scholars looking as far back as the Pauline epistles, took on an additional dimension with the epistolary novel, which evolved in the late Renaissance and continues to the present. Prime examples are the works of Samuel Richardson. He wrote (and printed himself) a how-to handbook on writing the personal letter (*Letters Written to and for Particular Friends*, 1741), much of which was realized in his seminal novel *Pamela* (1740–41). A century later, Anthony Trollope incorporated letters elaborately into many of his 47 novels, constituting one variation on the epistolary form in fiction; and Trollope, who worked for the British postal service, also illustrates how important the long personal letter became in the Victorian age. In the 20th century, Saul Bellow and John Barth are two American writers who have made complex use of the letter in literature. Barth's *Letters* (1979) is not only fiction but also essay in the most florid sense. Thus, in the last two centuries the distinction between the personal letter and more public forms of literary expression has become blurred almost beyond recognition. Some of the greatest writers have had their personal letters published as major works, often regarded as discussions of literature. An early example would be the letters of John Keats, which were originally personal, but which now appear in collections of essays on literary theory. Thus the ancient form continues to have an intriguing ambiguity of purpose and a vigorous potentiality in relation to the essay form.

DONALD M. HASSLER

Anthologies

The Faber Book of Letters, edited by Felix Pryor, London: Faber, 1988; Boston: Faber, 1989

The Letter Book: Selected, with an Introduction on the History and Art of Letter Writing, edited by George Saintsbury, London: Bell, 1922

Love Letters: An Anthology, edited by Antonia Fraser, London: Weidenfeld and Nicolson, 1976; New York: Knopf, 1977

Love Letters: An Anthology from the British Isles, 975–1944, edited by James Turner, London: Cassell, 1970

Love Letters: An Anthology of Passion, edited by Michelle Lovric, New York: Marlowe, 1994

The Oxford Book of Letters, edited by Frank Kermode and Anita Kermode, Oxford and New York: Oxford University Press, 1995

The Personal Art: An Anthology of English Letters, edited by Philip Wayne, London and New York: Longman Green, 1949

Postman's Horn: An Anthology of the Letters of Later Seventeenth-Century England, edited by Arthur Bryant, New York and London: Longman Green, 1936; revised edition, London: Home and Van Thal, 1946

Treasury of the World's Great Letters, from Ancient Days to Our Own Time, edited by Max Lincoln Schuster, New York: Simon and Schuster, 1940

Further Reading

Almeida, Teresa Sousa de, "Pour une théorie de la lettre au dix-huitième siècle," *Studies on Voltaire and the Eighteenth Century* 304 (1992): 863–66

Altman, Janet Gurkin, *Epistolarity: Approaches to a Form*, Columbus: Ohio State University Press, 1982

Altman, Janet Gurkin, "Epistolary Conduct: The Evolution of the Letter Manual in France in the Eighteenth Century," *Studies on Voltaire and the Eighteenth Century* 304 (1992): 866–69

Altman, Janet Gurkin, "Teaching the 'People' to Write: The Formation of a Popular Civic Identity in the French Letter Manual," *Studies in Eighteenth-Century Culture* 22 (1992): 147–80

Cherawatuk, Karen, and Ulrike Withaus, editors, *Dear Sister: Medieval Women and the Epistolary Genre*, Philadelphia: University of Pennsylvania Press, 1993

Classen, Albrecht, "Female Epistolary Literature from Antiquity to the Present: An Introduction," *Studia Neophilologica* 60, no. 1 (1988): 3–13

Drew, Elizabeth, *The Literature of Gossip: Nine English Letter Writers*, New York: Norton, 1964

Exler, Francis Xavier J., *The Form of the Ancient Greek Letter: A Study in Greek Epistolography* (dissertation), Washington, D.C.: Catholic University of America, 1923

Fantazzi, Charles, "The Evolution of Erasmus' Epistolary Style," *Renaissance and Reformation/Renaissance et Réforme* 13, no. 3 (1989): 263–88

Grassi, Marie Claire, "L'Art épistolaire français: XVIIIe et XIXe siècles," in *Pour une histoire des traités de savoir-vivre en Europe*, edited by Alain Montandon, Clermont Ferrand: Faculté des Lettres et Sciences Humaines de Clermont Ferrand, 1994

Henderson, Judith Rice, "Erasmus on the Art of Letter Writing," in *Renaissance Eloquence: Studies in the Theory and Practice of Renaissance Rhetoric*, edited by James J. Murphy, Berkeley: University of California Press, 1983

Howland, John W., *The Letter Form and the French Enlightenment: The Epistolary Paradox*, New York: Lang, 1991

Perelman, Les, "The Medieval Art of Letter Writing: Rhetoric as Institutional Expression of the Professions," in *Textual Dynamics of the Professions: Historical and Contemporary Studies of Writing in Professional Communities*, edited by Charles Bazerman and James Paradis, Madison: University of Wisconsin Press, 1991

Redford, Bruce, "'The converse of the pen': Letter Writing in the Age of Johnson," *Yale University Library Gazette* 59, nos. 1–2 (1984): 49–96

Robertson, Jean L., *The Art of Letter Writing: An Essay on the Handbooks Published in England During the Sixteenth and Seventeenth Centuries*, Liverpool: Liverpool University Press, 1942

Saliba, Jaimee R., "Regulating the I-You: Gender, Dialogue, and the Epistolary Text," *Papers on French Seventeenth-Century Literature* 21, no. 40 (1994): 177–85

Levi, Primo

Italian, 1919–1987

"It is not at all an idle matter trying to define what a human being is." So Primo Levi writes in *L'atrui mestiere* (1985; *Other People's Trades*). The larger and more intimate implications of this occupation form the basis for most of Levi's work.

Levi began his writing life as an essayist with *Se questo è un uomo* (1947; *If This Is a Man*), frequently described as a memoir, but really a series of linked essays describing his experience as a prisoner of Auschwitz during World War II, and analyzing a set of moral questions that arose from the unmediated culpability of his German captors and the Darwinian survival strategies of the inmates. Prior to his capture with the anti-fascist resistance in the Turin hills, Levi was beginning a career as a chemist. He tells us he had no literary pretensions before his experience at Auschwitz, though clearly he was well-educated and highly literate. The essay "Il canto di Ulisse" ("The Canto of Ulysses") in *If This Is a Man* is a virtual collage of literary allusion in which Levi displays – as he elsewhere discusses – the fact that the accoutrements of civilization, which were a burden and disadvantage in the Lagers (concentration camps), also occasionally helped to remind him of his continuing existence as a human being: "As if I also was hearing it for the first time: like the blast of a trumpet, like the voice of God. For a moment I forget who I am and where I am." "The Canto of Ulysses" is a *tour de force*, a major 20th-century essay, in its combination of the halting pain of first-person reminiscence, strategic quotation, fragmentary arrangement, and subtle attention to the interconnection of linguistic, literary, and moral considerations.

Levi frequently presents himself as a "witness" whose training in the sciences aids the scrupulous objectivity of his testimony. Indeed, a rigorous sense of logic and attention to detail runs through all of his work. Formally, this is perhaps most clear in *Il sistema periodico* (1975; *The Periodic Table*), a sequence of essays and stories organized by the elements, which have metaphorical or actual meaning in each piece. "Cerio" ("Cereum"), for example, ostensibly describes Levi and his friend Alberto's construction of lighter flints out of rods of cereum, an activity which purchased Levi two months of life in the Lager's black market. But as usual with Levi, the description of life in the camp is the largest subject within which complex subtextual material swirls. He begins "Cereum" with a sense of memory's mutability: "At a distance of thirty years I find it difficult to reconstruct the sort of human being that corresponded, in November 1944, to my name or, better, to my number: 174517," and proceeds to write a version of the friendship essay about the moral integrity of Alberto, ending darkly, even absurdly with the knowledge that Alberto's death was perversely bartered back in Italy: "Alberto did not return, and not a trace remains of him; after the end of the war a man from his town, half visionary and half crook, lived for a number of years on the money he made telling his mother false consolatory tales about him."

Levi committed suicide in 1987, his post-Holocaust battles for meaning and testimony exhausted by his sense that the Holocaust was already diminishing into a contextually compromised historicism. The last work he completed before death was the essay collection *I sommersi e i salvati* (1986; *The Drowned and the Saved* – also the title of the middle, literally central essay of *If This Is a Man*), which unifies the thematic complexities that marked his work from the beginning. In the earlier essay, Levi ponders the conundrums that inform all his work: how we are served by memory, and whether "it is necessary or good to retain any memory of this [the Lager's] exceptional human state"; the meaning of "two particularly well-differentiated categories among men – the saved and the drowned," and how these categories both can and cannot elucidate moral meaning outside of the concentration camp; the limits and possibilities of language for distorting and salvaging experience beyond ordinary limits. Here, as elsewhere, there is extraordinary tension in Levi's work between the logical,

rational, supposedly "objective" though morally essential processes of preserving memories of the camp, and the taxonomic (Levi is always fond of taxonomies) subjectivity he creates: Schepschel, Alfred L., Elias Lindzin, and Henri are the "saved" for whom Levi cannot conceal a deep distaste, despite his insistence on the moral qualification of evaluating the behavior of the victimized, broken men. And poignantly, Levi, too, is one of the "saved" for whom, as one moves through the essays, intellectual lucidity takes on the violence of a nightmare, a kind of hyperrationality which both undermines itself and threatens madness. His allusions to Dante's *Inferno*, therefore, seem horrifyingly appropriate in the summoning of pain both of and beyond this world. How does one understand a world in which "The worst survived, that is, the fittest; the best all died" ("La vergogna" ["Shame"])? Perhaps this is possible through a sometimes pathetically small sense that the victory of man's darkest impulses was incomplete. Certainly, Levi's consolations are never theological. He rejects any spiritually redemptive reading of the Holocaust since this tends to proffer a moral reading of survival. In a stunning moment at the end of "Ottobre 1944" in *If This Is a Man*, Levi reacts to Kuhn's prayer of thanks for not having been selected for the gas chamber and crematorium: "If I was God, I would spit at Kuhn's prayer." Hell can never be the best of all possible worlds.

In *The Drowned and the Saved*, Levi makes one last attempt to clarify his life's writing, and the essays in the collection reflect 40 years of refined and reconsidered humanistic assays into the experience of the Holocaust, the "concentrationary reality," as Levi calls it in "La zona grigia" ("The Gray Zone"). In *The Drowned and the Saved* Levi affirms his belief in the historical uniqueness of the Holocaust, while not completely separating or elevating it above subsequent horrors in Cambodia or South Africa. There are dangers in denying both the experience of history and the history of personal experience. Levi warns us that "Willingly or not we come to terms with power, forgetting that we are all in the ghetto, that the ghetto is walled in, that outside the ghetto reign the lords of death, and that close by the train is waiting." Levi is a furious cautionary whose sense of urgency poses a sometimes faint glimmer of hope balancing against jeremiadic despair. If, for Levi, our language can only grope to contain and explain horror, the essay is an important site for linguistic exploration, encompassing individual memory, cultural and historical testimony, formal, aesthetic, and moral possibility.

While the Holocaust was Levi's central and informing subject, he also wrote essays that venture lyrically into the natural world and childhood ("Tornare a scuola" [1985; "Going Back to School"], "'Le più liete creature del mondo'" [1985; "'The Most Joyful Creatures in the World'"], "Il fondaco del nonno" [1985; "Grandfather's Store"]), literary essays ("François Rabelais" [1985], "Scrivere un romanzo" [1985; "On Writing a Novel"], "Tradurre Kafka" [1983; "Translating Kafka"], "Dello scrivere oscuro" [1985; "On Obscure Writing"]), and the more general **familiar essay** ("Contro il dotore" [1985; "Against Pain"], "Bisogno di paura" [1985; "The Need for Fear"], "Del pettegolezzo" [1986; "About Gossip"]).

At their best, Levi's essays contain a philosophical intensity that might be compared to **Walter Benjamin**, but with a scientist's eye and a more singular, if complicated, sense of purpose.

DAVID LAZAR

Biography

Born 31 July 1919 in Turin. Studied at the University of Turin, degree in chemistry, 1941. Took part in the Italian Resistance during World War II, but was captured and held in Fossoli, then at Auschwitz concentration camp, 1944–45; returned to Italy, 1945. Industrial chemist, SIVA, Turin, 1945–47. Married Lucia Morpurgo, 1947: one son and one daughter. Contributor, *La Stampa* (The Press). Awards: Campiello Prize, 1963, 1982; Bagutta Prize, 1967; Prato Prize, 1975; Strega Prize, 1979; Viareggio Prize, 1982; Kenneth B. Smilen Award, 1985. Died (suicide) in Turin, 11 April 1987.

Selected Writings

Essays and Related Prose

Se questo è un uomo, 1947; as *If This Is a Man*, 1960, and as *Survival in Auschwitz: The Nazi Assault on Humanity*, 1961, translated by Stuart Woolf

Il sistema periodico, 1975; as *The Periodic Table*, translated by Raymond Rosenthal, 1984

L'altrui mestiere, 1985; as *Other People's Trades*, translated by Raymond Rosenthal, 1989

Racconti e saggi, 1986; as *The Mirror Maker: Stories and Essays*, translated by Raymond Rosenthal, 1989

I sommersi e i salvati, 1986; as *The Drowned and the Saved*, translated by Raymond Rosenthal, 1988

Other writings: collections of stories (including *La chiave a stella* [*The Monkey Wrench*], 1978; *Lilít e altri racconti* [*Moments of Reprieve*], 1981), the narrative *Se non ora, quando?* (1982; *If Not Now, When?*), and poetry.

Collected works edition: *Opere*, 3 vols., 1987–90.

Bibliography

Giffuni, Cathe, "An English Bibliography of the Writings of Primo Levi," *Bulletin of Bibliography* 50, no. 3 (1993): 213–21

Further Reading

Birkerts, Sven, *An Artificial Wilderness: Essays on 20th-Century Literature*, New York: Morrow, 1987

Böll, Heinrich, "Primo Levi and Saul Friedlander: Portrayals of Self and History," *Connecticut Review* 13, no. 1 (Spring 1991): 41–49

Camon, Ferdinando, *Conversations with Primo Levi*, Marlboro, Vermont: Marlboro Press, 1989

De Luca, Vania, *Tra Giobbe e i buchi veri: Le radici ebraiche dell'opera di Primo Levi*, Naples: Istituto Grafico Editoriale Italiano, 1991

Eberstadt, F., "Reading Primo Levi," *Commentary* (October 1985)

Epstein, Adam, "Primo Levi and the Language of Atrocity," *Bulletin of the Society for Italian Studies: A Journal for Teachers of Italian in Higher Education* 20 (1987): 31–38

Gilliland, Gail, "Self and Other: Christa Wolf's *Patterns of Childhood* and Primo Levi's *Se questo è un uomo* as Dialogic Texts," *Comparative Literature Studies* 29, no. 2 (1992): 183–209

Lowin, J., "Primo Levi's Unorthodox Judaism," *Jewish Book Annual* 45 (1987–88)

Patruno, Nicholas, *Understanding Primo Levi*, Columbia: University of South Carolina Press, 1995

Risk, Mirna, "Razionalità e coscenza etica di Primo Levi," *Italian Studies* 34 (1979): 122–31

Rudolf, Anthony, *At an Uncertain Hour: Primo Levi's War Against Oblivion*, London: Menard Press, 1990

Sodi, Risa, "The Memory of Justice: Primo Levi and Auschwitz," *Holocaust and Genocide Studies* 4, no. 1 (1989): 89–104

Sodi, Risa, *A Dante of Our Time: Primo Levi and Auschwitz*, New York: Lang, 1990

Sodi, Risa, "Primo Levi," in *Jewish Profiles: Great Jewish Personalities and Institutions of the Twentieth Century*, edited by Murray Polner, Northvale, New Jersey: Aronson, 1991

Styron, William, "Why Primo Levi Need Not Have Died," *New York Times*, 19 December 1988

Tesio, Giovanni, "Primo Levi," *Rassegna di Varia Umanità* 34 (1979): 657–76

Vincenti, Fiora, *Invito alla lettura di Primo Levi*, Milan: Mursia, 1973

Lewis, C. S.

British, 1898–1963

C. S. Lewis was the author of dozens of books in many different genres – literary criticism, children's stories, adult fantasies and novels, poetry, Christian apologetics (as allegory, autobiography, and broadcast). Probably best known as the creator of Narnia, a series of children's fantasy books, he is also one of the abler writers of the essay in the 20th century. Moreover, the distinctive Lewis style is consistent in occasional talks, apologetics, and literary criticism so that his work stands out among others' academic efforts.

Lewis' reputation as an essayist was made as a Christian apologist. During the Blitz of World War II he made four series of BBC broadcasts, from August 1941 to 1944. These radio talks, each ten minutes long, were intended to explain Christianity to the ordinary person; hence the qualities of the essay – conversational, simple, vivid, informative – were crucial and mask the breadth of references to learning. Already known for an allegorical tale, *The Pilgrim's Regress* (1933), *The Problem of Pain* (1940), and *The Screwtape Letters* (1942), originally published in the Manchester *Guardian*, Lewis in his radio talks presented the fundamentals of belief in a way especially suited to the time and audience. Response was enthusiastic, and Lewis became a popular figure, in both Britain and the United States. Almost immediately he published three volumes: *Broadcast Talks* (1942; also as *The Case for Christianity*), *Christian Behaviour: A Further Series of Broadcast Talks* (1943), and *Beyond Personality: The Christian Idea of God* (1944). A revised and enlarged edition appeared as *Mere Christianity* (1952), and continuing sales and testimonials of readers indicate its ongoing influence.

Lewis' style as an essayist, as well as a thinker, is clear in this work. Notable are the logical putting of a case and easy conversational quality. In the **preface** to *Mere Christianity* Lewis observes a distinction between talk and essay, explaining that he had expanded the contractions and recast sentences where he had voiced italics, "but without altering, I hope, the 'popular' and 'familiar' tone which I had all along intended." The "voice" of Lewis is consistent – direct and personable, with a clear argument presented with conviction combined with an evolving awareness of human limitation as his Christianity was more deeply experienced. The clear, and declared, antecedent for C. S. Lewis as an essayist is **G. K. Chesterton**, the great Edwardian essayist and Roman Catholic apologist. Lewis explains in *Surprised by Joy* (1955), a spiritual autobiography, that he first read Chesterton while in hospital recovering from wounds in World War I, when he was an aggressive atheist. Agreement about ideas was not the issue, but rather enjoyment, especially for "the humor which is not in any way separable from the argument but is rather (as Aristotle would say) the 'bloom' on dialectic itself." "[S]trange as it may seem," Lewis continued, "I liked him for his goodness." Further reading led to a conviction that "Chesterton had more sense than all the other moderns put together." Such crisp judgment is typical of Lewis, whose conviction about the rightness of his own point of view annoys many – as does Chesterton's. The two also share a delight in polemical argument, classical training, an extraordinary range of reading, and a relish of the good life, especially male company and friendship, and of many particularities of sense experience described with pleasure.

Lewis' essays combine a relentless Aristotelian logic – perhaps best deployed in *The Abolition of Man* (1943), ostensibly a reflection on education – with a use of metaphor that ranges from simple comparison to vision, carrying the argument more surely than logic would. He usually begins with something very ordinary, a little parable, like the quarrel in the opening of *Mere Christianity*, and then shows that the common experience has a universal basis; in this way he moves from particulars to moral absolutes. Analogy is a key technique in making abstract thought concrete, and often the analogy develops over several pages to produce the effect of proof. Association of ideas, not syllogism, determines the flow of a Lewis essay, which often includes fascinating and memorable digressions. Such strategies mask Lewis' Western habit of an either/or argument which fosters his extremes. Defenders of these limitations note that Lewis is competing against clever skeptics; opponents fault him for glibness and superficiality.

The Four Loves (1960) originated as radio talks in America. This late effort includes six chapters: "Introduction," "Likings and Loves for the Sub-Human," "Affection," "Friendship," "Eros," "Charity." As always there are clear definitions, often setting one view against another, and vivid parables; there is also a greater intensity of personal feeling and understanding, reflecting Lewis' late, brief marriage. The second **chapter** includes a long logical, systematic, and balanced consideration which could be considered a separate essay. As always, Lewis combines relaxed conversation with a careful progression of points to reach a conclusion stated with great conviction, having been presented with countless ordinary details and many references to literature and theology, and to Western culture.

A volume of *Selected Literary Essays* (1969) shows Lewis as the scholar who wrote about **William Morris**, Jane Austen, Rudyard Kipling, and Sir Walter Scott, as well as verse forms and medieval and Renaissance authors and texts; such writing made him famous as a literary critic and historian in several notable books. Written between 1932 and 1962, the essays reveal both the range of Lewis' knowledge and the consistency of his personal interests and style. The scholarly essays contain footnotes and less familiar references, but the manner closely resembles that of the broadcast essays – personal, conversational, excited by argument, assured. Lewis called his own selected collection of his essays *They Asked for a Paper* (1962), a title that suggests his response to challenges and reflects how much he sustained "an atmosphere of hopeful debate," a characteristic of the Edwardian intellectual life of his childhood,

while presenting himself as an anachronism who admired and loved the Middle Ages and Renaissance (which he saw as less antithetical than usually argued) and believed as a Christian in an age when few shared his values.

At the end of the 20th century Lewis' ideas require yet more vigor to convince a jaded audience, but the legacy of the essays is an alternate way of thinking embodied in the style as well as the statements.

VELMA BOURGEOIS RICHMOND

Biography

Clive Staples Lewis. Born 29 November 1898 in Belfast. Studied at Cherbourg School, Malvern, Worcestershire, 1911–13; Malvern College, 1913–14; privately, in Great Bookham, Surrey, 1914–17; University College, Oxford (Chancellor's English Essay Prize, 1921), 1917, 1919–23, B.A., 1922. Served as first lieutenant in the Somerset Light Infantry, 1917–19. Philosophy tutor and lecturer in English, University College, Oxford, 1924, and fellow and tutor in English, Magdalen College, Oxford, 1925–54; professor of medieval and Renaissance English, Cambridge University, 1954–63. Married Joy Davidman Gresham, 1956 (died, 1960): two stepsons. Awards: Gollancz Prize, 1937; Library Association Carnegie Medal, for *The Chronicles of Narnia*, 1957; honorary degrees from five universities; Honorary Fellow, Magdalen College, Oxford, 1955, University College, Oxford, 1958, and Magdalene College, Cambridge, 1963; Fellow, Royal Society of Literature, 1948, and British Academy, 1955. Died in Oxford, 22 November 1963.

Selected Writings

Essays and Related Prose
Rehabilitations and Other Essays, 1939
The Personal Heresy, with E. M. W. Tillyard, 1939
Broadcast Talks, 1942; as *The Case for Christianity*, 1943
Christian Behaviour: A Further Series of Broadcast Talks, 1943
The Abolition of Man; or, Reflections on Education (lectures), 1943
English Literature in the Sixteenth Century (Clark lectures at Trinity College, Cambridge), 1944
Beyond Personality: The Christian Idea of God, 1944
Transposition, and Other Addresses, 1949; as *The Weight of Glory, and Other Addresses*, 1949
Mere Christianity, 1952
The Four Loves, 1960
The World's Last Night, and Other Essays, 1960
Studies in Words, 1960
They Asked for a Paper, 1962
Of Other Worlds: Essays and Stories, edited by Walter Hooper, 1966
Studies in Medieval and Renaissance Literature, edited by Walter Hooper, 1967
Christian Reflections, edited by Walter Hooper, 1967
A Mind Awake: An Anthology of C. S. Lewis, edited by Clyde S. Kilby, 1968
Selected Literary Essays, edited by Walter Hooper, 1969
God in the Dock: Essays on Theology and Ethics, edited by Walter Hooper, 1970; as *Undeceptions: Essays on Theology and Ethics*, 1971
Fern-Seed and Elephants and Other Essays on Christianity, edited by Walter Hooper, 1975
On Stories and Other Essays on Literature, edited by Walter Hooper, 1982
First and Second Things: Essays on Theology and Ethics, edited by Walter Hooper, 1985
Present Concerns, edited by Walter Hooper, 1986
Timeless at Heart: Essays on Theology, edited by Walter Hooper, 1987

The Essential C. S. Lewis, edited by Lyle W. Dorsett, 1988
Christian Reunion and Other Essays, 1990

Other writings: the fiction series for children *The Chronicles of Narnia* (1950–56), an adult science-fiction trilogy (1938–45), the fables *The Screwtape Letters* (1942) and *The Great Divorce* (1945), poetry, works on literary history (including *The Allegory of Love*, 1936; *The Discarded Image*, 1964) and religion, autobiography (including *The Pilgrim's Regress*, 1933; *Surprised by Joy*, 1955; *A Grief Observed*, 1961), diaries, and correspondence.

Bibliographies

Christopher, Joe R., and Joan K. Ostling, *C. S. Lewis: An Annotated Checklist of Writings About Him and His Works*, Kent, Ohio: Kent State University Press, 1975
Hooper, Walter, "A Bibliography of the Writings of C. S. Lewis," in *Light on C. S. Lewis*, edited by Jocelyn Gibb, London: Bles, 1965; New York: Harcourt Brace and World, 1966: 117–60

Further Reading

Carpenter, Humphrey, *The Inklings: C. S. Lewis, J. R. R. Tolkien, Charles Williams, and Their Friends*, London: Allen and Unwin, 1978; Boston: Houghton Mifflin, 1979
Christopher, Joe R., *C. S. Lewis*, Boston: Twayne, 1987
Gibb, Jocelyn, editor, *Light on C. S. Lewis*, London: Bles, 1965; New York: Harcourt Brace and World, 1966
Hannay, Margaret Patterson, *C. S. Lewis*, New York: Ungar, 1981
Schakel, Peter J., and Charles A. Huttar, editors, *Word and Story in C. S. Lewis*, Columbia: University of Missouri Press, 1991
Walsh, Chad, *C. S. Lewis: Apostle to the Skeptics*, New York: Macmillan, 1949
Walsh, Chad, *The Literary Legacy of C. S. Lewis*, New York: Harcourt Brace Jovanovich, and London: Sheldon Press, 1979

Liang Yuchun

Chinese, 1906–1932

Liang Yuchun was given the nickname of "the Chinese Elia," but it would be more fitting to call him the Chinese "Citizen of the World." Though he never set foot outside China in his short lifetime, he was more universalist, at least in his authorial persona, than any other writer of his age; that is to say, his interest was in humanity, not in his countrymen, except in that they were human too. To encounter his essays for the first time is to experience nothing less than shock at the ease with which he transcended national barriers and communed with the best of humanity in other lands. He felt he needed to, to stay human himself.

Born in 1906 in Fujian province, Liang died of scarlet fever less than four years after graduating from Peking University with a degree in English. His country thereby lost a rare intelligence, a sensitive and generous soul, and the most fluent writer of *baihua* (the vernacular language) in the whole of the Republican period (1912–49). Those qualities are first-rate qualifications for an essayist, and indeed his work was immediately recognized as something special, but the fact that he produced only two volumes of essays (one posthumous) inevitably contributed to his subsequent relative neglect, which was compounded by the rapid politicization of Chinese literature: he was a "citizen of the world" before his country was ready for him. However, his essays have been reprinted in

Taiwan since the 1970s and in the People's Republic since the 1980s.

By his own confession, Liang was addicted to the English essay. He read the world's great novels with enjoyment, but once read they rested peacefully on his bookshelf, without being subjected to further "violent perturbation" at his hands. **Montaigne** and the whole succession of English essayists were, in contrast, his constant companions. While still an undergraduate he completed *Yingguo xiaopinwen xuan* (A selection of English essays, preface dated 1928), an annotated translation, with matching English text, of ten examples from **Joseph Addison** to Robert Lynd. He also wrote, in 1928, a startlingly perceptive appraisal of **Charles Lamb**, whom he regarded as the greatest of English essayists – hence the "Chinese Elia" tag. More volumes of English essays followed, as well as translations of English poetry and novels (including *Moll Flanders*). His own essays were published under the titles *Chunlao ji* (1930; Spring wine) and *Lei yu xiao* (1934; Tears and laughter).

From Liang's comments on the essayists selected for his anthologies it can be seen that he valued goodness in the author and acute and penetrating observation of life in his work. He found that the English essay told the truth, got behind appearances, and did battle with falsity and hypocrisy. In his own writing he followed suit. He also wrote on subjects popular with English essayists ("vagabonds," for example), though in his own way. If in style his work resembles that of any English essayist, it is **Hazlitt**'s rather than Lamb's: his words stream out seemingly under their own power, healthy, expressive words of the mother tongue. Like Hazlitt, too, he was given to standing conventional assumptions on their head: tears are preferable to laughter, the philosophy of death is more interesting than the philosophy of life, jovial people are not funny, and so on. On the other hand, he could also write in the droll style of the English "silver age," as on the pleasures of staying in bed.

To give a brief example of his work, "Mao gou" ("Cats and Dogs") is half droll, half serious. After saying how afraid he is of both animals, he associates them with the cities he knows:

> Shanghai is a dog. When you stand on the Bund and close your eyes, you may well visualize a vicious dog stretched out before you. Dogs represent the seamy side of reality. The darkness of reality in Shanghai makes you jumpy, as if there really is a mad dog at your heels. Peking, however, is a cat. It represents the fallen soul. Peking has a mustiness about it which makes people lax, not wanting to think or do anything, just content to stay put and muddle through life. It is as if a big cat has stamped a black mark on every soul, condemning them for eternity.

Other authors have expressed similar feelings, but none so imaginatively.

In sharp contrast with the healthiness of Liang's language is the morbidity of his thoughts. Looking up from the bottom of the heap, first as a student, then as a lowly lecturer, it is understandable that he should have been depressed by the pretense and pretentiousness of what he saw, but his pessimism was far more basic than that. In "Yige 'xinlike' de weixiao"

(A cynic's smile) he points out, "to see through people's masks is common enough, but what is the good, when you discover that compared to their masks people's true visages are so boring, so dull, so little fun?" – and that is just for starters. Given this dim view of existence, we find that unlike his beloved Charles Lamb, the wise, kindly light leading his readers through the dark vale, Liang offers only the analogy of "a spark between the darkness before and the darkness after" to describe our universe. The great and glorious compensation is that when he blows upon that spark it burns with as pure a flame as one could hope to find in any literature.

D. E. POLLARD

Biography

Born in 1906 in Minhou, Fujian province. Studied English literature at Peking University, 1924–28. Began publishing essays in liberal and left-wing magazines, from 1926. Lecturer in English (specializing in **Francis Bacon** and Charles Lamb), Jinan University, Shanghai, 1928. Returned to Beijing to work as a librarian, 1929. Possibly married, with one child. Died (of scarlet fever) in Beijing in 1932.

Selected Writings

Essays and Related Prose
Chunlao ji 1930
Lei yu xiao, 1934
Liang Yuchun sanwen ji (Liang Yuchun's collected prose), edited by Qin Xianci, 1979
Translation of essays in: *Renditions* 43 (1995): 124–32; *The Columbia Anthology of Modern Chinese Literature*, edited by Joseph S. M. Lau and Howard Goldblatt, 1995: 647–50

Other writings: translated from the English, including the anthology of English essays *Yingguo xiaopinwen xuan* (1928) and works by **Daniel Defoe**, Thomas Hardy, Joseph Conrad, and Nathaniel Hawthorne.

Further Reading

Qin Xianci, editor, *Liang Yuchun sanwen ji* (Liang Yuchun's collected prose), Taibei: Hongfan Bookstore, 1979 (contains essays on Liang by his contemporaries)

Liberté

French Canadian periodical, 1959–

For a long time newspapers were the only publishers in Canada. Poems, stories, shorter pieces, even novels appeared between news, **reportage**, advertisements, essays, and columns. The first literary movement in Quebec promoting post-Romanticism, nationalism, religious sensibility, folklore, and biographies published two cultural periodicals: *Les Soirées Canadiennes* (1861; Canadian evenings) and *Le Foyer Canadien* (1863; The Canadian hearth). Similar to them was *Le Terroir* (1909; The soil), founded by members of the École Littéraire de Montréal (Literary school of Montreal). On the opposite side was *Le Nigog* (1918), Modernist, open-minded, artistic, Parisian. Several years later, *Les Idées* (1935; The ideas), with its book **reviews** and classical criticism, was overtaken by the young, left-wing, Catholic, personalist *La Relève* (1934; The relief) and *La Nouvelle Relève* (1941; The new relief).

No journal or magazine is connected with the two important postwar literary or artistic groups: the Automatistes, whose leader was painter Paul-Émile Borduas, author of the manifesto *Refus global* (1948; Global refusal), and l'Hexagone, a cooperative workshop of young French-Canadian poets who would soon become the first true Quebecois writers, propelled by Gaston Miron, who began publishing poetry in 1953. During this time, the most influential journals among students and intellectuals were *Cité Libre* (Free city), founded in 1951 by Canada's future Prime Minister Pierre Elliott Trudeau and other lawyers, newspapermen, or trade unionists, and *Amérique Française* (French America), founded in 1941 as a wide laboratory of creative writing.

Liberté (Liberty) was founded in 1959 by Radio-Canada and National Film Board producers Hubert Aquin, **André Belleau**, Jacques Godbout, **Fernand Ouellette**, and editor Jean-Guy Pilon, who were or would soon be poets, novelists, and essayists. This new generation is highly representative of the so-called Quiet Revolution in the Province of Quebec. All friends, they were well-educated, cultured, modern readers, travelers, and members of the media. *Liberté* was neither school nor convent, but tavern, club, café.

Politically *Liberté* is centrally placed between the liberal, federalist, new Catholic *Cité Libre* and the separatist, socialist, atheistic, secular *Parti Pris* (1963–68; We affirm). *Liberté*'s contributors are freelance journalists more interested in arts, literature, and communications than in economics, Marxism, and other ideologies. They prefer their own fancy to intellectual vogue. They are acquainted with the wider world – Paris, New York, Algeria, Israel, Brazil, and so on – but they live, think, and write in Montreal. Open to the world through several issues, articles, and translations, *Liberté* is not an open-air theater – it has a basement, walls as well as doors and windows.

Writers on the staff include poets (Ouellette, Pilon) and novelists (Aquin, Godbout); all of them are essayists. Until 1969, no one was a professor or scholar. André Belleau would be the first, followed in the 1970s by young graduates from European (French) universities such as François Ricard and François Hébert, who became editors of *Liberté* after the long reign of Pilon and before that of Marie-Andrée Lamontagne, the current editor.

Liberté published issues about language, cinema, television, history, politics, and philosophy from a free, inventive, literary point of view. Jokes, paradoxes, parodies, and polemics are preferred to seriousness and heavy erudition. Professional critics and writers act as well-informed amateurs: Gilles Marcotte on music, **Pierre Vadeboncoeur** on painting, **Jacques Brault** on everyday life in town and country. *Liberté* has become a center, a laboratory for chronicles, essays, and *essayisme* in theory and practice.

Most of the best collections of essays produced by publishers HMH, l'Hexagone, and Boréal were first columns or articles in *Liberté*: for instance, Fernand Ouellette's *Les Actes retrouvés* (1970; Rediscovered acts) and *Écrire en notre temps* (1979; Writing in our time); and André Belleau's posthumous *Surprendre les voix* (1986; To catch the voices), in which he brings together fiction and essays. The younger generation – *La Génération lyrique* (1992) according to François Ricard's title, a multibiography or general description of anonymous baby-boomers, is represented by Ricard himself (*La Littérature contre elle-même* [1985; Literature against itself]) and sharp, controversial **Jean Larose**'s *La Petite Noirceur* (1987; The small darkness) and *L'Amour du pauvre* (1991; Love of the poor). Both Ricard and Larose read and write about society and social discourse, as well as reading and writing novels. This is the spirit of *Liberté*.

LAURENT MAILHOT

Further Reading

Beaulieu, André, and Jean Hamelin, *La Presse québécoise, des origines à nos jours*, Quebec City: Presses de l'Université Laval, 10 vols., 1973–90

Bélanger, André-J., *Ruptures et constantes: Quatre Idéologies du Québec en éclatement: La Relève, la JEC, Cité Libre, Parti Pris*, Montreal: HMH, 1977

Le Devoir issue on *Liberté*'s 25th anniversary, 5 November 1983

Ducrocq-Poirier, Madeleine, editor, *La Revue Liberté: Actes du colloque organisé par le Centre International d'Études Francophone de l'Université de Paris IV-Sorbonne et le Centre de Coopération Interuniversitaire Franco-Québécoise*, Montreal: L'Hexagone, 1990

Écrits du Canada Français issue on journals, 67 (1989)

Fortin, Andrée, *Passage de la modernité: Les Intellectuels québécois et leurs revues*, Quebec City: Presses de l'Université de Laval, 1993

Gauvin, Lise, *"Parti Pris" littéraire*, Montreal: Presses de l'Université de Montréal, 1975

Gauvin, Lise, "Les Revues littéraires québécoises de l'université à la contre-culture," *Études Françaises* 11, no. 2 (1975): 161–83

Mailhot, Laurent, "L'Action de *Liberté*," in his *Ouvrir le livre*, Montreal: L'Hexagone, 1992

Major, Robert, *"Parti Pris": Idéologies et littérature*, Montreal: HMH, 1979

Revue d'Histoire Littéraire du Québec et du Canada Français issue on journals, 6 (1983)

30 Ans de "Liberté": Index des noms (1959–1989), Montreal: University of Montreal Department of French Studies, 1990

Liebling, A. J.

American, 1904–1963

When critic and journalist A. J. Liebling died in 1963, a colleague at the **New Yorker** surveyed the heap of books and papers piled on and around Liebling's desk and concluded that they perfectly represented his eclectic interests in both life and writing. There was the Annual Report of the New-York Historical Society, the *American Racing Manual*, the collected works of **Albert Camus**, a guide to making beer, a travelogue on Tunisia, three volumes on boxing, and a month's issues of the Las Vegas *Sun*. Indeed, Liebling's interests and his writing ranged widely in a 28-year career at the *New Yorker* which established his reputation as a gifted and unique writer and reporter. His essays are regarded as a model for the wave of so-called New Journalists who came after him.

Liebling's quirky writing interests reflected a quirky personality and a varied career in journalism. Son of a New York furrier, he was raised on the Upper West Side and attended Dartmouth College, where he was expelled for skipping chapel. After finishing Columbia University's journalism program, he hired a bearded Norwegian to picket the New York *World*

with a sign that read, "Hire Joe Liebling." (The *World* didn't.) His brief stint at the New York *Times* ended when the sports editor fired him for repeatedly listing "Ignoto," Italian for unknown, as referee in New York-area basketball games. He briefly studied ancient history at the Sorbonne in Paris, where he developed a love for the city, a ripe appetite, and a taste for *haute cuisine*.

Back in the United States, Liebling found work first at the Providence *Journal* and *Evening Bulletin*. "I oozed prose over every aspect of Rhode Island life," he recalled. Later, in four years at the New York *World-Telegram* in the early 1930s, he honed his skills at writing feature articles, penning more than a thousand. In 1935 he began work at the *New Yorker* as one of the stable of editor Harold Ross' young writers. At the magazine, his home for the rest of his life, he considered himself and colleagues such as Alva Johnston, Meyer Berger, and Joseph Mitchell part of the *New Yorker*'s second generation of stylists.

Liebling's irreverent writing and thorough reporting, especially his gift for capturing New York's life in prose, quickly impressed Ross. Liebling loved the city and spent hours wandering its streets. He was fascinated with slang, what he called the "side-street New York language" of the city's backstreets, and he had a talent for re-creating it. In scores of colorful essays, he chronicled the rich and varied New York scene: Izzy Yereshevsky's Cigar Store, the opening of a new nightclub by Hymie the Tumbler, overly superstitious Italians, and down-and-out prizefighters. His New York stories were collected in *Back Where I Came From* (1938), *The Telephone Booth Indian* (1942), and *The Honest Rainmaker: The Life and Times of Colonel John R. Stingo* (1953).

His slangy, often funny first-person essays were noted for their exaggerated metaphors and unlikely allusions, which sometimes taxed a reader's knowledge of ancient history, one of Liebling's favorite subjects. A Liebling account of a Sugar Ray Robinson fight might include, as the New York *Times* once noted, "a delicate embroidery on a theme suggested by a medieval Arabian historian to whom he was partial." **Tom Wolfe** once described Liebling as a writer's writer with a following that was almost cultish.

Liebling wrote hundreds of articles for the *New Yorker*. "As time went on, he wrote with greater and greater elegance, and the journalism he was ostensibly doing somehow turned into the kind of writing that endures," wrote a *New Yorker* correspondent in an unsigned obituary (11 January 1964). His friend St. Clair McKelway said Liebling's writing – opinionated and stylish yet based on solid reporting – was part of "a new art form in American journalism" pioneered at the magazine (New York *Herald Tribune*, 29 December 1963). Liebling wrote and rewrote his pieces to perfection, and his confidence in his writing was legendary. He was said to present his finished work to the *New Yorker*'s editors with all the natural self-assurance of a child presenting crayon drawings to adoring parents. "Damn it," a competitor once said, "if I had just one per cent of Joe's self-confidence I'd have written 'War and Peace' by this time."

Liebling's *New Yorker* work included a stint as war correspondent. His trip home on a Norwegian tanker was chronicled in "Westbound Tanker," one of his best-known wartime pieces. He also covered the London Blitz for the *New Yorker* and followed the First Infantry Division in its invasions of North Africa and northern France. He was present at the liberation of Paris, the only city that rivaled New York in his affections. France valued his war reporting and in 1952 awarded him the cross of the Legion of Honor.

After the war, Liebling took over the *New Yorker*'s "Wayward Press" column, a forum for newspaper criticism that had been started by **Robert Benchley** in 1927 and published sporadically afterward. Liebling delighted in assailing reporters and newspapers for their foibles, reserving his harshest words for publishers. "As an observer from outside, I take a grave view of the plight of the press," Liebling wrote. "It is the weak slat under the bed of democracy." Liebling's press criticism, widely read and often quoted in trade journals of American newspapers, made him the best-known press critic of his generation. His press columns were collected in *The Wayward Pressman* (1947), *Mink and Red Herring* (1949), and *The Press* (1961).

DAVID R. DAVIES

Biography
Abbott Joseph Liebling. Born 18 October 1904 in New York. Studied at Dartmouth College, Hanover, New Hampshire, 1920–23; Columbia University School for Journalism, New York, B.Litt., 1925; medieval studies at the Sorbonne, Paris, 1926–27. Sports writer, New York *Times*, 1925–26; staff writer, Providence *Journal* and *Evening Bulletin*, 1926–30, New York *World*, 1930–31, and the New York *World-Telegram*, 1931–35. Married Anne Beatrice McGinn, 1934 (divorced, 1949). Staff writer, 1935–63, war correspondent in France, England, and North Africa, 1939–44, and columnist of "Wayward Press," 1946–63, the *New Yorker*. Married Lucille Hill Spectorsky, 1949 (divorced, 1959). Chevalier, Legion of Honor (France), 1952. Married the writer Jean Stafford, 1959. Died (of complications from viral pneumonia) in New York, 28 December 1963.

Selected Writings

Essays and Related Prose
Back Where I Came From, 1938
The Telephone Booth Indian, 1942
The Road Back to Paris, 1944
The Wayward Pressman, 1947
Mink and Red Herring: The Wayward Pressman's Casebook, 1949
Chicago: The Second City, 1950
The Honest Rainmaker: The Life and Times of Colonel John R. Stingo, 1953
The Sweet Science: A Ringside View of Boxing, 1956
Normandy Revisited, 1958
The Earl of Louisiana, 1961
The Press, 1961; revised edition, 1964
Between Meals: An Appetite for Paris, 1962
The Jollity Building, 1962
The Most of A. J. Liebling, edited by William Cole, 1963; as *The Best of A. J. Liebling*, 1965
Molly, and Other War Pieces, 1964
A Neutral Corner: Boxing Essays, edited by Fred Warner and James Barbour, 1990
Liebling at the New Yorker: Uncollected Essays, edited by James Barbour and Fred Warner, 1994

Further Reading
Core, George, "Stretching the Limits of the Essay," in *Essays on the Essay: Redefining the Genre*, edited by Alexander J. Butrym, Athens: University of Georgia Press, 1989: 207–20

Midura, Edmund M., *A. J. Liebling: The Wayward Pressman as Critic*, Lexington, Kentucky: Association for Education in Journalism, 1974
Sokolov, Raymond, *The Wayward Reporter: The Life of A. J. Liebling*, New York: Harper and Row, 1980
Toll, Seymour, "Liebling in Paris," *Sewanee Review* 93, no. 4 (Fall 1985): 554–73

Lima la horrible
by Sebastián Salazar Bondy, 1964

Lima la horrible (1964; Lima the horrible) represents the epitome of Sebastián Salazar Bondy's literary and journalistic career. During his short but productive life, Salazar Bondy (1924–65) focused on two concerns: the literary activity and development of Peru, and its political and social situation. *Lima la horrible* is an essay in book form, consisting of 11 **chapters**. It belongs to a wave of essays with the objective of defining the ethos of a nation and its peoples through introspective analysis. Psychoanalysis provided the apparatus with which Spanish American essayists scrutinized their continent, though most limited themselves to one country in their analysis. Only two well-known essays focused on cities: Salazar Bondy's *Lima la horrible* and **Ezequiel Martínez Estrada**'s *La cabeza de Goliat* (1940; The head of Goliath). These essays attempt to define the idiosyncrasy of Lima and Buenos Aires, both nonrepresentative capitals of their respective countries.

Within the Peruvian ambit, *Lima la horrible* belongs to a minority left-oriented movement whose most distinctive figure, **José Carlos Mariátegui**, was the founder of the Peruvian Socialist Party (1895–1930). After its publication, *Lima la horrible* was used by the leftist factions to awaken a social consciousness in Peru. It represents the harshest criticism ever undertaken against the Peruvian oligarchy. Salazar Bondy dissects, step by step, each facet of what he designates the Limean deceit, denouncing the ideology underlying the pyramidal system wherein the poor are throttled and the rich swell.

According to Salazar Bondy, Lima has successfully perpetuated the historical period in which, as the capital of a viceroyalty, it took delight in its exquisite luxuries, realized by the exploitation and ostracism of the native Peruvians. The aristocracy of yesterday ("hawkers who would buy titles") has become today's oligarchy. The caste that holds the economic and political reins of power in Peru has adopted and imposed as a national ideology a chimera that Salazar Bondy calls "Colonial Arcadia," in order to preserve its hegemony, denying a voice to both Indian and *mestizo* in the historical dialogue. Consequently, the Limean lacks authenticity. Salazar Bondy believes that, based on the invention of an archetype, Lima has fabricated a system of values and traditions that constitutes the Limean identity or *criollismo*. The *criollo* is an amalgam of appearances: he is so enmeshed in this act of representation that his true being has been all but lost.

If Lima's apogee was the vice-royal period, it successfully survives as a nostalgic reproduction, still overlooking the abysmal difference between the privileged and the indigent, the incongruity between myth and reality. Salazar Bondy demythologizes famous Limean figures such as Ricardo Palma, Saint Rosa de Lima, and Saint Martin de Porres. Ricardo

Palma, a renowned realistic writer, was the author, perhaps unintentionally, of the colonial chimera. By fusing fiction and history, Palma created the literary apparatus that asserts yesterday's glory and denies the present. As to the inherited image of the saints, it has been adulterated and transformed. The embellishment of their iconography is repeated in the Limean folklore as an affirmation of the beauty and luxury of a period, and not as an anomaly of the times, which would be what the two saints truly denote.

Another Peruvian source of pride Salazar Bondy deconstructs is the Cuzco School of Painting, the most famous in colonial times. According to the author, this school represents another mode used by the Spaniards to impose their own reality onto the Indians, in order to erase their native identity. If what was native and telluric formed part of a painting, it appeared to replace the European icons that signified evil. The psychological consequences were devastating. The identity crisis caused by this imposition is still reflected in two Peruvian expressions: *perricholista* and *huachafo*. Both embody the obsession with Otherness. The former refers to the lower-middle-class individual who foolishly assumes a disguise in real life in imitation of the upper class, rendering himself ridiculous and the target of endless derision. The latter defines the person who sells his mind and soul as an answer to the imperative desire to belong to the aristocracy. The difference between the two expressions is that the *huachafo* is too low in the social hierarchy ever to become an aristocrat, while the *perricholista* can become one if he pays the price.

A third figure from the Colonial Arcadia that Salazar Bondy analyzes is the *tapada*, or the mysterious colonial lady (she hides behind a shawl, exposing only one eye), the ironic pillar of a conservative society. She is repressed and almost illiterate, and her role in society was to be beautiful. She lived behind the shadow of a most desirable husband, rich and influential, vicariously enjoying his power. Salazar Bondy argues that the modern Limean woman has kept this role despite her education, mundane manners, and profession. Her goal has remained to achieve a marriage of convenience. This woman has not come to be an independent and emancipated individual because the chains from the past have not been broken; her situation represents another remnant of the colonial chimera.

Salazar Bondy begins and ends his essay by emphasizing the dramatic disjunction of Peru. The exploitation of and discrimination against ethnic groups, the growing belt of pauperization strangling Lima, make unbearable the prolongation of the Colonial Arcadia. The vote against the past, which Mariátegui would once have cast, becomes Salazar Bondy's. The antithesis of the Arcadia belongs to the youth who can and should initiate a dialogue between the present and its true reality.

VERÓNICA SAUNERO-WARD

Edition

Lima la horrible, 1964

Further Reading

Fox, Lucia, "Sebastián Salazar Bondy y las facetas de la tradición y cambio," in her *Ensayos hispano-americanos*, Caracas, 1966: 73–81

Fox, Lucia, *El rostro de la patria en la literatura peruana*, Buenos Aires: Continente, 1970: 32–37

Puccini, D., "Un libro escrito con rabia *Lima la horrible*," *Unión* 4, no. 4 (1965): 167–69

Tauro, Alberto, editor, *Enciclopedia ilustrada del Perú*, Lima: PEISA, 1987: 1861

Vargas Llosa, Mario, "Elogio de Sebastián Salazar Bondy," *Letras* 74–75 (1965): 187–89

Vargas Llosa, Mario, "Un mito, un libro y una casta *Lima la horrible*," *Revista de la Universidad de Mexico* 19–12 (1965): 12–13

Vargas Llosa, Mario, "Sebastián Salazar Bondy y la vocación del escritor en el Perú," *Revista Peruana de Cultura* 7–8 (1966): 25–54

Literary Theory and the Essay

Since so many of the precepts of contemporary literary theory bear an uncanny resemblance to the rhetorical and discursive conventions of the essay genre, it is surprising that criticism has failed to note, much less explain, such virtual mimicry. After all, both literary theory and the essay in the present day dismantle logical, temporal, and causal order, reject narrative closure, and posit the mediation of subjectivity as a constituent element of intellectual inquiry. Not only because of their closely aligned discursive and theoretical structures, but also because they both arise in the same period, the essay and modern literary theory naturally bear the signs of mutual influence. To determine, however, whether literary theory influenced the essay more or the essay literary theory would suppress the complex aesthetic, social, and economic entanglements between them. If we instead attempt to analyze this mutual development from the late 16th century to the present day as an ongoing series of responses to the transformation of aristocratic society into bourgeois culture, the rise of print capital and the subsequent growth of literacy and the public sphere, the birth of literary (and later theoretical) coteries, and finally the professionalization of literary theory in the university, we come to discover that literary theory and the essay are bound as much to each other as they are individually to the academy's intellectual and cultural production.

Because of the interdisciplinary force of postmodern and present-day literary theory, and because much of what we consider literary theory today evolves directly out of debates within theology, philosophy, and natural science, most often articulated and advanced in the essay, it is necessary to define literary theory for the purposes of this study in the broadest possible terms. Certainly both literary theorists and scholars of the essay have reached far back into the past to reclaim their heritage from writers and from among genres that predate the named existence of either of these relative latecomers to the literary marketplace.

The most obvious generic overlap between the essay and literary theory is the representation of the self in writing. Although such discursive representation is most comprehensively realized in autobiography, it has long been represented in Western philosophy by metaphors of writing. If for **Montaigne** the essay was an attempt to capture thought in the very process of formation, we must view his *Essais* (1580, 1588) as an early blueprint of cognition and subjectivity commensurate with the skeptical empiricism of early modernity. Such discursive models of cognition predate Montaigne:

Aristotle, for example, had envisaged the mind as a wax tablet, upon which empirical experience was imprinted. But Montaigne's model of subjectivity, like those that followed, was a writerly attempt to counter the threat that rationality posed for lived experience and the emotional realm of identity. Locke and **Hume** represented cognition as a *tabula rasa*, a blank sheet that stores an infinite number of sense impressions, while for Noam Chomsky the mind is like a block of veined marble, capable of preserving only a finite number of shapes. With his analogy of a "mystic writing pad," or palimpsest, **Freud** introduced a double level of consciousness, such that the writing pad's surface records an infinite number of impressions which, when lost to the surface (consciousness), are yet retained as trace impressions on the opaque under (unconscious) layer.

That the essay has not only been the vehicle of publication for these cognitive blueprints, but has also imitated their shapes, suggests the profound versatility of this genre: with the malleability of wax, the essay expands its discursive borders to encompass new forms of knowledge; like the *tabula rasa*, the essay can either begin anew, or, paradoxically, to use **Theodor W. Adorno**'s vivid metaphor, it can "reflect the child-like freedom that catches fire, without scruple, on what others have already done" ("Der Essay als Form" [1958; "The Essay as Form"]). In the case of Chomsky's marble, the essay by discursive shape-shifting takes the isomorphic form of that which it represents; finally, like the mystic writing pad, it can register meaning on more than one level, positing a complex model of human subjectivity. As these representations of the mind as metaphors of writing suggest, any attempt to formulate modern subjectivity in – or as – an act of writing will push the generic boundaries of writing itself to new limits.

If the essay maps the contours of writer in the process of thinking, as Adorno argues in "The Essay as Form," then the free and associative nature of its form has taught subsequent generations free thinking, liberating each generation from the received wisdom of its predecessors. It was hardly by chance, then, that the essay emerged in the Renaissance, the term itself announcing the rebirth of classical learning in theory, but proving its demise in practice. For **Bacon**'s method of science, grounded in experience rather than argument, undermined the tautologous system of Aristotle and the scholastics, irretrievably damaging the logic of syllogism. The new cosmology of Copernicus, Kepler, Galileo, and Newton, by denying the authority of Aristotle and renouncing Ptolemy's geocentric cosmos, made a decisive break with the dominion of classical authority. The Newtonian and Cartesian advancement in physics outstripped Pythagorean mathematics. And, finally, a prose revolution inaugurated by **Erasmus** and Rabelais, and brought to fruition by Montaigne, Bacon, Hobbes, and subsequent generations of philosopher essayists, eradicated the artificial symmetry of Ciceronian language, undermining, as it did so, the whole intricate structure of the correspondent universe.

In sum, the empirical sciences colluded with the essay to undermine the Renaissance world picture, positing in its stead a secular, materialist world view. We might trace in the skeptical empiricism of this new philosophy the antecedents to the postmodern theoretical essay, whose tendency toward authorial self-disclosure, anti-systematic thinking, and an insurgence against received tradition suggests that modern criticism,

although claiming to reinvent itself with every generation, is just another variation of an old form. **John Donne**'s poem *An Anatomy of the World* (1611) – depicting the Renaissance's anxiety that the age of new philosophy and exploration was tantamount to a postmortem dissection of the world – is often cited as an epigraph to modernity: "And new philosophy calls all in doubt . . ./And freely men confess that this world's spent . . ./'Tis all in pieces, all coherence gone."

Donne's lament for lost order echoes a refrain of high Modernism central to postmodern inquiry. Here are the fragments of **T. S. Eliot**'s *Wasteland* (1922), the signal Modernist allegory of the dangers of skepticism unrestrained. The unfixed nature of Donne's world, momentarily sliding between two philosophical cosmologies, would re-emerge as **Matthew Arnold**'s bleak summary of Victorian modernity: "one world dead/The other powerless to be born." **Roland Barthes**' point that the "writerly" and self-conscious textuality of the essay reflects a pre-mapped (pre-rational) world bears a striking, almost uncanny, resemblance to the self-awareness of Donne's prescient narrator at the brink of a new world: "It is *ourselves writing*, before the infinite play of the world . . . is traversed, intersected, stopped, plasticized by some singular system (Ideology, Genus, Criticism)." Barthes is, in part, alluding to the simultaneous birth of a new kind of subjectivity and the essay in the early modern period – both predicated upon the modern self-consciousness and intellectual anxiety produced in a time of disorder and cultural dissent. Such an argument is supported by Adorno's claim that the essay provides a glimpse of the potential for cognitive freedom before the fall of language into the reified grammar of instrumental reason. What Donne, the early Modernist Arnold, and the late Modernist Eliot would mourn, postmodern critics following the lead of Barthes and Adorno would eulogize. In short, what Barthes here celebrates as the pleasures of open-ended textuality is precisely the form and substance of the essay.

The expansion of the bourgeois public sphere in the 18th century, enabled by imperial affluence, was accompanied by an increase in leisure time, a boom in print culture, the birth of literary and philosophical societies, and the legislation of civic institutions, such as libraries and museums. Central to the development of intellectual culture and the advent of professional art criticism was the appearance of coffeehouses throughout Europe. Among London's literati, for example, Dryden's circle gathered at Will's – "the Wits' Coffee House," from which **Richard Steele** dated his literary articles in the *Tatler* – Joseph Addison presided over his "Little Senate" at Button's, and Marvell's and Pepys' circle frequented the Rota coffeehouse. These urban literary circles shaped the **critical essay** in the modern sense: from coffeehouse culture the essay borrowed the capricious rhythm of free thinking, the capacious and associative quality of conversation, the intrigue of eavesdropping, the intimacy and scandal of gossip, the delight of a chance encounter, and often the abruptness of a meeting postponed. At the center of one of the most influential coteries of the 19th century, the Transcendentalists' Club, **Ralph Waldo Emerson** would write in "Ecstasy and Eloquence" that the essay was the form in which "everything is admissible, philosophy, ethics, divinity, criticism, poetry, humor, fun, mimicry, anecdotes, jokes, ventriloquism," all the discursive practices of the "most liberal conversation."

During the 19th century, competing cultural ideologies and technological developments colluded in the birth of the modern critical essay, the most prominent forum for theoretical inquiry for the last two centuries. The Adams-powered platen press in the 1830s and the Wharfedale cylinder press of the 1860s revolutionized print culture. The ability to mass-produce printed material rapidly, cheaply, and more efficiently presaged a rise in the private press in both Britain and the United States. If Edward Cave could boast in 1741 that his *Gentleman's Magazine*, whose subscribers **Samuel Johnson** numbered at 10,000, was "read as far as the English language extends and . . . reprinted from several presses in Great Britain, Ireland and the Plantations," then the new portability of the private press a century later would do much to extend – this time by discursive rather than political imperialism – the former geographical boundaries of the English language. Moreover, by allowing writers greater artistic control over their work, the private press created a market that demanded increasingly innovative and specialized forms of written discourse, especially within the essay genre, as epitomized by the experimental writing of Emerson and his circle.

If mass production created a more widely informed reading public, and if academic institutions and a mid-century trend toward metropolitan libraries provided repositories for literature in regions with limited access to book markets, such changes were to be at odds with the growth of specialized knowledge and the increasing privatization of society following the major revolutions of the late 18th century. While a boom in print culture was establishing large international markets, the private press in league with a rise in philanthropic and philosophical societies was busy creating small, discrete, often regional, markets that would further compartmentalize knowledge and encourage cultural heterogeneity. In terms of specialized markets, **Frederick Douglass**' private press and anti-slavery newspaper, *North Star*, exemplify the entrepreneurial and "agitprop" spirit of a new age of *belles-lettres* in the U.S. A former slave and a tireless anti-slavery advocate, Douglass was one of the most prolific American essayists of the 19th century. More significant to the development of the critical language and recurring rhetorical patterns within coteries, however, is the way in which the various abolitionist campaigns, like those of Douglass' circle, collaborated with other coteries, such as the emerging transatlantic women's movement. These political coteries joined forces via the private press with reciprocal – often transatlantic – organizations to deploy genre-specific tropes and rhetorical structures endemic to their own partisan literature in a way similar to how philosophical and literary coteries engineered and exchanged increasingly insular lines of critical thought and private discourse. Such discourse would culminate in the modern theoretical essay, a subgenre rooted in a breakdown of "democratic" consensus and one which heralded the further departmentalization of knowledge.

The emergence of transcendentalism in 1836 was integral to this process, comprised as it was of many of the 19th century's most distinguished critical essayists: Amos Bronson Alcott, Cyrus Bartol, Ralph Waldo Emerson, **Margaret Fuller**, Theodore Parker, and **Henry David Thoreau**. It is hardly by chance that the transcendentalists, like the constituents in the various coteries of social reform, influenced and were in turn influenced by British intellectuals such as Matthew Arnold,

Charles Darwin, George Eliot, Francis Jeffrey, and **Thomas De Quincey**. Although sustained by continental philosophy, transcendentalism was America's first home-grown intellectual movement, one initiating seminal forms of social, religious, political, and literary criticism. Much of the transcendentalists' specialized philosophical inquiry evolved in private correspondence, personal **journal**s, and what Emerson called "liberal conversations." As a theoretical enterprise that merged in the critical essays of the Transcendentalists' Club, it anticipated the academic and artistic coteries of America's "lost generation," including T. S. Eliot, **Ezra Pound**, and Gertrude Stein, their elder contemporaries in the Bloomsbury Group, and the Modernist movements in whose circles these artists and critics moved. In the critical essay, inquiry sought a form commensurate with its philosophical and theoretical concerns. Nineteenth-century critical essayists worried about religion in a secular utilitarian society, played out the Hegelian obsession over the condition of the natural soul, and theorized the crisis of selfhood – or the human "prison of glass," as Emerson called it – in industrial modernity.

Through the *Dial* (1840–44), the transcendentalist magazine launched by Emerson and Margaret Fuller, and through a host of other journals, the transcendentalists helped to introduce the German idealism of **Goethe, Kant**, and **Schiller** into American and British intellectual life, paving the way for a bold philosophical transformation of the American university, one which would shape pedagogy on both sides of the Atlantic well into the 20th century. But these journals were not like the popular **periodical**s of the 18th century: their specialization and increasingly philosophical rhetoric distinguished them from the comparatively gentle moralizing and general accessibility of **Daniel Defoe**'s *A Review of the Affairs of France* (1704–13), Steele's *Tatler* (1709–11), Addison's and Steele's *Spectator* (1711–12, 1714), or even Johnson's *Rambler* (1750–52) and *Idler* (1758–60). Whereas the literary criticism of **Samuel Taylor Coleridge** and **William Hazlitt**, in league with the emerging museum and art gallery of their day, attempted to make every amateur a critic by institutionalizing aesthetic taste, the criticism of the next generation would become less accessible by its convoluted turn toward the ironies of Romantic self-expansiveness, such as the "flux of moods," as Emerson wrote in "Experience" (1844), that renders impossible the very notion of personal "identity." Played out in approaches to literature, the critical essay, in a single generation, prescribed its audience more narrowly.

At least one influential essayist offered a thinly veiled justification of the necessary complexity of literary criticism in an argument that praised and defended the convoluted prose of authorial genius. In 1826 William Ellery Channing published his influential essay, widely acclaimed among the London literati, on Milton's prose, arguing that "to be universally intelligible is not the highest merit. A great mind cannot, without injurious constraint, shrink itself to the grasp of common passive readers," but instead must write for the "gifted reader." In any event, the die was cast: the 19th century would professionalize and institutionalize both criticism and the critic. By the first quarter of the next century, art criticism was relegated to the university, making the critical essay the coin of the realm, just as it made Van Wyck Brooks, T. S. Eliot, **Lewis Mumford**, Ezra Pound, and Gertrude Stein the penultimate generation of the great freelance scholar. Hardly representative of a generation, such renowned essayists as **Irving Howe, Edmund Wilson,** and Alfred Kazin brought the tradition of freelance scholars to an end.

We can trace in the essay's continued proliferation and dispersion into highly specialized academic subgenres, the late 19th-century departmentalization of the university into – and the displacement of classical education by – the nascent disciplines of the human sciences and modern humanities, such as anthropology, sociology, psychology, English literature, and history. The pioneers of such new academic disciplines knew that the institutional authority and autonomy to which they aspired were predicated upon the semblance of scientific precision. Nowhere was the need for legitimation more keenly felt than in the humanities, long stigmatized by the early-century educational reform of the Benthamites, who demanded a more practical alliance between industry and higher education. The university was now running on borrowed time. In response to legislative pressure for utilitarian reform in academia, the faculty of Yale University had in 1828 issued a landmark defense of higher education, which, reprinted in Silliman's *American Journal of Science*, was widely circulated in the U.S. and abroad, and managed to stave off managerial and curricular reform until after the Civil War. Even as late as 1874, Charles Eliot Norton, one of the few surviving Brahminical academics who lived to see utility and morality again become the focus of popular education reform two generations later, wrote to **Thomas Carlyle** that "Fine Arts" could "show the political, moral, and social conditions which have determined the forms of the Arts, and . . . quicken . . . the youth of a land barren of visible memorials of former times, the sense of connection with the past and gratitude for the effort and labours of other nations and former generations." Rather than justifying the utility of literature, however, the emerging English departments, following the lead of the university as a whole, turned to the German model of higher education. In what was almost an open act of defiance against utilitarianism, English departments took refuge behind German idealism, especially the idealism of Kant as it was threaded through Coleridge, Carlyle, and the transcendentalists. Shaped by Arnold's *Culture and Anarchy* (1869) and emblematized in the title of the first chapter, "Sweetness and Light," this new aesthetic philosophy managed to hold the vocational model of education at bay for almost half a century, until the growth of industry and the consequent Taylorization of social institutions in the aftermath of World War I compelled pragmatic reform in the university. (Frederick Taylor's *The Principles of Scientific Management* [1911] promoted a system for increasing industrial output by rationalizing the production process.)

If, however, English departments had justified their work to society at large, they had yet to establish credibility or a niche within the new university. In an attempt to compete with the sciences, English programs developed increasingly formalist methods of analysis, drawing upon the structuralist work of pioneering anthropologists, linguists, and psychologists, such as **Freud,** Saussure, Jakobson, Lévi-Strauss, and Peirce. Armed with the interdisciplinary breadth of formalism, English departments strengthened their position in the new university by colonizing adjacent disciplines, incorporating the embryonic programs of linguistics, comparative literature, journalism,

speech, theater and dramatics, and technical and business writing. These disciplines would leave their mark upon literary theory and upon the essay as it was transformed and deployed as the material sign of authority within the academy. Its synthetic nature, mutability, and lack of a philosophical basis suggest the mutual influence of literary theory and the essay on the shape of modern critical inquiry. Moreover, from this perspective, Adorno's characterization of the critical essay as a genre that "swallows up the theories that are close by" not only becomes a telling commentary on the insatiable appetite of literary theory and the imperial tendencies of modern literary studies, but also accounts for George Ripley's bitter indictment of the 19th-century university for having deprived the "common mind" of all avenues of critical discourse. By the early part of this century, a group known as the "Young Americans," led by Lewis Mumford, were fighting an academic trend that had further distanced the critical essay from its democratic roots.

As the inchoate disciplines, subsumed by larger departments, began their struggle for individual autonomy, their authority was purchased in more rigorously specialized academic journals. Thus the struggle for academic legitimation and the interdepartmental skirmishes over disciplinary boundaries brought with them an increase in specialized, professional scholarly journals. Professionalization created communities of specialized readers, encouraging critics to produce the abstract conceptual languages that would culminate in contemporary literary theory. In broader terms, we return to T. S. Eliot's observation of a parallel development among the artistic communities both in and outside the academy, lamenting that the breakdown of aristocratic culture resulted in the critic or artist having to "talk to a coterie or to soliloquize." As academic and critical discourse specialized, it was the elasticity of the essay form that enabled the subsequent rise of arcane and idiosyncratic theory. Out of the university setting arose such seminal periodicals as *English Literary History, Philological Quarterly, PMLA,* and *Modern Language Review,* and from the artist colonies appeared such independent avant-garde and Modernist journals as Wyndham Lewis' *Blast* (London), the *Dial* (New York), Herwarth Walden's *Der Sturm* (Berlin), Pound's *Egoist* (London), Maiakovskii's futurist *LEF* (Russia), the **Nouvelle Revue Française** (New French review; Paris), *Poetry* (Chicago), *Ma* (Today; Budapest), the *Vorticist,* and the *Imagist* (London). If the new aesthetics proclaimed in these Modernist journals rejected the old traditions as exhausted and inadequate to the new conditions of modern urban life, they also enjoined critics to explore the formal properties of the discourses and media with which artists worked. Extensive self-scrutiny rapidly became the order of the day. Modernist theoretical experiments pressed the limits of language and representation, forcing the postmodern critical essay to dissolve the self in a play of signification.

If a new sense of chronic crisis, phenomenal challenges to fundamental beliefs, and its corollary threat to regulated selfhood and evolutionary destiny – and if new scientific ideologies that either undermined spiritual life or nourished its antithesis in unprecedented waves of millenarian anxiety – had given birth to the essay in the 16th century, then the heightened repetition of these pervasive themes at the turn of the 20th would finally bring the critical essay to maturity as the engine of politically engaged theoretical inquiry. Eliot's complaint about coteries registers an acceleration in competing and overlapping discourses aimed at serving different sociopolitical ends – even when the ends were one, the means were vigorously contested. Borrowing unevenly from their philosophical predecessors and from each other, these coteries shaped their new manifestoes in the critical essay, establishing it as the forum *par excellence* for theory's political intervention in this century. As higher education in Britain and the U.S. transformed from college to university in keeping with the Germanic model of education, it was assailed not only by the political and cultural reforms of the day, but also by intellectual dissenters from within and without. Critical of ivory tower "despots" and the "loyalty oaths" that bred elitism in the academy, the controversial intellectuals of the day nourished hopes of an alliance between university-level education and the populist insurgence in national politics.

The problem was locating middle ground. The "Young Americans," voicing the concerns of the young generation's liberal constituency, were repulsed by the lurid form of Arnoldian idealism that promoted the academy's political indifference on the one side, and the equally repugnant industrial materialism of Taylorization on the other. It was John Dewey, the most influential American philosopher of his generation, who first envisaged a union between Arnoldian aesthetics and industrial utilitarianism *vis-à-vis* "pragmatism," the new intellectual and humanist attitude that shaped his educational philosophy and national education reform through the first half of the century. Dewey and **William James** had transformed the pragmatism of their Harvard mentor C. S. Peirce, expanding it from the grammar of logic into an optimistic and progressive intellectual vision that traced its inspiration directly back to the Emersonian wellspring. Among the intellectuals, the fact that pragmatism had been authored by academics suggested hope for an easy alliance with university concerns. Its national appeal, however, lay in its ability to unite the bifurcated social attitudes that set industrial progress at odds with humanist (if sometimes motivated by *noblesse oblige*) concerns. Not only did Dewey's pragmatism pay homage to laissez-faire capitalism by the sense of everyday utility that the word itself conveyed, but just as importantly, it also played to the young liberal reformer's New England meliorism ultimately grounded in a Protestant *felix culpa*.

Because the Young Americans' own agenda was of a piece with Dewey's unified social vision, Emerson, not surprisingly, was to answer for both. Encouraged by Arnold's faith in the redemptive nature of art, the Young Americans, including Van Wyck Brooks, Randolph Bourne, and Waldo Frank, turned back to transcendentalism for answers to the spiritual and cultural crisis of modernity. Perceiving in the trend to departmentalize academic disciplines and institutionalize aesthetic criticism the increasing stratification of democratic culture, especially in the large urban centers, the Young Americans bitterly criticized the academy with the transcendentalist sentiment and missionary zeal of George Ripley, who had, 75 years earlier, warned Harvard theologian Andrews Norton that "the Sword of the Spirit is not wielded after the tactics of the university." Borrowing from their forebears the rhetoric of a jeremiad that indicted the university for withholding spiritual knowledge from "the common mind," as Ripley had put it,

only to place it "into the keeping of scholars," the Young Americans bitterly charged the academy with having erected an intellectual aristocracy to manage the production, accumulation, and distribution of knowledge, a flagrant violation of the democratic spirit of popular education.

Oddly, Mumford's circle seemed impervious to the irony that transcendentalism was itself complicit in making possible the university's philosophical monasticism. Now the Romantic idealism deployed by Ripley's circle to counter the institutionalizing forces of bureaucratic capitalism and technology was in the service of the very institution against which Ripley had railed. We are again reminded of the academy's consummate strategy for survival: it would incorporate the theories of its adversaries. As **Lionel Trilling** would observe, the quintessential 20th-century example of this lay in the university's absorption of the critical energies of avant-garde Modernism. After all, an aesthetic movement whose agenda was to force the intellectual or academic to the brink of what Trilling, in *Sincerity and Authenticity* (1972), described as the "abyss" of Western Civilization had instead become a footbridge across the chasm of its hypocrisy and cultural relativism. In a final turn of irony, one taking us as far back as Donne's cosmic rift, this same abyss would become the "mise en abîme" of Derridean deconstruction, a grand rupture to be opened up and celebrated as a site of postmodern tourism.

Such highly specialized discourse continued to drive a wedge between academic theorists and the wider reading public, the original consumers of the essay. This trend has only intensified in the postmodern age. Postwar European and American journals, such as *Tel Quel* (As is), *Les Temps Modernes* (Modern times), and *Critique* became the forum for critical thinking, and generated theoretical languages that by their esoteric nature often prescribed their audiences still more narrowly. The academy's rapid consumption and production of these languages, especially since the 1960s, was purchased at the price of greater isolation even from the educated reading public, just as the theoretical essay moves farther and farther from its bourgeois roots in the 18th-century public sphere and from its contemporary counterpart, the opinion essay of popular culture and mass media. This trend has pitted traditional academic humanists, the likes of William J. Bennett, Allan Bloom, Harold Bloom, Roger Kimball, Camille Paglia, Page Smith, and D'nesh D' Souza against the vanguard of cultural theory, a coalition comprised of, among others, poststructuralists, feminists, and Marxists. Thus, the last generation continues the feud of its predecessors, a feud grounded in the cultural pessimism of Arnold and Eliot, and one which restages in every generation the crisis of culture in a democratic society.

While pivotal as the form and forum for such debates, the essay is yet more intricately and deeply imbricated in the material foundation of the university. Although registering profound philosophical, ethical, and moral issues, the publications engendered in this feud – both by their production of institutional authority and by the print culture they generate – are the trusses undergirding the economic fabric of the academy. Moreover, few scholars or critics would deny the status of their reputation (based on publication) as a commodity in the academic marketplace or, on a larger scale, the value of an institution's reputation as the sum of all the individual reputations of its combined faculty. (As postmodern theorist Jacques Derrida's proclivity for economic metaphors suggests, theoretical scholarship has long been complicit with a bourgeois emphasis on investment – in this instance, on an institution's positive name-recognition and thus its ability to draw renowned scholars, whose publications become the capital in the next economic cycle.) If, however, as its etymology implies, criticism (and thus the essay) is generated in times of crisis, then there is something almost disingenuous in these generational debates. For, however high the theoretical stakes, we cannot forget that the crisis (the perennial "crisis in the humanities" staged in part for the benefit of an incredulous public) also re-enacts the literary discipline's struggle for professional legitimation. Perhaps not so disingenuous as caught between extremities, the literary academic must reconcile the social pressure to serve a utilitarian end in the tradition of Bentham and Taylor and the Arnoldian mandate to remain aloof from all forms of commercial or sectarian engagement. By failing to address the essay as a material component of academic life, scholars of the essay have failed to account for the genre's role in shaping institutional priorities, in, for instance, what many English literature scholars consider the emphasis on theory at the expense of literature in critical models subsequent to New Criticism.

In the eyes of intellectual liberals everywhere, the university had become just another example of the conglomerate trusts endemic to the late 19th and early 20th centuries, monopolies which undermined the democratic principles of intellectual exchange, competition, and fair play. For Mumford's circle and other like-minded liberals, the university had usurped the place of the large urban centers, whose heterogeneous terrain of wealth and poverty, of middle-class communities and perimeter slums, offered hope for a renewal of the self. This urban vitality was advanced in the essay on the levels of both form and function: while the essay served as a medium for the distribution of the social plan, the actual form of the essay came mimetically to illustrate the architectural design of the city and the new forms of human experience. Mumford, like **John Henry Newman**, in his influential essay "What Is a University?" (1873), saw the large urban center as a socially and culturally diverse campus, because, as Newman put it, "the newspapers, magazines, reviews, journals . . . the publishing trade, the libraries, museums, and academies, the learned and scientific societies, necessarily invest it with the functions of a University." Unlike Newman's, however, Mumford's vision was actualized in the practical and political blueprint of his life. If Mumford's attention to urban experience and the contingency of knowledge recalls the skeptical *flâneur* of the 18th-century **periodical essay**, and its re-emergence in the essays of Modernism, it is an atavism that surfaces again in the tone and tenor of postmodern critique.

The transformation of the critical essay and its efficacy as a force of intervention in the 20th century can never be fully appreciated, however, apart from an understanding of subject position in relation to political agency in the essay. Most philosophers and Modernist artists played up the age's Faustian parallels. The rapid advance of industry and technology, and the late 19th-century shift from agrarian markets to urban economies, nurtured a nagging worry that if mechanized repetition and assembly-line uniformity were the fruits of new

knowledge and greater progress, then selfhood and individuality were the Mephistophelian price exacted by the bargain. The intelligentsia represented the modern alienation from self and society with an increasing yet alternating sense of urgency and pessimism. As with every moment of crisis and social upheaval since the advent of modernity, the self was the primary site of ambivalence and anxiety for the critic. Not surprisingly, the counter-offensive against what was perceived as the dehumanizing forces of modernity was most effectively staged in the critical essay as it began to explore the linguistic constitution of subjectivity. Nowhere was this more vividly exemplified than in the reformist essays of Mumford, Brooks, and Bourne. The Young Americans, along with other intellectual radicals of their day, hoped to reintegrate the creative, irrational self in utilitarian society. Mumford's interdisciplinary scholarship foregrounded the "insurgent" subjectivity of the critical voice as a strategy for overcoming what Eliot called the "dissociation of sensibility," the schism between the rational and emotional self that is the essence of modern subjectivity. Inspired by Whitman's democratic poetics of the self and Patrick Geddes' "organic sociology," an anti-systemic movement in the sciences that yoked **Nietzsche**'s autobiographical critic with the intuition of Romanticism, Mumford's pungent essays against the assumed prestige and unquestioned authority of institutional criticism would, ironically, eventually foster the very academic-theoretical authority he so patently criticized: from Barthes' intensely autobiographical literary criticism to the Nietzschean rhetoric of poststructuralism, these postmodern projects, by their shared concerns with transcendentalism, would make apparent theory's atavistic tendency to treat recurring themes, especially the problem of finding an appropriate prose form for representing subjective experience.

By the 20th century, after the full flowering of science and technology, "periodical" would take on a new significance. The critical essay would now become periodical in its reproduction of reality as fragment. Simultaneous to the segregation of knowledge into university departments, the essay would similarly compartmentalize social experience, slicing everyday experience into clinical frames. In part, the program of the urban progressives was informed by the movement of naturalism and realism in art and literature at the turn of the century. Early on, under the guiding influence of **William Dean Howells**, whose authority emanated from his influential position as editor of the *Atlantic Monthly* (1871–81) and later as resident critic for *Harper's* (1886–92), American realism confronted what was perceived as the dangerous tendencies for a kind of national denial of social decay, as evidenced by the demand among a genteel audience for idealism or the clamor among the popular for romance. Realism in the essay took as its primary duty the presentation of moral and material poverty in society. If realism, by its close scrutiny of "pieces" of reality, could expose the hidden workings of power and thus demystify social hierarchies, it could also reify or "naturalize" these same social barriers (such as race, class, or gender) by the semblance of scientific legitimacy.

Measured against the background of fears about the loss of the self in a mechanized world, later realist essayists such as Upton Sinclair, Sinclair Lewis, **Mark Twain**, and **W. E. B. Du Bois** revised the moral realism of Howells into a politically engaged aesthetic. For instance, Du Bois formulated and propagated a new ideology of racial assertiveness whose contentious tone in the essay recalled the powerful jeremiad essays of Douglass, Martin Delaney, and James Redpath from the preceding century. As a humanitarian enterprise, Howells' early realism had flirted with a kind of Pelagianism popularized by the late 19th-century Social Gospel Movement, especially evident in his essays of the early 1890s; but under his aegis – until late in his career – realism had generally remained aloof from direct social engagement. Rather, it relied upon an aesthetics of observation, avoiding any emotionalism or social appeals that might be construed as partaking of the sentimental tradition, just then resurfacing and merging with a strain of realism in the form of early muckraking literature. As such, Howells' realism at the end of the last century bears a striking resemblance to the objective, clinical evaluations of Michel Foucault, whose scrupulously amoral historiography in the latter part of this century has been criticized for the sterility of its observation, evacuated as it is of subjective mediation. If Howells' realism had transformed the essay for a time from what George S. Hellman in his article "Later Essayists" (1933) called the "story essay" ("wherein the narrative element runs its gentle course over a bed of personal reflections and descriptive comment of individual flavour") to a prose style absent of any persona – a theory of detached observation – then the next generation of essayists would split the difference, advancing realism by fashioning and inserting an authorial persona that foregrounded what Mumford called "insurgent subjectivity." Such a revision would achieve its brilliant apotheosis in the autobiographical stand-point theories of the 1970s, and the politically engaged New Historicism in the American academy and Cultural Materialism in the British, and finally the confessional essayistic criticism that has emerged on both continents in the 1990s.

GREGORY S. JACKSON

Further Reading

Arnold, Matthew, *Culture and Anarchy*, Cambridge: Cambridge University Press, 1990; New Haven, Connecticut: Yale University Press, 1994 (original edition, 1869)

Banta, Martha, *Taylored Lives: Narrative Productions in the Age of Taylor, Veblen, and Ford*, Chicago: University of Chicago Press, 1993

Doody, Margaret Anne, *The Daring Muse: Augustan Poetry Reconsidered*, Cambridge and New York: Cambridge University Press, 1985

Eliot, T. S., *The Use of Poetry and the Use of Criticism*, London: Faber, 1980 (original edition, 1933)

Geertz, Clifford, *The Interpretation of Cultures*, New York: Basic Books, 1973

Good, Graham, "The Essay and Criticism," in his *The Observing Self: Rediscovering the Essay*, London and New York: Routledge, 1988: 176–86

Goodwin, James, *Autobiography: The Self Made Text*, New York: Twayne, 1993

Harrison, Thomas, *Essayism: Conrad, Musil, and Pirandello*, Baltimore: Johns Hopkins University Press, 1992

Jones, Richard Foster, *The Seventeenth Century: Studies in the History of English Thought and Literature from Bacon to Pope*, Stanford, California: Stanford University Press, 1951

Lukács, Georg, *The Theory of the Novel: A Historico-Philosophical Essay on the Forms of Great Epic Literature*, Cambridge, Massachusetts: MIT Press, and London: Merlin Press, 1971 (original German edition, 1920)

McCarthy, John A., *Crossing Boundaries: A Theory and History of Essay Writing in German, 1680–1815*, Philadelphia: University of Pennsylvania Press, 1989

McKeon, Michael, *The Origins of the English Novel, 1600–1740*, Baltimore: Johns Hopkins University Press, 1987

McMurtry, Jo, *English Language, English Literature: The Creation of an Academic Discipline*, Hamden, Connecticut: Archon, 1985

Obaldia, Claire de, *The Essayistic Spirit: Literature, Modern Criticism, and the Essay*, Oxford: Clarendon Press, and New York: Oxford University Press, 1995

Shuger, Debora, *Habits of Thought in the English Renaissance: Religion, Politics, and the Dominant Culture*, Berkeley: University of California Press, 1990

Sundquist, Eric J., *To Wake the Nations: Race in the Making of American Literature*, Cambridge, Massachusetts: Harvard University Press, 1993

Taylor, Charles, *Sources of the Self: The Making of Modern Identity*, Cambridge, Massachusetts: Harvard University Press, 1989

Liu Zongyuan

Chinese, 773–819

Liu Zongyuan achieved his reputation as a master essayist mainly because of his accomplishments in *guwen* (ancient prose). In its literary sense, *guwen* refers primarily to the prose style of the Confucian classics as well as to literary models dating from the Chinese antiquity to the Han era (206 BCE–220 CE). This style resurfaced in the eighth century as an intentional break with the parallel style which had dominated prose writing since the Six Dynasties period (420–589). Liu and his colleague Han Yu (768–824) fully developed the *guwen* style in the late eighth and early ninth centuries, and the two were in turn recognized by later generations as the two great Tang period (618–907) *guwen* stylists.

Liu shared with Han a similar literary-intellectual approach to *guwen*. Han saw the writing of *guwen* as both a literary practice and an effort to reflect values, "specifically the values that had guided the sages, the *shengren zhi tao* (the way of the sage) as they could be inferred from the textual tradition" (Peter Bol, 1992). Liu, too, considered that "*wen*, or literature, should illuminate the Tao" ("Da Wei Zhongli lun shidao shu" [Letter to Wei Zhongli on the Tao of being a teacher]). Unlike Han Yu, however, who restricted himself to the establishment and continuation of the system of the Confucian Tao, Liu Zongyuan's Tao can be best depicted as eclectic, incorporating the various intellectual values of his time such as Confucianism, Taoism, Buddhism, and legalism. In other words, Liu's Tao does not restate any specific doctrine but denotes in general the profound significance and multiple functions of literature, and even the sophisticated literary techniques with which literature should communicate. Following this consideration, Liu maintained that "literature has two Tao: 1) to phrase praise and blame based on the tradition of [documentary] compilation and interpretation; and 2) to convey allegorical or metaphorical expressions based on the tradition of [poetic] analogy and inspiration." This two-Tao theory formulated Liu's standards of essay writing, with the first Tao emphasizing the didactic and righteous content and flawless reasoning of an essay, and the second Tao emphasizing fluent, beautiful, and subtle rhetoric ("Yang Pingshi wenji houxu" [Postscript to the collected works of Yang Pingshi (Ling)]).

Liu Zongyuan's achievement in essay writing – over 500 pieces – was stimulated by his life experience. Like his fellow Tang literary figures, Liu considered his role primarily as a servant of the state. As Charles Hartman (1973) explains, "Only the agony and distress of a ruined or frustrated official career, as in the case of Liu [Zongyuan], could drive the [Tang] intelligentsia into serious literary pursuits." Liu's participation in an abortive political reform in 805 cost him his political career in the court. He was exiled as a marshal to Yongzhou, a southern prefectural seat a thousand miles south of the capital. A decade later, he was reassigned as a prefect to Liuzhou, a place even more remote, and eventually died there in 819. Liu's ten years in exile at Yongzhou contributed the most important part of his essay writing, which demonstrates "the range and the profundity of feelings that a traditional Chinese intellectual was able to attain in adverse circumstances" (Chen Yu-shih, 1988).

The most renowned among Liu's essays composed at Yongzhou are the nine "records of excursions" (youji). Liu's own despondency colored his view of the wild and luxuriant country landscapes with melancholy. Hence a grand metaphor pervades the entire group of essays, that of "spots of natural beauty isolated and neglected by their creator representing a good man who has been isolated and neglected by his friends and monarch" (William H. Nienhauser, 1973). Isolated in this barbarian place, Liu felt that he and the Yongzhou landscapes "would not once be able to dispose of their talents in the change of a hundred or even a thousand years" ("Xiao shicheng shan ji" [Record of the Mountain of Little Rock citadel]). The common destiny Liu shared with this landscape endeared him to nature and enabled him to find comfort and pleasure in nature's serenity. In his loneliness, he felt that only nature could touch his senses and communicate with his spirit. With this body of work Liu established youji as a subgenre and gained himself a position as a major stylist in Chinese literary history.

Another essay subgenre Liu Zongyuan developed at Yongzhou was the fable. Before Liu, the fable had often appeared merely as an illustrative part of Chinese philosophical writings; Liu was probably the first writer to treat it as a separate and viable literary genre. The 11 fables he composed at Yongzhou are mainly animal stories allegorized into moral or social criticism, often with philosophical dimensions. Among them the most famous are the San jie (Three cautionary fables), including "Linjiang zhi mi" (The deer of Linjiang), "Qian zhi lü" (The donkey of Guizhou), and "Yong mou shi zhi shu" (The rats of a certain family at Yongzhou), in which Liu satirizes three types of morally inferior people represented respectively by these animals. Their tragic endings also signify "the ultimate dominance of nature over human bias and the futility of man's desire to control his own fate" (Chen Yu-shih).

Liu's exile involved him with local people and sensitized him to their suffering. As a result, his biographical sketches break the conventional formula of recording only gentlemen's deeds and instead focus principally on the lives of ordinary people. His historical narratives often protest against social evils and corrupt government, as exemplified in three of his most-read biographies. "Bushe zhe shuo" (The snake catcher's lesson) relates the story of a man named Jiang whose family for three generations had accepted snake catching as an occupation in lieu of paying land tax. Both Jiang's grandfather and father were killed by poisonous snakes and Jiang himself only narrowly escapes death. When offered the opportunity to change his assignment back to tax-paying, however, Jiang is reduced to tears, saying "The misfortunes that come with this job are never so grievous as the misfortune that restoration of my taxes would be." "Guo Tuotuo zhuan" (The biography of Camel Guo) uses Guo's arboricultural skills as an allegory, arguing that governing people is like planting trees: "One has to follow their Heaven-bestowed characteristics and let their nature develop." Based on this Taoist principle, Liu criticizes rulers' intervention in people's lives. "Tong Ou Ji zhuan" (The biography of child Ou Ji) praises a courageous 11-year-old boy who alone thrashes two kidnappers. The story exposes the evil social phenomenon of abducting young children and selling them into slavery. Liu's biographical works also include over a dozen epitaphs of women, among them poor local young girls from the Yongzhou area.

Liu Zongyuan molded his guwen style by drawing upon a great range of earlier writings and writers. He transcended the boundaries of different genres and intellectual schools; hence it is difficult align him with any specific precursor. The vitality of the Guliang Commentary (of the Spring and Autumn Annals), the eloquence of the Confucian masters Mencius (c. 372–289 BCE) and Xun Zi (c. 313–238 BCE), the boundless imaginations in the Taoist classics Lao Zi and Zhuang Zi, the sentiments of Qu Yuan's (343–c. 278 BCE) grand poem Li sao (Encountering sorrow), and the purity of Sima Qian's (145–86 BCE) Shi ji (Records of the grand historian), all exerted great influence on his essays. Moreover, his political disquisitions absorbed the rigorous reasoning of Han Fei Zi's (?–233 BCE) legalistic works, and his records of excursions inherited the vivid descriptions and fresh rhetoric of Li Taoyuan's (?–527 CE) Shui jing zhu (Commentary on the classic of waters). Consequently, Liu's essays are full of changes in structure and meaning; as the Qing critic Liu Xizai (1978) comments: "Liu's compositions are like strange cliffs and peaks unfolding incessantly."

Many of Liu Zongyuan's friends regretted that he could never realize his political ambition. However, his colleague Han Yu considered the issue differently, contending that, had Liu Zongyuan not been in exile for so long, he would not have striven to compose literary works great enough to edify later generations. Indeed, any admirer of Liu Zongyuan would not exchange his literary achievements for any possible political achievements, even as a prime minister.

NANXIU QIAN

Biography

Courtesy name Zihou; also known as Liu Liuzhou. Born in 773; birthplace unknown (possibly Changan). Grew up in Changan; moved to Ezhou, 783, where his father was a judge. Studied privately, at a local family school, and possibly at the Imperial University. Passed the jinshi (civil service) exams, 793. Traveled in Binzhou, 793–95, then returned to Changan. Married Miss Yang, 796 (died, 798). Passed boxue hong ci exam, 798. Editor at the Jixian tian academy, from 798. Rectifier of characters, from 799; district defender to the magistrate of the Lantian district, c. 802–03; investigating censor, Changan, 803; vice bureau director, Ministry of Rites, 805. Participated in the abortive Wang Shuwen coup, 805: banished to Yongzhou as a marshal, 806–15; prefect, Liuzhou, 815–19. Died (probably of cholera) in Liuzhou, 28 November 819.

Selected Writings

Essays and Related Prose

Translations of essays in: *Chinese Classical Prose: The Eight Masters of the T'ang-Sung Period*, edited and translated by Shi Shun Liu, 1979: 103–31; *Inscribed Landscapes: Travel Writing from Imperial China*, translated by Richard E. Strassberg, 1994: 141–49

Other writings: poetry.

Collected works editions: *Liu Hedong ji*, 2 vols., 1974; *Liu Zongyuan ji*, edited by Wu Wenji, 4 vols., 1979.

Further Reading

Bol, Peter, *"This Culture of Ours": Intellectual Transitions in T'ang and Sung China*, Stanford, California: Stanford University Press, 1992

Chen Jo-shui, *Liu Tsung-yüan and Intellectual Change in T'ang China, 773–819*, Cambridge: Cambridge University Press, 1992

Chen Yu-shih, *Images and Ideas in Chinese Classical Prose: Studies of Four Masters*, Stanford, California: Stanford University Press, 1988

Duan Xingmin, *Liu Zihou yuyan wenxue tanwei* (Research into Liu Zongyuan's allegorical writings), Taibei: Wenjin chuban she, 1978

Gentzler, Jennings Mason, *A Literary Biography of Liu Tsung-yüan, 773–819* (dissertation), New York: Columbia University, 1966

Gu Yisheng, *Liu Zongyuan*, Shanghai: Zhonghua shuju, 1961

Hartman, Charles, "Alieniloquium: Liu Tsung-yüan's Other Voice," *Chinese Literature: Essays, Articles, and Reviews* 4, no. 1 (January 1982): 23–74

Huang Yunmei, *Han Yu, Liu Zongyuan wenxue pingjia* (A critical evaluation of the literary works of Han Yu and Liu Zongyuan), Jinan: Shangdon renmin chuban she, 1957

Liu Xizai, *Yigai* (A theoretical summary of art), Shanghai: Shanghai guji chuban she, 1978

Luo Liantian, *Liu Zongyuan shiji xinian ji ziliao leibian* (A chronological biography of Liu Zongyuan's life together with a classified compendium of reference materials), Taibei: Guoli bianyi guan zhonghua congshu bianshen weiyuan hui, 1981

Nienhauser, William H., Jr., Charles Hartman, and others, *Liu Tsung-yüan*, New York: Twayne, 1973

Shi Ziyu, *Liu Zongyuan nianpu* (A chronology of Liu Zongyuan's life and works), Wuhan: Hubei renmin chuban she, 1958

Shimizu Shigeru, "Ryuu soogen no seikatsu taiken to so no sansuiki" (Liu Zongyuan's life experience and his records of excursions in nature), *Chuugoku bungaku hoo* 2 (April 1955): 45–74

Spring, Madeline Kay, *A Stylistic Study of Tang Guwen: The Rhetoric of Han Yu and Liu Zongyuan* (dissertation), Seattle: University of Washington, 1983

Sun Changwu, *Liu Zongyuan zhuanlun* (A biographical account of Liu Zongyuan's life and works), Beijing: Zhonghua shuju, 1982

Wu Wenzhi, *Gudian wenxue yanjiu ziliao: Liu Zongyuan juan* (Materials for research on classical literature: volume on Liu Zongyuan), Beijing: Zhonghua shuju, 1964

Zhang Shizhao, *Liu wen zhiyao* (Essentials of Liu Zongyuan's writings), Beijing: Zhonghua shuju, 1974

Lopez, Barry

American, 1945–

With publication of the lyrical *Arctic Dreams: Imagination and Desire in a Northern Landscape* (1986) and his highly praised essay collection *Crossing Open Ground* (1988), Barry Lopez became a leading voice among writers who employ the art of the **nature essay** to express their concern for an endangered environment. His spare, clean, descriptive writing reveals an impressive understanding of natural history as he probes the often troublesome but necessary relationship between people and the real and mystical landscapes of nature. His topics reveal a scholar's grasp of the terminology of ornithology, mythology, marine biology, and anthropology as well as a gifted storyteller's knack for uncovering the wild longings of the human soul. In a review in the *Washington Post* (5 May 1988), T. H. Watkins writes that Lopez's essays validate his position "as one of the most fully involved and supremely articulate chroniclers of the land."

Lopez's popularity has increased commensurate with heightened public attention to potential hazards posed to oceans, wildlife, and forested lands by technology, urban sprawl and population growth. His individual appeal as a writer is also secured by the accessibility of his narrative style and personally involved approach to writing. His essays are widely published in such consumer-oriented journals as *Smithsonian*, *Harper's*, *Outside*, *Aperture*, and *National Geographic*, and in such scholarly publications as the **Georgia Review**, *Chouteau Review*, *Science*, and *Orion Nature Quarterly*. His essays have been included in anthologies, among them *On Nature* (1987), *This Incomperable Lande: A Book of American Nature Writing* (1989), *Wild Africa* (1993), *Major Modern Essayists* (1994), and *American Nature Writing* (1994 and 1995).

Lopez is an activist who endeavors to appeal to a general audience, writing from his own experience as a traveler and adventurer in a form characteristic of **Henry David Thoreau** and contemporary nature essayist **Edward Hoagland**. A running theme in Lopez's essays is the influence of the "exterior landscape" of nature, with its intricate relationship between what is discernible and what is ineffable, on the pattern of speculations, intuitions, and thoughts that take place in the "interior landscape" of the mind. In "Landscape and Narrative" (1984), Lopez explains that through narration, the storyteller "draws on relationships in the exterior landscape and projects them onto the interior landscape" to create a harmony "between the two landscapes" using all the storyteller's craft of syntax, mood, and figures of speech.

Lopez seeks through his attention to descriptive detail and his own participation to evoke epiphanies that foster a feeling of intimacy with the land and reveal a sense of place. "I am up to my waist in a basin of cool, acid-clear water," he writes in "Gone Back into the Earth" (1981). In "A Reflection on White Geese" (1982), there is the impression of a man of extreme patience writing about his own habitat, rather than as a visitor merely passing through on his way to somewhere else. "I sat there for three hours, studying the birds' landings and takeoffs, how they behaved toward each other on the water ... I am always struck anew in these moments, in observing such detail, by the way in which an animal slowly reveals itself." His use of metaphor and simile borrows from the attributes of the nature he writes about. In "Trying the Land" (1979), he writes, "We come downslope as graceless as boulders." Rather than using straightforward argument, he prefers to allow his truths to reveal themselves as if naturally encountered, as a child might wonder, in finding a piece of a raccoon's jaw in an alder thicket, how the animal had lived and died. In "Children in the Woods" (1982), Lopez writes that "everything found at the edge of one's senses" ultimately reveals how all things fit together to build an assurance of belonging.

Whether writing about ancient stone intaglios, explaining the reason behind the howling of wolves, or describing the snap and crack of an ice floe, Lopez expends considerable scholarly research and makes good use of his expert sources, which include botanists, biologists, naturalists, artists, and musicians. But he chooses to reveal the world of nature through the experience and eyes of his experts, rather than to rely solely on their academic expertise. In "A Presentation of Whales" (1980), a disturbing essay about the consternation that accompanies civilization's inability to cope with the enormity of natural processes, in this case the death of beached whales, the reader views through the eyes of a young biologist the horror of 41 rotting whales stretched for 500 yards nose to fluke. The young man sits on a dune awestruck and saddened but with the "rush of exhilaration, because there was so much information to be gathered." The seemingly incongruous blending of the mundane with the exotic sharpens the moments of illumination in Lopez's essays and creates for his readers new points from which to view the landscape.

But while there is a gentle, almost spiritually rambling tone to many of Lopez's essays, he can be confrontational and political, as he is in his extended essay *The Rediscovery of North America* (1990), which chides the incursion of Europeans into the New World to abuse the land, the people, and the diverse cultures. Still, he returns to the theme that nature, like art, offers the healing power of imagination: "We will always be rewarded if we give the land credit for more than we imagine, and if we imagine it as being more complex even than language." The thought reflects Lopez's view of literature in America. In an interview with Paul Pintarich of the Portland *Oregonian* (20 October 1994), Lopez, who lives in a cabin on the western slope of the Cascade Mountains near Eugene, Oregon, said he believes that many modern writers have been overly concerned with "interiors of the writer's mind. There is an utter disregard for the reader's imagination. Wherever our society is going, it will require an expansion of imagination."

PAUL L. WENSKE

Biography

Barry Holstun Lopez. Born 6 January 1945 in Port Chester, New York. Studied at the University of Notre Dame, Indiana, A.B., 1966, M.A. in teaching, 1968; University of Oregon, 1968–69. Married Sandra Landers, 1967. Full-time writer, from 1970. Associate at the Gannett Foundation, Columbia University, New York, from 1985; visiting writer or professor at various American universities, from 1985. Contributor to many journals and magazines; contributing editor, *North American Review*, from 1977, and *Harper's*, 1981–82 and from 1984. Awards: many, including the John Burroughs Medal and Christopher Medal, both for *Of Wolves and Men*, 1979; National Book Award and Christopher Medal, both for *Arctic Dreams*, 1986; Pacific Northwest Booksellers Award, for *Arctic Dreams*, 1987, and for fiction, 1995; Francis Fuller Victor Award, for *Arctic Dreams*, 1987; American Academy and Institute of Arts and Letters Award in Literature, 1987; Lannan Foundation Award, 1990; Governor's Award for Arts, 1990; honorary degrees from two universities.

Selected Writings

Essays and Related Prose
Desert Notes: Reflections in the Eye of a Raven, 1976
Arctic Dreams: Imagination and Desire in a Northern Landscape, 1986
Crossing Open Ground, 1988
The Rediscovery of North America, 1990

Other writings: fictional narratives, retellings of Native American tales, short stories, and a book about wolves (*Of Wolves and Men*, 1978).

Further Reading

Aton, Jim, "An Interview with Barry Lopez," *Western American Literature* 21, no. 1 (May 1986): 3–17
Bonetti, Kay, "An Interview with Barry Lopez," *Missouri Review* 11, no. 3 (1988): 59–77
Coles, Romand, "Ecotones and Environmental Ethics: Adorno and Lopez," in *The Nature of Things: Language, Politics, and the Environment*, edited by Jane Bennett and William Chaloupka, Minneapolis: University of Minnesota Press, 1993: 226–49
Lueders, Edward, editor, *Writing Natural History: Dialogues with Authors*, Salt Lake City: University of Utah Press, 1989
O'Connell, Nicholas, *At the Field's End: Interviews with Twenty Pacific Northwest Writers*, Seattle: Madrona, 1987
Paul, Sherman, *Hewing to Experience: Essays and Reviews on Recent American Poetry and Poetics*, Iowa City: University of Iowa Press, 1989
Ross, Daniel W., "Barry Lopez's Arctic Dreams: Looking into a New Heart of Darkness," *CEA Critic* 54, no.1 (Fall 1991): 78–86
Wild, Peter, *Barry Lopez*, Boise, Idaho: Boise State University Press, 1984

Lourenço, Eduardo

Portuguese, 1923–

Eduardo Lourenço is the quintessential Portuguese essayist, in the best tradition of the Iberian essay, somewhat reminiscent of elements of **José Ortega y Gasset** and **Miguel de Unamuno**. He was still in his twenties when he published a remarkable book of essays that would become a reference point both in his life and in the history of Portuguese intellectual life. *Heterodoxia I* (1949) reveals a heterodoxical mind balanced between the two forces pulling at Portuguese intellectuals, then and for the next four decades – Marxism and Catholicism. Lourenço carved out a space in which to build his own cohesive and powerful world view. Phenomenology and existentialism became the other two pillars of his edifice.

Lourenço's style possesses a distinct brilliance, whether he is in dialogue with the great European minds of his time or rethinking the key topics of Portuguese cultural history. His essays have graced a wide variety of publications, and his books are basically collections of essays organized thematically. *Poesia e metafísica* (1983; Poetry and metaphysics) collects pieces on the greatest Portuguese poets – Camões, Antero, and Pessoa, the last receiving special attention in seminal essays, some of them now standard. Another collection, *Ocasionais* (1984; Occasionals), gathers earlier essays whose unity lies not in the theme but in the style and mental attitude of their author. His topics in this volume range from Sade to Lorca, and from Gilberto Freyre's *luso-tropicalismo* to "Europe and Death."

Portugal and the path of Portuguese cultural history in relation to the rest of Europe (almost an obsession in Iberian essay writing for the last two centuries) has been one of Lourenço's major concerns. His bestseller *O labirinto da saudade: Psicanálise mítica do destino português* (1978; The labyrinth of *saudade*: mythical psychoanalysis of Portuguese fate) went through various editions throughout the 1980s. Its themes were dealt with from a more theoretical perspective in *Nós e a Europa, ou as duas razões* (1988; We and Europe, or the two reasons), for which Lourenço received the Charles Veillon European Essay Prize in 1988.

In the interview that opens a special issue of the journal *Prelo* dedicated to the study of his work, Lourenço explains the formative boundaries of his thought in the Portugal of the 1940s: "Of no little importance was the fact that I lived in a country and in a cultural atmosphere in which vital attitudes and spiritual or ideological choices were conditioned by the hegemonic presence of Catholicism, the creed, the ideology, almost the state religion and, even more important, the ancestral practice of the Nation. Out of that background, and as a kind of anti-church, emerged what one could grossly call Marxism, less important, there and then, as a political reality than as a sign of opposition to, and rejection of the official cultural discourse."

Explaining his turn from mainstream philosophy, in an interview entitled "As confissães de um místico sem fé" (The confessions of a mystic without faith) Lourenço says: ". . . it is true that my resistance to the philosophical temptation to engage in an absolute discourse found a basis in what is usually referred to as 'existentialism.' In the last analysis, it was the figure of *Philosophy* itself that at a given moment appeared to me suspect. Almost at the same time, my discovery of Pessoa and Kierkegaard took me in the same direction, one exemplifying the illusion of consciousness as 'consciousness of itself' existing ontologically; the other, the incommensurability of personal existence *vis-à-vis* any type of existence. In either case, the *end of philosophy*" (*Prelo*, 1984).

In the same interview, Lourenço explains the importance of literature in his life and thought: ". . . my disillusionment with philosophy . . . does not mean that I have encountered in literature the *truth* that in philosophy was denied to me. I encountered only a *reality* more in agreement with the general sentiment I look for in life and in the world, something which imposes itself precisely because in it (I speak of great literature) life manifests in terms of paradoxical (poetic) splendor the nature of our relationship with reality, which is *fictional*."

To the question of how Lourenço sees himself, since some literary critics consider him to be metaphysical, and some metaphysicians consider him to be literary, he replies: "I would like to deserve the always undeserved epithet of 'metaphysician' in the two senses the pseudo-Baptists attribute to it. Unfortunately, this is not the case. As a more adequate label, I accept that of *literato*, if that means love or passion for the written word (*imaginário*). However, the absence of idolatry in regard to that same *imaginário* perhaps will make me unjust with myself . . . I never desired, nor do I desire, any kind of status. The most I could accept is, vaguely, 'essayist,' if one considers form, and 'mystic without faith,' if one considers content" (*Prelo*, 1984).

The status of Lourenço among Portuguese intellectuals is unparalleled. His writings combine a wide range of qualities – from an encyclopedic familiarity with Western philosophy and intellectual history, literature and art, to a unique knowledge and understanding of Portuguese cultural history, as well as a passionate involvement in contemporary Portuguese and world wide political events. His youthful, contagious spirit contrasts with a controlled, tragic sense of life written in the vivid yet sage prose of a born writer and poet.

ONÉSIMO T. ALMEIDA

Biography

Born 23 May 1923 in São Pedro do Rio Seco. Studied at a military college, Lisbon; history and philosophy at the University of Coimbra, graduated 1946. Philosophy assistant, University of Coimbra, 1947–53; lecturer in Portuguese literature and culture, Universities of Hamburg, Heidelberg, and Montpellier, 1954–58; professor of philosophy, University of Bahia, Brazil, 1958–59; lecturer and associate professor, University of Nice, 1965–88; cultural attaché to the Portuguese Embassy, Rome, 1990; visiting professor, Brown University, Providence, Rhode Island, 1995. Married Annie Solomon: one son. Awards: Veillon European Essay Prize, 1988; Camões Prize; Ordem de Santíago de Espada; honorary degrees from two universities.

Selected Writings

Essays and Related Prose

Heterodoxia, 2 vols., 1949–67
O desespero humanista de Miguel Torga e o das novas gerações, 1955
Sentido e forma da poesia neo-realista, 1968
Fernando Pessoa revisitado: Leitura estruturante do drama em gente, 1973
Tempo e poesia, 1974
Os militares e o poder, 1975
Situação africana e consciência nacional, 1976
O fascismo nunca existiu, 1976
O labirinto da saudade: Psicanálise mítica do destino português, 1978
O complexo de Marx, ou, O fim do desafio português, 1979
O espelho imaginário, 1981
Poesia e metafísica: Camões, Antero, Pessoa, 1983
Ocasionais I, 1950–1965, 1984
Fernando, rei de Nossa Baviera, 1986
Nós e a Europa, ou as duas razões, 1988
O canto do signo, existência e literatura (1957–1993), 1994
Camões, 1525–1580, with Vasco Graça Moura, 1994
A Europa desen cantada, para uma mitologia europeia, 1994

Further Reading

"Eduardo Lourenço, o ensaísta criador," special section of *Jornal de Letras, Artes e Ideias* 16 (1996)
Gil, José, and Fernando Catroga, *O ensaísmo trágico de Eduardo Lourenço*, Lisbon: Relógio de Agua, 1996
Guimarães, Fernando, "Eduardo Lourenço: Entre a filosofia e a poesia," *Colóquio-Letras* 80 (July 1984): 86–90
Letras & Letras issue on Lourenço, 3, no. 27 (March 1990)
"Lourenço, Eduardo," in *Logos: Enciclopédia Luso-Brasileira de filosofia*, vol. 3, Lisbon and São Paulo: Verbo, 1991
"Lourenço, Eduardo," in *Dicionário do Estado Novo*, Lisbon: Círculo dos Leitores, 1996
Prelo: Revista da Imprensa Nacional-Casa da Moeda issue on Lourenço (May 1984)
Simões, João Gaspar, *Crítica V – Críticos e ensaístas contemporâneos (1942–1979)*, Lisbon: Imprensa Nacional-Casa de Moeda, 1983

Lu Xun

Chinese, 1881–1936

It was Lu Xun who introduced the best-known description of the **familiar essay** to China when he published a translation of the Japanese scholar Kuriyagawa Hakuson's *Chule xiangya zhi ta* (Out from the ivory tower) in 1925. Using Western sources, this work pictured the essay as a transcription of a good conversation around a winter fire among friends, in an atmosphere of slippered ease. Ironically, Lu Xun's own reputation as an essayist was of the opposite kind: that of a warlike, biting, often deadly polemicist.

Lu Xun had all the qualifications to be a good polemicist. On the personal level, he easily imagined himself slighted or traduced, and bore long grudges; he had a brilliant mind and, never having had a job which kept him busy, had devoted many years to reading Chinese history and literature, and through Japanese (he was a student in Japan from 1902 to 1909) to learning about the foreign experience, which gave him a superior stock of allusions and analogies. Moreover, under the imperial regime he had learned how to plan a composition and to use rhetorical devices. That he was able to mock and abuse the authorities without being arrested he owed to the relatively civilized regime in Beijing up to 1926, and subsequently to the protection of the International Settlement in Shanghai, which he moved to in 1927, as well as latterly to his nationwide fame.

The May Fourth movement (1919) was a kind of revolution against the "feudal" culture which the 1911 revolution had not seriously disturbed. As one of its pioneers, Lu Xun won his spurs as an essayist by laying into the establishment, and there was much in the conduct of national life to keep him embattled thereafter. When he joined the United Front around 1930 he committed himself to fight the Nationalist (Kuomintang) government until the end of his days. A great deal of his polemical work dealt of course with current affairs and needs lengthy footnotes for present-day readers, but his habit of relating current ills to perennial complaints and deep-rooted vices makes these writings appreciable without knowledge of the detail. Since China at that time was at the mercy of the colonial powers, especially Japan, the story that events told was one of weakness and subservience. This situation Lu Xun summed up in memorable words. Perhaps his most famous dictum was that China had only known two phases in its history: the one when its people were happy being slaves, the other when they were unhappy because they could not be slaves.

Lu Xun became known as dedicated to "hot abuse" and "cold sarcasm," but what raised his **polemical essays** above those of his contemporaries, aside from his powerful intellect, was his way of marshaling his words like troops on a battlefield, now feinting an attack, now feigning weakness, now holding, now retreating, finally springing a trap, all very much as the ancient manuals on the art of war recommended. The repetition of key phrases, with some variations (like Mark Antony's "an honourable man"), was one of his standbys, but patterns were rarely repeated. General characteristics of opponents were often subsumed in animal behavior (e.g. Pekinese dogs, packhounds, wasps), a trick he borrowed from

traditional satirical parables. His most flexible and reliable resource, however, was a more or less total command of the Chinese language, classical and modern: the ability to mix and switch registers was used very effectively to mock and shock. There is no doubt that as a polemicist Lu Xun was world class.

Though the greater part of Lu Xun's many volumes of miscellaneous essays were *littérature engagée*, he also displayed other sides. When in the mid-1920s he went through his dark night of the soul, the experience resulted in a collection of prose poems entitled *Ye cao* (1927; *Wild Grass*), which some regard as his finest work while others denigrate it as derivative. The tone seems to have been set by **Nietzsche**'s *Also sprach Zarathustra* (1883–85; *Thus Spoke Zarathustra*), to which Lu Xun was very attracted in early adulthood. Stark and barren landscapes, symbolic figures and images, and strange encounters and cryptic speeches dominate the collection.

More accessible are the backward-looking essays of *Zhao hua xi shi* (1928; Morning blossoms picked at eventide), which affectionately recall the background of his early life, and the more ruminative essays scattered throughout his collections, which are not without wit and humor. Though Lu Xun dissociated himself from the deliberate humor of the magazines that Lin Yutang was responsible for in the 1930s, he had a fund of wit which he used facetiously as well as cuttingly, as can be deduced merely from the title "You Zhongguo nüren de jiao tuiding Zhongguo ren de fei zhongyong, you youci tuiding Kong fuzi you weibing" (1933; To reach the conclusion from women's feet that Chinese people do not follow the golden mean, and thence further to conclude that Confucius suffered from his stomach). Humor of a generous kind can also be found in his work, though he was reluctant to admit it. A case in point is "A Jin" (1935), which takes its title from the name of the feisty woman servant who came to live and work opposite. Lu Xun was ideologically inclined to take the side of the working class, and had often written compassionately of the fate of weak and helpless females, but A Jin did not conform to type. He had to learn to give the house where she worked a wide berth, as she was in the habit of tossing things over her balcony, and the nights, when he did most of his writing, were disturbed by her lovers who came calling. Before she moved away he was forced to confess ruefully that this A Jin had made him revise beliefs he had cherished for the better part of his lifetime. The essay is one long complaint, but it is an index of its humanity that the reader feels that the author did not really regret his encounter.

Given that no one who writes as extensively as Lu Xun did can maintain consistent quality, the fact that so many of his essays bespeak a mind fully engaged to give of its considerable best makes it hard to dispute the claim common in his homeland that Lu Xun was 20th-century China's best essayist.

D. E. POLLARD

Biography

Born Zhou Shuren, 25 September 1881 in Shaoxing, Zhejiang province. Older brother of **Zhou Zuoren**. Studied at the Jiangnan Naval Academy, Nanjing, 1898–99; School of Mining and Railways, Nanjing, 1900–02; Japanese language at Kobun College, Japan, 1902–04; medicine at Sendai Medical School, Japan, 1904–06; continued private studies in Japan, 1906–09. Married Zhu An, 1906 (arranged by his mother; probably never consummated). Taught in

Hangzhou, 1909–10, and Shaoxing, 1910–11. Worked at the Ministry of Education, Beijing, 1912–26. Contributor to various journals, including *Xin qingnian* (New youth), from 1918. Lecturer in Chinese literature, Peking University, 1920–26, Beijing Women's Normal College, from 1923, Xiamen (Amoy) University, 1926, and Sun Yatsen University, Canton, 1927: resigned in protest at Jiang Kaishek's seizure of power. Lived in the International Settlement, Shanghai, from 1927. Founder, *Yusi* (Thread of conversation), 1924, and *Mangyuan* (The wilderness), 1925; cofounder, *Zhaohua she* (Dawn blossoms press), 1928; editor, *Benliu* (The torrent), 1928, and *Yiwen* (Translation), 1934. Founding member, League of Left-Wing Writers, 1930, China Freedom League, 1930, and member, League for the Defense of Civic Rights, 1933. Died in Shanghai, 19 October 1936.

Selected Writings

Essays and Related Prose
Refeng (Hot air), 1925
Huagai ji (Unlucky star), 2 vols., 1926–27
Fen (The grave), 1927
Zhao hua xi shi, 1928
Eryi ji (And that's that), 1928
Erxin ji (Two hearts), 1932
Sanxian ji (Three leisures), 1932
Wei ziyou shu (False freedom), 1933
Nanqiang beidiao ji (Mixed accents), 1934
Zhun fengyue tan (Pseudo-frivolous talk), 1934
Huabian wenxue (Fringed literature), 1936
Qiejieting zawen (Essays of Qiejieting), 3 vols., 1936
Selected Works, translated by Yang Xianyi and Gladys Yang, 4 vols., 1956–60
Silent China: Selected Writings, edited and translated by Gladys Yang, 1973
Translations of essays in: *The Columbia Anthology of Modern Chinese Literature*, edited by Joseph S. M. Lau and Howard Goldblatt, 1995: 587–600, and in *Renditions* 26 (1986): 125–31, and 31 (1989): 140–47

Other writings: the volume of prose poetry *Ye cao* (1927; *Wild Grass*), many short stories, a history of Chinese fiction, classical poetry, and correspondence. Also translated works from the German and Japanese.

Collected works editions: *Lu Xun xiansheng quanji*, 20 vols., 1938, revised edition, 1973, and supplements edited by Tang Tao, 2 vols., 1942–52; *Lu Xun quanji*, 10 vols., 1956–58; *Lu Xun quanji*, 16 vols., 1991.

Further Reading

Castro, Angela, *Three Early Essays of Lu Hsün* (M.Phil. dissertation), London: University of London, 1968
Lee, Leo Ou-fan, *Voices from the Iron House: A Study of Lu Xun*, Bloomington: Indiana University Press, 1987: 89–129
Pollard, David E., "Lu Xun's *Zawen*," in *Lu Xun and His Legacy*, edited by Leo Ou-fan Lee, Berkeley: University of California Press, 1985: 54–89

Lukács, Georg

Hungarian, 1885–1971

Georg Lukács was, first and foremost, an essayist. His career as an essayist was established primarily in the *Nyugat* (The west) and *Huszadik Szàzad* (The 20th century), the two leading journals of radical intellectuals in *fin-de-siècle* Budapest.

Lukács' essayist period of 1908 to 1911 yielded *A lélek és a formák* (1910; *Soul and Form*) and established his European reputation. The object of these essays is Lukács himself: engaging, ingenious, elusive, a virtuoso in flirting with roles – an ascetic, Faust, or Silenic-featured Socrates. Inspired by Lukács' tragic love affair with Irma Seidler, his immortal beloved, *Soul and Form* revolves around life, art, Eros, and philosophy – the compass points of the soul. In his essays, he appears a worthy disciple of **Montaigne**, Kierkegaard, and **Nietzsche**. In Montaigne, man's life – the random personal life as a whole – became problematic in the modern sense. Whereas Montaigne never transposed the problematic into the realm of the tragic, Lukács, caught between Eros and knowledge, celebrates the fatal, tragic solitude of Socratic souls, who, despite Eros, remain "servants and fanatics of their own development."

On a more intimate level, the essays in *Soul and Form* contain Kierkegaard's attitude of fascinated terror toward Eros. To Lukács, the object of Eros was not so much seduction or consummation as it was experimentation. In Socratic fashion, he approached Eros for the conquest of spirit rather than the conquest of the flesh. He faced the seductive possibilities of both Nietzsche, who claimed that none of the great philosophers – **Plato**, Spinoza, **Kant**, **Schopenhauer** – was married because marriage is an obstacle to fulfillment, and **Goethe**, whose love, as Lukács never failed to point out, gave birth to his spiritual drama *Iphigenie auf Tauris* (1802; *Iphigenia in Tauris*).

Not surprisingly, Lukács' essay "Über Sehnsucht und Form" (1911; "On Longing and Form"), reflecting on Plato's Eros, Dante's great love, Don Quixote, and the scorned heroes of Flaubert, caught **Thomas Mann**'s attention. In *Der Tod in Venedig* (1912; *Death in Venice*), Mann disputed Lukács' notion that "Socrates transformed his longing into a philosophy whose peak was eternally unattainable, the highest goal of all human longing: intellectual contemplation . . . In life [however], longing has to remain love: that is its happiness and its tragedy."

It may sound paradoxical that the essay, despite Lukács' renown as a Marxist system builder, remained his representative genre. In his essay on Kierkegaard, Lukács declared, "There is no system in life. In life there is only the separate and individual, the concrete. To exist is to be different." Influenced by Kierkegaard, Lukács the essayist disputed Hegel's claim that only art, religion, and philosophy reveal the absolute. In his famed triad, art–religion–philosophy, where art expresses the same "content" as religion and philosophy, but in a different "form," Hegel accords no recognition to the essay as a genre. By contrast, Lukács elevates the essay to an art form, designed to capture the absolute or permanent in the transitory, fugitive, and contingent, and distinguish it from the icy, final perfection of philosophy. Dissenting from Hegel, Lukács believes that the essay, as an art form, mediates between art and philosophy. The essayist, he said, poses questions: what is life, what is man, what is destiny? But questions are simply posed, not answered – the essayist does not supply "solutions" like the answers of science or, at purer heights, those of philosophy.

Like Montaigne, Lukács the essayist adapts his lofty intellect to the everyday detail of life, emphasizing it with ironic modesty. He sees the same irony, though in different form, in every text by every great essayist. In Plato, the greatest essayist in Lukács' definition, philosophy is underlined by the irony of the realities of life. According to Lukács, the life of Socrates, whose profound philosophical thoughts are interrupted by humor and irony, typifies the essay form. The essayist, modeled on Socrates, is preeminently a critic who, sent to proclaim and bring to light ideals and values, must judge every phenomenon by the scale of his own values. The essayist's right to create his judgment values from within himself, while offering no clear-cut answers, leads to Lukács' exalted claim: "The essay is a court, but (unlike in the legal system) it is not the verdict that is important, that sets the standards and creates precedent, but the process of examining and judging."

It is not surprising that some of Lukács' seminal essays, notably that on Laurence Sterne in *Soul and Form*, and "A lelki szegénységről" (1911; "On Poverty of Spirit"), are written in the form of Socratic dialogues. This approach presented problems when Lukács decided to pursue an academic career at Heidelberg. His friend and mentor, **Max Weber**, addressing the question whether Lukács was really an essayist and not a systematic thinker, was forthright: "I must be frank with you. A very good friend of yours, Emil Lask, is of the opinion that as a born essayist you will not be content with a systematic work, and that hence you should not habilitate [i.e. become qualified as a university lecturer]. The essayist is not one hair less of a disciplined systemizer, perhaps on the contrary. But he does not belong to the university, and he writes his work for his own salvation."

Lask's characterization of Lukács as a born essayist proved prophetic. His academic hopes dashed at Heidelberg, Lukács ultimately sought his own salvation in Budapest by joining the Hungarian Communist Party in 1918. His leap of faith stunned his friends, above all Weber. In his famous lectures entitled "Wissenschaft als Beruf" (1917; "Science as a Vocation") and "Politik als Beruf" (1919; "The Vocation of Politics"), delivered in Munich in January 1919, Weber took issue with Lukács who, he claimed, in turning Marxist failed to distinguish between the "ethic of responsibility" and the "ethic of ultimate ends."

What is instructive in the relationship of Weber and Lukács is that, despite their political differences, both remained essayists at heart. As one leading commentator of Weber put it, "If we regard the essay as the art-form suited to the twentieth century, then Weber is immediately placed alongside authors such as Georg Simmel, Robert Musil, and Georg Lukács, among others. They all shared the attempt to 'mediate,' to build bridges, and thereby open up new pathways" (Dirk Käsler, *Max Weber*, 1988).

Even as a Marxist, Lukács continued to write essays; in many ways, his Marxism constitutes the keynote of his character as a thinker. Thomas Mann, having read *Soul and Form*, observed that we have a particular right to "knowledge which we ourselves helped to create merely by our own existence." Lukács' own troubled existence in the hellish world of Stalin's Russia found relief, if not escape, in the essay. As Mann so perceptively put it, in response to Lukács' essays on Goethe's works in *Goethe és kora* (1946; *Goethe and His Age*), and on Mann's own intellectual and artistic development in *A polgár nyomában: A hetvenéves Thomas Mann* (1947; *Essays on Thomas Mann*), "This Communist [Lukács] who is deeply

concerned with the 'bourgeois heritage,' and who can write fascinatingly and intelligently about Raabe, Keller, or Fontane, had earlier discussed me with intelligence and respect."

During the Great Purges in Russia, where he had lived for many years, Lukács wrote essays on the tradition of the novel as exemplified in the works of Balzac, Stendhal, **Tolstoi**, Zola, and Gor'kii. These essays, written in the 1930s, appeared in *Essays über Realismus* (1948; *Studies in European Realism* and *Essays on Realism*), a landmark in 20th-century literary criticism. Whether Lukács writes on Balzac or Tolstoi, invariably he writes as an essayist from the perspective of a philosophical system. In his literary essays, he displays little of the subtlety and plasticity of Thomas Mann or **Virginia Woolf**. On the other hand, few modern critics can match Lukács' intellectual passion and philosophical vision for the literary tradition of European realism which he so admired and championed. Not unlike **Samuel Taylor Coleridge**, **T. S. Eliot**, or **Edmund Wilson**, intent on creating a new literary taste in conformity with their own artistic ideals, Lukács not only carried the torch for European realism, but became the uncompromising custodian or conscience of literary tradition. It is not without irony that Lukács – whose Marxist literary essays are steeped in German philosophy and metaphysics consisting of vocabulary and arguments the Anglo-Saxon literary world finds alien – accepted Eliot's dictum in "Tradition and the Individual Talent" (1919) that the poet and artist must transform the past in the light of the present.

In his greatest pre-Marxist essay, *Die Theorie des Romans* (1920; *The Theory of the Novel*), Lukács delineated the relationship between prose fiction and social reality, between the novel and time treated as a concrete historical medium. Lukács' historical-**philosophical essay**, formulating a new conception of time in the novel based on the Bergsonian concept of *durée* – the duration and expanse of time which the novel covers, dividing men into generations and integrating their actions in an historical-social context – also illustrates the formidable challenge Lukács the essayist presents to his English or American readers. The problems are twofold. For one thing, Lukács is rooted in the classics, especially Aristotle, his heritage is central European, and, reflecting his Jewish background, he approaches literature and writers from a universal, humanistic perspective, disregarding national, linguistic, and cultural boundaries. Moreover, there are Lukács' own convictions and tenor of thought, as well as his style of writing, which is complex, uncompromising, abstract, and displays little sensitivity or feeling for language and poetry. His profound intellect and erudition, which prefers the enunciatory style, full of gravity and depth, conveys finality and authority. Though Lukács' range of interest is immense, his essays are grounded in the conviction that criticism and philosophical discourse must establish a distance from *belles-lettres*, that an essayist who, like Nietzsche, turns his essays into a dazzling artistic performance betrays his vocation.

ARPAD KADARKAY

Biography

György Szegedy von Lukács. Born 13 April 1885 in Budapest. Studied at the University of Budapest, Ph.D., 1906; studied privately with Heinrich Rickert in Heidelberg, 1912–15. Joined the

Hungarian Communist Party, 1918. Married Gertrud Bortstieber, 1919. Commissar of Public Education, 1919: exiled from Hungary as a result. Associated with the Marx-Engels-Lenin Institute, Moscow, 1929–30; researcher, Institute of Philosophy, Soviet Academy of Sciences, Moscow, 1933–44. Returned to Hungary, 1945. Professor of aesthetics and cultural philosophy, University of Budapest, 1945–56. Minister of Culture, 1956. Awards: Kossuth Prize, 1955; Goethe Prize, 1970. Died in Budapest, 4 June 1971.

Selected Writings

Essays and Related Prose

(Lukács wrote in Hungarian and German; most works were published in both languages, but only first published edition listed here, regardless of its language)

A lélek és a formák (Kisérletek), 1910; enlarged edition, as *Die Seele und die Formen*, 1911; as *Soul and Form*, translated by Anna Bostock, 1974

Esztétikai kultúra, 1913

Taktika és ethika, 1919; as "Tactics and Ethics," in *Political Writings, 1919–1929*, translated by Michael McColgan, 1972

Die Theorie des Romans: Ein geschichtsphilosophischer Versuch über die Formen der grossen Epik, 1920; as *The Theory of the Novel: A Historico-Philosophical Essay on the Form of Great Epic Literature*, translated by Anna Bostock, 1971

Geschichte und Klassenbewusstsein: Studien über marxistische Dialektik, 1923; as *History and Class Consciousness: Studies in Marxist Dialectics*, translated by Rodney Livingstone, 1971

Balzac, Stendhal, Zola, 1945; part in *Studies in European Realism*, translated by Edith Bone, 1950, and in *Essays on Realism*, translated by David Fernbach, 1980

Goethe és kora, 1946; as *Goethe and His Age*, translated by Robert Anchor, 1968

Irodalom és demokrácia, 1947

A polgári filozófia válsága, 1947

A polgár nyomában: A hetvenéves Thomas Mann, 1947; as *Essays on Thomas Mann*, translated by Stanley Mitchell, 1964

A történelmi regény, 1947; as *The Historical Novel*, translated by Hannah and Stanley Mitchell, 1962

Schicksalswende, Beiträge zu einer deutschen Ideologie, 1948

Existentialisme ou marxisme?, 1948

A realizmus problémái, 1948

Új magyar kultúráért, 1948

Karl Marx und Friedrich Engels als Literaturhistoriker, 1948

Der junge Hegel: Über die Beziehungen von Dialektik und Ökonomie, 1948; as *The Young Hegel: Studies in the Relations Between Dialectics and Economics*, translated by Rodney Livingstone, 1975

Essays über Realismus, 1948; part in *Studies in European Realism: A Sociological Survey of the Writings of Balzac, Stendhal, Zola, Tolstoy, Gorki, and Others*, translated by Edith Bone, 1950, and in *Essays on Realism*, edited by Rodney Livingstone, translated by David Fernbach, 1980

Der russische Realismus in der Weltliteratur, 1949; enlarged edition, 1952; part in *Studies in European Realism: A Sociological Survey of the Writings of Balzac, Stendhal, Zola, Tolstoy, Gorki, and Others*, translated by Edith Bone, 1950, and in *Essays on Realism*, edited by Rodney Livingstone, translated by David Fernbach, 1980

Deutsche Realisten des 19. Jahrhunderts, 1951; as *German Realists in the Nineteenth Century*, edited by Rodney Livingstone, translated by Jeremy Gaines and Paul Keast, 1993

Puschkin-Gorki (Zwei Essays), 1952

Nagy orosz realisták; Kritikai realizmus; Szikra, 1952

Adalékok az esztétika történetéhez, 1953

Die Zerstörung der Vernunft, 1954; as *The Destruction of Reason*, translated by Peter Palmer, 1980

Schriften zur Literatursoziologie, edited by Peter Ludz, 1961

Deutsche Literatur in zwei Jahrhunderten, 1964

Die Grablegung des alten Deutschland: Essays zur deutschen Literatur des 19. Jahrhunderts, 1967

Writer and Critic, and Other Essays, edited and translated by Arthur D. Kahn, 1971

Political Writings, 1919–1929: The Question of Parliamentarianism and Other Essays, edited by Rodney Livingstone, translated by Michael McColgan, 1972; as *Tactics and Ethics: Political Essays, 1919–1929*, 1975

Marxism and Human Liberation: Essays on History, Culture, and Revolution, edited by E. San Juan, 1973

Politische Aufsätze, 1975

Kunst und objektive Wahrheit: Essays zur Literaturtheorie und Geschichte, 1977

Theory, Culture, and Politics, edited by Judith Marcus and Zoltan Tarr, 1989

The Lukács Reader, edited by Arpad Kadarkay, 1995

Collected works edition: *Werke*, 15 vols., 1962– (in progress).

Bibliography

Hartmann, Jürgen, in *Festschrift zum achtzigsten Geburtstag von Georg Lukács*, edited by Frank Benseler, Neuwied and Berlin: Luchterhand, 1965: 625–96

Further Reading

Bernstein, J. M., *The Philosophy of the Novel: Lukács, Marxism and the Dialectics of Form*, Minneapolis: University of Minnesota Press, and Brighton: Harvester, 1984

Congdon, Lee, *The Young Lukács*, Chapel Hill: University of North Carolina Press, 1983

Eagleton, Terry, *The Ideology of the Aesthetic*, Oxford: Blackwell, 1990

Feenberg, Andrew, *Lukács, Marx and the Sources of Critical Theory*, Totowa, New Jersey: Rowman and Littlefield, and Oxford: Robertson, 1981

Jameson, Frederic, *Marxism and Form: Twentieth-Century Dialectial Theories of Literature*, Princeton, New Jersey: Princeton University Press, 1971

Kadarkay, Arpad, *Georg Lukács: Life, Thought, and Politics*, Oxford and Cambridge, Massachusetts: Blackwell, 1991

MacIntyre, Alasdair, *Against the Self-Images of the Age: Essays on Ideology and Philosophy*, London: Duckworth, and New York: Schocken, 1971

Steiner, George, *George Steiner: A Reader*, New York: Oxford University Press, and Harmondsworth: Penguin, 1984

Wellek, René, *Four Critics: Croce, Valéry, Lukács, and Ingarden*, Seattle: University of Washington Press, 1981

M

McArthur, Peter

Canadian, 1866–1924

A prolific and popular writer whose oeuvre includes works of biography, biocriticism, fiction, and poetry, Peter McArthur is remembered most commonly as a humorist and for what he called his "country stuff": bucolic sketches closer to *causeries* than to formal essays. Although he published in such popular journals as the **Atlantic Monthly**, *Forum, Punch*, the New York *Sun*, and his own short-lived periodical, *Ourselves: A Magazine for Cheerful Canadians* (1910–12), his reputation was established primarily through his long association with two Canadian publications: the Toronto *Globe*, where his twice-weekly column appeared from 1909 to 1924, and the *Farmer's Advocate*, to which he contributed less regularly from 1910 to 1922. Indeed, his most popular books – *In Pastures Green* (1915), *The Red Cow and Her Friends* (1919), *The Affable Stranger* (1920), and *Around Home* (1925) – are compilations of these *Globe* and *Advocate* columns, arranged with some minor revisions by McArthur himself. (Two later and less popular compilations, *Familiar Fields* [1925] and *Friendly Acres* [1927], were arranged with editorial input from McArthur's son.)

Attracted to an idealistic and somewhat simplistic vision of Canada's rural past, McArthur was a dedicated promoter of agrarianism and the national myth of the heroic pioneer. His essays are casual and contemplative, structured as the first-person reflections of a contented farmer-philosopher and organized according to patterns drawn from farm life and from the natural world: a day on the farm, observations of seasonal changes in landscape, or the escapades of a familiar coterie of farm animals. Here McArthur celebrates rural living, idealizing the farm as "a place of peace, a place of refuge and a home" far removed from a modern world ravaged by the excesses of urbanization and industrialization, a deepening sense of personal alienation, rampant materialism, and social cleavage.

Never drawn to what he called "the cosmical moods" of a poet like Whitman or the natural theology of Wordsworth, McArthur constructs his philosophy on a kind of Bergsonian vitalism, a stance which, he believed, allowed him "to keep [his] feet on the earth – in good Canadian mud – even when indulging the wildest flights of imagination." An early Canadian proponent of the "back to the land" movement, a philosophical stance that leads to comparisons with such writers as William Cobbett and McArthur's own favorite, **Henry David Thoreau**, McArthur has a love of the land that is reinforced at every turn by pragmatism. Not only could a return to the farm ease the emotional and spiritual encumbrances of modern life, but it was also an efficacious means of guaranteeing all healthy workers a degree of annual self-subsistence.

On the other hand, McArthur is not one to suggest that all was sweetness and light on his farm; indeed, he frequently sharpens the homespun wisdoms of his farmer-philosopher to a satiric edge. But where such contemporaries as **Mark Twain** and **Stephen Leacock** are polished and witty commentators on the spirit of the day (or lack thereof), McArthur is often only unpleasant, his attacks heavyhanded. Moreover, his tendency on such occasions is to abandon the broad base of humanist concerns that characterizes his more successful pieces in order to focus instead on an increasingly familiar set of targets: a centralized banking system and a Bank Act which he saw as a threat to the economic stability of rural communities; the obscurantism of politicians and popular media; the ubiquitous "Big Interests" of commerce and industry; the human and economic costs of war; and the depopulation of farms and threat of an urban imperialism that drew future generations of farmers to lives of quiet desperation in city factories.

Of these so-called social essays, those collected in *The Affable Stranger* provide the most mature and thorough summary of McArthur's views. Organized around the trip of the titular "affable stranger," a man "willing to engage in conversation with any one who is willing to talk," they provide McArthur the opportunity to examine the various groups and ideologies struggling to gain or regain relevance following World War I, particularly those influencing Canadian-American relations. An ardent, yet tolerant and critical nationalist who some contemporary readers saw as excessively left-wing in his politics, McArthur remained wary of the "wild new politics" of communism, which he saw as impractical ("Prince Kropotkin's Cow"), and socialism, which he called the politics of "the Lotos-Eaters" ("Back to the Primitive"). At the same time he is fearful that any "nation that has been roused to a sense of power by the war will act swiftly and intolerantly without discriminating sufficiently between those who would reform society and those who would wreck it" ("The Elusive Insult"). His overall message in these essays is clear, albeit wishful: by wakening the dormant pioneer spirit of home-building and cooperation, humankind could successfully skirt the multitudinous hazards in its path.

Whether McArthur is recounting the farm escapades of Socrates the ram or railing against what he perceived to be the jingoism of American filmmakers ("Registering Reform," 1920), his style in almost all his essays is personal. Avoiding for the most part any hint of parochialism, his writing is marked by a genial, self-deprecating humor and reliance on what he purports to be firsthand knowledge and common sense. With an acknowledged "weakness for quotations" and allusion that assumes a literate and well-read audience, he also relies heavily and not so subtly on works of Poe, Shakespeare, Tennyson, Thoreau, various Romantic poets, and the Bible as "an easy way to get out of hammering out phrases and sentences to express ideas" ("Quotations," 1920). His writing, in this sense, becomes an odd, and at times mismatched, palimpsest of vernacular, historical, biblical, and cultural references which in the aggregate suggest that simplicity, even when associated with the peace and idealism of rural life, is neither simple nor without literary or artistic merit.

To the modern reader, McArthur's style, though never egregious, appears as his greatest weakness. Burdened by excessive and misplaced colloquialisms, faulty grammar, and meandering paragraphs, individual pieces often lapse into what Brandon Conron (1965) suggests is "sheer carelessness which cannot even be excused as 'homely charm'." Despite these limitations as a stylist, McArthur remains an important contributor to the development of the essay in *fin-de-siècle* Canada. Part light humorist, part rural nostalgist, and part populist farm advocate, McArthur was, in retrospect, always a sympathetic and articulate interpreter of Canada and the Canadian spirit at the beginning of a new century.

KLAY DYER

Biography

Born 10 March 1866 in Ekfrid Township, near Glencoe, Ontario. Studied at Strathroy Model School, teacher's certificate, 1887; taught for six months, then studied at the University of Toronto, 1888–89. Reporter, Toronto *Mail*, 1889–90; freelance journalist, New York, 1890–95, where he met Bliss Carman and the writer and critic Charles G. D. Roberts; editor, *Truth*, 1895–97. Married Mabel Waters, 1895: four sons and one daughter. Lived in England, 1902–04, writing for *Punch* and other journals and newspapers. Moved back to New York and briefly opened an advertising agency, 1904. Returned to Ekfrid family farm, 1909. Wrote for the Toronto *Globe*, 1909–24, and the *Farmer's Advocate*, 1910–22; editor, *Ourselves* farm magazine, 1910–12. Died in London, Ontario, 28 October 1924.

Selected Writings

Essays and Related Prose
To Be Taken with Salt: Being an Essay on Teaching One's Grandmother to Suck Eggs, 1903
In Pastures Green, 1915
The Red Cow and Her Friends, 1919
The Affable Stranger, 1920
Around Home, 1925
Familiar Fields, 1925
Friendly Acres, 1927
The Best of Peter McArthur, edited by Alec Lucas, 1967

Other writings: poetry, fiction, a study of Stephen Leacock (1923), and a biography of Sir Wilfrid Laurier (1919).

Further Reading

Conron, Brandon, "Essays 1880–1920," in *Literary History of Canada: Canadian Literature in English*, edited by Carl F. Klinck and others, Toronto: University of Toronto Press, 1976: 354–60 (original edition, 1965)
Deacon, William Arthur, *Peter McArthur*, Toronto: Ryerson Press, 1923
Lucas, Alec, Introduction to *The Best of Peter McArthur*, Toronto: Clarke Irwin, 1967
Lucas, Alec, *Peter McArthur*, Boston: Twayne, 1975
McNally, David, "Peter McArthur and Canadian Nationalism," *Ontario History* 64, no. 1 (1972): 1–10
Watt, F. W., "Peter McArthur and the Agrarian Myth," *Queen's Quarterly* 67, no. 2 (1960): 245–57
Wells, Kenneth, Introduction to *In Pastures Green* by McArthur, Toronto: Dent, 1948

Macaulay, Thomas Babington

British, 1800–1859

Thomas Babington Macaulay wrote histories, polemics, book reviews, and government reports rather than essays on subjects such as friendship or his own position in the world. Although his prose has distinct marks of a personality, he never exploits his emotions as a subject. He was a Whig politician, a Member of Parliament, active in the government of India, and a proponent of reform, but Macaulay engaged his issues by the requirement of a book review or an editor's assignment. As an historian, he is admired for his lively and interesting prose, but his underlying agenda enraged subsequent historians. As Jane Millgate (1973) notes, Whig historians "derive their historical patterns from the last item in a sequence of events" and trace the line backward, "disregarding all occurrences which that line does not intersect." Even his poetry – his book of verse was immensely popular, often reprinted and quoted – advocates his causes: a more open society dependent on commercial interests in England, a progressive view of English history, and faith in the English constitution.

Macaulay is sometimes called the first Victorian because he tames early 19th-century enthusiasm for the sublime, the mystic, and the distant by his practical sense of what ordinary humans can fathom. We live, with his essayist's voice, in the best of possible worlds, solidly in the middle way between fanatics of the left (the Puritans) and of the right (High Tories, Anglo-Catholics, and admirers of the Middle Ages). He probably wrote to an imagined audience composed, first, of his two beloved sisters. We overhear a conversation from an older brother, reaching and directing our thought in the best possible way. He expects his readers to catch allusions to Spenser, Dante, and Milton. Macaulay is always at our elbow with gentle nudges and not-so-innocent pushes. Courteously, he allows others in the room to listen. His prose, his focus, his sureness restore order in distracted minds. Gently he introduces good causes like votes for women, the rights of the Irish, the place of poetry. The voice is never shrill and always accommodating. His judgments are clear, assured, and firm. Macaulay aimed to attract novel readers and general readers high and low. How can this happy breed be but cheerful in the hands of a narrative voice that describes how "the long struggle between our sovereigns and their Parliaments . . .

bound up together the rights of the people and the title of the reigning dynasty"? He speaks to an American audience when he notes that the "British colonies rapidly became far mightier and wealthier than the realms which Cortes and Pizarro" added to Spain. Macaulay joyfully reels off the epic names and places of Celt, Saxon, and Norman until, presumably, we arrive at the First Reform Bill in 1832, when all is perfected.

Macaulay's judgments are distinct even in anonymous essays he wrote for the *Edinburgh Review*. Of Scottish ancestry himself, Macaulay disliked James Boswell but admired his biography of **Samuel Johnson**. His essay on Milton sent his readers to learning Italian so they could evaluate his comparison of the Protestant Milton to the Catholic Dante. His five biographical essays for the eighth edition of the *Encyclopaedia Britannica* (1854–59) define the form. Although an advocate of progress, he believed poetry and religion were best written and revealed in primitive times. He sought a literary tradition in opposition to the court or aristocratic literary history; his own time, manners, and truths seemed a triumph to him and to his audience.

Macaulay's essay style, on the surface, resembles his 18th-century predecessors. His sentences balance clause against clause, and phrase against phrase. He is fond of alliteration and witty lists: the austere Puritans thought it a "sin to hang garlands on a Maypole, to drink a friend's health, to fly a hawk, to hunt a stag, to play at chess, to wear lovelocks, to put starch into a ruff, to touch the virginals, to read the Fairy Queen." He is aphoristic, epigrammatic, and effortless. His play of wit is that of a serious person who causes laughter by his sure sense of conclusion. He mastered the art of the outrageous paradox, marveling that the boorish Boswell wrote the life of the hero Dr. Johnson. Macaulay's imagination could not see that Boswell created a fiction to dramatize his portrait of Johnson.

To his contemporaries Macaulay seemed arrogant, his firmness immature. He had a boy's joy and delight in exposing fallacies and follies, coupled with adult indignation. Nonetheless, like all good essayists, he is a good companion. **William Makepeace Thackeray** noted that Macaulay had, and revealed, a "brilliant intellect" with an "amazing variety and extent of learning" that produced essays "which all may so easily read." That ease is both the bane and the charm of Macaulay as essayist.

RICHARD C. TOBIAS

Biography

Born 25 October 1800 at Rothley Temple, Leicestershire. Studied at Aspenden Hall, Hertfordshire, 1814–18; Trinity College, Cambridge, 1818–22, B.A., 1822; Lincoln's Inn, London, admitted to the bar, 1826. Contributor, *Knight's Quarterly*, 1823, and the *Edinburgh Review*, 1825–44. Fellow of Trinity College, 1824–31. Commissioner of bankruptcy, 1828–30; Whig Member of Parliament for Calne, Wiltshire, 1830–32, Leeds, 1832–34, and Edinburgh, 1839–47 and 1852–56; commissioner, Board of Control, 1832–34; legal adviser to the Supreme Council of the East India Company, Calcutta, 1834–38; secretary of war in Melbourne's cabinet, 1839–41; paymaster-general in Russell's cabinet, 1846–47. Rector, University of Glasgow, 1849. Made Baron Macaulay of Rothley, 1857. Awards: Prussian Order of Merit, 1853; honorary degree from Oxford University. Died in London, 28 December 1859.

Selected Writings

Essays and Related Prose
Critical and Miscellaneous Essays, 5 vols., 1841–44; revised editions, 4 vols., 1857, 7 vols., 1859–61
Critical and Historical Essays Contributed to the Edinburgh Review, 3 vols., 1843; selections edited by Hugh Trevor-Roper, 1965
Speeches, 2 vols., 1853
Selections from Essays and Speeches, 2 vols., 1856
Biographical and Historical Sketches, 1857
The Miscellaneous Writings, 2 vols., 1860
Biographies by Lord Macaulay Contributed to the Encyclopaedia Britannica, 1863
Selected Writings, edited by John Clive and Thomas Pinney, 1972
The Letters, edited by Thomas Pinney, 6 vols., 1974–81; part as *Selected Letters*, edited by Pinney, 1982

Other writings: poetry (*Lays of Ancient Rome*, 1842) and *The History of England from the Accession of James II* (5 vols., 1848–61).

Collected works editions: *Works* (Albany Edition), 12 vols., 1898, reprinted 1980; *Works*, edited by Thomas F. Henderson, 9 vols., 1905–07.

Bibliographies
Pinney, Thomas, in *The Letters of Thomas Babington Macaulay*, vol. 6, Cambridge and New York: Cambridge University Press, 1981: 289–302
Potter, George Reuben, in *Macaulay*, London: Longman, 1959

Further Reading
Bryant, Arthur, *Macaulay*, London: Weidenfeld and Nicolson, and Lanham, Maryland: Barnes and Noble, 1979 (original edition, 1932)
Clive, John, *Macaulay: The Shaping of the Historian*, New York: Knopf, 1973
Clive, John, and Thomas Pinney, Introduction to *Selected Writings* by Macaulay, Chicago: University of Chicago Press, 1972
Clive, John, and Thomas Pinney, "Macaulay," in *Victorian Prose: A Guide to Research*, edited by David De Laura, New York: Modern Language Association of America, 1973: 29–30
Crosby, Christina, *The Ends of History: Victorians and "the Woman Question"*, London and New York: Routledge, 1991
Edwards, Owen Dudley, *Macaulay*, London: Weidenfeld and Nicolson, and New York: St. Martin's Press, 1988
Fisher, H. A. L., "The Whig Historians," in *Pages from the Past*, Freeport, New York: Books for Libraries, 1969: 40–92 (original edition, 1939)
Fraser, G. S., "Macaulay's Style as an Essayist," *Review of English Literature* 1, no. 4 (1960): 9–19
Geyl, Pieter, "Macaulay in His Essays," in his *Debates with Historians*, Gröningen: Wolters, 1955: 19–34
Hamburger, Joseph, *Macaulay and the Whig Tradition*, Chicago: University of Chicago Press, 1976
Levine, George, *The Boundaries of Fiction: Carlyle, Macaulay, Newman*, Princeton, New Jersey: Princeton University Press, 1968
Madden, William A., "Macaulay's Style," in *The Art of Victorian Prose*, edited by Madden and Georgè Levine, New York: Oxford University Press, 1968: 127–53
Millgate, Jane, *Macaulay*, London and Boston: Routledge and Kegan Paul, 1973
Svaglic, Martin J., "Classical Rhetoric and Victorian Prose," in *The Art of Victorian Prose*, edited by George Levine and William A. Madden, New York: Oxford University Press, 1968: 268–88

Trevelyan, G. O., *The Life and Letters of Lord Macaulay*, Oxford and New York: Oxford University Press, 2 vols., 1978 (original edition, 1876)

Weber, Ronald, "Singer and Seer: Macaulay on the Historian as Poet," *Papers on Language and Literature* 3 (1967): 210–19

McCarthy, Mary

American, 1912–1989

Mary McCarthy was a preeminent American literary figure for some 40 years. Well known for her biting, satiric novels and criticism, McCarthy, who moved within the circles of leading left-wing writers and intellectuals in the United States and Europe, can best be understood as an exceptional essayist. In terms of tone, style, and personal opinion, her numerous articles published in periodicals fit well within the essay form. Moreover, as one biographer, Doris Grumbach (1967), puts it, "McCarthy's fiction is very close to the spirit of the essay."

McCarthy began writing caustic book **reviews** for the *Nation* and the *New Republic* and ferocious theatrical criticism for the *Partisan Review* in the 1930s. She established a reputation for memorable glibness, writing of Tennessee Williams' *A Streetcar Named Desire* that "his work reeks of literary ambition as the apartment [in which the play is set] reeks of cheap perfume." McCarthy shifted to fiction at the insistence of **Edmund Wilson**, an influential critic who was the second of her four husbands. Her work overall offers a brilliant but somewhat unconventional and occasionally malicious look at American culture as seen through the eyes of the intellectual set with which she was identified. With cool intelligence and humor infused by a firm conviction of her own honesty and morality, she chronicles her personal involvement in and reaction to key social and political issues of her era, including sexual emancipation, communism, civic liberty, academic conformity, nuclear weapons, Vietnam, and Watergate. In a display of her depth of her knowledge, however, two of McCarthy's outstanding books lie in the field of cultural history (*Venice Observed*, 1956; *The Stones of Florence*, 1959).

Often drawn from autobiographical sources, many of the themes she developed in seven novels (published 1942–79) and various short stories were initially sketched in magazine articles. For example, McCarthy's most popular work, the best-selling novel *The Group* (1963), describes in scathing, sexually explicit detail the lives of eight graduates of Vassar College, where she obtained her bachelor's degree in 1933. Intended to be a partial parody, it portrays the women, thought to be thinly disguised versions of herself and her classmates, as they embrace or oppose ideas of political and social progress fashionable among intellectuals in the 1930s and 1940s. To a degree it draws on material presented in "The Vassar Girl" (1951), first published in *Holiday* and included in her most significant essay collection, *On the Contrary: Articles of Belief, 1946–1961* (1961). In "The Vassar Girl," McCarthy makes witty reference to scenes from her own anguished, orphaned childhood in Seattle and Minneapolis, which were later elaborated upon in her painful autobiography, *Memories of a Catholic Girlhood* (1957), itself mainly a collection of articles that appeared from 1946 to 1955 in the *New Yorker*. Some

critics called it her finest book. Along with two successive volumes of autobiography – *How I Grew* (1987) and *Intellectual Memoirs* (1992) – as well as fictional heroines who seemed much like herself, *Memories* served to mythologize her own life.

On the Contrary offers an overview of McCarthy's wide range of interests as an essayist. Divided into three sections, "Politics and the Social Scene," "Woman," and "Literature and the Arts," it displays her ability to dissect subjects ranging from comments in the United States on the assassination of Mahatma Gandhi to the work of contemporary playwrights and novelists. In one of her most provocative essays, "America the Beautiful: The Humanist in the Bathtub," originally published in 1947 in *Commentary*, she writes that the American experience rests on "a pseudo-equality, that is, in standardization, in an equality of things rather than of persons. The inalienable rights to life, liberty, and the pursuit of happiness appear, in practice, to have become the inalienable right to a bathtub, a flush toilet, and a can of Spam." Nevertheless, as Carol Brightman (1992) points out, McCarthy did not simply echo the prevailing left-wing view that capitalism had turned Americans into a nation of soulless consumers. Instead, she summed up in her epigrammatic style the conservative argument that consumerism represented an unobtainable dream of social equality: "We are a nation of twenty million bathrooms, with a humanist in every tub." In another essay, "The Fact in Fiction," based on lectures given in Europe in 1960, McCarthy argues that modern novelists, including herself, have become cut off from "common sense in terms of broad experience" and that, consequently, novels are dividing into component parts, the essay based on facts on the one hand, and the fictional tale on the other, instead of integrating the imagination with details of actual life.

As a writer, McCarthy was influenced by the classical education she had received in a convent school and an Episcopalian seminary in the state of Washington as well as at Vassar. To her Catholic upbringing she attributed her love of Latin, once commenting, "Writing with a Latinate turn, compressed, analytic, and yet having a certain extravagance or oratorical flourish sounded in my ears like a natural, spoken language" (*Current Biography*, 1969). At her death, the critic Elizabeth Hardwick was quoted as calling McCarthy's voice both "urbane and puritanical, an original and often daunting mixture" (*Time*, 6 November 1989).

MAURINE H. BEASLEY

Biography

Mary Therese McCarthy. Born 21 June 1912 in Seattle, Washington. Studied at the Annie Wright Seminary, Tacoma, Washington; Vassar College, Poughkeepsie, New York, A.B., 1933 (Phi Beta Kappa). Married Harold Johnsrud, 1933 (divorced, 1936). Book reviewer, the *Nation* and the *New Republic*; editor, Covici Friede publishers, New York, 1936–37; editor, 1937–38, and drama critic, 1938–62, *Partisan Review*. Married the writer Edmund Wilson, 1938 (divorced, 1946): one son. Taught or lectured at Bard College, Annandale-on-Hudson, New York, 1945–46 and 1986, Sarah Lawrence College, Bronxville, New York, 1948, University College, London, 1980, and Vassar College, 1982. Contributor to many journals and newspapers, including the *New York Review of Books*, the *Observer*, and the *Sunday Times*. Married Bowden Broadwater, 1946 (divorced, 1961), and James Raymond West,

1961. Lived in Paris and in Castine, Maine. Subject of a defamation suit by the writer Lillian Hellman: suit dropped after Hellman's death, 1984. Awards: three grants and fellowships; Edward MacDowell Medal, 1984; National Medal of Literature, 1984; First Rochester Literary Award, 1985; honorary degrees from six universities. Member, American Academy, National Institute of Arts and Letters. Died (of cancer) in New York, 25 October 1989.

Selected Writings

Essays and Related Prose
Sights and Spectacles, 1937–1956, 1956; enlarged edition, as Sights and Spectacles: Theatre Chronicles, 1937–1958, 1959; enlarged edition, as Theatre Chronicles, 1937–1962, 1963
Memories of a Catholic Girlhood (autobiography), 1957
On the Contrary: Articles of Belief, 1946–1961, 1961
The Humanist in the Bathtub, 1964
Vietnam, 1967
Hanoi, 1968
The Writing on the Wall and Other Literary Essays, 1970
Medina, 1972
The Seventeenth Degree (includes Vietnam, Hanoi, and Medina), 1974
The Mask of State: Watergate Portraits, 1974
Ideas and the Novel, 1980
Occasional Prose, 1985

Other writings: seven novels (The Company She Keeps, 1942; The Oasis, 1949; The Groves of Academe, 1952; A Charmed Life, 1955; The Group, 1963; Birds of America, 1971; Cannibals and Missionaries, 1979), short stories, two further volumes of autobiography (How I Grew, 1987; Intellectual Memoirs, 1992), and books of travel and cultural history.

Bibliographies
Bennett, Joy, and Gabriella Hochmann, Mary McCarthy: An Annotated Bibliography, New York: Garland, 1992
Goldman, Sherli, Mary McCarthy: A Bibliography, New York: Harcourt Brace and World, 1968

Further Reading
Brightman, Carol, Writing Dangerously: Mary McCarthy and Her World, New York: Clarkson Potter, 1992; London: Lime Tree, 1993
Gelderman, Carol, Mary McCarthy: A Life, New York: St. Martin's Press, 1988; London: Sidgwick and Jackson, 1989
Grumbach, Doris, The Company She Kept: A Revealing Portrait of Mary McCarthy, New York: Coward McCann, 1967; as The Company She Kept: A Study of Mary McCarthy, London: Bodley Head, 1967

Machiavelli, Niccolò
Italian, 1469–1527

Machiavelli's prolific and diverse output (poetry, novella, epigram, dialogue, letters, translation from Latin, biography, history, chronicle, political theory) typifies the activity of a Renaissance scholar steeped in knowledge of humanist classical culture. Unlike many humanists of his time, however, most of Machiavelli's writing has a political slant to it, with even literary works such as his famous play La mandragola (1518; The Mandrake) being susceptible to political interpretation.

Works in essay form – such as "Discorso sopra le cose di Pisa" (wr. 1499; "Discourse on Pisa"), "Del modo di trattare i popoli della Valdichiana ribellati" (wr. 1502; "On the Method of Dealing with the Rebellious Peoples of Valdichiana"), "Ritratti delle cose di Francia" (wr. 1512; "Description of French Affairs"), and Istorie fiorentine (wr. 1520, pub. 1532; The History of Florence) – though often more descriptive than evaluative, contain echoes of many of the precepts on history and politics to be found in his major political essays, Il principe (wr. 1513, pub. 1532; The Prince) and I discorsi (wr. 1517, pub. 1531; The Discourses). These precepts include his views on the need to learn from former historical eras and events, his attribution of Italy's contemporary social and political problems to the temporal power of the Papacy, and his aversion to the use of mercenary soldiers to fight on behalf of a ruler or a state. The fuller development of such notions in those major works has helped to make Machiavelli one of the key figures in the history of world social and political thought, though little weight was given to this area of his work by his contemporaries. Even when his political writings became more widely known in the second half of the 16th century, they were considered more dangerous than helpful, being placed on the Church Index of officially banned books in 1564 and attracting much odium for at least three centuries.

The 26 chapters of The Prince fall into the well-established Renaissance genre of the advice manual on how to rule, addressed to a prince by his humanist courtier. What distinguishes Machiavelli's manual from other such works, however, is the originality of the political principles it advances and its dual focus, which offers not only a general theoretical perspective but also contemporary practical advice. In order to illustrate the conclusions he has reached, Machiavelli draws upon examples from both ancient and more recent history and also taps into his own experience in government as a Florentine political administrator and diplomat beginning in 1498. In his prescriptions on statecraft, his first priority is the creation and maintenance of a strong independent state. The essential tool for the achievement of this is the practice of what he terms virtù. But far from requiring "virtue" in the conventional moral sense, Machiavelli's virtù does not demand that a ruler behave morally, but rather that he demonstrate political ability wherever this may lead in terms of actions – that he show, in Quentin Skinner's (1981) euphemistic formulation, "moral flexibility." Nor is Machiavelli afraid to enunciate the potentially dark consequences which the discovery of virtù carries with it. Its practitioner, he insists, must be cold and calculating, and not allow himself to be beset by moral scruples, feelings of guilt, or concern for abstractions such as right or justice. What must remain central is not any ethical sense but the capacity to govern successfully. As the great 19th-century writer Alessandro Manzoni explained: "Machiavelli did not want injustice ... he wanted what was useful, and he wanted it either with justice or with injustice." In this, The Prince, far from advocating any new political system or technique of government, was actually reflecting many of the ideas and practices already (and still) existing in political life, but its originality was in the attempt to arrange them clearly and unashamedly into a system and to bind them together in a conceptual framework.

Not that the writer's vision manages to be without internal contradictions. What emerges, for example, from Machiavelli's analysis in Chapter 8 of the actions of Agathocles, ruler of ancient Syracuse, is a description of horrifically immoral actions, which, though they seem to correspond to the writer's prescription for *virtù*, are emphatically denied such status. Indeed, some critics, like John Parkin (in *Niccolò Machiavelli's "The Prince": New Interdisciplinary Essays*, 1995), would argue that the work is informed by subliminal dialogue and the reader must proceed by "teasing out the contradictions and oppositions which function in his text." But even if we do not go this far, *The Prince* cannot be said to have the rigor of modern analytic political thought. It is not, as Maureen Ramsay (in *Niccolò Machiavelli's "The Prince": New Interdisciplinary Essays*, 1995) points out, "systematic or intellectually coherent enough" to be called political science and, like Machiavelli's other **treatise** works, offers ample scope for contemplation or disagreement on the part of the reader, thereby making it a fitting precursor to an essay genre that had yet to be seriously developed.

Machiavelli's other major essay, the much longer *Discourses*, has been seen by some as constituting something of a contradiction in the writer's thought. While *The Prince* upholds the need for strong dictatorial rule, *The Discourses* openly expresses support for republican government with active participation by a wider group of citizens. The apparent contradiction may be reconcilable in terms of a chronology whereby once a strong state is established by strong personal leadership, a wider, though equally strong, form of government may usefully follow at a later date. Whatever the case, the pre-imperial Roman Republic clearly arises from *The Discourses* as Machiavelli's favored political model.

What both works manifestly share is the appeal, whether in an absolute ruler or in republican leaders, to *virtù* and an insistence that human beings – selfish and prone to evil in Machiavelli's view – must be taken and governed as they are, not as we would like them to be. While throughout his writing Machiavelli explicitly rejects the doctrines and institutions of the established Church, he is also arguing, perhaps paradoxically, for one of Catholicism's central tenets – original sin – albeit from an empirical and secular perspective.

Machiavelli's style can be said to match the functionality of his message. It is characterized by a stark lexical economy and a conciseness of syntax in which concepts are compared and juxtaposed in formulations that can almost seem mathematical in their precision and their exclusion of embellishment. For all this the style, especially in *The Prince*, is not over-dry. It can even be vigorous and dramatic, eager and animated, and demonstrate the writer's gift for the vivid focusing image – e.g. the prince as a lion and a fox combined; fortune as a great river in flood, stoppable, however, by defensive human action informed by *virtù*.

Neither the attempts by modern scholars to view Machiavelli as a harbinger of democratic thought nor the popular concept of the man as the incarnation of evil reflect a balanced view of his writing. While it is true that what he wrote does not lend itself to a single monolithic interpretation, at the same time its significance cannot be stretched beyond all reasonable bounds, and we must above all take careful account of the times and their social and mental limitations. To do otherwise is not to shed light on the writer's thought but simply to misunderstand both the man and the historical context in which he operated.

HOWARD MOSS

Biography

Niccolò di Bernardo dei Machiavelli. Born 3 May 1469 in Florence. May have been involved in overthrowing the Savonarolist government, 1498; appointed head of the new government's Second Chancery, 1498, and secretary of an agency concerned with warfare and diplomacy, 1498–1512, visiting Cesare Borgia, 1502, Rome, 1503 and 1506, France, 1504 and 1510, and Germany, 1507–08; helped to set up a standing army, which reconquered Pisa, 1509. Medici family returned to power, 1512, ending the Florentine Republic; Machiavelli suspected of plotting against the Medici, and jailed and exiled to Sant'Andrea in Percussina, where he spent his remaining years and produced his major writings. Partly reconciled with the Medici in 1519 and given various duties, including writing a history of Florence. Hoped for a new government post when the Medici were deposed in 1527, but distrusted by the new republican government for previous association with the Medici. Died in Florence, 21 June 1527.

Selected Writings

Essays and Related Prose

I discorsi sulla prima deca di Tito Livio, 1531; edited by Corrado Vivanti, 1983, and Giorgio Inglese, 1984; as *The Discourses upon on the First Decade of T. Livius*, translated by Edward Dacres, 1636 (translation edited by Bernard Crick, 1971), Ninian Hill Thomson, 1883, and Allan H. Gilbert, 1946; as *The Discourses*, translated by Leslie J. Walker, 2 vols., 1950 (translation revised by Brian Richardson, edited by Bernard Crick, 1970)

Istorie fiorentine, 1532; as *The Florentine Historie*, translated by Thomas Bedingfield, 1595, M. K., 1674, and W. K. Mariott, 1909; as *The History of Florence*, translated by Henry Nevile, 1675, and Ninian Hill Thomson, 2 vols., 1906; as *The Florentine Histories*, translated by C. Edwards Lester, 1845; as *Reform in Florence*, translated by Allan Gilbert, 1946; as *Florentine Histories*, translated by Laura F. Banfield and Harvey C. Mansfield, Jr., 1988

Il principe, 1532; edited by Luigi Firpo, 1961, Brian Richardson, 1979, and Piero Melograni, 1991; as *The Prince*, translated by Edward Dacres, 1640; many subsequent translations, including by Allan H. Gilbert, 1946, Peter Rodd, 1954, George Bull, 1961, Daniel Donno, 1966, Robert A. Adams, 1977 (revised 1992), Harvey Claflin Mansfield, 1985, Russell Price, 1988, and David Wootton, 1995

The Historical, Political and Diplomatic Writings (includes *The History of Florence*; *The Prince*; *Discourse on Livy*; *Thoughts of a Statesman*; *Missions*; miscellaneous papers), translated by Christian E. Detmold, 4 vols., 1882

The Living Thoughts of Machiavelli (includes *Discourses on Livy*; *The Prince*; *Private Letters*), edited by Count Carlo Sforza, translated by Sforza and Arthur Livingston, 1940

The Portable Machiavelli, edited and translated by Peter E. Bondanella and Mark Musa, 1979

The Prince and Other Political Writings, edited and translated by Bruce Penman, 1981

Selected Political Writings, edited and translated by David Wootton, 1994

Other writings: the story *Novella di Belfagor arcidiavolo* (1545; *The Marriage of Belphegor*), three plays, a biography of Castruccio Castracani, and correspondence.

Collected works editions: *Opere*, edited by Sergio Bertelli and others, 4 vols., 1968–89; *The Chief Works and Others*, translated by Allan H. Gilbert, 3 vols., 1965, reprinted 1989.

Bibliographies

Bertelli, Sergio, and Piero Innocenti, *Bibliografia machiavelliana*, Verona: Valdonega, 1979

Fiore, Silvia Ruffo, *Niccolò Machiavelli: An Annotated Bibliography of Modern Criticism and Scholarship*, Westport, Connecticut: Greenwood Press, 1990

Further Reading

Anglo, Sydney, *Machiavelli: A Dissection*, London: Gollancz, 1969; New York: Harcourt Brace and World, 1970

Borsellino, Nino, *Niccolò Machiavelli*, Rome: Laterza, 1973

Chabod, Federico, *Machiavelli and the Renaissance*, Cambridge, Massachusetts: Harvard University Press, 1958

Colish, Marcia L., "The Idea of Liberty in Machiavelli," *Journal of the History of Ideas* 32 (1971): 323–50

Coyle, Martin, editor, *Niccolò Machiavelli's "The Prince": New Interdisciplinary Essays*, Manchester: Manchester University Press, and New York: St. Martin's Press, 1995

Fleischer, Martin, *Machiavelli and the Nature of Political Thought*, New York: Atheneum, 1972; London: Croom Helm, 1973

Gilbert, Felix, "The Humanist Conception of the Prince and *The Prince* of Machiavelli," *Journal of Modern History* 11 (1939): 449–83

Grazia, Sebastian de, *Machiavelli in Hell*, Princeton, New Jersey: Princeton University Press, and London: Harvester Wheatsheaf, 1989

Hale, J. R., *Machiavelli and Renaissance Italy*, New York: Macmillan, 1960; London: English Universities Press, 1966

Harriman, Robert, "Composing Modernity in Machiavelli's *Prince*," *Journal of the History of Ideas* 50 (1989): 3–29

Montano, Rocco, *Machiavelli: Valore e limiti*, Florence: Sansoni, 1974

Parel, Anthony, editor, *The Political Calculus: Essays on Machiavelli's Philosophy*, Toronto: University of Toronto Press, 1972

Pocock, J. G. A., *The Machiavellian Moment: Florentine Political Thought and the Atlantic Republican Tradition*, Princeton, New Jersey: Princeton University Press, 1975

Price, Russell, "The Senses of 'Virtù' in Machiavelli," *European Studies Review* 3 (1973): 315–45

Sasso, Gennaro, *Niccolò Machiavelli: Storia del suo pensiero politico*, Bologna: Il Mulino, 1980

Skinner, Quentin, *Machiavelli*, Oxford: Oxford University Press, and New York: Hill and Wang, 1981

Viroli, Maurizio, "Machiavelli and the Republican Idea of Politics," in *Machiavelli and Republicanism*, edited by Gisela Bock, Quentin Skinner, and Maurizio Viroli, Cambridge and New York: Cambridge University Press, 1990: 143–71

Whitfield, J. H., *Machiavelli*, Oxford: Blackwell, 1947; New York: Russell and Russell, 1965

Wood, Neal, "Machiavelli's Concept of 'Virtù' Reconsidered," *Political Studies* 15 (1967): 159–72

MacLennan, Hugh

Canadian, 1907–1990

Hugh MacLennan discovered his talent as an essayist relatively late in his writing career, and initially his motives for developing this talent were more financial than artistic. When the success of the novel *Two Solitudes* (1945) encouraged him to give up teaching and live by writing alone, it also made him a recognized authority on Canadian culture and where Canada stood in relation to Europe and the United States. Magazine editors were interested in having him express more directly the ideas behind his novels, and, needing money to supplement his income from fiction, MacLennan obliged. It was only gradually, however, that he came to see himself as an essayist, and even after he had won two Governor-General's Awards for nonfiction and developed a deep attachment to the essay form, he continued to think of himself as a novelist first.

MacLennan's idea of essay writing as a pleasant but relatively insignificant sideline, however reasonable in view of contemporary tastes, went against his natural abilities. Writing novels was always a struggle involving extensive drafting, rewriting, and editing; in contrast, writing essays came naturally to him so that, after a little practice, he was able to complete a good essay in only a couple of days. Also, the instructional bent which sometimes made MacLennan's novels seem too plainly dedicated to illustrating ideas for modern tastes proved an asset in his essays, where he excelled at explaining complex subjects lucidly and memorably. While his novels are of central importance in the development of modern Canadian literature, none is without significant flaws; more than a few of his essays, on the other hand, are excellent by any standard.

Although the three essay collections that MacLennan played a part in editing contain less than a quarter of the 400 or so essays he wrote, they serve well to represent both his development as a **familiar essay**ist and his growing affection for the form. *Cross Country* (1949) shows MacLennan experimenting with a variety of approaches. Several of the ten essays are analytical, fairly formal interpretations of Canadian and American society. MacLennan referred to them as "think pieces" in his introduction to the 1972 reissue of the book and attributed "their solemn, outdated style" to editorial expectations early in the Cold War. Although he exaggerates their stylistic faults, pieces like "The Canadian Character" and "On Discovering Who We Are" are long and, having originally been written as interpretive journalism rather than essays as such, designed to appeal mainly to the intellect. On the other hand, they are also timely, original, perceptive, and on the whole very readable. MacLennan's vocabulary, while extensive, is never obscure or any less accessible than his subjects require; his allusions and references are typically made understandable in context to the average educated reader. A few of the essays in *Cross Country* point to MacLennan's handling of the familiar essay later on. "An Orange from Portugal" and "Portrait of a City," which draw on memories of his youth in Halifax, are more subjective, emotional, and evocative than the analytical pieces, and "The Tyranny of the Sunday Suit" foreshadows the perceptive humor and more relaxed style of his later essays.

MacLennan's second collection, *Thirty and Three* (1954), shows him becoming much more comfortable with the familiar essay. His introduction explains that, in middle age, he has come to see the short essay as a form particularly suited to his temperament and has begun to value essays as a way of dealing with "all manner of things that fascinate and delight" which he could not fit into his novels. His subjects – favorite places, sports, small-town manners, public figures, essential qualities of humor – reflect the wide range of his enthusiasms and, taken together, the essays also afford as much insight into postwar Canadian experience as any of his novels. Most of the essays in *Thirty and Three* were published originally as regular monthly contributions to the *Montrealer* magazine, and they benefit from MacLennan's surer sense of audience. Writing for a local audience also required less background and interpretation and allowed him to get to the ideas he really wanted to express more directly than had been the case earlier. The tone is typically conversational, and writing in the first person has become MacLennan's usual practice. The narrative and descriptive skills he had developed through writing fiction are used to good advantage throughout the collection. Even when dealing with topics of public concern, like Prime Minister MacKenzie King – "neurotic son of a neurotic mother, full of quirks and strangeness, cautious as a turtle yet quick with intuition as any second-sighted Celt ... saved only from caricature by the fact that he happened to be a political genius" ("The Ghost That Haunts Us") – his views are more subjective and his style more lively than in *Cross Country*.

Most of the essays in *Scotchman's Return* (1960) were written during the mid- to late 1950s, a difficult but productive period in MacLennan's life during which his first wife's long illness finally ended in death. How deeply the loss affected him can be seen in his novel *The Watch That Ends the Night* (1959), but the emotional toll is much less apparent in his essays. Many are about education and literature, suggesting how important a part of his life his work with students at McGill University had become. By this time, writing essays had progressed from being primarily a way of making money to becoming a labor of love. His introduction refers to the essay as "the friendliest form of writing" and explains that "a desire for friendship" has made him "an addict of the form." *Scotchman's Return* includes some essays on lighter subjects – "let nobody pity them [the Scots] or wonder why they eat as they do. They prefer this diet because it gives them the pleasure of being miserable" ("By Their Foods . . .") – and MacLennan's quiet sense of humor is at work throughout, but the collection, on the whole, is more serious in tone than the one that preceded it. Significantly, the necessity of accepting things as they are is a recurring idea. We cannot "escape ourselves forever," he remarks in the opening essay ("Scotchman's Return"); "I am a prisoner of my own life," he concludes in the last ("Fifty Grand"). This mood of resignation contrasts with the characteristic impatience in MacLennan's earlier essays, but pervasive though it is, it is essentially positive – a mature acceptance of his own limitations and the inevitable faults of any human society rather than a sense of defeat. The best of these essays, the title piece and a series on Oxford University, are reflective, evocative, and nostalgic.

In addition to these three collections, MacLennan produced several nonfiction books with sections resembling essays. Of these, *Seven Rivers of Canada* (1961), which, much revised, formed the basis of *The Rivers of Canada* (1974), is by far the best. What began as travel writing – a magazine assignment to explore and write about major Canadian rivers – became much more to MacLennan. The geographical explorations provide starting points for reflections on the history and culture of the regions through which the rivers flow, as well as on their significance to the nation as a whole. In addition to being informative in a factual sense, the essays in *Rivers* are also deeply personal and bring together MacLennan's mature ideas about Canada. Particularly successful in its integration of narrative and descriptive illustration and abstract thinking, *Rivers* is arguably MacLennan's best nonfiction book.

MacLennan was dedicated to living fully, to seeing, experiencing, and understanding as much as he could, and, in his writing, to passing on what he had learned. An athlete, a perceptive critic of literature and other arts, a classical historian, and an astute observer of cultural, political, and economic changes in his times, he was able to write about an impressive variety of subjects with authority and original insight. Though he showed more compassion for the masses than confidence in their collective judgment, he wrote with a keen sense of social responsibility and reached out to inform as wide an audience as he could. His recurring concern with identity – individual, regional, and national – grew out of his conviction that a writer had to come to terms with his cultural roots, but his personal exploration of the subject had wider implications in that it played a central role in shaping national self-perception. MacLennan's essays will continue to be read, partly because many are excellent examples of the genre and partly also for the valuable insight they provide into Canadian consciousness as it evolved in the middle years of this century.

WILLIAM CONNOR

Biography

John Hugh MacLennan. Born in Glace Bay, Nova Scotia, 20 March 1907. Studied at Dalhousie University, Halifax, B.A., 1928; Rhodes scholar at Oriel College, Oxford, B.A., M.A., 1932; Princeton University, New Jersey, Ph.D., 1935. Taught Latin and history at Lower Canada College, Montreal, 1935–45. Married Dorothy Duncan, 1936 (died, 1957). Journalist and broadcaster, from 1945. Associate professor, 1951–67, professor of English, 1967–79, then professor emeritus, McGill University, Montreal. Elected to the Royal Society of Canada, 1953. Married Frances Walker, 1959. Awards: many, including the Governor-General's Award, for fiction, 1945, 1948, 1959, and for nonfiction, 1949, 1954; Royal Society of Canada Gold Medal, 1951; Lorne Pierce Medal, 1952; Molson Prize, 1966; Royal Bank of Canada Award, 1967, 1984; honorary degrees from 17 Canadian universities. Companion, Order of Canada, 1967. Died in Montreal, 7 November 1990.

Selected Writings

Essays and Related Prose
Cross Country, 1949
Thirty and Three, 1954
Scotchman's Return and Other Essays, 1960; as *Scotsman's Return and Other Essays*, 1961
Seven Rivers of Canada, 1961; revised edition, as *The Rivers of Canada*, 1974
The Other Side of Hugh MacLennan: Selected Essays Old and New, edited by Elspeth Cameron, 1978

Other writings: seven novels (*Barometer Rising*, 1941; *Two Solitudes*, 1945; *The Precipice*, 1948; *Each Man's Son*, 1951; *The Watch That Ends the Night*, 1959; *Return of the Sphinx*, 1967; *Voices in Time*, 1980).

Bibliography

Cameron, Elspeth, in *The Annotated Bibliography of Canada's Major Authors*, vol. 1, edited by Robert Lecker and Jack David, Downsview, Ontario: ECW Press, 1981

Further Reading

Buitenhuis, Peter, *Hugh MacLennan*, Toronto: Forum House, 1969

Cameron, Elspeth, Editor's Introduction to *The Other Side of Hugh MacLennan: Selected Essays Old and New*, Toronto: Macmillan, 1978

Cameron, Elspeth, *Hugh MacLennan: A Writer's Life*, Toronto: University of Toronto Press, 1981

Keith, W. J., "Novelist or Essayist? Hugh MacLennan and *The Watch That Ends the Night*," in *Hugh MacLennan: 1982*, edited by Elspeth Cameron, Toronto: University College Canadian Studies Programme, 1982

Lucas, Alec, *Hugh MacLennan*, Toronto: MacClelland and Stewart, 1970

MacLulich, T. D., *Hugh MacLennan*, Boston: Twayne, 1983

Morley, Patricia A., *The Immoral Moralists: Hugh MacLennan and Leonard Cohen*, Toronto: Clarke Irwin, 1972

Ryerson, Stanley B., "Hugh MacLennan's View of Social Class and Nationhood," in *Hugh MacLennan: 1982*, edited by Elspeth Cameron, Toronto: University College Canadian Studies Programme, 1982

Woodcock, George, *Hugh MacLennan*, Toronto: Copp Clark, 1969

MacMechan, Archibald

Canadian, 1862–1933

In his own day, Archibald MacMechan's place in Canadian letters rested largely on his various forms of essay writing; combined with his works of criticism, his essays constitute his main legacy to Canadian literary history. Lorne Pierce (*Unexplored Fields of Canadian Literature*, 1932), for instance, cites MacMechan as notable among Canadian essayists: "W. H. Blake, Sir Andrew Macphail and MacMechan . . . come nearest to the real essays . . . the easy inconsequence, grace, charm, sophistication and personal intimacy of the letter are all found in the essay, which may be defined as an epistle to the world of kindred spirits at large . . . The successful essay is a touchstone of urbanity, and only comes after long standing in the oak. Good talk sparkles and has a rich bouquet; the essay is that." Charles G. D. Roberts wrote in a letter (6 April 1929) to MacMechan: "I consider you our best essayist, – perhaps the best Canadian master of English prose."

MacMechan's essays are collected in three volumes: *The Porter of Bagdad and Other Fantasies* (1901), *The Life of a Little College* (1914), and *The Book of Ultima Thule* (1927). His essays have more in common with those of **Montaigne** or **Lamb** than with **Bacon** or **Arnold**: he wrote of Arnold's essays that "their length, their bellicosity, and their didacticism are against them. They are separate campaigns, battles, skirmishes, single combats, episodes in his life-long warfare against Philistines" (Montreal *Standard*, 28 June 1908). His own are characterized by a sense of leisure, nostalgia, and attention to homely details; often he adopts a gentle, humble persona: "the dreamer," "the summer boarder," "Grizzlebeard" are examples. The essay form was congenial in enabling him to combine scholarly accuracy with a personal, often dreamy style, the overall effect of which is an easy familiarity. *The Porter of Bagdad* essays are imitative of the later 19th-century English neo-Romanticism and Pre-Raphaelite style in their idealization of subject matter and their archaic diction. In this collection his characteristically undefined, nonspecific references to a favorite bit of landscape are the germ of what later becomes his very specific and articulate celebration of the province of Nova Scotia, his "Ultima Thule."

MacMechan's next collection, *The Life of a Little College, and Other Papers*, is concerned mainly with matters pertinent to academia – for example, "Tennyson as Artist," "Virgil," and MacMechan's best-known scholarly and critical essay, "The Best Sea-Story Ever Written," on *Moby-Dick*, originally published in 1899 and antedating general critical recognition by over two decades. This essay is notable for its attempt to identify the novel's "Americanization" (a lifelong preoccupation with MacMechan) and as a catalyst for his own *Headwaters of Canadian Literature* (1924). Here too is the germ of his affinity with matters pertaining to seafaring. (He privately noted that his collection of Maritime tales, *There Go the Ships* [1928], would be the work for which he would be longest remembered.)

The Book of Ultima Thule brings together essays written and published over the previous 27 years. As the title suggests, the collection is thematically centered: Nova Scotia is the basis for the literary landscape "Ultima Thule." Each essay explores a facet of an often idealized provincial scene. Possibly MacMechan is indebted to **Joseph Howe** for the idea of a remote, ideal place: Howe referred to Nova Scotia as "Little Paradise." "Dolcefar," MacMechan's coined name for Halifax in this collection, implies both sweetness and distance. The essays fall into two main categories: one focuses on Halifax and its landmarks, combining descriptive writing and historical fact; the other, characteristic of *The Porter of Bagdad*, has a fanciful quality and a speaker who is ostensibly a passive spectator writing reflectively of his surroundings. For the general reader, *The Book of Ultima Thule* provides an introduction to Nova Scotia's culture as perceived by a sensitive, articulate writer during the first quarter of the 20th century. Throughout there is a freshness of perception; possessing an outsider's eye (he reiterates the fact that he is a native of Ontario), MacMechan was keenly responsive to a way of life he saw vanishing in the province and was perhaps more apt to evaluate his surroundings than were its natives. His classical training, urbanity, and felicity of expression lift these essays out of mere regionalism.

JANET BAKER

Biography

Archibald McKellar MacMechan. Born 21 June 1862 in Berlin (now Kitchener), Ontario. Studied at Hamilton College Institute; University of Toronto, B.A., 1884; Johns Hopkins University, Baltimore, Ph.D., 1889. Married Edith May Cowan, 1889: three daughters. George Munro Professor of English Language and Literature, Dalhousie University, Halifax, 1889–1933. Book critic, Montreal *Standard*, 1907–33; coeditor, *University Magazine*, 1907–19. Elected to the Royal Society of Canada, 1926. Awards: Lorne Pierce Medal, 1931; honorary degree from the University of Toronto. Died in Halifax, 7 August 1933.

Selected Writings

Essays and Related Prose
The Porter of Bagdad and Other Fantasies, 1901
The Life of a Little College, and Other Papers, 1914
The Book of Ultima Thule, 1927

Other writings: the Canadian literary history *Headwaters of Canadian Literature* (1924), four books of provincial history (*Sagas of the Sea*, 1923; *Old Province Tales*, 1924; *There Go the Ships*, 1928; *Red Snow on Grand Pré*, 1931), and a posthumous book of poetry. Also edited editions of works by **Thomas Carlyle**, Tennyson, and others.

Further Reading

Conron, Brandon, "Essays 1880–1920," in *Literary History of Canada: Canadian Literature in English*, vol. 1, edited by Carl F. Klinck and others, Toronto: University of Toronto Press, 2nd edition, 1976 (original edition, 1965): 354–60
McBrine, R. W., "Archibald MacMechan, Canadian Essayist," *Dalhousie Review* 50 (1950): 23–33
Shortt, S. E. D., "Archibald MacMechan: Romantic Idealist," in his *The Search for an Ideal: Six Canadian Intellectuals and Their Convictions in an Age of Transition, 1890–1930*, Toronto: University of Toronto Press, 1976

Macphail, Andrew

Canadian, 1864–1938

A consummate stylist, Andrew Macphail first demonstrated unusual writing talent in 1891 when, as a graduating medical student at McGill University, he won an essay contest on vivisection sponsored by the American Humane Education Society, open to the English-speaking world, and juried by Harvard University medical professors. After further medical study in London, Macphail settled into the practice and teaching of medicine in Montreal. It was only after the death of his wife in 1902 that the balance of his commitments began to shift toward writing. In the next year he became editor of the *Montreal Medical Journal*, and in 1911 he became founding editor of the *Canadian Medical Association Journal*. The subject of his inaugural editorial in the national periodical was style in medical writing.

It was as an essayist that Macphail emerged as a Canadian literary figure. In 1905 he published *Essays in Puritanism*, a collection of studies on such figures as John Wesley and **Margaret Fuller**, whom he interpreted as representing or reacting against the faith. This book established Macphail's position as a serious writer; however, it also lacked unity, consisting of individual sketches originally delivered to a group of writers and painters in Montreal, the Pen and Pencil Club.

Four years later *Essays in Politics* was published. Focusing on Canada's role within the British Empire, Macphail emphasized the common ground of Canada and Great Britain, the growing maturity of Canada, and the need for it to assume more responsibility in such matters as imperial defense. "We cannot share in the glory of the Empire unless we share in its danger and, to put it bluntly, in the expense of it." He was unequivocally on the side of imperial federation, and against autonomy, in the public debate over Canada's future. With increasing trenchancy, he also criticized the advance of industry at the expense of agriculture, a trend he identified with materialism. The book was favorably noticed in Britain, and the Canadian Prime Minister, Sir Wilfrid Laurier, wrote to Macphail that he had read it "through & through."

In 1910 Macphail published *Essays in Fallacy*, consisting of critiques of modern trends in education, theology, and gender relations. His perspective was strongly traditionalist, and reflected his deep distrust of industrial civilization. He excoriated the phenomenon of "the American woman," by which he meant a social type not confined to the United States and not including most female Americans. This was woman removed from her "natural" role within the family, and the root cause of the removal was industrialization, which had taken outside the family the domestic tasks in which woman's nature would find fulfillment. In education, he condemned utilitarian values and emphasis on job training, which he attributed to the influence of industry and the acquiescence of educators. By also focusing on the alleged atrophy of craftsmanship and artistry which resulted from the confusion of education with training, and upon the potential in the modern process for dehumanization, his essay revealed the positive vision which lay behind his social criticism. His conservative social views increasingly occupied an equal position with his imperialism as a basis for his reputation and influence.

World War I had a major impact on Macphail, and initially he hoped that the war would cleanse and simplify modern civilization. Although almost blind in one eye, and about to turn 50, he insisted on enlisting for service at the front; he would eventually write the official history of the Canadian medical services during the conflict. His final collection of essays, *Three Persons* (1929), consisted of critical studies of Sir Henry Hughes Wilson, Edward Mandell House, and T. E. Lawrence, all three having emerged into public prominence during the course of the war. The book's distinctiveness lay in Macphail's method: in each case his only sources were the published reminiscences of the subject. There were enormous variations in tone as the three memoirists received radically different treatment.

Within Canadian letters, and for the genre of the essay in Canada, Macphail was important, as well, for his work as editor of the *University Magazine*, a quarterly he published out of his Montreal home, starting in 1907, the year he was appointed first professor of the history of medicine at McGill. His magazine addressed the educated reader, but it clearly reached beyond the small corps of academic professionals in Canada, for circulation approached 6000 at its peak; in Canada this was an unprecedented number for a quality quarterly and has not been matched since. The magazine provided such essayists as Maurice Hutton, **Archibald MacMechan**, **Stephen Leacock**, and Macphail himself with a forum. Macphail published 43 pieces in it, and all but one of his ten essays in *Essays in Politics* had originally appeared there. As an editor, he insisted on paying for submissions (usually 25 dollars), a policy MacMechan later described as "revolutionary." Macphail's absence during the war caused a decline in quality and circulation, which he was unable to reverse in 1919–20, and he discontinued the magazine.

Macphail was an exceptionally versatile author, who wrote in an authoritative tone on almost everything from aesthetics to science. The range of his writing made him the leading Canadian example of the "man of letters," who is distinguished from other members of the intelligentsia by his breadth and lack of an exclusive specialization. He attacked overspecialization even in medicine, which he identified particularly with American influences. In 1927 he published an essay titled "American Methods in Medical Education"; never fearing controversy, he had delivered it first to an American medical body. Although he experimented with many other genres, he never forsook the essay and, in his lifetime, it was as an essayist that he was best known. In 1932 he remarked to Lord Beaverbrook that "the essay form ... is my trade." His epigrammatic style, idiosyncratic perspectives, and ironic wit were especially well adapted to it. The function of his essays, in his view, was to make for "more correct ... thought."

IAN ROSS ROBERTSON

Biography
John Andrew McPhail; spelled his surname Macphail, from c. 1893. Born 24 November 1864 in Orwell, Prince Edward Island. Studied locally and at Prince of Wales College, Charlottetown, P.E.I.; taught for three years, then studied at McGill University, Montreal, B.A., 1888, M.D., 1891. Married Georgina Nightingale Burland, 1893 (died, 1902). Professor of medicine, University of Bishop's College, Montreal, 1893–1905; also practiced medicine for ten years; professor of the history of medicine, McGill University, 1907–37. Editor, *Montreal Medical Journal*, from 1903: merged it with another medical periodical and founded the *Canadian Medical Association Journal*, 1911; founding editor, the *University Magazine*, 1907–20. Served in the Canadian Army Medical Corps, 1915–19: made a Major. Knighted, 1918. Spent summers at family home in Orwell, where he conducted agricultural experiments. Died (after heart attacks) in Montreal, 23 September 1938.

Selected Writings

Essays and Related Prose
Essays in Puritanism, 1905
Essays in Politics, 1909
Essays in Fallacy, 1910
Three Persons, 1929

Other writings: a novel, poetry, the official history of the Canadian medical services in World War I, a work on the Bible in Scotland, and *The Master's Wife* (1939), a semi-autobiographical memoir of Prince Edward Island in his youth. Also translated *Maria Chapdelaine: A Romance of French Canada* by Louis Hémon (1921).

Bibliography
Robertson, Ian Ross, *Sir Andrew Macphail as a Social Critic* (dissertation), Toronto: University of Toronto, 1974: 368–83

Further Reading
Edgar, O. P., "Sir Andrew Macphail," *Queen's Quarterly* 54 (Spring 1947): 8–22
Leacock, Stephen, "Andrew Macphail," *Queen's Quarterly* 45 (Winter 1938): 445–52
Robertson, Ian Ross, *Sir Andrew Macphail as a Social Critic* (dissertation), Toronto: University of Toronto, 1974
Robertson, Ian Ross, "Andrew Macphail: A Holistic Approach," *Canadian Literature* 107 (Winter 1985): 179–86
Shortt, S. E. D., "Essayist, Editor, and Physician: The Career of Sir Andrew Macphail," *Canadian Literature* 96 (Spring 1983): 49–58

McPhee, John
American, 1931–

John McPhee is one of America's finest practitioners of literary nonfiction and, more specifically, of literary journalism. He became a staff writer for the *New Yorker* in the mid-1960s, shortly after it accepted his profile of Princeton basketball sensation Bill Bradley, and has been associated with the magazine ever since. Almost all of his published work – almost two dozen books, including four collections of shorter essays – has first appeared there. This association tells us much about McPhee's appeal: the *New Yorker* readership has traditionally come to the magazine not for the latest news or timely political opinion but for tasteful fiction and leisurely paced, highly literate feature articles. In McPhee they find the expositor *par excellence*, a deft handler of facts able to satisfy the educated nonspecialist's thirst for information on a wide range of topics: nature, education, geology, technology, nuclear physics, sports, art. His prose, however, is not simply a vehicle that efficiently delivers facts. As much as his expository precision, it is his strong sense of narrative and his eye for descriptive detail that make his essays engaging and his intense curiosity about his topics infectious.

Early profiles such as *A Sense of Where You Are* (1965), *The Headmaster* (1966), "A Roomful of Hovings" (1967), "A Forager" (1968), and "Twynam of Wimbledon" (1968) exemplify McPhee's attitudes and interests. The subjects of these essays – with the exception of the first, about Bradley – are not widely recognized, nor are they in any conventional sense heroes. But they are sympathetic figures, men whom McPhee openly admires, not only because they do work he considers worthwhile but because they are enthusiastically committed to what they do. Frank Boyden, the tireless headmaster of Deerfield Academy in Massachusetts, seems one part educator and three parts salesman, propagandist, and petty tyrant, yet even his shortcomings are treated with such fondness that McPhee's admiration for the man and his work evokes our own. By its end, we recognize in the essay a kind of modest, humanely balanced illustration of the great man theory. Rather than the great, though, McPhee's tastes more commonly tend toward the good; as his brief portrait of Robert Twynam shows, he can admire a groomer of grass as much as he does a groomer of young men. With an understated humor that lightens its tone but never disparages its subject, "Twynam of Wimbledon" makes the groundskeeper of the world's premier tennis tournament seem the consummate professional, scarcely noticed but nonetheless steadfast in his efforts to preserve Centre Court from invading bastard grasses, uncooperative weather, and, worst of all, toe-dragging tennis stars.

This sympathetic interest in people and their pursuits also shapes many of McPhee's longer essays, in which the central figures serve as topical experts and, at times, as moral touchstones. In *The Curve of Binding Energy* (1974), the ostensible topic is nuclear weapons, but the force of the book derives from McPhee's portrait of Theodore Taylor, the physicist who flunked out of graduate school only to become, almost accidentally, the designer of some of the world's most potent bombs. A tissue of persuasive argument, characteristically implicit, emerges through the subtle connections between narration and exposition, as the author weaves lucid explanations of nuclear physics together with amusing, sometimes disturbing vignettes of Taylor's past to suggest that pure science is as unpredictable as life, its results often uncontrollable. Perhaps more than any of McPhee's books, *The Curve of Binding Energy* seems intended to move as well as inform readers. It makes complex processes such as nuclear fusion, nuclear fission, and weapon design more accessible to the layperson, but also more alarming, by exposing the glib confidence with which scientists and government officials talk about controlling the awesome power of the atom.

Whether or not it is used suasively, exposition of the sort found in *The Curve of Binding Energy* is one of the most striking features in McPhee's prose. In essay after essay, he brings vividly before our eyes a wide range of technological processes and gizmos: the coloring of oranges in a packing house; the patient construction of a bark canoe; the "intricate rhomboids" of an experimental airship; the "rock jetties, articulated concrete mattress revetments, and other heavy defenses" used to shackle a growing river. Nature, too, is imaged sharply by McPhee's expository craft. In his four books on geology, *Basin and Range* (1981), *In Suspect Terrain* (1983), *Rising from the Plains* (1986), and *Assembling California* (1993), great geological formations and transformations are made clear to the mind's eye, often by metaphors that capture their most prominent features; they are "a rippled potato chip," a "snowball splatted against glass," "pieces cut from a wheel of cheese," or "Hershey's Kisses on a tray."

Many of McPhee's essays investigate environmental issues. In *Coming into the Country* (1977), the main focus is on Alaska's battles between developers and wilderness preservationists; in *The Control of Nature* (1989), on human attempts to contain water, lava, and mudslides; and in *Encounters with the Archdruid* (1971), on the radical environmentalist David Brower, President of the Sierra Club in the 1960s and 1970s. In each of these, the author's moderate stance on volatile issues is, again, suggested rather than argued. In the last, McPhee also makes greater use of himself as an actor in the drama he describes. Hiking and rafting through Colorado with a geologist, a government bureaucrat, and archdruid Brower, he serves as the facilitator for lively debate about wilderness and preservation. McPhee rarely talks about himself in *Encounters*, but we are always aware of his presence – as are his subjects, who often seem animated by his insatiable interest in their work.

In this use of himself as actor in his own nonfiction dramas, McPhee reveals his kinship with **New Journalism**. His quiet public profile and endearing ethos are very different from those of **Tom Wolfe**, **Norman Mailer**, or George Plimpton, but McPhee's reportage does draw on similar techniques. His choice of topics, for example, suggests a New Journalistic reluctance to grab the headlines, to go instead for the untold or behind-the-scenes story. Moreover, like other New Journalists, who scorn the idea of conducting a quick interview and then retreating to a desk, McPhee spends a long time with his subjects, hiking or boating with them, sometimes living with them before he essays to write their story. And for all his precision with facts and concern for accuracy, McPhee makes no pretense of keeping his journalistic distance; clearly, he selects topics for which he feels great affinity, and he openly demonstrates his affection for the people he profiles. It is this stance, at once leaning toward his subjects yet unbiased about the facts, that raises McPhee's journalism above the level of craft. Craft makes his reportage lucid; his sympathetic, trustworthy ethos turns reportage into nonfictive art.

BRIAN TURNER

Biography

John Angus McPhee. Born 8 March 1931 in Princeton, New Jersey. Studied at Princeton University, A.B., 1953; Magdalene College, Cambridge, 1953–54. Writer for *Robert Montgomery Presents* television show, 1955–56. Married Pryde Brown, 1957 (later divorced): four daughters. Associate editor, *Time* magazine, 1957–64; staff writer, the *New Yorker*, from 1964. Married Yoland Whitman, 1972: two stepsons and two stepdaughters. Ferris Professor of Journalism, Princeton University, from 1975. Awards: many, including the American Academy and Institute of Arts and Letters Award in Literature, 1977; Woodrow Wilson Award, 1982; John Wesley Powell Award, 1988; John Burroughs Medal, 1990; Walton Sullivan Award, 1993; honorary degrees from seven universities and colleges. Member, American Academy of Arts and Letters.

Selected Writings

Essays and Related Prose

A Sense of Where You Are: A Profile of William Warren Bradley, 1965
The Headmaster: Frank L. Boyden, of Deerfield, 1966
Oranges, 1967
A Roomful of Hovings and Other Profiles, 1968
The Pine Barrens, 1968
Levels of the Game, 1969
The Crofter and the Laird, 1970
Encounters with the Archdruid, 1971
Wimbledon: A Celebration, 1972
The Deltoid Pumpkin Seed, 1973
The Curve of Binding Energy, 1974
Pieces of the Frame, 1975
The Survival of the Bark Canoe, 1975
The John McPhee Reader, edited by William Howarth, 1976
Coming into the Country, 1977
Giving Good Weight, 1979
Basin and Range, 1981
In Suspect Terrain, 1983
Heirs of General Practice, 1984
La Place de la Concorde Suisse (in English), 1984
Table of Contents, 1985
In the Highlands and Islands, 1986
Rising from the Plains, 1986
The Control of Nature, 1989
Looking for a Ship, 1990
Assembling California, 1993
The Ransom of Russian Art, 1994
The Second John McPhee Reader, edited by Patricia Strachan and David Remnick, 1996

Further Reading

Core, George, "The Eloquence of Fact," *Virginia Quarterly Review* 54 (1978): 733–41
Espey, David, "The Wilds of New Jersey: John McPhee as Travel Writer," in *Temperamental Journeys: Essays on the Modern Literature of Travel,* edited by Michael Kowalewski, Athens: University of Georgia Press, 1992: 164–75
Giddens, Elizabeth, "An Epistemic Case Study: Identification and Attitude Change in John McPhee's *Coming into the Country,*" *Rhetoric Review* 11 (1993): 378–99
Howarth, William, Introduction to *The John McPhee Reader,* edited by Howarth, New York: Farrar Straus Giroux, 1976
Lounsberry, Barbara, "John McPhee's Levels of the Earth," in her *The Art of Fact: Contemporary Artists of Nonfiction,* New York: Greenwood Press, 1990: 65–106
Roundy, Jack, "Crafting Fact: Formal Devices in the Prose of John McPhee," in *Literary Nonfiction: Theory, Criticism, Pedagogy,* edited by Chris Anderson, Carbondale: Southern Illinois University Press, 1989: 70–92

Schuster, Charles, "Mikhail Bakhtin as Rhetorical Theorist," *College English* 47 (1985): 594–607

Smith, Kathy, "John McPhee Balances the Act," in *Literary Journalism in the Twentieth Century*, edited by Norman Sims, New York: Oxford University Press, 1990: 206–27

Terrie, Philip G., "River of Paradox: John McPhee's 'The Encircled River'," *Western American Literature* 23 (1988): 3–15

Turner, Brian, "Giving Good Reasons: Environmental Appeals in the Nonfiction of John McPhee," *Rhetoric Review* 13 (1994): 164–82

Vipond, Douglas, and Russell A. Hunt, "The Strange Case of Queen-Post Truss: John McPhee on Writing and Reading," *College Composition and Communication* 42 (1991): 200–10

Madariaga, Salvador de

Spanish, 1886–1978

Salvador de Madariaga can be considered a truly international European. Educated in Spain and France, he traveled extensively and lived in England for long periods of his life; he had assignments and held positions in Spain, England, France, and Switzerland; he wrote essays in their original form in Spanish, English, and French. After graduating from the School of Mines in Paris and briefly working at his profession in Madrid, he dedicated the rest of his life to the exercise of his intellectual interests, including journalism, as well as several years as a world public servant (the League of Nations), as a Spanish civil servant for the Spanish Republic (Ambassador in Washington and Paris), and as congressman and cabinet minister of justice and education. Because of his pacifist convictions he left Spain during the Civil War in order to work on a possible reconciliation between the contenders; he made a further attempt to broker a rapprochement between victors and vanquished in 1962. With the victory of General Franco in 1939, Madariaga established his residence in England, where he continued his intellectual work. He returned only briefly to Spain in 1976 after Franco's death. In sum, his life, his work, even the languages in which the ideas of this multifaceted personality were expressed in print bear the seal of European internationality.

Madariaga wrote essays for the most part, but he also wrote novels, drama, and poetry. He is mainly known for his essays of literary interpretation, as well as those analyzing Spanish culture, history, politics, and biography. His literary interest is apparent in *Shelley and Calderón* (1920), *The Genius of Spain* (1923), *Guía del lector del "Quijote"* (1926; *Don Quixote: An Introductory Essay in Psychology*), *De Galdós a Lorca* (1960; *From Galdós to Lorca*) – primarily the product of his years as professor of Spanish literature in Oxford, where he was a Fellow at Exeter College between 1928 and 1931. After the Spanish Civil War he returned to live in Oxford, where he pursued his intellectual interests.

The political essays are a corollary to Madariaga's work in public service. *Disarmament* (1929) is a consequence of his participation in the League of Nations, first as a member of the Press Division, later as head of the Disarmament Section. His interventions in Spanish politics and as a public servant of the Spanish government are compiled in *Discursos internacionales* (1934; International speeches). His ruminations on liberal democracy are part of *Anarquía y jerarquía* (1935; *Anarchy or Hierarchy*), where he admonishes both left and right that hierarchy is the very architecture of the state and must be saved. He distinguishes between liberty and democracy, the latter being defined as a set of practices that can be revised and adjusted.

However, Madariaga is best known internationally for his work interpreting Spanish culture, addressed to Spaniards as well as non-Spaniards. Beginning in 1930, he published *Spain: A Modern History* (1930), and went on to write a trilogy of biographies on Columbus, Cortés, and Bolívar. These were complemented by *The Rise of the Spanish American Empire* (1947) and *The Fall of the Spanish American Empire* (1947), where Madariaga elaborates a controversial explanation of why that empire fell. His theory of the emancipation of the Spanish kingdom in America is based on two principles. The first, of a biological nature, originates in the integration of Spaniards with the native population, resulting in a land that conquers its conquerors when the Creole stops feeling Spanish and begins to feel American. The second principle, of a legal nature, considers that Spanish America was a kingdom rather than a set of colonies. Therefore when the Spanish crown fell in Bayonne in 1808 during the Napoleonic wars, the kingdoms in America were left without a king. Had they promulgated Ferdinand VII as king, only then could they have remained a kingdom.

One of his most widely known essays, *Englishmen, Frenchmen, Spaniards* (1928), was inspired by Madariaga watching the English and French sort out their differences while he served as the disarmament chief in the League of Nations. He characterizes the English as people of action, the French as people of thought, and the Spanish as people of passion, with **Miguel de Unamuno** as the model for his assertion. His linguistic versatility (he was trilingual), which manifested itself in all of his work, can perhaps be observed most vividly in this instance. According to Madariaga the original text was written directly in English in the first part, in French for two chapters, and the rest in Spanish. By the same token, Madariaga states in his memoirs his preference for writing historical works in English because he felt he could exercise more discipline in his writing and be more objective.

Madariaga's essay discourse is more expository than argumentative, but as is proper in the nature of the essay, in trying to illuminate the reader there is an implied desire to promote acceptance or appreciation of the presented viewpoint. His essays originate in observation and intuitive knowledge, which provide the grounds for interpretation of the observed (as in *Englishmen, Frenchmen, Spaniards*). They also draw on personal experience (e.g. the political essays) or on reflection as well as documentation, with various degrees of objectivity and opinion in interpreting sources. Intuition plays an important part in some essays, with a degree of imagination that reveals intuitive finesse.

As an essayist Madariaga did not produce **treatises** or learned articles with critical apparatus. His essays are discourses in the true sense of the word. Being a generalist with a broad cultural and intellectual knowledge, he did not address a specialized readership or follow a specific methodology. His texts mirror the contemporary reader's world. He aimed to promote understanding among men, in an engaging form, expressed in flowing language but based on solid information, honest and acute observation, and intuition. His essays are knowledgeable, earnest, persuasive, written with skill and subtlety, and inspired by a spirit of controversy.

Madariaga was respected for his spirit of tolerance and conciliation. It has been said justly that he was a true universalist at home in the international society of world culture.

PILAR G. SÁENZ

Biography

Salvador Madariaga y Rojo. Born 23 July 1886 in La Coruña, Galicia. Studied at the Collège Chaptal, Paris, until 1906; École Polytechnique, Paris, 1906–08; École Supérieure des Mines, Paris, until 1911. Worked on railroads in Spain, 1911–16. Married Constance Helen Margaret Archibald, 1912 (died, 1970): two daughters. Staff member, the London *Times*, 1916–21. Staff member, 1921, head of Disarmament Section, 1922–27, and Spanish delegate, 1931–36, League of Nations, Geneva. Chair of Spanish literature, Oxford University, 1927–31, and from 1939. Spanish Ambassador to the United States, 1931, and France, 1932–34; minister of education, 1934, then minister of justice. Moved to England during the Spanish Civil War and lived there for most of his life. Married Emilie Szekely Rauman, 1970. Elected to the Royal Spanish Academy (received, 1976). Returned to visit Spain after Franco's death, 1976. Awards: Ere Nouvelle Prize; Europa Prize, 1963; Goethe Prize, 1967; honorary degrees from seven universities; Orders of Merit from several countries; Grand Cross, Legion of Honor (France); Knight Grand Cross of Order of the Republic (Spain). Died in Locarno, Switzerland, 14 December 1978.

Selected Writings

Essays and Related Prose

La guerra desde Londres (*Times* articles), 1918
Shelley and Calderón, and Other Essays on English and Spanish Poetry, 1920; as *Ensayos anglo-españoles*, 1922
The Genius of Spain, and Other Essays on Spanish Contemporary Literature, 1923
Guía del lector del "Quijote": Ensayo psicológico sobre el Quijote, 1926; as *Don Quixote: An Introductory Essay in Psychology*, 1934; revised edition, 1961
Englishmen, Frenchmen, Spaniards: An Essay in Comparative Psychology, 1928
Disarmament, 1929
Americans, 1930
Spain: A Modern History, 1930; as *España: Ensayo de historia contemporánea*, 1931; revised edition, 1934
Discursos internacionales, 1934
Anarquía y jerarquía, 1935; as *Anarchy or Hierarchy*, 1937
On Hamlet, 1948
Bosquejo de Europa, 1951; as *Portrait of Europe*, 1952
Essays with a Purpose, 1954
Presente y porvenir de Hispanoamérica, y otros ensayos, 1959
De Galdós a Lorca, 1960
Retrato de un hombre de pie, 1964; as *Portrait of a Man Standing*, 1968
Memorias de un federalista, 1967
Mujeres españolas, 1972
Obras escogidas: Ensayos, 1972
A la orilla del río de los sucesos (selected essays), 1975
Mi respuesta: Artículos publicados en la revista "Ibérica" (1954–1970), edited by Victoria Kent, 1982

Other writings: many novels, poetry, plays, biographies of Christopher Columbus (1940), Hernán Cortés (1941), and Simón Bolívar (1951), works on the Spanish American empire, and memoirs.

Further Reading

Benítez, Rubén, "Madariaga e Hispanoamérica," in *Studies in Honor of José Rubia Barcia*, edited by Roberta Johnson and Paul C. Smith, Lincoln: Nebraska Society of Spanish and Spanish-American Studies, 1982: 27–38

Caminals Gost, Rose, *Salvador de Madariaga and National Character* (dissertation), Barcelona: University of Barcelona, 1986

Carvalho, Joaquina de Montezuma, "¿Habrá sido Cristóbal Colón un mitómano?," *Norte* 364 (1991): 23–27

Cifo González, Manuel, "El tema de Cervantes en Ortega y Gasset: Meditaciones contrastadas con las de Américo Castro, Salvador de Madariaga, Ramiro de Maeztu y Azorín," *Cuadernos Hispanoamericanos* 403–05 (January–March 1984): 308–16

Cuence Toribio, Jose M., "Madariaga, historiador de la contemporaneidad," *Cuadernos Hispanoamericanos* 429 (1986): 141–46

Fawcett, Michael Leon, *Salvador de Madariaga: The Essays* (dissertation), Los Angeles: University of California, 1979

Sacks, Norman, "The Man Who Entered Through the Window: The Memoirs of Salvador de Madariaga," *Hispania* 59 (1976): 942–51

Sacks, Norman, "Salvador de Madariaga and George Orwell: Parallels and Contrasts," in *Estudios in Honor of Rodolfo Oroz-Santiago*, edited by Marino Pizarro Pizarro, Santiago: University of Chile, 1985: 285–97

Sacks, Norman, "Salvador de Madariaga's Interest in Language," in *East Meets West: Homage to Edgar C. Knowlton*, edited by Roger L. Hadlich and J. D. Ellsworth, Honolulu: University of Hawaii, 1988: 246–66

Torre, Guillermo de, "Rumbo literario de Salvador de Madariaga," *Revista de Occidente* 17 (1967): 368–69

Maeztu, Ramiro de

Spanish, 1874–1936

The life, work, and death of Ramiro de Maeztu, a member of the Generation of '98, are emblematic of the Spanish tragedy of the 1930s and of the European political radicalism of the decades between the two World Wars. Albeit author of a collection of romantic poems, a novel, and a play, Maeztu is best remembered in the history of Spanish literature for his journalistic essays, of which there are several thousand. His four most important books are comprised mainly of selections from his sociological essays and literary essays.

The political and literary ideas of his works of maturity, as well as the circumstances of his death – at the hands of left-wing militants in 1936 – rendered Maeztu a source of inspiration and propaganda for the official ideology of the Franco regime. He is best known in the English-speaking world, however, for his book *Authority, Liberty and Function in the Light of War* (1916), published in London and mentioned in the *Encyclopaedia Britannica* in the section devoted to Guild Socialism, together with Bertrand Russell and G. D. H. Cole.

A passionate speaker and polemicist, Maeztu published *Hacia otra España* (Toward a new Spain) in 1899, one year following the country's loss of its last colonies, Cuba and the Philippines. Most of the essays in the book discuss this disaster and present an analysis – in part lucid, in part impressionistic – of the causes of the loss. This work is representative of Maeztu as a member of the Generation of '98, whose proponents (Unamuno, Baroja, Azorín, Machado), shared the regenerationist and existential impulses which caused the Spanish defeat (by the United States) in 1898. In *Hacia otra España* he accuses the nation's intelligentsia, and in particular the media, of insensitivity to the national crisis; according to Maeztu the press not only ignored Spain's spiritual misery, but also contributed to its decadence through its excessive attention to bullfights, comedies, gossip, and all kinds of banality. Maeztu concentrates on regenerationist themes, arguing against the old aristocratic distaste for commerce and manual labor, and defending a capitalist creation of wealth followed by socialist distribution. His social critique, as we can see, lies more in the diagnosis of problems than in their solutions.

In 1905 Maeztu moved to London as a press correspondent interested in the union ideas then in vogue. This interest led to his second collection of essays, the above-mentioned *Authority, Liberty and Function*, which later appeared in Spanish as *La crisis del humanismo*. The book became an ideological bridge between his regenerationist phase and his final period of borderline fascism. In it he depicts the spiritual crisis of the Spanish writer who experienced an intensification of his Catholicism. From a nearly theocratic point of view, Maeztu analyzes the historical evolution of Renaissance humanism which, in his opinion, erroneously assumed man to be the "measure of all things" and thereby established the basis of the bureaucratic state. Such a state legitimizes its existence by means of a false premise: the naive idea that men are capable of accomplishing the best for themselves, without consideration of their "fallen" moral condition. Modern bureaucracy tends to feed itself and perpetuate the abuse of power delegated by the people. To fight the corruption of the radically secular, capitalist, or Marxist state, he proposes the creation of a system based on trade unions, which follows its own independent and professional hierarchies. Professional excellence would be – as in the Middle Ages – rewarded by means of an autonomous and hierarchical structure, rendering unnecessary any governmental mediation. Here Maeztu contributes to the sustaining ideology of Spanish fascism, both the most militant and idealist of the pre-Civil War era and the "National Catholicism" of the Franco dictatorship.

Of his third and most politically active phase which followed his return to Spain in 1919, two books are significant: *Don Quijote, Don Juan y la Celestina* (1926) and *Defensa de la Hispanidad* (1934; In defense of Hispanism). In the first, he claimed that Don Quixote represents the ideal of love, Don Juan the ideal of power, and the Celestina that of wisdom. But none of the three figures can be deemed complete because they lack what the other two have. Although Don Quixote is the most moral of the three, his love is ineffective because of his lack of wisdom and power. In *Defensa de la Hispanidad*, Maeztu's most original and mature work, he makes the claim that the moral and economic collapse of the Western powers and the Soviet Union following World War I clearly implicate the peoples of Hispanic language and culture as the moral reserve of the West. Spain's historical task thus consists of an acceptance of this type of "manifest destiny" and a resumption of its role as bearer of Christianity and civilization to both the decadent capitalist world and the brutal communist dictatorships.

Ramiro de Maeztu is indispensable to our understanding of the peculiarities of Iberian fascism, in both its nonracist character and its Catholic underpinnings. On the other hand,

Maeztu's thought contains elements characteristic of Anglo-Saxon culture (efficiency, work ethic), which are the result both of his family background (his mother was English) and of his residency in England and his visits to the U.S.

PEDRO MARIA MUÑOZ

Biography

Ramiro de Maeztu y Whitney. Born 4 May 1874 in Vitoria. Lived briefly in Paris, 1890–91, then joined his father in Cuba as administrator on his family's plantation. Upon death of his father, 1895, he returned to Spain (Bilbao) to live with his mother. Wrote for *El Parvenir Vascongado* (The Basque future), Bilbao, then moved to Madrid, 1897, and wrote for various newspapers and journals. Member of the Generation of 1898. Foreign correspondent in London, 1905–19, reporting from the Allied Front during World War I. Married Alice Mabel Hill, 1916: one son. Returned to Spain, 1919. Columnist, *El Sol*, from 1919. Became increasingly involved in activities of the extreme right. Ambassador to Argentina, 1927–30. Founder, *Acción Española* (Spanish action) fascist journal. Elected representative to Spanish Parliament, 1934. Elected to the Spanish Royal Academy, 1935. Refused to take advantage of connections and flee Spain at the onset of Civil War; jailed by Republican militia. Executed 29 October 1936.

Selected Writings

Essays and Related Prose

Hacia otra España, 1899
Authority, Liberty and Function in the Light of War, 1916; revised edition, as *La crisis del humanismo*, 1920
Don Quijote, Don Juan y la Celestina: Ensayos en simpatía, 1926
Defensa de la Hispanidad, 1934
La brevedad de la vida en nuestra poesía lírica, 1935
En vísperas de la tragedia, 1941
España y Europa, 1947
Ensayos, 1948
Frente a la República (articles published in *ABC*, 1931–36), edited by Gonzalo Fernández de la Mora, 1956
Liquidación de la monarquía parlamentaria, 1957
El nuevo tradicionalismo y la revolución social, 1959
Don Quijote o el amor: Ensayos en simpatía, 1964
Artículos periodísticos, 1975
Artículos desconocidos, 1897–1904, edited by E. Inman Fox, 1977
Liberalismo y socialismo: Textos fabianos, 1909–1911, 1984

Other writings: a novel, a play, poetry, and an autobiography.

Collected works edition: *Obras completas*, edited by Vicente Marrero, 1974.

Further Reading

Bancroft, Robert, "América en la obra de Ramiro de Maeztu," *Revista Hispánica Moderna* 13 (1947): 236–49
Díaz-Plaja, Guillermo, *Modernismo frente a Noventa y ocho*, Madrid: Espasa-Calpe, 2nd edition, 1966
Fox, E. Inman, "Ramiro de Maeztu y los intelectuales," *Revista de Occidente* 51 (1957): 369–77
Gómez Martínez, José Luis, "Ramiro de Maeztu, el hombre y su ideal," *Abside* 38 (1974): 196–201
González Cuevas, Pedro Carlos, "Ramiro de Maeztu frente a la segúnda república," *Historia* 16 (1987): 19–26
Lida, Clara, "Literatura anarquista y anarquismo literario," *Nueva Revista de Filología Hispánica* 19 (1970): 360–81
Marrero Suarez, Vicente, *Maeztu*, Madrid: Rialp, 1955
Marrero Suarez, Vicente, "Maeztu y el socialismo español," *Razón y Fe* 6 (1986): 277–90

Nozick, Martin, "An Examination of Ramiro de Maeztu," *PMLA* 69, no. 4 (pt. 1) (1954): 719–40

Rocamora, Pedro, "Ramiro de Maeztu y la generación del '98," *Arbor* 341 (1974): 7–22

Santervás, Rafael, "Maeztu y Ortega: Dos formas de Regeneracionismo: El poder y la ciencia," *Revista de Occidente* 96 (1989): 80–102

Sisto, David, "A Note on the Philosophy of Ramiro de Maeztu," *Hispania* 41 (1958): 457–59

Sobejano, Gonzalo, *Nietzsche en España*, Madrid: Gredos, 1967

Tellechea, J. Ignacio, and Laureano Robles, "Tres cartas de Maeztu a Miguel de Unamuno," *Cuadernos Salamantinos de Filosofía* 17 (1990): 559–91

Mailer, Norman

American, 1923–

Seer, savager, and sage describes Norman Mailer, the American writer who has expanded the boundaries of every nonfiction form he has assayed – including the essay. Mailer has published seven essay collections and won Pulitzer Prizes for two of his 15 book-length narrative essays (*The Armies of the Night: History as a Novel, the Novel as History*, 1968; *The Executioner's Song*, 1979). In truth, he has written more (and more innovative) nonfiction than fiction. More than any other American writer, Mailer has dared to place himself at the center of American political and cultural life and report back his observations. These have taken the form of lengthy and ambitious hybrid works which merge the **travel essay** and political essay (*Miami and the Siege of Chicago*, 1968; *St. George and the Godfather*, 1972; *Oswald's Tale*, 1995), the travel essay and the **science essay** (*Of a Fire on the Moon*, 1971), the travel essay and the sports essay (*King of the Hill*, 1971; *The Fight*, 1975), the cultural polemic and the literary **review** (*Advertisements for Myself*, 1959; *The Prisoner of Sex*, 1971; *Genius and Lust: A Journey Through the Major Writings of Henry Miller*, 1976), and the artist biography (*Marilyn: A Novel Biography*, 1973; *Of Women and Their Elegance*, 1980; *Portrait of Picasso as a Young Man: An Interpretive Biography*, 1995).

The novelist Norman Mailer began to find his voice as an essayist in the mid-1950s as an angry anti-establishment prophet of hip. As the self-proclaimed General Marijuana, he cofounded and named the *Village Voice*, one of the earliest underground American newspapers, in 1955, and proceeded to write a series of provocative essays that uncannily foreshadowed the 1960s. His controversial 1957 essay "The White Negro" predicted that "A time of violence, new hysteria, confusion and rebellion [would] . . . replace the time of conformity." His equally famous *Esquire* essay "Superman Comes to the Supermarket," written on the eve of the 1960 presidential election, is often credited with helping John F. Kennedy defeat Richard Nixon. Mailer's was one of the first voices against the Vietnam War, and his Pulitzer Prize-winning account of his arrest during a 1967 protest march on the Pentagon, *The Armies of the Night*, established forever the inescapable subjectivity of journalism and history – indeed of all nonfiction forms.

Because of this widely celebrated volume, Mailer is usually listed among the 1960s New Journalists. "I think if I started any aspect of the **New Journalism** – and I did," Mailer observed in 1980, "it was an enormously personalized journalism where the character of the narrator was one of the elements not only in telling the story, but in the way the reader would assess the experience." A related contribution is Mailer's innovative treatment of himself as a third-person "character" in his works, a technique he admits to borrowing from *The Education of Henry Adams* (1907). In *The Armies of the Night* Mailer depicts himself at various times as The Novelist, The Historian, The Participant, Mailer, and even as The Beast. In later works he is Aquarius (*Of a Fire on the Moon, St. George and the Godfather*), The Prize Winner, The Prisoner (*The Prisoner of Sex*), and Nommo, spirit of words (*The Fight*).

A gifted stylist, Mailer has been called a quick-change artist for his ability to alter his style to meet new artistic or intellectual goals. *The Executioner's Song*, Mailer's 1979 Pulitzer Prize-winning account of the macabre life and death of Utah murderer Gary Gilmore, confounded and delighted readers, not only because of Mailer's conspicuous absence as a character in the work and his equally uncharacteristic use of simple, even homespun metaphors, but because of his use of substitutionary narration, whereby he narrated the story in the accents and diction of his story's personae. Mailer has written on the Democratic and Republican presidential conventions since 1960; most recently he narrated part of his essay on the 1996 convention in a clipped imitation of the interior voice and diction of Republican presidential candidate Robert Dole: "Dole. Didn't sound like prosperity. More like a grim tomorrow. So Dole could see it. Had to bet the farm. His time had come. Bet the farm."

Mailer has always sought to address the national conscience, and so has published his essays in popular and men's magazines such as *Esquire*, *Playboy*, and (most recently) John F. Kennedy, Jr.'s *George*, as well as more intellectual journals like *Dissent*, *Commentary*, and the *New York Review of Books*. He is a Hegelian, and often will structure his works to pose a synthesis of warring oppositions ("The White Negro," 1957; *Cannibals and Christians*, 1966; *The Idol and the Octopus: Political Writings on the Kennedy and Johnson Administrations*, 1968; *St. George and the Godfather*; *Genius and Lust*). Within these works, he employs metaphors as probes of his subject and as a tool for enhancing intimacy with his readers as well as stimulating mental and social activity. Indeed, it is the forced intimacy of the metaphoric transaction that often causes disproportionate reactions to Mailer's essays –reactions usually of supreme admiration or distaste. Metaphor is coercive. One fails to make the (metaphoric) trip, or avoids intimate understanding, only if one fails to comprehend the metaphor. Because many of Mailer's metaphors are elaborate trips designed to stimulate or activate the reader, they naturally irritate those who do not wish to move – or be moved. On occasion, Mailer will compound this creative tension by verbally savaging his readers. He began his first *Village Voice* column in 1955 by stating: "That many of you are frustrated in your ambitions, and undernourished in your pleasures, only makes you more venomous." In his second column, he admonishes: "If you are not in the mood to think, or if you have no interest in thinking, then let us ignore each other until the next column. And if you do go on from here, please have the courtesy to concentrate."

Readers alienated by Mailer's verbal assaults often have difficulty recognizing that his most profound wish as a writer is
to bring life, to animate both individual bodies and the "body
politic" into greater being. He is thus more socially conscious
than is often credited. Mailer's own literary life is a model of
the regeneration he seeks for others and for the American
nation as a whole. He has described James T. Farrell's *Studs
Lonigan* (1934) as "the best single literary experience" of his
life, for Studs' working-class and lower-middle-class background were similar to his own. "Suddenly I realized you could
write about your life," Mailer told the *Paris Review* in 1964.
In terms of ideas, Mailer says he has gained more from **Karl
Marx** than from anyone else he has read. Marx, Mailer stresses,
"has something to say in every phrase."

Mailer followed Ernest Hemingway in creating a public
persona, and his early bullfight essays can be seen as direct
competition with "Papa." The Hemingway influence culminates in Mailer's volume *The Fight*, his artful reprise of
Hemingway's *Death in the Afternoon* in which Mailer achieves
renewed literary life for both Hemingway and himself through
Muhammad Ali. Mailer's work also shows the influence of
Walt Whitman (*Advertisements for Myself*) and Henry Miller.
In addition, *The Executioner's Song* can be read as Mailer's
Moby-Dick, with Gary Gilmore the white whale ultimately
eluding all social institutions and both Western and Eastern
voices.

Today a grey sage in his seventies, Mailer retains his intuitive, synthesizing daring. "Everything in society from the
largest social institution to those private intimate personal
moments, and the deepest mystical moments such as the onset
of death, might all be seen in their connections if one had the
courage to begin," he has observed. "You can never understand a writer until you find his private little vanity and mine
has always been that I will frustrate expectations. People think
they've found a way of dismissing me, but, like the mad butler
– I'll be back serving the meal."

BARBARA LOUNSBERRY

Biography

Norman Kingsley Mailer. Born 31 January 1923 in Long Branch,
New Jersey. Studied at Harvard University, Cambridge,
Massachusetts, 1939–43, S.B. (cum laude) in aeronautical
engineering, 1943; the Sorbonne, Paris, 1947. Married Beatrice
Silverman, 1944 (divorced, 1951): one daughter. Sergeant in the
United States Army, 1944–46. Married Adèle Morales, 1954
(divorced, 1961): two daughters. Contributing editor, *Dissent*,
1954; cofounder, 1955, and columnist, 1956, *Village Voice*;
columnist of "Big Bite," *Esquire*, 1962–63, and of "Responses
and Reactions," *Commentary*, 1962–63. Married Lady Jeanne
Campbell, 1962 (divorced, 1963): one daughter; married Beverly
Bentley, 1963 (divorced, 1979): two sons. Arrested for anti-war
protest at the Pentagon, October 1967. Member of the Executive
Board, 1968–73, and President, 1985–86, PEN American Center;
ran unsuccessfully for Mayor of New York City, 1969. Married
Carol Stevens, 1980 (divorced, 1980); married Barbara Norris
Church, 1980: three children. Awards: National Book Award,
for nonfiction, 1969; Pulitzer Prize, for nonfiction, 1969,
1980; MacDowell Medal, 1973; National Arts Club Medal,
1976; Emerson-Thoreau Medal, 1989; honorary degree from
Rutgers University. Member, American Academy,
1985.

Selected Writings

Essays and Related Prose
Advertisements for Myself, 1959
The Presidential Papers, 1963
Cannibals and Christians, 1966
The Bullfight, 1967
*The Idol and the Octopus: Political Writings on the Kennedy and
    Johnson Administrations*, 1968
The Armies of the Night: History as a Novel, the Novel as History,
    1968
*Miami and the Siege of Chicago: An Informal History of the
    Republican and Democratic Conventions of 1968*, 1968
Of a Fire on the Moon, 1971; as *A Fire on the Moon*, 1971
King of the Hill: On the Fight of the Century, 1971
The Prisoner of Sex, 1971
The Long Patrol: 25 Years of Writing, edited by Robert F. Lucid,
    1971
St. George and the Godfather, 1972
Existential Errands, 1972; in *The Essential Mailer*, 1982
Marilyn: A Novel Biography, 1973; enlarged edition, 1975
The Faith of Graffiti, 1974; as *Watching My Name Go By*, 1975
The Fight, 1975
Some Honorable Men: Political Conventions 1960–1972, 1976
*Genius and Lust: A Journey Through the Major Writings of Henry
    Miller*, 1976
The Executioner's Song: A True Life Novel, 1979
Of Women and Their Elegance, 1980
The Essential Mailer, 1982
Pieces and Pontifications, 1982
Oswald's Tale: An American Mystery, 1995
Portrait of Picasso as a Young Man: An Interpretive Biography,
    1995

Other writings: ten novels (*The Naked and the Dead*, 1948;
Barbary Shore, 1951; *The Deer Park*, 1955; *An American Dream*,
1965; *Why Are We in Vietnam?*, 1967; *A Transit to Narcissus*,
1978; *Ancient Evenings*, 1983; *Tough Guys Don't Dance*, 1984;
Harlot's Ghost, 1991; *The Gospel According to the Son*, 1997),
short stories, poetry, screenplays, and a play.

Bibliography
Adams, Laura, *Norman Mailer: A Comprehensive Bibliography*,
    Metuchen, New Jersey: Scarecrow Press, 1974

Further Reading
Adams, Laura, *Existential Battles: The Growth of Norman Mailer*,
    Athens: Ohio University Press, 1976
Adams, Laura, *Will the Real Norman Mailer Please Stand
    Up*, Port Washington, New York: Kennikat Press, 1974
Anderson, Chris, "Norman Mailer: The Record of a War," in his
    Style as Argument: Contemporary American Nonfiction,
    Carbondale: Southern Illinois University Press, 1987: 82–132
Begiebing, Robert J., *Acts of Regeneration: Allegory and Archetype
    in the Works of Norman Mailer*, Columbia: University of
    Missouri Press, 1980
Bloom, Harold, editor, *Norman Mailer: Modern Critical Views*,
    New York: Chelsea House, 1986
Braudy, Leo, editor, *Norman Mailer: A Collection of Critical
    Essays*, Englewood Cliffs, New Jersey: Prentice Hall, 1972
Bufithis, Philip H., *Norman Mailer*, New York: Ungar, 1978
Ehrlich, Robert, *Norman Mailer: The Radical as Hipster*, Metuchen,
    New Jersey: Scarecrow Press, 1978
Flaherty, Joe, *Managing Mailer*, New York: Coward McCann, and
    London: Michael Joseph, 1970
Foster, Richard, *Norman Mailer*, Minneapolis: University of
    Minnesota Press, 1968

Hellmann, John, "Journalism as Nonfiction: Norman Mailer's Strategy for Mimesis and Interpretation," in his *Fables of Fact: The New Journalism as New Fiction*, Athens: Ohio University Press, 1980: 35–65

Hollowell, John, "Mailer's Vision: History as a Novel, the Novel as History," in his *Fact and Fiction: The New Journalism and the Nonfiction Novel*, Chapel Hill: University of North Carolina Press, 1977: 87–125

Lennon, J. Michael, editor, *Critical Essays on Norman Mailer*, Boston: Hall, 1986

Lounsberry, Barbara, "Norman Mailer's Ages of Man," in her *The Art of Fact: Contemporary Artists of Nonfiction*, New York: Greenwood Press, 1990

Lucid, Robert F., editor, *Norman Mailer: The Man and His Work*, Boston: Little Brown, 1971

Manso, Peter, editor, *Mailer: His Life and Times*, New York: Simon and Schuster, 1985

Merrill, Robert, *Norman Mailer Revisited*, Boston: Twayne, 1992

Mills, Hilary, *Mailer: A Biography*, New York: Empire, 1982

Radford, Jean, *Norman Mailer: A Critical Study*, New York: Barnes and Noble, 1975

Stone, Albert E., "Factual Fictions: Experiments in Autobiography by Norman Mailer, Frank Conroy, Lillian Hellman," in his *Autobiographical Occasions and Original Acts: Versions of American Identity from Henry Adams to Nate Shaw*, Philadelphia: University of Pennsylvania Press, 1982: 265–324

Wenke, Joseph, *Mailer's America*, Hanover, New Hampshire: University Press of New England, 1987

Mallarmé, Stéphane

French, 1842–1898

In all his writing, prose or poetry, Stéphane Mallarmé is concerned less with what he terms the wonder of transposing a fact of nature than with extracting from it "the pure notion," so that whether his subject is theater or music, ballet or literature, he sets his reader the task of reading creatively, one that parallels the writer's need to penetrate the enigmas posed by social and natural phenomena. Originally published in a wide array of periodicals, from the American *Chap-Book* to the *Revue Wagnérienne* (Wagnerian review), from *La Plume* (The pen) to what he termed "the inimitable" *National Observer*, Mallarmé's essays subsequently appeared in volumes with such self-deprecating titles as *Divagations* (Ramblings), *Pages*, or, simply, *Prose*. The modesty of these titles is typical of him: while his essays are based on the unflinching premise of the supremacy of poetry and the value of the mind, they do not pontificate or condescend, but invite the reader to enter into a creative partnership, an intellectual debate. His jewel-like, often fragmentary, formulations are witty and suggestive rather than explicit and pedagogic, and the initial stimulus – a mime or a book, for instance – usually appears only briefly, transformed into the springboard for a far more wide-ranging meditation on art and thought.

Two pieces written in the 1860s reveal the revolutionary nature of his early aesthetic thinking and point forward to convictions he was to formulate more cryptically in later years. In "Hérésies artistiques – L'Art pour tous" (1862; Artistic heresies – art for all), the young poet argues that "all that is sacred and wishes to remain so envelops itself in mystery." Poetry alone is forced to use a language open to all, printed in the characters used by newspapers and political polemics rather than locked away behind the golden padlocks of old missals or the "inviolate hieroglyphs of papyrus rolls." Mallarmé's argument here moves poetry away from the didactic and sacerdotal role certain 19th-century poets had given it and toward the hermetic and the ludic that marks the Modernist concept of art.

His "Symphonie littéraire" (1865; Literary symphony) is a triptych, in which he responds to the work of three seminal poets of the time, **Baudelaire**, Théophile Gautier, and Théodore de Banville, not in the analytical mode of most contemporary critics but with the kind of passionate attempt to re-create each poet's imaginary vision that also marks the best of Baudelaire's literary criticism. Thus, for Baudelaire he imagines a landscape stripped of all vegetation except a few trees, "whose painful bark is an interweaving of exposed nerves: their *visible* growth is constantly accompanied, despite the strange immobility of the air, by a heart-rending complaint, like that of violins, which, when it reaches the end of each branch, trembles in musical leaves."

The same desire to enter into the intellectual and imaginary world of his subject marks the numerous pen portraits he wrote to celebrate contemporary poets, artists, and musicians. Typical of these is his evocation of his close friend, the novelist and playwright Auguste Villiers de l'Isle Adam. In this essay – which begins, famously, with the haunting sentence, "A man accustomed to dream comes here to speak of another, who is dead" – Mallarmé characteristically maintains a careful balance between the evocation of the individual, the author of *Axël* (1886) and *L'Ève future* (1886; Tomorrow's Eve) whose great desire, Mallarmé surmises, was to "reign," and his study of the writer as representative. Posing the question "Do we know what it means to write?" he offers an elliptical answer which allows the rest of his study of Villiers to be seen as an expanded response to the same challenge: "An ancient and very vague but jealous practice, whose meaning lies in the heart's mysteries." James McNeill Whistler, too, is at once presented as the archetypal painter, "the enchanter of a work of mystery, as tightly closed as perfection itself, which the mob would pass by without even feeling hostility toward it," and summed up in terms that brilliantly recall that arrogant, difficult, and highly gifted man: "a Dragon, battling, exulting, precious and worldly."

That oscillation between the apparent and the broader subject of an essay is also very much present in "Crayonné au théâtre" (1887; Scribbled in the theater) and in "Variations sur un sujet" (1895; Variations on a subject). Hamlet, for instance, is both Shakespeare's character and the "juvenile shadow of us all, thus embodying a myth." The ballerina is not "*a woman who dances*, for these combined reasons that she *is not a woman* but a metaphor resuming one of the elementary aspects of our form, dagger, chalice, flower, etc. and that *she does not dance*, suggesting, with a bodily writing, through the miracle of leaps and bounds, what in prose would take paragraphs of dialogue or description: she is a poem set free from all the paraphernalia needed by a scribe."

Best known, no doubt, among Mallarmé's essays are those written in response partly to the upsurge in popularity of Wagner's concept of art, and partly to the fashion for free verse. Initially given as lectures in Oxford and Cambridge, "La Musique et les lettres" (1894; Music and letters), together with its companion pieces, "Crise de vers" (1897; Crisis of poetry) and "Quant au livre" (1897; Concerning the book), has come to be regarded as a seminal text in the development of aesthetic thinking. Among the most challenging of his prose pieces, these meditations on the function of art contain some of Mallarmé's finest, if most elliptical, formulations on the function of the symbol, the role of personal experience, and the play of language. Since, Mallarmé argues, the poet is condemned to pursue black on white even when describing the luminosity of the stars against their black background, the reader is constantly invited to take the "dark lace" that art offers and make of it, from his or her own experience, vast networks containing a treasure trove of images. In order to illuminate truth, Mallarmé implies, one must put the lamp aside and work in darkness. That too is the task of the reader who embarks on Mallarmé's essays. While they can occasionally be precious in both senses of the word, they are above all challenging, stimulating, and endlessly rewarding.

ROSEMARY LLOYD

Biography

Born Étienne Mallarmé, 18 March 1842 in Paris. Studied at the Lycée Impérial, Sens, 1856–60, baccalauréat, 1860. Traveled to London, 1862–63. Married Marie Christina Gerhard, 1863: one son (died, 1879) and one daughter. Taught English in Tournon, 1863–66, Besançon, 1866–67, Avignon, 1867–70, Lycée Fontanes, Paris, 1871–74, Lycée Janson-de-Sailly, Paris, 1884–85, and Collège Rollin, Paris, 1885–93. Editor and contributor, La Dernière Mode (The last style), 1874–75. Elected to the French Academy, 1883. Liaison with Méry Laurent, late 1880s. Died (as a result of choking) at Valvins, 9 September 1898.

Selected Writings

Essays and Related Prose
Album de vers et de prose, 1887
Pages, 1891
Vers et prose, 1893
Divagations, 1897; edited by E. M. Souffrin, 1949
Selected Prose Poems, Essays and Letters, translated by Bradford Cook, 1956
Écrits sur le livre (selections), 1985

Other writings: several volumes of poetry (including L'Après-midi d'un faune [Afternoon of a Faun], 1876) and correspondence.

Collected works editions: Œuvres complètes (Pléiade Edition), edited by Henri Mondor and G. Jean-Aubry, 1945; Œuvres complètes, edited by Carl Paul Barbier and Charles Gordon Millan, vol. 1, 1983 (in progress; 3 vols. projected).

Bibliography

Morris, D. Hampton, Stéphane Mallarmé, Twentieth-Century Criticism (1901–1971) and (1972–1979), University: University of Mississippi Romance Monographs, 2 vols., 1977–89

Further Reading

Austin, Lloyd James, Poetic Principles and Practice, Cambridge: Cambridge University Press, 1987
Balakian, Anna, The Symbolist Movement: A Critical Appraisal, New York: New York University Press, 1977
Bersani, Leo, The Death of Stéphane Mallarmé, Cambridge: Cambridge University Press, 1982
Cohn, Robert Greer, Mallarmé's "Divagations": A Guide and Commentary, New York: Lang, 1990
Fowlie, Wallace, Mallarmé, Chicago: University of Chicago Press, 1953
Kravis, Judy, The Prose of Mallarmé: The Evolution of a Literary Language, Cambridge: Cambridge University Press, 1976
Lawler, James, The Language of French Symbolism, Princeton, New Jersey: Princeton University Press, 1969
Lloyd, Rosemary, Mallarmé: Poésies, London: Grant and Cutler, 1984
Marchal, Bertrand, La Religion de Mallarmé: Poésie, mythologie, et religion, Paris: Corti, 1988
Marvick, Louis Wirth, Mallarmé and the Sublime, Albany: State University of New York Press, 1986
Michaud, Guy, Mallarmé, Paris: Hatier, 1971
Millan, Gordon, The Throw of the Dice: The Life of Stéphane Mallarmé, London: Secker and Warburg, and New York: Farrar Straus Giroux, 1994
Paxton, Norman, The Development of Mallarmé's Prose Style, Geneva: Droz, 1968
St. Aubyn, Frederic Chase, Stéphane Mallarmé, Boston: Twayne, revised edition, 1989

Mallea, Eduardo

Argentine, 1903–1982

Although Eduardo Mallea is better known today by the general reading public as a novelist and short-story writer, the impact his essays had among Argentine readers in the 1930s and 1940s was extensive. His Historia de una pasión argentina (1937; History of an Argentine Passion), which became a bestseller soon after publication, received enthusiastic commentaries by the most promising writers of the period, like Horacio Rega Molina and Leopoldo Marechal, as well as laudatory reviews from well-known intellectuals, especially from the liberal sector of Argentine letters, such as Bernardo Canal Feijóo, José Bianco, and Luis Emilio Soto.

The history of Latin American essays shows, throughout the works of its major figures – **Andrés Bello, Domingo Faustino Sarmiento, José Martí, José Enrique Rodó, José Carlos Mariátegui,** and **José Vasconcelos,** to mention only a few – a constant intellectual effort to achieve a satisfactory formulation of what it means to be Latin American and a self-explanatory definition of the specificity of the New World (americanidad). Mallea's writings fit naturally into this broader tradition since the unity of his thinking comes from a permanent preoccupation with defining the essence of Argentina and leading his compatriots to a true understanding of argentinidad, a term coined by Ricardo Rojas in works like La restauración nacionalista (1909; Nationalist restoration), Blasón de plata (1912; Argentine blazon), La argentinidad (1916; Argentineness), and Eurindia (1924).

While other Latin American essayists dealt with regional issues such as the situation of the native population, the problem of colonial heritage, or the consequences of economic imperialism, Mallea approached the issue in less sociohistorical terms. In Conocimiento y expresión de la Argentina (Knowledge and expression of Argentina), the text of a lecture the author read in Italy in 1934 and that was published the following year under the imprint of the Argentine journal Sur (South), Mallea sustains the theory that, to be able to express themselves, Latin Americans need first to develop a form of self-consciousness that takes into account the particularities of their human condition. According to his description, Argentina is characterized by the presence of an immense plain and a small population. The blend of both factors results in the taciturn and melancholic mood that is usually attributed to Argentines. Although the necessary search for self-knowledge is thought to be less an individual quest and more a process in which all Argentines should be involved, only the members of an intellectual elite are really committed to attaining such a consciousness.

Mallea further developed these ideas in his next and most renowned essay, *History of an Argentine Passion*, a book-length text where autobiographical and narrative elements intertwine to advance the writer's insights about national identity. According to Mallea, during the first decades of the century Argentina went through a process of denaturalization, in which the people moved further and further away from the ideals of the founders of the country. The symptom of this "degeneracy" or "weakening" of true Argentine values is the lack of moral, historic, intellectual, and even human conscience that Mallea notices among the majority of his contemporaries. The reason for these changes is to be found in the blending of the traditional inhabitants and the most recent wave of immigrants, who introduced a different set of values, thus substituting authentic life with a representation of life, a superficially satisfactory existence oriented toward appearance and lacking in spirituality. As a consequence, there exist two Argentinas cohabiting the same space: one visible, which stands for unfounded values (artificiality, materialism, and shallowness), and another one, invisible, which preserves the genuine spirit of the country, its authentic though submerged ideals. Mallea believes that some members of the younger generation, such as himself, are deeply concerned with the present situation and are striving to recuperate the two main traits of Argentineness: its sense of giving and its devotion to freedom.

The essays contained in *Meditación en la costa* (1939; Meditation by the seaside), *El sayal y la púrpura* (1941; The sackcloth and the purple), and *La vida blanca* (wr. 1942, pub. 1960; The white life) are closely related to the same search for Argentina's true identity. The first, in the form of an introspective monologue, leads the essayist to the conclusion that Argentina, in its own process of national formation, was responding to European societal deformation which had been spreading for decades. Although recognizing the importance of economic prosperity, the writer reaffirms the idea that the key to a valid humanity is rooted in the nature and inner structure of the people.

In *El sayal y la púrpura* Mallea brings together several essays previously published in the journals *Sur* and *Realidad* (Reality). He analyzes different aspects of the contemporary situation: the widespread sensation of emptiness and failure that affects the world, the crisis of rationalism and the advent of existentialism, and the militant role of intellectuals who are supposed to assume responsibility for the destiny of humankind. Under these circumstances, it is time for America to rise up and share with the rest of the world its essential characteristics: simplicity, spontaneity, and humanity.

The metaphor of the title of *La vida blanca* is meant to express a colorless life, one of pretending rather than being.

This essay implies a different approach to Mallea's obsessive topic. The author takes stock of his former confidence in the spiritual qualities of the new Argentine generation, and comes to realize the futility of those expectations.

Belonging to an intellectualizing generation, Mallea developed a personal style that combines a rhetoric occasionally saturated with emotional overtones and a metaphorical and florid expression. At his best, Mallea is able to pursue his ontological quest in an exalted and deeply poetical style, but often his writing becomes wordy and overloaded with synonymous circumlocutions.

As an example of the work of a liberal intellectual, concerned with the definition of national identity and the condition of humankind in the modern world, Mallea's essays served as a literary model for an entire generation of Argentine writers. Historical distance, changes in interest and in the definition of social, historical, and ethical problems, and the radicalization of Argentine intellectuals have left his production on the margins of present concerns. Nevertheless, his writings continue to constitute a valuable document for the understanding of a major phase in Latin American cultural development.

DANIEL ALTAMIRANDA

Biography

Born 14 August 1903 in Bahía Blanca, Argentina. Studied law at the University of Buenos Aires. Cofounder, *Revista de América* (American review), 1921; contributed to several other journals, including *Sur*, from 1934; staff member, from 1928, and editor of literary supplement, 1931–35, *La Nación*. Traveled to Europe, 1928, 1934. Married Helena Muñiz Larreta, 1944. UNESCO delegate for Argentina, Paris, 1955–58, and New Delhi, 1956. Argentine Ambassador to France, 1955–58. Elected to the Argentine Academy of Letters, 1960. Awards: many, including First National Prize of Letters, 1945; Argentine Association of Writers Grand Prize of Honor, 1946; Grand National Prize of the Arts, 1970. Died in Buenos Aires, 12 November 1982.

Selected Writings

Essays and Related Prose

Conocimiento y expresión de la Argentina, 1935
Historia de una pasión argentina, 1937; as *History of an Argentine Passion*, translated by Myron I. Lichtblau, 1983
Meditación en la costa, 1939
El sayal y la púrpura, 1941
Notas de un novelista, 1954
La vida blanca, 1960
Las travesías, 2 vols., 1961–62
Poderío de la novela, 1965

Other writings: 10 novels (including *La bahía de silencio* [*The Bay of Silence*], 1940; *Todo verdor perecerá* [*All Green Shall Perish*], 1941), six collections of short stories, and two plays.

Collected works editions: *Obras completas*, 2 vols., 1961–65, and 1986– (in progress).

Further Reading

Earle, Peter G., and Robert G. Mead, *Historia del ensayo hispanoamericano*, Mexico City: Andrea, 1973
Lewald, H. Ernest, *Eduardo Mallea*, Boston: Twayne, 1977

Pintor Genaro, Mercedes, *Eduardo Mallea, novelista*, Río Piedras: University of Puerto Rico, 1976

Polt, John H. R., *The Writings of Eduardo Mallea*, Berkeley: University of California Press, 1959

Rivelli, Carmen, *Eduardo Mallea: La continuidad temática de su obra*, New York: Las Américas, 1969

Stabb, Martin S., *In Quest of Identity: Patterns in the Spanish American Essay of Ideas, 1890–1960*, Chapel Hill: University of North Carolina Press, 1967

Topete, José Manuel, "Eduardo Mallea y el laberinto de la agonía: *Historia de una pasión argentina*," *Revista Iberoamericana* 20, no. 39 (1955): 117–51

Villordo, Oscar Hermes, *Genio y figura de Eduardo Mallea*, Buenos Aires: Eudeba, 1973

Mandel'shtam, Osip

Russian, 1891–1938

Chronologically and thematically, Osip Mandel'shtam's essays reflect the three distinctive phases in his brief but intense life as a major poet and seminal figure in 20th-century Russian cultural life: the youthful prerevolutionary years as a student and Acmeist poet; the soul-searching and gradual turning away from verse to prose during the 1920s; and the mature years of the Stalinist 1930s as a time of spiritual renewal and rebellion, mental and physical hardship, arrest and exile, as well as his most complex and powerful essays and two-thirds of his verse. His output as both poet and essayist was slim, the result of artistic, personal, and political restrictions. Stylistically, two modes of expression dominate the essays: the dense metaphorical style evocative of the problematics of poetry and culture, and focused on "the word" (*logos*) as the condensed verbal manifestation of cultural continuity, and the polemical rhetoric invoked to assess and attack the state of contemporary arts, culture, and the literary establishment.

Mandel'shtam's career as an essayist began while a student of Romance languages and philosophy in Heidelberg. In 1910, his first essay, "François Villon," identified his mentors, Villon and Verlaine, with an "astronomical miracle" and epochal "mission" analogous to his own inchoate Acmeism. Praising their revolt against "artificial, hothouse poetry," he defined poetry's function as the actualization of the human experience in all its precision, vitality, and complexity, and juxtaposed the poet's capacity "to wield precise details" against the "suggestive hints" of the symbolists. Poetic craft, he claimed, made "the passing moment ... endure the pressure of centuries."

"François Villon" appeared along with his fellow Acmeists' prose and verse manifestos in 1913 in Nicolai Gumilev's Acmeist organ, *Apollon* (Apollo). Another essay, "Utro Akmeizma" (1913; "Morning of Acmeism"), emphasized semantic consciousness as the ultimate "reality," employed mathematical and architectural metaphors to "restrain" the "immense emotional excitement associated with works of art," and underscored both the historicity and continuity of art's highest forms, the "acme" of human creativity. The poet's synthesis of the common cultural experience into dynamic verbal forms, he asserted, reveals monuments of the past as impulses and vehicles of awe and surprise, concrete reminders of the "blessed legacy" of world culture conjoining the artists and monuments of all time.

"O sobesednike" (1913; "On the Addressee") presents Mandel'shtam's theory that a genuine poem is a letter to a future "providential addressee," while the prose essay engages the contemporary reader directly in a conscious interpretation of the world in motion: "the prose writer is compelled to stand 'higher' than ... society, since instruction is the central nerve of prose ..." Analytical skepticism is emphasized as a function of both logic and rhetoric.

Essays on the problematics of Russian culture begin with "Zametki o Shen'e" (1915; "Remarks on Chenier") and "Peter Chaadaev" (1915). The Russian philosopher's journey to the West and his independent decision to return home is reinterpreted as a paradigm of moral commitment for future Russian thinkers and writers. His vibrant self-image of the "*raznochinets*-author" (the *raznochintsi* were 19th-century Russian intellectuals who were not of noble origin) grows out of Chaadaev's ideal of his "sacred obligation" to express Russia's legacy of moral freedom.

If the early essays focus on the basic aesthetic and cultural vision of Acmeism, the poetics of cultural continuity and memory, and the expression of poetic freedom, those of the early 1920s raise the central question of the poet's relationship to the new Soviet age: the complexity of allegiance to the Revolution without sacrificing moral conscience and humanistic values. For example, "Slovo i kul'tura" (1921; "Word and Culture") seeks to redefine the role of culture in the new Soviet State, emphasizing its dependence on the "sacred power of the word." "Culture has become the church" and "cultural values ornament the State, endowing it with color, form, and if you will, gender." "O prirode slova" (1922; "On the Nature of the Word"), a paean to the Russian language, endeavors to synthesize the basic tenets of Acmeism with a broader, more metaphysically-oriented aesthetic vision, simultaneously broadening the role of civic and moral obligation. "Buria i natisk" (1923; "Storm and Stress") seeks to redefine the relationship between the culture of the recent past and the present, symbolism and futurism, by "knitting together the spines of two poetic systems, two poetic epochs."

Mandel'shtam is at his finest when his logic is discursive and indirect, his ideas correlated through rich and striking images rather than predetermined by patterns of logical subordination. A powerful interpretive design challenging the reader to rethink conventional concepts and prescribed paths grows out of his active engagement in the critical discourse of his argument and the seductive literariness of metaphor. For example, "Humanizm i sovremennost'" (1923; "Humanism and the Present") offers a conception of the ideal society, a new "social Gothic," which turns out to have the same structure as an ideal building or poem. An optimistic view of the Revolution is implicit in this ideal: just as the stone or the word must maintain and fulfill its individual creative self, so it must be a part of a collective "we," a social architecture, to best realize its potential. However, this vision of harmony is preceded by a prophetic warning: a contrasting cruel and formidable vision of inhumanity in human society, a recollection of epochs when individual life was crushed by the social architecture and treated as insignificant: "Assyrian prisoners swarm like baby chicks under the feet of an enormous king ..."

Mandel'shtam's Jewish thematics, which first emerge in the essays in 1926 ("Mikhoels," "Kiev"), are further developed in the 1930s in association with the image of the outsider, the "*raznochinets*-writer." Mikhoels, the spirit of Judaism, is described as "All the power of Judaism, all the rhythm of abstract ideas in dance . . . whose single motive is compassion for the earth – all this extends into the trembling of the hands, the vibration of the thinking fingers, animated like articulated speech."

The essays of the 1930s dramatically transform the view of the poet's place in society. Nadezhda Mandel'shtam, the poet's widow, credited his unpublishable jeremiad, "Chetvertaia proza" (wr. 1929–30; "Fourth Prose"), with returning the poet to health, reconfirming his faith in his creative powers, reasserting his demands for intellectual freedom, and paving the way for the verse of the *Voronezhskie tetradi* (wr. 1930–37; Voronezh notebooks) and the prose of "Puteshestvie v Armeniiu" (wr. 1930–32; "Journey to Armenia") and *Razgovor o Dante* (wr. 1933; "Conversation About Dante"). "Fourth Prose" gave new force to the self-image of the outsider and outcast as the voice of moral and spiritual freedom. The Jewish pathos and "compassion for the earth" is superimposed on the image of the "*raznochinets*-writer" and his ideal of moral freedom as "sacred obligation." Envisioning himself carrying his "Jewish staff" to Armenia, "the younger sister of the Jewish nation," as Chaadaev carried his staff to Rome, Mandel'shtam invokes the Mosaic law "Thou shalt not kill!" as his fundamental moral and aesthetic principle, excoriating and exorcising the entire literary establishment as the forces of death and destruction.

His last published essay, "Journey to Armenia," a philosophical travelogue, is simultaneously a hymn to the gift of life and language, the struggle against death, and the grace of spiritual resurrection. Armenia is his metaphor for Mediterranean or world culture and cultural memory.

"Conversation About Dante," Mandel'shtam's unique and intimate tribute to his Florentine mentor as the "first internal *raznochinets*," culminates his career as an essayist. It is his supreme apologia for poetic freedom and challenge to the establishment. Unpublishable until the mid-1960s, it reiterates and reformulates the poetics of cultural memory and cultural synchrony. Dense metaphors synthesizing physiological and philological essences reinvigorate his style, demonstrating precisely how the poet is "a master of the instruments of poetry" and how an impulse in the mind of the creative artist is realized as living verbal expression.

JANE GARY HARRIS

Biography

Osip Emil'evich Mandel'shtam. Born 15 January 1891 in Warsaw; moved to St. Petersburg as an infant. Studied at the Tenishev Commercial School, St. Petersburg, 1899–1907; studied in Paris, 1907–08; University of Heidelberg, 1909–10; attended meetings of **Viacheslav Ivanov**'s Bashnia (Tower) group and the St. Petersburg Society of Philosophy; enrolled at the University of St. Petersburg: never graduated. First poems published, 1910; joined the Guild of Poets, 1911. Married Nadezhda Iakovlevna Khazina, 1922. Translated Petrarch, Henri Barbier, Jules Romains, Old French literature, and other works. Traveled to Georgia and Armenia, April–November 1930. Moved to Moscow, December 1930. Lived in Koktebel', Summer 1933. Arrested twice: first for writing a poem critical of Stalin, May 1934: sentence of hard labor commuted to exile in Cherdyn and later Voronezh, ending 1937; second arrest for "counterrevolutionary activities," May 1938: sentenced to five years in a labor camp. Died in a transit camp at Vtoraia rechka, near Vladivostock, 27 December 1938 (official date on certificate).

Selected Writings

Essays and Related Prose
O poezii (On poetry), 1928
Prose, edited and translated by Clarence Brown, 1965; revised editions, 1967, and as *The Noise of Time and Other Prose Pieces*, 1986
Razgovor o Dante, edited by A. A. Morozov, 1967; as "Conversation About Dante," translated by Jane Gary Harris, in *The Complete Critical Prose and Letters*, 1979
Selected Essays, edited and translated by Sidney Monas, 1977
The Complete Critical Prose and Letters, edited by Jane Gary Harris, translated by Harris and Constance Link, 1979; as *The Collected Critical Prose and Letters*, 1991
Slovo i kul'tura: O poezii; Razgovor o Dante; Stat'i, retsenzii (Word and culture; On poetry; Conversation about Dante; articles, reviews) edited by S. Vasilenko, Iu. Freidin, and P. Nerler, 1987
Stikhotvoreniia; Perevody; Ocherki; Stat'i (Poetry; translations; essays; articles), 1990
Chetvertaia proza; Ocherki, sbornik (Fourth prose; essays; notebook), 1991

Other writings: several collections of poetry and five notebooks of poems unpublished during his lifetime.

Collected works editions: *Sobranie sochinenii*, edited by Gleb Struve and Boris Filippov, 1955, and in 4 vols., 1967–81; vol. 1 revised, 1967; vol. 2 revised, 1971; *Sochineniia*, edited by P. M. Nerler, 2 vols., 1990; *Sobranie sochinenii*, 4 vols., 1993–94.

Further Reading

Brown, Clarence, *Osip Mandelstam*, Cambridge: Cambridge University Press, 1973
Cavanagh, Clare, *Osip Mandelstam and the Modernist Creation of Tradition*, Princeton, New Jersey: Princeton University Press, 1995
Freidin, Gregory, *A Coat of Many Colors: Osip Mandelstam and His Mythologies of Self-Presentation*, Berkeley: University of California Press, 1987
Harris, Jane Gary, *Osip Mandelstam*, Boston: Twayne, 1988
Levin, Iu. I., "Zametki k Razgovor o Dante O. Mandel'shtama," *International Journal of Linguistics and Poetics* 15 (1972)
Mandel'shtam, Nadezhda, *Hope Against Hope: A Memoir*, New York: Atheneum, 1970; London: Harvill Press, 1971
Mandel'shtam, Nadezhda, *Hope Abandoned*, New York: Atheneum, and London: Harvill Press, 1974
Mandel'shtam, Nadezhda, *Kniga tret'ia*, Paris: YMCA Press, 1987
O. E. Mandel'shtam, *"I ty, Moskva, sestra moia, legka . . ." Stikhi, proza, vospominaniia, materialy k biografii: Venok Mandel'shtamu*, Moscow: Moskovskii Rabochii, 1990
Osip Mandel'shtam: K 100-letiiu so dnia rozhdeniia: Poetika i tekstologiia: Materialy nauchnoi konferentsii 27–29 dekabria 1991 g., Moscow: Gnosis, 1992
Pollak, Nancy, *Mandelstam the Reader*, Baltimore: Johns Hopkins University Press, 1995
Ronen, Omry, *An Approach to Mandelstam*, Jerusalem: Magnes Press, 1983
Ronen, Omry, "O 'russkom golose' Osipa Mandel'shtama," in *Tynianovskii sbornik: Piatye Tynianovskie chteniia*, Riga: Zinatne, 1994
Shtempel', N. E., "Mandel'shtam v Voronezhe," *Novyi Mir* 10 (1987): 207–34
Slovo i sud'ba: Osip Mandel'shtam: Issledovaniia i materialy, edited by P. Nerler and others, Moscow: Nauka, 1991

Stoletie Mandel'shtama: Materialy simpoziuma: Mandel'shtam Centenary Conference (SEES, London 1991), edited by Robin Aizlewood and Diana Myers, Tenafly, New Jersey: Hermitage Press, 1994

Zhizn' i tvorchestvo O. E. Mandel'shtama, edited by O. G. Lasunskii and others, Voronezh: Izd. Voronezhskogo Universiteta, 1990

Mann, Heinrich

German, 1871–1950

Like his more famous younger brother **Thomas Mann**, Heinrich Mann all his life accompanied his creative writing with the writing of essays. But unlike Thomas, Heinrich divided his interests roughly equally between literary-cultural essays and essays in which not only is a political viewpoint presented, but politics becomes the central theme. While Thomas remained firmly planted in the Germanic world, and found his materials primarily in the traditions of Weimar classicism (**Goethe, Schiller**), Romanticism, and the 19th century, Heinrich Mann's interests were cosmopolitan, oriented toward Western Europe, and especially toward France as the greatest exponent of Enlightenment and the liberal, later also socialist tradition. It is essential to understand this background when considering much of his essay output.

A second, even more crucial precondition for understanding these writings is an acquaintance with German history. Mann was an astute observer of sociopolitical as well as cultural and intellectual developments, a fearless polemicist, and a tireless activist. Over the span of his career, he moved from moderately conservative middle-class opinions to a strong commitment to democracy and various forms of socialism, even communism.

None of this is evident, however, in Mann's earliest essays, written between 1897 and 1904, though the pieces concerned with literature already show a preference for French writers. The 33 articles Mann wrote for the journal *Das zwanzigste Jahrhundert* (The 20th century) are surprisingly conservative and anti-Semitic, voiced in language closer to later Nazi polemics than to socialist humanism.

It is in the period between 1904 and the outbreak of World War I that a profound change in perspective in Mann's writing can be observed. Mann's transition to a strongly republican viewpoint is inspired partly, beginning in 1905, by his reading of **Rousseau**. In *Eine Freundschaft: Gustave Flaubert und George Sand* (1905; A friendship: Gustave Flaubert and George Sand) Mann begins his critique of bourgeois society, and initiates his series of positive examples of socially and morally engaged writers. "Französischer Geist" (1910; The spirit of France; later called "Goethe-Voltaire") draws a contrast between an Enlightenment France and a regressive Germany, a distinction that will become a constant in his essays. In "Geist und Tat" (1911; Spirit and action), a first high point in his essay oeuvre, Mann compares the dynamism, engagement, and moral standpoint of French literature represented by **Voltaire**, Rousseau, and Zola with the unpolitical, powerless, regressive literature of Germany exemplified by **Nietzsche**, Goethe, **Hofmannsthal**, Rilke, and George. The essay had an immediate impact on the expressionists, at the time the most

important group of progressive young writers, who read "Geist und Tat" as a call to arms against the prevalent ivory-tower mentality and politically compromised position of most writers. Mann became the most influential voice for a socially and politically engaged literature.

The outbreak of World War I confirmed what Mann had been warning against; the enthusiasm with which many people greeted the war in fact led to his most polemical writings about German culture in general, and the role of its writers in particular. It inspired Mann to write yet another defense of French over German values, "Zola" (1915), considered by many critics to be the most powerful of his essays. Using the earlier French period as a foil for present-day German conditions, Mann also indirectly attacks the exploitative attitudes of capitalists and industrialists which have led to the war. The essay caused a temporary rupture between the brothers Mann, since Thomas, who had written in defense of the war, felt personally attacked. Ultimately more important in this quarrel was the debate about the definition of the role of the modern writer; Thomas' denigrating term "Zivilisationsliterat" (cultural journalist) applied to his brother was soon worn as a badge of honor by Heinrich.

The ambivalent end of the war and the revolution of 1918 by necessity dictated that Heinrich would continue writing about political events. In a series of essays, collected in 1919 as *Macht und Mensch* (Power and the individual), Mann came out in defense of the fledgling Weimar Republic, in favor of socialism, and against what could soon be seen as restorative forces. Essays such as "Kaiserreich und Republik" (1919; Empire and republic) provide an analysis of the vanished empire in the light of idealist-utopian goals incorporated in the new constitution. Mann pleads for an end to class distinctions and capitalism, unfortunately making clear that he does not understand the complexities of the political situation; when it finally dawns on him that the restoration has already begun, his skepticism and despair become tangible in his essays. Thus, in the collection *Diktatur der Vernunft* (1923; The dictatorship of reason), Mann refers to the radicalism of both left and right ("Tragische Jugend" [1922; Tragic youth]), and rehearses the glaring contradictions of capitalism, the loss of freedom of the individual, and the fatal loss of faith in the possibility of democracy. Mann floats the idea of a "front of the people" against the forces of capitalism, and in an open letter to President Stresemann pleads for a "dictatorship of reason." Increasingly skeptical about conditions within Germany, he begins, partly inspired by his friendship with Felix Bertaux, to see in the cooperation between France and Germany the core of a new United States of Europe, the last possibility for peace and progress.

This period is characterized by a great variety in types of essayistic writings, from articles on major French authors such as Hugo, France, and Stendhal in the collection *Geist und Tat: Franzosen 1780–1930* (1931; Spirit and action: Frenchmen 1780–1930) to a large number of pieces for the newspaper *La Dépêche de Toulouse* (The Toulouse daily). Other political as well as cultural essays of this period were collected in *Sieben Jahre* (1929; Seven years), *Die geistige Lage* (1932; The intellectual situation), and *Das öffentliche Leben* (1932; Public life). In this period Mann became increasingly interested in popular culture as a counterweight to the elitist tendencies he observed around him.

Such considerations were of course overshadowed shortly by the growing power of National Socialism, which in 1933 led to his exile, first in France, then in the United States. Essays concerned with the struggles against fascism, written between 1932 and 1940, such as "Rüstung" (1932; Armament), "Die deutsche Entscheidung" (1932; The German decision), and "Hitler ist nicht Deutschland" (1932; Hitler is not Germany), appeared mostly in exile journals, but especially in Klaus Mann's *Die Sammlung* (The collection), published in Amsterdam. Perhaps the most important collection from this period, *Der Hass* (1933; Hatred), sets out to show how the cultivation of hatred as perpetrated by the Nazis must inevitably lead to the demise of civilization. Mann does not merely write polemical attacks on his enemies, however, but looks already beyond this phase in German history, and toward spiritual renewal.

Like many others, Mann was preoccupied by the question of guilt after World War II, writing about it in essays such as "Deutsche Schuld und Unschuld" (1943; German guilt or innocence), "Über Schuld und Erziehung" (1944; About guilt and education), and "Über den Widerstand" (1945; About the Resistance). "Lehren der deutsche Geschichte" (1949; Lessons of German history) and "Verfassung und reale Demokratie" (1947; Constitution and true democracy) reveal Mann's concern about the future of Germany. He was still involved with these questions when he debated a possible return to Germany: he was inclined to make East Germany his home, but his death on 12 March 1950 made a decision irrelevant.

Mann brought to the essay form some interesting personal elements. In his early essays, novelistic techniques are employed to enliven and dramatize the content; a typical example is the "Zola" essay. On other occasions his tone is factual, understated, even cool. The intellectual can always be felt, especially where an analysis of social or political dimensions is involved. On the other hand, he is never without passion where his convictions are concerned, and he often employs various forms of satire, from gentle to biting – as he does in his novels and novellas – to make his point. In collections such as *Der Hass* he excels at the quickly drawn portrait (in this case of prominent Nazis), whereas a distinctive rhetorical tone becomes audible in those essays which present arguments closest to his heart: those defending the ideals of the Enlightenment against all forms of obscurantism. Mann's range of writing is wide, the style always lively. The greatest impediment to its becoming more widely known is most likely its constant recourse to contemporary events and personalities not necessarily familiar to contemporary English-speaking readers.

AUGUSTINUS P. DIERICK

Biography

Luiz Heinrich Mann. Brother of the writer Thomas Mann. Born 27 March 1871 in Lübeck. Studied at a private preparatory school, Lübeck, until 1889; worked for a bookseller in Dresden, 1889–91, and a publisher in Berlin, 1891–92. Contracted tuberculosis and stayed in a sanatorium in Switzerland. Moved to Munich, 1894. Editor, *Das zwanzigste Jahrhundert*, 1894. Lived in France and Italy, 1895–96. Married Marie (Mimi) Kanová, 1914 (divorced, 1930): one daughter. Lecturer and journalist during the 1920s. Chair, Volksverband für Filmkunst, Berlin, 1928; president of literary section, Prussian Academy of the Arts, 1931–33 (dismissed).

Fled to France to escape the Nazi regime, 1933, and deprived of German citizenship; became a Czech citizen, 1936. Married Nelly Kroeger, 1939 (committed suicide, 1944). Moved to the United States, living in Los Angeles, 1940–49; writer, Warner Brothers film studios, Hollywood, 1940–41. Appointed president of the Academy of Arts, German Democratic Republic, Berlin, 1949. Awards: German Democratic Republic National Prize, 1949. Died (of a heart attack) in Santa Monica, 12 March 1950.

Selected Writings

Essays and Related Prose
Eine Freundschaft: Gustave Flaubert und George Sand, 1905
Macht und Mensch, 1919
Diktatur der Vernunft: Reden und Aufsätze, 1923
Sieben Jahre: Chronik der Gedanken und Vorgänge, 1929
Geist und Tat: Franzosen, 1780–1930, 1931
Die geistige Lage, 1932
Das öffentliche Leben, 1932
Das Bekenntnis zum Übernationalen, 1933
Der Hass: Deutsche Zeitgeschichte, 1933
Der Sinn dieser Emigration, 1934
Mut, 1939
Ein Zeitalter wird besichtigt, 1945
Politische Essays, edited by Hans Magnus Enzensberger, 1968
Verteidigung der Kultur: Antifaschistische Streitschriften und Essays, 1971

Other writings: many novels (including *Professor Unrat* [*The Blue Angel*], 1905; *Der Untertan* [*The Patrioteer*], 1918), plays, and correspondence.

Collected works editions: *Gesammelte Werke*, edited by Alfred Kantorowicz and Sigrid Anger, 18 vols., 1965–88 (in progress); *Gesammelte Werke*, 4 vols., 1969–71.

Bibliographies
Birr, Ewald, *Heinrich Mann*, Berlin: Stadtbibliothek, 1971
Zenker, Edith, *Heinrich-Mann-Bibliographie: Werke*, Berlin and Weimar: Aufbau, 1967

Further Reading
Banuls, André, *Heinrich Mann: Le Poète et la politique*, Paris: Klincksieck, 1966
Bornebusch, Herbert, "Schreiben für die Republik: Zu Heinrich Manns Essay 'Kaiserreich und Republik,'" *Neophilologus* 65 (1981)
Ebersbach, Volker, *Heinrich Mann: Leben, Werk, Wirken*, Frankfurt-on-Main: Röderberg, 1978
Exner, Richard, "Die Essayistik Heinrich Manns: Autor und Thematik," *Symposium* 13, no. 2 (1959)
Gockel, Heinz, "Heinrich Mann: Das Engagement des Essayisten," in *Heinrich Mann: Sein Werk in der Weimarer Republik*, edited by Helmut Koopmann and Peter-Paul Schneider, Frankfurt-on-Main: Klostermann, 1983
Haupt, Jürgen, "Zur Wirkungsgeschichte des Zivilisationsliteraten: Heinrich Mann und der Expressionismus," *Neue deutsche Hefte* 24 (1977)
Kammnitzer, Heinz, "Essays im Exil," *Neue deutsche Literatur* 8, no. 3 (1960)
Kantorowicz, Alfred, "'Zola'-Essay – 'Betrachtungen eines Unpolitischen': Die paradigmatische Auseinandersetzung zwischen Heinrich und Thomas Mann," *Geschichte in Wissenschaft und Unterricht* 11, no. 5 (1960)
Mörchen, Helmut, *Schriftsteller in der Massengesellschaft: Zur politischen Essayistik und Publizistik Heinrich und Thomas Manns, Kurt Tucholskys und Ernst Jüngers während der zwanziger Jahre*, Stuttgart: Metzler, 1973

Müller, Joachim, "Die kulturpolitische Position des Essayisten Heinrich Mann," *Wissenschaftliche Zeitschrift der Friedrich-Schiller-Universität Jena: Gesellschafts- und sprachwissenschaftliche Reihe* 23 (1974)

Roberts, Davis, "Heinrich Mann and the Essay," *Jahrbuch für internationale Germanistik* 8 (1976)

Vanhelleputte, Michel, "L'Essai de Heinrich Mann sur Zola," *Revue des Langues Vivantes* 29 (1963)

Wittig, Roland, *Die Versuchung der Macht: Essayistik und Publizistik Heinrich Manns im französischen Exil*, Frankfurt-on-Main: Lang, 1976

Wolff, Rudolf, editor, *Heinrich Mann: Werk und Wirkung*, Bonn: Bouvier, 1984

Wolff, Rudolf, editor, *Heinrich Mann: Das essayistische Werk*, Bonn: Bouvier, 1986

Mann, Thomas

German, 1875–1955

Thomas Mann was a prolific essayist, but hardly a great one. Given the prominence which discursive characters and narrators enjoy in his fiction, it is not surprising that throughout his long creative life he published essays in *propria persona*, sometimes on his own initiative, more often in response to invitations and commissions. These writings have never won the degree of recognition achieved by his imaginative works, for two main reasons.

The first is the prodigious self-centeredness of his imagination and intellect. Mann had an astonishingly limited set of basic preoccupations, rooted in his personal experience as a pathologically insecure, crypto-homosexual artist, hopelessly enamored of the professional solidity, social forms, and material comforts of the *haute bourgeoisie*. In his novels and stories, historical and social materials that had initially attracted him as allegorical vehicles for his idiosyncratic interests gained a density and momentum of their own as he wove them into narrative. The movement of his creative imagination was expansive: though the initial impetus always came from that narrow range of intimate concerns, the finished fictions engaged him, and have continued to engage readers across the globe, in worlds much broader and richer than his private preoccupations. When Mann took up the pen as an essayist, however, the movement tended to be in the opposite direction. He might indeed start with a subject at some remove from his private concerns; but inexorably, and sometimes with almost embarrassing swiftness, he managed to ignore or slough off all aspects of his theme which were not amenable to being used, or misused, as vehicles for his egregious lifelong fascination with his own problematic identity.

The second impediment to achievement as an essayist is embedded in the German cultural tradition itself. As a result of complex social and political pressures, German intellectual discourse since the Enlightenment has been marked by a cult of earnestness, which starved it of two of the chief nutrients on which the essay form thrived elsewhere: urbane wit and evenly matched polemic. Perhaps the most revealing of all Mann's essays is one he labored at during the first decade of the century, but never managed to finish, for which his working title was *Geist und Kunst*. *Kunst*, of course, means "art"; but the first word (meant here to be the antithesis of

Kunst) revealingly resists simple translation. In English, *Geist* means "spirit" or "mind" or "wit"; in French it is, apparently more straightforwardly, *esprit*. But where for a French essayist, displaying *esprit* unproblematically involves showing both penetration and agility of mind, a German writer with too light a touch has scant chance of being taken seriously. Mann's working notes for the *Geist und Kunst* project show him wrestling uncomfortably and, as always, self-consciously, with the notion that any intellectual dimension in a writer, whether visible in wit, analysis, or simple discursiveness, jeopardizes true artistic achievement. The writer who is in thrall to *Geist*, according to one strand in Mann's tangled drafts, is condemned to be a mere *Schriftsteller*, a scribbler who is doubtless entertaining to the trivial-minded, but who is debarred from the depths of intuitive insight and heights of national acclaim which belong to the *Künstler* unviolated by *Geist*. Mann was unusual in his time and place, not for entertaining this line of thought, but for being uneasy enough about it to be unable to carry his essay through to completion. For most of Mann's German contemporaries, writing that even gestured toward the ambience of French cultural urbanity belonged in a compartment signaled as suspiciously alien by the adoption of the word *feuilleton* to label it; and when Hermann Hesse, in *Das Glasperlenspiel* (1943; *The Glass Bead Game*), sought for a term to epitomize the alleged intellectual and moral triviality of 20th-century European culture, he chose "das feuletonistische Zeitalter," the Age of the *Feuilleton* or, as we might not too audaciously gloss it, the Era of the Essay.

The other distinctive dimension of the essay in other European countries and in America, its role in shaping opinion and policy through polemical exchange, was also impeded by distinctively German factors. There have been essay writers of great polemical gusto and talent in the German tradition: among others, **Lessing**, Heine, **Nietzsche**, and (in Austria) Karl Kraus; but they were unable to foster a genuine polemical tradition, partly because they lacked opponents able to engage with them on their own level, but more seriously because there was no real culture of public argument to give such exchanges a significant context. Until after World War II, the notion that open debate on issues of central importance between opposing parties united in a common wish to advance the public good is a sign of political health was alien to most Germans. What passed for polemic was more often malicious denunciation designed to have the opponent silenced by the powers that be; and responses to polemical attacks frequently took the form, not of telling counter-arguments, but of effusive and self-pitying indignation. Such writings justly perish with their immediate occasions.

A preponderance of indignation over argument is unfortunately all too visible in the complex of essays which Mann wrote in response to World War I, above all in the rambling *Betrachtungen eines Unpolitischen* (1918; *Reflections of a Nonpolitical Man*), where he belabors the contrast between Germanic "culture" and the decadent, commercial, technocratic "civilization" of the Western Allies. Even after Mann's dramatic renunciation of reactionary politics, first proclaimed in "Von deutscher Republik" (1922; "The German Republic"), his political writings in defense of democracy and what he calls "humanity" are generally heavily laden with *bien pensant* rhetoric and rather short on clarity of analysis or subtlety of argument (which is not to belittle the singular importance of his public stand against Hitler as a political phenomenon in its own right, quite independent of the literary quality of the writings that expressed it). He wrote lengthy pieces on his intellectual and artistic mentors: **Schopenhauer** – "Schopenhauer" (1938); Wagner –"Leiden und Grösse Richard Wagners" (1933; "Sufferings and Greatness of Richard Wagner"); and above all Nietzsche – "Nietzsches Philosophie im Lichte unserer Erfahrung" (1947; "Nietzsche's Philosophy in the Light of Recent History"); and in his later years he liked to bring a simplified version of the ideas of **Freud** to bear upon his main concerns – "Die Stellung Freuds in der modernen Geistesgeschichte" (1929; "Freud's Position in the History of Modern Thought"), "Freud und die Zukunft" (1936; "Freud and the Future"). His sustained attempts to live out what he called an *imitatio Goethe* were also partly conducted through a series of essays reinterpreting **Goethe**'s life in Mann's own image – "Goethe und Tolstoi" (1925; "Goethe and Tolstoy"), "Goethes Laufbahn als Schriftsteller" (1932; "Goethe's Career as a Man of Letters"), "Goethe und die Demokratie" (1949; "Goethe and Democracy"). Sadly, there is little in these writings that could be unreservedly recommended to someone seeking enlightenment about their ostensible subject matter. They provide ample insights into how Mann's imagination worked, but they do so largely because they fail to meet broader expectations about what essays with titles like these should offer.

MICHAEL BEDDOW

Biography

Paul Thomas Mann. Brother of the writer **Heinrich Mann**. Born 6 June 1875 in Lübeck. Studied at a gymnasium in Lübeck, 1899–94. Worked for an insurance company, Munich, 1894–95; military service, 1898–99. Married Katja Pringsheim, 1905: three daughters and three sons. Forced into exile by the Nazi regime, 1933, living in Switzerland, 1933–38; deprived of German citizenship, 1936; lived in Princeton, New Jersey, 1938–40, Santa Monica, California, 1940–52, and Kilchberg, Switzerland, 1952–55; became an American citizen, 1944. Awards: Bauernfeld Prize, 1904; Nobel Prize for Literature, 1929; Goethe Prize, 1949; Feltrinelli Prize, 1952; honorary degrees from many American and European universities. Died in Zurich, 12 August 1955.

Selected Writings

Essays and Related Prose

Friedrich und die grosse Koalition, 1915
Betrachtungen eines Unpolitischen, 1918; as *Reflections of a Nonpolitical Man*, translated by Walter D. Morris, 1983
Rede und Antwort: Gesammelte Abhandlungen und kleine Aufsätze, 1922
Bemühungen: Neue Folge der Gesammelten Abhandlungen und kleinen Aufsätze, 1925
Three Essays, translated by H. T. Lowe-Porter, 1929
Die Forderung des Tages: Reden und Aufsätze aus den Jahren, 1925–1929, 1930
Past Masters and Other Papers, translated by H. T. Lowe-Porter, 1933
Leiden und Grösse der Meister: Neue Aufsätze, 1935
Freud, Goethe, Wagner, translated by H. T. Lowe-Porter and Rita Matthias-Reil, 1937
Achtung, Europa! Aufsätze zur Zeit, 1938

Dieser Friede, 1938; as *This Peace*, translated by H. T. Lowe-Porter, 1938
Dieser Krieg, 1940; as *This War*, translated by Eric Sutton, 1940
Deutsche Hörer! 25 Radiosendungen nach Deutschland (radio broadcasts), 1942; as *Listen, Germany! 25 Radio Messages to the German People over the BBC*, 1943; enlarged edition, as *Deutsche Hörer! 55 Radiosendungen nach Deutschland*, 1945
Order of the Day: Political Essays and Speeches of Two Decades, translated by H. T. Lowe-Porter, Agnes E. Meyer, and Eric Sutton, 1942
Adel des Geistes: Sechzehn Versuche zum Problem der Humanität, 1945; enlarged edition, 1956
Essays of Three Decades, translated by H. T. Lowe-Porter, 1947
Neue Studien, 1948
The Thomas Mann Reader, edited by Joseph Warner Angell, 1950
Altes und Neues: Kleine Prosa aus fünf Jahrzehnten, 1953; revised edition, 1956
Versuch über Schiller, 1955
Nachlese: Prosa 1951–1955, 1956
Last Essays, translated by Richard and Clara Winston, Tania and James Stern, and H. T. Lowe-Porter, 1959
Addresses Delivered at the Library of Congress, 1942–1949, 1963
Wagner und unsere Zeit: Aufsätze, Betrachtungen, Briefe (collected writings on Wagner), edited by Erika Mann, 1963; as *Pro and Contra Wagner*, translated by Allan Blunden, 1985
Das essayistische Werk, edited by Hans Bürgin, 8 vols., 1968
Über deutsche Literatur: Ausgewählte Essays, Reden und Briefe, edited by Gerhard Steiner, 1968
Goethes Laufbahn als Schriftsteller: Zwölf Essays und Reden zu Goethe, 1982
Essays (in German), edited by Hermann Kurzke and Stefan Stachorski, 5 vols., 1993– (in progress)

Other writings: many novels (including *Buddenbrooks*, 1900; *Der Zauberberg* [*The Magic Mountain*], 1924; the Joseph tetralogy, 1933–43; *Doktor Faustus*, 1947; *Bekenntnisse des Hochstaplers Felix Krull* [*Confessions of Felix Krull, Confidence Man*], 1954), novellas (including *Der Tod in Venedig* [*Death in Venice*], 1912), diaries, and many volumes of correspondence.

Collected works editions: *Gesammelte Werke*, 14 vols., 1974; *Gesammelte Werke*, edited by Peter de Mendelssohn, 13 vols., 1980–90.

Bibliographies

Bürgin, Hans, *Das Werk Thomas Manns: Eine Bibliographie*, Frankfurt-on-Main: Fischer, 1959
Jonas, Klaus Werner, *Fifty Years of Thomas Mann Studies*, Minneapolis: University of Minnesota Press, 1955
Jonas, Klaus Werner, and Ilsedore B. Jonas, *Thomas Mann Studies*, vol. 2, Philadelphia: University of Pennsylvania Press, 1967
Matter, Harry, *Die Literatur über Thomas Mann: Eine Bibliographie 1898–1969*, 2 vols., Berlin: Aufbau, 1972
Wenzel, Georg, *Thomas Manns Briefwerk: Bibliographie gedruckter Briefe aus den Jahren, 1889–1955*, Berlin: Akademie, 1969

Further Reading

Exner, Richard, "Zur Essayistik Thomas Manns," *Germanisch-Romanische Monatsschrift* 43 (1962): 51–78
Koelb, Clayton, editor, *Thomas Mann's "Goethe und Tolstoi": Notes and Sources*, Tuscaloosa: University of Alabama Press, 1984
Lehnert, Herbert, *Nihilismus der Menschenfreundlichkeit: Thomas Manns "Wandlung" und sein Essay "Goethe und Tolstoi"*, Frankfurt-on-Main: Klostermann, 1991
Prater, Donald, *Thomas Mann: A Life*, Oxford and New York: Oxford University Press, 1995

Pütz, Peter, editor, *Thomas Mann und die Tradition*, Frankfurt-on-Main: Athenäum, 1971

Siefken, Hinrich, *Thomas Mann: Goethe – "Ideal der Deutschheit": Wiederholte Spiegelungen 1983–1949*, Munich: Fink, 1981

Siefken, Hinrich, "Der Essayist Thomas Mann," in *Text + Kritik: Sonderband Thomas Mann*, Munich: Edition Text + Kritik, 1982: 132–47

Reed, Terence J., *Thomas Mann: The Use of Tradition*, Oxford: Clarendon Press, 1974

Marías, Julián

Spanish, 1914–

Spanish essayist and philosopher Julián Marías came of intellectual age in Madrid in a cultural and literary milieu dominated by the philosophical menu and style of **José Ortega y Gasset** and his school and modulated by the literary canon of the Generation of 1898. He inherited from the former the theoretical premise that the efficacy of truth remains inseparable from aesthetic form and appeal; in the latter he found trans-theoretical confirmation of this doctrine, especially in such writers as the novelist and essayist **Azorín** and the poet Antonio Machado.

Marías describes an essential dimension of this literary doctrine as "page quality," which he understands not only as sustained stylistic creativity at the most localized and mundane level of discourse, but also as a strict aversion to any form of literary cliché or consensus. At its best this brave reliance on personal resources and the unexploited beauty of ordinary language rises to classic stylistic levels, as in the case of Ortega, Azorín, and Marías himself. Yet even in the flawed prose of the novelist Pío Baroja, Marías finds in the "incorruptible depths" of his personality a radical sincerity which he believes to be the true assurance of abiding literary relevance.

Within this same stylistic and doctrinal canon Marías himself writes with enormous power and apparent ease. Already an established philosophical author by 1951 when a relaxation of governmental censorship allowed him to begin a collateral career as a journalistic essayist, Marías soon gained a large and loyal following in such publications as *ABC*, *El País* (The country), *Blanco y Negro* (White and black), and, subsequently, Buenos Aires' *La Nación*. Although the majority of his journalistic articles remain uncollected, scores of his longer **philosophical essays** appear in such works as *Aquí y ahora* (1954; Here and now), *Ensayos de convivencia* (1955; Essays of coexistence), *El oficio del pensamiento* (1958; Essays of thought), *El tiempo que ni vuelve ni tropieza* (1964; Time which neither returns nor stumbles), *Al margen de estos clásicos* (1966; In the margin of these classics), *Nuevos ensayos de filosofía* (1968; New philosophical essays), and *Hispanoamérica* (1984). The excellence of his writing has been abundantly recognized with the award of both Spanish and international prizes.

Following the stylistic traditions of the master Spanish essayists, particularly Ortega, whose craft was shaped in the journalistic mold, Marías goes immediately to the heart of a problem and once centered on his theme pursues it with remarkable linguistic economy and grace, successfully blending modern popular themes and metaphors with vast classical erudition. Refreshingly free of postmodernist cant and exhibitionist pedantry, his style has been described by Lafuente Ferrari as "diamond-like" in its clarity and flawless brilliance.

Marías' essay style and doctrine converge in what he calls "narrative reason," that is, the notion that insofar as authentic ideas arise from and attach to human life, they also partake of its dynamic movement and internal illumination. Thus a narrative, plot-like quality characterizes his writings. Thematic movement, descriptive imagery, conceptual development, and ultimate human consequence pass before the reader in taut, dialectical sequence. Marías makes no concessions to extraneous abstractions and pomposities, much less to professional jargon and insider language, although he peppers his writings with fascinating *aperçus*. Deeply convinced of the seriousness of his topic and his methods, he does not slip into the defensive and self-indulgent introspection common to more timid essayists. His stylistic pace is too swift for him to second-guess himself. And yet for all this seriousness of purpose its register is broad enough to accommodate moments of humor, indignation, compassion, and, not infrequently, a fine sense of irony. His essays tend to evoke either enthusiasm or hostility, but almost never, it seems, indifference.

Although the essays of Marías presuppose the seamlessly articulated metaphysical foundation of human life as the "radical reality," each stands free and comprehensible on its own merits. Indispensable references to the underlying doctrinal base are couched in the language of common sense and contemporary experience. The result is a clear view into the depths of modern philosophical discourse and a cordial invitation to the general reader to join in the intellectual enterprise. For unlike those writers who claim universality but speak to no one in particular, Marías remains obedient to an abiding Spanish instinct by addressing real people in actual time and circumstances. Consequently few things that matter to this age have escaped his notice. With vigorous, crystalline language he has treated human problems and potentialities under such general rubrics as philosophy, ethics, sociology, historiography, technology, literary criticism, art, cinema, politics, and religion.

Perhaps **Salvador de Madariaga** best sums up Marías' stylistic qualities, which, as Buffon insisted, are also the man: "In him thought comes to light with such graceful ease that it seems that he is saying nothing new, yet everything is new and felicitous." As heir and defender of the Generation of 1898 and its successors, Marías takes his place in an illustrious line of philosophers, novelists, poets, and essayists who through their profound and eloquent commentary on the human condition have transformed the Spanish language into a polished instrument of contemporary discourse.

HAROLD RALEY

Biography

Julián Marías Aguilera. Born 17 June 1914 in Valladolid. Studied philosophy under Ortega y Gasset at the University of Madrid, degree in philosophy, 1936, Ph.D., 1951. Served in the Republican forces during the Spanish Civil War. Professor of philosophy, Aula Nueva, Madrid, 1940–48. Married Dolores Franco, 1941 (died, 1977): five sons (one died). Founder, with Ortega y Gasset, Instituto de Humanidades (Institute of the humanities), Madrid, 1948. Traveled widely, from 1951, in Europe and to the United States,

Canada, and South America. Lectured in Spain and Latin America, and taught or lectured at various universities in the U.S. Director, Seminario de Estudios de Humanidades (Seminary for studies in the humanities), Madrid, 1960–70. Founder, *Cuenta y Razón* (Account and reason), magazine of the Fundación de Estudios Sociológicos (Foundation for sociological studies). Elected to the Royal Spanish Academy, 1964. Member of Spanish Parliament, 1977–78. Professor of Spanish philosophy, University of Distance Learning, 1980–84. Awards: several, including John F. Kennedy Prize, 1964; Juan Palomo Prize, 1971; Gulbenkian Essay Award, 1972; Ramón Godó Lallana Prize, 1975–76; León Felipe Prize, 1979; Grand Cross (Argentina); honorary degrees from four universities; officer, Legion of Honor (France).

Selected Writings

Essays and Related Prose

Miguel de Unamuno, 1943; as *Miguel de Unamuno*, translated by Frances M. López-Morillas, 1966
San Anselmo y el insensato y otros estudios de filosofía, 1944
El método histórico de las generaciones, 1949; as *Generations: A Historical Method*, translated by Harold C. Raley, 1970
Aquí y ahora, 1954
Ensayos de teoría, 1954
Biografía de la filosofía, 1954; as *A Biography of Philosophy*, translated by Harold C. Raley, 1984
Ensayos de convivencia, 1955
La imagen de la vida humana, 1955; enlarged edition, 1971
Los Estados Unidos en escorzo, 1956; selections as *Modos de vivir: Un observador español en los Estados Unidos*, edited by Edward R. Mulvihill and Roberto G. Sánchez, 1964; in *America in the Fifties and Sixties: Julián Marías on the United States*, edited by Michael Aaron Rockland, translated by Blanche De Puy and Harold C. Raley, 1972
El intelectual y su mundo, 1956
La estructura social: Teoría y método, 1958; as *The Structure of Society*, translated by Harold C. Raley, 1987
El oficio del pensamiento, 1958
El tiempo que ni vuelve ni tropieza, 1964
Al margen de estos clásicos, 1966
Consideración de Cataluña (articles), 1966
Nuevos ensayos de filosofía, 1968
Análisis de los Estados Unidos, 1968; in *America in the Fifties and Sixties: Julián Marías on the United States*, edited by Michael Aaron Rockland, translated by Blanche De Puy and Harold C. Raley, 1972
Antropología metafísica: La estructura empírica de la vida humana, 1970; as *Metaphysical Anthropology: The Empirical Structure of Human Life*, translated by Frances M. López-Morillas, 1971
Visto y no visto: Crónicas de cine (cinema reviews), 2 vols., 1970
Philosophy as Dramatic Theory, translated by James Parsons, 1971
Sobre Hispanoamérica, 1973; revised edition, as *Hispanoamérica*, 1984
Literatura y generaciones, 1975
Cervantes clave española, 1990

Other writings: many works on philosophy.

Collected works edition: *Obras completas*, 10 vols., 1958–82 (incomplete).

Further Reading

Abellán, José Luis, "De cultura y filosofía española (II): Julián Marías y Manuel Granell," *Insula* 287 (1970): 10
Carpintero Capell, Heliodoro, *Cinco aventuras españolas: Aranguren, Ayala, Ferrater, Laín, Marías*, Madrid: Revista de Occidente, 1968
Donoso, Antón, *Julián Marías*, Boston: Twayne, 1982
Guy, Alain, "Julián Marías," in his *Les Philosophes espagnols d'hier et d'aujourd'hui: Époques et auteurs*, Toulouse: Privat, 1956: 330–39
Henares Martínez, Domingo, *Hombre y sociedad en Julián Marías*, Albacete: Diputación de Albacete, 1991
Homenaje a Julián Marías, Madrid: Espasa-Calpe, 1984
Raley, Harold, *Responsible Vision: The Philosophy of Julián Marías*, Clear Creek, Indiana: American Hispanist, 1980
Sarmiento, Edward, "The Mind of Julián Marías," *Tablet* 197 (30 June 1951): 515–17
Soler Planas, Juan, *El pensamiento de Julián Marías*, Madrid: Revista de Occidente, 1973
Vilar, Sergio, "Julián Marías and the Intelligentsia in Spain," *Books Abroad* 37 (1963): 252–60

Mariátegui, José Carlos

Peruvian, 1894–1930

As both his biography and his bibliography reveal, José Carlos Mariátegui is a genuine product of his time, and now considered one of the most original thinkers of the modern era. Mariátegui represents both branches (political and cultural) of the bifurcated Peruvian thought of the time and historical circumstances in which he lived and worked. He took an active part in the intellectual atmosphere that was shaping the Republic of Peru socially, politically, and culturally. At the national level, both political and cultural spheres meet in Mariátegui's special interest in indigenous, economic, and literary issues, a convergence masterfully portrayed by means of the essay, the genre for which he is best known. This is clear from reading his most celebrated work, *Siete ensayos de interpretación de la realidad peruana* (1928; *Seven Interpretative Essays on Peruvian Reality*), a text which has undergone more than 50 editions and several translations. In this corpus of seven essays, Mariátegui confronts the most important aspects of the Peruvian reality of his time, unearthing the past, unraveling the present, and composing a view of the future, all through his most original assessment of Marxist theory. The titles of these seven essays illustrate his particular perspective: "Esquema de la evolución económica" ("Outline of the Economic Evolution"), "El problema del indio" ("The Problem of the Indian"), "El problema de la tierra" ("The Problem of the Land"), "El proceso de la instrucción pública" ("Public Education"), "El factor religioso" ("The Religious Factor"), "Regionalismo y centralismo" ("Regionalism and Centralism"), and "El proceso de la literatura" ("Literature on Trial").

Mariátegui's visionary and active involvement in Peruvian economic, political, and cultural matters – as national and international columnist, and as founder of *Amauta*, one of Latin America's most prestigious critical forums – won him the reputation of being the first Marxist thinker of Latin America, as well as one of the most original interpreters of Marxist methodology, particularly as concerns possibilities for a more accurate portrayal of both Peruvian and other Latin American national realities. In this respect, he ranks with other outstanding intellectuals, such as **Antonio Gramsci** and **Georg Lukács**.

Mariátegui's original view of Marxism reflects the influence of the deep religious, mystical, and poetic insights characteristic of the first part of his life, a period mostly spent in poverty and solitary seclusion due to his weak constitution. These insights surface in his view of Marxism as a social revolutionary praxis that cannot rest solely on invariably applied, objective, and scientific precepts, as was originally envisaged by the orthodox line of Soviet Marxism. Mariátegui realized that the application of such a social theory cannot be detached from the particular historical, social, economic, geographical, and cultural circumstances of a given nation. Thus, upon his return from forced exile in Europe in 1923, he came to understand that a "religious factor," discovered within the popular masses, was part and parcel of "popular" behavior, as exhibited, for example, in such religious events as the Catholic procession. Mariátegui foresaw that if the masses could be imbued with the same mystical, mythical, and unifying fervor as that observed in these public acts, they could equally adopt such fervency in their pursuit of cultural and economic liberation from the feudal system that prevailed after their conquest and colonization by the Spanish crown.

Mariátegui's attempt to understand and portray Peruvian history and culture through the Marxist screen leads him to envision an indigenous socialism more in accordance with Peruvian historical circumstances, which he rightly perceived as being different from those of either Soviet and European countries, or even from those of other Latin American societies. For instance, he incisively points out that four-fifths of Peru's population consists of indigenous groups who contribute significantly to the Peruvian economy. Despite this indisputable fact, the indigenous population was not considered politically as a national group. Rather, the Peruvian nation had been viewed as made up mainly of white and Creole descendants of the conquering ruling class. Mariátegui rightly concluded that Peru was indeed constituted by several layered and separately coexisting sociocultural groups. One of these groups was the "modern feudalistic" Creole bourgeoisie, which subsisted mainly on trade with its European counterpart.

Mariátegui pondered the means of re-creating a modern "Tahuantinsuyo" (Peru) and concluded that it could only be accomplished by resorting to the imagination. This is the leading thrust of his famous seven essays, which deal not so much with economic problems as with those of culture, religion, and literature. Not surprisingly, Mariátegui even thought that in order better to portray Peruvian reality, it had to be re-created in the form of a novel – literature, he believed, is a key tool for the elucidation of the social and political reality of a nation. Nevertheless, torn between literary, ideological, and political conceptions, Mariátegui elected the essay as the form that provided him with the space to merge these keen and multifaceted visions.

Finally, Mariátegui's legacy lies in his recognition that Peruvian historical circumstances, more than academic or orthodox theory, demanded the allure of a myth that could initiate the transformation into a socialist society based on the collective and cultural constructs of historical Peru. In this regard, his visions echo those of the Spanish poet Antonio Machado in his realization that the path of a nation is not traced beforehand, but rather must be found within the nation itself. This is tantamount to a utopian project that must be undertaken by the peasantry and working class of Peru together, for, as Mariátegui believed, without them there could be neither vindication nor liberation. This process of

re-creation demanded Mariátegui's evolving a language capable of reflecting the new Peru he envisioned. This he endeavors to do by further elaboration of key terms and concepts such as feudalism, peasant socialism, civilization, and revolution as the process of liberation and struggle that must be undertaken by living immersed in a disarticulated society.

Mariátegui's literary conception and essayistic style are understandable given the autodidactic education and journalistic practice that placed him amid everyday sociopolitical and cultural Peruvian reality. From them he derives his free and influential style, divested of academic pretension and affectation. Mariátegui's originality allows us to label him, paraphrasing the Mexican essayist and Nobel Laureate **Octavio Paz**, "one of our true [Latin American] writers."

CIRO A. SANDOVAL-B.

Biography

Born 14 June 1894 in Moquegua, Peru. Copy boy at age 15, and journalist, from age 18, *La Prensa* (The press) newspaper, Lima; contributor to various journals, including *Variedades* (Varieties) and *Mundial* (Universal); journalist, *El tiempo* (The times) newspaper, 1918–19; cofounder, *Nuestra Época* (Our epoch), 1918, and *La Razón* (Reason), 1919. Traveled to Europe, 1919–23. Married Anna Chiappe, 1921: one son. Returned to Lima, 1923. Lecturer, González Prada People's University, and editor of its *Claridad* (Clarity), from 1923. Became ill partly as a result of overwork, and had leg amputated, 1923. Cofounder of Minerva publishing house, 1925, *Amauta* left-wing journal, 1926–30, and *Labor* newspaper, 1928–29. Cofounder, Peruvian Socialist Party, 1928, and Peruvian General Federation of Workers, 1929. Died in Lima, 16 April 1930.

Selected Writings

Essays and Related Prose

La escena contemporánea, 1925
Siete ensayos de interpretación de la realidad peruana, 1928; edited by Elizabeth Garrels, 1979; as *Seven Interpretative Essays on Peruvian Reality*, translated by Marjory Urquidi, 1971
Defensa del Marxismo, la emoción de nuestro tiempo, y otros temas, 1934
El alma national y otras estaciones del hombre de hoy, 1950
Ensayos escogidos, edited by Aníbal Quijano, 1956, and Augusto Salazar Bondy, 1971
Crítica literaria, 1969
Fascismo sudamericano: Los intelectuales y la revolución y otros artículos inéditos (1923–1924), 1975
Páginas literarias, edited by Edmundo Cornejo U., 1978
Invitación a la vida heroica (selection), edited by Alberto Flores Galindo and Ricardo Portocarrero Grados, 1989
Textos básicos (selection), edited by Aníbal Quijano, 1991

Other writings: political works, poetry, and two historical plays.

Collected works edition: *Ediciones populares de las obras completas*, 20 vols., 1959–70.

Further Reading

Aricó, José, editor, *Mariátegui y los orígenes del marxismo latinoamericano*, Mexico City: Siglo Veintuno, 1978
Becker, Marc, *Mariátegui and Latin American Marxist Theory*, Athens: Ohio University Center for International Studies, 1993

Belaúnde, Víctor Andrés, "En torno a los *Siete ensayos* de José Carlos Mariátegui," *La Realidad Nacional* (1980): 1–152

Flores Galindo, Alberto, *La agonía de Mariátegui*, Lima: Desco, 1980

Melis, Antonio, Albert Dessau, and Manfred Kossok, *Mariátegui: Tres estudios*, Lima: Amauta, 1971

Paz, Octavio, "A Literature of Convergences," in *Convergences: Essays on Art and Literature*, San Diego: Harcourt Brace Jovanovich, and London: Bloomsbury, 1987

Quijano, Aníbal, *Reencuentro y debate: Una introducción a Mariátegui*, Lima: Mosca Azul, 1981

Skirius, John, editor, *El ensayo hispanoamericano del siglo XX*, Mexico City: Fondo de Cultura Económica, 1981

Stabb, Martin S., "The New Humanism and the Left," in his *In Quest of Identity: Patterns in the Spanish American Essay of Ideas, 1890–1960*, Chapel Hill: University of North Carolina Press, 1967: 102–45

Tord, Luis Enrique, *El indio en los ensayistas peruanos, 1848–1948*, Lima: Unidas, 1978

Marivaux

French, 1688–1763

Marivaux built his early reputation on novels parodying classical forms and a mock epic in verse. In 1717, at age 30, he began publishing a series of articles in *Le Nouveau Mercure de France* (The new Mercury of France) entitled *Lettres sur les habitants de Paris* (Letters on the inhabitants of Paris), inspired by Charles Dufresny's *Amusements sérieux et comiques d'un Siamois* (1699; *Amusements Serious and Comical*) and to a lesser extent by **La Bruyère**'s *Caractères* (1688; *Characters*). Interesting for their portrayal of various aspects of Parisian life, they are even more so for his thoughts on the form he is adopting and for the way in which these reflections foreshadow the mature aesthetic of the essay he will put into practice in his essay masterpiece, *Le Spectateur Français* (The French spectator). Calling himself a "Théophraste moderne" (a modern Theophrastus) he declares the following traits to be essential to his manner of writing: a great number and variety of subjects; a mixture of the grave and the lighthearted; an ordering of subject matter that depends heavily on chance – for example, beginning with a subject that happens to be at hand, continuing more or less haphazardly, and concluding at whatever point he pleases; a free rein given to his nature as *un esprit libertin*, that is, one who hates constraint and prefers to follow his fancy and his natural bent; and finally, the freedom to please himself, since he has "no other object in mind than myself."

An important additional feature emerges from his philosophical reflections, *Pensées sur différents sujets* (Thoughts on different subjects), published two years later (1719) in the same periodical. This is his concept of "nature's sublime" as opposed to "man's sublime," a distinction with far-reaching implications for all Marivaux's work, theater and novel as well as essay. He compares the ordering of the various parts of a work to "an indivisible fabric . . . whose manner of taking shape we do not know, which is produced in us but not by us." Finished, polished, consciously controlled thought may be sacrificed in this kind of writing, but it is in the interests of something more valuable: thought-in-process, "thought taking shape under our

very eyes," as the great Marivaux scholar, Frédéric Deloffre (1967), describes it. Of all the affinities Marivaux has with **Montaigne** (some of which are obvious from the traits listed earlier), this power to create the impression of thought-in-the-making is probably the deepest.

From 1721 to 1724 Marivaux published a kind of "one-man periodical journal" in 25 issues or *feuilles*, each about ten pages long in the modern Garnier editions (1969, 1988), to which he gave the title *Le Spectateur Français*, honoring **Addison**'s and **Steele**'s *Spectator*, available in French translation since 1714. (The individual essays bear no titles.) His imitation of the *Spectator* is very free in nature; he uses the work as a springboard for innovation. What he seems to have valued most in the pioneer English essay work was its freedom of form, which encouraged him in his revolt against the hierarchy of genres inherited from 17th-century French classicism and in his propensity to literary experimentation. Once again, as in *Le Nouveau Mercure*, the element of chance plays a key role in composition. In the first *feuille* we find this striking self-description of his manner: "I know not how to invent, all I know is how to catch by surprise thoughts that chance causes to arise in me." The effect of *le naturel* continues to be faithfully sought by Marivaux, as when he aims to give a portrait truly resembling himself which is at the same time "a portrait of the human mind in its natural form" (a distinct echo of Montaigne). Clarifying a point that remained a bit puzzling in his *Lettres sur les habitants de Paris* – his relationship with his reader – he affirms on the one hand his intention of writing only for himself and on the other hand his need to engage his reader in a kind of dialogue. Giovanni Bonaccorso (1973) has shown how he provokes the reader, anticipates criticisms, answers critics whose objections to this or that point of his he has heard in salons and cafés – an approach that will also be characteristic of his two great novels, *La Vie de Marianne* (1731–42; *The Life of Marianne*) and *Le Paysan parvenu* (1734–35; *The Upstart Peasant*).

Abundant variety of matter and apparent randomness of form continue to be dominant features. There is much less sequentiality between issues than in the *Spectator*, Marivaux's trademark being the sudden interruption and change of subject. The many stories included in the *feuilles* (Montaigne also was fond of incorporating stories in his essays) are often unresolved or simply unfinished, the better, Marivaux argued, to stimulate the reader to reflect about them. The loose structures, full of fortuitous, unforeseen elements and discontinuities, suggest another important link between Marivaux's essays and his fiction. Whatever the source of his delight in such freedom of form – whether it was his fondness for "the surprises of improvisation" (Jean Rousset, 1962), his view of inconstancy in love (Robert Mauzi, 1960), or simply the coquettish play of author with reader (Felicia Sturzer, 1982; Henri Coulet and Michel Gilot, 1973) – this attitude lies at the heart of his essayist's art, and may be summed up in his remark, "Follow me, dear Reader. To tell the truth, I am not sure where I am going, but the pleasure lies in the journey itself."

In 1727 Marivaux produced his most unconventional and daring work, another "one-man journal," *L'Indigent Philosophe*, in which he uses as alter ego a pauper philosopher, or "philosopher bum," as Edward Greene (1961) has called him. The work was indeed so bold, in both form and content, that it first appeared anonymously. The seven *feuilles* comprising it constitute a much more unified and continuous whole than *Le Spectateur Français*. Presented by the author as a type of "Mémoires," the work reads, in fact, much like the "memoir-novels" of *The Life of Marianne* and *The Upstart Peasant*, except for its much smaller size. But its essayistic qualities are undeniable, as is the influence of Montaigne, greater here than in any of Marivaux's other works. Addison had spoken of the "wildness" of which the essay form was capable ("On Method in Discourse," *Spectator* no. 476). In *L'Indigent Philosophe* Marivaux goes beyond anything Addison might have imagined. In his foreword to the work he describes it as "an essay of what could be done by writing haphazardly whatever might strike the imagination."

A final one-man journal from Marivaux's pen, *Le Cabinet du Philosophe* (1734), consisting of 11 *feuilles*, adds little that is new to his concept or practice of the essay. He himself called it "detached pieces, fragments of thought on a great variety of subjects." It is hardly comparable in brilliance to its predecessors, and Greene is probably correct in surmising that Marivaux used the work as a receptacle for leftovers, miscellaneous notes, and the like.

Marivaux ranks among the greatest French and world essayists thanks to the highly personal kind of artful disorder (in reality a new kind of order) that he brought to the essay form as well as the variety and depth of his observations on human society and human nature. He is best known, perhaps, for his insights into the complexities of love, or for what one of his contemporary admirers called "the metaphysics of the heart." His genre, more precisely, is the *feuille périodique* or *essai journalistique*, short prose pieces best read in sequence, since they are not fully independent or autonomous and are not part of any "collections of essays" (the latter, in any case, being a more modern phenomenon). His achievement as an essayist, especially in affirming what he called his "libertinage d'idées" (following his fancy, more or less at random), was one of the fruits (the others being his fictional and theatrical creations) of his rebellion against the French classical aesthetics of the *anciens*. In the quarrel of Ancients and Moderns raging in his time he was a modern of the extreme avant-garde, challenging unceasingly, as Oscar Haac (1973) has pointed out, the "accepted mold" of literary theory and practice. His innovations embraced linguistic details such as vocabulary and syntax as well as larger forms, and the "disorder" of a sentence or paragraph in a given essay often presents a microcosm of the essay as a whole.

Marivaux's reputation as an essayist has been slow in establishing itself. The recognition of his genius in this field has more or less coincided with another important discovery: namely, that his total work forms an organic whole made up of three levels or zones of artistic inquiry, closely related and often intersecting, which correspond to the three genres – essay, fiction, theater – in which he excelled. Thus unlike Montaigne, the full-time essayist, or **Sainte-Beuve**, the essayist out of failure to succeed as poet and novelist, or many writers whose essays were a sideline, Marivaux incorporates the essay into the very heart of his literary enterprise, the exploration of human existence in all its mystery.

RICHARD M. CHADBOURNE

Biography

Pierre Carlet de Chamblain de Marivaux. Born Pierre Carlet, 4 February 1688 in Paris. Family moved to Riom in central France, 1699. Studied at the Faculty of Law, Paris, 1710–13 (moved permanently to Paris in 1712), law degree, 1721. Began writing plays, 1712; first used the name Marivaux c. 1712; name first published in full, 1716; published and/or produced over 30 comedies during his life. Married Colombe Bollogne, 1717 (died, probably 1723): one daughter. Took up journalism, from 1717, writing sketches for *Le Nouveau Mercure de France*; published the periodicals *Le Spectateur Français*, 1721–24, *L'Indigent Philosophe*, 1727, and *Le Cabinet du Philosophe*, 1734. Frequented salons, including those of Mesdames de Lambert, de Tencin, Geoffrin, and du Deffand. Lived with Mademoiselle de Jean, from 1744. Elected member, 1743, chancellor, 1750, and director, 1759, French Academy. Died in Paris, 12 February 1763.

Selected Writings

Essays and Related Prose

Lettres sur les habitants de Paris, in *Le Nouveau Mercure de France*, September 1717–August 1718
Pensées sur différents sujets, in *Le Nouveau Mercure de France*, April 1719
Lettres contenant une aventure, in *Le Nouveau Mercure de France*, December 1719–April 1720
Le Spectateur Français, 25 issues, July 1721–September 1724
L'Indigent Philosophe, 7 issues, 1727
Le Cabinet du Philosophe, 11 issues, January–April 1734
Journaux et œuvres diverses (Garnier Edition), edited by Frédéric Deloffre and Michel Gilot, 1969; revised edition, 1988

Other writings: over 30 comedies and one tragedy, journalism, and fiction (including two memoir-novels, *La Vie de Marianne* [*The Life of Marianne*], 11 vols., 1731–42; *Le Paysan parvenu* [*The Upstart Peasant*], 5 vols., 1734–35).

Collected works edition: *Œuvres complètes*, 12 vols, 1781.

Further Reading

Arland, Marcel, *Marivaux*, Paris: Gallimard, 1950
Badir, Magdy, and Vivien Bosley, editors, *Le Triomphe de Marivaux: A Colloquium Commemorating the Tricentenary of the Birth of Marivaux, 1688–1988*, Edmonton: University of Alberta Department of Romance Languages, 1989
Baldwin, Edward, "Marivaux's Place in the Development of Character Portrayal," *PMLA* 27 (1912): 168–87
Bonaccorso, Giovanni, "Le Dialogue de Marivaux avec ses lecteurs," *Cahiers de l'Association Internationale des Études Françaises* 25 (1973): 209–23
Chadbourne, Richard, "Marivaux's 'Libertinage d'Idées' in *Le Spectateur Français*," in *Man and Nature/L'Homme et la Nature*, edited by Nicholas Hudson and Rosena Davison, Edmonton: Canadian Society for Eighteenth-Century Studies, vol. 8, 1989
Chadbourne, Richard, "Discovering Marivaux the Essayist, or 'How many writers are there in Marivaux?'," in *Le Triomphe de Marivaux*, edited by Magdy Badir and Vivien Bosley, Edmonton: University of Alberta Department of Romance Languages, 1989
Coulet, Henri, and Michel Gilot, *Marivaux, un humanisme expérimental*, Paris: Larousse, 1973
Dédeyan, Charles, "Marivaux à l'école d'Addison et de Steele," *Annales de l'Université de Paris* 25 (1955): 5–17
Deloffre, Frédéric, "Etat présent des études sur Marivaux," *L'Information Littéraire* 16 (1964): 191–99
Deloffre, Frédéric, *Marivaux et le marivaudage, une préciosité nouvelle*, Paris: Colin, 1967
Ehrard, Jean, "Marivaux ou les chemins de la liberté," in his *Le XVIIIe Siècle, I: 1720–1750*, Paris: Arthaud, 1974

Gelobter, Hanna, *"Le Spectateur" von Pierre Marivaux und die englischen moralischen Wochenschriften*, Limburg: Limburger Vereinsdruckerei, 1936

Gilot, Michel, *Les Journaux de Marivaux: Itinéraire moral et accomplissement esthétique*, Paris: Champion, 2 vols., 1975

Greene, Edward, "Marivaux's Philosophical Bum," *L'Esprit Créateur* 1 (1961): 190–95

Greene, Edward, *Marivaux*, Toronto: University of Toronto Press, 1965

Haac, Oscar A., *Marivaux*, New York: Twayne, 1973

Jacœbée, Pierre, *La Persuasion de la charité: Thèmes, formes et structures dans les "Journaux et œuvres diverses de Marivaux"*, Amsterdam: Rodopi, 1976

Lagrave, Henri, *Marivaux et sa fortune littéraire*, Bordeaux: Ducros, 1970

Matucci, Mario, in *L'opera narrativa di Marivaux*, Naples: Pironti, 1962

Mauzi, Robert, "Le Mouvement et la vie de l'âme," in his *L'Idée du bonheur dans la littérature et la pensée françaises au XVIIIe siècle*, Paris: Colin, 1960

Poulet, Georges, "Marivaux," in his *Études sur le temps humain, II: La Distance intérieure*, Paris: Plon, 1952

Rousset, Jean, "Marivaux ou la structure du double registre," in his *Forme et signification: Essais sur les structures littéraires de Corneille à Claudel*, Paris: Corti, 1962

Roy, Claude, *Lire Marivaux*, Neuchâtel: La Baconnière, and Paris: Le Seuil, 1947

Sturzer, Felicia, "Exclusion and Coquetterie: First-Person Narrative in Marivaux's 'L'Indigent philosophe'," *French Review* 54 (1982): 471–77

Markov, Georgi

Bulgarian, 1929–1978

Georgi Markov began his career as a novelist, playwright, short story and screenplay writer, and literary critic. He was eventually drawn to nonliterary types of essays, such as social and political **pamphlets**, documentary articles, and **reviews**, partly by circumstance, partly because of his acute sense of social injustice. The publication of his first novel *Muzhe* (1962; Men) made him an instant literary star and Communist Party favorite. His later novels and plays, some of which were banned from publication – e.g. *Velikiat pokriv* (The great roof) and *Pokushitelite* (The assassins) – marked him, however, as a social iconoclast and political outcast. This alienation led him to defect to England, where he joined the Bulgarian section of the BBC World Service, and also wrote for the German radio station Deutsche Welle (German wave) and broadcast over Radio Free Europe. In these broadcasts he was harshly critical of the communist system. An accomplished literary critic who focused on the Bulgarian National Revival period (a century of growing national awareness between 1762 and 1878), he set out to write both **personal essays** and social and political commentaries. Following the tradition of his impressive literary predecessors and famous essayists Khristo Botev, Liuben Karavelov, and **Pencho Slaveikov**, he wrote powerful, heartfelt pamphlets in which he released years of pent-up thoughts and emotions.

Markov's output as a literary critic includes major studies of the Bulgarian poets Dimcho Debelianov and Geo Milev – *Dimcho Debelianov: Literaturen ocherk* (1962; Dimcho Debelianov: a literary sketch), *Geo Milev: Izbrani proizvedenia* (1971; Geo Milev: selected works). Both are extensive biographical and literary studies, at once illustrating the predominant form of literary essay of the socialist realism period and representing a significant departure from it. Both were issued by the finest publishers of literary criticism in Bulgaria, Bulgarski Pisatel' (Bulgarian writer) and the Institut za Bulgarska Literatura (Institute for Bulgarian literature at the Bulgarian Academy of Sciences) and exemplify the canon of literary criticism at its best. Markov follows the established model for literary essays of that period, demonstrating how history molds the individual, but he does not stop there. Contrary to some trends in literary criticism of the socialist-realism period, he does not present literary figures as solely the product of their social or historical medium. He does not deny the importance of individual sensibility or damn it as a literary flaw. He retains his professional integrity and moral dignity, treating the more personal side of literary works with understanding and respect. Moreover, he does not ascribe to these writers political aspirations and communist ideals they did not necessarily embrace. His greatest accomplishment in the literary essay remains his adherence to the truth in a society where personal and public history were rewritten to conform to the communist dogma.

Markov's nonliterary essays carry his professional honesty and civil candor to heights unimaginable to most of his contemporaries. In *Zadochni reportazhi za Bulgaria* (wr. in exile, pub. 1990; Broadcasts about Bulgaria), known in the West as *The Truth That Killed* (1983), and *Kogato chasovnitsite sa spreli: Novi zadochni reportazhi za Bulgaria* (wr. in exile, pub. 1991; New broadcasts about Bulgaria), he comes across as a captive sentenced to 40 years of silence who has finally broken loose and regained his right to speak. He confesses it is his "privilege and duty" to tell the world the truth about Bulgaria, that it is a "sovereign republic without sovereignty, a popular democracy without democracy, a country leading a lifeless social existence, numbed by heavyhanded police methods, a country having a faceless literature and crippled art." The two volumes comprise 167 short broadcast essays and include poignant political pamphlets, **critical essays**, historical surveys, humorous stories, sociological studies, brief portrait sketches, memoirs, and literary anecdotes. They are expressions which pour out the feelings and thoughts of a suffocated author. Form is unimportant, for form, metaphors, symbols, and allegories have come to signify to Markov the communist regime's weapons of deception. He felt it his duty to tell the truth without the usual literary embellishments or Party jargon, simple and unadorned.

In essays in *The Truth That Killed* – "Partia i rabota" ("The Party and Work"), "Biografia na vlasta" ("A Biography of the Regime"), "Nie te napravihme pisatel" ("We Made You into a Writer"), "Sreshti s Todor Zhivkov" ("Meetings with Todor Zhivkov") – Markov talks about those who parade as genuine believers in the communist utopia. These people humiliate and deprive others of all human rights, surround themselves with sycophants, and are incompetent, cynical, and hypocritical. They demoralize the people and ruin the country's economy. Filled with the sense of their divine invincibility, they go through life following the lifestyle of the world's most corrupt form of ruling autocracy. In essays such as "Porazheniata na kulta" (1984; "The Ravages of the Personality Cult"),

"Tsenzurna dialektika" (1984; "The Dialectic of Censorship"), "Zad fasadata na osmi mart" (1990; Behind the façade of Mother's Day), "Prostitutsiata" (1990; Prostitution), "Sled kulturnata revoliutsia" (1990; After the cultural revolution), "Zashto horata kradat" (1990; Why people steal), and "Zhenite na Varshava" (1990; The women of Warsaw), Markov analyzes phenomena such as the paranoid fear of the "enemy," the personality cult, the all-pervasive atmosphere of suspiciousness and apathy, Party patriotism, the system's reliance on self-censorship and informers, the disintegration of family relations and the exploitation of modern woman, the cheating of the country and the robbing of its people. He also depicts ordinary rank-and-file Bulgarians, who have survived hundreds of years of internal and external domination thanks to their common sense, down-to-earth realism, and ability to see through their rulers' hidden agendas. They have also miraculously retained a healing sense of humor, as expressed in essays like "Kiro i drugite" (1984; "Kiro and the Others"), "Da se prezhivee niakak" (1984; "To Endure Somehow"), and "Spasitelniat smiah" (1984; "The Saving Grace of Laughter").

Markov developed a theory of the perversion of language similar to that of **George Orwell**. He wrote to express his thoughts rather than demonstrate his commitment to the Party. He used words in their original meanings to tell the story of a people subjected to an unprecedented brainwashing through the use of an official "antilanguage," a highly developed and formal language of clichés adopted to misinform and distort the truth. Markov brought the Bulgarian language back to life, restoring its colorful vitality from the deadly kingdom of "black and white." Once again a voice, kindred to the well-known Bulgarian literary and public figures of the National Revival period, uttered the unthinkable "the king is naked," toppling from the communist Olympus all fake claims to freedom, independence, equality, and prosperity, as well as the Party's claim to absolute superiority and historical supremacy over all other forms of government. Markov went much further than the legendary tale: he actually explained in his essays that the king is not only naked, but also ugly and mean.

If Georgi Markov were Russian or Czech, he might be known as one of the best essayists from Eastern Europe. As it is, if he is known at all, it is because he was assassinated with a poisoned umbrella as an exile in London. This fact in itself is a testament to the power and importance of his writing for those who knew it and feared it. Bulgaria's Alistair Cooke and Aleksandr Solzhenitsyn broadcast his "letters from Bulgaria" in order to disclose the moral perversity of the politics of hate instilled by the communist *aparatchniks* in Bulgaria. Like Cooke, he reached the hearts and minds of millions of Bulgarians to tell them revealing stories about their country and their rulers. Like Solzhenitsyn, he had to suffer the consequences of his intelligence and moral integrity. And unlike anyone else, he had to pay for his essays with his life.

LILIA SAVOVA

Biography

Georgi Ivanov Markov. Born in 1929 in Sofia. Studied at the Polytechnic, Sofia, 1947–52, qualified as a chemical engineer. Imprisoned for political beliefs, 1950–51. Worked in a metallurgy factory, 1952–59, and as a chemical engineer. Began writing novels and plays. Elected to the Bulgarian Writers' Union, 1962. Left for

Italy after one performance (a preview) of his play *The Man Who Was Me*, June 1969; moved to England, 1971. Worked for the Bulgarian section of the BBC World Service, broadcasting a weekly column about British cultural life, and for Radio Free Europe, from 1975, and Deutsche Welle. Married Annabel Dilke (third marriage): one daughter. Awards: Bulgarian Literary Prize, for *Muzhe*; Edinburgh Festival Award, 1974. Died (after being stabbed with a poisoned umbrella, probably by the Bulgarian secret police) in London, 11 September 1978.

Selected Writings

Essays and Related Prose
The Truth That Killed, translated by Liliana Brisby, 1983; as *Zadochni reportazhi za Bulgaria*, 2 vols., 1990
Kogato chasovnitsite sa spreli: Novi zadochni reportazhi za Bulgaria, 1991

Other writings: three novels (including *Muzhe*, 1962), a thriller with David Phillips (*The Right Honourable Chimp*, 1978), plays, and works on Bulgarian literature.

Further Reading
Moser, Charles A., "Georgi Markov in the 1960s," *Slavonic and East European Review* 67, no. 3 (July 1989): 353–77
Smolyantisky, Solomon, "For the 70th [sic] Birthday of Georgi Markov: Probing Life," *Soviet Literature* 4, no. 397 (1981): 163–70
Todorov, Kalin, and Vladimir Bereanu, *Koi ubi Georgi Markov*, Sofia: Sibiia, 1991

Martí, José
Cuban, 1853–1895

José Martí's essays reveal a sense of urgency and precariousness appropriate to his brief life. In effect, the main body of his prose – of which some works are still being discovered – was journalistic in nature, targeted for quick publication in newspapers and magazines, although his essays consistently show a higher degree of regard for aesthetic values than typical journalistic work. The remainder – in fact, a large number – is dispersed among numerous **letters**, personal diaries and notes, other unpublished texts, and in patriotic speeches which were often improvised, then lost forever. In all his essays, regardless of the topic, Martí always reaffirms his anticolonialist, popular, and antiracist beliefs concerning the inherent equality of all human beings notwithstanding their physical differences. As one of his reflections exemplifies in "Mi raza" (1893; My race): "No man has any special right because he belongs to any specific race; just by saying the word man, we have already said all the rights." This statement can no doubt be directly linked with the Christian notion of the value of life; however, Martí's concept of morality does not disclose a religious affiliation; it is constructed of and integrates religious icons, ethics, and historical and social elements.

Martí consolidated his essay activities during the last 15 years of his life in New York (1880–95); starting in 1881 he sent regular contributions to important Spanish American newspapers such as *La Opinión Nacional* (Caracas) and *La Nación* (Buenos Aires). The excellent "Cartas de Nueva York" (Letters from New York) – his account of the American society of that period – is an example of this important work.

When Martí began his career, Spanish prose was lifeless and exhausted. Conscious of and concerned about the sense of beauty and with a fundamental fidelity to his perception of reality, Martí interpreted the essay as a literary genre that favors human causes, often patriotic and nationalistic. Thus, beginning in 1882 and even before the great masters of Spanish American Modernism, his essays display a new style, which ultimately translated into a profound revival of the literary prose of every Spanish-speaking nation. His essays of the early 1880s are free of superfluous baroque traits and anachronistic Romanticism; his prose is direct and agile, rich in content, endowed with power and color, as he defines the character of the ephemeral *Revista Venezolana* (1881; Venezuelan journal): "Simplicity as a condition is recommended, but this does not imply the exclusion of an elegant touch."

Martí's essays cannot be studied as a unified whole since plurality defines his style; there is a constant variation of styles appropriate to circumstances of the writing and to the audience. Thus, in the 1890s political and social influences led to a return to the long and complicated paragraph, and to the verbal exuberance that prevailed in his patriotic speeches to the exiled Cuban community of Tampa, Florida.

Martí's most emotionally expressive essays are about Cuba, its urgent need for freedom and its future problems, which he predicts with some accuracy. Beyond Cuba, as a greater nation, lies Spanish America; facing this region is North America, a source of anxiety and fear. As his devotion to the fight for his country's independence from Spain evolved, Martí identified in his most fundamental essay, *Nuestra América* (1891; "Our America"), the difference in structure and culture between the two Americas.

From a literary and ideological perspective, Martí can never be considered a subordinate or a mimic, dazzled by the splendor of European and North American culture. It is true that his essays display those intuitive, lyrical, and reflexive freedoms that, since the publication of the *Essais* by **Michel de Montaigne** in 1580, identify the essay as a legitimate and independent literary genre. But it is also true that the Spanish American essay assumes a specificity that is rooted in its themes and its pragmatic character. This in turn means that Spanish American essayists focus almost exclusively on the most immediate and pressing problems faced by their societies, as is exemplified by both Martí's writings and his life. The concrete achievement of his essays lies in the originality with which he is able to merge the aesthetic function with sociopolitical concerns in favor of the liberation of his country and "los pobres de la tierra" (the poor of the earth). His essays, although enriched with expressive literary artifacts, do not originate from literature, but from life.

FEDERICO A. CHACHAGUA

Biography
Born 28 January 1853 in Havana. Studied at the Instituto de Havana, 1866–69; University of Madrid, 1873; University of Saragossa, degree in law, 1873, degree in philosophy and letters, 1874. Worked on the underground periodicals *El Diablo Cojuelo* (The lame devil) and *La Patria Libre* (The free native land), and arrested for subversion, 1869: sentenced to six years' hard labor, but instead exiled to Spain, 1871; moved to Mexico, 1875.

Contributor, *Revista Universal* (Universal review), 1875–76, and cofounder, Alarcón Society, both in Mexico City. Married Carmen Zayas Bazán, 1876: one son. Taught language and philosophy in Guatemala, 1876–77. Returned to Cuba: worked in a law office, and taught literature at the Liceo de Guanabaco; arrested on suspicion of anti-government activity, and deported again to Spain, 1879. Traveled to the United States, and based in New York, 1880–95; journalist or foreign correspondent for various papers, including the New York *Sun*, c. 1880, *El Partido Liberal* (Mexico; The liberal party), *La Opinión Nacional* (Venezuela), from 1881, *La Nación* (Argentina), from 1882, *La República* (Honduras), from 1886, *El Economista Americano* (New York; The American economist), 1887, and *La Opinión Pública* (Uruguay), from 1889. Traveled to Venezuela and founded the *Revista Venezolana*, Caracas, 1881. Translator, Appleton publishers, New York, from 1882. Contributing editor, *La América* (New York), from 1883. Consul for Uruguay, New York, 1887–91. North American representative, Free Press Association of Argentina, from 1888. Founding editor, *La Edad de Oro* (The age of gold) children's magazine, 1889. Spanish teacher, Central High School, New York, 1890. Consul for Argentina and Paraguay, 1890–91, and Paraguay, from 1890. Founder, *Liga de Instrucción* (League of education), Tampa, Florida, 1891. In his last years deepened his involvement in Cuban revolutionary politics: cofounder, Cuban Revolutionary Party and the *Patria* (Native land) revolutionary journal, 1892; helped to organize the invasion of Cuba, 1895; named Major General of the Army of Liberation of Cuba. Killed in action, 19 May 1895.

Selected Writings

Essays and Related Prose
El presidio político en Cuba, 1871
La república española ante la revolución cubana, 1873
Guatemala, 1878
Artículos desconocidos (1883–84), 1930
The America of José Martí: Selected Writings, translated by Juan de Onís, 1953
Obras escogidas, edited by Rafael Esténger, 1953
Páginas de José Martí, edited by Fryda Schulz de Mantovani, 1963
Martí on the U.S.A., edited and translated by Luis A. Baralt, 1966
Martí, edited by Roberto Fernández Retamar, 1970
Sus mejores páginas, edited by Raimundo Lazo, 1970
Escritos desconocidos, edited by Carlos Ripoll, 1971
Ensayos sobre arte y literatura, edited by Roberto Fernández Retamar, 1972
Nuestra América, edited by Roberto Fernández Retamar, 1974, and Hugo Achugar, 1977
Inside the Monster: Writings on the United States and American Imperialism, edited by Philip S. Foner, translated by Foner, Elinor Randall, and others, 1975
Prosa escogida, edited by José Olivio Jiménez, 1975
Discursos selectos, 1977
On Education: Articles on Educational Theory and Pedagogy, and Writings for Children from the "Age of Gold", edited by Philip S. Foner, translated by Elinor Randall, 1979
Our America: Writings on Latin America and the Struggle for Cuban Independence, edited by Philip S. Foner, translated by Elinor Randall, 1979
On Art and Literature: Critical Writings, edited by Philip S. Foner, translated by Elinor Randall, 1982
Idearío, edited by Cintia Vitier and Fina García Marruz, 1987
Political Parties and Elections in the United States, edited by Philip S. Foner, translated by Elinor Randall, 1989
Ensayos y crónicas, edited by José Olivio Jiménez, 1995

Other writings: poetry, the novel *Amistad funesta* (1885), a play, stories for children, political works, and correspondence.

Collected works editions: *Obras completas*, edited by Gonzalo de Quesada y Miranda, 74 vols., 1936–53; *Obras completas* (Editorial de Ciencia Sociales edition), 27 vols., 1954; *Obras completas* (Nacional de Cuba edition), 27 vols., 1963–66.

Bibliographies

Blanch y Blanco, Celestino, *Bibliografía martiana (1954–63)*, Havana: Biblioteca Nacional, Departamento Colección Cubana, 1965

González, Manuel Pedro, *Fuentes para el estudio de José Martí: Ensayo de bibliografía clasificada*, Havana: Publicaciones del Ministerio de Educación, 1950

Peraza Sarausa, Fermín, *Bibliografía martiana (1853–1953)*, Havana: Comisión Nacional de Actos y Ediciones del Centenario, 1954

Ripoll, Carlos, *Índice universal de la obra de José Martí*, New York: Torres, 1971

Ripoll, Carlos, *Archivo José Martí: Repertorio Crítico; Medio siglo de estudios martianos*, New York: Torres, 1971

Further Reading

Cárdenas, Eliana, "José Martí y la identidad latinoamericana," *Plural: Revista Cultural de Excelsior* 11, no. 5 (1981): 16–24

Fernández Retamar, Roberto, *Introducción a José Martí*, Havana: Casa de las Américas, 1978

Schulman, Iván A., editor, *Nuevos asedios al modernismo*, Madrid: Taurus, 1987

Schulman, Iván A., *Relecturas martianas: Narración y nación*, Amsterdam: Rodopi, 1994

Terrazas Basante, Marcela, "Nuestra América y la otra América," *Cuadernos Americanos* 27 (May–June 1991): 137–43

Urrello, Antonio, *Verosimilitud y estrategia textual en el ensayo hispanoamericano*, Mexico City: Premiá, 1986

Martín Gaite, Carmen

Spanish, 1925–

Literary criticism, history, translations, adaptations of plays, television scripts, novels, short stories, poetry, and a one-act play: the literary forms Carmen Martín Gaite has cultivated attest to the range of her work. She is prone to blur the boundaries among these different forms, and her essays contain narrative, dramatic, and lyrical elements. The elasticity of the essay genre makes it a particularly suitable vehicle for Martín Gaite's blending of historical, literary, and linguistic interests. Her writing revolves around a core of abiding preoccupations: problems of communication in life and in literature, the complexity of emotional attachments, and the relationship between past and present. The single most important concern is the search for an interlocutor, or "La búsqueda de interlocutor," as she entitled a 1966 essay. In it she emphasized the primacy of our need for interlocution, arguing that both speech and writing originate in the desire to break out of our solitude and find an audience for our words. Speaker and writer alike seek to establish and maintain contact with a receptive listener or reader; the writer enjoys the advantage of being able to invent that ideal figure. Given the significance that interlocution holds for Martín Gaite, who is a brilliant and seductive conversationalist, it is no surprise that communication and accessibility are major goals of her essays.

Basic to the **familiar essay** is a relationship of intimacy between writer and reader, the former seeming to speak directly to the latter. Martín Gaite's writing frequently resembles speech. The voice heard is that of an intelligent, educated, cultured woman who was 11 when the Spanish Civil War broke out and who lived through the dreariness and repression of the postwar era. Many of her readers also have direct knowledge of that period, and shared experience constitutes a special bond between them and the writer. In *Usos amorosos de la postguerra española* (1987; Love and courtship customs in postwar Spain), which was awarded the Anagrama Essay Prize, Martín Gaite's recollections are complemented by extensive research, the result being a personal and carefully documented history that presents in essayistic form material previously elaborated in her novels. Quotations from publications of the time hold up to ridicule the restrictive ideology expressed by the more retrograde elements of society, and irony and humor underscore the absurdity of their moral strictures. Martín Gaite's gift for satire is evident in thumbnail sketches of Franco's wife and of Pilar Primo de Rivera, sister of the founder of the Falange and head of its Sección Femenina. Descriptions of the feminine ideal promulgated by the latter, courtship rituals, cinematic fare, and fashions make for a vivid and often poignant picture of what it was like to grow up female in the Spain of the 1940s.

A gendered perspective also informs *Desde la ventana: Enfoque femenino de la literatura española* (1987; From the window: feminine focus in Spanish literature). Martín Gaite's reflections on the significance of the window shed light on her own writing. Windows, which allow us to see without being seen, have traditionally been observation points for Spanish women, shut in and away from the world. Martín Gaite ventures the opinion, based on her own experience and her analysis of texts by a number of women, that a literary vocation is often born while standing at a window and longing for liberation and the opportunity to speak one's mind. Windows, she argues, impose a distinctive focus upon our perceptions and situate us in a concrete reality. Apropos of *A Room of One's Own*, Martín Gaite calls attention to the immediacy of **Virginia Woolf**'s writing, the significance of details, the charm of the humor, and the absence of pedantry, all of which characterize the Spanish author's writing and contrast with what she terms "the patriarchal methodology of learned men."

Martín Gaite's penchant for the unconventional and for transgressing generic boundaries is evident in *El cuento de nunca acabar* (1983; The never-ending tale), where literary theory is enlivened by personal anecdotes, conversational tone, and confidential manner. The subtitle *Apuntes sobre la narración, el amor y la mentira* (Notes on narration, love and lies) is reassuring in its suggestion that the book is not a learned **treatise** but a series of notes jotted down at odd moments. The inclusion of seven prologues hints at the leisurely pace of what is to follow and its digressive structure, but the jottings all bear upon the art of storytelling and are strategically positioned despite their seeming disorder. Like **Montaigne**, Martín Gaite conceives of the essay as a journey and persuades us that the ultimate destination is secondary to the pleasures encountered along the way. We, the readers, are cast in the role of traveling companions and conversational partners to whom she repeatedly stretches out her hand so as to make contact and invite us to engage in a **dialogue** with her. In the opening paragraph of *El cuento de nunca acabar* she compares the process of writing the book to embarking on a voyage along a river swollen by water from various tributaries (her previous works, other journeys, her first readings, youthful visions and desires) and fed by a subaqueous current (the conversations she has heard during her lifetime).

Phillip Lopate reminds us in *The Art of the Personal Essay* (1994) that the novel and the essay rose together and fed off each other as literary forms, and Martín Gaite relies on novelistic techniques in her essays, telling stories, incorporating dialogue, portraying characters, and painting scenes. The sense of her presence is strong, and yet the "I" that speaks in the essays, however much it may resemble that of the real-life author, draws upon her experiences, and invites identification of the writerly with the historical self, is in fact carefully constructed. The creation of a persona is one more strategy in the game of literature that Martín Gaite plays so well and with such relish. Although she is best known for her fiction, she is also a talented essayist, and this aspect of her writing is gaining increasing critical attention.

KATHLEEN M. GLENN

Biography
Born 8 December 1925 in Salamanca. Studied at the Feminine Institute of Salamanca; University of Salamanca, 1943–48, degree in romance philology, 1948; University of Madrid, doctorate, 1972. Married Rafael Sánchez Ferlosio, 1953 (divorced, 1987): one son and one daughter (both died). Writer-in-residence, University of Virginia, Charlottesville, 1982. Awards: Gijón Prize, 1954; Nadal Prize, 1957; National Prize for Literature, 1978; Anagrama Essay Prize, 1987; Booksellers' Guild Golden Book Award, 1987; Prince of Asturias Prize, 1988; Castile and León Prize for Letters, 1991; National Prize for Spanish Letters, 1994.

Selected Writings

Essays and Related Prose
Usos amorosos del dieciocho en España, 1972; as *Love Customs in 18th-Century Spain*, translated by Maria G. Tomsich, 1991
La búsqueda de interlocutor y otras búsquedas, 1973
El cuento de nunca acabar: Apuntes sobre la narración, el amor y la mentira, 1983
Usos amorosos de la postguerra española, 1987
Desde la ventana: Enfoque femenino de la literatura española, 1987
Agua pasada: Artículos, prólogos y discursos, 1993

Other writings: several novels (including *El balneario*, 1954; *Entre visillos* [*Behind the Curtains*], 1958; *Ritmo lento*, 1963; *Retahílas*, 1974; *El cuarto de atrás* [*The Back Room*], 1978; *Nubosidad variable*, 1992; *La Reina de las Nieves*, 1994), short fiction, and books for children.

Further Reading
Bergmann, Emilie L., "Narrative Theory in the Mother Tongue: Carmen Martín Gaite's *El cuento de nunca acabar*," in *Public Forums, Private Views: Spanish Women Writers and the Essay*, forthcoming
Brown, Joan Lipman, "Carmen Martín Gaite," in *Spanish Women Writers: A Bio-Bibliographical Source Book*, edited by Linda Gould Levine, Ellen Engelson Marson, and Gloria Feiman Waldman, Westport, Connecticut: Greenwood Press, 1993: 286–95
El Saffar, Ruth, "Shaping the Chaos: Carmen Martín Gaite and the Never-Ending Tale," *International Fiction Review* 11, no. 1 (1984): 25–30

Gómez Pérez, Angel Javier, "Pasos en busca de esa soledad" (review of *Usos amorosos del dieciocho en España*), *Nueva Estafeta* 42 (May 1982): 94–99
Pérez, Janet, "Spanish Women Writers and the Essay," *Siglo XX/20th Century* 4 (1986–87): 43–54
Pope, Randolph D., Amy Kaminsky, Andrew Bush, and Ruth El Saffar, "*El cuento de nunca acabar*: A Critical Dialogue," *Revista de Estudios Hispánicos* 22 (1988): 107–34
Sullivan, Constance A., "The Boundary-Crossing Essays of Carmen Martín Gaite," in *The Politics of the Essay*, edited by Ruth-Ellen Boetcher Joeres and Elizabeth Mittman, Bloomington: Indiana University Press, 1993

Martineau, Harriet
British, 1802–1876

Harriet Martineau's first literary success was a series of fables promoting utilitarian views, *Illustrations of Political Economy* (1832–34). The notoriety they attracted, particularly the controversy attached to her Malthusian views on family limitation, foreshadowed the pattern of her relationship with the reading public which lasted throughout her career. Like the *Illustrations of Political Economy*, Martineau's essays are generally motivated by a desire to instruct the reader and call on narrative and anecdotal material to make their points.

Deaf from childhood, she found solace in reading so that, at an early age, she became "a political economist without knowing it, and, at the same time, a sort of walking Concordance of Milton and Shakespeare." Compelled by a fall in the family's finances to earn an income, Martineau rejected urgings to eke out a living by needlework and chose instead "female authorship." Her consciousness of how she was marginalized by her gender and by her deafness, combined with the need to make her writing appeal to the widest possible audience, shaped her writing throughout her career.

One of her most interesting early essays, "Letter to the Deaf" (1834), sets out to advise deaf readers on how best to manage their disability. Although the essay affects to be unconcerned with the reactions "of those who do not belong to our fraternity," it implicitly encourages the hearing reader to take a more matter-of-fact approach to others' deafness. She urges the deaf to be as independent as possible and develop an active social life. The essay was seized upon and reprinted as a booklet for deaf readers by various charitable organizations concerned with the welfare of the deaf.

In the seven years following her first literary success Martineau consolidated her reputation with two books on her American travels, and a major novel, *Deerbrook* (1839). She was forced into retirement from London literary life by five years of illness until her symptoms seemed miraculously relieved by hypnosis. Her illness and dramatic recovery resulted in two important publications. *Life in the Sick-Room* (1844), a collection of essays which, like "Letter to the Deaf," was ostensibly addressed to "fellow-sufferers," examined the psychological aspects of prolonged illness. *Letters on Mesmerism* (1845) were based on the record she had made of the treatments which had relieved her illness. Martineau submitted the six essays to the *Athenaeum* in order to counter some of the gossip that had arisen. She was horrified when the *Athenaeum* appended editorial notes that attempted to discredit mesmerism in general and Martineau's experiences in particular. The war of words escalated when her brother-in-law, who had acted as her physician, published a **pamphlet** detailing the gynecological symptoms from which she had suffered and expressing skepticism about the cure. The episode illustrates not only Martineau's intensely personal approach, but also her willingness to take the risk of finding herself in the midst of virulent controversy.

Throughout her career Martineau continued to write on various aspects of political economy and to provide commentary on the political questions of the day. Her economic views, arguing for laissez-faire conservatism, were formed by her background in a textile manufacturer's family and endorsed by her early readings in political economy. This led her into conflict with **Dickens**, whose *Household Words* articles had been advocating better and safer factory conditions. Martineau weighed in on behalf of the manufacturers with a pamphlet, *The Factory Controversy: A Warning Against Meddling Legislation* (1855). John Chapman, in refusing the piece for publication in the *Westminster Review*, warned of her tendency to see factory owners as "a band of enlightened well-wishers."

On almost every other issue Martineau was progressive as well as outspoken. Her chief opportunity to influence both politicians and the general public came when she began writing leader articles for the *Daily News* in 1852. During the 14 years she was associated with the paper she wrote over a thousand articles on topical political events as well as broader issues such as women's rights and the abolition of slavery. She argued for better access to education for all, and for a less class-ridden education system since "our spirit of caste is quite broad enough without being extended into the kingdom of knowledge." Her 1864 article on the Contagious Diseases Bill (legislation allowing the detention and medical examination of women in military towns on the grounds that they might be prostitutes) launched the campaign against the proposed laws. When the law was finally repealed in 1871, her editor at the *Daily News* suggested to her that she had "done more than anyone else . . . to defeat the plan of the military." From the beginning of her tenure at the *Daily News* she had used her leaders to discuss women's legal situation. For example, her columns drew attention to the routine police use of the term "wife-beating," pointing out that the coining of the term indicated "the present prevalence of the ill usage of wives."

Martineau's essays are strikingly personal and direct. Even when writing obituary essays she is often refreshingly acerbic. In failing health and straitened circumstances at the end of her life, she was aided by *Daily News* staff who collected the obituary essays she had written on notable contemporaries. The resulting book was *Biographical Sketches* (1869), with its trenchant and vivid portraits of the many friends and foes she had so clearly observed throughout her remarkable career.

Martineau's polemical positions antagonized a number of her contemporaries such as **John Stuart Mill** and Dickens, but others held her in high regard. Elizabeth Barrett Browning admired her "lucid and able style," while **George Eliot** told one correspondent, "she is a *trump* – the only English woman that possesses thoroughly the art of writing."

Although many of Martineau's essays focus on the political and economic questions particular to her times, she remains one of the most accessible and appealing of 19th-century essayists. Despite the energy with which she promotes her opinions, she is disarmingly frank in her use of the essay as a means of exploration. As she noted at the outset of her career, "There is no education like authorship for ascertaining one's knowledge and one's ignorance."

GILLIAN THOMAS

Biography

Born 12 June 1802 in Norwich. Studied privately and at the Reverend Pervy's school, Norwich, 1813–15. In poor health throughout her life, and began to go deaf at age 12. Supported herself, her mother, and an aunt, first with needlework, then with writing. Contributor to the *Monthly Repository* Unitarian journal, 1820s. Traveled in the United States, 1834–36. Ill, possibly from a uterine tumor, and went to live near her doctor brother-in-law in Tynemouth, Northumberland, 1839–44: tried mesmerism as a cure, writing about her experience. Moved to Clappersgate, near Ambleside, Westmorland, 1845, where she met William Wordsworth and **Matthew Arnold**. Traveled to Palestine and Egypt, 1846–47. Contributor to *Household Words*, late 1840s, the *People's Journal*, the London *Daily News*, 1852–66, and *Edinburgh Review*, from 1859. Died in Clappersgate, 27 June 1876.

Selected Writings

Essays and Related Prose
The Faith as Unfolded by Many Prophets: An Essay Addressed to the Disciples of Mohammed, 1832
Life in the Sick-Room; or, Essays by an Invalid, 1844
Letters on Mesmerism, 1845
Household Education, 1849
Letters on the Laws of Man's Nature and Development, with Henry George Atkinson, 1851
Letters from Ireland, 1853
Biographical Sketches, 1869; revised edition, 1876
Harriet Martineau in the London Daily News: Selected Contributions, 1852–1866, edited by Elisabeth Sanders Arbuckle, 1994

Other writings: fiction (including the novel *Deerbrook*, 1839), the didactic tales *Illustrations of Political Economy* (1832–34), four children's novels, books on a variety of subjects such as travel, politics, and history, and a three-volume autobiography (1877).

Bibliography
Rivlin, J. B., *Harriet Martineau: A Bibliography of the Separately Printed Books*, New York: New York Public Library, 1946

Further Reading
David, Deirdre, *Intellectual Women and Victorian Patriarchy: Harriet Martineau, Elizabeth Barrett Browning, George Eliot*, Ithaca, New York: Cornell University Press, and London: Macmillan, 1987
Hoecker-Drysdale, Susan, *Harriet Martineau: First Woman Sociologist*, Oxford: Berg, 1992
Marks, Patricia, "Harriet Martineau: Fraser's Maid of [Dis] Honour," *Victorian Periodicals Review* 19 (1986): 28–34
Myers, Mitzi, "Unmothered Daughter and Radical Reformer: Harriet Martineau's Career," in *The Lost Tradition: Mothers and Daughters in Literature*, edited by Cathy N. Davidson and E. M. Broner, New York: Ungar, 1980: 70–80
Pichanick, Valerie Kossew, "An Abominable Submission: Harriet Martineau's Views on the Role and Place of Women," *Women's Studies* 5, no. 1 (1977): 13–32

Pichanick, Valerie Kossew, *Harriet Martineau: The Woman and Her Work, 1802–76*, Ann Arbor: University of Michigan Press, 1980

Thomas, Gillian, *Harriet Martineau*, Boston: Twayne, 1985

Webb, R. K., *Harriet Martineau: A Radical Victorian*, London: Heinemann, 1960

Martínez Estrada, Ezequiel

Argentine, 1895–1964

Ezequiel Martínez Estrada came to be the most important Argentine essayist of his generation, but could just as easily have become one of the country's leading poets. He received the active encouragement of Leopoldo Lugones, Argentina's leading *modernista* poet and a huge literary presence in the country, and subsequently won the Third National Prize for Literature for his poetry collection *Nefelibel* (1922). His motive for largely giving up poetry and opting for the essay as his definitive genre (he also wrote drama and short stories) can in great part be ascribed to his friendship with the reclusive Uruguayan writer Horacio Quiroga (one of Spanish America's finest exponents of the short story), which Martínez Estrada himself described in detail in *El hermano Quiroga* (1957; Brother Quiroga). As a consequence of that relationship, Martínez Estrada began to "write with his right hand," saying that it was Quiroga who "extinguished in me the dying lamp of poetry that had illuminated the dark paths of my youth ... He swept from me the final remnants of a deficient, academic education and [my] ignorant, schoolboyish acceptance of the deceitful opinion of the critics ..." Thus the essayist's encounter with Quiroga was an act of self-discovery and a confirmation that the "dark paths of his youth" in fact constituted a personality trait that was to last throughout his life.

In a literary career that comprised some 30 major essays, beginning in 1933 with *Radiografía de la pampa* (X-Ray of the Pampa), his most famous essay, and ending with his work on the 19th-century Cuban writer **José Martí**, he embarked upon a systematic demolition of Argentina's past and in particular what he saw as the shameful, collaborationist role of the country's writers and intellectuals in the creation and perpetuation of myths that traduced the real nature of Argentina's history and culture. This work, "the Bible of pessimism" as it came to be termed, set him apart from contemporaries such as **Eduardo Mallea** who, if sharing a sense of the polemical nature of the nation's cultural identity, formulated much less negative conclusions.

X-Ray of the Pampa offered an analysis of the region starting from the earliest colonial times, and ascribed the roots of cultural poverty and a deep spiritual malaise or "neurotic anguish" to the fruitless search for an El Dorado, to the failure to come to terms with the land, and to the development of a mixed Spanish-Indian society. That experience, according to Martínez Estrada, was to leave an indelible mark on the Argentine soul, and from it flowed the engendering of a false society, built as it was upon seriously flawed beginnings. The essay itself was not really an *essai* – neither the exposition of a reasoned hypothesis nor an implied dialogue with the reader – but rather a relentless deconstruction of Martínez Estrada's contemporary society that left little room for dissent.

The consequences of this position were twofold. First, so stark and unyielding was the essential message of *X-Ray of the Pampa* that the essayist found himself with few kindred spirits who were willing to share his analysis. Indeed he left few disciples, the most famous being H. A. Murena, whose principal essay *El pecado original de América* (1954; The Original Sin of America) reveals in its title the affinity with the master. Unlike, say, a **Jorge Luis Borges**, the greater part of Argentine youth of the day did not flock to Martínez Estrada's lectures and talks in search of direction and inspiration. This in turn led to the second consequence: the engendering in Martínez Estrada of a persecution complex, a conviction that publishers had ostracized him and shunned his work. He was in fact always ready to see himself as a biblical prophet (a modern-day Ezekiel) crying in the wilderness, as it were, of an Argentina that could not and would not heed his message. This conviction would remain with him and was a principal motive in his decision to seek temporary exile in Cuba in the early 1960s.

The irony of all this is that in the almost three decades from *X-Ray of the Pampa* to his departure for Cuba, Martínez Estrada went on to write (and publish) his best work in Argentina. These titles include *Sarmiento* (1946), *Los invariantes históricos en el "Facundo"* (1947; Historical invariables in the Facundo), *Muerte y transfiguración de Martín Fierro* (1948; The death and transfiguration of Martin Fierro), and the largely overlooked *Diferencias y semejanzas entre los países de la América Latina* (1962; Differences and similarities between the countries of Latin America). His chief bibliographer, Carlos Adam, following the essayist's recommendations, organized his writings under "literary," "historico-sociological," and "polemical" headings; examples of each would be *Realidad y fantasía en Balzac* (1964; Reality and fantasy in Balzac), *La cabeza de Goliat* (1940; The head of Goliath), and *Exhortaciones* (1957; Exhortations) respectively. While the essayist's output supports these classifications, it could equally be argued that at least until 1960 (the year of his departure for Cuba) his writings essentially stemmed from the same basic world view, which was expressed in *X-Ray of the Pampa* (grouped under the "historico-sociological" essays) and would appear in different types of essays, as is the case with this quote from *Para una revisión de las letras argentinas* (1967; Contributions to a revision of Argentine literature), which would fall under the "literary" category: "Self-betrayal is the central and radical problem of our lives ... the problem of our historical existence as a people, of a great nation having been misgoverned and impoverished yet with no awareness of the world in which it lives, nor of the peoples that coexist within it, nor of reality itself to which it hasn't yet resigned or adapted itself."

This message was to be repeated in various forms over the years, but Martínez Estrada could never persuade enough of his compatriots to accept it. He arrived in Cuba in 1960, at the invitation of the publishing house Casa de las Américas, an embittered expatriate. What no one counted on, including the essayist himself, was the effect the life and work of the legendary Cuban writer José Martí was to have upon him, lifting his spirits to heights of unusual optimism and self-confirmation, and causing him to write seven essays about Cuba and Martí. From this period are essays such as *El verdadero cuento* del *Tío Sam* (1963; The real story of Uncle Sam) and *Martí, revolucionario* (1967; Marti the revolutionary). Martínez Estrada was convinced that the latter, published posthumously, was the best work he had produced, a view not generally shared by critics, although there can be no doubt that his first-hand experience of Cuba between 1960 and 1962 (and visits to Mexico during the same period) in his view compensated to some degree for the tribulations and rejections he had perceived in earlier years in Argentina.

JAMES MAHARG

Biography
Born 14 September 1895 in San José de la Esquina, province of Santa Fe. Studied at the Colegio Avellaneda, Buenos Aires; largely self-taught. Worked for the General Post Office, Buenos Aires, 1915–46. Married Augustina Morriconi, 1921. Taught at the Colegio Nacional, University of La Plata, 1923–45. Traveled in Europe, 1927 and 1957, and Brazil, 1947. Founding member, and president, 1933–34 and 1942–46, National Society of Writers. Taught at the National University of the South, Bahía Blanca, from 1949. Suffered from a painful skin disease, a form of neurodermatitis, from 1952. Moved to Mexico, 1959, where he taught at the School of Political Science, National Autonomous University of Mexico. Lived in Cuba, 1960–62. Moved back to Bahía Blanca, 1962. Awards: five major Argentinian prizes, 1922–48; Casa de las Américas Prize, 1960. Died (of cancer) in Bahía Blanca, 3 November 1964.

Selected Writings

Essays and Related Prose
Radiografía de la pampa, 1933; edited by Leo Pollmann, 1991; as *X-Ray of the Pampa*, translated by Alain Swietlicki, 1971
La cabeza de Goliat, 1940
Sarmiento, 1946
Panorama de las literaturas, 1946
Nietzsche, 1947
Los invariantes históricos en el "Facundo", 1947
Muerte y transfiguración de Martín Fierro: Ensayo de interpretación de la vida argentina, 2 vols., 1948
El mundo maravilloso de Guillermo Enrique Hudson, 1951
Cuadrante del pampero, 1956
¿Qué es esto?, 1956
Exhortaciones, 1957
El hermano Quiroga, 1957
Las 40, 1957
Heraldos de la verdad: Montaigne-Balzac-Nietzsche, 1958
Diferencias y semejanzas entre los países de América Latina, 1962
El verdadero cuento del Tío Sam, 1963
En Cuba, y al servicio de la revolución cubana, 1963; as *Mi experiencia cubana*, 1965
Antología, 1964
Realidad y fantasía en Balzac, 1964
Martí, revolucionario, 1967
En torno a Kafka y otros ensayos, 1967
Para una revisión de las letras argentinas, edited by Enrique Espinoza, 1967
Leopoldo Lugones: Retrato sin retocar, 1968
Leer y escribir (selection), edited by Enrique Espinoza, 1969
Panorama de los Estados Unidos, edited by Joaquín Roy, 1985

Other writings: poetry, short stories, and plays.

Bibliography
Adam, Carlos, *Bibliografía y documentos de Ezequiel Martínez Estrada*, La Plata: National University of La Plata, 1968

Further Reading
Anderson Imbert, Enrique, "Kafka y Martínez Estrada," *Nueva Revista de Filología Hispánica* 36, no. 1 (1988): 467–76
Earle, Peter G., *Prophet in the Wilderness: The Works of Ezequiel Martínez Estrada*, Austin: University of Texas Press, 1971
Earle, Peter G., "Las soledades de Martínez Estrada," *Cuadernos Americanos* 7, no. 42 (November–December 1993): 148–56
Fernández Retamar, Roberto, "Desde el Martí de Ezequiel Martínez Estrada," *Cuadernos Americanos* 7, no. 42 (November–December 1993): 131–47
Maharg, James, *A Call to Authenticity: The Essays of Ezequiel Martínez Estrada*, University, Mississippi: Romance Monographs, 1977
Stabb, Martin S., *In Quest of Identity: Patterns in the Spanish American Essay of Ideas, 1890–1960*, Chapel Hill: University of North Carolina Press, 1967

Marx, Karl
German, 1818–1883

Intransigent, direct, mocking, and politically subversive, Marx ranks as one of the most powerful and distinctive voices Germany has produced. Its eloquence and conviction is the result of an activist approach to critique. Picking up where **Kant** and Hegel left off, Marx reformulates the theory-praxis problem in a revolutionary way. For him, change is no longer introduced by dogmatic assumptions; rather, it is through the critique of the old that the new becomes possible. Marx therefore calls for "the relentless critique of all that exists" (*Rheinische Zeitung*, 15 November 1844). This implies understanding oneself, i.e. the necessity of self-reflection (*Selbstverständigung*). Critique requires first and foremost a capacity for self-criticism. The unique mission and opportunity of the press call for it to make such critique possible.

Starting as a journalist, Marx combined a theoretical outlook with political engagement. Conceived as critical analyses of the dynamics of social forces, his articles forge the political essay into a tool for class struggle. Subverting in Hegelian fashion the hold of particular interests by exposing their internal contradictions, the essays take on repression, whatever its disguise, and exercise a power that goes beyond the mere fireworks they engender. Instead of merely offering a critique of the opposition, the analytic rigor of his essays destroys the claims of those in power, revealing their falseness as pretense. Identifying the moment of truth in such falseness, Marx's critique of ideology exposes the darker sides of exploitation.

In the age of Metternich's political reaction, Marx's first articles take Prussian censorship and the press laws to task. As he points out, method rather than its result creates the truth which can thereby resist all attempts at extraneous determination. To ignore this means to fall victim to the contradictions to which the denial of the self-defining constitution of truth would lead. Critique alone – as self-constituting court – is able to restrict itself. The parliament that desires to control freedom of the press indicts itself. Similarly, Marx's account of the debates on the law against theft of wood returns the blame which some legislators hoped to lay on the oppressed masses to those legislators themselves. In the final analysis, he argues, it is such legislation that threatens to undermine the very idea itself of law and state. Exposing the abuse in parliament's debates at every stage, Marx turns the tables in ingenious reversal: "The wood-thief has filched wood from the forest-owner, but the forest-owner has used the thief to filch the state itself" ("Debatten über das Holzdiebstahlsgesetz" [1842; "Debates on the Law on Thefts of Wood"]). Clearing up the ideological thicket, the literary strategy exposes the hypocritical character that lends exploitative fraud its friendly face.

Perhaps Marx's most accomplished essay, "Zur Judenfrage" (1844; "On the Jewish Question"), performs a precarious balancing act which displays most strikingly both the strength and limits of high-strung dialectics. A literary *pas de deux* of materialist and idealist thought, this essay pushes the discourse on emancipation to its brink. Its sheer density renders it at once opaque and translucent, light and heavyhanded, radical and superficial. Charged with the dynamics of dialectics, its sparkle has at the same time a blinding effect. Like Marx's other essays, it confronts readers with their own conceptual fixations. Argumentative irreducibility is enacted at the cost of the blind spot – Marx's Jewish self-hatred – around which the essay circles.

In 1848 Marx became editor-in-chief of the *Neue Rheinische Zeitung* (New Rhenish newspaper), Germany's mouthpiece for the 1848 Revolution. Marx saw his paper's task of recording and commenting on the course of political change as intricately linked on the local and international scale and as reflecting the stage world history had reached. The paper lasted only until May 1849, when the 1848 Revolution was finally thwarted. More astonishing is the fact that the paper could be published at all. Looking back on this period, Friedrich Engels recalls the editorial practice that created the newspaper's singular power to electrify the proletarian masses: "... thanks to the eight bayonet rifles and 250 shots of ammunition in the editor's office, and the typesetters' red Jacobin hats, our offices were known by the garrison's officers as a fort, too, that was not easily to be taken by a simple *coup de main*." As editor and journalist Marx himself more than once suffered the personal consequences of this struggle. As he described this experience: "... we were blessed at once with the advantages of feudal servitude, bureaucratic police protocol and the modern bourgeois legal brutality" (1849). Two months later, 19 May 1849, the last issue was printed in red ink.

With Engels Marx penned the *Manifest der Kommunistischen Partei* (1848; *The Communist Manifesto*), one of the single most influential texts written in the 19th century. Its manifesto style – clarity, brevity, and precision – carries the political essay to new heights. Its imagery has ever since informed and haunted the literary and political imagination. Designed to serve as the party's official missive, it demonstrates the unavoidable necessity for revolution. Between the suggestive opening, "A spectre is haunting Europe – the spectre of Communism," and the concluding call, "Working men of all countries, unite!" (the two single best-known lines in the manifesto), a forceful argument is launched arguing that the party is the only and irresistible agency capable of solving the world-historical mandate: to bring about the universal solution to oppression, the class-free society.

Four years later the 1851 December *coup d'état* by Louis Bonaparte marked an historical caesura that forced Marx to write his *Der achtzehnte Brumaire des Louis-Bonaparte* (1869; *The Eighteenth Brumaire of Louis Bonaparte*). To account for the surprising political backlash to the ideas in the wake of 1848, Marx resorts to the categories of tragedy and farce. Politics becomes a play whose farcical repetitions are ultimately free from historical ramifications. Yet where this theatrical staging sees only actors playing out their drama of politics, we find Marx attempting to solve the drama posed by his own theorizing. The model of tragedy/farce arrests history and reduces it to a loop. While Marx concedes the political its own sphere, the schedule of world history remains intact; enriched by breaks and interruptions, these farcical ruptures now corroborate what they seem to have jeopardized – the dignity of history. While Marx offers no argument to resolve this dilemma logically, the exposition of the essay provides the necessary space to act out what seems impossible to address otherwise.

While Marx continued his journalistic work as a sideline, the newspaper articles, which now solely served the purpose of a source of income, were toned down to the objective tone of technical reports. *Zur Kritik der politischen Ökonomie* (1859; *A Contribution to the Critique of Political Economy*) and *Das Kapital* (1867–95; *Capital*) are no longer essays but bring their project to completion. Informed by the praxis of critique, they retain some of the virtuoso dexterity that is the trademark of Marx's essays. Pointing beyond logical demonstration, the expository play in the later works is grounded in the evocative appeal to critical imagination.

WILLI GOETSCHEL

Biography

Karl Heinrich Marx. Born 5 May 1818 in Trier. Studied philosophy and law at the Universities of Bonn and Berlin, 1835–41; member of the "Doctorklub," a group of students interested in philosophy. Editor-in-chief, *Die Rheinische Zeitung*, Cologne, 1842–43: suppressed by the censor. Married Jenny von Westphalen, 1843: one son (died in youth) and three daughters. Moved to Paris, 1843, where he became lifelong friends with Friedrich Engels; coeditor, *Deutsch-Französische Jahrbücher* (German-French yearbook), Paris, 1843; expelled for writing anti-Prussian essays, and moved to Brussels, 1845, where he and Engels joined the Communist League. Returned to Cologne, 1848; editor, *Neue Rheinische Zeitung*, Cologne, 1848–49. Expelled from Germany and lived in London, from 1849; journalist for various newspapers, including *Neue Oder-Zeitung* (Breslau), 1855, Sheffield and London *Free Press*, 1855–56, and the *People's Paper* and *Wiener Presse* (Vienna), 1861–62; European correspondent for the New York *Daily Tribune* (many of these articles were actually written by Engels). Head, General Council of the International Working Men's Association, 1864–76. Died in London, 14 March 1883.

Selected Writings

Essays and Related Prose
(most works cowritten with Friedrich Engels)
Misère de la philosophie: Réponse à la philosophie de la misère de M. Proudhon, 1847; facsimile edition edited by Kikuji Tanaka, 1982; as *The Poverty of Philosophy*, translated by Harry Quelch, 1900
Manifest der Kommunistischen Partei, 1848; authorized English translation as *Manifesto of the Communist Party*, edited by Engels, translated by Samuel Moore, 1888; subsequent editions as

The Communist Manifesto, edited by Dirk J. Struik, 1971,
   Frederic L. Bender, 1988, and David McLellan, 1988
Der achtzehnte Brumaire des Louis-Bonaparte, 1869; as *The
   Eighteenth Brumaire of Louis Bonaparte*, translated by Daniel De
   Leon, 1898, and Eden and Cedar Paul, 1926
Selected Essays, translated by H. J. Stenning, 1926
"Die deutsche Ideologie," in *Historisch-kritische Gesamtausgabe,
   Werke, Schriften, Briefe*, vol. 5, edited by David Rjazanov and
   Vladimir Viktorovich Adoratskij, 1932; as *The German Ideology*,
   translated by S. Ryazanskaya, 1964
Basic Writings on Politics and Philosophy, edited by Lewis S. Feuer,
   1959
Economic and Philosophic Manuscripts of 1844, translated by
   Martin Milligan, 1959; edited by Dirk J. Stuik, 1969
Early Writings, edited and translated by T. B. Bottomore, 1963
Essential Writings, edited by David Caute, 1967
Articles from the Neue Rheinische Zeitung, 1848–49, edited by
   Bernard Isaacs, translated by S. Ryazanskaya, 1972
The Marx-Engels Reader, edited by Robert C. Tucker, 1972;
   revised, enlarged edition, 1978
Essential Writings, edited by Frederic L. Bender, 1972
Political Writings, edited by David Fernbach, 3 vols., 1973
Selected Writings, edited by David McLellan, 1977
The Essential Marx: The Non-Economic Writings, a Selection,
   edited and translated by Saul K. Padover, 1979
The Collected Writings in "The New York Daily Tribune", edited
   by A. Thomas Ferguson and Stephen J. O'Neil, 1980
The Portable Karl Marx, edited by Eugene Kamenka, 1983
Early Political Writings, edited and translated by Joseph O'Malley
   and Richard A. Davis, 1994
Later Political Writings, edited and translated by Terrell Carver,
   1996

Other writings: *Das Kapital* (1867–95; *Capital*), *Zur Kritik der
politischen Ökomonie* (1859; *A Contribution to the Critique of
Political Economy*), and many other political works.

Collected works editions: *Karl Marx, Friedrich Engels: Werke*, 43
vols., 1956–68; *Collected Works*, 47 vols., 1973–95 (in progress).

Bibliographies

Draper, Hal, *The Marx-Engels Register: A Complete Bibliography
   of Marx and Engels' Individual Writings*, New York: Schocken,
   1985
Eubanks, Cecil L., *Karl Marx and Friedrich Engels: An Analytical
   Bibliography*, New York: Garland, 1984 (original edition, 1977)
Neubauer, Franz, *Marx-Engels Bibliographie*, Boppard: Boldt,
   1979

Further Reading

Balibar, Etienne, *The Philosophy of Marx*, London and New York:
   Verso, 1995 (original French edition, 1993)
Bové, Paul, "The Metaphysics of Textuality: Marx's *Eighteenth
   Brumaire* and Nietzsche's Use and Abuse of History," *Dalhousie
   Review* 64 (1984): 401–22
Kemple, Thomas M., *Reading Marx Writing: Melodrama, the
   Market, and the "Grundrisse"*, Stanford, California: Stanford
   University Press, 1995
McLellan, David, *The Thought of Karl Marx: An Introduction*,
   London: Papermac, 1980 (original edition, 1971)
McLellan, David, *Karl Marx: A Biography*, London: Papermac,
   1995 (original edition, 1975)
Mehlman, Jeffrey, *Revolution and Repetition: Marx/Hugo/Balzac*,
   Berkeley: University of California Press, 1977
Said, Edward, "On Repetition," in his *The World, the Text, and
   the Critic*, Cambridge, Massachusetts: Harvard University Press,
   1983: 111–25

Massis, Henri

French, 1886–1970

Eloquent witness of the political, literary, intellectual, and
Catholic life in France during the first half of the 20th century,
Henri Massis is often dismissed today as a Catholic apologist
and a staunch defender of nationalism. Though dogmatic in
his moral and literary views, he must nonetheless be regarded
as one of the pioneers of the French essay as a contemporary
genre.

While Theodore Fraser (1986) states that the modern French
essayist can "... co nduct systematic investigations, spin theories, or simply speculate upon a myriad of topics and issues .
..," the *Anthologie des essayistes français contemporains* in
1929 defined the task of the essayist as being either to create,
to bring out, or to clarify ideas that serve as directives to an
epoch. As an influential figure in both the literary and the political world, Massis strove to do exactly that. In numerous essays
he often defended the traditional cultural, patriotic, and
Catholic values of France.

Massis began his prolific writing career during his Sorbonne
days, publishing, in his early twenties, *Comment Émile Zola
composait ses romans* (1906; How Émile Zola composed his
novels), *Le Puits de Pyrrhon* (1907; Pyrrho's well), a philosophical "*conte*" which he dedicated to Anatole France, and
La Pensée de Maurice Barrès (1909; The thought of Maurice
Barrès). This latter book was the first in which he took a political stand. Massis gained notoriety as early as 1911 when,
collaborating with his friend Alfred de Tarde under the pseudonym of Agathon, they published a widely debated essay on
the state of French university education, *L'Esprit de la nouvelle
Sorbonne* (The spirit of the New Sorbonne). Denouncing the
invasion of Germanic scientific methods into French university
pedagogy, Massis warned against the renunciation of traditional liberal arts education. He feared "'a progressive debasement of general culture' ... and the formation of a new kind
of person: not the *honnête homme* of the Renaissance tradition but the *esprit spécialiste*" (Fraser). In 1913, the year in
which Massis converted to Catholicism, he and de Tarde again
published under the same pseudonym the results of their
research on *Les Jeunes Gens d'aujourd'hui* (Young people of
today). Among the youth, they detected an anti-intellectual
tendency, a thirst for military action, a patriotic faith, an orientation toward Catholicism, and an anti-parliamentary attitude.
The monarchist Charles Maurras and his growing Action
Française movement welcomed their observation that there
seemed to be a nationalist renaissance in France.

Following the war, in 1919, Massis published the manifesto
"Pour un parti de l'intelligence" (In favor of intelligence), in
which he called for the restoration of the French spirit, of the
French state, and of the Catholic Church, as well as for the
revival of intellectual life in France through a national and
metaphysical awakening. However, Massis' postwar expectations for France and for a strong Catholic renewal were to be
disappointed.

Although never a member of the Action Française, Massis
did sympathize with this movement and became close to
Maurras, whose nationalist and traditionalist values he shared.
The founding of the *Revue Universelle* (Universal review) in

1920 by Maurras and Jacques Maritain proved a major event in the literary world. With Massis as editor, Jacques Bainville as director, and Jacques Maritain in charge of the philosophy section, the journal's stated mission was to rebuild the public spirit in France by means of the intellect, and by French thought to attempt a worldwide intellectual federation. With the journal as their vehicle, Massis and Maritain worked at instituting a Christian political philosophy, Maritain in making Thomism accessible to the French public through concepts and principles, Massis through criticism and literary applications.

In 1923, Massis' first volume of *Jugements* (Judgments) collected his essays on **Ernest Renan**, Anatole France, and Barrès and was dedicated to Maritain ("This testimony of our common hope in the metaphysical restoration"). His second volume of *Jugements*, with essays on **André Gide**, Romain Rolland, Georges Duhamel, and **Julien Benda**, appeared a year later. Uncompromisingly, Massis uncovered what he perceived to be the moral and ideological flaws in their writings. It was, he said, time to keep law and order in literature ("faire la police des lettres"). Massis particularly anathemized Gide, A. France, Rolland, and Benda, not only for having discredited but also for having corrupted the French tradition. Massis demanded that Christian values be strictly and absolutely followed in all areas of life, which he saw threatened by the changing values in postwar France. His particular aversion to Gide and his determination to battle the writer's influence on young French readers in an era of spiritual crisis were manifested as early as 1914 in an article for *L'Éclair* (Lightning) when he denounced "André Gide's perversity." Viewing Gide's theory of the gratuitous act as a "violation of all morality," his prose took on a vitriolic flavor. Massis repeatedly espoused Claudel's assessment of Gide that "le mal, ça ne compose pas" (evil does not create), not hesitating, in 1921, even to label Gide as the devil. Another article in 1929 described the "Faillite d'André Gide" (André Gide's failure).

In contrast, Massis' analysis of Marcel Proust was more benevolent. In his essay on *Le Drame de Marcel Proust* (1937; The drama of Marcel Proust), Massis attempted to uncover Proust's soul. Unlike Gide, Massis stated, Proust's fictional world did not destroy the moral universe. *D'André Gide à Marcel Proust* (1948; From André Gide to Marcel Proust) comprises incisive essays on both writers.

Other than his literary criticism, Massis' political essays may be best known today, especially his **treatise**, *Défense de l'Occident* (The defense of the West), published by Jacques Maritain in Plon's distinguished "Roseau d'Or" collection in 1927. Massis' ongoing concern to restore France's Christian and missionary vocation is manifested in his warnings against technological progress and what he perceived as the pernicious influence of Bolshevism, Oriental mysticism, and even Germanism, all of which he viewed as hostile to the Romano-Christian culture of France. These constant themes were echoed in Massis' essay collection of 1934, *Débats* (Debates), in his manifesto "Pour la défense de l'Occident et la paix en Europe" (1935; For the defense of the West and peace in Europe), written as a defense of Italy's invasion of Ethiopia, as well as in *La Guerre de trente ans* (1940; The Thirty Years' War), a collection of essays dedicated to the Franco-German problems. His *Découverte de la Russie* (1944; The discovery of Russia) serves as a kind of supplement to *Défense de l'Occident*, and

renews his warning against communist Russia and the danger of a potential union between Russia and a unified Germany. Postwar books such as *L'Allemagne d'hier et d'après-demain* (1949; Germany yesterday and the day after tomorrow), *L'Occident et son destin* (1956; The West and its destiny), as well as *L'Europe en question* (1958; Europe at stake) are all expressions of his apprehension regarding France's future spiritual direction.

Massis was personally acquainted with writers such as **Alain**, Henri Bergson, Barrès, **Charles Péguy**, Paul Claudel, France, Ernest Psichari, Henri Drouot, Maritain, **Georges Bernanos**, Maurras, Jean Cocteau, Robert Brasillach, to name but a few, and his recollections in *Maurras et notre temps* (1951; Maurras and our time) or in *Au long d'une vie* (1967; A lifetime) are of unique historical value regarding the evolution of literary and intellectual life in 20th-century France.

Massis employed the essay to defend Christian values, as well as France's Catholic mission and traditions. His output as literary critic, polemicist, and historian provoked heated debates in his time and had far-reaching influence. Massis did not indulge in posturing, and his style was never artificial. His writing was driven by deep personal convictions and ideals. These he tried to impress upon France's youth and intelligentsia in the hope that his country might lead Europe in a renewal of Catholic spirituality.

ASTRID HEYER

Biography

Born 21 March 1886 in Paris. Studied at the Lycées Condorcet and Henri IV (where he was taught by Alain), Paris; the Sorbonne, Paris. Married: one son. Military service, from 1905; also fought in World War I. Subeditor, *L'Opinion*, 1911–14. Converted to Catholicism, 1913. Editor, 1920–39, and director, 1939–44, *La Revue Universelle*; founder and editor, 1933 newspaper, 1929–34. Served under Vichy during World War II. Worked for Plon publishing house after the war. Elected to the French Academy, 1960. Award: French Academy Grand Prize for Literature, 1929. Died in Paris, 16 April 1970.

Selected Writings

Essays and Related Prose

Comment Émile Zola composait ses romans, 1906
Le Puits de Pyrrhon, 1907
La Pensée de Maurice Barrès, 1909
L'Esprit de la nouvelle Sorbonne, with Alfred de Tarde (jointly as Agathon), 1911
Les Jeunes Gens d'aujourd'hui, with Alfred de Tarde (jointly as Agathon), 1913
Romain Rolland contre la France, 1915
La Vie d'Ernest Psichari, 1916
Jugements, 2 vols., 1923–24; revised edition, 1929
En marge de "Jugements": Réflexions sur l'art du roman, 1927
Défense de l'Occident, 1927
Réflexions sur l'art du roman, 1927
Avant-Postes (chroniques d'un redressement), 1910–1914 (articles), 1928
Dix ans après: Réflexions sur la littérature d'après guerre, 1932
Débats, 1934
L'Honneur de servir, 1937
Le Drame de Marcel Proust, 1937
Chefs: Les Dictateurs et nous, 1939
Le Siège de l'Alcazar, with Robert Brasillach, 1939

La Guerre de trente ans, 1940
Les Idées restent, 1941
Découverte de la Russie, 1944
D'André Gide à Marcel Proust, 1948
L'Allemagne d'hier et d'après-demain, 1949
L'Occident et son destin, 1956
L'Europe en question, 1958
Visages des idées; À contre-courant; Thèmes et discussions, 1958
Salazar face à face, 1961
Barrès et nous, 1962

Other writings: works on politics, religion, and literature, and memoirs.

Further Reading

Archambault, Paul, *Jeunes Maîtres,* Paris: Bloud & Gay, 1926
Bernanos, Georges, *Correspondance inédite, 1904–1934: Combat pour la vérité,* Paris: Plon, 1971
Brasillach, Robert, *Notre Avant-guerre,* Paris: Plon, 1941
Calvet, J., *Le Renouveau catholique dans la littérature contemporaine,* Paris: Lanore, 1927
Christophe, Lucien, "Regards sur Henri Massis," *Revue Générale Belge* (May 1961): 17–41
Clouard, Henri, *Histoire de la littérature française: Du symbolisme à nos jours, de 1914 à 1940,* Paris: Albin Michel, 2 vols., 1947–49
Daudet, Léon, *Écrivains et artistes,* vol. 6, Paris: Capitole, 1929
Dubech, Lucien, *Les Chefs de file de la jeune génération,* Paris: Plon, 1925
Fraser, Theodore, *The French Essay,* Boston: Twayne, 1986
Griffiths, Richard, *The Reactionary Revolution: The Catholic Revival in French Literature 1870–1914,* New York: Ungar, 1965; London, Constable, 1966
Henri Massis, études, témoignages, textes et documents inédits, biographie et bibliographie, Paris: Nouvelles Éditions Latines, 1961
Itinéraires issue on Massis, 49 (January 1961)
Leitolf, Otto, "Die Gedankenwelt von Henri Massis," *Romanische Studien* 53 (1940):1–118
Maxence, Jean-Pierre, *Histoire de dix ans, 1927–1937,* Paris: Gallimard, 1939
Poulet, Robert, *Le Caléidoscope,* Lausanne: L'Âge d'Homme, 1982
Rebatet, Lucien, *Les Décombres,* Paris: Denoël, 1942
Séché, Alphonse, *Dans la mêlée littéraire (1900–1930),* Paris: Malfère, 1935
Thérive, André, *Opinions littéraires,* Paris: Bloud & Gay, 1925
Toda, Michel, *Henri Massis: Un témoin de la droite intellectuelle,* Paris: La Table Ronde, 1987

Maxim

As a literary genre the maxim exists chiefly as an elaboration of the proverb, perhaps with some element of commentary, or as the reduction of the predominantly French genre of "reflection." The only well-known work in whose title the term "maxim" occurs is **La Rochefoucauld**'s *Réflexions; ou, Sentences et maximes morales* (1665). There were other late 17th-century collections of **aphorisms** known as *maximes,* most notably those of La Rochefoucauld's close friend, the hypochondriac and devout Madame de Souvré, Marquise de Sablé, which were published with the *pensées* of Nicolas d'Ailly, canon of Lisieux, in the *Maximes et pensées diverses* of 1678.

The origin of the term "maxim" is obscure, but it appears to derive from the technical 15th-century *maxima propositio,*

the major premise of a syllogism in logic, generally stating a universally accepted axiom, such as "all dogs have four legs." The *maxima propositio* was followed, in a syllogism, by a minor premise ("this animal is a dog") and a conclusion ("therefore this animal has four legs"). Thus, the maxim acquired its connotations of meaning any aphoristically stated general truth. Its relation to the essay developed in the 16th century when authors such as **Erasmus** in his *Adagia* (1500; *Adages*), **Montaigne** in his *Essais* (1580, 1588), and a host of lesser-known writers in Latin and the major Western European vernaculars cited aphorisms or maxims in order to discuss or illustrate their meanings, applicability, aptness, or usefulness.

Erasmus constantly revised and augmented the *Adages* after the 1500 edition, which contained 818 proverbs with comments of a few lines on each, until the final total of over 4000 adages. Very often these are in the form of maxims, e.g. "Kings and fools are born, not made," "For the lazy it's always holiday," or "War is sweet to those who do not know it." In the 1515 edition Erasmus added, after every 500 adages, and under the guise of a commentary on the origin, meaning, and usefulness of some of them, long pieces of social **satire**, which today we would call essays.

The word "essay" did not, at this stage, denote a literary form, but meant "trial" or "test." However, several 16th-century authors, including Guillaume Budé and Étienne Dolet, inspired by Erasmus' success, interpolated sometimes lengthy passages of personal writing into what were ostensibly works of philological commentary. Montaigne's first two volumes of *Essais* were often reflections on the truth of aphorisms, or illustrations of their appositeness. The **chapters** were presented as forms of self-portrait, each supposedly testing the author's personal reaction to some statement about personal or social affairs, or dealing with some moral aspect of human nature. In fact, these chapters were really attempting something else: they were Montaigne's share of a peculiarly intimate **dialogue** with his reader, with falsification of such element of self-portraiture as there was.

Montaigne's essays, often bearing maxims as titles, cover such subjects as "The same end is reached by different means," "Our emotions carry us beyond ourselves," or "That our experience of what things are good and what are harmful depends on our opinion of them." The first chapter to break out of the bounds of the original form into a more obvious kind of speculation is titled with the Platonist maxim, "To philosophize is to learn how to die."

The development of the relationship between the maxim and the essay continued in the work of **Francis Bacon**, who borrowed the title of his 1597 *Essayes* from Montaigne, but whose work was rather a collection of "sentences" or maxims, with the subtitles *Religious Meditations* and *Places of Perswasion and Disswasion.* In 1612 Bacon increased the number of sentences from ten to 38, and in the 1625 edition to 58. They were also rewritten at greater length, thereby resembling more closely what we would now call essays.

After Bacon the maxim and the essay increasingly went their separate ways. A linking of the two did appear, however, in France in the work of La Rochefoucauld, the most famous of whose *maximes* was certainly the essay on *amour-propre,* first published in the third part of an anonymous *Recueil* in 1660. His manuscripts and the first edition of *Réflexions* contain items of much greater length than what we might now regard as appropriate in a maxim, and tend toward the essayistic. The work was first elaborated in the company of Madame de Sablé and her coterie, where the conversation was chiefly of moral matters, but also included health, devotion, and gastronomy. It is generally accepted that the manuscript tradition shows a progression from the maxims as recorded in the Liancourt manuscript, virtually at the moment of their discussion in Madame de Sablé's circle, through the pirated Dutch edition (1664), to the authentic first edition of 1665. This presumed progression displays a movement of reduction, from extended paragraphs to epigrammatic maxims, thus presenting the maxim as a distillation of essay-type pieces (of a kind similar to La Rochefoucauld's posthumously published *Nouvelles Réflexions* of 1693), rather than – as previously – a starting point for reflection.

From the late 17th century onward, the maxim continued its life as epigram or aphorism of moral prescription, leaving the essay to develop its various subforms. The two genres had come together splendidly in Erasmus, corresponded most closely in Montaigne and Bacon, and dissolved their relationship after the successive texts of La Rochefoucauld.

ANTHONY LEVI

Further Reading
Cavill, Paul, "Notes on Maxims in Old English Narrative," *Notes and Queries* 231, no. 2 (1986): 145–48
Chorney, Alexander Harry, *The English Maxim to 1756* (dissertation), Los Angeles: University of California, 1963
Clements, Pamela Jo, *The Prose Maxim in Old English: Aelfric and Wulfstan* (dissertation), Urbana: University of Illinois, 1984
Ford, Barbara J., "The Evocative Power of the Maxim: La Rochefoucauld and Proust," *Romance Notes* 25, no. 2 (1984): 169–74
Lafond, Jean, "Des Formes brèves de la littérature morale aux XVIe et XVIIe siècles," in his *Les Formes brèves de la prose et le discours discontinu*, Paris: Vrin, 1984
Lyons, John D., "Maxim and Narration in the Seventeenth Century," in *Proceedings of the Xth Congress of the International Comparative Literature Association*, edited by James J. Wilhelm and others, New York: Garland, 3 vols., 1985
Nemer, Monique, "Les Intermittences de la vérité: Maxime, sentence ou aphorisme: Notes sur l'évolution d'un genre," *Studi Francesi* 26, no. 3 (1982): 485–93
Rigolot, François, "Montaigne's Maxims: From the Discourse of Other to the Expression of Self," *L'Esprit Créateur* 22, no. 3 (1982): 8–18
Rosso, Corrado, "Maximen und Regeln: Von den Evangelien bis zur Gegenwart (Methodische Überlegungen)," in *Neuere Studien zur Aphoristik und Essayistik*, edited by Giulia Cantarutti and Hans Schumacher, Frankfurt-on-Main: Lang, 1986
Spackman, Barbara, "Machiavelli and Maxims," *Yale French Studies* 77 (1990): 135–55

Mazzini, Giuseppe

Italian, 1805–1872

Giuseppe Mazzini, the leading Italian patriot, political theorist, and critic, was born in 1805, the son of Giacomo Mazzini, a physician and participant in the Ligurian Jacobin movement,

and Maria Drago, a woman of strong Jansenist convictions who would exert an important influence on her son's work and ideas. Mazzini's literary talents developed early; in 1826, for instance, he submitted an article, "Saggio sul Dante Alighieri: 'Amor Patria'" ("Dante's Love of Country"), to the *Antologia*, considered the best Italian literary review of the time. The subject is significant, since Mazzini represented Dante as one of the earliest advocates of Italian unity; and although the article was at first rejected, it was later printed in that journal. In 1827 he received a degree in law and joined the Carbonari, continuing meanwhile to write articles on literary topics for publication in such journals as Francesco Guerrazzi's *L'Indicatore Livornese* (The Livornese indicator). A year later Mazzini assumed the editorship of a similar review, *L'Indicatore Genovese* (The Genoese indicator), in which several of his writings were published. One of his articles, on Sir Walter Scott, caused the small newspaper to be investigated by the police, the strong censorship of the period equating enthusiastic Romanticism with political extremism. Mazzini was, of course, quite involved in revolutionary activity at this time, and in 1830 was arrested for conspiracy and imprisoned in the fortress of Savona. After a short time he was allowed to choose exile and went to Marseilles. There he founded Giovine Italia (Young Italy), an organization dedicated to the unification of Italy as a republic, with Rome as its capital. By 1832, Mazzini's revolutionary and nationalistic ideas were well known throughout Italy. He left France the following year and moved to Switzerland, where he founded Young Europe as a broad international counterpart to Young Italy. Its purpose was to build a union of European republican nation-states, all based on the principles of equality and brotherhood and to be achieved by Mazzini's central formula of "thought and action." Forced to leave Switzerland after a failed political uprising, he went into exile in England, where he remained until 1848.

Settling in London, Mazzini continued writing and produced several incisive literary analyses of Dante, **Goethe**, Foscolo, Byron, **Carlyle**, and the Romantic movement. He also served as a correspondent for two liberal continental journals, the Paris-based *Le Monde* (The world) and the Swiss *Helvétie*, in which he gave lengthy observations on the social and political conditions in England as well as his first impressions on the politics of the working classes. During this period of exile he also made his living writing for **John Stuart Mill**'s *London and Westminster Review*, the *Monthly Chronicle*, the *British and Foreign Review*, *Tait's Edinburgh Magazine*, and the radical *People's Journal*. In that last periodical, in a series of six essays entitled "Thoughts upon Democracy in Europe," he traced the common utilitarian origins of various utopian movements of the time. When the revolutionary uprisings of 1848 erupted all over Europe, he returned to Italy where he experienced the attempt at insurrection in Milan and the establishment of the short-lived Roman Republic, serving as one of its governing triumvirs. Returning to England after the Republic's fall, Mazzini continued his prolific output of literary and political writings, which were aimed, in part, at building support and sympathy for the Italian cause among the British public. He also helped to organize unsuccessful uprisings in various parts of the Italian peninsula, but was opposed to the policy of those moderates who sought to tie Italy's unification to the Savoy monarchy.

In 1860 he published his major tome, *Doveri dell'uomo* (*The Duties of Man*), in which he outlined his main economic and social, as well as political, doctrines. In this work he urged the working classes in particular to abandon materialistic views such as Marxism and fulfill instead their obligations to God, the people, and the nation. In exile again in London from 1860 to 1868, Mazzini became a close friend of the poet A. C. Swinburne and the novelist George Meredith, both of whom used Mazzini and the central events of his life as themes in their works. Meredith's serialized *Vittoria* (1864–65) descried Mazzini at the height of his Romantic revolutionary career, and Swinburne's panegyric "Ode to Mazzini" (1857) and "Super Flumina Babylonis" (1869) praised him as the prophet who inspires his people to gain independence. Mazzini was also the subject of Robert Browning's poem, "The Italian in England," and his influence on English letters is further evident in the works of several of his British followers, including his translator Jessie White Mario and his biographer Emilie Ashurst Venturi. He was the inspiration for at least two novels, *Clara Hopgood* (1896) by William Hale White, in which his dealings with the British Chartist movement are described, and Benjamin Disraeli's *Lothair* (1870), which emphasizes the political disappointments of Mazzini's later years as well as his early idealism. The last four years of Mazzini's life were spent in Italy where he founded a new journal, *Roma del Popolo* (The people's Rome), and a working men's association while continuing to write countless articles and political tracts.

While Mazzini is best known for his political activism, the critical writings themselves form an important contribution to Italian Romanticism. They serve, moreover, to demonstrate the close connection that often existed in 19th-century Italy between new literary styles and elements of social and political activity. In an early essay on Italian literature, for instance, Mazzini asserted that the character of Italian poetry reflected that country's failure to produce independent and vital political movements, and called for the creation of a new Italian literature with "social man in action" as its theme. Additionally, he attacked Italy's writers for their constant servile admiration of the powerful, their tragic separation of literature from Italian national life, and their imitation of foreign literary schools and styles.

The significant essay on Dante which Mazzini wrote during his early career, describing him as a forerunner of Italian unity, is an essentially political interpretation of the poet's work. But it is still the result of Mazzini's fresh reading of the poetry itself rather than of a scholarly analysis of Dante's annotators or, as he puts it, "rummaging through the archives of monasteries." The essay recalls an appeal made earlier by Ugo Foscolo for a new criticism of Italy's greatest literary figure. In his study of Goethe and Byron, Mazzini sees the two writers as contrasting figures, each representing divergent intellectual views. "Goethe better expresses lives; Byron life. The one is more vast; the other more deep." Mazzini himself described poetry as an endeavor which has a religious, popular, and visionary purpose and, while praising much of the new Romantic literature of his age, rejected Romanticism's cult of the individual and the idea of art as a mere imitator of nature, or the formula "Art for art's sake." For this reason too, he placed Byron "far above" Wordsworth and **Coleridge**, whom he called "contemplative poets only, living remote from action

amid their mountains and lakes." His other incisive essays on the 16th-century Italian thinker Paolo Sarpi and on his own contemporaries, George Sand and Victor Hugo, are also written from this viewpoint. In a similar vein, he regarded historiography as having an essentially didactic purpose, the historian's role to be essentially that of "a prophet of a higher social end," quite in accord with his own guiding principle of "thought and action."

WILLIAM ROBERTS

Biography

Known as Joseph Mazzini while living in England. Born 22 June 1805 in Genoa. Studied privately; University of Genoa, from 1819, law degree, 1827. Editor, *L'Indicatore Genovese*, from 1828. Arrested and imprisoned for joining the Carbonari group of secret societies, 1830, and exiled to France, 1831, living in Marseilles; founder, Giovine Italia (Young Italy) political organization supporting Italian unification under republican form of government, 1831. Short liaison with Giuditta Sidoli: one child (died in infancy). Moved to Switzerland, 1833; founder, Young Switzerland and Young Europe (counterparts to Giovine Italia); expelled from Switzerland and France, and lived in London, 1837–48, where he wrote for various periodicals and newspapers, and became friends with Thomas and Jane Carlyle. Returned to Italy, 1848, to witness revolts, and became triumvir of short-lived Roman Republic; returned to England after Republic's fall; helped to organize unsuccessful uprisings in Milan, 1853, and Genoa, 1857; lived in London, 1860–68; lived in Lugano, from 1868, and secretly in Pisa. Founder, *Roma del Popolo*, 1871. Died in Pisa, 10 March 1872.

Selected Writings

Essays and Related Prose

Doveri dell'uomo, 1860; edited by Giuliana Limiti and Alda de Caprarriis, 1972, Paolo Rossi, 1972, and Giovanni Spadolini, 1990; as *The Duties of Man*, translated by Emilie A. Venturi, 1862, and Ella Noyes, in *The Duties of Man and Other Essays*, 1907
Essays: Selected from the Writings, Literary, Political and Religious (various translators), edited by William Clarke, 1887
"God and the People" ... Being Selections from the Writings, edited by C. W. Stubbs, 1891
Essays, edited by Bolton King, translated by Thomas Okey, 1894
The Duties of Man and Other Essays, translated by Ella Noyes, Thomas Okey, and L. Martineau, 1907
Selected Writings, edited by N. Gangulee, 1945
Dúna letteratura europea e altri saggi, edited by Paolo Mario Sipala, 1991

Other writings: correspondence.

Collected works editions: *Life and Writings of Joseph Mazzini*, 6 vols., 1864–70; *Scritti editi ed inediti* (Edizione Nazionale), 94 vols., 1906–43; *Opere*, edited by Luigi Salvatorelli, 2 vols., 1938.

Bibliography

Coppa, Frank J., and William Roberts, *Modern Italian History: An Annotated Bibliography*, Westport, Connecticut: Greenwood Press, 1990

Further Reading

Barr, Stringfellow, *Mazzini: Portrait of an Exile*, New York: Holt, 1935

Griffith, Gwilym O., *Mazzini: Prophet of Modern Europe*, New York: Fertig, 1970 (original edition, 1932)

King, Bolton, *The Life of Mazzini*, London: Dent, and New York: Dutton, 1902

Mack Smith, Denis, *Mazzini*, New Haven, Connecticut and London: Yale University Press, 1994

Morelli, Emilia, *L'Inghilterra di Mazzini*, Rome: Istituto per la Storia del Risorgimento Italiano, 1965

Roberts, William, *Prophet in Exile: Joseph Mazzini in England, 1837–1868*, New York: Lang, 1989

Salvemini, Gaetano, *Mazzini*, London: Cape, 1956; Stanford, California: Stanford University Press, 1957

Silone, Ignazio, *The Living Thoughts of Mazzini*, London: Cassell, and New York: Longman, 1939

Medical Essay

The history of medical narratives stretches back to the earliest days of medicine itself, with two streams sometimes interwoven: the case history and the first-person narrative of illness. Case histories have always been part of medical practice, though observations have always been informed by theory – whether the humoral theory of ancient and medieval medicine, the germ theory of 19th- and 20th-century medicine, or the emphasis on hormones and subcellular processes in the medicine of the last quarter of the 20th century.

Hippocrates, the leading figure in classic Greek medicine, advocated treating the individual rather than the disease, and treating the whole body rather than a part of it. Yet the humors theory attributed to Empedocles was incorporated into Hippocratic writings and, continuing through Aristotle and Galen, became the shaping theory throughout the Middle Ages (when the main interest was in the afterlife, and little attention was given to the human body) and even beyond. In the 17th century a return to Hippocratic medicine brought renewed interest in observing and talking with patients and thus a revival of the case history. In the 18th century, organized records were stressed, with the goal of collecting and classifying data. Only in the late 18th century, as diagnosis began to depend less on theory and more on observation, was the patient's narrative considered essential to diagnosis. Significantly, this period was also one of a major flowering of prose, when the narrative of the novel became accepted as a literary form. Coincidentally, as narrative gained cultural authority, so did the physician. Observing patients and compiling case histories was part of the 18th-century physician's training, and recorded observation played a major role as clinical medicine and statistics evolved.

In the movement toward the clinic as a vehicle for teaching, Michel Foucault (in *Naissance de la clinique* [1963; *The Birth of the Clinic*]) perceived a shift in the very epistemology of medicine, a shift to seeing – observation – as the basis for knowing, with the accompanying recording of what was seen. If the focus of medicine in the 18th century, then, was classification, in the 19th century the case history became more elaborate. A standard case history format was codified by the end of the century; it included identifying data, chief complaint, history of the present illness (HPI), patient's history, review of bodily systems, family history, and social history. The HPI required writing in sentences – thus contributing to an overall sense of coherence. Still, illness was somehow separated from the patient – at least for purposes of analyzing, classifying, and prescribing treatment.

In recent years, Lawrence Weed's "SOAP" approach has adopted a four-part medical history: "Subjective" details (the patient's history), "Objective" data (clinical observations, technological studies), "Assessments" (relying heavily on clinical observations and technical studies), and "Plans." In Weed's formula, personal history still retains the narrative element, but the language has become conventional as the structure has become prescribed, though the chief complaint is expected to be given in the patient's own words. The 20th century has seen the case record moving from the patient's history and the physical examination to reports of technical studies and imaging and then to intervention through technology. The contemporary case history has a seeming neutrality, even a lack of the humane – a lack that has spurred attempts to reinforce the history of the patient. However, as literary and linguistic theorists have demonstrated, no narrative is value-free; the medical case history, like any other narrative, is subject to the privileging of the author's voice and perspective.

Yet, even as the case history moved toward codification, the second stream of medical narrative continued, the tradition of personal accounts of illness. From medieval accounts of the massive spread of, and terrible suffering from, bubonic plague to **John Donne**'s and Izaak Walton's 17th-century accounts of illness, and **Samuel Johnson**'s account in the 18th century of his paralytic stroke, this genre has held the interest of the reading public. From the late 18th century through the 19th, illness narratives and books of popular advice had wide appeal. Among the Romantics, **Coleridge** wrote of his poetic depression and physical pain, **Thomas De Quincey** described the pains and dreams associated with his use of opium, and Coleridge's daughter Sara wrote of her own bouts of depression and confrontations with cancer. The Romantics wrote of Nature in grandiose terms as a sympathetic and protective force, though illness narratives such as Sara Coleridge's seemed to struggle with such a concept in the presence of real suffering.

In the later 19th century a case history was often used as a warning, particularly against the dangers of excesses, as well as advice on the virtues of moderation. "Nervous" tribulations were frequently the subject of medical essays in this period, which was fascinated by electrical explanations of the nervous system. In the tradition of tracing "nervous" maladies, and in a quest for understanding the whole patient through reconstructing the life story, **Sigmund Freud** effectively created a new science rooted in narrative, and in the course of this brought the case history to perhaps its highest artistic state. In Freud's hands, psychoanalysis was, indeed, more art than science as he led the patient (and the reader), in his terms, out of the forest and into the open space where all could be seen clearly as a whole, where dreams could be understood as, primarily, visual pastiches of experience. In his attempt to "decode" what the "dreamwork" had wrought, Freud took his readers through labyrinthine paths as he explored dreams in terms of the unconscious and of wish-fulfillments, and as he devised a whole new vocabulary for the workings of the unconscious: condensation, displacement, symbolic representation, and regression, for example. Freud's memorable tales of Dora and the Wolf Man, of the burning child who appears in his father's dream, and of his own young daughter's dreams of strawberries have enriched the history of the medical narrative and set precedents for contemporary medical essays.

With the increasing emphasis on the technical and on clinical language, the physician has become distanced from the narrative that seeks to present the patient as a whole. In the last quarter of the 20th century, however, the non-technical medical essay has achieved an unprecedented popularity. As a genre, the contemporary medical essay goes beyond the case history to explore the physician's voice and perspective, the physician becoming a persona who makes observations of patients, of medicine, of the world as seen through his or her eyes. As the medical essay attempts to present the human side of medicine, it returns to medicine as an art, attempting to replace or supplement the cold anonymity of the professional medical narrative. A good example is the work of **Lewis Thomas**, who began writing brief informal essays for the *New England Journal of Medicine* in 1971; their popularity has led to several collections, beginning with the award-winning *The Lives of a Cell: Notes of a Biology Watcher* (1974). Thomas brings his perspective as a clinician and epidemiologist to both medical and nonmedical subjects – from subcellular particles to the earth itself, considered as a kind of cell. He brings humor to his essays as he writes about our fascination with killing germs (especially our own) with antiseptic sprays that are given miraculous attributes in television commercials. Subjects ranging from medical history to warts, and to the way in which cells in the embryo "switch on," call forth Thomas' speculations and reveal his sense of wonder at life and its almost magical qualities.

The most sophisticated medical essays to emerge in the late 20th century often focus, as do many other literary and philosophical texts, on the role of language in conveying knowledge, emotion, and understanding. Thomas demonstrates his fascination with language, exploring the paradox that we can only consider language *through* language, using the brain to think about how the brain works. More literary and more seriously philosophical in his approach is **Oliver Sacks**, who also considers the role of language in medicine and attempts to break away from the fragmented, particularized approach to understanding as embodied in the Cartesian-Newtonian world view. This world view, accepted as modern medicine emerged, remains the basis for the analytical (and reductionist) breaking down of the medical condition into its component parts, isolating and treating the causative agent. Sacks has argued that medicine needs to turn to the everyday language – what he calls "metaphysical" language – that we use for things not measurable, and that modern medicine, ostensibly objective, and focusing on "subjects," carries dangers in that the war metaphors and notions of disease as alien and evil are not questioned. Narrative and drama, Sacks contends, are paths that lead back to the concrete; he looks to a holistic language to encompass both the individual patient and a larger view of the natural environment.

Sacks explores a variety of human conditions for their uniqueness and their instructiveness about the human body. In *Awakenings* (1973, revised 1976, 1982, 1991) he writes of patients who were brought back from unconscious states by the drug L-dopa, tracing with insight and sympathy the seeming return to life of these patients and also the relapse into arrested consciousness that many later experienced. In *The Man Who Mistook His Wife for a Hat* (1985), Sacks explores the often bizarre behavior of otherwise normal human beings whose perception of their surroundings is altered by neurological deficiencies – as in the case of the title character, who could deal with the world through singing, but who confused his foot with his shoe and seemed to confuse his wife's head with his hat. In other books he explores migraines as perceived today and throughout history, the culture of the deaf whose linguistic abilities are richly manifested in the visual language of Sign, and his own loss of proprioceptive awareness of self after a broken leg.

Richard Selzer employs in his writing the grotesque and the shocking, often juxtaposed with scenes of striking tenderness, to bring the reader into the realm of the living, bleeding human body. From the grotesquerie of the gangrenous limb upon which the patient had drawn a smiling face to the tenderness of a surgeon who slipped back (because the child's mother wanted her to be beautiful in the afterlife) to repair the cleft lip of a patient who died unexpectedly from anesthesia, Selzer explores the human body in all its decrepitude and beauty. Yet beneath Selzer's descriptions of grotesques there is an almost metaphysical quest (though he declares that he has come to believe there is only the flesh), a quest for meaning in the body, for what he calls "The Exact Location of the Soul." In Selzer's texts there is also a quest for meaning in what he does: he takes the word "doctor" to its Latin root meaning "leading" or "teaching" as he explains that he writes because he wants "to become a doctor."

Less philosophical than Sacks, and less focused on the grotesque than Selzer, but consciously admitting an element of mystery into his clinical tales, is Harold Klawans, who speculates half in jest in *Newton's Madness* (1990) on the effect of diagnosis on illness, with a nagging doubt that disease undiagnosed may not really be disease. Like Sacks, Klawans explores the human side of neurological disorders (in *Toscanini's Fumble* [1989] as in his other books) and provides notes to the medical literature; like Thomas, he pursues the etymology of words; like Selzer, he approaches life as *mysterium*, as something to be admired and not reducible to a neutral language.

These last three writers are representative of a number who tackle the many aspects of the "human" side of medicine. In addition, the late 20th century has also seen a resurgence of the first-person narrative of an individual's encounter with illness, though the focus has now come to include the health-care system. These narratives, or essays, though not structured in the manner of an essay written by a trained medical observer, have nevertheless contributed to a growing awareness of the importance of the medical essay and of its nature as a construct, rather than a straightforward presentation of objective fact. Although these "pathographies," as Anne H. Hawkins (1993) describes them, are often autobiographical, they may also be considered as indicative of the breadth in scope of the medical essay that has gained it such popularity in recent years.

Mary Ellen Pitts

Anthologies

Surgical Case-Histories from the Past, edited by Harold Ellis, London and New York: Royal Society of Medicine Press, 1994

Tenements of Clay: An Anthology of Medical Biographical Essays, edited by Arnold Sorsby, London: Friedmann, 1974; New York: Scribner, 1975

Further Reading

Ackerknecht, Erwin H., *A Short History of Medicine*, Baltimore: Johns Hopkins University Press, revised edition, 1982 (original edition, 1955)

Baron, Richard, "Bridging Clinical Distance: An Empathic Rediscovery of the Known," *Journal of Medicine and Philosophy* 6, no. 1 (1981): 5–23

Brody, Howard, *Stories of Sickness*, New Haven, Connecticut: Yale University Press, 1987

Charon, Rita, "To Render the Lives of Patients," *Literature and Medicine* 5 (1986): 58–74

Charon, Rita, "To Build a Case," *Literature and Medicine* 11, no. 1 (1992): 115–32

Engel, George I., "The Need for a New Medical Model: A Challenge for Biomedicine," *Science* 196 (1977): 129–36

Epstein, Julia, "Historiography, Diagnosis, and Poetics," *Literature and Medicine* 11, no. 1 (1992): 23–44

Hawkins, Anne Hunsaker, *Reconstructing Illness: Studies in Pathography*, West Lafayette, Indiana: Purdue University Press, 1993

Hilfiker, David, *Healing the Wounds: A Physician Looks at His Work*, New York: Pantheon, 1985

Hunter, Kathryn Montgomery, *Doctors' Stories: The Narrative Structure of Medical Knowledge*, Princeton, New Jersey: Princeton University Press, 1991

Mishler, Elliot G., *The Discourse of Medicine: Dialectics of Medical Interviews*, Norwood, New Jersey: Ablex, 1984

Psaty, Bruce M., "Literature and Medicine as a Critical Discourse," *Literature and Medicine* 6 (1987): 13–34

Rocher, Gregory de, "The Renaissance Wound: The Discourse of Power in Sixteenth-Century Medicine," *Romance Quarterly* 38, no. 2 (1991): 131–37

Meditation

Although today the literary genre of meditation is often supposed to be religious in origin, the term appears soon to have become the designation of a literary form in the late 14th-century secular context. As the written stimulus to a form of prayer, the term developed to indicate a more consciously reflective form of private spiritual activity than contemplation, and it then found conspicuous favor both as a speculative philosophical form, as in Descartes and later in Edmund Husserl, and as pre-Romantic and Romantic expressions of intimate personal feelings, as in **Rousseau**, who did not use the term to denote a genre, and Alphonse de Lamartine, who used the word in the title of his famous 1820 collection of poetry, *Méditations poétiques*.

Only subsequently was the word used of the work of stoic devotional reflections composed in solitude by the Roman ruler Marcus Aurelius (121–80 CE) during his military campaigns in the second century CE. His reflections, now known as the *Meditations*, are fragmentary jottings, often practical in tone, and possibly intended for the guidance of Aurelius' son, Commodus. They were highly prized, notably by **John Stuart**

Mill and **Ernest Renan**, for the way in which they subordinate stoicism to a love of humanity; but, in spite of the considerations they contain about God, matter, cause, practical reason or conscience, and the governance of the universe, they do not add up to a coherent universal philosophy. The aim of life for Marcus Aurelius was not so much happiness as tranquillity, to be found by living in accordance with nature, understood as human nature. Human beings are social, and conformity to their nature means that they should cultivate what Christians came to regard as the "cardinal" virtues – wisdom, justice, fortitude, and prudence. It is probably on account of their moral content that the reflections came later to be called the *Meditations*.

Before Descartes, the meditation had become a genre in works of devotion. *Meditations on the Passion* are among the English works of the early 14th-century English hermit Richard Rolle. In the *Spiritual Exercises* of Ignatius of Loyola, 16th-century founder of the Jesuit order, the prayerful considerations of mysteries taken from the life of Jesus, as recounted in the Gospel narratives, were known first as contemplations and then, no doubt to distinguish this form of prayer from less discursive types of mental activity directed toward the cultivation of religious devotion, they came to be known as meditations. That term was certainly in use in the Jesuit order shortly after its bull of foundation, dated 1540, and the verb "to meditate" occurs in the *Spiritual Exercises* themselves, of which a primitive form must have existed in writing by the later 1520s.

Meditations, often in written form, very quickly became part of the devotional heritage of Western Christendom, contrasting with the Church's official liturgical prayer, which was the chanting of the divine office, as well as with the contemplation described in the writings of some of the mystics. Discursive devotional meditations were published in huge quantities, and came to form the staple of interior prayer cultivated within the active orders of the Church, distinguished from the contemplative orders committed to the chanting of the divine office.

In post-Renaissance Europe the first significant use of the term "meditation" to denote a literary genre was by Descartes. He had conceived the project of writing what he called a "universal science" to elevate human nature to the highest perfection of which it was capable. Using the modish description "method," at that date replacing the term "art of," Descartes prefaced a small part of his planned undertaking with the important six-part *Discours de la méthode* (1937; *Discourse on Method*). He at first planned a philosophical system which he compared to a tree, with metaphysics as the roots, general physics and the physics of the animal and human kingdoms as the trunk, and mechanics, medicine, and ethics as the fruit. The metaphysics, already sketched in the fourth part of the *Discourse*, was elaborated in the six Latin meditations of 1641 demonstrating the existence of God and the immortality of the soul, the *Meditationes de prima philosophia in qua dei existentia et animae immortalitas demonstratur* (1641; Meditations on the first philosophy [metaphysics] in which the existence of God and the immortality of the soul are demonstrated). These, although supposed to have a practical bearing on the way life should be led, and intended finally to lead to an ethic, are overwhelmingly speculative rather than moral. They are increasingly concerned with the union in human beings of spiritual and bodily functions. Descartes' friend and correspondent, Marin Mersenne, communicated Descartes' meditations to other learned minds for comment, and Descartes' replies to the objections to his arguments prompted further objections, and further responses. The debate, which also concerned such religious topics as the action of grace in the soul and the nature of religious faith, became increasingly technical and recondite.

As a poetic genre, the meditation established itself with Lamartine's 1820 *Méditations poétiques*, the first major western European verse collection with the word "meditation" in the title. The 113-page octavo containing 24 odes and elegies was an immediate and huge success. Later works to use the term were in prose, like Guillaume Apollinaire's *Méditations esthétiques* (1913; *Aesthetic Meditations*) and **José Ortega y Gasset**'s *Meditaciones del Quijote* (1914; *Meditations on Quixote*), and were critical or philosophical.

Lamartine's volume struck a reverberating chord among a generation of educated young French people. It drew on the feelings exploited by Rousseau, **Goethe**, **Chateaubriand**, and Byron, emphasizing the grandeur and solitude of the individual, and parading in a reaction against the materialism of the Industrial Revolution the most intimate and inarticulate experience of the emotionally suppressed and bewildered. The imagery is always precise, the feelings nostalgic, vague, and associated with natural grandeur and personal sadness. The verse, in spite of its apparently nonchalant attitude to poetic technique, is in fact very careful, cultivating a musical fluidity, and giving the impression of nobility, loftiness, and a grandeur of spirit incompatible with anything petty, vulgar, or ungeneralized. In Lamartine, the meditation became the vehicle for the intense lyricism required by his immediate juniors.

Poetry, devotion, and philosophy have, then, all laid claim to the meditation as a subgenre, and the meditation did indeed become a form indigenous in all three realms. It has now, for some decades, been falling out of fashion as a serious literary form in all of them. Perhaps the most important 20th-century work with the term in the title, Husserl's *Méditations cartésiennes* (1931; *Cartesian Meditations*), takes up Descartes' usage of the word, using it in a deliberately archaic sense, and as a form in which to attack him. According to Husserl, Descartes' error was to situate the self in the "real world," whereas for Husserl the analysis of the self required a "phenomenological" reduction which excluded everything except mental intentionality. With Husserl the word "meditation" acquires an ironic sense.

ANTHONY LEVI

Further Reading

A great deal of the writing about meditative literature is devoted to poetry. The following items are a selection on prose.
Brumm, Ursula, "The Art of Puritan Meditation in New England," in *Studies in New England Puritanism*, edited by Winfried Herget, Frankfurt-on-Main: Lang, 1983
Lang, Berel, "Descartes and the Art of Meditation," *Philosophy and Rhetoric* 21, no. 1 (1988): 19–37
Nash, Jerry C., "The Christian-Humanist Meditation on Man: Denisot, Montaigne, Rabelais, Ronsard, Sceve," *Bibliothèque d'Humanisme et Renaissance* 54, no. 2 (1992): 353–71
Radcliffe, David Hill, *Meditations and Literary History, 1600–1750: Generic Mixture and Generic Change* (dissertation on Donne, Walton, Cowley, Defoe), Charlottesville: University of Virginia, 1987

Meditations

by Marcus Aurelius, c. 170–80 CE

If the Roman emperor Marcus Aurelius (121–80 CE) was not the philosopher-king that **Plato** envisioned, he was one of the few rulers who was also a philosopher. Deeply imbued with the doctrines of the Second Sophistic, a revival of Greek culture and thought in the second century CE, he cultivated the Stoicism of Epictetus, focusing on piety toward divine providence, duty, and self-sufficiency. "Constantly think of the Universe as one living creature, embracing one being and one soul," he admonished. "How it compasses all things with a single purpose, and how all things work together to cause all that comes to pass, and their wonderful web and texture." At the same time he resisted Stoic materialism, considering the human mind (*nous*) as distinct from the body. For Marcus Aurelius it was this mind, derived from the divine, that gave humans their agency to choose and act, and therefore commanded their obedience to duty. Failure to follow reason was both immoral and impious. It was in his *Meditations* that he most fully expressed and more fundamentally lived his Stoic piety, representing what R. B. Rutherford (1989) calls "his complex and humane response to the austerity and bleakness of Stoicism."

The exact nature and composition of the *Meditations* is not entirely certain. It was written in Greek, and internal evidence suggests that Marcus Aurelius worked on it during the last years of his life while on campaign along the marshlands of the Danube. The work was never "published," and was presumably preserved among his papers after his death by his family or scribes. It seems to have been unknown to his early biographers and chroniclers, the first reference to it only appearing two centuries later in an oration by the Greek philosopher and rhetorician Themistius. It was first printed in 1559 in Zurich by Andreas Gesner with a Latin translation by William Xylander. Thomas Gataker published the standard edition in 1652. Thereafter it has enjoyed a wide readership from poets to statesmen, appreciated both as an important document of the Later Stoa, and as a work of profound self-analysis and private devotion.

The *Meditations* contains 12 books. While Book I offers a clear organization and unity, Books II–XII do not. Nor is it evident how Books II–XII are structurally related to Book I. Thus while the themes, language, and aphoristic style remain consistent throughout, there is little sense that Marcus Aurelius is developing an argument or advancing a thesis. Each book may therefore be read as an independent work; the books are linked with one another through their common method and concerns. At the same time, it seems more than a collection of random thoughts or *pensées*. While various elements of the *Meditations* find parallels and prototypes in classical authors such as Plato, Lucretius, Horace, **Seneca**, Epictetus, and **Plutarch**, it does not fall neatly into any one literary category. Book I develops an autobiographical portrait, though Marcus

Aurelius presents himself indirectly through a series of memorials, expressing his gratitude to those who contributed to his success and to the formation of his character, from his grandfather and father, through his teachers, to the gods, who provided "good grandparents, good parents, a good sister, good masters, good intimates, kinfolk, friends, almost everything."

Some later commentators complain that Books II–XII lack philosophical rigor or originality. This, however, misunderstands the nature of the project. Marcus Aurelius is not so much writing a philosophical or moral **treatise** as engaging in a philosophical or spiritual exercise. The **aphorisms** of these later books tend to present a theme and variations in which he explores man's place in nature, the transience of his achievements, and human mortality. "All is ephemeral," he writes, "both what remembers and what is remembered." Given this condition, "What should be valued?" he asks – certainly not the clapping of hands or clicking tongues in approbation. Thus the rewards of glory amount to little. Extending the theme, he later adds, "Alexander the Great and his stable boy were leveled in death, for they were either taken up into the same life-giving principles of the Universe or were scattered without distinction into atoms." If the transience of things human tempers the fruits of glory, it also mitigates life's misfortunes. "Continually run over in mind men who were highly indignant at some event," he says, "men who attained the greatest heights of fame or disaster or enmity or of any kind of fortune whatever. Then pause and think: 'where is it all now?' Smoke and ashes and a tale that is told, or not so much as a tale." It is man's fate to die and be forgotten; to agonize over the inevitable is pointless. Thus through this rigorous self-interrogation, Marcus Aurelius confronts his pains and anxieties, teaching himself how to endure. By repeatedly examining human mortality from all its angles, weighing the implications of all possibilities, he is engaged in a process of spiritual care and therapy, a process described by Martha Nussbaum (1994) as important to Hellenistic ethics.

Philosophy for Marcus Aurelius is not an occupation so much as a preoccupation. If the *Meditations* does not represent an original contribution to Stoic doctrine, and if much of what it contains can be found in the writings of Epictetus and others, it remains nonetheless an eloquent reminder that the goal of philosophy is not merely to know the meaning of life, but to live it.

THOMAS L. COOKSEY

See also Classical Influences

Editions
Meditations, edited and translated by A. S. L. Farquharson (bilingual edition), 2 vols., 1944; translated by C. R. Haines (Loeb Edition), 1930, G. M. A. Grube and Maxwell Stanforth, 1964, and Roy Alan Lawes, 1984

Further Reading
Arnold, Matthew, "Marcus Aurelius," in his *Essays in Criticism: First Series*, London: Macmillan, 1865; Boston: Ticknor, 1866
Birley, Anthony, *Marcus Aurelius*, London: Batsford, and New Haven, Connecticut: Yale University Press, 1987 (original edition, 1966)
Brunt, P. A., "Marcus Aurelius in his *Meditations*," *Journal of Roman Studies* 64 (1974): 1–20
Farquharson, A. S. L., *Marcus Aurelius: His Life and His World*, Oxford: Oxford University Press, and New York: Salloch, 1951
Grant, Michael, *The Antonines: The Roman Empire in Transition*, London and New York: Routledge, 1994
Nussbaum, Martha C., *The Therapy of Desire: Theory and Practice in Hellenistic Ethics*, Princeton, New Jersey: Princeton University Press, 1994
Rutherford, R. B., *The Meditations of Marcus Aurelius: A Study*, Oxford: Clarendon Press, and New York: Oxford University Press, 1989
Stanton, G. R., "The Cosmopolitan Ideas of Epictetus and Marcus Aurelius," *Phronesis* 13 (1968): 183–95
Stanton, G. R., "Marcus Aurelius, Emperor and Philosopher," *Historia* 18 (1969): 570–87

Mencken, H. L.
American, 1880–1956

The essays of H. L. Mencken were critical of all aspects of American culture and influenced American thought for over 50 years, setting the standard for **satire** in his day, especially during the 15-year period following World War I and just prior to the start of the Great Depression. Walter Lippmann referred to Mencken as "the most powerful influence upon his whole generation of American people." As an essayist he reflected the same provocative and iconoclastic themes as in his work as a newspaper and magazine journalist, editor, author, and contributor to other works. By one estimate, he wrote nearly 3000 newspaper columns. Many of these began as literary criticism and were later advanced in essay form, appearing as part of his six-volume *Prejudices* series (1919–27). His essays are still widely read.

Mencken first gained recognition as a newspaperman at the Baltimore *Sun*, serving as editor, columnist, and political and war correspondent. He maintained his Baltimore residence throughout his life and, given many opportunities to relocate, argued: "The very richest man, in New York, is never quite sure that the house he lives in now will be his the next year ... the restlessness and unhappiness that go with it, make it almost impossible for anyone to accumulate the materials of a home" ("On Living in Baltimore," 1926). The course of Mencken's reporting career was cut short by a pro-German position he took during World War I, which proved an obstacle to his standing as a civil libertarian, a theme in many of his later essays. Mencken subsequently became author and columnist for "The Free Lance," gaining acclaim as a humorist, iconoclast, and agnostic, attacking moralists of every stripe and self-styled censors, the "smuthounds."

Two important early essays appeared first in the Baltimore *Sun* in 1917, in praise of critic James Gibbons Huneker and writer Joseph Conrad. Mencken became an agent of literary revolt during this period with essays contributed to a wide range of popular and select publications, thus reaching a large and diverse audience. These included conservative political journals, special interest periodicals, and high-brow publications. The *Nation* and the **New Yorker** printed his essays as well as *Cosmopolitan* and *Reader's Digest*. Later the *Yale Review* published "American Language" (1936), which became a consistent favorite among American instructors of literature.

Mencken's literary interests were stimulated by participation in a group calling itself the Saturday Night Club. This association spurred publication of his essays and short stories for popular magazines. *Short Stories* magazine was the principal outlet for his essays during this early period (1906–10), although others appeared in *Redbook* and *Frank Leslie's Popular Magazine*. At *Leslie's*, Mencken made the acquaintance of Ellery Sedgwick, an association that would create the stimulus for much of his prose nonfiction work. Shortly after Mencken returned to Baltimore from coverage of Berlin in 1917, Sedgwick asked him to write an article for the **Atlantic Monthly**; for a time after that Mencken devoted most of his energies to writing magazine articles.

Mencken coauthored two essays on medical issues with Baltimore physician Leonard Hirshberg which caught the attention of Theodore Dreiser, who invited a series on child care. Mencken declined the offer but submitted instead "The Slaughter of the Innocents" (1909), which he had ghost-written under Hirshberg's name. Dreiser ran that piece as part of a series, then began to correspond with Mencken. This resulted in their meeting in New York in 1908 and the invitation to write **humorous essays** for the *Bohemian* magazine. Dreiser also recommended Mencken as book reviewer for the New York literary monthly, *Smart Set*, which is often recognized as the turning point in his writing career. In the "Magazine of Cleverness," a subtitle Mencken despised, the new literary home offered a counterpoint to his own natural writing tendencies which emphasized a sense of the absurd and attacked the more ludicrous and bizarre aspects of American letters.

During the next decade at *Smart Set* Mencken estimated that he read 4000 books, reviewing major works by the likes of Upton Sinclair, Sinclair Lewis, **Henry James**, and even F. Scott Fitzgerald, whose first published story appeared in the magazine. As editor, Mencken published manuscripts by young American writers Zoë Akins, Eugene O'Neill, and Dorothy Parker. In this way he encouraged the growth of American literature and, at the same time, produced some of his best literary criticism, a calling he viewed as a combination of information and entertainment.

In 1914 Mencken assumed coeditorship of *Smart Set*, along with New York drama critic George Jean Nathan, later joining his partner in founding the *American Mercury*, giving him a sustained national readership. His work included *In Defense of Women* (1918), in which he attacked the institution of marriage, and "Treatise on Right and Wrong" (1934), for which he was widely assailed by critics. The "Days" trilogy constituting his autobiography was later published in the early 1940s from essays he had written for the *New Yorker*. Beginning with his childhood, or "Happy Days," as he dubbed them, Mencken credited his disposition to his upbringing in Baltimore, a satisfying, secure, and protected environment.

For Mencken, nothing about American culture was sacred. He savaged public figures with his satire, but focused unmercifully as well on general elements of the society he referred to as "Boobus Americanus." He often took the position that the average American had lost a love of liberty, become complacent and fainthearted, thereby inviting leadership by what he termed "cheer leaders, press agents, up-lifters." In politics, literature, and religion – those enterprises, according to Mencken, inclined to dullness – he strongly asserted that

each had reached unheard-of heights of stupidity in the United States. He expressed disgust for all manner of politicians, describing them as either master rogues or major bores. He likened Warren Harding's inaugural address to "dogs barking idiotically through endless nights." His classic, often-repeated line, upon hearing of the death of Calvin Coolidge, was "How can they be sure?" He referred to Franklin Roosevelt as "Franklin the First," or "Our Lord and Master," casting FDR alongside Woodrow Wilson and William Jennings Bryan as part of Mencken's "triumvirate of shame," labeling them respectively as "thief, liar and fool." His obituary of Bryan, "In Memoriam: WJB" (1926), evaluating the life work of the populist figure, written right after the Scopes-Monkey trial, stands as one of his famous and most frequently reprinted essays.

In his essay "On Being an American" (1922), Mencken lambasted virtually every immigrant ethnic group, castigating them as "second rate Englishmen," uncivilized and out of touch with their own national culture. In "Sahara of the Bozart" (1917), an essay written originally for the New York *Evening Mail*, he targeted especially the southern U.S. for its post-Civil War lack of culture. He then published his longest essay entitled "Puritanism as a Literary Force" (1917), which critiqued major literary figures and the influence of the British. He questioned whether intellectual life would exist at all in the U.S. were it not for regular imports from abroad, with London identified as the principal clearing house for new ideas. In "Three American Immortals" (1919) he revisited the promise of major American literary figures, including **Emerson**, Whitman, and Poe.

Mencken also condemned the limited accomplishments of those to come later, American writers preoccupied with the desires of their fellow men as opposed to the great bulk of serious writing by **Dostoevskii** and Dreiser, for example, in which the hero's battle ends in defeat, often oblivion. He added that on those rare occasions in which American literary figures have shown signs of enterprise, they have usually reacted to a hostility toward their ideas by departing for alien shores. Mencken observed no earnest pursuit of aesthetic passion in intellectual work but merely uninspiring and self-conscious efforts on a par with English music and German painting. These concerns were lost, he said, on an uncritical American public. He used **Shaw** as an example, "a blue nose" passed off to America as an Irish patriot.

Mencken consistently mocked American education. He maintained that most American scholars would be entirely lost if they were unable to borrow from others, adding that their limited mental capacity made it impossible for them to take on difficult enterprises. As a result, academic institutions were suffering from attempts to Americanize their curriculum. In "Criticism of Criticism of Criticism" (1919) he compared a professor with a theory to a dog with fleas. His assault on the style of Thorstein Veblen, entitled "Professor Veblen" (1919), and his comic evaluation of Columbia University President Nicholas Murray Butler – "He is a member of the American Academy himself, elected as a wet to succeed Edgar Allan Poe" ("Want Ad," 1919) – continue to delight readers.

As to his own motivation, Mencken said: ". . . an author, like any other so-called artist, is a man in whom the normal vanity of all men is so vastly exaggerated that he feels the sheer impossibility to hold it in. His overpowering impulse is to gyrate before his fellow men, flapping his wings and emitting defiant yells" ("The Fringes of Lovely Letters," 1926). He followed his own counsel and wrote his "yells" in the form of personal reminiscent essays, which remain among his most popular works.

MICHAEL D. MURRAY

Biography
Henry Louis Mencken. Born 12 September 1880 in Baltimore, Maryland. Studied at the Baltimore Polytechnic Institute, 1892–96. Worked in his father's cigar factory, 1896–99. Reporter or editor for several Baltimore papers, 1899–16; literary critic, 1908–23, and editor, with George Jean Nathan, 1914–23, *Smart Set*, New York; founder, with Nathan, *Parisienne, Saucy Stories*, and *Black Mask* pulp magazines, late 1910s, and *American Mercury* (also editor), 1923–33; war correspondent in Germany, 1916–18; literary adviser, Knopf publishers, New York, from 1917; columnist, New York *Evening Mail*, 1917–18, and of "The Free Lance," Baltimore *Sunpapers*, 1919–41 and 1948; contributor, Chicago *Tribune*, 1924–28, New York *American*, 1934–35, and the *Nation*, 1931–32. Married Sara Powell Haardt, 1930 (died, 1935). Suffered a stroke which impaired his speech, 1949. Awards: American Academy Gold Medal, 1950. Died (of heart failure) in Baltimore, 29 January 1956.

Selected Writings

Essays and Related Prose
A Book of Prefaces, 1917
In Defense of Women, 1918
Prejudices, 6 vols., 1919–27; *Prejudices: A Selection*, edited by James T. Farrell, 1958
Happy Days: 1880–1892, 1940
Newspaper Days: 1899–1906, 1941
Heathen Days: 1890–1936, 1943
The Vintage Mencken, edited by Alistair Cooke, 1955
A Carnival of Buncombe, edited by Malcolm Moos, 1956; as *On Politics*, 1960
The Bathtub Hoax, and Other Blasts and Bravos from the Chicago Tribune, edited by Robert McHugh, 1958
Smart Set Criticism, edited by William H. Nolte, 1968
The Young Mencken: The Best of His Work, edited by Carl Bode, 1973
A Choice of Days (selection), edited by Edward L. Galligan, 1980
The Impossible Mencken: A Selection of His Best Newspaper Stories, edited by Marion Elizabeth Rodgers, 1991

Other writings: *Ventures into Verse* (1903), *George Bernard Shaw* (1905), *The Philosophy of Friedrich Nietzsche* (1908), *The Artist: A Drama Without Words* (1912), *A Little Book in C Major* (1916), *Damn! A Book of Calumny* (1918), *The American Language* (1919 and later revisions and supplements), memoirs (including *Thirty-Five Years of Newspaper Work: A Memoir*, edited by Fred Hobson, Vincent Fitzpatrick, and Bradford Jacobs, 1994), diaries, and correspondence.

Bibliographies
Adler, Betty, and Jane Wilhelm, *H. L. M.: The Mencken Bibliography*, Baltimore: Johns Hopkins University Press, 1961
Adler, Betty, *The Mencken Bibliography: A Ten-Year Supplement, 1962–1971*, Baltimore: Enoch Pratt Free Library, 1971
Bulsterbaum, Allison, *H. L. Mencken: A Research Guide*, New York: Garland, 1988
Fitzpatrick, Vincent, *HLM: The Mencken Bibliography, a Second Ten-Year Supplement, 1972–1981*, Baltimore: Enoch Pratt Free Library, 1986

Frey, Carroll, *A Bibliography of the Writings of H. L. Mencken*, Folcroft, Pennsylvania: Folcroft, 1969 (original edition, 1924)
Porter, Bern, *H. L. Mencken: A Bibliography*, Pasadena, California: Geddes Press, 1957

Further Reading
Angoff, Charles, *H. L. Mencken: A Portrait from Memory*, New York: Yoseloff, 1956
Bode, Carl, *Mencken*, Carbondale: Southern Illinois University Press, 1969
Boyd, Ernest, *H. L. Mencken*, New York: McBride, 1925
Cooke, Alistair, "The Baltimore Fox: An Appraisal by a British Journalist of a Writer with an Inimitable Style," *Saturday Review*, 10 September 1955; from Cooke's Introduction to *The Vintage Mencken*, edited by Cooke, New York: Vintage, 1955
Cooke, Alistair, "The Last Happy Days of H. L. Mencken," *Atlantic Monthly* 197 (May 1956): 33–38
Dorsey, John, editor, *On Mencken*, New York: Knopf, 1980
Douglas, George H., *H. L. Mencken: Critic of American Life*, Hamden, Connecticut: Archon, 1978
Downs, Robert B., "The Great Debunker," in his *Books That Changed America*, New York: Macmillan, 1970
Farrell, James T., "Dr. Mencken: Criticus Americanus," in his *Reflections at Fifty and Other Essays*, New York: Vanguard Press, 1954; London: Spearman, 1956
Goldberg, Isaac, *The Man Mencken: A Biographical and Critical Survey*, New York: Simon and Schuster, 1925
Hecht, Ben, "About Mencken," in his *Letters from Bohemia*, Garden City, New York: Doubleday, 1964
Kemler, Edgar, *The Irreverent Mr. Mencken*, Boston: Little Brown, 1950
Kummer, Frederic Arnold, "Something Must Have Happened to Henry," *Bookman* 65 (June 1927)
Leary, Lewis, "H. L. Mencken: Changeless Critic in Changing Times," in *The Young Rebel in American Literature*, edited by Carl Bode, London: Heinemann, 1959; New York: Praeger, 1960
Manchester, William, *Disturber of the Peace: The Life of H. L. Mencken*, Amherst: University of Massachusetts Press, 1986 (original edition, 1951)
Mayfield, Sara, *The Constant Circle: H. L. Mencken and His Friends*, New York: Delacorte Press, 1968
Nolte, William H., *H. L. Mencken: Literary Critic*, Middletown, Connecticut: Wesleyan University Press, 1966
Rubin, Louis D., "H. L. Mencken of the Baltimore Sunpapers," *Virginia Quarterly Review* 71 (Spring 1995)
Stenerson, Douglas C., *H. L. Mencken: Iconoclast from Baltimore*, Chicago: University of Chicago Press, 1971
William, W. H. A., *H. L. Mencken*, Boston: Twayne, 1977
Williams, Michael, "Mencken's Bible for Boobs," *Commonweal*, 2 April 1930

Mendelssohn, Moses
German, 1729–1786

Moses Mendelssohn plays a central role in the genesis of modern German literary criticism. Destined to become a rabbi and trained in Talmudic scholarship, Mendelssohn arrived as a young student in Berlin. Introduced to the arts and sciences, he soon became involved in the enlightened circles of Berlin's young literati. There he met **Lessing**, whose friendship became a lifelong inspiration. Forced to support himself and later his family, he began as a tutor, but was soon made manager and eventually partner of the silk factory of his students' father.

Mendelssohn's extramural education, his autodidactic genius, and the conversational tone of intellectual life may all have contributed to the essayistic and refined fashion of his writing.

Defining his own discursive terrain, he began as author of *Philosophische Gespräche* (1755; Philosophical dialogues), *Briefe über die Empfindungen* (1755; Letters on sensations), and its sequel "Rhapsodie" (1761). These **philosophical essays** introduce a new, civil tone to metaphysics. Conceived as **dialogues**, they not only bring fresh air to the stuffy quarters of philosophy but are accessible to a larger public. Mendelssohn thus transformed philosophy into a concern shared by all which, therefore, must transcend the narrow confines of academia and address itself to the public. The prevailing view is to see Mendelssohn as nothing more than a representative of popular philosophy, occupied more with disseminating knowledge than with rethinking it. Yet such a view ignores the deeper implications the choice of the essay as a literary genre entails for philosophy itself. In staging philosophical arguments as dialogues, the discourse of philosophy changes its format, but also its priorities, interests, and concerns. Paradoxically, it seems that Mendelssohn was engaged in a philosophically more challenging enterprise when he chose to compose essays. Reformulating philosophical arguments in the form of dialogues was a matter of recontextualized philosophy, allowing the validity of its own presuppositions to be examined in an unassuming manner. The essay genre – **Hume** and **Shaftesbury** were his most prominent models – allowed Mendelssohn to engage in intellectual debate at the social and institutional margins without falling prey to the mechanisms of exclusion. It also provided the means to reformulate philosophy as a discourse outside the exclusive framework of Christian theology, in which the Leibniz-Wolffian school of philosophy of 18th-century Germany was still deeply imbedded.

With his innovative essay form Mendelssohn emerged as Germany's leading literary critic. As coeditor, consultant, and single most prolific contributor to the **review** journals his friend Friedrich Nicolai published – *Bibliothek der schönen Wissenschaften und der freyen Künste* (1757–59; Library of the humanities and the liberal arts), *Briefe die neueste Literatur betreffend* (1758–61; Letters on contemporary literature), and *Allgemeine deutsche Bibliothek* (1765–84; Universal German library) – he was instrumental in forging German literary criticism into a powerful participant in the public sphere. Departing from the practice of assessing literature, poetry, and drama according to preconceived standards, Mendelssohn's reviews acknowledged the poetics of each work within its own cultural and poetological setting, appreciating each on its own specific terms. According to Mendelssohn, the critic's task does not consist of applying fixed rules and standards so much as it consists of presenting, as a public advocate, each case to the public, which in turn is expected to serve as judge. As facilitator of this process, the literary critic's essays aim at transparency, attempting to trace the most subtle sensations, reflections, emotions, and feelings in experiencing literature and fine arts. In so doing the critic creates the necessary forum for discussing aesthetic experience. This makes it possible for the public to realize its task as the ultimate judge in art and literature.

Mendelssohn was one of the most sophisticated comparatists of the 18th century, thoroughly versed in biblical literature, Homer, Dante, Shakespeare, French and German literature, and equipped with a rare sensibility for aesthetic quality and philosophical reasoning; his reviews established the standards that served as frames of reference to aesthetic theorists like **Kant**, **Herder**, **Goethe**, Karl Philipp Moritz, and **Schiller**.

In *Jerusalem, oder über religiöse Macht und Judentum* (1783; *Jerusalem, or, On Religious Power and Judaism*), Mendelssohn presents the question of Jewish emancipation as a central issue for modern culture; the plea for equal rights and social acceptance are expressed in a style and rhetoric typical of Mendelssohn. These essayistic strengths make *Jerusalem* stand out from the literary landscape of its era as a uniquely powerful work.

The "German Socrates" – as Mendelssohn was called after the rewriting of **Plato**'s *Phädon* (1767) brought him international fame – redefined the philosophical essay and the review as new forms in which conflicting interests could be expressed and the demand for aesthetic autonomy justified. Mendelssohn's writing was celebrated for its fluidity, precision, civility, and stylistic beauty, and it assumed paradigmatic importance for critics and poets alike. Mendelssohn's aesthetic theory introduced its themes in an aesthetically pleasing form: versatile enough both to respond to aesthetic expectations and to adhere to the disipline that informs the discourse of philosophy. Mendelssohn participated in the Enlightenment debate in the 1780s with a series of pieces addressing the role of Enlightenment. They are short and concise interventions, programmatic essays forcefully arguing for the collaborative search for truth and the best for society.

WILLI GOETSCHEL

Biography

Born 6 September 1729 in Dessau. Studied the Bible and the Talmud under Rabbi David Fränkel, following him to Berlin, 1743, and studying at his Talmud Academy. Private tutor, from 1750. Met and became friends with Lessing, 1753. Accountant, then assistant to a silk merchant, from 1754, and part owner of the factory on his death, from 1768. Founder, with Friedrich Nicolai, *Bibliothek der schönen Wissenschaften und der freyen Künste*, 1757, and with Nicolai and Lessing, *Briefe die neueste Literatur betreffend*, 1758. Married Fromet Gugenheim, 1762: five children, one of whom was the father of Felix Mendelssohn (two others died). Awards: Prussian Academy Prize, 1763. Died in Berlin, 4 January 1786.

Selected Writings

Essays and Related Prose
Briefe über die Empfindungen, 1755
Philosophische Gespräche, 1755
Philosophische Schriften, 1761; revised edition, 1771, 1777
Abhandlung über die Evidenz in metaphysischen Wissenschaften, 1764
Phädon, oder über die Unsterblichkeit der Seele, 1767; edited by Dominique Bourel, 1979; as *Phædon; or, The Death of Socrates*, translated by Charles Cullen, 1789
Schreiben an den Herrn Diaconus Lavater zu Zürich, 1770; as *Letter of Moses Mendelssohn, to Deacon Lavater*, translated by Frederick Henry Hedge, 1821, and in *Memoirs of Moses Mendelssohn*, 1825

Jerusalem, oder über religiöse Macht und Judentum, 1783; as
Jerusalem: A Treatise on Ecclesiastical Authority and Judaism,
translated by M. Samuels, 1838; as *Jerusalem: A Treatise on
Religious Power and Judaism*, translated by Isaac Leeser, 1852;
as *Jerusalem, or, On Religious Power and Judaism*, edited by
Alexander Altmann, translated by Allan Arkush, 1983
Morgenstunden; oder, Vorlesungen über das Daseyn Gottes, 1785;
edited by Dominique Bourel, 1979
Abhandlung von der Unkörperlichkeit der menschlichen Seele, 1785
Moses Mendelssohn an die Freunde Lessings, edited by Johann
Jakob Engel, 1786
Abhandlungen über das Kommerz zwischen Seele und Körper, 1788
Kleine philosophische Schriften, 1789
*Aufsätze über jüdische Gebete und festfeier aus archivalischen
Akten*, edited by L. E. Borowski, 1791
Jerusalem, and Other Jewish Writings, edited and translated by
Alfred Jospe, 1969
Moses Mendelssohn: Selections from His Writings, edited and
translated by Eva Jospe, 1975
Schriften über Religion und Aufklärung, edited by Martin Thom, 1989

Other writings: books on Judaism, and correspondence. Also
translated **Rousseau**, and with others translated the Torah.

Collected works editions: *Sämmtliche Werke*, 12 vols., 1819–25;
Gesammelte Schriften, edited by Ismar Elbogen, Julius Guttmann,
Eugen Mittwoch, and others, 22 vols., 1974– (in progress).

Bibliographies

Albrecht, Michael, "Moses Mendelssohn: Ein Forschungsbericht,
1965–1980," *Deutsche Vierteljahrsschrift für
Literaturwissenschaft* 57 (March 1983): 64–159
Meyer, Hermann M. Z., *Moses Mendelssohn Bibliographie*, Berlin:
de Gruyter, 1965

Further Reading

Albrecht, Michael, Eva J. Engel, and Norbert Hinske, editors, *Moses
Mendelssohn und die Kreise seiner Wirksamkeit*, Tübingen:
Niemeyer, 1994
Altmann, Alexander, *Moses Mendelssohn: A Biographical Study*,
London: Routledge and Kegan Paul, and Tuscaloosa: University
of Alabama Press, 1973
Altmann, Alexander, *Die trostvolle Aufklärung: Studien zur
Metaphysik und politischen Theorie Moses Mendelssohns*,
Stuttgart and Bad Cannstatt: Frommann-Holzboog, 1982
Arkush, Allen, *Moses Mendelssohn and the Enlightenment*, Albany:
State University of New York Press, 1994
Engel, Eva J., "Moses Mendelssohn: His Importance as a Literary
Critic," *Lessing Yearbook* supplement (1982): 259–73
Goetschel, Willi, "Moses Mendelssohn und das Projekt der
Aufklärung," *Germanic Review* 71 (1996): 163–75

Menéndez y Pelayo, Marcelino

Spanish, 1856–1912

Marcelino Menéndez y Pelayo is the earliest Spanish historian
of literature, culture, and ideas whose erudition and theories
must still be taken into account by contemporary researchers.
From an early age he demonstrated prodigious academic
ability, studying with the most significant Spanish university professors of the time in Barcelona, Valladolid, and
Madrid. This resulted in a Ph.D. in 1875 from the University
of Madrid, governmental fellowships for research in Portugal,

Italy, and France, and, following public competitive exams, in
being named to the chair of literature at that university in the
autumn of 1878.

Unfortunately Menéndez y Pelayo grew up and came to
intellectual maturity in the years of civil war and fierce
ideological and religious contention before, during, and after
the period marked by the 1868 expulsion of the Bourbon
monarchy from Spain and its 1875 restoration. Hence, while
his first essays of the early 1870s were always notable for their
learning, they also revealed a conservative but nationalistic
Catholic ideology which represented to Menéndez y Pelayo the
great tradition of what made Spain Spain; nonetheless, this
course simultaneously estranged him from liberals (centered
around the Krausists – followers of the German philosopher
Karl Christian Friedrich Krause) and ultramontanists.

As was typical among intellectuals and writers in the Spain
of the 1870s, Menéndez y Pelayo began publishing scholarly
essays in such leading national and regional journals and magazines as *La Ilustración Española y Americana* (Spanish and
American illustration), *Revista Histórico-Latina* (Latin-histor-
ical review), *La España Católica* (Catholic Spain), *Revista
Europea* (European review), *La Tertulia* (The gathering), and
Revista Cántabro-Asturiana (Cantabria-Asturias review).

Of Menéndez y Pelayo's great multi-volume projects, two
especially were received in their time as products of the charged
ideological rivalries. *La ciencia española* (1879, 1887–88;
Spanish science), which became a three-volume work, always
retained the imprint of its birth as a series of polemical **letters**
published in *Revista de España* (Spanish review) in 1876. The
essay-letters attacked the notion that the Spanish Inquisition
and Monarchy destroyed the possibility of European-style
science and progress in Spain. Moreover they introduced
and analyzed physical scientists, philosophers, and medical
researchers who were little remembered in the 19th century,
but who flourished in Spain during the previous three centuries
and deserved notice.

The second polemical work is the famous and frequently
reprinted *Historia de los heterodoxos españoles* (1880–81,
1911–32; History of Spanish heretics). It began as a series
of interpretative biographical sketches during Menéndez y
Pelayo's student days, but reached three volumes during its
first publication and eventually extended to seven. In their final
form the individual studies – which range from Roman times
on the Iberian Peninsula to the middle of the 19th century –
became integrated into a major, albeit partisan study of cults,
schools, and individuals whose thought differed from that of
orthodox Catholicism as established through Church Councils
and papal pronouncements.

The publication in 23 volumes between 1982 and 1991 of
letters written by Menéndez y Pelayo and to him from all parts
of Europe and the Americas, and the 1982 conference and
its proceedings, *Menéndez y Pelayo: Hacia una nueva imagen*
(1983; Menéndez y Pelayo: toward a new image), gave a
productive orientation to contemporary use and evaluation of
the writer's work and place in Spanish culture and thought.
The collection acknowledges his polemical and ideological
dimensions, and hence emphasizes that considerable part of
his work not limited by bias and partisanship.

STEPHEN MILLER

Biography

Born 3 November 1856 in Santander. Studied at the Universities of Barcelona, Valladolid, and Madrid, Ph.D., 1875, and at the major libraries in Portugal, France, and Italy. Professor of literary history, University of Madrid, 1878–98. Elected to the Royal Spanish Academy of the Language, 1881. Elected member, 1883, librarian, 1893–95, and director, 1910–12, Royal Spanish Academy of History. Director, National Library, Madrid, from 1898. Deputy to Spanish Parliament for Mallorca, 1884, and Saragossa, 1891, and senator representing the University of Oviedo, 1893–95, and the Royal Spanish Academy of the Language, 1899–1912. Died in Santander, 19 May 1912.

Selected Writings

Essays and Related Prose

Estudios sobre escritores montañeses, 1877
La ciencia española, 1879; revised, enlarged edition, 3 vols., 1887–88
Historia de los heterodoxos españoles, 3 vols., 1880–81; revised, enlarged edition, 7 vols., 1911–32
Calderón y su teatro, 1881
Estudios de crítica literaria, 5 vols., 1884–1908
Ensayos de crítica filosófica, 1892
Estudios sobre el teatro de Lope de Vega, 6 vols., 1919–27

Other writings: works on classical and Spanish literature, aesthetics, history, and correspondence (collected in *Epistolario*, edited by Manuel Revuelta Sañudo, 23 vols., 1982–91). Also edited part of the edition of Lope de Vega's works (1890–1912).

Collected works edition: *Obras completas* (Edición Nacional), edited by Enrique Sánchez Reyes, 70 vols., 1940–57.

Bibliographies

Simón Díaz, José, *Estudios sobre Menéndez y Pelayo*, Madrid: Instituto de Estudios Madrileños, 1954
Simón Díaz, José, "Bibliografía de y sobre Menéndez y Pelayo, 1939–1955," *Arbor: Revista General de Investigación y Cultura* 34, nos. 127–28 (July–August 1956): 536–59

Further Reading

Artigas y Ferrando, Miguel, *La vida y la obra de Menéndez y Pelayo*, Saragossa: Heraldo de Aragón, 1939
Calzada Rodríguez, Luciano de la, *La historia de España en Menéndez y Pelayo*, Murcia: University of Murcia, 1957
Donoso, Armando, *Menéndez y Pelayo y su obra*, Santiago: University of Chile Press, 1913
Gili Gaya, Samuel, *Sobre la "Historia de las ideas estéticas en España" de Menéndez y Pelayo*, Santander: Sociedad Menéndez y Pelayo, 1956
Lázaro Carreter, Fernando, *Menéndez y Pelayo: Su época y su obra literaria*, Salamanca: Anaya, 2 vols., 1962
Revuelta Sañudo, Manuel, *La biblioteca de Menéndez y Pelayo*, Santander: Sociedad Menéndez y Pelayo, 1982
Revuelta Sañudo, Manuel, editor, *Menéndez y Pelayo: Hacia una nueva imagen*, Santander: Sociedad Menéndez y Pelayo, 1983
Sainz Rodríguez, Pedro, *Menéndez y Pelayo, ese desconocido*, Madrid: Fundación Universitaria Española, 1975
Santovena Setién, Antonio, *Marcelino Menéndez y Pelayo: Revisión crítico-biográfica de un pensador católico*, Santander: University of Cantabria, 1994

Merton, Thomas

American, 1915–1968

One of the most prolific American Catholic writers of the 20th century, Thomas Merton produced a supple, contemplative prose style that grew out of his contemplative life as a Cistercian monk. Or it could be said that the prose style preceded the lifestyle, for the nature of Merton's writing was established well before he became a priest and a monk. In an era when the American essay was becoming almost embarrassingly intimate, Merton's own prose, though it could be called "personal" in style, exhibited a personalism that de-emphasized the value of the self. Even his spiritual autobiography, *The Seven Storey Mountain* (1948), which by its nature must focus on himself, is not so much self-conscious as conscious that the self is an illusion. "Free by nature," begins the second sentence in the book, "in the image of God, I was nevertheless the prisoner of my own violence and my own selfishness, in the image of the world into which I was born." In all his writing, Merton's spirituality is inseparable from his style.

For readers, however, the connection between Merton's contemplative prayer and his writing must be heavily qualified. Merton thought of contemplation as the "cloud of unknowing" imagined by an anonymous 14th-century mystic, a prayer carefully devoid of images. Yet *writing* that is emptied of images is very dull, and almost invariably bad. Hence even the most transcendent and abstract spiritual experiences appear in Merton's prose in concrete images. The saint's radical freedom in God he expresses this way in *Seeds of Contemplation* (1949): "A door opens in the center of our being and we seem to fall through it into immense depths which, although they are infinite, are all accessible to us." Even the "cloud of unknowing" and "the dark night of the soul" are themselves images in writing, for all that they represent an imageless contemplation.

Merton's prose is capable of abstraction, of course, and he is capable of abstract thought. In a lengthy paragraph critiquing Marxism, which very quickly turns to a personal critique of **Marx**, Merton writes, in prose filled with generalities as vague as those of the worst Marxist rhetoric, about the terrible effects of Marx's "bourgeois and Jewish conscience" on the world. But just as the connections Merton makes are about to collapse into their own abstraction, he ends the paragraph with a picture that focuses as sharply on Marx as on the "effects" Merton has asserted: "Because Marx raged at himself and everyone else and wore out a path in his carpet walking up and down the room cursing his boils, there are now twenty million persons in Soviet forced labor camps" (*The Monastic Journey*, 1977). What had been abstract assertion is now realized in a verbal diptych.

Though his formal theological writings can be as involuted in thought and style as those of Thomas Aquinas, whom Merton revered, his attempts to popularize contemplative life, or to explain it to a lay audience, could be simple and aphoristic. Thus, in attempting to counter a Manichaean tendency in religion, the error of valuing only spirit and scorning material reality, Merton crossed Alexander Pope's "Everything that is, is right" with William Blake's "Everything that lives is holy" to say "Everything that is, is holy," a chapter title in

Seeds of Contemplation. (Blake in fact was an important influence in Merton's thought and writing, and his "Proverbs of Hell" in *The Marriage of Heaven and Hell* [1793] may be a source of Merton's own aphoristic style.)

Merton's **aphorisms**, however, are not presented as proverbs, disembodied snippets of wisdom. They always arise naturally as incandescent condensations of the point he is moving toward in the paragraph. "The spiritual life is first of all a *life*" (*Thoughts in Solitude*, 1958). "All true love is a death and a resurrection in Christ" (*Disputed Questions*, 1960). "The devil believes in God but he has no God" (*No Man Is an Island*, 1955). "To *see* your hope is to abandon hope" (*The New Man*, 1961). "As long as we are in this world, our life in Christ remains hidden" (*The Living Bread*, 1956). "When a myth becomes a daydream it is judged, found wanting, and must be discarded" (*Conjectures of a Guilty Bystander*, 1966). Yet sentences like these differ from proverbs and folk sayings in that their meanings are not self-contained: they need to be unfolded in the sentences that surround them. By themselves they either make no sense or seem incomplete.

Though most of his prose tends toward the theological, Merton's essays touch on any number of subjects, primarily literary and art criticism (his early training was in art, his graduate studies in literature) and politics. Since his vocation as a writer preceded his vocation as a priest, and since he considered both to be literally calls from God, Merton maintained a keen interest in the role of literature and art in the culture of the 20th century. Thus an essentially religious book, *Disputed Questions*, begins with a 20,000-word chapter on the Russian novelist Boris Pasternak, with whom Merton had corresponded in the years just before Pasternak's death.

As well known for his poetry as his prose, Merton displays the poet's ear for prose rhythm. In a random passage in his journal *Conjectures of a Guilty Bystander* Merton attributes to Gregory the Great a break from the classical style in medieval Latin toward a rhythm that simplified medieval prose the way Gregorian chant simplified medieval music. There is no doubt that a little of Gregory's simplified prose rhythms also crept into Merton's writing, especially since he tells us that he spent a year of his novitiate reading Gregory's *Moralia*. One of the wonders of Merton's prose is that it sounds very contemporary while yet echoing in rhythm, diction, and, of course, doctrine, the great writers of Catholic antiquity.

JOHN R. HOLMES

Biography

Born 31 January 1915 in Prades, France. Brought to the United States, 1916; returned to France, 1925, then lived in England, from 1928, and back in the U.S., from 1934; became a U.S. citizen, 1951. Studied at Clare College, Cambridge, 1933–34; Columbia University, New York, 1935–38, B.A., 1938, M.A., 1939. Instructor in English, Columbia University, 1938–39, and St. Bonaventure University, New York, 1939–41. Cistercian monk at the Abbey of Our Lady of Gethsemani, near Bardstown, Kentucky, 1941–68: ordained priest, 1949, master of scholastics, 1951–55, master of novices, 1955–65, and lived as a hermit in the grounds of the monastery, 1965–68. Awards: Mariana Griswold Van Rensselaer Award, 1939; Catholic Literary Award, 1949; Catholic Writers Guild Golden Book Award, 1951; Columbia University Medal for Excellence, 1961; Pax Medal, 1963; honorary degree from one university. Died (accidentally electrocuted) in Bangkok, Thailand, 10 December 1968.

Selected Writings

Essays and Related Prose
What Is Contemplation?, 1948
Seeds of Contemplation, 1949; revised edition, as *New Seeds of Contemplation*, 1962
The Ascent to Truth, 1951
Bread in the Wilderness, 1953
No Man Is an Island, 1955
The Living Bread, 1956
The Silent Life, 1957
Thoughts in Solitude, 1958
Spiritual Direction and Meditation, 1960
Disputed Questions, 1960; selection as *The Power and Meaning of Love*, 1976
The Behavior of Titans, 1961
The New Man, 1961
A Thomas Merton Reader, edited by Thomas P. McDonnell, 1962
Life and Holiness, 1963
Seeds of Destruction, 1964
Seasons of Celebration, 1965
Mystics and Zen Masters, 1967
Zen and the Birds of Appetite, 1968
Faith and Violence: Christian Teaching and Christian Practice, 1968
The Climate of Monastic Prayer, 1969; as *Contemplative Prayer*, 1969
The True Solitude: Selections from the Writings, edited by Dean Walley, 1969
Opening the Bible, 1970; revised edition, 1983
Contemplation in a World of Action, 1971
Thomas Merton on Peace, 1971; revised edition, as *The Nonviolent Alternative*, edited by Gordon C. Zahn, 1980
Spiritual Direction and Meditation; and, What Is Contemplation?, 1975
Thomas Merton on Zen, 1976
Ishi Means Man: Essays on Native Americans, 1976
The Monastic Journey, edited by Patrick Hart, 1977
Love and Living, edited by Naomi Burton Stone and Patrick Hart, 1979
Thomas Merton on St. Bernard, 1980
Introductions East and West: The Foreign Prefaces, edited by Robert E. Daggy, 1981; revised, enlarged edition, as *Honorable Reader: Reflections on My Work*, edited by Daggy, 1989
The Literary Essays, edited by Patrick Hart, 1981
"Monks Pond": Thomas Merton's Little Magazine, edited by Robert E. Daggy, 1989
Thomas Merton, Spiritual Master: The Essential Writings, edited by Lawrence S. Cunningham, 1992
Passion for Peace: The Social Essays, edited by William Shannon, 1995

Other writings: poetry, volumes of autobiography (including *The Seven Storey Mountain*, 1948; as *Elected Silence*, 1949), and several volumes of journals and correspondence.

Bibliographies

Breit, Marquita, *Thomas Merton: A Bibliography*, Metuchen, New Jersey: Scarecrow Press, 1974
Dell'Isola, Frank, *Thomas Merton: A Bibliography*, Kent, Ohio: Kent State University Press, 1975

Further Reading

Bailey, Raymond, *Thomas Merton on Mysticism*, New York: Doubleday, 1975
Furlong, Monica, *Merton, a Biography*, New York: Harper and Row, 1980; London: SPCK, revised edition, 1995

Kramer, Victor A., "Thomas Merton's Published Journals: The Paradox of Writing as a Step Toward Contemplation," *Studia Mystica* 3 (1980): 3–20

Kramer, Victor A., "Merton's Affirmation and the Affirmation of Merton: Writing About Silence," *Review* 4 (1982): 295–334

Kramer, Victor A., *Thomas Merton*, Boston: Twayne, 1984

Labrie, Ross, *The Art of Thomas Merton*, Fort Worth: Texas Christian University Press, 1979

McInerny, Dennis Q., *Thomas Merton: The Man and His Work*, Spencer, Massachusetts: Cistercian Publications, 1974

Twomey, Gerald, editor, *Thomas Merton: Prophet in the Belly of a Paradox*, New York: Paulist Press, 1978

Woodcock, George, *Thomas Merton, Monk and Poet: A Critical Study*, Vancouver: Douglas and McIntyre, Edinburgh: Canongate, and New York: Farrar Straus Giroux, 1978

Meynell, Alice

British, 1847–1922

In 1919, Theodore Maynard wrote of Alice Meynell that "of all the prose writers of the Twentieth Century, she is the one most certain of immortality." Though we might question Maynard's prescience today, Meynell was widely regarded as one of the most important essayists of her day due to the remarkable quantity and quality of her essays. Although critical and scholarly commentary on Meynell has been sparse since her death, her essays are still insightful, elegant, and vivid, and cover a wide range of subjects from literary criticism to women's suffrage to English grammar to children. A disciplined Catholic spiritualism pervades her outlook, but it is not dogmatic or overbearing and not nearly so evident as it is in her more private poetry, for which she was also much admired. Her skills as a poet inform much of her prose writing in its precise diction, elaborate style, and figurative language, but also in its perception of life, particularly in the opening lines of "The Rhythm of Life" (1889), her impressive early essay on the regularity – what Meynell calls the "periodicity" – of human existence: "If life is not always poetical, it is at least metrical." Such an opening sentence shows Meynell's mastery of the lead, the attention-grabber necessary in journalism, and of the well-put, surprising, witty observation. Indeed, her essays are a unique blend of literary sophistication and journalistic observation and accessibility. From her early journalistic writing to the end of her career, Meynell considered herself a professional writer who demanded her own personal standards of excellence, and her essays bear the mark of an incisive cultural critic writing for and about the age in which she lived. In her insistence upon the important contribution of women in society, she is also, in the essay, **Virginia Woolf**'s most immediate precursor.

Most of Meynell's essays first appeared in periodicals such as the *Scots Observer*, the *Saturday Review*, the **Spectator**, and particularly the *Pall Mall Gazette*, for which Meynell wrote a weekly column from 1893 to 1898. Her column, "The Wares of Autolycus," named after both the thief of Greek mythology and the endearing pedlar in Shakespeare's *The Winter's Tale*, "a snapper-up of unconsidered trifles," was intended initially for women readers of the *Pall Mall Gazette*, which was both a newspaper and literary review; but the column soon broadened in its appeal to include a larger family audience, and

Meynell became recognized for writing insightful essays on children. Most of her important essays first appeared here, and the column's title, most likely provided by the editors, suggests that Meynell's purpose in the column was to reconsider the familiar and seemingly insignificant elements of everyday life. Her literary and aesthetic writing appealed to a well-read, sophisticated, but general audience; she wrote critical introductions to popular collections of poets such as Elizabeth Barrett Browning (1896, 1916), William Wordsworth (1903), **Percy Bysshe Shelley** (1903), Robert Herrick (1905), William Cowper (1905), Christina Rossetti (1906), William Blake (1911), and others. Interestingly, Meynell wrote commentaries on (at the time) less familiar women writers of the Romantic period, who are currently being reincorporated into the literary canon, such as Anna Seward and Joanna Baillie, in *The Second Person Singular* (1921), and **Mary Wollstonecraft** and Elizabeth Inchbald, published in the posthumous collection *Essays of Today and Yesterday* (1926). Throughout her career, Meynell revised and collected her essays for ten volumes published to much popular and critical acclaim. Several of these editions have been reprinted since her death. During her lifetime, she earned the admiration of other writers such as Francis Thompson, Coventry Patmore, George Meredith, **G. K. Chesterton**, and Aubrey De Vere, with whom she became close, often intimate, friends. Meynell clearly became part of the contemporary literati, but her writing, though polished and sophisticated, maintained the accessibility and relevance that made her column so widely read in the 1890s.

Meynell's essays on language bear the influence of **Johnson**, **Hazlitt**, and **Arnold**. They reveal a degree of linguistic analysis uncommon in popular journalism of the time but typical of her steadfast belief in the importance of grammar as a cornerstone of cultural stability. Her essay "Composure" (1891) is based on her belief that language itself is educative in the linguistic recognition of the disparity between the word and the thing it represents but teaches us to recognize this through the development of vocabulary: "Shall not the Thing more and more, as we compose ourselves to literature, assume the honour, the hesitation, the leisure, the reconciliation of the Word?" For Meynell, linguistic and semantic gulfs are not so much problems as they are essential aspects of learning. In "The Little Language" (1909), she writes of the felicitous character, intimacy, and locality of dialect, with characteristic metaphorical acuity: "Dialect is the elf rather than the genius of place, and a dwarfish master of the magic of local things." "A Corrupt Following" (1921) blames Gibbon for the degradation of the English language during the 19th century in what Meynell sees as his influential but imprecise and ungrammatical stylistic vulgarity. In her much admired essay "The Second Person Singular" (1921), she finds in grammar the heritage of English culture and laments its recent decline, using contemporary usage of the pronoun "you" as an example of "the slovenliness of our civilization in the practice of the inflexions of grammar." Meynell followed her own example in the fastidious precision and polish of her writing.

Meynell's voice, however, does not lose its vitality in its precision. On the contrary, she considers life not in its random collisions and cacophonies but in its ordered continuities and in its wayfaring spirit. She sees life through a poetic prism of refracted light and color, as in the invasion of pastoral green in the urban landscape described in the opening passage of "Ceres Runaway" (1906) or in the corrective spectrum of "The Colour of Life" (1895), which she points out is not the color of blood – "Red is the colour of violence, or of life broken open, edited, and published" – but the color of the body, "the covered red," in its various shades under the lamp of nature.

Meynell's vitality and soulfulness are what attracted readers to her loving depictions of growing children, for instance, in "The Child of Tumult," "The Child of Subsiding Tumult," both from her third book of essays *The Children* (1897), "The Influential Child," from *Childhood* (1913), and others inspired by her own son and, later, her grandchildren, which provided invaluable insight on the development and care of personalities before Maslow and Spock. The essays on childhood are central to all of Meynell's prose work because childhood is the foundation of the human life explored in one way or another in all of the other essays. As she wrote in "The Illusion of Historic Time," an essay on adult perception of contracted time, "Childhood is itself Antiquity – to every man his only Antiquity."

DANIEL ROBINSON

Biography
Born Alice Christina Gertrude Thompson, 11 October 1847 in Barnes, southwest London. Studied with her father and tutors in England and Italy. Moved with family to the Isle of Wight, 1866. Converted to Roman Catholicism, 1868. Married Wilfrid Meynell, 1877: seven children (one other died in infancy). Contributor to many journals, including the *Spectator*, the *Scots Observer*, Edinburgh (later the *National Observer*, London), the *Saturday Review*, the *Art Journal*, and the *Tablet*; editor, with Wilfrid Meynell, the *Pen*, 1880, the *Weekly Register*, 1881–99, and *Merry England*, from 1883; weekly columnist of "The Wares of Autolycus," 1893–98, and art critic, 1902–05, *Pall Mall Gazette*, London; lectured in the United States, 1901–02. Associated with other writers, including Coventry Patmore, George Meredith, and G. K. Chesterton. Moved to Greatham, Sussex, 1911. Elected Fellow, Royal Society of Literature, 1914. Died in London, 27 November 1922.

Selected Writings

Essays and Related Prose
The Rhythm of Life and Other Essays, 1893
The Colour of Life and Other Essays on Things Seen and Heard, 1896
The Children, 1897
London Impressions, 1898
The Spirit of Place and Other Essays, 1899
Ceres Runaway and Other Essays, 1909
Mary, the Mother of Jesus: An Essay, 1912; revised edition, 1923
Childhood, 1913
Essays, 1914
Hearts of Controversy, 1917
The Second Person Singular and Other Essays, 1921
Essays of Today and Yesterday (selected essays), 1926
Essays, edited by Francis Meynell, 1947
The Wares of Autolycus: Selected Literary Essays, edited by P. M. Fraser, 1965

Other writings: six collections of poetry, religious books, and biographies of William Holman Hunt and John Ruskin.

Bibliographies
Alice Meynell, 1847–1922: Catalogue of the Centenary Exhibition, London: National Book League, 1947
Connolly, Terence L., "Alice Meynell: A Short-Title List of Poetry, Essays, Miscellaneous Works, Anthologies, Translations, Editings and Introductions," in *Alice Meynell Centenary Tribute, 1847–1947*, edited by Connolly, Boston: Humphries, 1948: 41–72

Further Reading
Badeni, June, *The Slender Tree: A Life of Alice Meynell*, Padstow, Cornwall: Tabb House Press, 1981
Connolly, Terence L., editor, *Alice Meynell Centenary Tribute, 1847–1947*, Boston: Humphries, 1948
Maynard, Theodore, *Carven from the Laurel Tree*, Freeport, New York: Books for Libraries Press, 1967 (original edition, 1918)
Meynell, Viola, *Alice Meynell: A Memoir*, London: Cape, and New York: Scribner, 1929
Moore, Virginia, *Distinguished Women Writers*, Port Washington, New York: Kennikat Press, 1968 (original edition, 1934)
Tuell, Anne Kimball, *Mrs. Meynell and Her Literary Generation*, St. Clair Shores, Michigan: Scholarly Press, 1970 (original edition, 1925)
Vogt, Elizabeth L., *Honours of Mortality: The Career, Reputation and Achievement of Alice Meynell* (dissertation), Lawrence: University of Kansas, 1989

Mill, John Stuart
British, 1806–1873

John Stuart Mill published many essays, some as articles in periodical journals, many collected and separately published, some as **pamphlets**, and others as monographs. His first publications were two **letters** in 1822 for an evening newspaper, the *Traveller*. His earliest writing was in an epistolary style, formal and argumentative, for a faceless audience of readers. However, his topics were not merely topical, since he sought to advance the liberal cause of free inquiry into any subject; he signed his earliest writings as "Wickliffe," to associate himself with the continuing reformist spirit of John Wycliffe.

Mill sought to emulate the lucid, transparent style of classical 18th-century British authors, such as **Jonathan Swift**, Edward Gibbon, and the early Jeremy Bentham. His compositions were analytical, taking apart the elements of ideas suffering from loose and ill-defined usage, such as "Nature" (wr. 1854, pub. 1874). Mill's intellectual heroes were authors of Greek history and philosophy, and it was from the model of classical Greek (which he began learning at the age of three) that he took his cue for precision of expression.

There has never been a want of readers for Mill's writings, from his first audience to today. Whether his subject has been political reform or biography, logic or autobiography, he has had responsive and responsible readers. His most frequently chosen form of essay was the **review** article for periodicals, from the *Westminster Review* in 1823 to *Fraser's Magazine* and the *Fortnightly Review* in the last decade of his life. Mill collected some of these articles as *Dissertations and Discussions* (1859), to which he added later essays for new editions in 1867 and again in 1875.

As a polemicist and practicing politician, Mill was an advocate for moderation in tone, even while promoting radical ideas of utilitarianism and agnostic materialism. Indeed, his tone and style both aimed for balance, to assuage skeptical readers whose prejudices he often took apart. He had a passion for the Socratic **dialogue**, cast in the Aristotelian form of a dissertation. To establish an intellectual dialectic within which he could pursue a common truth through the many-sidedness of experience, he would often set one argument against another, much as in a debate. Thus did he compose his two significant essays on the influences of Jeremy Bentham (1838) and **Samuel Taylor Coleridge** (1840), illustrating the complementary virtues of their seemingly different methods and philosophies: Bentham wanted to know the truth of things, Coleridge the meaning of them. These two great teachers brought together for Mill the logic of both induction and deduction. "They were the two great seminal minds of England in their age," he wrote.

Having learned from his father and Jeremy Bentham the power of syllogistic reasoning and deductive logic, Mill had to discover from another the way to truth by experience and induction. An important resource for this purpose was Alexis de Tocqueville's study *Democracy in America*, which Mill reviewed for the *London and Westminster Review* when it was translated into English in 1835 (vol. 1) and 1840 (vol. 2). As with other works which he admired, Mill quoted long passages from the volumes under review, and sought to present the case for the author's argument in both positive and negative lights. At a time when many English writers (such as **Matthew Arnold**) were pointing to America as a place of anarchy, Mill found in its political experiment a great laboratory for optimism. This was reinforced by the analysis Tocqueville made from his observations while living in America. Mill found in this work much of the evidence he sought for his belief that democracy required something more than an identifying of interests between the government and the governed, something more than "the greatest happiness for the greatest number," as Bentham had taught. A vital democracy needed a means for representing the interests of minority groups as well as those of the majority. Otherwise, America demonstrated through Tocqueville, individuals and minority groups would suffer from the tyranny of a majority exercising its authority as mere "public opinion." Mediocrity would then reign in a democratic state. These are faults, not of democracy, as Tocqueville would have it; instead, Mill says, they are the consequences of a triumphant commercial spirit in the progress of "civilization."

His major essay, by his own assessment, is the work *On Liberty*, which he wrote with the assistance of his wife, Harriet Taylor, and which he published in 1859, soon after her death. This was a long exposition of the value central to modern civilization, a value whose power was threatened by the very forces to which it gave birth. If democracy were indeed a result of majority rule, when sheer numbers would prevail, then democracy might annihilate the possibility for continuing intellectual progress. If truth were protean in experience and its meaning a function of its rich variety, then democracy might suffocate truth and choke life of its meaning. Following a great English tradition which includes John Locke's *Letters on Toleration* (1689–92) and John Milton's *Areopagitica* (1644), *On Liberty* analyzes and champions the idea of liberty as a condition for the meaning of life in every individual's experience of it. From liberty of thought to liberty of expression, there is a logical progression toward liberty of action, when

individuality proceeds to its fullest realization. There is, however, no liberty where there is no tolerance for the liberty of others; liberty endures only so long as it extends to all. Mill entertains the possibility of social values prevailing over individual ones, but concludes that "the worth of a State, in the long run, is the worth of the individuals composing it."

The one individual about whom John Stuart Mill knew the most was himself; he composed an essay on his own mental development in the *Autobiography*, published posthumously by his stepdaughter in 1873. This work is a complex narrative which Mill wrote in three different stages of his life. The first draft he composed soon after his marriage in 1851, the second he revised over three years after his wife's death in 1858, and the last version he completed in 1869. Among the several notable features of this work are Mill's estimate of his father, his tribute to his wife, and his psychological self-analysis. It is this last feature which has most consistently attracted reader interest, because it lies at the center of the book, as a crisis in the young man's mental life. Drawing upon his later reading of the English Romantic poets Wordsworth and Coleridge, as well as upon his friendship with and respect for **Thomas Carlyle**, Mill deftly dramatized the incidents of 1826, when he discovered an emptiness of spirit which he had to fill to become a whole human being. He realized that reasoning required feeling, that utility of means without an end to life would be meaningless. He found integrity in a balancing of individuality with circumstances, subjectivity with objectivity, analysis with synthesis.

While he was author of many other important essays, such as *A System of Logic* (1843), *Principles of Political Economy* (1848), and *The Subjection of Women* (1869), Mill remains best known for his essay *On Liberty* and his *Autobiography*. In all his writings, he labored for clarity of expression and never sought a rhetorical style of ornamentation or self-conscious display. Nevertheless, some distinctive characteristics of metaphor and imagery communicate forcefully, with aesthetic pleasure, the ideas carried by his style. For example, Coleridge and Bentham created movements of influence which were "two concentric circles which the shock given by them is spreading over the ocean of mind." Liberty of individuality lost to State interests would produce "a State which dwarfs its men" until it finds "that with small men no great thing can really be accomplished." Reading the works of 18th-century master writers, Mill "lost the jejuneness of my early compositions; the bones and cartilages began to clothe themselves with flesh, and the style became, at times, lively and almost light."

RICHARD D. McGHEE

Biography

Born 20 May 1806 in London. Studied privately with his father; studied law, 1822–23. Lived in southern France with the family of Jeremy Bentham's brother Samuel, 1820–21. Worked for the East India Company, London, 1823–58. Founding member, the Unitarian Society, 1823–26. Contributor to various journals, including the *London and Westminster Review*, the **Edinburgh Review**, and the *Monthly Repository*. Experienced a mental crisis, 1826. Met Harriet Hardy Taylor, 1831, carried on a platonic relationship with her until her husband's death (1849), and married, 1851 (she died, 1858). Lived in Avignon, France for part of each year, after 1858.

Liberal Member of Parliament for Westminster, 1865–68. Rector, University of St. Andrews, Fife, 1866. Died in Avignon, 7 May 1873.

Selected Writings

Essays and Related Prose

A System of Logic, Ratiocinative and Inductive, 2 vols., 1843
Essays on Some Unsettled Questions of Political Economy, 1844
Principles of Political Economy, with Some of Their Applications to Social Philosophy, 2 vols., 1848; edited by W. J. Ashley, 1909, and Jonathan Riley, 1994
Thoughts on Parliamentary Reform, 1859; revised, enlarged edition, 1859
On Liberty, 1859; edited by R. R. McCallum, 1946, Gertrude Himmelfarb, 1982, Stefan Collini, with *The Subjection of Women* and *Chapters on Socialism*, 1989, and John Gray and G. W. Smith, 1991
Dissertations and Discussions, Political, Philosophical, and Historical, 4 vols., 1859–75
Considerations on Representative Government, 1861; in *Three Essays*, 1912
Utilitarianism, 1863
England and Ireland (pamphlet), 1868
The Subjection of Women, 1869; edited by Stanton Coit, 1906, Mary Warnock, with *A Vindication of the Rights of Woman* by Mary Wollstonecraft, 1986, Susan Moller Okin, 1988, and Stefan Collini, with *On Liberty* and *Chapters on Socialism*, 1989
Chapters and Speeches on the Irish Land Question, 1870
Autobiography, 1873
Nature, The Unity of Religion, and Theism: Three Essays on Religion, 1874
Socialism, 1879; as *Chapters on Socialism*, edited by Stefan Collini, with *On Liberty* and *The Subjection of Women*, 1989, and Jonathan Riley, 1994
Early Essays, edited by J. W. M. Gibbs, 1897
Mill on Bentham and Coleridge, edited by F. R. Leavis, 1950
Prefaces to Liberty: Selected Writings, edited by Bernard Wishy, 1959
Essays on Politics and Culture, edited by Gertrude Himmelfarb, 1963
Essays on Literature and Society, edited by J. B. Schneewind, 1965
Literary Essays, edited by Edward Alexander, 1967
Essays on Sex Equality, with Harriet Taylor Mill, edited by Alice S. Rossi, 1970
Essays on Poetry, edited by F. Parvin Sharpless, 1976
On Politics and Society, edited by Geraint L. Williams, 1976
Utilitarianism and Other Essays, edited by Alan Ryan, 1987
On Liberty and Other Essays, edited by John Gray, 1991

Other writings: works on philosophy, politics, and sociology, and correspondence.

Collected works edition: *Collected Works*, edited by F. E. L. Priestley, F. E. Minecka, John M. Robson, and others, 33 vols., 1963–93.

Bibliographies

Laine, Michael, *Bibliography of Works on John Stuart Mill*, Toronto: University of Toronto Press, 1982
MacMinn, Ney, and others, *Bibliography of the Published Writings of John Stuart Mill*, Evanston, Illinois: Northwestern University, 1945

Further Reading

Briggs, Asa, *Victorian People: A Reassessment of Persons and Themes, 1851–67*, Chicago: University of Chicago Press, revised edition, 1970

Donagan, Alan, "Victorian Philosophical Prose: J. S. Mill and F. H. Bradley," in *The Art of Victorian Prose*, edited by George Levine and William A. Madden, New York: Oxford University Press, 1968
Halévy, Élie, *The Growth of Philosophic Radicalism*, London: Faber, 1928; Boston: Beacon Press, 1955
Himmelfarb, Gertrude, *On Liberty and Liberalism: The Case of John Stuart Mill*, New York: Knopf, 1974
Himmelfarb, Gertrude, *The De-Moralization of Society: From Victorian Virtues to Modern Values*, New York: Knopf, 1995
Levi, William Albert, "The Value of Freedom: Mill's Liberty (1859–1959)," *Ethics* 70 (1959): 37–46

Miłosz, Czesław

Polish/American, 1911–

For a writer who declares poetry to be his first vocation, Czesław Miłosz's essayistic output is remarkable. He is the author of about a dozen volumes of essays published after World War II both in Polish and in translation. Before the war, as a member of the poetic group Żagary (Brushwood), he was involved in heated literary debates carried in Vilnius and Warsaw periodicals. These articles – manifestos rather than essays – reveal the seeds of Miłosz's views on literature which the poet cultivates consistently in his later works: the condemnation of purely aesthetic and narcissistic trends in literature in the name of the metaphysical and ethical dimension of artistic creation; attacks on the formalism of the poetic avant-garde in the name of poetry which expresses the personality of a poet and his philosophy of the world; and criticism of socially committed poetry from a position of Christian personalism. In his juvenilia there are also traces of Miłosz's persisting distaste for any form of nationalism, anti-Semitism, and ideological indoctrination. These concerns gain particular importance in his analysis of certain aspects of the Polish cultural tradition in *Rodzinna Europa* (1959; *Native Realm*), the poet's autobiography, and of communism in *Zniewolony umysł* (1953; *The Captive Mind*).

Miłosz writes essayistic books rather than collections of essays. Most combine biographical memoirs, historical and literary analyses, poetic descriptions, poems and translations, notes and thoughts on literature, philosophy, and culture, as well as arresting portraits of other writers. This formal diversity illustrates Miłosz's lifelong search, in both his poetry and his prose, for more elastic forms than those existing in the literary canon. The search reflects not only his need for formal experimentation but most importantly his religious or metaphysical aspiration – the source of a fundamental tension in his works – to reach beyond the describable toward the essence of things. In his Nobel Prize lecture of 1980, Miłosz calls this aspiration "a quest for reality." It is also a quest for a harmonious solution to "the contradiction between being and action, or, on another level, a contradiction between art and solidarity with one's fellow men." The poet believes in the redemptive power of art and treats it as a "moral discipline" and a moral obligation in the world suffering from a metaphysical crisis and a loss of historical memory.

Miłosz's thoughts develop from personal digressions and fragments, which he anchors in individual and historical details drawn from centuries of cultural heritage. The scope of his intellectual reflection is enormous: from language and its use as a creative medium, through contemplation of the essence of poetry and the obligations of poets, to Hegelianism, Catholicism, and the nature of evil. In *Ziemia Ulro* (1977; *The Land of Ulro*), a book regarded as Miłosz's philosophical testament, he analyzes the hermetic, metaphysical systems of his intellectual mentors: William Blake (from whom Miłosz borrows the title of his book), Oskar V. de L. Miłosz, and Emanuel Swedenborg. He devotes many pages to the works of the Polish poet Adam Mickiewicz, and "the Romantic crisis of European culture" (so termed by **Stanisław Brzozowski**, another intellectual patron who is the subject of the book-length study, *Człowiek wśród skorpionów* [1962; Man among scorpions]). His thoughts on **Fedor Dostoevskii** and **Simone Weil** (expanded in *Emperor of the Earth*, 1977), on Witkacy (i.e. Stanisław Witkiewicz) and **Witold Gombrowicz** are part of a broader discourse on the history of ideas and religion (with a particular interest in Manichaeism, with which the poet admits particular fascination). In *Widzenia nad Zatoką San Francisco* (1969; *Visions from San Francisco Bay*), Miłosz's essays on contemporary American culture, including his polemics with Herbert Marcuse, Henry Miller, Robinson Jeffers, and Allen Ginsberg, are also a springboard for the reflections on his most important topic: the relationship between nature, history, art, and religion.

Miłosz's intellectual fascinations stem from his own preoccupation with the most important dilemmas of Western civilization: the irrevocable failure of secular humanism; the ontological disinheritance of mind described as "the mind torn between the certainty of man's insignificance in the immensity of a hostile universe, and an urge, born of wounded pride, to endow man with preeminence" (*The Land of Ulro*); and the dramatic and incurable split – initiated by "the three sinister figures: Bacon, Locke, Newton, the unholy trinity" – between the laws of science and the inner life of man.

The combination of autobiographical facts and reflections on the readings gives Miłosz's essays a highly personalized tone. He speaks in a multitude of voices: the Eastern European exile and the American professor, the Polish poet and the native of Lithuania, the historian of ideas, the Catholic, the skeptical intellectual, and the catastrophist. The dialogic character of his essays helps to paint a complex spiritual portrait of an author who tries to reconstruct his own intellectual, poetic, and ethical lineage. Fascinated by the essence of Being (he opens *The Land of Ulro* with symptomatic words: "Who was I? Who am I now, years later . . .?"), Miłosz examines his own life in its historical, political, cultural, and social contexts. He objectifies personal spiritual experiences to find the meaning of human existence and of history – his acknowledged obsession. In fact, he often searches for the essence of man in his historicity.

Miłosz, the interpreter of cultures, historical experiences, and ideas, does not write for a wide circle of readers. His essays are dense and intellectually demanding, requiring the reader to make a smooth leap from the description of a casual encounter or detail to the recognition of a general truth which takes contradictions and paradoxes into account. He employs an austere eloquence and a rigorous intellect in his lucid sallies and multilayered reflections. His prose develops through digressions and circumventing descriptions. However, the reader who is willing to meander through his thoughts finds in Miłosz's personal, philosophical, and interpretive essays a unique and profoundly spiritual insight into the "peculiar aspirations of humankind."

TAMARA TROJANOWSKA

Biography

Born 30 June 1911 in Szetejnie, Lithuania. Studied at the University of Stefan Batory, Vilnius, M. Juris., 1934; studied in Paris, 1934–35. Cofounder, *Żagary* literary journal, 1931. Worked for Polish National Radio, 1936–39. Participated in clandestine cultural life during World War II. Worked for the Polish Diplomatic Service, Washington, D.C. and Paris, 1945–50. Defected to the West, 1951; lived in Paris, 1951–60, then moved to the United States. Taught Slavic languages and literatures, University of California, Berkeley, 1960–78, then emeritus. Became a U.S. citizen, 1970. Awards: many, including the European Literary Prize, 1953; Kister Award, 1967; Neustadt International Prize, 1978; Nobel Prize for Literature, 1980; National Medal of Arts, 1989; honorary degrees from five universities. Member, American Academy of Arts and Sciences, and American Institute of Arts and Letters.

Selected Writings

Essays and Related Prose

Zniewolony umysł, 1953; as *The Captive Mind*, translated by Jane Zielonko, 1953
Kontynenty, 1958
Rodzinna Europa, 1959; as *Native Realm: A Search for Self-Definition*, translated by Catherine S. Leach, 1968
Ogród wśród skorpionów, 1962
Widzenia nad Zatoką San Francisco, 1969; as *Visions from San Francisco Bay*, translated by Richard Lourie, 1982
Prywatne obowiązki, 1972
Emperor of the Earth: Modes of Eccentric Vision, 1977
Ziemia Ulro, 1977; as *The Land of Ulro*, translated by Louis Iribarne, 1984
Ogród nauk, 1979
Nobel Lecture, 1981
Świadectwo poezji: Sześć wykładów o dotkliwości naszego wieku, 1983; as *The Witness of Poetry*, 1983
Poszukiwania: Wybór publicystyki rozproszonej 1931–1983 (selected essays), 1985
Zaczynając od moich ulic, 1985; as *Beginning with My Streets: Essays and Recollections*, translated by Madeline G. Levine, 1991
Metafizyczna pauza, 1989
Rok myśliwego, 1990; as *A Year of the Hunter*, translated by Madeline G. Levine, 1994
Szukanie ojczyzny, 1992

Other writings: many volumes of poetry (collected in translation in *The Collected Poems 1931–1987*, 1988) two novels (*Zdobycie władzy* [*The Seizure of Power*], 1955; *Dolina Issy* [*The Issa Valley*], 1955), and studies of writers and literature. Also translated poets from the Polish, and edited anthologies of poetry.

Collected works edition: *Dzieła zbiorowe*, 6 vols., 1980–85 (in progress).

Bibliography

Volynska-Bogert, Rimma, and Wojciech Zalewski, *Czesław Miłosz: An International Bibliography, 1930–1980*, Ann Arbor: University of Michigan Department of Slavic Languages and Literatures, 1983

Further Reading

Brodsky, Joseph, "Presentation of Czesław Miłosz to the Jury," *World Literature Today* 3 (1978)

Bruno, Eva, "Czesław Miłosz: Barn av Europa och andra dikter Tolkning frou amerikanska," *Artes* 3 (1979)

Coleman, Alexander, "The Still Point in Miłosz's *Native Realm*," *World Literature Today* 3 (1978)

Contoski, Victor, "Czesław Miłosz and the Quest for Critical Perspective," *Books Abroad* 1 (1973): 35–41

Czarnecka, Ewa, and Aleksander Fiut, *Conversations with Czesław Miłosz*, San Diego: Harcourt Brace Jovanovich, 1987

Czesław Miłosz: A Stockholm Conference, September 9–11, 1991, edited by Nils Ake Nilsson, Stockholm: Almqvist & Wiksell International, 1992

Danilewicz-Zielińska, Maria, *Szkice o literaturze emigracyjnej*, Paris: Instytut Literacki, 1978: 192–212

Fiut, Aleksander, Czesława Miłosza autoportret przekorny, Cracow: Wydawnictwo Literackie, 1988

Gombrowicz, Witold, *Diary*, vol. 1, Evanston, Illinois: Northwestern University Press, 1988: 56–58

Iribarne, Louis, "The Human Thing: Encomium for Czesław Miłosz," *World Literature Today* 3 (1978): 365–68

Jeleński, Konstanty A., "Miłosz et Gombrowicz," *La Discordance* 1 (1978): 14–16

Poznawanie Miłosza, edited by Jerzy Kwiatkowski, Cracow: Wydawnictwo Literackie, 1985

Scherer, Olga, "The Ulro Through San Francisco Bay," *World Literature Today* 3 (1978): 395–99

Walicki, Andrzej, *Zniewolony umysł po latach*, Warsaw: Czytelnik, 1993

Mitford, Mary Russell

British, 1787–1855

Mary Russell Mitford's contribution to the genre of the essay was the "sketch" of rural life. Through it she created a vision of rural England that had enormous influence through the 19th century and up to the present. These essays were originally published serially in the early 1820s in a magazine for "ladies" and then collected in five volumes under the title *Our Village* (1824–32). Complete editions and selections were reprinted throughout the 19th and 20th centuries, often with deliberately quaint illustrations by well-known illustrators. This form of the essay continues to be almost ubiquitous throughout the English-speaking world, and beyond, as the "country life" column in newspapers and magazines.

The ideological and cultural influence of *Our Village* in its time and since was in creating an image of rural England as predominantly middle-class, virtually free of both the landed gentry and the rural laboring class who in fact formed most of rural society. Mitford also makes her rural England seem socially and culturally essential, central, and authentic in ways that urban England is not. This representation of rural life enabled Mitford to accomplish two important ideological and cultural tasks for her predominantly urban, middle-class readership. First, it contributed significantly to a broad movement to expropriate or redefine in middle-class terms the spaces historically dominated by the middle class' social rivals – the landed gentry and the laboring classes. Second, it enabled generations of readers to ignore responsibility for the actual misery and injustice of both rural and urban life under agrarian and industrial capitalism.

Mitford's form of the essay as rural sketch was a response to the cultural, social, and political conflicts of her time. There were movements among many local gentry and middle-class professionals in various parts of Britain and its colonies to celebrate domestic and local life. These movements were designed partly to resist the cultural, social, economic, and political hegemony of the metropolis. They were also designed to give cultural expression and validation to economic revolutions and accompanying cultural renaissances in the Midlands, East Anglia, and the North of Britain, and in Scotland, Ireland, and some overseas colonies. Mitford's essay-sketches were, however, written against the cultures and associated class interests of both the metropolis and the regions. Her semi-fictionalized village is clearly situated in the southern "home counties," somewhere between the metropolis of London and its provincial or regional rivals. If the metropolis is identified with courtly aristocratic culture and vulgar middle-class commercialism and the provinces with pushing and pretentious middle-class enterprise, then "our village" is left to occupy a gentrified middle-class space.

It is also a feminine, or feminized space. "Our village" is a place of domestic and local action, relationships, and knowledges, which were conventionally gendered "feminine." It is a politicized place, too. Celebration of the domestic and local, in literature and such newly popular amateur middle-class arts as watercolor and the graphic sketch, was designed to contrast with the public and political sphere. The latter was still represented as occupied by a decadent and incompetent ruling upper class and dangerously rebellious lower classes, as a scene of social, cultural, and political conflict inimical to "authentic" subjectivity and the "domestic affections." In the aftermath of the French Revolution and similar upheavals elsewhere in Europe and its colonies, from Ireland to the West Indies, the domestic and local were increasingly represented as the nursery of authentic subjectivity and the domestic affections, and a refuge from the apparently unresolvable conflicts of the public sphere.

Mitford represents the feminine yet politicized middle-class world of "our village" through domestic settings, description of local topography, flora and fauna, characters, daily life, and community activities, and narratives of domestic and local relationships. She uses a pictorial form of representation, often invoking the analogy of the graphic sketch and framing her representations as if they were pictures. Like her contemporary essayist, **Charles Lamb**, she uses an insistently personal and even idiosyncratic narrative mode, conversational style, and intimate tone. Such writing would have been read at the time as feminine, despite the fact that the voice in Mitford's essays seems to be that of a man. Equally important is what is marginalized in her essays. The metropolis remains, somewhat menacingly, over the horizon. Rural economic and political protest, such as the Luddite violence of the 1810s, is virtually excluded. The historic hierarchical class relations and increasing class alienation of the revolutionary aftermath are minimized, treated with light humor, or shown to be overcome by love, domestic affection, and community feeling. In short, "our village" is a fantasy, but Mitford authenticates it by treating it with techniques that would then have been considered realistic.

Mitford discloses two important sources for her invention of this rural England in the essay-sketch. The first of these is the Rev. Gilbert White's *The Natural History and Antiquities of Selborne* (1788), an anecdotal and personal description of the countryside and flora and fauna of his rural parish in Hampshire. Like Mitford's fictionalized village, White's Selborne is a space for the exercise of a particular kind of middle-class culture, though a masculine one – the local scientific, archaeological, and antiquarian researches of a man in one of the elite "learned professions." White's Selborne, like Mitford's village, is also virtually free of both the landed gentry and the rural poor. The other source named in *Our Village* is Jane Austen, represented by Mitford as a realistic portrayer of village life similar to herself. The publication history and influence of White's book and Austen's novels were similar to Mitford's essay-sketches. Together, *Our Village*, *The Natural History and Antiquities of Selborne*, and Austen's novels comprise the canonical texts of an embourgeoisement of rural England with considerable and continuing cultural and political influence, for better and for worse.

GARY KELLY

Biography

Born 16 December 1787 in Alresford, Hampshire. Family moved to Lyme Regis for a year, mid-1890s, then London; lived in Reading, Berkshire, 1797–1820. Won £20,000 in the lottery when she was ten. Studied at the Abbey School, London, 1798–1802. Lived in Three Mile Cross, Hampshire, 1820–51, and Swallowfield, Berkshire, 1851–55. Contributor to journals, from 1821. Friends with Elizabeth Barrett Browning. Granted Civil List pension, 1837. Died in Swallowfield, 9 (some sources say 10) January 1855.

Selected Writings

Essays and Related Prose

Our Village: Sketches of Rural Character and Scenery, 5 vols., 1824–32; edited by John Squire, 1936, and Anne Scott-Thomas, 1987
Belford Regis; or, Sketches of a Country Town, 3 vols., 1835
Recollections of a Literary Life; or, Books, Places, and People, 3 vols., 1852; as *Recollections and Selections from My Favourite Poets and Prose Writers*, 1883

Other writings: poetry, plays, fiction, and many letters, including to Elizabeth Barrett Browning.

Bibliography

Hart, R. J., *Mary Russell Mitford, 16 December 1787–9 January 1855: A Bibliography* (dissertation), Chicago: American Library Association, 1981

Further Reading

Astin, Marjorie, *Mary Russell Mitford: Her Circle and Her Books*, London: Douglas, 1930
Coles, W. A., "Magazine and Other Contributions by Mary Russell Mitford and T. N. Talfourd," in *Studies in Bibliography: Papers of the Bibliographical Society of the University of Virginia*, Charlottesville: University of Virginia Bibliographical Society, 1959: 218–26
Croker, Thomas Crofton, *My Village, Versus "Our Village"*, London: Fisher Fisher and Jackson, 1833
Horn, Pamela, "Alresford and Mary Russell Mitford," *Hatcher Review* 3, no. 22 (Autumn 1986): 86–94
Owen, J. C., "Utopia in Little: Mary Russell Mitford and Our Village," *Studies in Short Fiction* 5 (Spring 1968): 245–56

Pigrome, Stella, "Mary Russell Mitford," *Charles Lamb Bulletin* 66 (April 1989): 53–62
Roberts, W. J., *Mary Russell Mitford: The Tragedy of a Blue Stocking*, London: Melrose, 1913
Watson, Vera, *Mary Russell Mitford*, London: Evan, 1949

Momaday, N. Scott

American, 1934–

N. Scott Momaday is often recognized as the author of the Pulitzer Prize-winning novel, *House Made of Dawn* (1968). But since that initial novel, Momaday has gained increasing notoriety as one of America's most important essayists – a reputation that was established by the publication of *The Way to Rainy Mountain* (1969) and *The Names: A Memoir* (1976), the latter often being referred to as a Native American version of Alex Haley's *Roots*. Besides these autobiographical collections, Momaday has written numerous scholarly and journalistic pieces, and, during 1972 and 1973, produced 86 short essays on a variety of topics for *Viva, Northern New Mexico's Sunday Magazine*. It is, however, Momaday's exploration of his Kiowa Indian heritage and identity that have gained him the most critical and popular attention as an essayist.

The issues of subjectivity and identity explored in Momaday's work place him squarely in the postmodern essay tradition, but, as several scholars have observed, Momaday's racial heritage gives these personal and literary issues a cultural urgency. Although Momaday spent much of his childhood in American Indian communities – Kiowa, Navajo, and Jemez – the traditional religion and language of these cultures had mostly vanished due to a century-long campaign of violence, oppression, and assimilation waged by the U.S. government. Momaday thus had limited access to tribal traditions, even though his father was full-blooded Kiowa. Along with his mother, who was of Anglo-American descent, Momaday's father raised him in an educated, middle-class home environment protected from the often intense poverty and despair of reservation life. Still, his parents modeled a deep connection to American Indian culture, and taught Momaday the importance of maintaining his Kiowa identity in the face of its extinction. Much of Momaday's essay writing thus illustrates the difficult yet important process of resurrecting elements of a tribal heritage within a modern, individualistic sense of identity.

Momaday's treatment of nature and landscape in his essays also represents a unique blending of cultural perspectives. Like his Kiowa ancestors, Momaday sees his physical and spiritual existence as being deeply influenced by the "remembered earth," particularly the desert Southwest where he grew up and the Great Plains where the Kiowa tribe once flourished. Momaday's "native vision" of the natural world – his belief that it is made up not only of "objects and forms, but also of essences and ideals" ("A Vision Beyond Time and Place," 1971) – reveals the influence of the American transcendental tradition of nature writing. However, his physical journey through his home landscapes and his close observation of natural detail become particularly crucial given that so much of Kiowa material culture has vanished. Ultimately, in his essays, the landscape represents the most significant physical remnant of Kiowa culture to which he can attach his personal identity.

The issue of identity, for Momaday, is also an issue of language, and he has used his essay writing to create and sustain a persona that reflects both his Kiowa and Anglo-American heritage. His literary voice, while crafted in written English, often contains the oral, storytelling characteristics of the Kiowa tradition. In *The Way to Rainy Mountain*, for instance, Momaday divides each short essay into three distinct voices – each isolated into a separate paragraph and font – to articulate historical, mythical, and personal narratives. In this way Momaday emphasizes at once his personal connection to, and distance from, Kiowa legend and history. The essays in *The Names*, however, represent a more seamless weaving together of tribal history, ancestral legends, and personal recollections into a unified vision of self. He accomplishes this at the sentence level, slipping in and out of different tenses, using cyclical, dream-like imagery, and moving quickly from a Kiowa storytelling voice ("It happened so:") to an Anglo-American sense of personal history ("I was thirteen years old"). Examples like these from "My Horse and I" are found throughout this essayistic memoir, and together create a reading experience in which Anglo and Indian, past and present, dream and reality, landscape and imagination coalesce.

Momaday's emphasis on a kind of writing that is "very much like speaking aloud to an audience" links him not only to the Kiowa oral tradition, but also to the tradition of the **familiar essay** exemplified by such writers as **Montaigne, Virginia Woolf**, and **E. B. White** – all of whom used conversational language to create the sense of a personal presence in their essays. Momaday can also be seen as an important voice among modern Western American essay writers – including **Wallace Stegner**, Momaday's teacher at Stanford – who have often emphasized the interconnectedness of self, language, and landscape. The influence of poet Yvor Winters, his tutor at Stanford, and novelist William Faulkner, whom he met while attending the University of Virginia, can also be discerned in Momaday's use of lyrical language, disjunctive time-plots, and multiple voices in his nonfiction prose.

Just as important, however, is the influence of his Kiowa grandmother, and other American Indian voices, who first introduced him to the legends of tribal culture and the beauty of the native language. Critic Matthias Schubnell (1985) claims that the central value of Momaday's writing resides in this ability to "bridge the gap between cultures and join literary and artistic traditions." If so, much of the value of his essays can be traced to the complexity of the personal journey which has so often informed them – a pilgrimage which, as Momaday himself has said, contains "many journeys in the one."

JOHN T. PRICE

Biography

Navarre Scott Momaday. Born 27 February 1934 in Lawton, Oklahoma. Studied at the Augusta Military Academy; University of New Mexico, Albuquerque, A.B., 1958; Stanford University, California (creative writing fellow, 1959), A.M., 1960, Ph.D., 1963. Married Gaye Mangold, 1959 (later divorced): three daughters. Taught English and comparative literature at the University of California, Santa Barbara, 1963–69, University of California, Berkeley, 1969–73, Stanford University, 1973–82 and from 1985, and University of Arizona, Tucson, 1982–85; visiting writer or teacher at various universities and institutions, 1970–85. Member of the Board of Trustees, Museum of the American Indian, New York, from 1978. Married Regina Heitzer, 1978 (later divorced): one daughter. Awards: many, including the Pulitzer Prize, for *House Made of Dawn*, 1969; American Academy Award, 1970; Mondello Prize (Italy), 1979; Western Literature Association Award, 1983; honorary degrees from nine universities.

Selected Writings

Essays and Related Prose
The Journey to Tai-Me, 1967; enlarged edition, as *The Way to Rainy Mountain*, 1969
The Names: A Memoir, 1976

Other writings: two novels (*House Made of Dawn*, 1968; *The Ancient Child*, 1989) and poetry.

Further Reading

Ballassi, William, John F. Crawford, and Annie O. Eysturoy, editors, *This Is About Vision: Interviews with Southwestern Writers*, Albuquerque: University of New Mexico Press, 1990
Blaeser, Kimberly, "*The Way to Rainy Mountain*: Momaday's Work in Motion," in *Narrative Chance: Postmodern Discourse on Native American Indian Literatures*, edited by Gerald Vizenor, Albuquerque: University of New Mexico Press, 1989: 39–54
Bloodworth, William, "Neihardt, Momaday, and the Art of Indian Autobiography," in *Where the West Begins: Essays on Middle Border and Siouxland Writing*, edited by Arthur R. Huseboe and William Geyer, Sioux Falls, South Dakota: Center for Western Studies Press, 1978: 152–60
Brumble, H. David, "*The Way to Rainy Mountain* and the Traditional Forms of American Indian Autobiography," in *Approaches to Teaching Momaday's The Way to Rainy Mountain*, edited by Kenneth M. Roemer, New York: Modern Language Association of America, 1988: 41–46
Lincoln, Kenneth, "Word Senders: Black Elk and N. Scott Momaday," in his *Native American Renaissance*, Berkeley: University of California Press, 1983: 82–121
Lincoln, Kenneth, "Tai-Me to Rainy Mountain: The Makings of American Indian Literature," *American Indian Quarterly* 10, no. 2 (Spring 1986): 101–17
Martin, Calvin, editor, *The American Indian and the Problem of History*, New York: Oxford University Press, 1987
Popovich, J. Frank, "Landscape, Tradition, and Identity in *The Way to Rainy Mountain*," *Perspectives on Contemporary Literature* 12 (1986): 13–19
Prampolini, Gaetano, "'Many Journeys in the One': *The Way to Rainy Mountain* and N. Scott Momaday's Literary Work," in *Native American Literatures*, edited by Laura Coltelli, Pisa, Italy: SEU, 1994: 3–30
Schubnell, Matthias, *N. Scott Momaday: The Cultural and Literary Background*, Norman: University of Oklahoma Press, 1985
Strelke, Barbara, "N. Scott Momaday: Racial Memory and Individual Imagination," in *Literature of the American Indians*, edited by Abraham Chapman, New York: New American Library, and London: New English Library, 1975: 348–57
Thompson, Craig B., *Speaking of Identities: The Presentation of American Indian Experience* (dissertation), San Diego: University of California, 1993
Trimble, Martha Scott, *N. Scott Momaday*, Boise, Idaho: Boise State College, 1973
Woodard, Charles L., *Ancestral Voice: Conversations with N. Scott Momaday*, Lincoln: University of Nebraska Press, 1989

Monsiváis, Carlos

Mexican, 1938–

Carlos Monsiváis' contribution to Mexican cultural and intellectual life is truly outstanding. His numerous publications have appeared in newspapers as well as academic journals since the late 1960s. He is highly regarded as a polemicist, advocate, and thinker who has had a powerful influence on the present generation of Mexican artists. He has involved himself in almost every aspect of Mexican intellectual and artistic production: as a narrator, translator, radio director, and commentator, as well as a literary, film, and art critic.

However, it is his essays that are considered to be his most original and perceptive contribution to the critical study and analysis of Mexican society. His early book *Días de guardar* (1970; Days to keep) traces the beginning of the fateful events of the student rebellion on 2 October 1968, which would culminate in the tragic massacre of Tlatelolco. With irony and biting humor, Monsiváis places the calendar of Mexican national celebrations under a radically different and critical light.

In the essay *Nuevo catecismo para indios remisos* (1982; New catechism of remiss Indians), Monsiváis scrutinizes Catholic ethics and faith, especially devotion to the saints, and uncovers the ambivalence, contradictions, and hypocrisy of Mexico's Catholic Church, with its predominantly orthodox mentality. Through contrast, irony, and juxtaposition of catechistic texts and fragments of the saints' lives, Monsiváis reveals the self-negating practices of a church almost solely interested in fulfilling its temporal interests even at the expense of its most fundamental principles.

Amor perdido (1977; Lost love) is Monsiváis' most important and influential work. In this essay on Mexican history he displays valuable critical and analytical abilities, developing a language full of rich metaphor, penetrating humor, and sharp imagery. Armed with an impressive capacity to reveal a variety of ideological perspectives and events, he approaches the main sociohistorical material with a kaleidoscope of viewpoints drawn from documents and well-informed witnesses. In the process, he constantly challenges the "official version" of events and rewrites important segments of Mexican history and cultural life, with profound implications for its future.

Parading through the pages of *Amor perdido* are a number of "consecrated" historical characters and events of Mexican history, society, and culture. These characters include those belonging to the middle and upper-middle classes and those who have risen from the poorer strata of Mexican society. They have left their mark, negative and positive, on Mexican life, especially those who were present in the pages of "popular" contemporary chronicles. However, the individuals and events themselves take second place in the essay to the dynamics of their multiple interrelationships within the context of their times and values. Monsiváis' approach sends the reader in search of meaning as it is generated through the different layers of text, providing the possibility of alternative readings of the characters and events portrayed.

In *Amor perdido* multiple components of an important event are spatially and temporally collapsed into the present moment and the act of reading; in doing so the interpretation resists being anchored solely on a master narrative of events and characters and goes beyond to embrace new and revealing contexts. In reconstructing events Monsiváis uses cinematic techniques, including fragmentation, flashbacks, interior monologues, and image superimposition; as he explains, the text is aimed at "the operational center of memory . . . [the one that keeps] melted, dislocated, mixed images . . ."

The spatio-temporal collapse of historical events and figures enforces a multilateral or "vertical" reading rather than the unilateral or "horizontal" approach that uses chronology as a pointer. Thus, the historical event, the historical protagonist, president, union leader, cultural leader, and the "popular" movie idol are scrutinized from a variety of different and converging perspectives, and through the use of personal diaries, **letters**, declarations, manifestos, and interviews granted to the media. Other versions of characters come from witnesses (favorable and antagonistic), friends, relatives, coworkers, and lovers, and through evaluations made by critics or commentators. All of this information is enveloped in an agile language which presents a dynamic version of individuals and events so that myth, history, legend, criticism, and even rumor are allowed to play a role in a number of possible interpretations.

Monsiváis' process establishes a new textual order by radically reassembling events, characters, and contexts and retrieving them from the "official" version. By isolating character and event from context, the official version was able to glorify or condemn those individuals or events from a prejudiced point of view. Monsiváis' method allows the possibility of different interpretations by a reader who now has at his or her disposal a more complex and complete version of the historical and institutional circumstances.

Amor perdido ultimately sends the literary essay back to its most effective origins as a potent, amusing, fascinating, and forceful "chronicle," powerfully written yet accessible to all. In this light, the essay is designed to inform, criticize, and reveal while simultaneously producing an enjoyable reading experience through the effective integration of narrative and film techniques. Essays such as *Amor perdido* are catalysts that have awakened popular interest in the important subjects and events raised within their pages.

Because of its breadth and innovative techniques, *Amor perdido* is to the essay what Gabriel García Márquez's *Cien años de soledad* (1967; *One Hundred Years of Solitude*) has been to the narrative in terms of its exploration of the possibilities of communication, enjoyment of reading, and multiplicity of interpretation.

ANTONIO URRELLO

Biography

Born 4 May 1938 in Mexico City. Studied at the National Autonomous University of Mexico, Mexico City, 1955–60; Centro Mexicano de Escritores, 1962–63 and 1967–68; Center for International Studies, Harvard University, Cambridge, Massachusetts, 1965. Editor, *Medio Siglo* (Mid-century), 1956–58, and *Estaciones* (Stations), 1957–59; contributor to various Mexican newspapers and journals, including *Sucesos*, *Futuro*, *Política*, *Proceso*, *Novedades*, *El Día*, *Excelsior*, *Uno Más Uno* (One plus one), *La Jornada* (The journey), *Siempre* (Always), and *Plural*. Director of the program *Voz Viva de México* (Living voice of Mexico), Radio Universidad, 1961–62. Taught at the University of

Essex, Colchester, 1970–71, and the National Autonomous University of Mexico, from 1972. Awards: National Prize for Journalism, 1978, 1993; Jorge Cuesta Prize; Mazatlán Prize, 1989; Club de Periodistas Prize for Journalism, 1994; Villaurrutia Prize, 1995; honorary degrees from three universities.

Selected Writings

Essays and Related Prose
Principados y potestades, 1968
Días de guardar, 1970
Amor perdido, 1977
Nuevo catecismo para indios remisos, 1982
Celia Montalván (te brindas voluptuosa e impudente), 1983
De qué se rié el licenciado, 1984
María Izquierdo, 1986
Entrada libre: Crónicas de la sociedad que se organiza, 1987
Escenas de pudor y liviandad, 1988
El género epistolar: Un homenaje a manera de carta abierta, 1991
Rostros del cine mexicano, 1993
Por mi madre bohemios, 1993
Los mil y un velorios, 1993
A través del espejo: El cine mexicano y su público, 1994
Los rituales del caos, 1995

Other writings: works on Mexican art and culture, and an autobiography (1966). Also edited anthologies of Mexican prose and poetry, including *La poesía mexicana del siglo XX* (1966) and *A ustedes les consta: Antología de la crónica en México* (1979).

Further Reading
Cossío, María Eugenia, "El diálogo sin fin de Monsiváis," *Hispanic Journal* 5, no. 2 (Spring 1984): 137–43
Duncan, J. Ann, *Voices, Visions, and a New Reality: Mexican Fiction Since 1970*, Pittsburgh: University of Pittsburgh Press, 1986: 31–33, 200, 220
Ocampo de Gomez, Aurora Maura, and Ernesto Prado Velázquez, *Diccionario de escritores mexicanos*, Mexico City: National Autonomous University of Mexico, 1967: 235–36
Sefchovich, Sara, *México: País de ideas, país de novelas*, Mexico City: Grijalbo, 1987: 43–45, 245–47, 251–53
Urrello, Antonio, "*Amor perdido*: Inversión de la dicotomía y montaje de sus mecanismos," in his *Verosimilitud y estrategia textual en el ensayo hispanoamericano*, Mexico City: Premiá, 1986: 112–33

Montaigne, Michel de

French, 1533–1592

In 1571 at the age of 38 Michel de Montaigne, an aristocrat of the minor landed nobility, withdrew from public life to his château in southwestern France in order to devote his remaining years, in the company of the "Muses," to a life of calm, freedom, and leisure, as well as respite from the civil wars of religion. Shortly thereafter he began writing what he called, by a somewhat strange name that was destined to have an immensely influential future, his *Essais*. Except for interruptions in order to travel and to serve as mayor of Bordeaux and as political negotiator, this project occupied him until his death 20 years later. The *Essais* consist of three books, published in 1580 (I and II), 1588 (III plus numerous additions to I and II), and posthumously in 1595. His literary

apprenticeship had been slight: his only previous publication of any importance had been a translation into French of the Latin *Book of Creatures or Natural Theology* by the Spanish theologian Raymond Sebond, which would serve as the basis for his longest and least characteristic (though philosophically very important) essay, "Apologie de Raimond Sebond" ("Apology for Raymond Sebond"). Since his aim in writing the *Essais* was a highly personal one ("domestic and private" is how he describes the work in his foreword "Au lecteur" ["To the Reader"]), this was a type of writing – in fact it was one of the few types of writing – considered suitable for a "gentleman" (i.e. nobleman) of his day. Far from viewing himself as a literary artist, he wrote that he was "less a maker of books than of anything else" ("De la ressemblance des enfants aux pères" ["Of the Resemblance of Children to Fathers"]); his purpose was greater self-knowledge and knowledge of human nature in order to live more wisely.

His desire to write was also fired by the memory of his friendship with the late poet and political writer, Étienne de La Boétie. No longer able to converse or to correspond with his dearest friend, he felt the need to address his thoughts to others, to potential readers who might serve as surrogates for La Boétie. Thus the essay as he initially conceived it had something in it of both the **letter** to an ideal friend and the **dialogue** with an ideal friend, echoing two forms of discursive writing inherited from classical antiquity, two "forerunners" of the essay. This aspect goes a long way toward explaining the unique liveliness, the "irrepressible vivacity" (**Virginia Woolf**, 1925) of the *Essais*. But La Boétie left an even greater mark on the work: Book I not only contains the justly famous tribute to the deceased friend, "De l'amitié" ("Of Friendship"), but also is structured as a "literary tomb" for him, the individual essays being compared to "fantastic paintings" (*grotesques*) surrounding and adorning what he considered the true masterpiece, La Boétie's sonnets, located at the exact center of Book I.

But why the title *Essais*, and what models, if any, did Montaigne draw upon? It is clear that he did not begin with the kind of long, **personal essay** characteristic of the later books, especially Book III. The great pioneer Montaigne scholar, Pierre Villey, in tracing Montaigne's progress from the beginning "toward the personal essay," revealed that he not so much began with the essay as grew into it. "Villey has shown that the form of the Essays stems from the collections of exempla, quotations, and aphorisms which were a very popular genre [that] helped to spread humanistic material" (Erich Auerbach, 1946). The evolution of his essays "epitomizes the general evolution of the form from the commonplace book [as these collections were known in England] to independent reflections" (Douglas Bush, *English Literature in the Earlier Seventeenth Century, 1600–1660*, 1945). Montaigne's earliest essays are generally very short and thick enough with quotations from classical and other writers (without any indication of sources) for him to remark of them, in his inimitable earthy style, that they "smell a bit foreign" ("Sur des vers de Virgile" ["On Some Verses of Virgil"]). But he also asserted that despite these "borrowed incrustations" he "does not speak the mind of others except to speak [his] own mind better" ("De l'institution des enfants" ["Of the Education of Children"]). Patrick Henry (1987) has pointed out that readers today stand in relation to Montaigne as he stood in relation to his sources, challenged by him, as he was by them, to develop our own thought in reading him.

It is important to note also – and this has great bearing on the future of the essay – that Montaigne carries such learning with a grace, charm, and human appeal seldom found in works of specialized knowledge, and was very conscious of doing so. "Authors communicate with the people by some special extrinsic work [i.e. authoritative credentials]; I am the first to do so by my entire being, as Michel de Montaigne, not as a grammarian or a poet or a jurist" ("Du repentir" ["Of Repentance"]). He thus initiated, for the immediate future, "a worldly literature breaking with specialized learning, the literature of *l'honnête homme* [the cultivated gentleman]" (Hugo Friedrich, 1949), and for the long run, the destiny of the essay as a vehicle of humanistic learning.

No real models existed for Montaigne's essays. There was for him no "anxiety of influence," as Harold Bloom would call it. He was very conscious of being a pioneer: "It is the only book of its kind, a book with a wild and eccentric plan" ("De l'affection des pères aux enfants" ["Of the Affection of Fathers for Their Children"]). Montaigne himself includes among works encouraging him in the development of the essay: Horace's verse *Epistles*, with their free-wheeling form; **Plutarch**'s *Moral Essays*, works "in which he forgets his theme, in which his subject is found only incidentally, quite smothered in foreign matter" ("De la vanité" ["Of Vanity"] – the reference is to "The Demon of Socrates"); **Seneca**'s *Epistles*, which were for Montaigne like Plutarch's essays, "detached pieces that do not demand the obligation of long labor, of which I am incapable . . . For they have no continuity from one to the other" ("Des livres" ["Of Books"]); and **Plato**'s *Dialogues*, especially the *Phaedrus*, a "fantastic motley," in which Plato lets himself be "tossed in the wind, or *seem to be*" ("Of Vanity" – italics added). An important "anti-model" or "anti-essay," so to speak, was **Cicero**, with his boring "prefaces, definitions, partitions . . . logical and Aristotelian arrangements . . . [and] long-winded preparations" ("Of Books").

Andreas Blinkenberg (in *Mélanges de linguistique et de littérature romanes offerts à Mario Roques*, 1950) claims that Montaigne may have chosen his unfamiliar title, *Essais*, *because* of its lack of precision. From the Low Latin *essagium* (cf. Italian *saggio* and Spanish *ensayo*), *essai* or *coup d'essai* originally meant the apprentice artisan's work as distinct from the master's. By extension it came to mean any "testing," "trying out," "trial," or "probing." For Montaigne what is involved is his own "self-testing," the testing of his judgment, his mind, indeed of his whole being as it is pitted against various problems: "As for the natural faculties that are in me, of which this book is the essay . . ." ("Of the Education of Children"); or again, he calls his writing "the record of the essays of my life" ("De l'expérience" ["Of Experience"]). He appears not to have used the term in its later sense of a *literary* form or genre, in fact calling the divisions of his book not *essais* but *chapitres* (chapters) or *contes* (stories). His concept of the essay as a testing of one's powers guaranteed that the subject matter of the essay would be without limitation, infinitely open-ended, the generator of "infinis essais" ("number-less essays" – "Considération sur Ciceron" ["A Consideration upon Cicero"]). The suitability of any subject to self-testing is also supported by his philosophical belief that all subjects are mysteriously related to one another: "Any topic is fertile for me. A fly will serve my purpose . . . for all subjects are linked with one another" ("On Some Verses of Virgil").

We have touched on Montaigne's relatively novel "dialogic" or "dialectical" relationship with his reader (explored further by Patrick Henry). An even more radical departure from literary tradition is his relationship with his own book. "I am myself the matter of my book" ("To the Reader"); "I study myself more than any other subject. That is my metaphysics and my physics" ("Of Experience"). He goes even further in stating that he and his book are one, using a theological term from the Nicene Creed: his book is "consubstantial with its author" ("Du démentir" ["Of Giving the Lie"]). He both shapes his book, by virtue of his art, and is shaped by it in his life and nature. But we must be careful not to oversimplify the complex meaning of the "self" for Montaigne. Far from portraying himself "entire and wholly naked," his "respect for the public" ("To the Reader"), especially on the part of the gentleman that he was, placed limits on his candor. **Jean-Jacques Rousseau** wrote his *Confessions* (1782–89) in part to show the way beyond what he considered the disappointing reticences of the *Essais*. Montaigne's example taught future essayists that the essay is not expected to be self-revelatory in the same manner as the intimate **journal** or the confession. In addition to his silences he often adopts "protective masks" to hide his most daring thoughts and indulges in "artful proceedings" and "subterfuges" concerning his innermost self (Jacob Zeitlin, Introduction to *The Essays of Michel de Montaigne*, 1934). As well, he acknowledges the inevitable amount of "adornment" that occurs in any self-portrait: "Painting myself for others, I have painted my inward self with colors clearer than my original ones" ("Of Giving the Lie").

Furthermore, the self that one finds in his essays is never solipsistic or narcissistic but has been broadened to include many other "voices." Dialogue occurs not only with his reader and with the authors he quotes but also with himself, in what Donald Frame (1969) calls "the constant inner dialogue of the self-portrayer." How can this be otherwise, since Montaigne has said, "I presented myself to myself for argument and subject" ("Of the Affection of Fathers for Their Children")? The most famous of his assertions that his "self" was not to be narrowly construed is his oft-quoted statement, "Each man bears the entire form of man's estate" ("Of Repentance"). In other words, his habit of self-observation qualified him for observing others and seeking knowledge of "man in general" ("On Books"), but to attain such knowledge is another matter. Underlying the *Essais* is his perception of reality as constant flux, perpetual motion: "I do not portray being, I portray passing" ("Of Repentance"). "The essay according to Montaigne," writes Jean Starobinski (1982), is "the pursuit [of a self] that is by definition unattainable." His use of the prepositions *de* (of) and *sur* (on) in so many of his titles arises less from respect for classical usage (Cicero, Seneca, *et al.*) or from modesty than from his conviction that *no* subject can be grasped in its totality: "For I do not see the whole of anything; *nor do those who promise to show it to me*" ("Of Experience" – italics added).

The critic's attempt to describe the method and art of the *Essais* is helped immensely by the fact that this very subject lies at the heart of the book: "I write of myself and of my writings as of my other actions, because my theme turns in upon itself" ("Of Experience"). "The *Essais* are their own developed commentary" (Friedrich) – and, one should add, "their own best commentary." The typical essayist's habit of reflecting on his or her own art thus begins with Montaigne himself. Almost all his characteristic features of form and style flow logically from his desire to capture in writing that "marvellously vain, diverse, and undulating object that is the human being" ("Par divers moyens on arrive à pareille fin" ["By Diverse Means We Arrive at the Same End"]). A disorderly process at best, we might believe; but beneath the apparent disorder of the surface lies a new kind of order, a new kind of rhetoric which critics have come more and more to discover (Richard Sayce, Michel Baraz, Floyd Gray). "The very notion of order acquires a different sense in each truly original creation" (Baraz, 1961). For every passage of the essays calling attention to their formlessness there is a corresponding one inviting us to discover their hidden form. Citing Plato and Plutarch as precursors, Montaigne writes: "My ideas follow one another, but sometimes it is from a distance, and look at each other, but with a side-long glance" ("Of Experience"). And again: "It is the inattentive reader who loses my subject, not I" ("Of Experience"). Starobinski shows that "the form 'essayed' by Montaigne approximates as fully as possible the absence of form [*l'informe*]."

Emerson's (1850) description of Montaigne's style has become famous: he found it "wild and savoury as sweet fern" and added, "Cut these words and they would bleed; they are vascular and alive; they walk and run." Montaigne's finest translator, Donald Frame, has summed up the essential features of his style (in his translation of *The Complete Essays*, 1958): the "vivid bold images; the epigrammatic word play; the meandering, associative order, disdainful of logical connectives; the obscenity, which is a studied protest against man's rejection of the body." Montaigne's style is both "familiar" and "poetic." "The speech I love is a simple natural [*naïf*] speech, the same on paper as in the mouth . . . remote from affectation, irregular, disconnected and bold; each bit [*chaque lopin*] making a body in itself" ("Of the Education of Children"). **Albert Thibaudet** (1963) coined the term "lopinisme" to describe this style, arguing that it corresponded to a view of reality as fragmented and discontinuous. Humor is also an essential ingredient of this style, as it will be of the subsequent essay, especially of the English essay. This "humorous and familiar style" ("A Consideration upon Cicero") was actually Montaigne's very original adaptation into French of a literary mode going back to Seneca in Latin and to Plato in Greek, the so-called "Attic prose," which fought traditional rhetoric with a new rhetoric and preferred "the forms that express the energy and labor of minds seeking the truth . . . to the forms that express a contented sense of the enjoyment and possession of it" (Morris Croll, 1966). As important as the familiar, conversational aspect of Montaigne's style is its poetic quality, which will also leave its mark on future essayists, from **Sir Thomas Browne** to Emerson, Virginia Woolf and beyond. Plato's *Dialogues* were his supreme example here; it is clear that he intended his own prose to be moved by a similar "demon" (operating often on a subconscious level): "I love the poetic gait, by leaps and gambols. It is an art, as Plato says, light, flighty, demonic" ("Of Vanity"). Perhaps the most striking of his poetic qualities is his extensive use of imagery, first singled out for praise by the great critic **Sainte-Beuve**, who called his style "a perpetual metaphor, constantly renewed," and attempted, with varying degrees of success, to imitate it in his own essays. More recently, Thibaudet and his disciple Floyd Gray (1958) have conducted perceptive analyses of Montaigne's imagery.

Montaigne is the creator of the essay, of whom his numerous followers might say, as Haydn, speaking for the composers of his day, said of Handel, "He is the master of us all." He also, quite extraordinarily for the inventor of a literary form, remains its greatest exponent, which may explain why he is both imitable and inimitable. His successors learned from him: the inexhaustible potentiality of the self as subject, testing itself against an infinite variety of subjects; the role of chance in the selection of subjects; the use of the essay as "a literary device for saying almost everything about anything" (Aldous Huxley, 1958); the essay as vehicle for the process, rather than the end results, of thought: "For we are born to quest after truth; to possess it belongs to a greater power" ("De l'art de conférer" ["Of the Art of Discussion"]); and the replacement of logical thought by "free association artistically controlled" (Huxley). But there are also distinct limits to Montaigne's influence, including certain unique features of his *Essais*: the role of La Boétie in their genesis; the presence of three "strata" in the definitive text (the original plus additions), which enhance in a unique way the overall impression of artful disorder; the "façade titles" of many essays, designed to trick the censor into missing the hidden, heterodox, or otherwise subversive subject (Patrick Henry); and the special way in which quotations are absorbed into the text. His towering stature as a writer may also have intimidated imitators; does one "imitate" Shakespeare? His profound skepticism about the possibility of "fashioning a consistent and solid fabric" out of a person ("De l'inconstance de nos actions" ["Of the Inconsistency of Our Actions"]) is not shared by all essayists; but, together with his claim to portray not "being" but "passing . . . from day to day, from minute to minute," this view of human nature may have influenced such great modern novelists as Flaubert, Proust, Joyce, and Woolf (Sayce, Starobinski). But all, especially all essayists, would find it hard not to agree with **Nietzsche**'s magnificent tribute: "That such a man has written adds to the pleasure of having lived on earth."

RICHARD M. CHADBOURNE

Biography

Michel Eyquem de Montaigne. Born 28 February 1533 at Château de Montaigne, near Bordeaux. Studied privately (spoke in Latin at home); Collège de Guyenne, Bordeaux, c. 1539–46; philosophy at the University of Bordeaux, from 1546; probably studied law, possibly in Toulouse or Paris. Councillor at the Cour des Aides, Périgueux, 1554, transferred to Bordeaux, 1557, where he became friends with Étienne de La Boétie (died, 1563). Married Françoise de la Chassaigne, 1565: one daughter (four others died in infancy). Inherited the domain of Montaigne upon father's death, 1568; resigned magistracy, 1570. Suffered from kidney stones, from 1578, and traveled to Switzerland, Germany, and Italy, 1580–81, staying at various spas. Mayor of Bordeaux, 1581–85. Friendship with Marie de Gournay, from 1588. Died (from kidney stones) at Château de Montaigne, 13 September 1592.

Essay Collections

Essais, 2 vols., 1580; revised, enlarged edition, 3 vols., 1588; edited by Marie de Gournay (definitive edition), 1595; facsimile of 1580 edition reprinted, 2 vols., 1976; facsimile of 1588 edition reprinted, 3 vols., 1987

Modern editions: (Municipal Edition) edited by Fortunat Strowski and others, 5 vols., 1906–33, Pierre Villey, 3 vols., 1930–31 (revised by V.-L. Saulnier, 2 vols., 1965), Jean Plattard, 6 vols., 1931–33, Maurice Rat, 3 vols., 1941, Pierre Michel, 3 vols., 1966, Alexandre Micha, 3 vols., 1969, and Claude Pinganaud, 1992.

Translations in English: as *Essays*, translated by John Florio, 1603 (reprinted 1965), Charles Cotton, 3 vols., 1685–86 (revised by William Carew Hazlitt, 1842, and Blanshard Bates, 1949), George B. Ives, 4 vols., 1925, E. J. Trechmann, 2 vols., 1927, Jacob Zeitlin, 3 vols., 1934–36, Donald M. Frame, 1958, and M. A. Screech, 1991.

Selections in French: edited by J. Carol Chapman and François J.-L. Mouret, 1978.

Selections in English: edited and translated by Donald M. Frame, 1943, also a bilingual edition edited and translated by Frame, 1963; translated by J. M. Cohen, 1958; edited by Walter Kaiser, translated by John Florio, 1964; edited and translated by M. A. Screech, 1993.

Other writings: diary of a journey to Switzerland, Germany, and Italy.

Collected works editions: *Œuvres complètes*, edited by Armand Armaingaud, 12 vols., 1924–41; *Œuvres complètes* (Pléiade Edition), edited by Albert Thibaudet and Maurice Rat, 1962; *The Complete Works*, translated by Donald M. Frame, 1957.

Bibliographies

Henry, Patrick, "Bibliography of Works Cited," in his *Montaigne in Dialogue*, Saratoga, California: Anma Libri, 1987

Sayce, Richard A., and David Maskell, *A Descriptive Bibliography of Montaigne's Essais, 1580–1700*, London: Bibliographical Society/Modern Humanities Research Association, 1983

Strawn, Richard R., and Samuel F. Will, "Michel Eyquem de Montaigne," in *A Critical Bibliography of French Literature*, vol. 2, edited by Alexander H. Schutz, Syracuse, New York: Syracuse University Press, 1956

Tannenbaum, Samuel A., *Michel de Montaigne (A Concise Bibliography)*, New York: S. A. Tannenbaum, 1942

Further Reading

Auerbach, Erich, "L'Humaine Condition," in his *Mimesis: The Representation of Reality in Western Literature*, Princeton, New Jersey: Princeton University Press, 1953 (original German edition, 1946)

Baraz, Michel, "Sur la structure d'un essai de Montaigne," *Bibliothèque d'Humanisme et de Renaissance* 23 (1961): 265–81

Boase, Alan M., *The Fortunes of Montaigne: A History of the Essays in France, 1580–1669*, London: Methuen, 1935; New York: Octagon, 1970

Bowman, Frank, *Montaigne: Essays*, London: Edward Arnold, 1965

Bulletin de la Société des Amis de Montaigne, 1913–

Burke, Peter, *Montaigne*, Oxford: Oxford University Press, 1981

Croll, Morris, "Attic Prose: Lipsius, Montaigne, Bacon," in his *Style, Rhetoric, and Rhythm: Essays*, edited by J. Max Patrick and others, Princeton, New Jersey: Princeton University Press, 1966

Emerson, Ralph Waldo, "Montaigne; or the Skeptic," in his *Representative Men (Collected Works of Ralph Waldo Emerson*, vol. 4), Cambridge, Massachusetts: Belknap Press of the Harvard University Press, 1987 (original edition, 1850)

Frame, Donald, *Montaigne in France, 1812–1852*, New York: Octagon, 1970 (original edition, 1940)

Frame, Donald M., *Montaigne's Discovery of Man: The Humanization of a Humanist*, New York: Columbia University Press, 1955

Frame, Donald M., *Montaigne: A Biography*, New York: Harcourt Brace and World, 1965

Frame, Donald M., *Montaigne's Essais: A Study*, Englewood Cliffs, New Jersey: Prentice Hall, 1969

Friedrich, Hugo, *Montaigne*, Berkeley: University of California Press, 1991 (original German edition, 1949)

Good, Graham, "Montaigne: The Growth of Experience," in his *The Observing Self: Rediscovering the Essay*, London and New York: Routledge, 1988: 26–42

Gray, Floyd, *Le Style de Montaigne*, Paris: Nizet, 1958

Gray, Floyd, "The Unity of Montaigne in the *Essais*," *Modern Language Quarterly* 22 (1961): 79–86

Henry, Patrick, *Montaigne in Dialogue*, Saratoga, California: Anma Libri, 1987

Huxley, Aldous, Preface to his *Collected Essays*, New York: Harper, 1958; London: Chatto and Windus, 1960

Kellermann, Frederick, "Montaigne, Reader of Plato," *Comparative Literature* 8 (1956): 307–22

Pouilloux, Jean-Yves, *Lire les Essais de Montaigne*, Paris: Maspéro, 1969

Sainte-Beuve, Charles-Augustin, in his *Port-Royal*, vol. 1, Paris: Gallimard, 1952 (original edition, 1840)

Sainte-Beuve, Charles-Augustin, "Montaigne," in his *Causeries du lundi*, vol. 4, Paris: Garnier Frères, 1927 (article originally published 1851)

Sayce, Richard, "L'Ordre des Essais de Montaigne," *Bibliothèque d'Humanisme et de Renaissance* 8 (1946): 129–36

Sayce, Richard A., *The Essays of Montaigne: A Critical Exploration*, London: Weidenfeld and Nicolson, 1972

Schon, Peter M., *Vorformen des Essays in Antike und Humanismus*, vol. 1, Wiesbaden: Mainzer Romantische Arbeiten, 1954

Screech, M. A., *Montaigne and Melancholy: The Wisdom of the Essays*, London: Duckworth, 1983

Starobinski, Jean, "Montaigne on Illusion: The Denunciation of Untruth," *Daedalus* 108 (1979): 85–101

Starobinski, Jean, *Montaigne en mouvement*, Paris: Gallimard, 1982; as *Montaigne in Motion*, Chicago: University of Chicago Press, 1985

Telle, E. V., "À propos du mot 'essai' chez Montaigne," *Bibliothèque d'Humanisme et de Renaissance* 30 (1968): 225–47

Thibaudet, Albert, *Montaigne*, Paris: Gallimard, 1963

Villey, Pierre, *Les Sources et l'évolution des Essais de Montaigne*, Paris: Hachette, 2 vols., revised edition, 1933

Woolf, Virginia, "Montaigne," in her *The Common Reader, First Series*, edited by Andrew McNeillie, London: Hogarth Press, and New York: Harcourt Brace Jovanovich, 1984 (original edition, 1925)

Montale, Eugenio

Italian, 1896–1981

When he received the Nobel Prize for Literature in 1975, Eugenio Montale saw his work as a poet rewarded. In the speech he gave in Stockholm – "È ancora possibile la poesia?" ("Is Poetry Still Possible?") – he made a point of reminding his audience that he was also a librarian, translator, literary and musical critic, and even unemployed after his publicly stated lack of belief in the fascist regime. Montale was first and foremost a free and independent man, even before being the most important Italian poet of the 20th century. The man and his work were both to be honored by the Republic of Italy when Montale was made a senator for life in 1967.

Ossi di sepia (1925; *Cuttlefish Bones*), Montale's first poetry collection, already revealed his metaphysical despair. Against the descriptive background of his native Liguria, between seascapes and arid landscapes, Montale explored both the seriousness and the absurdity of the world. He expressed himself entirely in negativity, denial, passivity, and ultraconservatism, using a new poetic language that came close to prose but deliberately stopped short by playing with sounds derived largely from his musical youth. We immediately see the clean break he made when faced with the rhetoric of D'Annunzio or Carducci on the one hand, and the futurists' experimentations of the period on the other. His contemporaries bracketed him with the negative poetry of **Leopardi**, or the esoteric tendencies of Ungaretti or Quasimodo. But as one collection followed another, the critics were to discover that Montale's poetry went beyond conventions. He, in turn, influenced a number of Italian poets after him.

At the same time as writing poetry, Montale early on embarked on a career as a journalist. In 1920 he began working for *L'Azione* (The action). Two years later he founded the short-lived magazine *Primo Tempo* (First time). In 1925, in the columns of *L'Esame* (The examination), he published "Omaggio a Italo Svevo" (Homage to Italo Svevo), after making a passionate discovery of that author, whom he was to meet the following year. Over more than 40 years, through essays, articles, or lectures, Montale was to wage an unceasing battle as a critic to give the novelist from Trieste a place in Italian literature. These various writings were brought together in *Lettere con gli scritti di Montale su Svevo* (1966; Letters and writings by Montale on Svevo).

In 1929, after a spell with the publisher Bemporad, Montale was appointed director of the scientific and literary body Vieusseux, the famous Florentine cultural institute. He was dismissed from his post nine years later for refusing to join the fascist party. There then began a period of intense work for various magazines such as *Solaria* and *Letteratura* (Literature) that made clear their cultural opposition to the regime in power and advocated openness to international literature at a time when national self-sufficiency was recommended. In these and other magazines, Montale published short critical essays on poetry and prose (reprinted in *Sulla poesia* [1976; On poetry]).

At the end of the war, Montale began contributing to *Il Corriere della Sera* (The evening courier), writing for it for nearly 30 years. It was his column in the daily paper which made the poet known to the public. He was, of course, writing journalism in prose, but even so, the same autobiographical and stylistic background was visible here as in his poetry, though more clearly articulated, and occasionally softening tragedy and metaphysical agonizing with a degree of humor. Most of these pieces, critical or factual, were collected in *La Farfalla di Dinard* (1956, 1960; *The Butterfly of Dinard*) and *Auto da fé* (1966). Subtitled *Cronache in due tempi* (Chronicles in two times), this latter collection of pieces clearly demarcates the two stages of Montale's cultural and militant activity. In the immediate postwar years, he was questioning the relationship between fascism and literature, the moral value of art and its need to be independent, and the loneliness of the artist.

In a later period, he placed art within a technological and industrial society, denouncing the boredom of mass art, artistic utilitarianism, and fashionable, commercialized art. Without undue bitterness, and denouncing sterile nostalgia, Montale grew uneasy about the role of art and the artist in a constantly changing world. Even in an earlier short essay ("Stile e tradizione" [1925; Style and tradition]) reprinted in the collection, Montale, while defining his idea of a poetic art, is already questioning the links between literature and society.

Other articles were collected in *Nel nostro tempo* (1972; *Poet in Our Time*) and *Trentadue variazioni* (1973; 32 variations). *Prime alla Scala* (1981) brings together Montale's writings about music. *Fuori di casa* (1969; Away from home), on the other hand, is a collection of various pieces written between 1946 and 1964, when he was abroad, mostly for *Il Corriere della Sera*. From these journeys in Europe, New York, and the Middle East, Montale brought back slices of life and ideas; the accounts of the real world sometimes provided material for poetry.

Not only in his poetic writings, but in his articles and essays as well, "Montale's poetic heart continued to beat beneath the lucid and ironic mask of ideological and cultural polemic, behind occasional dips into literary criticism" (Marco Forti, 1974).

CHRISTINE MASUY

Biography
Born 12 October 1896 in Genoa. Studied at schools in Genoa to age 14; studied opera singing under Ernesto Sivori. Infantry officer in the Italian army, 1917–19. Met Rusilla Tanzi (La Mosca), 1926, maintained close relationship for many years, and married, 1963 (La Mosca died, 1963). Founder, with others, *Primo Tempo* literary journal, Turin, 1922. Staff member, Bemporad publishers, Florence, 1927–28. Curator of book collection, Vieusseux cultural institute, Florence, 1929–38. Worked or wrote for *La Fiera Letteraria* (The literary fair), 1938–48, *Il Mondo* (The world), 1945–48, *Il Corriere della Sera*, 1948–73, and *Corriere d'Informazione* (The information courier), 1955–67. Life member of the Italian Senate, from 1967. Awards: several, including Marzotto Prize, 1956; Feltrinelli Prize, 1962; Nobel Prize for Literature, 1975; honorary degrees from four universities. Died in Milan, 12 September 1981.

Selected Writings

Essays and Related Prose
La Farfalla di Dinard (autobiographical sketches), 1956; revised edition, 1960; as *The Butterfly of Dinard*, translated by G. Singh, 1970
Auto da fé: Cronache in due tempi, 1966
Lettere con gli scritti di Montale su Svevo (includes letters), 1966
Fuori di casa, 1969
La poesia non esiste (cultural burlesques), 1971
Nel nostro tempo, edited by Riccardo Campa, 1972; as *Poet in Our Time*, translated by Alastair Hamilton, 1972
Trentadue variazioni, 1973
Sulla poesia, edited by Giorgio Zampa, 1976
Selected Essays, edited and translated by G. Singh, 1978
Prime alla Scala, edited by Gianfranca Lavezzi, 1981
The Second Life of Art: Selected Essays, edited by Jonathan Galassi, 1982

Other writings: many collections of poetry.

Bibliography
Barile, Laura, *Bibliografia montaliana*, Milan: Mondadori, 1977

Further Reading
Almansi, Guido, *Eugenio Montale: The Private Language of Poetry*, Edinburgh: Edinburgh University Press, 1977
Avalle d'Arco, Silvio, *Tre saggi su Montale*, Turin: Einaudi, 1970
Barbuto, Antonio, *Eugenio Montale*, Rome: Edizioni dell'Ateneo, 1972
Becker, Jared, *Eugenio Montale*, Boston: Twayne, 1986
Cambon, Glauco, *Eugenio Montale*, New York: Columbia University Press, 1972
Cataldi, Pietro, *Montale*, Palermo: Palumbo, 1991
Contini, Gianfranco, *Una lunga fedeltà: Scritti su Eugenio Montale*, Turin: Einaudi, 1974
Forti, Marco, *Montale*, Milan: Mondadori, 1974
Luperini, Romano, *Montale o l'identità negata*, Naples: Liguori, 1984
Manacorda, Giuliano, *Montale*, Florence: La Nuova Italia, 1969
Marasco, Armida, editor, *Per Eugenio Montale: Gli interventi nella stampa quotidiana*, Galatina: Congedo, 1982
Martelli, Mario, *Eugenio Montale: Introduzione e guida allo studio dell'opera montaliana: Storia e antologia della critica*, Florence: Le Monnier, 1982
Nascimbeni, Giulio, *Montale*, Milan: Longanesi, 1969
Ramat, Silvio, *Montale*, Florence: Vallecchi, 1965
Ramat, Silvio, *L'acacia ferita e altri saggi su Montale*, Venice: Marsilio, 1986
Singh, G., *Eugenio Montale: A Critical Study of His Poetry, Prose, and Criticism*, New Haven, Connecticut: Yale University Press, 1973

Montalvo, Juan

Ecuadorian, 1832–1889

Juan Montalvo, like **Domingo Faustino Sarmiento** and **José Martí**, is one of the many 19th-century Latin American figures who made little distinction between literary and political activity. Born in a poor and backward country like Ecuador, Montalvo was obliged to be involved in the clamor of national public life, even though he really wanted to be a writer in the classical Spanish style. He attempted to establish this style in *Capítulos que se le olvidaron a Cervantes* (1895; Chapters that Cervantes forgot), his "imitation of an inimitable book" – a curious and early example of metafiction in a hybrid form of narrative and essay.

Montalvo's spiritual background is fundamentally European; he spoke English, French, and Italian and spent several years in France, Italy, and Spain. He was a melancholy man, weighed down by depression; it is not surprising that in Europe he found comfort and an aesthetic orientation in Romanticism and the friendship of Alphonse de Lamartine and other European writers.

Nevertheless, despite his European connections Montalvo is remembered as the formidable adversary of Gabriel García Moreno, the ultraconservative Ecuadorian despot whose existence shaped Montalvo's; the relationship is reminiscent of that between Sarmiento and the Argentine dictator Juan Manuel de Rosas. It was another of those rivalries that branded with fire the historical and intellectual process of the continent. When Montalvo returned to Ecuador in 1860, García Moreno had just taken power. Montalvo immediately wrote him an open letter that demonstrates his magnificent insolence, his splendid prose, and his great liberal zeal: "If at some time I resign myself to take part in our miserable affairs, you and any other whose political conduct is hostile to the liberties and rights of the people will find in me an enemy, and no ordinary one." In 1866 he began publishing his magazine, *El Cosmopolita* (The cosmopolitan), in which many of his **treatises** and political **pamphlets** appeared. This magazine is the first of four – the others are *El Regenerador* (The regenerator), *El Espectador* (The spectator), and the series *Las Catilinarias* (in reference to Catiline, the powerful man attacked by **Cicero** in a famous work; Montalvo used the name to give his political denunciations a classical echo) – that may properly be considered among his works, as they were in large part the result of his sole personal efforts. They contain numerous essays that demonstrate the mastery of his style and his persistent preoccupations.

The mature phase of Montalvo's career is characterized by political exile, travels in Europe, and prolific intellectual output, which produced major works such as *Siete tratados* (1882–83; Seven treatises) and *Geometría moral* (1902; Moral geometry), as well as the *Capítulos* mentioned above. Although his main theme as an essayist is politics, he also deals with culture, morality, and his personal life and tribulations. He was a vehement propagandist, with Olympian gestures and violent hatreds, distinguished by a sharp and vigorous tongue suffused with the best of Latin oratory and the Spanish classics. He knew how to lash out and he used his voice responsibly, as demonstrated by the ardent *Catilinarias* (which is not really a periodical, but a work published in installments) and the varied *Siete tratados*. The title of the latter book is as deceptive as that of *Geometría moral*. The first is a collection of reflections and **meditations** on various themes rather than a book that sets out a rigorous doctrine; the second, which contains some narrative efforts, is a type of discourse on love illustrated by great ancient and modern figures, from Pericles to **Goethe**.

As a political thinker Montalvo was not very original; rather, he moralized around common themes such as welfare, justice, education, honesty, and respect for the popular will. He was a passionate liberal whose radical anticlericalism was exacerbated by the strict Catholicism of García Moreno. He considered religion and dictatorship as almost indistinguishable, and in this way he contributed to the anticlerical tradition that developed in 19th-century Latin America. He firmly believed in individual heroism as a providential driving force of history, and the saints in his pantheon were Napoleon, Washington, and Bolívar. His way of confronting these themes and linking them with other digressions and confessions is closer to that of the English essayists (particularly **Bacon** and **Carlyle**) than any other Latin American writer apart from **Andrés Bello**. With his diverse interests, he is a model of the antithetic forms characteristic of Latin American Romanticism: subjectivity and social humanitarianism. However, he lacked a modern conception of history: for him it was only a source of famous examples to be imitated. Nor was he sensitive to the popular and local trends that other Spanish American prose writers were contributing to the written language: he was an innate purist.

But Montalvo had the essayist's essential attitude: the ability to react, almost spontaneously, to the constant challenge presented to him by the interweaving of his personal experience and the political world. The urgency of his task never prevented him from being a refined and delicate artist, even when he was hurling insults. He is one of the most elegant prose writers the Americas have produced; his skill with expressive forms, the memorable pithiness of his phrases, the visual sparkle and rhythmic persistence of his images, make him a precursor of the essay as it was to be cultivated by *modernismo*: an art form.

JOSÉ MIGUEL OVIEDO
translated by Richard Shaw

Biography

Born 13 April 1832 in Ambato, Ecuador. Studied in Quito, master's degree in philosophy, 1851. Secretary of the Ecuadorian legation, Paris, from 1857; returned to Ecuador because of illness, 1860. Editor, *El Cosmopolita*, 1866–69. Exiled for writings, 1869, and lived in Ipiales, Colombia, 1869–76. Editor, *El Regenerador*, 1876–78. Traveled again to Europe, 1879, living in Paris for one year before returning to Ipiales. Lived in Paris, 1881–89. Editor, *El Espectador*, 1886–88. Liaison with Augustine-Catherine Contoux: one son. Died (of pleurisy, probably suffering from tuberculosis) in Paris, 17 January 1889.

Selected Writings

Essays and Related Prose

Las Catilinarias series, 1880–82; in 2 vols., 1925
Siete tratados, 2 vols., 1882–83; edited by José L. Abellán, 1977
Mercurial eclesiástica: Libro de las verdades, 1884
El Espectador (periodical), 3 vols., 1886–88; in 1 vol., 1927
El Cosmopolita (periodical), 1894; in 2 vols., 1923
Capítulos que se le olvidaron a Cervantes, 1895
Inéditos y artículos escojidos, 1897
Lecturas, edited by Juan de D. Uribe, 1898
Geometría moral, 1902
El Regenerador (periodical), 2 vols., 1928
Ensayos, narraciones y polémica, 1945
Lecciones de libertad (selection), 1958
Cartas y lecturas, edited by Galo Martinez Acosta, 1964
Ensayos, 1975
Las Catilinarias, El Cosmopolita, El Regenerador (selection), edited by Benjamín Carrión, 1976
Selections from Juan Montalvo, translated by Frank MacDonald Spindler and Nancy Cook Brooks, 1984

Other writings: a play and short stories.

Collected works edition: *Obras completas*, 10 vols., 1969–70.

Bibliography

Naranjo, Plutarco, and Carlos Rolando, *Juan Montalvo: Estudio bibliográfico*, Quito: Casa de la Cultura Ecuatoriana, 2 vols., 1966

Further Reading

Actas del Colegio de Besançon issue on Montalvo (1976)
Agramonte, Roberto D., "Preámbulo a los *Siete tratados* de Montalvo," *Círculo: Revista de Cultura* 19 (1990): 39–46
Anderson Imbert, Enrique, *El arte de la prosa en Juan Montalvo*, Mexico City: El Colegio de México, 1948

Carrión, Benjamín, *El pensamiento vivo de Montalvo*, Buenos Aires: Losada, 1961
Coloquio internacional sobre Juan Montalvo (14–22 July 1988), Quito: Fundación Friedrich Naumann, 1989
Crawford, W. Rex, *A Century of Latin-American Thought*, Cambridge, Massachusetts: Harvard University Press, 1961: Chapter 6
Miño, Reinaldo, *Juan Montalvo, polémica y ensayo*, Guayaquil, Ecuador: Claridad, 1990
Naranjo, Plutarco, *Ensayos sobre Montalvo*, Quito: Casa de la Cultura Ecuatoriana, 1985
Pérez, Galo René, *Un escritor entre la gloria y las borrascas: Vida de Juan Montalvo*, Quito: Banco Central de Ecuador, 1990
Roig, Arturo Andrés, *El pensamiento social de Montalvo*, Quito: Tercer Mundo, 1984
Sacoto Salamea, Antonio, *Juan Montalvo, el escritor y el estilista*, Cuenca, Ecuador: Casa de la Cultura Ecuatoriana "Benjamín Carrión," 2 vols., 1987
Zaldumbide, Gonzalo, *Montalvo y Rodó*, New York: Instituto de Españas en los Estados Unidos, 1938

Montherlant, Henry de

French, 1896–1972

Henry de Montherlant is best known as a playwright and novelist, one of the finest that 20th-century France has produced. Mirroring the themes of the major fictional and dramatic works, his essays, though couched in the same precise, formal French and like them mediated through a style characterized by sustained eloquence and austere elegance, are more in the nature of occasional writings.

They divide into two broad periods of production. The first category comprises the essays written in response to World War I, and the second group consists of writings inspired by the approach of, and subsequent responses to, the outbreak of World War II. In neither category, however, do we find essays which might be called "political," either in a general way, or in the narrower sense of being devoted to the propagation of a particular program. Montherlant's approach is always that of the aloof commentator, an attitude described in a famous 1915 essay by one of his mentors, Romain Rolland, as a stance "au-dessus de la mêlée" (above the hurly-burly).

Montherlant began his career as an essayist with *La Relève du matin* (The morning relief), completed in 1918 but not published until two years later. It consisted mainly of reflections on his schooldays at a single-sex Roman Catholic private *collège* or high school. As a result it was hailed as a Catholic work, but Montherlant was all his life an agnostic for whom (in the plays especially) Catholicism was a source of inspiration rather than a matter of personal belief. What Montherlant admired about his school was its cult of physical strength and of what, rather grandiloquently, he termed "virile brotherhood."

The same theme recurs in *Chant funèbre pour les morts de Verdun* (1924; Dirge for the Verdun dead), consisting mainly of newspaper articles he wrote in his capacity as secretary of the fund to build an ossuary on the site of the Douaumont fortress, where so many soldiers fell in the defense of France during World War I. In this book, and in a companion volume *Mors et vita* (1932; Death and life), he celebrated courage and self-sacrifice, seeking in the cult of sport in general and of competitive games in particular to recapture the atmosphere of exalted activity and virile comradeship that he had seen manifested in war.

Most critics agree that the lead article in *Aux fontaines du désir* (1927; At the fountains of desire), an essay entitled "Syncrétisme et alternance" (Syncretism and alternation), sums up Montherlant's thinking and indeed the whole of his work in this genre. The absurdity which, in common with many French writers of his generation, he sees at the root of the human condition is for him a natural state of affairs, a fact of life, neither to be luxuriated in nor to be deplored. Humankind is at once capable of great evil and self-destruction (hence the necessity to build a charnel house at Douaumont in order to preserve the human remains exhumed from the battlefield) and of great courage and sacrifice (as demonstrated in the patriotic willingness, despite the enormous cost, to stand and fight at Verdun). Wisdom for Montherlant lies in accepting these extremes; a healthy balance must be struck between Angel and Beast, the empire of the senses and the world of the mind. Only mediocrity is to be eschewed at all costs. The writer must embrace all facets of human life and not stand on the sidelines as a mere observer: Montherlant was, after all, a near-contemporary of those soldier-writers *par excellence*, Ernest Hemingway and André Malraux. This period of Montherlant's essay output closes with the publication of a collection of writings devoted mainly to the extensive travels he undertook between the wars, *Un voyageur solitaire est un diable* (A lone traveler is a devil), completed earlier but not published until 1945.

The second period opens with *Service inutile* (1935; Useless service), a more overtly political collection – with the reservation mentioned above – than the preceding books. This was followed by *L'Équinoxe de septembre* (1938; The September equinox), *Le Solstice de juin* (1941; The June solstice), and *Textes sous une occupation* (1953; Texts under an occupation). These essays got Montherlant into trouble after the war, since they were felt to have exalted the swastika and denigrated French defense efforts. Montherlant's fastidious, ironic manner was partly to blame; after all, to argue, as he did, that purely out of self-respect one must serve a cause even though one knows it to be useless ("idealism requires service; realism exposes its pointlessness"), was hardly likely to endear him to the Resistance. As Lucille Becker (1970) explains, his actions cut him off from the mainspring of French life: "Montherlant's generation had hailed him principally as a moralist, but the postwar generation, unable to accept his overwhelming pessimism and nihilism, turned to writers like André Malraux, Jean-Paul Sartre, and Albert Camus, who had been actively engaged in the struggle for freedom." When young people threw in their lot with the Resistance, she says, Montherlant was conspicuous by his absence.

Like all French moralists since **Montaigne**, Montherlant used the essay to explore his own developing ideas, for instance his thinking on suicide, "the last act by which a man can show that he dominates life and is not dominated by it"; it therefore comes as no surprise that he carefully chose the moment of his own death, shooting himself when it was clear to him that he was going blind. He had first contemplated suicide in 1935, so it can hardly be considered an impulsive act on his part.

Montherlant's philosophy, as expounded over the years in successive volumes of essays with striking consistency and continuity, can be summed up as follows. In a world where all is confusion and incoherence, and where nothing makes sense, human beings have no great task to perform but rather a single injunction to obey: that of extracting maximum physical pleasure from life. The instruments that enable humankind to do this are intelligence, lucidity, and a calm, unshakable agnosticism. Wisdom consists in annulling reasons for suffering. Since the world cannot be changed, it is we humans who must adapt to it: the intelligence contemplates the world and its occupants in order to plot a safer passage through it.

Far from being depressing, Montherlant's thought is marked by a kind of stoical cheerfulness. Not only did he foresee death at his own hand, he also anticipated, and was not perturbed by, the eventual eclipse of his writings. He knew that they were the product of a particular time (the early 20th century) and of a specific place (intellectual Paris). He did not flatter himself that they would survive in the same way as had the work of his admired Greeks and Romans. On the contrary, he endorsed **Paul Valéry**'s sobering pronouncement: "nous autres civilisations, nous savons maintenant que nous sommes mortelles" (we civilizations now know that we are mortal).

JOHN FLETCHER

Biography

Henry Marie Joseph Millon de Montherlant. Born 21 April 1896 in Paris. Studied at the Collège Sainte-Croix, Neuilly-sur-Seine, 1910–12: expelled; baccalauréat in philosophy, 1913; law at the Institut Catholique, Paris, 1912–13; failed law examinations. Served in the French army, 1916–18: wounded; interpreter for the American forces, 1918–19. Worked to build ossuary at Douaumont, 1920–24. Traveled several times to North Africa, from 1926, and lived there, 1931–32. War correspondent with French infantry, 1939–40; war correspondent, *Marianne* weekly, c. 1941; worked for the Red Cross, 1942–45. Began gradually to go blind, from 1959. Elected to the French Academy, 1960. Awards: Northcliffe Prize (England), for novel, 1934; French Academy Grand Prize for Literature, for novel, 1934; Grand Prize for Colonial Literature (refused), 1934. Died (suicide by gunshot) in Paris, 21 September 1972.

Selected Writings

Essays and Related Prose
La Relève du matin, 1920; revised edition, 1933
Les Olympiques (includes essays, poems, and short stories on sports), 2 vols., 1924
Chant funèbre pour les morts de Verdun, 1924
Aux fontaines du désir, 1927
Troisième Olympique, 1929
La Petite Infante de Castille, 1929
Hispano-moresque, 1929
Pour une vierge noire, 1930
Mors et vita, 1932
Service inutile, 1935; revised edition, 1952
Flèche du sud, 1937
L'Équinoxe de septembre, 1938
La Possession de soi-même, 1938
Le Solstice de juin, 1941
La Paix dans la guerre, 1941
Sur les femmes, 1942

Croire aux âmes, 1944
Un voyageur solitaire est un diable, 1945
L'Art et la vie, 1947
Notes sur mon théâtre, 1950
España sagrada, 1951
Textes sous une occupation (1940–1944), 1953
Carnets (1930–1944), 1957
Selected Essays, edited by Peter Quennell, translated by John
    Weightman, 1960
Essais (Pléiade Edition), 1963
*Discours de réception de M. Henry de Montherlant à l'Académie
    Française*, 1963
Va jouer avec cette poussière: Carnets, 1958–1964, 1966
Le Treizième César, 1970
Tous feux éteints (carnets), 1975

Other writings: nine novels (including *Les Célibataires* [*The
Bachelors*], 1934; *Les Jeunes Filles* [*The Girls*] tetralogy, 1936–39),
many plays (including *La Reine morte* [*Queen After Death*], 1942;
Malatesta, 1946; *Le Maître de Santiago* [*The Master of Santiago*],
1947; *Port-Royal*, 1954), and several volumes of diaries.

Further Reading
Becker, Lucille, *Henry de Montherlant: A Critical Biography*,
    Carbondale: Southern Illinois University Press, 1970
Cruickshank, John, *Montherlant*, Edinburgh: Oliver and Boyd, 1964
Johnson, Robert B., *Henry de Montherlant*, New York: Twayne,
    1968

Moral Essay

The moral essay is one in which the author attempts to
prescribe the attitudes and forms of behavior that will lead
to a virtuous life and a just society. Narrowly defined, the
moral essay speaks directly of issues of character – courage,
compassion, loyalty, truthfulness, and so on. When **Francis
Bacon** commends sagacity or **Samuel Johnson** derides indolence, we know we are in the presence of the moral essay.
However, the moral essay may exhibit a less didactic tone,
particularly in its more modern manifestations. **Joan Didion**
insists, in her essay "Why I Write" (1976), that any act of
writing always results in "an imposition of the writer's sensibility on the reader's most private space." Thus, the moral
essay can suggest appropriate attitudes and behavior by indirect means – including personal narrative – as well as through
overt moralizing.

Precedents of the moral essay can be seen clearly in the prose
of **Plutarch** and **Seneca**, particularly in the latter's *Epistles to
Lucilius*. The rediscovery of classical sources in the Renaissance
led to a resurgent interest in moral deliberation that was not
limited to theological study. **Michel de Montaigne** often draws
on classical sources in writing his *Essais* (1580, 1588);
however, he deviates from the pattern of the medieval *leçon
morale* by subordinating the authority of the classical views to
his own observations and experiences. Although Montaigne's
opinions are sometimes strikingly unorthodox, the themes of
many of his essays – cruelty, vanity, honesty, courage –
certainly belong in the tradition of the moral essay.

The 17th century engendered more narrowly **religious
essays**. **Sir William Cornwallis the Younger** (*Essayes*, 1600–
01), Owen Felltham (*Resolves*, 1620), and **Sir Thomas Browne**

(*Religio Medici*, 1642) all found the essay an ideal vehicle for
moral and spiritual reflection. After the Restoration, the moral
essay, as practiced by Abraham Cowley and **Sir William
Temple**, returned to general reflections on life in the style of
Montaigne. Another powerful influence on the tradition of the
moral essay was the revival of the Theophrastan **character
sketch** (modeled on his *Characters*), such as Joseph Hall's
Characters of Vertues and Vices (1608). In France **Jean de La
Bruyère** turned his *Caractères* (1688) into biting satire,
attacking not so much the morals as the manners of the day.

The moral essay soon found a place in the popular gazettes
that prospered during the 18th century. **Richard Steele** and
Joseph Addison wrote serious essays on topics such as death,
education, and loyalty for the *Tatler* and the *Spectator*.
However, their principal contribution to the moral essay was
in the tradition of La Bruyère's *Caractères*. Their use of wit
and **satire** to expose the foibles of the vain, the indolent, and
the incompetent had a lasting impact on popular essayists. In
America, **satiric essays** modeled on those of Addison and Steele
were popularized in James Franklin's *New-England Courant*
and by his brother **Benjamin Franklin** in the *Pennsylvania
Gazette*.

The latter half of the 18th century was perhaps the pinnacle
for the moral essay. The desire of the rising middle class for
social improvement resulted in a ready market for **pamphlet**s,
sermons, and moral **treatise**s of every kind. The preeminent
practitioner of this art was Samuel Johnson, who found in his
Rambler and *Idler* essays an ideal form for his moral and
philosophical inquiry. Although Johnson is not humorless in
his essays, he evinces a formality of style and a high moral
purpose in most of his work. His writing on diligence,
prudence, piety, and simplicity retains the manner, if not the
dogma, of earlier pietist writers.

The moral essay was taken up in the 19th century by the
reformers in England, such as **Thomas Carlyle**, **John Stuart
Mill**, **Matthew Arnold**, and T. H. Huxley. Although diverse
in their opinions, all of these writers challenged the established
order in some way: Carlyle was an outspoken critic of the
philistinism of the commercial class; Mill was a leading voice
for liberalism in both intellectual and political causes; Arnold
championed the role of culture as the principal impetus toward
moral action in society; and Huxley was the leading advocate
of abandoning the classical model of education for one founded
on science. Even those essayists whose social agenda was rather
traditional, such as **John Henry Newman**, were writing in reaction to the tides of change around them.

In America, the moralist tradition of the Puritans – of
William Bradford, Cotton Mather, Jonathan Edwards – was
passed on to the transcendentalists. **Ralph Waldo Emerson**'s
essays draw heavily on Christian notions of charity and service,
but are infused with a reverence for nature and a belief in
personal revelation (e.g. "The Oversoul," 1848). In one of the
most influential moral essays of all time, Emerson's disciple
Henry David Thoreau argues for the supremacy of individual
conscience over legal authority in his essay on "Civil
Disobedience" (1849).

The moralist tradition has been preserved in British letters
in the 20th century by essayists such as **G. K. Chesterton** and
C. S. Lewis, both of whom laid claim to specifically Christian
morals. More broadly, essayists such as **E. M. Forster** and

George Orwell appeal to a sense of good manners and fair play. It is difficult to name any major American essayist of the 20th century who could be considered a Johnsonian moralist. However, a moral vision clearly underpins most of the essayists working for social change, whether appealing for civil rights (**James Baldwin**, Martin Luther King, Jr., **Alice Walker**) or preservation of the environment (**Wendell Berry, Annie Dillard, Edward Hoagland**).

Some critics have seen the essay as a literary form in decline because of its close connection to Enlightenment ideals, which have increasingly come under question. How can the essay appeal to universal values when those shared values have seemingly disintegrated into cultural pluralism? The counter-response is that the recognition of a pluralistic society has created an even greater need for an exploratory form of the essay that can lead to mutual understanding and cooperative social action. Thus, the contemporary moral essay is less likely to make dogmatic pronouncements based on unchanging doctrines, and more likely to attempt to construct a moral consensus through ongoing dialogue.

DAVID W. CHAPMAN

Further Reading
Bush, Douglas, *English Literature in the Earlier Seventeenth Century, 1600–1660*, Oxford: Clarendon Press, 1962 (original edition, 1945)
Didion, Joan, "Why I Write," *New York Times Book Review*, 6 December 1976
Fort, Keith, "Form, Authority, and the Critical Essay," *College English* 32 (1971): 629–39
Lukács, Georg, "On the Nature and Form of the Essay," in his *Soul and Form*, Cambridge, Massachusetts: MIT Press, 1974 (original German edition, 1911)
O'Neill, John, "The Essay as a Moral Exercise: Montaigne," *Renaissance and Reformation* 9 (1985): 209–18
Quinby, Rowena Lee, *The Moral-Aesthetic Essay in America* (dissertation), West Lafayette, Indiana: Purdue University, 1984
Rucker, Mary, "The Literary Essay and the Modern Temper," *Papers on Language and Literature* 11 (1975): 317–35
Spellmeyer, Kurt, "Common Ground: The Essay in the Academy," *College English* 51 (1989): 262–76
Trimbur, John, "Essayist Literacy and the Rhetoric of Deproduction," *Rhetoric Review* 9 (1990): 72–86
Voitle, Robert, *Samuel Johnson, the Moralist*, Cambridge, Massachusetts: Harvard University Press, 1961
Zeiger, William, "The Exploratory Essay: Enfranchising the Spirit of Inquiry in College Composition," *College English* 47 (1985): 454–66

Morley, Christopher

American, 1890–1957

Although he is known to many readers as the author of a successful novel (*Kitty Foyle*, 1939) and two minor fictional classics (*Parnassus on Wheels*, 1917; *The Haunted Bookshop*, 1919), and published 16 volumes of poetry between 1912 and 1955, Christopher Morley was perhaps best known in his own time to the American public as an essayist who produced 18 volumes of essays, many of them previously appearing in periodicals as varied in approach as the **Atlantic Monthly**, *Coronet*, the *American Mercury*, the *Bookman*, *Commonweal*, the Manchester *Guardian*, and the *Saturday Review of Literature*.

Because much of his career was spent as a journalist, almost all of his essays were written as columns for the magazines and newspapers by whom he was employed. In an effort to appeal to the wide audience of these periodicals, he wrote on a broad variety of topics. Some of his essays were written in part to advance the literary careers and publicize the works of close literary associates and friends such as Heywood Broun, Don Marquis, Robert Cortes Holiday, and H. M. Tomlinson. Others deal with modern writers whom Morley deeply respected: **Hilaire Belloc**, Joseph Conrad, Rupert Brooke, and **George Santayana**, among others. One of his best collections in which he deals with literature and its relationship to life is *Inward Ho!* (1923). In these pieces, which had originally appeared as columns in the New York *Evening Post*, he provides enlightened, sensitive, and sensible literary criticism on authors as diverse as **Bacon**, Keats, **Tolstoi**, **Yeats**, and Carl Sandburg. In one set of essays in *Plum Pudding* (1921), he writes about the ideal reader, Walt Whitman, the making of a poet, and a renowned professor of literature, Francis Barton Gummere.

All of his essays may well have been written for Morley's "Perfect Reader," whom he describes in an essay by the same title: "Oh, the Perfect Reader! There is not an illusion that he misses; in all those lovely printed words he sees the subtle secrets that a lesser soul would miss. He (bless his heart!) is not thinking how he himself would have written it; his clear, keen, outreaching mind is intent only to be one in spirit with the invisible and long-dead author ... And as long as there are Perfect Readers, who read with passion, with glory, and then speed to tell their friends, there will always be, ever and anon, a Perfect Writer."

Morley's essays consequently tend to be quite personal, as he writes about people, places, and things he has known intimately, a quality which makes his writing still attractive. He writes easily about small events which might otherwise escape the attention of most observers but which take on added significance when treated by a perceptive writer with an engaging style.

In other essays Morley is fascinated with local Americana. In many pieces he describes locations with a great deal of fondness. In the Philadelphia area, for example, he lovingly treats many obscure and well-known places such as Dooner's Tavern, Independence Hall, Little Italy, and Walt Whitman's home in nearby Camden. He can write with equal poignance about New York City as he describes various places with which he has pleasant associations; Madison Square Garden, Vesey Street, St. Paul's Churchyard, McSorley's Saloon, and the New York subway take on a piquancy which makes even the commonplace seem special.

Morley also wrote **travel essays** in which he tells of his excursions in England, France, Canada, and the Caribbean, as well as his fascination with great ocean liners upon which he had voyaged. Often he makes associations between the places themselves and their literary and historical significance. As he wrote in "The Sense of Place" (*The Ironing Board*, 1949), "Only from that humble footing, companionship with things of sight and touch, can the mind rise to larger vantage. The Place may be anywhere and happens by chance ... Any place is dear where a human mind rose above the joy and torture of the flesh and said its triumphant word."

Morley's essays are polished, sophisticated, and highly personal, much in the tradition of the **personal essay** of **Addison** and **Steele** and **Lamb**. While Morley and his work have been neglected by the reading public in the very late 20th century, they still admirably fulfill the classical requirement of pleasing both the mind and the heart.

ROBERT C. STEENSMA

Biography
Christopher Darlington Morley. Born 5 May 1890 in Haverford, Pennsylvania. Family moved to Baltimore, 1900. Studied at Haverford College, B.A., 1910; Rhodes scholar in modern history at New College, Oxford, 1910–13. Staff member, Doubleday Page and Co., from 1913. Married Helen Booth Fairchild, 1914: four children. Editor, *Ladies' Home Journal*, 1917; columnist, Philadelphia *Evening Public Ledger*, 1917; cofounder and columnist, the *Saturday Review of Literature*, 1924–41, and New York *Evening Post*, 1920–23; editorial board member, Book-of-the-Month Club, 1926–54. Suffered a stroke, 1951, which incapacitated him for the rest of his life. Died in Roslyn Heights, New York, 28 March 1957.

Selected Writings

Essays and Related Prose
Shandygaff, 1918
Mince Pie: Adventures on the Sunny Side of Grub Street, 1919
Travels in Philadelphia, 1920
Pipefuls, 1920
Plum Pudding, 1921
The Powder of Sympathy, 1923
Inward Ho!, 1923
Religio Journalistici, 1924
Forty-Four Essays, 1925
Safety Pins and Other Essays, 1925
The Romany Stain, 1926
Essays (selection), 1928
Off the Deep End, 1928
The Child and the Book, 1929
Internal Revenue, 1933
Shakespeare and Hawaii (lectures), 1933
Christopher Morley's Briefcase, 1936
Streamlines, 1936
History of an Autumn, 1938
Letters of Askance, 1939
Morley's Variety: A Selection from the Writings, edited by Louis Greenfield, 1944
The Ironing Board, 1949
Prefaces Without Books: Prefaces and Introductions to Thirty Books, edited by Herman Abromson, 1970

Other writings: eight novels (*Parnassus on Wheels*, 1917; *The Haunted Bookshop*, 1919; *Where the Blue Begins*, 1922; *Thunder on the Left*, 1925; *Human Being*, 1932; *Kitty Foyle*, 1939; *Thorofare*, 1942; *The Man Who Made Friends with Himself*, 1949), short stories, poetry, plays, and the autobiography *John Mistletoe* (1931). Also edited two editions of *Bartlett's Familiar Quotations*.

Bibliographies
Lee, Alfred P., *A Bibliography of Christopher Morley*, Garden City, New York: Doubleday Doran, 1935
Lyle, Guy R., and Henry Tatnall Brown, Jr., *A Bibliography of Christopher Morley*, Washington, D.C.: Scarecrow Press, 1952

Further Reading
Hughes, Babette, *Christopher Morley*, Seattle: University of Washington Chapbooks, 1927
Wallach, Mark I., and Jon Bracker, *Christopher Morley*, Boston: Twayne, 1976

Morris, William
British, 1834–1896

William Morris' essays comprise a small part of his prolific literary work; nevertheless, they are the most significant of his works in clarifying the essential relationship Morris perceived between art and society and between art and politics. Less well known in literary circles than his poetry, translations, and prose romances, Morris' essays profoundly influenced the socialist movement in England during his lifetime, and they have continued to raise important questions about the crassness of commercialism, the exploitation of nature, the destructive separation of the worker from the pleasure of creation, and the inevitability of social collapse given the current state of Western society. Many of **John Ruskin**'s themes reappear in Morris' essays, which also owe much of their exhortative style to Ruskin. Both the subject matter and the style of Morris' essays were also greatly influenced by his translation of Icelandic sagas and his vision of medieval Icelandic culture as epitomizing the integration of art into society. The substance of Morris' essays also grew out of his reading of **John Stuart Mill** and **Karl Marx**.

Written between 1877 and 1894, Morris' essays, for the most part, were first delivered as lectures and then published in **periodicals** or as **pamphlets**; some were then reprinted in collections. Many of his essays and lectures were first published only in the 20th century. In addition, Morris wrote about 500 editorials and signed articles for *Justice* and *Commonweal*, a socialist newspaper he edited from 1884 to 1890.

Best known during his lifetime as author of the four-volume narrative poem *The Earthly Paradise* (1868–70), Morris turned to essays in the late 1870s when he began to involve himself in such political issues as the "Eastern Question," the conflict between Russia and other nations over control of the Ottoman Empire, a conflict which threatened to involve Great Britain, an ally of Turkey, in war against Russia. This early political issue and Morris' indignation at the methods being used to restore ancient buildings stimulated him to begin writing essays, lectures, and newspaper articles. As he became more and more involved in the socialist movement in England, he turned almost exclusively to writing nonfiction prose. In his attacks on the methods of restoring medieval buildings, Morris echoes Ruskin's *The Nature of Gothic* (1853). In his essay "The Beauty of Life" (1880), Morris pays homage to Ruskin's "eloquence" and influence, and in a Ruskinesque vein, writes that "down to very recent days everything that the hand of man touched was more or less beautiful: so that in those days all people who made anything shared in art, as well as all people who used the things so made; that is, *all* people shared in art." In this important essay, Morris identifies his cause as "the Democracy of Art, the ennobling of daily and common work," and holds up the promise of an enlightened society in which art would be "made by the people and for the people, a joy to the maker and the user." For Morris, the greatest art was also political, as he explains in "The Revival of Handicraft" (1888): "... it is impossible to exclude socio-political questions from the consideration of aesthetics."

Morris' style, like Ruskin's, is often expostulatory, instructive, and zealous, punctuated with rhetorical questions and parallel phrasing. In "Art and the Beauty of the Earth" (1881), for example, Morris exhorts his audience to protect the beauty of the earth, following his exhortation with a rhetorical question: "... it is this reasonable share in the beauty of the earth that I claim as the right of every man who will earn it by due labour; a decent house with decent surroundings for every honest and industrious family; that is the claim which I make of you in the name of art. Is it such an exorbitant claim to make of civilization?" In some of his lectures clearly directed to a working-class audience, Morris uses fairly simple diction and organization, often showing the process through which he has puzzled ideas out, for example, in "Useful Work v. Useless Toil" (1884), where he states that:

> ... the first thing as to the work done in civilization and the easiest to notice is that it is portioned out very unequally amongst the different classes of society. First, there are people – not a few – who do no work, and make no pretence of doing any. Next, there are people and very many of them, who work fairly hard, though with abundant easements and holidays, claimed and allowed; and lastly there are people who work so hard that they may be said to do nothing else than work, and are accordingly called the "working classes"...

When Morris is writing for a well-educated class or specialists, as in "How We Live and How We Might Live" (1885) and "Whigs, Democrats and Socialists" (1886), his diction, sentence structure, and allusions correspond to the ability of his audience to understand. Some essays on the history and practice of particular arts, such as "On the Artistic Qualities of the Woodcut Books of Ulm and Augsburg in the Fifteenth Century" (1895), clearly challenge all but the most erudite readers. The socialist lectures appeal on a primary level to the largely uneducated audience Morris was addressing, and as such feature much repetition, second-person references, and simple organization; but on a secondary level, their allusions, especially to history and art, make them seem simultaneously intended for a more sophisticated readership.

Recently Morris' essays have received more critical attention, part as the result of a critical revival in Morris studies which began in the 1970s and has accelerated steadily. The additional interest being paid to his essays also reflects the modern interest in nonfiction that has coincided with the rise of cultural studies. Early views of Morris as an escapist who sought refuge in an idealized medieval world have been re-evaluated; what has emerged from this study is a recognition of Morris' complexity as a writer who has much to say to the modern world.

LINDA A. JULIAN

Biography

Born 24 March 1834 in Walthamstow, Essex. Studied at Marlborough College, Wiltshire, 1848–51; privately, 1852–53; Exeter College, Oxford, 1853–55, B.A., 1856, M.A., 1875. Articled to G. E. Street's architectural firm, Oxford and London, 1856. Founding editor, *Oxford and Cambridge Magazine*, 1856. Painter, 1857–62: friend of members of the Pre-Raphaelite Brotherhood, including Dante Gabriel Rossetti and Edward Burne-Jones; founder, with Rossetti, Burne-Jones, and others, Morris Marshall Faulkner & Co. design firm, London, 1861–74, later Morris & Co., 1874–96. Married Jane Burden, 1859: two daughters. Lived in Bexley, Kent, 1861–65, and in London, from 1865. Traveled in Iceland, 1871 and 1873. Examiner, South Kensington School of Art, later the Victoria and Albert Museum, London, 1876–96. Public lecturer on art, architecture, and socialism, 1877–96. Founder, Kelmscott Press, London, 1890–96. Treasurer, National Liberal League, 1879; member, Democratic Federation, 1883, then the Socialist League, from 1884: editor of its journal *Commonweal*, 1884–90, and League delegate to the International Socialist Working-Men's Congress, Paris, 1889; founding member, Hammersmith Socialist Society, 1890. Died in Hammersmith, west London, 3 October 1896.

Selected Writings

Essays and Related Prose
Hopes and Fears for Art: Five Lectures, 1882
Lectures on Art, 1882
Signs of Change: Seven Lectures, 1888
Socialist Platform (collected pamphlets), with others, 1888; revised edition, 1890
The World of Romance, Being Contributions to the Oxford and Cambridge Magazine, 1856, 1906
The Unpublished Lectures, edited by Eugene D. LeMire, 1969
The Ideal Book: Essays and Lectures on the Arts of the Book, edited by William S. Peterson, 1982
Political Writings, edited by A. L. Morton, 1984
Socialist Diary, edited by Florence Boos, 1985
Political Writings: Contributions to Justice and Commonweal, 1883–1890, edited by Nicholas Salmon, 1994

Other writings: poetry, fiction (including the two prose dream narratives *A Dream of John Ball*, 1888, and *News from Nowhere*, 1890), works on socialism, letters, and translations of Old Icelandic and Norse sagas.

Collected works edition: *Collected Works*, edited by May Morris, 24 vols., 1910–15; supplement, as *William Morris: Artist, Writer, Socialist*, edited by May Morris, 2 vols., 1936.

Bibliographies
Aho, Gary L., *William Morris: A Reference Guide*, Boston: Hall, 1985
Briggs, R. C. H., *Handlist of the Public Addresses of William Morris*, Dublin: Dolmen Press, 1961
Scott, Temple, *A Bibliography of the Works of William Morris*, London: Bell, 1897
Walsdorf, John J., *William Morris in Private Press and Limited Editions: A Descriptive Bibliography of Books by and About Morris, 1891–1981*, Phoenix, Arizona: Oryx, and London: Library Associaton, 1983

Further Reading
Faulkner, Peter, *Against the Age: An Introduction to William Morris*, London and Boston: Allen and Unwin, 1980
Gallasch, Linda, *The Use of Compounds and Archaic Diction in the Works of William Morris*, Berne: Lang, 1979
Harvey, Charles, and Jon Press, *William Morris: Design and Enterprise in Victorian Britain*, Manchester: Manchester University Press, 1991

Kocmanova, Jessie, "The Living Language of William Morris," *Brno Studies in English* 9 (1970): 17–34

Lewis, Peter, editor, *William Morris: Aspects of the Man and His Work* (proceedings of the 1977 conference on William Morris held at the Loughborough University of Technology), Loughborough: Loughborough Victorian Studies Group, 1978

MacCarthy, Fiona, *William Morris: A Life for Our Time*, London: Faber, 1994; New York: Knopf, 1995

Thompson, E. P., *William Morris: Romantic to Revolutionary*, London: Merlin Press, 1977; New York: Pantheon, 1978 (original edition, 1955)

Thompson, Paul, *The Work of William Morris*, Oxford: Clarendon Press, 1991 (original edition, 1967)

Thompson, Paul, *Why William Morris Matters Today: Human Creativity and the Future World Environment*, London: William Morris Society, 1991

Muir, Edwin

British, 1887–1959

Edwin Muir is remembered primarily for his work as poet and as translator with his wife Willa of the novels of Franz Kafka. Muir first came to prominence, however, as essayist and reviewer for the *New Age* under the editorship of A. R. Orage in the second decade of the century. The success of *We Moderns* (1918), his collected short essays, or **aphorisms**, as he called them, won him a contract with the American *Freeman* magazine, which enabled him to leave Britain in 1921 for his first taste of Europe and of freedom as a writer. Although he began to write poetry during that European experience and increasingly saw poetry as his chosen *métier*, he continued to contribute essays to periodicals both literary and general, and alongside his work as translator of European fiction, it was as an essayist and reviewer that he made a modest living throughout his life. For Muir, books were a "starting-point for an enquiry into the human spirit," as he expressed it in the essay "A Plea for Psychology in Literary Criticism" (1921). His literary and **review** essays were therefore never divorced from life, but became meditations on life, social and spiritual. The best of these essays have been collected in book form over the years, although several collections are now out of print. They deserve to be better known for the perspectives they provide on the culture of their times and for the insight they provide into Muir the poet.

The early *We Moderns* was written under the pseudonym "Edward Moore" and was later rejected by Muir for its Nietzschean assertiveness. Although he called the series "aphorisms," many of the pieces are more akin to essays in miniature or expanded *pensées*. Muir's talents were more suited to an expanded reflection or **meditation** than to the short, witty statement typical of the true aphoristic form. Yet even in this largely uncharacteristic collection, one can recognize the Muir of the later poetry and essays: in the concern with the Fall of Man and Original Sin and the effect of such a doctrine on human lives; in the meditations on realism in contemporary art and the consequent loss of the classical concern with what he saw as the essence of art, the "eternal problem." As critic, Muir stands apart from the mainstream of criticism this century, rejecting the scientific move toward formal analysis and allying himself with the tradition of Renaissance humanism

with its emphasis on the imagination and the moral purpose of art – to teach by delighting. He saw literature as having an emancipating role, such as he himself had experienced through his contact with the *New Age*, and his exemplars were the English and German Romantic poets and the late 19th-century critic and poet **Matthew Arnold**.

Muir's affinity with Europe and European writers was an early feature of his essay writing. His travels in the early 1920s took him to Prague and Dresden, and from there he sent to the *Freeman* "sketches" giving his responses to his new environment and short essays on European writers such as **Dostoevskii**, Ibsen, and **Nietzsche**. He was the first writer to introduce Hölderlin to an English-speaking public, his early essay "A Note on Friedrich Hölderlin" appearing in the *Scottish Nation* in September 1923. This was followed by further essays on the German poet in the 1930s, which were later collected in *Essays on Literature and Society* (1949, revised and enlarged 1965). His interest in Hölderlin was life-long. Like Muir himself, Hölderlin "approached the mystery of time and eternity through the imagination . . . the mystery itself, not any particular manifestation of it, was his theme; and what he made out of it was a mythology," as Muir described it in the late essays. The *Freeman* essay "North and South" (1922) demonstrates his interest in **Goethe** and Heine and the preoccupation with *Sehnsucht*, longing for a lost land, which was to feature so prominently in his own *First Poems* (1925). These European essays were collected in *Latitudes* (1924).

In contrast to the European *Latitudes*, Muir's next essay collection, *Transition* (1926), focused on contemporary writers in England such as **T. S. Eliot**, **Virginia Woolf**, James Joyce, **Aldous Huxley**, and **D. H. Lawrence**. Although he was never happy with what he considered Lawrence's "nihilism" and at that point in time considered Eliot more interesting as critic than poet, Muir was remarkably acute in his contemporaneous perception of the significant writers of the period. His *Transition* essay on James Joyce was reproduced with variations in several periodicals of the time, including the *Calendar of Modern Letters* and the *Nation*, and was included in *James Joyce: The Critical Heritage*, edited by Robert H. Deming in 1970.

In the mid-1930s, family circumstances brought Muir back to Scotland; this period saw him engaging more fully in the contemporary debates about Scottish cultural identity. Although never as committed culturally to Scotland as the poet Hugh MacDiarmid (i.e. Christopher Murray Grieve), with whom he quarreled over the question of the viability of Scots as a literary language, Muir's Scottish essays and reviews of this period furthered an understanding of Scotland's social and cultural situation.

Muir's final and most mature collections of essays are *Essays on Literature and Society* and *The Estate of Poetry*, a series of meditations on poetry in the modern world given at Harvard University between 1955 and 1956 and published posthumously in 1962. He had spent the immediate post-1945 years in Prague as Director of the British Council and had witnessed both the brief movement of the Czechs toward freedom and self-determination after the defeat of the Nazis and the extinguishing of that freedom when the Communists took charge in 1948. *Essays on Literature and Society*, like his poetry collection *The Labyrinth* (1949), took its impulse from what he called in *An Autobiography* (1954) "the single, disunited world" of mid-20th-century Europe, which he contrasted in the essay "Robert Henryson" with the lost philosophical coherence of a past age of faith. These essays give voice to his belief in the imagination and in the need for imagination in a world increasingly dominated by technology and adherence to machine-like progress. This "artificial world which we have made of the world" and the changing relationship between poet and public are the themes of *The Estate of Poetry*, which takes a more pessimistic view of the capacity of poetry as we have known it to survive in the modern world. Yet Muir's understanding that it is through the imagination that we can comprehend both art and society is itself a pointer to survival. His situation in an inclusive humanist tradition of criticism and art give his essays a new relevance at the end of the century in their recall of the poet from the periphery to the center of the human stage.

MARGERY PALMER MCCULLOCH

Biography

Born 15 May 1887 in Deerness, Mainland Island, Orkney. Studied at a school on Wyre, Orkney, and at Kirkwall Burgh Grammar School, Orkney. Family moved to Glasgow, 1901. Clerk for a shipbuilding firm, Glasgow, 1902–18. Lectured at the National Guild League, Glasgow, from 1916, and helped publish the *Guildsman*; wrote series of "We Moderns," 1918, and staff member, *New Age*, London, 1919–21. Married Wilhelmina Anderson (i.e. the writer Willa Muir), 1919: one child. Moved to London, 1919; lived in Prague, 1921–22, then Dresden and Hellerau; traveled in Italy, returning to Britain, 1924; lived in the south of France, 1926–27, in southern England, 1927–35, and St. Andrews, Fife, 1935–40. Book reviewer, the *Listener*, 1933–45; coeditor, *European Quarterly*, 1934. Worked for the British Council in Edinburgh, 1941–45, Prague, 1945–48, and Rome, 1949–50. Warden, Newbattle Abbey College, Dalkeith, 1950–55; Charles Eliot Norton Professor of Poetry, Harvard University, Cambridge, Massachusetts, 1955–56; retired to Swaffham Prior, near Cambridge, U.K., 1956. Awards: Foyle Prize, 1950; Heinemann Award, 1953; Frederick Niven Literary Award, 1953; Russell Loines Award, 1957; Saltire Society Prize, 1957; German Academy Voss Prize, 1958; honorary degrees from five universities. Commander, Order of the British Empire (CBE), 1953; Fellow, Royal Society of Literature, 1953. Died in Swaffam Prior, 3 January 1959.

Selected Writings

Essays and Related Prose

We Moderns: Enigmas and Guesses (as Edward Moore), 1918; as Edwin Muir for the first U.S. edition, 1920
Latitudes, 1924
Transition: Essays on Contemporary Literature, 1926
The Structure of the Novel, 1928
Essays on Literature and Society, 1949; revised, enlarged edition, 1965
The Estate of Poetry (Norton lectures), 1962
Uncollected Scottish Criticism, edited by Andrew Noble, 1982
Selected Prose, edited by George Mackay Brown, 1987
The Truth of the Imagination: Some Uncollected Reviews and Essays, edited by P. H. Butter, 1988

Other writings: poetry, three novels, and an autobiography (1940, revised 1954). Also translated, with Willa Muir, many German-language writers, including works by Kafka.

Bibliographies

Mellown, Elgin W., *Bibliography of the Writings of Edwin Muir*, Tuscaloosa: University of Alabama Press, 1964; revised edition, London: Vane, 1966; supplement, Tuscaloosa: University of Alabama Press, and London: Kaye and Ward, 1970
Mellown, Elgin W., and Peter C. Hoy, *A Checklist of Writings About Edwin Muir*, Troy, New York: Whitston, 1971

Further Reading

Akros issue on Muir, 6, no. 47 (August 1981)
Blackmur, R. P., "Edwin Muir: Between the Tiger's Paws," *Kenyon Review* 21, no. 2 (1959): 419–36
Butter, P. H., *Edwin Muir: Man and Poet*, Edinburgh: Oliver and Boyd, and New York: Barnes and Noble, 1966
Chapman issue on Muir, 9, no. 6 (Summer 1987)
Gardner, Helen, *Edwin Muir*, Cardiff: University of Wales Press, 1961
Gaskill, P. H., "Edwin Muir and Goethe," *Proceedings of the English Goethe Society* 48 (1978): 22–51
Gaskill, P. H., "Edwin Muir as Critic of Hölderlin," *Forum for Modern Language Studies* 14 (1978): 345–64
Gaskill, P. H., "Edwin Muir: The German Aspect," *Lines Review* 69 (June 1979): 14–20
Gaskill, P. H., "Edwin Muir in Hellerau," *Scottish Literary Journal* 11 (May 1984): 45–56
Hoffman, Daniel, *Barbarous Knowledge: Myth in the Poetry of Yeats, Graves and Muir*, New York: Oxford University Press, 1967
McCulloch, Margery, "Edwin Muir's Scottish Journey 1935–80," *Scottish Review* 17 (February 1980): 47–52
McCulloch, Margery, "Inter-War Criticism," in *The History of Scottish Literature Volume 4: Twentieth Century*, edited by Craig Cairns, Aberdeen: Aberdeen University Press, 1987: 119–32
McCulloch, Margery, *Edwin Muir: Poet, Critic and Novelist*, Edinburgh: Edinburgh University Press, 1993
MacLachlan, C. J. M., and D. S. Robb, editors, *Edwin Muir: Centenary Assessments*, Aberdeen: Association for Scottish Literary Studies, 1990
Marshall, George, *In a Distant Isle: The Orkney Background of Edwin Muir*, Edinburgh: Scottish Academic Press, 1987
Mellown, Elgin W., *Edwin Muir*, Boston: Twayne, 1979
Muir, Willa, *Belonging: A Memoir*, London: Hogarth Press, 1968
Raine, Kathleen, "Edwin Muir: An Appreciation," *Texas Quarterly* 4, no. 3 (Autumn 1961): 233–45
Robertson, Ritchie, "'Our Generation': Edwin Muir as Social Critic, 1920–22," *Scottish Literary Journal* 9, no. 2 (December 1982): 45–65
Robertson, Ritchie, "Edwin Muir as Critic of Kafka," *Modern Language Review* 79, no. 4 (July 1984): 638–52

Muir, John

American, 1838–1914

Mountaineer, traveler, naturalist, activist, and essayist, John Muir is perhaps more than any other single person the progenitor of modern American environmentalism. At a time when Americans were hungry for accounts of the wilderness, his **nature essays** offered the public affectionate firsthand descriptions of America's natural beauty and at the same time alerted them to the environmental threat of expanding urbanization. Shifts in public attitudes were not the only consequence of his paeans to nature. A series of essays in the *Atlantic Monthly* (later published as *Our National Parks*, 1901) is thought to have been the driving force behind the Congressional bill establishing the National Park system. Muir's writing also articulated, less as a theory than through intuitions based on years of close and disciplined observation, some of the ecological principles that would become fundamental to later environmentalists. But perhaps the greatest reason for Muir's appeal and continuing relevance is that his vision of nature as having value in and of itself offers a powerful, ethically responsible alternative to the still predominant view of nature as a consumer commodity. "No dogma taught by the present civilization," he argued in the early essay "Wild Wool" (1875; later included in *Steep Trails*, 1918), "seems to form so insuperable an obstacle in the way of a right understanding of the relations which culture sustains to wildness as that which regards the world as made especially for the uses of man."

Muir filled some 60 journals with the observations he made during years of hiking in and studying the wilderness. Drawing heavily on these, he wrote dozens of sketches and essays for local newspapers and for popular American magazines such as *Century*, *Overland Monthly*, and the *Atlantic Monthly*, many of which were later revised for inclusion in his books. In spite of this considerable output, Muir found writing very difficult. Recording observations in personal **journal**s was one thing; reporting them to the public, quite another. When he had to address a broader audience, words came to him "slow as a glacier." *The Mountains of California* (1894), his first and possibly his best book, was published only when he was in his mid-fifties. His difficulties can to some extent be attributed to the rhetorical situation in which he, like many nature writers since, found himself. To evoke in the American public an *active* interest in nature, to take them out of their expanding cities and make them realize the need for limits on urban growth, Muir knew he had to revivify what Americans had come to take for granted; yet in using language to achieve this he risked drawing their attention to words rather than living things. The paradox of nature writing clearly frustrated him: "No amount of word-making will ever make a single soul to know these mountains," he complained. "One day's exposure to mountains is better than cartloads of books."

The attempt both to inform and to move his readers was not always successful. In some essays, Muir's sustained descriptions of nature may seem tedious to the modern sensibility, and his scientific reportage dry; in others, his attempts to convey his awe in the face of nature's wonders seem somewhat inflated and altogether too dependent on eager intensifiers and superlatives. Seldom does his prose possess the balance, grace, and fluidity evident in the writing of that other great 19th-century American naturalist, **Henry David Thoreau**. Yet there are also many passages in which it does achieve an appealing simplicity, where Muir's spare diction and syntax so effectively convey his joy in nature that they elicit our own. When the snow falls in the High Sierra, he writes in *The Mountains of California*, "The rough places are then made smooth, the death and decay of the year is covered gently and kindly, and the ground seems as clean as the sky." Anthropomorphic descriptions in the same book suggest an affection for all things natural and exemplify Muir's belief that everything has a life and purpose of its own. Great rocks "lean back in majestic repose" or "advance their brows in thoughtful attitudes . . . their feet set in pine-groves" and "bathed in floods of singing water"; as the glaciers retreat, pine-trees "march" up the "sun-warmed moraines" in "long, hopeful files."

Along with his keen and affectionate eye for detail, Muir's ethos is the source of power in his essays. He is a kind of *sotto voce* John the Baptist, his occasional anger at tourists and distaste for the "pathetic and silly" gardens of civilization always softened by the pleasure he takes in snow and rainstorms, rocks and rivers, sequoia trees and wild sheep. The American essayist **Edward Hoagland** has said of Muir, "At rock bottom, love was what he was about." Yet he is also about joy, and about the heightened consciousness that encounters with nature can bring us. At times, the reader feels not only the extraordinary exuberance of the man but the deep bond he had with the American wilderness – as, for example, when he tells us, in *My First Summer in the Sierra* (1911), of shuffling along a three-inch rocky ledge high over the rushing Merced River, his mouth stuffed with bitter artemisia leaves "to prevent giddiness"; or when he recounts, in *The Yosemite* (1912), how he slowly ascended a mountain, sunk waist-deep in snow and almost "out of sight" in some places, only to find himself "riding an avalanche" down, his body "moderately embedded on the surface or at times a little below it." Passages like these make Muir a nature writer still worth reading. At his best, he is like the grasshopper described in *My First Summer in the Sierra*: a "crisp electric spark of joy enlivening the massy sublimity of mountains like the laugh of a child."

BRIAN TURNER

Biography

Born 21 April 1838 in Dunbar, Scotland. Moved with his family to the United States, 1849, settling in Wisconsin. Studied at the University of Wisconsin, until 1863. Walked from Indiana to New Mexico, 1867, to California, 1868, and into Yosemite Valley, where he remained six years. Married Louise Wanda Strentzel, 1880: two daughters. Learned horticulture from his father-in-law and ran a fruit ranch, Alhambra Valley, California, 1881–91. Campaigned to establish Yosemite National Park, 1890, and eventually became an acknowledged leader of the forest conservation movement in the U.S. Took President Theodore Roosevelt on a camping trip in Yosemite, 1903: as a result Roosevelt set aside 148 million acres of additional forest reserves. Awards: honorary degrees from four universities. Member, American Academy of Arts and Sciences. Died in Los Angeles, 24 December 1914.

Selected Writings

Essays and Related Prose

The Mountains of California, 1894; enlarged edition, 1911; edited by Robert C. Baron, 1988
Our National Parks, 1901; enlarged edition, 1909
The Yosemite, 1912
Articles by John Muir, Published in the Century Magazine, Atlantic Monthly, the Outlook, 1890 to 1912, 1916
A Thousand-Mile Walk to the Gulf, edited by William Frederic Badè, 1916
Travels in Alaska, 1917
Steep Trails, edited by William Frederic Badè, 1918
Studies in the Sierra, 1950; revised edition, edited by William E. Colby, 1960
The Wilderness of John Muir (selection), 1954
Trails of Wonder: Writings on Nature and Man, edited by Peter Seymour, 1972
Wilderness Essays, 1980

The Yosemite and Beyond: Writings from the Years 1863 to 1875,
edited by Robert Engberg and Donald Wesling, 1980
Muir Among the Animals: The Wildlife Writings, edited by Lisa
Mighetto, 1986
South of Yosemite: Selected Writings, edited by Frederic R. Gunsky,
1988
In Nature's Heart: The Wilderness Days, edited by James Randklev,
1991

Other writings: *Stickeen* (1909), the story of a dog, nature writing
on glaciers and mountains, journals, and autobiographies (*The Story
of My Boyhood and Youth*, 1913; *My First Summer in the Sierra*,
1911).

Collected works editions: *Writings* (Manuscript Edition), edited by
William Frederic Badè, 10 vols., 1916–24; *The Eight Wilderness
Discovery Books*, 1992.

Further Reading

Cohen, Michael P., *The Pathless Way: John Muir and American
Wilderness*, Madison: University of Wisconsin Press, 1984
Elder, John C., "John Muir and the Literature of Wilderness,"
Massachusetts Review 22 (1981): 375–86
Fleck, Richard F., *Henry Thoreau and John Muir Among the
Indians*, Hamden, Connecticut: Archon, 1985
Fox, Stephen, *The American Conservation Movement: John Muir
and His Legacy*, Madison: University of Wisconsin Press, 1985
Hoagland, Edward, Foreword to *Steep Trails* by Muir, San
Francisco: Sierra Club, 1994
Jones, Holway R., *John Muir and the Sierra Club: The Battle for
Yosemite*, San Francisco: Sierra Club, 1965
Nash, Roderick, *Wilderness and the American Mind*, New Haven,
Connecticut: Yale University Press, 1967
Oelschlaeger, Max, *The Idea of Wilderness: From Prehistory to the
Age of Ecology*, New Haven, Connecticut: Yale University Press,
1991
Orovec, Christine, "John Muir, Yosemite, and the Sublime
Response: A Study in the Rhetoric of Preservationism," *Quarterly
Journal of Speech* 67 (1981): 245–58
Tallmidge, John, "John Muir and the Poetics of Natural
Conversion," *North Dakota Quarterly* 59 (1991): 62–79
Turner, Frederick, *Rediscovering America: John Muir in His Time
and Ours*, San Francisco: Sierra Club, 1985

Mumford, Lewis

American, 1895–1990

Lewis Mumford was born in 1895 to a lower-middle-class
family in Queens, New York, and his career as a social critic
and public intellectual spans the greater part of the 20th
century. The largely self-educated Mumford wrote over 30
books of criticism, history, fiction, and autobiography – most
of which are still in print – and more than a thousand essays
and reviews. He contributed regular and often influential essays
to the *New Republic*, the *Dial*, the *Nation*, the **New Yorker**,
and many other journals. Despite his avocation as a freelance
scholar with few university ties, Mumford's eclectic work
helped inaugurate several academic disciplines and specialized
fields, including the social history of technology, architectural
and urban planning, and American studies. Drawing on
anthropology, cultural and political history, sociology, literature, political economy, and philosophy, Mumford's work
synthesizes older fields of intellectual inquiry into a coherent,
"organic" whole. Mumford's essays shaped policy debates
in public arenas as diverse as urban and regional planning,
ecology, and nuclear disarmament; for these efforts he was
awarded numerous honors, including the National Book
Award, the National Medal for Literature, and the Smithsonian
Institution's Hodgkins Gold Medal for groundbreaking,
cross-disciplinary scholarship linking the sciences and the
humanities.

Like the "Young American" critics Van Wyck Brooks,
Waldo Frank, and Randolph Bourne with whom he is often
associated, Mumford locates the modern crisis of individual
identity at the crossroads of aesthetics and politics. Shaped by
diverse traditions and individuals including Patrick Geddes,
Henri Bergson, continental *Lebensphilosophie*, American pragmatism, and "insurgent" "American Scholars" such as Walt
Whitman, **Ralph Waldo Emerson**, and **Henry David Thoreau**,
Mumford's biologically grounded, vitalist sociology sought to
reverse **T. S. Eliot**'s modern "dissociation of sensibility" by
joining the intellectually abstract to the physically palpable.
Mumford harshly criticized the European Enlightenment that
had both excluded the irrational and the sacred from cultural
analysis and privileged the untrammeled development of technological rationality at the expense of craftsmanship and
creativity. With his Modernist contemporaries, Mumford
exposed the enlightened rationalism of the Victorian age to a
relentless moral critique, countering its confidence in objective
science with a renewed emphasis on subjectively lived experience. Mumford deplored the one-sided development of the
individual's capacities in capitalist modernity and argued
passionately for an Emersonian reconstruction of the individual, investing the Rousseauvian essay of self-inventory with
the republican virtue of a Roman moralist. Mumford's essayistic persona declaims a new American jeremiad, prophesying
a renewal of cultural and social life merging the best aspects
of premodern tradition – the individual's imbeddedness in
regional communities and shared memory of a collective past
– with the potential for material abundance offered by modern
industrial society.

Mumford – following **John Ruskin** – posits architecture and
city planning as the cultural practices that most prominently
represent society's aspirations and spiritual essence. The
"usable history" of American architectural and literary tradition provides a possible resource for renewal, for rooting social
life in the "total situation" of its biological and cultural
complexity rather than the merely "artful system of concepts"
characteristic of academic criticism. The early ground-breaking
essays on American culture – *Sticks and Stones* (1924),
The Golden Day (1926), *Herman Melville* (1929), and *The
Brown Decades* (1931) – identify in the "Golden Day" of the
American literary and architectural renaissance a potentially
redemptive link between the technological present and the
organic past. "Towards Modern Architecture" (1922), an early
and influential essay, lauds the early "Brown Decades" architecture of Henry Hobson Richardson, John Wellborn Root,
and Louis Sullivan for clearing away "the truckloads of ornament and bric-a-brac" characteristic of Victorian aesthetics,
thus preparing the way for Frank Lloyd Wright's exemplary
Modernist innovations. For Mumford, Wright's architectural
compositions – especially the early buildings which explored
"the beauty of earth colors and natural finishes: the manifold

possibilities of glass ... the principles of horizontal composition" – would serve as aesthetic allegories of the potential for a Romantic reintegration of self and society.

Not unlike the Renaissance humanists who inspired him, Mumford reasons by analogy. His synoptic "Renewal of Life" series – *Technics and Civilization* (1934), *The Culture of Cities* (1938), *The Condition of Man* (1944), and *The Conduct of Life* (1951) – surveys the rise of the modern "megamachine" – the impersonal, bureaucratic structures of technological modernity characterized by "exactitude in measurement ... abstract mechanical system ... [and] compulsive regularity" – and the resulting diminution of the unpredictably vital elements in human life. Similarly, *The City in History* (1961) narrates the moral and cultural decline of the European city, praising the organic synthesis of medieval town planning and decrying the "enlightened" geometrical abstraction of the modern age: "There could be no sharper contrast between the two orders of thinking, the organic and the mechanical, than here: the first springs out of the total situation; the other simplifies the facts of life for the sake of an artful system of concepts, more dear to the mind than life itself." By allowing us to glimpse the workings of an exemplary mind unfettered by artful systems, Mumford's version of the post-Romantic Modernist essay rhetorically suggests an escape from the structures of instrumental reason that trap the individual in a "megamachine" of his own devising. Inductive, intuitive, and sweeping in scope, Mumford's often **treatise**-length essays contribute to that signal Modernist tradition we might call the mythology of secular redemption.

A profound sense of personal loss animates Mumford's **critical essays** and scholarly essays. In a typical passage, Mumford writes that "the city I once knew so intimately has been wrecked; most of what remains will soon vanish; and therewith scattered fragments of my own life will disappear in the rubble that is carted away." Gone was the "brownstone" New York of his childhood and with it disappeared the "diagrammatic neatness" of old New York's tightly-knit "small town" social fabric, aesthetic harmony, and "moral stability." New York is for Mumford both a proper subject for essayistic reflection and itself a living essay. In "Yesterday's City of Tomorrow" (1962), striking the plangent moral and epistemological pose familiar to the essay genre since its inception, Mumford notes with sorrow that "the freedom of movement, the change of pace, the choice of alternative destinations, the spontaneous encounters, the range of social choices ... in fact, the multifarious life of a city, have been traded away for expressway, parking space, and vertical circulation."

The lyrical, autobiographical quality that permeates Mumford's work suggests the debt his social criticism owes to the essay form itself. If the New York of Mumford's fondly remembered childhood presented itself as a spectacle "to gladden [his] eyes and beckon [his] legs to ramble" – the rhetoric of the urban *flâneur* familiar to the essay since **Addison** and **Steele** – contemporary city design encourages neither aesthetic reflection nor unrehearsed exploration. For Mumford, the uncritical celebration of technology culminating in the skyscraper, the empty architectural abstractions of Le Corbusier's Modernism, and the reliance on new forms of transportation such as the automobile to the exclusion of foot traffic, devalue individuals and local communities, who become

merely idiosyncratic obstacles for the architects and planners of the modern city. To the same degree that old New York inspired enriching aesthetic experiences and lyrical, essayistic responses with its sporadic rhythms and spontaneous encounters, the bureaucratically regimented cities of the future would produce only anomic despair. Further, with the Cold War expansion of the military industrial complex and the rise of a new "Pentagon of power" (the "financial, industrial, scientific, military, and educational experts"), and the dropping of the atomic bomb on Hiroshima threatening the possibility of global apocalypse, Mumford cautiously qualified his earlier hopes for a potentially humane deployment of technology as he saw the worst tendencies in the culture of modern "technics" magnified.

Despite the general disillusionment of his later work, however, Mumford continued until the final moments of his life to struggle against the pessimism of his own intellect: "The renewal of life is the great theme of our age, not the further dominance ... of the machine ... In short, we must take *things* into our own hands ... And in the end, proudly reversing Blake's dictum, we shall, I hope, be able to say: *Art elevated, imagination affirmed, peace governs the nations.*"

MATTHEW TITOLO

Biography
Born 19 October 1895 in New York City. Studied at the City College of New York, 1912–17; Columbia University, New York, 1915–16; New School for Social Research, New York, 1919. Served in the U.S. army, 1918–19. Assistant editor, *Fortnightly Dial*, 1919. Married Sophia Wittenberg, 1921: one son (killed in action during World War II) and one daughter. Taught at the New School for Social Research, 1925, Dartmouth College, Hanover, New Hampshire, 1929–35, Columbia University, 1931–35, Stanford University, California, 1942–44, North Carolina State University, Raleigh, 1948–52, University of Pennsylvania, Philadelphia, 1951–56 and 1959–61, Massachusetts Institute of Technology, Cambridge, 1957–61 and 1973–75, University of California, Berkeley, 1961–62, and Wesleyan University, Middletown, Connecticut, 1962–64. Contributing editor, the *New Republic*, 1927–40; architectural critic and columnist of "Sky Line," the *New Yorker*, 1931–63; also contributed to various other journals. Awards: many, including the National Book Award, for *The City in History*, 1962; Presidential Medal of Freedom, 1964; Emerson-Thoreau Medal, 1965; American Academy of Arts and Letters Gold Medal in Belles Lettres, 1971; Hodgkins Gold Medal, 1971; National Book Committee National Medal for Literature, 1972; Prix Mondial, 1976; honorary degrees from two universities. Died in Amenia, New York, 26 January 1990.

Selected Writings

Essays and Related Prose
Sticks and Stones: A Study of American Architecture and Civilization, 1924
The Golden Day: A Study of American Experience and Culture, 1926; as *The Golden Day: A Study in American Literature and Culture*, 1933
Herman Melville, 1929; revised edition, 1962
The Brown Decades: A Study of the Arts in America, 1865–1895, 1931
Technics and Civilization, 1934
The Culture of Cities, 1938
The South in Architecture, 1941
The Condition of Man, 1944
City Development: Studies in Disintegration and Renewal, 1945

*Values for Survival: Essays, Addresses, and Letters in Politics and
    Education*, 1946
The Conduct of Life, 1951
The Arts in Renewal, 1951
Art and Technics (lectures), 1952
The Human Prospect, edited by Harry T. Moore and Karl W.
    Deutsch, 1955
*From the Ground Up: Observations on Contemporary Architecture,
    Housing, Highway Building, and Civic Design*, 1956
The City in History, 1961
The Highway and the City, 1963
The Urban Prospect, 1968
*Interpretations and Forecasts, 1922–1972: Studies in Literature,
    Biography, Technics, and Contemporary Society*, 1973
*Architecture as a Home for Man: Essays for "Architectural
    Record"*, edited by Jeanne M. Davern, 1975
Findings and Keepings, 1914–1936, 1975
The Lewis Mumford Reader, edited by Donald L. Miller, 1986

Other writings: works on town planning, cities, and architecture.

Bibliography

Newman, Elmer S., *Lewis Mumford: A Bibliography, 1914–1970*,
    New York: Harcourt Brace Jovanovich, 1971

Further Reading

Blake, Casey Nelson, *Beloved Community: The Cultural Criticism of
    Randolph Bourne, Van Wyck Brooks, Waldo Frank and Lewis
    Mumford*, Chapel Hill: University of North Carolina Press, 1990
Carrithers, Gale H., Jr., *Mumford, Tate, Eiseley: Watchers in the
    Night*, Baton Rouge: Louisiana State University Press, 1991
Hughes, Thomas P., *American Genesis: A Century of Invention and
    Technological Enthusiasm, 1870–1970*, New York: Viking, 1989
Hughes, Thomas P., and Agatha C. Hughes, *Lewis Mumford: Public
    Intellectual*, New York: Oxford University Press, 1990
Miller, Donald L., *Lewis Mumford: A Life*, New York: Weidenfeld
    and Nicolson, 1989
Miller, Donald L., editor, *The Lewis Mumford Reader*, Athens:
    University of Georgia Press, 1995 (original edition, 1986)

Murdoch, Walter

Australian, 1874–1970

Successive reprints of collections under new titles testify to the popularity of Walter Murdoch's essays, which are regarded as models of relaxed, lucid writing in which insight and thought are brought to a great variety of accessible but not mundane topics. Among the best known of his first essays, published in 1891 in the Melbourne journal the *Australian Weekly*, are "The Worst Hundred Books" and "Thackeray and Meredith." In the former he combined critical insight with dry humor to encourage the general reader to look at literary texts with new interest; in the latter he took up his lifetime mission to make European literature a familiar possession of middle-class Australians who might not have had a university education. The essay was to Murdoch in the nature of vocation; he wrote in the essay "On Doors": "I am one who believes that the essay, if not the highest form of literature, is the most difficult of all; that a good essay is harder to write than a good novel; that the great essayists are rarer than the great poets; that we are likely to see another Shakespeare sooner than another Montaigne."

Murdoch's style changed very little over the years, remaining witty, wry, and unselfconsciously urbane, and displaying on occasions a wonderful aptitude for parody. Aware that his early writing in newspapers and journals from the 1890s might look "dowdy and old-fashioned," he nevertheless retained in all his work the same liberal, critical, and often skeptical stance based on a respect for broad humanist principles and essentially British values. Tempered by a shrewd wit that appealed to the educated Australian reader, Murdoch's essays reflected a transitional stage in Australian intellectual life from a conscious appeal to English ideas and tastes to a more confident Australian outlook. Murdoch's apparent failure to appreciate the directions and achievement perceptible in Australian writing from the 1930s led to criticism from some younger academics. Yet Murdoch espoused originality and "Australianism," and looked kindly on the Jindyworobak poets who sought to replace the dependence of Australian poetry on European models with closer ties to Australian landscape and Aboriginal culture. As a critic of contemporary Australian writing, Murdoch said little of permanent interest, but his respect for reasoned ideas and the language in which they are expressed remain relevant.

The critic A. A. Phillips (*Meanjin*, 1969) saw Murdoch as a master of "the art of good-humored devastation." Whether his subject was literary or related more generally to middle-class culture, he defended the habit of sober questioning and seeing things steadily and in perspective. His ability to steer a commonsense middle course in intellectual and moral questions should not be seen as mediocrity, a state which his writing and radio broadcasts persistently attacked. His attitude is summed up in the motto he wrote for himself: "Amid a world of sceptred sham/ Be this my humble aim, at least;/ To seem the sort of beast I am/ And not some other sort of beast."

Murdoch's conversational, intimate engagement with the reader has been compared to that of **Charles Lamb** and usually renders palatable his tendency to unpretentious moralizing and admonishing. His best-known essays include "A Question Settled" (1931), "The Book and the Island" (1934), "The Pink Man's Burden" (1936), and "The Art of Controversy" (1931). Murdoch's essay "The Enemies of Literature" (1907), delivered as a presidential address to the Melbourne Literature Society, drew from the poet Bernard O'Dowd his famous credo, "Poetry Militant."

Murdoch's conservatism, however, was so mild that he seldom aroused controversy, and in "The Pink Man's Burden" he describes the class who believes that there are two sides to every question and "to which I have the misfortune to belong; the mild people, the moderate people, whose colour is about half-way between the stainless white of the Tory and the vivid and flaming red of the Revolutionary; the pink people, in short." Refusing to promulgate any point of view other than that there are many, Murdoch gave few answers but encouraged readers both to question and to find their own answers. When the questions raised in his essays touched on religion, Murdoch often found himself attacked by professional theologians, but his infinite courtesy in reply disarmed hostility. His essays are cultured but not cultivated, and learned without being academic. His writing is never anti-intellectual but implicitly and explicitly expresses faith in common sense and in the ability of average people to arrive at sound and hard decisions should they apply themselves to big questions.

Murdoch's essays often drew on European literature and culture, but were recognized as expressions of Australian intellectual and social ideals. As the writer and critic Mary Durack wrote in 1969, Murdoch's essays were part of "his fight for the use of clear and precise language, for the development of informed opinion, for tolerance and consideration towards his fellow men, and for the right of the individual to be himself within the framework of his own personality."

ELIZABETH PERKINS

Biography

Walter Logie Forbes Murdoch. Uncle of the press baron Sir Keith Murdoch; great-uncle of the media tycoon Rupert Murdoch. Born 17 September 1874 in Pitsligo, Aberdeenshire, Scotland. Came to Australia at age ten. Studied logic and philosophy, University of Melbourne, B.A., 1895; M.A., 1897. Earliest essays appeared, under pseudonyms including Diogenes, Nick O'Teen, and Elzevir, in the *Australian Weekly* and the *Argus* and other journals and newspapers, from 1891. Tutor near Beaufort, Victoria, 1895; taught at Hamilton Academy, Victoria, 1896, and Warrnambool College, Victoria, 1901–03. Married Violet Catherine Hughston, 1897. Lecturer in English, University of Melbourne, from 1904. Founding editor, *Trident*, 1907–09. Foundation Chair of English, 1912–39, and chancellor, 1943–48, University of Western Australia. Companion, Order of British Empire (CBE), 1939. Knighted, 1964. Second university in Western Australia named after him. Died in South Perth, 30 July 1970.

Selected Writings

Essays and Related Prose
Loose Leaves, 1910
Speaking Personally, 1930
Saturday Mornings, 1931
Moreover, 1932
The Wild Planet, 1934
The Two Laughters, 1934
Lucid Intervals, 1936
Collected Essays, 1938
The Spur of the Moment, 1939
Steadfast: A Commentary, 1941
Selections, 1941
72 Essays: A Selection, 1947
Answers, 1953; as *My 100 Answers*, 1960
Selected Essays, 1956
Walter Murdoch and Alfred Deakin on Books and Men: Letters and Comments, 1900–1918, edited by John A. La Nauze and Elizabeth Nurser, 1974

Other writings: the collection of poetry *Anne's Animals* (1921), the history *The Struggle for Freedom* (1903), and a biography of Alfred Deakin (1923). Also edited *The Oxford Book of Australasian Verse* (1918).

Bibliographies
Crag, G., "A Walter Murdoch Bibliography," *Meanjin* 9, no. 1 (1950)
Hergenhan, Laurie, and Martin Duwell, editors, *The ALS Guide to Australian Writers: A Bibliography, 1963–1990*, St. Lucia: University of Queensland Press, 1992

Further Reading
Durack, Mary, "Walter Murdoch: The Man in the Mirror," *Meanjin* (1969)
Green, H. M., *A History of Australian Literature*, revised by Dorothy Green, Sydney: Angus and Robertson, 2 vols., 1984
La Nauze, John A., *Walter Murdoch: A Biographical Memoir*, Carlton: Melbourne University Press, 1977

Musil, Robert
Austrian, 1880–1942

Robert Musil published many essays during his lifetime in which he dealt with contemporary issues concerning the visual arts, sciences, politics, religion, theater, motion pictures, literature, social and economic conditions of women, nationalism, and empiricism. He was also highly active as a theater and art critic, as his large output of **reviews** demonstrates. As a trained physicist and engineer, Musil dealt with a wide range of human issues by combining analytical with inspirational and mystical thinking, and thus challenged his contemporaries with radically different views about life. As an essayist Musil established himself as a central figure of European intellectual discourse, although with the rise of National Socialism and the barbarous culture of Nazi Germany in the 1930s and 1940s he was increasingly marginalized, and died, almost forgotten, at the height of World War II.

In his famous fragmentary novel *Der Mann ohne Eigenschaften* (1930–43; *The Man Without Qualities*) Musil explicitly outlines the meaning of the essay for the future of Western culture at large: the essay facilitates the study of any object from many different angles, without necessarily discussing it to its full extent; otherwise the object would be reduced to a label and thus lose its individual contours. Relativity plays a major role in Musil's thinking: a murderer, for example, could be either considered as such and tried by the courts, or seen as a national hero and celebrated. In Musil's eyes every human being is given an infinite number of possibilities for his or her life and can pursue a plurality of connections with other people and objects. The "unwritten poem" serves as a metaphor for the powerful impact of emotions, intuitions, and sensations on reality. Morality is a matter of definition and social circumstances, not an absolute value. Modern sciences (particularly psychology) indicate, as Musil emphasizes, the breaking up of traditional values, injecting into them a plethora of new meanings. The essayist is not a philosopher in the narrow sense of the word, but explores through narrative alternatives the framework and conditions of life.

As Musil suggests, the modern world has lost its sense of logic and order; only the essay can capture the essential thoughts and ideas in the inner life of a human being and give expression to the chaotic conditions of existence. Essayists assume a position between religion and science, between a poem and an intellectual argument, and between scholarship and literature. The essayist does not strive for truth as such, nor does he create fiction, but rather searches for a conviction and for the potentiality of his own being.

In *The Man Without Qualities* the crucial realization of what life's meaning might be occurs shortly before Book Two when Ulrich learns that his father has died. According to the narrator the modern world has lost the sense for the epic and its narrative continuum, whereas the lyric offers nothing but an illusionary refuge. Life can no longer be represented by either literary genre, instead appearing as a dimension of endless and forever intertwining threads, which form the basic elements of the essay.

Not surprisingly, Musil never managed to complete *The Man Without Qualities*, and exhausted himself in trying without much success to pull together the whole work, a huge collection of essays in itself. Musil's tragic error lay in not seeing that his expressly stated goal to conquer the world by "force of mind and spirit" was in stark contradiction to the idea of the essay as the primary foundation of the literary treatment of reality. Novelistic narration is still a major force in Musil's masterpiece, but both **aphorisms** and essayistic passages increasingly replace the traditional reliance on fictional elements. Its title indicates the extent to which the author has understood that the modern world can no longer be represented in illusionary fiction, but finds its appropriate expression in the paradox of the man without qualities.

Musil's farsightedness and modernity is documented not only in his essayistic novel, but also in his large number of essays. In fact, through his essays, which he had hoped to publish in a collection in 1926, he searches for the new man and a new society that will rise in the wake of the technological and scientific revolution in the first half of the 20th century. Musil had written only two technical articles and his doctoral dissertation on Ernst Mach when he joined the public debate about the relationship between sickness and art with the essay "Das Unanständige und Kranke in der Kunst" (1911; "The Obscene and Pathological in Art"). Here he takes the side of those people suppressed and persecuted by the authorities, particularly because his moral and intellectual relativism opened his eyes to alternative views.

Because of his thorough training as a scientist, his critical writing is strongly influenced by scientific discourse and pure rationality. In his essay "Das Geistliche, der Modernismus und die Metaphysis" (1912; "The Religious Spirit, Modernism, and Metaphysics") Musil argues that modernity was simply the result of injecting religion with bourgeois reason, of discarding emotions, and of ignoring rationality as the prime goal of the modern world. He laments the loss of the soul which may be the corresponding element to *ratio*, and recommends exploring the spiritual life with the same tools scientists use to study the objective world.

Musil also examined the political structure and culture of the Austrian Empire with its artificially sustained aristocratic system and idealization of the monarchy. In his postwar essay "Buridans Österreicher" (1919; "Buridan's Austria") Musil observes Austria's longstanding dilemma between forming a federation of nations in the Danube region (Balkan) or joining the German Reich. He maintains satirically that Austria was populated by 50 million intellectuals and 1000 working-class people, whereas the ratio was the opposite in Germany. In this and other essays he formulates many ideas which later were incorporated in *The Man Without Qualities*. The same applies to his studies on morality, pathology, mathematics, metaphysics, nationalism, poetry, and sciences.

The outstanding feature of all of Musil's essays is their analytic precision and high level of rational penetration into a problem, be it the church, the state, modern literature, or a combination of any of these elements. Musil's literary works

such as his narratives (*Die Verwirrungen des Zöglings Törless* [1906; *Young Törless*], *Drei Frauen* [1924; Three women, translated as *Five Women*], *Nachlass zu Lebzeiten* [1936; *Posthumous Papers of a Living Author*]) and his dramatic texts (*Die Schwärmer* [1921; *The Enthusiasts*] and *Vinzenz und die Freundin bedeutender Männer* [1924; Vinzenz and the girlfriend of important men]) strongly reflect the essayist and mathematician in the writer who also attempts to understand the human soul, mystical experiences, love, and other areas of the irrational mind. Musil coined the phrases "ratioid" and "nicht-ratioid" for the opposition between these two dimensions of human epistemology. Consequently he also investigated the differences between "civilization" and "culture," between nation and individual. But his main interest as an essayist was to discuss the course of world history, the future development of humankind, the revolution of science and morality, and the essence of history.

Musil's style is that of both scientist and moralist. He despised the glorification of feelings without studying them with the rational eye of a mathematician. Hence he opted for the essay as the most important literary form in the 20th century because in it he could combine science and mysticism, or rationality and emotions. Whereas physics and the other natural sciences had forged ahead of their time, neither morality nor ethics, neither aesthetics nor spirituality had kept up with the transitions of the early 20th century. With his essays Musil attempted to inject the moral world with the same investigative and analytical tools as were employed in laboratories ("Politische Bekenntnisse eines jungen Mannes" [1913; Political confessions of a young man]). Whereas science had made the development of the modern world possible, the arts and literature had not progressed and were in strong need of reform. The essay, as a genre, was for Musil one feasible avenue toward this goal.

Simultaneously Musil was very interested in modern art forms and art media, as his essays on film ("Ansätze zu einer neuen Ästhetik" [1925; "Toward a New Aesthetic"]), on the relationship between literature and psychology, and on individual avant-garde poets ("Zu Kerrs 60. Geburtstag" [1927; On Kerr's 60th birthday]) indicate. He also treated the various literary genres, stylistic features, and themes in his essays, examined the situation of women in modern society ("Die Frau gestern und morgen" [1929; "Women Yesterday and Tomorrow"]), but always searched for a combination of natural science (mathematics) with the world of emotions, or, put differently, scientific analysis with the essay.

Although Musil never gained broad acceptance as an essayist and social and ethical philosopher, his critical writing represents the avant-garde of modern literature and still awaits public recognition.

ALBRECHT CLASSEN

Biography

Robert Edler von Musil. Born 6 November 1880 in Klagenfurt, Austria. Studied engineering at the Technische Hochschule, Brno, 1898–1901; military service, 1901–02; assistant researcher at the Technische Hochschule, Stuttgart, 1902–03; studied philosophy, psychology, and mathematics at the University of Berlin, 1903–05, Ph.D., 1908. Contributor to various journals and newspapers throughout his life. Married Martha Marcovaldi, 1911. Librarian,

Technische Hochschule, Vienna, 1911–14; editor, **Die neue Rundschau** (The new review), Berlin, 1914. Captain in the Austrian army, 1914–16: hospitalized, 1916, and editor of army newspaper, 1916–18. Head of the education office, 1918–19, and consultant, 1920–22, Defense Ministry; worked in the press section of the Office of Foreign Affairs, Vienna, 1919–20. Lived in Berlin, 1931–33, Vienna, 1933–38, and Zurich and Geneva, 1938–42. Awards: Kleist Prize, 1923; City of Vienna Prize, 1924. Died (of a stroke) in Geneva, 15 April 1942.

Selected Writings

Essays and Related Prose

Der Mann ohne Eigenschaften (novel), 3 vols., 1930–43; as *The Man Without Qualities*, translated by Ernst Kaiser and Eithne Wilkins, 3 vols., 1953–60, and Sophie Wilkins, 2 vols., 1995
Tagebücher, Aphorismen, Essays und Reden (vol. 2 of *Gesammelte Werke*), edited by Adolf Frisé, 1955
Das hilflose Europa: Drei Essays, 1961
Theater: Kritisches und Theoretisches, edited by Marie-Louise Roth, 1965
Selected Writings, edited by Burton Pike, 1986
Precision and Soul: Essays and Addresses, edited and translated by Burton Pike and David S. Luft, 1990
Kleine Prosa, Aphorismen, Autobiographisches; Essays und Reden, Kritik (part of *Gesammelte Werke*), edited by Adolf Frisé, 1978
Der literarische Nachlass (CD-Rom), edited by Friedbert Aspetsberger, Karl Eibl, and Adolf Frisé, 1992

Other writings: another novel (*Die Verwirrung des Zöglings Törless* [*Young Törless*], 1906), short stories (including *Nachlass zu Lebzeiten* [*Posthumous Papers of a Living Author*], 1936), novellas, two plays, and correspondence.

Collected works edition: *Gesammelte Werke*, edited by Adolf Frisé, 3 vols., 1952–57, revised edition, 2 vols., 1978.

Bibliographies

Arntzen, Helmut, *Musil-Kommentar sämtlicher zu Lebzeiten erschienener Schriften ausser dem Roman "Der Mann ohne Eigenschaften"*, Munich: Winkler, 1980: 279–310
Arntzen, Helmut, *Musil-Kommentar zum Roman "Der Mann ohne Eigenschaften"*, Munich: Winkler, 1982: 450–80
King, Lynda J., "Robert Musil Bibliography 1976/1977," *Musil-Forum* 4 (1978): 104–16
Mae, Michiko, "Robert-Musil-Bibliographie 1977–1980," *Musil-Forum* 6 (1980): 239–58
Mae, Michiko, "Robert Musil-Bibliographie: Ergänzungsbibliographie 1980–1983," *Musil-Forum* 9 (1983): 183–220
Rogowski, Christian, *Distinguished Outsider: Robert Musil and His Critics*, Columbia, South Carolina: Camden House, 1994
Thöming, Jürgen C., *Robert-Musil-Bibliographie*, Bad Homburg: Gehlen, 1968

Further Reading

Arntzen, Helmut, *Satirischer Stil: Zur Satire Robert Musils im "Mann ohne Eigenschaften"*, Bonn: Bouvier, 1970 (original edition, 1960)
Corino, Karl, *Robert Musil: Leben und Werk in Bildern und Texten*, Reinbek: Rowohlt, 1988
Dinklage, Karl, Elisabeth Albertson, and Karl Corino, editors, *Robert Musil: Studien zu seinem Werk*, Reinbek: Rowohlt, 1970
Harrison, Thomas, *Essayism: Conrad, Musil, and Pirandello*, Baltimore: Johns Hopkins University Press, 1992
Hickman, Hannah, editor, *Robert Musil and the Literary Landscape of His Time*, Salford, Lancashire: University of Salford Department of Modern Languages, 1991
Hochstätter, Dietrich, *Sprache des Möglichen: Stilistischer Perspektivismus in Robert Musils "Der Mann ohne Eigenschaften"*, Frankfurt-on-Main: Athenäum, 1972
Kaiser, Gerhard R., *Proust, Musil, Joyce: Zum Verhältnis von Literatur und Gesellschaft am Paradigma des Zitats*, Frankfurt-on-Main: Athenäum, 1972
Luft, David S., *Robert Musil and the Crisis of European Culture, 1880–1942*, Berkeley: University of California Press, 1980
Payne, Philip, *Robert Musil's "The Man Without Qualities": A Critical Study*, Cambridge and New York: Cambridge University Press, 1988
Pfeiffer, Peter C., *Aphorismus und Romanstruktur: Zu Robert Musils "Der Mann ohne Eigenschaften"*, Bonn: Bouvier, 1990
Renier-Servranckx, Annie, *Robert Musil*, Bonn: Bouvier, 1972
Roth, Marie-Louise, *Robert Musil: Ethik und Ästhetik*, Munich: List, 1972
Venturelli, Aldo, "Die Kunst als fröhliche Wissenschaft: Zum Verhältnis Musils zu Nietzsche," *Nietzsche-Studien* 9 (1980): 302–37
Willemsen, Roger, *Robert Musil: Vom intellektuellen Eros*, Munich: Piper, 1985

Mutafov, Chavdar

Bulgarian, 1899–1954

Chavdar Mutafov is the first Bulgarian writer to conceptualize how 20th-century spirituality was transformed by the mechanization of human life. His vision of the new epoch in the development of European civilization is ambiguous, however. In his essays and public lectures on fine arts and dance and on the new-born arts of cinema, poster design, and caricature, he appreciates the economic plenitude and the inevitable changes imposed on European culture by mass production. At the same time, Mutafov's works of fiction suggest that he was very aware that this new phenomenon would have dangerous side effects on humanity.

Mutafov's pioneer position as an advocate of Modernism in interwar Bulgaria resulted to a great extent from the circumstances of his life. During his studies in Munich (engineering 1908–14, and architecture 1923–25) he was fascinated with the avant-garde. Afterwards, in Bulgaria, he combined his work as a professional architect and writer with a genuine and enduring interest in the implications of the impetuous development of technology.

Mutafov considered promoting avant-garde ideas among Bulgarian intellectuals and a mass audience as an important cultural mission. The numerous talks on modern art, cinema, music, and industrial design that he gave throughout the country honed his expositional skills for his essays (published mainly in the popular interwar Bulgarian literary-cultural monthly *Zlatorog* [Goldenhorn]). Mutafov realized that, if his essays were to be read by a general audience, they had first and foremost to inform, and to persuade not by means of mere rhetoric, but by objective representation and analysis of factual data. Thus he usually begins by locating the topic in its natural Western European environment, and only then proceeds to discuss its Bulgarian analogues. "Peizazhut i nashite khudozhnitsi" (1920; Landscape painting and our painters) is schematically typical: Mutafov starts with general statements on the relation between the world of art and the real world, goes on to reflect on the function of the soul as a mediator between the two worlds, and finally presents the cultural phenomenon – landscape painting – as an expression of man's philosophical relation to existence, a kind of "metaphysics of art." Only after this setting is completed does he portray a few then popular Bulgarian painters and inquires into Bulgarian Modernist art as an organic part of European Modernism.

"Peizazhut i nashite khudozhnitsi" is also representative of Mutafov's holistic approach to whatever phenomenon of culture he analyzes, but "Liniiata v izobrazitelnoto izkustvo" (1920; Line in visual art) and "Plakatut" (1921; Poster) are exemplary in this respect. These essays are concerned with the phenomena Bulgarians were to become aware of much later. The former presents a brief history of visual art through the development of the symbolism of line; the latter is devoted to the idiosyncrasy of the perception of the poster as a kind of decorative art, a combination of the banal and the artful which becomes possible only in an urban environment. In both cases Mutafov is concerned with the unique new features of the objects under scrutiny, analyzing them comprehensively. Both essays reveal a writer who has mastered succinctness to perfection.

Compared to that of other Bulgarian essay writers, Mutafov's style seems strikingly objective and condensed, sometimes even elliptical, and by the same token dry and alien to the Bulgarian rhetorical tradition. Perhaps the only exception is his essay "Zeleniiat kon" (1920; The green horse), a passionate manifesto and defense of expressionism and of what Kandinskii calls "inner necessity" in art.

During the 1920s Mutafov was one of the most interesting and ambiguous figures in Bulgarian cultural life. Although not always appreciated by his audience, which was in principle suspicious of the "anti-realistic" Western fashions, Mutafov managed to popularize his "ultramodern absurdities and eccentricities," as his all-encompassing vision of the modern times was called by some homespun critics (*Hiperion*, 1928). Mutafov's works of fiction – expressionistic short stories, grotesques, and "impressions," and the "decorative novel" *Diletant* (1926; Dilettante) – greatly complicate this vision. They testify to his awareness of the dehumanizing side of mass production and disclose the limitations of Modernism in its search for entirely new artistic expression; consequently, they were even less understood by the public.

Mutafov might have been a leading figure among Bulgarian expressionists were it not for their central concern with social issues, which interested Mutafov only through the prism of the ultimate existential questions. Despite his pro-Western orientation, he did not become a leader of the pro-Western trend in Bulgarian cultural life either. While adherents of the West stated that Romantic subjectivism should set the vectors for the Europeanization of Bulgarian literature and art, Mutafov

was convinced that the time for the objectification of the self had come. He remained a "dangerously premature pioneer in a sleepy culture," as Dimitur Avramov summarized Mutafov's position in Bulgarian intellectual life ("Podraniliiat modernist" [1972; The premature Modernist]).

Under communism the ideology of "socialist realism," the only officially permitted critical approach, excluded Mutafov, along with other "ideologically incorrect writers," from the group of published authors, as well as from the surveys and textbooks on Bulgarian literature and art. In fact, Mutafov was the only Bulgarian writer to be officially designated as an author with a fascist orientation (*Rechnik na Bulgarskata literatura* [1970; Dictionary of Bulgarian literature]), without any supporting evidence. In the 1990s the interest in Mutafov's output has grown, and in 1993 a selection of his essays was published for the first time.

Even without taking into consideration Mutafov's courage to publicize ideas from the urbane culture of Western Europe in a basically agrarian Bulgaria, his vision of modern spirituality impresses us with its integrity and potential. Mutafov realized that no matter how backward his native country was after World War I, its culture could not remain unaffected by the birth of technological civilization in Western Europe. In this respect he clearly differed from both those who maintained the idea of "unique native art" (*rodno izkustvo*) and those who believed that Bulgarian culture should be open only to the classical models of Western literature and art.

KATIA MITOVA-JANOWSKI

Biography
Born 19 September 1899 in Sevlievo. Studied civil engineering, 1908–14, and architecture, 1923–25, in Munich. Worked as a professional architect. Contributor to various journals, including *Vezni* (Libra), *Zlatorog*, and *Demokraticheski pregled* (Democratic review). Associated with the pro-West group Strelets (Archer), which included Konstantin Gulabov, Atanas Dalchev, Ivan Mirchev, and other poets and artists: editor of its journals *Iztok* (East) and *Strelets*. Married Fani Popova-Mutafova. Under communism, unpublished and subject to censorship. Died in Sofia, 10 March 1954.

Selected Writings

Essays
Izbrano, 1993

Other writings: the novel *Diletant* (1926), short stories, and grotesques.

Further Reading
Avramov, Dimitur, "Podraniliiat modernist" and "Buntât na ekspresionizma," in his *Dialog mezhdu dve izkustva*, Sofia: Bulgarski Pisatel, 1993

N

Nashe, Thomas

English, 1567–1601

There is general consent about the qualities of Nashe's prose: one of the most original Elizabethan writers, he is a master of **satire** and polemic, capable of immense energy, invention, and reckless subversion. As an essayist he has perhaps been overshadowed by **Francis Bacon** and assigned the generically vague title of "pamphleteer." However, Nashe is an essayist in the etymological sense of the word: he *attempts* an argument or persuasive encounter with his readers. Above all his contribution to the essay is coextensive with his humanistic commitment to rhetoric as performance. The meaning of his work is to be found not in sober epigrams or sententiae but in the movement and vitality of the prose, in the display of his compositional skill.

Like his fellow University Wits Nashe generally wrote for a commercial market, demonstrating an unerring ability to combine a talent to entertain with an eye for fashion. In doing this his tone varies from scatological wit to moral censure. From his earliest work he betrays a debt to the complaint tradition of William Langland and John Skelton, but differs from contemporary moralists such as Philip Stubbes and Stephen Gosson by embracing the excesses of linguistic and literary invention. Robert Greene bestowed him with the title "young Juvenall" and Nashe himself declared that "of all the stiles I most affect and strive to imitate Aretines," a reference to the scandalous satire of Aretino, whose work was translated in the 1580s.

In *The Anatomy of Absurdity* (1589), he adopts a euphuistic style, but in later work he establishes a more distinctive literary texture. The turning point came when he was commissioned to provide a counterblast to the popular but subversive Marprelate **pamphlets**. In *An Almond for a Parrot* (1590) he found his *métier*, the controversial essay-pamphlet in which he could range freely and scurrilously through numerous topics, deploying his exuberant invention to the fullest. From this point onward his literary career was dominated by verbal skirmishing. Nashe appropriated Marprelate's "extemporall vein," his tactics of savage invective, direct address to the reader, the juxtaposition of serious arguments with anecdote, swift colloquial banter, moral fable, and gross hyperbole; he personalized this with learned allusions, a knowledge of popular ballads and prophecies as well as journalistic curiosity.

The great flyting with Gabriel Harvey, an argument inherited from Greene, allowed Nashe to deflate a living version of one of the types he wrote against elsewhere. Harvey, who practiced a well-known and hyperbolically overbearing conceit, was also an advocate of Ramist logic and occultism. Nashe attacked each of these positions in *Strange News* (1592) and *Have with You to Saffron-Walden* (1596). While Harvey wrote with a florid academicism espousing elegance and decorum, Nashe was forever his guttersnipe rival, adopting a low style replete with comic neologisms to counter Harvey's intellectual "inkhorn terms." Confident in his skills, Nashe uses the essay form as an arena for the settling of scores, transporting his readers through diversions of literary allusion, direct insult, and amplifications of gratuitous vulgarity. These are evident in his mock biography of Harvey and his warning that if he "take[s] truth's part . . . I will prove truth to be no truth, marching out of thy dung-voiding mouth." When Harvey complains that Nashe insulted his father's occupation of rope maker, Nashe replies that if he were so attacked he would "have proved it by syllogistry to be one of the seven liberal sciences." As ever, Nashe's concern is rhetorical power and the plenitude of wit.

In *Pierce Penilesse* (1592), an improvisatory and comical complaint to the Devil, Nashe considers the vices of his time, mixing an admonitory vision of the seven deadly sins with a defense of the theater and satires on foreigners and the fashions of Londoners. The text is composed of an agitated profusion of images which relentlessly generate effects of movement and are never allowed to settle into tonal rigidity. There is little time for the establishment of a consistent viewpoint; for example, although the description of Dame Niggardize begins in the manner of a homiletic admonition, this is soon lost in a welter of specific detail, making it impossible to define the figure so simply.

Such rhetorical indulgence is exemplified in his masterpiece, *Lenten Stuffe* (1599), an extended *tour de force* which takes the form of a rhapsodic mock encomium celebrating the town of Yarmouth and its staple product, the red herring or kipper. Commencing with a history of Yarmouth, blending contemporary observation with antiquarian detail, he moves on to a celebration of this humble fish, wresting it to the center of almost every conceivable enterprise. Extemporizing a series of anecdotes, including a comic rendition of *Hero and Leander*, Nashe elevates the kipper to heroic heights; demonstrating how it miraculously sustains the thriving population of Yarmouth in the midst of a barren environment, he presents it as a source of wealth, beauty, and adventure exceeding that of Helen since it "draweth more barques to Yarmouth Bay than her beauty did to Troy." The ostensible theme of this comic masterpiece, the red herring, is what it figuratively suggests: a false trail. Insofar as it has a motivation, *Lenten Stuffe* affirms the power of invention to elicit vitality and profusion from a world of scarcity and poverty.

In other works Nashe reveals darker compulsions. His discourse on apparitions, *The Terrors of the Night* (1594), commences with rationalistic refutations of occultist views: ". . . there are no true apparitions," he argues. However, it soon lapses into fragmentary and doom-laden **meditations** on dreams and spirits. Nashe is also drawn to the corruptions of Elizabethan London in *Christ's Tears over Jerusalem* (1593) where he "disinherites" his wit and presents a morbid and obsessive meditation on apocalypse, fixated on the question, "What has immortalitie to do with this muck?" This catalogue of almost pathological descriptions of monstrous births, tortured criminals, plagues, and famines lacks Nashe's characteristic exuberance, but what remains is a compositional method based on analogy, since the images of the agonized body form a correlative to spiritual deformity. Although Nashe shortly returned to his verbal brawl with Harvey, this sense of decay and corruption is never entirely absent from his writing.

Nashe's scatalogical moralism and rhetorical prowess are clearly at odds with the Baconian plain style and the conception of the essay that were to dominate the 17th century. In his capacity to wander constructively and entertainingly Nashe suggests **Montaigne**'s description of the essay as a "bundling up of so many different things." Although original and powerful, Nashe's influence on the essay is difficult to assess. Changes in taste combined with the ban imposed on printed satire in 1599 (following official disquiet over Nashe and Harvey's quarrel) meant that the qualities of Nashe's writing could not easily be reproduced. The virtues of his prose were inherited instead by the dramatists. The energy and invention of many theatrical characters, including Shakespeare's saturnalian Falstaff, bear more than a passing resemblance to the spirit of Tom Nashe.

DARRELL HINCHLIFFE

Biography
Born in 1567 in Lowestoft, Suffolk. Moved to Harling, Norfolk, 1573. Studied at St. John's College, Cambridge, 1582–88, B.A., 1586. Arrived in London, 1588, and became involved with a group of writers known as the University Wits, including Thomas Lodge, John Lyly, Thomas Watson, George Peele, Matthew Roydon, and Robert Greene; Greene appointed Nashe to write the **preface** for his *Menaphon*, 1589. Employed, along with other writers, by Archbishop Whitgift as a paid government propagandist to write retorts to the subversive but popular Puritan satirical *Martin Marprelate* tracts, 1589. Engaged in a continuing dispute with Richard and Gabriel Harvey, 1590s: suppressed by Archbishop Whitgift as part of his blanket ban on satire, 1599. Used a succession of patrons, including Lord Strange, Archbishop Whitgift, Robert Cotton, and Sir George Carey. Lived on the Isle of Wight to escape counter-attacks on his satirical writing, 1592/93–94; forced to flee London because of the satire *The Isle of Dogs*, written with Ben Jonson, 1597; returned to London by early 1599. Died in 1601.

Selected Writings

Essays and Related Prose
(Many anti-Marprelate writings were once attributed to Nashe, but authorship no longer certain)

Preface to *Menaphon* by Robert Greene, 1589
The Anatomy of Absurdity, 1589
An Almond for a Parrot, 1590; edited by J. Petheram, 1846
"Somewhat to Reade from Them That List," Preface to *Astrophel and Stella* by Sir Philip Sidney, 1591
Strange News, 1592; facsimile reprint, 1969
Pierce Penilesse, His Supplication to the Devil, 1592; facsimile reprint, 1969; edited by J. Payne Collier, 1842, reprinted 1966, and G. B. Harrison, 1966
Christ's Tears over Jerusalem, 1593; facsimile reprint, 1970
The Terrors of the Night; or, A Discourse of Apparitions, 1594
Have with You to Saffron-Walden, 1596; facsimile reprint, 1971; edited by J. P. Collier, 1870
Lenten Stuffe, 1599; facsimile reprint, 1971
Selected Writings, edited by Stanley Wells, 1964
The Unfortunate Traveller and Other Works, edited by J. B. Steane, 1972

Other writings: the fiction work *The Unfortunate Traveller* (1594), the poem "A Choice of Valentines," and the plays *Summer's Last Will and Testament* (1592), *Dido, Queene of Carthage*, with Christopher Marlowe (1594), and *The Isle of Dogs*, with Ben Jonson (1597).

Collected works edition: *Works*, edited by Ronald B. McKerrow, 5 vols., 1904–10, revised edition, edited by F. P. Wilson, 5 vols., 1958.

Bibliographies
Johnson, R. C., "Thomas Nashe 1941–1965," in *Elizabethan Bibliographies Supplements* 5, edited by Charles A. Pennel, London: Nether Press, 1968
Tannenbaum, Samuel A., *Thomas Nashe: A Concise Bibliography*, New York: Scholars' Facsimiles and Reprints, 1941

Further Reading
Anselment, Raymond A., *"Betwixt Jest and Earnest": Marprelate, Marvell, Swift and the Decorum of Religious Ridicule*, Toronto: University of Toronto Press, 1979
Barber, C. L., "The May-Games of Martin Marprelate," in his *Shakespeare's Festive Comedy*, Princeton, New Jersey: Princeton University Press, 1972 (original edition, 1959)
Crewe, Jonathan, *Unredeemed Rhetoric: Thomas Nashe and the Scandal of Authorship*, Baltimore: Johns Hopkins University Press, 1982
Hibbard, G. R., *Thomas Nashe: A Critical Introduction*, Cambridge, Massachusetts: Harvard University Press, and London: Routledge and Kegan Paul, 1962
Hutson, Linda, *Thomas Nashe in Context*, Oxford: Clarendon Press, and New York: Oxford University Press, 1989
Lewis, C. S., *English Literature in the Sixteenth Century, Excluding Drama*, Oxford: Oxford University Press, 1973: 410–16 (original edition, 1954)
McGinn, Donald J., "Nashe's Share in the Marprelate Controversy," *PMLA* 59 (1944): 952–84
McGinn, Donald J., "The Allegory of the 'Beare' and the 'Foxe' in Nashe's *Pierce Penilesse*," *PMLA* 61 (1946): 431–53
McGinn, Donald J., "A Quip from Thomas Nashe," in *Studies in the English Renaissance Drama*, edited by Josephine Bennet, Oscar Cargill, and Vernon Hall, London: Peter Owen and Vision Press, and New York: New York University Press, 1959: 172–88
Mackerness, E. D., "*Christ's Teares* and the Literature of Warning," *English Studies* 33 (1952): 251–54
McPherson, David C., "Aretino and the Harvey-Nashe Quarrel," *PMLA* 84 (1969): 1551–58
Nicholl, Charles, *A Cup of News: The Life of Thomas Nashe*, London and Boston: Routledge and Kegan Paul, 1984
Perkins, David, "Issues and Motivations in the Harvey-Nashe Quarrel," *Philological Quarterly* 39 (1960): 224–30

Rhodes, Neil, *Elizabethan Grotesque*, London and Boston: Routledge and Kegan Paul, 1980

Salyer, Sandford M., "Hall's Satires and the Harvey-Nashe Controversy," *Studies in Philology* 25 (1928): 149–70

Schafer, Jurgen, *Documentation in the O.E.D.: Shakespeare and Nashe as Test Cases*, Oxford: Clarendon Press, and New York: Oxford University Press, 1980

Steane, J. B., Introduction to *The Unfortunate Traveller and Other Works* by Nashe, edited by Steane, Harmondsworth: Penguin, 1972

Summersgill, Travis L., "The Influence of the Marprelate Controversy upon the Style of Thomas Nashe," *Studies in Philology* 48 (1951): 145–60

Thomas, Sidney, "New Light on the Nashe-Harvey Quarrel," *Modern Language Notes* 68 (1948): 481–83

Nature Essay

The nature essay is a heterogeneous form that draws on travel narrative, philosophy, landscape description, environmental reporting, outdoor and recreational writing, natural and local history, autobiography and diary, prose fiction, and other genres. Strict boundaries cannot be drawn around the nature essay, which undergoes constant metamorphosis as it migrates through various historical and cultural contexts. The form's aesthetic and literary dimensions are as variable as the rhetorical and political ends it can serve. Just as the word "nature" ranges in meaning to encompass many different ways of viewing and living in the world, the nature essay is not a monolithic tradition but a body of writings linked by a loose family resemblance.

Its history in English can be traced back at least as far as the 17th century to, for example, **Sir William Temple**'s genteel reflections upon gardens, country life, and Epicurean philosophy in "Upon the Gardens of Epicurus" (1690). Temple connected classical philosophy to the pleasures of a specifically English rusticity, returning home, "after so much ramble into ancient times and remote places," to contemplate the excellence of English apples, peaches, and grapes.

Neither Gilbert White's *The Natural History and Antiquities of Selborne* (1788) nor *The Grasmere Journals* (wr. 1800–03) of Dorothy Wordsworth are, strictly speaking, books of essays: White made use of an epistolary structure, addressing his careful observations of the world around him to two other English naturalists, while Dorothy Wordsworth recorded notebook entries on the places and people of Grasmere valley. Both, however, provided models for later writers who sought to combine precise description of a specific locale with a carefully wrought, but seemingly spontaneous, prose style.

Most nature writing since the 19th century has explored, either directly or indirectly, the supposed rift between nature and culture. The assumptions that underlie this persistent dualism are often subverted, or at least subjected to fresh examination. Some critics see the nature essay as basically oppositional, a reaction to the rise of modern industrial society and mechanistic science. Many nature writers, however, take positions in harmony with modern scientific perspectives. Key concepts derived from science that have influenced nature writing include *Ökologie* (ecology), introduced by the German biologist Ernst Heinrich Häckel in 1866, and "ecosystem" (an interdependent system of living organisms) coined by the British ecologist A. G. Tansley in 1935. The influence of Darwinian evolutionary biology has been enormous, and a complex intertextual relation exists between **Darwin**'s writings and those of W. H. Hudson, **John Burroughs**, and many others.

Although 19th- and early 20th-century nature essayists often rejected scientific taxonomies and laboratory methods, the rise of a new natural history had an impact on thinking about nature. Canadian nature writing found an important early exponent in Catharine Parr Traill, whose botanical observations appeared in *Studies of Plant Life in Canada; or, Gleanings from Forest, Lake and Plain* (1885). Like other writers of the period, Traill filtered scientific writing through a late Romantic literary sensibility (plant ecology first emerged as a discipline at around this time). Closer to our own time, **Aldo Leopold**'s essayistic *A Sand County Almanac* (1949) advanced the idea of a "land ethic," to promote the "integrity, beauty, and stability of the biotic community," along with a conservation aesthetic, intended to heighten awareness "of the natural processes by which the land and the living things upon it have achieved their characteristic forms (evolution) and by which they maintain their existence (ecology)." Writers such as Leopold and Rachel Carson deploy (and, in some ways, revise) the authority of scientific discourses to support a position sometimes called "ecocentrism."

The nature essay is often viewed as an essentially American genre, a tradition inspired by the 19th-century writers **Henry David Thoreau**, John Burroughs, and **John Muir**, as well as by the enormous diversity and beauty of the American landscape itself. Although it is occasionally stigmatized as "subliterary" or as a minor genre, a substantial body of criticism and analysis has nevertheless sprung up around the nature essay. It is of central importance for understanding the relation of the self to the land, and the particular spatial configurations that shape American experience. In general American nature writing tends to combine description of particular localities with personal narratives and passages of philosophical reflection. The problem of representing the self in relation to a nonhuman natural world has occupied many nature essayists. Questions of identity, solitude, and human subjectivity repeatedly surface in American writers from Mary Austin to Gretel Ehrlich.

The American nature essay rose to new prominence during the 19th century. Thoreau's identification of nature with "absolute freedom and wildness, as contrasted with a freedom and culture merely civil" ("Walking," 1862) set the tone for a good deal of later writing. His sense of the "wild" as a space located outside civilization, where civilization can nevertheless discover and somehow preserve itself resonates throughout American culture for the next 100 years and more. John Burroughs, who was famous in his own lifetime and the author of many books of nature essays, played a key role in bringing the Thoreauvian tradition into the 20th century. He embraced a poetics of nature writing that valued careful observation and the power of language to defamiliarize ordinary experience: "The writer's style, the quality of mind he brings," he wrote, "is the vase in which his commonplace impressions and incidents are made to appear so beautiful and significant" ("A Sharp Lookout," 1886). Through both his writings and his work as an activist, John Muir had a direct impact on the political climate of his day, becoming an important voice in the conservation movement. All three of these writers, it should be noted, were energetic walkers and hikers (one of Muir's books is titled *A Thousand-Mile Walk to the Gulf*, 1916), and their work has affinities with the literary excursion or "ramble."

Interest in the form has revived since the 1970s, and some observers claim that the nature essay, particularly in the United States, has entered a new golden age, linked to the growth of ecology movements and green politics. A very selective list of contemporary American nature essayists would include **Annie Dillard, Barry Lopez, John McPhee,** Peter Matthiessen, **Wallace Stegner,** David Quammen, Terry Tempest Williams, and Ann Zwinger.

ALVIN SNIDER

Anthologies

American Nature Writing series, edited by John A. Murray, San Francisco: Sierra Club Books, 3 vols., 1994–96 (and ongoing)
Another Wilderness: New Outdoor Writing by Women edited by Susan Fox Rogers, Seattle: Seal Press, 1994
Great American Nature Writing, edited by Joseph Wood Krutch, New York: William Sloane Associates, 1950
The Norton Book of Nature Writing, edited by Robert Finch and John Elder, New York: Norton, 1990
A Republic of Rivers: Three Centuries of Nature Writing from Alaska and the Yukon, edited by John A. Murray, New York: Oxford University Press, 1990
This Incomperable Lande: A Book of American Nature Writing, edited by Thomas J. Lyon, Boston: Houghton Mifflin, 1989
Three Centuries of Nature Writing from Africa, edited by John A. Murray, New York: Oxford University Press, 1993

Further Reading

Bryant, Paul, "Nature Writing and the American Frontier," in *The Frontier Experience and American Literature*, edited by David Mogen, Mark Busby, and Bryant, College Station: Texas A & M University Press, 1989
Buell, Lawrence, *The Environmental Imagination: Thoreau, Nature Writing, and the Formation of American Culture*, Cambridge, Massachusetts: Harvard University Press, 1995
Cason, Jacqueline Johnson, "Nature Writer as Storyteller: The Nature Essay as a Literary Genre," *CEA Critic* 54, no. 1 (1991): 12–18
Farr, Moira, "The Death of Nature Writing," *Brick* 47 (1993): 16–27
Fritzell, Peter A., *Nature Writing and America: Essays upon a Cultural Type*, Ames: Iowa State University Press, 1990
Keith, W. J., *The Rural Tradition: A Study of the Non-Fiction Prose Writers of the English Countryside*, Toronto: University of Toronto Press, 1974; as *The Rural Tradition: William Cobbett, Gilbert White and Other Non-Fiction Prose Writers of the English Countryside*, Hassocks, Sussex: Harvester Press, 1975
Lyon, Thomas J., "The Nature Essay in the West" and "The Western Nature Essay Since 1970," both in *A Literary History of the American West*, edited by Max Westbrook and James H. Maguire, Fort Worth: Texas Christian University Press, 1987
Lyon, Thomas J., "Nature Writing as a Subversive Activity," *North Dakota Quarterly* 59, no. 2 (1991): 6–16
MacLulich, T. D., "Reading the Land: The Wilderness Tradition in Canadian Letters," *Journal of Canadian Studies* 20 (1985): 29–44
Manning, Peter J., "Reading and Writing Nature," *Review* 15 (1993): 175–96
Murray, John, and others, "The Rise of Nature Writing: America's Next Great Genre?" *Manoa* 4, no. 2 (1992): 73–96
Raglon, Rebecca, *American Nature Writing in the Age of Ecology: Changing Perceptions, Changing Forms* (dissertation), Kingston, Ontario: Queen's University, 1989
Raglon, Rebecca, "Voicing the World: Nature Writing as a Critique of the Scientific Method," *Canadian Review of American Studies* 22, no. 1 (1991): 23–32
Slovic, Scott, *Seeking Awareness in American Nature Writing: Henry Thoreau, Annie Dillard, Edward Abbey, Wendell Berry, Barry Lopez*, Salt Lake City: University of Utah Press, 1992

Die neue Rundschau
German periodical, 1890–1945, 1950–

The monthly literary journal *Die neue Rundschau* (The new review) has a remarkable place in German literary and cultural history, particularly during the period between 1933 and 1945. The Berlin journal was first published by Samuel Fischer in 1890 and thereafter by Fischer and his son-in-law, Gottfried Bermann Fischer, until 1936 when Bermann Fischer, who was Jewish, was forced into exile by the National Socialists; Peter Suhrkamp became responsible for the general operation of the *NR* and the Fischer publishing company at this time. Although Bermann Fischer established another publishing company in exile, Suhrkamp kept the Fischer name for the publishing company and the *NR* until the National Socialists forced him in 1942 to replace Fischer's name with his own.

The legacy of the *NR* was left to Suhrkamp, who had been made Editor-in-Chief in 1933 by Samuel Fischer. Suhrkamp remained remarkably true to the initial format of its founders, directing the *NR* to the same readership of intellectuals and artists with a similar mix of literature and criticism. Essays and critical commentary were crucial to the *NR*, and many issues included **journal** entries, **letters**, travelogues, and memoirs in addition to essays on politics and culture. In the earliest years of Fischer's journal, the *Neue deutsche Rundschau*, as the periodical was then called, was associated with naturalism and with the establishment of the Freie Bühne, analogous to the Théâtre Libre in France. Fischer's journal included works by Richard Dehmel, Hermann Hesse, **Hugo von Hofmannsthal, Thomas Mann,** and Jakob Wassermann, as well as foreign writers such as **Yeats** and Hemingway. Suhrkamp continued to feature many of these writers even as the National Socialists blacklisted them and, in 1944, imprisoned Suhrkamp on charges of high treason. During the period of National Socialist control Suhrkamp published works by 122 blacklisted authors, a number that exceeded all other publishers in Germany from 1933 to 1945 (Dietrich Strothmann, 1960). The *NR* also published other "unerwünschte" (unwanted) writers, in National Socialist terminology, such as Alfred Döblin, Alfred Kerr, Harry Graf Kessler, Annette Kolb, and Siegfried Kracauer.

The *NR* provided one of the few forums (albeit limited) for Modernist literature in Nazi Germany. The *NR* was also one of only a few journals which dared comment critically upon the social and political conditions of the period. The journal featured discussions ranging from considerations of film and literary genres to Suhrkamp's musings on social conditions under the National Socialists. Thomas Mann's seminal essay on Richard Wagner and the implications of the composer's music for modern art appeared in the *NR* in 1933.

Although Suhrkamp continued to contribute works to the *NR* and to exert control over its operations through 1944, he was editor of the journal only until 1937. Subsequent editors included Wolfgang von Einsiedel, Karl Korn, Hans Paeschke, and Gerhard Aichinger. Suhrkamp's own contributions to the *NR* were among the most critical of life in Germany under the National Socialists. In 1942–43 his episodic works "Der Zuschauer" (The spectator) and "Tagebuch eines Zuschauers" (Journal of a spectator) detailed the dissolution of Germany. There were no editorials per se in the *NR*, though a section entitled "Anmerkungen" (Notes) at the end of the journal did sometimes include discussion of political conditions, in addition to remarks concerning new books and up-and-coming authors. Suhrkamp's and his editors' stance toward fascism, however, is best seen in works such as "Der Zuschauer," and the resolve to publish essays and works of fiction by "unacceptable" writers despite boycotts, censorship, and increasing surveillance by the authorities. Suhrkamp's clear-sighted assessment of conditions as well as his publication of Jewish writers under assumed names ultimately led to trumped-up charges of high treason. He was arrested in 1944 and imprisoned in the Sachsenhausen concentration camp. He was released by the authorities in 1945 but health problems contracted during his imprisonment, including a lung infection and a spinal injury, led to his death in 1959.

The high quality of the *NR* was also a result of efforts by Oskar Loerke and Hermann Kasack. Loerke had been a reader for Samuel Fischer since 1917; when Loerke died in 1941, Kasack became chief reader of the *NR*. Both men contributed essays and fiction to the journal and many of their works have figured greatly in the reestablishment of German literary studies after the war. After Suhrkamp's imprisonment, Kasack was placed in charge of the *NR*. Despite Suhrkamp's attempts to maintain the standards of the journal, and the expertise of his editorial staff, the economic situation and the National Socialists' programmatic policies of censorship and intimidation constrained the *NR*. The cost of paper led in 1939 to a reduced typeface, and by 1944 the periodical was forced to appear in quarterly rather than monthly issues. By 1940 issues of the *NR* contained works almost solely by German authors. There was also a dramatic change in the kind of material printed. Instead of works by Mann and Hesse, essays on Caesar, German military history, and the barbarism of the British became common. At this time, too, jingoistic advertisements, and even quotations from Hitler, appeared regularly in the journal. In an attempt to erase all signs of Jewish culture, National Socialist authorities demanded in 1942 that Fischer's name be removed as publisher.

By the end of the war the *NR* had been discontinued. Five years later, Bermann Fischer, who had returned to Germany, regained ownership of the *NR* and began publishing the journal in monthly issues. The journal continues to be published today, providing influential literary and cultural commentary. Although Suhrkamp was not associated with the *NR* after the war, he was the first to receive a license to publish in the British sector of Berlin under the Allies' elaborate licensing procedure, and his publishing house has become one of the most successful in the postwar period, even after his death.

CHRISTOPHER P. MCCLINTICK

Anthology
Der goldene Schnitt: Grosse Essayisten der Neuen Rundschau, 1890–1960, edited by Christoph Schwerin, Frankfurt: Fischer, 1960

Further Reading
Kasack, Hermann, "Bild eines Verlegers," in his *Mosaiksteine: Beiträge zu Literatur und Kunst*, Frankfurt: Suhrkamp, 1956: 309–16
Schwarz, Falk, "Literarisches Zeitgespräch im Dritten Reich: Dargestellt an der Zeitschrift *Neue Rundschau*," *Börsenblatt für den Deutschen Buchhandel* 51 (1971): 1409–1508
Strothmann, Dietrich, *Nationalsozialistische Literaturpolitik: Ein Beitrag zur Publizistik im Dritten Reich*, Bonn: Bouvier, 1960
Voit, Friedrich, *Der Verleger Peter Suhrkamp und seine Autoren*, Kronberg/Ts.: Scriptor, 1975

New Journalism

The term "New Journalism" is most often associated with the work of certain American literary journalists who came to prominence in the 1960s. The phrase, however, also recalls a style of 1960s cultural politics which challenged not merely traditional journalism, but also fiction and the essay genre.

Tom Wolfe, the most outspoken advocate of the form, credits New York writer Pete Hamil with the first use of the term. In 1965, Hamil approached a New York editor with the idea of doing an article called "The New Journalism" about writers such as Gay Talese, who was writing exquisitely crafted feature articles for the New York *Times* and *Esquire*, and Jimmy Breslin, a colorful feature writer/columnist for the dying New York *Herald Tribune*. These writers were employing many devices of literature (scenes, dialogue, interior monologue, symbolic detail) in the service of nonfictional subjects. By the end of the decade a throng of both new and established writers had published popularly and critically acclaimed volumes in this form, including Wolfe (*The Kandy-Kolored Tangerine-Flake Streamline Baby*, 1965; *The Electric Kool-Aid Acid Test*, 1968; *The Pump House Gang*, 1968); Truman Capote (*In Cold Blood*, 1965); Hunter S. Thompson (*The Hell's Angels*, 1966); George Plimpton (*Paper Lion*, 1966); **Joan Didion** (*Slouching Towards Bethlehem*, 1968); **Norman Mailer** (the Pulitzer Prize-winning *The Armies of the Night: History as a Novel, the Novel as History*, 1968; *Miami and the Siege of Chicago*, 1968); Talese (*New York – A Serendipiter's Journey*, 1961; *The Overreachers*, 1963; *The Bridge*, 1965; *The Kingdom and the Power*, 1969); and Breslin (*Can't Anybody Here Play This Game?*, 1963).

In his 1973 manifesto and anthology *The New Journalism*, Wolfe described the literary hierarchy in the 1960s. The lowest rungs, he claimed, were the domain of the "lumpenprole" journalists. Essayists or "men-of-letters" held middle status, and the novelist reigned as the most esteemed of all writers. The New Journalism challenged this hierarchy by collapsing it, by, in effect, bringing the techniques of all three forms together into one ambitious hybrid genre. "What interested me was not simply the discovery that it was possible to write accurate nonfiction with techniques usually associated with novels and short stories," stated Wolfe. "It was the discovery that it was possible in non-fiction, in journalism, to use any literary device, from the traditional dialogisms of the essay to stream-of-consciousness, and to use many different kinds simultaneously, or within a relatively short space . . . to excite the reader both intellectually and emotionally."

The New Journalism challenged the image of the essayist as "a literary gentleman with a seat in the grandstand" (Wolfe, 1973). Wolfe believed most nonfiction writers adopted this "century-old British" mindset without even recognizing it. New journalists dared essayists to come down from the grandstand and mingle with their subjects. They also called for more than "vivid description plus sentiment," the forte of the familiar essayist. Instead they favored the kind of thorough reporting that made possible the re-creation of "scenes." Implicit, too, was a call for expansion of the subject matter deemed worthy of the essayist's attention. The unnoticed and ignored gained the spotlight along with the celebrated, as did a range of emerging cultural lifestyles – including the drug and rock-and-roll cultures.

Most stultifying of all to Wolfe and his colleagues, however, was the genteel voice of the polite essayist – a hushed voice "like a radio announcer at a tennis match." The essay had room, they insisted, for the "hectoring narrator," the narrator speaking in the voice and accents of his subjects, the narrator inhabiting many points of view – narrators, in short, engaged in "apostrophes, epithets, moans, cackles, anything" (Wolfe, 1973). Such stress on technical virtuosity represented a shift in emphasis from the traditional essay which often featured a didactic tone. "One of the greatest changes," Wolfe noted, "has been a reversal of this attitude – so that the proof of one's technical mastery as writer becomes paramount and the demonstration of moral points becomes secondary."

The legacy of the New Journalism, therefore, is not insubstantial. The major New Journalists of the 1960s have continued publishing in the genre, making what began as a youth movement now the domain of venerated literary lions. David Eason (1990) has offered a helpful distinction between "realist" New Journalists such as Talese, Wolfe, and Capote, who believe "reality" can be discovered and revealed, and "Modernist" New Journalists like Mailer, Didion, and Thompson, who describe "what it feels like to live in a world where there is no consensus about a frame of reference to explain 'what it all means'." A second generation of such writers is also established, headed by "Modernists" **Annie Dillard** (*Holy the Firm*, 1977; *Teaching a Stone to Talk*, 1982) and William Least Heat-Moon (*The Blue Highways*, 1982; *PrairyErth*, 1991), and "realists" Tracy Kidder (*The Soul of a New Machine*, 1981; *House*, 1985; *Among School Children*, 1989; *Old Friends*, 1993) and Melissa Fay Greene (*Praying for Sheetrock*, 1991; *The Temple Bombing*, 1996). Their works today, however, are more likely to be categorized as literary or artful nonfiction than as New Journalism.

Wolfe's efforts to define an identifiable school of writing have only partially succeeded. He has acknowledged that few of the writers he lauded in his manifesto wanted to be part of his "raggedy band": Hunter Thompson insisted he was not a New Journalist but a "gonzo journalist," a tongue-in-cheek term for his own patented mix of paranoia, black humor, and hyperbole; Talese said he was simply writing "stories with real names"; Capote called his *In Cold Blood* a "nonfiction novel";

and Mailer used the term "true life novel" for his 1979 Pulitzer Prize-winning *The Executioner's Song*. By calling his hybrid form "New," however, Wolfe spurred scholars to document what is now seen as a long tradition of literary journalism extending from **Defoe** through to the present.

This research now locates the New Journalism of the 1960s as one of the peaks of this long tradition. As a style of 1960s cultural politics, it forced journalists, essayists, and fiction writers to reexamine established views of subject matter, form, and authorial role. In collapsing the boundaries between journalism, fiction, and the essay it enlarged each of these forms and raised important questions regarding the ways in which experience is organized and recorded.

BARBARA LOUNSBERRY

Anthologies

The New Journalism, edited by Tom Wolfe and E. W. Johnson, New York: Harper and Row, 1973

New Journalism, edited by Marshall Fishwick, Bowling Green, Ohio: Bowling Green University Popular Press, 1975

The New Journalism: A Historical Anthology, edited by Nicolaus Mills, New York: McGraw Hill, 1974

Further Reading

Anderson, Chris, *Style as Argument: Contemporary American Nonfiction*, Carbondale: Southern Illinois University Press, 1987

Connery, Thomas B., "Discovering a Literary Form," in *A Sourcebook of American Literary Journalism: Representative Writers in an Emerging Genre*, edited by Connery, Westport, Connecticut: Greenwood Press, 1992

Eason, David, "The New Journalism and the Image-World," in *Literary Journalism in the Twentieth Century*, edited by Norman Sims, New York and Oxford: Oxford University Press, 1990

Hellmann, John, *Fables of Fact: The New Journalism as New Fiction*, Urbana: University of Illinois Press, 1981

Hersey, John, "The Legend on the License," *Yale Review* 70 (Fall 1980): 1–15

Hollowell, John, *Fact & Fiction: The New Journalism and the Nonfiction Novel*, Chapel Hill: University of North Carolina Press, 1977

Johnson, Michael L., *The New Journalism: The Underground Press, the Artists of Nonfiction, and Changes in the Established Mode*, Lawrence: University Press of Kansas, 1971

Lounsberry, Barbara, *The Art of Fact: Contemporary Artists of Nonfiction*, Westport, Connecticut: Greenwood Press, 1990

Macdonald, Dwight, "Parajournalism, or Tom Wolfe and His Magic Writing Machine," *New York Review of Books*, 26 August 1965: 3–5

Murphy, James E., *The New Journalism: A Critical Perspective*, Lexington, Kentucky: Association for Education in Journalism, 1974

Pauly, John J., "The Politics of the New Journalism," in *Literary Journalism in the Twentieth Century*, edited by Norman Sims, New York and Oxford: Oxford Univrsity Press, 1990

Sims, Norman, editor, *The Literary Journalists*, New York: Ballantine, 1984

Talese, Gay, "Origins of a Nonfiction Writer," in *The Literature of Reality*, edited by Talese and Barbara Lounsberry, New York: HarperCollins, 1996

Weber, Ronald, *The Reporter as Artist: A Look at the New Journalism Controversy*, New York: Hastings House, 1974

Weber, Ronald, *The Literature of Fact: Literary Nonfiction in American Writing*, Athens: Ohio University Press, 1980

Wolfe, Tom, *The New Journalism*, New York: Harper and Row, 1973 (includes an anthology, edited by Wolfe and E. W. Johnson)

Zavarzadeh, Mas'ud, *The Mythopoeic Reality: The Postwar American Nonfiction Novel*, Urbana: University of Illinois Press, 1976

The New Yorker

American magazine, 1925–

The *New Yorker* is one of America's longest running and most successful journals. The publication began as a humor magazine, and many readers still find the cartoons its most distinctive feature. However, the *New Yorker*'s success is based on more than its cartoons; its success is attributable to Harold Ross, the founding editor of what became America's wittiest and most sophisticated magazine. After only three changes in editor-in-chief in its history, it generally retains this reputation, much of which is derived from the journal's high-quality essays.

Only Ross, who claimed "I'll hire *anybody*" and who early on proved that statement, would have hired Ross. His connection with the Thanatopsis Literary and Inside Straight Club (Alexander Woollcott, Franklin P. Adams, George S. Kaufman, **Robert Benchley**, and Dorothy Parker) led to his founding of the magazine. Through this group Ross met Raoul Fleischmann, a millionaire baker, who agreed to provide $150,000 for Ross' proposed journal.

The early months were almost fatal for the *New Yorker*. Fifteen thousand copies of the 21 February 1925 inaugural issue were sold, but by late April circulation had dropped to 8000, and by August it had fallen to 2700. Ross and Fleischmann declared the magazine defunct, then changed their minds. The budget was cut, Fleischmann supplied more money, and 60,000 dollars was allocated for advertising. Finally, though, it was Ellin MacKay's essay "Why We Go to Cabarets, A Post-Debutante Explains" in the first year's Thanksgiving issue which saved the magazine. MacKay created a Park Avenue audience with her essay about why young women from New York's high society went to nightclubs rather than contend with stag lines at private parties.

With minor variations, the *New Yorker*'s format has remained constant. The first textual material, "Of All Things," contained the magazine's prospectus, followed by the "Talk of the Town" section. Other departments in the beginning were "Profile," "The Story of Manhattan-Kind," and "Behind the News." Lois Long created the "Tables for Two" and "On and Off the Avenue" columns. The nightclub gossip of the former and the good taste of the latter, a buying guide, attracted readers and provided the journal with stability.

After the premiere issue, "The Talk of the Town" was the first editorial content until "Goings on About Town" was moved to the front in December 1925. Beginning with this issue, the names of "Advisory Editors" (Ralph Barton, Marc Connelly, Irving Kaufman, Alice Duer Miller, Parker, and Woollcott, who was replaced by Hugh Wiley) were printed above the "Talk of the Town" title. The role of Ross' managing editor was filled by many men labeled "Jesuses" and "Geniuses": Joseph M. March, M. B. Levick, Arthur Samuels, Bernard A. Bergman, Stanley Walker, Ik Shuman, Philip D. Hoyt, and St. Clair McKelway.

Until 1969, no masthead or table of contents was included in the magazine. There is still no identification of the editor-in-chief or of fiction, nonfiction, or art editors, and even after a table of contents was added, contributors' names were not listed for years. In fact, one of the attractions of the *New Yorker* was the guessing game prompted by the printing of authors' names at the conclusions of their contributions. Readers either turned to the end of a piece to see who wrote it or tried to determine authorship from the topic and style. The placing of the writer's name at the end remained in force until quite recently, even when the information was eventually placed in the table of contents; the names now appear at the beginning of the articles.

Items in the table of contents fall into four categories: regular departments and various kinds of reporting (on politics, or theater, dance, film, music, art, and book **review**s); personal experiences and reflections; works of fiction; and poems. Except for advertising, the first content in today's *New Yorker* is "Comment," followed by "In the Mail," "Goings on About Town" (a listing of events in New York City), review sections, other departments on an irregular basis, poetry, and "casuals," as Ross called the periodical's prose pieces.

The *New Yorker*'s format reflects its editorial philosophy. No blurbs appear on the cover to grab a reader's attention (although this policy may be in the process of changing, with blurbs printed on a half-cover wrap for issues sold at newsstands and abroad). Little color has been used in the magazine, though more and more is being featured, mostly in advertisements. The black and white pages are clean and quiet, as is the prose, and there are no subheads, an approach devised by make-up editor Carmine Peppe.

Ross never catered to an audience. He contended that he would not edit his journal "for the old lady in Dubuque" because "An editor prints only what pleases him – if enough people like what he likes, he is a success." In the *New Yorker*'s prospectus he declared that the magazine would "be a reflection in word and picture of metropolitan life. It will be human. Its general tenor will be one of gaiety, wit, and satire, but it will be more than a jester. It will not be . . . radical or highbrow. It will be . . . sophisticated . . . It will hate bunk . . . Its integrity will be above suspicion." In the editorial statement in the premiere issue, Ross said that the *New Yorker* would have "a serious purpose but . . . not [be] . . . too serious in executing it. It hopes . . . to keep up with events of the day." The magazine would "publish facts that it will have to go behind the scenes to get, but it will not deal in scandal for the sake of scandal."

The chief element in the *New Yorker*'s success was Ross' editing: "Use the rapier, not the bludgeon," he advised. To help his writers hone their prose, he edited it meticulously; manuscripts were returned with lists of numbered comments that sometimes were as long as the manuscripts. Ross also established a special department to check every fact. Four-letter obscenities and sexual connotation were barred.

Ross had misgivings about his management abilities. To overcome this he was willing to hire almost anybody. Employees were brought in high on the editorial ladder, regardless of their experience. Most worked down to a more suitable level or left the magazine, but for 26 years Ross attracted and fostered the most important American humorists, who knew or found out how to make the magazine a success. He not only allowed his talented staff to perform, he forced them to reach their potential.

William Shawn served as editor-in-chief for 30 years, having replaced Ross in January 1952. Born Chon (he changed the spelling so readers would not think that he was Chinese), he had minimal journalistic experience when he joined the magazine as Ross' hand-picked successor, and he perpetuated the characteristics established by his predecessor. Both men developed writers under their tutelage, albeit in different ways. Whereas Ross was a stickler for details, the intellectually inquisitive Shawn was concerned with whether an author said what he intended to say. Shawn was also more politically oriented than Ross – it was he who convinced Ross to devote an entire issue to John Hersey's 30,000-word "Hiroshima" (1946), and during Vietnam and Watergate the New Yorker, particularly in "Notes and Comments," spoke out against immorality.

Humor diminished under Shawn, though he may not have been at fault. In the mid-1940s, Ross bemoaned the dwindling of humor and the increasing "grim stuff." Times, taste, and authors change, and the world of World War II and after was not amenable to the happy-go-lucky humor of the early New Yorker. There is still humor, but entire humorous essays are rare. Indeed, the magazine has become increasingly political, and increasingly liberal.

The major categories of essays for which the journal is noted are the profiles (biographical portraits), personal reminiscences, and reviews of the arts. New Yorker casuals are characterized by humane, cultivated, erudite, sensitive qualities. The style is lyrical softness. Authors assume an unhurried, gentle, relaxed, urbane prose. If they sometimes appear dilettantish, they are not foppish, silly, or stupid; quiet as opposed to ranting, they are amused, yet wistful; they are romantic; they are wise but at times innocently foolish. Many of America's important writers have contributed to the journal. The list contains a Who's Who of American humorists in the mid-20th century: Benchley, S. N. Behrman, Sally Benson, Clarence Day, Ralph Ingersoll, Nunnally Johnson, Kaufman, Ring Lardner, Long, **H. L. Mencken**, Parker, **S. J. Perelman**, Leonard Ross, Thorne Smith, Jean Stafford, Frank Sullivan, **James Thurber, E. B. White**, Woollcott. Among the most famous pieces were Day's "Life with Father" (1935) and Ruth McKenney's "My Sister Eileen" (1936) series.

Additionally, many other distinguished authors' works have appeared in the New Yorker: Sherwood Anderson, **James Baldwin**, Rachel Carson (The Silent Spring), John Cheever, Robert M. Coates, Clifton Fadiman, F. Scott Fitzgerald, Ernest Hemingway, Shirley Jackson ("The Lottery" caused a major brouhaha in 1948), **A. J. Liebling, Mary McCarthy**, John McNulty, **Lewis Mumford**, Irwin Shaw, **Rebecca West, Edmund Wilson**. Samuel Beckett's Catastrophe was published in the New Yorker, as have been over 100 pieces each by Truman Capote, John O'Hara, and J. D. Salinger. The high quality continues with works by Wright Morris, Alice Adams, and Calvin Trillin. Regular contributors have included Brendan Gill, Penelope Gilliatt, and John Lahr (on drama), Pauline Kael and Terrence Rafferty (on film), Molly Panter-Downes ("Letter from London"), Edith Oliver, and George Steiner.

Of all of the writers who have contributed to the New Yorker, three have made the biggest imprint and are most representative of the journal's tone: White, Thurber, and Perelman. White, who joined the staff in 1926, may have had the greatest influence. He was responsible for much of the editing and helped Ross establish the style that until lately characterized the prose. Famed for his essays and children's novels, he is renowned as well for his revised edition of William Strunk, Jr.'s The Elements of Style (1959). Possibly more important than White's editorial skills were his "Talk of the Town" contributions, particularly "Notes and Comments," for this section set the tone for the New Yorker's content and approach. White's "Notes and Comments," Thurber says in The Years with Ross (1959), "left its firm and graceful imprint on American letters and . . . exerted its influence upon local, or even wider, affairs." The format and the success of the "Talk of the Town" demonstrate how well Ross chose those who shared his vision and were equipped to execute it. In the 1924 prospectus, he stated, "There will be a personal mention column – a jotting down in the small-town newspaper style of the comings, goings and doings in the village of New York. This will contain some josh and some news value." During White's 11 years as department head, he provided what Ross wanted. The Ross-White tradition continued when Russell Maloney took over the "Talk of the Town" editorship in 1935. David Kuhn is the current "Talk of the Town" editor, yet even today the department retains much of the flavor introduced by White, that of a small-town newspaper reporting on events in a folksy way, implying writer/reader familiarity and a sharing of beliefs. Unfortunately, the editorial "we," which used to be used throughout, has been replaced by an ego-centered "I," an indication of a new philosophical approach.

Thurber's impact on the New Yorker was immeasurable. He, too, joined the magazine in its formative period, in 1927, and as an active, long-time editorial staffer, he was a primary factor in determining the journal's style. Most important, however, were his model 364 casuals and 307 drawings. "The Secret Life of Walter Mitty" (1939), a classic fantasy, became the most famous piece of fiction ever published in the New Yorker.

Perelman's relationship with the New Yorker was different from that of White and Thurber. His contribution came in the form of his casuals. Between 1930 and 1979, Perelman contributed 278 casuals, and his writing came to define New Yorker humor. His style, drawing on American frontier humor and Yiddish theater, combined careful structuring, "lapidary prose," a massive vocabulary, refined exuberance, and a sense of literalism about clichés filtered through a sense of parody in pieces described by White as having "a lead sentence . . . that was as hair-raising as the first big dip on a roller coaster." Among Perelman's more popular essays were his "Cloudland Revisited" series of 22 reminiscences (1948–53) which began with "Into Your Tent I'll Creep."

Like its writers, the New Yorker audience is urbane, intelligent, cosmopolitan, and affluent. With the editorial appointment of the British, former Vanity Fair editor Tina Brown in October 1992, however, a transformation occurred. In Brown's new incarnation, the magazine's contents and tone have shifted, as has its audience. When the New Yorker was established, the editorial and advertising departments were assigned physically separate offices; Ross did not want the advertising department to have any opportunity to influence the editorial department. He was particular about what products could be advertised in his journal as well. James Playsted Wood (1971) noted the *New Yorker* restrictions on advertising: "no exaggeration, superlatives, or innuendoes. It eschews feminine hygiene, bad breath, body odors, and patent medicines. It will picture nothing which is worn beneath a woman's slip." Comparing this policy with Brown's four-letter-word-sprinkled essays and lingerie ads is instructive in light of the magazine's recently diminished reputation. However, possibly because of the large amount of publicity generated specifically about Brown's editorial decisions, the *New Yorker*'s circulation jumped from 628,104 in June 1992 to its present level of 833,672. This has not occurred without sacrificing much of the traditional style and character which distinguished the journal – evident in the placement of the authors' names, added color, increased advertising, less humor, and the nature of the articles. In 1994–95, timely pieces on topics such as O. J. Simpson, a pro-Hillary Clinton puff, and an attack on Newt Gingrich are representative of the Brown approach.

If longevity, circulation, and advertising revenue were insufficient to demonstrate the success and importance of the *New Yorker*, the journal has received serious attention from major periodicals, and books and chapters in books have been written about the magazine that the Bombay *Times* calls part of American social history and the *Spectator* labels "an important part not only of American culture but of Western culture generally." The *Saturday Review* attributed the *New Yorker*'s success to Ross' sense of perfection, the "number and variety of items in each issue," and the "complexity of action" behind the magazine's weekly publication (an outgrowth of Ross' traits combined with a wide audience and broadening of subject matter). Ross' love for accuracy produced attention to detail not usually found elsewhere. This instilled a feeling of good workmanship complemented and emphasized by the editorial care given to the writing style. The result was that for the majority of the 20th century, the *New Yorker* was the primary force in redefining the essay in America.

STEVEN H. GALE

Further Reading

Blow, Richard, and Ari Posner, "Are You Completely Bald? Adventures in Fact Checking," *New Republic*, 26 September 1988: 23
Brilliant, Richard, *Portraiture*, Cambridge, Massachusetts: Harvard University Press, and London: Reaktion, 1991
Cullather, James L., "Has the Laughter Died? Musings on the *New Yorker*'s Business Ethics Cartoons," *Business Horizons* 26 (March–April 1983): 30–33
Cullather, James L., "Musings II: Revisiting the *New Yorker*'s Business Ethics Cartoons," *Business Horizons* 29 (May–June 1986): 23–27
Gale, Steven H., "Thurber of *The New Yorker*," *Studies in American Humor* issue on Thurber, 3, no. 1 (Spring 1984): 11–23
Gale, Steven H., "The New Yorker," in *American Humor Magazines and Comic Periodicals*, edited by David E. E. Sloane, Westport, Connecticut: Greenwood Press, 1987: 179–91
Gale, Steven H., "James Thurber," in *Popular World Fiction, 1900–Present*, vol. 4, edited by Walton Beacham and Suzanne Niemeyer, Washington, D.C.: Beacham, 1987: 1524–38
Gale, Steven H., "James Thurber," in *American Short-Story Writers, 1910–1945, Second Series*, edited by Bobby Ellen Kimbel, *Dictionary of Literary Biography* vol. 102, Detroit: Gale Research, 1991: 319–34
Gill, Brendan, *Here at the New Yorker*, New York: Random House, 1975
Kramer, Dale, *Ross and the New Yorker*, Garden City, New York: Doubleday, 1951
McPhee, John, "The New Yorker Index 1992," *New Yorker*, 22 February 1993: 81–102
Mott, Frank Luther, *A History of American Magazines*, Cambridge, Massachusetts: Harvard University Press, 5 vols., 1938–68
The New Yorker Staff, "Remembering Mr. Shawn," *New Yorker*, 28 December 1992/4 January 1993: 134–45
The New Yorker Twenty-Fifth Anniversary Album, 1925–1950, New York: Harper and Row, 1951
Peterson, Theodore, *Magazines in the Twentieth Century*, Urbana: University of Illinois Press, revised edition, 1964
Thurber, James, *The Years with Ross*, Boston: Little Brown, 1959
Wood, James Playsted, *Magazines in the United States*, New York: Ronald Press, 3rd edition, 1971

Newman, John Henry

British, 1801–1890

It is a curious paradox that, while John Henry Newman was essentially an "occasional" writer who wrote comparatively few books as such, nevertheless two of his most famous book-length works contain the word "essay" in their titles: *An Essay on the Development of Christian Doctrine* (1845) and *An Essay in Aid of a Grammar of Assent* (1870). In fact, the *Development of Christian Doctrine* was never finished, so in that sense it remains an "essay" or attempt at a larger work; while the dry and abstract opening of the *Grammar of Assent* is so unlike Newman's usual personal manner as to remind us that the intention to sit down to write a **treatise** was far from his normal method of proceeding. This can be seen by comparing it with his other chief philosophical work, the *Oxford University Sermons* (1843), where he adumbrates some of his most original ideas in the form of some brilliantly stimulating essays, albeit ostensibly **sermons** on Scripture texts. Indeed, the concluding sermon, "The Theory of Developments in Religious Doctrine," which took an hour and a half to deliver, is based on simple and familiar words from the New Testament ("Mary kept all these things, and pondered them in her heart"), but is in fact a theological essay that is arguably a better and clearer exposition of his views than the full-length book which it anticipated.

It is hardly a cause for surprise that Newman never wrote, or even contemplated writing, a work of spirituality. Rather, it is to his sermons, preached for specific occasions and to specific congregations, that we must turn for the most concentrated expression of his thoughts on the spiritual life. As well as the more intellectual *Oxford University Sermons*, there were nine volumes of Anglican sermons published, as opposed to only two volumes for the Catholic period, when, except on more formal occasions, he preached extempore from notes rather than read from a prepared text as he had done as the Vicar of the University Church of St. Mary's in Oxford. There, Sunday by Sunday, his eyes fixed on his manuscript, he had read out those expositions of the Scripture readings which made such a profound impression on those who heard him, although they were delivered without any attempt at oratorical effect: apart from the legendary low, musical voice and lengthy pregnant pauses, the effect came totally from the words. Again, the style was conversational rather than rhetorical as the preacher, on the one hand, drew out the thought of the Greek Fathers which had so influenced him but which sounded so unfamiliar a note in the context of Victorian Protestantism; and, on the other hand, seemed to look into the very souls of his hearers with his extraordinarily keen insight into the nature of fallen humanity.

The *Oxford University Sermons* remain Newman's most seminal writings, where he not only sketched out some of his most important philosophical and theological ideas, but where he also, in the course of his explorations of the human mind, anticipated the essays and lectures that constitute *The Idea of a University* (1873), which is still the classic work on a liberal education, but which, far from being a systematic treatise, bears all the marks of its "occasional" genesis. The first part of the book consists of the *Discourses on the Scope and Nature of University Education* (1852), only half of which were actually delivered, that were commissioned by the church authorities to justify a Catholic university. The second part comprises the *Lectures and Essays on University Subjects* (1859), which Newman wrote in the course of establishing and presiding over the new Catholic University of Ireland. Nowhere better than in *The Idea of a University* do we see the force of Gerard Manley Hopkins' comment that when Newman wrote, what he was essentially doing was to think aloud, so that his prose is really that of cultured conversation – and therefore, one might add, admirably fitted to the literary form of the essay.

Newman has been called the greatest controversialist in English literature – a point which relates not only to the "occasional" nature of so many of his writings but also to the fact that he is never more himself than when he is arguing and debating with real or imagined opponents. This enables him in his *Lectures on Certain Difficulties Felt by Anglicans* (1850) and even more in his *Lectures on the Present Position of Catholics in England* (1851) to display his considerable powers as a satirist, powers which had first flowered in print in the **letters** he had written as an Anglican to the *Times* on *The Tamworth Reading Room* (1841).

Again, when we look at his theological work, we can see why his brother Francis thought Newman could have been a formidable barrister, for in so many of his writings, which take the form of **tracts**, **review** articles, or lengthy letters intended for publication, he is either attacking or defending a thesis. Thus the three most important of his Catholic works are the article "On Consulting the Faithful in Matters of Doctrine" (1859), the *Letter to the Rev. E. B. Pusey* (1866) on Mariology, and the *Letter to the Duke of Norfolk* (1875) on papal infallibility. Similarly, in his Anglican period his two principal theological works were first delivered as *Lectures on the Prophetical Office of the Church* (1837) and as *Lectures on Justification* (1838) before they were published as books. His own contribution to the Oxford or Tractarian Movement had begun with some historical, polemical articles for the *British Magazine* on *The Church of the Fathers* (1840), which began appearing in October 1833, a month before the first of the *Tracts for the Times*, some of which Newman also wrote. His other more important Tractarian writings include: the essay "On the Introduction of Rationalistic Principles into Revealed Religion," first published as *Tract 73* (1835); "Holy Scripture in Its Relation to the Catholic Creed," first given as lectures and then mostly published as *Tract 85* (1838); and the article "Prospects of the Anglican Church," originally "The State of Religious Parties" (1839).

Voluminous as Newman's writings are, it is remarkable how few of the volumes were first written as full-length books. Instead, the vast majority consist of collections of articles, essays, lectures, letters, sermons, and tracts. It is indeed as though Newman required the stimulus of a particular occasion, a particular point of view to advocate or attack, or a particular opponent, before he could put pen to paper.

IAN KER

Biography

Born 21 February 1801 in London. Studied at Ealing School, London, 1808–16; Trinity College, Oxford, 1817–22, B.A., 1820. Fellow, Oriel College, Oxford, 1822–45. Ordained in the Anglican church, 1824; curate, St. Clement's, Oxford, 1824–26; vicar, St. Mary's, Oxford, 1828–43. Began the Oxford (Tractarian) Movement, with John Keble and E. B. Pusey, 1833: left it, 1842. Editor and contributor, *Tracts for the Times*, 1833–41; coeditor, *A Library of the Fathers of the Holy Catholic Church* series, from 1838. Joined the Roman Catholic Church, 1845; ordained priest, 1847. Established the Oratory of St. Philip Neri, Birmingham, 1848, and founded the attached boys' school. Rector, Catholic University of Ireland, Dublin, 1851–58. Editor, the *Rambler* Catholic journal, 1859. Made a Cardinal, 1879. Doctor of Divinity, Rome, 1850. Honorary Fellow, Trinity College, Oxford, 1878. Declared Venerable, 1991. Died in Birmingham, 11 August 1890.

Selected Writings

Essays and Related Prose
Tracts for the Times, anonymously published by Newman and others, 1833–41
Parochial Sermons, 6 vols., 1834–42; edited by W. J. Copeland, 6 vols., 1868; vol. 2 as *Sermons for the Festivals*, edited by Vernon Stanley, 1904
Lectures on the Prophetical Office of the Church, 1837
Lectures on Justification, 1838
The Church of the Fathers, 1840
The Tamworth Reading Room: Letters on an Address by Sir Robert Peel, 1841
Sermons, Bearing on Subjects of the Day, 1843; edited by W. J. Copeland, 1869
Sermons, Chiefly on the Theory of Religious Belief Preached Before the University of Oxford, 1843; enlarged edition, as *Fifteen Sermons Preached Before the University of Oxford, Between A.D. 1826 and 1843*, 1872
Plain Sermons by Contributors to Tracts for the Times, vol. 5, 1843; edited by W. J. Copeland, 2 vols., 1808
An Essay on the Development of Christian Doctrine, 1845; edited by G. Wiegel, 1960
Discourses Addressed to Mixed Congregations, 1849
Lectures on Certain Difficulties Felt by Anglicans in Submitting to the Catholic Church, 1850; revised edition, 1857
Lectures on the Present Position of Catholics in England, 1851; edited by J. J. Daly, 1942
Discourses on the Scope and Nature of University Education, 1852; revised edition, 1859

The Office and Work of Universities, 1856; as University Sketches, edited by G. Sampson, 1902; edited by Michael Tierney, 1964

Sermons Preached on Various Occasions, 1857

Lectures and Essays on University Subjects, 1859

Letter to the Rev. E. B. Pusey, D.D. on His Recent Eirenicon, 1866

An Essay in Aid of a Grammar of Assent, 1870; edited by Ian Ker, 1985

Miscellanies from the Oxford Sermons and Other Writings, 1870

Two Essays on Scripture Miracles and on Ecclesiastical, 1870

Essays Critical and Historical, 2 vols., 1872

Historical Sketches, 3 vols., 1872–73

The Idea of a University (includes Discourses on the Scope and Nature of University Education and Lectures and Essays on University Subjects), 1873; edited by Ian Ker, 1976, and Frank M. Turner, 1996

Tracts Theological and Ecclesiastical, 1874

A Letter to the Duke of Norfolk on the Occasion of Mr. Gladstone's Recent Expostulations, 1875

Stray Essays and Controversial Points, 1890

Essays and Sketches, edited by C. F. Harrold, 1948

Sermons and Discourses, edited by C. F. Harrold, 2 vols., 1949

Faith and Prejudice and Other Unpublished Sermons, edited by C. S. Dessain, 1956; as Catholic Sermons, 1957

A Newman Companion to the Gospels: Sermons, edited by Armel J. Coupet, 1966

The Genius of John Henry Newman: Selections from His Writings, edited by Ian Ker, 1989

Sermons, 1824–1843, edited by Vincent Ferrer Blehl, 2 vols., 1991–93

Selected Sermons, edited by Ian Ker, 1994

Other writings: the autobiography Apologia Pro Vita Sua (1865), poetry, and over 30 volumes of correspondence.

Collected works edition: Works (Uniform Edition), 41 vols., 1908–18.

Bibliographies

Blehl, Vincent Ferrer, John Henry Newman: A Bibliographical Catalogue of His Writings, Charlottesville: University Press of Virginia, 1978

Griffin, John R., John Henry Newman: A Bibliography of Secondary Sources, Front Royal, Virginia: Christendom Publications, 1980

Further Reading

Gilley, Sheridan, Newman and His Age, London: Darton Longman and Todd, 1990

Helmling, Steven, The Esoteric Comedies of Carlyle, Newman, and Yeats, Cambridge and New York: Cambridge University Press, 1988

Holloway, John, The Victorian Sage: Studies in Argument, London: Macmillan, 1953; New York: Norton, 1965

Houghton, Walter E., The Art of Newman's "Apologia", New Haven, Connecticut: Yale University Press, and London: Oxford University Press, 1945

Ker, Ian, John Henry Newman: A Biography, Oxford and New York: Oxford University Press, 1988

Ker, Ian, The Achievement of John Henry Newman, London: Collins, and Notre Dame, Indiana: University of Notre Dame Press, 1990

Levine, George, The Boundaries of Fiction: Carlyle, Macaulay, Newman, Princeton, New Jersey: Princeton University Press, 1968

Peterson, Linda H., Victorian Autobiography: The Tradition of Self-Interpretation, New Haven, Connecticut: Yale University Press, 1986: Chapter 4

Prickett, Stephen, Romanticism and Religion: The Tradition of Coleridge and Wordsworth in the Victorian Church, Cambridge and New York: Cambridge University Press, 1976: Chapters 6 and 7

Tillotson, Geoffrey, and Kathleen Tillotson, Mid-Victorian Studies, London: Athlone Press, 1965

Ngugi wa Thiong'o

Kenyan, 1938–

Ngugi wa Thiong'o has always insisted that his essays should be read alongside his novels: "... they have been products of the same moods and touch on similar questions and problems" (Homecoming, 1972). They indeed accompany the works of fiction as they trace the history of men and ideas in East Africa, from the hopeful days of independence to the later questioning of ways of asserting a truly African culture. They also trace the evolution of a novelist who is also a professor of literature and an international literary and political figure, required to address meetings in many parts of the world. His five collections to date reflect the change in the function of Ngugi's essays as his public itself changes. Homecoming: Essays on African and Caribbean Literature, Culture, and Politics (1972) consists of texts written from a university perspective. The author analyses the works of Chinua Achebe, Wole Soyinka, and George Lamming, at the same time proposing to widen the curriculum. The relevance of literature in the cultural life and educational system of a newly independent country is foremost in his mind. Art has a function to fulfill; "The Writer in a Changing Society" is representative of this central preoccupation, echoing Achebe's famous line, "The novelist is a teacher."

Writers in Politics (1981) was written between 1970 and 1980, accompanying the publication of Petals of Blood (1977). The latter is a committed novel which is a fierce indictment of injustice in Kenyan society, yet the writer knows that the masses in whose name he intends to speak will not have access to his book in English. He reiterates the question: "... what is the relevance of literature to life?" but this time does not think that a change in school reading lists will be enough to solve problems. While the first collection is marked by the thinking of Frantz Fanon, Writers in Politics is more clearly Marxist, with references to other world literatures such as that of North Korea.

Two events radicalized his approach even further. First, in December 1977 he was detained for a year without charges after the production of a play in his original language Gikuyu was promptly banned by the regime; the experience is related in Detained (1981), both an autobiography and a meditation. Second, in 1982, an attempted coup took place in Nairobi: while order was restored, Ngugi was not allowed to return to his country and was forced to remain in exile. Barrel of a Pen: Resistance to Repression in Neo-Colonial Kenya (1983) is an angry account of the way opposition is quashed; parallels are drawn with the liberation struggles of the Mau Mau period. Recent events, with photographic documents about the banned play and detained students, figure prominently in the book, yet even when using these images of violent conflict, Ngugi still pursues his reflection on the part played by oral and written art in "National Identity and Imperialist Domination: The Crisis of Culture in Africa Today."

The book that follows is a meditation on the central problem of the choice between English or African languages for literature. By 1980 Ngugi had decided to write his fiction in Gikuyu. On this topic, Decolonising the Mind: The Politics of Language in African Literature (1986) collects essays which were mostly delivered as university lectures. The focus of the work is clear, and the debate is set at a consistently high level. This volume is an important contribution to the discussion of cultural assertion in the face of various types of domination.

The most recent volume, *Moving the Centre: The Struggle for Cultural Freedoms* (1993), gathers texts which for the most part were first spoken addresses at various occasions, often of a political nature. It covers no new ground in its attack on the hegemony of a new multinational order. Ngugi asks for action and cultural resistance: the title, a kind of retort to V. S. Naipaul's more inward-looking *Finding the Centre* (1984), proposes a shift away from the neo-colonial metropolis to a world where a plurality of centers would engage in a fruitful dialogue.

Many of these essays are historical landmarks, mapping the development and the assertion of an African world view. Ngugi is an intellectual novelist, a theoretician who with exacting honesty takes pains to analyze his position in an explicit, sometimes dogmatic corollary to his works of art. The essays clarify the issues, whereas the polyphonic novels allow room for debate, complexity, and contradiction. His essays are always extremely clear, even didactic, with logical developments and well-organized structures, often giving examples in the shape of parables. At his worst, and particularly in the last volume, Ngugi can give a reductive political **sermon**, often reiterating ideas expressed in other Marxist-inspired writings. At his best, however, he can summon all the resources of spoken rhetoric: he is a compelling speaker, and several essays are given life by rhythmic assertions and sarcastic questioning, a polemic mode that carries a great deal of energy. In many ways, once the political immediacy recedes, the texts with the most appeal are of two kinds: the pieces of literary criticism, which are among the best by an African writer, and the most personal moments, the "grains of sand" which, being intimate, reveal the vulnerable human being, the man whose love of life is the profound motivating source of so much didactic energy. "Matigari, and the Dreams of One East Africa," an essay from *Moving the Centre* devoted to the identity of East Africa, has at its core a description of a fishing party in Dar es Salaam. The evocation of the tastes, the smells, the voices of Tanzania so close to inaccessible Kenya across the border contains the pleasures and the pain of the exile. Such passages display the best qualities of the fictional prose as well as the firm intellectual control of the essays. As such they are likely to endure beyond the time and place that occasioned them.

JACQUELINE BARDOLPH

Biography
Originally wrote as James T. Ngugi. Born 5 January 1938 in Kamiriithu, near Limuru, Kiambu District. Studied at Alliance High School, Gikuyu; Makerere University College, Kampala, Uganda, 1959–63, B.A., 1963; Leeds University, Yorkshire, 1964–67, B.A., 1964. Married Nyambura, 1961: five sons and three daughters. Columnist of "As I See It," early 1960s, and reporter, 1964, Nairobi *Daily Nation*; editor, *Zuka*, Nairobi, 1965–70; lecturer in English, University College, Nairobi, 1967–69; fellow in creative writing, Makerere University, Kampala, 1969–70; visiting lecturer, Northwestern University, Evanston, Illinois, 1970–71; senior lecturer, associate professor, and chair of the Department of Literature, University of Nairobi, 1972–77. Imprisoned under the Public Security Act, 31 December 1977–12 December 1978. Was

staying in London in 1982 when an attempted coup in Kenya made it impossible for him, a well-known opponent to the regime, to return to his country: lived for six years in London; taught at Yale University, New Haven, Connecticut, 1989–92, and New York University, from 1992; also gives lectures and talks in various universities and at conferences around the world. Awards: East African Literature Bureau Award, 1964.

Selected Writings

Essays and Related Prose
Homecoming: Essays on African and Caribbean Literature, Culture, and Politics, 1972
Writers in Politics, 1981
Barrel of a Pen: Resistance to Repression in Neo-Colonial Kenya, 1983
Decolonising the Mind: The Politics of Language in African Literature, 1986
Moving the Centre: The Struggle for Cultural Freedoms, 1993

Other writings: four novels in English (*Weep Not, Child*, 1964; *The River Between*, 1965; *A Grain of Wheat*, 1967; *Petals of Blood*, 1977), short stories (*Secret Lives*, 1975), two novels originally in Gikuyu (*Devil on the Cross*, 1982; *Matigari*, 1989), the autobiographical *Detained: A Writer's Prison Diary* (1981), and several plays, alone or in collaboration.

Bibliography
Sicherman, Carol, *Ngugi wa Thiong'o: A Bibliography of Primary and Secondary Sources, 1957–1987*, London and New York: Zell, 1989

Further Reading
Cook, David, and Michael Okenimpke, *Ngugi wa Thiong'o: An Exploration of His Writings*, London: Heinemann, 1983
Sicherman, Carol, *Ngugi wa Thiong'o, the Making of a Rebel: A Source Book in Kenyan Literature and Resistance*, London and New York: Zell, 1990

Nietzsche, Friedrich
German, 1844–1900

Friedrich Nietzsche was perhaps the most influential writer at the end of the 19th century. He wrote in an innovative, fragmentary style for a small group of friends and like-minded "free spirits" who were not beholden to any ideology or afraid of looking into the abyss of the unknown and uncontrollable. He described himself as dynamite rather than as merely human and is best known for his re-evaluation of all values. The prophet Zarathustra's self-description in *Also sprach Zarathustra* (1883–85; *Thus Spoke Zarathustra*) applies to the author himself: "I move about among mankind as among the fragments of the future, of that future which I envision. That is the object of my writing and striving: I write as poetry and bring together into a whole that which is fragment and enigma and horrible accident." Some readers even make him responsible for the "death of God," although he was only observing the general movement in the 19th century from traditional beliefs (myth) to a trust in science, commerce, and industry. His essayistic stance is dictated by resistance to those growing tendencies and by his desire for renewed vigor. The latter explains why his writing is largely subtitled a philosophy of/for the future.

Nietzsche's writing can be divided roughly into three phases. The first corresponds to his development as a professor of classical philology in Basle. It consists of the influential essay *Die Geburt der Tragödie* (1872; *The Birth of Tragedy*) and the celebrated essay collection *Unzeitgemässe Betrachtungen* (1873–76; *Untimely Meditations*). The latter includes "David Strauss, der Bekenner und Schriftsteller" (1873; "David Strauss, the Confessor and the Writer"), "Vom Nutzen und Nachteil der Historie für das Leben" (1874; "On the Advantage and Disadvantage of History for Life"), "Schopenhauer als Erzieher" (1874; "Schopenhauer as Educator"), and "Richard Wagner in Bayreuth" (1876). His cultural criticism is directed against "theoretical man," that is, against the scientific positivism and industrialization of the 19th century, in the manner of **Ralph Waldo Emerson** and **Arthur Schopenhauer**, whom he greatly admired. Optimism, democracy, and logic are for Nietzsche signs of declining vitality, while logical inconsistency is valued positively. With its nonscientific images and constructions, art appears as an instrument of resistance in his struggle against the myth-destroying rationalism of Socrates.

The second phase includes the collections *Menschliches, Allzumenschliches* (1878–80; *Human, All Too Human*), *Morgenröthe* (1881; *Daybreak*), and *Die fröhliche Wissenschaft* (1882; *The Gay Science*) and represents the power of negation in preparing the ground for new possibilities. Nietzsche attempts here a new conception of science and a re-evaluation of the relationship between art and knowledge. Chemistry, the historicity of natural events which Nietzsche once considered as a disciplinary field, replaces the timeless world myth. The breaking down into elements displaces the sense of an organic whole. Nietzsche emerges here as the radical skeptic, psychologist, and analyst.

The third phase begins already with the end of *The Gay Science* with its scorn of numbers and calculation, continuing through *Zarathustra*, *Jenseits von Gut und Böse* (1886; *Beyond Good and Evil*), "Der Fall Wagner" (1888; "The Case of Wagner"), *Götzen-Dämmerung* (1889; *Twilight of the Idols*), and *Ecce homo* (wr. 1888, pub. 1908), to the late essays *Der Antichrist* (1895; *The Antichrist*) and *Nietzsche contra Wagner* (1889). (Several volumes of posthumously published fragments, among them the so-called *Der Wille zur Macht* [1901; *The Will to Power*], were penned throughout his life and therefore do not necessarily belong to the late phase.) Everywhere is heard the call for a transvaluation of all values, Nietzsche's great metaphysical essay. In this phase art is rehabilitated as the necessary counterweight to the devitalizing influence of knowledge: "Art is the great enabler of life, the great temptress to life, the great stimulant of life" (*The Gay Science*). In the third phase the love of lies and masks dominates because Nietzsche has recognized that life is impossible without falsification.

For Nietzsche art and intellectual inquiry thus went hand in hand. Despite his deep love of music, his own preferred art form was aphoristic and essayistic in nature. In the essay and late preface to his *Birth of Tragedy*, "Versuch einer Selbstkritik" (1886; "Essay in Self-Criticism"), he laments the fact that he was not bold enough in 1872 to adopt a new tone of discourse, one sparked by the language of poetry and free of the bonds of Kantian and Schopenhauerean categories. The regret is due to the fact that *The Birth of Tragedy* was his first attempt at seeing science through the eyes of the artist and art from the perspective of life itself. His entire opus is an attempt to read life, art, and science as if they were all texts open to interpretation. That attitude led to the "untimely meditations" dispersed throughout his opus: "Untimely," as he explains in the essay "On the Advantage and Disadvantage of History," because he argued that his age was marked by loss, frailty, and deficiency rather than strength and vigor.

Nietzsche's writing is exemplary for the intimate, albeit uneasy nexus of philosophy and literature. A fundamental quality of his writing and thinking is the ever-present perspectivism, a point emphatically made in the essayistic **preface** to *Beyond Good and Evil* where he calls perspectivism "the fundamental condition of all life." Since polyperspectivism lies at the center both of the quest for truth and of literariness, it is not surprising that Nietzsche is claimed as a model by continental philosophers and literary critics alike. Some even claim that literature holds the most promise for shedding light on some of the toughest epistemic problems.

Life for Nietzsche was literature, since the asceticism of his writings is both the motivation for and the result of perspectivism (Alexander Nehamas, 1985). The world is comprehended as if it were a text; in fact, Nietzsche viewed his own life as a text in the making. The only abstraction possible is that of perspectivism as the ruling principle of existence with its partial and fragmented views of things. All is only a series of shifting masks, of lies about the world and the self. The meaning of those partial views is constructed by the author and his reader in dynamic interplay, for the reader is not given a detailed road map of the author's constructed text, just the principle of perspectivism. Nietzsche eschewed straight-line approaches and required the reader's creative participation.

To do justice to Nietzsche as essayist, then, one must take his mode of writing fully into account. Behind that mode of writing is a philosophical attitude toward the world and the self. Essentially, it asks what can be said about the world, the self, and the future. Since Nietzsche considered human beings to be so many fragments of an unrealized future, his task as a writer and philosopher was to advance the organic unfolding of those fragmentary natures into full constructs. Philosophy always contains an element of autobiography, as do works of art. *Ecce homo* is an especially apt example of this alignment. Key is Nietzsche's self-conscious experimentation with genre mixing, of which the chief characteristics are fragmentation and hyperbole. The latter is variously guised as exaggeration, extravagance, errancy, and quest. Its underlying concern seems to be whether writing motivates thought or thought motivates writing. The hyperbole so favored by Nietzsche is a response to Socrates' preferred method of understatement (litotes). In any event, the reader is constrained to enact meaning and to "do" philosophy. The Romantic roots of this manner of thinking and writing are clear (cf. **Friedrich Schlegel**). All this questioning movement is related to the project of essayism. No wonder, then, that Nietzsche is widely acclaimed as a classical essayist. While his preferred genre is the **aphorism**, many of those so-called aphorisms are, in fact, essays.

In the long essay *The Birth of Tragedy*, Nietzsche early on formulates his essential stance and attitude toward truth, life, art, and ultimately writerliness. Fundamental is the tension between the natural Apollonian forces of harmony and ordering on the one hand and the Dionysian powers of intoxication and disruption on the other. Like **Heinrich von Kleist** before him, Nietzsche laments the loss of natural movement through the rise of self-consciousness. The dance metaphorically symbolizes the coordination of these dialectical forces and insures humankind's participation in a higher commonality with nature (cf. *Human, All Too Human*). In the essay "Über Wahrheit und Lüge im aussermoralischen Sinne" (1873; "On Truth and Lies in an Extra-Moral Sense") Nietzsche explicitly contends that humankind can live in a semblance of peace, security, and consistency only by losing its self-conscious sense of subjectivity as an "artistically creative subject." There is no causal relationship between subject and object, only an aesthetic one; that is, one of nuance and approximation, of "rough translation into a totally foreign tongue" – in other words, that of the dance. Thus one can never achieve the "right" perspective, for the right perspective is the one which is never present and ever-fleeting. Obviously this balancing act of shifting perspectives is the essence of life, art, and the act of writing. The dancing motif reflects the interpenetration of poetic creation and reflective moment to the point where they become indistinguishable.

Nietzsche's opus is rich with essayistic assessments of this relationship between science and poetry. A few examples will have to suffice. *The Gay Science, Zarathustra, Beyond Good and Evil, Zur Genealogie der Moral* (1887; *A Genealogy of Morals*), and *Twilight of the Idols* contain numerous essays in the garb of aphorisms. In *The Gay Science* we find, for instance, no. 357: "Zum alten Problem: 'was ist deutsch?'" ("On the Old Problem: What Is German?"); no. 366: "Angesichts eines gelehrten Buches" ("Encounter with a Scholarly Book"); no. 377: "Wir Heimatlosen" ("We Homeless People"); no. 381: "Zur Frage der Verständlichkeit" ("On Incomprehensibility"). In *Zarathustra* the chapters "Von der Erlösung" ("On Redemption"), "Vom Vorübergehen" ("On Passing By"), and "Vom Geist der Schwere" ("On the Spirit of Heaviness") are excellent examples of rhapsodic essays. Especially telling is Zarathustra's remark in "On the Spirit of Heaviness": "Ein Versuchen und Fragen war all mein Gehen." The German is full of ironic playfulness and ambiguity, for "Versuchen" is an "attempting" or "essaying"; "Fragen" is the skeptical attitude of questioning toward all encounters on one's travels through life; and the classic metaphor of the private, leisurely walk in essayistic writing is echoed in "mein Gehen." Thus, the translation might read: "Attempting and questioning was my whole progression."

This attitude is further mirrored in *Beyond Good and Evil*, in particular aphorisms nos. 44, 188, 203, 208, 224, and 230 with their numerous, tentative solutions, and invitation to think things through. They all have more in common with the style and tone of the essay than with the laconic aphorism. The themes, style, and length of the pieces cited are classically essayistic. The same holds true for the involvement of the reader in seemingly personal **meditations** upon weighty as well as seemingly trivial subjects.

Finally, in aphorism no. 381 of *The Gay Science* Nietzsche explains his "aphoristic" style once more as the most appropriate for the expression of his ideas. He believes namely that his writings are designed to stimulate and uplift the reader. His approach to profound problems, he states, is the way one approaches a cold bath: jump in quickly and get out quickly. The genuine attitude of the philosopher, Nietzsche adds, is that of a dancer: "The dance, namely, is his ideal, also his art, finally also his devoutness, his divine service." Here he succinctly summarizes not only his own style of writing but also the essence of the essayistic attitude. Nietzsche viewed the relationship between scientific inquiry and art, philosophy, and life, in the manner of a true essayist.

JOHN A. MCCARTHY

See also Philosophical Essay

Biography

Friedrich Wilhelm Nietzsche. Born 15 October 1844 in Röcken. Studied at Pforta School, 1858–64; philosophy and theology at the University of Bonn, 1864–65; University of Leipzig, 1865–67, Ph.D., 1869. Became friends with Richard Wagner, 1868. Chair of classical philology, University of Basle, 1869–79: retired because of ill health. Volunteer in the army medical service, 1867–68. Gave up Prussian citizenship, 1869, and remained stateless for the rest of his life. Traveled often to Sils Maria, Nice, and Italy, 1879–89. Suffered from mental illness for the last 11 years of his life. Died in Weimar, 25 August 1900.

Selected Writings

Essays and Related Prose

Die Geburt der Tragödie aus dem Geiste der Musik, 1872; as *Die Geburt der Tragödie; oder, Griechentum und Pessimismus*, 1886; as *The Birth of Tragedy*, translated by William A. Haussmann, 1909, Francis Golffing, 1956, Walter Kaufmann, 1967, and Shaun Whiteside, 1993

Die Philosophie im tragischen Zeitalter der Griechen, 1873; as *Philosophy in the Tragic Age of the Greeks*, translated by Marianne Cowan, 1962

Unzeitgemässe Betrachtungen, 4 vols., 1873–76; as *Unmodern Observations: Thoughts Out of Season*, translated by Anthony M. Ludovici, 1909; as *Untimely Meditations*, translated by R. J. Hollingdale, 1983; as *Unfashionable Observations*, translated by Richard T. Gray, 1995

David Strauss, der Bekenner und der Schriftsteller, 1873

Vom Nutzen und Nachteil der Historie für das Leben, 1874; as *The Use and Abuse of History*, translated by Adrian Collins, 1949; as *Of the Advantage and Disadvantage of History for Life*, translated by Peter Preuss, 1980

Schopenhauer als Erzieher, 1874; as *Schopenhauer as Educator*, translated by James W. Hillesheim and Malcolm B. Simpson, 1965

Richard Wagner in Bayreuth, 1876

Menschliches, Allzumenschliches: Ein Buch für freie Geister, 3 vols., 1878–80; complete edition, 1886; as *Human, All Too Human: A Book for Free Spirits*, translated by Alexander Harvey, 1908, Helen Zimmern and Paul V. Cohn, 2 vols., 1909–11, Marion Faber and Stephen Lehmann, 1984, and R. J. Hollingdale, 1986

Morgenröthe, Gedanken über die moralischen Vorurteile, 1881; enlarged edition, 1887; as *The Dawn of Day*, translated by Johanna Volz, 1903, and J. M. Kennedy, 1974; as *Daybreak: Thoughts on the Prejudices of Morality*, translated by R. J. Hollingdale, 1982

Die fröhliche Wissenschaft, 1882; enlarged edition, 1887; as *The Joyful Wisdom*, translated by Thomas Common, 1910; as *The Gay Science*, translated by Walter Kaufmann, 1974

Also sprach Zarathustra: Ein Buch für Alle und Keinen, 4 vols., 1883–85; revised edition, 1892; as *Thus Spoke Zarathustra: A Book for All and None*, translated by Alexander Tille, 1896, Thomas Common, 1898, Marianne Cowan, 1957, R. J. Hollingdale, 1961, and William Kaufmann, 1966

Jenseits von Gut und Böse: Vorspiel einer Philosophie der Zukunft, 1886; as *Beyond Good and Evil: Prelude to the Philosophy of the Future*, translated by Helen Zimmern, 1909, Marianne Cowan, 1955, William Kaufmann, 1966, and R. J. Hollingdale, 1973

Zur Genealogie der Moral: Eine Streitschrift, 1887; as *A Genealogy of Morals*, translated by William A. Haussmann, 1897, Horace B. Samuel, 1910, and Francis Golffing, 1956; as *On the Genealogy of Morals*, translated by William Kaufmann and R. J. Hollingdale, 1967, and Carole Diethe, 1994

Götzen-Dämmerung; oder, Wie man mit dem Hammer philosophirt, 1889; as *Twilight of the Idols*, translated by Thomas Common, 1896, Anthony M. Ludovici, 1911, and R. J. Hollingdale, 1968

Der Antichrist: Fluch auf das Christenthum, 1895; as *The Antichrist*, translated by Thomas Common, 1896, H. L. Mencken, 1920 (reprinted 1988), P. R. Stephenson, 1928, and R. J. Hollingdale, 1968

Nietzsche contra Wagner: Aktenstücke eines Psychologen, 1889; as *Nietzsche contra Wagner*, translated by Thomas Common, 1896

Der Wille zur Macht, edited by P. Gast and Elisabeth Förster-Nietzsche, 1901; as *The Will to Power*, translated by Anthony M. Ludovici, 2 vols., 1909–10, and R. J. Hollingdale and Walter Kaufmann, 1968

Ecce homo: Wie man wird – was man ist, edited by Raoul Richter, 1908; as *Ecce Homo: How One Becomes What One Is*, translated by Anthony M. Ludovici, 1911, and R. J. Hollingdale, 1979

The Portable Nietzsche, edited by Walter Kaufmann, 1954
Basic Writings, edited by Walter Kaufmann, 1968
A Nietzsche Reader, edited by R. J. Hollingdale, 1977
Nietzsche Selections, edited by Richard Schacht, 1993
Hammer of the Gods: Selected Writings, edited and translated by Stephen Metcalf, 1996

Other writings: poetry, notebooks, and correspondence.

Collected works editions: *Werke: Grossoktavausgabe*, edited by the Nietzsche Archive, 15 vols., 1894–1904; *The Complete Works*, edited by Oscar Levy, various translators (as listed after individual works above), 18 vols., 1909–11; *Sämtliche Werke: Kritische Studienausgabe*, edited by Giorgio Colli and Mazzino Montinari, 15 vols., 1967–86; *Complete Works* (Stanford Edition), edited by Ernst Behler, 1994– (in progress).

Bibliography

Reichert, Herbert W., and Karl Schlechta, *International Nietzsche Bibliography*, Chapel Hill: University of North Carolina Press, revised edition, 1968 (original edition, 1960)

Further Reading

Allison, David B., editor, *The New Nietzsche: Contemporary Styles of Interpretation*, New York: Dell, 1977
Del Caro, Adrian, *Nietzsche contra Nietzsche: Creativity and the Anti-Romantic*, Baton Rouge: Louisiana State University Press, 1989
De Man, Paul, "Rhetoric of Tropes (Nietzsche)," in his *Allegories of Reading: Figural Language in Rousseau, Nietzsche, Rilke and Proust*, New Haven, Connecticut: Yale University Press, 1979: 103–18
Derrida, Jacques, *Spurs: Nietzsche's Styles*, Chicago: University of Chicago Press, 1979 (original French edition, 1978)
Fleischer, Margot, *Der "Sinn der Erde" und die Entzauberung des Übermenschen: Eine Auseinandersetzung mit Nietzsche*, Darmstadt: Wissenschaftliche Buchgesellschaft, 1993

Heller, Erich, *The Importance of Nietzsche: Ten Essays*, Chicago: University of Chicago Press, 1988
Holub, Robert, *Friedrich Nietzsche*, New York: Twayne, and London: Prentice Hall International, 1995
Kofman, Sarah, *Nietzsche and Metaphor*, Stanford, California: Stanford University Press, and London: Athlone Press, 1993 (original French edition, 1972)
Magnus, Bernd, Stanley Stewart, and Jean-Pierre Mileur, *Nietzsche's Case: Philosophy as/and Literature*, New York and London: Routledge, 1993
Nehamas, Alexander, *Nietzsche: Life as Literature*, Cambridge, Massachusetts: Harvard University Press, 1985
Pütz, Peter, "Nietzsche: Art and Intellectual Inquiry," in *Nietzsche: Imagery and Thought: A Collection of Essays*, edited by Malcolm Pasley, Berkeley: University of California Press, and London: Methuen, 1978: 1–32
Solomon, Robert C., editor, *Nietzsche: A Collection of Critical Essays*, Notre Dame, Indiana: University of Notre Dame Press, 1980
Staten, Henry, *Nietzsche's Voice*, Ithaca, New York: Cornell University Press, 1990
Stern, J. P., "Nietzsche and the Idea of Metaphor," in *Nietzsche: Imagery and Thought: A Collection of Essays*, edited by Malcolm Pasley, Berkeley: University of California Press, and London: Methuen, 1978: 65–81
Williams, W. D., "Nietzsche's Masks," in *Nietzsche: Imagery and Thought: A Collection of Essays*, edited by Malcolm Pasley, Berkeley: University of California Press, and London: Methuen, 1978: 82–103

Nouvelle Revue Française

French periodical, 1908–14, 1919–43, 1953–

The *Nouvelle Revue Française* (New French review) began publishing at the end of 1908, at first as a literary review, though its character changed radically as its editorial policy and contents became politicized in the 1930s. The dominating mind behind the foundation, the early aims, and the editorial policy of the *NRF* was that of **André Gide**, a leading member of the avant-garde who, like the painters surrounding Picasso at the same time, had in the early years of the 20th century turned away from the cultural movement we know as symbolism. The prepublication announcement of the *NRF* said that it aspired to be the review of the generation "which immediately followed symbolism." It was to take the position once held by the *Mercure de France* (Mercury of France) and the Natanson brothers' *Revue Blanche* (White review). Gide had published in the symbolist *L'Ermitage* (The hermitage) and in the *Revue Blanche*, and had been literary editor for the latter for six months. He had introduced his brother-in-law, Marcel Drouin, to both reviews, and had come to know his Belgian admirer André Ruyters and the writer Henri Ghéon. This quartet formed the core of the founding group of the *Nouvelle Revue Française*, soon enlarged to form a sextet with Jean Schlumberger and Jacques Copeau.

This group had practically taken over the Belgian periodical *Antée* when Gide's play *Le Roi Candaule* (*King Candaules*) failed after one performance in Berlin; at the same time, *Antée* nearly merged with the still symbolist *La Phalange* (The phalanx). The group, by now regarding itself as Gide's team, began planning its review, and the first number was published in November 1908. Gide objected to two of the articles and to the way his own "Notes" had been treated, wanting the review to reflect a corporate view, while some of the others preferred to make it a forum for debate. The editorial group split on the issue, broke up, and a new group, consisting only of Gide, Schlumberger, and Copeau, announced a second number for 1 February 1909. The series ran for 68 numbers until interrupted by World War I, a new series beginning with no. 69 on 1 June 1919.

The title of the new review was deliberately nationalistic, as the prevailing fashion demanded. Recently founded titles had included the daily version of *L'Action Française* (French action) and *La Patrie Française* (French homeland). Memories of the Franco-Prussian war were still vivid, and the Dreyfus affair, like the strong alliance of radical socialism with nationalism in **Charles Péguy**, testified to the strength of nationalist feeling in France. The price of the review was fixed sufficiently high to enable it to accommodate longer pieces. The chief editorial problems it faced concerned the difficulty of finding sufficiently brief texts of high literary quality, and Gide's meticulous perfectionism, leading to fastidiousness with proofs and frequently late submission of material. The first three numbers contained in three parts Gide's first undoubted masterpiece, *La Porte étroite* (*Strait Is the Gate*), perhaps best described as a novella. It was shot through with delicate inlays of irony and refined psychological nuance, with multiple references to the intricacies of intellectual debate in France during the century's first decade.

Schlumberger's essay "Considérations" in the first number tried hard to reconcile the intention not to let the review become the mouthpiece of a coterie with the desire to make it the product of the "strong unity of a group." The review was largely apolitical, but liberally pro-Dreyfus, while, like Péguy, remaining patriotic. Serious work inspired by Catholic conviction did not prevent the attempt to insulate aesthetic from moral values. The keynote was the liberal, civilized treatment of all serious literature, philosophy, and cultural attitudes, although the review has been criticized for not noticing what was occurring in the political world or in the world of the visual arts, and for not noticeably encouraging new nonliterary talent. It did indeed miss the revolution in painting occurring in Montmartre, the strong anti-symbolist reaction in all the arts, and the impact of Sergei Diaghilev on French culture. It was *Le Figaro* which published the futurist manifesto.

The *NRF* prospered, and founded its own in-house publishing company, largely to insure the availability of offprints. Issues quickly reached 185 pages, and the publishing house, at first known by the NRF initials, became in 1911 "Éditions Gallimard" when the review's publishing committee sold out to its publishing manager. The review adapted well to France's cultural life in the 1920s. It sponsored the Pontigny literary workshops of Paul Desjardins, and helped Copeau, who was training the great actor-producers Louis Jouvet and Charles Dullin at the Vieux-Colombier. After World War I Gide, still the guiding figure, began to hand over the review's direction to Jacques Rivière, and its writers came to include Louis Aragon, André Breton, Marcel Jouhandeau, François Mauriac, Paul Morand, and, briefly, Marcel Proust.

During the 1930s the major cultural constraint acting on French intellectuals was the apparent choice in Europe between fascism, as it had appeared in Hitler's Germany, Mussolini's Italy, and Franco's Spain, and the communism which took its inspiration from the Russian Revolution. The *NRF*, necessarily reflecting the need for France to choose between the conflicting ideologies which might pull the European economies out of their depression, gradually became more important for its famous chronicle of cultural events in France than for its prose writing. Jean Paulhan, director from 1935, nevertheless continued to find and publish work during that period from the best of France's available literary talent.

The *NRF* ceased publication in June 1940, the month in which Paris was taken by German troops. It was reopened under the editorship of the pro-Nazi Pierre-Eugène Drieu la Rochelle in November 1940, but drifted too far toward an admiration for Stalinist communism to please the occupying authorities, and was discontinued in June 1943. By that date few of its former authors were willing to be published in its pages, and Drieu la Rochelle, eventually to commit suicide, had become disillusioned by Hitler. However, in 1953 the *NRF* began publication once more, under the title *La Nouvelle Nouvelle Revue Française* (the clumsy second *Nouvelle* was eventually dropped), edited by Paulhan and the journalist and critic Marcel Arland. Since then it has continued to attempt to maintain high standards and to serve as the barometer of French culture.

ANTHONY LEVI

Anthologies

L'Esprit NRF: 1908–1940 (selections), edited by Pierre Hebey, Paris: Gallimard, 1990
La Nouvelle Revue Francaise: Études et travaux, edited by Claude Martin, Lyons: University of Lyons II Center for Gide Studies, 9 vols., 1975– (in progress)

Further Reading

Angles, Auguste, *André Gide et le premier groupe de la "Nouvelle Revue Française"*, Paris: Gallimard, 3 vols., 1978–86
Cabanis, José, *Dieu et la "Nouvelle Revue Française": 1909–1949*, Paris: Gallimard, 1994
Cornick, Martyn, *Intellectuals in History: The "Nouvelle Revue Française" Under Jean Paulhan, 1925–1940*, Amsterdam and Atlanta: Rodopi, 1995
Hebey, Pierre, *La NRF des années sombres: Juin 1940–juin 1941, des intellectuels à la dérive*, Paris: Gallimard, 1992
Lacouture, Jean, *Une adolescence du siècle: Jacques Rivière et la "Nouvelle Revue Française"*, Paris: Seuil, 1994
Morino, Lina, *La "Nouvelle Revue Française" dans l'histoire des lettres*, Paris: Gallimard, 1939
Naughton, Helen T., editor, *The Critics of the "Nouvelle Revue Française"*, L'Esprit Créateur special issue, 14, no. 2 (1974)

Novalis

German, 1772–1801

Georg Philipp Friedrich von Hardenberg, who adopted the pen name Novalis, is universally considered the prototypical German Romantic. The magical idealism he developed in his literary writings remains one of the enduringly great aesthetic accomplishments of the culture of German-speaking countries. Like his poetry and novels, the few essay-like writings composed by Novalis during his short life profoundly influenced German-speaking writers of the calibre of Joseph von Eichendorff, Rainer Maria Rilke, Hermann Hesse, and **Thomas Mann**, to name just a few. These works contain Novalis' inchoate attempt to develop a speculative and aesthetic synthesis of reality, which his literary writings later brought to a higher level of fruition. He dreamed of achieving a "magical" unification of major dimensions of human existence, encompassing such realms as the marital, political, historical, and mystical. In his essays, Novalis envisages a pantheistic harmonization of these constellations that springs from his perception of the mythic power of poetry to evoke and illuminate the absolute Ego (*Ich*), which constitutes the ground of nature.

Novalis' first published prose work was a loose series of philosophical fragments entitled "Blütenstaub" (1798; "Pollen"). These fragments originally appeared in the Schlegel brothers' journal *Athenäum*. Each short piece in this collection is written in a prose style that synthesizes abstract philosophical insights with a richly layered poetic language. Novalis' intention in composing these speculative vignettes was not that of elaborating a systematic argument. It reflected, on the contrary, an attempt to provide poetic spirits – those endowed with the potential to discover a higher metaphysical vocation in life – with a series of hieroglyphic messages, whose symbolic content emanates from the transcendent realm of the Absolute Ego. This notion derives from **Johann Gottlieb Fichte**'s *Grundlage des gesammten Wissenschaftslehre* (1794; *The Science of Knowledge*), a philosophical work that exerted a profound influence on Novalis' speculative thinking.

For Novalis, the soteriological purpose of the tiny essay fragments in "Pollen" lay in aiding higher spirits to discover "[den] Weg nach Innen": the esoteric spiritual path leading to the numinous, inner depths of the soul. In this sphere the soul enters into mystical communion with the true essence of nature: the universal Mind which constitutes the Being of the eternal universe. In opposition to Fichte's idealism, however, Novalis views this epiphany not as a rationalistic *Amor intellectualis Dei*, but as an eminently transcognitional intuition. Novalis affirms that in the *ecstasis* of this beatific contemplation, the human soul apprehends the fundamental ideality of nature's hypostatic essence. It thus becomes overwhelmed by a mystic yearning (*Sehnsucht*) to transform the external, material world: the tenebrous realm of the Fichtean Non-Ego (*Nicht-Ich*). Its spiritual vision causes the soul to endeavor to transfuse this dark, ultimately irreal sphere of sensually conditioned determinacy (*Bestimmtheit*) with the intelligible refulgence that radiates from its infinite ontological source. Thus, according to Novalis' reinterpretation of Fichtean metaphysics, their experience of the Fichtean Absolute Ego impels the chosen spirits who attain enlightenment ethically and poetically to strive to transfigure the external world, reinvesting the domain of the *Nicht-Ich* with the ideal presence of the Absolute.

Another series of essay fragments, entitled "Glaube und Liebe" (1798; Faith and love), contains Novalis' chiliastic reflections on politics. A dominant impetus of this work consists in the latter's utopian vision of the ideal monarch. For Novalis, monarchy represents an essential stage in the spiritual development of humanity toward a state of being in which each individual will embody the higher virtues of Platonic love and enlightened rationality. This universal spirituality is destined ultimately to supersede all forms of human government. Novalis embraces the notion that democracy reflects a higher theory of government than monarchy. However, he also expresses the belief that European humanity is not yet ethically prepared to assume the full freedom of individual self-determination prerequisite to realizing this higher order. Novalis avers that if the people are not given an education that promotes their appropriation of higher virtues, democratic government will inevitably degenerate into mobocracy. On this basis, present-day kings in Europe have an important ethical role to fulfill in terms of their ability to assume a status as avatars of pantheistic virtues, such as enlightened tolerance, Christ-like gentleness, and the Spinozan intellectual love of God. By providing such an example, rulers can evoke the higher moral and intellectual nature dormant in the hearts of their subjects. This will prepare humanity for a chiliastic age in which government will be rendered unnecessary, inasmuch as all human beings will live by the law of Christ. Hence, in Novalis' view, a king's power should not be based on military might or political force, but on his divine calling as a moral and spiritual guide for his subjects.

Novalis' most coherent essay bears the title "Die Christenheit, oder Europa" (wr. 1799, pub. 1826; "Christianity or Europe"). In this work, the poet articulates a theory of history whose culmination lies in a quasi-Hegelian realization of humanity's universal spiritual unity and peace. This represents a historical symphony divided into three major movements. The first resides in Novalis' vision of a utopian Middle Ages. Here European civilization basked in the spiritual light flowing from the Catholic religion. In this age, European humanity dwelt in a state of harmonious unity with God and the Church. According to Novalis' fairytale description of the medieval period, the Pope, like the rulers of Europe in general, represented a spiritual father of the people whose power was vouchsafed him by Christ. While the light of Christ reigned throughout Europe in the personage of the Pope, humanity remained in a state of universal peace. However, a necessary stage of humanity's historical development came in the form of a break-up of the ecclesiastical and political harmony that pervaded the Middle Ages.

The Reformation and Enlightenment periods of European history signified humanity's loss of the spiritual peace and security it had formerly enjoyed. One of the historical reasons for this loss lay in the preponderance, during the Middle Ages, of the communal spirit over that of the individual. This latter principle was rightfully posited and developed during the Reformation. This development proceeded, in particular, through Luther's insistence upon the unmediated personal communion between the individual believer and the *lux vera* of Christ. Like the Protestant Reformation, modern natural science, which flourished during the Enlightenment, enhanced the life of the individual in its endeavor to promote human happiness by transforming nature. However, the dangers inherent in these historical phases of humankind's development manifested themselves in the form of modern science's reduction of the spirit of the Bible to the letter of the text. This exegetical reductionism was complemented by the rationalist endeavors of science during the Enlightenment to dissect and mathematically analyze the living beauty of divine nature. This coldly analytical approach to the world sought to displace the pantheistic spirit of the universe with its mechanistic conception of nature. But the passionate aspirations of the French Revolution, which for Novalis marked the culmination of the Enlightenment as well as its end, paved the way for humanity to rid itself of the austere and spiritless rationality of the epoch of science, preparing it for a coming age. In this period humanity would once again worship the Holy Virgin and the saints in an epiphany of universal holiness and poetry. Indeed, Novalis predicts that, in this final age of history, an ecumenical Christianity will harmonize the earth's religions into a state of all-encompassing peace and mystic adoration of the transcendent Christ. In contrast to the Middle Ages, however, this millennial period – humankind's historical and spiritual apotheosis – will be characterized not only by the individual's harmony with the community of humanity in general, but also by the individual soul's *unio mystica* with the divine. In consonance with the Book of the Apocalypse, Novalis specifies that the capital of the universal society at the end of history will be Jerusalem.

While Novalis' essay on the ultimate meaning and purpose of history was neglected by his immediate contemporaries, it became viewed, not long after his death, as a manifesto of German Romanticism's utopian-religious idealism concerning the historical vocation of humanity. The essay also came to exemplify German Romanticism's fascination with Catholicism and the Middle Ages. Furthermore, it foreshadowed later attempts, such as those of Max Scheler in the 20th century, to develop a philosophical agenda intended to provide European humanity with a renewed vision of higher, platonistic values leading to the possibility of cultural and spiritual rebirth.

RODNEY TAYLOR

Biography

Born Georg Philipp Friedrich Leopold von Hardenberg, 2 May 1772 in Oberwiedstedt, Thuringia. Studied under **Schiller** at the University of Jena, 1790–91; University of Leipzig, 1791–93; University of Wittenberg, 1794; law degree, 1794; Mining Academy, Freiberg, 1797–99. Became friends with Friedrich Schlegel, Ludwig Tieck, and other early Romantics. Engaged to Sophie von Kühn, 1795 (died, 1797). Actuary for Kreisamtmann Just, Tennstedt, 1795–97; assistant in salt works, Weissenfels, 1796–97, 1799–1801; associated with Bergakademie, Freiberg, 1797–99. Engaged to Julie von Charpentier, 1798. Died (of tuberculosis) in Weissenfels, 25 March 1801.

Selected Writings

Essays and Related Prose

"Blütenstaub," *Athenäum* 1 (April 1798): 70–106; selections as "Pollen," translated by Alexander Gelley, in *German Romantic Criticism*, edited by A. Leslie Willson, 1982

"Glauben und Liebe, oder der König und die Königin," *Jahrbücher der Preussischen Monarchie unter der Regierung von Friedrich Wilhelm III* 2 (July 1798): 269–86

"Die Christenheit, oder Europa," in *Schriften*, edited by Ludwig Tieck, 1826; as "Christianity or Europe," translated by Charles E. Passage, in *Hymns to the Night and Other Selected Writings*, 1960

Fragmente, edited by Otto Michel, 1947(?)

Hymns to the Night and Other Selected Writings (includes poetry and aphorisms), translated by Charles E. Passage, 1960

"Selected Aphorisms and Fragments," translated by Alexander Gelley, in *German Romantic Criticism*, edited by A. Leslie Willson, 1982: 62–83

Pollen and Fragments: Selected Poetry and Prose, translated by Arthur Versluis, 1989

Other writings: poetry (including *Hymnen an die Nacht* [*Hymns to the Night*], 1800) and the unfinished novel *Heinrich von Ofterdingen*.

Collected works editions: *Schriften*, edited by Friedrich Schlegel and Ludwig Tieck, 2 vols., 1802; *Schriften*, edited by Paul Kluckhohn and Richard Samuel, 5 vols., 1975, revised edition, edited by Samuel, Hans-Joachim Mähl, and Gerhard Schulz, 1977–88.

Bibliography

Samuel, Richard, *Novalis: Der handschriftliche Nachlass des Dichters: Zur Geschichte des Nachlasses*, Gerstenberg: Hildesheim, 1973

Further Reading

Hiebel, Friedrich, *German Poet, European Thinker, Christian Mystic*, Chapel Hill: University of North Carolina Press, 1954
Neubauer, John, *Novalis*, Boston: Twayne, 1980
Von Molnár, Geza and Jochen Schulte-Sasse, *Romantic Vision, Ethical Context: Novalis and Artistic Autonomy*, Minneapolis: University of Minnesota Press, 1987

Novikov, Nikolai

Russian, 1744–1818

Military officer, commissioner under Catherine II for the drafting of a new code of law, journalist, literary critic, social critic, satirist, translator at the College of Foreign Affairs, publisher, an idealist with strong moral convictions, a good organizer and businessman, Freemason but staunchly Russian Orthodox, the Metropolitan of Moscow having said that he wished all Christians were like him: Nikolai Novikov was a complete man of the Enlightenment without being Voltairean. When Novikov began his writing and publishing activity in the late 1760s, satirical journals of the English type such as the *Tatler* and the *Spectator* of **Addison** and **Steele** were popular in Russia. Catherine the Great was herself the sponsor and regular contributor to one such journal called *Vsiakaia Vsiachina* (1769; Odds and ends); in response to this rather harmless publication, which limited its satirical attacks to the question of vice in general, Novikov launched *Truten'* (1769–70; The drone), a satirical review concerned with the realities of Russian life: the lack of education, the insufficiency of mere Church learning, the brutality of serfdom. It published editorials, **letters** to the editor, replies to "Granny" (the Empress), and articles under names such as those by Mr. Drone, the fictitious editor standing idly aloof from the affairs of the world, an editor "not altogether qualified for the business I have undertaken." Then there was Mr. Perochinov (pencil sharpener), Pravoliubov (the lover of truth), who used to mock Madame Miscellany for not knowing Russian well (the Empress was of German origin), Chistoserdov (pure heart), and Mr. Nedoum (perplexed): "I do not know why the air here is so very different from that in England. There wise men go mad, while here, those without reason are thought intelligent." After *Truten'* came other satirical reviews: *Pustomelia* (1770; The chatterbox, or tattler), *Zhivopisets* (1772–73; The painter), and *Koshelek* (1774; The purse). In them Novikov trained the reader to appreciate the nuances of social behavior. Ideas and opinions were never served up plain: readers were not meant to be passive, but were drawn into a new relationship by being invited to participate in the journal's activities. However, these journals were also the beginning of social criticism in Russia and as a result were all suppressed.

Novikov also wrote serious works, establishing new traditions in Russia. In 1772 he published *Opyt istoricheskogo slovaria o rossiiskikh pisateliakh* (An essay at an historical dictionary of Russian writers), the first work of its kind in Russia, which did much to popularize writers of the day such as Denis Fonvizin, Fedor Aleksandrovich Emin, and V. N. Maikov. In another historical work, *Drevniaia rossiiskaia biblioteka* (1773–75; The ancient Russian library), Novikov tried to emphasize the greatness and civility of Russia's past in order to reply to the Russian and foreign (especially French) detractors of the Motherland, who saw it as a backward country: "It is useful to be acquainted with the customs, mores and way of life of other peoples in other times . . . it is shameful to look down on one's own fellow countrymen." Novikov was dissatisfied with the French influence on the Russian noble class and wrote "not everything here, thank God, has yet been contaminated by France."

In 1775 Novikov became a Freemason: ". . . I had no bearings nor any foundation on which I might build spiritual peace and so without prior deliberation I fell into the Freemasons." This marked the beginning of a religious phase in his writing. His review *Utrennii Svet* (1777–80; Morning light) carried none of the **satire** of the earlier reviews, but was moral and educational: ". . . hold up to individuals, many of them as fickle as butterflies, the mirror of truth, and guide them along the path from the superficial and corporal aspect of man to the very essence of his inner being."

In 1779 Novikov moved from St. Petersburg to Moscow, where he successfully ran the Moscow University Press. His office was a combination of publisher, hospital, and pharmaceutical laboratory, which treated the poor for free. In Moscow he also became more involved with the Freemasons and operated a secret Freemason press, the Tipograficheskoi Kompanii (Typographical company), eventually leading to his arrest and death sentence in 1792, which was later changed to 15 years' imprisonment. However, he was released in 1796 after the death of the Empress, with the order that he could not go back to writing or publishing.

Novikov was a great admirer of classical literature and did much to promote it in Russia. He also published many Western works by Shakespeare, **Rousseau, Lessing, Diderot, Voltaire,** Beaumarchais, **Swift**, Milton, Pope, and others. His later Moscow reviews, such as *Moskovskoe Ezhemesiachnoe Izdanie* (1781; Moscow monthly) and *Vecherniaia Zaria* (1782; Evening light), were a mixture of moral lessons and teaching on the immortality of the soul together with political, geographical, and historical matters.

Novikov's writing style was simple and straightforward, and not particularly original. The central ideas in his writings, apart from his satirical social criticism, were the harmony and beauty of creation, as well as the belief that each individual contains a spiritual light, but a light that has been obscured by evil deeds. Novikov also had a talent for popularizing ideas. He saw art as therapeutic and beneficial: "those sisters poetry and art do not hinder, but rather aid us in our internal development." He was the first writer in Russia to be concerned with the raising of children – "when the rearing of children has reached the acme of perfection, everything else will be made easy" – and began publishing a series of books for them. He helped to spread culture, learning, and a civic consciousness to the most remote regions of Russia. Through his essays and publications, Novikov helped to instruct an entire generation of Russian nobility.

ANDRIUS VALEVIČIUS

Biography

Nikolai Ivanovich Novikov. Born 8 May 1744 at Tikhvinskoe-Avdot'ino family estate, near Bronnitsii. Studied at the Moscow University gymnasium for the nobility, 1755–60. Served in the Izmailovskii Regiment, 1762–67; secretary with Catherine II's Legislative Commission for the drafting of a new code of laws, 1767–69. Editor and main contributor, *Truten'*, 1769–70, *Pustomelia*, 1770, *Zhivopisets*, 1772–73, and *Koshelek*, 1774. Joined the Freemasons, and became an adherent of Rosicrucianism, 1775. Publisher, *Sanktpeterburgskie Uchenie Vedomosti* (St. Petersburg academic news), 1777, and *Utrennii Svet*, 1777–80; moved to Moscow, 1779, where he published several journals and newspapers, including the *Moskovskie Vedomosti* (Moscow morning news), 1779–89, *Ekonomicheskii Magazin* (The economic magazine), 1780–89, *Moskovskoe Ezhemesiachnoe Izdanie*, 1781, *Vecherniaia Zaria*, 1782, *Gorodskaia i Derevenskaia Biblioteka* (Town and country library), 1782–86, *Pokoyashchisia Trudoliubets* (The diligent at rest), 1784–85, and *Detskoe Chtenie Dlia Serdtsa i Razuma* (Children's reading for heart and mind), 1785–89; publisher, Moscow University Press, 1779–89; founder, Tipograficheskoi Kompanii publishing house, 1784–91. Married Aleksandra Iegorovna Rimskaia-Korsakova (died, 1791), 1781: one son and one daughter. Arrested for supposedly publishing illegal works (a culmination of his fall from favor with Catherine II), 1792, and sentenced to 15 years' imprisonment; held in prison until the death of Catherine II, 1796: after his release not allowed to resume publishing or journalism; retired to his family estate. Died (of a stroke) at Tikhvinskoe-Avdot'ino family estate, 12 August 1818.

Selected Writings

Essays and Related Prose
Truten', 1769–70; edited by P. A. Iefremov, 1865, and A. S. Suvorin, 1902
Pustomelia, 1770; edited by A. N. Afanas'ev, 1858
Zhivopisets, 1772–73; edited by P. A. Iefremov, 1864, and A. S. Suvorin, 1900
Koshelek, 1774; edited by A. N. Afanas'ev, 1858, and A. S. Suvorin, 1900
Satiricheskiie zhurnalii N. I. Novikova: Truten' 1769–1770; Pustomelia 1770; Zhivopisets 1772–1773; Koshelek 1774, edited by P. N. Berkov, 1951

Other writings: *Opyt istoricheskogo slovaria o rossiiskikh pisateliakh* (1772), the serial *Drevniaia rossiiskaia biblioteka* (1773–75), and satirical short stories (1782).

Collected works edition: *Izbrannie sochineniia*, edited by I. V. Malishev and L. B. Svetlov, 1961.

Bibliography
Stepanov, V. P., and Iu. V. Stennik, in *Istoriia russkoi literaturi XVIII veka: Bibliograficheskii ukazatel'*, Leningrad, 1968: items 5686–6168

Further Reading
Jones, W. Gareth, "Novikov's Naturalized *Spectator*," in *The Eighteenth Century in Russia*, edited by G. Garrard, Oxford: Clarendon Press, 1973: 149–65

Jones, W. Gareth, *Nikolay Novikov: Enlightener of Russia*, Cambridge: Cambridge University Press, 1984

Leonard, Gerald Irwin, *Novikov, Shcherbatov, Radishchev: The Intellectual in the Age of Catherine the Great* (dissertation), Binghamton: State University of New York, 1980

McArthur, Gilbert H., *The Novikov Circle in Moscow, 1779–1792* (dissertation), New York: University of Rochester, 1968

McArthur, Gilbert H., "Freemasonry and Enlightenment in Russia: The Views of N. I. Novikov," *Canadian-American Slavic Studies* 14, no. 3 (1980): 361–76

Monnier, André, *Un publiciste frondeur sous Catherine II: Nicolas Novikov*, Paris: Institut d'Études Slaves, 1981

Okenfuss, Max J., "The Novikov Problem: An English Perspective," in *Great Britain and Russia in the Eighteenth Century: Contacts and Comparisons*, edited by A. G. Cross, Newtonville, Massachusetts: Oriental Research Partners, 1979

Webster, William Mark, *Novikov, Freemasonry and the Russian Enlightenment* (Master's dissertation), Montreal: McGill University, 1987

Weinbaum, Alexandra, *N. I. Novikov (1774–1818): An Interpretation of His Career and Ideas* (dissertation), New York: Columbia University, 1975

Zenkovsky, V. V., *A History of Russian Philosophy*, vol. 1, London: Routledge and Kegan Paul, 1953

O

Ocampo, Victoria

Argentine, 1890–1979

Victoria Ocampo was educated at home in subjects considered suitable for the daughter of a wealthy, conservative family living in rigidly patriarchal Argentina. Though not expected to have a career, she read widely and traveled in Europe, becoming fluent in French, English, and Italian. Soon after an early, disastrous marriage, Ocampo rebelled against her circumscribed life by having a scandalous affair, leaving the church, and embarking on a life of intellectual independence.

While Argentina in the early 1900s was an inauspicious time and place for a woman to establish a writing career, she used her beauty, charm, and wealth, as well as a network of important friends, to found the literary journal *Sur* (South) in 1931, and, two years later, the publishing house Sur. Thereafter she was assured a place to publish her hundreds of essays. From the beginning she met opposition from the isolationist military government and the Catholic Church, each of which was at odds with her liberal, international intellectualism. In 1953 she was imprisoned for 26 days by the Peronist regime. This defining experience served as the backdrop for her "El hombre del látigo" (1957; "The Man with the Whip").

Ocampo used essays as a way to clarify her life and beliefs, often as a vehicle to challenge male authority and to promote the cause of women. She approached topics with a personal style, using the familiar "you" to address a reader she expected to be active, a "common reader" who read for pleasure and was part of a well-informed, intellectual elite. Her essays are characterized by enthusiasm, intensity, frequent digressions, and occasional playfulness. They are often dialectic and reflective. Graphic metaphors, sarcasm, and a slightly ironic humor mark her work. For example, she characterized commentators on Dante as "that numerous and terrible band of guards . . . [who stand] armed with aggressive erudition on the threshold of each canto, brandishing their often contradictory interpretations like pitchforks . . ." (*De Francesca a Beatrice* [1921; From Francesca to Beatrice]).

Ocampo's ten volumes of essays, *Testimonios* (1935–77; Testimonies), cover many subjects, among them people (Gandhi, T. E. Lawrence, Mussolini), books (by Shakespeare, Proust, Malraux), and films (*The Bicycle Thief, Wuthering Heights, The Grapes of Wrath*). Only a small fraction of her total output has been translated into English.

Her earliest essays (1920–33) challenged male authority in a variety of ways. She took on erudite male scholars in *De Francesca a Beatrice*. In "Babel" (1920), she took an iconoclastic look at the biblical story, suggesting that God had played "a dirty trick" on humankind by making possible multiple interpretations for any given word. She went on to question "equality," as "a big word, swollen with emptiness, that we toss around a lot . . ." She chided **Ruskin** for his condescending tone and for not allowing the reader to think for himself ("Al margen de Ruskin" [1920; A note on Ruskin]). She took exception to **Ortega y Gasset**'s chauvinism and his portrayal of woman as man's passive muse ("Contestación a un epílogo de Ortega y Gasset" [1928; Reply to an epilogue by Ortega y Gasset]). From the beginning, Ocampo pushed hard against the limits of what a woman, at that time and place, could articulate in an essay.

Her most important essays are on women, generally and specifically, whether real or fictional, from Emily Brontë, Gabriela Mistral, and Indira Gandhi to Lady Chatterley and Ma Joad. After Ocampo met **Virginia Woolf** in 1934 she became politically active in the struggle for women's rights in Argentina and wrote as a declared feminist. Her essays stressed the need to improve women's education ("La mujer, sus derechos y sus responsabilidades" [1936; "Woman, Her Rights and Her Responsibilities"]), she called on women to express themselves, especially in writing ("La mujer y su expresión" [1936; "Woman and Her Expression"]), and she took a liberal approach to many issues, among them divorce, abortion, prostitution, and illegitimacy.

Inspired and encouraged by Woolf's books and by extensive correspondence with her, Ocampo wrote essays about Woolf from a fresh, intimate perspective ("Virginia Woolf en mi recuerdo" [1941; "Virginia Woolf in My Memory"]). She also wrote interpretations of Woolf's works (*Orlando, To The Lighthouse, A Room of One's Own, A Writer's Diary*), which Sur had introduced to Latin American readers in Spanish translation.

While Ocampo fervently championed women's rights, a tolerant, constructive understanding supported her feminism. She did not see men as the enemy, she regarded mothers as all-important in their work of molding their children, and she envisioned the ideal marriage as a partnership of equals based on love and mutual respect ("Pasado y presente de la mujer" [1966; "Woman's Past and Present"]). But she was not blind to the problems of men or marriage, criticizing men for their love of war and their adherence to a double standard; she warned women that they should not try to live through either their children or their husbands.

Ocampo's substantial contributions brought her honors from around the world, including an honorary degree from Harvard in 1967. Perhaps the greatest tribute was her admission in 1977 into the previously all-male Argentine Academy of Letters, an honor she had been consciously or unconsciously aiming toward all her life. As contemporary scholars begin to explore essays by Latin American women, an active interest has developed in Ocampo and her role as a feminist writer and a key figure in the intellectual history of Latin America.

PATRICIA OWEN STEINER

Biography
Victoria Ocampo de Estrada. Born 7 April 1890 in Buenos Aires. Studied privately with tutors and at the Sorbonne, Paris. Married at age 22 (later separated). Founder, *Sur* literary journal, from 1931, and Sur publishing house, from 1933. Manager, Teatro Colon, Buenos Aires, 1933. Cofounder, 1936, and president, 1936 and 1938, Argentine Union of Women. Imprisoned briefly for opposition to Perón regime, 1953. Elected to the Argentine Academy of Letters, 1977. Awards: Argentine Society of Writers Grand Prize of Honor, 1950; Alberti y Sarmiento Prize, 1967; honorary degree from Harvard University. Officer, Legion of Honor (France); Commander, Order of the British Empire (CBE). Died in San Isidro, Argentina, 27 January 1979.

Selected Writings

Essays and Related Prose
De Francesca a Beatrice a través de la Divina comedia, 1921
Testimonios, 10 vols., 1935–77; 4th vol. as *Soledad sonora*, 1950
Domingos en Hyde Park, 1936
338171 T.E., 1942; as *338171 T.E. (Lawrence of Arabia)*, translated by David Garnett, 1963
El viajero y una de sus sombras (Keyserling en mis memorias), 1951
Virginia Woolf en su diario, 1954
Tagore en las barrancas de San Isidro, 1961
Victoria Ocampo: Against the Wind and the Tide (also contains a critical study of Ocampo), translated by Doris Meyer, 1979
Autobiografía (includes *El archipiélago*; *El imperio insular*; *La rama de Salzburgo*; *Viraje*; *Versailles-Keyserling, Paris-Drieu*; *Sur y Cía*), 6 vols., 1979–84; selections edited by Francisco Ayala, 1991

Other writings: plays. Also translated works by William Faulkner, **Graham Greene**, D. H. Lawrence, **Albert Camus**, Colette, Dylan Thomas, and John Osborne.

Bibliographies
Adam, Carlos, "Bio-bibliografía de Victoria Ocampo," *Sur* 346 (1980): 125–79
Foster, David William, "Bibliography of Writings by and About Victoria Ocampo, 1890–1979," *Revista Interamericana de Bibliografía* 30, no. 1 (1980): 51–58

Further Reading
Greenberg, Janet Beth, *The Divided Self: Forms of Autobiography in the Writing of Victoria Ocampo* (dissertation), Berkeley: University of California, 1986
Guiñazú, Maria Cristina Arambel, "'Babel' and *De Francesca a Beatrice*: Two Founding Essays by Victoria Ocampo," in *Reinterpreting the Spanish American Essay: Women Writers of the 19th and 20th Centuries*, edited by Doris Meyer, Austin: University of Texas Press, 1995

Meyer, Doris, *Victoria Ocampo: Against the Wind and the Tide* (also includes translations of essays), New York: Braziller, 1979
Meyer, Doris, "Letters and Correspondence in the Essays of Victoria Ocampo," *Revista* 42, no. 2 (1992): 233–40
Meyer, Doris, "Victoria Ocampo, Argentine Identity, and the Landscape of Essay," *Review: Latin American Literature and Arts* 48 (Spring 1994): 58–61
Meyer, Doris, "Victoria Ocampo and Spiritual Energy," in *A Dream of Light and Shadow: Portraits of Latin American Women Writers*, edited by Marjorie Agosín, Albuquerque: University of New Mexico Press, 1995
Meyer, Doris, "The Early (Feminist) Essays of Victoria Ocampo," *Studies in 20th Century Literature* 20 (1996): 41–64
Molloy, Sylvia, "The Theatrics of Reading: Body and Book in Victoria Ocampo," in her *At Face Value: Autobiographical Writing in Spanish America*, Cambridge and New York: Cambridge University Press, 1991
Pratt, Mary Louise, "Don't Interrupt Me: The Gender Essay and Conversation and Countercanon," in *Reinterpreting the Spanish American Essay: Women Writers of the 19th and 20th Centuries*, edited by Doris Meyer, Austin: University of Texas Press, 1995
Sarlo, Beatriz, "Decir y no decir: Erotismo y represión," in her *Una modernidad periférica: Buenos Aires 1920 y 1930*, Buenos Aires: Nueva Visión, 1988

Odobescu, Alexandru
Romanian, 1834–1895

It is difficult to say whether any Romanian writings before 1800 can be described as "essays," even though homiletic and aphoristic publications may display some essayistic features. However, soon after 1800 the conversational and **familiar essay** became very popular, often combined with other marginal, half-literary, or playful genres. Thus Dinicu Golescu (1770–1830) and Nicolae Filimon (1819–65) among others used the travelogue as a vehicle for moral and intellectual reflection. Vasile Alecsandri (1818–90) mixed semi-fantastic narrative with gentle irony upon the foibles of a transitional society, and his friends Ion Ghica (1867–97) and Costache Negruzzi (1808–68) used the epistolary form as their preferred mode for presenting social customs and moral and economic reflections under a literary guise. Essays of literary criticism in institutionalized forms began with I. Heliade Radulescu (1802–72) and, more clearly, with Titu Maiorescu (1840–1917). Even more frequent than these genres was the "physiognomy," portraits of social customs and character types subjectively captured; a leading practitioner of this genre was Mihail Kogălniceanu (1817–91). The choice of the essay as a preferred vehicle was largely due to its flexibility, which was convenient for the insecurities of writers in a fragile and peripheral society.

More than any of the above-mentioned contemporaries, Alexandru Odobescu inscribes himself in the Western modes of the essay. His chief work of this kind was *Pseudo-cynegeticos, sau fals tratat de vinatoare* (1875; Pseudo-kynegeticos, or a false treatise on hunting). Originally this work was intended as a **preface** to a genuine textbook guide to the craft of hunting (written by a friend), but it became too long and was consequently published separately. It is a charming, whimsical, and ironic mosaic of references to hunting in many literatures (classical and modern) and arts, but it also contains personal reminiscences, natural descriptions (one of them, particularly famous, evokes the charm of the plains of Southern Wallachia), and is interspersed with passages from folktales and folk poetry. Odobescu relied heavily on intertextuality and on the contrasting effects obtained by juxtaposing local Romanian materials with quotes from Greek and Latin, as well as French, German, and English authors. Etymologies that we might now call "deconstructive" are used as connective elements. The style is ornate and digressive, with mock-pompous passages, yet it always manages to remain conversational, with intimate addresses to the friend whose work he was supposed to preface. The last chapter is left blank and bears the title "the reader's favorite chapter." Light sarcastic allusions to the social and cultural state of Romania appear as asides. The general message of the essay is the jovial and amiable praise of a quiet, contented life in the company of natural and literary beauty.

Odobescu's manner is expressed equally well in *Cîteva ore la Snagov* (1862; A few hours spent in Snagov). Snagov is a small village by a lake near Bucharest, at the time itself nothing more than a small and sleepy capital city. Odobescu is particularly interested in Snagov monastery, the eldest parts of which date from the 15th century. Humorously self-deprecating erudition, enchantment in the face of the surrounding landscape, and nostalgic historical evocation are combined with a barely noticeable narrative line. Odobescu skips nonchalantly from romanticized history to a consideration of the best way to dress and cook the tasty fish inhabiting the lake by the monastery.

In some ways Odobescu is a belated Romantic, resuming the manner of **Charles Lamb**, **Leigh Hunt**, or even Karl Julius Weber, in his search for the playful side of erudition and knowledge. From another point of view his writings are in line with those of his (particularly French) symbolist and aesthetic contemporaries, giving voice to a kind of impressionistic humanism linked to an elite readership of taste and education. Finally, it cannot be denied that, despite his essentially cosmopolitan orientation, Odobescu responded with some subtlety to the appeal of national glorification, whether in its historical past, in the exaltation of the Romanian landscape, or in the highlighting of traditional folk music and storytelling. He was effective and eloquent in promoting national values and images precisely because he did not avoid placing them in the light of cosmopolitan taste; it is also fair to add that he thus tacitly undermined the emerging rhetoric of localist chauvinism. Odobescu differs from other Romanian contemporaries precisely in having chosen the frivolous discourse of the conversational essay, in which all these threads are pleasingly woven together.

VIRGIL NEMOIANU

Biography

Son of general Ion Odobescu. Born in Bucharest, 23 June 1834. Studied at a lycée in Paris, baccalauréat, 1853; literature and archaeology at the University of Paris, graduated 1855. Married Saşa Prejbeanu, 1858: one daughter; often apart from his wife, and had affairs with other women. Cabinet minister for education, 1863; head clerk, Ministry of Foreign Affairs, 1865; prosecutor, Court of Appeal. Traveled in Switzerland and Italy, 1870, in connection with his discovery and description of the "Petroasa treasure," a collection of objects made from precious metals, of Gothic origin, found on Romanian territory; also traveled to several other countries, including Denmark and Turkey. Opposed the tendency toward artificially latinizing the literary language. Elected to the Romanian Academy, 1870. Professor of archaeology, University of Bucharest, from 1874. Secretary of the Romanian legation, Paris, 1882. Principal of a teacher-training institute, Bucharest; principal of the National Educational Institute, 1892. Died (suicide by morphine overdose) in Bucharest, 10 November 1895.

Selected Writings

Essays and Related Prose
Cîteva ore la Snagov, 1862; edited by G. Pienescu, 1961
Pseudo-cynegeticos, sau fals tratat de vinatoare, 1875; edited by G. Pienescu, 1961
Pagini regăsite, edited by G. Şerban, 1965
Note de călătorie, edited by Corneliu Popescu, 1981

Other writings: short stories, several dozen scholarly articles, an anthology of folktales and one of folk poetry, and a history of archaeology (1877). Also translated both literary and scholarly works.

Collected works editions: *Opere complete*, 4 vols., 1906–19; *Opere*, edited by Tudor Vianu, 2 vols., 1955; *Opere*, 12 vols., 1965–92 (in progress).

Further Reading

Curticapeanu, Doina, *Odobescu, sau lectura formelor simbolice*, Bucharest: Minerva, 1982
Manolescu, Nicolae, *Introducere in opera lui Alexandru Odobescu*, Bucharest: Minerva, 1976
Păcurariu, Dumitru, *A. I. Odobescu*, Bucharest: ESPLA, 1966
Pandele, Rodica, editor, *Alexandru Odobescu: Antologie critica*, Bucharest: Eminescu, 1976

Oliphant, Margaret
British, 1828–1897

Though better known as a novelist, Margaret Oliphant, one of the most prolific Victorian writers, was an influential critic and **periodical essay**ist. Her articles appeared in a range of journals, including *St. James's Gazette*, *Cornhill Magazine*, *Contemporary Review*, *Fraser's Magazine*, and the *Spectator*.

However, it was her long association with *Blackwood's Edinburgh Magazine* that afforded her the most powerful platform. Over a period of more than 40 years from June 1854 to almost the end of her life Oliphant was *Blackwood's* major literary reviewer, her critical output encompassing fiction, biography, history, religion, poetry, and works of reference. Less frequently she reviewed art exhibitions and the theater, while also publishing travel sketches, biographical essays, and social commentary. Her nonfiction books, particularly biographies and cultural histories, share some of the stylistic features of her periodical articles, but she did not seek to republish those essays in book form.

Oliphant's productivity affected both her work and her reputation. In her lifetime she was irritated by any praise of what after her death was characterized as her "marvellous industry," even though she herself described her position at *Blackwood's* as a "sort of general utility woman in the Magazine" (*Annals of a Publishing House*, vol. 3, 1898). She frequently had several pieces within one issue. Her descriptive sketches – sharpened by witty asides and her ability to conjure up an animated crowd scene, constantly switching perspective from the panoramic to the close-up – have a lively sense of ambience. Her work was usually produced at speed and is inevitably uneven in quality. At its best it offers perceptive judgments of literature and a sharply observed assessment of her society. A vein of irony enlivens her commentary and often renders problematic what are on the surface conformist opinions.

Though more radical in her sympathies than the Tory *Blackwood's*, Oliphant's working relationship with John Blackwood proved successful professionally and socially. Her readers were the educated, relatively conservative middle class, and she envisaged herself addressing a mainly masculine audience. Some critics argue that she adopted a male voice. Certainly she occasionally referred to herself as if to a man, and for one of her series of discursive commentaries ("The Old Saloon," January 1887–December 1892) took on a persona writing from the distinctly male space of *Blackwood's* original library; it should be noted, however, that she also wrote elsewhere under the sobriquet "A Dowager." In many of her essays the writer's sex is indeterminate. *Blackwood's* policy of anonymity suited her, and she strongly maintained the advantage of anonymity for critics since it liberated them from "embarrassing difficulties" when discussing the work of acquaintances ("The Rev. W. Lucas Collins," 1887).

Oliphant's voice can be at once self-deprecatory and authoritative. Admitting her judgment to be "uninstructed" she yet delivers it in the magisterial first-person plural – "Speaking as one of the unlearned, a heathen man and a publican, we yet shudder at ourselves when we say . . ." ("London in January," 1886). Her tone shifts between familiar alliance with the reader and formal discourse. Essays opening with an authoritative statement on the general then glide into the conversational or focus upon the particular. So a literary **review** ("Sensation Novels," 1862) is launched from the state of the nation: "Ten years ago the world in general had come to a singular crisis in its existence. The age was lost in self-admiration." Her review essays give scope for broad discussion of cultural trends, commonly covering works by diverse authors or an assessment of a writer's oeuvre, dealing with different branches of the arts, or, like "The Literature of the Last Fifty Years" (1887), offering a retrospective assessment.

It is unfortunate that Oliphant's critical capabilities are today often characterized by her negative view of *Jude the Obscure* ("The Anti-Marriage League," 1896). The distinctive, acerbic tone of her writing makes her an easy target for selective quotation, but as some scholars have recently urged, her views are more complex than such quotations suggest. Even where she regarded a subgenre as having a vitiating influence, as she did with both the sensational novel, whose Count Fosco and Magdalens "make the worse appear the better cause" ("Sensation Novels"), and the fiction of the "alarming revolution" following "the invasion of *Jane Eyre*," she praised genius where she found it. Wilkie Collins she rated highly and *Jane Eyre* she considered "one of the most remarkable works of modern times" ("Modern Novelists, Great and Small," 1855; see also "The Sisters Brontë," 1897).

Equally, her views on the Woman Question, which have been regarded as conservative, even antifeminist, cannot be accurately gauged from the antisuffrage remarks in the earlier essays ("Laws Concerning Women," 1856; "The Condition of Women," 1858; "The Great Unrepresented," 1866). Oliphant did not trust the power of the law to right women's wrongs, and maintained the importance and dignity of a mother's responsibilities; but she approved of education for women, and over the decades modified her opinions (e.g. "The Grievances of Women," 1880). In her review of the novel *Ideala* ("The Old Saloon," 1889) she referred sympathetically to "the singular and scarcely recognised revolution which has taken place in the position of women during the last generation."

Oliphant's commentaries on the visual arts emphasized a society which creates and consumes art as much as the art itself. The value of making art accessible to the people as a whole, the dangers of private patronage, the role of the gallery in national life, the relationship of art to commercial interests, and the effects of industrialization and social change, were constant themes (e.g. "Art in May," 1875; "The Royal Academy," 1876).

Oliphant's own art was produced, not in a quiet study, or cloistered library, but amid the reality of everyday domestic life. This sense of commonplace experience colored her theory of the arts. Thus her notion of the tragic was integrally linked to the idea of disillusionment in ordinary life. "Hamlet is the greatest instance of that disenchantment . . . about the bitterest pang of which the soul is capable" ("Hamlet," 1879).

Blackwood's effusive obituary tribute – "the most accomplished periodical writer of her day" – indicates Oliphant's contemporary influence in that genre, an influence which modern critics are now reassessing.

BARBARA MARY ONSLOW

Biography

Born Margaret Oliphant Wilson, 4 April 1828 in Wallyford, Midlothian. As a child lived in Lasswade, near Edinburgh, Glasgow, and Liverpool. No formal education. Published her first novel, 1849. Married Francis Wilson Oliphant (a cousin), 1852 (died, 1859): two daughters (one died in infancy, the other in youth) and four sons (two died in infancy, two in adulthood). Moved to London, 1852. Contributor to various journals, primarily *Blackwood's Edinburgh Magazine*, from 1854. Traveled to Italy for her husband's health, 1859; moved to Edinburgh, 1860, Ealing, London, 1861, and Italy, Switzerland, and France, 1863–65; lived in Windsor, Berkshire, from 1865. From 1868 her brother Frank and his family became increasingly dependent on her financially. Traveled to Jerusalem, 1890. Moved to Wimbledon, south London, 1896. Died in Wimbledon, 25 June 1897.

Selected Writings

Essays and Related Prose

(Most of Oliphant's essays have not yet been published in book form.)
Historical Sketches of the Reign of George II, 2 vols., 1869
Historical Sketches of the Reign of Queen Anne, 1894; as *Historical Characters*, 1894

Other writings: many novels, biography, an autobiography, and a history of *Blackwood's* publishing house.

Bibliographies

Clarke, John Stock, *Margaret Oliphant: A Bibliography*, St. Lucia: University of Queensland Department of English, 1986

Houghton, Walter E., editor, *The Wellesley Index to Victorian Periodicals 1824–1900*, Toronto: University of Toronto Press, 5 vols., 1966–89: "Bibliographies of Contributors" lists Oliphant's essays and criticism in those periodicals covered by the index

Further Reading

Colby, Robert A., and Vineta Colby, "Mrs. Oliphant's Scotland: The Romance of Reality," in *Nineteenth-Century Scottish Fiction*, edited by Ian Campbell, Manchester: Carcanet, and New York: Barnes and Noble, 1979: 89–104

Colby, Vineta, and Robert A. Colby, *The Equivocal Virtue: Mrs. Oliphant and the Victorian Literary Market Place*, Hamden, Connecticut: Archon, 1966

Jay, Elisabeth, *Mrs. Oliphant: "A Fiction to Herself": A Literary Life*, Oxford: Clarendon Press, and New York: Oxford University Press, 1995

Kramer, Dale, "The Cry That Binds: Oliphant's Theory of Domestic Tragedy," in *Margaret Oliphant: Critical Essays on a Gentle Subversive*, edited by D. J. Trela, Selinsgrove, Pennsylvania: Susquehanna University Press, 1995: 147–64

Trela, D. J., "Two Margaret Oliphants Review George Eliot," *George Eliot – George Henry Lewes Studies* (September 1993): 37–60

Trela, D. J., "Introduction: Discovering the Gentle Subversive," in *Margaret Oliphant: Critical Essays on a Gentle Subversive*, edited by Trela, Selinsgrove, Pennsylvania: Susquehanna University Press, 1995: 11–27

Williams, Merryn, *Margaret Oliphant: A Critical Biography*, Basingstoke: Macmillan, and New York: St. Martin's Press, 1986

Williams, Merryn, "Feminist or Anti-Feminist? Oliphant and the Woman Question," in *Margaret Oliphant: Critical Essays on a Gentle Subversive*, edited by D. J. Trela, Selinsgrove, Pennsylvania: Susquehanna University Press, 1995: 165–80

On the Sublime

by "Longinus," written probably c. 1st century CE

On the Sublime – to accept the usual English translation of υψοσ (*hypsos*) – must be taken on its own terms, as we know nothing for certain of its author, not even his (assuming a male) name. The earliest manuscript, which dates from 10th-century Paris, ascribes the work to "Dionysius or Longinus," but internal evidence suggests that it was written in the 1st century CE, and there is no early evidence about the authorship. However, it became one of the most respected and discussed pieces of classical literary criticism, and, with its translation into English in the mid-17th century, helped to give at least temporary currency to a critical concept that eventually paved the way for Romanticism.

Its argument is presented in the lively form of a **letter** to a friend, Terentianus, on its topic, apparently in answer to an account recently published, and now lost, by one Cecilius. Longinus – to use the conventional if unsubstantiated name – sets out to correct this account, and does so in a cogent manner, with plenty of illustrations from his favorite authors, particularly Homer. The tone is relaxed, as that of a well-informed mind communicating with an equal.

Longinus begins by asserting his central assumption, taken to be shared by Terentianus, that "sublimity consists in a certain excellence and distinction in expression, and that it is from this source alone that the greatest poets and historians have acquired their preeminence and won for themselves an eternity of fame." The emphasis is on the power of this "elevated language" to "entrance" rather than persuade its hearers, for Longinus has in mind an audience rather than a readership, and an audience for both poetry and oratory – his examples are taken from both areas with equal authority. This idea of the "entrancement" (or, in other translations, "transporting") of the listeners is central to the whole argument, for it is asserted to be the power that raises the sublime beyond the qualities to be found in ordinary oratory or poetry. Longinus confronts the question that this might be expected to give rise to – is there an art of the sublime, and can one develop it in oneself? – and answers affirmatively: though nature provides the basic energies that carry the sublime, its exponent needs to know how to avoid errors which spoil the effect, such as frigidity, bombast, puerility, and emotionalism.

From this starting point, Longinus goes on to discuss his topic under five headings, giving a clear sense of a developing argument. The first two qualities are said to be largely innate: "the ability to form grand conceptions" is derived from "nobility of soul"; and "the stimulus of powerful and inspired emotion" comes only to those who train themselves to receive it, partly by "imitation and emulation of the great historians and poets of the past," particularly Homer and **Plato**. The other qualities discussed are more technical. The third is "the proper formation of ... figures of thought and figures of speech," which are considered through a range of technical terms – adjuration, asyndeton, inversion, polyptoton, periphrasis – in a way that makes them all clear to the reader. The fourth source is "the creation of a noble diction," considered in terms of language and imagery, although the section includes an interesting digression on the idea that genius is never flawless, while mediocrity may be. The final section concerns "the arrangement of the words in the due order," and is particularly emphatic on the power of rhythm to "entrance" its hearers.

On the Sublime ends with a lively coda, in which Longinus speculates – rather in the spirit of our own postmodernist day – on why, with so many competent men in public life, there are so few "sublime and transcendent natures," so that contemporary literature exhibits "a great and world-wide dearth." One argument is that this is because of the destruction of Roman democracy in the replacement of the Republic by the Empire. Longinus' view is rather that it is because of the domination of society by the love of money ("a disease that makes us petty-minded") and the love of pleasure ("an utterly ignoble attribute"). This contributes to the overall liveliness of the piece, which reads less like academic literary criticism and more like the reflections of a highly intelligent and well-informed general reader (or listener).

The work breaks off with a promise to examine in more detail the importance of the emotions in literature, and especially the sublime. Although that discussion does not survive, there is enough in what does to have inspired much subsequent discussion, particularly in late 18th-century England, with **Edmund Burke**'s *Philosophical Enquiry into ... the Sublime and Beautiful* (1757) as the best-known response. Critics seeking to find an explanation and justification of the power, as well as the sanity, of art found the term "sublime" helpful in their quest. There is a resurgence of interest in the idea today, expressed in books like Peter De Bolla's *The*

616   ON THE SUBLIME

Discourse of the Sublime (1989), as criticism strives to answer the same questions about power in writing, now in a context in which the idea of the unconscious plays a significant part.

On the Sublime is usually described as a piece of literary criticism, or even (in the *Oxford Companion to English Literature*) as a **treatise**. The latter term is misleading, and literary criticism can be conducted in a variety of modes, including the poem, as Horace (e.g. **Poetic Art**) and Pope (e.g. **Essay on Criticism, Essay on Man**) show. While it may be appropriate to consider Aristotle's *Poetics* a treatise, the informal tone and the personal address of *On the Sublime* reveal it to be a precursor of the essay, however much its central sections aspire to the rigors of categorization. The last section, with its sudden shift into consideration of contemporary cultural debates, as they would now be termed, is evidence that we are in the presence of a writer untrammeled by external considerations, with the essayist's taste for the immediate and the personal.

PETER FAULKNER

See also Classical Influences

Editions

On the Sublime, edited by A. O. Prickard, 1906, revised edition, 1946, and D. A. Russell, 1964; translated by J. Hall, 1652; many subsequent translations, including by A. O. Prickard, 1906, W. H. Fyfe (Loeb Edition), in *Demetrius on Style*, 1927, G. M. A. Gruber, 1957, D. A. Russell, 1965, and T. S. Dorsch, 1965

Further Reading

Brody, Jules, *Boileau and Longinus*, Geneva: Droz, 1958
Coleman, Dorothy, "Montaigne and Longinus," *Bibliothèque d'Humanisme et Renaissance* 47, no. 2 (1985): 405–13
Costa, Gustavo, "Longinus's Treatise on the Sublime in the Age of Arcadia," *Nouvelles de la République des Lettres* 1 (1981): 65–86
De Bolla, Peter, *The Discourse of the Sublime: Readings in History, Aesthetics and the Subject*, Oxford: Blackwell, 1989
Guerlac, Suzanne, "Longinus and the Subject of the Sublime," *New Literary History* 16, no. 2 (Winter 1985): 275–97
Hamashita, Masahiro, "Genealogy of the Aesthetics of the Sublime: To Addison and Shaftesbury," *Kobe College Studies* 38, no. 3 (March 1992): 102–27
Henn, Thomas R., *Longinus and English Criticism*, Cambridge: Cambridge University Press, 1934
Logan, J.-L., "Montaigne et Longin: Une Nouvelle Hypothèse," *Revue d'Histoire Littéraire de la France* 83, no. 3 (1983): 355–70
Macksey, Richard, "Longinus Reconsidered," *MLN* 108, no. 5 (December 1993): 913–34
Monk, Samuel Holt, *The Sublime: A Study of Critical Theories in XVIII-Century England*, Ann Arbor: University of Michigan Press, 1960 (original edition, 1935)

d'Ors, Eugenio

Spanish, 1881–1954

Eugenio d'Ors, Catalan philosopher and essayist, was to a lesser extent a novelist and playwright. There are two distinct periods of his work, the first written in Catalan and identified with his native region of Catalonia, the second turned toward Castile and written in Spanish after his alienation from the Catalans.

The Catalan period of his life and work was of primary importance to the Catalan *Renaixença* (Renaissance), a time of great political and literary splendor in Catalonia. D'Ors' cultural and political activism began in 1898, when he first used the pen name Xenius, and ended in 1920, when he broke with Puig i Cadafalch, then President of the Mancomunitat of Catalonia, where d'Ors had served as Secretary of Education.

Through the prestigious newspaper *La Veu de Catalunya* (The Voice of Catalonia) he began publishing his "glosses," brief essays in which d'Ors gave his readers a probing and incisive series of "quotidian blows in favor of culture," as **José Ortega y Gasset** would say. He reported on current news in the world of culture (philosophy, art, literature, politics) while also striving to extract the essential and profound within the framework of time as a lasting and flexible concept.

It is hard to classify the glosses strictly as essays, given their concise form prescribed by a daily press publication. They are a hybrid form between learned articles and general information, combining observation and invention, being more subjective than objective, more arbitrary than impartial, more literary than scholarly. They are expository rather than argumentative, with a felicitous intuition verging on the poetic.

The *glosari* were seminal in the development of d'Ors' ideology into a coherent system. For instance, d'Ors formed the notion of *catalanidad* (what it is to be Catalan) in a selection of glosses, which became the novel *La ben plantada* (1911; The woman of fine physique). In it the heroine Theresa personifies harmony, culture, tradition, and classicism – all virtues exalted by the cultural and political Catalonia of the early 1900s. Thus Theresa became a symbol of all that was considered the essence of being Catalan.

D'Ors proposed that man is an interplay of work and play based on two principles: that philosophy is not pure contemplation but inscribed in action, and that, in turn, contemplation is conceived as open to action and must embrace a dualistic conception of values that compares and contrasts power with resistance, spirit with matter, will with reality. Reason must draw from both nature and history to become a genuine power that can perceive the individual and concrete as well as the general and abstract. The synthesis of the former and the latter is embodied in the Catalan concept of *seny* (common sense or measure).

D'Ors formulated a philosophical interpretation of history, proposing a new view of the traditional philosophy of history. His aim was to explain, organize, and systematize history according to certain unchanging values of culture manifested over the course of time. *La ciencia de la cultura* (1964; Science of culture) charts d'Ors' creation of a philosophy of history and a theory of historiography. He acknowledges that his conception of history as both flowing and cyclical has antecedents in the philosophy of **Plato**, Giambattista Vico, **Nietzsche**, and Spengler. He makes a distinction between civilization and culture, with a theoretical approach that is philosophical as well as sociological, and gives as antecedents the work of sociologist Benjamin Kidd, who applies biological discoveries to sociology, Houston S. Chamberlain as a pioneer in systematizing the concept of culture, Leon Frobenius and his formulation of the "spirit of each culture," and the relativism of Oswald Spengler.

D'Ors formulated the problem of culture in its theoretical aspect within his "systematics of culture," and in its formal character as "morphology of culture"; he applied his newly conceived system to a series of "epiphanies" or successive manifestations along the history of culture. Thus he conceived of culture as a systematic entity where history is examined not descriptively but in a vital and constitutive form. He introduced the term "eon" or "historic constant," a living and archetypal category inserted in the fabric of history, in the contingent flow of events. Among the "pure eons" are language, virility and femininity, classicism and baroque, Rome and Babel. This conceptualization reflects the vision of reality within a dual system in which the universe is framed in a gigantic synoptic scheme.

Morphology of culture is defined as the close relation between spiritual content (idea) and formal manifestation (form). One of d'Ors' most felicitous examples is the pair of values Cupola-Monarchy, elicited by the visual image of St. Peter's cupola in Rome and the corresponding concept of the monarchic institution of the papacy. Within this morphological formulation, dual corresponding schemes can be found in nature and art, nature and human customs, and botany and architecture, among many other examples. D'Ors claimed that his morphology of culture establishes theoretical and general principles that are simultaneous and symmetrically valid in areas of knowledge that were never before related.

D'Ors' aesthetic criticism is rooted in his system of the science of culture and is structured within a scheme of figurative thought. He wrote several essays and innumerable glosses on painters, whether Spanish, French, Italian, Dutch, or his contemporary Catalans. However, of all his essays dealing with aesthetics the best known is *Tres horas en el Museo del Prado* (1923; *Three Hours in the Prado Museum*). Ostensibly he aimed to provide the visitor with an itinerary giving information and a clear and rational classification, but in reality the book is an illustrated expository of d'Ors' aesthetic ideas. He selects subjectively but preserves some constant guiding norms by using the principles of the morphology of culture and tectonics, which he advocated in all his art criticism.

PILAR G. SÁENZ

Biography

Eugenio d'Ors Rovira. Used the pseudonym Xenius. Born 28 September 1881 in Barcelona. Studied at the University of Barcelona, law degree, 1905; the Sorbonne, Paris; University of Madrid, Ph.D. in philosophy, 1913. Lived in Catalonia and wrote in Catalan for the first half of his life, then broke with the Catalan government, 1920, moved to Madrid, and wrote mainly in Castilian. Contributor to various journals and newspapers, from 1899; correspondent in Paris for *La Veu de Catalunya*, from 1906, where he began publishing *glossaris* (glosses); also published *glosario* in *ABC*, 1923–31, *El Debate*, 1932–34, and *Arriba España* (Above Spain), 1937–39. Elected Secretary of Education in the Union of Catalonia, 1917–20 (dismissed). Lived on and off in Paris, 1927–37; Spanish representative to the Institute of Intellectual Cooperation, League of Nations, 1927. Elected to the Royal Spanish Academy, 1928. Elected general director of fine arts and perpetual secretary, Institute of Spain. Lectured in Europe and South America. Awards: honorary degree from Coimbra University. Died in Villanova i Geltrù, Barcelona, 1954.

Selected Writings

Essays and Related Prose

Glosari, 5 vols., 1907–16
El Valle de Josafat, 1921
El nuevo glosario, 7 vols., 1921–23
Tres horas en el Museo del Prado, 1923; as *Three Hours in the Prado Museum*, translated by John Forrester, 1954
Cinco minutos de silencio, 1925
Las ideas y las formas, 1928
Cuando ya esté tranquilo, 1930
La tradición, 1939
Jardín botánico, 1940
Teoría de los estilos, y Espejo de la arquitectura, 1944
Del barroco, 1945
Arte de entreguerras, 1946
Nuevo glosario (Glosario completo, 1920–43), 3 vols., 1947–49
La palabra en la onda: Glosas para la radio, 1950
Glosari (1906–1910) (most complete collection of *glosari* in Catalan), 1950

Other writings: the novel *La ben plantada* (1911), other fiction, plays, philosophical works, and art criticism.

Bibliography

Amorós, Andrés, *Eugenio d'Ors, crítico literario*, Madrid: Prensa Española, 1971: 241–48

Further Reading

Aguilera Cerni, Vicente, *Ortega y d'Ors en la cultura artística española*, Madrid: Ciencia Nueva, 1966
Amorós, Andrés, *Eugenio d'Ors, crítico literario*, Madrid: Prensa Española, 1971
Aranguren, José Luís, *La filosofía de Eugenio d'Ors*, Madrid: Espasa-Calpe, 1981 (original edition, 1945)
Benítez Claros, Rafael, "Eugenio d'Ors y la ciencia de la cultura," *Cuadernos del Idioma* 1 (1965): 129–38
Díaz Plaja, Guillermo, *Lo social en Eugenio d'Ors y otros estudios*, Barcelona: Cotal, 1982
Ferrán, Jaime, "El diálogo con Europa de Miguel de Unamuno y Eugenio d'Ors," in *Spanish Thought and Letters in the Twentieth Century*, edited by Germán Bleiberg and E. Inman Fox, Nashville: Vanderbilt University Press, 1966: 193–99
Ferrater Mora, José, "D'Ors: Sentido de una filosofía," in his *Obras selectas*, vol. 1, Madrid: Revista de Occidente, 1969: 189–97
Guy, Alain, *Les Philosophes espagnols d'hier et d'aujourd'hui*, Toulouse: Privat, 1956: 167–72
Guy, Reine, "Cultura y unidad según Eugenio d'Ors," *Cuadernos Hispanoamericanos* 300 (1975): 694–98
Hina, Horst, "Eugenio d'Ors, precursor del estructuralismo," *Cuadernos del Sur* 11 (1972): 194–209
Jardí Casany, Enric, *Tres diguem-ne desarrelats: Pijoan, Ors, Gaziel*, Barcelona: Selecta, 1966
Jardí Casany, Enric, *Eugenio d'Ors*, Barcelona: Aymá, 1967
Jiménez Moreno, Luís, *Práctica del saber en filósofos españoles: Gracián, Unamuno, Ortega y Gasset, Eugenio d'Ors, Tierno Galván*, Barcelona: Anthropos, 1991
López Quintas, Alfonso, *El pensamiento filosófico de Ortega y d'Ors, una clave de interpretación*, Madrid: Guadarrama, 1972
Muro Romero, Pedro, "La teoría de la forma de Eugenio d'Ors," *Archivo Hispalense* 55 (1972): 63–77
Ortega y Gasset, José, "Sobre la fenomenología de Eugenio d'Ors," *Revista de Occidente* 108 (1990): 13–28
Resina, Joan Ramón, "Eugenio d'Ors y la obra continua," *Annali Instituto Universitario Orientale* 28 (1986): 321–36
Resina, Joan Ramón, "Barcelona ciutat en la estética de Eugenio d'Ors," *Revista Hispánica Moderna* 43 (1990): 167–78

Sáenz, Pilar G. Suelto de, *Eugenio d'Ors: Su mundo de valores estéticos*, Madrid: Plenitud, 1969

Sáenz, Pilar, *The Life and Works of Eugenio d'Ors*, Troy, Michigan: International Book Publishers, 1983

Ortega y Gasset, José

Spanish, 1883–1955

José Ortega y Gasset is Spain's greatest **philosophical essay**ist, and arguably one of the finest essayists of the 20th century in any language. Most of his writings (now collected in 12 thick volumes) were originally published in Spain's leading newspapers and journals, or delivered as lectures in his philosophy classes or in public venues. These writings are remarkable for their thematic diversity, intellectual verve, and stylistic brilliance. Ortega practiced many subtypes of the essay: note, gloss, **review**, prologue, fragment, thesis, article, **meditation**, lecture, **dialogue**, and biographical sketch. A voracious reader with panoramic interests, he wrote about an astounding range of subjects, from art to zoology. Specialized studies of literary, philosophical, or political aspects of Ortega's thought abound, but the magnitude and diversity of his oeuvre, and the partial truncation of his career by the Spanish Civil War and its aftermath, have delayed a fuller appreciation of his work. If antihumanist trends since the 1960s have partly eclipsed Ortega's existential humanism, excellent recent studies by Cerezo Galán (1984), Gray (1989), and others have made important strides in demonstrating the continuing relevance of Ortega's thought.

Coming of age around the turn of the century, Ortega embraced the project of Francisco Giner de los Ríos and Joaquín Costa to regenerate and modernize Spain by emulating the scientific ethos of more advanced European countries. In his various roles of essayist, critic, journalist, editor, lecturer, teacher, and political leader, Ortega carried on his mission of bringing Spanish culture up to the European "height of the time." He armed himself for this mission by extended periods of study in German universities and by wide reading in the classics, in European literature, philosophy, and history, and in contemporary science. From 1910 to 1936 he held the chair in metaphysics at the University of Madrid. He disseminated, both in his own works and through the *Revista de Occidente* (1923–36; Western review), the latest ideas of German philosophers **Georg Simmel**, Edmund Husserl, Max Scheler, and other leading European thinkers of the day. Ortega not only imported European philosophy into Spain; he also exported his own "Spanish interpretation of the world" to the international reading public.

Ortega shared many of the aesthetic and literary preoccupations of **Miguel de Unamuno** and José Martínez Ruiz (i.e. **Azorín**), his immediate predecessors from the Generation of 1898, especially their efforts to reinterpret Spanish culture by way of recovering authentic national values. But Ortega and his generation (that of 1914) distanced themselves from the mythologizing tendencies of the preceding generation, advocating a more rigorous and optimistic approach to national regeneration. To Unamuno's brooding Romanticism and "tragic sense of life," Ortega opposed his own "sportive" and "festive" sense of life, adopting such bold personae as hunter, archer, bullfighter, explorer, and navigator in his essays. One key to Ortega's style and its appeal is that his essays constantly enact his contention that each person's life is an adventure, with its urgent mission and stakes: to succeed or fail at realizing one's destiny. By dramatizing the hazards and pleasures he encountered in his own inquiries, Ortega hoped to incite readers to take up and develop the issues under discussion.

His wish to address contemporary Spanish readers where they lived led him to publish his ideas in the form of newspaper articles rather than systematic **treatises**. As he revealed in "Prólogo para alemanes" (1934; Prologue to Germans), he had never written for humanity at large, but had chosen to address only Spanish-speaking readers, with whom he could carry on an intimate conversation. Cordial without being familiar in tone, his limpid Castilian prose often echoes the rhythms and colloquial flavor of Madrid speech. He was a charismatic lecturer and orator, and his personal warmth and expressiveness are apparent throughout his writings. But Ortega's relation to the reader was not always one of straightforward dialogue. In "Ni vitalismo ni racionalismo" (1924; Neither vitalism nor rationalism), Ortega wrote that, since he had not been blessed with subtle, philosophically inclined readers, his strategy had been to "seduce the reader to philosophy by lyrical means." He added that this strategy had been successful enough to allow him to take the next step of "speaking philosophically about philosophy." In fact, Ortega never stopped using rhetorical means to entice the reader and to dramatize his ideas.

Chief among the distinctive qualities of his prose is a lavish use of metaphor. From his early writings on, he theorized about the nature and uses of metaphor in art, philosophy, and ordinary language. He aptly uses a metaphor to define the trope's cognitive function: "Metaphor is a supplement to our intellective arm, and represents, in logic, the fishing pole or the rifle." Other favorite rhetorical figures are paradox, irony, oxymoron, chiasmus, hyperbole, personification, and digression. Ortega's knowledge of classical and modern literature, the sciences, and visual arts supplied his fertile imagination with a rich lexicon and copious source of analogy and allusion. He is fond of coining ingenious neologisms, and of embellishing a passage with a well-chosen foreign expression. The effect is occasionally precious, but never pedantic. Ortega presumes not an erudite reader, only an intelligent and curious one. His phrasing is felicitous, his exposition lucid – he calls clarity "the courtesy of philosophers." He has a gift for concise definitions, and for clinching a point with a memorable **aphorism**.

Ortega's thought evolves organically, as the continuous elaboration of themes broached early in his career. His mature work can be divided into three periods, according to biographical and thematic developments: 1914–27, 1927–36, and 1936–55. In the first period, extending from the publication of his first book, *Meditaciones del Quijote* (1914; *Meditations on Quixote*) to his encounter with **Martin Heidegger**'s *Sein und Zeit* (1927; *Being and Time*), Ortega explores the role of circumstance and perspective in human life, and works out his philosophy of "vital reason." In a long prologue to *Meditations on Quixote*, he sets forth his lifelong essayistic program, inviting his compatriots to join him in "the negation of decrepit Spain" and in "experiments toward a new Spain." In his view, hatred and rancor had dulled Spaniards' spirits, leaving them isolated and unable to appreciate their surroundings. He proposes "new ways of looking" which would reconnect individuals to their world, rescuing marginal phenomena from oblivion and restoring an authentic scale of values. Ortega offers his "essays in intellectual love" as "salvations," or redemptive integrations of self and milieu: "The reabsorption of circumstance is the concrete destiny of man . . . I am myself plus my circumstance, and if I do not save it, I cannot save myself." This is the vital core of Ortega's philosophy, expressing the "radical reality" to which he returns throughout his writings: life as a ceaseless, intense dialogue between oneself and one's environment.

Despite its belletristic presentation, the program adumbrated in this early work went beyond literary criticism. Ortega approaches Cervantes' great novel, *Don Quixote* – the ostensible subject of his meditation – obliquely, as a pretext, for he has bigger game in view: a new metaphysics of human life. As Philip Silver (1978) has shown, Ortega's "new ways of looking" amounted to a "mundane phenomenology" aimed at giving each individual's concrete sensory experience of the world its due, and thereby avoiding what he considered the intellectualist error of transcendental phenomenology, as expounded by his German contemporary, Edmund Husserl.

In the same prologue, Ortega gives a much-quoted if equivocal definition of the essay. Although his essays are motivated by philosophical desires, "they are not philosophy, which is science. The essay is science, minus the explicit proof." It is not that the essayist lacks such proof: "it is a matter of intellectual honor not to write anything susceptible of proof without possessing the latter beforehand." But the essayist elects for stylistic reasons to withhold "the rigid mechanical apparatus of proof," which he commands no less than the philosopher or scientist, so as not to interrupt the flow or conceal from the reader "the inner warmth with which the thoughts were conceived." By reducing the distinction between essay and science to rhetorical strategy, Ortega seems to minimize or gloss over possible differences of method, scope, and subject matter. This is an instance of what Thomas Mermall (1994) calls a fundamental tension between the rhetorical nature of Ortega's writings and their epistemic claims: he somehow intended his essays to be at once circumstantial and systematic.

In *El tema de nuestro tiempo* (1923; *The Modern Theme*), Ortega attends to the biological basis of culture and proposes a synthesis of vitalism and rationalism. Human life, having both spiritual and biological aspects, is governed by countervailing imperatives: "Man, a living being, must be good – commands the cultural imperative. The good must be human, lived: that is, compatible with human life – orders the other imperative, the vital one." Modernity, according to Ortega, has made two opposite and unsuccessful attempts to resolve the antinomy of life and culture – first rationalism (which he calls "the irony of Socrates") and then, in response, relativism ("the irony of Don Juan"). The first denies life to save culture; the second reacts by denying the objective value of culture, thus making way for life. Ortega considers these to be two "complementary forms of blindness," and argues that the task of his time is to seek a third way. "Pure reason" must yield to "vital reason."

In his "La doctrina del punto de vista" ("Doctrine of the Point of View"), the final essay of *The Modern Theme*, Ortega argues that perspectivism can break the impasse of rationalism and relativism in the sphere of knowledge, or "the acquisition of truths." The question is, how can truths, by definition "eternal, unique and invariable," be apprehended by ephemeral human subjects? According to rationalism, the knowing subject must be an unchanging, transparent medium which can receive reality without deforming it. Relativism, recognizing that human beings do not meet those criteria, holds trans-individual knowledge to be a vain project. For Ortega, the subject is not a "pure I," the transparent medium posited by rationalists, but neither does the subject's perception of reality deform it, as relativists claim. Rather, the subject is likened to a sieve or net which, placed in a current, retains some things and lets others pass. Thus, the knowing subject selects but does not distort reality. When two individuals look at the same landscape from different vantage points, they see different scenes: each sees something which eludes the other's point of view. To infer from this that one or both views must be false or illusory would be to posit a third, ideal landscape, independent of any definite point of view – the persistent "utopian" error of rationalist philosophy. There is no such "archetypal landscape," declares Ortega. Reality, like a landscape, lends itself to an infinite number of perspectives, each one true and authentic as far as it goes.

Ortega was well aware that perspectivism, while sanctioning the individual point of view, does not answer the question of how there can be "eternal and invariable" truths. He apparently felt it necessary to reinvent an absolute point of view which would synthesize all partial viewpoints. "By juxtaposing everyone's partial views, it would be possible to weave them together and attain the universal and absolute truth." He ends the essay on a distinctly "utopian" note: the sum of all individual viewpoints would be "God . . . the symbol of the vital torrent through whose infinite nets the universe gradually passes . . . mankind is the visual organ of divinity." It may be argued that Ortega solved the problem of relativism more satisfactorily in his many evocative essays devoted to the Spanish landscape, in which he showed how provincial perspectives may be overcome through travel, comparison, and dialogue. He also explored the implications of perspective in aesthetics and the arts in a number of seminal essays, including his well-known "La deshumanización del arte" (1925; "The Dehumanization of Art").

Ortega reached the height of his powers during the intense second period (1927–36), which saw the fruition of such important works as *La rebelión de las masas* (1930; *The Revolt of the Masses*), *Misión de la universidad* (1930; *Mission of the University*), *Goethe desde dentro* (1932; Goethe from within), and "Historia como sistema" (wr. 1935, pub. 1936 as "History as a System"), as well as dozens of influential political articles and speeches. He also gave three important series of lectures not published until after his death: *¿Qué es filosofía?* (given 1929, pub. 1958; *What Is Philosophy?*), *Unas lecciones de metafísica* (given 1932–33, pub. 1966; *Some Lessons in Metaphysics*), and *En torno a Galileo* (given 1933, pub. 1956; On Galileo, translated as *Man and Crisis*).

In *The Revolt of the Masses*, his most famous and influential work, Ortega extends the sociological diagnosis of modernity that he had begun in previous works of the 1920s. The initial symptom of the problem – "the fact of agglomeration" – is registered as the realization that public places are now filled by teeming masses. The instruments of civilization, and the refined pleasures once reserved for the few, are suddenly to be found in the possession of the "multitude." The crowd, which had previously stayed in the background of the social stage, has advanced to the footlights and assumed the starring role: "There are no longer protagonists; there is only the chorus." Contrary to a common misunderstanding, Ortega's "elitism" is not a defense of inherited privilege; his opposition between "select minorities" and masses does not correspond to the distinction between "upper" and "lower" classes. By select minorities, Ortega means those who wish to excel and therefore make high demands on themselves, living in the service of ideals. Mass man, by contrast, demands nothing of himself and is quite content to be like everyone else. The distinction is between "noble life and common life, or effort and inertia." In Ortega's view, human society is always "aristocratic" in this sense – a dynamic unity of relatively inert masses led by creative minorities – or it ceases to be a society. Unlike its 19th-century counterpart, which respected law and followed the lead of qualified minorities, the modern mass is a "hyperdemocracy" which rejects any appeal to higher standards and ideals, and imposes its will through direct action or violence. The mediocre, commonplace mind "has the effrontery to proclaim the right to vulgarity and to impose it everywhere." Minorities have abdicated their role, leaving the masses to rule civil society but without the vision or capacity to rule. Lacking a vital program or compelling moral code, European societies are demoralized and adrift.

Ortega is not simply retelling Spengler's pessimistic version of Western decline. He takes the new prominence of the masses first as a sign that the general quality of human life has risen dramatically. The average man represents history's field of action; "he is to history what the sea-level is to geography." The advent of the masses represents a dramatic surge of human potentiality, an ambiguous success story, resulting from the previous century's "noble experiment" at combining liberal democracy with what Ortega dubs "technicism" – itself the offspring of the marriage of industrial capitalism and science. Unfortunately, the masses, like spoiled children, have inherited the fruits of these experiments but not the heroic effort and inventive spirit required to produce and sustain them. The result is paradoxical: "the modern world is a civilized one; its inhabitant is not." Mass man is "a primitive who has slipped through the wings onto the age-old stage of civilization." His prototype, ironically, is the average man of science, widely regarded as the finest flower of European civilization. The increasing specialization mandated by scientific research has produced a new and paradoxical species, the "learned ignoramus" – a human type with myopic, fragmentary vision; a new "barbarian" whose complacency and narrowness are a betrayal of the scientific ideal of integrated knowledge.

But the greatest danger facing European civilization, Ortega writes prophetically, is that of state intervention. The contemporary state is, like science, one of the glories of European culture, whose very success has created the conditions for a possible reversion to barbarism. Failing to see the state as the delicate human artefact it is, created and sustained by political values and civic virtues whose preservation requires vigilance and effort, the masses instead view it as an anonymous instrument for the realization of their every whim. The grave danger in this tendency is "the absorption of all spontaneous social effort," the crushing of creative minorities, and the "bureaucratization of existence" by the State. Means and ends are reversed: "the people are converted into fuel to feed the mere machinery which is the State. The skeleton devours the flesh around it. The scaffolding becomes the owner and tenant of the house." Ortega's prophecy has been amply fulfilled in this century, by totalitarian regimes of left and right. His study concludes on another prophetic note, envisioning a new vital project – the unification of Europe – which might avoid the dangers, and reap the potential, symbolized by the revolt of the masses.

This transitional period saw both the zenith and the nadir of Ortega's involvement in Spanish politics. For a generation he had been at the forefront of liberal intellectual reformers, leading the call in 1930 for the replacement of Spain's tottering parliamentary monarchy by a democratic Republic. After serving for a year as an elected representative to parliament at the beginning of the Second Republic (1931–32), Ortega grew disillusioned with the polarized political situation, withdrew, and kept a pointed silence about Spanish politics from then on.

In Ortega's evolving thought of this period, "historical reason" subsumed "vital reason" as he meditated on the historical dimension of human life. After reading Heidegger's great work, Being and Time, Ortega reaffirmed (but never really fulfilled) his earlier commitment to presenting his work as a philosophical system. He occasionally reminded his readers that his own early works had anticipated many of Heidegger's central ideas. Nelson Orringer (1979) has shown that in fact many of Ortega's main aesthetic and philosophical concerns were heavily indebted to his early readings in German thought. Ortega's influences, however, were always imaginatively transformed by his unique vision and idiom. For example, one of his root metaphors – life as shipwreck – is an ancient Greek one. Ortega does not invoke the pathos of shipwreck to suggest the absurdity or hopelessness of man's fate. In "Pidiendo un Goethe desde dentro" (1932; "In Search of Goethe from Within") Ortega uses the metaphor to stress the human need for action and invention, for an urgent, vital project, in order to survive. "To be shipwrecked is not to drown." He equates culture to the swimming motions which the drowning individual makes to save himself. "The consciousness of shipwreck, being the truth of life, is already salvation. This is why I no longer believe in any thoughts but those of the shipwrecked."

During the third and final period, from the outbreak of the Civil War (and his decade-long self-exile) until his death, Ortega continued to publish and lecture, and to work on his announced major treatises on history, society, and philosophy – leaving them unfinished, to be published posthumously as El hombre y la gente (1957; Man and People), La idea de principio en Leibniz y la evolución de la teoría deductiva (1958; The Idea of Principle in Leibnitz and the Evolution of Deductive Theory), and Sobre la razón histórica (1979; Historical Reason). In these rewarding works – which are for the most part distillations or elaborations of earlier themes rather than new departures – Ortega probes the growing sense of crisis in European thought, especially the erosion of faith in reason. One cause of the crisis is the failure of modern philosophy and science to give an adequate account of human nature. In *Historical Reason*, delivered originally as lectures in Buenos Aires (1940) and Lisbon (1944), Ortega explains this failure and announces a new mode of thought to remedy it. "Man has no nature; what he has is history; because history is the mode of being of the entity that is constitutionally, fundamentally, mobility and change." Man, an "unknown" whose existence cannot be fixed or quantified, only interpreted, "will not be discovered in the laboratories. The hour of the historical sciences is at hand. Pure reason . . . must be replaced by narrative reason . . . This narrative reason is historical reason." When Ortega left Spain in voluntary exile in 1936, he lost the immediate contact with the Spanish public on which the dynamism of his style and thought had depended. While leaving him freer to work on his long-promised systematic works, his relative isolation could only adversely affect the character and pace of his production.

Some critics have reproached Ortega for being "only" a great stylist, a creator of metaphors, instead of becoming the systematic philosopher he aspired to be. His principal virtues are admittedly synoptic and heuristic, not systematic; they are those of the discoverer and trailblazer, not those of the colonizer or city-builder. But the tension between his literary vocation and his philosophical aspirations needs no apology, for it is the source of his unique mode of essaying. His philosophy of "authentic life" – life as an ever-renewed process of self-invention, of discovering one's necessary task in the crucible of circumstances – is precisely what he practiced in his incandescent essays.

R. LANE KAUFFMANN

Biography

Born 9 May 1883 in Madrid. Studied at a Jesuit school in Miraflores, Málaga, 1891–97; University of Deusto, Bilbao, 1897–98; University of Madrid, 1898–1904, degree, 1902, Ph.D. in philosophy, 1904; Universities of Berlin, Leipzig, and Marburg, 1905–07. Professor of psychology, logic, and ethics, Escuela Superior del Magisterio, Madrid, 1908–10. Founder, *Faro*, Madrid, 1908. Married Rosa Spottorno Topete, 1910: three children. Professor of metaphysics, Central University of Madrid, 1910–29 (resigned in protest against the military dictator Miguel Primo de Rivera) and 1930–36. Elected to the Royal Spanish Academy of Moral and Political Sciences, 1914. Cofounder, League of Political Education, 1914. Founder, *España* review, 1915–23, and *Revista de Occidente*, 1923–36, and cofounder, *El Sol* (The sun), 1917. Founder, with **Ramón Pérez de Ayala** and Gregorio Marañón, Agrupación al Servicio de la República (Group at the Service of the Republic), 1931; deputy for the province of León, Constitutional Assembly, Second Spanish Republic, and Civil Governor of Madrid, 1931–32. Self-imposed exile in France, the Netherlands, Argentina, and Portugal, 1936–41; professor of philosophy, University of San Marcos, Lima, from 1941; returned to Spain, 1945. Founder, with Julián Marías, Institute of the Humanities, Madrid, 1948–50. Lectured frequently in Germany, Switzerland, and the United States, 1950–55. Awards: Gold Medal of City of Madrid; honorary degrees from two universities. Died in Madrid, 18 October 1955.

Selected Writings

Essays and Related Prose
Meditaciones del Quijote, 1914; as *Meditations on Quixote*, translated by Evelyn Rugg and Diego Marín, 1961

Personas, obras, cosas, 1916; as *Mocedades*, 1973
El Espectador: Colección de ensayos filosóficos y literarios, 8 vols., 1916–34; in 1 vol., 1943
El tema de nuestro tiempo, 1923; as *The Modern Theme*, translated by James Cleugh, 1933
La deshumanización del arte: Ideas sobre la novela, 1925; as *The Dehumanization of Art and Notes on the Novel*, translated by Helene Weyl, 1948; in *Velázquez, Goya and The Dehumanization of Art*, edited by Christine Bernard, translated by Alexis Brown and others, 1972
Tríptico (on Mirabeau, Kant, and Goethe), 3 vols., 1927–33
Misión de la universidad, 1930; as *Mission of the University*, translated by Howard Lee Nostrand, 1944
La rebelión de las masas, 1930; *The Revolt of the Masses*, translated by J. R. Carey, 1932, and Anthony Kerrigan, 1986
La redención de las provincias y de la decencia nacional (articles), 1931
Goethe desde dentro, 1932
Ensimismamiento y alteración; Meditación de la tecnica, 1939; first essay as "The Self and the Other," translated by Willard R. Trask, in *Partisan Review*, 1952; second essay as "Man the Technician," translated by W. Atkinson, in *History as a System and Other Essays Toward a Philosophy of History*, 1961
El libro de las misiones (includes *Misión del bibliotecario*; *Misión de la universidad*; *Miseria y esplendor de la traducción*), 1940; first essay as *The Mission of the Librarian*, translated by James Lewis and Ray Carpenter, 1961
Teoría de Andalucía y otros ensayos, 1942
History as a System and Other Essays, translated by Helene Weyl, 1946
En torno a Galileo, 1956; as *Man and Crisis*, translated by Mildred Adams, 1958
Meditación de la técnica, 1957
Ensayos escogidos, 1957
El hombre y la gente, 1957; as *Man and People*, translated by Willard R. Trask, 1957
Kant, Hegel, Dilthey, 1958
Meditación del pueblo joven, 1958
¿Qué es filosofía?, 1958; as *What Is Philosophy?*, translated by Mildred Adams, 1960
La idea de principio en Leibniz y la evolución de la teoría deductiva, 1958; as *The Idea of Principle in Leibnitz and the Evolution of Deductive Theory*, translated by Mildred Adams, 1971
History as a System and Other Essays Toward a Philosophy of History, translated by W. Atkinson, 1961
Misión del bibliotecario y otros ensayos afines, 1962
Unas lecciones de metafísica, 1966; as *Some Lessons in Metaphysics*, translated by Mildred Adams, 1970
The Dehumanization of Art, and Other Essays on Art, Culture and Literature, 1968
Velázquez, Goya and The Dehumanization of Art, edited by Christine Bernard, translated by Alexis Brown and others, 1972
Escritos políticos, 3 vols., 1973
Pasado y porvenir para el hombre actual (selected speeches), 1974
Sobre la razón histórica, 1979; as *Historical Reason*, translated by Philip W. Silver, 1984
Ensayos sobre la "Generación del 98" y otros escritores españoles contemporáneos, 1981
Meditación de la técnica, y otros ensayos sobre ciencia y filosofía, 1982
Misión de la universidad y otros ensayos sobre educación y pedagogía, 1982
Meditaciones sobre la literatura y el arte, edited by E. Inman Fox, 1987

Other writings: philosophical works.

Collected works editions: *Obras completas*, 11 vols., 1946–69, and 12 vols., 1983.

Bibliographies

Donoso, Anton, and Harold C. Raley, *José Ortega y Gasset: A Bibliography of Secondary Sources*, Bowling Green, Ohio: Bowling Green State University, 1986

Rukser, Udo, *Bibliografía de Ortega: Estudios Orteguianos 3*, Madrid: Revista de Occidente, 1971

Further Reading

Cerezo Galán, Pedro, *La voluntad de aventura: Aproximamiento crítico al pensamiento de Ortega y Gasset*, Barcelona: Ariel, 1984

Copleston, Frederick, "Ortega y Gasset and Philosophical Relativism," in his *Philosophers and Philosophies*, New York: Barnes and Noble, 1976

Dust, Patrick H., editor, *Ortega y Gasset and the Question of Modernity*, Minneapolis: Prisma Institute, 1989

Gaos, José, *Sobre Ortega y Gasset y otros trabajos de historia de las ideas en España y la América española*, Mexico City: Imprenta Universitaria, 1957

Graham, John T., *A Pragmatist Philosophy of Life in Ortega y Gasset*, Columbia: University of Missouri Press, 1994

Gray, Rockwell, *The Imperative of Modernity: An Intellectual Biography of José Ortega y Gasset*, Berkeley: University of California Press, 1989

Gray, Rockwell, "Ortega y el ensayo (I–II)," article published in two parts, *El País*, 8–9 June 1992

McClintock, Robert, *Man and His Circumstances: Ortega as Educator*, New York: Teachers College Press, 1971

Marías, Julián, *Ortega y Gasset: Circumstance and Vocation*, Norman: University of Oklahoma Press, 1970

Marichal, Juan, "La singularidad estilística de Ortega," in his *Teoría e historia del ensayismo hispánico*, Madrid: Alianza, 1984

Mermall, Thomas, "Entre *epísteme* y *doxa*: El trasfondo retórico de la razón vital," *Revista Hispánica Moderna* 47 (1994)

Morón Arroyo, Ciriaco, *El sistema de Ortega y Gasset*, Madrid: Alcalá, 1968

Nicol, Eduardo, *El problema de la filosofía hispánica*, Madrid: Tecnos, 1961

Orringer, Nelson, *Ortega y sus fuentes germánicas*, Madrid: Gredos, 1979

Ouimette, Victor, *José Ortega y Gasset*, Boston: Twayne, 1982

Regalado García, Antonio, *El laberinto de la razón: Ortega y Heidegger*, Madrid: Alianza, 1990

Rodríguez Huéscar, Antonio, *José Ortega y Gasset's Metaphysical Innovation: A Critique and Overcoming of Idealism*, Albany: State University of New York Press, 1995

Rossi, Alejandro, and others, *José Ortega y Gasset*, Mexico City: Fondo de Cultura Económica, 1984

Senabre Sempere, Ricardo, *Lengua y estilo de Ortega y Gasset*, Salamanca: Universidad de Salamanca, 1964

Silver, Philip W., *Ortega as Phenomenologist: The Genesis of "Meditations on Quixote"*, New York: Columbia University Press, 1978

Orwell, George

British, 1903–1950

Although George Orwell is probably best known for the two novels he wrote late in his life, *Animal Farm* (1945) and *Nineteen Eighty-Four* (1949), his reputation as an essayist clearly ranks with the finest of the 20th century. His achievement is something of an anomaly given the artistic and cultural movements of the 1930s and 1940s when he produced the majority of his essays. At a time when the Modernists were struggling to produce a new aesthetic and traditionalists were reviving classical forms, a writer who willingly sacrificed the literary integrity of his work for political purposes must have seemed altogether beyond the pale.

In "Why I Write" (1946), a landmark essay on the writer's life, Orwell examines the motives behind literary production, including sheer egoism, aesthetic enthusiasm, historical impulse, and political purpose. To some degree, he finds these various impulses to be beyond the writer's control. His own natural inclination would have led him to write less polemical works, but the exigencies of his time – deprivation of human rights in the British Empire, massive unemployment among the working classes in England, the rise of fascism in Europe – made it impossible for him to retreat to the novel of manners or elegiac poetry. His experience in the Spanish Civil War was pivotal in driving him to sublimate his literary ambitions to political necessity. He was also transparent about the nature of his political motives: "Every line of serious work that I have written since 1936 has been written, directly or indirectly, against totalitarianism and for democratic Socialism."

However, Orwell did not think that political writing was necessarily devoid of artistic merit. In his own writing, he clearly distinguished rapidly produced newspaper articles and **reviews** from more significant essays that combined political purpose and aesthetic enthusiasm. Instead of identifying writers as essayists or journalists, Orwell's tendency is to connect the essay to the conditions of publication. He produced a steady stream of "potboilers" for most of his life which were written primarily for the money, including the radio scripts he produced for the BBC during World War II. Interspersed with these ephemeral creations were the carefully crafted essays written for important journals such as *Adelphi*, *Horizon*, and the **Partisan Review**.

Of course, writing that is motivated by political purpose can potentially undermine the aesthetic achievement of the text. In "Why I Write" Orwell recalls a conversation with one of his critics about *Homage to Catalonia* (1938), his book on the Spanish Civil War. The majority of the book describes Orwell's experiences as a foot soldier in a badly disorganized army. His depiction of the war has the qualities we associate with a great novel: vivid description, interesting characters, suspenseful action. However, the political purpose which motivated his writing was the need to alert the West to the betrayal of the ordinary soldiers and workers by their duplicitous leaders. For this reason, Orwell spends a chapter in the book describing the political in-fighting among the various Marxist factions in the war. Orwell's critics argued that this chapter should have been omitted in order to maintain the artistic integrity of the book. Orwell believed passionately that to delete this chapter would have undermined the whole purpose of the book.

Still, the aesthetic failure of *Homage to Catalonia* led Orwell to look for new ways to "fuse political purpose and artistic purpose into one whole." His search led him to examine the work of many canonical writers who were "political" to one degree or another. In "Charles Dickens" (1940), Orwell noted that although everyone is sure that **Dickens** is politically motivated, no one can be sure what his politics are. He is claimed by both Marxists and Christians, proletariat and bourgeoisie. He is assumed to be a reformer, but he is as cynical about reformers as he is about capitalists and landowners. In essence, Dickens' political philosophy can be summed up as behaving decently toward one another. In this essay Orwell clearly stipulates that "all art is propaganda," but he quickly adds "not all propaganda is art." One of the things that defines the great writer, he believes, is the ability to avoid the party line, to write honestly and independently. The eccentricity, and even inconsistency, of Dickens' work is a sign of his genius.

Orwell takes up this theme again in "Politics vs. Literature" (1946), his examination of **Jonathan Swift**'s moral philosophy as expounded in *Gulliver's Travels*. Orwell was a great admirer of Swift's work, and no one can read *Animal Farm* without recognizing Orwell's indebtedness to Swift's **satire**. On the other hand, Swift's Tory politics were completely antithetical to an avowed socialist. Can such literature be "good" if it espouses a false world view? For Orwell the answer is clearly "yes." He argues first that what represents a false world view can only be understood within the political possibilities of a particular age. But beyond this, Orwell is willing to separate artistic achievement from political progressivism: "The views that a writer holds must be compatible with sanity, in the medical sense, and with the power of continuous thought: beyond that what we ask of him is talent, which is probably another name for conviction." It is worth noting that Orwell considers talent to be virtually synonymous with conviction. For him a writer need not possess the "correct" world view, but he must hold some view with conviction in order to succeed as an artist.

Perhaps even more problematic for Orwell as a writer was the nature of his own political convictions. He was well aware that most art was inherently elitist and aristocratic. Good books were produced by and for the upper classes. As a proponent of "democratic Socialism" what sort of "art" was possible for the serious writer? Orwell grappled with this dilemma in many of his major essays.

One consequence of his socialist position was a tendency to savage the cultural elite. Yeats is a fascist ("W. B. Yeats," 1943); H. G. Wells is out of touch with reality ("Wells, Hitler and the World State," 1941); Shaw writes "cracker-mottoes" ("Rudyard Kipling," 1946); Salvador Dalí is decadent ("Benefit of Clergy," 1946); even Gandhi comes in for some criticism ("Reflections on Gandhi," 1949). On the other hand, he often defends the most unlikely heroes. He rehabilitates Kipling, who was, without doubt, a "jingo Imperialist," but who spoke the language of the common people. In fact, Orwell identifies a whole genre of what he calls "good bad poetry." In essence, this is poetry that gives pleasure to the masses; it is a "graceful monument to the obvious." Even more remarkably, Orwell defends the German broadcasts of P. G. Wodehouse, which were considered treasonous by many British citizens. As someone who had dedicated his life against fascism, how could Orwell defend a German sympathizer during the war? Furthermore, how could he defend Wodehouse's novels, which seemed tailor-made for Orwell's socialist critique? At first, such a defense must seem pure perversity on Orwell's part. More likely, however, is that Orwell sees in Wodehouse a harmless dupe, much less guilty of abetting the enemy than his accusers, many of whom had cheered the policy of appeasement in 1938.

Perhaps Orwell's sympathy for Wodehouse sprang from his own sense of culpability as an officer in the Indian Imperial Police in Burma. Some of his best essays reflect upon his experience in Burma. One of his earliest essays, "A Hanging"

(1931), is a chilling description of the death of a Burmese native and the inhumanity of his executioners. "Shooting an Elephant" (1936) displays Orwell's self-loathing as a British officer who is trapped between his hatred of the Empire, which is clearly morally indefensible, and his hatred of the people, who take every opportunity to humiliate their oppressors. The irony of the essay is that he ultimately shoots the elephant, not because it represents a real threat, but "solely to avoid looking a fool." The dilemma of those serving the Empire is also the theme of Orwell's early novel, *Burmese Days* (1934).

Another theme running through many of Orwell's essays is his sympathy for the lower classes. After returning from Burma, Orwell more or less deliberately plunged into a life of poverty. These experiences were recorded in *Down and Out in Paris and London* (1933). One of Orwell's last essays is also drawn from his experience when taken ill in France. "How the Poor Die" (wr. 1946, pub. 1950) describes the degrading medical treatment given to the destitute in public hospitals. Even after Orwell resumed middle-class life, he often disguised himself as a tramp in order to understand the hardships of the lower class. His experiences are recorded in articles such as "The Spike" (1931) and "Common Lodging Houses" (1932). Some of them were included in his 1935 novel, *A Clergyman's Daughter*. Ultimately, they led to his first popular success, *The Road to Wigan Pier* (1937), a description of unemployed laborers in the north of England.

One other recurring theme in Orwell's essays is his attachment to childhood. In his weekly articles for the *Tribune*, he sometimes returned to childhood pleasures, as in his "Thoughts on the Common Toad" (1946) and "A Good Word for the Vicar of Bray" (1946). He was also one of the earliest critics to consider the effect of popular children's literature on the formation of political principles. His review of "Boys' Weeklies" (1940), though erring in some factual details, argues that the stories contained in such papers are all tracts for conservative, if not fascist, points of view. It is perhaps fitting that his last major essay, "Such, Such Were the Joys" (wr. 1947, pub. 1953), treats the subject of his boarding school education. In this essay, many of Orwell's lifelong themes – contempt for authority, sympathy for the oppressed, and a love of simple pleasures – readily coalesce.

Orwell's principal contribution to the essay was his unification of political purpose and human sympathy into a genre that was largely divided between ideological diatribe on the one hand and sentimental recollection on the other. As a stylist, he contributed unforgettable passages of prose. No one who has watched Orwell's elephant die can soon forget it: "He neither stirred nor fell, but every line of his body had altered. He looked suddenly stricken, shrunken, immensely old, as though the frightful impact of the bullet had paralyzed him without knocking him down."

The early criticism of Orwell, coming in the political climate of the Cold War, was frequently devoted to illuminating Orwell's vision of the totalitarian state. Contemporary studies of Orwell have focused more on the effects of technology on human privacy and the connections between language and bureaucratic institutions of all kinds. His essay "Politics and the English Language" (1946) is considered foundational to understanding the influence of language on political decision-making. He argues forcefully that political chicanery not only debases language, but that bad habits of language undermine the political process. His view that language is not morally neutral – expounded both here and in the "Newspeak" addendum to *Nineteen Eighty-Four* – has had a profound impact on both the practice of the essay and the nature of political discourse in our times.

DAVID W. CHAPMAN

Biography

Born Eric Arthur Blair, 25 June 1903 in Motihari, Bengal. Moved with mother and sister to England, 1904. Studied at St. Cyprian's, Eastbourne, Sussex, 1911–16; Wellington School, Somerset, 1917; Eton College, Berkshire, 1917–21. Member of the Imperial Indian Police in Burma, 1922–27. Lived in London, 1927 and 1930–31, and Paris, 1928–29; teacher and bookshop clerk, 1929–36. Reviewer for the *New English Weekly*, 1935–36, *Time and Tide*, 1940–41, the *Tribune*, 1940–47 (literary editor, 1943–45), and *Horizon*, 1940–49. Married Eileen O'Shaughnessy, 1936 (died, 1945): one adopted son. Shopkeeper, Wallingford, Hertfordshire, 1936–40. Went to Spain as a journalist and served in the United Marxist Workers' Party militia in Catalonia, 1937: wounded in the neck. Served in the Home Guards, 1940–43. Columnist of "London Letter," *Partisan Review*, New York, 1941–46; coeditor, Searchlight Books series, Secker and Warburg publishers, London, 1941–42; talks producer in the Empire Department, BBC, London, 1941–43; contributor, the *Observer*, London, 1942–49 (war correspondent, 1945); columnist, Manchester *Evening News*, 1943–46. Lived on Jura, Hebrides Islands, Scotland, 1946–47. Married Sonia Mary Brownell, 1949. Died (of tuberculosis) in London, 21 January 1950.

Selected Writings

Essays and Related Prose
Inside the Whale, and Other Essays, 1940
The Lion and the Unicorn: Socialism and the English Genius, 1941
Critical Essays, 1946; as *Dickens, Dali and Others: Studies in Popular Culture*, 1946
The English People, 1947
Shooting an Elephant, and Other Essays, 1950
England, Your England and Other Essays, 1953; as *Such, Such Were the Joys*, 1953
A Collection of Essays, 1954
The Orwell Reader: Fiction, Essays, and Reportage, edited by Richard H. Rovere, 1956
Selected Essays, 1957; as *Inside the Whale and Other Essays*, 1965
Collected Essays, 1961
Decline of English Murder and Other Essays, 1965
The Collected Essays, Journalism, and Letters, edited by Sonia Orwell and Ian Angus, 4 vols., 1968
The Penguin Essays of George Orwell, 1984

Other writings: six novels (*Burmese Days*, 1934; *A Clergyman's Daughter*, 1935; *Keep the Aspidistra Flying*, 1936; *Coming Up for Air*, 1939; *Animal Farm*, 1945; *Nineteen Eighty-Four*, 1949) and three volumes of reportage (*Down and Out in Paris and London*, 1933; *The Road to Wigan Pier*, 1937; *Homage to Catalonia*, 1938).

Bibliographies
Hammond, J. R., "Select Bibliography," in his *A George Orwell Companion*, London: Macmillan, and New York: St. Martin's Press, 1982: 266–74
Meyers, Jeffrey, and Valerie Meyers, *George Orwell: An Annotated Bibliography of Criticism*, New York: Garland, 1977

Further Reading
Aldritt, Keith, *The Making of George Orwell: An Essay in Literary History*, New York: St. Martin's Press, and London: Arnold, 1969

Atkins, John, *George Orwell: A Literary Study*, London: Calder, and New York: Ungar, 1971 (original edition, 1955)
Bal, Sant Singh, *George Orwell: The Ethical Imagination*, New Delhi: Arnold-Heinemann, and Atlantic Highlands, New Jersey: Humanities Press, 1981
Bolton, W. F., *The Language of 1984: Orwell's English and Ours*, Knoxville: University of Tennessee Press, and Oxford: Blackwell, 1984
Gardner, Averil, "Orwell the Essayist," in her *George Orwell*, Boston: Twayne, 1987: 80–95
Good, Graham, "George Orwell: Myth and Counter-myth," in his *The Observing Self: Rediscovering the Essay*, London and New York: Routledge, 1988: 152–75
Gross, Miriam, editor, *The World of George Orwell*, London: Weidenfeld and Nicolson, 1971; New York: Simon and Schuster, 1972
Hammond, J. R., "The Essays," in his *A George Orwell Companion*, London: Macmillan, and New York: St. Martin's Press, 1982: 187–227
Harris, Harold J., "Orwell's Essays and 1984," *Twentieth Century Literature* 4 (1959): 154–61
Kubal, David L., *Outside the Whale: George Orwell's Art and Politics*, Notre Dame, Indiana: University of Notre Dame Press, 1972
Meyers, Jeffrey, *A Reader's Guide to George Orwell*, London: Thames and Hudson, 1975; Totowa, New Jersey: Littlefield Adams, 1977
Meyers, Jeffrey, editor, *George Orwell: The Critical Heritage*, London and Boston: Routledge and Kegan Paul, 1975
Oldsey, Bernard, and Joseph Browne, editors, *Critical Essays on George Orwell*, Boston: Hall, 1986
Patai, Daphne, *The Orwell Mystique: A Study in Male Ideology*, Amherst: University of Massachusetts Press, 1984
Rees, Richard, *George Orwell: Fugitive from the Camp of Victory*, London: Secker and Warburg, and Carbondale: Southern Illinois University Press, 1961
Wemyss, Courtney T., and Alexej Ugrinsky, editors, *George Orwell*, Westport, Connecticut: Greenwood Press, 1987
Williams, Raymond, *Orwell*, London: Collins, 1971; as *George Orwell*, New York: Viking, 1971
Williams, Raymond, editor, *George Orwell: A Collection of Critical Essays*, Englewood Cliffs, New Jersey: Prentice Hall, 1974
Woodcock, George, *The Crystal Spirit: A Study of George Orwell*, Boston: Little Brown, 1966; London: Cape, 1967
Zwerdling, Alex, *Orwell and the Left*, New Haven, Connecticut: Yale University Press, 1974

Ouellette, Fernand

French Canadian, 1930–

Fernand Ouellette is that young man who, in the 1960s, without any technical knowledge of music, simply because he profoundly loved the works of Edgard Varèse, wrote to him, talked with him in New York, and wrote a biography that is still one of the mainstays of the Varèse bibliography (*Edgard Varèse*, 1966). This is how Ouellette has always worked, in all the literary genres he has practiced – poetry, novel, essay – with a kind of calculated temerity, forging ahead without any regard for the commonplace or the strictures of narrow professionalism. "Stuck between rapture and darkness," he wrote in his second book of essays, *Journal dénoué* (1974; Untied journal), "I have learned not to care about the fear of ridicule. I have accustomed my intelligence to make jumps, to take risks, like a tight-rope walker." "How does he dare?" a

Paris critic wrote in response. What he dared, in *Journal dénoué*, was to reveal how he managed to escape a traditional fear of life and love, while at the same time immensely enlarging his grasp of modern thought by reading such writers as Rainer Maria Rilke, Friedrich Hölderlin, **T. S. Eliot**, Pierre-Jean Jouve, and Søren Kierkegaard. What he asked from the authors he read was not simply culture, but a kind of salvation.

Ouellette is a passionate writer, sometimes to the point of candor. In his essays he remains true to the poetic nature he revealed in *Les Heures* (1987; The hours), one of his most celebrated books of poems; yet his essays are not purely impressionistic. His book on the German poet **Novalis**, for instance, entitled *Depuis Novalis* (1973; Since Novalis), sprang from a course he taught with his friend **André Belleau** at the University of Quebec in Montreal. His numerous essays on painters, a subject that increasingly preoccupies him, bear the mark of serious documentation. Ouellette's essays are all more or less autobiographical, sometimes directly, as in *Journal dénoué*, but more often, as the years go by, as part of a spiritual quest. It would not be excessive to say that the light he discovers (or rather pursues) in the paintings of Vermeer or Matisse is the same mystical light he talks about in his more explicitly **religious essays**.

Ouellette's spiritual quest informs his consideration of the world in which he lives, the larger world with its tragedies of war, torture, hunger, and lack of freedom, as well as his own small world of Quebec, which concerns him deeply. His contributions to public debate, though not numerous, have been important. An ardent nationalist, he has written against bilingualism, arguing that it would lead to the victory of English over French in Quebec. When terrorism broke out in the 1960s, taking a number of innocent victims, he lashed out against all forms of violence. Those essays were published first in the magazine *Liberté*, of which he was one of the founders, and were reprinted in a book entitled, significantly, *Écrire en notre temps* (1979; Writing in our time). Poetry itself, a frequent subject in Ouellette's essays, is deeply rooted in "our time." Poetry is not a refuge from the issues of the contemporary world, nor should it necessarily be concerned with these issues. Poetry signifies hope and the survival of hope, giving humans, speaking beings, a possible future.

Ouellette's voice is grave, noble, and earnest, and speaks about the essential themes of human thought: love, death, language, and God. His essays do not read like **treatises**. They are, as he has said, "flashes of lightning, fragments of a foreign time, desperate leaps out of form." Ouellette has often used the word "fulgurance" (fulguration) to describe the inner movement of his poetry. The same term can be applied to his essays.

GILLES MARCOTTE

Biography

Born 24 September 1930 in Montreal. Studied at the Collège Séraphique, Ottawa, 1943–47; social sciences at the University of Montreal, licence, 1952. Book sales representative, 1953–60; scriptwriter for the National Film Board of Canada, 1955–59. Married Lisette Corbeil, 1955. Director for the radio network of Société Radio-Canada, 1960–91. Cofounder, *Liberté*, 1959, and of the International Quebecois Meeting of Writers, 1972. Awards:

France-Quebec Prize, for biography, 1966; Governor-General's Award, for nonfiction (refused), 1970, for fiction, 1985, and for poetry, 1987; France-Canada Prize, for poetry, 1972; *Études Françaises* Prize, for nonfiction, 1974; David Prize.

Selected Writings

Essays and Related Prose
Les Actes retrouvés, 1970
Depuis Novalis: Errance et gloses, 1973
Journal dénoué, 1974
Écrire en notre temps, 1979
Ouvertures, 1988
Commencements, 1992
En forme de trajet, 1996

Other writings: three novels (*Tu regardais intensément Geneviève*, 1978; *La Mort vive*, 1980; *Lucie ou un midi en novembre*, 1985), poetry, and a biography of Edgard Varèse (1966).

Further Reading

Bilodeau, François, *Action et errance: Les Essais de Fernand Ouellette*, Montreal: McGill University, 1984
Mailhot, Laurent, "Récit-Essai: Le *Journal dénoué* de Fernand Ouellette," in his *Ouvrir le livre*, Montreal: L'Hexagone, 1992: 205–12 (article originally published, 1975)
Nepveu, Pierre, "Fernand Ouellette: La Lumière hors d'elle-même," in *L'Essai et la prose d'idées au Québec*, Montreal: Fides, 1985: 711–22

Ouyang Xiu

Chinese, 1007–1072

Known as one of the eight great prose stylists of the Tang and Song dynasties, Ouyang Xiu is remembered for both his output and his influence upon the course of literary history. More than any other single writer, Ouyang was responsible for developing a new expressiveness in expository prose, setting prose writing of the Northern Song era on a course markedly different from that of earlier periods.

Ouyang's voluminous literary production contains expository prose in a large number of distinct genres, including the **letter**, **preface**, record or inscription (*ji*), farewell, tomb inscription, colophon, "poetry talks," "calligraphy exercises," and the thesis or discourse (*lun*). Ouyang produced dozens of pieces in each of these forms. While the *lun* is the closest approximation of the Western "essay," any general consideration of Ouyang's achievement as an essayist must take his work in all of these forms into account. Whatever its origin or utilitarian purpose, Ouyang utilized each form to develop and express his thinking on diverse topics in the manner of the essayist.

Standard evaluations of Ouyang in literary histories identify him as the leader of an 11th-century stylistic revival known as the "ancient prose movement" (*guwen yundong*). A complex event in the intellectual history of the period, this "movement" had ethical and political dimensions that made it far more than merely a matter of aesthetic preference for one type of prose style over another. Ouyang and his supporters were dissatisfied with the vogue of parallel prose in their day, a style that required language to be cast in a series of paired statements exhibiting rigid grammatical parallelism between the two members and a diction that was heavily reliant upon recondite and elaborate tropes and literary allusion. While not denying that such a style had its place, "ancient prose" adherents decried the requirement that it be used by candidates for the civil service examinations (jinshi) and, by extension, throughout the written documentation produced in the huge imperial bureaucracy.

Parallel prose, or the "current style," as it was called, was attacked as intellectually stultifying or, worse still, morally degenerate: it encouraged attention to scintillating ornamentation at the expense of stress upon the fundamental Confucian values which writing should serve. The "ancient style" alternative that Ouyang and others championed was supposedly a return to the nonparallel rhythms and "unadorned" diction of the Tang statesman Han Yu, which could itself be traced back to ancient classics such as Mencius and The Book of Rites. The defining moment of the movement came in 1057 when Ouyang was appointed to administer the highest examinations. He failed all those who wrote their answers in parallel prose and honored instead young men who showed their mastery in the ancient style. This event is credited with effecting a change in examination standards thereafter, and in seriously weakening, if not ending, the ascendancy of the "current style" for decades to come.

The controversy described here, while undoubtedly real, tends to be exaggerated in modern accounts, the rivalries too sharply drawn. What also tends to be distorted in standard literary histories is the huge gulf between the expository tone and style of Ouyang's writing and that of his supposed model, the prose of Han Yu. As with most archaizing movements in Chinese aesthetics, while the slogan may have been "return to the past," what in fact took place was the development of a new style. To be sure, Ouyang did write essays, such as his "Pengdang lun" (1044; "On Factions") and "Ben lun" (1042; "On Fundamentals"), which project an image of him as a staunch Confucian moralist, much in the tradition of the conventional image of Han Yu. But as soon as one moves beyond these anthology pieces and begins to explore the full corpus of Ouyang's prose works, a very different impression is formed.

Ouyang managed to cultivate a level of flexibility and informality in expository prose quite unlike what had been previously achieved. A reading of his compositions set against those of any of the great Tang masters, even **Liu Zongyuan**, will reveal a relaxation of the high seriousness of earlier centuries in Ouyang's style. This key innovation was already recognized in Ouyang's time by Su Xun, an important figure in his own right. Su Xun likened Han Yu's writing to a mighty river which flows with a great surge and conceals terrifying water monsters in its depths, so that anyone who ventures to its banks and gazes into its murky depths shrinks back in fear. Ouyang's prose he likened instead to a meandering stream, twisting supplely this way and that, never hurried or belabored or intimidating.

Ouyang's fondness for injecting himself and his own feelings into his prose pieces is an important factor in his distinctive tone. In prefaces, studio records, and even grave inscriptions, Ouyang does not hesitate to speak personally and openly about his feelings for the person or object under consideration. The result is a tone in prose that verges on the lyrical, something that had never been accomplished on any sustained level by previous writers. Ouyang's most celebrated compositions, the autobiographical "Zuiweng ting ji" (1046; "The Old Drunkard's Pavilion") and "Liuyi jushi zhuan" (1070; "Biography of Recluse Six-Ones") exemplify this tone, albeit with a special playfulness. Although a detailed study has yet to be done, the particular features of Ouyang's diction and prose rhythm surely also contribute to his tone. Avoiding archaic language, Ouyang strove for a "plain and bland" (pingdan) style, as he did in poetry as well. Consequently, the language of his essays is unexpectedly close to that of Five Dynasties and Song period anecdotal writing (biji), which may have influenced Ouyang.

Among the compositions with the greatest literary merit one common trait stands out. Ouyang is adept at selecting a particular object or site (a rock, a studio, a zither, a painting) and writing about his relationship with the subject in a way that endows it with multiple layers of significance or meaning. This method is a departure from the simpler technique of prose parable, widespread in Tang writings, in which the symbolism of the subject eclipses all other meanings. Here too, an affinity may be detected between this richness of meaning in Ouyang's prose and what we normally expect to find in personal, lyric poetry.

Ouyang Xiu was the first of a number of Northern Song dynasty figures known for their multiplicity of interests and accomplishments in philosophy, classical studies, historiography, poetry, and literary prose. While his output in these other fields is certainly important, and particularly so in the two poetic forms (shi and ci), it is arguably as a prose stylist that he was most innovative and most influential. **Su Shi**, his protégé, became a greater poet, Sima Guang a more important historian, Zheng Yi a more seminal thinker, and Wang Anshi a more original and ambitious, if controversial, statesman. But no writer of the time matched the richness of Ouyang's collected prose or developed so distinctive a style.

RONALD EGAN

Biography

Born in 1007 in Mianzhou prefecture (now Mianyang, Sichuan). Moved to Suizhou as a boy. Studied privately; passed the qualifying exams for one of the imperial colleges in Kaifeng, 1028, and the jinshi (civil service) exams, 1030. Married, 1031 (wife died, 1033): one child; married Miss Yang (died, 1035). Prefectural judge, Luoyang, 1031–34; collator of texts, Imperial Library, Kaifeng, from 1034 and 1040–43. Exiled to Yiling for supporting Fan Zhongyan's criticism of the court, 1035. Married Miss Xue, 1037. Magistrate, Qiande, 1038–40; policy critic, then drafting official, from 1043; part of a group of liberals who promoted the Minor Reform, 1043. Exiled on a technicality, 1045, after charges of incest (for which he was acquitted three times) damaged his reputation; governor of Chuzhou, 1045–48, Yangzhou, 1048–49, and Yingzhou, 1049–52; returned to Kaifeng, 1054; various government appointments, including to the Bureau of Academicians, from 1054; compiler of the official history of the Tang dynasty, from 1054; assistant chief minister, 1061–67. Accused of incest with his daughter-in-law, 1067: acquitted but again his reputation was damaged, and he requested a transfer; governor, Bozhou, 1067–68; retired from government service, 1071. Died in Yingzhou, Anwei province in 1072.

Selected Writings

Essays and Related Prose
Ouyang Xiu sanwen xuan (Collected essays), edited by Chen
Bixiang, 1990
Translations of essays in: *Chinese Classical Prose: The Eight
Masters of the T'ang-Sung Period*, edited and translated by Shi
Shun Liu, 1979: 141–209; *The Literary Works of Ou-yang Hsiu
(1007–72)* by Ronald Egan, 1984: Chapter 2 and the Appendix;
Inscribed Landscapes: Travel Writing from Imperial China,
translated by Richard E. Strassberg, 1994: 162–67

Other writings: poetry, songs, and works on history.

Collected works editions: *Ouyang Wenzhong gong ji*, 1933; *Ouyang
Xui quan ji*, 2 vols., 1961.

Further Reading
Egan, Ronald C., *The Literary Works of Ou-yang Hsiu (1007–72)*,
Cambridge: Cambridge University Press, 1984
Liu, James J. Y., *Ou-yang Hsiu: An Eleventh Century Neo-
Confucianist*, Stanford, California: Stanford University Press, 1967
(original Chinese edition, 1963)
Locke, Marjorie A., *The Early Life of Ou-yang Hsiu and His
Relation to the Rise of the Ku-wen Movement of the Sung
Dynasty* (dissertation), London: University of London, 1951
Yan Jie, *Ouyang Xiu nianpu*, Nanjing: Nanjing chubanshe, 1989

Ozick, Cynthia
American, 1928–

Cynthia Ozick explores many forms in her several hundred
essays, including the literary **review**, biographical sketch, editorial, travelogue, and autobiography. Several topics occur again
and again in her essays, such as feminism, **Henry James'** literary
influence, what it means to be a writer, of both nonfiction and
fiction, and, most importantly for Ozick, what it means to be
a Jewish writer in 20th-century America. Her nonfiction has
been published in a wide variety of magazines and journals,
from the *New Yorker*, *Ms.*, and the *New York Times Book
Review* to *Judaism*, *Commentary*, and the *Partisan Review*.
Despite Ozick's being better known for her novels and short
stories, critics increasingly analyze her collections of essays in
their studies of her fiction. She continues to contribute
frequently to periodicals, and clearly desires her essays to be
accepted as separate entities from her fiction. In the **preface**,
entitled "Forewarning," to *Metaphor & Memory* (1989), she
writes that it is "plain foolishness" for readers to think that
"the stories were 'illustrations' of the essays" or that "the
essays expressed the ideational (or even at times the ideological) matrix of the stories."

Whether Ozick writes for a general or more specialized readership, she makes several consistent assumptions about her
audience. For example, though many of her essays were originally composed as speeches, she assumes a kind of intellectual crossover, an attentiveness, between a hearing and a
reading audience. Furthermore, her formal style reveals her
belief that authorial expertise is neither divisive nor distancing,
but rather expected by those who read nonfiction prose. Her
tone is authoritative, didactic, at times even polemical, yet
she assumes an openmindedness, a willingness to explore the

unknown, in her audience. Her broad literary and historical
knowledge, and especially her learned readings of the Torah
and Pentateuch, act as a foundation for her readers and herself,
and she teaches rather than declaims. Ozick seems to believe
that both the writing and reading of an essay are parts of a
journey, and she makes the journey along with her readers. She
writes in the foreword to *Art and Ardor* (1983) that the
"only nonfiction worth writing – at least for me – lacks
the summarizing gift, is heir to nothing, and sets out with
empty pockets from scratch."

Two of Ozick's best-known pieces on Judaism illustrate
several characteristics of her approaches to the essay. In her
preface to "Toward a New Yiddish" (1970) in *Art and Ardor*,
Ozick states that "my own striving is to be one thing all the
time, and to everyone; not to have one attitude or subject
matter (or imagining or storytelling) for one kind of friend and
another for another kind." Though the essay argues that "there
are no major works of Jewish imaginative genius written in
any Gentile language," Ozick's selection of the essay for *Art
and Ardor* suggests that she assumes her Gentile as well as her
Jewish readers will be open to her revolutionary ideas. Her
purpose in the essay is to encourage Jews to develop a central
liturgical language, by and for Jews, that will allow them to
develop in the Diaspora a Jewish oeuvre. She responds to her
own ideas in "Bialik's Hint" (1983), altering them slightly, to
conclude that a new language is not what is necessary – what
is needed for Jews to accomplish a new literature is to replicate the combination of the Hebraic and the Platonic that
produced the Jewish holiness of study in a new assimilation
of Hebrew and Enlightenment thought – "for Enlightenment
ideas of skepticism, originality, individuality, and the assertiveness of the free imagination to leach into what we might call
the Jewish language of restraint, sobriety, moral seriousness,
collective conscience." Her shift in thought does not contradict her desire to be the same person to all people; rather, it
expresses the kind of openness that marks the capacity of writer
and reader to learn.

Even Ozick's more polemical style, reminiscent of **Mary
Wollstonecraft**, in her feminist essays belies the conclusion that
she writes for the converted. For example, in "Previsions of
the Demise of the Dancing Dog" (1972), Ozick argues that
"the enlightenment has, for women, and especially by women,
not yet occurred"; however, in "The Hole/Birth Catalogue"
(1972), written for *Ms.*, she rails against the idea that anatomy
is destiny; and in "Literature and the Politics of Sex: A
Dissent," written for the same magazine, she emphatically
distances herself from the "new" feminism. In the latter essay,
she objects to the term "woman writer," believing that it
further solidifies the intellectual disenfranchisement of women
that classical feminism struggled to dissipate. Ozick might
choose to modify her ideas over time; but she will not give an
audience what it expects, and her voice is often tough, cheer-
less, and demanding.

In her essays on contemporary writers, such as Saul Bellow,
John Cheever, and **John Updike**, Ozick's tone recalls **William
Hazlitt's** – opinionated, cranky, educated, and above all,
unapologetic. Her explorations of literary figures from the past,
however, take the forms of introduction, recovery, or rediscovery, and in them her tone is affectionate, her didactic
style easier and more forgiving of her audience's unfamiliarity

with her subject. In "What Henry James Knew" (1993), for example, one of her many essays on the most influential writer of her career, she explores the effect of James' theatrical failure, *Guy Domville* (1894), upon his later novels, in which he "looked freely into the Medusan truth." In "Sholem Aleichem's Revolution" (1988), she historicizes Yiddish, and explains Aleichem's revolutionary insistence that the language be taken seriously. In "More than Just a Victorian" (1995), she avers that late 20th-century readers reject Anthony Trollope because he understands them too well.

In "Metaphor and Memory" (1986), Ozick explicitly discusses the morality she believes should undergird any enterprise, including writing. Intellectual passion is the hallmark of Ozick's esoteric essays, lyricism that of her rare personal reflections. When freed from the constraints of erudition, Ozick's writing soars, and the "metaphorical concentration" she believes allows all "strangers to imagine the familiar hearts of strangers" emerges unbidden. In her eulogy to Bernard Malamud (1986), she writes that after a telephone conversation with him, she felt she "had been blessed, anointed, by an illumination of generosity fetched up out of the marrow of human continuity." In her memoir, "Alfred Chester's Wig" (1992), Ozick characterizes the instructor at New York University who pits Chester and her against one another in Freshman Composition as a "sly, languid, and vainglorious Roman emperor presiding over the bloody goings on in the Colosseum of his classroom, with the little green buds of Washington Square Park just beginning to unfold below the college windows." Finally, in her childhood recollection, "A Drugstore in Winter" (1982), Ozick recalls how one year Pelham Bay "froze so hard that whole families, mine among them, crossed back and forth to City Island, strangers saluting and calling out in the ecstasy of the bright trudge over such a sudden wilderness of ice."

Joseph Epstein (1984) uses the adjectives "brilliant, quirky, profound, outrageous" to describe the pieces in *Art and Ardor*, while Sarah Blacher Cohen (1990) finds that some of the essays in *Metaphor & Memory* are the "illuminations" Ozick strives to achieve. Yet each of these writers views the essays through the lens of the fiction. Ozick's ongoing and varied composition of essays elicits the hope that they will continue to be collected, and that they will some day be viewed by their own light.

SIOBHAN CRAFT BROWNSON

Biography

Born 17 April 1928 in New York City. Studied at New York University, B.A. (cum laude) in English, 1949 (Phi Beta Kappa); Ohio State University, Columbus, M.A., 1950. Married Bernard Hallote, 1952: one daughter. Taught at New York University, 1964–65, and Indiana University, Bloomington, 1972; distinguished artist-in-residence, City College, New York, 1981–82; Phi Beta Kappa Orator, Harvard University, Cambridge, Massachusetts, 1985. Awards: many, including the Wallant Award, 1972; B'nai B'rith Award, 1972; Jewish Book Council Epstein Award, 1972, 1977; American Academy of Arts and Letters Award, 1973; Hadassah Myrtle Wreath Award, 1974; Lamport Prize, 1980; honorary degrees from 11 universities and institutions.

Selected Writings

Essays and Related Prose

Art and Ardor, 1983
Metaphor & Memory, 1989
What Henry James Knew, and Other Essays on Writers, 1993
Portrait of the Artist as a Bad Character, and Other Essays on Writing, 1996
Fame & Folly, 1996
A Cynthia Ozick Reader, edited by Elaine M. Kauvar, 1996

Other writings: three novels (*Trust*, 1966; *The Cannibal Galaxy*, 1983; *The Messiah of Stockholm*, 1987), short stories, poetry, and a play.

Bibliography

Currier, Susan, and Daniel J. Cahill, "A Bibliography of Writings by Cynthia Ozick," *Texas Studies in Literature and Language* (Summer 1983)

Further Reading

Cohen, Sarah Blacher, "The Fiction Writer as Essayist: Ozick's *Metaphor & Memory*," *Judaism* 39 (Summer 1990): 276–81
Epstein, Joseph, "Cynthia Ozick, Jewish Writer," *Commentary* 77 (March 1984): 64–69
Pinsker, Sanford, "Jewish Tradition and the Individual Talent," in *Cynthia Ozick*, edited by Harold Bloom, New York: Chelsea House, 1986
Pollitt, Katha, "The Three Selves of Cynthia Ozick," in *Cynthia Ozick*, edited by Harold Bloom, New York: Chelsea House, 1986
Strandberg, Victor, *Greek Mind/Jewish Soul: The Conflicted Art of Cynthia Ozick*, Madison: University of Wisconsin Press, 1994

P

Paine, Thomas

British/American, 1737–1809

Thomas Paine was a pioneer in popular rhetoric, a form of discourse most familiar now in advertising, which he employed primarily in support of the natural rights of humankind, but he is best known for his association with the American and French Revolutions and for his rejection of conventional Christianity. Although this last position was common among his Enlightenment contemporaries, it was the ruin of Paine. He was a serious writer, never humorous, whose plainness and lack of pretense, were it not for allusions to contemporary issues, more closely resemble good political discourse of the 20th century than of his own, especially in his most famous work *The Rights of Man* (1791–92).

Paine was nearly 40 when he became an overnight sensation with his first published work, *Common Sense* (1776), a **pamphlet** which urged the American colonies to consider the rightness of separation from England. He spent the next two decades basking in the glow of various revolutionary fires, although he personally objected to violent overthrow and viewed revolution as ideally a "natural selection" in government. While in France, he nearly lost his life in a failed defense of Louis XVI on these grounds. Controversy followed him wherever he went, inviting a popular form of personal attack at the time; his biography is, unfortunately, a part of all readings of Paine. Political enemies funded the first Paine biography with money provided by an English MP after the publication of the first half of *The Rights of Man*. It suggests that he was cruel to his mother, killed his first wife, abandoned his second, drank excessively, and did not wash. Although cleverly written, it is neither history nor biography, and has colored all subsequent Paine scholarship. Controversy surrounding *The Rights of Man* culminated in a conviction on charges of treason for too nearly suggesting the overthrow of the English monarchy to some readers, although modern readers will have difficulty seeing it.

With the publication of the first part of his statement of personal belief, *The Age of Reason* (1794–95), Paine's infamy was complete. He lost his popularity in America, the only country he claimed as his own, a final, deeply ironic failure as an essayist in a lifetime of spectacular success in that genre. Immediately after his death, a large body of unpublished work was probably destroyed by a former French revolutionary out of combined loyalty to Paine and to the Catholic Church, to which she had converted while caring for Paine in his old age. A fire destroyed the rest several years later. Near the end of the 19th century, the first editor of Paine's collected works ended his biography of Paine with a call for world government and religious tolerance in a style reminiscent of Paine's own, the first scholarly testament to the power Paine continues to wield with readers.

The basic elements of the Paine myth – the scurrilous biography, the late-life apostasy, the legions of loyal Paineites – have always overshadowed the essayist Paine. It goes without saying that any serious appreciation of the simple logic of his essays – all of it intended as public discourse and unrelated to the controversies which followed him to the grave – should absolutely exclude the "life" of Thomas Paine, especially since the private Paine is lost with the lost papers.

All that remains of the popular Paine are the opening lines of the first installment of what is now collectively referred to as *The American Crisis* (1776–83): "These are the times that try men's souls . . ." With this essay, Paine invented an American identity and with it the possibility of an American nationalism necessary in times of war. These lines, written to rouse disheartened soldiers in General Washington's army, have reappeared in wartime speeches of commanding generals ever since, although Paine's personal political views were idealistic and pacifist, founded on the idea of the people's right to establish or re-establish their own government based on present need rather than on either tradition or the fundamental notion of "might makes right." His philosophy proved impractical, even to himself in the end when he failed to influence the French with his rhetoric of reconciliation, a realization which lent much of the bitterness to *The Age of Reason*.

At the height of his powers, Paine produced the immensely popular *The Rights of Man* in support of the French and in response to **Edmund Burke**'s *Reflections on the Revolution in France* (1790). Unlike the philosopher Burke, Paine approached the essay form as a populist means to current ends rather than as a literary form in the service of philosophy. Although he succeeded, according to relative sales of the two documents, he did not do justice to the subtleties of Burke's argument. While Burke addressed a social and political elite with the power of England's literary past behind him, Paine produced rhetoric that inflamed a broader readership, choosing what proved to be a superior moral high road.

Now that the argument no longer matters, Paine's is clearly the superior rhetoric, although Burke is of course the superior philosopher, as Paine was neither systematic nor profound in his thinking. Without exception, his well-circulated works set off a storm of print reaction. Much of this reaction, both contemporary and in the large body of subsequent scholarship, suggests a linguistic counterpoint – an unmistakable mirroring of Paine's style – resembling face-to-face argumentation (in which disputants tend toward the code of the strongest speaker), unlike the strictly rule-bound style of formal debate taught in the university system which had produced Burke. Olivia Smith suggests in *The Politics of Language* (1984) that the keen awareness of audience which characterized Paine's prose is even more apparent in *The Rights of Man* than in his American writing because Paine studied Burke's use of himself as a narrative device, noting his broadly drawn images as well as his frequent attention to his readers. Whether or not Paine was constructing himself in this document as the ideal opponent to Burke, only Paine knew, but his relationship to his audience is clear. He set up two audiences – on the one side his larger audience, to whom he speaks sometimes boldly, sometimes patiently, the rhetorician using his skill to inspire a range of emotions according to his will. On the other is Edmund Burke, whom he repeatedly challenges to respond to his response. The effect of the clearly distinct audiences is to strengthen the voice of Paine himself and to place the reading audience always in the position of taking up the dialectic in opposition to a common foe.

CLARA SPEER

Biography

Born 29 January 1737 in Thetford, Norfolk, England. Studied at grammar school until age 13. Apprentice to his father in the staymaker trade; privateer at sea, 1756; staymaker, London, 1756–57, Kent, 1758–60, and Norfolk, 1766. Married Mary Lambert, 1759 (died, 1760). Excise officer, Thetford, 1761, Lincolnshire, 1762–65 (dismissed), and Sussex, 1768–74 (dismissed for organizing a demand for a pay rise); usher, London, 1766–68. Married Elizabeth Ollive, 1771 (legally separated, 1774; died, 1808). Traveled to Philadelphia, 1774; editor, *Pennsylvania Magazine*, Philadelphia, 1775–76; contributor, *Pennsylvania Journal*. Secretary, Continental Congress committee to negotiate treaty with the Indians, 1777, and the committee on foreign affairs, 1777–79; clerk, Pennsylvania Assembly, 1779–81; secretary on a mission to France to raise money for George Washington's army, 1781. Lived in Bordentown, New Jersey, and on a farm near New Rochelle, New York, 1783–87; lived in England and France, from 1787. Tried in absentia for treason (over *The Rights of Man*) and outlawed from England, 1792. Made a French citizen by the French Assembly, 1792; member of the National Convention, for Pas de Calais, 1792, as part of Gironde group, which supported the banishment rather than death of Louis XVI; at the fall of the Girondists he was deprived of French citizenship and imprisoned, 1793–94; resumed seat in Convention, 1795, and lived in Paris until 1802. Returned to the U.S., 1802, and lived in New Jersey, New Rochelle, and New York City, 1802–09. Awards: honorary degree from the University of Pennsylvania. Died in New York City, 8 June 1809.

Selected Writings

Essays and Related Prose

Common Sense, 1776; revised edition, 1776; edited by Isaac Kramnick, 1976
The American Crisis, 13 nos., 1776–83
The Rights of Man: Being an Answer to Mr. Burke's Attack on the French Revolution, 2 vols., 1791–92; edited by Henry Collins, 1969, Arthur Seldon, 1969, Eric Foner, 1985, and Gregory Claeys, 1992

The Age of Reason: Being an Investigation of True and Fabulous Theology, 2 vols., 1794–95
Selections from the Writing of Thomas Paine, edited by Carl Van Doren, 1922
Representative Selections, edited by Harry Hayden Clark, 1944
Common Sense and Other Political Writings, edited by Nelson F. Adkins, 1953
The Thomas Paine Reader, edited by Michael Foot and Isaac Kramnick, 1987
Political Writings, edited by Bruce Kuklick, 1989
Rights of Man, Common Sense, and Other Writings, edited by Mark Philp, 1995

Other writings: works on history and politics.

Collected works editions: *Life and Works*, edited by William M. Van der Weyde, 10 vols., 1925; *Complete Writings*, edited by Philip S. Foner, 2 vols., 1945; *Collected Writings* (Library of America Edition), 1995.

Bibliographies

Aldridge, A. O., "Thomas Paine: A Survey of Research and Criticism Since 1945," *British Studies Monitor* 5 (1974): 3–29
The Thomas Paine Collection at Thetford: An Analytical Catalogue, Norwich: Norfolk County Library, 1979
Wilson, Jerome, "Thomas Paine in America: An Annotated Bibliography, 1900–1973," *Bulletin of Bibliography* 31 (1974): 133–51, 180

Further Reading

Aldridge, A. Owen, *Man of Reason: The Life of Thomas Paine*, Philadelphia: Lippincott, 1959; London: Cresset Press, 1960
Aldridge, A. Owen, *Thomas Paine's American Ideology*, Newark: University of Delaware Press, 1984
Butler, Marilyn, editor, *Burke, Paine, Godwin and the Revolution Controversy*, Cambridge and New York: Cambridge University Press, 1984
Conway, Moncure Daniel, *The Life of Thomas Paine*, New York: Putnam, 1892; London: Watts, 1909
Dyck, Ian, editor, *Citizen of the World: Essays on Paine*, London: Helm, 1987; New York: St. Martin's Press, 1988
Fennessy, R. R., *Burke, Paine, and the Rights of Man*, The Hague: Nijhoff, 1963
Foner, Eric, *Tom Paine and Revolutionary America*, New York: Oxford University Press, 1976
Fruchtman, Jack, Jr., *Thomas Paine: Apostle of Freedom*, New York: Four Walls Eight Windows, 1994
Keane, John, *Tom Paine: A Political Life*, Boston: Little Brown, and London: Bloomsbury, 1995
Philp, Mark, *Thomas Paine*, Oxford: Oxford University Press, 1989
Powell, David, *Tom Paine, The Greatest Exile*, London: Croom Helm, 1985
Smith, Olivia, *The Politics of Language, 1791–1819*, Oxford: Clarendon Press, and New York: Oxford University Press, 1984
Wilson, Jerome D., and William F. Ricketson, *Thomas Paine*, Boston: Twayne, revised edition, 1989 (original edition, 1978)

Palmer, Nettie

Australian, 1885–1964

Nettie Palmer is one of the most important Australian writers who emerged between the 1920s and the 1940s, but where her contemporaries were novelists, dramatists, or poets, she worked almost exclusively within the essay form, the book review, and the journal. She was self-effacing and self-critical, considering that her writing was of minor importance compared with that of the "creative writer," but it has stood the passage of time much better than that of many of her contemporaries. Her lively style went hand in hand with an exceptional critical shrewdness. While she was underrated in her time, her posthumous reputation has continued to grow.

Like her husband **Vance Palmer**, Nettie Palmer was concerned with breaking down entrenched colonial attitudes that refused to consider local writing on its own merits. She wanted to encourage an intellectual, critical approach to Australian writing and increase the writer's sense of an audience. She wrote on a range of topics such as the Australian accent, suburbs, Australian English, surfing, Italian immigrants, and wooden houses. But she also wanted Australian writers to keep in touch with the great currents of world literature and not to become enclosed in the limited world of the merely local. University educated, Nettie Palmer spoke French and German, had studied Greek and Latin and later took up Spanish to study South American literature, seeing important analogies between the Australian and South American situations.

Her first extended publication (apart from two early volumes of verse) was *Modern Australian Literature, 1900–1923* (1924), a milestone in the study of 20th-century Australian writing. Throughout the 1920s she contributed literary essays to major Australian newspapers and the weekly *Bulletin*, her main aim being to introduce women writers like Mary Gilmore and Katharine Susannah Prichard to as wide an audience as possible. In 1929 she began contributing a personal column to *All About Books*, but her most important essays appeared in the *Illustrated Tasmanian Mail*. In those articles there is a conscious but flexible and unstrained merging of overseas and local writers. She brought the same quality of attention to bear on the poetry of John Shaw Neilson as on **Thomas Mann's** *Der Zauberberg* (1924; *The Magic Mountain*) or Osbert Sitwell's *England Reclaimed* (1927). Most of the best-known English, American, and Australian writers of the time are mentioned in her columns. Within the limits of weekly and fortnightly literary journalism and working within the belletristic tradition of the 1920s (less deliberately politicized than her work in the late 1930s), she was able to produce much relevant criticism and alert, lively comment. She dealt with a wide range of authors, including Spenser, **Goethe**, Ibsen, Strindberg, **Yeats**, Hardy, **Lawrence**, Sigrid Undset, Proust, Joyce, **Pound**, and O'Neill. Most of this work remained uncollected during her lifetime though some of it appeared in slightly different form in her journal *Fourteen Years* (1948). Her opinions could be trenchantly independent. Writing of **Aldous Huxley** in April 1929 she judges *Point Counter Point* to be glittering journalism, claiming that Huxley is a writer of ingenuity rather than imagination, and that his skeptical materialism puts him on the side and in the service of the philistines.

For all her absorption in the European tradition, Nettie Palmer took every opportunity to discuss the work of Australian writers and their particular situation. She insisted that Australian culture was still at the stage where writers had to interpret and humanize the country and give the lie to D. H. Lawrence's statement that "Australia is a country with no word written across it yet." Palmer wanted to see a movement in Australian writing away from a prolonged colonialism to an independent and autonomous literary tradition. No one wrote more forcefully than she about the literary situation in Australia in her time: she pointed to the poor publishing conditions, the lack of weekly and monthly reviews which are indispensable to the growth and nourishment of a sound literary culture, the unavailability or inaccessibility of Australian books, the impossibility of a writer making a living purely as an author, the indifference to local work, the stifling censorship laws. She had a marked gift for focusing on the significant writers and issues of her time. In her best essays she did not merely serve Australian literature, she contributed to it.

Fourteen Years: Extracts from a Private Journal, 1925–1939 was originally published in an edition limited to 500 copies, a fact that reveals much about the condition of Australian literary production at the time. A collection of some of Palmer's best writing, it contains character studies and portraits of figures as different as Barbara Baynton, Christina Stead, Shaw Neilson, and Henry Handel Richardson, among many others; nature notes and observations of places ranging from Barcelona to Paris, London to Green Island and Melbourne. Miles Franklin compared Nettie Palmer with Mary Collum and Lady Gregory; **A. D. Hope** wrote of *Fourteen Years* that "it gave the impression, rare in Australian literature before the present day, of a really professional writer in the European sense." There is no other volume quite like it in Australian writing.

VIVIAN SMITH

Biography

Born Janet Gertrude Higgins, 18 August 1885 in Sandhurst (now Bendigo), Victoria. Studied at the University of Melbourne, 1905–09, B.A., 1909, M.A., 1912; traveled to Europe to study modern languages in Marburg, Berlin, and Paris, 1910–11, then returned to Australia. Returned to London, 1914. Married Vance Palmer (died, 1959), 1914: two daughters. Staying at Tregastel, Brittany when war was declared, 1914; returned to Australia, 1915. Literary journalist and essayist, 1920–35, contributing to various journals, including the *Argus*, *All About Books*, the Brisbane *Courier*, the *Bulletin*, the *Illustrated Tasmanian Mail*, and the *Australian Woman's Mirror*. Traveled to Europe again, 1935–36. Active in the Spanish Relief Committee during the Spanish Civil War. Died in Melbourne, 19 October 1964.

Selected Writings

Essays and Related Prose

Modern Australian Literature, 1900–1923, 1924
Henry Bournes Higgins: A Memoir, 1931
Talking It Over, 1932
Fourteen Years: Extracts from a Private Journal, 1925–1939, 1948
Henry Handel Richardson: A Study, 1950
The Dandenongs, 1952
Bernard O'Dowd, with Victor Kennedy, 1954
Nettie Palmer: Her Private Journal Fourteen Years, Poems, Reviews and Literary Essays, edited by Vivian Smith, 1988

Other writings: poetry and correspondence.

Bibliography

Smith, Vivian, "Nettie Palmer: A Checklist of Literary Journalism, 1918–1936," *Australian Literary Studies* 6, no. 2 (October 1973): 190–96

Further Reading

Hope, A. D., "The Prose of Nettie Palmer," *Meanjin* 18 (1959): 22–27

Hope, A. D., "End of an Age" (obituary article), *Australian*, 24 October 1964; reprinted in his *Native Companions*, Sydney: Angus and Robertson, 1974

Jordan, Deborah, "Towards a Biography of Nettie Palmer," *Hecate* 6, no. 2 (1980): 6–72

Jordan, Deborah, "Nettie Palmer as Critic," in *Gender, Politics and Fiction*, edited by Carole Ferrier, St. Lucia: University of Queensland Press, 1985

Jordan, Deborah, "Nettie Palmer: The Writer as Nationalist," in *Double Time: Women in Victoria – 150 Years*, edited by Marilyn Lake and Farley Kelly, Ringwood: Penguin, 1985

Modjeska, Drusilla, *Exiles at Home: Australian Women Writers, 1925–1945*, Sydney: Angus and Robertson, and London: Sirius, 1981

Serle, Geoffrey, *The Creative Spirit in Australia: A Cultural History*, Richmond, Victoria: Heinemann Australia, 1987

Smith, Vivian, "Vance and Nettie Palmer: The Literary Journalism," *Australian Literary Studies* 6, no. 2 (October 1973)

Smith, Vivian, *Vance and Nettie Palmer*, Boston: Twayne, 1975

Stewart, Douglas, "Conversation Piece," *The Bulletin*, 3 August 1949

Tipping, Marjorie, "Remembrance of Palmers Past," *Overland* 100 (1985): 10–18

Palmer, Vance

Australian, 1885–1959

Vance Palmer was the leading man of letters of his generation in Australia as well as poet, novelist, dramatist, and short story writer, but his reputation as an essayist, literary journalist, social commentator, and key figure in the development of Australian culture in the first half of the 20th century has received less attention than it deserves. He tried to bring breadth, flexibility, and maturity to the Australian theme by never losing touch with what was happening in writing and thought abroad and by trying where possible to incorporate it into the Australian situation. He understood and affirmed the close relationship between a national literature and national experience. Palmer believed that it is the business of the artist to create interest in the life around him. "Art is really the interpretation of the inner life of his surroundings. There must be no seeing through English spectacles. Our art must be original as our fauna and flora are original" (*Steele Rudd's Magazine*, 1905).

Palmer's first important London recognition came through the journal *New Age*, where some of his early sketches were published. On his return to Australia Palmer was associated with the journal *Fellowship* in the pursuit of a national identity. In the March 1917 issue "A Note on Joseph Furphy" was a determined effort to promote a relaunch of Furphy's 1903 novel *Such Is Life*. Palmer was convinced that the recognition of this novel was intimately related to the status of Australian culture as a whole and a large part of his writings as an essayist is devoted to establishing a canon of Australian writers. From his return from World War I until the late 1930s, and subsequently in his articles and **reviews** for the Australian Broadcasting Commission, his essays aimed at enhancing the quality of Australian cultural life. A quiet note of social

criticism is rarely absent. Early essays draw on visits to France and Ireland; others respond to the situation of American writers like Sherwood Anderson and Ambrose Bierce, **H. L. Mencken** and Robert Nathan, later to Hemingway and Faulkner. Palmer noted points of comparison between the situation of writers in America and Australia, agreeing with his wife **Nettie Palmer** in 1930 that "Australia in literary matters, is probably where America stood a century ago."

Some of his most interesting essays are those on the conditions of literary production in the Australia of his time. He objected to the way novelists had to address a public overseas; he complained that "There is practically no criticism of such literary work as is produced in Australia, and consequently no responsive public" (1923) and that "there is no critically informed and alert public in Australia" (1925). Palmer saw literature as a unifying force in society with a power to change life.

World War II precipitated a new national awareness and inspired Palmer to produce three books, tributes to figures of the past who had directly or indirectly influenced his life and the course of Australian culture. *National Portraits* (1940) is a series of essays devoted to those pioneers who had originated ideas and tapped springs that were later to enrich the public life. It celebrates those men of vision who fought against the intellectual timidity that went with "colonialism" in all its forms. Arranged chronologically, the essays as a whole present an outline of the country's history, and illustrate one of Palmer's major preoccupations: the need for Australia to become a home to the imagination.

By 1940 Palmer was coming to be considered the leading figure in Australian letters and more and more of the official tasks of warden of Australian culture fell to him. He was asked to assemble a commemorative volume in honor of A. G. Stephens, whose policy on the "Red Page" of the *Bulletin* and in the *Bookfellow* he had so admired – to "stimulate Australian writing, to assess its value, and to connect it with the main stream of European culture." *Frank Wilmot* (1942) is a tribute to one of the most popular poets of his time. Palmer saw the Australian writer's task as the transformation of the environment – "to water the dry soil of this country to give it richer life" and he valued Wilmot's contribution to this end.

The Legend of the Nineties (1954) stands at the head of the numerous inquiries that have since been made into the Australian tradition and the formation of a distinctive national character. As a study of the aspiration toward a specifically Australian outlook and the emergence of a recognizable Australian identity, the book is more valuable for the questions it raises than for any answers it proposes. It remains an essential text of its time.

VIVIAN SMITH

Biography

Edward Vivian Palmer. Born 28 August 1885 in Bundaberg, Queensland. Youth spent in a succession of outback country towns. Studied at Ipswich Grammar School, Queensland, 1899–1901. Traveled to London for the first time, 1905, returning to Australia via Finland, Russia, and Japan, 1907. Tutor in Abbieglassie, near Mitchell, Queensland, 1909. Traveled to London again, 1910, returning to Australia via the United States and Mexico, 1912. Married Janet Gertrude Higgins (i.e. the writer Nettie Palmer),

1914: two daughters. Served in the Australian Imperial Forces, 1918. Associated with the Pioneer Players, Melbourne, 1922–23. Traveled to London and New York, 1931, and France, England, and Spain, 1936. Delegate to the World Peace Conference, Helsinki, 1955. Died in Melbourne, 15 July 1959.

Selected Writings

Essays and Related Prose
National Portraits, 1940; enlarged edition, 1954
A. G. Stephens: His Life and Work, 1941
Frank Wilmot, 1942
Louis Esson and the Australian Theatre, 1948
The Legend of the Nineties, 1954
Intimate Portraits and Other Pieces, edited by H. P. Heseltine, 1969

Other writings: 16 novels, five volumes of short stories, plays, and poetry.

Further Reading

Barnes, John, "The Man of Letters," *Meanjin* 18 (1959): 193–205
Barnes, John, editor, *The Writer in Australia: A Collection of Literary Documents, 1856 to 1964*, Melbourne: Oxford University Press, 1969
Barnes, John, Introduction to *An Australian Selection*, Sydney: Angus and Robertson, 1974
Heseltine, Harry P., *Vance Palmer*, St. Lucia: University of Queensland Press, 1970
Indyk, Ivor, "Vance Palmer and the Social Function of Literature," *Southerly* (September 1990): 346–58
Smith, Vivian, *Vance Palmer*, Melbourne: Oxford University Press, 1971
Smith, Vivian, *Vance and Nettie Palmer*, Boston: Twayne, 1975
Walker, David, *Dream and Disillusion: A Search for Australian Cultural Identity*, Canberra: Australian National University Press, 1976

Paludan, Jacob

Danish, 1896–1975

Jacob Paludan had established himself as both a poet and a novelist before, relatively late in his career, he came to the essay. Qualified as a pharmacist, Paludan had an unusual background. He moved to Ecuador for two years after completing his training in Denmark. From there, via New York, he returned to Denmark. In his novels and indeed later in his critical work he is a conservative who voices skepticism about culture in the United States. Thus he stood in opposition to his Danish contemporaries Tom Kristensen and Johannes V. Jensen, who admired American technology and traveled several times to the U.S.

When asked what Paludan's major contribution has been, a student of Danish literature will answer the novel *Jørgen Stein* (1932–33). In this important work and other novels, Paludan is a social critic in much the same way as Henrik Pontoppidan, Nobel Prize winner in 1917, had been a critic of the social situation in Denmark. As an essayist, however, Paludan's attitude changed over time. To begin with, his essays reflected his somewhat rigid approach to and analysis of culture. Later, however, while remaining an essentially conservative thinker, Paludan became more flexible and less dogmatic, no longer making sweeping condemnations of American or Danish culture, but rather addressing himself to small details in Danish life and letters. It is at times startling to find the gentle essayist of the war and postwar eras to be the same writer as the abrasive critic of the 1920s and 1930s.

Paludan's career as an essayist began with the volume *Feodor Jansens jeramiader* (1927; The jeremiads of Feodor Jansen). Paludan claimed he was the editor rather than the author of the volume; there was, however, no other candidate for the position of Jeremiah. Ten essays make up the jeremiads section; they read like traditional essays on subjects such as newspapers, friendship, the new youth, and poets. The last part of the volume is entitled "Jansen og det kvindelige" (Jansen and the feminine); here there are clear echoes of Paludan's dislike of life in the United States. In particular, in evincing his skepticism concerning feminism, Paludan makes several disputable statements, declaring, for instance, that women attach themselves to people, and men to objects. Another of his odd observations is that young women do not need friends, and that friendship with men exists only once they are older. "What the young woman needs is admirers!" he claims. What Paludan must have thought of these ideas in later decades, when his essays were more charitable, benevolent, and good-natured, is a matter of conjecture.

In contrast to this first collection of essays, Paludan's later essays turn to other subjects, often situations in the natural world, and his experiences and reflections. His essays in the 1960s are easier to read, more general in nature, but with little point. We read them in the same way we read his memoirs like *Siden de spørger – og andre omkredsninger* (1968; Since you are asking and other roundabout ways). The collection *Mørkeblåt og sort* (1965; Dark blue and black) to an extent sums up the author's work with an abundance of **aphorisms** Paludan described as a rough mosaic.

Paludan's work as a journalist gave him access to a large audience, permitting him to submit short articles and essays to periodicals, newspapers, and journals for several decades. While some of his essays may seem dated today, they are nevertheless the testimony of an eyewitness, of a thinking man, whose concern is his country and its future.

P. M. MITCHELL

Biography

Jacob Stig Henning Paludan. Born 7 February 1896 in Copenhagen. Trained as a pharmacist, qualified 1918. Traveled to Ecuador and the United States, 1920–21. Literary critic for various newspapers, after 1925, including *Dagens Nyheder* (Daily news), *Politiken*, and *Århus Stiftstidende*; editor, Hasselbalchs Kulturbibliotek, from 1940. Founding member, Danish Academy. Awards: several, including Holberg Medal, 1939; Danish Academy Prize, 1964. Died in Copenhagen, 26 September 1975.

Selected Writings

Essays and Related Prose
Feodor Jansens jeramiader, 1927
Aaret rundt: Trykt og utrykt, 1929
Tanker og bagtanker, 1937
Som on intet var hændt, 1938
Smaa apropos'er, 1943

Søgende aander: Redegørelse og debatter, 1943
Facetter, 1947
Han gik ture, 1949
Skribenter på yderposter: Redegørelser og debatter, 1949
Retur til barndommen, 1951
Fremad til nutiden, 1953
Sagt i korthed, 1929–1954, 1954
Bøger, poeter og stilister, 1954
Litterært selskab, 1956
Glæde over Danmark, 1958
Røgringe, 1959
Landeveje og tankeveje: Udvalgte essays fra 30 aar, 3 vols., 1963
Mørkeblåt og sort, 1965
Skrivebord og stjernehimmel, 1972

Other writings: several novels (including *De vestlige veje*, 1922; *Søgelys*, 1923; *En vinter lang*, 1924; *Fugle omkring fyret* [*Birds Around the Light*], 1925; *Markerne modnes*, 1927; *Jørgen Stein*, 1932–33), a collection of poetry, and four volumes of memoirs.

Bibliography
Benthien, Børge, *Jacob Paludan, en bibliografi*, Copenhagen: Gyldendal, 1980

Further Reading
Danske digtere i det 20.aarhundrede, vol. 1, edited by Ernst Frandsen and Niels Kaas Johansen, Copenhagen: Gyldendal, 1951: 331–52
Frederiksen, Emil, "Der Essayist und Prosaverfasser Jacob Paludan," *Ausblick: Zeitschrift für Deutsch-Skandinavische Beziehungen* (1964): 43–44
Frederiksen, Emil, *Jacob Paludan*, Copenhagen: Gyldendal, 1966
Hallar, Søren Christian, *Jacob Paludan*, Copenhagen: Hasselbalch, 1927
Heltberg, Niels, "Jacob Paludan," *American-Scandinavian Review* 40, no. 2 (1952): 142–45
Profiler: Jacob Paludan et al., Copenhagen: Andersen, 1944
Smith, Johannes, "En fornem pen-i dansk skrivekunst," *Perspektiv* 3 (April 1956)

Pamphlet

According to **George Orwell**, a pamphlet is "a short piece of polemical writing, printed in the form of a booklet and aimed at a large public." Orwell differentiates the pamphlet from similar productions of the press, "such as leaflets, manifestoes, memorials, religious tracts, circular letters, instructional manuals," and so forth, by emphasizing its oppositionality: "in essence it is always a protest." In many cases, however, neat distinctions such as Orwell's are impossible to draw. Pamphlets are thus considered in this essay as writings printed and circulated so as to have an immediate political or social impact, and therefore to influence public opinion.

The English word "pamphlet" entered the vernacular in the 15th century: William Caxton, for example, refers to "many dyuerse paunflettis and bookys" (*Oxford English Dictionary*). Bibliographers, emphasizing form over function, tend to define pamphlets according to the number of pages they contain, the type of binding used, or other physical features. Before 1610 English printers often used black-letter (or Gothic) type for news pamphlets, a typeface generally reserved for ballads,

proclamations, and other publications intended for a wide audience (D. C. Collins, 1943). Pamphlet writing rose in importance with the growth of the letterpress and later declined with the appearance of newspapers and magazines. Usually associated with the essay and the medium of nonfiction prose, the term "pamphlet" has nevertheless been applied historically to forms such as plays, poems, and romances. When James Boswell remarked to **Samuel Johnson** that "a pamphlet meant a prose piece," Johnson retorted, "No, sir. A few sheets of poetry unbound are a pamphlet, as much as a few sheets of prose" (Boswell's *Life of Samuel Johnson*, 1779). The pamphlet's relation to specific forms of writing is complex and varies according to circumstance. A sense of the pressure of historical events and a spirit of relentless critique are almost always discernible in anything describable as a pamphlet.

Pamphleteering generally thrives in an atmosphere of controversy, in relatively open political cultures where a literate public creates a market for timely and inexpensive printed materials that address contemporary issues. The London bookseller George Thomason made a collection of materials on the English civil wars that included more than 20,000 items, many of them pamphlets. During the Fronde in France (1648–52) more than 5000 political pamphlets appeared (called *mazarinades* after their usual subject, Cardinal Mazarin), and had a measurable effect on public discourse. Pamphlets are not invariably a product of protest movements or popular consciousness. In his study of Dutch pamphlets in the 17th century, Craig Harline (1987) shows a political elite working to control pamphleteering and thus shape the climate of opinion. In 17th-century England the word "pamphlet" was sometimes used pejoratively to suggest invective or violent and irresponsible public discourse. A 1610 pamphlet, *Martin Mark-All, Beadle of Bridewell* denounced Thomas Dekker as "an upstart pamphlet maker and a most iniuirious and Satiricall Libeller," and Dekker's writings as "malitious and iniurious Pamphlets" (quoted in Sandra Clark's *The Elizabethan Pamphleteers*, 1983). The French word *pamphlet* (lampoon, **satire**), introduced in the late 17th century, retains something of this association with aggressive rhetoric. As one might assume, one legacy of the French Revolution is a large body of pamphlet literature, now housed in the collections of the Bibliothèque Nationale and the British Library.

While most English pamphlets of the 17th and 18th centuries are rarely read today except by specialists, John Milton's *Areopagitica* (1644), written to contest a parliamentary order forbidding the publication of unlicensed books and pamphlets, remains a canonical work. No less appreciated for its "literary" merits is **Jonathan Swift**'s *A Modest Proposal for Preventing the Children of Poor People from Being a Burthen to Their Parents or the Country, and for Making Them Beneficial to the Publick* (1729). This brilliantly ironic defense of cannibalism as a remedy for overpopulation, however, had a less immediate impact on contemporary events than Swift's Drapier's Letters (1724). The historical circumstances behind the Drapier's Letters at first might seem parochial and unpromising – a struggle between the Irish Revenue Commissioners and the London government over the minting of copper coins in Ireland. Yet Swift's writing here was quietly devastating in its indictment of British policy: "Our neighbours, whose understandings are just upon a level with ours (which perhaps are none of the brightest) have a strong contempt for most nations, but especially for Ireland" (Letter 4). Another 18th-century movement for independence from colonial rule produced **Thomas Paine's** 1776 pamphlet *Common Sense*, the great success of which can be measured by its circulation (100,000 copies sold in three months). Paine's admirer William Cobbett veered from the radical views he advocated while in England (and to which he reverted upon his return) to a career in the United States that made him a fierce partisan of the British monarchy and a relentless critic of democracy, republicanism, and Paine. In a series of pamphlets written between 1794 and 1800 Cobbett infused his newly acquired Toryism with satirical indignation. These and other examples bear witness to the pamphlet writer's motivation as being a desire to intervene in public affairs, often in contentious times.

The pamphlet played a significant role in the development of modern political life, engaging public debate and challenging the practices of secrecy and censorship. Sharon Achinstein (1994) argues that 17th-century pamphleteers and polemicists in England contributed to the formation of a new type of political subject. Milton wrote both his poetry and his pamphlets in the context of a widely shared project to instruct the reading public in techniques of interpretation and textual resistance. Until mass media and advertising took its place, the pamphlet remained an important vehicle for shaping public opinion and expressing political dissent.

ALVIN SNIDER

See also Polemical Essay

Anthologies

British Pamphleteers (vol. 1: *From The Sixteenth Century to the French Revolution*; vol. 2: *From the French Revolution to the Nineteen-Thirties*), edited by George Orwell, London: Wingate, 2 vols., 1948–51
Political Pamphlets, edited by A. F. Pollard, London: Kegan Paul Trench Trubner, 1897
The Women's Sharp Revenge: Five Women's Pamphlets from the Renaissance, edited by Simon Shepherd, London: Fourth Estate, and New York: St. Martin's Press, 1985

Bibliographies

Catalogue of the Pamphlets, Books, Newspapers, and Manuscripts Relating to the Civil War, the Commonwealth, and Restoration, London: British Museum Department of Printed Books (Thomason Collection), 1908
Lindsay, Robert O., and John Neil, *French Political Pamphlets, 1547–1648* (microfilm), New Haven, Connecticut: Research Publications, 1978; supplement, 1981

Further Reading

Achinstein, Sharon, *Milton and the Revolutionary Reader*, Princeton, New Jersey: Princeton University Press, 1994
Adams, Thomas R., *American Independence: The Growth of an Idea: A Bibliographical Study of the American Political Pamphlets Printed Between 1764 and 1776*, Providence, Rhode Island: Brown University Press, 1965
Ahrens, Rudiger, "The Political Pamphlet: 1660–1714: Pre- and Post-Revolutionary Aspects," *Anglia* 109, nos. 1–2 (1991): 21–43

Balcque, Antoine de, "La Dénonciation publique dans la presse et le pamphlet (1789–1791)," *Studies on Voltaire and the Eighteenth Century* 287 (1991): 261–79
Birn, Raymond, "The Pamphlet Press and the Estates General of 1789," *Studies on Voltaire and the Eighteenth Century* 287 (1991): 56–59
Clark, Sandra, *The Elizabethan Pamphleteers: Popular Moralistic Pamphlets, 1580–1640*, Rutherford, New Jersey: Fairleigh Dickinson University Press, 1983
Collins, D. C., *A Handlist of News Pamphlets, 1590–1610*, London: Southwest Essex Technical College, 1943
Harline, Craig E., *Pamphlets, Printing, and Political Culture in the Early Dutch Republic*, Dordrecht: Nijhoff, 1987
Sawyer, Jeffrey K., *Printed Poison: Pamphlet Propaganda, Faction Politics, and the Public Sphere in Early Seventeenth-Century France*, Berkeley: University of California Press, 1990
Smithers, James R., "Propaganda and Theater: Authorial Intent and Audience Response to Political Pamphlets, 1550–1650," *Cahiers du Dix-Septième* 5, no. 2 (1991): 179–94

Pardo Bazán, Emilia

Spanish, 1851–1921

Emilia Pardo Bazán was an extremely prolific writer, with almost two dozen novels and hundreds of short stories to her credit. Her writing career spans several literary periods, including realism, naturalism, and Spanish Modernism, and her work reflects the changing values and literary styles of late 19th- and early 20th-century Spain. In addition to her narrative production, she also cultivated biography and various forms of the essay, including literary criticism, travel literature, social commentary, and critique. The leading Spanish feminist of the 19th century and one of the most important women writers of all of Spanish literature, she is a polemical figure who enjoyed the limelight but also exhibited the anxiety that typifies many women writers of the period as they test the limits of traditional patriarchal society. In a Spain that lagged behind the rest of Europe in industrial and social modernization, Pardo Bazán's feminist writings and her active participation in international feminist congresses and campaigns created considerable opposition and required the elaboration of a complex public persona in order to counter public disapproval and condemnation. Her novels and essays display a dual rhythm of rebellion and submission, but under the guise of acquiescence there can usually be found a dissonant or ambiguous voice that allows for an alternative and more defiant reading.

Nineteenth-century writers as well as many contemporary critics classify Pardo Bazán as a conservative, Catholic writer and approach her essays from this perspective. Pardo Bazán clearly encouraged such a view at different times in her writing career, invoking her Catholic faith and traditional Spanish values as a shield against accusations of radicalism. However, her defense of free will, her repudiation of determinist philosophies, and her invocations of nationalist or class privilege also reflect a feminist impulse and a desire to liberate women from essentialist definitions and reformulations of female inferiority under the guise of Darwinism and biological determinism. This double-voicing begins as early as 1877 in her "Reflexiones científicas contra el darwinismo" (Scientific reflections against Darwinism) and continues in her later essays and her literary criticism.

Pardo Bazán's much-cited *La cuestión palpitante* (The burning question), which originally appeared as a series of articles between 1881 and 1883 in *La Época* and then as a book in 1883, studies the naturalist movement initiated by Émile Zola in France and offers a moderate defense of the movement as it evolved in Spain. Critics have generally studied the ensuing polemic as an exclusively literary event; however, Pardo Bazán's text represents much more than a cautious acceptance of literary naturalism and exerts an important influence on questions of art and literature as well as on broader issues of social and political transformation. The text exploits the discursive complexity of essay writing, inserting multiple and often contradictory voices and interweaving them in order to give expression to silenced or muted social and political issues that underpin the debate on literary naturalism. These include the fear of social and sexual revolution and the connections between these two 19th-century phenomena.

The presence of a female speaker in a national polemic in itself altered the terms of the debate and brought to the foreground issues of female access to public space, female sexuality, and radical social transformation, all of which had been avoided assiduously by writers in the period following the First Spanish Republic (1873–74). *La cuestión palpitante* provoked numerous responses among Spanish writers on the left and the right, as male writers struggled with their own and their readers' fears of a breakdown of the established social and sexual order. In this and all of her essays, Pardo Bazán employs a number of strategies to deflect anticipated criticism and opposition to a female speaker. She makes abundant use of quotations drawn from male writers and canonical works to enhance her authority, adopts an epistolary or fictional form to minimize the effect of a single speaker, or attempts to efface her personality and sexuality through the use of scientific and historical discourse.

Many of Pardo Bazán's better-known essays deal directly with topics of female emancipation, as in "La mujer española" (1907; The Spanish woman), "La educación del hombre y la de la mujer" (1892; The education of men and of women), "Del amor y la amistad" (1892; On love and friendship), and "La cuestión académica" (1891; The question of the Academy). In these texts the complex tension between the establishment of an authoritative textual voice and deference to the authority of the reader becomes even more acute as the female speaker, more or less disguised behind an impersonal narrator, attempts to move the primarily male reader to an acceptance of male-female equality. Like all essayists, Pardo Bazán makes use of contemporary discourse but also seeks to channel it in new directions and reveal its inconsistencies. The essays that argue for women's rights invoke 19th-century liberal values and language with frequent allusions to human rights, to a belief in the individual capacity for improvement, and to the value of scientific discovery. However, they also seek to deconstruct these discourses and expose the irrational fears that undergird contemporary definitions of women. Through a continual interweaving of multiple and contradictory voices and discourses drawn from 19th-century Spanish and European culture and the introduction of a new female voice that interjects irony, mockery, exaggeration, and other dissonant perspectives, Pardo Bazán moves the late 19th-century Spanish essay toward a new and more modern form.

MARY LEE BRETZ

Biography

Born 16 September 1851 in La Coruña, Galicia. Self-educated. Married José Quiroga, 1868 (separated, 1885): two daughters and one son. Traveled to Paris, London, Italy, and Austria, 1871–72; moved to Madrid, 1886, where she frequented court and artistic circles and opened her own salon. Contributor to various periodicals, including *La Ciencia Cristiana* (The Christian science), 1876–81, *La Revista Compostelana* (The review of Compostela), 1876–77, *La Época*, from 1881, *La Ilustración Artística* (The artistic illustration), from 1886, *El Imparcial*, 1887–1920, *España Moderna*, 1889–90, *Blanco y Negro* (Black and white), 1895–1920, *La Lectura*, 1901–05, *La Ilustración Española*, from 1908, *La Esfera* (The sphere), from 1910, *Los Contemporáneos*, from 1914, *Raza Española* (The Spanish race), 1919–21, and *ABC*; founding editor, *El Nuevo Teatro Crítico* (The new critical theater), 1891–93. First female president, literary section of the Atheneum, Madrid, 1906. Made countess, 1908. Advisor to the Ministry of Education, 1910. Professor of Romance literature, University of Madrid, 1916. Founder, Women's Library. Died in Madrid, 12 May 1921.

Selected Writings

Essays and Related Prose

La cuestión palpitante, 1883; edited by Carmen Bravo-Villasante, 1966, and José Manuel González Herrán, 1988
De mi tierra, 1888
Mi romería, 1888
Al pie de la Torre Eiffel, 1889
Los poetas épicos cristianos, 1894
Cuarenta días en la exposición, 1901
Por la Europa católica, 1902
De siglo a siglo, 1902
El lirismo en la poesía francesa (lectures), 1926
La mujer española y otros artículos feministas, edited by Leda Schiavo, 1976
Crónicas en "La Nacion" de Buenos Aires (1909–1921), edited by Cyrus DeCoster, 1994

Other writings: 19 novels (including *Los pazos de Ulloa* [*The House of Ulloa*], 1886; *La madre naturaleza*, 1887; *Una cristiana* [*A Christian Woman*], 1890; *La quimera*, 1905; *La sirena negra*, 1908; *Dulce dueño*, 1911), short stories, plays, and works on literary criticism and history.

Collected works editions: *Obras completas*, 43 vols., 1891–1926, and edited by Federico Carlos Sainz de Robles, 3 vols., 1964.

Bibliographies

Clémessy, Nelly, *Emilia Pardo Bazán como novelista*, vol. 2, Madrid: Fundación Universitaria Española, 1982: 831–922
Scari, Robert M., *Bibliografía descriptiva de estudios críticos sobre la obra de Emilio Pardo Bazán*, Valencia: Albatros/Hispanófila, 1982

Further Reading

Bravo-Villasante, Carmen, *Vida y obra de Emilia Pardo Bazán*, Madrid: Revista de Occidente, 1962
Bretz, Mary Lee, *Voices, Silences and Echoes: A Theory of the Essay and the Critical Reception of Naturalism in Spain*, London: Tamesis, 1992

Clémessy, Nelly, *Emilia Pardo Bazán como novelista*, Madrid: Fundación Universitaria Española, 2 vols., 1982

El Saffar, Ruth, "Emilia Pardo Bazán," in *Spanish Women Writers: A Bio-Bibliographical Source Book*, edited by Linda Gould Levine, Ellen Engelson Marson, and Gloria Feiman Waldman, Westport, Connecticut: Greenwood Press, 1993: 378–88

Lissorgues, Yvan, editor, *Realismo y naturalismo en España en la segunda mitad del siglo XIX*, Barcelona: Anthropos, 1988

Pattison, Walter, *El naturalismo español*, Madrid: Gredos, 1969

Pattison, Walter, *Emilia Pardo Bazán*, New York: Twayne, 1971

Torre, Guillermo de, *Del 98 al barroco*, Madrid: Gredos, 1965

Partisan Review

American journal, 1934–

Partisan Review was founded by William Phillips and Philip Rahv in 1934. It entered the arena of American left-wing cultural and political controversies with a verve and energy that immediately distinguished it as a political and cultural voice in the struggles over who spoke for the new literary radical left. Impatient with and yet attracted to indigenous American liberalism, populism, and bohemianism, and restless with the views expressed in journals such as the proletarian *New Masses*, *Partisan Review* began as a literary adjunct to the communist John Reed Club, whose mandate was to recognize unknown writers and artists with proletarian leanings. *Partisan Review* immediately announced itself as the inheritor of proletarian impulses and the prophetic voice for the future of new literary values. Its audience would be those who should be affected by the class struggles and upheavals sweeping through industrial societies, and those who would challenge the uneven control of the bourgeoisie over cultural values.

However, the twists and turns of communist cultural policies around propaganda and realism, the Spanish Civil War, Stalinism and its cruelties, the precarious nature of Trotskyism, the rise of the American New Deal, and the necessity to interpret Modernist writers both to themselves and to the new generation caused the editors to reconsider their allegiance to the John Reed style of populism. *Partisan Review* suspended publication in 1936 and joined with *Anvil* as a monthly, *Partisan and Anvil*, beginning what would become the intellectual trademark of the magazine: to criticize leftist politics from the vanguard Modernist position of a literary and radical culturalism that would accommodate American circumstances.

In 1937 the journal suspended publication, severed any residual connection to the Communist Party, and refashioned itself almost immediately as an independent quarterly under the editorial guardianship of Phillips and Rahv, Fred Dupee, Dwight Macdonald, **Mary McCarthy**, and George L. K. Morris. Fearing conformist leftism, it identified itself in a 1937 Editorial Statement with a larger historical project that would place the "accent chiefly on culture and its broader social determinants." While there were compelling political reasons for changing the journal's outlook to one critical of Stalinism and the bureaucratic academicism of the organized left, besides the more urgent need to fight against fascism and philistinism in culture and politics, the *Partisan Review*'s concern was to speak in a truly American cultural idiom that would register the changes in American culture through literary values not usurped by ideology. This need to identify with American culture continued to plague the journal's identity crises and editorial policies until the 1990s.

During and after World War II *Partisan Review* overcame its political alliances of the 1930s by developing a following among serious readers literate and hungry for avant-garde controversies and Modernist experiments. The rapidly fading dependency on realism and proletarian tendencies gave way to the new literary values of **T. S. Eliot**, **André Gide**, and William Faulkner, finally fulfilling the call to "independence in politics as well as art" (Editorial Statement, 1937). In retrospect it may be possible to overestimate the influence of *Partisan Review* on the sensibilities and self-image of the American cultural left; however, it is difficult to underestimate the journal's sense of its own importance and influence. During the war the struggle over fascism, pacifism, and rapprochement with the reactionary Modernist politics of figures like Eliot or **Ezra Pound** brought its defense of the mystifying Modernist styles into stark political relief. Its readership during and after the war may have been 10,000, but its influence was certainly wider, causing Richard Hofstadter (1963) to declare that it was the "house organ of the American intellectual community."

During the war the journal's inner circle was broken when Dwight Macdonald's pacifism clashed with the muted acceptance of the war by Phillips, Rahv, and the art critic Clement Greenberg. Typical of its frequent symposia is the wartime discussion, given the ambiguously traitorous sounding title, "The Failure of Nerve" (1943), in which religion, existentialism, and science become entangled with the issue of whether loyalty to the war effort can be defended. The wartime "London Letter" (1940), a column written by **George Orwell**, D. S. Savage, and others, forged a link to British intellectuals' ideological agonizing over commitment to the war, and whether pacifism, anarchism, and anti-fascism were objectively pro-Hitler or self-serving.

It was only after the war that the journal began to take on the voice of the American "intellectual community," that the accent of the "New York intellectual" became authoritative, if somewhat priggish. New York was a crossroads to Europe, to dissent, to immigrant cultures, to history, and to a barbed independence that gave its writers a style of mind and sense of publicity and purpose that defined its name and aura. Its phases since the war have mirrored the changes in the fortunes and tendencies of American left cultural politics.

In the 1950s the nervous loyalty to the crusade against fascism, the affluence of postwar reconstruction, and the unraveling of socialism forced *Partisan Review* to confront the "age of conformism." The attempt to find and defend any positive value of American democracy was complicated by the ravages of McCarthyism and the barbaric nature of cold war communism and capitalism. The road of accommodation to the perceived demands of its audience can be marked by the flags of some of its symposia and exchanges: "The Situation of American Writing," 1939; "Colloquium About Liberalism," 1948; "Religion and Intellectuals," 1950; "Our Country and Our Culture," 1952; "This Age of Conformity," 1954; "The Crisis in Communism," 1957; "The Negro Writer in America," 1958; "The Cold War and the West," 1962; "What's Happening to America," 1967; "On the New Cultural Conservatism,"

1972; "Writers in Exile," 1984; "The Politics of Political Correctness," 1993. The journal's rapprochement with American culture is clearly part of its history.

After the 1960s, the notorious critiques of kitsch and conformism that gave the journal a nuanced position against mass culture were turned into an often heavy-handed critique of the countercultural generation who formed part of the self-consciously democratic culture of late capitalism. Struggles for and against the student movement divided the editorial board and its writers. As *Partisan Review*'s audience aged and moved on from the necessary difficulties of Modernism against its enemy, indifference, massmindedness, and conformity, the journal's engagement with a clearly defined audience grew problematic, and its responses to the new generation's political preoccupations were quarrelsome and defensive.

Originally *Partisan Review*'s editors and writers were not part of university life. The formative intellectual personality can best be characterized by a tone of detachment from the academy, and its incorrigible, often gnarled defense of experimental Modernism and socialism gave its intellectuality a quality that distinguished it from other journals like the genteel *Kenyon Review* and *Southern Review*. It debated the American New Criticism, Russian formalism, surrealism, film, Modernism and the novel, psychoanalysis and culture, Sartrean existentialism, the self and society, and diverse theories of alienation. The journal published a range of independent intellectuals like C. Wright Mills, Paul Goodman, Harold Rosenberg, **Hannah Arendt**, Karl Jaspers, and **Lionel Trilling**, whose preoccupations were perhaps most typical of its intellectual style. It was an organ for the essays and prose of writers like Stephen Spender, **James Baldwin**, **Edmund Wilson**, Saul Bellow, Vladimir Nabokov, **Norman Mailer**, Philip Roth, Mary McCarthy, Diana Trilling, and Alfred Kazin. These writers defined Modernism as a total cultural condition, not simply a literary movement. Often its own contributors attacked the journal as if its parental voice were the center of the entire intellectual world (Leslie A. Fiedler, 1956; Norman Podhoretz, 1979).

As wide-ranging as the modern themes appeared to be, some questions seemed superficially addressed. Jews and the Holocaust, race and segregation, Jewish intellectual identity, and the fate of the labor movement were considered but not with adequate depth. Often *Partisan Review* was simply "keeping abreast" but losing ground to more culturally avant-garde positions (Harvey Teres, 1996). For Russell Jacoby (1987), however, the New York intellectuals were doomed to be "the last intellectuals," who no longer had a public role after the 1950s.

In the 50th anniversary edition of *Partisan Review* (1984), the founding editor, William Phillips, mused that the New Left was "a complex of outworn Marxist notions, vaguely progressive ideas, trendy causes like environmentalism and various liberation movements, sympathy for something called the Third World, pacifism, anti-Americanism, an obsessive fear of nuclear power." Struggling to keep *Partisan Review* from becoming a neoconservative journal, it spoke for a new calling – a new liberalism – which would "examine each issue on its own," perhaps reflecting, in the name of social responsibility, the very fragmentation that the early passionate calling to Modernism wanted to understand and heal.

Today the original incentives toward a revolutionary critique of capitalism would appear distant, instead giving ground to a critique of how democratic values have declined. The powerful incentive for its readers is not to identify with its 1930s' anti-capitalism or its postwar critique of the American system, but to remain closer to the mainstream of American intellectual life and to excavate some fragments of ethics from the tradition. In this *Partisan Review* is indistinguishable from other small journals. However, the proliferation of books on its history and significance by both its founding writers and the next generation who observe it from afar indicates that it retains its presence, not only as one of the longest lasting journals on the American scene, but as a cultural institution whose history reflects the American struggle for an intellectually respectable left identity.

JERALD ZASLOVE

Anthologies

The Partisan Reader: Ten Years of Partisan Review, 1934–1944, New York: Dial Press, 1946

The New Partisan Reader, 1945–1953, edited by William Phillips and Philip Rahv, New York: Harcourt Brace, 1953

The Partisan Review Anthology, edited by William Phillips and Philip Rahv, New York: Holt Rinehart and Winston, 1962

Writers & Politics: A Partisan Review Reader, edited by Edith Kurzweil and William Phillips, Boston: Routledge and Kegan Paul, 1983

Partisan Review: The 50th Anniversary Edition, edited by William Phillips, New York: Stein and Day, 1985

A Partisan Century: Political Writings from Partisan Review, edited by Edith Kurzweil, New York: Columbia University Press, 1996

Further Reading

Bloom, Alexander, *Prodigal Sons: The New York Intellectuals and Their World*, New York and Oxford: Oxford University Press, 1986

Cooney, Terry A., *The Rise of the New York Intellectuals: Partisan Review and Its Circle*, Madison: University of Wisconsin Press, 1986

Fiedler, Leslie A., *An End to Innocence: Essays on Culture and Politics*, New York: Stein and Day, 1972 (original edition, 1955)

Fiedler, Leslie A., "*Partisan Review*: Phoenix or Dodo?" *Perspectives USA* 16 (Spring 1956)

Gilbert, James Burkhart, *Writers and Partisans: A History of Literary Radicalism in America*, New York: Columbia University Press, 1992 (original edition, 1968)

Greenberg, Clement, *Art and Culture*, Boston: Beacon Press, 1989 (original edition, 1961)

Guilbaut, Serge, *How New York Stole the Idea of Modern Art: Abstract Expressionism, Freedom, and the Cold War*, Chicago: University of Chicago Press, 1983

Hoffman, Frederick J., Charles Allen, and Carolyn F. Ulrich, *The Little Magazine: A History and a Bibliography*, Princeton, New Jersey: Princeton University Press, 1946

Hofstadter, Richard, *Anti-Intellectualism in American Life*, New York: Knopf, 1963; London: Cape, 1964

Hook, Sidney, "The Radical Comedians: Inside *Partisan Review*," *American Scholar* (Winter 1984–85): 45–61

Howe, Irving, *A Margin of Hope: An Intellectual Autobiography*, San Diego: Harcourt Brace Jovanovich, 1982; London: Secker and Warburg, 1983

Jacoby, Russell, *The Last Intellectuals: American Culture in the Age of Academe*, New York: Basic Books, 1987

Kazin, Alfred, *New York Jew*, New York: Knopf, and London: Secker and Warburg, 1978

Krupnick, Mark, *Lionel Trilling and the Fate of Cultural Criticism*, Evanston, Illinois: Northwestern University Press, 1986

McCarthy, Mary, *Intellectual Memoirs: New York, 1936–1938*, New York: Harcourt Brace Jovanovich, 1992

Macdonald, Dwight, *The Root Is Man: Two Essays in Politics*, Alhambra, California: Cunningham Press, 1953

Macdonald, Dwight, *Against the American Grain*, New York: Random House, 1962; London: Gollancz, 1963

Phillips, William, *A Partisan View: Five Decades of the Literary Life*, New York: Stein and Day, 1983

Podhoretz, Norman, *Breaking Ranks: A Political Memoir*, New York: Harper and Row, 1979; London: Weidenfeld and Nicolson, 1980

Rahv, Philip, *The Myth and the Powerhouse*, New York: Farrar Straus Giroux, 1965

Rosenberg, Harold, *Discovering the Present: Three Decades in Art, Culture, and Politics*, Chicago: University of Chicago Press, 1973

Teres, Harvey, *Renewing the Left: Politics, Imagination, and the New York Intellectuals*, New York and Oxford: Oxford University Press, 1996

Trilling, Lionel, *The Opposing Self: Nine Essays in Criticism*, New York: Harcourt Brace Jovanovich, 1979; Oxford: Oxford University Press, 1980 (original edition, 1955)

Trilling, Lionel, *The Last Decade: Essays and Reviews, 1965–1975*, edited by Diana Trilling, New York: Harcourt Brace Jovanovich, 1979; Oxford: Oxford University Press, 1982

Wald, Alan M., *The New York Intellectuals: The Rise and Decline of the Anti-Stalinist Left from the 1930s to the 1980s*, Chapel Hill: University of North Carolina Press, 1987

Wilford, Hugh, *The New York Intellectuals: From Vanguard to Institution*, Manchester: Manchester University Press, and New York: St. Martin's Press, 1995

Pascal, Blaise

French, 1623–1662

Although known primarily as a scientist, mathematician, and religious apologist, Blaise Pascal can also justly be seen as a major essayist. Much of his written output consists of polemical exchanges and discourses.

The work that distinguishes him above all as an essayist is the *Lettres provinciales* (*The Provincial Letters*). Appearing initially as a series of **pamphlet**s between January 1656 and June 1657, the 18 **letter**s were first published together, under the pseudonym of Louis de Montalte, in 1657. The reason for anonymity resulted from the highly flammable debate between two leading Catholic sects, the Jesuits (who had the support of the King, Louis XIV) and the Jansenists (whom Pascal was trying to defend).

The Jansenists (never officially accepted by the Catholic Church) were named after Cornelius Jansenius (1587–1638), a Flemish theologian and Bishop of Ypres, whose posthumously published *Augustinus* (1640) was an attempt to vindicate the teaching of St. Augustine against the doctrines of more recent Jesuit theologians. The Jansenists, situated initially at a convent near Paris, known as Port-Royal des Champs, and then also in Paris itself at Port-Royal, based their beliefs on the doctrine of original sin. They argued that, since the Fall in the Garden of Eden, all humankind has been corrupted by sin. Their objection to the Jesuits stemmed from what they saw as the over-reliance of the Jesuits on human free will, to the detriment of divine grace.

At the beginning of 1656, a defender of those at Port-Royal was badly needed. Antoine Arnauld, a leading theologian at Port-Royal, was about to be censured by the Sorbonne for taking a stand on five so-called heretical propositions which were allegedly to be found in Jansenius' *Augustinus*. However, with the risk of imprisonment which the Port-Royal sympathizers ran if they were discovered to be the authors of any attack on the Jesuits, it was difficult to find someone who could champion their cause. Pascal turned out to be the ideal person. At that time he was famous only for his mathematical and scientific gifts, and was not known for his links with Port-Royal; it was therefore easier for him to preserve his anonymity. Another great advantage was that, because he was not trained as a theologian, he could write with a freshness and immediacy that was appealing and understandable to a wider audience, not simply to those interested in the intricacies of the religious debate. It is this seeming spontaneity which has maintained the appeal of *The Provincial Letters* to this day.

The letters can be divided into two main groups: letters 1–10 and letters 11–18. In the first group, we find an interplay between a naive persona (often referred to as the Louis de Montalte figure) writing to his friend in the provinces, a Jansenist friend, and some Jesuit priests. By employing the interview technique (especially in letters 4–10), Pascal manages to make the Jesuits condemn themselves with their own words. He also achieves this by the highly selective quotation of various Jesuit writers. The comedy of the situation is heightened by the contrast between Pascal's portrayal of an irascible and buffoon-like Jesuit central figure and the quietly knowing and reasonable Jansenist friend. Much of the debate in the early letters surrounds the Jesuits' use of terms like "proximate power" and "sufficient grace," which, according to Pascal, enabled them to explain away their pursuit of morally reprehensible lives. Whereas the Jesuits believed that human beings had sufficient grace within them to be saved, Pascal followed the more rigorous idea of "efficacious grace," where God alone is seen as capable of bestowing grace upon human beings. Pascal had elaborated upon these ideas in his *Écrits sur la grâce* (wr. c. 1657–58; Writings on grace), in which he contrasts the "disciples of St. Augustine" (Jansenists) with the Calvinists and the Jesuits (or "Molinists," as he calls them, named after the Spanish Jesuit theologian, Molina).

In letters 11–18, all pretense of a real exchange between different personae is dropped. The speaker (now much more knowledgeable) engages in direct polemic with the Jesuits as a whole. In the final two letters (17–18), the attack is directed specifically at Père Annat, one of the leading Jesuits and the King's spiritual confessor. The reason for the shift in emphasis in letter 11 onward stemmed from the fact that the Jesuits themselves had launched a vigorous counterattack against the author of *The Provincial Letters*, and Pascal felt it necessary to respond more directly to accusations that he was making fun of religion by writing such satirical pamphlets.

Many other shorter works also mark Pascal as an essayist. In addition to a large number of scientific **treatise**s, there exist several writings on religious or related topics. Even the **preface** to his treatise on the vacuum, written in 1651 (long before his definitive conversion in 1654), contains a discussion of religious issues. In it he compares the value of recent research, where the use of reason (as in scientific experiments) is paramount, with other forms of knowledge, where the importance of tradition or authority (as in theology) is stressed.

Between 1654 and 1656, Pascal wrote a number of significant short works. A document, known as the "Mémorial," which was found sewn into Pascal's clothing after his death, testifies to the conversion experience he underwent on the night of 23–24 November 1654. Another work that can be linked to the conversion, the "Entretien avec Monsieur de Saci" (wr. c. 1655; Conversation with Monsieur de Saci), contains an account by Nicolas Fontaine of the conversation Pascal had soon after his conversion with his spiritual director, Isaac Le Maistre de Saci, on the subject of the worldly writers **Montaigne** and Epictetus. Although first published only in 1728, the "Entretien" is generally accepted as authentic, and it is probable that Fontaine based his account on a written text (now lost) by Pascal. Another work, "De l'esprit géométrique" (wr. c. 1655; On the geometrical mind), concentrates on different kinds of reasoning and reveals the influence of Descartes (much of whose philosophy Pascal would refute in his later religious writings). There is an interesting subsection of "De l'esprit géométrique" entitled "De l'art de persuader" (On the art of persuasion), in which Pascal considers the importance of different persuasive methods, acknowledging moreover that rational methods are often less persuasive than those that appeal to the heart or will. He was to develop these ideas in his most celebrated work, the posthumously published *Pensées* (1670).

Because the *Pensées* remained uncompleted at Pascal's death, it is uncertain what form the work would have taken. However, there is some evidence to suggest that Pascal would have juxtaposed different kinds of discourse, including fragmentary writings, **maxim**s, letters, and **dialogue**. It is significant that Montaigne's *Essais* (1580, 1588) were a major influence on the *Pensées*, as the disparate ordering of the former can be discerned to some extent in the latter. However, one of Pascal's major purposes in writing the *Pensées* was to try and convince the non-believers and skeptics of his day, many of whom were admirers of Montaigne, of the necessity of religion, and Pascal deliberately attempts to distance himself from what he sees as the extreme egotism of Montaigne.

A number of longer passages in the *Pensées* constitute essays in their own right. The most notorious (and most widely interpreted) section is that known as the Wager, where Pascal uses various mathematical arguments to convince the reader of the necessity to bet in favor of the existence of God. One long passage on the "disproportion de l'homme" (disproportion of man) depicts man as caught between two extremes of infinity and nothingness. Another section chronicles the debate between pyrrhonists (or skeptics) and dogmatists (or rationalists). The conflict between these leading sects is used by Pascal to demonstrate the contradictions which abound in human philosophy, contradictions which he argues can only be resolved by a recognition of original sin. Pascal also discusses at length the dangers of "divertissement" (diversion), showing how the quest for entertainment distracts humans from reflecting upon their wretched state. The long fragments devoted to the three orders (material, intellectual, and spiritual) are typical of his methods in other extracts, where he speaks of a "renversement continuel du pour au contre"

(constant swing from pro to contra). In the passages devoted to "raison des effets" (cause and effect), for example, he considers the different attitudes of a varied range of people to appearances, showing how different kinds of people come to the same conclusion but for different reasons.

Pascal writes at length in the *Pensées* on the "puissances trompeuses" (deceptive powers) which cloud man's self-awareness and which can even create their own world, named by Pascal as "une seconde nature" (a second nature). Prominent among these are imagination, which has the strength to form its own ideal of such abstract notions as beauty, justice and happiness, self-love (*amour-propre*), which turns man away from love for God, and custom or habit, which plays a large part in determining social attitudes or choice of employment. Other long essay-like passages include those on the concupiscences (influenced by Augustine), human justice (largely influenced by Montaigne), and that known as "le mystère de Jésus" (the mystery of Jesus), where Pascal uses prosopopoeia to depict Christ as speaker in the fragment. Other essays in the *Pensées*, like those on miracles, might have been intended for separate publication.

Among Pascal's lesser-known writings, there are a number of essays, such as "Sur la conversion du pécheur" (wr. c. 1653; Upon the sinner's conversion), which charts the different stages a sinner might encounter on the path toward recognition of God, and "Trois discours sur la condition des grands" (wr. c. 1650; Three discourses on the condition of men of noble estate), in which Pascal advises a young nobleman on the implications of his rank.

Pascal's confrontational style has earned him many enemies as well as admirers over the centuries since his death. Significantly, Pascal himself has been the subject of essays by writers as diverse as **Voltaire, Chateaubriand, Valéry,** and **T. S. Eliot.**

NICHOLAS HAMMOND

See also Pensée

Biography

Born 19 June 1623 in Clermont-en-Auvergne (now Clermont-Ferrand). Moved with family to Paris, 1631, and to Rouen, 1640. Studied privately, tutored mostly by father. Scientist and mathematician; invented the "Pascaline," a machine performing mathematical calculations, 1642–52, and conducted experiments with the vacuum, 1646–48. Converted to Jansenism, 1646. Returned to Paris on father's second retirement, 1647; had second conversion, 23–24 November 1654, a mystical experience he described in the "Mémorial" document of faith, which was found sewn in his doublet on his death. Made occasional retreats to Jansenist community at Port-Royal des Champs, from 1655. Worked on a public transportation system for Paris, 1660–62. Died in Paris, 19 August 1662.

Selected Writings

Essays and Related Prose

Lettres provinciales (18 letters), January 1656–June 1657; in book form (as Louis de Montalte), 1657; edited by Louis Cognet, 1965, and Michel Le Guern, 1987; as *The Provincial Letters*, translated by William Andrews, 1744, Thomas M'Crie, 1847, and A. J. Krailsheimer, 1966

Pensées de M. Pascal sur la religion, et sur quelques autres sujets, edited by Étienne Périer, 1670, revised edition, 1684, Voltaire (Condorcet Edition), 1778, A. P. Faugère, 1844, Louis Lafuma,

2 vols., 1947, Georges Brunet, 1956, Louis Marin, 1969, and Philippe Sellier, 1976; as *Discours sur la religion, et quelques autres sujets*, edited by Emmanuel Martineau, 1992; selections edited by André Comte-Sponville, 1992; many translations, including by J. Walker, 1688, H. F. Stewart, 1950, John Warrington, 1960, J. M. Cohen, 1961, Martin Turnell, 1962, A. J. Krailsheimer, 1966, and Honor Levi, 1995
Great Shorter Works of Pascal, translated by E. Cailliet and John C. Blankenagel, 1948
Selections, edited by Richard H. Popkin, 1989
The Mind on Fire (selections; various translators), edited by James M. Houston, 1989
Selected Readings, edited by Robert Van De Weyer, 1991

Other writings: scientific works and a life of Jesus.

Collected works editions: *Œuvres complètes*, edited by Léon Brunschvicg, 14 vols., 1904–14; *Œuvres complètes* (Pléiade Edition), edited by Jacques Chevalier, 1954; *Œuvres complètes* (Intégrale Edition), edited by Louis Lafuma, 1963; *Œuvres complètes*, edited by Jean Mesnard, 4 vols., 1964–92 (in progress).

Bibliographies

Heller, Lane M., and Thérèse Goyet, *Bibliographie Blaise Pascal (1960–1969)*, Clermont-Ferrand: Adosa, 1989
Maire, Albert, *Bibliographie générale des œuvres de Blaise Pascal*, Paris: Giraud-Badin, 5 vols., 1925–27

Further Reading

Croquette, Bernard, *Pascal et Montaigne: Étude des réminiscences des Essais dans l'œuvre de Pascal*, Geneva: Droz, 1974
Davidson, Hugh M., *Blaise Pascal*, Boston: Twayne, 1983
Hammond, Nicholas, *Playing with Truth: Language and the Human Condition in Pascal's Pensées*, Oxford: Clarendon Press, 1994
Krailsheimer, A. J., *Pascal*, Oxford and New York: Oxford University Press, 1980
Mesnard, Jean, *Les Pensées de Pascal*, Paris: Société d'Édition d'Enseignement Supérieur, 1993 (original edition, 1976)
Norman, Buford, *Portraits of Thought: Knowledge, Methods and Styles in Pascal*, Columbus: Ohio State University Press, 1988
Parish, Richard, *Pascal's Lettres provinciales: A Study in Polemic*, Oxford: Clarendon Press, 1989
Rex, Walter E., *Pascal's Provincial Letters: An Introduction*, London: Hodder and Stoughton, 1977
Wetsel, David, *Pascal and Disbelief: Catechesis and Conversion in the Pensées*, Washington, D.C.: Catholic University of America Press, 1994

Pater, Walter

British, 1839–1894

Most of Walter Pater's work appeared initially in leading Victorian periodicals such as the *Westminster Review*, the *Fortnightly Review*, *Macmillan's Magazine*, and similar publications. With the exception of his novel *Marius the Epicurean* (1885), the volumes that were published in Pater's lifetime, for example *Studies in the History of the Renaissance* (1873), or posthumously edited, for example *Greek Studies* (1895), were thematically related collections of **periodical** essays or similar pieces, such as introductions and lectures. Moreover, even *Marius* was an "ideological" or "critical" novel, resembling a group of essays tied together by an ancillary plot. Indeed, Pater's second, incomplete novel, *Gaston de Latour* (1896), appeared serially as a historical romance in *Macmillan's*, but its **chapter** on Giordano Bruno was printed initially in the *Fortnightly* as an essay. Pater felt that the essay, lying between lyric poetry and the didactic **treatise**, was the "characteristic literary type of our own time, a time so rich and various in special apprehensions of truth, so tentative and dubious in its sense of their *ensemble*, and issues," as he says in *Plato and Platonism* (1893). For the famous Renaissance essayist **Montaigne**, the genre, says Pater, provided "precisely the literary form necessary to a mind for which truth itself is but a possibility, realisable not as general conclusion, but rather as the elusive effect of a particular personal experience."

Pater produced studies not only of Montaigne, but also of such eminent English essayists as **Sir Thomas Browne** and **Charles Lamb**. Sainte-Beuve's *Portraits contemporains* (1846; Contemporary portraits) probably supplied Pater with the "imaginary portraits" label for his fiction, though portraiture is the characteristic form of Pater's nonfictional essays as well. Pater's pen portraits of real or imaginary figures – literary writers, artists, mythological figures, and political rulers – depict the living personality behind cultural productions, epitomizing particular historical phases, philosophic schools, and works of art. In his portraits, the accent is on finely discriminated "sensations and ideas" (the subtitle of *Marius*) – that is, on perception and the fleeting impression rather than on action or dialogue. This critical or analytic turn of mind is associated with a Romantic or Wordsworthian sense that eye and ear subjectively half-create the world they perceive. Pater agreed with Flaubert and Stendhal that prose was greatly superior to poetry for inquiring into those elusive *mouvements de cœur*, nuances of a consciousness conscious of itself.

Despite successive stages of composition and revision that often seemed to involve a disproportionate effort for the results obtained, Pater's texts contain a certain irreducible core of factual and grammatical error as well as rhetorical ambiguity. Perhaps his private emotional tensions resisted final formulation in the logic and rhythm-phrases of prose. Yet Pater's essays do achieve a unique "imaginative sense of fact," a "vision within," as he defined his purpose in "Style" (1888); accordingly, they radically revise the Victorian positivist-utilitarian prose standards of mimetic objectivity and rhetorical persuasion.

The customary synopsis of Pater's style as precious, over-refined, artificial, or exotic is perhaps more fantasy than fact. His two most famous "purple panels," both in his first book, *The Renaissance*, are passages on the sinister Mona Lisa in "Leonardo da Vinci" (1869), in which he imagines Lady Lisa to be "older than the rocks among which she sits; like the vampire, she has been dead many times, and learned the secrets of the grave"; and on aesthetic experience in the volume's Conclusion (1868), in which Pater advises young men to seek the quickening "passion" of art, "to burn always with this hard, gemlike flame."

Many readers familiar with these early essays are not acquainted, for example, with his portrait of the historical memoirist and *femme fatale*, Margaret of Navarre, in a diptych of essays on poisonous love in his late work, *Gaston de Latour*. **Oscar Wilde** had sent Pater a copy of his play, *Salomé* (perhaps because Pater earlier had given Wilde a book by Flaubert that suggested the topic), and accordingly Pater began his portrait of Margaret on a "moon-lit street," reminiscent of the sensuously charged moon in Wilde's play. Wilde's predatory princess and her trophy on a silver shield either echoes or is echoed in Margaret's relic of a beheaded lover. Describing the pallor of the princess, "like white lilac or roses in winter," Pater's paradoxes catch something of her ambiguous beauty and the fate of Narcissus to which her beholders are driven: "there was almost oriental blue richness, blackness, in the king-fisher wings or waves of hair which over-shadowed *ce beau visage blanc* so abundantly, yet with lines so jealously observed along the proud, firm, smooth flesh, making you think, by its transparent shadows, of cool places around – yes! around dangerously deep water-pools, amid a great heat. Like such water, the black eyes surprised you by their clear dark blue, when in full sunlight for a moment, as the trees opened above." Often in Pater's prose, the larger unities of book, essay, paragraph, or sentence dissolve in qualifications, digressions, postponements, and delays as Pater works toward a final impression left vibrating in consciousness – here, Margaret's dark blue eyes as perilous pools. This aggregate image through which all the other ideas rush anticipates what **Ezra Pound** in "Vorticism" (1914) called "a radiant node or cluster" that records "the precise instant when a thing outward and objective transforms itself, or darts into a thing inward and subjective." In Pater's essays, we have a mind watching itself in motion; hunting its aesthetic equivalent within hesitant, exquisitely adjusted prose; and aspiring to permanence in "a fragment of perfect expression."

GERALD MONSMAN

Biography

Walter Horatio Pater. Born 4 August 1839 in London. Studied at King's School, Canterbury, 1853–58; Queen's College, Oxford, 1858–62, B.A. in classics, 1862. Tutor in Oxford, 1862–64; elected to the Old Mortality, an essay society in Oxford, 1863; Fellow, from 1864, and tutor, until 1883, Brasenose College, Oxford, M.A., 1865. Traveled to Italy for the first time, 1865, and lived in Rome, 1882, 1883. Contributor to various journals, from 1866, including the *Westminster Review* and the *Fortnightly Review*. Associated with the Pre-Raphaelites, particularly Swinburne, from 1869. Lived in London, 1885–93, and Oxford, 1893–94. Awards: honorary degree from the University of Glasgow, 1894. Died in Oxford (of rheumatic fever), 30 July 1894.

Selected Writings

Essays and Related Prose

Studies in the History of the Renaissance, 1873; revised edition, as *The Renaissance*, 1877; revised editions, 1888, 1893; edited by Donald L. Hill, 1980, Adam Phillips, 1986, and William E. Buckler, in *Three Major Texts*, 1986
Imaginary Portraits, 1887; edited by William E. Buckler, in *Three Major Texts*, 1986
Appreciations, with an Essay on Style, 1889; revised edition, 1890; edited by William E. Buckler, in *Three Major Texts*, 1986
Plato and Platonism: A Series of Lectures, 1893
Greek Studies: A Series of Essays, edited by Charles L. Shadwell, 1895
Miscellaneous Studies: A Series of Essays, edited by Charles L. Shadwell, 1895

Essays from The Guardian, 1896
Uncollected Essays, 1903
Sketches and Reviews, 1919
Selected Works, edited by Richard Aldington, 1948
Essays on Literature and Art, edited by Jennifer Uglow, 1973
Selected Writings, edited by Harold Bloom, 1974
Three Major Texts, edited by William E. Buckler, 1986

Other writings: two novels (*Marius the Epicurean*, 1885; *Gaston de Latour* [unfinished], 1896, revised edition edited by Gerald Monsman, 1995).

Collected works edition: *Works*, 10 vols., 1910.

Bibliographies

Court, Franklin E., *Walter Pater: An Annotated Bibliography of Writings About Him*, De Kalb: Northern Illinois University Press, 1980
Wright, Samuel, *A Bibliography of the Writings of Walter Pater*, New York: Garland, and Folkestone: Dawson, 1975

Further Reading

Block, Ed, "Walter Pater's 'Diaphaneite' and the Pattern of Reader Response in the Portrait Essay," *Texas Studies in Literature and Language* 25 (1983): 427–47
Buckler, William E., *Walter Pater: The Critic as Artist of Ideas*, New York: New York University Press, 1987
Chandler, Edmund, "Pater on Style," *Anglistica* 20 (1958): 1–100
Court, Franklin E., "Walter Pater's Impressionism: A 'New Line' in English Prose," in *Der englische Essay: Analysen*, edited by Horst Weber, Darmstadt: Wissenschaftliche Buchgesellschaft, 1975: 263–74
Donoghue, Denis, *Walter Pater: Lover of Strange Souls*, New York: Knopf, 1995
Duffy, John J., "Walter Pater's Prose Style: An Essay in Theory and Analysis," *Style* 1 (1967): 45–63
Fletcher, Ian, *Walter Pater*, London: Longman, revised edition, 1971 (original edition, 1959)
Fraser, G. S., "Walter Pater: His Theory of Style, His Style in Practice, His Influence," in *The Art of Victorian Prose*, edited by George Levine and William Madden, New York: Oxford University Press, 1968: 201–23
Inman, Billie A., "Pater's Appeal to His Readers: A Study of Two of Pater's Prose Styles," *Texas Studies in Literature and Language* 14 (1973): 643–66
Monsman, Gerald, "Walter Pater: Style and Text," *South Atlantic Quarterly* 71 (1972): 106–23
Monsman, Gerald, *Walter Pater*, Boston: Twayne, 1977
Monsman, Gerald, "Introduction: On Reading Pater," in *Walter Pater: An Imaginative Sense of Fact*, edited by Philip Dodd, London: Cass, 1981: 1–11; also in *Prose Studies* 4 (1981): 1–11
Seiler, R. M., editor, *Walter Pater: The Critical Heritage*, London and Boston: Routledge, 1980
Zangwill, Israel, "Pater and Prose," in his *Without Prejudice*, London: Fisher Unwin, and New York: Century, 1896: 207–19

Paz, Octavio

Mexican, 1914–

Octavio Paz is the author of many shorter and book-length essays of literary and multifaceted cultural analysis; these studies are often centered on Mexico, but are not limited to that country. For many years now the first publication in Spanish of his essays, whether collections of shorter pieces or books, has been quickly followed by translation into the principal European languages. Paz's most important current editorial position is as founder in 1976 of the monthly magazine *Vuelta* (Return), titled to mark his return to Mexico from voluntary exile following the 1968 government massacre of protesting students in the Tlatelolco district of Mexico City. In *Vuelta*, as contributor and editor, Paz publishes literary, artistic, political and **historical essays** by leading writers and intellectuals from all over the world.

The central theme of Paz's essays and, indeed, of much of his writing, is a dialectic between the fact of the individual's solitude and its need for suprapersonal reality. Paz views the individual as alone by virtue of the totally solitary manner of birth and death; all else is the Other. He seems to have come to this basic notion in the process of writing his first and perhaps most famous essay, *El laberinto de la soledad* (1950; *The Labyrinth of Solitude*). There he states: "The Mexican and his Mexicanism must be defined as separation and negation." This notion, with time, is not limited to the Mexican context; rather it becomes in Paz's view a hallmark of human life. Paz then points to how the Mexican reacts to his solitude: his life can also be defined "as a search, a desire to transcend this state of exile." As Paz's thought evolves, this search becomes another hallmark of human beings as they try to communicate, to form community, to make society and life a communion through understanding and love.

Given Paz's self-image as being primarily a poet, and only secondarily an intellectual who writes essays and scholarly studies, it may not be surprising that he sees poetry as one of the ways in which humankind may best transcend its solitude. In "La otra orilla" ("The Other Shore"), an essay contained in his 1956 book *El arco y la lira* (*The Bow and the Lyre*), Paz suggests succinctly how poetry may create such experience: "Poetic rhythm does not fail to offer analogies to mythical time; the image, to mystical utterance; participation, to magical alchemy and religious communion. Everything leads us to insert the poetic act into the realm of the sacred." He believes that poetry and religion "spring from the same source and that it is not possible to dissociate the poem from its pretension to change man without the risk of turning the poem into an inoffensive form of literature." Paz notes that the public festivals which are so much a part of Hispanic life on both sides of the Atlantic Ocean, and which have their roots in popular, pre-Christian religions, are also a striving to overcome solitude and engage in communion.

As a theorist of cultural identity and difference, for example in both *The Labyrinth of Solitude* and the later *Sor Juana Inés de la Cruz; o, Las trampas de la fe* (1982; *Sor Juana, or, The Traps of Faith*), Paz may be at his best when he compares and contrasts Hispanic and Anglo-Saxon culture in the Old and New Worlds. In addition to his explanation of the more positive role of public festivals in Hispanic culture than in Anglo-Saxon, Paz's analysis of the reasons for the traditional – not necessarily contemporary – Hispanic rejection of the scientific method based on criticism and reason is especially compelling. Most interesting is the way he links this issue to the different cultures' positions in the Reformation and Counter Reformation.

At the same time, Paz is keenly aware that an increasingly dominant theme in the Hispanic world is the acceptance of the cultural models of post-industrial societies. In *Postdata* (1970; *The Other Mexico*) and the 1975 interview "Vuelta a *El laberinto de la soledad*" (Return to *The Labyrinth of Solitude*), Paz reacts to such sociohistorical change in Mexico. Subsequently he discusses the conflicts created, for instance in the Miskito Indian homelands of Nicaragua or in the Mexican state of Chiapas, when pressure builds on underdeveloped Hispanic and third-world countries to reach the levels of material prosperity and political maturity which developed countries have achieved as part of their organic evolution.

While Paz takes very seriously the specific themes, issues, and problems treated in his essays, it may be argued that there is something more important to him than the content of any of his essays: the commitment to disinterested observation and thought guided by critical reason. For Paz human life and history are totally dynamic. He habitually approaches his subject by means of a historical study, and identifies the ongoing synthesis of new and old which is the history of the entity being considered. The fact of change and the need to understand its direction and consequences make the method of critical thought more important than any specific subject to be studied.

STEPHEN MILLER

Biography

Born 31 March 1914 in Mexico City. Studied at the National Autonomous University of Mexico, Mexico City, 1932–37. Stayed in Spain during Civil War, 1937 (on Republican side). Founder or editor of the literary journals *Barandal* (The railing), 1931, *El Popular*, late 1930s, *Taller* (Studio), 1938–41, *El Hijo Pródigo* (The prodigal son), 1943–46, and *Plural*, 1971–75, later *Vuelta*, from 1976. Married Elena Garro, 1937 (later divorced): one daughter. Won Guggenheim Award to study and travel in the United States. Worked for the Mexican Embassy, Paris, 1946 and 1959–62, and Tokyo, 1951 and 1953–58; Mexican ambassador to India, 1962–68 (resigned). Married Marie José Tramini, 1964. Taught at various American and British universities, 1968–72. Awards: many, including the Jerusalem Prize, 1977; Critics' Prize (Spain), 1977; National Prize for Letters, 1977; Grand Aigle d'Or (Nice), 1979; Yoliztli Prize, 1980; Cervantes Prize, 1981; Heinse Medal (Germany), 1984; Gran Cruz de Alfonso X el Sabio, 1986; Ingersoll Foundation T. S. Eliot Award, 1987; Nobel Prize for Literature, 1990.

Selected Writings

Essays and Related Prose

El laberinto de la soledad, 1950; revised edition, 1959; edited by Enrico Mario Santí, 1993; as *The Labyrinth of Solitude: Life and Thought in Mexico*, translated by Lysander Kemp, 1961, enlarged edition, 1985

El arco y la lira: El poema, la revelación poética, poesía e historia, 1956; revised edition, 1967; as *The Bow and the Lyre: The Poem, the Poetic Revelation, Poetry and History*, translated by Ruth L. C. Simms, 1973

Las peras del olmo, 1957

Cuadrivio, 1965

Los signos en rotación, 1965

Puertas al campo, 1966

Claude Lévi-Strauss; o, El nuevo festín de Esopo, 1967; as *Claude Lévi-Strauss: An Introduction*, translated by J. S. and Maxine Bernstein, 1970

Corriente alterna, 1967; as *Alternating Current*, translated by Helen Lane, 1973

Marcel Duchamp; o, El castillo de la pureza, 1968; as *Marcel Duchamp; or, The Castle of Purity*, translated by Donald Gardner, 1970

México: La última década, 1969

Conjunciones y disyunciones, 1969; as *Conjunctions and Disjunctions*, translated by Helen Lane, 1974

Postdata, 1970; as *The Other Mexico: Critique of the Pyramid*, translated by Lysander Kemp, 1972

Traducción: Literatura y literalidad, 1971

Las cosas en su sitio: Sobre la literatura española del siglo XX, with Juan Marichal, 1971

Los signos en rotación y otros ensayos, edited by Carlos Fuentes, 1971

El signo y el garabato, 1973

Apariencia desnuda: La obra de Marcel Duchamp, 1973; as *Marcel Duchamp: Appearance Stripped Bare*, translated by Rachel Phillips and Donald Gardner, 1978

La búsqueda del comienzo: Escritos sobre el surrealismo, 1974

Los hijos del limo: Del romanticismo a la vanguardia, 1974; as *Children of the Mire: Modern Poetry from Romanticism to the Avant-Garde*, translated by Rachel Phillips, 1974, revised, enlarged edition, 1991

Teatro de signos/Transparencias, edited by Julián Ríos, 1974

The Siren and the Seashells and Other Essays on Poets and Poetry, translated by Lysander Kemp and Margaret Sayers Peden, 1976

Xavier Villaurrutia en persona y en obra, 1978

In/Mediaciones, 1979

México en la obra de Octavio Paz, edited by Luis Mario Schneider, 1979; enlarged edition, 4 vols., 1987

El ogro filantrópico: Historia y política, 1971–1978, 1979; as *The Philanthropic Ogre*, translated by Lysander Kemp, Yara Milos, and Rachel Phillips, 1985

Sor Juana Inés de la Cruz; o, Las trampas de la fe, 1982; as *Sor Juana: Her Life and World*, and as *Sor Juana, or, The Traps of Faith*, translated by Margaret Sayers Peden, 1988

Sombras de obras: Arte y literatura, 1983

Tiempo nublado, 1983; as *One Earth, Four or Five Worlds: Reflections on Contemporary History*, translated by Helen Lane, 1985

Hombres en su siglo y otros ensayos, 1984; as *On Poets and Others*, translated by Michael Schmidt, 1986

Convergences: Essays on Art and Literature, translated by Helen Lane, 1987

Primeras letras (1931–1943), edited by Enrico Mario Santí, 1988

La otra voz, 1990; as *The Other Voice: Essays on Modern Poetry*, translated by Helen Lane, 1991

Essays on Mexican Art, translated by Helen Lane, 1993

Itinerario, 1993

The Double Flame: Essays on Love and Eroticism, translated by Helen Lane, 1996

Other writings: many collections of poetry, a play, and works on literature and culture.

Bibliographies

Foster, David William, in *Mexican Literature: A Bibliography of Secondary Sources*, Metuchen, New Jersey: Scarecrow Press, 1992

Valencia, Juan O., and Edward Coughlin, *Bibliografía selecta y crítica de Octavio Paz*, Cincinnati: University of Cincinnati, 1973

Verani, Hugo J., *Octavio Paz: Bibliografía crítica*, Mexico City: National Autonomous University of Mexico, 1983

Further Reading

Antípodas issue on Camilo José Cela, Gabriel García Márquez, and Paz, 4 (December 1992): 171–250

Gullón, Ricardo, "The Universalism of Octavio Paz," *Books Abroad* (October 1972)

Jiménez Cataño, Rafael, *Octavio Paz: Poética del hombre*, Pamplona: EUNSA, 1992

Montoya Ramírez, Enrique, coordinator, *Octavio Paz* (week's conference on Paz in Madrid, 9–12 May 1988, at the Instituto de Cooperación Iberoamericana), Madrid: Cultura Hispánica, 1989

Ruy Sánchez, Alberto, *Una introducción a Octavio Paz*, Mexico City: Planeta, 1990

Wilson, Jason, *Octavio Paz: A Study of His Poetics*, Cambridge: Cambridge University Press, 1979

Wilson, Jason, *Octavio Paz*, Boston: Twayne, 1986

Péguy, Charles

French, 1873–1914

Charles Péguy, a poet as well as an essayist and by turns an ardent socialist and Christian, was never less than an idealist. Of peasant stock from Orléans, although not so working-class as he pretended, Péguy won a series of scholarships and finally gained admission on his third attempt in 1894 to the exclusive École Normale Supérieure in Paris. His study was nicknamed "Utopia" by his fellow students and, influenced by the socialist leader Jean Jaurès, Péguy's later essays were all to be devoted, if not exclusively to planning an ideal society, at least to denouncing the injustices and errors of that in which he lived. Péguy was not academically successful, failed his final agrégation, which would have given him a job for life, and experienced serious economic deprivation.

When Émile Zola published his celebrated newspaper article *J'accuse* on 13 January 1898, attacking the army's cover-up by falsifying the evidence against the Jewish Alfred Dreyfus, who had been accused of betraying French military secrets to Germany, Péguy met with Zola and summoned other French socialists to support him. In 1898, he opened a commercially disastrous bookshop which became the Dreyfusard headquarters, and began his series of essays on the Dreyfus affair which were published in the *Revue Blanche* (White review).

While remaining a non-Marxist socialist, but after breaking with the socialist hierarchy who wished to control his activities, Péguy founded in 1900 the famous *Cahiers de la Quinzaine* (Fortnightly notebooks), a review which was itself to become a movement of political and moral reform, although never a financial success throughout its 15 series and 229 numbers. He boasted that, as a movement, the *Cahiers* were "a perfectly free association of people who all believe in something," but subscriptions rarely rose above 1000. Péguy published a glittering list of political essayists, and the *Cahiers* remain an important source for materials not available elsewhere in their full texts. Publication ceased only with the outbreak of World War I in 1914.

Although his emphasis was to change as Péguy moved toward a Christian synthesis combining social justice, civilized values, and the anti-materialism of Henri Bergson, there is a sense in which he never strayed far from an initial series of preoccupations. His whole life was spent exploring ever more deeply – chiefly in his *Cahiers* essays – the major themes of education, history, the implications of the Dreyfus affair, French national pride, Bergson's philosophy, and Christianity. The movement is from anti-rationalism and anti-positivism, expressed in Péguy's hostility to **Hippolyte Taine** and a host of prominent French academics who adopted Taine's "method" and anti-clericalism, toward a growing patriotism and national pride. The mysterious, the religious, and the poetic seemed to Péguy to be beyond the reach of the idol erected in the name of science.

As the anti-clerical elements gathered strength within the French administration around the turn of the century, laicizing the educational system and exiling religious orders, even democracy – linking itself with declericalization and scientism – became suspect to Péguy. By 1908 he had moved closer to Catholicism – in company, it should be said, with a whole group of other important French writers, although at that date in France socialism was considered to be virtually incompatible with Catholicism on account of the materialism and the determinism associated with it.

By 1908 too, Péguy clearly foresaw the approaching European conflict. He was alarmed by the danger of mystiques and ideals being transformed into political stances and ideologies. Péguy never discontinued his essays, but more of his energy during the immediate prewar years went into his poetic production, investigating the Christian mysteries of suffering, sacrifice, and salvation, and defining as the best quality in French culture its developed sense of the heroic. His own death, leading his company at Villeroy in September 1914, was the result of taking a risk so perverse that it resembled the acting out of an heroic fantasy.

The attitudes to be found in Péguy's essays are based on an artisan background, a love of rural French life, with its deeply ingrained Catholicism, the poverty and ordinariness of his experience, and his undisciplined search for spiritual answers which made him vulnerable to idealistic mystiques. Stylistically, his essays are unpolished, often rambling, invariably overextended, and weakened by his tendency to pursue topics with only a tangential bearing to his main theme. His treatment of major themes may be much enriched in the process, but it is often difficult to follow, as Péguy rarely relates the side issues to the main themes with adequate explicitness.

He was nonetheless a great writer, made so by an originality deriving from the honesty, integrity, and idealism which refused to follow intellectual fashion, or to link attitudes which had no intrinsic connection. A stalwart Dreyfusard, he nevertheless believed in the mystic force of the nationalistic French tradition, an attitude normally associated with the military.

ANTHONY LEVI

Biography

Charles Pierre Péguy. Born 7 January 1873 in Orléans. Studied at the lycée in Orléans, 1885–91, baccalauréat, 1891; Lycée Lakanal, Sceaux, 1891–92; military service, 1892–93; Collège de Sainte-Barbe, Paris, 1893–94, licence in philosophy, 1894; École Normale Supérieure, Paris, 1894–95, 1896–97. Contributor to the *Revue Socialiste*, from 1896, and the *Revue Blanche*, 1899. Married Charlotte-Françoise Baudouin, 1897: three sons (one born after Péguy's death) and one daughter. Owner of a socialist bookshop in the Latin Quarter, 1898, turning it into a cooperative to avoid bankruptcy, 1899; founder and editor, *Les Cahiers de la Quinzaine*, 1900–14. Served in the army during World War I. Killed in the Battle of the Marne, near Villeroy, 5 September 1914.

Selected Writings

Essays and Related Prose

Cahiers de la Quinzaine, 15 vols., 1900–14
Basic Verities: Prose and Poetry, translated by Ann and Julien Green, 1943
Men and Saints: Prose and Poetry, translated by Ann and Julien Green, 1947
Temporal and Eternal, translated by Alexander Dru, 1958
Œuvres en prose (Pléiade Edition), edited by Marcel Péguy, 2 vols., 1957–59
Œuvres en prose complètes (Pléiade Edition), edited by Robert Burac, 3 vols., 1987–92

Other writings: a play and a long poem about Joan of Arc, two mysteries (religious plays), and other poetry.

Collected works editions: *Œuvres complètes*, 20 vols., 1916–55; *Œuvres complètes*, edited by Jean Bastaire, 10 vols., 1974.

Bibliography

Vergine, Pia, *Studi su Péguy: Bibliografia critica ed analitica (1893–1978)*, Lecce: Milella, 1982

Further Reading

Bastaire, Jean, *Péguy l'inchrétien*, Paris: Desclée, 1991
Burac, Robert, *Charles Péguy, la révolution et la grâce*, Paris: Laffont, 1994
Charles Péguy et la Critique Littéraire, Australian Journal of French Studies 1 (1973)
Delaporte, Jean, *Connaissance de Péguy*, Paris: Plon, revised edition, 2 vols., 1959
Dru, Alexander, *Péguy*, London: Harvill Press, 1956; New York: Harper, 1957
Finkielkraut, Alain, *Le Mécontemporain: Péguy, lecteur du monde moderne*, Paris: Gallimard, 1991
Guyon, Bernard, *Péguy*, Paris: Hatier, 1960
Halévy, Daniel, *Péguy and "Les Cahiers de la Quinzaine"*, London: Dobson, 1946; New York: Longman Green, 1947 (original French edition, 1919)
Jussem-Wilson, N., *Charles Péguy*, London: Bowes and Bowes, 1965
Laichter, František, *Péguy et ses Cahiers de la Quinzaine*, Paris: Maison des Sciences de l'Homme, 1985
Porché, François, *Charles Péguy et ses Cahiers*, Paris: Bloch, 1914
Rolland, Romain, *Péguy*, Paris: Albin Michel, 2 vols., 1944
St. Aubyn, F. C., *Charles Péguy*, Boston: Twayne, 1977
Schmitt, Hans A., *Charles Péguy: The Decline of an Idealist*, Baton Rouge: Louisiana State University Press, 1967
Servais, Yvonne, *Charles Péguy: The Pursuit of Salvation*, Cork: Cork University Press, and Westminster, Maryland: Newman Press, 1953
Tardieu, Marc, *Charles Péguy, biographie*, Paris: Bourin, 1993
Villiers, Marjorie, *Charles Péguy: A Study in Integrity*, New York: Harper, 1965

Pensée

The use of the French word *pensée* (literally, thought) to designate a literary genre necessarily brings to mind the *Pensées* of **Blaise Pascal**, the only major work to have the term in its title. Pascal did not choose it himself, and was not responsible for the publication of the fragments posthumously collected, arranged, very heavily edited, and issued as the *Pensées de M. Pascal sur la religion, et sur quelques autres sujets* (1670;

Thoughts of M. Pascal on religion, and on some other subjects). The word *pensée*, like *portrait* and *maxime* (**maxim**), then underwent a certain vogue during the decade following 1670.

In French, *pensée* also occurs as the title of a work of **aphorisms** composed by the Abbé Nicolas d'Ailly, tutor to Mme. de Longueville's children, and published in 1678 with the *maximes* of Madeleine de Souvré, as *Maximes et pensées diverses* (Maxims and diverse thoughts). D'Ailly's *pensées* were for the most part much shorter than the disjointed paragraphs which Pascal's family had stitched together. As a genre, therefore, the *pensée* blended with the aphorism, although, like *maxime*, it had a tendency to develop into a lengthier, more speculative elaboration of a simple idea. The equivalent English "thought" experienced a considerable popularity some decades later, appearing, for instance, in John Locke's *Some Thoughts Concerning Education* (1693) and the posthumous *Some Thoughts on the Conduct of the Understanding in the Search for Truth* (1762). His usage was followed by **Mary Wollstonecraft** in her *Thoughts on the Education of Daughters* (1787).

The only work known to posterity as *pensées* remains Pascal's mass of fragments, heterogeneous both in form and in content. It is, essentially, no more than notes relevant to the possible redaction of a book about a series of problems concerned with human nature and its weaknesses, Christian devotion, and theology. Some of the fragments are notes for a work of religious apologetic which we are told Pascal intended to write, though this may have been planned rather as some more general religious work about the human condition. It was clearly abandoned, and the notes were never meant for publication as fragments, nor given any title by Pascal.

After his death, Pascal's friends and family, led by his sister Gilberte, constructed a sequentially coherent work from some of the fragments more obviously conducive to devotion, containing sharp insights into the predicament of the human individual in the cosmos, with the individual seen as at once so important, because rational, yet also as physically insignificant. Pascal's family, however, had also carefully gathered together every discoverable scrap of paper on which he had written, and a copy of the fragments, now lost, was made exactly as he left them. This copy was at least twice recopied with meticulous exactness, and the two copies made from it still exist, as do the original fragments as pasted onto a large sheet of paper and partly arranged into files by Pascal himself. Many editions of the *Pensées* have appeared, most based on some conjectural structure which, it is speculated, Pascal would have adopted. More recent editions have, with increasing success, reproduced the fragments as Pascal actually left them in what is known as the second of the two copies made from the lost original, but which is certainly the earlier of the two.

It is no doubt unusual for a literary genre to have been constituted virtually in its entirety by a single work; but the contents of Pascal's fragments are so profound, disparate, and difficult, while displaying so many changes of intention and offering so many ambiguities of interpretation, that it has become inappropriate to use the term *pensées* to describe any lesser collection of aphorisms. Some of Pascal's fragments are movingly lyrical, some witty and ironic, some quite polished passages of cadenced prose extended over a page or two. Some are addressed to a reader, while some are merely notes on how

a projected book might, at different moments, have been composed. The overwhelming probability is that Pascal at no time envisaged the publication of a work in aphoristic form. It is, on the contrary, plain that he was tempted both by the **dialogue** form and by an epistolary exchange. (The forms were brilliantly combined in Pascal's *Lettres provinciales* [1656–57; *The Provincial Letters*].)

It does, however, remain pertinent to draw attention to the meaning that the word *pensée* had acquired in the context of Descartes' *Discours de la méthode* (1637; **Discourse on Method**). Descartes memorably used the verb *penser* in the fourth part of the *Discourse*, when discussing how he could know that something existed from his awareness of his own existence – "Je pense, donc je suis" (I think, therefore I am) – going on to conclude that he knew himself to be a spiritual substance whose nature was simply to think. But he also used "pensée" in the first paragraph of the first part of the *Discourse*, when distinguishing between the power of judgment, the *raison* or *bon sens* equal in all human beings, and the *esprit*, the power of the application of thought, which distinguishes the brilliant from the less talented.

Although the *Discourse* was not widely disseminated, it showed that the *pensée*, as a form of spiritual power, was not universally equal among human beings, but could refer to a spiritual capacity of much wider significance. *Pensées*, for Descartes and for Pascal's editors, were not aphorisms so much as an indication of a totality of spiritual powers, which is what made it as apposite a title as any for the diversified collection of fragments Pascal's editors published. His contemporaries rightly saw the *Pensées* as containing some of the most penetrating comments on human nature and behavior known to their culture. They may have understood the fragments incorrectly, falsified and simplified their purpose, and incensed historians by the liberties they took with the text and its arrangement. But it is difficult to know what other word in the French language would more aptly have indicated the nature of its content.

ANTHONY LEVI

Further Reading

Hammond, Nicholas, *Playing with Truth: Language and the Human Condition in Pascal's Pensées*, Oxford: Clarendon Press, 1994

Jaouen, Françoise, *Discours aphoristique et pensée minimaliste: Le Classicisme en petits morceaux* (dissertation), Berkeley: University of California, 1991

Mesnard, Jean, *Les Pensées de Pascal*, Paris: Société d'Édition d'Enseignement Supérieur, 1993 (original edition, 1976)

Perelman, S. J.

American, 1904–1979

S. J. Perelman's prolific output of essays, plays, and film and screen credits attests to his extraordinary versatility as a writer who enjoyed the challenge of moving from one genre to another. Of all his works, however, his essays in the popular, sophisticated magazines of his day, including the **New Yorker**, *Holiday*, *Life*, and the *Saturday Evening Post*, gave him a wide and devoted audience of readers.

At age 13 he wrote an essay entitled "Grit" which won him first prize in a writing contest. Published in *American Boy* magazine, the essay extols the virtues of big-city taxi drivers. At Classical High School, his essay "Why I Am an Atheist" caused a stir because of its accomplished prose but the controversial topic deterred the judges from awarding him the Anthony Medal for first prize.

Entering Brown University in Providence, Perelman planned to pursue his artistry as a cartoonist, but could not resist sending in short humorous pieces to the Brown *Daily Herald*. He developed a column called the "Genial Cynic" and began signing his name S. J. P., the habit of using only his initials becoming his trademark. Eventually he wrote essays for the Brown literary magazine, *Casements*, and distinguished himself with "The Exquisite: A Divagation" (May 1924). From this experience he moved on to writing college humor essays, collected and published with Quentin Reynolds in *Parlor, Bedlam, and Bath* (1930). Then, in 1931, he began a lifelong association with the *New Yorker*.

Perelman's genius for **satire** and his facility with language appeared early, and his admirers in the Algonquin Circle, which included Dorothy Parker, Heywood Broun, and **Robert Benchley**, placed him at the center of New York's top magazine writers of the day. But his reputation did not stop there. F. Scott Fitzgerald wrote of Perelman's work that "Sid had an exquisite tact in prose." Such a comment would surely have pleased Perelman, who always thought of himself as a writer rather than a humorist.

Perelman's first important collection of essays, *Strictly from Hunger* (1937), contains 24 *New Yorker* essays, including a parody of Constance Garnett's translation of **Dostoevskii** entitled "A Farewell to Omsk." Robert Benchley's foreword reports that "Perelman took over the dementia praecox field and drove us all to writing articles on economics for the *Commentator*."

Perelman also wrote essays for the *Saturday Evening Post*, producing a popular column, "A Child's Garden of Curses, of the Bitter Tea of Mr. P." A new collection of essays for Random House, *The Dream Department* (1943), earned him the title "the funniest man in America." Another collection of 46 *New Yorker* essays appeared in *Crazy like a Fox* (1944), followed by *Keep It Crisp* (1946). This volume contains a parody of Raymond Chandler's popular detective novels, "Farewell, My Lovely Appetizer," and captured the critics' attention. No subject was sacred. Perelman even poked fun at Bennett Cerf, editor at Random House, with "No Dearth of Mirth – Fill Out the Coupon." *Time* magazine (12 August 1940) reported that next to Edgar Allan Poe and "not excepting Henry Miller," Perelman was "the most proficient surrealist in the United States."

His commercial breakthrough came with the publication of *Westward Ha! or, Around the World in Eighty Clichés* (1948). The book sold 60,000 copies, twice any previous book's sales, and featured work focusing on his new passion for travel and satirizing resorts of the rich and famous. Perelman began to emphasize travel satire as *Holiday* magazine sponsored his travels to Madagascar and Europe. Of his stay in London, he writes in "Call and I Follow, I Follow!" that "The clientele, picturesque without being intrusive, consists in the main of dehydrated colonials with saffron faces, bishops in gaiters, and

elderly spinsters who still cling to ruching and avian headgear." Every locale provided fodder for parody. Other essays feature adventures in St. Augustine, Hollywood, Las Vegas, and a dude ranch in Arizona. His travels netted him a tropical bird he named Cyrano, who became the subject of "Look, My Toucan" (1957), in which Perelman describes the bird's raucous yelling and the effect on his Bucks County Farm neighbors.

Perelman's Home Companion (1955) is a collection of earlier and out-of-print works, while *The Road to Miltown* (1957) features a **review** by Dorothy Parker in which she notes that Perelman stands alone as a humorist. *The Most of S. J. Perelman* (1958) provides the most comprehensive collection of his **humorous essays**, 96 in all covering a period of 38 years. *The Rising Gorge* (1961) includes Perelman's *New Yorker* trip to the East Coast of Africa and several **travel essays** written for *Redbook*. He continued his adventures in the Balkans, recounting them in *Chicken Inspector no. 23* (1966) and *Baby, It's Cold Inside* (1970).

Perelman, like his Algonquin contemporaries, was a "screwball wit," with a delightful sense of the cliché and the ability to use mimicry as an art. His mastery of language gave him the power to create satires and parodies that cut to and revealed the human heart.

ADELAIDE P. AMORE

Biography

Sidney Joseph Perelman. Born 1 February 1904 in Brooklyn, New York. Studied at Brown University, Providence, Rhode Island, 1921–24, B.A., 1925. Contributor, *Judge* magazine, 1924–29, *College Humor* magazine, 1929–30, and the *New Yorker*, from 1931; also contributor to many other journals and magazines, including the *Saturday Evening Post*, *Life*, *McCall's*, *Redbook*, *Holiday*, and *Travel and Leisure*. Married Laura West, 1929 (died, 1970): one son and one daughter. Wrote plays for Broadway and screenplays, including two for the Marx Brothers. Lived in London, 1970–72. Awards: New York Film Critics Award, 1956; Academy Award (Oscar), for screenplay, 1957; Writers Guild West Award, for screenplay, 1957; Special National Book Award, 1978; honorary degree from Brown University. Member, American Academy of Arts and Letters. Died in New York, 17 October 1979.

Selected Writings

Essays and Related Prose

Dawn Ginsbergh's Revenge, 1929
Parlor, Bedlam, and Bath, with Q. J. Reynolds, 1930
Strictly from Hunger, 1937
Look Who's Talking!, 1940
The Dream Department, 1943
Crazy like a Fox, 1944
Keep It Crisp, 1946
Acres and Pains, 1947
The Best of S. J. Perelman, 1947
Westward Ha! or, Around the World in Eighty Clichés, 1948
Listen to the Mocking Bird, 1949
The Swiss Family Perelman, 1950
The Ill-Tempered Clavichord, 1952
Perelman's Home Companion, 1955
The Road to Miltown; or, Under the Spreading Atrophy, 1957; as *Bite on the Bullet*, 1957
The Most of S. J. Perelman, 1958
The Rising Gorge, 1961

Chicken Inspector no. 23, 1966
Baby, It's Cold Inside, 1970
Vinegar Puss, 1975
Eastward Ha!, 1977
The Last Laugh, 1981
That Old Gang o' Mine: The Early and Essential S. J. Perelman,
   edited by Richard Marschall, 1984

Other writings: several plays (including the musical *One Touch of
Venus*, with Ogden Nash, 1943), screenplays (including *Monkey
Business*, with Will. B. Johnstone, 1931; *Horse Feathers*, 1932;
Around the World in Eighty Days, with James Poe and John
Farrow, 1956), and correspondence.

Bibliographies

Gale, Steven H., *S. J. Perelman: An Annotated Bibliography*, New
   York: Garland, 1985
Toombs, Sarah, "S. J. Perelman: A Bibliography of Short Essays,
   1932–1979," *Studies in American Humor* 3, no. 1 (Spring 1984):
   83–97

Further Reading

Fowler, Douglas, *S. J. Perelman*, Boston: Twayne, 1983
Gale, Steven H., *S. J. Perelman: A Critical Study*, Westport,
   Connecticut: Greenwood Press, 1987
Gale, Steven H., editor, *S. J. Perelman: Critical Essays*, New York:
   Garland, 1992
Herrmann, Dorothy, *S. J. Perelman: A Life*, New York: Putnam,
   1986; London: Simon and Schuster, 1988
Pinsker, Sanford, "Perelman: A Portrait of the Artist as an Aging
   New Yorker Humorist," *Studies in American Humor* 3, no. 1
   (Spring 1984): 47–55
Teicholz, Tom, *Conversations with S. J. Perelman*, Jackson:
   University Press of Mississippi, 1995

Pérez de Ayala, Ramón

Spanish, 1880–1962

Although Ramón Pérez de Ayala is best known for his novels,
the genre he practiced all his adult life was the essay. Most of
his essays were short magazine articles which showed keen
observation, immense knowledge, and individual, occasionally
polemical, ideas. Ayala believed that **Bacon**, **Montaigne**, and
Hume had cultivated the true essay, the kind published in the
Spectator. The Spanish author took pleasure in that English
title, which reflects the true spirit of the essayist: one who
observes attentively in expectation. Ayala often chose lesser
labels for these conversations with his readers – *apostillas*
(marginal notes), *divagaciones* (musings), *pequeños ensayos*
(little essays). Despite the brevity of these writings and Ayala's
denigration of their importance, the reader always learns something from his entertaining chats, about literature, international
or Spanish politics, travel, art, or war as seen from the trenches.
His words are carefully chosen, often evincing his extensive
knowledge of classical Latin and Greek. His style is personal,
yet measured; erudite, yet seldom snobbish; entertaining while
informing. One technique Ayala uses is an apparent wandering
from the topic announced in the title, only to draw upon that
"tangential information" as a key illustration of a difficult
concept. In an article written soon after his arrival in Argentina,
his desire to communicate with his audience is clear; he

celebrates a large number of **letters** from readers, praising,
questioning, and even suggesting topics for future essays. This,
he said, was unheard of in Spain, where he received few letters,
and those few were injurious or insulting.

Pérez de Ayala published in at least 16 leading magazines
in Spain and Latin America, among them the pro-Republican
España, *Nuevo Mundo* (New world), *El Imparcial*, *La
Tribuna*, and Argentina's *La Prensa* (The press). Ayala was a
war correspondent for the last during World War I; those
essays comprise *Hermann, encadenado: Notas de un viaje a
los frentes del Isonzo, la Carnia y el Trentino* (1917; Herman
in chains: notes on a trip to the front lines of Isonzo, la Carnia
and il Trentino). He was also a correspondent for the Spanish
newspaper *ABC* during his exile in Argentina (1940–54), as
well as after his return to Spain in 1954. Because of the
disparate nature of these publications (on two continents, in
so many sources, and over a wide range of topics), Ayala's
editors face a monumental task in collecting and publishing
his essays.

Spaniards were treated to Pérez de Ayala's personal observations of other countries in several volumes of collected
essays. In *El país del futuro* (1959; The country of the future),
Ayala reports his observations of the United States during two
visits (1913–14, 1919–20). His *Tributo a Inglaterra* (1963;
Tribute to England) collects articles written about and from
England, and *Crónicas londinenses* (1958; London chronicles)
includes his newspaper articles written during his visit in 1908.
Ancient Greece is the focus of *Viaje entretenido al país del
ocio: Reflexiones sobre la cultura griega* (1975; Entertaining
journey to the land of leisure: reflections on Greek culture).
Fábulas y ciudades (1961; Fables and cities) considers the
educational importance of fables for all ages and the origins
of great cities. Ayala proves that neither archaeologists nor
anthropologists have answered the question of how cities begin,
subsequently offering his own theories.

A majority of Ayala's essays treat two themes: literature
(especially drama and the novel) and politics. In *Política y toros*
(1918; Politics and bulls), he analyzes the Spanish perspective
of the world, indicating that the Spaniard believes himself to
be an expert on both politics and the bullfight. Ayala, however,
calls Spain uncivilized, for, unlike any civilized nation, Spain
has neither resolved nor stated its political problems. In a
later collection, *Escritos políticos* (1967; Political writings),
editor Paulino Garagorri includes Ayala's denunciation of
Primo de Rivera's dictatorship and his welcoming the fall of the
monarchy and the beginning of the Second Republic.

Spanish or international letters and history are explored in
Ante Azorín (1964; In the presence of Azorín), *Amistades y
recuerdos* (1961; Friendships and remembrances), *Nuestro
Séneca y otros ensayos* (1966; Our Seneca and other essays),
Principios y finales de la novela (1958; Beginnings and
ends of the novel), *Divagaciones literarias* (1958; Literary
musings), and *Más divagaciones literarias* (1960; More literary musings). In *Las máscaras* (1917–19; Masks), his famous
two-volume collection of theatrical criticism and **reviews**, Ayala
criticized and analyzed the leading Spanish playwrights of his
day, at times heavyhandedly. In later years, he revised some
of his more vitriolic reviews, especially on Benavente. He did,
however, continue to appreciate most drama which followed
classical and Aristotelian principles.

From the other essays on literature, one can glean Ayala's theory of the novel. He stated, for example, that the essay and the novel are the culmination of the development of genres; classicism is likewise the zenith of literary movements. Ayala believed that the novel must present many (perhaps even contradictory) viewpoints in order to portray three-dimensional reality by one-dimensional description. Although the novel's purpose is communication, and therefore content must be privileged, style is still important, though it should never be used solely for decorative effect. The plot, he stated, is merely melodramatic if it is founded on a conflict between good and evil. Instead, the best plot presents the confrontation of two or more just causes. The best topics for novels, therefore, are love and tolerance.

Miscellaneous collections cover all the above topics as well as art, education, and geography. Among these are *Pequeños ensayos* (1963; Little essays), *Apostillas y divagaciones* (1976; Marginal notes and musings), *Tabla rasa* (1963; The table cleared), and *Las terceras de ABC* (1976; The third page of ABC). The latter's title refers to Pérez de Ayala's essays appearing on that Madrid newspaper's third page. *El libro de Ruth* (1928; The book of Ruth) is an anthology of essays extracted from Ayala's novels.

Pérez de Ayala contributed significantly to Spaniards' understanding of themselves and the world for nearly 50 years. It is only fitting, therefore, that he should be appreciated for his most constant genre, the essay.

EUNICE DOMAN MYERS

Biography

Born 9 August 1880 in Oviedo, Asturias. Studied at the Jesuit school in Gijón, 1890–94; University of Oviedo, 1896–1902, law degree; University of Madrid, 1902. Contributor to *Helios*, 1903–04; London correspondent, *El Imparcial*, 1908. Traveled to Germany, 1912, and the United States, 1913–14. Married Mabel Rick, 1913: two sons. War correspondent for *La Prensa* (Buenos Aires), 1916; contributor to Madrid newspapers while in the U.S., 1919–20. Elected to the Royal Spanish Academy, 1928. Founder, with **José Ortega y Gasset** and Gregorio Marañón, Agrupación al Servicio de la República (Group at the service of the Republic), 1931. Spanish ambassador in London, 1931–36 (resigned); lived in Biarritz and Paris, 1936–39, returning to Spain at the end of the Civil War. Lived in Buenos Aires, 1940–54; worked for a time at the Spanish Embassy, Buenos Aires; returned to Spain, 1954. Contributor, *ABC*, 1954–62. Awards: Mariano de Cavia Prize, for journalism, 1922; National Literature Prize, 1926; Juan March Prize, 1960; honorary degree from the University of London. Died in Madrid, 5 August 1962.

Selected Writings

Essays and Related Prose

Hermann, encadenado: Notas de un viaje a los frentes del Isonzo, la Carnia y el Trentino, 1917
Las máscaras, 2 vols., 1917–19
Política y toros, 1918
El libro de Ruth: Ensayos en vivo, 1928
Selections from Pérez de Ayala (in Spanish), edited by Nicholson B. Adams and Sterling A. Stoudemire, 1934
Principios y finales de la novela, 1958
Divagaciones literarias, edited by José García Mercadal, 1958
Crónicas londinenses, 1958; edited by Agustín Coletes Blanco, 1985

El país del futuro: Mis viajes a los Estados Unidos, 1913–1914, 1919–1920, edited by José García Mercadal, 1959
Más divagaciones literarias, edited by José García Mercadal, 1960
Amistades y recuerdos, 1961
Fábulas y ciudades, 1961
Tabla rasa, 1963
Pequeños ensayos, edited by José García Mercadal, 1963
Tributo a Inglaterra, edited by José García Mercadal, 1963
Ante Azorín, edited by José García Mercadal, 1964
Nuestro Séneca y otros ensayos, edited by José García Mercadal, 1966
Escritos políticos, edited by Paulino Garagorri, 1967
Viaje entretenido al país del ocio: Reflexiones sobre la cultura griega, edited by José García Mercadal, 1975
Apostillas y divagaciones, edited by José García Mercadal, 1976
Las terceras de ABC, 1976
Artículos y ensayos en los semanarios "España," "Nuevo Mundo," y "La Esfera", edited by Florencio Friera Suárez, 1986

Other writings: nine novels (*Tinieblas en las cumbres*, 1907; *A.M.D.G.*, 1910; *La pata de la raposa* [*The Fox's Paw*], 1912; *Troteras y danzaderas*, 1913; *Belarmino y Apolonio*, 1921; *Luna de miel, luna de hiel* [*Honeymoon, Bittermoon*], 1923; *Los trabajos de Urbano y Simona*, 1923; *Tigre Juan*, 1926; *El curandero de su honra*, 1926), novellas, poetry, and a play.

Collected works edition: *Obras completas*, edited by José García Mercadal, 4 vols., 1964–69.

Bibliographies

Best, Marigold, *Ramón Pérez de Ayala: An Annotated Bibliography of Criticism*, London: Grant and Cutler, 1980
Bibliografía de Ramón Pérez de Ayala en la Biblioteca Pública de Oviedo (Bibliografía para un centenario), Oviedo: Biblioteca Pública, 1980
Fernández, Pelayo H., "Bibliografía sobre Ramón Pérez y Ayala," in his *Estudios sobre Ramón Pérez y Ayala*, Oviedo: Instituto de Estudios Asturianos, 1978: 153–93

Further Reading

Bobes Naves, María del Carmen, and others, *Homenaje a Ramón Pérez de Ayala*, Oviedo: University of Oviedo Department of Literary Criticism, 1980
Campbell, Brenton Kay, "The Esthetic Theories of Ramón Pérez de Ayala," *Hispania* 50, no. 3 (September 1967): 447–53
Campbell, Brenton Kay, "Free Will and Determinism in the Theory of Tragedy: Pérez de Ayala and Ortega y Gasset," *Hispanic Review* 37 (July 1969): 375–82
Feeny, Thomas, "Subjectivity in the Dramatic Criticism of Pérez de Ayala," *Revista de Estudios Hispánicos* 17, no. 1 (January 1983): 55–64
Fernández, Pelayo H., editor, *Simposio internacional Ramón Pérez de Ayala*, Gijón: Flores, 1981
Fernández, Pelayo H., "Bergson y Pérez de Ayala: Teoría de lo cómico," *Cuadernos Americanos* 248, no. 3 (May–June 1983): 103–09
Fernández Avelló, Manuel, "Ramón Pérez de Ayala y el periodismo," *Boletín del Instituto de Estudios Asturianos* 42 (April 1961): 37–56
García Calderón, Francisco, "Ramón Pérez de Ayala y la política española," in *La herencia de Lenín y otros artículos*, Paris: Garnier, 1929: 153–61
González del Valle, Luis T., *El canon: Reflexiones sobre la recepción literaria-teatral (Pérez de Ayala ante Benavente)*, Madrid: Huerga & Fierro, 1993
Insula issue on Pérez de Ayala, 404–05 (July–August 1980)
Myers, Eunice D., "Tradition and Modernity in Pérez de Ayala's Literary Theories," *Crítica Hispánica* 2, no. 2 (1980): 157–66

O'Brien, MacGregor, *El ideal clásico de Ramón Pérez de Ayala en sus ensayos en la Prensa de Buenos Aires*, Oviedo: IDEA, 1981

Pérez Ferrero, Miguel, *Ramón Pérez de Ayala*, Madrid: Publicaciones de la Fundación Juan March, 1973

Rand, Marguerite C., *Ramón Pérez de Ayala*, New York: Twayne, 1971

Sallenave, Pierre, "La estética y el esencial ensayismo de Ramón Pérez de Ayala," *Cuadernos Hispanoamericanos* 234 (June 1969): 601–15

Sallenave, Pierre, "Ramón Pérez de Ayala, teórico de la literatura," *Cuadernos Hispanoamericanos* 82, no. 244 (April 1970): 178–90

Suarée, Octavio de la, Jr., *Sociedad y política en la ensayística de Ramón Pérez de Ayala*, New York: Contra Viento y Marea, 1982

Villanueva, Darío, editor, *La novela lírica*, vol. 2, Madrid: Taurus, 1983

Weber, Frances Wyers, *The Literary Perspectivism of Ramón Pérez de Ayala*, Chapel Hill: University of North Carolina Press, 1966

Periodical Essay

In a general sense, the term "periodical essays" may be applied to any grouping of essays that appear serially. **Charles Dickens** once referred to himself as a "periodical essayist," and various 20th-century columnists whose syndicated work appears with some frequency might be given this designation. The term "periodical essay" appears to have been first used by George Colman the Elder and Bonnell Thornton in their magazine the *Connoisseur* (1754–56). By the time it occurred to them to use these two words to describe the form of publication in which they were engaged, serial essays which shared a number of characteristics with the *Connoisseur* had been published (in England especially) for half a century. So numerous were these serials, so persistent a feature of the reading diet of people throughout English society during nearly the entire century, and so natural did it seem to an 18th-century author to develop a periodical essay series or at least to contribute a paper or two to a series established by another writer, that any discussion of the periodical essay is most appropriately situated in this period.

The confluence of three separate cultural developments appears to have caused the emergence of the periodical essay form early in the 18th century. The first of these was the rise of publications that conveyed news, commentary, and (frequently) political propaganda to the general reading public. Governmental licensing controls over publishing had been allowed to lapse in the latter years of the 17th century, and by the end of the first decade of the 18th a variety of publications, most appearing weekly or two to three times per week, were serving a wide reading audience. **Daniel Defoe** estimated the total national weekly circulation of such periodicals at 200,000 in 1711, and the sharing of papers at coffeehouses and within families doubtless created a larger audience even then. The second development was the rise of the informal essay at the same time, undoubtedly influenced by the writings of **Montaigne** as well as by the recognition that particular kinds of prose style might be more appropriate to some discourses than to others. Ephraim Chambers' entry on the essay in his *Cyclopaedia* (1728) refers to "sudden, occasional Reflexions, which are to be wrote much at the Rate, and in the Manner a Man thinks . . ." A third factor contributing to

the popularity of this form was the 18th-century fondness for pseudonymous writing – the adoption of fictitious personae appropriate to the expression of particular views. **Jonathan Swift** and **Richard Steele** are only two of the most visible practitioners of this technique; it is also to be found employed with similar energy by hundreds of other writers.

The formal properties of the periodical essay were largely defined through the practice of **Joseph Addison** and Steele in their two most widely read series, the *Tatler* (1709–11) and the *Spectator* (1711–12, 1714). Many characteristics of these two papers – the fictitious nominal proprietor, the group of fictitious contributors who offer advice and observations from their special viewpoints, the miscellaneous and constantly changing fields of discourse, the use of exemplary **character sketch**es, **letters** to the editor from fictitious correspondents, and various other typical features – existed before Addison and Steele set to work, but these two wrote with such effectiveness and cultivated such attention in their readers that the *Tatler* and *Spectator* served as the models for periodical writing in the next seven or eight decades. Unlike their contemporary Defoe, whose **Review of the Affairs of France** (1704–13) moved to more general cultural topics from a central engagement with political issues, Addison and Steele devoted themselves to matters of style, fashion, behavior, opinion, and manners characteristic of middle-class life; it was this rapidly growing and prospering audience that established so solid a readership for periodical essays in several successive generations.

A listing of the most successful and influential 18th-century periodical essays would be a very long one. When the popularity of the form was at its height in the middle and later years of the century, the leading series included: **Henry Fielding**'s *Covent Garden Journal* (1752); **Samuel Johnson**'s *Rambler* (1750–52) and *Idler* (1758–60); John Hawkesworth's *Adventurer* (1752–54), to which Johnson also contributed; the *World* (1753–56), which Edward Moore conducted in collaboration with Horace Walpole, the **Earl of Chesterfield**, and Richard Owen Cambridge; the *Connoisseur* (1754–56) of Coleman and Thornton; **Oliver Goldsmith**'s "Chinese Letters" in the *Public Ledger* (1760), which he published separately as *The Citizen of the World* two years later; and Henry Mackenzie's *Mirror* (1779–80) and *Lounger* (1785–87).

One measure of the popularity of periodical essays was the emergence of an entirely new and separate periodical form, designed to allow readers better access to such literature: in 1731, Edward Cave's *Gentleman's Magazine* was established as a monthly collection of the best periodical essays from the previous month. Cave and his staff printed digests of the essays they selected in the interests of gentlemen who wished to keep abreast of the latest periodical commentary but simply did not have sufficient time to read it all as it appeared. Ultimately, the form evolved in ways that integrated it into the general conventions of literary publication; that is, the essay series was continued until sufficient numbers had been published to make up two- or four-volume sets. In 1764, when William King published as *The Dreamer* a group of essays (infused with all the qualities of the periodical essay form) which had never been published serially, the serial form may be said to have reached historical closure. Wonderful essays continued to be written – by gifted new writers such as **Charles Lamb** and by others who perpetuated the stylistic and topical qualities that had made the periodical essay so important. But such essays came to readers as preformed collections in bookshops or lending libraries, rather than as segments of discourse delivered to readers as a regular feature of their daily lives.

JAMES M. KUIST

See also Topical Essay

Bibliography

Weed, Katherine Kirtley, and Richmond Pugh Bond, *Studies of British Newspapers and Periodicals from Their Beginning to 1800: A Bibliography*, Chapel Hill: University of North Carolina Press, 1946

Further Reading

Bateson, F. W., "Addison, Steele, and the Periodical Essay," in *Dryden to Johnson*, edited by Roger Lonsdale, New York: Bedrick, 1987
Black, Jeremy, *The English Press in the Eighteenth Century*, Philadelphia: University of Pennsylvania Press, 1987
Bond, Richmond Pugh, *Studies in the Early English Periodical*, Chapel Hill: University of North Carolina Press, 1957
Bond, Richmond Pugh, *Growth and Change in the Early English Press*, Lawrence: University Press of Kansas, 1969
Graham, Walter, *English Literary Periodicals*, New York: Nelson, 1967 (original edition, 1930)
Marr, George Simpson, *The Periodical Essayists of the Eighteenth Century*, New York: Appleton, 1924
Watson, Melvin Roy, "The *Spectator* Tradition and the Development of the Familiar Essay," *English Literary History* 13 (1946): 189–215
Watson, Melvin Roy, *Magazine Serials and the Essay Tradition, 1746–1820*, Baton Rouge: Louisiana State University Press, 1956
Wiles, R. M., *Serial Publication in England Before 1750*, Cambridge: Cambridge University Press, 1957

Periodicals

The periodical publication of journals, reviews, and magazines is a phenomenon of Western European culture closely tied to the evolving hegemony of secular science and especially technology in the 17th century. During the 16th century, print had replaced manuscript as the primary mode for circulating philosophical and scientific ideas, expanding and in some senses actually creating the idea of a "community of scholars," an abstract notion whose real impact as an historic event is best witnessed in the continental effect of the publication of Galileo's manuscripts. One can safely agree with Elizabeth Eisenstein's assertion in *The Printing Press as an Agent of Change* (1979) that the medium and not the message was the subject of the trials of Galileo. At any rate, the development of serialization in learned printing created a mode of communication eventually constructed around the essay because of its discursive predisposition toward scrutiny and knowledge. Periodical writing adds to these distinctive attributes of the essay temporal and spatial qualities that came to define the way in which European culture views knowledge. The serial nature of periodicals contributes significantly to the modern concept of learning as tentative and utilitarian. With each week and each month, new ideas appear to alter the contours of or entirely displace those that came before them. Learning is no longer limited to the learned or the specialist as journals and reviews expand their circulation and accessibility, with the result that the simple pursuit of knowledge for its own sake steadily gives way to knowledge for the sake of its useful application to industry, trade, and economics. It is thus no great exaggeration to say that periodicals both initially defined and subsequently fostered mass communication and international media, seminal attributes of Modernism.

The two works usually cited as the first examples of the periodical appeared respectively in France and England in the same year, 1665; however, Denis de Sallo's *Le Journal des Savants* came out in Paris in January, predating Henry Oldenburg's London publication of the *Philosophical Transactions of the Royal Society* (March 1665) by two months. These were quickly followed by a number of imitations and plagiarisms across Europe, of which the most important and independent offspring was *Il Giornale de' Letterati* (The journal of letters), first published in Rome in 1668 and continued through 1675, when it was reconceived and issued as a new series until 1769. Among the attempts at periodical journalism before 1665 in both France and England, the best – and perhaps the first – is the *Bureau d'Addresse*, which was edited and printed by Théophraste Renaudot between 1633 and 1642 and was composed entirely of summaries of the current activities in the sciences and literature, much of the information garnered through court gossip and correspondence. Jean Loret's *Muse Historique* ran through 1651 in Paris and spawned a London imitator in 1656 called the *Sportive Wit: The Muses Merriment*, both interesting early examples of what Walter Graham (1926) identifies as the "periodical of amusement." This category of serial publication has its early master later in the century when Peter Motteux, the Huguenot journalist and professional writer, began to issue in France his journal *Le Mercure Galant* (1672-1724; The gallant Mercury; then *Le Mercure de France*, 1724-1965), which dealt in articles about court news and gossip. In January 1692 Motteux started the English-language *Gentleman's Journal*, more or less a miscellany of domestic and foreign news, questions and answers on history and philosophy, and news of the learned world, particularly abstracts of learned publications. The *Gentleman's Journal* averaged 64 pages with each issue and was a substantial forerunner of the later achievements in this kind of format, Edward Cave's *Gentleman's Magazine* (1731) and the Edinburgh-based *Scots Magazine* (1739). Still, at its inception, the periodical eschewed commentary and analysis in favor of abstracts and summaries, which is certainly the hallmark of both the *Journal des Savants* and the *Philosophical Transactions*. Only with the 1690s, and particularly in England, did the periodical become the focus of public debate and controversy, a development brought about in part by the innovative combination of the polemical style of the **pamphlet** with the learned periodical's objective of conveying scientific and philosophical knowledge.

Two aspects of 17th-century English prose writing contribute significantly to the emergence of what the modern reader would recognize as the periodical style: the pamphlet wars during and after the Civil War, especially those dealing with Protestant controversy; and the evolution of **character sketch**es from their modern beginning in Joseph Hall's refashioning of the **Characters** of Theophrastus in his *Characters of Vertues and Vices* (1608), with its subsequent secular cousin, Sir Thomas Overbury's enormously successful and influential characterization in *A Wife* (1613). What develops steadily in both kinds of writing is a sensitivity to voice, and especially a rhetoric that takes up the intense awareness of the private self which characterizes the essay from its inception at the hand of **Montaigne** and applies that language of intimate experience and personal belief to a very public kind of work, the political and religious pamphlet. Character writing like that of Hall, Overbury, and John Webster, however, lacked any kind of genuinely psychological element of the sort that makes Montaigne's *Essais* compelling. This rhetorical development can be located in the religious pamphlets of self-examination popular among Protestants, of which the finest example is, perhaps, **John Donne**'s *Devotions upon Emergent Occasions* (1624), which takes the tradition of the spiritual autobiography into its most psychologically self-conscious mode.

By the 1680s, a type of periodical writing began to appear in which contemporary issues and controversies were addressed not in the cold language of abstract and summary but in the rhetorical heat of journalistic **dialogue**. Roger L'Estrange can be said to have pioneered this format in his periodical the *Observator* (1681–87), with its "dialogue papers" in which various characters debate issues in dramatic voices. Perhaps the most eccentric and compelling of L'Estrange's imitators is Charles Leslie, whose *Rehearsal* (1704–09) was structured around the editor's debates with a character called simply "the Countryman" who posed controversial questions concerned with contemporary issues of Church and State, emulating L'Estrange's question-and-answer format. Leslie was a Tory who began his periodical in direct response to John Tutchin's Whig revival of the *Observator* in 1702. This partisanship in journalism, growing out of the political divisions, left over from the Civil War, did much to advance the characterization of voice in periodical writing by establishing an implicit tradition of political identification and opposition in the majority of journalistic undertakings. The paradigm is evident in what are probably the earliest examples of journalism in English, the royalist paper *Mercurius Aulicus* (January 1643) and its opposition response *Mercurius Britannicus* (August 1643). This dialectic in the English periodical press was continued in such 18th-century publications as George Ridpath's Whig *Flying-Post* (1695–1731) and Abel Roper's Tory *Post-Boy* (1695–1736). In part, the domination of the English-language periodical as the exemplary model across Europe can be traced to this volatile format of partisan controversy in the public periodical press in England. The instability of the social experiment of religious tolerance in England after the Civil War, with its explicit protagonist-antagonist relationship between Anglican and Dissenter, Tory and Whig, created a literary model for public debate that quickly presented itself in the three most influential examples of this genre: the *Athenian Gazette* (1690–97), the *Tatler* (1709–11), and the *Spectator* (1711–1712, 1714).

Throughout the 17th century in Europe, there was a sharp division between what we have called "learned" and "amusement" journals, particularly in evidence when we contrast the *Philosophical Transactions* and its professional readership with something like the *News from Parnassus*, first issued 2 February 1680, which was written in the style of a *roman-à-clef*, as a sort of political entertainment, in part a parody of the Spanish novelist and essayist Francisco de Quevedo, whose work *Los sueños* (1627; *Visions*) had been translated by Roger L'Estrange in 1667. John Dunton, however, saw a way to bring together the popular and the professional periodical press in his *Athenian Gazette*, begun 17 March 1690 and printed thereafter twice weekly on Saturdays and Tuesdays. Dunton assembled a "Society of Athenian Gentlemen," more or less a parody of the Royal Society that included, along with Dunton himself, the mathematics teacher Richard Sault, the Church of England divine Samuel Wesley (father of John and Charles Wesley), the polymath John Norris and, on occasion, **Daniel Defoe**. The *Gazette* set out "to endeavour the Answering any reasonable Question which should be proposed." Here for the first time knowledge was applied not abstractly but in response to the specific needs of readers; Dunton openly described this method as one that mixed common sense with scholarly research. The *Gazette* listed sources from Aristotle to the *Philosophical Transactions* among its resources. The content ranged from the admirably eclectic to the bizarrely arcane, including essays on natural science, theology, mathematics, and Hebrew and Greek grammar alongside folklore, domestic truisms, and advice for the lovelorn. The paper was printed as two columns on a folio half-sheet and often answered a dozen questions, although single-issue topics did occur. The writing was not yet fully evolved into the periodical style of **Addison** and **Steele**, but it was recognizably essayistic and employed polemic and opinion in a way unlike any previous periodical.

Of especial interest is Dunton's awareness of his readership. He identified a significant number of women among his following and quickly produced a special issue for the female reader which appeared on the first Tuesday of every month, becoming the first periodical published specifically for women. Dunton's format combined the dissemination of knowledge and information with opinion and analysis, producing a critical journal which was at the same time the first "democratic" periodical, intended for a broadly representative readership in terms of gender, class, religion, and education. His question-and-answer practice took the dialogue technique in periodical writing to its next step where the readers themselves engaged directly in the discourse; Dunton established a convention that became the letter to the editor in the *Tatler* and *Spectator* and remained a staple rhetorical tactic in periodicals from the **Rambler** through to the **Atlantic Monthly**.

John Dunton had many emulators, beginning within months of his first *Athenian Gazette* when Jean de la Crose published his monthly *History of Learning* (July 1691). Retitled *Works of the Learned*, this periodical continued until 1712 and followed Dunton in breaking with the use of abstracts to convey information about the book world. De la Crose is credited with being the first journalist to offer his reader actual **review**s and critical articles. Peter Motteux took the further step of publishing original work by a wide range of contributors in his previously mentioned *Gentleman's Journal* (1692–94), described by George Sherburn (in *The Restoration and the Eighteenth Century*, 1948) as "more like a modern magazine than any other periodical for years to come." The last of the innovators of the 1690s was Edward (Ned) Ward, whose *London Spy* (1698–1700) took characterization and voice outside of the question-and-answer, letter to the editor, and dialogue models into the realm of true personae. In each issue, Ward used a stereotypical character like the Quack or the Gossip to take his readers into the day-to-day activities of London life. His language is colloquial, even coarse and brutal at times, but Ward made human interest stories and the business of the city street a category of information just as desirable to the reader and profitable to the publisher as the knowledge of the scholars or the news of government strategies. The best periodical writing of the 1690s is distinguished by its evocation of voices representative of the spectrum of urban life. Periodicals now spoke in recognizably contemporary and individual ways, sounding Tory or Whig, high or low, and increasingly reflecting national characteristics. A critically informed voice that was private at its origin but public in its effect was one of the significant contributions made by Dunton's *Athenian Gazette* to the periodical style; it remained, however, for Richard Steele and Joseph Addison to create the illusion of informed conversation and in so doing bring the **periodical essay** to its fulfillment in the *Tatler* and the *Spectator*.

If the 1690s had been a period of frenetic innovation in periodical writing, the first decade of the 18th century was one of proliferation. There were 21 periodicals in London in 1702, increasing to 31 in 1707 and 50 in 1711 when the *Spectator* made its appearance. Most of these were irregular and short-lived publications, struggling to define a market as reliable and lucrative as the one that served Dunton's *Athenian* for seven years. Richard Steele made the next significant impact upon that market with the **Tatler**, which ran to 271 numbers, sold for a penny – although the first four issues were offered free to engage an immediate readership – and was offered to the public three times a week, on the days when the London mail coaches left for the country. For all of its stylistic innovations, the *Tatler* is obviously just as important for its acute business sense, using the now common strategy of the loss leader to attract a market and attaching itself to a readership outside of London to extend that market as far as possible through – in Steele's words – "the convenience of the post." In its way, the *Tatler* was the first periodical to use national identity as both a selling and an editorial point, resolving as the first paper declares to settle "a correspondence in all parts of the known and knowing world," which amounted to the coffeehouses of London, perhaps the first journalistic designation of that urban precinct as "the City." Steele wrote 188 *Tatlers*, Addison 42, with contributions from other sources filling out the run. The *Tatler* combined the streetwise observations of Ned Ward's *London Spy* with review writing after the fashion of Motteux and editorializing in the manner Defoe had initiated with his *Review of the Affairs of France* (1704–13). But it is the moral tone and literariness of the *Tatler* that signify its originality. Steele fashioned the periodical essay in journalism by combining the intimacy of the essay form as derived from Montaigne with the dramatic personae which had gradually evolved into the journalistic voices of the popular press. Steele's persona in the *Tatler*, Isaac Bickerstaff, spoke with the inflections of a city gentleman; he sounded as if he were speaking to the reader over a fashionable cup of coffee. He was the first

voice of the editor, informed, erudite, but at ease with his authority. It was a rhetorical innovation that seized the imagination of the reading public – and sold very well.

Like the *Tatler*, the **Spectator** was a folio half-sheet, but it appeared daily between 1 March 1711 and 6 December 1712, running to a total of 555 numbers with the writing shared by Addison and Steele. Addison resumed publication on his own 18 June 1714, producing another 80 papers through 20 December 1714. The *Spectator* was one of the few periodicals to survive Bolingbroke's half-penny tax and consequently sold at twopence, twice the cost of the *Tatler*. A more intellectually ambitious periodical than any of its predecessors, the *Spectator* developed the **critical essay** to a sophisticated degree through Addison's papers on Milton's *Paradise Lost* and other literary topics. It also continued to employ and enhance the persona of the worldly editor whose subtle, informed, and often ironic voice guides the reader with patriarchal authority; where Steele's Bickerstaff was part of the world he moved in and seemed to feel its moral dilemmas, Addison's Mr. Spectator is often detached, his stoicism at times giving way to cynicism. The success of Addison's rhetorical methods in the *Spectator* encouraged wide imitation, notably Eliza Haywood's *Female Spectator*, and was the inspiration for **Samuel Johnson**'s resurrection of the periodical essay in his **Rambler** (1750–52), as well as the Edinburgh periodicals of the late 18th century, the *Mirror* (1779–80) and the *Lounger* (1785–87). On the continent, the *Spectator* was widely translated and established the standard for several generations of essayists, its greatest impact appearing in the work of the French encyclopedists, especially **Voltaire** and **Diderot**.

After Addison, there were few gentlemen journalists. Hack writing paid the bills for most, not the least among whom were Samuel Johnson and **Benjamin Franklin**. Johnson along with Daniel Defoe charted the career of the professional periodical writer in his own life. In fact, Johnson and Defoe between them created and brought to its highest form the art of literary journalism, Johnson as a political conservative and Defoe as a socialist. Both contributed in very different ways to the development of the magazine, which Ben Franklin then took up in the United States. Defoe, traveling and writing journalism in France, Scotland, and Holland, essentially invented foreign correspondence in the modern sense of that term, and was the founder, editor, and sole contributor to *A Review of the Affairs of France* (1704–13), a periodical appearing three times a week and dedicated to bringing England to a mature understanding of international politics. Defoe developed a Scottish edition of the *Review* in 1709 while he was in Edinburgh editing and writing for the *Edinburgh Courant* and the *Scots Postman*. His politically savvy style did much to advance the polemical style in periodical writing.

Samuel Johnson, in turn, developed a political awareness in his journalism through his work for the publisher Edward Cave, whose *Gentleman's Magazine*, begun in 1731, had the most significant overseas influence of any English periodical after the *Spectator*. The *Gentleman's Magazine* had an average circulation of some ten thousand readers throughout the 18th century; Johnson contributed to it as a hack writer for several years, chiefly as the "author" of its accounts of the speeches and transactions of the Houses of Parliament under the allegorically disguised heading, "Senate of Lilliput." The essay style Johnson adopted in his early journalism for the *Gentleman's Magazine* reached its fulfillment in his three subsequent periodical ventures: the **Rambler** (1750–52); the *Universal Chronicle*, a newspaper for which he wrote a column under the title of "**The Idler**," in all producing a further 104 essays; and the **Adventurer** (1752–54), edited by John Hawkesworth, the other great English periodical writer of the mid-18th century, whose career began with the *Gentleman's Magazine*.

The 1740s saw a surge in magazine production outside of England but especially in the American colonies. Following the example of the *Gentleman's Magazine* and the equally successful *Scots Magazine* (launched in 1739 as a monthly in Edinburgh and published without interruption to this day), such periodicals as the Italian *Novelle Letterarie* (1740–70; Literary news) began to appear on the continent, distinguished in large part by their attempts to emulate the impartiality of the English magazine format. However, the most significant flourishing took place across the Atlantic, mostly because the suppression of the press in Catholic Europe blocked periodical publication on the continent. In the American colonies, the first magazines were founded in turn by Benjamin Franklin and John Webbe. The proposal for Franklin's *General Magazine* appeared early in 1740 and he employed Webbe as an editorial assistant. Webbe then abruptly abandoned Franklin and published his own proposal for the *American Magazine* on 30 October 1740. Webbe brought out his periodical first, on 13 February 1741, followed three days later by Franklin's. Both monthlies failed after six issues, neither being able to generate a subscription list which was the financial foundation of Cave's *Gentleman's Magazine*. Only after the American Revolution did the magazine market become stable. In 1788 Noah Webster revived Webbe's *American Magazine* and in the next year published the *New York Magazine* (1789). Charles Brockden Brown, the first professional journalist in the United States and a successful novelist, launched his *Monthly Magazine and American Review* the same year, but circulation remained a problem, as he wrote in his May issue: ". . . it is impossible to arrest the attention of those attached to the active scene of business." Only Mathew Carey's *American Museum*, with a readership of 1200, could sustain a viable circulation.

For whatever reason, Protestants seem to have been the driving force in periodical publication from its beginning in the late 17th century. This is true even in the examples of French journalism where the Huguenot writers Peter Motteux and Jean de la Crose were the chief innovators before their exile to England. The tradition of religious commentary in Protestantism, with its emphasis on the voice of the individual, may well have contributed to the direction taken by periodical writing in English; certainly the English Protestant press took Montaigne's essay in a very different direction as a model for journalism.

Further supporting this argument is the example of Scottish periodical writing, which from the 1770s became the source for the most striking new developments and which by the early 19th century had redirected and reinvigorated the form. William Smellie and Gilbert Stuart began this renaissance in periodical publication with their *Edinburgh Magazine and Review* (1773–76), which radically altered the reviewing technique then prevalent in such English magazines as the *Monthly Review* and the *Critical Review*. Smellie and Stuart wrote reviews which continued over several issues and in which they never hesitated to express their personal positions on politics and literary taste. They attacked as they criticized and created in the process a public outcry that eventually closed down their magazine. Their style, however, served as an example for the Scottish periodicals of the subsequent generation, especially the great arbiter of literary taste, the **Edinburgh Review** (1802–1929) and the mercurial and innovative **Blackwood's Edinburgh Magazine**, established by the publisher William Blackwood in 1817. Published by John Constable and edited by Francis Jeffrey, Henry Brougham, and Sydney Smith, the *Edinburgh Review* made and broke literary careers and, unlike the *Gentleman's Magazine*, openly espoused a political position. But it was *Blackwood's*, under the direction of John Gibson Lockhart, James Hogg, and John Wilson, which brought new energy to periodical publication by reviving the satirically aggressive stance of Smellie and Stuart. *Blackwood's* had a flippant, even nasty, quality to its writing which generated a significant readership and numerous libel suits, in every way reminiscent of the *Edinburgh Magazine and Review*. It also revived the dialogue journalism of early 18th-century periodicals with particular success in its "Noctes Ambrosianae," a series of fictional conversations set in a pub and touching on various issues of life and literature with each of the magazine's editors adopting a different persona. Together with John Murray's **Quarterly Review**, launched in February 1809 with Walter Scott as its chief contributor, this revival of the literary periodical at Scottish hands had its influence on England with the founding of the *London Magazine* (1820), the *Westminster Review* (1824), and *Fraser's Magazine* (1830), the forerunner of *Punch* (1841).

Increasingly in the 19th century across Europe and in the United States, speciality magazines began to define the periodical. In Britain, there were the important radical and labour publications where the political nature of the English periodical most fully expressed itself. Beginning with the anti-London activist paper the Manchester *Herald* (1792–93), the best efforts of this kind were William Cobbett's *Evening Post* (1820) and *Leader* (1850–60), the first periodical truly for the working man. In Italy, the periodical marketplace was much disrupted until well into the 19th century when three influential specialist publications took root, the *Annali di Matematica* (1867; Annals of mathematics), the *Nuovo Giornale Botanica* (1869; New botanical journal), and the *Giornale di Filologia Romanza* (Journal of romance philology), which continued to publish into the 20th century. In France, the 19th century saw the burgeoning of art periodicals, most prominently *L'Art* (1875–1907). This weekly was international in its coverage and historically inclusive. So dominant was its adjudication of public taste that it effectively marginalized Impressionism in France when it damned the movement in all its works and artists in a famous review of the crucial impressionist exhibition in 1876. *L'Art* inspired the English language periodical the *Artist* (1880–1902), a monthly directed mostly at an audience of artists and dealers to which **Oscar Wilde**, **John Ruskin**, and James McNeill Whistler contributed.

Musical periodicals have been a particular strength in German publishing from their appearance in the 19th century. Of the early examples, the most distinguished and longest running was Robert Schumann's *Neue Zeitschrift für Musik* (New journal for music), founded in 1834 and renamed *Zeitschrift für Musik* in 1920 when it was taken over by the Leipzig publisher Steingraber. Once a trendsetting periodical, it became traditional and reactionary in the 1930s. Many German musical periodicals tended to be popular publications, reflecting public taste and responding to political pressures, unlike the esoteric and specialized art magazines in France. *Die Musik*, established by Bernard Schuster in 1901, was the most successful of the periodicals intended for a wide and inclusive readership. It was remarkable for its variety and attention to jazz but was silenced for political reasons in 1934. Still, the dominant periodicals for musicology have been German and were oriented entirely toward the specialist. In the 1920s, periodicals began to treat seriously the new influences of jazz and experimental music. Of these, *Melos* was among the first to appear, launched in 1920 by the Berlin conductor Hermann Scherchen and designed to focus on contemporary music.

In the 20th century, the periodical has spread to every literate culture and has become a crucial shaper of national identities. The present format is still recognizably derived from the first efforts of Jean de la Crose, Peter Motteux, and Edward Cave, and in its unmistakably European sensibility, the periodical's worldwide proliferation is a lasting reminder of colonialism. Still, if the business of the periodical has usually been to create or impose community and identity on its readers, it is also within its power to dissolve community and recover identity. Periodicals, in this sense – whatever their apparent special interest, however obscure their literary or scientific bias, and despite the seeming eccentricity of their material – are always political organs. This is most obvious today in the editorial work of writers like the pan-African historian Paul Zeleza, founder of the *Odi*, the bilingual Malawian quarterly, and in *Brick*, the international literary magazine re-established by the Sri Lankan-Canadian Michael Ondaatje in the 1980s, which now specializes in creative nonfiction, a genre invented by Daniel Defoe.

At their best, periodicals have taken the modern genre of the essay and used its rhetoric of private scrutiny to fashion a public discourse that emulates conversation. The illusion in periodical writing is a simple but powerful one: the reader hears the voice of the essayist as part of a public dialogue which imparts an identity – social, national, professional – to all who acknowledge and participate in it. The best periodicals are eclectic in appearance only; they contain a wealth of information about the world through correspondence from many sources, but that variety is brought to uniformity by the authority of editorial opinion and political bias. The first British periodical of an international character, the *Strand* (1891–1958), with its contributions from writers across Europe, Russia, and the Americas and its combination of articles and stories, essays and fiction, was finally a testimony to the political triumph of the Commonwealth and died with the passing of that political moment. So too with the great American periodicals of the 20th century, *Harper's* (1850–), the **Atlantic Monthly** (1857–) and the **New Yorker**

(1925–) – they represent a political moment that will also pass. Essentially, the periodical is distinguished from its poor cousin the miscellany by its political identity; it is the literary expression of the European attraction to hegemonies.

STEPHEN W. BROWN

Further Reading
Bond, Donovan H., and W. Reynolds McLeod, editors, *Newsletters to Newspapers: Eighteenth-Century Journalism*, Morgantown: West Virginia University School of Journalism, 1977
Cowan, R. M. W., *The Newspaper in Scotland*, Glasgow: Outram, 1946
Downie, J. A., and Thomas N. Corns, editors, *Telling People What to Think: Early 18th-Century Periodicals from the Review to the Rambler*, London: Cass, 1993
Gardair, Jean-Michel, *Le "Giornale de' Letterati" de Rome, 1668–1681*, Florence: Olschki, 1984
Graham, Walter, *The Beginnings of English Literary Periodicals*, New York: Octagon, 1972 (original edition, 1926)
Griffiths, Dennis, editor, *The Encyclopedia of the British Press, 1422–1992*, London: Macmillan, and New York: St. Martin's Press, 1992
Harris, Michael, editor, *Journal of Newspapers and Periodical History* (1984–)
Harris, Michael, and Alan Lee, editors, *The Press in English Society from the Seventeenth to Nineteenth Centuries*, Rutherford, New Jersey: Fairleigh Dickinson University Press, and London: Associated University Presses, 1986
Hughes, Linda K., and Michael Lund, *The Victorian Serial*, Charlottesville: University Press of Virginia, 1991
Mott, Frank Luther, *A History of American Magazines*, Cambridge, Massachusetts: Harvard University Press, 5 vols., 1930–57
Rogers, Pat, *Literature and Popular Culture in Eighteenth Century England*, Brighton: Harvester Press, and Totowa, New Jersey: Barnes and Noble, 1985
Sutherland, James, *The Restoration Newspaper and Its Development*, Cambridge and New York: Cambridge University Press, 1986

Personal Essay

The personal essay is what most people mean when they consider the essay as a genre. It has the characteristics usually mentioned in defining the essay generally: an informal style, a casual, meandering structure, a conversational tone, the clear imprint of the author's personality, and a tendency toward subjects Phillip Lopate (1994) has dubbed "the familiar and the domestic, the emotional middle of the road." Most of the great essayists have been masters of the personal essay, from the genre's founder **Montaigne** onward.

It is useful to define the personal essay by comparing it to its close relations. The label is often used interchangeably with the **familiar essay**, but where the familiar essay is characterized by its everyday subject matter, the personal essay is defined more by the personality of its writer, which takes precedence over subject. On the other hand, the personal essayist does not place himself firmly center stage, as does the **autobiographical essay**ist; the autobiographical element of the personal essay is far less calculated. The writer's presence is not secondary, but his approach is usually humble, and often self-deprecating and wryly humorous. The personal essay is an exploration of self only insofar as it translates into universal experience. In the best personal essays, the reader senses what Lopate calls a "shiver of self-recognition."

The personal essay began with Montaigne, though he referred to the **letters** of **Seneca** – informal, intimate **dialogues** with the self – as influential precursors. It is Montaigne the man we look for and marvel at in his essays: his unabashed presentation of self, warts and all, and his deftness at drawing us into his experience and making it our own. His writing possesses three qualities essential to the personal essay: honesty, intimacy, and a definitive point of view. In a personal essay the reader must trust the writer to tell his story as truthfully as possible; the narrator cannot be unreliable. In addition, the writer sets up a kind of dialogue with the reader, creating an intimate bond of understanding. As Seneca addressed his letters to a friend, so Montaigne wrote with his late friend La Boétie in mind. Finally, Montaigne's strong, clear point of view permeates his essays without being didactic or self-righteous.

As with the history of the essay in general, the personal essay leapt from France to England, with some continental variations, before finding a strong place in American letters, particularly in the 20th century. It can be found in elements of the **periodical essays** of **Addison** and **Steele**, before reaching what many believe was its most glorious representation in the writings of **William Hazlitt** and, to a lesser degree, **Charles Lamb**. It was picked up by **Ralph Waldo Emerson** and **Henry David Thoreau** in mid-19th-century America, and shared in the 20th century between England and America in writers such as **Max Beerbohm**, **Virginia Woolf**, **H. L. Mencken**, **George Orwell**, **E. B. White**, **James Baldwin**, and **Joan Didion**, among many others.

Many of today's essays, particularly in the United States, are suffused with the personal; indeed, Carl Klaus (1995) has pointed out that the former courtesies and conventions of restraint in the personal essay have been all but abandoned for the practice "to speak out, to let it all hang out, to come out, to bear witness, to testify, to talk back, to be heard." Intimate self-revelation has taken the place of the kind of genteel entertainment that was all personal essayists aspired to in the past. However, Klaus believes that while discretion may have been abandoned, so has the class-consciousness of earlier generations, the linking of personality with social demeanor. The personal essay is no longer a bourgeois, middle-class phenomenon, but a truly universal expression.

The subject matter of personal essays traditionally concerns common things, tending, as Lopate puts it, toward "a taste for littleness." Human relations with family and friends is a frequent topic, as are childhood reminiscences, and the consideration of pastimes such as travel, walking, and sheer idleness. While the personal essayist often has a serious point to make, it is rare that the essay's subject will be overtly political, with the exception perhaps of Orwell, one of the few writers consistently to maintain a balance between the personal and the political.

The tone of the personal essay is usually light, often nostalgic without being sentimental, gently humorous, rarely didactic. Its finest practitioners are often middle-aged, perhaps, as Lopate suggests, "because it is the fruit of ripened experience, which naturally brings with it some worldly disenchantment, or at least realism." Its structure is rambling, intuitive and organic rather than logical and rigid. It reflects the inner, often contradictory workings of the mind; it is, as **Theodor W. Adorno** described the essay in general, a reflection of "man thinking."

One of the finest examples of the personal essay is E. B. White's classic "Once More to the Lake" (1941), also one of the most anthologized of all essays. Ostensibly a comparison of White's childhood experience at a lake in summer with a return trip to the lake he made as an adult with his young son, it is really a meditation on growing up, the passing of time, the nature of memory, and the recognition of mortality. Gentle and self-deprecating ("I guess I remembered," he undercuts himself), White is nonetheless ruthless in his recognition of his desire to be young again, to the point where he feels he cannot tell where his son's experience at the lake begins and his own ends. While the tone is light and lovingly descriptive, the essay is almost unbearably sad, without being self-pitying. Detailed in its depiction of White's boyhood memories, it is yet not exclusive but speaks to the reader of the common human experience.

Joseph Epstein (1997) describes the personal essay as the "freest form in all of literature." It "is able to take off on any tack it wishes, building its own structure as it moves along, rebuilding and remaking itself – and its author – each time out." Its continuing popularity today may stem from its being "the ideal form for ages of transition and uncertain values."

THERESA WERNER

Anthologies

The Art of the Personal Essay: An Anthology from the Classical Era to the Present, edited by Phillip Lopate, New York: Doubleday, 1994
Intimate Exile: Personal Essays, edited by Rosellen Brown, *Ploughshares* 20, nos. 2–3 (Fall 1994)
The Norton Book of Personal Essays, edited by Joseph Epstein, New York: Norton, 1997

Further Reading

Epstein, Joseph, Introduction to *The Norton Book of Personal Essays*, edited by Epstein, New York: Norton, 1997
Klaus, Carl H., "Embodying the Self: Malady and the Personal Essay," *Iowa Review* 25, no. 2 (1995): 177–92
Lopate, Phillip, Introduction to *The Art of the Personal Essay: An Anthology from the Classical Era to the Present*, edited by Lopate, New York: Doubleday, 1994
Repplier, Agnes, "The American Essay in Wartime," *Yale Review* 7, no. 2 (January 1918): 249–59
Zeiger, William, "The Personal Essay and Egalitarian Rhetoric," in *Literary Nonfiction: Theory, Criticism, Pedagogy*, edited by Chris Anderson, Carbondale: Southern Illinois University Press, 1989: 301–14

Philosophical Essay

Philosophy has been closely linked to the essay since the genre's inception. Both of the essay's founding fathers, **Michel de Montaigne** and **Francis Bacon**, attempted to endow it with a philosophical status despite the diametrically opposed stances they took in their treatment of the genre. Montaigne was the first to use the term "essay," in the title of his *Essais* (1580,

1588), not only to designate a literary composition but also to stress the significance of the term's original meaning, "trial" or "attempt." Montaigne saw the essay more as an ongoing process of discovery, while Bacon saw it more as a didactic, finished reflection – the subtitle to the latter's *Essayes* (1597, 1612, 1625) being "Practical and Moral Advice." Nonetheless, both conceived of the essay as fundamentally philosophical in nature.

This shared conception was at least in part a result of their times, which introduced extreme philosophical doubt about human nature and man's place in the universe. The end of the 16th century was marked by great political and social unrest, which saw the collapse of scientific doctrines long accepted as truths – notably, Copernicus' toppling of Ptolemaic astronomy. From the beginning, then, and indeed throughout its history, the philosophical orientation of the essay has been fundamentally a skeptical one. Not surprisingly, both Montaigne and Bacon were attracted to the philosophical doctrine of skepticism, which can be traced to the ancient philosopher Pyrrhon of Elis (c. 365–c. 270 BCE) and his disciple Sextus Empiricus (fl. c. 200 CE), whose works were published with a Latin translation by Henri Estienne in about 1560 – well within the lifetimes of both Bacon and Montaigne. The skeptics developed a systematic demonstration that man is deceived by both empirical evidence and reason. Unlike the nihilist, the skeptic reserves judgment and describes the world as a detached observer. While Montaigne's subjective presence is felt often in his practice of the essay, his fundamental skepticism led him to question human nature and the solidity of the self or a central "I" – what Descartes later called *cogito*.

According to Stanley Cavell (1988), skepticism's fundamental tenet – which underlies the philosophical essay – is paradoxical: it implies the quest for the "ordinary," the "everyday," and the "human," which at the same time it seeks to deny and transcend. With the German Romantic Jena School's conception of "fragment" as an unsystematizable form of writing, the essay becomes even more closely associated with skepticism's contradictory tendencies. German Romantics, notably **Friedrich Schlegel**, wrote extensively on skepticism and the fragment. Indeed, Schlegel's notion of "fragment" bears a striking affinity to the essay. Philippe Lacoue-Labarthe and Jean-Luc Nancy (1988) maintain in their reading of Schlegel's *Athenäum* fragments (1798–1800) that the fragment, like the essay, reflects a similar paradox: "subjective" and "objective" modes are virtually inextricable. This conflation of opposites has its roots in the Romantics' notion that writing is meant to enact its subject.

Writing in the mid- to late 19th century, **Ralph Waldo Emerson** and **Friedrich Nietzsche** were heavily indebted to the Romantic Jena School tradition, and both continued to link the essay with the fragment and with unsystematic philosophy. According to Emerson, every superior being "belongs" to the skeptical class which Montaigne represents. Like skepticism, which attempts to maintain a "middle ground" between extremes, transcendentalism aimed to find a balance between realism and idealism, and thus fuse the everyday with the sublime. Much influenced by Emerson's "skeptical" spirit, Nietzsche's aphoristic writings bear striking similarities to both the fragment and the essay. Indeed, Zarathustra, Nietzsche's "alter-ego," seems to embody skepticism with his *Ja-sagen*,

which is neither affirmation nor negation, but which belongs to a paradoxical third category that shuns extremes as well as definitions. Following the German Romantics' example, both Emerson and Nietzsche conceived of content and form as a single entity, and their writings as the very enactment of their lives. For Emerson, the essay was "*essaying to be*": it was the enactment of the process of accommodation between the world and the "I," and thus it became the act of consciousness realizing itself. Similarly, in Nietzsche's work, form and content remain inextricable, and the writer/philosopher becomes inseparable from Zarathustra.

In the 20th century, the philosophical essay has moved further away from ideas of the self, and become more critical and more self-conscious, in so far as it is obsessed with language, discourse, and methodology. The broader intellectual context of the modern essay is no longer that of Montaigne's times, nor even that of Emerson's and Nietzsche's. Whereas Montaigne refused to separate himself from method, or the living subject from the experienced object, the modern essay is much more fragmented and attenuated. Schooled in the German Romantic tradition, and writing before and after World War I, Central European writers such as **Robert Musil**, Rudolf Kassner, **Georg Lukács**, and **Georg Simmel** conceived the essay as the perfect synthesis of seemingly contradictory elements such as form and content, science and art, and ethics and aesthetics. To them, the essay had to fulfill a "sacred" mission: to provide the world with a spiritual orientation it had long been lacking. In *Die Seelen und die Formen* (1911; *Soul and Form*), written before he joined the Communist Party, Lukács maintained that the essayist is by nature a precursor to a greater figure or system, a John the Baptist who goes out to preach in the wilderness about another who is yet to come. According to Lukács, the modern essayist can no longer pose his questions directly, as Montaigne did, but must necessarily use a "mediating medium." In other words, he must consider all the ways *others* pose their questions before formulating his own. By underlining this preoccupation with style and methodology, Lukács linked the modern essay with criticism, and raised a debate that continues today – between those who view the essay as art and those who view it as criticism.

This debate on the status of the essay has, in turn, stimulated two divergent schools of thought – the Frankfurt School of the mid-20th century, and the French poststructuralists of the late 20th century. Both groups reject Lukács' Hegelian-Marxist validation of totality and system, and conceive the modern, philosophical essay more as a fragmentary mode that refuses the ontological priorities of systems and their privileging of the timeless over the historical, and the universal over the particular. Although the two schools continue the essay's philosophical tradition, they diverge mainly in their respective views of essayistic "fragmentation." For the German theorists, such as **Walter Benjamin** and **Theodor W. Adorno**, still working, in a sense, within a humanist-idealist tradition, the fragmentary nature of the essay serves to decenter the self, so that the subject may experience the object without dominating it. For the French poststructuralists, however, who take this process a step further, essayistic fragmentation serves to eliminate all vestiges of Cartesianism and humanism from the text. Indeed, they pronounce the subject anachronistic, and the author dead.

While the German thinkers ascribe to the essay the heroic role of defending critical and creative thought against reason, as embodied in systems, the French have resisted identifying their writings with any established genres, questioning even the very notion of genre. Indeed, they have at times distanced themselves from the essay especially, mistrusting a discourse that encourages self-representation, whether in the traditional role of the Cartesian *cogito*, or in the more congenial guise of Montaigne's essays. Despite such objections, the French theorists, as well as the Frankfurt School thinkers, still belong in the tradition of the philosophical essay. Indeed, it is revealing that both Michel Foucault and **Roland Barthes**, who criticized bourgeois individualism in their early works, made the self a central concern in their late works. Both paid a final homage to the essay as well. Foucault, for example, describes the essay, in *L'Usage des plaisirs* (1984; Use of pleasure), as the "living substance of philosophy ... an exercise of oneself in the activity of thought."

With its avowed fragmentariness and its unmethodological method, the philosophical essay is inherently a pluralistic and interdisciplinary genre. At once art and criticism, literature and philosophy, imagination and reason, its task is not to stay within well-charted boundaries, nor to shuttle back and forth across these boundaries, but rather to reflect on and to challenge them.

ALINA C. HUNT

Further Reading

Adorno, Theodor W., "The Essay as Form," *New German Critique* 32 (Spring 1984): 151–71 (original German article published 1954)

Atkins, Douglas G., *Estranging the Familiar: Toward a Revitalized Critical Writing*, Athens: University of Georgia Press, 1992

Butrym, Alexander J., editor, *Essays on the Essay: Redefining the Genre*, Athens: University of Georgia Press, 1989

Cavell, Stanley, *In Quest of the Ordinary: Lines of Skepticism and Romanticism*, Chicago: University of Chicago Press, 1988

Harrison, Thomas, *Essayism: Conrad, Musil, and Pirandello*, Baltimore: Johns Hopkins University Press, 1992

Jay, Martin, *The Dialectical Imagination: A History of the Frankfurt School and the Institute of Social Research, 1923–1950*, Boston: Little Brown, and London: Heinemann, 1973

Joeres, Ruth-Ellen Boetcher, and Elizabeth Mittman, editors, *The Politics of the Essay: Feminist Perspectives*, Bloomington: Indiana University Press, 1993

Lacoue-Labarthe, Philippe, and Jean-Luc Nancy, *The Literary Absolute: The Theory of Literature in German Romanticism*, Albany: State University of New York Press, 1988

Lukács, Georg, *Soul and Form*, Cambridge, Massachusetts: MIT Press, 1974 (original German edition, 1911)

Snyder, John, *Prospects of Power: Tragedy, Satire, the Essay and the Theory of Genre*, Lexington: University Press of Kentucky, 1991

The Physiology of Taste

by Brillat-Savarin, 1825

Jean-Anthelme Brillat-Savarin (1755–1826) is known almost exclusively as the author of the witty and urbane *Physiologie du goût* (1825; The Physiology of Taste). He was a lawyer and judge by profession, and his previous work included an essay on political economy (*Vues et projets d'économie*

politique [1802; Views and projects of political economy]), one on legal theory (*Fragments d'une théorie judiciaire* [1808; Fragments of a judicial theory]), and another on duelling (*Essai historique et critique sur le duel* [1819; Historical and critical essay on the duel]). While intelligent and erudite, these writings enjoyed little contemporary success, and are virtually forgotten today.

For the last quarter of his life, however, he had worked in near total secrecy on another project. In late 1825, a few months before his death, Brillat-Savarin published his magnum opus – anonymously, at his own expense, and to the great surprise of even his closest friends. Entitled *Physiologie du goût; ou, Méditation de gastronomie transcendante* (*The Physiology of Taste; or, Meditations on Transcendental Gastronomy*), it soon became immensely popular; numerous editions have followed, in many languages. Brillat-Savarin's influence has likewise been enormous. For better or worse, his example has, in large measure, spawned the innumerable volumes of "food writing" which now crowd the shelves of bookstores.

As its full title suggests, Brillat-Savarin's essay pretends to be both a scientific treatise (*physiologie*) and a philosophical rumination (*méditation*). With mock seriousness, the self-proclaimed "professor" tries his hand at codifying the new "science" of gastronomy, and in so doing touches upon an astounding variety of subjects related to food, its preparation, consumption, and, most of all, enjoyment. Indeed, little seems to escape Brillat-Savarin's omnivorous pen: from the culinary eccentricities of ancient Rome, to the effects of different foods on dreams, to the best way to cook an unusually large turbot.

The *Physiology* opens with four introductory sections, including "Aphorisms of the Professor" and "The Author's Preface." The main body of the essay is made up of 30 "meditations" (e.g. "On Appetite"; "Theory of Frying"; "On Gourmandism"). These are followed, in turn, by a brief "Transition," a substantial section of "Varieties" and, finally, a "Parting Salute to the Gastronomers of the Old and New Worlds."

Brillat-Savarin's opening **aphorism**s – billed as "a preamble to his work and ... a lasting foundation for the science of gastronomy" – have indeed remained the best-known and most-quoted part of the *Physiology*. Twenty in all, they include such perennial favorites as "Tell me what you eat, and I shall tell you what you are." In the "Author's Preface," Brillat-Savarin deals, most notably, with his style: while asking indulgence for his digressiveness and "garrulity," he begs not to be considered a simple "compiler"; he also defends his frequent use of foreign words and neologisms.

Most of Brillat-Savarin's 30 **meditation**s are made up of several smaller sections (e.g. "Definition of Taste," "Turkey Lovers," "Inevitable Longevity of Gourmands"). Typically, a meditation proceeds from ostensibly serious, scholarly-sounding developments on the history and theory of gastronomy (entitled "Origin ..." "Definition ..." or "Analysis ..."), to more lighthearted, digressive, and often autobiographical musings (entitled "Anecdote," "Reflection," "Sketch," or "Portrait"). This tendency informs the entire *Physiology* as well, for even when Brillat-Savarin's prose seems at its most serious, a wellspring of mirth lies just beneath the surface. Finally, in the "Varieties," Brillat-Savarin abandons any "scientific" pretense, unleashing a veritable flood of witty observations, amusing anecdotes, and other such *hors d'œuvre*. As he explains, these could not fit into his earlier, "theoretical" expositions, but are entertaining and worth writing nonetheless. No doubt the most emblematic of these wide-ranging and thoroughly heterogeneous "Varieties" is a brief section entitled, simply, "Miscellanea."

In its digressiveness, its amiable verbosity, and its largely unsystematic encyclopedism, Brillat-Savarin's *Physiology* belongs to a French tradition of the essay beginning with **Montaigne**. As a supposedly "scientific" and "philosophical" treatise, moreover, it parodies influential works by certain late 18th- and early 19th-century thinkers. These include, most notably, the Enlightenment sensationalist Étienne Bonnet de Condillac's *Traité des sensations* (1754; *Treatise on the Sensations*), which owes a great deal to Locke, and the *idéologue* P. J. G. Cabanis' *Rapports du physique et du moral de l'homme* (1802; *On the Relationship Between the Physical and Moral Aspects of Man*), which seeks to ground psychology in physiology.

Written at a time when cooking was becoming increasingly professionalized, and when the restaurant was becoming a major force in French culture, the *Physiology* also belongs to an emerging body of writing on culinary arts and gastronomy: from Karl Friedrich von Rumohr's *Geist der Kochkunst* (1823; *The Essence of Cookery*) to Marie-Antonin Carême's *L'Art de la cuisine française au XIXe siècle* (1828; The art of French cooking in the 19th century) to Alexandre Dumas' *Grand Dictionnaire de cuisine* (1873; *Dictionary of Cuisine*), to name but a few. Yet the author to whom Brillat-Savarin is most often compared remains the nearly forgotten Alexandre-Balthazar-Laurent Grimod de la Reynière, who wrote *Le Manuel des amphitryons* (1808; The almanac of Amphytryons) and *L'Almanach des gourmands* (1803; The almanac of gourmands), and edited a short-lived *Journal des gourmands et des belles* (Journal of gourmands and beauties) years before the *Physiology of Taste* was published. While commentators generally hail Grimod's originality as the inventor of new forms (i.e. the gastronomic treatise, guide, and periodical), Brillat-Savarin is considered by far the superior stylist.

Indeed, from the 19th century to the present, Brillat-Savarin has often been celebrated for his style. Balzac (1835) attributes the *Physiology*'s rapid success to the "savor" (*saveur*) of its style; **M. F. K. Fisher**, in the introduction to her 1949 translation, admires the "simplicity" and "restrained discretion" of Brillat-Savarin's "straightforward" yet gently "tongue in cheek" style; **Roland Barthes** (1975) characterizes the professor's language as "gourmande"; and Jean-François Revel (1982) hails his discovery of an "amiable style." Yet to see Brillat-Savarin solely as a stylist is to underestimate the philosophical depth of his work. Gastronomy, for Brillat-Savarin, is an eminently *human* pursuit: eating for pleasure, not just sustenance, is what separates us from the beasts. In the largest sense, then, *The Physiology of Taste* is an eloquent apology of epicureanism, a celebration of *savoir-vivre* – the art of living well. It is that most rare of books, for, as M. F. K. Fisher wrote in 1949, it succeeds in articulating "a well-balanced expression of one thinking man's attitude toward life."

MICHAEL D. GARVAL

Editions

Physiologie du goût; ou, Méditation de gastronomie transcendante, 1825; many subsequent editions, including those edited by Michel Guibert, 1975, and Jean-François Revel, 1982; translated under many titles, including *The Handbook of Dining* (1859), *Gastronomy as a Fine Art* (1877), *A Handbook of Gastronomy* (1884), and *The Philosopher in the Kitchen* (1970), but most often as *The Physiology of Taste; or, Transcendental Gastronomy*, translated by Fayette Robinson, 1854, and as *The Physiology of Taste; or, Meditations on Transcendental Gastronomy*, translated by M. F. K. Fisher, 1949

Further Reading

Balzac, Honoré de, "Brillat-Savarin (Extrait de la Biographie Universelle, tome 59)," in *Œuvres complètes*, vol. 23, Paris: Club de l'Honnête Homme, 1956 (original piece, 1835)

Barthes, Roland, "Lecture de Brillat-Savarin," in *Physiologie du goût* by Brillat-Savarin, edited by Michel Guibert, Paris: Hermann, 1975

Boissel, Thierry, *Brillat-Savarin, 1755–1826: Un chevalier candide*, Paris: Presses de la Renaissance, 1989

MacDonogh, Giles, *Brillat-Savarin: The Judge and His Stomach*, London: Murray, and Chicago: Dee, 1992

Revel, Jean-François, "Brillat-Savarin ou le style aimable," introduction to *Physiologie du goût* by Brillat-Savarin, Paris: Flammarion, 1982

Picón-Salas, Mariano

Venezuelan, 1901–1965

Before Mariano Picón-Salas, the Venezuelan literary tradition had produced several prominent essayists: **Andrés Bello**, Simón Rodríguez, Rufino Blanco Fombona, and Manuel Díaz Rodríguez. As was the case with his predecessors, not only did Picón-Salas attempt to reconcile nationalistic and purely aesthetic concerns in his work, but his direct involvement in politics proved to be decisive for the evolution of his career. When he was a young man, his liberal convictions strengthened in response to the atrocities of Juan Vicente Gómez's dictatorship (1909–35). In 1922, escaping the repressive and stagnant atmosphere of his homeland, Picón-Salas settled in Chile, where he obtained an advanced degree in history and later worked as a university professor until Gómez's death. This first international experience gave the young writer a truly continental scope, which continued to expand throughout his life. In 1948, he had to abandon Venezuela again after the overthrow of Rómulo Gallegos and, once democracy was restored years later, served as ambassador to Mexico, UNESCO, and Brazil.

Picón-Salas' works may be roughly defined by setting them within a Latin American literary and artistic trend that prevailed from the 1910s to the 1950s and has been called *mundonovismo* (from *Nuevo Mundo* – "New World") by some critics or, simply, *americanismo* ("Latin Americanism"). At the end of the Hispanic Modernist era (which began in the 1880s and started to decline in 1916, after the death of its leader, **Rubén Darío**), some poets and prose writers felt the need to compensate for what they considered to be an excessive cosmopolitanism among the Modernists. The *mundonovistas*' reaction against what they saw as escapism, occasional political indifference, and egotistical distance from the problems of the Latin American masses was full of irony, and they soon tried to distinguish themselves from their predecessors by depicting Modernists as irresponsible inhabitants of ivory towers. In contrast, the *mundonovistas* described themselves as incarnations of the voice of the people or as pedagogues whose basic aim was to educate their fellow countrymen and prepare them for modern political reform and material progress. As simplistic as this ideology may sound, it was sometimes combined with true stylistic mastery or solid erudition. In fact, some of the most respectable Spanish American writers in the first half of the 20th century were, at one time or another, *mundonovistas*, including the novelists José Eustasio Rivera and Ricardo Güiraldes, the poets Gabriela Mistral, Nicolás Guillén, and Pablo Neruda, and the essayists **Alfonso Reyes**, **Pedro Henríquez Ureña**, **José Carlos Mariátegui**, and **Eduardo Mallea**. Rómulo Gallegos' novels, as well as Arturo Uslar Pietri's and Picón-Salas' essays, are the best Venezuelan contributions to a movement that deeply shaped the first half of the 20th century in all of Latin America.

The topics chosen by Picón-Salas were always related to the definition of a continental identity, a goal he sometimes attained by portraying exemplary historical personages, as in *Miranda* (1946), *Pedro Claver: El santo de los esclavos* (1950; Pedro Claver: the saint of the slaves), and *Simón Rodríguez* (1953). At times he studied aspects of an isolated nationality, as in *Intuición de Chile* (1935; Intuiting Chile), *Comprensión de Venezuela* (1949; Understanding Venezuela), and *Gusto de México* (1952; Savoring Mexico). Finally, he tried to grasp the totality of the New World essence in classic essays such as *De la Conquista a la Independencia: Tres siglos de historia cultural latinoamericana* (1944; *A Cultural History of Spanish America, from Conquest to Independence*) and *Europa-América: Preguntas a la esfinge de la cultura* (1947; Europe/America: questions for the sphinx of culture).

Although his first book, *Buscando el camino* (1920; In search of a path), was still permeated by the *modernista* exquisiteness of vocabulary and syntax, Picón-Salas' work opposes the egocentrism he attributed to the turn-of-the-century intellectuals. Interestingly enough, his belief that the essayist must act as a social conscience soon clashed with his own conception of the essay as a genre. In fact, on some occasions Picón-Salas acknowledged **Montaigne** as the *patrono de los ensayistas* (patron saint of the essayists), which forced him to try to explain why the French author insisted on referring to his inner world. This desperate endeavor produced shallow and unconvincing conclusions in short texts such as "En torno al ensayo" (1954; On the essay), where Picón-Salas asserts that "Montaigne described in himself the supreme chaos of his time." It is, however, precisely the tension Picón-Salas felt between his private life and his public obligations that fuels the volume considered to be his masterpiece, *Regreso de tres mundos* (1959; Returning from three worlds), an autobiographical essay that synthesizes his philosophy and his Latin Americanist passion. In this work the representation of the essayistic "I" splits into many different subpersonalities that do not always co-exist harmoniously: the young man from the Venezuelan Andes, the human being, the intellectual, the man from the 20th century, the ambassador, and others. The result is a poignant and dramatic polyphony of viewpoints that

surprisingly subverts the monotonous magisterial attitudes typical of other *mundonovistas* less concerned about the contradictions inherent in their aesthetics.

Juan Liscano, Francisco Rivera, Guillermo Sucre, and Óscar Rodríguez Ortiz, the best Venezuelan essayists of the second half of the 20th century, have always avoided assuming the role of the voice of the people, perhaps taking into account the problematic example set earlier by Picón-Salas, who, nevertheless, is still revered as one of the most influential writers Venezuela has produced.

MIGUEL GOMES

Biography

Born 26 January 1901 in Mérida. Studied privately with a tutor; studied law at the Central University of Venezuela, Caracas, 1920–22; moved to Chile, 1922, living in Santiago for 13 years; studied history in Santiago. Librarian and history professor. Returned to Caracas, 1936. Appointed chargé d'affaires, Prague, 1936–37. Professor in Santiago, 1937–38. Lived in Caracas for four years. Founder and editor, *Revista Nacional de Cultura* (National review of culture); also contributed to *El Nacional*, *Cultura Universitaria*, *Sardio*, and other journals and newspapers. Traveled to the United States and taught at various colleges and universities, 1942–44. Founder, Faculty of Philosophy and Letters, Central University of Venezuela, Caracas, 1946. Venezuelan ambassador to Colombia, 1947–48, Brazil, 1958–59, UNESCO, Paris, 1959–62, and Mexico, 1962. Organized founding of the Instituto Nacional de Cultura y Bellas Artes (National institute of culture and fine arts), Caracas, 1964 (founded 1965 after his death). Awards: National Prize for Literature, 1954. Member, National Academy of History. Died in Caracas, 1 January 1965.

Selected Writings

Essays and Related Prose
Buscando el camino, 1920
Hispano-América, posición crítica, 1931
Intuición de Chile y otros ensayos en busca de una conciencia histórica, 1935
Formación y proceso de la literatura venezolana, 1940
1941: Cinco discursos sobre pasado y presente de la nación venezolana, 1940
De la Conquista a la Independencia: Tres siglos de historia cultural latinoamericana, 1944; as *A Cultural History of Spanish America, from Conquest to Independence*, translated by Irving A. Leonard, 1962
Europa-América: Preguntas a la esfinge de la cultura, 1947
Comprensión de Venezuela, 1949; revised edition, 1955
Dependencia e independencia en la historia hispanoamericana, 1952
Gusto de México, 1952
Suramérica, 1953
Crisis, cambio, tradición: Ensayos sobre la forma de nuestra cultura, 1955
Ensayos escogidos, edited by Juan Loveluck, 1958
Regreso de tres mundos: Un hombre en su generación, 1959
Los malos salvajes: Civilización y política contemporáneas, 1962; as *The Ignoble Savages*, translated by Herbert Weinstock, 1965
Hora y deshora: Temas humanísticos, Nombres y figuras, Viajes y lugares, 1963
Suma de Venezuela: Antología de páginas venezolanas, 1966
Viejos y Nuevos Mundos, edited by Guillermo Sucre, 1983
Las formas y las visiones: Ensayos sobre arte, edited by Juan Carlos Palenzuela, 1984

Other writings: novels, works on Spanish American cultural history, three biographies, travel, and autobiography.

Further Reading

Azzario, Esther A., *La prosa autobiográfica de Mariano Picón-Salas*, Caracas: Equinoccio, 1980

Gomes, Miguel, *Poéticas del ensayo venezolano del siglo XX*, Cranston, Rhode Island: Inti, 1996: 121–38

Morin, Thomas D., *Mariano Picón Salas*, Boston: Twayne, 1979

Rodríguez Ortiz, Óscar, "Picón Salas y la imaginación del presente," in *Placebo*, Caracas: Fundarte, 1990: 74–80

Rosenblat, Ángel, "Mariano Picón-Salas: El estilo y el hombre," *Thesaurus* 20 (1965): 201–12

Sucre, Guillermo, Prologue to *Viejos y Nuevos Mundos* by Picón-Salas, Caracas: Ayacucho, 1983: ix–xli

Uslar Pietri, Arturo, "El regreso de los mundos de Mariano Picón-Salas," in his *En busca del Nuevo Mundo*, Mexico City: Fondo de Cultura Económica, 1969: 161–67

Plato

Greek, c. 429/427–347 BCE

If Plato is unambiguously one of the greatest philosophers in history, his relation to the art of prose is paradoxical. In **dialogues** such as the *Protagoras* and *Gorgias*, he expresses his suspicion of rhetoric. Yet throughout his works, he demonstrates a masterful command of rhetorical modes, figures, and register, from the formal oration to the colloquial conversation. In works such as the *Ion* and the second and third books of the *Republic*, he attacks the power and pretension of literature. Yet his works are realistic dramas, choreographing action and dialogue with the fluency of a playwright. Out of the historical Socrates, he creates one of the most memorable and well-formed characters in Western literature. Finally, in works such as the *Cratylus* and *Phaedrus*, he articulates his mistrust of written language. Yet Plato was one of the best stylists of classical Attic Greek prose. Even long works such as the *Republic* show the care and intricacy of a sonnet. Noting that Plato had a reputation for revision, the ancient critic Dionysus of Halicarnassus observed wryly that "up to his eightieth year Plato never ceased combing and curling and every way braiding his own dialogues."

The dialogue developed out of Plato's ambivalence about the limits of written language. The genre imitates the form of the dialectic, preserving the dynamic and open-ended character of conversation. One ancient commentator noted that "just as dialectic compels the soul to reveal the labors it undergoes . . . so also the dialogue may compel the reader to assent to the things said . . ." At the same time, it allows Plato to explore issues while suspending any final judgment on his own part. Plato himself is noticeably absent in most of the dialogues.

Plato's philosophical and literary activities extend over a period of 50 years. His works fall into two categories: the **letters** and the dialogues. Of the letters, 13 are extant. Most are addressed to Dionysus the Tyrant of Syracuse, or to Dionysus' son and successor, Dion, and are concerned with political advice and Plato's aspirations for creating a philosopher-king. Of the dialogues, 26 can be firmly attributed to Plato, with several others of questionable authorship. Looking at shifts in philosophical doctrine and stylistic evidence, scholars divide them loosely into three periods, roughly bounded by his voyages from Athens to Sicily. Thus the *Apologia*, *Crito*, *Laches*, *Lysis*, *Charmides*, *Euthyphro*, *Hippias minor*, *Protagoras*, *Gorgias*, *Ion*, and perhaps *Hippias major* belong to the early period before his first trip around 387 BCE. The *Meno*, *Phaedo*, *Republic*, *Symposium*, *Phaedrus*, *Euthydemus*, *Menexenus*, and *Cratylus* belong to the middle period, the years of the Academy from 388 to 367 BCE. The late period falls between a second trip to Sicily around 367 and a third trip around 361, and includes the *Parmenides*, *Theaetetus*, *Sophist*, *Politicus* (*Statesman*), *Timaeus*, *Critias*, *Philebus*, and *Laws*.

The dialogues of the first period generally feature Socrates in debate with some antagonist. These tend to focus on moral issues, in which the interlocutor, after whom the dialogue is named, makes a statement, and is then interrogated by Socrates. They are marked by the use of argument and counterargument, and represent the purest form of the Socratic method, the elenctic debate, a *via negationis* in which Socrates moves toward some understanding or truth by determining what he does not know, even if he cannot establish with certainty what he does know. Both the method and the moral themes closely reflect those attributed to the historical Socrates, but even at this early stage Plato plays an active role in shaping the material. This is evident, for example, when one compares Plato's version of the *Apology*, Socrates' defense of himself, with the account given by Xenophon.

The dialogues of the middle period take on a different tone. The animated and often hostile format of the debate gives way to more leisurely conversations. In turn, Socratic ignorance and dialectic give way to long stretches of exposition. The *Symposium*, for instance, Plato's famous examination of love, is in the form of a succession of encomia by a group of friends at a drinking party. Although morality and virtue are important, these dialogues are more concerned with metaphysical issues, including an examination of love, language, and the afterlife. They also develop Plato's theory of forms (or ideas). The work of the third period extends the tendencies of the middle period; the figure of Socrates moves to the background in the *Sophist* and the *Politicus*, and disappears altogether in the *Laws*, replaced by an interlocutor simply identified as "the Athenian." In these late works, Plato is primarily concerned with questions of knowledge, and a critical re-examination of his early ontological doctrines.

The importance of Plato's dialogues was recognized almost immediately. References and allusions to almost every one of them can be found among ancient writers. More importantly, Plato's dialogues created the genre, influencing all subsequent philosophical dialogues from **Cicero**'s *Tusculanae disputationes* (47–44 BCE), Thomas More's *Utopia* (1516), and George Berkeley's *Three Dialogues Between Hylas and Philonus* (1713), to **Giacomo Leopardi**'s *Operette morali* (1827; *Essays and Dialogues*), to mention some of the best. While this genre has spawned many imitators, none has surpassed Plato's command of language, the profundity of his thought, or the power of his dramatic invention. If Plato is one of the greatest philosophers, he is also one of the most eloquent.

THOMAS L. COOKSEY

See also Classical Influences

Biography

Born c. 429–427 BCE probably in Athens (possibly in Aegina). Met Socrates c. 407 and became his disciple; after Socrates' execution, 399, Plato went with other Socratic disciples to Megara, then traveled for 12 years, visiting Egypt, Sicily, 390–388, where he met Dionysius I of Syracuse, and Italy, where he met Archytas of Tarentum; began teaching pupils near the grove of Academus outside Athens, 388, and continued until his death; summoned to court of Dionysius II of Syracuse by Dion, the ruler's uncle, 366–365, and by Dionysius II himself, 362–361. Died in Athens in 347 BCE.

Selected Writings

Essays and Related Prose (dialogues in chronological order)

Hippias minor, edited by George Smith, 1895; translated by Floyer Sydenham, 1767, and Robin Waterfield, 1987

Hippias major (authorship questionable), edited by Dorothy Tarrant, 1928; translated by Floyer Sydenham, 1767, Paul Woodruff, 1982, and Robin Waterfield, 1987

Laches, edited by M. T. Tatham, 1888 (reprinted 1966), and F. G. Plaistowe, translated by T. R. Mills, 1898; translated by W. R. M. Lamb (Loeb Edition), 1924, Rosamund Kent Sprague, 1973, and Iain Lane, 1987

Charmides, edited by Richard F. Hipwell, 1951; translated by Rosamund Kent Sprague, 1973, T. G. and G. S. West, 1986, and Donald Watt, 1987

Ion, edited by George Smith, 1895, St. George Stock, 1909, and J. M. Macgregor, 1912; translated by Percy Bysshe Shelley, in *The Banquet of Plato and Other Pieces*, 1887, W. R. M. Lamb (Loeb Edition), 1925, Lane Cooper, 1938, W. H. D. Rouse, 1956, Paul Woodruff, 1983, and Trevor J. Saunders, 1987

Protagoras, edited by James and A. M. Adam, 1981; several translations, including by W. R. M. Lamb (Loeb Edition), 1924, W. K. C. Guthrie, 1956, B. A. F. Hubbard, 1982, Patrick Coby, 1987, and Stanley Lombardo and Karen Bell, 1992

Euthyphro, edited by C. E. Graves, revised edition, 1935, and C. J. Emlyn-Jones, 1991; several translations, including by Lane Cooper, 1941, Basil Wrighton, 1948, W. D. Woodhead, 1953, John Warrington, 1963, R. E. Allen, 1970, and G. M. A. Grube, 1986

Apologia, edited by Edward Henry Blakeney, 1929, Robin Barrow, 1977, and John Burnet, 1977; many translations, including by Lane Cooper, 1941, Basil Wrighton, 1948, W. H. D. Rouse, 1956, John Warrington, 1963, R. E. Allen, 1980, G. M. A. Grube, 1986, and Thomas C. Brickhouse, 1989

Crito, edited by John Burnet, 1977, and James Adam, 1988; many translations, including by Lane Cooper, 1941, Basil Wrighton, 1948, W. H. D. Rouse, 1956, John Warrington, 1963, A. D. Woozley, 1979, R. E. Allen, 1980, and G. M. A. Grube, 1986

Phaedo, edited by C. J. Rowe, 1994; many translations, including by Lane Cooper, 1941, Basil Wrighton, 1948, G. M. A. Grube, 1977, John Burnet, 1979, and R. Larson, 1980

Gorgias, edited by E. R. Dodds, 1959, revised edition, 1990; translated by W. R. M. Lamb (Loeb Edition), 1932, Lane Cooper, 1938, W. Hamilton, 1960, Terence Irwin, 1980, and D. J. Zeyl, 1986

Meno, edited by R. S. Bluck, 1961, and A. Sesonske and N. Fleming, 1965; several translations, including by W. R. M. Lamb (Loeb Edition), 1924, W. K. C. Guthrie, 1956, W. H. D. Rouse, 1956, R. W. Sharples, 1985, and G. M. A. Grube, 1986

Lysis, translated by W. R. M. Lamb (Loeb Edition), 1932, David Bolotin, 1979, Donald Watt, 1987, and Benjamin Jowett and E. O'Connor, 1991

Menexenus, edited and translated by T. R. Mills, 1902; several translations, including by Percy Bysshe Shelley, in *The Banquet of Plato and Other Pieces*, 1887, and A. S. Way, 1934

Euthydemus, edited by G. H. Wells, 1881, and E. H. Gifford, 3 vols., 1905; translated by W. R. M. Lamb, 1924, Rosamund Kent Sprague, 1972, and Robin Waterfield, 1987

Cratylus, edited by G. Pasquali, 1908; translated by Thomas Taylor, 1793

Symposium, edited by R. G. Bury, 1973, and K. J. Dover, 1980; many translations, including by W. R. M. Lamb (Loeb Edition), 1932, Lane Cooper, 1938, W. H. D. Rouse, 1956, R. Larson, 1980, Tom Griffith, 1986, A. Nehamas and Paul Woodruff, 1989, R. E. Allen, 1991, and Robin Waterfield, 1994

Republic, edited by James Adam, revised by D. A. Rees, 2 vols., 1963, and Allan Bloom, 1968; several translations, including by P. Shorey (Loeb Edition), 2 vols., 1930–35, W. H. D. Rouse, 1956, I. A. Richards, 1966, G. M. A. Grube, 1974, revised by C. D. C. Reeve, 1992, Richard W. Sterling and William C. Scott, 1985, and Robin Waterfield, 1993

Parmenides, translated by A. E. Taylor, 1934, Francis M. Cornford, 1939, John Warrington, 1961, R. E. Allen, 1983, and Glenn R. Morrow and John M. Dillon, 1987

Theaetetus, edited by Lewis Campbell, 2nd edition, 1883; several translations, including by H. N. Fowler (Loeb Edition), 1921, Seth Benardete, 1986, and Robin Waterfield, 1987

Phaedrus, edited by W. H. Thompson, 1868; several translations, including by Lane Cooper, 1938, Robin Waterfield, 1982, and C. J. Rowe, 1986

Sophist, translated by H. N. Fowler (Loeb Edition), 1921, Francis M. Cornford, 1935, A. E. Taylor, 1961, John Warrington, 1961, and Seth Benardete, 1986

Statesman, translated by H. N. Fowler (Loeb Edition), 1925, A. E. Taylor, 1961, John Warrington, 1961, and Seth Benardete, 1986; as *Politicus*, translated by J. B. Skemp, 1952

Philebus, translated by F. Sydenham, 1767, R. Hackforth, 1945, A. E. Taylor, 1956, J. C. B. Gosling, 1975, and Robin Waterfield, 1982

Timaeus, edited by Christopher Gill, 1980; several translations, including by R. G. Bury (Loeb Edition), 1929, A. E. Taylor, 1929, Francis M. Cornford, 1937, and John Warrington, 1965

Critias, edited by C. Gill, 1981; translated by A. E. Taylor, 1929, and H. D. P. Lee, 1971

Laws, edited by E. B. England, 2 vols., 1921; translated by R. G. Bury (Loeb Edition), 2 vols., 1926, A. E. Taylor, 1934, Trevor S. Saunders, 1970, and Thomas L. Pangle, 1988

[Dialogues], edited by John Burnet, 5 vols., 1900–07; edited and translated by R. E. Allen, 3 vols., 1985–96; translated by Benjamin Jowett, 4 vols., 1868–71, Henry Cary, 1900, H. N. Fowler and others (Loeb Edition), 12 vols., 1914–29; *Collected Dialogues* (including *Letters*), edited by Edith Hamilton and Huntington Cairns, translated by Lane Cooper and others, 1961

The Portable Plato (selected dialogues), translated by Benjamin Jowett, 1948; edited by Scott M. Buchanan, 1977

The Death of Socrates: An Interpretation of the Platonic Dialogues, translated by Basil Wrighton, 1948

Socratic Dialogues (selection), edited and translated by W. D. Woodhead, 1953

Great Dialogues of Plato, edited by Eric H. Warmington and Philip G. Rouse, translated by W. H. D. Rouse, 1967; revised edition, 1970

Five Dialogues, translated by G. M. A. Grube, 1986

Early Socratic Dialogues, edited by Trevor J. Saunders, translated by Saunders, Iain Lane, Donald Watt, and Robin Waterfield, 1987

The Roots of Political Philosophy: Ten Forgotten Socratic Dialogues, edited and translated by Thomas L. Pangle, 1987

Collected works editions: *Works*, translated by Thomas Taylor and Floyer Sydenham, 5 vols., 1804, reprinted 1995– (in progress); *Platonis opere* (Clarendon Edition), edited by E. A. Duke and others, 1995– (in progress).

Bibliographies

McKirahan, Richard D., *Plato and Socrates: A Comprehensive Bibliography, 1958–1973*, New York: Garland, 1978

Saunders, Trevor J., *A Bibliography on Plato's "Laws," 1920–1970, with Additional Citations Through May 1975*, New York: Arno Press, 1976

Further Reading

Brandwood, Leonard, *The Chronology of Plato's Dialogues*, Cambridge: Cambridge University Press, 1990

Brickhouse, Thomas C., and Nicholas D. Smith, *Plato's Socrates*, New York and Oxford: Oxford University Press, 1994

Frede, M., "Plato's Arguments and the Dialogue Form," in *Oxford Studies in Ancient Philosophy*, supplement, edited by Julia Annas and Robert H. Grimm, Oxford: Clarendon Press, and New York: Oxford University Press, 1988: 201–19

Friedländer, Paul, *Plato: An Introduction*, Princeton, New Jersey: Princeton University Press, 1973 (original edition, 1928)

Grube, G. M. A., *The Greek and Roman Critics*, Toronto: University of Toronto Press, and London: Methuen, 1965

Guthrie, W. K. C., *A History of Greek Philosophy*, Cambridge: Cambridge University Press, 4 vols., 1962–71

Hadas, Moses, *Ancilla to Classical Reading*, New York: Columbia University Press, 1961 (original edition, 1954)

Havelock, Eric A., *Preface to Plato*, Cambridge, Massachusetts: Harvard University Press, 1982 (original edition, 1962)

Irwin, Terence, *Plato's Ethics*, New York and Oxford: Oxford University Press, 1995

Kahn, C. H., "Did Plato Write Socratic Dialogues?" *Classical Quarterly* 31 (1981): 305–20

Lesky, Albin, *A History of Greek Literature*, New York: Crowell, and London: Methuen, 1966 (original German edition, 1959)

Morgan, Michael L., *Platonic Piety: Philosophy and Ritual in Fourth-Century Athens*, New Haven, Connecticut and London: Yale University Press, 1990

Vlastos, Gregory, editor, *Plato: A Collection of Critical Essays*, Garden City, New York: Anchor, and London: Macmillan, 2 vols., 1972

Vlastos, Gregory, *Socrates: Ironist and Moral Philosopher*, Ithaca, New York: Cornell University Press, and Cambridge: Cambridge University Press, 1991

Plutarch

Greek, c. 46–c. 120/125 CE

Although Plutarch was Greek, he was as familiar with the history and culture of Rome as he was with that of his native land. A disciple of **Plato** and Aristotle, he nevertheless had his own views of humanity and expressed them in his works. He was a prolific and varied writer who produced two extensive collections of essays, *Moralia* (*Morals*) and *Vitae parallelae* (Parallel lives; translated simply as *Lives*).

The *Morals* reveals Plutarch's personal interests as well as his scholarly knowledge of a wide range of subjects. Using the forms of **dialogue, letter,** and diatribe, he is ever the lecturer on human weaknesses and problems, but always with an optimistic turn of mind that provides the reader with the solace that such weaknesses and problems do have answers if one will just look for them. These essays are a pleasure to read not only for their style, but also for their wide variety of topics, such as the education of children, how to distinguish between flattery and true friendship, the significance of Isis and Osiris in Egyptian mythology, the genius of Socrates, rules for husband and wife, the eating of meat, whether water or fire is more useful, and superstition. Although some are long and can be difficult to read, they nevertheless reflect a broad familiarity with literature and history and a keen insight into many human concerns, both esoteric and practical. Often referred to as a "physician of the soul," Plutarch probably wrote more on moral topics than any other writer of ancient times.

As interesting as *Morals* may be, however, it is the *Lives* for which Plutarch is best known. These are biographical essays on illustrious Greeks and Romans produced in successive books probably between 105 and 115 CE. The essays are paired, one Greek and one Roman. Plutarch's primary concern is not with history or politics specifically, but with the personal aspects of his subjects, particularly the ways their qualities and virtues might serve as guides for himself and his readers. "It was for the sake of others that I first began to write biographies," he says, "but I find myself continuing to do it for my own."

Although he understood human nature well, Plutarch had in him more than a touch of the romantic. An accomplished storyteller, he seeks to reflect the truth in his essays, at least as he sees it. Admitting, for example, that "nothing can be said of Lycurgus, the lawgiver of Sparta, which is not open to dispute," he goes on to say that he will nevertheless "endeavor to write a history of his life, following the statements which are least contradicted and depending upon the authors who are most worthy of belief." In this way, then, Plutarch approaches all of the *Lives*.

While the subjects of Plutarch's *Lives* left their imprints on their times, he writes about them from his own moral point of view. Like most biographers, he does not try to hide that perspective, thus adding to the interest and readability of the *Lives*. Plutarch seeks to bring out those aspects of his characters' lives that, while they may seem minor in some cases, are in his mind just as important as heroic exploits in illustrating virtues and vices. "I must," he says, "be allowed to dwell especially on things that express the souls of these men, and through them portray their lives, leaving it to others to describe their mighty deeds and battles."

Not only does Plutarch skillfully balance Greek with Roman, he also balances the weaknesses and strengths, as he sees them, of his subjects. Themistocles, on the one hand, might be an ambitious person hungry for fame and a keen moneymaker; yet on the other, he was liked by all the people, "for he called every citizen by name, and would act as a safe and a fair judge in private disputes between citizens."

When he comes to Alexander and Caesar, Plutarch finds himself with "such an abundance of material that I shall make no other preface but to beg my readers not to complain of me if I do not relate all their celebrated exploits . . . I am writing not histories but lives, and a man's most conspicuous achievements do not always reveal best his strength or his weakness." Likening himself to a portrait painter, he points out that he must be allowed to go beyond the mere faces of his subjects and to "dwell especially on things that express the souls of these men." That statement probably best describes the strategy and the goal that Plutarch had in writing the *Lives*.

Although Plutarch is ever the moralist in the *Lives*, he presents an education in Greek and Roman history that surpasses any other extant ancient work. That the work has been read and has influenced other writers for almost 2000 years attests not only to the superb research and tremendous effort that Plutarch put into its creation, but also the vitality and spirit of his narrative style and to his love for humankind.

WILTON ECKLEY

See also Classical Influences

Biography

Born Lucius (?) Mestrius Plutarchus, c. 46 CE in Chaeronea, Boeotia, central Greece. Studied in Athens, mid-60s. Married Timoxena: at least four sons and one daughter. Lectured in Rome and visited Egypt; priest at Delphi, and helped revive the shrine there; held numerous municipal posts in Chaeronea; possibly made a procurator by the emperor Hadrian. Died c. 120–25 CE.

Selected Writings

Essays and Related Prose

Moralia, edited by H. Wegehaupt and others, 1925–; as *Morals*, various translators, 5 vols., 1684–94, revised by W. W. Goodwin, 5 vols., 1874–78; also translated by Frank G. Babbitt and others (Loeb Edition), 15 vols., 1927–69, and Harold Cherniss, 1976; selections translated by T. G. Tucker and A. O. Prickard, 2 vols., 1913–18, Rex Warner, 1971, Robin Waterfield, 1992, and Donald Russell, 1993

Vitae parallelae, edited by K. Ziegler and C. Lindskog, 8 vols., 1926–39, revised edition, 4 vols., 1957–80, and by Robert Flacelière and others, 1957–; as *Lives*, translated by Thomas North, 1579; edited in translation by John Dryden, 5 vols., 1683–86, revised by A. H. Clough, 1900; also translated by Oliver Goldsmith and Joseph Collyer, 5 vols., 1762 (abridged version), J. and W. Langhorne, 6 vols., 1770, and Bernadotte Perrin (Loeb Edition), 11 vols., 1914–26; selections translated by G. Long, 5 vols., 1844–48, W. R. Frazer, 1906, Aubrey Stewart and G. Long, 1906, C. E. Byres, 1907, T. G. Tucker, 1913, Moses Hadas, 1957, Rex Warner, 1958 (revised edition, 1972), Ian Scott-Kilvert, 1960–73, and Richard J. A. Talbert, 1988

Further Reading

Barrow, R. H., *Plutarch and His Times*, London: Chatto and Windus, and Bloomington: Indiana University Press, 1967

Berry, Edmund, *Emerson's Plutarch*, Cambridge, Massachusetts: Harvard University Press, 1961

DeLacey, Phillip, "Biography and Tragedy in Plutarch," *American Journal of Philology* 73 (April 1952): 159–71

Gianakaris, C. J., *Plutarch*, New York: Twayne, 1970

Helmbold, W. C., and E. N. O'Neil, *Plutarch's Quotations*, Baltimore: American Philological Association, 1959

Jones, Christopher P., *Plutarch and Rome*, Oxford: Clarendon Press, 1971

Oakesmith, John, *The Religion of Plutarch*, London and New York: Longman Green, 1902

Rose, H. J., *Introductory Essays to the Roman Questions of Plutarch*, New York: Arno Press, 1975 (original edition, 1924)

Russell, D. A., *Plutarch*, New York: Scribner, and London: Duckworth, 1973

Stadter, P. A., *Plutarch's Historical Methods: An Analysis of the Mulierum Virtutes*, Cambridge, Massachusetts: Harvard University Press, 1965

Tracy, H. L., "Notes on Plutarch's Biographical Method," *Classical Journal* 37 (1941–42): 213–21

Trench, Richard C., *Plutarch: His Lives and His Morals*, London: Macmillan, 1873

The Poetic Art

by Horace, written c. 12–8 BCE

The centrality of the poetic epistle to the Pisos by Horace (65–8 BCE), *Epistula ad Pisones*, popularly known as *Ars poetica* or *The Poetic Art*, to Western literary theory is partly adduced by the number of concepts and phrases from it that have passed into standard usage by critics, often unacknowledged. Whenever we speak of a misplaced eloquence as a "purple patch," or of epic poets beginning "*in medias res*"; whenever we speak of poetry's purpose to "delight and instruct," or excuse a poet's error by saying that "Homer nods," or refer to the revision process as taking the writing "back to the anvil," we are borrowing from Horace's *Ars poetica*.

Ars poetica is cast in the form of a *sermo*, or verse epistle, which gives the poem a remarkably conversational style. It seems to ramble, as conversation does, though many readers have discerned a structure beneath the apparent randomness. If an early commentator was right in asserting that the work originated as an informal commentary on the maxims of Neoptolemus of Parium, then that may account for its unstructured appearance. Addressed to the aristocratic Piso family, a father and two sons (although there is some debate as to which Pisos are meant), the verse essay offers practical advice on poetry to would-be poets. It is important to keep in mind the practical nature of its putative intention, for while it has rightly taken its place as a classic of literary criticism, it pretends to be more of a how-to manual for writers.

The admonitory nature of the work heightens its sense of audience. Many lines are simple imperatives: "Don't begin like this"; "let no god intervene"; "handle your Greek models day and night." Periodic vocatives keep the intended audience in the text, referring to all three as "Pisos," "writers," or "Sons of Pompilius." Horace's frequent use of second-person pronouns and verb forms creates an intimate tone, especially when he uses the *vos* to distinguish his chosen readers from the rabble, as in his discussion of Plautus, whom "your ancestors praised" though "you and I know how to tell crudity from wit."

Yet as much as these techniques contributed to conversational effect, and as much as *Ars poetica* is ultimately a poem and not a treatise, it yields to most readers a coherent rhetorical structure beneath the seemingly random talk. Because his transitions are gradual, and bridge topics by seeming to apply now to the preceding, now to the following, the divisions in Horace's treatise are not universally agreed upon. But allowing some leeway of a few lines in either direction, general sections can be distinguished. The first 40 lines are an introduction of sorts, but introduce a critical principle of unity. The would-be poet is advised to leave out of his poem any element that is inconsonant with the poem as a whole. Lines 40–118 discuss order and style: Horace rejects a reigning dictim against neologisms, though he urges caution in coining new words; metrical patterns should be appropriate to the poetic type; the poet must truly feel what he wants his reader to feel.

Lines 119–294 suggest how to organize larger poems, and categorize their generic types. Much of the structural advice echoes Aristotle's *Poetics*: begin in the middle of the action; insure a beginning, middle, and end; keep violence offstage; avoid the artificial *deus ex machina*. The poet's models for subject and meter should be Greek, says Horace; revise carefully over a long period of time. The final section, lines 295 to the end, entertains specific questions about literary criticism. This section begins with Horace's relinquishing of the title of poet, in order to introduce the distinction between poet and critic – an irony since, as a work of criticism, the letter to the

Pisos takes a writer's point of view rather than a critic's. After a lament that Romans can count money better than poetic meter, Horace lays down his famous principle: poetry must delight and instruct. He admits, however, that even Homer fails to delight at times; it is inevitable in longer poems.

The concluding pronouncements (if indeed the poem as we have it is complete) concern revision: the Pisos are enjoined to put each work away for nine years, to avoid making public something that will embarrass them later; the poem should be "returned to the anvil" for reshaping. The issue of revision brings in the controversy of art versus nature: is the hard work of revision necessary for a work of genius? Is poetic skill inborn or acquired? To Horace, both innate genius and craftsmanship are needed to make great poetry.

The poem ends rather abruptly with a satiric attack on mad poets who inflict their poetry on unwilling readers. The suddenness of the ending has led many readers to consider the poem a fragment, yet the end comes no more suddenly than the ends of Horace's other epistles; the abruptness is a part of the conversational style. When we consider also that *The Poetic Art* is longer than any other poem by Horace, there is no reason to believe that we do not have the whole of it.

The sound, practical advice in Horace's *Poetic Art* dominated literary theory in Europe into the 19th century. It continues to exert a strong influence, and its easy, intimate style makes it more accessible to the modern audience than virtually any other classical essay.

JOHN R. HOLMES

See also Classical Influences

Editions
Ars poetica, edited and translated by A. F. Watt, 1905, and edited by C. O. Brink, 1971; as *Ars poetica*, translated by H. R. Fairclough (Loeb Edition), 1926, R. C. Trevelyan, 1940, Burton Raffel, 1974, and Niall Rudd, 1989; as *The Poetic Art*, translated and adapted by C. H. Sisson, 1975

Further Reading
Brink, C. O., *Horace on Poetry*, Cambridge: Cambridge University Press, 1963
Commager, Steele, *The Odes of Horace: A Critical Study*, New Haven, Connecticut: Yale University Press, 1962
Costa, C. D. N., editor, *Horace*, London: Routledge and Kegan Paul, 1973
Fraenkel, Eduard, *Horace*, Oxford: Clarendon Press, 1957
Lee, M. Owen, *Word, Sound, and Image in the Odes of Horace*, Ann Arbor: University of Michigan Press, and Toronto: Clark Irwin, 1969
Rudd, Niall, *The Satires of Horace: A Study*, Berkeley: University of California Press, and Cambridge: Cambridge University Press, 1966
West, David Alexander, *Reading Horace*, Edinburgh: Edinburgh University Press, 1967

Polemical Essay

Bernard Quémada (1980) noted that in the essay, the subject matter is treated through successive approaches, and generally by using methods or viewpoints that are put to a test. Marc Lits (1994) has pointed out that this idea of the confrontation of different approaches is an essential characteristic of the genre, more important and relevant than the notions of modesty or superficiality usually advanced. In considering the polemical essay, we are brought back to the analysis carried out by Dominique Maingueneau in *Sémantique de la polémique* (1983). Polemic constitutes a means for reinforcing its own enclosure by exposing itself to an imagined, threatening Other. Polemic, like other forms of the essay, would appear to operate in a discursive niche of confrontation, openness, and redefinition.

As Marc Angenot (1982) observed, polemic, like the **pamphlet** or the **satire**, presupposes the demonstration of a thesis and the refutation or disqualification of an opposing thesis. In this sense, polemical and other essay forms would appear to share common ground. If polemic commits itself, it is because the polemicist presupposes – whatever the gap separating the views at issue – that the opposing argument is underpinned by shared premises, on the basis of which it can be refuted. It is in this manner that polemic marks itself out from satirical prose. Satire deliberately denies a contrary view any rational basis. Although both satire and polemic, to varying degrees, imply a persuasive function and an aggressive function, the polemicist, however hostile he shows himself or herself to be, must technically be able to construct the antithesis, and rework his or her assertions in order to achieve the intended effect of rejection.

Among the many variations of the essay, the place successfully taken by the polemical essay is directly linked to the development of journalism. The work of **Joseph Addison** and **Richard Steele** on the *Spectator* is traditionally cited as the defining moment in the development, during the 18th century, of the essay as a periodical-based genre. When it became part of journalism, the essay became lighter, less philosophical and serious. The rapid growth of the press was henceforth to give many essayists an opportunity to express themselves in the political and satirical arenas. Taking France as an example, from the Third Republic to May 1968, and considering the Dreyfus affair on the way, a tradition of violent confrontations has been forged, with close links to the press. Among the outstanding French polemical writers, mention might be made of Henri de Rochefort, Émile Zola, Léon Daudet, Édouard Drumont, Louis-Ferdinand Céline, and **Jean-Paul Sartre**. But it must also be acknowledged that although current editorial pages have, to a certain extent, replaced the polemical essay, the genre has, additionally, experienced a certain loss of vitality. By going back to **Julien Benda**'s *La Trahison des clercs* (1927; *The Treason of the Intellectuals*), Marc Angenot has shown that here we may uncover what characterizes the existential position of the modern pamphleteer: a feeling of detachment with regard to a set of perverse and scandalous practices, in which resentment and twilight prophetism are combined. On a formal level, everything indicates the neutral objectivity typical of the cognitive essay. Perhaps this formal neutrality, for journalism, too, has replaced outright polemic.

BENOÎT GREVISSE

Bibliography
Baskerville, Edward J., *A Chronological Bibliography of Propaganda and Polemic Published in English Between 1553 and 1558*, Philadelphia: American Philosophical Society, 1979

Further Reading

Angenot, Marc, *Contribution à la parole pamphlétaire: Typologie des discours modernes*, Paris: Payot, 1982

Barbey d'Aurevilly, Jules, *Journalistes et polémistes, chroniqueurs et pamphlétaires*, Geneva: Slatkine Reprints, 1968 (original edition, 1895)

Bertaut, Jules, *Chroniqueurs et polémistes*, Paris: Sansot, 1906

Billy, André, *Les Écrivains de combat*, Paris: Les Œuvres Représentatives, 1931

Boyce, Benjamin, *The Polemic Character, 1640–1661: A Chapter in English Literary History*, Lincoln: University of Nebraska Press, 1955

Burgess, Glenn, "Protestant Polemic: The Leveller Pamphlets," *Parergon* 11, no. 2 (1993): 45–67

Corns, Thomas N., "Archetypal Mystification: Polemic and Reality in English Political Literature, 1640–1750," *Eighteenth-Century Life* 7, no. 3 (1982): 1–27

Corns, Thomas N., "The Literature of Controversy: Polemical Strategy from Milton to Junius," *Prose Studies* 9, no. 2 (1986)

Daudet, Léon, *Flammes: Polémiques et polémistes*, Paris: Grasset, 1930

Dominique, Pierre, *Les Polémistes français depuis 1789*, Paris: La Colombe, 1962

Kerbrat-Orecchioni, Catherine, *L'Énonciation de la subjectivité dans le langage*, Paris: Colin, 1980

Lits, Marc, *L'Essai*, Brussels: Hatier, 1994

Maingueneau, Dominique, *Sémantique de la polémique: Discours religieux et ruptures idéologiques au XVIIe siècle*, Lausanne: L'Âge d'Homme, 1983

Moore, Evelyn Knopp, *Lessing's Theory of Polemic* (dissertation), Urbana: University of Illinois, 1990

Propaganda in England and France: Polemic, Art, and Literature, edited by James Leheny, *Eighteenth-Century Life* 7, no. 3 (1982)

Quémada, Bernard, *Trésor de la langue française: Dictionnaire de la langue du XIXe et du XXe siècle (1789–1960)*, vol. 8, Paris: CNRS, 1980

Revel, Jean-François, *Qu'est-ce que la polémique?*, Paris: Pauvert, 1966

Thrash, Cheryl Haines, *The Polemical Body in Seventeenth-Century Toleration Tracts* (dissertation), Atlanta: Emory University, 1992

Watson, George, *The Certainty of Literature: Essays in Polemic*, New York: St. Martin's Press, 1989

Polish Essay

The beginnings of the Polish essay can be traced back to Renaissance secular moral **treatises**. Mikołaj Rej (1505–69) with *Wizerunek własny żywota człowieka poczciwego* (1558; A faithful image of an honest man) and Łukasz Górnicki (1527–1603) with *Dworzanin Polski* (1566; The polish courtier) initiated a productive trend in Polish nonfiction prose that is concerned with the moral and intellectual perfection of man. The 17th century contributed to laying the foundations of the essay genre with a few original works, all of which were published for the first time only in the 19th century: Jan Chryzostom Pasek's (c. 1636–c. 1701) *Pamiętniki* (wr. 1690–95, pub. 1839; *Memoirs*), Stanisław Żółkiewski's (1547–1620) diary, entitled *Początek i progres wojny moskiewskiej* (wr. 1612, pub. 1833; Beginning and progress of the Muscovite war), and King Jan Sobieski's (1629–96) **letters** to his French-born wife Mariette, *Listy do Marysieńki* (wr. 1664–83, pub. 1823; Letters to Marysienka). In a distinctively critical and often satirical tone, the Renaissance theme of human perfection was pursued in Enlightenment essays published in the popular social-political and cultural magazine *Monitor* (1765–85).

With early Romanticism, the first refined Polish essayist and literary critic appeared: Maurycy Mochnacki (1804–34), known for his study *O literaturze polskiej w wieku dziewiętnastym* (1830; On Polish literature in the 19th century). Although in mature Romanticism prose was supplanted by poetry and drama, this period was also important for the genre of the essay. It was a time of the accumulation of problems and issues bound up with national identity which were to inspire essay writers in the 20th century. This period was dominated spiritually by the so-called "Wielka Emigracja" (Great emigrants) in Paris (after the November Uprising of 1831, 6000 of its leaders were forced into exile), responsible for creating the model of the émigré writer: one who is sensitive to the present and obligated to the future of his homeland. Polish messianism and nationalism as a uniting force in the period from the Third Partition of Poland (1795) until its liberation (1918) and the image of the poet as a prophet and spiritual leader of the nation are Romantic themes still vital in the public discourse.

At the beginning of the 20th century the Romantic ideals were reconsidered and revised by essayists like **Stanisław Brzozowski** (1878–1911), Tadeusz Żeleński (**Boy**) (1874–1941), and Karol Irzykowski (1873–1944). In his *Legenda Młodej Polski* (1910; Legend of young Poland), Brzozowski criticized Polish neo-Romanticism for its "lazy" aestheticism and decadence of the will, which he viewed as a revival of the weaknesses of Romanticism. According to Brzozowski (influenced by **Marx** and **Nietzsche**), it was the will to persuade and to change society – that is, the "strong side" of Polish Romanticism – which was to be cherished. The entertaining French-style essays of Boy-Żeleński (the translator of **Montaigne**'s *Essais* into Polish) challenged Polish Romantic myths from the "common sense" point of view. Irzykowski in his *Walka otreść* (1929; The struggle for contents) opposed both Żeleński's cult of "real life" as a point of reference for literature and the theory of pure form advocated by Stanisław Ignacy Witkiewicz (1885–1939). Against these, Irzykowski urges writers to go beyond unquestioned meanings and to remove the "masks" that hide reality. These three authors represent different styles in essay writing. The witty and elegant essays of Boy-Żeleński, popular among liberals and anticlericals, are considered to be an influential promotion of French rationalist thought and of the French incarnation of the essay genre. Brzozowski in his turn was, above all, an intricate thinker concerned with ultimate questions of human existence; consequently, his was a serious, laconic style with broad allusions and no jesting whatsoever. To Irzykowski, the essay was mainly a vehicle for detailed critical analysis, incompatible with any generalizations or wittiness. Subsequently, the Polish essay developed within the wide and fruitful space between Boy-Żeleński and Brzozowski.

The interwar period favored the genre of the essay in two ways. On the one hand, after centuries of struggle for national independence, Poland was liberated in 1918 and the pressure of the national problem was diminished. The attention of Polish essayists then switched to a variety of cultural and philosophical problems peculiar to European civilization. On the other hand, the classical orientation of the high school educational system of the first decade of the 20th century, preserved after World War I, created a fertile environment for the emergence of both writers and a readership with humanistic erudition. **Jerzy Stempowski's** (1893–1969) work is the best example of this new stage in the development of the Polish essay. In the interwar period Stempowski was published in all the popular literary and cultural journals, with writings on the relation between literature (especially the avant-garde) and the ongoing economic and social changes (*Chimera jako zwierzę pociągowe* [1933; Chimera as a beast of burden]; *Literatura wokresie wielkiej przebudowy* [1935; Literature in the period of great rebuilding]). His main concern, however – the decline of European civilization – was spelled out later, in the volume *Eseje dla Kasandry* (1961; Essays for Cassandra). Two interwar essayists – Bolesław Miciński (1911–43) and Stanisław Vincenz (1888–1971) – were the most truthful to the spirit of Stempowski's essays. Miciński, an antagonist of academic philosophy, took his own metaphysical experiences as subject matter for his essays. His *Podróże do piekieł* (1938; Journeys to hell) and *Portret Kanta* (1947; Portrait of Kant) are built around great historical figures of European thought, mythology, and literature and are influenced by Freudian psychology. Vincenz, who wrote essays on Homer and Dante as well, is known mainly for his three-volume book *Na wysokiej połoninie* (vol. 1, 1936; *On the High Uplands*; vols. 2 and 3 were published in the 1970s), a collection of stories and myths of the Carpathian Huculs written in the spirit of Homeric epic. Vincenz's narrative is a characteristic example of the so-called "talk" or *gawenda* style of storytelling, similar to the Russian *skaz*, viewed by **Czesław Miłosz** and Marta Wyka as a typically Polish feature of the essay. Jan Parandowski (1895–1978) popularized the ancient heritage of European civilization through adaptations of Greek mythology, the *Iliad*, and the *Odyssey*, and through his **travel essays** *Rzym czarodziejski* (1924; The enchanting Rome) and *Dwie wiosny* (1927; Two springs). He also penned one of the best examples of the biographical essay, *Król życia* (1930; The king of life), about Oscar Wilde.

In the interwar period, with its abundance of cultural events, literary periodicals, and visions for the future of independent Poland, the essay ceased to be an auxiliary form of expression for poets and novelists and began to enjoy its "full rights" as a genre with well-developed varieties: the literary, **historical**, biographical, or **philosophical essay**, the memoir, and the manifesto. Polish essayists saw themselves as members of the international community of humanists, called upon to preserve and popularize the European cultural heritage and to apply its standards to their contemporary culture. Most of them felt as much citizens of Europe as Poles. They lived in different countries, but wrote mainly in Polish, and for the Polish public. Poets and novelists, philosophers and painters – all reached for the genre of the essay to present their innovative theories of literature and art. Stanisław Ignacy Witkiewicz, a painter, playwright, novelist, and philosopher, promoted his avant-garde doctrine on the pure form in art in *Nowe formy w malarstwie i wynikające stąd nieporozumienia* (1919; On the new forms in painting and on the resulting misunderstanding) and *Szkice estetyczne* (1922; Essays on aesthetics), and especially in his prophetic anticipation of the theater of the absurd, *Teatr:*

Wstęp do czystej formy w teatrze (1923; Theater: introduction to pure form in the theater). Bruno Schulz (1892–1942), whose cycles of poetic stories are the most original phenomenon in interwar prose, also published an essay about poetry as a regeneration of the elemental myths hidden within the words themselves ("Mityzacja rzeczywistości" [1936; Mythologizing reality]) and essays on contemporary Polish and foreign authors, among which are his particularly persuasive interpretations of **Gombrowicz** and Kafka. The logician and painter Leon Chwistek (1884–1944), in his essay *Wielość rzeczywistości* (1921; The plurality of reality), elaborated on the idea that there are four kinds of non-interfering realities expressed by different artistic approaches (primitivist, naturalist, impressionist, and futurist).

In 1939, after only two decades of independence, the western border of Poland was invaded by the German army and its eastern border by the Russians. World War II (which took six million Polish lives) again thrust Polish culture into an abnormal situation. The rethinking of the experience of war and occupation, of the German and Russian concentration camps, and of the Holocaust naturally came to dominate postwar prose. However, the critical consequence that the war and the subsequent establishment of communist rule had for literary culture was the division of Polish writers once more, as in the 19th century, into an émigré wing and a domestic wing. They faced different social environments, wrote for different readerships, saw their calling differently, and chose different genres to fulfill their intellectual responsibilities and their artistic cravings.

Paradoxically, this situation, unfavorable for the national literature as a whole, in exile brought about the golden age of the Polish essay. Stempowski (now under the pseudonym Pawel Hostowiec), Miciński, and Vincenz reflected on the decadence of European civilization, seeking the cure for it in antiquity. The decline of humanistic values is one of the leading themes of the essays of **Czesław Miłosz** (1911–), who emphasizes the moral dimensions of this crisis. Along with the originality of Miłosz's essays, the peculiar development of the contemporary Polish essay is manifest in **Witold Gombrowicz's** (1904–69) *Dziennik* (1953–69; *Diary*) and **Gustaw Herling-Grudziński's** (1919–) *Dziennik pisany nocą* (1969–; Journal written at night, translated as *Volcano and Miracle*), both published by the Paris-based émigré monthly *Kultura* (1947–; Culture). Although the overwhelmingly playful element in Gombrowicz's "diary" and the erudite reflections in Grudziński's "journal" represent two opposite approaches to the writing of nonfiction, both authors exemplify one of the main genre characteristics of the essay – subjectivity. The **journal** form they employ is to some extent a matter of convenience (they write for a monthly magazine), but it also allows them to exploit fully another peculiarity of the essay – its link with the spirit of the present time. Both journals can be read as a process of self-construction of the narrator's image (including some mystification) and as a response to the most urgent problems of contemporary European culture, of Poland under communist rule, and of Eastern European intellectuals in exile. The potential of this "hybrid" between the essay and the diary was revealed by Miłosz in *Rok Myśliwego* (1990; *A Year of the Hunter*), Aleksander Wat (1900–67) in *Mój wiek* (wr. 1963–65, pub. 1977; *My Century*), Andrzej Bobkowski

(1913–61) in *Szkice piórkiem* (1957; Sketches with a quill), Kazimierz Wierzyński (1894–1969) in *Moja prywatna Ameryka* (1966; My private America), and Marek Hłasko (1934–69) in *Piękni dwudziestoletni* (The beautiful 20 year old), published in the second half of the 1960s in *Kultura*.

The circumstances of exile – a familiar Romantic theme – were discussed by most Polish émigré writers. Some of them, like Gombrowicz and Herling-Grudziński, were inclined to see their situation in a positive light. Gombrowicz considered the exile of the artist to be a universal problem; Herling believed that a writer in exile, being free to express himself, is much better off than a writer under totalitarian rule. Czesław Miłosz in his *Nobel Lecture* (1980) and other essays is concerned with the dramatic choices and compromises forced onto a writer in exile. The most critical of these compromises is, of course, the language – an issue discussed by **Stanisław Barańczak** (1946–) in a few of his essays collected in *Breathing Under Water* (1990). Józef Wittlin (1896–1976) in "Blaski i nędze wygnania" (1957; "Sorrow and Grandeur of Exile") discusses both the positive and the negative sides of the problem. Exile does not seem to be so unbearable to the philosopher **Leszek Kołakowski** (1927–), who responded by becoming a citizen of the world, convincingly demonstrated by his essays in *Modernity on Endless Trial* (1990). This also holds true for the theater critic **Jan Kott** (1914–), who published the representative English selection of Polish essays *Four Decades of Polish Essays* (1990).

Until 1978, when *samizdat* (underground publishing) rendered émigré literature accessible to the domestic audience, the reception of émigré publications was relatively limited. In the 1980s, however, the presence of émigré essayists on the home literary market became one of the important motors of the movement toward the abolition of the communist system. In their native country, authors in exile were read as moral authorities. The process of uniting two wings of Polish literature, however, took more than a decade, for the whole system of literary and moral values had to be revised. Several essayists who remained in Poland during the communist era (although some were eventually forced to emigrate in the 1980s) survived the test of the new epoch: the poet and master of the travel essay **Zbigniew Herbert** (1924–), Kazimierz Wyka (1910–75), Mieczysław Jastrun (1903–83), who wrote on literature, the science-fiction writer and philosopher Stanisław Lem (1921–), and the historian and politician Adam Michnik (1946–).

At the end of the 20th century the essay genre is a vital trend in Polish literature – now finally united – and enjoys the constant attention of a wide readership. Along with poetry, the essay represents Polish culture abroad and is the preferred form for discussion of the cultural and moral problems of the period of transition to a free market economy.

KATIA MITOVA-JANOWSKI

Anthology
Four Decades of Polish Essays, edited by Jan Kott, Evanston, Illinois: Northwestern University Press, 1990

Further Reading
Danielewicz Zielińska, Maria, *Szkice o literaturze emigracyjnej*, Wrocław: Zakład Narodowy im. Ossolińskich–Wydawnictwo, 1992

Kott, Jan, Introduction to *Four Decades of Polish Essays*, edited by Kott, Evanston, Illinois: Northwestern University Press, 1990
Miłosz, Czesław, *The History of Polish Literature*, Berkeley: University of California Press, 1983
Olejniczak, Józef, "Esej i dziennik na emigracji," in *Literatura emigracyjna, 1939–1989*, vol. 1, edited by Józef Garliński and others, Katowice: Ślask, 1994: 226–60
Wyka, Maria, editor, *Polski essej: Studia*, Cracow: Universitas, 1991

Portuguese Essay

Francisco Sanches (c. 1550–1623) could be considered the first Portuguese essayist, despite the fact that he moved to France while still a youth. Sanches was a contemporary of **Montaigne** (who incidentally was his cousin), and his *Quod nihil scitur* (*That Nothing Is Known*) was published in Lyons in 1581. In this book-length essay he defends a form of skepticism which provoked strong reactions from 17th-century German theologians, who considered him the most (potentially) destructive of the skeptics.

Carta de guia de casados (1651; *The Government of a Wife, or, Wholesome and Pleasant Advice for Married Men*) by Francisco Manuel de Mello (1608–66) can also be read as a volume of essays. Written in colloquial style, though tempered with a baroque spirit and humor, it is a collection of considerations about aspects of married life. Father Manuel Bernardes' (1644–1710) five-volume *Nova floresta* (1706–28; New forest) includes, among his serene, short prose writings, authentic essays. Father António Vieira (1608–97), a Jesuit who spent most of his life in Bahia, Brazil, is a master of Portuguese prose. His baroque style is more temperate than the exuberant expressions commonly associated with baroque art. Vieira is a master of language and rhythm, playing with the emotions of his audience, and combining great clarity with an often sinuous, even cunning, logic. Many of his *Sermões* (Sermons), 15 volumes published between 1679 and 1699, together with some of his **letters** – particularly those in which he emerges as a staunch defender of the Brazilian Indians – as well as some of his reports could easily take their place in a collection of classic essays.

Francis Bacon had his admirers in Portugal. The physician Jacob de Castro Sarmento suggested to King John V that *Novum organum* (1620) be translated into Portuguese. Another admirer, Luís António Verney (1713–92), became, in the words of Sílvio Lima, author of a book-length essay on the nature of the essay, "a propagandizer of the critical essayism of modernity" by virtue of his *Verdadeiro método de estudar* (1746; True method of studying). The same can be said of the physician Ribeiro Sanches (1699–1783) and his *Cartas sobre a educação da mocidade* (1746; Letters on the education of youth). Both Verney and Sanches were considered "estrangeirados" (literally, "foreignized") by their Portuguese contemporaries for their "un-Portuguese" views. Verney in particular was a harsh critic of a culture he felt was immersed in an excessive baroque taste, with its nefarious impact on letters, thought, and education. He chastised baroque writing for being hollow, obscure, and illogical, and advocated the introduction of modern ideas in Portugal.

The state of the nation *vis-à-vis* Central and Northern Europe became a fertile ground for national reflections in the first half of the 19th century. Alexandre Herculano (1810–77) wrote pieces on political, historical, educational, literary, and moral topics which easily qualify as essays. Collected in his *Opúsculos* (1873–1908; Minor works), they provide a good window from which to observe Portugal's battles in the process of adjusting its institutions to the times. In the second half of the century, *Causas da decadência dos povos peninsulares* (1871; Causes of the decline of the Iberian people), a long essay by Antero de Quental (1842–91), mentor of the formidable "1870 generation," stands out. It sketches the history of the Iberian peoples after the Counter-Reformation, and identifies the moral, political, and economic causes of the Iberian Peninsula's backwardness compared with the rest of Europe. Quental wrote other remarkable essays, such as *Tendências gerais da filosofia na segunda metade do século XIX* (1890; General trends in philosophy in the second half of the 19th century), as well as others on literary and philosophical themes. Oliveira Martins (1845–94) wrote extensively with the same concerns as Herculano and Antero. His collection of essays *A Inglaterra de hoje* (1893; England today) is a telling document of the cultural differences between the Portuguese and the English, and how he envisioned a modernization of Portugal that could avoid what he considered to be the pitfalls of British civilization.

Eça de Queiroz (1845–1900), the most admired of Portuguese fiction writers, was a member of Quental's group. Several volumes of his collected works – *A correspondência de Fradique Mendes* (1900; The correspondence of Fradique Mendes), *Cartas de Inglaterra* (1905; Letters from England), *Notas contemporâneas* (1909; Contemporary notes), and *Crónicas de Londres* (1945; London chronicles) – are precious collections of social commentary by a master of irony, wit, and elegant prose. Fialho de Almeida (1857–1911) is another example of a prolific writer with many pieces in his five-volume *Os gatos* (1889–94; The cats) fitting the essay genre; its topics range from theater and literature to social commentary.

Leonardo Coimbra (1883–1936), a philosopher with his own grand conception of life known as creationism, independently conceived but with significant links to Henri Bergson's philosophy, wrote about love and death, joy, pain, and grace; the liberal and the reactionary spirit; experimental reason; man and destiny; the spirit and war. A synthesis of his view can be found in *O criacionismo: Esboço de um sistema filosófico* (1912; Creationism: a synthesis of a philosophical system). The mind of this original essayist can also be appreciated in his *A alegria, a dor e a graça* (1916; Joy, pain, and grace). The poet Teixeira de Pascoaes (1877–1952), in part under Coimbra's influence, wrote numerous short essays attempting to depict the traits of the collective Portuguese soul, which he thought was best captured by the concept of *saudade*, a bittersweet feeling of nostalgia for a lost, or a not-yet-found world, a longing for an absent love. Some of his collected essays on the topic were collected in the volume *A Saudade e o saudosismo* (1988; *Saudade* and saudosism).

The essay was also cultivated by members of the Modernist group *Orpheu*, with Fernando Pessoa (1888–1935) as its greatest representative. Known above all as a poet and creator of a constellation of heteronyms, Pessoa also wrote short essays, most of them unfinished or briefly sketched. His *Livro do desassossego* (The Book of Disquiet), written under the name Bernardo Soares, appeared for the first time only in 1982, almost 50 years after the author's death. The work is a collection of prose manuscripts resembling **Nietzsche**'s work; its many entries are condensed essays, outlines of ideas to be developed, although the overall structure and style of the book make it most like an intimate diary. Its contents, though, point to reflections on the broken self, the absence of meaning – "Today I suddenly experienced an absurd but quite valid sensation. I realized, in an intimate lightning flash, that I am no one. No one, absolutely no one ... And I, truly, I am the center that doesn't exist except as a convention in the geometry of the abyss; I am the nothingness around which this movement spins ..."

In the first half of the 20th century, António Sérgio (1883–1969) stands out as the great cultivator of the genre. The title of his eight volumes of *Ensaios* (1920–58) is a conscious affiliation with Montaigne and Bacon. A rationalist who wanted to use reason to change the Portuguese mentality from obscurantism to rationalism, he revisited historical myths in order to extricate what he felt were the hard realities his countrymen had to confront.

After Sérgio, the genre proliferated, multiplied in a rich and diversified variety of themes and styles. In this century most major Portuguese writers have written essays, mostly in the literary field. In this respect, the best tradition of the genre as practiced by **T. S. Eliot**, Edgar Allan Poe, **E. M. Forster**, **Aldous Huxley**, Charles Baudelaire, George Bernard Shaw, Edmund Wilson, and **Paul Valéry**, to name a few, has plenty of cultivators among Portuguese literary figures. Sílvio Lima (1904–93) was the author of the remarkable and influential *Ensaio sobre a essência do ensaio* (1944; Essay on the essence of the essay). For Lima, an essay is an exercise in personal critical thinking about universal realities. During his times and in subsequent years, names like Vitorino Nemésio (1901–78), Jorge de Sena (1919–78), **Vergílio Ferreira** (1916–), David Mourão-Ferreira (1927–), and José Régio (1901–69) became associated with the genre, together with others whose work privileged the essay format – Joaquim de Carvalho (1892–1958), **Eduardo Lourenço** (1923–), António José Saraiva (1917–93), Joel Serrão (1919–), Manuel Antunes (1918–85), Jacinto do Prado Coelho (1920–84), Oscar Lopes (1917–), José Marinho (1904–75), and Vitorino Magalhães Godinho (1918–).

In the last years of the Salazar-Caetano dictatorship, which ended in 1974, the essay became heavily politicized. Cinema joined literature as a main topic, but both were simply a pretext for social and political commentary. During the years immediately following the so-called "April 25th Revolution," literature was somewhat abandoned and the essay became doctrinal, with prose heavily weighted with Marxist jargon. Little by little, however, the voices of the established writers re-emerged. Reviewing for the journal *Colóquio-Letras* a decade of the Portuguese essay (1974–84), Eduardo Prado Coelho recognizes that a narrow definition of essayism would certainly include Eduardo Lourenço – without a doubt the great essayistic presence of the post-April 25th period – Vergílio Ferreira, some works by Jorge de Sena, two or three books by António José Saraiva, the dispersed reflections of

Father Manuel Antunes, or Nuno Teixeira Neves, some of the cultural interventions of Miguel Serras Pereira, but little else. Most of these authors had established their reputations before the arrival of the democratic state in 1974.

It was only in the early 1980s that literature recovered its importance in Portugal, and Portuguese authors actually began to receive in their own country attention unmatched in any previous period. An assessment of the last decade leaves us with most of the same names at the top of the list, if we are to consider the essay in the strict sense. An important shift occurred in the Portuguese literary scene, however: the academicization of the essay. The proliferation of conferences, national as well as international, standardized Portuguese writing according to the international norms of the academic paper. In effect, only the old generation continued cultivating the old-fashioned essay: Lourenço, Ferreira, Saraiva, and de Sena.

The cultural and literary historian António José Saraiva had a creative mind which did not allow him to remain within the straitjacket of professional scholarship. He wrote freely and loved toying with the ideas of great thinkers and writers. A good example of his essay writing was published in 1990, three years before his death. A tertúlia ocidental (Western literary group) is a pleasant excursion into the lives and thought of renowned figures of the "1870 generation." Other studies, both old and more recent, such as Poesia e drama (1990; Poetry and drama) and the two volumes of A cultura em Portugal (1981–83; Culture in Portugal), a series of essays on late medieval and early modern Portuguese cultural and literary themes, or Ser ou não ser arte (1973; To be or not to be art), and Filhos de Saturno (1980; Children of Saturn), on political topics, confirm his brilliance as an essayist.

Jorge de Sena, a superb poet of the generation of Ferreira and Lourenço, wrote in every genre (close to 100 books published despite his premature death at 58), including numerous essays, which reflect his desire to write about everything. In spite of his death, he is alive and well in his works, which continue to be published thanks to the energy of his wife, Mécia de Sena. In 1992, another volume appeared for the first time: Amor e outros verbetes (Love and other words), a collection of entries written upon request for the Encyclopaedia Britannica and other reference works. In the introduction, Mécia de Sena explains that the volume contains the Portuguese version of the pieces rather than the cut and edited versions which appeared in English. She refers to incidents with the editors and criticizes the peculiar demands of English writing, which she calls "non-style" and which Jorge de Sena had classified as "mono-style." The pieces in this volume are excellent examples of his particular style – an outpouring of facts, woven with comments, asides, and tangents which sometimes last for pages, but always with a fascinating force conducting the reader through the labyrinths of a great mind.

Among the recent volumes of Sena's posthumously published works is the impressive collection of essays O dogma da Trindade poética (Rimbaud) e outros ensaios (1994; The dogma of poetic trinity (Rimbaud) and other essays). The sheer range of topics is impressive – Rimbaud, Cavafy, Antonio Machado, T. S. Eliot, **Sartre**, Rilke, Ungaretti, expressionism, Modernism, Don Juan, and Garcilaso, among others. Sena's torrential style is both refreshing and overwhelming.

An original, hard-to-classify essayist, with a paradoxically modern classical prose and a penchant for venturing into uncommon territory in Portuguese letters (e.g. virtue, tolerance, God, Latin comedy) is Agostinho da Silva (1906–94). Two good collections of his writings – essays in the strictest sense – are Dispersos (1988; Dispersals) and Considerações e outros textos (1988; Considerations and other texts).

Of the younger generation, Eduardo Prado Coelho (1944–), Arnaldo Saraiva (1939–), and José Augusto Seabra (1937–), also academics and scholars, are three excellent cultivators of the genre, publishing their pieces in the literary and cultural supplements of major newspapers. Prado Coelho has published two volumes of a journal which is really a reader's response to books – Tudo o que não escrevi (1992–94; Everything that I did not write), a title taken from Ludwig Wittgenstein. Most of the entries, though, are essays on a variety of contemporary debates ranging from literature to philosophy and the arts. Saraiva is a heterodoxical writer who writes in an engaging style about topics from national anthems and graffiti to advertisements, epigraphs, and polemics, as can be found in his Literatura marginal/izada – Novos ensaios (1980; Marginalized literature – new essays), a delightful collection in the best tradition of the forefathers of the genre. Seabra's subjects are more conventional, and his style more academic.

The list of essayists could be longer, particularly as the boundary between the essay and the scholarly study further breaks down. Other important writers of essays include Luís de Sousa Rebelo (1922–), Natália Correia (1923–), José Enes (1924–), Eugénio Lisboa (1930–), Fernando Cristóvão (1929–), Maria Alzira Seixo (1941–), Vasco Graça Moura (1942–), José-Augusto França (1922–), João Medina (1939–), Alexandre Pinheiro Torres (1923–), Isabel Allegro de Magalhães (1942–), Boaventura de Sousa Santos (1941–), Silvina Rodrigues Lopes (1950–), Fernando Guimarães (1928–), António Ramos Rosa (1924–), João Barrento (1940–), and Diogo Pires Aurélio (1946–).

Those familiar with the contemporary Portuguese literary scene may find this survey rather conservative, keeping to established figures of the older generations, and short on women writers. While this is indeed the case, the reason may be that the essay seems to be an offspring of maturity. Presently, the members of the younger generation of men and women (there has been a considerable increase in the female presence in Portuguese literature since 1974) are either in the process of establishing academic careers (and thus writing scholarly papers) or writing excellent newspaper articles and crónicas (a favorite genre in Portugal, lighter than the essay) for such dailies as Diário de Notícias, and O Público, and the weeklies Expresso and Jornal de Letras, and have not yet published books collecting their best pieces.

ONÉSIMO T. ALMEIDA

Further Reading

Coelho, Eduardo Prado, "Ensaio," Colóquio-Letras 78 (March 1984): 43–54

Coelho, Jacinto do Prado, editor, Dicionário de literatura, 5 vols., Porto: Figueirinhas, 1981 (original edition, 1956–60)

Lima, Sílvio, Ensaio sobre a essência do ensaio, Coimbra: Arménio Amado, 1944

Logos: Enciclopédia Luso-Brasileira de filosofia, Lisboa and São Paulo: Verbo, 1989

Saraiva, António José, and Oscar Lopes, *História da literatura Portuguesa*, Porto: Porto Editora, 1996 (original edition, 1949)

Pound, Ezra

American, 1885–1972

Ezra Pound, the most prolific essayist among his Modernist contemporaries, wrote from within an astonishingly wide range of allusion, yet his thematic interests remain relatively narrow. It is only a slight exaggeration to say that after *The Spirit of Romance* (1910), he wrote only endless installments – many brilliant – of two extended essays. Pound is initially concerned with poetry and its place in society, and then, beginning around 1924, with the ways economic systems promote or debase culture. Pound's cultural criticism is almost always aimed at establishing the proper grounds for poetry's growth and appreciation. Whatever their particular occasion, the essays exude polemical intensity, for Pound seldom took up his pen without meaning to argue or instruct. **T. S. Eliot**, in his introduction to *The Literary Essays of Ezra Pound* (1954), writes, "Mr. Pound has never valued his literary criticism except in terms of its literary impact."

The discoverer of James Joyce and the champion of Eliot, Ford Madox Ford, and Henri Gaudier-Brzeska, Pound can lay claim to being the inventor of Anglo-American Modernism, or at least its greatest impresario. Largely through the medium of the **personal essay**, Pound exerted substantial influence on the arts of painting and sculpture, as well as literature, and took intelligent notice of music. The "Treatise on Harmony" (1924) and the two essays on Arnold Dolmetsch (1918) are still of interest.

Beginning as a late Victorian admirer of Browning and the early **Yeats**, steeped in the traditions of European poetry, Pound was transformed by the destruction, waste, and stupidity of World War I into a radical stylist and eccentric economic and aesthetic theorist. The same experiences turned him toward the fascism of Mussolini, whom he naively believed would be interested in the economic theories of Social Credit. The fullest and most coherent of Pound's political writings is "Jefferson and/or Mussolini" (1935). The least coherent and most noxious of his fascist statements are to be found in the radio scripts of the early 1940s, broadcast over Rome radio. Pound's real passion, however, was always the arts, and his fondest hope in the 1920s and 1930s was that fascism could establish the sort of society in which the arts could flourish. He was, obviously, wrong; at the same time, his error was shared by many intellectuals in England and America.

Something of Pound's characteristic tone during this period can be heard in the very brief "The Constant Preaching to the Mob" (1916), which argues that poetry is not "entertainment," but a mode of feeling crucial to the functioning of a healthy society. After quoting and translating from Old English four lines of "The Wanderer," Pound remarks that "Such poems are not made for after-dinner speakers ... Still it flatters the mob to tell them that their importance is so great that the solace of lonely men, and the lordliest of arts, was created for their amusement." Pound, like Eliot, is an unashamed elitist with no use for the common reader except to decry his ignorance.

No Modernist poet relied so heavily upon the genre of the essay as Pound. Throughout his life he employed it to promote poetry as the highest and most exclusive of the arts, and to defend it against sentimentality and the fuzzy thinking that results, he believed, from economic and political corruption. The mature style of Pound's poetry is highly essayistic, his essays poetic. In both genres he makes extensive use of juxtaposition, which he called "the ideographic method," an idea derived from the work of the Orientalist Ernest Fenollosa. Donald Davie (*Pound*, 1975) sees what he calls an intellectual "rhythm" in the way Pound juxtaposes the materials of his art. In both poetry and prose, Pound's technical innovations were always designed to achieve what he called "hardness." In "Credo" (1918) he writes, "I believe in technique as the test of a man's sincerity."

Expatriate from his early twenties, Pound saw American culture as smugly sentimental and isolated from the traditions that make the arts possible. In "What I Feel About Walt Whitman" (1909) Pound writes that his great predecessor was "an exceedingly nauseating pill," but admits that "he accomplished his mission." "His crudity is an exceeding great stench," Pound added, but later, in the brief lyric "A Pact" (1915), admits Whitman had "broken the new wood." Much the same can be said of Pound himself. It is hard to overestimate the effect of Pound's poetics on American and British poets of the second half of the 20th century.

Pound's literary reputation rests on his poetry, but the greater part of his influence has been transmitted through the essays. Generations of poets have been instructed in the tenets of their art by the *ABC of Reading* (1934), which evolved from a cluster of key essays from the 1920s. Among these, "Credo" and "A Retrospect" (1918) may be said to have established Modernist poetic technique. In "The Prose Tradition in Verse" (1913), Pound can be said to have created the academic literary taste of the 20th century. Virtually all Pound's famous mottos are to be found in these three brief pieces. "An image is that which presents an intellectual and emotional complex in an instant of time" from "A Few Don'ts" (1913) launched imagism as a literary movement. By 1918, Pound is definitely propounding a system of composition. In "Credo" he writes, "Rhythm – I believe in an 'absolute rhythm,' that is in poetry which corresponds exactly to the emotion or shade of emotion to be expressed ... Symbols – I believe the proper and perfect symbol is the natural object ... Technique – I believe in technique as the test of a man's sincerity ..." In "A Retrospect," he offers the following three prescriptions for poetry: "1. Direct treatment of the 'thing' whether subjective or objective. 2. To use absolutely no word that does not contribute to the presentation. 3. As regarding rhythm: to compose in the sequence of the musical phrase, not in the sequence of the metronome."

Pound's most influential essay may be a "translation." He compiled *The Chinese Written Character as a Medium for Poetry* (comp. 1914; pub. 1936) from the notes of Ernest Fenollosa. It is hard to distinguish where Fenollosa leaves off and Pound begins. In any event, Pound's meditations on the Chinese character, which he and Fenollosa supposed less distant from the processes of both human thought and the natural world, gave rise to imagism as a literary movement, as well as to *Cathay* (1915), a collection of Pound's versions of Chinese poems. As a poet Pound is justly famous for creating a different analogue in English – almost a separate version of the language – for each writer he "brought over"; he seems to have done the same for Fenollosa's fragmentary prose.

The *ABC of Reading* formalizes the doctrines of the early essays and adds an extensive syllabus. Its theoretical underpinnings are taken over from *The Chinese Written Character*. Throughout Pound addresses himself to the poet who wishes to become part of the tradition, as well as to the reader who aspires to an adequate understanding of the canon. The *ABC of Reading* presents the reader with Pound the pedagogue. It also exhibits the paradoxical relations of Romantic and scientific modes of thought in Pound's criticism.

Confronted with the body of Pound's work, especially in prose – full of screeds against his countrymen and venomous reviews of his contemporaries – the reader encounters a similar paradox. Pound's fascism is nauseating, certainly, and his elitism, while it avoids Eliot's religiosity, seems rooted in an equally untenable vision of the social world. Against these deficits is counterbalanced the beauty of Pound's music, his genius for polemic, his astonishing literary energy on behalf of other writers, and a profound personal integrity.

JOSEPH DUEMER

Biography

Ezra Weston Loomis Pound. Born 30 October 1885 in Hailey, Idaho. Studied at the University of Pennsylvania, Philadelphia, 1901–03 and 1907–08, M.A. in Romance languages, 1906; Hamilton College, Clinton, New York, 1903–05, Ph.B., 1905. Lived in Venice, 1908, London, 1908–21, Paris, 1921–24, and Rapallo, Italy, 1924–45. Contributor or editor, *New Age*, from 1911, *Poetry*, 1912–19, *New Freewoman* (later the *Egoist*), 1913–14, *Blast*, 1914, *Little Review*, 1917–19, *Athenaeum*, 1920, the *Dial*, 1920–23, the *Exile*, 1927–28, *Il Mare* (The sea), 1932–40, and *New English Weekly*, 1932–35. Married Dorothy Shakespear, 1914: one son; also had one daughter with Mary Rudge. Made broadcasts over Rome Radio critical of United States involvement in World War II, from 1940, and as a result jailed by the U.S. army, 1945, first near Pisa, but then found mentally unsound and committed to St. Elizabeth's Hospital, Washington, D.C., 1946–58. Returned to Italy and lived mainly in Venice, 1958–72. Awards: Bollingen Prize, 1949; Harriet Monroe Award, 1962; honorary degree from Hamilton College. Died in Venice, 1 November 1972.

Selected Writings

Essays and Related Prose

The Spirit of Romance: An Attempt to Define Somewhat the Charm of the Pre-Renaissance Literature of Latin Europe, 1910
Pavannes and Divisions, 1918
Instigations, 1920
Make It New, 1934
ABC of Reading, 1934
The Chinese Written Character as a Medium for Poetry, edited from a work by Ernest Fenollosa, 1936
Polite Essays, 1937
Guide to Kulchur, 1938; as *Culture*, 1938
Literary Essays, edited by T. S. Eliot, 1954
Pavannes and Divagations, 1958
Impact: Essays on Ignorance and the Decline of American Civilization, edited by Noel Stock, 1960

Selected Prose, 1909–1965, edited by William Cookson, 1973
Ezra Pound and Music: The Complete Criticism, edited by R. Murray Schafer, 1977
"Ezra Pound Speaking": Radio Speeches of World War II, edited by Leonard W. Doob, 1978
Ezra Pound and the Visual Arts, edited by Harriet Zinnes, 1980
Ezra Pound and Japan: Letters and Essays, edited by Sanehide Kodama, 1987
Ezra Pound's Poetry and Prose: Contributions to Periodicals, edited by Lea Baechler, A. Walton Litz, and James Longenbach, 1991

Other writings: many volumes of poetry (primarily *The Cantos*, from 1925), works on literary criticism and culture, and much correspondence. Also translated work from the Japanese, Chinese, and Italian.

Bibliographies

Ezra Pound Criticism, 1905–1985: A Chronological Listing of Publications in English, Marburg: University of Marburg Library, 1991
Gallup, Donald, *Ezra Pound: A Bibliography*, Charlottesville: University Press of Virginia, revised edition, 1983 (original edition, 1963)
Ricks, Beatrice, *Ezra Pound: A Bibliography of Secondary Works*, Metuchen, New Jersey: Scarecrow Press, 1986

Further Reading

Coyle, Michael, "Determining Frontiers: T. S. Eliot's Framing of the Literary Essays of Ezra Pound," *Modern Language Quarterly* 50, no. 3 (September 1989): 248–72
Harmon, William, "Pound's Earlier Critical Writings on Cultural Time and Value," and "Pound's Later Critical Writings on Cultural Time and Value," in his *Time in Ezra Pound's Work*, Chapel Hill: University of North Carolina Press, 1977: 3–23, 24–43
Harris, Natalie, "A Map of Ezra Pound's Criticism," *Southern Review* (Summer 1983): 548–72
Knapp, James F., *Ezra Pound*, Boston: Twayne, 1979
Longenbach, James, *Stone Cottage*, Oxford: Oxford University Press, 1988
McLuhan, Marshall, "Ezra Pound's Critical Prose," in *Ezra Pound: A Collection of Essays to Be Presented to Ezra Pound on His Sixty-Fifth Birthday*, edited by Peter Russell, London: Nevill, 1950; New York: Haskell, 1968
Ruthven, K. K., *Ezra Pound as Literary Critic*, London and New York: Routledge, 1990
Wellek, René, "Ezra Pound's Literary Criticism," *Denver Quarterly* 11 (1976): 1–20

Preface

A preface, formally considered, is a preliminary part of a book or long essay, and in this physical sense it shares, with introductions, forewords, dedications, and prolegomena, an initiatory and, in some cases, participatory relation to the text it precedes, commending either the work, the reader who takes it up, or the author who wrote it. Although Greek and Roman rhetoricians identified the recurrent topoi of classical prefaces or *exordia* (i.e. the conventional forms of modesty designed to create the transparent public persona of the writer), the modern preface, reflecting changing conceptions of the author as a representable, private, individuated self, is nongeneric, and so resists precise description. A preface may confine itself to the factual circumstances surrounding a work, its development, and publication (like **Dickens'** prefaces to "the Original Edition, 1837" and "the Cheap Edition, 1847" of *The Pickwick Papers*) or range in memoir fashion over the history of its reception (like his preface to "the Charles Dickens Edition, 1867" of that work). **Henry James** used the 18 prefaces written for the New York Edition of his works to say about his own and others' writing "what he hoped all his life the critics would say for him" (Leon Edel, *Henry James: The Master, 1901–16*, 1972), while **George Bernard Shaw**'s prefaces are a reader's supplement to the ideas (perhaps not fully realized) in the staged productions of his plays. Paradoxically, the most famous prefaces are those that transcend the usual secondary status of the preface and become independent **critical essays** – Conrad's preface to *The Nigger of the Narcissus* (1897), for instance, or Wordsworth's preface to the *Lyrical Ballads* (1798). John Dryden, who wrote dedications, prologues, a celebrated essay, and a discourse, as well as prefaces, and whose use of the latter term is more precise than most, nevertheless remarks in his "Preface to *The Fables*" (1700) that "the nature of a preface is rambling, never wholly out of the way, nor in it."

In general, prefaces state what (for one reason or another) cannot be stated in the works they accompany – the author's motivation, assumptions, and self-imposed regulations, the credentials of authorship or authority. The preface is the place where the private author may introduce himself to the public to gain its attention and acceptance. In early periods, when writers depended upon the patronage of an aristocratic minority, this function was accomplished in dedications, but as the reading public became more anonymous, writers had to establish a less specific relationship with their more general audience. The preface allowed the author to engage his or her readers on some common ground, to assume for the moment the mask of a reader in a mutual project of understanding or, more formally (as Dryden does in the preface to *The Fables*), in a judicial appeal to a jury.

Prefaces of works of nonfiction are more narrowly focused on the work than on the author. Here the preface becomes a metadiscourse rather than a **familiar essay**. The author appears to step outside his work in order to prepare the reader for what is to follow. Such prefaces pretend to begin at the beginning, to say in advance what has not yet been said, and perhaps even to answer as yet unspoken objections to what is still to come. But in fact, a preface is retrospective, not anticipatory; it is written after the work it precedes and in some manner introduces. Equivocally anterior and exterior to the works that prompt them, prefaces thus tend to cancel themselves out. "Preceding what ought to be able to present itself on its own," Jacques Derrida observes, "the preface falls like an empty husk, a piece of formal refuse ..." Paradoxically, Derrida's deconstruction of the preface appears itself in a preface to his *La Dissémination* (1972; *Dissemination*), where it conceals its prefatory nature behind a series of alternative labels – "*Hors Livre*," "Outwork," "*Hors d'œuvre*," "Extratext," "Foreplay," etc.

The suspicion of bad faith and superfluousness that hovers about prefaces is not new. Aristotle, in the *Rhetoric*, observed that "Introductions are popular with those whose case is weak ... it pays them to dwell on anything rather than the actual facts of it." Since the 18th century, at least within the world of *belles-lettres*, the preface has become a form of apology and an object of parody. Laurence Sterne may serve as the modern exemplar. Near the middle of *Tristram Shandy* (1759–67), the putative author pauses to remark: "All my heroes are off my hands; 'tis the first time I have had a moment to spare, – and I'll make use of it, and write my preface ... No, I'll not say a word about it [the book], – here it is, – in publishing it, – I have appealed to the world, – and to the world I leave it; – it must speak for itself." Tristram only resumes his story after a further ten pages, however.

GEORGE WASSERMAN

Further Reading
Auerbach, Erich, "Germinie Lacerteux," in his *Mimesis: The Representation of Reality in Western Literature*, Princeton, New Jersey: Princeton University Press, 1953 (original German edition, 1946)
Blodgett, E. D., A. G. Purdy, and S. Totosy de Zapetnek, editors, *Prefaces and Literary Manifestoes*, Edmonton: University of Alberta, 1990
Curtius, Ernst Robert, *European Literature and the Latin Middle Ages*, Princeton, New Jersey: Princeton University Press, 1990: especially Chapter 5 (original German edition, 1948)
Derrida, Jacques, "Outwork, Prefacing," in his *Dissemination*, Chicago: University of Chicago Press, 1981 (original French edition, 1972)
Dunn, Kevin, *Pretexts of Authority: The Rhetoric of Authorship in the Renaissance Preface*, Stanford, California: Stanford University Press, 1994
Edelstein, Marilyn Joan, *At the Threshold of the Text: The Rhetoric of Prefaces to Novels* (dissertation), Buffalo: State University of New York, 1984
Georgulis, Christine, *"This is a true story": Fiction Disguised as Fact in the Prefaces of Late Seventeenth- and Eighteenth-Century French and English Prose Works* (dissertation), New York: City University of New York, 1988
Janson, Tore, *Latin Prose Prefaces: Studies in Literary Conventions*, Stockholm: Almqvist & Wiksell, 1964
Jullien, Dominique, "La Préface comme auto-contemplation," *Poétique* 21, no. 84 (1990): 499–508
Navarette, Ignacio, "The Preface as a Platform for Theories of Translation," *Publishing History* 16 (1984): 21–32
Shale, Michele Magnin, *Metamorphosis of the Preface: A Diachronic Study of Prefaces of French Novels* (dissertation), San Diego: University of California, 1986
Tatlock, Lynne, "The Process of Recognition in Satire and Realism: The Prefaces of Seventeenth-Century Novels as a Guide to Author-Intention," *Colloquia Germanica* 18, no. 3 (1985): 238–47
West, Catherine Jones, *La Mise en jeu de l'autorité dans la préface du roman* (dissertation), Chapel Hill: University of North Carolina, 1989

Priestley, J. B.
British, 1894–1984

Over the course of a long and generally successful career, J. B. Priestley was a journalist, novelist, playwright, travel writer, radio broadcaster, biographer, and autobiographer. It was as an essayist that Priestley first established himself, however, and the essay – particularly the **familiar essay** – was a genre to which he frequently returned.

Priestley's first articles were published in local newspapers in his native Yorkshire while he was still in his teens, but his life as an author really commenced in the early 1920s when, following service in World War I and taking a degree at Cambridge, he began publishing essays in periodicals such as the *London Mercury*, the *Nineteenth Century*, the *Outlook*, and the *Cambridge Review*. He later called these early essays "mostly literary exercises," saying that although he "took great pains with them," they were like a musician's practice pieces and therefore inconsequential. Priestley's earlier essays are less focused than his mature pieces and exhibit a somewhat imitative and florid prose style; however, they are more than the "exercises" he dismissed them as, but are in fact well-crafted and articulate essays. One of the most noteworthy characteristics of Priestley's prose is its consistency – from the essays in the 1922 collection *Papers from Lilliput* to the short pieces collected in *Outcries and Asides* (1974) his prose is marked by a consistent tone of good humor, with unostentatious erudition and a sense imparted of a genial and unpretentious narrative persona.

Priestley called the short essay his "favourite literary form," and it was the familiar essay in the tradition of **Montaigne** and **Hazlitt** that Priestley made his own. Although he contributed critical articles to the **Times Literary Supplement** beginning in the 1920s, and was to turn to more **polemical essays**, primarily in the *New Statesman*, after World War II, Priestley saw the familiar essay as the only legitimate essay. Although most of his essays were issued in collected form, most originally appeared in periodicals. Priestley believed that an essayist who writes frequently for the same periodical develops a certain rapport with the reader; the essayist "tends to lose a certain stiffness, formality, self-consciousness that would inevitably make its appearance if he were writing a whole book at a time." This easy relationship with the audience was important, Priestley felt, because "the real essayist has no subject, or if you will, has every subject in the world at his command, for the simple reason that his business is to talk about himself or express the relation between any subject and himself" (introduction to the anthology *Essayists Past and Present*, 1925). The audience Priestley wrote for was the "middle brow" audience. Although he assumes a certain level of knowledge of classical and contemporary literature, Priestley despised literary snobs, particularly academics, the "dons yapping at your feet."

Priestley continually alludes to Romantic authors, especially **Lamb** and Hazlitt, and there are some clear traces of influence to be found in terms of theme and treatment. The gently quizzical treatment of the eccentric acquaintance in Priestley's "The Editor" (1922) has echoes of Lamb's similar subject in his "Captain Jackson" (1823). "The Ring" (1932), Priestley's essay on the old boxing hall in the Blackfriars Road, has several echoes of Hazlitt's 1822 essay "The Fight," both in subject matter, treatment, and general tone. He called Hazlitt "my favourite, my model author, and the only one who directly influenced my writing" (*William Hazlitt*, 1960). Although the direct allusions and echoes of the Romantics become fewer in the later essays, as Priestley developed his own voice and themes further, he remains grounded in this tradition of the Romantic familiar essay.

The topics and themes of Priestley's essays are numerous: reflections on contemporary media (newspapers, radio, and later television); commentary on music, theater, and popular entertainment; remarks on the writing process and the profession of authorship; and many pieces musing on aspects of the English national character or recounting impressions of travel or the incidents of domestic life. All of these are typical of the English familiar essay, but there are certain threads, ideas, and themes throughout which are distinctive to Priestley.

As a novelist and playwright, Priestley was interested in the nature of subjective reality, returning often to the ideas of time and human understanding of reality; these are frequent themes in his essays as well. Often, Priestley seeks to evoke the sense of transience, of the just vanished moment in depictions of the ephemeral nature of reality. The theme of impermanence is worked out in essays such as "A Vanished Lodging" (1931), which describes Priestley's response to news that his college in Cambridge was pulling down the cramped, "elfin" back gate lodge where he had lived in "the queerest rooms in all the University." Now that the physical place he associates most strongly with his university experience is no more, he no longer feels connected to that past, declaring "I'll to the Cam no more, the laurels all are cut." Priestley explores the nature of dreams, and the shifting nature of apprehended reality in essays like "The Dream" (1922), "The Berkshire Beasts" (1927), and "Midsummer Day's Dream" (1927). The first is a nightmarish description of a dream of pursuit and danger, reminiscent of **Thomas De Quincey**'s descriptions of his opium dreams. In it, and in "The Berkshire Beasts," a more whimsical account of an absurd dream, Priestley reflects on how the internal logic of dreams gives them a reality that, by implication, calls into question how authentic our perceptions in our waking moments are, a speculation he returns to in essays like "Midsummer Day's Dream," where he describes the dream-like quality that can occur in the actual world. "The Strange Outfitter" (1928) is notable for being a nightmare rendition of another of Priestley's favorite subjects, his difficulty in shopping for clothing. He discusses the seemingly random nature of insight in "A Road and Some Moods" (1922), of how "we realise the beauty and blessing of life itself only in rare, inexplicable moments, and then most keenly," an idea he was to express again in "The Moments" (1966), where he describes how the "great blue bottle of happiness" comes upon us suddenly, seemingly unconnected to our physical reality, and we realize that our perceptions are shaped by "influences beyond our understanding." In "This Insubstantial Pageant" (1923), he remarks that ideas "have a trick of taking to themselves some of the glamour of the time when they were first conceived," that we may continue to cling to a foolish intellectual position merely because it was adopted when we were experiencing a period of happiness. The subjective nature of apprehension is also addressed in this essay, as Priestley describes how, in just the right light, from just the right angle, London becomes a place of ethereal beauty.

Although Priestley wrote a number of book **review**s and essays on literary topics, he eschewed the critical or scholarly approach of those whom he frequently disparaged as "Eng. Lit. types." His choice of subjects in *The English Comic Characters* (1925) and *Figures in Modern Literature* (1924) is generally canonical, and here, as in his other literary essays, he is less concerned with critical analysis and more intent on presenting a subjective "appreciation" of the work or author discussed. This approach is exemplified in the brief pieces on art, music, and theater in *Particular Pleasures* (1975), tellingly subtitled *Being a Personal Record of Some Various Arts and Many Different Artists*. Priestley argued for a literature which was "extroverted" rather than "introverted," believing that works of art should meet some need, spiritual or otherwise, for the reader, and should not be evaluated on narrow, programmatic grounds. Thus, in the ironic "Those Terrible Novelists" (1925) he laments what he saw as the "motiveless sneering and confounding" of writers in the 1920s, a concern echoed in "The Outsider" (1956), a critique of John Osborne's *Look Back in Anger* and what Priestley saw in the postwar Angry Young Men as a fruitless alienation, "poisoned by an embittered egoism." Writing in "Disturbing" (1967), Priestley again critiques contemporary playwrights and novelists for exacerbating contemporary problems, creating works that sought to "disturb" a reading public already disturbed by the myriad problems of the day. Rather than valuing literature which spoke to the common reader, Priestley argues, among contemporary critics and authors "a new snobbery of pessimism" had arisen. He frequently criticized what he saw as the arrogance of academic literary critics, who he remarked "seem to regard themselves as the ferocious theologians and grand inquisitors of art" ("Another Revolution," 1957).

Although committed to a form of liberal socialism throughout his life, Priestley despised ideologues, declaring in *Outcries and Asides* that the "Iron Maidens of our age are ideologies, whether of the Left or Right." He was also ambivalent about the writer's role in the political arena, calling it in his autobiographical *Margin Released* (1962) a world that the writer enters "without confidence and probably with loathing." While recognizing that the writer is a citizen, with the same rights and duties as any other, he believed that the professional writer should be wary of engaging in political activities, recognizing the danger of what he called the "ego-swelling ham Theatre" of political speaking. Despite this professed wariness of political action, Priestley wrote many polemical pieces, becoming increasingly politicized during and immediately following World War II. His pamphlet *Letter to a Returning Serviceman* (1945), for example, is somewhat Marxist in orientation, sharing the then common sentiment that Britain was obliged to rebuild after the war along socialist lines. In the 1950s Priestley became a director of the *New Statesman*, helping to shape its development as a "conscience" for the governing Labour Party. He wrote many articles for the journal, the most notable probably being "Britain and the Nuclear Bombs" (1957), in which he cogently refutes many of the arguments for Britain continuing to maintain a nuclear arsenal, arguing for the moral superiority that unilateral nuclear disarmament would bring. It is this article which is widely recognized as instigating the formation of the Campaign for Nuclear Disarmament. Another of his *New Statesman* pieces, the frequently anthologized "Wrong Ism" of 1966, is a critique of current geopolitics, notably of nationalism, which Priestley likened to "the rotten meat between the two healthy slices of bread" that were regionalism and internationalism.

Priestley has not fared well at the hands of critics, and his contemporary reputation is negligible, with most of his works being out of print or difficult to obtain. At his peak, he was dismissed by critics such as F. R. Leavis and **Virginia Woolf**

as a mere popular novelist; but he was never a deliberate "best-seller" author. In *Margin Released* he writes that "I am too conventional for the avant-garde, too experimental for Aunt Edna . . . a lowbrow to highbrows, a highbrow to lowbrows." A few of his essays continue to be anthologized, although the majority are neglected. He should be considered important to serious students of the English essay, however – as Susan Cooper notes in her preface to Priestley's *Essays of Five Decades* (1968), his essays reflect and helped shape a crucial stage of the development of this literary form, the transition from the "graceful and discursive" familiar essay that Priestley inherited from the Edwardians to the "more genuinely personal framework and mind" of the modern English essay.

JAN PETER F. VAN ROSEVELT

Biography
John Boynton Priestley. Born 13 September 1894 in Bradford, Yorkshire. Worked for wool traders, 1910–14. Served with the Duke of Wellington's and Devon regiments, 1914–19. Studied at Trinity Hall, Cambridge, 1919–21, B.A. in history, 1921. Married Patricia Tempest, 1919 (died, 1925): two daughters. Journalist and reviewer for various newspapers and periodicals, including the *New Statesman*, from 1922. Married Mary Wyndham Lewis, 1926 (divorced, 1952): two daughters and one son. Founder, English Plays Ltd., a production company for his own work; director, Mask Theatre, London, 1938–39; broadcaster of "Postscripts" for the BBC, 1940–41. Chair, president, or member of various organizations and conferences concerning theater; U.K. delegate to UNESCO conferences, 1946–47. Moved to Kissing Tree House, Warwickshire, 1959. Awards: James Tait Black Memorial Prize, 1930; Ellen Terry Award, 1948; honorary degrees from three universities; Order of Merit, 1977. Died at Kissing Tree House, 14 August 1984.

Selected Writings

Essays and Related Prose
Papers from Lilliput, 1922
Brief Diversions, 1922
I for One, 1923
Figures in Modern Literature, 1924
The English Comic Characters, 1925
Essays of To-day and Yesterday, 1926
Talking, 1926
Open House: A Book of Essays, 1927
Apes and Angels: A Book of Essays, 1928; as *Too Many People and Other Reflections*, 1928
The Balconinny and Other Essays, 1929
Self-Selected Essays, 1932
Postscripts (radio broadcasts), 1940; as *All England Listened*, 1968
Letter to a Returning Serviceman, 1945
The Secret Dream: An Essay on Britain, America, and Russia, 1946
Delight, 1949
All About Ourselves and Other Essays, edited by Eric Gillett, 1956
Thoughts in the Wilderness, 1957
The Art of the Dramatist, 1957
William Hazlitt, 1960
Man and Time, 1964
The Moments, and Other Pieces, 1966
Essays of Five Decades, edited by Susan Cooper, 1968
Over the Long High Wall: Some Reflections and Speculations on Life, Death, and Time, 1972
Outcries and Asides, 1974
Particular Pleasures, Being a Personal Record of Some Various Arts and Many Different Artists, 1975
English Humour, 1976

Other writings: many plays (including *Dangerous Corner*, 1932; *Laburnum Grove*, 1933; *Eden End*, 1934; *I Have Been Here Before*, 1937; *When We Are Married*, 1938; *An Inspector Calls*, 1945; *The Linden Tree*, 1947), novels (including *The Good Companions*, 1929; *Angel Pavement*, 1930; *Bright Day*, 1946; *Lost Empires*, 1965), a few short stories, one collection of poetry, works on literature and politics, and several volumes of autobiography (including *Margin Released*, 1962). Also edited the anthology *Essayists Past and Present* (1925).

Bibliography
Day, Alan Edwin, *J. B. Priestley: An Annotated Bibliography*, Stroud: privately printed, 1980

Further Reading
Atkins, John, *J. B. Priestley: The Last of the Sages*, London: Calder, 1981
Braine, John, *J. B. Priestley*, London: Weidenfeld and Nicolson, 1978
Brome, Vincent, *J. B. Priestley*, London: Hamilton, 1988
DeVitis, A. A., and Albert E. Kalson, *J. B. Priestley*, Boston: Twayne, 1980
Hughes, David, *J. B. Priestley: An Informal Study of His Work*, London: Rupert Hart-Davis, 1958

Pritchett, V. S.

British, 1900–1997

For the greater part of the 20th century V. S. Pritchett almost singlehandedly preserved the tradition of the English man of letters. A professional writer, Pritchett composed successful travel books, autobiographies, and biographies, but he is best known for his short stories and for his literary essays, which have appeared, primarily in the *New Statesman*, since 1926.

Pritchett's literary essays are not those of a rigorous academic critic, and his ideas reflect no philosophical or literary dogma. They are the informal literary reflections of a widely read and intelligent "common reader," for whom each book is a new experience requiring an individual response, one that usually involves summary, description, and evaluation. Although Pritchett's criticism is eclectic, certain broad themes underlie much of it.

One of Pritchett's principal concerns is the historical aspect of books and their authors. Believing that "one of the obligations of the critic is to possess himself of the eyes with which a novelist's contemporaries read him" ("The Shocking Surgeon," 1946), Pritchett often begins an essay by describing a scene representative of a book or an author, as in a stagecoach ride ending in crash and chaos to introduce the scientific romances of H. G. Wells ("The Scientific Romances," 1946) or his long, novelistic description of London's East End as a foreign city to introduce the work of Arthur Morrison ("An East End Novelist," 1946). The other aspect of Pritchett's historical approach is his belief that the relevance of older works to contemporary readers should be stressed. In his **preface** to *In My Good Books* (1942) Pritchett emphasizes that the best works of fiction "are those in which the cries of an age are like echoes of our own ... We hold up the crystal sphere; we see ourselves in miniature reflection and, perhaps, if our minds are not too literal, we may also see our future."

Thus in an essay on Fielding's *Jonathan Wild* Pritchett finds the mock biography "the perfect medicine for the present time" because it treats contemporary subjects, while in novels "the news is already absorbed and digested. We see our situation at a manageable remove" ("An Anatomy of Greatness," 1942). Literature, in **Ezra Pound**'s phrase, is news that stays news, so that "Tyranny abroad, corruption at home – that recurrent theme of the eighteenth-century satirists who were confronted by absolute monarchy and the hunt for places – is our own."

Another common Pritchett approach is the biographical. Many of Pritchett's essays are reviews of literary biographies, and he uses these works as a springboard to discuss the subject's background and surroundings that influence the writing. For Pritchett the "death of the author" has not occurred, and when useful he will discuss Eugène François Vidocq's flamboyant life as a criminal and policeman, Thomas Day's personality as that of "a crank who is the guide to all cranks, the pattern of the tribe" ("The Crank," 1946), or the effects of Synge's and Joyce's respective return to and escape from Ireland, as necessary to a full understanding of their work. For Pritchett the *living* novel, as he titled one of his collections, is written by living writers.

A third avenue of Pritchett's criticism is more technical. A notable writer of novels and short stories himself, Pritchett can knowledgeably and effectively comment on certain literary aspects of a writer's art with professional insight. In his discussion of *Sons and Lovers*, for instance, Pritchett defines **Lawrence**'s originality as the ability to write "from within – from inside the man, the woman, the tree, the fox, the mine" ("Sons and Lovers," 1946). Lawrence's characters and settings are "grasped with both hands, with mind and senses. The impersonal novelist has gone ... the people, the trees, the mines, the fields, the kitchens come physically upon the page."

These brief insights, rather than sustained criticism, are the most notable and valuable aspects of Pritchett's literary essays, and such insights can be found almost at random in them. Pritchett provides the germ of an idea in brief, provocative statements, for instance that Sheridan Le Fanu "might be described as the Simenon of the peculiar" ("An Irish Ghost," 1946), that for the lower middle class life as described in *The Diary of a Nobody*, "Reality was the joke, its awful, dreary grayness" ("The Nobodies," 1942), or that *The Ring and the Book* is not an epic poem but "a great Victorian novel, or, more accurately, the child of a misalliance between poetry and the novel" ("A Victorian Misalliance," 1942). Pritchett then briefly discusses the idea but pays his readers the compliment of assuming that they can pursue such considerations for themselves.

A final aspect of Pritchett's criticism is its enormous range and inclusiveness. Pritchett's literary essays include discussions of the literature of many countries, not just England, and like his near contemporary **Virginia Woolf** he is as interested in the cranks, iconoclasts, and eccentrics of literature as he is in its major figures. In Pritchett's work a Peacock, Le Fanu, Jerome, or **Perelman** is responded to as readily and intelligently as a Joyce or **Mann**.

This wide range of literary interests, together with his concern with literary biography and his relatively simple style, may make Pritchett seem a rather old-fashioned figure in an era dominated by scholarly approaches and sometimes arcane literary theory, and like his nearest American equivalent **Edmund Wilson**, Pritchett has not always appealed to the academic specialist. However, he did not write for the academic specialist, but for the nonspecialist intelligent reader, and those readers who persevere through the enormous volume of Pritchett's *Complete Collected Essays* (1990) will acquire, in a highly informative and entertaining way, a broad knowledge of both the major and the minor currents of world literature.

JOHN H. ROGERS

Biography

Victor Sawdon Pritchett. Born 16 December 1900 in Ipswich, Suffolk. Studied at Alleyn's School, Dulwich, London. Worked in the leather trade in London, 1916–20, and in various trades in Paris, 1920–32. Correspondent for the Boston *Christian Science Monitor* in Ireland and Spain, 1923–26; critic, from 1926, and director, 1946–78, *New Statesman*, London. Married Dorothy Rudge Roberts, 1936: one son and one daughter. Held lectureships and visiting professor and writer-in-residence posts at various American universities as well as at Cambridge University, 1953–81. President, PEN English Centre, 1970, International PEN, 1974–76, and Society of Authors, from 1977. Elected Fellow, 1969, and Companion of Literature, 1987, Royal Society of Literature. Knighted, 1975. Awards: Heinemann Award, 1969; PEN Award, 1974; W. H. Smith Award, 1990; Silver Pen Award, 1990; honorary degrees from four universities. Commander, Order of the British Empire (CBE), 1968. Died in London, 21 March 1997.

Selected Writings

Essays and Related Prose
In My Good Books, 1942
The Living Novel, 1946; revised, enlarged edition, 1964
Books in General, 1953
The Working Novelist, 1965
George Meredith and English Comedy (Clark lectures), 1970
The Myth Makers: Essays on European, Russian, and South American Novelists, 1979
The Tale Bearers: Essays on English, American, and Other Writers, 1980
A Man of Letters: Selected Essays, 1985
At Home and Abroad, 1989
Lasting Impressions: Selected Essays, 1990; as *Lasting Impressions: Essays, 1961–1987*, 1990
The Complete Essays, 1991; as *Complete Collected Essays*, 1991

Other writings: five novels (*Clare Drummer*, 1929; *Shirley Sanz*, 1932 [published in the U.S. as *Elopement into Exile*]; *Nothing like Leather*, 1935; *Dead Man Leading*, 1937; *Mr. Beluncle*, 1951), many volumes of short stories, two volumes of autobiography, and books on travel and literary criticism.

Further Reading

Baldwin, Dean R., *V. S. Pritchett*, Boston: Twayne, 1987
Borkland, Elmer, "V. S. Pritchett," in his *Contemporary Literary Critics*, London: Macmillan, and New York: St. Martin's Press, revised edition, 1982: 452–57 (original edition, 1977)
Kermode, Frank, "Books in General," *New Statesman and Nation*, 19 March 1965: 455–56
Lewis, Peter, "Loner with a Master's Touch," *Daily Telegraph*, 14 December 1980: 21
Marcus, Stephen, "An Ideal Critic," *New York Review of Books*, 8 October 1964: 12–15
Marks, Harry S., "V. S. Pritchett," in *British Novelists, 1930–1959*, *Dictionary of Literary Biography*, vol. 15, part 2, Detroit: Gale Research, 1983: 464–71
Maxwell, William, "The Two Merlins," *The New Yorker*, 29 August 1970: 77–78
Vidal, Gore, "Secrets of the Shell," *New York Review of Books*, 28 June 1979: 6–7

Propaganda

Propaganda has so broad a meaning that it is almost impossible to define on the basis of specific literary values that may be recognized in traditional literary forms like the **sermon, treatise**, or **tract**. Historical contexts are critical in understanding what propaganda is, what its uses are, and how it is perceived by its analysts and proponents. Historians agree that the origin of the term dates from the Catholic Church's *Congregatio de propaganda fide* in 1622, which sanctioned missionary projects throughout the world. However, definitions of propaganda vary depending on the contexts in which opinion forms. Propaganda, then, may have a neutral or descriptive meaning, or it may be used, as it tends to be in modern times, with negative connotations. René Wellek's classic *Theory of Literature* (1949) argues that "The term 'propaganda' is loose and needs scrutiny. In popular speech, it is applied to doctrines viewed as pernicious and spread by men whom we distrust. The word implies calculation, intention, and is usually applied to specific, rather than restrictive doctrines or programmes." Wellek claims, as would many literary theorists, that literature as art is opposed to propaganda; yet if we argue that all writers sincerely attempt to influence, then all writing may be "propaganda."

Wellek's views are influenced by propaganda as a problem in the function of literature in the period after World War I, when the partisanship and political engagement of writers were linked to social movements, and questions of ethics and belief in literary interpretation were on the agenda. Instructive was **T. S. Eliot**'s turn to Christian culture as a solution to democratic individualism, collectivism, and fascism. Eliot's essays like "Journalism and Literature" (1931) and "Christianity and Society" (1939) attempt to answer the question of belief and unbelief versus disinterested truth. Eliot even says that Dante and Lucretius are "good propagandists" ("Poetry and Propaganda," 1930).

But if rhetorical persuasion cannot be equated with propaganda, can there be both "positive" propaganda and "negative" propaganda? Even an authority on propaganda like Harold Lasswell (1959) can define it ahistorically as a neutral technique: propaganda is "in the broadest sense . . . the technique of influencing human action by the manipulation of representations" in different media. How deliberate the manipulation may be is clearly a problem in defining what it is. We can see that propaganda in this sense touches other literary forms, since it cuts across genres, including didactic and educational essays which may contain many rhetorical or literary conventions. However, this still does not distinguish it from other vehicles or ideologically oriented cultural attitudes like myths or belief systems which also frame truths.

We may define "soft" propaganda minimally as an instrument of persuasion and manipulation of public opinion which coerces truth by claiming universality for its views. Propaganda in this sense would be distinguished from education, which assumes that the listener is rational, can understand several points of view, and will make up his or her mind on the basis of the evidence. Yet a recent commentator on propaganda, Lucy Lippard (1980), argues the reverse, namely that propaganda is a function of knowledge itself: feminists "... have to keep in the back of our minds that we wouldn't have to use the denigrated word 'propaganda' for what is, in fact, education, if it weren't consistently used against us." She argues that quality, objectivity, and neutrality in art "belong to them," and that "Feminism has potentially changed the terms of propaganda as art by being unashamed of its obsessions and political needs, and by confirming the bonds between individual and social experience."

The difficulty of defining propaganda is such that it is often tempting to look for its origins in ancient and medieval cultures. For example, it might be claimed that **Plato**'s *Republic* is propaganda for or against the state or that the Homeric epics or Greek drama contain propagandistic elements that praise the laws or the rule of tyrants. We could say that the poems of Hesiod or the *Iliad* and *Odyssey*, and similarly Dante or Milton, use fixed conventions and styles that appropriate the responses and expectations of the listener. However, even though belief, ritual, religion, and the symbols may exist as separate spheres for the modern reader, the syncretic, artistic forms of ancient genres do not allow us to claim that they are used as propaganda, even though they may reinforce belief or faith in the gods. At the same time, it is fair to say that Aristophanes in Athens and Horace in Rome parodied the popularization of literature and the debasing of the word. This indicates that political demagoguery is a feature of the ancient world.

The humanist movements that dramatically separate politics from religion from the 14th to the 18th centuries constitute another phase in understanding the problematic political origin of propaganda. In the Middle Ages literary and rhetorical techniques in both high and low culture were dependent on the degree of literacy and education in the secular institutions of society. The rise of a reading public from the 14th to the 19th centuries in Europe led to an explosion of **pamphlet**s, broadsides, and polemical tracts of a personal, heretical, and dissenting nature. These later became a feature of the revolutionary traditions in France, England, and Germany in the late 18th and 19th centuries. Already in the 16th century Rabelais, **Montaigne**, and **Erasmus** were writing in the humanist tradition that draws out the relationship of power to the increasing consciousness of absolutism. The English humanism of Sir Thomas More's *Utopia* (1516) is a particularly striking example of schooling and education defended as higher goods that are tied to social issues. Milton's *Areopagitica* (1644) constructs freedom of speech against intolerance, but at the same time propagandizes against popery.

But More's *Utopia*, **Edmund Burke**'s *Reflections on the Revolution in France* (1790), and the political essays of Wyndham Lewis like *The Art of Being Ruled* (1926), or even **Nietzsche**'s *Also sprach Zarathustra* (1883–85; *Thus Spoke Zarathustra*), are more than mere ideas. They insist that ideas change the world and that using a personal language in essayistic form can change the reader's convictions about reality. Propagandists seem to be intoxicated by ideas and language.

Humanistic propaganda is typically concerned about social justice, the welfare of the poor, the injustices of man, and the inequalities associated with religion and monarchy. The techniques used are not just emotional expressions. Humanist essays contain elements like name-calling, ridicule, and degrading invective, judgments about the motivations of enemies, blasphemy, and caustic sarcasm formed in the crucible of the dissenting traditions. The audience would be familiar with satirical, polemical, hortatory, and parodic styles of speech. Indeed, oaths, curses, and rhetorical inversions are used by "good" and "bad" propagandists to travesty enemies, and the false "truths" of opponents. To subvert the mind of the reader and build up one's own case is considered fair. Learning and preaching are not easily separated, but to the polemicist the pedantry of official speech is open game.

If propaganda comes from those who control the means of persuasion, like the intelligentsia, it can also be used by those who do not fit into the dominant world view. Indeed, it can be argued that with the rise of printing in the mid-15th century, combined with the spread of the Reformation with its emphasis on literacy and schooling, a new audience was created which would be open to both religious and secular demagoguery. By appealing to the base motives of the powerful, the propagandist attempts to psychologize about motives and builds up the status and esteem of those who are outside of the cultured and educated classes in order to make them feel like insiders. Both Calvin's and Luther's treatises use sacred texts in order to open a new audience to the criticism of doctrinal and theological values; since many of the new readers were members of the commercial classes, both leaders and addressees were familiar with vernacular speech.

As the bearers of social transformation, the new classes were particularly prone to the crises that accompanied economic and political change. Clerical forces not only "propagated the faith," they also attempted to combat change and the spread of knowledge. Galileo, Copernicus, and Bruno are vivid examples of the effects of "positive" clerical propaganda used against secular thought. Censorship in France and most of Europe was official policy from the 14th century to the French Revolution. If propaganda is placed in the context of the humanist tradition it can be seen as a subset of institutional discourses, a medium in which ideas are used to change the beliefs of others and above all to promote action or conversion in ways that not only represent the truth, but demand action on behalf of truth.

Propaganda only began to assume negative attributes in the 19th century, well beyond the time when the "propagation of the faith" was a neutral activity of a benign church. In the aftermath of the French Revolution, workers' movements, educational and abolitionist movements, along with the missionizing zeal of Catholic and Protestant churches, created conditions for mobilizing opinion for ideological causes. It was clear that traditional cultural or normative ethics could be attacked in the name of coercing audiences on behalf of religious or political truths.

The pamphlets, screeds, and manifestos written in the revolutionary times of the 18th and 19th centuries show us that sedition and censorship are two sides of the propaganda coin. However, seen from the perspective of the manipulation of public opinion during times when the fragmentation of communal values occurs, it is clear that propaganda and censorship are the children of the marriage of rising literacy and democratic movements. The propagandist assumes an attitude that people in masses cannot reason for themselves and are basically irrational. This permits writers to degrade an enemy and use indirect suggestion rather than argue with reasonable auditors. The formation of social movements and publics within modern nation-states gives rise to special interests which attempt to mobilize opinion and solidarity for their causes. The rise of new classes and groups – the masses are open to movements for reform, reeducation, and politicizing – leads to the development of literary and rhetorical tools for the manipulation of the mind and emotions in ways that go beyond mere rational persuasion.

Propaganda became both a public issue and a writer's issue in England and America during World War I. Following the religious and colonial wars of the 19th century, when nationalism appeared to be an answer to the upheavals and transformations of social movements, new ideological conditions prevailed. World War I was fought on the basis of loyalty to national identity, and propaganda became an official arm of governments for maintaining national unity against the dark European "Central Powers." Appropriating writers for war-making causes marked a shift from the previous centuries when writers decried nationalism and xenophobia. England's propaganda machine in World War I affected writers as diverse as **Henry James**, H. G. Wells, Ford Madox Ford, and John Galsworthy, who enlisted themselves on the side of England's cause. Other writers, however, like **D. H. Lawrence** ("Education of the People," 1920) and **E. M. Forster** ("Two Cheers for Democracy," 1951), opposed the use of propaganda to bring the masses in line with war-making.

In modern times propaganda is almost always associated with the political coercion of opinion, war-making, and the militarization of society. This explains why avant-garde writers and artists are often associated with propaganda or are attracted by the techniques that encourage art to achieve a direct relationship to society. "Agitprop" – the most conscious of propagandistic movements in art and literature in the 1930s in the Soviet Union and Germany – is a term coined expressly to sanction the connection between publicity, agitation, and propaganda.

It is easy to see how in modern times propaganda is associated with advertising and brainwashing, because propaganda is now assumed to be deliberate manipulation. The "hidden persuaders" of the advertising and consumer industries successfully create conditions for obedience to official values and organizational behavior. Jacques Ellul (1965) argues that language and imagery condition and absorb individuals into the mechanical reproduction of reality. However, advertising as well as the written text, images, and the daringly graphic designs of agitprop can entertain as well as lure willing spectators into hostile attitudes toward an enemy. Yet folk songs and popular songs, proverbs, and political songs are themselves vehicles for propaganda. Propaganda uses slogans that scapegoat members of a class, race, or ethnic community as the enemy who is outside the boundaries of the human community. Both sophisticated and simplistic, psychologically loaded techniques like caricature, distortion, displacement, and sexual stereotyping demonize foreigners and outsiders. At the same time,

techniques of propaganda can be used to control how information is disseminated. Noam Chomsky (1988), following in the tradition of **John Stuart Mill**, Alexis de Tocqueville, Harold Lasswell, and Jacques Ellul, coined the phrase "manufacturing consent" to describe how Western governments, newspapers, and the media propagate the official line by developing sophisticated verbal and documentary techniques that deceive a public unable to distinguish political policy from expedience. The democratic obligations to educate and enlighten about controversial political and cultural issues are evaded.

The historical and political forces that create the genre "propaganda" are clear. But the relationship to the essay as a form of thought may be elusive. While propaganda is often associated with social transformation and revolution or counter-revolution, it is useful to remember that propaganda is not only a genre of writing, but a framework which helps us understand and become aware of the relationship between language, reason, and coercion. Historically, intellectuals and writers have been attracted to the issues raised by propaganda. Intellectuals interpret reality and criticize reason; thus they often find themselves searching for ways to identify forces in society which criticize absolutist political domination. Writers often seek approval and power and join the forces that control ideas or promote hostility.

Propaganda can be described as a tool for establishing the consensual basis for new alliances in society. This is not a new tactic. **Addison**'s and **Steele**'s journals or Jean-Paul Marat's agitational pamphlets can promote a rationalist view of the world in order to secure new modes of consent among those who are out of power, just as the enemies of power, like **William Godwin** or Percy Bysshe Shelley, plead for a higher rationality. Critics of official thought, like **Jonathan Swift** in "An Essay upon the Art of Political Lying" (1710) and *A Modest Proposal* (1729) or **George Orwell** in "Politics and the English Language" (1946), object to the use of language that cajoles, threatens, frightens, or obsequiously praises authority or mass-mindedness. Shelley's "A Defence of Poetry" (1821), the essays of Bertolt Brecht on partisanship and commitment in the 1930s, **H. L. Mencken**'s tirades against mediocrity and conformism in language, while anchored to different political alignments, are sophisticated analyses of the culture of official speech, because they are aware of the illiberal influence the manipulation of language can have among both the educated and the uneducated. For them publicists are "legislators" who must be responsible to the people, and their essays do not shy away from passionate criticism of the standardization of thought that swallows up and digests reason.

Agitprop under communism – often called the propaganda of the deed – or lurid Nazi anti-Semitic propaganda, or war propaganda in England and America, shared the common end of coercing ideological realignment by projecting a powerful enemy in the name of maintaining power. Propaganda appeals to the purity and superiority of those groups who are struggling against forces which are deemed capable of annihilating the self-identified good or just cause. Propaganda should be understood as a cross-generic phenomenon embedded within a variety of forms and genres that may be equally popular, plebeian, or official. In attempting to bring the reader to a point where acting, performing, or changing consciousness and identity can be effected in the name of powerful forces of social and cultural transformation, propaganda is framed by the platitudes and clichés of prejudice and conventional wisdom, but its essence lies in its function as a discourse between preconstructed audiences and images of audiences. The social consequences of propaganda reveal the objectives of propaganda, namely that by subjecting truth to coercive forms, a crisis of legitimation in the nature of citizenship (and particularly, belonging) is precipitated. Essays which harbor propagandistic elements, or can be clearly identified as propaganda, should make the reader consider whether it is possible to entrust the enlighteners with our minds and souls.

JERALD ZASLOVE

Further Reading

Adorno, Theodor W., "Anti-Semitism and Fascist Propaganda," in his *The Stars Come Down to Earth and Other Essays on the Irrational in Culture*, edited by Stephen Crook, London and New York: Routledge, 1994 (article originally published 1946)

Bauman, Zygmunt, *Legislators and Interpreters: On Modernity, Post-Modernity, and Intellectuals*, Ithaca, New York: Cornell University Press, and Cambridge: Polity Press, 1987

Brecht, Bertolt, *Brecht on Theatre*, edited by John Willett, New York: Hill and Wang, and London: Methuen, 1992 (original edition, 1964)

Buitenhuis, Peter, *The Great War of Words: British, American, and Canadian Propaganda and Fiction, 1914–1933*, Vancouver: University of British Columbia Press, 1987

Chomsky, Noam, *American Power and the New Mandarins*, New York: Pantheon, and London, Chatto and Windus, 1969

Chomsky, Noam, *Manufacturing Consent: The Political Economy of the Mass Media*, New York: Pantheon, 1988; London: Vintage, 1994

Darnton, Robert, and Daniel Roche, editors, *Revolution in Print: The Press in France, 1775–1800*, Berkeley: University of California Press, 1989

Eliot, T. S., "Poetry and Propaganda," *Bookman* 70, no. 6 (February 1930)

Ellul, Jacques, *The Technological Society*, New York: Knopf, 1964 (original French edition, 1954)

Ellul, Jacques, *Propaganda: The Formation of Men's Attitudes*, New York: Vintage, 1973 (original edition, 1965)

Elshtain, Jean Bethke, *Women and War*, Chicago: University of Chicago Press, 1995 (original edition, 1987)

Godzich, Wlad, *The Culture of Literacy*, Cambridge, Massachusetts: Harvard University Press, 1994

Graff, Harvey, *The Legacies of Literacy: Continuities and Contradictions in Western Culture and Society*, Bloomington: Indiana University Press, 1987

Habermas, Jürgen, *The Structural Transformation of the Public Sphere: An Inquiry into a Category of Bourgeois Society*, Cambridge, Massachusetts: MIT Press, and London: Polity Press, 1989 (original German edition, 1962)

Hauser, Arnold, "Propaganda, Ideology and Art," in *Aspects of History and Class Consciousness*, edited by Istvan Meszaros, London: Routledge and Kegan Paul, 1971

Hilvert, John, *Blue Pencil Warriors: Censorship and Propaganda in World War II*, St. Lucia, Queensland: University of Queensland Press, 1984

Jackall, Robert, editor, *Propaganda*, New York: New York University Press, 1995

Jacoby, Russell, *Dogmatic Wisdom: How the Culture Wars Divert Education and Distract America*, New York: Doubleday, 1994

Kracauer, Siegfried, *From Caligari to Hitler: A Psychological History of the German Film*, Princeton, New Jersey: Princeton University Press, 1974 (original edition, 1947)

Lasswell, Harold, "Propaganda," in *Encyclopedia of the Social Sciences*, vol. 11, edited by Edwin R. A. Seligman and Alvin Johnson, New York: Macmillan, 1959

Lippard, Lucy R., "Some Propaganda for Propaganda," *Heresies* 3, no. 1 (1980): 35–39

MacKenzie, John, *Propaganda and Empire: The Manipulation of British Public Opinion, 1880–1960*, Manchester: Manchester University Press, 1984

Mencken, H. L., *The American Language: An Inquiry into the Development of English in the United States*, New York: Knopf, 1980 (original edition, 1919; original 3rd revised edition, 1923)

Messinger, Gary S., *British Propaganda and the First World War*, Manchester: Manchester University Press, and New York: St. Martin's Press, 1992

Mumford, Lewis, *The Myth of the Machine: The Pentagon of Power*, New York: Harcourt Brace Jovanovich, 1964

Orwell, George, "Politics and the English Language," in *The Collected Essays, Journalism and Letters of George Orwell*, vol. 4, edited by Sonia Orwell and Ian Angus, London: Secker and Warburg, and New York: Harcourt Brace World, 1968 (essay originally published 1946)

Rosenberg, Bernard, and David Manning White, editors, *Mass Culture: The Popular Arts in America*, New York: Free Press, and London: Collier Macmillan, 1964 (original edition, 1957)

Scott, William G., and David K. Hart, *Organizational America*, Boston: Houghton Mifflin, 1979

Thompson, E. P., *The Making of the Working Class*, London: Gollancz, 1980 (original edition, 1963)

Tocqueville, Alexis de, *Democracy in America*, New York: Knopf, 1993 (original French edition, 1835–40)

Williams, Raymond, *The Long Revolution*, Westport, Connecticut: Greenwood Press, 1975 (original edition, 1961)

Williams, Raymond, *Writing in Society*, London: Verso, 1983

Pushkin, Aleksandr

Russian, 1799–1837

Less well known than his unparalleled poetry and pioneering imaginative prose, Aleksandr Pushkin's essays, advocating supple language and a modern approach to literature, emerged from the crucible of the critical and journalistic polemic of his times. Pushkin wrote over 100 essays, critical fragments, rebuttals, notes, and reviews which in content are literary, theoretical, polemical, autobiographical, biographical, critical, historical, political, and satirical. The majority are short in length and brilliantly concentrated. Most remained in draft form and over half were published posthumously due to repressive censorship and the restrictive political situation. Friends learned of his ideas through discussion, the familiar letter, or circulation in manuscript form.

While Pushkin's primary focus is on the issues of literature as an institution (classical, Romantic, and incipient realistic), as well as language, the readership, and publication, his concern for social, political, and historical issues is always present, at times in the form of circumspect discourse within other contexts. Indeed, some scholars perceive Pushkin's notes as sketches toward an autobiography in lieu of the memoirs that were destroyed following the ill-fated Decembrist Rebellion in 1825.

Foremost in the remarkably erudite Pushkin's focus is literature – Russian and foreign, particularly French, German, English, and classical – with increasing attention given to history, primarily to revolutions and cultural conflicts – from the Time of Troubles (1598–1613) to contemporary issues. His voice is that of the vanguard of the cultured elite, often years ahead of the times. In fact, his essays lend legitimacy to a nascent genre in Russian letters. John Bayley (1986) calls Pushkin's "sense" of literature "dazzling" with "an unerring feeling for what makes a really great genius," arguing that "Pushkin the artist is as detached and objective about a work of art – his own or another's – as is Pushkin the critic." Pushkin's first known essay, "Moi zamechaniia ob russkom teatre" (wr. 1820; "My Observations on the Russian Theater"), advocates professionalism on the boards. The first published essay, "Pismo k izdateliu *Syna otechestva*" (pub. 1824; "Letter to the Publisher of *Son of the Fatherland*"), tactfully subdues a polemic on Romanticism versus classicism concerning Pushkin's poem, *Bakhchisaraiskii fontan* (*The Fountain at Bakhchisarai*), between his friend Prince Viazemskii and M. A. Dmitriev by maintaining that Romanticism finds resistance only in Western Europe.

Pushkin's overarching concern is the unsuitability for modern abstract reasoning of contemporary Russian prose, despite the merits of Nikolai Karamzin's literary and historical writings. Accordingly, Pushkin's first article on literature, "O proze" (wr. 1822; "On Prose"), promotes "accuracy and brevity" as the premier merits of prose and demands abundant ideas and thoughts. As in his poetry, the semantic and metaliterary, political, and personal levels of discourse are often encoded in the primary narrative. Paul Debreczeny (1983) finds that Pushkin's expository prose is closest in language to his imaginative prose. In fact, the language and conceits of poetry and prose often intertwine and complement each other, as in his rebuttal poem "Moia rodoslovnaia" ("My Genealogy") and the essay "Oproverzhenie na kritiki" (wr. 1830; "Refutation of Criticisms").

Few of Pushkin's essays were published until his confidant Baron Anton Delvig founded the *Literaturnaia Gazeta* (1830–35; Literary gazette). Fifteen of Pushkin's 18 contributions filling the critical void deplored in his "O zhurnal noi kritike" (pub. 1830; "On Journalistic Criticism") were anonymous or pseudonymous. Pushkin contends that some literary works, lacking sophisticated criticism, "appear, live, and die without receiving due evaluation." He seeks critical interpretation rather than evaluative generalization of good versus bad. Nor are the critics the final judges, although reading them explains their relations among themselves and with the writers ("Razgovor o kritike" [draft undated; pub. 1884; "Conversation About Criticism"]). Pushkin founded *Sovremennik* (The contemporary) in 1836 to generate quality literature and criticism and to raise the aesthetic and critical awareness of his primarily upper-class readership after the authorities closed *Literaturnaia gazeta*. Six of his approximately 20 essays appeared anonymously in *Sovremennik* to circumvent the Tsar's growing censorship.

Pushkin's crisp, elegant, and precise style is informed by his Romantic leanings and Westernizing tendencies, on the one hand, and is part of the best of the Russian literary tradition, on the other, drawing from the wellspring of Russian chronicles and the vernacular. His precise yet nuanced vocabulary embraces foreign words and phrases for concepts lacking Russian equivalents. Pithy sayings, proverbs, and quotes, often

in other languages, liven his cogent narrative. Many essays are responses, such as the unequivocal and reasoned "O prichinakh, zamedlivshikh khod nashei slovesnosti" (wr. 1824; "On the Factors That Delayed the Progress of Our Literature"), which lays the blame on the overwhelming use of French by the upper class, on Russian writers, and on the increasing influence of scholarly and scientific language. Pushkin's objective of creating the institution of literary criticism and essays is at the fore of his **polemical essay** "Vozrazhenie na stat'iu A. Bestuzheva 'Vzgliad na russkuiu slovesnost' v techenie 1824 i nachala 1825 godov" (pub. 1834; "Objection to A. Bestuzhev's Article 'A View on Russian Literature During 1824 and the Beginning of 1825'").

Crafting his essays as instructive models, Pushkin underscores the nascency of Russian literary criticism in "'Istoriia poezii' S. P. Shevyreva" (wr. 1836; "S. P. Shevyrev's 'History of Poetry'"). He further addresses the question in "O poezii klassicheskoi i romanicheskoi" (wr. 1825; "On Classical and Romantic Poetry") by articulating that form (genre) determines which of the two schools poetry belongs to and rather broadly assigns to classicism all genres emanating from the Greeks. He credits the troubadours with inventing new genres, rhymes, and Romantic poems unfamiliar to the ancients. Acknowledging his friend's mind, learning, and literary grace in "Vozrazhenie na stat'i Kiukhelbekera v *Mnemozine*" (wr. 1825–26; "Objection to Kiukhelbeker's Articles in *Mnemosyne*"), Pushkin goes on to illuminate several of his errors concerning the superiority of classical genres over Romantic ones; he also defines the aesthetic categories of the beautiful and maps out the theoretical conditions of inspiration and imagination. Ernest J. Simmons (1935) ranks Pushkin's critical judgments on English literature with those of Keats for keenness of perception and farsighted veracity.

Without compromising his integrity of thought in fulfilling Emperor Nicholas' commissioned "O narodnom vospitanii" (wr. 1828; "On Public Education"), Pushkin shifts the responsibility for the "recent events" (the December Rebellion) onto insufficient enlightenment and morality as well as onto foreign influences that find fertile ground in poorly educated minds. He introduces several criticisms, such as the preoccupation with advancement and the insular patriarchal education of young nobles by their social inferiors. He hints at his own situation, as in other essays. This essay exemplifies Pushkin's advocacy of the Lancaster method of mutual teaching, of abolishing both corporal punishment and examinations, the latter by then having become a clandestine business for professors. Republican concepts, he argues to an autocratic emperor, should be part of the curriculum, the better to undermine their allure of novelty. While Pushkin seems fascinated by democratic republicanism and the American experience, he also perceives the faults of and the tendency to idealize both the natural state of life (James Fenimore Cooper, **Chateaubriand**) and the United States, as shown in his essay "Dzhon Tenner" (1836; "John Tanner").

Censorship receives oblique attention in a commentary on an ultra-conservative inveighing against seditious and amoral foreign literature in "Mnenie E. E. Lobanova o dukhe slovesnosti, kak inostrannoi, tak i otechestvennoi" (1836; "E. E. Lobanov's Opinion on the Spirit of Foreign and National Literature"). Pushkin parries Lobanov's call for the censor "to penetrate all designs of writers" by quoting rules restricting judgment to the text's actual meaning rather than its alleged intent.

In "Frakiiskie elegii: Stikhotvoreniia Viktora Tepliakova" (1836; "Thracian Elegies: The Poems of Viktor Tepliakov") Pushkin expounds an enriching tenet of Russian poetics – imitation as faith in one's own ability to discover new worlds by following in the footsteps of genius and the desire to study one's model in order to give it new life.

Pushkin's essays were published gradually as the political situation permitted, many in 1855, 1885, even as late as 1930; consequently their influence on the Russian essay was kept to a minimum, while **Vissarion Belinskii** and others reigned supreme. No sizable study of Pushkin's essays exists, although several recent publications discuss them. Instead Pushkin's essays are used in biographical studies and as sources for elucidating his imaginative writing.

SONIA I. KETCHIAN

Biography

Born 8 June 1799 in Moscow. Studied at the Imperial lycée, Tsarskoe Selo, near St. Petersburg, 1812–17. Member of the Arzamas literary society. Civil servant, St. Petersburg, 1817–20. Exiled in southern Russia and Pskov province, for unpublished political poems, 1820–26, then returned to St. Petersburg. Visited his brother Lev and friends who were fighting the Turks in the Russian Army in Transcaucasia, 1829. Married Natalia Goncharova, 1831. Founding editor, *Sovremennik*, 1836–37. Died (following a duel) in St. Petersburg, 11 February 1837.

Selected Writings

Essays and Related Prose

The Critical Prose, edited and translated by Carl R. Proffer, 1970
Pushkin on Literature, edited and translated by Tatiana Wolff, 1971; revised edition, 1986
Pushkin-kritik, edited by E. N. Lebedev and V. S. Lysenko, 1978

Other writings: poetry, the novel-in-verse *Eugene Onegin* (1831), the drama-in-verse *Boris Godunov* (1831), the novel *Kapitanskaia dochka* (1836; *The Captain's Daughter*), short stories (including *Pikovaia dama* [*The Queen of Spades*], 1834), and correspondence (collected in *Letters*, edited and translated by J. Thomas Shaw, 3 vols., 1963).

Collected works editions: *Polnoe sobranie sochinenii*, 17 vols., 1937–49, reprinted 1994– (in progress); *Polnoe sobranie sochinenii*, edited by B. V. Tomashevskii, 10 vols., 1977–79.

Bibliographies

Bibliografiia proizvedenii A. S. Pushkina i literatura o nem, 1886–99, 1918–57, Moscow/Leningrad, 8 parts, 1949, 1952–60
Pushkiniana 1900–10 and *1911–17*, Leningrad, 2 vols., 1929, 1937
Wreath, P. J., and A. I. Wreath, "Alexander Pushkin: A Bibliography of Criticism in English: 1920–75," *Canadian-American Slavic Studies* (Summer 1976): 279–304

Further Reading

Bayley, John, "In Search of Pushkin," in *Pushkin on Literature*, edited and translated by Tatiana Wolff, Stanford, California: Stanford University Press, and London: Athlone Press, revised edition, 1986
Debreczeny, Paul, *The Other Pushkin: A Study of Alexander Pushkin's Prose Fiction*, Stanford, California: Stanford University Press, 1983
Driver, Sam, *Pu(kin: Literature and Social Ideas*, New York: Columbia University Press, 1989
Frank, Semion, "Pushkin kak politicheskii myslitel'," in *Pushkin v russkoi filisofskoi kritike: Konets XIX-pervaia polovina XX vv*, edited by R. A. Gal'tseva, Moscow: Kniga, 1990
Levkovich, Ia. L., *Avtobiograficheskaia proza i pis'ma Pushkina*, Leningrad: Nauka, 1988
Petrunina, N. N., *Proza Pushkina: Puti evoliutsii*, Leningrad: Nauka, 1987
Simmons, Ernest J., *English Literature and Culture in Russia (1553–1840)*, New York: Octagon, 1964 (original edition, 1935)
Todd, William Mills III, *The Familiar Letter as a Literary Genre in the Age of Pushkin*, Princeton, New Jersey: Princeton University Press, 1976

Q

The Quarterly Review

British periodical, 1809–1967

The *Quarterly Review* originated in opposition to the Whiggish *Edinburgh Review*, whose success as a weighty and popular journal dealing with every aspect of contemporary culture added substance to its liberal politics, a fact unwelcome to supporters of a distinctly conservative administration. The *Edinburgh*'s decisive offense was to publish in 1808 a vigorously radical article by Henry Brougham on the Spanish insurrection against the French invaders. It was insufficiently enthusiastic about the war itself, and this was felt to make the establishment of a truly patriotic review imperative. The *Quarterly*, however, turned out to be very much a conservative organ, and contributors like **Robert Southey**, who had a radical past and prided himself on his free and fearless thinking, were sometimes indignant at the way their reviews were "gelded" to tone them down. This was not just in connection with sensitive political or theological questions. **Charles Lamb** wrote a sympathetic **review** of Wordsworth's *Excursion*, and was distressed to find, when he read the published text, that it had been altered beyond recognition. As he put it in a letter to Wordsworth, "Every warm expression is changed for a nasty cold one . . . The eyes are pulled out and the bleeding sockets are left."

The editor who performed these mutilations was William Gifford, according to **Hazlitt** a "low-bred, self-taught man" who was formed in the school of "anti-Jacobin" journalism, savaging any manifestation of liberality or intimation of reforming sentiment. This was the reason for the notorious review by John Wilson Croker of Keats' *Endymion* (1818): the poet was an associate of **Leigh Hunt**, the editor of the radical Sunday newspaper the *Examiner*, so inevitably the poem had to consist of "the most incongruous ideas in the most uncouth language."

In 1826 the *Quarterly* was taken over by Walter Scott's son-in-law J. G. Lockhart, but the Gifford mode continued to feature in the reviews written or revised by Croker, in his heavily sarcastic notice of Tennyson's 1833 volume, for example, but perhaps most strikingly in his revision of a review by P. H. Stanhope, Lord Mahon, of a book by the Whig politician Lord John Russell on the causes of the French Revolution. Stanhope included his own version of the review in a collection of **historical essays** published in 1849. It is a temperately critical analysis. But the review in the *Quarterly* for April 1833,

though it retains large fragments of the original text, is transformed into a scurrilously abusive party-political polemic.

All this may seem to reinforce the early 19th-century liberal consensus that the *Quarterly* was a brutal bully hired by a corrupt establishment. But like the *Edinburgh*, a large proportion of the review essays dealt with a wide range of topics likely to be of interest to the intelligent reader. Walter Scott's contributions are invariably magnanimous, not least when reviewing (anonymously of course, and with some editorial enhancements) his own *Tales of My Landlord* (1817). His essay on the Culloden Papers (1816) is a moving lament for the Highland clearances. The number that contained Croker's attack on *Endymion* included an article on Egyptian antiquities which helped to inspire Keats' vision of the temple of Moneta in the second version of *Hyperion*. Many of Southey's articles on the state of the poor are pioneering formulations of the concerns of Victorian social reformers, and when a late 20th-century publisher attempted to illustrate the Victorian social conscience in a score or so volumes of reprints of contemporary **periodical essays**, the *Quarterly* featured extensively.

The ethos of the *Quarterly* in mid-century is perhaps best illustrated by Benjamin Disraeli's *Coningsby* (1844), with its satirical portrait of Croker in the appalling Mr. Rigby – author of many "slashing" pieces in the *Quarterly Review* – and its idealized mentor for the hero in Sidonia, who had "exhausted all the sources of human knowledge" and was master of the learning of every nation: precisely the impression that writers tried to create when adopting the reviewers' "we." **John Ruskin**, for one, provides a pleasant example of this in one of his rare excursions into reviewing, when he made Lord Lindsay's history of Christian art the occasion for his own wide-ranging survey (1847).

At their best, reviews in the *Quarterly* convey a vivid sense of public discussion in the more conservative parts of British society. There is a fine review of *Vanity Fair* and *Jane Eyre* by Lady Eastlake (1848), which has usually been cited as an illustration of Victorian moral outrage with its allegation that Charlotte Brontë's novel breathes the spirit of disaffection and revolution that has threatened the social fabric in Britain and abroad. But the reviewer's frank avowal of how disturbing readers find *Jane Eyre*, enabling normally reticent English people to drop their defenses in unwontedly uninhibited discussion, is a conscious and perceptive tribute to Brontë's literary power.

The *Quarterly* took an intelligent part, from a conservative angle, in most of the major Victorian controversies. William

Ewart Gladstone appeared as a formidable critic of Roman Catholicism, while Bishop Wilberforce was the reviewer chosen for **Darwin**'s *Origin of Species*. W. J. Courthope contributed his view of the debate on culture initiated by **Matthew Arnold** ("Modern Culture," October 1874), and it was writers like himself, with Francis Turner Palgrave and Churton Collins, who did much to establish the canon that initially dominated the teaching of literature in British universities. The process may be usefully examined in the pages of the *Quarterly*.

The review continued publication until 1967, and perhaps retained its preeminent position at least until the early years of the century. Latterly it became just one periodical among many, but its very survival for over a century and a half is in itself deeply impressive.

GEOFFREY CARNALL

Further Reading

"The Centenary of the *Quarterly Review*," *Quarterly Review* 210 (1909): 731–84; 211 (1909): 279–324

Graham, Walter J., *Tory Criticism in the "Quarterly Review" 1809–53*, New York: AMS Press, 1970 (original edition, 1921)

Koss, Stephen, *The Rise and Fall of the Political Press in Britain*, vol. 1: *The Nineteenth Century*, London: Hamilton, 1981

L., C. E., "Retrospect: Nos. 1–500, *Quarterly Review*," *Quarterly Review* 253 (1929): 1–17

"Musings Without Method: The Quarterly Review – Its Origins – The Slashing Article – The Reigns of Gifford and Lockhart," *Blackwood's Edinburgh Magazine* 173 (1903): 100–17

Shattock, Joanne, *Politics and Reviewers: "The Edinburgh" and "The Quarterly" in the Early Victorian Age*, Leicester: Leicester University Press, 1989

Shine, Hill, and Helen Chadwick Shine, *The Quarterly Review Under Gifford: Identification of Contributors, 1809–24*, Chapel Hill: University of North Carolina Press, 1949

R

The Rambler

British periodical, 1750–1752

Samuel Johnson stands at the crossroads between the Renaissance and the Modern period, and so played a crucial part in the development of the essay. There can be no doubt that Johnson found the essay an especially congenial literary form. As its origin in the French word *essai* suggests, the essay is an informal "attempt" to say something worthwhile. In an essay one was not promising much, only that one was trying; this more relaxed generic tone suited Johnson well. Above all, the essay as a literary form offered him freedom: it had no set agenda, no rules about topic, no prescribed length, and no required content.

Looking back, Johnson considered the achievements of **Montaigne** in the 16th century, of **Francis Bacon** in the 17th, and of **Addison** and **Steele** in the early 18th. When, however, his chance came to follow in the footsteps of his predecessors in the middle of the 18th century he chose instead to develop the essay in a somewhat new direction. The result was what James Boswell would later call "bark and steel for the mind," and what Walter Jackson Bate (1955) would describe as "the closest anticipation of Freud to be found in psychology or moral writings before the twentieth century."

Johnson's chance to do something significant with the essay form came after he had been at work for two or three years on his *Dictionary*, which would appear in 1755. Financially strapped, he was unable to keep up with his many expenses. At this fateful juncture he was approached by a trio of London booksellers. Edward Cave, John Payne, and Joseph Bouquet offered him the chance to become the author of a new set of **periodical essays** which they were hoping could match or surpass the earlier successes of the *Tatler* (1709–11) and *Spectator* (1711–12, 1714). Johnson was to be paid two guineas per essay, and there were to be two essays each week. This would provide him with four extra guineas each week, or with slightly over 200 guineas in extra annual income – a not insignificant sum of money for a writer who only a year earlier had accepted the sum total of 15 guineas for the rights to his great poem *The Vanity of Human Wishes*. The offer from the booksellers was irresistible.

Johnson thus found himself in early March 1750 committed to producing two essays each week – one to be published on Tuesday, the other on Saturday – indefinitely. They were to address important issues of the day, though Johnson was by no means sure just what those would be. Consequently, he designated himself "the Rambler," undoubtedly to allow himself as much flexibility as possible when it came to choosing his subjects. However, as Steven Lynn (1992) has suggested, his title may also have been drawing attention to a religious meaning in his work. It is clear enough that Johnson conceived of himself as a pilgrim soul on a journey toward God. But it is equally clear that he did not have the same sense of clear direction which had guided those who thought of themselves as pilgrims in earlier times. It was his lot here on earth to be but a rambler.

Johnson eventually brought his project to a conclusion in *Rambler* no. 208, published on 14 March 1752, just before the death of his beloved wife Tettie on 17 March 1752. During the two years that he devoted to the *Rambler* there were only four occasions when he allowed someone else to compose one of the essays, though others had been responsible for a few small parts of other essays.

Apparently the *Rambler* was not a great financial success initially. The sale of individual folio numbers, we are told, never went much beyond 500. However, even when they were first being published in **pamphlet** form some of the individual essays did enjoy a much wider circulation than the numerical count would indicate, for they were reprinted in country newspapers and monthly magazines. Individual numbers of the *Rambler* sold for two pence each, so simple arithmetic would tell us that Johnson's financial backers at first lost money on this venture. However, it is also true that, in one of the odder turns of literary history, the reputation of the *Rambler* began to grow almost immediately among the British reading public. Not long after Johnson ceased publishing there was enough demand for a collected edition of the *Rambler* essays, printed in a duodecimo edition. Before Johnson's death in 1784, there were to be ten authorized editions of the collected *Ramblers*, and even more by the end of the 18th century.

Though Johnson's reputation as the author of the *Rambler* papers would soon be overshadowed by his great achievement with the *Dictionary*, most members of the brilliant social and intellectual set surrounding him in his later years first came to know and admire him as "the Rambler." Young James Boswell is but one instance of someone who was not looking for "Dictionary" Johnson when he came to London in 1762: he was instead seeking out the author of the *Rambler* papers.

It is not easy to assess Johnson's overall achievement in the *Rambler* essays. The 204 essays mostly or entirely by him cover a wide range of topics and ideas. To a great extent, what any individual reader will value in these essays will almost certainly depend upon what he or she is looking for. Johnson is perhaps most admired as a teacher of wisdom, and it is not hard to find essays that exemplify the kind of Johnsonian wisdom that has long been valued. *Rambler* no. 32 on the value of patience under extreme duress is mentioned admiringly by most who have read carefully through the essays. Boswell mentions no. 54 on the death of a friend and no. 110 on the value of penance as two that had a profound effect on him. No. 25 urging us to overcome feelings of timidity in the pursuit of excellence is yet another essay that continues to be widely admired.

Essays of other types are also still appreciated. Johnson does make a few attempts at humor. The most successful of these is probably no. 117, which contains a tongue-in-cheek argument in praise of a garret's beneficial effects on writing. Other essays tell stories, a few extending to more than one number: the story of Misella, for example (nos. 170 and 171), or that of Seged (nos. 204 and 205). Misella's tale illustrates Johnson's remarkable sensitivity to the plight of women, particularly to the horrors of prostitution. The story of Seged is commonly read as an early version of *Rasselas, Prince of Abyssinia*, one of Johnson's most celebrated literary works, which he published in 1759. On the whole, though, he is not especially successful as a storyteller in the *Rambler* essays.

Much easier to admire are the essays devoted to what we now call literary criticism. Praise for *Rambler* no. 60, which sketches out Johnson's theory of biography, has been almost universal. It was a major inspiration for Boswell, who quotes from it extensively at the beginning of his own much-heralded biographical work, *The Life of Samuel Johnson* (1791). There can be little doubt that Boswell found its carefully chiseled prescriptions and shrewd observations on biography as a literary form sufficient justification for doing things with biography that had never been done before. *Rambler* no. 4 contains an early argument on behalf of moral fiction, and is frequently cited as one of the first serious efforts to come to terms with the new literary form we now call the novel. *Rambler* no. 92 is an especially valuable contribution to our theoretical understanding of poetry. In it Johnson takes up the question of the relationship between sound and sense. After examining numerous illuminating examples he concludes that the intimacy of the relationship between the two has been wildly exaggerated. Whatever the essence of great poetry may be, it must lie in something other than sound. Other critical essays beyond these – on Milton, on pastoral poetry, on the "rules" for writing – are also of considerable value.

The *Rambler* continues to be of interest for a variety of reasons. Its essays reveal to us how one of the best writers in English employed the form at an important moment in its development. Some consider ideas of storytelling, while others make still valid points about issues in literary theory and criticism. Perhaps, though, most significantly, a surprising number of the *Rambler* essays still offer a wisdom that most of us can make use of in our daily lives.

JOHN J. BURKE, JR.

Editions

The Rambler, 208 nos., 20 March 1750–14 March 1752; in 6 vols., 1752; in *The Works of Samuel Johnson* (Yale Edition), vols. 3–5, edited by Walter Jackson Bate and Albrecht B. Strauss, 1969; selections in *Essays from the Rambler, Adventurer, and Idler*, edited by Walter Jackson Bate, 1968

Further Reading

Alkon, Paul K., *Samuel Johnson and Moral Discipline*, Evanston, Illinois: Northwestern University Press, 1967

Bate, Walter Jackson, *The Achievement of Samuel Johnson*, New York: Oxford University Press, 1955

Bloom, Edward A., "Symbolic Names in Johnson's Periodical Essays," *Modern Language Quarterly* 13 (1952): 333–52

Bloom, Harold, "Dr. Samuel Johnson, the Canonical Critic," in his *The Western Canon: The Books and School of the Ages*, New York: Harcourt Brace Jovanovich, 1994; London: Papermac, 1995: 183–202

Boswell, James, *Boswell's Life of Johnson, Together with Boswell's Journal of a Tour to the Hebrides and Johnson's Diary of a Journey into North Wales*, edited by George Birkbeck Hill, revised by L. F. Powell, 6 vols., Oxford: Clarendon Press, 1934–64: especially vol. 2: 212–26

Burke, John J., Jr., "Excellence in Biography: *Rambler* No. 60 and Johnson's Early Biographies," *South Atlantic Bulletin* 44, no. 2 (May 1979): 14–34

Clifford, James L., *Dictionary Johnson: Samuel Johnson's Middle Years*, New York: McGraw Hill, 1979

Damrosch, Leopold, "Johnson's Manner of Proceeding in the *Rambler*," *ELH* 40 (1973): 70–89

Greene, Donald, *Samuel Johnson*, Boston: Twayne, revised edition, 1989

Hagstrum, Jean, "Johnson and the *Concordia Discors* of Human Relationships," in *The Unknown Samuel Johnson*, edited by John J. Burke, Jr. and Donald Kay, Madison: University of Wisconsin Press, 1983: 39–53

Lynn, Steven, *Samuel Johnson After Deconstruction: Rhetoric and "The Rambler"*, Carbondale: Southern Illinois University Press, 1992

Olson, Robert, *Motto, Contest, Essay: The Classical Background of Samuel Johnson's "Rambler" and "Adventurer" Essays*, Lanham, Maryland: University Press of America, 1984

Rogers, Pat, *Johnson*, Oxford and New York: Oxford University Press, 1993

Selden, Raman, "Deconstructing the *Ramblers*," in *Fresh Reflections on Samuel Johnson*, edited by Prem Nath, Troy, New York: Whitston, 1987: 269–82

Wharton, T. F., *Samuel Johnson and the Theme of Hope*, London: Macmillan, 1984

Wiles, R. M., "The Contemporary Distribution of Johnson's *Rambler*," *Eighteenth-Century Studies* 2 (1968): 155–71

Ranke, Leopold von

German, 1795–1886

Prussian historian Leopold von Ranke is generally regarded as the founder of modern historiography. While the 20th century has produced a substantial number of German historians who are also interesting as essayists, there was a paucity of such in Ranke's day. The great or near-great can, indeed, be counted on one hand: Mommsen, Friedrich Christoph Dahlman, Heinrich von Treitschke, and Alfred Dove, as well as Ranke himself. Though he apparently never wrote consciously as an essayist – even though the genre had established itself as such by the mid-19th century in Germany, with such writers as **Herman Grimm** and Karl Hillebrand and fellow historians Georg G. Gervinus, Otto Gildemeister, and Theodor Mommsen – Ranke did write a number of shorter works that could well qualify as essays. These were often in the form of **dialogues**, intended as **prefaces** to his major works, or were otherwise relatively informal and briefer works without the usual formidable scholarly apparatus characteristic of Ranke's major writings.

Ranke's essayistic writings, though by definition not displaying the meticulous and distanced craftsman, are nonetheless perfectly consistent with the tenor, predispositions, and general style of his most famous scholarship, *Die Römischen Päpste* (1834–36; *The History of the Popes*), *Deutsche Geschichte im Zeitalter der Reformation* (1839–47; *History of the Reformation in Germany*), and other works. Notably, there are no significant changes in the style, tenor, or general purport of Ranke's essays over the course of an extensive stretch of time.

Essayistic compositions sometimes occur as parts of longer works, such as the oft-excerpted pieces from the *Vorträge* (lectures) for the benefit of King Maximilian II of Bavaria – for instance, "Wie der Begriff Fortschritt in der Geschichte aufzufassen sei" (1854; How the concept of progress in history should be understood) and "Was von den sogenannten leitenden Ideen in der Geschichte zu halten sei" (1854; What should one think of the so-called leading ideas in history); such contributions show the best side of Ranke as essayist. Two even briefer pieces from the same series, "Die nordamerikanische Revolution" (1854; The North American revolution) and "Die französische Revolution" (1854; The French Revolution), though displaying the careful historian reluctant to make easy generalizations unsupported by mountains of data and detail, yet reveal the more relaxed and expansive essayist who implicitly assumes an understanding between himself and his reader that the author is not writing for archival record.

While Ranke edited and wrote most of the contributions for a journal he founded, the *Historische-politische Zeitschrift* (Historical-political journal), this work is hardly a mine for those exploring Ranke as essayist: its primary purpose was to function as an organ for the policies of the Prussian government. The journal did, however, contain his two most important contributions to the essay: "Das politische Gespräch" (1836; "A Dialogue on Politics") and "Die grossen Mächte" (1832; "The Great Powers").

In "A Dialogue on Politics" the character of Friedrich is patently the writer's spokesman, while the figure of Karl is representative of Ranke's friend, the renowned Prussian jurist Friedrich Karl Savigny. It examines, among other themes: the political situation in the 1830s; the nature of the state; the state *vis-à-vis* political parties; the varying role of the army according to the form of state it serves; states considered as individual personalities; the duties and limitations of government; and the relationship between church and state. Seemingly under the influence of **Johann Gottfried Herder**, Giambattista Vico, and **Edmund Burke**, Ranke maintains that each state has its unique personality and *Zeitgeist* (a term popularized by but not originating with Ranke) and, consequently, reforms – no matter how attractive in theory – should never be arbitrarily imposed upon an existing state. Moreover, the individual citizen gains his full development as a human being only through his life within the state. Based upon this rootedness of the citizen in a particular state, the continued vitality of

European civilization itself is made possible. The past, therefore, should never be judged from the perspective of the present or with criteria by which epochs are evaluated according to their contribution to some notion of progress. This form of historicism, while certainly intended in part to refute such politically engaged historians as Gustav Droysen and Heinrich von Sybel, surely had the dominant political thought of Hegel as its primary target. Moreover, unlike some of his fellow historians (e.g. Friedrich Christoph Schlosser, Karl von Rotteck, Gervinus, and **Thomas Babington Macaulay**), Ranke felt that the historian should be a technician rather than a moralizing judge "distributing praise and blame" (Pieter Geyl, 1958).

Written consistently in the tone of a broadminded and free-wheeling discussion, the dialogue is lively, realistic, and often compelling, never stepping out of its guise and degenerating into a dissertational style. It comes as no surprise that Ranke regards drama as the most effective literary means for gaining insight into the human heart. Peter Gay (1974) comments on this: "In Ranke, the shaping hand of the literary artist is never far from the constructive effort of the historian." Frequent use is made of the rhetorical question and what Gay calls the "counterfactual alternative." Lyricism, smoothness, and breadth are characteristic, but – perhaps surprisingly, given the frequent use of irony – there is little genuine humor.

The second of Ranke's most important essays, "The Great Powers," is a wide-ranging survey of those European powers – England, France, Austria, Prussia, and Russia – among whom a political and cultural, seemingly perpetual, competition serves to keep the balance of power (and thus the civilization) of Europe in a healthy condition. Everything, Ranke asserts, is secondary to the authority of the state, while foreign policy is the state's most important function. Although not as lively a piece as "A Dialogue on Politics," this earlier work must be regarded as one of the most perceptive and instructive contributions to the subject during the author's lifetime.

Ranke's **letters**, diaries (*Tagebücher*), and notebooks also contain much that can be classified as essayistic in nature. Unfortunately, little scholarly attention has been paid to these sources as contributions to the genre. In them can be found occasional statements of belief, attitude, and feeling – ruminations and speculations rather than tightly reasoned arguments, e.g. on the nature of history, its place among other academic disciplines, the primacy of political history (almost to the exclusion of everything else), and the importance of the great historical figure (the "Great Man" theory of history).

Beyond the considerations of theme and content in Ranke's essays, there is always the compelling excellence of his style and form. It seems that Ranke took the preceding century's Buffon to heart ("le style est l'homme même" [style is the man himself]) and believed that it was only through style that a writer – especially the historian – could rise above the prosaic role of reporter and recorder (Gay). He took obvious pleasure in his role as a historical commentator and speculator, a disposition eminently appropriate for the accomplished essayist.

ROBERT V. SMYTHE

Biography

Born 21 December 1795 in Wiehe, Kursachen. Studied at the Schulpforta, near Naumburg; University of Leipzig, 1816–17, doctoral degree, 1817. Taught history at the gymnasium in Frankfurt-on-Oder, 1818–24; chair of history, University of Berlin, 1825–71, where he taught **Jacob Christoph Burckhardt**. Traveled and studied in Italy, 1828–31. Editor, *Historische-politische Zeitschrift*, 1832–36. Ennobled, 1865. Died in Berlin, 25 May 1886.

Selected Writings

Essays and Related Prose

Über die Epochen der neueren Geschichte: Neunzehn Vorträge für König Maximilian von Bayern, edited by Alfred Dove, 1888, and Theodor Schieder and Helmut Berding, 1971
Zeitbilder und Charakteristiken, edited by Alexander Eggers, 1918
Ausgewählte Schriften, edited by Friedrich Ramhorst, 1918
Volkssagenforschung: Vorträge und Aufsätze, 1935
Geschichte und Politik: Ausgewählte Aufsätze und Meisterschriften, edited by Hans Hofmann, 1942
Weltgeschichtliches Lesebuch, edited by Fritz Ernst, 1957
The Theory and Practice of History, edited by Georg G. Iggers and Konrad von Moltke, translated by von Moltke and Wilma A. Iggers, 1973

Other writings: many volumes on history, particularly on the 16th and 17th centuries, as well as an unfinished history of the world (*Weltgeschichte*, 16 vols., 1881–88) and a history of the popes (1834–36), diaries, and correspondence.

Collected works editions: *Sämtliche Werke*, 54 vols. (in 29 vols.), 1867–90; *Gesamtausgabe* (German Academy Edition), edited by Erich Marcks and others, 1925– (in progress).

Bibliography

Helmolt, Hans F., *Ranke-Bibliographie*, Leipzig: Dykschen, 1910

Further Reading

Barnes, Harry Elmer, *A History of Historical Writing*, New York: Dover, revised edition, 1962 (original edition, 1937)
Gay, Peter, *Style in History*, New York: Norton, 1988 (original edition, 1974)
Gay, Peter, and V. G. Wexler, editors, *Historians at Work*, vol. 3, New York: Harper and Row, 1975
Geyl, Pieter, *Debates with Historians*, New York: Meridian, 1958: especially Chapter 1, "Ranke in the Light of the Catastrophe"
Gilbert, Felix, *History, Politics or Culture? Reflections on Ranke and Burckhardt*, Princeton, New Jersey: Princeton University Press, 1990
Guillard, Antoine, *Modern Germany and Her Historians*, Westport, Connecticut: Greenwood Press, 1970 (original French edition, 1915)
Iggers, Georg G., *The German Conception of History*, Middletown, Connecticut: Wesleyan University Press, 1968
Iggers, Georg G., and James M. Powell, editors, *Leopold von Ranke and the Shaping of Historical Disciplines*, Syracuse, New York: Syracuse University Press, 1990
Kohn, Hans, editor, *German History: Some New German Views*, Boston: Beacon Press, and London: Allen and Unwin, 1954: especially "Ranke and Burckhardt" by F. Meinecke
Krieger, Leonard, *Ranke: The Meaning of History*, Chicago: University of Chicago Press, 1977
Rohner, Ludwig, *Deutsche Essays: Prosa aus zwei Jahrhunderten*, vol. 1, Berlin and Neuwied: Luchterhand, 1968

Read, Herbert

British, 1893–1968

Sir Herbert Read, knighted by Winston Churchill in 1953 "for services to literature," is one of the most enigmatic of the modern essayists who interpreted Modernist aesthetic values and styles to a reluctant English literary culture. Of those who established their mark in the vanguard movements of English literary circles during the period between World Wars I and II, and in spite of his over 60 books, Read remains one of the forgotten, even though his reputation in the 1950s placed him alongside well-known cultural-literary critics such as **Matthew Arnold**, **William Morris**, **Paul Valéry**, **T. S. Eliot**, and **George Orwell**. Read became visible after World War I as a young poet and defender of the newest Modernism. Along with more notorious Modernists like Georges Sorel, **Friedrich Nietzsche**, Henri Bergson, **Ezra Pound**, James Joyce, T. E. Hulme, Wyndham Lewis, and T. S. Eliot, Read identified himself with the dissident movements in literary and cultural values. Inspired by the convergence of the visual arts and letters and philosophy in continental movements, he founded a journal, *Arts and Letters* (1917), which joined Modernism to the criticism of the philistine bourgeoisie and the mass culture encroaching on England.

His editing of T. E. Hulme's notebooks for A. R. Orage's *The New Age* (1922) and Hulme's *Speculations* (1924) helped secure Read's solidarity with Eliot and the *Criterion*, to which Read began contributing in 1922. Read's long association with Eliot, whom he first met in 1917, remains even today not easy to assess. Both writers published and encouraged other writers – Read at Routledge and Kegan Paul, Eliot at Faber and Faber – and both writers were not afraid to relate ethical and cultural values to forgotten literary figures or emergent artistic movements. But Eliot's conservative Christianity and Read's anarchism and his commitment and engagement to a political outlook, as well as his affirmation of the creative nature of the unconscious self, separated them into intellectually opposed camps. What often joins them in a common cause is the necessity to come to terms with the Romantic principle of imagism translated into the impersonality of form in poetry.

Read's essays in the 1930s, whether polemical, austere, or personal, were written in a style accessible to the reader searching for new insights into modern life through the surrealist journals that linked art and surrealism to the radical and politically changing cultures in Spain, Germany, England, and Russia. In the 1930s alone Read published over 400 essays and books. Socialism versus barbarism was on the agenda, and being engaged with the "contemporary" was a required stance. Placed against the smaller number of Eliot's essays, which are written in an imperious, scholastic style, or Orwell's journalistic plain speaking, Read may sound remote, didactic, or tendentious. But his work avoided mannerism and maintained diversity, including essays on art exhibitions, literature, education, social action, and aesthetics; all together it numbers well over 1100 publications and reveals a protean intelligence in his public essays and an introspective lyrical turn in his autobiographical writings.

Read was a philosophical anarchist and outspoken pacifist during World War II, and his defense of craft-based work and syndicalist working habits marks his entire outlook and must be associated even with his essays championing Wordsworth, **Shelley**, and **Coleridge**. This development of the ideology of Romanticism would inevitably stamp him as an outsider in the face of Eliot and Pound's objectivism and classicism. Read's visionary side was infused with the mystique of nonviolent anarchism, guild and revolutionary socialism, and the mythology of place, especially the northern English landscape, symbolized in his essayistic Blakean novel, *The Green Child: A Romance* (1935), which was puzzled over by Jung and admired by a range of literary and artistic fellow travelers of Modernism and mysticism, including the writer **Kenneth Rexroth**, and artists of the Dynaton Group around Wolfgang Paalen. Read's lifelong admiration first for Freud and then for Jung allowed him to place the unconscious into a direct relationship with the artistic process. By linking inorganic imagery to abstraction, and empathy to the human need for primal form, and both with the drive for aesthetic freedom, he provided readers with a unique intellectual context for a social consciousness that is different, if not absent, from many of his contemporaries, for example F. R. Leavis, Christopher Caudwell, or, later, Raymond Williams.

Just as his attempt to set standards for understanding modern art did not appeal to later cultural critics like Raymond Williams, Read's association with the anarchists of the Freedom Press group puzzled the sensibilities of traditional leftists like Stephen Spender. Read's advocacy of anarchism and of education through art, and his lingering lifelong admiration for Hegel, **Schiller**, and **Marx** reinforced his belief that alienation was a condition of modern life that could not be resolved through Eliot's Christian stoicism or religion. In his essays on industrial design he drew parallels between a utopian vision of a human-scale, abstract technology, and primitive and children's art, which are also abstract and sensual. His desire to see our nature through depth psychology that reveals the inner biological basis of form informs his 1920s essays as well as the psychoanalytically informed essays on aesthetics in the postwar period. But ultimately Read focuses his moral disgust for the ugliness of industrialism on the systems that grind individuals down into robotic dependency on the state. He pilloried the English (*Poetry and Anarchism*, 1938) for failing to understand literary values that were not simply culturally acceptable values, and his **pamphlet** essay "To Hell with Culture: Democratic Values Are New Values" (1941) became the cornerstone essay for other works like *The Politics of the Unpolitical* (1943) and *The Education of Free Men* (1944).

Read's lucid prose was neither academic nor fashionably belletristic, but was suffused with an energetically pamphleteering, albeit feuilletonist quality that brought together analysis, defiance, and acquaintance with the work at hand. He ultimately scorned the Bloomsbury literati, and his defense of surrealism and "degenerate art" in little journals like *Axis*, *Minotaur*, *Southern Review*, or *Circle* identified him as a spirited voice addressing apologists for bourgeois culture in the name of the outsiders and aesthetically dispossessed. At the same time his reviews in publications like the *Times Literary Supplement*, the *Nation*, *Adelphi*, the *Listener*, *Horizon*, and *Architectural Review* gave him license, guerrilla-like, to speak patiently and intelligently about the cultural contradictions beween insider, official culture, and artistic innovation and experiment.

Often labeled a highbrow Modernist voice, or primarily a poet (George Woodcock, 1972), Read, like his counterparts in the United States, **Lionel Trilling** or Clement Greenberg, came to be seen as an apologist for liberal values – one who sought the assimilation of modern literature and art into the mainstream. Yet his work is too broad in scope for these reductions. His prose style is deceptively and consciously personal without imposing the voice of his private "personality." Hating the stridency of a Wyndham Lewis, he stands with **Swift**, **Hazlitt**, Coleridge, **Nietzsche**, **Tolstoi**, **Lawrence**, and **Freud** – those writers who do not cater to the common reader as "a passive recipient of pleasures for which he pays a fair market price" (*English Prose Style*, 1928) or to the often decadent manner of being leisurely, tasteful, and unconcerned. In the final analysis, he sees himself as a psychologist of the soul. In this, a Romantic attachment to both scientific analysis and the desire to dissect the realities of modern life, where science and art both conflict and coincide, Read consciously adopted the persona of the diagnostician, discoverer, and psychologist as the basis of the essay form. In *Collected Essays in Literary Criticism* (1938), his introduction boldly states that psychoanalytic depth psychology is necessary for understanding literary creation, and that through the psychoanalytic domain we understand the place of the irrational in an irrational age. He writes: "I have been gradually drawn towards a psychological type of literary criticism because I have realized that psychology, more particularly the method of psycho-analysis, can offer explanations of many problems connected with the personality of the poet, the technique of poetry, and the appreciation of the poem." One of the first in England to advance and develop this perspective in the mid-1920s, and at home as a Romantic in an anti-Romantic age, he recognized that he wrote against the grain of the expectations of an age limited to traditional moral ideas about realism in art. As a crusader for contemporary art Read never lost touch with the Romantic idea that art is in a sense speaking to us as moderns.

JERALD ZASLOVE

Biography
Herbert Edward Read. Born 4 December 1893 at Muscoates Grange, Kirbymoorside, Yorkshire. Studied at the University of Leeds, 1911–14. Served in the army, 1915–18, fighting in France and Belgium: made captain, 1917; mentioned in dispatches; Military Cross, Distinguished Service Order, 1918. Founder, with Frank Rutter, *Arts and Letters*, 1917–20 (during the war via correspondence and when on leave). Married 1) Evelyn Roff; 2) Margaret Ludwig; four sons and one daughter. Assistant principal of the Treasury, London, 1919–22. Assistant keeper of ceramics and stained glass, Victoria and Albert Museum, London, 1922–31. Contributor, the *Criterion*, 1922–39, editor, *Burlington Magazine*, 1933–39, and editor, English Master Painters series, from 1940. Watson Gordon Professor of Fine Arts, University of Edinburgh, 1931–33; Sydney Jones Lecturer in Art, University of Liverpool, 1935–36; Leon Fellow, University of London, 1940–42; Charles Eliot Norton Professor of Poetry, Harvard University, Cambridge, Massachusetts, 1953–54. Knighted, 1953. Fellow, Center for Advanced Studies, Wesleyan University, Middletown, Connecticut, 1964–65. Awards: Erasmus Prize, 1966; honorary degrees from four universities. Honorary fellow, Society of Industrial Artists; Foreign Corresponding Member, Académie Flamande des Beaux Arts, 1953; Foreign Member, Royal Academy of Fine Arts, Stockholm, 1960; Honorary Member, American Academy of Arts and Letters, 1966. Died at Stonegrave house, Yorkshire, 12 June 1968.

Selected Writings

Essays and Related Prose

Reason and Romanticism: Essays in Literary Criticism, 1926
English Prose Style, 1928
The Sense of Glory: Essays in Criticism, 1929
Julien Benda and the New Humanism, 1930
Wordsworth, 1930
Art Now, 1933
The Innocent Eye, 1933
Henry Moore, Sculptor, An Appreciation, 1934
Essential Communism, 1935
Art and Society, 1936
In Defence of Shelley and Other Essays, 1936
Collected Essays in Literary Criticism, 1938; as *The Nature of Literature*, 1956
Poetry and Anarchism, 1938
To Hell with Culture: Democratic Values Are New Values, 1941
Education Through Art, 1943
The Politics of the Unpolitical, 1943
The Education of Free Men, 1944
A Coat of Many Colours: Occasional Essays, 1945; revised edition, 1956
The Grass Roots of Art, 1947
The Philosophy of Modern Art: Collected Essays, 1952
The True Voice of Feeling, 1953
Anarchy and Order: Essays in Politics, 1954
The Tenth Muse: Essays in Criticism, 1957
The Forms of Things Unknown: Essays Toward an Aesthetic Philosophy, 1960
A Letter to a Young Painter, 1962
The Contrary Experience: Autobiographies, 1963
To Hell with Culture, and Other Essays on Art and Society, 1963
Art and Alienation: The Role of the Artist in Society, 1967
Essays in Literary Criticism: Particular Studies, 1969
A One-Man Manifesto and Other Writings for Freedom Press, edited by David Goodway, 1994

Other writings: poetry (including *The End of a War*, 1933), three radio plays, the novel *The Green Child* (1935), works on art history and literature, and a book on English prose style.

Bibliographies

Gerwing, Howard, and Michael W. Pidgeon, *A Checklist of the Herbert Read Archive*, Victoria, British Columbia: University of Victoria McPherson Library, 1969
Read, Benedict, and David Thistlewood, in *Herbert Read: A British Vision of World Art*, edited by Read and Thistlewood, Leeds: Leeds City Art Galleries, 1993

Further Reading

Goodway, David, editor, *Herbert Read*, Liverpool: University of Liverpool Press, 1997
Hortmann, Wilhelm, *Wenn die Kunst stirbt*, Duisberg: Braun, 1976
Ideologies of Britishness in Post-War Art and Culture, Collapse special issue, 1 (1994)
Keel, John Siegfried, *The Writings of Herbert Read and Their Curricular Implications* (dissertation), Madison: University of Wisconsin, 1960
King, James, *The Last Modern: A Life of Herbert Read*, London: Weidenfeld and Nicolson, and New York: St. Martin's Press, 1990
Read, Benedict, and David Thistlewood, editors, *Herbert Read: A British Vision of World Art*, Leeds: Leeds City Art Galleries, 1993
Skelton, Robin, editor, *Herbert Read: A Memorial Symposium*, London: Methuen, 1970

Thistlewood, David, *Herbert Read: Formlessness and Form: An Introduction to His Aesthetics*, London and Boston: Routledge and Kegan Paul, 1984
Treece, Henry, editor, *Herbert Read: An Introduction to His Work by Various Hands*, London: Faber, 1944; Port Washington, New York: Kennikat Press, 1969
Woodcock, George, *Herbert Read: The Stream and the Source*, London: Faber, 1972

Religious Essay

In some ways, the term "religious essay" is an oxymoron, since "religious" is commonly used to suggest faithful devotion or orthodox certainty while as Graham Good suggests in *The Observing Self: Rediscovering the Essay* (1988), the essay tends to explore "inconsistencies" rather than reinforce existing systems. Yet the essay, like much literature in the West, has deep roots in Christian tradition and practice. Although in "Über Form und Wesen des Essays" ("On the Nature and Form of the Essay") in *Die Seele und die Formen* (1911; *Soul and Form*), **Georg Lukács** saw medieval German mystics as a source of the essay form, medieval writers drew on a tradition of confession, apology, and polemic begun by early Church Fathers such as Augustine of Hippo. In his *Confessions* (wr. 397–98 CE), Augustine initiated a tradition of reflection on experience that placed the subjective "I" in a dynamic **dialogue** with both God and the reader.

Before the Reformation, that dialogue usually took place within a framework of doctrinal certainty, yet, in the 12th to 14th centuries, visionaries such as Julian of Norwich and Catherine of Siena affirmed the authority of subjective experience. Graham Good, like other critics, describes the essay using terms that reflect its roots in this tradition: it is concerned with "illumination" rather than with "the accumulation of knowledge," it substitutes a subjective "configuration" of experience for the "figura" of a received system, and its structure is "provisional" rather than "providential." While medieval mystical texts foreshadowed this emphasis on subjective vision, the essay genre came into being as the mystics' world was passing away.

The Reformation provided later essayists with strong models of religious texts in the vernacular, including translations of Scripture, polemical **treatises**, and **sermons**. Vernacular translations of the Bible, including Martin Luther's (completed in 1534) and the English Authorized Version (1611) helped to produce the "plain style." In Germany, Luther's religious prose also made its mark. Works like *Von der Freiheit eines Christenmenschen* (1520; *The Freedom of a Christian*) provided later writers with a model of a ruggedly plain style, which gained force from its use of popular idiom.

Perhaps the Reformation's greatest gift to the essay and to religious prose was its elevation of the sermon to the center of religious life among Protestants and Dissenters. In *The English Sermon, 1550–1660* (1976) Martin Seymour-Smith notes that from 1550 to 1850 the sermon was "one of the main vehicles for current reflections about the way of the world," exerting an important influence on prose, particularly in England. The word "sermon," which comes from a Latin root meaning "talk" or "speech," denotes a discourse, usually based on a text of Scripture, designed to present religious instruction or exhortation in oral form. Although from the 16th to the 19th centuries most sermons were written out, the fact that they were intended to be spoken shaped their length and rhetorical techniques. Like the essay, the sermon explores a limited subject, is relatively brief, and often is structured as an unfolding reflection on received tradition in the light of individual experience. The plain style coming into being at the end of the 17th century owes much to the ways sermons sought to communicate complex ideas in accessible language. In addition, while the sermon was an oral form, sermons were often printed and thus read by a wide audience. In the 16th century, the lucid prose of Thomas Cranmer's *Book of Homilies* (1547) and the carefully crafted sermons of Hugh Latimer, who, Seymour-Smith suggests, seemed to "invite his listeners casually into the ramifications of his mind," were influential.

In the 17th century, the meditative tradition shaped both the sermon and the prose essay. In "Meditative Poetry" (1971), Louis L. Martz states that by the 17th century, European Christians had developed a widely accepted method of **meditation** as "interior drama" in which the individual examined himself or herself, engaged in a dialogue with God, and imaginatively re-created the scenes of Christ's life. This tradition shaped the dramatic preaching of **John Donne** as well as his prose "meditations" and "devotions." **Sir Thomas Browne** embodied his attempt to sort out his beliefs in *Religio Medici* (1642) and in *Hydriotaphia, or Urn Burial* (1658), ornate prose essays that delight in paradox and depict the believing writer as "that great and true *Amphibium*, whose nature is disposed to live ... in divided and distinguished worlds." These words embody one of the central patterns enacted by religious essayists as they dramatized tensions in their experiences of faith and doubt in an increasingly rational and secular world.

Alongside the subjective drama of the meditative tradition, a number of other patterns developed during the 17th century. The sermons of Lancelot Andrewes contributed to the popularity of a witty, metaphysical style, ornate and linguistically playful, which is sometimes labeled "euphuistic." In pamphlets such as *Areopagitica* (1644), John Milton forged a rhetoric of argument that is ordered yet imaginative, grounding his arguments equally in faith in a providential God and in the experience of the questing individual. In France, Jacques Benigne Bossuet's sermons and prose writings created a polemic model that was balanced, dignified, and courteous, while clothing important ideas in simple language. While his fellow countryman **Blaise Pascal** is best known for the fragmentary *Pensées* (1670), his *Lettres provinciales* (1656–57; *The Provincial Letters*) exemplify another strategy for the religious essayist in his satirical dramatization of a plain Frenchman's questioning of a Jesuit official. The pattern of aphoristic and fragmentary reflection in the *Pensées* influenced many 20th-century religious essayists.

In colonial America, existing patterns of meditation, spiritual autobiography, preaching, and polemic were reshaped by what Reverend Samuel Danforth called the "errand into the wilderness." In "Religion and Literature" (1988), Lynn Ross-Bryant notes that the Bible was a central literary model and suggests that the plain style's reliance on "clear, concrete images" demanded that writers bring the details of their everyday experience in the New World into their prose. She

also argues that the utopian aspirations of early religious settlers made the jeremiad an important pattern for American writers, since it not only examines the failures of the covenant people, but reasserts their providential relationship to God. This sense of providential mission is apparent in Increase Mather's "An Essay for the Recording of Illustrious Providences" (1684), which follows the format of a scientific treatise, suggesting that the language and prose strategies of the new sciences were already reshaping the way religious writers examined the evidence for their faith. Jonathan Edwards best exemplifies the resulting combination of observing intellect and mystical faith in the prose of his sermons, treatises, narratives, and reflections. The spiritual autobiography of his "Personal Narrative" (wr. 1739?–42?) and the visionary exposition of *A Divine and Supernatural Light* (1734) suggest two central patterns for North American religious writing.

By Edwards' day, in England as well as in America, the plain style and the rational epistemology of the scientific era dominated religious discourse. While the sermon was still an important form, it had become increasingly plain and direct. In *The English Sermon, 1650–1750* (1976) C. H. Sisson describes the sermon in the new style as "on the whole, shorter than the old; it made three good points and sent people home to their dinner. Above all, it said nothing that would strike sensible people as out of the way ..." At the same time, the burgeoning popular periodical press made the essay a major means of disseminating information and opinion. In the periodical presses, the essay began to replace the **pamphlet** as a means of public debate on religious issues, as is evidenced by the many responses to **David Hume**'s skeptical consideration of revelation and the supernatural in "On Miracles" (1748).

While many who saw their faith as endangered by rationalism and empiricism attempted to respond by using rational arguments and natural law analogies, another sort of religious essay flourished under the influence of writers like William Law. His *A Serious Call to a Holy and Devout Life* (1728) kept alive an affective, mystical, and pietistic approach to faith which flowered in the evangelical revivals later in the century. This strain of religious writing favored confessional modes, emphasizing spiritual autobiography shaped by patterns of self-scrutiny, conversion and epiphany, and pilgrimage or spiritual quest.

Both skeptical demythologizing and spiritual pilgrimage were important 19th-century modes of dealing with issues of faith. By the 19th century, the essay had gained a cultural authority that enabled the essayist to assume the role of sage or prophet. Many 19th-century essays stretch the boundaries of the genre by incorporating narrative and extending its length. In England, writers such as **Samuel Taylor Coleridge** and **Thomas Carlyle** sought to redefine received Christian tradition. From his "Religious Musings" (wr. 1794–96) to *Aids to Reflection* (1825), Coleridge, who "never yet read even a Methodist's 'Experience in a Gospel Magazine' without receiving instruction and amusement," sought to create a tolerant faith grounded in experience, intuition, and process. In *Sartor Resartus* (1833–34) Carlyle combined the techniques of autobiography, novel, and essay to embody his sense of the need for a "natural supernaturalism" to counter the spiritually and morally deadening force of mechanistic views of the universe. In contributions to *Tracts for the Times*, which was published between 1833 and 1841, and in works like *Essay in Aid of a Grammar of Assent* (1870), **John Henry Newman** set another pattern, addressing questions of faith and belief in ways intended to restore confidence in religious orthodoxy. Newman's learning, his elegant style, and his successful embodiment of his own motto, *cor ad cor loquitur* (heart speaking to heart), gained him a wide reading audience.

On the continent and in the United States, 19th-century religious writers used a variety of essay forms to explore their religious crises and to reshape the language of conviction for an increasingly skeptical world. In the United States, **Ralph Waldo Emerson** combined the sage's office with oratorical techniques in his *Essays, First Series* (1841) and *Essays, Second Series* (1844). In works like "The Divinity School Address," "Self-Reliance," and "The Oversoul," Emerson rejected orthodoxy, redefining the sacred in terms of complete, honest personhood, harmony with the natural, and the spontaneous, oracular utterances of the "Orphic" voice. In Russia, **Lev Tolstoi** described the crisis which led him to reject orthodox religion in *Ispoved'* (1884; *A Confession*) and went on to construct a gospel ethic stripped of supernaturalism in *V chem moia vera?* (1884; *What I Believe*). In Denmark, Søren Kierkegaard's essays were both theologically and stylistically innovative, creating a genre of religious essay that combines theological reflection and imaginative construction in *Enten-Eller* (1843; *Either/Or*) and *Stadier paa Livets Vej* (1845; *Stages on Life's Way*). He is one of the first writers to explore what he called the "existential" sense of man's tragic situation in a universe that seems entirely at odds with man's spirit.

The dilemma Kierkegaard named has been central for many 20th-century religious essayists. **Albert Camus** used the essay to explore philosophical and moral questions, creating a sort of theology without God. In Spain, **Miguel de Unamuno**'s essays, like his fiction, explore the tensions between reason and faith in the context of a strongly Catholic culture. In such works as *Del sentimiento trágico de la vida* (1913; *The Tragic Sense of Life*) he explored living in uncertainty.

The 20th century has also been rich in the work of writers who, like Newman, find it possible to embrace some sort of religious orthodoxy or supernatural religion. Early in the century, **G. K. Chesterton** and **Hilaire Belloc** both used the weapon of laughter to defend Roman Catholic orthodoxy. During and after World War II, English popular essayists **C. S. Lewis** and Dorothy L. Sayers created a vigorous Christian apologetic grounded in humor, reason, and the experience of everyday life. French essayists **Simone Weil** and Pierre Teilhard de Chardin responded to the challenges of skeptical science, social tyranny, and human need; their posthumously published works exerted a strong influence, particularly in America. Teilhard sought to recover the consciousness of the world as a "divine milieu," while in works like *Attente de Dieu* (1950; *Waiting for God*), Weil embraced a faith grounded in identification with the suffering outsider. Dietrich Bonhoeffer, executed by the Nazis in 1943, provided the model of a reasoned, devout, and deeply moral faith in his posthumously published *Letters and Papers from Prison* (1953).

For essayists in the Jewish tradition, the Holocaust has provided a literal and metaphorical crisis of faith which demands a theological answer. Abraham Joshua Heschel and Elie Wiesel, two notable writers in this tradition, attempt to synthesize Eastern European and Western experience and ideas. Heschel's essays present the "pathos" of God in order to reinvent the ground on which 20th-century rationalists can meet the Divine. Wiesel explores the mystery of suffering in journalistic essays and fictional narratives that have earned him the label of "a modern Job."

In the United States, the 20th century has seen a lively variety of writers on religious topics, with several patterns emerging. **Thomas Merton** and Henri J. M. Nouwen exemplify the revival of the contemplative tradition in essays that combine spiritual autobiography with moral and spiritual guidance. **Wendell Berry** and **Annie Dillard** have embodied a strong spiritual response to the natural world, coupled with a keen sense of moral responsibility, and, in Dillard's case, a soaring, magical prose style. Frederick Buechner and Madeleine L'Engle have taken fresh looks at old spiritual paradigms, through the lens of the joys and pains of ordinary life. Walker Percy examined the malaise of modern life and diagnosed the need for a renewal of belief to fill the vacuum created by skepticism, technological advancement, and materialism. The sheer variety and energy of these voices suggest that the United States has remained open to belief, fulfilling the dream of another influential American essayist, **William James**, who declared in *The Will to Believe* (1897) that "Religious fermentation is always a symptom of the intellectual vigor of a society" and urged his readers in a pluralistic society to continue to take "the risk of belief."

LINDA MILLS WOOLSEY

Further Reading

Cline, Dorothy Peake, *The Word Abused: Problematic Religious Language in Selected Prose Works of Swift, Wesley, and Johnson* (dissertation), Newark: University of Delaware, 1991

Cockshut, A. O. J., *Anglican Attitudes: A Study of Victorian Religious Controversies*, London: Collins, 1959

Frye, Roland M., *Perspective on Man: Literature and the Christian Tradition*, Philadelphia: Westminster Press, 1961

Gordon, Mary, editor, *Spiritual Quests: The Art and Craft of Religious Writing*, Boston: Houghton Mifflin, 1988

Gunn, Giles B., editor, *Literature and Religion*, London: SCM Press, 1971

Hudson, Elizabeth K., "English Protestants and the Imitatio Christi, 1580–1620," *Sixteenth Century Journal* 19, no. 4 (1988): 541–88

Jarrett-Kerr, Martin, *Studies in Literature and Belief*, London: Rockliff, 1954

Kantra, Robert A., "Undenominational Satire: Chesterton and Lewis Revisited," *Religion and Literature* 24, no. 1 (1992): 33–57

Keeble, N. H., *The Literary Culture of Nonconformity in Later Seventeenth-Century England*, Leicester: Leicester University Press, 1987

Link-Salinger, Ruth, editor, *Of Scholars, Savants, and Their Texts: Studies in Philosophy and Religious Thought*, New York: Lang, 1989

McDiarmid, John, "Humanism, Protestantism, and English Scripture, 1533–1540," *Journal of Medieval and Renaissance Studies* 14, no. 2 (1984): 121–38

Panikas, George Andrew, *Mansions of the Spirit: Essays in Literature and Religion*, New York: Hawthorn, 1967

Reedy, Gerard S. J., *The Bible and Reason: Anglicans and Scripture in Late Seventeenth-Century England*, Philadelphia: University of Pennsylvania Press, 1985

Ruland, Vernon, *Horizons of Criticism: An Assessment of Religious-Literary Options*, Chicago: American Library Association, 1975

Sasek, Lawrence A., *The Literary Temper of the English Puritans*, Baton Rouge: Louisiana State University Press, 1961

Scott, Nathan, *Modern Literature and the Religious Frontier*, New York: Harper, 1958

Shuger, Debora K., *Sacred Rhetoric: The Christian Grand Style in the English Rhetoric*, Princeton, New Jersey: Princeton University Press, 1988

Smith, Nigel, *Perfection Proclaimed: Language and Literature in English Radical Religion, 1640–1660*, Oxford: Clarendon Press, and New York: Oxford University Press, 1989

Willey, Basil, *More Nineteenth-Century Studies: A Group of Honest Doubters*, London: Chatto and Windus, and New York: Columbia University Press, 1956

Renan, Ernest

French, 1823–1892

Although Ernest Renan is probably best known for his *L'Avenir de la science* (1890; *The Future of Science*), his history of Judeo-Christian origins (especially *Vie de Jésus* [1863; *The Life of Jesus*]), and his autobiography, *Souvenirs d'enfance et de jeunesse* (1883; *Recollections of My Youth*), the several hundred articles he wrote over a period of some 40 years – notably for the **Revue des Deux Mondes** (Review of two worlds) and the **Journal des Débats**, and collected in seven books and part of two others – form an important cross-section of his oeuvre and are among his finest works. It is in these essays, furthermore, that we best encounter Renan in the many sides of his personality: the scholar proficient as archaeologist, epigraphist, philologist, and historian; the tireless and joyful traveler; the political analyst and acute critic of contemporary affairs; the "penseur," as the French call their thinkers who are not systematic or professional philosophers; and the marvelously gifted prose writer. The essays' importance is enhanced by the fact that Renan was very conscious of their belonging to a "new literary genre" (preface, *Études d'histoire religieuse*), a type of writing that he considered, in fact, characteristic of his century and of its best literary efforts.

Renan's essay production may be roughly divided into three periods: the inartistic, combative journalism of the 1840s; the mature, artistically sensitive criticism of the 1850s, 1860s, and early 1870s; and the somewhat frivolous pieces of his late years, from about 1876 to his death in 1892. In this last phase one still finds, exceptionally, a few of his greatest essays.

From 1848 to 1850, in the pro-revolutionary, republican, socialist *Liberté de Penser: Revue Philosophique et Littéraire*, the brilliant young scholar of Semitic languages took his first bold journalistic strides into two fields that were to interest him permanently: the history of religion and contemporary political and religious questions. In a partisan polemical spirit, the former Catholic seminarian, who had abandoned orthodox faith under the pressure of rationalism and biblical criticism, attacks clericalism and defends liberalism in a crude, dogmatic style (not without real vigor) as different from his mature style as night from day. That he had **Pascal**'s brilliant polemic against the Jesuits, the *Lettres provinciales* (1657; *The Provincial Letters*; signed "Louis de Montalte"), in mind as a model is shown by his use of the pseudonym "Ernest de Montalte" for one of the most caustic **satiric essay**s of the series.

The stylistic revisions that Renan made in these articles when he published them in later essay collections reveal in striking fashion the evolution of his style and its growth into the subtly refined, artistic, often poetic prose of his mature manner. This profound change, coinciding with his elevation of the *article de revue* into a "new literary genre," was due in part to the influence of his mentor, the great historian of medieval France, Augustin Thierry, and to that of such purists and advocates of classical French prose style as his sister, Henriette, and the editor of the *Journal des Débats*, Ustazade de Sacy (both this journal and the *Revue des Deux Mondes* had much higher literary standards than the *Liberté de Penser*); but above all it was due to the aesthetic awakening he experienced as the result of his academic mission to Italy in 1849–50. He had also discovered, thanks largely to Thierry, that refinement of form was inseparable from force of argument, even in historical and philosophical writing.

The first fruit of his literary conversion, at age 34, was the *Études d'histoire religieuse* (1857; *Studies of Religious History*), a landmark in the history of the French essay, which introduces a number of features that will remain characteristic of Renan's essay art. In his hands the essay, already given a new dignity by the choice of the word "study" in the title, becomes a supreme instrument of "vulgarisation," even "haute vulgarisation," as the French call it (as distinct from mere "popularisation"), or the art of rendering erudition accessible to the common reader. (**Sainte-Beuve** had paved the way with his humanization of *literary* scholarship.) Renan's subjects include religions of antiquity, Judaism, Christianity, Islam, Calvin, Unitarianism, neo-Hegelianism, and religious art. Criticism, with its synthesis of the "sentiment religieux" ("religious sense," as distinct from dogmas and creeds) and scholarly historical analysis, has become nothing less than "an original form of creation peculiar to our age" (preface). Although the *Études* may be read independently of one another, the author, very conscious of the need to provide a truly unified and organic whole (preface), arranges them with an eye to the thematic structure of the book as a whole.

These formal features are continued and perfected in Renan's second collection, the *Essais de morale et de critique* (1859; *Moral and critical essays*), which surpass the *Études* and may well be his greatest essay work. It consists of an important **preface** followed by 13 essays, divided roughly into two parts: the first, a series of critical portraits aiming to define the originality of his own generation (the generation of 1848) by comparing it with the preceding one (the Romantic), represented by a philosopher (Victor Cousin), a religious writer (Félicité Robert de Lamennais), and a historian (Thierry); and the second, using history as a springboard, a moral and political critique of the Second Empire. The main theme, giving coherence to the different essays, is "the establishing of freedom by way of the regeneration of the individual conscience" (preface). Resistance, in the name of an intellectual and moral elite, is urged against middle-class mediocrity and vulgarity and against the tyranny of the centralized, bureaucratic state. Various examples of forces counteracting materialism culminate in the final essay, the famous "Poésie des races celtiques" (Poetry of Celtic races). Renan, as a Breton, makes of his Celtic inheritance from a "golden age" of idealism and spirituality the supreme symbol of resistance to what he calls "an age of lead and tin."

The essayist's method here is to employ an intricate pattern, almost rhythmical in nature, of abstract thought, concrete detail, anecdote, poetic image, and reflection, subtly suggesting his message more often than he directly states it. It is the method of "grasping one's object by way of successive approximations" (this last term was taken up by Renan's admirer, **Charles Du Bos**, to become the title of his own essay masterpiece, *Approximations* [1922–37]). The style, with its subtle harmonies and its "slow and calm manner of breathing" (Jules Renard), for the most part appeals less to the eye than to the ear – and to the moral sense.

By contrast, Renan's two subsequent essay volumes, the *Questions contemporaines* (1868; Contemporary questions) and *La Réforme intellectuelle et morale* (1871; Intellectual and moral reform), deal in a much more direct and vigorous style with political problems in the broadest sense, including education, and with proposed solutions. The first is a sober critique of the Second Empire in its final phase, while the second is a zealous, provocative, at times apocalyptic vision of the ills of a France seeking to recover from its defeat in the Franco-Prussian War. "Reactionary" as *La Réforme* is, in its pushing of the elitist thesis of the *Essais* to authoritarian if not proto-fascist extremes, it makes more exciting reading than the *Questions* and contains some of Renan's most prophetic writing. In both books he has mastered the art of conferring on essays written for specific political occasions ("écrits de circonstance") a more universal, permanent interest and value; at his best he ranks with such great political essayists as Walter Bagehot and Lord Acton.

Renan's **philosophical** essays, though only four in number, form a significant part of his total philosophical work. Three, composed in the 1860s, appeared as "fragments" in *Dialogues et fragments philosophiques* (1876; *Philosophical Dialogues and Fragments*), and the fourth, "Examen de conscience philosophique" (Examination of philosophical conscience), one of his greatest essays, is the concluding piece in his final book, *Feuilles détachées* (Detached leaves), published in the year of his death in 1892. To come to these from his political essays is to leave "importunate truths" expressed in forceful prose for a tenuous verbal music expressive of their author's belief that philosophy, apart from its usefulness as a handmaid of history and science, and especially in that branch of it known as metaphysics, is essentially a form of poetry. Renan's famous "play of ideas" occurs to some extent in these essays, but for a freer, more unpredictable, more "essayistic" form of such play one must turn to what he called the "conversations between the different lobes of [his] brain" in the **dialogues**, where he reveals himself to be a worthy successor of **Plato** and Malebranche. As a philosophical essayist he is perhaps less great than **Emerson** (with whom he had a remarkable affinity, as noted by Bland Blanshard, 1984), **George Santayana**, or Bertrand Russell.

In his final period Renan produced four essay collections, if we include the "oral essays" of the *Discours et conférences* (1887; Speeches and lectures), containing one of his most famous and most lastingly relevant pieces, "Qu'est-ce qu'une nation?" (What is a nation?). On the whole these collections of "songeries crépusculaires" (twilight musings), as Maurice

Barrès called them in *Huit Jours chez M. Renan* (1913), contain a greater number of charming trifles and miscellaneous bits of erudition and fewer of the polished, deliberate essays of the kind to which the earlier Renan has accustomed us. He seems to have felt that the heyday of such "grands articles" had passed. The style has become somewhat facile and flaccid. Nor is the "renanisme" that marks many of these pieces – the attitude of a Gallic Buddha smiling ironically at the spectacle of a world that should not be taken too seriously – to everyone's taste. The *Nouvelles études d'histoire religieuse* (1884; New studies in religious history, translated as *Studies in Religious History*) is a superficial successor to the great *Études* of 1857. The *Mélanges d'histoire et de voyages* (1878; Miscellany of historical and travel essays), on the other hand, is a neglected book containing several fine specimens of historiography in the best Renanian tradition as well as a great **travel** essay, "Vingt Jours en Sicile" (20 days in Sicily). This essay, based on his trip to a learned congress in Palermo in 1875, is a beautiful, sensuous recapturing of youthful spirit on the part of the aging and ailing scholar; it corresponds in his work to the place held by **Montaigne**'s "Sur des vers de Virgile" (1588; "On Some Verses of Virgil") in his *Essais*. Exceptionally fine essays are also still found in the *Feuilles détachées*, with its lovely play on words of the title – autumnal pages detached from the tree of his work; leaves falling from the tree of his life; his death anticipated with serene detachment. In reality the book offers the last variation on the Renanian theme of the "poetry of the self," and is offered as a sequel to his *Recollections of My Youth*. It rises to a fitting culmination in his final essay, a philosophical last testament and summing up of his deepest beliefs, the "Examen de conscience philosophique." An important counterweight to the skepticism and frivolity of *renanisme* itself, it is also nothing less than Renan's "De l'expérience" (Montaigne, 1588; "On Experience").

Renan as an essayist learned much from Sainte-Beuve's *Portraits* and *Lundis*, although he had serious reservations about their author as a thinker. It was Sainte-Beuve, on the other hand, who with no less modesty than critical acumen singled out his younger contemporary as "the master of a new genre," that is, the "article de revue." In his essays in religious history Renan succeeded in annexing that field into the realm of literature (Brunetière, *Cinq lettres sur Renan*, 1904). The breadth of his essays, equaled in France only by those of Sainte-Beuve and Montaigne (who surpasses them both), is derived not only from his extraordinarily broad learning and culture, but also and even more from his lifelong insistence on representing multiple and contradictory points of view, on "not letting a single component of humanity stifle any other" (*Fragments intimes et romanesques* [1914; Intimate and fictional fragments]). His essays faithfully reflect the "fabric woven of contradictions" that he exulted in being. He also enriched his essay work by combining subjective and objective points of view. Like Sainte-Beuve, he avoided deeply personal disclosures à la Montaigne, reserving these, again like Sainte-Beuve, for his intimate notebooks. He reproached his contemporaries "for being too subjective, too wrapped up in themselves," a criticism that would seem to augur poorly for a would-be essayist. Yet, paradoxically, like Sainte-Beuve, he succeeded in speaking meaningfully of himself while at the same time being "absorbed in the object, that is, in all that lies before us, the world, nature, history" (preface, *Feuilles détachées*). Among essayists who learned from his example are, in France, Anatole France, Émile Faguet, Jules Lemaître, **Paul Bourget**, Charles Du Bos; abroad, **Matthew Arnold**, **Walter Pater**, George Santayana.

RICHARD M. CHADBOURNE

Biography
Ernest Joseph Renan. Born 28 February 1823 in Tréguier, Brittany. Studied at the École Ecclésiastique, Tréguier, 1832–38; seminary of Saint-Nicolas du Chardonnet (run by Abbé Dupanloup), Paris, 1838–41, and seminaries at Issy, 1841–43, and Saint-Sulpice, 1843–45; tutor, 1845–48; studied privately for licence in letters, 1846, agrégation in philosophy, 1848, and doctorate in letters, 1852. Contributor to *Liberté de Penser* and *Journal de l'Instruction Publique*, late 1840s, *Journal des Débats*, early 1850s, and *Revue des Deux Mondes*, from 1853. Sent by government to classify manuscripts of major Italian libraries, 1849–50; lived with his sister Henriette in Paris, from 1851; worked for the manuscript section, Bibliothèque Nationale, Paris, 1851–60. Elected to the Académie des Inscriptions et Belles-Lettres, 1856. Married Cornélie Scheffer, 1856: one daughter (died in infancy) and one son. Led archaeological expedition to Phoenicia (Syria), 1860, and Palestine, 1861, where Henriette died of malaria. Professor of Hebrew, Collège de France, Paris, 1862–64 and from 1870 (administrator, from 1883). Traveled to Egypt and the Upper Nile, 1864. Assistant director of manuscripts department for the Imperial Library, 1864. Founded collection of Semitic inscriptions, *Corpus Inscriptionum Semiticarum*, and named secretary of the Société Asiatique, 1867. Ran unsuccessfully as liberal candidate for deputyship in district of Meaux, 1869. Elected to the French Academy, 1878. Award: Volney Prize, 1847; Officer, 1880, Commander, 1884, and Grand Officer, 1888, Legion of Honor. Died (of pneumonia and heart trouble) in Paris, 2 October 1892.

Selected Writings

Essays and Related Prose
Études d'histoire religieuse, 1857; as *Studies of Religious History*, translated by O. B. Frothingham, 1864
Essais de morale et de critique, 1859
Questions contemporaines, 1868
La Réforme intellectuelle et morale, 1871
Dialogues et fragments philosophiques, 1876; as *Dialogues philosophiques*, edited by Laudyce Rétat, 1992; as *Philosophical Dialogues and Fragments*, translated by Râs Bihâri Mukharjî, 1883
Mélanges d'histoire et de voyages, 1878
Nouvelles études d'histoire religieuse, 1884; as *Studies in Religious History*, translated by William M. Thomson, 1886
Discours et conférences, 1887
Feuilles détachées, 1892
La Réforme intellectuelle et morale et autres écrits (selection), edited by Alain de Benoist, 1982
Renan histoire et parole, œuvres diverses (selection), edited by Laudyce Rétat, 1984

Other writings: a book on the future of science (1890), a seven-volume history of the origins of Christianity (*Les Origines du christianisme*, 1863–82), a history of the people of Israel (1887–93), other works on religion, the autobiography *Souvenirs d'enfance et de jeunesse* (1883; *Recollections of My Youth*), *Drames philosophiques* (1888), and a book about his sister Henriette (1862). Also translated several books of the Bible from Hebrew.

Collected works edition: *Œuvres complètes*, edited by Henriette Psichari, 10 vols., 1947–61.

Bibliography
Girard, Henri, and Henri Moncel, *Bibliographie des œuvres de Ernest Renan*, Paris: Presses Universitaires de France, 1923

Further Reading
Arnold, Matthew, "M. Renan," in his *Essays in Criticism, Third Series*, Folcroft, Pennsylvannia: Folcroft, 1969 (original edition, 1910)
Babbitt, Irving, "Renan," in his *The Masters of Modern French Criticism*, Boston and New York: Houghton Mifflin, 1912
Blanshard, Bland, "Ernest Renan," in his *Four Reasonable Men: Marcus Aurelius, John Stuart Mill, Ernest Renan, Henry Sidgwick*, Middletown, Connecticut: Wesleyan University Press, 1984
Chadbourne, Richard, "Renan or the Contemptuous Approach to Literature," *Yale French Studies* 2 (1949): 96–104
Chadbourne, Richard, "Renan as Prophet of the European and World Future," *American Society of Legion of Honor Magazine* 22 (1951): 299–309
Chadbourne, Richard, "Renan's Revision of His *Liberté de Penser* Articles," *PMLA* 66 (1951): 927–50
Chadbourne, Richard, "Renan and Sainte-Beuve," *Romanic Review* 44 (1953): 127–35
Chadbourne, Richard, *Ernest Renan as an Essayist*, Ithaca, New York: Cornell University Press, 1957
Chadbourne, Richard, *Ernest Renan*, New York: Twayne, 1968
Darmsteter, James, "Ernest Renan," *New World* 2 (1893): 401–33
"Ernest Renan," in *Nineteenth-Century Literary Criticism*, vol. 26, edited by Janet Mullane and Robert Wilson, Detroit: Gale Research, 1990: 361–428
Guéhenno, Jean, *Aventures de l'esprit*, Paris: Gallimard, 1954
Guérard, Albert, "Renan," in his *French Prophets of Yesterday*, London: Unwin, and New York: Appleton, 1913
James, Henry, "Renan's *Dialogues and Philosophic Fragments*," in his *Literary Reviews and Essays on American, English, and French Literature*, edited by Albert Mordell, New York: Twayne, 1957 (original article published 1876)
Monod, Gabriel, *Les Maîtres de l'histoire: Renan, Taine, Michelet*, Paris: Calmann-Lévy, 1894
Mott, Lewis, *Ernest Renan*, New York and London: Appleton, 1921
Neff, Emery, "History as Art: Renan, Burckhardt, Green," in his *The Poetry of History*, New York: Columbia University Press, 1947
Peyre, Henri, "Ernest Renan, critique littéraire," *PMLA* 44 (1929): 288–308
Pommier, Jean, *Renan, d'après des documents inédits*, Paris: Perrin, 1923
Psichari, Henriette, *Renan d'après lui-même*, Paris: Plon, 1937
Sainte-Beuve, Charles-Augustin, "M. Ernest Renan," in his *Nouveaux Lundis*, vol. 2, Paris: Lévy, 3rd edition, 1870
Sainte-Beuve, Charles-Augustin, "*Vie de Jésus* par M. Ernest Renan," in his *Nouveaux Lundis*, vol. 6, Paris: Lévy, 1872
Saintsbury, George, "Ernest Renan," *Fortnightly Review* 27 (1880): 625–43
Smith, Colin, "The Fictionalist Element in Renan's Thought," *French Studies* 9 (1955): 30–41
Smith, Colin, "Renan's Final Cosmology," *Forum for Modern Language Studies* 14 (1978): 231–46
Wardman, H. W., *Ernest Renan: A Critical Biography*, London: Athlone Press, 1964
Wardman, H. W., "L'Esprit de finesse and Style in Renan," *Modern Language Review* 59 (1964): 215–24
Wilson, Edmund, "Decline of the Revolutionary Tradition: Renan," in his *To the Finland Station: A Study in the Writing and Acting of History*, New York: Harcourt Brace, and London: Secker and Warburg, 1940

Reportage

Theories of contemporary journalism and literature reveal a variety of sometimes contradictory definitions of the term "reportage," which is often used in relation to the essay broadly conceived. Two distinct traditions exist for defining the nature of reportage. First, there is the journalistic perspective, restricting the term to a subgenre of reporting. Second, there is the literary perspective, particularly discussed in relation to the **New Journalism**.

From the Latin *reportare* (to bring news, to announce, to report), the word "reportage" is generally used in Romance languages to refer to an enriched variation of what in standard journalistic English is known as the news story, meaning a piece of direct, informative reporting, as opposed to comment (editorials and columns). This system of dividing all journalistic work into two categories (news and comment) reflects the success of American-led theory in journalism schools. In other cultural traditions, especially Southern Europe and until very recently Latin America, "news" is considered as at least three different variations of informative journalism. First, there are stories, second reportage, and third a hybrid category using terms derived from the word "chronicle."

In modern journalism two elements distinguish a pure news story from reportage: the purpose of the "lead-in," and the language and structure. In a pure news story, the lead-in summarizes the main points of the news by answering the so-called five "W" questions (Who, What, Where, When, and Why); the lead-in of a piece of reportage attempts to attract the attention of the reader and presents a wider stylistic range: an epigram, an ironic fact, the use of color and contrast, a question, or a relevant quotation. The main body of an item of reportage, as well as the traditional news story, has at last three kinds of approach: the fact story (a series of facts in descending importance), the action story (initial event, then follow-up with details, then return to the initial event with additional arguments, etc.), and the "quote" story (lead, quotation, new summary of context, documentation, more quotation, etc.). Models of fact story and action story are the items in news magazines such as *Time* and *Newsweek*.

What in continental Europe is called "in-depth" reportage corresponds to the American "in-depth reporting," also known as interpretative reporting, and even investigative reporting. Its distinctive ingredients are the provision of background, a human element to the story, a degree of explanation and clarification, and an attempt to help the reader understand the underlying significance of the events.

Theorists of journalism also comment on related subgenres such as the French *chronique*, related to the American "column" and therefore belonging to the realm of opinion, along with the editorial. In contrast, the Spanish *crónica* and the Italian *cronaca* are considered as hybrid subgenres, lying somewhere between the column and the story, and retain as their goal the provision of information. A standard definition of *crónica* includes direct and immediate narration, which evaluates the chronological progression of an event. Such elements are also the primary criteria for the inclusion of certain texts in English anthologies of reportage, for example the writings of Xenophon, Marco Polo, Amerigo Vespucci, Bartolomé de Las Casas, and Garcilaso de la Vega, as well as recent accounts by such distinguished writers as **George Bernard Shaw**, **George Orwell**, Stephen Crane, John Reed, and John Steinbeck, and nonprofessional writers such as Hitler's general Erwin Rommel and the astronaut Neil Armstrong.

It is not surprising, therefore, that a wide variety of writing is routinely catalogued as reportage by publishers and libraries. First, there is the work of the practitioners of New Journalism, a school or trend that is not really so "New" since it corresponds to what is also called "literary journalism." Contextual evidence questions the "journalistic" nature of the best of New Journalism: though many typical examples of the trend have appeared in newspapers or magazines, they might just as easily have been published as books. However, literary journalists do have to follow certain procedures, such as researching the topic, maintaining an interwoven structure, reporting the facts accurately, keeping a sense of responsibility, and often adding an element of symbolism.

In its widest sense, reportage also includes nonsyndicated columnists as well as some of the classic syndicated journalists, writers who exhibit a personal style that transcends the standard formats pursued by editors. The term "reportage" could also embrace the work of some of the best Pulitzer Prize winners, and take in some of the more elaborate varieties of the journalistic form more usually known as the feature.

All the variations of reportage have certain characteristics in common with the essay. First, they usually reflect the author's own concerns and personality. Second, they express a greater interest in the human elements than in the facts of the newsworthy events themselves. They are more attracted to aspects of what in the Spanish tradition is called the *intrahistoria*, the daily activities of ordinary people, than the milestones of official history. Third, the structure and style show a degree of flexibility that obviates the need to use the inverted pyramid (in which facts are presented in descending order of importance) prevalent in standard informative newspaper writing. Finally, they attempt to persuade the reader of a particular stance even as they claim objectivity in the presentation of facts. It could be said that the essay and reportage share similar characteristics and constraints, the most apparent being the opinion-prone and author-centered nature of the writing.

JOAQUÍN ROY

See also Journalism and the Essay

Anthologies

The Best of Granta Reportage, London: Granta/Penguin, and New York: Viking Penguin, 1994
The Faber Book of Reportage, edited by John Carey, London: Faber, 1987; as *Eyewitness to History*, Cambridge, Massachusetts: Harvard University Press, 1987
The New Journalism, edited by Tom Wolfe and E. W. Johnson, New York: Harper and Row, 1973
A Sourcebook of American Literary Journalism: Representative Writers in an Emerging Genre, edited by Thomas B. Connery, Westport, Connecticut: Greenwood Press, 1992

Further Reading

Copple, Neale, with Emily E. Trickey, *Depth Reporting: An Approach to Journalism*, Englewood Cliffs, New Jersey: Prentice Hall, 1964
Foley, Barbara, *Telling the Truth: The Theory and Practice of Documentary Fiction*, Ithaca, New York: Cornell University Press, 1986

Frus, Phyllis, *The Politics and Poetics of Journalistic Narrative: The Timely and the Timeless*, Cambridge and New York: Cambridge University Press, 1994

Geisler, Michael, *Die literarische Reportage in Deutschland: Möglichkeiten und Grenzen eines operativen Genres*, Königstein: Scriptor, 1982

Hernadi, Paul, *Beyond Genre: New Directions in Literary Classification*, Ithaca, New York: Cornell University Press, 1972

Rothmeyer, Karen, *Winning Pulitzers: The Stories Behind Some of the Best News Coverage of Our Time*, New York: Columbia University Press, 1991

Scholes, Robert, and Carl H. Klaus, *Elements of the Essay*, New York: Oxford University Press, 1970

Winterowd, W. Ross, *The Rhetoric of the "Other" Literature*, Carbondale: Southern Illinois University Press, 1990

Wolfe, Tom, *The New Journalism* (includes an anthology edited by Wolfe and E. W. Johnson), New York: Harper and Row, 1973

Repplier, Agnes

American, 1855–1950

In her "happy half century" as an essayist, Agnes Repplier produced 18 volumes of essays. She placed the first of her Lamb-like "conversations" in the *Atlantic Monthly* in 1886 and continued to appear regularly in the *Atlantic* and other outlets of higher journalism, such as the *Century Magazine* and *Harper's*, until the late 1930s.

Repplier used what she called "the light essay" to explore such specific and seemingly random subjects as mirrors, dogs, letters, diaries, spinsters, cakes and ale, as well as topics as abstract and diverse as superstition, education, pleasure, ennui, Christianity, humor, and war. Of her many subjects the two she returned to the most were those that made up the title of her first book – *Books and Men* (1888) – with the "men" usually being authors.

Repplier was an autodidact. Though she would eventually receive honorary degrees from Notre Dame, Pennsylvania, Princeton, Yale, and Columbia, her formal education ended when her rebelliousness got her expelled from convent school at the age of 15. The many allusions and quotations in her essays testify to the fact that she read voraciously and always with a pencil in hand. Her essays flow from the tradition of the commonplace book. An early (1894) and anonymous reviewer in the *Atlantic* cited them as examples of "the bookish essay," a "harvest of book-browsings" that makes "no attempt at criticism beyond the report of the effect of a volume upon the personality of the essayist." Such a summary statement overstates the case, but Repplier's displays of knowledge are sometimes intrusive. Witness for example the piling up of (often obscure) allusion in this single sentence:

> Actaeon flying as a stag from the pursuit of his own hounds; Circe's swinish captives groveling at their troughs; Björn turned into a bear through the malice of his stepmother, and hunted to death by his father, King Kring; the swans of Lir floating mournfully on the icy waters of the Moyle; the *loup-garou* lurking in the forest of Brittany, the *oborot* coursing over the Russian steppes; Merlin sleeping in the gloomy depths of Broceliande, and

> Raknar buried fifty fathoms below the coast of Helluland, are alike the victims of "woven and of waving hands," whether the spell be cast by an outraged divinity, or by the cruel hand of a malignant foe." ("On the Benefits of Superstition," 1888)

Repplier does not so much criticize literature as talk about her reading, which ranged widely in the Latin classics and the established canons of both France and England. She offers impressions, but does not build a system. She is often enthusiastic, sometimes acerbic, but never a true theoretician.

Repplier's essays ramble, but Repplier' style is always polished and energetic. Her tone is at once companionable and ironic, gentle and biting. She wrote often on humor – e.g. "A Plea for Humor" (1891), "Wit and Humor" (1893), "Humor: English and American" (1894), "The Mission of Humor" (1912), "Cruelty and Humor" (1920), "The American Laughs" (1924), and "The Unconscious Humor of the Movies" (1931) – and though she criticized the tendency in both individuals and nations to hold the humor of others in disdain, she herself favored the English brand of wit and drollery. She expects, even requires, an alert reader. Of motion pictures, which she termed a "kind of amplified and diversified Punch and Judy show, depending on incessant action and plenty of hard knocks," she wrote, "Even the animals – dogs, donkeys and pigs – are subject to catastrophes that must wreck their confidence in life" ("The American Laughs"). Of the snobbery of colonial Philadelphia Anglicans who were willing to forego their privileges as British subjects in order to have their way with the Quakers, she noted, "The ardent churchman felt no sacrifice too great for the coveted privilege of correcting his neighbor's misdemeanors" (*Philadelphia: The Place and the People*, 1898).

Her humor was her saving grace, for her opinions were firmly held and often unpopular. Her irony was as self-deprecating as it was wicked. Unmarried herself, she wrote essays on "The Spinster" (1904) and "Three Famous Old Maids" (1895) – e.g. "Miss Austen, Miss Edgeworth, Miss Mitford." She was a political conservative and devout Catholic, but did not shirk from alluding to her own weakness for drink ("The Strayed Prohibitionist," 1920), though it should be noted that she wrote with equal enthusiasm about tea (*To Think of Tea!*, 1932). She was less evenhanded with other topics. Her attacks on feminists, pacifists, and other reformers were always uncompromising and sometimes contemptuous. Immigrants were holding America back. Liberals were pessimists who lacked "sympathy with man and with his work, with the beautiful and imperfect things he has made of the chequered centuries" ("Consolations of a Conservative," 1920).

She saw herself as a classicist and a patrician whose task it was to defend literary tradition, that "little band of authors who, unknown to the wide careless world, remain from generation to generation the friends of a few fortunate readers" (introduction to the biography *James Howell*, 1907). If she could choose one "happy half century," she said, it would be the one that straddled 1800. For her, this meant that the essay should be Lambian. She recognized the obstinacy of such a position, but persisted. As early as 1894 she allowed that "the essay may die, but just now it possesses a lively and encouraging vitality" ("The Passing of the Essay"). To prove her point, she cited the popularity of seven particular essayists. Unfortunately, three of them were already dead and two more would die within the year. By 1918, she was admitting defeat: "The personal essay, the little bit of sentiment or observation, the lightly offered commentary which aims to appear the artless thing it isn't – this exotic, of which Lamb was a rare exponent, has withered in the blasts of war" ("The American Essay in War Time").

Repplier's version of the **personal essay** may have been narrow and antiquated, but she practiced it with enough energy, wit, and style that James Gray in *American Non-Fiction: 1900–1950* (1952) credits her with keeping it "alive almost without aid far into the 1930's."

NED STUCKEY-FRENCH

Biography

Born 1 April 1855 in Philadelphia. Studied at the Convent of the Sacred Heart, Philadelphia: expelled at age 10; Eden Hall Sacred Heart convent, Torresdale, Pennsylvania, 1867–70; Miss Agnes Irwin's School, Philadelphia, 1870–71: expelled. Lived primarily in Philadelphia; traveled a great deal in Europe. Contributor to many journals, from 1881, including *Catholic World* and the *Atlantic Monthly*. Friends with other writers, including **Oliver Wendell Holmes** and Walt Whitman. Awards: Laetare Medal, 1911; American Academy of Arts and Letters Gold Medal, 1935; honorary degrees from five universities. Died in Philadelphia, 15 December 1950.

Selected Writings

Essays and Related Prose

Books and Men, 1888
Points of View, 1891
Essays in Miniature, 1892
Essays in Idleness, 1893
In the Dozy Hours, and Other Papers, 1894
Varia, 1897
Philadelphia: The Place and the People, 1898
The Fireside Sphinx, 1901
Compromises, 1904
A Happy Half-Century, and Other Essays, 1908
Americans and Others, 1912
Counter-Currents, 1916
Points of Friction, 1920
Under Dispute, 1924
Times and Tendencies, 1931
To Think of Tea!, 1932
In Pursuit of Laughter, 1936
Eight Decades: Essays and Episodes, 1937

Other writings: the autobiography *In Our Convent Days* (1905) and biographies. Also edited *A Book of Famous Verse* (1892).

Further Reading

"Contemporary Essays," *Atlantic Monthly* 73 (February 1894): 265
Flanagan, John T., "A Distinguished American Essayist," *South Atlantic Quarterly* 44 (1945): 162–69
Hall, James Norman, "A Word for the Essayist," *Yale Review* 32 (September 1942): 50–58
Pattee, Fred Lewis, *A History of American Literature Since 1870*, New York: Century, 1915: 428–32
Pattee, Fred Lewis, *The New American Literature, 1890–1930*, New York: Century, 1930: 434–35
Repplier, Emma (Mrs. Lightner Witmer), *Agnes Repplier: A Memoir*, Philadelphia: Dorrance, 1957
Rickenbacker, William F., "Agnes Repplier Revisited," *Modern Age: A Quarterly Review* 36, no. 4 (Summer 1994): 341–50
Stokes, George Stewart, *Agnes Repplier: Lady of Letters*, Philadelphia: University of Pennsylvania Press, and London: Oxford University Press, 1949

Rêverie

It is irony rather than paradox that the French genre of *rêverie* should have been born of the rationalist 18th century, the *siècle des lumières*, which saw the emergence of scientific rationalism as the supreme authority in philosophy. Yet that was the period during which was also born what with hindsight we have decided to call "pre-Romanticism," a movement connected with the cultivation of tenderness, the expression of feeling, and concern with the nonlogical, irrational forms of human experience, including *rêves* or dreams. The connection between the French Romantic movement and pre-Romanticism is actually tenuous, but a continuity is apparent in the increasing interest in mental states, of which the *rêverie* represents one type, existing outside the sphere of strict logic and relaxing the enforcement of strict rational control.

As a mental event, the *rêverie*, to which the English "daydream" is merely an approximation, represents only a moderated relaxation of rational control, such as used to be cultivated chiefly by imaginative artists and their followers in developing their sensitivity to nature and beauty, in search of aesthetic stimulus or satisfaction. Our inadequate vocabulary for dealing with such phenomena nonetheless allows us to distinguish the realm of imagination, in which the *rêverie* explores with some degree of realism the meaning of emotional experience, together with any possible alternative forms which it might take, from the realm of mere fantasy, in which all degree of conscious control or logical coherence can be jettisoned.

The *rêverie* as a genre is an extension of the *rêve*, which came into prominence when **Diderot** used *Le Rêve de d'Alembert* (*D'Alembert's Dream*) as the title of the second and most poetic of the three **dialogue**s he wrote in August 1769, when toward the end of his life he had time at last to return to philosophy. The dialogue is probably the most imaginatively powerful of all Diderot's works, and also that which most successfully unites literature with philosophy. It concerns the awakening of *sensibilité* in hitherto inert matter when, under the impetus of an external stimulus like warmth, the "soul" becomes the organic principle unifying a living and sentient being, and the directing force of its growth. The *Rêve* was released in Autumn 1782 to Grimm's private fortnightly newsletter to subscribing heads of European courts. A run of the **letters** was later gathered together and published as the *Correspondance littéraire* (16 vols., 1829).

The most famous set of *rêveries* in French, **Rousseau**'s *Les Rêveries du promeneur solitaire* (1782; *Reveries of the Solitary Walker*), was a very late confessional work, largely provoked by rumors of his death in 1776. It was intended to be a sequel to the *Confessions* (wr. 1764–70, pub. 1782–89). The choice of titles raises some complex issues. Rousseau, in spite of the apparent formality of some of his works, was not a polished writer, and the informality of tone indicated by the *rêverie*, and underlined by the reference to the solitude of the unsupported thinker in the title, is not an affectation. The late confessional writings, including the *Confessions* themselves, are not among Rousseau's more powerful works, and the light in which he wished to present himself distorts the truth. Nevertheless, his title denotes a touch of boastful independence. The *Rêveries*, even if apparently little more than an epilogue to the *Confessions*, are idealized visions, often of serious philosophic interest, although also frequently set off by some trivial anecdote, experience, or incident. But they are the visions of one who attempted to live his life in a mental solitude unconstrained by the intellectual pressures which society imposed on its members. They were, then, in an unusually full sense, Rousseau's own visions.

Rousseau's 1960 editor, Henri Roddier, claims that the *Rêveries* inspired the literary form of both the intimate **personal essay** and the ostensibly private diary written for publication. The *rêverie* as a genre certainly belongs to the category of self-revelatory, often fictionalized, autobiography. The genre did move toward fiction, apparently in order to allow serious philosophical and social principles to be presented in the tentative guise of a fantasy.

The form's next important author, Étienne Pivert de Senancour, who once applied to the government for support to lead his life as a solitary thinker, suppressed his first two books, signed "Rêveur des Alpes," written in 1792 and 1793. Best known for his novel *Oberman* (1804), he nonetheless composed a *Rêveries sur la nature primitive de l'homme* (Reveries on the primitive nature of man) in 1799, to be reworked in 1809, and again, simply as *Rêveries*, in 1833. In 1834, shortly after the appearance of Rousseau's *Rêveries*, Senancour published *Libres méditations d'un solitaire inconnu* (Free meditations of a solitary unknown) less hostile to Christianity than his previous work had been, but still looking for guiding principles in human and physical nature. Intellectually Senancour's life was dominated by the need to balance nature's menace against the therapeutic effects it exercised on the sensibility and to weigh the protection afforded by civil society against the constraints it imposed.

With the full-blooded Romanticism of the 1820s the *rêverie*, like the **meditation**, went out of fashion as a genre. It was essentially a pre-Romantic form, but it contained several works which constitute literary apexes of that movement in France.

ANTHONY LEVI

Further Reading
Much of the literature on the *rêverie* concerns specific examples and specific authors, particularly Rousseau (see the Further Reading under his entry).

Bachelard, Gaston, *The Poetics of Reverie: Childhood, Language, and the Cosmos*, New York: Orion, 1969 (original French edition, 1960)
Morrisey, Robert J., *La Rêverie jusqu'à Rousseau: Recherches sur un topos littéraire*, Lexington, Kentucky: French Forum, 1984
Tripet, Arnaud, *La Rêverie littéraire: Essai sur Rousseau*, Geneva: Droz, 1979

Review

Genetically, the genre of the review is closely related to the essay. The family resemblance points to their common origin. While Montaigne's *Essais* can be understood both as an examination of the self and as a running commentary of books that reviews the entire tradition as such, the review is like the essay's younger sibling.

In the 17th century, reviews emerged at the moment when correspondence between scholars, philosophers, and scientists no longer satisfied the demands for communication of a growing intellectual community. As a response, **Pierre Bayle** began in 1684 his journal *Nouvelles de la République des Lettres* (News from the Republic of Letters). Twenty years earlier, in 1665, Denis de Sallo initiated *Le Journal de Sçavans* (The journal of the educated), the pioneering model for 18th-century review journals. The *Journal* was just a few months ahead of the Royal Society's *Philosophical Transactions*, founded the same year. In Germany, the *Acta Eruditorum* followed in 1682, and from 1688 to 1690 was published Christian Thomasius' *Freymüthige Gedancken oder Monats-Gespräche* (Frank thoughts or monthly entertainments), the first review journal in German.

While the first review journal began in France, it was in Germany, and, by way of the importation of German Romanticism, in Britain, that the review gained importance as an independent literary genre. Among the multitude of literary forms the great essayists of 17th- and 18th-century France employed, book reviews in effect did not exist. It was not until the arrival of Romanticism that reviewing took hold in France. While encyclopedias served as the new medium in France, the review of books and periodicals took center stage in 18th-century Germany. Whereas intellectual life in France was reduced to small coteries in Paris which made the writing of reviews obsolete, cultural life in Germany and Britain remained largely decentralized and dependent on the flow of printed news. And while the Parisian pecking order secured some stability, decentralized republics of letters established discursive order by way of mutual critical reviewing.

It was not long before the new book reviewing, advertising, and often self-advertising industry was taken to task. In 1714, Thomasius launched another journal, his *Auffrichtige und Unpartheyische Gedancken über die Journale, Extracte und Monaths-Schrifften* (Honest and impartial thoughts about the journals, excerpts, and monthly periodicals) just for the purpose of such meta-reviewing. With the increase of publications, it became more and more necessary to maintain an overview of the book market, which, in the 18th century, expanded exponentially.

From 1739, the *Göttingische Gelehrten Anzeigen* reviewed publications in all fields. In 1749 Ralph Griffiths started the *Monthly Review*, and in 1756 Tobias Smollett introduced fierce competition with his *Critical Review*, which counted **Samuel Johnson**, **David Hume**, **Oliver Goldsmith**, and later **Samuel Taylor Coleridge** among its contributors. With the emergence of literature as a field in its own right, and an onslaught of fiction produced for mass consumption, the demand for review journals exclusively dedicated to literature led to specialized periodicals. With Friedrich Nicolai's

Bibliothek der schönen Wissenschaften und schönen Künste (1757–65; Library of the humanities and fine arts), *Briefe die neueste Literatur betreffend* (1758–61; Letters on contemporary literature), and *Allgemeine deutsche Bibliothek* (1765–1806; Universal German library), reviews broke ground for modern German literary criticism and aesthetic theory. The *Allgemeine Literaturzeitung* (1785–; Universal literary news) became the organ for Kantian philosophy. Here, **Schiller** published his reviews which shaped the program for the canon of German literature he envisaged. The publication of *Athenäum*, edited by the **Schlegel** brothers in 1798, announced a shift in literary criticism to the newly discovered subjectivity. **Novalis'** remark, "the review is complement to the book," commented on the new critical significance the review had gained. In 1826, Hegel's two-decade-old project, the *Jahrbücher für wissenschaftliche Kritik* (Yearbook for critical humanities), was realized. Its turn away from the Romantics carried the mark of Hegel, who turned the review into full-fledged philosophical critique, reflecting upon the theoretical implications of the stand the author under review takes.

Until the Revolution, publishers in France were dependent on the tightly regulated granting of printing privileges. It was thus only after the Revolution that review journals proliferated. In Britain, the *English Review* (1783–) was absorbed in 1796 into the *Analytical Review* (1788–99) which, however, won a reputation not for its abstracts but for its radical opinions. In 1793, the *British Critic* joined the scene. The *Edinburgh Review* (1802–1929) set a new style and became the model of all British reviews of the 19th century. Independent from the book trade, it took on the review of publications in all fields in a liberal, challenging, and critical fashion. More than merely a Whig party organ, it was so successful that it led in 1809 to the establishment of a counter journal, the *Quarterly Review*, which by 1820 was a distinctly conservative periodical. Among the 60 British periodicals carrying reviews in the first quarter of the 19th century, the *Edinburgh* and the *Quarterly* were the leaders.

By the early 19th century, the basic types of reviews had been introduced, from the abstract to lengthy studies of the books at hand, which could also become merely the pretext for independent essays associated with the subjects of the books reviewed. Anonymity of reviewer was customary. The *Jahrbücher für wissenschaftliche Kritik* was the first to have articles signed with full names; before then, reviews had been either unsigned or signed with a letter or symbol. Contributors could be identified only by insiders. Protected by anonymity, reviews could be impartial and objective, or simply a disguise to promote one's opinions or own works. However, shameless self-promotion or favorable reviews of friends under the shield of anonymity could lead to the erosion of trust and reputation. As early as 1778, the author of *Anfangsgründe der Rezensirkunst* (Introduction to the art of reviewing) joked that the only difference between an author of pasquinades and a reviewer was that the latter could not be sued.

Today reviewing has become an industry in its own right, crucial for library acquisition and the dissemination of information. But, interestingly, while scholarly publishing has become subject to explicit control mechanisms, reviews have escaped such examination. Reviews have remained an arena for debate, and abuse of the freedom they offer is regrettable. Yet to

"referee" them would in the end abolish their distinguishing characteristics. Self-regulation is crucial to the review, even where it seems to set up its writer as judge. The best practitioners of the Enlightenment and Romantic reviews, from **Moses Mendelssohn** to **Lessing** to Hegel, kept close to the review's relative, the essay, in that they aimed not to judge and sentence, but to contextualize and examine the books under review to provide sufficient analysis for the readers to judge for themselves. This, it could be argued, is still the ultimate criterion for what makes a good review.

While book reviews are now considered *de rigueur* for a serious intellectual paper, changes in the wake of the electronic revolution will have far-reaching consequences; to the extent that books as we know them disappear, reviews in print form will become anachronistic. For the time being, London's *Times Literary Supplement*, the New York *Times Book Review*, and especially the *New York Review of Books* may – in the English-speaking world – serve as reliable trend spotters. Sophisticated readers may wish to turn to the richly diverse market of print media to satisfy their need for current reviews. No single paper can claim any longer to cover book production in its entirety.

Willi Goetschel

Further Reading

Carlsson, Anni, *Die deutsche Buchkritik von der Reformation bis zur Gegenwart*, Berne and Munich: Francke, 1969

Clive, John Leonard, *Scotch Reviewers: The Edinburgh Review, 1802–1815*, London: Faber, 1957

Drewry, John E., *Writing Book Reviews*, Westport, Connecticut: Greenwood Press, 1974

Hayden, John O., *The Romantic Reviewers, 1802–1824*, London: Routledge and Kegan Paul, and Chicago: University of Chicago Press, 1969 (original edition, 1945)

Morgan, Peter F., *Literary Critics and Reviewers in Early 19th-Century Britain*, London: Croom Helm, 1983

Roper, Derek, *Reviewing Before the "Edinburgh," 1788–1802*, London: Methuen, and Newark: University of Delaware Press, 1978

Rowland, Herbert, and Karl J. Fink, editors, *The Eighteenth Century German Book Review*, Heidelberg: Winter, 1995

Walford, A. K., editor, *Reviews and Reviewing: A Guide*, London: Mansell, and Phoenix, Arizona: Oryx Press, 1986

A Review of the Affairs of France
British periodical, 1704–13

This **periodical** was conducted by **Daniel Defoe**, it is thought singlehandedly, from 19 February 1704 until the end of July 1712. The original title, *A Weekly Review of the Affairs of France and of All Europe, as Influenced by That Nation*, was changed to *A Review of the Affairs of France and of All Europe, with Observations on Transactions at Home* later in the year, and then, at the beginning of 1706, to *A Review of the State of the English Nation*. Only the first eight numbers appeared weekly. Thereafter, the periodical was published twice a week for about a year, and then three times a week. Beginning in August 1712, a new series entitled simply the *Review* appeared twice a week until 11 June 1713. The entire body of writing Defoe produced in this journalistic enterprise amounts to some 5610 pages.

Such a sustained performance required unusual gifts of mind and personal resourcefulness. Defoe – whose fertile imagination and grasp of the mechanisms of publication led him in the early 1720s to produce a flurry of prose fiction which constitutes in certain ways the beginning of the modern novel – happened to possess such qualities. He was ideally positioned during these years to carry forward a periodical concerning itself with the variety of issues of which the general reading public was conscious. The energetic Defoe probably served as a publicist for both political parties at different times (depending on the issue and the pay), perhaps even for both at the same time. Certainly he was well placed to get information, and he had a nose for issues that mattered. His commentary in the *Review* was often pungent, dismaying or angering those whose partisanship he offended. To the reader distanced by time from the issues about which Defoe was writing, however, the *Review* is a fascinating serialization of one person's thoughts on public affairs during an intriguing epoch.

The dominating feature of the *Review* throughout its history was the essay, about 1200–2000 words in length, spread across the columns of the front page and most of its verso. Advertisements for a range of patent medicines and cosmetics along with books and **pamphlets** filled in whatever space was free of other text (and were not insignificant sources of revenue for the periodical). At certain times, primarily in 1704 and 1705, Defoe ran a feature responding to the personal questions of his (real or imagined) readers. In these years it was called "Advice from the Scandalous Club . . . Being a Weekly History of Nonsense, Impertinence, Vice and Debauchery." There was sometimes the added juicy suggestion that the column was translated from a French original. Here Defoe touched on subjects such as courtship, marital relationships, problems arising in domestic life, habits such as smoking, and religious practices of both priesthood and laity. He ran these columns at first as monthly supplements, then as a feature he called the "Little Review." It appears to have been quite popular with Defoe's readers, but his packaging of it and decision to discontinue it indicate that he regarded the *Review* primarily as a medium for his broader discourse as an essayist.

Defoe used his opportunity in writing the *Review* to address many subjects to which he returned throughout his career as a journalist: the distribution of wealth, aristocratic privilege, workhouses and public policies related to human need, charitable institutions, the theater and other public entertainments. The nominal purpose of the periodical – to consider questions about relations with France – framed many papers on the conduct of military operations, on the actions of individual military leaders, and on Marlborough, Charles XII of Sweden, and Queen Anne. He wrote on issues related to union with Scotland, on a variety of subjects having to do with the church, and on a broad variety of economic matters. Defoe's essays in the *Review* are marked by the flow of ideas and energetic rhetoric which is characteristic of his prose: "Land is a fund of wealth, that's true; but trade is the fund of land, from your trade springs your land's wealth . . . What was the land in Barbados good for when the island was unpossessed by us? It was as rich as now, the fund was there – but that trade gave that fund a value. It was a fund and no fund – a fund of nothing; and take trade from that island now, with all its

wealth, and what will it be good for still? Will it feed and employ 60,000 Negroes, &c., in a place of but 25 leagues round?" (1 May 1711).

Defoe's *Review* was one of the principal factors in the establishment of the **periodical essay** form in 18th-century England. Certainly other periodicals developed features and methods of distribution which were as important as those used by Defoe, and doubtless later essayists chose as models the papers of **Addison** and **Steele** more consciously than those of Mr. Review. Addison and Steele took as their audience the middle and upper-middle classes of English society, and their subject matter was largely significant in its cultural implications. Defoe seems to have felt that he was writing for the world at large, and he was by nature far more interested in economics, politics, and history than he was in aesthetics, behavior, or style. His discourse as an essayist is characteristically argumentative rather than conversational, and he experimented very little with the adoption of various points of view which entertained readers of the personae – from the Spectator club to Mr. Rambler and his friends – who ostensibly conducted so many of the other periodicals of the age. With wonderful consistency, however, over more than a decade, Defoe produced essay after essay on a range of topics which were certainly important enough concerning daily life in England. His readers then – and now – have in his *Review* the work of one of England's most significant essayists.

JAMES M. KUIST

Editions
Defoe's Review, facsimile edition, edited by Arthur Secord, 23 vols., 1938; index to this edition by William L. Payne, 1948; selection as *The Best of Defoe's "Review": An Anthology*, edited by Payne, 1951

Further Reading
Backscheider, Paula R., *Daniel Defoe: Ambition and Innovation*, Lexington: University Press of Kentucky, 1986
Backscheider, Paula R., *Daniel Defoe: His Life*, Baltimore: Johns Hopkins University Press, 1989
Dobree, Bonamy, "Some Aspects of Defoe's Prose," in *Pope and His Contemporaries: Essays Presented to George Sherburn*, edited by James L. Clifford and Louis A. Landa, Oxford: Clarendon Press, 1949
Dobree, Bonamy, "The Writing of Daniel Defoe," *Journal of the Royal Society of Arts* 108 (1960): 729–42
Graham, Walter, *English Literary Periodicals*, New York: Nelson, 1967 (original edition, 1930)
James, E. Anthony, *Daniel Defoe's Many Voices: A Rhetorical Study of Prose Style and Literary Method*, Amsterdam: Rodopi, 1972
Matchen, D., "Daniel Defoe's Rhetorical Art in the *Review*," *College Language Association Journal* 4 (1982): 427–46
Moore, John R., *Daniel Defoe: Citizen of the Modern World*, Chicago: University of Chicago Press, 1958
Novak, Maximillian E., "Defoe's Use of Irony," in his *The Uses of Irony: Papers on Defoe and Swift*, with Herbert J. Davis, Los Angeles: Clark Memorial Library, 1966
Payne, William L., *Mr. Review: Daniel Defoe as Author of "The Review"*, New York: King's Crown Press, 1947

Revista de Occidente

Spanish journal, 1923–

Revista de Occidente (Western review), an international journal of humanistic inquiry, was founded in 1923 by the Spanish philosopher **José Ortega y Gasset**. Its publication history is divided into four distinct periods, the first of which runs from the year of its founding to 1963, the second from 1963 to 1975, the third from 1975 to 1977, and the fourth from 1980 to the present. In addition to continuity of name, the magazine's four stages are linked by their shared commitment to providing the cultured, though not necessarily erudite, reader of Spanish with a cosmopolitan variety of rigorously conceived writings on contemporary issues in the arts, humanities, social sciences, and physical sciences. They are unified by the pursuit of the ideals displayed in *Revista de Occidente*'s first epoch prior to the outbreak of the Spanish Civil War, when the charismatic Ortega himself controlled the journal's editorial agenda.

Ortega's audacious aim in founding *Revista de Occidente* was, as Evelyne López Campillo (1972) has said, to create "a journal that would bring the Spanish reader up to date on all the new ideas in every domain of culture." For Ortega, becoming intellectually "up to date" meant becoming highly conversant not only with the ideas and attitudes of the outstanding contemporary thinkers of Spain, but more importantly, with those of the finest intellectuals of Europe. Almost from the time he began publishing articles in his family's newspaper, *El Imparcial* (The impartial), in 1904, Ortega had repeatedly advocated the need to "regenerate" a decadent Spain through the adoption of foreign, mainly European, ideas. As he said in his 1910 speech, "La pedagogía social como programa político" (Social pedagogy as political program), "Regeneration is the desire; Europeanization is the means of satisfying it."

In the period previous to the founding of *Revista de Occidente*, during which Ortega wrote hundreds of newspaper articles, participated in the founding of four journals and one newspaper – *Faro* (1908–09; Beacon), *Europa* (1910; Europe), *España* (1915–24; Spain), *El Espectador* (1916–34; The spectator), and *El Sol* (1917–37; The sun) – and published his celebrated *Meditaciones del Quijote* (1914; *Meditations on Quixote*) and *España invertebrada* (1921; *Invertebrate Spain*), he conceived of the process of Europeanization largely in terms of the goal of radically transforming Spain's political culture. By 1923, however, his doubts about the possibility of effecting such profound political change in his country (which had come to light as early as 1916 when he founded *El Espectador* as a self-styled refuge from political speculation) led Ortega to adopt an intellectual approach that was markedly less "Spanish" and "political" in its focus. The most immediate fruits of this new, more "universalist" orientation, which would only be reinforced by the fear of falling foul of the censorship of the Primo de Rivera dictatorship (September 1923–January 1930), are the appearance, in the summer of that year, of the essay "El tema de nuestro tiempo" (The modern theme), in which he outlines what would later become his concept of ratiovitalism, and the first issue of *Revista de Occidente*.

Within months of its debut, **Ernst Robert Curtius** compared the *Revista de Occidente* favorably with the *Nouvelle Revue Française* (New French review), the *Criterion*, and the *Neue Rundschau* (The new review), widely considered to be the most prestigious cultural journals in Europe at that time. A look at its impressive list of collaborators would appear to confirm this judgment. From the German-speaking countries, which supplied the largest number of foreign contributors, came articles from, among many others, Carl Jung, **Thomas Mann**, Max Scheler, **Georg Simmel**, Albert Einstein, and Werner Heisenberg. From the English-speaking world there were contributions from **Aldous Huxley**, Bertrand Russell, **George Santayana**, Joseph Conrad, William Faulkner, Sherwood Anderson, **D. H. Lawrence**, and Eugene O'Neill. Notable collaborators from other European countries included Jean Cocteau, Luigi Pirandello, **Benedetto Croce**, and Johan Huizinga.

Because *Revista de Occidente* did so much to promote the work of trans-Pyrenean luminaries within Spain, it is possible to overlook its important role in stimulating home-grown cultural production. In the magazine's foundational period, Ortega's famous *tertulia*, or discussion group, held regularly in the editorial offices of the *Revista de Occidente*, was, in the eyes of many, the epicenter of Spanish intellectual life. This gathering, together with the *Revista*'s allied publishing company (the purpose of which was to make the latest developments of intellectual thought in other countries available in Spanish translation) and, of course, the magazine itself, did much to promote the development of what became arguably the most cosmopolitan and widely read generation of Spanish intellectuals since the country's vaunted Golden Age in the 16th and 17th centuries. Included in this impressive group of young writers were Rafael Alberti, Vicente Aleixandre, Dámaso Alonso, Max Aub, **Francisco Ayala**, **Américo Castro**, Luis Cernuda, **Rosa Chacel**, Federico García Lorca, Ramón de la Serna, Jorge Guillén, Benjamin Jarnés, Gregorio Marañón, José Antonio Maravall, **Ramón Pérez de Ayala**, and **María Zambrano**. Ortega had also originally hoped to encourage the broad participation of Latin American intellectuals in *Revista de Occidente*. Though important Latin American figures such as **Jorge Luis Borges**, Pablo Neruda, **Eduardo Mallea**, **Victoria Ocampo**, **Alonso Reyes**, and Torres Bodet did contribute articles to the journal, the vision of creating a truly pan-Hispanic intellectual forum was never fully realized.

What Ortega did undoubtedly accomplish with *Revista de Occidente*, however, was to create an institution which greatly furthered the process of more fully integrating what he liked to call the "select minorities" of Spanish society into the larger, and perhaps more intellectually demanding, context of modern European culture.

THOMAS S. HARRINGTON

Anthologies

La recepción de lo nuevo: Antología de la Revista de Occidente (1923–1936), edited by Magdalena Mora, *Revista de Occidente* special issue, 146–47 (July–August 1993)
Selección y recuerdo de la Revista de Occidente, Madrid: Revista de Occidente, 1950

Further Reading

Calvet, Rosa, "Literatura francesa en la *Revista de Occidente* I," *Epos* 3 (1987): 303–28

Calvet, Rosa, "Literatura francesa en la *Revista de Occidente* II," *Epos* 4 (1988): 437–67

Desde Occidente: 70 años de Revista de Occidente, Madrid: Grupo Endesa, 1993

Escudero, Javier, "La segunda época de *Revista de Occidente* (1963–1975): Historia y valoración," *Hispania* 77, no. 2 (May 1994): 185–96

López Campillo, Evelyne, *La Revista de Occidente y la formación de minorías, 1923–1936*, Madrid: Taurus, 1972

McClintock, Robert, *Man and His Circumstances: Ortega as Educator*, New York: Columbia Teachers College Press, 1971

Niedermayer, Franz, *José Ortega y Gasset*, New York: Ungar, 1973 (original German edition, 1959)

Sabugo Abril, A., "Pasión politica e intelectualidad creadora: De la revista *España* a *Revista de Occidente*," *Cuadernos Hispanoamericanos* 403–05 (January–March 1984): 583–601

Segura Covarsi, Enrique, *Indice de la Revista de Occidente*, Madrid: Instituto "Miguel de Cervantes" del Consejo Superior de Investigaciones Científicas, 1992

Vicente, Arie, "Nación, raza y razones, en el ensayo español de los años 30 al 45," *Cuadernos de Aldeeu* 7, no. 1 (April 1991): 67–85

Revue des Deux Mondes

French journal, 1829–

The *Revue des Deux Mondes: Journal des Voyages* (Review of two worlds: journal of voyages) was founded in 1829 with a capital of 550,000 francs, and then sold by its two founders, Prosper Mauroy and Ségur-Dupeyron, to the printer Auffray. In 1831 Auffray, educated at the well-known Parisian Lycée Louis-le-Grand, installed as editor a former school friend, François Buloz. Before taking this position Buloz had worked on a biographical dictionary and as a typesetter and proofreader. He was the true creator of the *Revue des Deux Mondes*, turning it into the weightiest literary organ of 19th-century France. When he began editing the *RDM* the circulation was 350; when he retired in 1874 it was 18,000. By 1914 it had reached 40,000.

Buloz was a martinet with a fundamentally kind heart and a genius for promoting the often young and generally radical writers whom he allowed to provoke political and social reactions from his staid but cultivated readership. He was a moderate liberal who reined in his progressive contributors before they could seriously frighten his readers, pandering to the weighty, diffuse, and ponderous style they preferred. It was a way of alleviating their bourgeois anxieties, quite justifiable in the second quarter of the 19th century, while promoting political and social attitudes generally just left of center, although occasionally also just to its right. The editorial attitude of the review became markedly more conservative after the 1848 Revolution.

On his appointment Buloz continued for a while to publish accounts of travel, then dropped the "Journal des Voyages" from the review's title and changed its focus to matters of literary and philosophical interest. Buloz himself wrote nearly nothing, but was an immensely hard worker and had an almost infallible sense of public feeling. He was fortunate when Victor Hugo introduced him to **Sainte-Beuve**, whom Hugo wanted to review his novel, *Notre-Dame de Paris*. Sainte-Beuve had left the Saint-Simonian *Le Globe* in April 1831, and Buloz

published a first piece by him on 15 June that year, followed by a second in August, taking the critic onto the staff and relying on him to draw up policy statements in Buloz's name. It was Sainte-Beuve who wrote the statement published in March 1833 to the effect that the review had no philosophical, religious, social, or aesthetic commitment, but believed in the evidence afforded by accumulated historical fact, and looked forward to "the future goal, the great social unity . . . toward which the age is clearly moving."

In 1834 the company owning the *RDM* also acquired the *Revue de Paris*, founded by Louis Véron in 1829. Buloz, who became director of the Comédie-Française while still editing the *RDM*, was also made editor of the *Revue de Paris*, making him virtual dictator of serious periodical literature in France. He used the *Revue de Paris* to publish his second-rank material not quite suitable for the *RDM*.

It was largely through Sainte-Beuve that Buloz came into contact with the circle of young Romantics surrounding Charles Nodier and then Hugo, and it was partly through Sainte-Beuve that Buloz recruited his famous galaxy of authors: Hugo, Prosper Mérimée, Gustave Planche, George Sand, Alfred de Vigny, Alphonse de Lamartine, Étienne Pivert de Senancour, Marceline Desbordes-Valmore, Heinrich Heine, and Alfred de Musset. Few contributed anything that could properly be called essays, but it was Buloz who invented the famous editorial criterion of accepting nothing not so written that he could understand it. He sent back a piece on **Kant** by Victor Cousin, France's major philosopher, on the grounds that it was incomprehensible. Buloz's insistence on structured argument and simplicity of line was one of the great forces shaping the development of the essay as a literary genre in 19th-century France.

From 1845, when the previous owners retired, all the shares in the holding company of the *RDM* passed into the hands of Buloz, his immediate family, and his authors. From the beginning he had put the review behind the July monarchy inaugurated in 1830, despite the strong blandishments of François Guizot, who was backed by the *Journal des Débats* (Journal of debates). Although the launching of the cheap press in 1836 forced Buloz to seek out novelists for serialization in his columns, the *RDM* remained virtually unchanged, with essays on serious social and political topics next to pieces in the more imaginative genres. It forged ahead after the decline of the *feuilleton* from about 1846. After the Revolution of 1848, the review published authors whose attitudes were more reactionary than those favored earlier by Buloz, although the cautious new conservatism did not prevent him from publishing selected essays of **Hippolyte Taine**, in spite of his radical determinism, and did not go far enough to allow him to yield to pestering by the right-wing Catholic legitimist dilettante, Barbey d'Aurevilly. The *RDM* went on to publish a whole group of important authors – including **Ernest Renan**'s middle-brow essays – and it is a tribute to Buloz that they considered it an honor to have appeared in the review.

Buloz was succeeded as editor by his son Charles, who himself died in 1893, and was succeeded by **Ferdinand Brunetière**, introduced to the review by **Paul Bourget** in 1875. Politically the review remained liberal conservative, although now also republican, favoring in literature the Parnassian school as represented by Sully Prudhomme, José-Maria de Heredia, and Charles-Marie Leconte de Lisle. It published

Anatole France alongside Bourget, François Coppée, Pierre Loti, René Bazin, and Guy de Maupassant. In the Dreyfus affair the *RDM* was uncommitted.

During the first decade of the 20th century until the eve of World War I the importance of the *RDM* diminished even as its circulation was increasing. During World War II it was hostile to the occupying forces and was obliged to suspend publication. In reappeared in 1948, becoming strongly Gaullist in 1958, but never won back the dominant position in French culture it had enjoyed under Buloz.

ANTHONY LEVI

Further Reading

Broglie, Gabriel de, *Histoire politique de la "Revue des Deux Mondes" de 1829 à 1979*, Paris: Perrin, 1979
Cent ans de vie française à la "Revue des Deux Mondes", *Revue des Deux Mondes* centenary issue (1929)
Du Val, Thaddeus Ernest, *The Subject of Realism in the "Revue des Deux Mondes" (1831–1865)* (dissertation), Philadelphia: University of Pennsylvania, 1936
Furman, Nelly, *La "Revue des Deux Mondes" et le romantisme, 1831–1848*, Geneva: Droz, 1975

Rexroth, Kenneth

American, 1905–1982

Kenneth Rexroth was primarily a poet and translator who occasionally wrote essays and book reviews. Although he believed that poets should write prose only for money, he took the writing of his commissioned assignments seriously. Altogether he wrote over 400 essays, book reviews, and newspaper columns. Most were on literary topics, but Rexroth also wrote authoritatively on modern art, jazz, religion, the Orient, and contemporary society. Regardless of the topic, the essays and reviews are all marked by his strong opinions on aesthetics, morality, and community.

In the introduction to his first collection, *Bird in the Bush* (1959), Rexroth wrote that his essays "are not criticism but journalism. It is my hope that they may find a modest place in what critics call a 'tradition' – the tradition of [James Gibbons] Huneker, [H. L.] Mencken, [Edmund] Wilson." The writers he cites each wrote on social as well as artistic issues, for a mass audience in popular magazines, all the while expressing unpopular opinions. Like them, Rexroth expressed his often radical views in popular magazines such as the *Nation*, the *Saturday Review*, the New York *Herald Tribune*, and *Art News*. Like his predecessors, Rexroth used these organs to bring a middle-class audience news of the avant-garde in jazz and art and literature, as well as of social movements such as those of the Beats in the 1950s and the hippies in the 1960s and 1970s.

The voice in the essays is instantly recognizable as Rexroth's – lucid, learned, anecdotal, sometimes dogmatic ("Baudelaire was the greatest poet of the capitalist epoch. Does anyone doubt this?" from "Unacknowledged Legislators and 'Art pour art'," 1958), and informed by a strong sense of aesthetic, political, and social values. An autodidact himself, Rexroth assumed an equal desire for education and information on the part of his audience. For instance, he wrote long essays on such recondite topics as alchemy, gnosticism, and Hasidism. His anecdotal manner stems from his frequent personal involvement with the issues of his essays ("Recently police activity began to impinge upon my own life" from "The Heat," 1966) or to develop a sense of immediacy, if not of a somewhat truculent authority ("As [Charles] Mingus once said to me . . ." or "I knew Bird [Charlie Parker] pretty well . . ." from "Some Notes on Jazz," 1957). But behind the lightly worn learning and the occasional swaggering is a deeply felt and frequently stated view that modern civilization has gone dreadfully wrong.

Rexroth believed that "organized society in our epoch simply has nothing good about it. It is a deadly fraud from start to finish" ("The Ennobling Revulsion," 1957). Human beings, he felt, are alienated from their work, their fellow beings, and themselves. He ranks **Mark Twain**'s *Huckleberry Finn* as one of the world's greatest novels primarily because of the book's "realization that the official version of anything is most likely farce and that all authority is based on fraud" ("Would You Hit a Woman with a Child?," 1957). A home-grown anarchist-socialist, Rexroth emphasized the virtues of community and cooperation. His book-length essay, *Communalism* (1974), is an examination of attempts at cooperative living from Neolithic times to the present.

Believing that "Literary criticism can play its role in social change" ("The Art of Literature," 1974), Rexroth felt that "official high-brow culture," as evinced in specialized academic journals and critical reviews, was "the enemy" of true culture, communication, and change ("Disengagement: The Art of the Beat Generation," 1957). But although regarded as a father figure and spokesperson for the Beat Generation of the 1950s, Rexroth was highly critical of that ostensibly rebellious movement, finding it aimless, without principle, and ultimately conformist. To Rexroth, true revolutionaries, unlike the escapist Beats and the later hippies, work vigorously – in art and life – to overthrow the "social lie" of church, state, and capitalism ("Revolt: True and False," 1958).

Although Rexroth's best essays present the spectacle of a thoroughly engaged intelligence attempting to explain the cultural manifestations of the middle years of the 20th century, perhaps his most lasting prose works are the 101 short essays collected in *Classics Revisited* (1968) and *More Classics Revisited* (1989). First published in the *Saturday Review*, these brief essays seek to distill the essence of enduring literary works while giving a sense of their social and moral importance. In his introduction Rexroth declared that "The greatest works of imaginative literature . . . objectify the crucial history of the subjective life. They make reality, nature, out of man."

In these short essays the traditional classics are discussed – Homer and Sophocles, Shakespeare and **Tolstoi**, Mark Twain. But also – and long before the academics he detested began their debates on the canon – Rexroth included masterpieces from around the world: the Finnish *Kalevala*, the Icelandic *Njal's Saga*, the Hindu *Mahabharata* and *Bhagavad-Gita*, Murasaki Shikibu's *The Tale of Genji*, the Chinese novel *The Dream of the Red Chamber*, and the poetry of Tu Fu. In his essays, as well as in the poetry to which he devoted his life, Rexroth's proved an early and resonant voice for an increasingly multicultural time.

CHARLES L. O'NEILL

Biography

Born 22 December 1905 in South Bend, Indiana. Studied at the Art Institute, Chicago; Art Students League, New York. Married Andree Dutcher, 1927 (died, 1940). Active in libertarian and anarchist movements during the 1930s and 1940s, San Francisco; orderly, San Francisco County Hospital, 1939–45. Married Marie Kass, 1940 (divorced, 1948). Conscientious objector during World War II. Cofounder, Pacifica Foundation, 1949. Married Marthe Larsen, 1949 (divorced, 1961): two daughters. Involved with the Beat writers, 1950s. San Francisco correspondent for the *Nation*, 1950s; book reviewer and critic, the *New York Times*; columnist, San Francisco *Examiner*, 1958–68, *San Francisco Magazine*, and *San Francisco Bay Guardian*, from 1968. Taught at San Francisco State College, 1964, University of Wisconsin, Madison, and University of California, Santa Barbara, from 1968. Married Carol Tinker, 1974. Awards: several fellowships and grants; Shelley Memorial Award, 1958; Copernicus Award, 1975. Member, American Academy and National Institute of Arts and Letters, 1969. Died (as the result of a stroke) in Montecito, California, 6 June 1982.

Selected Writings

Essays and Related Prose

Bird in the Bush: Obvious Essays, 1959
Assays, 1961
Classics Revisited, 1968
The Alternative Society: Essays from the Other World, 1970
With Eye and Ear, 1970
American Poetry in the Twentieth Century, 1971
The Elastic Retort: Essays in Literature and Ideas, 1973
Communalism: From Its Origins to the Twentieth Century, 1974
World Outside the Window: The Selected Essays, edited by Bradford Morrow, 1987
More Classics Revisited, edited by Bradford Morrow, 1989

Other writings: many volumes of poetry, a play, and the autobiographies *An Autobiographical Novel* (1966) and *Excerpts from a Life* (1981). Also translated poetry from the Japanese, Chinese, Spanish, Greek, Latin, and French.

Bibliography

Hartzell, James, and Richard Zumwinkle, *Kenneth Rexroth: A Checklist of His Published Writings*, Los Angeles: University of California Friends of the UCLA Library, 1967

Further Reading

Bartlett, Lee, *Kenneth Rexroth*, Boise, Idaho: Boise State University, 1988
Beach, Joseph Warren, *Obsessive Images: Symbolism in Poetry of the 1930s and 1940s*, edited by William Van O'Connor, Minneapolis: University of Minnesota Press, 1960
Foster, Richard, "With Great Passion, a Kind of Person," *Hudson Review* 13, no. 1 (Spring 1960): 149–54
Foster, Richard, "Lucubrations of an Outside Insider," *Minnesota Review* 3, no. 1 (Fall 1962): 130–33
Gibson, Morgan, *Kenneth Rexroth*, New York: Twayne, 1972
Hamalian, Linda, *A Life of Kenneth Rexroth*, New York: Norton, 1991
Kazin, Alfred, "Father Rexroth and the Beats," *Reporter* 22 (3 March 1960): 54–56
Lipton, Lawrence, *The Holy Barbarians*, New York: Messmer, 1959; London: Allen, 1960
Mills, Ralph J., "Recent Prose," *Poetry* 102, no. 4 (July 1963): 270
Montague, John, "American Pegasus," *Studies* 48 (Summer 1959): 183–91
Parkinson, Thomas, "Phenomenon or Generation," in *A Casebook on the Beat*, edited by Parkinson, New York: Crowell, 1961

Reyes, Alfonso

Mexican, 1889–1959

Alfonso Reyes was one of the leading essayists from Mexico – indeed, from all of Latin America – during the first half of the 20th century. His literary production excelled in quantity (comprising 24 large volumes in his *Obras completas* [1955–91; Complete works]), in breadth of scope, and in quality. While his vast output lacks the exotic originality of **Jorge Luis Borges**, for instance, Reyes' eloquent essays reveal an extensive knowledge of the classic Greco-Roman world and, at the same time, of pre-Hispanic indigenous Mexico, along with past and present literatures of Spain, France, England, Germany, and Latin America. Reyes' stylistic versatility in several genres – novels, short stories, poems, and plays – is obvious, but it is unquestionably in his essays that the broad humanism of his production is most evident. They range from brief, casual, impressionistic sketches to well-composed, serious, precise studies – and yet all are personal in spirit.

Reyes published his first book, the collection of essays titled *Cuestiones estéticas* (1911; Aesthetic questions), when he was only 21. It contained unusually penetrating and far-reaching comparative studies of aesthetic approaches from ancient to modern periods. Its immediate success augured well for the work to follow, as Reyes became the undisputed dean of Mexican letters, writing prodigiously for the next 48 years and influencing generations of writers in his native land and elsewhere in Latin America.

An accomplished linguist, Reyes reveled in puns and wordplay. Among charming works in a light vein were essays on razor blades (used ones, no less), onions, and flies, published in popular journals and various collections. On a more sober level, along with his interest in the complexities of Greek and Roman classical texts, Reyes maintained a consuming fascination with European (especially Spanish) and Latin American (especially Mexican) literature. He wrote insightful essays on authors as diverse as **Goethe**, **Stéphane Mallarmé**, **Oscar Wilde**, and **George Bernard Shaw**, but his major European passion was for Iberian figures, ranging from Miguel de Cervantes and Pedro Calderón de la Barca to **Miguel de Unamuno** and **José Ortega y Gasset** – all examined in his scholarly *Capítulos de literatura española* (1939–45; Chapters in Spanish literature).

Reyes resided for many years outside of Mexico, in France and Spain, as well as in both Argentina and Brazil as the Mexican ambassador. Yet despite the years of absence, he was a devoted student of his native land, its origins and character. From his youth Reyes was caught up in a search for Mexican identity and the influences of the conquered indigenous and the conquering Spanish cultures on the development of Mexico. The genesis of this interest may have been his membership as a young man of the Ateneo de la Juventud (Atheneum of youth), an organization which had as one of its tasks a search for national identity (necessary because of, among other things, Mexico's multiple cultural heritage).

In the prologue he wrote for a Mexican film, *Raíces* (Roots), Reyes announced: "Mexico is at once a world of mystery and clarity: clarity in her landscape, mystery in the souls of her people." This statement was written after decades of endeavors by Reyes to scrutinize carefully, if not to dispel, this mystery.

In the essay "México en una nuez" (1944; "Mexico in a Nutshell"), he described concisely the development of colonial Mexico: "During three centuries the races mixed as they pleased, and the colony was governed and maintained through a miracle of respect for the monarchic idea and through religious submission to the categories of the state ... Meanwhile a new nation – with Indians underneath, the Spaniards on top, and the arrogant and domineering creoles and the astute and subtle mestizos in the middle – was quietly being evolved."

Much earlier in *Visión de Anáhuac* (1917; *Vision of Anahuac*) Reyes presented colorful, poetic depictions of ancient Tenochtitlan (now modern Mexico City), whose mansions and palaces, zoos and gardens, and perhaps most impressive of all, giant marketplace left the Spanish invaders dazzled. Recent archaeological studies of this magnificent ancient site have expanded and refined details about it, yet none has surpassed the cogency or beauty of Reyes' descriptions.

Over the years Reyes became more concerned with questions concerning the relative importance of regional and universal expressions of culture; he came to view the significance of Mexican cultural and artistic values as contributing to a universal art and culture. During the 1930s he developed this philosophy of culture in such collections of essays as *Discursos por Virgilio* (1931; Discourses about Virgil) and *Homilia por la cultura* (1935; Homily for culture), while during the 1940s his concerns shifted to issues of social philosophy in books like *Norte y sur* and *Los trabajos y los días* (1944; Works and days).

In later years Reyes wrote a series of essays on strictly literary topics, published in such works as *La experiencia literaria* (1942; Literary experience) and *Letras de la Nueva España* (1948; Letters of the New Spain). There were also a whole series of essays on Greek and Roman philosophy, religion, and literature in his *Obras completas*, many of which appeared in a wide variety of journals but were not published originally in book form.

Special mention must be made of *El deslinde* (1944; Demarcation), Reyes' most developed, systematic elaboration of literary theory. It was based on four lengthy "lessons on the science of literature" he presented at the College of St. Nicholas in Morelia, Michoacán in 1940. In several essays Reyes established the differences between literature with and without an extrinsic purpose ("pure literature and service literature") as well as within the disciplines of science, mathematics, history, and theology. This was clearly his scholarly *tour de force*.

If there is a weakness in Reyes' writings, it is a tendency at times to oversimplify, and to rely on poetic license. This may be because he was so prolific – perhaps if he had written less he would have written better.

Unfortunately for non-Spanish-literate readers very few of Reyes' essays have been translated into English, with ten appearing in *The Position of America, and Other Essays* (1950) and 12 included in *Mexico in a Nutshell, and Other Essays* (1964). Each volume is composed of essays from a wide variety of sources dating from 1915 to 1948. This dearth of sources in English is unfortunate, for Reyes' works are a vital part of a rich literary tradition.

JOHN H. HADDOX

Biography

Born 17 May 1889 in Monterrey, Mexico. Moved to Mexico City, 1906; part of the Centennial Generation lecture society, and the Ateneo de la Juventud literary society; cofounder and secretary, 1912, School of Higher Studies, National Autonomous University of Mexico, Mexico City, where he also took a law degree, 1913. Married: at least one child. Second secretary of the Mexican legation in France, 1913; moved to Spain because of the war, 1914; editor of cultural section, *El Sol* (The sun) newspaper; second, then first secretary of the Mexican legation in Spain, 1920–24; diplomat in Paris, 1924–27; Mexican ambassador to Argentina and Brazil, Buenos Aires and Rio de Janeiro, from 1927. Publisher, *Monterrey* literary bulletin, Rio de Janeiro, 1930–37. Returned to Mexico City, 1939. Cofounder, El Colegio Nacional, Mexico City, 1945; professor, College of St. Nicholas, Morelia, Michoacán, 1940, and the National Autonomous University of Mexico, Mexico City, 1941. Helped to form, and honorary president, 1954, Fédération des Alliances Françaises, Mexico. Elected director, Mexican Academy of the Language, 1957. Awards: National Prize in Literature, 1945. Died (of a heart attack) in Mexico City, 27 December 1959.

Selected Writings

Essays and Related Prose

Cuestiones estéticas, 1911
Cartones de Madrid, 1917; edited by Juan Velasco, 1988
El suicida, 1917
Visión de Anáhuac, 1917; as *Vision of Anahuac*, translated by Harriet de Onís, in *The Position of America, and Other Essays*, 1950, and translated by Charles Ramsdell, in *Mexico in a Nutshell, and Other Essays*, 1964
Retratos reales e imaginarios, 1920
El cazador: Ensayos y divagaciones, 1911-1920, 1921
Simpatías y diferencias, 5 vols., 1921–26
Calendario, 1924
Cuestiones gongorinas, 1927
Discursos por Virgilio, 1931
Tren de ondas (1924-32), 1932
Horas de Burgos, 1932
Homilia por la cultura, 1935
Las vísperas de España, 1937
Aquellos días (1917-1920), 1938
Mallarmé entre nosotros, 1938
Capítulos de literatura española, 2 vols., 1939–45
La crítica en la edad ateniense, 1941
Pasado inmediato, y otros ensayos, 1941
La antigua retórica, 1942
La experiencia literaria, 1942
Última Tule, 1942
El Brasil y su cultura, 1944
Los trabajos y los días, 1934-1944, 1944
El deslinde: Prolegómenos a la teoría literaria, 1944
Dos o tres mundos: Cuentos y ensayos (includes stories), edited by Antonio Castro Leal, 1944
Norte y sur (1925-1942), 1944
Tentativas y orientaciones, 1944
Letras de la Nueva España, 1948
Entre libros, 1912-1923, 1948
Junta de sombras: Estudios helénicos, 1949
Tertulia de Madrid, 1949
De viva voz, 1920-1947, 1949
Sirtes (1932-1944), 1949
The Position of America, and Other Essays, edited and translated by Harriet de Onís, 1950
Ancorajes, 1951
Trazos de historia literaria, 1951
Medallones, 1951
Marginalia, 3 vols., 1952–59
Memorias de cocina y bodega, 1953

De la antigüedad a la edad media, 1954
Trayectoria de Goethe, 1954
Quince presencias 1915–1954, 1955
Estudios helénicos, 1957
Las burlas veras, 2 vols., 1957–59
A campo traviesa, 1960
Al yunque, 1944–1958, 1960
Antología: Prosa, teatro, poesía, 1963
Mexico in a Nutshell, and Other Essays, translated by Charles
   Ramsdell, 1964
Universidad, política y pueblo, edited by José Emilio Pacheco,
   1967
Ensayos (selection), edited by Roberto Fernández Retamar,
   1968
Monterrey (Correo literario de Alfonso Reyes) (facsimile edition),
   1980
Última tule y otros ensayos, edited by Rafael Gutierrez Girardot,
   1991

Other writings: many volumes of poetry, several novels, prose
narratives, plays, memoirs, and correspondence. Also translated
Homer's *Iliad* (1951).

Collected works edition: *Obras completas,* edited by Reyes and
Ernesto Mejía Sánchez, 24 vols., 1955–91.

Bibliography
Robb, James Willis, *Repertorio bibliográfico de Alfonso Reyes,*
   Mexico City: National Autonomous University of Mexico, 1974

Further Reading
Cepeda Adan, Luis, and others, *Comiendo con Reyes: Homenaje a
   Alfonso Reyes,* Mexico City: Posada, 1986
Olguín, Manuel, *Alfonso Reyes, ensayista: Vida y pensamiento,*
   Mexico City: Andrea, 1956
Perea, Hector, *España en la obra de Alfonso Reyes,* Mexico City:
   Fondo de Cultura Económica, 1965
Robb, James Willis, *Patterns of Image and Structure in the Essays
   of Alfonso Reyes* (abstract of a dissertation), Washington, D.C.:
   Catholic University Press of America, 1958
Robb, James Willis, *El estilo de Alfonso Reyes,* Mexico City: Fondo
   de Cultura Económica, 1965
Robb, James Willis, *Estudios sobre Alfonso Reyes,* Bogotá: El
   Dorado, 1976

Rich, Adrienne
American, 1929–

Adrienne Rich is one of the most influential self-identified
lesbian feminists of 20th-century America. Her writing reflects
the development of feminist thought, and documents events
in the history of the women's movement. Her talents as an
essayist have been acknowledged mainly in this context, as
distinct from her poetry. Throughout her decades of work
as a writer-activist, Rich uses essays, speeches, conference
papers, magazine articles, book reviews, and personal reflections to articulate with stunning complexity issues of women's
liberation, individual identity, and the role of poetry. She has
collected these writings in three volumes: *On Lies, Secrets, and
Silence: Selected Prose, 1966–1978* (1979), *Blood, Bread,
and Poetry: Selected Prose, 1979–1985* (1986), and *What Is
Found There: Notebooks on Poetry and Politics* (1993). Rich

introduces each piece with information about its first publication (or delivery). She also supplies updated facts, sketches out
controversies that particular passages evoke, and cites references for further reading. Her prose complements her poetry
by expanding upon metaphors epitomizing her hopes for the
future.

On Lies, Secrets, and Silence contains Rich's first essays
about the damaging effects of patriarchy, which she sees as a
product of a gynophobic splitting of thought from emotion.
Rich resists this division by bringing personal experience back
into the political realm. Relying heavily on the wisdom of
Virginia Woolf, she envisions communities of women that will
create a politics of addressing women's questions. She discusses
issues surrounding daycare, education, safety from violence,
and the politics of birth control and of housework. Her essays
on education connect sexism with other systems of oppression,
while motherhood becomes a central social and political issue
in "The Antifeminist Woman" (1972). (This essay inspired her
to write a separate prose volume on the ideology of motherhood under patriarchy, *Of Woman Born: Motherhood as
Experience and Institution,* 1976). Rich also resurrects female
writers as mentors for women who are unearthing the unspeakable elements of their lives, since "women's minds cannot grow
to full stature, or touch the real springs of our power to alter
reality, on a diet of masculine ideology" ("Conditions for
Work: The Common World of Women," 1976.)

Patriarchal dualisms create other divisions (gay/straight,
white/black) which Rich scrutinizes in her second anthology,
Blood, Bread, and Poetry. Her formulation of feminist issues
now foregrounds their connections to racism, class-blindness,
and anti-Semitism. She quotes and reviews the work of black
feminists, and credits the civil rights movement as a model
for the women's movement. She also focuses on issues of
lesbian identity and history; "Compulsory Heterosexuality
and Lesbian Existence" (1980), her most famous essay, documents a breakthrough in sexual politics: the recognition of
how patriarchal culture uses the assumption that everyone is
heterosexual to disempower women. In the second half of the
book, Rich interrogates her position and privileges as a United
States citizen, leading ultimately to "Notes Toward a Politics
of Location" (1984). Location encompasses all the differences
among women, men, places, times, cultures, conditions, class,
and movements that contribute to one's perspective. This
formulation refines her earlier ideas about acknowledging
individual experience in a political sphere.

Rich moves from a revolutionary social agenda in early
essays toward the ostensibly narrower purpose of examining
poetry and politics in her third anthology, *What Is Found
There.* As she compiles excerpts about poetic power from
diverse authors and from her own reflections, her scope widens
to encompass poetry in prisons, malls, public art, and everyday
epiphanies. Her vision grows global as she contends that the
most exciting recent poetry comes from indigenous, mestiza/o,
and women's poetry movements in all the Americas, the
Caribbean, the Pacific Islands, New Zealand, and Australia, as
well as Europe and Africa ("What If?," 1993). Unfortunately,
as Rich attempts to interweave the political concerns of more
people from more places, her writing loses focus. In the middle
of reading any given essay, it can be hard to isolate the original thematic issue.

Rich's later writings seem scattered – not because she is trying to deal with too many issues (her earlier writings prove that she is eminently capable of combining breadth and subtlety), but rather because the format of many selections reads like an imprecise gathering of **journal** fragments, with few connecting arguments or commentaries on quotations. The powerful, direct rhetoric that characterizes her earlier anthologies is sadly diffused by this profusion of information. Her earlier experiments with alternative styles seem more deliberate. The psychoanalytically rich "Women and Honor: Some Notes on Lying" (1975) discusses relationships in an elegantly impressionistic format; in "Split at the Root: An Essay on Jewish Identity" (1982), Rich meanders through time and circumstance to explore her Jewish heritage. Episodic writing is well suited for these reflections, but the wide-ranging political goals of her most recent volume fall between the cracks of this writing style. Although an open format best matches Rich's political vision, it is not purposeful enough to support her convictions.

The most astonishing element of Rich's essays is an ever more exacting vision of politics. When she returns to topics in order to develop her thoughts further, her self-criticism is fearless. In one particularly lucid example, Rich describes an audience's reactions to her statement that "It is the lesbian in us who is creative, for the dutiful daughter of the fathers in us is only a hack" ("It Is the Lesbian In Us . . .," 1976). Recounting the various opinions becomes an occasion to reevaluate her assertion. Rich notes that "I probably oversimplified the issue, given limits of time, and therefore obscured it. This experience made me more conscious than ever before of the degree to which, even for lesbians, the word lesbian has many resonances." As she goes on to describe some possibilities, Rich discards any solution that implies an escape from radical complexity ("The Meaning of Our Love for Women Is What We Have Constantly to Expand," 1977). Here, as in her writing in general, the essays indicate a continuing exploration, not a destination.

KAREN SCHIFF

Biography

Adrienne Cecile Rich. Born 16 May 1929 in Baltimore. Studied at Radcliffe College, Cambridge, Massachusetts, A.B. (cum laude), 1951 (Phi Beta Kappa). Married Alfred H. Conrad, 1953 (died, 1970): three sons. Taught at the YM-YWHA Poetry Center Workshop, New York, 1966–67, Swarthmore College, Pennsylvania, 1966–68, Columbia University, New York, 1967–69, City College of New York, 1968–75, Brandeis University, Waltham, Massachusetts, 1972–73, Douglass College, New Brunswick, New Jersey, 1976–78, Cornell University, Ithaca, New York, 1981–85, San Jose State University, California, 1985–86, and Stanford University, California, 1986–93; visiting professor at various colleges and universities. Columnist, *American Poetry Review*, 1972–73; coeditor, *Sinister Wisdom*, 1980–84; member of the editorial collective, *Bridges: A Journal for Jewish Feminists and Our Friends*, from 1989. Awards: many, including several grants and fellowships; Yale Series of Younger Poets Award, 1951; Ridgely Torrence Memorial Award, 1955; American Academy Award, 1961; *Poetry* magazine Bess Hokin Award, 1963; *Poetry* magazine Eunice Tietjens Memorial Prize, 1968; Shelley Memorial Award, 1971; National Book Award, 1974; Ruth Lilly Prize, 1986; Elmer Holmes Bobst Award, 1989; honorary degrees from seven colleges and universities.

Selected Writings

Essays and Related Prose

On Lies, Secrets, and Silence: Selected Prose, 1966–1978, 1979
Blood, Bread, and Poetry: Selected Prose, 1979–1985, 1986
What Is Found There: Notebooks on Poetry and Politics, 1993
Adrienne Rich's Poetry and Prose: Poems, Prose, Reviews, and Criticism, edited by Barbara Charlesworth Gelpi and Albert Gelpi, 1993

Other writings: many collections of poetry (including *Diving into the Wreck*, 1973; *The Dream of a Common Language*, 1980; *A Wild Patience Has Taken Me This Far*, 1981; *The Fact of a Doorframe*, 1984; *Your Native Land, Your Life*, 1986; *Time's Power*, 1989; *An Atlas of the Difficult World*, 1991; *Dark Fields of the Republic*, 1995), two plays, and *Of Woman Born: Motherhood as Experience and Institution* (1976).

Further Reading

Cooper, Jane Roberta, editor, *Reading Adrienne Rich: Reviews and Re-Visions, 1951–81*, Ann Arbor: University of Michigan Press, 1984
Diaz-Diocaretz, Myriam, *The Transforming Power of Language: The Poetry of Adrienne Rich*, Utrecht: HES, 1984
Diaz-Diocaretz, Myriam, *Translating Poetic Discourse: Questions of Feminist Strategy in Adrienne Rich*, Amsterdam and Philadelphia: Benjamins, 1985
Farwell, Marilyn R., "Adrienne Rich and an Organic Feminist Criticism," *College English* 39 (October 1977): 191–203
Flowers, Betty S., "The 'I' in Adrienne Rich: Individuation and the Androgyne Archetype," in *Theory and Practice of Feminist Literary Criticism*, edited by Gabriela Mora and Karen S. Van Hooft, Ypsilanti, Michigan: Bilingual Press, 1982: 14–35
Griffin, Susan, and Beverly Dahlen, *Skirting the Subject: Pursuing Language in the Works of Adrienne Rich*, Uppsala: Uppsala University, 1993
Keyes, Claire, *The Aesthetics of Power: The Poetry of Adrienne Rich*, Athens: University of Georgia Press, 1986
Ratcliffe, Krista, *Anglo-American Challenges to the Rhetorical Traditions: Virginia Woolf, Mary Daly, Adrienne Rich*, Carbondale: Southern Illinois University Press, 1996
Templeton, Alice, *The Dream and the Dialogue: Adrienne Rich's Feminist Poetics*, Knoxville: University of Tennessee Press, 1994

Richler, Mordecai

Canadian, 1931–

Mordecai Richler has been a working essayist since the 1950s, appearing in virtually every major Canadian, British, and American journal. Over that time, he has written most often about politics and social customs, travel and sports, Jews and Gentiles. He has also regularly reviewed books. Throughout, the touchstone has been his growing up on Montreal's largely Jewish and working-class St. Urbain Street, which has also been central to his fiction. His success as an essayist has frequently supported that fiction, which remains the work on which he clearly wishes his reputation to rest. But Richler writes essays not merely to make a living: the genre affords him the obvious pleasure of exercising his "sense of the ridiculous."

Although Richler has appeared in journals like the *New York Review of Books* and the *New Statesman*, he has often written for larger audiences (in *Playboy* and *Inside Sports*, for example). Throughout, his voice has been that of a sane man in a world only intermittently sane. His ideal reader, although never surprised by human nonsense, is still astonished by its variety. Critics have sometimes complained that Richler's work lacks enough of a moral center to be satiric; indeed, he is more likely to puncture the ridiculous than offer remedies. In Richler's work there is no overarching political or religious "Truth," but simply the individual, doing his best by family and friends.

Richler's style reflects the broad audience he has written for: it is readable, smart, and occasionally bawdy, a mix of learning and street talk. It is also funny. A review of Gay Talese's *Thy Neighbor's Wife* (1990) quotes an understandably breathless Talese on the life of the penis – "endlessly searching, sensing, expanding, probing, penetrating, throbbing, wilting, and wanting more." To which Richler adds: "And not to quibble, but merely to introduce a personal note, in my case, it also pisses." Discussing Canadian uneasiness that the world is always happening elsewhere, he notes that "the Canadian kid who wanted to be prime minister wasn't thinking big" ("The October Crisis, or Issue Envy in Canada," 1984).

Richler's Jewishness is seldom absent from his work. His essays, however, do not deal in chicken soup *yiddishkeit* but in the absurdities of the comfortable Jewish middle class making its way in North America. He lets *The Encyclopedia of Jews in Sports*, for example, self-destruct simply by quoting the jacket copy ("A noteworthy contribution to mankind's quest for knowledge"); he then suggests it may be a precursor to other bar mitzvah presents such as a "compilation of Famous Jewish Homosexuals, Professional and Amateur, Throughout History." An essay on the Catskills (a resort area with a mostly Jewish clientele) characterizes one hotel as "a Disneyland with knishes," then deftly recounts how a militant black civil rights singer (inexplicably booked into the "All Star Friday Nite Revue") is asked to sing "Tzena Tzena," a popular Hebrew folksong – which he does.

Richler's writing about Jews, is, in fact, highly sympathetic – indeed, with a hair trigger look-out for anti-Semites. But like Philip Roth, he has not been especially popular with the pillars of the Jewish community: "'Why,' I was once asked ... 'does everybody adore Sholem Aleichem, but hate your guts?'" ("Hemingway Set His Own Hours," 1990). For Richler, of course, Jewish ridiculousness is merely a subgenre of the much larger human variety. It just happens to be the kind he knows best.

Richler has also written much about Canadian politics. As Quebec has become ever more nationalistic, he has attacked its laws which sharply limit the public display of any language but French. For Richler, these laws do not protect French culture (as their defenders claim) but instead are merely spiteful and xenophobic. *Oh Canada! Oh Quebec!* (1992) begins with a self-appointed language vigilante solemnly taking photographs of a restaurant menu written illegally in English. Elsewhere, Richler comments that "when thousands of flag-waving nationalists march through the street roaring 'Le Québec aux Québécois!' they do not have in mind anybody named Ginsburg. Or MacGregor, come to think of it." Not surprisingly, Richer has himself become a target of Quebec nationalists, who see his attacks (especially in non-Canadian publications) as the typical arrogance and treachery of English

Montreal. It is a very public debate, and quite a nasty one, with Richler characteristically dismissing one editorial denunciation of him as "the sort of letter many write in anger but have the wit not to mail" (*Oh Canada! Oh Quebec!*).

Canadian nationalism fares little better, especially cultural nationalism. As English Canada has itself become increasingly fixed on expressing its own distinctiveness, Richler has criticized that expression as mere anti-Americanism, parochialism, or greed masquerading as love of country: "The nationalists [were] ... determined to win through legislation, for the second-rate but homegrown writer, what talent alone had hitherto denied him: an audience, applause" ("Pourquoi Pas – A Letter from Ottawa," 1984). Not for Richler is it ever enough to be "world famous in Canada" ("The October Crisis, or Issue Envy in Canada").

Richler, to repeat, wishes his reputation to rest with his fiction, not his essays, most of which were written to deadlines. Nonetheless, as several collections show, his essays lose surprisingly little of their bite, even years after their targets have been forgotten. If those targets sometimes seem sent by Central Casting solely for his amusement and laceration, they are, Richler would no doubt remind us, not his invention but the world's.

ARNOLD KELLER

Biography

Born 27 January 1931 in Montreal. Studied at Baron Byng High School, Montreal, 1944–49; Sir George Williams University, Montreal, 1949–51. Lived in Europe, 1951–52 and 1954–72. Worked for the Canadian Broadcasting Corporation, 1952–53. Married Florence Wood, 1959: three sons and two daughters. Writer-in-residence, Sir George Williams University, 1968–69; visiting professor, Carleton University, Ottawa, 1972–74; judge, Book-of-the-Month Club, 1972–88; columnist of "Books and Things," *GQ* magazine; regular columnist, *Saturday Night* magazine. Awards: several, including the University of Western Ontario President's Medal, for nonfiction, 1959; *Paris Review* Award, 1968; Governor-General's Award, for fiction and nonfiction, 1968, and for fiction, 1971; Berlin Film Festival Golden Bear, for screenplay, 1974; Jewish Chronicle-Wingate Award, 1981; Commonwealth Writers Prize, 1990.

Selected Writings

Essays and Related Prose
Hunting Tigers Under Glass: Essays and Reports, 1968
Shovelling Trouble, 1972
Notes on an Endangered Species and Others, 1974
The Great Comic Book Heroes and Other Essays, edited by Robert Fulford, 1978
Home Sweet Home: My Canadian Album, 1984
Broadsides: Reviews and Opinions, 1990
Oh Canada! Oh Quebec! Requiem for a Divided Country, 1992
This Year in Jerusalem, 1994

Other writings: nine novels (*The Acrobats*, 1954 [published in the U.S. as *Wicked We Love*]; *Son of a Smaller Hero*, 1955; *A Choice of Enemies*, 1957; *The Apprenticeship of Duddy Kravitz*, 1959; *The Incomparable Atuk*, 1963 [published in the U.S. as *Stick Your Neck Out*]; *Cocksure*, 1968; *St. Urbain's Horseman*, 1971; *Joshua Then and Now*, 1980; *Solomon Gursky Was Here*, 1989), short stories, screenplays, and books for children.

Bibliography

Darling, Michael, "Mordecai Richler: An Annotated Bibliography," in *The Annotated Bibliography of Canada's Major Authors*, vol. 1, edited by Robert Lecker and Jack David, Downsview, Ontario: ECW Press, 1979

Further Reading

Brenner, Rachel Feldhay, *Assimilation and Assertion: The Response to the Holocaust in Mordecai Richler's Writing*, New York: Lang, 1989

Brenner, Rachel Feldhay, "A. M. Klein and Mordecai Richler: The Poetics of the Search for Providence in the Post-Holocaust World," *Studies in Religion* 19, no. 2 (1990): 207

Craniford, Ada, *Fiction and Fact in Mordecai Richler's Novels*, Lewiston, New York: Mellen Press, 1992

Darling, Michael, editor, *Perspectives on Mordecai Richler*, Toronto: ECW Press, 1986

Davidson, Arnold E., *Mordecai Richler*, New York: Ungar, 1983

Greenstein, Michael, "Breaking the Mosaic Code: Jewish Literature vs. the Law," *Mosaic* 27, no. 3 (1994): 87

Henighan, Stephen, "Myths of Making It: Structure and Vision in Richler and Beauchemin," *Essays on Canadian Writing* 36 (Spring 1988): 22–37

Iannone, Carol, "The Adventures of Mordecai Richler," *Commentary* 89 (June 1990): 51–53

McNaught, Kenneth, "Mordecai Richler Was Here," *Journal of Canadian Studies* 26 (Winter 1991–92): 141–43

McSweeney, Kerry, *Mordecai Richler and His Works*, Toronto: ECW Press, 1984

Ramraj, Victor J., *Mordecai Richler*, Boston: Twayne, 1983

Sheps, G. David, editor, *Mordecai Richler*, Toronto and New York: McGraw Hill Ryerson, 1971

Woodcock, George, *Mordecai Richler*, Toronto: McClelland and Stewart, 1970

Rodó, José Enrique

Uruguayan, 1871–1917

"Superbly irritating," "insufferable," "admirable," "stimulating," are some of the qualifiers offered by the Mexican writer **Carlos Fuentes** in his prologue to *Ariel*, the best known of José Enrique Rodó's literary works and one of the most influential pieces in the field of the Latin American essay. Despite its brevity, it has had a lasting impact on the evolution of Latin American literature in general, and Latin American thought in particular.

Ariel may be irritating to some contemporary readers, for Rodó writes in a rhetorical fashion that defies the attention of today's readers. This style is the culmination of *modernismo*, whose towering figures were Nicaragua's **Rubén Darío** and Cuba's **José Martí**. While they deserve a special place in Latin American literary history mainly as poets, Rodó is the quintessential *pensador*, a prototype of the French *philosophe* and the clearest example of the Latin American thinkers who dedicated themselves almost exclusively to the craft of the essay.

Ariel was published in 1900 when Rodó was only 29, but the author had achieved enough maturity to grasp the political context resulting from the Spanish-American War and the warning signals of unstoppable U.S. dominance of the hemisphere. The literary setting was staged by *modernismo*, a Latin American intellectual movement that elevated literary standards to a level never before reached in the Spanish language. By the first decade of the 20th century, *modernismo* had captured the philosophical approach of idealism, substituting it for positivism, which had dominated the social and political arena since the demise of Romanticism. The application of Comte's philosophy of "order and progress" to guarantee Latin American development was the logical crowning touch of the search for a cultural and political model proposed by Rodó's most direct predecessor, **Domingo Faustino Sarmiento**. His search for civilization and his proposal that the United States be used as a model to replace the remaining traces of Spain's influence is exactly what Rodó invites the reader to reject in *Ariel*.

The essay narrates a seminar-style lecture given by a professor, and uses symbolic characters borrowed principally from literary classics. From Shakespeare's *The Tempest* (1610) Rodó takes Prospero and the angel, Ariel. In **Montaigne**'s *Essais* (1580, 1588) Caliban appears in the role of a cannibal, who was mentioned by Christopher Columbus in his *Diary*, and is later revamped in **Ernest Renan**'s *Caliban: Suite de la Tempête* (1878), alongside a transformed Prospero more to Rodó's taste. While Shakespeare made Caliban out to be a savage, Renan painted him as a deformed main character, contrasting sharply with Ariel, the son of air, representing a fading spirituality. With brief mentions of Calibán by Darío in one poem and by the Argentine writer Paul Groussac in a speech in the emblematic year of 1898, Rodó provides the final warning for Latin American survival facing Caliban, who represents a culture based on utilitarianism, democratic mediocrity, and material goal-seeking. Rodó pays tribute to a number of aspects of North American culture ("although I do not love them, I admire them"). However, he stresses the need to recover the roots of the Latin American way of being – a more spiritual, authentic, Mediterranean, classical Greek sense of civilization, represented by Ariel. While he recognizes "the grandeur and power of work" and the role of curiosity, philanthropy, and industry in the United States, he invites Latin American youth to adopt an authentic model of beauty, quality, and good taste that he insists are part of an innate Hispanic heritage.

While criticism of the negative aspects of Latin American societies is absent in *Ariel*, Rodó can claim that his aristocratic attitude is paradoxically a precedent for the harsher literature that the regionalists would generate in the first decades of this century. He will also be recognized as the initiator, along with Martí and Darío, of an anti-imperialist literature, a permanent subgenre of both Latin American literature and a more sophisticated chapter of Latin American thought known as *dependencia* theory. Rodó's dichotomy reappeared in a variety of books during the course of the century, until its repudiating character was transformed into a positive symbol of mestizo culture by Cuban writer Roberto Fernández Rematar in *Caliban* (1971).

Since *Ariel*, the resulting negative consequence of the use or abuse of the work is called *arielismo*, a pervading trend that consists of a Latin American moral and spiritual superiority, rejecting measures of modern development, and consistently blaming the United States for all the ills of Latin America. Venezuelan journalist Carlos Rangel aptly summarized this trend in his bestseller *Del buen salvaje al buen revolucionario* (1976; *The Latin Americans: Their Love-Hate Affair with the U.S.*).

The lasting impact of *Ariel* explains the irritating overuse of Rodó's lines or key words such as *arielista* or *rodoniano*. Without reading the book or mentioning the author, presidents during inaugurations, diplomats in international conferences, editorialists in search of contrasting arguments, and professors seeking to impress students have used (and still use) Rodó's best-known phrases to make a point.

Besides the specificity of *Ariel*'s impact on both Latin American intellectual history and its place in the evolution of the Latin American essay, Rodó's lasting legacy as an essayist is best illustrated by his use of variations of the genre, as expressed in his philosophically oriented books and in his works as a literary critic. The most outstanding example of the first is *Motivos de Proteo* (1909; *The Motives of Proteus*), a more global proposal for intellectual enrichment. Its motto is a correction of D'Annunzio's "To reform or to die" into "reformarse es vivir" (to reform oneself is to live). Its form is a variable structure of essays, prose poems, anecdotes, and parables in prose.

As a literary critic using the form of the essay, Rodó's best-known work is *El mirador de Próspero* (1913; Prospero's outlook), a compendium of articles, lectures, speeches, literary comments, and travel columns. In this book Rodó elevates each variation of essayistic prose to the highest level attempted in Latin America. However, as with *Ariel*, the dense declamatory nature of his writings made his style a progressively less attractive example for future generations.

JOAQUÍN ROY

Biography

Born 15 July 1871 in Montevideo, Uruguay. Studied privately, and at the Escuela Elbio Fernández. Cofounder, *Revista Nacional de Literatura y Ciencias Sociales* (National review of literature and social sciences), 1895–97. Professor of literature, University of Montevideo, 1898–1902. Elected to the House of Representatives, 1902–05 (resigned) and 1908–14. Contributor to *La Nación*, Buenos Aires, from 1907, and traveled to Europe as its correspondent, 1916. Fell ill in Genoa, Fall 1916. Died (of abdominal typhus and nephritis) in Palermo, 1 May 1917.

Selected Writings

Essays and Related Prose

La vida nueva, I: "El que vendrá" and "La novela nueva", 1897
La vida nueva, II: Rubén Darío, 1899
Hombres de América, 1899
La vida nueva, III: Ariel, 1900; edited by Leopoldo Alas (Clarín), 1948, Gordon Brotherston, 1967, Raimundo Lazo, 1968, Ángel Rama, 1976, and Abelardo Villegas, 1982; as *Ariel*, translated by F. J. Stimson, 1922, and Margaret Sayers Peden, 1988
Motivos de Proteo, 1909; as *The Motives of Proteus*, translated by Ángel Flores, 1928
El mirador de Próspero, 1913
Bolívar, 1914
Cinco ensayos, 1915
El camino de Paros (meditaciones y andanzas) (European travel notes), 1918
Los últimos movitos de Proteo, edited by Dardo Regules, 1932
Parábolas, y otras lecturas, 1935
La tradición intelectual argentina, edited by Rafael Alberto Arrieta, 1939
Ideario, edited by Luis Alberto Sánchez, 1941
La América nuestra, edited by Arturo Ardao, 1977

Collected works editions: *Obras completas*, edited by José Pedro Segundo and Juan Antonio Zubillaga, 4 vols., 1945–58, and Emir Rodríguez Monegal, 1957, revised edition, 1967.

Bibliography

Scarone, Arturo, *Bibliografía de Rodó*, Montevideo: Imprenta Nacional, 2 vols., 1930

Further Reading

Albarrán Puente, Glicerio, *El pensamiento de José Enrique Rodó*, Madrid: Cultura Hispánica, 1953
Benedetti, Mario, *Genio y figura de José Enrique Rodó*, Buenos Aires: University of Buenos Aires, 1966
Benedetti, Mario, *Rodó, el pionero que quedó atrás*, Montevideo: La República, 1991
Bollo, Sarah, *Sobre José Enrique Rodó*, Montevideo: Imprenta Uruguaya, 1951
Bosco de Bullrich, Nieves, *La imaginación del signo*, Buenos Aires: Vinciguerra, 1993
Costabile de Amorin, Helena, *Rodó, pensador y estilista*, Washington, D.C.: Organization of American States, 1973
Crow, John A., "Ariel and Caliban," in his *The Epic of Latin America*, Berkeley: University of California Press, revised edition, 1980: 675–97 (original edition, 1946)
Earle, Peter G., and Robert G. Mead, Jr., "José Enrique Rodó (1871–1917)," in their *Historia del ensayo hispanoamericano*, Mexico City: Andrea, 1973: 61–64
García Morales, Alfonso, *Literatura y pensamiento hispánico de fin de siglo: Clarín y Rodó*, Seville: University of Seville, 1992
Gómez-Gil, Orlando, *Mensaje y vigencia en José Enrique Rodó*, Miami: Universal, 1992
González Maldonado, Edelmira, *El arte del estilo en José Enrique Rodó*, San Juan, Puerto Rico: Edil, 1968
Guevara, Dario C., *Magisterio de dos colosos: Montalvo, Rodó*, Quito: Minerva, 1963
Langhorst, Frederick Hart, *Three Latin Americans Look at Us: The United States as Seen in the Essays of José Martí, José Enrique Rodó and José Vasconcelos* (dissertation), Atlanta: Emory University, 1976
Lauxar, B., *Rubén Darío y José Enrique Rodó*, Montevideo: Agencia General de Librería y Publicaciones, 1924
Martínez Durán, Carlos, *José Enrique Rodó, en el espíritu de su tiempo y en la conciencia de América: Homenaje al maestro de América en el centenario de su nacimiento, 1871–1971*, Caracas: Central University of Venezuela, 1974
Pereda, Clemente, *Magna patria, Rodó: Su vida y su obra*, Caracas: Imprenta Universitaria, 1973
Pérez Petit, Víctor, *Rodó: Su vida, su obra*, Montevideo: Garcia, 1937 (original edition, 1918)
Simón, Luis, *José Enrique Rodó*, San José, Costa Rica: Ministry of Culture, Youth, and Sports, 1985
Torres Ríoseco, Arturo, "José Enrique Rodó and His Idealistic Philosophy," in his *Aspects of Spanish-American Literature*, Seattle: University of Washington Press, 1963: 31–50
Zaldumbide, Gonzalo, *José Enrique Rodó*, Montevideo: Garcia, 1944 (original edition, 1919)

Rousseau, Jean-Jacques

French (Swiss-born), 1712–1778

Jean-Jacques Rousseau published nothing that could be called an essay, in the sense that even his late confessional works, although obviously personal in tone, as the essay must be, are not written in the objective style demanded by the essay form. However, Rousseau's earlier, often polemical works of philosophical speculation, even when called *discours* (discourses), present their case in a form nearer to essay than to **treatise**, and the longer works like *Julie; ou, La Nouvelle Héloïse* (1761), ostensibly a novel, and *Émile; ou, De l'éducation* (1762), ostensibly a treatise on education, each contain speculative passages which could easily be regarded as self-contained essays. Neither confines itself to the form in which it starts. Sometimes Rousseau disguises an essay as a **letter**, as to d'Alembert on the theater (1758). Both the *Discours sur les sciences et les arts* (1750; *A Discourse on the Arts and Sciences*) and the *Discours sur l'origine et les fondements de l'inégalité parmi les hommes* (1755; *A Discourse on the Origin of Inequality*) were actually written as prize essays for the Dijon Academy, and *Du contrat social* (1762; *The Social Contract*) itself, the 18th century's best-known treatise on political philosophy, is speculative and personal enough to be categorized more suitably as an essay.

Rousseau never wanted to write. He had no formal education, and his consciousness of a lack of grace about his person, clothing, dress, appearance, and manners always eroded his self-confidence. He established for himself the circumstances of life which allowed him to think out as far as possible from first principles – without intellectual or social constraints from outside – the major truths about God, humanity, nature, life, art, education, love, society, and death. The focus of his interest was emotionally inspired activity of all sorts. He was aware that the results of his work were part theory, part dream, never completely coherent or even internally consistent.

Until he was 37, Rousseau had written nothing except libretti for his own music. Then, in the summer of 1749, the Dijon Academy announced a prize to be offered for an essay on the subject, "Has the progress of the arts and sciences contributed to the purification of morals?" Rousseau changed the title to include the possibility that they had contributed rather to their corruption, wrote *A Discourse on the Arts and Sciences*, and won the prize. He later said that what he wrote in the first flush of inspiration was the oration of Fabricius, at the end of the first part of the published discourse, in which he laments the decadence wrought by luxury and science. The essay ends with a plea to strive for simplicity, virtue, and obedience to the inner voice of conscience.

The second, better-known *Discourse on the Origin of Inequality*, on the origins and basis of inequality among human beings, is the most powerful of Rousseau's early works, although in response to the invitation to write about both the origins and the basis it moves bewilderingly from an historical account of the development of human social organization to the discussion of constitutional principles. Essentially Rousseau's point of view is moral, extrapolating primitive human innocence from what is artificial and morally corrupt in the present state of society. He does not yearn for an impossible return to humanity's primitive state, prior to the creation of society and morality, but points to the fact that the social order at present rests, and always has rested, on relations of subservience between those who should be equals. He draws on the tradition established by Hugo Grotius (1583–1645) that human liberty, unlike goods which can be bought and sold, is inalienable by contract. The need for corporate activities, like hunting and cultivating the soil, created both society and ownership, so that Rousseau does not need to presuppose that society was created by a contract, which could become binding only by virtue of the morality which was itself the result of the existence of society.

Rousseau's most famous essay is the unsatisfactory *Social Contract*, a work he himself came to think needed rewriting. Its four books are devoted respectively to the nature of society, the nature of sovereignty, the different forms of government, and the administrative institutions appropriate to each. The published text of 1762 can be seen to have grown out of an earlier article on political economy, out of other material prepared for the "Institutions politiques" abandoned in 1758, and out of the Geneva manuscript of *The Social Contract* itself. The definitive text sets out from the premise that, since we are born free, our subjection to government must be the result of free assent to a social pact with our fellows. The famous opening declaration, "Man is born free and everywhere is in chains," must refer to political freedom, although the second sentence understands freedom in a moral sense: "A man may believe himself the master of others and yet be more enslaved than they are."

Rousseau is here going no further than the natural law school of political theorists derived from Justinian's *Digest* through Aquinas and Grotius to Samuel Pufendorf. What is new in Rousseau is the inalienability of political liberty, even by the contract, an idea which Rousseau took from the Calvinist Johannes Althusius' *Politica* (1603). Rousseau's essay begins from the eighth chapter of the second book to be heavily dependent on Montesquieu's *De l'esprit des lois* (1748; *The Spirit of Laws*), whose reliance on the Roman concept of virtue Rousseau incorporates, and whose argument he quite closely follows, although his social philosophy is by no means the same.

In fact, Rousseau's desire to follow John Locke and the English liberals clashes with his fundamental concepts of moral and political liberty, so that there are several inconsistencies in his argument, as in the need he sees for a legislator, in society's right to impose the death penalty, in his admission that his democratic ideal was unattainable, and in the notion of civil liberties, where he allows that when the individual can be forced to follow the general will, "he will be forced to be free." Rousseau argues against Locke that the social contract can have only one form, and, unlike Montesquieu and **Voltaire**, he was uncompromisingly republican. He was, however, clearly thinking only of small societies in which corruption was not necessarily endemic, like Corsica and Geneva.

Like *The Social Contract*, Rousseau's *Émile* further draws out the principles implicit in the first two discourses. *Émile* only begins as a treatise on education, eventually turning into a *Bildungsroman*, but it contends that a child is born innocent and is educated through its feelings, and at least the work's earlier portion can be regarded as an essay, as no doubt can the nationalistic *Considérations sur le gouvernement de la Pologne* (1782; *Considerations on the Government of Poland*) – not, however, intended for publication.

Only by stretching the meaning of the term essay to include a mixture of anecdote and intimate personal confidence can *Les Rêveries du promeneur solitaire* (1782; *Reveries of the Solitary Walker*) be said to belong to the genre. The ten *promenades* are a mixture of anecdote and confessional introversion, very possibly an attempt to ward off the paranoia which they describe, and with which Rousseau felt himself threatened. They were written in the wake of the psychological crisis he suffered after his readings of the autobiographical *Confessions* were banned, and are not polished literary pieces, but indications of varying moods, certainly of greater psychological and biographical than literary interest. The eighth starts with a reference to "meditating" on his soul's feeling in all the situations he has experienced, and it is perhaps better to look on the *Reveries* as **meditation**s or "rêveries" (daydreams) than to regard them as essays, since they lack formal structure. There are philosophical reflections throughout the text, as on the mutability of things, but they seldom warrant being referred to as insights, however interestingly they reveal Rousseau's own intimate feelings.

Rousseau took the essay very near the genre of formal treatise, keeping it distinct only through intrusive personal speculation. His frequent exploitation of the **dialogue**, epistolary, and fictional forms showed that he needed a genre which openly admitted the expression of speculative opinions based on personal feelings and allowed play to his imagination. Nonetheless, the two discourses and *The Social Contract* are genuine essays, however marginal their influence on the development of the essay as a literary form in France, especially once pre-Romantics such as **Chateaubriand** gave full rein to the expression of their views, even on abstract, theoretical subjects, as inspired by personal feeling.

ANTHONY LEVI

Biography

Born 28 June 1712 in Geneva. Apprenticed to an engraver, 1725–28. Left Geneva to travel, 1728; converted to Catholicism in Turin, 1728; lived with or near Madame de Warens, Annecy and Chambéry, 1729–42, then moved to Paris. Secretary to the French Ambassador to Venice, 1743–44. Began liaison with Thérèse Levasseur, 1745 (married her, 1768): five children (all given to foundling hospital). Music copyist, 1750s; returned to Geneva, reverted to Protestantism, and regained citizenship, 1754; moved to Montmorency, 1756; condemned for religious unorthodoxy, 1762, and fled to Switzerland, first to Neuchâtel, 1762–65, then to Bienne, 1765; renounced Geneva citizenship, 1763; visited England, 1766–67; lived in Paris, from 1770; moved to Ermenonville, 1778. Award: Dijon Academy Prize, for *Discours sur les sciences et les arts*, 1749. Died (of apoplexy) in Ermenonville, 2 July 1778.

Selected Writings

Essays and Related Prose

Discours sur les sciences et les arts, 1750; edited by George R. Havens, 1946, and Gérald Allard, 1988; as *A Discourse on the Arts and Sciences*, translated anonymously, 1752, and by Roger D. and Judith R. Masters, in *The First and Second Discourses*, 1964, and Victor Gourevitch, 1986

Discours sur l'origine et les fondements de l'inégalité parmi les hommes, 1755; edited by Bertrand de Jouvenal, 1982, Jean Starobinski, 1989, and Gérald Allard, 1993; as *A Discourse on the Origin of Inequality*, translated by G. D. H. Cole, 1952, Roger D. and Judith R. Masters, in *The First and Second Discourses*, 1964, Maurice Cranston, 1984, Victor Gourevitch, 1986, Donald A. Cress, 1992, and Franklin Philip, 1994

Discours sur l'économie politique, 1758; edited by Barbara de Negroni, 1990; as *Discourse on Political Economy*, edited by Roger D. Masters, translated by Judith R. Masters, 1978, and Christopher Betts, 1994

Lettre à d'Alembert sur les spectacles, 1758; edited by M. Fuchs, 1948; as *A Letter to M. d'Alembert*, translated anonymously, 1759, and by Allan Bloom, in *Miscellaneous Writings*, 1960

Du contrat social; ou, Principes du droit politique, 1762; edited by C. E. Vaughan, 1918, and Jean-Pierre Siméon, 1977; as *A Treatise on the Social Compact*, translated anonymously, 1764; as *The Social Contract*, with *The Discourses*, translated by G. D. H. Cole, 1913, translation revised by J. H. Brumfitt and John C. Hall, 1973; as *On the Social Contract*, edited by Roger D. Masters, translated by Judith R. Masters, 1978; as *Of the Social Contract, or, Principles of Political Right*, with *Discourse on Political Economy*, translated by Charles M. Sherover, 1984; as *On the Social Contract*, translated by Donald A. Cress, 1987; as *The Social Contract*, translated by Christopher Betts, 1994

Lettres écrites de la montagne, 1764

Essai sur l'origine des langues, 1781; edited by Charles Porset, 1976, Pierre-Yves Bourdil, 1987, and Catherine Kintzler, 1993; as *On the Origin of Language*, translated by John H. Moran and Alexander Gode, 1966

Considérations sur le gouvernement de la Pologne, 1782; as *Considerations on the Government of Poland*, translated by Willmoore Kendall, 1947, and Frederick Watkins, 1953

Les Rêveries du promeneur solitaire, 1782; edited by Marcel Raymond, 1948, and John S. Spink, 1948; as *The Reveries of the Solitary Walker*, translated anonymously, 1783; as *The Reveries of a Solitary . . .*, translated by John Gould Fletcher, 1927; as *Reveries of the Solitary Walker*, translated by Peter France, 1979

Political Writings, edited and translated by Frederick Watkins, 1953

The First and Second Discourses, edited by Roger D. Masters, translated by Roger D. Masters and Judith R. Masters, 1964

Lettres philosophiques, edited by Henri Gouhier, 1974

The First and Second Discourse Together with the Replies to Critics; and Essay on the Origins of Languages, edited and translated by Victor Gourevitch, 1986

Basic Political Writings, edited and translated by Donald A. Cress, 1987

Selections, edited and translated by Maurice Cranston, 1988

Political Writings: New Translations, Interpretive Notes, Backgrounds, Commentaries, edited by Alan Ritter and Julia Conaway Bondanella, translated by Bondanella, 1988

Other writings: fictional works (including *Julie; ou, La Nouvelle Héloïse*, 1761; *Émile; ou, De l'éducation*, 1762), two volumes of autobiography (*Les Confessions*, 1782–89), a pastoral opera, correspondence, and philosophical and political works.

Collected works editions: *Œuvres complètes* (Pléiade Edition), edited by Bernard Gagnebin and Marcel Raymond, 4 vols., 1959–69 (out of projected 5); *Œuvres complètes* (Intégrale Edition), edited by Michel Launay, 3 vols., 1967–71; *The Collected Writings* (various translators), edited by Roger D. Masters and Christopher Kelly, 3 vols., 1990–92 (in progress).

Bibliographies

McEachern, Jo-Ann, *Bibliography of the Writings of Jean-Jacques Rousseau to 1800*, Oxford: Voltaire Foundation, 2 vols., 1989–93

Senelier, Jean, *Bibliographie générale des œuvres de Jean-Jacques Rousseau*, Paris: Presses Universitaires de France, 1949

Trousson, R., "Quinze Années d'études rousseauistes," *Dix-Huitième Siècle* 9 (1977)

Further Reading

Blum, Carol, *Rousseau and the Republic of Virtue*, Ithaca, New York: Cornell University Press, 1986

Broome, J., *Rousseau: A Study of His Thought*, London: Edward Arnold, 1963

Cranston, Maurice, *Jean-Jacques Rousseau*, London: Allen Lane, 2 vols., 1983–91 (in progress; 3 vols. projected)

Crocker, Lester G., *Jean-Jacques Rousseau: The Quest (1712–1758)* and *The Prophetic Voice (1758–1778)*, New York: Macmillan, 2 vols., 1968–73

Derathé, Robert, *Jean-Jacques Rousseau et la science politique de son temps*, Paris: Librairie Philosophique, 2nd edition, 1970

Guéhenno, Jean, *Jean-Jacques Rousseau*, London: Routledge and Kegan Paul, and New York: Columbia University Press, 2 vols., 1966

Havens, George R., *Jean-Jacques Rousseau*, Boston: Twayne, 1978

Masters, Roger D., *The Political Philosophy of Rousseau*, Princeton, New Jersey: Princeton University Press, 1976

Melzer, Arthur M., *The Natural Goodness of Man: On the System of Rousseau's Thought*, Chicago: University of Chicago Press, 1990

Miller, James, *Rousseau, Dreamer of Democracy*, New Haven, Connecticut and London: Yale University Press, 1984

Rozanov, Vasilii

Russian, 1856–1919

Renowned as both a leading religious thinker and an innovative Russian stylist, Vasilii Rozanov has often been called the most remarkable writer among Russian philosophers. His first published work, *O ponimanii* (1886; On the understanding), was a neo-Slavophile philosophical **tract**. His literary reputation, however, was established with the publication in 1891 of the long essay *Legenda o velikom inkvizitore F. M. Dostoevskogo* (*Dostoevsky and the Legend of the Grand Inquisitor*), which dealt with the implications of Ivan Karamazov's parable for modern Russia, whose current historical experience and fate Rozanov conceived in apocalyptic terms. After this initial success, Rozanov expressed his philosophical, political, and religious ideas almost exclusively in essays and in shorter, more topical journalistic articles, principally in Suvorin's conservative newspaper *Novoe Vremia* (The new times), but also in papers of different political stripes under numerous pseudonyms.

Rozanov's ideas, particularly his mystical religious understanding of sexuality and procreation as man's main link to God and the transcendent world, appeared in his oeuvre from the late 1890s on, giving it a kind of internal consistency. Nevertheless, his essay production and the often contradictory ideological positions he espoused, often within the same essay, led to his being accused of what for the Russian essayists of the period were the greatest of sins: lack of all principle and intellectual dishonesty. Rozanov was considered dangerous for the reader by such diverse figures as Leon Trotskii, Petr Struve, and **Vladimir Solov'ev** because the volatility of his ideas was expressed in often beautiful and always hypnotic verbal magic.

Not only were Rozanov's ideas fresh and even outrageous, he, like **Lev Shestov**, had a genius for **aphorism**, and his often paradoxical and humorous witticisms make his oeuvre a gold mine for the compiler of quotable quotes. Realizing this near the end of his life, Rozanov created in Russia what was hailed by some as a new genre – a species of free-form writer's notebook in which he claims to register his immediate thoughts, to give the words that ceaselessly flowed through his mind full and immediate expression. These late works – *Uedinennoe*

(1912; *Solitaria*), *Opavshie list'ia* (1913–15; *Fallen Leaves*), and *Apokalipsis nashego vremeni* (1917–18; "The Apocalypse of Our Times") – contain a variety of materials, from aphorisms and anecdotes to personal letters and short stories, as well as a number of brilliant short essays. They were hailed as surpassing literary achievements, albeit of a new kind, and have secured Rozanov's reputation as one of the greatest writers of the Silver Age (1890–1920), a period of unparalleled brilliance in Russian arts and letters.

Called the Russian **Nietzsche** in part because of his aphoristic and fragmentary writings, Rozanov was the pioneer of the fragmentary literary form in Russian Modernism. Its influence has been great in the 20th century – on Aleksei Remizov, Velimir Khlebnikov, the experimental prose of **Osip Mandel'shtam** and **Viktor Shklovskii**, Andrei Siniavskii (Abram Tertz), and most recently the late Soviet and post-Soviet cult figure Venedikt Erofeev. In the English-language tradition Rozanov most strongly influenced **D. H. Lawrence** in his writer's notebooks. Almost all these writers have acknowledged Rozanov's direct and decisive influence on their writings, most in essay form, Erofeev by making Rozanov a literary character.

Besides their fragmentary character, these last works are undoubtedly polyphonic. The mode of writing is not only "motley," as some have claimed, it is the often cacophonous colloquy of at least eight discrete voices, each with its own point of view, peculiar language, and recognizable style. These Rozanovian personae can be categorized as: the Prophet of Doom – poetic mouthpiece of Rozanov's Old Testament affinities and apocalyptic foreboding; the Fervent Mystic – a voice of religious, often pagan ecstasy; the Mentor – formulator of morals often in aphoristic form; the Objective Critic – the standard, restrained, serious essayistic voice; the Confessor – source of all manner of intimate detail about Rozanov's feelings and personal and family life; the Homebody – Rozanov's version of the views and feelings of the lower-middle-class Russian Everyman; the Gossip – an often vicious *ad hominem* critic of contemporary people and events; and the Buffoon, who is **Dostoevskii**'s Fedor Karamazov, or Lebedev from *Besy* (1872; *The Possessed*), suddenly let loose in a literary essay (Anna Lisa Crone, 1978). Rozanov appears to have taken literally **Montaigne**'s claim that he was a different person at every moment, and to have realized its implications in these last texts, as well as in the unfinished *Mimiletnoe* (Fleeting things).

Yet the voices combining in a free-for-all in Rozanov's late works were already familiar to the Russian reader from his essays. In his earlier essays in the 1890s his prose was dominated by the authoritative, often erudite voice of the Objective Critic; only the ideas were polemical, provocative, or new. As time went on he increasingly flouted the decorum of the essay genre with the introduction of everything from irrational mystical outbursts, to emotional and "unseemly" attacks on societal mainstays such as Russian Orthodoxy, Christ and Christianity, and marital and divorce laws, to gossipy attacks on respected cultural figures (Solov'ev, **Lev Tolstoi**, Nikolai Chernyshevskii). The very manner of writing became as controversial as the contradictory collection of ideas Rozanov espoused.

Reading Rozanov from the late 1890s on, one senses the presence of two or more voices in his essays – usually both ideologically and stylistically incompatible. Rozanov claimed he respected all ideas and believed there was a grain of truth in all positions; he enjoyed "giving expression" to these various Russian points of view, all of which he wanted to feel and experience. In a modern way Rozanov comes close to saying that his whole essayistic and literary enterprise was only about writing, about the music of words, their articulation and resonance, and that he had a physiological need to converse, mutter, and commit his verbal rambling to written form. He built a mysticism around the individual's word, his voice, pronunciation, and even handwriting being expressions of unrepeatable personality. A poet's sense of words as bearers of a unique human spirit far outweighed interest in the word as a tool for other ends; Mandel'shtam was the first, after Rozanov himself, to point out that placing too much emphasis on the semantic aspect of Rozanov's words was the surest way to misunderstand him. Rozanov, of course, thrived on self-contradiction, an almost baroque clashing of opposing ideas. Yet his essayistic prose does not submit well to structural analysis in terms of mere binary oppositions. Cavalier in his attitude toward fact and fiction, truth and lies, and all manner of serious moral categories, Rozanov sets up oppositions dialectically in essays and proceeds to subvert and destroy them himself. This makes the mature Rozanov a prime subject for deconstructionist treatment as he often takes the first steps at deconstructing the meaning and form of his utterances himself. Truth for Rozanov was "an omelet"; the more ideological and/or semantic "eggs" one cracked and mixed into it, the better. Subverting a dialectical opposition, Rozanov shied away from satisfying or elegant synthesis or resolution. For him it was enough to challenge received ideas and provoke an open dialogue inside his reader's mind as long as the language in which he did so was powerful and satisfied his aesthetic requirements.

Rozanov wrote in this internally contradictory way about almost every issue of interest to Russians in the period between 1891 and 1919. The briefest list of his essay collections reveals an almost unprecedented variety of topics. Perhaps his greatest achievement was to subject almost every received notion to doubt and negative scrutiny and to expose the relativism of most ideas and judgments. This exposé of the emotional and irrational motives behind even the most rational of human thoughts was coupled with his constant elevation of the mystical and irrational sides of the human psyche. For this Rozanov was idolized as the messenger of a new, deeper Russian truth and detested as a cynical nihilist. He was so hated by the Left that he was rendered a nonperson in Soviet Russian letters, and his works and studies about him went unpublished from the early 1920s to the later 1980s. Since 1988 this fascinating essayist has been published in Russia again, generating considerable public and scholarly interest in his work.

Unlike Shestov, who used rational argument and systematic means to demolish rationalism, Rozanov began as a more standard essay writer and slowly through a proliferation of voices and multiple points of view came to a complex and intermittently rational/irrational relativism. But whether one deals with the serious Rozanov or the more scandalous and outrageous Rozanov, his polyphonic style was so unique that Dmitrii Merezhkovskii, quoting him in *Bol'naia Rossiia* (1910; Sick Russia), could say with conviction: "These lines were written anonymously. But there is no need to name their author, because every reader knows that there is only one man in Russia who could have authored them – Vasilii Vasil'evich Rozanov."

ANNA LISA CRONE

Biography

Vasilii Vasil'evich Rozanov. Born 2 May 1856 in Vetluga. Studied history and philosophy at Moscow University, graduated 1880. Taught at gymnasiums in Simbirsk, Elets, Belyi, and Viaz'ma, 1880–1893. Married Apollinariia Suslova, 1880 (separated, 1886: she refused to divorce him); companion of Varvara Rudneva, from 1889: five children. Worked in the Office of State Control, 1893. Contributor to various journals, from 1893, including *Novoe Vremia*, *Mir Iskusstva* (World of art), *Russkii Vestnik* (Russian herald), *Rosskoe Obozvenie* (Russian review), and *Novyi Put'* (The new way). Died in Sergiev Posad, 5 February 1919.

Selected Writings

Essays and Related Prose

O ponimanii, 1886
Mesto khristianstva v istorii (The place of Christianity in history), 1890
Legenda o velikom inkvizitore F. M. Dostoevskogo, 1891 (in periodical); 1894 (in book form); as *Dostoevsky and the Legend of the Grand Inquisitor*, translated by Spencer E. Roberts, 1972
Teoriia isoricheskogo progressa i upadok (The theory of historical progess and decline), 1892
Sumerki prosveshcheniia (The twilight of enlightenment), 1893 (in periodical); 1899 (in book form)
Literaturnye ocherki (Literary sketches), 1899
Religiia i kul'tura (Religion and culture), 1899
Priroda i istoriia (Nature and history), 1900
V mire neiasnogo i nereshennogo (In the world of the obscure and unsolved), 1901
Semeinyi vopros v Rossii (The family problem in Russia), 2 vols., 1901
Okolo tserkovnykh sten (Around the church walls), 2 vols., 1906
Ital'ianskie vpechatleniia (Italian impressions), 1909
Kogda nachal'stvo ushlo (When the authorities went away), 1910
Tiomnii lik (The dark face), 1911; part as "Sweetest Jesus and the Bitter Fruits of the World," translated by Spencer E. Roberts, in *Four Faces of Rozanov: Christianity, Sex, Jews and the Russian Revolution*, 1978
Liudi lunnogo sveta, 1911; as "People of the Moonlight," translated by Spencer E. Roberts, in *Four Faces of Rozanov: Christianity, Sex, Jews and the Russian Revolution*, 1978
Uedinennoe, 1912; as *Solitaria*, translated by S. S. Koteliansky, 1927
Opavshie list'ia, 2 vols., 1913–15; vol. 1 as *Fallen Leaves, Bundle One*, translated by S. S. Koteliansky, 1929
Literaturnie izgnanniki (Literary exiles), 1913
Sredi khudozhnikov (Among artists), 1914
Oboniatel'noe i osiazatel'noe otnoshenie evreev k krovi (The attitude of the Jews toward the smell and touch of blood), 1914
Iz vostochnykh motivov (From Eastern motifs), 1916–17
Apokalipsis nashego vremeni, 1917–18 (in periodical); part as "The Apocalypse of Our Times," translated by S. S. Koteliansky, in *Solitaria*, 1927, and by Spencer E. Roberts, in *Four Faces of Rozanov: Christianity, Sex, Jews and the Russian Revolution*, 1978
Four Faces of Rozanov: Christianity, Sex, Jews and the Russian Revolution, translated by Spencer E. Roberts, 1978

Collected works edition: *Sobranie sochinenii*, edited by A. N. Nikoliukina, 1994– (in progress).

Bibliography
Gollerbakh, E., in *V. V. Rozanov: Zhizn' i tvorchestvo*, Paris: YMCA Press, 1976 (original edition, 1922)

Further Reading
Crone, Anna Lisa, *Rozanov and the End of Literature: Polyphony and the Dissolution of Genre in "Solitaria"*, Würzburg: Jal, 1978

Crone, Anna Lisa, "V. V. Rozanov and the Russian Art of Autobiography," in *Autobiographical Statements in Modern Russian Literature*, edited by Jane Gary Harris, Princeton, New Jersey: Princeton University Press, 1990

Gulyga, Arseni, "'The anguish of being Russian': A Note on the Life and Works of Vasilii Rozanov," *Glas: New Russian Writing* 6 (1993): 184–200

Hutchings, Stephen C., "Breaking the Circle of the Self: Domestication, Alienation and the Question of Discourse Type in Rozanov's Writings," *Slavic Review* 52, no. 1 (Spring 1993): 67–86

Kaulbach, Z. K., *The Life and Works of V. V. Rozanov* (dissertation), Ithaca, New York: Cornell University, 1973

Poggioli, Renato, *Rozanov*, London: Bowes and Bowes, 1957; New York: Hillary House, 1962

Putnam, George F., "Vasilii V. Rozanov: Sex, Marriage and Christianity," *Canadian Slavic Studies* 5 (1971): 301–26

Ruskin, John
British, 1819–1900

John Ruskin was a prolific essayist who, like his intellectual and stylistic mentor **Thomas Carlyle**, railed against many of the advances of modern society. Many of his major works were epistolary or delivered as lectures, making generic classification problematic; nevertheless, the wide range of Ruskin's interests may be viewed as a series of interrelated essays. As an art critic and social economist Ruskin defined the relationship between art and society and between the worker and society in novel ways, influencing figures as diverse as Proust and Gandhi. In a rapidly changing world, in which workers were becoming alienated from the works they produced and science was competing with art and literature as a source of knowledge and spiritual sustenance, Ruskin championed art as both ethical teacher and moral yardstick against which society could be measured.

The publication of volume one of *Modern Painters* in 1843 launched Ruskin's career as "sage" and intellectual guide for his era. Expanding on ideas espoused in uninspired essays written while Ruskin was a student at Oxford, *Modern Painters* began as a defense of Turner's landscape painting against the charge that it was untrue to nature. The five volumes of *Modern Painters* (1843–60) became an ambitious series of essays on the social context in which art is produced and which in turn mirrors the society that produces it. Art, therefore, appeals to the intellect as well as to the aesthetic sensibility. In accordance with his lofty aims, Ruskin employs a formal and literary prose in the first three volumes of *Modern Painters*. He is a master at exemplifying major points through succinct examples. In illustrating the connection between art's power to evoke great thought, as well as its capacity to give aesthetic pleasure, Ruskin states in volume three: "A finished work of a great artist is only better than its sketch if the sources of pleasure belonging to colour and realization – valuable in

themselves – are so employed as to increase the impressiveness of the thought."

The writing of *Modern Painters* was interrupted by the creation of two of Ruskin's most important works, *The Seven Lamps of Architecture* (1849) and the three volumes of *The Stones of Venice* (1851–53). *The Seven Lamps* is largely a theoretical work applying many of the standards of art to architecture. Ruskin, in great part, attempts to resolve the apparent dichotomy between architecture's practical restraints and what should be one of its important aims: the imitation of nature. In *The Stones of Venice* he applies theoretical considerations to Venetian architecture. No doubt influenced by his recent visit to Northern Italy in 1849, where he made many sketches of Venice's famous buildings, *The Stones of Venice* contains Ruskin's characteristic attention to detail and a luxuriant "painterly" prose, syntactically harmonious, full of minute descriptions of the forms and colors of the city. His "portrait" of Piazza San Marco demonstrates his rich prose:

> . . . for beyond those troops of ordered arches there rises a vision out of the earth, and all the great square seems to have opened from it in a kind of awe, that we may see it far away; – a multitude of pillars and white domes, clustered into a long low pyramid of coloured light; a treasure-heap, it seems, partly of gold, and partly of opal and mother-of-pearl, hollowed beneath into five great vaulted porches, ceiled with fair mosaic, and beset with sculpture of alabaster, clear as amber and delicate as ivory, – sculpture fantastic and involved, of palm leaves and lilies, and grapes and pomegranates, and birds clinging and fluttering among the branches, all twined together into an endless network of buds and plumes . . .

Ruskin admittedly had little reading in economic theory, but his philosophical assumptions about the relationship between art and morality led him naturally into the field. Believing that only a spiritually nourishing environment could lead to great art, Ruskin opposed Bentham's *laissez-faire* economic doctrines as morally debilitating. In a series of forceful but sometimes illogical essays published in *Cornhill Magazine*, Ruskin contests the popular view that man is selfishly motivated in pursuit of his economic interests. The public was infuriated by many of Ruskin's assertions and publication of the essays was terminated. The essays were later collected in *Unto This Last* (1862), which many years after its publication became a popular and influential work.

Several books followed, which were collections of essays and lectures Ruskin delivered to a variety of audiences, including his students at Oxford. They demonstrate an impressive eclecticism and intellectual prowess, but also a self-indulgence and lack of logic which may have been caused by several bouts of mental illness suffered during the later years of his life.

Ruskin's views were often extreme, exalting minor artists and vilifying others such as Whistler, who won a libel suit against him. His strict evangelical upbringing, his daily reading in the Bible, and his frustrated personal life have all been offered as causes of his sermon-like prose; but his breadth of knowledge and his masterful use of language to help us "see" mark him as a unique essayist of the English language.

ROBERT ZWEIG

Biography

Born 8 February 1819 in London. Studied at Christ Church, Oxford, 1836–40, 1842, B.A., 1842, M.A., 1843. Married Euphemia Chalmers Gray, 1848 (marriage annulled, 1854). Lived mainly in Venice, 1849–53. Wrote annual review catalogues for Royal Academy exhibitions, 1855–59 and 1875; taught drawing, Working Men's College, London, 1850s; lectured throughout England, 1855–70; catalogued Turner bequest to the National Gallery, London, 1857–58; teacher, Winnington Hall girls' school, from 1857; Rede Lecturer, Cambridge University, 1867; first Slade Professor of Fine Art, Oxford University, 1869–79 and 1883–84. Founder of a drawing school in Oxford, 1870, a school in Camberwell, London, Whitelands College, Chelsea, London, St. George's Museum, Walkley, near Sheffield, and the Guild of St. George, 1871 (wrote the guild's journal *Fors Clavigera*, 1871–74). Bought Brantwood house, by Coniston Lake, 1871, and lived there from 1889. Suffered first of several mental breakdowns, 1878. Awards: honorary degrees from Cambridge and Oxford Universities; Honorary Fellow, Corpus Christi College, Oxford, 1871; Honorary Member, Royal Society of Painters in Water-Colours, 1873; Fellow, Royal Geological Society, Royal Zoological Society, and Royal Institute of British Architects. Died at Coniston, 20 January 1900.

Selected Writings

Essays and Related Prose

Modern Painters, 5 vols., 1843–60; abridged edition, edited by David Barrie, 1987
The Seven Lamps of Architecture, 1849
The Stones of Venice, 3 vols., 1851–53; selections edited by Arnold Whittick, 1976, and Jan Morris, 1981
Lectures on Architecture and Painting, 1854
The Political Economy of Art (two lectures), 1857; enlarged edition, as "A Joy for Ever", 1880
The Two Paths, Being Lectures on Art and Its Application to Decoration and Manufacture, 1859
Unto This Last: Four Essays on the First Principles of Political Economy, 1862; edited by J. D. C. Monfries and G. E. Hollingsworth, 1931, and Lloyd J. Hubenka, 1967
Sesame and Lilies: Two Lectures, 1865
The Ethics of the Dust: Ten Lectures to Little Housewives on the Elements of Crystallisation, 1866; edited by R. O. Morris, 1914
The Crown of Wild Olive: Three Lectures on Work, Traffic, and War, 1866; edited by W. F. Melton, 1919
Time and Tide, by Weare and Tyne: Twenty-Five Letters to a Working Man of Sunderland on the Laws of Work, 1867; edited by P. Kaufman, 1928
The Queen of the Air: Being a Study of the Greek Myths of Cloud and Storm, 1869
Lectures on Art, 1870; revised edition, 1887
Fors Clavigera: Letters to the Workmen and Labourers of Great Britain, 8 vols., 1871–84
Munera Pulveris: Six Essays on the Elements of Political Economy, 1872
Aratra Pentelici: Six Lectures on the Elements of Sculpture, 1872
The Eagle's Nest: Ten Lectures on the Relation of Natural Science to Art, 1872
Love's Meinie: Lectures on Greek and English Birds, 3 vols., 1873–81
Ariadne Florentina: Six Lectures on Wood and Metal Engraving, 3 vols., 1873–75
Val D'Arno: Ten Lectures on the Tuscan Art Directly Antecedent to the Florentine Year of Victories, 1874
Proserpina: Studies of Wayside Flowers, 10 vols., 1875–86
Deucalion: Collected Studies of the Lapse of Waves, and Life of Stones, 9 vols., 1875–83
Mornings in Florence, Being Simple Studies of Christian Art for English Travellers, 6 vols., 1876–77

Arrows of the Chace, Being a Collection of Scattered Letters Published Chiefly in the Daily Newspapers, 1840–1880, edited by A. D. O. Wedderburn, 2 vols., 1880
On the Old Road: A Collection of Miscellaneous Essays, 1834–1885, edited by A. D. O. Wedderburn, 2 vols., 1885; revised edition, 3 vols., 1899
Verona and Other Lectures, edited by W. G. Collingwood, 1894
Lectures on Landscape, 1897
The Lamp of Beauty: Writings on Art, edited by Joan Evans, 1959; revised editions, 1980, 1995
The Genius of Ruskin: Selections, edited by John D. Rosenberg, 1963
Ruskin Today (selections), edited by Kenneth Clark, 1964
The Art Criticism, edited by Robert L. Herbert, 1964
The Literary Criticism, edited by Harold Bloom, 1965
Unto This Last, and Other Writings, edited by Clive Wilmer, 1985
The Social and Economic Works, 6 vols., 1994
Selected Writings, edited by Philip Davis, 1995

Other writings: the three-volume autobiography *Praeterita* (1886–89) and many volumes of correspondence.

Collected works edition: *Works* (Library Edition), edited by E. T. Cook and A. D. O. Wedderburn, 39 vols., 1903–12, reprinted in microfiche, 1986.

Bibliographies

Beetz, Kirk H., *John Ruskin: A Bibliography, 1900–1974*, Metuchen, New Jersey: Scarecrow Press, 1976
Cate, George Allan, *John Ruskin: A Reference Guide*, Boston: Hall, 1988
Wise, Thomas J., and James P. Smart, *A Complete Bibliography of the Writings in Prose and Verse of John Ruskin, LL.D.*, London: privately printed, 2 vols., 1889–93

Further Reading

Helsinger, Elizabeth K., *Ruskin and the Art of the Beholder*, Cambridge, Massachusetts: Harvard University Press, 1982
Hewison, Robert, *John Ruskin: The Argument of the Eye*, Princeton, New Jersey: Princeton University Press, and London: Thames and Hudson, 1976
Hilton, Tim, *John Ruskin: The Early Years*, New Haven, Connecticut and London: Yale University Press, 1985
Hunt, John Dixon, *The Wider Sea: A Life of John Ruskin*, New York: Viking, and London: Dent, 1982
Kirchhoff, Frederick, *John Ruskin*, Boston: Twayne, 1984
Rosenberg, John D., *The Darkening Glass: A Portrait of Ruskin's Genius*, New York: Columbia University Press, 1961; London: Routledge and Kegan Paul, 1963
Rosenberg, John D., "Style and Sensibility in Ruskin's Prose," in *The Art of Victorian Prose*, edited by George Levine and William Madden, New York: Oxford University Press, 1968: 177–200

Russian Essay

In Russian letters the essay genre has a weak tradition. This fact is reflected in the absence of an exact, single-word translation for the genre known in English as the essay. Other words such as *opyty* (experiments), *ocherk* (sketch), *etiudy* (studies), *zapiski* (notes), *rassuzhdenie* (thoughts), and *pouchenie* (instruction) only partially cover the requirements of the genre, which S. I. Ozhegov in his Russian dictionary *Slovar' Russkogo iazyka* (1952) defines as a "short prose work of any style on a personal theme which is treated subjectively and usually not exhaustively."

Although the reasons why a tradition never developed can be partially explained by the absence of the genre in early modern Russian literature, one can claim with certainty that the essay as employed by **Montaigne** appeared in Russia very late. Although the first translation of Montaigne into Russian was published in 1803, and between 1806 and 1808 there appeared two short articles about him, the genre "essai," translated as *opyty*, never set down deep roots. The Russian word *esse* did not appear until the middle of the 19th century. Thus, instead of borrowing directly, Russian authors molded this foreign form to their own particular needs and desires. Instead of "essays," Russian writers cultivated literary criticism, political writing, and philosophical speculation.

A study of the essay in Russian culture poses certain problems for scholars, due to the dearth of secondary literature on the subject. The main danger lies in the identification and classification of the genre. Since a broad variety of hybrid literary forms can fall under the rubric "essay" in Russia, there is no consensus about what exactly constitutes an essay. At present scholars are obliged to make independent choices based on criteria which have emerged from Western definitions of the genre. For our purposes, we identify those works which belong to one of three categories – the political essay, the meditative or **philosophical essay**, and the **critical essay**. By identifying the essay's qualities, it may be possible to locate those normative features characteristic of the Russian experience with this literary form.

The genre as it is known in the West came late to Russia, appearing only in the second half of the 18th century. It bears clear marks of its derivation from Western European sources. While literary genres similar to the essay certainly appeared earlier – polemical works and religious apologetics – medieval conventions remained longer in Russian literature than in the West. Russian writing was characterized by thematic topoi and formal conventions, which lasted with few exceptions up to the 17th century. Thus, we may distinguish between the essay as it was practiced in the West (at least by the time of the Renaissance), in which the concrete views of an individualized author were expressed, and those in which the identity of the author was unknown or reflected a conventionalized persona, a monk, a benevolent ruler, or a courtier. In such works the subject matter lacked the personal, meditative quality or the critical bite we associate with the genre.

In the first half of the 18th century the term "essay" did not appear, nor is it easy to identify works belonging to the genre. The classification of genres in classicism, the leading literary style, offered philosophical writing primarily in the form of "odes" or "epistles." Moreover, subjectivism in general was not characteristic of classicism, which was founded rather on rules and norms. The leading writers in the 18th century, Mikhail Lomonosov (1711–65), Vasilii Trediakovskii (1703–69), and Aleksandr Sumarokov (1718–77), authored **treatises** on the rules of writing poetry. In such prose works the authors tried to present an objective and authoritative view.

Writing which resembled essays appeared in the satirical journals which proliferated in the early part of the reign (1762–96) of Catherine the Great. These journals, while based on foreign, especially English models such as the *Tatler*,

Spectator, and *Guardian*, were adapted to Russian conditions. Catherine sponsored her own journal and challenged others to follow suit. The most interesting were **Nikolai Novikov's** (1744–1818) *Truten'* (1769–70; The drone), Aleksandr Sumarokov's (1717–77) *Trudoliobivaia Pchela* (1759; Worker bee), and Catherine's own *Vsiakaia Vsiachina* (1769; Odds and ends). In these journals the authors published short instructive writings in which they mocked social conditions and criticized universal human foibles. New scholarship has shown that such criticism was not rebellious in intent as was previously thought, but rather was governed by the conventions of satirical journals. These journals, however, did provide a forum for a kind of discourse in which a subjective treatment of intellectually lively subjects could find expression.

The final quarter of the 18th century reflected the growing intensity of political concerns. As Russia's critical intelligentsia formed, it began to demand a political voice, and several major writers of the period – Prince Mikhail Shcherbatov (1733–90), Denis Fonvizin (1745–92), and Aleksandr Radishchev (1749–1802) – penned political articles in which each tried to describe the proper and most propitious means for governing the state. For example, in his essay *O povrezhdenii nravov v Rossii* (1786–89; *On the Corruption of Morals in Russia*), Prince Shcherbatov argued in favor of the rights of the hereditary nobility and "ancient Russian virtues" against the interests of the court and its "western-aping" habits. Similarly, Denis Fonvizin, in his "Rassuzhdenie o neprimennykh gosudarstvennikh zakonakh" ("Discourse on the Indispensable Laws of the State"), advised the new tsar Paul to shun favoritism and tyrannical rule and create inalterable laws that would bring harmony and stability.

Aleksandr Radishchev, the famed author of the fictional *Puteshestvie iz Peterburga v Moskvu* (1790; *A Journey From St. Petersburg to Moscow*), also argued forcefully for revolution in his "Beseda o tom, chto est' syn otechestva" (1789; Conversation about who is his nation's son). Here he railed against serfdom, denouncing the unchecked power of landowners over their human chattel and the illegitimate source of political power in Russia. While the authors delivered serious criticism of Russia's political system, their presentation of arguments and use of vocabulary from a variety of disciplines link these works with the political essay.

At the end of the 18th and beginning of the 19th centuries, Romanticism replaced classicism as the leading literary sensibility. A change occurred in social and artistic consciousness, the subjective "I" becoming an important source for creative writing. This new tendency gave a strong impetus to essay writing. Sentimentalism gradually destroyed the genre system of classicism; new genres with the potential for confessional narratives appeared (to a great degree influenced by **Jean-Jacques Rousseau's** *Confessions* [1782–89]). A variety of travel narratives – journeys, walks, and travel notes (*puteshestvie, progulki, putevye zametki*) – permitted the expression of personal, spontaneous impressions. In addition, in 1803 Montaigne's essays were translated and served as a blueprint for many Russian authors.

Nikolai Karamzin (1766–1826) reflected the ethic of sentimentalism, especially its rationalistic and didactic character. For example, in his essay "Nechto o naukakh, iskusstvakh i prosveshchenii" (1793; A bit about the sciences, arts, and

Enlightenment), he polemicizes with Rousseau, who had said in one of his discourses that "the sciences ruin morals." Karamzin argued that enlightenment, science, and art possess an enormous instructive significance. Karamzin also wrote political articles for the journal *Vestnik Evropy* (The messenger of Europe) in which he analyzed the political situation of Europe before the French Revolution and the wars France waged in Europe and Africa. Karamzin held a conservative position, arguing for the preservation of religion and the restoration of the monarchy. He offered a utopian picture of Europe and the world, employing the stylistic manner typical of sentimentalist aesthetics.

The spirit of Romanticism, known as the "Golden Age" of Russian poetry, was conducive to producing Russia's first serious literary criticism. In newly established journals, *Poliarnaia Zvezda, Aglaia, Msemodia,* and *Literaturnaia Gazeta* (Literary gazette), Vasilii Zhukovskii (1783–1852), Aleksandr Bestuzhev-Marlinskii (1797–1837), Dmitrii Venevitinov (1805–27), Vil'gelm Kiukhel'beker (1797–1846), O. M. Somov (1793–1833), and Kondratii Ryleev (1795–1825), set forth aesthetic criteria with which they judged the most recent poetic creations. Principally, they emphasized the artistic expression of the author's unique personality. Furthermore, critics applauded the appearance of their favored works of poetry, viewing them in a national cultural context. Thus appeared the literary survey, critical articles adumbrating the trends in Russian literary life.

Vasilii Zhukovskii is often considered the originator of Russian Romanticism in poetry, but he was also an important critic. Many of Zhukovskii's critical articles, however, have a programmatic character and served as manifestoes of Romanticism. As a translator he made available the philosophical essays of David Hume, such as "On Simplicity and Refinement in Writing," "On Tragedy," and "Of Eloquence." In his own "Rafaeleva 'Madonna'" (1824; Raphael's Madonna), Zhukovskii described his view of the Romantic artist, setting forth his impressions of the painting. He claimed that inspiration from on high is the source of the writer's art and the author is a prophet or messenger of divine knowledge.

A critical figure in Russian essay writing is Konstantin N. Batiushkov (1787–1855). In his first collection entitled *Opyty v stikhakh i proze* (1817; Essays in verse and prose – the title imitates Montaigne's book, and he takes the epigraph from him), he includes prose texts from a variety of genres: the **letter**, speech, travelogue, philosophical essay, and critical article. In his essay "Nechto o poete i poezii" (1816; A bit about the poet and poetry), Batiushkov depicted the sentimental poet, claiming that art, or spiritual experience, should correspond to real life. In his famous essay, "Progulka v Akademiiu khudozhestv" (1814; A walk to the Academy of Arts), Batiushkov expressed his aesthetic viewpoint, taking as his touchstone the culture of antiquity. From this position, he evaluated the Renaissance and contemporary Russia, illustrating his patriotism with praise for the achievements of national culture.

Petr A. Viazemskii (1792–1878) also penned a number of important essays. The majority were written for monthly journals and can be seen as critical reflections on literary events of the time. Despite the subjectivity of most of his critical opinions, these essays were important in instigating a critical appreciation of literature. Examples are "O Derzhavin" (1816; On Derzhavin), "Sonety Mitskevicha" (1829; Mickievich's sonnets), and "O duxe partii; o literaturnoi aristokratii" (1830; On the spirit of parties; on literary aristocracy).

During this period Russian literary criticism played a central role in literary life, becoming a permanent feature of the political and literary journals. Bestuzhev-Marlinskii's survey articles on Russian literature for 1823 and 1824–25 and Vil'gelm Kiukhel'beker's "O napravlenii nashei poezii osobenno liricheskoi v poslednee desiatiletie" (On the direction of our poetry especially lyrical during the last decade) are representative examples. These articles have common traits with the essay, since the authors freely express their views on literature, literary life, and society. As B. Egorov writes in *On the Craft of Literary Criticism* (1980), "For criticism of the post-Karamzinian epoch, in the period of the birth of a romantic method, a state of chaos, an intentional disconnectedness of ideas and subjects was very characteristic. The powerful intrusion of the subjective voice of the critic contributed to such discursiveness."

As a writer of essays, the greatest of Russian poets **Aleksandr Pushkin** (1799–1837) was prolific. Pushkin's essays are characterized by a broadness of theme, clarity of thought, and richness of philosophical speculation. In them he expounds on history, philosophy, education, literature, and poetry. As a literary critic, Pushkin observed the subtleties of literary craft, judging with precision the best and worst of the literature of his day. He wrote about his friends, the poets Evgenii Batiushkov and Baron Delvig, and expressed his views on literary life with critical articles on Nikolai Polevoi, Mikhail Zagoskin, and Ivan Krylov. Pushkin also offered thoughtful reflections on poetic inspiration and the role of literature in society in such essays as "O literaturnoi kritike" (1830; "On Literary Criticism") and "Trebuet li publika izveshcheniia" (1830; "Does the Public Demand Instruction?"). He wrote on history and historiography with **review**s of the *Dictionary of Saints* and in his famous letter (1836) to Petr Chaadaev.

Often called the father of Russian philosophy, Chaadaev (1794–1856) wrote philosophical essays, which he presented in the form of a fictional correspondence. His *Filosoficheskie pis'ma* (*Philosophical Letters*) consisted of eight letters, only one of which was published in his lifetime, appearing in the journal *Teleskop* in 1836. In this essay, Chaadaev levied all his critical anger at his native land, juxtaposing inferior Russia to a superior Western civilization. Russia, Chaadaev complained, having never experienced the Renaissance and Reformation, lacked the civilizing experiences of the West, the emblem of which he considered the Roman Catholic Church. Although Chaadaev overstated his case, the questions he posed about the meaning of Russia's history and its relations to the West would become central to the two main philosophical movements of the 19th century, the Slavophiles and the Westernizers.

The great Russian writer Nikolai Gogol' (1809–52) also wrote a variety of essays. His early attempts at the genre are contained in the volume *Arabeski* (1835; *Arabesques*). Part of the volume deals with aesthetic problems: "Ob arkhitekture" ("On Architecture"), "Skul'ptura, zhivopis', muzyka" ("Sculpture, Painting, Music"), and "Poslednii den' Pompei" ("The Last Day of Pompei"). The other section is connected with Gogol's university teaching. In "O srednikh vekakh" ("On the Middle Ages") he disputed Enlightenment thinkers, who considered the Middle Ages a primitive period, and the Romantics, who idealized it. In "Vzgliad na sostavlenie Malorossii" ("A View on the Formation of Little Russia") and "O Malorossiiskikh pesniakh" ("On Little Russian Songs"), Gogol' revealed his interest in Ukrainian national culture and folklore.

Among the Westernizers – individuals whose value system was oriented toward ideas originating in the West – **Vissarion Belinskii** (1811–48) was the most important literary critic and essayist; he contributed to the development of the profession of literary criticism. He was passionate and personally engaged with his subject, and his prose reflects this involvement. As the literary historian Leonid Grossman put it (in *Vissarion Belinsky*, 1954), "Belinsky's primary and favorite form is criticism as speech, criticism as lecture, criticism as conversation. Concentrating on the main intonation of his writings, we can truly imagine him standing on a tribunal before a large audience which he instructs, educates, convinces and entertains with his talk. This is a critic-orator."

While the political views of a writer were important to Belinskii, aesthetics also mattered a great deal. In part, in his articles on Pushkin (1843–46), he was responsible for canonizing Pushkin as the national poet; in his article "O russkoi povesti i povestiakh g. Gogolia" (1835; On the Russian story and Gogol's stories) he crowned Gogol' the leader of the "Natural School." In his annual review of the year's events in Russian literature (starting in 1841), Belinskii drew a portrait of the epoch, while presenting theoretical issues about literature. In addition to claiming that literature was an expression of the national spirit, Belinskii promulgated his theoretical position that literature is "thinking in images." Besides seeking out the political "ideals" in a literary work, Belinskii also "emphasized the dialectical unity of content and form and the indivisibility of progress and historical development" (B. F. Egorov, in *Russkie pisateli, 1800–1917*, 1992). Thus, he believed in the transforming role of literature in the general and inexorable improvement of humanity. This commitment to progress led Belinskii into a polemic with Gogol', and in one of the most influential essays of Russian intellectual history, "Pis'mo k Gogoliu" (1847; "Letter to N. V. Gogol'"), which because of censorship could not be published in Russia, Belinskii condemned the tyranny of tsarism, the unfreedom of serfdom, and Gogol's own misdirected and unfortunate religious conservatism.

In addition to Belinskii, the "men of the 1840s" included distinguished writers such as **Aleksandr Herzen** (1812–70), Mikhail Bakunin (1814–76), **Ivan Turgenev**, Nikolai Stankevich (1813–40), and Timofei Granovskii (1813–55). Herzen became the most illustrious and was a master of the political essay. Despite having been born into great wealth, early in his life Herzen became enamored with the ideals of socialism. After having been exiled twice within Russia for his views, he left Russia voluntarily in 1847. However, it was in emigration that he was to play his greatest role. As the editor and primary writer for his journal, *Kolokol* (1857–67; The bell), which was smuggled back into Russia, Herzen influenced government policy in the years just before and after the emancipation of the serfs in 1861.

In *Kolokol* Herzen published political essays such as "Moskva i Peterburg" (1857; Moscow and Petersburg), "Zapadnye knigi" (1857; Western books), "Very Dangerous" (1859; original title in English), and "Lishnie liudi i zhelcheviki" (1860; Superfluous men and revolutionaries). He railed against the illusions of Slavophilism, while criticizing the radicals for not considering the significance of the liberals of the 1840s (of whom Herzen was one) in the struggle against tsarism. Furthermore, in response to witnessing the revolutions of 1848 in Europe and to his own experiences in Russia, Herzen wrote two books composed of essays, *Pis'ma iz Frantsii i Italii* (1847–52; *Letters from France and Italy, 1847–1851*) and *S togo berega* (first published in German, 1850, in Russian, 1855; *From the Other Shore*). In these deftly written, philosophically astute, and personally engaged articles, Herzen spurned the radicals, rejecting the view that history is progressing inexorably to a predestined or purposeful end. He considered that personalities rather than abstract ideas make history.

Another fine essay writer among the Westernizers was the novelist **Ivan Turgenev** (1818–83). Although he wrote only a few essays, they are important as reflections of the conflicts between the "men of the 1840s" and the revolutionaries of the 1860s. The most important of them is "Gamlet i Don Kikhot" (1860; "Hamlet and Don Quixote"), in which Turgenev describes two basic human types. Hamlet represents a person paralyzed by self-doubt and reflection, someone socially useless or "superfluous." Don Quixote, on the contrary, is "completely devoted to his ideal, for which he is prepared to sacrifice everything, including his life. It is true that this ideal is sometimes based on fantasy or illusion, so much so that Don Quixote may appear to be a madman. But this does not in any way diminish its purity or sincerity, or Don Quixote's determination and strength of will" (Leonard Schapiro, *Turgenev: His Life and Times*, 1978). Like his novels, Turgenev's essays had a powerful effect on society, since they appeared with perfect timing at a moment of social convulsion.

Protests against the Westernizers were levied by their intellectual antitheses, the Slavophiles, who widely employed the philosophical essay. Thoroughly Western in their education and sensibility, Ivan Kireevskii (1808–56) and Aleksei Khomiakov (1804–60) used references from European literature, history, and philosophy in order to promulgate their view of Russia as unique from the West. At the start of his career, in his own journal *Evropeets* (The European), Kireevskii wrote "Deviatnadtsatyi vek" (1832; The 19th century), perhaps the most absorbing essay of his time. In it he treated the intellectual movements of the 18th and 19th centuries in Europe from the viewpoint of a "conservative favorably disposed toward the West," criticizing European irreligiosity but "happy for the return of religion to its rightful central place" (Peter K. Christoff, *An Introduction to Nineteenth-Century Russian Slavophilism*, 1972).

Later Kireevskii, together with Khomiakov, would articulate the basic premises of the Slavophile doctrine. In philosophical articles such as Kireevskii's "O neobkhodimosti i vozmozhnosti novykh nachal dlia filosofii" (1856; On the necessity and possibility of new principles in philosophy) and Khomiakov's "O sovremennykh iavleniiakh v oblasti filosofii"

(1859; On contemporary trends in the area of philosophy), the two thinkers indicated the differences between Russia and the West. The West, they held, was based on rationalism and religious agnosticism, while the Russian people were religious in their essence. Furthermore, while in Europe the single individual's well-being was the central goal, Russia was based on principles of unity and inclusion. For these reasons, the latter was superior spiritually, while Europe languished in moral turpitude.

The division between the followers of the Slavophiles and the Westernizers widened in the tumultuous years following the abolition of serfdom in 1861. The conflict grew in part because of the uncompromising attitude of the nihilists, who demanded nothing less than the overthrow of the tsar. Nevertheless, these same nihilists, extremist in their political program, were powerful critics, enormously influential on the thought and behavior of subsequent generations of radicals. **Nikolai Chernyshevskii** (1828–89), for example, depicted positive heroes useful for public emulation. Furthermore, these radical social critics, such as Chernyshevskii himself, Nikolai Dobroliubov (1836–61), and Dmitrii Pisarev (1840–68), intended to incite the reader's anger about the wrongs of Russia's social structure and to provoke action on behalf of political change. Thus, for reasons of censorship, essays purporting to be literary criticism were actually sociopolitical tracts in disguise. Incidentally, Pisarev also wrote educational essays on popular science, transmitting to a Russian audience the ideas of positivism, utilitarianism, and educational reform.

Among the next generation of critics, Apollon Grigor'ev (1822–64) reflected the influence of both the Westernizers and the Slavophiles. Practicing a type of reading he called "organic criticism," Grigor'ev saw a work of art as a complicated whole, an entity in which the depiction of life emerges from the author's inner vision. The artist is seen as a prophet or clairvoyant who "opens the mysteries of life" and reveals their relationship with eternal ideals. In critical essays such as "O pravde i iskrennosti v iskusstve" (1856; On truth and honesty in art), Grigor'ev creatively interpreted Russia's poets as sharp observers of reality and metaphysical visionaries.

During the 1860s, the novelist **Fedor Dostoevskii** (1821–81) wrote many articles about Russia's social, political, and psychological character. Many of his journalistic articles he signed under the heading "A Writer's Diary," and these have been republished in separate volumes. As editor and owner of his own journals *Vremia* (1861–63; Time) and *Epokha* (1864–65; Epoch), and as editor of *Grazhdanin* (1873–78; The citizen), Dostoevskii had an outlet for his philosophical deliberations about Western civilization and Russia in the years following the liberation of the serfs. Opposing the nihilists, Dostoevskii advocated, in the words of R. L. Belknap (in *Handbook of Russian Literature*, edited by Victor Terras, 1985), "not a Slavophile repudiation of the West as such, nor a denial of the need to better the lot of Russia's poor, and certainly not any sympathy with the ideals of Russian aristocrats, bureaucrats, or plutocrats, but a doctrine that he and his associates called *pochvennichestvo*, or 'grassroots.' They argued that Peter the Great's Westernization had enriched Russia, but that now Russia must turn to the wisdom of its rural past if it is to say its own word in the history of mankind."

One feature of Dostoevskii's essays, however, is contradictory and morally disconcerting. In his essays a shrill voice sometimes expresses deep resentment against religions other than Russian Orthodoxy and ethnic races other than Russian. The objects of Dostoevskii's wrath include Jews, Poles, and Germans. He does not appear to have had much patience with those elements of society which were different or contrary to his idealistic vision of a theocratic Russia.

Lev Tolstoi (1828–1910) wrote his essays primarily in the periods of retreat from fiction writing. The first period of essays follows Tolstoi's return to his estate, Iasnaia Poliana, after feeling snubbed by Petersburg's professional intellectuals. There he began to write a periodical describing his theory of education and the practical results of his work as a teacher of peasant children in his own school. Twelve issues of *Iasnaia Poliana* appeared between 1862 and 1863. Tolstoi articulated his ideas most strikingly in "Komu u kogo uchit'sia pisat', krest'ianskim rebiatam u nas, ili nam u krest'ianskikh rabiat?" (1862; "Who Should Learn to Write from Whom, the Peasant Children from Us, or We from the Peasant Children?"). In the years of writing *Anna Karenina* (1875–77) and thereafter, Tolstoi became engaged in a struggle to remodel Christianity, and expressed his new religious outlook in book-length didactic treatises aimed at attracting readers to his views of nonresistance to evil, the abolition of private property, and the utility of art for moral edification: *Tak chtozhe nam delat'?* (1888; *What to Do?*), *Tsarvtso Bozhie vnutri vas* (1893–94; *The Kingdom of God Is Within You*), and *Chto takoe iskusstvo?* (1898; *What Is Art?*).

The other great realist, Anton Chekhov (1860–1904), was not a prolific essayist, although his articles, letters to the editor, and reviews make entertaining reading. In part, this can be explained by Chekhov's ability to treat contemporary problems in his fiction; nonfiction therefore held less interest for him. Nevertheless, he did complete *Iz Sibiri* (1890; From Siberia) and *Ostrov Sakalin* (1895; A Journey to Sakalin), that "remarkable book," made up of separate essays about the social, economic, and medical conditions of Russia's Far East. In addition, Chekhov also published exposés of social problems and sketches of contemporaries: for example, essays on Sarah Bernhardt (1881), I. A. Mel'nikov (1893), N. N. Figner (1893), and "Novoe vremia" (1894), a letter to the editor of *The New Times*.

A contemporary of Chekhov and a brilliant intellectual, **Vladimir Solov'ev** (1853–1900) was a remarkable essayist and gifted stylist. Inspired by Slavophile thought, Solov'ev was a religious philosopher who created his own Christian world view by uniting boundless faith in the divinity with a tremendous respect for science and human creativity. Among his most famous philosophical essays are "Obshchii smysl iskusstva" (1890; "The General Meaning of Art") and *Smysl liubvi* (1892–94; *The Meaning of Love*). His personality and thought were extremely influential for poets and philosophers associated with the younger symbolists.

During the 1880s and 1890s the positivist school of literary criticism dominated the "thick" journals. The leader of the movement, Nikolai Mikhailovskii (1842–1904), was a fine essayist and an important figure, since his blending of utilitarianism, individual egoism, and populism influenced revolutionary thought of the time. In the 1890s, however, a new school of writers arose who attacked the general confidence in rationalism and political collectivism in the name of artistic creativity and Nietzschean apolitical individualism. At times called Russian decadents or symbolists, Dmitrii Merezhkovskii (1865–1941), Zinaida Gippius (1869–1945), and Valerii Briusov (1873–1924) were energetic writers and self-advertisers who for at least a decade devoted their energies to spreading the new aesthetic until it became the leading artistic movement in Russia.

The best statement of the tenets of this new movement can be found in Merezhkovskii's programmatic essay "O prichinakh upadka i o novykh techeniiakh sovremennoi russkoi literatury" (1893; On the reasons for the decline and the new trends in contemporary Russian literature). Briusov also wrote **polemical essays** against those intellectual movements antagonistic to symbolism – positivism, materialism, and political conservatism; for example, "Kliuchi tain" (1904; The keys of mysteries) and "Sovremennye soobrazheniia" (1905; Contemporary thoughts). Later Briusov began to write about the necessity of considering the real world, not simply the inner experiences of the authors. In addition, Briusov wrote many important critical essays about Russian literature, especially on the poetry of Aleksandr Pushkin, for example in "Stikhotvornaia technika Pushkina" (1915; Pushkin's verse techniques).

The 1905 Revolution was the central event of the first decade of the 20th century and it became a major theme for writers. For example, at the same time that the centrist and leftist parties were wresting from the tsar the right to establish the Duma, an elected legislature, a group of intellectuals, notably **Viacheslav Ivanov** (1866–1949) and Georgii Chulkov (1879–1939), wrote political essays advocating "misticheskom anarkhizme" (mystical anarchy). Later, addressing the unfulfilled expectations of the Revolution, seven non-Marxist philosophers published a collection of essays entitled *Vekhi: Sbornik statei o russkoi intelligentsii* (1909; *Landmarks: A Collection of Essays on the Russian Intelligentsia*). These political essays by Nikolai Berdiaev (1874–1948), Sergei Bulgakov (1871–1944), **Mikhail Gershenzon** (1869–1925), Semion Frank (1877–1950), A. Kistiakovskii (1868–1920), Petr Struve (1870–1944), and Aleksandr Izgoev (1872–1935) had a scandalous success; the volume incited over 200 published responses within the first year alone. Although the contributors disagreed among themselves about a positive solution for Russia's problems, they joined forces to criticize the revolutionary intelligentsia's moral maximalism and indifference to truth, beauty, or knowledge, independent of its use for the political cause.

This period of cultural flowering, known to scholars as the "Silver Age" (1890–1920), also featured excellent essay writers among the religiously-minded intelligentsia. Of special interest are **Vasilii Rozanov** (1856–1919) and **Lev Shestov** (1866–1938). In his essays Rozanov treated the issues of Christianity, Judaism, the Russian idea, and his own biography, blending them together in a surprising and idiosyncratic way (in his personal life he was friendly with both anti-Semites and Jews, educated philosophers and peasant artists). His erratic, "irrational" views are matched by a bizarre, personal writing style. Breaking down genre barriers, in his greatest books, *Uedinennoe* (1912; *Solitaria*) and *Opavshie list'ia* (1913–15; *Fallen Leaves*), Rozanov included short essays on a variety of topics, which he treated with his characteristic shifting of intonation, from irony to complete seriousness in a single breath.

Lev Shestov was one of Russia's greatest essay writers because of his clear and limpid style. Writing about literature and philosophy, Shestov created his own approach, organizing his essays around an analysis of his subjects' biographies. Influenced by **Nietzsche**, Shestov claimed that creation emerges from personal tragedies, and that authors try to hide their horrifying experiences or transform them in fiction. It is up to the critic, therefore, to reconstruct the artist's psychological condition. Shestov masterfully applied his subjective method to the study of Shakespeare, Dante, Dostoevskii, Tolstoi, Chekhov, Pushkin, the Greek philosophers, and the heroes of the Bible.

The poet **Aleksandr Blok** (1880–1921) is also well known for his essay writing. He wrote especially on social and political problems in essays such as "Narod i intelligentsia" (1909; "The People and Intelligentsia"), "Intelligentsiia i revoliutsiia" (1918; "The Intelligentsia and Revolution"), and "Krushenie gumanizma" (1921; "The Collapse of Humanism"). In these works Blok expressed doubts about the value of the humanist tradition and revealed an attraction for the apocalypse, which would bring a conclusion to the unjust and spiritually incomplete world. Thus, Blok fatally embraced the Bolshevik putsch which brought Lenin to power. Blok's position was a sign to the entire intelligentsia, and the historian Ivanov-Razumnik (1878–1946) in the journal *Skifii* (1917–18; Scythians) expressed the view that intellectuals had fully to accept the October Revolution as a *fait accompli*.

Another group of writers and thinkers, however, interpreted the Bolshevik Revolution as nothing less than unlawful violence. In 1918, under the direction of Petr Struve, a group of religious philosophers and political liberals (the core group from *Landmarks* plus several other thinkers, minus Gershenzon) contributed essays to *De profundis*, a volume which was intended to provide a theoretical repudiation of Bolshevism.

Maksim Gor'kii (i.e. Aleksei Peshkov, 1868–1936) was at once a powerful political writer and an important literary critic. In his early years he wrote revolutionary manifestoes, awakening the world proletariat to action (1905–06). In the period during which he resided in Capri (1906–13), Gor'kii published many articles of literary and social criticism. He attacked decadence, individualism, and trounced the leading Russian authors, while praising the ideals of socialism and the virtues of the working class in essays such as "Razrushenie lichnosti" (1909; "The Destruction of the Individual"), "O Karamozovshchine" (1913; "About Karamazovism"). In the revolutionary years, Gor'kii published two books of articles, *Revoliutsiia i kul'tura* (1918; Revolution and culture) and *Nesvoevremennye mysli* (1917–18; *Untimely Thoughts*), in which he argued for the preservation of cultural values and called for the popularization of knowledge and culture for the masses. After the Revolution, in emigration, Gor'kii continued to write critical articles, working as an editor of the journal *Dialogue*.

The early years of Bolshevik rule are paradoxical in that, while intellectuals in Petersburg and Moscow were literally starving, there occurred a vibrant flowering in the arts. Given the desire to understand the social changes which had taken place since the Revolution, much of the creative energy in literature took the form of philosophical speculation and literary criticism. In weekly issues of the *Letopis' Doma Literatorov* (1918–21; Chronicle of the house of writers), famous intellectuals such as Vladislav Khodasevich (1886–1939), Fedor Kuzmin (1875–1936), **Viktor Shklovskii** (1893–1984), Aleksandr Blok, and new talents, Evgenii Zamiatin (1884–1937), Mikhail Zoshchenko (1895–1958), and Benedikt Livshits (1881–1939), published their works. During this period Viacheslav Ivanov and Mikhail Gershenzon created their masterpiece, *Perepiska iz dvukh uglov* (1921; *Correspondence Across a Room*). Although the work consists of 14 letters, each is in itself a self-contained essay about the purpose of history, metaphysics, and the Russian Revolution. The book has an interesting history, since the two authors actually lived together in a sanitorium and sent letters "across a room."

While the October Revolution offered communist writers such as Leon Trotskii (1879–1940), Nikolai Bukharin (1888–1938), and Anatolii Lunacharskii (1875–1933) an advantage in getting into print, they did not have exclusive control over publishing during the 1920s. The relative freedoms of the period permitted other writers to emerge. Among the nondogmatic communists, the best essayist was Aleksandr Voronskii (1884–1943), who published his critical articles on Soviet literature in the thick journal he edited, *Krasnaia Nov'* (1921–27; Red virgin soil). Voronskii was something of a sore point for the dogmatists, since he was adamant that Soviet literature had to offer more than merely a message: it should also be aesthetically and formally "beautiful."

In the 1920s and 1930s the Acmeist poets Anna Akhmatova (1889–1966) and **Osip Mandel'shtam** (1891–1938) offered excellent examples of the genre. Mandel'shtam impressed readers with his essays on the idea of Acmeism – "François Villon" (1913) – and poetic language – "O prirode slova" (1922; "About the Nature of the Word") and "Utro akmeizma" (1922; "Morning of Acmeism"). He also revealed in part the mysteries of poetic creation with "Razgovor o Dante" (1933; "Conversation About Dante"). Simultaneously, Akhmatova's various essays on Pushkin, while scholarly and well-written, also reveal in cryptic ways her own creative process. The author Evgenii Zamiatin (1884–1937) also wrote essays in which he expressed his observations and thoughts on the problem of literature in a totalitarian state. In part he argued against censorship and ideological dogmatism in articles such as "Zavtra" (1920; Tomorrow) and "O segodniashem i sovremennom" (1924; On today and the contemporary).

In post-revolutionary Russia literary scholars such as Viktor Shklovskii offered personal reflections, sociological observations, and insights about literature in short prose works which were collected in *Gamburgskii schet* (1928; Hamburg account). His student **Lidiia Ginzburg** (1902–90) also penned synthetic essays in which she joined personal reminiscences and thoughts on literature; these have been published recently in *Chelovek za pis'mennym stolom* (1989; A person at the writing table).

The exile from Russia in the 1920s of so many leading intellectuals brought about a split between Soviet and émigré literature. Despite the difficulties of life in emigration, intellectual life was surprisingly multifarious and vivacious. In the 1920s collections of essays appeared in which émigré movements such as Eurasianism and Smena Vekh (Changing of the signposts) publicized their ideological credo. In addition, émigré journals such as *Vozrozhdenie* (Resurrection), *Put'* (The way), and *Dni* (Days) were established, and the best writers, poets, and philosophers wrote for them. Among the finest essayists of the period were Vladimir Nabokov (1899–1977), Vladislav Khodasevich (1886–1939), Georgii Adamovich (1884–1972), Georges Florovsky (1893–1979), Mark Aldanov (1886–1957), and Prince Dmitrii Sviatopolk-Mirskii (1890–1939). During World War II the most important émigré journals were *Novyi Zhurnal* (New journal) and *Novoe Russkoe Slovo* (New Russian word).

During the post-Stalinist "Thaw" (1954–62) in Soviet Russia, essay writing was heralded by Il'ia Ehrenburg (1891–1967), who published a book of literary-critical articles and essays, *Frantsuzskie tetradi* (1958; French notebooks). During this period, **Andrei Siniavskii** (1925–97), writing in Russia under the pseudonym Abram Tertz, published his critical essay "Chto takoe sotsialisticheskii realizm" (1959; *On Socialist Realism*), which, although published abroad, was a brilliant critique of the Soviet policy of engendering literature "by dictate." In many senses, the Thaw period was a time for revelations of the horrors of the past, a period of literary education rather than a rebirth for Russian letters.

In the "Third Wave" of emigration from Russia (1970–80s), the essay form was dominated by émigré novelists who contributed to the journals appearing in the West and in Israel: Aleksandr Zinov'ev (1922–), Vasilii Aksenov (1932–), Vladimir Voinovich (1932–), and Iuz Alezhkovskii (1929–). The exception to this rule was the poet **Joseph Brodsky** (1940–96), who published two excellent collections of essays in English, *Less than One* (1986) and most recently *On Grief and Reason* (1995). Brodsky's command of English and insights into the essay form display a mastery rarely encountered.

The 1980s ushered in the era of *glasnost*, political reform from above and new "openness" in the arts. The essay form found practitioners in new or newfangled reformist journals, *Argumenty i Faktii* (Arguments and facts), *Ogonek* (Little flame), and *Znamia* (The banner), among others. Among the popular essayists during the period, Lev Anninskii (1934–), Natal'ia Ivanova, Dmitrii Likhachev (1906–) – the doyen of Russian scholarship – and Viktor Erofeev were perfect barometers for the mood of the liberal intelligentsia.

In the new postcommunist world the spectrum of intellectual life has broadened considerably, and the essay form is finding ever greater use among religious thinkers, academic philosophers, literary critics, muck-raking journalists, economists, and culture-watchers of all types. While it is difficult to make predictions about the pathways of literary life, signs from the past indicate that the critical, philosophical, and political essays are alive and kicking in all directions in present-day Russia.

BRIAN HOROWITZ

Further Reading

Brown, William Edward, *A History of 18th Century Russian Literature*, Ann Arbor, Michigan: Ardis, 1980

Segel, Harold B., *The Literature of 18th-Century Russia*, New York: Dutton, 2 vols., 1967

Todd, William Mills III, *The Familiar Letter as a Literary Genre in the Age of Pushkin*, Princeton, New Jersey: Princeton University Press, 1976

S

Sabato, Ernesto

Argentine, 1911–

Ernesto Sabato is one of the most important thinkers and essayists of Latin America. His works deal mainly with life's contradictions, where the dichotomy between flesh and spirit is presented as the central source of man's existential problem. Sabato's academic background is in mathematics and physics. In 1938 he was working at the Curie Laboratory in Paris when the first experiments with nuclear energy were conducted. This experience precipitated a personal crisis, which made him eventually abandon science and devote his life to literature. Foreseeing the horrible and destructive future of nuclear energy, Sabato became one of the main critics of science and scientific knowledge, defending the power of intuitive knowledge as humanity's main source of understanding. His three novels and several books of essays are primarily a development of this idea. As an essayist Sabato has developed his own style of short, highly ironic and concise commentaries, dealing with one problem at a time, but organized in a collection through which a common problem or theme runs.

His first collection of essays was *Uno y el universo* (1945; One and the universe), a series of short essays on different topics ranging from the "astronomic lens" to "truth and beauty." This book is composed of 75 sections that as a whole investigate different aspects of the relationship between humankind and the world. In this book Sabato presents his position *vis-à-vis* science and the course of technological advances, which, as he sees it, are taking us down the road to automatization and destruction. *Uno y el universo* was his first contribution to the literary world, and like most of his subsequent publications was polemical and controversial.

Hombres y engranajes (1951; Men and gears) was his second book of essays, written three years after the publication of *El túnel* (1948; *The Tunnel*), the novel that made him a famous writer in Latin America. The four parts of the book analyze the development of the human spirit since the Renaissance, outlining the changes that took place in man's view of the world, and how these changes have affected our perception and our hopes. In the second part, "El universo abstracto" (The abstract universe), Sabato discusses the role of abstract reasoning in the current crisis, and how reason has become the new god, the omnipotent force able to control and explain all human reactions. In the end, reason fails us as a way of understanding our role in life, and humans rebel in response.

Rebellion is the topic of the third part of the book, where Sabato writes about the Romantic revolution, Marxism, and existentialism, the three most important "revolts of human intellectual history," as he calls them. The fourth and final section deals with the role of the arts and letters in the crisis. Literature is for Sabato the only road to the secrets of life, the only sincere and direct access to our most intimate fears and deepest secrets. Art and literature are therefore the only way we can face ourselves and surpass the crisis of the modern world.

Two years later Sabato published *Heterodoxia* (1953; Heterodoxy), a collection of philosophical comments on gender and sexuality, the writer and the artist, the human condition and the irrational mind. The polemical nature of the book aroused many favorable opinions but also evoked critical reactions, including a reply by **Victoria Ocampo** that led to the end of their friendship and of Sabato's collaboration with *Sur* (South), the most important literary journal of Argentina.

El escritor y sus fantasmas (1963; The writer and his phantoms) is perhaps his most important book of essays. In this volume Sabato presents his concept of art as "the only means to reintegrate man's divided self" and the novel as "the comprehensive genre able to articulate reason and intuition." The book attempts to answer the question of why, how, and for what purpose fictions are written, and serves as a spiritual guide for aspiring authors. Literature is for Sabato an exploration of the unconscious. While the essay is a rational contemplation of the world, it is the novel, with all its ambiguities and contradictions, which is the genre that can best express human essence and true nature. Only behind the masks of fiction can writers say what they really think about the things that truly matter to them.

Among Sabato's other publications should be mentioned *Tres aproximaciones a la literatura de nuestro tiempo* (1968; Three approaches to the literature of our times). The three essays included in this book address three different concepts of literature, as exemplified by Alain Robbe-Grillet, **Jorge Luis Borges**, and **Jean-Paul Sartre**. From the pure objectivism of the *nouveau roman*, to the intellectual games of Borges, to the politically *engagé* literature of Sartre, Sabato dissects each of these positions with his characteristic irony and wit, outlining their values as well as their pitfalls. At times Sabato's constant criticism might seem unreasonable, but a careful reading of his works shows that he is always looking for the existential experience behind the abstraction, always interested in how art and science, knowledge and intuition, affect human lives.

That is the center of his analysis, the main idea he has been working with for 50 years throughout his novels and essays.

NICASIO URBINA

Biography

Author has chosen not to use an accent on his surname. Born 24 June 1911 in Rojas, Argentina. Studied at the Colegio Nacional, 1924–28; National University of La Plata, 1929–37, Ph.D. in physics, 1937; Joliot-Curie Laboratory, Paris, 1938; Massachusetts Institute of Technology, Cambridge, 1939. Married Matilde Kuminsky-Richter, 1934: two sons. Professor of theoretical physics, National University of La Plata, 1940–45: dismissed because of conflict with the government. Executive post with UNESCO, 1947 (resigned after two months). Editor, *Mundo Argentino* (Argentine world), from 1955. Director of cultural relations, Ministry of Foreign Relations and Culture, 1958–59 (resigned). Chair, National Commission on the Disappearance of Persons, 1984. Awards: several, including Buenos Aires Municipal Prize, for essay collection, 1945; Argentine Writers' Society Sash of Honor, 1945, and Grand Prize, 1974; Institute of Foreign Relations Prize (West Germany), 1973; Consagració Nacional Prize, 1974; Prix du Meilleur Livre Étranger (France), 1977; Gran Cruz al Mérito Civil (Spain), 1979; Gabriela Mistral Prize, 1984; Cervantes Prize, 1985; Jerusalem Prize, 1989. Chevalier, Order of the Arts and Letters (France), 1964; Chevalier, 1979, and Commander, 1987, Legion of Honor (France).

Selected Writings

Essays and Related Prose

Uno y el universo, 1945
Hombres y engranajes: Reflexiones sobre el dinero, la razón y el derrumbe de nuestro tiempo, 1951
Heterodoxia, 1953
El otro rostro del peronismo: Carta abierta a Mario Amadeo, 1956
El caso Sábato: Torturas y libertad de prensa – Carta abierta al Gral. Aramburu, 1956
Tango: Discusión y clave, 1963
El escritor y sus fantasmas, 1963
Tres aproximaciones a la literatura de nuestro tiempo: Robbe-Grillet, Borges, Sartre, 1968
Itinerio, 1969
La convulsión política y social de nuestro tiempo, 1969
Obras: Ensayos, 1970
Claves políticos, 1971
La cultura en la encrucijada nacional, 1973
Apologías y rechazos, 1979
La robotización del hombre y otras páginas de ficción y reflexión, 1981
Nunca más: Informe de la Comision Nacional sobre la Desaparicion de Persona, 1985
The Writer in the Catastrophe of Our Time, translated by Asa Zatz, 1990

Other writings: three novels (*El túnel* [*The Tunnel*], 1948; *Sobre héroes y tumbas* [*On Heroes and Tombs*], 1961; *Abaddón, el exterminador* [*The Angel of Darkness*], 1974).

Bibliographies

Urbina, Nicasio, "Bibliografía crítica completa de Ernesto Sabato, con un índice temático," *Revista de Critica Literaria Latinoamericana* 14, no. 27 (1988): 117–222; also in *Pre-Texto* 19: 1–84
Urbina, Nicasio, "Bibliografia crítica comentada sobre Ernesto Sabato con un indice temático," *Hispania* 73 (1990): 953–77

Further Reading

Benedetti, Mario, "Ernesto Sabato como crítico practicante," in his *Letras del continente mestizo*, Montevideo: Arca, 1967: 47–50
Brushwood, J. C., "Ernesto Sabato: *Hombres y engranajes*," *Books Abroad* 26, no. 3 (1952): 281–82
Catania, Carlos, *Sabato: Entre la idea y la sangre*, San José: Editorial Costa Rica, 1973
Correa, Maria Angelica, *Genio y figura de Ernesto Sabato*, Buenos Aires: University of Buenos Aires, 1971
Dellepiane, Ángela B., "Dialogo con Ernesto Sabato," *El Escarabajo Deoro* 5 (1962): 4–6, 20
Dellepiane, Ángela B., "Sabato y el ensayo hispanoamericano," *Asomante* 22, no. 1 (1966): 47–59
Dellepiane, Ángela B., *Ernesto Sabato: El hombre y su obra*, New York: Las Américas, 1968
Fernandez Suarez, Alvaro, "Ernesto Sabato: *Heterodoxia*," *Sur* 204 (1951): 129–32
Fernandez Suarez, Alvaro, "Ernesto Sabato: *Hombres y engranajes*," *Sur* 204 (1951): 71–74
Giacoman, Helmy F., editor, *Los personajes de Sabato*, Buenos Aires: Emece, 1972
Giacoman, Helmy F., editor, *Homenaje a Ernesto Sabato*, New York: Las Américas, 1973
Oberhelman, Harley Dean, *Ernesto Sábato*, New York: Twayne, 1970: especially Chapter 2, "Sabato the Essayist"
Ocampo, Victoria, "Carta a Ernesto Sabato," *Sur* 211–12 (1952): 166–69
Ocampo, Victoria, "Correspondencia sobre 'La metafisica del sexo'," *Sur* 213–14 (1952): 161–64
Petrea, Mariana D., *Ernesto Sabato: La nada y la metafísica de la esperanza*, Madrid: Porrúa Turanzas, 1986
Urbina, Nicasio, "La lectura en la obra de Ernesto Sabato," *Revista Iberoamericana* 53, no. 141 (1987): 823–36
Urbina, Nicasio, *La significacion del genero: Estudio semiotico de las novelas y ensayos de Ernesto Sabato*, Miami: Universal, 1992
Vázquez Bigi, A. M., editor, *Epica dadora de eternidad: Sabato en la crítica americana y europea*, Buenos Aires: Sudamericana/Planeta, 1985

Sacks, Oliver

British, 1933–

Oliver Sacks is a physician gifted in seeing the concrete, individual plights of patients and exploring his insights in **medical essays** that lead the reader to perceive the marvelous in the mundane, the beautiful in the twisted and suffering, the meaning in the individual rather than a disease possessing an individual. He is best known for his 1985 collection of essays entitled *The Man Who Mistook His Wife for a Hat, and Other Clinical Tales* and for his 1973 book *Awakenings*, based on his work with post-encephalitic patients; this volume led to a British documentary and subsequently became the basis for an American film starring Robin Williams and Robert De Niro.

Sacks' first book, *Migraine* (1970), foreshadows his sensitivity to patients. A scholarly study accessible to the educated public, the book explores case histories that reveal Sacks' concern for the individual. He sees migraine as an event that is not just physical, but "emotional and symbolic" as well. He also carefully traces records of the illness and describes cases from history, such as the visions of the medieval mystic Hildegard of Bingen, whose drawings he reproduces to complement the text.

In *Awakenings*, Sacks' "clinical tale" comes of age as he characterizes Parkinsonism and describes the pandemic of "sleeping-sickness" of 1916–17 that left thousands of patients in a Parkinsonian state of suspended animation often lasting many years. Sacks' work in the late 1960s, administering the drug L-dopa to patients whose consciousness had often remained suspended since their youth, led to stunning "awakenings." Some remained trapped in an earlier time, unable to realize that 40 years had passed. The patients' responses varied, with some able to adapt and find new lives, while others regretted being brought into a strange new world, and some tragically relapsed. What sets Sacks apart as an essayist is his sensitivity to the human plight of these individuals, quoting the patients' observations and sympathetically describing them.

Sacks' central essay in *Awakenings*, "Perspectives," exemplifies his wide reading not only in medical texts but in literature and philosophy, all of which he weaves into his commentary on the L-dopa experiment. Contending that we can fight our own maladies by inner strength, Sacks turns to everyday language, to what he calls "metaphysical" terms we use for things that are not measurable. In explaining the resources this language provides, Sacks eloquently explores the effects of metaphors on modern medicine and its patients; he notes the destructive effects of the mechanistic world view – traceable to Newton, Locke, and Descartes – that has reduced human beings to mechanisms and systems that can be measured with a misled notion of objectivity. In place of the reductionist approach of modern medicine, Sacks extols a language that includes both the individual patient and a larger view of nature, both the particular and the general. Fragmenting human beings in order to explain, measure, and cure is, for Sacks, a form of blindness in modern medicine.

Sacks' widely read *The Man Who Mistook His Wife for a Hat* describes unique patients with unexpected neurological deficits, such as that of the title character, a music professor for whom faces had become puzzles and the world a muddle of abstractions. While he retained his musical abilities, his perceptual abilities waned so that once, searching for his hat, he placed his hand on his wife's head as if to pick it up. In his **preface**, Sacks laments the decline of the clinical tale since the 19th century, comparing such tales to classical fables, for both have heroes, battles, martyrs, and archetypes. He suggests that we need to look for new symbols and myths, such as are richly represented in narratives of the sick. Here he describes himself as both "a naturalist and a physician," "a theorist and dramatist" who is intrigued not only by science by also by the "romantic." Sympathetic observation and dramatization characterize Sacks' approach to the essay, just as his wide readings in literature and in neurology characterize his style.

A Leg to Stand On (1984) is Sacks' account of his own experience as a patient. He describes his encounters with aloof members of the medical community who refuse to accept his damaged proprioceptive sense after a fall. For Sacks, a broken leg simply ceased to be there; his existential horror is juxtaposed to his physicians' impatience with something that cannot be "measured." Sacks details his own turn toward a new philosophical and medical position, requiring an archetypal journey/narrative, a reading of an old volume on neurosurgery on a train ride, and an avowed determination to embrace "the ideal of a humane medicine," a "heretical" science.

In *Seeing Voices* (1989) Sacks explores the world of the deaf, which he treats as a "culture" to avoid terms of "dysfunction" or "disease." Approaching this marginalized culture, Sacks reveals not only the neurological potential among deaf people, but the equally exciting latent potential for all human beings. As he explores the visual potential of American Sign Language, Sacks investigates the possibilities for the hearing culture to expand both left-brain and right-brain capabilities through Sign. In Sign's linguistic use of space Sacks finds a challenging extra dimension.

Finally, in *An Anthropologist on Mars* (1995), Sacks pursues not only clinical tales, but personal follow-ups that give insight into the individuals he describes, all of whom have experienced some inexplicable neurological condition: Tourette's syndrome – in which the individual compulsively touches him/herself, others, or objects, and often swears unexpectedly, but can function calmly while singing, flying a plane, or performing surgery – and autism – in which the individual may be isolated from other human beings but may have a remarkable talent, as for instance a young man who can draw in minute detail buildings he saw days or even years ago.

In all his texts, Sacks' focus is on how the anomaly affects the individual. His interest is more than clinical: it extends to the patient's potential and relationship with the larger world, and what we can learn about ourselves from those whose neurological experiences are outside the norm. In these penetrating explorations of alternative worlds, Sacks demonstrates a concern for empathy, the role of language, and the role of the individual in the greater whole.

MARY ELLEN PITTS

Biography

Oliver Wolf Sacks. Born 9 July 1933 in London. Studied at St. Paul's School, London; Queen's College, Oxford, B.A., 1954; Middlesex Hospital, London, M.A., B.M., B.Ch., 1958. Intern in medicine, surgery, and neurology, Middlesex Hospital, 1958–60; moved to the United States, 1960; rotating intern, Mt. Zion Hospital, San Francisco, 1961–62; resident in neurology, University of California, Los Angeles, 1962–65. Fellow in neuropathology and neurochemistry, 1965–66, instructor in neurology, 1966–75, assistant professor, 1975–78, associate professor, 1978–85, and clinical professor of neurology, from 1985, Albert Einstein College of Medicine, Bronx, New York; consultant neurologist, Bronx State Hospital, from 1966, and at the Little Sisters of the Poor, New York. Fellow, American Academy of Neurology. Awards: Hawthornden Prize, for *Awakenings*, 1974; Felix Mart-Albanez Award, 1987; American Psychiatric Association Oskar Pfister Award, 1988; Guggenheim Fellowship, 1989; Harold D. Vursell Memorial Award, 1989; Odd Fellows Award, 1990; University of Southern California Scriptor Award, 1991; honorary degrees from four universities.

Selected Writings

Essays and Related Prose

Awakenings, 1973; revised editions, 1976, 1982, 1991
The Man Who Mistook His Wife for a Hat, and Other Clinical Tales, 1985
An Anthropologist on Mars: Seven Paradoxical Tales, 1995

Other writings: a book on migraines (1970), *A Leg to Stand On* (1984), a memoir about being a patient, and *Seeing Voices: A Journey into the World of the Deaf* (1989).

Further Reading

Comprone, Joseph, "Reading Oliver Sacks in a Writing-Across-the-Curriculum Course," *Journal of Advanced Composition* 8, nos. 1–2 (1988): 158–66

Hawkins, Anne Hunsaker, "Oliver Sacks' *Awakenings*: Reshaping Clinical Discourse," *Configurations* 1, no. 2 (1993): 229–45

Hawkins, Anne Hunsaker, "The Myth of Cure and the Process of Accommodation: Reconsidering *Awakenings*," *Medical Humanities Review* (Spring 1994): 9–21

Kusnetz, Ella, "The Soul of Oliver Sacks," *Massachusetts Review* 33, no. 2 (1992): 175–98

McRae, Murdo William, "Oliver Sacks' Neurology of Identity," in *The Literature of Science: Perspectives on Popular Scientific Writing*, edited by Murdo William McRae, Athens: University of Georgia Press, 1993: 97–110

Pitts, Mary Ellen, "Reflective Scientists and the Critique of Mechanistic Metaphor," in *The Literature of Science: Perspectives on Popular Scientific Writing*, edited by Murdo William McRae, Athens: University of Georgia Press, 1993: 249–90

Pitts, Mary Ellen, "Toward a Dialectic of the Open End: The Scientist as Writer and the Revolution Against Measurement," *Centennial Review* 38, no. 1 (1994): 179–204

Sainte-Beuve, Charles-Augustin

French, 1804–1869

Sainte-Beuve's earliest essays appeared from 1824 to 1835 in several Parisian periodicals: the newspapers *Le Globe* and *Le National*, and the reviews *Revue de Paris* (Paris review) and *Revue des Deux Mondes* (Review of two worlds). They were published in book form posthumously in 1874–75 and given the title *Premiers lundis* by his editor to associate them with what in the meantime had become his most famous essay collections, the *Causeries du lundi* (1851–62; *Monday Chats*) and *Nouveaux lundis* (1863–70; New Mondays). As a former medical student, trying to earn his living as a journalist-critic, Sainte-Beuve found that his true ambition was to become a great poet and perhaps a great novelist as well. It was clear from these first pieces, which he called "my gropings and beginnings," that he sought to use the books given him to review, which covered a great variety of subject matter, as the pretext for his own thought and – even more unusual – for his own artistic expression. His aim was to bring his subjects to life, as vividly as possible, to "paint" or "depict" them (the verb *peindre* recurs frequently), emulating not other critics so much as the novelists he admired, such as Sir Walter Scott and James Fenimore Cooper. Something highly original was stirring here: no critic had ever spoken of his ambition "to depict mankind in all its variety of passions and circumstances," like Shakespeare, Molière, or Scott, allowing himself, like them, "to be transformed into an infinite number of characters" ("Mort de Walter Scott" [1832; Death of Walter Scott]).

Between 1829 and 1846 Sainte-Beuve pursued two parallel, overlapping, and interdependent vocations: that of the critic and that of the poet/novelist. During these remarkably productive years he published his first and most famous verse volume (in reality a mixture of prose and verse), *Vie, poésies et pensées de Joseph Delorme* (1829; Life, poetry, and thoughts of Joseph Delorme), followed by three more books of verse; his only completed novel, *Volupté* (1834); and three series of critical essays, *Portraits littéraires* (1844; Literary portraits), *Portraits*

de femmes (1844; *Portraits of Celebrated Women*), and *Portraits contemporains* (1846; Contemporary portraits), in the *Revue de Paris* and the *Revue des Deux Mondes*. That he eventually abandoned poetry and fiction in favor of criticism was due less to his lack of success in these genres (he in fact enjoyed a modest success) than to his greater success as a critic and to his awareness (he was his own best critic) that he would never achieve the greatness he aspired to as poet and novelist. However, he made up for this loss by applying his imaginative gifts to his critical essays, in which erudition became imbued with poetic feeling, as several of his more astute contemporaries, including Victor Hugo, recognized.

The *Portraits* embrace a rich variety of primarily literary topics: authors both major and minor, professional writers as well as marginal ones who left nothing more than memoirs or letters. Literary criticism is broadened to include the study of human behavior traditionally associated in France with "le moraliste" (the student of *mores*, of *mœurs*). Literary opinions, Sainte-Beuve wrote to a friend, mattered much less to him than reflections on "life itself, its purpose, the mystery of our own heart, the nature of happiness and holiness." In the *Portraits of Celebrated Women* he states: "Literary criticism is never anything more for the mind of moralist bent than a point of departure, an opportunity."

His method in these essays is primarily biographical and combines both the objective, impartial, sometimes clinical approach that he called "physiology" (assimilated perhaps from his medical studies) with poetic expression ("hidden poetry" is his term) of a somewhat elegiac nature. The fictionist's art is also sometimes put to use, as when he calls the essay on Madame de Charrière one of his "little short stories with a single character." In the second of his essays on **Diderot** (*Portraits littéraires*) he describes the process of re-creating his character-models and how it should ideally culminate in the magic moment when "analysis disappears into the act of creation, the portrait speaks and lives, one has found the man" (almost as often it is "the woman"). In overall form there is little resemblance in these pieces, or in other essays of the author, to the artful disorder or studied randomness of **Montaigne**, **Marivaux**, or the English essayists, for these qualities were alien to his basically neoclassical taste and sense of order. Nor did the intimate first-person style of the "**personal**" or "**familiar**" essay appeal to him. For his self-revelations one must turn to his poetry or to *Volupté*, or to his superb intimate **journals**, the *Cahiers* (wr. 1834–47, pub. 1973), selections of which have appeared under the titles *Pensées et maximes* (1955) and *Mes Poisons* (1926), admired and emulated by **Cyril Connolly** in his *The Unquiet Grave* (1945). In the *Portraits*, as in his other essays, self-revelations are very subtly and indirectly presented. The style tends to be involved syntactically, is sometimes labored or clumsy, and is heavily laden with metaphors and other images; but at its best it is highly readable; the use of spatial images (topographical, landscape) in the analysis of his subjects is an original, striking feature.

Had Sainte-Beuve published only the *Portraits* his stature as an essayist of the first rank would be secure. However, in 1849, at age 45, he renewed himself in extraordinary fashion by launching a series of articles appearing each Monday in various journals and reviews, first in *Le Constitutionnel* (The constitutional) and then in *Le Moniteur* (The monitor), *Le Temps* (The times), and the *Revue des Deux Mondes*. They were interrupted only by his death in 1869. These *Causeries du lundi* and *Nouveaux lundis* (their titles in book form) consist of no less than 28 volumes containing roughly 600 separate titles and almost 400 different topics. Based for the most part on publications the critic was given to review, the majority concern French literature and history, especially contemporary works and those of the two preceding centuries. Others deal with Greco-Roman antiquity and English, German, Italian, and Spanish authors. Writers great and small are found beside royalty, aristocrats, magistrates, diplomats, statesmen, soldiers, women of polite society (*femmes du salon*), saints, and scientists, to name but a few, providing only that these "non-professional" writers left something worth reading. Women continue to figure prominently. The thematic range is also extraordinarily wide: purely literary or aesthetic questions form merely part of a vast inquiry into the nature of the writer (**Thibaudet** [1936] calls this Sainte-Beuve's "Comédie littéraire") and into the broader human drama of the "Comédie humaine." Not unlike his arch-enemy and rival, Balzac, he carried whole societies in his head.

Several new elements not characteristic of the *Portraits* are introduced into the *Lundis*. The style, as promised in the title *Causeries*, is more "oral," more "conversational," less laden with imagery, sharper and wittier than in the *Portraits* (in his **preface** the essayist describes it as "more concise and more unencumbered"). This "spoken" manner Jean Bonnerot (in *Bibliographie de l'œuvre de Sainte-Beuve*, vol. 3) attributes to the fact that the critic dictated many of these pieces to his secretary or "talked them out" before giving them a final form. Another new feature is the more authoritative tone, as the essayist, citing the examples of Nicolas Boileau, **Samuel Johnson**, and Jean-François de La Harpe, asserts his right to be a judge and an arbiter of taste, especially in regard to contemporary works. Finally, the *critique-peintre* and *critique-moraliste* are now enriched by the addition of the *critique-naturaliste*, a "naturalist of minds" whose aim is to found "the natural history of literature," the classification of writers according to species, the "science of minds." The assimilation of literary criticism to a science, however, takes place within distinct limits determined by the ultimately elusive and mysterious nature of creative genius. Criticism itself continues to be viewed by Sainte-Beuve as a form of creation (see "Diderot," *Causeries*, vol. 3) in which the critic, paradoxically, "disappears" into his subjects, taking on their nature ("metamorphosis" is the term Sainte-Beuve uses), while at the same time sketching his own "profile" (his "apotheosis").

Sainte-Beuve's greatness as an essayist lies in his raising the periodical article, in the form of the **critical essay**, to a new level of creative power rivaling (as his admirer **Matthew Arnold** understood) all but the greatest of poets or novelists. The "Tenth Muse," Thibaudet calls it. Among readers whom he influenced are such other essayists as **Ernest Renan, Henry James**, George Saintsbury, and **Edmund Wilson**. Sainte-Beuve had few models on which to draw: chiefly **Plutarch**'s *Lives*, **Johnson**'s *Lives of the Poets* (1779–81; known most probably by reputation), **Fontenelle**'s biographical sketches or *éloges*, and Diderot's art criticism. He devoted several fine essays to Montaigne, whom he acknowledged as one of his "masters,"

but eschewed Montaigne's type of self-portraiture and his capricious form. His collected essays, as remarkable for their sustained level of quality and readability as for their quantity, represent one of the most extraordinary feats in the history of journalism. Although they may be dipped into anywhere and read independently of one another, their author recommended that they best be read in the order of their appearance, so as to grasp the evolution of his thought and his revisions of opinion.

RICHARD M. CHADBOURNE

Biography

Born 23 December 1804 in Boulogne-sur-Mer. Studied at the Institut Landry and the Collège Charlemagne, Paris, 1818–21; Collège Bourbon (now the Lycée Condorcet), Paris, 1821–23, baccalauréat in letters, 1823; studied medicine in Paris, from 1823, baccalauréat in science, 1824. Contributor to many journals, from 1824, including *Le Globe, Revue de Paris*, and *Revue des Deux Mondes*. Close friends with Victor Hugo, 1827–34, and had an intermittent affair with Hugo's wife Adèle, 1832–36. Lectured in Lausanne, 1837–38, Liège, 1848, Collège de France, Paris, 1854–55, and the École Normale Supérieure, Paris, 1857–61. Appointed *conservateur*, Bibliothèque Mazarine, Paris, 1840–48. Elected to the French Academy, 1844. Columnist of "Les Lundis," appearing in various periodicals, 1849–69. Made member of the Senate, 1865. Health deteriorated after an operation to ease an obstruction of the bladder, 1869. Died in Paris, 13 October 1869.

Selected Writings

Essays and Related Prose

Critiques et portraits littéraires, 1832; enlarged edition, 5 vols., 1836–39
Portraits de femmes, 1844; as *Portraits of Celebrated Women*, translated by Harriet W. Preston, 1868; in *Essays on Men and Women*, edited by William Sharp, translated by William Matthews and Harriet W. Preston, 1890
Portraits littéraires, 2 vols., 1844; edited by Gérald Antoine, 1993
Portraits contemporains, 2 vols., 1846; enlarged editions, 3 vols., 1855, and 5 vols., 1869–71
Causeries du lundi, 15 vols., 1851–62; revised edition, 15 vols., 1857–62; enlarged edition, 16 vols., 1882–85; as *Causeries du lundi*, translated by E. J. Trechmann, 8 vols., 1909–11; selection as *English Portraits*, translated anonymously, 1875; selection as *Monday Chats*, edited and translated by William Matthews, 1877; selections edited by George Saintsbury, 1885
Derniers portraits littéraires, 1852
Nouveaux lundis, 13 vols., 1863–70
Essays (selection), translated by Elizabeth Lee, 1869(?)
Premiers lundis, 3 vols., 1874–75
Chroniques parisiennes (1843–1845), 1876
Select Essays, translated by A. J. Butler, 1890
Essays on Men and Women, edited by William Sharp, translated by William Matthews and Harriet W. Preston, 1890
Portraits of Men, translated by Forsyth Edeveain, 1891
Portraits of the Eighteenth [Seventeenth] Century, Historic and Literary, translated by Katharine Wormeley and George Burnham Ives, 4 vols., 1904–05
Œuvres, edited by Maxime Leroy, 2 vols., 1951–56
Selected Essays, edited and translated by Francis Steegmuller and Norbert Guterman, 1963
Literary Criticism, edited and translated by Emerson R. Marks, 1971

Other writings: poetry, the novel *Volupté* (1834), a five-volume history of Port-Royal (1840–59), correspondence, and journals.

Bibliographies

Bonnerot, Jean, *Bibliographie de l'œuvre de Sainte-Beuve*, Paris: Giraud-Badin, 4 vols., 1937–52

Bonnerot, Jean, *Un demi-siècle d'études sur Sainte-Beuve, 1904–1954*, Paris: Les Belles Lettres, 1957

Phillips, E. M., "The Present State of Sainte-Beuve Studies," *French Studies* 5 (1951): 101–25

Regard, Maurice, "Esquisse d'un état présent des études sur Sainte-Beuve," *Information Littéraire* 11 (1959): 139–48

Further Reading

Arnold, Matthew, "Sainte-Beuve," in his *Complete Prose Works*, vol. 5, edited by R. H. Super, Ann Arbor: University of Michigan Press, 1965 (article originally published 1869)

Babbitt, Irving, "Sainte-Beuve," in his *The Masters of Modern French Criticism*, New York: Farrar Straus, 1963

Billy, André, *Sainte-Beuve, sa vie et son temps*, Paris: Flammarion, 2 vols., 1952

Bradford, Gamaliel, *A Naturalist of Souls: Studies in Psychography*, New York: Dodd Mead, 1917

Chadbourne, Richard, "Symbolic Landscapes in Sainte-Beuve's Early Criticism," *PMLA* 80 (1965): 217–30

Chadbourne, Richard, "La Comédie humaine de Sainte-Beuve," *Études Françaises* 9 (1973): 15–26

Chadbourne, Richard, "Criticism as Creation in Sainte-Beuve," *L'Esprit Créateur* 14 (1974): 44–54

Chadbourne, Richard, *Charles-Augustin Sainte-Beuve*, Boston: Twayne, 1977

Chadbourne, Richard, "Sainte-Beuve and Samuel Johnson," *Transactions of the Samuel Johnson Society of the Northwest* 9 (1980): 1–14

James, Henry, "Sainte-Beuve's Portraits," "Sainte-Beuve's First Articles," and "Sainte-Beuve's English Portraits," in his *Literary Reviews and Essays*, edited by Albert Mordell, New York: Grove Press, 1957 (articles originally published 1868, 1875, 1875)

Lehmann, A. G., *Sainte-Beuve: A Portrait of the Critic, 1804–1842*, Oxford: Clarendon Press, 1962

MacClintock, Lander, *Sainte-Beuve's Critical Theory and Practice After 1849*, Chicago: University of Chicago Press, 1920

Molho, Raphaël, *L'Ordre et les ténèbres, ou La Naissance d'un mythe du XVIIe siècle chez Sainte-Beuve*, Paris: Colin, 1972

Mott, Lewis, *Sainte-Beuve*, New York: Appleton, 1925

Regard, Maurice, *Sainte-Beuve, l'homme et l'œuvre*, Paris: Hatier, 1960

Richard, Jean-Pierre, "Sainte-Beuve et l'objet littéraire," in his *Études sur le romantisme*, Paris: Seuil, 1970

Thibaudet, Albert, "Sainte-Beuve," in his *Histoire de la littérature française de 1789 à nos jours*, Paris: Stock, 1936

Saint-Évremond

French, 1614–1703

Saint-Évremond displayed in both his life and his essays the studied negligence of an unpedantic scholar. He was an Epicurean and a skeptic, and serves as a transitional figure between the libertine circles of free thought in the 17th century, and the philosophical writers of the Enlightenment, who saw in him one of their precursors.

In his privileged youth as a Norman noble, he entered into contact with Gassendi, the famous libertine thinker, who was one of his preceptors and who influenced his thought profoundly. Throughout his life Saint-Évremond cultivated the company of the great minds of his age, including Heinsius, Spinoza, and Vossius, especially during his long exile in London. During this time he maintained a lively correspondence with major thinkers and writers throughout Europe, which provided him an international forum and cosmopolitan outlook on the issues of his time.

Saint-Évremond's consciously cultivated, negligent style is apparent in both the form his writings took, that of **letter**s and essays, and the fact that he did not publish any of his non-theatrical works, although friends and associates oversaw the printing of several editions of various pieces during his lifetime. He was not systematic in his thought or his approach to various subjects, but was guided by the occasion of the writing of a letter or observation, and by the course of his own reflections. In many ways he represents a 17th-century **Montaigne**, who served as a primary source of influence and whose essays Saint-Évremond enjoyed and often read. He can be considered a moralist, in that he often meditated in his texts on aspects of human conduct and analyzed emotional states. He created prose portraits, sometimes of real figures, sometimes imaginary, which often illustrate a point of morality, although he remained a detached observer rather than an ardent preacher.

His highly developed wit and refinement characterize him as a fine example of polite French society in the second half of the 17th century. His "Conversation du maréchal d'Hocquincourt avec le Père Canaye" (wr. 1654, pub. 1687; Conversation between the Maréchal d'Hocquincourt and Father Canaye) continues many of the themes and critical attacks found in Pascal's *Lettres provinciales* (1657; *The Provincial Letters*). Saint-Évremond revealed his mistrust of religious dogma and intolerant rigidity in theological issues. He saw in the dispute between Jesuits and Jansenists a power struggle more than a religious conflict, and found fault with both sides. Although highly skeptical in matters of religion, especially in terms of doctrine and institution, Saint-Évremond did display a genuine admiration for Christianity and discreet morality in certain aspects of his life and works.

Rather than lamenting the uncertainty and misery of humankind's condition, Saint-Évremond chose a life of diversion, according to the dictates of an aristocratic *honnêteté* and the principles of good taste. He cultivated the social virtues of good deeds, charity, and friendship, placing importance on individual acts of this world, rather than an ascetic rejection of society. Although acknowledging that it is nearly impossible to know oneself, Saint-Évremond held consistently throughout his writings that humankind is neither entirely good nor entirely evil, and that in order to account for human behavior and morality the coexistence of the noble and the base must be seen as a fundamental aspect of humanity. This view, which stresses the confusion of qualities and constant change in human behavior, is more characteristic of a baroque perspective on reality, and of the historians from classical antiquity, rather than the French classical view of a more static unity having distinct components which was promoted during the second half of the 17th century.

If Saint-Évremond's preference for the earthly pleasures of fine food, good art, and sensual pleasure appears egotistical, it is nonetheless a sincere and overt choice. It has none of the deception and hypocrisy of the contemporaries he observed, who, like Molière's Tartuffe, feigned public indifference to worldly pleasures only to hide privately indulged passions. He saw realistically, perhaps even somewhat cynically, that reputation and virtue are often quite separate, and that few people are truly devout or honorable, despite their claims. Instead, he accepts people for what they are: imperfect, powerless, fickle. A tacit optimism informs much of Saint-Évremond's writing, which insists that life is worth living, and that people basically have merit.

Many of his works contain insights into contemporary matters of literary criticism. In the early 1660s he wrote an essay critical of *Alexandre le Grand* (1665; Alexander the Great), one of Racine's first tragedies. Saint-Évremond believed that Racine incorporated too many modern elements into his depiction of characters and situations taken from antiquity, whereas Corneille, whom he preferred, retained more of a sense of the nations and historical periods represented in his tragedies.

Moral and literary criteria for excellence were closely connected, as is evident in his judgments of contemporary authors. While literature is a major diversion and source of pleasure, it requires a great degree of accuracy in its depiction of human traits and actions. The ideal subject is the civilized person, whose tastes and rationality are explored in a psychological, especially theatrical, approach. He did not care much for poetry. He rejected the novelistic, fantastic aspects of certain texts. Referred to as the Petronius, the Arbiter of Taste, of his time, Saint-Évremond also rejected many of the constraints imposed upon contemporary authors, although he did agree that Christian subjects should not appear on the stage. Whereas in general he admired Corneille's work, he found that *Polyeucte* (1642) would have made a beautiful **sermon**, but was instead a miserable tragedy. His opinions on good taste were shaped by his immense reading from antiquity, as well as by the French *précieux* and writers of the first half of the century and also by English critics, especially Hobbes.

Saint-Évremond was widely read in ancient history, especially Roman, and held firm views on the proper writing and use of history both on the stage and in cultured society. In his "Réflexions sur les divers génies du peuple romain dans les différents temps de la République" (1662; Reflections on diverse characteristics of the Romans during various phases of the Republic) he attempted to discover what really transpired in antiquity, reacting against prevailing credulity and simplistic views. Many of his insights are penetrating, and his portraits of various historical figures still stir the imagination. His call for accuracy in historical writing was unusual for its time, and did not gain wide acceptance or practice until at least a century later. His erudition in matters of Roman history also influenced his political philosophy, which was mainly republican.

Despite his ardent passion for Roman history, he took the position of a Modern in the quarrel of the Ancients and the Moderns. His great admiration for antiquity did not change the fact that he saw in his own times more discontinuity than similarity with the past. He could not understand why contemporary French authors would strive so hard to imitate authors from antiquity, setting them as the standard, when so much had changed, and generally for the better, in the interval.

His views on women are ambiguous, and depend on the context of their expression. These gentle creatures were worthy of serving his own personal pleasure, but regarded in his essays as full of faults. Responsible for much court intrigue, they are vain and weak, and easily persuaded to error. But such comments reveal a general criticism of all human conduct. Women are scarcely inferior to men, who suffer from the same defects. In fact, he is astonished that women are excluded from so many human affairs, since many of them are "wiser and more capable than men" ("Observations sur Salluste et sur Tacite" [1668; Observations on Sallust and Tacitus]). In taking the position that those who wish to bar women from public life are blinded by self-interest and error, Saint-Évremond was certainly stating a minority opinion for his time.

Saint-Évremond wrote for his own pleasure, and considered pleasure an essential element of human existence. He developed the notion of good taste in many of his essays, which discussed the interplay of several contributing factors: delicacy, good sense, and naturalness. His writing is marked by a witty intelligence and conversational informality, rather than a systematic approach to issues or an exposition of profound ideas. It is uniquely personal in its observations, while conveying a representative picture of Saint-Évremond's libertine and *honnête* milieu.

By the urbane tone and unpretentious style of his texts, which contain witty observations and intelligent comments on issues of human conduct, Saint-Évremond, living in exile in London, originated the form of the essay which was to be practiced in 18th-century England. In his essays he was rarely paradoxical in his own views, in spite of the many seemingly contradictory aspects of life he discussed, and never superficial. His apparent nonchalance was a pose, creating an ironic distance between himself and the material of his essays. He discounted the importance of these little texts, which he alluded to frequently as "bagatelles," but their influence was widespread at the time, and for a century later.

ALLEN G. WOOD

Biography
Charles de Marguetel de Saint-Denis, Seigneur de Saint-Évremond. Born 5 January 1614. Studied at the Jesuit Collège de Clermont, Paris, from 1623; University of Caen, 1628; Collège d'Harcourt, Paris, 1628–29. Career in the army: ensign, 1630, lieutenant, 1637, and in the Duc d'Enghien's Guards, 1642, wounded in the knee at Nördlingen, 1645, and made maréchal de camp, 1652. Imprisoned in the Bastille for offending Mazarin, 1653; exiled for satirizing government policy, 1661: lived in Nantes, 1661, London, 1662–65; Holland, 1665–70, and London, 1670–1703; governor of Saint James's Park, 1698. Died in London, 20 September 1703.

Selected Writings

Essays and Related Prose
Œuvres meslées, 1668; revised editions, 2 vols., 1689, 5 vols., 1690–94, 5 vols., 1705, 3 vols., 1709, 5 vols., 1726, and 5 vols., 1739; edited by Charles Giraud, 3 vols., 1865
Miscellaneous Essays, translated by John Dryden and others, 2 vols., 1692–94
The Works, translated anonymously, 2 vols., 1700
Critique littéraire, edited by Maurice Wilmotte, 1921
Œuvres en prose, edited by René Ternois, 4 vols., 1962–69
Lettres, edited by René Ternois, 2 vols., 1967–68
Textes choisis, edited by Alain Niderst, 1970

Other writings: plays (unperformed), poetry, and correspondence.

Collected works editions: Œuvres, 10 vols., 1740; edited by René de Planhol, 3 vols., 1927.

Further Reading

Baker, S. R., "The Rhetoric of Self Presentation in Saint-Évremond," *French Literature Series* 19 (1992): 19–27

Barnwell, Henry T., *Les Idées morales et critiques de Saint-Évremond*, Paris: Presses Universitaires de France, 1957

Bouysse, Patrice, "Essai sur la jeunesse d'un moraliste: Saint-Évremond (1614–1661)," *Papers on French Seventeenth-Century Literature* 14 (1987): 1–346

Hope, Quentin M., *Saint-Évremond, the "Honnête Homme" as a Critic*, Bloomington: Indiana University Press, 1962

Lanniel, J. M., "Un scepticisme nuancé de regret, Saint-Évremond et la dévotion," *Dix-Septième Siècle* 93 (1971): 13–25

Rosmarin, Leonard A., *Saint-Évremond, artiste de l'euphorie*, Birmingham, Alabama: Summa, 1987

Schmidt, Albert-Marie, *Saint-Évremond, ou L'Humanisme impur*, Paris: Cavalier, 1932

Taittinger, Claude, *Saint-Évremond, ou Le Bon Usage des plaisirs*, Paris: Perrin, 1990

Viala, A., "Saint-Évremond ou les regards de l'exilé," in *Horizons européens de la littérature française au XVIIe siècle*, edited by Wolfgang Leiner, Tübingen: Narr, 1988: 345–52

Wolfe, P., "Sincérité et insincérité dans la 'Conversation de M. le maréchal d'Hocquincourt'," *Papers on French Seventeenth-Century Literature* 10, no. 18 (1983): 213–20

Saltykov-Shchedrin

Russian, 1826–1889

Mikhail Evgrafovich Saltykov (pen name "Shchedrin") was a prominent figure in the literary world of Russia from the 1850s to the 1880s. In his widely read satirical writings he maintained a consistent criticism of the political establishment and society of his time. His work was published mainly in the journals *Sovremennik* (The contemporary) and *Otechestvennye Zapiski* (Fatherland notes) – of the latter he was an editor from 1868 to 1884. All that he wrote related to some aspect of contemporary social or political life and was of a radical tendency, in keeping with the tone of the journals to which he contributed. He had an unusually broad experience of Russian conditions, gained partly from his many years' service as a provincial official, and he was an authoritative commentator on officialdom, the state of society of all classes in town and country, and the political attitudes of the government and of the conservative, liberal, and radical intelligentsia. Critical of most things, he promoted no particular ideology or faction: in his works he was simply concerned, he said, with depicting "those features which make Russian life not altogether comfortable."

Saltykov wrote principally in two modes: the discursive essay and the illustrative narrative sketch; both modes were often employed in the same piece. He made use of various other forms – the diary (*Dnevnik provintsiala v Peterburge* [1872; Diary of a provincial in Petersburg]), **letters** (*Pis'ma o provintsii* [1868–70; Letters on the provinces]; *Pis'ma k teten'ke* [1881–82; Letters to Auntie]), the mock historical chronicle (*Istoriia odnogo goroda* [1869–70; *The History of a*

Town]), and fables in prose (*Skazki* [1869–86; *Fables*]), as well as parodic documents and dramatic interludes. In some works he adopts the persona of a character who is the object of his **satire**, and writes in the first person (*Ubezhishche Monrepo* [1878–79; The haven of Mon Repos]; *Sovremennaia idilliia* [1877–83; A contemporary idyll]). His discursive essays are written in the heavyweight manner favored in 19th-century Russian journalism and generally require close reading to follow the laboriously developed argument. In contrast, the narrative sketches, which were his forte, are pointed and lively; here, in particular, his robust humor and pungent irony come to the fore. Saltykov had the gift of encapsulating in a single character or brief narrative episode some fundamental aspect of the conduct or psychology of a social group; this ability is exemplified in his fables, each of a few pages, which together provide a convenient summary of the principal themes which he treats in the score or so of his sketch-cycles.

Saltykov's numerous journal contributions can only loosely be termed "essays." Few of them give a complete, one-off treatment of a topic. His general practice was to develop a subject in a succession of pieces published over a period of months (the journals for which he wrote appeared monthly) or, in some cases, considerably longer. Each item would make a point, explore a facet of a theme; between one piece and the next there might, or might not, be a sequential link. When the cycle was completed, it was published separately under the title designated at the outset. Some cycles are of variegated content and individual items can be read separately, but in others it is necessary for full comprehension to read each part in the context of the whole.

Saltykov used a wide range of styles and had an impressive command of the different registers of the Russian language. In his discursive articles the style is dense and often ponderous, with long periods, complex syntax, and weighty formal vocabulary; he employs the various rhetorical devices commonly found in publicistic writing (e.g. questions to introduce declarative statements, inversions, anaphora). This manner is not infrequently lightened by an overt or underlying irony, and the tone is occasionally broken by some unexpected linguistic incongruity. The narrative sketches are distinguished by the lively variety of the characters' speech modes – Saltykov could reproduce precisely the speech of bureaucrats, gentry, merchants, peasants, lawyers, journalists, priests, men-about-town; he was also an accomplished parodist, as he demonstrates with his imitations of ancient chronicles, official documents, academic dissertations, and the discourses of conservative and liberal publicists. Fantasy and the grotesque play a part in some of his brightest works. As well as the Russian of his day, he makes use of Church Slavonic in biblical phrases, French (particularly as a social marker in his sketches), and school Latin tags.

A feature of Saltykov's writing was his employment of aesopic language. This was necessitated by the stringent censorship that operated in his time. For an "oppositionist" writer, as Saltykov was, it required much ingenuity to convey his views in such a way as to avoid infringing the censorship regulations. This aesopic language involved the use of circumlocution, oblique reference, and a variety of allusive denominators: e.g. *serdtseved* ("sounder of hearts") for a police officer assessing political reliability, or *vnezapnosti* ("suddennesses") for acts of administrative repression. Such terms of reference became conventional in Saltykov's writings and were readily understood by the initiated reader. The relatively subversive content of much that Saltykov wrote, presented in this encoded form, created a kind of conspiratorial bond between the author and his readers which he valued highly. Unfortunately, the tactical obfuscation practiced by him creates for the modern reader a formidable barrier, additional to that presented by most readers' unfamiliarity with the historical context in which he wrote. English translations of Saltykov's works, except for his novel *Gospoda Golovlevy* (1875–80; *The Golovlevs*), are understandably few.

I. P. FOOTE

Biography

Mikhail Evgrafovich Saltykov. Born 27 January 1826 in Spas-Ugol, Tver province. Studied at the Moscow Pension for the Nobility; the Tsarskoe Selo lycée (the Aleksandr Lycée, from 1844), St. Petersburg, graduated 1844. Civil servant, War Ministry, from 1844. Exiled to Viatka for "subversive" writing, 1848–55, though he continued to be employed as a government official. Married Elizaveta Apollonovna Boltina, 1856: one daughter and one son. Worked for the Ministry of the Interior, St. Petersburg, 1856–58; vice-governor, Riazan, 1858–60, and Tver, 1860–62. Left government service to pursue journalism full-time, 1862, publishing mainly in *Sovremennik*, 1862–64. Rejoined government service, 1864, working at Penza, 1865–66, Tula, 1866–67, and Riazan, 1867–68. Coeditor, *Otechestvennye Zapiski*, 1868–84; also contributor to various other journals. Died in St. Petersburg, 10 May 1889.

Selected Writings

Cycles of Sketches and Related Prose

(published in cycles mainly in *Sovremennik* and *Otechestvennye zapiski*)
Gubernskie ocherki, 1856–57; part as *Tchinovnicks*, translated by Frederic Aston, 1861
Satiry v proze (Satires in prose), 1859–62
Priznaki vremeni (Signs of the times), 1863–71
Pompadury i pompadurshi (Pompadours and pompadouresses), 1863–74; as *The Pompadours: A Satire on the Art of Government*, translated by David Magarshack, 1985
Pis'ma o provintsii, 1868–70
Gospoda Tashkenttsy (Gentlemen of Tashkent), 1869–72
Blagonamerennye rechi (Well-intentioned speeches), 1872–76
V srede umerennosti i akkuratnosti (In the world of moderation and precision), 1874–77
Ubezhishche Monrepo, 1878–79
Za rubezhom (In foreign parts), 1880–81
Pis'ma k teten'ke, 1881–82
Pestrye pis'ma (Variegated letters), 1884–86
Selected Satirical Writings (in Russian), edited by I. P. Foote, 1977

Other writings: the novels *Gospoda Golovlevy* (1875–80; *The Golovlevs*), and *Sovremennaia idilliia* (1877–83), the novel/diary *Dnevnik provintsiala v Peterburge* (1872), the mock historical chronicle *Istoriia odnogo goroda* (1869–70; *The History of a Town*), *Skazki* (1869–86; *Fables*), and the fictionalized autobiography *Poshekhonskaya starina* (1887–89; Old times in Poshekhonie).

Collected works edition: *Sobranie sochinenii*, edited by S. A. Makashin and others, 20 vols., 1965–77.

Bibliographies

Baskakov, B. N., *Bibliografiia literatura o M. E. Saltykove-Shchedrine, 1918–1965*, Moscow and Leningrad: Nauka, 1966
Baskakov, B. N., in *Saltykov-Shchedrin, 1826–1876: Stat'i, materialy, bibliografiia*, Leningrad: Nauka, 1976: 391–428
Dobrovol'skii, L. M., *Bibliografiia literatury o M. E. Saltykove-Shchedrine, 1848–1917*, Moscow: Izd-vo Akademii Nauk SSR, 1961
Foote, I. P., "M. E. Saltykov-Shchedrin in English: A Bibliography," *Oxford Slavonic Papers* 22 (1989): 89–114

Further Reading

Blankoff, Jean, *La Société russe de la seconde moitié du XIXe siècle: Trois témoignages littéraires: M. E. Saltykov-Ščedrin, Gleb Uspenskij, A. F. Pisemskij*, Brussels: Éditions de l'Université de Bruxelles, 1972
Draitser, E. A., *Techniques of Satire: The Case of Saltykov-Shchedrin*, Berlin and New York: de Gruyter, 1994
Foote, I. P., "Quintessential Saltykov: *Ubezhishche Monrepo*," *Oxford Slavonic Papers* 12 (1979): 84–103
Sanine, Kyra, *Saltykov-Chtchédrine: Sa vie et ses œuvres*, Paris: Université de Paris Institut d'Études Slaves, 1955
Strelsky, N., *Saltykov and the Russian Squire*, New York: AMS Press, 1966 (original edition, 1940)

Sanders, Scott Russell

American, 1945–

Scott Russell Sanders began his career as a literary critic (publishing a book on **D. H. Lawrence** in 1973) and as a writer of fiction, including science fiction, but since the early 1980s when his essays began appearing regularly in the *North American Review* and especially since the publication of his second book of essays, *The Paradise of Bombs*, which won the Associated Writing Programs Award for Creative Nonfiction when it appeared in 1987, he has focused his attention on the **personal essay**. Between 1987 and 1995 he published three more collections of essays, and his first, *In Limestone Country* (1985), was reissued.

In addition to his many personal essays, Sanders has also written widely on the form of the essay. In his **prefaces** and essays on writing – e.g. "The Singular First Person" (1988), "Speaking a Word for Nature" (1991), "The Writer in the University" (1995), and "Writing from the Center" (1995) – he has turned his skills as a literary critic on himself and his form, gaining, as a result, a reputation as one of America's foremost theoreticians of the essay.

Sanders continues to publish essays in the *North American Review* and other literary quarterlies – e.g. the **Georgia Review**, *Gettysburg Review*, *Kenyon Review*, *Michigan Quarterly Review*, and *Sewanee Review*. He has also published in large circulation magazines such as **Harper's** and appeared twice (1987, 1993) in *The Best American Essays* yearly anthology. He also takes seriously his responsibility, as a teacher and writer, to the academic and writing communities, and has published position pieces in the organs of the Association of Departments of English and the Associated Writing Programs.

If Sanders can be said to have a central topic, it is place. His titles and subtitles regularly testify to this preoccupation. *In Limestone Country* collects 13 pieces on life around the southern Indiana quarries that have produced the stone for many of America's most famous buildings, including the Pentagon and the Empire State Building. *Staying Put: Making a Home in a Restless World* (1993) and *Writing from the Center* (1995) focus on the geography – spiritual, emotional, and artistic – of the American Midwest. Even the expansively titled *Secrets of the Universe* (1991) returns to the center with its subtitle – *Scenes from the Journey Home*. "Every work of literature," he has written, "is the drawing of a charmed circle, since we can write about only a piece of the world" ("Speaking a Word for Nature").

Sanders' concerns with place, landscape, and home have led logically to a passionate commitment to nature writing. Several of his essays have appeared in magazines associated with the environmental movement (*Orion*, *Parabola*, and the *Sierra Club Wilderness Calendar*). He has also edited the writings of ornithologist and painter John James Audubon (1986) and written about his life (1984). His nature writing is scientifically informed – he began his university education studying physics, though he later switched to literature – but always accessible to the general reader. He has characterized his project as an attempt to explore the connections between writing and landscape, and the writer and his or her locale. His work can be seen as part of the re-emergence of nature writing in America, and he has expressed his admiration in many ways for the work of contemporaries such as **Wendell Berry**, **Barry Lopez**, Robert Finch, Terry Tempest Williams, Leslie Marmon Silko, Gretel Ehrlich, Richard Nelson, and John Haines.

Besides environmentalism, Sanders' political concerns include the struggles for justice, women's rights, and peace. He usually writes on these larger issues by connecting them to a personal experience such as serving jury duty ("Doing Time in the Thirteenth Chair," 1987), growing up on an Ohio arsenal ("At Play in the Paradise of Bombs," 1987), discussing feminism with a female friend ("The Men We Carry in Our Minds," 1987), or traveling to the Soviet Union ("Living Souls," 1991).

Though he has written movingly about many public issues, his work has achieved perhaps its most powerful effects when he has confronted dark themes that are at once more private and universal – death, love, and the tangle of guilt and shame within families. His most anthologized essays deal with his father's death ("The Inheritance of Tools," 1986) and his father's drinking ("Under the Influence," 1989). In these essays, Sanders' careful, polished style becomes infused with the details of memory and the energy of emotion, and they open up into the full and dramatic honesty he believes to be the province of the essay. His intention as an essayist is to "pay my respects to a minor passage of history in an out-of-the-way place" and "speak directly out of my life into the lives of others" ("The Singular First Person").

In search of such directness, Sanders writes in a familiar, accessible style. Yet, as befits someone who began as and remains a fiction writer, his essays are full of scene, narration, and dialogue. He wears humor lightly, reveals himself with self-deprecation, and often achieves immediacy by means of the present tense and precise imagery: "Ticktock. The judge assures us that we should be finished in five days, just in time for Christmas. The real jurors exchange forlorn glances. Here I sit, number thirteen, nobody looks my way. Knowing I am stuck here for the duration, I perk up, blink my eyes. Like the bear going over the mountain, I might as well see what I can see" ("Doing Time in the Thirteenth Chair").

Sanders, who has taught literature at Indiana University since 1971, also displays in his essays the wide reading of an English professor. An awareness of audience, however, helps him vary the ways in which he employs his allusions. In pieces addressed to fellow academics and writers, he may mention **Theodor W. Adorno**, Jacques Derrida, and Paul de Man (for instance in "The Writer in the University"), and two of his four collections of essays have included endnotes; but when writing for a wider audience, as he usually does, Sanders explains his allusions, keeps them biblical, or confines himself to the unpacking of clichés – "Solid as a rock, we say. Build your foundations upon stone, we say. But of course the rocks are not fixed" ("Digging Limestone," 1985).

Sanders has described his texts as expeditions, the sniffings of a hunting dog, and an amateur's raids into the realms of experts, but, finally, somewhat less figuratively, as "essays, by which I mean they are experiments in making sense of things, and . . . personal, by which I mean the voice speaking is the nearest I can come to my own voice" (introduction to *The Paradise of Bombs*).

NED STUCKEY-FRENCH

Biography
Born 26 October 1945 in Memphis, Tennessee. Studied at Brown University, Providence, Rhode Island, B.A. in English, 1967; Cambridge University, 1967–71, Ph.D., 1971. Married Ruth Ann McClure, 1967: one daughter and one son. Literary editor, *Cambridge Review*, 1969–71. Taught English at Indiana University, Bloomington, from 1971. Awards: several fellowships; Penrod Award, for *In Limestone Country*, 1986; Associated Writing Programs Award for Creative Nonfiction, for *The Paradise of Bombs*, 1987; American Library Association Award, for *Bad Man Ballad*, 1987; PEN Syndicated Fiction Award, 1988.

Selected Writings

Essays and Related Prose
In Limestone Country, 1985
The Paradise of Bombs, 1987
Secrets of the Universe: Scenes from the Journey Home, 1991
Staying Put: Making a Home in a Restless World, 1993
Writing from the Center, 1995

Other writings: three novels (*Terrarium*, 1985; *Bad Man Ballad*, 1986; *The Engineer of Beasts*, 1988), short stories, children's books, *D. H. Lawrence: The World of the Major Novels* (1973), and a fictional account of the life of John James Audubon (*Wonders Hidden*, 1984).

Further Reading
Stafford, Kim R., "In Short: *The Paradise of Bombs*," *New York Times Book Review*, 24 May 1987: 13
Stuttaford, Genevieve, "Nonfiction: *Secrets of the Universe: Scenes from the Journey Home* by Scott Russell Sanders," *Publishers Weekly* 238, no. 44 (October 1991): 74
Stuttaford, Genevieve, "Nonfiction: *Writing from the Center* by Scott Russell Sanders," *Publishers Weekly* 242, no. 34 (August 1995): 54
Walzer, Kevin, "Staying Put: The Invisible Landscape of Scott Russell Sanders's Nonfiction," *Journal of Kentucky Studies* 11 (September 1994): 117–25

Santayana, George

Spanish/American, 1863–1952

Idiosyncratic and paradoxical, George Santayana has been a largely neglected figure among modern philosophical essayists for several reasons: he had no homeland with colleagues and a following (though he taught for many years at Harvard); his essays on aesthetics (for which he is probably best remembered) are in some cases difficult and in many ways elusive, if not obscure; and, finally, his deliberate failure to create anything like a complete system of thought has perhaps kept a dedicated coterie or school of "Santayanans" from forming. Nonetheless, Santayana is a fascinating essayist with challenging insights, a beautiful (if at times florid) writing style, a disarming honesty (which is the source of certain contradictory facets of his thought), and on occasion an ability to penetrate to the very depth of wisdom.

Born in Madrid (his mother was Scottish, his father Spanish), Santayana came to the United States when he was nine. He spoke no English on arrival and continued to converse in Spanish at home even after he learned the new language, though he was to become a master stylist in it and all of his books would be written in English. He lived in the United States for 40 years and taught there until he was 50 years old, yet he never admitted being more than an alien in the United States and (at times) a friendly observer. Santayana once commented that his Americanism (discussed, among other places, in his volume of essays *Character and Opinion in the United States*, 1920) was two-sided – one involuntary and one voluntary. The first of these was due simply to the fact that he was sent to the U.S. and lived there not through free choice. The second, voluntary side, he said was due to his American friendships, which were more numerous, loyal, and sympathetic than any others of his life.

The spirit of Santayana's philosophy was summarized in his earliest book, *The Sense of Beauty* (1896), when he writes: "To have imagination and taste, to love the best, to be carried by the contemplation of nature to a vivid faith in the ideal, all this is more, a great deal more, than any science can hope to be. The poets and philosophers who express this aesthetic experience and stimulate the same function in us by their example, do a greater service to mankind and deserve higher honor than the discoverers of historical truth." This is clearly the purpose and meaning of all his later work.

He emphasized on numerous occasions that his primary concern was with values, both ethical and aesthetic, and believed that such areas were too complex and difficult for any one theory or system to explain. He insisted that there is no "snug" universe, not even a rational one in any simple sense. Rejecting all orthodoxies, Santayana regarded philosophy as an art of sorts whose practice is valued as life-enhancing and significant; and while he felt that no system of thought is to be trusted, all systems may be used if they produce a degree of understanding. Further, he argues in *Interpretations of Poetry and Religion* (1900) that the human mind has five senses providing data, a moderate power of understanding to interpret the sensory data, and "A passionate fancy to overlay that interpretation." This "passionate fancy" is the human imagination, which compensates for the limitations of understanding by opening up vistas and filling in outlines.

In the essay "A General Confession" (1940), Santayana also proclaims that critical reflection has freed him from "the horrid claim" of his ideas having literal truth. He comments: "Mind does not come to repeat the world but to celebrate it" and "All is a tale told, if not by an idiot, at least, by a dreamer; but it is far from signifying nothing." Thus, as Santayana explains in *The Sense of Beauty*, art arises in response to our need for entertainment through our senses and imagination. Here he emphasizes that the pleasure accompanying sensuous and/or imaginative activity is real and basic. Humans gain positive and immediate pleasure when experiencing certain objects, associating pleasure with these objects. Santayana believed this association is the ground for attributing beauty to the objects experienced instead of recognizing that the term "beauty" has its origin in the experiences themselves, in a person's senses and feelings. Beauty is most accurately described as "objectified pleasure"; Santayana explained that aesthetic pleasure takes us directly to the object at the same time as the bodily organ is stimulated. He thus writes, "Beauty is an emotional element, a pleasure of ours, which we nevertheless regard as a quality of things."

The most significant aspect of Santayana's **philosophical essays** is clearly his enthusiastic emphasis on the value of art, beauty, imagination, and human creativity. He once commented that the arts "are employments of our freedom after the work of life is done and the terror of it is allayed" – but clearly he did not see the enjoyment of art and the appreciation of beauty as an escape from life. On the contrary, they are essential elements in any life but the most spiritually and culturally impoverished. Without the development of aesthetic taste, our experiential lives will become nothing but, as he puts it, "drowsy reverie relieved by nervous thrills."

JOHN H. HADDOX

Biography

Born Jorge Agustín Nicolás de Santayana, 16 December 1863 in Madrid. Moved to the United States, 1872. Studied at Boston Latin School, from 1874; Harvard University, Cambridge, Massachusetts, 1882–86, A.B., 1886, A.M. (Walker Fellow in Germany and England), 1888, Ph.D., 1889; King's College, Cambridge, 1896–97. Taught at Harvard University, 1889–1912; Hyde Lecturer, the Sorbonne, Paris, 1905–06. Moved to Europe, 1912, living in England, France, then primarily in Rome, 1925–52. Spencer Lecturer, Oxford University, 1923. Awards: Royal Society of Literature Benson Medal, 1928; Columbia University Butler Gold Medal, 1945; honorary degree from the University of Wisconsin. Member, American Academy. Died in Rome, 26 September 1952.

Selected Writings

Essays and Related Prose

Interpretations of Poetry and Religion, 1900
Three Philosophical Poets: Lucretius, Dante and Goethe, 1910
Winds of Doctrine: Studies in Contemporary Opinion, 1913
Egotism in German Philosophy, 1916; as *The German Mind: A Philosophical Diagnosis*, 1968
Character and Opinion in the United States, 1920
Little Essays, edited by Logan Pearsall Smith, 1920
Soliloquies in England and Later Soliloquies, 1922
Dialogues in Limbo, 1925; enlarged edition, 1948
The Genteel Tradition at Bay, 1931
Some Turns of Thought in Modern Philosophy: Five Essays, 1933

Obiter Scripta: Lectures, Essays, and Reviews, edited by Justus
   Buchler and Benjamin Schwartz, 1936
*The Idea of Christ in the Gospels; or, God in Man: A Critical
   Essay*, 1946
*Dominations and Powers: Reflections on Liberty, Society, and
   Government*, 1951
Essays in Literary Criticism, edited by Irving Singer, 1956
The Idler and His Works, and Other Essays, edited by Daniel Cory,
   1957
The Genteel Tradition: Nine Essays, edited by Douglas L. Wilson,
   1967
*Animal Faith and Spiritual Life: Previously Unpublished and
   Uncollected Writings*, edited by John Lachs, 1967
George Santayana's America: Essays on Literature and Culture,
   edited by James Ballowe, 1967
Selected Critical Writings, edited by Norman Henfrey, 2 vols., 1968
The Birth of Reason and Other Essays, edited by Daniel Cory,
   1968
*Santayana on America: Essays, Notes, and Letters on American
   Life, Literature, and Philosophy*, edited by Richard C. Lyon,
   1968
Physical Order and Moral Liberty: Previously Unpublished Essays,
   edited by John and Shirley Lachs, 1969

Other writings: the novel *The Last Puritan* (1935), poetry, many
books on philosophy (including *The Sense of Beauty*, 1896; *The
Life of Reason*, 5 vols., 1905–06; *Reason and Art*, 1922; *Scepticism
and Animal Faith*, 1923; *Realms of Being*, 4 vols., 1927–40),
correspondence, and three volumes of autobiography (1944–53).

Collected works editions: *Works* (Triton Edition), 15 vols.,
1936–40; *Works*, edited by William G. Holzberger and Herman J.
Saatkamp, Jr., 4 vols., 1986–94 (in progress).

Bibliography

Saatkamp, Herman J., Jr., and John Jones, *George Santayana: A
   Bibliographical Checklist 1880–1980*, Bowling Green, Ohio:
   Bowling Green University Philosophy Documentation Center,
   1982

Further Reading

Arnett, Willard E., *Santayana and the Sense of Beauty*, Bloom-
   ington: Indiana University Press, 1955
Cory, Daniel, *Santayana: The Later Years: A Portrait with Letters*,
   New York: Braziller, 1963
McCormick, John, *George Santayana: A Biography*, New York:
   Knopf, 1987
Schilpp, Paul Arthur, editor, *The Philosophy of George Santayana*,
   La Salle, Illinois: Open Court, 1971 (original edition, 1940)

Sarmiento, Domingo Faustino

Argentine, 1811–1888

Domingo Faustino Sarmiento, one of 19th-century Latin
America's most accomplished essayists, also had a distinguished career in education and government, culminating in
his term as Argentina's President from 1868 to 1874. No other
leader of that century accomplished more to benefit the masses
through promotion of technology, social and economic reform,
and universal public schooling.

Until the age of 28 this autodidact in languages and
new ideas resided in Argentina's isolated Andean province of
San Juan, which was nearly devoid of libraries, educational

institutions, and newspapers. Exiled to Chile in 1840, he found
instant success as a journalist with his forceful writing style
and stellar intelligence. In the next 15 years he wrote several of
his most acclaimed book-length essays, which are a written
testimony of his impassioned personal life and his participation
in the turbulent social and political events of his time. From
1854 until the end of his life he lived primarily in Buenos Aires,
the country's capital, where he combined his chosen profession
of journalist – or "public writer" – with a long succession of
positions in government and public administration.

Writing for Sarmiento was largely a means of furthering a
worthy social cause. He disdained poetry and fictional narrative, but found the essay to be a valuable tool for his ideological struggles. The 53 volumes of his *Obras completas*
(Complete works) unite the short essays written for the daily
or weekly press throughout his long career of public service:
costumbrista (essays on customs or personality types), sketches,
reviews of books and theater productions, all with reformist
intention; his 1842 polemic in defense of Romanticism and
against classicism; promotional pieces for public education,
highways, innovative industrial practices, and trade; studies on
the impact of governmental policies for immigration or the sale
of public lands; and considerations on constitutional and political issues. Also included in the *Obras completas* are his longer
essays, which circulated widely in book form, and are variously classified as literature, biography and autobiography,
travel commentary, and sociological and political studies.

Since the greater part of Sarmiento's essays were first
published in the press, it is not surprising that the style, tone,
and focus of these writings were influenced by that medium.
His was political writing at its best, conceived in the passion
of polemic and intended to move the reader to action. Logic
and system were often sacrificed in favor of effect. He
wrote with the "performative" goal of altering reality rather
than merely describing it. Writing for him was a type of action,
and its impact on the reader was often as important as what
it said. Critics have called attention to how Sarmiento's
emotional or irrational "intent" overshadows a conscious or
prescribed "intention," how he dynamically incorporates his
own person into the narration, and how his prose persuades
through affective rather than logical conduits. For these and
other reasons literary anthologies often place Sarmiento's name
at the head of Latin America's Romantic literary tradition.

Yet Sarmiento's essayistic prose defies such easy classification. His defense of Romantic literature in the 1842 polemics
in Chile was primarily a means of shaking up that country's
complacent intellectual elite, whose members still ignored the
fertile literary and ideological contributions emanating from
Western Europe since the late 18th century. Romanticism,
Sarmiento believed, already belonged to a preterite age.
Nevertheless, he recognized the insurrectional value of that
literature in the face of tradition, and was conscious of the
need for writers of his own age to forge an original expression that would agitate on behalf of liberal institutions and
material progress. In this respect he embraced the dictum
accredited to Victor Hugo, that Romanticism was nothing less
than liberalism in literature. So although certain characteristics of his essayistic writing were undeniably "Romantic," it
was a Romanticism at the service of progress. Early on he and
his renowned cohorts of the Argentine Generation of 1837

labeled this orientation *socialista* – not to be confused with the collectivist and proletarian orientation that Engels and **Marx** later lent to the term – which they borrowed from the writings and thought of Claude-Henri de Rouvroy, the Count of Saint-Simon, who was a precursor of positivism.

This pre-positivist orientation found expression in Sarmiento's style. For example, one passage of his most acclaimed work, *Facundo; o, Civilización y barbarie* (1845; *Life in the Argentine Republic in the Days of the Tyrants; or, Civilization and Barbarism*) portrays the emotional author-protagonist who is moved to tears upon observing the intense religious devotion of a cattle rancher living in the isolated countryside. Reason, however, finally prevails when the narrator, now sounding like a social scientist, ends the passage with an explanation of how the barbaric countryside causes a degeneration in the people's religious practices and in their social institutions in general. A similar procedure is observed with Sarmiento's description of a pampa storm: few writers have captured in more forceful words the destructive power of nature over humble humanity. But then there is an abrupt stylistic transition: "Romantic" prose is followed immediately by a physiological explanation, perhaps influenced by the theories of galvanism, whereby untamed nature activates the "electrical fluid" in man's brain, arouses his passions, and clouds his reason. Sarmiento then concludes the passage by underlining how the untamed physical setting is a major contributor to the stunted intellectual faculties of the rural inhabitant. Here again, the writer initially builds toward the reader's "Romantic" appreciation and then destroys it. Other examples could also be given of positivistic literary stratagems whereby rationality predominates over emotion and science over Romanticism. On the written page and in his public career Sarmiento always placed literature and the essay at the service of politics.

One could argue that, on account of this tolerance of textual contradiction and propensity for stylistic movement, Sarmiento exemplifies well the model of writing offered by the essayist who baptized the genre, **Michel de Montaigne**. For both, the process of writing was in itself a search for truth whereby different ideas would be registered, treated, digested, and discarded. Neither feared self-contradiction and ideological or stylistic inconsistency. But here the similarities end. Whereas Montaigne wrote for himself and a small coterie of readers, Sarmiento wrote primarily for the public forum. With justification his detractors have called attention to Sarmiento's ideological expediency whereby writing was his form of denying or overwhelming other interpretations and making his own ideas prevail.

Facundo was composed, in the author's own words, in a "rapture of lyricism" for publication by installments in Chile's weekly press before circulating throughout the Río de la Plata region (Argentina, Uruguay, Paraguay, and southern Brazil) in book form. The essay unites three highly contrasting sections. The first, inspired by sociological or ethnographic theory and heavily flavored by the biases and idiosyncratic beliefs of the author, attempts to account for the state of Argentine society after 20 years of devastating civil skirmishes. As such, four successive chapters of this first section focus on the region's landscape of endless pampas; the psychology of rural inhabitants that resulted from their residence in that primitive environment; the social institutions arising in that physical setting and in accordance with the particular values and orientations of its inhabitants; and the historical events of recent years that were the product of all the geographical, psychological, and social factors previously discussed. Within these chapters Sarmiento includes memorable *costumbrista* passages that romantically portray character types of the Argentine pampas: the pathfinder, the cattle hand, the bad gaucho, and the singer. The work's second section, which is Sarmiento's subjective incursion into biography and romantically rendered history, re-creates in negative terms the events surrounding the life and exploits of the Promethean *caudillo*, or charismatic rural leader, Juan Facundo Quiroga. The work's third section, excluded entirely from the English translation, analyzes the tyrannical practices of the Buenos Aires dictator, Juan Manuel de Rosas.

Over the years critics have disputed the work's generic classification on account of the wide range of materials treated. The term "essay" was not then in current usage. Sarmiento himself characterized the work as a form of "poem, political pamphlet, history." Informed readers have agreed about only two issues: the intense impact of Sarmiento's forceful prose, and the immense influence of this uneven and untidy essay over thought and politics, and subsequent conceptual writing, in Argentina and Latin America.

Three other essays merit consideration here. First, *Viajes en Europa, África y América* (1849–51; Travels through Europe, Africa, and America), which compiles the long **letters** that Sarmiento wrote during his extensive travels a few years earlier. The work features penetrating observations of customs and practices flavored by familiarity with a not insignificant number of written sources. Also important is *De la educación popular* (1849; About public education), only one of many studies he published to promote free and universal schooling for the masses of his continent. The work unites observations and studies of educational systems across northern Europe, and presents the author's own practical plan for implementing such practices in the South American republics. More important for literary readers is *Recuerdos de provincia* (1843; Memories of provincial life), demonstrating Sarmiento's considerable talents as historian and describer of customs. With autobiographical focus, the work venerates the personages and progressive institutions that prevailed in San Juan's patriarchal society at the time of his youth.

WILLIAM H. KATRA

Biography

Born 15 February 1811 in San Juan, Argentina. Studied at the Escuela de la Patria, San Juan, 1817–19; moved to the province of San Luis with his uncle, 1825, and tutored by him. Lieutenant with the Unitarist forces against General Facundo Quiroga's army, captured and held for four months, 1829–30, then escaped briefly to Chile; returned to San Juan, then fled again to Chile, 1831, where he taught in Los Andes, worked in a store, and in a silver mine in northern Chile. Had one daughter (possibly by María de Jéus del Canto), 1832. Contracted typhoid fever and allowed to return to San Juan, 1836. Founder, Colegio para Señoritas, San Juan, 1839; copublisher, *El Zonda* newspaper, 1839. Imprisoned for conspiracy and almost executed, but saved by intervention of governor and exiled to Chile again, 1840. Founder, *El Progreso* newspaper, Santiago, early 1840s. Traveled to Europe and the

United States to inspect educational systems, 1845–47. Married
Benita Martínez Pastoriza, 1848 (separated, 1862): one son
(probably his). Lived mostly in Buenos Aires, from 1854. Appointed
minister of Mitre, 1860; governor of the province of San Juan,
1862–64 and 1874. Leader in the repression of the Peñalosa
rebellion, 1863–64. Argentine ambassador to the United States,
1865–68. President of the Argentine Republic, 1868–74. Appointed
director of schools, Province of Buenos Aires, 1875, minister of
Avellaneda, 1879, and general superintendent of Argentine schools,
1881. Unsuccessful candidate for President, 1879. Died in Asunción,
Paraguay, 11 September 1888.

Selected Writings

Essays and Related Prose
Recuerdos de provincia, 1843; edited by Guillermo Ara, 1966
Civilización y barbarie: Vida de Juan Facundo Quiroga, 1845; as
  Facundo; o, Civilización y barbarie en las pampas argentinas,
  1868; edited by Emma Susána Speratti Piñero, 1972, Jorge Luis
  Borges, 1974, Luis Ortega Galindo, 1975, Nora Dottori and
  Silvia Zanetti, 1977, and Robert Yahni, 1990; as *Life in the
  Argentine Republic in the Days of the Tyrants; or, Civilization
  and Barbarism*, translated by Mrs. Horace Mann, 1868
Viajes en Europa, África y América, 2 vols., 1849–51; edited by Delia
  S. Etcheverry, 1940, Alberto Palcos, 1955, and Javier Fernández,
  1993; part as *Travels in the United States in 1847*, translated by
  Mrs. Horace Mann, 1868, and Michael A. Rockland, 1970; part as
  Travels: A Selection, translated by Inés Muñoz, 1963
De la educación popular, 1849; as *Educación común*, 1855; edited
  by Gregorio Weinberg, 1987
Discursos populares, 1927
Idearo, edited by Luis Alberto Sánchez, 1943, and Bernardo
  Movsichoff, 1988
A Sarmiento Anthology, edited by Allison Williams Bunkley,
  translated by Stuart Edgar Grummon, 1948
Sarmiento: A través de sus mejores páginas, edited by Andrés
  Iduarte and James F. Shearer, 1949
Cartas y discursos políticos, edited by José P. Barreiro, 1963

Other writings: many political works, biographies of Abraham
Lincoln and Benjamin Franklin, memoirs, and correspondence.

Collected works editions: *Obras*, edited by Augusto Belín Sarmiento,
53 vols., 1885–1903; *Obras completas*, 53 vols., 1948–56.

Bibliography
Becco, Horacio Jorge, "Bibliografía de Sarmiento," *Humanidades*
  37, no. 2 (1961): 119–44

Further Reading
Anderson Imbert, Enrique, *Genio y figura de Sarmiento*, Buenos
  Aires: University of Buenos Aires, 1967
Barrenechea, Ana María, "Notas al estilo de Sarmiento," *Revista
  Iberoamericana* 41–42 (1956): 275–94
Borello, Rodolfo, "*Facundo*: Heterogeneidad y persuasión,"
  Cuadernos Hispanoamericanos 263–64 (1972): 283–302
Bunkley, Allison Williams, *The Life of Sarmiento*, Princeton, New
  Jersey: Princeton University Press, 1952
Carilla, Emilio, *Lengua y estilo en Sarmiento*, La Plata: National
  University of La Plata, 1964
Crowley, Frances G., *Domingo Faustino Sarmiento*, New York:
  Twayne, 1972
Gálvez, Manuel, *Vida de Sarmiento: El hombre de autoridad*,
  Buenos Aires: Emecé, 1945
Halperín Donghi, Tulio, Prologue to *Campaña en el Ejército
  Grande Aliado de Sud América* by Sarmiento, Mexico City:
  Fondo de Cultura Económica, 1958: xx–xxvi

Jitrik, Noé, *Muerte y resurrección de "Facundo"*, Buenos Aires:
  Centro Editor de América Latina, 1968
Jones, Cyril Albert, *Sarmiento: "Facundo"*, London: Grant and
  Cutler, 1974
Katra, William H., "Discourse Production and Sarmiento's Essayistic
  Style," in *Simposio el ensayo hispánico: Actas*, edited by Isaac
  Jack Levy and Juan Loveluck, Columbia: University of South
  Carolina, 1984
Katra, William H., *Sarmiento: Public Writer (Between 1839 and
  1852)*, Tempe: Arizona State University Institute of Latin
  American Studies, 1985
Katra, William H., "*Facundo* as Historical Novel," in *The
  Historical Novel in Latin America: A Symposium*, edited by
  Daniel Balderston, Gaithersburg, Maryland: Hispamérica, 1986:
  31–46
Katra, William H., *Sarmiento de frente y perfil*, New York: Lang,
  1993
Katra, William H., "Sarmiento in the United States," in *Sarmiento:
  Author of a Nation*, edited by Tulio Halperín Donghi and others,
  Berkeley: University of California Press, 1994
Katra, William H., *The Argentine Generation of 1837: Echeverría,
  Alberdi, Sarmiento, Mitre*, Rutherford, New Jersey: Fairleigh
  Dickinson University Press, 1995
Lugones, Leopoldo, *Historia de Sarmiento*, Buenos Aires: Babel,
  1931 (original edition, 1910)
Martínez Estrada, Ezequiel, *Sarmiento*, Buenos Aires: Argos, 1956
Palcos, Alberto, *Sarmiento: La vida, la obra, las ideas, el genio*,
  Buenos Aires: Emecé, 1962 (original edition, 1929)
Patton, Elda Clayton, *Sarmiento in the United States*, Evansville,
  Indiana: University of Evansville Press, 1976
Pomer, León, "Sarmiento, el caudillismo y la escritura histórica,"
  Cuadernos Hispanoaméricos: Los complementarios 3 (1989):
  7–37
Rockland, Michael A., Introduction to *Travels in the United States
  in 1847* by Sarmiento, Princeton, New Jersey: Princeton
  University Press, 1970
Rojas, Ricardo, *El profeta de la pampa: Vida de Sarmiento*, Buenos
  Aires: Losada, 1945
Salomon, Noël, "À propos des éléments 'costumbristas' dans le
  Facundo de D. F. Sarmiento," *Bulletin Hispanique* 52 (1968):
  342–412
Verdevoye, Paul, *Domingo Faustino Sarmiento: Éducateur et
  publiciste (entre 1839 et 1852)*, Paris: Institut des Hautes Études
  de l'Amérique Latine, 1963

Sartre, Jean-Paul
French, 1905–1980

Jean-Paul Sartre is largely responsible for our image of the
postwar French intellectual – a man of letters who is not merely
that, but an "écrivain engagé" or "committed writer," putting
his thoughts into action in the political vanguard. It was
Sartre's intellectual versatility and his frenetic energy as a writer
and activist that allowed him to assume this leading role. His
essays are only one dimension of a prodigious written output
(Sartre is said to have averaged 20 pages a day throughout his
life), including philosophical **treatise**s, biographies, plays,
novels, political journalism, and scripts for film, radio, and
television, in addition to diaries and **letters**.

While Sartre wrote some of his most important work before
and during World War II – including the novel *La Nausée*
(1938; *Nausea*) and the treatise *L'Être et le néant* (1943; *Being
and Nothingness*) – it was in the immediate postwar period
that he leapt to fame. In 1945 he delivered his famous lecture

"L'Existentialisme est un humanisme" (published 1946; "The Humanism of Existentialism") and founded *Les Temps Modernes* (Modern times). The original editorial committee of this journal headed by Sartre included such prominent figures as Raymond Aron, Maurice Merleau-Ponty, **Simone de Beauvoir**, and the surrealist Michel Leiris. It immediately became a focal point for intellectual and political controversies, and while Sartre normally left its day-to-day editing to others, his association with the journal helped guarantee a lasting audience for his essays. These essays, which range in length from two-page editorial pieces to short books, originally appeared in *Les Temps Modernes*, in other journals and newspapers, and often as **prefaces** to books by other writers; many are collected in the ten volumes of *Situations* (1947–76). They can be divided broadly into essays in social and political commentary, literary and artistic criticism, biography, and philosophy.

The breadth of Sartre's concerns and his literary inclinations are clearly in evidence in his philosophical texts. His first philosophically significant essay is "La Transcendance de l'égo" (1937; "The Transcendence of the Ego"). While this essay is written for an audience versed in the technical terminology of Edmund Husserl's phenomenology, the literary and anecdote-loving side of Sartre makes refreshing appearances, as when he refers to Rimbaud or tells the story of a "young bride [who] was in terror, when her husband left her alone, of sitting at the window and summoning the passersby like a prostitute." Sartre shows a talent here for memorable phrases, and he uses straightforward and effective philosophical terms, such as "the I and the me."

Sartre's talent for vivid explanation (which he does not always employ as much as one would wish) was no doubt enhanced by his experience as a teacher of philosophy in French schools. Sartre also knows how to capture the attention of his audience, as when he begins "La République du silence" (1944; "The Republic of Silence") with the shocking line, "We were never more free than under the German Occupation." (What Sartre means is that under the occupation "each gesture had the weight of a commitment.")

"The Humanism of Existentialism" is Sartre's best-known essay, although he could hardly have expected that it would gain such fame. The opening of the essay ("I should like on this occasion to defend existentialism against some charges which have been brought against it") indicates that it was not intended as the primary manifesto of existentialism, but as a response to specific criticisms Sartre's philosophy had recently received from enemies on the right and the left. However, the essay was composed just as the label "existentialism" was gaining its vogue, and it provides a convenient definition for the term: existentialism is the position in which for human beings, "existence precedes essence." In other words, "first of all, man exists, turns up, appears on the scene, and, only afterwards, defines himself." Phrases such as this succeed in condensing some major themes of the abstruse *Being and Nothingness* into clear, colloquial terms. This essay exercised a seemingly irresistible power, as it provoked heated responses from both critics and admirers, including **Martin Heidegger**'s important "Brief über den Humanismus" (1947; "Letter on Humanism"). The power of Sartre's essay is due partly to its accessible language and vivid examples, partly to the confidence with which he enters into debate with his

contemporaries, and partly to the overconfidence which leads him into some provocative yet unsubstantiated positions (in particular, his sketch of an existentialist ethics of freedom, which he himself came to see as premature).

"Présentation des *Temps Modernes*" (1945; "Introducing *Les Temps Modernes*") is an important source for Sartre's theory of the committed writer. (The theory is developed at greater length in "Qu'est-ce que la littérature?" [1947; "What Is Literature?"].) In "Introducing *Les Temps Modernes*," Sartre analyzes literary production in terms of the writer's involvement in a community, arguing that the myth of the disengaged author who bears no responsibility for his or her surroundings is a bourgeois illusion. Like it or not, "we have only this life to live, amid *this* war, and perhaps *this* revolution." Thus, aesthetes such as Proust are denounced as "accomplice[s] of bourgeois propaganda." Those who try to write for the ages rather than the moment, says Sartre in a direct and elegant line, "have allowed their lives to be stolen from them by immortality." The ambition of *Les Temps Modernes*, as described here, is nothing less than to produce a new, emancipatory vision of human existence. To this end, the journal was to publish criticism, fiction, poetry, journalism, history, and even psychiatric studies.

The theory of "committed writing" views aesthetic and political analyses as complementary parts of a unified attempt to understand and influence one's world; nevertheless, we can place Sartre's postwar essays on a spectrum which ranges from the primarily aesthetic to the primarily political. The aesthetic end of the spectrum can be illustrated by "Le Séquestré de Venise" (1957; "The Venetian Pariah"), an essay which also displays Sartre's biographical techniques and hints at his political views. Here Sartre writes on Tintoretto in a carefully crafted style that arouses the reader's curiosity from the beginning of the essay: "Nothing. His life is an enigma: a few dates, a few facts, and then the cackling of ancient writers. But courage: *Venice speaks to us.*" Pouring his imagination into the biographical details that have come down to us, Sartre produces a vivid series of sketches of the painter's life and personality – often speculating well beyond the documented evidence ("Never during his entire life did he allow himself an indulgence, a dislike, a preference, or even the comfort of a dream"). At the same time, Sartre investigates numerous aspects of Tintoretto's relation to his society, its material conditions and its authorities, driving home his point that human beings are situated – or to put it in existentialist terms, "the painter knows full well that he will not leave the world, that even if he could, he would bear with him everywhere the Nothingness that transpierces him." This essay is notable for some of Sartre's most flamboyant and enigmatic descriptions of art: for example, "every artifice should be employed to replace the *representation* by a hollow participation of the spectator in the spectacle, so that horror and tenderness would thrust men against their images and, if possible, into their midst, so that desire, burning all the fires of perspective, would discover the *ersatz* of divine ubiquity – the immediate presence of flesh; the logic of the heart."

At the political end of the spectrum one finds Sartre's most polemical pieces of writing. These plunge energetically into controversial questions of their day – the war in Algeria, the Vietnam War, the student movement of 1968 – and analyze these events from a decidedly left-wing perspective, while usually avoiding any brand of Marxist orthodoxy ("Introducing *Les Temps Modernes*" had promised that the journal would not serve the interests of any particular party, and Sartre was never comfortable aligning himself with a dogma). Many of these political essays remain thought-provoking today, but they are susceptible to two apparently contradictory flaws: unnecessarily technical verbiage and overly simplistic analysis. A case in point is the late essay "Élections, piège à cons" (1973; "Elections: A Trap for Fools"). Here Sartre uses a substantial dose of jargon that stems from his *Critique de la raison dialectique* (1960; *Critique of Dialectical Reason*): for example, "One finds serialization in the practico-inert field." (Fortunately, he promptly explains this particular bit of jargon with a straightforward example of a man who by driving a car "becomes no more than one driver among others.") As the title of this essay indicates, it is an unabashedly propagandistic piece, in the sense that it exhorts its readers to choose a clear good over a clear evil. While Sartre cites many facts in the process of criticizing liberal democratic institutions, his positive vision of an alternative to electoral politics is strikingly vague – in fact, he himself describes the utopian concept of "legitimate power" as "embryonic, diffuse, unclear even to itself." Sartre concludes with a call to "organize the vast anti-hierarchic movement which fights institutions everywhere." A subtle mind such as Sartre's could not fail to note the ironic incongruity of a call to organize an anti-organizational force – but the propagandistic tenor of the essay seems to rule out any acknowledgment of this irony.

It was Sartre's goal to combine careful crafting of words with political activism: "Introducing *Les Temps Modernes*" cautions that "in 'committed literature,' *commitment* must in no way lead to a forgetting of *literature*." But it can be argued that there is a tension between Sartre the writer and Sartre the political activist, and that his growing emphasis on political effectiveness tended to come at the expense of careful editing of his prose. Not all of Sartre's essays will stand the test of time. However, they were not written for the future; they are the products of a writer consciously situated in a time and place.

RICHARD POLT

Biography

Jean-Paul Charles Aymard Sartre. Born 21 June 1905 in Paris. Studied at the Lycée Montaigne, 1913–15, and Lycée Henri IV, Paris, 1915–22, baccalauréat, 1922; Lycée Louis-le-Grand, Paris, 1922–24; École Normale Supérieure, Paris, 1924–29, agrégation in philosophy, 1929; studied phenomenology at the Institut Français, Berlin, 1933–34. Began a lifelong relationship with Simone de Beauvoir, 1929. Military service, 1929–31. Taught at lycées in Le Havre, Laon, and Paris, 1931–44. Worked in the army meteorological section during World War II: captured, 1940, repatriated and returned to France, 1941. Founding editor, with Beauvoir, *Les Temps Modernes*, from 1945. Member, Rassemblement Démocratique Révolutionnaire (Democratic revolutionary assembly), 1948–49. Editor, *La Cause du Peuple* (The cause of the people), from 1970, *Tout* (Everything), 1970–74, *Révolution*, 1971–74, and *Libération*, 1973–74. Awards: New York Drama Critics Circle Award, 1947; Grand Novel Prize, 1950; Omegna Prize (Italy), 1961; Nobel Prize for Literature, 1964 (refused); honorary degree from the University of Jerusalem, 1976; Foreign Member, American Academy of Arts and Sciences. Died (of oedema of the lungs) in Paris, 15 April 1980.

Selected Writings

Essays and Related Prose

Situations 1–10, 10 vols., 1947–76; selections published under various titles, translated by Bernard Frechtman, 1949, Annette Michelson, 1955, S. W. Allen, 1963, Benita Eisler, 1965, Martha H. Fletcher and John R. Kleinschmidt, 1968, Irene Clephane, 1969, John Mathews, 1974, and Paul Auster and Lydia Davis, 1977
Essays in Aesthetics, edited and translated by Wade Baskin, 1963
Essays in Existentialism, edited and translated by Wade Baskin, 1967
The Writings of Jean-Paul Sartre, vol. 2: *Selected Prose*, edited by Michel Contat and Michel Rybalka, translated by Richard C. McCleary, 1974
"What Is Literature?" and Other Essays, 1988

Other writings: four novels (*La Nausée* [*Nausea*], 1938; *L'Âge de raison* [*The Age of Reason*], 1945; *Le Sursis* [*The Reprieve*], 1945; *La Mort dans l'âme* [*Iron in the Soul*], 1949), a collection of stories (*Le Mur* [*The Wall*], 1939), ten plays (including *Les Mouches* [*The Flies*], 1943; *Huis clos* [*No Exit*], 1944; *Les Séquestrés d'Altona* [*The Condemned of Altona*], 1959), screenplays, biographies of Flaubert and Genet, and books on existentialism (including *L'Être et le néant* [*Being and Nothingness*], 1943) and literature.

Bibliographies

Contat, Michel, and Michel Rybalka, *The Writings of Jean-Paul Sartre*, vol. 1: *A Bibliographical Life*, Evanston, Illinois: Northwestern University Press, 1974
Gabel, Gernot U., *Sartre, a Comprehensive Bibliography of International Theses and Dissertations, 1950–1985*, Hürth-Efferen: Gemini, 1992
Lapointe, François H., and Claire Lapointe, *Jean-Paul Sartre and His Critics: An International Bibliography 1938–1980*, Bowling Green, Ohio: Bowling Green State University, revised edition, 1981
Nordquist, Joan, *Jean-Paul Sartre: A Bibliography*, Santa Cruz, California: Reference and Research Services, 1993
Rybalka, Michel, and Michel Contat, *Sartre: Bibliography, 1980–1992*, Bowling Green, Ohio: Bowling Green State University, 1993
Wilcocks, Robert, *Jean-Paul Sartre: A Bibliography of International Criticism*, Edmonton: University of Alberta Press, 1975

Further Reading

Adereth, Maxwell, *Commitment in Modern French Literature: A Brief Study of "littérature engagée" in the Works of Péguy, Aragon, and Sartre*, London: Gollancz, 1967; as *Commitment in Modern French Literature: Politics and Society in Péguy, Aragon, and Sartre*, New York: Schocken, 1968
Bauer, George H., *Sartre and the Artist*, Chicago: University of Chicago Press, 1969
Champigny, Robert, *Stages on Sartre's Way, 1938–1952*, Bloomington: Indiana University Press, 1959
Halpern, Joseph, *Critical Fictions: The Literary Criticism of Jean-Paul Sartre*, New Haven, Connecticut and London: Yale University Press, 1976
Hayman, Ronald, *Writing Against: A Biography of Sartre*, London: Weidenfeld and Nicolson, 1986; as *Sartre: A Life*, New York: Simon and Schuster, 1987: especially Chapter 15 on the immediate postwar period
Jameson, Fredric, *Sartre: The Origins of a Style*, New Haven, Connecticut: Yale University Press, 1961
La Capra, Dominick, *A Preface to Sartre*, Ithaca, New York: Cornell University Press, 1978

McCleary, Richard C., "Translator's Preface" to *The Writings of Jean-Paul Sartre*, vol. 2: *Selected Prose*, edited by Michel Contat and Michel Rybalka, Evanston, Illinois: Northwestern University Press, 1974

Poster, Mark, *Existential Marxism in Postwar France: From Sartre to Althusser*, Princeton, New Jersey: Princeton University Press, 1975

Suhl, Benjamin, *Jean-Paul Sartre: The Philosopher as a Literary Critic*, New York: Columbia University Press, 1970

Thody, Philip, *Jean-Paul Sartre: A Literary and Political Study*, London: Hamilton, 1960

Ungar, Steven, Introduction to *"What Is Literature?" and Other Essays* by Sartre, Cambridge, Massachusetts: Harvard University Press, 1988

Satire

Satire is a literary response to life in the city: its basic cynicism and especially its political nature seem to require an urban culture to spawn and thrive. There are other less sophisticated kinds of verbal and literary vitriol; flyting and invective, what might best be described as creative name calling, occur almost universally, but satire proper derives from a parodic association between literature and the hypocrisy of civil behavior. While the term itself has its etymological roots in the Latin *satura*, meaning "a full or mixed dish" in the sense of a cacophonous variety, the Greeks had a rich satiric tradition, especially evident in the Athenian Old Comedy, which played scatologically with the pretentious behavior of particular contemporary citizens recognizable to the audience. Aristophanes' lampoons on Socrates and Euripides are prominent examples. The great Roman poets Horace and Juvenal set the literary standards for European satire, their best work being much imitated models, even well into the 20th century. They also lend their names to the two essential types of satire: Horatian is the gentler kind, which exposes human folly to correct it and thus strengthens the social fabric; Juvenalian is harsh, even abusive, and sees little chance of social progress. Horace and Juvenal use language that is colloquial and immediate, and most importantly, like Aristophanes', their subjects are actual and contemporary people and current issues. These remain the distinguishing elements of satire: it is colloquial, immediate, and recognizably real in style and subject.

In a peculiar way, satire's generic qualities and social motives are very close to those of the essay. The satirist, like the essayist, is intensely aware of his or her subjectivity and attempts to engage the reader on a personal and even conversational level. In both genres, the dominant impression is one of immediacy, of a face-to-face exchange in which opinion and interpretation take precedence over fact and objectivity. The attitude is casual, however charged with message, and the whole has about it the feel of the marketplace or coffeehouse. The wit, worldliness, and sophistication of the satirist declare his urbanity; this is not the familiar mode of a pastoral country cousin. Both satirist and essayist assume a sophisticated literacy in their readers, relying on the reader's abilities to recognize cultural allusions and to detect subtle variations in literary voice and tone.

Gilbert Highet identified three satiric modes in his *Anatomy of Satire* (1962): monologue, parody, and narrative. Each has a long literary pedigree and finds practitioners in, respectively: **Jonathan Swift**, whose *A Modest Proposal* (1729) is among the best examples of a satiric monologue; Robert Burns, who used parody with uncanny precision in "Holy Willie's Prayer" (wr. 1785, pub. 1799); and Rabelais, whose *Gargantua and Pantagruel* (1532–34) influenced most subsequent satiric narratives, especially mock travels. These three satirists, however different the cultural objectives of their work, have one thing in common: they share with most satirists a talent for observing the excesses and absurdities of those social conventions designed specifically to control human behavior. Satire in this way is almost always political, focusing as it does on the methods by which the group and the individual impose restrictions on human appetites and ambitions. Just as the satirist takes up a position outside the norm to observe critically the human scene, so the satiric voice or persona usually represents a position of alienation or otherness. At the very least, the satirist is set apart because of a disenchantment with the way things are; often that isolation is the result of the more intense emotional experience of the satirist's anger and hatred. That is certainly true of those satiric narratives that also pass so easily for children's literature: Carlo Collodi's *Le avventure di Pinocchio* (1883; *The Adventures of Pinocchio*), Lewis Carroll's *Alice in Wonderland* (1865), and Frank Baum's *Wizard of Oz* (1900). The child's perspective is easily made into one of bewilderment, frustration, and separation. Similarly, the traveler, whether Homer's Odysseus or Swift's Gulliver, makes a ready satiric persona because of his naturally alien condition. Naivety and credulity are also necessary elements of much satiric narrative, however complex and ironic their contributions.

Sometimes, it is the narrator or the satirist's chief character who is the credulous ingenue, as in **Voltaire**'s *Candide* (1759), or much of the recent work of the Australian novelist, Elizabeth Jolley; in other cases, the credulity of the reader is manipulated and exploited by the satirist, as in the work of **Mark Twain**, or hoax literature such as **Daniel Defoe**'s *The Shortest Way with the Dissenters* (1702) and **Denis Diderot**'s *La Religieuse* (1796). The effect of most satire is to create in the reader not just a sense of doubleness, of the world's duplicity and falseness, but of outright separation, an experience that truth is, ironically, not enlightening but disabling, that the reality of social conventions is wholly at odds with moral and ethical goodness. Innocence, naivety, openness, and honesty are all risky postures in satire; the satirist assumes such attitudes only ironically and invites the reader to adopt them only to be humiliated. Satiric irony at its extreme leaves the reader in a position of "enlightened isolation": we see truths about our society but in acknowledging those insights we are made to feel ashamed of our own hypocritical social identity. In summary, great satire is seldom constructive.

Swift's notoriously cutting observation, that man is an animal only capable of reason, is a disturbingly double-edged sword. To the Horatian satirists, it suggests that humanity, with the prodding of a little critical laughter at itself, may be nudged into more reasonable if not wholly rational behavior. But to the Juvenalian, humanity's mere capacity for reason is an unattainable condition, the promise of sensibleness and justice which exists only to reveal and deride the human animal for the vain and foolish thing it is. The darker ironic tendencies of satire and its necessary, if parasitic, relationship to a sophisticated and literate culture predispose it well to the genre of the essay, with its narrative self-consciousness, its tradition of sharp social observation, and especially its sensitivity to the ephemerality of meaning and language.

STEPHEN W. BROWN

See also Satiric Essay

Anthologies

English Satire: An Anthology, edited by Norman Furlong, London: Harrap, 1946

The Naked Emperor: An Anthology of International Political Satire, edited by Barbara Fultz, New York: Penguin, 1970

Satire: A Critical Anthology, edited by John David Russell and Ashley Brown, Cleveland: World, 1967

Satire: An Anthology , edited by Ashley Brown and John L. Kimmey, New York: Crowell, 1977

Further Reading

Guilhamet, Leon, *Satire of the Transformation of Genre*, Philadelphia: University of Pennsylvania Press, 1987

Highet, Gilbert, *The Anatomy of Satire*, Princeton, New Jersey: Princeton University Press, 1962

Paulson, Ronald, editor, *Satire: Modern Essays in Criticism*, Englewood Cliffs, New Jersey: Prentice Hall, 1971

Pollard, Arthur, *Satire: The Critical Idiom*, London: Methuen, 1970

Rawson, Claude, editor, *English Satire and the Satiric Tradition*, Oxford: Blackwell, 1984

Rosenheim, Edward W., Jr., *Swift and the Satirist's Art*, Chicago: University of Chicago Press, 1963

Sullivan, J. P., editor, *Satire: Critical Essays on Roman Literature*, London: Routledge and Kegan Paul, 1963

Satiric Essay

The essay is a literary mode peculiarly well disposed to **satire**. Both the *Encomium moriae* (1511; *The Praise of Folly*) by **Erasmus** and the *Utopia* (1516) of Sir Thomas More employed a politically sensitive irony to set old and new world views of the moral life against one another. While not satiric in any way, **Machiavelli**'s *Discorsi* (1531; *Discourses*) and **Francis Bacon**'s *Essayes* (1597, 1612, 1625), in the unwavering critical scrutiny they brought to bear on their subjects, indicated the direction satire was to take in the form of the essay; Machiavelli and Bacon, from their respectively suspicious and skeptical perspectives, were engaged in the business not so much of providing as of criticizing knowledge. The analytical revisionism of the Renaissance, by questioning the authority of received learning and by drawing attention to the limitations and problems surrounding all human ways of knowing, assumed a critical posture akin to the traditional position of the satirist. While Machiavelli and Bacon cannot be described as satirists, their methodology is latently satiric in its essential skepticism.

It is **Montaigne** who fully developed the essay's potential as a vehicle for satire, and in so doing made satire a crucial way of seeing and analyzing the world. The evolution of prose into the primary medium of literary expression in Renaissance Europe altered the nature of satire radically, with its novel emphasis on the written word and on the solitary and silent business of reading. Montaigne's *Essais* (1580, 1588) illustrate this new dynamic exquisitely. He wrote much about the act of reading, about his own critical and intellectual engagement with other texts and authors; in this he drew attention to the word as its own reality, to the way in which literature, reading, and intellectual reflection create a space apart from nature where the human personality experiences itself. Critical self-awareness is the source of the ironic epiphanies that characterize Montaigne's satiric essays. This sort of satire is especially evident in "Des cannibales" (1580; "Of Cannibals"), where the object of ironic analysis is finally not the anthropological truth about cannibals, but the literary ambiguity of texts and especially the slipperiness of meaning that allows the European to disguise himself and his culture, using language deliberately to render truth incognito. In the final paragraph of the essay, Montaigne complains about the impediment that inaccurate translation places in the path of understanding, blaming the stupidity of a translator for his difficulty in getting the answers he wants from a certain chieftain among the cannibals: "I spoke with one of them a long time but I had an interpreter who followed me badly and was so unresponsive to my ideas that I had little pleasure from it." Montaigne's reading of various texts about the New World aboriginals becomes a satire on the inhumanity of European governance in areas where cannibalism is institutionalized. But his ultimate satiric concern here is with the language by which moral neglect is disguised as necessary policy rather than with the actions themselves. Flawed interpretations, intellectual impatience, and the failure, often deliberate, to grasp and express meaning with clarity become the ultimate joke in Montaigne's essay: politically self-serving language cannibalizes meaning and denies all access to truth. The satiric essay, as Montaigne rendered it, provides a means for regurgitating truth through the ironic manipulation of texts. "Of Cannibals" is the seminal example of the satiric essay: it becomes the very thing it satirizes, duping the unwary reader into mistaking its purposes while using a clever parody of contemporary accounts of the Americas to expose European political duplicity.

Practitioners of the form after Montaigne continued to employ kinds of parody to disguise their subversive objectives, often with such success that their satires were mistaken by the majority of their first readers for straightforward essays. Two of the more remarkable instances of this sort are **Daniel Defoe**'s *The Shortest Way with the Dissenters* (1702) and **Jonathan Swift**'s *A Modest Proposal for Preventing the Children of Poor People from Being a Burthen to Their Parents or the Country* (1729), both savage satires written in the guise of domestic political **pamphlets**. In *The Shortest Way* Defoe set out to expose the Anglican Church's repressive policies against dissenting denominations by assuming a High Church persona and arguing for more severe restrictions and punishments, insisting that "if the Gallows instead of the Counter, and the Gallies instead of the Fines, were the Reward of going to a Conventicle, to preach or hear," then few if any Englishmen would profess dissenting beliefs or survive to witness them. Defoe succeeded only in outraging both his fellow Dissenters and the authorities because his ironies were too acute; neither side could see the humor in so devastatingly naked an exposure of actual repression. At its best, the satiric essay simply states the truth with an authority and a zeal for precision that almost recalls Bacon's scientific method. Nowhere is that mock authority and ironic precision more disturbingly manipulated than in *A Modest Proposal*. Swift assumes the voice of a Tory gentleman to suggest that the English aristocracy encourage their Irish subjects to sell their own children as delicacies for the upper-class table, even going so far as to include recipes for this new epicurean delight. Swift's debt to Montaigne's "Of Cannibals" is an obvious one, but his own essay has assumed a transcendent place as the model for the ultimate reach of satiric irony, the phrase "a modest proposal" becoming a synonym for irony itself.

The extreme responses elicited by both Defoe and Swift from their readers have less to do with the obvious use of exaggeration and hyperbole in their essays than with the way in which both writers ironically manipulate the public discourse in their parody of recognizable political texts. These essays try to deceive their readers into overlooking their blatant ironies by closely imitating the language and emulating the rhetoric of the propagandists they intend to expose. Satiric essays are thus often more interested in humiliating readers by exposing our inattentiveness to the meaning of written language and our deafness to the tone of printed texts than in attacking their political foes. The danger that satiric essays warn about is the danger of the print medium itself, the power of a text-based culture to disarm the moral sensitivity of the reader by usurping the individual's reflective identity. That realization compels two satiric personae as unlike as Miguel de Cervantes' Don Quixote and Anthony Burgess' Alex (*A Clockwork Orange*, 1962) to destroy, respectively, the printing press and the typewriter that have imprinted their textual identities.

Bringing enlightenment through humiliation and empowering the reader through victimization are the paradoxical objectives that unite satiric essays as different as those of Francisco Gómez de Quevedo y Villegas (*Los sueños* [1627; *Visions*]), Laurence Sterne (*A Political Romance*, 1759), Victor Hugo (*Napoléon le Petit*, 1852), and **Mark Twain** (*To the Person Sitting in Darkness*, 1901). Even in the less ironic work of a **William Makepeace Thackeray** or an **S. J. Perelman**, the focus is still on the ambiguous nature of written language itself in its capacity to dull us to social inequalities and political injustice. By drawing the reader's attention to the dangerous inadequacies of language through entrapping that reader in a text of unexpected bewilderment, the satiric essay is ultimately an instruction in the fine and dangerous art of reading itself.

STEPHEN W. BROWN

Further Reading

Elliott, Robert C., *The Power of Satire*, Princeton, New Jersey: Princeton University Press, 1960

Nokes, David, *Raillery and Rage*, Brighton, Sussex: Harvester Press, and New York: St. Martin's Press, 1987

Paulson, Ronald, *The Fictions of Satire*, Baltimore: Johns Hopkins University Press, 1967

Rawson, Claude, editor, *English Satire and the Satiric Tradition*, Oxford: Blackwell, 1984

Tave, Stuart M., *The Amiable Humorist*, Chicago: University of Chicago Press, 1960

Scandinavian Essay

1. Introduction

The genesis of the essay in Scandinavia is not a Northern phenomenon. Its origin and inspiration came from the English moral weeklies of the early 18th century such as **Addison**'s and **Steele**'s *Tatler* and *Spectator*. Dano-Norwegians and Swedes became familiar with the **moral essay** primarily through translation into French or German, if not directly through the original English.

By the same token, the evolution of the essay in Scandinavia is not a unified phenomenon. Although the presumed homogeneity of the region sometimes engenders the hope of a common literature, each country has pursued its own path. While it is true that Denmark, Norway, and Sweden have inherited some shared experiences by dint of foreign literary influences and mutual political and cultural circumstances, the essay has more than any other genre retained its national character.

Notwithstanding, the essay in Scandinavia – linguistically speaking – can be traced to a single country; it was in Sweden, with the appearance in 1732 of **Olof von Dalin**'s (1708–63) journal *Then Swänska Argus* (1732–34; The Swedish Argus), that the Scandinavian essay began. The Swedish essay in turn heralded the rise of the Danish essay in the hands of Norwegian-born **Ludvig Holberg** (1684–1754), whose *Moralske Tanker* (*Moral Reflections*) appeared in 1744, a dozen years after the demise of *Then Swänska Argus*. Unlike Holberg, who after *Moral Reflections* wrote five volumes of epistles (1748–54), Dalin did not continue along the same lines for the remainder of his life. Thus while his Swedish *Argus* had some impact on Danish literature, its limited range – in both subject matter and the duration of publication – meant that it did not enjoy the international popularity or influence of Holberg's essays. Dalin's journal may have appeared first, but Holberg's essays found a greater and more lasting place in literary history.

2. The Danish Essay

In point of fact, Ludvig Holberg was not Denmark's first essayist. His essays were preceded by those of Christian Falster (1690–1752), who wrote three volumes of essays in Latin entitled *Amoenitates philologicæ* (1729–32; The pleasance of learning) in a neoclassical style. His themes are diverse; most are, however, scrupulously areligious. For both Danish writers, personal experience, moral philosophy, and the value of knowledge and philosophy are essential. While Holberg is still read today, Falster, whose essays were not translated into Danish until 1919, is only of historical interest.

By contrast, Holberg's *Moral Reflections* were translated into Dutch, French, Swedish, and German, while the *Epistles*, of which there are over 540, filling some 2000 pages, were translated into German, Dutch, and partially into Russian. *Moral Reflections* and the *Epistles* are complementary: the earlier work comprises the serious literary essay in the classical tradition (with echoes of Lucilius, **Cicero**, and **Seneca**), while the latter evinces a blend of **satire** and moral philosophy more aligned with **Montaigne**. Irony and parody became Holberg's main literary devices in addressing his public. His essays are of a dual nature: they reflect, on the one hand, individual experience, and demonstrate, on the other, the notion of common experience. The entertaining expert and occasional dilettante shows that he is well-read and informed on diverse subjects.

As the instigator setting the course of the Danish essay and the epistle, Holberg drew on foreign sources. It is difficult to speak of the essay tradition in Denmark – then or now – without taking account of foreign models. Both classical and French elements dominated the Danish essay up until Holberg's death in 1754. In the latter half of the 18th century, Denmark was more and more influenced by the English *Spectator* tradition. Twentieth-century Danish essays have likewise demonstrated a dependence on English and American authors.

Following Holberg's death, the Danish essay lived on in the spirit of the English moral weeklies. Jørgen Riis' *Den Danske Spectator* (1744–45; The Danish spectator) and *Anti-Spectator* (1744–45) were short-lived but nevertheless popular, inspiring a number of foreign-language *Spectator* publications. Among the most prominent were Johann E. Schlegel's *Der Fremde* (1745), La Beaumelle's *La Spectatrice Danoise* (1749), and J. A. Cramer's *Der Nordische Aufseher* (1758–61). Subsequently, another Danish-language publication, Jens Schielderup Sneedorff's (1724–64) *Den Patriotiske Tilskuer* (1761–63; The patriotic spectator), continued the tradition.

By the close of the 18th century, the essay in Denmark had been transformed from an expression of the neoclassical spirit into a sociopolitical undertaking which relied on the genre's ability to affect opinion and taste. The sudden change of emphasis can be ascribed to an enlarged audience and its increasingly bourgeois character. Eighteenth-century essays generally represented the learned class and in some cases, the learned elite. The transition from a theological to a secular society led, moreover, to new literary applications of the essay. Although the *Spectator* tradition was often the model for the popular Danish essay, the classical essay – the epistle in particular – remained the genuine representative of the genre. Toward the close of the 18th century, however, the epistle receded as a medium. The source of intimacy associated with epistolary dialogue became less and less compelling for both essayist and reader. Simultaneously, writers of essays developed a powerful sense of individualism and a diminished need to be morally instructive. What, then, had previously grounded itself in didactics transformed into an expression of individual experience. The resulting **personal essay** has since become the most practiced type of essay in Denmark. Whether Danish essayists describe life at home or abroad, they characteristically (and often ambivalently) express from an individual point of view what it is to be Danish and to live within Denmark's borders.

During the first half of the 19th century, a number of Danish writers excelled as masters of prose, but few as essayists *per se*. The primary emulator of English essayists was Johan Ludvig Heiberg (1791–1860), whose *Københavns Flyvende Post* (1827–37; The Copenhagen flying mail) includes **critical essays** which are both aesthetic and political. In considering the development of the Danish essay during the previous century, it becomes clear how the genre's purpose and emphasis changed with the times – namely, from a genre preoccupied with tangible concerns to issues more esoteric in nature. The

change can be explained in part by the reaction to Denmark's political and ideological confrontations with Prussia. The Danish essay was no longer exclusively the domain of the privileged and learned; well-established critics of lesser means now took it upon themselves to give it new life. As a result, the essay gradually lost its entertaining quality; in its place emerged the serious **treatise** and **polemical essay**.

Georg Brandes (1842–1927) is recognized as one of Denmark's principal essayists. He was, however, less an essayist than a master of polemic. In contrast to Holberg, who looked back to well-versed authorities of antiquity, Brandes turned to spokesmen of an empirical spirit consonant with his own age. Brandes' particular blend of essay and polemic was symptomatic of works labeled "essay" during the first decades of the 20th century. Religion, morals, ethical values, and the limits and responsibilities of science provided the basis of public opinion through which modern essayists were inspired. As a result, essays in Denmark became for a time less artistic and more topical. Once again, the journal took on the role as the leading medium for the essay.

Just after World War II, a group of aspiring critics and poets identifying themselves as "Heretics" contributed to a journal entitled *Heretica* (1948–53). Internationally oriented, they concerned themselves with the condition of modern man. The essay, along with the lyric, was the primary genre of the journal's first years. In this and like-minded literary journals, Danish writers appeared side by side with representatives from an international array of poets and essayists, Rainer Maria Rilke, **William Butler Yeats**, Pablo Neruda, Bertrand Russell, and **James Baldwin** among them.

Heretica, and the essays it contained, brought new impulses for other genres and set the tone for the Danish essay in subsequent years. Despite the Danish essayists' collective vision to improve society through the aesthetic qualities of language, stylistically they remained individuals as they contributed to the evolution of what is referred to as the literary essay. The final decade of the 19th century had experienced a rejuvenation of the literary essay, which became popular among modern-day moral philosophers and stylists. The Danish literary essay acquired some new supporters of the genre who saw it not only as a literary form, but also as a tool for enacting social change. Today, one typically finds a blend and an exchange of philosophy and fiction in the Danish literary essay.

During the second half of the 20th century, an increasing number of essay collections by individual Danish authors have appeared. **Jacob Paludan** (1896–1975), known as the essayist who in modern times has done the most for the genre, fuses the subjective and the objective in a free-wheeling style. His essays have been likened to "jaunts." Critics like Paludan have enthusiastically examined the nature and form of the Danish essay. **Per Lange** (1901–91) is best remembered for his characterization of the essay in "Om Essayets Form" (On the art of the essay). The critic Conrad Raun gave an account of the Danish essay in 1958 in the literary journal *Vindrosen* (Wind rose). Increased consciousness of the genre no doubt led to its use by social critics from the 1950s to the 1970s. For some writers of prose fiction such as **Villy Sørensen** (1929–), the essay is employed as a means of explaining that which has been concealed in the metaphors of imaginative literature, making symbols of human values perceptible when other genres have failed.

The youngest representatives of the Danish essay tend to hold their readers at a distance. Unlike their predecessors, they are not inclined to instruct. These aesthetically disposed essayists are often engaged critics, whose primary concerns are the interrelationships between ethics and art.

3. The Norwegian Essay

Ludvig Holberg, the father of Danish literature, is conventionally referred to by Norwegian literary historians as the first Norwegian essayist. Holberg's internationalism and air of modernity extended to continental Europe. Although it may be argued that the contemporary Norwegian essay is in some ways still reflective of European culture, most essays from Norway are oriented toward the country's national character and its concern for national identity. The dominance of Danish language and culture in Norway hindered the cultivation of an autonomous Norwegian essay. Following its political independence from Denmark in 1814 and the accompanying campaign for written Norwegian, the country witnessed the strengthening of the Norwegian essay. However, it has still not entirely emancipated itself from the didactic function and pedagogical tone it acquired through the patriotic efforts of the 1830s and 1840s.

Not unlike essayists in Sweden and Denmark, Norwegian essayists have concentrated on descriptions of nature and on essays which portray national literature. Some of the country's leading essayists – Hans Ernst Kinck (1865–1926), **Nils Kjær**, and Arne Garborg (1851–1924) – provide outstanding examples of a nationally oriented literature with an awareness of landscape and language. Of particular interest has been the Norwegian essayist's portrayal of contemporary Norwegian writers; **Gunnar Heiberg**'s (1857–1929) characterization of Henrik Wergeland and Knut Hamsun's (1859–1952) characterization of Henrik Ibsen are but two examples. The abstract quality often associated with the essay is consequently less visible in the Norwegian essay. In keeping with Norway's new national awareness, Norwegian essays have often resulted from internal social conflicts. Because of the popularity of this kind of writing, the social value of such pieces has from time to time dominated artistic elements. Particularly during the 1960s and 1970s, the Norwegian essay took on the character of monologue and polemic.

While in Denmark the essay has sometimes exposed the Danes' ambivalence toward their country, in Norway it has worked to create a mode of expression compatible with efforts to establish cultural unity. Linguistically, this is observed in the essays of Asmund Vinje (1818–70) in his periodical *Dølen* (1858–70; The dalesman). With his *Spectator*-like treatment of topics such as education, folklore, politics, and philosophy, Vinje found a conversational style which complemented his efforts to promote the written Norwegian language *nynorsk*, which was based on western Norwegian dialects. The continuation of the tradition, using the essay to strengthen nationalism, can be observed in the epistles and essays of the so-called 20th-century Vinje, Tor Jonsson (1916–51).

The essay has affected Norwegian literature in another way. This point was made clear by **Nils Kjær** (1870–1924), who represents the last chapter of the era of Norway's literary dependence on Denmark. In 1895, Kjær wrote in the journal *Tidssignaler* (Signs of the times) that the critical essay was about to supersede the novel as the dominant genre. There, he points to the French writer **Paul Bourget** as an example of a belletrist and philosopher who considers the **critical essay** to be an organic whole – that is, more than merely a literary **review**. According to Kjær, the growing popularity of the essay in Norway just before the turn of the century could be ascribed to new expectations and a thirst for intellectual growth by readers. More and more, the Norwegian public looked to literature less for entertainment than for intellectual stimulation. Kjær found a further explanation for the essay's popularity in the critics' changed perception of their goals and means. Contrary to **Hippolyte Taine**, the new Norwegian essayist wrote with the conviction that criticism is art and not science. Norwegian essays at the turn of the century reveal their authors' individual personalities. In Kjær's words, those essayists sought to create "*sjælemonographier*" (monographic accounts of the soul) rather than "*kulturbilleder*" (pictures of civilization).

4. The Swedish Essay

Notwithstanding the fact that individual Swedish authors wrote essays during the 18th century, there was no organized effort then to further the genre in Sweden. To the brief list of 18th-century Swedish essays belongs Count Johan Thuresson Oxenstierna (1666–1733), whose *Recueil de pensées du Comte J. O. sur divers sujets* (1720–21; Collection of thoughts of Count Johan Oxenstierna on diverse subjects) attracted international attention. Oxenstierna has been referred to as "the Montaigne of the North"; the allusion is to the authors' similar choice of topics, their use of quotations, and the general disposition of their works. *Pensées* was printed 18 times in French, but it was not translated into Swedish until 1767.

Swedish-language epistles can first be identified with *En gammal mans bref till en ung printz* (1756; An old man's letter to a young prince) by Carl Gustaf Tessin (1695–1770). The Swedish-language tradition continued, mostly in the form of *Spectator* literature. Even before Olof von Dalin's *Then Swänska Argus*, Sweden could boast of Carl (1703–61) and Edvard (1704–67) Carleson's *Sedolärande Mercurius* (1730–31; Didactic Mercury). In both of these publications, the essays were usually character portrayals. Following the cessation of *Then Swänska Argus*, a number of Swedish moral weeklies appeared. Parallel with the moral weeklies emerged essays in the form of literary criticism. *Den Swänska Mercurius* (1755–61, 1763–65; The Swedish mercury) of Carl Christoffer Gjörwell (1731–1811) can be described as the beginning of Swedish literary criticism published on a daily basis and in brief essays.

The early 19th century is represented by P. D. A. Atterbom (1790–1855), Johan Erik Rydkvist (1800–77), and Louis Gerhard de Geer (1818–96). Rydkvist's journal *Heimdall* (1828–32) was English- and French-inspired at a time when the Swedish cultural climate was dominated by Germany. Associated with the **familiar essay**, and an admirer of **Francis Bacon**, de Geer produced pieces such as "Om dans" (On dance) and "Om konversation" (On conversation).

During the so-called "breakthrough" of modern literature in the 1870s and 1880s, increasing influence from France was evident. **Sainte-Beuve** and Paul Bourget inspired Swedish literary essayists; Atterbom's *Litterära karakteristiker I–II*

(1870; Literary characteristics) was largely influenced by Sainte-Beuve. Both writers tended to create psychological portraits, using anecdotes and, at times, fictional enhancements of authors' lives. In response to Atterbom, the number of literary, biographical, and **historical essays** increased in Sweden during the 1890s. The development of the Swedish essay during the latter half of the 19th century took its cues from Sainte-Beuve, as well as Taine and Brandes. Other noted essayists of this period are Gustav af Geijerstam (1858–1909) (*Ur samtiden* [1883; From our times]) and Ola Hansson (1860–1925) (*Literära silhouetter* [1885; Literary silhouettes]). Both works are compendia of literary portraits. Hansson, in particular, concentrated on the development of the critical-biographical essay as a literary form. Metaphor and lyric quality are essential elements in his writing. Sweden's general awareness of the essay as a genre can be accredited to Hansson's essays.

The dominant Swedish essayist during the period between 1890 and 1906 was Oscar Levertin (1862–1906), whose principal essay collection, *Diktare och drömmare* (1898; Poets and dreamers), reveals his distrust of contemporary movements. While some of his essays approach prose fiction, they retain personal elements which are identified with the essay.

Levertin's successor was Frederik Böök (1883–1961). Although he attracted considerable attention for his affinity with Nazism, his essays nevertheless inspired aspiring essayists, and by doing so pointed to the role of the genre in shaping political opinion. As an essayist, Böök can be characterized as a critic and moralist who was dedicated to Germany and to nationalism. His major work, *Essayer och kritiker* (1913–23; Essays and criticism), is a multi-volume collection of works often on literary topics and literary figures.

Most contemporary Swedish essayists evince a close familiarity with modern journalism and prose fiction. Characteristically, Levertin's essays demonstrate an affinity with descriptive metaphor and hypotactic associations. Analogies often reveal a relationship to art. All of this contributes to essays in which subjectivity replaces fact. Even an essayist as ideologically attuned as Böök revealed a sensitivity to symbolism.

Frans G. Bengtsson (1894–1954) is recognized as the most widely read Swedish essayist. His style is largely associative, but also archaic and imitative. He is a master of the informal essay, holding his own with French and English essayists. Stylistically, Bengtsson is an anglophile, writing in the tradition of **Charles Lamb, Thomas Carlyle,** and **Thomas Babington Macaulay.** Bengtsson succeeds in mastering parallelism through the use of comic and musical elements. Analogies, anecdotes, and quotations create an ironic but also sympathetic pastiche.

During the second period in the development of the Swedish essay (1907–19), the essay emerged as a new form of expression, and developed dramatically. This growth can in part be attributed to a change in the structure of the reading public. Collections of literature and theater criticism increased. Some essayists and critics in Sweden felt that the term essay should be reserved for the literary essay. Even those who accepted the term "essay" recognized two forms: the aesthetic on the one hand, and the nationalistic on the other.

In Sweden, the term "essay" came to be used as a subtitle for literary, historical, and **philosophical essays.** "Essay" was accepted, for example, by Ola Hansson when he changed the name of his "silhouettes" to "essays," and by Ellen Key (1849–1924) when she described her pieces in *Människor* (1899; Man) as "essayer." During the decade between 1920 and 1930, however, consciousness of the essay in Sweden decreased, for various political and economic reasons. At the same time, however, new forms of the essay such as the **travel essay,** descriptions of nature, and the historical essay gained popularity.

Over time, the essay has taken on many styles in Sweden. Inspired by **Rousseau,** Carl Jonas Love Almqvist (1793–1866) produced lengthy essays on national character. August Strindberg (1849–1912) wrote essays on cultural and social problems. **Vilhelm Ekelund** (1880–1949) gave expression to his search for truth and beauty in a long series of aphoristic essays. The 1930s saw a rash of critical essays in short-lived periodical publications such as *Spektrum,* the *Fönstret* (Window), and *Fronten.*

The essay flourished among 19th- and 20th-century Swedish speakers in Finland. In its origins, the Finland-Swedish essay can be traced to Johan Ludvig Runeberg (1804–77), who as an essayist wrote principally about Finland's political and social conflicts and the problems of literary criticism, and to Johan Vilhelm Snellman (1806–81), who despite his Finnish sympathies wrote in Swedish against Sweden.

A number of Swedish essays in Finland can be described as discourses on aesthetics, as self-portrayals, and as self-analyses. Literary journals have played an important role in the reception of the essay, as literary criticism was thought to be edifying. Viktor Rydberg (1828–95) was known for what is called the extended controversial essay or polemic. Elmer Diktonius (1896–1961) mastered the "conversational essay." The critical essay is associated with Rabbe Enckell (1903–74). In general, however, the Swedish essay in Finland has remained local and historical, as it reflects literary history and national concerns.

5. Conclusion

As with other genres, it may be argued that the essay in individual Scandinavian countries is marked by certain affinities. The Danish essay might be called the subjective, **personal essay;** the Norwegian essay, the essay of national character; the Swedish essay, the literary essay. Scandinavia's production of essays has also been affected by conditions outside the realm of literature; for example, the historian must consider the effects of the world wars on book production, the ensuing climate of intellectual debate, and the influence of the press. And in all three countries, the cultural and literary journal has played a role in keeping the essay alive in the minds of readers. The essay has not, however, been a traditional genre in all parts of Scandinavia. In fact, the only Icelandic writer who can be identified as an essayist is Guðmundur Finnbogason (1873–1944), one-time national librarian of Iceland. Women make up a proportionately small number of essayists; the largest group is represented by Sweden. In some literary histories the term "essay" is not even indexed. In others, the essay is generally treated as an author's secondary preoccupation; little effort is made to clarify the relationship between the essay and other genres. Although the essay is much discussed, it is relegated to the less important corners of secondary and university instruction. Nevertheless, there are superficial efforts to insure the future of the essay. Editors of anthologies of

Scandinavian essays tend to comb and excerpt every major author's oeuvre.

To address the future of the essay in Scandinavia implies that solutions must be found to make it relevant to a wide range of readers, to portray ordinary and universal experience. In an essay entitled "Essayn," the Swedish writer Sven Lindqvist writes that the traditional gentleman's essay must lose its elitism. In order to survive as an art form, it must speak to both the joys and the sorrows of life, and it must be instructive.

P. M. MITCHELL
VIVIAN GREENE-GANTZBERG

Anthology
Norske essays, edited by Carl F. Engelstad, Oslo: Gyldendal, 1967

Further Reading
Billeskov Jansen, F. J., *Holberg som epigrammatiker og essayist*, Copenhagen: Munksgaard, 2 vols., 1938–39

Engelstad, Carl F., "Innledning," in *Norske essays*, edited by Engelstad, Oslo: Gyldendal, 1967

Grepstad, Ottar, "Det nynorske essayet fra a ti Aa," *Vinduet* 36, no. 3 (1982): 24–34

Grepstad, Ottar, editor, *Essayet i Norge: Fjorten riss av ein tradisjon*, Oslo: Norske Samlaget, 1982

Hågg, Göran, *Övertalning och underhallning: Den svenska essaistiken, 1890–1930*, Stockholm: Wahlström & Widstrand, 1978

Sandersen, Vibeke, *Essayet – Oprøret og tradition*, Copenhagen: Gyldendal, 1975

Sandersen, Vibeke, *Essayet – Filosofi og fiktion*, Copenhagen: Gyldendal, 1977

Schoolfield, George, "The Literary Essay in Finland," in *The Nordic Mind: Current Trends in Scandinavian Literary Criticism*, edited by Fred Egholm Andersen and John Weinstock, Lanham, Maryland: University Press of America, 1986: 103–10

Schiller, Friedrich von

German, 1759–1805

Although Friedrich von Schiller is principally known as a dramatist, he also produced a substantial body of critical and theoretical writings during the course of his career, some of which might be described as essays. The term "essay" requires some qualification, however, if it is to be applied to Schiller's work: his theoretical writings are never familiar or personal in tone and he is never concerned with trivia or with capturing the fleeting impressions of ordinary human existence. His vision is consistently broad and grand – but it is given life and energy through the dynamic, rhetorical style and organizational skills of the born dramatist, and underpinned by a distinctly practical concern (whether explicit or implicit) with how literary works can be put together effectively, and with the role they fulfill in the world.

Schiller's earliest surviving prose works, dating from his school days at Duke Karl Eugen's academy in Stuttgart, already exhibit the essential characteristics of his mature work. They include two speeches on the nature of virtue, composed for festive occasions at court and delivered by Schiller himself in 1779 and 1780. These display a confident, even exuberant, mastery of rhetorical structures and devices, and the ability to present an argument with persuasive forcefulness. Schiller's medical writings from the same period offer an interesting contrast to these party pieces, with a more sober tone and a coolly analytical approach. His later prose works derive their particular strength from a combination of these qualities: a highly analytical method sustained by often breathtaking stylistic virtuosity.

During the 1780s, alongside his early plays, Schiller produced a number of occasional pieces for journals, including two short essays on the theater and a number of **reviews** (among them reviews of Goethe's *Egmont* in 1788 and *Iphigenie* in 1789). The themes and stylistic features of later prose works are variously prefigured in these pieces, but it was not until the early 1790s, when he was professor of history at the University of Jena, that Schiller began to investigate aesthetic and philosophical issues in greater depth, inspired by his study of **Kant**. The result was a number of shorter **treatises**: two essays on tragedy ("Über den Grund des Vergnügens an tragischen Gegenständen" [1792; On the reason for our enjoyment of tragic subjects] and "Über die tragische Kunst" [1792; On the art of tragedy]), essays on the sublime and on pathos ("Vom Erhabenen" and "Über das Pathetische," which appeared in *Neue Thalia* in 1793), and an investigation into the nature of beauty ("Über Anmut und Würde" [1793; On grace and dignity]). Even amid the abstract speculations of these philosophical works the dramatic practitioner is constantly apparent: the analysis of tragic or literary effects veers repeatedly toward discussion of how these effects are to be achieved in practice.

Schiller's momentous meeting with **Goethe** in July 1794, the beginning of their decade-long friendship, proved to be a catalyst in terms of his own work, provoking a deeper investigation of aesthetic questions and inspiring a personal creative renaissance. In 1794 and 1795, under the impetus of this new association, Schiller produced his two major theoretical essays, *Briefe über die ästhetische Erziehung des Menschen* (*On the Aesthetic Education of Man*) and the treatise *Über naive und sentimentalische Dichtung* (*On the Naive and Sentimental in Literature*).

The *Aesthetic Education* began as a series of **letters** addressed to the patron who had intervened with financial assistance in 1791, when serious illness and poverty were threatening to bring Schiller's career to an untimely end. These early letters were destroyed in a fire in Copenhagen in February 1794 and in the Fall of the same year Schiller started work on a revised version, which was published in three installments in the journal *Die Horen* (The muses) in 1795. Two hundred years after their composition there is still much in these 27 letters that speaks directly to a modern readership. The early letters establish the basis of the argument, with Schiller's contention that aesthetic matters are not a peripheral issue but fundamental for the harmonious development of both society and the individual. This section of the work culminates in the tremendous fifth and sixth letters, which survey the current lamentable state of humanity: individuals torn between imagination and intuition on the one hand, and science and abstraction on the other; a fragmented society where people are just cogs in a larger machine, unable to develop fully as individuals.

Schiller's resonant condemnation of a world in which progress is attained at the expense of individual wholeness is extremely effective; echoes of his argument can be heard distinctly in **Freud**'s *Das Unbehagen in der Kultur* (1930; *Civilization and Its Discontents*). The later letters examine the concept of beauty, and argue that art has a vital function in enabling society and individuals to develop their full moral potential, through its ability to reconcile the basic drives underlying human existence (e.g. material and form, the finite and the infinite, sensation and reflection).

Much of Schiller's argument is clearly still pertinent today, when the distances between different areas of human endeavor and the chasms of ignorance between isolated specialist fields appear greater and their implications more terrifying than ever. Other aspects of the work may seem more historically specific – Schiller's contention, for example, that artists should turn to the Greek classics for inspiration, as a counterbalance to the stultifying conventions of the contemporary cultural scene. Yet all of it is compelling: the driving, dramatic style of presentation gives the writing immense force and presence, even where the author is dealing in abstractions. Schiller's ideal aesthetic resolution of the fundamental tensions in human existence has its stylistic equivalent in the beautiful, almost architectonic structures of his language.

Schiller's second major theoretical treatise, *On the Naive and Sentimental in Literature*, was begun at the same time as the *Aesthetic Education* and also appeared in installments in *Die Horen*, in 1795 and 1796. This work owes even more to the stimulating effect of Schiller's friendship with Goethe. It is no more familiar in tone than any of his other prose works, but it is, in a very profound way, thoroughly an "essay": in it Schiller is implicitly testing and defining himself (an archetypally "sentimental" or reflective writer) against literary traditions and ideals, and against his much-admired friend (an archetypal "naive" genius). In a letter to Wilhelm von Humboldt (7 September 1795), Schiller reveals that his examination of the "naive" in literature had necessarily forced upon him the question of how he could still claim to be a writer despite having no feeling of kinship with the ancient Greeks. Through this treatise he is effectively defining and validating his position as a modern writer.

The presentation of the argument in this treatise also has more traditional essay-like qualities: Schiller did not start out with an overall plan, but let the argument evolve as he progressed. He begins with an examination of the "naive" as if this is his only object of inquiry, moving on to consider the contrasts between the "naive" and "sentimental" modes (between nature and culture, feeling and thought, the finite and the infinite). This leads into an extended examination of different genres and writers. The essay ends with a more general application of the central categories to "realists" and "idealists" as human archetypes.

After 1795 Schiller devoted himself to his dramatic compositions (the plan for the Wallenstein trilogy was already under way); the correspondence with Goethe became his principal arena for literary discussion, and he produced little in the way of published theoretical writing – just the small essay on epic and dramatic poetry written jointly with Goethe, and a **preface** to *Die Braut von Messina* (1803; *The Bride of Messina*) on the use of the chorus in tragedy. All Schiller's theoretical writings, and especially those of the 1790s, display the consummate rhetorical and constructional skills of this master dramatist; the two major treatises formed a basis for, and a prelude to, the great dramatic works he produced in the following decade.

SUSAN MACKERVOY

Biography
Johann Christoph Friedrich von Schiller. Born 10 November 1759 in Marbach am Neckar, Württemberg. Studied law and medicine at the military academy of Duke Karl Eugen of Württemberg (i.e. the Karlsschule), Stuttgart, 1773–80, graduated as a regimental doctor, 1780. First play, *Die Räuber* (*The Robbers*), performed January 1782; left Württemberg because his writing displeased the Duke, 1782. Contracted to write for the National Theater, Mannheim, 1783–84. Editor, *Die Rheinische Thalia* (later *Die Thalia* and *Die Neue Thalia*), 1785–93; joined the Körner circle, Leipzig, then Dresden, from 1785. Professor of history, University of Jena, 1789–91: resigned because of ill health. Married Charlotte von Lengefeld, 1790: two sons and two daughters. Founder and editor, *Die Horen*, 1794–97. He refused professorship in Tübingen, 1795. Lived in Weimar, after 1799, and several plays produced under Goethe's direction at the Hoftheater. Ennobled by Emperor Franz II, 1802. Died in Weimar, 9 May 1805.

Selected Writings

Essays and Related Prose
Briefe über die ästhetische Erziehung des Menschen, in *Die Horen*, 1795; edited by Wolfgang Düsing, 1981; as "Upon the Aesthetic Culture of Man," in *The Philosophical and Aesthetic Letters and Essays*, translated by J. Weiss, 1845; as *On the Aesthetic Education of Man*, translated by Reginald Snell, 1954, and Elizabeth M. Wilkinson and L. A. Willoughby, 1967
Über naive und sentimentalische Dichtung, in *Die Horen*, 1795–96; edited by W. F. Mainland, 1950; as "On Simple and Sentimental Poetry," in *Essays Aesthetical and Philosophical*, 1875; as *On the Naive and Sentimental in Literature*, translated by Helen Watanabe O'Kelly, 1981
The Philosophical and Aesthetic Letters and Essays, translated by J. Weiss, 1845
Aesthetical Writings, translated by Charles J. Hempel, in *Schiller's Complete Works*, vol. 2, 1861
Essays Aesthetical and Philosophical (various translators), 1875
Essays and Letters, translated by A. Lodge, E. B. Eastwick, and A. J. W. Morrisson, 1901
Aesthetical and Philosophical Essays, translated anonymously, edited by Nathan Haskell Dole, 2 vols., 1902
Essays (various translators), edited by Walter Hinderer and Daniel O. Dahlstrom, 1993

Other writings: 18 plays (including *Don Carlos*, 1787; *Wallenstein* plays, 1798–99; *Maria Stuart*, 1800; *Wilhelm Tell* [*William Tell*], 1804), poetry (including *An die Freude* [*Ode to Joy*], 1786), fiction, histories of the Low Countries and of the Thirty Years' War, and letters.

Collected works editions: *Works* (Bohn Standard Library), 4 vols., 1847–49; *Werke* (Nationalausgabe), edited by Julius Petersen, Gerhard Fricke, and others, 1943– (in progress); *Werke und Briefe*, edited by Klaus Harro Hilzinger and others, 6 vols., 1988–95 (in progress; 12 vols. projected).

Bibliographies
Vulpius, W., *Schiller-Bibliographie 1893–1958*, Weimar: Arion, 1959; supplements by Vulpius, 1967, P. Wersig, 1977, and Roland Bärwinkel and others, 1989; other supplements in *Jahrbuch der Deutschen Schillergesellschaft*.

Further Reading

Meyer, Hermann, "Schillers philosophische Rhetorik," *Euphorion* 53 (1959): 91–128

Reed, T. J., *The Classical Center: Goethe and Weimar, 1775–1832*, Totowa, New Jersey: Barnes and Noble, 1980; Oxford: Oxford University Press, 1986

Staiger, Emil, *Friedrich Schiller*, Zurich: Atlantis, 1967

Üding, Gert, *Schillers Rhetorik: Idealistische Wirkungsästhetik und rhetorische Tradition*, Tübingen: Niemeyer, 1971

Wilkinson, Elizabeth M., and L. A. Willoughby, Introduction to their translation of *On the Aesthetic Education of Man* by Schiller, Oxford: Clarendon Press, 1982 (original translation, 1967)

Schlegel, Friedrich

German, 1772–1829

Brother of August Wilhelm (the great Sanskritist and Shakespeare scholar), contemporary of **Goethe, Schiller,** Ludwig Tieck, and **Madame de Staël,** and influenced by his predecessors **Lessing, Herder,** and **Kant,** Friedrich Schlegel was one of history's great practitioners of the essay form. While he wrote in many other genres, his other best-known works were collections of **aphorism**s, in part probably inspired by S. R. N. Chamfort's revival of the form. His critical masterpiece is generally agreed to be "Über Goethe's *Meister*" (1798; "On Goethe's *Meister*"), though an earlier essay, "Über das Studium der griechischen Poesie" (1797; "On the Study of Greek Poetry"), aroused much interest, inspired as it was by Schiller's famous piece, *Über naive und sentimentalische Dichtung* (1795–96; *On the Naive and Sentimental in Literature*).

Schlegel developed further Herder's earlier efforts to relate ancient and modern literature, using Herder's insights into Shakespeare and historical relativism, and learning much from neoclassicists like Johann Winckelmann and Lessing, however much of their thought he also rejected. In 1797, Schlegel published his first collection of aphorisms in the journal *Lyceum der schönen Künste* (Lyceum of the fine arts), introducing central ideas about "romantische Poesie" from earlier conceptions of the character of modern literature as "interessant." Three years later, the *Gespräch über die Poesie* (Dialogue on Poetry) was published, and became known as Schlegel's manifesto of Romanticism.

By this time, Schlegel had begun to believe that the preoccupations of earlier critics with the differences between ancient literature (Greek, Latin, Hebrew) and modern writings had obscured the more important fact of their similarities. The tendency to revile and devalue modern literary works, forms, and styles in the 18th century in favor of ancient ones had begun to falter, as Herder, Johann Georg Hamann, August Wilhelm Schlegel, Tieck, and others began to perceive the appropriateness of new art for new eras – hence the centrality of Herder's "historical relativism." Yet, while other early writings of Schlegel's, including "Über Lessing" (1797; "On Lessing"), "Über die Unverständlichkeit" (1800; "On Incomprehensibility"), "Athenäum Fragmente" (1798; "Athenaeum Fragments"), and "Ideen" (1800; "Ideas"), functioned to gain a new appreciation for modern literature, using Shakespeare's works as a touchstone, Schlegel also established this evaluation by a new means. His writings reveal a dawning awareness that, in spite of all the differences – now perceived as valuable innovations and beauties, instead of fallings away from a classical ideal – there were central similarities between ancient and modern art and literature. Even further, Schlegel came to believe that these similarities were expressive of whatever those characteristics are which we feel to be "aesthetic" qualities, and which lead to "aesthetic" experiences. Thus, the earlier effort to understand better the "essentially modern" in literature led instead to a better appreciation of the "essentially aesthetic." Eventually, the adverb "essentially" was dropped, and a historical, relative view of art, literature, and the aesthetic was fully developed, in which Schlegel and other contemporaries like **Novalis,** Tieck, Jean Paul (Richter), and Karl Solger explored the way concepts like "Romantic irony," "self-criticism," and "self-development" could contribute to an open-ended, non-absolutist, non-essentialist aesthetic theory. The essays, fragments, and other writings of these German Romantic ironists – as they are often known – combined with writings in England by their friend **Coleridge** and, later, **Shelley,** laid the theoretical grid for much modern critical theory, starting with the Russian formalists and leading, through Mikhail Bakhtin, the New Critics, and structuralism, to both deconstruction and new historicism. For the Romantic ironists, deconstructive ideas and historicist-relativist ideas would hardly seem as antagonistic as they are made out to be today. Schlegel's concept of "Romantic irony" was, in large part, an attempt to show that historical and textual criticism are not antagonists, and not even alternative approaches, but necessary complements in any critical discussion of a work of art.

Schlegel's essays, as well as his fragments, his novel *Lucinde* (1799), and his other writings proceed in the main through a playful, witty, and nonsequential mode which defies traditional essay forms and audience expectations. Much like Shelley, Schlegel released the energies of extended metaphors, symbols, images, and apparently anecdotal, miscellaneous asides to create a new kind of development which defied the reason while intriguing the imagination. Digressions, absurd asides, and other disruptions led to the juxtaposition of themes, styles, and manners not normally seen in such a relation, so that the usual discursive prose of the essay is turned into rhetorical fireworks, and the essay – the criticism – itself becomes a work of art. Like Coleridge with his *Biographia Literaria* (1817) or Shelley with "A Defence of Poetry" (1821), Schlegel nurtured a form of literary criticism which sought not to reveal objective truths or best interpretations of literary works. These writers sought to achieve a criticism which was so illuminating about how works of art delight the reader that it became a work of art itself. This is a case of "Romantic irony" in its most exemplary form. It led to such concepts as "self-cultivation" and "self-development," ideas about which Schiller and Goethe had also written or in which they had also been interested. However, these two giants rejected, in the main, formulations that the younger, rebellious generation gave them.

Such central aesthetic concepts about the self were based on the Socratic/Platonic emphasis on self-knowledge: "Know thyself" as the end not only of philosophy, but also of art and its sister, religion. Schlegel's essays, as well as his fragments and novel, were designed as implicit **dialogues,** functioning to draw the reader into the thinking and imagining processes embodied in the text. This dialogic trait helps to prevent the reader both from extracting notional truths in a subservient way and from being condescending. Schlegel's ironic (self-implicating) narrative structures gradually reveal to the reader that the "content" of all works of criticism/art/philosophy can be said metaphorically to be self-cultivation and self-knowledge. Moreover, as Novalis added, without a thorough knowledge of ourselves we can never understand others. This self-knowledge, however, is described by means of concepts of layers and strata with no center; like an onion, we peel away layer after layer. Schlegel described self-development as "eternal agility": endless, purposeless play, with art as a central initiator – for both artist and reader – of opportunities for partaking in a feast of intense self-experiencing, which alone leads to a knowledge of the world.

Other characteristics of Schlegel's essay form involved techniques of "indirect communication" – adopted with ironic intensity by Kierkegaard some decades later. Based on ideas discussed above, indirect communication is at the center of Schlegel's aesthetics, and is demonstrated in his essay style, whereby in speaking and writing about one thing – some specific subject matter – he is actually speaking and writing about language, speaking, and writing. Since language is so fundamental to human consciousness, this leads to Schlegel's indirect subject matter, the human mind and the reader as specific occasion of that mind. Yet, while individuality is one focus of Schlegel's attention in his fragments and essays, it is situated in that quintessentially communal, social experience, namely literature. Through an emphasis upon *Sympoesie* and *Gesellschaft* or community, Schlegel's essays often do actually succeed in demonstrating what he set out to expound in them.

KATHLEEN M. WHEELER

Biography

Carl Wilhelm Friedrich von Schlegel. Born 10 March 1772 in Hanover. Studied at the University of Göttingen, 1790–91; University of Leipzig, 1791–94. Apprenticed to a banker in Leipzig, 1788; moved to Dresden, 1794, and Berlin, 1797. Contributor, *Deutschland*, 1797, and **Der Teutsche Merkur** (The German Mercury), cofounder and editor, with his brother August Wilhelm Schlegel, **Athenäum**, 1798–1800. Lecturer, University of Jena, 1800–01. Lived in Paris, 1802–04. Founding editor, *Europa* journal, 1803–05. Married Dorothea Veit (née Mendelssohn; daughter of **Moses Mendelssohn**), 1804. Lived in Cologne, 1804–07. Converted to Catholicism, 1808. Moved to Vienna, 1808. Administrator, Austrian government diplomatic service, 1809; served in the Austrian army, 1809–10. Cofounder and editor, *Deutsches Museum* (German museum) periodical, 1812–13. Appointed by Metternich as member of Austrian delegation to the Bundestag, Frankfurt, 1815–18. Editor, *Concordia* journal, 1820–23. Died (of a stroke) in Dresden, 12 January 1829.

Selected Writings

Essays and Related Prose

Die Griechen und Römer: Historische und kritische Versuche über das Klassische Alterthum, 1797
Gespräch über die Poesie, in *Athenäum*, 1800; as *Dialogue on Poetry*, with *Literary Aphorisms*, edited and translated by Ernst Behler and Roman Struc, 1968
Über die Sprache und Weisheit der Indier, 1808; edited by E. F. K. Koerner, 1977; as "On the Language and Philosophy of the Indians," in *The Aesthetic and Miscellaneous Works of F. von Schlegel*, translated by E. J. Millington, 1849

Über die neuere Geschichte (lectures), 1811; translated by Lyndsey Purcell and R. H. Whitelock, in *A Course of Lectures on Modern History*, 1849
Geschichte der alten und neuen Literatur, 1812; as *Lectures on the History of Literature, Ancient and Modern*, translated by J. G. Lockhart, 2 vols., 1818
Philosophie des Lebens (lectures), 1828; as *The Philosophy of Life, and Philosophy of Language*, translated by A. J. W. Morrison, 1847
Philosophie der Geschichte (lectures), 2 vols., 1829; as *The Philosophy of History*, translated by James Burton Robertson, 2 vols., 1835, revised edition, 1846
Philosophische Vorlesungen, insbesondere über Philosophie der Sprache und des Wortes, 1830
The Aesthetic and Miscellaneous Works, translated by E. J. Millington, 1849
A Course of Lectures on Modern History: To Which Are Added Historical Essays on the Beginning of Our History, and on Caesar and Alexander, translated by L. Purcell and R. H. Whitelock, 1849
Kritische Schriften, edited by Wolfdietrich Rasch, 1956
Kritische Fragmente, edited by Wolfdietrich Rasch, 1956; as "Critical Fragments," in *Lucinde and The Fragments*, translated by Peter Firchow, 1971
Literary Notebooks, 1797–1801 (in German), edited by Hans Eichner, 1957
Dialogue on Poetry; Literary Aphorisms, edited and translated by Ernst Behler and Roman Struc, 1968
Lucinde and The Fragments (includes the novel *Lucinde*; "Critical Fragments"; "Athenaeum Fragments"; "Ideas"; "On Incomprehensibility"), translated by Peter Firchow, 1971
Philosophical Fragments, translated by Peter Firchow, 1991

Other writings: the novel *Lucinde* (1799), a play, poetry, and correspondence.

Collected works edition: *Kritische Friedrich-Schlegel-Ausgabe*, edited by Ernst Behler and others, 28 vols., 1958–95.

Bibliography

Deubel, Volker, "Die Friedrich-Schlegel-Forschung, 1945–1972," *Deutsche Vierteljahrsschrift* 47 (1973): 48–181

Further Reading

Dieckmann, Liselotte, "Friedrich Schlegel and the Romantic Concepts of the Symbol," *Germanic Review* 34 (1959): 276–83
Eichner, Hans, "The Supposed Influence of Schiller's 'Naive and Sentimental Poetry' on Friedrich Schlegel's 'Über das Studium der griechischen Poesie'," *Germanic Review* 30 (1955): 260–64
Eichner, Hans, "Friedrich Schlegel's Theory of Romantic Poetry," *PMLA* 71 (1956): 1018–41
Eichner, Hans, *Friedrich Schlegel*, New York: Twayne, 1970
Henel, H., "Friedrich Schlegel und die Grundlagen der modernen literarischen Kritik," *Germanic Review* 20 (1945): 81–93
Immerwahr, R., "The Subjectivity or Objectivity of Friedrich Schlegel's Poetic Irony," *Germanic Review* 26 (1951): 173–91
Immerwahr, R., "Friedrich Schlegel's 'On Goethe's *Wilhelm Meister*'," *Monatshefte* 49 (1957): 1–22
Lange, Victor, "Friedrich Schlegel's Literary Criticism," *Comparative Literature* 7 (1955): 289–305
Szondi, Peter, "Friedrich Schlegel und die romantische Ironie: Mit einem Anhang über Ludwig Tieck," *Euphorion* 48 (1954): 397–411
Walzel, Oskar, *German Romanticism*, New York and London: Putnam, 1932 (original German edition, 1908)
Wheeler, K. M., Introduction to *German Aesthetic and Literary Criticism: The Romantic Ironists and Goethe*, edited by Wheeler, Cambridge: Cambridge University Press, 1984: 1–27

Schopenhauer, Arthur

German, 1788–1860

Arthur Schopenhauer presented in his major philosophical work, *Die Welt als Wille und Vorstellung* (1819; *The World as Will and Representation*), a consistent, rationally defended pessimism unique in the history of Western thought. Published when he was 30, *The World as Will and Representation* is the centerpiece and point of reference of all his other writings. Written in a nonacademic style that is lucid, direct, and immediate, it is a philosophical book that hardly needs explication. Because of his focus on "the problem of existence" Schopenhauer has been linked to existential philosophy. His Olympian, ironic, and spiritually aristocratic tone presents the message that existence is the expression of an insatiable, pervasive will generating a terrible world of conflict and suffering, senselessness, and futility. The "will to live" perpetuates this dreadful cosmic spectacle, and the goal of one who sees through the deceptive illusions of life is the *denial* of this powerful will to live.

Schopenhauer wrote a number of purely **philosophical essays** which, in effect, were supplements to *The World as Will and Representation*. In his essay *Über den Willen in der Natur* (1836; "On the Will in Nature"), he presents a dark portrait of the brutality and cruelty in the natural world based on the studies of naturalists, a theme replicated in film and television in recognizable Schopenhauerian tones. Another philosophical essay, "Über die Freiheit des menschlichen Willens" (*Essay on the Freedom of the Will*) was awarded a prize in 1839 by the Scientific Society of Trondheim in Norway. In 1841 he combined this essay with another entitled "Über das Fundament der Moral" (*The Basis of Morality*) and had the two published in a single volume under the title *Die beiden Grundprobleme der Ethik* (The two fundamental problems in ethics).

Schopenhauer's influence can be traced to some of the themes of the music dramas of one of his earliest admirers, the composer Richard Wagner, to the development of the theory of the unconscious in Eduard von Hartmann's *Philosophie des Unbewussten* (1869; *The Philosophy of the Unconscious*), and (both positively and negatively) to the philosophy of **Nietzsche**. Given the depiction of humankind as under the sway of an unconsciously operative irrational will, which is manifested in a primal "will to live" and in the "sexual impulse," as well as related features of his thought, it has often been said that **Freud**'s dynamic theory of the individual owes much to Schopenhauer's writings.

Toward the end of his life Schopenhauer produced a remarkable collection of work, *Parerga und Paralipomena: Kleine philosophische Schriften* (1851; *Parerga and Paralipomena: Short Philosophical Essays*). The Greek terms in his ill-chosen title for "popular" essays suggest surplus, supplementary writings, matters left over. In these essays on a variety of topics Schopenhauer reveals himself as the Romantic ironist, the moral idealist, who repeatedly reminds humankind of its selfishness, egotism, hypocrisy, and malice. His cynicism toward humanity is expressed sharply, economically, and with sardonic wit. Always, he seeks to look beneath the civil, social "mask" or *persona* in order to reveal the often unattractive inner, willful ego.

In "Psychologische Bermerkungen" (1851; "Psychological Observations") he remarks that "Our temperament is so *despotic* that we are not satisfied unless we draw everything into our own life, and force all the world to agree with us." In the same spirit, in one of his better essays, "Unser Verhalten gegen Andere betreffend" (1851; "Our Relations to Others") Schopenhauer proclaims that "Most men are so thoroughly subjective that nothing really interests them but themselves." With characteristic directness he accepts as given that "In savage countries they eat one another, in civilized they deceive one another." Seeing himself as a wise and shrewd observer of his species, as a "man of the world," Schopenhauer issues *sangfroid* critical judgments throughout his lucid and cutting essays. In "Über die Menschlichkeit" (1851; "Human Nature") he judges what Freud will later merely describe: ". . . it is *Schadenfreude*, a mischievous delight in the misfortunes of others, which remains the worst trait in human nature."

In his notorious essay, "Über die Weiber" (1851; "Of Women"), Schopenhauer both reveals cultural attitudes toward women in his time and adds his own bitter misogyny. Here his vaunted "objectivity" fails him, no doubt due to the lifelong bitter hostility between himself and his mother, a woman who was totally unresponsive to him and coldly rejecting. Aside from occasional lapses of crankiness and blunt prejudices, most of Schopenhauer's essays have persuasive power, caustic humor, and depth of insight. His "Über den Selbstmord" (1851; "On Suicide") reveals his compassionate side and the essays in the section *Aphorismen zur Lebensweisheit* (*The Wisdom of Life*) in *Parerga and Paralipomena* advise the development of the inner world, the cultivation of personal qualities that fuel spiritual growth or what he sometimes calls "the higher self." When he is truly objective and calm, Schopenhauer does attain an austere, impressive wisdom.

In the long essay "Die Ehre" (1851; "Honor"), Schopenhauer's social criticism satirically demolishes the then reigning "code of honor" or modern version of "knightly honor," characterizing it as "the child of pride and folly." He brings to this essay, as he does to all his writings, an extensive breadth of cultural knowledge. His familiarity with French, Spanish, and English (a language which he spoke fluently and wrote fairly well) gave Schopenhauer an unusual cosmopolitan perspective which informs his accessible essays.

Although it is included in the second volume of *The World as Will and Representation*, "Metaphysik der Geschlechtsliebe" ("The Metaphysics of the Love of the Sexes") has often been extracted as a separate essay. In it love is ultimately reduced to the physical satisfaction of the "sexual impulse" and romantic, erotic attachments are described as being in the service of nature, the "will to live," and the reproductive interest of the species. For Schopenhauer, apart from the basic desire for existence, "the love of life," the "sexual impulse" is the most powerful, most pervasive, motive in human existence. Nature is said to attain its goal, procreation, by implanting the illusion in individuals that they are satisfying their own desires while it is the aim of the species that is served.

In an appendix to the discussion on the metaphysical understanding of sexuality added to the third edition of *The World as Will and Representation*, Schopenhauer, at the age of 71, added a discussion about the then volatile subject of male homosexuality. Despite disapproval of the practice, he points to its prevalence and discusses it with the coolness and objectivity of the student of human nature. He even speculates, like some recent sociobiologists, that homosexuality may have a natural developmental purpose: diverting adolescents and the elderly away from reproductive activity. In this instance, as in many others, we see a daring thinker who already anticipates not only Freud's idea of the "life-instinct" (*eros*) and the centrality of libido in human life, but who also presents the rudiments of a Darwin-like evolutionary theory in his conceptions of the perpetual struggle for existence in nature, attraction in sexual selection, the intellect as a "tool" of the will to live, and much more.

Throughout the essays comprising *Parerga and Paralipomena* Schopenhauer typically illustrates many of his pointed judgments by citations from dramas, novels, from **Baltasar Gracián**'s *The Oracle* (which he translated into German), **Montaigne, La Rochefoucauld,** Georg Christoph Lichtenberg, **Plato, Seneca,** and numerous other figures in world literature and philosophy. He was an intellectual internationalist who had great appreciation for languages and cultures other than his own.

Although his writings were generally ignored (Schopenhauer claimed they were subject to "a conspiracy of silence") during most of his lifetime, in the last decade of his life he began to receive recognition internationally and, in Germany, despite the powerful negations of his metaphysics, he was surprisingly popular for a time.

Schopenhauer expresses his literary-philosophical knowledge in a clear, appealing, unpedantic way that invites the reader into a realm of cultivated, civilized, though often harsh and opinionated, discourse. Because of his honesty, his penetration of the veils that conceal the tragic aspect of existence, and his psychological insights Schopenhauer's essays still have the power to startle, sting, and charm. In his writings a polyphonic rhythm of ideas expresses the ultimate symphony of a cosmic Romantic-ironic pessimism.

GEORGE J. STACK

Biography
Born 22 February 1788 in Danzig (now Gdańsk). Apprenticed to merchants in Danzig, 1804, and Hamburg, 1805–07, with the expectation that he would take over his father's business; however, after father's death, terminated apprenticeship and enrolled in a gymnasium in Gotha, 1807; studied science and philosophy at the University of Göttingen, 1809–11; philosophy at the University of Berlin, 1811–13. Lived in Dresden, 1814–18. Lectured at the University of Berlin, 1820. Lived in Frankfurt, 1833–60. Awards: Trondheim Scientific Society Prize (Norway), 1839. Died (of a heart attack) in Frankfurt-on-Main, 21 September 1860.

Selected Writings

Essays and Related Prose
Über die vierfache Wurzel des Satzes vom zureichenden Grunde, 1813; revised, enlarged edition, 1847; edited by Julius Frauenstädt, 1864, and Michael Landmann and Elfriede Tielsch, 1957; as "On the Fourfold Root of the Principle of Sufficient Reason," translated by Mrs. Karl Hillebrand, in *Two Essays*, 1889, and by E. F. J. Payne, 1974
Über das Sehn und die Farben (treatise), 1816; enlarged edition,

1854; edited by Julius Frauenstädt, 1870; chapter 1 as "On Vision," translated by E. F. J. Payne, in *The Fourfold Root of the Principle of Sufficient Reason*, 1974
Über den Willen in der Natur, 1836; revised, enlarged edition, edited by Julius Frauenstädt, 1867; as *The Will in Nature*, translated anonymously, 1877, reprinted 1982; as "On the Will in Nature," translated by Mrs. Karl Hillebrand, in *Two Essays*, 1889
Die beiden Grundprobleme der Ethik (includes "Über die Freiheit des menschlichen Willens"; "Über das Fundament der Moral"), 1841; revised, enlarged edition, 1860; first essay as *Essay on the Freedom of the Will*, translated by Konstantin Kolenda, 1960; second essay as *The Basis of Morality*, translated by Arthur Brodrick Bullock, 1903, and as *On the Basis of Morality* by E. F. J. Payne, 1965
Parerga und Paralipomena: Kleine philosophische Schriften, 2 vols., 1851; as *Parerga and Paralipomena: Short Philosophical Essays*, translated by E. F. J. Payne, 2 vols., 1974; selections translated by T. Bailey Saunders in various collections, including *Studies in Pessimism*, 1890 (also translated by William M. Thomson, 1896), *The Art of Literature*, 1890, *Religion: A Dialogue, and Other Essays*, 1899, and *Essays from the Parerga and Paralipomena*, 1951; selection as *Essays and Aphorisms*, edited and translated by R. J. Hollingdale, 1970
Select Essays, translated by Garritt Droppers and C. A. P. Dachsel, 1881
Aphorismen zur Lebensweisheit (from *Parerga und Paralipomena*), 1886; edited by L. W. Winter, 1966, and Rudolf Marx, 1968; selections as *The Wisdom of Life* and *Counsels and Maxims*, translated by T. Bailey Saunders, 1890
Two Essays (includes "On the Fourfold Root of the Principle of Sufficient Reason"; "On the Will in Nature"), translated by Mrs. Karl Hillebrand, 1889
Selected Essays, translated by Ernest Belfort Bax, 1891
The Art of Controversy, and Other Posthumous Papers, edited and translated by T. Bailey Saunders, 1896
On Human Nature: Essays (Partly Posthumous) in Ethics and Politics, edited and translated by T. Bailey Saunders, 1897
Essays, translated by Mrs. Rudolf Dircks, 1897
Complete Essays, translated by T. Bailey Saunders, 1942
Philosophical Writings, edited by Wolfgang Schirmacher, 1994

Other writings: the philosophical treatise *Die Welt als Wille und Vorstellung* (1819; *The World as Will and Representation*) and several volumes of manuscript fragments.

Collected works editions: *Sämtliche Werke*, edited by Julius Frauenstädt, 6 vols., 1873–74, revised and enlarged by Arthur Hübscher, 7 vols., 1937–41.

Bibliographies
Cartwright, David, "An English-Language Bibliography of Works on Schopenhauer," *Schopenhauer-Jahrbuch* 68 (1987): 257–66
Hübscher, Arthur, *Schopenhauer-Bibliographie*, Stuttgart and Bad Cannstatt: Fromann-Holzboog, 1981

Further Reading
Copleston, Frederick C., *Schopenhauer, Philosopher of Pessimism*, London: Burns Oates and Washbourne, 1946
Fox, Michael, editor, *Schopenhauer: His Philosophical Achievement*, Brighton: Harvester Press, 1980
Gardiner, Patrick, *Schopenhauer*, Harmondsworth: Penguin, 1971 (original edition, 1963)
Hamlyn, David W., *Schopenhauer: The Arguments of the Philosophers*, London: Routledge, 1980
Hamlyn, David W., "Schopenhauer and Freud," *Revue Internationale Philosophique* 42 (1988): 5–17

Hübscher, Arthur, *The Philosophy of Schopenhauer in Its Intellectual Context: Thinker Against the Tide*, Lampeter, Dyfed: Mellen Press, 1989 (original German edition, 1982)

Janaway, Christopher, *Schopenhauer*, Oxford and New York: Oxford University Press, 1994

Magee, Bryan, *The Philosophy of Schopenhauer*, Oxford: Clarendon Press, 1983

Safranski, Rudiger, *Schopenhauer and the Wild Years of Philosophy*, London: Weidenfeld and Nicolson, 1989; Cambridge, Massachusetts: Harvard University Press, 1990 (original German edition, 1987)

Snow, James, "Schopenhauer's Style," *International Philosophical Quarterly* 33, no. 4 (December 1993): 401–12

Taylor, Richard, "Schopenhauer," in *A Critical History of Western Philosophy*, edited by D. J. O'Connor, New York and London: Collier-Macmillan, 1964

Zimmern, Helen, *Arthur Schopenhauer: His Life and Philosophy*, London: Allen and Unwin 1932 (original edition, 1876)

Schröder, Rudolf Alexander

German, 1878–1962

For the first half of his life Rudolf Alexander Schröder was a profusely productive poet whose verse was shaped by *fin-de-siècle* aestheticism, and by a stylistic versatility that is indebted to the canon of European classics. Above all, he cultivated a talent for absorbing and reactivating a diverse array of historical forms (odes, elegies, sonnets). Thus he saw himself as a creative assimilator of time-honored literary and artistic models rather than as a critical innovator. His predilection for refinement, and indeed his sense of cultural superiority, derived from his social status – he came from a patrician merchant family in Bremen – and reflect the social values of the German *haute bourgeoisie* at the century's end: faith in a broad humanistic education, retreat from public controversies into inwardness and a dignified style of leisure, promotion of the arts as a way to foster civic sociability. The privileges of wealth and talent are employed most legitimately, in other words, when they serve the conciliatory purposes of moderation and continuity.

This attitude of conservative guardianship is sustained by an essentially aesthetic response to the uncertainties of life, experienced both as private contradictions and as the encounter with sociopolitical controversies. Schröder did not really question, much less abandon, this orientation when, during the mid-1920s as a belated reckoning with the consequences of World War I, he curtailed his lyrical output significantly in favor of essays, articles, and speeches – and of his work as an architectural designer. It was his program after 1918 to contribute toward the preservation of a national culture that he felt was being threatened with obliteration from many different directions. The rhetorical approach he thought best suited for such a task reflects two seemingly contradictory features of his personality: the self-conscious elitism of the connoisseur, and a strong need for recognition, even for public acclaim. Schröder was never a haughty loner like his friend **Rudolf Borchardt,** or a melancholy recluse like the cautiously admired Rilke. Rather, he found in the classical literature of Europe and in the company of conservative artists a world of congenial sociability into which he could easily enter. And he always valued the appreciation of a discriminating audience.

Consequently, his essayistic prose often recaptures the style of knowledgeable colloquies in which a small group of people explore a variety of agreeable topics and concerns. They may not always arrive at a consensus, but they never argue dialectically or with polemical sharpness. Such a manner of presentation, for all its erudition and authoritative command over the material at hand, proceeds with graceful, or at least effortless and at times casual, naturalness. Its ease only rarely slips into folksiness, or assumes the egalitarian voice of intimacy. It does keep its distance but eschews at the same time anything more forceful than a slight hint of confrontational acerbity. Schröder never employs harsh tropes or strident metaphors, never uses sarcasm. He is clearly uncomfortable with irony and bathos. His preferred mode of expression is a gently didactic tone, learned, with touches of wisdom, and free as much as possible from pedantry. It is a diction that allows his readers and listeners to share their preceptor's delight in his pleasurable duties. His writing, in other words, is not driven by any sense of urgency, nor is it animated by a struggle with incongruities or by the perplexity of multiple viewpoints.

This was possible only because Schröder remained distant from politics or social problems, both during the turbulent years of the Weimar Republic and under the dictatorship of the Third Reich. Such aloofness from the tensions of public life and from ideological hostilities was voluntary and not the consequence of a defiantly powerless capitulation before a ruthless enemy. It accorded easily with his concept of history and with his distaste for the immediacy of mundane problems. While the fate of German democracy and ultimately the future of Europe was at stake, Schröder sought to reassert the indelible values of the Western cultural tradition, for example, by giving four different lectures on bibliophilism (1929) and by translating Homer, **Cicero,** the complete poetry of Horace and Virgil, the classics of French drama (especially Racine and Molière), and after 1945 the plays of **T. S. Eliot.** But there is no hint in any of his work, including over 150 essays, nearly all of which deal with poets and their environment, that any Modernist author or recent aesthetic debate or even the great writers of the 19th century attracted his attention. Among his contemporaries there is almost no one but **Hugo von Hofmannsthal,** perhaps the closest of his acquaintances, who elicited more than a few courteous observations, and this only *post mortem*, in the form of five commemorative appreciations. The rest of German (and world) literature might well have ended with Hölderlin, Brentano, and Jean Paul.

It should come as no surprise, then, that Schröder's interests did not fluctuate or expand significantly, either after 1936, when he moved from his native Bremen to the village of Bergen (Upper Bavaria), or after 1945 when he was greatly in demand as a speaker at memorial and other festive occasions. His response to the Nazi regime, whose favors he never courted, was an intensified search for spiritual assurances, which brought him close to the members of Martin Niemöller's Bekennende Kirche (Confessing church) and to the existentialist theology of Karl Barth. As a lay preacher (*Lektor*) in the Evangelical-Lutheran Church (1942–53) he wrote and delivered some 90 **sermons,** all meditative and consolatory; his few public statements that included a political message (for example, "Horaz als politischer Dichter" [1935; Horace as a political poet], "Dichter und Volk" [1937; Poet and people], or "Christentum und Humanismus" [1942; Christianity and humanism]) were formulated in such cautiously general terms as to give no specific offense or encouragement. This was inevitable because Schröder's concept of *Geist* (spirit or intellect) has little regard for the impermanence of earthly things. His attention, rather, is focused on the eternal and on those emanations both of the Holy Spirit and of the human mind which have withstood the ravages of time. Most prominent in Schröder's purview of timeless values are the piety expressed, for example, in baroque church hymns (he wrote essays on six of their authors), and the humanistic universalism he attributed to the genius of **Goethe**.

MICHAEL WINKLER

Biography

Born 26 January 1878 in Bremen. Studied architecture, art history, and music at the University of Munich, 1897–99. Cofounder, *Die Insel*, 1899. Lived in Paris, from 1901, and Berlin, 1905–08. Architectural designer, until 1931. Lay preacher for the Evangelical-Lutheran Church, 1942–53; appointed member of the Protestant Church Synod, 1948. Awards: several, including the Lessing Prize, 1947; Bremer Literature Prize, 1959; honorary degrees from five European universities. Died in Bad Wiessee, Bavaria, 22 August 1962.

Selected Writings

Essays and Related Prose

Die Aufsätze und Reden, 2 vols., 1939
Meister der Sprache, 1953
Über die Liebe zum Menschen, edited by Johannes Pfeiffer, 1966
Aphorismen und Reflexionen, edited by Richard Exner, 1977

Other writings: many volumes of poetry. Also translated Homer, Virgil, and others.

Collected works edition: *Gesammelte Werke*, 8 vols., 1952–65.

Bibliography

Adolph, Rudolf, *Schröder Bibliographie*, Darmstadt: Winter, 1953

Further Reading

Adolph, Rudolf, editor, *Leben und Werk von Rudolf Alexander Schröder*, Frankfurt-on-Main: Suhrkamp, 1958
Noltenius, Rainer, *Hofmannsthal, Schröder, Schnitzler: Möglichkeiten und Grenzen des modernen Aphorismus*, Stuttgart: Metzler, 1969
Tgahrt, Reinhard, and others, editors, *Rudolf Borchardt, Alfred Walter Heymel, Rudolf Alexander Schröder: Eine Ausstellung des Deutschen Literaturarchivs im Schiller-Nationalmuseum, Marbach am Neckar*, Munich: Kösel, 1978

Science Essay

Science has been part of the subject matter of the essay for as long as the essay has been a distinct genre. In the 20th century, the science essay has developed primarily as a means of informing the general public about scientific theories and what it means to be a scientist. These essays often use personal reflection as a means to teach, use a story to make a case, and discuss major cultural and scientific questions by relating episodes of the authors' lives. **Loren Eiseley**, one of the foremost science essayists of the 20th century, writes in his autobiography, *All the Strange Hours: The Excavation of a Life* (1975), of creating "the concealed essay, in which personal anecdote was allowed gently to bring under observation thoughts of a more purely scientific nature." The science essay is also characterized by its use of comparisons and allusions to familiarize the reader with the sometimes esoteric details of the scientific information being discussed. Usually there is an emphasis on style, as poetic devices and rhetorical figures focus the reader on the language of the message.

Montaigne, in his innovation of the essay genre, did much to make the form amenable to the concerns of science and natural history. In his essays he frequently functioned as an ethnographer or anthropologist, as in "Des cannibales" (1580; "Of Cannibals") and "De l'usage de se vestir" (1580; "Of the Custom of Wearing Clothes"). In both essays, he recounts information without judging, and explains his abstract, philosophical ideas through appeals to specific examples, often from his own life. Many contemporary science essayists also use their own lives as examples and starting points for their essays. Montaigne also established the essay as a genre characterized by a skeptical and ironic attitude toward old ideas and an interest in new knowledge. He celebrated diversity and backed it up with a multiplicity of quotations. The essay, as Montaigne conceived it, helped engender the scientific method, and the essay genre that developed is permeated with natural history subjects and underpinned by a sense of the importance of the trial and error of scientific inquiry.

The originator of the essay form in English, **Francis Bacon**, apparently conceived of his *Essayes* (1597, 1612, 1625) as a way of presenting knowledge. Although the subtitle of his book of essays is *Counsels, Civill and Morall*, he also included scientific information about agriculture in "Of Plantations" and "Of Gardens." Both Montaigne and Bacon wrote about the medical practices of their time and included information about ways to live a healthy life. In such essays Bacon functioned as a teacher; in doing so he effectively utilized the persuasive power of the essay. The essay as Bacon wrote it allowed the presentation of facts and observations without the drawing of conclusions. His *Essayes* are laden with quotations and short narratives, which are not personal, but instead "represent the discussion of a man, not involved in a private reverie or confession, but involved in public debate or address" (Otis Winchester and Winston Weathers, 1968). The science essay has throughout time been associated with public debate on issues of scientific controversy.

In the 18th century the term "science" came to acquire the definition it has today. Most educated men had some interest in natural history, science, and medicine. The 18th-century essayists included scientific topics among those they wrote about, a notable example being **Samuel Johnson**'s "On Birth, Health, and Diligence" (1753). Most scientific writing was aimed at the educated populace rather than specialists, and many of the articles included in the *Philosophical Transactions* of the Royal Society of London would today be considered science essays rather than scientific articles.

In England, the first collection of natural history essays – Gilbert White's *The Natural History and Antiquities of*

Selborne – was published in 1788. White's essays were to prove widely influential. His writings are full of poetic quotations, literary and biblical allusions, and he merges scientific diction with his own Augustan style. His stated aim in the author's "Advertisement" was "to bring his readers a greater appreciation of the wonders of the creation and to enlarge the stock of scientific knowledge." White's prominent place in the history of nature writing has been characterized by **Joseph Wood Krutch** in *Great American Nature Writing* (1950): "White was the student of natural history who used the materials of science in the composition of a work which became belles-lettres because these materials, treated intimately rather than with complete detachment, take on emotional significance."

In the 19th century, science fundamentally changed people's conception of the universe and their place in it. While specialized scientific publications did exist, and became more significant for the professional scientist, the majority of scientific information and debate was disseminated in general literary publications. The debate between two prominent American scientists, Asa Gray and Louis Agassiz, on the validity of Darwin's *On the Origin of Species* (1859) was waged in the **Atlantic Monthly**. When science became controversial to the average citizen, scientists took advantage of the popular press to present ideas and opinions. **T. H. Huxley** is perhaps the preeminent scientist of the 19th century concerned with the presentation of scientific ideas to the emerging literate population; his prose ranks him as one of the best stylists of that century. His principal technique was to take a specific, commonplace object, such as a piece of chalk, and use it as an example by which the public could learn to appreciate and understand the scientific mode of apprehending the world.

Twentieth-century science essayists have continued the pedagogic tradition, engaging the public in scientific debate, and personalizing science through autobiography. Almost every significant 20th-century scientist, from **Sigmund Freud** and Albert Einstein to James D. Watson and Stephen Hawking, has written essays aimed at the general public. In addition, many academic scientists write in the genre to extend their own teaching beyond the classroom, examples being **Lewis Thomas**, Jeremy Bernstein, **Stephen Jay Gould**, Freeman Dyson, Harold J. Morowitz, and Gerald Weismann. Essays on scientific subjects have also engaged nonspecialist writers such as **John McPhee**, K. C. Cole, and Diane Ackerman. All of these writers produce essays that blend scientific fact and documentation with philosophical discussion and evocative, even emotional description as their hallmarks.

DIANE DOWDEY

Anthologies

The Faber Book of Science, edited by John Carey, London: Faber, 1995

From Sea to Space: An Anthology of Scientific Prose, edited by J. D. Stephenson and A. R. Moon, London: Edward Arnold, 1962

Great American Nature Writing, edited by Joseph Wood Krutch, New York: Sloane, 1950

Science in Writing: A Selection of Passages from the Writings of Scientific Authors, edited by Thomas Rice Henn, London: Harrap, 1960; New York: Macmillan, 1961

The Scientific Background: A Prose Anthology, edited by A. Norman Jeffares, London: Pitman, 1958

A Treasury of Scientific Prose: A Nineteenth-Century Anthology, edited by Howard Mumford Jones and I. Bernard Cohen, Boston: Little Brown, 1963; as *Science Before Darwin: A Nineteenth-Century Anthology*, London: Deutsch, 1963

Further Reading

Bazerman, Charles, "The Writing of Scientific Non-Fiction," *Pre-Text: A Journal of Rhetorical Theory* 5, no. 1 (1984): 39–74

Beer, Gillian, "Parable, Professionalization, and Literary Allusion in Victorian Scientific Writing," *AUMLA* 74 (1990): 48–68

Black, Joel Dana, "The Scientific Essay and Encyclopedic Science," *Stanford Literature Review* 1, no. 1 (1984): 119–48

Dowdey, Diane, *Literary Science: A Rhetorical Analysis of an Essay Genre and Its Tradition* (dissertation), Madison: University of Wisconsin, 1984

Findlen, Paula, "Jokes of Nature and Jokes of Knowledge: The Playfulness of Scientific Discourse in Early Modern Europe," *Renaissance Quarterly* 43, no. 2 (1990): 292–331

Gates, Barbara, "Retelling the Story of Science," in *Victorian Literature and Culture*, edited by John Maynard, Adrienne Munich, and Sandra Donald, New York: AMS Press, 1993

Gross, Alan G., *The Rhetoric of Science*, Cambridge, Massachusetts: Harvard University Press, 1990

Harre, Rom, "Some Narrative Conventions of Scientific Discourse," in *Narrative in Culture: The Uses of Storytelling in the Sciences, Philosophy, and Literature*, edited by Christopher Nash, London: Routledge, 1990

Rousseau, G. S., "Science Books and Their Readers in the Eighteenth Century," in *Books and Their Readers in Eighteenth-Century England*, Leicester: Leicester University Press, and New York: St. Martin's Press, 1982

Selzer, Jack, editor, *Understanding Scientific Prose*, Madison: University of Wisconsin Press, 1993

Winchester, Otis, and Winston Weathers, *The Prevalent Forms of Prose: The Popular Article, the Professional Article, the Personal Essay, the Formal Essay, the Criticial Review*, Boston: Houghton Mifflin, 1968

Sei Shōnagon
Japanese, c. 965–?

Sei Shōnagon's *Makura no sōshi* (*The Pillow Book*) is a hybrid work whose combination of narrative sketches, desultory reflections, and categorical lists was held in generic limbo, known by its author and title or simply as "book" from the time of its composition in the late 10th century to 1774. It was not until then that the essayist Ban Kōkei labeled it *zuihitsu*, the Japanese transcription of a Chinese word that means "following the brush," the equivalent of "essay" in Japanese. *The Pillow Book* fits the literal sense of essay, reading like a series of trials in various styles and subjects, and evokes the essayistic feeling of close and unpredictable contact with the authorial world. From these pages we know what was considered unthinkable, vulgar, precious, and sane in her milieu.

The courtly Heian period was known for its women writers. While schooling meant the continental classics for men, who employed a form of Chinese to write poetry and record important matters, women of the aristocracy wrote largely in the vernacular, using a simplified syllabic writing system. *Kana*, alternatively called *onnade*, or the "woman's hand," eliminated the need for most Chinese graphs. Sei was a master of the vernacular, with its agglutinative forms, honorifics, elliptical phrasing, and paratactic structures. Her lyric passages flow with rhythmic asymmetry. Although literate females knew the Chinese tradition, if mostly through translation (China was the source of Japan's writing system, and added depth to its literary heritage), it was considered inappropriate to flaunt such knowledge. The greater ease with which women could express themselves, and the greater poignancy of their lives in a society that felt the ideal love affair should end in the woman's abandonment, have been credited for women's monumental achievements in belles-lettres.

Sei Shōnagon is the least retiring of these writers. Eager to display her Chinese learning, she uses allusions with such dexterity that it requires committees of men to match her. In vernacular poetry as well she informs us that her talent earned admiration among her peers, not to mention her social betters. Whereas resignation to their fates seems to motivate women characters in the fiction of the time, Sei portrays the triumph and insouciance of ladies who cajole the opposite sex and revel in the outcome, even when they are left behind. Her own relations with men feature stinging repartee rather than tears. Above all, Sei evinces wit and good taste, frequently judging things okashi, a term of approbation whose meanings include "delightful," "splendid," and "fascinating." Her satire on the clumsy lover who knocks his cap askew while taking his leave in the pre-dawn darkness is delicious; her pronouncements on the ultimate in various kinds of experience, such as the memories provoked by old letters, strike home and incite the reader to join in a game of enumeration.

Much of the impetus for her composition comes from Sei's mistress, Empress Teishi or Sadako (ruled 977–1000). Court-related events in the work span the years 986 to 1000, including the period of Sei's service from 993 until the untimely death of her patron. Part of the empress' ammunition in the polygamous struggles of the court was the literary accomplishment of her retinue. Sei never hesitates to enhance the reputation of her patron, who thus appears wiser, fairer, and more amusing than any contemporary. Considering Sei's own middling rank, such favoritism is inevitable, but it reminds us that she was writing as a representative of the ideals of a salon as much as an individual. The authority of this group underlies her confident tone.

The meaning of "pillow book" has been extensively debated, but it appears to refer to the inclusion of lists featuring "song pillows" (utamakura), place names established in the poetic tradition. Hills, trees, plants, bridges, temples, and poetry collections themselves are some of the topics Sei covers. Many items seem to form elegant puns, reinforcing another theory that her prototypes included Chinese compendia of witty sayings, such as the miscellany of Li Shang-yin (813–58). The makura may be a chronicle of all that mattered in her circle, and may have been meant to stimulate admiration and conversation among readers, but her work has also been said to resist the act of reading. Its amorphousness presents a challenge to linear comprehension and to fixed notions of the female gender. In her text Sei (or a later emendator) protests her shame that the work has come to light, but also notes its favorable reception – not surprising, she comments, given her perverse habit of disliking what others enjoy. Such modesty is characteristic of East Asian authors, and in no way contradicts her love of attention.

The Pillow Book received less notice over the centuries than classic tales, yet it was copied often enough to produce complicated variants. There are two main divisions, into texts that group similar segments together and texts of random order. Scholars believe the random texts are closest to the original, while the classificatory texts represent medieval redactors' aims to make the content on Heian era customs more accessible. A critique voiced by a group of women, the Mumyōzōshi of about 1220, aligns The Pillow Book with Genji monogatari (The Tale of Genji) as a moving work. Medieval anecdotes of Sei's comeuppance are evidence for a popular view of her as too strident and self-promoting. With the introduction of printing and the spread of education from the 17th century, The Pillow Book was widely read and parodied. A recent translation into the patois of fashionable young Japanese women uses exclamation points liberally, capturing the flavor that has so captivated readers. Only the sharp tongue of the woman author kept it from being a premier textbook. Although the notion of antiquarian interest would have appalled Sei (who preferred what was up-to-the-minute), that, combined with her prose style, regarded as the purest in the native language, eventually established the work as a pedagogical model. Generations of Japanese have been vastly enriched by imagining how Sei meant them to complete her opening words, "In spring, it is dawn . . ."

LINDA H. CHANCE

Biography
Real name unknown. Born c. 965 in Kyoto. Daughter of Kiyohara no Motosuke, governor of Higo, a member of the middle aristocracy. May have briefly married Tachibana no Norimitsu; may have had a son. Lady-in-waiting to Empress Teishi (Sadako), c. 993–1000. May have married Fujiwara no Muneyo, a much older man who died before her. Had one daughter. May have become a Buddhist nun. Legends of her extensive travel in later years are unsubstantiated. Probably died at Tsukinowa (her father's residence), Kyoto.

Selected Writings

Essays and Related Prose
Makura no sōshi, edited by Tanaka Jūtarō (fully annotated), 5 vols., 1983, and Watanabe Minoru, 1991; as The Pillow Book, edited and translated by Ivan Morris, 1967, abridged vol., 1991; selections translated by Arthur Waley, 1928

Other writings: poetry.

Further Reading
Bowring, Richard, Murasaki Shikibu: Her Diary and Poetic Memoirs, Princeton, New Jersey: Princeton University Press, 1982
Marra, Michele, "Mumyōzōshi: Introduction and Translation," Monumenta Nipponica 39, nos. 2–4 (Summer/Autumn/Winter 1984): Part 1: 115–45; Part 2: 281–305; Part 3: 409–34
Morris, Ivan, The World of the Shining Prince: Court Life in Ancient Japan, New York: Kodansha International, 1994 (original edition, 1964)
Morris, Mark, "Sei Shōnagon's Poetic Catalogues," Harvard Journal of Asiatic Studies 40, no. 1 (June 1980): 5–54
Okada, H. Richard, Figures of Resistance: Language, Poetry and Narrating in The Tale of Genji and Other Mid-Heian Texts, Durham, North Carolina: Duke University Press, 1991

Sarra, Edith, "A Poetics of the Gaze in *Makura no sōshi*," in *The Desire for Monogatari*, Proceedings of the Second Midwest Research/Pedagogy Seminar on Japanese Literature, edited by Eiji Sekine, West Lafayette, Indiana: Purdue University, 1994: 21–30

Selzer, Richard

American, 1928–

Richard Selzer's essays have appeared regularly for the past three decades in upscale magazines and are familiar, often painfully so, to American college students enrolled in analytical writing courses. His **medical essays**, densely written musings upon the meaning of life, are ideally suited to exercises in interpretation, and classroom uses have surely produced a loyal readership among the young and literate. Readers who approach Selzer uninstructed do best to savor the sound and balance in his use of language, and appreciate the challenge within the occasional impenetrable passage as one would if it were poetry, into which he sometimes slips. Selzer is a retired surgeon and Yale School of Medicine professor, but he has been an essayist as well since the early 1970s. His audience is not narrowly confined to colleagues, despite the fact that his vocabulary is occasionally obscurely latinate, and his approach to subject matter clinical and often bloody, as if he were filling a chart, but using the language of Wordsworth to do it.

Although Selzer shuns the plain prose expected of the essayist, his form is conventional and recognizable despite his florid but skilled use of language. He usually chooses and frames single ideas in ways reminiscent of **Thomas Carlyle** at his most whimsical, usually allowing for very plain Carlylean titles. Had Carlyle been a surgeon, he would surely have found in surgery what Selzer has found – a sticky, warm world where dying and dignity, suffering and silence are alliterative ideas and language holds the key to all philosophy. Like Carlyle, he does not attempt to be popular in his views and occasionally stretches his relationship with readers by blending moral analysis with twisted diction. He is a writer who claims to care more about truth than consequences, although consequences to essayists exist on a different plane from those faced by surgeons, a point clearly not lost on him.

Selzer anticipates readers who would note the professional dichotomy by never questioning himself in his professional role, when to do so would be inconvenient, even in the early essays written while he was still a practicing surgeon. In his essay "Abortion" (1974), he registers his disapproval of this practice through a deliberately artless shift to second person in which he describes the horror of a pedestrian who finds that he has stepped on a fetus, dropped from an overloaded garbage truck in a bag labeled "hazardous wastes." "I am a surgeon," he says, abruptly shifting to the first person, turning his back on the "Street of the Dead Fetuses" and the discomfited reader, who shares the knowledge that the second person is only grammatically distanced from Citizen Selzer while he proceeds to distance Dr. Selzer from the unnamed procedure. "I do not shrink from the particularities of sick flesh. Escaping blood, all the outpourings of disease – phlegm, pus, vomitus, even those occult meaty tumors that terrify – I see as blood, disease, phlegm, and so on. I touch them to destroy them. But I do not make symbols of them. I have seen, and I am used to seeing. Yet there are paths within the body that I have not taken, penetralia where I do not go. Nor is it lack of technique, limitation of knowledge that forbids me these ways." From this explanation he proceeds to an abortion, which he has asked to witness. It is a late-term abortion, the mother a smiling, presumably healthy, bystander. He describes the procedure in lurid detail, placing the fetus in the central role, a conventional tragic hero. By the end, however, he is classic Selzer, immersed in his art, emotionally connected to the essayist, but completely estranged from the surgeon. "And who would care to imagine," he asks no one, "that trapped within the laked pearl and a dowry of yoke would lie the earliest stuff of dram and memory?"

Selzer is impossible to read casually; however, he can be read for the pleasure of working through his thoughts. There are no indifferent readers or mixed reviews. The positive reviews are glowing, the negative vituperative, as has often been the case with essayists whose work falls in and out of fashion, but never fades. Joel Howell of the *New England Journal of Medicine*, a representative Selzer reader, identifies Selzer as a type, a scientist by trade who is by nature a poet and philosopher, and who succeeds in science only because of his ability to believe in his own power to dismiss the possibility of either order or chaos: "There are surgeons," he writes, "capable of surrendering to romantic awe and wild philosophical speculation after confronting the body's pulsating internal labyrinth, and who are driven to name the unnameable." Selzer illustrates this type with a passage from his book on his own experience with Legionnaires' Disease, *Raising the Dead* (1993), in which he imagines an uncomfortable confrontation between himself a dying patient and himself the doctor: "There is the sadness of a toad in his hazel eyes. The familiar landmarks by which he could once be identified are no longer to be seen: the zygomatic circles surmounting the cheeks, the iliac crests, the tapered phalanges. He has become something I would not want to touch."

One among many sources of difficulty to Selzer's readers are the unexplained medical terms, many of them hopelessly obscure, which are not in lay dictionaries and can be frustrating for the reader who wants clarification. This is not the reader Selzer wishes to keep. The physician who knows the language gets no more out of this passage from "The Exact Location of the Soul" (1974) than the nonspecialist: "Women are physics and chemistry. They are matter. It is their bodies that tell of the frailty of men. Men have not their cellular, enzymatic wisdom. Man is albuminoid, proteinaceous, laked pearl; woman is yolky, ovoid, rich. Both are exuberant bloody growths. I would use the defects and deformities of each for my sacred purpose of writing, for I know that it is the marred and scarred and faulty that are subject to grace."

CLARA SPEER

Biography

Born 24 June 1928 in Troy, New York. Studied at Union College, Schenectady, New York, B.S., 1948; Albany Medical College, M.D., 1953; Yale University, New Haven, Connecticut, 1957–60. Married Janet White, 1955: two sons and one daughter. Practiced general surgery in New Haven, from 1960; associate professor of surgery, Yale School of Medicine; fellow of Ezra Stiles College. Contributor to various periodicals and magazines, including *Antaeus*, *Redbook*, *Harper's*, *Esquire*, and *American Review*. Awards: National Magazine Award, for essay, 1975; honorary degrees from four colleges and universities.

Selected Writings

Essays and Related Prose
Mortal Lessons: Notes on the Art of Surgery, 1976
Confessions of a Knife, 1979
Letters to a Young Doctor, 1982
Taking the World in for Repairs, 1986

Other writings: two collections of short stories (*Rituals of Surgery*, 1974; *Imagine a Woman and Other Tales*, 1990), the memoir *Down from Troy: A Doctor Comes of Age* (1992), and a book about his bout with Legionnaires' Disease (*Raising the Dead*, 1993).

Bibliography
Stripling, Mahala Yates, "Richard Selzer: A Checklist," *Bulletin of Bibliography* 47, no. 1 (March 1990): 3–8

Further Reading
Anderson, Charles M., *Richard Selzer and the Rhetoric of Surgery*, Carbondale: Southern Illinois University Press, 1989
Davis, Robert Leigh, "The Art of Suture: Richard Selzer and Medical Narrative," *Literature and Medicine* 12, no. 2 (Fall 1993): 178–93
Elbow, Peter, "The Pleasures of Voice in the Literary Essay: Explorations in the Prose of Gretel Ehrlich and Richard Selzer," in *Literary Nonfiction: Theory, Criticism, Pedagogy*, edited by Chris Anderson, Carbondale: Southern Illinois University Press, 1989: 211–34
Josyph, Peter, *What One Man Said to Another: Talks with Richard Selzer*, East Lansing: Michigan State University Press, 1994
Morris, David B., "Beauty and Pain: Notes on the Art of Surgery," *Iowa Review* 11, nos. 2–3 (Spring–Summer 1980): 124–30
Peschel, Enid Rhodes, "Eroticism, Mysticism, and Surgery in the Writings of Richard Selzer," *Denver Quarterly* 16, no. 1 (Spring 1981): 87–98
Schuster, Charles I., "The Nonfiction Prose of Richard Selzer: An Aesthetic Analysis," in *Literary Nonfiction: Theory, Criticism, Pedagogy*, edited by Chris Anderson, Carbondale: Southern Illinois University Press, 1989: 3–28
Tavormina, M. Teresa, "Richard Selzer: The Rounds of Revelation," *Literature and Medicine* 1 (1982): 61–72
Whittier, Gayle, "Richard Selzer's Evolving Paradigms of Creativity," *Centennial Review* 33, no. 3 (Summer 1989): 278–301

Seneca

c. 4 BCE–65 CE

The life of Lucius Annaeus Seneca the Younger often seems at variance with his Stoic philosophy. A rich and ambitious man who praised frugality and moderation, he was the moral tutor of the Roman Emperor Nero. When the Emperor Claudius was alive, Seneca celebrated his clemency in his essay *De clementia*, then ridiculed him posthumously in his satirical *Apocolocyntosis* ("Pumpkinification"). Thus, although Seneca never set himself up as a model of rectitude, even suggesting that his *Epistulae morales* were an exchange between two moral invalids, readers as early as Tacitus have admired the style more than the man.

Seneca was a prolific writer; his prose works fall into five groups, though they share much with regard to form, style, and content. These include the ten *Dialogi*, such as the early *Ad Marciam de consolatione* ("To Marcia on Consolation") and *De ira* ("On Anger"), and the later *De otio* ("On Leisure") and *De providentia* (*Providence*); the two longer **treatises**, *De clementia* (*On Clemency*) and *De beneficiis* (*On Benefits*); the seven extant books of *Naturales quaestiones* (*Natural Questions*); the *Apocolocyntosis*; and the 124 *Epistulae morales ad Lucilium* (*Epistles* or *Letters to Lucilius*). With the exception of the comic *Apocolocyntosis*, whose rich display of different styles makes it one of the few extant examples of Roman *satura* (**satire**) as defined by Quintilian, all of Seneca's prose works are modeled on the form of the **letter**. Though they differ in tone and intimacy, each presents Seneca writing to a friend, family member, or disciple with the intention of moral instruction or consolation. Parallels have been drawn with his contemporary, St. Paul. The epistolary style also shapes the *Dialogi*, which are really one-sided monologues. Even the *Natural Questions*, which discuss the workings of nature and various natural phenomena, are addressed to Lucilius. This epistolary form hints at the origins and nature of Senecan style.

European and English prose styles tend to fall into one of two camps: the Ciceronian and the Senecan. The former is complex and rich, formed of cadenced periodic sentences; the latter is spare and abrupt, marked by the so-called "exploded period," a series of independent statements set down in simple sentences or clauses linked by coordinating conjunctions. The result is lapidary and epigrammatic. Caligula described it as "sand without lime"; **Thomas Babington Macaulay** complained that it was "like dining on nothing but anchovy sauce." The difference between the Ciceronian and Senecan styles emerges from the difference between a rhetoric aimed at oratorical performance in the Forum, and one intended for written expression, in a world where free speech was limited. **Cicero**'s repetitions and cadences are meant for the ears of a general audience, Seneca's understatement, irony, and paradox for the eyes of a reader.

Stoic philosophy informs most of Seneca's written works. For him the great paradox of the human condition is not between life and death, but between fate (*fatum*) and chance (*fortuna*). The measure of human happiness is not the achievement of pleasure, but the ability to accept suffering and the dictates of fate. Since we have little control over what we must endure, the concern is rather with *how* to endure. So saying, misfortune is that which allows the good person to show his moral worth, for he endures well, while the bad person does not. We must learn not only to understand correctly, but to act correctly, achieving self-command. Too often we are the slaves of our appetites. Attacking greed, avarice, and covetousness (*gula*, *avaritia*, and *luxuria*) in his *Consolatio ad Helviam* ("Consolation to Helvia"), he complains that in Rome, "they vomit to eat and eat to vomit." While Seneca's writings are deeply philosophical, they are not for the most part philosophical treatises, systematically developing a logical argument. Rather, as one commentator suggests, Seneca is a preacher, focusing on one or two themes in each letter, then reiterating them in a series of vivid and memorable variations in order to hammer home his point.

Seneca had an immediate and continuous influence as both philosopher and writer. If early Church fathers such as Lactantius were hostile to the materialism of Stoicism, others such as Jerome appreciated Seneca's moral doctrine. In the Middle Ages, he exemplified philosophy, exerting a profound influence on medieval thinkers as diverse as John of Salisbury, Bernard of Clairvaux, St. Bonaventure, and Dante, who referred to him in the *Inferno* as "Seneca morale." The development of printing led to a resurgence of interest in Seneca's work, and Erasmus of Rotterdam produced the first critical edition in 1515. Humanists such as **Erasmus**, Sir Thomas More, Justus Lipsius, and John Calvin, as well as later Renaissance writers such as **Montaigne** and **Francis Bacon**, admired both his independence of mind and conciseness of style, positing him as the model of anti-Ciceronian eloquence. Among later philosophers, Seneca's influence can be found in moral thinkers such as Spinoza, **Rousseau**, and **Emerson**, and especially among various existentialists from Kierkegaard and **Nietzsche** to **Heidegger** and Paul Tillich. Among later writers, Shakespeare, Quevedo, and Racine frequently quote him, and Pope, **Hazlitt**, **Wilde**, T. S. Eliot, and **H. L. Mencken** draw on his style.

THOMAS L. COOKSEY

See also Classical Influences

Biography

Lucius Annaeus Seneca. Born c. 4 BCE in Corduba (now Cordoba, Spain). Taken to Rome as an infant. Studied grammar and rhetoric, then various schools of philosophy, in Rome. Married Pompeia Paulina: one son (died, 41 CE). Lived in Egypt for health reasons, returning to Rome c. 31 CE. Elected *quaestor* (financial administrator), 30s. Exiled to Corsica for alleged adultery with Julia Livilla, sister of Caligula and niece of Claudius, 41–49. Tutor to Nero, designated *praetor* (judicial officer), 50, and adviser and minister to Nero, with Burrus, 54–62; consul, 56; retired on Burrus' death, 62. Forced to commit suicide for supposed participation in Pisonian conspiracy, near Rome, 65 CE.

Selected Writings

Essays and Related Prose

De beneficiis, edited by C. Hosius, 1914; as *On Benefits*, translated by Aubrey Stewart, 1887
De clementia, edited by C. Hosius, 1914; as *On Clemency*, translated by Aubrey Stewart, 1899
De providentia, as *Providence*, translated by W. B. Langsdorf, 1900
Dialogi, edited by E. Hermes and others, 3 vols., 1898–1907, and by L. D. Reynolds, 1977
Epistulae morales, edited by L. D. Reynolds, 2 vols., 1965; as *Letters* (Loeb Edition; bilingual), edited and translated by R. M. Gummere, 3 vols., 1917–25; as *Morals*, translated by Roger L'Estrange, 1678, and by J. W. Basore (Loeb Edition), 3 vols., 1928–35; selections as *The Epistles*, translated by T. Morell, 1786; as *Select Letters of Seneca*, translated by W. C. Summers, 1910; as *Seneca's Letters to Lucilius*, translated by E. Phillips Barker, 2 vols., 1932; as *Letters from a Stoic*, translated by Robin Campbell, 1969
Naturales quaestiones, edited by P. Oltramare, 1929, and Harry M. Hines, 1981; as *Natural Questions*, translated by Thomas H. Corcoran (Loeb Edition), 2 vols., 1971–72
Minor Dialogues, translated by Aubrey Stewart, 1899
Moral Essays (Loeb Edition), 3 vols., 1928–35

Moral and Political Essays (selection), edited and translated by J. W. Basore, M. Cooper, and J. F. Procopé, 1995

Other writings: eight tragedies (and a further two attributed to him) and poetry.

Collected works edition: *Works*, 19 vols., 1981–84.

Bibliography

Motto, Anna L., and John R. Clark, *Seneca: A Critical Bibliography, 1900–1980: Scholarship on His Life, Thought, Prose and Influence*, Amsterdam: Hakkert, 1989

Further Reading

Arnold, Edward Vernon, *Roman Stoicism*, London: Routledge and Kegan Paul, 1958 (original edition, 1911)
Bourgery, Abel, *Sénèque prosateur: Études littéraires et grammaticales sur la prose de Sénèque le philosophe*, Paris: Les Belles Lettres, 1922
Canter, Howard Vernon, *Rhetorical Elements in the Tragedies of Seneca*, Urbana: University of Illinois Press, 1925
Coleman, Robert, "The Artful Moralist: A Study of Seneca's Epistolary Style," *Classical Quarterly* 24 (December 1974): 276–89
Costa, C. D. N., editor, *Seneca – Greek and Latin Studies: Classical Literature and Its Influence*, London and Boston: Routledge and Kegan Paul, 1974
Croll, Morris, *Style, Rhetoric, and Rhythm*, edited by J. Max Patrick, Princeton, New Jersey: Princeton University Press, 1966
Currie, H. M., "The Younger Seneca's Style," *Bulletin of the Institute of Classical Studies* 13 (1966): 76–87
Griffin, Miriam T., *Seneca: A Philosopher in Politics*, Oxford: Clarendon Press, 1992 (original edition, 1976)
Hutchinson, G. O., *Latin Literature from Seneca to Juvenal*, Oxford: Clarendon Press, and New York: Oxford University Press, 1993
Motto, Anna Lydia, *Seneca*, New York: Twayne, 1973
Sørensen, Villy, *Seneca: The Humanist at the Court of Nero*, Chicago: University of Chicago Press, and Edinburgh: Canongate, 1984 (original Swedish edition, 1976)
Williamson, George, *The Senecan Amble: A Study in Prose from Bacon to Collier*, Chicago: University of Chicago Press, and London: Faber, 1951

Sermon

Like essays, sermons vary a great deal in kind, but are generally prose pieces of moderate length. Both forms consider a variety of topics, with an attempt at explanation or definition, and are frequently anecdotal, with occasional personal elements, and significant deployment of narrative. A key distinction is that sermons are initially speeches – albeit fully crafted and often published – usually delivered from a pulpit as part of a religious service or sometimes in a civic context. While essays are occasionally moralizing, the sermon always is. Moreover, the sermon characteristically employs formal rhetorical devices to secure an immediate response from an audience. Writing out and memorizing were a common preparation, but the words of skillful preachers could be *ex tempore dicendi*, where reporters recorded and then submitted the text for the preacher's correction before publication in circulating collections. Printed publication, by the author or by others, was determined to preserve the texts. The sermon can be regarded, then, as a precursor of the essay, derived from a secular classic tradition and establishing a European style of explanation, subsequently developed by the essay.

Elements of form and style come from the Greek tradition of rhetoric, most notably the *Rhetoric* of Aristotle (384–22 BCE) and also Isocrates (436–338 BCE), largely through the great Latin writings. St. Augustine (354–430 CE) had identified, in *De doctrina Christiana* (*On Christian Doctrine*), respectable authorities, those not tainted by pagan Rome's immorality. This followed centuries of conflict, epitomized by St. Jerome's dream of God's declaration, "Thou art not a Christian, but a Ciceronian." Augustine admired Marcus Tullius **Cicero** (106–43 BCE), who followed Isocrates and was most influential in Western traditions; *De inventione*, along with the pseudo-Ciceronian *Rhetorica ad herennium*, and parts of the *De oratore*, were the basis of rhetorical theory during the Middle Ages, known through commentaries as well as the texts. Since Jesus urged a Christian duty to "Preach to all nations," homilists needed guidelines for organizing subject matter and devices for eloquent persuasion. There is no medieval parallel for secular speaking, because the Church assumed the role of popular oratory that was part of classical experience. Techniques in the early centuries of Christianity are suggestive of those of informal essayists, with an almost conversational style and directness analogous to St. Paul's *Epistles*. In the 13th century emerges the *ars praedicandi*, rules for a "university style" of sermon; many specialized manuals explained how to construct a sermon, beginning with a theme (quotation from Scripture) and a statement of purpose, then dividing and amplifying to explain and introduce authorities. This description suggests dialectical argument, but an awareness of the audience kept the sermon from rigid scholastic design. Robert of Basevorn's *Forma praedicandi* (wr. 1322; *The Form of Preaching*) illustrates such concern with oral discourse, both in its theory and as an easy personal style that later informs the essay. Masters of rhetoric distinguished two media (oral and written), but as Brunetto Latini observed in *Tresor* (wr. 1266), "the precepts are common to both." Renaissance emphasis upon antiquity reaffirmed classical traditions of rhetoric, which remain crucial to many modern sermons, while other popular styles developed.

St. Augustine, Gregory the Great, and the Venerable Bede were significant writers of Latin sermons, widely available in the popular homiliary of Paul the Deacon (c. 720–c. 799). The customary transcription of sermons into Latin obscures their delivery in the vernacular. Among Anglo-Saxons is Ælfric (c. 955–c. 1012), prose stylist and scholar, whose reputation rests on two volumes of *Catholic Homilies* and the *Lives of the Saints*, each containing about 40 sermons. Exegetical explanations of typology, allegory, symbols, and full development of illustrative narratives combine with a memorable style, whose balance and alliteration are models of elegance. Ælfric's contemporary Wulfstan (d. 1023) also selected Latin passages about his topic, translated them, and then developed his comments on ethical and religious ideas, often, as in the "Sermon of Wolf to the English," about evil days, the lack of loyalty, and sins that caused the Danish persecution. Questions, exclamations, repetition, and other rhetorical devices achieve a high emotional pitch and show dependence on Cicero, with little realistic detail.

Preaching in English continued after the Norman Conquest, but the sermon became especially important with the guidelines for instruction of the Fourth Lateran Council (1215). Many manuals explained logical ways to treat themes, with subdivisions and proper citations, and the use of authorities. Preaching was basic for the two mendicant orders, the Franciscans and Dominicans, who brought religion directly to the people, giving more time to the sermon than to other parts of services. A number of collections survive, like the *Northern Homily Cycle* (c. 1300), along with manuals and handbooks of *exempla*. Among 34 collections made from 1250 to 1350 is the Franciscan *Gesta Romanorum*, which contains edifying and amusing stories, alphabetically arranged by themes and cross-referenced, derived from many sources. Sermons by John Wycliffe (c. 1324–84) and his followers seek a more direct return to biblical text, an emphasis upon the literal sense. The Lollard sermon has a greater simplicity of style and concentration upon argument, often becoming polemical in addressing church abuses and thus more resembling a **satiric essay**. Chaucer's *Pardoner's Tale* (wr. c. 1387–1390s) explicitly presented as an example of preaching, explores this popular medieval art, combining the importance of oral delivery and audience, arguments about sin – well illustrated with examples and buttressed by authorities – and illustration of a text (greed is the root of evil) with the exciting story of the three rioters. Similarly, John Mirk's *Festial* (early 15th century), a collection of homilies assigned to Sundays and feasts, combines explanation of Scripture and feast with lively stories to illustrate the theme.

Renaissance sermons were highly intellectual and valued entertainment; with **pamphlets** and **treatises**, they were read like essays. Among distinguished preachers were Lancelot Andrewes, Jeremy Taylor, and **John Donne**, famous for their delivery and art. Taylor's rich style and melody combined with violent imagery and learning, and *The Eniautos* (1653–55) is an illustrious collection. Andrewes' *Sermons*, designed for the court and a theologically sophisticated audience, were published shortly after his death in 1626 by the king's command. Andrewes' style is difficult; sentences are long but logically constructed, laced with Latin, and more concerned with exegesis than personal comment and exhortation. Such severity and intellectualism are also characteristic of Donne, but the Dean of St. Paul's is also powerfully emotional, revealing, as in his poetry, many unresolved conflicts. Over 160 of Donne's sermons have been preserved, many published in his lifetime. Donne's "baroque" manner includes extraordinary metaphors – from science and new exploration – questioning, wordplay, repetition, puns, and a rootedness in the physical world that appeals instantly to both sensibilities and mind.

Coexistence of worldliness with Anglican preaching continued in the 18th century, as the essay became an established genre. Laurence Sterne published seven small volumes, albeit at a time when religious oratory lacked literary distinction. Another clergyman, **Jonathan Swift**, published **tracts** and **satires** to urge the moral reform that in earlier centuries would have been communicated through sermons. A lay writer like **Samuel Johnson** wrote in the style and manner of sermons in many essays in the *Rambler* (1750–52) which are infused with high moral purpose and urge physical and spiritual health. The alternative popular evangelical sermons of John Wesley indicate further a drawing away from formalism.

In the 19th century preaching, especially "university sermons" at Oxford, enjoyed another glorious age as Victorian audiences responded to the eloquence of John Keble, Edward Pusey, and most notably **John Henry Newman**. Their theological arguments and compelling presentation sparked religious reform, as secular essays urged a change in attitude. Newman's clear and logical analyses, knowledge of history, and mastery of scripture, all presented with elegance and warmth, have survived as the preaching of Charles Kingsley, chaplain to Queen Victoria, and **Matthew Arnold** have not. In an age of emerging skepticism, Newman's extraordinary skill in making Christianity concretely realized without resorting to emotional rhetoric was to be as inspiring in his several published volumes of sermons as when first heard in his silvery voice. Their literary skill and persuasion show again an affinity with the essay.

Notable authors of sermons in the 20th century include Swiss theologian Karl Barth and American popular broadcaster Fulton Sheen. Ronald Knox sustained the English sermon of clarity and elegance. Part of the Oxford tradition, Knox moved from Anglicanism to Roman Catholicism, as had Newman. His two volumes, *Pastoral Sermons* (1960) and *Occasional Sermons* (1960), show the same knowledge of scripture, theology, history, and literature, and the careful organization around text and theme that go back to classical traditions of rhetoric. Knox follows the teaching method of expounding parables and miracles, typically finishing with a precise definition. His sense of audience leads to a conversational style, enriched with contemporary allusions and often humorous. Like many other distinguished sermons, these show the agility of mind, the searching self-analysis, and seriousness of purpose that characterize essays seeking to elucidate a topic of great importance to the author.

VELMA BOURGEOIS RICHMOND

See also Religious Essay

Anthologies

Lollard Sermons, edited by Gloria Cigman, n.p.: Early English Text Society, 1989
The Puritan Sermon in America, 1630–1750, edited by Ronald A. Bosco, Delmar, New York: Scholars' Facsimiles and Reprints, 4 vols., 1978

Further Reading

Coleman, Janet, "Memory, Preaching and the Literature of a Society in Transition," in *English Literature in History, 1350–1400: Medieval Readers and Writers*, London: Hutchinson, 1981
Davidson, Edward H., "'God's well-trodden foot-paths': Puritan Preaching and Sermon Form," *Texas Studies in Literature and Language* 25, no. 4 (1983): 503–27
Fedderson, Kim Murray, *The Rhetoric of the Elizabethan Sermon* (dissertation), York, Ontario: York University, 1985
Heffernon, Thomas J., "Sermon Literature," in *Middle English Prose: A Critical Guide to Major Authors and Genres*, edited by A. S. G. Edwards, New Brunswick, New Jersey: Rutgers University Press, 1984
Hudson, Anne, *The Premature Reformation: Wycliffite Texts and Lollard History*, Oxford: Clarendon Press, and New York: Oxford University Press, 1988
Jacoebee, W. Pierre, "The Classical Sermon and the French Literary Tradition," *Australian Journal of French Studies* 19, no. 3 (1982): 227–42
Miller, Joseph M., Michael H. Prosser, and Thomas W. Benton, editors, *Readings in Medieval Rhetoric*, Bloomington: Indiana University Press, 1973
Murphy, James J., editor, *Three Medieval Rhetorical Arts*, Berkeley: University of California Press, 1971
Murphy, James J., *Rhetoric in the Middle Ages: A History of Rhetorical Theory from Saint Augustine to the Renaissance*, Berkeley: University of California Press, 1981
Owst, G. R., *Literature and Pulpit in Medieval England*, Oxford: Blackwell, 1966 (original edition, 1933)
Reedy, Gerard S., "Essential Studies of the Restoration Anglican Sermon," *Restoration* 2, no. 2 (1978): 14–16
Rivers, Cheryl, "The Jeremiad as Political Sermon," in *Amérique révolutionnaire*, edited by Jean Béranger and Jean-Claude Barat, Bordeaux-Talence: Maison des Sciences de l'Homme d'Aquitaine, 1976

Serrès, Michel

French, 1930–

To read Michel Serrès is to set sail on an essayistic, poetic, and philosophical journey of discovery and recovery of the history of sciences, human nature, and knowledge. Serrès was born in Agen, in his beloved Valley of Garonne, and later became a naval officer. He coined numerous maritime metaphors on his journeys on board military ships, at the same time developing a very different perspective of the earth and humanity, which led him to his cherished field: philosophy. This itinerary explains the tropological language that surfaces in his nature-oriented, essayistic writings, such as *Détachement* (1983; *Detachment*) – which he subtitles *Apologue* – and *Le Contrat naturel* (1990; *The Natural Contract*), in which he views earth as a spaceship that humanity must steer wisely. Here his philosophical views against violence, inspired by his reading of **Simone Weil**, gather a momentum that permeates all his work, influencing his exchange of maritime journeys for revolutionary ones across the archipelago of knowledge. He sees his exploratory passages as "re-educating revolutions" (*La Traduction* [1974; *Translation*]). These explorations were widened at L'École Normale Supérieure, where Serrès completed his doctorate in philosophy and the history of science in 1968. Since that time he has been best viewed as a philosopher-poet, which reflects his penchant for the pursuit of synthesis out of the complexity of humanity's inherited knowledge.

Serrès' essayistic methodology and approach to philosophy are epitomized by free thinking and random searching for passages and connections across the sciences, a Hermes-like method he deems essential to creativity. It is not by chance that he chooses the Greek god/messenger Hermes (Mercury/angel messenger in Roman tradition) as the pilot of his intellectual journeys. Serrès elects this symbol of the "power to communicate, to connect" (by the magic power of Hermes' wand), a power which he also perceives in our contemporary mass media. Under Hermes' aegis Serrès launched his five-volume series *Hermès: La Communication* (1968; Communication), *L'Interférence* (1972; Interference), *La Traduction* (1974; Translation), *La Distribution* (1977; Distribution), and *Le Passage du Nord-Ouest* (1980; The Northwest passage) – a series reflected in his subsequent writings, a complete Hermesian/Serrèsian system in itself.

These exploratory and revolutionary journeys provide us with the opportunity to reconsider the modern essay as a genuine locus of cultural *mestizaje* (adaptation), a view that springs from one of Serrès' most constructive philosophical metaphors: that of the "educated third" (*Le Tiers-instruit*, 1991). Serrès wants his readers to understand this metaphor as the philosophy of cultural adaptation, a metaphor that echoes Hermes' ability to transport cultural values from one place to another. Culture, for Serrès, stands as the foundation of human civilization; he sees its significance as comparable, for example, to a "plate tectonics" theory for understanding humanity's development.

While he visualizes humanity as passing from local through global frontiers (*The Natural Contract*) – a movement that parallels that of the essay – Serrès hopes cultural adaptation will return humanity to the original sense of philosophy as love of wisdom, as the urgently needed confluence of the soft and the hard sciences (humanities and natural sciences). This confluence, Serrès believes, is needed in order to reverse the regrettable departure of science from the humanistic sphere as brought about by the "scientization and technologization" of modern Western society. It is at this confluence that Serrès foresees the main role and responsibility for the philosopher and writer toward the humanistic disciplines.

As for the possibilities for such cultural *mestizaje* to crystallize, Serrès reconsiders and redefines the fundamental physical constructs of time and space, as the primordial ambience where fruitful and countless contacts between diverse entities and principles may develop, beyond the positivistic and reductionist frontiers of hegemonic specialization. Here he acknowledges his debt to the poetic vision of Lucretius (c. 100–55 BCE) in his *De rerum natura* (*On The Nature of Things*). This Latin poet and philosopher gave Serrès insight into the existence of principles such as that of the *clinamen* (inclination), "the smallest conceivable condition," that sets in motion the creative processes of the turbulent universe (*La Naissance de la physique dans le texte de Lucrèce* [1977; The birth of physics in the text of Lucretius]). Like Lucretius, Serrès envisions an ontological and structural grounding for a theory of systems, and the intricate series of processes of exchange, within and across countless systems. Thanks to these systemic interrelations, it is possible for Serrès to link, for instance, the processes of language, communication, and life. In turn, this structural vision allows us to perceive the poetic sense of Serrès' philosophy, for poetry gives us an image of the world and its being in time and space. Serrès' vision here may concur with that of **Octavio Paz**, who believes that poetry is what manifests itself in/as the poem, that very space from which things emerge out of the creative turbulence of chaos, and which we can perceive as an infinite array of kaleidoscopic images, colors, and a holographic dance of fractals. This connection helps explain Serrès' illuminating statement that "philosophy is profound enough to make us understand that literature [poetry] is even more so" (*Stéphan Bureau rencontre Michel Serrès*, Radio Québec, 1993).

The principal aim of these philosophical and poetic connections is the search for innovative, creative ways of solving problems in the perception of knowledge, and in the portrayal of what is called reality, as Serrès clarifies in a series of interviews with philosopher and anthropologist Bruno Latour, published as *Éclaircissements* (1992; *Conversations on Science, Culture, and Time*). As Serrès explains, the rationale for his essayistic methodology of comparative connections and interferences is that legitimate knowledge is disseminated everywhere, with no one claiming exclusive rights or possession. Accordingly, argues Serrès, there is as much logic and reason to be found in the essays of **Michel de Montaigne** as in poetry, physics, or biochemistry. Equally, there can be as much unreason scattered throughout the sciences as there may be found in myth and dream (*Conversations on Science, Culture, and Time*). Serrès echoes Montaigne's essayistic method when he states, for instance, that where philosophy cannot go, literature very well can. This is indeed an apology for the humanities, as well as a denial that science is the only illuminating sun of truth (paraphrasing Kepler).

As a philosopher-poet and humanist, Serrès also seeks a space for the senses, especially the spirit of beauty. Thus he feels that the soft sciences (humanities) provide us with that sense of "earthly residence" (Pablo Neruda), whereas the hard sciences such as mathematics – the very language both Leibniz and Serrès see as central to the study of a philosophy of communication – are the most effective means of dealing with the luminous spirit embodied in human rationality. Serrès regards philosophy as an enterprise in which the new culture will reconcile, not only exact sciences and humanities, but also the most advanced rational knowledge, ethics, and spiritual uneasiness (*Statues*, 1987).

CIRO A. SANDOVAL-B.

Biography

Born 1 September 1930 in Agen. Studied at the École Normale Supérieure, Paris, agrégation in philosophy and the history of science, 1968. Professor of philosophy and the history of science at the Sorbonne, Paris, Stanford University, California, and the Institut de France, Paris. Elected to French Academy, 1990. Editor, *Dominos*, from 1993. President, Association pour le Corpus Philosophique de la Langue Française (Association for the philosophical body of the French language).

Selected Writings

Essays and Related Prose

Hermès I–V, 5 vols., 1968–80; selections as *Hermes: Literature, Science, Philosophy* (various translators), edited by Josué V. Harari and David F. Bell, 1982
Jouvences sur Jules Verne, 1974
Feux et signaux de brume, Zola, 1975
Auguste Comte: Leçons de philosophie positive, 1975
La Naissance de la physique dans le texte de Lucrèce: Fleuves et turbulences, 1977
Le Parasite, 1980; as *The Parasite*, translated by Lawrence R. Schehr, 1982
Genèse: Récits métaphysiques, 1982; as *Genesis*, translated by Genevieve James and James Nielson, 1995
Rome: Le Livre des fondations, 1983; as *Rome, the Book of Foundations*, translated by Felicia McCarren, 1991
Détachement: Apologue, 1983; as *Detachment*, translated by Genevieve James and Raymond Federman, 1989

Les Cinq Sens, 1985

Statues: Le Second Livre des fondations, 1987

L'Hermaphrodite: Sarrasine sculpteur, 1987

Le Contrat naturel, 1990; as *The Natural Contract*, translated by
   Elizabeth MacArthur and William Paulson, 1995

Le Tiers-instruit, 1991

*Discours de réception à l'Académie française et réponse de Bertrand
   Poirot-Delpech*, 1991

La Légende des anges, 1993; as *Angels: A Modern Myth*, translated
   by Francis Cowper, 1995

Les Origines de la géométrie, 1993

Atlas, 1994

Les Messages à distance, 1995

Éloge de la philosophie en langue française, 1995

Other writings: works on philosophy, literature, and science.

Bibliography
"Bibliographie des travaux de Michel Serrès," *Critique* 380 (January
   1979): 121–25

Further Reading
Auzias, Jean-Marie, *Michel Serrès, philosophe occitan*, Mussidan:
   Fédérap, 1992

Crahay, Anne, *Michel Serrès: La Mutation du cogito: Genèse du
   transcendantal objectif*, Paris: Éditions Universitaires, and
   Brussels: De Boeck University, 1988

Michel Serrès: Interférences et turbulences, *Critique* issue on Serrès,
   35, no. 380 (1979)

Serrès, Michel, and Bruno Latour, *Michel Serrès with Bruno Latour:
   Conversations on Science, Culture, and Time*, Ann Arbor:
   University of Michigan Press, 1995 (original French edition, 1992)

Sévigné, Madame de

French, 1626–1696

Saint-Simon, himself a great essayist, wrote that Madame de Sévigné "knew a great deal about all kinds of things without ever wishing to give the appearance of it." It is this combination of insight and modesty for which she is perhaps best known. Her fame as a writer is particularly remarkable because she never published any literary work during her lifetime. Rather, her renown stems from her surviving letters, over a thousand in all, the majority of which were addressed to her much loved daughter, Madame de Grignan (1646–1705), who in 1671 moved with her husband from Paris to Provence. The first published collection of her letters appeared in 1725.

Although the letters of Madame de Sévigné can be regarded on one level as a series of letters to relatives and friends, they represent on another level essential documents and highly literate essays on a wide variety of subjects relating to 17th-century France. A major source of debate among literary critics has been whether she should be considered as simply a letter writer or as an epistolary author. Some view her work as purely private communication between individuals, but others see the letters as one of the few means available to a woman at that time to express herself as a writer. By writing to her daughter, they argue, she was able to create a certain kind of textual persona. Whichever way we may view her output, it is incontrovertible that the acuteness of her observation permeates all the letters. In this context, although she does not take up and

pursue subjects in the comprehensive way many essayists do, there are three categories of observation to which her letters give rise: historical, literary, and social.

Of the historical letters, the most significant are the 14 letters written between November 1664 and January 1665 to Simon Arnauld de Pomponne on the trial of their mutual friend Nicolas Fouquet. Fouquet had been Minister of Finance under Cardinal Mazarin, but, after the latter's death in 1661, Colbert (the future Minister of Commerce and Internal Affairs) collaborated with the king, Louis XIV, to arrest Fouquet on the charge of financial maladministration. Not only can Madame de Sévigné's letters on the trial be seen as an account of a significant historical event but, more importantly, she focuses on the human aspects of the drama, relating the emotions and responses of the leading participants and evoking both pathos and humor. Other historical events, such as wars and political marriages, are similarly suffused with her personal observations and accounts of other people's reactions. In her famous description of the public execution in 1676 of the murderess Madame de Brinvilliers, for example, Madame de Sévigné concentrates on both the event and her own limited view of the proceedings.

Throughout the letters, Madame de Sévigné displays a broad literary knowledge. She quotes from a wide variety of authors and was herself closely acquainted with leading writers of the day such as **La Rochefoucauld** and especially Madame de Lafayette. Not only does she observe many interesting literary and religious debates, such as the dispute between the Jesuits and the Jansenists (with whom she had close ties), but she also acts as literary critic both of writers who are little known today, like Ménage, Segrais, and Coulanges, and of well-known writers like Molière, Corneille, Racine, and La Fontaine. Her literary judgment does not always concur with that of posterity, as is shown in her unfavorable comments on some plays by Racine.

Madame de Sévigné's social observation is perhaps most particularly acute, as she is always keen to point out the absurdity of certain appearances and pretensions. She is a close observer of court life as well as life in the country, where she had a home at Les Rochers in Brittany. But, besides the vignettes of 17th-century life, her perception of human relationships extends beyond the age in which she lived. The mother-daughter relationship that manifests itself in the vast majority of the letters provides a unifying structure to the correspondence, and her expressions of love and pain at her daughter's absence are readily comprehensible to all ages. Moreover, her prime wish was to entertain her daughter in her letters, and this is demonstrated in her highly inventive use of language. At times she creates suspense by purposefully withholding information until the end of a letter, while at others she invents dialogues and even includes messages from other people, such as her friend Corbinelli or her son Charles de Sévigné. Although most letters display her effervescence and continual good humor, occasionally her observations contain a deep sense of sadness, for example at the death of La Rochefoucauld or at the suicide of Vatel, the king's chef. Little mention is made of her husband, Henri de Sévigné, who was killed in 1651 in a duel over his mistress, Madame de Gondran, but the pain of his infidelity and the rigors of having been widowed at the age of 25 are briefly evoked.

Madame de Sévigné has been widely praised, for both the seeming spontaneity and the extreme artfulness of her style. In many ways her writing can be compared to that of the theater: she creates vivid scenarios in which several characters play different roles, she herself operating as both spectator and actress. In the Fouquet letters, for example, she describes the actions and words of the leading participants as well as the response of the onlookers, including herself. But she can also be viewed as an essayist in her own right, as it was through her letters that she was able to discuss and comment upon the society in which she lived.

NICHOLAS HAMMOND

Biography

Marie de Rabutin Chantal, Marquise de Sévigné. Born 5 February 1626 in Paris. Studied privately with tutors. Married Henri, Baron and Marquis de Sévigné, 1644 (killed in a duel, 1651): one daughter and one son. Frequented salons, and met many literary figures, becoming close friends with Madame de Lafayette. Wrote at least 1100 letters during her life, many to her daughter Françoise-Marguerite, Comtesse de Grignan. Died (possibly of pneumonia or influenza) at Grignan, 17 April 1696.

Letters

Lettres choisies de Mme. la marquise de Sévigné, 1725
Lettres de Marie Rabutin-Chantal, marquise de Sévigné, 2 vols., 1726
Recueil des lettres de Mme. la marquise de Sévigné, edited by D.-M. Perrin, 6 vols., 1734–37
Lettres de Mme. de Sévigné, de sa famille et de ses amis, edited by M. Monmerqué, 14 vols., 1862–68
Lettres inédites de Mme. de Sévigné, 2 vols., 1876
Letters (selection), edited by Richard Aldington, translated anonymously, 2 vols., 1927
Lettres (Pléiade Edition), edited by Émile Gérard-Gailly, 3 vols., 1953–57
Letters (selection), edited and translated by Violet Hammersley, 1955
Selected Letters, edited and translated by H. T. Barnwell, 1960
Correspondance de Mme. de Sévigné (Pléiade Edition), edited by Roger Duchêne, 3 vols., 1972–78
Lettres (selection), edited by Bernard Raffali, 1976
Selected Letters, translated by Leonard Tancock, 1982
Lettres choisies, edited by Roger Duchêne, 1988

Further Reading

Allentuch, Harriet, *Madame de Sévigné: A Portrait in Letters*, Baltimore: Johns Hopkins University Press, 1963
Duchêne, Roger, *Madame de Sévigné, ou, La Chance d'être une femme*, Paris: Fayard, 1982
Duchêne, Roger, *Madame de Sévigné et la lettre d'amour*, Paris: Klincksieck, revised edition, 1992
Farrell, Michèle Longino, *Performing Motherhood: The Sévigné Correspondence*, Hanover, New Hampshire: University Press of New England, 1991
Gibson, Wendy, *Women in Seventeenth-Century France*, New York: St. Martin's Press, and London: Macmillan, 1989
Hawcroft, Michael, "Historical Evidence and Literature: Madame de Sévigné's Letters on the Trial of Fouquet," *The Seventeenth Century* 9, no. 1 (1994): 57–75
Papers on French Seventeenth-Century Literature issue on Madame de Sévigné, 8 (1981): 1–162
Recker, Jo Anne Marie, *"Appelle-moi Pierrot": Wit and Irony in the Lettres of Madame de Sévigné*, Amsterdam and Philadelphia: Benjamins, 1986

Shaftesbury, Earl of

English, 1671–1713

Anthony Ashley Cooper, the Third Earl of Shaftesbury, was among the most widely read and influential writers of his era. A man of aristocratic bearing whose delicate health restricted his involvement in the public domain, Shaftesbury did not court fame through authorship. Unlike a number of his contemporaries, he disdained to engage in controversy, and he did not share in the Augustan propensity to display his talents in the various poetic genres as well as in prose. His fame derived wholly from his essays, and almost entirely from those he published as a collection in one book, the *Characteristicks of Men, Manners, Opinions, Times*, which appeared in 1711, two years before his death.

The *Characteristicks* represents Shaftesbury's gathering of essays he had written over the previous decade into a coherent and purposeful single text. At least one essay had appeared without his authorization, and his fastidiousness as a stylist compelled him to pay attention to the text of what must have occurred to him would be the ultimate collected edition of his writings. Besides such stylistic emendations, he restructured his texts to some degree, to enhance the clarity or to reduce the formality of his discourse. To complete the book, he wrote and published for the first time a long essay he called "Miscellaneous Reflections" on the earlier essays. Though he continued to write after publishing this book, and these and other pieces appeared posthumously, the *Characteristicks* had already established Shaftesbury's influence and reputation in England and on the continent. Eleven editions of the book had been published in England alone by 1790.

To his own and subsequent generations, Shaftesbury was known primarily as a philosopher. Though they cannot be said to originate with him, his ideas about the perfection of the universe, the innate goodness of man, and the natural human endowment with moral sentiment gave wide popular circulation to basic deistic treatments of the universe and the nature of man; the many writers and theologians who attacked him did so to get at these ideas. Shaftesbury's notions about poetry, music, architecture, and taste, while not presented systematically in his essays, also made him a contributor to the aesthetic discourse of his age. His comments on enthusiasm, which he disdained in religious behavior but admired as a constituent of the poetic imagination, helped to awaken English poets to the beauties of nature and the significance of the sublime.

As an essayist, Shaftesbury represents well the ease and grace of early 18th-century English prose. Though conservative in his taste and rather doctrinaire about the Rules, Shaftesbury cultivated a clear, relaxed style of discourse based (as he says in his "Advice to an Author") on the conversation of "good company, and people of the better sort." The *Characteristicks* presents blocks of argument developed with such leisure and rhetorical restraint that one is not aware of reading argumentation at all. Through conjunctive elements and bits of narrative he controls transitions of thought easily, and varies masterfully the levels of usage in his address to explicit or imagined readers. Consider the stylistic control of this passage from his essay on "enthusiasm":

We have a notable instance of this freedom in one of our sacred authors. As patient as Job is said to be, it cannot be denied that he makes bold enough with God, and takes his providence roundly to task. His friends, indeed, plead hard with him, and use all arguments, right or wrong, to patch up objections, and set the affairs of providence upon an equal foot. They make a merit of saying all the good they can of God, at the very stretch of their reason, and sometimes quite beyond it. But this, in Job's opinion, is flattering God, accepting of God's person, and even mocking him. And no wonder.

At its best, Shaftesbury's prose flows easily along a reader's consciousness with a quality which may perhaps best be called (to use one of his favorite terms) "serenity": "Whoever has been an observer of action and grace in human bodies must of necessity have discovered the great difference in this respect between such persons as have been taught by nature only, and such as by reflection and the assistance of art have learnt to form those motions which on experience are found the easiest and most natural" ("Advice to an Author"). Such passages – particularly those articulating ideas about virtue and the goodness of the Divine Being – awakened wide admiration for Shaftesbury in his own age (except in the realm of theological controversy), at home and abroad. Both **Diderot** and **Herder** read him with pleasure, and Montesquieu named him, with **Plato**, Malebranche, and **Montaigne**, among "the four great poets." The tough-minded Elizabeth Carter spoke of rising from the *Characteristicks* with her mind full of "beauties, and love, and harmony, but all of a divine and mysterious nature."

In the 19th and 20th centuries, Shaftesbury's reputation has waned – along with the subject matter, it must be said, with which his essays are principally concerned. Readers who discover the *Characteristicks*, however, now some three centuries after the first publication, are likely to agree (at the least) with John M. Robertson's assessment in the introduction to his edition of these essays (1900), still the only complete modern edition of the work: "Given fair play, the *Characteristicks* can still hold their own with most of the books with which they competed in their generation."

JAMES M. KUIST

Biography

Anthony Ashley Cooper, Third Earl of Shaftesbury. Born 26 February 1671 at Wimborne St. Giles, Dorset. Studied privately in Dorset, under the influence of John Locke; Winchester College, 1682–84; privately in London, from 1686. Toured the continent, 1687–89, then returned to look after his family and estate. Whig Member of Parliament for Poole, 1695. Suffered from asthma for the rest of his life. Stayed in Rotterdam, 1697, 1698–99, and 1703–04. Lived in Chelsea, south London, 1699–1709. Married Jane Ewer, 1709: one son. Moved to Reigate, 1709; moved to Italy for his health, 1711. Died in Chiaia, near Naples, 15 February 1713.

Selected Writings

Essays and Related Prose

Inquiry Concerning Virtue in Two Discourses, 1699; facsimile reprint, 1991; edited by David Walford, 1977
A Letter Concerning Enthusiasm, 1708; edited by Richard B. Wolf, 1988

Sensus Communis: An Essay on the Freedom of Wit and Humour, 1709
Characteristicks of Men, Manners, Opinions, Times, 3 vols., 1711; revised edition, 1714; edited by John M. Robertson, 2 vols., 1900, reprinted 1964

Other writings: works on philosophy and moral behavior, and correspondence.

Collected works edition: *Complete Works, Selected Letters and Posthumous Writings* (in English, and translated into German), edited by Gerd Hemmerich and Wolfram Benda, 6 vols., 1981–93 (in progress).

Further Reading

Aldridge, Alfred Owen, "Shaftesbury and the Deist Manifesto," *Transactions of the American Philosophical Society* 41 (1951): 297–385
Crane, R. S., "Suggestions Toward a Genealogy of the Man of Feeling," *Journal of English Literary History* 1 (1934): 205–30
Markley, R., "Style as Philosophical Structure: The Contexts of Shaftesbury's *Characteristicks*," in *The Philosopher as Writer: The Eighteenth Century*, edited by Robert Ginsberg, Selinsgrove, Pennsylvania: Susquehanna University Press, 1987
Moore, C. A., "The Return to Nature in the English Poetry of the Eighteenth Century," *Studies in Philology* 14 (1917): 257–86
Tuveson, Ernest L., "The Importance of Shaftesbury," *Journal of English Literary History* 20 (1953): 267–99
Tuveson, Ernest L., "Shaftesbury and the Age of Sensibility," in *Studies in Criticism and Aesthetics, 1660–1800: Essays in Honor of Samuel Holt Monk*, edited by Howard Anderson and John S. Shea, Minneapolis: University of Minnesota Press, 1967

Shaw, George Bernard

Irish, 1856–1950

George Bernard Shaw is best known for his plays, but at the end of his life he reproved one of his biographers for thinking of him only as a playwright: "For every play I have written I have made hundreds of speeches and published big books on Fabian Socialism" (*Sixteen Self Sketches*, 1949). Shaw actually began his career making speeches from soapboxes to anyone who would listen, and his style is predominantly a speaking one: forceful, witty, frequently paradoxical, and yet straightforward enough to be understood at one brisk reading. On the negative side, this does not leave much scope for personal emotion, and the shock statements and paradoxes can lead to oversimplification and brightly polished half-truths. Yet Shaw is seldom merely superficial; rather, he makes serious points in a witty manner.

Shaw first published book **reviews**, going on to review music, theater, and painting. He also wrote more generally on the arts, notably when discussing Ibsen and Wagner. He reminisced on his own career (though guardedly) and about people he had known. He added long **prefaces** to his plays, expanding on the ideas they presented. The majority of his writings are, in the wider sense, political – on how society should be organized. They often originated as speeches and then appeared as articles, **pamphlets**, books, and even lengthy **letters** to the editor. Nearly all of Shaw's prose is journalism, in the sense that it is based on "what everybody is thinking about (or ought to be thinking about) at the moment of writing" (preface to *The Sanity of Art*, 1908). Most journalism loses its significance as time passes and circumstances change; many of Shaw's articles do not read as independent literary essays because they are tied to a particular event or situation, such as a dramatic performance. However, other articles – a small proportion of his great output, but still enough to fill a sizable book – have outlasted the topics that prompted them, and survive as literature. These topics are usually biographical, artistic, or (most commonly) political.

Despite a reputation for self-promotion, Shaw seldom writes directly about his own personal experiences. There are the *Self Sketches*, but these are curiously unrevealing about his feelings and not very interesting as essays. However, his pen portraits of others are valuable, partly because many of the people are well known – **William Morris, Oscar Wilde, H. G. Wells** – but also because many have a personal tone usually missing in Shaw's writing. His affection is evident in the essays on Morris (1899), the editor H. W. Massingham (1925), and the drama critic William Archer (1927). Of the last he says: ". . . after more than forty years, I have not a single unpleasant recollection." His response to H. G. Wells' furious public criticisms of Shaw and other leaders of the Fabian Society (which aimed at gradual socialism) is typical of Shaw's ability to be hard-hitting and yet genuinely affable, partly, as he says elsewhere, by "the art of softening a touchy point by a stroke of humorous exaggeration" (1899).

Biography is combined with the discussion of art, particularly when Shaw describes the leading actors of his period and their performances. He wages a long campaign against actor-director Henry Irving who, Shaw claims, altered Shakespeare's plays so drastically that they were unrecognizable. He makes the same criticism of Herbert Beerbohm Tree, but good-naturedly: "As far as I could discover, the notion that a play could succeed without any further help from the actor than a simple impersonation of his part never occurred to Tree. The author, whether Shakespeare or Shaw, was a lame dog to be helped over the stile by the ingenuity and inventiveness of the actor-producer" (1920). The success of Shaw's plays, without being rewritten by the actors, simply "bewildered" Tree.

Shaw is always willing to speak against the majority, and prepared to praise where others condemn. He strongly defends **Henry James'** ill-fated play *Guy Domville*, and defends Wilde against the fashionable charge that his plays are facile (1895): "As far as I can ascertain, I am the only person in London who cannot sit down and write an Oscar Wilde play at will." He does share the majority view on **Dickens**, and a pretended letter of complaint from the Rev. Stiggins about the Wellers of *Pickwick Papers*, "sensual, ribald, and unseemly" (1887), brings out the perennial attraction of Dickens' characters. His introduction to *Hard Times* (1913) anticipates **Orwell**'s more famous essay ("Charles Dickens," 1940) in many important points, examining the novel as announcing a major shift in Victorian perceptions of society.

The political essays are usually tied to contemporary situations, but some address wider topics. "War Delirium" (from the preface to *Heartbreak House*, 1919) is a study of how, in World War I, "the ordinary war-conscious citizen went mad," and what this reveals of human nature. It combines a balanced, humanitarian view with trenchant judgments. "Fools exulted

in 'German losses.' They were our losses as well. Imagine exulting in the death of Beethoven because Bill Sykes dealt him his death blow!" "Democracy" (1929) has similar qualities but the tone is lighthearted: Parliament is compared to a hot-air balloon that touches down briefly once every five years. "The Crime of Poverty" (1912) and "Death of an Old Revolutionary Hero" (1905) use sustained irony that, in the latter, becomes **satire**. The "revolutionary hero" has opposed all the reforms of the 19th century, however worthy, on the grounds that they did not go far enough. Shaw, the gradualist socialist, makes fun of "all or nothing" men. As usual, his genial skepticism allows him to be highly critical and yet open-minded and entertaining.

RALPH STEWART

Biography

Born 26 July 1856 in Dublin. Studied at various schools in Dublin, 1867–69. Worked for an estate agent in Dublin, 1871–76, then moved to London. Ghost writer for a music critic, 1876–77 and 1881; wrote serialized novels and literary and art criticism for various magazines and newspapers, 1879–83. Joined the Fabian Society, 1884, becoming a member of the executive committee, 1885–1911. Music, art, or drama reviewer for various journals, sometimes using the pseudonyum Corno di Bassetto for his music reviews, 1885–98. Helped to establish the London School of Economics, 1895. Playwright: first play, *Widowers' Houses*, produced 1892. Vestryman and councillor, Borough of St. Pancras, London, 1897–1903. Married Charlotte Payne-Townshend, 1898 (died, 1943). Lived mainly at country home in Ayot St. Lawrence, Hertfordshire, from 1906. Cofounder, the *New Statesman*, 1913. Awards: Nobel Prize for Literature, 1926; Irish Academy of Letters Medal, 1934; Academy Award (Oscar), for screenplay, 1939. Died in Ayot St. Lawrence, 2 November 1950.

Selected Writings

Essays and Related Prose

The Quintessence of Ibsenism, 1891; revised, enlarged edition, 1913
Dramatic Opinions and Essays, 2 vols., 1906
The Sanity of Art, 1908
Music in London, 1890–1894, 3 vols., 1931
Our Theatre in the Nineties, 3 vols., 1931
London Music in 1888–89, 1937
Sixteen Self Sketches, 1949
Plays and Players: Theatre Essays, edited by A. C. Ward, 1952
Shaw on Theatre: Sixty Years of Letters, Speeches, and Articles, edited by E. J. West, 1958
Major Critical Essays, 1958
Dramatic Criticism, 1895–98, edited by John F. Matthews, 1959
Shaw on Shakespeare, edited by Edwin Wilson, 1961
The Religious Speeches, edited by Warren Sylvester Smith, 1963
Shaw on Language, edited by Abraham Tauber, 1963
Selected Non-Dramatic Writings, edited by Dan H. Laurence, 1965
Shaw on Religion, edited by Warren Sylvester Smith, 1967
The Road to Equality: Ten Unpublished Lectures and Essays, 1884–1918, edited by Louis Crompton and Hilayne Cavanaugh, 1971
Nondramatic Literary Criticism, edited by Stanley Weintraub, 1972
Practical Politics: Twentieth-Century Views on Politics and Economics, edited by Lloyd J. Hubenka, 1976
Shaw and Ibsen: Bernard Shaw's The Quintessence of Ibsenism, and Related Writings, edited by J. L. Wisenthal, 1979
Shaw's Music: The Complete Musical Criticism, edited by Dan H. Laurence, 3 vols., 1981

Agitations: Letters to the Press, 1875–1950, edited by Dan H. Laurence and James Rambeau, 1985
Book Reviews: Originally Published in the Pall Mall Gazette from 1885 to 1888, edited by Brian Tyson, 1991
The Drama Observed, edited by Bernard F. Dukore, 1993
The Complete Prefaces, edited by Dan H. Laurence and Daniel J. Leary, 2 vols., 1993–95

Other writings: many plays (including *Arms and the Man*, 1894; *Candida*, 1897; *Mrs. Warren's Profession*, 1898; *Man and Superman*, 1903; *Major Barbara*, 1905; *Pygmalion*, 1914; *Heartbreak House*, 1919; *Saint Joan*, 1924), five complete novels, screenplays, correspondence (published in *Collected Letters*, edited by Dan H. Laurence, 4 vols., 1965–88), diaries, and autobiography. Also edited (and contributed two essays to) *Fabian Essays in Socialism* (1889).

Collected works edition: *Works* (Standard Edition), 37 vols., 1931–50.

Bibliographies

Haberman, Donald C., J. P. Wearing, and Elsie B. Adams, *G. B. Shaw: An Annotated Bibliography of Writings About Him*, De Kalb: Northern Illinois University Press, 3 vols., 1986–87
Laurence, Dan H., *Bernard Shaw: A Bibliography*, Oxford: Clarendon Press, and New York: Oxford University Press, 2 vols., 1983

Further Reading

Barber, George S., "Shaw's Contributions to Music Criticism," *PMLA* 72 (December 1957): 1005–17
Barr, Alan P., "Diabolonian Pundit: G. B. S. as Critic," *Shaw Review* 11 (January 1968): 11–23
Breuer, Hans-Peter, "Form and Feeling: George Bernard Shaw as Music Critic," *Journal of Irish Literature* 11 (September 1982): 74–102
Fromm, Harold, *Shaw and the Theater in the Nineties: A Study of Shaw's Dramatic Criticism*, Lawrence: University of Kansas Press, 1967
Gassner, John, "Shaw as a Drama Critic," *Theatre Arts* 35 (May 1951): 26–29, 91–95
Glicksberg, Charles I., "The Criticism of Bernard Shaw," *South Atlantic Quarterly* 50 (January 1951): 96–108
Hadsel, Martha, "The Uncommon-Common Metaphor in Shaw's Dramatic Criticism," *Shaw Review* 23 (September 1980): 119–29
Hill, Eldon C., *George Bernard Shaw*, Boston: Twayne, 1978
Irvine, William, "G. B. Shaw's Musical Criticism," *Musical Quarterly* 32 (July 1946): 319–32
King, Carlyle, "G. B. Shaw on Literature: The Author as Critic," *Queen's Quarterly* 66 (Spring 1959): 135–45
Shenfield, M., "Shaw as a Music Critic," *Music and Letters* 39 (October 1958): 378–84
Silverman, Albert H., "Bernard Shaw's Shakespeare Criticism," *PMLA* 72 (September 1957): 722–36
Smith, J. Percy, "Superman Versus Man: Bernard Shaw on Shakespeare," *Yale Review* 42 (Autumn 1952): 67–82

Shelley, Percy Bysshe

British, 1792–1822

If Percy Bysshe Shelley regarded poets as unacknowledged legislators, it was in the medium of prose that he explicitly formulated this creed. In the small body of essays, **prefaces**, and fragments that form his prose corpus, Shelley treats religion, morals, politics, and literature not as separate critical concerns but as aspects of a cultural totality constructed by and constructing his role as a poet – a role far removed from that of the "ineffectual angel" described by some later readers. Indeed, Shelley's last and best-known essay, "A Defence of Poetry" (1821), defines poetry in explicitly functional terms as culturally mediated expression that "communicates itself to others, and gathers a sort of reduplication from that community." Whether as poet or polemicist, idealist or skeptic, Shelley writes as an engaged citizen.

Shelley's first public appearances as an author explore two poles of the expressive resources available to a prose writer. His first two prose publications, "The Necessity of Atheism" (1811) and "An Address to the Irish People" (1812), emerge from the philosopher's closet and the hustings respectively. Its mild, reasoned tenor notwithstanding, the first resulted in Shelley's expulsion (along with a friend) from Oxford. While the second effected no practical result beyond bringing home to its author the volatility of religious issues, it demonstrates a grasp of the plain style so effectively employed by radical writers like **Thomas Paine** and William Cobbett. The same year Shelley published "An Address" he also made an intervention on behalf of press freedoms in "A Letter to Lord Ellenborough," addressed to the judge who had recently convicted a bookseller and publisher for publishing Thomas Paine's *The Age of Reason*. The "Letter" speaks with what Blake terms "the voice of honest indignation," adeptly assuming the persona of an Englishman asserting his outrage at an infringement of traditional liberties ("Whom has he injured? What crime has he committed?").

An alternation between philosophical and popular modes characterizes Shelley's subsequent prose – a dichotomy reflecting a division among his poems as well. The common threads running through all of these works, however, are an engagement with the social good – whether it concerns diet ("Essay on the Vegetable System of Diet," wr. 1814–15) or political suffrage ("A Proposal for Putting Reform to the Vote Throughout the Kingdom," pub. 1817) – and a rational public voice. While its author was sometimes portrayed by contemporaries as a self-dramatizing young Werther figure, Shelley's prose eschews the personal, idiosyncratic, and often confessional impulses of the Romantic essay as practiced by **Lamb, De Quincey,** and **Hazlitt.** Shelley was a child of the Enlightenment and his essays reflect the encyclopedic cultural purview and the rational vantage of 18th-century moral philosophy. His writing is learned, employing even the most recondite classical references with ease, and capable of philosophical sophistication, treating fundamental questions in pieces like "Essay on Love" (wr. c. 1818) and "Essay on Life" (wr. c. 1812–14), for instance, with rigorous economy of exposition ("The words, *I, you, they* are not signs of any actual difference subsisting between the assemblage of thoughts thus indicated, but are merely marks employed to denote the different modifications of the one mind"). The work is fully engaged as well, directing its energies of inquiry to the most immediate issues affecting daily life. For Shelley, as a poet, these issues are ultimately implicated in the status and function of poetry in an age when the dominant modes of inquiry were rational in nature. In 1820, his friend Thomas Love Peacock published a witty essay entitled *The Four Ages of Poetry*, in which Peacock argues that poetry has outlived its usefulness: "It can never make a philosopher, nor a statesman, nor in any class of life an useful or rational man. It cannot claim the slightest share in any one of the comforts and utilities of life of which we have witnessed so many and so rapid advances." In reply, Shelley wrote "A Defence of Poetry" – his best-known essay and, along with Wordsworth's preface to the *Lyrical Ballads* (1800), a central critical document of English Romanticism. Taken together, both essays clearly look back to the Elizabethan controversy sparked by Stephen Gosson's *School of Abuse* (1579), an angry attack on poetry that provoked Sir Philip Sidney to write his famous **Defence of Poesy** (1595). Where Gosson takes the moralistic line of puritanism, however, Peacock argues from the bloodlessly practical perspective of utilitarianism. What makes Shelley's reply so effective is that it, too, proceeds from the principle of utility – albeit a much less reductive version.

Like Peacock's essay, which traces poetry's decline as a cultural force from its vital role in primitive heroic cultures to its puerile decadence at present, Shelley's "Defence" is conceived on the model of the Enlightenment cultural survey. It starts out from the premise that "poetry is connate with the origin of man," arguing for the priority of imagination over reason. Shelley's method is by turns logical and declamatory, alternating rational exposition ("Reason is the enumeration of quantities already known; imagination is the perception of the value of those quantities, both separately and as a whole") with rhetorical figures ("Reason is to imagination as the instrument to the agent, as the body to the spirit, as the shadow to the substance"). Shelley uses the term "poet" in its broadest sense as an originator of knowledge, a category necessarily including "all the authors of revolutions in opinion." This argument – that it is through new figures of speech, new modalities of language, that new ways of thinking emerge – is what validates the heightened, declamatory language employed in the essay by Shelley when he speaks in the persona of the legislator/seer the essay itself celebrates: "[Poetry] is at once the centre and circumference of knowledge; it is that which comprehends all science, and that to which all science must be referred. It is at the same time the root and blossom of all other systems of thought; it is that from which all spring, and that which adorns all." Rather than arguing against utility, then, the essay argues against a narrow conception of utility, and awards the civic laurel to poetry in the service of a higher utility.

JAMES MULVIHILL

Biography
Born 4 August 1792 at Field Place, near Horsham, Sussex. Studied at Syon House Academy, Isleworth, Middlesex, 1802–04; Eton College, Berkshire, 1804–10; University College, Oxford, 1810–11: expelled for the pamphlet *The Necessity of Atheism*. Eloped with Harriet Westbrook, and married, 1811 (died, 1816): one daughter and one son. Visited Ireland, 1812; lived in Lynmouth, Devon, Tremadoc, Wales, near Windsor, and on the continent, 1812–15. Left Harriet Westbrook for Mary Wollstonecraft Godwin (i.e. the writer Mary Shelley), daughter of **William Godwin** and **Mary Wollstonecraft**, 1814, and married her after Westbrook's death, 1816: two sons and one daughter. Lived in Geneva, 1816, Great Marlow, Buckinghamshire, 1817, and Italy, from 1818. Drowned in a sailing accident in the Mediterranean, in the Gulf of Spezia near Lerici, 8 July 1822.

Selected Writings

Essays and Related Prose
Essays, Letters from Abroad, Translations, and Fragments, edited by Mary Shelley, 2 vols., 1840
The Prose Works, edited by H. Buxton Forman, 4 vols., 1880
Prose Works, edited by Richard Herne Shepherd, 2 vols., 1888
Shelley's Prose, or, The Trumpet of a Prophecy, edited by David Lee Clark, 1954; corrected edition, 1988
Selected Poetry and Prose, edited by Alasdair D. F. Macrae, 1991
The Necessity of Atheism, and Other Essays, 1993
The Prose Works, vol. 1, edited by E. B. Murray, 1993
Poems and Prose, edited by Timothy Webb and George E. Donaldson, 1995

Other writings: poetry, two romances, and the verse drama *Prometheus Unbound* (1820).

Collected works editions: *The Complete Works*, edited by Roger Ingpen and Walter Edwin Peck, 10 vols., 1926–30; *The Bodleian Shelley Manuscripts*, editor-in-chief Donald H. Reiman, 21 vols., 1986–95.

Bibliographies
Dunbar, Clement, *A Bibliography of Shelley Studies, 1823–1950*, New York: Garland, 1976
Engelberg, Karsten Klejs, *The Making of the Shelley Myth: An Annotated Bibliography of Criticism of Percy Bysshe Shelley 1822–1860*, London: Mansell, and Westport, Connecticut: Meckler, 1988
Erdman, David, *The Romantic Movement: A Selective and Critical Bibliography*, New York: Garland, 10 vols., 1982– (in progress)

Further Reading
Cameron, Kenneth Neill, *The Young Shelley: Genesis of a Radical*, New York: Macmillan, 1950; London: Gollancz, 1951
Cameron, Kenneth Neill, *Shelley: The Golden Years*, Cambridge, Massachusetts: Harvard University Press, 1974
Dawson, P. M. S., *The Unacknowledged Legislator: Shelley and Politics*, Oxford: Clarendon Press, 1980
Delisle, Fanny, *A Study of Shelley's A Defence of Poetry: A Textual and Critical Evaluation*, Salzburg: University of Salzburg Institute for English Language and Literature, 1974
Hoagwood, Terence Allan, *Skepticism and Ideology: Shelley's Political Prose and Its Philosophical Context from Bacon to Marx*, Iowa City: University of Iowa Press, 1988
Keach, William, *Shelley's Style*, New York: Methuen, 1984
Scrivener, Michael, *Radical Shelley: The Philosophical Anarchism and Utopian Thought of Percy Bysshe Shelley*, Princeton, New Jersey: Princeton University Press, 1982
Verkoren, Lucas, *A Study of Shelley's Defence of Poetry: Its Origin, Textual History, Sources, and Significance*, New York: Haskell House, 1970 (original edition, 1937)

Shestov, Lev
Russian, 1866–1938

Perhaps the greatest stylist among Russian philosophers, Lev Shestov was in the main a writer of essays. His earliest works – *Shakespeare i ego kritik Brandes* (1898; Shakespeare and his critic Brandes), *Dobro v uchenii Gr. Tolstogo i Nietzsche filosofiia i propoved'* (1900; "The Good in the Teaching of

Tolstoy and Nietzsche: Philosophy and Preaching"), and *Dostoevskii i Nietzsche: Filosofiia tragedii* (1903; "Dostoevsky and Nietzsche: The Philosophy of Tragedy") – bridged the disciplines of philosophy and literary criticism. Shestov's first fully philosophical work, *Apofeoz bespochvennosti* (1905; The apotheosis of groundlessness, translated as *All Things Are Possible*), is, like much of his subsequent philosophical writing, comprised of small aphoristic clusters, similar to those in **Nietzsche**'s *Der Antichrist* (1895; *The Antichrist*) or *Morgenröthe* (1881; *The Dawn of Day*), and contains brief essays of under five pages in length. *All Things Are Possible* reveals Shestov's major theme: belief in the revelation of a divine mystical being who can be known only through faith, which for Shestov "is not a lower form of cognition." Shestov conceives of the history of Western philosophy as the struggle between Athens – the rationalizing, secularizing spirit from Aristotle, through Thomas Aquinas, Descartes, Spinoza, Leibniz, **Kant**, and Hegel, and including materialist positivism and Marxism – and Jerusalem – the mystical faith in the God revealed in the Old and New Testaments.

Many of Shestov's early essays were collected in the books *Nachala i kontsii* (1908; Beginnings and endings, translated as *Penultimate Words and Other Essays*) and *Velikie kanunii* (1910; Great vigils). *Vlast' kliuchei: Potestas clavium* (1923; The power of the keys, translated as *Potestas Clavium*) was the first collection of Shestov's essays to appear abroad and was followed by a host of essays in the Parisian émigré journals *Sovremennye Zapiski* (Contemporary notes) and *Russkie Zapiski* (Russian notes). His late books *Na vesakh Iova* (1929; *In Job's Balances*), *Kierkegaard i eksistentsialnaia filosofiia* (1939; *Kierkegaard and the Existential Philosophy*), and *Afiny i Ierusalim* (wr. 1938, pub. 1951; *Athens and Jerusalem*) reiterate ideas that were already present in Shestov's earlier work, but are generally considered more dialectical and cogent presentations of those same views.

Shestov called attention to his own affinities with existentialism and has been classified as an existentialist, most notably by Nikolai Berdiaev. This is because he assumes the viewpoint of the human individual and champions his unhindered search for truth over and against any and all rational laws and ideological systems, be they materialist-positivistic, rational ethics, or rationalized religion – from Spinoza to **Solov'ev**. Shestov, of course, does not reject the knowledge of modern science for practical life, but dismisses it as totally useless for man's spiritual quest. His anti-moralist stance was evident in his early book on **Lev Tolstoi** and Friedrich Nietzsche, where he takes the side of the German thinker against Tolstoyan "preaching."

Despite the frequent label of "existentialist" and the influence he undoubtedly exerted on both Christian and atheistic existentialist philosophers in France, where he taught at the Sorbonne for many years, there is ample reason to view Shestov's thought as even more theocentric than man-centered. The shape of Shestov's own philosophical quest led him to focus primarily on God, specifically on defending the mystical God of his "Jerusalem" from philosophy's rationalist constructions. Anything anthroposophizing in relation to God is demeaning and inadequate, including all the constructions of Western philosophy. With God and for God literally "all things are possible"; all the laws of science can be invalidated at any

moment. God can be felt and "known" only by nonrationalist, mystical means. Zenkovsky (in *A History of Russian Philosophy*, 1953) has characterized Shestov as "a *believing consciousness*, rare for its sustained and lucid quality." The sympathetic reader of Shestov will discover writing focused on the utter "otherness" and mystical nature of the deity and the ways of knowing God. Shestov provokes more interest in God and the things beyond immediate experience than most existentialist writers, even religious ones.

Philosophically an irrationalist like Nietzsche, or rather an anti-rationalist, Shestov uses a highly rational and clear discourse to demolish rationalism and its necessary laws in any and all forms he finds in the history of human thought. Unlike his irrationalist contemporary in Russia, **Vasilii Rozanov**, Shestov does not resort to poetic lines, prose poetry, illogicality, or mystical whimsicality. A mystical thinker at base, he uses razor-sharp logic to demolish, piece by piece, the manifold tenets of the whole Western philosophical tradition. Shestov's statements are striking and bold, often formulated as paradoxes. Yet there is a constant tension between his clear, logical, rational language and the actual thoughts expressed. Zenkovsky sees Shestov in the grips of rationalism, struggling against its hold upon him throughout his life. In *In Job's Balances* Shestov writes, "One can and must sacrifice everything to find God." Zenkovsky describes the philosopher as sacrificing the baggage of Western philosophical culture on the altar of his mystical faith.

The fact that his discourse is constantly calling attention to its own inadequacy, and the harm caused by the tradition from which such language derives, makes Shestov's work stronger in negation than in affirmation. All his works deal overwhelmingly with the destruction of what is inadequate to express the mystical positive content of revelation; however, they come up short as expressors of his positive faith.

It appears that Shestov accepted the revelations of the Old and New Testaments and felt that religion and philosophy must begin from the mystical truth revealed in the Bible. Shestov wishes to free man not only *from* rationalism, but also *for* his own creative spiritual activity. Divulging the positive content of Shestov's own mystical faith, even if it were possible in rational discourse, would counter one of the main purposes of his writing. He wishes to provoke creative religious thought in others, not supplant their old customary ways of thinking with an explicit philosophy of his own. In this he is like Nietzsche who wanted to make man aware of his radical freedom from the strictures of dogmatic Christianity and its morality.

To his credit, Shestov has an uncanny ability to see rationalism and its delimiting power in writers and systems that are not usually thought of in such terms. He is ever pitting the individual against the idea and defending God from human definition. Thus in his article "Prorocheskii dar. k dvadtsatipiatiletiiu smerti Dostoevskogo" (1908; "The Gift of Prophecy: For the 25th Anniversary of Dostoevsky's Death") he attacks **Dostoevskii**, much as Nietzsche had, for his retreat from irrational "Truth" into a web of Orthodox and nationalist constructs. His essay on Anton Chekhov, the "poet of hopelessness," "Tvorchestvo iz nichego: A. P. Chekhov" (1908; "Creation from Nothing"), shows the pessimistic side of a thoroughgoing hatred of ideology. There are few societal or religious-moral sacred cows which escape Shestov's powerful and often ironic attack, for any rational system, even rationalized religion, is faithless secularism for Shestov.

ANNA LISA CRONE

Biography

Born Lev Isaakovich Shwarzmann, 13 February 1866 in Kiev. Studied mathematics, then law at Moscow University, 1884–89; University of Kiev, degree in law, 1889. Managed the family textile business, 1892–94. Went abroad, 1896, living in Italy and Switzerland, 1897–1914. Married Anna Eleasarovna Beresovskii, 1897: two daughters. Lived in Moscow, 1914–18; professor of philosophy, University of Kiev, 1918–19. Moved to Switzerland, 1920, then Paris, 1921. Member, Russian Academic Group, Paris, from 1921; Professor of Russian, Institut d'Études Slaves, the Sorbonne, Paris, from 1922. Died in Paris, 20 November 1938.

Selected Writings

Essays and Related Prose

Shakespeare i ego kritik Brandes, 1898
Dobro v uchenii Gr. Tolstogo i Nietzsche filosofiia i propoved', 1900; as "The Good in the Teaching of Tolstoy and Nietzsche: Philosophy and Preaching," translated by Bernard Martin, in *Dostoevsky, Tolstoy and Nietzsche*, 1969
Dostoevskii i Nietzsche: Filosofiia tragedii, 1903; as "Dostoevsky and Nietzsche: The Philosophy of Tragedy," translated by Bernard Martin, in *Dostoevsky, Tolstoy and Nietzsche*, 1969
Apofeoz bespochvennosti, 1905; as *All Things Are Possible*, translated by S. S. Koteliansky, 1920
Nachala i kontsii, 1908; as *Anton Tchekhov and Other Essays*, 1916, as *Penultimate Words and Other Essays*, 1916, and as *Chekhov and Other Essays*, 1966
Velikie kanunii, 1910
Vlast' kliuchei: Potestas clavium, 1923; as *Potestas Clavium*, translated by Bernard Martin, 1968
Na vesakh Iova, 1929; as *In Job's Balances: On the Sources of the Eternal Truths*, translated by Camilla Coventry and C. A. Macartney, 1932
Kierkegaard i eksistentsialnaia filosofiia, 1939; as *Kierkegaard and the Existential Philosophy*, translated by Elinor Hewitt, 1969
Afiny i Ierusalim, 1951; as *Athens and Jerusalem*, translated by Bernard Martin, 1966
Umozrenie i oktrovenie: Religioznaia filosofia Vladimira Solov'eva i drugie statii, 1964; as *Speculation and Revelation*, translated by Bernard Martin, 1982
Tolko veroi – Sola fide, 1966
Dostoevsky, Tolstoy and Nietzsche, translated by Bernard Martin, 1969
A Shestov Anthology, edited by Bernard Martin, 1970

Collected works edition: *Sochineniia*, edited by A. V. Akhutina, 2 vols., 1993.

Bibliographies

Baranoff, Nathalie, *Bibliographie des œuvres de Léon Chestov*, Paris: Institut d'Études Slaves, 1975
Baranoff, Nathalie, *Bibliographie des études sur Léon Chestov*, Paris: Institut d'Études Slaves, 1978

Further Reading

Baranoff, Nathalie, *Vie de Léon Chestov*, Paris: La Différence, 2 vols., 1991–93
Davison, R. M., "Lev Shestov: An Assessment," *Journal of European Studies* 11, no. 4 (December 1981): 279–94

Jones, Malcolm, "Shestov on Chekhov," in *Russian Writers on Russian Writers*, edited by Faith Wigzell and Robin Aizlewood, Oxford: Berg, 1994
Kline, George L., "Religious Existentialisms: Shestov and Berdyaev," in his *Religious and Antireligious Thought in Russia*, Chicago: University of Chicago Press, 1968
Patterson, David, "Shestov's Second Dimension," *Slavic and East European Journal* 22 (1978): 141–52
Shein, Louis J., *The Philosophy of Lev Shestov (1866–1938): A Russian Religious Existentialist*, Lampeter, Dyfed and Lewiston, New York: Edwin Mellen Press, 1991
Valevičius, Andrius, *Lev Shestov and His Times: Encounters with Brandes, Tolstoy, Dostoevsky, Chekhov, Ibsen, Nietzsche and Husserl*, New York: Lang, 1993
Wernham, James, *Two Russian Thinkers: An Essay in Berdyaev and Shestov*, Toronto: University of Toronto Press, 1968

Shklovskii, Viktor

Russian, 1893–1984

Viktor Shklovskii began his career as a futurist. Strongly attracted to the poetry of Vladimir Maiakovskii and Velimir Khlebnikov, he enthusiastically joined their crusade against the tenets of realism and symbolism. In his essay entitled *Voskreshenie slova* (1914; "Resurrection of the Word"), Shklovskii provided a theoretical basis for the work of the futurists, advancing the idea that futurist poetry emancipated words from their traditional significance and restored them to perceptibility by calling attention to their sounds. This essay is usually regarded as the cornerstone of the movement eventually known as Russian formalism.

Shklovskii showed the essay to the eminent scholar Baudouin de Courtenay, who introduced Shklovskii to his most brilliant linguistics students, Lev Iakubinskii and Evgenii Polivanov. Tired of analyzing ancient texts, they were intrigued by the possibility of applying their techniques to the language of futurist poetry. Together with Shklovskii they formed the nucleus of Opoiaz (Society for the study of poetic language), and were subsequently joined by Osip Brik, Boris Eikhenbaum, and Iurii Tynianov. Before long, the group's interest in futurist poetry broadened into an interest in the specific nature of verse language as a whole. Collections of their essays were published in 1916, 1917, and 1919. The 1919 collection contained Shklovskii's seminal articles "Iskusstvo kak priem" (Art as device) and "Sviaz' siuzhetnykh priemov s obshchimi priemami stilia" (The connection between plot devices and general stylistic devices), in which he enunciated the theoretical principles that laid the foundation for the formalist school of criticism.

Next Shklovskii set out to rescue literature from the critics who insisted on treating it as a mirror of society or the author's life. Discarding the conventional dichotomy of form and content, he substituted the dichotomy of form and material. He insisted that a work of literature, in all its component parts – hero, plot, motif – is form and only form. In one of the provocative formulations for which he was famous, he proclaimed, "A work of literature does not exceed the sum of its stylistic devices."

Literature restores outworn words, objects, and genres to perceptibility. To describe that process, Shklovskii coined two terms that subsequently gained wide currency: *ostranenie* (estrangement) and *zatrudnennoe postroenie* (obstructed form). Estrangement includes all the techniques by which a writer renders the material unfamiliar, such as the use of a peculiar narrative viewpoint (e.g. a child or a horse); obstructed form refers to the process by which a writer dismantles the material and arranges it into conspicuous verbal patterns.

In his essay on **Vasilii Rozanov** (1921), Shklovskii completed his theoretical edifice with a new hypothesis about the dynamics of literary history that drew upon his theory of perception. At any given time, literary forms exist in a complex hierarchy. As a dominant form ceases to elicit perception, it is replaced by one of the subordinate forms in the hierarchy. In other words, a major new writer originates not from the dominant predecessor, but from the minor genres and writers in the literary hierarchy of the time. As Shklovskii phrased it, "In the history of art, the legacy is transmitted not from father to son, but from uncle to nephew."

The seminal essays Shklovskii produced after the Revolution were collected in his landmark book, *O teorii prozy* (1925, 1929; *Theory of Prose*). He found in the work of Rozanov, Laurence Sterne, and **Andrei Belyi** not only ideal subjects for his theories, but models for his own prose. Influenced by Rozanov's rebellion against "tidy," cohesive literature, Shklovskii cultivated a deliberate stylistic and compositional nonchalance: a conversational tone, the use of ironic epigraphs, and a cavalier disregard of logical composition. Sterne taught him numerous methods for distorting the proportions of a work by using chronological shifts and digressions. From Belyi, Shklovskii learned how to lay bare the components of a work and to unify those components with a substratum of repeated images.

In his style Shklovskii obtained striking effects in a variety of ways. He interspersed literary language with slang and conversational idioms. He chose images that juxtaposed startlingly dissimilar items. He renounced the paragraph as a means of organizing a cluster of related material: instead, he either assembled incongruous ideas in the same paragraph or resorted to the one-sentence paragraph, which became his trademark.

After the Revolution, Shklovskii propagated the doctrines of formalism in countless essays and lectures, working with special intensity as mentor to a brilliant group of young writers who called themselves the Serapion Brothers. Threatened by arrest for his heretical views and activities, he fled to Berlin in Spring 1922. There he published an essay on Charlie Chaplin and a book called *Literatura i kinematograf* (1923; Literature and cinematography), in which he applied his theories about literature to the new medium. After his return to the Soviet Union in Fall 1923, he worked closely with the important film directors of the 1920s, especially Sergei Eisenstein, whose theories of montage owe something to Shklovskii's influence.

During the late 1920s, as the Communist Party imposed tight controls on art and literature, Shklovskii abandoned his early insistence on intricate forms and irony. Invoking his theory of perception, he asserted that the new Russian reader had ceased to respond to those forms and now preferred documentary literature. Accordingly, Shklovskii led the exploration and refinement of such genres as the newspaper article, the *feuilleton*, and the essay – forms that would dominate the Russian literary scene during the 1930s. He retained his much maligned dedication to formal analysis, but enlarged his scope to include the impact of society on the formation of literature.

In 1930 Shklovskii published his controversial essay "Pamiatnik nauchnoi oshibke" (A monument to scientific error), which has been widely misinterpreted as his unconditional surrender to the Party's demand for orthodoxy in art. In fact, this essay took the position that the charges against the formalists apply only to the initial stage of their movement. Shklovskii argued that after 1924, the formalists evolved a more sophisticated approach to literature that included recognition of social and economic factors. He concluded the essay by flatly refusing to declare himself a Marxist.

Throughout the 1930s, 1940s, and 1950s, Shklovskii was pilloried by Marxist critics for his alleged adherence to the heresies of formalism. Finally, however, he was able to publish his critical masterpiece, *Khudozhestvennaia proza: Razmyshleniia i razbory* (1959, 1961; Artistic prose: reflections and analyses), in which he re-established himself as a superb comparativist with a series of essays on his old favorites: Shakespeare, Boccaccio, Cervantes, **Fielding**, Sterne, and **Dickens**, along with the Russian writers **Tolstoi**, Chekhov, and Sholokhov. In 1966, Shklovskii expanded this book by adding essays on Gogol', **Pushkin**, and **Dostoevskii** and changing the title to *Povesti o proze: Razmyshleniia i razbory* (Tales about prose: reflections and analyses).

In 1970, at the age of 77, Shklovskii published *Tetiva: O neskhodstve skhodnogo* (Bowstring: on the dissimilarity of the similar), which one reviewer described as "the champagne of criticism" (*TLS*, 15 October 1971). In this book Shklovskii moved beyond the confines of the individual text into a sort of **meditation** on the essence of literature: the sources of unity, the shaping role of the author, the tension between component parts, and the deformation of fact by literary form.

The revolution Shklovskii led against hackneyed language, form, and thought in all the arts made a powerful contribution to the brilliant achievements of Russian art during the early part of the 20th century. He also left an indelible imprint on the schools of criticism that followed Russian formalism.

RICHARD SHELDON

Biography

Viktor Borisovich Shklovskii. Born in St. Petersburg, 6 February 1893. Studied philology at St. Petersburg University. Married Vasilisa Kordi, 1909 (later divorced): two children. Cofounding member, Opoiaz (Society for the study of poetic language), 1916. Joined the Social Revolutionaries and fought against both the White Guard and the Bolsheviks during the Civil War, 1917. Professor, Institute of Art History, St. Petersburg, 1920–21. Fled to Berlin to avoid arrest for anti-Bolshevik activities, Spring 1922; after receiving an amnesty, returned to Russia, Fall 1923, and settled in Moscow, where he spent the rest of his life. Never forgiven by the Communist Party for his activities, both literary and nonliterary, during the 1920s. Hounded by the Marxist critics virtually all his life. War correspondent during World War II; consultant to Sergei Eisenstein in the making of the film *Ivan the Terrible*, 1944. Married Serafima Narbut after World War II. Awards: State Prize, 1979. Died in Moscow, 5 December 1984.

Selected Writings

Essays and Related Prose

Voskreshenie slova, 1914; as "Resurrection of the Word," translated by Richard Sherwood, in *Russian Formalism*, edited by Stephen Bann and John E. Bowlt, 1973: 41–47

Rozanov, 1921; as "Plotless Prose: Vasilii Rozanov," translated by Richard Sheldon, *Poetics Journal* 1 (January 1982): 3–23
Razvertyvanie priema (The elaboration of the device), 1921
Tristram Shendi Sterna i teoriia romana, 1921; as "Sterne's Tristram Shandy and the Theory of the Novel," translated by Richard Sheldon, *Review of Contemporary Fiction* (Spring 1981): 190–211
Khod konia, 1923
Literatura i kinematograf, 1923
O teorii prozy, 1925; revised, enlarged edition, 1929; as *Theory of Prose*, translated by Benjamin Sher, 1990
Udachi i porazheniia Maksima Gor'kogo (Successes and failures of Maksim Gor'kii), 1926
Piat' chelovek znakomykh (Five acquaintances), 1927
Tekhnika pisatel'skogo remesla (The technical devices of the writer's craft), 1927
Gamburgskii schet (Hamburg account), 1928
Mater'ial i stil' v romane L'va Tolstogo Voina i mir (Material and style in Lev Tolstoi's novel "War and Peace"), 1928
Matvei Komarov: Zhitel' goroda Moskvy (Matvei Komarov: inhabitant of the city of Moscow), 1929
Kratkaia no dostovernaia povest' o dvorianine Bolotove (A short but reliable tale about the nobleman Bolotov), 1930
Podenshchina (Day labor), 1930
Poiski optimizma (In search of optimism), 1931
Chulkov i Levshin (Chulkov and Levshin), 1933
Zhizn' khudozhnika Fedotova (The life of the artist Fedotov), 1936
Kapitan Fedotov (Captain Fedotov), 1936
Marko Polo, 1936; revised edition, in *Istoricheskie povesti i rasskazy*, 1958; revised edition, as *Zemli razvedchik (Marko Polo)*, 1969; revised edition, in *Sobranie sochinenii*, vol. 2, 1974
Zametki o proze Pushkina (Remarks on Pushkin's prose), 1937
Dnevnik (Diary), 1939
O Maiakovskom (About Maiakovskii), 1940; revised edition, in *Sobranie sochinenii*, vol. 3, 1974; as *Maiakovskii and His Circle*, translated by Lily Feiler, 1972
Minin i Pozharskii (Minin and Pozharskii), 1940
Vstrechi (Encounters), 1944
O masterakh starinnykh (About the masters of old), 1951; revised, enlarged edition, 1953
Zametki o proze russkikh klassikov: O proizvedeniiakh Pushkina, Gogolia, Lermontova, Turgeneva, Tolstogo, Chekhova (Remarks on the prose of the Russian classics), 1953; revised, enlarged edition, 1955
Povest' o khudozhnike Fedotove (A tale about the artist Fedotov), 1955; revised edition, in *Istoricheskie povesti i rasskazy*, 1958; revised, enlarged edition, 1965
Za i protiv: Zametki o Dostoevskom (Pro and con: remarks on Dostoevskii), 1957; revised edition, in *Sobranie sochinenii*, vol. 3, 1974
Istoricheskie povesti i rasskazy (Historical tales and sketches), 1958
Khudozhestvennaia proza: Razmyshleniia i razbory, 1959; revised, enlarged edition, 1961; enlarged edition, as *Povesti o proze: Razmyshleniia i razbory*, 2 vols., 1966
Zhili-byli: Vospominaniia, memuarnye zapisi, povesti o vremeni: S kontsa XIX veka po 1962 (Once upon a time: reminiscences, memorial notes, tales about the era), 1964; revised, enlarged edition, 1966
Za sorok let: Stat'i o kino (In the course of 40 years: articles about film), 1965
Staroe i novoe: Kniga stat'ei o detskoi literature (The old and the new: a book of articles about children's literature), 1966
Tetiva: O neskhodstve skhodnogo, 1970
Eisenshtein, 1973
Energiia zabluzhdeniia: Kniga o siuzhete (The energy of delusion: a book about plot), 1981
Za shest'desiat let: Raboty o kino (In the course of 60 years: pieces on film), 1985
Gamburgskii schet: Stat'i, vospominaniia, esse (1914–1933) (Hamburg account: articles, reminiscences, essays), 1990

Other writings: experimental memoirs (including *Zoo: Pis'ma ne o lyubvi, ili Tret'ya Eloiza* [*Zoo, or Letters Not About Love*], 1923; *Sentimental'noe puteshestvie: vospominaniia 1917–1922* [*A Sentimental Journey*], 1923), over two dozen screenplays, and a biography of Lev Tolstoi (1963–67).

Collected works edition: *Sobranie sochinenii*, 3 vols., 1973–74.

Bibliographies

Berman, D. A., and L. A. Verolainen, "Viktor Borisovich Shklovskii," in *Russkie sovetskie prozaiki*, vol. 6, pt. 1, Moscow: Kniga, 1969: 229–89
Galushkin, A. Yu., "Novye materialy k bibliografii V. B. Shklovskogo," *De Visu* 1 (January 1993): 64–77
Sheldon, Richard, *Viktor Shklovskii: An International Bibliography of Works by and About Him*, Ann Arbor, Michigan: Ardis, 1977

Further Reading

Galan, F. M., "Film as Poetry and Prose: Viktor Shklovskii's Contribution to the Poetics of Cinema," *Essays in Poetics* 9 (1984): 95–104
Gifford, Henry, "Viktor Shklovskii," *Grand Street* (Autumn 1988): 94–110
Grits, Teodor, "The Work of Viktor Shklovskii," in *Third Factory* by Shklovskii, Ann Arbor, Michigan: Ardis, 1977: 91–121 (original edition, 1927)
Haber, Edythe C., "Bulgakov and Shklovskii: Notes on a Literary Antagonism," in *New Studies in Russian Language and Literature*, edited by Anna Lisa Crone and Catherine V. Chvany, Columbus, Ohio: Slavica, 1987: 151–58
Mitchell, Stanley, "From Shklovskii to Brecht: Some Preliminary Remarks Toward a History of the Politicization of Russian Formalism," *Screen* 15 (Summer 1974): 74–80; see also Ben Brewster's article, "From Shklovskii to Brecht: A Reply": 81–102
Nicholas, Mary A., "Formalist Theory Revisited: On Shklovskii's 'On Pil'nyak'," *Slavic and East European Journal* 36, no. 1 (Spring 1992): 68–83
Segre, Cesare, "Viktor Shklovskii, or the Structures of Pity," in *Semiotics and Literary Criticism*, The Hague: Mouton, 1973: 133–44
Sheldon, Richard, "Shklovskii, Gor'kii and the Serapion Brothers," *Slavic and East European Journal* 12, no. 1 (Spring 1968): 1–13
Sheldon, Richard, "Making Armored Cars and Novels: A Literary Introduction," in *A Sentimental Journey* by Shklovskii, Ithaca, New York: Cornell University Press, 1984: ix–xxv (original edition, 1970)
Sheldon, Richard, Introduction to *Zoo, or Letters Not About Love* by Shklovskii, Ithaca, New York: Cornell University Press, 1971: xiii–xxxiii
Sheldon, Richard, "The Formalist Poetics of Viktor Shkovskii," *Russian Literature Tri-Quarterly* 2 (Winter 1972): 351–71
Sheldon, Richard, "Viktor Shklovskii and the Device of Ostensible Surrender," *Slavic Review* 34, no. 1 (March 1975): 86–108
Sheldon, Richard, "Shklovskii and Mandelshtam," in *Russian and Slavic Literature*, edited by Richard Freeborn, R. R. Milner-Gulland, and Charles A. Ward, Columbus, Ohio: Slavica, 1976: 396–406
Sheldon, Richard, "The Itinerary of Viktor Shklovskii's *A Sentimental Journey*," in *Norwich Symposia on Russian Literature and Culture*, vol. 3, Northfield, Vermont: The Russian School, forthcoming
Sherwood, Richard, "Viktor Shklovskii and the Development of Early Formalist Theory on Prose Literature," in *Russian Formalism*, edited by Stephen Bann and John E. Bowlt, Edinburgh: Scottish Academic Press, and New York: Barnes and Noble, 1973: 26–40

Steiner, Peter, "The Praxis of Irony: Viktor Shklovskii's *Zoo*," in *Russian Formalism, a Retrospective Glance: A Festschrift in Honor of Victor Erlich*, edited by Robert Louis Jackson and Stephen Rudy, New Haven, Connecticut: Yale University Center for International and Area Studies, 1985

Thompson, Ewa M., "V. Shklovskii and the Russian Intellectual Tradition," in *Aspects of Modern Russian and Czech Culture*, edited by Arnold McMillin, Columbus, Ohio: Slavica, 1989

Simmel, Georg

German, 1858–1918

Georg Simmel belongs, together with Emile Durkheim and **Max Weber**, to the founding fathers of modern sociology. From the 1890s onward, the essay plays a prominent role in his work. In addition to a rich production of essays published in newspapers, magazines, and journals, Simmel's academic writings illustrate the central role the essay assumes in his new method of sociology. Suspicious of system-building tendencies, Simmel fashions the essay into the suitable genre for his thought. Combining a Nietzschean critique of culture with a *fin-de-siècle* sensibility for symbolism and the wary post-Kantian soberness that outlines the aesthetics of *Neue Sachlichkeit* (new objectivism), he engages in a search for the typical forms of social interaction.

Given the fragmentary, fluid, and dynamic nature of the social sphere, Simmel argues that sociology can gain a firm hold of its subject only if its aesthetic qualities receive due attention. Sociology as a discipline must, therefore, methodologically reflect the aesthetic moment in the production of knowledge. Sociology, then, is not so much a science that depends on new facts; rather, in reconstructing the rules of their social relevance, it reinterprets facts critically. Less interested in society (*Gesellschaft*) per se, sociological reflection attends to the laws of association that form social relations (*Vergesellschaftung*). "Drawing a new line through the facts which are otherwise well known" creates perspectives which lead to new interpretations of the laws that govern social relations.

Looking at the dynamic, ever-differentiating process of social associations, Simmel distinguishes the content from the form of social interactions. While recognition of social forms reveals the laws of interhuman action, the distinction between content and form operates in areas where there are no fixed rules. Instead, aesthetic intuition leads the way to discovery. Any attempt at laying bare "pure forms of human behavior" hinges, therefore, on an "intuitive procedure," i.e. "a special focus of the gaze." Consequently, even Simmel's textbook study *Soziologie* (1908; *Sociology*) is replete with fragments woven into a text that combines precise observations of the trivial with high-powered theorizing. Instead of a system, this approach offers vistas and highlights where the forms of associations that inform social experience appear in sharp profile: ". . . human association is continuously constituted, dissolved and constituted anew, a perpetual flowing and pulsating that concatenates the individuals." Because instances of individual behavior represent crystallized forms of social interdependences, the method of knowledge production itself must reflect this. In describing the dynamics of human relations in their diverse, expanding, and often conflicting paths, Simmel reflects at the same time on the method with which to tackle the restless fluidity of the social sphere: "At every moment such threads are spun, dropped, resumed, replaced, and interwoven with others." This is exactly how Simmel's essays themselves proceed.

The specificity of the individual event, sign, interaction, or exchange is, as a part, always connected to the whole, which it represents in its own manner. This unity of the social sphere, tentative and precarious as it may be, provides in all its fragility a common denominator for interpreting social laws. The essay takes advantage of this epistemological given as it launches an analysis that feeds off the unified but open-ended nature of human experience. It knows itself to be carried by the recognition that "from each point on the surface of existence – however closely attached to the surface it might seem – one may drop a sounding into the depths of the psyche so that almost all the most banal externalities of life finally are connected with the ultimate decisions concerning the meaning and style of life."

This new approach redefines the scope of the essay. A whole new range of phenomena now comes into focus. Fashion, coquetry, conversation, communication, secrecy, discretion, competition, subordination, thankfulness, loyalty, jewelry, poverty, gender, acting, and landscapes and cityscapes now all become objects of the sociologist's concern. In his essays on the handle, the bridge and the door, the rose, money, clothing and jewelry, Simmel turns to cultural artifacts which, at the intersection of interhuman relations, highlight the functioning of the social weave. Exposing the purely functional aspects of these social constructions, these essays bring out the formal codes of what constitutes society as a whole. With the bridge that connects the two sides of a river, humans fashion nature in their own minds' image, inscribing social forms onto the landscape. Likewise, the door connects to what it separates; clothing and jewelry expose what they obscure. As a result, social functions rather than the nature and materiality of the world determine human behavior, which thus assimilates everything to its own needs as it casts the categorical net of forms of social associations over the world. Probing the conditions of the possibility of such social associations, Simmel's essays abound with intellectual playfulness. Their self-referential turn relies on the literary nature of the essay.

Simmel's observations on the adventurer, the artist, the stranger, the traveler who enjoys ruins and the Alps, make manifest the essayist as theorist of margins and marginal existence. Like them, he travels the overwhelming realm of experience. His insights are only as good as the categories he brings into play. Like the adventure, the essay enacts the accidental coincidence which – marginal to existence as it may present itself – connects directly to the heart of life. As the continuum of the social sphere expands in all directions, sociology's procedure is the lucky gaze that, directed at infinitely reflecting mirrors, guides an enriched understanding.

Wherever the essay picks up a single thread in the fabric of appearances, it is sure to interconnect with the whole, a kind of "aesthetic pantheism," as Simmel calls it: "Every point contains within itself the potential of being redeemed to absolute aesthetic importance. To the adequately trained eye, the totality of beauty, the complete meaning of the world as a whole, radiates from every single point." With Simmel, the essay thus becomes the genre in which the intellectual and the existential conflict of modernity – the loss of mediation between individual and universal – finds its critical form.

WILLI GOETSCHEL

Biography
Born 1 March 1858 in Berlin. Studied history and psychology at the University of Berlin, Ph.D., 1881. Outside lecturer in philosophy, 1885–1900, and professor extraordinarius, 1900–14, University of Berlin; professor of philosophy, University of Strasbourg, 1914–18. Married Gertrud Kinel, 1890. Died in Strasbourg, 26 September 1918.

Selected Writings
Essays and Related Prose
Kant: Sechzehn Vorlesungen, 1904
Die Probleme der Geschichtsphilosophie, 1905; as *The Problems of the Philosophy of History: An Epistemological Essay*, edited and translated by Guy Oakes, 1977
Soziologie, 1908; as *The Sociology of Georg Simmel*, edited and translated by Kurt H. Wolff, 1950; part as *Conflict*, translated by Wolff, and *The Web of Group Affiliations*, translated by Reinhard Bendix, 1955
Philosophische Kultur: Gesammelte Essays, 1911; revised edition, 1919
Der Krieg und die geistigen Entscheidungen: Reden und Aufsätze, 1917
Lebensanschauung: Vier metaphysische Kapitel, 1918
Schulpädagogik: Vorlesungen, edited by Karl Hauter, 1922
Zur Philosophie der Kunst: Philosophische und kunstphilosophische Aufsätze, 1922
Fragmente und Aufsätze, aus dem Nachlass und Veröffentlichungen der letzten Jahre, edited by Gertrud Kantorowicz, 1923
Brücke und Tür: Essays des Philosophen zur Geschichte, Religion, Kunst, und Gesellschaft, edited by Michael Landmann, 1957; as *Das Individuum und die Freiheit*, 1984
The Conflict in Modern Culture, and Other Essays, translated by K. Peter Etzkorn, 1968
Das individuelle Gesetz: Philosophische Exkurse, edited by Michael Landmann, 1968
On Individuality and Social Forms: Selected Writings, edited by Donald N. Levine, 1971
Georg Simmel: Sociologist and European (selections), edited by P. A. Lawrence, translated by D. E. Jenkinson, 1976
Essays on Interpretation in Social Science, edited and translated by Guy Oakes, 1980
Vom Wesen der Moderne: Essays zur Philosophie und Ästhetik, edited by Werner Jung, 1990

Other writings: works on sociology and philosophy (including *Philosophie des Geldes* [*The Philosophy of Money*], 1900), coquetry, and German writers.

Collected works editions: *Gesammelte Werke*, 1958– (in progress); *Gesamtaugabe*, edited by Otthein Rammstedt, 9 vols., 1988–95 (in progress).

Bibliography
Gassen, Kurt, *Georg Simmel 1858–1918: A Collection of Essays*, edited by Kurt H. Wolff, Columbus: Ohio State University Press, 1959: 357–75

Further Reading
Adorno, Theodor W., *Noten zur Literatur*, edited by Rolf Tiedemann, Frankfurt-on-Main: Suhrkamp, 1981 (original edition, 1958–65)
Axelrod, Charles D., "Toward an Appreciation of Simmel's Fragmentary Style," *Sociological Quarterly* 18 (1977): 185–96
Böhringer, Hannes, and Karlfried Gründer, editors, *Ästhetik und Soziologie um die Jahrhundertwende: Georg Simmel*, Frankfurt-on-Main: Klostermann, 1976
Christen, Matthias, "Essayistik und Modernität: Literarische Theoriebildung in Georg Simmels Philosopher Kultur," *Deutsche Vierteljahrsschrift* 66 (1992): 129–59
Coser, Lewis A., "Georg Simmel's Style of Work: A Contribution to the Sociology of the Sociologist," *American Journal of Sociology* 63 (1958): 635–40
Dahme, Heinz-Jürgen, and Otthein Rammstedt, editors, *Georg Simmel und die Moderne: Neue Interpretationen und Materialien*, Frankfurt-on-Main: Suhrkamp, 1984
Davis, Murray S., "Georg Simmel and the Aesthetics of Social Reality," *Social Forces* 51 (1973): 320–29
Frisby, David, *Sociological Impressionism: A Reassessment of Georg Simmel's Social Theory*, London: Heinemann, 1981
Frisby, David, *Fragments of Modernity: Theories of Modernity in the Work of Simmel, Kracauer and Benjamin*, Cambridge: Polity Press, 1985
Gassen, Kurt, and Michael Landmann, editors, *Buch des Dankes an Georg Simmel: Briefe, Erinnerungen, Bibliographie*, Berlin: Duncker & Humblot, 1993 (original edition, 1958)
Kracauer, Siegfried, *Georg Simmel, Das Ornament der Masse*, Frankfurt-on-Main: Suhrkamp, 1977
Liebeschütz, Hans, *Von Georg Simmel zu Franz Rosenzweig: Studien zum Jüdischen Denken im deutschen Kulturbereich*, Tübingen: Mohr, 1970
Susman, Margarete, *Die geistige Gestalt Georg Simmels*, Tübingen: Mohr, 1959
Weinstein, Deena, and Michael A. Weinstein, *Postmodern(ized) Simmel*, London and New York: Routledge, 1993

Siniavskii, Andrei
Russian, 1925–1997

The essay played a vital role in the career of Andrei Siniavskii in each of his identities – that of a scholar, writing academic pieces under his own name, and as a belletrist, employing the pseudonym Abram Tertz. The latter pieces, in particular, are intimately connected with his fiction, providing insights about both the technique and the thematic concerns that predominate in his prose.

The critical pieces Siniavskii produced under his own name prior to his 1965 arrest lack the stylistic inventiveness of his stories, but they already reveal him as a probing and sensitive critic, most notably in the long introduction he wrote for a major 1965 collection of Boris Pasternak's poetry. Siniavskii's sensitivity to Pasternak's use of language, as evidenced by his incisive comments on the stylistic and tonal aspects of the poetry, as well as his emphasis on Pasternak's imagery and philosophical concerns, can, in retrospect, be seen as signaling his own interests as a writer. Perhaps surprisingly, much of his early writing was on a stalwart of socialist realism, **Maksim Gor'kii**, whose final, unfinished novel was the subject of his dissertation, part of which appeared as "O khudozhestvennoi strukture romana *Zhizn' Klima Samgina*" (1958; On the artistic structure of *The Life of Klim Samgin*).

Siniavskii's political sympathies during the early 1960s show up more clearly in the attitude he displays to the then current literature. Thus, besides his enthusiastic piece on Pasternak, he offers a warm appreciation of Anna Akhmatova's more recent poetry on the occasion of her 75th birthday ("Raskovannyi golos" [1964; "The Unfettered Voice"]). Conversely, when writing on those who strongly supported the repressive aspects of Soviet literary life, he could be merciless. "O novom sbornike Anatoliia Sofronova" (1959; "On a Collection of Verses by Anatoly Sofronov") concludes with an excerpt from Vladimir Maiakovskii's original and powerful poetry of the 1920s to highlight the imitative and pallid nature of Sofronov's verse.

One of the earliest works to be signed Abram Tertz is the programmatic essay "Chto takoe sotsialisticheskii realizm" (1959; *On Socialist Realism*). Here his lively and witty manner partly masks a very serious purpose: to undermine the dogma that had by then ruled Soviet literature for a quarter of a century. In part he objects to the deadening effect of the realistic manner that was imposed on Soviet writers so that their works would be accessible to the masses, but more broadly he points to logical inconsistencies in the very terminology: why should "realism" necessarily be "socialist"? In fact, he goes on to point out that Marxism (and, by extension, communism) is not unlike a religious movement in its efforts to direct belief, and that by trying to make writing portray a future ideal society its advocates are calling for something that is closer to Romanticism than realism. Further, by forcing writers into a mode that is not of their own making, socialist realism results in simplistic, static, and ultimately uninteresting literature.

Mysli vrasplokh (1965; *Unguarded Thoughts*), also by "Abram Tertz" in the pre-arrest period, at first resembles a seemingly random collection of ideas and **aphorism**s, but upon closer inspection turns out to focus on a handful of themes – most notably, the nature of sexuality, which is not treated positively, and belief in God, which is. The work is thus important for treating two topics of concern to Siniavskii/Tertz elsewhere as well, while in both form and content it also signals his interest in the turn-of-the-century philosopher **Vasilii Rozanov**, later the subject of Siniavskii's study, *"Opavshie list'ia" V. V. Rozanova* (1982; Rozanov's "Fallen Leaves"). Furthermore, the fragmentary structure serves as a precursor of *Golos iz khora* (1973; *A Voice from the Chorus*), a much longer work constructed from the material in **letter**s that Siniavskii sent to his wife while in prison. *Voice*, seen by some critics as a kind of autobiography, contains material based on his prison experience along with his views on literature, the nature of art, and a host of other themes. Siniavskii thus develops what might be termed an "anti-narrative" essay, which freely mingles a variety of forms and jumps seemingly arbitrarily from topic to topic; it requires the reader's active participation to derive the broader themes and a sense of coherence.

Two other essays published after his emigration to France in 1973, and under the name Abram Tertz, have proved to be Siniavskii's most controversial: *Progulki s Pushkinym* (1975; *Strolls with Pushkin*) and *V teni Gogolia* (1975; *In Gogol's shadow*). The former in particular led to sharp protests by émigré figures in the West when it was first published, and then by Soviet critics when it finally appeared in the Soviet Union during the period of *glasnost*. Siniavskii's detractors were disturbed by his iconoclastic treatment of Russia's greatest writer; what they seemed to miss, or refused to accept, is that a "demythologizing" of **Pushkin** was precisely the point of the essay: only in this way could Siniavskii discover the essence of Pushkin's true significance for subsequent literature (and for himself).

The remainder of Siniavskii's work from his period abroad can be roughly divided into two categories: 1) sociopolitical commentary on the Soviet Union and on current developments in Russian political and intellectual life, and 2) a renewal of his earlier career as literary critic. The latter includes, besides his essay on Rozanov, articles on a wide range of figures in 20th-century Russian literature: Zoshchenko, Remizov, and, once again, Gor'kii, who is now, understandably, treated less reverently than before (cf. "Roman M. Gor'kogo *Mat'* kak rannii obrazets sotsialisticheskogo realizma" [1988; Gor'kii's novel *Mother* as an early model of socialist realism]). The first group opens with his "Literaturnyi protsess v Rossii" (1974; "The Literary Process in Russia"), in which he notes that the Soviet state's very efforts to control writers had the perverse effect of heightening their influence, often against the state's interests. He has also written about his own experiences as a dissident and about the resurgence of Russian nationalism; several essays in which he attempts to define the essential features of Bolshevism form the basis of his book *Soviet Civilization* (1990), to date published only in translation.

While on the surface Siniavskii had two identities as an essayist – the relatively straightforward commentary that he signed under his own name and the more literary type of essay that appeared under the pseudonym Abram Tertz – his concerns were similar in both guises: to examine the ideals and strivings of the artist, to explore issues of freedom and oppression, and to understand the nature of the creative urge.

BARRY P. SCHERR

Biography

Andrei Donatovich Siniavskii. Born 8 October 1925 in Moscow. Studied at Moscow University, literature degree, 1949, doctorate, 1952. Married Maria Rozanova-Kruglikova: one son. Senior research follow, Gor'kii Literary Institute, Moscow, until 1965; lecturer in Russian literature, Moscow University, until 1960, and at the Theater Studio, Moscow Art Theater, until 1965. Reviewer for *Novyi Mir*, early 1960s. Arrested for supposed anti-Soviet writings published abroad, 1965: sentenced to seven years' hard labor, 1966; released, 1971, and allowed to emigrate to France, 1973. Professor of Russian, the Sorbonne, Paris, 1973–94. Cofounder and coeditor, *Sintakis* (Syntax) literary journal and publishing house. Russian citizenship restored, 1990. Died in Paris, 25 February 1997.

Selected Writings

Essays and Related Prose

"Chto takoe sotsialisticheski realizm," 1959; as *On Socialist Realism*, translated by George Dennis, 1961

"Thought Unaware," 1965; as *Mysli vrasplokh*, 1966; as *Unguarded Thoughts*, translated by Manya Harari, 1972

For Freedom of Imagination, translated by Laszlo Tikos and Murray Peppard, 1971

Golos iz khora, 1973; as *A Voice from the Chorus*, translated by Kyril FitzLyon and Max Hayward, 1976

Progulki s Pushkinym, 1975; as *Strolls with Pushkin*, translated by Catharine Theimer Nepomnyashchy and Slava I. Yastremski, 1993

V teni Gogolia, 1975
Soviet Civilization: A Cultural History, translated by Joanne
   Turnbull, 1990

Other writings: three novels (*Sud idet* [*The Trial Begins*], 1960;
Liubimov [*The Makepeace Experiment*], 1963; *Spokoinoi nochi*
[*Goodnight!*], 1984), a collection of short stories, and a study of
Vasilii Rozanov (1982).

Collected works edition: *Sobranie sochinenii*, 2 vols., 1992.

Further Reading

Aucoutourier, Michel, "Writer and Text in the Works of Abram
   Terc (An Ontology of Writing and a Poetics of Prose)," in
   *Fiction and Drama in Eastern and Southeastern Europe:
   Evolution and Experiment in the Postwar Period*, edited by
   Henrik Birnbaum and Thomas Eekman, Columbus, Ohio: Slavica,
   1980
Dalton, Margaret, *Andrei Siniavskii and Julii Daniel': Two Soviet
   "Heretical" Writers*, Würzburg: Jal, 1973
"A Discussion of Abram Tertz's Book *Strolls with Pushkin*,"
   Russian Studies in Literature 28, no. 1 (1991–92): 63–88
Fanger, Donald, "Conflicting Imperatives in the Model of the
   Russian Writer: The Case of Tertz/Sinyavsky," in *Literature and
   History: Theoretical Problems and Russian Case Studies*, edited
   by Gary Saul Morson, Stanford, California: Stanford University
   Press, 1986: 111–24
Hayward, Max, Introduction to *A Voice from the Chorus* by Tertz,
   New Haven, Connecticut and London: Yale University Press,
   1995 (original edition, 1976)
Holmgren, Beth, "The Transfiguring of Context in the Work of
   Abram Terts," *Slavic Review* 50 (1991): 965–77
Kolonosky, Walter F., "Andrei Siniavskii: The Chorus and the
   Critic," *Canadian-American Slavic Studies* 9 (1975): 352–60
Levitt, Marcus C., "Siniavskii's Alternative Autobiography: *A Voice
   from the Chorus*," *Canadian Slavonic Papers* 33, no. 1 (1991):
   46–61
Lourie, Richard, *Letters to the Future: An Approach to Sinyavsky-
   Tertz*, Ithaca, New York: Cornell University Press, 1975
Murav, Harriet, "The Case Against Andrei Siniavskii: The Letter
   and the Law," *Russian Review* 53 (1994): 549–60
Nepomnyashchy, Catharine Theimer, Introduction to *Strolls with
   Pushkin* by Siniavskii (Abram Tertz), New Haven, Connecticut:
   Yale University Press, 1993
Nepomnyashchy, Catharine Theimer, *Abram Tertz and the Poetics
   of Crime*, New Haven, Connecticut and London: Yale University
   Press, 1995
Nussbaum, Andrew J., "Literary Selves: The Tertz-Sinyavsky
   Dialogue," in *Autobiographical Statements in Twentieth-Century
   Russian Literature*, edited by Jane Gary Harris, Princeton, New
   Jersey: Princeton University Press, 1990: 238–59
Pomerants, G., "Urok medlennogo chteniia," *Oktiabr'* 6 (1993):
   178–83
Rozanova, Mariia, "On the History and Geography of This Book
   [*Strolls with Pushkin*]," *Russian Studies in Literature* 28, no. 1
   (1991–92): 89–98
Rubinshtein, Natalia, "Abram Terts i Aleksandr Pushkin," *Vremia i
   My* 9 (1976): 118–33
Sandler, Stephanie, "Sex, Death and Nation in the *Strolls with
   Pushkin* Controversy," *Slavic Review* 51 (1992): 294–308
Shafarevich, Igor', "The Emigration Phenomenon," *Russian Studies
   in Literature* 28, no. 1 (1991–92): 45–55
Solzhenitsyn, Aleksandr, ". . . Koleblet tvoi trenozhnik," *Vestnik
   Russkogo Khristianskogo Dvizheniia* 142 (1984): 133–52
Tikos, Laszlo, and Murray Peppard, Introduction to *For Freedom of
   Imagination* by Siniavskii, New York: Holt Rinehart and
   Winston, 1971

Slaveikov, Pencho

Bulgarian, 1866–1912

Pencho Slaveikov can be considered the father of the Bulgarian
essay. Not only did he institute the genre of the essay in
Bulgarian literature, but he also outlined the essential features
of its future physiognomy: a highly critical approach to the
phenomena of national cultural life, an ambition to mediate
in the process of the Bulgarian appropriation of Western
European spiritual values, and a twofold mission – to inform,
and to influence public opinion on all momentous subjects.
The tradition of essay writing that Slaveikov initiated during
the first decade of the 20th century was fully internalized
by the interwar readership through the publication, in the
1920s, of seven volumes of his works (edited by the literary
historian and essayist Boian Penev), three of which contain his
most representative essays. Slaveikov's essays are also considered by critics to be an insightful guide to his own poems,
which occupy an eminent position as part of the intellectual
trend in Bulgarian poetry.

Born into the family of Petko R. Slaveikov (a poet, publicist, and explorer of Bulgarian folklore heritage), Pencho
Slaveikov extracted as good an education as he could in his
native country (which in 1878 had just been liberated, after
almost five centuries, from the Ottoman yoke) and supplemented it in Leipzig, where he studied philosophy, aesthetics,
and literature (1892–98). German philosophy – mainly
Nietzsche, Schopenhauer, and his professors J. Folkelt and W.
Wundt – deeply influenced his views. Slaveikov's aesthetic
taste bears the marks of his thorough acquaintance with the
works of **Goethe,** Heine, Kierkegaard, and Ibsen. This general
perspective allowed him to look at the cultural and political
life of his native Bulgaria with the eye of an outsider.

The target of Slaveikov's harsh criticism included both works
of contemporary authors and the activity of popular cultural
and political figures of the time (such as Ivan Vazov, who is
commonly recognized as "the patriarch of Bulgarian literature") as well as the freshly created mythology of the heroic
period of the fight for national independence (e.g. Khristo
Botev, the national symbol of a poet-revolutionary). The
driving force behind Slaveikov's criticism was his conviction
that an artist's good intentions and sincerity would not
compensate for a lack of artistic merit and that the application of provincial criteria to the emerging modern literature in
Bulgaria could only harm its development and kill whatever
of value had been born within it ("Bulgarskata poeziia: Predi,
sega" [1906; Bulgarian poetry: before, and now]). According
to Slaveikov, there were three main sources from which
Bulgarian artists should seek models and criteria: Bulgarian
oral poetry, as preserved in the folklore; the great achievements of other Slavic literatures (e.g. **Pushkin, Tolstoi,** and
Mickiewicz); and German literature, especially its spiritual
loftiness and refinement.

Slaveikov believed that it was not the written religious
texts (which reveal Byzantine provenance), but the Bulgarian
oral tradition that best mirrored the national character and
creativity and could serve as fertile ground for literature in
independent Bulgaria ("Bulgarskata narodna pesen" [1904;
Bulgarian folksong]; "Narodnite liubovni pesni" [1902; Love

folksongs]). An important part of Slaveikov's own poetry as well as his highly appreciative essays on the works of two Bulgarian symbolist writers – Peio Iavorov and Petko Todorov, both greatly influenced by folklore – is a practical confirmation of his vision of the unity between the centuries-old oral tradition and the beginnings of written literature in the 19th century.

While looking at the foreign literary examples as models for Bulgarian literature, Slaveikov was fully aware of the impossibility of directly transplanting them into the Bulgarian context. Bulgarian writers and readers should, Slaveikov believed, form their taste on the greatest achievements of European literature; imitations of German and Russian poets, however, received nothing but Slaveikov's scornful rejection. To Slaveikov, translation was the most beneficial way of overcoming the distance between the young Bulgarian literature and the European literary models. His essays on the reception of Heine's and Pushkin's poetry in Bulgaria (he also planned to write his doctoral thesis on Heine in Russia) disclose a mature conception of translation as a natural way of adopting alien ideas and literary forms.

As an enthusiastic reader of Nietzsche's *Also sprach Zarathustra* (1883–85; *Thus Spoke Zarathustra*), Slaveikov often takes as a point of departure the charisma of the writer (as in his essays on Nietzsche, Goethe, Pushkin, and Tolstoi). The originality of a work of art, Slaveikov maintains, comes from the greatness of the writer's personality: "One cannot question a personality, one only needs to understand it" ("Zaratustra," 1920). Nevertheless, the lack of great personalities did not prevent Slaveikov from outlining a vivid picture of Bulgarian cultural life with its weaknesses and its promise ("Natsionalen teatur" [1910; National theater]; also his **reviews** of the Bulgarian literary and cultural journals). Slaveikov promotes the idea of the enlightened and creative leading figure (be it the editor of a journal or the director of a theater) with the highest aesthetic standards and the civic courage to pursue them. As a director of the National Theater (1908–09) and the National Library (1909–11), and as an editor at large of the literary journal *Misul* (Thought) (1892–1907), Slaveikov embodied this ideal and was loved by the talented and the inspired, but also hated by the mediocre.

Slaveikov's conviction that literature and art should stay as far as possible from political struggles ran counter to the 19th-century Bulgarian understanding of the "utilitarian" role of literature and, in particular, of poetry which was supposed to serve as an instrument in politics. Slaveikov consistently followed this view in all his activities; along with his austerity as a critic, this contributed to his lonely position in Bulgarian culture during his life. Communist scholars, applying the Marxist methodology to his output, felt obliged to emphasize the "contradictions" in his aesthetic views and the "negative impact of idealistic philosophy" on his thought. Nevertheless, traces of Slaveikov's refining influence can be detected in the whole subsequent development of the essay in Bulgaria.

KATIA MITOVA-JANOWSKI

Biography

Born 27 April 1866 in Triavna. Studied philosophy, aesthetics, and literature at the University of Leipzig, 1892–98. In poor health for most of his life, from 1884. Member of the literary group Misul,

which emerged around the literary-cultural journal *Misul* (1892–1907) and included Peio Iavorov and Petko Todorov. Worked as a teacher; deputy director, 1901–09, and director, 1909–11, National Library, Sofia; director, National Theater, 1908–09: dismissed because of his attacks on the government. Companion of Mara Belcheva, from 1903. Died (as the result of a long-term chronic disease) at Lake Como, Italy, 28 May 1912.

Selected Writings

Essays and Related Prose
Izbrani proizvedeniia, vol. 2, 1955
Suchineniia, vol. 2, edited by Angel Todorov and Boris Delchev, 1966

Other writings: poetry (including the unfinished *Kurvava pesen* [wr. 1911–13, pub. 1919–20]).

Collected works editions: *Subrani suchineniia*, edited by Boian Penev, 7 vols., 1928; *Subrani suchineniia*, edited by Boris Delchev, 8 vols., 1958–59.

Bibliography
Furnadzhieva, Elena Georgieva, *Pencho Slaveikov: Bibliografiia*, Sofia, 1966

Further Reading
Hinrichs, Jan Paul, "On the Language of Penčo Slavejkov," in *Dutch Studies in South Slavic and Balkan Linguistics*, edited by A. A. Barentsen, B. M. Groen, and R. Sprenger, Amsterdam: Rodopi, 1987
Sarandev, Ivan, *Pencho Slaveikov: Esteticheski i literaturno-kriticheski vuzgledi*, Sofia: Bulgarski Pisatel, 1977

Sociological Essay

Although sociology narrowly defined as the contemporary academic science of society has its roots in the French Enlightenment, the sociological impulse in contemporary criticism across the academic disciplines might best be considered a direct descendant of the great British and American essayists of the 19th century. From the Romantics to the organicist sociology of **Lewis Mumford** and his circle, from **Matthew Arnold**, **Thomas Carlyle**, and **John Stuart Mill** to contemporary New Historicism, the sociological critic has been, with some notable exceptions, first and foremost a "public moralist." Although empirical sociology has long held prestige in the university, more broadly influential still has been the cooptation of sociological techniques and presumptions in interdisciplinary work across the humanities and social sciences. While the constellation of race, class, and gender as the *sine qua non* of the contemporary sociological essay owes much of its force to a century of empirical research and synthesis, few critics have noted that the shape of social criticism in the 20th century has been deeply informed by generic constraints. The short sociological essay – with strong links to the academic article and scholarly monograph – has exerted a powerful, if subtle, influence on contemporary discussions of culture across the academic disciplines and outside the academy. In short, the social sciences, cultural criticism, and the history of literature share common historical ancestors.

Georges Bataille's short-lived Collège de Sociologie exemplified the newly perceived link between the personal and the political in the sociological essay, which began in the 20th century to reject the common, public language of "bourgeois" social science and Arnoldian critique. Anticipating the movement away from the broad national voice of the public intellectual in the latter half of the century – a national voice on the model of the New York intellectuals, and on Thomas Carlyle, **John Ruskin**, and John Stuart Mill before them – the Collège de Sociologie, whose members included sociologists, anthropologists, and philosophers, began to explore cryptic themes in an increasingly autobiographical idiom. Bataille's "sacred sociology," intended to dissolve the borders between the self and the society in which it is embedded, suggests the essayistic tenor in 20th-century sociological criticism. The self-reflexive textuality of the essay, represented in the work of Bataille and many admirers by a juxtaposition of rhetorical registers, literary styles, and authorial voices, signifies a turn toward the irrational and unrepresentable as sources of sociological concern. In *Visions of Excess: Selected Writings, 1927–1939* (1985), for example, a posthumous collection of his sociological essays written in the new style, Bataille writes, "It is clear that the world is purely parodic, in other words, that each thing seen is the parody of another, or is the same thing in a deceptive form." In its abandonment of academic decorum in favor of frank description and painfully personal detail, and in its insistence on the fundamental absurdity of social relations, the French sociological essay continued to estrange itself further from the **critical essays** of the popular press. A whole generation of Anglo-American critics – especially in the 1970s and 1980s – followed its example.

An anticipation of this new sociology was provided in 1923, when the anthropologist Marcel Mauss, a powerful influence on Georges Bataille and his generation, published his widely read "Essay on the Gift," which distinguished between "primitive" gift economies and modern exchange economies, attributing to the former the nobility of gift-giving without reserve, and to the latter the stain of mass society and capitalist calculation. This distinction, so important to 20th-century intellectual life, with its Romantic hostility to utilitarianism, undergirded both social progressivism, such as that of Lewis Mumford and his circle, and neo-Luddite reactions against mass society, as expressed earlier in England by Thomas Carlyle and in America by John Crowe Ransom, Robert Penn Warren, Allen Tate, and the other Southern agrarian essayists. In sum, the new Nietzschean trend in sociological criticism experimented with interdisciplinary forms such as collage and free writing to gain access to the "primitive" forces buried by the psychological defense mechanisms symptomatic of civilization's discontents.

As Julia Kristeva writes of the new intellectual milieu that developed out of the shambles of post-1945 French political culture, "what has emerged in our postwar culture, after the wave of totalitarianism, is these peculiar kinds of speeches and *jouissance* directed against the equalizing Word ... This is something ignored by the machinery of politics, including that on the left, which has been caught up in a large history that excludes the specific histories of speech, dreams and *jouissance*" (quoted in Bensmaïa, 1987). We might take Kristeva's words here as describing a general intellectual crisis of

authority that has haunted social criticism for the last 50 years. As the micropolitics of language displaced the "metanarrative" concerns with large-scale radical transformation – "the equalizing Word" – the sociological essay adapted itself to accommodate these new intellectual priorities. Not unlike the Modernist aesthetic experiments from which contemporary literary and social theory has drawn much of its inspiration, the form of the sociological essay began to reflect its intellectual content and political orientation. Further strengthening the link between the essay's form and its content, the insurgency of the critical voice, gently encouraged in the North Atlantic tradition by **Ralph Waldo Emerson** and the British and American Romantics, urgently demanded by the trans-Atlantic slave narratives – whose authors had "written themselves into being" – and righteously declaimed by the Young Americans, the insurgent voice became a commonplace in social and cultural theory by the last quarter of the 20th century. Taking Modernist experiments as paradigms for the limits of language and representation, and resisting the reification of everyday speech into stereotype and newspaper banality – **Roland Barthes'** "necrosis in language" – many postwar intellectuals began to reject the worn-out and cliché-ridden language of the public sphere, a language which had been the medium of the critical essay since the public sociologists of the 19th century gave the genre wide currency.

Setting the trend for intellectual life on both sides of the Atlantic, and temporarily rescuing the oppositional potential of the cultural avant-garde from academic complacency, French intellectuals in the last quarter of the century have argued that literary Modernism's self-reflexive experimentalism demonstrated sophisticated, albeit highly encrypted, insights into the mechanics of language and desire – insights they would later elaborate into fully fleshed-out theories of discourse and society. In fact, we might see in the poststructural essay of social criticism only the most recent version of the self-reflexive, exploratory tradition of writing begun in the 16th century with the birth of the early modern essay. Julia Kristeva notes the link between social criticism, methodology, and the essay genre when she remarks that "when thought concedes its debt to language – and that is the case, well before structuralism, within the French essayistic tradition – the speaking subject is thrown into Infinity conceived as the power and ruse of the Word."

The insights of 20th-century French philosophers and sociologists have been borne out by other major intellectual traditions as well. In "Der Essay als Form" (1958; "The Essay as Form"), for example, Frankfurt School critical theorist **Theodor W. Adorno** argues that the seeming self-contradictions and paradoxes of the essay genre itself expose the reified rationality at the heart of positivistic social science. For Adorno, the essay's rambling and unmethodical method reproduces the rational mind's own hidden capricious rhythms, employing a dialectical language that doubles back on itself at every turn. Adorno writes: "... doubt about the unconditional priority of method was raised, in the actual process of thought, almost exclusively by the essay. It does justice to the consciousness of non-identity, without needing to say so, radically un-radical in refraining from any reduction to a principle, in accentuating the fragmentary, the partial rather than the total." The heterodox essay genre, Adorno argues, rejects the metaphysical distinction between form and content, culture and nature, likewise abandoning the philosophical search for origins characteristic of both science and theology. Further, according to Adorno, the essay's refusal to indulge itself in the illusion of unmediated representation characteristic of much sociology casts doubt on the spurious certainties and common-sense ideologies that reproduce the status quo. **Georg Lukács** provides a similar justification for the essay as an inherently critical genre in a **letter** to Leo Popper later published as "Über Form und Wesen des Essays" (1911; "On the Nature and Form of the Essay"): "the essay has to create from within itself all the preconditions for the effectiveness and validity of its vision. Therefore two essays can never contradict one another: each creates a different world . . ."

On the essay, then, traditions of social criticism as divergent as the Frankfurt School of critical theory and French post-structuralism concur. For Adorno and Lukács, as for Kristeva and Barthes, both critical theory and the essay similarly collude in the critique of ideology as it is transmitted by aesthetic form and scholarly method. From this perspective, then, poststructuralism's hostility to narrative closure and emphasis on difference and dissemination, combined with the Frankfurt School's critique of instrumental reason, lends the re-emergence of the essay genre in postwar criticism an air of inevitability.

Following the war, first in France, then across the Atlantic, the linguistic turn of social critique – underscored by the Althusserian, and later, Foucauldian emphasis on the social constitution of subjectivity – further placed the sociological essay at the eye of the university's political storm. As theorists on both sides of the Atlantic fought to prevent their own critical work from ironically coalescing into new dogma, increasingly idiosyncratic, autobiographical rhetoric made its way into academic life. The performative aspects of thought now began to vie for an intellectual respectability formerly reserved for the disembodied, system-building Enlightenment as the foundation for a new sociological scholarship; this trend would culminate in poststructuralism, postmodernism, and the New Historicism. As Roland Barthes' own work suggests, the essay genre, which encourages critical self-reflection with its ready-made tradition of writerly texts *par excellence*, is perhaps the best resource for postmodern social critics obsessed with the operations of discursive power on the level of the individual.

If a certain strain of sociological criticism has encouraged essayistic self-exploration, broader political developments have also renewed the essay's lease as the most appropriate prose forum for theoretical inquiry across the disciplines. The rise of "new social movements" in and outside the academy in the late 1960s – including civil rights, feminism, environmentalism, and many others – has demanded theoretical cartographies supple enough to map out the intricate relationships between the personal and the political. From the revolution of the Modernist word and Kristevan "écriture feminine" to the materialist sociology of British cultural studies, a wide variety of "standpoint theories" of gender, race, and class have commanded academic center stage since the late 1970s. As with previous eras, the essay has proved itself the most durable and pliable testing ground for interrogating the sociological limits and boundaries of subjectivity. In perhaps the most notable recent example of aesthetic form abetting intellectual

and political function, the sociological essay has accompanied the flourishing of contemporary feminism, aiding its efforts to rewrite and rework a masculine cultural tradition to suit properly feminist ends. Further, since (as philological scholars have been fond of pointing out) the essay has no "legitimate" patrilineage, the genre opens up new discursive space for the reinvention and revision of the Western tradition which continues apace in the Anglo-American academy. Citing **Virginia Woolf**, one of the most influential essayists for academic feminism, Rachel Blau du Plessis underscores this observation in the influential collection *New Feminist Essays on Virginia Woolf* (1981): "Writers know their text as a form of intimacy, of personal contact, whether conversations with the reader or with the self. Letters, journals, voices are sources for this element . . . [I] see 'no reason why one should not write as one speaks, familiarly, colloquially' expressing the porousness and non-hierarchic stances of intimate conversation in both structure and function." The intimacy and porousness of conversation, justifiably lauded here as a principle of feminist textuality, suggests the dialogic coffeehouse of the 18th-century public sphere as readily as it does the art of liberal conversation praised by Emerson.

Finally, revising and extending the tradition of the essayistic public sphere of the 19th century, the 1990s have brought a spate of confessional, conversational, popular sociological texts such as *Daughters* (1994) by Gerald Early, Patricia Williams' *The Alchemy of Race and Rights* (1991), Alice Kaplan's *French Lessons* (1993), Nancy K. Miller's *Getting Personal* (1991), and Mike Rose's *Lives on the Boundary* (1989). These narratives signal a return of the sociological critic as public intellectual. While social theory narrowly defined remains largely opaque, despite its putative links to public concerns, these autobiographical narratives dismantle the opposition between the public and the private, the personal and the political, contributing to a broader tradition of cultural critique of which social theory is one element. Continuing in the tradition of the trans-Atlantic slave narratives, the reformist sociology of Lewis Mumford and his circle, and the **New Journalism** of the 1960s, this most recent revival of essayism in sociological criticism may at first appear novel, but is in fact as old as the essay form itself.

MATTHEW TITOLO

Further Reading

Adorno, Theodor W., "The Essay as Form," in his *Notes to Literature*, vol. 1, New York: Columbia University Press, 1991 (original German essay published 1958)

Bataille, Georges, *Visions of Excess: Selected Writings, 1927–1939*, edited and translated by Allan Stoekl, Minneapolis: University of Minnesota Press, 1985

Bensmaïa, Réda, *The Barthes Effect: The Essay as Reflective Text*, Minneapolis: University of Minnesota Press, 1987 (original French edition, 1986)

Gross, John, *The Rise and Fall of the Man of Letters: A Study of the Idiosyncratic and the Humane in Modern Literature*, London: Weidenfeld and Nicolson, and New York: Macmillan, 1969

Lepenies, Wolf, *Between Literature and Science: The Rise of Sociology*, Cambridge and New York: Cambridge University Press, 1988 (original German edition, 1985)

Lukács, Georg, "On the Nature and Form of the Essay," in his *Soul and Form*, Cambridge, Massachusetts: MIT Press, 1974 (original German essay published 1911)

Nisbet, Robert, *Sociology as an Art Form*, London: Heinemann, and New York: Oxford University Press, 1976

El Sol

Spanish newspaper, 1917–1939

The morning daily newspaper *El Sol* (The sun) was first published in Madrid on 1 December 1917. Its lifespan can be divided into three clearly defined parts. Only during the first period, from the paper's appearance in 1917 to 25 March 1931, did it play a major role in restoring Spain's political culture, as well as in shaping the concept of journalism itself. On that latter date its founder, the Basque civil engineer Nicolás María de Urgoiti, was removed by the monarchist shareholders who owned a majority of the company's stock. These were the days immediately preceding the proclamation of the Second Spanish Republic. During the five years of that regime's tenure (April 1931 to July 1936), when frequent changes in ownership and management took place, *El Sol* ceased to be a major factor in shaping Spanish public opinion, although it maintained its high standards in news reporting. The third period in the life of *El Sol*, through the Spanish Civil War, ended with General Franco's entrance into Madrid. Limited to a secondary role among the Madrid newspapers and with a circulation of merely 25,000, *El Sol* was at that time controlled by Spain's Communist Party. In spite of this ideological reversal, the paper held to the same editorial format. Consequently, *El Sol*'s intellectual history developed almost exclusively during the first of the three periods mentioned above. The main editors and contributors of Urgoiti's *El Sol* also founded with him *Crisol* (1931–32; Crucible) and *Luz* (1932–34; Light), two newspapers loyal to the policies of the famous daily.

El Sol's unique role in the history of the Spanish press has its roots in the paper's foundational purpose, to be instrumental in a cultural renewal involving the whole of Spanish society. "Renovación" (renewal) is indeed the key word for *El Sol*. After the national disaster of 1898, several attempts were made to promote publications that might help reduce the gap between the country's slow cultural progress and the demand for modernization. This is the Europeanization of Spain proposed by the philosopher **José Ortega y Gasset** in such media as the newspaper *El Imparcial* (The impartial) and the weekly review *España*. Ortega became the main contributor to *El Sol*, as well as the mentor of its political stance; it is in the daily that he published as serials some of his most renowned works, such as *España invertebrada* (1921 [book form]; *Invertebrate Spain*) and *La redención de las provincias* (1931 [book form]; The redemption of the provinces).

Within this framework Urgoiti tried to encourage, in the realm of culture, the modernization project that he had previously launched successfully as a civil engineer, by promoting the rationalization of Spain's paper industry. It was from among the industrialists of this special area that Urgoiti obtained most of the funds for the publication of the newspaper, a

circumstance that would eventually cost him control over the daily. It was one thing to accept economic rationalization, but something else to admit political modernization and promote a more European Spain. (For instance, *El Sol* did not report on bullfights: a strong statement, since bullfights were the most popular pastime in Spain.)

In the process of implementing his project of renewal, Urgoiti was active on three fronts. On the technical level, he produced a newspaper which was up-to-date in its business structure, as well as in the distribution and management of the different sections and even in establishing its own news agency (Febus). Second, he recruited with an open mind contributors to the journal, from a wide range of thinkers of different political persuasion, but committed, as he was, to promoting modernization. Finally, he made clear that *El Sol* would promote reform by dealing in depth with the political problems of the country while maintaining a position of strict independence from the control or influence of political parties or the administration. This attitude meant, in the daily's first period, a firm defense of the allies' cause during World War I, within the polemical climate of neutral Spain.

The management of *El Sol* operated on two levels. As in any other daily, an editorial board, presided over by the directors (Félix Lorenzo and Manuel Aznar between 1917 and 1931), managed the day-to-day running of the paper, always under the supervision of Urgoiti. The editorial position and the analysis of important questions raised in the political and intellectual fields were discussed within a restricted circle – called "la tertulia de *El Sol*" or, humorously, "Olympus" – which included Urgoiti and his principal intellectual advisers: Ortega, in the first place, and other prominent figures such as Luis de Zulueta and Francisco Grandmontaigne. The group of regular contributors on the payroll of *El Sol* comprised most of the outstanding thinkers and writers of the time: Ortega, **Américo Castro**, **Salvador de Madariaga**, Gregorio Marañón, Luis Araquistáin, Fernando de los Ríos, Ramón Gómez de la Serna, **Ramiro de Maeztu**, Gabriel Miró, Ernesto Giménez Caballero, Luis Olariaga, **Ramón Pérez de Ayala**, Eduardo Gómez de Baquero, Ricardo Baeza. The weight of this important intellectual component is reflected in the front page articles and editorials, the latter accompanied by humorous cartoons, usually by Luis Bagaría. Likewise noteworthy is the sensitivity and care apparent in the section devoted to book reviews and reports of cultural events.

Like previous attempts at cultural renewal, *El Sol*'s influence was restricted by the fact that the public interested in a product of such high quality was limited. In an attempt to remedy this problem, it was decided to publish *La Voz* (The voice), an evening daily of a more popular nature. It first appeared on 1 July 1920, and became *El Sol*'s companion through all its vicissitudes until the extinction of both papers in 1939. However, they had widely different readers. In 1926 *La Voz* was selling 110,000 copies against the 80,000 sold by *El Sol*; the evening daily's success, however, was mostly confined to Madrid, while only 20 percent of the morning paper's output was sold in the capital, with the remaining 80 percent sold in the provinces – a fact that underscores *El Sol*'s role in shaping public opinion on a national level.

In its early days, when Europe was aflame with World War I or immersed in postwar tension, *El Sol* stood for a democratization of the Spanish monarchy. Later it greeted with positive expectations the rise to power of General Primo de Rivera, who ruled from 1923 to 1930. The initial hope expressed in *El Sol*, based on the suppression of political corruption, was soon frustrated, however, and gave way to serious questioning of the need for political change. Finally in 1930, after the fall of the dictator, when the political line followed by King Alfonso XIII had reached a point of no return, *El Sol* published an article by Ortega that became famous for its closing line, "Delenda est monarchia," forecasting the imminent demise of the regime. The price Urgoiti paid for this announcement was his exile from *El Sol*. Paradoxically, when Spain's regime changed 20 days later, the newspaper, now separated from its founder, main contributors, and editorial board, adhered enthusiastically to the republic. The founding project of cultural renewal was, however, irretrievably lost. The conservative owners appointed Manuel Aznar as director, trying unsuccessfully to establish a bridge with the past. After August 1932, the newspaper executive and entrepreneur Antonio Miquel took over the firm and for some time supported the policies of the republican leader **Manuel Azaña**. Miquel's failure led to a new political line with Fernando Vela as director, beginning in February 1934. Throughout these changes, *El Sol* was losing both money and readers. In July 1934, no more than 5000 copies were sold in Madrid. In the words of the historian Gonzalo Redondo (1970), it was the closing issue of Urgoiti's *El Sol* on 25 March 1931 that was really "the final issue of the newspaper."

ANTONIO ELORZA
MARÍA SOLEDAD CARRASCO

Further Reading

Aubert, Paul, and Jean Michel Desvois, "*El Sol*, un grand quotidien atypique (1917–1939)," in *Typologie de la presse hispanique*, edited by D. Bussy Genevois, Rennes: Presses Universitaires de Rennes 2, 1986

Cabrera, Mercedes, *La industria, la prensa y la política: Nicolás María de Urgoiti (1869–1951)*, Madrid: Alianza, 1994

Cabrera, Mercedes, María Soledad Carrasco, Rafael Cruz, and Antonio Elorza, "Las fundaciones de Nicolás María de Urgoiti: Escritos y archivos," *Estudios de Historia Social* 24–25 (January–June 1983): 267–471

Redondo, Gonzalo, *Las empresas políticas de Ortega y Gasset*, Madrid: Rialp, 2 vols., 1970

Soloukhin, Vladimir

Russian, 1924–

As a young writer Vladimir Soloukhin earned his living by turning out essays for the popular journal *Ogonek* (Little flame) on topics chosen by his editors. Little of enduring interest remains from these early efforts. His career as a serious essayist began in the early 1960s, after, as he has written, his "eyes were opened" to the Soviet regime's distortion of Russia's pre-Soviet past.

The scope and technique of Soloukhin's mature work cannot be understood without reference to the Communist Party's literary apparatus and its methods of rewarding, punishing,

and censoring writers. The same agencies that awarded him the State Prize of the Russian Republic in 1979 and the Red Banner of Labor on his 60th birthday in 1984, and that elevated him to high office in the Writers' Union and enabled him to travel widely outside the U.S.S.R., would also censure journals publishing his more offensive essays, and threatened him with expulsion from the Party and from the Writers' Union for having written and published the series of short essays *Nenapissanye rasskazy* (1985; Stories not written). And when the essays collected under the title *Vremia sobirat' kamni* (1980; A Time to Gather Stones) were published as a book, all 70,000 copies were sent to library reserve collections, so as not to fall into the hands of readers.

The essays of his mature years are almost all devoted to the same theme – that of recovering a past discarded and derided by Lenin's heirs. The task of bringing that past to the Soviet reader leads Soloukhin to test the essay's capacity for concealing offending truths in ostensibly acceptable discourse.

Mikhail Epstein has observed (*After the Future*, 1995) that the essay approaches its subject obliquely. This is true of Soloukhin's essays, where paradox must take the place of forthright assertion of propositions. Thus in *Poseshchenie Zvanki* (1975; A visit to Zvanka) he finds the remains of the poet Gavriil Romanovich Derzhavin re-interred by the Soviet authorities under a tombstone identifying him as "an Actual Privy Councillor and Bearer of Many Decorations." This is the same Derzhavin who provided Russia's greatest field marshal with the epitaph "Here Lies Suvorin." The contrast speaks eloquently, if obliquely, of the decline in the literary climate.

It is characteristic of Soloukhin's essays that they begin on one theme, which turns out to be merely a device facilitating passage to the real theme. *Chernye doski* (1966; *Searching for Icons in Russia*) begins with the theme of collecting as an avocation, but eventually the reader sees that the real topic is the role of religious art in traditional Russian culture. Similarly, *A Time to Gather Stones* begins with a discussion of the Optina Pustyn Monastery's importance for the writings of Dostoevskii and Tolstoi, whereas the real subject of the essay is the institution of elders within Russian monasticism. *Bol'shoe Shakhmatovo* (1979; Greater Shakhmatovo) begins with reference to plans for marking the centenary anniversary of Aleksandr Blok's birth. In fact, the essay celebrates the liberal intelligentsia of pre-revolutionary Russia, a class incorrectly and unfairly dismissed in the Soviet period, Soloukhin notes, as "idlers and spongers." In *Poseshchenie Zvanki* a recollection of seeing the ruins of Derzhavin's estate is the pretext for an analysis of the intricate structure used by the poet in the construction of his ode to God.

In "Rasskazat' i skazat'" (1976; Telling and saying) Soloukhin ponders what distinguishes works of a genius, such as Pushkin, from those of Mel'nikov-Pecherskii, a writer of far less talent. Great writers, he suggests, possess the quality of *fokusirovka*: the ability to reduce complex subjects to vivid images possessing immediate relevance to authentic life experiences. The term and the concept are characteristic of Soloukhin's own work in the essay genre, especially in *Kameshki na ladone* (A handful of pebbles), miniature essays contributed to journals on a continuing basis and periodically printed in book form (1977, 1982, 1988). An enormous salmon being consumed at dinner in a portrait of Aleksei

Tolstoi becomes in Soloukhin's essay the objective representation of a writer who would leave the freedom and poverty of exile in order to prostitute his talent for Stalin's regime. A visit to Joan of Arc's parish church at Domrémy reveals that the list of priests serving there since the 13th century contains fewer names than the list of chairmen in the troubled 50 years of the collective farm that consumed Soloukhin's home village. In *Bol'shoe Shakmatovo* Soloukhin evokes early communism's cultural nihilism by creating the image of village schoolchildren working out math problems on the back of handwritten manuscripts of Aleksandr Blok's poems, looted from his family's manor house before it was burned to the ground during Lenin's campaign of terror against "class enemies."

Soloukhin's orientation toward his audience is that of Everyman on a voyage of discovery and self-discovery. In "Sovkhoz im. Lenina. Dom kul'tury" (1984; The house of culture at the Lenin Soviet farm), devoted to an exhibition of paintings by Konstantin Vasil'ev, Soloukhin refers to himself as a *verkhogliad* (a slang term meaning "superficial observer"). Yet he affirms the importance of the amateur when, after listening to professional academic artists dismiss Vasil'ev's work as primitive and transparent, he recalls seeing a queue of 500 people waiting in inclement weather to see the artist's work at an exhibition held on a remote collective farm. What the experts did not see, concludes Soloukhin, was Vasil'ev's gift of spiritual resonance (*odukhotvorennost'*) with the Russian people's innermost aspirations.

When Soloukhin was able to reduce his output of essays and begin writing fiction, the sensation, he has noted, was similar to that of removing heavy work boots and donning track shoes. The burden undertaken by the essayist is derived from the essay's "capaciousness" (*emkost'*), its appetite for taking on features of all literary genres, in order to mediate between life and life's sciences. In Soloukhin's late and post-Soviet essays, such as *Drevo* (1991; The tree), *Pri svete dnia* (1992; In the light of day), and *Solenoe ozero* (1994; Salt lake), the genre plays host to a wide assortment of expository devices in efforts to re-create in the reader's imagination a vision of the past with the power and capacity to explain Russia's 20th-century experiences.

HARRY WALSH

Biography

Vladimir Alekseevich Soloukhin. Born 14 June 1924 in Alepino Stavrovskii, Vladimir region. Studied at the Vladimir Engineering Technicum, 1938–42, graduated in tool mechanics; Gorkii Literary Institute, Moscow, 1946–51. Served in the army, until 1945. Married Rosa Soloukhin. Feature writer, *Ogonek*. Joined the Communist Party, 1952. Member of the board of the Union of Soviet Writers, 1958–75; member of the editorial staff, Molodaia Gvardiia publishing house, Moscow, 1964–81. Awards: State Prize for Literature, 1979; Red Banner of Labor, 1984.

Selected Writings

Essays and Related Prose
Vladimirskie Proselki, 1958; as *A Walk in Rural Russia*, translated by S. Miskin, 1966
Veter stranstvii (The wind of traveling), 1960
S liricheskikh pozitsii (From lyrical points of view), 1965

Pis'ma iz russkogo muzeia (Letters from the Russian museum); *Chernye doski*; *Vremia sobirat' kamni*, 1966; *Chernye doski* as *Searching for Icons in Russia*, translated by Paul Falla, 1971; enlarged edition of *Vremia sobirat' kamni*, 1980; as *A Time to Gather Stones*, translated by Valerie Z. Nollan, 1993
Tret'ia okhota (Third hunt), 1968
Poseshchenie Zvanki, 1975
Slovo zhivoe i mertvoe (o vremeni i o sebe) (The word living and dead [about time and self]), 1976
Kameshki na ladoni, 3 vols., 1977–88
Bol'shoe Shakmatovo, 1979
Volshebnaia palochka (Magical cane), 1983
Sozertsanie chuda (The contemplation of a miracle), 1984
Bedstvie s golubiami, 1984
Nenapissanye rasskazy, 1985
Chitaia Lenina (Reading Lenin), 1989
Rasstavanie s idolom (Parting with the idol), 1991
Drevo, 1991
Pri svete dnia, 1992
Solenoe ozero, 1994

Other writings: several novels (including *Smekh za levym plachom* [*Laughter over the Left Shoulder*], 1988), poetry, and many works of Russian "village prose."

Collected works edition: *Sobranie sochinenii*, 10 vols., 1995– (in progress).

Further Reading
Brown, Deming, *Soviet Russian Literature Since Stalin*, Cambridge: Cambridge University Press, 1978
Dunlop, John, "Ruralist Prose Writers in the Russian Ethnic Movement," in *Ethnic Russia in the U.S.S.R.: The Dilemma of Dominance*, edited by Edward Allworth, New York: Pergamon Press, 1980: 80–88
Givens, John, Review of Soloukhin's *A Time to Gather Stones*, *Slavic Review* 54 (Spring 1995): 245–46
Turkov, Andrei, "Energy and Talent," *Soviet Literature* 6, no. 435 (1984): 103–06

Solov'ev, Vladimir
Russian, 1853–1900

Vladimir Solov'ev is recognized as Russia's leading religious philosopher of the 19th century. He was also an important poet, whose thought and manner exerted a powerful influence on the most important religious symbolists, **Aleksandr Blok**, **Viacheslav Ivanov**, and **Andrei Belyi**. There is in fact probably no non-Marxist thinker in 20th-century Russia who was not profoundly influenced by Solov'ev.

Solov'ev was inspired by the mystical religious intuition of a being of resplendent beauty, which he called "Bozhestvennaia Sofiia" (Divine Sophia) and "Sofiia Premudrost'" (Divine Wisdom); his philosophical thought is a synthesis of Christian dogmatism with Eastern, particularly Russian, mysticism, the natural sciences, and rationalist idealist philosophy. One of the most erudite men of his day, Solov'ev undertook advanced study in both philosophy and the natural sciences. His prose style included discourses in both these disciplines, and in time took on a markedly poetic quality. In his mature essays Solov'ev increasingly used literary examples, and even poetry (particularly of those he considered "philosopher-poets") along with and at times in lieu of rational argument.

His early, more academic philosophical works – his M.A. thesis *Krizis zapadnoi filosofii* (1874; *The Crisis in Western Philosophy*), his doctoral dissertation *Kritika otvlechennykh nachal* (1880; A critique of abstract principles), and his neo-Slavophile book *Filosofskie printsipy tsel'nogo znaniia* (1877; The philosophical foundations of integral knowledge) – are written in the Russian rendition of Hegelian discourse, the so-called "school language." Solov'ev became less satisfied with that language over time. He was one of the greatest philosophical stylists. The historian of philosophy V. V. Zenkovsky (1953) writes of Solov'ev's philosophical idiom: "He always wrote with astonishing clarity, precision and vividness. Diffuseness is totally alien to him. In this respect Solovyov is extremely close to the French philosophical style. There was in Solovyov's very mode of thinking a penchant for rationalism, logical constructions and a dialectical binding together of heterogeneous ideas. These were the external peculiarities of Solovyov's creative activity which often made him a slave of his own mode of thinking and writing." Solov'ev was a mystical religious philosopher who wished to integrate all areas of intellectual endeavor with intuitive feeling. He himself remarked that he could always find adequate words for his thoughts, but never for his feelings.

A number of his essay-length works are publicistic, treating the reunification of the Eastern and Western churches and national and political divisions within Russia. He was also a bitterly sardonic polemicist, as seen in his essays attacking **Vasilii Rozanov** and his **review**-attacks on the fledgling symbolist movement led by Valerii Briusov. His reputation as a great essayist, however, rests on his religious lectures about the meaning of **Dostoevskii**'s life and work (1881–83), his religious and philosophical *Chteniia o Bogochelovechestve* (1877–81; *Lectures on Godmanhood*), and his numerous aesthetically oriented essays written from the late 1880s to the end of his life.

The young Solov'ev knew Dostoevskii, and different critics have suggested that he was the living prototype for Ivan or Aliosha Karamazov. Solov'ev's important essays in this late period include five that are united under the title *Smysl liubvi* (1892–94; *The Meaning of Love*), as well as "Krasota v prirode" (1889; Beauty in nature), "Obshchii smysl iskusstva" ("The General Meaning of Art"), "O liricheskoi poezii" (1895; On lyric poetry), "Poeziia F. Tiutcheva" (1895; The poetry of F. Tiutchev), and the brilliant unfinished cycle of essays entitled *Osnovy teoreticheskoi filosofii* (1897–99; part translated as "Foundations of Theoretical Philosophy"). One of his more interesting late works, *Tri razgovora o voine, progresse, i konste istorii* (1900; *War, Progress, and the End of History*) is in Platonic **dialogue** form. It concludes with the fascinating "Kratkaia povest' ob Antikhriste" ("Short Tale of the Antichrist"), a brilliant reworking of Ivan Karamazov's prose poem "Legenda o velikom inkvizitore" ("The Legend of the Grand Inquisitor") in Dostoevskii's *Brat'ia Karamazovy* (1880; *The Brothers Karamazov*). The Grand Inquisitor figure in this apocalyptically tinged work was an attack on Tolstoian rationalized religion, yet after Rozanov's suggestion it has often been viewed as Solov'ev's self-parody of his own attempts to unite the churches, a task which consumed him in the 1880s.

In his essay "The General Meaning of Art," Solov'ev asserts the great importance of aesthetics: "For their genuine realization Truth and the Good must become a creative force in the human subject, transforming – not only reflecting, reality . . . the light of reason can not be limited to knowledge alone, but the meaning of life must be incarnated in a new, more suitable reality . . . Real art, in essence – any sensible portrayal of an object or phenomenon from the point of view of its ultimate (teleological) state, i.e., in the light of the world's future, is a work of art." He finds a practical example of this consciously created in the poetry of Fedor Tiutchev and unconsciously in that of Afanasii Fet. In his essay on Tiutchev (1895) Solov'ev writes: "The action of ideal beings on us, which produces in us both intellectual contemplation (Schelling's *intellektuelle Anschauung*) and the creation of their ideal forms or ideas is called inspiration. This action takes us out of our usual center, raises us to a higher sphere, makes us ecstatic." In "On Lyric Poetry" he writes: ". . . for sensitive people . . . love poems like those here [of Fet] can serve as a better affirmation of mystical truths than any possible 'school proofs'."

In his great late essays, therefore, Solov'ev is clearly trying to bridge the disciplines of natural science, mystical religion, and aesthetics/poetic art. His writing style presents a somewhat polyphonic mixture of the discourses of the three disparate fields. The cacophony of natural science proofs and statistics and the exalted Romantic style are particularly sharp in the seminal essays "Beauty in Nature" and *The Meaning of Love*, so much so that Konstantin Mochul'skii (1936) was moved to comment: "The poet [in Solov'ev] conquers the natural scientist and pure lyricism invades a very scientific scholarly exposition. Solov'ev felt 'the heavenly life of flowers' very deeply . . . After a lyrical digression the author returns to 'realities,' i.e., to zoology and the evolution of species, quoting Darwin."

The attempt to integrate such different discourses in one essayistic style in Solov'ev was occasioned by the fact that for most of his intellectual life Westernized Russian intellectuals, his main audience, were profoundly uninterested in idealistic philosophy and even less moved by mystical religion. Scholarly and natural science discourses were used for their authority with his rather hostile readership. Thus while his point of view is extremely antipositivist, the positivist "idiom" of the "other" is coopted by Solov'ev as a means of overcoming the (for him) only apparent contradiction between Reason and Faith. The preponderance of nonmystical discourse in the **philosophical essays** and books of this mystic, and his lifelong crusade to systematize and rationalize the faith, led Zenkovsky to remark that "Solovyov characterized Russian religious thought from without." This is less and less true in his late aesthetic essays, where the action of beauty on human individuality becomes virtually the cornerstone of philosophy.

Having achieved in his early philosophical works a lucid academic style, Solov'ev went on to abandon it for the mixed, often poetic discourse of his later years. His late essays, both in form and in their championing of the philosopher-poet and theurgic art, laid the foundation for the artistic essay of the next generation of poet-artists, particularly Ivanov and Belyi. Solov'ev's late aesthetic-philosophical essays were the precondition of Belyi's prophecy: "From now on philosophy and poetry will go hand in hand . . . after the crisis in philosophy

... it was inevitable that art should come forth to take the place of philosophy as the guiding light of mankind" ("Magiia slov" [1910; "The Magic of Words"]).

ANNA LISA CRONE

Biography

Vladimir Sergeevich Solov'ev. Born 28 January 1853 in Moscow. Studied natural sciences, philosophy, and history at Moscow University, 1869–73, M.A. in history, 1874; Moscow Theological Academy, 1873–74; St. Petersburg University, Ph.D., 1880. Lecturer, Moscow University, 1875; studied at the British Museum, London, July–October 1875; traveled to Egypt, November 1875–March 1876; gave a series of public lectures, 1877–81: in one lecture advocated clemency for Alexander II's assassins: reprimanded by the Minister of Public Education, and as a result voluntarily resigned lectureship and abandoned his university career. Full-time writer, from 1881. Editor (also contributor) of the philosophical sections of the Brockhaus-Efron Encyclopedia, from 1891. Traveled again to Europe and Egypt, 1898. Died near Moscow, 13 August 1900.

Selected Writings

Essays and Related Prose

Chteniia o Bogochelovechestve, 1877–81; as Lectures on Godmanhood, translated by Peter Zouboff, 1948; revised edition, as Lectures on Divine Humanity, edited by Boris Jakim, 1995

Dukhovye osnovy zhizni, 1884; as God, Man and the Church, translated by Donald Attwater, 1938

L'Idée russe, 1888; Russian edition, 1909

La Russie et l'église universelle, 1889; Russian edition, 1911; as Russia and the Universal Church, translated by H. Rees, 1948

Smysl liubvi, 1892–94; as The Meaning of Love, translated by Jane Marshall, 1945, revised by Thomas R. Beyer, Jr., 1985

Opravdanie dobra, 1897; as Justification of the Good: An Essay in Moral Philosophy, translated by Natalie Duddington, 1918

Osnovy teoreticheskoi filosofii, 1897–99; part as "Foundations of Theoretical Philosophy," translated by Vlada Tolley and James Scanlan, in Russian Philosophy, vol. 3, 1965: 99–134

Tri razgovora o voine, progresse, i konste istorii, i kratkaia povest' ob Antikhriste (Three conversations . . .), 1900; as War, Progress, and the End of History, Including a Short Tale of the Antichrist, translated by Alexander Bakshy, 1915, revised by Thomas R. Beyer, Jr., 1990

A Solovyov Anthology, edited by S. L. Frank, translated by Natalie Duddington, 1950

Other writings: poetry, three plays, literary criticism, philosophical works, and encyclopedia articles. Also translated **Schiller**, Heine, Virgil, Petrarch, Dante, Mickiewicz, Longfellow, and Tennyson.

Collected works editions: Sobranie sochinenii, 2nd edition, edited by Sergei M. Solov'ev and Ernest L. Radlov, 10 vols., 1911–14, revised edition, 12 vols., 1966–70.

Bibliography

Sidorov, S. A., Bibliografiia rabot o Vl. Solov'eve, n.p.: Obshchestvo Pamyati Vladimira Solov'eva (Vladimir Solov'ev society), 1916

Further Reading

Cioran, Samuel D., Vladimir Soloviev and the Knighthood of the Divine Sophia, Waterloo, Ontario: Wilfred Laurier University Press, 1977

Kline, George L., "Russian Religious Thought," in 19th Century Religious Thought in the West, vol. 2, edited by Ninian Smart and others, Cambridge: Cambridge University Press, 1985: 208–17

Mochul'skii, Konstantin, V. S. Solov'ev, Paris: YMCA Press, 1951 (original edition, 1936)

Sutton, Jonathan, The Religious Philosophy of Vl. Solovyov: Towards a Reassessment, Basingstoke: Macmillan, and New York: St. Martin's Press, 1988

Zenkovsky, V. V., A History of Russian Philosophy, vol. 2, New York: Columbia University Press, 1953: 469–531

Zernov, N., Three Russian Prophets: Khomiakov, Dostoevsky, Soloviev, London: S.C.M. Press, 1944; Gulf Breeze, Florida: Academic International Press, 1973

Sønderby, Knud

Danish, 1909–1966

Knud Sønderby came to be known as a novelist, an essayist, and, to a lesser degree, a dramatist. He was also a prolific journalist. Many of the works included in essay collections appeared first in Danish newspapers as chronicles in essay form. His first collection of essays, Grønlandsk sommer (1941; Greenland summer) appeared ten years after his debut novel. This essay collection, which signaled Sønderby's transition to the essay, was followed by five principal collections, the last appearing posthumously in 1969. While some critics regard his essays as less significant than his fiction, others see them as a rejuvenation of his oeuvre. Indeed, Midt i en jazztid (1931; In the middle of a jazz age), his best-known novel on the crisis of the Danish youth, presages some of the underlying themes of his essays. The perspective of the young served as Sønderby's most effective medium in imparting the Danish character of his work. His subdued tone and casual style also suggest the influence of his narrative works.

Not unlike the novelist, the essayist Sønderby is an analytical observer. Major themes in Sønderby's essays embrace the interplay of past and present, the imminence of death, and man's concept of time; other work, in large part semi-autobiographical, portrays the disillusionment of the 1920s.

Notwithstanding the personal tone of his essays, Sønderby's perspective lends a special character to the relationship between the essay and its public. His jeg ("I") is not exact; it is, rather, an image of him as an observer. His reader is not left with the egotistical indulgences of the author, but afforded insight into how that author's images are perceived. The reader is held at a distance, permitting us to observe how Sønderby observes. His essays are filled with minute detail, chronicling the landscape, man, and the animal world. His point of departure is often specifically Danish, but he can also render pristine descriptions of life abroad. The seemingly insignificant phenomena of everyday life, such as a facial expression or a flower, acquire a sensory quality in his prose. His reader feels, smells, and hears. Accordingly, his language shows more than it tells. At times, Sønderby's language can be taut and subtle; at other times it is humorous and light.

In the collections Hvidtjørnen (1950; The Hawthorn) and Gensyn med havet (1957; Rendezvous with the sea), there is a gradual movement from a specific situation to a more encompassing contemplation of memories about the Danish landscape. Sønderby's digressions, imprecise expressions, and wordplay are reiterated in Det danske land (1952; This Danish land), a collection of essays by various writers which he edited with Otto Gelsted. In his contribution he combines epic and descriptive styles in order to bring his reader closer to the landscape.

The proliferation of Sønderby's essays precludes their remaining within the confines of the traditional essay. He preferred to think of his prose pieces as *myter* (myths), like those of Johannes Vilhelm Jensen. While Sønderby's prose fiction is often critical and pessimistic in tone, his essays are artistic and optimistic. By transgressing space and time, the essays speak encouragingly to man's common values.

VIVIAN GREENE-GANTZBERG

Biography

Born 10 July 1909 in Esbjerg, Denmark. Studied at the Øregaard Gymnasium, graduated 1927; law at the University of Copenhagen, law degree, 1935. Journalist, including film reviewer, for several Copenhagen newspapers, 1930s–1940s. Secretary to the director, Government Committee for Greenland, 1935. Solicitor, 1936–37. Married, 1940. Founding member, Danish Academy, 1960. Died in Thy, 8 August 1966.

Selected Writings

Essays and Related Prose
Grønlandsk sommer, 1941
Forsvundne somre, 1946
Hvidtjørnen, 1950; as *The Hawthorn*, translated by Reginald Spink, 1966
Gensyn med havet, 1957
De blå glimt, 1964; as *The Blue Flashes*, translated by Reginald Spink, 1966
The Blue Flashes; The Hawthorn; Danish Harbours, translated by Reginald Spink, 1966
De danske havne: Efterladte essays, edited by Inge Sønderby and Mogens Knudsen, 1969
Danmarkskortet: Udvalget essays om landskaber og mennesker, edited by Inge Sønderby and Mogens Knudsen, 1970

Other writings: four novels (*Midt i en jazztid*, 1931; *To mennesker mødes*, 1932; *En kvinde er overflødig*, 1936; *De kolde flammer*, 1940), plays, and memoirs. Also coedited (and contributed to) the anthology *Det danske land* (1952).

Bibliographies
Gadman, Peter, in *Knud Sønderbys forfatterskab*, Copenhagen: Vinten, 1976
Hellum, Dan, *Knud Sønderby: Bibliografi og produktionsregistrant, 1925–74*, Copenhagen: Danmarks Biblioteksskole, 1976

Further Reading
Bager, Poul, *Fylde og tomhed: Om Knud Sønderbys forfatterskab*, Copenhagen: Gyldendal, 1984: 167–76
Bjørnvig, Thorkild, *Digtere*, Copenhagen: Gyldendal, 1991
Gadman, Peter, *Knud Sønderbys forfatterskab*, Copenhagen: Gyldendal, 1976
Kaas Johansen, Niels, in *Danske digtere i det 20. aarhundrede*, vol. 2, edited by Kaas Johansen and Ernst Frandsen, Copenhagen: Gyldendal, 1951: 451–64
Sandersen, Vibeke, *Essayet – oprør og tradition*, Copenhagen: Gyldendal, 1975: 55–64
Svendsen, Hanne Marie, "Livsstil og klasseforskel," in *Tilbageblik på 30'erne: Litteratur, teater, kulturdebat*, vol. 1, Copenhagen: Vendelkær, 1967: 80–93
Wamberg, Niels Birger, "Knud Sønderbys gratie," *Vinduet* 17 (1963): 86–89

Sontag, Susan

American, 1933–

Susan Sontag's label "the Dark Lady of American Letters" refers to more than her physical features. From her persistent championing of European writers and thinkers to her refusal to ally herself with any particular school of thought, Sontag is usually considered an outsider by American academia – respected for her sharp intelligence but treated warily. In part this may be because she has been so critical of the approach that modern academics take to art. Sontag demands nothing less than a revamping of the way we perceive art; to some this may be too demanding and threatening a shift in perspective.

In Sontag's first collection, *Against Interpretation and Other Essays* (1966), the title essay (first pub. 1964) and "On Style" (1965) together serve as a position statement from which Sontag has never deviated. In them she discusses the way we look at art and the distorting nature of modern interpretation, in which we no longer see works of art as simply existing, but look for their underlying meanings. This act of interpretation ignores the true nature of art. As Sontag explains in "On Style," "A work of art encountered as a work of art is an experience, not a statement or an answer to a question. Art is not only about something; it is something. A work of art is a thing *in* the world, not just a text or commentary *on* the world." Rejecting interpretation, she advocates what she calls in the title essay "transparence," which means "experiencing the luminousness of the thing in itself, of things being what they are."

Crucial to approaching art experientially is the abandonment of the distinction between content and form, a distinction which usually privileges content over form and further encourages the search for meaning. Sontag contends that style and content are so intricately interwoven that they cannot be disentangled without damaging the integrity of the artwork. Separating art into different levels implies a hierarchy, whereas a transparent surface reveals everything at once; there are no hidden depths or meanings. In other words, style is a part of content, and content a part of style; the "meaning" of art lies in the experiencing of both together without analysis.

The other essays in *Against Interpretation* either extend Sontag's initial argument into specific areas of culture, such as in her famous essay "Notes on 'Camp'" (1964), or provide examples of how that argument might be applied, for instance in essays on theater, film, and European authors and thinkers like Nathalie Sarraute, **Georg Lukács**, and **Simone Weil**.

Sontag's second collection, *Styles of Radical Will* (1969), confirmed her reputation as a major, but controversial, intellectual force in the U.S. In it she writes again on theater and film, on European thinkers such as **Walter Benjamin** and **E. M. Cioran**, and on pornography. Also included is "The Aesthetics of Silence" (1967), a restatement of Sontag's thesis against interpretation, this time focusing on what the spectator should bring to the contemplation of art: silence. In the ideal meeting between art and viewer, Sontag explains, "The spectator would approach art as he does a landscape. A landscape doesn't demand from the spectator his 'understanding,' his imputations of significance, his anxieties and sympathies; it demands, rather, his absence, it asks that he not add anything to it. Contemplation, strictly speaking, entails self-forgetfulness on the part of the spectator: an object worthy of contemplation is one which, in effect, annihilates the perceiving subject."

The act of perception is given book-length treatment in one of Sontag's best-known works, *On Photography* (1977). Sontag finds in photography the ideal art form for her pursuit of transparency. Because photography has a leveling effect on its subject matter (i.e. anything can be photographed and so nothing is privileged) and is so prolific in society that it destroys the boundaries and definitions of art, the viewer can approach a photograph freely with no expectation of discovering what it means; its transparency is anticipated.

Given Sontag's suspicion of levels of meaning, it is not surprising that her own writing style is clear, unfussy, and free of metaphors. She is also careful to remove herself from the text, even from a work like the extended essay *Illness as Metaphor* (1978), which considers the symbolic meanings attached to tuberculosis in the 19th century and cancer in the 20th. Sontag wrote *Illness as Metaphor* after she herself had cancer, but avoided the easy temptation of mentioning her own experience, only referring to it briefly in the later *Aids and Its Metaphors* (1989), which extends her argument to include Aids.

Throughout her essays, most of Sontag's references are to Europeans, to the point where she can appear scathing and condescending about her fellow countrymen. Certainly in "What's Happening in America" (1967), she is very negative about the state of her country. Her sensitivity and alliance to the European intellectual tradition display the generalist nature of her work and her position as a universal intellectual. Monika Beyer has called her "a free-floating commentator on the general culture, unaffiliated to specific interest groups or institutions" (Liam Kennedy quoting Beyer, 1995).

However, as Liam Kennedy points out, despite acting as a free agent, Sontag has long been associated with the "New York intellectuals" of the 1960s, particularly through her connection with the *Partisan Review*, which she idolized as a youth and began contributing to in 1961. The New York intellectuals advocated cultural criticism and intellectual generalism, and used the essay form as the most appropriate genre in which to explore ideas. Kennedy feels that "It is no accident Sontag should find herself most at home with the essay form, self-consciously manipulating its provisional and performative features, using it to 'try out' ideas. She favours disjunctive forms of argument: aphoristic and epigrammatic modes of critical expression are widely applied in her writings."

In 1992 Sontag published her third novel, *The Volcano Lover*, and since then has declared that she will concentrate on writing fiction rather than essays. Perhaps she feels she has made her point; it is now up to her readers and admirers to apply to her fiction the approach to art she has advocated since "Against Interpretation" and has herself so successfully applied throughout her oeuvre.

THERESA WERNER

Biography
Born 16 January 1933 in New York City. Studied at the University of California, Berkeley, 1948–49; University of Chicago, 1949–51, B.A., 1951; Harvard University, Cambridge, Massachusetts,

1954–57, M.A., 1955; St. Anne's College, Oxford, 1957. Married Philip Rieff, 1950 (divorced, 1958): one son. Taught English, philosophy, or religion at the University of Connecticut, Storrs, 1953–54, Harvard University, 1955–57, City College of New York and Sarah Lawrence College, Bronxville, New York, 1959–60, and Columbia University, New York, 1960–64. Editor, *Commentary*, New York, 1959; also contributor to various other periodicals, including *Partisan Review*, *New York Review of Books*, **Atlantic Monthly**, *Nation*, and **Harper's**. Also directed several plays and films. Awards: several fellowships; American Academy Ingram Merrill Foundation Award, 1976; National Book Critics Circle Award, 1977; Academy of Sciences and Literature Award (Germany), 1979. Member, American Academy, 1979; Officer, Order of Arts and Letters (France), 1984.

Selected Writings

Essays and Related Prose
Against Interpretation and Other Essays, 1966
Styles of Radical Will, 1969
On Photography, 1977
Illness as Metaphor, 1978
Under the Sign of Saturn, 1980
A Susan Sontag Reader, 1982
Aids and Its Metaphors, 1989

Other writings: three novels (*The Benefactor*, 1963; *Death Kit*, 1967; *The Volcano Lover*, 1992), short stories, the play *Alice in Bed* (1993), and screenplays.

Further Reading

Hardwick, Elizabeth, Introduction to *A Susan Sontag Reader*, New York: Farrar Straus Giroux, 1982; Harmondsworth: Penguin, 1983

Jeffords, Susan, "Susan Sontag," in *Modern American Critics Since 1955*, edited by Gregory S. Jay, *Dictionary of Literary Biography*, vol. 67, Detroit: Gale Research, 1988

Kennedy, Liam, *Susan Sontag: Mind as Passion*, Manchester: University of Manchester Press, 1995

Poague, Leland, *Conversations with Susan Sontag*, Jackson: University Press of Mississippi, 1995

Sayres, Sohnya, *Susan Sontag: The Elegiac Modernist*, New York: Routledge Chapman and Hall, 1989; London: Routledge, 1990

Sørensen, Villy

Danish, 1929–

Recognized as contemporary Denmark's most significant philosopher, Villy Sørensen also enjoys a reputation as an accomplished writer of fantastic tales, short stories, and criticism. In an interview in 1966, Sørensen pointed to the related themes of his fiction and essays and confessed that he began to write philosophically in order to explain what he had said in other ways. When asked whether there is a line between his essays and his fiction, he replied that while there are different ways to express oneself, what one expresses remains the same. Sørensen ended his remark with the reminder that the reading public of the 1950s understood and discussed symbols less than they did a decade later. He had initially turned to the essay out of a practical need to be understood.

Following his debut in 1953 with the collection of symbolic tales entitled *Sære fortællinger* (*Strange Stories*), Sørensen proceeded to pursue in nonfiction themes of division and dualism as they affect the individual and society. In several of his essays he attacks totalitarian tendencies which endanger the development of individual personality. To a large extent, both his fiction and his essays deal with the consequences of man's metaphorical "fall" (*faldet*) from grace which signaled the breakdown of values and man's inability to act. In interpreting the "fall" in the context of contemporary society, Sørensen lends his oeuvre a cyclical character.

Although Sørensen had written short prose pieces as a member of the group of young philosophically inspired writers identified as Heretikere (Heretics), he did not publish his first collection of essays until 1959. In *Digtere og dæmoner* (Poets and demons), Sørensen takes up an underlying theme also identifiable in his fiction: the contradiction between the absolute and the abstract. In doing so, he offers interpretations and evaluations as a literary, aesthetic, and social critic. The presence of opposites in the dialectical concept of man, in the conflict of myth and the critical denial of myth, and in the discrepancies of ontological versus societal determinants of man's environment define the contradictory texture of Sørensen's essays.

The irony that Sørensen does not consider himself an essayist ("I do not regard myself as anything described by a word ending in -ist. Neither philosophically nor artistically") and yet composes works which reflect the characteristics of the essay suggests not so much his refusal to identify with other authors of this genre as it does his individuality as a writer and thinker and his ambition to employ the genre consistent with his own goals. Notwithstanding, the titles of his collections of essays and the tone of the individual works seem to justify the use of the term "essay." *Hverken – eller* (1961; Neither – nor), *Uden mål – og med* (1973; With and without a goal), and *Den gyldne middelvej* (1978; The golden mean) all suggest the noncommittal attitude assumed by the essayist. Moreover, Sørensen's consciousness of the requisites of the essay are now revealed in his diaries. In contemplating the nature of the goals of *Digtere og dæmoner*, for example, Sørensen uses not only the term *essay*, but *essaysamling* (collection of essays) and *essaybog* (essay book) as well. In his struggle to create "the book," he reminded himself that a work which comprises a collection of essays must have organic cohesion.

Sørensen's readers view him in large part as an author of essays grouped around themes, reflecting the recognition of opposites. He addresses the contrasting relationships between art and democracy, natural science and psychology, as well as the interplay of power, morality, and nature. Although Sørensen's thinking is grounded in the classical tradition, at the same time it reflects his personal thoughts as well as current debate. Sørensen's concern for society's development takes the form of social criticism. He admonishes not only with respect to the welfare of Denmark ("Det indre Danmarksbillede" [Denmark from within]), but that of Europe as well ("Det faldne Europe" [Fallen Europe]).

As a writer of essays, Sørensen understands how to intimate knowledge without tiring his readers. He is free of provincialism and sees as one of his goals awakening the sensitivity of his readers to critical thinking. He does not deny the pedagogical vein of his writing; in fact, he emphasizes that irony and pedagogy have always been compatible. Moreover,

Sørensen expresses himself in an accessible manner, using humor as one of his most effective tools.

A good example of his essay style can be found in "Den frie vilje" (Free will), which appeared in the literary and cultural journal *Perspektiv* (Perspective) in 1957–58. In it he echoes **Montaigne** and **Ludvig Holberg**, employing the dialectic of gallantry to present his views as the nobleman who circumvents war by keeping his sword in the sheath. For him, the essay essentially becomes a test of strength, a proving ground; he fluctuates between argument and counterargument, examination and reexamination. As soon as he exhausts one perspective, he turns the discussion toward another. Characteristically, "Den frie vilje" contemplates man's relationship to freedom, guilt, and predestination by juxtaposing divergent means of interpretation, but offers no solution to its inherent problems.

In this and other essays, Sørensen's prose is charged by his use of puns, his attention to hidden meanings, and his fascination with paradox. His leaning toward the essay as a genre grew partly out of his need to clarify his fiction and partly out of his recognition of the crisis of his time. No longer able to identify a unifying culture in Denmark or Europe, he sought to break the silence of his generation. His criticism of contemporary society made him a dominant figure in postwar Danish culture. Inspired by **Søren Kierkegaard**, Carl Jung, and Hermann Broch among others, he found in the essay a means of questioning the materialism and rationalism of the day.

VIVIAN GREENE-GANTZBERG

Biography

Born 13 January 1929 in Frederiksberg, near Copenhagen. Studied at the Vestre Borgerdydskole, graduated 1947; philosophy at the University of Copenhagen, 1947–51, and the University of Freiburg, Baden, 1952–53. Editor, with Klaus Rifbjerg, *Vindrosen* (Wind rose), 1959–63; editor, *På Vej* (En route), 1978–81, and Gyldendal Kulturbibliotek, 1987–91. Awards: many, including the Danish Critics Prize, 1959; Danish Academy Prize, 1962; Gyldendal Prize, 1965; Nathansen Award, 1969; Holberg Medal, 1973; Brandes Prize, 1973; Steffens Prize, 1974; Nordic Council Prize, 1974; Amalienborg Prize, 1977; Hans Christian Andersen Award, 1983; Swedish Academy Nordic Prize, 1986; Poul Henningsen Prize, 1987; Wilster Prize, 1988; honorary degree from the University of Copenhagen. Member, Danish Academy.

Selected Writings

Essays and Related Prose
Digtere og dæmoner: Fortolkninger og vurderinger, 1959
Hverken – eller: Kritiske betragtninger, 1961
Uden mål – og med: Moralske tanker, 1973
Den gyldne middelvej og andre debatindlaeg fra 70'erne, 1978
Demokratiet og kunsten, 1989
Den frie vilje, 1992

Other writings: several collections of short stories and retold Nordic myths, philosophical works, and diaries. Also translated **Erasmus**, Kafka, and Hermann Broch.

Bibliography
Sønderiis, Ebbe, *Villy Sørensen: En ideologisk analyse*, Kongerslev: GMT, 1972

Further Reading

Claussen, Claus, editor, *Digtere i forhør*, Copenhagen: Gyldendal, 1966: 11–34

Petersen, Ulrich Horst, "Om (nogle af) Villy Sørensens historier," in his *Frihed og tabu: Essays*, Copenhagen: Gyldendal, 1971: 108–66

Rossel, Sven, "Villy Sørensen: Mythologist, Philosopher, Writer," *World Literature Today* 65 (1991): 41–45

Schnack, Arne, "Den sørensenke dialektik," *Vindrosen* 4 (1965)

Southey, Robert

British, 1774–1843

Robert Southey thought of himself primarily as a poet, but the bulk of his writing is prose. His "reactionary" image is only partially correct. In his youth he had been a committed radical, and as a mature man he was rather more liberal than his erstwhile friends **Coleridge** and Wordsworth. While *The Life of Nelson* (1813) is indeed a work imbued with nationalistic rhetoric and pride, and Southey's opposition to an extension of civil rights to Roman Catholics (as well as his colonialist convictions) was unabashed, it is also true that his writings of journalistic history usually send mildly reformist messages, compatible with a benevolently ironic kind of Enlightenment ideology: he opposed anti-Semitism, supported the secret ballot, and protested against the conditions of the industrial proletariat.

Southey's gravitation toward the essay can be seen even in some of his poems such as "The Battle of Blenheim" (1798) or, in a more humorous vein, "Snuff" or "The Pig" (both 1799). It comes to full fruition in *The Doctor* (1834–47), a novel in name only, but in its substance an excellent connecting link between the English **familiar essay** of the 18th century and the newer, more whimsical, and more erudite developments that had been initiated by contemporaries such as **Charles Lamb, Leigh Hunt,** and **William Hazlitt.** Written in the tradition of Sterne's *Tristram Shandy*, the text (unfinished at the time of Southey's mental decline and death) further deconstructs or even explodes any novelistic framework. The different **chapters** become conversational essays, and as digressions gain full autonomy inside the text. Southey's impressive but disorderly and subjective erudition allows him to switch nonchalantly from disquisitions on topographical etymology to comments on equitation and horse-raising, from witty associative examinations of the symbolism of the letter "D" to loud admiration for folk superstitions, lore, or obsessions. Besides these we find anecdotes, homilies, genre sketches, exercises in the whimsical and the absurd, and Southey's ambition to distill "wine into alcohol," i.e. to develop symptomatology into a substitute for grave and systematic informational intake. *The Doctor* is a work in which a kind of philosophy of detail is worked out by concrete illustration; the book turns into an encyclopedia of the essay, bringing under one roof the different kinds of texts that had been the object of experimentation by other Romantics. There are also intriguing signs that (despite his patriarchal ideology) Southey was trying to approach by indirection a kind of feminine discourse (a fact to which he himself alludes several times) stripped of logocentric impositions.

More conventionally essayistic writings are those in which, by the late 1820s and early 1830s, Southey gives expression to his vision of a "traditional" England, a pre-capitalist and pre-modern, Horatian construct: a harmonious, modestly self-satisfied environment in which contact with nature could be preserved at all times, with the admission of slow and carefully selected movements toward progress. It is surprising how many of the key themes of Victorian England in general (and of Disraeli's "progressive conservatism" in particular) are clearly outlined in Southey's sociopolitical essays.

At the opposite end of the essayist spectrum is the short, dry notation of odd facts (*Omniana*, 1812; *Common-Place Book*, posthumously pub. 1849–51). Southey is overwhelmed by and enthusiastic about the explosive expansion of knowledge in history, geography, the natural sciences, and the humanities that occurred at the turn of the century. He plunges deep into this sea of knowledge, coming up with various objects and episodes which he holds up to attention. These are expected to have an eloquence of their own, so that readers can draw their own conclusions. The rhetoric of strange facts also becomes a kind of subjective alternative to the vast ordering and disciplinary systems emerging in Southey's time.

A consistently anti-canonical streak in Southey's intellectual make-up also connected him with essayistic attitudes. He turned happily toward the margins of Europe and the West (Portugal, Brazil, Wales), chose Indian and Arabic themes for some of his main epic poems, and lauded (with a puzzled smile) the "uneducated," trivial, and "low-class" poets: "water-poets," "old servants," men and women alike.

For all such preferences of taste, temperament, and ideology, it is obvious that a generic vehicle of ambiguity and multiple meanings, unsuited to definitive statements, was a sheer necessity for Southey. The continuing scholarly indifference to and public ignorance of him is strange, regrettable, and unjustified.

VIRGIL NEMOIANU

Biography

Born 12 August 1774 in Bristol. Studied at Westminster School, London, 1788–92: expelled for publishing a **satire** on corporal punishment in the school paper; Balliol College, Oxford, 1793–94, where he met and became friends with Samuel Taylor Coleridge; also studied law, 1797. Married Edith Fricker, 1795 (died, 1837): one daughter (another died in infancy) and one son. Lived in Portugal, 1795–96 and 1800–01, and at Westbury, near Bristol, 1798–99. Began writing **reviews,** from 1796, for journals including the *Monthly Magazine, Morning Post, Critical Review, Annual Review,* and **Quarterly Review.** Settled near William Wordsworth at Greta Hall, Keswick, 1803. Formed with Wordsworth and Coleridge the so-called "Lake School," the most structured expression of early English Romanticism. Poet Laureate, 1813–43. Received a government pension, 1835. Married Caroline Ann Bowles, 1838. Died (of a stroke) at Greta Hall, 21 March 1843.

Selected Writings

Essays and Related Prose

Letters Written During a Short Residence in Spain and Portugal, 1797; revised edition, 1799; revised edition, as *Letters Written During a Journey in Spain, and a Short Residence in Portugal,* 2 vols., 1808

Letters from England: By Don Manuel Alvarez Espriella, 2 vols., 1807

Omniana, or Horae Otiosiores, with Samuel Taylor Coleridge, 2 vols., 1812; edited by Robert Gittings, 1969

Vindiciae Ecclesiae Anglicanae: Letters to Charles Butler, Comprising Essays on the Romish Religion and Vindicating the Book of the Church, 1826

Sir Thomas More; or, Colloquies on the Progress and Prospects of Society, 2 vols., 1829–31

Essays, Moral and Political, 2 vols., 1832

Selections from the Prose Works, edited by I. Moxon, 1832; as *The Beauties of the Prose Works*, 1833

The Doctor, 7 vols., 1834–47 (vols. 6 and 7 edited by John Wood Warter)

Common-Place Book, edited by John Wood Warter, 4 vols., 1849–51

Select Prose, edited by Jacob Zeitlin, 1916

The Contributions of Robert Southey to the Morning Post, edited by Kenneth Curry, 1984

Other writings: poetry (including the long epic poems *Thalaba the Destroyer*, 1801; *The Curse of Kehama*, 1810; *Roderick, the Last of the Goths*, 1814), two plays, works of history, biographies of Nelson (1813), Wesley (1820), and Cowper (1835), journals, and much correspondence.

Bibliography

Curry, Kenneth, *Robert Southey: A Reference Guide*, Boston: Hall, 1977

Further Reading

Bernhardt-Kabish, Ernest, *Robert Southey*, Boston: Twayne, 1977

Curry, Kenneth, *Southey*, London and Boston: Routledge and Kegan Paul, 1975

Dowden, Edward, *Southey*, New York: Harper, 1980 (original edition, 1879)

Simmons, Jack, *Southey*, London: Collins, 1945; New Haven, Connecticut: Yale University Press, 1948

Raimond, Jean, *Robert Southey: L'Homme et son temps, l'œuvre, le rôle*, Paris: Didier, 1968

Sovremennik

Russian journal, 1836–1866

Founded by the poet **Aleksandr Pushkin** in 1836, *Sovremennik* (The contemporary) became one of the most successful and influential liberal journals of 19th-century Russia. Like the other so-called "thick journals" of the period, *Sovremennik* appealed to an increasingly broad readership by offering a mixture of contents, ranging from political essays to literary reviews and essays, to works of poetry and imaginative prose. Its political slant was always of a liberal, "Westernizing" tendency – that is, it advocated adapting to Russian society Western intellectual currents and the basic position of Western reform movements – but after 1856, when the radical critic **Nikolai Chernyshevskii** assumed the primary duties as editor, *Sovremennik* became the vehicle for political writings of the extreme socialist left.

Sovremennik went through three major phases in its 30-year career. The first of these, from 1836 to 1846, was its least successful, as the journal lost circulation and influence due to a combination of ineffective editorship and oppressive literary censorship. Although Pushkin had conceived of *Sovremennik*

as a liberal political literary journal, he died after the journal's first year, having produced only four issues. After his death and the political scandal surrounding it the journal became even more subject to scrutiny by the censorship department of Tsar Nicholas I. The editorship passed to the hands of Piotr Pletnev, Pushkin's good friend and a professor of literature at the University of St. Petersburg. Under Pletnev *Sovremennik* became a strictly literary journal containing memoirs, short stories, and lyric poetry. Although by publishing some of these texts in *Sovremennik* – particularly the works of Nikolai Gogol' and of the poet Fedor Tiutchev, as well as the posthumous works of Pushkin – Pletnev was performing an important service for the Russian reading public, on the whole he and his editors were offering fare not to the taste of Russian readers, who had outgrown (as they thought) lyric poetry and demanded instead greater realism from their writers. In 1846 Pletnev sold the journal to Nikolai Nekrasov and Ivan Ivanovich Panaev, under whose editorship *Sovremennik* became the most influential liberal journal in Russia.

Nekrasov's acquisition of *Sovremennik* (Panaev's contribution was essentially financial) launched the journal's second period of ever-increasing influence and financial success, which lasted from 1847 to 1855. The first issue under Nekrasov (January 1847) contained contributions by the best-known names of Russian literature in the 19th century: poetry by Nekrasov, prose by **Ivan Turgenev** and **Fedor Dostoevskii**, political writings of **Aleksandr Herzen**, and literary criticism by **Vissarion Belinskii**. Subsequent issues would contain early works of such writers as **Lev Tolstoi** and Ivan Goncharov; almost every significant figure in Russian literature of this period appeared on the pages of *Sovremennik* under Nekrasov's editorship.

The tone of *Sovremennik* in these years was heavily influenced by the legacy of Belinskii, the leading social and literary critic of the 1840s. Indeed, Belinskii had been involved in Nekrasov and Panaev's original plans to take over Pletnev's dwindling *Sovremennik* as a move to undermine, or at least to counterbalance, the influence of the primary Westernizer journal, *Otechestvennye Zapiski* (Fatherland notes): Belinskii had been its editor and main contributor, yet by 1846 he wished to break from it and establish a rival journal. Before his death in 1848 Belinskii published in *Sovremennik* two important articles surveying Russian literature in the years 1846 and 1847.

Despite the participation of Russia's foremost writers and liberal-minded thinkers, the material published in *Sovremennik* was severely restricted by the censorship committee until the death of Tsar Nicholas I in 1855. The role of official censorship in tsarist Russia – no less than in the Soviet Union – cannot be underestimated. After the revolutionary movements that swept Europe in 1848, censorship in Russia interfered with all publications to an even greater extent than before. As a result, the editors of *Sovremennik* had to be satisfied with publishing mild social criticism as it appeared in works of fiction; the most talented author of this type of writing was Turgenev (whose *Zapiski okhotnika* [1852; *A Sportsman's Notebook*] and other short fiction were published in *Sovremennik* in their entirety), although the works of the young Dostoevskii and the translated works of **Charles Dickens** also served this purpose.

After Nicholas' death and the ascension to the throne of his more liberal-minded son, the "Reformer-Tsar" Alexander II, censorship in Russia enjoyed a respite, albeit a brief one. With Alexander's reign the third phase of *Sovremennik*'s activity began, characterized by the radical socialist politics of its primary editors and contributors, Chernyshevskii and Nikolai Dobroliubov. Nekrasov was still the editor-in-chief of the journal, and indeed remained so until it was shut down in 1866; however, after 1856 he increasingly entrusted the editorial duties to his young protégé, Chernyshevskii, whose willingness and ability to work full-time for the journal had greatly impressed the older man as much as his critical abilities.

With Chernyshevskii's editorship the tone of *Sovremennik* changed tremendously. A particularly prevalent social issue which was aired in the journal's pages was that of Russian serfdom. On the eve of the emancipation of the serfs, Chernyshevskii, Dobroliubov, and their followers refused to support the Tsar's reform efforts and persistently published articles comparing serfdom in Russia to slavery in the United States; it is significant in this regard that the first Russian translation of Harriet Beecher Stowe's abolitionist novel *Uncle Tom's Cabin* appeared in the 1857 issues of *Sovremennik*. Typically, when the Emancipation Decree was finally passed in 1861 there was no mention of it at all in *Sovremennik*: Nekrasov as well as Chernyshevskii and Dobroliubov realized that the Tsar and his ministers had done the minimum they thought possible, and that it was the landowners and not the peasants who benefited from the "reform."

Although a large part of the journal was still devoted to *belles-lettres*, the literature of this period had a strong and undisguised dimension of social and political criticism, earning the label "literature of accusation" (*oblichitel'naia literatura*). Although the more moderate liberal writers such as Turgenev and Lev Tolstoi continued to publish in its pages, clashes over politics became increasingly frequent. In 1858 a final break occurred between the liberals and radicals. Although as a result of this conflict *Sovremennik* lost many of its most celebrated contributors, its profits increased tremendously as the Russian reading public proved eager to read about the issues addressed in this newly radical journal. Turgenev's novel *Nakanune* (1860; *On the Eve*) was published in *Sovremennik*, yet the critical review of it by Dobroliubov, a dogmatic article entitled "Kogda zhe pridet nastoiashchii den'?" (1860; "When Will the Real Day Come?"), which has since become a classic of Russian revolutionary writing, so alarmed Turgenev that he attempted to have it withdrawn. When Chernyshevskii published the review anyway, which deliberately misinterpreted Turgenev's novel in order to cast a more revolutionary reading on it, Turgenev broke with the editors of *Sovremennik* for good.

Thanks to the radical politics of their contributions, Chernyshevskii and Dobroliubov's *Sovremennik* suffered increasing pressure from the censor. In 1862 it was shut down for eight months when Chernyshevskii was arrested for inciting student and peasant disturbances. Finally in 1866, after its editors printed Chernyshevskii's revolutionary novel *Chto delat'?* (1863; *What Is to Be Done?*), which he wrote in prison, *Sovremennik* was closed down.

The significance of *Sovremennik* for 19th-century Russian literature and social thought cannot be overstressed. In its 30 years of circulation the major liberal debates and ideas – not to mention some of the most important works of Russian literature – were aired in its pages. The well-known historical division of intellectual "fathers and sons" (made famous in Turgenev's novel of that name) is best documented by reading *Sovremennik*: this is the break of the "men of the sixties" (Chernyshevskii, Dobroliubov, and their followers) from the "men of the forties" (Belinskii, Herzen, and others), whose aesthetic liberalism was not to the taste of the more practical-minded younger generation. Among the most important essays in Russian thought and criticism that appeared for the first time in *Sovremennik* are Belinskii's above-mentioned "surveys" of Russian literature. These two articles both supported *Sovremennik*'s political agenda by stressing the social significance of works of Russian literature, and alarmed the liberal editors by criticizing the "humanist" ideas of Russian Westernizers and insisting on a unique Russian national identity (P. V. Annenkov, 1968). In 1860 "Gamlet i Don Kixot" ("Hamlet and Don Quixote"), Turgenev's celebrated characterization of Russian literary heroes, appeared. It quickly became a classic **treatise** on the Russian character. In it Turgenev identifies two primary "types" of hero in Russian literature: the "Hamlet" type, or intellectual, who thinks and reasons but is incapable of action, and the "Don Quixote" type, a dreamer, who alone is capable of effective action, however foolish he at times appears. In *Sovremennik*'s final years the most important critical reviews to appear were by Dobroliubov, particularly his reading of Turgenev's novel, "When Will the Real Day Come?," and his classic characterization of the "illness" of the Russian intelligentsia, "Chto takoe Oblomovshchina?" (1859; "What Is Oblomovitis?").

CATHERINE O'NEIL

Further Reading

Annenkov, P. V., *The Extraordinary Decade: Literary Memoirs*, edited by Arthur P. Mendel, Ann Arbor: University of Michigan Press, 1968

Berlin, Isaiah, *The Russian Thinkers*, edited by Henry Hardy and Aileen Kelly, London: Hogarth Press, and New York: Viking Press, 1978

Birkenmayer, Sigmund S., *Nikolaj Nekrasov: His Life and Poetic Art*, The Hague and Paris: Mouton, 1968

Corbet, Charles, *Nekrasov, l'homme et le poète*, Paris: Institut d'Études Slaves, 1948

Granjard, Henri, *Ivan Tourguenev et les courants politiques et sociaux de son temps*, Paris: Institut d'Études Slaves, 1954

Hare, Richard, *Pioneers of Russian Social Thought*, London: Oxford University Press, 1951

Harper, Kenneth E., "Criticism of the Natural School in the 1840's," *American Slavic and East European Review* 15 (1956): 400–14

Herzen, Alexander, *My Past and Thoughts*, Berkeley: University of California Press, 1982 (original translation, 1973)

Lampert, Evgeny, *Sons Against Fathers: Studies in Russian Radicalism and Revolution*, Oxford: Clarendon Press, 1965

Nikitenko, Aleksandr, *The Diary of a Russian Censor*, abridged, edited, and translated by Helen Saltz Jacobson, Amherst: University of Massachusetts Press, 1975 (original Russian edition, 1893)

Svyatopolk-Mirsky, Dmitry Petrovich, *A History of Russian Literature*, edited by Francis J. Whitfield, London: Routledge and Kegan Paul, 1949; New York: Knopf, 1964 (original edition, 1926–27)

Venturi, Franco, *Roots of Revolution: A History of the Populist and Socialist Movements in Nineteenth Century Russia*, London: Weidenfeld and Nicolson, 1960

Woehrlin, William F., *Chernyshevskii: The Man and the Journalist*, Cambridge, Massachusetts: Harvard University Press, 1971

Soyinka, Wole

Nigerian, 1934–

Though best known as a playwright, 1986 Nobel laureate Wole Soyinka has also written numerous volumes of fiction, autobiography, and poetry, as well as over a thousand pages of dense, often difficult literary and cultural criticism. The majority of his essays are widely scattered throughout numerous small journals and obscure newspapers, and so can be difficult to locate. As a result, his best-known and most influential essays are those which are available in three volumes of collected essays: *Myth, Literature and the African World* (1976) and *Art, Dialogue and Outrage: Essays on Literature and Culture* (1988) bring together a number of his most important essays on literary criticism and aesthetic theory, while more recently *The Open Sore of a Continent* (1996) puts together in book form a series of Soyinka's public lectures which examine the present political crisis in Nigeria.

Obi Maduakor (1986) has commented that "Soyinka's literary essays are, to some extent, one large essay. His critical prejudices were formed quite early in his career, and both the early and later essays are crisscrossed by related threads of thought." This is due as much to Soyinka's persistence in examining and re-examining a limited set of issues and concerns, as to the way in which his essays are produced: almost all of them were originally written for lectures or conferences, and older essays are frequently "cannibalized" and used in the writing of newer ones. Hence ideas and phrases often recur in several essays; it is difficult to locate a "master-text" on any given issue that Soyinka discusses. Instead, reference must be made to a series of essays which, for all of their surface similarities, involve surprising about-faces and seemingly contradictory changes of position – inversions which Biodun Jeyifo (1988) attributes to Soyinka's deliberate attempt "almost" to bring about aporias in his writing.

The majority of Soyinka's essays, like those of **Chinua Achebe**, attempt to establish and argue for a certain vision of the possibilities of African literature. The polemical, passionate, explosive, and oppositional style of his writing has placed him at the center of a number of controversies over the form and function of African writing. Famously, he has been cast in the role of the most outspoken critic of *négritude*, a position most closely associated with the work of Senegalese writer (and past President) Léopold Senghor and the *bolekaja* ("come down and fight") critics associated with Chinweizu. In essays such as "The Future of African Writing" (1960), "From a Common Back Cloth" (1963), "Neo-Tarzanism: The Poetics of Pseudo-Tradition" (1975), and the final section of *Myth, Literature and the African World*, Soyinka's case against *négritude* emerges. He is critical of both its philosophical and its aesthetic failings. Philosophically, he believes that "*négritude*'s reference points took far too much coloring from European ideas even

while its messiahs pronounced themselves fanatically African" (*Myth*). Instead of developing a genuinely African ontology, Soyinka sees *négritude* as simply affirming one of the central Eurocentric prejudices against Africans: Europeans are rational and intellectual, while Africans are emotive and intuitive. Aesthetically, *négritude* encourages "a mounting narcissism which involved contemplation of the contrived self in the supposed tragic grandeur of the cultural dilemma" (*Myth*). Soyinka discusses this failing of *négritude* in detail in "And After the Narcissist?" (1966), in which he accuses Senghor of a self-absorption which negates the kind of social action which African literature should ideally promote. For Soyinka, it is only when African fiction achieves a level of "indifferent self-acceptance," as it does for him in the fiction of Achebe, that African literature becomes "authentic" – no longer, as Soyinka famously says, a "tiger" interested only in its "tigritude," but a literature able to deal effectively with all aspects of contemporary African reality.

Soyinka's criticism of *négritude* is in danger of seeming both unfair and overly dismissive unless it is understood in the context of his more general positions on writing and literature. His attack on *négritude* is analogous to the criticisms he has launched against the other favorite target of his ripostes – Marxist literary criticism. In "Who's Afraid of Elesin Oba?" (1977) and "The Critic and Society" (1980), he makes his distaste for the artificial imposition of any ideology on literature – whether in the form of *négritude*'s invocation of a past African pastoral idyll or the Marxist promise of an African utopia to come – abundantly clear. For Soyinka, "the practical effects of literary ideology on the creative process lead to predictability, imaginative constraint and thematic excisions" because literature consists of the "essentially fluid operations of the creative mind upon social and natural phenomena" (*Myth*). The constraint of having to produce literature within a predetermined ideological system leads to bad, useless, and irrelevant writing which inaccurately represents the conditions and problems of modern African culture. He argues repeatedly for the autonomy of the writer – an autonomy that does not exclude the social relevance of the writer so much as it insures his or her honest reflection of social experience.

Soyinka's major achievement is perhaps to be found in the collection of interrelated essays entitled *Myth, Literature and the African World*. In "The Fourth Stage: Through the Mysteries of Ogun to the Origin of Yoruba Tragedy" (originally pub. 1973), he outlines a theory of tragedy uniquely rooted in African representations of experience and reality; this theory, combined with the other essays in *Myth*, becomes the basis of an entire mythopoeic aesthetics unique in African literature. His aesthetic theory, which takes its inspiration both from Yoruba mythology (most importantly, the gods Ogun, Sango, and Obatala) and from a confrontation with **Friedrich Nietzsche**'s *Die Geburt der Tragödie* (1872; *The Birth of Tragedy*), is notoriously complex and detailed, and resists any simple summary. By comparing the nature of Yoruba tragedy with European models of tragedy and the very different role of hubris in the story of the Yoruba gods, Soyinka produces a theory of tragedy which is anti-mimetic and anti-realistic, and finds its power and symbolic depth in ritual and myth. The significance of the "fourth stage," the transitional passage between being and non-being, human and non-human, life and death, is that it is here that Ogun sacrifices his being, and tragedy arises. It is useful to consider Soyinka's own plays through the aesthetics he proposes here; and in general, all of his essays may be seen as in some way offering commentaries and assessments of his own vast literary production.

IMRE SZEMAN

Biography

Born Akinwande Oluwole Soyinka, 13 July 1934 in Abeokuta. Studied at the Government College, Ibadan, 1946–50; University College, Ibadan, 1952–54; University of Leeds, Yorkshire, 1954–57, B.A. in English. Married: several children. Worked for the Royal Court Theatre, London, 1957–59; founding director, Masks Theatre, Lagos, 1960, and Orisun Theatre, Ibadan, 1964; research fellow in drama, University of Ibadan, 1961–62; lecturer in English, University of Ife, 1963–64, and senior lecturer in English, University of Lagos, 1965–67. Coeditor, *Black Orpheus*, 1964. Imprisoned for political reasons by the Federal Military Government, Lagos and Kaduna, 1967–69. Artistic director and head of the Department of Theatre Arts, University of Ibadan, 1969–72; fellow, Churchill College, Cambridge, 1973–74, visiting professor, University of Ghana, Legon, 1973–74, University of Sheffield, 1974, Yale University, New Haven, Connecticut, 1979–80, and Cornell University, Ithaca, New York, 1986; professor of comparative literature and head of the Department of Dramatic Arts, University of Ife, 1975–85. Editor, *Transition* (later *Ch'indaba*) magazine, Accra, Ghana, 1975–77. Nigerian passport seized, 1994: began living in France. Accused of treason by the Nigerian government, 1997. Awards: many, including the John Whiting Award, 1967; Nobel Prize for Literature, 1986; Benson Medal, 1990; Mondello Prize, 1990; honorary degrees from seven universities and colleges. Fellow, Royal Society of Literature; Member, American Academy of Arts and Letters, and the Academy of Arts and Letters of the German Democratic Republic; Commander, Federal Republic of Nigeria, 1986, Legion of Honor (France), 1989, and the Order of Merit (Italy), 1990; Akogun of Isara, 1989; Akinlatun of Egbaland, 1990.

Selected Writings

Essays and Related Prose
Myth, Literature and the African World, 1976
The Critic and Society, 1982
This Past Must Address Its Present (Nobel lecture), 1986
Art, Dialogue and Outrage: Essays on Literature and Culture, 1988; revised, enlarged edition, 1993
The Open Sore of a Continent: A Personal Narrative of the Nigerian Crisis, 1996

Other writings: many plays (including *The Road*, 1965; *Madmen and Specialists*, 1970; *Death and the King's Horseman*, 1975), radio plays, two novels (*The Interpreters*, 1965; *Season of Anomy*, 1973), poetry, the prison diary *The Man Died* (1972), and memoirs.

Bibliographies

Gibbs, James, Ketu H. Katrak, and Henry Louis Gates, Jr., *Wole Soyinka: A Bibliography of Primary and Secondary Sources*, Westport, Connecticut: Greenwood Press, 1986
Okpu, B., *Wole Soyinka: A Bibliography*, Lagos: Libriservice, 1984

Further Reading

Adelugba, Dapo, *Before Our Very Eyes: Tribute to Wole Soyinka*, Ibadan: Spectrum, 1987
Appiah, Anthony Kwame, "Myth, Literature and the African World," in *Wole Soyinka: An Appraisal*, edited by Adewale Maja-Pearce, Oxford and Portsmouth, New Hampshire: Heinemann, 1994
Black American Literature Forum issue on Soyinka, edited by Henry Louis Gates, Jr., 22, no. 3 (Fall 1988)
Booth, James, *Writers and Politics in Nigeria*, London: Hodder and Stoughton, 1981
Chinweizu, Onwuchekwa Jemie, and Ihechukwu Madubuike, *Toward the Decolonization of African Literature*, Enugu: Fourth Dimension, 1980; Washington, D.C.: Howard University Press, 1983; London: KPI, 1985
Crow, Brian, "Soyinka and His Radical Critics: A Review," *Theatre Research International* 12, no. 1 (Spring 1987): 61–73
Gibbs, James, editor, *Critical Perspectives on Wole Soyinka*, Washington, D.C.: Three Continents Press, 1980; London: Heinemann, 1981
Gibbs, James, *Wole Soyinka*, Basingstoke: Macmillan, 1986
Irele, Abiola, *The African Experience in Literature and Ideology*, London: Heinemann, 1981
Jeyifo, Biodun, "Wole Soyinka: A *Transition* Interview," *Transition* 42 (1973): 62–64
Jeyifo, Biodun, *The Truthful Lie: Essays in a Sociology of African Drama*, London: New Beacon, 1985
Jeyifo, Biodun, "Introduction: Wole Soyinka and the Tropes of Disalienation," in *Art, Dialogue and Outrage* by Soyinka, Ibadan: New Horn Press, and New York: Pantheon, 1988: ix–xxix
Jones, Eldred Durosimi, *The Writing of Wole Soyinka*, London: Heinemann, revised edition, 1983 (original edition, 1973)
Literary Half-Yearly issue on Soyinka, edited by James Gibbs, 28, no. 2 (July 1987)
Maduakor, Obi, *Wole Soyinka: An Introduction to His Writing*, New York: Garland, 1986
Moore, Gerald, *Wole Soyinka*, London: Evans, 1978 (original edition, 1971)
Research in African Literatures issue on Soyinka, edited by James Gibbs, 14, no. 1 (Spring 1983)
Senghor, Léopold Sédar, "*Négritude*: A Humanism of the Twentieth Century," in *The Africa Reader: Independent Africa*, edited by Wilfred Cartey and Martin Kilson, New York: Random House, 1970
Wright, Derek, *Wole Soyinka Revisited*, New York: Twayne, 1993

Spanish Essay

Strict criteria based on the Montaignean model yield scant results if they are used in a search for essays through the corpus of Spanish literature. Since 711 Spain has been the Western frontier between the two great branches of Western civilization, Christendom and Islam. The intellectual consequence may be intuited in Lotario's admonition to Anselmo in *Don Quixote* (Part I, Ch. 33): "It seems to me, Anselmo, that thine is just now the temper of mind which is always that of the Moors, who can never be brought to the error of their creed by quotations from the Holy Scriptures, or by reasons which depend upon the examination of the understanding or are founded upon the articles of faith, but must have examples that are palpable, easy, intelligible, capable of proof, not admitting of doubt, with mathematical demonstrations that cannot be denied, like, '*If equals be taken from equals, the remainders are equal*'." Cervantes depicts the Muslim mind as having progressed no further than the third Common Notion of Euclid's *Elements of Geometry*, whereas the Christian engages in intellectual speculation. Hence the former has remained stuck in Euclidean space whereas the latter can ponder the indivisibility of infinity because he has been indoctrinated in the Athanasian Creed, which posits that the Father, Son, and Holy Ghost are uncreated, illimitable, and eternal and yet there are not three, but only one uncreated, illimitable, and eternal.

We now know that the Moors never went beyond their invention, *al-jabr* (algebra), and fell into intellectual oblivion while the Christians developed what Oswald Spengler calls the Faustian mathematics of capitalism, as well as, of course, the essay, a creation of secularized Christendom (also known as Western Civilization). But Cervantes was more broad-minded than his nation's rulers. Scientific advances were reserved for the rest of Europe whereas in Spain people were denounced to the Inquisition for being mathematicians. Saint Teresa (1515–82), whose *El castillo interior, o Tratado de las moradas* (1588; Interior Castle) is deemed by José Luis Gómez-Martínez (1981) to be a model of the spiritual essay, writes in the penultimate chapter of her autobiography: "While reciting the psalm 'Quicumque vult' [i.e. the Athanasian Creed] I was given to understand the manner in which there were one God and three persons, so clearly, that I was awed and greatly consoled. It benefited me greatly in understanding the greatness of God and his wonders, and when I think of the Holy Trinity or when it comes up, it seems that I understand how it can be, and it brings me much contentment." In Spain, then, engaging in *especulación del entendimiento* (examination of the understanding) with respect to the indivisibility of infinity appears limited to mystical experience; intellectual speculation in general posed considerable danger.

Owing to this danger, the Spanish mind is usually too cautious to divagate publicly. When a reforming elite acquires power, as during the 18th-century Enlightenment, the consciousness of its role induces it to keep its distance. (An exception to this habit occurs when the intellectual elite is marginalized, as were the early Liberals and the Generation of 1898.) The Spaniard presents a courteous exterior but his interior is hermetically sealed, so that digression and wearing one's heart on one's sleeve, important Montaignean criteria, are rare in Spanish literature. Yet the elegance, wit, and subtlety found in Spain's nonfictional prose more than compensate for this reticence.

When the danger seemed to dissipate, personal opinions were revealed in a manner untypical of Montaignean equanimity. Thus, the great novelist Pío Baroja (1872–1956), addressing his fellow Basques in his collection of essays entitled *Las horas solitarias* (1918; The solitary hours), judges the mentality of his compatriots in his usual caustic manner: "When one sees a Moor holding one book containing the whole truth, one understands that his race will never produce a Kant or a Newton. The majority of Spaniards, and almost all Basques, are Moors who, instead of carrying the Koran, bear in their spirit the doctrine of Father Astete." The Jesuit Gaspar Astete's (1537–1601) *Doctrina Cristiana* (1599; Christian doctrine) was one of the most widely translated and enduring Spanish works of all time.

It is appropriate, then, to broaden the concept of the essay by speaking of subgenres in which we find works that possess specific literary qualities: mystical essays, biographical essays, **satiric essays**, political, literary, social, journalistic, and philosophical essays. Even though the purist may categorize some as **treatises** and others as newpaper articles, they truly possess artistic quality. Moreover, the masterpieces of Spanish literature are often in hybrid genres.

Because it is the only subgenre offering real continuity for several centuries, the feminist essay merits consideration apart from the chronological arrangement used for the rest of the genre. We can begin with the seven "Prohemios" (Proems) placed by Álvaro de Luna (1388?–1453) at the head of his *Libro de las claras y virtuosas mujeres* (1446; Book of famous and virtuous women), dedicated to the queen. Its author, who seems to have been in correspondence with Joan of Arc, states that women should be allowed to do battle if they wish, and argues that woman is not more responsible than man for the Fall. Another important 15th-century work in this vein is the *Triunfo de las donas* (Triumph of the ladies) by Juan Rodríguez de la Cámara (c. 1390–c. 1450) who, among other topics, argues that it is woman who evinces the superiority of humankind to the animals because, unlike their females, she looks heavenward during coitus. Not until the early 18th century, however, do we find a truly modern feminist treatise, *Defensa de la mujer* (Defense of woman), by the most famous of all Spanish essayists, the Benedictine monk **Benito Jerónimo Feijóo y Montenegro** (1676–1764). **Josefa Amar y Borbón** (1749–1833) was the first Spanish woman to write feminist essays. The 19th century brings us *La mujer* (1860; The woman), a book of feminist articles by the Cuban-born poet Gertrudis Gómez de Avellaneda (1814–73), a book and an article by Concepción Sáiz (1850–?), and Concepción Arenal's (1820–93) *La mujer del porvenir* (1868; The woman of the future), which antedates by one year **John Stuart Mill**'s *The Subjection of Women*. Because her father spent most of his life as a political prisoner, Arenal was brought up completely by women. In the first edition of her book she argues for the ordination of women to the priesthood and civil rights for the fair sex, though not political rights, fearful that it would double the number of assassinations and thus leave children totally rather than half-orphaned. After being informed of the peaceful results of female suffrage in parts of the United States, she changed her position on this point. Arenal was followed as leader of the feminist movement by the great novelist Countess **Emilia Pardo Bazán** (1851–1921), who, as a faithful Catholic, opposed feminine ordination, and, as a fairly conservative monarchist, opposed universal male suffrage as well because the latter would theoretically allow all males to subjugate all females. In truth, it did not bother her to have the political privileges of the moneyed classes maintained. A dozen years after her death the liberals finally agreed to enfranchise women who then, influenced by the priests, voted them out of power. The most outstanding feminist essayists of the 20th century are María de Maeztu y Whitney (1882–1948) and Carmen Díaz de Mendoza, Countess of San Luis (?–1929).

Antecedents of the essay appear early, as Spain was the first land in Europe to replace Latin with the vernacular in expository prose, partly in order to accommodate Jewish translators of Arabic books. King Alfonso the Learned (1221–84) encouraged the enrichment of Castilian in order to make it suitable for the many important treatises whose redaction he supervised. Oriental literature translated from Arabic sources under his aegis influenced his nephew, Don Juan Manuel

(1282–1349?), whose treatises on the education of princes, *Libro de los estados* (wr. c. 1330; Book of estates), and on the meaning of life, *Balaam y Josafat*, exhibit a tolerant pragmatism anticipating the humanist basis of the essay. In the kingdom of Aragon, Ramon Llull (i.e. Raymond Lully, 1232–1315) and Francesch Eximenis (1340–1409), the medieval precursors of the mystic essay, wrote in Catalan.

The biographical essay was initiated in the 15th century with *Generaciones y semblanzas* (Generations and portraits) by Fernán Pérez de Guzmán (1376–1460) and *Claros varones de Castilla* (1486; Famous men of Castile) by Hernando del Pulgar (1436–93). These pithy sketches of the outstanding figures of the 15th century display unusual expressiveness in manifesting the authors' psychological intuition, for example, in Pérez de Guzmán's depiction of his uncle, the statesman, diplomat, and scholar Pero López de Ayala (1332–1407) who, as a historiographer, is comparable to his model, Livy. Of great interest likewise are his sketches of three bishops, the first of noble blood, the second of peasant stock, and the third, Pablo de Santa María, Bishop of Burgos, a converted Jew who had been Grand Rabbi of that city. His son (born before his conversion) Alonso de Cartagena (1384–1456), also bishop of Burgos like his father, authored the *Respuesta al Marqués de Santillana* (1444; Reply to the Marquise of Santillana), considered by Juan Marichal (1957) to be the first essay written in Castilian.

Two famous Renaissance thinkers who left Spain wrote their treatises in Latin. Juan Luis Vives (1492–1540) held important posts in England but, as a faithful Catholic, left because of his opposition to Henry VIII's divorce; his *De subventione pauperum* (1526; *Concerning the Relief of the Poor*) supposedly marks the beginning of the so-called Protestant ethic. Miguel Servet (1511–53), a forerunner of William Harvey in researching the circulation of the blood, authored *De Trinitatis erroribus* (1531; *On the Errors of the Trinity*), which eventually led to his burning at the stake in Geneva by Calvin and to his esteem among Unitarians. The writings of Erasmists like the Valdés brothers, Alfonso (1490–1532) and Juan (1501?–41), Pedro Mexía (1497–1551), Cristóbal de Villalón (c. 1505–58), and Antonio de Torquemada (fl. 1553–70) cannot really be called essays, but they strongly influenced the genre, and some of them were translated into English in their day. Closer to the genre are works by Antonio de Guevara (1480?–1545), whose *Reloj de príncipes* (1529; *The Dial of Princes*) was widely translated. Its most appreciated item is "El villano del Danubio" ("The Peasant of the Danube"), a fictional appeal to a Roman emperor, a veiled allegory, in **Américo Castro**'s opinion, of the manner in which the Indians were being treated by the Spaniards. The antithetical rhetoric of Guevara distances his work from the essay genre, especially in *Menosprecio de corte y alabanza de aldea* (1539; Scorn for the city and praise for the country), which has not been translated into English, although another work was passed off on the British public with this title and authorship. If we admit that the pseudo-epistolary genre is a variant of the essay, then his *Epístolas familiares* (1539–41; *Golden Epistles*), many of which likewise have not been translated, are essays in the most humanistic sense of the word. It may puzzle the contemporary mind to learn that Guevara was, among other things, an Inquisitor, one of the many honors bestowed upon him which he could hardly turn down. Yet we must remember that what

characterizes Spanish Renaissance thought is the attempt to Christianize humanism, as evidenced in the didactic prose of Fray Luis de Granada (1504–88), a precursor of Saint Teresa and Fray Luis de León (1527–91).

The baroque period provides us with an anti-Machiavellian treatise, *Política de Dios y gobierno de Cristo* (wr. 1617, pub. 1626; Politics of God and government of Christ), by the great poet and picaresque novelist Quevedo (1580–1645), and his ascetic treatise, *La cuna y la sepultura* (1635; The cradle and the grave). Quevedo's writing is always cited as a model of *conceptismo* (style laden with figures of thought), as opposed to the *culteranismo* (style laden with rhetorical figures) of the poet Luis de Góngora y Argote (1561–1627). In this respect the Jesuit **Baltasar Gracián** (1601–58) is a follower of Quevedo. His *Criticón* (1651–57; *The Critick*) may be deemed a hybrid of novel and essay, but other works, such as *El héroe* (1637; *The Hero*), *El político D. Fernando el Católico* (1640; The politician Fernand the Catholic), and *El discreto* (1646; The discreet man, translated as *The Complet Gentleman*) fall more closely within the essay genre.

The advent of the Bourbons in the 18th century brought about a long-needed process of renovation and modernization to lift the country from Habsburg decadence. At the beginning of the Spanish Enlightenment the genre was dominated by Feijóo, although some of the writings of **Diego de Torres Villarroel** (c. 1694–1770) can be considered **satiric essays**. In the second half we find the incorruptible statesman **Gaspar Melchor de Jovellanos** (1744–1811), some of whose best work was composed during his political imprisonment. The first person is sparingly used in the expository prose of the Age of Reason, but personal revelation emerges at times in the work of the pre-Romantic **José Cadalso** (1741–82). His *Cartas marruecas* (wr. 1789, pub. 1793; Moroccan letters), inspired formally by Montesquieu's *Lettres Persanes* (1730; *Persian Letters*) but ideologically by **Oliver Goldsmith**'s *The Citizen of the World* (1762), is a hybrid of essay and epistolary novel, with three correspondents rather than Montesquieu's two, and traditional enemies rather than inhabitants of a distant nation. Cadalso's *Los eruditos a la violeta* (1772; The pseudo-intellectuals), on the other hand, is a long satiric essay directed at pedantry. Among the many other meritorious works advocating national reform and modernization, one example is the *Cartas sobre los obstáculos que la naturaleza, la opinión y las leyes oponen a la felicidad pública* (1808; Letters on the obstacles that nature, opinion, and laws raise against public prosperity) by the economist and minister Francisco Cabarrús (1752–1810) written from prison in 1795, arguing that freedom is necessary for economic development. In the epistolary genre, mention must be made of the **letters** and impressions of foreign travel, especially to England, of the great playwright Leandro Fernández de Moratín (1760–1828), which in many instances border on the essay. It must also be pointed out that in the 18th century the renovation and perfection of the means of expression were of great concern to reformers, so that excellence of expository style gave treatises the status of literature. Hence the writings of men like the cultural historian Juan Pablo Forner (1756–97), the philologers Gregorio Mayáns y Síscar (1699–1781) and Lorenzo Hervás y Panduro (1735–1809), the aesthetician Esteban de Arteaga (1747–98), the rhetorician Antonio de Capmany (1742–1813), and the art critic Antonio Ponz (1725–92) may be included within the essay genre.

The period following the Napoleonic occupation was characterized by growing progressive and liberal agitation, cruelly repressed by traditionalist tyranny. As ecclesiastical authorities were sufficiently influential to suppress the drama and the novel, a genre known as *costumbrismo*, emulating French writers like Victor Jouy, made its way into newspapers to describe local color, plentiful in a growing capital to which peasants from various parts of Spain, with their peculiar dress, speech, and habits, were migrating in large numbers. The genre culminated in a collection entitled *Los españoles pintados por sí mismos* (1843–44; The Spaniards, painted by themselves). Some of its practitioners, like Ramón de Mesonero Romanos (1803–82), were able to inject social criticism into their often witty sketches, but all were outshone by the Romantic suicide **Mariano José de Larra** (1809–37), who passed off his subtle barbs of political **satire** as *costumbrismo*. Mention should also be made of the *Letters from Spain* (1822), political essays written in English by the exiled poet José María Blanco White (1775–1841). It has been argued that Romanticism came late to Spain owing to rigid censorship during the reign of Ferdinand VII. Its displacement of neoclassicism was marked by a literary controversy between Juan Nicolás Böhl von Faber (1770–1863) and Antonio Alcal Galiano (1789–1865).

The Romantics were followed by the disciples of Julián Sanz del Río (1814–69), who brought back from his studies in Germany the philosophy of Karl Christian Friedrich Krause, whose "panentheism" suited the reforming efforts of the somewhat mystical mentality of the post-Romantic generation. Unlike the Enlightenment reformers, the followers of *Krausismo*, distrustful of the corrigibility or efficacy of governmental institutions, placed their hopes on the perfectibility of man. By making beauty equivalent to truth and goodness, the Krausists, as Juan López-Morillas (1956) points out, confused metaphysics, aesthetics, and epistemology. From their harmonic rationalism, apparently derived from Pythagorean ideas about music, they concluded that only by the study of art, which reveals the secret galleries of the genuine collective spirit, can history be truly humanized and point the way to universal harmony. Identifying epic poetry with homogeneous and unified culture, and lyric poetry with cultural bankruptcy, pluralist variety, and discordant multiculturalism, Krausists looked forward to a period of reconciliation and harmony brought about by dramatic poetry. Hence they raised the level of respect for belletristic endeavor, an attitude completely new to Spain, and paved the way for the re-examination of its history through its literature, a process that culminated decades later in the work of Américo Castro.

When the Krausists were barred from teaching at the universities, Francisco Giner de los Ríos (1839–1915) founded in 1876 the Institución Libre de Enseñanza (Independent secondary school), which contributed a renewed concept of education to Spain, freeing it from the current practice of indoctrination. The school's Sunday morning field trips, scheduled at the same time as the church **sermons**, constituted an astonishing innovation in Spanish pedagogy. Giner's *Estudios sobre educación* (1886; Studies on education) antedate many of John Dewey's ideas. In this collection can be found "La crítica espontánea de los niños en bellas artes" (The spontaneous criticism of children in the fine arts), describing a field trip to the school of fine arts, which had recently received from Italy plaster casts of sculptures by Donatello and della Robbia; these had just been unpacked and were lying pell-mell on the floor. Giner asked his class which they preferred and why. The gist of the children's conversations, eventually resulting in a shift of preference from della Robbia to Donatello, is masterfully recounted in Giner's essay. Also of great interest are his *Estudios literarios* (1866; Literary studies), *Estudios de literatura y arte* (1876; Studies of literature and art), *Estudios sobre artes industriales* (1892; Studies on industrial arts), and *Cartas literarias* (1878–79; Literary letters).

According to López-Morillas, *Krausismo* went through three stages, the first being an exposition of its doctrines by Sanz del Río; the second, their application and hence adaptation by Giner, Francisco Fernández y González (1833–1917), and others, especially Francisco Canalejas (1834–83), whose optimism differentiates him from his colleagues' meliorism; and the third, represented by Manuel de la Revilla (1846–81) and Urbano González Serrano (1848–1904), in whose thought the philosophy of Krause has been considerably diluted by the influence of positivism, evolutionism, determinism, and neo-Kantianism. This third generation of Krausists also had to recognize that the dramatic poetry of Romanticism was out of fashion and being replaced by the novel, thus casting doubt on the poetic predictions of their doctrine. Undoubtedly *Krausismo* had a lasting influence much beyond its time, for example on **Unamuno**'s concept of *intrahistoria* and on the *Galerías* of Antonio Machado's poetry. At variance with *Krausismo*, Catholic traditionalism is represented by the diplomat Juan Donoso Cortés (1809–53), whose *Ensayo sobre el catolicismo, el liberalismo, y el socialismo* (1851; *Essay on Catholicism, Liberalism and Socialism*) enjoyed some popularity in Germany, by the Thomist Jaime Balmes (1810–48), and by the great literary historiographer **Marcelino Menéndez y Pelayo** (1856–1912), the Krausists' most able opponent.

It sometimes happens that persons famous for other genres are not thought of as essayists, even though some of their writings may be more genuinely essayistic than those of colleagues known as practitioners of the genre. Such is the case with the great orator Emilio Castelar (1832–99), who is represented in a well-known collection of the world's famous orations. His *Recuerdos de Italia* (1872; Recollections of Italy, translated as *Old Rome and New Italy*) and *Un año en París* (1875; A year in Paris) are undeservedly forgotten. Castelar, who argued all his life for social justice, combined an impeccable aesthetic appreciation of architecture with a keen understanding of its dwellers. His insight into the character of the inhabitants of various Italian cities is extraordinary. When dealing with Rome, he spends more time on, of all places, the ghetto than on any other. But then, it was his speech in the 1869 Cortes that brought religious freedom to Spain.

The novelists of the latter part of the 19th century are known as the Generation of 1868, this being the date of a revolution that temporarily dethroned the Bourbons and brought about the short-lived reign of Amadeo of Savoy and the equally short-lived First Republic. Among these novelists we find two outstanding essayists in addition to Emilia Pardo Bazán. Juan Valera (1824–1905), besides his novels, is known for some beautiful short stories and an extraordinary erudition, evident in his literary and **historical essays**. Valera was a Platonist repelled by the excesses of the Romanticism prevalent in his youth as well as the positivism in vogue during his mature years, and his moderation served him well in his profession as a diplomat. Valera also excels in the epistolary genre, closely allied to the essay. His witty comments about the upper classes of the lands where he served constitute an eternal source of amusement. In his *Cartas desde Rusia* (Letters from Russia), composed at the beginning of his diplomatic career when he accompanied the Duque de Gor on a mission to St. Petersburg, he pokes gentle fun at the duke, at one of his colleagues, at the disparity between the classes, at Russian customs, and at the ugliness of the Russian aristocracy while also admiring their luxury and deploring their tyranny. On the other hand, as a moderate monarchist, in his letters from Washington he expresses some disdain for "the Great Republic," whose capital had no palaces, and makes hilarious comments about American politicians and the courtship customs of their unchaperoned daughters.

Quite different from Valera's Andalusian wit is the mixture of irony and sentimentality found in the great Asturian novelist Leopoldo Alas, "Clarín" (1852–1901), whose sarcastic "paliques" (chitchats) against intellectual and ecclesiastical backwardness and the mediocrity of literary figures favored by the politicized Royal Academy induced even more vicious attacks from those he ridiculed. When he criticized the Spanish navy for its ineptitude, evidenced by an inexcusable accident, his diminutive stature provided a pretext for turning down a challenge to a duel by angered officers. His *Folletos literarios* (1886–91; Literary pamphlets) are of similar tenor. When he was quoted as saying that contemporary Spain only had two and a half poets, Clarín, being asked who was the half-poet, named Manuel de la Revilla. When the latter attacked him in return, Clarín put out a *folleto literario* entitled *A 0,50 poeta* (1889; At 0.50 a poet). As a republican, he also directed unjust and nasty barbs at the conservative Catholic Countess Pardo Bazán for her feminism.

Reacting to the loss of the remnants of empire as the result of its war with the United States, a group of young writers to whom one of their members, "**Azorín**," gave the name of the "Generation of '98," set out radically to re-examine and alter the Spanish mentality, still immobilized in the ideology developed during the nation's former glory. Inspired in part by the provocative attitude of Clarín and the caustic exasperation of Larra, whose fame they revived by a much-touted visit *en masse* to his grave, this generation periodically enjoyed greater freedom to impugn intellectual routinarianism than any previous one. In the essays of **Miguel de Unamuno** (1864–1936), who yearned to be the *intranquilizador de España*, we witness the writer's eagerness to provoke hostile reaction. And some of the 66 articles comprising *Las horas solitarias* by the great novelist Pío Baroja can almost be called a hybrid of the essay and the temper tantrum. On the other hand, their contemporary, José Martínez Ruiz, "**Azorín**" (1873–1967), observes the Spanish scene with melancholy, tolerance, and resignation. The great poet Antonio Machado (1875–1939), fictitiously imitating what **Plato** did for Socrates, composed a long memoir of the thoughts of a nonexistent teacher, *Juan de Mairena* (1936), which must be called an essay for lack of a better word. The Nobel Prize-winning

neurologist Santiago Ramón y Cajal (1852–1934) also published valuable essays on the possibility of scientific renewal in Spain.

Two other important essayists of this generation are **Ángel Ganivet** (1864–98) and **Ramiro de Maeztu** (1875–1936), both of whose analyses of the causes of the Spanish character have been superseded by the work of the philologist and historian **Américo Castro** (1885–1972), greatly influenced in his approach by the ideas of Wilhelm Dilthey.

The generation following that of '98, named *novecentistas* by one of its members, **Eugenio d'Ors** (1881–1954), includes the physician Gregorio Marañón (1887–1960), who produced extraordinary essays about life in the 16th and 17th centuries from the viewpoints of the history of medicine and Jungian psychology, and the erudite diplomat and novelist, **Ramón Pérez de Ayala** (1880–1962), whose essays are far more measured than those of the Generation of '98. Indeed, there was bound to be a reaction to the belligerency of Unamuno, and it came with **José Ortega y Gasset** (1883–1955), internationally recognized for his *La deshumanización del arte* (1925; *The Dehumanization of Art*) and *La rebelión de las masas* (1930; *The Revolt of the Masses*), the latter greatly influenced by Oswald Spengler, although a couple of comments regarding the German thinker evince a careless reading on Ortega's part. His essay on love attempts to rebut Stendhal's *De l'amour* (1822; *Love*) whose author, according to Ortega, was incapable of being in love. Conversely, Ortega, who never produced any fiction, fancied himself a literary critic, in which guise he proved himself incapable of appreciating the art of a great contemporary novelist, Gabriel Miró (1879–1930), some of whose *costumbrista* sketches surpass this subgenre's 19th-century models. Another great novelist, Ramón Gómez de la Serna (1888–1963), internationally known for his *greguerías*, produced several surrealist sketches which fit this subgenre. In this generation we should also mention the humorists Wenceslao Fernández Flórez (1885–1964) and Julio Camba (1882–1962), whose essays about the United States were widely read in his day, and **Manuel Azaña** (1880–1940), author of literary essays and President of the Republic.

The sobering experience of the Civil War injected a cautious tone into the genre. The new generation has been divided into the categories of Traditional Humanists, who sought harmony and compatibility among different viewpoints, Liberal Catholic Humanists, and Socialist Humanists. The term "Medical Humanist," used to characterize Ramón y Cajal and Marañón, was now applied to Pedro Laín Entralgo (1908–), who is also, with the philosophers **Xavier Zubiri** (1898–1983) and Juan Rof Carballo (1905–), a Conservative Humanist. José Luis Aranguren (1909–) is a Traditional Humanist who, along with the political scientist, philosopher, and late Mayor of Madrid **Enrique Tierno Galván** (1918–86), belongs to Socialist Humanism.

The end of the Franco era, the attainment of stability and democratic institutions, and the integration of Spain into the European Community have all provided the freedom to facilitate a flowering of literature and new ideas. Some of the émigrés who had returned during a mitigation of the regime's severity rejoined those who had remained. This group includes students of Ortega, like the cosmopolitan philosophers **Julián Marías** (1914–) and José Ferrater Mora (1912–), **María**

Zambrano (1904–91), Joaquín Xirau (1895–1946), and José Gaos (1902–69), as well as the poets Luis Felipe Vivanco (1907–75) and Pedro Salinas (1891–1951), the diplomat **Salvador de Madariaga** (1886–1978), and the novelists Benjamín Jarnés (1888–1949), **Francisco Ayala** (1906–), **Rosa Chacel** (1898–1994), and **Carmen Martín Gaite** (1925–), along with scholars who combine literary criticism and historiographic method, like José Antonio Maravall (1911–86). Juan Marichal (1922–) argues in one of the essays of *La voluntad de estilo* (1957; The will for style) that a new sensitivity among the caste of 15th-century *conversos* (descendants of Jews) is at the bottom of the origins of the Spanish essay. The Nobel Prize-winning novelist Camilo José Cela y Trulock (1916–) has composed two book-length essays about his travels through Spain on foot and by donkey. We cannot fail to mention the immensely popular and witty but erudite *El español y los siete pecados capitales* (1966; *The Spaniard and the Seven Deadly Sins*) and books with similar titles about other nations, including France and the United States, by Fernando Díaz-Plaja (1918–), not to be confused with the literary historiographer Guillermo Díaz-Plaja (1909–).

An overview of the Spanish essay reveals that some epochs were quite fruitful while others were almost barren, depending on the political situation. Certainly no period was as fiercely anti-intellectual as the Ominous Decade (1823–43) when, in 1827, the professors of the University of Cervera, most of whom belonged to the clergy, sent to the king an exposition stating that "the dangerous novelty of reasoning lies far from our minds." At other times Spaniards enjoyed relative freedom. Yet the specter of possible repression never failed to haunt the minds of writers, who consequently preferred to express themselves in poetry or prose fiction that contained allegorical levels. In the words of Blanco White found in *El Español* of January 1811, "Peoples subjected to governments that do not allow free expression possess the liveliness of deaf-mutes to make themselves understood by signs." Consequently, in order to put ideas in a mild form acceptable to censorship, some essayists may have made themselves appear more conservative than they really were at heart. Their influence might have been swept aside after a loosening of the reins, but they still deserve respect when we view them in their historical context. Conversely, as a result of revolution or national disaster, new generations engaged in bursts of passion, whose literary expression should also be accepted in its historical context. As Marichal puts it, "In the case of Spain, the essayist's articulation with contemporaneous society is much more changeable [than in Great Britain], and hence, in our essays, the continuity of literary manner characteristic of the English is not as observable. The Spanish essay will prove its worth if we approach it while keeping in mind that relative social stability and political freedom are by no means universal."

PIERRE L. ULLMAN

Anthologies

Antología del feminismo, edited by Amalia Martín-Gamero, Madrid: Alianza, 1975

El concepto contemporáneo de España: Antología de ensayos (1895–1931), edited by Ángel del Río and M. J. Benardete, Buenos Aires: Losada, 1946

El ensayo español del siglo veinte, edited by Donald W. Bleznick, New York: Ronald Press, 1964

Ensayos españoles, edited by Guido Mazzeo, Englewood Cliffs, New Jersey: Prentice Hall, 1973

The Modern Spanish Essay, edited by Alfred Rodríguez and William Rosenthal, Waltham, Massachusetts: Blaisdell, 1969

Further Reading

Alborg, Juan Luis, *Historia de la literatura española*, Madrid: Gredos, 5 vols., 1966–96

Ferrater Mora, José, *Ortega y Gasset*, New Haven, Connecticut: Yale University Press, revised edition, 1973 (original edition, 1957)

Gómez-Martínez, José Luis, *Teoría del ensayo*, Mexico City: Universidad Nacional Autónoma, 2nd edition, 1992 (original edition, 1981)

López-Morillas, Juan, *The Krausist Movement and Ideological Change in Spain, 1854–1874*, Cambridge: Cambridge University Press, 1981 (original Spanish edition, 1956)

Marichal, Juan, *La voluntad de estilo*, Barcelona: Seix Barral, 1957; revised, enlarged edition, as *Teoria e historia del ensayismo hispánico*, Madrid: Alianza, 1984

Mermall, Thomas, *The Rhetoric of Humanism: Spanish Culture After Ortega y Gasset*, Jamaica, New York: Bilingual Press, 1976

Río, Ángel del, *Historia de la literatura española*, New York: Holt Rinehart Winston, revised edition, 2 vols., 1963 (original edition, 1948)

Salinas y Serrano, Pedro, *Reality and the Poet in Spanish Poetry*, Baltimore: Johns Hopkins Press, 1940

Spanish American Essay

The essay, a protean form that **Alfonso Reyes** deemed the centaur of the genres, has assumed many shapes and roles in Latin America. Most critics agree that the literary essay was born in Spanish America toward the end of the 18th century as the voice of the Independence movements. The form it acquired did not faithfully follow its European precursors but assumed a *sui generis* model that reflected the realities of the new world. The Spanish American literary essay is the axis which has aligned the history of every country on the continent. Thus, intellectuals have utilized it as a means to examine, explicate, and theorize about the fate of the Spanish Americas as a whole. In the 20th century it has been instrumental in defining a distinctive Spanish American identity and the ethos of most countries. This does not imply that other types of essay have not been cultivated; however, the literary essay that ideologically follows the genesis of Spanish America is the most representative of the genre. Furthermore, most Latin American literati bring into their writing an eclectic intellectual baggage because of the multiple roles they play within the framework of their countries' circumstances: i.e. they are statesmen, physicians, professors, engineers, or philosophers whose work reflects their background. As a consequence, the literary essay can have, for example, strong philosophical or scientific overtones, in either style or content.

The first essayistic texts that dealt with ideals of independence date from the last decades of the 18th century. American and French revolutionary texts were smuggled in by educated *criollos* (Spaniards born in America), who translated and published them clandestinely. The news about the American and French revolutions and the Enlightenment ideals behind them created social and political unrest, which was reflected in the literature of the time. In exile, the Peruvian Jesuit Juan Pablo Vizcardo (1748–98) wrote *Carta dirijida a los españoles americanos por uno de sus compatriotas* (1792; Letter directed to the American Spaniards by one of their compatriots), in which he expressed his urgent conviction for an independent America. In Colombia, Camilo Torres (1766–1816) wrote *El memorial de agravios* (1809; A brief of offenses) against the Spaniards, and the Argentine Mariano Moreno (1778–1811), one of the translators of **Rousseau**'s *Contrat social*, defended free trade in *Representación a nombre de los hacendados* (1809; Representation in the name of the ranchers). Two Mexican writers come to mind in this period: José Servando Teresa de Mier (1763–1827), a Dominican, patriot, and adventurer, and José Joaquín Fernández de Lizardi (1776–1827). Teresa de Mier was persecuted by the Spaniards throughout his life because of his liberal thought and writings. He published *Relación de lo que sucedió en Europa al Doctor Don Servando Teresa de Mier después que fue trasladado allá por resultas de lo actuado contra él en México, desde julio de 1795 hasta octubre de 1805* (1820; Report of what happened to Doctor Don Servando Teresa de Mier after he was sent there as a consequence of what was done against him in Mexico from July 1795 to October 1805), *Apología* (1820; Apology), and *Memorias* (1820; Memoirs). The last was written in Spain and reflects Teresa de Mier's intense nationalism. Fernández de Lizardi wrote under the pen name of El Pensador Mexicano (The Mexican thinker). He founded various newspapers, including *El Pensador Mexicano* (1812–14), *Alacena de Frioleras* (1815–16; Cupboard of trinkets), *El Conductor Eléctrico* (1820; The electric conductor), and *Conversaciones del Payo y el Sacristán* (1824–25; Conversations between the peasant and the sacristan). Throughout his writings, Fernández de Lizardi disseminated the new ideals of independence as he criticized the political and social situations of the day. In Chile, the friar Camilo Henríquez (1769–1825) started the newspapers *La Aurora de Chile* (1812; The dawn of Chile) and *El Monitor Araucano* (1813; The Araucan monitor), in which he offered liberal reflections. Once exiled in Argentina, he published *Ensayo* (Essay), about demarcated radicalism, and "El catecismo de los patriotas" (1812; The patriots' catechism), in which he expressed his deep trust in reason as the means to eliminate ignorance and superstition in the colonies.

Another outstanding personality of this period is the Ecuadorian Javier Eugenio de Santa Cruz y Espejo (1747–95), son of an Indian and a *mestizo* woman. An erudite physician and liberal patriot, he was the subject of racial discrimination. Santa Cruz y Espejo devoted his life's work to denouncing the inequalities and injustices that plagued the colonies. He wrote political speeches and social criticism in a sarcastic style, as well as dialogues and scientific articles. Some appeared in the newspaper he founded, *Primicias de la cultura de Quito* (1792; First fruits of culture in Quito). Other works include *El nuevo Luciano de Quito o despertador de los ingenios* (1779; The new Luciano of Quito or the one who awakens talents), *Marco Porcio Catón* (1780), *Reflexiones . . . acerca de un método seguro para preservar a los pueblos de las viruelas* (1785; Reflections . . . on a safe method to protect people from smallpox), and *Defensa de los curas de Riobamba* (1786; Defense of the priests from Riobamba).

Simón Bolívar (1783–1830), the Venezuelan liberator of Bolivia, Peru, Venezuela, Colombia, and Ecuador, left a great essayistic legacy. Among his most important texts are "Record of the Enemy's Crimes and Reasons for Total War" (1813), a reflection about his mission of freedom, "Manifiesto de Cartagena" (1812; Cartagena manifesto), "Carta de Jamaica" (1815; Jamaica Letter), and "Discurso en el Congreso de Angostura" (1819; Speech at the Congress of Angostura). In these works, Bolívar examined how the course of Spanish American history shifted from a potential future full of hope and enthusiasm to one of disillusion and dismay as internal wars in the newly independent Venezuela and Colombia threatened to halt the liberation of South America before it was accomplished. Bolívar believed that Enlightenment principles and ideals conflicted with the idiosyncrasy of the new nations by reason of their ethnic composition and past history. In "Carta de Jamaica" Bolívar confesses: "Good and perfectly representative institutions are not suitable for our nature, customs and present intelligence." In "Discurso en el Congreso de Angostura" he offers this caution: "Let us keep in mind that our people is not the European, nor the North American, but a composition of Africa and America rather than an emanation of Europe; since even Spain itself is not really European because of its African ascent, its institutions and their nature." Bolívar's solution to the reigning anarchy was the implementation of an authoritarian and despotic government. His *a priori* condemnation to failure of the new republics, because of a biological and historical determinism, became a recurrent motif in Latin American thought which has persisted to the modern day.

Another Venezuelan, **Andrés Bello** (1781–1865), devoted his life to the intellectual development and education of the new republics. In London he founded the literary magazines *Biblioteca Americana* (1823; American library) and *El Repertorio Americano* (1826–27; American repertoire), through which he tried to elaborate an Americanist cultural program. An adoptive son of Chile – where he spent most of his life – Bello wrote some of his most important works there: *Gramática de la lengua castellana, destinada al uso de los americanos* (1847; A Spanish grammar designed to be used by Americans), *Principios de derecho de gentes* (1832; Principles of international law), *Código civil de la república de Chile* (1855; Civil code of Chile), and *Filosofía del entendimiento* (1881; Philosophy of the Understanding).

Early in the second half of the 19th century, the failure of the independent regimes was evident. Freedom had only changed the surface of an infrastructure that had taken the Spaniards three centuries to build. The Romantic wave of the 19th century brought with it an infusion of liberalism, love for what was autochthonous, and a firm commitment to change the Spanish American reality through popular education and progress. The United States provided an example of a republican system, at least until its imperialistic intentions were revealed. Argentina was the first country to have a serious literary circle, Asociación de Mayo (May association), formed by young liberal intellectuals, most of them educated in Paris. Among this group was Esteban Echeverría (1805–51), who imported to the new continent the Romantic ideology from

France even before it had reached Spain. Another member, Juan Bautista Alberdi (1810–84), anti-Romantic but an Americanist at heart, advocated the institution of laws that responded to the unique needs of Argentina and that were not imitations of foreign laws. He authored *Bases y puntos de partida para la organización política de la República Argentina* (1852; Foundations and points of departure for the political organization of the Argentine republic), *El crimen de la guerra* (wr. c. 1880s, pub. 1915; *The Crime of War*), *Estudios económicos* (1916; Economic studies), and *Cartas Quillotanas* (1853; *Quillotanas* letters).

The most important intellectual among the Argentine Romantics was undoubtedly **Domingo Faustino Sarmiento** (1811–88). Not only did he become the president of his country, but his works influenced future essayists throughout the continent. Sarmiento was a fervent admirer of the U.S. democratic system, writing biographies of Abraham Lincoln and **Benjamin Franklin**. When Sarmiento lived in Chile, he started *El Progreso* (early 1840s; Progress), in which he interpreted Argentina's past and present circumstances. He firmly believed that education was the key to progress and that the Spanish heritage, as well as the American natives, greatly impeded development. Recent critical readings of *Civilización y barbarie: Vida de Juan Facundo Quiroga* (1845; *Life in the Argentine Republic in the Days of the Tyrants; or Civilization and Barbarism*) show that Sarmiento discriminated against the native elements of his country by outlining the quest for progress in Argentina as "a struggle between the European civilization and the Indian savagery, between intelligence and matter." In 1849 he wrote *De la educación popular: Bases y puntos de partida para la organización política de la República Argentina* (Of popular education: foundations and starting points for the political organization of Argentina). In one of his last works, *Conflictos y armonía de las razas en América* (1883; Conflict and harmony of the races in America), Sarmiento examined the racial characteristics of Spanish America from a positivist point of view.

José Victorino Lastarria (1817–88) represented Romantic thought in Chile. For Lastarria, literature was the best medium for intellectuals to identify the true national ethos, and he passionately advocated a national literature. His *Investigaciones sobre la influencia social de la conquista y del sistema colonial de los españoles en Chile* (1844; Research on the social influence and colonial system of the Spaniards in Chile) attacked the feudal system that the Spaniards imposed on the new continent for three centuries, and specifically targeted its major representatives: the Church and the army. In the texts Lastarria published under the title *Miscelánea histórica y literaria* (1868; Historical and literary miscellany), he argued that progress required the modernization of every aspect of the complex organism that comprises a country. Chile, therefore, needed a drastic change from the past, a total awakening of consciousness, education, and spiritual evolution in order to succeed in the future. Another Chilean intellectual who shared Lastarria's ideas was Francisco Bilbao (1823–65). *Sociabilidad chilena* (1844; Chilean sociability) examined the benefits of a liberal system as opposed to a conservative one; Chile was under a conservative regime for two decades during Bilbao's lifetime. Other works by Bilbao included *La América en peligro* (1862; America in danger), and *El*

evangelio americano (1864; American gospel). He always tried to demonstrate that the conservatism inherited from colonial times would only lead to backwardness.

Within the northern countries in South America, the Ecuadorian **Juan Montalvo** (1832–89) stands out as a major man of letters and eminent essayist. He spent most of his life in exile in Colombia, Panama, and Europe as a result of his ferocious and open denunciation of two of the presidents of his country: Gabriel García Moreno and Ignacio de Veintimilla. Montalvo is considered one of the best examples of the Spanish American essayist, achieving a perfect balance between analysis, feeling, and imagination. His work exposed the ills that afflicted his country, and expressed his political and social creed. From the pages of the newspapers he founded, *El Cosmopolita* (1866–69; The cosmopolitan) and *El Regenerador* (1876–78; The regenerator), he lashed out against the despots, clergy included, who ruled his country. A rebel, Montalvo was unafraid of polemics. Once, when he came back from one of his forced exiles to Europe, he wrote to the president of Ecuador, Gabriel García Moreno: "A few years living away from my beloved country, in the process of learning about and abhorring the despots in Europe, have taught me, at the same time, to know and scorn the petty tyrants of Spanish America. If for some reason I decide to take part in our poor dealings, you, and any other whose conduct would be hostile to the freedom and rights of a country, would have in me an enemy, and not a meek one." His most important works are *Siete tratados* (1882–83; Seven treatises), *Capítulos que se le olvidaron a Cervantes* (1895; Chapters that Cervantes forgot), *Geometría moral* (1902; Moral geometry), published after his death, and the periodical *Las Catilinarias* (1880–82; Catilinarians), written against the Ecuadorian president Ignacio de Veintimilla.

In Mexico José María Luis Mora (1794–1850) published liberal, anti-clerical, and anti-military essays. He held the colonial powers responsible for the rampant backwardness and ignorance of Mexico; he advocated popular education, civil rights, and, overall, progress, as long as it was pursued on nonviolent terms. Some of Mora's publications include *México y sus revoluciones* (1836; Mexico and its revolutions) and *Obras sueltas* (1837; Miscellaneous works). Cuba is represented during this period by José Antonio Saco (1797–1879) and José de la Luz y Caballero (1800–62), the latter a disciple of the former. Both devoted themselves to education. The podium was for them a vehicle for their nationalistic and liberal ideas, since Cuba had not yet obtained its independence. Saco published the three-volume *Colección de papeles científicos, históricos, políticos, y de otros ramos* (1858–59; A collection of scientific, historical, political, and other papers), and an unfinished work, *Historia de la esclavitud* (1875–77; History of slavery). Luz y Caballero's life production was compiled in *Escritos literarios* (Literary writings) in 1946.

The intellectuals' neoclassic and Romantic ideas did little to pull Spanish America out of chaos, and disillusion reigned among them. The aversion to the Spanish legacy proved insufficient to eradicate its idiosyncrasy. The positivisim of Auguste Comte and Herbert Spencer proved more effective. Mexican statesman and physician Gabino Barrera (1818–81) applied Comte's three states to Mexican history. The theological state was the colonial era, the metaphysical state was the period of independence and the years that followed, and the positivist state was the present. Religious beliefs, spirituality, and intuition were replaced by a deep faith in scientism. Although there were definite liberal changes, like those of Benito Juárez in Mexico, progress was viewed from the perspective of a privileged social class. The Indian, African, and *mestizo* groups were at the periphery of progress. In Mexico, positivist thought was represented by Justo Sierra (1848–1912). A historian, statesman, and poet, Sierra also advocated development through public education. Some of his works are the "Prólogo" he wrote to *Poesías* by Manuel Gutiérrez Nájera (1896), *México, su evolución social* (1900–02; *Mexico, Its Social Evolution*), and *Juárez, su obra y su tiempo* (1905; Juarez, his work and his times).

A major intellectual who held a more humanist view of positivism was the Puerto Rican **Eugenio María de Hostos** (1839–1903). Though he was born on the island, his work was committed to the continent. He participated in the political life of Spain, but when he realized that the independence of the Antilles was not an issue there, he returned to the U.S., where he traveled extensively, spreading a message of freedom, civilization, and independence for Puerto Rico. He established himself in Chile until his death. Hostos published *Moral social* (Social morality) in 1888. His style tends to be positivist – devoid of feeling and following a logical structure – but his speeches, the most renowned in Spanish America, were more lyrical. The speech given in 1884 at the Escuela Normal of Santo Domingo has been called by Antonio Caso "a masterpiece of moral thought in Spanish America."

The Cuban sociologist, educator, philosopher, and literary critic Enrique José Varona (1849–1933) yearned, as Hostos did, for the independence of his country. Unlike Hostos, Varona witnessed the liberation of the island, but also the disenchantment that came later. Some of his works are compiled in *Conferencias filosóficas* (1880; Philosophical lectures), *Discursos literarios y filosóficos* (1883; Literary and philosophical studies), *Seis conferencias* (1885; Six lectures), *Artículos y discursos* (1891; Articles and speeches), *Desde mi belvedere* (1907; From my belvedere), and *Violetas y ortigas* (1917; Violets and nettles).

In Peru, the poet and writer Manuel González Prada (1848–1918) was prominent during this time, becoming a public figure after Peru's disastrous defeat at the hands of Chile in the Pacific War. His speeches harangued his compatriots to wake up to their reality. González Prada was a positivist in that he believed only science could alleviate the ills inherited from the Colony. His prose is devoid of intimacy and strongly rejects the purity of Castilian Spanish, following the usage in Peru. González Prada was also the first to call attention to the absence of the Indian population in the national plans. A defender of the underdog and an enemy of Peruvian conservatism, he did not find much support in his country. Some of his major works are *Pájinas libres* (1894; Free pages), *Horas de lucha* (1908; Hours of struggle), and *El tonel de Diógenes* (1945; The barrel of Diogenes).

The Colombian Carlos Arturo Torres (1867–1911), an educator, statesman, journalist, literary critic, and poet, left behind an essayistic body of work with strong positivist overtones. In *Idola fori* (1910), he discussed in a scientific manner the consequences of the transplantation of European ideas to Latin America. Other essays are *Literatura de ideas* (1911; Literature of ideas), *Estudios de crítica moderna* (1917; Studies on modern criticism), and *Estudios ingleses* (1907; English studies).

Positivism was later joined by socioanthropological ideas that claimed to interpret the social and cultural development of a race according to their biological grouping. One of the European racial theorists who was widely read in Latin America, Gustave Le Bon, maintained that, just as there were physical racial traits, there were immutable psychosomatic traits that shaped the make-up of a national character. Thus, the concept of superior and inferior races emerged. An inferior race could experience positive but superficial changes through education and refinement, but the essence of its inferiority would never change. The explicit racism of this branch of sociology and social evolutionism found ready followers in Spanish America. Indian and African groups were considered pernicious elements that blocked progress in their countries, and those of mixed race were considered even worse. The only solution to this "malady" was a greater European migration to counteract the other two races. Deploying medical terminology, the essayists diagnosed the "sickness" of the continent. In Argentina, Agustín Álvarez (1857–1914), published his *Manual de patología política* (1899; Handbook of political pathology). That same year, the Venezuelan César Zumeta (1860–1955) published *El continente enfermo* (The sick continent). In 1903 the Argentine Carlos Octavio Bunge (1875–1918) literally followed Le Bon's ideas, applying them to the continent in *Nuestra América* (Our America). In 1905, his compatriot Manuel Ugarte (1878–1951) authored *Enfermedades sociales* (Social maladies). Ironically, most of the rest of his extensive essay production expressed strong socialist tendencies. In 1909, the Bolivian Alcides Arguedas (1879–1946) condemned Bolivia in *Pueblo enfermo: Contribución a la psicología de los pueblos hispanoamericanos* (1909; Sick country: contribution to the psychology of the Spanish American countries). In his last edition of 1934, Arguedas agreed that pedagogy was Bolivia's only salvation, though it would never make illustrious men out of the Indians. Francisco García Calderón (1883–1953) was a Peruvian writer who concurred with the intellectuals mentioned above and who published mostly in French. His main piece, *Les Démocraties latines de l'Amérique* (1912; The Latin democracies of America), focused on the question of race, taking for granted that the non-European groups were inferior to those from the old continent. The racism and snobbism of this work should not cloud his other more humanist essays. Another prolific thinker of this school was the Argentine José Ingenieros (1877–1925), who, though a socialist, persisted in explaining the ills of Spanish America through the heterogeneity of superior and inferior races peopling it. He wrote *La simulación en la lucha por la vida* (1903; The simulation in the struggle for life), *El hombre mediocre* (1913; The mediocre man), and *Psicología genética* (1911; Genetic psychology).

Almost simultaneous with this somber and depressing view of Spanish America, a more spiritualist and aestheticist movement arose, highlighting humanist values, intuition, spiritualism, and a new respect for the Latin-Spanish tradition. The Peruvian Ricardo Palma (1833–1919) glorified the colonial era in *La bohemia de mi tiempo* (1887; The bohemian of my time) and the Mexican Guillermo Prieto (1818–97) recalled the past in *Memorias de mis tiempos 1828–1853* (1906; Memoirs of my times 1828–53). Spiritualist tendencies made room for a literary movement called *Modernismo* (Modernism; not to be confused with the European Modernism), in which language and form bloomed anew. Even though poetry was the primary Modernist genre, the essay was invigorated stylistically and ideologically. The Cuban **José Martí** (1853–95) is considered the precursor of this movement, an outstanding representative of this humanist reaction to the problems of Spanish America and a hero to his country. He cultivated all genres, including journalism and translation. A renovator of Spanish prose and verse, he wrote in renowned newspapers like *La Nación* of Buenos Aires, *El Partido Liberal* (The liberal party) in Mexico and *La Opinión Nacional* of Caracas among others. Concern for his country and its independence was the main thread of key articles collected in *El presidio político en Cuba* (1871; The political prison in Cuba), *La república española ante la revolución cubana* (1873; The Spanish republic in view of the Cuban revolution), and in Martí's war journal. *Guatemala* (1878) represents a more mature prose – rhythmic and chromatic – and *Poema del Niágara* (1882; Poem to Niagara) laments the spiritual destitution and the constant change humanity undergoes. In "Nuestra América" (1891; Our America), he left behind the immortal words: "There is no battle between civilization and savagery, but between false erudition and nature." True to his convictions, Martí joined the Cuban army and soon died in a skirmish.

The Mexican poet Manuel Gutiérrez Nájera (1859–95), a prominent member of the *Modernista* (Modernist) movement like Martí, created the chronicle, a type of refined, mundane, frivolous, and poetic conversation published in the major newspapers of Mexico. He began the *Revista Azul* (Blue review), whose articles were paradigms of the French Belle Epoque. The Uruguayan poet Julián J. Casal (1889–1954) wrote journalistic articles on literary and artistic topics, as well as contributing to the chronicle. The Nicaraguan **Rubén Darío** (1867–1916) founded the *Modernista* movement. A true aesthete, Darío was a poet and fiction writer, as well as a journalist. His journalistic work, published in major newspapers in various cities, was gathered later. *Los raros* (1896; The rare ones) is a collection of essays about literary personalities. His various trips in Europe and Spanish America allowed him to write *Peregrinaciones* (1901; Peregrinations). Besides aesthetic thematics, Darío was also concerned with the U.S. imperialist attitude toward the continent. Many countries had succumbed: Mexico, the Central American countries, Colombia, and the *coup fatal*, the Spanish-American war that determined the destiny of the Antilles. His last essays – included in two of his final collections, *La caravana pasa* (1902; The caravan goes by) and *Tierras solares* (1904; Solar lands) – are permeated with melancholy and disillusion.

The Uruguayan writer and professor **José Enrique Rodó** (1871–1917) was the greatest representative of the Modernist essay. His readings of the classics and the philosophers of his time allowed him to develop a theory of meritocracy, although talent, as a measure of superiority, did not take into account the pyramidal structure of the Spanish American societies where the underprivileged were deprived of any education. Rodó had unyielding faith in a free and protean spirit. In his masterpiece *Ariel* (1900), he defended Spanish American spiritualism over the United States' pragmatic perspective on life. His philosophy was to return to Latin roots and to the humanist legacy the Spaniards brought to America. He coined the phrase "the colossus of the north" to refer to the United States. Other works are *Motivos de Proteo* (1909; The Motives of Proteus), *El mirador de Próspero* (1913; The outlook of Prospero), and *El camino de Paros* (1918; The way to Paros). Other *Modernista* writers include Rodó's disciple Carlos Nin Frías (1882–1937), the Colombians Carlos Arturo Torres and Baldomero Sanín Cano (1861–1957), the Guatemalan Enrique Gómez Carrillo (1873–1927), and the Venezuelans Manuel Díaz Rodríguez (1871–1927) and Rufino Blanco Fombona (1874–1944), the latter a multifaceted writer who later became a critic of this movement.

Two other ideological currents reacted against positivism. A group of young Mexican writers – Ateneo de la Juventud (Atheneum of youth) – looked for new answers under the guidance of the Dominican **Pedro Henríquez Ureña** (1884–1946). Hostos' follower and Rodó's admirer, Henríquez Ureña led the group in the study of the irrationalists. He believed that in every historical crisis Spanish America faced, its spirit remained unharmed and sound. The continent could become its own utopia, for it was only beginning to forge its future. Henríquez Ureña's message to the Ateneo de la Juventud could be summarized in his own words:

> The universal man we dream of, the kind our America aspires to, will not be an outcast, will enjoy everything, will appreciate all hues, but will belong to his land; his land and not others', the land will give him the intense flavor of what is native, and that will be his best preparation to taste that which has a genuine flavor and a true character. Universality does not mean being an outcast: in a utopian world, character differences born of the climate, language and traditions should not disappear; but all of these differences, instead of signifying division and discordance, should be combined into diverse hues of human unity. Never uniformity, the ideal of sterile imperialistic systems; yes to unity, as a harmony of the multi-unanimous peoples' voices. (*La utopía de América: Patria de la justicia* [1925; America's utopia: country of justice])

His major works are *Ensayos críticos* (1905; Critical essays), *Literary Currents in Latin America* (1945), *Historia de la cultura en la América Hispana* (1947; A history of Spanish American culture), and his most notorious text, *Seis ensayos en busca de nuestra expresión* (1928; Six essays in search of our expression).

Great essayists and philosophers followed Henríquez Ureña: the Mexican **Alfonso Reyes** (1889–1959), for example, ranked by many as the best prose writer of the continent. Some of his outstanding collections of essays are *Visión de Anáhuac* (1917; Vision of Anahuac), *Ancorajes* (1951; Anchorages), *El cazador* (1921; The hunter), *Última Tule* (1942; Last Tule), *Discursos por Virgilio* (1931; Discourses about Virgil), and *Letras de la Nueva España* (1948; Letters of the New Spain). Antonio Caso (1883–1946) is remembered as the keen philosopher of the Ateneo and for his masterpiece, *La existencia como economía, como desinterés y como caridad* (1919; Existence as economy, as selflessness and as charity). He also published *Discursos a la nación mexicana* (1922; Speeches to the Mexican nation) and *El peligro del hombre* (1942; The danger of man). **José Vasconcelos** (1882–1959), the essayist most influenced by the Mexican Revolution, dreamed of a cosmic, Spanish American conglomerate of races. Absorbed in the triumph of the revolution, and in the energy that emanates from aestheticism, he believed it would be the fifth and most superior race. These ideas are expressed in *La raza cósmica* (1925; The cosmic race), *Indología* (1927; Indianology – Vasconcelos' term), and *Ulises criollo* (1935–39; A Mexican Ulysses).

In the Andean countries, a spiritualist movement instilled with telluric overtones was the response to the racism of scientism. In Bolivia, Franz Tamayo (1879–1956) rejected Alcides Arguedas' predeterminism and exalted the individual will in *Creación de la pedagogía nacional* (1910; The creation of a national pedagogy). Fernando Díez de Medina (1908–90), statesman, journalist, and writer, was active in the nationalization of the mines (Bolivia's main export was tin) and helped design the agrarian reform. He defended the Indian character and the magical powers that the earth exercises on humans. His major essays are *Nayjama* (1950) and *El velero nacional* (1935; The national sailing vessel). In *Thunupa* (1947), based on an Aymaran legend, Díez de Medina described the main god's son as a cosmogonic numen, the regenerative spirit of the Andean peoples. Guillermo Francovich's (1901–90) *Pachamama* (1942) also exalted the telluric forces of the earth and their influence on humans. In Argentina, Ricardo Rojas (1882–1957), in *La restauración nacionalista* (1909; The national restoration), *La argentinidad* (1916; The Argentine ethos), and *Eurindia* (1924) followed the idealism of Martí, Rodó, and Vasconcelos, and constructed an aesthetic foundation for the Argentine culture. Rojas' solution for Argentina, and for the rest of the continent, was a synthesis of the different traditions that coexisted into a firmer, more cohesive one. Another Argentine, Manuel Gálvez (1882–1962), followed Rojas' ideas in *El diario de Gabriel Quiroga* (1910; The diary of Gabriel Quiroga), *El solar de la raza* (1913; The ancestral home of the race), and *Este pueblo necesita . . .* (1934; This country needs . . .).

In Peru, Marxist beliefs were entangled with the idealism of the irrationalists. The most important figure is **José Carlos Mariátegui** (1894–1930), who, following González Prada's *indigenismo*, advocated Indian human and civil rights. He founded *Amauta* (1926–30; Wise man), the best radical and influential magazine on the continent. In his *Siete ensayos de interpretación de la realidad peruana* (1928; *Seven Interpretative Essays on Peruvian Reality*), Mariátegui found in the Inca civilization a harmonious paradigm of religion, economy, culture, and government for Peru. Antenor Orrego (1892–1960) was the founder and director of *El Norte* (1922; The north), a left-oriented newspaper from Trujillo, and a regular collaborator of *Amauta*. He wrote *El pueblo continente* (1939; The people of the continent), where he emphasized the need to learn every aspect of the evolution of the Spanish American world, so as to differentiate it better from the European one. Luis E. Valcárcel (1891–?) followed the same tenets in three essays: *Del ayllu al imperio* (1925; From the Ayllu to the empire), *Tempestad en los Andes* (1927; Storm in the Andes), and *Ruta cultural del Perú* (1945; Cultural route of Peru).

Toward the second half of the century, the essay focused on the individual. Influenced by psychoanalysis, the Spanish American intelligentsia examined man as a microcosm of his country. At the same time it regarded him from a universal perspective, as a citizen of the world. As Emilio Uranga says in *Análisis del ser del mexicano* (1952; Analysis of the Mexican being): "It is not a question of interpreting that which is Mexican, that which gives us our identity as human, but rather the reverse – of interpreting that which is human as Mexican." The Mexican Samuel Ramos (1897–1959) authored *El perfil del hombre y la cultura en México* (1934; *Profile of Man and Culture in Mexico*), a deep analysis of the national "personality" stemming from its "childhood" experiences or the experiences related to the traumatic encounter between the Indians and the conquistadores. **Octavio Paz** (1914–), in one of his most famous essays, *El laberinto de la soledad* (1950; *The Labyrinth of Solitude*), analyzed the Mexican ethos by reinterpreting history. The Mexican man, a product of his history, is an orphan, devoid of reality, covered with masks that constantly redefine him. He is alone: "We are finally alone. As all men are. Like them, we live in a world of violence, of simulation and of the self-effacing: that which is a tight solitude, if it defends us it oppresses us, and when it hides us it disfigures and mutilates us. If we tear away these masks, if we open up, if, ultimately, we confront ourselves, we start to live and to truly think . . . There, in the open solitude, hands of other solitary fellow men await us, and for the first time, in our history, we are contemporaries of all men." Many essays in the same vein as *Labyrinth* followed, some published in the famous review *Filosofía y Letras*: Emilio Uranga's "Análisis del ser mexicano" (Analysis of the Mexican being), Jorge Carrión's "Mito y magia del mexicano" (1952; The Mexican's myth and magic) and "De la raíz a la flor del mexicano" (1952; From the Mexican's root to the flower). **Carlos Fuentes** (1928–) wrote *París: La revolución de mayo* (1968; Paris: the May revolution) on the Mexican army's massacre of students at Tlatelolco, *Tiempo mexicano* (1971; Mexican time), and *Nuevo tiempo mexicano* (1994; A new time for Mexico), among others.

Guatemala, las líneas de su mano (1955; Guatemala, the lines in her hand) by **Luis Cardoza y Aragón** (1904–92) explored and interpreted the history of his country in a passionate, lyrical, and objective manner. In Cuba, Fernando Ortiz (1881–1969) started his literary career with a positivist approach, but later, in *Contrapunteo cubano del tabaco y del azúcar* (1940; Cuban counterpoint between tobacco and sugar), he presented a complete analysis of the economic and social structures of Cuba. He coined the term "transculturation," which signified the clash between diverse cultures and their interpenetration at an equal level. The founding of the leftist review *Avance* (1927) brought together essays like Jorge Mañach Robato's (1898–1961) "Indagación del choteo" (1928; Inquiry about *choteo*), in which he analyzed the Cuban character, as well as Juan Marinello's (1899–1977) "Sobre la inquietud cubana" (1929; About Cuban anxiety) and "Americanismo y cubanismo literario" (1932; Americanism and literary Cubanism). The Puerto Rican Antonio S. Pedreira (1899–1939) stated in *Insularismo* (1934) that the Puerto Rican soul, fragmented by its history, sought integration. However, his essay is heavily tinted with geographical and biological determinism. In Colombia, Eduardo Caballero Calderón (1910–) published *Suramérica, tierra del hombre* (1944; South America, land of man) and *Americanos y europeos* (1957; Americans and Europeans), in which he questioned Latin American identity. **Germán Arciniegas** (1900–) was a prolific essayist deeply involved with the continent's destiny. Some of his collections include *El estudiante de la mesa redonda* (1932; The round table student), *América, tierra firme* (1937; America, inland), *Biografía del Caribe* (1945; A biography of the Caribbean), and *El continente de los siete colores* (1965; The seven-colored continent).

The Venezuelan **Mariano Picón-Salas** (1901–65) was one of the first essayists to point out the weaknesses of scientism in *Buscando el camino* (1920; In search of a path). His major essays are *Intuición de Chile y otros ensayos en busca de una conciencia histórica* (1935; An intuition of Chile and other essays in search of a historical conscience), *De la Conquista a la Independencia* (1944; *A Cultural History of Spanish America, from Conquest to Independence*), *Comprensión de Venezuela* (1949; Understanding Venezuela), and *Europa – America, preguntas a la esfinge de la cultura* (1947; Europe – America; questions for the sphinx of culture). The Ecuadorian Jorge Carrera Andrade (1903–78) followed the same path in *Viajes por países y libros* (1965; Travels through countries and books) and *El volcán y el colibrí* (1970; The volcano and the hummingbird). In Chile two major essayists deal with this theme: Benjamín Subercaseaux (1902–73) with *Chile o una loca geografía* (1940; Chile or a crazy geography), and Luis Durand (1895–1954) in *Presencia de Chile* (1942; Chile's presence). Sebastián Salazar Bondy's (1924–1965) *Lima la horrible* (1964) is a systematic and poignant analysis of Lima as perpetuator of the ills of the Colonial period in Peru. Mario Vargas Llosa's (1936–) essays *Políticos peruanos: Palabras, palabras, palabras, 1820–1989* (1989; Peruvian politicians: words, words, words, 1820–1989) and *Desafíos a la libertad* (1994; Challenges to freedom) reflect on the destiny of Peru.

Existentialism was a definite influence on the Argentine essays written by a generation concerned with the essence of human beings and the Argentine ethos. A great pessimism permeated their work. Among the most important of these essayists is **Ezequiel Martínez Estrada** (1895–1964), whose socialist perspective, tinted with existentialism, perceived a failing Argentina. He considered his country to be invisible and inauthentic. Its nature was hostile, its citizens hid behind masks, and Buenos Aires was a corrupt capital which grew too fast. Its artificial world alienated humans from what was true and natural. His most important essays are *Radiografía de la pampa* (1933; *X-Ray of the Pampa*), *La cabeza de Goliat* (1940; The head of Goliat), and *Muerte y transfiguración de Martín Fierro* (1948; The death and transfiguration of Martin Fierro). Carlos Alberto Erro (1903–68) did not share Martínez Estrada's bleakness, but he tried to define *criollismo* (that which is representative of the culture), *argentinidad*, and eventually, *americanidad* as universal concepts. **Eduardo Mallea** (1903–82), an agonist but not a pessimist, believed there were two Argentinas: a visible one which was superficial, selfish, cruel, and held false values, and an invisible one which believed in true values and was honest and generous. This dichotomy could be seen in human beings as well as in the land. His major works are *Conocimiento y expresión de la Argentina* (1935; Knowledge and expression of Argentina), *Historia de una pasión argentina* (1937; History of an Argentine passion), and *El sayal y la púrpura* (1941; The rough cloth and the imperial cloth). Héctor A. Murena (1923–75) concludes this existentialist interpretation with *El pecado original de América* (1954; The original sin of America). Murena asserted that the Spanish American, dispossessed of a history, was alienated from Western history and tried to find his place in someone else's world. A postmodernist, Julio Cortázar (1911–84), was a major innovator of the Spanish American essay. Within his oeuvre, the collections *La vuelta al día en ochenta mundos* (1967; *Around the Day in Eighty Worlds*) and *Último round* (1969; Last round), as well as *Nicaragua, tan violentamente dulce* (1983; *Nicaraguan Sketches*), are the most representative of the ideological essay. Silvina Bullrich (1915–), also Argentinean, penned *La Argentina contradictoria* (1986; Argentina, the contradiction).

The Cuban revolution left a profound impression on the Spanish American intelligentsia. The Uruguayan Eduardo Galeano (1940–) analyzed the history of the continent following the method of dialectical materialism in *Las venas abiertas de América Latina* (1971; *The Open Veins of Latin America*). He wrote: "Underdevelopment is not a stage of development. It is its consequence. The Latin American underdevelopment arises from a foreign development, and continues to feed it. Powerless, and agonizing since it was born, the system's role is that of international servitude . . ." Another Uruguayan, Mario Benedetti (1920–), who has lived most of his life in Cuba, believed Latin America is a political term not defined by a language or a culture, but by whatever is not of the United States. He wrote *El país de la cola de paja* (1960; The country with the straw tail) and *Crónicas del 71* (1972; Chronicles of 1971). In *Calibán: Apuntes sobre la cultura en nuestra América* (1971; *Caliban and Other Essays*), the Cuban Roberto Fernández Retamar (1930–) analyzed the exploitation of Latin America by imperialist powers. The Bolivian Marcelo Quiroga Santa Cruz (1931–80), who was assassinated by a repressive military government, wrote *Desarrollo con soberanía* (1967; Development with sovereignty), *Lo que no debemos callar* (1968; What we cannot say), and most importantly, *El saqueo de Bolivia* (1973; Bolivia's plundering). The antithesis of these essays is *Del buen salvaje al buen revolucionario* (1976; From the good savage to the good revolutionary, translated as *The Latin Americans, Their Love-Hate Relationship with the United States*) by the Venezuelan Carlos Rangel (1929–), who returned to the idea that Spanish American history was one of total failure. Comparing Spanish America's progress to that of the United States, he attributed the difference to the attitude toward the native population of America: the Anglo culture alienated Native Americans while the Spaniards incorporated the Indian and black ethnic groups into their society, making them the major work force.

Women have not figured largely in the history of the Latin American literary essay, perhaps because of their disenfranchisement from the source of political and economic power. While several women writers have written exemplary essays, their concerns are often gender politics, education, and literary issues rather than the question of Latin American identity *per se*. Among women writers whose oeuvre includes outstanding essays are the Mexicans Yolanda Oreamuno (1916–56), **Rosario Castellanos** (1925–74), Elena Poniatowska (1933–), and Margo Glantz (1930–); the Argentines **Victoria Ocampo** (1890–1979) and Alfonsina Storni (1892–1938); the Chileans Gabriela Mistral (1889–1957) and Julieta Kirkwood; the Peruvians Flora Tristan (1803–44) and Magda Portal (1901–89); the Venezuelan Teresa de la Parra (1889–1936); the Costa Rican Carmen Naranjo (1931–); the Cuban Lydia Cabrera (1900–91); and the Puerto Rican Rosio Ferré (1938–).

The literary essay that chronicles the birth and development of the Spanish American countries is a unique form born of the realities of the continent. Although it adheres to the literary currents that were cultivated in the Western hemisphere, the essay acquired a shape of its own by becoming the political, social, and literary mouthpiece of the young continent. As the 21st century approaches, the Spanish American essayist is no longer so concerned with defining the essence of the Latin American people, now that its universality is irrefutable; as a genre, the essay continues to be the best tool for self-examination and self-criticism for a continent that is constantly redefining itself. According to Mario Vargas Llosa (in an interview with José Oviedo, Mexican TV, March 1997), Latin American writers would be irresponsible if they were not concerned with the political fabric of their homelands. As privileged citizens of countries where a large sector of the population is illiterate, they should participate directly or indirectly in the political life of the nation. Some essayists who continue to act as witnesses of their national and continental reality include the Mexicans Elena Poniatowska and **Carlos Monsiváis** (1938–), the Chilean Ariel Dorfman (1942–), the Argentines Joan José Sebreli (1930–), Blas Matamoro (1942–), and María Elena Rodríguez de Magis, and the Peruvian Julio Ortega (1942–).

VERÓNICA SAUNERO-WARD

Anthologies

El ensayo hispanoamericano del siglo XX, edited by John Skirius, Mexico City: Fondo de Cultura Económica, 1994 (original edition, 1981)

Rereading the Spanish American Essay: Translations of 19th and 20th Century Women's Essays, edited by Doris Meyer, Austin: University of Texas Press, 1995

Further Reading

Castañón, Adolfo, "La ausencia ubicua de Montaigne: Ideas para una historia del ensayo hispanoamericano," *Vuelta* 16, no. 184 (March 1992): 35–38

Chachagua, Freddy, and Gleider Hernández, "El discurso crítico hegemónico y crítico marginal en la genealogía del ensayo hispanoamericano," *Confluencia* 8–9, nos. 1–2 (Spring–Fall 1993): 63–79

Concejo, Pilar, "Localismo y universalidad en el ensayo hispanoamericano," *Cuadernos Hispanoamericanos* 387 (September 1982): 631–38

Earle, Peter G., "El ensayo hispanoamericano: Del modernismo a la modernidad," *Revista Iberoamericana* 48, nos. 118–19 (January–June 1982): 47–57

Earle, Peter G., and Robert G. Mead, *Historia del ensayo hispanoamericano*, Mexico City: Andrea, 1973

Fernández, Teodosio, *Los géneros ensayísticos hispanoamericanos*, Madrid: Taurus, 1990

Fernández Retamar, Roberto, "Para una teoría de la literatura hispanoamerica," in his *Para una teoría de la literatura hispanoamericana y otras aproximaciones*, Havana: Casa de las Américas, 1975

Gómez Martínez, Jose Luis, *Teoría del ensayo*, Salamanca: Ediciones Universidad de Salamanca, 1981

Levy, Kurt, and Ellis Keith, editors, *El ensayo y la crítica literaria en Iberoamérica*, Toronto: University of Toronto, 1970

Marichal, Juan, *Teoría e historia del ensayismo hispánico*, Madrid: Alianza, 1984

Martínez-Echazabal, Lourdes, "Positivismo y racismo en el ensayo hispanoamericano," *Cuadernos Americanos* 2, no. 3 (1988): 121–29

Meyer, Doris, editor, *Reinterpreting the Spanish American Essay: Women Writers of the 19th and 20th Centuries*, Austin: University of Texas Press, 1995

Oviedo, José Miguel, "The Modern Essay in Spanish America," in *The Cambridge History of Latin American Literature*, volume 2: *The Twentieth Century*, edited by Roberto González Echevarría and Enrique Pupo-Walker, Cambridge and New York: Cambridge University Press, 1996: 365–424

Ripoll, Carlos, *Conciencia intelectual de América: Antología del ensayo hispanoamericano*, New York: Torres, 1974 (original edition, 1966)

Sacoto, Antonio, "El ensayo como género," in *El indio en el ensayo de la América española*, New York: Las Américas, 1971

Sacoto, Antonio, "El ensayo hispanoamericano contemporáneo," *Cuadernos Americanos* 2, no. 3 (1988): 107–20

Shumway, Nicolas, "The Essay in Spanish South America: 1800 to Modernismo," in *The Cambridge History of Latin American Literature*, volume 1: *Discovery to Modernism*, edited by Roberto González Echevarría and Enrique Pupo-Walker, Cambridge and New York: Cambridge University Press, 1996: 556–89

Stabb, Martin S., *In Quest of Identity: Patterns in the Spanish American Essay of Ideas, 1890–1960*, Chapel Hill: University of North Carolina Press, 1967

Stabb, Martin S., *The Dissenting Voice: The New Essay of Spanish America, 1960–1985*, Austin: University of Texas Press, 1994

Stabb, Martin S., "The Essay of Nineteenth-Century Mexico, Central America, and the Caribbean," in *The Cambridge History of Latin American Literature*, volume 1: *Discovery to Modernism*, edited by Roberto González Echevarría and Enrique Pupo-Walker, Cambridge and New York: Cambridge University Press, 1996: 590–607

Urrello, Antonio, *Verosimilitud y estrategia textual en el ensayo hispanoamericano*, Mexico City: Premiá, 1986

Zum Felde, Alberto, *El problema de la cultura americana*, Buenos Aires: Losada, 1943

Zum Felde, Alberto, *Indice crítico de la literatura hispanoamerica: Los ensayistas*, Mexico City: Guarania, 1954

The Spectator

British periodical, 1711–12, 1714

In the *Spectator*, **Joseph Addison** and **Richard Steele** combined their talents and interests to produce a series of **periodical** essays that both established and defined the genre, rendering it more elegant, social, and edifying than ever before (or since). This **periodical** is distinguished by its high social topics, its formal and detached style, and its abstract and polite vocabulary. Its authors were witty, trenchant, perspicuous, and edifying, while its readers were assumed or encouraged to be attentive, literate, well-informed, and contemplative. Six days a week between March 1711 and December 1712 the *Spectator* exhibited and promoted common sense, decorum, discretion, equanimity, good nature, good taste, politeness, and virtue.

These qualities still enrich its pages, even for those readers who no longer regard them as essential to human happiness and a well-ordered polity.

Addison's boast, in the *Spectator* no. 10, that there were already 3000 papers distributed every day, with some 60,000 readers, suggests how well and how quickly the publication took hold. He promised this sizable, thoughtful, and, above all, new readership that he would endeavor on their behalf "to enliven Morality with Wit, and to temper Wit with Morality," to the considerable advantage of their "Virtue and Discretion." Few periodicals, before or since, have concerned themselves with the virtue and discretion of their readers. Fewer still would have deftly balanced a figure drawn from the forging of swords in a sentence calculated to remind acute readers of the differences between "wit," which is lively and cutting, but brittle, and "morality," which is weighty, divisive, and sturdy.

In the same paper, "Mr. Spectator," the bland but pleasant and serviceable persona that Addison and Steele adopted, announced his ambition to have it said of him that, whereas Socrates "brought Philosophy down from Heaven, to inhabit among Men," he himself had "brought Philosophy out of Closets and Libraries, Schools and Colleges, to dwell in Clubs and Assemblies, at Tea-Tables, and in Coffee-Houses." Those unsocial, masculine, and pedantic places to which "Philosophy" (i.e. love of thinking, wisdom) had previously been confined were bookish, isolated, sparse, and argumentative. The places in which the *Spectator* proposed to make wisdom shine are, instead, social, pleasurable, conversible, and polite. Two of them, the Assemblies and the Tea-Tables, were frequented by women, and Addison and Steele presumed to discuss the concerns and behavior of women in many issues. It must be admitted, however, that the overall air of the *Spectator* is that of the male coffeehouse, into the workings, concerns, and assumptions of which we are given many vivid glimpses. Some 50 different coffeehouses are mentioned by name and location, and many of them are visited or described.

These places call attention to the *Spectator*'s delicate and pervasive sociability, its concentration on the social realm, where representative individuals enter into select company. The essays deal with characters rather than identities, and with sets and clubs rather than private concerns or confusions. When Addison and Steele write about such psychological abstractions as jealousy, envy, zeal, and ambition (as they often do), it is with their social consequences in mind, and it is the reactions of others that the essays develop. Other essays pay sustained attention to the workings of such social abstractions as shame, derision, modesty, impertinence, impudence, cheerfulness, and esteem. Even courting and married couples, the most numerous characters of all, show themselves in public, where Mr. Spectator and others can observe them. Those who stay in their homes and contribute to the paper write of follies and extravagances, misfortunes and visits, rather than of intimacies.

Mr. Spectator might have done well to include two other places that his essays refer to and discuss repeatedly: the print shop and the theater. He relied on the first, of course, to print and distribute papers to an audience that, by definition, took printing very seriously. Books are quoted at the beginning of every paper, and quoted or referred to throughout most of them. Fewer journals have ever been more literate, in the exact sense of that word.

And when they weren't reading, subscribers seem to have been attending or thinking about the theater. A good many of the essays are, in effect, theater criticism, whether discussions of Tragedy (nos. 39, 40, 42, 44) or critiques of single plays (e.g. no. 270, on Beaumont and Fletcher's *The Scornful Lady*). Others deplore the new fashion for opera or puppets, which offend against the *Spectator*'s insistence on language that makes sense, or correct the techniques of actors or the manners of the audience. Many other issues invoke passing references to plays or the theater. In no. 370 Steele quotes the motto above the stage in Drury Lane: "the whole World acts the Player." "It is, with me [he continues], a Matter of the highest Consideration what Parts are well or ill performed, what Passions or Sentiments are indulged or cultivated, and consequently what Manners and Customs are transfused from the Stage to the World, which reciprocally imitate each other."

Its continuing popular success is confirmed by a series of collected editions of the individual papers. The first collection was issued by subscription early in 1712. All seven volumes of the 555 original papers were out by 1713. There were innumerable reprints in the 18th century, and seven new editions thereafter, culminating with the definitive Clarendon Edition edited by Donald Bond in 1965. In 1714 Addison tried to revive the *Spectator*, writing 25 papers himself, and enlisting such contributors as Eustace Budgell, Thomas Tickell, and four or five others to compile 80 papers in all, generally agreed to be inferior to the original 555.

The readership that Addison estimated amounts to about 15 percent of the population of London; there is also contemporary evidence of scattered readers in Dublin, Scotland, Boston, and Sumatra. Glimpses of this readership may be had from the correspondents, real or imaginary, and the advertisements in the original papers, as well as the subscription list to the collected volumes. In his introduction to the Clarendon Edition, Bond quotes a personal advertisement from no. 297 in which we get a vivid glimpse of people we would like to think of as regular readers of the *Spectator*: "A Person in a white Cloth Suit, laced with Silver, who handed two Ladies out of the Box in the Gallery of the Play-house in Drury-lane, on Wednesday last, is desired to come this Day, without fail, to the Abby Church in Westminster, betwixt 3 and 4 in the Afternoon." Bond also summarizes the list of subscribers to the 1712–13 collected edition in some detail, enumerating members of the Peerage, the Church, and the university (the names Isaac Newton and Godfrey Kneller figure in these lists), but also prominent bankers, merchants, and civil servants. The list also includes the names of 36 women.

The commercial nature of the venture is apparent not only in the authors' attention to audience and sales, but also in the increasing number of advertisements for such things as books, plays, housing, and clothing. The business acumen of the two essayists carries over into the celebration of merchants (e.g. no. 174) and a gentle preference for Sir Andrew Freeport, with his eye for the main chance and the bottom line, over Sir Roger de Coverley's outmoded, and landed, patriarchy. But the businessmen, like the gallants, the prostitutes, the servants, and the actors and actresses in the *Spectator*, are all uncommonly articulate and polite.

Several features of the *Spectator* which render it of importance to literary history complicate its status as a collection of essays: its joint, or rather divided, authorship; its reliance on **letters** from readers to form part of the content (Steele incorporated outside contributions into many of the papers he wrote, though it is probable that he and Addison wrote some of the letters themselves, and edited the content of others); its construction of a fictional "club," with the personalities, opinions, and, occasionally, actions of the members becoming the focus of a single essay (e.g. no. 517, on the death of Sir Roger); its frequent veering from essay into narrative, with a story drawn from the past (e.g. no. 349, of Moluc) or imported from afar (e.g. no. 11, of Inkle and Yarico), or a representative and usually cautionary fiction featuring emblematic rather than particularized characters (e.g. "Constantia" and "Theodosius" in no. 164).

Twenty-six papers emanate from a visit to Sir Roger's country estate and report and reflect on the social life of the countryside. Eighteen papers analyze the importance of *Paradise Lost*; six consider, seriously but wittily, wit in the empirical philosophy of Locke; and 11 delve into the psychology and aesthetics of the imagination. The Saturday papers, by Addison, ponder serious topics such as devotion and death; other numbers reflect soberly on what can only be called the human condition – one that has not changed noticeably since these essays were written: "Since we cannot promise our selves constant Health, let us endeavour at such a Temper as may be our best Support in the Decay of it" (no. 143).

Generally, however, the *Spectator* wrote about courtship and marriage, follies and extravagances, disappointments and impertinences, and other large, human concerns. It made the ordinary and social workings of the human body and the human mind its daily topic. What men and women wore and said, read, gossiped, quarreled or bantered about, how they greeted friends and treated strangers – these are its concerns, all vividly presented, thoughtfully developed, and eloquently expressed. The language used in public (and in letters) by real and imagined contemporaries of the original readers is one of the most frequent and fruitful of the *Spectator*'s concerns. Whole essays are given over to appraising the social and semantic value of conversations, trivial or empty expressions, the conventional utterances of courtship, swearing, "ingenious Ribaldry" (no. 155), and a principled distrust of pedantry and "cant," wherever they are uttered (e.g. no. 147).

For Addison and Steele the essay was a social collaboration, not just between themselves and the other occasional contributors, but with their readers, who supplied them with materials, correspondence, and, sometimes, whole papers. (See no. 46, for an outline of topics and materials for future papers, supposedly mislaid in a coffeehouse!) Their style, as we have seen, is formal, witty, abstract, and elaborate. They delight in antithetical paragraphs contrasting wise and foolish behavior, and in extended examples, allegories, and analogies which set the reader's mind to work along clearly marked paths: "A modest Man preserves his Character, as a frugal Man does his Fortune; if either of them live to the Height of either, one will find Losses, the other Errours which he has not Stock by him to make up" (no. 206).

The authors frequently comment on their own style and methods: "When I make Choice of a Subject that has not been treated of by others, I throw together my Reflections on it without any Order or Method, so that they may appear rather in the Looseness and Freedom of an Essay, than in the Regularity of a Set Discourse. It is after this manner that I shall consider Laughter and Ridicule in my present Paper" (no. 249). Though emphasizing the relaxed structure of the essay, this statement also reminds us of Mr. Spectator's willingness to reflect, his consciousness of the work of others, his assortment of subjects, his attention to connections within an essay, and his overriding concern with abstractions that entail moods, attitudes, and behavior.

Subsequent writers admired and emulated the *Spectator*. It became a model from which **Voltaire**, **Benjamin Franklin**, and Giuseppe Baretti learned to write elegant English. In his *Lives of the Poets* (1779–81) **Samuel Johnson** praised Addison because "He not only made the proper use of wit himself, but taught it to others; and from his time it has been generally subservient to the cause of reason and truth" and for a "middle style . . . on grave subjects not formal, on light occasions not groveling" and that is pure, exact, and easy. **Thomas Babington Macaulay**, writing in the *Edinburgh Review* (1843), praised Addison as one who had "reconciled wit and virtue," though Macaulay and his contemporaries had a diminished conception of those two entities, as, indeed, do we. Nevertheless, the *Spectator* continues to be read, admired, and studied.

ALAN T. MCKENZIE

Editions

The Spectator, written and edited by Joseph Addison and Richard Steele, nos. 1–555, 1 March 1711–6 December 1712; second series (by Addison alone), nos. 556–635, 18 June–20 December 1714; edited by Gregory Smith (Everyman Edition), 4 vols., 1907, reprinted 1979, and by Donald F. Bond (Clarendon Edition), 5 vols., 1965; selection, as *Critical Essays from "The Spectator,"* edited by Bond, 1970

Further Reading

Bateson, F. W., "Addison, Steele, and the Periodical Essay," in *Dryden to Johnson*, edited by Roger Lonsdale, London: Sphere, revised edition, 1986; New York: Bedrick, 1987: 117–35

Bloom, Edward A., and Lillian D. Bloom, *Addison's Sociable Animal: In the Market Place, on the Hustings, in the Pulpit*, Providence, Rhode Island: Brown University Press, 1971

Bloom, Edward A., and Lillian D. Bloom, editors, *Addison and Steele: The Critical Heritage*, London: Routledge, 1980

Bloom, Edward A., Lillian D. Bloom, and Edmund Leites, editors, *Educating the Audience: Addison, Steele, and Eighteenth-Century Culture*, Los Angeles: University of California William Andrews Clark Memorial Library, 1984

Bloom, Lillian D., "Addison's Popular Aesthetic: The Rhetoric of the 'Paradise Lost' Papers," in *The Author in His Work: Essays on a Problem in Criticism*, edited by Louis L. Martz and Aubrey Williams, New Haven and London: Yale University Press, 1978: 263–81

Bond, Donald F., "The First Printing of the *Spectator*," *Modern Philology* 47 (1950): 164–77

Bond, Donald F., "Addison in Perspective," *Modern Philology* 54 (1956): 124–28

Damrosch, Leopold, Jr., "The Significance of Addison's Criticism," *SEL* 19 (1979): 421–30

Elioseff, Lee A., *The Cultural Milieu of Addison's Literary Criticism*, Austin: University of Texas Press, 1963

Furtwangler, Albert, "Mr. Spectator, Sir Roger and Good Humour," *University of Toronto Quarterly* (Fall 1976): 31–50

Furtwangler, Albert, "The Making of Mr. Spectator," *Modern Language Quarterly* 38 (1977): 21–39

Ketcham, Michael G., *Transparent Designs: Reading, Performance, and Form in the Spectator Papers*, Athens: University of Georgia Press, 1985

Knight, Charles A., "'The Spectator's' Generalizing Discourse," *Prose Studies* 16 (1993): 44–57

Knight, Charles A., "'The Spectator's' Moral Economy," *Modern Philology* 91 (1993): 161–79

Lewis, C. S., "Addison," in *Essays on the Eighteenth Century Presented to David Nichol Smith in Honour of His Seventieth Birthday*, Oxford: Clarendon Press, 1945; New York: Russell and Russell, 1963

McCrea, Brian, *Addison and Steele Are Dead: The English Department, Its Canon, and the Professionalization of Literary Criticism*, Newark: University of Delaware Press, 1990

McKenzie, Alan T., "Into Company and Beyond: The Passions in 'The Spectator'," in his *Certain, Lively Episodes: The Articulation of Passion in Eighteenth-Century Prose*, Athens: University of Georgia Press, 1990: 89–117

Saccamano, Neil, "The Sublime Force of Words in Addison's 'Pleasures'," *ELH* 58 (1991): 83–106

Watson, Melvin R., "The Spectator Tradition and the Development of the Familiar Essay," *ELH* (1946): 189–215

Zeitz, Lisa M., "Addison's 'Imagination' Papers and the Design Argument," *English Studies* 73 (1992): 493–502

The Spectator

British periodical, 1828–

From its beginning in 1828, the *Spectator* has consistently been regarded as one of the most influential weeklies in Britain. Its founders, Robert Rintoul, Douglas Kinnaird, and Joseph Hume, targeted an independent-thinking readership, "chiefly . . . the men of culture who like to listen to all sides of controversies, provided the argument is conducted with fairness and moderation" (1 May 1858); to a great extent, those people – men and women – continue to make up its readership. The first issue of the paper (5 July 1828) described itself thus:

> The tone and character of the *Spectator*, the variety of its contents, and even its external form, peculiarly fit it for the use of respectable families. Its plan is entirely new, comprising (1) the whole news of the week; (2) a full and impartial exhibition of all the leading politics of the day; (3) a separate discussion of interesting topics of a general nature, with a view to instruction and entertainment at the same time; (4) a department devoted to literature, consisting of independent criticisms of the new books, with specimens of the best passages; (5) dramatic and musical criticism; (6) scientific and miscellaneous information.

Its early tradition of intellectual quality was a result not only of its resolute political independence, but also of the continuity provided by the long-term stewardship of its first four editors: Rintoul (1828–58), Meredith Townsend and Richard Holt Hutton (1861–97), and John St. Loe Strachey (1897–1925). Its quality may also owe something to the fact that those editors were also the proprietors, a situation which assured editorial independence. Since Strachey, some proprietors have also served as editor, but more often than not the two positions have been separate. Modern-era editors have changed with more frequency, too; the only long-term 20th-century editor has been J. Wilson Harris (1932–53).

Although Rintoul wrote very little for the paper during his editorship, he established what became known as the "*Spectator* style," and through careful selection of his writers, judicious editing, and sheer force of will he put out a weekly newspaper that, with few exceptions, read as if it were written by a single individual. The *Spectator* style consisted of well-reasoned, simply written articles that, as Rintoul wrote to William Blackwood, exhibited "straightforwardness, and the preference of plain, strong sense to affected finery or to Cockney simplicity" (**Margaret Oliphant**, 1897). The political articles were informed by Rintoul's liberal-radical leanings, and the literary criticism leaned toward a conservative, utilitarian view of the place of literature in society. The *Spectator*'s most influential essays under Rintoul included the series in support of the Reform Bill of 1832 and Anti-Corn Law legislation in 1846, and of Edward Gibbon Wakefield's scheme for emigration reform in the 1840s.

Although the *Spectator* regularly lost money through its early years, by 1840 the circulation had risen to a respectable 3500 per week and it began paying dividends. Perhaps the paper's marketability and the quality of the writing under Rintoul can best be judged by what happened after he sold the paper to Benjamin Moran in 1858. Moran installed Thornton Hunt as editor, and for the next three years Moran's *Journal* (1948) recorded mounting losses as the circulation declined. Hunt tried to stamp his imprint on the paper, much as Rintoul had, but was unable to create a new *Spectator* style; instead, the paper lost much of its political influence through its support of pro-slavery factions in the United States, and, despite the publication of several occasional essays by Hunt's famous father **Leigh Hunt**, did not seem to have a consistent literary position.

Townsend's purchase of the paper from Moran, and his eventual partnership with Hutton, marked the beginning of a new *Spectator* style. The two re-established Rintoul's independent liberal-radical political position and added to it an emphasis on theological questions. They also improved the quality of the paper's literary criticism, jettisoning Rintoul's utilitarianism for a more art-centered approach. But the two did not try to produce a paper consistent in style; on the contrary, Hutton's essays were described by **Virginia Woolf** as a "voice which is as a plague of locusts – the voice of a man stumbling drowsily among loose words, clutching aimlessly at vague ideas" (*The Common Reader*, 1925), while Townsend's were described as "nervous, vivid, almost violent" (William Beach Thomas, 1928). Still, as Robert Blake said, "if their styles were diverse, unity was preserved by their common ideology" (1978). Townsend and Hutton were joined by some of the leading essayists of the day, including Francis Power Cobbe, Thomas Hughes, Walter Bagehot, Edmund Gosse, John Morley, Emily Faithful, Julia Wedgwood, **Matthew Arnold**, and A. C. Swinburne.

Under Hutton and Townsend, the *Spectator*'s most important political essays were those in support of the North during the American Civil War (a position which caused a momentary decline in circulation), the series attacking the Disraeli government over the Bulgarian atrocities, and those in opposition to Irish Home Rule. Hutton also wrote a number of important theological essays, which he later collected and published. A tone of high seriousness marked most of the

Spectator's essays; it was often noted that the paper was almost totally devoid of a sense of humor during the last half of the 19th century.

Strachey, who succeeded Hutton and Townsend as editor and proprietor, wrote most of the leaders and a large number of literary **reviews** during his first 15 years as editor. His regular contributors, including J. B. Atkins, Stephen Gwynn, C. J. Cornish, and Lord Cromer, did not approach the quality of earlier writers. However, Strachey doubled the paper's circulation from 11,000 to 22,000 in his first five years by producing simple, direct prose in support of such diverse issues as free trade, state-controlled alcohol sales, and Rudyard Kipling's poetry and prose. Unfortunately he worked himself into a serious illness toward the end of World War I and had to cut back his literary and editorial contributions to the *Spectator*. Circulation plunged to just over 13,000 in 1922, and Strachey turned over the operational control of the editorial office to Sir Evelyn Wrench. In 1925, upon Strachey's retirement, Wrench took over as both proprietor and editor.

Through the next three decades the *Spectator* maintained its respected position among the British weeklies. J. Wilson Harris continued the tradition of liberal independence politically while promoting a rather traditional critical position in the arts. He also increased circulation to a high of 53,500 in 1946. From the 1960s on, the *Spectator* has continued to provide a combination of thoughtful political essays and irreverent social criticism, seizing a position that Christopher Booker (1978) has described as midway between Anarchic Reaction and Boring Triviality. Its circulation reached 94,000 at its 150th anniversary in 1978, and its contributors included Richard Ingrams, Auberon Waugh, Richard West, Patrick Marnham, Jeffrey Bernard, Taki, and Michael Heath, who were also the core contributors to the notorious *Private Eye*.

Speaking of the *Spectator*'s readers in 1975, George Hutchinson said: "There is, I believe, a durable if not permanent minority who like and value good writing, considered, unhurried argument and sound information presented at substantial length when occasion requires, free from irrelevance and invested with the independent expert authority frequently encountered among their contributors" (Robert Blake). The reader Hutchinson described sounds remarkably like the *Spectator* reader in 1828. Clearly, Rintoul's formula succeeded beyond what even he might have imagined.

RICHARD D. FULTON

Further Reading

Atkins, J. B., "St. Loe Strachey's *Spectator*," *Spectator*, special supplement, 15 May 1953: xxx

Blake, Robert, "A History of the *Spectator*," *Spectator*, 23 September 1978: 30–35

Booker, Christopher, "An Untimely Obituary," *Spectator*, 23 September 1978: 37–39

Colby, Robert A., "'How It Strikes a Contemporary': The 'Spectator' as Critic," *Nineteenth Century Fiction* 11 (June 1956): 182–206

Escott, T. H. S., *Masters of English Journalism*, Folcroft, Pennsylvania: Folcroft, 1970 (original edition, 1911)

Fulton, Richard D., "*Spectator*," in *British Literary Magazines*, vol. 2, edited by Alvin Sullivan, Westport, Connecticut: Greenwood Press, 1986

Fulton, Richard D., "*Spectator*," in *British Romantic Prose Writers, 1789–1832*, 2nd series, edited by John R. Greenfield, *Dictionary of Literary Biography*, vol. 110, Detroit: Gale Research, 1991

Grant, James, *The Metropolitan Weekly and Provincial Press*, vol. 3 of *The Newspaper Press*, London and New York: Routledge, 1872

Graves, C. L., "The *Spectator* in the Eighties and Nineties," *Spectator*, centennial supplement, 3 November 1928: 16–17

Harrop, A. J., "Rintoul and Wakefield," *Spectator*, centennial supplement, 3 November 1928: 10–11

Hogben, John, *Richard Holt Hutton of 'The Spectator'*, Edinburgh: Oliver and Boyd, 1899

Jump, John D., "Matthew Arnold and the *Spectator*," *Review of English Studies* 25 (1949): 61–64

Leroy, Gaylord C., "Richard Holt Hutton," *PMLA* 56 (1941): 809–40

Oliphant, Margaret, *Annals of a Publishing House: William Blackwood and His Sons, Their Magazine and Friends*, New York: AMS Press, 3 vols., 1974 (original edition, 1897–98)

"The 6,000th *Spectator*," *Spectator*, 25 June 1943: 586–87

"The Spectator," *Nation and Athenaeum* 44 (November 1928): 168–69

Strachey, Amy, *St. Loe Strachey: His Life and His Paper*, London: Gollancz, 1930

Strachey, John St. Loe, *The Adventure of Living: A Subjective Autobiography*, London: Hodder and Stoughton, and New York: Putnam, 1922

Tener, Robert H., "Richard Holt Hutton," *Times Literary Supplement*, 24 April 1959: 241

Tener, Robert H., "Swinburne as Reviewer," *Times Literary Supplement*, 25 December 1959: 755

Tener, Robert H., "The *Spectator* Records, 1874–1897," *Victorian Newsletter* 17 (1960): 33–36

Tener, Robert H., "Spectatorial Strachey," *Times Literary Supplement*, 31 December 1964: 1181

Thomas, William Beach, *The Story of the Spectator, 1828–1928*, London: Methuen, 1928

"The Truth Behind the Facts," *Spectator*, 23 September 1978: 3

Staël, Madame de

French, 1766–1817

In her most important book of essays, *De la littérature considérée dans ses rapports avec les institutions sociales* (1800; *The Influence of Literature upon Society*) and *De l'Allemagne* (1810; *Of Germany*), Germaine Necker, Baroness of Staël von Holstein can be considered a feminist *avant la lettre*, founder of the sociology of literature, and the first historian of comparative history. In her essays she reveals the spirit of the contemporary European movements she came to know during several exiles as a major opponent of Napoleon. The emerging Romantic generation in particular impressed her considerably. Already in *The Influence of Literature upon Society* she transformed the opposition between Christian medieval Romanticism and classicism as stated by August Wilhelm Schlegel in his Berlin lectures into an opposition between German folk literature and the classical tradition, discovering along the way the importance of Nordic literature as well as the tension between Northern and Southern within the history of European culture. Contemporary German literature was considered a necessary model for the renewal of French literature. Madame de Staël emphasized the institutional status of literature, considering the literary text as the expression of society and its history, although society was still understood in the sense of a leading social class. She believed the emergence of new literary classes to be a consequence of the emancipation of society from the monarchical system that resulted from the French Revolution. Freedom and emancipation were the new values of literature.

The sociological emphasis of her essays was inherited from the Enlightenment, especially from Montesquieu's theory of climates and the idea of the influence of literature on religion, habits, and law put forward by Marmontel, whose writings Madame de Staël linked to a Rousseauvian concept of perfectibility. Because of Marmontel's heritage, René Wellek, for instance, denies the originality of Madame de Staël. Her capacity for coherently synthesizing different sources is obviously a heritage of the Enlightenment, and already Vico, **Lessing**, and **Herder** had perceived the influence of people's moral and social habits on literature. Nevertheless, Madame de Staël focused on the importance of extraliterary factors such as nationality, history, and social institutions in an organic way, claiming a more dynamic theory of literature which takes into account historical processes and adapts classic normative poetics to contemporary needs. Methodologically, the sociology proposed by Madame de Staël is obviously not modern, since it does not include the consideration of economic factors. Moreover, her concept of history is not historically differentiated. The idea of perfectibility inherited from **Rousseau** only concerns the ideal of education, and her vision of nations is incomplete (especially concerning Spain). The aim of her essays is nonetheless not the establishment of universal history, but the position of French literature in relation to the literatures of other countries. Her comparative analysis of literary history corresponds with the purpose of defining national character through comparison with representative traditions such as classical literature.

In *De l'Allemagne*, a more meticulous work about German culture, de Staël plays the role of opinion leader for European intellectuals. Through the portraits and reportages (in the sense of modern interviews) as well as résumés of books contained in these essays, Madame de Staël influenced the image of Germans in France and throughout Europe. The emerging Romantic generation in Germany is presented as an idyllic republic of poets and erudite people working enthusiastically on the establishment of modern thinking during the crisis of the ancient social structures in Europe. Her image of Germans was partially a compendium of French common opinions, but more interesting than these stereotypes are her sociological arguments. She attributed what she saw as Germans' lack of taste and *esprit* as well as their inaccurate linguistic style (all of this in spite of their profound intellectual work) to both the nonexistence of a capital and the separation of court life and intellectuals.

Madame de Staël's essayistic style is extremely personal, resulting from discussions within the literary gatherings at her family residence at Coppet on Lake Geneva. Her portraits, particularly in *De l'Allemagne*, are a casual "montage" of impressions, a detailed reportage including quotations from texts (which she translated), as well as a mixture of information and meditations about German philosophy and religion and about questions on literary theory, though she did not examine music and the arts.

VITTORIA BORSÒ

Biography

Anne Louise Germaine Necker, Baronne de Staël von Holstein. Born 22 April 1766 in Paris. Studied privately at home. Grew up attending her mother's salon. Married Baron Eric Magnus de Staël von Holstein, 1786 (separated, 1800; he died, 1802): one daughter (died in infancy). Opened her own salon, 1787. Affair with Count Louis de Narbonne, 1788–93: two sons. Moved to Coppet on Lake Geneva for part of each year, from 1790; fled to England during the Revolution, 1793. Affair with Benjamin Constant, from 1795: one daughter probably fathered by Constant. Exiled by Napoleon, 1795–96; reopened her salon in Paris, 1797; traveled often to Italy, Austria, Germany, Russia, Sweden, and England, from 1803; exiled by Napoleon for *De l'Allemagne*, 1810. Married Jean Rocca secretly, 1811, publicly, 1816: one son. Lived in England, 1813–14; returned to Paris after Napoleon's defeat, 1814. Died (after a stroke) in Paris, 14 July 1817.

Selected Writings

Essays and Related Prose

Lettres sur les ouvrages et le caractère de Jean-Jacques Rousseau, 1788; revised edition, 1789
Réflexions sur le procès de la reine, 1793
Réflexions sur la paix, 1795; edited by C. Cordié, 1945
De l'influence des passions sur le bonheur des individus et des nations, 1796; edited by Michel Tournier, 1979; as *A Treatise on the Influence of the Passions upon the Happiness of Individuals and Nations*, translated anonymously, 1798
Essai sur les fictions, 1796; edited by Michel Tournier, 1979
De la littérature considérée dans ses rapports avec les institutions sociales, 2 vols., 1800; edited by Paul Van Tieghem, 1959, and Gérard Gengembre and Jean Goldzink, 1991; as *A Treatise on Ancient and Modern Literature*, translated anonymously, 1803; as *The Influence of Literature upon Society*, translated anonymously, 1812
De l'Allemagne, 1810; edited by Jean de Pauge and Simone Balayé, 1958
Réflexions sur le suicide, 1813; as *Reflections on Suicide*, translated anonymously, 1813
Essais dramatiques, 1821
Madame de Staël on Politics, Literature, and National Character, translated by Morroe Berger, 1964
An Extraordinary Woman: Selected Writings, translated by Vivian Folkenflik, 1987

Other writings: two dramas-in-verse (*Sophie*, 1790; *Jane Grey*, 1790), two novels (*Delphine*, 4 vols., 1802; *Corinne*, 3 vols., 1807), two volumes of short stories, a play, books on the French Revolution and on cultural comparisons between France and Germany, and many volumes of correspondence.

Collected works edition: *Œuvres complètes*, edited by Auguste-Louis de Staël, 17 vols., 1820–21.

Bibliographies

Longchamp, F.-C., *L'Œuvre imprimée de Mme. Germaine de Staël*, Brussels: Mondeanum, 1966
Schazmann, Paul-Émile, *Bibliographie des œuvres de Madame de Staël*, Paris and Neuchâtel: Attinger, 1938

Further Reading

Balayé, Simone, *Madame de Staël: Lumières et liberté*, Paris: Klincksieck, 1979
Balayé, Simone, *Madame de Staël: Écrire, lutter, vivre*, Geneva: Droz, 1994
Besser, Gretchen Rous, *Germaine de Staël Revisited*, New York: Twayne, 1994

Diesbach, Ghislain de, *Madame de Staël*, Paris: Perrin, 1983

Gutwirth, Madelyn, Avriel Goldberger, and Karyna Szmurlo, editors, *Germaine de Staël: Crossing the Borders*, New Brunswick, New Jersey: Rutgers University Press, 1991

Herold, J. Christopher, *Mistress to an Age: A Life of Mme. de Staël*, Indianapolis: Bobbs Merrill, 1958; London: Hamilton, 1959

Hogsett, Charlotte, *The Literary Existence of Germaine de Staël*, Carbondale: Southern Illinois University Press, 1987

Isbell, John Claiborne, *The Birth of European Romanticism: Truth and Propaganda in Staël's "De l'Allemagne," 1810–1813*, Cambridge: Cambridge University Press, 1994

Posgate, Helen B., *Madame de Staël*, New York: Twayne, 1968

Winegarten, Renée, *Mme. de Staël*, Leamington Spa: Berg, 1985

Steele, Richard

English, 1672–1729

Along with Daniel Defoe and his schoolmate, friend, and coadjutor, **Joseph Addison**, Steele stands as one of the inventors and masters of the **periodical essay**. After attending Charterhouse School and Christ Church, Oxford, and a stint in the Life Guards and Coldstream Guards, Steele, in the first decade of the 18th century, had a successful career as a playwright and political writer. He garnered several lucrative state offices, including the post of Gazetteer. But, as was the case throughout his life, he struggled financially as he pursued gentlemanliness, spending more than he earned.

On 12 April 1709, Steele published the first number of the *Tatler*, hoping it would be a moneymaker. As in the earlier *Gazette* (1707–10), Steele reprinted news items, but the *Tatler* achieved popularity, even fame, because it also offered an essay, frequently a gently ironic comment upon contemporary manners and mores. Steele took the name for the persona of the *Tatler*, Isaac Bickerstaff, from **Jonathan Swift**'s Bickerstaff papers (1708–09). Steele's friendship with Swift, however, would soon fall victim to the divisions in British society created by the War of the Spanish Succession and the disputes between landed men and moneyed men, between Tories and Whigs that erupted during the ministry of Robert Harley, Earl of Oxford. Swift became Harley's chief propagandist; Steele became one of Harley's most visible and vociferous opponents.

In the years 1710 to 1714, Steele passionately defended the Duke of Marlborough's war policy, repeatedly accusing the Oxford ministry of threatening the Protestant Succession as it attempted to negotiate a peace with France. In October 1710, the Oxford ministry stripped Steele of his Gazetteership. He responded to his financial loss by starting the *Spectator*, the first number appearing on 1 March 1711. Addison, who had not written for the *Tatler* until the 18th number, had also lost state offices and wrote for the *Spectator* from its inception.

The *Spectator* claimed "an exact neutrality" in political matters, but political discord intensified, as the Oxford ministry attempted to remove Marlborough and to conclude peace negotiations. By 1712, Steele wished to comment directly upon events; hence the journal concluded its first run on 6 December 1712 (Addison would later revive it). The following March, Steele began publishing the *Guardian*, which was followed in October by the *Englishman*, both journals claiming to defend

traditional English liberties threatened by the conditions of the Peace of Utrecht. Steele's political commentary became so controversial that, in 1714, he was expelled from Parliament and prosecuted for publishing seditious libels. With the death of Queen Anne and the Hanoverian Succession, however, Steele returned to political favor. He was awarded the Royal Patent for Drury Lane Theatre, and his last periodical, the *Theatre* (1720), concerned itself principally with matters of theater government and with establishing a model for comedy to replace that of the Restoration stage.

As Steele sought a large audience, so he avoided the Juvenalian satire of Swift, preferring to take a more Horatian tack, emphasizing social consensus and the importance of good nature. Steele tries to direct his **satire** at groups rather than at individuals, and he always seeks a temperate tone. Perhaps the best example of this is the most famous *Spectator* character created by Addison and Steele, Sir Roger de Coverley, a landed man and a Tory, the political opposite of Steele. Yet as he is characterized throughout the journal, most notably in a series of papers by Addison in which Mr. Spectator visits Sir Roger in the country, de Coverley acts with admirable if old-fashioned good will. He falls asleep at church services after requiring all other members of the congregation to remain awake; at the assizes he makes an irrelevant speech about a legal matter that he does not understand. He appears in equal parts superannuated and admirable.

As part of his campaign to shape manners (and to build a large following), Steele takes clarity as one of his great objects. "Hard and crabbed Words" (*Tatler* no. 2) are to be avoided, lest they alienate readers. In the *Tatler* no. 212, a **letter** from "Plain English" requests an explanation of a term, "*Simplex Munditis*," used in an earlier essay. Although Addison and Steele were both cultivated, even (at least in Addison's case) learned men, Steele, rather than jesting about his correspondent's lack of education, patiently offers the explanation required. "Plain English" sets the standard to which Steele aspires. Papers in both the *Tatler* and the *Spectator* open with epigrams from the classical languages, but it is a rare paper that, at some point, does not gloss the epigram in English.

As part of this pursuit of clarity, Steele attacks punning as a device for "Men of small Intellects" (*Spectator* no. 504) and characterizes the conversational counterpart of punning – "biting" – as one symptom of a "Decay in Conversation," as a technique in the "Art" of "being unintelligible in Discourse" (no. 12). He returns to the topic of biting in no. 504, dismissing it as an act of conversational duplicity and associating it with criminals. He claims that "a Biter is one who thinks you a Fool, because you do not think him a Knave."

Despite his attacks upon verbal artifice – ambiguity, punning, biting – Steele relishes extended explanatory analogies. While he strives always to eliminate "double meanings" from his diction, he makes persistent use of allegory, so long as the allegory maintains an unambiguous and fixed correspondence between the characters and objects it describes and the virtues or vices they represent; for Steele "fable" and "allegory" are synonymous. He uses allegory in its simplest form, the *roman à clef*, by inventing imaginary kingdoms that comment directly upon life in Great Britain.

Having established an analogy, Steele is loath to drop it; rather he will return to it and eliminate any ambiguity. In a series of *Tatler* papers on the evils of gambling, he opens by alerting his readers that an allegory will follow: "*Aesop* has gain'd to himself immortal Renown for figuring the Manners, Desires, Passions, and Interests of Men, by Fables of Beasts and Birds; I shall in my future Accounts of our modern Heroes and Wits vulgarly call'd *Sharpers*, imitate the Method of that delightful Moralist" (no. 59). He then compares sharpers to a "Pack of Dogs," and, in subsequent numbers, categorizes the different species of "Curs," even as he notes the similarities between a dog kennel and a gambling house. The last paper of the series (no. 76) describes the "Curs" as threatening the very being of the state because they illicitly acquire property, the basis of commonwealth in Steele's Whiggish political thinking.

This last paper expands the relevance of the allegory and also links this series to ten papers in which Steele (along with Addison) compares the morally dead to the physically dead and urges many in his audience to consider if they should turn themselves in to "Upholders" (undertakers) for burial. Letters come in from upholders who defend the honor of their profession and from readers who wonder about their moral health, and Steele uses these to keep the topic alive, to refine our sense of what moral deadness actually is. At first, the comparison of the morally and the physically dead is witty, even ironic; the word "dead" is briefly ambiguous. But Steele never leaves his readers in this condition. He elaborates the analogy until it becomes familiar, even, as correspondents join in, conversational.

Steele frequently returns to comparisons and restates them. Statements like "In my last *Thursday*'s paper I made mention of" (*Spectator* no. 227) and "I shall reserve this Subject for the Speculation of another Day" (*Spectator* no. 275) bind the papers together. They also allow Steele to become his own interpreter. Steele – whose life was a busy blend of politics, attempts at commerce, and active socializing – was not above using such cross-referencing to ease his writing load. That load, heavy in the *Tatler*, which was published thrice-weekly, doubled in the *Spectator*. While the provenance of letters to the *Spectator* remains an open question, and some of the letters clearly were written by Addison and Steele, others come from actual correspondents. Correspondence both keeps issues going and helps to refine them. Thus, in the *Spectator* no. 268, a correspondent writes, "Your Discourse of the 29th of *December* [no. 201] on Love and Marriage is of so useful a kind, that I cannot forbear adding my Thoughts to yours on that Subject." While what evidence we have shows that Steele used few letters as they were submitted, he did study them carefully, occasionally changing or improving them, so they could fit into a series of his devising.

The question of the respective contributions of Addison and Steele to the two great journals has been raised frequently and, in the 19th century, was pursued with remarkable intensity. **Thomas Babington Macaulay** in an 1843 essay on Addison praised him for bringing "suavity and moderation" to the political and literary conflicts of the early 18th century, even as he dismissed Steele: "His writings have been well compared to those light wines which, though deficient in body and flavour, are yet a pleasant drink if not kept too long, or carried too far." Steele, however, found his defenders. John Forster ("Sir Richard Steele," 1855) claimed that his stories

"have all the warmth as well as brevity of unpremeditated accounts," and that "the beauties as well as the defects of his style" follow from his mastery of the "colloquial." Austin Dobson (1886), citing **Leigh Hunt**, judged Steele's humor to be "so cheerful and good-natured, so frank and manly that . . . 'I prefer open-hearted Steele with all his faults to Addison with all his essays'." The contrast between Addison's suavity and Steele's sentimentality recurs in 19th- and 20th-century criticism. W. J. Courthope (*Addison*, 1901) mediates the two positions by describing Addison as an improver of "the opportunity which Steele affords him." In this view, the impetuous and impecunious Steele opens territory that the urbane Addison cultivates.

Steele had a remarkably busy life. His work as an essayist stands with his work as a playwright and critic; his literary career stands with numerous other public activities – be they as grand as speaking in Parliament or as mundane as fending off debt collectors. Seeking to gain income from his essays, Steele was closely attuned to his audience, necessarily sensitive to changes in the reading public in the early 18th century. Perhaps his greatest achievement was his offering, in the *Tatler* and the *Spectator* most notably, a mediation between landed men and moneyed men, between the aristocracy and the bourgeoisie, between tradition and change. In the breadth of his activities and his sympathies, he helped to define polite behavior for a middle class that was just coming into being and did not yet define itself as such.

BRIAN MCCREA

Biography

Born in Dublin; baptized 12 March 1672. Studied at Charterhouse, London, where he met Joseph Addison, 1684–89; Christ Church, Oxford, 1690; Merton College, Oxford, 1691–92. Served in the Life Guards, 1692–95, and as a captain in the Coldstream Guards, 1695–97; secretary to Lord Cutts, 1696–97; stationed at the Tower of London, by 1700, and in Lord Lucas' regiment at Landguard Fort, Suffolk, 1702–05. Fathered an illegitimate daughter. Married Margaret Stretch, 1705 (died, 1706). Served Prince George of Denmark (Queen Anne's husband), 1706–08. Married Mary Scurlock, 1707 (died, 1718): two sons and two daughters. Gazetteer, and editor, the *Gazette*, 1707–10. Founding editor of several periodicals, including the *Tatler*, 1709–11, the *Spectator* (with Addison), 1711–12, the *Guardian*, 1713, the *Englishman*, 1713–14, the *Lover*, 1714, the *Reader*, 1714, *Town-Talk*, 1715–16, the *Tea-Table*, 1716, *Chit-Chat*, 1716, the *Plebeian*, 1719, and the *Theatre*, 1720. Member of Parliament for Stockbridge, Hampshire, 1713–14 (expelled), Boroughbridge, Yorkshire, 1715, and Wendover, Buckinghamshire, 1722; on Hanoverian succession, held various appointed positions, including governor of the Theatre Royal, Drury Lane, 1714–24. Knighted, 1715. Died in Carmarthen, Wales, 1 September 1729.

Selected Writings

Essays and Related Prose

The Tatler, nos. 1–271, 12 April 1709–2 January 1711; edited by Donald F. Bond, 3 vols., 1987; as *The Lucubrations of Isaac Bickerstaff, Esq.*, edited by John Nichols, 6 vols., 1786
The Spectator, written and edited with Joseph Addison, nos. 1–555, 1 March 1711–6 December 1712; edited by Gregory Smith (Everyman Edition), 4 vols., 1907, reprinted 1979, and by Donald F. Bond (Clarendon Edition), 5 vols., 1965; selection, as *Critical Essays from "The Spectator,"* edited by Bond, 1970

The Guardian, with others, nos. 1–175, 12 March–1 October 1713; edited by John Calhoun Stephens, 1982

The Englishman, nos. 1–57, 6 October 1713–15 February 1714; second series, nos. 1–38, 11 July–21 November 1715; edited by Rae Blanchard, 1 vol., 1955

The Reader, nos. 1–9, 22 April–10 May 1714

The Lover, nos. 1–40, 25 February–27 May 1714; edited by W. Lewin, 1 vol., 1887

Town-Talk, nos. 1–9, 17 December 1715–15 February 1716

Chit-Chat, nos. 1–3, March 1716

The Plebeian, nos. 1–4, 14 March–6 April 1719

The Theatre, nos. 1–28, 2 January–5 April 1720; edited by John Loftis, 1962

Periodical Journalism 1714–1716: The Lover, The Reader, Town Talk, Chit-Chat, edited by Rae Blanchard, 1959

Selections from the Tatler and the Spectator, edited by Angus Ross, 1982

Other writings: four plays, occasional verse, and correspondence (collected in *The Correspondence of Richard Steele*, edited by Rae Blanchard, 1968).

Further Reading

Bloom, Edward A., and Lillian D. Bloom, editors, *Addison and Steele: The Critical Heritage*, London: Routledge, 1980

Bond, Richmond P., *The Tatler: The Making of a Literary Journal*, Cambridge, Massachusetts: Harvard University Press, 1971

Dobson, Austin, *Richard Steele*, London: Longman Green, and New York: Appleton, 1886

Goldgar, Bertrand A., *The Curse of Party: Swift's Relations with Addison and Steele*, Lincoln: University of Nebraska Press, 1961

Ketcham, Michael G., *Transparent Designs: Reading, Performance, and Form in the Spectator Papers*, Athens: University of Georgia Press, 1985

McCrea, Brian, *Addison and Steele Are Dead: The English Department, Its Canon, and the Professionalization of Literary Criticism*, Newark: University of Delaware Press, 1990

Winton, Calhoun, *Captain Steele: The Early Career of Richard Steele*, and *Sir Richard Steele, M.P.: The Later Career*, Baltimore: Johns Hopkins University Press, 2 vols., 1964–70

Stegner, Wallace

American, 1909–1993

During a writing career that stretched over half a century, from his first novel, *Remembering Laughter* (1937), to his last book of essays, *Where the Bluebird Sings to the Lemonade Springs* (1992), and his death in 1993, Wallace Stegner produced 13 novels (one of which won the Pulitzer Prize in 1972), three volumes of short stories, three historical and biographical works, and seven collections of essays. Although Stegner is best known to most readers for his fiction, many critics believe that his reputation as an essayist will eventually be just as strong.

Having spent his high school and college years, as well as the first years of his teaching career, in Salt Lake City, Stegner was well equipped to write *Mormon Country* (1942), a book which remains in print and continues to sell over 50 years after its first publication. In 28 essays he writes about the culture and history of a religious group often misunderstood, deftly weaving the religious beliefs and practices, history, culture, and personalities of a distinctly American denomination into an engaging book. A reading of these essays makes

it clear that Stegner highly respected the strength and faith of these people even though he did not share their theology.

Wolf Willow (1962), whose subtitle is *A History, a Story, and a Memory of the Last Plains Frontier*, is an interesting blend of 19 essays in which Stegner deals with his youthful years from 1914 to 1920 in southern Saskatchewan. It is a loving evocation of the last years of the Canadian frontier in which he studies the relationship between the people and the harsh land in which they live. The town of Whitemud (actually East End) comes through in these pieces, Stegner says near the end of the book, as "a seedbed, as good a place to be a boy and as unsatisfying a place to be a man as one could well imagine."

The Sound of Mountain Water (1969) contains 14 essays written over a period of more than three decades dealing with the American West, its history, local color, and culture. Two of the essays, "At Home in the Fields of the Lord" and "Born a Square," are among his best, the first dealing with the author's experience in growing up as a "Gentile" (i.e. non-Mormon) in Salt Lake City, the second with the difficulties of writers from the American West trying to find their way in a literary world dominated by East Coast editors and publishers who know and care little about the West.

American Places (1981), lavishly illustrated with color photographs by the eminent American photographer Eliot Porter, is a collection of 14 essays Stegner wrote with his son Page (himself a well-known writer) dealing with North American human and natural history, the relationship between Americans and their environment, and the people themselves, sometimes told in the words of America's explorers and immigrants. Stegner wrote eight of the essays himself and collaborated with Page on one.

One Way to Spell Man (1982), like *American Places*, was published after Stegner had retired from Stanford University, where he had directed one of America's most distinguished creative writing programs. The book is a collection of 16 essays written over 30 years from the 1950s onward and previously published in a variety of quality magazines and as editorial introductions to literary works. In these pieces Stegner writes about the relationship of the arts to our understanding of the world around us, the craft of fiction, the problems of the young writer, the superfluity of four-letter words, adulthood, the seeking of excellence and pleasure, Canadian culture, the photography of Ansel Adams, and conservation. Three other essays are critical analyses of novels: Owen Wister's *The Virginian*, Walter Van Tilburg Clark's *The Ox-Bow Incident*, and A. B. Guthrie's *The Big Sky*. All of these essays, like his others and his fiction, are infused with the spirit of Stegner's statement in his **preface**: "I am terribly glad to be alive; and when I have wit enough to think about it, terribly proud to be a man and an American, with all the rights and privileges that those words connote; and most of all I am humble before the responsibilites that are also mine. For no right comes without a responsibility, and being born luckier than most of the world's millions, I am also born more obligated."

Where the Bluebird Sings to the Lemonade Springs (1992), Stegner's last book-length publication, brings together 16 essays previously published in magazines and books. He writes about, among other things, his migrant childhood in Canada and the American West, his relationship with his mother,

Western American aridity, conservation, and the art of fiction; he also provides **critical essays** on George R. Stewart and John Steinbeck.

Stegner's essays, like his fiction, are strongly permeated with a moral sense. Whether writing about the beliefs and folk ways of a Mormon village in southern Utah, the place of a library in a civilization, or the art of fiction, Stegner believes that things matter.

ROBERT C. STEENSMA

Biography

Wallace Earle Stegner. Born 18 February 1909 in Lake Mills, Iowa. Studied at the University of Utah, Salt Lake City, A.B., 1930; University of Iowa, Iowa City, A.M., 1932, Ph.D., 1935; University of California, Berkeley, 1932–33. Married Mary Stuart Page, 1934: one son. Taught at Augustana College, Rock Island, Illinois, 1934, University of Utah, 1934–37, University of Wisconsin, Madison, 1937–39, Harvard University, Cambridge, Massachusetts, 1939–45, and Stanford University, California, 1945–71; also visiting lecturer or writer-in-residence at various universities and institutions. Staff member, Bread Loaf Writers' Conference, Vermont, from 1939. Editor, Houghton Mifflin publishers, 1945–53. Chair, National Parks Advisory Board, 1965–66. Editor-in-chief, *American West*, 1966–68. Awards: many, including several fellowships; O. Henry Award, 1942, 1950, 1954; Houghton Mifflin Life-in-America Award, 1945; Anisfield-Wolf Award, 1945; Pulitzer Prize, for *Angle of Repose*, 1972; Western Literature Association Award, 1974; National Book Award, 1977; Los Angeles *Times* Kirsch Award, 1980; honorary degrees from seven universities. Died in Santa Fe, New Mexico, 13 April 1993.

Selected Writings

Essays and Related Prose

Mormon Country, 1942
Wolf Willow: A History, a Story, and a Memory of the Last Plains Frontier, 1962
The Sound of Mountain Water, 1969
American Places, with Page Stegner, photographs by Eliot Porter, 1981
One Way to Spell Man, 1982
The American West as Living Space, 1987
Where the Bluebird Sings to the Lemonade Springs: Living and Writing in the West, 1992

Other writings: 13 novels (including *The Big Rock Candy Mountain*, 1943; *Angle of Repose*, 1972; *The Spectator Bird*, 1976; *Crossing to Safety*, 1987), short stories, biographies of John Wesley Powell (1954) and Bernard De Voto (1974), and works on history, especially the American West.

Bibliography

Colberg, Nancy, *Wallace Stegner: A Descriptive Bibliography*, Lewiston, Idaho: Confluence Press, 1990

Further Reading

Anthony, Arthur, editor, *Critical Essays on Wallace Stegner*, Boston: Hall, 1982
Benson, Jackson J., *Wallace Stegner: His Life and Work*, New York: Viking Penguin, 1996
Lewis, Merrill, and Lorene Lewis, *Wallace Stegner*, Boise, Idaho: Boise State College, 1972
Robinson, Forrest G., and Margaret G. Robinson, *Wallace Stegner*, New York: Twayne, 1977

Steinhardt, N.
Romanian, 1912–1989

N. Steinhardt belongs to a remarkable generation of Romanian essayists and philosophers (Generation '27) whose intellectual journey began in the late 1920s and first peaked in the 1930s. Among Steinhardt's friends at the time were Mircea Eliade, Eugène Ionesco, and **E. M. Cioran**, who later made brilliant careers abroad. Influenced by the predominant existentialist *Zeitgeist*, these young Romanian intellectuals were obsessed with authenticity, saw culture and life as indissolubly linked, and were familiar with the main intellectual debates of the time. Steinhardt's friendship with other distinguished essayists and philosophers who remained in Romania – Constantin Noica, Alexandru Paleologu, Mihai Sora, Sergiu Al. George, Dinu Pillat – had a lasting influence on his intellectual and spiritual life.

These similarities notwithstanding, Steinhardt's own destiny was a singular one, in many respects a coincidence of opposites. A Jew who converted to Eastern Orthodox Christianity, a writer and monk dividing his time between the cultural attractions of Bucharest and the contemplative atmosphere of Rohia monastery, an enlightened "nationalist" who loved the traditions of his country but also felt comfortable on the streets of London or in the gardens of Chevotogne monastery, Steinhardt considered himself a *franc-tireur*, a "liberal conservative," and a "dilettante." In his essays he mixed moral and aesthetic considerations and ignored the often rigid canons of academic literary criticism and philosophy. His works – published in the most distinguished Romanian journals such as *Revista Fundaţiilor Regale* (The journal of royal foundations), *Viaţa Românească* (Romanian life), *Secolul 20* (The 20th century), *Steaua* (The star), *Familia* (The family), and *Vatra* (The hearth) – range from theological essays to nonacademic literary criticism. Among his most beloved authors were **G. K. Chesterton, Charles Dickens**, Nikolai Berdiaev, **Charles Péguy**, and Mircea Eliade; his admiration was for the France of **Blaise Pascal, Simone Weil**, and Léon Bloy rather than that of René Descartes, **Jean-Paul Sartre**, and Michel Foucault.

A lover of liberty and an opponent of unconditional obedience and dogmatism, Steinhardt was rightly called by one of his fellows "the samurai of Romanian literary criticism." His eccentric profile stirred controversy and admiration; after the Revolution of 1989 he became almost a cult figure. Unexpected associations of ideas, the propensity to reconsider unduly ignored writers, the rejection of the ethics/aesthetics dichotomy – these were among the characteristics that formed the core of his personality as an essayist. The aim of art, Steinhardt once wrote (echoing Andrei Tarkovskii), is to prepare humans for death; culture cannot be separated from ethics simply because there is no hiatus between life and books. Furthermore, he believed that the key to understanding art and literature is to cherish all their forms and manifestations. The more one admires and loves, Steinhardt once wrote, the happier one is. Admiring, however, requires understanding otherness, overcoming one's own solitude, and sharing in the communion with others. The intellectual knows how to go beyond himself and is fascinated with human diversity. An intellectual, Steinhardt claims, does not read what interests him, he is simply interested in anything he reads.

Steinhardt's iconoclastic nature was powerfully conveyed in his first book, *In genul tinerilor* (1934; In the manner of young-sters), a collection of highly entertaining essays-pastiches published under the pseudonym Antisthius (taken from **La Bruyère**'s *Caractères*), in which he mocks the verbosity and style of his friends' writings. Steinhardt's later essays were deeply influenced by an experience he had at a critical moment in his life. During his imprisonment for political reasons (1959–64), he converted to Eastern Orthodox Christianity. Entering this new world, he discovered joy as the eternal theme of Christianity and came to learn the value of courage and inner liberty. The book that would bring him posthumous fame, *Jurnalul fericirii* (1991; The diary of happiness), describes Steinhardt's *saison en enfer* and was unanimously hailed as a revelation, combining irony and wit, vernacular language and sophisticated philosophical and theological references. The *Jurnalul*, along with the seminal essay "Secretul 'Scrisorii pier-dute'" (1975; The secret of "The lost letter") and the posthu-mously edited **sermons** (which are, in fact, brilliant oral essays full of theological insight and persuasion), can be considered the most refined literary expressions of Steinhardt's outlook, with forays into literature, ethics, religion, politics, and the philosophy of culture. His important essay-manifesto on liberty, "Taina libertății" (1987; The mystery of liberty), is a momentous apology of political courage and a firm denunci-ation of voluntary servitude.

The fascination with Steinhardt's essays comes not only from his ideas, but also from his profoundly original and persua-sive style. His is a *fröhliche Wissenschaft* (gay science) aiming at a wide audience with an appetite for wisdom rather than entertainment. Provocative ideas, rhetorical twists, and a ludic style captivate his readers, while skillful paradoxes and a nondidactic, nonsystematic approach couched in a peculiar, sometimes archaic vocabulary convey puzzling ideas and connections worthy of any great French moralist. Steinhardt's writings are always warm and joyful, pathetic and enthusiastic, never formal or dry; an "ideal reader" himself interested in philosophy and thrillers, theology and physics, literature and history, Steinhardt was driven by the concupiscence of know-ledge, yet he never forgot that all systems and theories are relative, partial, questionable, and uncertain. The breadth and variety of his interdisciplinary interests are indeed astonishing: he cherished classical as well as contemporary authors and had a special predilection for unduly forgotten – it is tempting to say second-rank – authors. His topics range from liberty to false idealism, from exile to physics experiments, from contem-plation to the new French quantitative historiography. He wrote with equal interest, competence, and sympathy on Michelangelo Antonioni and **Voltaire**, Dickens and Barbusse, Eliade and Beaumarchais, Daudet and Aitmatov, Maria Callas and **Dostoevskii**, Kurt Gödel and **Thomas Mann**, Mateiu Caragiale and Marshall McLuhan. Writing on Chesterton, he celebrated the mystery of life and the value of fidelity. From Marcel Jouhandeau he learned the joy of life, while Péguy and **Henry de Montherlant** taught him the value of courage. Reading Cervantes, Dickens, and John Galsworthy was for Steinhardt an occasion to note that writing a novel is a hap-pening in itself in which authors themselves gradually discover their characters. Milton reinforced one of his older beliefs that the writer must not be detached from history and contingency.

Finally, writing on Sinclair Lewis was an opportunity to meditate, in the wake of Alexis de Tocqueville, on democratic conformity and the need to swim against the current.

To account for the puzzling breadth of Steinhardt's writ-ings, one should bear in mind that in his view the essay is much more than literary criticism or learned scholarship: it is a "happening," a sophisticated and subtle form of commen-tary and meditation aiming at a "second creation." Steinhardt preferred what he called a "field analysis" to a more detailed exegesis focusing exclusively on the text. He believed that every work of art is surrounded by a halo similar to that found around everyone; the essayist must study this halo and attempt to translate its aura into words. In Steinhardt's view, to be an essayist one must learn the "art of admiration"; writing an essay amounts to composing a hymn in praise of the original work. This requires much more than hermeneutic skills: a calling is needed that combines attention to detail with synthetic intuition and empathy. Steinhardt was never wary of quoting Werner Heisenberg to the effect that the observer always influences the observed phenomenon; in a similar manner, the essayist interferes with the works he admires, thus creating new meanings. He cannot limit his interests, for he is "condemned" to universalism and an unending quest. The essayist is expected to be cultivated and intelligent, attentive and moderate, enthusiastic and capable of admiration, ambi-tious and daring.

AURELIAN CRĂIUȚU

Biography

Born in 1912 in Bucharest. Studied law at the University of Bucharest, law degree, 1934, Ph.D., 1936. Visited France and England, 1937–39. Contributor to various journals, including *Revista Fundațiilor Regale*, 1940s. Imprisoned for political reasons, 1959–64. Began to publish again, 1976. Entered the Rohia monastery, Maramures (northern Romania), 1980, but continued to be active in literary circles. Died March 1989.

Selected Writings

Essays and Related Prose

In genul tinerilor (as Antisthius), 1934
Essai sur une conception catholique du judaisme, with E. Neuman, 1935
Illusions et réalités juives, with E. Neuman, 1936
Între viață si cărți, 1976
Incertitudini literare, 1980
Geo Bogza: Un Poet al efectelor, Exaltării, Grandiosului, Solemnității, Exuberanței și Pateticului, 1980
Critică la persoana întîi, 1983
Escale în timp și spațiu, 1987
Prin alții spre sine: Eseuri vechi si noi, 1988
Jurnalul fericirii, edited by V. Ciomoș, 1991
Monologul polifonic, edited by V. Bulat, 1991
Daruind vei dobîndi (sermons), 1992; enlarged edition, 1994
Primejdia mărturisirii, edited by I. Pintea, 1993
Cartea împărtășirii, edited by I. Vartic, 1995

Further Reading

Alexandru, Ioan, "Elogiu simplității," *Flacăra*, 3 April 1980
Ierunca, Virgil, "N. Steinhardt și 'dreapta socotința'," in his *Subiect și predicat*, Bucharest: Humanitas, 1993
Lovinescu, Monica, "N. Steinhardt la 70 ani," in her *Unde scurte III*, Bucharest: Humanitas, 1994: 342–44

Lovinescu, Monica, "*Escale in timp si spatiu,*" in her *Unde scurte IV*, Bucharest: Humanitas, 1995: 356–61

Grigurcu, Gheorghe, "N. Steinhardt ori samuraiul critic," in his *Între critici*, Cluj: Dacia, 1983: 140–43

Grigurcu, Gheorghe, "Creştinismul în tratare liberă," *Viaţa Românească* 9 (1991): 93–99

Mecu, Nicolae, "Portret al artistului la bătrîneţe," *Revista de Istorie si Teorie Literară* 40, nos. 1–2 (1992): 57–69

Negoiţescu, Ion, "Predicile lui N. Steinhardt," *Transilvania* 1–2 (1993): 113–14

Negoiţescu, Ion, "N. Steinhardt, escale în timp şi spaţiu," in his *Scriitori contemporani*, Cluj: Dacia, 1994: 413–16

Simuţ, Ion, "Destinul unei cărţi, cartea unui destin," in his *Incursiuni în literatura actuală*, Oradea: Cogito, 1994: 306–13

Stempowski, Jerzy

Polish, 1893–1969

The major part of Jerzy Stempowski's output consists of thousands of pages of articles, **letters**, and *feuilletons*, yet its kernel is the essay. The selection of texts *Eseje dla Kassandry* (1961; Essays for Cassandra), prepared by the author himself, and the posthumously published volume *Od Berdyczowa do Rzymu* (1971; From Berdyczow to Rome) constitute merely a fourth of Stempowski's output.

From among the prewar essays, particular attention should be given to the **pamphlet** *Pan Jowialski i jego spadkobiercy* (1931; Mr. Jowialski and his heirs), which at first appears to be a critical study of the comedies of the Polish comic playwright Aleksandr Fredro. In fact it is a critique of the policies of Marshal Józef Piłsudzki, the consequences of which Stempowski, who had access to ministerial cabinets, could observe from close up. Stempowski revealed his intentions in his **preface** to the essay, in which he cautions that "to read a little bit more than the author actually wrote is the normal task of the reader, who maintains the perennial illusion of the ever-new richness of old literature." An excellent essay about the Western European avant-garde in art, "Chimera jako zwierzę pociągowe" (1933; Chimera as a beast of burden), written around the same time, was particularly important in gaining Stempowski recognition as an essayist. In it he uncovers the hidden relationships between the economic processes of the first quarter of the 20th century and the "literary currents vital for European Bohemia": "Lautréamont, Rimbaud, Dostoevskii, Nietzsche created in loneliness, yet they opposed the whole world. Surrealists write as a school; they are encouraged and applauded by a certain elite in the audience, and, besides, by a crowd of snobs and nouveaux-riches."

A major subject of Stempowski's essays is the crisis and decline of European civilization, as, for example, in "Esej dla Kassandry" (1950; "Essay for Cassandra"), "Rubis d'Orient" (1954), and "Czytając Tukidydesa" (1957; Reading Thucydides). In invoking the mythological persona of Cassandra, Stempowski presents portraits of people who turned out to be perceptive in their "prophecies" regarding the future of Europe. In common with the daughter of Priam, they had been pushed aside and misunderstood by their own contemporaries. The end of the essay leaves no room for doubt: "If Europe, ruined by so many insanities, is to avoid annihilation, her population must learn to foresee more accurately the results of its actions, and it can no longer afford to ignore those who possess this gift." In the text alluding to Thucydides' *Peloponnesian War*, Stempowski uses a similar artistic device, accepting that the present can be investigated in an interesting way if we assume the perspective of past generations. Moreover, human fate likes to repeat itself; the nature of man does not change. The words of **Ernst Jünger** quoted at the beginning of the essay are telling: "The great world theater has a small cast. In historical costumes, with the languages from different epochs on their lips, they always play the same characters. They star in a couple of perennial conflicts."

Apart from the crises of European culture, two other important themes appear in Stempowski's essays. The first is ancient culture and the world of its values. An excellent testimony to the fertility of ancient culture is the essay about Stempowski's sojourn during World War II in the mountains, in "the hiding-place of smugglers" who, quite unexpectedly, offered him a box full of old books. Having found Ovid's *Metamorphoses* and Virgil's *Bucolics* and *Georgics*, Stempowski once again discovered the charm of the unforgettable verse: "In the smugglers' hideout," he writes, ". . . I was struck for the first time by the realistic and psychological content of the *Bucolics*. An exile departing from his native land instinctively clings to the soil, absorbs it with his eyes as if to preserve it forever in memory . . . This perspective is the secret of Virgil and the source of the timeless appeal of the *Bucolics*" ("Księgozbiór przemytników" [1948; "The Smugglers' Library"]).

The second theme of Stempowski's essays is man's attitude toward nature. Stempowski was fascinated with the world of nature and, like the 17th- and 18th-century writers and thinkers, with the various attempts to humanize it. These essays are full of brilliant descriptions of landscapes, roads, gardens, and parks. The deep melancholy which permeates Stempowski's observations has as its source the conviction that humanized nature – as a result of wars, cultural changes, and changes in customs – has strayed far from its original state. His *La Terre Bernoise* (1954), written in French, is an attempt to transpose Virgil's *Bucolics* and *Georgics* into the form of an essay. "In Europe," Stempowski writes in the book's introduction, "nature in its pure state exists only in high mountains, among the rocks and snow. Below, the surface of earth was reshaped many times by man's hand in accordance with his tastes and needs. In this way landscape becomes part of civilization. The economic structure, ideas, as well as the history of society find their reflection in it."

Along with Bolesław Miciński, Stempowski was one of the first writers to introduce the essay into Poland; scarcely an essayist in Poland has not been influenced by him. Among those who influenced Stempowski himself were Marcel Proust and **Simone Weil**, as well as writers like Tacitus, who tried to combine a succinctness of form with a precision of thought without, however, breaking the connection with the experiences of past generations. Stempowski was primarily interested in demonstrating that the experiences of the past were not in vain, and that cultural continuity should be preserved – even at the expense of originality.

KRZYSZTOF KOZŁOWSKI
translated by Zbigniew Janowski

Biography

Born 10 December 1893 in Cracow. Studied philosophy at Jagiellonian University, Cracow, 1911; medicine in Munich, 1912, and Zurich, 1915; philosophy, 1915, and history and literature, 1916, University of Berne. Contributor to various periodicals, particularly the Paris-based Polish émigré magazine *Kultura*, from 1918, and the London émigré weekly *Wiadomości Literackie* (Literary news), from 1929; correspondent for the Polish press in Paris, Geneva, and Berlin following World War I. Diplomatic courier, Ministry of Foreign Affairs, 1919; volunteer in the Polish-Bolshevik war, 1920; worked for the Polish Chamber of Council, 1926. Taught at the National Institute of Theater Art, Warsaw, 1935–39. Left Poland for Switzerland, 1939; lived in Berne, 1940–69. Published *Notatnik niespiesznego przechodnia* (Notes of a leisurely passerby), a series of essays in *Kultura*, from 1954. Used the pseudonym Paweł Hostowiec. Died in Berne, 4 October 1969.

Selected Writings

Essays and Related Prose

Pielgrzym, 1924
Pan Jowialski i jego spadkobiercy, 1931
Dziennik podróży do Austrii i Niemiec, 1946
La Terre Bernoise, 1954
Eseje dla Kassandry, 1961; "Essay for Cassandra" and "The Smugglers' Library" translated by Jarosław Anders, in *Four Decades of Polish Essays*, edited by Jan Kott, 1990
Od Berdyczowa do Rzymu, 1971
Listy z ziemi berneńskiej, 1974
Eseje, edited by Wojciech Karpiński, 1984
Szkice Literackie, vol. 1: *Chimera jako zwierzę pociągowe*; vol. 2: *Klimat życia i klimat literatury*, edited by Jerzy Timoszewicz, 1988
Listy do Jerzego Giedroycia, edited by Andrzej Stanisław Kowalczyk, 1991
W dolinie Dniestru i inne eseje ukraińskie; *Listy o Ukrainie*, edited by Andrzej Stanisław Kowalczyk, 1993

Other writings: memoirs.

Further Reading

Czapski, J., "Przy Sybillach-królowych," *Kultura* 11 (1961)
Czapski, J., "Jerzy Stempowski," *Kultura* 12 (1969)
Herling-Grudziński, Gustaw, "Wyjście z milczenia," *Kultura* 11 (1961)
Jeleński, K. A., "Paweł Hostowiec czyli o wysiłku wyobraźni," *Kultura* 11 (1961)
Kowalczyk, A. S., "Podróż do Europy: Dzienniki Jerzego Stempowskiego," *Znak* 11–12 (1986)
Kowalczyk, A. S., "Wobec kryzysu Europy: Powojenna eseistyka Jerzego Stempowskiego," *Pamiętnik Literacki* 2 (1987)
Miciński, Bolesław, *Pisma: Eseje, artykuły, listy*, edited by Anna Micińska, Cracow: Znak, 1970
Miłosz, Czesław, "Proza," *Kultura* 11 (1961)
Stempowski, Stanisław, *Pamiętniki, 1870–1914*, Wrocław: Wydawnictwo Polskiej Akademii Nauk, 1953
Terlecki, Tymon, "Pan Jerzy," *Kultura* 12 (1969)
Terlecki, Tymon, *Rzeczy teatralne*, Warsaw: Państwowe Wydawnictwo Naukowe, 1984
Timoszewicz, Jerzy, "Wstęp do 'teatru masowej konsumpcji' Stempowskiego," *Dialog* 9 (1981)
Timoszewicz, Jerzy, "'Pamiętnik Teatralny' . . . jest w czasach Piasta i Rzepichy": Teatr w listach Jerzego Stempowskiego, Wrocław, 1989
Tomkowski, Jan, *Jerzy Stempowski*, Warsaw: Interim, 1991
Weintraub, W., "Klasyk polskiej eseistyki," *Tygodnik Powszechny* 33 (1984)
Wyka, M., "Esej jako autobiografia: O Jerzym Stempowskim," *Pismo* 4 (1983)
Zieliński, J., "Tragik w czapeczce," *Odra* 7–8 (1985)

Stephen, Leslie

British, 1832–1904

Leslie Stephen may be unique in having been represented in two important fictional works – Meredith's *The Egoist* (1879), in which he appears as the walker and rationalist Vernon Whitford, and his daughter **Virginia Woolf**'s *To the Lighthouse* (1927), where he is the patriarchal philosopher, Mr. Ramsay. (He is also celebrated in a memorial sonnet by his friend Thomas Hardy.) These two accounts take us toward the man of Victorian rectitude and energy, whose views can seem advanced in 1879 and antiquated in 1927. Reading Stephen's numerous essays today we can find good grounds for both judgments.

Stephen's mental horizons were formed by his reading in philosophy, mostly in the 18th-century tradition that culminated in utilitarianism and the thought of **John Stuart Mill**. This, allied with Darwinism, destroyed the muscular Evangelical Christianity which had enabled Stephen to take orders and become a Fellow of Trinity College, Cambridge, where he had established close bonds with his students by encouraging athletic activities, especially rowing and walking. When, having resigned his Fellowship, he moved to London in 1864 with the aim of making a living by writing, he first edited the *Alpine Journal*. His first book of essays, *The Playground of Europe* (1871), consists of accounts of Alpine ascents.

The kind of play represented by walking and climbing was a serious matter (well discussed in Anne D. Wallace's *Walking, Literature, and English Culture*, 1993). In a later essay, "In Praise of Walking" (1902), Stephen links walking to thinking: "The true walker is one . . . to whom the muscular effort of the legs is subsidiary to the 'cerebration' stimulated by the effort; to the quiet musings and imaginings which arrive most spontaneously as he walks, and generate the intellectual harmony which is the natural accompaniment to the monotonous tramps of his feet." This is a typical Stephen sentence: ponderous, thoughtful, grounded in experience – its rhythm that which Virginia Woolf famously ascribed to "the masculine sentence" in *A Room of One's Own* (1929). Stephen certainly sought "intellectual harmony," and found it in the British philosophical tradition of empiricism already mentioned, to which his major books are devoted.

His essays deal with similar subject matter, from *Essays on Freethinking and Plainspeaking* (1873) onward. The very title invokes a characteristic attitude, that of a man – one of his favorite adjectives is "manly" – who knows his own mind and will let *us* know too. He was an important contributor to the free-thought movement of the late 19th century. "Poisonous Opinions" from *An Agnostic's Apology* (1893) puts the matter succinctly, within its historical view of the development of religion – "A vigorous religion is a superstition which has enslaved a philosophy" (Stephen is capable of the memorable **aphorism**) – and its distant hope for a condition in which "philosophy might be the ally instead of the slave of religion." Meanwhile, however, in Christian England, it was to secular philosophy that Stephen gave his forceful allegiance. His many lectures to London ethical societies are collected in the two volumes of *Social Rights and Duties* (1896).

However, Stephen was not a philosopher, but rather what we would now call a historian of ideas, of a moralizing kind characteristic of his age. He read widely in English literature, and more of his essays concern imaginative writers than philosophers proper. What Stephen is always interested in is lines of thought, especially relating to ethics. The several volumes of *Hours in a Library* (1874–79) and *Studies of a Biographer* (1898–1902) display his range, going back to **John Donne** and **Sir Thomas Browne** but focusing most often on the 18th and early 19th centuries, and typically concerned with "Carlyle's Ethics" in the former and "Pope as a Moralist" and "Wordsworth's Ethics" in the latter. On all occasions Stephen attempts to be fair-minded, setting each writer's work in a historical context, carefully surveying it, and trying accurately to portray its particular qualities to see how valuable these might be to a reader looking for sources of enlightenment and moral guidance. He makes no distinction between a writer and his (or occasionally her) work. He is never flippant, seldom amusing, but always sensible. His strength and limitations are well suggested by the terms of his praise of Joseph Butler: "an honest and brave man – honest enough to admit the existence of doubts, and brave enough not to be paralysed by their existence." Honesty and courage are Stephen's admirable but inflexible moral and intellectual ideals. This cast of mind served him well in his numerous contributions (378 in all, amounting to some thousand pages) to the *Dictionary of National Biography*, of which he was the first editor; in these he developed the capacity to provide summarizing accounts of his chosen subjects, relating personality to achievement with consistent clarity and confident authority.

To set Stephen's essays by the side of his daughter's, with their engaging vivacity and flexibility, is an illuminating way of approaching the relationship of Victorianism to Modernism.

PETER FAULKNER

Biography
Born 28 November 1832 in London. Studied at Eton College, Berkshire; private tutors, from 1848; King's College, London; Trinity College, Cambridge, 1851–54, B.A., 1854. Fellow, Trinity College, 1854–64. Visited the United States, 1863, meeting and becoming friends with James Russell Lowell and Oliver Wendell Holmes, Jr.; visited again in 1868 and 1890. Moved to London, 1864. Married Minny Thackeray, 1867 (died, 1875): one daughter. Editor, *Alpine Journal*, 1868–72, and *Cornhill Magazine*, 1871–82; contributor to many journals and periodicals, including the *Saturday Review*, *Pall Mall Gazette*, *Nation* (New York), *Fraser's Magazine*, and *Fortnightly Review*. Married Julia Duckworth, 1878 (died, 1895): two daughters, including the writer Virginia Woolf and the artist Vanessa Bell, two sons, and three stepchildren. Editor (and contributor of 378 entries), *Dictionary of National Biography*, 1882–90: toward the end of the project suffered from nervous exhaustion. President, London Library, 1892. Elected member, British Academy, 1902. Knighted, 1902. Awards: honorary degrees from four universities. Died in London, 22 February 1904.

Selected Writings

Essays and Related Prose
Sketches from Cambridge, by a Don, 1865
The Playground of Europe (Alpine essays), 1871; revised edition, 1894; edited by H. E. G. Tyndale, 1936
Essays on Freethinking and Plainspeaking, 1873

Hours in a Library, 3 vols., 1874–79; enlarged edition, 3 vols., 1892
An Agnostic's Apology, and Other Essays, 1893
Social Rights and Duties (lectures), 2 vols., 1896
Studies of a Biographer, 4 vols., 1898–1902
Men, Books and Mountains: Essays, edited by S. O. A. Ullmann, 1956
Selected Writings in British Intellectual History: Leslie Stephen, edited by Noël Annan, 1979

Other writings: *History of English Thought in the Eighteenth Century* (1876), biographies of British literary figures and other works on literature, and memoirs.

Bibliography
Fenwick, Gillian, *Leslie Stephen's Life in Letters: A Bibliographical Study*, Aldershot: Scolar Press, and Brookfield, Vermont: Ashgate, 1993

Further Reading
Annan, Noël, *Leslie Stephen: His Thought and Character in Relation to His Time*, London: MacGibbon and Kee, 1951; revised edition, as *Leslie Stephen: The Godless Victorian*, London: Weidenfeld and Nicolson, and New York: Random House, 1984
Bicknell, John W., "Leslie Stephen," in *Victorian Prose Writers After 1867*, edited by William B. Thesing, *Dictionary of Literary Biography*, vol. 57, Detroit: Gale Research, 1987
Grosskurth, Phyllis, *Leslie Stephen*, London: Longman Green, 1968
Hyman, Virginia, "Late Victorian and Early Modern: Continuities in the Criticism of Leslie Stephen and Virginia Woolf," *English Literature in Transition* 23, no. 3 (1980): 144–54
Leavis, Q. D., "Leslie Stephen: Cambridge Critic," in *A Selection from "Scrutiny"*, vol. 1, edited by F. R. Leavis, Cambridge: Cambridge University Press, 1968: 22–31
Maitland, Frederick William, *The Life and Letters of Leslie Stephen*, Bristol: Theommes, 1991 (original edition, 1906)
Maurer, Oscar, Jr., "Leslie Stephen and the *Cornhill Magazine*," *University of Texas Studies in English* 32 (1953): 67–95
Orel, Harold, "Leslie Stephen," in *Victorian Literary Critics*, London: Macmillan, 1984
Schmidt, Barbara Ann, "In the Shadow of Thackeray: Leslie Stephen as the Editor of the *Cornhill Magazine*," in *Innovators and Preachers: The Role of the Editor in Victorian England*, edited by Joel Wiener, Westport, Connecticut: Greenwood Press, 1985: 77–96
Zink, David, *Leslie Stephen*, New York: Twayne, 1972

Stevenson, Robert Louis
British, 1850–1894

During his 20 years as a writer Robert Louis Stevenson turned his hand to nearly every possible genre: novel, short story, drama, poems for children and adults, history, biography and essays. Fiction and essays form the bulk of his work, and they are almost evenly balanced. Furthermore, Stevenson's essays and fiction share each other's conspicuous characteristics. The essays are filled with narrative and with fictive images of military action and adventure; the stories are marked by passages of sententious meditation.

Essays came first, with Stevenson using the form as a self-imposed apprenticeship in which he taught himself to write "as men learn to whittle" ("A College Magazine," 1887), deliberately modeling his own structure and style on essayists of the past such as **Lamb** and **Hazlitt**. Stevenson's first three collections were travel books, an especially attractive form for the beginning writer, since travel provides a ready-made structure, while leaving many opportunities for digression. These essays are gracefully written and sound much alike, the work of a writer learning how to say things without yet having much to say. Stevenson's main task in these early essays was to invent his own character, which he presents as a sympathetic, mildly bohemian onlooker who invites but resists involvement in the affairs that he observes.

After these travel books, Stevenson published three collections of mixed essays during the next decade: *Virginibus Puerisque* (1881), *Familiar Studies of Men and Books* (1882), and *Memories and Portraits* (1887). Several essays in *Virginibus Puerisque*, written while Stevenson was in his twenties, purvey solemn nonsense about marriage and old age. But in others written at the same time, notably "Æs Triplex" (first pub. 1878), he is both graceful and convincing on the need to face life with courage. His own ill health, which had already brought him to the brink of death several times, enabled him to write with real power on a subject that could easily become trite and sentimental. "Walking Tours" (first pub. 1876) generalizes the themes of the earlier travel books and helped to establish a new cultural role, that of the young man tramping the roads of Europe by himself – but never too far from a friendly inn – meditating as he goes on life and the surrounding scenery. "Walking Tours" is the precursor of the many essays and poems written on this subject by a host of British and American authors from the 1880s to World War I.

The essays in *Familiar Studies* and *Memories and Portraits* coincide with Stevenson's development as a writer of fiction. In addition to the shared characteristics mentioned above, some of these essays also create characters who prefigure types that Stevenson would explore more fully in his stories. The two essays on Robert Burns and François Villon (both in *Familiar Studies*) are excellent examples. Stevenson castigates Burns as a drunkard and womanizer, but at the same time he sees him as a tragic figure, constantly striving to act responsibly even though he was beaten down by overwhelming flaws. He is like the reluctant wrongdoers of "Markheim" and *Kidnapped* (1886), perhaps even a bit like Dr. Jekyll. Villon fascinated Stevenson as a charming but utterly ruthless villain. He later published two short stories in which Villon figures as a character, but one can also see in Stevenson's version of Villon preliminary sketches of Long John Silver and the Master of Ballantrae.

Even more interesting cross-connections between Stevenson as an essayist and as a writer of fiction are to be found in "A Gossip on Romance" (1882) and "A Humble Remonstrance" (1884), both in *Memories and Portraits*. Most critical writing about Victorian fiction concentrates upon the Jamesian view that fiction is a kind of history, that its important dimension is the temporal, and that its value depends upon the intensity of the author's impressions of life. Stevenson insists that fiction imitates speech, not life, and that romances differ from novels because they depend upon place and incident. Their important dimension is the spatial. "A Humble Remonstrance" was actually addressed to **Henry James** himself, but despite this disagreement – or even because of it – the two writers became close personal friends.

Many other essays in these books as well as in *Across the Plains* (1892) are almost secular **sermons**. They express a moral code that might be described as "quixotic stoicism," emphasizing scrupulous honesty (especially in money matters), endurance of misfortune without complaint, but also grand, heroic gestures in the face of fate.

Stevenson's essays are written in highly wrought prose marked by a precise, even precious vocabulary and carefully controlled cadences. Sometimes, it must be admitted, he strikes attitudes. It is important to recognize that for Stevenson style – even flamboyant style – was a moral quality. Partly this is a matter of financial probity, insuring that the author gives honest value for money received. But there is also in his writing a firm belief that grand, heroic gestures can be performed in words as well as in deeds.

In 1888 Stevenson began several years of travel in the South Pacific, where he lived for the last six years of his life. *In the South Seas* (1896), the last of his travel books, was originally a series of newsletters recounting his voyages. In early books Stevenson had often given the impression of provoking whimsical incidents so as to have something to write about. Here there was no need to do so: exotic sights and bizarre events surrounded him. In these essays, however, Stevenson resisted all temptations to florid or precious writing. The style is lean and muscular throughout – the same style Stevenson was developing for his last novels, *The Ebb-Tide* (1894) and *Weir of Hermiston* (1896).

Special mention must be made of "Father Damien: An Open Letter to the Reverend Dr. Hyde of Honolulu," published in 1890. The previous year Stevenson had visited the leper colony founded by Father Damien, a Belgian missionary in Hawaii, and had been greatly moved by the heroism of Damien and his followers. A year later Stevenson chanced to read a letter in a religious newspaper brutally criticizing the late Father Damien. Immediately he leaped to Damien's defense in a letter which is a masterpiece of warm-hearted but cool-headed invective. For once Stevenson had found a topic that required the highest pitch of his rhetorical skills. Indeed, he later wondered if he had been too harsh, but fortunately he never revised this open letter; it remains one of the most effective diatribes in English literature.

During the 20 years after his death in 1894, Stevenson's reputation as an essayist was caught up in the vogue for sentimental whimsy that marked British and American literary taste at the turn of the century. In the 1920s and 1930s taste changed; Stevenson suffered from the reaction against sentimentality, and his reputation plunged. However, later generations have reconsidered Stevenson's writing, and it is now possible to see his essays as the work of a professional craftsman who could rise above his own desire to be charming. At their best, the essays manifest the twin virtues of beautiful prose and a generous heart.

PETER HINCHCLIFFE

Biography

Robert Louis Balfour Stevenson. Born 13 November 1850 in Edinburgh. In bad health throughout his life, particularly with hemorrhaging lungs and possibly tuberculosis. Studied at the University of Edinburgh, 1867–72; studied law in the office of Skene Edwards and Gordon, Edinburgh: admitted to the Scottish bar, 1875. Lived mainly in France, 1875–79, the United States, 1879–80 and 1887–88, Scotland, 1881–82, various places in Britain, France, and Switzerland, 1882–84, and Bournemouth, 1884–87. Contributor, *Cornhill Magazine*, London, 1876–82. Married Fanny Osbourne, 1880: two stepchildren. Sailed to the South Pacific islands, 1888; settled at Vailima, Samoa, 1890. Died (of a stroke) at Vailima, 3 December 1894.

Selected Writings

Essays and Related Prose
An Inland Voyage, 1878; edited by Wilbur L. Cross, with *Travels with a Donkey*, 1924, and Trevor Royle (with *The Silverado Squatters*), 1984
Edinburgh: Picturesque Notes, 1879
Travels with a Donkey in the Cévennes, 1879; edited by Wilbur L. Cross, with *An Inland Voyage*, 1924, and Trevor Royle (with *The Silverado Squatters*), 1984
Virginibus Puerisque and Other Papers, 1881
Familiar Studies of Men and Books, 1882
The Silverado Squatters: Sketches from a Californian Mountain, 1883; edited by Trevor Royle, with *An Inland Voyage* and *Travels with a Donkey*, 1984
Memories and Portraits, 1887
Across the Plains, with Other Memories and Essays, edited by Sidney Colvin, 1892
The Amateur Emigrant from the Clyde to Sandy Hook, 1895
In the South Seas, 1896
Essays and Criticism, 1903
Essays of Travel, 1905
Essays in the Art of Writing, 1905
The Pentland Essays (selections), 1913
Selected Essays, edited by H. G. Rawlinson, 1923
Essays, edited by Malcolm Elwin, 1950
The Mind of Robert Louis Stevenson: Selected Essays, Letters, and Prayers, edited by Roger Ricklefs, 1963
From Scotland to Silverado; Comprising The Amateur Emigrant, The Silverado Squatters and Four Essays on California, edited by James D. Hart, 1966
The Lantern Bearers and Other Essays, edited by Jeremy Treglown, 1988
The Scottish Stories and Essays, edited by Kenneth Gelder, 1989
Travels with a Donkey in the Cévennes, and Selected Travel Writings, edited by Emma Letley, 1992

Other writings: many short stories and novels (including *Treasure Island*, 1883; *The Strange Case of Dr. Jekyll and Mr. Hyde*, 1886; *Kidnapped*, 1886), plays, poetry (including *A Child's Garden of Verses*, 1885), books on history and travel, and correspondence (collected in *Letters*, edited by Bradford A. Booth and Ernest Mehew, 1994–[in progress]).

Collected works editions: *The Works* (Edinburgh Edition), edited by Sidney Colvin, 28 vols., 1894–98; Vailima Edition, edited by Lloyd Osbourne and Fanny van de Grift Stevenson, 26 vols., 1922–23; Tusitala Edition, 35 vols., 1924; South Seas Edition, 32 vols., 1925.

Bibliographies
Bethke, Frederick J., *Three Victorian Travel Writers: An Annotated Bibliography of Criticism on Mrs. Frances Milton Trollope, Samuel Butler, and Robert Louis Stevenson*, Boston: Hall, 1977
McKay, George L., *The Stevenson Library: Catalogue of a Collection of Writings by and About Robert Louis Stevenson*, New Haven, Connecticut: Yale University Press, 6 vols., 1951–64
Prideaux, W. F., *A Bibliography of the Works of Robert Louis Stevenson*, revised by F. V. Livingston, London: Hollings, 1918
Swearingen, Roger G., *The Prose Writings of Robert Louis Stevenson: A Guide*, London: Macmillan, and Hamden, Connecticut: Archon, 1980

Further Reading
Aldington, Richard, *Portrait of a Rebel: The Life and Work of Robert Louis Stevenson*, London: Evans, 1957
Balfour, Graham, *The Life of Robert Louis Stevenson*, London: Methuen, and New York: Scribner, 2 vols., 1901
Bell, Ian, *Robert Louis Stevenson: Dreams of Exile*, London: Headline, 1993
Calder, Jenni, *R. L. S.: A Life Study*, London: Hamilton, 1980
Calder, Jenni, editor, *The Robert Louis Stevenson Companion*, Edinburgh: Harris, 1980
Calder, Jenni, editor, *Stevenson and Victorian Scotland*, Edinburgh: Edinburgh University Press, 1981
Chesterton, G. K., *Robert Louis Stevenson*, London: Hodder and Stoughton, 1927; New York: Dodd Mead, 1928
Daiches, David, *Robert Louis Stevenson*, Norfolk, Connecticut: New Directions, 1947
Eigner, Edwin M., *Robert Louis Stevenson and Romantic Tradition*, Princeton, New Jersey: Princeton University Press, 1966
Furnas, J. C., *Voyage to Windward: The Life of Stevenson*, New York: Sloane, 1951; London: Faber, 1952
Greene, Graham, "From Feathers to Iron," in his *The Lost Childhood and Other Essays*, London: Eyre and Spottiswoode, 1951; New York: Viking, 1952
Hammond, J. R., *A Robert Louis Stevenson Companion: A Guide to the Novels, Essays and Short Stories*, London: Macmillan, 1984
McLynn, Frank, *Robert Louis Stevenson*, London: Hutchinson, 1993
Maixner, Paul, editor, *Robert Louis Stevenson: The Critical Heritage*, London and Boston: Routledge and Kegan Paul, 1981
Noble, Andrew, editor, *Robert Louis Stevenson*, London: Vision, and Totowa, New Jersey: Barnes and Noble, 1983
Rankin, Nicholas, *Dead Man's Chest: Travels After Robert Louis Stevenson*, London: Faber, 1987
Riedel, F. C., "A Classical Rhetorical Analysis of Some Elements of Stevenson's Essay Style," *Style* 3 (1968): 182–99
Smith, Janet Adam, editor, *Henry James and Robert Louis Stevenson: A Record of Friendship and Criticism*, London: Hart Davis, 1948; Westport, Connecticut: Hyperion Press, 1979
Swinnerton, Frank, *R. L. Stevenson: A Critical Study*, London: Secker and Warburg, 1914; New York: Kennerley, 1915

Strachey, Lytton
British, 1880–1932

A prolific essayist, Lytton Strachey first gained widespread fame and notoriety as the iconoclastic author of *Eminent Victorians* (1918), four miniature biographies of Cardinal Manning, Florence Nightingale, Thomas Arnold, and General Charles Gordon. Previously portrayed in the standard "two fat volumes" of Victorian biography which Strachey abhorred as inartistic and disorganized hagiographies at best, these four icons of the Catholic Church, medical humanitarianism, educational and moral reform, and military adventure respectively were brilliantly and wittily exposed by Strachey as all too human, obsessive, and dysfunctional, the wonder lying not in their perfection but in the fact that, given their imperfections, they had affected their era so markedly and achieved so much.

Strachey's contemporary audience, for the most part, was ready to relish a work that, in the words of Richard Altick (1995), "turned an entire past society into a laughing stock." Disillusioned by the horrors of World War I, profoundly mistrustful of the establishment, and desperately seeking some psychologically understandable rationale for recent events, many of Strachey's readers welcomed the opportunity these essays offered to reject and ridicule the late Victorian institutions that could be viewed as leading to the war to which Strachey was a conscientious objector. Although works by such earlier writers as **George Bernard Shaw**, H. G. Wells, **G. K. Chesterton**, and **Max Beerbohm** had already presented critical views of the Victorians, Strachey's detractors tend to blame his work for spawning scores of later "popularized" or "jazz-age biographies," those overfictionalized and underresearched essays and book-length lives written by hacks, would-be wits, and professional de-bunkers. Such imitators damaged his reputation and fostered an image still current in some minds today of Strachey as a careless and superficial cynic.

Even most of Strachey's detractors, however, agree that his essays are eminently readable, while one of his latest and most able defenders, Barry Spurr (1995), points out that relatively recent scholarly treatments of Strachey's subjects tend intentionally or not to endorse Strachey's conclusions and to confirm the breadth and depth of his knowledge – for example, in Strachey's treatment of Cardinal Manning and **John Henry Newman** in *Eminent Victorians*. Moreover, Strachey's paradoxical and arresting pronouncements such as that near the opening of the **preface** to *Eminent Victorians* – "ignorance is the first requisite of the historian" – may well imply an ironic and sophisticated consciousness of the psychological complexities of his subjects, of the ambiguities and inadequacies of language and reason, and of the impossibility, in many instances, of attaining an absolute or finite conception of truth. Certainly these three concerns remain central for writers and scholars today. While Strachey stressed the importance of stringent selectivity and brevity in his biographical and **historical essays**, these ideals are certainly not those currently in vogue for scholarly biographers, as Michael Holroyd's excellent two-volume biography (1967–68) of Strachey himself demonstrates. But Strachey's emphasis on careful scholarship, discriminating treatment and organization, and an elegant, engaging style are still the hallmarks of the best modern biographies.

A leading figure of the Cambridge Apostles and subsequently of the Bloomsbury Group, Strachey also demonstrated his exceptional skills as a literary critic and prose stylist in the host of essays and **reviews** he contributed during his early career to the *Spectator*, the *Independent Review*, *New Quarterly*, *Athenaeum*, and the *Edinburgh Review* as well as in his first book, *Landmarks in French Literature* (1912). Here Strachey's high estimation of such writers as Pope, Gibbon, **Voltaire**, and Racine is clear. Thus the early key influences on his prose are Augustan and Victorian. His voice conveys the polished aristocratic authority of an elite; but his perspective is that of the homosexual, oppressed and suppressed, by turns indirect, hostile, melancholic, and often ironic. Strachey evolves an idiom that Spurr dubs "Camp Mandarin" – a witty parody of an elite mode, used to undermine the conventional views of the mandarins through incongruity and exaggeration. He uses a variety of rhetorical techniques, such as alliteration,

triplets, Latinate vocabulary, and biblical allusion, in this way: Florence Nightingale "seems hardly to distinguish between the Deity and the Drains" (*Eminent Victorians*); the "holiness of the Middle Ages embodied itself in prayer, asceticism, and dirt" ("Lady Mary Wortley Montagu," 1907); Dr. North is described as "meticulous in the true sense of the word" ("The Life, Illness and Death of Dr. North," 1927); Carlyle as prophet cannot rival the reputation of Isaiah and Jeremiah who, unlike Carlyle, "have had the extraordinary good fortune to be translated into English by a committee of Elizabethan bishops" ("Carlyle," 1928).

Later longer works by Strachey like *Queen Victoria* (1921) and *Elizabeth and Essex* (1928) continue to demonstrate the vivid novelistic qualities and psychological interest in character of his earlier essays, but some of his best work is in his collections of **critical essays**, many of which are characterized by the quality and artistry that Strachey, a pleasing and anxious being himself, recognized and so admired in John Aubrey's *Brief Lives* (1669–96): "the pure essentials – a vivid image, on a page or two, without explanations, transitions, commentaries, or padding. This is what Aubrey gives us; this, and one thing more – a sense of the pleasing, anxious being who, with his odd old alchemy, has transmuted a few handfuls of orts and relics into golden life" ("John Aubrey," *Portraits in Miniature*, 1931).

ANNE SKABARNICKI

Biography

Born 1 March 1880 in Clapham, south London. Studied at Abbotsholm School, Derbyshire, 1893; Leamington College, until 1897; Liverpool University College, 1897–99; Trinity College, Cambridge, 1899–1903, B.A. in history, 1903. Met Thoby Stephen, Clive Bell, and Leonard Woolf at Cambridge, the latter two becoming, with Strachey, part of the Bloomsbury Group, along with **Virginia Woolf, E. M. Forster**, painters Vanessa Bell and Duncan Grant, economist John Maynard Keynes, art critic Roger Fry, and others. Conscientious objector during World War I. Met the painter Dora Carrington, 1915: lived with her on and off in a mainly platonic relationship in Tidmarsh, Berkshire, from 1917, and at Ham Spray house, Berkshire, from 1924; they were joined by Ralph Partridge, who married Carrington, 1919. Died (of cancer of the stomach) at Ham Spray house, 21 January 1932.

Selected Writings

Essays and Related Prose
Eminent Victorians, 1918
Books and Characters: French and English, 1922
Pope: The Leslie Stephen Lecture for 1925, 1925
Portraits in Miniature and Other Essays, 1931
Characters and Commentaries, 1933
Literary Essays (part of the Uniform Edition of works), 1943
Biographical Essays (part of the Uniform Edition of works), 1943
Spectatorial Essays, 1964
The Really Interesting Question and Other Papers, edited by Paul Levy, 1972
The Shorter Strachey, edited by Michael Holroyd, 1980

Other writings: *Landmarks in French Literature* (1912), a biography of Queen Victoria (1921), a study of Queen Elizabeth I and the Earl of Essex (1928), a play, and a collection of poetry.

Collected works edition: Uniform Edition, 6 vols., 1949.

Bibliography

Edmonds, Michael, *Lytton Strachey: A Bibliography*, New York: Garland, 1981

Further Reading

Altick, Richard, "Eminent Victorianism," *American Scholar* 64 (Winter 1995): 81–89

Beerbohm, Max, *Lytton Strachey*, Cambridge: Cambridge University Press, and New York: Knopf, 1943

Ferns, John, *Lytton Strachey*, Boston: Twayne, 1988

Holroyd, Michael, *Lytton Strachey: A Critical Biography*, London: Heinemann, 2 vols., 1967–68; New York: Holt Rinehart, 1968; revised edition, as *Lytton Strachey: A Biography*, London: Penguin, 1971

Holroyd, Michael, *Lytton Strachey: The New Biography*, London: Chatto and Windus, 1994; New York: Farrar Straus Giroux, 1995

Kallich, Martin, *The Psychological Milieu of Lytton Strachey*, New York: Bookman Associates, 1961

Merle, Gabriel, *Lytton Strachey (1880–1932): Biographie et critique d'un critique et biographe*, Paris: Champion, 2 vols., 1980

Sanders, C. R., *Lytton Strachey: His Mind and Art*, New Haven, Connecticut: Yale University Press, 1957

Scott-James, R. A., *Lytton Strachey*, London: Longman, 1955

Spurr, Barry, *A Literary-Critical Analysis of the Complete Prose Works of Lytton Strachey (1880–1932): A Re-Assessment of His Achievement and Career*, Lewiston, New York, and Lampeter, Dyfed: Mellen Press, 1995

Srinivasa Iyengar, K. R., *Lytton Strachey: A Critical Study*, London: Chatto and Windus, 1939

Yu, Margaret M. S., *Two Masters of Irony: Annotations on Three Essays by Oscar Wilde and Lytton Strachey*, Folcroft, Pennsylvania: Folcroft, 1974 (original edition, 1957)

Su Shi

Chinese, 1037–1101

Su Shi continued the efforts of his patron, **Ouyang Xiu**, in advocating *guwen* (ancient prose) in the Song era (960–1279). His own practice of *guwen* essay writing made him the leading stylist of his time. He was thus perceived by later generations as one of the eight *guwen* masters of the Tang and Song periods, along with Han Yu, **Liu Zongyuan**, Ouyang Xiu, his father Su Xun, brother Su Zhe, and two other Song essayists Wang Anshi and Zeng Gong.

Like Han Yu and Ouyang Xiu, Su Shi emphasized the connection between literature and the Tao. Unlike them, however, Su Shi's understanding of the Tao turned away from his predecessors' focus on the Confucian Tao and more or less followed the tradition that Tao is what things rely upon to be themselves, and myriad patterns are attested to (Guo Shaoyu, 1957). As Peter Bol (1992) points out, "The first line of the Tao te ching, 'the tao that can be spoken of is not the constant tao,' seems to be in the back of Su's mind throughout, although he never cites it." For Su Shi, the Tao encompasses many things, including both historical categories of human affairs and objects perceived by human beings, and can be "brought on" only through close studies of them ("Ri yu" [On finding an analogy for the sun]). Literature, then, provided the best way to transport the Tao to other people by making things "comprehensible" in words, which can discriminate shapes, colors, tastes, sounds, and movements. By doing so, literature

introduces particular cases of human practice for the reader to intuit – rather than define – the meaning, or the Tao, embodied in everything. Understandably, the literati should strive to acquire knowledge and polish their literary and artistic skills in order to grasp the subtleties of things as if "binding the wind and catching the shadow" ("Yu Xie Minshi tuiguan shu" [Letter to Judge Xie Minshi]).

Su himself provides the best example in using literature and art to reflect the fundamental principles underlying the phenomenal world. As a result, his accomplishments mark the peak of almost every field of Song intellectual life: Confucian, Taoist, and Buddhist scholarship, poetry, calligraphy, painting, and essay writing. The huge body of his essays – over 3000 pieces – covers every possible subgenre, varying from political disquisitions to historical comments, literary and art **reviews**, **philosophical essays**, travelogues, biographies, epitaphs, **character sketches**, botanical and zoological articles, medical and pharmacological notes, and even cookery entries. Taken together they reflect Su's effort to understand the world by various means and his eagerness to share his findings with his audience.

Two important features characterize Su Shi's style. First, a philosophical touch often flavors his essays, resulting from his tireless pursuit of the Tao. He even ushers reasoning into his travelogues, generally a descriptive and sentimental genre, to abstract epistemological or moral truth from his observation of natural scenery. For instance, "Shizhong shan ji" ("Stone Bells Mountain") recounts a moonlit boat outing he conducted in order to find out the origin of the name "Stone Bells." The account of the search is accompanied by a vivid description of various sounds echoing among the grotesquely shaped rocks. This surreal presentation of an audiovisual symphony finally leads to a rational conclusion – the importance of achieving knowledge through investigation and sharing that knowledge accurately.

Secondly, Su's essays contain such unrestrained vitality that they burst any conscious boundaries and flow along their own natural tracks. As he himself puts it: "My writing is like ten thousand barrels of spring water, gushing from the ground, choosing no specific outlet. On level ground, it floods and covers thousands of miles in a day without the least effort. Turning and twisting with the mountains and rocks, it takes its forms from whatever it encounters, unpredictably. All that can be foretold is that it always goes where it should go, and it always stops where it cannot but stop" ("Zi ping wen" [Criticism of my own essays]). This tendency, again, comes from his understanding of literature's function of communicating the Tao. Since each thing in the world follows its own course, literature should not yield to any single rule, but instead conform to what it is intended to reflect, just as water "takes its forms from whatever it encounters."

Su Shi's sincerity toward the truth in life and the world, however, set him at odds with contemporary trends, whether political or scholastic. Although he attained his *jinshi* degree – the highest in the civil service examination system – at the age of 20 and thus gained the attention of the emperor, he never really remained within the center of political power. All his life he was in continual exile and demotion, often through accusations fabricated by his enemies upon intentional misreading of his literary works. Despite these dismal experiences, Su manifested "a transcendental outlook that rose above momentary human sorrow" (Chang Kang-i Sun, in *The Indiana Companion to Traditional Chinese Literature*, 1986), best expressed in his two-rhyme prose (*fu*) entitled "Chibi fu" ("The Red Cliff"). Linking the vicissitudes of human life and history with the natural rhythms of change – the progression of the seasons, the waxing and waning of the moon, the flowing of the water – as illustriously described in these two masterpieces, Su Shi merged transient human life with the perpetual process of nature. Thus he transcended mundane trivialities and found serenity in dissolving himself into nature's fluid eternity.

Among a great range of previous writers who had influenced him, Su Shi drew the most inspiration from the Taoist philosopher Zhuang Zi (c. 369–c. 286 BCE). In addition to his assimilation of Zhuang Zi's philosophical axioms, Su Shi also emulated his great capability of accurately expressing his meanings with words. As his brother Su Zhe recollected: ". . . then he [Su Shi] read the Zhuang Zi. He said with a sigh, 'Previously, when I perceived something of what was within me, my mouth was unable to put it into words. Now I have seen the Zhuang Zi and grasped my own mind'" ("Wangxiong Zizhan duanming muzhi ming" [Epitaph for my late elder brother Zizhan]; Bol).

Already a model essayist for his contemporaries during his lifetime, Su Shi's influence grew even stronger after his death. His style directly affected the civil service examination system in the Southern Song period (1127–1279). A common saying of the time proclaimed that "If one is familiar with Su Shi's essays, he will eat mutton (he will be able to pass the civil examinations and will thereupon live a wealthy life); if not, he can only eat vegetable soup (he will not be able to pass the civil examinations and hence will live poorly)" (Cheng and Wu, 1991). His reputation reached its zenith in the Ming period (1368–1644), when the Tang-Song School essayists canonized his works and Ming literati in general regarded him as the most celebrated of all men of letters. The wealth of folktales and jokes he had incorporated in his own essays also found their way to the public. His fascinating personality, his great achievements in art and literature, and his benevolent governing made him a legendary hero in popular culture, which in turn increased his literary glamor. Su Shi has attracted one of the largest audiences in Chinese literary history.

NANXIU QIAN

Biography

Courtesy name Su Zizhan; studio name Su Dongpo. Born 8 January 1037 in Meishan, Sichuan province. Married Wang Fu, 1054 (died, 1065). Passed *jinshi* (civil service) exams, 1057, and decree exams, 1061. Notary, Fenxiang, 1062–64. Married Wang Runzhi, 1068 (died, 1093). Vice prefect, Hangzhou, 1071–73, and prefect, Mizhou, 1074–76, and Xuzhou, 1077–79. Arrested for slandering the emperor and court, 1079, and exiled to Huangzhou, 1080–84; prefect, Dengzhou, 1085; Hanglin academician, 1086–88 and 1091; prefect, Hangzhou, 1089–90, Yingzhou and Yangzhou, 1091–92, and Dengzhou, 1093. Exiled again, to Huizhou, 1094–97, and Hainan Island, 1097–1100, then pardoned. Also a calligrapher and painter. Died in Changzhou, 28 July 1101.

Selected Writings

Essays and Related Prose

Selections from the Works of Su Tung-p'o, translated by Cyril Drummond Le Gros Clark, 1931
The Prose-Poetry of Su Tung-p'o, translated by Cyril Drummond Le Gros Clark, 1935
Jingjin Dongpo wenji shilüe (Annotated selection of prose), edited by Lang Ye, 1979
Su Shi wenji (Collected essays), edited by Kong Fangli, 6 vols., 1986
Translations of essays in: *Chinese Classical Prose: The Eight Masters of the T'ang-Sung Period*, edited and translated by Shi Shun Liu, 1979: 232–85; *Inscribed Landscapes: Travel Writing from Imperial China*, translated by Richard E. Strassberg, 1994: 185–94

Other writings: poetry.

Collected works editions: *Su Dongpo ci*, edited by Cao Shuming, 1968; *Su Shi shiji*, edited by Kong Fanli, 1982.

Further Reading

Bol, Peter, *"This Culture of Ours": Intellectual Transitions in T'ang and Sung China*, Stanford, California: Stanford University Press, 1992
Chen, Yu-shih, *Images and Ideas in Chinese Classical Prose: Studies of Four Masters*, Stanford, California: Stanford University Press, 1988
Cheng Qianfan and Wu Xinlei, *Liang Song wenxue shi* (The literary history of the Norhern Song and the Southern Song), Shanghai: Shanghai guji chuban she, 1991
Dongpo yanjiu luncong (Studies of Su Dongpo), Chengdu: Sichuan wenyi, 1986
Egan, Ronald C., *Word, Image, and Deed in the Life of Su Shi*, Cambridge, Massachusetts: Harvard University Council on East Asian Studies and Harvard-Yenching Institute, 1994
Fuller, Michael, *The Road to East Slope: The Development of Su Shi's Poetic Voice*, Stanford, California: Stanford University Press, 1990
Grant, Beata, *Mount Lu Revisited: Buddhism in the Life and Writings of Su Shih*, Honolulu: University of Hawaii Press, 1994
Guo Shaoyu, *Zhongguo wenxue piping shi* (History of Chinese literary criticism), Shanghai: Xin wenyi chuban she, 1957
Hatch, George C., "Su Shih," in *Sung Biographies*, vol. 3, edited by Herbert Franke, Wiesbaden: Steiner, 1976: 900–68
Lin, Yu-tang, *The Gay Genius: The Life and Times of Su Tungpo*, New York: Day, 1947; London: Heinemann, 1948
Liu, James J. Y., *Chinese Theories of Literature*, Chicago: University of Chicago Press, 1975
Liu Naichang, editor, *Su Shi wenxue lunji* (Collected studies on Su Shi's writings), Jinan: Qilu shushe, 1982
Liu Xizai, *Yigai* (A theoretical summary of art), Shanghai: Shanghai guji chuban she, 1978
Ma Jigao, *Song-Ming lixue yu wenxue* (Neo-Confucianism and literature in the Song and Ming periods), Changsha: Hunan shifan daxue chuban she, 1989
March, Andrew L., *Landscape in the Thought of Su Shih* (dissertation), Seattle: University of Washington, 1964
Su Zhe, "Wangxiong Zizhan duanming muzhi ming" (Epitaph for my late elder brother Zizhan), in *Su Zhe ji, Nuancheng houji*, no. 22, Beijing: Zhonghua shuju, 1990: 1117–28
Yu Xinli, *Su Dongpo de wenxue lilun* (The literary theories of Su Dongpo), Taibei: Xuesheng shuju, 1981
Zeng Zaozhuang, *Su Shi pingzhuan* (Critical biography of Su Shi), Chengdu: Sichuan renmin chuban she, 1981

Sur

Argentine periodical, 1931–1980

Modeled on the examples of two renowned European cultural magazines, the *Nouvelle Revue Française* (New French review) and the *Revista de Occidente* (Western review), the journal *Sur* (South) has been a decisive factor in 20th-century Argentine intellectual history, enjoying an unusually long publishing life of over 40 years. Rather than a manifesto or a formal declaration of principles, the first issue in Summer 1931 opened with a letter to the American writer Waldo Frank from **Victoria Ocampo**, founder and financer of the publication. This letter, in the form of a personal recollection of the many conversations between the two writers about the need to publish a new, American journal, defines its purpose in rather vague terms: to study the problems that are essentially linked to America without ignoring Europe. Two years later, issue no. 8 ends with a brief note, a "Notícula," complementing this idea. It states that the journal is original, not an imitation of any other Argentine magazine, and that it will strive to include writings by talented young people who are prepared to explore new areas of thinking and who display an authentic consciousness of the spiritual misery of contemporary times. To fulfill these self-imposed requirements, the journal provided translations of significant contemporary works originally written in French or English, essays devoted to analyzing the relationship of the intellectual to society, and innumerable articles and notes whose goal was to familiarize the readership with current trends in a cosmopolitan form of high culture.

There is no general agreement on what factors should be taken into account to establish the different stages of the history of *Sur*. Nevertheless, it is helpful to combine the incorporation of new figures who became decisive in the development of the journal with the impact of major external events. During the earliest period (1931–38), Ocampo's literary preferences and opinions predominated. This explains the proliferation of the essay over poetry and fiction, and the use of an undefined notion of "taste" as the measure of literary value. The second period began with the designation of José Bianco as editor-in-chief, whose presence would affect *Sur*'s editorial practice by giving more space to creative writing. Although Bianco continued his activity until 1961, a third period opened in 1948 with the acceptance of a younger generation of contributors, which included Julio Cortázar, Enrique Pezzoni, and the controversial Héctor Alberto Murena. The final period of the magazine corresponds to the 1960s, when changes in socioeconomic conditions and in the intellectual field, both in Argentina and in Latin America, seriously challenged the vitality of a deeply liberal cultural project.

The essay was the dominant form in the 1930s and, for both European contributors such as **Aldous Huxley** and Jacques Maritain, and local writers, the prevailing subject was the answer of intellectuals to the different crises of the period. The *Sur* group conceived the role of intellectuals in the social context as shapers of ideas, but without committing themselves to any particular ideology. Thus they are responsible for working in the abstract domain of ideas, in a "third position" that allows them to reflect on reality without getting involved in it.

Although the magazine was founded as a nonpolitical enterprise, changes in the international and local situation forced the members to define their position, frequently against the interests and desires of the Argentine government and society at large. The journal did not involve itself in any form of concrete political action. However, it never concealed its points of view, in particular when events raised moral questions. For instance, facing the Spanish Civil War, the initial reaction was somewhat ambivalent but, after the execution of the poet Federico García Lorca, the magazine openly supported the cause of the Republicans. Similarly, at the beginning of World War II, *Sur* published a declaration entitled "Nuestra actitud" (September 1939; Our attitude) which sided with the Allies. As for national issues, the magazine expressed an internationalist and mainly liberal orientation against the prevailing Catholic nationalism of the 1930s and a sustained oppositional criticism *vis-à-vis* the populist presidencies of Juan Domingo Perón (1946–55).

The list of contributors who published in *Sur* throughout its history is certainly impressive, including almost all the significant names in Argentine culture up to the mid-1950s. Enrique Anderson Imbert, Adolfo Bioy Casares, Bernardo Canal Feijóo, Carlos Alberto Erro, **Eduardo Mallea, Ezequiel Martínez Estrada, Ernesto Sabato**, and Juan José Sebreli are only a few of the renowned signatures to be found in the pages of the journal. Nevertheless, its two major figures are Victoria Ocampo, with her continuous ambition to preserve a secure space for high culture, and **Jorge Luis Borges**, the first member of the original *Sur* group to receive international recognition and who went on to become a leading figure in contemporary literature.

Memorable special issues included "La guerra" (October 1939; The war), "La guerra en América" (December 1941; The war in America), "La paz" (July 1945; Peace), "Cuaderno San Martín dedicado a los derechos del hombre" (1950; San Martin notebook devoted to human rights), and "Por la reconstrucción nacional" (November–December 1955; In favor of national reconstruction). *Sur* also published several homage issues: **Domingo Faustino Sarmiento** (1938), **Paul Valéry** (1945), **Pedro Henríquez Ureña** (1946), Mahatma Gandhi (1948), **George Bernard Shaw** and **André Gide** (1951), Sor Juana Inés de la Cruz (1951), Rainer Maria Rilke (1953), **José Ortega y Gasset** (1956), and William Shakespeare (1964).

Sur was the publication in Argentina most vilified by its detractors, and most praised by its supporters. It remains a perfect example of the ideological tensions of Argentine cultural history. Those who believe that its pages were merely manifestations of the cultural project of an enlightened minority who lived completely cut off from the general history of the country are countered by hundreds of pages filled with the reactions of those associated with *Sur* to questions of Argentina's social reality. Those who consider that there is nothing for Argentine culture to produce after *Sur* must accept the abundant example of those who never had access to its pages.

The death in 1979 of Victoria Ocampo, the slow break-up of her team of talented collaborators, along with the profound changes that took place among Argentine intellectuals beginning in the mid-1950s are factors that determined the disappearance of this prestigious and influential review in 1980.

DANIEL ALTAMIRANDA

Further Reading

Bastos, María Luisa, "Escrituras ajenas, expresión propia: *Sur* y los *Testimonios* de Victoria Ocampo," *Revista Iberoamericana* 110–11 (1980): 123–37

King, John, *Sur: A Study of the Argentine Literary Journal and Its Role in the Development of a Culture, 1931–1970*, Cambridge: Cambridge University Press, 1986

Lafleur, Héctor, Sergio Provenzano, and Fernando Alonso, *Las revistas literarias argentinas (1893–1967)*, Buenos Aires: Centro Editor de América Latina, 2nd edition, 1968

Matamoro, Blas, *Genio y figura de Victoria Ocampo*, Buenos Aires: Eudeba, 1986: 201–308

Méndez, Jesús, "The Origins of *Sur*, Argentina's Elite Cultural Review," *Revista Interamericana de Bibliografía* 31, no. 1 (1981): 3–15

Romano, Eduardo, "Julio Cortázar frente a Borges y el grupo de la revista *Sur*," *Cuadernos Hispanoamericanos* 364–66 (1980): 106–38

Zuleta, Emilia de, "Letras españolas en la revista *Sur*," *Revista de Archivos, Bibliotecas y Museos* 80, no. 1 (1977): 113–45

Susman, Margarete

German, 1872–1966

Margarete Susman was one of the first women writers in Germany resolute and powerful enough to enter what was in her time still considered the exclusive grounds of male competence: philosophy, theology, and cultural criticism. While even progressive movements like critical theory seldom encouraged women writers except in auxiliary positions, and the role of women in existential and phenomenological schools of thought came at the cost of being typecast in subservient roles, Susman, who lived much of her life in Switzerland, succeeded in what for a short time was a uniquely liberal climate to establish herself as a distinct voice.

A student and close friend of **Georg Simmel**, she followed him in recognizing even in the least important object "its relation to the truly human" and its importance for what she called "the great themes, that is, the being of the soul, life, death, time, eternity, transcendence, and immanence" ("Erinnerungen an Simmel" [1958; Reminiscences of Simmel]). Simmel's playful attitude to the deepest problems of existence liberated and inspired Susman, and her younger friends and fellow students Bernhard Groethuysen, Martin Buber, and Ernst Bloch, to rely in a more assured way on their own capacity for subjective intuition. Mentor, friend, and philosophical support, Simmel changed with his own "marginal" writing the philosophical climate and ascribed to the essay its own theoretical dignity.

While Susman had published in 1901 a volume of poetry which she soon withdrew, and a second one in 1907, her career as a writer did not really begin until 1907 when she became a regular contributor to the *Frankfurter Zeitung* (The Frankfurt news), run by Heinrich Simon. Her first essay, "Judentum und Kultur" (1907; Judaism and culture), a book **review**, announces in its title the two main themes she would pursue throughout her writing.

While Simmel provided the intellectual backing for the kind of essayistic approach Susman would embark on, she developed her own distinctive style. Replacing Simmel's rapid, associative, and suggestive thinking with a contemplative, introspective mode, her essays as well as her book-length studies reflect a thinking that self-consciously rests in itself. Designed as appreciative interpretations, her essays observe, listen, and strive to find sense in, or rather make sense of, the abundance of historical figures, and social, political, and intellectual trends and events that shape her time. Tracing the Gestalt or mental images of individuals and intellectual-historical constellations, Susman presents interpretative sketches that provide a framework to express her concern with culture as well as reflect on the individual's creativity and the role of self-determination in history.

Her essay "Vom Sinn unserer Zeit" (1931, revised 1965; On the meaning of our time) is typical in determining the stand her writings take. There she notes "that [the human] is the only being known to us that searches for the meaning of its life." The fact that, as she claims, no other historical period has been further away from an answer to that question marks the searching yet firmly grounded perspective of her essays. While a definite answer of who and what we are may be undiscoverable, the recognition that we are always in search of it reminds us of the value of self-examination and self-judgment, as encouraged by the reflective character of the essay.

Spanning the full range of the cultural history of humanity, Susman's essays link the diversity of their topics to the central quest for the meaning and determination of existence. Questions of religion, history, and cultural imagination receive their specific urgency from this core concern, and give the essays their philosophical stringency and cohesion. This is achieved, however, at the expense of concrete specificity. Abstract and lofty, Susman's essays occupy the problematic space between the material and the metaphysical, the factual and the ideal. In a unique fashion, her writing takes on the mediation between these extremes in the seemingly free realm of pure thought. It performs a critical move that navigates the discursive deadlock of contemporary philosophy.

With *Das Buch Hiob und das Schicksal des jüdischen Volkes* (The Book of Job and the destiny of the Jewish people) Susman presents her most ambitious essay, a pioneering contribution to Jewish reconstruction in the wake of Auschwitz. Published in 1946 and revised in 1948, and addressing the challenge of the foundation of the State of Israel, this essay examines the single most haunting challenge of modern times: the systematic extermination of the Jewish people in the midst of modern civilization. It is in the format of an essay, a search for answers to the unanswerable, that Susman envisions a possibility of engaging with the past. For, she argues, it is only by way of responding in the present and future that we are able to produce – retrospectively and without fatally rationalizing the irrational – a "sense" of the past. Through reconnecting with the message of biblical Judaism, Susman suggests, Jewish life after Auschwitz receives its meaning, for it is the encounter with the biblical that makes it possible to confront convincingly the modern.

Gestalten und Kreise (1954; Figures and circles) is Susman's final collection of essays on key figures in intellectual history, including seminal studies on **Moses Mendelssohn, Goethe,** Kafka, and Franz Rosenzweig. Contemplative and often meditative, these essays bring to a formal conclusion her attempt to comprehend the great themes by way of careful and empathic interpretations of individuals in their specificity.

WILLI GOETSCHEL

Biography

Born 14 October 1872 in Hamburg. Studied at a school in Zurich; Arts Academy, Düsseldorf; studied in Paris, Munich, 1898–1900, and Berlin, c. 1901, where she studied under Georg Simmel. Married Eduard von Bendemann, 1906 (divorced, 1928): one son. Book critic and literary contributor, *Frankfurter Zeitung*, 1907–33. Moved to Zurich, 1933. Joined the socialist-religious circle of the theologian Leonhard Ragaz. Government restricted her political writings, so she published some work in newspapers and magazines under the pseudonym "Reiner." Awards: City of Zurich Prize, 1944; Swiss Literary Association Prize, 1954; Swiss-Jewish Communal Association Prize, 1955; honorary degree from the University of Berlin. Died in Zurich, 16 January 1966.

Selected Writings

Essays and Related Prose

Frauen der Romantik, 1929
Das Buch Hiob und das Schicksal des jüdischen Volkes, 1946; revised edition, 1948
Gestalten und Kreise, 1954
Vom Geheimnis der Freiheit: Gesammelte Aufsätze, 1914–1964, edited by Manfred Schlösser, 1965
Das Nah- und Fernsein des Fremden: Essays und Briefe, edited by Ingeborg Nordmann, 1992

Other writings: six volumes of poetry, literary criticism, works on the philosophy of religion, particularly concerning Jewish questions, and memoirs (1966).

Further Reading

Für Margarete Susman: Auf gespaltenem Pfad, Darmstadt: Erato, 1964
Goetschel, Willi, "Margarete Susman," in *Helvetische Steckbriefe 47 Schriftsteller aus der deutschen Schweiz seit 1800*, edited by Zürcher Seminar für Literaturkritik and Werner Weber, Zurich: Artemis, 1981: 247–53
Goldschmidt, Hermann Levin, Preface to *Das Buch Hiob* by Susman, Frankfurt-on-Main: Jüdischer Verlag, 1996
Nordmann, Ingeborg, "Nachdenken an der Schwelle von Literatur und Theorie: Essayistinnen im 20. Jahrhundert," in *Deutsche Literatur von Frauen*, vol. 2, edited by Gisela Brinker-Gabler, Munich: Beck, 1988: 364–79

Swift, Jonathan

Irish, 1667–1745

Jonathan Swift's essays are public writings by a public man and intended for public effect. They are the work of someone deeply involved in the life of his time, reflecting his immersion in politics, the Church, and Ireland. Because much of Swift's writing in all of these areas is so closely related to the events of his day, most of it is now read only by specialists, but several of his essays – primarily those in which he does not speak in his own voice but creates a distinct persona to present his often bleak views – transcend the occasions that prompted them and retain a lasting interest.

Although Swift's essays concern a wide variety of subjects, certain norms and beliefs underlie all of them. He was a firm believer in the *via media*, the "middle way" between political and religious extremes, and in the necessity of employing common sense in one's approach to highly divisive issues.

Those who adopted an extreme view of church or state were subject to Swift's most slashing **satire**, for, as he wrote to his friend John Arbuthnot, "I could never let people run mad without telling and warning them sufficiently."

Perhaps the least read of all Swift's writings are the political essays and **pamphlets**, which were written for a specific purpose. When Swift shifted his allegiance from the Whigs to the Tories in 1710 he found that "their great difficulty lay in the Want of some good Pen to keep up the Spirit raised in the People, to assert the Principles, and justify the Proceedings of the new Ministers." Of the several pamphlets and 33 essays Swift contributed to the *Examiner*, most can be reduced to the theme that Tories are preferable to Whigs. Swift's only political writing of current interest is his *The Conduct of the Allies* (1711), and that not for its political message but because in this pamphlet he began to use an assumed character, in this case a supposedly impartial narrator who objectively presents "facts" concerning the disgraceful behavior of England's allies during the War of the Spanish Succession, facts intended to induce the English public to accept the peace the Tories desired. Swift does not employ satire and irony in this work, but he does lie quite successfully, so successfully indeed that according to G. M. Trevelyan Swift did more in this pamphlet "to settle the immediate fate of parties and of nations than did ever any other literary man in the annals of England."

Much of Swift's religious writing is also little read today, but his "Sentiments of a Church of England Man" (1708) is an essential statement of Swift's political and religious principles, primarily that the great evil to be avoided is arbitrary power; the supreme power must be invested in the whole people, and those who wish to "preserve the Constitution entire in Church and State" will avoid extreme Whiggery for the sake of the Church and extreme Toryism for the sake of the State. The ideas presented are those of a typical Swift narrator, a man who wishes to do his country service by "unbiasing his mind as much as possible, and thus endeavouring to moderate between the rival powers." A further attack on religious extremism is conveyed in "The Mechanical Operation of the Spirit" (1704), an example of what Ricardo Quintano (1936) has termed "three-dimensional irony." In two-dimensional irony what is said is directly opposite to what is meant; in the three-dimensional irony of "The Mechanical Operation" the narrator arrives at a perfectly sound conclusion, but the initial premise and all the reasoning resulting from it are completely wrong. The narrator analyzes religious enthusiasm, described as "a lifting up of the soul or its faculties above matter," by describing the three traditional ways of "ejaculating the soul": inspiration, from above; possession, from below; and the natural process of strong conjunctions or passion. To these methods the narrator now adds a fourth, "purely an effect of artifice and mechanic operation," the self-induced trance in which all religious belief and practice becomes a matter of distilled vapors. "The Mechanical Operation of the Spirit" and the "Argument Against Abolishing Christianity" (1708), in which the narrator argues for the preservation of the Christian religion not as a religious experience but as a social necessity, are two of Swift's best satires, illustrating both the effectiveness and dangers of the form. Readers aware of the nature of satire can easily discern the serious religious thought underlying both, but Swift always believed, no doubt correctly, that a misreading of such works led to the charges of irreligion that plagued him throughout his life.

Satire was perhaps a less dangerous weapon when employed in the service of Ireland, and Swift's Irish writings were so strong that they made him the unlikeliest of Irish patriotic heroes. Having clearly outlined the problems confronting Ireland in his *Short View of Ireland* in 1727, to no effect whatever, Swift returned to these problems in *A Modest Proposal* of 1729, an essay often considered the best sustained satire in the English language, demonstrating Swift's satiric technique at its best. In form the modest proposal is a formal Aristotelian argument, but used for perverted purposes. The persona who makes this proposal may be Swift's best use of the imagined narrator, who presents himself as a man of reason and good will with a great love for his country. The narrator proceeds modestly, methodically, and objectively to suggest that Irish poverty can be ameliorated by the sale of infants for food, remarking that "a very knowing American" of his acquaintance has assured him that "a young healthy child well nursed is at a year old a most delicious, nourishing, and wholesome food, whether stewed, roasted, baked, or boiled." With relentless and horrifying logic the narrator calmly outlines the many benefits of his scheme, all the while protesting that cruelty "hath always been with me the strongest objection against any project, how well soever intended." Throughout the essay the narrator's economic scheme reduces humans to the level of beasts, the way, Swift implies, that the Irish are actually treated by their landlords and by the English. In a country where aged and diseased poor people "are every day dying and rotting by cold and famine, and filth and vermin, as fast as can be reasonably expected" and in which young laborers are "now in almost as hopeful a condition" because they cannot find work and in any case are too weak from starvation to do any, why not make a metaphor literal: if the English and absentee landlords continue to devour the Irish people, why not their children as well?

The true horror of *A Modest Proposal* lies in the bland understatement with which it is presented, a narrative pose sustained until the very end of the essay when Swift's savage indignation blasts forth as the narrator, responding to possible objections, urges his opponents to "first ask the parents of these mortals whether they would not at this day think it a great happiness to have been sold for food at a year old in this manner I prescribe, and thereby have avoided such a perpetual scene of misfortunes as they have since gone through by the oppression of landlords, the impossibility of paying rent without money or trade, the want of common sustenance, with neither house nor clothes to cover them from the inclemencies of the weather, and the most inevitable prospect of entailing the like or greater miseries upon their breed forever."

Perhaps the most astonishing aspect of this performance is that *A Modest Proposal*, in common with a few of Swift's other works, notably the fourth book of *Gulliver's Travels* (1726), retains its power to upset, disturb, anger, and shock contemporary readers. Swift would surely have been pleased that as recently as 1984 Peter O'Toole's reading of *A Modest Proposal* at the reopening of the Gaiety Theatre in Dublin was greeted with cries of "disgusting" and "offensive," followed by the departure of several members of the audience.

Such controversy has always been associated with Swift. During the late 18th century and throughout the 19th he was frequently regarded as a monster in both his personal and literary lives. The 20th century has responded more favorably to him; today his reputation has probably never been higher, partly because of the dedicated work of recent scholars who have added greatly to our understanding of Swift's satiric methods and underlying seriousness of purpose. Another, more visceral reason for Swift's greater popularity has surely been the horrors of the 20th century itself. Satires that describe religion as a social rather than spiritual activity, that warn of the dangers of religious and political extremism, and above all that ironically advocate the methodical destruction of large numbers of humans for the economic prosperity of the state, may have been written in the 18th century, but speak directly to our own.

JOHN H. ROGERS

See also Satiric Essay

Biography

Born 30 November 1667 in Dublin. Studied at Kilkenny Grammar School, 1674–82; Trinity College, Dublin, 1682–89, B.A., 1686, M.A., 1692. Secretary to **Sir William Temple** at Moor Park, Farnham, Surrey, 1689–95 and 1696–99; ordained in the Church of Ireland (Anglican), Dublin, 1695; vicar of Kilroot, 1695–96, and Laracor, from 1700; prebendary, St. Patrick's Cathedral, Dublin, 1701; emissary for the Irish clergy in London, 1707–09. Contributor of the "Bickerstaff Papers," 1708–09, and to the *Tatler*; editor, the *Examiner*, 1710–11. Renounced the Whigs and joined the Tories when they came to power, 1710. Cofounder, the Scriblerus Club, 1713–14. Returned to Ireland, 1714. Dean, St. Patrick's Cathedral, 1713–42. Married Esther (Stella) Johnson, c. 1716 (died, 1728). Visited London, 1726 and 1727. Awards: honorary degree from University of Dublin. Died in Dublin, 19 October 1745.

Selected Writings

Essays and Related Prose

(selection; many pamphlets and letters individually published)
Esquire Bickerstaff's Most Strange and Wonderful Predictions for the Year 1708, 1708
The Accomplishment of the First of Mr. Bickerstaff's Predictions, 1708
Bickerstaff redivivus; or, Predictions for the Year 1709, 1709
A Vindication of Isaac Bickerstaff Esq. Against What Is Objected to Him by Mr. Partridge, 1709
The Examiner, nos. 13–45, 2 November 1710–14 June 1711; in *Swift vs. Mainwaring: "The Examiner" and "The Medley"*, edited by Frank H. Ellis, 1985
A Modest Proposal for Preventing the Children of Poor People from Being a Burthen to Their Parents or the Country, and for Making Them Beneficial to the Publick, 1729; edited by Charles Beaumont, 1969
Prose Works, edited by Herbert Davis and others, 14 vols., 1939–68
The Writings of Jonathan Swift (selection), edited by Robert A. Greenberg and William Bowman Piper, 1973
Swift's Irish Pamphlets, edited by Joseph McMinn, 1991
The Intelligencer, with Thomas Sheridan, edited by James Woolley, 1992
A Modest Proposal and Other Satires, 1995

Other writings: the satires *A Tale of a Tub* (1704) and *Gulliver's Travels* (1726), poetry, many works on politics, and correspondence (collected in *The Correspondence*, edited by Harold Williams, 5 vols., 1963–65).

Collected works editions: *The Works*, edited by Thomas Sheridan, 17 vols., 1784, revised edition edited by John Nichols, 24 vols., 1812; *Works*, edited by Sir Walter Scott, 19 vols., 1814.

Bibliographies

Landa, Louis A., and J. E. Tobin, *Jonathan Swift: A List of Critical Studies Published from 1895 to 1945*, New York: Octagon, 1974 (original edition, 1945)

Rodino, Richard H., *Swift Studies, 1965–1980: An Annotated Bibliography*, New York: Garland, 1984

Stathis, James J., *A Bibliography of Swift Studies, 1945–1965*, Nashville: Vanderbilt University Press, 1967

Teerink, Herman, *A Bibliography of Writings of Jonathan Swift*, The Hague: Nijhoff, 1937; revised edition, edited by Arthur H. Scouten, Philadelphia: University of Pennsylvania Press, 1963

Further Reading

Bullitt, John M., *Jonathan Swift and the Anatomy of Satire*, Cambridge, Massachusetts: Harvard University Press, 1953

Craik, Henry, *The Life of Jonathan Swift*, London: Murray, 1882

Davis, Herbert, *Jonathan Swift: Essays on His Satire and Other Studies*, New York: Oxford University Press, 1964

Downie, J. A., *Jonathan Swift: Political Writer*, London and Boston: Routledge and Kegan Paul, 1984

Ehrenpreis, Irvin, *Swift: The Man, His Works, and the Age*, Cambridge, Massachusetts: Harvard University Press, 3 vols., 1962–83

Ewald, William Bragg, Jr., *The Masks of Jonathan Swift*, Cambridge, Massachusetts: Harvard University Press, and Oxford: Blackwell, 1954

Ferguson, Oliver W., *Swift and Ireland*, Urbana: University of Illinois Press, 1962

Landa, Louis, *Swift and the Church of Ireland*, Oxford: Clarendon Press, 1954

Nokes, David, *Jonathan Swift, a Hypocrite Reversed: A Critical Biography*, Oxford and New York: Oxford University Press, 1985

Price, Martin, *Swift's Rhetorical Art: A Study in Structure and Meaning*, New Haven, Connecticut: Yale University Press, 1953

Quintano, Ricardo, *The Mind and Art of Jonathan Swift*, London: Oxford University Press, 1936

Quintano, Ricardo, *Swift: An Introduction*, London: Oxford University Press, 1955

Rosenheim, Edward, *Swift and the Satirist's Art*, Chicago: University of Chicago Press, 1963

Watkins, W. B. C., *Perilous Balance: The Tragic Genius of Swift, Johnson, and Sterne*, Princeton, New Jersey: Princeton University Press, 1939

Williams, Kathleen, *Jonathan Swift and the Age of Compromise*, Lawrence: University of Kansas Press, 1958; London: Constable, 1959

T

Taine, Hippolyte

French, 1828–1893

Born a century later, Taine would have been a university professor, though given the extent of his interests – philosophy, psychology, literature, art, sociology, history – it is hard to know in which discipline: "Theory," perhaps, or "Cultural Studies." He was a brilliant student at the École Normale Supérieure, taught philosophy for a year at a collège, and wrote a doctoral thesis on La Fontaine. But his anti-clericalism, his hostility to the dominant *spiritualiste* school of French philosophy, his adherence to the views of Spinoza, and his interest in Hegel made him anathema to the university establishment. At the age of 24 he took the decision to become an outlaw (he uses the English word): he would leave the university and live from his pen as a journalist and essayist.

He began with **review** articles for the *Revue de l'Instruction Publique* (Review of public education), on French writers – classical (**La Bruyère**) or contemporary (Michelet). Soon he was writing for the more prestigious *Revue des Deux Mondes* (Review of two worlds) and the *Journal des Débats* (Journal of debates). All of his books were made up from articles first published in these journals or in the lighter *Vie Parisienne* (Parisian life), so that, while he gave the specific title *Essais* to the three volumes of collected articles (and to the monographs on La Fontaine and Livy), there is a sense in which all his work is that of an essayist.

His *Histoire de la littérature anglaise* (1863–64; *History of English Literature*), for example, began life as essays on particular authors (first **Macaulay**, then **Dickens**, Chaucer, Shakespeare, Bunyan, **Thackeray**, Milton, and others). In the *History*, the essays are considerably revised and become **chapters**, ordered chronologically. For the collection Taine writes his famous introduction, claiming that literature is the best source for the historian, and gives the book unity by treating English literature as a case study demonstrating his claim. Even in his major work, *Les Origines de la France contemporaine* (1875–93; *The Origins of Contemporary France*), he often proceeds by set-piece portraits such as those on the Jacobins or Napoleon Bonaparte.

Those essays that were not organized into works like the *History of English Literature* or *Les Philosophes classiques du XIXe siècle* (1857, 1868; Classical philosophers of the 19th century) were collected under the title (borrowed from Macaulay) of *Essais de critique et d'histoire* (Critical and historical essays). The first of these collections appeared in 1858 with a **preface** describing and defending his "scientific" theory of criticism. Most of the essays in these three volumes (*Essais*; *Nouveaux essais*, 1865; *Derniers essais*, 1894) are devoted to one author. A typical Taine essay attempts to explain an individual in terms of one dominant theme, or *faculté maîtresse*, which structures the life and the work. It also places the subject within a social and historical context (derived, he says, from the individual's race, milieu, and moment). Taine is a structuralist *avant la lettre*, with the structuralist's tendency to downplay randomness, contradiction, and flux. His essays are brilliant demonstrations: one idea is developed, sometimes overdeveloped, and everything hangs together – in the life and in the work – in the essay. The early article on La Bruyère is a good example: in portraying him Taine uses the discrepancy between his social status and the aristocratic milieu in which he lived, to explain his acerbity.

But there are two levels to Taine: one is this structuralist emphasis on system, evident in the prefaces and the unifying "key" he provides for each subject. The other is his own deeply felt and lived experience of contradiction – his Romanticism at odds with his positivism. The great pleasure of reading Taine's essays comes from reading between (or above) the lines, of glimpsing the subjective behind the "scientific" objectivity, the conflicts and dilemmas behind the claims of unity. Taine was a highly emotional man who disliked displaying his emotions directly in public writing. And yet his essays are full of discreet personal "confessions" – either clear statements of fundamental preference ("I prefer De Musset to Tennyson") or statements about his subject which are in fact statements about himself. The essay on Balzac (1858) is certainly a brilliant and influential account of a controversial contemporary, but it is also a depiction of Taine's own experience of stress and financial struggle as a writer and of his own divided feelings about modernity. It would not be an exaggeration to say that Taine writes about different authors in order to explore different aspects of his own experience; and his experience is of conflict and tension rather than of resolution.

This restrained self-disclosure is most affecting in the last essays, which are deeply felt **meditations** on how posterity remembers the achievements of a lifetime. They are a kind of testament about death and the inevitability of failure. At this period, Taine is of the age when funerals begin – of his father-in-law, old friends such as Édouard de Suckau and Anatole Prévost-Paradol – above all of his mother (his father had died when Taine was 13). The theme is *Ubi sunt?* – What is left of those who lived, struggled, and died? For the vast majority the answer is, he says, nothing save a name on a tombstone. Even writers leave little more. These late essays are elegiac obituaries of minor figures: Louis de Loménie, the historian whom he succeeded at the French Academy; Marcelin (Émile Planat), his school friend and editor of the *Vie Parisienne*; Frantz Woepke the orientalist, another friend; Ernest Bertin, editor of the *Débats*; George Sand; **Sainte-Beuve** himself, who claimed to have left a portrait of himself in 50 volumes of essays devoted to others.

Of Marcelin Taine writes that the 25 volumes of his *Vie Parisienne* "only show the lesser part of his thoughts; this is the fate of most men; very few fulfill their nature completely." Will Marcelin be remembered? The newspaper, together with a book of essays, "is all that remains of him together with his memory in the minds of four or five friends who will not live long. Woepke, who most deserved to live, was the first to die. We walk close behind them on the path which vanished beneath their feet. It is collapsing beneath us; each day we sink deeper and we are already up to our knees in the same earth which covers them."

When he writes these essays Taine is, along with **Ernest Renan**, the most famous intellectual in France, but he knows that writers who are not creative artists have their modest afterlife only in encyclopedias. And he is resigned to that fate.

COLIN EVANS

Biography

Hippolyte Adolphe Taine. Born 21 April 1828 in Vouziers, the Ardennes. Studied at the Collège Bourbon, Paris, 1841–48, baccalauréat, 1848; École Normale Supérieure, Paris, 1848–51, doctorate in letters, 1853. Taught at a collège in Nevers and a lycée in Poitiers, 1851–52, then private tutor. Contributor to various periodicals, from 1850s, including the *Revue de l'Instruction Publique*, *Revue des Deux Mondes*, and *Journal des Débats*. Suffered often from fatigue, from 1857. Admissions examiner in history and German, Military Academy of Saint-Cyr, 1863–66; professor of aesthetics and art history, École des Beaux-Arts, Paris, 1864–84. Married Thérèse Denuelle, 1868: one daughter and one son. Lectured at Oxford University, 1871. Elected to the French Academy, 1878. Awards: French Academy Prize, for essay, 1855; honorary degree from Oxford University. Member, Legion of Honor, 1866. Died in Paris, 5 March 1893.

Selected Writings

Essays and Related Prose

Essai sur les Fables de La Fontaine, 1853; as *La Fontaine et ses fables*, 1861
Essai sur Tite-Live, 1856
Les Philosophes français du XIXe siècle, 1857; as *Les Philosophes classiques du XIXe siècle*, 1868
Essais de critique et d'histoire, 1858
Histoire de la littérature anglaise, 4 vols., 1863–64; definitive edition, 5 vols., 1872; as *History of English Literature*, translated by Henri Van Laun, 2 vols., 1871
Philosophie de l'art, 1865; as *Lectures on Art*, translated by John Durand, 2 vols., 1875
Nouveaux essais de critique et d'histoire, 1865; one essay as *Balzac: A Critical Study*, translated by Lorenzo O'Rourke, 1906
Notes sur Paris: Vie et opinions de M. Frédéric-Thomas Graindorge, 1867; as *Notes on Paris*, translated by J. A. Stevens, 1875

Notes sur l'Angleterre, 1872; as *Notes on England*, translated by W. Fraser Rae, 1872, and Edward Hyams, 1957
Derniers essais de critique et d'histoire, 1894

Other writings: *Les Origines de la France contemporaine* (6 vols., 1875–93; *The Origins of Contemporary France*), works on the history of art, travel books on the Pyrenees and Italy, studies on **John Stuart Mill**, Charles Dickens, and **Thomas Carlyle**, and volumes of correspondence.

Bibliographies

Giraud, Victor, *Bibliographie critique de Taine*, Paris: Hachette, 1902
Smith, H., "The Taine Centennial: Comment and Bibliography," *MLN* 44 (1929): 437–45
Thieme, Hugo P., "The Development of Taine Criticism Since 1893," *MLN* 17 (1902): 71–82, 140–53

Further Reading

Charlton, D.G., *Positivist Thought in France During the Second Empire, 1852–1870*, Oxford: Clarendon Press, 1959
Evans, Colin, *Taine: Essai de biographie intérieure*, Paris: Nizet, 1975: especially 173–308
Evans, Colin, "Taine and His Fate," *Nineteenth-Century French Studies* 6, nos.1–2 (Fall–Winter 1977–78): 118–28
Léger, François, *Monsieur Taine*, Paris: Critérion, 1993
Nordmann, Jean-Thomas, *Taine et la critique scientifique*, Paris: Presses Universitaires de France, 1992
Weinstein, Leo, *Hippolyte Taine*, New York: Twayne, 1972

The Tatler
British periodical, 1709–1711

The *Tatler* was a collaborative effort: the authorial mask of Isaac Bickerstaff was a satiric invention of **Jonathan Swift**'s, whose pseudonymous pamphlet *Predictions for the Year 1708* pilloried the astrologer John Partridge. In the last issue, no. 271 of 2 January 1711, **Joseph Addison**'s role is acknowledged, although his anonymity is preserved: "The Hand that has assisted me in those noble Discourses upon the Immortality of the Soul, the glorious Prospects of another Life, and the most sublime Idea's of Religion and Virtue, is a Person too fondly my Friend ever to own them." The editor credits his friend with providing "the finest Strokes of Wit and Humour in all Mr. *Bickerstaff*'s Lucubrations." But the design and execution of the *Tatler* are principally the work of **Richard Steele**, as he himself reveals in the same number.

Steele had been a successful comic playwright, experience that served him well in his role of drama critic and theatrical commentator in the *Tatler*. He had also served as editor of the London *Gazette*, and so had prepared himself for the rigors of producing a thrice-weekly newspaper. Although the *Tatler* is now revered as a literary magazine and as a prototype both for the single-author, pseudonymously published journals to follow (the ***Spectator*** and the ***Rambler*** being probably the most famous examples) and for the magazine miscellanies such as the *Gentleman's* that held a dominant place in the popular press for most of the 18th century, Steele initially conceived of the *Tatler* as a newspaper, in competition with the *Gazette*, the *Daily Courant*, and *Post Boy*. As such, it reported, under the heading "St. James's Coffee-house," on foreign and domestic news, as well as fulfilling its stated purpose "to expose the false Arts of Life, to pull off the Disguises of Cunning, Vanity, and Affectation, and to recommend a general Simplicity in our Dress, our Discourse, and our Behaviour."

The *Tatler* essays are an invaluable record of the geography, politics, manners, and artistic achievement of early 18th-century England. Collectively, they offer a sort of walking tour of London, highlighted by visits to Westminster Abbey, the Tower, St. Paul's Cathedral, Bethlehem Hospital, and the Old Bailey. In its function as an almanac, the paper records notable calendar events and the weather, and comments on events of local notoriety such as the State Lottery of 1710, which "turned a Tax into a Diversion."

As an instrument of social reform, the paper advocated moderation: avoidance of extremes in custom and fashion, and adherence to reason and benevolence. The "Censor" takes on an unholy parade of "drunkards," gamblers, rakes, atheists, pugilists, swearers, and those who unjustifiably wear the mantle of "men of wit." For the lovelorn, the paper serves as a sort of marriage counselor preaching the virtues of patience and domestic harmony and avoidance of libertinism. For its more erudite readers, the paper comments on the virtues of classical learning, holding up Homer, Virgil, Horace, and **Cicero** for special praise and commending modern authors such as Shakespeare and Milton for their good taste.

For his first number of 12 April 1709, Steele as "Isaac Bickerstaff, Esq." announced the organizational plan for the journal. He would be a sort of domestic correspondent, sorting into various categories material that issued from founts of news and gossip in London. For verisimilitude, he used the names of actual coffeehouses and other places of social congregation. Under the heading "White's Chocolate-house" would appear all matter concerning "Gallantry, Pleasure, and Entertainment." These entries tended to be personality sketches – some of them "characters" in the 17th-century sense, some of them thinly veiled, recognizable figures. The anecdotes ostensibly illustrated some moral point. The entry for the first number is a character of a "very pretty Gentleman" who has been smitten by the sight of a young Lady passing by in a coach – and who thenceforth lets his passions "maul" him. No. 21 for 28 May 1709 provides contrasting characters of a "Man of Conversation" and his pale imitation, the "Pretty Fellow." No. 25 for 7 June 1709 takes on one of Steele's favorite targets for his satirical moralizing, the "fatal folly" of duelling.

Will's Coffee-house would serve as the forum for commentary on the subject of poetry. This feature also provides theater historians with invaluable information on the staging and performances of contemporary plays such as Jonson's *Volpone* and *The Alchymist*, Wycherley's *The Country-Wife*, Dryden's *All for Love*, Farquhar's *The Recruiting Officer*, and Centlivre's *The Busie Body*. The first number reviews a production of Congreve's *Love for Love*, a benefit performance for Thomas Betterton, who was nearing the end of his life and whom Steele esteemed as the preeminent British actor of his era. The **review** applauds the "all-star" cast of Mrs. Barry, Mrs. Bracegirdle, and Mr. Dogget, all veteran players. From the columns under this heading comes a wealth of critical commentary on contemporary performers, dramatic authors, audiences, the plays themselves, and the general state of British theater.

Miscellaneous material appeared under the heading "From my own apartment." No. 1 carries on Swift's joke about Mr. Partridge, whose death is reannounced: "I therefore give all Men fair Warning to mend their Manners, for I shall from Time to Time print Bills of Mortality; and I beg the Pardon of all such who shall be named therein, if they who are good for Nothing shall find themselves in the Number of the Deceased." No. 167 for 4 May 1710 offers a memorial tribute to Betterton. Bickerstaff has particular praise for Betterton's Othello: "The wonderful Agony which he appeared in, when he examined the Circumstance of the Handkerchief in *Othello*; the Mixture of Love that intruded upon his Mind upon the innocent Answers *Desdemona* makes, betrayed in his Gesture such a Variety and Vicissitude of Passions, as would admonish a Man to be afraid of his own Heart."

Clearly, the places of origin revealed in the headings appealed directly to a coffeehouse readership. In its advertisement for the first issue, the *Tatler* specifies its intended audience. The paper is "principally intended for the Use of Politick Persons, who are so publick-spirited as to neglect their own Affairs to look into Transactions of State." But the paper also quickly signals its moralizing intent by satirizing its coffeehouse constituency, much as it would castigate all manner of vice and folly: "Now these Gentlemen, for the most Part, being Persons of strong Zeal and weak Intellects, It is both a Charitable and Necessary Work to offer something, whereby such worthy and well-affected Members of the Commonwealth may be instructed, after their Reading, WHAT TO THINK." The editor also promises material designed for the "Fair Sex, in Honour of whom I have invented the Title of this Paper."

No. 229 for 26 September 1710 hints at the extraordinary popular reception of the *Tatler*, which drew the praise and condemnation of "The Town" as well as a slew of imitators: "Should I lay down my Paper, What a Famine would there be among the Hawkers, Printers, Booksellers, and Authors? . . . I have been *annotated*, *retattled*, *examined*, and *condoled*" by admirers, critics, and plagiarists. Clearly the tone, organization, and subject matter left a lasting impression, exemplified by borrowings in virtually all of the *Tatler*'s journalistic offspring.

In No. 162, at the end of the first year of publication, Bickerstaff assigns himself the title "Censor of Great Britain." In so doing he defined what has become known as "Augustan" satire: "making frequent Reviews of the People," looking "into the Manners of the People," and "punishing Offences according to the Quality of the Offender." The *Tatler*'s moral assignment was to chastise folly and to punish vice, a censorious function associated with the Scriblerians and early 18th-century **satire** in general.

Early 18th-century writing was frequently collaborative and normally anonymous or pseudonymous. Attribution problems facing those attempting to sort out who contributed which essays to the *Tatler* are similar to those facing students of virtually any writing of this period. Typically, there is a lack of reliable evidence to determine confidently which essays are Steele's, Addison's, or other contributors'. About 200 of the 271 issues have been ascribed to Steele. Controversy remains over whether to accept Thomas Tickell's record of Addison's contributions in the first collected edition of Addison's works (1721), although Tickell was said to have asked Steele to identify them.

Twentieth-century critics have largely followed the judgment of late 18th-century writers who found in Addison and the *Spectator* the apotheosis of wit and morality and who deemed the *Tatler* a decidedly inferior forebear. The *Tatler*, as its name suggests, was certainly more topical in content and chatty in style than the *Spectator*, seldom reaching the latter's philosophical complexity. Yet, in part because of its topicality and diversity in voice and subject, the *Tatler* provides literary historians access to the period probably unmatched by any other single source.

RICHARD C. TAYLOR

See also Periodical Essay

Editions

The Tatler, nos. 1–271, 12 April 1709–2 January 1711; edited by Donald F. Bond, 3 vols., 1987

The Lucubrations of Isaac Bickerstaff, Esq., edited by John Nichols, 6 vols., 1786

Further Reading

Bond, Richmond P., *The Tatler: The Making of a Literary Journal*, Cambridge, Massachusetts: Harvard University Press, 1971

Winton, Calhoun, *Captain Steele: The Early Career of Richard Steele*, Baltimore: Johns Hopkins University Press, 1964

Temple, Sir William

English, 1628–1699

Sir William Temple's career as an essayist began in his early twenties while he was on the continent after leaving Cambridge without completing his degree. During his years as a political figure and as a retired diplomat at his magnificent estates at Sheen and Moor Park, Temple continued to work in the essay form, producing works on a wide variety of topics.

The early essays, written and left untitled before 1652, were printed for the first time in 1930 by G. C. Moore Smith (*The Early Essays and Romances*) and were given titles in 1940 by Homer Woodbridge (*Sir William Temple: The Man and His Work*). Their titles are indicative of their content: "Of the Inconstancy and Variety of Our Judgements," "Of Reverie and Idle Fancy," "Of Fortune and Content," "Of Envy and Jealousy," "Of Stained Honor," and "That Virtue Is Not the Mean of Vices."

For the next 20 years or so, while he was occupied with political affairs such as the negotiation of the Triple Alliance and the marriage of William of Orange to Mary Stuart, he seems to have neglected the essay. But in 1673 he began publishing essays, some of which ran to book length, starting with *Observations upon the United Provinces of the Netherlands*. In 1680 appeared the first part of his *Miscellanea*, which contained "A Survey of the Constitutions and Interests of the Empire, Sweden, Denmark, Spain, Holland, France, and Flanders," "Upon the Original and Nature of Government," "Upon the Advancement of Trade in Ireland," "Upon the Conjuncture of Affairs in October 1673," "Upon the Excesses of Grief," and "Upon the Cure of the Gout by Moxa." The second part of the *Miscellanea* (published in 1690 and augmented in 1692) contained "Upon the Gardens of Epicurus," "Of Poetry," "Of Heroic Virtue," and "An Essay upon the Ancient and Modern Learning." The remainder of his essays appeared in *Miscellanea, The Third Part*, edited by **Jonathan Swift** (who served as Temple's secretary for the last ten years of his life) and published in 1701 after Temple's death in 1699; it included "Of Popular Discontents," "Of Health and Long Life," and "Some Thoughts upon Reviewing the Essay of Ancient and Modern Learning."

Several scholars have noted the influence of **Montaigne** on both the style and content of the early essays in their openness, ardor, and personal tone. The essays also anticipate political, literary, and philosophical ideas found in his more mature works, as well as his distrust of modern learning, later manifested in the famous essay on ancient and modern learning. The ideas found in the early essays were to be refined and polished by Temple's travel, reading, and experience over the next several decades.

In his essays on politics Temple demonstrates his belief that people are more or less the same in all times and places except for those differences brought about by climate. In the major essay "Upon the Original and Nature of Government," he holds to the idea that the origin of government is to be found in the family; thus he subscribes to the patriarchal theory of government's beginnings as it emerged in the Old Testament, **Plato**, Aristotle, Jean Bodin, and Sir Robert Filmer. In the essay on the Netherlands Temple reveals his deep respect for the Dutch and their civilization. The "Survey" reflects his interest in diverse European cultures and his analysis of the dangers posed to peace by Louis XVI. In essays on Ireland Temple discusses the difficult relationship between England and Ireland and proposes remedies that might ease the deplorable conditions in the latter nation. In "Of Popular Discontents" Temple identifies and analyzes the causes of political unrest, believing that these will never disappear until "all Men are wise, good, and easily contented."

His essays on culture are better known. "Upon the Gardens of Epicurus" discusses Epicureanism and its appeal to the philosophical mind, traces the history of gardens from Eden to Rome and northern Europe, and shows how they enable people to "enjoy the Ease and Freedom of a private Scene, where a Man may go his own Way and his own Pace, in the common Paths or Circles of Life." The essays "Of Health and Long Life" and "Upon the Cure of the Gout by Moxa" illustrate Temple's distrust of science and his belief that good health is essential to "Tranquility of Mind, and Indolence of Body." "Of Poetry" deals with the origin and history of poetry, the nature of poetic inspiration, style, versification, folklore, and the relationship of poetry to prose, romance, and satire. It is one of the more important critical documents of 17th-century England.

Temple's most famous essay is "An Essay upon the Ancient and Modern Learning," which embroiled him in the Ancients–Moderns controversy that had originated on the continent. Basically Temple took the side of the Ancients, dismissing the accomplishments of the Moderns in almost all areas. "Some Thoughts upon Reviewing the Essay of Ancient and Modern Learning" amplifies some of the points made in the earlier essay.

Temple's overriding philosophy in the essays seems to be embodied in two famous quotations: "When all is done, Human Life is, at the greatest, and the best but like a froward Child, that must be play'd with and humour'd a little to keep it quiet till it falls asleep, and then the Care is over" ("Of Poetry"); and that everything that people pursue for happiness "are baubles, besides old wood to burn, old wine to drink, old friends to converse with, and old books to read" ("An Essay upon the Ancient and Modern Learning").

Temple's influence and reputation as a stylist emerged in the early 18th century when **Swift**, Pope, John Hughes, and Leonard Welsted held him in high esteem. Swift, for example, said that Temple "has advanced our English Tongue, to as great a perfection as it can well bear." Later, **Samuel Johnson** was to praise Temple as "the first writer who gave cadence to English prose."

ROBERT C. STEENSMA

Biography

Born 25 April 1628 in Blackfriars, London. Studied at Emmanuel College, Cambridge, left 1648. Traveled on the continent for four years. Married Dorothy Osborne 1654 (died, 1695): nine children (only two survived childhood, and they died before their father). Member of the Irish Parliament for Carlow, 1661; moved to England, 1663; served the Crown on various diplomatic missions in Europe, including effecting the Triple Alliance between England, Holland, and Sweden, 1668; awarded a baronetcy, 1666. Retired to his estate at Sheen, 1668–74. Visited The Hague: formalized peace between England and the Netherlands, 1674, and arranged the marriage between William of Orange and Mary Stuart, 1677. Retired again to his estate at Moor Park, near Farnham, Surrey, 1680. Died at Moor Park, 27 January 1699.

Selected Writings

Essays and Related Prose
Observations upon the United Provinces of the Netherlands, 1673; edited by George N. Clark, 1932, reprinted 1972
Miscellanea, 2 vols., 1680–90; vol. 3 edited by Jonathan Swift, 1701
Essays, edited by J. A. Nicklin, 1903
Upon the Garden of Epicurus, with Other 17th-Century Garden Essays, edited by A. F. Sieveking, 1908
Essays on Ancient and Modern Learning and on Poetry, edited by J. E. Spingarn, 1909, and Martin Kämper (in English and German), 1995
The Early Essays and Romances, edited by G. C. Moore Smith, 1930
Three Essays, edited by F. J. Fielden, 1939
Five Miscellaneous Essays, edited by Samuel Holt Monk, 1963

Other writings: poetry, romances, *An Introduction to the History of England* (1695), and correspondence.

Collected works edition: *The Works*, 2 vols., 1720.

Further Reading

Allen, R. J., "Swift's Earliest Political Tract and Temple's Essays," *Harvard Studies* 19 (1937)
Kirk, Clara Marburg, *Sir William Temple: A Seventeenth-Century "Libertin"*, New Haven, Connecticut: Yale University Press, and London: Oxford University Press, 1932
Steensma, Robert C., *Sir William Temple*, New York: Twayne, 1970
Woodbridge, Homer E., *Sir William Temple: The Man and His Work*, New York: Modern Language Association, and London: Oxford University Press, 1940

Der Teutsche Merkur

German periodical, 1773–1810

Der Teutsche Merkur (The German Mercury) was an 18th-century German periodical, founded in 1773 and principally edited by **Christoph Martin Wieland**; it was renamed *Der neue Teutsche Merkur* during the period of the French Revolution. Usually issued in monthly numbers, the *TM* was one of the longest-lived (38 years) and most influential journals of the age. Its founder – who established the periodical in loose imitation of the *Mercure de France* just a few months after settling in Weimar – anticipated that it would serve a twofold purpose: as an educational medium for his melioristic classical-humanistic ideas and as a source of income that would support him and his family independent of patrons. A secondary, though not insignificant, desire was that such a public forum might aid in spreading the editor's fame as a poet and novelist. Significantly, Wieland was to shift the emphasis away from his French model's concern with the theater to ideas and opinions of a broader nature (John A. McCarthy, 1979), especially to contemporary cultural, social, and political affairs.

As both owner and chief editor of the *TM*, Wieland regarded the entrepreneurial aspect of his role "as if I were an honest weaver or cobbler supporting myself and my family upon the fruits of my handiwork" (A. W. Kurtz, 1956). One of Wieland's critics, Claude Miquet (1990), makes a convincing case, however, that both entrepreneur and Enlightener were united in the person of the editor and that the commercial aspect of Wieland's enterprise was far from being its most important. In any event, various **prefaces** and addresses to subscribers during the first few years of the journal's life clearly reveal Wieland's assumption of an audience whose attention and favor must be carefully courted, if his principal goals of instruction and stimulation to thought were to be achieved. In the preface to the first number (January 1773), for example, he avers that only articles of a superior character would be allowed entry, although he also intends to include trifles: "Trivialities, too, can be interesting, and good taste and the heart can often profit more from such than from a heavy-handed seriousness . . . Nonetheless, these articles will for the most part be appropriate for the intellect of those who think or for the heart of those who feel."

The novice publisher had great hopes for his venture and wished to reach as large a portion of the reading public as possible, rather than to concentrate on the interests and tastes of a small, elite group. Early on he tried to capitalize on the new-found German patriotism generated by the young Storm and Stress poets, and to make a transregional, integrative appeal to those speakers of German either outside of or otherwise indifferent to the old Reich (S.-A. Jørgensen and others, 1994). Also consonant with this attempt to gain a larger readership was the accommodation he made in 1777 to subscribers who had complained about the recent removal of a feature entitled "Logogryphen und Rätsel" (Logographs and puzzles): he conceded that he had been too long prejudiced against such slight divertissements and announced his intention of restoring the feature. A year later he renewed his pledge to spare his readers "dry treatises" and, rather, to provide "essays that will nourish the mind and incite to thought."

Generally, Wieland aimed for his journal to combine a classical-humanist spirit with matters of interest to the German reading public; the principal means of realizing his goals were the cultivation of "social intercourse and critical insight" (Jørgensen). Moreover, and in contrast to other famous periodicals of the age, such as **Schiller**'s *Die Horen* (The muses) and the Schlegel brothers' *Athenäum*, the project was by no means intended to embody any specific literary, philosophical, or cultural program (Friedrich Sengle, 1949). Repeatedly, in the early years, Wieland asseverated that his publication would be successful – in both an entrepreneurial and a more spiritual sense – only insofar as it retained the interest of the average reader. Success, he believed, could best be attained through a nonpartisan, serious, and assiduous search for truth in which the writer and his reader would be firmly and equally allied. Not the least ingredient in this formula for success was the editor's intention to engage only the best German thinkers as contributors.

Several of Wieland's critics have concluded that in the end the *TM* was not a school for high-minded idealists, and that it hardly met the high hopes of some of those early enthusiasts who greeted its first appearance as a possible counter to the *Allgemeine Deutsche Bibliothek* (Universal German library), published by the hide-bound and widely resented German Enlightenment philosopher Friedrich Nicolai (cf. **Moses Mendelssohn**). Nonetheless, the journal enjoyed an unprecedented success upon first appearance. An initial run of 2500 had to be augmented by a second printing, and even though the next year saw subscriptions drop to 2000, this figure was unparalleled for the time. Ten years after its inception, the number of subscribers had fallen by another 500 or so, with a steady decline thereafter to 800 by 1798. Not until the Romantic age, however, when Wieland redirected his editorial interests, did the *TM* come to an irreversible end (Sengle).

In spite of the journal's popular success in the early years, many among the German intelligentsia of the late 18th century were sorely disappointed by the *TM*'s lack of commitment to criticism, one of the two or three most significant areas of interest during the period. Wieland's failure to persevere with criticism – despite the promises to his initial subscribers – is explained by some of his later commentators as stemming from faintheartedness in the face of a possible public withdrawal of support for the journal, not least from his disinclination to assume the role of critic in the first place. Compounding this lack of full dedication was the editor's often annoying practice of deleting or otherwise altering material from his contributors that he thought either harshly critical, offensive, or beyond the competence of his subscribers. While this practice was inconsonant with the originally announced intention to include a section entitled "Umständliche Beurteilung neuer Bücher" (Detailed criticism of new books), the journal did sometimes offer true and decisive literary criticism in the late 1770s, especially during Johann Heinrich "Mephistopheles" Merck's tenure as coeditor. Moreover, while it is perhaps a moot point whether **Kant**'s revolutionary epistemology and writings on aesthetics would have found extensive commentary in the *TM* without the spur of K. L. Reinhold, Wieland's son-in-law and Kant enthusiast, there is little doubt on the editor's part that philosophical contributions which might tax the patience of the general audience had to be handled with circumspection. Prudence was also exercised with contributions in the areas of political philosophy, including those from prominent statesmen of the time – and for essentially the same reason: the disinclination to publish something that might be construed as unfair partisanship. This policy of noncommittal neutrality was to change, at times drastically, during the era of the French Revolution. Even so, articles on such subjects as art history and musicology, Shakespeare, theoretical physics and chemistry, archaeology, and orientalism found good representation in the journal (Thomas Starnes, 1994).

Wieland's interest in the French Revolution was prepared long beforehand by his general preoccupation with matters French. Indeed, as Sengle has pointed out, Wieland propagandized throughout the history of the *TM* for France as the best model for the Germans to follow in their efforts to achieve a higher civilization. The French, he argued, simply had the most modern and most exemplary of those European cultures that were based on classical antiquity. In fact, he enthusiastically opened the pages of his journal to French affairs in the decade of the 1780s, publishing, for example, a series of essays on French women writers, and several articles on balloon flight in France (especially by the brothers Montgolfier). During the 1790s the *TM* stood out among the periodicals of the age in placing the French Revolution center stage in reports and observations. Moreover, Wieland's journal offered the most percipient and intelligible commentary among popular and widely-read German periodicals. Indeed, Wieland's own contributions on the questions raging around that event – e.g. democracy vs. monarchy; how the Germans should react to the Revolution; what would be its upshot – constitute by far the most important and interesting matter in the *TM* during the 1790s. They were also among Wieland's own most forthright and lasting contributions to the essay genre: for example, his acceptance of only one part (*fraternité*) of the Revolutionary triadic slogan, and his famous Napoleon prophecy (McCarthy, 1979). However, he eventually felt himself incapable of comprehending the events sweeping over his old European order, and finally turned away from French affairs to devote himself to the translation of works from classical antiquity, and with that the establishment, in 1796, of another journal, the *Attisches Museum* (Attic museum).

Though Hans Wahl (1914) – as Sengle maintains – has made a sincere effort to show that the *TM* was a well-integrated whole during most of its existence, the journal was, nonetheless, not "the development of a program of a living idea, and displayed rather a constantly changing relationship between the publisher and his age." In tracing its history, Sengle notes that the first three years were relatively balanced, with the editor even attempting to fulfill his responsibility as critic, though ironically and with stiff resistance to the clamorous demands and challenges of the Storm and Stress poets. In the second half of the 1770s, the journal was stamped primarily by Merck's literary criticism, Wieland's essayistic ruminations on the nature of art, and the inclusion (usually in serial form) of his own poetry and literary works such as the romance tale *Oberon* (1780). The 1780s witnessed something of an ebb tide, with criticism giving way to all manner of popular subjects (e.g. divination, magnetism, travelogues, magic); this preoccupation is countered only somewhat by **Johann Gottfried Herder**'s brief appearance as contributor in 1781–82.

Beginning c. 1783, in his fifties, Wieland fell into a profound resignation concerning both his literary career generally and the fortunes of the *TM* specifically. As noted, the French Revolution revivified him. In the second half of the 1790s, however, he began more and more to leave the direction of his journalistic enterprise to others, notably F. J. Bertuch, a Weimar publisher and writer, and K. A. Böttiger, antiquarian director of the Weimar Gymnasium and later head of the Dresden Museum. One of the most notable contributions during the final years of the periodical was Wieland's essay on euthanasia (1805). The journal appeared for the last time in 1810.

Ultimately the *TM*'s importance inheres essentially in its longevity as a vehicle for the spread of popular culture, for the many important essays that Wieland himself contributed, and for its list of supporting contributors and coeditors (among them **Goethe** and Schiller, Herder, the Schlegel brothers, Reinhold, Ludwig Gleim, Merck, and **Novalis**). Goethe noted in 1825, long after the journal's demise, that "all the upper classes owe their style and taste to Wieland" (McCarthy, 1979). While the journal began in large part as a commercial enterprise, it provided a valuable service for the general reading public in German-speaking lands in bringing that public to a greater awareness of the world outside the limited perspective of strictly German experience. Perhaps more important than any particular contribution made by the editor himself was the pervasive spirit of curiosity, openness, and toleration which he consistently and fervently tried to inculcate in his audience. Always dominant in his mind as editor and writer was the need to spur his readers to intelligent thought and discussion. In opening his journal to virtually all areas of popular interest, and even frequently – in spite of his misapprehensions as an entrepreneur – to controversial political questions and philosophical subjects, he most of all strove to educate his fellow Germans to a citizenship as true Europeans.

ROBERT V. SMYTHE

Further Reading

Jørgensen, S.-A., H. Jaumann, John A. McCarthy, and H. Thomé, *Christoph Martin Wieland: Epoche, Werk, Wirkung*, Munich: Beck, 1994

Kurtz, A. W., *C. M. Wieland and the "Teutscher Merkur"* (dissertation), College Park: University of Maryland, 1956

McCarthy, John A., *Christoph Martin Wieland*, Boston: Twayne, 1979

McCarthy, John A., "The Poet as Journalist and Essayist: Chr. M. Wieland, Part One – A Descriptive Account," *Jahrbuch für internationale Germanistik* 12, no. 1 (1980): 104–38

Miquet, Claude, *C. M. Wieland: Directeur du "Mercure Allemand"*, 1773–89, Berne and New York: Lang, 1990

Schulze, Volker, "*Der Teutsche Merkur (1773–1810)*," in *Deutsche Zeitschriften des 17. bis 20. Jahrhunderts*, edited by Heinz-Dietrich Fischer, Pullach: Dokumentation, 1973

Sengle, Friedrich, *Wieland*, Stuttgart: Metzler, 1949

Starnes, Thomas C., *Der Teutsche Merkur: Ein Repertorium*, Sigmaringen: Thorbecke, 1994

Wahl, Hans, *Geschichte des Teutschen Merkur*, Berlin: Mayer & Müller, 1914

Wieland, Christoph Martin, *Wieland's Werke*, edited by Heinrich Düntzer, Berlin: Hempel, 1879

Thackeray, William Makepeace

British, 1811–1863

William Makepeace Thackeray's career as an essayist spanned 30 years and can be divided into two eras: early (1833–47) and late (1860–63), with an interval (1847–60) in which his novels (beginning with *Vanity Fair*), took precedence. George Saintsbury (1931), one of the few commentators who gives as much space to Thackeray's essays as to his novels, rates his last collection, *Roundabout Papers* (1863), as one of the best of the 19th century.

Exactly which is Thackeray's first publication has never been definitively determined. Leaving Cambridge without graduating and the law without articling, he had fallen into casual journalism as a means of supporting his apprenticeship to the fine arts in Paris during the mid-1830s. Ultimately it was his essayistic loiterings with "the Fraserians" that brought him a living. In *Fraser's Magazine*, the most high-spirited magazine of the day, he published his first famous satiric series, *The Yellowplush Correspondence* (1837–38). Yellowplush's purlieus are those of fashionable Regency London below-stairs, rather like *Vanity Fair* misspelled. This is not the poverty of **Dickens**' London slums but rather the straits of those who, like **Defoe**'s heroes, fall in and out of credit. *Fraser's*, with its abusive and boisterous severity, was the special vehicle of this satiric voice. **Leslie Stephen** in the *Dictionary of National Biography* bemoans this "practice common to the literary class of the time," known as "personality." The 1830s "personality" dates much of Thackeray's first decade as a writer, and because of this rowdy element, his writing from this time is not what later readers think of as the **familiar essay** along the lines of **Addison** and **Steele**.

Thackeray reprinted some of this 1830s journalism as two volumes of *Comic Tales and Sketches* "edited and illustrated by Michael Angelo Titmarsh" (1841). He used the same pseudonym for the tourist narrator of *The Paris Sketch Book* (1840). What is confusing is that "Titmarsh" becomes the voice for both Thackeray's essays and fiction. He is the author of *The Second Funeral of Napoleon* (1841) and *The Chronicle of the Drum* (1841), *The Irish Sketch-Book* (1843), *Notes of a Journey from Cornhill to Grand Cairo* (1846), and two longer narratives, *Mrs. Perkins's Ball* (1847) and *Our Street* (1848). Thackeray used other pseudonyms as well – Ikey Solomons, Our Fat Contributor, Jeames de la Pluche – and in these narratives, satire emerges as much from the burlesque voices of the characters as from the stories they tell. This is what makes it difficult to say sometimes what genre Thackeray is working in. Eventually Titmarsh was to step aside, and Thackeray and his "Pen and Pencil Sketches of English Society" finally took center stage in *Vanity Fair* (1847–48), with this and the novel *Pendennis* (1849–50) representing the apogee of Thackeray's journalistic career. *The Book of Snobs*, first published in *Punch* as "The Snobs of England, by One of Themselves" (1846–47) – with its "University Snobs," "Dining-out Snobs," and snobs of the literary, military, clerical, and aristocratic kinds – was but a prelude to his sketches of English society in *Vanity Fair*. After *Vanity Fair*, the fiction work *The History of Samuel Titmarsh and the Great Hoggarty Diamond* (1849) is advertised as being by "W. M. Thackeray,

Author of 'Pendennis,' 'Vanity Fair,' &c." Thus the pseudonym of the journalist is used alongside the real-life identity of the author – which is finally seen to be that of the novelist.

The English Humourists of the Eighteenth Century (1853) follows naturally from the novel *Henry Esmond* (1852). Standing alone, the lectures from the *English Humourists* series are more satisfactory as essays than the Titmarsh spoofs, which require the context of the pages of the *Fraser's* club of the 1830s to achieve their effect. The parodies, too, in *Punch's Prize Novelists* (1853) of Ainsworth, Disraeli, Bulwer, and others lose their point when detached from the 1840s.

Thackeray is calculated to have written 380 pieces for *Punch* alone during the years between 1842 and 1851. However, in the early 1860s, his name is most associated with the *Cornhill Magazine*, of which he was the first editor; its covers were the same yellow as his novels. His lecture series *The Four Georges* was first printed in a periodical format in the *Cornhill* (July–October 1860) as "Sketches of Manners, Morals, Court, and Town Life," then as a book later that year. Meanwhile, in between the novels *The Newcomes* (1853–55) and *The Virginians* (1858–59), his publishers put together four volumes of *Miscellanies: Prose and Verse* (1855–57). After *The Four Georges*, the next and final collection of Thackeray's papers in his lifetime was *Roundabout Papers* (1863), a reprint of his essays from the *Cornhill*. Leslie Stephen's characterization of the *Cornhill* essays may stand as a description of Thackeray's essay writing at its best: "They are models of the essay which, without aiming at profundity, gives the charm of playful and tender conversation of a great writer." As an essayist for the six-shilling magazine market of the 1830s, Thackeray acted out the role of the fashionable young Regency buck; presiding over the editorship of a new-style shilling magazine in the 1860s, he protected his readers' domestic sensibilities from those Regency adventures with the watchful eye of the Victorian paterfamilias.

KATHRYN CHITTICK

Biography

Born 18 July 1811 in Calcutta. Sent to England, 1817. Studied at the Charterhouse, London, 1822–28; Trinity College, Cambridge, 1829–30; studied law at Middle Temple, London, 1831–32. Traveled in Europe and visited Goethe in Weimar, 1831–32. Owner and editor, *National Standard*, London, 1833–34. Lived in Paris, and studied painting, 1834–37. Married Isabella Gethin Shawe, 1836 (declared insane, 1840, and confined from 1842): three daughters (one died in infancy). Paris correspondent for London *Constitutional*, 1836–37; contributor to many magazines and newspapers, including the *Times* and *Fraser's Magazine*, from 1837, and *Punch*, 1842–54; reviewer for the *Morning Chronicle*, mid-1840s. Lecturer on English humorists and on Hanoverian monarchs, in Britain and the United States, 1851–57. Editor, *Cornhill Magazine*, London, 1859–62. Died in Kensington, London, 24 December 1863.

Selected Writings

Essays and Related Prose
The Yellowplush Correspondence, 1838
An Essay on the Genius of George Cruikshank, 1840
The Paris Sketch Book, 2 vols., 1840
Comic Tales and Sketches, 2 vols., 1841

The Irish Sketch-Book, 2 vols., 1843
Notes of a Journey from Cornhill to Grand Cairo, 1846
The Book of Snobs, 1848; complete edition, 1852; edited by John Sutherland, 1978
Miscellanies: Prose and Verse, 2 vols., 1849–51
Punch's Prize Novelists, The Fat Contributor, and Travels in London, 1853
The English Humourists of the Eighteenth Century: A Series of Lectures, 1853; revised edition, 1853
Miscellanies: Prose and Verse, 4 vols., 1855–57
The Four Georges: Sketches of Manners, Morals, Court, and Town Life, 1860
Roundabout Papers, 1863
Early and Late Papers, edited by J. T. Fields, 1867
The Orphan of Pimlico and Other Sketches, Fragments and Drawings, 1876
Loose Sketches, An Eastern Adventure, 1894
The Hitherto Unidentified Contributions to Punch, edited by M. H. Spielmann, 1899
Writings in the National Standard and the Constitutional, edited by Walter Thomas Spencer, 1899
Stray Papers: Being Stories, Reviews, Verses, and Sketches 1821–47 [sic: should be 1829], edited by Lewis Melville, 1901
The New Sketch Book, Being Essays from the Foreign Quarterly Review, edited by R. S. Garnett, 1906
Contributions to the Morning Chronicle, edited by Gordon N. Ray, 1955
Drawn from Life: The Journalism, edited by Margaret Forster, 1984

Other writings: many novels (including *Vanity Fair*, 1847–48; *Pendennis*, 1849–50; *Henry Esmond*, 1852; *Barry Lyndon*, 1852–53; *The Newcomes*, 1853–55; *The Virginians*, 1858–59), books of drawings, and correspondence.

Collected works editions: *The Oxford Thackeray*, edited by George Saintsbury, 17 vols., 1908; *Works*, edited by Peter L. Shillingsburg, 1989– (in progress).

Bibliographies
Flamm, Dudley, *Thackeray's Critics: An Annotated Bibliography of British and American Criticism, 1836–1901*, Chapel Hill: University of North Carolina Press, 1967
Goldfarb, Sheldon, *Thackeray: An Annotated Bibliography, 1976–1987*, New York: Garland, 1989
Olmsted, John C., *Thackeray and His Twentieth-Century Critics: An Annotated Bibliography, 1900–1975*, New York: Garland, 1977

Further Reading
Eddy, Spencer L., *The Founding of the Cornhill Magazine*, Muncie, Indiana: Ball State University Press, 1970
Ferris, Ina, *William Makepeace Thackeray*, Boston: Twayne, 1983
Harden, Edgar F., "The Writing and Publication of Thackeray's *English Humourists*," *Papers of the Bibliographical Society of America* 76, no. 7 (1982): 197–207
Kiely, Robert, "Victorian Harlequin: The Function of Humor in Thackeray's Critical and Miscellaneous Prose," in *William Makepeace Thackeray: Critical Views*, edited by Harold Bloom, New York: Chelsea House, 1987
Monsarrat, Ann, *An Uneasy Victorian: Thackeray the Man, 1811–1863*, London: Cassell, 1980
Oram, Richard W., "'Just a little turn of the circle': Time, Memory, and Repetition in Thackeray's *Roundabout Papers*," in *William Makepeace Thackeray: Critical Views*, edited by Harold Bloom, New York: Chelsea House, 1987
Pantucková, Lidmila, *W. M. Thackeray as a Critic of Literature*, Brno: Purkyne University Press, 1972

Ray, Gordon N., *Thackeray*, London: Oxford University Press, and New York: McGraw Hill, 2 vols., 1955–58

Saintsbury, George, *A Consideration of Thackeray*, New York: Russell and Russell, 1968 (original edition, 1931)

Segel, Elizabeth, "Thackeray's Journalism: Apprenticeship for Writer and Reader," *Victorian Newsletter* 57 (Spring 1980): 23–27

Thibaudet, Albert

French, 1874–1936

When Albert Thibaudet died in 1936, he left unfinished his most important work, the *Histoire de la littérature française de 1789 à nos jours* (*French Literature from 1795 to Our Era*), posthumously published in the year of his death. It was innovative in treating authors strictly according to generations rather than slotting them into genres or movements. Thibaudet's agrégation was in geography, and his initial training continued to color his later literary criticism, which was to remain dependent on an awareness, unusual for his time, of the way in which imaginative literature and literary criticism were rooted in the place, date, and circumstances of their composition. Thibaudet taught at a number of lycées before becoming professor of French literature at Geneva. Most of his essays and **reviews**, subsequently gathered as *Réflexions* on literature, on the novel, and on literary criticism, were first published in the **Nouvelle Revue Française** (New French review).

Thibaudet first became prominent with *La Poésie de Stéphane Mallarmé* (1912). This book was followed by one on Flaubert in 1922, which is still regarded as a standard work; Thibaudet went on to publish essays on **Valéry**, Fromentin, Amiel, Verlaine, and Rimbaud in 1923 and 1924, and a book on Stendhal in 1931. In the context of his contribution to the essay form, his most important work is the set of six lectures delivered in 1922 at the Théâtre du Vieux-Colombier, subsequently published separately in a series of journals before being collected into a single volume and published in 1930 as *Physiologie de la critique* (Physiology of criticism). They are an important landmark in the development of the essay not only on account of their own form, but also for what they say about the nature of the **critical essay**.

Formally, Thibaudet's critical essays pick up where those of **Sainte-Beuve** left off, developing Sainte-Beuve's journalistic impressionism by adding academic structure and rigor. Thibaudet regarded *la critique*, by which he means literary criticism as a genre produced by a body of professional specialists, as a 19th-century creation which he assumed had not yet, in 1922, reached the peaks of which it was capable. Thibaudet felt that the literary-critical essay was a genre gestated by the post-revolutionary emergence in France of a properly professional academic body no longer nurtured and subsequently controlled by the church. Its inaugurators had been the generation of professors around 1830, François Guizot, Victor Cousin, and Abel-François Villemain, abetted by the newly emergent body of professional journalists, whose precursors and models had been the 18th-century writers **Voltaire** and **Diderot** in their roles as pamphleteers. Academic criticism was exemplified for Thibaudet by Désiré Nisard, director of the

École Normale Supérieure from 1857 to 1867, while the journalistic literary-critical essay had originally been developed by Sainte-Beuve, only subsequently adopted as the object of an academic cult.

The literary-critical essay for Thibaudet was necessarily historical, "cutting a section in a slice of duration," and could be bred only from the interaction of opposing coexistent attitudes. At least in Thibaudet's mind, the dual academic and journalistic parentage of literary criticism made the essay its appropriate form. His own criticism is at its best when expressed in essay form, partly because the chronological dimension which he considers essential forces the critic to limit the content of a piece to precisely defined individual points if criticism is not to degenerate into survey.

Thibaudet's individual essays on criticism are limited to a single point of view often applied to more than one author or critic and invariably contextualized historically. They do not eschew harshness toward such predecessors as Émile Faguet, Jules Lemaître, and **Ferdinand Brunetière**, but are often deeply perceptive in their understanding of great authors, like **Montaigne**, and frequently cogent in the analysis of such complex matters as the nature of historical criticism and the inevitability of changes in evolving attitudes toward the past. Nonetheless, they are kept conversational in tone.

Thibaudet himself draws attention to his tone, sometimes flagrant in its irony. He also makes it plain by employing a register of language which is sometimes provocatively colloquial. His model is Montaigne, whose *Essais* he notes are the work of someone who, having early lost "the only friend with whom he could really converse" – referring to Montaigne's close friendship with Étienne de La Boétie – had to write about "everything and nothing, and above all about himself" to free himself from the tensions imposed by his environment and his way of life. From Montaigne's one-sided conversation, with the reader as interlocutor, derived an early example of what Thibaudet regarded as model criticism. It is true that *Essais* does not mean "essays," but something like experiments or attempts. However, there is in Thibaudet's mind an equation, apparent in the text of the *Physiologie de la critique*, between criticism, the essay genre, and a conversational tone. Thibaudet's contribution to the literary-critical essay is precisely to insist on its conversational tone and sinuosity of approach on the model of Montaigne, as it cuts and labels its historical section through the troughs as well as the peaks of literature.

ANTHONY LEVI

Biography

Born 1 April 1874 in Tournus, Burgundy. Studied at the Lycée Henri IV, Paris, where he was taught by Henri Bergson, agrégation in history and geography; University of Dijon, licence in philosophy, 1894. Traveled to Greece, 1902–03. Taught French at the Universities of York and Uppsala; chair in French literature, University of Geneva, 1924–36. Contributor, *Nouvelle Revue Française*, 1911–36. Died in Geneva, 16 April 1936.

Selected Writings

Essays and Related Prose

Le Liseur des romans, 1925
Physiologie de la critique, 1930

Réflexions sur le roman, 1938
Réflexions sur la littérature, 2 vols., 1938–40
Réflexions sur la critique, 1939

Other writings: a book on Bergsonism (1923), *Histoire de la littérature française de 1789 à nos jours* (1936; *French Literature from 1795 to Our Era*), works on Montaigne, Mallarmé, Flaubert, Valéry, Stendhal, and other writers, and a sociological study of French intellectuals. Also edited editions of works by Flaubert and Montaigne.

Further Reading

Davies, John C., *L'Œuvre critique d'Albert Thibaudet*, Geneva: Droz, and Lille: Giard, 1955
Devaud, Marcel, *Albert Thibaudet: Critique de la poésie et des poètes*, Fribourg: Éditions Universitaires, 1967
Glauser, Alfred, *Albert Thibaudet et la critique créatrice*, Paris: Boivin, 1952
Nouvelle Revue Française issue on Thibaudet (July 1936)
O'Neill, James, *The Critical Ideas of Albert Thibaudet* (dissertation), Ann Arbor: University of Michigan, 1942

Thomas, Lewis

American, 1913–1993

Lewis Thomas, biologist and physician, won a literary reputation with *The Lives of a Cell: Notes of a Biology Watcher*, a collection of essays which received the National Book Award in 1974. He followed this with five more essay collections, *The Medusa and the Snail* (1979), *Late Night Thoughts on Listening to Mahler's Ninth Symphony* (1983), *The Youngest Science: Notes of a Medicine-Watcher* (1983), *Et Cetera, Et Cetera: Notes of a Word-Watcher* (1990), and *The Fragile Species* (1992). His essays began appearing monthly in the *New England Journal of Medicine* in 1971, each with an allotted length of about 1000 words. It was at the suggestion of Joyce Carol Oates that he first collected and published some of these in one volume. His essays subsequently came out in the *New York Review of Books* and other journals and magazines.

Thomas' essays are the musings of a medical expert at ease. Shrewd and technical on the one hand, graceful and humanistic on the other, they read like a busman's holiday: at the end of the day's work, the scientist relaxes in his den and reflects – not as a professional, but as an ordinary citizen. Each essay relies on his special knowledge of biology and the medical profession, and ranges philosophically – now whimsically, now critically, sometimes grimly – over issues confronting an educated person in the second half of the 20th century. The human need for society, the fragility and the resiliency of life, the bomb, the abuse of drugs, the healthcare system, personal identity, national defense, the possibility of life on other planets, and dying – these are among the many issues he explores. His optimism is seasoned in his essays by a Yankee practicality. He criticizes defense spending and offers down-to-earth reasons for funding pure research. He excoriates the notion of acceptable losses in a nuclear war and soberly counts the social and personal costs of heroin addiction.

Underlying all these issues, Thomas' major theme is the unity of life. Individuality is an affectation or an illusion: human beings are not so much individuals as collections of autonomous life forms and, on a larger scale, participants in

a huge life mass – unplanned, perhaps, but nevertheless orderly. Thomas' wonder at the natural world echoes that of **Loren Eiseley**.

Thomas' style is readable and charming. He brings to his craft a love of language and a gift for artfully reducing formidable technical concepts to everyday conversation. He can substitute a common expression for a technical term with such a touch of the poetic that the new expression not only translates, but domesticates. In "On Societies as Organisms" (1971), for example, he explains that a few termites together behave randomly, but a larger number coordinate their efforts: "As more join in, they seem to reach a critical mass, a quorum . . ." To describe the isolation of single cells before they reach this critical mass, he again makes the arcane familiar: "At first they are single amebocytes swimming around, eating bacteria, aloof from each other, untouching, voting straight Republican." The folksy reference activates a whole neighborhood of recognizable images, allowing the reader to feel at home and at ease with a technical concept.

Literary allusions dot his essays. In "Vibes" (1972), questioning how a life form attains a unique identity, he punctuates a chemical analysis with a droll allusion to Shakespeare: "any set of atoms, if arranged in precisely the same configuration, by whatever chemical name, might smell as sweet." Such allusions soften the edges of Thomas' expertise.

In a longer passage, too, Thomas may introduce an exotic term and gradually make it not only understandable, but as homely as one's own backyard. This is the lead paragraph of "A Fear of Pheromones" (1972):

> What are we going to do if it turns out that we have pheromones? What on earth would we be doing with such things? With the richness of speech, and all our new devices for communication, why would we want to release odors into the air to convey information about anything? We can send notes, telephone, whisper cryptic invitations, announce the giving of parties, even bounce words off the moon and make them carom around the planets. Why a gas, or droplets of moisture made to be deposited on fence posts?

This merging of the technical with the commonplace is typical of Thomas' witty, urbane style and emblematic of his vision of universal harmony.

A lover not only of words, but also of music, Thomas makes one of his most charming assertions, again uniting the worlds of the scientific and the humane, in "Ceti" (1972), when he considers what message humankind might best broadcast into outer space to identify ourselves to possible other life forms: "I would vote for Bach, all of Bach, streamed out into space, over and over again. We would be bragging, of course, but it is surely excusable for us to put the best possible face on at the beginning of such an acquaintance."

Thomas' style often recalls that of **Montaigne**, whom he cites along with 17th-century literary lights. Like theirs, his writing is aphoristic ("Language is what childhood is for") and, despite his scientific and political sophistication, he always sounds like an amateur, a curious mind flying by the seat of its pants.

WILLIAM ZEIGER

See also Medical Essay; Science Essay

Biography

Born 25 November 1913 in Flushing, New York. Studied at Princeton University, New Jersey, B.S., 1933; Harvard University, Cambridge, Massachusetts, M.D., 1937. Intern, 1937–39, and fellow, 1941–42, Boston City Hospital; resident in neurology, Neurological Institute, New York, 1939–41. Married Beryl Dawson, 1941: three daughters. Served in the U.S. Naval Reserve, 1941–46. Visiting investigator, Rockefeller Institute for Medical Research, 1942–46; taught pediatrics, medicine, and/or pathology at Johns Hopkins University, Baltimore, 1946–48, Tulane University, New Orleans, 1948–50, University of Minnesota, Minneapolis, 1950–54, New York University, 1954–69, Yale University, New Haven, Connecticut, 1969–73, and Cornell School of Medicine, New York, 1973–93; president and chief executive officer, 1973–80, and chancellor, 1980–83, Memorial Sloan-Kettering Cancer Center, New York. Also worked at or attached to various hospitals. Contributor to many journals and magazines, including *Science*, *Saturday Review of Science*, and *Nature*; columnist of "Notes of a Biology Watcher" in the *New England Journal of Medicine*, from 1971. Member, American Academy and Institute of Arts and Letters, 1984. Awards: many, including the National Book Award, for *The Lives of a Cell*, 1974; Modern Medicine Distinguished Achievement Award, 1975; American Academy and Institute of Arts and Letters Award, 1980; American Book Award, for *Medusa and the Snail*, 1981; Association of American Physicians Kober Medal, 1983; American Association of Pathologists Gold Headed Cane Award, 1988; Albert Lasker Public Service Award, 1989; New York Academy of Science John Stearns Award for Lifetime Achievement, 1991; honorary degrees from eight universities and colleges. Died (of Waldenström's Disease) in New York, 3 December 1993.

Selected Writings

Essays and Related Prose

The Lives of a Cell: Notes of a Biology Watcher, 1974
The Medusa and the Snail: More Notes of a Biology Watcher, 1979
Late Night Thoughts on Listening to Mahler's Ninth Symphony, 1983
The Youngest Science: Notes of a Medicine-Watcher, 1983
The Wonderful Mistake: Notes of a Biology Watcher (includes *The Lives of a Cell* and *The Medusa and the Snail*), 1988
Et Cetera, Et Cetera: Notes of a Word-Watcher, 1990
A Long Line of Cells: Collected Essays, 1990
The Fragile Species, 1992

Further Reading

Gould, Stephen Jay, "Calling Dr. Thomas," in his *An Urchin in the Storm: Essays About Books and Ideas*, New York: Norton, and London: Penguin, 1987
Medawar, Peter, *The Threat and the Glory: Reflections on Science and Scientists*, edited by David Pyke, Oxford: Oxford University Press, and New York: HarperCollins, 1990
Nemerov, Howard, "Lewis Thomas, Montaigne, and Human Happiness," in his *New and Selected Essays*, Carbondale: Southern Illinois University Press, 1985
Oates, Joyce Carol, "Beyond Common Sense," *New York Times Book Review*, 26 May 1974: 8–9
Rosenblatt, Roger, "Lewis Thomas," *New York Times Magazine*, 21 November 1993: 50–53
Shiring, Joan, "Recommended: Lewis Thomas," *English Journal* (December 1984): 55–56
Zinsser, William, editor, *Inventing the Truth: The Art and Craft of Memoir*, Boston: Houghton Mifflin, revised, enlarged edition, 1995 (original edition, 1987)

Thoreau, Henry David

American, 1817–1862

Henry David Thoreau, best known to modern readers for *Walden* (1854), was better known to his contemporaries as a political activist and naturalist whose essays were often outgrowths of his public lectures. Modern readers have the advantage of access to his **journals**, which also shed light on his development as an essayist. The journals, in a wooden box made by Thoreau, are stored in the J. Pierpont Morgan Library, and reveal the seeds of all of his published essays.

The essay was Thoreau's primary genre. Even *Walden* and *A Week on the Concord and Merrimack Rivers* (1849) include separately composed essays inserted within the narrative. His posthumously published *The Maine Woods* (1864) and *Cape Cod* (1865) are likewise essays stitched together to form book-length studies. His early training as an essayist began at Harvard in the rhetoric classes of Edward Tyrrel Channing. Twenty-three essays and the text of six speeches submitted to Channing survive, ranging in subject from the joys of wandering in the woods to an attempt at defining moral excellence, subjects that would continue to interest Thoreau.

Three general subjects provide the focus for most of Thoreau's essays: a scientifically precise examination of nature; the relationship between government and individual citizens; and the joy of traveling, particularly by foot or canoe. There are occasional forays into other areas, such as his appreciative examination of "Thomas Carlyle and His Works" (1847), or his matrimonial advice to his friend H. G. O. Blake in "Love" (1865) and "Chastity and Sensuality" (1865). But nature, individual freedom and responsibility, and the joy of perambulation remain his focal points. In the longer works, Thoreau often addresses all three.

Nature provided the subject for his first published essay, "Natural History of Massachusetts" (1842), ostensibly a book **review** of a study of the flora and fauna of the state. Only the last five paragraphs of the essay actually deal with the study under review, the rest of the essay being Thoreau's own observations. He includes poetry, describes the Merrimack River, and discusses the best technique for spear-fishing, among other diverse subjects, concluding that the study he is reviewing lacks detail and accuracy.

Thoreau's fascination with his natural surroundings is reflected in many of his essays dealing primarily with other subjects. Toward the end of his life he returned to examining the woods and wildlife around Concord. "The Succession of Forest Trees" (1860) explains why an oak forest grows up whenever a pine forest is cut down, and that a pine forest will return when the hardwoods are cut. His theories, based on his own observations while wandering around Concord, and contradicting theories of the time, would be proven correct by researchers nearly a century later. He rhapsodizes about the colors of Fall foliage in "Autumnal Tints" (1862), the variations found in "Wild Apples" (1862), and the tranquillity found in "Night and Moonlight" (1863), the last essay left unrevised for publication when Thoreau died. "Autumnal Tints" began as art work. Thoreau intended to trace a leaf from various hardwoods growing around Concord. He would then paint each tracery with the tints he observed in the Fall.

Discovering the process to be slow and tedious, he decided to paint the leaves with words.

Thoreau was also noted by his contemporaries for his speeches and essays concerning the relationship between an individual and the demands of government. The Mexican War and the institution of slavery precipitated "Resistance to Civil Government" (1849), often reprinted with the title "Civil Disobedience." The war ended before the publication of the essay, but Thoreau left in the references to imperialism because, for him, they represent a type of misgoverning that calls for resistance. He recommends disobeying unjust laws, and then drawing attention to the injustice by accepting the punishment. Honest citizens, seeing someone punished unjustly, would then be motivated to change the laws. Thoreau's concept of passive resistance to injustice later inspired Mahatma Gandhi and Martin Luther King, Jr. among other activists.

The issue of slavery precipitated other essays as well. Thoreau argues in "Slavery in Massachusetts" (1854) that local abolitionists were misguided when they condemned slavery in the South while living in and paying taxes to the Commonwealth of Massachusetts where the Fugitive Slave Act was being enforced, returning escaped slaves to their owners. Most controversial, though, are his three essays supporting and defending John Brown's raid on the armory at Harper's Ferry in an attempt to provide arms and impetus for a slave rebellion. No uprising occurred, and the fighting led to the deaths not only of several of Brown's followers, but also of U.S. Marines and innocent civilians, including a free Negro living in the town. Many readers have pointed out that Thoreau's defense of Brown appears to contradict his earlier advocacy of passive resistance. Thoreau apparently felt no contradiction, arguing that separating slaves from slave-holders through force was a form of self-defense for people unable to protect themselves. In "A Plea for Captain John Brown" (1860), delivered as a speech three times before publication, Thoreau defends Brown as a man living by principle rather than by public opinion. Brown's unyielding commitment to a personal ideal is apparently the trait that motivated Thoreau's admiration. He continues that much of the harsh public reaction was the result of hypocritical coverage by the newspapers, which called for an end to slavery but then objected to direct means of achieving that end. The essays "Martyrdom of John Brown" (1860) and "The Last Days of John Brown" (1860) were also aimed at swaying public opinion, the latter essay primarily a eulogy following Brown's execution.

Thoreau's final essay, "Life Without Principle" (1863), published posthumously, returns to a less immediate but more enduring vision of how individuals must resist conformity, rejecting conventional wisdom in order to search for truth. He warns that working for money alone will never bring happiness, and advocates following pursuits that are self-improving, using the gold rushes in California and Australia to illustrate the mindless pursuit of wealth. He attacks his contemporaries' fascination with news and gossip, suggesting that this compulsion masks an inner vacuum. Thoreau argues that taking an interest in one's own life eliminates the need to live vicariously through gossip. His attempt to separate himself from society and find "higher laws" through self-awareness is recounted in Walden, and his final essay quietly demands that others follow this example.

A third area that drew Thoreau's attention was leisure traveling. For him, travel and sightseeing were synonymous, the goal generally much less significant than the path. His essays "A Walk to Wachusett" (1843), "A Winter Walk" (1843), and "Walking" (1862) all deal with his favorite means of locomotion and his favorite area, the countryside around Concord. Carefully observed natural details fill the essays. In "Walking" Thoreau notes that thinking about anything other than your immediate surroundings as you walk defeats the purpose of the exercise, adding that a minimum of four hours walking was a daily requirement for his physical and emotional health.

Thoreau's posthumous longer works describing his travels resulted from editors tying several essays together. The Maine Woods, Cape Cod, and A Yankee in Canada (1866) were compiled in this manner. The first two sections of The Maine Woods were published earlier, "Ktaadn and the Maine Woods" in Union Magazine (1848), and "Chesuncook" in the Atlantic Monthly (1858). He was revising "The Allegash and the East Branch" when he died. The three essays describe three separate camping trips into the Maine woods, noting how this area was changing as the woods were cut to provide farmland. Sophia Thoreau, his sister, and Ellery Channing, a close friend, made the decision to combine the two previously published essays with the unfinished essay as a single volume. They made the same decision concerning three related essays dealing with three separate visits to Cape Cod. The first three of the five essays that make up A Yankee in Canada were published in Putnam's Magazine in 1853. When the editor, George William Curtis, changed parts of the essays without Thoreau's consent, the author refused to provide the final two essays.

The travel essays and nature essays combine prose and poetry. Thoreau often quoted Shakespeare, Milton, Wordsworth, and other English poets, but more often, the poetry was Thoreau's own. The political writing, polemical in tone and intent, only occasionally includes verse. Allusions to other works, including Hindu writings and works by his fellow transcendentalists, are frequent. Latin phrases and quotations are generally followed by Thoreau's translation.

In "Walking" Thoreau attempts to explain the derivation of "sauntering," suggesting that the word comes either from beggars claiming they needed alms to go to the Holy Land, Sainte Terre, or from sans terre, people who wandered because they were without land. In any case, sauntering is an apt description for the organization of most of Thoreau's essays. Occasionally he attempts to impose an order on his thoughts. In "A Winter Walk" he divides the essay into sections corresponding to the different parts of the day on which the walk occurred. The second halves of "Wild Apples" and "Autumnal Tints" are divided by types of trees, but no true pattern is imposed throughout these essays. Thoreau liked to allow his thoughts to saunter, and his pen followed behind, recording, adjusting, and adding commentary. This style is a reflection of his journal, where the primary pattern is simply chronological; he recorded his thoughts as they came to him, each thought provoked by an earlier experience or expression, and leading into whichever new direction seemed, at the moment, to be promising. His essays were carefully, and often significantly revised, but this meandering organization usually remained.

In "Thomas Carlyle and His Works" (1847) Thoreau laments that too many readers treat Carlyle's thoughts with such seriousness that they miss his humor. The same might be said for Thoreau's readers, though the Concord writer's style is more accessible. With the exception of the John Brown essays, Thoreau's wry sense of humor permeates his writing, through the use of wordplay, understatement, and mild ironies. In *Cape Cod*, for example, he notes that stages, in order to cross the sand, had tires five inches wide: "The more tired the wheels, the less tired the horses." Thoreau describes in *The Maine Woods* attempting to discover if moose shed their antlers annually. The only antlers he found, though, had "a head attached to them, and I knew they did not shed their heads more than once in their lives." In "The Succession of Forest Trees" he notes that he has trespassed on his neighbors' property so regularly that he could often tell them shortcuts across their property unknown to them. In *A Yankee in Canada*, he points out that the only thing he brought back from Canada was a cold.

Finally, his writing often relies on hyperbole. When he writes in "Resistance to Civil Government" that "any man more right than his neighbors constitutes a majority of one already," he uses extremes to provoke thought and reaction. His journals as well as his published essays exploit this technique frequently, though as he grew older he tended more toward description and less toward dialectic.

Thoreau found the essay to be the most compatible genre for his thoughts. Even *Walden*, ostensibly a book-length study of a year living in the woods, contains within it several set pieces from Thoreau's journals on subjects such as "Reading" and "The Pond in Winter." *A Week on the Concord and Merrimack Rivers* has a well-known essay on friendship inserted in the description of the canoe trip. Thoreau preferred to record and test his ideas in his journal, and then carefully develop and revise them. A short form such as an essay allowed him to focus more directly, seeing his entire work through a narrower lens. Longer works could always be created by combining several shorter works. Thoreau often found poetry a compatible genre for the same reasons, but his talents were more suited to essays. Among 19th-century American essayists, only **Emerson** has received comparable attention. Thoreau's published essays, combined with his multivolume journals, show a rich and detailed understanding of nature, a commitment to individual freedom and independence of thought, an optimistic evaluation of human nature, and a clarity of expression few writers can approach.

TIMOTHY J. EVANS

Biography
Born David Henry Thoreau, 12 July 1817 in Concord, Massachusetts. Studied at Concord Academy, 1828–33; Harvard University, Cambridge, Massachusetts, 1833–35 and 1836–37, graduated 1837. Teacher in Canton, Massachusetts, 1835–36, and at Center School, 1837 (resigned after two weeks). Contracted tuberculosis, 1835, suffering from recurring bouts throughout his life. Worked in his father's pencil factory, 1837–38, 1844, and 1849–50. Ran Concord Academy and taught there, 1838–41; curator, 1838–43, and regular lecturer, from 1848, Concord Lyceum. Contributor, the *Dial*, 1840–44. Lived with Ralph Waldo Emerson, 1841–43, and with Emerson's family, 1847; tutor to William Emerson's sons, Staten Island, New York, 1843. Lived in a cabin at Walden Pond, near Concord, 1845–47. Jailed for refusing to pay poll tax (in protest against slavery), 1846. Land surveyor, from 1848. Died in Concord, 6 May 1862.

Selected Writings

Essays and Related Prose
A Week on the Concord and Merrimack Rivers, 1849; edited by Walter Harding, 1963
"Resistance to Civil Government," in *Aesthetic Papers* (journal), 1849; as "Civil Disobedience," in *A Yankee in Canada*, 1866; edited by Walter Harding, 1967, William Rossi, 1983, revised edition, as *Resistance to Civil Government*, 1992
Walden; or, Life in the Woods, 1854; edited by Walter Harding, 1968, Philip Van Doren Stern, 1970, William Rossi, 1983, revised edition, 1992, and Christopher Bigsby, 1995
Excursions, edited by Ralph Waldo Emerson, 1863
The Maine Woods, edited by Sophia E. Thoreau and William Ellery Channing, 1864; edited by Dudley C. Lunt, 1950
Cape Cod, edited by Sophia E. Thoreau and William Ellery Channing, 1865; edited by Thea Wheelright, 1971
A Yankee in Canada, with Anti-Slavery and Reform Papers, edited by Sophia E. Thoreau and William Ellery Channing, 1866
Walden, and Other Writings, edited by Joseph Wood Krutch, 1962
The Portable Thoreau, edited by Carl Bode, 1964
Thoreau's Vision: The Major Essays, edited by Charles R. Anderson, 1973
Civil Disobedience, and Other Essays, 1993
Political Writings, edited by Nancy L. Rosenblum, 1996

Other writings: journals, poetry, and correspondence.

Collected works editions: *Complete Works* (Concord Edition), edited by H. G. O. Blake, 5 vols., 1929; *Writings* (Princeton Edition), edited by William L. Howarth, 7 vols., 1971–93 (in progress).

Bibliographies
Borst, Raymond R., *Henry David Thoreau: A Descriptive Bibliography*, Pittsburgh: University of Pittsburgh Press, 1982
Boswell, Jeanetta, and Sarah Crouch, *Thoreau and the Critics: A Checklist of Criticism 1900–1978*, Metuchen, New Jersey: Scarecrow Press, 1981
Harding, Walter, and Jean Cameron Advena, editors, *A Bibliography of the Thoreau Society Bulletin Bibliographies, 1941–1969: A Cumulation and Index*, Troy, New York: Whitston, 1971
Howarth, William L., *The Literary Manuscripts of Henry David Thoreau*, Columbus: Ohio State University Press, 1974
Scharnhorst, Gary, *Henry David Thoreau: An Annotated Bibliography of Comment and Criticism Before 1900*, New York: Garland, 1992

Further Reading
Borst, Raymond R., editor, *Thoreau Log: A Documentary Life of Henry David Thoreau, 1817–1862*, New York: Macmillan, 1992
Buell, Lawrence, *The Environmental Imagination: Thoreau, Nature Writing, and the Formation of American Culture*, Cambridge, Massachusetts: Harvard University Press, 1995
Canby, Henry S., *Thoreau*, Boston: Houghton Mifflin, 1939
Harding, Walter, *The Days of Henry Thoreau: A Biography*, Princeton, New Jersey: Princeton University Press, 1992 (original edition, 1965)
Harding, Walter, "Adventures in the Thoreau Trade," *American Scholar* 61 (Spring 1992): 277–89
Harding, Walter, and Michael Meyer, *The New Thoreau Handbook*, New York: New York University Press, 1980
Krutch, Joseph Wood, *Henry David Thoreau*, New York: Dell, 1965 (original edition, 1948)
Leary, Lewis, "Henry David Thoreau," in *Eight American Authors*, edited by James Woodress, New York: Norton, 1971

Matthiessen, F. O., *American Renaissance: Art and Expression in the Age of Emerson and Whitman*, London: Oxford University Press, 1968 (original edition, 1941)

Meyers, Michael, *Several More Lives to Live: Thoreau's Political Reputation in America*, Westport, Connecticut: Greenwood, 1977

Myerson, Joel, editor, *Emerson and Thoreau: The Contemporary Reviews*, Cambridge: Cambridge University Press, 1992

Richardson, Robert D., Jr., *Henry Thoreau: A Life of the Mind*, Berkeley: University of California Press, 1986

Salt, Henry S., *The Life of Henry David Thoreau*, Fontwell: Centaur, 1993 (original edition, 1890)

Sattelmeyer, Robert, *Thoreau's Reading: A Study in Intellectual History with Bibliographical Catalogue*, Princeton, New Jersey: Princeton University Press, 1988

Sayre, Robert F., *Thoreau and the American Indians*, Princeton, New Jersey: Princeton University Press, 1977

Schofield, Edmund A., and Robert C. Baron, *Thoreau's World and Ours: A Natural Legacy*, Golden, Colorado: North American Press, 1993

Shanley, J. Lyndon, *The Making of Walden*, Chicago: University of Chicago Press, 1957

Thurber, James

American, 1894–1961

James Thurber experimented in many types of writing during his career. His journalistic contributions to the **New Yorker** magazine, where almost all of his best work first appeared, include several pieces concerning eccentric places and individuals of New York City for the magazine's "Talk of the Town" section and "Where Are They Now," a series of pieces concerning once famous individuals now little known and emphasizing the ironic contrast between great early fame and later and lengthy anonymity. In both series Thurber provides the new and odd perspective on seemingly familiar events, places, and persons that marks most of his major work. Thurber also contributed numerous essays on dogs, including such memorable sketches as "Memorial" (1942) and "Snapshot of a Dog" (1935) that offer admirable examples of how to achieve sentiment while avoiding sentimentality. Thurber's most important contributions to the essay, however, were a certain character and a certain style. Although neither was completely original with Thurber, he popularized them and became their most influential employer.

Thurber's best-known character is the Little Man beset by insignificant but impenetrable obstacles, a character introduced into American humor by **Robert Benchley**. Several of Thurber's early pieces, such as "The Gentleman Is Cold" (1935), in which Thurber is defeated by an overcoat which does not fit and has lost its buttons, and "My Memories of D. H. Lawrence" (1936), in which the person at the railroad station Thurber assumes to be **Lawrence** turns out to be George R. Hopkins, owner of a paper factory in Fitchburg, Massachusetts, are pure Benchley, whose self-mockery is more successful than Thurber's. Thurber's real success in and distinctive contribution to this area of humor derives from his attention to the Little Man's inner life, an inner life which adds the dimension of wild fantasy.

The most famous example of this flight into fantasy is the short story "The Secret Life of Walter Mitty" (1942), but

Thurber employs the same kind of figure in his **Personal essays**. In many essays some optical or auditory signal precipitates headlong flights into the fantastic, into what **John Updike** termed "the enchantment of misapprehension." Thurber, almost completely blind, wrote that "The kingdom of the partly blind is a little like Oz, a little like Wonderland . . . Anything you can think of, and a lot you would never think of, can happen there." In such a world, described in "The Admiral at the Wheel" (1936), common objects "blur into fantasy" as Thurber, without his glasses, sees such remarkable sights as "a gay old lady with a gray parasol walk right through the side of a truck," and an electronic welder is transformed into "a radiant fool setting off sky-rockets by day."

The other major confusion in Thurber's world is that of language, as strange remarks lead him to even stranger imaginings. When his maid Margaret has trouble with the "doom-shaped" part of his refrigerator, Thurber wonders if he is still in the real world. When another maid, Della, announces "They are here with the Reeves," the ensuing conversation reaches such a level of insanity that "only Lewis Carroll could have understood her completely." When the handyman Barney Haller announces "Dis morning bime by . . . I go hunt grotches in de voods," Thurber finds that "If you are susceptible to such things, it is not difficult to visualize grotches. They fluttered into my mind: ugly little creatures, about the size of whippoorwills, only covered with blood and honey and the scrapings of church bells" ("The Black Magic of Barney Haller," 1935). Language thus leads Thurber into a linguistically anarchic wonderland where communication falters and fantasy begins.

Perhaps the best summation of Thurber's approach is "A Ride with Olympy" (1942), his description of a drive down a mountain road in France. The situation is at once terrifying and farcical. As they proceed down the steep road the American writer tries to explain, in very bad French, the essentials of the automobile to a Russian boat specialist whose French is equally lacking. Both the ride and the conversation spin wildly out of control so that "whereas we had been one remove from reality to begin with, we were now two, or perhaps three, removes."

Three removes from reality is the location of most of Thurber's best work, which appeared roughly from the mid-1920s through the beginning of World War II. Thurber's postwar essays, written for a world he no longer understood and thoroughly detested, too often become mere wordplay or unrefined and virulent objections to contemporary life. These later essays, together with the passage of time, have seriously damaged the reputation of a writer who during his life was generally considered the greatest American humorist since **Mark Twain**. Also damaging were his overuse of the remarks of black maids and the deep misogyny underlying Thurber's obsessive theme of the war between men and women, which badly date some of his work.

What seems unlikely to date are Thurber's use of fantasy and his style. Developed under the tutelage of **E. B. White** and Harold Ross, editor of the *New Yorker*, Thurber's style is the deceptively simple prose of a journalist of genius. Its lightness, clarity, and understatement make his writing endlessly flexible, able to encompass a vast array of subjects and emotions, often far from humorous ones. His ability to imbue almost any situation, from the ridiculous to the tragic, with humor make Thurber, in Adam Gopnik's (1994) phrase, the "light stylist of the heavy heart."

JOHN H. ROGERS

See also Humorous Essay

Biography

James Grover Thurber. Born 8 December 1894 in Columbus, Ohio. Studied at Ohio State University, Columbus, 1913–14 and 1915–18. Code clerk, American Embassy, Paris, 1918–20; reporter, the Columbus *Dispatch*, 1920–24, Chicago *Tribune* (Paris edition), 1925–26, and New York *Evening Post*, 1926–27. Married Althea Adams, 1922 (divorced, 1935): one daughter. Wrote for the *New Yorker*, from 1927. Married Helen Wismer, 1935. Awards: several, including the Library Association Prize, for children's picture book, 1943; Laughing Lions of Columbia University Award for Humor, 1949; American Library Association Liberty and Justice Award, 1957; Antoinette Perry Special Award, 1960; honorary degrees from three universities. Died (of pneumonia) in New York, 2 November 1961.

Selected Writings

Essays and Related Prose
The Owl in the Attic and Other Perplexities, 1931
The Seal in the Bedroom and Other Predicaments, 1932
My Life and Hard Times, 1933
The Middle-Aged Man on the Flying Trapeze: A Collection of Short Pieces, 1935
Let Your Mind Alone! and Other More or Less Inspirational Pieces, 1937
My World – and Welcome to It, 1942
The Thurber Carnival, 1945
The Beast in Me, and Other Animals: A New Collection of Pieces and Drawing About Human Beings and Less Alarming Creatures, 1948
The Thurber Album: A New Collection of Pieces About People, 1952
Thurber Country: A New Collection of Pieces About Males and Females, Mainly of Our Own Species, 1953
Alarms and Diversions, 1957
Lanterns and Lances, 1961
Credos and Curios, 1962
Vintage Thurber, 2 vols., 1963

Other writings: the satire *Is Sex Necessary?*, with E. B. White (1929), books for children, books of drawings, fables, two plays, a memoir about *New Yorker* editor Harold Ross (*The Years with Ross*, 1959), and correspondence.

Bibliographies
Bowden, Edwin T., *James Thurber: A Bibliography*, Columbus: Ohio State University Press, 1968
Toombs, Sarah Eleanora, *James Thurber: An Annotated Bibliography of Criticism*, New York: Garland, 1987

Further Reading
Bernstein, Burton, *Thurber: A Biography*, New York: Dodd Mead, and London: Gollancz, 1975
Black, Stephen A., *James Thurber: His Masquerades*, The Hague and Paris: Mouton, 1970
Fensch, Thomas, editor, *Conversations with James Thurber*, Jackson: University Press of Mississippi, 1989
Gale, Steven H., "Thurber of *The New Yorker*," *Studies in American Humor* 3, no. 1 (Spring 1984): 11–23

Gopnik, Adam, "The Great Deflator," *New Yorker*, 27 June–4 July 1994: 168–76
Grauer, Nell A., *Remember Laughter: A Life of James Thurber*, Lincoln: University of Nebraska Press, 1994
Holmes, Charles S., *The Clocks of Columbus: The Literary Career of James Thurber*, New York: Atheneum, 1972; London: Secker and Warburg, 1973
Holmes, Charles S., editor, *Thurber: A Collection of Critical Essays*, Englewood Cliffs, New Jersey: Prentice Hall, 1974
Kenney, Catherine M., *Thurber's Art of Confusion*, Hamden, Connecticut: Archon, 1984
Kinney, Harrison, *James Thurber: His Life and Times*, New York: Holt, 1995
Long, Robert Emmet, *James Thurber*, New York: Continuum, 1988
Morsberger, Robert, *James Thurber*, New York: Twayne, 1964
Tobias, Richard C., *The Art of James Thurber*, Athens: Ohio University Press, 1969

Tierno Galván, Enrique

Spanish, 1918–1986

In the **preface** to *Sobre la novela picaresca y otros escritos* (1974; On the picaresque novel and other writings) Tierno Galván lists three major obstacles to his intellectual development during the early years of the Franco regime: scholasticism, existentialism, and the influence of the Generation of 1898. Against such formidable heritage, Tierno's essays form a stark contrast to the principal intellectual currents of post-Civil War Spain and constitute a rejection of the Spanish and European humanistic traditions. The author repeatedly and systematically impugns the hallowed categories of personalism, subjectivism, and mental or inner life (*intimismo*), in the name of a thorough and absolute secularization of society based on the principles of utility, efficiency, and material well-being. Indeed, while his distinguished contemporaries **Xavier Zubiri**, Pedro Laín Entralgo, and **Julián Marías** were involved in such issues as transcendence, the essence of Spain, or the philosophy of **José Ortega y Gasset**, Tierno was reading the works of Spinoza, Gottlob Frege, and Wittgenstein, whose *Tractatus logico-philosophicus* he translated into Spanish. An early interest in neopositivism soon led Tierno to embrace a Marxist view of society, which during the 1960s he cloaked in the presumably neutral language of neopositivist sociology. With the publication of *Razón mecánica y razón dialéctica* (1969; Mechanical reason and dialectical reason), an openly Marxist agenda informs his essays and political activities, first as opposition figure representing the Social Democratic Party of Spain, and eventually as mayor of Madrid. The author often stated that his intellectual mission was to educate the Spanish people's social intelligence. The first step toward this goal consists in destroying the assumptions of Western humanism, which include metaphysics and subjectivism: "I believe that subjectivism (*intimidad*) is the greatest obstacle to material and spiritual happiness ... By subjectivism I mean the psychic space from which we oppose the world" (*La realidad como resultado* [1957; Reality as result]).

Tierno's style and temper may be traced to the essays of **Francis Bacon**. Although separated in time and space, both writers share a distinct method and program for the reform of philosophy. Like the father of the English essay, Tierno too criticizes the erroneous and misleading habits of mind that obstruct the aims of genuine science. Both share a distaste for metaphysics, favor demonstration over invention, and lament the intellectual's inadaptability to the world. The Englishman's stylistic influence is particularly evident. Tierno appropriates Bacon's observation in *The Advancement of Learning* that "The aphorism cannot be made but of the pith and heart of the sciences." Inspired by Wittgenstein's *Tractatus* Tierno penned his first major work in the form of some 200 **aphorisms** with the title *La realidad como resultado* – a trenchant critique of metaphysics and an apology for the verification principle.

Tierno's aphoristic style stands out against the often prolix, digressive, and anecdotal essays of his contemporaries. Essentially, the aphorism is for Tierno an epistemological tool of maximum intellectual rigor, economy, and precision. Thinking through aphorisms involves a series of independent, spaced enunciations that convey truth in a compact, atomized form. Distrustful of systematic demonstrations on a grand scale, the author finds the aphorism especially suitable to the fragmentary view of knowledge and the simultaneity of experience that characterize modernity.

The author's essays may be divided into both formal and informal categories. The formal works, marked generally by an aphoristic style, reflect Tierno's commitment to the neopositivist and Marxist principles of sociological analysis (e.g. *La realidad como resultado*; *Conocimiento y ciencias sociales* [1966; Knowledge and the social sciences]). The informal essays, in line with the moralist tradition of the early **Marx** and **Nietzsche**, show a critical consciousness directed toward the transformation of the social order within the framework of a revolutionary ideology. To accomplish his political and ethical aims Tierno favors the rhetorical strategy of dissociation. This consists of a series of shocking antitheses, often oxymoronic, designed to disrupt the associations inherited from humanist and personalist modes of thought. Thus, one finds expressions such as "the trivial is destiny" (*Desde el espectáculo a la trivialización* [1961; From spectacle to trivia]); "philosophy should be a vulgar discipline" (*Acotaciones a la historia de la cultura occidental en la edad moderna* [1964; Marginal notes on the history of modern Western culture]); "the scientific control of human relations will lead to happiness"; "The world is not the dwelling place of man" (*Diderot como pretexto* [1965; Diderot as a pretext]). This last statement speaks of the author's concern for "the destiny of the species" rather than that of the individual or the person.

Following Wittgenstein, Tierno believes that whereof one cannot speak one should remain silent; he nevertheless accepts the existence of the mysterious and assigns literature and the arts the task of expressing the ineffable, provided that such expression is confined to the finite and the mundane. In *¿Qué es ser agnóstico?* (1975; What is an agnostic?) he writes in the hope that "a new type of man will appear, for whom nothing finite will be alien." In this brave new world humankind will have abjured transcendence. Free from the dualisms and scissions imposed by the humanist tradition, individuals will be reconciled with their species: "No agnostic can be an end in himself, but only as part of the world as the objective expression of the species." Installed in a finite world as its home, humanity will live in "serenity without resignation."

The forceful, vital, iconoclastic style of Tierno's essays surprised Spanish intellectuals of the Franco era, most of whom had ignored or severely marginalized the currents of logical positivism and Marxism. By eschewing the rhetorical habits of his contemporaries – exordium, digression, personal anecdote, metaphoric transposition – Tierno's terse, economic style will be remembered as the antipode to the essayistic tradition of **Unamuno** and Ortega y Gasset.

THOMAS MERMALL

Biography

Born 8 February 1918 in Madrid. Fought with the Republican forces, and cofounder of the Socialist Party of the Interior (later the Popular Socialist Party), during the Spanish Civil War. Studied for law degree, 1942, and doctorate in law, 1945. Married Encarnación Pérez Relaño: one son. Professor of political science at the Universities of Murcia, 1948–53, and Salamanca, 1953–65, then dismissed: reinstated after Franco's death, 1976; visiting professor at various universities in the United States. Acquitted on charges of trying to overthrow Franco, 1961. Defense lawyer for political defendents, late 1960s–early 1970s. Elected president of the Social Democratic Party of Spain, 1978. Elected mayor of Madrid, 1979–86. Died (of cancer) in Madrid, 20 January 1986.

Selected Writings

Essays and Related Prose

La realidad como resultado, 1957
Desde el espectáculo a la trivialización, 1961
Tradición y modernismo (lectures), 1962
Acotaciones a la historia de la cultura occidental en la edad moderna, 1964
Humanismo y sociedad, 1964
Diderot como pretexto, 1965
Conocimiento y ciencias sociales, 1966
Razón mecánica y razón dialéctica, 1969
Escritos, 1950–1960, 1971
La rebelión juvenil y el problema en la universidad, 1972
Sobre la novela picaresca y otros escritos, 1974
¿Qué es ser agnóstico?, 1975
Idealismo y pragmatismo en el siglo XIX español, 1977
Bandos del Alcalde, 1986

Other writings: works on Spanish philosophy and literature.

Further Reading

Díaz, Elías, *Pensamiento español en la era de Franco: 1939–1973*, Madrid: Tecnos, 1983
Marichal, Juan, *El nuevo pensamiento político español*, Mexico City: Finisterre, 1966
Mermall, Thomas, *The Rhetoric of Humanism: Spanish Culture After Ortega y Gasset*, New York: Bilingual Press, 1976: 85–107
Sistema: Revista de ciencias sociales issue on Tierno Galván, 71–72 (June 1986), particularly articles by Elías Díaz and Raúl Morodo

Times Literary Supplement

British periodical, 1902–

Originally a weekly section of the *Times* newspaper, the *Times Literary Supplement* has gradually become one of the most popular and respected critical voices in the English-reading world. Its prototype, a penny **periodical** called the *Literary*

Times, appeared in 1863 and ran for 11 numbers from 14 March to 23 May. Later, in 1897, as the *Times* found it hard to review a satisfying number of books, a new and entirely separate journal, *Literature*, was created. It lasted only four and a half years, barely managing to take the pressure off the daily newspaper. Eventually, the first issue of the *TLS* appeared on 17 January 1902 and was presented as an occasional supplement when Parliament was sitting and political news took up most of the newspaper's pages. It would "appear as often as may be necessary in order to keep abreast with the more important publications of the day."

The first issue consisted of eight pages. Mostly devoted to literary **reviews**, it also contained pieces on science, art, drama, music, and chess, as well as separate listings of forthcoming and recently published books. Soon after the creation of the supplement, its first editor, Sir James Thursfield (1902), was replaced by Bruce Richmond (1902–38), who during his long tenure gave the *TLS* many of its distinctive traits and helped it evolve from its initially uncertain state. Although Parliament adjourned for Whitsuntide on 16 May 1902, the supplement went on and, over the years, it grew steadily in size, becoming a separate publication on 12 March 1914. Richmond favored anonymity of reviewers, which was to remain one of the peculiar and most debated traits of the *TLS*, and he attracted authoritative contributors, often assigning them specific fields and topics. In its early days, the periodical owed much of its steady success and reputation to Richmond's choice of reviewers, including Arthur Clutton-Brock, A. T. Quiller-Couch, and Andrew Lang, and foremost literary figures such as Henry Rider Haggard, **Henry James**, Edith Wharton, George Gissing, and Austin Dobson. Publication was not interrupted by the outbreak of World War I in 1914. On the contrary, during wartime, the *TLS* grew in length and gave more prominence to some of its distinctive features: the presence of original poetry, the **letters** to the editor, and a more extensive book list at the back.

In the 1920s the *TLS* became established as an authoritative critical organ, also thanks to the new reviewers contacted by Richmond. **Virginia Woolf** had first been invited to write a piece in 1905 and became a regular contributor from 1908 onward. Between then and her death in 1941 she wrote more than 220 articles, many of which were reprinted in her later collections of essays such as *Granite and Rainbow* (1958). At about the same time, Richmond contacted **T. S. Eliot**, securing him as the reviewer for studies of Renaissance drama and 17th-century poetry from 1919 to 1935. Many of Eliot's famous essays originally appeared as lead-reviews in the *TLS*, such as "Ben Jonson" (13 November 1919), "Andrew Marvell" (31 March 1921), and "The Metaphysical Poets" (20 October 1921). Other famous contributors from this period include **Herbert Read**, Richard Aldington, George Trevelyan, Edmund Blunden, and John Middleton Murry.

In 1922, possibly considering the profits of the *TLS* too small, Lord Northcliffe, the owner of the *Times*, decided that the number for 13 April would be the last. However, the periodical continued to appear regularly, for this order had not reached all the departments concerned, while in August the same year Lord Northcliffe became ill and died. Nonetheless, publication was temporarily interrupted during the general strike of 1926, with another minor interruption occurring

during the great freeze-up of Winter 1947. By the time Bruce Richmond retired in 1938, the *TLS* had reached its own specific identity. From its uncertain beginnings it had grown into a highly respected, weekly journal of criticism, devoted to the discussion of books of different subjects, although literature still prevailed, and also including shorter reviews, **critical essays**, a section of letters, and extensive book listings. Richmond was replaced by David L. Murray (1938–45) who started a largely unsuccessful campaign of modernization in order to increase the readership. The front page was given up to an illustration and the long essay was moved to the middle. After some internal troubles, Murray left, his place being taken by Stanley Morison (1945–48), who threw out many of the new features and reinstated the long front-page essay. Morison's editorship marked a new increase in circulation figures, a development partly the result of the paper-rationing policy adopted during World War II: whereas many daily newspapers abandoned their pages on book reviews because of paper shortage, the *TLS* remained the only medium providing an adequate coverage of books in this period.

In 1948 Morison was replaced by Alan Pryce-Jones (1948–59), whose task would be to guide the paper through the extended postwar period. In particular, he introduced new contributors such as Anthony Powell, who became fiction editor, and increased the presence of original poetry, while also starting the practice of special issues on a selected topic. His editorship was followed by those of Arthur Crook (1959–74) and John Gross (1974–81). On 7 June 1974 the practice of anonymous reviewing was abolished. Between December 1978 and November 1979 the *TLS* stopped publication during the one-year closure of Times Newspapers and, after the acquisition of the group by Rupert Murdoch's News International plc in 1981, the paper's archives became open to the public.

In recent times, during the editorships of Jeremy Treglown (1982–90) and Ferdinand Mount (1991–), publishing goals have varied little from those of Richmond's days. The *TLS* continues to aim at a broad audience of well-informed, general readers whose numbers have swelled, especially in the United States. From its beginnings the *TLS* has covered books about art and architecture, literature both in English and in foreign languages, literary criticism and theory, music, history and anthropology, politics, women's studies, economics, and reference books. Recent changes in editorial policy include more frequent coverage of politics and the arts and an increase in the number of long essays. At present the *TLS* reviews around 2000 books and the listings include some 6000 titles a year, thus remaining unique in its attempt to cover the whole publishing waterfront. Other important prerogatives include the fact that it is a weekly publication, whereas its most respectable competitors, the *New York Review of Books* and the *London Review of Books*, appear slightly less than fortnightly and mainly concentrate on modern literature and political issues. Circulation figures of the *TLS* have always oscillated between 20,000 and 45,000, settling halfway between these extremes in the mid-1980s.

As a "journal of record," the *TLS* has influenced other literary journals, most notably T. S. Eliot's *Criterion* and, more recently, the *New Review*, *Quarto*, and the *London Review of Books*. Despite its authority, it has attracted criticism mainly aimed at its policy of anonymity and its failure to review important texts such as **D. H. Lawrence**'s *The Rainbow* in 1916 and James Joyce's *Ulysses* in 1922. Over the years, the *TLS* has also been accused of anti-Americanism, of upholding liberal-humanist tenets based on "civilized judgment" and "civilized man," and of repressing freedoms of sexual behavior and expression. Nonetheless, the history of the *TLS* has been largely characterized by independence of opinion, and its pages have hosted a varied spectrum of critical and political voices. The success and authority enjoyed by the *TLS* result from its meeting comprehensively the demands of the critic, the scholar, and the general reader, and as such it holds a special place among reviewing periodicals in the English-speaking world.

DIEGO SAGLIA

Further Reading
Bateson, F. W., "Organs of Critical Opinion: IV. *The Times Literary Supplement*," *Essays in Criticism* 7 (1957): 349–62
Bradshaw, David, "Lonely Royalists: T. S. Eliot and Sir Robert Filmer," *Review of English Studies* 46 (1995): 375–79
Eliot, T. S., "Bruce Lyttelton Richmond," *Times Literary Supplement*, 13 January 1961: 17
Graham, Walter, *English Literary Periodicals*, New York: Nelson, 1930
Grigg, John, *The History of the Times*, vol. 6: *The Thomson Years, 1966–1981*, London: Times Books, 1994
Gross, John, "Naming Names," *Times Literary Supplement*, 7 June 1974: 610
Gross, John, "The *TLS* and the Modern Movement," in *The Modern Movement: A TLS Companion*, edited by Gross, London: Harvill, and Chicago: University of Chicago Press, 1992: xi–xxiii
Kirkpatrick, B. J., "Virginia Woolf: Unrecorded *Times Literary Supplement* Reviews," *Modern Fiction Studies* 38 (1992): 279–301
McDonald, Iverach, *The History of the Times*, vol. 5, London: Times Books, 1984
"The Times Literary Supplement: A Record of Its Beginnings," *Times Literary Supplement*, 18 January 1952: 33–39
Treglown, Jeremy, "Literary History and the *Lit. Supp.*," *Yearbook of English Studies* 16 (1986): 132–49
Wood, Adolf, "A Paper and Its Editors," *Times Literary Supplement*, 17 January 1992: 14–15
Yearbook of English Studies literary periodicals issue, edited by C. J. Rawson, 16 (1986)

Tolstoi, Lev

Russian, 1828–1910

Lev Tolstoi was one of the world's greatest novelists; he was also perhaps the world's leading exponent of literary realism. In his total oeuvre essays do not bulk large; no critic of his work would put him forward as primarily a practitioner of the essay. Nor, had one explained to Tolstoi what literary critics mean by the term "essay," would he likely have acknowledged that certain of his shorter works are essays; indeed, he would probably have said that the essay (at least of the belletristic variety) was an effete luxury, and that there was no need in literature for a literary genre of that sort.

Most of Tolstoi's slim production of essays belong to his final, post-conversion period, and are concerned with religion or art. Following his conversion to his own form of Christianity

in the 1880s, Tolstoi altered almost completely his manner of writing. Formerly his style had shown an exemplary realism, with a striving to give descriptive detail and to supply as consistent a narrative point of view as possible. His later manner, in both fiction and nonfiction, is simpler and more direct, a sermon-like style notable for its total authority, such that it is virtually impossible to doubt the author even when he utters patent absurdities. Tolstoi the objective chronicler has metamorphosed into Tolstoi the single-minded preacher. The new style is almost free from rhetoric, quite beautiful, without excessive lyricism, but with a note of stern command that cannot escape our notice.

Prominent among Tolstoi's "essays" is his celebrated confession *Ispoved'* (1884; *A Confession*). Though it is worthy, in both content and form, to rank with the famous examples of the genre by St. Augustine (cf. **Confessions**) or **Rousseau**, it also fits well into the essay form: though recounted in the first person, it is obviously about Everyman; though it contains many narrative elements, these are softened, generalized, and permeated with a lyric introspection. Thus, although Tolstoi did not choose to write essays as such, we may at least call him an essayist *manqué*.

Tolstoi's *Confession* is an outpouring of his celebrated religious conversion, which is usually dated as taking place in 1881 and 1882, though its roots may be found far earlier, for instance in Levin's doubts and his impulse toward suicide described in the closing pages of Tolstoi's novel *Anna Karenina* (1875–77). Despite its simplified but refined style, there can be little doubt that Tolstoi's *Confession* is close to the events of his life; we must wonder if there were not an attempt on Tolstoi's part to "live literature" as well as to "reflect life in literature." Tolstoi had always sought to bring life and literature together, as Boris Eikhenbaum tried to show (1922): in his early period of literary realism Tolstoi used the techniques of realism mentioned above; in his final period he dropped or constrained the customary techniques of fiction, unifying and compressing the authorial voice to give it the closest tie to life.

Tolstoi's *Confession*, like those of St. Augustine or Rousseau, tells the story of his life, but life perceived almost solely as a quest for salvation. Wherever he searches, Tolstoi's quest is frustrated, and he is dogged by anxiety and a compulsive urge to suicide. Only when he abandons that in which he seems to excel – money, noble rank, knowledge, literary fame, science – can he dispel his fear and set out on the true path. Finally, he confirms his insights by studying the life of the peasantry around him – the peasants who seem deficient only in what he himself has excelled in.

If Tolstoi had written only this single essay, one that has some claim, indeed, to be his masterpiece, he would be celebrated as an essayist. However, besides his *Confession*, he also wrote a handful of shorter essays on questions of religion and morality.

Tolstoi created what was for him a new style, which could be applied to **meditations** on moral and spiritual concerns. Just as the fiction Tolstoi wrote after his conversion – *Smert' Ivana Ilyicha* (1886; *The Death of Ivan Ilyich*) or *Khoziain i rabotnik* (1895; *Master and Man*) – is itself full of essay-like passages concerned with man's quest for salvation, so Tolstoi's nonfictional style also changed. Paradoxically, he himself criticized his earlier masterpieces as worthless in that they seemed to be trying to teach when he had nothing to teach. But now that he had, he began to teach with a vengeance.

Tolstoi likewise employed this new style in a handful of essays on art, a subject almost as important to him as religion, since art, he supposed, might either lead man to salvation or tempt him to perdition. The major and most famous of these, *Chto takoe iskusstvo?* (1898; *What Is Art?*), is too polemical to be called an essay, but an earlier attempt to deal with the question, "Ob iskusstve" (1889; "On Art"), is certainly an essay in that it largely eschews forceful persuasion for reflection. Tolstoi tells us that he came to his subject because of the importance generally conceded to art and artistic interpretation by so many people; thus he does not begin with a view of art's unimportance and powerlessness in daily life, a perhaps more common starting point. He also perceives fully the ambiguity and ambivalence of art: motivated by the best of reasons, works of art can in fact do great harm by representing as true a false way of life.

It is tempting to ask why Tolstoi did not write more essays. In spite of all the power and authority of a story like *The Death of Ivan Ilyich*, which some have even called Tolstoi's masterpiece, the essay form may strike us as equally or more appropriate to the character of his ideas after his conversion. The essay remained closer and more faithful to those ideas; it did not compromise them with characters or objects drawn from our external world. It remained purer; this purity and the consistency it fostered could well have been attractive to the author as well as the reader.

WILLIAM E. HARKINS

Biography

Lev (Leo) Nikolaevich Tolstoi. Born 9 September 1828 at Iasnaia Poliana family estate, near Tula. Studied privately with tutors; studied Eastern languages, then law, Kazan University, 1844–47. Inherited estate, 1847, and lived there (with extended periods of absence) throughout his life. Served in the Russian Army, 1852–56. Lived in St. Petersburg, from 1856, frequenting literary circles and meeting leading writers and critics. Traveled abroad, 1857 and 1860–61. Studied European educational systems, established a school on his estate for the children of his serfs, 1859–62, wrote and published *Iasnaia Poliana* journal outlining his theories on education, 1862–63, and wrote and compiled materials for a complete elementary education course: published it as the primer *Azbuka*, 1872, revised as *Novaia azbuka*, 1875, and widely used thereafter in Russian schools. Married Sof'ia Andreevna Bers, 1862: 13 children (nine survived to adulthood); also had a son by one of the peasants on his estate. Suffered increasingly from depression and suicidal thoughts, until his conversion to his own version of Christianity, early 1880s; most of his subsequent writings concerned religious themes and were banned or censored. Excommunicated from the Russian Orthodox Church, 1901. Died (of pneumonia and resulting heart failure) at Astapovo railway station, 20 November 1910.

Selected Writings

Essays and Related Prose

Ispoved', 1884; edited by A. D. P. Briggs, 1994; as *A Confession*, translated anonymously, 1885, and by Jane Kentish, in *A Confession and Other Religious Writings*, 1987
V chem moia vera, 1884; as *My Religion*, translated by Huntington Smith, 1885; as *What I Believe*, translated by Constantine Popoff, 1885

In Pursuit of Happiness, translated by Aline Delano, 1887
O zhizni, 1888; as *Life*, translated by Isabel F. Hapgood, 1888; as *On Life*, translated by Mabel and Agnes Cook, 1902
Tsarstvo Bozhie vnutri vas, 2 vols., 1893–94; as *The Kingdom of God Is Within You*, translated by Constance Garnett, 2 vols., 1894
Chto takoe iskusstvo?, 1898; as *What Is Art?*, translated by Charles Johnston, 1898, and Aylmer Maude, 1930
Tak chtozhe nam delat'?, 1902; as *What to Do?*, translated by Isabel F. Hapgood, 1887; uncensored edition, 1888
Essays and Letters, translated by Aylmer Maude, 1903
Ne mogu molchat', 1908; translated as "I Cannot Be Silent," in *I Cannot Be Silent: Selection from Tolstoy's Non-Fiction*, edited by W. Gareth Jones, 1989
On Life and Essays on Religion, translated by Aylmer Maude, 1934
The Kingdom of God, and Peace Essays, translated by Aylmer Maude, 1936
Recollections and Essays, translated by Aylmer Maude, 1937
Essays from Tula, translated by Evgeny Lamport, 1948
Why Do Men Stupefy Themselves?, and Other Writings, translated by Aylmer Maude, 1975
Tolstoy on Education: Tolstoy's Educational Writings, 1861–62, edited by Alan Pinch and Michael Armstrong, translated by Pinch, 1982
The Lion and the Honeycomb: The Religious Writings, edited by A. N. Wilson, translated by Robert Chandler, 1987
Writings on Civil Disobedience and Non-Violence, translated by Aylmer Maude and Ronald Sampson, 1988
The Gospel According to Tolstoy, translated by David Patterson, 1992

Other writings: many novels (including *Voina i mir* [*War and Peace*], 1863–69; *Anna Karenina*, 1875–77; *Smert' Ivana Ilyicha* [*The Death of Ivan Ilyich*], 1886), plays, stories, and works on religious issues.

Collected works editions: *Polnoe sobranie sochinenii*, edited by V. Chertkov and others, 90 vols., 1928–58; *Oxford Centenary Edition*, edited by Aylmer Maude, translated by Aylmer and Louise Maude, 21 vols., 1928–37; *Sobranie sochinenii*, edited by S. A. Makashina, 12 vols., 1980–87.

Bibliographies

Egan, David R., and Melinda A. Egan, *Leo Tolstoy: An Annotated Bibliography of English Language Sources to 1978*, Metuchen, New Jersey: Scarecrow Press, 1979
Sheliapina, N. G., and others, *Bibliografiya literatury o L. N. Tolstom*, Moscow: Isd-vo Vses. knizhnoi palaty, vol. 1, 1960; Moscow: Kniga, vols. 2–5, 1965–90

Further Reading

Christian, R. F., *Tolstoy: A Critical Introduction*, Cambridge: Cambridge University Press, 1969
Eikhenbaum, Boris, *The Young Tolstoi*, Ann Arbor, Michigan: Ardis, 1972 (original Russian edition, 1922)
Gustafson, Richard F., *Leo Tolstoy, Resident and Stranger: A Study in Fiction and Theology*, Princeton, New Jersey: Princeton University Press, 1986
Lavrin, Janko, *Tolstoy: An Approach*, London: Methuen, 1944; New York: Macmillan, 1946
Maude, Aylmer, *The Life of Tolstoy*, Oxford and New York: Oxford University Press, 1987 (original edition, 1908–10)
Simmons, E. J., *Leo Tolstoy*, Boston: Little Brown, 1946; London: Lehmann, 1949
Steiner, George, *Tolstoy or Dostoevsky: An Essay in the Old Criticism*, London: Faber, 1980; Chicago: University of Chicago Press, 1985 (original edition, 1959)
Troyat, Henri, *Tolstoy*, New York: Harmony, and Harmondsworth: Penguin, 1980 (original French edition, 1965)

Topical Essay

The topical essay is generally one written in response to a newsworthy event, and hence has within it the ephemerality of daily journalism. What distinguishes it from regular journalism is often its attention to prose style, and just as often its search for wisdom within the facts of the event being written about. Often the news event is the pretext for the essay rather than the true or ultimate topic of engagement.

The term "topical essay" is not commonly used. More often, essays of this type have been termed "periodical essays" or, since the 1960s, "literary journalism." Newspaper and magazine columns frequently fall into this category as well. No matter the name, though, the 20th century has seen a surge of essays written in response to world events well outside the writers' lives. With the coming of World War I, the formerly popular and dominant familiar essay came under attack as too genteel, too irresponsible, too lacking in the insight and wisdom that a contemporary readership craved and even needed to help it make sense of an increasingly chaotic world. **Agnes Repplier**, in her 1918 essay "The American Essay in Wartime," argued that the "leisure and reflection" that had long been key to the personality of the essay was no longer justifiable. "To write essays in these flaming years," she claimed, "one must have a greater power of detachment than had Montaigne or Lamb."

Yet, the roots of the topical essay are in the 18th century, in English newspapers which routinely combined current news with sharp political commentary. In the early 1700s, there were upwards of 18 newspapers being published in London – including **Daniel Defoe**'s *A Review of the Affairs of France* (1704–13), which combined news, political moderation, wit, and social comment, and helped mold the audience for the more famous series of topical essays in **Joseph Addison**'s and **Richard Steele**'s *Tatler* (1709–11) and *Spectator* (1711–12, 1714). Steele referred to himself and Addison as "weekly Historians," and their essays won broad acclaim for their vivid depictions of the social life of the period. They were criticized as being trivial (by **Jonathan Swift**, for example), but both men, seeking to bring "philosophy out of the Closets and Libraries, Schools and Colleges," believed that to sell their papers they had to base their "lucubrations" on areas of current interest. Many critics today, however, argue that the political, social, and religious topics in Addison and Steele's essays are outdated only in matters of style, and that the insights offered in them pushed them well beyond the limited life of ephemeral journalism. Numerous imitations sprang up after Addison and Steele, including, most famously, **Samuel Johnson**'s *Rambler* (1750–52) and *Idler* (1758–60).

In the 19th century **Ivan Turgenev**'s "Kazn' Tropmana" (1870; "The Execution of Tropmann") was a forerunner of literary journalism; the writer implicated himself in the barbarity as a semi-willing voyeur of the public guillotining. (**George Orwell** made the same sort of portrayal in "A Hanging" [1931] and "Shooting an Elephant" [1936] – both essays intended to criticize British imperialism.) Other 19th-century literary journalists include **Mark Twain** and Stephen Crane. In the 20th century the form became defined by pieces such as Ernest Hemingway's reporting on bullfighting, Joseph

Mitchell's portraits of characters from the Bowery and the Fulton Fish Market in Manhattan, **A. J. Liebling**'s essays on boxing, and **James Agee**'s *Let Us Now Praise Famous Men* (1941). Many of these writers chose as their subjects what may have seemed at the time common and ordinary – not at all topical. Yet their essays often captured the feel of their times in ways that more autobiographical or **Personal essays** rarely did. Much of John Steinbeck's writing in the late 1930s, for instance, was devoted to reports on the Dust Bowl migrants, which would "break the story hard enough so that food and drugs can get moving . . ." His literary journalism was a tool for his advocacy.

When the **New Journalism** became popular in the early 1960s (the term "New Journalism" later gave way to "literary journalism"), it was led by profiles for the commercial magazines. Gay Talese's "Frank Sinatra Has a Cold" (1962), perhaps one of the most durable of those pieces, illustrates how a reporter uses scenes and dialogue and evocative description to teach readers not only about the essay's nominal subject – Sinatra – but also, in this case, about the world of entertainment in the 1950s and 1960s, as well as about the uses and abuses of charisma, money, and power. Talese, like many other New Journalists of that decade, wrote in the third person, in order to signify that, though his presence is on every page, he is not the subject of his essay.

Norman Mailer's *The Armies of the Night* (1968), which tells of an antiwar march on the Pentagon in 1967, focuses on the nominal event in a larger cultural context as "a paradigm of the twentieth century." Mailer, who took part in the protest, makes his own character dominant, as a way of arguing that the historian/topical essayist must become a novelist who invents the meaning of the event in an act of self-definition.

The dreamlike nature of American reality in the 1960s also led Hunter S. Thompson, in reports such as *Fear and Loathing in Las Vegas* (1971), to describe a culture in which the real has become saturated with the fantastic, a culture in which the American Dream has become the hedonistic pursuit of "the now." **Joan Didion** described her 1968 volume of reportage, *Slouching Towards Bethlehem*, as a confrontation with the "evidence of atomization, the proof that things fall apart," and as an attempt "to come to terms with [the] disorder" of the 1960s in America and, more specifically, in California. Many such writers – Didion, Mailer, Thompson, **Tom Wolfe** – have continued to be essayists with their fingers on the topical, as in Didion's *After Henry: Sentimental Journeys* (1992), written in response to the rape and murder of a jogger in New York City's Central Park and the subsequent media coverage.

Topical essayists are often by necessity **travel essay**ists, with the writer going in search of the story. Hence poet and journalist James Fenton put himself in Saigon ("The Fall of Saigon," 1985); foreign correspondent John Simpson wrote from China ("Tiananmen Square," 1989); Didion traveled to El Salvador and brought back a harrowing account of the troubles occurring there (*Salvador*, 1983).

It has also often been the ambition of newspaper columnists to be topical essayists – writers who can address current events factually but in a way that captures the essay's traditional depth of reflection and personality. Perhaps all columnists can trace their roots and influences back to Addision and Steele.

In America, writers such as **Benjamin Franklin** contributed to this tradition – Franklin, for instance, with his columns written under the pen name Silence Dogood. **Thomas Paine** gave the discordant American colonies a unifying voice, filling *Pennsylvania Magazine* with topical pieces in which his radical temper was evident in his attacks on imperial misrule. Eighty-five essays written by Alexander Hamilton, James Madison, and John Jay, originating as columns in New York newspapers and coming to be called *The Federalist*, defended the drafting of the U.S. Constitution in 1787–88; perhaps no more influential collection of newspaper articles has appeared. William Lloyd Garrison, editor of the abolitionist weekly the *Liberator*, was one of the best-known columnists arguing the antislavery cause in the 1830s to 1860s. In a more social vein, Fanny Fern, the first female American columnist, wrote satirical columns on literary, political, and social issues.

In 20th-century America, **H. L. Mencken**, who often commented upon current social and political issues, led the way as an influential topical essayist. **E. B. White** had great popularity with his "One Man's Meat" column in *Harper's* magazine – a column in which he often responded to war reports from Europe. Walter Lippmann, who described writing columns as "a puzzled man making notes . . . drawing sketches in the sand, which the sea will wash away," worked within that ephemerality to become one of the most influential columnists. More recently, columnists who have the required feeling for facts and technical agility, but who have also imbued their writings with enough essayistic qualities to give them greater permanence than the usual run of daily journalism, include Russell Baker, Molly Ivins, Ellen Goodman, and Anna Quindlen.

DAN ROCHE

Anthologies
The Best of Granta Reportage, London: Granta/Penguin, and New York: Viking Penguin, 1994
Literary Journalism: A New Collection of the Best American Nonfiction, edited by Norman Sims, New York: Ballantine, 1995
Pundits, Poets, and Wits: An Omnibus of American Newspaper Columnists, edited by Karl E. Meyer, New York: Oxford University Press, 1990

Further Reading
[See also Further Reading in the entry on New Journalism]
Sims, Norman, *The Literary Journalists*, New York: Ballantine, 1984
Sims, Norman, editor, *Literary Journalism in the Twentieth Century*, New York and Oxford: Oxford University Press, 1990

Torres Villarroel, Diego de

Spanish, c. 1694–1770

In the canon of 18th-century Spanish literature, the works of Diego de Torres Villarroel represent the antithesis of Enlightenment reason and a model of the baroque with all its linguistic intricacies. Torres Villarroel realizes this endeavor by blending humor, common sense, and personal observation into a series of works that reveal the attitude of the commoner. Unlike many of his contemporaries, who relied on encyclopedic didacticism, this author allows the foibles and frailties of human nature to be the catalysts for his commentary. As Russell Sebold (1963) suggests, Torres Villarroel was "one of the most humane spirits and because of this the most tormented there is among the Catholic writers of Spain."

The two works that reflect clearly the disposition of Torres Villarroel and his essay style are *Visiones y visitas con Francisco de Quevedo* (1727–28; Visions and visits with Francisco de Quevedo) and *Vida, ascendencia, nacimiento, crianza y aventuras* (1743–58; Life, lineage, birth, upbringing, and adventures; translated as *The Remarkable Life of Don Diego*). Speaking of the author, Ivy McClelland (1976) observes that ". . . his witness to mass-minded suspicion and incomprehension is of supreme value to historians attempting to examine the reason for any country's resistance to scientific common sense; for it is the lesser scholars – such as Torres – who represent the ordinary state of mind of the ordinary man and make history three-dimensional. Torres is as stimulatingly alive as Feijóo. But he lived his life on the reverse side of eighteenth-century Enlightenment." These works offer the reader two significant viewpoints regarding Torres Villarroel's attitude toward his own person and toward society at large.

The prologue to *Visiones y visitas* provides an excellent example of how the worlds of the author and the reader come together. First, Torres Villarroel treats his reader as a friend by using the familiar *tú* form of address. Under the guise of friendship and familiarity, readers are bombarded with a series of twisted, bombastic remarks. Each comment is carefully couched in humor as if to lull them and dull the senses. However, lying just below the surface Torres Villarroel subtly suggests that his discourse will bite and tear at the very fabric of his readers' moral, intellectual, and physical reality. More important, Torres Villarroel insinuates that his perspective, which is conveyed through this series of "dreams," will prove beneficial to his readers. Thus, he warns that anyone determined to read the work should also be willing to reflect on what is said. The author asks only that readers willingly suspend all prejudice and by so doing find wholesome doctrine that will protect them from the vices of the times. Immediately following this invitation, Torres Villarroel states that some readers lack the depth and ability to understand his writings. He greatly fears his readers because too often they approach his work with "evil intentions," "only grasp at trivialities," and "censure" the style and the tone of his writing without understanding the message. Furthermore, he chastises them for their intellectual indiscretion. He warns that if they wish to "nibble away" at his writing, they must first learn to speak and write correctly. However, if the reading public relies only on what they have learned at the knees of their mothers or wet nurses, they should stay clear of the author's "dreams," or they might get burned.

From the playful tone of the discourses the reader might assume that Torres Villarroel's primary purpose is to amuse. However, beneath the playful façade there is a harsh and direct criticism of society. To accomplish his task, Torres Villarroel relies on the power and subtlety of **satire**. With this rhetorical device in hand he corrupts the sanctity of long-held traditions and subverts the newly adopted methodologies of the

Enlightenment. Whether intentionally or not, Torres Villarroel espouses the need for introspection and self-criticism. The examination of oneself appears to be an integral part of both *Visiones y visitas* and *Remarkable Life*. More important, the introspection the author recommends to his reader is equally applicable to himself.

Torres Villarroel's *Remarkable Life* is a parody of confessional works by religious figures such as St. Augustine and Santa Teresa. In this work he relies heavily on the frequent reference to his own unworthiness and ignorance. Like Cervantes, who often imbued his foolish characters with sagelike wisdom, Torres ridicules his own persona in order to speak more clearly the truths he sees being ignored by society. Interestingly, he opens the prologue to *Remarkable Life* with both a critique of the confessional autobiography and a self-defense: "You will say (as if I were listening), as soon as you take in your hand this paper, that in Torres there is no virtue, humility nor amusement to write his life, rather the pure impudence, the strong roguery and the insolent philosophy of a rascal who has made a living making fun of himself and enjoys teasing and creating an uproar among the people of the world. And I will say that you are right, like I am a Christian." Here the reader notes that there is no denial of Torres Villarroel's motivation for writing, only an affirmation. From the outset of the work, Torres Villarroel takes control of the reader and dictates how the work is to be interpreted. It can be assumed that he does this with the intention of distracting the reader away from the harsh criticisms he scatters throughout the work.

Torres Villarroel represents an important cog in the literary mechanism of Spanish Enlightenment. McClelland states clearly, "When Feijóo, the empiric scholar, and Torres, the dilettante, confronted each other in battle they exteriorized their epoch's conflicts of misunderstanding that affected the speed of change." More important, Torres Villarroel rediscovered the power of the word and used it to reveal the conflict of his internal and external worlds.

ALVIN F. SHERMAN, JR.

Biography
Baptized 18 June 1694 in Salamanca. Traveled and worked variously in Spain and Portugal, 1713–15. Took minor orders, 1715, then abandoned clerical career, though later ordained, 1745. Studied at the University of Salamanca, 1718–20. Began publishing almanacs (*Almanaques y Proviósticos*) under the name "El Gran Piscator Salmantino," 1720s. Chair of mathematics, University of Salamanca, 1726–32 and 1734–51: banished for involvement in a criminal case, 1732–34, then obtained royal pardon. Died in Salamanca, 19 June 1770.

Selected Writings

Essays and Related Prose
Visiones y visitas con Francisco de Quevedo, 3 vols., 1727–28; edited by Russell P. Sebold, 1966
La barca de Aqueronte, 1731; edited by Guy Mercadier, 1969
Los desahuciados del mundo, 3 vols., 1736–37; edited by Manuel María Pérez, 1979
Vida, ascendencia, nacimiento, crianza y aventuras, 6 vols., 1743–58; edited by Federico de Onís, 1912, Guy Mercadier, 1972, and Dámaso Chicharro, 1980; as *The Remarkable Life of Don Diego*, translated by W. C. Atkinson, 1958

Other writings: almanacs, works about mathematics, poetry, and plays.

Collected works edition: *Obras completas*, 15 vols., 1794–99.

Further Reading
Aguilar Pinal, Francisco, "Pronósticos de Torres Villarroel en México y Perú," in *Homenaje a Noel Salomon: Ilustración española e independencia de América*, edited by Alberto Gil Novales, Barcelona: University of Barcelona, 1979: 345–53
Ettinghausen, Henry, "Torres Villarroel's Self-Portrait: The Mask Behind the Mask," *Bulletin of Hispanic Studies* 55 (1978): 321–28
Fernández Cifuentes, Luis, "Autobiography and Print: The Negotiation of Authorship in Eighteenth-Century Spain," *Journal of Interdisciplinary Literary Studies* 5, no. 1 (1993): 3–21
Ilie, Paul, "Grotesque Portraits in Torres Villarroel," *Bulletin of Hispanic Studies* 45 (1968): 16–37
Ilie, Paul, "Franklin and Villarroel: Social Consciousness in Two Autobiographies," *Eighteenth-Century Studies* 7 (1974): 321–42
Ilie, Paul, "Dream Cognition and the Spanish Enlightenment: Judging Torres Villarroel," *Modern Language Notes* 101, no. 2 (1986): 270–97
Kahiluoto Rudat, Eva M., "Imagination and Popular Humor in Torres Villarroel's *Visiones y Visitas*," in *Pen and Peruke: Spanish Literature of the Eighteenth Century*, edited by Monroe Z. Hafter, Ann Arbor: University of Michigan Department of Romance Languages, 1992: 73–86
McClelland, I. L., *Diego de Torres Villarroel*, Boston: Twayne, 1976
Marichal, Juan, "Torres Villarroel: Autobiografía burguesa al hispánico modo," *Papels de Son Armadans* 36 (1965): 297–306
Mercadier, Guy, "¿Cuándo nació Diego Torres de Villarroel?," *Insula* 18, no. 197 (1963): 14
Peset Reig, Mariano, and José L. Peset Reig, "Un buen negocio de Torres Villarroel," *Cuadernos Hispanoamericanos* 279 (1973): 514–36
Sebold, Russell P., "Mixtificación y estructura picarescas en la *Vida de Torres Villarroel*," *Insula* 18, no. 204 (1963): 7, 12
Varela, Antonio, "Narration and Theme in *Vida* of Diego de Torres Villarroel," *American Hispanist* 4, nos. 34–35 (1979): 5–7
Zavala, Iris M., "Utopia y astrología en la literatura popular del setecientos: Los almanaques de Torres Villarroel," *Nueva Revista de Filología Hispánica* 33, no. 1 (1984): 196–212
Zavala, Iris M., *Lecturas y lectores del discurso narrativo dieciochesco*, Amsterdam: Rodopi, 1987

Tract

A tract has come to be distinguished from its cognate *tractate* because of its brevity, its religious, moral, and/or political character, its hortatory, often highly emotional style – calculated to win converts rather than to stimulate discussion or analysis – and its suitability for widespread distribution. The American Tract Society (ATS) in 1824 proclaimed that "a plain didactic essay on a religious subject may be read by a Christian with much pleasure," but warned that those for whom tracts are designed "will fall asleep over it. There must be something to allure the listless to read, and this can only be done by blending entertainment with instruction." Copying the style, if not the content, of increasingly popular novels, romances, and adventure stories, tract writers employed brisk pacing, sprightly dialogue, and narrative situations that the reader, imagined as lower-class and poorly educated, either would be likely to face or might fantasize about facing. Thanks to this formula, coupled with modern printing and distribution techniques, the ATS has estimated that from 1800 to 1825 100 million copies of tracts were published worldwide, with titles such as "Stop That Thought," "The Blaspheming Sailor Reclaimed," and "Twenty-Two Reasons for Not Being a Roman Catholic."

While Evangelicals strove to convey a simple creed to a mass audience, a group of Anglo-Catholic reformers led by **John Henry Newman** employed tracts differently. Although these members of the so-called Oxford Movement became known as Tractarians because of their *Tracts for the Times* (1833–41), only Newman wrote tracts in the narrow sense, possibly because he was an avid reader of them. The others, including John Keble and Edward Pusey, instead wrote learned **treatise**s. In any case, what the Tractarians sought was a "middle way" in the Church of England between the extremes of Protestantism and Catholicism. In the last and most famous of the series, Tract 90, Newman tried to remove all obstacles blocking the recognition that Anglican teaching was apostolic and Catholic in nature. The tract was censored by the Church, and Newman became a Roman Catholic a few years later.

Somewhat paradoxically, given the response to Tract 90 and the virulent anti-Catholicism of the evangelical tracts, the *Catholic Homilies* (wr. c. 985–95) of Abbot Ælfric are perhaps the earliest specimens of the genre in English literature. Ælfric used these vernacular homilies both to embolden the English, who were facing renewed onslaughts from the Vikings, and to educate those in the clergy who did not know Latin well enough to understand basic Christian theology. John Wycliffe greatly influenced medieval theology with tracts known as the *Summa de ente* (wr. c. 1370; Treatise on being), which challenged the dominant philosophical nominalism of the 14th century. Religion and politics merged in the tracts of Martin Luther, including *De captivitate Babylonica* (The Babylonian captivity of the Church) and *An den Christlichen Adel deutscher Nation* (An address to the Christian nobility of the German nation), both of 1520, the latter of which alleged wickedness and corruption in the Catholic Church and proposed reforms in Church and nation. Other 16th-century writers who tackled theological and political issues in tracts include Sir Thomas More, John Fisher, and William Tyndale. The anonymous author or authors who took the name "Martin Marprelate" wrote a rollicking series of tracts (1588–89), which have been called the best prose satires of the Elizabethan age; such noted writers as John Lyly and **Thomas Nashe** responded with tracts attacking Marprelate's rough handling of England's bishops. Tracts poured from the press during the English Civil War and subsequent Commonwealth era (1642–60). Bookseller George Thomason collected some 23,000 items, mostly tracts, which are now bound and housed at the British Library. One of the most prolific tract writers was John Milton, whose *Of Reformation Touching Church Discipline in England* (1641), among others, attacked the English bishops. Milton's early tracts shed considerable light on his later, more famous writings, as is the case with **Jonathan Swift** in the early 18th century.

In the last decade of the 18th century, as England began to be flooded with revolutionary **pamphlet**s such as **Thomas Paine**'s *Rights of Man* (1791–92) as well as penny pamphlets and ballads, socialite-turned-evangelical writer Hannah More was asked by the Bishop of London to undertake countermeasures. "To teach the poor to read, without providing them with *safe* books," she wrote at the time, "has always appeared to me an improper measure." She began contributing to, and overseeing, the *Cheap Repository of Moral and Religious Tracts* (1795–98). Two million copies of these thrice-monthly tracts were distributed in the first year, largely among the poor and needy by wealthy people who purchased subscriptions. Contributors besides More included Henry Thornton, John Newton, and William Mason. The tracts have been derided as banal and stuffed with mindless reactionary politics, but careful study by Susan Pedersen (1986) has shown that most of the tracts attack general evils, from drunkenness to slavery, and "defy a simple political explanation."

Largely because of the project's success, the London Religious Tract Society was formed in 1799, and one year later the first organized distribution of tracts began in America. Over time, employees of the American Tract Society began going from house to house furnishing tracts to anyone unable to buy them. This activity and related practices quickly spread around the world. David Sonenschein (1982) calculated that there were 4000 tracts in circulation from 43 known tract publishers, with total printings well into the billions. Despite this success, and the fact that Hannah More as much as anyone else made the written word accessible to new readers, the reputation of the tract has undergone serious erosion since her time. For instance, while 19th-century tracts promoted such commendable causes as the abolition of slavery, in the 20th century the genre is often associated with intolerance and bigotry, as in the outpourings of such racist groups as the Citizens' Councils during the American Civil Rights movement. At its best, though, as A. G. Newell wrote (1966), the tract "elevated a species of ephemeral journalism into a genuine kind of creative literature."

STEVEN EPLEY

See also Religious Essay

Anthologies
The Marprelate Tracts 1588, 1589, edited by William Pierce, London: Clarke, 1911
Tracts on Liberty of Conscience and Persecution, 1614–1661, New York: Franklin, 1966 (original edition, 1846)

Further Reading
The American Tract Society Documents, 1824–1925, New York: Arno Press, 1972
Brown, Ford K., *Fathers of the Victorians: The Age of Wilberforce*, Cambridge: Cambridge University Press, 1961
Carlson, Leland H., "Martin Marprelate: His Identity and His Satire," in *English Satire: Papers Read at a Clark Library Seminar, January 15, 1972*, edited by Leland and Ronald Paulson, Los Angeles: William Andrews Clark Memorial Library, 1972: 1–53
Cook, Richard I., *Jonathan Swift as a Tory Pamphleteer*, Seattle: University of Washington Press, 1967
Ffinch, Michael, *Cardinal Newman: The Second Spring*, San Francisco: Ignatius Press, and London: Weidenfeld and Nicolson, 1991
Jay, Elisabeth, editor, *The Evangelical and Oxford Movements*, Cambridge and New York: Cambridge University Press, 1983
Lindholt, Paul J., "The Significance of the Colonial Promotion Tract," in *Early American Literature and Culture: Essays Honoring Harrison T. Meserole*, edited by K. Z. Derounian Stodola, Newark: University of Delaware Press, 1992

Myers, Mitzi, "Hannah More's Tracts for the Times: Social Fiction and Female Ideology," in *Fetter'd or Free? British Women Novelists, 1670–1815*, edited by Mary Anne Schofield and Cecilia Macheski, Athens: Ohio University Press, 1986: 264–84

Newell, A. G., "Early Evangelical Fiction," *Evangelical Quarterly* 38 (1966): 3–21

Nord, David Paul, *The Evangelical Origins of Mass Media in America, 1815–1835*, Columbia, South Carolina: Association for Education in Journalism and Mass Communications, 1984

Nord, David Paul, "Systematic Benevolence: Religious Publishing and the Marketplace in Early Nineteenth-Century America," in *Communication and Change in American Religious History*, edited by Leonard I. Sweet, Grand Rapids, Michigan: Eerdmans, 1993: 239–69

Pedersen, Susan, "Hannah More Meets Simple Simon: Tracts, Chapbooks, and Popular Culture in Late Eighteenth-Century England," *Journal of British Studies* 25 (1986): 84–113

Poole, Kristen, "Saints Alive! Falstaff, Martin Marprelate, and the Staging of Puritanism," *Shakespeare Quarterly* 46 (1995): 47–75

Sales, Roger, *English Literature in History, 1780–1830: Pastoral and Politics*, London: Hutchinson, 1983: especially Chapter 1, "The Propaganda of the Victors"

Sonenschein, David, "Sharing the Good News: The Evangelical Tract," *Journal of American Culture* 5 (1982): 107–21

Spinney, G. H., "Cheap Repository Tracts: Hazard and Marshall Edition," *Library* 20 (1939): 295–340

Travel Essay

The nature of travel, often prolonged and unpredictable, is perhaps at odds with the concision of the essay form. Traveling lends itself to fragmentary modes – **letters**, notebooks, **journals** – which somehow swell to fill long books. Observations on manners, morals, and monuments; autobiographical and anecdotal digressions; the flow of narrative incident, reminiscence, and analysis – all seem to require leisurely and expansive treatment.

None of the earliest travel writers appears to have written in a form that could safely be called an essay. Herodotus produced a *History of the Persian Wars*, and Pausanius wrote a guidebook for second-century Roman travelers in Greece. The Venetian Marco Polo recounted his travels to China, and the medieval Berber, Ibn Battuta, told of visiting most of the known world. Explorers of the 15th and 16th centuries, including Christopher Columbus, Amerigo Vespucci, Bernal Díaz del Castillo, and Sir Walter Ralegh kept journals and wrote letters describing the marvels they encountered. But none of them, it seems, wrote travel essays.

Montaigne's famous essay, "Des cannibales" (1580; "Of Cannibals"), does not narrate his own travels, but reflects on the customs of different cultures, and the relative nature of barbarism: "each man calls barbarism whatever is not his own practice." (Montaigne also kept a *Journal de Voyage en Italie* which was not published until 1774.) **Francis Bacon**'s essay "Of Travel" (1625) advises young men what to see, and recommends keeping a diary. In 1763 Richard Hurd published "On the Uses of Foreign Travel," a dialogue concerning the value of travel.

In the 18th century nearly every major writer tried his hand at writing a travel book – **Defoe, Fielding,** Smollett, Sterne, **Johnson,** Boswell, **Goethe** – but well-known travel essays are in short supply. In 1792 William Gilpin published his *Three Essays: On Picturesque Beauty; On Picturesque Travel; and on Sketching Landscape*. One might argue that the letters of Lady Mary Wortley Montagu, written in Turkey from 1716 to 1718, should count as travel essays. Wife of the British ambassador to Turkey, Lady Mary sent home hundreds of polished and witty letters, each a mini-essay about some aspect of Turkish life. Her trenchant observations on the contrasting merits of Turkish and British society place her among the most celebrated travel writers.

The great essayist **William Hazlitt** wrote "On Going a Journey" (1822), which extols the pleasures of traveling alone: "the soul of a journey is liberty." In 1826 he published a series of essays, *Notes of a Journey Through France and Italy*; though he calls travel a splendid dream, he concludes that "our affections must settle at home."

The Victorians' appetite for travel books has probably never been equaled, but they tended to devour multi-volume tomes rather than succinct essays. Richard Burton alone produced 43 volumes of travel, and none of the era's classics – Frances Trollope's *Domestic Manners of the Americans* (1832), Alexander Kinglake's *Eōthen, or, Traces of Travel Brought Home from the East* (1844), Charles Doughty's *Travels in Arabia Deserta* (1888), and Mary Kingsley's *Travels in West Africa* (1897) – is short. If the definition of the essay can be stretched once again to include letters, Isabella Bird's best-known work, *A Lady's Life in the Rocky Mountains* (1879), recounts in a series of lively vignettes her adventures in the American West.

Leslie Stephen's delightful mountaineering essays in *The Playground of Europe* (1871) were originally written for the *Alpine Journal*. **Robert Louis Stevenson**'s *Essays of Travel* were collected in 1905, yet he is better known for his charming account of *Travels with a Donkey in the Cévennes* (1879). Rudyard Kipling wrote *Letters of Travel (1892–1913)* (1920), a series of newspaper articles describing his visits to North America, Japan, and Egypt; later he published *Brazilian Sketches* (1927) and *Souvenirs of France* (1933).

Although the most popular 19th-century American travel writer, **Mark Twain**, wrote mainly long, humorous travel books – *Innocents Abroad* (1869), *Roughing It* (1872), *A Tramp Abroad* (1880) – other American authors produced admirable travel essays. **Ralph Waldo Emerson** visited England twice, in 1833 and 1847, and later published *English Traits* (1856) on topics such as manners, character, the aristocracy, and universities. For most travelers, personal experience forms the basis of their narratives, but Emerson preferred analysis to autobiography. His essays are prone to sweeping generalizations: "the one thing the English value is pluck."

Unlike Emerson, who claimed to travel unwillingly, **Henry James** was an inveterate and passionate traveler. He published several volumes of travel essays: *Transatlantic Sketches* (1875), *Portraits of Places* (1883), and *A Little Tour in France* (1884, revised 1900); some travel essays reappeared in *English Hours* (1905) and *Italian Hours* (1909). James was familiar with Europe from childhood, and fascinated by the contrast between the Old World and the New. Like many of his novels, his travel sketches take Europe as both location and theme. He brought a wide culture to his travels, yet his purpose was not to instruct: "I write these lines with the full consciousness of having no information whatever to offer." Instead he offered reminiscences and impressions, discriminating observations and sophisticated judgments, all in an urbane, cosmopolitan style.

D. H. Lawrence wrote a series of essays about his long stay in Italy, published in 1916 as *Twilight in Italy*. A restless traveler in search of a home, Lawrence lived in over a dozen countries and produced several more travel books, including *Sea and Sardinia* (1921), *Mornings in Mexico* (1927), and *Etruscan Places* (1932). Other important figures in 20th-century English travel are Evelyn Waugh, **Graham Greene**, Peter Fleming, Robert Byron, Freya Stark, Eric Newby, Patrick Leigh Fermor, Dervla Murphy, Jonathan Raban, and Bruce Chatwin. The best-known contemporary English travel essayist is Jan Morris, author of numerous collections including *Places* (1972), *Travels* (1976), *Journeys* (1984), and *Among the Cities* (1985).

Shiva Naipaul's *Beyond the Dragon's Mouth: Stories and Pieces* (1984) contains a number of his travel essays about England, India, Africa, and the Caribbean. V. S. Naipaul's travel writing includes an essay on the Ivory Coast, "The Crocodiles of Yamoussoukro," originally published in the **New Yorker** and reprinted in *Finding the Center* (1984).

In the United States, postwar travel essays are varied. **James Baldwin**'s "Stranger in the Village" (1953) recounts his experience as the first black man to appear in a Swiss village. The *New Yorker* frequently publishes travel essays: those by Berton Roueché were collected under the title *Sea to Shining Sea: People, Travel, Places* (1985), while a selection of Calvin Trillin's **humorous essays** came out in 1989 as *Travels with Alice*. Paul Theroux has made the persona of the grouchy rail traveler instantly recognizable; *The Great Railway Bazaar* (1975) was the first of many satiric travel books, and Theroux's travel essays appear in a wide variety of publications. Tim Cahill writes irreverent adventure travel articles for *Outside* and other magazines; two collections of his essays are *Jaguars Ripped My Flesh: Adventure Is a Risky Business* (1987) and *A Wolverine Is Eating My Leg* (1989).

Although the self-contained formal essay may not be best adapted to encompass the sprawling variety and multitudinousness of travel, the genre continues to flourish, often disguised as letters, sketches, impressions, portraits, or dispatches. Currently, travel essays of one sort or another appear in a wide range of newspapers and magazines; occasional issues of *Granta* are devoted to travel writing by contemporary authors.

HEATHER HENDERSON

Anthologies
A Book of Travellers' Tales, edited by Eric Newby, London: Collins, 1985; New York: Viking, 1986
Ladies on the Loose: Women Travellers of the 18th and 19th Centuries, edited by Leo Hamalian, New York: Dodd Mead, 1981
The Norton Book of Travel, edited by Paul Fussell, New York: Norton, 1987
The Spirit of Place: An Anthology of Travel Writings, edited by Michael Venter, Oxford and New York: Oxford University Press, 1992
A Taste for Travel: An Anthology, edited by John Julius Norwich, London: Macmillan, 1985; New York: Knopf, 1987

Travel Literature Through the Ages: An Anthology, edited by Percy G. Adams, New York: Garland, 1988

Further Reading
Adams, Percy G., *Travel Literature and the Evolution of the Novel*, Lexington: University Press of Kentucky, 1983
Batten, Charles L., Jr., *Pleasurable Instruction: Form and Convention in Eighteenth-Century Travel Literature*, Berkeley: University of California Press, 1978
Brown, Sharon Rogers, *American Travel Narratives as a Literary Genre from 1542 to 1832: The Art of a Perpetual Journey*, Lampeter, Dyfed, and Lewiston, New York: Mellen Press, 1993
Caesar, Terry, *Forgiving the Boundaries: Home as Abroad in American Travel Writing*, Athens: University of Georgia Press, 1995
Campbell, Mary B., *The Witness and the Other World: Exotic European Travel Writing 400–1600*, Ithaca, New York: Cornell University Press, 1988
Cocker, Mark, *Loneliness and Time: British Travel Writing in the Twentieth Century*, London: Secker and Warburg, and New York: Pantheon, 1992
Curley, Thomas M., *Samuel Johnson and the Age of Travel*, Athens: University of Georgia Press, 1976
Foster, Shirley, *Across New Worlds: Nineteenth-Century Women Travellers and Their Writings*, New York and London: Harvester Wheatsheaf, 1990
Frawley, Maria H., *A Wider Range: Travel Writing by Women in Victorian England*, Rutherford, New Jersey: Fairleigh Dickinson University Press, 1994
Fussell, Paul, *Abroad: British Literary Travelling Between the Wars*, New York and Oxford: Oxford University Press, 1980
Kowalewski, Michael, editor, *Temperamental Journeys: Essays on the Modern Literature of Travel*, Athens: University of Georgia Press, 1992
Lawrence, Karen R., *Penelope Voyages: Women and Travel in the British Literary Tradition*, Ithaca, New York: Cornell University Press, 1994
Middleton, Dorothy, *Victorian Lady Travelers*, New York: Dutton, and London: Routledge and Kegan Paul, 1965
Munter, Robert, and Clyde L. Grose, *Englishmen Abroad: Being an Account of Their Travels in the Seventeenth Century*, Lampeter, Dyfed and Lewiston, New York: Mellen Press, 1986
Porter, Dennis, *Haunted Journeys: Desire and Transgression in European Travel Writing*, Princeton, New Jersey: Princeton University Press, 1991
Pratt, Mary Louise, *Imperial Eyes: Travel Writing and Transculturation*, London: Routledge, 1992
Russell, Mary, *The Blessings of a Good Thick Skirt: Women Travellers and Their World*, London: Collins, 1988
Stowe, William W., *Going Abroad: European Travel in Nineteenth-Century American Culture*, Princeton, New Jersey: Princeton University Press, 1994

Treatise

Conventionally scientific, historical, or philosophical in theme, the treatise (from the Latin *tractatus*) is a text of variable length (sometimes of book length), which *treats* some particular topic by way of a formal, methodical exposition. As a description, account, or report of some topic under investigation, its literary effect today is secondary to its seriousness of purpose; but an earlier tradition also held the treatise to be a story, tale, or narrative, as in the stories of Chaucer's *Canterbury Tales*.

Once the major literary medium of scholasticism, the treatise is a nonfictional literary text that shares a border with the formal essay, and may thus be best understood by way of a comparison with the general essay form. The latter is an expository text organized into relatively short prose, readable in one sitting, and articulating the author's perception through an associative and open-ended synthesis of rigorous method and imaginative literature. The treatise, on the other hand, is a literary text in which the author typically retreats behind the methodological principles of logic and rationalism, of the syllogism and systematic objectivity. Continuous control and verification of results and conclusions are the goal in the discourse of a treatise. Critical approach, rigorous methodology, and a high degree of specialization, expertise, and seriousness – as evident in the avoidance of chance, subjectivity, and imaginative play – all characterize the treatise and distinguish it from the essay.

The innovation in a treatise's subject is generally not marked by its style, which restricts itself to reporting, describing, and deducing. In contrast, the originality of an essay, particularly the informal, occasional, or **familiar essay**, often proceeds from its form, structure, style, and tone, even though the essay may contain no new factual truths. Not only does the treatise proceed logically from steadfast premises, but the conventional treatise presents its truths as accomplished facts, as logical conclusions. It aims for completeness, remains with the matter at hand, and follows singlemindedly its explicit purpose, often to the point of pedantry.

The treatise reports or treats results obtained empirically or deductively. Neither aesthetic nor rhetorical principles of style contribute to its value; in fact, they may detract from it. Often, elaboration of form has been viewed with a good deal of suspicion as artistry attained at the expense of objectivity, rigor, precision, and scientific truth. Indeed, it could be said that when sophisticated and varied form and style occupy a prominent position in matters of structure, the text has changed from being a treatise to being an essay. Moreover, the closed, systematically ordered communication between writer and reader is monologic in a treatise, and does not involve the reader as a partner or respondent in its discourse. And the truths a treatise implies must exist beyond all doubt for both the writer and the reader: doubtful observations must be excluded from the treatise's realm.

Clearly, the methodological and rhetorical disparities between treatise and essay are a reflection of differences in the readership of these two literary forms. While the treatise instructs the specialized reader in scientific "truth," the essay persuades and entertains, by way of congenial conversation, the general reader of general interests.

RALPH W. BUECHLER

Further Reading

Burnett, Mark Thornton, "Masters and Servants in Moral and Religious Treatises, c. 1580–c. 1642," in *The Arts, Literature, and Society*, edited by Arthur Marwick, London and New York: Routledge, 1990

Dubrow, Heather, *Genre*, London: Methuen, 1982

Feyerabend, Paul, *Against Method: Outline of an Anarchistic Theory of Knowledge*, London and New York: Verso, 3rd edition, 1993 (original edition, 1975)

Kruse, Joseph, "Traktat," in *Reallexikon der deutschen Literaturgeschichte*, vol. 4, edited by Klaus Kanzog and Achim Masser, Berlin: de Gruyter, 1981

Lewalski, Barbara Kiefer, editor, *Renaissance Genres: Essays on Theory, History and Interpretation*, Cambridge, Massachusetts: Harvard University Press, 1986

Trilling, Lionel

American, 1905–1975

Though he wrote at least one masterful short story, a timely and respected novel, and books on two major authors, Lionel Trilling may be strongest in the essay form. His strong sense of "self" is suited to the compact and intense first-person expression of the essay. His first-person point of view is characteristically plural for the reasons he self-consciously outlines in the **preface** to his third collection, *Beyond Culture* (1965), and the compactness of his essays often embraces extensive complexity. Nevertheless, the short form geared to strong statements about modern culture, rather than strict literary criticism or theory, is Trilling's hallmark. Further, despite his embracing the trendy Freudian thought of mid-century and his frequent evoking of the vaunted liberalism of New York intellectuals (the jeremiahs of our time), Trilling as essayist and cultural critic is strangely anachronistic. He is best at his version of **Matthew Arnold**'s moves toward general ideas of humanness. He is even reminiscent of a moralist like the **Samuel Johnson** whose mentors had advised "first get general principles." Hence Trilling is often dismissed both by more practical liberals and by more incisive critics of modern literature as old-fashioned and even stuffy. But his several dozen strong essays remain in print as a voice for the old human values of opposition and struggle.

Learning again from Arnold and maybe even from Dr. Johnson himself, Trilling consciously analyzes his own high seriousness of both intent and rhetoric when he talks about his use of "we" in the short prefatory essay to his third collection. He gently wants to nudge what he calls "the temper of our age" toward the serious contemplation of selfhood and value. Similarly, in the important preface to his first collection *The Liberal Imagination* (1950), which won him immediate fame as a cultural critic, Trilling defines the nature of and the reasons for another key characteristic of his style – his continual folding back on himself with qualification and complexity. He points out that one role for the liberal thinker is to simplify issues in order to move toward progress; but it is that move to simplification and system that he continually opposes. His essays as a whole, as well as the separate parts of essays, demonstrate the reality for Trilling of variety and complexity and of the heroic benefits derived from oppositions, even within the self, so that in the end any first-person plural consensus becomes buried in time and complexity. In other words, Trilling's old-fashioned commitment to broad human values, with a full awareness of how complex those might be, places him in constant opposition to the practical movements of his own time.

One of Trilling's heroes of selfhood is the poet John Keats, but his essay on Keats that heads his second collection, *The Opposing Self* (1955), is not about the poetry but rather the **letters**. Similarly, his exciting early essay on Wordsworth's "Intimations of Immortality," which has helped many with the ode over the years, strangely is not much about the poetry itself but rather about ideas. Trilling admitted that he preferred the 19th-century novel, in which social ideas are more important than the language experimentation of Modernist novels; this preference is more evidence of his commitment to a general humanism.

Finally, then, there is an abstractness and, perhaps, an honest and self-conscious anachronism at the heart of Trilling's work with the essay. He is at odds with himself. If he were primarily known for his fiction, or even as a crafty poet (and Trilling is capable of very crafty writing), he might seem more concrete and fixed to his readers. Instead Trilling achieved fame in the essay by acknowledging the essay almost as a secondary form. He qualifies and opposes himself at the same time that he insists on our need to commit to society and to literature. Thus, somewhere between the poignancy of a **personal essay**ist such as Lamb and the practicality of a new thinker such as **Freud**, Trilling's several collections of essays waver as the cultural criticism of a qualified and qualifying man. For him this civility is part of being a gentleman. He was indeed a gentle man.

DONALD M. HASSLER

Biography
Born 4 July 1905 in New York. Studied at Columbia University, New York, 1921–26, B.A., 1925, M.A., 1926, Ph.D., 1938. Worked for the *Menorah Journal*, New York, 1923–31; taught at the University of Wisconsin, Madison, 1926–27, Hunter College, New York, 1928–34, and Columbia University, 1932–75; visiting professor or Fellow, Oxford University, 1964–65, Harvard University, Cambridge, Massachusetts, 1969–70, and All Souls College, Oxford, 1972–73. Married Diana Rubin (i.e. the writer Diana Trilling), 1929: one son. Member of the editorial board, *Kenyon Review* and *Partisan Review*. Awards: Mark Van Doren Award; Thomas Jefferson Award; Brandeis University Creative Arts Award; honorary degrees from eight universities. Member, American Academy of Arts and Sciences, 1951. Died in New York, 5 November 1975.

Selected Writings

Essays and Related Prose
The Liberal Imagination: Essays on Literature and Society, 1950
The Opposing Self: Nine Essays in Criticism, 1955
A Gathering of Fugitives, 1956
Beyond Culture: Essays on Literature and Learning, 1965
Sincerity and Authenticity (lectures), 1972
The Last Decade: Essays and Reviews, edited by Diana Trilling, 1979
Prefaces to the Experience of Literature, 1979
Speaking of Literature and Society, edited by Diana Trilling, 1980

Other writings: the novel *The Middle of the Journey* (1947), short stories, and books on Matthew Arnold and **E. M. Forster**.

Collected works edition: *Works* (Uniform Edition), edited by Diana Trilling, 12 vols., 1978–80.

Bibliographies
Barnaby, Marianne Gilbert, "Lionel Trilling: A Bibliography, 1926–1972," *Bulletin of Bibliography* (January–March 1974): 37–44
Leitch, Thomas M., *Lionel Trilling: An Annotated Bibliography*, New York: Garland, 1993

Further Reading
Anderson, Quentin, Stephen Donadio, and Steven Marcus, editors, *Art, Politics, and Will: Essays in Honor of Lionel Trilling*, New York: Basic Books, 1977
Boyers, Robert, *Lionel Trilling: Negative Capability and the Wisdom of Avoidance*, Columbia: University of Missouri Press, 1977
Chace, William M., *Lionel Trilling: Criticism and Politics*, Stanford, California: Stanford University Press, 1980
French, Philip, *Three Honest Men: Edmund Wilson, F. R. Leavis, Lionel Trilling: A Critical Mosaic*, Manchester: Carcanet, 1980
Krupnick, Mark, *Lionel Trilling and the Fate of Cultural Criticism*, Evanston, Illinois: Northwestern University Press, 1986
Scott, Nathan A., Jr., *Three American Moralists: Mailer, Bellow, Trilling*, Notre Dame, Indiana: University of Notre Dame Press, 1973
Shoben, Edward Joseph, Jr., *Lionel Trilling*, New York: Ungar, 1981
Tanner, Stephen L., *Lionel Trilling*, Boston: Twayne, 1988
Trilling, Diana, *The Beginning of the Journey*, New York: Harcourt Brace Jovanovich, 1993

Trottier, Pierre
French Canadian, 1925–

First known as a poet with *Le Combat contre Tristan* (1951; The fight against Tristan), Pierre Trottier is a writer of memory, roots, erudition, and culture, no less than a man of professional travels and life in old foreign cities (Moscow, Jakarta, Paris, Lima). His poems from Russia are obsessed with exile, strangeness, origins, identity, and differentiation. *Les Belles au bois dormant* (1960; The beauties in the sleeping woods) are not fairytales but a gallery of women and men (widow, virgin, private soldier, rebel with or without a cause) of all conditions. *Sainte-Mémoire* (1972; Saint Memory) is a collection of returns and reconsiderations: to Oedipus, Don Quixote, Canadian winter, the concept of zero as scratch or as starting point. Time must not only be (re)collected, but corrected; his apparent simplicity, legibility, is a catch.

The 17 short essays of *Mon Babel* (1963; My Babel) deal with lost paradises and new horizons throughout Greek, French, and English classics. Trottier tries to translate, to adapt his Canadian or North American situation in space and time. He connects ideas as he opposes and links landscapes, seasons, ages, sexes. He contrasts cold, clear, sunny Canadian winters with wet, cloudy, dull European winters. He looks at the white plains with the eyes of a nonfigurative painter, Paul-Émile Borduas, chief of the Automatistes group and author of *Refus global* (1948; Global refusal), an influential manifesto against the Dark Ages ("la grande Noirceur") of conservatism, clericalism, and academicism.

Un pays baroque (1979; A baroque country) is lively, tortuous, witty, and moving. From the scholastic, self-styled "Status questionis" to an open conclusion called "Ephphata," it contains 13 assorted essays, sketches, monologues, comedies, parodies, and morality plays, with a blithe mix of Latin, Greek, Aramaic, Amerindian titles, proverbs, and slogans. Canada is seen as a paradoxical country on account of its geophysics, geopolitics, history, and no-story; it is a railway, a seaway, a highway *a mari usque ad mare* (from sea to sea) along the border of the United States.

Trottier's most recent collection of essays, *Ma dame à la licorne* (1988; My lady of the unicorn), is his most autobiographical, full of dreams, readings, and encounters. "Nostalgia taught me curiosity," he says. This book is a celebration of woman as mother of life, myth, language, and art. Before being born in (and from) a country, every man comes from (and in) a woman.

Trottier's wor(l)d trip is a love trip among Latin and Russian etymologies, encompassing Jivago, Malenkov, Molotov, but most of all *doucha* (soul) and *doukh* (spirit). Trottier's essays are also, often, pieces of poetry in prose.

LAURENT MAILHOT

Biography

Born 21 March 1925 in Montreal. Studied at the Jesuit Collèges de Sainte-Marie and Jean-de-Brébeuf, B.A., 1942; Law School of the University of Montreal, law degree, 1945. Secretary to the Chamber of Commerce, Montreal; joined the Department of External Affairs, Ottawa, 1949: diplomatic posts in Moscow, 1951–54 and 1970–73, Jakarta, 1956–57, London, 1954–61, and Paris, 1964–68. Married Barbara Theis, 1952: two daughters and one son. Associated with the Center for International Affairs, Harvard University, Cambridge, Massachusetts; Ambassador to Peru, 1973–76; diplomatic adviser to the Governor-General of Canada, 1976–79; Ambassador to UNESCO, 1969–84. Awards: David Prize, 1963; Society of Men of Letters Prize, for poetry, 1964. Member, Royal Society of Canada, 1978.

Selected Writings

Essays and Related Prose
Mon Babel, 1963
Un pays baroque, 1979
Ma dame à la licorne, 1988

Other writings: many collections of poems, collected in *Sainte-Mémoire* (1972) and *En vallées closes: Poèmes 1951–1986* (1989).

Bibliography

Hamel, Réginald, John Hare, and Paul Wyczynski, *Dictionnaire des auteurs de langue française en Amérique du Nord*, Montreal: Fides, 1989: 1308–09

Further Reading

Archambault, Gilles, "*Mon Babel*, de Pierre Trottier," in *Livres et auteurs canadiens 1963*, Montreal: Jurmonville, 1964: 87–89
Dorais, Fernand, "*Mon Babel*, essai de Pierre Trottier," in *Dictionnaire des œuvres littéraires du Québec*, vol. 4, edited by Maurice Lemire, Montreal: Fides, 1984: 584–85
Grandpré, Pierre de, "*Mon Babel*, de Pierre Trottier," in his *Dix Ans de vie littéraire au Canada français*, Montreal: Beauchemin, 1966: 234–41
Marcotte, Gilles, "Diplomate, essayiste et poète: Pierre Trottier . . ." *Québec* (October 1964): 92–95
Morency, Jean, "*Un pays baroque*, essai de Pierre Trottier," in *Dictionnaire des œuvres littéraires du Québec*, vol. 6, edited by Maurice Lemire, Montreal: Fides, 1994: 864–65
Pavelich, Joan, *Pierre Trottier, poète et essayiste* (M.A. dissertation), Montreal: University of Montreal, 1979
Vachon, Georges-André, "Pour une morale du risque," *Québec* (October 1964): 126–27

Tsvetaeva, Marina

Russian, 1892–1941

Marina Tsvetaeva's prose has always been to some extent the naughty stepchild of her poetry. Even after she had gained recognition as a world-class poet, a distinction dating from 1960, if not before, her prose continued to be regarded as "painfully pretentious and obscure" (D. S. Mirsky, *A History of Russian Literature*, 1960). Despite the hostile critical reception, she produced a sizable body of prose covering a wide range of nonfictional genres. Among these, perhaps the best known are her autobiographical sketches, especially her masterful trilogy "Dom u Starogo Pimena" (1933; "The House at Old Pimen"), "Mat' i muzyka" (1935; "My Mother and Music"), and "Moi Pushkin" (1937; "My Pushkin"), but they also include memoirs, travel sketches, diaries, and prose portraits of her famous contemporaries in the Silver Age of Russian literature, such as Maximilian Voloshin ("Zhivoe o zhivom" [1933; "A Living Word About a Living Man"]), **Andrei Belyi** ("Plennyi dukh" [1934; "A Captive Spirit"]), and Valerii Briusov ("Geroi truda" [1925; A hero of labor]). They appear as genres more familiar to Western readers (the book **review** and the ***feuilleton***), as well as some brilliant and highly idiosyncratic forays into literary history and criticism: an appreciation of her beloved contemporary Pasternak ("Svetovoi liven'" [1922; "A Downpour of Light"]), a comparison of Pasternak and Maiakovskii ("Epos i lirika sovremennoi rossii" [1932; "Epic and Lyric in Contemporary Russia"]), and theoretical essays ("Iskusstvo pri svete sovesti" [1932; "Art in the Light of Conscience"], "Poet i vremia" [1932; "The Poet and Time"], and "Poety s istoriei i poety bez istorii" [1934; "Poets with a History and Poets Without a History"]).

Tsvetaeva's prose covers nearly the entire span of her creative career. As J. Marin King's ground-breaking translations (published in *A Captive Spirit*, 1980) indicate, it can be divided into three periods with some overlap. The first period extends from 1917 to 1921 and contains predominantly diaries and prose sketches culled from her experiences in the Russian Revolutions of 1917 and the Civil War. The second (1922 to 1932) is devoted to essays on poets and writers, the nature of creativity, and the ethics of writing. The third period extends from 1934 to 1937. During this period myth and memory merged to produce the most memorable of the prose portraits as well as the landmark autobiographical sketches. As King also indicates, the thematic and chronological continuity among the autobiographical sketches suggests that Tsvetaeva viewed them not independently but as **chapters** of an autobiography.

Undoubtedly the main reason why Tsvetaeva's prose did not initially receive the recognition it deserved is its extreme difficulty. Hers is a powerful prose that delights in flexing its muscles. In its terseness it resembles a form of personal shorthand. Transitions are replaced by dashes linking unrelated, even antithetical ideas. Paragraphs are reduced to a single sentence, and sentences to a single word. The reduction of the text to its smallest structural unit is a deliberate Tsvetaevan strategy. For her, the word is not an empty signifier but a repository of sound, and sound generates meaning. This is demonstrated by her favorite technique of taking a single word and from it deriving an entire chain of auditory and thematic associations. Unfortunately, these chains of association are often so personal that they leave the uninitiated reader bewildered.

The question of Tsvetaeva's relationship to her reader has received much critical attention because it was unique, even in the age of formal experimentation in which she wrote. Although a great admirer of **Montaigne** and **Sainte-Beuve**, she has neither their discursive style nor their critical distance. Instead she adopts an uncompromising attitude toward her reader, keeping up a rapid-fire barrage of indicatives, interrogatives, direct address, and interpolated asides representing either her own "alternate" voice or the reader's assumed reply. From this, both **Joseph Brodsky** (1986) and Angela Livingstone (introduction to Tsvetaeva's *Art in the Light of Consciousness*, 1992) conclude that her style is dialogic, while King emphasizes that it has the sound and rhythm of a live human voice. This too is a deliberate strategy on Tsvetaeva's part. She provokes the reader into joining her in the spirit of "cocreation": ". . . what is reading if not deciphering, interpreting, drawing out something secret, something behind the lines, beyond the limits of words. (Not to mention the difficulties of syntax!) Reading is – above all – co-creating" ("Poet o kritik" [1926; "The Poet on the Critic"]).

No less unique is the structure of her essays, which strikes us by its lack of inductive argument. She typically begins by stating a paradox. She then develops one branch of the paradox as far as possible. Returning to her point of origin, she develops the opposite branch until she reaches a point where the two meet, like a pair of clasped arms. In the process, she consistently elevates the level of argument until she reaches a conclusion, most often couched in the form of an **aphorism**. Tsvetaeva was addicted to aphorisms, and hers are particularly rewarding: "Every poet is essentially an émigré . . . émigré from the Kingdom of Heaven and from the earthly paradise of nature . . . An émigré from immortality in time, a non-returner to his *own* heaven" ("The Poet and Time").

Tsvetaeva wrote the bulk of her prose in emigration and published in various Russian émigré periodicals based in Prague, Berlin, and Paris: *Volia Rossii* (Russia's will), *Chisla* (Dates), *Poslednie Novosti* (The latest news), *Sovremennye Zapiski* (Contemporary annals), to name but a few. The process was far from smooth: her longer essays were subjected to brutal editorial cuts, and two projected book-length collections, the one of her Civil War diaries, the other of her **critical essays**, never materialized for lack of a publisher. Ironically, it was her prose that ultimately shaped her fate in emigration. Her scathing attack of 1926 on the Russian émigré literary establishment, "The Poet on the Critic," caused an outraged community to ostracize her, thus depriving her of an audience. Only since the 1980s has her stature as a brilliant memoirist and profound essayist been conclusively established.

LAURA D. WEEKS

Biography

Marina Ivanovna Tsvetaeva. Born 26 September 1892 in Moscow. Studied at schools in Switzerland and Germany, and at the Sorbonne, Paris. Married Sergei Efron, 1912 (executed, 1939): two daughters (one starved to death) and one son. Trapped in Moscow for five years after the 1917 Revolution; left Russia, 1922, for Berlin, Prague, and finally Paris, 1925; returned to Russia, 1939, but officially ostracized and unable to publish. Died (suicide by hanging) in Elabuga, 31 August 1941.

Selected Writings

Essays and Related Prose
Proza, 1953
Izbrannaia proza v dvukh tomakh, 1917–1937, 2 vols., 1979
A Captive Spirit: Selected Prose, translated by J. Marin King, 1980
Proza, edited by A. A. Saakiants, 1989
Ob iskusstve (On art), 1991
Gde otstypaetsia liubov' (Where love renounces), 1991
Art in the Light of Conscience: Eight Essays on Poetry, translated by Angela Livingstone, 1992

Other writings: ten volumes of poetry and much correspondence.

Collected works editions: *Stikhotvoreniia i poemy v piati tomakh*, edited by Alexander Sumerkin and Viktoria Schweitzer, 5 vols., 1980–90; *Sobranie sochinenii*, 7 vols., 1994–95.

Bibliography
Gladkova, Tatiana, and Lev Mnukhin, *Bibliographie des œuvres de Marina Tsvetayeva*, Paris: Institut d'Études Slaves, 1982

Further Reading
Baer, Joachim T., "Three Variations on the Theme 'Moi Pushkin': Briusov, Akhmatova, Tsvetaeva," *Transactions of the Association of Russian-American Scholars in the U.S.A.* 20 (1987): 163–83
Brodsky, Joseph, "A Poet and Prose," in his *Less than One: Selected Essays*, New York: Farrar Straus Giroux, and London: Viking, 1986
Chester, Pamela, "Engaging Sexual Demons in Marina Tsvetaeva's 'Devil': The Body and the Genesis of the Woman Poet," *Slavic Review* 53, no. 4 (1994)
Feiler, Lily, *Marina Tsvetaeva: The Double Beat of Heaven and Hell*, Durham, North Carolina: Duke University Press, 1994
Feinstein, Elaine, *A Captive Lion: The Life of Marina Tsvetayeva*, London: Hutchinson, and New York: Dutton, 1987
Forrester, Sibelan, "Marina Tsvetaeva as Literary Critic and Critic of Literary Critics," in *Russian Writers on Russian Writers*, edited by Faith Wigzell and Robin Aizelwood, Oxford: Berg, 1994
Gifford, Henry, "Joseph Brodsky on Marina Tsvetaeva," in *Russian Writers on Russian Writers*, edited by Faith Wigzell and Robin Aizelwood, Oxford: Berg, 1994
Karlinsky, Simon, *Marina Tsvetaeva: The Woman, Her World and Her Poetry*, Cambridge: Cambridge University Press, 1985
Knapp, Liza, "Tsvetaeva's Two Goncharovas," in *Cultural Mythologies of Russian Modernism: From the Golden Age to the Silver Age*, edited by Boris Gasparov, Robert P. Hughes, and Irina Paperno, Berkeley: University of California Press, 1992
Korkina, Elena, "'Pushkin i Pugachev': Liricheskoe rassledovanie Mariny Tsvetaevoi," in *Marina Tsvetaeva: One Hundred Years: Papers from the Tsvetaeva Centenary Symposium*, edited by Viktoria Schweitzer and others, Berkeley, California: Berkeley Slavic Specialties, 1994
Kroth, Anya M., "The Poet and Time in Marina Tsvetaeva's Philosophical Essays," in *Russian Literature and American Critics: In Honor of Deming B. Brown*, edited by Kenneth N. Brostrom, Ann Arbor: University of Michigan Department of Slavic Languages and Literatures, 1984
Lossky, Véronique, *Marina Tsvetaeva: Un Itinéraire poétique*, Paris: Solin, 1987

Mnatsakanova, Elizaveta, "O roli detskogo vospominaniia v psikhologii khudozhestvennogo tvorchestva: Na primere prozy Mariny Tsvetaevoi i dvukh otryvok iz romana F. M. Dostoevskogo 'Brat'ia Karamazovy'," *Wiener Slawistischer Almanach* 19 (1982): 325–49

Schweitzer, Viktoria, *Tsvetaeva*, edited and annotated by Angela Livingstone, London: Harvill Press, 1992; New York: Farrar Straus Giroux, 1993

Smith, Alexandra, "The Cnidus Myth and Tsvetaeva's Interpretation of Pushkin's Love for N. Goncharova," *Essays in Poetics* 14, no. 2 (1989): 83–102

Taubman, Jane A., *A Life Through Poetry: Marina Tsvetaeva's Lyric Diary*, Columbus, Ohio: Slavica, 1989

Turgenev, Ivan

Russian, 1818–1883

Apollon Grigor'ev, a 19th-century Russian critic, complained that Ivan Turgenev set no straight course and consequently was "subject to all winds, the stirrings of a breeze" and its gossamer waftings. What was a shortcoming for Grigor'ev is serendipity for the modern reader, for without a manifest ideology and program Turgenev became the sensitive eye and ear of his era. He was attuned to the most subtle changes in societal temperature and weather. Though only two of his 28 volumes of works and **letters** are composed of essays and other articles, these range in subject from the psychic life of a dog ("Pegaz" [1871; Pegasus]), to coverage and analysis of the Franco-Prussian War, to an appreciation of the ruins of the temple of Zeus discovered in Pergamon in 1878. Turgenev produced travel articles, **reviews** of literature, music, and art, cultural commentary, ethnographic sketches, **reportage**, reminiscences of famous friends, and obituaries, as well as a currently archaic form, the prepared speech for significant occasions – an oral essay. In a highly politicized time in Russian history the above appeared in diverse magazines and newspapers such as the *Russkii Vestnik* (Russian courier), *Vestnik Evropy* (Courier of Europe), *Sovremennik* (The contemporary), *Novoe Vremia* (New times), *Spb Vedomosti* (St. Petersburg news), *Nedelia* (The week), *Moskovskii Vestnik* (Moscow courier), and even the *Zhurnal Okhoty i Konnozavodstva* (Hunter's and horseman's journal).

Turgenev saw himself as living during an era of transition in Russian culture and history (Vospominanie ob A. A. Ivanove" [1861; "Reminiscences of Ivanov"]). For him Russia was a powerful nation but in an embryonic state of unformed corporate institutions and unattended tensions. He was at once very Russian and an exemplar of a European-wide high culture. Turgenev was fluent in Russian, French, and German, knew English and Italian, and read in the classical languages. So proficient was he in French that he could differentiate between the dialects of Provence and Gascony. He was well versed in the principal European traditions of literary criticism and the serious essay of social and political commentary, citing numerous French practitioners of the craft and especially valuing **Gotthold Ephraim Lessing** in German and **Thomas Babington Macaulay** in English. He was an astute critic of the arts, knowledgeable in technique, historical significance, and effect. In many respects he prefigures his younger

contemporary, **Walter Pater**. With such scope Turgenev naturally eschewed the utilitarian notion of a writer being driven by a particular agenda or by the projection of his own ideas into his art ("Po povodu *Otsov i detei*" [1869; "On *Fathers and Sons*"]).

Turgenev's first true essay, "Les i step'" (1849; "The Forest and the Steppe") – published first in *Sovremennik* and then as an appendage to his *Zapiski okhotnika* (1852; *A Sportsman's Sketches*) – began a tradition of reflections on the significance of human life and its meaning. It deals specifically with immutable nature, the transience of the manifest, and the obscurity of the transcendent. This theme casts a constant shadow over his dominant idealism. Like most intellectuals of the time Turgenev believed in universal progress, both material and spiritual, thus revealing his Hegelian inheritance and the fruits of his philosophical studies in Berlin. Literature (and literary criticism) to him was the royal road to understanding culture and the self. Turgenev held this belief perhaps more fervently than either **Dostoevskii** or **Tolstoi**, who themselves embraced alternative systems as well. Art for Turgenev was not so much for entertainment as it was for the education of sensibility, although there is some dissonance between his views of literature as keeper of civic consciousness (the 1860s) and intimate salon literature (1830s and 1840s), as exemplified in "Literaturnyi vecher u P. A. Pletneva" (1869; "A Literary Evening at Pletnev's"). Scrupulously dispassionate and evenhanded in his reminiscences, he praises both Timofei Granovskii and Nikolai Stankevich for their accomplishments, though he adores the first and is cool toward the second. In "Vospominaniia o Belinskom" (1869; "Reminiscences on Belinskii") he praises love of country while discrediting chauvinism and self-styled defenders of the motherland. In another essay Turgenev reveals a subtle psychological sense that sees the notorious Jean Baptiste Tropmann ("Kazn' Tropmana" [1870; "The Execution of Tropmann"]) on the morning of his execution as giving a bravura "stage performance" to the assembled distinguished witnesses and thus keeping himself from disintegrating into hysterics. After the beheading none of the company feels that an act of justice has taken place.

Of the greats, Turgenev esteems **Pushkin** (e.g. his speech at the dedication of the monument to Pushkin in 1881, a major event in the history of Russian culture), Shakespeare (a speech at the celebration in 1864 of the 300th anniversary of Shakespeare's birth), and Gogol' ("Gogol'," 1869), with a caveat for his retrogressive piety. Authenticity, enlightenment, freedom, and courage are the traits he values in the artist and the citizen. He praises Pushkin's classical sense of measure and harmony but sees it as devalued by his contemporaries.

Turgenev lived in the post-Christian world of the intelligentsia but with the residual gift of having the Enlightenment and Christian ethics as sources of his values. He professed an aesthetic humanism which was an anachronism to many of his contemporaries. He believed that the engagement with art took the self into a meta-reality where choices, explorations, and seductions had no external constraining consequences. The self is thereby liberated from its linear public life and becomes free to make radical choices, run risks, assume alien identities, and spar with powerful opponents. It returns from this world aware of styles and choices which are normally closed to it. Thus exploring the ambiguity and multiplicity of meaning in art makes us intellectually agile, physically elegant, and spiritually tolerant.

GEORGE S. PAHOMOV

Biography

Born 9 November 1818 in Orel. Studied at Moscow University, 1833–34; University of St. Petersburg, 1834–37; University of Berlin, 1838–41; completed his master's exam in St. Petersburg, 1842. Civil servant, Ministry of the Interior, 1843–45. Intimate friendship with Pauline Garcia-Viardot, traveling to France with her and her husband, 1845–46 and 1847–50. Had a daughter by one of his serfs. Arrested and confined to his estate for writing a commemorative article on Gogol's death, 1852–53. Left Russia to live in Western Europe, 1856, first in Baden-Baden, then Paris with the Viardots, 1871–83. Doctor of Civil Laws: Oxford University, 1879. Died in Bougival, near Paris, 3 September 1883.

Selected Writings

Essays and Related Prose

Literaturnye i zhiteiskie vospominaniia, 1874; revised edition, 1880; as Literary Reminiscences and Autobiographical Fragments, translated by David Magarshack, 1958

Other writings: many novels (including Zapiski okhotnika [A Sportsman's Sketches], 1852; Rudin, 1856; Dvorianskoe gnezdo [A Nest of the Gentry], 1859; Nakanune [On the Eve], 1860; Ottsy i deti [Fathers and Sons], 1862), novellas (including Pervaia liubov' [First Love], 1860), stories, plays (including Mesiats v derevne [A Month in the Country], 1869), poetry, and correspondence.

Collected works editions: Polnoe sobranie sochinenii i pisem, 28 vols., 1960–68; Polnoe sobranie sochinenii i pisem, edited by M. P. Alekseev, 30 vols., 1978.

Bibliographies

Waddington, Patrick, A Bibliography of Writings by and About Turgenev Published in Great Britain up to 1900, Wellington, New Zealand: Victoria University of Wellington Department of Russian, 1985

Yachnin, Rissa, and David H. Stam, Turgenev in English: A Checklist of Works by and About Him, New York: New York Public Library, 1962

Zekulin, Nicholas G., Turgenev: A Bibliography of Books, 1843–1982 by and About Ivan Turgenev, Calgary, Alberta: Calgary University Press, 1985

Further Reading

Costlow, Jane T., Worlds Within Worlds: The Novels of Ivan Turgenev, Princeton, New Jersey: Princeton University Press, 1990

Freeborn, Richard, Turgenev: The Novelist's Novelist, Westport, Connecticut: Greenwood Press, 1978 (original edition, 1960)

Gifford, H., "Turgenev," in Nineteenth-Century Russian Literature: Studies of Ten Russian Writers, edited by J. L. I. Fennell, Berkeley: University of California Press, and London: Faber, 1973

Granjard, Henri, Ivan Tourguénev et les courants politiques et sociaux de son temps, Paris: Institut d'Études Slaves, 1954

Hellgren, Ludmila, Dialogue in Turgenev's Novels: Speech-Introductory Devices, Stockholm: Almqvist & Wiksell, 1980

Jackson, R. L., "The Root and the Flower: Dostoevsky and Turgenev: A Comparative Esthetic," Yale Review (Winter 1974): 228–50

Jackson, R. L., "The Turgenev Question," Sewanee Review 93 (1985): 300–09

Kagan-Kans, Eva, Hamlet and Don-Quixote: Turgenev's Ambivalent Vision, The Hague: Mouton, 1975

Ledkovsky, Marina, The Other Turgenev: From Romanticism to Symbolism, Würzburg: Jal, 1973

Lednicki, Waclaw, Bits of Table Talk on Pushkin, Mickiewicz, Goethe, Turgenev and Sienkiewicz, The Hague: Nijhoff, 1956

Peterson, Dale E., The Clement Vision: Poetic Realism in Turgenev and James, Port Washington, New York: Kennikat Press, 1975

Ripp, Victor, Turgenev's Russia: From "Notes of a Hunter" to "Fathers and Sons", Ithaca, New York: Cornell University Press, 1980

Schapiro, Leonard, Turgenev: His Life and Times, Oxford: Oxford University Press, and New York: Random House, 1978

Seeley, Frank Friedeberg, Turgenev: A Reading of His Fiction, Cambridge: Cambridge University Press, 1991

Waddington, Patrick, Turgenev and England, London: Macmillan, 1980; New York: New York University Press, 1981

Waddington, Patrick, Ivan Turgenev and Britain, Oxford: Berg, 1995

Walicki, A., "Turgenev and Schopenhauer," Oxford Slavonic Papers 10 (1962): 1–17

Wilson, Edmund, Introduction to Literary Reminiscences and Autobiographical Fragments by Turgenev, New York: Farrar Straus and Cudahy, 1958; London: Faber, 1959

Twain, Mark

American, 1835–1910

Mark Twain produced a considerable number of essays during his long writing career. But since he frequently combined fictional and nonfictional elements in his short works, Twain's writing, as his editors have often noted, cannot always be easily classified according to traditional literary categories such as the short story or essay, making it difficult at times precisely to determine his output within a specific genre. His versatility as an essayist is shown by the broad range of essay forms he mastered: travel letters, sketches, articles, memoirs, literary and art criticism, social and political commentary, and philosophical treatises. Writing on an astonishing variety of topics, ranging from such trivial matters as curing a cold or riding a bicycle to the major cultural and social issues of his time, Twain attracted a large and diverse audience. His essays appeared in various newspapers and in magazines with a wide readership, including the Galaxy and Harper's, as well as in the more prestigious and literary publications such as the Atlantic Monthly and the North American Review.

Twain's immense skill as a humorist greatly contributed to his popular appeal and became a hallmark of his writing style, which is also distinguished by his innovative use of narrative and rhetorical devices and an ability to render with accuracy and clarity the physical and emotional texture of places and events. His "Sandwich Islands" letters (1873), for example, vividly describe the exotic life and customs of the Hawaiians while humorously exposing the ways the missionaries and the American government have corrupted their idyllic existence. Annexation is necessary, Twain ironically declares, so that "we can afflict them with our wise and beneficent government." In "Queen Victoria's Jubilee" (1897), Twain presents a detailed portrait of another world – the pomp and pageantry of an English royal procession. He varies the narrative structure of this essay by incorporating the device of an imaginary account, told by a "spiritual correspondent," of the procession celebrating Henry V's victory at Agincourt in 1415 to reflect upon England's material progress and growth as a world power in the 19th century.

Writing on diverse social and political issues in his **polemical essays**, Twain used his talent as a satirist artfully to reveal and attack various forms of hypocrisy, injustice, and oppression. Though his views are not always consistent, he is recognized today as an important social commentator and reformist. Particularly effective in these essays is the way in which Twain creates satiric irony by his skillful control of point of view. Narrating "The Czar's Soliloquy" (1905) and "King Leopold's Soliloquy" (1905) in the form of a dramatic monologue, Twain condemns the political evils caused by despotism by having the rulers ironically reveal their crimes while attempting to defend themselves. This device works especially well in the latter essay in which Leopold's exploitation of the Congo, which included the murder, mutilation, and enslavement of millions of Congolese, is forcefully documented in the reports he reads. Oblivious to the truth this material contains, Leopold develops ridiculous and self-serving arguments to refute the charges against him.

One of the most important ways Twain uses point of view to create **satire** in his essays, and one which has received considerable critical attention, is the development of fictional narrators to express views that are in opposition to his own. The speaker in "Disgraceful Persecution of a Boy" (1870), whom John Gerber (1962) identifies as an example of the "Moralist" in his seven categories of masks Twain assumes, describes how society and its institutions condition its members to accept and perpetuate injustices against the Chinese; yet he ironically fails to recognize that racism and the evils it causes are wrong. Believing, instead, that a boy who was arrested on his way to Sunday school for stoning a Chinaman was doing the "high and holy thing" society taught him, the speaker is outraged because the boy is being unjustly punished for doing his "duty."

Although Twain continued to use elements of the comic tradition he learned from the Southwest humorists during his early years as a journalist (e.g. burlesque, exaggeration, and narrative poses), his later polemical and **philosophical essays** have more affinity with the invective style of **Swift** and **Voltaire**. Speaking in his own voice rather than using a persona in "To the Person Sitting in Darkness" (1901), Twain produced his finest satire of imperialism by masterfully interweaving numerous rhetorical devices into the pattern of his argument: metaphors, puns, allusions, symbolism, irony, and understatement. Using the metaphor of the "Blessings-of-Civilization Trust" to represent the Western governments and the Christian missionaries, he develops a lengthy discussion of how their exploitation of the Chinese, South Africans, and Filipinos has become so blatant that the people in darkness are beginning to see "more light than . . . was profitable for us." With Swiftian irony, Twain presents his modest proposal to solve this problem by recommending that Trust return to the former practice of concealing its true motives under the guise of offering the people the "blessings of civilization" so it "can resume Business at the old stand."

Firmly committed to the principles of realism in his own writing, Twain also used them when judging the literary merit of other authors. In a skillfully developed and **humorous essay**, Twain presents a devastating attack on James Fenimore Cooper's Leatherstocking novels (despite his failure to appreciate the conventions of romantic fiction) for their lack of verisimilitude in characterization, plot action, and dialogue, and for Cooper's verbose and inaccurate style ("Fenimore Cooper's Literary Offences," 1895). In contrast, he praises **William Dean Howells'** "sustained" achievement as a great stylist; and in his insightful analysis of nonfiction passages written by his fellow realist, Twain reveals the qualities he sought in his own prose: "clearness, compression, verbal exactness, and unforced and seemingly unconscious felicity of phrasing" ("William Dean Howells," 1906). In addition, Twain exhibits his ability to marshal evidence, uncover faulty reasoning and logic, and expose pretentious and dishonest writing in his carefully crafted essay attacking Edward Dowden's biography of **Percy Bysshe Shelley** ("In Defense of Harriet Shelley," 1894).

Although Twain has long been recognized as a major literary artist, his essays have not been given as much critical attention as those written by other important 19th-century American novelists such as **Henry James** and William Dean Howells. This is due in part to the topical nature of some of his writing and the difficulty at times of classifying his short fictional and nonfictional works. However, the literary importance of his essays, particularly the later ones, continues to be re-evaluated (e.g. William Macnaughton, 1979). Furthermore, the work being done by the Mark Twain Project in publishing the definitive editions of Twain's writing should greatly contribute to the reassessment of his accomplishments in all genres – including the essay.

RONALD J. BLACK

See also Satiric Essay

Biography

Born Samuel Langhorne Clemens, 30 November 1835 in Florida, Missouri. Moved to Hannibal, Missouri, 1839. Printer's apprentice and typesetter for Hannibal newspapers, 1847–50, and worked on the Hannibal *Journal*, 1850–52; printer and typesetter in St. Louis, New York, and Philadelphia, for the Keokuk *Saturday Post*, Iowa, 1853–56, and in Cincinnati, 1857. Apprentice river pilot on the Mississippi, 1857–58, and pilot, 1859–60; secretary to his brother in Nevada, and worked as a goldminer, 1861. Staff member, Virginia City *Territorial Enterprise*, Nevada, 1862–64; wrote for newspapers in San Francisco and Sacramento, 1864–69. Visited the Sandwich Islands, 1866, and France, Italy, and Palestine, 1867. Editor, Buffalo *Express*, 1869–71. Married Olivia Langdon, 1870 (died, 1904): one son and three daughters. Moved to Hartford, Connecticut, and became associated with Charles L. Webster Publishing Company, 1884; invested in the Paige typesetter and went bankrupt, 1894. Lived mainly in Europe, 1896–1900, New York, 1900–07, and Redding, Connecticut, 1907–10. Awards: honorary degrees from three universities. Member, American Academy of Arts and Letters, 1904. Died in Redding, 21 April 1910.

Selected Writings

Essays and Related Prose

A Curious Dream and Other Sketches, 1872
Sketches, 1874
Sketches, New and Old, 1875
Punch, Brothers, Punch! and Other Sketches, 1878

How to Tell a Story and Other Essays, 1897; revised edition, 1900
The Man That Corrupted Hadleyburg and Other Stories and Essays, 1900
My Début as a Literary Person, with Other Essays and Stories, 1903
Speeches, edited by F. A. Nast, 1910, and Albert Bigelow Paine, 1923
What Is Man? and Other Essays, 1917
Travels with Mr. Brown, Being Heretofore Uncollected Sketches Written for the San Francisco Alta California in 1866 and 1867, edited by Franklin Walker and G. Ezra Dane, 1940
Traveling with the Innocents Abroad: Mark Twain's Original Reports from Europe and the Holy Land, edited by Daniel Morley McKeithan, 1958
Life as I Find It: Essays, Sketches, Tales, and Other Material, edited by Charles Neider, 1961
The Complete Essays, edited by Charles Neider, 1963
Collected Tales, Sketches, Speeches, and Essays (Library of America), edited by Lewis J. Budd, 2 vols., 1992
Tales, Speeches, Essays, and Sketches, edited by Tom Quirk, 1994
Selected Writings of an American Skeptic, edited by Victor Doyno, 1995

Other writings: 15 novels (including *The Adventures of Tom Sawyer*, 1876; *The Adventures of Huckleberry Finn*, 1884; *A Connecticut Yankee at King Arthur's Court*, 1889), short stories, and many volumes of travel writing.

Collected works editions: *The Writings* (Definitive Edition), edited by Albert Bigelow Paine, 37 vols., 1922–25; *Works* (Iowa-California Edition), edited by John C. Gerber and others, 8 vols., 1972–93 (in progress).

Bibliographies

Johnson, Merle, *A Bibliography of the Works of Mark Twain*, New York: Harper, revised edition, 1935 (original edition, 1910)
McBride, William M., *Mark Twain: A Bibliography of the Collections of the Mark Twain Memorial and the Stowe-Day Foundation*, Hartford, Connecticut: McBride/Publisher, 1984
Rodney, Robert H., editor, *Twain International: A Bibliography and Interpretation of His Worldwide Popularity*, Westport, Connecticut: Greenwood Press, 1982
Tenney, Thomas Asa, *Mark Twain: A Reference Guide*, Boston: Hall, 1977

Further Reading

Baetzhold, Howard G., "Samuel Langhorne Clemens," in *American Literary Critics and Scholars, 1850–1880*, edited by John W. Rathbun and Monica M. Grecu, *Dictionary of Literary Biography* vol. 64, Detroit: Gale Research, 1988: 34–47
Bellamy, Gladys Carmen, *Mark Twain as a Literary Artist*, Norman: University of Oklahoma Press, 1950
Budd, Louis J., *Mark Twain: Social Philosopher*, Bloomington: Indiana University Press, 1962
Ferguson, De Lancey, *Mark Twain: Man and Legend*, Indianapolis: Bobbs Merrill, 1943
Foner, Philip, *Mark Twain: Social Critic*, New York: International Publishers, 1958
Gerber, John C., "Mark Twain's Use of the Comic Pose," *PMLA* 77 (June 1962): 297–304
Gibson, William M., *The Art of Mark Twain*, New York: Oxford University Press, 1976
Krause, Sydney J., *Mark Twain as Critic*, Baltimore: John Hopkins University Press, 1967
Macnaughton, William R., *Mark Twain's Last Years as a Writer*, Columbia: University of Missouri Press, 1979
Neider, Charles, *Mark Twain*, New York: Horizon Press, 1967

Tynan, Kenneth

British, 1927–1980

The popular image of Kenneth Tynan has been one of a cultural and social *provocateur*, a reputation stemming from his various gestures on behalf of the sexual revolution of the 1960s, notably the erotic revue he devised with others, *Oh! Calcutta!* (1969). Of far greater significance, though, was his contribution to British theater as the most respected and influential of postwar theater critics, and as the first literary manager of Britain's National Theatre, working under Laurence Olivier. Underlying all of these activities was the fundamental skill which he deployed in all his areas of interest – his ability to write strikingly expressive prose. This was underpinned by his sheer love of language, a passion ingrained at an early age – in 1944, the precocious 16-year-old described himself as a "soft old word fancier," advising a close friend to "worry about words; they are the only consistent elements in your life. as remy de gourmont [*sic*] said, 'ideas are well enough until you are twenty; after that only words will do.'"

Tynan's early **letters** and articles for school and university magazines reveal an omnivorous intelligence using an eclectic array of verbal means – from puns and clerihews to French quotations and Latin tags – to recount his personal experiences, to elaborate his constantly changing views on literature and the world, and, most tellingly, to document keenly his avid theater-going. These early writings show him constantly searching for the precise phrase both to represent his state of mind as spectator and to bring alive the material characteristics of performances.

His student notes and writings resulted in his first book of theatrical observations, *He That Plays the King* (1950), published when he was 23. He became a fulltime theater critic, after coming down from Oxford, until the early 1960s. His prose of that period consists largely of short pieces of around 1000 words – perhaps too short to be normally considered as essays. Yet Tynan developed a style of rich compression, which probed and scraped away the generalized impressions typical of so much writing in the genre, to achieve a muscular directness and concreteness of evocation. Cumulatively, the **reviews** also constitute a larger exploration of the nature of performance *per se* and an affirmation of Tynan's belief in the importance of theater in the overall cultural fabric. (The appropriation of Hazlitt's title *A View of the English Stage* for his 1975 compilation of reviews – perhaps an act of both audacity and deference – suggests their essayistic ambition.) It could be said that these individual pieces are essay-like in their depth of examination and in their grounding of the writer's subjective view in persuasive terms of debate. In reviews of actors, comics, and other performers, his prose displays a kind of filmic rhythm, swooping in for close-ups before drawing away to restore balance and an overarching perspective. This is evident even in an early review, of Olivier as Shakespeare's Richard III (1944), where Tynan homes in on the voice – "slick, taunting, and curiously casual; nearly impersonal, 'smooth as sleekstone', patting and pushing each line into place. Occasionally he lets out a gurgling, avuncular cackle, a good-humoured snarl: and then we see the over-riding mephitic good humour of the man" – before panning out to consider the overall interpretation as exemplifying "Blake's conception of active, energetic evil," with analogies to Sidney's elegiacs and **Gor'kii**'s *Lower Depths*.

Tynan's writing grew more versatile as his theatrical experience deepened. While the wit, use of apposite phrase, and crystalline precision of description remained constant, his style grew in flexibility, and his responses – in accordance with his gradual assumption of idealist/socialist ideas about the perfectibility of humankind – were increasingly adumbrated by a greater sense of social and political concern, reflected particularly in his admiration for Bertolt Brecht. Stylistically, he could resort both to playful pastiche (as in his affectionate Runyonesque review of the musical *Guys and Dolls*, 1952) and to pointed parody (in his "Slamm's Last Knock," 1958, a mock-Beckettian two-hander bemoaning the increasingly fatalistic *ennui* of Beckett's characters), while also making bold and confident claims for works he championed. Welcoming Beckett's *Waiting for Godot* (1955), he stated that "it forced me to re-examine the rules which have hitherto governed the drama; and having done so, to pronounce them not elastic enough"; and he eulogized John Osborne's *Look Back in Anger* (1956) for presenting "post-war youth as it really is," famously concluding: "I doubt if I could love anyone who did not wish to see *Look Back in Anger*. It is the best young play of its decade."

On taking up his post at the National Theatre, Tynan gave up regular theater reviewing. His writings thenceforward were of a more occasional, but more varied, nature. In the athletic metaphor he used on several occasions, the short-distance "sprinting" of the reviews increasingly came to be replaced by the "middle-distance" running of essay-features. The subdivisions of his collection *Tynan Right and Left* (1967) – "Theatre," "Cinema," "People," "Places," and "Comments and Causeries" – usefully summarize the fields of all his longer writing. Earlier pieces tend to be commentaries on theatrical subjects – overviews of the careers of actors, writers, and directors, considerations of theater styles (e.g. "Prose and the Playwright," "The Lost Art of Bad Drama," 1954), and unashamedly partisan interventions in larger cultural debates, such as lobbying for the establishment of a National Theatre ("The National Theatre: A Speech to the Royal Society of Arts," 1964) and the removal of theater censorship ("The Royal Smut-Hound," 1965). These articles appeared in a variety of publications, including the *Harper's Bazaar*, the *Observer*, the **New Yorker**, *Playboy*, and *Holiday*.

The form of essay in which Tynan came to specialize, however, was the profile-essay – the portrait of an outstanding individual who was either an epitome of his or her type or, very often, considered by Tynan to be *sui generis*. The earlier of these were more obviously logical extensions of his theatrical and cinematic experiences, allowing him to synthesize instances of performance into larger characterizations of an individual's style and significance, while also supplying biographical and anecdotal sidelights. But the profile-essay especially allowed him to take the notion he elaborated of "high definition performance" – "supreme professional polish, hard-edged technical skill . . . the hypnotic saving grace of high and low art alike, the common denominator that unites tragedy, ballroom dancing, conversation and cricket" – and apply it to a wide range of people, taking in other expressive artists (writers, matadors, jazz musicians, film directors, television personalities), pursuing the attributes of the performative in both an individual's public and private lives.

Of all the publications to which Tynan contributed profiles, none was more important to him than the **New Yorker**, the magazine which the teenage Tynan revered in provincial Birmingham as representing the peak of American urbanity and sophistication, and whose style under its editor Harold Ross he lauded in 1951 as "pungent and artless, innocently sly, superbly explicit: what one would call low-falutin'." Collaborating now with William Shawn, Ross' successor, Tynan spent much of his last years writing his longest profiles for the *New Yorker*. The magazine's image and scope of interest was, in some quarters, then deemed somewhat conservative (essays such as Tynan's 1966 "Meditations on Basic Baroque," on the erotic history of the female bottom, understandably appeared elsewhere – despite its references to James Joyce, François Villon, Henry Vaughan, and **Edmund Burke**!). More importantly, however, Tynan shared the *New Yorker*'s high sense of writerly discipline, admiring its punctiliousness enough to spend hours in discussion with the editor and his staff over phraseology.

In the **preface** to *Show People* (1980) – the collection of his final, longer *New Yorker* profiles – Tynan offered a context for his writing, and, in characteristically witty vein, an explicit defense of the essay form: "Many critics maintain that the essay is an inferior form . . . Out of the window – if these experts are right – goes Montaigne. To the bonfire with William Hazlitt, closely followed by Max Beerbohm, Sainte-Beuve and John Aubrey . . . and into the garbage goes Samuel Johnson's *Lives of the Poets*, perhaps the finest book of profile-essays ever written . . . Any theory that regards works like these as second-class . . . is transparently dotty."

While not comparing himself to all the "masters" he cited, he felt he might "go a couple of rounds" with **Charles Lamb**. The pieces that follow – on writer Tom Stoppard, actor Ralph Richardson, television star Johnny Carson, silent-film actress Louise Brooks, and comedian Mel Brooks – tackle high and low culture with equal verve, in each case mapping out the contours of a distinctive terrain. Tynan's profiles vary in tone and orientation – here, for example, the Louise Brooks piece is a kind of homage to a forgotten star and personal idol, the Mel Brooks piece delves into the relationship of comedy, fear, and ambition, and the Stoppard article is an extended musing on writing, style, and political commitment. But, while all include many examples of "vintage" Tynan, in his reportage of personal encounters (performances, dinner parties, interviews, letters), such elements are subtly worked into a widening and deepening perspective. A profile often begins obliquely, by virtue of apparently unrelated anecdotes or random information; then essential biographical information is lightly introduced, and thereafter the portrait is built up incrementally, as a shape and thesis emerge. The profile is rounded out by quotations from others on the subject and the deployment of a battery of cultural references. The most marked contrast with the shorter writings is the cooler, analytical quality that emerges in a more measured pace; the sprinting, dazzling prose is calmed by direct, yet always elegantly written, exposition and by pertinent, well-grounded comment.

At Tynan's funeral, Tom Stoppard summarized the potency of Tynan's writing as resting in "his paragraphs – paragraphs were the units of his prose, not sentences," written to "outlast the witness." While this quality contributes to the exceptional eloquence of his theater reviews, nowhere is the comment more apposite than in regard to the later profile-essays. It is ultimately in this sense of creating a permanence for the ephemeral through the written word, so that the prose fascinates even when its subject may be only dimly familiar to the reader, that Tynan lays claim to a place in the history of the modern essay.

MARK HAWKINS-DADY

Biography
Kenneth Peacock Tynan. Born 2 April 1927 in Birmingham. Studied at King Edward's School, Birmingham, 1938–45; Magdalen College, Oxford, 1945–48, B.A. in English, 1948. Director, Lichfield repertory theater company, 1949; director, 1950, and actor, 1951, London. Married Elaine Brimberg Dundy, 1951 (divorced, 1964): one daughter. Drama critic for the *Spectator*, 1951–52, the *Evening Standard*, 1952–53, and the *Daily Sketch*, 1953–54; drama critic, 1954–58 and 1960–63, and film critic, 1964–66, the *Observer*; script editor, Ealing Films, London, 1956–58; drama critic, 1958–60, and feature writer, 1976–80, the *New Yorker*; editor, *Tempo* television arts program, 1961–62; literary manager, 1963–69, and literary consultant, 1969–73, National Theatre of Britain, London. Married Kathleen Halton, 1967: one daughter and one son. Moved to California for health reasons, 1976. Died (of emphysema) in Santa Monica, California, 26 July 1980.

Selected Writings

Essays and Related Prose
He That Plays the King: A View of the Theatre, 1950
Persona Grata, 1953
Curtains: Selections from the Drama, Criticism and Related Writings, 1961; as *Tynan on Theatre*, 1964
Tynan Right and Left, 1967
A View of the English Stage, 1944–63, 1975
The Sound of Two Hands Clapping, 1975
Show People: Profiles in Entertainment, 1980
Profiles, edited by Kathleen Tynan and Ernie Eban, 1989

Other writings: books on Alec Guinness (1953) and bull fighting (1955), radio plays, theater adaptations, and correspondence. Also collaborated on the revue *Oh! Calcutta!* (1969).

Further Reading
Kihn, Patricia Lenehan, *Kenneth Tynan and the Renaissance of Post-War British Drama* (dissertation), Detroit: Wayne State University, 1986
Tynan, Kathleen, *The Life of Kenneth Tynan*, London: Weidenfeld and Nicolson, and New York: Morrow, 1987

U

Unamuno, Miguel de

Spanish, 1864–1936

Unamuno is, along with **José Ortega y Gasset**, one of the most prolific, versatile, and original minds in modern European literature, and Spain's most eminent thinker. Patriarch of the so-called Generation of 1898, he achieved eminence as novelist, poet, philosopher, and dramatist. The sheer volume and thematic diversity of his essayistic output – over seven hefty volumes – is staggering. Unamuno engaged every major discipline in the human sciences (especially the fields of philosophy, religion, history, linguistics, literary criticism, and politics), and practiced a variety of the types and subgenres of the essay – among them the **treatise**, autobiography, diary, **letter, meditation**, speech, **dialogue, aphorism, travel essay,** and confession. A classical philologist by training (he was professor of Greek and became rector of the University of Salamanca), Unamuno was equally well-versed in Catholic and Protestant theology, and 19th-century scientific theories and philosophical systems.

Studies of Unamuno continue unabated, with each generation of scholars finding new dimensions to his personality and work. Religious, existential, and linguistic orientations of past decades have been steadily enriched in recent years with deconstructive and rhetorical studies, Jungian analysis, and gender perspectives. Along with the traditional image of Unamuno as an intellectual gadfly who challenged the conventional religious beliefs and practices of his day, there has emerged a picture of him as a Modernist with a keen insight into the nature and function of language as both the instrument and the subject of philosophical inquiry. Although a lapsed Catholic and crypto-atheist, Unamuno was unwilling to abandon theological inquiry or the comforts of religious belief, and made the unremitting struggle between reason and faith and a hunger for immortality the cornerstone of his thought and the subject for his best known book-length essays. These are principally *Del sentimiento trágico de la vida* (1912; *The Tragic Sense of Life*), *Cómo se hace una novela* (1927; How a novel is made), and *La agonía del cristianismo* (1925, 1931; *The Agony of Christianity*).

Unamuno's career as essayist began in 1886 under the spell of positivism, leading him to embrace briefly the aims of Marxist socialism (1894–97). During these early years he contributed to the socialist press of his native Bilbao commentaries and exhortations on momentous political and economic issues of the day. He gradually evolved into a liberal and by 1917 became openly anti-Marxist; yet even during his brief commitment to scientific socialism Unamuno looked upon Marxism more as a moral and humanitarian ideal compatible with Christian values than as an economic theory or blueprint for violent revolution. A disenchantment with the utopian ideals of science and the narrow logic of positivism, exacerbated by a wrenching religious crisis in 1897, broke Unamuno's trust in social engineering and in the ability of the great rationalist philosophical systems to address and satisfy humankind's deepest longings.

Influenced by Kierkegaard and liberal Protestantism, Unamuno's essays probe deeply and dramatically into the meaning and possibility of being Christian in a secular age. But unlike Kierkegaard, Unamuno renounced any ultimate metaphysical security and exploited the tensions and contradictions inherent in a modern religious sensibility. Although at times he would defend the simple, genuine, untutored faith of Everyman, more often than not he was bent on sowing doubt. Thus critics have long accepted both the contemplative, reflective Unamuno in search of harmony and peace, exemplified by *En torno al casticismo* (1895; On authentic tradition), and a passionate, paradoxical Unamuno determined to shake public apathy and undermine intellectual complacency and dogmatism. This temper is typified by *Vida de don Quijote y Sancho* (1905; *The Life of Don Quixote and Sancho*) and "Sobre la europeización (Arbitrariedades)" (1906; On becoming Europeans). Although it is risky to categorize Unamuno ideologically, his essays are, as a rule, rhetorical strategies devised to challenge the commonplaces of his day, provoke readers into a state of uncertainty, and encourage self-scrutiny. A Christian existentialist beset by disbelief, he urged that individuals create, in the crucible of doubt, the meaning and purpose of their lives and induced them, in line with his paradoxical and "tragic sense of life," to wager on personal immortality without renouncing rational inquiry.

Unamuno confronts his reader directly and openly, appealing to the concerns of the concrete "man of flesh and bone" and not just to scholars and intellectuals. The tone of his essays is familiar and engaging, but often aggressive and abrasive. He does not, however, apologize for any breach of decorum, but admits candidly that he is not a pleasant fellow ("A mis lectores" [1909; To my readers]): it is better to be disliked and admired for boldness and honesty than liked for toeing the line of conventional thought. Indeed, the author acknowledges that he may shout and rant and even offend, but this may be the only way, he believes, to "wake up the sleeper." A strident individualism and personalism, given to gesture and histrionics, characterize Unamuno's persona. He is not content, like **Montaigne**, to be the multifaceted subject of his book, but in addition orchestrates a dramatic interplay of conflicting and contradictory selves in tones both shrill and grave, dispensing indignation, scorn, reverence and irreverence, prophecy, advice, or simply engagement in intellectual games and wordplay. And yet, very often, Unamuno's essays are a model of reasonableness and common sense – a term uncongenial to his thought. Thus, on the one hand, he can belittle Cervantes as a poor devil, unaware of the significance of his own creation, condemn the French for their *joie de vivre*, or rail in mawkish self-pity against the dictator Primo de Rivera for offenses to his person more imaginary than real. On the other hand, his articles written during the Spanish Republic (1931–36) are eminently sensible, balanced, and fair, revealing a liberal who welcomed and supported the secular legislation of the new government, yet wished to preserve some traditional religious values that he saw threatened by extremists. Unamuno never failed to extend his personal drama to a preoccupation with the historical and spiritual destiny of Spain. This patriotic concern ranges from earnest and informed criticism of social injustices based on economic exploitation to a total indifference to such issues in the name of spiritual values; in this vein he would extol the dignity of an idealized Spanish peasantry as a counter-example to European materialism ("La vida es sueño" [1898; Life is a dream]).

Unamuno's evolution as an essayist may be illustrated by attention to a few representative works. It is instructive to begin with *En torno al casticismo*, which appeared in 1895 as a series of five essays in *La España Moderna* (Modern Spain) and in book form in 1902. It reflects the author's faith in the idea of progress and the redeeming power of science. Influenced by such diverse sources as Hegel, Spencer, **Darwin**, and the Spanish mystic Fray Luis de León, Unamuno argues mainly by analogy and dialectic for unity and harmony within diversity in the historical development of Spanish identity. This is to be achieved by a reconciliation of perennial opposites such as personal/collective, temporal/eternal, Spain/Europe. The most important of these dualities is history/intra-history; that is, the tension between the transitory, superficial dimension of Spanish life and the deep and lasting values of the people. Unamuno elaborates the dynamics of these concepts with analogies derived from biological and geological metaphors.

After the religious crisis of 1897, Unamuno lost faith in the explanatory power of science and the great rationalist systems and under the influence of Kierkegaard began to explore the domain of inwardness. At this point one finds a significant turn in Unamuno's style, mainly the displacement of analogy by the extensive use of paradox. Whereas analogy reflected the author's will to harmonize opposites, and dialectic promoted a reconciliation of local and universal themes, paradox reveals a mind bent on dissociation and contradiction. Pithy oxymorons and extravagant puns, conceits and etymological games serve to dramatize the author's existential anguish and to frustrate in the reader the process of expected associations. Perhaps the most widely used and effective trope in the agonistic Unamuno is the chiasmus, in which a phrase is repeated in reverse order and the relations between the same or similar words yield a wide range of semantic possibilities.

Typical chiastic paradoxes in Unamuno are: "I seek peace in war and war in peace"; "The word hypocrite designates in Greek an actor . . . But if a hypocrite is an actor the actor, surely, is no hypocrite"; "Just as our death is an unbirthing, so our birth is an undying."

The transition from rationalism to voluntarism, from analogy to existential paradox is evident in "Sobre la europeización." Here, for example, the terms of the opposition Spain/Europe, which in *En torno al casticismo* were harmoniously interdependent, are now polarized with their respective values redefined and ultimately reversed. The "European" cultural categories of logic, science, progress, and the celebration of life are rejected in the name of arbitrariness, passion, and the wisdom derived from the Spanish people's meditation on death. As if to mock his own previous penchant for harmonious analogies, Unamuno now writes in neat chiastic equations: "Wisdom is to science what death is to life or, if you will, wisdom is to death what science is to life."

In *The Life of Don Quixote and Sancho* Unamuno fuses Nietzschean voluntarism with traditional Spanish cultural values. In this passionate dissection of Cervantes' masterpiece the heroic and tragic knight assumes the virtues of Christ, becoming an outcast who in his loneliness and will to create new spiritual values is defeated by a world of philistines and materialists. Unamuno's text is, in the words of Martin Nozick (1982), "a tapestry of ingenious paradoxes, diatribes, poetic prose, and arbitrary conclusions drawn from the best-known episodes of the original." Some of these qualities are evident in the first sentence of the work: "You ask me, my good friend, if I know of a way to unchain a delirium, a vertigo, any kind of madness upon these poor, peaceful, orderly masses who are born, eat, sleep, reproduce and die."

Perhaps the most original of Unamuno's essayistic endeavors is *Cómo se hace una novela*, a hybrid of autobiography, essay, and fiction. Written in the confessional mode, with tones of an anguished exile, the narrative voice is consubstantial with the self-reflective author, who occasionally splits off into his double as a character in a fictional autobiography. The dualistic themes of history/fiction, authenticity/role playing, life/art dominate this work, in which fictional techniques are subordinated to the essay. Finally, *The Agony of Christianity*, also written in exile, intensifies the religious tenor of *The Tragic Sense of Life* with biblical parables and paradoxes, "tragic plays on words" from St. Paul and **Pascal**, and especially with an allegory of the death of God, sustained by the erotic language of mysticism. Unamuno emphasizes here the inherent contradictions of Christianity, its fate in a highly secularized culture which he predicts will absorb and bastardize faith and ultimately put an end to the "agony" of Christianity.

In his heroic search for truth Unamuno despairs, oscillates, wavers between the rational and the affective without relinquishing either reason or faith. His best-known essays alternately affirm and negate contraries in perpetual tension. His "rhetoric of existence," to use Allen Lacy's (1967) apt expression, engages the great topics of modern philosophical discourse, creating truth from doubt and doubt from truth.

THOMAS MERMALL

Biography

Miguel de Unamuno y Jugo. Born 29 September 1864 in Bilbao. Studied at the Colegio de San Nicolás and the Instituto Vizacaíno, Bilbao, 1875–80; philosophy at the University of Madrid, 1880–84, Ph.D., 1884. Private tutor in Bilbao, 1884–91. Married Concepción [Concha] Lizárraga Ecénarro (died, 1934), 1891: ten children. Professor of Greek, 1891–1924, rector, 1900–14 (dismissed) and 1934–36, and professor of the history of the Spanish language, 1930–34, University of Salamanca. Exiled to the Canary Islands for publicly criticizing the dictatorship of Primo de Rivera, 1924; lived in Paris, 1924, and Hendaye, 1925–30; returned to Spain, 1930. Placed under house arrest for criticism of Franco government, 1936. Awards: Cross of the Order of Alfonso XII, 1905; honorary degrees from two European universities. Died in Salamanca, 31 December 1936.

Selected Writings

Essays and Related Prose

Tres ensayos, 1900
En torno al casticismo, 1902
De mi país, 1903
Vida de don Quijote y Sancho, 1905; as The Life of Don Quixote and Sancho, translated by Homer P. Earle, 1927; as Our Lord Don Quixote, translated by Anthony Kerrigan, 1967
Mi religión y otros ensayos breves, 1910; as Perplexities and Paradoxes, translated by Stuart Gross, 1945
Soliloquios y conversaciones, 1911
Por tierras de Portugal y de España (travel articles), 1911; edited by Manuel García Blanco, 1972
Contra esto y aquello, 1912
El porvenir de España, with Ángel Ganivet, 1912
Del sentimiento trágico de la vida en los hombres y en los pueblos, 1912; as The Tragic Sense of Life in Men and in Peoples, translated by J. E. Crawford Flitch, 1921
Ensayos, 7 vols., 1916–18; revised edition, 2 vols., 1942; part as Essays and Soliloquies, translated by J. E. Crawford Flitch, 1925
Andanzas y visiones españolas (travel articles), 1922
L'Agonie du christianisme, 1925; as La agonía del cristianismo, 1931; as The Agony of Christianity, translated by Pierre Loving, 1928, Kurt F. Reinhardt, 1960, and Anthony Kerrigan, in The Agony of Christianity and Essays on Faith, 1974
Cómo se hace una novela, 1927; edited by Paul R. Olson, 1977
Dos artículos y dos discursos, 1930; edited by David Robertson, 1986
Ensayos y sentencias (selection), edited by Wilfred A. Beardsley, 1932
Cuenca ibérica, 1943
Paisajes del Alma, 1944
La enormidad de España, 1945
Algunas consideraciones sobre la literatura hispano-americana, 1947
Visiones y comentarios, 1949
De esto y de aquello, 4 vols., 1950–54
España y los españoles, edited by Manuel García Blanco, 1955
Inquietudes y meditaciones, 1957
Mi vida y otros recuerdos personales, 2 vols., 1959
Pensamiento político, edited by Elias Díaz, 1965
La vida literaria, 1967
El gaucho Martín Fierro, 1967
La agonía del cristianismo, Mi religión, y otros ensayos, 1967
Desde el mirador de la guerra, edited by Louis Urrutia, 1970
The Agony of Christianity and Essays on Faith, edited by Anthony Kerrigan and Martin Nozick, translated by Kerrigan, 1974
Escritos socialistas: Artículos inéditos sobre el socialismo, 1894–1922, edited by Pedro Ribas, 1976
Artículos olvidados sobre España y la primera guerra mundial, edited by Christopher Cobb, 1976
En torno a las artes: Del teatro, el cine, las bellas artes, la política y las letras, 1976
Crónica política española (1915–1923), edited by Vicente González Martín, 1977

República española y España republicana (1931–1936), edited by Vicente González Martín, 1979
Artículos y discursos sobre Canarias, edited by Francisco Navarro Artiles, 1980
Ensueño de una patria: Periodismo republicano, 1931–36, edited by Victor Ouimette, 1984
El resentimiento trágico de la vida: Notas sobre la revolución y guerra civil españolas, 1991
Artículos en "La nación" de Buenos Aires, 1919–1924, edited by Luis Urrutia Salaverri, 1994

Other writings: several novels (including Paz en la guerra [Peace in War], 1897; Niebla [Mist], 1914; Abel Sánchez, 1917; San Manuel Bueno, 1933), poetry, plays, and theological works.

Collected works edition: Obras completas, edited by Manuel García Blanco, 16 vols., 1951–58.

Bibliographies

Fernández, Pelayo H., Bibliografía crítica de Unamuno 1888–1975, Madrid: Porrúa, 1976
Valdés, Mario James, and María Elena de Valdés, An Unamuno Source Book: A Catalogue of Readings and Acquisitions, with an Introductory Essay on Unamuno's Dialectical Enquiry, Toronto: University of Toronto Press, 1973

Further Reading

Blanco Aguinaga, Carlos, El Unamuno contemplativo, Mexico: Nueva Revista de Filología Hispánica, 1959
Butt, J. W., "Unamuno's Idea of Intrahistoria: Its Origins and Significance," in Studies in Spanish Literature and Art Presented to Helen F. Grant, edited by Nigel Glendinning, London: Tamesis, 1972: 13–24
Cerezo-Galán, Pedro, Las máscaras de lo trágico: Filosofía y tragedia en Miguel de Unamuno, Madrid: Trotta, 1996
Ferrater Mora, José, Unamuno, a Philosophy of Tragedy, Berkeley: University of California Press, 1962 (Spanish edition, 1957)
Franz, Thomas, The Word in the World: Unamuno's Tragic Sense of Language, Athens, Ohio: Strathmore, 1987
Ilie, Paul, Unamuno: An Existential View of Self and Society, Madison: University of Wisconsin Press, 1967
Jurkevich, Gayana, The Elusive Self: Archetypal Approaches to the Novels of Miguel de Unamuno, Columbia: University of Missouri Press, 1991
Lacy, Allen, Miguel de Unamuno: The Rhetoric of Existence, The Hague: Mouton, 1967
La Rubia-Prado, Francisco, Alegorías de la voluntad: Pensamiento orgánico, retórica y deconstrucción en la obra de Miguel de Unamuno, Madrid: Libertarias/Prodhufi, 1996
Marías, Julián, Miguel de Unamuno, Cambridge, Massachusetts: Harvard University Press, 1966 (Spanish edition, 1943)
Marichal, Juan, Teoría e historia del ensayismo hispánico, Madrid: Alianza, 1984: Chapter on Unamuno
Mermall, Thomas, "The Chiasmus: Unamuno's Master Trope," PMLA 105 (1990): 245–55
Navajas, Gonzalo, Miguel de Unamuno: Bipolaridad y síntesis ficcional, Barcelona: PPU, 1988
Nozick, Martin, Miguel de Unamuno, New York: Twayne, 1971
Nozick, Martin, Miguel de Unamuno: The Agony of Belief, Princeton, New Jersey: Princeton University Press, 1982
Olson, Paul, "Unamuno's Lacquered Boxes: Cómo se hace una novela and the Ontology of Writing," Revista Hispánica Moderna 36 (1970–71): 186–99
Orringer, Nelson R., Unamuno y los protestantes liberales (1912): Sobre las fuentes de "Del sentimiento trágico de la vida", Madrid: Gredos, 1985
Regalado García, Antonio, El siervo y el señor: La dialéctica agónica de Miguel de Unamuno, Madrid: Gredos, 1968

Updike, John

American, 1932–

Though noted primarily for his novels, John Updike has made a significant contribution to American letters through his work as an essayist. Beginning with his appointment to the staff of the *New Yorker* magazine after returning from graduate studies in England in 1955, Updike has written speculative pieces on American society, book **reviews** on works by his countrymen and writers from around the world, reminiscences, travelogues, parodies, and criticism of literature and art. The bulk of his work has appeared originally in the *New Yorker* and other popular or highbrow American magazines such as the *Saturday Evening Post*, *New Republic*, **Harper's**, and the **American Scholar**. During the 1980s and 1990s he has contributed introductions and commentaries to anthologies and reprints of important works by other writers. In the five collections issued between 1965 and 1991, he expands his published materials to include several speeches given before local and national forums. Taken *in toto*, these nonfiction pieces provide a surprisingly useful gloss on the literary vision of one of America's most prolific and successful fiction writers of the 20th century.

Clearly the majority of Updike's nonfiction has been occasional, prompted by an invitation to contribute to a publication or for a special event. His reviews of contemporary literature run into the hundreds, and he considers the opportunity to produce reviews and essays an important corollary to his work as a novelist and short-story writer. "One accepts editorial invitations," he remarks in the **preface** to *Odd Jobs* (1991), "in the hopes of learning something, or of extracting from within some unsuspected wisdom. For writing educates the writer as it goes along." How one uses the education gained through such writing is, Updike admits with wry self-deprecation, another matter: "My purpose in reading has ever secretly been not to come and judge but to come and steal." Certainly these literary exercises have benefited Updike in his novels, but his erudition shows also in the wide range of tasks he has undertaken with facility. Among the writers whose works he has reviewed are Americans Philip Roth, Saul Bellow, **Annie Dillard**, Kurt Vonnegut, Donald Barthelme, Joyce Carol Oates, and William Least Heat Moon; British writers Iris Murdoch, **Cyril Connolly**, and Margaret Drabble; Europeans Robert Pinget, Michel Tournier, Raymond Queneau, **Umberto Eco**, Milan Kundera, Yuri Trifonov, Evgenii Evtushenko, and Elena Bonner; Latin Americans Gabriel García Márquez, Mario Vargas Llosa, and Isabel Allende. Regardless of the author he reviews, Updike speaks with authority, making pertinent connections to other works by his subject and others. Throughout his career as a literary journalist, Updike follows the **maxim** set down by **T. S. Eliot** in "Tradition and the Individual Talent" (1919), that a new work should be measured against the body of literature it joins and which it changes by its appearance. In doing so, not only does he display his knowledge, but – more importantly – he reveals much of his own literary credo. In writing about his contemporaries Updike makes a clear case for his own literary values: accuracy in presenting one's subject, felicity in style, precision in describing both external circumstance and inner feelings, and

a deep understanding of and sympathy for the flawed creatures who make up the human race, regardless of national allegiance or ethnic origin.

In his less formal pieces, Updike often strikes the pose of the gentle satirist, poking fun at American life and customs; nor does he exempt himself from criticism. Whether writing about baseball, postal envelopes, or an imaginary visit to the planet Minerva, he is able to capture people, places, and events with a clarity of vision that brings them to life for readers. Even in pieces which seem to have no great moral, political, or sociological import, Updike takes great pains to see that readers share the experience about which he has chosen to write. While there may be no great lessons to impart, readers are nevertheless heartened – even delighted – to have an opportunity to find before them a little bit of the American scene, with all its foibles and idiosyncracies.

Although his subjects vary widely, Updike writes with a consistent voice throughout all his nonfiction. Seldom does he become too effusive in his praise, and even less seldom does he stoop to mean-spirited castigation. He does not begrudge others their fame or financial success. He recognizes, even celebrates, the ordinary life he sees around him. He is remarkably forgiving of mistakes by others, and he frequently asks readers to recognize and forgive his own misapprehensions, perceived or real. The "I" of Updike's essays is genuine, direct, and sympathetic – in the original sense of the word: capable of entering into a fellow-feeling with his subjects, whatever their profession.

LAURENCE W. MAZZENO

Biography

John Hoyer Updike. Born 18 March 1932 in Shillington, Pennsylvania. Studied at Harvard University, Cambridge, Massachusetts, A.B. (summa cum laude), 1954; Knox Fellow, Ruskin School of Drawing and Fine Arts, Oxford, 1954–55. Married Mary Pennington, 1953 (marriage later dissolved): two daughters and two sons. Staff reporter, 1955–57, and frequent contributor, the *New Yorker*. Married Martha Bernhard, 1977. Awards: many, including the National Book Award, 1964; Foreign Book Prize (France), 1966; MacDowell Medal, 1981; Pulitzer Prize, 1982, 1991; American Book Award, 1982; National Book Critics Circle Award, for fiction, 1982, 1990, and for *Hugging the Shore*, 1984; Union League Club Abraham Lincoln Award, 1982; National Arts Club Medal of Honor, 1984; National Medal of the Arts, 1989. Member, American Academy and Institute of Arts and Letters, 1976.

Selected Writings

Essays and Related Prose
Assorted Prose, 1965
Picked-Up Pieces, 1975
Hugging the Shore: Essays and Criticism, 1983
Just Looking: Essays on Art, 1989
Odd Jobs: Essays and Criticism, 1991

Other writings: 17 novels (*The Poorhouse Fair*, 1959; four Rabbit novels, 1960–90; *The Centaur*, 1963; *Of the Farm*, 1965; *Couples*, 1968; *A Month of Sundays*, 1975; *Marry Me*, 1976; *The Coup*, 1978; *The Witches of Eastwick*, 1984; *Roger's Version*, 1986; *S.*, 1988; *Memories of the Ford Administration*, 1992; *Brazil*, 1994; *In the Beauty of the Lilies*, 1996), many collections of short stories and poetry, two plays, and the memoir *Self-Consciousness* (1987).

Bibliography
De Bellis, Jack, *John Updike: A Bibliography, 1967–1993*, Westport, Connecticut: Greenwood Press, 1994

Further Reading
Bloom, Harold, editor, *John Updike*, New York: Chelsea House, 1987
Burchard, Rachael C., *John Updike: Yea Sayings*, Carbondale: Southern Illinois University Press, 1971
Detweiler, Robert, *John Updike*, Boston: Twayne, revised edition, 1984
Donoghue, Denis, "The Zeal of a Man of Letters," *New York Times Book Review*, 18 September 1983: 1, 30–31
Greiner, Donald J., *The Other John Updike: Poems, Short Stories, Prose, Play*, Athens: Ohio University Press, 1981
Hamilton, Alice, and Kenneth Hamilton, *The Elements of John Updike*, Grand Rapids, Michigan: Eerdmans, 1970

Hunt, George W., *John Updike and the Three Great Secret Things: Sex, Religion, and Art*, Grand Rapids, Michigan: Eerdmans, 1980
Kenner, Hugh, "Jobs Well Done: *Odd Jobs*," *National Review*, 17 February 1992: 52–54
Macnaughton, William R., editor, *Critical Essays on John Updike*, Boston: Hall, 1982
Newman, Judie, *John Updike*, London: Macmillan, and New York: St. Martin's Press, 1988
Riggan, William, "Shallow Drafts: John Updike's *Hugging the Shore*," *World Literature Today* 58 (Summer 1984): 380–83
Schwartz, Sandford, "Top of the Class," *New York Review of Books*, 24 November 1983: 26–30, 35
Simon, John, "Plying a Periplus," *New Republic*, 21 November 1983: 34–37
Trevor, William, "Discourse Most Eloquent Musing: *Odd Jobs*," *Spectator*, 8 February 1992: 29–30
Wolcott, James, "The Price of Finesse," *Harper's* 267 (September 1983): 63–66

V

Vaculík, Ludvík

Czech, 1926–

Ludvík Vaculík came to literature as a member of the Czech Communist Party and Party journalist; he belonged to that wing of the Party which worked in the late 1960s for democratic reform. His second novel, *Sekyra* (1966; *The Axe*), is an extremely personal account of his disillusionment as a Party journalist with the socialist order.

Vaculík took part in the Czechoslovak struggle for democracy and independence from the grasp of Soviet power; he composed the major manifesto of the liberation movement, "Dva tisíce slov" (1968; Two thousand words). But the invasion of Czechoslovakia by Soviet forces in August 1968 brought his exclusion from the Party and, though he was not arrested at the time, he was deprived of his opportunity to publish, as either a journalist or a writer of fiction. Still, all literary avenues were not closed to him, since a substantial literature of *samizdat* had grown up in Czechoslovakia, with typewriters and carbon paper used to produce works of literature at home, without censorship. Vaculík soon placed himself at the head of this effort, known in Czechoslovakia under the name of the largest group of these home-produced publications as Petlice ("the padlock"). He also published abroad, which remained technically legal in Czechoslovakia. *Morčata* (in German, 1971, in Czech, 1973; *The Guinea Pigs*), his third novel, is a surreal, Kafkaesque fantasy of man's calculated inhumanity to defenseless pets, an obvious allegory of totalitarian dictatorship.

In spite of the fact that Vaculík possessed outlets for publication, he had no income and no way of dealing with the repressive Czechoslovak regime, which eventually did imprison him for several months. His earlier work suggested that journalism was the answer: why not revive a traditional Czech form of free journalistic expression? And, since even in *samizdat* writings he was hardly free to express everything he wished, why not employ the traditional Czech literary techniques of irony and understatement to make his points by indirection?

Vaculík proceeded to revive the traditional Czech *feuilleton*, a form cultivated with success by Jan Neruda and **Karel Čapek**. The Czech *feuilleton* is a kind of newspaper column, which can be more or less journalistic in style and manner, or more or less literary. At times it approaches the essay in its length, preoccupation with style and stylistic devices, and introspective

manner. Vaculík's *feuilletons* are probably less essay-like than certain of Karel Čapek's, but their use of irony and understatement and their introspection fully entitle us to call them essays.

Vaculík sought literary action, for effectively he was leading a political crusade. He organized a network of Petlice correspondents who exchanged home-produced *feuilletons*, editing them in collections that could be circulated at home or sent abroad for publication.

He produced his own *feuilletons* in cycles of roughly 12 per year. Beginning in 1976, he began each annual cycle with a piece called "Jaro je tady" (Spring is here), presumably a reference to the "Prague Spring," the name by which the Czech struggle for liberation that took place in Spring 1968 was known. Similarly, each annual cycle includes a piece on "August" (*srpen*), the monthly anniversary of the Soviet invasion which crushed Czech liberties in 1968. The "Spring" pieces do contain the lyricism about nature we might expect, as well as an appeal to a paganesque mythology of creative growth and strength. However, in neither case is there a sense of commemoration of a political movement or of the anniversaries of the events they mark.

The use of devices such as irony or understatement is so traditional in Czech literature that positive meanings, expected and called for in other patriotic and democratic literature, are fully present and comprehensible, despite the absence of literal statements. The "Spring" pieces at once recall the Prague Spring to the attentive Czech reader. Moreover, understated irony makes possible the inversion of other value systems: the *feuilleton* "Šálek kávy při výslechu" (1977; "A Cup of Coffee with My Interrogator") shows the secret police interrogator treating the author with the utmost kindness and consideration, while the author replies with the greatest tact and delicacy; these inversions actually serve to suggest the real brutality of the moment depicted.

The "narrative" or "story" type of this *feuilleton* is less common for Vaculík than a "lyric" type more typical of the essay. This has already been illustrated in the cycle of "Spring" *feuilletons*. Others are lyric meditations, e.g. "Poznámky o statečnosti" (1978; On heroism), which reflects on whether one would have the heroism to go to prison for personal beliefs. This problem is posed as purely hypothetical, though it must have been very real for its author. Another lyric meditation, despite minimal "story" elements, is "Feuilleton o 1. Máji 1975" (1975; The first of May), which takes its start from Neruda's similarly named *feuilleton*, hailing the emerging triumph of the working class, but ending bathetically with the all-powerful communist president Husák attempting to speak over a broken loudspeaker that perversely remains silent.

Vaculík's *feuilletons* lost some of their urgency and significance after December 1989, when the Czechs and Slovaks asserted their independence. Still, the new Republic was dogged by many political and social problems; throughout these he has continued to produce his *feuilletons* at the same pace. He has thus revived for his people a leading Czech literary genre, one full of understatement and irony, a genre that has lasted well into the time of the re-creation of a new young democratic republic.

WILLIAM E. HARKINS

Biography

Born 23 July 1926 in Brumov, Moravia. Studied at the Commerce Academy for International Business, 1944–46; High School for Social and Political Sciences, Prague, 1946–51, B.S., 1951. Worked in a Bata shoe factory, Zlin and Zurc, 1941–43; teacher, until 1949, and tutor, 1950–51. Member of the Communist Party, 1946–68: expelled. Married Marie Komárková, 1949: three sons. Editor, Rudé Pravo publishers, 1953–57, *Beseda Venkovské Rodiny* (Native rural journal) 1957–59, *Literární Noviny* (Literary journal), 1966–69, and *Literární Listy* (Literary papers), 1968–69; worked for Czechoslovak Radio, Prague, 1959–66; organizer of Edice Petlice (Padlock editions) *samizdat* publishing. Arrested and imprisoned for giving an interview to the BBC, 1973. Awards: Československý Spisovatel (publishers) Award, 1967; George Orwell Prize, 1976.

Selected Writings

Essays and Related Prose

Milí spolužáci! Vybor písemných prací, 1939–1979, 2 vols., 1986
A Cup of Coffee with My Interrogator: The Prague Chronicles,
    translated by George Theiner, 1987
Jaro je tady: Fejetony z let, 1981–1987, 1988
Srpnový rok: Fejetony z roku 1988, 1989
Stará dáma se baví, 1990
Jak se dela chalpec, 1993

Other writings: four novels (*Rušný dům*, 1963; *Sekyra* [*The Axe*], 1966; *Morčata* [*The Guinea Pigs*], in German, 1971, in Czech, 1973; *Český snář*, 1980).

Further Reading

Harkins, William E., "The New Czechoslovak Feuilleton – A Literary Genre Revived," *Ulbandus Review* 1, no. 2 (Spring 1978): 50–57
Liehm, Antonin J., *The Politics of Culture*, New York: Grove Press, 1968: 181–201
Liehm, Antonin J., "Ludvík Vaculík and His Novel *The Axe*," in *Czech Literature Since 1956: A Symposium*, edited by William E. Harkins and Paul I. Trensky, New York: Bohemica, 1980: 91–102

Vadeboncoeur, Pierre

French Canadian, 1920–

In 1960, the first year of what has been called the Quiet Revolution in Quebec, Pierre Vadeboncoeur published an epoch-making essay entitled "La Ligne du risque" (The path of risk) in *Écrits du Canada Français* (Writings from French Canada). In it Vadeboncoeur pleaded for a renewal, or rather a transformation of the spiritual tradition of French Canada, following in the footsteps of the painter Paul-Émile Borduas. The latter had published in 1948 a manifesto called *Refus global* (Global refusal). Influenced by surrealism, this seminal document raged against the religious and nationalist narrowness of Quebec thought. "Borduas," wrote Vadeboncoeur, "was the first to break radically. He broke totally. He did not break in order to break; he did it to be alone and without witness before truth. Our spiritual history begins with him."

In the 1960s, Vadeboncoeur worked for the Confédération des Syndicats Nationaux (Confederation of National Trade Unions), and in the collection *La Ligne du risque* (1963) launched a vigorous attack against American unionism, which had become a part of the capitalist system instead of a revolutionary force. Thus, in this first book, we find two major aspects of the author's thought: an emphasis on spiritual values, and a dedication to social reform. A third aspect was to emerge a few years later, in 1970, with the publication of an autobiographical narrative, *Un amour libre* (A free love), in which Vadeboncoeur describes the relationship between father and son and reflects on love and private life. Running through these two books is the common theme of freedom. Spiritual life, social combat, art, and love are all paths to freedom, and one can not be separated from the others.

In the years that followed, Vadeboncoeur's main preoccupation became political, that of promoting the independence of Quebec. At the beginning of the 1950s, he had been one of the founders of the magazine *Cité Libre* (Free city), along with his friends Pierre Elliott Trudeau and Gérard Pelletier, who were later to become, respectively, Prime Minister and Minister in the federal government. As the years passed by, Vadeboncoeur became more and more estranged from them, and found that his ideal of freedom could not be attained if the people of Quebec remained in the Canadian Confederation. He became a polemicist, lashing out at the federal system, the domination of the English language, and the subservience of so many French Canadians – including some of his former friends – to what he considered a certain form of colonialism perpetrated by the Anglophone power structure.

Then, in 1978, a major change occurred in Vadeboncoeur's career. With the publication of a long essay entitled *Les Deux Royaumes* (The two realms), he broke with his polemical brochures, and went back, beyond the magazine *La Ligne du Risque*, to the very first essays he had published in the 1940s in *La Nouvelle Relève* (The new awakening). He took leave from his union duties, deciding to devote all his time and efforts to writing. "There are two realms," he wrote, "the one irreducible to the other, and the first human truth consists in knowing that fact . . . I have always known that, more or less consciously. That knowledge had been obscured by the occupations of life, until I came to suffer more and more from our epoch's raw existentialism." Recognizing the coexistence of these two realms – the social and the spiritual – Vadeboncoeur opted decisively for the second, at about the same time as did, in France, the "nouveaux philosophes," Bernard-Henri Lévy, Philippe Nemo, and others. This meeting of minds is not, of course, without historical significance.

Vadeboncoeur has not changed his intense, terse style, reminiscent sometimes of the best prose works of **Charles Péguy.** If anything, his style has become purer in the books that followed, in which he wrote mainly, if not exclusively, about art – whether his own daughter's drawings or the Centre Pompidou in Paris (a splendid essay) – and love, that kind of human but almost mystical love that is strengthened by absence. Vadeboncoeur was a powerful essayist; he has become a prosateur: a prose writer in the strongest sense of the word, an artist of prose writing, one among very few.

GILLES MARCOTTE

Biography
Born 28 July 1920 in Strathmore, near Montreal. Studied at the Collèges Jean-de-Brébeuf and Sainte-Marie, 1938–40; law at the University of Montreal, licence, 1943. Civil servant, journalist, and translator, 1943–50; legal adviser to the Confederation of National Trade Unions, 1950–75. Full-time writer, from 1975; contributor to various journals, including *Cité Libre, Liberté, Situation, Maintenant* (Now), and *Parti Pris* (We affirm). Awards: Liberté Prize, 1970; Duvernay Prize, 1971; David Prize, 1976; City of Montreal Grand Prize for Literature, for *Les Deux Royaumes,* 1978; France-Quebec Prize, for *Trois Essais sur l'insignifiance,* 1984; Canada-Suisse Prize, for *L'Absence,* 1987; Canada-Communauté Française de Belgique Prize, 1994.

Selected Writings

Essays and Related Prose
La Ligne du risque, 1963
L'Autorité du peuple, 1965
Lettres et colères, 1969
La Dernière Heure et la première, 1970
Un amour libre, 1970
Indépendances, 1972
Un génocide en douce: Écrits polémiques, 1976
Chaque jour, l'indépendance, 1978
Les Deux Royaumes, 1978
To Be or Not to Be, That Is the Question (text in French), 1980
Trois essais sur l'insignifiance, 1983
L'Absence: Essai à la deuxième personne, 1985
Essais inactuels, 1987
Essai sur une pensée heureuse, 1989
Le Bonheur excessif, 1992
Gouverner ou disparaître, 1993
Dix-sept tableaux d'enfant: Étude d'une métamorphose, 1994

Further Reading
Arbour, Rose Marie, "Vadeboncoeur et le féminisme," *Possibles* 8, no. 1 (1983): 181–89
Beaudoin, Réjean, editor, *Un homme libre: Pierre Vadeboncoeur,* Montreal: Leméac, 1974
Beaulieu, Victor-Lévy, "Pour saluer Pierre Vadeboncoeur," *Liberté* 12, no. 4 (July–August 1970): 3–11
Dumont, François, "L'Essai littéraire québécois des années quatre-vingt: La Collection 'Papiers collés'," *Recherches Sociographiques* 33, no. 2 (1992): 323–35
Leloup, Béatrice, *Les Images dominantes dans les essais de P. Vadeboncoeur,* Montreal: McGill University, 1981
Liberté issue on Vadeboncoeur, 21, no. 6 (November–December 1979)
Mailhot, Laurent, "D'un amour libre à un pays libéré, ou de l'autorité de l'enfant à celle du peuple," in his *Ouvrir le livre,* Montreal: L'Hexagone, 1992: 195–204 (article originally published 1972)
Melançon, Benoît, "La Fiction de l'Amérique dans l'essai contemporain: Pierre Vadeboncoeur et Jean Larose," *Études Françaises* 26, no. 2 (Autumn 1990): 31–39
Przychodzen, Janusz, "L'Essai québécois contemporain: L'Être spéculaire," *La Licorne* 27 (1993): 205–18
Roy, Paul-Émile, *Pierre Vadeboncoeur: Un homme attentif,* Montreal: Méridien, 1995
Vachon, Stéphane, "Problématique d'une nouvelle forme: L'Essai-Pamphlet au Quebec," *Itinéraires et Contacts de Culture* 6 (1985): 47–57
Vigneault, Robert, "Pierre Vadeboncoeur: L'Énonciation dans le discours de l'essai," in *L'Écriture de l'essai,* Montreal: L'Hexagone, 1994: 133–59 (article originally published 1982)
Vigneault, Robert, "Pierre Vadeboncoeur: La Promotion littéraire du dualisme," in *L'Écriture de l'essai,* Montreal: L'Hexagone, 1994: 110–33 (article originally published 1985)

Valéry, Paul
French, 1871–1945

Form, for Paul Valéry, was of central importance. Many of the intricately crafted poems in his collection *Charmes* (1922; Magic spells) not only richly demonstrate this critical preference but, as his many quips against the cult of Romantic "inspiration" tirelessly remind us, make formal qualities more meaningful than so-called content itself – the structure of the tides as opposed to the mere foam of events on the surface of the sea. Of the many verbal genres that occupied him throughout his long writing life, from poem, prose poem, drama, or mock Socratic dialogue on the one hand, to **aphorism** or fragmentary analysis on the other, where stands the essay in this self-imposed hierarchy of intellectual worth?

In Valéry's own eyes, seemingly low on the list, however prolific an essayist he was to become. He tended to associate it with a conventional, rhetorically-led expression – as loose, by virtue of its discursive prose fabric, as mere walking to dancing, its very ease of comprehensibility a cause for suspicion (this the heritage of the symbolist cult of suggestive difficulty led by his friend and mentor, **Stéphane Mallarmé**). He valued instead, next to the polished voice of a poem with its power to integrate the different "speeds" of mental discovery, the brief but concentrated jottings of his private notebooks, the *Cahiers* (wr. 1894–1945), written at dawn before the more public commitments of the day.

Devoted for the most part to influential writers and thinkers – Descartes, **Pascal,** Goethe, Bergson, **Nietzsche,** Mallarmé – and often stemming from his eminent position at the French Academy, many of the essays of the several volumes of *Variété* (Variety) were occasioned by circumstance, even their scope and subject matter imposed. So much in demand did Valéry become, in fact, for everything from literary **preface** to inaugural discourse, that he referred to himself wearily in a letter to **André Gide** as the "Bossuet of the Third Republic." First published as a collection by the *Nouvelle Revue Française* (New French review) in 1924 and subsequently extended in four further volumes (1929–44) under the subject groupings of literary, philosophical, quasi-political, aesthetic, educational, and poetic (chronological grouping was considered by Valéry to be no more than systematic disorder), the essays of *Variété* nonetheless develop, for all their "varied" range of interests, the single, personal interest at the heart of his thinking: the functioning of the human mind, not the least our capacity for a kind of mental gymnastics or unifying self-awareness brought to bear on sensibility and even consciousness itself. *Introduction à la méthode de Léonard de Vinci* (1919; *Introduction to the Method of Leonardo da Vinci*), where a specific genius, the Renaissance "polymath" Leonardo, is characteristically used to typify a principle of the creative imagination, is but one example of such an interest in human possibility; or, again, "Crise de l'esprit" (1919; "The Spiritual Crisis"), where the same theme of a "fiduciary" partnership between knowledge and individual freedom is extended to a prophetic examination of international relations, including the possible decline of the West through an excess of rationality. "We civilizations now know that we are mortal" is the famous first sentence of this open **letter** first published in English in the *Athenaeum*, or, in a companion piece, "I wrote the other day that peace is the war which admits in its process acts of love and creation."

From analysis of the revelatory mental processes involved in poetic composition, to the conditions of the modern world which make wars as predictable as avoidable, there is not one subject on which Valéry does not bring to bear his uniquely subversive method of assumed naivety (a "Robinson Crusoe" approach, as he called this favored method of banning all untested, secondhand knowledge from his empirical island), and, indeed, his peculiar clarification or "surgical cleansing" of a problem by attending first to its possible origin in words ("le nettoyage de la situation verbale"). The phrase itself, memorable like the walking/dancing analogy for its characteristic blend of precision and suggestion, can be found in the paradoxically well-crafted "Poésie et pensée abstraite" (1939 [the Zahrahoff lecture at Oxford University]; "Poetry and Abstract Thought"). It was one of many essays to become, to the post-symbolist generation and far beyond Valéry's death in 1945, a source of almost biblical pronouncement on fundamental principles of aesthetic criticism (music, painting, and sculpture as much as literature) or – with his usual reflexive curiosity toward the trinity of mind, body, and world which, contrary to so much metaphysical thinking, he saw as the source, limit, and goal of all things human – on the hidden role of language in civilization and thought.

Here the reader may feel that, far from intellectual elitism, a sustained impatience with unnecessary detail informs Valéry's notorious scorn for the would-be exhaustive or "encyclopedic" form of essay or lecture (that same impatience with a "naturalistic" aesthetic of accumulated detail which underlies his in some ways misguided attack on the novel as a true literary form). Wary of metaphysics and philosophical systems, and relegating the political to the realm of myth and dream, these and many of the pieces in parallel collections such as *Maîtres et amis* (1927; Masters and friends), *Regards sur le monde actuel* (1931, 1945; *Reflections on the World Today*), *Souvenirs poétiques* (1947; Poetic memories), or *Vues* (1948; Views) radiate a boldly simple wisdom capable of empowering the general reader with the virtues and rewards of the analytic: a ceaselessly vigilant, single-minded "voice" in which protest and a sense of renewed potentiality combine.

To return, then, to the creative tension between public and private, subject and object, unitary and fragmentary,

undoubtedly present at the heart of Valéry's extended prose writing: much of his reluctant later fulfillment as essayist is derived, it would seem, from the fertile surprise of "finding himself involved in an unaccustomed order of thought . . ." – in other words, from the challenge posed by the public dimension itself. At a far remove from the cult of pure potentiality symbolized by his fictitious monster of the intellect, Monsieur Teste, the externalizing commitment of the essay could be said to produce at its best a wonderfully agile balance of specific and general, enabling him to expand the intense but cryptic perceptions of the notebooks and even to breach, Leonardo-like in the process, the falsely watertight divisions of Science and Art. However ostensibly alien to the tradition of personal confession (what more boring than to read the essays of **Montaigne**, he complains in the *Cahiers*), the essays frequently begin with some lively, personal anecdote concerning his reading (his notorious love-hate relationship with the 17th-century Christian apologist Pascal, for instance) and, at the risk of a certain unrepentant monotony of focus, take delight in rediscovering the "natural flow of thought" temporarily disrupted by the initial demand. There is in the poet something of the potter's art of accommodating the unexpected, he suggests in the early piece, "Au sujet d'Adonis" (1921; "Adonis"), to be used as the preface to an admired edition of La Fontaine's fables, where the goals of pleasure and instruction combine.

With its focus on a "poetics" of mental life, the essay might be seen, finally, as an empathetic mode of discourse particularly suited to Valéry's ability to remain detached from his subject while reidentified through generality itself. This is exemplified in, for instance, "Fragment d'un Descartes" (1925; "Sketch for a Portrait of Descartes" – note yet another defiantly non-definitive title) where, moving as usual from personal anecdote to general perception, he conveys the excitement of Descartes' first encounter with the seed of intellectual possibility to determine the rest of his life, if not the development of the whole of Western thought: a moment of crisis and mathematical insight we cannot but link with Valéry's own formative crisis in 1892, the famous night of the storm when he felt himself divided in two, observer and observed, and decided to devote himself to the analysis of affectivity rather than its passive experience. Far from weakening objectivity, such passionate involvement in universality cannot but appear to strengthen the power of his argument: a disarmingly persuasive polemic full of grace, wit, and humor, if not without its moments of perversely "anti-literary" obstinacy (the notorious essay on Proust, for example, where he denies having read his great novel at all).

Valéry dedicated his reflections on the modern world to "those who adhere to no system or political party and who, therefore, are still at liberty to question what is in doubt and [a typically probing twist to the incipient cliché] not free to deny what is beyond question." In valuing the freedom to question the most cherished conviction (religious, political, or otherwise), and in exploiting the implicit dialogue with his reader as a means of questioning the role of received ideas in his own thought, he characteristically revivifies the primary sense of the term "essay" as the French *essayer* – "to attempt," or, in this case, to struggle against the damaging closure of a form of metaphysical thinking parasitic on language alone. In my ignorance lies my strength – the Cartesian "cogito" turned on its head? We are back, moreover, to the theme of formal difficulty (Leonardo's "hostinato rigore"). It is in this sustained devotion to the pursuit of the shadow at the heart of light that Valéry, essayist and attempter of the impossible (for how can thought itself not betray the fluid, he seems to asks through the very form of the essay), might be said to reveal the Modernism underlying his classical achievement, but also, no less valuably, to vindicate the values of critical lucidity and stylistic balance kept alive by a limpid use of French prose still largely unrivaled to this day.

CHRISTINE CROW

Biography

Ambroise Paul Toussaint Jules Valéry. Born 30 October 1871 in Cette (now Sète). Studied at a lycée in Montpellier, 1887–88, baccalauréat, 1888; University of Montpellier, 1888–92, law degree, 1892. Military service, 1889–90. Worked in the War Office, 1897–1900; private secretary to Édouard Lebey, director of the Agence Havas press association, Paris, 1900–22. Married Jeannie Gobillard, 1900: two sons and one daughter. Coeditor, *Commerce* literary review, 1924–32. Elected to the French Academy, 1925. Administrator, Centre Universitaire Méditerranéen, Nice, from 1933; chair of poetics, Collège de France, Paris, 1937–45. Awards: honorary degree from Oxford University. Chevalier, 1923, Officer, 1926, and Commander, 1931, Legion of Honor. Died in Paris, 20 July 1945.

Selected Writings

Essays and Related Prose

Introduction à la méthode de Léonard de Vinci, 1919; as *Introduction to the Method of Leonardo da Vinci*, translated by Thomas McGreevy, 1929
Fragments sur Mallarmé, 1924
Variété 1–5, 5 vols., 1924–44; first 2 vols., as *Variety*, translated by Malcolm Cowley and William Aspenwall Bradley, 1927–38
Études et fragments sur le rêve, 1925
Essai sur Stendhal, 1927
Maîtres et amis, 1927
Poésie: Essais sur la poétique et le poète, 1928
Divers essais sur Léonard de Vinci, 1931
Regards sur le monde actuel, 1931; revised, enlarged edition, 1945; as *Reflections on the World Today*, translated by Francis Scarfe, 1948
Calepin d'un poète: Essais sur la poétique et le poète, 1933
Discours aux chirurgiens, 1938
Tel quel (fragments from notebooks), 2 vols., 1941–43
Mauvaises pensées et autres, 1942
Souvenirs poétiques, 1947
Vues, 1948
Écrits divers sur Stéphane Mallarmé, 1950
Cahiers, 29 vols., 1957–61; Pléiade Edition edited by Judith Robinson, 2 vols., 1973–74; *Cahiers, 1894–1914*, edited by Nicole Celeyrette-Pietri and Judith Robinson-Valéry, 5 vols., 1987–94 (in progress)
An Anthology (includes essays, poetry, and dialogues), edited by James R. Lawler, 1977

Other writings: poetry, three plays, and correspondence.

Collected works editions: *Collected Works*, edited by Jackson Mathews, 15 vols., 1957–75; *Œuvres* (Pléiade Edition), edited by Jean Hytier, 2 vols., 1975–77.

Bibliographies

Davis, Ronald, and Raoul Simonson, *Bibliographie des œuvres de Paul Valéry, 1895–1925*, Paris: Plaisir de Bibliophile, 1926
Karaiskis, Georges, and François Chapon, *Bibliographie des œuvres de Paul Valéry*, Paris: Blaizot, 1976

Further Reading

Austin, Lloyd James, "The Genius of Paul Valéry," in *Wingspread Lectures in the Humanities*, Racine, Wisconsin: Johnson Foundation, 1966
Benoist, Pierre-François, *Les Essais de Paul Valéry, vers et prose*, Paris: Pensée Moderne, 1964
Bowie, Malcolm, Alison Fairlie, and Alison Finch, editors, *Baudelaire, Mallarmé, Valéry: New Essays in Honour of Lloyd Austin*, Cambridge: Cambridge University Press, 1982
Crow, Christine, *Paul Valéry: Consciousness and Nature*, Cambridge: Cambridge University Press, 1972
Crow, Christine, *Paul Valéry and Maxwell's Demon: Natural Order and Human Possibility*, Hull: University of Hull, 1972
Crow, Christine, *Paul Valéry and the Poetry of Voice*, Cambridge: Cambridge University Press, 1982
Franklin, Ursula, *The Rhetoric of Valéry's Prose "Aubades"*, Toronto: University of Toronto Press, 1979
Gifford, Paul, *Valéry, Charmes*, Glasgow: Glasgow University Press, 1995
Grubbs, Henry A., *Paul Valéry*, New York: Twayne, 1968
Ince, W. N., *The Poetic Theory of Paul Valéry: Inspiration and Technique*, Leicester: Leicester University Press, 1961
Ince, W. N., *Paul Valéry: Poetry and Abstract Thought* (an inaugural lecture delivered at the University of Southampton, 24 May 1973), Southampton: University of Southampton, 1973
Lawler, James, *The Poet as Analyst: Essays on Paul Valéry*, Berkeley: University of California Press, 1974
Mackay, Agnes, *The Universal Self: A Study of Paul Valéry*, Glasgow: Maclellan, 2nd edition, 1980 (original edition, 1961)
Nash, Suzanne, *Paul Valéry's "Album de vers anciens": A Past Transfigured*, Princeton, New Jersey: Princeton University Press, 1983
Pickering, Robert, *Paul Valéry, poète en prose*, Paris: Lettres Modernes, 1983
Robinson, Judith, "Dreaming and the Analysis of Consciousness in Valéry's *Cahiers*," French Studies 16, no. 2 (April 1962): 101–23
Scarfe, Francis, *The Art of Paul Valéry: A Study in Dramatic Monologue*, London: Heinemann, 1954
Stimpson, Brian, *Paul Valéry and Music*, Cambridge: Cambridge University Press, 1984
Suckling, Norman, *Paul Valéry and the Civilized Mind*, London: Oxford University Press, 1954
Virtanen, Reino, *L'Imagerie scientifique de Paul Valéry*, Paris: Vrin, 1975
Whiting, Charles, *Paul Valéry*, London: Athlone Press, 1978

Varchi, Benedetto

Italian, 1503–1565

Varchi's writing encompasses, in true Renaissance fashion, a wide variety of genres and forms, both fictional and nonfictional: lyric and pastoral poetry, comic theater, translations from Latin and Greek texts, literary commentary and editing, artistic theory, commemorative oration, dialogue, philology, and history. His major work, the *Storia fiorentina* (wr. 1547, pub. 1721; Florentine history), was commissioned by his patron, Cosimo de' Medici, ruler of Florence. Its 16 short books take the form of a series of essays commenting on the period from 1527 to 1538. They have been judged harshly by some for their praise of Cosimo and his family, said to be dictated by the writer's position as a Medici courtier and dependent. Varchi's admiration for his benefactor, however, can also be seen as an expression of the general esteem in which Cosimo was held by 16th-century humanists for his wide culture, his patronage of the arts, and his undoubted and much-prized quality of *virtù* (energy). Whatever the case, the *Storia* is a work of conscientious and systematic research demonstrating that concern of Renaissance historians, first found in Petrarch and illustrated later in contemporaries of Varchi such as **Machiavelli** and **Guicciardini**, not merely to trust received views or accept what previous historians had written, but to use and check evidence from a full range of sources: histories, chronicles, private memoirs, official documents, and, in Varchi's case, personal knowledge and experience of facts and individuals. But while from this angle the *Storia* bears favorable comparison with the work of Varchi's more illustrious contemporaries, and is indeed itself a useful historical source book, it lacks the theoretical framework, the evaluative vigor and the wider European or at least pan-Italian dimension to be found in the writing of, say, Machiavelli. Yet this makes it more of an "open" work, engaging more with the reader than other similar works of the period. Its alternations between, on the one hand, well-marshaled fact and analysis and, on the other, accumulations of events and opinions which seem to tumble out without order, hierarchy, or stylistic unity make it a hybrid more typical of earlier Renaissance historiography. At the same time – and this too raises questions in the mind of the reader – it can tend toward the mere erudition or chronicle characteristic of later Counter-Reformation writers such as Vincenzo Borghini or Scipione Ammirato.

In these **historical essays** Varchi is something of a transition figure between Renaissance and Counter-Reformation, and indeed a marked hostility to certain aspects of the spirit of the Counter-Reformation is to be found in the aversion to clerical involvement in politics very forcefully expressed in the *Storia*. In contrast, his essay work on artistic theory shows that in this area he had to a large extent completed the transition from the Platonist eclecticism characteristic of Renaissance artistic thought to the more rigid Aristotelian conventions of the new era, which divided learning into the two distinct categories of art and science and further insisted on the division of art into discrete forms and genres, each governed by its own rules and proprieties. His *Due lezzioni* (1549; Two lectures), initially delivered to the Accademia Fiorentina in 1546, consist of a pedestrian analysis of a Michelangelo sonnet followed by a somewhat sterile discussion on which of the two artistic forms, painting and sculpture, holds primacy over the other, leading Baxter Hathaway (1962) to describe Varchi as "one of the more timid and unoriginal of the Aristotelians." His *Orazione funerale ... nell'essequie di Michelangelo Buonarroti* (1564; Funeral oration for Michelangelo) is, in its expression, equally illustrative of the rhetorical excess which characterized the Counter-Reformation, the oration form being, as Peter M. Brown (1974) puts it, "thoroughly decadent, the plaything of erudition and of the pedestrian rhetoric of the *letterato*." However, it would be wrong to see his Aristotelianism, of which he was, in Umberto Pirotti's words,

"a clear and elegant popularizer," as entirely formal and monolithic, since, as his collected lectures on philosophy and aesthetics published in 1590 (*Lezzioni*) show, his theorizing raises significant contradictions between intellect and religious dogma, even if, like most of his contemporaries, he then leaves them serenely unresolved.

The vogue for rhetoric also found expression in the linguistic disputes that raged in 16th-century Italy, in particular the famous *questione della lingua* ("language question"), in which Varchi was a significant figure. His essay in dialogue form about written Italian, *L'Ercolano* (wr. 1565, pub. 1570; The dialogue of Ercolano), is his best-known work and, perhaps because of the more practical nature of the issue, shows greater originality of thought and insight than his writings on artistic theory. He steers a middle course between the two main theories current at the time: the one championed by Pietro Bembo which maintained that the "correct" language to be cultivated by writers was the archaic literary tongue of 14th-century Florence found in Dante, Petrarch, and Boccaccio; and the other, supported by such figures as Claudio Tolomei and Annibal Caro, which argued that "correct" Italian was that currently used in Florence for spoken purposes. The *Ercolano*, while providing a comprehensive survey of the whole question, shows great admiration for Bembo and his views, which as the century wore on were finally to prevail. But at the same time Varchi is concerned to reconcile Bembo's prescriptions with a perceived need for making modern usage play a part in the language of literary composition. In this attempt to apply the linguistic lesson of the old writers to the contemporary idiom, Varchi is taking up the theme much present in his artistic theory of the relationship between art (in this case the 14th-century language) and nature (practical modern usage). The claim he lays in this work to systematic analysis of the topic and the evidence relating to it is not, however, fulfilled. He does present an impressive wealth of exemplification, but it is not always appropriately ordered, and the effectiveness of his arguments is not infrequently diminished by digressions and obvious factual errors. Yet it cannot be denied that this is somewhat counterbalanced by his vigor of argument in support of convictions which are manifestly deeply held and which, in the light of modern knowledge about language, can sometimes be seen to be both perceptive and prophetic.

HOWARD MOSS

Biography

Born 1503 in Florence. Studied jurisprudence in Pisa, from 1521; qualified as notary, but main interest was in literature and humanist studies; learned Greek with Pietro Vettori and translated many Latin and Greek authors; taught himself Provençal and translated a Provençal grammar into Italian. Banished from Florence for supporting the Republicans, 1530, and went into exile with the Strozzi family to escape Medici rule. Traveled widely in Italy, including to Bologna, Padua, and Venice. Recalled to Florence, 1543, by Cosimo I de' Medici, who appointed him state historiographer; received into the Florentine Academy, 1543, and consul, from 1553; changeable relationship with his patrons the Medici, falling in and out of favor several times; finally became one of Cosimo's leading acolytes and was commissioned by him to write a recent history of Florence and to compose orations. Died in 1565.

Selected Writings

Essays and Related Prose

Due lezzioni, 1549
Orazione funerale . . . nell'essequie di Michelangelo Buonarroti, 1564
L'Ercolano (dialogue), 1570; edited by Maurizio Vitale, 1979
Lezzioni, 1590
Lezione su Dante e prose varie, 1590; edited by Giuseppe Aiazzi and Lelio Arbib, 2 vols., 1841
Storia fiorentina, 1721; edited by Gaetano Milanesi, 3 vols., 1857–58

Other writings: poetry and a play. Also translated many classical works.

Collected works edition: *Opere*, 2 vols., 1834; *Opere*, edited by Antonio Racheli, 2 vols., 1858–59.

Further Reading

Bonora, Ettore, "Il purismo fiorentino e la nuova filologia," in *Storia della letteratura italiana*, vol. 4, edited by Emilio Cecchi and Natalino Sapegno, Milan: Garzanti, 1966: 607–26
Brown, Peter M., *Lionardo Salviati: A Critical Biography*, London: Oxford University Press, 1974: especially 80–93
Hathaway, Baxter, *The Age of Criticism: The Late Renaissance in Italy*, Ithaca, New York: Cornell University Press, 1962
Izzo, Herbert J., "The Linguistic Philosophy of Benedetto Varchi, Sixteenth-Century Florentine Humanist," *Language Sciences* 40 (1976): 1–7
Manacorda, Guido, *Benedetto Varchi: L'uomo, il poeta, il critico*, Rome: Polla, 1976 (original edition 1903)
Montevecchi, Alessandro, *Storici di Firenze: Studi su Nardi, Nerli, e Varchi*, Bologna: Patron, 1989
Papuli, Giovanni, *Benedetto Varchi: Logica e poesia*, Manduria: Lacaita, 1970
Pirotti, Umberto, "Benedetto Varchi e la questione della lingua," *Convivium* 28 (1960): 257–342
Pirotti, Umberto, "Aristotelian Philosophy and the Popularization of Learning: Benedetto Varchi and Renaissance Aristotelianism," in *The Late Italian Renaissance, 1525–1630*, edited by Eric Cochrane, London: Macmillan, and New York: Harper and Row, 1970: 168–208
Pirotti, Umberto, *Benedetto Varchi e la cultura del suo tempo*, Florence: Olschki, 1971
Quiviger, Francis, "Benedetto Varchi and the Visual Arts," *Journal of the Warburg and Courtauld Institutes* 50 (1987): 219–24
Rossi, Sergio, "Varchi, Michelangelo e la disputa sul 'Primato' delle arti," in his *Dalle botteghe alle accademie: Realtà sociale e teorie artistiche a Firenze dal XIV al XVI secolo*, Milan: Feltrinelli, 1980: 89–122
Vitale, Maurizio, Introduction to *L'Ercolano* by Varchi, Milan: Cisalpino-Goliardica, 1979 (reprint of 1804 Milan edition)
Vitale, Maurizio, *La questione della lingua*, Palermo: Palumbo, 1984: 90–94 (original edition 1960)
Ward, Michael T., "Benedetto Varchi as Etymologist," *Historiographia Linguistica* 16 (1989): 235–56
Ward, Michael T., "Benedetto Varchi and the Social Dimensions of Language," *Italica* 68 (1991): 176–94
Weinberg, Bernard, *A History of Literary Criticism in the Italian Renaissance*, Chicago: University of Chicago Press, 1961

Vasconcelos, José

Mexican, 1882–1959

Activist philosopher, political figure (once a candidate for the Mexican presidency), and educational administrator (among other things, secretary of public education in his native land for four years), José Vasconcelos was also a prolific essayist, producing dozens of books and numerous uncollected essays which appeared in diverse periodicals.

If it can be said that Parmenides was being-intoxicated and that Spinoza was God-intoxicated, it can just as well be said that Vasconcelos was unity-intoxicated, possessed by a desire to achieve a comprehension of the whole of reality – not by abstracting generalities from individual differences, but by seeking what he termed a "synthesis of the heterogeneous," wherein all aspects of reality would be unified while still remaining diverse. As a result it can be difficult to understand or appreciate single essays in isolation. Vasconcelos' words are often like notes, his essays like musical passages, even at times like whole movements of a symphony, and are more meaningful considered together than by themselves.

Among the many works he penned were four volumes of autobiography; a number of aesthetics-centered works, the most important of which were *El monismo estético* (1918; Aesthetic monism), *Tratado de metafísica* (1929; Treatise on metaphysics), *Ética* (1932; Ethics), *Estética* (1935; Aesthetics), and *Lógica organica* (1945; Organic logic); several collections of essays on sociopolitical topics, including *La raza cósmica* (1925; The cosmic race), *Indología* (1927; Indianology – Vasconcelos' term), and *Bolivarismo y Monroísmo* (1934; Bolivarism and Monroism); and a collection of highly original essays on educational theory and practice entitled *De Robinsón a Odiseo* (1935; From Robinson [Crusoe] to Odysseus).

Vasconcelos affirmed that the major achievements of his homeland were in the realm of the arts – poetry, music, painting, sculpture, and architecture. Hence when he concentrated on aesthetics in his philosophy he felt he was reflecting a dominant feature of Mexican life. Further, he was, in the traditional Spanish phrase, *un hombre de carne y hueso* (a man of flesh and bone), a philosopher who sought truth as the fruit of a total experience – sensory, intellectual, volitional, emotional; he sought the "whole" truth as a "whole" person, and this total experience is aesthetic. In *Tratado de metafísica* Vasconcelos used the example of a gardener who, amidst the splendor of a rose garden, sets himself to counting the bushes. However, as soon as he does so the most profound and stirring aspects of the place are shattered. As with the rose garden, so too is the philosophical conception of the universe of a person whose vision is narrowed to the realm of the mathematical.

Even in his ethics, Vasconcelos' approach was aesthetic. He pointed out that to create a work of beauty the artist gives a special form to some matter, such as the arrangement of sounds in a symphony or of shapes and colors in a painting. Our human acts and the events and circumstances of our lives are a kind of matter to which we can give a form. Thus in *Ética* Vasconcelos wrote that in a heroic action or a saintly work, ethics and aesthetics become one, with the hero or the saint creating a life of beauty.

The task of achieving a system of unity-with-diversity in his aesthetic philosophy was also the principal problem in Vasconcelos' social and political thought – in both domestic concerns within Mexico (as in *La raza cósmica* and especially in *Indología*, where he discussed questions concerning human unity and racial and cultural diversity) and international (especially inter-American) issues (as in *Bolivarismo and*

Monroísmo, where he sought the integration of the diverse nations of Latin America in an exemplary union).

To project his comprehensive view of reality Vasconcelos employed a "poetic" method of exposition. He explained that the poet, as an artist, recognizes the essential role of the emotions in the cognitive process and is precisely the artist who employs a discursive language by means of which this process can be elaborated and explicated. Thus Vasconcelos remarked in his *Ética* that a philosopher must be "a poet with a system," pointing out that the insights of the poet are necessary in order to grasp reality; the philosopher organizes such insights in the writing of essays.

While his essays are often attractive and stimulating, Vasconcelos' scholarship can be suspect (with, for example, slight care taken about properly identifying his sources). Moreover, a number of his poetic passages are at times decidedly obscure; the reader may glimpse poetic insights without being able to discover the philosopher's system. However, such objections concerned Vasconcelos little since he saw himself as an inventor, a creative essayist, and not as a pedantic philosopher.

José Vasconcelos was a complex, passionate figure who, despite his academic weaknesses, is one of the major philosopher-essayists of modern Latin America.

JOHN H. HADDOX

Biography
Born 28 February 1882 in Oaxaca. Studied in the United States; law at the Escuela Nacional de Jurisprudencia, Mexico City, graduated 1905. Married Serafina Miranda (later died), 1909: one son and one daughter. Cofounder, Ateneo de la Juventud (Atheneum of youth), Mexico City, 1909–14. Official post in the Progressive Constitutional Party; official representative for Francisco Madero in Washington, D.C., 1910–11; arrested and briefly imprisoned after Madero's assassination, 1913. Traveled in Peru and the United States, 1915–20. Rector, National Autonomous University of Mexico, Mexico City, 1920–21. Secretary of public education, 1920–24; unsuccessful candidate for Governor of the State of Oaxaca, 1924. Traveled in Europe, from 1925, and taught at various universities in the U.S. Unsuccessful candidate for President of Mexico, 1929. Traveled in Central America, Europe, and the U.S. for ten years; returned to Mexico, 1938. Director, National Library and the Library of Mexico. Founding member, El Colegio de México. Married Esperanza Cruz, 1942: one son. Died (of a heart attack) in Mexico City, 30 June 1959.

Selected Writings

Essays and Related Prose
El monismo estético, 1918
Divagaciones literarias, 1919
Estudios indostanicos, 1920
Artículos: Libros que leo sentado y libros que leo de pié, 1920
Ideario de acción, 1924
La raza cósmica, 1925
Aspects of Mexican Civilization (lectures), with Manuel Gamio, 1926
Indología, 1927
Tratado de metafísica, 1929
Pesimismo alegre, 1931
Ética, 1932
Bolivarismo y Monroísmo: Temas iberoamericanos, 1934
Hispanoamérica frente a los nacionalismos agresivos de Europa y Norteamérica (lectures), 1934

De Robinsón a Odiseo: Pedagogía estructurativa, 1935
Estética, 1935
Qué es el comunismo, 1936
Qué es la revolución, 1937
El realismo científico (lectures), 1943
El viento de Bagdad: Cuentos y ensayos, 1945
Lógica organica, 1945
Discursos, 1920–1950, 1950
Temas contemporáneos, 1955
En el ocaso de mi vida, 1957
Cartas políticas, edited by Alfonso Taracena, 1959
Letanías del atardecer, 1959
Pesimismo heroico, 1964
Antología de textos sobre educación, edited by Alicia Molina, 1981

Other writings: three plays, works on Mexican history, sociology, and education, biographies of important Mexicans, and the autobiographical series *Ulises criollo* (1935–39; *A Mexican Ulysses*).

Collected works edition: *Obras completas*, 4 vols., 1957–61.

Bibliography
Foster, David William, "A Checklist of Criticism on José Vasconcelos," *Los Ensayistas* 14–15 (1983): 177–212

Further Reading
Basave Fernández del Valle, Augustín, *La filosofía de José Vasconcelos*, Madrid: Cultura Hispánica, 1958
Cárdenas Noriega, Joaquín, *José Vasconcelos, 1882–1982: Educador, político y profeta*, Mexico City: Océano, 1982
De Beer, Gabriella, *José Vasconcelos and His World*, New York: Las Américas, 1966
Fernández MacGregor, Genaro, *Vasconcelos*, Mexico City: Ediciones de la Secretaría de Educación Pública, 1942
Giordano, Jaime A., "Notas sobre Vasconcelos y el ensayo hispanoamericano del siglo veinte," *Hispanic Review* 41 (1973): 541–54
Haddox, John, *Vasconcelos of Mexico, Philosopher and Prophet*, Austin: University of Texas Press, 1967
Robb, James Willis, "José Vasconcelos y Alfonso Reyes: Anverso y reverso de una medalla," *Los Ensayistas* 16–17 (1984): 55–65
Taracena, Alfonso, *José Vasconcelos*, Mexico City: Porrúa, 1982

Vidal, Gore
American, 1925–

Although Gore Vidal distinguished himself first as a novelist, he has become one of America's most prolific essayists, perhaps because the essay allows him to pursue most easily what he admits is his "only serious interest" as a writer: "the subversion of a society that bores and appals me." Toward this goal, he has produced work that has been collected in 11 volumes, the first, *Rocking the Boat*, appearing in 1962, the latest, *United States*, in 1992. While the majority of the essays originally appeared in journals, magazines, and newspapers such as the *New York Review of Books*, the *Nation*, and the *Reporter*, Vidal's opinions also found voice in less predictable forums like *Zero* and *Architectural Digest*.

As the titles of the journals in which Vidal's essays appeared might indicate, he writes about literature, issues of national interest, and the people he has known. In fact, in *United States*, which draws from essays published during the preceding 40 years, Vidal separates the essays into three categories: "State of the Art," "State of the Nation," and "State of Being." As these groupings indicate, Vidal regards himself as a critic of literature, government, and society.

Critics of his work generally agree that Vidal's essays about literature represent him at his best, even though the majority of these essays are not weighty: arguing, for example, the influence of films on modern fiction or denouncing academic novels. They are, however, usually bright, witty, and filled with pithy metaphors. He accuses John O'Hara of detailing his characters' spending habits "with the zest of an Internal Revenue man examining deductions for entertainment" and **Henry James** of "giving us monsters on a grand scale" in his late fiction. Evaluating Herman Wouk, Vidal quotes a passage and concludes, "This is not at all bad, except as prose." When he approves of a writer or a work, his appraisals ring with wit and insight. His disapproval, characterized frequently as "bitchy," stings with biting **satire**.

Satire is, indeed, his preferred mode. More negative than positive in his evaluation of the "state of the nation," Vidal attacks government regulations, bureaucracy, and "the Bank," specifically Chase Manhattan Bank; but he explains that this shorthand also refers to all those who have "ownership of the United States." This group includes Democrats, Republicans, and the press. In a manner that critics often classify as superficial and frequently vindictive, Vidal condemns the policies and/or personal behavior of most 20th-century presidents, characterizing Harry Truman as "the president who did us the most harm" and Jack Kennedy as sexually selfish – "not much interested in giving pleasure to his partner." Although surely liberal in his sentiments, Vidal proposes reforms which most people, liberal or otherwise, might have difficulty endorsing, either for their naivety or for their inhumanity. Supporting the legalization of illegal drugs and substances, he justifies his position on the bases that legalization would remove the Mafia from the drug picture and that if people want to kill themselves, the government should not try to stop them. After the Reagan election, Vidal called for a coalition of "faggots," Jews, and blacks since the do-gooders wished to place all of them "in the same gas chambers." Richard Brookhiser's hostile review of United States in the New Criterion (September 1993) dismisses these political essays, saying, "When Vidal exerts himself, he rises to the average."

His essays on "State of Being" accommodate work that does not fit neatly into the other two categories. Pieces such as "On Flying" (1985), which recalls Vidal's first experience with an airplane at the age of four and moves to a lesson on the history of flight and famous aviators; "Tarzan Revisited" (1963), which summarizes the Tarzan story with the purpose of exploring human fascination with and personal dreams of adventure; and several essays which might serve as a travel guide for the uninitiated – "Nasser's Egypt" (1963), "Mongolia!" (1983), and "At Home on a Roman Street" (1985) – are included in this section. Like most of Vidal's essays, these pieces incorporate not only his personal views but also references to people, places, and experiences from his own life.

Vidal's family provides him with a wealth of material. His maternal grandfather was Thomas Pryor Gore, one of the first two senators from Oklahoma. He was related to Jackie Kennedy through one of his mother's marriages. Even though Vidal admits in Palimpsest, his 1995 book-length memoir, that "I had never wanted to meet most of the people that I had met and the fact that I never got to know most of them took dedication and steadfastness on my part," he claims an acquaintance with a large number of political and literary figures in his essays. Being a novelist, essayist, screenwriter, and playwright and having also run for Congress twice, Vidal met and worked with prominent people in politics, the entertainment industry, and literary circles. He freely uses these connections in his essays, frequently sharing anecdotes from his personal and working relationships with the famous and infamous. In fact, we might classify his style as conspiratorial name-dropping. Readers learn of the business dealings and the sexual, drinking, and personal habits of the notorious; family skeletons emerge from the closets. John F. Kennedy, Henry James, Tennessee Williams, F. Scott Fitzgerald, Theodore Roosevelt, Anaïs Nin, and many others become human in the most negative sense with Vidal's revelations. While these anecdotes personalize and invigorate Vidal's views, they also frequently trivialize them. As Robert Kiernan (1982) observes, "the essays are more interesting for their quips, their anecdotes, and their satirical exaggerations than for the spine of essayistic logic that these bend to their will. The essays . . . are a banquet of canapes. They may leave one hungry . . . but the canapes are so tasty withal that more conventional fare seems unflavored." While Vidal accuses some authors and reviewers of "book chat," he himself may be guilty of "people chat." However, Vidal without the conspiratorial revelations would hardly be Vidal.

GLORIA GODFREY JONES

Biography

Eugene Luther Gore Vidal, Jr. Born 3 October 1925 in West Point, New York. Studied at Los Alamos School, New Mexico, 1939–40; Phillips Exeter Academy, New Hampshire, 1940–43. Warrant officer in the U.S. Army, 1943–46. Editor, E. P. Dutton publishers, New York, 1946. Lived in Antigua, Guatemala, 1947–49. Member of the advisory board, *Partisan Review*, 1960–71. Democratic-Liberal candidate for Congress, New York, 1960; member, President's Advisory Committee on the Arts, 1961–63. Lived in Italy, 1967–76. Co-chair, New Party, 1968–71. Awards: Mystery Writers of America Award, for television play, 1954; Cannes Film Critics Award, for screenplay, 1964; National Book Critics Circle Award, for criticism, 1983; National Book Award, for *United States*, 1993.

Selected Writings

Essays and Related Prose
Rocking the Boat, 1962
Sex, Death, and Money, 1968
Reflections upon a Sinking Ship, 1969
Homage to Daniel Shays: Collected Essays, 1952–1972, 1972; as
    Collected Essays, 1952–1972, 1974; as *On Our Own Now*, 1976
Matters of Fact and of Fiction: Essays, 1973–1976, 1977
Sex Is Politics and Vice Versa, 1979
The Second American Revolution and Other Essays, 1976–1982,
    1982; as *Pink Triangle and Yellow Star, and Other Essays*, 1982
Armageddon? Essays, 1983–1987, 1987
At Home: Essays, 1982–1988, 1988
A View from the Diners Club: Essays, 1987–1991, 1991
Screening History (lectures), 1992
United States: Essays, 1951–1991, 1992

Other writings: 23 novels (including *The City and the Pillar*, 1949; *Washington, D.C.*, 1967; *Myra Breckinridge*, 1968; *1876*, 1976; *Lincoln*, 1984), three crime novels as Edgar Box, a collection of short stories, many plays, television plays, and screenplays, and the memoir *Palimpsest* (1995).

Bibliography

Stanton, Robert J., *Gore Vidal: A Primary and Secondary Bibliography*, Boston: Hall, and London: Prior, 1978

Further Reading

Abbott, Sean, "Book Sales, Prizes, Tenure, and Riotous Times at Bread Loaf: An Interview with Gore Vidal," *At Random* 12 (Fall 1995): 43–45
Auchincloss, Louis, *The Style's the Man: Reflections on Proust, Fitzgerald, Wharton, Vidal and Others*, New York: Scribner, 1994
Baker, Susan, *Gore Vidal: A Critical Companion*, Westport, Connecticut: Greenwood Press, 1997
Brookhiser, Richard, "State of the Essay?," *New Criterion* 12, no. 1 (September 1993): 80–83
Dick, Bernard F., *The Apostate Angel: A Critical Study of Gore Vidal*, New York: Random House, 1974
Kiernan, Robert F., *Gore Vidal*, New York: Ungar, 1982
Macaulay, Stephen, *Gore Vidal, or, A Vision from a Particular Position*, Rockford: Rockford Institute, 1982
White, Ray Lewis, *Gore Vidal*, New York: Twayne, 1968

Voltaire

French, 1694–1778

When it was suggested to President de Gaulle that **Jean-Paul Sartre** should be sent to prison, he answered, "One does not send Voltaire to the Bastille." Voltaire is now remembered as a national conscience for human rights. De Gaulle's gesture may have been generous, but it was also cautious: in 1726 Voltaire became a cumbersome prisoner visited by such a flow of admirers that the worried authorities found it preferable to free him promptly (Jean Orieux, 1978).

Voltaire enjoyed European fame early in life. His official reputation was built on poetry and tragedies (now forgotten); his influential essays were regularly condemned as seditious, and they caused him numerous imprisonments and exiles. Voltaire published them in Switzerland and in the Low Countries whenever he expected scandals. Anonymous authorship, denied authorship, and pretense of collective authorship were some of his protective strategies. Eventually Voltaire always returned to Paris, where he finally became a member of the French Academy (in 1746), while his tragedies gave him introductions at the French court. He could have become a minister, had he not been cultivating his humorous **pamphlets** and essays. He also visited Frederick II of Prussia, and his entire library was purchased by Catherine II of Russia.

At the time of his 1726 stay at the Bastille, Voltaire was deemed the successor of Racine and enjoyed a budding courtier career. This imprisonment was a humiliating experience caused by France's rigid stratification of society according to ranks of birth. When released, Voltaire was banished to England (1726–28), where he wrote his first essays in English: the *Essay upon Epic Poetry* and *Essay upon the Civil Wars in France*,

published in 1727, when he began composing the *Letters Concerning the English Nation* (1733). In the latter, it is apparent that he perceived fewer barriers between occupations in England, where statesmen, religious leaders, writers, and scientists could be found in the same family and treated with equal respect. Indeed, one man could freely combine such functions, as William Penn and **Francis Bacon** had. Voltaire believed that individuals ought to cultivate all their talents, and reacted against divides of caste and specialization. For this reason, he later objected to d'Alembert's *Encyclopédie* in which many specialists (including himself) had juxtaposed ideas. He preferred **Pierre Bayle**'s *Dictionnaire historique et critique* (1697; *An Historical and Critical Dictionary*), richer in its interdisciplinary insight because it issued from one mind. In his essays, Voltaire explored all branches of knowledge, and mobilized all his resources and erudition to the evaluation of human accomplishments, measured independently from national prejudice.

In addressing the English public, Voltaire adopted the stance of the ingenuous visitor judging the country according to the baffling standards of France, standards far more arbitrary, foolish, and immoral than what England had to offer. England was not free of foibles either, and English readers reflected on the historical foundations of their sociopolitical structure with Voltaire. The English *Letters* became a British bestseller. The *Lettres philosophiques* (1734) was not merely their translation. Voltaire abandoned his playful tone but retained his humor, refusing to adopt Pascalian pessimism. French readers were meant to discover a society far more advanced than theirs in the domain of personal liberties. In France, the book was considered to be "a bomb against the Ancien Regime" (Gustave Lanson, 1966).

In the *Lettres*, Voltaire used both countries to give a sense of relativity to the living conditions in each regime, suggesting that ideas molded lifestyles. English political stewardship favored commerce, which benefited each citizen as well as the country's economic health. England's humanitarian mission was apparent in its free circulation of merchandise, and of medical and scientific knowledge. Bacon, Newton (whom Voltaire translated), and Locke, who sometimes "dares affirm, but also to doubt," are the founders of experimental science which deduces from the objective world instead of fitting it into a conceptual mold. Voltaire's enthusiasm for English literature (Shakespeare, **Swift**, Pope) echoed the admiration he felt for Milton in his *Essay upon Epic Poetry*, and it paralleled the relationship of experimental science to nature: the poetical genius of England resembles a strong, uneven tree which would perish under strict geometrical pruning, just as a French geometrical hierarchy would kill the prosperity and strength produced by England's free societal system. From then on, the Voltairean essay may be understood as an attack against erroneous or limiting thoughts.

In the 12th **letter**, Voltaire introduced a concept of history which he developed in his most important essay, the *Essai sur l'histoire générale et sur les mœurs et l'esprit des nations* (1756, 1761–63; *Essay on the Manner and Spirit of Nations, and on the Principal Occurrences in History*), begun in June 1741 as history lessons for Madame du Châtelet. Early versions were shared among Voltaire's friends, and one was published in 1753 without Voltaire's approval. The *Essay* constitutes the first modern comparative history of civilizations, including Asia, and a history of the human mind. Instead of repeating the succession of kings and battles tied to legendary incidents, Voltaire means to discover a given society through its ideas, domestic life, arts, and monetary systems. In the events he presents, he seeks the contrast between causes and effects, rather than their relationships. He does not write to defend a thesis: the part on America contains opposing information; Chapter 39 includes a paragraph of questions to which Voltaire finds no satisfying answer; Chapter 51 concludes that "A reasonable mind, while reading history, is almost strictly busy refuting it." Louis Trénard (1979) estimates that after the *Essay*, history was no longer a compilation, a hagiography, or a moralizing enterprise – doubt and inconclusiveness became permissible. As the king's historiographer, Voltaire came to realize that documents are evaluated according to our best judgment, which remains relative, being reduced to our analysis of probabilities and bound by the literary category of verisimilitude. This is also the truth which the Voltairean essay seeks to explore. Like the essayist, the historian sorts through information without necessarily finding definite answers. Another innovative aspect of Voltairean history is that the chivalric hero is rejected for the "good administrator" who protects liberties in order for society to prosper. This is also his self-appointed role as essayist and his ideal for the "philosopher-king."

One of these important liberties is religious tolerance. Voltaire expressed great sympathy for tolerant England in the first eight *Lettres philosophiques*, reiterated in the *Essay on the Manner and Spirit of Nations*. The *Dictionnaire philosophique* (*The Philosophical Dictionary*), published in Paris in 1764, was immediately condemned there, in Geneva, and in Amsterdam, and was burned in the bonfire that consumed the young Chevalier de la Barre, tortured and condemned to death because he had neglected to take off his hat while passing a bridge where a sacred statue was exposed. Voltaire denied authorship of the *Dictionary* while secretly augmenting the volume until 1769. His suspicion of systematic (potentially dogmatic) thinking led him to give in to the new fashion of alphabetized works: the *Dictionary* (called *La Raison par alphabet* [Reason by the alphabet] in the 1769 edition) does not display dissertations, explanations, or argumentations. His pieces are short, incisive, polemical; they are parodies, tales, **meditations**. In a letter of 1760, Voltaire defined it as a "dictionary of ideas," as an intimate piece where he would consign his thoughts about this world and the next one. Yet (even in his memoirs) Voltaire never fell into the "ridicule of talking to oneself about oneself." He wrote to promote tolerance, to dispel mistakes, "to act." To that end, he limits the pages of his "portable" *Dictionary*. He compares the *Dictionary* to the Bible, which would have produced fewer converts, Voltaire argues, had it been multivolumed. Made to instruct and distract, the *Dictionary* may be opened anywhere and read out of sequence. Voltaire eventually introduced it as a dialogical book: it is "more useful" when "the readers produce the other half." The allusory and brief nature of his articles encouraged readers to participate in their message. The mood of the articles (mostly anti-clerical) alternates between false compliance with established norms, indignation, laughter, and ridicule, all aimed at provoking a contagious or opposing reaction.

The nine volumes of the *Questions sur l'Encyclopédie* (1770–72; Questions about the Encyclopedia) are the longest piece of writing by Voltaire, written and dictated when he was old and sick. The articles vary in length from a hundred words to over 50 pages. The *Questions* is a summation of Voltairean thought, including an important section on religion and religious history from the *Dictionary* and formerly in the *Lettres*. Voltaire adds more literary appreciations, and gathers many fragments and hitherto independent pieces on natural and political sciences, legal systems, and commerce. According to Ulla Kölving, editor of the most recent collected works edition begun in 1983, Voltaire is more of a relativist than ever and finds no certainty but in the existence of God, "master of the Universe."

When compared to **Montaigne** and **Pascal**, Voltaire appears more optimistic about humanity and the progress of knowledge. His essays are never composed in a frame of solitude and isolation. Montaigne writes as a recluse in his square tower, and Pascal rejects society in his longing expectation for God's kingdom, while the suggestive Voltairean essay addresses the reason and emotions of his readers, who are called upon to shape humanity's happier destiny. Voltaire never becomes moralizing or misanthropic: his arguments and indignation always express a faith in humanity and in the possibility of earthly contentment. In the article "Genesis" of his *Dictionary*, Voltaire rejects the notion of a lost golden age or Paradise: he claims that if Adam was cultivating the "garden of delights" before he was condemned to cultivate his "fields," gardener simply became farmer and his new task does not seem that much worse, nor that bad. Adam dutifully tends his piece of land, as did Voltaire, the happy Candide and Zadig.

SERVANNE WOODWARD

Biography
Born François Marie Arouet, either 21 February (as Voltaire contended) or 21 November (according to baptismal record of 22 November) 1694 in Paris. Studied at the Collège Louis-le-Grand, Paris, 1704–11; studied law, 1711–13. Secretary to the French ambassador in Holland, 1713; articled to a lawyer, 1714. Arrested and exiled from Paris for five months, 1716, and imprisoned in the Bastille, 1717–18 (after which he used the name Voltaire), for satiric writings, and 1726, for quarrel with the Chevalier de Rohan-Chabot; lived in England, 1726–29; lived at the Château de Cirey with Madame du Châtelet, 1734–36 and 1737–40 (took refuge in Holland, 1736–37). Ambassador-spy in Prussia, 1740, Brussels, 1742–43, and at the court of King Stanislas, Lunéville, 1748; historiographer to Louis XV, 1745–50; elected to the French Academy, 1746; courtier with Frederick II of Prussia, Berlin, 1750–53; lived in Colmar, 1753–54, Geneva, 1754–55, Les Délices, near Geneva, 1755–59, and at Ferney, 1759–78; visited Paris and received a triumphant welcome, 1778. Member, Royal Society (London), Royal Society of Edinburgh, 1745, and Academy of St. Petersburg, 1746. Died in Paris, 30 May 1778.

Selected Writings

Essays and Related Prose
Essay upon Epic Poetry, 1727; as *L'Essai sur la poésie épique*, 1765; as *Essay on Epic Poetry: A Study and an Edition*, edited by Florence D. White, 1915, reprinted 1970; part as *Essay on Milton*, edited by Desmond Flower, 1954
Essay upon the Civil Wars in France, translated anonymously, 1727; as *Essai sur les guerres civiles de France*, 1729

Letters Concerning the English Nation, translated by John Lockman, 1733; as *Lettres écrites de Londres sur les Anglais*, and as *Lettres philosophiques*, 1734; edited by Gustave Lanson and A.-M. Rousseau, 2 vols., 1964, and Frédéric Deloffre, 1986; as *Letters on England*, translated by Leonard Tancock, 1980; edited (in English) by Nicholas Cronk, 1994

Essai sur la nature du feu, 1739

Essai sur l'histoire générale et sur les mœurs et l'esprit des nations, 7 vols., 1756, revised edition, 8 vols., 1761–63; as *Essai sur les mœurs et l'esprit des nations et sur les principaux faits de l'histoire depuis Charlemagne jusqu'à Louis XIII*, edited by René Pomeau, 2 vols., 1963; as *The General History and State of Europe*, translated by Sir Timothy Waldo, 1754; as *An Essay on Universal History*, translated by Mr. Nugent, 1759, revised 1782; as *Essay on the Manner and Spirit of Nations, and on the Principal Occurrences in History*, translated anonymously, 1780

Traité sur la tolérance, 1763; edited by René Pomeau, 1989; as *A Treatise on Toleration*, translated by David William, 1779; in *A Treatise on Toleration and Other Essays*, translated by Joseph McCabe, 1994

Dictionnaire philosophique portatif, 1764; revised edition, 1765 (and later editions): revisions include *La Raison par alphabet*, 2 vols., 1769, and *Questions sur l'Encyclopédie*, 9 vols., 1770–72; edited by Julien Benda and Raymond Naves, 1961, and Béatrice Didier, 1994; as *The Philosophical Dictionary for the Pocket*, translated anonymously, 1765; as *Philosophical Dictionary*, translated by H. I. Woolf, 1945, Peter Gay, 2 vols., 1962, and Theodore Besterman, 1971

Essai historique et critique sur les dissensions des Églises de Pologne, 1767

Voltaire and the Enlightenment (selection), translated by Norman L. Torrey, 1931

Selections, edited by George R. Havens, revised edition, 1969

Voltaire on Religion (selection), edited and translated by Kenneth W. Applegate, 1974

Selections (various translators), edited by Paul Edwards, 1989

A Treatise on Toleration and Other Essays, translated by Joseph McCabe, 1994

Political Writings (various translators), edited by David Williams, 1994

Dictionnaire de la pensée de Voltaire par lui-même, edited by André Versaille, 1994

Other writings: several works of fiction (including the novellas *Zadig*, 1748, and *Candide*, 1759), plays, poetry, and philosophical works.

Collected works editions: *Œuvres complètes* (Kehl Edition), 70 vols., 1784–89, and on CD-ROM (Chadwyck-Healey); *Œuvres complètes*, edited by L. Moland, 52 vols., 1877–85; *Complete Works* (in French), edited by Theodore Besterman and others, 135 vols., 1968–1977; *Complete Works/Œuvres complètes*, edited by Ulla Kölving, 35 vols., 1983–94 (in progress; 84 vols. projected).

Bibliographies

Barr, Mary Margaret H., *A Century of Voltaire Study: A Bibliography of Writings on Voltaire, 1825–1925*, New York: Institute of French Studies, 1929; supplements in *Modern Language Notes* (1933, 1941)

Barr, Mary Margaret H., and Frederick A. Spear, *Quarante Années d'études voltairiennes: Bibliographie analytique des livres et articles sur Voltaire, 1926–1965*, Paris: Colin, 1968

Bengesco, Georges, *Voltaire: Bibliographie de ses œuvres*, Paris: Rouveyre & Blond, vol. 1, and Perrin, vols. 2–4, 1882–90; index by Jean Malcolm, Geneva: Institut et Musée Voltaire, 1953

Candaux, Jean Daniel, "Voltaire: biographie, bibliographie et éditions critiques," *Revue d'Histoire Littéraire de la France* 79 (1979): 296–319

Vercruysse, Jérôme, "Additions à la bibliographie de Voltaire, 1825–1965," *Revue d'Histoire Littéraire de la France* 71 (1971): 676–83

Further Reading

Aldridge, A. Owen, "Problems in Writing: The Life of Voltaire," *Biography: An Interdisciplinary Quarterly* 1, no. 1 (1978): 5–22

Besterman, Theodore, *Voltaire*, London: Longman, and New York: Harcourt Brace and World, 1969

Brumfitt, John-Henry, "Voltaire Historian and the Royal Mistress," in *Voltaire, the Enlightenment and the Comic Mode: Essays in Honor of Jean Sareil*, edited by Maxine G. Cutler, New York: Lang, 1990: 11–26

Ferenczi, Laszlo, "Voltaire: Le Critique historiographe," *Acta Literaria Academiae Scientiarum Hungaricae* 16 (1974): 140–51

Ferenczi, Laszlo, "Le *Discours* de Bossuet et l'*Essai* de Voltaire," in *Les Lumières en Hongrie, en Europe centrale et en Europe orientale*, edited by Béla Köpeczi, Budapest: Akadémiai Kiadó, 1984: 187–91

Lanson, Gustave, *Voltaire*, New York: Wiley, 1966

Lavallée, Louis, "De Voltaire à Mandrou: Études et controverses autour du *Siècle de Louis XIV*," *Canadian Journal of History/Annales Canadiennes d'Histoire* 12 (1977): 19–49

Madeleine, L.-H., "L'*Essai sur les mœurs et l'esprit des nations*: Une histoire de la monnaie?," in *Mélanges Pomeau*, Oxford: Voltaire Foundation, vol. 2, 1987: 577–92

Monch, Walter, "Voltaire et sa conception de l'histoire: Grandeur et insuffisance," *Travaux de Linguistique et de Littérature* 17, no. 2 (1979): 47–58

O'Meara, Maureen F., "Towards a Typology of Historical Discourse: The Case of Voltaire," *MLN* 93 (1978): 938–62

Orieux, Jean, *Voltaire ou la royauté de l'esprit*, Paris: Flammarion, 1978

Penke, Olga, "Réflexions sur l'histoire: Deux histoires universelles des Lumières françaises et leurs interprétations hongroises," *Studies on Voltaire and the Eighteenth Century* 264 (1989): 993–96

Pomeau, René, editor, *Voltaire en son temps*, Oxford: Voltaire Foundation, 5 vols., 1985–94

Renwick, John, *Voltaire et Morangiés 1772–1773, ou Les Lumières l'ont échappé belle*, Oxford: Voltaire Foundation, 1982

Richter, Peyton, *Voltaire*, Boston: Twayne, 1980

Rivière, M.-S., "Voltaire's Use of Larrey and Limiers in *Le Siècle de Louis XIV*: History as a Science, an Art, and a Philosophy," *Forum for Modern Languages Studies* 25, no. 1 (1989): 34–53

Roger, Jacques, *Les Sciences de la vie dans la pensée française du XVIIIe siècle*, Paris: Colin, 1963

Trénard, Louis, "La Place de Voltaire dans l'historiographie française," *Kwartalnik Histrii Nauki i Techniki* 24 (1979): 509–22

Vignery, Robert J., "Voltaire as Economic Historian," *Arizona Quarterly* 31 (1975): 165–78

Wade, Ira O., *The Intellectual Development of Voltaire*, Princeton, New Jersey: Princeton University Press, 1969

Walters, Robert L., "Chemistry at Cirey," *Studies on Voltaire and the Eighteenth Century* 58 (1967): 1807–27

Williams, David, "Voltaire's 'true essay' on Epic Poetry," *Modern Language Review* 88, no. 1 (January 1993): 46–57

W

Walker, Alice

American, 1944–

Alice Walker has published two collections of her prose, *In Search of Our Mothers' Gardens* (1983) and *Living by the Word* (1988). Together they form a rich compendium of speeches, book and movie **reviews**, travelogues, memoirs and **journal** entries, **letters**, historical reflections, and essays proper. Many pieces are reprinted from the feminist monthly magazine *Ms.*, where Walker was a contributing editor beginning in 1974. Others originally appeared in publications ranging from *Black Scholar* to the *Socialist Review*.

Walker is best known for her work as a novelist. Her 1982 novel *The Color Purple* won the Pulitzer Prize and an American Book Award, and was made into a movie by Steven Spielberg. It also sparked a series of public controversies, some of which she recounts in her essays. Though her nonfiction prose collections have been less well known in the mass market, a few individual essays are commonly anthologized, notably "Beauty: When the Other Dancer Is the Self" (1983), "In Search of Our Mothers' Gardens" (1974), and "Am I Blue?" (1986). These selections epitomize themes that pervade her essays: identity, self-esteem, connection to one's ethnic and artistic roots, the health of the soul in all living beings, and the interconnection of oppressions.

Walker investigates these themes while writing about a variety of social concerns, and the anthologies reveal her political development. Starting with her first published essay ("The Civil Rights Movement: What Good Was It?," 1967), she takes up her pen in support of civil rights and black pride, using personal memories to support her philosophies. One lecture, "Oppressed Hair Puts a Ceiling on the Brain" (1987), discusses Walker's realization that letting her hair grow out naturally would be a crucial step in her political and spiritual development. Her narratives are not exclusively self-referential; she uses other writers' ideas to augment her rhetoric. For example, "In Search of Our Mothers' Gardens" argues that if black women want to be writers, they need rooms of their own as **Virginia Woolf** prescribed.

In her early essays, Walker often uncritically invokes white writers while calling for a black feminist politics based in essentialism – the idea that blacks can relate to oppression because they are black. In later writings, her perspective becomes more courageous, complicated, and internally consistent: Walker explores her own mixed ethnicity and encourages all people to explore their own complex genealogies. Many essays reflect on the position of blacks in the historically charged American South, where she herself grew up. Walker has continued to write about race in essays published after these anthologies; in 1994 the *Monthly Review* printed a 1992 speech called "The Story of Why I Am Here: or, A Woman Connects Oppressions."

The strategy of connecting oppressions gains weight as Walker's philosophy develops. She ties race to gender by coining the now famous term "womanist," its primary definition being "A black feminist or feminist of color" (and its most pithy summation being "Womanist is to feminist as purple is to lavender"). From her concerns with racism and feminism in her early work, she works toward an understanding of Native Americans, homosexual freedom, respect for the poor and for the oppressed citizens of other nations. An all-encompassing spirituality motivates her related efforts to save the trees, animals, and the earth. Oppression in any form, she implies, is of importance to anyone who is capable of concern.

Walker experiments with different rhetorical techniques to make social issues into compelling reading. She often juxtaposes quotations from many writers in quick succession, which allows her to give voice to many perspectives. Quotations from her own journals appear alongside excerpts from newspapers, student essays, or poetry, with selected words italicized for editorial emphasis.

Walker also makes political points in the process of telling a story. For instance, her essay about journeying with her mother to look at Flannery O'Connor's childhood home, only a few miles from her own childhood home in Eatonton, Georgia, is a wry, wise reflection on how race and class can influence a writer's financial and critical success ("Beyond the Peacock: The Reconstruction of Flannery O'Connor," 1972). The chronicle of a trip to China examines social dynamics in mental "snaps" that form a verbal photo album ("A Thousand Words: A Writer's Pictures of China," 1985).

The conversational, loosely connected tone of these essays is that of a storyteller recounting favorite tales. Walker sometimes even recycles the same event in more than one essay, shaping the details to fit the occasion. The storytelling metaphor reflects Walker's veneration for Zora Neale Hurston, an early 20th-century black novelist, folklorist, and anthropologist whose accounts of southern black storytelling gave Walker the confidence to write from her own experiences of growing up black in the South. In her loving essays about

Hurston, Walker honors her ancestors through writing, also showing how artistic expression itself is part of her legacy from black southern women.

Perhaps because she is writing for social change, Walker's essays are generally – and sometimes disingenuously – optimistic. Ending with an uplifting resolution is one way to register hope for the future, and to activate others to work toward a better world. Her optimism also reads as a pleasant ramble through the author's mind, but her good-humored attitude about any experience can ring false, especially when it obscures political realities of the situation at hand.

Just as Walker's individual essays generally end optimistically, her anthologies build toward a holistic sense of connection. At the end of *In Search of Our Mothers' Gardens*, Walker focuses on a sense of wholeness that she finds in herself through her relationship with her daughter. With a child to tend and love, Walker feels connected to a lineage of women. At the end of *Living by the Word*, she communes with trees, whose fate she sees as being tied to the future of all living beings on the earth. It is fitting that her essay anthologies culminate in a garden, a search for which has inspired her to write, and the love of which now motivates her to continue fighting for justice.

KAREN SCHIFF

Biography

Alice Malsenior Walker. Born 9 February 1944 in Eatonton, Georgia. Studied at Spelman College, Atlanta, 1961–63; Sarah Lawrence College, Bronxville, New York, 1963–65, B.A., 1965. Voter registration and Head Start program worker, Mississippi, and with the New York City Department of Welfare, mid-1960s. Married Melvyn R. Leventhal, 1967 (divorced, 1976): one daughter. Taught at Jackson State College, Mississippi, 1968–69, Tougaloo College, Mississippi, 1970–71, Wellesley College, Massachusetts, 1972–73, University of Massachusetts, Boston, 1972–73, and Yale University, New Haven, Connecticut, after 1977; Distinguished Writer, University of California, Berkeley, Spring 1982; Fannie Hurst Professor, Brandeis University, Waltham, Massachusetts, Fall 1982. Contributing editor, *Ms.* magazine, from 1974. Cofounder and publisher, Wild Trees Press, Navarro, California, 1984–88. Awards: several grants and fellowships; American Scholar Prize, for essay, 1967; Lillian Smith Award, for poetry, 1973; American Academy Rosenthal Award, 1974; American Book Award, 1983; Pulitzer Prize, 1983; O. Henry Award, 1986; Langston Hughes Award, 1989; California Governor's Arts Award, 1994; honorary degrees from two universities.

Selected Writings

Essays and Related Prose

In Search of Our Mothers' Gardens: Womanist Prose, 1983
Living by the Word: Selected Writings 1973–1987, 1988
The Same River Twice: Honoring the Difficult: A Meditation on Life, Spirit, Art, and the Making of the Film, "The Color Purple," Ten Years Later, 1996
Anything We Love Can Be Saved, 1997

Other writings: five novels (*The Third Life of Grange Copeland*, 1970; *Meridian*, 1976; *The Color Purple*, 1982; *The Temple of My Familiar*, 1989; *Possessing the Secret of Joy*, 1992), two collections of short stories (*In Love and Trouble*, 1973; *You Can't Keep a Good Woman Down*, 1981), poetry (including *Once*, 1968; *Revolutionary Petunias and Other Poems*, 1973; *Horses Make a Landscape Look More Beautiful*, 1984; *Her Blue Body Everything We Know*, 1991), and books for children.

Bibliographies

Banks, Erma Davis, and Keith Byerman, *Alice Walker: An Annotated Bibliography, 1968–1986*, New York: Garland, 1989
Kirschner, Susan, "Alice Walker's Nonfictional Prose: A Checklist, 1966–1984," *Black American Literature Forum* 18, no. 4 (Winter 1984): 162–63
Pratt, Louis H., and Darnell D. Pratt, *Alice Malsenior Walker: An Annotated Bibliography 1968–1986*, Westport, Connecticut: Meckler, 1988

Further Reading

Allan, Tuzyline Jita, "A Voice of One's Own: Implications of Impersonality in the Essays of Virginia Woolf and Alice Walker," in *The Politics of the Essay: Feminist Perspectives*, edited by Ruth-Ellen Joeres and Elizabeth Mittman, Bloomington: Indiana University Press, 1993: 131–47
Bloom, Harold, editor, *Alice Walker*, New York: Chelsea House, 1989
Carter, Nancy Corson, "Claiming the Bittersweet Matrix: Alice Walker, Sandra Cisneros, and Adrienne Rich," *Critique* 35, no. 4 (1994): 195–204
Fernald, Anne, "A Room, a Child, a Mind of One's Own: Virginia Woolf, Alice Walker and Feminist Personal Criticism," in *Virginia Woolf: Emerging Perspectives*, edited by Mark Hussey and Vara Neverow, New York: Pace University Press, 1994: 245–51
Gates, Henry Louis, Jr., and K. A. Appiah, editors, *Alice Walker: Critical Perspectives Past and Present*, New York: Amistad, 1993
Grimes, Dorothy, "Womanism," in *Global Perspectives on Teaching Literature: Shared Visions and Distinctive Visions*, edited by Sandra Ward Lott, Maureen S. G. Hawkins, and Norman McMillan, Urbana, Illinois: National Council of Teachers of English, 1993: 65–75
Wincell, Donna Hasty, *Alice Walker*, New York: Twayne, 1992

Weber, Max

German, 1864–1920

Max Weber is remembered as a founding father of sociology, as a major contributor to our sense of what distinguishes modern societies from earlier human cultures, and as a political theorist whose analysis of bureaucracies in particular remains fundamental to discussion of the functioning of modern states. But it is unlikely that he was thought of in his own lifetime as an exemplary stylist. What distinguished him from his contemporaries as a writer on human affairs was precisely his insistence that the rhetoric of persuasion should not be allowed to interfere with a clear sense of investigative method; for that reason he acquired a reputation for stylistic asceticism. His keen sense of methodology was related in turn to the interdisciplinary nature of sociological inquiry in his day, as well as to his awareness of the provisional nature of the assumptions on which the inquiries of the human sciences are inescapably based. It is this combination of features – the sense that Weber was working in the interstices between formal disciplines and his self-consciousness about proceeding on provisional terms – that makes it appropriate to regard him in retrospect as an important contributor to the genre of the essay. Indeed it was as "collected essays" on social and economic history, on the sociology of religion, and on the methodology of the humanities, that his best-known works have come down to us.

Weber studied law and economics, and did his early research on medieval business organizations and on the agrarian economy of ancient Rome. He was also active in liberal politics at various times of his life, and his mature writings present the reader with an oft-noted paradox: he was a man of action who nevertheless insisted that political value judgments should be excluded from academic writing, and he was an assiduous scholar who nevertheless expressed firmly-held convictions in his works. The origins of the paradox can again be found in the circumstances of his time. The methodological essays which Weber began to publish when he became one of the principal editors of the journal *Archiv für Sozialwissenschaft und Sozialpolitik* (Archive for social science and social policy) in 1903 show him to be fighting a battle on two fronts. On the one hand he was opposing those who believed it was possible for scholarship to be conducted from a position of "ethical neutrality" (which they tended to equate with their own world view); on the other hand he was opposing those who believed that it was possible for each academic subject to determine its own set of normative values from within its subject area. When he formulated his famous proposition that academic inquiry should be "value-free," it was in order to draw a clear distinction between the specific tasks of investigation which an academic discipline can perform and the necessarily diverse perspectives which individual members of society, with their various cultural backgrounds and personal motives, bring to the evaluation of the results of empirical research.

For Weber it was axiomatic that there could be no absolute "objectivity" in the study of human societies because the nature of the analysis involved was dependent upon the material selected for investigation and on the perceptions of the investigator. The discipline of sociology, he argued, needed to proceed by a method of self-critique which moved from the initial construction of analytical concepts, through the expansion of horizons by empirical research, to the refinement and reformulation of theoretical premises. The form of explanation for human behavior that the sociologist was seeking to arrive at was concerned not only with a sense of the determining forces at work in the society in question, but much more with the effort to understand empathically the *meaning* that human beings attached to their actions in the historical circumstances of that society.

Weber's most famous work, *Die protestantische Ethik und der Geist des Kapitalismus* (1904, revised 1920–21; *The Protestant Ethic and the Spirit of Capitalism*), has been subject to some misunderstanding in the Anglo-Saxon world, either because it is too readily assumed that Weber is working within a German idealist tradition and looking to explain material phenomena in terms of the agency of a spirit, or because it is interpreted (e.g. by translator Talcott Parsons) as conceiving of an attitude of Protestant asceticism as a necessary precondition for "modernization" processes in general. In reality Weber was seeking to describe the distinctive ethical principles by which leading capitalist figures of the post-Reformation period organized their lives and their trading opportunities, and the role these principles had played in shaping "the cosmos of the modern economic order" as it had established itself in Western Europe and North America. (In the original 1904 version of the text, incidentally, Weber's scrupulousness on this point led him to put inverted commas around the word "spirit" in his title.) At the same time it is clear that what motivated his investigation of this theme was a strong personal sense that the moral demands of what a previous age had conceived as a "calling" had subsequently become manifest in the technical and economic conditions of an industrial age, and in doing so had imposed social constraints on the lives of those who came after.

By the standards of later scholarship, the range and scope of Weber's projects no doubt appear exceedingly ambitious (the process of increasing specialization which he described as an irreversible feature of modern knowledge has continued relentlessly since his day). But his essays retain the vigor of a pioneering interdisciplinary inquiry conducted with a keen sense of methodological rigor. As he extended his inquiries into the social dimensions of the world's major religions, he used his findings in one area to illuminate and qualify his view of another. Whether he was describing the emergence of the conditions of "modernity" for the European society of his own day, the economic organization of Mediterranean societies in antiquity, or the implications of oriental religions for social behavior and the economic role of individuals, Weber was using the flexibility of the essay form to express his differentiated sense of how the interaction between mentality and practice affected the specific circumstances of historical developments.

DAVID MIDGLEY

Biography

Born 21 April 1864 in Erfurt, Thuringia. Studied at the Universities of Heidelberg, 1882–83, Strasbourg, 1883–84, Berlin, 1884–85 and 1886–89, Ph.D., 1889, and Göttingen, 1885–86; called to the bar in Berlin. University lecturer in law, University of Berlin, 1892–94. Married Marianne Schnitger, 1893. Professor of economics, University of Freiburg, 1894–96, University of Heidelberg, 1896–1903, and University of Munich, 1919–20. Suffered a nervous breakdown, 1898, and unable to work until 1902. Coeditor, *Archiv für Sozialwissenschaft und Sozialpolitik*, from 1903; editor, *Grundriss der Sozialökonomik* (Outline of social economics), from 1907; cofounder, German Society for Sociology, 1910. Died (of pneumonia) in Munich, 14 June 1920.

Selected Writings

Essays and Related Prose

Gesammelte Aufsätze zur Religionssoziologie, 3 vols., 1920–21; parts as: *The Protestant Ethic and the Spirit of Capitalism*, translated by Talcott Parsons, 1930; *The Religion of China: Confucianism and Taoism*, edited and translated by Hans H. Gerth, 1951, abridged version, as *Confucianism and Taoism*, translated by M. Alter and J. Hunter, 1984; *The Religion of India: The Sociology of Hinduism and Buddhism*, edited and translated by Gerth and Don Martindale, 1958; *On Ancient Judaism*, edited and translated by Gerth and Ned Polsky, 1949, and as *Ancient Judaism*, translated by Gerth and Martindale, 1952

Gesammelte politische Schriften, 1921; enlarged edition, edited by Johannes Winckelmann, 1958

Gesammelte Aufsätze zur Wissenschaftslehre, 1922; enlarged edition, edited by Johannes Winckelmann, 1951

Gesammelte Aufsätze zur Sozial- und Wirtschaftsgeschichte, 1924; as *The Agrarian Sociology of Ancient Civilizations*, translated by R. I. Frank, 1976

Gesammelte Aufsätze zur Soziologie und Sozialpolitik, 1924

Essays in Sociology, edited and translated by Hans H. Gerth and C. Wright Mills, 1946

Schriften zur theoretischen Soziologie, zur Soziologie der Politik und Verfassung, edited by Max Graf zu Solms, 1947

Aus den Schriften zur Religionssoziologie, edited by Max Graf zu Solms, 1948

The Methodology of the Social Sciences, edited and translated by Edward A. Shils and Henry A. Finch, 1949

Soziologie, weltgeschichtliche Analysen, Politik, edited by Johannes Winckelmann, 1955; revised, enlarged edition, 1960

Selections, edited by S. M. Miller, 1963

Staat; Gesellschaft; Wirtschaft, edited by Ludwig Heieck, 1966

Selections in Translation, edited by W. G. Runciman, translated by E. Matthews, 1978

Political Writings, edited by Peter Lassman and Ronald Speirs, 1994

Other writings: works on sociology and economics (including *Wirtschaft und Gesellschaft* [*Economy and Society*], 1922), and correspondence.

Collected works edition: *Gesamtausgabe*, edited by Horst Baier and others, 1984– (in progress; 33 vols. projected).

Bibliographies

Murvar, Vatro, *Max Weber Today – An Introduction to a Living Legacy: Selected Bibliography*, Brookfield: University of Wisconsin-Milwaukee Max Weber Colloquia and Symposia, 1983

Riesebrodt, Martin, in *Prospekt der Max Weber-Gesamtausgabe*, Tübingen: Mohr, 1981

Seyfarth, Constans, and Gert Schmidt, *Max Weber Bibliographie: Eine Dokumentation der Sekundärliteratur*, Stuttgart: Enke, 1977

Further Reading

Beetham, David, *Max Weber and the Theory of Modern Politics*, Cambridge: Polity Press, 1985 (original edition, 1974)

Butts, S., "Parsons' Interpretation of Weber: A Methodological Analysis," *Sociological Analysis and Theory* 7 (1977): 227–41

Cohen, J., L. E. Hazelrigg, and W. Pope, "De-Parsonizing Weber: A Critique of Parsons' Interpretation of Weber's Sociology," *American Sociological Review* 40 (1975): 229–40

Eldridge, J. E. T., "Introductory Essay: Max Weber – Some Comments, Problems and Continuities," in *The Interpretation of Social Reality* by Weber, London: Michael Joseph, 1970; New York: Scribner, 1971

Green, Bryan S., *Literary Methods and Sociological Theory: Case Studies of Simmel and Weber*, Chicago: University of Chicago Press, 1988

Hennis, Wolfgang, *Max Weber: Essays in Reconstruction*, London: Allen and Unwin, 1988

Käsler, Dirk, *Max Weber: An Introduction to His Life and Work*, Cambridge: Polity Press, 1988 (original German edition, 1979)

Kaye, H. L., "Rationalisation as Sublimation: On the Cultural Analyses of Weber and Freud," *Theory, Culture and Society* 9, no. 4 (1992): 45–74

Lepenies, Wolf, *Between Literature and Science: The Rise of Sociology*, Cambridge: Cambridge University Press, 1988 (original German edition, 1985)

Lichtblau, Klaus, and Johannes Weiss, Introduction to *Die Protestantische Ethik und der "Geist" des Kapitalismus* by Weber, Bodenheim: Athenäum/Hain/Hanstein, 1993

Mitzman, Arthur, *The Iron Cage: A Historical Interpretation of Max Weber*, New York: Knopf, 1970

Mommsen, Wolfgang J., *Max Weber and German Politics, 1890–1920*, Chicago: University of Chicago Press, 1984; Cambridge: Polity Press, 1992 (original German edition, 1956)

Mommsen, Wolfgang J., *The Political and Social Theory of Max Weber*, Chicago: University of Chicago Press, and Cambridge: Polity Press, 1989

Tribe, Keith, editor, *Reading Weber*, London and New York: Routledge, 1989

Turner, Bryan S., *Max Weber: From History to Modernity*, London and New York: Routledge, 1992

Wagner, Gerhard, and Heinz Zipprian, editors, *Max Webers Wissenschaftslehre: Interpretation und Kritik*, Frankfurt: Suhrkamp, 1994

The Week

Canadian periodical, 1883–1896

Issued from the Toronto offices of C. Blackett Robinson on 6 December 1883, the first weekly number of the *Week* included a masthead announcing it as an independent "Canadian Journal of Politics, Society, and Literature" and a prospectus promising to "endeavor faithfully to summarize the intellectual, social and political movements of the day." Edited in its inaugural year by Canadian writer and critic Charles G. D. Roberts, *The Week* established itself as one of the most successful and influential **periodicals** published in Victorian Canada. Taking seriously the terms of its mission statement, it accepted contributions of varying intellectual rigor and quality from writers representing a broad spectrum of taste and political opinion. Although many contributions may be considered essays in only the most general sense, they marked the first appearance of many feature and shorter articles which were later collected as "essays" and which continue to be cited as important early examples of Canadian essay writing.

The *Week* gained much of its formative energy from the presence and pen of Goldwin Smith, a one-time Regius Professor of History at Oxford who emigrated in 1871. Already well known as a political commentator to audiences on both sides of the Atlantic, he was also known to Canadian readers through his involvement in establishing two other popular journals: the *Canadian Monthly and National Review* (1872–78) and the *Bystander* (1880–83, 1889–90). A prolific and sharp-tongued writer whose contributions often appeared under the familiar and somewhat ironic journalistic pseudonym "A Bystander," Smith was anything but a chance spectator of world affairs. In terms of international affairs, he used his regular "Current Events and Opinions" columns to comment on such controversial issues as Irish Home Rule (he was against it), the prohibitionist movement (which he equated with "compulsory teetotalism"), and the emancipation of women (of which he was intolerant). Closer to home, Smith wrote passionately on many of the early questions of nationhood, including immigration policies, coeducation at Canadian universities, government grants for railway construction, and the proposed changes to the international copyright laws.

Two other essayists who figured prominently in the pages of the *Week* had close personal, political, and professional ties with Smith: Graeme Mercer Adam and Theodore Arnold Haultain had been involved in Smith's other publishing ventures and shared many of his ideas; Haultain, in fact, went on to become Smith's private secretary and literary executor. Whereas Smith wrote primarily about political and social issues, Adam and Haultain turned their pens to topics of a cultural and literary nature. If diversity and the ideal of nonpartisanship were founding principles of the *Week*, cosmopolitanism was the order of the day in cultural commentaries. Dedicated to the wholesome edification of their literate, largely middle-class readership and to "stimulating our national sentiment, guarding our national morality, and strengthening our national growth," writers in the *Week* set out to cultivate a distinctly Old World standard of literary and cultural criticism. Accordingly, laudatory essays on such "model" writers and thinkers as **Matthew Arnold, George Eliot,** and Sir Walter Scott become commonplace, providing readers with a guide to the best that was being thought and said in the world as well as a kind of Old World datum against which to judge their burgeoning national literature. Indeed, this sense of broad moral purpose underpinned the contents and the tone of *The Week*. As Brandon Conron (1965) suggests: "Though differing widely in interests and style, the writers of these pieces had one quality in common; the assumption, whether tacit or expressed, that their work had literary value, even when their purposes were dictated by politics or religion, and their methods by the editorial, the feature article, or the regular column."

Although Smith's input and critical standards had a lasting influence on the periodical's own standards, his contributions decreased in number and regularity after its first few years. The *Week* continued to flourish, attracting a coterie of important writers from throughout central Canada, including William Dawson LeSueur, who wrote on a variety of cultural and scientific topics; William Douw Lighthall, who contributed to a series of "Views of Canadian Literature" (1894); **Archibald MacMechan,** whose contributions are perhaps closest to the formal essay; and Roberts, who continued to contribute following his tenure as editor. The latter's "Notes on Some of the Younger American Poets" (1884), a harsh denunciation of experimentalist poetry in general and Walt Whitman in particular, set the tone for subsequent discussions of contemporary poetry.

Another important contribution of the *Week* to the development of the essay in Canada was its role as a forum for a number of important Canadian women writers. Among these were Agnes Maule Machar, a moderate social reformer who wrote under the pseudonym "Fidelis," who contributed literary **review** essays as well as nature sketches ("Our Woods in Spring," 1886) and essays on issues of particular import to women, including education ("The Higher Education of Women," 1889) and the National Council of Women of Canada; Susie Frances Harrison ("Seranus"), who sought to promote Canada and Canadian culture in her essays and regular music column in the 1880s; and Agnes Ethelwyn Wetherald, whose four-part series on "Some Canadian Literary Women" (1888) is of particular interest to modern scholars.

Of the women who found an outlet for their writing in the *Week*, it is Sara Jeannette Duncan who has been called the periodical's "liveliest and most urbane writer" (Claude Bissell, 1950). Besides offering her opinions on such diverse subjects as the ubiquitous issue of "International Copyright" (1886) and contemporary tastes in fiction ("Literary Pabulum," 1887), Duncan wrote regular reviews and commentaries on all aspects of culture and society, including art and Canadian literature. Structured most commonly as *causeries* and gathered under such varied titles as "Saunterings," "Afternoon Tea,"

and "Ottawa Letter," her contributions are impressive for their breadth and variety. An articulate crusader against what she saw as the potentially stultifying conservatism and provincialism of her readers, Duncan was, in retrospect, an especially important bellwether of the future of literary and cultural criticism in Canada.

When the *Week* ceased publication in November 1896, Canada lost a publication that had played a seminal role in shaping the country's intellectual and literary environment.

KLAY DYER

Further Reading
Bentley, D. M. R., *A Checklist of Literary Materials in "The Week" (Toronto, 1883–1896)*, Ottawa: Golden Dog Press, 1978
Bissell, Claude T., "Literary Taste in Central Canada During the Late Nineteenth Century," in *Twentieth Century Essays on Confederation Literature*, edited by Lorraine McMullen, Ottawa: Tecumseh Press, 1976 (article originally published, 1950)
Conron, Brandon, "Essays 1880–1920," in *Literary History of Canada: Canadian Literature in English*, 2nd edition, edited by Carl F. Klinck and others, Toronto: University of Toronto Press, 1976: 354–60 (original edition, 1965)

Weil, Simone

French, 1909–1943

As she lay dying from tuberculosis and self-imposed starvation, Simone Weil continued to write. During those last months, she pointed to Shakespeare's fools as models for the writer, declaring that only the dispossessed are truly free to speak the truth. Her writing is grounded in her own pursuit of a voluntary poverty, isolation, and exile that would free her to speak this fool's truth. Many readers have pondered whether these impassioned, lucid, and **critical essays** are the work of a holy fool or just a plain fool. She has been seen as a saint, a madwoman, a failure, a genius. Yet even her detractors grant her a place as an important political and religious writer, although she published only a handful of essays during her lifetime.

For Weil, writing was resistance and the essay was a means of action. Her essays and **journals** read like a series of **letters** from the front, in which a creative, tough-minded, passionate, philosophically trained mind bears witness to the horrors of exploitation, unemployment, and war. Her productivity is astonishing – 16 volumes in a posthumous collected edition edited by André A. Devaux and Florence de Lussy. For the most part this work is fragmentary, unfinished, unrevised – a series of sketches. Yet her style is often powerful when it reflects the sort of "nakedness" Weil admired – a resistance to ideology, ornament, and rationalizations.

Her work falls into two phases, separated by a period of transition in which disillusionment with human ability gives way to faith in a hidden God. Essays and journals of the first period, from 1931 to 1936, explore the problems of her era from a revolutionary-political vantage point, while the writings of 1938 to 1943 are permeated by the religious reflection engendered by her "waiting for God." Both the political and religious writings are characterized by unconventional challenges to economic, social, and spiritual ideologies and institutions.

Believing that idolatry – a clinging to a particular dogma – is a chief danger of intellectual life, Weil adopts the stance of outsider, speaking with the voice of the loyal adversary and often employing paradox and dialectic. Her prose, particularly in the last decade, enacts her ideals of attention (*attention*) and waiting (*attente*) by remaining grounded in experience and resisting closure.

Weil's plain and often aphoristic style reflects the influence of her teacher, the French philosopher Emile Auguste Chartier, better known by his pen name **Alain**. He trained his students to think critically by assigning them *topoi*, take-home essay examinations. These essays developed Weil's preference for short, straightforward, precise prose forms and schooled her in an inductive method. For Weil, induction came to mean contact with real situations – visiting a mine before writing about miners, harvesting grapes before writing about agricultural workers. Weil's early essays, published in Alain's *Libre Propos* (Free *propos* [remarks]), clearly reflect his anarchistic and pacifistic influence. But Alain's brilliant pupil soon began to demonstrate intellectual independence, embracing activism and criticizing democratic liberalism, Marxism, and totalitarianism with equal vigor.

As a teacher at a girls' school, Weil practiced voluntary poverty and devoted her spare time to political activism, basing her work for the *Tribune Républicaine* on her experiences in the teacher's union, among the unemployed, and with mine workers. This resulted in a growing critique of **Marx**'s lack of awareness of working conditions and of the impact of technology. In *Simone Weil: An Introduction to Her Thought* (1982), John Hellman suggests that after the apprenticeship writing of these years, Weil found the traditional political essay too narrow in scope.

Weil's insistence on writing anchored in experience gave power to her political thought despite her failure – or deliberate refusal – to systematize. For the next two decades Weil's writing forms a sort of ongoing journal of a mind evolving in response to historical reality – strikes, war, the resistance movement, the rise of Hitler. As events unfold, the essays and journal entries provide an impassioned eyewitness account.

Writing in *L'Express* (1951), **Camus** called her "the only great spirit of our time." A philosopher by training and a political activist by choice, she also became a major spiritual writer. Essays growing out of a 1932 visit to Germany demonstrate Weil's willingness to report what she saw – even when it ran counter to leftist expectations. But Weil's 1934 *Réflexions sur les causes de la liberté et de l'oppression sociale* (pub. posthumously 1980; Reflections concerning the causes of liberty and social oppression) shows more clearly the strength of her moralist stance. Despite its oversimplifications, undeveloped sketches, and preaching tone, Camus praised this essay, comparing Weil to Marx.

The 1934–36 journals of Weil's experiences of factory work and of the Spanish Civil War form a turning point, as romanticized views of worker solidarity and heroism give way to disillusionment, particularly as she witnesses disorder, incompetence, and brutality in Spain. These journals confirm her declaration in the 1934 *Réflexions*: "From human beings, no help can be expected."

Yet the journals, letters, and essays of the late 1930s and early 1940s record an experience of help from another quarter. Simone Weil had not sought for God, but seeking truth, felt that God came to her. In *Simone Weil: A Modern Pilgrimage* (1987) Robert Coles suggests that Weil's 1942 "Spiritual Autobiography," is, like Augustine's **Confessions**, "a performance for God." While Weil shares Augustine's apologetic bent and sense of being God-directed, the differences between the two are instructive. While Augustine weaves a highly ornamented, architectural, epic narrative, Weil's spiritual autobiography is stripped down, focused, and couched in the form of a letter to a friend. While Augustine narrates a journey from opposition and exile to acceptance and homecoming, Weil's apologia is the story of one who loves God but remains in exile. Seeking to embody "a truly incarnated Christianity," she rejects membership in a Church whose anathema sit aligns it with totalitarian forces threatening to engulf her world. In Weil's narrative, a procession of fishermen's wives in Portugal shows the young woman who has "received forever the mark of the slave" as a factory worker the nature of Christianity as "preeminently the religion of slaves." Her later experiences at Assisi and Solesmes, along with George Herbert's "Love" and the paternoster, re-create a pattern common to mystic spiritual autobiography – a sense of an overpowering reality at once hidden, intimate, and beautiful, ordering the cosmos, and reordering the self. Like Augustine, Weil's pursuit of truth results in rejecting ideologies and embracing God. "Christ," she says in the "Autobiography," "likes us to prefer truth to him because, before being Christ, he is truth. If one turns aside from him to go toward the truth, one will not go far before falling into his arms."

As her faith dawned, Weil studied Greek poetry and Gregorian music, writing about Antigone for a plant newspaper and finding in *The Iliad* a metaphor for a world obsessed with power. With the collapse of France in 1940, she wrote for the Resistance, contributing to *Les Cahiers du Sud* (Notebooks from the south) and scribbling schemes for parachuting nurses to the front. The daughter of agnostic, assimilated Jews, Weil vehemently denied her Jewishness and refused to confront the plight of the Jews, focusing instead on workers and on colonial oppression. Yet in *Simone Weil: An Introduction* (1994) Heinz Abosch suggests that her mature writing reflects elements of her Jewish heritage in her insistence on connecting thought and action, her mysticism, her prophetic social stance, and her focus on God's unity and hiddenness.

L'Enracinement (1949; *The Need for Roots*), written as she was dying in England in 1943, embodies Weil's characteristic merging of political, moral, and theological reflections on the problems of her time. Drafted as a plan for France's future, it is a series of essays linked by the metaphor of rootedness as she examines the "needs of the soul" and calls for a social order grounded in a "spiritual core" of physical labor. In *The Need for Roots* the polarities of Weil's thought are evident as she veers between the moralist's authoritarian need for order and the individual's anarchistic thirst for freedom, wrestling to speak a Fool's holy and unvarnished truth.

LINDA MILLS WOOLSEY

See also Autobiographical Essay; Religious Essay

Biography

Born 3 February 1909 in Paris. Studied at the Lycée Fénelon, 1920–24, and Lycée Victor Duruy, Paris, 1924–25, baccalauréat, 1925; Lycée Henri IV (where she was taught by Alain), Paris, 1925–28; École Normale Supérieure, Paris, 1928–31, agrégation in philosophy, 1931. Suffered from violent headaches, from 1930. Taught philosophy in various schools in Le Puy, Auxerre, Roanne, Bourges, and Saint-Quentin, 1931–38; factory worker for Renault, Alsthom, and Carnaud, 1934–35. Volunteer with the Republicans in the Spanish Civil War, 1936. Converted from Judaism to Christianity, 1938. Lived with her parents in Paris, Vichy, and Marseilles, 1939–42. Contributor, *Les Cahiers du Sud*, 1940. Fled from Nazi occupation to the United States, then England, 1942; worked for the Ministry of the Interior in De Gaulle's Free French movement, 1943. Died (of tuberculosis and self-neglect) in Ashford, Kent, 24 August 1943.

Selected Writings

Essays and Related Prose

La Pesanteur et la grâce (Gustave Thibon's selection from the Marseilles Notebooks), 1947; as *Gravity and Grace*, translated by Arthur Wills, 1952, and Emma Craufurd, 1952
L'Enracinement: Prélude à une déclaration des devoirs envers l'être humain, 1949; as *The Need for Roots*, translated by Arthur Wills, 1952
Attente de Dieu (letters and articles), 1950; as *Waiting for God*, translated by Emma Craufurd, 1951
La Connaissance surnaturelle (notebooks), 1950; translated by Richard Rees in *First and Last Notebooks*, 1970
Cahiers, 3 vols., 1951–56; enlarged edition, 1970; as *The Notebooks of Simone Weil*, translated by Arthur Wills, 2 vols., 1956
Intuitions préchrétiennes (writings on Greek philosophy), 1951; as *Intimations of Christianity Among the Ancient Greeks*, translated by Elisabeth Chase Geissbuhler, 1957
La Condition ouvrière (factory journal and articles), 1951; part translated by Richard Rees, in *Seventy Letters*, 1965
Lettre à un religieux, 1951; as *Letter to a Priest*, translated by Arthur Wills, 1954
La Source grecque, 1953; part translated by Elisabeth Chase Geissbuhler, in *Intimations of Christianity Among the Ancient Greeks*, 1957, and by Richard Rees in *On Science, Necessity and the Love of God*, 1968
Oppression et liberté, edited by Albert Camus, 1955; as *Oppression and Liberty*, translated by Arthur Wills and John Petrie, 1958
The Iliad; or, The Poem of Force (pamphlet), translated by Mary McCarthy, 1956
Écrits de Londres et dernières lettres, 1957; part translated by Richard Rees, in *Selected Essays*, 1962
Leçons de philosophie, 1959; as *Lectures on Philosophy*, translated by Hugh Price, 1978
Écrits historiques et politiques (short articles), 1960
Pensées sans ordre concernant l'amour de Dieu (articles), 1962; part translated by Richard Rees, in *Seventy Letters*, 1965
Selected Essays, 1934–43, translated by Richard Rees, 1962
Seventy Letters, translated by Richard Rees, 1965
Sur la science (letters and articles), 1966; part translated by Richard Rees, in *On Science, Necessity and the Love of God*, 1968
On Science, Necessity and the Love of God, translated by Richard Rees, 1968
First and Last Notebooks, translated by Richard Rees, 1970
The Simone Weil Reader, edited by George A. Panichas, 1977
Réflexions sur les causes de la liberté et de l'oppression sociale, 1980
An Anthology, edited by Siân Miles, 1986
Formative Writings, 1929–41, edited and translated by Dorothy T. McFarland and Wilhemina van Ness, 1987

Other writings: philosophical and mystical works.

Collected works edition: *Œuvres complètes* (Pléiade Edition), general editors André A. Devaux and Florence de Lussy, 5 vols., 1988–94 (in progress; 16 vols. projected).

Bibliography

Little, Janet Patricia, *Simone Weil: A Bibliography*, London: Grant and Cutler, 1973; supplement, 1979

Further Reading

Abosch, Heinz, *Simone Weil: An Introduction*, New York: Pennbridge, 1994
Allen, Diogenes, *Three Outsiders: Pascal, Kierkegaard, and Simone Weil*, Cambridge, Massachusetts: Cowley, 1983
Cabaud, Jacques, *Simone Weil: A Fellowship in Love*, New York: Channel Press, 1964
Coles, Robert, *Simone Weil: A Modern Pilgrimage*, Reading, Massachusetts: Addison Wesley, 1987
Hardwick, Elizabeth, "Simone Weil," in *Bartleby in Manhattan, and Other Essays*, New York: Random House, 1983
Hellman, John, *Simone Weil: An Introduction to Her Thought*, Waterloo, Ontario: Wilfrid Laurier University Press, 1982; Philadelphia: Fortress Press, 1984
Lichtheim, George, "Simone Weil," in his *Collected Essays*, New York: Viking, 1973
McFarland, Dorothy T., *Simone Weil*, New York: Ungar, 1983
Miłosz, Czesław, "The Importance of Simone Weil," in his *Emperor of the Earth: Modes of Eccentric Vision*, Berkeley: University of California Press, 1977
Murdoch, Iris, "On 'God' and 'Good'," in *Revisions: Changing Perspectives in Moral Philosophy*, edited by Stanley Hauerwas and Alasdair MacIntyre, Notre Dame, Indiana: University of Notre Dame Press, 1983
Petrement, Simone, *Simone Weil: A Life*, New York: Schocken, 1988 (original French edition, 1973)
Rees, Richard, *Simone Weil: A Sketch for a Portrait*, Carbondale: Southern Illinois University Press, and London: Oxford University Press, 1966
Sontag, Susan, "Simone Weil," in her *Against Interpretation, and Other Essays*, New York: Anchor, 1990 (original edition, 1966)
Springstead, Eric, *Affliction and the Love of God: The Spirituality of Simone Weil*, Cambridge, Massachusetts: Cowley, 1986
White, George Abbott, editor, *Simone Weil: Interpretations of a Life*, Amherst: University of Massachusetts Press, 1981

Die weissen Blätter

German periodical, 1913–1920

The literary review *Die weissen Blätter* (The white pages) was one of the three prominent journals of the expressionist movement. This periodical introduced itself as the "voice of the younger generation," whose purpose was to be engaged with all areas of contemporary life. In its relatively short history it published many of the essential texts of German Modernism, including all genres of *belles-lettres* as well as general essays on political and cultural issues. The last pages of each number were interspersed with advertisements and contained a section of news items, topical notes, commentaries, and polemics. The visual arts played only a minor role (represented largely by

Ludwig Meidner's portrait drawings) and disappeared altogether in 1917. The emphasis throughout was on literary quality rather than on experimental novelty. On principle, *Die weissen Blätter* encouraged the interplay of various progressive influences, and did not allow any one personality or avant-garde theory to dominate its program. Its editors were averse to any form of militancy. They also rejected the kind of idiosyncratic diversity that made their principal competitors, Franz Pfemfert's *Die Aktion* (The action) and Herwarth Walden's *Der Sturm* (The storm), more provocative and aggressive, but in the end also more doctrinaire.

The intellectual sponsors of *Die weissen Blätter* did have a specific agenda, however. They saw their new publication as a direct challenge to the well-established monthly forum of S. Fischer Verlag, *Die neue Rundschau* (The new review), which reflected the literary tastes and cultural preferences of the liberal and moderately conservative bourgeoisie. Their model was the **Nouvelle Revue Française** (New French review). Financial independence and solid honoraria were guaranteed by the generosity of Erik Ernst Schwabach, a wealthy student of German literature in Berlin, who is listed as the periodical's first official publisher. Otto Flake served as his literary adviser but was soon replaced by the more experienced Viennese *littérateur* Franz Blei. In January 1914 the publisher Kurt Wolff took charge as manager of both the journal and an affiliated book publishing venture, Verlag der Weissen Bücher, in Leipzig. After members of this staff were called up for military service in the war, their friend René Schickele, an accomplished man of letters from a small town in Alsace, became the new editor-in-chief.

In September 1915 patriotic groups in Berlin falsely accused Schickele of espionage for France and the Office of War Censorship in Munich tried to have the police investigate his activities. He emigrated to Switzerland, where he made preparations to move the journal to Zurich. For the time between April 1916 and July 1917, he found a new publisher in the firm of Rascher & Cie., who had offices in Zurich and Leipzig. This prevented direct interference by the German authorities and saved, for example, the important antiwar issue of May 1916 from confiscation. But the threat of expulsion from a neutral country made further precautions necessary: in July 1918 the editorial office was moved to Berne-Bümpliz and Schickele assumed sole personal responsibility for the next six issues of volume 5 (1918). He did have the support, however, of both the cultural attaché at the German Embassy, Harry Graf Kessler, and the wealthy art critic and dealer Paul Cassirer, who published the journal during its final two years in Berlin, after June 1920 also serving as its editorial director.

Die weissen Blätter was usually published on the 15th of every month. Sold at a reasonable price, the first issues, in octavo, had between 98 and 120 pages, plus 16 (and proportionately more) pages, numbered separately, of advertisements and commentary. This more-than-respectable size, and the initial circulation of some 3000 copies, were steadily reduced during the war years until, in 1918, they had shrunk to about one third of the original. Henceforth, the inclusion of longer works of literature was inadvisable, and political debates as well as cultural critiques had to be limited severely.

Though the very name of these "white pages" signaled an editorial policy of unbiased openness, even of a self-conscious innocence *in politicis*, this aversion to providing a platform for sectarian propaganda did not imply, even before the war, a complete withdrawal from agitation on behalf of specific programs. On the whole, however, the review remained remarkably consistent in its emphasis on literature. It espoused at first a vague and idealistic "socialism without functionaries" (in contributions by such diverse writers as Eduard Bernstein, Ernst Bloch, Martin Buber, Georges Duhamel, Rosa Luxemburg, Carlo Mierendorff, and Anna Siemsen), with Schickele editorially advocating "a government formed by the majority of comrades who have learned to live physically and mentally without using coercion, without applying force" (January 1919). Aside from a dutiful commitment to democracy (for example, "Die Pflicht zur Demokratie" [November 1916; The duty to support democracy]) and to a rejuvenated humanism (discussed in issues from April 1916 until July 1917), a Christian federalism appeared to promise the best hope for Europe's future.

Lead articles as early as 1913 speak out in favor of pacifism, which more and more became Schickele's credo. He also, and immediately, supported the aims of an organization of intellectuals, *Clarté: Internationale de la Pensée* (Clarity: international thought) which Henri Barbusse and his friends had founded in May 1919; he published their statutes (December 1919) and principles ("Leitsätze von Clarté"; Guiding principles of Clarté) in March 1920, but distanced himself from their communist sympathies.

Three essay highlights in the journal may be singled out: first, **Heinrich Mann**'s reaction against his brother **Thomas Mann**'s war euphoria in his treatise "Zola" (November 1915), a plea for the truth of the mind (*Geist*) as superior to the rights of the state and a celebration of the democratic artist as the true politician; second, Schickele's "Der Mensch im Kampf" (Man's struggle), his first editorial (April 1916), a condemnation of the intellectuals' betrayal of political morality and a call for European unity in the fight for new fatherlands; and finally, his "Revolution, Bolschewismus und das Ideal" (December 1918; Revolution, bolshevism, and the ideal), a defense of utopian idealism and an appeal for moral change ("Menschenverwandlung") in the face of revolutionary violence.

"Die Verwandlung" ("The Metamorphosis") is also the title of the most famous piece of fiction published in *Die weissen Blätter* (February 1915), i.e. Kafka's story. Other prominent contributions include **Gottfried Benn**'s scene "Ithaka" (March 1914), Hasenclever's play *Der Sohn* (April–June 1914; The son), the dramatization of a father-son conflict, and Heinrich Mann's *Madame Legros* (March 1916). Novellas by Sternheim, Edschmid, and Leonhard Frank exemplify the best of prose fiction; Franz Werfel and J. R. Becher are the lyrical poets most frequently represented. Max Brod's *Tycho Brahes Weg zu Gott* (Tycho Brahe's Road to God), serialized between January and June 1915, tried to undo what damage the journal's reputation for literary integrity had suffered when it accepted Gustav Meyrink's tale of fantasy horror, *Der Golem* (December 1913–August 1914), which became an international bestseller.

Die weissen Blätter published with principled imagination and often under difficult conditions, but it did not survive the immediate postwar years. Its demise can be blamed on the political and social uncertainties of that time and on the need of expressionist writers to find new directions. But it was the impact of inflation, most of all, and the collapse of the literary market that made it impossible to sustain an independent literary journal of high quality.

MICHAEL WINKLER

Further Reading

Göbel, Wolfram, "Der Kurt Wolff Verlag 1913–1930; mit einer Bibliographie des Kurt Wolff Verlages und der ihm angeschlossenen Unternehmen," *Archiv für Geschichte des Buchwesens* 15 (1976): 521–962, and 16 (1977): 1299–1456

Haase, Horst, *Die Antikriegsliteratur in der Zeitschrift "Die weissen Blätter"* (dissertation), Berlin: Humboldt University, 1956

Hellack, Georg, "René Schickele und die *Weissen Blätter*: Ein Beitrag zur Geschichte expressionistischer Zeitschriften," *Publizistik* 8 (1963): 250–57

Raabe, Paul, *Die Zeitschriften und Sammlungen des literarischen Expressionismus*, Stuttgart: Metzler, 1964

Raabe, Paul, editor, *Index Expressionismus: Bibliographie der Beiträge in den Zeitschriften und Jahrbüchern des literarischen Expressionismus, 1910–1925*, vol. 13, Nendeln, Liechtenstein: Kraus-Thomson, 1972: cols. 1976–2058

West, Rebecca

British, 1892–1983

One of Rebecca West's first essays as a young columnist for the suffragist weekly the *Freewoman* was a spirited attack on Mrs. Humphry Ward, then a bulwark of the literary establishment. While Mary Ward might seem to modern readers an easy target, in 1912 such an attack required considerable daring. The essay was one of the first to be written under her pseudonym – an impulsive borrowing from Ibsen's *Rosmersholm*. In many respects both the irreverence toward an established icon and the *nom de plume* she selected typify the essay writing stance she adopted at the outset of her career. While West never lost what her last literary editor described as her "unmistakable pounce," the objects of her scorn shifted as she herself became transformed into an establishment figure who by the end of her career occupied a cultural position not unlike that enjoyed by Mrs. Humphry Ward before World War I.

In her early essays in the *Freewoman*, and later in the socialist newspaper the *Clarion*, she developed a style which was to be the hallmark of her essays throughout her career. She plainly took enormous pleasure in using her pithy and epigrammatic style to skewer her political opponents with devastating dismissals. Sir William Anson, for example, was, "an anti-feminist too uninteresting to be really dangerous," while Mrs. Humphry Ward's assertion that a laborer could easily feed a family of five on 18 shillings a week represented that novelist's "one real flash of imagination." Recognizing the demands of newspaper journalism, she made sure that an arresting opening sentence began each essay. She was somewhat frustrated by the narrow topicality required by partisan political journalism, but despite this, several essays from this period stand out as being of lasting significance and value. Her 1913 essay on the suffragist Emily Davidson, who had endured numerous imprisonments and forcible feeding and been killed when she threw herself in front of the king's horse at the Derby, remains one of the most eloquent essays of moral outrage produced in English. While the essays in the *Freewoman* and the *Clarion* provide an outstanding record of the struggle for women's suffrage, West's finest essay on the period is "A Reed of Steel," her 1933 essay on Emmeline Pankhurst.

During the 1920s, after publishing two novels and a critical study of **Henry James**, West turned her attention to literary criticism with a book of more ambitious literary essays, *The Strange Necessity* (1928). In her essay on Joyce's *Ulysses*, West clearly sees herself as an admirer and defender of Joyce, paying what is intended as a tribute to the structure of that novel by organizing her essay around a day spent in Paris, paralleling the single day in Dublin which bounds Joyce's novel. But West's reading of the novel seems superficial. The essay strives for profundity, but merely stumbles through mazes of inverted sentences and subordinate clauses. The essay on Lawrence is stronger because she returns to her strong suit of biographical rather than textual criticism.

West's awkwardness with *Ulysses*, despite her avowed admiration, marks an unease with the avant-garde which was increasingly to shape her aesthetic judgments. In "Kafka and the Mystery of Bureaucracy" (1957) she dismissed *Metamorphosis* as "another absurd avant-garde story," yet in the essay as a whole she develops a sophisticated and complex investigation of Kafka's relationship with bureaucracy. In a 1964 BBC interview West said, "What I chiefly want to do when I write is to contemplate character . . . This is an inborn tendency in me." While the comment might seem to bear more directly on her work as a novelist, it underlines her strength as an essayist. Whether in her literary or political essays she writes with a surer hand in delineating character than in dealing with abstractions.

West's skill as a novelist merges with her growing preoccupation with the nature of evil in her essays reporting on trials. Her essay, "Greenhouse with Cyclamens I" (1955), on the closing sessions of the Nuremberg trials, attempts not only to convey some impression of the Nazi leaders facing sentencing but also to make a broader statement about life in postwar Germany and even the German character. Despite its rhetorical flourishes, the essay falters in fulfilling its ambitious intent partly because of the inadequacy of the overarching "greenhouse" metaphor and partly because, in trying to convey the sense of evil exuded by the Nazis, West falls back on facile suggestions of sexual perversity, so that Goering is "like a madam in a brothel," Streicher, "a dirty old man of the sort that gives trouble in parks," and so on. During the postwar years West was intensely preoccupied with the theme of political betrayal and wrote about nearly every major trial concerning the Official Secrets Act. Her essays on the treason trial of William Joyce ("Lord Haw-Haw"), whose wartime broadcasts from Germany had been intended to undermine British morale, were first published in the **New Yorker** and later appeared in her best-known book *The Meaning of Treason* (1947).

West's writing had become widely known in the United States during World War II principally through her essays in *Harper's* on everyday life under wartime conditions. American journals such as the *New Yorker* gave her the opportunity to develop a subject without severe length restrictions. Her political views were also increasingly in step with the anticommunist fervor that gripped postwar America. In 1947 *Time* magazine put her on the cover and described her as "one of the greatest of living journalists." She even defended the McCarthy hearings in a series of four essays called "The Facts Behind the Witch Trials" for the *Sunday Times* in Spring 1954 in which she claimed, "It would be a strange Government indeed that felt no curiosity when faced with such intimations of disorder."

Although West was aptly described by **Kenneth Tynan** in 1954 as "the best journalist alive," and although she had a voracious appetite for documentary evidence, the hand that shapes West's reportage is always that of a novelist whose sense of character, of drama, of moral tensions takes precedence over mere fact.

GILLIAN THOMAS

Biography
Born Cicily Isabel Fairfield, 21 December 1892 in London. Grew up in London and Edinburgh. Studied at George Watson's Ladies' College, Edinburgh; Royal Academy of Dramatic Art, London, 1909–10. Briefly an actress, 1911, with a role in Ibsen's *Rosmersholm*, from which she adopted the name Rebecca West. Liaison with the writer H. G. Wells, 1913–23: one son. Contributor to various journals and newspapers, from 1912, including the *Freewoman*, *New Freewoman* (later the *Egoist*), *Clarion*, *New Statesman and Nation*, *New Republic*, New York *Herald-Tribune*, *Time and Tide*, *New Yorker*, and *Harper's*. Married Henry Maxwell Andrews, 1930 (died, 1968). Lived in Buckinghamshire, 1930–68, and London, 1968–83. Talks supervisor, BBC, London, during World War II; Terry Foundation Lecturer, Yale University, New Haven, Connecticut, 1956. Awards: Royal Society of Literature Benson Medal, 1966; honorary degrees from two universities; Member, Order of St. Sava (Yugoslavia), 1937; Fellow, 1947, and Companion of Literature, 1968, Royal Society of Literature; Chevalier, Legion of Honor (France), 1957; Honorary Member, American Academy of Arts and Letters, 1972; Commander, Order of the British Empire (CBE), 1949; Dame Commander, Order of the British Empire (DBE), 1959. Died in London, 15 March 1983.

Selected Writings

Essays and Related Prose
The Strange Necessity: Essays and Reviews, 1928
Ending in Earnest: A Literary Log, 1931
The Meaning of Treason, 1947; revised edition, 1952; second revised edition, as *The New Meaning of Treason*, 1964
A Train of Powder, 1955
The Court and the Castle (Yale Terry lectures), 1957
The Young Rebecca: Writings of Rebecca West, 1911–1917, edited by Jane Marcus, 1982

Other writings: eight novels (*The Return of the Soldier*, 1918; *The Judge*, 1922; *Harriet Hume*, 1929; *The Thinking Reed*, 1936; *The Fountain Overflows*, 1956; *The Birds Fall Down*, 1966; *This Real Night*, 1984; *Sunflower*, 1986), novellas, short stories, biographies of St. Augustine and Henry James, *Black Lamb and Grey Falcon* (1941), a book about Yugoslavia and Europe in the 1930s, and *1900* (1982), a social history of that year.

Bibliographies
Hutchinson, George, *A Preliminary List of the Writings of Rebecca West, 1912–1951*, Folcroft, Pennsylvania: Folcroft, 1973 (original edition, 1957)

Packer, Joan, *Rebecca West: An Annotated Bibliography*, New York: Garland, 1991

Further Reading
Deakin, Motley F., *Rebecca West*, Boston: Twayne, 1980
Glendinning, Victoria, *Rebecca West: A Life*, London: Weidenfeld and Nicolson, and New York: Knopf, 1987
Marcus, Jane, "A Speaking Sphinx," *Tulsa Studies in Women's Literature* 2, no. 2 (1983): 151–54
Seeley, Tracy, "Woolf and Rebecca West's Fiction Essays," *Virginia Woolf Miscellany* 39 (1992): 6–7
Wolfe, Peter, *Rebecca West, Artist and Thinker*, Carbondale: Southern Illinois University Press, 1971

White, E. B.
American, 1899–1985

Widely regarded as one of America's finest essayists, E. B. White is often credited with restoring the informal essay to a place of respect. While he also wrote children's books, poetry, editorials, a famous style manual, and some well-received short fiction, White's position in American literature is secured by the charming **personal essays** he published in the *New Yorker* and *Harper's* magazine from the 1920s through the 1960s. In collections of essays such as *One Man's Meat* (1942), *The Second Tree from the Corner* (1954), *The Points of My Compass* (1962), and *Essays of E. B. White* (1977), White demonstrates what many critics consider America's most engaging 20th-century essay style in the personal or Montaignean tradition.

Among critics, White is frequently identified as this century's most exemplary personal essayist. He is most frequently commended for the music and architecture of his paragraphs, the subtle rhythm and pace of his sentences, and the elegant yet colloquial diction of his comfortable yet intense essaying voice. The terms commonly used to describe White's essay persona are "modest," "sincere," "gentle," and "precise." His highly esteemed prose style makes him a great favorite among anthologizers of essay texts for college English composition courses. Among his most frequently anthologized essays are "The Ring of Time" (1956), "Death of a Pig" (1948), "Once More to the Lake" (1941), and his tribute to **Thoreau**, "A Slight Sound at Evening" (1954).

While some find fault with his tendency to adopt the voice of the entertainer who takes a homey and self-deprecating stance in addressing commonplace subjects, most reviewers find White to be a serious, even passionate advocate of social causes ranging from civil rights to ecology. Warren Beck and Eudora Welty, among others, defend White as a strong individualist, an intellectually and morally rigorous writer who does not trivialize or avoid dark and divisive issues.

White began writing poetry and short fiction as a boy in Mount Vernon, New York, winning three literary prizes and being published in *St. Nicholas Magazine* before his 15th year. From 1917 to 1921 he studied at Cornell University, where he developed his journalistic skills as editor of the *Cornell Daily Sun*. White earned a degree in English, studying literature and writing, most notably under the direction of Professor Will Strunk, whose "little book" of precepts about writing

White would, in 1959, revise and expand into *The Elements of Style*. This manual has achieved enormous popularity for its succinct and bold advice for writers, being continuously in print over three decades, used in college courses and as a stylistic bible by a generation of freelance writers.

After leaving Cornell, White embarked on brief, unrewarding careers as a newspaper reporter for United Press syndicate and the Seattle *Times*. He would later write several engaging essays about this "unrooted period" of his life, most notably "Years of Wonder" (1961), dealing with his naive wandering in Alaska, and "Farewell, My Lovely" (1936), a celebration of the eccentricities of the Model T Ford which White and a friend drove across the continent the year after graduation.

Returning to New York City in 1923, White took a job for which he was temperamentally ill-suited, working for an advertising agency while submitting humorous sketches and poetry to newspapers. Fortuitously for White, just at the time he determined to make his living as a writer of essays and short humor pieces, a new magazine appeared under the editorship of Harold Ross and his assistant, Katherine Sergeant Angell. Impressed with several light sketches or "casuals" which White submitted, Ross offered White a job as staff writer for the *New Yorker*. White, who would marry Katherine upon her divorce in 1929, established a literary home for himself at the *New Yorker*, making his mark on that urbane and witty magazine while writing for it in several capacities for most of the next 50 years.

At the *New Yorker* White resisted the discipline of the traditional desk job, cherishing his personal freedom and avoiding normal office hours while cultivating many literary friendships. Among the writers with whom White and his wife developed social and professional relationships at the *New Yorker* were Dorothy Parker, **Robert Benchley**, Alexander Woollcott, and **Stephen Leacock**. Most notably, White collaborated with his sometime office mate **James Thurber**, whose cartooning talents were discovered by White as he retrieved doodles and scribblings from the wastebasket they shared. White collaborated with Thurber on *Is Sex Necessary?* (1929), a parody on contemporary sex advice books. Together White and Thurber established the clever, bemused editorial tone for which the *New Yorker* is known. They also pioneered such magazine subgenres as "Notes and Comments" and the "newsbreak," filling in small portions of white space between the magazine's articles with brief, logically and typographically flawed excerpts from other publications, to which White and Thurber would add comic oneliners. White published two collections of these: *Ho-Hum: Newsbreaks from the New Yorker* (1931) and *Another Ho-Hum* (1932).

At various times through the 1930s, White wrote essays, notes and comments, light verse, cartoon captions, and editorial columns for the *New Yorker*, as well as short comic sketches which he called "preposterous parables." A collection of sketches was published in 1938 under the title *Quo Vadimus?* Ever self-deprecating and irregular in his work habits, White referred to his position at the *New Yorker* as that of "office boy deluxe." When offered the editorship of the competing *Saturday Review* in 1936, he declined the position.

Although he had been making his living as a magazine prose writer, White felt a strong attraction to poetry. Most of his poetic output is, however, considered by critics to be light verse. He published his first volume of poems, *The Lady Is Cold*, in 1929, and followed it with another volume, *The Fox of Peapack and Other Poems*, in 1938. Following his poetic muse and suffering from a nervous condition, White resigned from his job at the *New Yorker* in 1937 to devote himself to a long, serious, autobiographical poem which never materialized. White would later use some material from this failed poem in his essay "Zoo Revisited" (1954).

Having moved from New York to a saltwater farm in Maine, White lived as an amateur farmer while writing a monthly column for *Harper's*. These collected essays, featuring White's rural experiences, were published in 1942 as *One Man's Meat*. Critics hailed this as White's best book to date, characterizing him as a 20th-century approximation of Montaigne and Thoreau. Later that year, Ross coaxed White back into working for the *New Yorker*, asking him to focus on patriotic wartime themes. Sent to cover the San Francisco Conference that led to the foundation of the United Nations, White became an enthusiastic editorial supporter of postwar internationalism, publishing an idealistic collection of essays devoted to world government under the title *The Wild Flag* (1946).

Throughout White's career, he celebrated two seemingly contradictory themes: human interdependence and an almost Thoreauvian commitment to individualism. His is a lyrical prose voice, both moderate and insistent, with a clearly moral foundation in American principles of liberty and justice. The personal ethics which pervade the essays become evident in the published *Letters of E. B. White* (1976). These **letters** reveal, among other telling autobiographical details, that White refused a guaranteed offer of $20,000 from the Book of the Month Club for *The Second Tree from the Corner* because he could not tolerate a six months' delay in publication of what he considered to be timely and **topical essays**.

White, sometimes dismissed as a writer of children's books (including the classics *Stuart Little* [1945] and *Charlotte's Web* [1952]), magazine humor pieces, and unprepossessing **familiar essays**, has earned a wide and affectionate following. Employing such comic devices as parody, colloquial dialogue, personification of animals, and understatement, White built an enduring reputation as a serious and humane essayist who succeeded with humor and good grace.

DALE E. HASKELL

Biography

Elwyn Brooks White. Born 11 July 1899 in Mount Vernon, New York. Studied at Cornell University, Ithaca, New York (editor, *Cornell Daily Sun*, 1920–21), 1917–21, A.B., 1921. Private in the U.S. army, 1918. Reporter, Seattle *Times*, 1922–23; advertising copywriter, Frank Seaman Inc. and Newmark Inc., New York, 1924–25; contributing editor, *New Yorker*, 1926–37 and from 1943. Married Katharine Sergeant Angell, 1929 (died, 1977): one son and two stepchildren. Columnist of "One Man's Meat," *Harper's*, 1938–43. Awards: several, including Page One Award for Literature, for *The Second Tree from the Corner*, 1954; American Academy Gold Medal, for essays, 1960; Presidential Medal of Freedom, 1963; American Library Association Wilder Award, for children's book, 1970; National Medal for Literature, 1971; Pulitzer Special Citation, 1978; honorary degrees from seven American colleges and universities. Member, American Academy. Died in North Brooklin, Maine, 1 October 1985.

Selected Writings

Essays and Related Prose

Every Day Is Saturday, 1934
Quo Vadimus? or, The Case for the Bicycle (sketches), 1938
One Man's Meat, 1942
World Government and Peace: Selected Notes and Comment 1943–1945, 1945
The Wild Flag: Editorials from the New Yorker on Federal World Government and Other Matters, 1946
Here Is New York, 1949
The Second Tree from the Corner (includes poetry), 1954
The Points of My Compass: Letters from the East, the West, the North, the South, 1962
An E. B. White Reader, edited by William W. Watt and Robert W. Bradford, 1966
Essays of E. B. White, 1977
Writings from the New Yorker, 1927–1976, edited by Rebecca M. Dale, 1990

Other writings: the satire *Is Sex Necessary?*, with James Thurber (1929), the handbook of style *The Elements of Style*, with William Strunk, Jr. (1959), three novels for children (*Stuart Little*, 1945; *Charlotte's Web*, 1952; *The Trumpet of the Swan*, 1970), two collections of poetry, and correspondence (collected in *Letters of E. B. White*, edited by Dorothy Lubrano Guth, 1976).

Bibliographies

Anderson, A. J., *E. B. White: A Bibliography*, Metuchen, New Jersey: Scarecrow Press, 1978
Hall, Katherine R., *E. B. White: A Bibliographic Catalogue of Printed Materials in the Department of Rare Books, Cornell University Library*, New York: Garland, 1979

Further Reading

Beck, Warren, "E. B. White," *College English* 7 (April 1946): 367–73
Dennis, Nigel, "Smilin' Through," *New York Review of Books*, 27 October 1977: 42–43
Elledge, Scott, *E. B. White: A Biography*, New York: Norton, 1984
Epstein, Joseph, "E. B. White, Dark and Lite," *Commentary* 81 (April 1986): 48–56
Fuller, J. W., *Prose Style in the Essays of E. B. White* (dissertation), Seattle: University of Washington, 1959
Grant, Thomas, "The Sparrow on the Ledge: E. B. White in New York," *Studies in American Humor* 3 (Spring 1984): 23–33
Haskell, Dale E., *The Rhetoric of the Familiar Essay: E. B. White and Personal Discourse* (dissertation), Fort Worth: Texas Christian University, 1983
Heldreth, Leonard G., "'The Pattern of Life Indelible': E. B. White's 'Once More to the Lake'," *CEA Critic* 45 (November 1985): 31–34
Howarth, William, "E. B. White at the New Yorker," *Sewanee Review* 93 (Fall 1985): 574–83
Platizky, Roger S., "'Once More to the Lake': A Mythic Interpretation," *College Literature* 15 (Spring 1988): 171–79
Plimpton, George, and Frank H. Crowther, "The Art of the Essay I: E. B. White," *Paris Review* 48 (Fall 1969): 65–88
Quigley, Michael, *"The Germ of Common Cause": History, Rhetoric, and Ideology in the Essays of E. B. White* (dissertation), Eugene: University of Oregon, 1989
Root, Robert L., Jr., editor, *Critical Essays on E. B. White*, New York: Hall, and Oxford: Maxwell Macmillan International, 1994
Sampson, Edward, *E. B. White*, New York: Twayne, 1974
Schott, Webster, "E. B. White Forever," *New Republic*, 24 November 1962: 23–24
Smith, Kenneth Alan, *Contesting Discourses in the Essays of Virginia Woolf, James Baldwin, Joan Didion, and E. B. White* (dissertation), Iowa City: University of Iowa, 1993
Tanner, Stephen L., "E. B. White and the Theory of Humor," *Humor: International Journal of Humor Research* 2 (1989): 43–53
Thurber, James. "E. B. W.," *Saturday Review of Literature*, 15 October 1938: 1+
Updike, John, "Remarks on the Occasion of E. B. White Receiving the 1971 National Medal for Literature," in his *Picked-Up Pieces*, New York: Knopf, 1975; London: Deutsch, 1976: 434–47
Weales, Gerald, "The Designs of E. B. White," *New York Times Book Review*, 24 May 1970: 2+
Welty, Eudora, "Dateless Virtues," *New York Times Book Review*, 25 September 1977: 43+

Wieland, Christoph Martin

German, 1733–1813

While Christoph Martin Wieland is best known to the non-German world for his novels, romances, and didactic tales in verse, he was also among the first and most prominent of those writers, such as **Gotthold Ephraim Lessing**, **Johann Gottfried Herder**, and **Georg Forster**, who inaugurated the German essay in the 18th century. This distinction can be ascribed in part to Wieland's ownership and direction of the longest-lived journal of the age, the *Teutscher Merkur* (The German Mercury), but also, more fundamentally, to his own creativity and enterprise as an essayist.

By his nature, background, and experience Wieland was eminently suited for his role as one of Germany's first essayists. As has been well observed of him as a stylist, he possessed many of those qualities that most essayists in the European literatures seem to share: a sociable manner of expression, a habit of directly engaging the reader in a common enterprise, the wish both to make himself understandable and to incite the reader to independent thought (Fritz Martini, 1967). Certain other predispositions and habits of mind further equip him exceptionally for the role of essayist: a humane relativism, an openness to all sources of knowledge and truth, and a sincere willingness to give a fair hearing to views different from his own. For most of his career Wieland ardently held to a melioristic outlook; in so doing he became, along with Lessing and **Moses Mendelssohn**, one of the most important literary representatives of the German Enlightenment.

There was hardly a question agitating his era that did not find expression in Wieland's essayistic writings, and specific essay topics extend over a wide reach: Graecomania, Shakespeare, **Rousseau**, balloon flight, the plan for an academy, patriotism, the French Revolution, cosmopolitanism, animal magnetism, the Enlightenment, Sturm und Drang (Storm and stress) aesthetics, ethics, political philosophy, everyday life. The great variety of his output can best be schematized under the broad divisions of cultural, political, philosophical, religious, and literary, with the first two categories preponderant. Three fairly distinct periods in Wieland's career as essayist evolved: early (1750–63), middle (1764–87), and late (1788–1813).

Wieland's essayistic writings up to 1755 are pervaded by pietism and exuberant idealism, usually finding expression in the form of categorical assertiveness; accordingly, a sermonizing and rather imperious attitude toward the reader is the dominant tone. Additionally, there is an occasional Anacreontic ornamentation, especially in those pieces cast in verse. Though there are only four or five essays in the earliest and extremely pietistic years, it is nonetheless significant that these works constitute much of Wieland's entire literary productivity during that period. "Timoklea: Ein Gespräch über scheinbare und wahre Schönheit" (1755; Timoklea: a conversation on apparent and genuine beauty) and its companion piece, "Theages; oder Unterredung von Schönheit und Liebe" (1758; Theages; or conversation on beauty and love), are the two principal achievements in these early years.

As early as his 21st year a marked change occurs in the form, temper, and content of Wieland's work. The shift begins after his departure from his patron, the critic and aesthete Johann Jakob Bodmer, is furthered by his friendship with the poet J. G. Zimmermann and a reading of the **Earl of Shaftesbury**, and becomes virtually complete under the influence of the Francophile Count Friedrich Stadion. The middle years of Wieland's career (1764–87), then, witness both the maturity of his thought on philosophical, political, historical, and literary subjects and the full development of his skills as an essayist. Especially with his founding of the *Teutscher Merkur* in 1773, he had available a medium for expressing his confrontation with new developments in political and cultural affairs.

During the middle period he wrote over 50 essays. Among the most notable of those pieces on philosophical or religious topics are "Was ist Wahrheit?" (1778; "What Is Truth?"); "Über den Hang, an Magie und Geistererscheinungen zu glauben" (1781; On the inclination to believe in ghostly apparitions); "Antworten und Gegenfragen auf die Zweifel und Anfragen eines vorgeblichen Weltbürgers" (1783; Answers and counterquestions to the doubts and inquiries of a would-be cosmopolite); "Über religiöse Toleranz" (1783; On religious tolerance); and "Über den freien Gebrauch der Vernunft in Glaubenssachen" (1788; On the free use of reason in religious matters). "What Is Truth?," written five years after **Kant**'s sanguine observations in "Was ist Aufklärung?" (1773; "What Is Enlightenment?"), is probably the most frequently reprinted of all of Wieland's essays. Though the work is not demonstrably an intentional counter to Kant's piece, Wieland confidently and persuasively states his case on the subject of humankind's future with an optimism as cautious and diffident as that of his famous contemporary. A considerable portion of the middle years is also devoted to the relationship between religious and political matters, perhaps best represented by "Gedanken über eine alte Aufschrift" (1772; Thoughts on an old inscription), one of the most persuasive and well-crafted pieces of the entire period.

Wieland wrote approximately a dozen essays of a political nature during these 20-odd years, the best of which are "Das göttliche Recht der Obrigkeit" (1777; The divine right of kings); "Über die Rechte und Pflichten der Schriftsteller" (1785; On the rights and duties of authors), one of his most vigorous essays, dealing with the freedom of the press; and "Eine Lustreise ins Elysium" (1787; A pleasure trip to Elysium). "Das göttliche Recht der Obrigkeit," which outdoes even Hobbes in its advocacy of the ancient political principle, unsurprisingly

provoked the wrathful distaste of many of Wieland's more progressive and optimistic contemporaries and evidently cost the *Merkur* no few subscribers. Much of this opposition failed to recognize Wieland's perception of a fine line between unworkable idealism and brutal realism. Throughout his career, Wieland preferred a practical and skeptical empiricism that grants hope to the possibility of reform and progress (John A. McCarthy [in Jørgensen], 1994). His interest in historical topics was impelled for the most part by a search for historical parallels with his own age: the lessons of the past, he assumed, are often relevant to the problems of the present and can thus serve as a guide for the future.

Wieland consistently held an adamant conviction that *belleslettres* constituted the most effective means for advancing the humanistic ideals of the European Enlightenment. He frequently addressed in a direct and sustained way questions concerning the nature and essence of literature – especially such theories as were current in the period between the baroque and Romantic periods (McCarthy [in Jørgensen], 1994). Most of the more important of his essays on these matters are contained in a series of articles written in the 1770s and early 1780s, among others: "Der Eifer, unserer Dichtkunst einen National-Charakter zu geben" (1773; The enthusiasm for giving a national character to our literature); "Wenn sie fortfahren, die Teutschen des 18. Jahrhunderts für Enkel Tuiskons anzusehen" (1773; If they continue to regard the Germans of the 18th century as descendants of Tuiskon); "Der Geist Shakespears" (1773; The Shakespearean spirit); "Über das Schauspiel *Götz von Berlichingen mit der eisernen Hand*" (1773; On the drama *Götz von Berlichingen*); "Unterredungen zwischen W** und dem Pfarrer zu ***" (1775; Conversations between W** and the Pastor of ***); "Gedanken über die Ideale der Alten" (1777; Thoughts on the ideals of the Ancients); *Briefe an einen jungen Dichter* (1782–84; Letters to a young poet) (McCarthy [in Jørgensen], 1994).

While it can be reasonably asserted that Wieland's writings on literary and cultural themes deserve as firm a place in the literary history of the 18th century as those of Johann Joachim Winckelmann, Lessing, and **Schiller** (McCarthy [in Jørgensen], 1994), in his role as reviewer during the 1770s and 1780s he revealed his weakest side. In fact, there exists only a handful among the dozens of **reviews** in these two decades that can qualify as essays, the piece on Goethe's *Götz von Berlichingen* being the most notable. Tone and general style are, at best, straightforward, at worst, lackluster. The relatively unimportant contributions that Wieland brought to his role of reviewer had more to do with his wishes, as editor of the *Merkur*, to avoid harsh or otherwise imperious judgments, whether his own or those of his many contributors. At the same time this policy served the ultimate purpose of establishing and maintaining a good tone in his journal. Moreover, severe criticism would almost necessarily imply an inconsistency with Wieland's constant and avowed aspiration to entertain multiple perspectives (McCarthy [in Jørgensen], 1994).

Essayistic writings in the late period (1788–1813) are with few exceptions devoted to topics connected with the Revolution in France. The form in which Wieland expresses his thoughts on these topics is generally dialogic, while the tone is principally apprehensive and monitory. The most noteworthy of these serious writings are "Das Geheimnis des Kosmopoliten-Ordens" (1788; The secret of the order of cosmopolites); "Über deutschen Patriotismus" (1793; On German patriotism); *Neue Göttergespräche* (1791; New dialogues of the gods, translated as *Dialogues of the Gods*); "Für und Wider" (1793; Pro and contra); and "Betrachtungen über die gegenwärtige Lage des Vaterlandes" (1793; Observations on the present condition of the homeland). Fritz Martini regards this last essay as a unique masterpiece of Wieland's dialectic thought. The 13th dialogue of the *Dialogues of the Gods* deserves particular comment for its expression of Wieland's general attitude toward the French Revolution, its employment of a favorite form – the **dialogue** – and its surprising use of historical parallelism. While the latter is a favorite device throughout his career, it is used here with striking variation: the past (represented by various rulers and divinities) is conjured to comment upon and judge the present; human history is hailed before the bar of transhistorical reason, as it were, and forced to testify against itself. "Gespräche unter vier Augen" (1793; Tête-à-têtes), a culmination of several earlier works advancing the thesis that rule by the stronger, however unpalatable as a political principle, is nonetheless a historically established fact (McCarthy, 1979), was Wieland's last major essay on the Revolution.

Most of the common methods of setting forth an argument, such as inductive or deductive reasoning, precatory appeals, the invocation of authority, and the presupposition of reader agreement (*ad hominem* and *ad populum*), are found in abundance throughout the middle and late periods of Wieland's career in essay writing. Two types of argumentation, however – the dialectic and the rhetorical question – are both his preferred and his most accomplished devices.

As has often been remarked, Wieland was hardly akin to the more militant spirit of a Lessing or Herder; thus he only occasionally advances an adamantly polemical viewpoint. The desire, indeed the felt necessity, to shun severe criticism was part of his pacific nature, and he generally opted for a nonconfrontational and neutral ambiguity over harsh judgment. Such an attitude easily led, of course, to the charge – unfair, but leveled by contemporaries and later critics alike – that he was a trimmer and waverer. Wieland himself was clearly aware of and explicitly acknowledged his vulnerability on this count. In any event, his tone and temper in expressing his ideas, whether affirmative, negative, or indecisive, can be bitter, witty, dour, lighthearted, indignant, ironic, wry, resigned. Regardless of his stylistic disposition in a given work, however, he is consistently lucid and eminently readable. As one of the true founders of the German essay, he continues – almost two centuries after his death – both to reward careful and reflective study and to entertain and educate the casual reader.

ROBERT V. SMYTHE

Biography

Born 5 September 1733 in Oberholzheim, near Biberach. Studied privately with Johann Wilhelm Baumer, 1748–49; enrolled at the University of Erfurt, 1749–50. Engaged to his cousin Sophie Gutermann (i.e. the novelist Sophie von La Roche, 1750 (broken off, 1753, but remained friends throughout his life). Began a course in jurisprudence, University of Tübingen, 1750, but wrote poetry rather than studying law. Lived as guest of the scholar Johann Jakob Bodmer, Zurich, 1752–54; tutor in Zurich and Berne, 1754–60. Engaged to Julie Bondeli, 1759 (broken off). Senator and acting town clerk, Biberach, 1760. Married Dorothea von Hillenbrand, 1765 (died, 1801): eight daughters and four sons (two other children died in infancy). Appointed privy councillor of Mainz, 1769, and of Saxony, 1772. Professor of philosophy, University of Erfurt, 1769–72; tutor to the sons of Dowager Duchess Anna Amalia of Sachsen-Weimar, 1772–74. Cofounder and editor, *Der Teutsche Merkur* (later *Der neue Teutsche Merkur*), 1773–96. Became lifelong friends with **Goethe**, from 1775. Elected to the Prussian Academy of Science, 1787. Founder, *Attisches Museum* (Attic museum), 1796. Lived on the Ossmannstedt country estate, near Weimar, 1797–1803, then returned to Weimar. Awards: Legion of Merit (France), 1808; Cross of Saint Anna (Russia), 1808. Died in Weimar, 20 January 1813.

Selected Writings

Essays and Related Prose
Sympathien, 1756
Sammlung prosaischer Schriften, 2 vols., 1764
Beyträge zur Geheimen Geschichte des menschlichen Verstandes und Herzens (includes fiction), 1770
Prosaische Schriften, 2 vols., 1771–72; revised edition, 2 vols., 1785
Dialogues, translated anonymously, 1775
Neue Göttergespräche, 1791; part as *Dialogues of the Gods*, translated by William Taylor, 1795
Meine Antworten: Aufsätze über die Französische Revolution 1789–1793, edited by Fritz Martini, 1983
Politische Schriften: Insbesondere zur Französischen Revolution, 3 vols., 1988

Other writings: several novels (including *Die Geschichte des Agathon* [The History of Agathon], 1766–67), poetry (including the verse romance *Oberon*, 1780), and correspondence. Also translated works by Shakespeare, Horace, Lucian, and **Cicero**.

Collected works editions: *Sämtliche Werke*, edited by Heinrich Duntzer, 40 vols., 1867–79; *Gesammelte Schriften* (Berlin Academy of Science Edition), edited by Bernard Seuffert and others, 1909– (in progress; 100 vols. projected); *Werke*, edited by Fritz Martini and Hans Werner Seiffert, 5 vols., 1964–68; *Werke*, edited by Gonthier-Louis Fink and others, 1986– (in progress).

Bibliographies

Ottenbacher, Viia, "Wieland-Bibliographie, 1983–1988," *Wieland-Studien*, vol. 1, Sigmaringen: Thorbecke, 1991
Steinberger, Julius, *Bibliographie der Wieland-Übersetzungen*, Göttingen: Selbstverlag, 1930
Günther, Gottfried, and Heidi Zeilinger, *Wieland-Bibliographie*, Berlin and Weimar: Aufbau, 1983

Further Reading

Ermatinger, Emil, *Die Weltanschauung des jungen Wieland*, Frauenfeld: Huber, 1907
Fink, Gonthier-Louis, "Wieland et la Révolution française," *Revue d'Allemagne (Hommage à Robert Minder)* 5 (1973): 497–522
Haas, Gerhard, *Essay*, Stuttgart: Metzler, 1969
Jørgensen, S.-A., H. Jaumann, John A. McCarthy, and H. Thomé, *Christoph Martin Wieland: Epoche, Werk, Wirkung*, Munich: Beck, 1994
Just, Klaus Günther, "Essay," in *Deutsche Philologie im Aufriss*, vol. 1, edited by W. Stammler, Berlin: Schmidt, 1966: columns 1897–1948
McCarthy, John A., "Wieland as Essayist," *Lessing Yearbook 8* (1976): 125–39
McCarthy, John A., *Christoph Martin Wieland*, Boston: Twayne, 1979

McCarthy, John A., "The Poet as Journalist and Essayist: Chr. M. Wieland, Part One – A Descriptive Account," *Jahrbuch für internationale Germanistik* 12, no. 1 (1980): 104–38

McCarthy, John A., "The Poet as Essayist II," *Jahrbuch für internationale Germanistik* (1981): 74–137

Martini, Fritz, "C. M. Wieland und das 18. Jahrhundert," in *Festschrift Paul Kluckhohn und Hermann Schneider*, Tübingen: Möhr, 1948

Martini, Fritz, "Nachwort" to *Werke* by Wieland, vol. 3, Munich: Hanser, 1967

Meesen, H. J., "Wielands Briefe an einen jungen Dichter," *Monatshefte* 47 (1955): 193–208

Meyer, Verena, *C. M. Wieland und die geschichtliche Welt*, Zurich: Buchdruckerei Akeret, 1944

Rehder, Helmut, "Die Anfänge des deutschen Essays," *Deutsche Vierteljahrsschrift für Literaturwissenschaft und Geistesgeschichte* 40 (1966): 25–42

Rohner, Ludwig, *Der deutsche Essay: Materialien zur Geschichte und Ästhetik einer literarischen Gattung*, Neuwied and Berlin: Luchterhand, 1966

Schulze, Volker, "Der Teutsche Merkur (1773–1810)," in *Deutsche Zeitschriften des 17. bis 20. Jahrhunderts*, edited by Heinz-Dietrich Fischer, Pullach: Dokumentation, 1973

Seiffert, Hans W., "Die Idee der Aufklärung bei Christoph Martin Wieland," *Wissenschaftliche Annalen* 2 (1953): 678–89

Sengle, Friedrich, *Wieland*, Stuttgart: Metzler, 1949

Stamm, Israel S., "Wieland and Sceptical Rationalism," *Germanic Review* 33 (1958): 15–29

Starnes, Thomas C., *Der Teutsche Merkur: Ein Repertorium*, Sigmaringen: Thorbecke, 1994

Tietze, Wilhelm, "Wieland der Mensch und der Schriftsteller," *Die Literatur* 43 (1940–41): 275–79

Vogt, Oskar, "'Der goldene Spiegel' und Wielands politische Ansichten," *Forschungen zur neueren Literaturgeschichte* 26 (1904): 1–101

Wahl, Hans, *Geschichte des Teutschen Merkur*, Berlin: Mayer & Müller, 1914

Weyergraf, Bernd, *Der skeptische Bürger: Wielands Schriften zur Französischen Revolution*, Stuttgart: Metzler, 1972

Wilde, Oscar

Irish, 1854–1900

If Oscar Wilde had written nothing but essays and **dialogues**, he would be well known for them now. But until recently, his plays, his novel *The Picture of Dorian Gray* (1891), and above all the myth of his life have overshadowed his essays. His important contemporaries were more clear-sighted: **Pater** ("A Novel by Mr. Oscar Wilde," 1891) described Wilde as carrying on, "more perhaps than any other writer, the brilliant critical work of Matthew Arnold." **Yeats** ("Oscar Wilde's Last Book," 1891) drew attention to the literary aspect of Wilde's work: "*Intentions* hides within its immense paradox some of the most subtle literary criticism we are likely to see for many a long day."

Wilde by no means confined his nonfiction work to a traditional essay form: he enjoyed stretching the notional limits of genres, typically presenting his theory of Shakespeare's sonnets as a short story in "The Picture of Mr. W. H." (1889) or condensing a whole theory of art into a series of epigrams as "A Preface to *Dorian Gray*" (1891). He also harked back to older forms, and some of his most striking essays followed **Plato**, Sidney, or Dryden by adopting the dialogue form with a new, almost postmodern self-consciousness.

His first notable essay is "L'Envoi," an introduction to a volume of poems by his friend Rennell Rodd, the American publication of which he orchestrated in 1882. "L'Envoi" is effectively a manifesto for "the modern romantic school," a clear commitment to art for art's sake, a deliberate departure from **Ruskin**'s teaching, always essentially moral, in favor of a purely aesthetic ideal. This is the young Wilde's first call for "personality and perfection," his open commitment to "Greek things," his first notable dismissal of the Victorian ideals of sincerity and constancy. It is full of Paterian echoes, although Pater is nowhere mentioned; arguably by this time Wilde had wholeheartedly made some of Pater's ideas his own, and was assembling his own rich brew of the masters who were to be lasting influences, such as **Ralph Waldo Emerson**, apostle of individualism, and Théophile Gautier, precursor of art for art's sake.

Before the theatrical success which seemed to mark the end of his financial problems, Wilde was a hard-working literary man, writing articles and book **reviews**; many of these anonymous and apparently ephemeral publications deserve to be valued as literary essays. Richard Ellmann published a selection of them along with the better-known essays and dialogues in *The Artist as Critic: Critical Writings of Oscar Wilde* (1969). Outstanding among these is "A Chinese Sage," in which Wilde encounters Chuang Tzu, a Chinese Taoist philosopher of the fourth century BCE, and in him recognizes a contemporary and a fellow thinker. Chuang Tzu also preached inaction, contemplation, and the uselessness of all useful things. Wilde welcomes this paradoxical and subversive critic of wealth, moralizing, and good intentions, this proponent of "the ideal of self-culture and self-development"; this master joined Wilde's amalgam of inspirations, with a lasting influence on his thought. But when considering his major essays and dialogues, it is pointless to look for masters: Wilde is in his own literary element, inventive, creative, witty, and invariably speaking in what is now his own voice.

His two major literary-theoretical works are the poised and witty dialogues "The Decay of Lying" (1889) and "The Critic as Artist" (1890). Neither has yet received full critical treatment, though they have been annotated in detail in *The Oxford Authors Oscar Wilde* (1989). The protagonists of "The Decay of Lying" are two fashionable young men, the leader Vivian being exceptionally well read and happy to display esoteric learning. The success of the dialogues is in their self-consciousness: here, Vivian forecasts "a new Renaissance of Art," and reads out and discusses a paper he is writing. He goes on to "prove" that Art never expresses anything but itself, that all bad art comes from returning to Life and Nature, and that "Life imitates Art far more than Art imitates Life." In "The Critic as Artist," Gilbert convinces a doomed Ernest that Criticism is the superior part of creation, and that the critic must not be fair, rational, and sincere, but possessed of "a temperament exquisitely susceptible to beauty." Gilbert praises the possibilities of the dialogue form, in which, as the luckless Ernest points out, a critic "can invent an imaginary antagonist, and convert him when he chooses by some absurdly sophistical argument."

The Soul of Man Under Socialism (1891) is a more traditional essay on wider themes, dealing with notions of power and authority, anarchy and individualism, and "the great actual Individualism latent and potential in mankind generally." Here Wilde takes an airily optimistic view of the road to the socialist future and, while writing fraternally of the teachings of Christ, rejects the ideal of self-sacrifice and pain in favor of joy as the door to perfection.

There is a major change of direction in Wilde's writing in 1897, stemming from his reaction to his prison experiences and mainly involving his closer acquaintance with the realities of pain. When he was at last allowed pen and paper in H.M. Prison, Reading, after more than 19 months of deprivation, solitary confinement, and hard labor, Wilde had become inclined to take opposite views on the potential of humankind toward perfection. *De Profundis* (1905), written while he was in prison, is many things: it can be read as dramatic monologue, autobiography, elegy, love **letter**, and of course as essay. It was first published when Robert Ross extracted what seemed to him to be appropriate passages for publication, and it is clear that Wilde saw it as destined at least in parts for a wider audience than its addressee, Lord Alfred Douglas. Among other things, it enacts the essay he contemplates here, on Christ "as the precursor of the Romantic movement in life."

Arguably his two most powerful late essays are those which share the tone and passion of *The Ballad of Reading Gaol* (1898) – the two long letters he wrote to the *Daily Chronicle* (1897, 1898), which were printed under the titles "The Case of Warder Martin, Some Cruelties of Prison Life" and "Don't Read This if You Want to Be Happy Today." The optimum audience for these letters, as for the *Ballad*, was the widest possible readership, united only in the collective recognition of cruelty and of guilt.

ISOBEL MURRAY

Biography
Oscar Fingal O'Flahertie Wills Wilde. Born 16 October 1854 in Dublin. Studied at Portora Royal School, Enniskillen, County Fermanagh, 1864–71; Trinity College, Dublin, 1871–74; Magdalen College, Oxford, where he was taught by Walter Pater and John Ruskin, 1874–78, B.A., 1878. Moved to London, 1878; art reviewer, 1881; lectured in the United States and Canada, 1882; lived in Paris, 1883; lectured in Britain, 1883–84. Married Constance Lloyd, 1884 (separated, 1893; died, 1898): two sons. Regular contributor, *Pall Mall Gazette* and the *Dramatic Review*, mid-1880s; editor, *Woman's World*, London, 1887–89. Sued the Marquess of Queensberry for slander, 1895, but evidence at the trial revealed his relationship with Queensberry's son, Lord Alfred Douglas, and he was prosecuted for offenses to minors: sentenced to two years' hard labor in Wandsworth prison, London, then Reading Gaol, 1895–97. On release lived under the name Sebastian Melmoth in Berneval, near Dieppe, then in Paris. Allowed into the Roman Catholic Church on his deathbed. Died (of cerebral meningitis) in Paris, 30 November 1900.

Selected Writings

Essays and Related Prose
Intentions, 1891
"The Soul of Man Under Socialism," in *Fortnightly Review*, 1891; in book form, as *The Soul of Man*, 1895; as *The Soul of Man Under Socialism*, 1912
De Profundis, expurgated edition, edited by Robert Ross, 1905; revised edition, 1909; suppressed portion published, 1913; published in full in *The Letters*, edited by Rupert Hart-Davis, 1962; edited by Peter Forster, 1991

The Portable Oscar Wilde, edited by Richard Aldington, 1946; revised edition, edited by Aldington and Stanley Weintraub, 1981
Essays, edited by Hesketh Pearson, 1950
Selected Essays and Poems, 1954; as *De Profundis and Other Writings*, 1973
Literary Criticism, edited by Stanley Weintraub, 1968
The Artist as Critic: Critical Writings, edited by Richard Ellmann, 1969
Oxford Notebooks: A Portrait of Mind in the Making, edited by Philip E. Smith II and Michael S. Helfand, 1989
The Oxford Authors Oscar Wilde (selections), edited by Isobel Murray, 1989
The Soul of Man, and Prison Writings, edited by Isobel Murray, 1990
Aristotle at Afternoon Tea: The Uncollected Oscar Wilde, edited by John Wyse Jackson, 1991

Other writings: eight plays (including *Lady Windermere's Fan*, 1892; *Salomé*, 1893; *A Woman of No Importance*, 1893; *An Ideal Husband*, 1895; *The Importance of Being Earnest*, 1895), the novel *The Picture of Dorian Gray* (1891), fairytales, and poetry.

Complete works editions: *Works*, edited by Robert Ross, 4 vols., 1908–10; *Complete Works*, edited by Vyvyan Holland, 1948, reprinted 1989; *Works*, edited by Merlin Holland, 3 vols., 1993.

Bibliographies
Fletcher, Ian, and John Stokes, "Oscar Wilde," in *Anglo-Irish Literature: A Review of Research*, edited by Richard J. Finneran, New York: Modern Language Association of America, 1976
Fletcher, Ian, and John Stokes, "Oscar Wilde," in *Recent Research on Anglo-Irish Writers*, edited by Richard J. Finneran, New York: Modern Language Association of America, 1983
Mason, Stuart, *A Bibliography of Oscar Wilde*, London: Laurie, 1914
Mikhail, E. H., *Oscar Wilde: An Annotated Bibliography of Criticism*, London: Macmillan, and Totowa, New Jersey: Rowman and Littlefield, 1978

Further Reading
Bashford, Bruce, "Oscar Wilde as Theorist: The Case of *De Profundis*," *English Literature in Transition* 28, no. 4 (1985): 395–406
Beckson, Karl, editor, *Oscar Wilde: The Critical Heritage*, London: Routledge and Kegan Paul, and New York: Barnes and Noble, 1970
Beckson, Karl, *London in the 1890s: A Cultural History*, New York: Norton, 1992
Dyson, A. E., "Oscar Wilde: Irony of a Socialist Aesthete," in his *The Crazy Fabric: Essays in Irony*, London: Macmillan, and New York: St. Martin's Press, 1965
Ellmann, Richard, *Oscar Wilde*, London: Hamilton, 1987; New York: Knopf, 1988
Kohl, Norbert, *Oscar Wilde: The Works of a Conformist Rebel*, Cambridge and New York: Cambridge University Press, 1989
Murray, Isobel, "Oscar Wilde's Absorption of 'Influences': The Case History of Chuang Tzu," *Durham University Journal* 64, no. 1 (1971): 1–13
Murray, Isobel, "Oscar Wilde and Individualism: Contexts for *The Soul of Man*," *Durham University Journal* 83, no. 2 (1991): 195–207
Sandulescu, C. George, editor, *Rediscovering Oscar Wilde*, Gerrards Cross, Buckinghamshire: Smythe, 1993
Schiff, Hilda, "Nature and Art in Oscar Wilde's 'The Decay of Lying'," *Essays and Studies* (1965): 83–102
Shewan, Rodney, *Oscar Wilde: Art and Egotism*, London: Macmillan, and New York: Barnes and Noble, 1977

Small, Ian, *Oscar Wilde Revalued: An Essay on New Materials and Methods of Research*, Greensboro, North Carolina: ELT Press, 1993

Thomas, J. D., "The Intentional Strategy in Oscar Wilde's Dialogues," *English Literature in Transition* 12, no. 1 (1969): 11–20

Wilson, Edmund

American, 1895–1972

During his long career as a man of letters, Edmund Wilson produced hundreds of individual essays and several dozen published volumes of nonfiction prose. His broad interests included the Dead Sea Scrolls, the privations of Kentucky coalminers during the Depression, Iroquois and Zuni tribal culture, the development of the Soviet Union, and almost all aspects of European and American literature in the 19th century and the first half of the 20th. His work varies in length from brief book **reviews** to long scholarly books like *Patriotic Gore* (1962), his 800-page study of the literature of the American Civil War.

While his **reportage**, travel writing, and posthumously published diaries and notebooks have all been widely read and reviewed, his most prolific and important work is surely his literary criticism. This criticism was consistently and unfashionably a discussion "of literature in relation to life and of life in relation to history" ("Re-examining Dr. Johnson," 1944), foregrounding biographical, moral, political, and historical contexts at a time when academic literary scholarship was largely dominated by New Critical formalism.

Since he never found academic employment congenial, Wilson earned his living as a journalist, beginning with a brief period on the staff of *Vanity Fair* in 1920. He placed significant work in the *Dial*, the *Nation*, **Atlantic Monthly**, and **Partisan Review**, but three other periodicals published the bulk of his work. From 1921 to 1941 he was associated with the *New Republic*, which published parts of *To the Finland Station* (1940), his literary history of the European Left from Michelet to Lenin; many of the long literary essays later collected in *The Triple Thinkers* (1938) and *The Wound and the Bow* (1941); and most of the book reviews that make up *The Shores of Light* (1952). In 1943 he joined the **New Yorker**, where he first published most of the book reviews later collected in *Classics and Commercials* (1950), *The Bit Between My Teeth* (1965), and the posthumous *The Devils and Canon Barham* (1973). It was also in the *New Yorker* that he initially published much of *Europe Without Baedeker* (1947), his postwar tour of England, Italy, and Greece, *The Scrolls from the Dead Sea* (1955), and *Apologies to the Iroquois* (1960). In the last years of his life, he lent his prestige to the fledgling *New York Review of Books*, publishing there nine essays, including "The Fruits of the MLA" (1968), his influential indictment of American academic literary scholarship.

In his 1943 essay, "Thoughts on Being Bibliographed," Wilson outlined the circuitous way his work developed. He first sought reporting assignments or books to review on subjects that interested him, then combined these short articles into longer essays, and finally grouped essays for publication as books. His "preliminary sketches" are, he says, "tentative," and after being "exposed to criticism and correction," may be "contradicted by my final conclusions." His bibliographers are further tested by his habit of republishing revised, expanded, or recombined versions of his books whenever possible, sometimes with significantly revised titles, sometimes not. Given their complex publishing histories, Wilson's books and essays sometimes seem too loosely structured, but his individual sentences and paragraphs are much more carefully worked out. The generally unsympathetic chapter on Wilson in Stanley Edgar Hyman's *The Armed Vision* (1948) concedes his ability "to work the most recondite material into simple and comprehensible English." His prose style shows an old-fashioned fondness for Latinate diction and formal sentence structure coupled with forceful declarative statements. He hated jargon and imprecision, avoiding them himself and attacking them in other authors, as in "A Postscript to Fowler: Current Clichés and Solecisms" (1963). His style has often been described as conversational, but the conversation is dominated by one highly opinionated voice; Wilson's several attempts at **dialogue** (e.g. "The Delegate from Great Neck," 1924) resulted in one character virtually smothering the other.

Though perhaps a rather domineering conversationalist, Wilson had a strong sense of what his reader needed to know and what that reader might find interesting. Indeed his major complaint about academic literary critics was their impoverished sense of audience: at best, they wrote for small groups of fellow specialists, at worst, simply to create scholarly credentials with no readers in mind whatsoever. Wilson, on the other hand, worked hard to make his considerable erudition accessible and interesting to the broad audience that read the *New Yorker*. While he was an accomplished linguist, who taught himself Hebrew, Russian, and Hungarian after learning several less exotic languages, he almost always translates quotations into English. He is also quite happy to provide plot summaries of books he is discussing whenever he thinks they might be helpful. So, for example, in "Dickens: The Two Scrooges" (1941), he summarizes *Little Dorrit* but not *A Christmas Carol*. He also quotes at length from his sources, in part at least to convey their style and flavor; this habit grew with time, and quotations in *Patriotic Gore* can be ten pages long.

In addition to his very different sense of audience, Wilson was separated from most academic critics of his time by his emphasis on biographical and historical context and his corresponding failure to focus on textual analysis. Discussing *Axel's Castle* (1931), Wilson's study of literary Modernism and its roots in symbolism, Delmore Schwartz (1942) complains that when Wilson comes to the "technical working, the craftsmanship and the unique forms," of literary works, he becomes "impatient and hurried," so *Axel's Castle* "is not a book for writers."

Instead of form, Wilson looked at what led the author to produce the work and what the work has to say to us. He was very broadly a psychological critic: for example, the essays in *The Wound and the Bow*, drawing their theme from Sophocles' play about the wounded archer Philoctetes, show how psychological wounds are inseparable from the achievements of writers like Kipling, **Dickens**, and Hemingway. His criticism is also historical, both because he re-creates for his readers the historical environments of the writers he discusses and because he seeks origins and traces developments. *To the Finland Station*, for example, seeks the origin of modern socialism in the bourgeois French Revolution, and *Patriotic Gore* shows, among other things, the evolution of New England Puritanism from the Calvinist orthodoxy of Harriet Beecher Stowe's father to the agnosticism of Justice Oliver Wendell Holmes, Jr. He was also a rhetorical critic since the literature he studied included memoirs, diaries, speeches, **letters**, and histories at a time when most critics defined literature more narrowly as fiction, poetry, and drama. Implicit or explicit in all Wilson's criticism is a moral message for his reader, as in the conclusion to *Axel's Castle*, where we are warned against literary Modernism's tendency to retreat from the problems of society.

While Wilson himself always addressed society's problems, his messages sometimes split between progressive and reactionary elements. In the 1920s he championed literary Modernism, and in the next decade he was a sympathetic student of Marx and Lenin. By the early 1960s he was attacking the U.S. government's role in the Cold War, and he was an early opponent of the war in Vietnam. He often seemed at war with his own past: a descendant of Cotton Mather but consistently hostile to the Christian religion; a patrician WASP but also a rabid Anglophobe. Yet he never seemed at home in the 20th century either. He hated typewriters, radios, televisions, and movies; he never learned to drive an automobile. In 1956 he proclaimed, "I have lately been coming to feel that, as an American, I am more or less in the eighteenth century – or at any rate, not much later than the early nineteenth" (*A Piece of My Mind*, 1956). He had never had much sympathy for American popular culture and by the 1950s had lost interest in the younger writers; his later essays frequently lament the fact that some useful volume has gone out of print. The last book he published during his lifetime was *Upstate* (1971), a series of elegiac meditations by a country gentleman who has retreated to his ancestral home in Talcottville, New York. For Alfred Kazin, who knew him well, Wilson was "the great anachronism."

The biographical emphasis in his writing has led to predictable comparisons with **Plutarch** and **Sainte-Beuve**, but Wilson himself pointed to his discovery as a schoolboy of **Hippolyte Taine** as the origin of his method ("A Modest Self-Tribute," 1952). He acknowledged a certain debt to both **Marx** and **Freud** in the development of his approach ("The Historical Interpretation of Literature," 1940), but he followed them in only a very general way. His broad humanism has suggested parallels with **Matthew Arnold**, and he expressed admiration for **Henry James** and George Saintsbury. Another essayist he admired and resembled is **Samuel Johnson**. They reached nearly opposite conclusions on political and religious questions, but they were both guided by vigorous, skeptical common sense, both hated cant, and both delivered their opinions with great confidence and in clear but formal language. They both wrote on the lives of the poets and defined literature broadly to give full weight to nonfictional prose. Wilson's focus on biography and history and his interest in nonfictional prose often made his criticism look old-fashioned during his lifetime, but today his work seems far more current than that of the New Critics. He still gets very modest attention in the

universities, but the new interest in context and rhetorical analysis may well lead to a revival of interest in his impressive body of work.

WILLIAM F. NAUFFTUS

Biography

Born 8 May 1895 in Red Bank, New Jersey. Studied at Princeton University, New Jersey (member of the editorial staff, 1913–15, and managing editor, 1915–16, *Nassau Literary Magazine*), 1912–16, A.B., 1916. Reporter, New York *Evening Sun*, 1916–17. Served in the U.S. army, 1917–19. Contributed to or edited *Vanity Fair*, New York, 1920–23, *New Republic*, 1921–41, and *New Yorker*, 1943–48, and frequently thereafter. Married 1) Mary Blair, 1923 (divorced, 1928): one daughter; 2) Margaret Canby, 1930 (died, 1932); 3) **Mary McCarthy**, 1938 (divorced, 1946): one son; 4) Elena Thornton, 1946: one daughter. Awards: several, including the American Academy Gold Medal, for nonfiction, 1955; Presidential Medal of Freedom, 1963; MacDowell Medal, 1964; Emerson-Thoreau Medal, 1966; National Medal for Literature, 1966. Died in Talcottville, New York, 12 June 1972.

Selected Writings

Essays and Related Prose

Axel's Castle: A Study in the Imaginative Literature of 1870–1930, 1931
The American Jitters: A Year of the Slump, 1932; as *Devil Take the Hindmost*, 1932; enlarged edition, as *The American Earthquake: A Documentary of the Twenties and Thirties*, 1958
Travels in Two Democracies, 1936
The Triple Thinkers: Ten Essays on Literature, 1938; enlarged edition, as *The Triple Thinkers: Twelve Essays on Literary Subjects*, 1948
To the Finland Station: A Study in the Writing and Acting of History, 1940
The Wound and the Bow: Seven Studies in Literature, 1941
The Boys in the Back Room: Notes on California Novelists, 1941
Europe Without Baedeker: Sketches Among the Ruins of Italy, Greece, and England, 1947
Classics and Commercials: A Literary Chronicle of the Forties, 1950
The Shores of Light: A Literary Chronicle of the Twenties and Thirties, 1952
Eight Essays, 1954
The Scrolls from the Dead Sea, 1955; revised edition, as *The Dead Sea Scrolls, 1947–1969*, 1969; enlarged edition, as *Israel and the Dead Sea Scrolls*, 1978
A Literary Chronicle, 1920–1950, 1956
Red, Black, Blond and Olive: Studies in Four Civilizations, 1956
A Piece of My Mind: Reflections at Sixty, 1956
Apologies to the Iroquois, 1960
Patriotic Gore: Studies in the Literature of the American Civil War, 1962
The Cold War and the Income Tax: A Protest, 1963
O Canada: An American's Notes on Canadian Culture, 1965
The Bit Between My Teeth: A Literary Chronicle of 1950–1965, 1965
A Prelude: Landscapes, Characters, and Conversations from the Earlier Years of My Life, 1967
Upstate: Records and Recollections of Northern New York, 1971
A Window on Russia, 1972
The Devils and Canon Barham: Ten Essays on Poets, Novelists, and Monsters, 1973
Letters on Literature and Politics, 1912–1972, edited by Elena Wilson, 1977
The Nabokov-Wilson Letters, 1940–1971, edited by Simon Karlinsky, 1979

The Portable Edmund Wilson, edited by Lewis M. Dabney, 1983
From the Uncollected Edmund Wilson, edited by Janet Groth and
    David Castronovo, 1995

Other writings: the novel *I Thought of Daisy* (1929), the short
stories *Memoirs of Hecate County* (1946), plays, poetry, and
notebooks and diaries (collected in five books, four edited by Leon
Edel, 1975–86, the last by Lewis M. Dabney, 1993). Also edited
*The Shock of Recognition: The Development of Literature in the
United States Recorded by the Men Who Made It* (1943).

Bibliography
Ramsey, Richard David, *Edmund Wilson: A Bibliography*, New
    York: Lewis, 1971

Further Reading
Aaron, Daniel, Introduction to *Letters on Literature and Politics,
    1912–1972* by Wilson, edited by Elena Wilson, New York: Farrar
    Straus Giroux, 1977: xv–xxix
Castronovo, David, *Edmund Wilson*, New York: Ungar, 1984
Dabney, Lewis M., "Edmund Wilson and *The Sixties*," in *The
    Sixties* by Wilson, New York: Farrar Straus Giroux, 1993:
    xxi–lxvii
Edel, Leon, "A Portrait of Edmund Wilson," in *The Twenties* by
    Wilson, New York: Farrar Straus Giroux, and London:
    Macmillan, 1975: xvii–xlvi
Epstein, Joseph, "Bye-Bye, Bunny," *Hudson Review* 47, no. 2
    (Summer 1994): 235–48
Frank, Charles P., *Edmund Wilson*, New York: Twayne, 1970
Groth, Janet, *Edmund Wilson: A Critic for Our Time*, Athens: Ohio
    University Press, 1989
Hyman, Stanley Edgar, "Edmund Wilson and Translation in
    Criticism," in his *The Armed Vision: A Study in the Methods of
    Modern Literary Criticism*, New York: Knopf, 1948: 19–48 (this
    chapter was deleted from later editions)
Levin, Harry, "Edmund Wilson: The Last American Man of
    Letters," *Times Literary Supplement*, 11 October 1974: 1128–30
Meyers, Jeffrey, *Edmund Wilson: A Biography*, Boston: Houghton
    Mifflin, 1995
Paul, Sherman, *Edmund Wilson: A Study of Literary Vocation in
    Our Time*, Urbana: University of Illinois Press, 1965
Schwartz, Delmore, "The Writing of Edmund Wilson," *Accent* 2
    (Spring 1942): 177–86
Wain, John, editor, *Edmund Wilson: The Man and His Work*, New
    York: New York University Press, 1978; as *An Edmund Wilson
    Celebration*, Oxford: Phaidon, 1978

Wolf, Christa

German, 1929–

The famous "German-German literary debate" (deutsch-
deutscher Literaturstreit) on the political function of literature
was sparked in the Summer of 1990 following the publication
of Christa Wolf's *Was bleibt* (What remains). The mere fact
that a short narrative by a single – though established – author
could provoke such a widespread debate involving a substantial number of German intellectuals is a sign of Wolf's importance. The question arose as to whether and to what degree
Wolf had supported the East German government and, as a
consequence, whether or not her writings should be taken seriously. The debate was an indication of how intellectuals on
both sides of the iron curtain found themselves disoriented in
the face of German reunification and the termination of the

Cold War. Even today, many of these uncertainties remain
unresolved, and Wolf continues to symbolize those controversial questions that reach beyond the ethical and aesthetic
dimensions of literature and seek instead to find a new direction and orientation in a world where the idea of political
utopia has fallen into disrepute. Though Wolf has often been
accused of aligning herself with the restrictive socialist government of the GDR, her essayistic writings do contain critical
elements which stretched the limits imposed by the censors.

In her early collection of essays, *Lesen und Schreiben* (1972;
The Reader and the Writer), Wolf, a trained Germanist, reflects
on the role of literature. The introductory essay, "Lesen und
Schreiben" (1968; "Reading and Writing"), explains that the
prose genre is in particular danger of becoming obsolete in an
ever-changing world filled with scientific innovation, where it
is increasingly difficult to reserve time and space for dreams
and fantasies, vital for the development of the individual in
society. She concludes that the task of the author as individual
creator is to support and facilitate the tradition of human interaction by writing prose: "Prose can expand the limits of what
we know about ourselves. It keeps alive in us the memory of
a future which we cannot disown, on pain of destruction."
This memory of a future is what has made Wolf's essayistic
writings relevant for political as well as literary debates to this
day, well beyond the restrictive label of "GDR literature."

In her detailed essay on the almost forgotten Romanticist,
Karoline von Günderrode (1978), Wolf describes Romanticism
as a movement of change that reached "a new way of looking
at things" by overcoming "dry rationalism." Wolf thus goes
beyond describing the problems of a female author in a time
of uncertainty and turmoil. "Günderrode's generation, like all
who live in transitional periods, had to create new patterns
which later generations would use as models, stencils, warnings, slogans, in literature as in life." Wolf identifies with many
of the ideas of German Romanticism and considers herself as
one of those later generations who would use the patterns
developed by the Romantics. Her narrative *Kein Ort, Nirgends*
(1979; *No Place on Earth*) investigates the lives of Romantic
writers including Günderrode and sets up a clear parallel to
her own time. This work is a critique of the Enlightenment
that deviated from the traditional Marxist-Leninist interpretation of intellectual history. In contrast to the Marxist critique
of Romanticism, evident for instance in much of **Georg Lukács'**
writings, Wolf does not consider Romanticism to be an escapist
movement leading to irrationalism, decadence, and fascism.
Rather, she echoes the disappointment in the "totalitarian"
nature of the Enlightenment, as suggested in 1947 by Max
Horkheimer and **Theodor W. Adorno** in their *Dialektik der
Aufklärung* (1947; *Dialectic of Enlightenment*), though with a
different outcome. Wolf describes the writings and the early
death of Günderrode – an icon for other Romantics – as a
result of the repressive society she had to endure. In light of
the expatriation of East German poet Wolf Biermann in 1976
by the GDR government, which Wolf perceived as a serious
crisis for the role of the artist in the GDR, her depiction of
Günderrode can be seen as Wolf's self-censored but critical
assessment of contemporary GDR society.

Wolf's essays also include treatments of various authors
from different times, such as **Schiller**, Georg Büchner, **Thomas
Mann**, **Max Frisch**, and Anna Seghers, as well as numerous

lectures on her own experiences as an author, and even one on psychosomatic medicine. The recent Nazi Germany past, which Wolf experienced as a child, is embedded in many of her essays. When writing on other authors, she is generally more interested in the personal side of their writings, their emotions, and the nuances to be found between the lines, rather than in an abstract interpretation of their works. This approach is reflected in the style of her essays, a unique mixture of contemplation, linguistic force, self-confidence, and questioning, and distinguishes her from other essayists of her time.

Wolf often responds to questions others have posed or are likely to pose, perpetuating a dialogue with society. The most significant example of this tendency can be found in the essays accompanying her successful novel *Kassandra* (1983; *Cassandra*). Despite the somewhat misleading subtitle of the German edition, "Poetik-Vorlesungen" (Lectures on poetics), which suggests normative instructions on writing, Wolf wants her readers to witness the process of reflexive thought that led her to the creation of an aesthetic entity. By allowing the reader to participate in such an intimate process, Wolf retains the Marxist desire to reduce the alienation between art and recipient, as well as between individual and society. It is this keen interest in the individual readers themselves that marks Wolf as an outstanding critic and essayist of this century.

AGNES C. MÜLLER

Biography

Born 18 March 1929 in Landsberg an der Warthe, Germany (now Gorzow, Poland). Secretary to mayor of Gammelin, 1945–46. Studied at the Universities of Jena and Leipzig, 1949–53, diploma, 1953. Member of the Communist Party, 1949–89 (resigned). Married Gerhard Wolf, 1951: two daughters. Technical assistant, East German Writers' Union, 1953–59; editor, *Neue deutsche Literatur*, 1958–59; reader for Mitteldeutscher Verlag publishers, Halle, 1959–62, and Velag Neues Leben, Berlin; resident writer in a freight car manufacturing company, 1959–62; candidate member of central committee, SED, 1963–67. Awards: several, including Heinrich Mann Prize, 1963; National Prize, 1964; Raabe Prize, 1972; Fontane Prize, 1972; Büchner Prize, for essays, 1980; Schiller Prize, 1983. Member, Academy of Arts, Berlin.

Selected Writings

Essays and Related Prose

Lesen und Schreiben: Aufsätze und Betrachtungen, 1972; as *The Reader and the Writer*, translated by Joan Becker, 1977
Fortgesetzter Versuch: Aufsätze, Gespräche, Essays, 1979
Lesen und Schreiben: Neue Sammlung, 1980
Voraussetzungen einer Erzählung: Kassandra (includes the novel *Kassandra* and four lectures on the novel), 1983; as *Cassandra: A Novel, and Four Essays*, translated by Jan van Heurck, 1984
Die Dimension des Autors: Essays und Aufsätze, Reden und Gespräche, 1959–1985, 2 vols., 1986; part as *The Fourth Dimension: Interviews with Christa Wolf*, translated by Hilary Pilkington, 1988
The Author's Dimension: Selected Essays, edited by Alexander Stephan, translated by Jan van Heurck, 1993
Auf dem Weg nach Tabou: Texte 1990–1994, 1994

Other writings: seven novels (*Nachdenken über Christa T.* [*The Quest for Christa T.*], 1968; *Kindheitsmuster* [*A Model Childhood*], 1976; *Kein Ort, Nirgends* [*No Place on Earth*], 1979; *Kassandra* [*Cassandra*], 1983; *Störfall: Nachrichten eines Tages* [*Accident: A Day's News*], 1987; *Sommerstück*, 1989; *Medea*, 1996), novellas, and short stories.

Bibliography

Geist, Rosemarie, and Maritta Rost, "Auswahlbibliographie," in *Christa Wolf: Ein Arbeitsbuch: Studien-Dokumente-Bibliographie*, edited by Angela Drescher, Frankfurt-on-Main: Luchterhand, 1989: 415–536

Further Reading

Fries, Marilyn Sibley, editor, *Responses to Christa Wolf*, Detroit: Wayne State University Press, 1989
Kuhn, Anna K., editor, *Christa Wolf's Utopian Vision: From Marxism to Feminism*, Cambridge: Cambridge University Press, 1988
Love, Myra N., *Christa Wolf: Literature and the Conscience of History*, New York: Lang, 1991
Smith, Colin E., *Tradition, Art and Society: Christa Wolf's Prose*, Essen: Die Blaue Eule, 1987

Wolfe, Tom
American, 1930–

Tom Wolfe's essays are as flamboyant as his dress. His signature white suits, stepped collar vests, and spats reveal his homage to – and gentle tweaking of – the English Victorian man-of-letters tradition he has elaborated; yet his high-speed, highly exclamatory, exuberantly punctuated writing style marks him all-American and late 20th century. Wolfe is best known as a chronicler of American popular culture, which he renders in a sophisticated essay-and-reportage form he has christened "the **New Journalism**." Today he is increasingly recognized, not only as one of America's leading prose stylists, but as a social critic (and satirist), although he demurs at the latter label.

From the beginning of his newspaper and magazine article writing career, Wolfe's range has been impressive. He wrote hundreds of traditional feature articles for the Springfield (Massachusetts) *Union* (1956–59), Washington *Post* (1959–62), and New York *Herald Tribune* (1962–66) before a 1963 assignment to cover the California custom car culture for *Esquire* magazine led to "There Goes (Varoom! Varoom!) That Kandy-Kolored Tangerine-Flake Streamline Baby," Wolfe's breakthrough article in his dazzlingly punctuated kinetic style. Since then, he has written profiles of cultural heroes, portraits of cultural lifestyles, **travel essays** (such as "Las Vegas (What?) Las Vegas (Can't Hear You! Too Noisy) Las Vegas!!!!," 1964), and political **satire**. Wolfe is best understood as a cultural critic. He has made a career of challenging establishment views, of being the bad boy of arts and letters. His early assault on the **New Yorker** and its venerable former editor, William Shawn, in the 1965 articles "Tiny Mummies" and "Lost in the Whichy Thicket," occasioned spirited defenses of that magazine. His attacks on the worlds of art and architecture in two book-length essays, *The Painted Word* (1975) and *From Bauhaus to Our House* (1981), have stirred similar debates. A wicked phrasemaker, Wolfe has seen his terms "radical chic" and "the right stuff" become part of the cultural landscape, as has his name for the 1970s, "the me decade." Like **Max Beerbohm**, Wolfe illustrates many of his essays and has published an entire collection of satirical drawings entitled *In Our Time* (1980).

Although holding a doctoral degree in American studies from Yale University, Wolfe has eschewed academic writing for the wider, general audience which reads newspapers and popular magazines. This audience has made him a bestselling writer. He was a contributing editor to *New York* magazine through 1976 and remains to this day a contributing editor to the men's magazine *Esquire*. Indeed this graduate of (then) all-male Washington and Lee University in Virginia is most at home celebrating masculine heroes.

The components of Wolfe's distinctive writing style can be traced to his reading. He borrowed several narrative techniques and his dynamic punctuation from a group of early 20th-century Soviet writers (Evgenii Zamiatin, Boris Pilniak, and the Serapion Brothers), whom he read in translation at Yale. In *We* (1924), the novel upon which **George Orwell** based *1984*, Zamiatin often breaks off thoughts with a dash in mid-sentence and uses many exclamation points. This style attempts to imitate the human mind, which operates, not in elegant sentences, but in fragmentary, often emotional, fits and starts. Wolfe's kinetic style should be seen as his attempt to imitate sensory and cognitive processes – and to decrease the distance between author, reader, and subject. Through frenetic fragments and picturesque punctuation he tries to give readers a vicarious sense of the experience he is re-creating, be it the rush of psychedelic drugs (*The Electric Kool-Aid Acid Test*, 1968), or supersonic space travel (*The Right Stuff*, 1979). This highly sensory style matches best with highly sensory subjects.

Wolfe joined these narrative techniques with others gleaned from fellow New York journalists in the early 1960s. His 1973 anthology *The New Journalism*, which argues that the New Journalism "can no longer be ignored in an artistic sense," identifies four traits which characterize the form: scene-by-scene construction; dialogue in full; third-person point of view; and the detailing of status life. Wolfe acknowledges that he learned to write scenes from Gay Talese and dialogue from Jimmy Breslin. His penchant for what he calls "status detail" can be traced to Honoré de Balzac, who enjoyed dropping the names of furniture into his novels. Social status and social humiliation are prominent themes in Wolfe's writings; his brilliant capturing of details of dress and decor allows him to pinpoint his subjects precisely in the social strata.

Wolfe's most original stylistic trait, however, is his extension of **Henry James'** notions of point of view. Wolfe acknowledges that he tries to create his scenes from a triple perspective: the subject's point of view, that of other people watching, and his own. His technical virtuosity in shifting among these conflicting perspectives, often from sentence to sentence, adds to the postmodern zest of his writing. No essayist switches point of view more rapidly than Wolfe. However, this rapid-fire multiple perspective carries with it certain risks. It tends to frustrate readers seeking to isolate Wolfe's own view of his subjects. Wolfe relishes this confusion. As John Hellmann (1981) has noted, Wolfe's "insistent choices of hyperbolic, kinetic, or baroque words and phrases make his descriptions as much an assault as a representation . . . These stylistic traits work like those of the cubists to break up the reader's usual modes of perception."

Wolfe does, however, possess a social vision. He was raised in the Presbyterian Church, and uniting all his work is his lament for waning Protestant morality (*The Right*[eous] *Stuff*),

and his implicit call for its renewal. Wolfe's inspired transformation of that oldest of American literary forms, the Puritan **sermon**, into Menippean satire represents an intelligent man's recognition of the unpopularity of his old-fangled, Calvinistic views were he to express them forthrightly in his own voice in the traditional forms of the formal or familiar essay. Let the bonfire of vanities burn, Wolfe cries instead, for he is an American jeremiah in camouflage, both criticizing vice and encouraging American expansion and revolution toward grace.

BARBARA LOUNSBERRY

Biography

Thomas Kennerly Wolfe, Jr. Born 2 March 1930 in Richmond, Virginia. Studied at Washington and Lee University, Lexington, Virginia, A.B. (cum laude), 1951; Yale University, New Haven, Connecticut, Ph.D., 1957. Wrote for the Springfield *Union*, Massachusetts, 1956–59, Washington *Post*, 1959–62, New York *Herald Tribune*, 1962–66, and New York *World Journal Tribune*, 1966–67; contributing artist, *Harper's*, 1978–81. Married Sheila Berger, 1978: one daughter and one son. Awards: several, including the American Book Award, 1980; National Book Critics Circle Award, 1980; Columbia/Columbus Award, for journalism, 1980; John Dos Passos Award, 1984; President Award, 1993; honorary degrees from 11 universities.

Selected Writings

Essays and Related Prose
The Kandy-Kolored Tangerine-Flake Streamline Baby, 1965
The Pump House Gang, 1968; as *The Mid-Atlantic Man and Other New Breeds in England and America*, 1969
The Electric Kool-Aid Acid Test, 1968
Radical Chic & Mau-Mauing the Flak Catchers, 1970
The Painted Word, 1975
Mauve Gloves and Madmen, Clutter and Vine, and Other Stories, 1976
The Right Stuff, 1979
From Bauhaus to Our House, 1981
The Purple Decades: A Reader, 1982

Other writings: the novel *The Bonfire of the Vanities* (1987) and the collection of drawings *In Our Time* (1980). Also edited the anthology *The New Journalism* (1973).

Further Reading

Anderson, Chris, "Tom Wolfe: Pushing the Outside of the Envelope," in his *Style as Argument*: *Contemporary American Nonfiction*, Carbondale: Southern Illinois University Press, 1987: 8–47
Cohen, Ed, "Tom Wolfe and the Truth Monitors: A Historical Fable," *Clio* 16 (Fall 1986): 1–11
Dundy, Elaine, "Tom Wolfe . . . But Exactly, Yes!," *Vogue*, 15 April 1966: 124, 152–55
Gilder, Joshua, "Creators on Creating: Tom Wolfe," *Saturday Review*, April 1981: 40, 42–44
Hellmann, John, "Reporting the Fabulous: Representation and Response in the Work of Tom Wolfe," in his *Fables of Fact*: *The New Journalism as New Fiction*, Urbana: University of Illinois Press, 1981: 101–25
Hollowell, John, "Life in Edge City: Wolfe's New Journalism," in his *Fact & Fiction: The New Journalism and the Nonfiction Novel*, Chapel Hill: University of North Carolina Press, 1977: 126–46

Kallan, Richard A., "Tom Wolfe," in *A Sourcebook of American Literary Journalism: Representative Writers in an Emerging Genre*, edited by Thomas B. Connery, Westport, Connecticut: Greenwood Press, 1992

Lounsberry, Barbara, "Tom Wolfe's Negative Vision," *South Dakota Review* 20 (Summer 1982): 15–31

Lounsberry, Barbara, "Tom Wolfe's American Jeremiad," in her *The Art of Fact: Contemporary Artists of Nonfiction*, Westport, Connecticut: Greenwood Press, 1990: 37–64

Macdonald, Dwight, "Parajournalism, or Tom Wolfe and His Magic Writing Machine," *New York Review of Books*, 26 August 1965: 3–5

Macdonald, Dwight, "Parajournalism II: Wolfe and *The New Yorker*," *New York Review of Books*, 3 February 1966: 18–24

Sheed, Wilfrid, "A Fun-House Mirror," *New York Times Book Review*, 3 December 1972: 2, 10

Stull, James N., "The Cultural Gamesmanship of Tom Wolfe," *Journal of American Culture* 14 (Fall 1991): 25–30

Weber, Ronald, "Subjective Reality and Saturation Reporting," in his *The Literature of Fact: Literary Nonfiction in American Writing*, Athens: Ohio University Press, 1980: 89–110

Zavarzadeh, Mas'ud, "The Contingent *Donnée*: The Testimonial Nonfiction Novel," in his *The Mythopoeic Reality: The Postwar American Nonfiction Novel*, Urbana: University of Illinois Press, 1976: 131–53

Wollstonecraft, Mary

British, 1759–1797

Author prior to 1790 only of a conventional work in the conduct book genre and a semi-confessional novel, Wollstonecraft's practice as a reviewer for the *Analytical Review* prepared her entry into the male arena of political debate with *A Vindication of the Rights of Men* (1790), one of the earliest replies to **Edmund Burke**'s *Reflections on the Revolution in France* (1790). This **polemical essay**, largely a personal attack on Burke despite its claim to offer a reasoned critique (and thus succumbing to the same emotionalism and rhetorical excess it condemns in his text), is of interest mainly in so far as it anticipates the sociopolitical analysis of the more famous *A Vindication of the Rights of Woman* (1792) that followed.

Addressing herself to middle-class women as those most susceptible to reformation, Wollstonecraft sets out in the *Rights of Woman* to inspire a "revolution in female manners" and to attack justifications of women's subordinate status whether biblically derived or in the more insidious contemporary form of a Rousseauvian eroticized idealization of feminine submissiveness. Wollstonecraft bases her defense of women's rights on the claim that women like men were created free moral agents endowed with reason. Their inferiority and subordinate status are neither natural nor divinely ordained but a product of social conditioning. While conceding that women in their present state are inferior to men – indeed, reduced to "a state of degradation" – Wollstonecraft blames it on a misconceived education that prepares girls to become the objects of male desire rather than independent rational beings fit for their vital moral and social role as mothers. Rational education is therefore the primary and most urgently needed right she claims for women. (Her more radical claims – the rights to political representation and economic independence through work

outside the home – are buried in the final chapters.) In condemning the infantilization of middle-class and aristocratic women and in adumbrating the vices produced by dependence, miseducation, and the overdevelopment of sensibility at the expense of reason, Wollstonecraft does not herself entirely avoid the misogyny she is attempting to combat. Her anger is directed as much at women (whom she condemns for colluding in their own oppression) as at their oppressors. Her stress on maternal duty combined with her attack on romantic love (informed by an awareness of its role in disguising women's subordinate status) lead her, as modern critics have noted, to deny women's sexual needs. While attempting to free women from the influence of writers like Rousseau who have made them "objects of pity," Wollstonecraft offers as sternly puritanical a message as any conduct book.

Digressive, repetitive, and rambling in organization, the *Rights of Woman* is not always easy reading. At its best it has an urgent energy and incisiveness, but it often declines into **sermon** or harangue. However, despite its undeniable flaws and limitations, it remains a work of major significance as the first feminist manifesto, far ahead of its time in its political and psychological insights and its call for the moral, intellectual, and economic autonomy of women.

While her two-year stay in France led to *An Historical and Moral View of the Origin and Progress of the French Revolution* (1794), a defense of the Revolution despite the excesses of the Terror, it was a Scandinavian journey that inspired the work which, after the *Rights of Woman*, is Wollstonecraft's best claim to interest the modern reader: *Letters Written During a Short Residence in Sweden, Norway, and Denmark* (1796). Often characterized as an odd mix of genres, combining elements of the tour, the epistolary novel, and the confession, it is precisely through its elision of generic boundaries that *A Short Residence* has survived. Presented in the guise of **letters** to an unnamed but clearly faithless lover (Gilbert Imlay, whose legal interests Wollstonecraft was representing in a Norwegian court case), the book is a series of essays in miniature, linked by the journey narrative and moving easily from the experiences of the day to the larger concerns that preoccupy the writer. Permitting the combination of social analysis and subjective response, moral reflection and personal revelation, inviting the associative and the spontaneous as principles of composition, the travel genre and epistolary form gave free play to Wollstonecraft's talents and interests, liberating her from the constraints of the masculine political discourse she had sought with only partial success to emulate in her polemical writings. The situation of deserted mother and infant daughter caught the sympathy of contemporary readers while coloring both Wollstonecraft's observation of Scandinavian society and her descriptions of the Northern landscape. It was this latter aspect, as well as the novelty of an account of a region hitherto unexplored in the travel literature of the period, that captivated **William Godwin**, William Wordsworth, and **Robert Southey** and influenced **Samuel Taylor Coleridge**'s "Kubla Khan" (wr. 1797, pub. 1816). While often couched in the conventional language of the sublime, at its best Wollstonecraft's attempt to convey the "romantic" character of the landscape blends observation and introspection in a manner that anticipates the Romantic exploration of self and nature.

A Short Residence was in some sense her personal vindication, not only in its self-justifying declarations of virtuous love and maternal duty as she tries to come to terms with her situation as cast-off mistress and single mother, but in its self-portrait of a woman who can ask "men's questions" while revealing a mother's tenderness, who has eschewed the conditioned frailty of her sex (so vigorously denounced in the *Rights of Woman*) and its concomitant need for protection, while retaining a feminine sensibility and refinement. That this independence has not freed her from emotional need becomes increasingly evident in the final letters and the abrupt and desperate ending.

Despite the recognition she achieved with these two works, Wollstonecraft's untimely death in childbirth and the subsequent publication of Godwin's ill-judged revelations of her life effectively curtailed any influence she might have had upon her contemporaries as writer or analyst. But the re-examination of her work in recent decades has not only established her as a significant figure in her time, it has also contributed importantly to new ways of viewing that era.

ANN PEARSON

Biography

Born 27 April 1759 in London. Lived in Beverley, Yorkshire, 1768–73, London, 1774–75 and 1777, and Laugharne, Wales, 1776. Paid companion, Bath, 1778–80; ran, with her sisters and a friend, a school in Islington, then Newington Green, London, 1784–86; governess in Mitchelstown, County Cork, 1786–87. Translator and reader for the radical publisher Joseph Johnson, and reviewer and editorial assistant for his journal the *Analytical Review*, London, 1787–92 and 1797. Lived in France, reporting on the French Revolution, 1792–95. Liaison with Gilbert Imlay, 1793–95: one daughter. Traveled in Scandinavia, 1795, then returned to England. Married William Godwin, 1797: one daughter (the writer Mary Shelley). Died (of septicemia after childbirth) in London, 10 September 1797.

Selected Writings

Essays and Related Prose
A Vindication of the Rights of Men, 1790; revised edition, 1790; facsimile reprint, 1960; edited by Sylvana Tomaselli, with *A Vindication of the Rights of Woman*, 1995
A Vindication of the Rights of Woman, 1792; revised edition, 1792; edited by Charles W. Hagelman, Jr., 1967, Gina Luria, 1974, Miriam Brody Kramnick, 1975, Carol H. Poston, 1975, Ulrich H. Hardt, 1982, Mary Warnock, with *The Subjection of Women* by John Stuart Mill, 1986, Ashley Tauchert, 1995, and Sylvana Tomaselli, with *A Vindication of the Rights of Men*, 1995
Letters Written During a Short Residence in Sweden, Norway, and Denmark, 1796; edited by Carol H. Poston, 1976; as *A Short Residence in Sweden, Norway, and Denmark*, edited by Richard Holmes, 1987

Other writings: two novels, the polemical work *Thoughts on the Education of Daughters* (1787), a book about the French Revolution (1794), and correspondence.

Collected works edition: *Works*, edited by Janet Todd and Marilyn Butler, 7 vols., 1989.

Bibliography
Todd, Janet, *Mary Wollstonecraft: An Annotated Bibliography*, New York: Garland, 1976

Further Reading
Alexander, Meena, *Women in Romanticism: Mary Wollstonecraft, Dorothy Wordsworth and Mary Shelley*, Basingstoke: Macmillan, and Savage, Maryland: Barnes and Noble, 1989
Conger, Syndy McMillen, *Mary Wollstonecraft and the Language of Sensibility*, Rutherford, New Jersey: Fairleigh Dickinson University Press, 1994
Cox, Stephen, "Sensibility as Argument," in *Sensibility in Transformation: Creative Resistance to Sentiment from the Augustans to the Romantics,* edited by Syndy McMillen Conger, Rutherford, New Jersey: Fairleigh Dickinson University Press, 1990
Finke, Laurie A., "A Philosophic Wanton: Language and Authority in Wollstonecraft's *A Vindication of the Rights of Woman*," in *The Philosopher as Writer: The Eighteenth Century*, edited by Robert Ginsberg, Selinsgrove, Pennsylvania: Susquehanna University Press, 1987
Ellison, Julie, "Redoubled Feeling: Politics, Sentiment, and the Sublime in Williams and Wollstonecraft," *Studies in Eighteenth-Century Culture* 20 (1990): 197–215
Ferguson, Moira, and Janet Todd, *Mary Wollstonecraft*, Boston: Twayne, 1984
Guralnick, E. S., "Rhetorical Strategy in Mary Wollstonecraft's *A Vindication of the Rights of Woman*," *Humanities Association Review* 30, no. 3 (1989): 174–85
Jones, Vivien, "Women Writing Revolution: Narratives of History and Sexuality in Wollstonecraft and Williams," in *Beyond Romanticism: New Approaches to Texts and Contexts 1780–1832*, edited by Stephen Copley and John Whale, London and New York: Routledge, 1992
Kaplan, Cora, "Pandora's Box: Subjectivity, Class, and Sexuality in Socialist Feminist Criticism," in *Making a Difference: Feminist Literary Criticism*, edited by Gayle Green and Coppelia Kahn, London and New York: Methuen, 1985
Kelly, Gary, *Revolutionary Feminism: The Mind and Career of Mary Wollstonecraft*, London: Macmillan, and New York: St. Martin's Press, 1992
Moore, Jane, "Plagiarism with a Difference: Subjectivity in 'Kubla Khan' and *Letters Written During a Short Residence in Sweden, Norway, and Denmark*," in *Beyond Romanticism: New Approaches to Texts and Contexts 1780–1832*, edited by Stephen Copley and John Whale, London and New York: Routledge, 1992
Myers, Mitzi, "Mary Wollstonecraft's *Letters Written . . . in Sweden*: Toward Romantic Autobiography," *Studies in Eighteenth-Century Culture* 8 (1979): 165–85
Parks, George B., "The Turn to the Romantic in the Travel Literature of the Eighteenth Century," *Modern Language Quarterly* 25 (1964): 22–33
Poovey, Mary, *The Proper Lady and the Woman Writer: Ideology as Style in the Works of Mary Wollstonecraft, Mary Shelley, and Jane Austen*, Chicago: University of Chicago Press, 1984
Wilson, Anna, "Mary Wollstonecraft and the Search for the Radical Woman," *Genders* 6 (1989): 88–101
Yaeger, Patricia, *Honey-Mad Women: Emancipatory Strategies in Women's Writing*, New York: Columbia University Press, 1988

Woolf, Virginia
British, 1882–1941

Virginia Woolf's output as an essayist was prodigious: in addition to two lengthy feminist monographs, she produced over 500 **pamphlets**, articles, **reviews**, and notices. The breadth and variety of her essays are likewise impressive, expanding well beyond the literary review-essay to encompass **travel essays**, autobiography, art reviews (on drama, painting, film, and photography), and commentaries on aspects of culture and society – even extending to cookery. The new critical attention being given to Woolf's essays and the increasing tendency to read them in relation to one another (stimulated both by Andrew McNeillie's publication of the complete essays and by a general resurgence of interest in nonfictional forms) is contributing to the ongoing revision of earlier constructions of Woolf as a Modernist confined to subjective reality and aesthetic form. While evidencing Woolf's abiding interest in the issues of writing, reading, and publication, the essays reveal an approach that is firmly grounded in a recognition of social, material, and historical contexts.

Woolf's career as an essayist was established primarily in the *Times Literary Supplement* and consolidated through the two volumes of *The Common Reader* published by the Hogarth Press in 1925 and 1932. While contributing as well to periodicals aimed at a more select and literary audience – such as T. S. Eliot's *Criterion* – Woolf also published in more popular journals such as *Vogue* and the *Atlantic Monthly*, and in the feminist weeklies *Woman's Leader and the Common Cause* and *Time and Tide*. The diverse audience she thus addressed has an important bearing on Woolf's style as an essayist; as she herself wrote, writer and reader are bound together in a collaborative and symbiotic relation: "twins indeed, one dying if the other dies, one flourishing if the other flourishes" ("The Patron and the Crocus," 1924). The reader in her text is well read and literate but not necessarily of the educated or privileged class; if the **letters** she received from individual readers are indicative of her general audience, she was read not only by members of the male establishment but by students, aspiring writers, housewives (particularly wives of academics), school teachers, and members of the working class (including at least one bus conductor).

Addressing herself to such a large "patronage," Woolf separates herself from the increasingly professionalized character of English studies and reaches beyond the male upper-class literati. Nevertheless, she expects a high intellectual level in her readership. Her French remains untranslated; she assumes a broad cultural and historical knowledge and a familiarity with the texts she discusses. However, such assumptions of knowledge are unlikely to block an understanding of her essays; meanings are contextually lucid and the presumed familiarity with the subject simply allows her to leap immediately to a level of provocative ideas which can serve as either foreword or afterword to a reading of the text.

Woolf's self-identification as a "common reader" and her assumption of an informed but nonspecialist audience are reflected in connections between her style and that of the familiar essay. Her vocabulary, while extensive, is never obscure or uncommon: the essay, she writes, is the form of literature "which least calls for the use of long words" ("The Modern Essay," 1922). Her reader is directly addressed, in a conversational tone: "Let us watch Miss Frend trotting along the Strand with her father" ("Lives of the Obscure," 1924). Her ideas develop frequently through narrative and metaphor: **Defoe** presents us with "a plain earthenware pot" ("Robinson Crusoe," 1926); **Addison**, with "pure silver" ("Addison," 1919). Mrs. Carlyle's letters emit a "crooning domestic sound like the purring of a kitten or the humming of a tea-kettle"

("Geraldine and Jane," 1929). Unlike the formalist critic, Woolf rarely quotes from her reading; furthermore, when she does provide quotations, it is to present the text in its own voice, rather than to pursue detailed textual analysis.

These stylistic elements help to produce the normal speaking voice of the **familiar essay**, as opposed to the authoritative voice of the formal essay. This personal voice enables an approach, like that of the familiar essay, that is speculative and open-ended rather than definitive and conclusive. But Woolf's characteristic handling of multiple viewpoints is complex and challenging, figured in skillful ironies and subtle shifts in discourse and in voice. She does not employ the direct confrontation of argument but instead leads the reader to "inhabit" differing points of view. The resemblance of this style to the discourse of the "proper lady" has led some critics to dismiss the seriousness of the essays, citing Woolf's own reservations about the "Victorian game of manners" ("A Sketch of the Past," wr. 1939–40, pub. 1976). Recent readings, however, tend to emphasize the dialogic nature of Woolf's style and its subversive and revisionary effect. Instead of adopting a stable point of view, the essays enact a continual questioning of opinion, in a manner which Woolf once referred to as her "turn & turn about method" (*Diary* II, 13 June 1923). By emphasizing such rhetorical twists, critics now propose that Woolf foregrounds the ideological assumptions that underlie any construction of "knowledge." She is thus seen to be as concerned with the process of interpreting as she is with interpretations. Her Modernism is still linked to subjectivity; the difference is that instead of identifying Woolf with an ahistorical and aestheticized approach to reality, most critics now see her as engaged with the social and political implications of attitudes and beliefs. As a woman, she is seen to use her perspective as an outsider to critique the assumptions underlying the dominant patriarchal ideologies of her time; in a broader sense, she can be seen to situate all views in terms of their historical, national, or gendered contexts.

Given Woolf's foregrounding of the problematic nature of knowledge, it is not surprising that the essayist with whom she appears to be aligned most sympathetically is **Montaigne**. Woolf celebrates his multiplicity, his contradictoriness, his provisionality, his inconclusiveness; adopting his own travel metaphor, she describes his focus on the process of his thinking in a way that could describe her own essays: "the journey is everything" ("Montaigne," 1924). But whereas Woolf is drawn to Montaigne's self-positioning and self-questioning, encapsulated in his question "Que scais-je?," her style is informed as well by her interest in more overtly dramatized forms, from the Platonic **dialogues** ("Art and Life," 1909; "On Not Knowing Greek," 1925), to Walter Landor's *Imaginary Conversations* ("Landor in Little," 1919), or George Moore's reconstructed conversations with Mr. Gosse or Mr. Balderston ("Winged Phrases," 1919). Noting, however, that these dialogues are often, in effect, situated within the one voice, Woolf herself sought a more oppositional and contestatory form and experimented in dramatizing strongly divergent points of view ("Mr. Conrad: A Conversation," 1923). While ultimately rejecting fictionalized debates because too much of the essay had to be devoted to the creation of characters, she nevertheless frames her essays around oppositional views, often installing the dominant or conventional view and then proceeding, through a dialogic process, to position and examine it. Again recalling Montaigne, these shifts produce a structure of rambling circularity as opposed to the logical linearity of the dominant Western rhetorical mode.

But while Woolf's style has much in common with the familiar essay, her essays do not fit easily into any category. It may be best to regard them as a hybrid form, as befitting a writer who did not herself believe in discrete genres. On the one hand, her style is informed by the "great tradition" of canonical prose writers, with affinities to such writers as **Johnson, Hazlitt, Lamb, De Quincey,** and **Pater,** in addition to Montaigne. On the other hand, Woolf's essays are equally consanguineous with the alternative tradition of diaries, letters, and memoirs which women had used to record their thoughts.

There is another interesting "split" in her writing that is perhaps even more significant. While her commitment to a common readership and her rejection of an authoritative voice link her essays in style and approach to the familiar essay and forms of everyday writing, the literary issues that she addresses connect her essays in content with the academic professional article beginning to emerge. Her discussions of specific writers are framed by larger academic questions about the significance of tradition, the standards used to interpret and evaluate it, and the assumptions encoded in these standards. She addresses problems concerning the inclusion or exclusion of non-canonical works, the effect on a writer of outer circumstances, and the relation between writer and audience. But though Woolf's approach to these issues is as compelling as Eliot's, her manner of writing was overshadowed by Eliot's impersonal and doctrinal discourse, which came to exert a strong formative influence on the academic article in English studies. Thus in the years after her death, despite the attention she herself devoted to lost or forgotten works of literature, her own essays suffered the fate of being marginalized themselves.

The situation at the end of the century has substantially reversed, and Woolf's essays tend to attract more attention now than Eliot's. In this light, it is salutary to recall the strongly positive reception of Woolf's essays by her contemporaries, many of whom considered them to be her finest work. Reviewers praised her combination of "historical sense" with "wideness of sympathy," of "keen analysis" with a "synthesizing humanity," of "the science of criticism" with "the insight of the novelist." All of these comments testify to Woolf's ability to integrate the intellectual and the personal, but it was Olive Heseltine in the *Daily News* (4 August 1925) who most evocatively captured this strength: in an appropriately Woolfian image, Heseltine summed up *The Common Reader* as "a marriage of true minds consummated between a wood nymph and a don."

MELBA CUDDY-KEANE

Biography

Daughter of the writer **Leslie Stephen.** Born 25 January 1882 in London. No formal education; studied privately. Lived in Bloomsbury, London, 1904-15 and 1924-39, Richmond, Surrey, 1915-24, and maintained Monks House, Rodmell, near Lewes, Sussex, 1919-41. Published some 500 essays in periodicals and collections, beginning 1905. Associated with a group later known as the Bloomsbury Group, which included writers **E. M. Forster** and **Lytton Strachey,** painters Vanessa Bell (her sister) and Duncan

Grant, economist John Maynard Keynes, art critic Roger Fry, and others. Married the writer Leonard Woolf, 1912. Founder, with Leonard Woolf, Hogarth Press, Richmond, Surrey, later London, from 1917. Awards: Femina-Vie Heureuse Prize, 1928. Subject to mental breakdowns throughout her life. Died (suicide by drowning) in Rodmell, 28 March 1941.

Selected Writings

Essays and Related Prose
The Common Reader, 1925; edited by Andrew McNeillie, 1984
A Room of One's Own, 1929
The Common Reader, second series, 1932; U.S. publication as *The Second Common Reader,* 1932; edited by Andrew McNeillie, 1986
Three Guineas, 1938
The Death of the Moth and Other Essays, 1942
The Moment and Other Essays, 1947
The Captain's Death Bed and Other Essays, 1950
Granite and Rainbow, 1958
Contemporary Writers, edited by Jean Guiguet, 1965
Collected Essays, edited by Leonard Woolf, 4 vols., 1966-67
Moments of Being: Unpublished Autobiographical Writings, edited by Jeanne Schulkind, 1976
Books and Portraits: Some Further Selections from the Literary and Biographical Writings, edited by Mary Lyon, 1977
Women and Writing, edited by Michèle Barrett, 1979
The Essays, edited by Andrew McNeillie, 4 vols., 1986-94 (in progress)
A Woman's Essays: Selected Essays, vol. 1, edited by Rachel Bowlby, 1992
The Crowded Dance of Modern Life: Selected Essays, vol. 2, edited by Rachel Bowlby, 1993

Other writings: nine novels (*The Voyage Out,* 1915, revised edition, 1920; *Night and Day,* 1919; *Jacob's Room,* 1922; *Mrs. Dalloway,* 1925; *To the Lighthouse,* 1927; *Orlando,* 1928; *The Waves,* 1931; *The Years,* 1937; *Between the Acts,* 1941), short stories, a biography of Roger Fry, six volumes of correspondence, five volumes of diaries, and **journals.** Also translated **Dostoevskii** and **Tolstoi.**

Bibliographies

Kirkpatrick, Brownlee Jean, *A Bibliography of Virginia Woolf,* London: Hart-Davis, 1957; revised edition, 1967; 2nd revised edition, Oxford: Oxford University Press, 1980; 3rd revised edition, forthcoming
McNeillie, Andrew, *An Annotated Critical Bibliography of Virginia Woolf,* Totowa, New Jersey: Barnes and Noble, 1983
Majumdar, Robin, *Virginia Woolf: An Annotated Bibliography of Criticism, 1915-1974,* New York: Garland, 1976
Rice, Thomas Jackson, *Virginia Woolf: A Guide to Research,* New York: Garland, 1984

Further Reading

Bishop, Edward, "The Essays: The Subversive Process of Metaphor," in his *Virginia Woolf,* London: Macmillan, 1991: 67-78
Brewster, Dorothy, "The Uncommon Reader as Critic," in her *Virginia Woolf,* New York: New York University Press, 1962; London: Allen and Unwin, 1963
Caughie, Pamela, "Virginia Woolf as Critic," in her *Virginia Woolf and Postmodernism: Literature in Quest and Question of Itself,* Urbana: University of Illinois Press, 1991: 169-93
Cuddy-Keane, Melba, "The Rhetoric of Feminist Conversation: Virginia Woolf and the Trope of the Twist," in *Ambiguous Discourse: Feminist Narratology and British Women Writers,* edited by Kathy Mezei, Chapel Hill: University of North Carolina Press, 1996: 137-61

Delord, J., "Virginia Woolf's Critical Essays," *Revue des Langues Vivantes* 29 (1963)

Dusinberre, Julie, "Virginia Woolf and Montaigne," *Textual Practice* 5 (1991): 219–41

Fernald, Anne, "*A Room of One's Own*, Personal Criticism, and the Essay," *Twentieth Century Literature* 40 (Summer 1994): 165–89

Goldman, Mark, *Virginia Woolf as a Literary Critic*, The Hague: Mouton, 1976

Good, Graham, "Virginia Woolf: Angles of Vision," in his *The Observing Self: Rediscovering the Essay*, London: Routledge, 1988: 112–34

Johnson, Georgia, "The Whole Achievement in Virginia Woolf's *The Common Reader*," in *Essays on the Essay: Redefining the Genre*, edited by Alexander J. Butrym, Athens: University of Georgia Press, 1989

Kronenberger, Louis, "Virginia Woolf as Critic," in *The Republic of Letters: Essays on Various Writers*, New York: Knopf, 1955

Meisel, Perry, *The Absent Father: Virginia Woolf and Walter Pater*, New Haven, Connecticut: Yale University Press, 1980

Pacey, Desmond, "Virginia Woolf as a Literary Critic," *University of Toronto Quarterly* 18 (April 1948): 234–44

Richter, Harvena, "Hunting the Moth: Virginia Woolf and the Creative Imagination," in *Virginia Woolf: Revaluation and Continuity*, edited by Ralph Freedman, Berkeley: University of California Press, 1980

Rosenberg, Beth Carole, *Virginia Woolf and Samuel Johnson: Common Readers*, New York: St. Martin's Press, 1995

Sharma, Vijay L., *Virginia Woolf as Literary Critic: A Revaluation*, New Delhi: Arnold-Heinemann, 1977

Steele, Elizabeth, *Virginia Woolf's Literary Sources and Allusions: A Guide to the Essays*, New York: Garland, 1983

Steele, Elizabeth, *Virginia Woolf's Rediscovered Essays: Sources and Allusions*, New York: Garland, 1987

Wellek, René, "Virginia Woolf as Critic," *Southern Review* 13 (1977): 419–37

Wright, Judith

Australian, 1915–

Judith Wright has long been recognized as an outstanding modern Australian poet; she can also be claimed as the leading woman of letters of her time. Her work as an essayist is a major contribution to the understanding of Australian culture.

Wright's first full-length collection, *Preoccupations in Australian Poetry* (1965), is devoted to the main figures in Australian poetry from colonial times to the 1950s, with most attention focused on Charles Harpur, Henry Kendall, Adam Lindsay Gordon, Barcroft Boake, Christopher Brennan, Hugh McCrae, John Shaw Neilson, Kenneth Slessor, R. D. FitzGerald, James McAuley, and **A. D. Hope**. There had been earlier survey histories and articles on Australian poetry, but no poet before Wright had turned to the Australian theme with such intense commitment. She was the first modern poet to write with passionate engagement about the colonial poets; she stimulated a whole new generation to look in depth at the work of Harpur and Neilson and to reread and write Australia afresh.

Preoccupations sprang out of her acute consciousness of what she called "Australia's double aspect." In these essays she was moved to explore ways in which "a society of transplanted Europeans in a new country started to make their separate contribution in the world." She examines the ways in which Australian poets coped with the problems facing them in their time and place, in relation to both their own country and its emergence into nationhood, and the main stream of Western thought and writing. She shows, for instance, how Charles Harpur was influenced by Wordsworth, what Kendall owed to Harpur, and the growth and meaning of the bush in Australian writing. Her opinions are subtle, forceful, and pointed: "Kendall . . . is not the 'first Australian poet' . . . but the poet of his own desperate struggle and final self mastery"; O'Dowd "gives no hint of possessing a pair of eyes." She notes in McCrae "an inability to grow beyond his own youth"; and of poets before Brennan, "their Australianism was inescapable, a straitjacket." Each essay is full of sharp particular judgments and probing insights.

Wright explores two impulses in early Australian writing and experience. One sees Australia as a place of exile, remote from the old world and the source countries from which Australians have come; the other sees it as a land of opportunity for the development of a radically new kind of society. No other book on Australian poetry has covered so much so fully in so concentrated a space. Wright believes that "the true function of art and culture is to interpret us to ourselves, and to relate us to the country and the society in which we live." Since *Preoccupations* was published, much more scholarly work has appeared on all the poets dealt with, and a whole new generation of poets of the quality and variety of Les Murray, Geoffrey Lehmann, and Kevin Hart has emerged, but it is not the kind of book that can be superseded.

As a leading poet and intellectual, Wright was frequently asked to lecture, and in 1975 she collected her addresses and speeches in *Because I Was Invited*. She returns again and again to the poets who have most engaged her – Harpur, Brennan, and Neilson – but ranges widely from Australian poetry after Pearl Harbor to the voices of Aboriginal poets. There are also essays on the teaching of poetry in which Wright criticizes universities and schools for their failure or inability to introduce students to the pleasures of the poetic text.

Wright believes the poet should be concerned with national and social problems. Her urgent commitment to questions of ecology and conservation and the questions of Aboriginal Australia and the need for a land treaty have been the focus of her most recent concerns. New ways of reading the past and a fuller understanding of Aboriginal Australia are important aspects of present-day culture: Judith Wright's essays have been at the forefront of its development.

VIVIAN SMITH

Biography
Judith Arundell Wright. Born 31 May 1915 in Armidale, New South Wales. Studied at Sydney University, from 1934. Traveled in Britain and Europe, 1937–38. Secretary and clerk, 1938–44; university statistician, University of Queensland, St. Lucia, 1944–48. Married J. P. McKinney (died, 1966): one daughter. Commonwealth Literary Fund Lecturer, Australia, 1949 and 1962; Honors Tutor in English, University of Queensland, 1967. Began fight to conserve the Great Barrier Reef, 1967, and continued conservation campaign work. Member, Australia Council, 1973–74. Awards: several fellowships; Grace Leven Prize, 1950, 1972; Australia-Britannica Award, 1964; Robert Frost Memorial Award, 1977; Australian World Prize, 1984; Queen's Medal for Poetry, 1992; honorary degrees from seven universities.

Selected Writings

Essays and Related Prose
Charles Harpur, 1963
Preoccupations in Australian Poetry, 1965
Henry Lawson, 1967
Because I Was Invited, 1975
The Coral Battleground, 1977
The Cry for the Dead, 1981
We Call for a Treaty, 1985
Born of the Conquerors: Selected Essays, 1991
Going on Talking, 1992

Other writings: many collections of poetry, a collection of short stories, and books for children.

Bibliography
Walker, Shirley, *Judith Wright*, Melbourne: Oxford University Press, 1981

Further Reading
Strauss, Jennifer, *Judith Wright*, Melbourne: Oxford University Press, 1995
Thomson, A. K., editor, *Critical Essays on Judith Wright*, Brisbane: Jacaranda, 1968
Walker, Shirley, *Flame and Shadow: A Study of Judith Wright's Poetry*, St. Lucia: University of Queensland Press, 1991

Y

Yeats, William Butler

Irish, 1865–1939

William Butler Yeats, though best known for his poems and plays, composed a significant body of essays and **reviews** illuminating his own work by applying his views concerning appropriate literary content and style to the work of other writers. His reviews cover half a century, beginning with a review of "The Poetry of Sir Samuel Ferguson" (1886) and concluding with one of "Poems: by Margot Ruddock with Prefatory Notes on the Author" (1936). They promoted Irish nationalism, the development of an Irish national theater, and the use of Irish folklore to develop a new and vigorous symbolism, among other subjects.

The essays primarily offer an expanded discussion of the attitudes found in his reviews, particularly the relationship Yeats felt existed between the supernatural or occult and literary symbolism. His essay "Magic" (1901) describes his participation in seances, and his belief that he could send and receive images telepathically. This ability, he felt, existed because all people are linked through the supernatural. He had briefly described a seance in "Invoking the Irish Fairies" (1892) to suggest that folklore was not just imaginative, but reflective of a storyteller's connection to the occult. In "Symbolism in Painting" (1898) and the companion essay "The Symbolism of Poetry" (1900), he uses Jungian concepts of archetypes to explain why great poets and painters use symbols that have nearly universal effectiveness. He states in "The Philosophy of Shelley's Poetry" (1900) that any writer sensitive to the supernatural will share "the sudden conviction that our little memories are but a part of some great Memory that renews the world and men's thoughts age after age, and that our thoughts are not, as we suppose, the deep, but a little foam upon the deep." The connection between artist and audience that makes symbolism resonate is explained, to Yeats, by our common link to the supernatural, not by genetics or other scientifically explainable means.

Yeats therefore preferred the Romantics and the symbolist writers to the Victorians, arguing in "The Symbolism of Poetry" that Tennyson was hobbled by "brooding over scientific opinion." The Romantics, with their emphasis on nature for inspiration, were more sensitive to the occult forces that Yeats associated with forests, lakes, and other natural settings. He particularly admired **Shelley** and Blake, the latter as much for his painting as for his poetry. Shelley is a central example

in "The Symbolism of Poetry," as well as the focus of "The Philosophy of Shelley's Poetry" and "Prometheus Unbound" (1932). Blake is examined in detail in "William Blake and the Imagination" (1897) and "William Blake and His Illustrations to *The Divine Comedy*" (1924). Blake also provides frequent illustrations for Yeats in many of his shorter reviews. Yeats credits both poets with forming their own mythology, and, as poet-philosophers, using this myth to explain matters gained through intuition, not taught through science. In "William Blake and the Imagination" he describes Blake as "a man crying out for a mythology, and trying to make one because he could not find one to his hand." Yeats, of course, would also create his own mythology to provide a context for his symbols.

Among his contemporaries, Yeats most admired the symbolists and the Irish writers who were attempting to use Irish folklore to provide texture to their narrative poems. In "The Celtic Element in Literature" (1902) he associates folklore with an appreciation of nature. He argues that people close to nature are always aware of the supernatural, whereas people who rely on science and technology and live huddled in cities have lost their awareness of the occult. He credits the works of Standish O'Grady with first showing him how Irish folklore was a rich vein for inspiration. He describes in "A General Introduction for My Work" (1937) first discovering O'Grady's work as a teenager. Yeats attempted to provide greater visibility for Irish writers in a series of four articles in the *Bookman* on Irish National Literature (July–October 1895). The essay "Poetry and Tradition" (1907), written on the occasion of the death of John O'Leary, is the most complete explanation of Yeats' belief that he, and others, could reform Irish poetry by "keep[ing] unbroken the thread up to [Henry] Grattan which John O'Leary had put into our hands . . ." Grattan, as one of the founders of the Irish Parliament, represented the Irish nationalism that Yeats promoted as a source for inspiration.

The theater also fascinated Yeats. He argues in "The Theatre" (1899) that dramatic writers needed to use small, intimate theaters, and write plays for small, intellectually discriminating audiences. Such plays would not be successful in larger settings, but could build a loyal audience. In the same year he helped begin the Irish Literary Theatre, and became connected with the Abbey Theatre in 1904. Many of his review articles dealt with programs at the Abbey.

In his essays and reviews, Yeats' style is direct and robust. In "The Symbolism of Poetry" Yeats notes that we have little record of what Shakespeare discussed when talking with other writers and actors, but that they must have talked about drama. Writing, for Yeats, was an all-consuming passion, leaving no other suitable topics for discussion. His essays, therefore, tend to be polemical as he weaves his interests in art, poetry, drama, Irish nationalism, and the occult into interconnected patterns. For Yeats, an awareness of the supernatural was necessary for producing great works of literature, and such literature develops the national pride he promoted. He uses quotations extensively in his discussions; in many cases more than half the text of an essay is quoted examples. Yeats wrote in "The Symbolism of Poetry" that great writers "have had some philosophy, some criticism of their art; and it has often been this philosophy, or this criticism, that has evoked their most startling inspiration . . ." For readers interested in the inspiration of Yeats' poems and plays, his essays are a valuable resource.

TIMOTHY J. EVANS

Biography

Born 13 June 1865 in Sandymount, County Dublin. Studied at Godolphin School, Hammersmith, London, 1875–80; Erasmus Smith School, Dublin, 1880–83; Metropolitan School of Art, Dublin, 1884–86; Royal Hibernian Academy School, 1886. Lived mainly in London, from 1887, spending part of each year in Ireland, 1890–1921. Cofounder of the Rhymers' Club, London, 1891, and member of the Yellow Book group; helped found the Irish Literary Society, London, 1891, and the National Literary Society, Dublin, 1892. Met Lady Gregory, 1896, and thereafter spent many of his summer holidays at her home in Sligo. Cofounder, with Lady Gregory, Edward Martyn, and George Moore, Irish Literary Theatre, 1899 (the Irish National Theatre Society at the Abbey Theatre, Dublin, from 1904); director of the Abbey Theatre, 1905–39. Editor, *Beltaine*, 1899–1900, *Samhain*, 1901–08, and the *Arrow*, 1906–09. Lectured in the United States, 1903–04, 1913, 1919–20, and 1932. Married Georgiana Hyde-Lees, 1917: one daughter and one son. Lived in Oxford, 1920–21, and Ireland, mainly Dublin, from 1922. Senator of the Irish Free State, 1922–28. Awards: Nobel Prize for Literature, 1923; honorary degrees from four universities. Died in Cap Martin, France, 28 January 1939.

Selected Writings

Essays and Related Prose
Discoveries: A Volume of Essays, 1907
Poetry and Ireland: Essays, with Lionel Johnson, 1908
Essays (Collected Works 4), 1924
Essays 1931 to 1936, 1937
On the Boiler (essays and poetry), 1939
Essays and Introductions, 1961
Uncollected Prose, edited by John P. Frayne and Colton Johnson, 2 vols., 1970–76
Prefaces and Introductions: Uncollected Prefaces and Introductions by Yeats to Works by Other Authors and to Anthologies Edited by Yeats, edited by William H. O'Donnell, 1988
Vision Papers, edited by George Mills Harper and Mary Jane Harper, 3 vols., 1992
Writings on Irish Folklore, Legend and Myth, edited by Robert Welch, 1993
Later Essays (vol. 5 of The Collected Works), edited by William H. O'Donnell and Elizabeth Bergmann Loizeaux, 1994

Other writings: poetry, many plays, and correspondence (collected in *The Collected Letters*, edited by John Kelly and Eric Domville, 3 vols., 1986–94 [in progress]).

Collected works edition: *The Collected Works*, edited by Richard J. Finneran and George Mills Harper, 8 vols., 1989–94 (in progress).

Bibliographies

Jochum, K. P. S., *W. B. Yeats: A Classified Bibliography of Criticism*, Urbana: University of Illinois Press, 1990 (original edition, 1978)
Wade, Allan, *A Bibliography of the Writings of Yeats*, London: Hart-Davis, 1951; revised edition by Russell K. Alspach, 1968

Further Reading

Ellmann, Richard, *Yeats: The Man and the Masks*, New York: Norton, 1978; Oxford: Oxford University Press, 1979 (original edition, 1948)
Ellmann, Richard, *The Identity of Yeats*, New York: Oxford University Press, and London: Faber, 1964 (original edition, 1954)
Finneran, Richard J., editor, *Critical Essays on W. B. Yeats*, Boston: Hall, 1986
Gwynn, Stephen L., editor, *Scattering Branches*, New York and London: Macmillan, 1940; as *William Butler Yeats: Essays in Tribute*, Port Washington, New York: Kennikat Press, 1965
Hall, James, and Martin Steinmann, editors, *The Permanence of Yeats*, New York: Macmillan, 1950
Henn, Thomas R., *The Lonely Tower: Studies in the Poetry of W. B. Yeats*, London and New York: Methuen, 1979 (original edition, 1950)
Hone, Joseph M., *W. B. Yeats, 1865–1939*, London and New York: Macmillan, 1962 (original edition, 1942)
Jeffares, A. Norman, *W. B. Yeats: Man and Poet*, New York: St. Martin's Press, 1996 (original edition, 1949)
Jeffares, A. Norman, *A Commentary on the Collected Plays of W. B. Yeats*, Stanford, California: Stanford University Press, and London: Macmillan, 1975
Jeffares, A. Norman, *A New Commentary on the Poems of W. B. Yeats*, Stanford, California: Stanford University Press, and London: Macmillan, 1984
Marcus, Phillip L., *Yeats and the Beginning of the Irish Renaissance*, Syracuse, New York: Syracuse University Press, 1987 (original edition, 1970)
O'Neill, Charles, "The Essay as Aesthetic Ritual: W. B. Yeats and *Ideas of Good and Evil*," in *Essays on the Essay: Redefining the Genre*, edited by Alexander J. Butrym, Athens: University of Georgia Press, 1989
Skelton, Robin, and Ann Saddlemyer, editors, *The World of W. B. Yeats: Essays in Perspective*, Dublin: Dolmen Press, and Seattle: University of Washington Press, 1965
Tuohy, Frank, *Yeats*, London and New York: Macmillan, 1976
Whitaker, Thomas R., *Swan and Shadow: Yeats's Dialogue with History*, Washington, D.C.: Catholic University of America Press, 1989 (original edition, 1964)

Yuan Hongdao

Chinese, 1568–1610

Yuan Hongdao, who with his brothers founded the Gongan school of writers (Gongan being their native home) at the end of the 16th century, and enjoyed considerable fame – touched with notoriety – in his lifetime, was restored to prominence in the early 1930s by modern prose writers who were seeking a native ancestry for their compositions, their sights having previously been set on foreign genres such as essays, sketches, and *belles-lettres*. To them Yuan Hongdao both advocated and exemplified individualism and contemporaneity in a culture that was basically conformist and backward-looking. He is still well represented in recent anthologies of classical prose.

Yuan Hongdao was an effective communicator, playing his part in propagating the school's philosophy of *xingling* (native sensibility). This derived from the doctrine of *tongxin* (the childlike mind) of their mentor, Li Zhi (1527–1602), which advocated remaining naive and unspoilt, looking on the world with fresh eyes, unclouded by convention or tradition, and exploring one's own interests; expression would thus be freed from the trammels of conventional rhetoric and habitual rhythms. As the school all agreed, they lived in their own times, so should write for their own times, and let the dead bury the dead. But Yuan Hongdao's great personal contribution to the development of Chinese prose was not in originality of thought but in translating an attitude to life and literature into practices that clearly worked and that others could learn from, through pouring new wine into old bottles (biographical and scenic sketches), and extending the range of subjects that could be written about entertainingly (e.g. vulgar pursuits, riffraff).

Youji (travelogues, scenic descriptions) bulk largest in Yuan's prose, reflecting his joy in traveling. From the great variety of these compositions it is possible to see the virtue of the Gongan school approach to literature. The writings are all inspirational and unexpected. Yuan may give a full description of the scene that met the travelers' eyes (Chinese scholars usually made these outings in a group), but equally the interest may be in a story that is attached to the place, or what happened to the party, or may simply focus on a joke someone made. In other words, the shaping force is subjectivism: whatever took his fancy, whatever made the deepest impression, is what went down on paper, regardless of any plan or overview.

To take a standard scene description as an example of his work, "Manjing youji" (An excursion to the Brimful Well) records a visit to a famously big well about a mile outside the walled city of Beijing, made in 1599 when Yuan had a post in the capital. The long view of the distant hills, the middle view of the surrounding fields and dykes, and the close-ups of the well itself are not given in any ordered way, but by abrupt switching, and are described either by elaborate similes or in highly condensed four-character phrases. The soft contours of the hills are likened to a woman's high coiffure, freshly combed into place; the shine on the surface of the well, from which the "skin" of ice has just melted, is compared to the "cold glint" that shoots from a silver mirror when its box is opened. Compactness is achieved by exploiting the grammatical flexibility of Chinese words, mostly by using nouns as verbs: so fellow trippers are classed as "spring-and-tea-ists" (those who drink tea made with spring water), "goblet-and-song-ers" (those who quaff wine and sing), and "red-attire-and-hack-ers" (colorfully dressed women riding docile horses). This kind of freshness of conception and fluidity of language betokens a true liberation from convention, a release of the brakes on the mind.

More celebrated and much more exuberant is Yuan's "Hu Qiu ji" (1596; Tiger Hill), which describes the droves of people streaming out of the city of Suzhou on the night of the Mid-Autumn Festival to enjoy the full moon from Tiger Hill. Syntactically isolated strings of words are used like splashes of color to convey the carnival atmosphere, and to plunge the writer from his normal elevation into the mêlée. The high point is the amateur singing competition, in which contestants are eliminated until "one man alone takes the stage, and there is a deathly hush. His voice is like a thin strand of hair. It cuts through the air and pierces the clouds. A single syllable is drawn out for nearly a quarter of an hour. Birds are arrested in flight, and strong men break down in tears."

It is, however, typical of Yuan Hongdao to undercut his own lyricism, as in "Tian Chi" (1596; The pool of heaven) when, after waxing enthusiastic about the beauties of nature, he asks his pageboy, "Isn't that fine?" and the pageboy answers, "I'm dog tired, what's fine about it?" This kind of deflation is not calculated to startle the reader, but inherent in his dedication to truthfulness to experience, and his complete openmindedness about what should go into a composition. It is in that spirit that he writes entertainingly about ant fights and spider fights, beggars and drunkards, dreams and uncanny happenings. Openmindedness also allowed him to rate folk songs above refined poetry and popular novels above the classics.

But if he was dedicated to truthfulness, it was the truthfulness of the moment. Where Yuan gains in inspiration, he loses in lack of reflection. In other ways, too, he displayed the vices of his virtues: wittiness spills over into facetiousness, freedom into license. Convention is, after all, a useful restraint. If the conventions of accepted standards are rejected, there normally remains the restraining influence of (conventional) unseen readers; but Yuan Hongdao wrote, besides for his own pleasure, for a small coterie of like-minded people; there were no readers "out there" to take into account. However, genius always exacts a price, and we read Yuan with great enjoyment for what he was, with few regrets about what he was not.

D. E. POLLARD

Biography

Style (assumed on reaching manhood) "Zhonglang." Born 1568 in Gongan. Passed the *juren* (provincial) exams, 1588, and the *jinshi* (civil service) exams, 1592. Held government offices sporadically (retiring frequently), including as a magistrate, Wu district (Suzhou), 1595–96, secretary, Ministry of Rites, 1600 and from 1606, positions with the Ministry of Personnel, 1608, vice director, then director, Bureau of Evaluations, 1608–09, and chief examiner of the *juren* exams, Shanxi, 1609. Cofounder, with his brothers, Putao she (Grape society), Chongguo Temple, Beijing, 1598. Lived in a religious community, Gongan, 1600. Died in Shashi, Hubei Province, 22 October 1610.

Selected Writings

Essays and Related Prose
The Pilgrim of the Clouds: Poems and Essays by Yuan Hung-tao and His Brothers, translated by Jonathan Chaves, 1978
Translations of essays in *Inscribed Landscapes: Travel Writing from Imperial China*, translated by Richard E. Strassberg, 1994: 305–12

Other writings: poetry, a historical romance, a play adaptation, and diaries.

Collected works edition: *Yuan Zhonglang quan ji*, 1629, reprinted 1976.

Further Reading

Hong Mingshui, *Yüan Hung-tao and the Late Ming Literary and Intellectual Movement* (dissertation), Madison: University of Wisconsin, 1974

Pollard, D. E., Appendix on the Gongan School, in his *A Chinese Look at Literature: The Literary Values of Chou Tso-jen in Relation to the Tradition*, London: Hurst, 1973: 158–66

Yang Depen, *Yuan Zhonglang ji wenxue si siang* (The literary thought of Yuan Hongdao), Taibei, 1976

Z

Zambrano, María

Spanish, 1904–1991

María Zambrano wrote little other than essays, whether books or journalistic articles. Despite the rarity of Spanish women essayists and philosophers, Zambrano decided early that her life's role was as a thinker, and she chose as her vehicle the **philosophical essay**. She left more than 200 articles and 28 books, especially impressive considering the gender and culture barriers she faced in pre-Civil War Spain and postwar exile in Cuba, Mexico, and Puerto Rico. Republican affiliations and exile combined with gender and her essentially esoteric work to keep Zambrano relatively unknown during the Franco dictatorship; until the final years, exiles' works and most critical studies on them were prohibited by Spanish censors. Nevertheless, when Zambrano finally returned to Spain in 1984, conditions had changed radically. In 1981 she received the Prince of Asturias national literary prize, and significant official and critical recognition continued throughout her remaining life; she became the first woman and first philosopher to receive the Cervantes Prize, ten million pesetas awarded by the Association of Spanish Language Academies, constituting the most significant recognition available to writers in the Spanish-speaking world. Honoring a lifetime's intellectual accomplishments, the Cervantes Prize distinguishes "conspicuous contributions to enriching the Spanish cultural patrimony."

Zambrano's selection surprised many: she had written no bestsellers and was little known to general readers, having besides her essays only some poems and a rather essayistic text – memoir or novelized autobiography – *Delirio y destino* (wr. mid-1950s, pub. 1989; Delirium and destiny), set during 1929 and 1930, the intellectually stimulating days of Spanish vanguardism when Zambrano was deciding her own future. Despite *Bildungsroman* traits, reflecting Zambrano's youthful philosophical training and her relationship with her teacher, leading Spanish philosopher **José Ortega y Gasset**, this lyric discourse combines history, memoir, philosophy, and literature. *Delirio y destino*, like *Los intelectuales en el drama de España* (1937; Intellectuals in Spain's drama [i.e. the Civil War]), depicts the rich cultural ambience of the famed Generation of 1927 – poets García Lorca, Vicente Aleixandre, Rafael Alberti – and Zambrano's friendships with others: Luis Cernuda, Miguel Hernández, **Rosa Chacel**, and various disciples of Ortega.

Zambrano's earliest essay volume, *Nuevo liberalismo* (1930; New liberalism), builds upon work by her father, the idealistic socialist pedagogue Blas Zambrano, an enduring influence, and figures among her most political writing. Simultaneously she worked on her doctoral dissertation treating individual salvation in Spinoza, and began publishing commentaries on Ortega's works. Zambrano's apprenticeship teaching of metaphysics prefigures another constant theme, differentiating her thought from Ortega's. Zambrano's incipient philosophy appears in "Hacia un saber del alma" (1937; Toward a knowledge of the soul), expanded and published separately in 1950. Her early connotations of soul approximate spirit or human subjectivity, and are without the mystical-religious aspects that later appeared. Early influences of Scheler give way to **Heidegger**. Bergson influenced Zambrano's concepts of time, the historical, intuition, and her essentially lyric, personal, philosophical style. Heidegger contributed to her rejection of philosophical rationalism and scientific reason, to her notions of being-in-the-world, "dwelling," letting things speak, and her fusion of style and thinking as she diverged from Ortega. Philosopher-poet Antonio Machado anticipates her vision of poetry as philosophy or vice versa: Zambrano's *Filosofía y poesía* (1939; Philosophy and poetry) and *Pensamiento y poesía en la vida española* (1939; Thought and poetry in Spanish life) explain the poetic initiation of the philosopher via an intuition of "poetic reason." Rhetoric aside, Zambrano's "reason" resembles no prior rationalism but rather revelation connected to desire.

Zambrano's youthful verse appeared in major **periodicals** and she wrote on contemporary poets, anticipating her theoretical explorations of poetry's relation to epistemological epiphanies. This concept, plus her mystic metaphysics and pervasively lyric discourse, significantly influenced contemporary poets. Zambramo had a long academic career and was affiliated with major universities in South and Central America and Europe. Her philosophical/literary-critical exegeses included *La España de Galdós* (1959; Galdós' Spain), *El freudismo, testimonio del hombre actual* (1940; Freudianism: testimony to contemporary man), and *El pensamiento vivo de Séneca* (1944; Seneca's living thought). Her wartime works attest to her suffering over the war in Europe: *Isla de Puerto Rico (Nostalgia y esperanza de un mundo mejor)* (1940; Puerto Rico, nostalgia and hope of a better world) and *La agonía de Europa* (1945; Europe's agony).

Among Zambrano's longest works, *El hombre y lo divino* (1955; Man and divinity) uses poetic reason to elucidate religious experience, studying the meaning of gods, the sacred, sacrifice, and human attitudes toward the unknown future. Her concept of destiny, within contemporary existential parameters, resembles Ortega's "plenitude," later becoming nearly synonymous with vocation. Zambrano once commented that the title of *El hombre y lo divino* would aptly suit her complete work, a prescient observation *vis-à-vis* later texts.

Dreams become prominent in Zambrano's thought in the mid-1950s. "Los sueños y el tiempo" (1958; Dreams and time), further elaborated in *El sueño creador* (1965; Creative dreaming), and considers time's role in human life, viewing dream-time and dreaming as near atemporal passivity, revelatory of time's origination. Zambrano's dream-theory synthesizes relationships between dreams and the creative word, tragedy, religion, poetry, philosophy, and the novel, appearing also in *Los sueños y el tiempo* (1992; Dreams and time) and *España, sueno y verdad* (1965; Spain, dream and truth), whose ostensible topics are predominantly literary, revealing intertextual debts to Calderón's vision of life as a dream, waking as death. *Claros del bosque* (1977; Clearings in the forest), whose title alludes to the wood near Lake Leman where Zambrano once lived, treats being, presence and reality, concealment and revelation, all united by ontological concerns and the concept of passive epiphany. Other pivotal ideas involve the word (*logos*) and dawn. *De la aurora* (1986; Concerning dawn) presents the *logos* as an inevitable point of departure. Zambrano concentrates on the subjective, within a mystical or gnostic tradition, privileging intuition and advocating the reform of understanding via awareness of the irrational and intuitive, things neither objective nor intelligible in abstract reason. Man constitutes an enigma, something to be deciphered or realized (vocation), resembling existential notions of man as project.

Zambrano's career demonstrates the fallacy of considering woman and philosopher inherently contradictory, but her relative obscurity until the decade before her death did not encourage translations or critical works. Zambrano's major prizes during the 1980s have spurred recent critical attention, mostly in Spanish, but translations have begun and she will be better known in the next century than in her own.

JANET PÉREZ

Biography

Born 25 April 1904 in Vélez-Málaga. Studied philosophy under Ortega y Gasset and **Xavier Zubiri** at the University of Madrid, 1924–28, Ph.D., 1928. Taught in Madrid, 1930–36; wrote for the **Revista de Occidente**, *Cruz y Raya* (Cross and line), and *Hora de España* (Hour of Spain). Married Alfonso Rodríguez Aldave, 1936 (separated, 1948): one daughter (died, 1972). Lived in Chile, 1936–37; on return to Spain worked actively on behalf of the Republic. Exiled from Spain, 1939; taught at the Universities of Havana, 1940–43, and Puerto Rico, 1943–46; lived in Paris, 1946–49, Havana, 1949–53, Rome, 1953–64, France, 1964–80, and Geneva, 1980–84; returned to Spain, 1984. Awards: Prince of Asturias Prize, 1981; Cervantes Prize, 1988; honorary degree from the University of Málaga. Died in Madrid, 1991.

Selected Writings

Essays and Related Prose
Nuevo liberalismo, 1930
Los intelectuales en el drama de España, 1937; enlarged edition, 1977

Filosofía y poesía, 1939
Pensamiento y poesía en la vida española, 1939
El freudismo, testimonio del hombre actual, 1940
Isla de Puerto Rico (Nostalgia y esperanza de un mundo mejor), 1940
El pensamiento vivo de Séneca, 1944
La agonía de Europa, 1945
Hacia un saber sobre el alma, 1950
El hombre y lo divino, 1955
Persona y democracia: La historia sacrificial, 1958
La España de Galdós, 1959; enlarged editions, 1982, 1989
El sueño creador: Los sueños, el soñar y la creación por la palabra, 1965
España, sueno y verdad, 1965; enlarged edition, 1982
La tumba de Antígona, 1967
Claros del bosque, 1977
El nacimiento: Dos escritos autobiográficos, 1981
Andalucía, sueño y realidad, 1984
Senderos, 1986
De la aurora, 1986
Notas de un método, 1989
Algunos lugares de la pintura, edited by Amalia Iglesias, 1989
Antología temática y crítica, edited by Jesús Moreno Sanz, 1989
Los bienaventurados, 1990
Los sueños y el tiempo, 1992
La razón en la sombra, edited by Jesús Moreno Sanz, 1993

Other writings: poetry and the memoir *Delirio y destino* (1989).

Bibliography
"Bibliografía de y sobre María Zambrano," *Anthropos* 70–71 (1987): 82–93

Further Reading
Abellán, José Luis, "María Zambrano: La 'razón poética' en marcha," in *Filosofía española en América (1936–1966)*, Madrid: Guadarrama, 1967: 169–89

Aranguren, J. L., "La palabra de María Zambrano," *Cuadernos Hispanoamericanos* 413 (1984): 21–23

Azcoaga, Enrique, "María Zambrano y lo poético," *Cuadernos Hispanoamericanos* 413 (1984): 159–72

Donahue, Darcy, "National History as Autobiography: María Zambrano's *Delirio y destino*," *Monographic Review* 9 (1993): 116–24

Janés, Clara, "La palabra poética de María Zambrano," *Cuadernos Hispanoamericanos* 413 (1984): 183–87

Laffranque, Marie, "De la guerre à l'exil: María Zambrano et le Sénéquisme des années 40," in *Femmes-philosophes en Espagne et en Amérique Latine*, Paris: Centre National de la Recherche Scientifique, 1989: 27–55

López Castro, Armando, "El pensar poético de María Zambrano," *Cuadernos Hispanoamericanos* 413 (1984): 75–79

Muñoz Victoria, Fernando, "Sueño y creación," *Anthropos* 70–71 (1987): 119

Muñoz Victoria, Fernando, editor, *María Zambrano o la metafísica recuperada*, Vélez-Málaga: Delegación de Cultura del Ayuntamiento, 1982

Ortega Muñoz, J. F., "La crisis de Europa en el pensamiento de María Zambrano," *Religión y Cultura* 25, no. 108 (1979): 41–69

Pérez, Janet, "'Circunstancia,' Reason and Metaphysics: Context and Unity in the Thought of María Zambrano," in *Public Forums/Private Views: Spanish Women Writers and the Essay*, edited by Kathleen M. Glenn and Mercedes Mazquiarán de Rodríguez, forthcoming

Rof Carballo, Juan, "María Zambrano," *Cuadernos Hispanoamericanos* 413 (1984): 24–31

Salinero Portero, José, "María Zambrano en algunas revistas hispanoamericanas entre 1938 y 1964," *Cuadernos Hispanoamericanos* 413 (1984): 134–58

Savater, Fernando, "Angustia y secreto: El diálogo entre filosofía y poesía en la reflexión de María Zambrano," *Cuadernos del Norte* 8 (1981): 10–13

Subirats, Eduardo, "Intermedio sobre filosofía y poesía," *Anthropos* 70–71 (1987): 94–99

Valente, José Angel, "María Zambrano y 'El sueño creador'," *Insula* 238 (1966): 1, 10

Zea, Leopoldo

Mexican, 1912–

Among the practitioners of the essay of Latin American cultural identity, Leopoldo Zea emerges as one of the outstanding figures of the 20th century. From his seminal essay, "En torno a la filosofía americana" (1942; On American philosophy), until now, his work exemplifies and marks the stages that Latin American thought has followed, from attempts to recuperate cultural patrimony to the articulation, beginning in the 1960s, of a discourse of liberation. Because of the geographic distribution of his essays, their content, and, above all, the repercussion and influence of his ideas, Zea is a continental essayist. A prolific writer, author of dozens of books of essays, he stands out equally as a leader of the Latin Americanist movement and as an untiring motivator and organizer of meetings of intellectuals in various Latin American countries. His essays are difficult to classify; they pertain to what came to be called in the 1980s "cultural studies." His concerns, however, have remained constant: they are reflections on the problem of identity and on the structures that govern the unavoidable interculturality of Latin American peoples. Thus, the context of his work is Latin America, but his national vocation (Mexico) and his regional vocation (Latin America) develop within a Western cultural context and within an explicit search for the liberation of the human being.

Zea became known as an essayist in the early 1940s, principally through two continentally recognized Mexican magazines: *Cuadernos Americanos* (American notebooks) and *Filosofía y Letras* (Philosophy and letters). In the first, which stands out for the aesthetic quality of its essays, he brings forward his most influential ideas; for the second, which is more specialized, he was acclaimed by the academic community for his profound thinking. However, both magazines reveal one of the distinctive attributes of his style: the depth of the theme must not affect the clarity of the exposition. Zea writes for an educated public, but he does so without the technical vocabulary of the specialist. His first major book, *El positivismo en México* (1943; *Positivism in Mexico*), is an early example of his affiliation with what we now refer to as cultural studies; it is an interdisciplinary work written with the depth of the specialist, with the stylistic concern of the artist, and above all, with the reflective spirit of the essayist who essentially initiates a **dialogue**. Zea questions and deconstructs logocentric assumptions, especially those that have attempted to impose European perspectives, which in Latin America seemed to perpetuate a situation of cultural colonization.

Zea's work first emerges in dialogue with that of **Ortega y Gasset** and afterwards with that of **Heidegger** and Hegel; but the roots of his ideas really lie in the Latin American essay tradition of Simón Bolívar, **Andrés Bello**, Juan Alberdi, and, most of all, **José Martí**, all of whom form an intimate part of his intellectual context. Even though we cannot speak of stages, in the sense of ruptures, in Zea's essayistic production, we can trace in his works the same process that has governed Latin American thought during the second half of the 20th century. Zea subscribes to José Martí's assertion that "Barricades of ideas are worth more than barricades of stone" ("Nuestra América" [1891; "Our America"]). For this reason, in his first essays, such as *Positivism in Mexico* and *Dos etapas del pensamiento en Hispanoamérica* (1949; *The Latin-American Mind*), Zea concerns himself with the recovery of the Latin American intellectual legacy. He discovers the dimensions of Latin America's colonial reality and initiates a process of deconstruction of the diverse colonial structures through the essays later collected in seminal works such as *Conciencia y posibilidad del mexicano* (1952; Consciousness and possibility for the Mexican), *América como conciencia* (1953; America as consciousness), *Latinoamérica y el mundo* (1960; *Latin America and the World*).

The political, economic, and cultural globalization of the 1960s instigated his reflection on the structures of intercultural dialogue that seem to stratify relations among men: according to Zea, the terms "first and third world," "developed and underdeveloped" nations, "center and periphery" have resulted in a division among human beings as "men and pseudo-men." In these cultural structures, Zea recognizes renovated forms of colonialism that he is committed to denouncing. He published during these years reflections that would later give rise to the formulation of a liberation ideology, expressed in works such as *La filosofía americana como filosofía sin más* (1969; The American philosophy as philosophy), *La esencia de lo americano* (1971; The essence of the American), *Dependencia y liberación en la cultura latinoamericana* (1974; Dependence and liberation in Latin American culture), and *Dialéctica de la conciencia americana* (1976; Dialectic of the American consciousness). This period coincided with intense Latin American cultural movements: hence the impact of Latin American fiction and the opening it created by reintegrating European writing to its regional context and giving rise in the Western world to the writings of other regions – Africa and Asia – which until then had remained marginalized. During the same period there was a resurgence of liberation theology as a philosophy that focuses the mission of religious institutions on regional necessities. In this context, Zea's essays, collected in books such as *Discurso desde la marginación y la barbarie* (1988; Discourse on marginalization and barbarism) and *Filosofar a la altura del hombre* (1993; To philosophize at the height of man), question the assumed universality of European philosophical thought in order to deconstruct it. Zea finds that "to know oneself equal by being distinct is, precisely, the essence of the social relation between individuals and nations . . . [which] permits human beings, or nations, to recognize themselves in another as a fellow human being and thus as an equal."

JOSÉ LUIS GÓMEZ-MARTÍNEZ

Biography

Leopoldo Zea Aguilar. Born 30 June 1912 in Mexico City. Studied at the National Autonomous University of Mexico, Mexico City, Ph.D., 1944. Associated with *Tierra Nueva* (New earth), 1940–42. Taught philosophy at the Escuela Nacional Preparatoria, Mexico City, 1942–47, the National Autonomous University of Mexico, Villa Obregon, 1944–76 (then emeritus professor), and El Colegio de México, from 1946. Married Elena Prado Vertiz, 1943 (divorced, 1977): four daughters and two sons. Head of department of intellectual cooperation and university studies, Secretary of Public Education, 1953–54; secretary of permanent commission, UNESCO, Consejo Consultivo, 1953–54; director of cultural relations, and special deputy and plenipotentiary, Secretary of Exterior Relations, 1960–66. Lectured at many universities and government institutions throughout the world. Contributor to various journals. Editor of *México y lo mexicano* series of essays. Married Elena Rodríguez Ozán, 1982. Editor, *Cuadernos Americanos*, from 1987. Awards: many, including the Justo Sierra Prize, 1944; National Arts and Sciences Prize, 1980; Gran Cruz de Alfonso X el Sabio (Spain), 1984; honorary degrees from several universities; Commander, Legion of Honor (France).

Selected Writings

Essays and Related Prose

El positivismo en México, 1943; as *Positivism in Mexico*, translated by Josephine H. Schulte, 1974
Apogeo y decadencia del positivismo en México, 1944
En torno a una filosofía americana, 1945
Ensayos sobre filosofía en la historia, 1948
Dos etapas del pensamiento en Hispanoamérica: Del romanticismo al positivismo, 1949; as *The Latin-American Mind*, translated by James H. Abbott and Lowell Dunham, 1963
Conciencia y posibilidad del mexicano, 1952
La filosofía como compromiso y otros ensayos, 1952; edited by Liliana Weinberg de Magis and Mario Magallón, 1991
América como conciencia, 1953
El Occidente y la conciencia de México, 1953; as *Mexican Consciousness and Its Role in the West*, edited by Amy A. Oliver, translated by Michelle B. Butler and Michael A. Ervin, 1993
La conciencia del hombre en la filosofía: Introducción a la filosofía, 1953
La filosofía en México, 2 vols., 1955
América en la conciencia de Europa, 1955
Esquema para una historia de las ideas en Iberoamérica, 1956
Del liberalismo a la revolución en la educación mexicana, 1956
Las ideas en Iberoamérica en el siglo XIX, 1957
América en la historia, 1957; as *The Role of the Americas in History*, translated by Sonja Karsen, 1992
La cultura y el hombre de nuestros días, 1959
Latinoamérica y el mundo, 1960; as *Latin America and the World*, translated by Frances K. Hendricks and Beatrice Berler, 1969
Dos ensayos: Del liberalismo a la revolución en la educación mexicana; Problema cultural de América Latina, 1960
Antología del pensamiento social y político de América Latina, 1964
El pensamiento latinoamericano, 1965
Latinoamérica en la formación de nuestro tiempo, 1965
La filosofía americana como filosofía sin más, 1969
Latinoamérica: Emancipación y neocolonialismo, 1971
La esencia de lo americano, 1971
Dependencia y liberación en la cultura latinoamericana, 1974
Dialéctica de la conciencia americana, 1976
Filosofía y cultura latinoamericanas, 1976
Latinoamérica: Tercer mundo, 1977
Filosofía de la historia americana, 1978
Simón Bolívar, 1980
Latinoamérica en la encrucijada de la historia, 1981
Sentido de la difusión cultural latinoamericana, 1981
Latinoamérica, un nuevo humanismo, 1982

Discurso desde la marginación y la barbarie, 1988
Descubrimiento e identidad latinoamericana, 1990
Regreso de las carabelas, 1993
Filosofar a la altura del hombre, 1993

Also edited many anthologies on Mexican culture and Latin American thought.

Further Reading

Cerutti Guldberg, Horacio, "La polémica entre Salazar Bondy y Leopoldo Zea," in his *Filosofía de la liberación latinoamericana*, Mexico City: Fondo de Cultura Económica, 1983: 161–68
Fornet-Betancourt, Raúl, editor, *Für Leopoldo Zea, Para Leopoldo Zea*, Aachen: Augustinus-Buchhandlung, 1992
Gómez-Martínez, José Luis, "La crítica ante la obra de Leopoldo Zea," *Anthropos* 89 (1988): 36–47
Gómez-Martínez, José Luis, *Pensamiento de la liberación*, Madrid: EGE, 1995
Gracia, Jorge J. E., "Zea y la liberación latinoamericana," in *América Latina, historia y destino: Homenaje a Leopoldo Zea*, vol. 2, Mexico City: National Autonomous University of Mexico, 1992: 95–106
Guadarrama González, Pablo, "Urdimbres del pensamiento de Leopoldo Zea frente a la marginación y la barbarie," *Cuadernos Americanos* 36 (1992): 51–64
Hale, Charles A., "Sustancia y método en el pensamiento de Leopoldo Zea," *Historia Mexicana* 20, no. 2 (October–December 1970): 285–304
Kourím, Zdeněk, "La obra de Leopoldo Zea: Los últimos 25 años," in *Filosofar a la altura del hombre* by Zea, Mexico City: National Autonomous University of Mexico, 1993: 31–71
Lipp, Solomon, *Leopoldo Zea: From "Mexicanidad" to a Philosophy of History*, Waterloo, Ontario: Wilfrid Laurier University Press, 1980
Lizcano, Francisco, *Leopoldo Zea: Una filosofía de la historia*, Madrid: Cultura Hispánica, 1986
López Díaz, Pedro, *Una filosofía para la libertad: La filosofía de Leopoldo Zea*, Mexico City: Costa-Amic, 1989
Medin, Tzvi, *Leopoldo Zea: Ideología y filosofía de América Latina*, Mexico City: National Autonomous University of Mexico, 1992
Mues de Schrenk, Laura, "El problema de nuestra identidad en el pensamiento de Leopoldo Zea," in *América Latina, historia y destino: Homenaje a Leopoldo Zea*, vol. 2, Mexico City: National Autonomous University of Mexico, 1992: 247–56
Nogueira Dobarro, Ángel, and others, "Leopoldo Zea: Filosofía de la historia latinoamericana como compromiso," *Anthropos* 89 (1988): 1–64
Oliver, Amy, "Values in Modern Mexican Thought," *Journal of Value Inquiry* 27 (1993): 215–30
Rippy, Merrill, "Theory of History: Twelve Mexicans," *Americas* 17, no. 3 (January 1961): 223–39
Roig, Arturo Andrés, "La filosofía de la historia mexicana," in his *Teoría y crítica del pensamiento latinoamericano*, Mexico City: Fondo de Cultura Económica, 1981: 186–97
Sauerwald, Gregor, "Leopoldo Zea und die Philosophie der Befreiung," in *América Latina, historia y destino: Homenaje a Leopoldo Zea*, vol. 2, Mexico City: National Autonomous University of Mexico, 1992: 341–54
Schutte, Ofelia, "The Master-Slave Dialectic in Latin America: The Social Criticism of Zea, Freire, and Roig," *The Owl of Minerva* 22 (1990): 5–18
Schutte, Ofelia, "The Humanity of Mestizaje and the Search for Freedom: Zea, Roig, and Miró Quesada on Consciousness," in her *Cultural Identity and Social Liberation in Latin American Thought*, Albany: State University of New York Press, 1993: 109–39
Weinberg de Magis, Liliana, "Leopoldo Zea: América como sentido," in *América Latina, historia y destino: Homenaje a Leopoldo Zea*, vol. 2, Mexico City: National Autonomous University of Mexico, 1992: 415–526

Zhang Dai

Chinese, 1597–1689

Zhang Dai is one of the quintessential voices of the literati culture of the late Ming dynasty. A master of the "prose miniature" (*xiaopin wen*), he was one of a number of iconoclastic writers who espoused the values of individualism in opposition to various modes of literary orthodoxy based on imitation of past models and a narrow Confucian moralism. This movement in prose and poetry arose in the latter half of the 16th century with such spokesmen as the three Yuan brothers, especially **Yuan Hongdao** (1568–1610), Li Zhi (1527–1602), Tang Xianzu (1550–1617), Zhong Xing (1574–1624), and Xu Wei (1521–93). Rejecting the official culture of their time, they argued for personal authenticity and uniqueness in expression and also promoted a wider sense of literature which included popular forms such as the novel and drama. In a culture where literature is usually read in connection with the facts of the author's life, Zhang Dai's writings are especially autobiographical and reflect the growth of self-consciousness characteristic of the progressive writers of the 17th century. The works for which he is best remembered were all written after the fall of the Ming dynasty in 1644, a catastrophic event which left him destitute in middle age and deprived of his privileged status as the talented scion of an old, established family of high officials. Despite the conservative shift in taste under the new Manchu rulers, Zhang Dai's writings continued to espouse the individualism of the late Ming. They preserve the details of a lost, antebellum era of taste and pleasure while articulating a coherent aesthetics which has had continuous appeal for Chinese intellectuals.

Zhang Dai's prose writings, only a small portion of which have been preserved, can be divided into three groups – historical writing, miscellaneous works, and reminiscences – as well as into those written before the fall of the Ming and those written afterwards. Zhang's historical writings are in the form of biographies with expository essays introducing each category of people. Zhang considered these works his most formal, and as his public legacy which was originally intended to influence current political opinion and, later, to pass judgment on the age. The earliest of his historical works was *Gujin yilie zhuan* (1628; Biographies of righteous martyrs past and present), which contains more than 400 exemplary biographies of righteous heroes and scholars who resisted political oppression, from the Zhou down through the Ming dynasties. It was written during a particularly turbulent period to oppose eunuch factions at court who instituted purges of reformist scholars. It reveals Zhang's talent for incisive, rounded portraits, which would reappear later in many of his reminiscences.

His major historical work took four decades to complete and was written in two parts. Part 1 of *Shigui shu* (1655; A history in a stone casket), begun in 1628, made use of over 400 sources, many from his family archives, to compile a history of the Ming from the Hongwu through the Tianqi reigns (1368–1627). Part 2, known as *Shigui shu houji* (A continuation of a history in a stone casket), was begun in the early Kangxi era when Zhang was asked to aid in the compilation of the official history of the Ming dynasty. This enabled him to gain access to new archival material about the last reign

and the loyalist regimes. It continues the story down through the Chongzhen era (1628–44) and the loyalist regimes of the Southern Ming, which continued briefly to resist the Manchus. Also organized according to the grouped biography format, its topics include politics, economics, culture, and military, ethnic, and foreign affairs.

Zhang's miscellaneous works include a wide range of formats such as **prefaces**, afterwords, **letters**, encomia, essays, travel writing, biographies, and epitaphs – including his own, which he prematurely composed at the age of 68. Most of those that survive are preserved in *Langhuan shiwenji* (Collected poetry and prose from the Langhuan garden), first printed in 1877. They not only reveal his aesthetic opinions, family background, and self-views, but also indicate his extensive social relations with many of the outstanding scholars of the time. Two collections of reminiscences, *Xihu xunmeng* (1671; In search of my dreams of West Lake) and *Taoan mengyi* (c. 1685; Dream-like memories from the studio of contentment), remain the basis of Zhang's later literary fame. *Xihu xunmeng* contains 72 pieces organized as a more formal record of famous places around West Lake in Hangzhou, a glittering cultural center he first visited as a child of six and had not seen in 28 years. Among the sites recalled were many destroyed in the Manchu conquest, including his own estate. First printed in the Kangxi era (1662–1722), it is the only one of his works included by the orthodox bibliographers of the Manchu Qing dynasty in the official *Siku quanshu* (1773–82; The complete collection of the four libraries). *Taoan mengyi*, first printed during the Qianlong era (1736–95), is an entertaining miscellany of 123 prose miniatures reminiscing about people, places, objects, customs, and the pleasures of the first half of Zhang's life before the fall of the Ming. Each piece averages only about several hundred ideographs and manages to encapsulate a curious facet of a vanished world as witnessed by an independent and, occasionally, irreverent eye.

Zhang Dai's espousal of individualism was founded on a view of literature as a vehicle for expressing the unique character of the writer. In his reminiscences, this was principally articulated through his choice of subject matter, aesthetic judgments, and linguistic style. Among his best-known pieces are portraits of artisans and performers, a group of low social status outside the canon of traditional biography, whose members he exalted as icons of authenticity and genius. The illiterate storyteller Liu Jingting, for example, who briefly gained influence at the court of the ill-fated Nanjing Restoration of the Ming in 1645, is recalled as a masterful teller of tales whose consummate artistry was in stark contrast to his ugly appearance. In his travel pieces, Zhang often focused on tangential aspects of a place outside the conventional decorum of representation such as the prostitutes of Yangzhou, the matchmakers at West Lake, or the extravagant inns at the pilgrimage site of Mount Tai. A connoisseur of a wide range of arts and pleasures, he admired the obsessive pursuit of artistic ideals, advocating the cultivation of taste as the path to self-realization while frequently deriding the vulgarity of conventional standards of beauty. In another well-known piece about viewing the summer moon at West Lake, Zhang created a typology of society based on the manners and self-consciousness of different groups of holiday tourists, particularly lampooning those who never look at the moon but only at others enviously looking at them. After visiting the garden of the merchant Yu Wu and praising its ingenuity, Zhang dismissed the excessive piling up of expensive rocks at a more famous garden and remarked that it would have been better to design the latter around two odd-shaped rocks which had been discarded.

Zhang's own aesthetics emerge as a highly personal kind of sophistication which appreciated the finest in both elite and popular culture. He found particular value in the marginal, the genuine, the marvelous experience, and in the unique perception. Like most Chinese literati, his ideals contain moral implications, and he managed to convey a broad, ethical awareness while eschewing Confucian didacticism. His reminiscences have the appearance of random sketches intended to reproduce a sense of the spontaneous experiences of a former life well lived, an arrangement that has been termed "cherished disorder" (Stephen Owen, 1986). This autobiographical self embraced the contradictions of the world, the passions aroused by memory, and the despair of his old age. Though occasionally tinged with nostalgia, these pieces are thoroughly realistic in their focus on concrete detail and recapture a world rich in the unexpectedly fascinating, often deflating the serious with humor. His linguistic style in his most characteristic pieces is eclectic and peppered with novelty, especially in *Taoan mengyi*. For example, he exploited archaic features of classical Chinese in dialogue, such as using nouns as verbs, and liked to combine the repetitive rhythms of colloquial oral storytelling with lofty diction. Zhang valued above all evocativeness. His terse but suggestive description, choppy syntax, and telling observations sought to achieve a mode of literary essentialism which could preserve for eternity his own qualities of animation, curiosity, intelligence, and broadmindedness.

RICHARD E. STRASSBERG

Biography
Courtesy name Zongzi and, later, Shigong; studio name Taoan. Born 1597 in Shanyin (now Shaoxing), Zhejiang province. Descended from a prominent family of officials and scholars. As a youth traveled extensively with his father and uncles, meeting many of the leading writers and artists of the late Ming period and gaining attention as a prodigy. Failed the *jinshi* (civil service) exams several times, and renounced a public career; wrote historical works in an effort to revive the faltering Ming dynasty. After the Manchu invasion and fall of the Ming, 1644, briefly joined the ill-fated regime of the Ming pretender Prince Lu, 1645, but soon resigned and went into hiding for two months when the Manchu forces conquered Shaoxing. Lost his property in the civil war and lived in reduced circumstances for the rest of his life as a reclusive Ming loyalist. Refused to support the new Qing dynasty and devoted himself to completing his history of the Ming. Died near Shaoxing in 1689.

Selected Writings

Essays and Related Prose
(Most of Zhang Dai's works were not printed and have not survived. Below are listed the principal surviving works and collections.)
Gujin yilie zhuan (Biographies of righteous martyrs), 1628
Shigui shu, 1655
Xihu xunmeng, 1671; edited by Sun Jiasui, 1984

Taoan mengyi, c. 1685; edited by Zhou Xianqing, 1985
Langhuan shiwenji, 1877; edited by Xia Xianchun, 1991
Shigui shu houji (A continuation of a history in a stone casket), 1959
Sishu yu (Encounters in reading the Four Books), 1985
Yehangchuan (Night-time sailing), edited by Liu Yaoen, 1987
Translations of essays in: *The Columbia Anthology of Traditional Chinese Literature*, edited by Victor Mair, New York: Columbia University Press, 1994: 594–98; *Inscribed Landscapes: Travel Writing from Imperial China*, translated by Richard E. Strassberg, Berkeley: University of California Press, 1994: 335–51

Other writings: poetry and memoirs.

Further Reading
A Ying, "Langhuan wenji" (On collected prose from the Langhuan garden), in his *Haishi ji* (Collected mirages), Shanghai: Beixin shuju, 1936: 155–69
Nienhauser, William H., Jr., "Chang Tai," in *The Indiana Companion to Traditional Chinese Literature*, edited by Nienhauser, Bloomington: Indiana University Press, 1986: 220–21
Owen, Stephen, *Remembrances: The Experience of the Past in Classical Chinese Literature*, Cambridge, Massachusetts: Harvard University Press, 1986: 134–41
Xia Xianchun, *Mingmo qicai – Zhang Dai lun* (On Zhang Dai, a genius of the late Ming), Shanghai: Shanghai shehuikexueyuan chubanshe, 1989
Zhang Dihua, "Zhang Dai," in *Zhongguo dabaike quanshu: zhongguo wenxue* (The Chinese encyclopedia: Chinese literature), vol. 2., Beijing and Shanghai: Zhongguo dabaike quanshu chubanshe, 1986: 1231

Zhou Zuoren
Chinese, 1885–1967

Zhou Zuoren owed his prominence in the New Literature movement, which took off around 1919, to his education in "Western learning" under the patronage of the imperial government. Like his brother **Lu Xun**, he had spent long years in Japan as a student, where he had been among the few in the Chinese contingent to interest himself seriously in Western culture and literature. Wedded to Western humanism, and equipped with a knowledge of English as well as easy access to Japanese scholarship (which was the first to channel knowledge of Western trends to the Orient), his was a voice that his compatriots, especially the younger ones, wanted to hear. In literature he above all championed the cause of the essay, as a vehicle for sane and civilizing discourse.

Zhou's first important pronouncement on the essay, however, emphasized the aesthetic aspect, in order to point out that the essay could stand as an art form alongside poetry and fiction, rather than being simply a medium for controversy, although at that stage he was no stranger to controversy himself. In "Mei wen" (1922; Belles-lettres) Zhou looked to Western paragons, especially English essayists, whose work was an extension of their personality. He commended in particular their "genuineness," a quality sadly lacking in contemporary Chinese compositions. "Genuineness" was to remain for Zhou a *sine qua non*; however, from roughly 1930 onward his attention was focused almost exclusively on the compositions of his own Chinese tradition known as *xiaopin wen* ("little form" compositions), a free form that the educated elite had used down the ages to express their private thoughts and feelings and record their own experiences, released from the obligation to speak "on behalf of the sages." For most of Chinese history this kind of essay had been regarded only as a diversion, at certain times as the authentic voice of literature. **Yuan Hongdao** and **Zhang Dai** represented the latter standpoint, and Zhou was responsible in no small measure for their revival. But whether English or Chinese, and whatever label it was given, the true essay excluded service to any cause; to be written by individuals for individuals, it displayed man in all his humors and diversity, but since it put a premium on "naturalness" and "sincerity," in this diversity there was community: it was the ideal medium for a "literature of humanity." This did not mean, of course, that the essay was limited to discussing man and his works: it extended to the world of creation in which man found himself.

Zhou Zuoren published over two dozen books of essays, naturally not all of the same kind. From initially applying "scientific common sense" (derived largely from Western sociology, psychology, and anthropology) to issues of the day and his own country's habits and practices, he tended more and more toward bookishness and isolation, having persuaded himself that literature was "useless" and that any attempt to prove otherwise would only cause pointless "vexation of spirit" – as well as court danger. Perhaps unwittingly, Zhou described what was to become his typical manner as an essayist as early as 1923, when he distinguished two types of writer produced by his home province of Zhejiang: the one magisterial, trenchant in judgment, pungent in expression (which fits Lu Xun), the other mild and gentlemanly, easy and unaffected, given to mixing the amusing and the serious (which fits himself).

The essay "Shuili de dongxi" (1930; Things in the water) fairly represents the image projected by Zhou in mid-career. Its subject is the superstition in his home district of many waterways concerning "river ghosts," spirits of the drowned who seek release for themselves by drowning others, who will become their substitutes. Unlike the common run of ghosts, these are rather attractive in appearance: they take the form of "little people" who may be seen playing in groups on the river banks, until they are disturbed, when they "plop" into the water like frogs. Zhou thinks these river ghosts may have something in common with the "river lads" (*kappa*) of Japanese superstition, a kind of demon who also pulls people under water. Up to this point he has treated the subject as an amusing curiosity, an item of folklore personalized by reference to his own childhood recollections, and told with many apologies for imprecision and disclaimers of authority. But finally he feels he has to draw a moral, like the essayists of old, and explains that his real interest is not in the ghosts but in their connection with the mundane world of the people who believe in such things, which he hopes Chinese sociologists will investigate. This is indeed a "gentlemanly" essay. It apologizes for trespassing on the reader's attention, is elaborately unassuming, and exhibits unprofessional vagueness (as illustrated by the title). By fitting into the Chinese tradition of scholarly "notes" on regional customs, and using wholly Chinese language structures (as opposed to the Europeanized Chinese already in vogue), it disguises the fact that in presentation it

is more like the quizzical type of English essay popular in the early 20th century than any *xiaopin wen*.

But if "Shuili de dongxi" was the kind of essay most readers of the time associated with Zhou Zuoren, it was not one of his best. His finest essays combine a similar sort of relaxed humor with deep sadness, most often over the cruelty of ignorance, whether directed against the self or others. In another essay on a related theme, "Gui de shengzhang" (1934; The aging of ghosts), he collects from written sources a number of contradictory anecdotes on the question of whether or not ghosts continue to age in the spirit world, culminating in long excerpts from the diary of a gentleman who corresponded via a planchette with members of his family who died, until even those spirits departed and left him more alone than ever. This transition from the mildly amusing to the equally ridiculous but profoundly affecting shows Zhou Zuoren in his true colors, all mannerisms shed. Despite his evident superiority to his matter, he evinces no trace of condescension: honest foolishness is treated with polite respect; pain is shared. No admiration is demanded from his reader, with whom he shares his knowledge and thoughts on equal terms, and enters into a closer relationship and talks of more serious things as the "conversation" progresses. Fortunately for the reader, Zhou always has things to say that we never knew before, so far-reaching was his curiosity and learning; hence, even when his style becomes excessively dry, as it did in the 1940s, reading him remains a real education.

D. E. POLLARD

Biography

Also wrote under the names Zhitang and Yaotang. Younger brother of the essayist Lu Xun. Born 16 January 1885 in Shaoxing, Zhejiang province. Studied at the Jiangnan Naval Academy, Nanking, 1901; studied in Japan, 1906–11. Married Habuto Nobuko, 1909 (died, 1962): one son and two daughters (one died in youth). Returned to Zhejiang province, 1911, and worked in the educational service, teaching English in Shaoxing; professor of literature, from 1917, and dean of the department of Japanese literature, from 1931, Peking University. Contributor to various journals, including *Xin qingnian* (New youth), from 1918, *Xiaoshuo yuebao* (Short story monthly), from 1921, *Yuzhou feng* (The cosmic wind), *Lunyu* (Analects), from 1932, and *Renjian shi* (This human world); founding member, Wenxue yanjiu hui (Literary association), 1921, and *Yusi* magazine, 1924. One of the leaders in the May Fourth movement for intellectual reform. Collaborated with the Japanese invaders during the Sino-Japanese war (1937–45): commissioner of education, North China, 1940–43; after the war tried for collaboration by the Chinese government and imprisoned, 1945–49, then pardoned. Lived in Beijing for the rest of his life. Died in Beijing in 1967.

Selected Writings

Essays and Related Prose
Ziji de yuandi (One's own garden), 1923; enlarged edition, 1928
Yutian de shu (A rainy day book), 1925
Yishu yu shenghuo (Art and life), 1926
Tan long ji (Speaking of dragons), 1927
Tan hu ji (Speaking of tigers), 2 vols., 1928
Yong ri ji (Passing the time), 1929
Kanyun ji (Gazing at the clouds), 1932
Ku yu zhai xu bawen (Prefaces and postscripts from the Driving Rain Studio), 1934

Ye du chao (Notes from night reading), 1934
Ku cha suibi (Bitter tea essays), 1935
Ku zhu za ji (Bitter bamboo jottings), 1936
Feng yu tan (Wind and rain), 1936
Gua dou ji (Melons and beans), 1937
Bingzhu tan (Talks by candlelight), 1940
Yaotang yulu (Jottings by Yaotang), 1941
Yao wei ji (Bitter taste), 1942
Shufang yijiao (A corner of the library), 1944
Bingzhu hou tan (More talks by candlelight), 1944
Yaotang zawen (Random essays of Yaotang), 1944
Ku kou gan kou (Bitter and sweet), 1944
Lichun yiqian (Before spring), 1945
Guoqu de gongzuo (Past work), 1959
Zhitang yiyou wenbian (Zhitang's writings during 1945), 1961
Zhitang huixiang lu (Zhitang's memoirs), 1970
Translations of essays in: *Renditions* 26 (1986), and in *The Columbia Anthology of Modern Chinese Literature*, edited by Joseph S. M. Lau and Howard Goldblatt, 1995: 601–15

Other writings: poems, a textbook on the history of European literature (1918), a book on the sources of modern Chinese literature (1932), works on his brother Lu Xun, and correspondence.

Further Reading

Pollard, D. E., "Chou Tso-jen and Cultivating One's Garden," *Asia Major* 11, no. 2 (1965): 180–98
Pollard, D. E., *A Chinese Look at Literature: The Literary Values of Chou Tso-jen in Relation to the Tradition*, London: Hurst, 1973
Qian Liqun, *Zhou Zuoren zhuan* (A life of Zhou Zuoren), Beijing: Shiyu wenyi chubanshe, 1990
Wolff, Ernst, *Chou Tso-jen*, New York: Twayne, 1971
Zhang Tierong, *Zhou Zuoren pingyi* (A balanced view of Zhou Zuoren), Tianjin: Tianjin renmin chubanshe, 1996

Zubiri, Xavier

Spanish, 1898–1983

Xavier Zubiri's lofty reputation in the Spanish-speaking world, and among Catholic philosophical circles elsewhere, is based primarily on his skill as an essayist – and on his personal presence as a teacher, at least for those who were fortunate enough to attend the courses he taught both as a university professor and as a private citizen. Zubiri's most important essays are contained in a single volume, *Naturaleza, historia, Dios* (1944; *Nature, History, God*). As Zubiri explains in his introduction to the English translation of the book, these essays belong to only one period of his intellectual development. In this period, Zubiri is concerned especially with the question of what philosophy has been and should be. His later thought is based on an understanding of philosophy as metaphysics, that is, an investigation of the fundamental principles of real beings as such and of the human relation to reality; this period culminates in the treatise *Sobre la esencia* (1962; *On Essence*) and his trilogy of works on intelligence (1980–83). Zubiri's essays, then, are especially suited to provoke reflection on the nature of the philosophical enterprise itself. They succeed thanks to his integration of diverse philosophical and scientific traditions and his conjunction of an accessible style with wide-ranging knowledge and profound reflection.

Zubiri's ideas and style display an unusually felicitous combination of the Catholic metaphysical tradition with a respect for the existential context of metaphysical thought. On the one hand, he is thoroughly grounded in medieval philosophy and its ancient sources; on the other hand, his sensitivity to philosophy as an enterprise carried out by human beings in specific personal and historical circumstances is reminiscent of **Heidegger** or **Ortega y Gasset**, both of whom were Zubiri's teachers. The concluding words of "Sócrates y la sabiduría griega" (1940; "Socrates and the Greek Idea of Wisdom") elegantly express this harmony between historical and philosophical understanding: "The history of philosophy is not culture or philosophic erudition. It is finding oneself with other philosophers in the things about which one philosophizes." A number of Zubiri's essays are deft, economical portraits of great philosophers which focus on these thinkers' concepts of philosophy itself (in addition to the essays in *Nature, History, God*, see *Cinco lecciones de filosofía* [1963; Five lessons in philosophy]).

Zubiri brings a fresh approach to time-honored philosophical topics, as in his influential treatment of the problem of God under the rubric of *religación*, or our essential tie to the source of our own existence. Zubiri also breathes new life into a traditional theme when, in "Nuestra situación intelectual" (1942; "Our Intellectual Situation"), he considers the time-honored, even time-worn scholastic concept of truth as "an *agreement* of thought with things." In Zubiri's hands, this concept becomes an occasion for diagnosing the contemporary intellectual malaise – the "profoundly paradoxical situation" in which, as he claims at the outset of the essay, scientists find themselves today. Zubiri explores the concept of "agreement" systematically but never drily, and closes with phrases worthy of the best existentialist manifestos: "But if, by a supreme effort, man is able to fall back upon himself, he will sense the ultimate questions of existence pass by his unfathomable depth like *umbrae silentes* [silent shadows]."

Zubiri's essays manifest a wide range of knowledge acquired in his studies with the outstanding philosophers, physicists, mathematicians, biologists, and linguists of his day. However, he is particularly wary of confusing philosophy with "a brilliant 'apprenticeship' of books or a splendid course of grand lectures" – that is, a mere display of encyclopedic erudition ("Our Intellectual Situation"). The scientific and historical facts Zubiri cites are always in the service of a philosophical problem. Thus, although his essays can accurately be described as dense, theirs is a rich rather than a ponderous density. Rather than arguing at length for a narrow thesis, Zubiri covers a great deal of ground by attacking the fundamental questions and bringing out their relationships. No words go to waste in his essays, but many topics are touched on only briefly, with a reluctant parenthetical note that the problem cannot be addressed adequately at this point. This style makes his writings suggestive and stimulating.

The richness of Zubiri's essays does not prevent them from being accessible to beginners. For instance, "¿Qué es saber?" (1935; "What Is Knowledge?") begins with a humble example: "Suppose that we are shown a cup of wine." Zubiri's pedagogical experience is illustrated in this essay and others by the skill with which he introduces readers to successively deeper levels of the problem, using phrases such as "here new difficulties arise" and "neither is this sufficient." His style is also enlivened by well-turned phrases: "science is not a simple addition of truths which man *possesses*, but rather the unfolding of an understanding possessed by truth" ("Our Intellectual Situation").

It is Zubiri's ability to make philosophical questions come alive, and to use his learning to sharpen rather than to blunt the force of these questions, that accounts for the distinctive power of his essays.

RICHARD POLT

Biography

Xavier Zubiri Apalátegui. Born 4 December 1898 in San Sebastián. Studied under Ortega y Gasset at the University of Madrid, Ph.D. in philosophy, 1921; University of Louvain; Gregorian University, Rome, Ph.D. in theology, 1920; studied independently in Europe, including under Husserl and Heidegger, 1928–31; other teachers included the mathematician Zermelo, the physicists Erwin Schrödinger and Louis de Broglie, and the philologist Jaeger. Chair of the history of philosophy, University of Madrid, 1926–36: taught at the Catholic Institute and the Sorbonne, Paris, 1936–39; chair of the history of philosophy, University of Barcelona, 1940–42; taught privately in Barcelona and Madrid, from 1945. Died in Madrid, 21 December 1983.

Selected Writings

Essays and Related Prose
Ensayo de una teoría fenomenológica de juicio (doctoral thesis), 1923

Naturaleza, historia, Dios, 1944; as *Nature, History, God*, translated by Thomas B. Fowler, Jr., 1981
Sobre la esencia, 1962; as *On Essence*, translated by A. Robert Caponigri, 1980
Cinco lecciones de filosofía, 1963
Inteligencia sentiente, 1980
Siete ensayos de antropología filosófica, 1982
Inteligencia y logos, 1982
Inteligencia y razón, 1983

Other writings: works on philosophy and religion.

Further Reading

Caponigri, A. Robert, Introduction to *On Essence* by Zubiri, translated by Caponigri, Washington, D.C.: Catholic University of America Press, 1980
Ferrater Mora, José, "The Philosophy of Xavier Zubiri," in *European Philosophy Today*, edited by George L. Kline, Chicago: Quadrangle, 1965
Homenaje a Xavier Zubiri, Madrid: Moneda y Crédito, 2 vols., 1970
Ramírez, C., *The Personalist Metaphysics of Xavier Zubiri* (dissertation), Washington, D.C.: Georgetown University, 1969
Rovaletti, Maria Lucrecia, editor, *Hombre y realidad: Homenaje a Xavier Zubiri (1898–1983)*, Buenos Aires: University of Buenos Aires Press, 1985
Wilhelmsen, Frederick D., *The Metaphysics of Love*, New York: Sheed and Ward, 1962

INDEXES

TITLE INDEX

This index lists all the titles in the Essays and Related Prose sections of the entries on individual writers. The name in parentheses directs the reader to the appropriate entry, where fuller information is given. The date given is that of first publication; revised titles and English-language translations are listed, with their dates.

A brasileiro entre os outros hispanos (Freyre), 1975
A campo traviesa (Reyes), 1960
A condição humana e outras temas (Freyre), 1972
À contre-courant (Massis), 1958
A educação pela noite (Cândido), 1987
A Europa desen cantada (Lourenço), 1994
A. G. Stephens (Vance Palmer), 1941
A la orilla del río de los sucesos (Madariaga), 1975
À margem da história (Cunha), 1909
A Propos of Lady Chatterley's Lover (Lawrence), 1930
A través del espejo (Monsiváis), 1994
Aaret rundt (Paludan), 1929
Abälard und Heloise (Feuerbach), 1834
Abbotsford and Newstead Abbey (Irving), 1835
ABC of Color (Du Bois), 1964
ABC of Reading (Pound), 1934
Abenteuerliche Herz (Jünger), 1929
Abhandlung über den Ursprung der Sprache (Herder), 1772
Abhandlung über die Evidenz in metaphysischen Wissenschaften (Mendelssohn), 1764
Abhandlung von der Unkörperlichkeit der menschlichen Seele (Mendelssohn), 1785
Abhandlungen über das Kommerz zwischen Seele und Körper (Mendelssohn), 1788
Abinger Harvest (E. M. Forster), 1936
Abolition of Man (Lewis), 1943
Absence (Vadeboncoeur), 1985
Absence of Myth (Bataille), 1994
Abyss Deep Enough (Kleist), 1982
Ação cultural para a liberdade (Freire), 1976
Accepting the Universe (Burroughs), 1920
Accomplishment of the First of Mr. Bickerstaff's Predictions (Swift), 1708
Account of My Hut (Kamo no Chōmei), 1955

Accursed Share (Bataille), 1988
Ach Europa! (Enzensberger), 1987
Achtung, Europa! (Thomas Mann), 1938
Achtzehnte Brumaire des Louis-Bonaparte (Marx), 1869
Acotaciones a la historia de la cultura occidental en la edad moderna (Tierno Galván), 1964
Acres and Pains (Perelman), 1947
Across the Plains (Stevenson), 1892
Actes retrouvés (Oullette), 1970
Actuelles (Camus), 1950
Ad Hoc (Jünger), 1970
Adages (Erasmus), 1539
Adagia (Erasmus), 1500
Adalékok az esztétika történetéhez (Lukács), 1953
Addresses to the German Nation (Fichte), 1914
Adel des Geistes (Thomas Mann), 1945
Adieux (Beauvoir), 1984
Adonis and the Alphabet (Aldous Huxley), 1956
Adrastea (Herder), 1801
Adventurer (Johnson), 1752
Advertisements for Myself (Mailer), 1959
Aesthetic as Science of Expression and General Linguistic (Croce), 1909
Aesthetic as the Science of Expression and of the Linguistic in General (Croce), 1992
Aesthetic Relation of Art to Reality (Chernyshevskii), 1953
Aesthetic Theory (Adorno), 1984
Affable Stranger (McArthur), 1920
Afiny i Ierusalim (Shestov), 1951
Aforisme reflecţii (Călinescu), 1984
African Literature (Gordimer), 1972
Afrika zhdet menia (Belyi), 1984
After Henry (Didion), 1992
After 1903 - What? (Benchley), 1938
After Strange Gods (T. S. Eliot), 1934
Aftermath (Belloc), 1903
Afternoons in Utopia (Leacock), 1932

Against Interpretation (Sontag), 1966
Against Pure Reason (Herder), 1993
Against Racism (Du Bois), 1985
Against the Current (Leont'ev), 1969
Age of Reason (Paine), 1794
Agenda (Azorín), 1959
Agitations (Shaw), 1985
Agnostic's Apology (Stephen), 1893
Agonía de Europa (Zambrano), 1945
Agonía del cristianismo (Unamuno), 1931
Agonie du christianisme (Unamuno), 1925
Agony of Christianity (Unamuno), 1928
Agony of Flies (Canetti), 1994
Agrarian Sociology of Ancient Civilizations (Weber), 1976
Agua pasada (Martín Gaite), 1993
Agudeza y arte de ingenio (Gracián), 1648
Aids and Its Metaphors (Sontag), 1989
Aids to Reflection in the Formation of a Manly Character (Coleridge), 1825
Ainsi soit-il (Gide), 1952
Al margen de estos clásicos (Marías), 1966
Al margen de los clásicos (Azorín), 1915
Al pie de la Torre Eiffel (Pardo Bazán), 1889
Al yunque (Reyes), 1960
Alarms and Discursions (Chesterton), 1910
Alarms and Diversions (Thurber), 1957
Albergo Empedocle (E. M. Forster), 1971
Album de vers et de prose (Mallarmé), 1887
Além do apenas moderno (Freyre), 1973
Alemanes en la conquista de América (Arciniegas), 1941
Aleph borgiano (Borges), 1987
Alessandro Manzoni (Croce), 1930
Alfonso XIII (Darío), 1921
Algunas consideraciones sobre la literatura hispano-americana (Unamuno), 1947
Algunos lugares de la pintura (Zambrano), 1989
Alhambra (Irving), 1832
Alhos e bugalhos (Freyre), 1978
All About Ourselves (Priestley), 1956
All England Listened (Priestley), 1968

GENERAL INDEX

Page numbers in **bold** indicate subjects with their own entries.

NOTES ON ADVISERS
AND CONTRIBUTORS

Adams, Stephen M. Assistant professor of English, Westfield State College, Massachusetts. Adviser, Honors College, University of Missouri, Columbia. Author of "Some Current Publications" in *Restoration: Studies in English Literary Culture, 1660–1700*. **Essays:** Daniel Defoe; *The Examiner*.

Almeida, Onésimo T. Professor and chair, Department of Portuguese and Brazilian Studies, Brown University, Providence, Rhode Island. Editor of *Gávea-Brown*, and member of the editorial board of *Santa Barbara Portuguese Studies*. Author of *Mensagem – Uma tentativa de reinterpretação* (1987), *Açores, açorianos, açorianidade* (1989), and of articles in *Hispania, Bulletin of Hispanic Studies, Colóquio-Letras, Ideologies and Literature, Europe, Revista Brasileira de Filosofia, Revista de Comunicação e Linguagens, Cultura-História e Filosofia*, and other journals. Editor of *Lisbon in Manhattan* by José Rodrigues Miguéis (1985). **Essays:** Vergílio Ferreira; Eduardo Lourenço; Portuguese Essay.

Altamiranda, Daniel. Assistant visiting professor, Arizona State University, Tempe. Author of articles in *Romanistisches Jahrbuch, Incipit*, and *Paresédor & Diferentes*. Editor of *Basta callar* by Pedro Calderón de la Barca (1995); coeditor of *Literatura española: Una antología* (1995). **Essays:** Eduardo Mallea; *Sur*.

Alter, Nora M. Assistant professor of German, film, and media studies, University of Florida, Gainesville. Author of *Vietnam Protest Theatre: Staging the Television War in the US and Abroad, 1965–1979* (1996) and chapters in books and articles in journals on film, theater, and the essay film. **Essay:** Essay Film.

Amana, Harry. Associate professor, School of Journalism, University of North Carolina, Chapel Hill. Author of articles in the *Journalism Quarterly, CLIO Among the Media*, and entries in *History of the Mass Media in the United States: An Encyclopedia* (1977) and *American Magazine Journalists, Dictionary of Literary Biography*. **Essays:** James Baldwin; Frederick Douglass.

Amore, Adelaide P. Professor of English and women's studies and director of English secondary education, Southern Connecticut State University, New Haven. Editor of the book review section, *Connecticut English Journal*. Author of *Models of Teaching English* (1981), six articles in *The Oxford Companion to Women's Writing in the United States* (1994), two articles in *Reference Guide to English Literature* (1991), four articles in the journal *The Leaflet*, and many columns on women's issues from a feminist point of view for the New Haven *Register*. Editor of *A Woman's Inner World: Selected Poetry and Prose of Anne Bradstreet* (1983) and *Oroonoko* by Aphra Behn (1987). **Essays:** Margaret Fuller; S. J. Perelman.

Anderson, Chris. Associate professor of English, Oregon State University, Corvallis. Author, editor, or coeditor of eight books, including *Style as Argument: Contemporary American Nonfiction* (1987), *Literary Nonfiction* (1989), *Free/Style: A Direct Approach to Writing* (1992), and a book of personal essays, *Edge Effects: Notes from an Oregon Forest* (1993).

Angyal, Andrew J. Professor of English, Elon College, North Carolina. Author of biographies of Loren Eiseley (1983), Lewis Thomas (1989), and Wendell Berry (1995), "Loren Eiseley's Immense Journey: The Making of a Literary Naturalist" in *The Literature of Science* (1993), and articles in the *CLA Journal, South Carolina Review, Christianity and Literature, Robert Frost Review*, and *Poe Studies*. **Essays:** Wendell Berry; Loren Eiseley.

Atwan, Robert. Founder and series editor of *The Best American Essays*. Author of essays and reviews in many national publications, including the New York *Times*, Los Angeles *Times, Atlantic Monthly, National Review, Kenyon Review*, and *Iowa Review*, as well as articles on literature and psychology in *Research Communications in Psychology* and *Psychiatry and Behavior*, and critical essays in several published volumes. Editor or coeditor of many college textbooks in composition and literature, including *The Harper American Literature* (1987), *Popular Writing in America* (1974), *Why We Write, Our Times*, and *The Writer's Presence*. American editor of *Openings: Original Essays by Contemporary Soviet and American Writers* (1990). Coeditor of two collections of poetry inspired by the Bible, *Chapters into Verse* (1993) and *Divine Inspiration*.

Baker, Janet. Associate professor of English, Saint Mary's University, Halifax, Nova Scotia. **Essay:** Archibald MacMechan.

Bardolph, Jacqueline. Professor, University of Nice. Author of *Ngugi wa Thiong'o, l'homme et l'œuvre* (1991), "Language Is

Courage (*The Satanic Verses*)" in *Reading Rushdie: Perspectives on the Fiction of Salman Rushdie*, edited by D. M. Fletcher (1994), and 60 articles in various journals, mainly on Nuruddin Farah, V. S. Naipaul, and East African literature. Editor of *Short Fiction in the New Literatures in English* (1990). **Essay:** Ngugi wa Thiong'o.

Beasley, Maurine H. Professor of journalism, University of Maryland, College Park. President of the Assocation for Education in Journalism and Mass Communication, 1993–94. Formerly staff writer, Washington *Post*. Corresponding editor of *Journalism History*. Author (with Sheila Gibbons) of *Taking Their Place: A Documentary History of Women and Journalism* (1993), *Eleanor Roosevelt and the Media: A Public Quest for Self-Fulfillment* (1987), and *White House Press Conferences of Eleanor Roosevelt* (1983). **Essay:** Mary McCarthy.

Bedani, Gino. Head of Italian Department and dean of Faculty of Arts and Social Sciences, University of Wales, Swansea. Italian editor of *Romance Studies*. Author of *Vico Revisited: Orthodoxy, Naturalism and Science in the "Scienza Nuova"* (1989), *Politics and Ideology in the Italian Workers' Movement* (1995), and articles in *Italian Studies*, *Quinquereme*, and *Lettera*. Editor of and contributor to *The Italian Lyric Tradition* (1993). **Essay:** Benedetto Croce.

Beddow, Michael. Professor of German, University of Leeds. Author of *Thomas Mann's Doctor Faustus* (1994). **Essay:** Thomas Mann.

Black, Ronald J. Professor of English, McKendree College, Lebanon, Illinois. Author of an entry on George Meredith in *Victorian Prose Writers After 1867*, *Dictionary of Literary Biography* vol. 57 (1987), and articles in the *Literary Magazine Review*, *McKendree Review*, *American Comparative Literature Association Newsletter*, and *CEA Critic*. **Essay:** Mark Twain.

Blinderman, Charles. Professor of English and adjunct professor of biology, Clark University, Worcester, Massachusetts. Author of *Biolexicon: A Guide to the Language of Biology* (1990), *The Piltdown Inquest* (1987), and articles in the *Journal of Popular Culture*, *Journal of Church and State*, *Journal of the History of Ideas*, and *Perspectives in Biology and Medicine*. **Essay:** T. H. Huxley.

Block, Ed, Jr. Associate professor of English, Marquette University, Milwaukee, Wisconsin. Associate editor, 1990–95, and editor, since 1995, *Renascence*. Author of *Rituals of Dis-Integration: Romance and Madness in the Victorian Psychomythic Tale* (1993), "Experience, Existence, and Mystery: Biblical Ideas of Justice in Postcolonial Fiction" in *Postcolonial Literature and the Biblical Call for Justice*, edited by Susan V. Gallagher (1993), and "Gadamer, Christian Tradition, and the Critic" in *Renascence* (1989). Editor of *Critical Essays on John Henry Newman* (1992). **Essay:** Thomas Carlyle.

Bonadeo, Alfredo. Professor emeritus of Italian, University of California, Santa Barbara. Member of the editorial board, *Studi Italiani*. Author of *D'Annunzio and the Great War* (1995) and "Guicciardini on War and Conquest" in *Il Pensiero Politico* 14 (1981). **Essay:** Francesco Guicciardini.

Borsò, Vittoria. Professor, Romanisches Seminar, Heinrich Heine University, Düsseldorf. Author of *Metapher: Erfahrungs- und Erkenntnismittel: Die Wirklichkeitskonstitution im franzö- sischen Roman des XIX. Jahrhunderts* (1985), *Mexiko jenseits der Einsamkeit: Versuch einer interkulturellen Analyse* (1994), and many articles in published volumes and journals. **Essays:** Michel Butor; Madame de Staël.

Brady, Maura. Former instructor and Ph.D. candidate in English literature, University of Iowa, Iowa City. **Essay:** James Agee.

Bretz, Mary Lee. Professor and chair of Spanish, Rutgers University, New Brunswick, New Jersey. Author of *Voices, Silences and Echoes: A Theory of the Essay and the Critical Reception of Naturalism in Spain* (1992), *Concha Espina* (1980), *La evolución novelística de Pío Baroja* (1979), and articles on 19th- and 20th-century Spanish literature in *Anales de la Literatura Española Contemporánea*, *Hispanic Journal*, *Symposium*, *Revista Canadiense de Estudios Hispánicos*, and other journals. **Essays:** Azorín; Ángel Ganivet; Emilia Pardo Bazán.

Brown, Stephen W. Professor of English and master of Champlain College, Trent University, Peterborough, Ontario. Author of a forthcoming biography of William Smellie, and many articles on 17th–20th-century literatures of England, Scotland, and Australia. Editor of a forthcoming collection of 18th-century Scottish essays on literary and scientific topics. **Essays:** *The Adventurer*; Biography and the Essay; Critical Essay; Encyclopedias and the Essay; Historical Essay; Periodicals; Satire; Satiric Essay.

Brownley, Martine Watson. Professor of English, Emory University, Atlanta. Author of *Clarendon and the Rhetoric of Historical Form* (1985). Editor of *Two Dialogues* by Clarendon (1984), *Complete History of England* by Tobias Smollett (forthcoming) and coeditor of *Mothering the Mind* (1984). **Essay:** Character Sketch.

Brownson, Siobhan Craft. Graduate student in English, University of South Carolina, Columbia. **Essay:** Cynthia Ozick.

Bruce, Michael. Lecturer, Goldsmiths College, University of London. British editor of the *Scriblerian* (Temple University, Pennsylvania), 1983–89. Author of articles in *The Hanoverian Encyclopedia* (1995) and *European Bibliography of Resources in English Studies* (1995). **Essays:** An *Essay of Dramatic Poesy*; An *Essay on Criticism*.

Buechler, Ralph W. Associate professor of German, University of Nevada, Las Vegas. Author of *Science, Satire, and Wit: The Essays of Georg Christoph Lichtenberg* (1990) and articles in *German Quarterly*, *Monatshefte*, *Seminar*, *Selecta*, and other journals. **Essays:** Aphorism; Hans Magnus Enzensberger; Georg Forster; Treatise.

Burke, John J., Jr. Professor of English and director of English honors, University of Alabama, Tuscaloosa. Author of *Signs and Symbols in Chaucer's Poetry* (1981), *The Unknown Samuel Johnson* (1983), *Boswell's "Life of Johnson": New Questions, New Answers* (1985), *Fresh Reflections on Samuel Johnson* (1987), *New Light on Boswell* (1992), and articles in *CLIO, Studies in Eighteenth-Century Culture, Philological Quarterly, Studies in the Novel, South Atlantic Review*, and the *Age of Johnson*. **Essay:** The Rambler.

Bush, William. Professor emeritus of French, University of Western Ontario, London. Member of the editorial advisory board, *Twentieth-Century Literature*. Author of *Souffrance et expiation dans la pensée de Bernanos* (1962), *L'Angoisse du mystère: Essai sur Bernanos et M. Duine* (1966), *Genèse et structures d'Un mauvais rêve: Bernanos et "le cercle enchanté"* (1982), *George Bernanos* (1969), *Genèse et structures de Sous le soleil de Satan d'après la manuscrit Bodmer* (1988). Editor of the critical editions of *Sous le soleil de Satan* by George Bernanos (1982) and *Relation du martyre des seize Carmélites de Compiègne* (1993) by Marie de l'Incarnation; editor of the Bernanos section of *A Critical Bibliography of French Literature* (1980). **Essay:** Georges Bernanos.

Butrym, Alexander J. Professor emeritus of English, Seton Hall University, South Orange, New Jersey. Editor of *Essays on the Essay: Redefining the Genre*, 1989.

Carballo, Robert. Associate professor of English and graduate coordinator, Millersville University, Pennsylvania. Author of articles in the *Angelus, American Benedictine Review, Faith and Reason, Humanitas, Neohelicon: Acta Comparationis Litterarium*. **Essay:** Matthew Arnold.

Carnall, Geoffrey. Honorary fellow (formerly reader in English literature), Department of English Literature, University of Edinburgh. Author of *Robert Southey and His Age* (1960) and *The Mid-Eighteenth Century* (vol. 8 of the *Oxford History of English Literature*), with John Butt (1979). **Essays:** The Edinburgh Review; The Quarterly Review.

Chachagua, Federico A. Ph.D. candidate in Latin American culture and literature, University of British Columbia, Vancouver. Author of articles in *Alba de America* and *Confluencia*. **Essay:** José Martí.

Chadbourne, Richard M. Professor emeritus of French, University of Calgary, Alberta. Author of *Ernest Renan as an Essayist* (1957), *Ernest Renan* (1968), *Charles-Augustin Sainte-Beuve* (1977), "A Puzzling Literary Genre: Comparative Views of the Essay" in *Comparative Literature Studies* (1983), and articles on various French essayists in *Man and Nature, French Literature Series*, and *PMLA*. **Essays:** French Essay; Marivaux; Michel de Montaigne; Ernest Renan; Charles-Augustin Sainte-Beuve.

Chance, Linda H. Associate professor of Japanese language and literature, University of Pennsylvania, Philadelphia. Author of *Formless in Form: Kenkō, Tsurezuregusa, and the Rhetoric of Japanese Fragmentary Prose* (1997), and articles in *Journal of the American Oriental Society* and *Journal of Comparative Literature and Aesthetics*. **Essays:** Japanese Essay; Kenkō; Sei Shōnagan.

Chapman, David W. Associate professor of English, Samford University, Birmingham, Alabama. Editor of *Alabama English*, since 1992; consulting reader of *English Journal*, since 1992, *College Composition and Communication*, since 1990, and *Journal of Advanced Composition*, since 1990. Author of *The Power of Writing*, with Lynn Waller (1994, revised 1995) and articles in *Rhetoric Review, Journal of Advanced Composition*, and *ADE Bulletin*. **Essays:** Chapter; Moral Essay; George Orwell.

Chittick, Kathryn. Associate professor of English, Trent University, Peterborough, Ontario. Member of the editorial board of *English Studies in Canada* and the forthcoming Oxford University Press *Dickens Companion*. Author of *The Critical Reception of Charles Dickens, 1833–1841* (1989), *Dickens and the 1830s* (1990), and articles in *Nineteenth-Century Fiction* and the *Dickensian*. **Essay:** William Makepeace Thackeray.

Classen, Albrecht. Professor of German studies, University of Arizona, Tucson. Editor of *Tristania* and *Synopsis*, coeditor of *Mediaevisktik*, and member of the advisory board of *Fifteenth-Century Studies*. Author of *Zur Rezeption norditalienischer Kultur des Trecento im Werk Oswalds von Wolkenstein* (1987), *Utopie und Logos* (1990), *Autobiographische Lyrik des europäischen Spätmittelalters* (1991), *The German Volksbuch* (1995), and about 120 articles in various journals. Editor of *Eroticism and Love in the Middle Ages* (1994), *Das deutsche Mittelalter in seinen Dichtungen* (1994), *Canon and Canon Transgression* (1993), *Women as Protagonists and Poets in the German Middle Ages* (1991), and *Medieval German Literature* (1989). Translator of works by Moriz von Craun (1992) and of *Tristans als Mönch* (1994). **Essays:** Jacob Christoph Burckhardt; Ernst Robert Curtius; Robert Musil.

Clowes, Edith W. Professor of Russian and comparative literature and director of the program in comparative literature, Purdue University, West Lafayette, Indiana. Author of *Russian Experimental Fiction: Resisting Ideology After Utopia* (1993), *The Revolution of Moral Consciousness: Nietzsche in Russian Literature* (1988), and articles in *Slavic and East European Journal, Russian Literature, Russian Review, Critique, Modern Language Journal*, and *Soviet Studies*. Editor of *Doctor Zhivago: A Critical Companion* (1995), *Between Tsar and People: Educated Society and the Quest for Public Identity in Late Imperial Russia* (1991), and *Maxim Gorky: A Reference Guide* (1987). **Essays:** Fedor Dostoesvkii; Aleksandr Herzen.

Connor, William. Associate professor of English and associate dean of arts, University of Alberta, Edmonton. Author of *Influential Writing* (1995) and *Harbrace College Workbook for Canadian Writers* (1988, revised edition 1990), and articles in *Canadian Literature, Studies in Canadian Literature, World Literature Written in English*, and other journals. Contributing editor to *The Harbrace Anthology of Literature* (1993). **Essays:** Robert Benchley; Canadian Essay (English); Robertson Davies; Roderick Haig-Brown; Hugh MacLennan.

Cooksey, Thomas L. Associate professor of English and philosophy, Armstrong Atlantic State University, Savannah, Georgia. Author of "The Labyrinth in the Monad: Possible Worlds in Borges and Leibniz" in *The Comparatist* (1993), "The Central Man of the World: The Victorian Myth of Dante" in *Studies in Medievalism* (1992), six entries in *Encyclopedia of Romanticism* (1992), and three entries in *Dictionary of Literary Biography* vol. 110 (1991). **Essays:** *Discourse on Method*; Giacomo Leopardi; *Meditations*; Plato; Seneca.

Cope, Kevin L. Professor of English and comparative literature, Louisiana State University, Baton Rouge. Editor of the journal *1650–1850: Ideas, Aesthetics, and Inquiries in the Early Modern Era*. Author of *Criteria of Certainty* (1990), *Enlightening Allegory* (1993), *Compendious Conversations* (1992), and over 70 articles on the British Restoration and 18th century. **Essay:** Dialogue.

Crăiuțu, Aurelian. Ph.D. candidate, Department of Politics, Princeton University, New Jersey. Adviser to Humanitas publishing house, Bucharest. Author of an article in *East European Constitutional Review* (1995). Translator into Romanian of *Cartesian Meditations* by Edmund Husserl. **Essay:** N. Steinhardt.

Crone, Anna Lisa. Associate professor of Russian language and literature, University of Chicago. Member of the editorial board of *Russian Language Journal*. Author of *Rozanov and the End of Literature* (1978), *New Studies in Russian Language and Literature* (1986), and about 50 articles on many Russian authors. Russian author for *World Book Encyclopedia*. **Essays:** Vasilii Rozanov; Lev Shestov; Vladimir Solov'ev.

Crow, Christine. Honorary reader in French, University of St. Andrews, Scotland. Author of *Paul Valéry, Consciousness and Nature* (1972), *Paul Valéry and Maxwell's Demon* (1972), *Paul Valéry and the Poetry of Voice* (1982), *Miss X or the Wolf Woman* (1990), and articles in *French Studies, Modern Languages Review, Forum for French Studies, Bulletin des Études Valéryennes,* and *Lines Review*, as well as in *Taking Reality by Surprise*, edited by Susan Sellers (1991) and *Tea and Leg-Irons: New Feminist Readings from Scotland*, edited by Caroline Gonda (1992). **Essay:** Paul Valéry.

Cuddy-Keane, Melba. Associate professor of English and humanities and Northrop Frye Scholar, University of Toronto at Scarborough. President of the Virginia Woolf Society, 1994–96; member of the associate editorial board of *Woolf Studies Annual*, since 1994. Author of articles in *Contemporary Literature, Cultural Critique, Journal of Modern Literature, PMLA, South Carolina Review, Studies in the Novel, Ambiguous Discourse*, edited by Kathy Mezei (1996), *Re: Reading, Re: Writing, Re: Teaching Virginia Woolf*, edited by Eileen Barrett and Patricia Cramer (1995), *Virginia Woolf: Texts and Contexts*, edited by Eileen Barrett and Beth Rigel Daugherty (1996), and *Encyclopedia of Contemporary Literary Theory*, edited by Irene R. Makaryk (1993). **Essay:** Virginia Woolf.

Daniel, Dalia. Member of the Department of English/Rhetoric, Southern Methodist University, Dallas. Author of two volumes of poetry, *Flowers of Being* (1976) and *Noia* (1995), and articles in *World Literature Today, Hebrew Studies,* and *Hebrew Abstracts*. **Essay:** Hannah Arendt.

Darby, David. Assistant professor of German and comparative literature, University of Western Ontario, London. Inaugural editor of *Arachné: An Interdisciplinary Journal of Language and Literature*. Author of *Structures of Disintegration: Narrative Strategies in Elias Canetti's Die Blendung* (1992), and articles and reviews in *Neophilologus, Modern Austrian Literature, Seminar, Textual Practice, Monatshefte, Études Littéraires,* and *Literary Research*. Editor of a forthcoming anthology of critical essays on Elias Canetti. **Essay:** Elias Canetti.

Daugherty, Sarah B. Professor of English, Wichita State University, Kansas. Member of the editorial board of the *Henry James Review*. Author of *The Literary Criticism of Henry James* (1981) and articles on Henry James and William Dean Howells in the *Henry James Review, Harvard Library Bulletin, American Literary Realism, Dictionary of Literary Biography,* and *A Companion to Henry James Studies*, edited by Daniel M. Fogel (1993). **Essays:** William Dean Howells; Henry James.

Davidson, Pamela. Lecturer, School of Slavonic and East European Studies, University of London. Member of the editorial board of Harwood Academic Publishers' Studies in Russian and European Literature series. Author of *The Poetic Imagination of Vyacheslav Ivanov: A Russian Symbolist's Perception of Dante* (1989), *Viacheslav Ivanov: A Reference Guide to Literature* (1996), and many articles on Ivanov in *Oxford Slavonic Papers, Cahiers du Monde Russe,* and various published volumes. **Essay:** Viacheslav Ivanov.

Davies, David R. Assistant professor of journalism, University of Southern Mississippi, Hattiesburg. **Essay:** A. J. Liebling.

Davis, Duane H. Assistant professor of philosophy, Ball State University, Muncie, Indiana. Author of articles in *Merleau-Ponty Vivant*, edited by Martin C. Dillon (1991), *Journal of the British Society for Phenomenology,* and *Josephinum Journal of Theology*. Editor of *The Dehiscence of Responsibility: Merleau-Ponty's Later Thought and Its Practical Implications* (1997). **Essay:** Simone de Beauvoir.

de Paolo, Charles. Professor of English, Manhattan City College, City University of New York. Author of *Coleridge's Philosophy of Social Reform* (1987) and articles in *Encyclopedia of Time* (1994) and in *CLIO, Theoria,* and other journals. **Essays:** Samuel Taylor Coleridge; Leigh Hunt.

Dierick, Augustinus P. Associate professor and chair, Department of German, University of Toronto. Associate editor of *Canadian Journal of Netherlandic Studies*. Author of *German Expressionist Prose: Theory and Practice* (1987), *Gottfried Benn and His Critics: Major Interpretations* (1992), and articles in *Modern Austrian Literature, Neophilologus, Orbis Litterarum, Seminar, Germanic Review,* and *Mosaic*. **Essays:** Gottfried Benn; Heinrich Mann.

Doebeling, Marion. Assistant professor of German and humanities, Reed College, Portland, Oregon. Author of *Theodor Fontane im Gegenlicht* (1996) and an article on Fontane in *Germanic Review*. **Essay:** Walter Benjamin.

Dowdey, Diane. Associate professor of English and director of composition, Sam Houston State University, Huntsville, Texas. Author of *The Researching Reader* (1990), *Constructing Rhetorical Education* (1992), and articles in the *Journal of Technical Communication* and *Markham Review*. **Essays:** Stephen Jay Gould; Science Essay.

Duemer, Joseph. Associate professor of humanities, Clarkson University, Potsdam, New York. Poetry editor of the *Wallace Stevens Journal*, and associate editor of the journal's poetry series. Author of the poetry collections *Customs* (1988) and *Static* (1995), the chapbooks *Fool's Paradise* (1980) and *The Light of Common Day* (1985), and poems in *American Poetry Review*, *Iowa Review*, *Antioch Review*, *New England Review*, *Mid-American Review*, and *Poetry Northwest*. Editor of *Dog Music* (1996). **Essay:** Ezra Pound.

Dyer, Klay. Ph.D. candidate, University of Ottawa. Author of the introduction to *The Untempered Wind* by Joanna Ellen Wood (1994), "Passing Time and Present Absence: Looking to the Future in *In the Village of Viger*" in *Canadian Literature* (1994), and reviews in the *Journal of Canadian Poetry*. **Essays:** Joseph Howe; Peter McArthur; *The Week*.

Earle, Peter G. Professor emeritus, University of Pennsylvania, Philadelphia. Member of the editorial/advisory boards of *Hispanic Review*, *Revista Hispánica Moderna*, and formerly of *Los Ensayistas* and *Latin American Literary Review*. Author of *Unamuno and English Literature* (1960), *Prophet in the Wilderness: The Works of Ezequiel Martínez Estrada* (1971), *Historia del ensayo hispanoamericano*, with Robert G. Mead, Jr. (1973), *Gabriel García Márquez* (1981), and many articles in *Hispanic Review*, *Insula*, *Cuadernos Americanos*, *Sur*, *Hispania*, *Ideas/Imágenes*, the encyclopedia *Latin American Writers* (1989), and *A History of Literature in the Caribbean* vol. 1 (1994).

Eckley, Wilton. Professor of liberal arts, Colorado School of Mines, Golden. Author of *The American Circus* (1984), *Herbert Hoover* (1980), *T. S. Stribling* (1975), *Harriette Arnow* (1974), and *Guide to e e cummings* (1969), and some 40 articles and essays on literature and history in various journals. **Essays:** Benjamin Franklin; Plutarch.

Egan, Ronald. Professor of Chinese and chair, Program in East Asian Languages and Cultural Studies, University of California, Santa Barbara. Author of *Word, Image, and Deed in the Life of Su Shi* (1994), *The Literary Works of Ou-yang Hsiu (1007–72)* (1984), and several articles in the *Harvard Journal of Asiatic Studies*. Translator of a work by Ouyang Xiu in *The Columbia Anthology of Traditional Chinese Literature*, edited by Victor Mair (1994). **Essay:** Ouyang Xiu.

Eichner, Hans. Professor emeritus of German, University of Toronto. Member of the advisory board of *Arbitrium*, *Zeitschrift für Germanistik*, and other journals. Author of *Thomas Mann: Eine Einführung in sein werk* (1953, revised 1961), *Four Modern Authors: Mann – Rilke – Kafka – Brecht* (1964), *Friedrich Schlegel* (1970), and *Deutsche Literatur im klassisch-romantischen Zeitalter, 1. Teil* (1990). Editor of *Kritische Friedrich-Schlegel-Ausgabe*, vols. 2–6, 16 (1961–81), *"Romantic" and Its Cognates: The European History of a Word* (1972), *Ausgewählte Schriften* by Johann Georg Hamann (1994), and other volumes. **Essay:** *Athenäum*.

Eile, Stanisław. Senior lecturer in Polish, School of Slavonic and East European Studies, University of London. Author of *Modernist Trends in Twentieth-Century Polish Fiction* (1996) and articles in *New Literary History*, *Soviet Jewish Affairs*, *Revue des Études Slaves*, and other journals. **Essay:** Stanisław Brzozowski.

Elorza, Antonio. Professor and chair, Department of the History of Ideas, Universidad Complutense, Madrid. Author of *La razón y la sombra: Una lectura política de Ortega y Gasset* (1984), *La ideología liberal en la Ilustración española* (1970), *La modernización política de España* (1989), and *La religione política* (1996). **Essay:** *El Sol*.

Elsworth, John. Professor of Russian studies, University of Manchester. Author of *Andrey Bely* (1972) and *Andrey Bely: A Critical Study of the Novels* (1983). **Essay:** Andrei Belyi.

Emig, Rainer. Lecturer, School of English, University of Wales, Cardiff. Author of *Modernism in Poetry: Motivations, Structures and Limits* (1995). **Essay:** Cyril Connolly.

Engel, Sandra A. Head of the Humanities Department, Mohawk Valley Community College, Utica, New York. Author of articles in the *Journal of Basic Writing*, *Negative Capability*, *English Journal*, *Moving Out*, and the St. Petersburg *Times*. **Essay:** Edward Hoagland.

Epley, Steven. Assistant professor of English, Samford University, Birmingham, Alabama. Author of several book reviews in *Envoi: A Review Journal of Medieval Literature*. **Essay:** Tract.

Evans, Colin. Reader in French, University of Wales, Cardiff. Author of *Taine: Essai de biographie intérieure* (1975), *Language People* (1988), and *English People* (1993). Editor of *Developing University English Teaching* (1995). **Essay:** Hippolyte Taine.

Evans, Timothy J. Professor of English, Richard Bland College of the College of William and Mary, Petersburg, Virginia. Contributing bibliographer to CCCC *Annual Annotated Bibliography of Composition and Rhetoric*. Member of the board of editorial consultants, *Victorian Institute Journal*. Author of entries on Paul Theroux and Anthony Trollope in the *Dictionary of Literary Biography* (1979, 1987). **Essays:** Henry David Thoreau; William Butler Yeats.

Fakundiny, Lydia. Senior lecturer, Department of English, Cornell University, Ithaca, New York. Editor of *The Art of the*

Essay (1991). Author of *The Restorationist, Text One: A Collaborative Fiction by Jael B. Juba*, with Joyce Elbrecht (1994). Editor of *Discoveries*, a journal of distinguished student writing from the Cornell writing program. **Essays:** Autobiographical Essay; Sir William Cornwallis the Younger; Washington Irving.

Farrar, Jennifer. Instructor in Spanish, Kennesaw State University, Georgia. **Essay:** Rosario Castellanos.

Faulkner, Peter. Reader, University of Exeter. Editor of the *Journal of the William Morris Society*, since 1987. Author of *Modernism* (1973), *Angus Wilson: Mimic and Moralist* (1983), and *Yeats* (1987). Editor of *Selected Poems of William Morris* (1993). **Essays:** *On the Sublime*; Leslie Stephen.

Faulkner, Robert K. Professor of political science, Boston College. Member of the board of editors of *Polity*. Past president of the New England Political Science Association. Author of *Francis Bacon and the Project of Progress* (1993), *Richard Hooker and the Politics of a Christian England* (1981), *The Jurisprudence of John Marshall* (1968), chapters in *The End of "Isms"?* (1994), *The Constitution and Justice* (1989), *Reason and Republicanism: Thomas Jefferson's Legacy of Liberty* (1996), and articles in *Political Studies, Interpretation, American Political Science Review, Polity, William and Mary Quarterly*, and other journals. **Essay:** Francis Bacon.

Ferns, John. Professor of English, McMaster University, Hamilton, Ontario. Member of the editorial board of the *Hopkins Quarterly*. Author of *A. J. M. Smith* (1979) and *Lytton Strachey* (1988). Editor, with Brian Crick, of *Studies in Literature and the Humanities* by George Whalley (1985). **Essay:** E. K. Brown.

Fletcher, John. Professor of European literature, University of East Anglia, Norwich. General editor of Calder and Boyars publishers' Critical Appraisals Series, 1974–80. Author of *The Novels of Samuel Beckett* (1964), *Claude Simon and Fiction Now* (1975), *Novel and Reader* (1980), and *Alain Robbe-Grillet* (1983). **Essays:** Albert Camus; Henry de Montherlant.

Foote, I. P. Formerly university lecturer in Russian, Oxford University; emeritus fellow, Queen's College, Oxford. Joint editor of the *Oxford Slavonic Papers*, 1972–91, and the *Slavonic and East European Review*, 1980–90. Author of articles on Saltykov-Shchedrin in *Forum for Modern Language Studies, Oxford Slavonic Papers*, and *Slavonic and East European Review*. Editor of *Selected Satirical Writings* by Saltykov-Shchedrin (1977). Translator of works by Saltykov-Shchedrin, Lermontov, and Tolstoi. **Essay:** Saltykov-Shchedrin.

Fulton, Richard D. Dean of Faculty, Clark College, Vancouver, Washington. Editor of *Victorian Periodicals Reviews*. Author of *Union List of Victorian Serials* (1985) and many articles and reviews. Editor of *A British Studies Sampler* (1994) and the American Slavery issue of *Nineteenth-Century Contexts*. **Essay:** *The Spectator*.

Gale, Steven H. Endowed chair in the humanities, Kentucky State University, Frankfort. General editor of Garland Publishers' Garland Studies in Humor. Founder and series coeditor, *Pinter Review*. Author of books and bibliographies on Harold Pinter, S. J. Perelman, and David Mamet, and dozens of articles in books and journals. Editor of *Encyclopedia of American Humorists* (1988) and *Encyclopedia of British Humorists* (1995). **Essay:** *The New Yorker*.

García Monsivais, Blanca M. Professor, Universidad Autónoma Metropolitana, Iztapalapa, Mexico. Member of the editorial board of *Signos* and *Acciones Textuales*. Author of *El ensayo mexicano en el siglo XX* (1995) and articles in various journals. **Essay:** Carlos Fuentes.

Garval, Michael D. Assistant professor of French, North Carolina State University, Raleigh. Author of "Balzac's Archival Rival" in *Nineteenth Century French Studies* and "The Rise and Fall of the Literary Movement in Post-Revolutionary France" in *Selected Proceedings of the 1993 International Association of Word and Image Studies Conference*. **Essay:** *The Physiology of Taste*.

Gilfillan, Daniel D. Ph.D. candidate, Department of Germanic Literature, University of Oregon, Eugene. Author of articles in *Praxis* and the *German Quarterly*. **Essay:** Alfred Andersch.

Glenn, Kathleen M. Professor of Romance languages, Wake Forest University, Winston-Salem, North Carolina. Coeditor of *Anales de la Literatura Española Contemporánea*; member of the editorial board of *Letras Peninsulares*, and of the advisory board of the Society of Spanish and Spanish-American Studies. Author of *The Novelistic Technique of Azorín* (1973), *Azorín* (1981), and articles in *Anales de la Literatura Española Contemporánea, Revista de Estudios Hispánicos, Hispanófila, Romance Notes, Letras Peninsulares, Catalan Review, Monographic Review, Romance Languages Annual*, and other journals. **Essay:** Carmen Martín Gaite.

Goetschel, Willi. Associate professor of German, Columbia University, New York. Author of *Constituting Critique: Kant's Writing as Critical Praxis*, translated by Eric Schwab (1994) and articles in the *Germanic Review, Babylon, Telos, Weimarer Beiträge*, and in various books. Editor of *Perspektiven der Dialogik* (1994) and *Werke* by Hermann Levin Goldschmidt (9 vols., 1993–). **Essays:** Gotthold Ephraim Lessing; Karl Marx; Moses Mendelssohn; Review; Georg Simmel; Margarete Susman.

Gomes, Miguel. Assistant professor, University of Connecticut, Storrs. Author of *El poso de las palabras: Ensayos críticos* (1990). Editor of *Antología poética de Oswald de Andrade* (1988) and the forthcoming *Estética del modernismo* and *Estética hispanoamericana del siglo XIX*. **Essay:** Mariano Picón-Salas.

Gómez-Martínez, José Luis. Research professor of Spanish, University of Georgia, Athens. Editor of *Los Ensayistas* and *Anuario Bibliográfico*; member of the editorial board of *Concordia: Internationale Zeitschrift für Philosophie, Estudios*

Interdisciplinarios de América Latina y el Caribe, South Atlantic Review, and *Cuyo: Anuario de Historia de la Filosofía Argentina y Americana*. Author of *Américo Castro y el origen de los españoles* (1975), *Teoría del ensayo* (1980), *Bolivia: Un pueblo en busca de su identidad* (1988), *Ortega y Gasset y la formación de una conciencia iberoamericana* (1996), and over 100 articles in various journals. **Essays:** Cuadernos Americanos; Eugenio María de Hostos; Leopoldo Zea.

Good, Graham. Professor of English, University of British Columbia, Vancouver. Author of *The Observing Self: Rediscovering the Essay* (1988).

Greene-Gantzberg, Vivian. Associate professor of Germanic languages, University of Maryland, College Park. Author of *Herman Bang oj det fremmede* (1992) and "Ludvig Holberg and German-Speaking Europe," in *Ludvig Holberg: A European Writer*, edited by Sven Hakon Rossel (1994). Editor of *Udenrigspolitisk journalistik* by Herman Bang (1990). **Essays:** Gunnar Heiberg; Nils Kjær; Per Lange; Scandinavian Essay; Knud Sønderby; Villy Sørensen.

Grevisse, Benoît. Member of the Department of Communications, Catholic University of Louvain, Belgium. **Essay:** Polemical Essay.

Gutiérrez, Carlos M. Teaches at Arizona State University, Tempe. Author of *Dejémonos de cuentos* (1994) and "Bibliografía del cervantismo finisecular" in *Estudios de Literatura* (1995). **Essay:** José Luis González.

Haddox, John H. Professor of philosophy, University of Texas, El Paso. Member of the editorial board of the *Southwestern Journal of Philosophy* and the Texas Western Press. Author of *Vasconcelos of Mexico: Philosopher and Prophet* (1967), *Antonio Caso: Philosopher of Mexico* (1971), chapters in *Religion in Latin American Life and Literature* (1980), *Integrated Studies* (1982), *Profit and Responsibility* (1985), *El APRA y lo ideología a la praxis* (1989), and articles in 17 journals. **Essays:** Alfonso Reyes; George Santayana; José Vasconcelos.

Hagberg, Garry L. Associate professor of philosophy, Bard College, Annandale-on-Hudson, New York. Author of *Art as Language: Wittgenstein, Meaning, and Aesthetic Theory* (1995), *Meaning and Interpretation: Wittgenstein, Henry James, and Literary Knowledge* (1994), and articles in *Philosophy, British Journal of Aesthetics, Journal of Aesthetics and Art Criticism, Philosophical Investigations, Journal of Aesthetic Education, Mind, Philosophy and Literature*, and other journals in philosophy and aesthetics. **Essay:** *An Essay Concerning Human Understanding*.

Hammond, Nicholas. Fellow, Gonville and Caius College and lecturer in French, University of Cambridge. Author of *Playing with Truth: Language and the Human Condition in Pascal's Pensées* (1994) and several articles on 17th-century French literature. Coeditor of *Dissertations contre Corneille* by l'Abbé D'Aubignac (1995). **Essays:** Blaise Pascal; Madame de Sévigné.

Harkins, William E. Professor emeritus of Slavic languages, Columbia University, New York. Author of *The Russian Folk Epos in Czech Literature* (1951), *A Modern Czech Grammar* (1953), *Karel Čapek* (1962), and entries in the *Dictionary of Russian Literature* (1957). Editor of *Anthology of Czech Literature* (1953) and of American contributions to the *Sixth International Congress of Slavists* vol. 2 (1968). **Essays:** Karel Čapek; Lev Tolstoi; Ludvík Vačulik.

Harman, Mark. Visiting faculty, University of Pennsylvania, Philadelphia. Author of articles in the *Sewanee Review, Georgia Review, German Quarterly*, and newspapers such as the Los Angeles *Times*, Boston *Globe*, and Irish *Times*. Editor of *Robert Walser Rediscovered: Stories, Fairy-Tale Plays, and Critical Responses* (1985). Translator of *Soul of the Age: Selected Letters (1896–1962)* by Hermann Hesse (1991). **Essay:** Heinrich von Kleist.

Harrington, Thomas S. Assistant professor of Spanish, Trinity College, Hartford, Connecticut. Author of *The Pedagogy of Nationhood: Concepts of National Identity in the Iberian Peninsula, 1874-1925* (1994) and "Laying the Foundations for an Integrated and Multi-Polar Approach to the Study and Teaching of Peninsular Culture: Labanyi and Graham's *Spanish Cultural Studies*: An Introduction" in *Siglo XX/Twentieth Century* 14, nos. 1–2 (1996). **Essays:** El Espectador; Revista de Occidente.

Harris, Jane Gary. Professor of Russian, University of Pittsburgh. Member of the editorial boards of *Essays in Poetics, Slavic and East European Journal*, and other journals. Author of *Osip Mandelstam* (1988) and *Autobiographical Statements in 20th-Century Russian Literature* (1990). Editor and cotranslator of *The Complete Critical Prose and Letters* by Mandel'shtam, 1979 (as *The Collected Critical Prose and Letters*, 1991). **Essay:** Osip Mandel'shtam.

Haskell, Dale E. Associate professor of English, Southeast Missouri State University, Cape Girardeau. Director, Southeast Missouri Writing Project. Associate editor of *Cape Rock*. Author of articles in *English Journal* and *Missouri English Bulletin*, and poetry in *Aethlon, Kentucky Poetry Review, Wisconsin Review, Rectangle, Cape Rock*, and other journals. **Essays:** M. F. K. Fisher; E. B. White.

Hassler, Donald M. Professor of English, Kent State University, Ohio. Editor of *Extrapolation*, since 1990. Author of *Erasmus Darwin* (1974), *Comic Tones in Science Fiction* (1982), *Patterns of the Fantastic* (1983), *Hal Clement* (1982), *Death and the Serpent* (1985), and *Isaac Asimov* (1991). Editor of *The Letters of Arthur Machen and Montgomery Evans* (1993). **Essays:** Letter; Lionel Trilling.

Hawkins-Dady, Mark. Freelance editor and writer. Author of articles on drama and the performing arts in *New Theatre Quarterly, John Osborne: A Casebook*, edited by Patricia Denison (1997), and various reference books. Editor of the *International Dictionary of Theatre* vols. 1-2 (1992-94) and *Reader's Guide to Literature in English* (1996). **Essay:** Kenneth Tynan.

Henderson, Heather. Associate professor of English, Mount Holyoke College, South Hadley, Massachusetts. Book review editor of the *Dickens Quarterly*, 1991–94; trustee of the Dickens Society, 1993–95. Author of *The Victorian Self: Autobiography and Biblical Narrative* (1989), "The Travel Writer and the Text" in *Temperamental Journeys: Essays on the Modern Literature of Travel* (1992), and articles in the *African Literature Association Bulletin, Cycnos, New Orleans Review, Victorians Institute Journal, Publishing History*, and other journals. Coeditor of the Victorian section of the *HarperCollins Anthology of British Literature* (1997). **Essay:** Travel Essay.

Hendon, Paul. Lecturer, University of Exeter. **Essay:** W. H. Auden.

Hergenhan, Laurie. Professor of Australian literature, University of Queensland, Brisbane. Series editor of the University of Queensland Press Australian Authors series. Editor of *Australian Literary Studies*, since 1963. Author of *Unnatural Lives: Studies in Australian Fiction About the Convicts* (1983), *No Casual Traveller: C. Hartley Grattan and Australia – U.S. Connections* (1995), and numerous articles on English and particularly Australian literature in various journals. Editor of *A Colonial City: High and Low Life: Selected Journalism* by Marcus Clarke (1972), *Penguin Literary History of Australia* (1988), *The ALS Guide to Australian Writers*, with others (1993), and *Changing Places: Australian Writers in Europe, 1960–1990*, with Irmtraud Petersson (1994). **Essay:** Marcus Clarke.

Heseltine, Harry. Formerly rector and professor of English, Australian Defence Force Academy, University of New South Wales, Canberra. Author of *The Uncertain Self: Essays in Literature and Criticism* (1986), *Annals of Australian Literature*, with Joy Hooton (2nd edition 1992), and other books on Australian literature. Editor of *The Penguin Book of Australian Verse* (1972) and *The Penguin Book of Australian Short Stories* (1976). **Essay:** Australian Essay.

Hesse, Douglas. Professor of English, Illinois State University, Normal. Editor of *WPA: Writing Program Administration*. Author of chapters in *Literary Nonfiction*, edited by Chris Anderson (1989), *Essays on the Essay: Redefining the Genre*, edited by Alexander J. Butrym (1989), *Narrative as Argument, Rebirth of Rhetoric* (1992), *Short Story Theory at a Crossroads* (1989), *Writing Theory and Critical Theory* (1994), and articles in the *Journal of Advanced Composition, Rhetoric Review, College Composition and Communication*, and *English Journal*. **Essay:** British Essay.

Heyer, Astrid. Part-time faculty member, Department of French, University of Western Ontario, London. Author of articles on Georges Bernanos in the *Chesterton Review, Revue des Lettres Modernes, Renascence*, and of a chapter in *A Critical Bibliography of French Literature: The Nineteenth Century*, edited by David Baguley (1994). Translator of articles by William Bush, Kathryn Brush, and Wolfgang Kemp. **Essay:** Henri Massis.

Hinchcliffe, Peter. Associate professor, St. Jerome's College, University of Waterloo, Ontario. Fiction editor of the *New Quarterly*. Author of articles in the *University of Toronto Quarterly, Journal of Canadian Fiction, English Studies in Canada*, and *Profiles in Canadian Literature*. **Essay:** Robert Louis Stevenson.

Hinchliffe, Darrell. Lecturer in literature, Staffordshire University, Stoke-on-Trent. **Essay:** Thomas Nashe.

Holman, Petr. Professor, Institute of Czech Literature, Academy of Sciences, Prague. Author of two books about Otokar Březina (1992, 1993). Editor of a collection of essays by Březina (1996) as well as other documents. **Essay:** Otokar Březina.

Holmes, John R. Associate professor of English, Franciscan University of Steubenville, Ohio. Author of articles in *Early American Literature* and *Studia Mystica*. Editor of the forthcoming *Letters of Charles Brockden Brown*. **Essays:** *The Anatomy of Melancholy*; Cicero; Thomas Merton; *The Poetic Art*.

Holý, Jiří. Scientific worker, Institute of Czech Literature, Academy of Sciences, Prague. Author of five books on Czech literature and writers. **Essay:** Václav Havel.

Horowitz, Brian. Assistant professor of Russian, University of Nebraska, Lincoln. Book review editor of *Soviet Post-Soviet*. Author of *The Myth of Alexander Pushkin in Russia's Silver Age* (1996) and articles on Mikhail Gershenzon and book reviews in various journals. **Essays:** Mikhail Gershenzon; Russian Essay.

Howells, Bernard. Lecturer in French, King's College, London. Author of articles in *French Studies, Romanic Review, Revista di Letterature Moderne e Comparate, Études Baudelairiennes*, and chapters in *Écrire la peinture* (1991) and *Ideology and Religion* (1989). **Essay:** Charles Baudelaire.

Hunt, Alina C. Lecturer, University of North Carolina, Greensboro. Author of "Toward an Unfinalizable Dialogue: Robert Musil's Essayism and Bakhtinian Dialogism" in *College Literature* (May 1995), "Robert Musil's Utopian Essayism: An Unresolvable Dialectics" in *MIFLC Review* (March 1995), and "Nineteenth-Century Utopian Visions and the Arcades of Paris" in *Constructions* (1990). **Essay:** Philosophical Essay.

Ives, Maura. Associate professor of English, Texas A&M University, College Station. Author of *George Meredith's Essay on Comedy and Other New Quarterly Magazine Publications* (1997), an entry on Meredith in the *Encyclopedia of British Humorists*, edited by Steven H. Gale (1995), and articles in *Literature in the Marketplace* (1995), *Keeping the Victorian House* (1995), and the journals *Studies in Bibliography* and *Papers of the Bibliographical Society of America*. **Essay:** An Essay on Comedy.

Jackson, Gregory S. Lecturer, Department of English, University of California, Los Angeles. Author of various articles on 18th- and 19th-century British and American literature and culture. **Essays:** Charles Darwin; Erasmus; Literary Theory and the Essay.

Janowski, Zbigniew. Ph.D. candidate, Committee on Social Thought, University of Chicago. Coeditor of the Philosophy Plus series for Pero Publishing House, Sofia, Bulgaria. Author of several book reviews and of articles in *Kultura, Arka,* and *Panorama.* **Essays:** Julien Benda; Boy-Żelenski; Leszek Kołakowski.

Jones, Gloria Godfrey. Assistant professor of English, Winthrop University, Rock Hill, South Carolina. Author of articles in the *Explicator* and *CEA Critic,* and in *Language Variation in North America,* edited by Wayne Glowka and Donald Lance (1993). **Essay:** Gore Vidal.

Jonson, Jep C. Graduate student in English, University of South Carolina, Columbia. Editorial assistant of *Studies in Scottish Literature.* Author of an entry on John Watson (Ian Maclaren) in the *Dictionary of Literary Biography* vol. 156 (1996) and an article on Robert Burns in *Studies in Scottish Literature.* **Essay:** John Eglinton.

Julian, Linda A. Associate professor of English and chair of the Department of English, Furman University, Greenville, South Carolina. Author of *Strategies for Teaching Writing* (4th edition, 1996), "The Impact of Icelandic Sagas on the Socialist Aesthetics of William Morris" in *Pre-Raphaelite Art in Its European Context,* edited by Susan Casteras and Alicia Faxon (1995), and entries on Mary Louisa Molesworth and G. S. Street in *British Short Fiction Writers, 1880–1914,* edited by William B. Thesing, *Dictionary of Literary Biography* vol. 135 (1994). **Essays:** Charles Dickens; William Morris.

Kadarkay, Arpad. Professor of political theory, University of Puget Sound, Tacoma, Washington. Author of *George Lukács: Life, Thought and Politics* (1991) and *Human Rights in American and Russian Political Thought* (1982). Editor and translator of *The Lukács Reader* (1995). **Essay:** Georg Lukács.

Karcz, Andrzej. Ph.D. candidate, Department of Slavic languages and literature, and lecturer and language instructor in Russian and Polish, University of Chicago. Author of articles in the *Polish Review* and various Polish journals. **Essay:** Zbigniew Herbert.

Katra, William H. Faculty member, University of Wisconsin, Eau Claire. Author of *"Contorno": An Argentine Journal of Literature and Politics* (1987), *Sarmiento: Public Writer (Between 1839 and 1852)* (1985), *Sarmiento de frente y perfil* (1993), and *The Argentine Generation of 1837: Echeverría, Alberdi, Sarmiento, Mitre* (1995). **Essay:** Domingo Faustino Sarmiento.

Kauffmann, R. Lane. Associate professor of Spanish and humanities, Rice University, Houston. Member of the editorial board of *Transculture.* Author of articles in *Essays on the Essay: Redefining the Genre,* edited by Alexander J. Butrym (1989), *The Interpretation of Dialogue,* edited by Tullio

Maranhão (1990), and *Divergencias y unidad: Perspectivas sobre la generación del 98 y Antonio Machado,* edited by John P. Gabriele (1990), in various conference proceedings, and in the journals *Diogène, Diacritics, L'Esprit Créateur, Philological Quarterly, Telos, Inti: Revista de Literatura Hispánica,* and the *New Scholar.* **Essay:** José Ortega y Gasset.

Keely, Karen A. Teaching fellow and Ph.D. candidate, Department of English, University of California, Los Angeles. Editorial assistant of *Signs: Journal of Women in Culture and Society,* 1990–91. **Essays:** The American Scholar; The Georgia Review.

Kehlen, John Pavel. Ph.D. candidate, Committee on Social Thought, University of Chicago; has also taught several courses on Japanese and Chinese literature. **Essay:** Kamo no Chōmei.

Keller, Arnold. Associate professor and director of the writing program, University of Victoria, British Columbia. Member of the review board of *McGill Journal of Education.* Author of *When Machines Teach* (1987), *English Simplified* (latest edition 1995), and articles in *McGill Journal of Education* and *Computers and Education.* **Essay:** Mordecai Richler.

Kelly, Gary. Professor of English, Keele University, Staffordshire. Author of *The English Jacobin Novel, 1780–1805* (1976), *English Fiction of the Romantic Period, 1789–1830* (1989), *Revolutionary Feminism: The Mind and Career of Mary Wollstonecraft* (1991), and *Women, Writing, and Revolution, 1790–1827* (1992). General editor, *Longman's History of Women's Writing in English.* **Essay:** Mary Russell Mitford.

Kelsall, Malcolm. Professor of English, University of Wales, Cardiff. Advisory editor of the *Byron Journal.* Author of *Christopher Marlowe* (1981), *Congreve* (1981), *Studying Drama* (1985), *Byron's Politics* (1987), and *The Great Good Place: The Country House and English Literature* (1992). Editor of *Encyclopedia of Literature and Criticism* (1990). **Essay:** Joseph Addison.

Ker, Ian. Tutor, Campion Hall, and member of the theology faculty, Oxford University; dean of graduate research, Maryvale Institute, Birmingham. Author of *John Henry Newman: A Biography* (1988) and *The Achievement of John Henry Newman* (1990). Editor of *The Idea of a University* by Newman (1976). **Essay:** John Henry Newman.

Ketchian, Sonia I. Research fellow, Harvard University Russian Research Center, Cambridge, Massachusetts. Author of *The Poetry of Anna Akhmatova: A Conquest of Time and Space* (1986) and *The Poetic Craft of Bella Akhmadulina* (1993). Editor of *Anna Akhmatova, 1889–1989* (1993), *Studies in Russian Literature in Honor of Vsevolod Setchkarev,* with Julian W. Connolly (1986), and *In the Shadow of the Fortress: The Genocide Remembered* by Bertha Nakshian Ketchian (1988). **Essay:** Aleksandr Pushkin.

Kieser, Rolf. Professor, City University of New York. Author of *Englands Appeasementpolitik und der Aufstieg des Dritten*

Reiches im Spiegel der britischen Presse (1933–1939) (1964), *New Functional German*, with Max Kirch (1967), *Max Frisch: Das literarische Tagebuch* (1975), *Erzwungene Symbiose: Thomas Mann, Robert Musil, Georg Kaiser und Bertolt Brecht im Schweizer Exil* (1984), *Olga Plümacher-Hünerwadel: Eine vergessene Lenzburger Philosophin* (1990), and *Benjamin Franklin Wedekind: Biographie einer Jugend* (1990). Editor of *Novels, Plays, Essays* by Max Frisch (1989). **Essay:** Max Frisch.

Kline, George L. Milton C. Nahm Professor Emeritus of Philosophy, Bryn Mawr College, Pennsylvania. Past president of the Hegel Society of America and the Metaphysical Society of America. Consulting editor of the *Journal of the History of Ideas, Studies in East European Thought* (formerly *Studies in Soviet Thought*), and *Russian Studies in Philosophy* (formerly *Soviet Studies in Philosophy*). Author of *Spinoza in Soviet Philosophy* (1952) and *Religious and Anti-Religious Thought in Russia* (1968). Coeditor of and contributor to *Russian Philosophy* (3 vols., 1965). Translator of *A History of Russian Philosophy* by V. V. Zenkovsky (2 vols., 1953) and *Selected Poems* by Joseph Brodsky (1973). **Essay:** Konstantin Leont'ev.

Knapp, Gerhard P. Professor of German and comparative literature, University of Utah, Salt Lake City. Member of the editorial board of *Amsterdamer Beiträge zur neueren Germanistik*, since 1993. Published extensively on 19th- and 20th-century German and comparative literature, philosophy, and sociology. Author and coauthor of 17 books, including *The Art of Living: Erich Fromm's Life and Works* (1989) and *Friedrich Dürrenmatt* (1993), and 60 articles and 118 reviews/critiques. Editor and coeditor of 12 anthologies and critical editions. **Essay:** Friedrich Dürrenmatt.

Koepke, Wulf. Formerly distinguished professor of German, Texas A&M University, College Station. Coeditor of *Exilforschung* and *Herder Yearbook*. President of the International J. G. Herder Society, 1985–90. Author of *Erfolglosigkeit* (1977), *Lion Feuchtwanger* (1983), *Johann Gottfried Herder* (1987), and *Understanding Max Frisch* (1990). Editor of *J. G. Herder: Innovator Through the Ages* (1984). **Essays:** Johann Gottfried Herder; Ricarda Huch.

Koppisch, Michael S. Professor of French and chair, Department of Romance and Classical Languages, Michigan State University, East Lansing. Member of the editorial advisory committee of *Studies in Early Modern France*. Author of *The Dissolution of Character: Changing Perspectives in La Bruyère's Caractères* (1981) and articles in *Seventeenth-Century French Literature*. Coeditor of *Approaches to Teaching Molière's Tartuffe and Other Plays* (1995). **Essay:** Jean de La Bruyère.

Kozłowski, Krzysztof. Ph.D. candidate, Zakład Teatru i Filmu, Poznań, Poland. Author of article in *Czytanie Herberta* (1995). **Essay:** Jerzy Stempowski.

Kuharski, Allen J. Assistant professor of theater studies, Swarthmore College, Pennsylvania. Founding associate editor of *Periphery: Journal of Polish Affairs*, since 1994;

performance review editor of *Theatre Journal*, since 1995. Author of articles in *Themes in Drama, San Francisco Review of Books, Theatre Journal, Dialog, The Theatre in Poland/Le Théâtre en Pologne, 2B: Polish American Academic Quarterly, New Theatre Quarterly, Yale/Theater*, and *Periphery*. **Essay:** Jan Kott.

Kuist, James M. Professor of English, University of Wisconsin, Milwaukee. Author of *The Nichols File of The Gentleman's Magazine* (1982), *The Works of John Nichols* (1970), and articles in *PMLA, Studies in Bibliography*, and the *South Atlantic Quarterly*. Editor of *Cursory Observations on the Poems Attributed to Rowley* by Edmond Malone (1968). **Essays:** *The Idler*; Periodical Essay; *A Review of the Affairs of France*; Earl of Shaftesbury.

Larkin, Edward T. Associate professor of German, University of New Hampshire, Durham. Author of *War in Goethe's Writings: Representation and Assessment* (1992) and articles in *Unterrichtspraxis, Michigan Germanic Studies*, and the *Dictionary of Literary Biography*. **Essay:** Johann Gottlieb Fichte.

Lazar, David. Associate professor and director of creative writing, Ohio University, Athens. Associate editor of the *Ohio Review*. Author of articles in the *Southwest Review, Denver Quarterly, Quarterly West, Seattle Review, Aperture, Mississippi Valley Review*, and other journals. Editor of *Conversations with M. F. K. Fisher* (1992). **Essays:** Hubert Butler; Natalia Ginzburg; Primo Levi.

Levi, Anthony. Formerly Buchanan Professor of French Language and Literature, University of St. Andrews, Scotland. Author of the *Guide to French Literature* (2 vols., 1992–94) and several other books on French literature. Editor of *Humanism in France at the End of the Middle Ages and in the Early Renaissance* (1970) and critical editions of *In Praise of Folly* by Erasmus (1971) and *Pensées and Other Writings* by Pascal (1995). **Essays:** Ferdinand Brunetière; *Feuilleton*; Bernard de Fontenelle; André Gide; *Journal des Débats*; La Rochefoucauld; Maxim; Meditation; *Nouvelle Revue Française*; Charles Péguy; *Pensée*; *Rêverie*; *Revue des Deux Mondes*; Jean-Jacques Rousseau; Albert Thibaudet.

Lits, Marc. Professor, Department of Communication, University of Louvain, Belgium. Author of *L'Essai* (1994), *Le Roi est mort: Émotion et médias* (1994), *La Peur, la mort el les médias* (1993), *Le Roman policier* (1993), and *Pour lire le roman policier* (1989). **Essays:** Roland Barthes; E. M. Cioran; Umberto Eco.

Livingston, Donald W. Professor of philosophy, Emory University, Atlanta. Author of *Hume's Philosophy of Common Life* (1984). Editor of *Liberty in Hume's History of England*, with Nicholas Copredi (1990) and *David Hume, Philosopher of Society, Politics, and History*, with Marie Martin (1991). **Essay:** David Hume.

Lloyd, Rosemary. Professor of French, Indiana University, Bloomington. Author of *Baudelaire et Hoffmann* (1979), *The*

Land of Lost Content (1992), and *Closer and Closer Apart* (1995). Editor of the *Literary Criticism* (1981), *Letters* (1986), and *Prose Poems* and *La Fanfarlo* (1991) by Charles Baudelaire, *Poésies* (1984) and *Letters* (1988) by Stéphane Mallarmé, *Madame Bovary* by Gustave Flaubert (1990), and *Master Pipers* by George Sand (1994). **Essays:** Remy de Gourmont; Stéphane Mallarmé.

Lonergan, Jennifer. Teacher of English language and literature. Author of six entries in the forthcoming *Reference Guide to Russian Literature* and three entries in the forthcoming *Peoples of Evasion*. **Essay:** Nikolai Chernyshevskii.

Lopate, Phillip. Adams Professor of English, Hofstra University, Hempstead, New York. Juror for the Pulitzer Prize, National Book Award, and Association of Writing Programs contest. Editor of *The Art of the Personal Essay* anthology (1994). Author of two volumes of essays, *Bachelorhood* (1981) and *Against Joie de Vivre* (1989), the memoir *Being with Children* (1975), two novels, *Confessions of Summer* (1979) and *The Rug Merchant* (1987), and the poetry collection *The Daily Round* (1976).

Lorenzo-Rivero, Luis. Professor of Spanish, Portuguese, and comparative literature, University of Utah, Salt Lake City. Author of *Larra: Técnicas y perspectivas* (1988), *Estudios literarios sobre Mariano J. de Larra* (1986), *Larra: Lengua y estilo* (1977), *Estudios de literatura española moderna* (1976), *Larra y Sarmiento* (1968), and various articles. Editor of *Macías* by Mariano José de Larra (1990). **Essay:** Mariano José de Larra.

Lounsberry, Barbara. Professor of English, University of Northern Iowa, Cedar Falls. Author of *The Writer in You* (1992) and *The Art of Fact: Contemporary Artists of Nonfiction* (1990). Editor of *Writing Creative Nonfiction: The Literature of Reality*, with Gay Talese (1995). **Essays:** Joan Didion; Oliver Wendell Holmes; Norman Mailer; New Journalism; Tom Wolfe.

Lynn, Steven. Professor and director of freshman English, University of South Carolina, Columbia. Author of *Samuel Johnson After Deconstruction* (1992), *Texts and Contexts* (1994), and articles in *Eighteenth-Century Studies*, *College English*, and *Age of Johnson*. **Essay:** Samuel Johnson.

McCarthy, John A. Professor of German and comparative literature, Vanderbilt University, Nashville, Tennessee. Editorial board member and reader for the *Lessing Yearbook*, *Goethe Yearbook of North America*, *Seminar*, *Studies in 18th-Century Culture*, *Eighteenth-Century Studies*, *German Quarterly*, and *Internationale Forschungen zur Allgemeinen & Vergleichenden Literaturwissenschaft*. Author of *Crossing Boundaries: A History and Theory of Essay Writing in Germany, 1680–1815* (1989), *Christoph Martin Wieland: Epoche – Werk – Wirking*, with others (1994), *Christoph Martin Wieland* (1979), "Wieland as Essayist" in *Lessing Yearbook 8* (1976), "The Philosopher as Essayist: Leibniz and Kant" in *The Philosopher as Writer*, edited by R. Ginsburg (1987), "Reviewing Nation: The Review and the Concept of Nation" in *The 18th-Century*

German Book Review, edited by H. Rowland and K. J. Fink (1995), "Rewriting the Role of the Author: On the 18th Century as the Age of the Author" in *Leipziger Jahrbuch für Geschichte des Buchwesens 5* (1995), and numerous other essays on German literature and comparative literature. **Essays:** German Essay; Friedrich Nietzsche.

McClintick, Christopher P. Teaches at Vanderbilt University, Nashville, Tennessee. Author of articles in *Seminar*, *Michigan Germanic Studies*, and the collection *The Future of German Studies in North America*. **Essays:** *Die Akzente*; *Die Fackel*; *Die Grenzboten*; *Die neue Rundschau*.

McCrea, Brian. Professor of English, University of Florida, Gainesville. Member of the editorial board of the *South Atlantic Review*. Author of *Henry Fielding and the Politics of Mid-Eighteenth-Century England* (1981), *Addison and Steele Are Dead: The English Department, Its Canon, and the Professionalization of Literary Criticism* (1990), and *College Writing* (1985). **Essays:** Henry Fielding; Richard Steele.

McCulloch, Margery Palmer. Lecturer in Scottish literature, University of Glasgow. Author of *The Novels of Neil M. Gunn: A Critical Study* (1987), *Edwin Muir: Poet, Critic and Novelist* (1993), chapters in *History of Scottish Literature* (1987), *Byron and Scotland* (1989), *Edwin Muir: Centenary Assessments* (1990), *Études Ecossaises* (1992), and *Scotland and the Slavs* (1993), and articles in *Studies in Scottish Literature*, *Scottish Literary Journal*, *English Review*, *Cencrastus*, *Chapman*, *Modern Language Review*, *Pen International*, *Studies in Hogg and His World*, and other journals. Editor of *The Man Who Came Back: Essays and Short Stories* by Neil M. Gunn (1991). **Essay:** Edwin Muir.

McDonagh, Josephine. Lecturer in English, Birkbeck College, University of London. Author of *De Quincey's Disciplines* (1994). Coeditor of *Political Gender: Texts and Contexts* (1994). **Essays:** Thomas De Quincey; George Eliot.

McGhee, Richard D. Dean, College of Arts and Sciences, Arkansas State University. Author of *Guilty Pleasures: William Wordsworth's Poetry of Psychoanalysis* (1993), *John Wayne: Actor, Artist, Hero* (1990), *Henry Kirke White* (1981), and *Marriage, Duty and Desire in Victorian Poetry and Drama* (1980). **Essays:** *An Essay on the Principle of Population*; John Stuart Mill.

McKenzie, Alan T. Professor of English, Purdue University, West Lafayette, Indiana. Author of *Certain, Lively Episodes: The Articulation of Passion in Augustan Prose* (1990), *Sent as a Gift: Eight Correspondences from the Eighteenth Century* (1993), an entry on the Earl of Chesterfield in *British Prose Writers, 1660–1800, Second Series*, edited by Donald T. Siebert, *Dictionary of Literary Biography* vol. 104 (1991), and articles in *Eighteenth-Century Studies*, *The Eighteenth Century: Theory and Interpretation*, *Georgia Review*, *Harvard Library Bulletin*, and *1650–1850: Ideas, Aesthetics, and Inquiries in the Early Modern Era*, among other places. **Essays:** Earl of Chesterfield; *The Spectator*.

Mackervoy, Susan. Freelance writer and translator, London. **Essay:** Friedrich von Schiller.

McLaren, John. Professor of humanities, Victoria University of Technology, Footscray, Australia. Editor of *Overland* literary magazine, since 1993, and *Australian Book Review*, 1978–86. Author of *Writing in Hope and Fear* (1996), *New Pacific Literatures* (1993), and *Australian Literature: An Historical Introduction* (1989). **Essay:** Dorothy Green.

Maharg, James. Associate professor of Spanish and Portuguese, University of Illinois, Chicago. Author of *A Call to Authenticity: The Essays of Ezequiel Martínez Estrada* (1977), *Los primeros modernistas* (1983), *José Ortega y Gasset* (1992), and articles in *Revista de Occidente, Cuadernos Hispanoamericanos, Luso-Brazilian Review,* and *Bulletin of Hispanic Studies.* **Essay:** Ezequiel Martínez Estrada.

Mahoney, John L. Thomas F. Rattigan Professor of English, Boston College. Author of *The Logic of Passion: The Literary Criticism of William Hazlitt* (1981), *The Whole Internal Universe: Imitation and the New Defense of Poetry in British Criticism, 1660–1830* (1986), and articles in the *Wordsworth Circle, European Romantic Review,* and *British Journal of Aesthetics.* Coeditor of *Coleridge, Keats, and the Imagination* (1990). **Essay:** William Hazlitt.

Mailhot, Laurent. Professor, Department of French studies, University of Montreal. Editor of *Études Françaises,* 1979–87; member of the editorial board of the Presses de l'Université de Montreal Bibliothèque du Nouveau Monde series. Author of *La Littérature québécoise* (1974), *La Poésie québécoise des origines à nos jours,* with P. Nepveu (1981), *Ouvrir le livre* (1992), and other books. Editor of *Essais québécois, 1837–1983: Anthologie littéraire,* with Benoît Melançon (1984). **Essays:** Canadian Essay (French); Lionel Groulx; *Liberté;* Pierre Trottier.

Marcotte, Gilles. Formerly Professor, University of Montreal. Author of *Une Littérature qui se fait* (1962), *Le Roman à l'imparfait* (1976), *La Prose de Rimbaud* (1983), *L'Amateur de musique* (1992), and *Littérature et circonstances* (1989). **Essays:** Fernand Ouellette; Pierre Vadeboncoeur.

Masuy, Christine. Member of the Department of Communication, Catholic University of Louvain, Belgium. **Essays:** Italo Calvino; Eugenio Montale.

Matiko, Beverly J. Associate professor of English and communication, Andrews University, Berrien Springs, Michigan. Author of the entry on *Pilgrim at Tinker Creek* by Annie Dillard in *MasterPlots II: Women's Literature* (1995), and of forthcoming entries in *Masterplots* on *The Chosen* and *My Name Is Asher Lev* by Chaim Potok. **Essay:** Annie Dillard.

Mayer, Sigrid. Professor of German, University of Wyoming, Laramie. Author, with W. Eggers, *Ernst Cassirer: An Annotated Bibliography* (1988). Editor, with Anselm Dreher, of *Drawings and Words, 1954–1977* (1983) and *Etchings and Words, 1972–1982* (1985), both by Günter Grass. **Essay:** Günter Grass.

Mazzeno, Laurence W. President, Alvernia College, Reading, Pennsylvania. Managing editor, 1986–88, and editor, 1988–92, of *Nineteenth-Century Prose;* managing editor and book review editor of the *Arnoldian,* 1980–86; consulting editor of *Masterplots* (12 vols., 1996). Author of *The British Novel, 1670–1832* (1997), *Victorian Poetry* (1995), *The Victorian Novel* (1989), and *Herman Wouk* (1994). **Essay:** John Updike.

Melançon, Benoît. Adjunct professor, University of Montreal. Member of the editorial board of *Discours Social/Social Discourse.* Author of *Diderot épistolier* (1996) and articles in *Spirale, Jeu, Études Françaises, Littérales,* and *Voix et Images.* Editor of *Essais québécois, 1837–1983: Anthologie littéraire,* with Laurent Mailhot (1984). **Essays:** André Belleau; Jacques Brault; Canadian Essay (French); Jean Larose; Jean Le Moyne.

Mermall, Thomas. Professor of Spanish, Brooklyn College and Graduate School, New York. Member of the editorial board of *Los Ensayistas,* 1978–88, and *Journal of Interdisciplinary Studies,* since 1994. Author of *The Rhetoric of Humanism: Spanish Culture After Ortega* (1975), *Las alegorías del poder en Francisco Ayala* (1984), and articles on Unamuno, Ortega y Gasset, Francisco Ayala, and other Spanish writers in *Bulletin of Hispanic Studies, Hispanic Review, PMLA, Insula, Revista Canadianese de Estudios Hispánicos,* and other journals. **Essays:** Enrique Tierno Galván; Miguel de Unamuno.

Midgley, David. University lecturer in German, Cambridge University. Author of *Arnold Zweig* (1980) and articles on various German writers and intellectuals in *German Life and Letters, German Quarterly, Oxford German Studies, Zeitschrift für deutsche Philologie,* and *Jahrbuch für internationale Germanistik.* Editor of *The German Novel in the Twentieth Century* (1993). **Essays:** Sigmund Freud; Max Weber.

Mihăilescu, Călin-Andrei. Associate professor of comparative literature and Spanish, University of Western Ontario, London. Editor of "Recherche littéraire/Literary research" in the *Journal of the International Comparative Literature Assocation.* Author of articles in *Style, Texte, Comparatist, Euresis, Revista Canadiense de Estudios Hispánicos,* and other journals. Editor of *Fiction Updated: Theories of Fictionality, Narratology and Poetics* (1996). **Essay:** George Călinescu.

Miller, Anthony. Senior lecturer in English, University of Sydney. Author of articles in the *Sidney Newsletter, Studies in Philology,* and *English Literary Renaissance.* Editor of editions of Shakespeare's *Richard III* (1989) and *Julius Caesar* (1995). **Essays:** *The Defence of Poesy; An Essay on Man.*

Miller, Stephen. Professor of Spanish and director of graduate studies in modern and classical languages, Texas A&M University, College Station. Member of the editorial board of *Romance Quarterly* and *Antípodas.* Author of *El mundo de Galdós: Teoría, tradición y evolución del pensamiento socioliterario galdosiano* (1983) and *Del realismo/naturalismo al modernismo: Galdós, Zola, Revilla y Clarín (1870–1901)* (1993). Coeditor of *Critical Studies on Gonzalo Torrente Ballester* (1988) and *Critical Studies on Armando Palacio*

Valdés (1993). Guest editor of *Antípodas* special issue: *Three Hispanic Nobels: Camilo José Cela, Gabriel García Márquez, Octavio Paz* (1992). **Essays:** Marcelino Menéndez y Pelayo; Octavio Paz.

Mitchell, P. M. Adjunct professor of modern languages, Cornell University, Ithaca, New York. Author of *A Bibliographical Guide to Danish Literature* (1951), *A History of Danish Literature* (1957 and later revisions), *Vilhelm Grønbech* (1978), *Daguerreotypes and Other Essays*, with W. D. Paden (1979), *Henrik Pontoppidan* (1979), and many other books. Editor of *Anthology of Danish Literature*, with F. J. Billeskov Jansen (1972) and of several volumes of the *Ausgewählte Werke* by Johann Christoph Gottsched (1975–95). Editor and translator of *Selected Essays* (1955) and *Moral Reflections and Epistles* (1991) by Ludvig Holberg. **Essays:** Frans G. Bengtsson; Olof von Dalin; Ludvig Holberg; Jacob Paludan; Scandinavian Essay.

Mitova-Janowski, Katia. Ph.D. candidate, Committee on Social Thought, University of Chicago. Editor-in-chief of *Panorama* Bulgarian quarterly magazine, 1990–94; editor of *Puls* Bulgarian literary and cultural weekly, 1987–90; coeditor of the Philosophy Plus series for Pero Publishing House, Sofia, Bulgaria. Author of a collection of poetry (1994), articles in *Literaturna Misal, Plamak, Slavic Literatures in Bulgaria*, and other journals, and prefaces to books by Polish writers. Translator of works by various Polish writers. **Essays:** Stanisław Barańczak; Bulgarian Essay; Gustaw Herling-Grudziński; Chavdar Mutafov; Polish Essay; Pencho Slaveikov.

Monsman, Gerald. Professor of English, University of Arizona, Tucson. Author of *Pater's Portraits* (1967), *Walter Pater* (1977), *Walter Pater's Art of Autobiography* (1980), *Confessions of a Prosaic Dreamer* (1984), *Olive Schreiner's Fiction* (1991), and two articles in *Blackwood's Magazine*. Editor of *Gaston de Latour: The Revised Text* by Walter Pater (1995). **Essay:** Walter Pater.

Moss, Howard. Lecturer in Italian, University of Wales, Swansea. Former editor of the *Bulletin of the Society for Italian Studies* and the *Journal of the Association of Italian Studies*. Author of articles in *Italian Studies, Italica, Forum Italicum, Il Politico, Comparative Literature, Italian Quarterly, Rivista dell'Aipi, Italianist*, and *Bulletin of the Society for Italian Studies*. **Essays:** Antonio Gramsci; Niccolò Machiavelli; Benedetto Varchi.

Motta, Vanna. Tutorial fellow in Italian, University of Wales, Cardiff. **Essay:** Carlo Cattaneo.

Müller, Agnes C. Recent Ph.D. candidate, Vanderbilt University, Nashville, Tennessee. Author of articles in *Chaotische Nachrichten* and *New German Review*. **Essays:** Theodor W. Adorno; Max Bense; Peter Hamm; Christa Wolf.

Mulvihill, James. Associate professor of English, University of Alberta, Edmonton. Consultant on the Norton Readers. Author of *Thomas Love Peacock* (1987) and articles in *Studies in Romanticism, SEL, Keats-Shelley Journal, Nineteenth-Century Literature*, and other journals. **Essays:** William Godwin; Percy Bysshe Shelley.

Muñoz, Pedro Maria. Assistant professor of Spanish literature, Winthrop University, Rock Hill, South Carolina. Author of *Guia cultural del mundo hispánico* (1992) and articles and book reviews in *Hispania, España Contemporánea, Letras Peninsulares*, and other journals. **Essays:** Baltasar Gracián; Ramiro de Maeztu.

Murray, Isobel. Senior lecturer in English, University of Aberdeen. Author of many articles on Oscar Wilde; editor of critical editions of Wilde's *The Picture of Dorian Gray* (1976), *Wilde's Complete Shorter Fiction* (1979), *The Oxford Authors Oscar Wilde* (1989), and *The Soul of Man, and Prison Writings* (1990). Author of *Ten Modern Scottish Novels*, with Bob Tait (1984) and articles on Scottish writing. **Essay:** Oscar Wilde.

Murray, Michael D. Professor and chair, Department of Communication, University of Missouri, St. Louis. Member of the editorial advisory board of *Journalism History* and *Communication Research Reports*. Author of *The Political Performers* (1994) and *Television in America* (1997). **Essay:** H. L. Mencken.

Musgrove, Brian. Head, Department of Humanities, University of Southern Queensland, Toowoomba. Coeditor of *Coppertales* journal of rural arts. Author of *Signifying Others* (1992). Director of the documentary films *D. H. Lawrence and the Culture Industry* (1985) and *Making Shakespeare* (1988). **Essay:** D. H. Lawrence.

Myers, Eunice Doman. Associate professor of Spanish, Wichita State University, Kansas. Author of articles on Ramón Pérez de Ayala, Rosa Chacel, Manuel Ferrand, Ana María Matute, and other women writers in several books and in the journals *Crítica Hispánica, Perspective on Contemporary Literature, Hispanic Journal, Hispania, Letras Femenina, Monographic Review*, and *Letras Peninsulares*. Coeditor of *Continental, Latin-American and Francophone Women Writers* (1987). **Essay:** Ramón Pérez de Ayala.

Naufftus, William F. Associate professor of English, Winthrop University, Rock Hill, South Carolina. Author of an entry on Thomas Babington Macaulay in *Victorian Prose Writers Before 1867*, edited by William B. Thesing, *Dictionary of Literary Biography* vol. 55 (1987). Editor of *British Short Fiction Writers, 1880–1914: The Romantic Tradition, Dictionary of Literary Biography* vol. 156 (1995). **Essay:** Edmund Wilson.

Nemoianu, Virgil. William J. Byron Distinguished Professor of Literature, Catholic University of America, Washington, D.C. Secretary general of the International Comparative Literature Association. Author of *The Taming of Romanticism: European Literature and the Age of Biedermeier* (1984), *A Theory of the Secondary: Literature, Progress, and Reaction* (1989), *Micro-Harmony: The Growth and Uses of the Idyllic Model in Literature* (1977), and articles in the *Times Literary Supplement, PMLA, Modern Language Notes, Poetics Today*, and other journals. Coeditor of *Play, Literature,*

Religion (1992) and *The Hospitable Canon* (1991). **Essays:** Chateaubriand; Ernst Jünger; Alexandru Odobescu; Robert Southey.

O'Neil, Catherine. Postdoctoral student, University of Chicago. **Essay:** *Sovremennik.*

O'Neill, Charles L. Assistant professor, Division of the Humanities, St. Thomas Aquinas College, Sparkill, New York. Author of "Violence and the Sacred in Seamus Heaney's *North*" in the forthcoming *Seamus Heaney: The Consciousness of the Artist*, edited by Catherine Malloy, "Paul Muldoon's *Madoz*: A Mystery and the Romantic Poets" in *Wordsworth Circle* (1993), and "Haunting the Ordinary: Tess Gallagher and Irish Poetry" in *Poetry Society of America* (1993). **Essays:** Kenneth Burke; Kenneth Rexroth.

Onslow, Barbara Mary. Lecturer in English, University of Reading. Author of the second ten-year index of *Victorian Periodicals Review*, several articles including those on 19th-century British women writers, literature as journalism, and 19th-century prose and journalism in *Reader's Guide to Literature in English* (1996), and "Deceiving Images, Revealing Images: Portraits of Romance and Reality in Victorian Women's Writing" in *Victorian Poetry* (Autumn/Winter 1995). **Essays:** *Blackwood's Edinburgh Magazine*; Margaret Oliphant.

Oviedo, José Miguel. Trustee professor, University of Pennsylvania, Philadelphia. Author of *Mario Vargas Llosa: La invención de una realidad* (1970, revised 1977), *Escrito al margen* (1982, revised 1987), *La niña de New York: Una revisión de la vida erótica de Jorge Martí* (1989), *Breve historia del ensayo hispanoamericano* (1991), and "The Modern Essay in Spanish America" in *The Cambridge History of Latin American Literature, Volume 2: The Twentieth Century*, edited by Roberto González Echevarría and Enrique Pupo-Walker (1996). Editor of *Antología crítica del cuento hispanoamericano* (2 vols., 1989–92). Contributing editor to the Library of Congress *Handbook of Latin American Studies*. **Essays:** Jorge Luis Borges; Juan Montalvo.

Pahomov, George S. Professor of Russian language and literature, Bryn Mawr College, Pennsylvania. Editor and translator for Kingston Press; editor of *Transactions*. Author of *In Earthbound Flight: Romanticism in Turgenev* (1983) and numerous articles on writers such as Zhukovskii, Pushkin, Turgenev, Chekhov, Bunin, and Elagin in various journals. Editor and translator of *Istoriia Rossii*, vol. 4, by Vladimir Solov'ev (1996). **Essay:** Ivan Turgenev.

Park, Pamela. Associate professor of French, Idaho State University, Pocatello. Author of "Description and Evaluation of an Academic Year in a French *Lycée*, 1992–1993" in *"Hands On" Language* (1994) and "Imagination et ennui dans *Lamiel*" in *Stendhal Club* 118 (1988). **Essay:** Jean-Louis Guez de Balzac.

Pavich, Paul Nicholas. Professor of English, Fort Lewis College, Durango, Colorado. Author of *Where the West Begins* (1978), *Joseph Wood Krutch* (1989), and articles in *Earthly Words:*

Essays on Contemporary American Nature and Environmental Writers (1994), *Western American Literature, Southwestern American Literature,* and *Western Humanities Review.* Editor, with Agnes Picotte, of *Dakota Texts* and *Speaking of Indians* by Ella Deloria (1979). **Essay:** Joseph Wood Krutch.

Pearson, Ann. Lecturer, University of British Columbia, Vancouver. **Essay:** Mary Wollstonecraft.

Pebworth, Ted-Larry. William E. Stirton Professor in the Humanities and professor of English, University of Michigan, Dearborn. Assistant editor of *Seventeenth-Century News.* Author of 12 books and 76 articles on 17th- and 20th-century authors. Textual coeditor of *The Variorum Edition of the Poetry of John Donne* (8 vols., 1995–). Coeditor, *The Wit of Seventeenth Century Poetry* (1995). **Essay:** John Donne.

Pérez, Janet. Horn Professor of Spanish and associate graduate dean, Texas Tech University, Lubbock. Editor of the *Monographic Review/Review Monografica,* since 1985; member of the editorial board of *Letras Femeninas, Hispanófila, Anales de la Narrativa Española Contemporánea, Letras Peninsulares, Siglo XX/Twentieth Century,* and other journals. Editor for Spain, Twayne World Authors Series. Author of *The Major Themes of Existentialism in the Works of Ortega y Gasset* (1970), *Ana María Matute* (1971), *Miguel Delibes* (1972), *Novelistas femeninas de la postguerra española* (1983), *Gonzalo Torrente Ballester* (1984), *Women Writers of Contemporary Spain* (1988), *Modern and Contemporary Spanish Women Poets* (1995), and 175 articles and chapters in books. Editor of *Critical Studies on Gonzalo Torrente Ballester,* with Stephen Miller (1988) and *Dictionary of Literature of the Iberian Peninsula,* with Maureen Ihrie (2 vols., 1993). **Essays:** Francisco Ayala; Rosa Chacel; María Zambrano.

Perkins, Elizabeth. Associate professor of English, James Cook University of North Queensland, Townsville. Founding editor of *LINQ* (Literature in North Queensland). Author of *The Plays of Alma De Groen* (1994). Editor of *The Poetical Works* (1984) and *Stalwart the Bushranger with The Tragedy of Donohoe* (1987) by Charles Harpur. **Essays:** A. D. Hope; Walter Murdoch.

Piggott, Jill. Ph.D. candidate, Drew University, Madison, New Jersey. Author of articles in *The Female Tradition in Southern Literature,* edited by Carol S. Manning (1993), *American Transcendental Quarterly,* and *Southern Literary Journal.* **Essay:** Nadine Gordimer.

Pitts, Mary Ellen. Professor and head, Department of English, Western Kentucky University, Bowling Green. Author of *Toward a Dialogue of Understanding: Loren Eiseley and the Critique of Science* (1995), "Reflective Scientists and the Critique of Mechanistic Metaphor" in *The Literature of Science: Perspectives on Popular Scientific Writing,* edited by M. William McRae (1993), and "Toward a Dialectic of the Open End: The Scientist as Writer and the Revolution Against Measurement" in *Centennial Review* 38, no. 1 (1994). **Essays:** Aldo Leopold; Medical Essay; Oliver Sacks.

Pollard, D. E. Professor of translation, Chinese University of Hong Kong. Editor of *Renditions*, since 1989. Author of *A Chinese Look at Literature* (1973) and coauthor *Colloquial Chinese* (1982). Coeditor of *An Encyclopedia of Translation: Chinese-English, English-Chinese* (1995). **Essays:** Chinese Essay; Liang Yuchun; Lu Xun; Yuan Hongdao; Zhou Zuoren.

Polt, John H. R. Professor emeritus of Spanish, University of California, Berkeley. Member of the editorial board of *Dieciocho*. Author of *The Writings of Eduardo Mallea* (1959), *Jovellanos and His English Sources: Economic, Philosophical, and Political Writings* (1964), *Gaspar Melchor de Jovellanos* (1971), and *Batilo: Estudios sobre la evolución estilística de Meléndez Valdés* (1987), and articles and reviews in *Anales de Literatura Española*, *Hispanic Review*, *Dieciocho*, *Revista Iberoamericana*, *Studies in Eighteenth-Century Culture*, and other journals. **Essay:** Gaspar Melchor de Jovellanos.

Polt, Richard. Assistant professor of philosophy, Xavier University, Cincinnati, Ohio. Author of articles in *Auslegung*, *Journal of the British Society for Phenomenology*, and the forthcoming *Dictionary of Existentialism*, edited by Haim Gordon. **Essays:** Ludwig Feuerbach; Martin Heidegger; Jean-Paul Sartre; Xavier Zubiri.

Polukhina, Valentina. Professor of Russian literature, Keele University, Staffordshire. Author of *Joseph Brodsky: A Poet for Our Time* (1989), *Brodsky Through the Eyes of His Contemporaries* (1992), and *The Dictionary of Brodsky's Tropes* (1995). Editor of *Brodsky's Poetics and Aesthetics* (1990) and *Brodsky's Genres* (1995). **Essay:** Joseph Brodsky.

Post, Jonathan F. S. Professor of English, University of California, Los Angeles. Member of the editorial board of the *Huntington Library Quarterly*, since 1995. Author of *Henry Vaughan: The Unfolding Vision* (1982), *Sir Thomas Browne* (1987), and many articles and reviews in *Renaissance Literature*. Editor of *George Herbert in the Nineties* (1996). **Essay:** Sir Thomas Browne.

Price, John T. Graduate instructor, University of Iowa, Iowa City. Author of "Personal Connections to the Midwest" in *The Updated Literary History of the American West* (1996). **Essay:** N. Scott Momaday.

Pucci, Suzanne R. Associate professor of French, University of Kentucky, Lexington. Advisory editor of *Eighteenth-Century Studies*, since 1995. Author of *Diderot and a Poetics of Science* (1986), various chapters in books, and articles and reviews in journals. Editor of *Diderot in the Wake of Modern Critical Thought*, special issue of *L'Esprit Créateur* (1984). **Essay:** Denis Diderot.

Pursglove, Michael. Senior lecturer in Russian, University of Exeter. Author of *The New Russia* (1995) and *D. V. Grigorovich: The Man Who Discovered Chekhov* (1987). Editor of editions of *Childhood* (1993), *Anton; The Peasant: Two Stories of Serfdom* (1991), and *Sebastopol Stories* (1994) by Lev Tolstoi. **Essay:** Vladimir Giliarovskii.

Qian, Nanxiu. Assistant professor of Chinese literature, Rice University, Houston. Cotranslator from classical to modern Chinese of *An Abridged Translation of the Shih-shuo hsin-yu* (1989). Author of articles in *T'ang Studies*, *Literary Review*, and other journals. Coeditor of *A Guide to Chinese Culture* (1986). **Essays:** Liu Zongyuan; Su Shi.

Rae, Patricia. Assistant professor of English, Queen's University, Kingston, Ontario. Author of *The Practical Muse: Pragmatism and Inspiration in Hulme, Pound, and Stevens* (1996) and articles in *Comparative Literature*, *ELH*, *Southern Review*, and *English Studies in Canada*. **Essay:** William James.

Raley, Harold. Dean, College of Arts and Humanities, Houston Baptist University. Author of *José Ortega y Gasset: Philosopher of European Unity* (1971), *Responsible Vision: The Philosophy of Julian Marías* (1980), *José Ortega y Gasset: A Bibliography of Secondary Sources*, with Antón Donoso (1986), "Phenomenological Life: A New Look at the Philosophic Enterprise in Ortega y Gasset" in *Analecta Husserliana* (1989), and other studies. **Essays:** Manuel Azaña; Julián Marías.

Rapport, Nigel. Professor in social anthropology, University of St. Andrews. Author of *Talking Violence: An Anthropological Interpretation of Conversation in the City* (1987), *Diverse World Views in an English Village* (1993), and *The Prose and the Passion: Anthropology, Literature and the Writings of E. M. Forster* (1994). **Essay:** E. M. Forster.

Richmond, Velma Bourgeois. Professor of English, Holy Names College, Oakland, California. Author of *Muriel Spark* (1985), *Geoffrey Chaucer* (1992), *The Popularity of Medieval Romance* (1975), *Laments for the Dead in Medieval Narrative* (1965), *The Legend of Guy of Warwick* (1995), and many articles. **Essays:** Hilaire Belloc; *The Confessions*; C. S. Lewis; Sermon.

Ritchie, Daniel E. Professor of English, Bethel College, St. Paul, Minnesota. Author of *Reconstructing Literature in an Ideological Age* (1996), "Desire and Sympathy, Passion and Providence: The Moral Imaginations of Burke and Rousseau" in *Burke and the French Revolution* (1992), and "The Story of Robinson Crusoe and the Stories of Scripture" in *Journey to the Celestial City* (1995). **Essay:** Edmund Burke.

Roberts, William. Professor of history, Fairleigh Dickinson University, Rutherford, New Jersey. Member of the advisory panel for modern European history for the National Endowment for the Humanities. Author of *Sicily: An Informal History* (1992), *Modern Italian History: An Annotated Bibliography* (1990), and *Prophet in Exile: Joseph Mazzini in England* (1989). **Essay:** Giuseppe Mazzini.

Robertson, Ian Ross. Professor of history, University of Toronto at Scarborough. Author of *The Tenant League of Prince Edward Island, 1864–1867: Leasehold Tenure in the New World* (1996), chapters in *The Atlantic Region to Confederation: A History* and *Canadian History: A Reader's Guide, Volume 1: Beginnings to Confederation*, and articles in the *Dictionary of Canadian Biography*, *Acadiensis*, *Canadian Literature*, and *The Island Magazine*. **Essay:** Andrew Macphail.

Robinson, Daniel. Ph.D. candidate, University of South Carolina, Columbia. Author of "From 'Mingled Measure' to 'Ecstatic Measures': Mary Robinson's Poetic Reading of 'Kubla Khan'" in *Wordsworth Circle* (1995) and "Reviving the Sonnet: Women Romantic Poets and the Sonnet Claim" in *European Romantic Review* (1995). **Essay:** Alice Meynell.

Roche, Dan. Teacher of nonfiction writing, University of Central Arkansas, Conway. Author of *Love's Labors: A Man's Memoir of Marriage and Remarriage* (1996) and articles in the *North American Review*, *Ohio Journal*, and the *Slate*. **Essays:** American Essay; *The Atlantic Monthly*; Familiar Essay; *Harper's*; Topical Essay.

Rogers, John H. Professor of English, Vincennes University, Indiana. Author of entries on Thomas Love Peacock in *British Romantic Poets*, Horace Smith in *British Romantic Novelists*, William Maginn in *British Romantic Prose Writers*, and Sir John Hawkins in *Eighteenth-Century Biographers*. Associate editor of *British Literary Characters: The Novel* (vol. 2) and editor of *British Short Fiction Writers, 1915–1945*, *Dictionary of Literary Biography* (1996). **Essays:** Max Beerbohm; V. S. Pritchett; Jonathan Swift; James Thurber.

Rojas, Lourdes. Associate professor of Spanish and director of Africana and Latin American studies, Colgate University, Hamilton, New York. Author of *La mujer, desmitificación y novela* (1990), "La indagación desmitificadora en la poesía de Rosario Castellanos" in *Revista/Review InterAmericana* 12, no. 1 (1982), "At the Crossroads: Latinas' Affirmation of Life in *Getting Home Alive* by Rosario Morales" in *Breaking Boundaries: Latinas' Writing and Critical Essays* (1988), and "Intruders and Usurpers: Latin American Women Essayists" with N. Sternbach, in *The Politics of the Essay: Feminist Perspectives*, edited by Ruth Ellen Joeres and Elizabeth Mittman (1993). **Essays:** Andrés Bello; Pedro Henríquez Ureña.

Rosengrant, Judson. Independent scholar. Compiler of a bibliography on Lidiia Ginzburg in *Russian Review* (1995). Editor and translator of *On Psychological Prose* (1991) and *On Lyric Poetry* (forthcoming) by Ginzburg. Author of several articles in *Russian Review*, *Style*, *Slavic and East European Journal*, *Canadian-American Slavic Studies*, and other journals. Editor and translator of works by Iurii Olesha, Fazil Iskander, and Edward Limonov. **Essay:** Lidiia Ginzburg.

Rosevelt, Jan Peter F. van. Graduate teaching assistant, University of South Carolina, Columbia. Associate prose editor of *Yemassee*. Author of an entry on Michael Arlen in *British Short Fiction Writers, 1915–1945*, edited by John H. Rogers, *Dictionary of Literary Biography* (1996), and "Dining with *The Ambassadors*" in the *Henry James Review* 15, no. 3 (1994). **Essay:** J. B. Priestley.

Rowe, Noel. Lecturer in English, University of Sydney. Author of *Modern Australian Poets* (1994) and articles and poetry in *Southerly*, *Voices*, *Pacifica*, *Meridian*, *Quadrant*, *Phoenix Review*, and *The Oxford Book of Australian Religious Poetry* (1994). **Essay:** Vincent Buckley.

Roy, Joaquín. Professor of international studies and Latin American literature, University of Miami. Literary director of *Letras de Oro*, since 1986. Director of the Iberian Studies Institute, since 1986, and the European Community Research Institute, since 1990. Author of *Julio Cortázar ante su sociedad* (1974), *Narrativa y crítica de Nuestra América* (1978), *Ezequiel Martínez Estrada, Panorama de los Estados Unidos* (1985), *ALA: Periodismo y literatura* (1986), *Camilo José Cela: Homage to a Nobel Prize* (1991), and *El pensamiento demócratacristiano* (1993). **Essays:** Germán Arciniegas; Rubén Darío; Journalism and the Essay; Reportage; José Enrique Rodó.

Sáenz, Pilar G. Professor of Spanish, George Washington University, Washington, D.C. President of the Ibero-American Society for Eighteenth-Century Studies. Author of *Eugenio d'Ors: Su mundo de valores estéticos* (1969), *The Life and Works of Eugenio d'Ors* (1983), contributions to *Women Writers of Spain: An Annotated Bio-Bibliograpical Guide* (1986) and *Dictionary of Literature of the Iberian Peninsula*, edited by Janet Pérez and Maureen Ihrie (2 vols., 1993), and articles in *Insula*, *Papeles de Son Armadans*, *Thesaurus*, *Hispanófila*, *Duquesne Hispanic Review*, and *Dieciocho*. **Essays:** Américo Castro; Salvador de Madariaga; Eugenio d'Ors.

Saglia, Diego. Tutor, School of European Studies, University of Wales, Cardiff. Author of articles in the *Byron Journal*, *Studies in the Novel*, *Textus: English Studies in Italy*, and *Byron and Spain: Itinerary in the Writing of Place* (1996). **Essay:** *Times Literary Supplement*.

Sandoval-B., Ciro A. Assistant professor of Spanish and comparative studies, Michigan Technological University, Houghton. Author of "Michel Serrès' Philosophy of the 'Educated Third': Hermesian Confluences Among the Humanities, Science, and Technology" in *Philosophy Today* (Summer 1995), "Rafael Catala: Un Hermes para la Cienciapoesia Latinoamericana" in *Rafael Catala: Del Circulo cuadrado a la cienciapoesia: Hacia una nueva poetica latinoamericana*, edited by Luis A. Jimenez (1994). Coeditor of *Jose Maria Arguedas: A Comparative Reconsideration* (1996). **Essays:** Aldous Huxley; José Carlos Mariátegui; Michel Serrès.

Saunero-Ward, Verónica. Part-time professor of Spanish and Italian, College of Santa Fe, New Mexico. Author of eight articles in the *New Mexican*, and articles in *ALEPH* and *Bolivia Studies*. **Essays:** *Lima la horrible*; Spanish American Essay.

Savova, Lilia. Professor of English, Indiana University of Pennsylvania. Author of *English for the Eleventh Grade of the English Language Schools* (1984), *English for the Tenth Grade* (1993), and *English for the Eighth Grade of the National School for Ancient Languages and Civilizations* (1987). **Essay:** Georgi Markov.

Schell, Richard. Professor of English, Laurentian University, Sudbury, Ontario. Joint editor of the Yale Edition of *The Shorter Poems of Edmund Spenser*. **Essays:** *Areopagitica*; Northrop Frye.

Scherr, Barry P. Professor of Russian, Dartmouth College, Hanover, New Hampshire. Author of *Russian Poetry: Meter, Rhythm, and Rhyme* (1986), *Maxim Gorky* (1988), and articles in *Slavic and East European Journal*, *International Journal of Slavic Linguistics and Poetics*, *Style*, *Slavic Review*, *Russian Language Journal*, and *Russian Literature*. Coeditor of *Russian Verse Theory* (1989) and *A Sense of Place: Tsarskoe Selo and Its Poets* (1993). **Essays:** Maksim Gor'kii; Andrei Siniavskii.

Schiff, Karen. Ph.D. candidate in comparative literature and literary theory, University of Pennsylvania, Philadelphia. Author of "Finding the Reader in *The Waves*: Bernard's Dinner Party" in *Re: Reading, Re: Writing, Re: Teaching Virginia Woolf*, edited by Eileen Barrett and Patricia Cramer (1995) and "Taking a Tangent on Saussure and Derrida: Conceptualizing Signification and *Différence* Through a Graph of the Tangent Function" in *Constructions* 8 (1993). **Essays:** Adrienne Rich; Alice Walker.

Schwab, Eric. Ph.D. candidate in German, Yale University, New Haven, Connecticut. Translator of *Constituting Critique: Kant's Writing as Critical Praxis* by Willi Goetschel (1994). Editor of an issue of *ARTlies*, 1994. **Essay:** Immanuel Kant.

Sheldon, Richard. Chair, Russian Department, Dartmouth College, Hanover, New Hampshire. Compiler of *Viktor Shklovskii: An International Bibliography of Works by and About Him* (1977). Author of "Shklovskii, Gor'kii and the Serapion Brothers" in *Slavic and East European Journal* 12, no. 1 (Spring 1968), "The Formalist Poetics of Viktor Shkovskii" in *Russian Literature Tri-Quarterly* 2 (Winter 1972), "Viktor Shklovskii and the Device of Ostensible Surrender" in *Slavic Review* 34, no. 1 (March 1975). Translator and editor of Shklovskii's *A Sentimental Journey* (1970), *Zoo, or Letters Not About Love* (1971), *Third Factory* (1977), and various articles. **Essay:** Viktor Shklovskii.

Sherman, Alvin F., Jr. Associate professor of Spanish and assistant dean of graduate studies and research, Idaho State University, Pocatello. Author of *Mariano José de Larra: A Directory of Historical Personages* (1992) and articles in *Crítica Hispánica*, *Dieciocho*, *Anales de Literatura Española*, *Ojáncano*, and *Ariel*. **Essays:** Benito Jerónimo Feijóo y Montenegro; Diego de Torres Villarroel.

Simmons, James R., Jr. Ph.D. candidate, University of South Carolina, Columbia. Author of entries in the *Dictionary of Literary Biography*, *American National Biography*, and *Reference Guide to American Literature*, and articles in *English Language Notes*, *Brontë Society Transactions*, the *Dickensian*, and *Victorian Studies*. **Essay:** G. K. Chesterton.

Skabarnicki, Anne. Associate professor of English, Royal Military College of Canada, Kingston, Ontario. Editor of the *Carlyle Studies Annual*, since 1992. Member of the editorial advisory board for the University of California Press' Selected Carlyle Project. Author of articles in the *Carlyle Studies Annual*, *Nineteenth-Century Prose*, and *Scotia*. Coeditor of a forthcoming volume of Carlyle's political and social essays. **Essay:** Lytton Strachey.

Sloane, David A. Associate professor of Russian, Tufts University, Medford, Massachusetts. Author of *Aleksandr Blok and the Dynamics of the Lyric Cycle* (1988) and articles in the *Slavic and East European Journal*, *Russian Literature*, *Ulbandus Review*, *Tolstoy Studies Journal*, *Harvard Ukrainian Studies*, and in several conference proceedings, festschrifts, and other collections. **Essay:** Aleksandr Blok.

Smith, Christopher. Reader in French, School of Modern Languages, University of East Anglia, Norwich. Author of *Jean Anouilh: Life, Work and Criticism* (1985), *Atalante, Bikinis and Calvados* (1985), and many articles in journals. Editor of *France et Grande Bretagne* (1990) and *Dramatic Works* by Jean de la Taille (1972). **Essays:** Georges Bataille; Paul Bourget.

Smith, Vivian. Reader in English, University of Sydney. Widely published poet and critic. Author of *Vance and Nettie Palmer* (1975), *The Poetry of Robert Lowell* (1974), *Selected Poems* (1985), *New Selected Poems* (1995), and other works. Editor of the *Letters of Vance and Nettie Palmer* (1977) and *Nettie Palmer: Her Private Journal Fourteen Years, Poems, Reviews and Literary Essays* (1988). **Essays:** Nettie Palmer; Vance Palmer; Judith Wright.

Smythe, Robert V. Assistant professor of German, University of Memphis. Author of *Mustersätze und Grammatik*, with Chas. Long (textbook; 1975) and a review in the *Lessing Jahrbuch* (1994). **Essays:** Leopold von Ranke; *Der Teutsche Merkur*; Christoph Martin Wieland.

Snider, Alvin. Associate professor, University of Iowa, Iowa City. Author of *Origin and Authority in Seventeenth-Century England: Bacon, Milton, Butler* (1994). **Essays:** Nature Essay; Pamphlet.

Soledad Carrasco, María. Professor emerita, Hunter College, City University of New York. Author of *El moro de Granada en la literatura* (1956), *The Moorish Novel* (1976), and *El moro retador y el moro amigo (Estudios sobre fiestas y comedias de moros y cristianos)* (1996). **Essay:** El Sol.

Sondrup, Steven P. Professor of comparative literature, Brigham Young University, Provo, Utah. Editor of *Scandinavian Studies* and the *Bulletin of the International Comparative Literature Association*. Author of "The Poetry of Ecstatic Vision" in *Edith Södergran and Klagar Olson* (1995), *Vers Konkordanz zu Goethes Faust, Erster und zweiter Teil* (2 vols., 1986–89), *The Poetry and Prose of Östen Sjöstrand* (1988), and *Hofmannsthal and the French Symbolist Tradition* (1976). **Essays:** Vilhelm Ekelund; Hugo von Hofmannsthal.

Speer, Clara. Instructor, College of Santa Fe, New Mexico. Editorial assistant for the World Shakespeare Bibliography. **Essays:** Thomas Paine; Richard Selzer.

Spurr, Barry. Senior lecturer in English literature, University of Sydney. Author of *The Word in the Desert* (1995), *The Poetry of Kenneth Slessor* (1995), *The Poetry of Wilfred Owen* (1993), *Literature and Spirituality* (1993), *The Poetry of Coleridge* (1993), "Eliot and the Seventeenth Century" in

Hellas, "Eliot's Longer Poems" in *Sydney Studies in English*, "Lytton Strachey's Essayist's Art" in *Prose Studies*, and many other books and articles. **Essay:** T. S. Eliot.

Stack, George J. Professor emeritus of philosophy, State University of New York, Brockport. Author of *Berkeley's Analysis of Perception* (1970), *On Kierkegaard* (1976), *Kierkegaard's Existential Ethics* (1977), *Sartre's Philosophy of Social Existence* (1978), *Lange and Nietzsche* (1983), *Nietzsche and Emerson* (1992), *Nietzsche: Man, Knowledge, Will to Power* (1994), and 160 articles in various journals. **Essays:** Ralph Waldo Emerson; Arthur Schopenhauer.

Staines, David. Professor of English, University of Ottawa. General editor of the New Canadian Library; editor of *Journal of Canadian Poetry*. Author of *Tennyson's Camelot: The Idylls of the King and Its Medieval Sources* (1982), *Beyond the Provinces: Literary Canada at Century's End* (1995). Editor of *Stephen Leacock: A Reappraisal* (1986) and Leacock's *My Financial Career and Other Follies* (1993). Translator of *The Complete Romances of Chrétien de Troyes* (1990). **Essay:** Stephen Leacock.

Steensma, Robert C. Professor of English, University of Utah, Salt Lake City. Author of *Sir William Temple* (1970), *Dr. John Arbuthnot* (1979), and articles in *College English*, *US Naval Institute Proceedings*, *Naval War College Review*, *Western American Literature*, *Rocky Mountain Review*, *Shakespeare Newsletter*, and other journals. **Essays:** *The Compleat Angler*; Bernard De Voto; Graham Greene; Christopher Morley; Wallace Stegner; Sir William Temple.

Steiner, Patricia Owen. Writer and translator, Ann Arbor, Michigan. Author of a forthcoming biography of Victoria Ocampo. Translator of *The Banners of the Champions: An Anthology of Medieval Arabic Poetry from Andalusia and Beyond*, with James Bellamy (1989), *Don Segundo Sombra*, with Ricardo Guiraldes (1995), and various articles from the Spanish. **Essay:** Victoria Ocampo.

Stewart, Ralph. Member of the English Department, Acadia University, Wolfville, Nova Scotia. Author of "Richard III, Josephine Tey, and Some Uses of Rhetoric" in *Clues* 12, no. 1 (1991), "Swift and the Authorship of Creichton's Memoirs" in *Scottish Historical Review* (1993), and entries on Bertrand Russell and John Lehmann in the *Dictionary of Literary Biography* vol. 100 (1990). Editor of *A History of the Church of Scotland* by James Kirkton (1993). **Essay:** George Bernard Shaw.

Stone, Staci L. Ph.D. candidate, University of South Carolina, Columbia. Assistant editor of *Yemassee*. **Essay:** Maria Edgeworth.

Strassberg, Richard E. Professor of Chinese, University of California, Los Angeles. Translator of *Inscribed Landscapes: Travel Writing from Imperial China* (1994). **Essay:** Zhang Dai.

Stuckey-French, Ned. Recent Ph.D. candidate in American literature, University of Iowa, Iowa City. Author of articles and reviews in the *Harvard Advocate*, *Iowa Review*, *Modern Fiction Studies*, *Walt Whitman Encyclopedia*, and *Walking Magazine*. **Essays:** American Essay; W. E. B. Du Bois; William H. Gass; Humorous Essay; Agnes Repplier; Scott Russell Sanders.

Suchoff, David. Associate professor of English, Colby College, Waterville, Maine. Author of *Critical Theory and the Novel* (1994). Cotranslator of *The Imaginary Jew* by Alain Finkielkraut (1994). **Essay:** Irving Howe.

Szeman, Imre. Graduate student, Literature Program, Duke University, Durham, North Carolina. Founding editor of *Prosthesis: A Graduate Journal of Theory and Criticism*. Author of the forthcoming "Spectral Spaces/The Time of Marx" in *theory@buffalo*, "Disappearing Nations: Atom Egoyan's Canada" in *Constructing Nations, Constructing Selves*, edited by Lynn Domina and Peter Naccarato (1997), "Heidegger's Neighbourhood and Philosophy's Landscape" in *Re-Naming the Landscape*, edited by Bruce Butterfield and Jurgen Kleist (1994), and "Tracing Lines of Flight: *Masala* and Multiculturalism" in *Reverse Shot* 1, no. 2 (May 1994). **Essays:** Chinua Achebe; Wole Soyinka.

Taylor, Richard C. Associate professor of English, East Carolina University, Greenville, North Carolina. Author of *Goldsmith as Journalist* (1993) and articles in *Philological Quarterly*, *Review of English Studies*, *Modern Philology*, *Studies in English Literature*, *Comparative Drama*, *English Language Notes*, *Review*, and *Concerns*. **Essays:** Oliver Goldsmith; *The Tatler*.

Taylor, Rodney. Associate professor of German, Truman State University, Kirksville, Missouri. Author of *Perspectives on Spinoza in Works by Schiller, Büchner, and C. F. Meyer: Five Essays* (1995) and other books, and articles in the *Michigan Germanic Studies*, *Deutsche Vierteljahrsschrift*, *Seminar*, and other journals. **Essay:** Novalis.

Tesser, Carmen Chaves. Professor of Romance languages, University of Georgia, Athens. Member of the editorial board of *The Eighteenth Century: A Current Bibliography*, since 1993, and *MIFLC Review*, since 1992. Author (as Carmen C. McClendon) of *Dissertations in Hispanic Languages and Literatures, 1967–76*, with James R. Chatham (1981), the forthcoming *Um modelo de discurso femenino: A obra de Lya Luft*, and many articles (also as Carmen Chaves Tesser). Editor (as Carmen C. McClendon) of *Brasil: Os ultimos quarenta años* (1985) and *Brazil in the Eighties*, with M. Elizabeth Ginway (1990). Editor (as Carmen Chaves Tesser) of *The Forgotten Centuries: Europeans and Indians in the American South, 1513–1704*, with Charles M. Hudson (1994). Translator of *The Island of the Dead* by Lya Luft, with Betty Jean Craige, (1986) and the forthcoming *Tradition Matters: Modern Gaúcho Identity in Brazil* by Ruben George Oliven. **Essays:** Josefa Amar y Borbón; José Cadalso; Antônio Cândido; Euclides da Cunha; Paulo Freire; Gilberto Freyre.

Thomas, Gillian. Professor of English, Saint Mary's University, Halifax, Nova Scotia. Author of *Harriet Martineau* (1985) and

A Position to Command Respect: Women and the Eleventh Britannica (1992). **Essays:** Harriet Martineau; Rebecca West.

Titolo, Matthew. Ph.D. candidate in Victorian literature and critical theory, and teaching associate, University of California, Los Angeles. Author of articles on intellectual and cultural history, Victorian literature, the history of slavery, and critical theory. **Essays:** Classical Influences; Lewis Mumford; Sociological Essay.

Tobias, Richard C. Professor of English, University of Pittsburgh. Member of the editorial board of *Victorian Poetry, Modern Language Studies,* and *Victorian Institute Journal.* Author of *Art of James Thurber* (1969), *T. E. Brown* (1971), and *Bibliographies of Studies of Victorian Literature, 1975–85* (1991). **Essay:** Thomas Babington Macaulay.

Trojanowska, Tamara. Assistant professor, Department of Slavic Languages and Literatures, University of Chicago. Coauthor of *Quest for a New Theatre* (1988) and author of articles in *Canadian Slavonic Papers, Dialog,* and other journals. **Essays:** Witold Gombrowicz; Czesław Miłosz.

Turner, Brian. Assistant professor of rhetorical criticism and composition, University of Winnipeg, Manitoba. Author of articles in *Rhetoric Review, Journal of Teaching Writing, Teaching English in the Two-Year College,* and *Inkshed.* **Essays:** John McPhee; John Muir.

Ullman, Pierre L. Professor emeritus of Spanish, University of Wisconsin, Milwaukee. Author of *Mariano de Larra and Spanish Political Rhetoric* (1971) and many articles on Spanish literature. **Essay:** Spanish Essay.

Urbina, Nicasio. Associate professor, Department of Spanish and Portuguese, Tulane University, New Orleans. Author of *La significación del género: Estudio semiótico de las novelas y ensayos de Ernesto Sabato* (1992), bibliographies of Sabato in *Revista de Crítica Literaria Latinoamericana* 14, no. 27 (1988) and *Hispania* 73 (1990), *La estructura de la novela nicaragüense: Análisis narratológico* (1995), a collection of poetry (1995), a collection of short stories (1991), and many articles in journals. **Essay:** Ernesto Sabato.

Urrello, Antonio. Professor of Hispanic and Italian studies, University of British Columbia, Vancouver. Author of *José María Arguedas* (1974), *Verosimilitud y estrategia textual en el ensayo hispanoamericano* (1986), *La poesía de Quebec* (1994), and several articles in journals. Editor of *One Hundred Years of Solitude: Critical Perspectives* (1987). **Essay:** Carlos Monsiváis.

Valevičius, Andrius. Professor, Faculty of Theology, Ethics, and Philosophy, University of Sherbrooke, Quebec. Author of *From the Other to the Totally Other: The Religious Philosophy of Emmanuel Levinas* (1988), *Lev Shestov and His Times: Encounters with Brandes, Tolstoy, Dostoevsky, Chekhov, Ibsen, Nietzsche and Husserl* (1993), and "Le Sense de l'histoire dans la pensée russe" in *Écrits du Canada Français* 75 (1992). **Essays:** Vissarion Belinskii; Arthur Buies; Nikolai Novikov.

van der Laan, James M. Associate professor of German, Illinois State University, Normal. Coeditor of *Transculture.* Author of articles in the *Germanic Review, Euphorion, Deutsche Vierteljahrsschrift, Seminar, History of European Ideas, Neophilologus, Lessing Yearbook,* and *Gutenberg Jahrbuch.* **Essay:** Johann Wolfgang von Goethe.

Villafañe, Camille. Doctoral student, Arizona State University, Tempe. **Essay:** Luis Cardoza y Aragón.

Walker, Charlotte Zoë. Professor of English and women's studies, State University of New York, Oneonta. Author of the novel *Condor and Hummingbird* (1987) and short stories in various journals and collections. Editor of *Sharp Eyes: John Burroughs and American Nature Writing: A Collection of Essays* (1997). **Essay:** John Burroughs.

Walsh, Harry. Associate professor of Russian, University of Houston. Author of articles in *Religion and Literature, CLIO, Slavic and East European Journal, Slavonic and East European Review, Russian Language Journal, Comparative Literature Studies,* and other journals. **Essay:** Vladimir Soloukhin.

Wasserman, George. Professor emeritus, Russell Sage College, Troy, New York. Author of *Samuel Butler and the Earl of Rochester: A Reference Guide* (1986), *Roland Barthes* (1981), *Samuel "Hudibras" Butler* (1976, revised 1989), *John Dryden* (1964), and articles in the *Philological Quarterly, English Literary History, Studies in English Literature, Modern Language Quarterly,* and other journals. Editor of *Hudibras: The Second Part (1663)* by Butler (1993). **Essays:** Characters; Preface.

Weeks, Laura D. Independent scholar. Formerly chair, Russian Department, Wheaton College, Norton, Massachusetts. Author of articles in the *Slavic Review* and *Russian Review.* Editor of *Study Guide to The Master and Margarita* (1996). **Essay:** Marina Tsvetaeva.

Wenske, Paul L. Assistant professor of journalism, William Allen White School of Journalism and Mass Communications, University of Kansas, Lawrence. Journalist writing for various papers, including the *Daily Oklahoman,* Kansas City *Star and Times,* Washington *Post,* Miami *Herald,* and Boston *Globe,* as well as the *National Law Journal* and *Ingram's Magazine.* **Essay:** Barry Lopez.

Werner, Theresa. Freelance writer and editor, London. **Essays:** Personal Essay; Susan Sontag.

West, Alan G. H. Ph.D. candidate in English literature, University of Ottawa. **Essay:** Richard Jefferies.

Whalen, Terry. Professor of English, Saint Mary's University, Halifax, Nova Scotia. Author of *Bliss Carman and His Works* (1983), *Charles G. D. Roberts and His Works* (1989), *Philip Larkin and English Poetry* (1986), and articles on late 19th-century and 20th-century British, American, and Canadian authors in various journals. Editor of *The Atlantic Anthology: Critical Essays* (1985). **Essay:** Bliss Carman.

Wheeler, Kathleen M. University lecturer, Faculty of English, Cambridge University. Author of *Explaining Deconstruction* (1996), *A Critical Guide to Twentieth-Century Women Novelists* (1996), *"Modernist" Women Writers and Narrative Art* (1994), *Romanticism, Pragmatism and Deconstruction* (1993), *Sources, Processes and Methods in Coleridge's Biographia Literaria* (1980), *The Creative Mind in Coleridge's Poetry* (1981), and *German Aesthetic and Literary Criticism: The Romantic Ironists and Goethe* (1984). **Essay:** Friedrich Schlegel.

Wilson, Keith. Professor and chair, Department of English, University of Ottawa. Author of a wide range of books and articles on 19th- and 20th-century literature, including *Thomas Hardy on Stage* (1995). Editor of the forthcoming Penguin Modern Classics edition of Hardy's *The Mayor of Casterbridge*. **Essay:** A. C. Benson.

Winkler, Michael. Professor of German studies, Rice University, Houston. Author of *Stefan George* (1970), *George-Kreis* (1972), *Einakter und kleine Dramen des Jugendstils* (1974), *Deutsche Literatur im Exil, 1933–1945: Texte und Dokumente* (1977), *Phantastische Erzählungen der Jahrhundertwende* (1982), *Deutschsprachige Exilliteratur: Studien zu ihrer Bestimmung im Kontext der Epoche 1930 bis 1960* (1984), and *Exilliteratur, 1933–1945* (1989). **Essays:** Rudolf Borchardt; Hermann Grimm; Rudolf Alexander Schröder; *Die weissen Blätter*.

Wood, Allen G. Associate professor of French, Purdue University, West Lafayette, Indiana. Editor for French of *Purdue Studies in Romance Literature* and the Purdue University Monographs in Romance Languages. Author of *Literary Satire and Theory* (1985) and over 20 articles on 17th-century French literature. **Essays:** Alain; Pierre Bayle; Saint-Évremond.

Woodward, Servanne. Assistant professor of French, University of Western Ontario, London. Author of *Diderot and Rousseau's Contributions to Aesthetics* (1991) and articles in *Romance Languages Annual*, *Diderot Studies*, *Revue Marivaux*, *Diogène*, *Essays in French Literature*, *Comparative Literature Studies*, and other journals. **Essays:** Charles Du Bos; Voltaire.

Woolsey, Linda Mills. Professor of English, King College, Bristol, Tennessee. Author of entries on Jane Porter and Anna Maria Porter, Thomas De Quincey, the *London Magazine*, and *Tait's Edinburgh Magazine* in the *Dictionary of Literary Biography*, and articles in *The Image of Crime*, edited by Steven Kaplan and Will Wright (1991) and *Tennessee Philological Bulletin*. **Essays:** Journal; Religious Essay; Simone Weil.

Zaslove, Jerald. Professor of English and humanities, Simon Fraser University, Burnaby, British Columbia. Author of over 30 essays and monographs, including *Jeff Wall* (1990), contributions in the books *Recharting the '30s* (1996) and *Herbert Read: Centenary Reassessments*, edited by David Goodway (1997), and articles in *Telos*, *Public*, *Collapse*, *West Coast Review*, *Recovering Literature*, *Boston Journal of Education*, and *Open Letter*. **Essays:** *Partisan Review*; Propaganda; Herbert Read.

Zeiger, William. Assistant professor of English, Slippery Rock University, Pennsylvania. Author of "The Exploratory Essay" in *College English* (1985), "Freedom of Imagination" in *The Critical Writing Workshop*, edited by Toni-Lee Capossela (1993), and "The Personal Essay and Egalitarian Rhetoric" in *Literary Nonfiction*, edited by Chris Anderson (1989). **Essays:** Apothegm; Charles Lamb; Lewis Thomas.

Zweig, Robert. Professor of English, Manhattan Community College, City University of New York. Author of entries on the dramatic unities, Victorian poetry, Victorian literary criticism, and poetry in *The Encyclopedia of Time* (1995), and "Death in Love: Rossetti and the Victorian Journey Back to Dante" in *Sex and Death in Victorian Literature* (1990). **Essay:** John Ruskin.